LEGACY STANDARD BIBLE

DAILY READING BIBLE

STEADFAST BIBLES

LEGACY STANDARD BIBLE

Typesetting by 2K / DENMARK.
Printed in Korea ◊ 28 27 26 25 24 / 1 2 3 4 5

STEADFAST BIBLES
Is a division of
THREE SIXTEEN PUBLISHING

Southern California

978-1-63664-415-8 978-1-63664-416-5 978-1-63664-417-2

Discover more about the LSB including the entire text online as well as videos
& articles from the team of scholars discussing the translation process at:

LSBible.org

INTRODUCTION

Most Christians understand that daily Bible reading would be a great benefit to their walks with the Lord, yet few develop this vitally important spiritual habit. We live in a fast-paced society with a long list of tasks and distractions all vying for our attention. But for our spiritual survival, we must make reading the Bible a priority.

Jesus said, "Man shall not live on bread alone, but on every word that proceeds out of the mouth of God" (Matthew 4:4). Just like we cannot survive and grow without physical food, Christians cannot live without a regular intake of the spiritual food of the Word.

Reading the Bible in a year may seem like an intimidating goal, but in your hands you hold a proven method to help you with this rewarding journey. Scripture reminds us that there is wisdom in having a plan before beginning a task (cf. Proverbs 24:27).

The *LSB Daily Reading Bible* provides an easy-to-read plan that will help you go through the entire Bible in one year! Each day lays out four refreshing portions of Scripture, which can be read in under 15 minutes. Each week includes a quote from godly men and women, to encourage you on your journey.

Over 150 years ago, Charles H. Spurgeon, called the "Prince of Preachers", gave a sermon with seven principles for getting the most benefit when reading the Bible. We've included a brief summary of his sermon so you can get the most out of reading God's Word.

1. Read & Depend

> *In order to properly understand the holy Word we need to have the Holy Spirit to be His own expositor ... the divine Author, who must know His own meaning, is ever ready to lead you into its meaning. He dwells in you and shall be with you, and Christ Jesus said, "When he, the Spirit of truth is come, he shall lead you into all truth."*

It is an incredible gift that the Father would send the Holy Spirit to live inside of Christians and to directly teach us. God desires all Christians to understand the truth. We need the Spirit of truth in order to truly understand what He has spoken in His Word. So, remember to pray and ask God to help you depend on the Spirit before, during, and after reading the Bible.

2. Read & Meditate

> *For lack of meditation the truth runs by us, and we miss and lose it. Our treacherous memory is like a sieve, and what we hear and what we read runs through it and leaves but little behind ... I often find it very profitable to get a text as a sweet morsel under my tongue in the morning and to keep the flavor of it, if I can, in my mouth all the day.*

When reading the Bible, you may find it easy to forget what you just read. So, it is important that we meditate on what we read. Unlike pagan meditation, which focuses on emptying the mind, biblical meditation involves pondering the truth over and over again—like a cow chewing the cud. The righteous man in Psalm 1:2 "meditates [on His Word] day and night." As you read, slow down, make observations, and jot down questions. It is a good habit to ponder the Word throughout the day and into the night.

3. Read & Apply

See what precepts are binding upon yourself, and then, as a child of God, be your feet swift to run in the way of His commandments. ... Do with the Bible as the sick man does with the doctor's prescription. Follow it by personally doing what it bids you.

The Bible tells us when we apply God's Word to our lives, He makes us more like Jesus. This process is called sanctification, and it is motivated by God's loving work in our hearts (cf. Psalm 119:32). James 1:22 warns us about not consistently obeying His Word: "But become doers of the word, and not merely hearers who delude themselves." Jesus, our great Physician (cf. Luke 5:31), has given us a prescription for our spiritual sicknesses through His Word, so it is for our good to obey Him.

4. Read & Practice

The world will learn better and will more likely be brought to know Christ when the lives of Christians are better, and when the Bible of the Christian life shall be more in accordance with the Bible of Christian doctrine! God, make us holy, sanctify us, spirit, soul, and body, and then we shall be made finely serviceable both to the church and to the world.

As God's ambassadors we must purposefully apply His truth to our lives and show others what it means to belong to Him (2 Corinthians 5:20). As we are more saturated in His Word, we can then carry out His will within His church, our homes, our workplaces, and our communities. Consider how to practice what you read in your daily life.

5. Read & Pray

A text is like a treasure chest which is locked, and prayer is the key to open it, and then we get God's treasure. ... To only read is unprofitable, to pray without reading is not so soul enriching, but when the two run together, they are like the horses in the chariot, and they speed along right merrily.

The Bible is a treasure more valuable than gold (Psalm 19:10), and God freely offers it to us. Since the Word of God belongs to Him, we must ask Him by prayer to give it to us and to plant it in our hearts. So, pray like the Psalmist: "Open my eyes, that I may behold wonderful things from Your law" (Psalm 119:18).

6. Read & Try

Try what you hear, try what you profess, try what you read. ... If you ever have a doctrine of God in your mind, find out the text or texts which prove it! If there should happen to be other texts which seem to point the other way, do not cut and pare any of them down, but accept all and wait until the Spirit reveals wherein they really agree! Scripture is not to fit your opinions, but your opinions to conform to the blessed word!

It is good to "try" (that is, "test") what we hear, believe, and read. The Bible encourages Christians to examine our own beliefs and the beliefs of others by looking to the Scriptures (cf. Acts 17:11). Although written across thousands of years and by dozens of authors, God's Word never contradicts itself. When we read Scripture and hard questions arise, we should pray for God's help. As we discipline ourselves to study the Word, over time the questions may continue, but the answers will often be revealed as we make every effort to anchor our lives to the truth of the Bible (cf. Deuteronomy 29:29).

7. Read & Tell Out

> *When you have read for an hour or so, spend another half hour in communicating to a child, or a servant, or a seeker, or to some bed ridden saint, the thing that has enriched and helped you. ... if you have been brought into personal contact with divine truth, let it be the first impulse of your soul to—"Tell to the sinners round What a dear Savior you have found."*

As you read, telling others about what you've been learning from the Lord helps set the minds of your family members, coworkers, and friends on heavenly things and the saving love of Jesus (cf. Colossians 3:1-4). Finding creative ways to talk about what you have been reading is one of the best ways to share the hope of the gospel (Romans 15:4).

To read the entire sermon from Charles H. Spurgeon and to find other free resources to help with Bible memorization, visit the Free Resources tab at 316Publishing.com.

EXPLANATION OF GENERAL FORMAT FOR THIS EDITION

CAPITALIZED WORDS are used to provide helpful information. Personal pronouns are capitalized when pertaining to Deity. The word "Law" is capitalized when pertaining to Mosaic Law.

ITALICS are used in the text to indicate words that are not found in the original Hebrew, Aramaic, or Greek but are implied by it, or are sometimes necessary for correct English. There are also special cases of italics referring to words that actually are in the original text. Italic "began" mentioned in GREEK TENSES (found in the complete LSB Foreword) is one example, where "began" communicates the grammatical tense of a verb. Another is italic possessive pronouns for Greek articles ("the" in Greek) used as possessive pronouns, a common feature in the Greek language. "*His* good pleasure," literally: "the good pleasure" in Phil 2:13 is an example. The purpose of the italic in this case is to inform the reader that the expected Greek word (the Greek possessive pronoun) is not found in the original text, but is represented by another word (the article) in the original text.

SMALL CAPS in the New Testament are used in the text to indicate Old Testament quotations or references to Old Testament texts. Variations of Old Testament wording are found in New Testament citations depending on whether the New Testament writer translated from a Hebrew text, used existing Greek or Aramaic translations, or paraphrased the material. It should be noted that modern rules for the indication of direct quotation were not used in biblical times, and the ancient writer would use exact quotations or references to quotation without any specific indication of them.

ASTERISKS are used to mark verbs that are historical presents in the Greek grammar and have been translated with an English past tense in order to conform to modern usage. The translators recognized that in some contexts the present tense seems more unexpected and unjustified to the English reader than a past tense would have been. But Greek authors frequently used the present tense for the sake of heightened vividness, thereby transporting their readers in imagination to the actual scene at the time of occurrence. However, the translators felt that it would be wise to change these historical presents to English past tenses.

BRACKETS in text indicate words probably not in the original writings.

The complete LSB Foreword can be found at read.LSBible.org.

TABLE OF CONTENTS

The *LSB Daily Reading Bible* is designed to systematically take you through the entire Bible. Each day has a selected passage of Scripture from the Old Testament, Psalms, Proverbs, and New Testament. Each of these four passages are in the order they appear in the Bible with no repetition. This means that the flow of each day's reading will continue from what came the day before, helping you better understand the context and the truth that God is speaking to you. Additionally, every seven days, you will find a quote from godly men and women to encourage you on your journey.

Do not feel restricted to use this Bible in only one particular way. Here are a few ideas for your consideration:

1. **Read the whole Bible in one year** by reading one day each day. You may choose to read all four passages at once or perhaps split them up throughout the day. For example, you may choose to start your mornings with the shorter Psalms and Proverbs readings and then sit down in the evening to read the Old Testament and New Testament portions.

2. **Read the whole Bible in two years** by reading the Old Testament and Proverbs passages one year and then the New Testament and Psalms passages the next year.

3. **Read starting in the middle of the year**. For example, if you are picking up this book on June 9th, begin your journey on June 9th rather than waiting until January 1st.

4. **Read along with your church or family**. You may want to give copies as gifts to your friends and family so you will be encouraged as you grow from God's Word together through the same passages.

MONTHS

TABLE OF CONTENTS

BOOKS OF THE BIBLE

The Old Testament

The New Testament

JANUARY 1

Genesis 1:1–2:25

1 In the beginning God created the heavens and the earth. 2 And the earth was formless and void, and darkness was over the surface of the deep, and the Spirit of God was hovering over the surface of the waters. 3 Then God said, "Let there be light"; and there was light. 4 And God saw that the light was good; and God separated the light from the darkness. 5 And God called the light day, and the darkness He called night. And there was evening and there was morning, one day.

6 Then God said, "Let there be an expanse in the midst of the waters, and let it separate the waters from the waters." 7 So God made the expanse and separated the waters which were below the expanse from the waters which were above the expanse; and it was so. 8 And God called the expanse heaven. And there was evening and there was morning, a second day.

9 Then God said, "Let the waters below the heavens be gathered into one place, and let the dry land appear"; and it was so. 10 And God called the dry land earth, and the gathering of the waters He called seas; and God saw that it was good. 11 Then God said, "Let the earth sprout vegetation, plants yielding seed, *and* fruit trees on the earth bearing fruit after their kind with seed in them"; and it was so. 12 And the earth brought forth vegetation, plants yielding seed after their kind, and trees bearing fruit with seed in them, after their kind; and God saw that it was good. 13 And there was evening and there was morning, a third day.

14 Then God said, "Let there be lights in the expanse of the heavens to separate the day from the night, and let them be for signs and for seasons and for days and years; 15 and let them be for lights in the expanse of the heavens to give light on the earth"; and it was so. 16 So God made the two great lights, the greater light to rule the day, and the lesser light to rule the night, and *also* the stars. 17 And God placed them in the expanse of the heavens to give light on the earth, 18 and to rule the day and the night, and to separate the light from the darkness; and God saw that it was good. 19 And there was evening and there was morning, a fourth day.

20 Then God said, "Let the waters swarm with swarms of living creatures, and let birds fly above the earth across the face of the expanse of the heavens." 21 And God created the great sea monsters and every living creature that moves, with which the waters swarmed after their kind, and every winged bird after its kind; and God saw that it was good. 22 Then God blessed them, saying, "Be fruitful and multiply, and fill the waters in the seas, and let the birds multiply on the earth." 23 And there was evening and there was morning, a fifth day.

24 Then God said, "Let the earth bring forth living creatures after their kind: cattle and creeping things and beasts of the earth after their kind"; and it was so. 25 God made the beasts of the earth after their kind, and the cattle after their kind, and every creeping thing of the ground after its kind; and God saw that it was good.

26 Then God said, "Let Us make man in Our image, according to Our likeness, so that they will have dominion over the fish of the sea and over the birds of the sky and over the cattle and over all the earth and over every creeping thing that creeps on the earth." 27 And God created man in His own image, in the image of God He created him; male and female He created them. 28 God blessed them, and God said to them, "Be fruitful and multiply, and fill the earth, and subdue it; and have dominion over the fish of the sea and over the birds of the sky and over every living thing that creeps on the earth." 29 Then God said, "Behold, I have given to you every plant yielding seed that is on the surface of all the earth, and every tree which has *the* fruit of *the* tree yielding seed; it shall be food for you; 30 and to every beast of the earth and to every bird of the sky and to every thing that creeps on the earth which has life, *I have given* every green plant for food"; and it was so. 31 And God saw all that He had made, and behold, it was very good. And there was evening and there was morning, the sixth day.

2 Thus the heavens and the earth were completed, and all their hosts. 2 And on the seventh day God completed His work which He had done, and He rested on the

seventh day from all His work which He had done. 3 Then God blessed the seventh day and sanctified it, because on it He rested from all His work which God had created in making *it.*

4 These are the generations of the heavens and the earth when they were created, in the day that Yahweh God made earth and heaven. 5 Now no shrub of the field was yet in the earth, and no plant of the field had yet grown, for Yahweh God had not caused it to rain upon the earth, and there was no man to cultivate the ground. 6 But a stream would rise from the earth and water the whole surface of the ground. 7 Then Yahweh God formed man of dust from the ground and breathed into his nostrils the breath of life; and so the man became a living being. 8 And Yahweh God planted a garden in Eden, toward the east; and there He placed the man whom He had formed. 9 And out of the ground Yahweh God caused to grow every tree that is desirable in appearance and good for food; the tree of life also in the midst of the garden, and the tree of the knowledge of good and evil.

10 Now a river went out of Eden to water the garden; and from there it divided and became four rivers. 11 The name of the first is Pishon; it is the one that went around the whole land of Havilah, where there is gold. 12 Now the gold of that land is good; the bdellium and the onyx stone are there. 13 And the name of the second river is Gihon; it is the one that went around the whole land of Cush. 14 And the name of the third river is Tigris; it is the one that went east of Asshur. And the fourth river is the Euphrates.

15 Then Yahweh God took the man and set him in the garden of Eden to cultivate it and keep it. 16 And Yahweh God commanded the man, saying, "From any tree of the garden you may surely eat; 17 but from the tree of the knowledge of good and evil, you shall not eat from it; for in the day that you eat from it you will surely die."

18 Then Yahweh God said, "It is not good for the man to be alone; I will make him a helper suitable for him." 19 And out of the ground Yahweh God had formed every beast of the field and every bird of the sky, and He brought *each* to the man to see what he would call it; and whatever the man called a living creature, that was its name. 20 And the man gave names to all the cattle and to the birds of the sky and to every beast of the field; but for Adam there was not found a helper suitable for him. 21 So Yahweh God caused a deep sleep to fall upon the man, and he slept; then He took one of his ribs and closed up the flesh at that place. 22 And Yahweh God fashioned the rib, which He had taken from the man, into a woman, and He brought her to the man. 23 Then the man said,

"This one finally is bone of
my bones,
And flesh of my flesh;
This one shall be called Woman,
Because this one was
taken out of Man."

24 Therefore a man shall leave his father and his mother, and cleave to his wife; and they shall become one flesh. 25 And the man and his wife were both naked and were not ashamed.

Psalm 1:1–6

1 How blessed is the man who does not
walk in the counsel of the wicked,
Nor stand in the way of sinners,
Nor sit in the seat of scoffers!
2 But his delight is in the law of Yahweh,
And in His law he meditates
day and night.
3 And he will be like a tree *firmly*
planted by streams of water,
Which yields its fruit in its season
And its leaf does not wither;
And in whatever he does,
he prospers.

4 The wicked are not so,
But they are like chaff which
the wind drives away.
5 Therefore the wicked will not
rise in the judgment,
Nor sinners in the congregation
of the righteous.
6 For Yahweh knows the way
of the righteous,
But the way of the wicked will perish.

Proverbs 1:1–7

1 The proverbs of Solomon the son of David, king of Israel:
2 To know wisdom and discipline,
To understand the sayings
of understanding,

3 To receive discipline *that*
leads to insight,
Righteousness, justice,
and equity,
4 To give prudence to the simple,
To the youth knowledge
and discretion;
5 Let the wise man hear
and increase in learning,
And a man of understanding
will acquire guidance,
6 To understand a proverb
and an enigma,
The words of the wise
and their riddles.

7 The fear of Yahweh is the
beginning of knowledge;
Ignorant fools despise wisdom
and discipline.

Matthew 1:1–25

1 The book of the genealogy of Jesus Christ,
the son of David, the son of Abraham:
2 Abraham was the father of Isaac,
and Isaac was the father of Jacob,
and Jacob was the father of Judah
and his brothers.
3 And Judah was the father of Perez
and Zerah by Tamar,
and Perez was the father of Hezron,
and Hezron was the father of Ram.
4 And Ram was the father of
Amminadab,
and Amminadab was the father of
Nahshon,
and Nahshon was the father of
Salmon.
5 And Salmon was the father of Boaz
by Rahab,
and Boaz was the father of Obed by
Ruth,
and Obed was the father of Jesse.
6 And Jesse was the father of David
the king.

And David was the father of Solomon
by the *wife* of Uriah.
7 And Solomon was the father of
Rehoboam,
and Rehoboam was the father
of Abijah,
and Abijah was the father of Asa.
8 And Asa was the father of
Jehoshaphat,
and Jehoshaphat was the father
of Joram,
and Joram was the father of Uzziah.
9 And Uzziah was the father of Jotham,
and Jotham was the father of Ahaz,
and Ahaz was the father of Hezekiah.
10 And Hezekiah was the father
of Manasseh,
and Manasseh was the father
of Amon,
and Amon was the father of Josiah.
11 And Josiah was the father of Jeconiah
and his brothers, at the time of
the deportation to Babylon.

12 And after the deportation to Babylon:
Jeconiah was the father of Shealtiel,
and Shealtiel was the father
of Zerubbabel.
13 And Zerubbabel was the father
of Abihud,
and Abihud was the father of Eliakim,
and Eliakim was the father of Azor.
14 And Azor was the father of Zadok,
and Zadok was the father of Achim,
and Achim was the father of Eliud.
15 And Eliud was the father of Eleazar,
and Eleazar was the father of
Matthan,
and Matthan was the father of Jacob.
16 And Jacob was the father of Joseph the
husband of Mary, by whom Jesus was
born, who is called Christ.
17 Therefore all the generations from
Abraham to David are fourteen genera-
tions; and from David to the deportation to
Babylon, fourteen generations; and from
the deportation to Babylon to the Christ,
fourteen generations.
18 Now the birth of Jesus Christ was as
follows: when His mother Mary had been
betrothed to Joseph, before they came
together she was found to be with child by
the Holy Spirit. 19 And Joseph her husband,
being a righteous man and not wanting to
disgrace her, planned to send her away
secretly. 20 But when he had considered
this, behold, an angel of the Lord appeared
to him in a dream, saying, "Joseph, son of
David, do not be afraid to take Mary as your
wife; for the One who has been conceived in
her is of the Holy Spirit. 21 And she will bear
a Son; and you shall call His name Jesus, for
He will save His people from their sins."
22 Now all this took place in order that what

was spoken by the Lord through the prophet
would be fulfilled, saying, 23 “BEHOLD, THE
VIRGIN SHALL BE WITH CHILD AND SHALL
BEAR A SON, AND THEY SHALL CALL HIS NAME
IMMANUEL,” which translated means,
“GOD WITH US.” 24 And Joseph got up from
his sleep and did as the angel of the Lord
commanded him, and took *Mary* as his wife,
25 but kept her a virgin until she gave birth to
a Son; and he called His name Jesus.

JANUARY 2

Genesis 3:1–4:26

3 Now the serpent was more crafty than
any beast of the field which Yahweh
God had made. And he said to the woman,
“Indeed, has God said, ‘You shall not eat
from any tree of the garden’?” 2 And the
woman said to the serpent, “From the fruit
of the trees of the garden we may eat; 3 but
from the fruit of the tree which is in the
midst of the garden, God said, ‘You shall
not eat from it, and you shall not touch it,
lest you die.’” 4 And the serpent said to the
woman, “You surely will not die! 5 For God
knows that in the day you eat from it your
eyes will be opened, and you will be like
God, knowing good and evil.” 6 Then the
woman saw that the tree was good for food,
and that it was a delight to the eyes, and that
the tree was desirable to make *one* wise, so
she took from its fruit and ate; and she gave
also to her husband with her, and he ate.
7 And the eyes of both of them were opened,
and they knew that they were naked; and
they sewed fig leaves together and made
themselves loin coverings.

8 Then they heard the sound of Yahweh God
walking in the garden in the cool of the day,
and the man and his wife hid themselves from
the presence of Yahweh God in the midst of
the trees of the garden. 9 Yahweh God called
to the man and said to him, “Where are you?”
10 And he said, “I heard the sound of You in the
garden, and I was afraid because I was naked;
so I hid.” 11 And He said, “Who told you that
you were naked? Have you eaten from the tree
of which I commanded you not to eat?” 12 And
the man said, “The woman whom You gave *to*
be with me, she gave to me from the tree, and I
ate.” 13 Then Yahweh God said to the woman,
“What is this you have done?” And the woman
said, “The serpent deceived me, and I ate.”
14 And Yahweh God said to the serpent,

“Because you have done this,
Cursed are you more than
any of the cattle,
And more than every beast of the field;
On your belly you will go,
And dust you will eat
All the days of your life;
15 And I will put enmity
Between you and the woman,
And between your seed and her seed;
He shall bruise you on the head,
And you shall bruise him on the heel.”

16 To the woman He said,

“I will greatly multiply
Your pain and conception,
In pain you will bear children;
Your desire will be for your husband,
And he will rule over you.”

17 Then to Adam He said, “Because you
have listened to the voice of your wife and
have eaten from the tree about which I
commanded you, saying, ‘You shall not eat
from it’;

Cursed is the ground because of you;
In pain you will eat of it
All the days of your life.
18 “Both thorns and thistles it
shall grow for you;
And you will eat the plants of the field;
19 By the sweat of your face
You will eat bread,
Till you return to the ground,
Because from it you were taken;
For you are dust,
And to dust you shall return.”

20 Now the man called his wife’s name
Eve, because she was the mother of all *the*
living. 21 Then Yahweh God made garments
of skin for Adam and his wife, and He
clothed them.

22 Then Yahweh God said, “Behold, the
man has become like one of Us to know
good and evil; and now, lest he send forth his
hand and take also from the tree of life and
eat and live forever”— 23 therefore Yahweh
God sent him out from the garden of Eden,
to cultivate the ground from which he was
taken. 24 So He drove the man out; and at
the east of the garden of Eden He stationed
the cherubim and the flaming sword which

turned every direction to guard the way to
the tree of life.

4 Now the man knew his wife Eve, and she
conceived and gave birth to Cain, and
she said, "I have gotten a man with *the help
of* Yahweh." 2 And again, she gave birth to his
brother Abel. Abel was a keeper of flocks,
but Cain was a cultivator of the ground. 3 So
it happened in the course of time that Cain
brought an offering to Yahweh of the fruit of
the ground. 4 Abel, on his part, also brought
of the firstborn of his flock and of their fat
portions. And Yahweh had regard for Abel
and for his offering; 5 but for Cain and for his
offering He had no regard. So Cain became
very angry, and his countenance fell. 6 Then
Yahweh said to Cain, "Why are you angry?
And why has your countenance fallen? 7 If
you do well, will not *your countenance* be
lifted up? And if you do not do well, sin is
lying at the door; and its desire is for you,
but you must rule over it." 8 Then Cain spoke
to Abel his brother; and it happened when
they were in the field, that Cain rose up
against Abel his brother and killed him.

9 Then Yahweh said to Cain, "Where is
Abel your brother?" And he said, "I do not
know. Am I my brother's keeper?" 10 And
He said, "What have you done? The voice
of your brother's blood is crying out to Me
from the ground. 11 And now, cursed are
you from the ground, which has opened
its mouth to receive your brother's blood
from your hand. 12 When you cultivate the
ground, it will no longer yield its strength to
you; you will be a vagrant and a wanderer on
the earth." 13 And Cain said to Yahweh, "My
punishment is too great to bear! 14 Behold,
You have driven me this day from the face
of the ground; and from Your face I will
be hidden, and I will be a vagrant and a
wanderer on the earth, and it will be that
whoever finds me will kill me." 15 So Yahweh
said to him, "Therefore whoever kills Cain,
vengeance will be taken on him sevenfold."
And Yahweh appointed a sign for Cain, so
that no one who found him would strike
him.

16 Then Cain went out from the presence
of Yahweh and settled in the land of Nod,
east of Eden.

17 Then Cain knew his wife, and she
conceived and gave birth to Enoch; and he
built a city and called the name of the city
Enoch, after the name of his son. 18 Now to
Enoch was born Irad, and Irad was the father
of Mehujael, and Mehujael was the father of
Methushael, and Methushael was the father
of Lamech. 19 And Lamech took for himself
two wives: the name of the one was Adah,
and the name of the other, Zillah. 20 And
Adah gave birth to Jabal; he was the father
of those who live in tents and *have* livestock.
21 And his brother's name was Jubal; he was
the father of all those who play the lyre and
pipe. 22 As for Zillah, she also gave birth to
Tubal-cain, the forger of all implements of
bronze and iron; and the sister of Tubal-cain
was Naamah.

23 And Lamech said to his wives,
"Adah and Zillah,
Hear my voice,
You wives of Lamech,
Give ear to my word,
For I have killed a man for striking me;
And a boy for wounding me;
24 If Cain is avenged sevenfold,
Then Lamech seventy-sevenfold."

25 Then Adam knew his wife again; and
she gave birth to a son and named him
Seth, for *she said*, "God has set for me
another seed in place of Abel, for Cain
killed him." 26 And to Seth, to him also,
a son was born; and he called his name
Enosh. Then *men* began to call upon the
name of Yahweh.

Psalm 2:1–6

1 Why do the nations rage
And the peoples meditate
on a vain thing?
2 The kings of the earth take their stand
And the rulers take counsel together
Against Yahweh and against
His Anointed, *saying*,
3 "Let us tear their fetters apart
And cast away their cords from us!"

4 He who sits in the heavens laughs,
The Lord mocks them.
5 Then He speaks to them in His anger
And terrifies them in His fury, *saying*,
6 "But as for Me, I have installed My King
Upon Zion, My holy mountain."

Proverbs 1:8–9

8 Hear, my son, your father's discipline
And do not abandon your
mother's instruction;

9 For they are a garland of
grace for your head
And ornaments about your neck.

Matthew 2:1–23

2 Now after Jesus was born in Bethlehem of Judea in the days of Herod the king, behold, magi from the east arrived in Jerusalem, saying, 2 “Where is He who has been born King of the Jews? For we saw His star in the east and have come to worship Him.” 3 And when Herod the king heard *this*, he was troubled, and all Jerusalem with him. 4 And gathering together all the chief priests and scribes of the people, he was inquiring of them where the Christ was to be born. 5 And they said to him, “In Bethlehem of Judea; for this is what has been written by the prophet:

6 ‘And you, Bethlehem,
land of Judah,
Are by no means least among
the leaders of Judah;
For out of you shall come
forth a Leader
Who will shepherd My
people Israel.’”

7 Then Herod secretly called the magi and carefully determined from them the time the star appeared. 8 And he sent them to Bethlehem and said, “Go and search carefully for the Child; and when you have found *Him*, report to me, so that I too may come and worship Him.” 9 Now after hearing the king, they went their way; and behold, the star, which they had seen in the east, was going on before them until it came and stood over *the place* where the Child was. 10 And when they saw the star, they rejoiced exceedingly with great joy. 11 And after coming into the house they saw the Child with Mary His mother; and they fell to the ground and worshiped Him. Then, opening their treasures, they presented to Him gifts of gold, frankincense, and myrrh. 12 And having been warned in a dream not to return to Herod, the magi departed for their own country by another way.

13 Now when they had departed, behold, an angel of the Lord *appeared to Joseph in a dream, saying, “Get up! Take the Child and His mother and flee to Egypt, and remain there until I tell you; for Herod is going to search for the Child to destroy Him.”

14 So Joseph got up and took the Child and His mother while it was still night, and departed for Egypt. 15 And he remained there until the death of Herod, in order that what had been spoken by the Lord through the prophet would be fulfilled, saying, “Out of Egypt I called My Son.”

16 Then when Herod saw that he had been tricked by the magi, he became very enraged, and sent and slew all the male children who were in Bethlehem and all its vicinity, from two years old and under, according to the time which he had carefully determined from the magi. 17 Then what had been spoken through Jeremiah the prophet was fulfilled, saying,

18 “A voice was heard in Ramah,
Weeping and great mourning,
Rachel weeping for her children;
And she was refusing to
be comforted,
Because they were no more.”

19 But when Herod died, behold, an angel of the Lord *appeared in a dream to Joseph in Egypt, saying, 20 “Get up, take the Child and His mother, and go into the land of Israel; for those who sought the Child’s life are dead.” 21 So Joseph got up, took the Child and His mother, and came into the land of Israel. 22 But when he heard that Archelaus was reigning over Judea in place of his father Herod, he was afraid to go there. Then after being warned *by God* in a dream, he departed for the district of Galilee, 23 and came and lived in a city called Nazareth, so that what was spoken through the prophets would be fulfilled: “He shall be called a Nazarene.”

JANUARY 3

Genesis 5:1–6:22

5 This is the book of the generations of Adam. In the day when God created man, He made him in the likeness of God. 2 He created them male and female, and He blessed them and named them Man in the day when they were created.

3 When Adam had lived 130 years, he became the father of *a son* in his own likeness, according to his image, and named

him Seth. 4 Then the days of Adam after he
became the father of Seth were 800 years,
and he became the father of *other* sons and
daughters. 5 So all the days that Adam lived
were 930 years, and he died.

6 And Seth lived 105 years and became the
father of Enosh. 7 Then Seth lived 807 years
after he became the father of Enosh, and he
had *other* sons and daughters. 8 So all the
days of Seth were 912 years, and he died.

9 And Enosh lived 90 years and became
the father of Kenan. 10 Then Enosh lived 815
years after he became the father of Kenan,
and he became the father of *other* sons and
daughters. 11 So all the days of Enosh were
905 years, and he died.

12 And Kenan lived 70 years and became
the father of Mahalalel. 13 Then Kenan
lived 840 years after he became the father
of Mahalalel, and he became the father of
other sons and daughters. 14 So all the days
of Kenan were 910 years, and he died.

15 And Mahalalel lived 65 years and
became the father of Jared. 16 Then Maha-
lalel lived 830 years after he became the
father of Jared, and he became the father of
other sons and daughters. 17 So all the days
of Mahalalel were 895 years, and he died.

18 And Jared lived 162 years and became
the father of Enoch. 19 Then Jared lived 800
years after he became the father of Enoch,
and he became the father of *other* sons and
daughters. 20 So all the days of Jared were
962 years, and he died.

21 And Enoch lived 65 years and became
the father of Methuselah. 22 Then Enoch
walked with God 300 years after he became
the father of Methuselah, and he became
the father of *other* sons and daughters.
23 So all the days of Enoch were 365 years.
24 Enoch walked with God; and he was not,
for God took him.

25 And Methuselah lived 187 years and
became the father of Lamech. 26 Then
Methuselah lived 782 years after he became
the father of Lamech, and he became the
father of *other* sons and daughters. 27 So all
the days of Methuselah were 969 years, and
he died.

28 And Lamech lived 182 years and
became the father of a son. 29 Now he called
his name Noah, saying, "This one will give
us rest from our work and from the pain of
our hands *arising* from the ground which
Yahweh has cursed." 30 Then Lamech lived
595 years after he became the father of
Noah, and he became the father of *other*
sons and daughters. 31 So all the days of
Lamech were 777 years, and he died.

32 And Noah was 500 years old, and
Noah became the father of Shem, Ham,
and Japheth.

6 Now it happened, when men began to
multiply on the face of the land, and
daughters were born to them, 2 that the sons
of God saw that the daughters of men were
good *in appearance*; and they took wives for
themselves, whomever they chose. 3 Then
Yahweh said, "My Spirit shall not strive with
man forever because he indeed is flesh;
nevertheless his days shall be 120 years."
4 The Nephilim were on the earth in those
days, and also afterward, when the sons of
God came in to the daughters of men, and
they bore *children* to them. Those were
the mighty men who *were* of old, men of
renown.

5 Then Yahweh saw that the evil of man
was great on the earth, and that every intent
of the thoughts of his heart was only evil
continually. 6 And Yahweh regretted that
He had made man on the earth, and He was
grieved in His heart. 7 And Yahweh said, "I
will blot out man whom I have created from
the face of the land, from man to animals to
creeping things and to birds of the sky; for
I regret that I have made them." 8 But Noah
found favor in the eyes of Yahweh.

9 These are the generations of Noah. Noah
was a righteous man, blameless among
those in his generations; Noah walked with
God. 10 And Noah became the father of three
sons: Shem, Ham, and Japheth.

11 Now the earth was corrupt before
God, and the earth was filled with violence.
12 And God saw the earth, and behold, it was
corrupt; for all flesh had corrupted their way
upon the earth.

13 Then God said to Noah, "The end of
all flesh has come before Me; for the earth
is filled with violence because of them;
and behold, I am about to destroy them
with the earth. 14 Make for yourself an
ark of gopher wood; you shall make the
ark with rooms, and you shall cover it
inside and out with pitch. 15 Now this is
how you shall make it: the length of the
ark 300 cubits, its breadth 50 cubits, and
its height 30 cubits. 16 You shall make a

window for the ark, and complete it to
one cubit from the top; and set the door of
the ark in the side of it; you shall make it
with lower, second, and third decks. 17 As
for Me, behold I am bringing the flood of
water upon the earth, to destroy all flesh
in which is the breath of life, from under
heaven; everything that is on the earth
shall breathe its last. 18 But I will establish
My covenant with you; and you shall enter
the ark—you and your sons and your wife
and your sons' wives with you. 19 And of
every living thing of all flesh, you shall
bring two of every *kind* into the ark, to
keep *them* alive with you; they shall be
male and female. 20 Of the birds after their
kind, and of the animals after their kind,
of every creeping thing of the ground after
its kind, two of every *kind* will come to you
to keep *them* alive. 21 As for you, take for
yourself some of all food which is edible,
and gather *it* to yourself; and it shall be
for food for you and for them." 22 Thus
Noah did; according to all that God had
commanded him, so he did.

Psalm 2:7–12

7 "I will surely tell of the
decree of Yahweh:
He said to Me, 'You are My Son,
Today I have begotten You.
8 'Ask of Me, and I will surely give the
nations as Your inheritance,
And the ends of the earth
as Your possession.
9 'You shall break them with
a rod of iron,
You shall shatter them like
a potter's vessel.'"

10 So now, O kings, show insight;
Take warning, O judges of the earth.
11 Serve Yahweh with fear
And rejoice with trembling.
12 Kiss the Son, lest He become angry,
and you perish *in* the way,
For His wrath may soon be kindled.
How blessed are all who
take refuge in Him!

Proverbs 1:10–19

10 My son, if sinners entice you,
Do not be willing.
11 If they say, "Come with us,
Let us lie in wait for blood,
Let us ambush the innocent
without cause;
12 Let us swallow them alive like Sheol,
And whole, as those who
go down to the pit;
13 We will find all *kinds* of
precious wealth,
We will fill our houses with spoil;
14 Cast in your lot with us,
We shall all have one purse,"
15 My son, do not walk in the
way with them.
Withhold your feet from their pathway,
16 For their feet run to evil
And they hasten to shed blood.
17 For it is no use that a net is spread
In the sight of any bird;
18 But they lie in wait for their own blood;
They ambush their own lives.
19 So are the paths of everyone
who is greedy for gain;
It takes away the life of its possessors.

Matthew 3:1–17

3 Now in those days John the Baptist
*came, preaching in the wilderness of
Judea, saying, 2 "Repent, for the kingdom
of heaven is at hand." 3 For this is the one
referred to by Isaiah the prophet, saying,
"THE VOICE OF ONE CRYING
IN THE WILDERNESS,
'MAKE READY THE WAY OF THE LORD,
MAKE HIS PATHS STRAIGHT!'"
4 Now John himself had a garment of camel's
hair and a leather belt around his waist; and
his food was locusts and wild honey. 5 Then
Jerusalem was going out to him, and all
Judea, and all the district around the Jordan;
6 and they were being baptized by him in the
Jordan River, as they confessed their sins.
7 But when he saw many of the Pharisees
and Sadducees coming for his baptism, he
said to them, "You brood of vipers, who
warned you to flee from the wrath to
come? 8 Therefore bear fruit in keeping with
repentance; 9 and do not suppose that you
can say to yourselves, 'We have Abraham for
our father'; for I say to you that from these
stones God is able to raise up children to
Abraham. 10 And the axe is already laid at
the root of the trees; therefore every tree
that does not bear good fruit is cut down
and thrown into the fire.
11 "As for me, I baptize you with water for
repentance, but He who is coming after me

is mightier than I, and I am not fit to remove His sandals; He will baptize you with the Holy Spirit and fire. 12 His winnowing fork is in His hand, and He will thoroughly clear His threshing floor; and He will gather His wheat into the barn, but He will burn up the chaff with unquenchable fire."

13 Then Jesus *arrived from Galilee at the Jordan *coming* to John to be baptized by him. 14 But John tried to prevent Him, saying, "I have need to be baptized by You, and do You come to me?" 15 But Jesus answered and said to him, "Permit *it* at this time; for in this way it is fitting for us to fulfill all righteousness." Then he *permitted Him. 16 And after being baptized, Jesus came up immediately from the water; and behold, the heavens were opened, and he saw the Spirit of God descending like a dove *and* coming upon Him, 17 and behold, *there was* a voice out of the heavens saying, "This is My beloved Son, in whom I am well-pleased."

JANUARY 4

Genesis 7:1–8:22

7 Then Yahweh said to Noah, "Enter the ark, you and all your household, for you *alone* I have seen *to be* righteous before Me in this generation. 2 You shall take with you of every clean animal by sevens, a male and his female; and of the animals that are not clean, two, a male and his female; 3 also of the birds of the sky, by sevens, male and female, to keep *their* seed alive on the face of all the earth. 4 For after seven more days, I will send rain on the earth forty days and forty nights; and I will blot out from the face of the land every living thing that I have made." 5 And Noah did according to all that Yahweh had commanded him.

6 Now Noah was six hundred years old when the flood of water came upon the earth. 7 Then Noah and his sons and his wife and his sons' wives with him entered the ark because of the water of the flood. 8 Of clean animals and animals that are not clean and birds and everything that creeps on the ground, 9 by twos they came to Noah into the ark, male and female, as God had commanded Noah. 10 Now it happened after the seven days, that the water of the flood came upon the earth. 11 In the six hundredth year of Noah's life, in the second month, on the seventeenth day of the month, on this day all the fountains of the great deep split open, and the floodgates of the sky were opened. 12 Then the rain came upon the earth for forty days and forty nights.

13 On this very day Noah and Shem and Ham and Japheth, the sons of Noah, and Noah's wife and the three wives of his sons with them, entered the ark, 14 they and every beast after its kind, and all the cattle after their kind, and every creeping thing that creeps on the earth after its kind, and every bird after its kind—every fowl, every winged creature. 15 So they came to Noah into the ark, by twos of all flesh in which was the breath of life. 16 And those that entered, male and female of all flesh, entered as God had commanded him; and Yahweh closed *it* behind him.

17 Then the flood came upon the earth for forty days, and the water multiplied and lifted up the ark, so that it rose above the earth. 18 And the water prevailed and multiplied greatly upon the earth, and the ark went on the surface of the water. 19 And the water prevailed more and more upon the earth, so that all the high mountains under all the heavens were covered. 20 The water prevailed fifteen cubits higher, and the mountains were covered. 21 And all flesh that moved on the earth breathed its last, that is birds and cattle and beasts and every swarming thing that swarms upon the earth, as well as all mankind. 22 All in whose nostrils was the breath of the spirit of life—of all that was on the dry land—died. 23 Thus He blotted out every living thing that was upon the face of the land, from man to animals to creeping things and to birds of the sky, and they were blotted out from the earth; and only Noah remained, and those that were with him in the ark. 24 And the water prevailed upon the earth 150 days.

8 Then God remembered Noah and all the beasts and all the cattle that were with him in the ark; and God caused a wind to pass over the earth, and the water subsided. 2 Also the fountains of the deep and the floodgates of the sky were closed, and the rain from the sky was restrained;

3 and the water receded from the earth,
going *forth* and returning, and at the end
of 150 days the water decreased. 4 In the
seventh month, on the seventeenth day of
the month, the ark rested upon the moun-
tains of Ararat. 5 Now the water decreased
steadily until the tenth month; in the tenth
month, on the first day of the month, the
tops of the mountains appeared.
6 Then it happened at the end of forty
days, that Noah opened the window of the
ark which he had made; 7 and he sent out a
raven, and it went out *flying* back and forth
until the water was dried up from the earth.
8 Then he sent out a dove from him, to see
if the water was abated from the face of the
land; 9 but the dove found no resting place
for the sole of its foot, so it returned to him
into the ark, for the water was on the surface
of all the earth. Then he stretched out his
hand and took it and brought it into the ark
to himself. 10 Then he waited yet another
seven days; and again he sent out the dove
from the ark. 11 And the dove came to him
toward evening, and behold, in its beak was
a freshly picked olive leaf. So Noah knew
that the water was abated from the earth.
12 Then he waited yet another seven days
and sent out the dove; but it did not return
to him again.
13 Now it happened in the six hundred
and first year, in the first *month,* on the
first of the month, the water was dried up
from the earth. Then Noah removed the
covering of the ark and looked, and behold,
the surface of the ground was dried up. 14 In
the second month, on the twenty-seventh
day of the month, the earth was dry. 15 Then
God spoke to Noah, saying, 16 "Go out of the
ark, you and your wife and your sons and
your sons' wives with you. 17 Bring out with
you every living thing of all flesh that is with
you, birds and animals and every creeping
thing that creeps on the earth, that they
may swarm on the earth, and that they
may be fruitful and multiply on the earth."
18 So Noah went out, and his sons and his
wife and his sons' wives with him. 19 Every
beast, every creeping thing, and every bird,
everything that moves on the earth, went
out by their families from the ark.
20 Then Noah built an altar to Yahweh
and took of every clean animal and of every
clean bird and offered burnt offerings on the
altar. 21 And Yahweh smelled the soothing
aroma; and Yahweh said to Himself, "I will
never again curse the ground because of
man, for the intent of man's heart is evil
from his youth; and I will never again strike
down every living thing as I have done.
22 "While all the days of the earth *remain,*
Seedtime and harvest,
And cold and heat,
And summer and winter,
And day and night
Shall not cease."

Psalm 3:1–4

1 O Yahweh, how my adversaries
have become many!
Many are rising up against me.
2 Many are saying of my soul,
"There is no salvation for
him in God." Selah.
3 But You, O Yahweh, are a
shield about me,
My glory, and the One
who lifts my head.
4 I was calling to Yahweh with my voice,
And He answered me from
His holy mountain. Selah.

Proverbs 1:20–22

20 Wisdom shouts in the street,
She gives forth her voice in the square;
21 At the head of the noisy
streets she calls out;
At the entrance of the gates in the
city she utters her sayings:
22 "How long, O simple ones, will
you love simplicity?
And scoffers delight in scoffing
And fools hate knowledge?

Matthew 4:1–25

4 Then Jesus was led up by the Spirit into
the wilderness to be tempted by the
devil. 2 And after He had fasted forty days
and forty nights, He then became hungry.
3 And the tempter came and said to Him, "If
You are the Son of God, command that these
stones become bread." 4 But He answered
and said, "It is written, 'MAN SHALL NOT LIVE
ON BREAD ALONE, BUT ON EVERY WORD THAT
PROCEEDS OUT OF THE MOUTH OF GOD.'"
5 Then the devil *took Him into the holy
city and had Him stand on the pinnacle of the
temple, 6 and *said to Him, "If You are the Son
of God, throw Yourself down; for it is written,

'He will command His angels
concerning You';
and
'On *their* hands they will bear You up,
Lest You strike Your foot
against a stone.'"
7 Jesus said to him, "Again, it is written, 'You
shall not put the Lord your God to the
test.'"
8 Again, the devil *took Him to a very
high mountain and *showed Him all the
kingdoms of the world and their glory;
9 and he said to Him, "All these things I will
give You, if You fall down and worship me."
10 Then Jesus *said to him, "Go, Satan! For
it is written, 'You shall worship the Lord
your God, and serve Him only.'" 11 Then
the devil *left Him; and behold, angels came
and *began to* minister to Him.
12 Now when *Jesus* heard that John had
been taken into custody, He departed into
Galilee; 13 and leaving Nazareth, He came
and lived in Capernaum, which is by the sea,
in the region of Zebulun and Naphtali, 14 in
order that what was spoken through Isaiah
the prophet would be fulfilled, saying,
15 "The land of Zebulun and
the land of Naphtali,
By the way of the sea, beyond the
Jordan, Galilee of the Gentiles—
16 The people who were sitting in
darkness saw a great Light,
And those who were sitting in the
land and shadow of death,
Upon them a Light dawned."
17 From that time Jesus began to preach
and say, "Repent, for the kingdom of heaven
is at hand."
18 Now as *Jesus* was walking by the Sea of
Galilee, He saw two brothers, Simon who was
called Peter, and Andrew his brother, casting
a net into the sea; for they were fishermen.
19 And He *said to them, "Follow Me, and I
will make you fishers of men." 20 And imme-
diately they left their nets and followed Him.
21 And going on from there He saw two other
brothers, James the *son* of Zebedee, and John
his brother, in the boat with Zebedee their
father, mending their nets; and He called
them. 22 And immediately they left the boat
and their father, and followed Him.
23 And Jesus was going throughout all
Galilee, teaching in their synagogues and
preaching the gospel of the kingdom, and
healing every kind of disease and every kind
of sickness among the people.
24 And the news about Him spread
throughout all Syria; and they brought to
Him all who were ill, those suffering with
various diseases and pains, demoniacs,
epileptics, paralytics; and He healed them.
25 And large crowds followed Him from
Galilee and the Decapolis and Jerusalem and
Judea and *from* beyond the Jordan.

JANUARY 5

Genesis 9:1–10:32

9 And God blessed Noah and his sons and
said to them, "Be fruitful and multiply,
and fill the earth. 2 And the fear of you and
the terror of you will be on every beast of
the earth and on every bird of the sky; with
everything that creeps on the ground, and
all the fish of the sea, into your hand they
are given. 3 Every moving thing that is alive
shall be food for you; as *with* the green
plant, I give all to you. 4 However, flesh with
its life, *that is*, its blood, you shall not eat.
5 Surely I will require your lifeblood; from
every living thing I will require it. And from
every man, from each man's brother I will
require the life of man.
6 "Whoever sheds man's blood,
By man his blood shall
be shed,
For in the image of God
He made man.
7 "As for you, be fruitful and multiply;
Swarm on the earth and multiply in it."
8 Then God spoke to Noah and to his
sons with him, saying, 9 "As for Me, behold,
I establish My covenant with you and with
your seed after you; 10 and with every living
creature that is with you, the birds, the cat-
tle, and every beast of the earth with you;
of all that comes out of the ark, even every
beast of the earth. 11 Indeed I establish My
covenant with you; and all flesh shall never
again be cut off by the water of the flood,
and there shall never again be a flood to
destroy the earth." 12 Then God said, "This
is the sign of the covenant which I am giving
to be between Me and you and every living
creature that is with you, for all successive

generations; 13 I put My bow in the cloud, and
it shall be for a sign of a covenant between
Me and the earth. 14 And it will be, when I
bring a cloud over the earth, that the bow
will be seen in the cloud, 15 and I will remem-
ber My covenant, which is between Me and
you and every living creature of all flesh; and
never again shall the water become a flood to
destroy all flesh. 16 So the bow shall be in the
cloud, and I will look upon it, to remember
the everlasting covenant between God and
every living creature of all flesh that is on
the earth." 17 And God said to Noah, "This
is the sign of the covenant which I have
established between Me and all flesh that
is on the earth."

18 Now the sons of Noah who went out of
the ark were Shem and Ham and Japheth;
and Ham was the father of Canaan. 19 These
three *were* the sons of Noah, and from these
the whole earth was scattered abroad.

20 Then Noah began *to be* a man of the
land and planted a vineyard. 21 And he
drank of the wine and became drunk and
uncovered himself inside his tent. 22 Then
Ham, the father of Canaan, saw the naked-
ness of his father and told his two brothers
outside. 23 But Shem and Japheth took the
garment and laid it upon both their shoul-
ders and walked backward and covered the
nakedness of their father; and their faces
were turned backward, so that they did not
see their father's nakedness. 24 Then Noah
awoke from his wine, and he knew what his
youngest son had done to him. 25 So he said,

"Cursed be Canaan;
A servant of servants
He shall be to his brothers."

26 And he said,
"Blessed be Yahweh,
The God of Shem;
And let Canaan be his servant.
27 "May God enlarge Japheth,
And let him dwell in the tents of Shem;
And let Canaan be his servant."

28 And Noah lived 350 years after the
flood. 29 So all the days of Noah were 950
years, and he died.

10 Now these are the generations of
Shem, Ham, and Japheth, the sons
of Noah; and sons were born to them after
the flood.

2 The sons of Japheth *were* Gomer and
Magog and Madai and Javan and Tubal and
Meshech and Tiras. 3 The sons of Gomer
were Ashkenaz and Riphath and Togarmah.
4 The sons of Javan *were* Elishah and Tarsh-
ish, Kittim and Dodanim. 5 From these the
coastlands of the nations were separated
into their lands, every one according to his
tongue, according to their families, into
their nations.

6 The sons of Ham *were* Cush and Mizraim
and Put and Canaan. 7 The sons of Cush *were*
Seba and Havilah and Sabtah and Raamah
and Sabteca; and the sons of Raamah *were*
Sheba and Dedan. 8 Now Cush was the father
of Nimrod; he began to be a mighty one on
the earth. 9 He was a mighty hunter before
Yahweh; therefore it is said, "Like Nimrod
a mighty hunter before Yahweh." 10 The
beginning of his kingdom was Babel and
Erech and Accad and Calneh, in the land
of Shinar. 11 From that land he went out to
Assyria and built Nineveh and Rehoboth-Ir
and Calah, 12 and Resen between Nineveh
and Calah; that is the great city. 13 Mizraim
was the father of Ludim and Anamim and
Lehabim and Naphtuhim 14 and Pathrusim
and Casluhim (from whom came the Philis-
tines) and Caphtorim.

15 Canaan was the father of Sidon, his
firstborn, and Heth 16 and the Jebusite and
the Amorite and the Girgashite 17 and the
Hivite and the Arkite and the Sinite 18 and
the Arvadite and the Zemarite and the
Hamathite; and afterward the families of the
Canaanite were scattered. 19 The border of
the Canaanite extended from Sidon as you
go toward Gerar, as far as Gaza; as you go
toward Sodom and Gomorrah and Admah
and Zeboiim, as far as Lasha. 20 These are
the sons of Ham, according to their families,
according to their tongues, by their lands,
by their nations.

21 Also to Shem, the father of all the
children of Eber, *and* the older brother of
Japheth, children were born. 22 The sons of
Shem *were* Elam and Asshur and Arpach-
shad and Lud and Aram. 23 The sons of Aram
were Uz and Hul and Gether and Mash.
24 Arpachshad was the father of Shelah;
and Shelah was the father of Eber. 25 Now
two sons were born to Eber; the name of the
one *was* Peleg, for in his days the earth was
divided; and his brother's name *was* Joktan.
26 And Joktan was the father of Almodad and
Sheleph and Hazarmaveth and Jerah 27 and
Hadoram and Uzal and Diklah 28 and Obal

and Abimael and Sheba 29 and Ophir and
Havilah and Jobab; all these were the sons
of Joktan. 30 Now their settlement extended
from Mesha as you go toward Sephar, the
hill country of the east. 31 These are the
sons of Shem, according to their families,
according to their tongues, by their lands,
according to their nations.
32 These are the families of the sons of
Noah, according to their generations, by
their nations; and out of these the nations
were separated on the earth after the flood.

Psalm 3:5–8

5 I lay down and slept;
I awoke, for Yahweh sustains me.
6 I will not be afraid of ten
thousands of people
Who *all* around have set
themselves against me.

7 Arise, O Yahweh; save me, O my God!
For You have struck all my
enemies on the cheek;
You have shattered the
teeth of the wicked.
8 Salvation belongs to Yahweh;
Your blessing *be* upon Your
people! Selah.

Proverbs 1:23–27

23 "Turn to my reproof,
Behold, I will pour out
my spirit on you;
I will make my words known to you.
24 "Because I called and you refused,
I stretched out my hand and
no one paid attention;
25 And you neglected all my counsel
And were not willing to
accept my reproof;
26 I will also laugh at your disaster;
I will mock when your dread comes,
27 When your dread comes like a storm
And your disaster comes
like a whirlwind,
When distress and anguish
come upon you.

Matthew 5:1–26

5 Now when Jesus saw the crowds, He
went up on the mountain; and after He
sat down, His disciples came to Him. 2 And
He opened His mouth and *began to* teach
them, saying,

3 "Blessed are the poor in spirit, for theirs
is the kingdom of heaven.

4 Blessed are those who mourn, for they
shall be comforted.

5 Blessed are the lowly, for they shall
inherit the earth.

6 Blessed are those who hunger and
thirst for righteousness, for they shall
be satisfied.

7 Blessed are the merciful, for they shall
receive mercy.

8 Blessed are the pure in heart, for they
shall see God.

9 Blessed are the peacemakers, for they
shall be called sons of God.

10 Blessed are those who have
been persecuted for the sake of
righteousness, for theirs is the
kingdom of heaven.

11 "Blessed are you when *people* insult you
and persecute you, and falsely say all kinds
of evil against you because of Me. 12 Rejoice
and be glad, for your reward in heaven is
great; for in the same way they persecuted
the prophets who were before you.
13 "You are the salt of the earth; but if
the salt has become tasteless, how will it
be made salty *again*? It is no longer good
for anything, except to be thrown out to be
trampled under foot by men.
14 "You are the light of the world. A city
set on a hill cannot be hidden; 15 nor does
anyone light a lamp and put it under a
basket, but on the lampstand, and it gives
light to all who are in the house. 16 Let your
light shine before men in such a way that
they may see your good works, and glorify
your Father who is in heaven.
17 "Do not think that I came to abolish
the Law or the Prophets; I did not come
to abolish but to fulfill. 18 For truly I say
to you, until heaven and earth pass away,
not the smallest letter or stroke shall pass
from the Law until all is accomplished.
19 Whoever then annuls one of the least of
these commandments, and teaches others
to do the same, shall be called least in the

kingdom of heaven; but whoever does and teaches *them*, he shall be called great in the kingdom of heaven.

20 "For I say to you that unless your righteousness surpasses *that* of the scribes and Pharisees, you will not enter the kingdom of heaven.

21 "You have heard that the ancients were told, 'YOU SHALL NOT MURDER' and 'Whoever murders shall be guilty before the court.' 22 But I say to you that everyone who is angry with his brother shall be guilty before the court; and whoever says to his brother, 'Raca,' shall be guilty before the Sanhedrin; and whoever says, 'You fool,' shall be guilty *enough to go* into the fiery hell. 23 Therefore if you are presenting your offering at the altar, and there remember that your brother has something against you, 24 leave your offering there before the altar and go; first be reconciled to your brother, and then come and present your offering. 25 Make friends quickly with your opponent at law while you are with him on the way, so that your opponent may not hand you over to the judge, and the judge to the officer, and you be thrown into prison. 26 Truly I say to you, you will not come out of there until you have paid up the last quadrans.

JANUARY 6

Genesis 11:1–12:20

11 Now the whole earth had the same language and the same words. 2 And it happened as they journeyed east, that they found a plain in the land of Shinar and settled there. 3 Then they said to one another, "Come, let us make bricks and burn *them* thoroughly." And they had brick for stone, and they had tar for mortar. 4 And they said, "Come, let us build for ourselves a city, and a tower whose top *will reach* into heaven, and let us make for ourselves a name, lest we be scattered over the face of the whole earth." 5 Then Yahweh came down to see the city and the tower which the sons of men had built. 6 And Yahweh said, "Behold, they are one people, and they all have the same language. And this is what they have begun to do. So now nothing which they purpose to do will be impossible for them. 7 Come, let Us go down and there confuse their language, so that they will not understand one another's language." 8 So Yahweh scattered them from there over the face of the whole earth; and they stopped building the city. 9 Therefore its name was called Babel, because there Yahweh confused the language of the whole earth; and from there Yahweh scattered them over the face of the whole earth.

10 These are the generations of Shem. Shem was 100 years old and became the father of Arpachshad two years after the flood; 11 and Shem lived 500 years after he became the father of Arpachshad, and he became the father of *other* sons and daughters.

12 And Arpachshad lived 35 years and became the father of Shelah; 13 and Arpachshad lived 403 years after he became the father of Shelah, and he became the father of *other* sons and daughters.

14 And Shelah lived 30 years and became the father of Eber; 15 and Shelah lived 403 years after he became the father of Eber, and he became the father of *other* sons and daughters.

16 And Eber lived 34 years and became the father of Peleg; 17 and Eber lived 430 years after he became the father of Peleg, and he became the father of *other* sons and daughters.

18 And Peleg lived 30 years and became the father of Reu; 19 and Peleg lived 209 years after he became the father of Reu, and he became the father of *other* sons and daughters.

20 And Reu lived 32 years and became the father of Serug; 21 and Reu lived 207 years after he became the father of Serug, and he became the father of *other* sons and daughters.

22 And Serug lived 30 years and became the father of Nahor; 23 and Serug lived 200 years after he became the father of Nahor, and he became the father of *other* sons and daughters.

24 Nahor lived 29 years and became the father of Terah; 25 and Nahor lived 119 years after he became the father of Terah, and he became the father of *other* sons and daughters.

26 And Terah lived 70 years and became the father of Abram, Nahor, and Haran.

27 Now these are the generations of Terah.
Terah became the father of Abram, Nahor,
and Haran; and Haran became the father
of Lot. 28 And Haran died in the presence
of Terah his father in the land of his birth,
in Ur of the Chaldeans. 29 Abram and Nahor
took wives for themselves. The name of
Abram's wife was Sarai; and the name of
Nahor's wife was Milcah, the daughter of
Haran, the father of Milcah and the father
of Iscah. 30 And Sarai was barren; she had
no child.

31 And Terah took Abram his son, and
Lot the son of Haran, his grandson, and
Sarai his daughter-in-law, his son Abram's
wife; and they went out together from Ur of
the Chaldeans in order to go to the land of
Canaan; and they came as far as Haran and
settled there. 32 And the days of Terah were
205 years; and Terah died in Haran.

12 And Yahweh said to Abram,
"Go forth from your land,
And from your kin
And from your father's house,
To the land which I will show you;
2 And I will make you a great nation,
And I will bless you,
And make your name great;
And so you shall be a blessing;
3 And I will bless those who
bless you,
And the one who curses
you I will curse.
And in you all the families of
the earth will be blessed."

4 So Abram went forth as Yahweh had
spoken to him; and Lot went with him.
Now Abram was seventy-five years old
when he departed from Haran. 5 So Abram
took Sarai his wife and Lot his brother's
son, and all their possessions which
they had accumulated, and the persons
which they had acquired in Haran, and
they departed to go forth to the land of
Canaan; thus they came to the land of
Canaan. 6 And Abram passed through the
land as far as the site of Shechem, to the
oak of Moreh. Now the Canaanite *was* then
in the land. 7 Then Yahweh appeared to
Abram and said, "To your seed I will give
this land." So he built an altar there to
Yahweh who had appeared to him. 8 Then
he proceeded from there to the mountain
on the east of Bethel, and he pitched his
tent with Bethel on the west and Ai on the
east; and there he built an altar to Yahweh
and called upon the name of Yahweh.
9 And Abram journeyed on, continuing
toward the Negev.

10 Now there was a famine in the land;
so Abram went down to Egypt to sojourn
there, for the famine was severe in the
land. 11 And it happened as he drew near
to entering Egypt, that he said to Sarai his
wife, "Now behold, I know that you are a
woman beautiful in appearance; 12 and it
will be when the Egyptians see you, that
they will say, 'This is his wife'; and they will
kill me, but they will let you live. 13 Please
say that you are my sister so that it may
go well with me because of you, and that
I may live on account of you." 14 Now it
happened when Abram came into Egypt,
that the Egyptians saw that the woman was
very beautiful. 15 And Pharaoh's officials
saw her and praised her to Pharaoh; and
the woman was taken into Pharaoh's
house. 16 Therefore he treated Abram well
because of her; and sheep and oxen and
donkeys and male and female servants and
female donkeys and camels came into his
possession.

17 But Yahweh struck Pharaoh and his
house with great plagues because of Sarai,
Abram's wife. 18 Then Pharaoh called Abram
and said, "What is this you have done to me?
Why did you not tell me that she was your
wife? 19 Why did you say, 'She is my sister,'
so that I took her for myself as a wife? So
now, here is your wife, take her and go." 20 So
Pharaoh commanded *his* men concerning
him; and they sent him away with his wife
and all that belonged to him.

Psalm 4:1–3

1 Answer me when I call,
O God of my righteousness!
You have relieved me in *my* distress;
Be gracious to me and hear my prayer.

2 O sons of men, how long will my
glory become a reproach?
How long will you love what is
worthless and seek
falsehood? Selah.
3 But know that Yahweh has set apart
the holy one for Himself;
Yahweh hears when
I call to Him.

Proverbs 1:28–33

28 "Then they will call on me,
but I will not answer;
They will seek me earnestly
but they will not find me,
29 Because they hated knowledge
And did not choose the fear of Yahweh.
30 "They were not willing to
accept my counsel,
They spurned all my reproof.
31 "So they shall eat of the
fruit of their way
And be satisfied with their
own devices.
32 "For the turning away of the
simple will kill them,
And the complacency of fools
will destroy them.
33 "But he who listens to me
shall dwell securely
And will be at ease from
the dread of evil."

Matthew 5:27–48

27 "You have heard that it was said, 'YOU
SHALL NOT COMMIT ADULTERY'; 28 but I say to
you that everyone who looks at a woman to
lust for her has already committed adultery
with her in his heart. 29 But if your right eye
makes you stumble, tear it out and throw
it from you; for it is better for you to lose
one of the parts of your body, than for your
whole body to be thrown into hell. 30 And
if your right hand makes you stumble, cut
it off and throw it from you; for it is better
for you to lose one of the parts of your body,
than for your whole body to go into hell.
31 "Now it was said, 'WHOEVER SENDS HIS
WIFE AWAY, LET HIM GIVE HER A CERTIFICATE
OF DIVORCE'; 32 but I say to you that everyone
who divorces his wife, except for the reason
of sexual immorality, makes her commit
adultery; and whoever marries a divorced
woman commits adultery.
33 "Again, you have heard that the ancients
were told, 'YOU SHALL NOT MAKE FALSE VOWS,
BUT SHALL FULFILL YOUR VOWS TO THE LORD.'
34 But I say to you, make no oath at all, either
by heaven, for it is the throne of God, 35 or by
the earth, for it is the footstool of His feet, or
by Jerusalem, for it is THE CITY OF THE GREAT
KING. 36 Nor shall you make an oath by your
head, for you cannot make one hair white
or black. 37 But let your statement be, 'Yes,
yes' *or* 'No, no'; anything beyond these is
of the evil one.
38 "You have heard that it was said, 'AN EYE
FOR AN EYE, AND A TOOTH FOR A TOOTH.' 39 But
I say to you, do not resist an evil person;
but whoever slaps you on your right cheek,
turn the other to him also. 40 And if anyone
wants to sue you and take your tunic, let
him have your garment also. 41 And whoever
forces you to go one mile, go with him two.
42 Give to him who asks of you, and do not
turn away from him who wants to borrow
from you.
43 "You have heard that it was said, 'YOU
SHALL LOVE YOUR NEIGHBOR and hate your
enemy.' 44 But I say to you, love your ene-
mies and pray for those who persecute you,
45 so that you may be sons of your Father
who is in heaven; for He causes His sun to
rise on *the* evil and *the* good, and sends
rain on *the* righteous and *the* unrighteous.
46 For if you love those who love you, what
reward do you have? Do not even the tax
collectors do the same? 47 And if you greet
only your brothers, what more are you doing
than others? Do not even the Gentiles do the
same? 48 Therefore you are to be perfect, as
your heavenly Father is perfect.

JANUARY 7

Genesis 13:1–14:24

13 So Abram went up from Egypt to the
Negev, he and his wife and all that
belonged to him, and Lot with him.
2 Now Abram was very rich in livestock,
in silver and in gold. 3 And he went on his
journeys from the Negev as far as Bethel,
to the place where his tent had been at the
beginning, between Bethel and Ai, 4 to the
place of the altar which he had made there
formerly; and there Abram called upon the
name of Yahweh.
5 Now Lot, who was going with Abram,
also had flocks and herds and tents. 6 And
the land could not sustain them while
living together, for their possessions were
so abundant that they were not able to live
together. 7 And there was strife between
the herdsmen of Abram's livestock and
the herdsmen of Lot's livestock. Now the

Canaanite and the Perizzite were living then in the land.

8 So Abram said to Lot, "Please let there be no strife between you and me, nor between my herdsmen and your herdsmen, for we are brothers. 9 Is not the whole land before you? Please separate from me; if *to* the left, then I will go to the right; or if *to* the right, then I will go to the left." 10 Then Lot lifted up his eyes and saw all the valley of the Jordan, that it was well watered everywhere—*this was* before Yahweh destroyed Sodom and Gomorrah—like the garden of Yahweh, like the land of Egypt as you go to Zoar. 11 So Lot chose for himself all the valley of the Jordan, and Lot journeyed eastward. Thus they separated from each other. 12 Abram lived in the land of Canaan, while Lot lived in the cities of the valley and moved his tents as far as Sodom. 13 Now the men of Sodom were evil and sinners, exceedingly so, against Yahweh.

14 And Yahweh said to Abram, after Lot had separated from him, "Now lift up your eyes and look from the place where you are, northward and southward and eastward and westward; 15 for all the land which you see, I will give it to you and to your seed forever. 16 And I will make your seed as the dust of the earth, so that if anyone can number the dust of the earth, then your seed can also be numbered. 17 Arise, walk about the land through its length and breadth; for I will give it to you." 18 Then Abram moved his tent and came and lived by the oaks of Mamre, which are in Hebron, and there he built an altar to Yahweh.

14 And it happened in the days of Amraphel king of Shinar, Arioch king of Ellasar, Chedorlaomer king of Elam, and Tidal king of Goiim, 2 *that* they made war with Bera king of Sodom, and with Birsha king of Gomorrah, Shinab king of Admah, and Shemeber king of Zeboiim, and the king of Bela (that is, Zoar). 3 All these came as allies to the valley of Siddim (that is, the Salt Sea). 4 Now for twelve years they had served Chedorlaomer, but the thirteenth year they rebelled. 5 So in the fourteenth year Chedorlaomer and the kings that were with him, came and struck the Rephaim in Ashteroth-karnaim and the Zuzim in Ham and the Emim in Shaveh-kiriathaim, 6 and the Horites in their Mount Seir, as far as El-paran, which is by the wilderness. 7 Then they turned back and came to En-mishpat (that is, Kadesh). And they struck all the country of the Amalekites, and also the Amorites, who were living in Hazazon-tamar. 8 And the king of Sodom and the king of Gomorrah and the king of Admah and the king of Zeboiim and the king of Bela (that is, Zoar) came out; and they arranged *themselves* for battle against them in the valley of Siddim, 9 against Chedorlaomer king of Elam and Tidal king of Goiim and Amraphel king of Shinar and Arioch king of Ellasar, four kings against five— 10 now the valley of Siddim was full of tar pits—and the kings of Sodom and Gomorrah fled, and they fell into them; but those who remained behind fled to the hill country. 11 Then they took all the possessions of Sodom and Gomorrah and all their food supply and departed. 12 They also took Lot, Abram's nephew, and his possessions and departed; now he was living in Sodom.

13 Then a fugitive came and told Abram the Hebrew. Now he was dwelling by the oaks of Mamre the Amorite, brother of Eshcol and brother of Aner, and these were in a covenant with Abram. 14 So Abram heard that his relative had been taken captive, and he led out his trained men, born in his house, 318 *in number*, and went in pursuit as far as Dan. 15 And he divided his *men* against them by night, he and his servants, and struck them and pursued them as far as Hobah, which is north of Damascus. 16 And he brought back all the possessions, and he also brought back his relative Lot with his possessions and also the women and the people.

17 Then after he came back from striking down Chedorlaomer and the kings who were with him, the king of Sodom went out to meet him at the valley of Shaveh (that is, the King's Valley). 18 And Melchizedek king of Salem brought out bread and wine; now he was a priest of God Most High. 19 Then he blessed him and said,

"Blessed be Abram of God Most High,
Possessor of heaven and earth;
20 And blessed be God Most High,
Who has delivered your
enemies into your hand."

Then he gave him a tenth of all. 21 And the king of Sodom said to Abram, "Give

the people to me, but take the possessions
for yourself." 22 Then Abram said to the
king of Sodom, "I have raised my hand
to Yahweh God Most High, possessor of
heaven and earth, 23 that I will not take a
thread or a sandal strap or anything that
is yours, so that you would not say, 'I have
made Abram rich.' 24 I will take nothing
except what the young men have eaten,
and the share of the men who went with
me, Aner, Eshcol, and Mamre; let them
take their share."

Psalm 4:4–8

4 Tremble, and do not sin;
Ponder in your heart upon
your bed, and be still. Selah.
5 Offer the sacrifices of righteousness,
And trust in Yahweh.

6 Many are saying, "Who will
show us good?"
Lift up the light of Your face
upon us, O Yahweh!
7 You have put gladness in my heart,
More than when their grain
and new wine abound.
8 In peace I will both lie down and sleep,
For You alone, O Yahweh, make
me to abide in safety.

Proverbs 2:1–5

2 My son, if you will receive my words
And treasure my commandments
within you,
2 To make your ear pay
attention to wisdom,
Incline your heart to
discernment;
3 For if you call out for understanding,
Give your voice for discernment;
4 If you seek her as silver
And search for her as for
hidden treasures;
5 Then you will understand
the fear of Yahweh
And find the knowledge of God.

Matthew 6:1–18

6 "Beware of doing your righteousness
before men to be noticed by them;
otherwise you have no reward with your
Father who is in heaven.
2 "Therefore, when you give to the poor,
do not sound a trumpet before you, as the
hypocrites do in the synagogues and in the
streets, so that they may be glorified by
men. Truly I say to you, they have their
reward in full. 3 But when you give to the
poor, do not let your left hand know what
your right hand is doing, 4 so that your
giving will be in secret; and your Father
who sees *what is done* in secret will reward
you.
5 "And when you pray, you are not to be
like the hypocrites; for they love to stand
and pray in the synagogues and on the street
corners so that they may be seen by men.
Truly I say to you, they have their reward in
full. 6 But you, when you pray, go into your
inner room, and when you have shut your
door, pray to your Father who is in secret,
and your Father who sees *what is done* in
secret will reward you.
7 "And when you are praying, do not use
meaningless repetition as the Gentiles do,
for they suppose that they will be heard for
their many words. 8 Therefore, do not be like
them; for your Father knows what you need
before you ask Him.
9 "Pray, then, in this way:
'Our Father who is in heaven,
Hallowed be Your name.
10 'Your kingdom come.
Your will be done,
On earth as it is in heaven.
11 'Give us this day our daily bread.
12 'And forgive us our debts, as we also
have forgiven our debtors.
13 'And do not lead us into
temptation, but deliver us from
the evil one. [For Yours is the
kingdom and the power and
the glory forever. Amen.']
14 "For if you forgive others for their
transgressions, your heavenly Father will
also forgive you. 15 But if you do not forgive
others, then your Father will not forgive
your transgressions.
16 "Now whenever you fast, do not put on
a gloomy face as the hypocrites *do*, for they
neglect their appearance so that they will
be noticed by men when they are fasting.
Truly I say to you, they have their reward
in full. 17 But you, when you fast, anoint
your head and wash your face 18 so that
your fasting will not be noticed by men,
but by your Father who is in secret; and
your Father who sees *what is done* in secret
will reward you.

Resolved, to study the Scriptures so steadily, constantly and frequently, as that I may find, and plainly perceive myself to grow in the knowledge of the same.

— JONATHAN EDWARDS

JANUARY 8

Genesis 15:1–16:16

15 After these things the word of Yahweh came to Abram in a vision, saying,

"Do not fear, Abram,
I am a shield to you;
Your reward shall be very great."

2 And Abram said, "O Lord Yahweh, what will You give me, as I go on being childless, and the heir of my house is Eliezer of Damascus?" 3 And Abram said, "Since You have given no seed to me, behold, one born in my house is my heir." 4 Then behold, the word of Yahweh came to him, saying, "This one will not be your heir; but one who will come forth from your own body, he shall be your heir." 5 And He brought him outside and said, "Now look toward the heavens, and number the stars, if you are able to number them." And He said to him, "So shall your seed be." 6 Then he believed in Yahweh; and He counted it to him as righteousness. 7 And He said to him, "I am Yahweh who brought you out of Ur of the Chaldeans, to give you this land to possess it." 8 And he said, "O Lord Yahweh, how may I know that I will possess it?" 9 So He said to him, "Bring Me a three year old heifer, and a three year old female goat, and a three year old ram, and a turtledove, and a young pigeon." 10 Then he brought all these to Him and split them into parts down the middle and laid each part opposite the other; but he did not split apart the birds. 11 Then the birds of prey came down upon the carcasses, and Abram drove them away.

12 Now it happened that when the sun was going down, a deep sleep fell upon Abram; and behold, terror *and* great darkness fell upon him. 13 Then *God* said to Abram, "Know for certain that your seed will be sojourners in a land that is not theirs, and they will be enslaved and mistreated four hundred years. 14 But I will also judge the nation to whom they are enslaved, and afterward they will come out with many possessions. 15 As for you, you shall go to your fathers in peace; you will be buried at a good old age. 16 Then in the fourth generation they will return here, for the iniquity of the Amorite is not yet complete."

17 Now it happened that the sun had set, and it was very dark, and behold, *there appeared* a smoking oven and a flaming torch which passed between these pieces. 18 On that day Yahweh cut a covenant with Abram, saying,

"To your seed I have given this land,
From the river of Egypt as far as the great river, the river Euphrates:

19 the Kenite and the Kenizzite and the Kadmonite 20 and the Hittite and the Perizzite and the Rephaim 21 and the Amorite and the Canaanite and the Girgashite and the Jebusite."

16 Now Sarai, Abram's wife, had borne him no *children*, and she had an Egyptian servant-woman whose name was Hagar. 2 So Sarai said to Abram, "Now behold, Yahweh has shut my *womb* from bearing *children*. Please go in to my servant-woman; perhaps I will obtain children through her." And Abram listened to the voice of Sarai. 3 And after Abram had lived ten years in the land of Canaan, Abram's wife Sarai took Hagar the Egyptian, her servant-woman, and gave her to her husband Abram as his wife. 4 So he went in to Hagar, and she conceived. Then she saw that she had conceived, so her mistress became contemptible in her sight. 5 And Sarai said to Abram, "May the violence done to me be upon you. I gave my servant-woman into your embrace, but she saw that she had conceived, so I became contemptible in her sight. May Yahweh judge between you and

me." 6 But Abram said to Sarai, "Behold, your
servant-woman is in your hand; do to her
what is good in your sight." So Sarai afflicted
her, and she fled from her presence.

7 Now the angel of Yahweh found her by
a spring of water in the wilderness, by the
spring on the way to Shur. 8 And he said,
"Hagar, Sarai's servant-woman, where
have you come from and where are you
going?" And she said, "I am fleeing from
the presence of my mistress Sarai." 9 Then
the angel of Yahweh said to her, "Return to
your mistress and humble yourself under
her hands." 10 Moreover, the angel of
Yahweh said to her, "I will greatly multiply
your seed so that they will be too many to
be counted." 11 And the angel of Yahweh said
to her further,

"Behold, you are with child,
And you will bear a son;
And you shall call his name Ishmael,
Because Yahweh has heard
your affliction.

12 "And he will be a wild donkey
of a man,
His hand *will be* against everyone,
And everyone's hand *will*
be against him;
And he will dwell in the face
of all his brothers."

13 Then she called the name of Yahweh who
spoke to her, "You are a God who sees"; for
she said, "Have I even remained alive here
after seeing Him?" 14 Therefore the well was
called Beer-lahai-roi; behold, it is between
Kadesh and Bered.

15 So Hagar bore Abram a son; and Abram
called the name of his son, whom Hagar
bore, Ishmael. 16 Now Abram was eighty-six
years old when Hagar bore Ishmael to him.

Psalm 5:1–7

1 Give ear to my words, O Yahweh,
Consider my meditation.
2 Give heed to the sound of my cry
for help, my King and my God,
For to You I pray.
3 O Yahweh, in the morning,
You will hear my voice;
In the morning I will order *my prayer*
to You and *eagerly* watch.

4 For You are not a God who
delights in wickedness;
Evil does not sojourn with You.
5 The boastful shall not stand
before Your eyes;
You hate all workers of iniquity.
6 You destroy those who
speak falsehood;
Yahweh abhors the man
of bloodshed and deceit.
7 But as for me, in the abundance
of Your lovingkindness I
will enter Your house,
At Your holy temple I will
worship in fear of You.

Proverbs 2:6–9

6 For Yahweh gives wisdom;
From His mouth *come* knowledge
and discernment.
7 He stores up sound wisdom
for the upright,
A shield to those who walk in integrity,
8 To guard the paths of justice,
And He keeps the way of His holy ones.
9 Then you will understand
righteousness and justice
And equity—every good track.

Matthew 6:19–34

19 "Do not store up for yourselves
treasures on earth, where moth and rust
destroy, and where thieves break in and
steal. 20 But store up for yourselves trea-
sures in heaven, where neither moth nor
rust destroys, and where thieves do not
break in or steal; 21 for where your treasure
is, there your heart will be also.

22 "The eye is the lamp of the body; so
then if your eye is clear, your whole body
will be full of light. 23 But if your eye is bad,
your whole body will be full of darkness. If
then the light that is in you is darkness, how
great is the darkness!

24 "No one can serve two masters; for
either he will hate the one and love the other,
or he will be devoted to one and despise the
other. You cannot serve God and wealth.

25 "For this reason I say to you, do not
be worried about your life, *as to* what you
will eat or what you will drink; nor for your
body, *as to* what you will put on. Is not life
more than food, and the body more than
clothing? 26 Look at the birds of the air, that
they do not sow, nor reap nor gather into
barns, and *yet* your heavenly Father feeds
them. Are you not worth much more than
they? 27 And which of you by worrying can

add a single cubit to his life span? 28 And
why are you worried about clothing?
Observe how the lilies of the field grow; they
do not toil nor do they spin, 29 yet I say to
you that not even Solomon in all his glory
clothed himself like one of these. 30 But if
God so clothes the grass of the field, which
is *alive* today and tomorrow is thrown into
the furnace, *will He* not much more *clothe*
you? You of little faith! 31 Do not worry then,
saying, 'What will we eat?' or 'What will we
drink?' or 'What will we wear for clothing?'
32 For all these things the Gentiles eagerly
seek; for your heavenly Father knows that
you need all these things. 33 But seek first
His kingdom and His righteousness, and all
these things will be added to you.

34 "So do not worry about tomorrow; for
tomorrow will worry about itself. Each day
has enough trouble of its own.

JANUARY 9

Genesis 17:1–18:33

17 Now it happened that when Abram
was ninety-nine years old, Yahweh
appeared to Abram and said to him,

"I am God Almighty;
Walk before Me and be blameless,
2 so that I may confirm My covenant
between Me and you,
And that I may multiply
you exceedingly."

3 Then Abram fell on his face, and God spoke
with him, saying,

4 "As for Me, behold, My
covenant is with you,
And you will be the father of
a multitude of nations.
5 "And no longer shall your
name be called Abram,
But your name shall be Abraham;
For I have made you the father
of a multitude of nations.

6 "And I will make you exceedingly fruitful,
and I will make nations of you, and kings
will go forth from you. 7 And I will establish
My covenant between Me and you and your
seed after you throughout their generations
for an everlasting covenant, to be God to you
and to your seed after you. 8 And I will give
to you and to your seed after you, the land
of your sojournings, all the land of Canaan,
for an everlasting possession; and I will be
their God."

9 God said further to Abraham, "Now as
for you, you shall keep My covenant, you
and your seed after you throughout their
generations. 10 This is My covenant, which
you shall keep, between Me and you and
your seed after you: every male among you
shall be circumcised. 11 And you shall be cir-
cumcised in the flesh of your foreskin, and
it shall be the sign of the covenant between
Me and you. 12 And every male among you
who is eight days old shall be circumcised
throughout your generations, one who is
born in the house or one who is bought with
money from any foreigner, who is not of
your seed. 13 A *servant* who is born in your
house or who is bought with your money
shall surely be circumcised; thus shall My
covenant be in your flesh for an everlasting
covenant. 14 But an uncircumcised male
who is not circumcised in the flesh of his
foreskin, that person shall be cut off from
his people; he has broken My covenant."

15 Then God said to Abraham, "As for Sarai
your wife, you shall not call her name Sarai,
but Sarah *shall be* her name. 16 And I will
bless her, and indeed I will give you a son
by her. Then I will bless her, and she shall
be *a mother of* nations; kings of peoples will
come from her." 17 Then Abraham fell on his
face and laughed and said in his heart, "Will
a son be born to a man one hundred years
old? And will Sarah, who is ninety years old,
bear *a son*?" 18 And Abraham said to God,
"Oh that Ishmael might live before You!"
19 But God said, "No, but Sarah your wife
will bear you a son, and you shall call his
name Isaac; and I will establish My covenant
with him for an everlasting covenant for
his seed after him. 20 As for Ishmael, I have
heard you; behold, I will bless him and will
make him fruitful and will multiply him
exceedingly. He shall become the father of
twelve princes, and I will make him a great
nation. 21 But My covenant I will establish
with Isaac, whom Sarah will bear to you
at this season next year." 22 So He finished
talking with him, and God went up from
Abraham.

23 Then Abraham took Ishmael his son,
and all who were born in his house and all

who were bought with his money, every male among the men of Abraham's household, and circumcised the flesh of their foreskin in the very same day, as God had spoken with him. [24] Now Abraham was ninety-nine years old when he was circumcised in the flesh of his foreskin. [25] And Ishmael his son was thirteen years old when he was circumcised in the flesh of his foreskin. [26] In the very same day Abraham was circumcised, and Ishmael his son. [27] Now all the men of his household, who were born in the house or bought with money from a foreigner, were circumcised with him.

18 Then Yahweh appeared to him by the oaks of Mamre, while he was sitting at the tent door in the heat of the day. [2] And he lifted up his eyes and looked, and behold, three men were standing nearby; he saw, and he ran from the tent door to meet them, and he bowed himself to the earth, [3] and he said, "My Lord, if now I have found favor in Your sight, please do not pass Your servant by. [4] Please let a little water be brought and wash your feet, and rest yourselves under the tree; [5] and let me bring a piece of bread, that you may refresh your hearts; after that you may pass on, since in such a manner you have passed *by* your servant." And they said, "So you shall do, as you have said." [6] So Abraham hurried into the tent to Sarah and said, "Hurry, prepare three seahs of fine flour, knead *it*, and make bread cakes." [7] Abraham also ran to the herd and took a tender and choice calf and gave *it* to *his* young man, and he hurried to prepare it. [8] Then he took curds and milk and the calf which he had prepared, and placed *it* before them; and he was standing by them under the tree, and they ate.

[9] Then they said to him, "Where is Sarah your wife?" And he said, "There, in the tent." [10] And He said, "I will surely return to you at this time next year; and behold, Sarah your wife will have a son." And Sarah was listening at the tent door which was behind him. [11] Now Abraham and Sarah were old, advanced in age; Sarah was past childbearing. [12] And Sarah laughed to herself, saying, "After I am worn out, shall I have pleasure, my lord being old also?" [13] And Yahweh said to Abraham, "Why did Sarah laugh, saying, 'Shall I indeed bear *a son,* when I am *so* old?' [14] Is anything too difficult for Yahweh? At the appointed time I will return to you, at this time next year, and Sarah will have a son." [15] Then Sarah denied *it* however, saying, "I did not laugh"; for she was afraid. And He said, "No, but you did laugh."

[16] Then the men rose up from there and looked down toward Sodom; and Abraham was walking with them to send them off. [17] Now Yahweh said, "Shall I conceal from Abraham what I am about to do, [18] since Abraham will surely become a great and mighty nation, and in him all the nations of the earth will be blessed? [19] For I have known him, so that he may command his children and his household after him, that they keep the way of Yahweh to do righteousness and justice, so that Yahweh may bring upon Abraham what He has spoken about him." [20] So Yahweh said, "The outcry of Sodom and Gomorrah is indeed great, and their sin is exceedingly grave. [21] I will go down now and see whether they have done entirely according to its outcry, which has come to Me; and if not, I will know."

[22] Then the men turned away from there and went toward Sodom, while Abraham was still standing before Yahweh. [23] Then Abraham came near and said, "Will You indeed sweep away the righteous with the wicked? [24] Suppose there are fifty righteous within the city; will You indeed sweep *it* away and not spare the place for the sake of the fifty righteous who are in it? [25] Far be it from You to do such a thing, to put to death the righteous with the wicked, so that the righteous and the wicked are *treated* alike. Far be it from You! Shall not the Judge of all the earth do justice?" [26] So Yahweh said, "If I find in Sodom fifty righteous within the city, then I will spare the whole place on their account." [27] And Abraham answered and said, "Now behold, I have ventured to speak to the Lord, although I am *but* dust and ashes. [28] Suppose the fifty righteous are lacking five, will You destroy the whole city because of five?" And He said, "I will not destroy *it* if I find forty-five there." [29] Then he spoke to Him yet again and said, "Suppose forty are found there?" And He said, "I will not do *it* on account of the forty." [30] Then he said, "Oh may the Lord not be angry, and I shall speak; suppose thirty are found there?" And He said, "I will not do *it* if I find thirty there." [31] And he said, "Now behold, I have ventured to speak to the Lord;

suppose twenty are found there?" And He
said, "I will not destroy *it* on account of the
twenty." 32 Then he said, "Oh may the Lord
not be angry, and I shall speak only this
once; suppose ten are found there?" And
He said, "I will not destroy *it* on account of
the ten." 33 And as soon as He had finished
speaking to Abraham, Yahweh departed,
and Abraham returned to his place.

Psalm 5:8–12

8 O Yahweh, lead me in Your
righteousness because of my foes;
Make Your way straight before me.
9 There is nothing reliable
in their mouth;
Their inward part is destruction *itself*.
Their throat is an open grave;
They flatter with their tongue.
10 Hold them guilty, O God;
By their own devices let them fall!
In the abundance of their
transgressions thrust them out,
For they are rebellious against You.

11 But let all who take refuge
in You be glad,
Let them ever sing for joy;
And may You shelter them,
That those who love Your
name may exult in You.
12 For it is You who blesses the
righteous one, O Yahweh,
You surround him with favor
as with a large shield.

Proverbs 2:10–22

10 For wisdom will enter your heart
And knowledge will be
pleasant to your soul;
11 Discretion will keep you,
Discernment will guard you,
12 To deliver you from the way of evil,
From the man who speaks
perverse things;
13 From those who forsake the
paths of uprightness
To walk in the ways of darkness;
14 Who are glad to do evil
And they rejoice in the
perversity of evil;
15 Whose paths are crooked,
And who are devious in their tracks;
16 To deliver you from the
strange woman,
From the foreign woman who
flatters with her words;
17 Who forsakes the close
companion of her youth
And forgets the covenant of her God;
18 For her house sinks down to death
And her tracks *descend* to the dead;
19 All who go to her will not return,
And they will not reach
the paths of life.
20 So that you will walk in the
way of good men
And keep to the paths of the righteous.
21 For the upright will dwell in the land
And the blameless will remain in it;
22 But the wicked will be cut
off from the land
And the treacherous will be
torn away from it.

Matthew 7:1–29

7 "Do not judge, so that you will not be
judged. 2 For with what judgment you
judge, you will be judged; and with what
measure you measure, it will be measured to
you. 3 And why do you look at the speck that
is in your brother's eye, but do not notice the
log that is in your own eye? 4 Or how can you
say to your brother, 'Let me take the speck
out of your eye,' and behold, the log is in your
own eye? 5 You hypocrite, first take the log out
of your own eye, and then you will see clearly
to take the speck out of your brother's eye.
6 "Do not give what is holy to dogs, and
do not throw your pearls before swine, lest
they trample them under their feet, and turn
and tear you to pieces.
7 "Ask, and it will be given to you; seek,
and you will find; knock, and it will be
opened to you. 8 For everyone who asks
receives, and he who seeks finds, and to
him who knocks it will be opened. 9 Or
what man is there among you who, when
his son asks for a loaf, will give him a stone?
10 Or if he asks for a fish, he will not give
him a snake, will he? 11 If you then, being
evil, know how to give good gifts to your
children, how much more will your Father
who is in heaven give what is good to those
who ask Him!
12 "Therefore, in all things, whatever you
want people to do for you, so do for them,
for this is the Law and the Prophets.
13 "Enter through the narrow gate; for the
gate is wide and the way is broad that leads

to destruction, and there are many who enter through it. 14 For the gate is narrow and the way is constricted that leads to life, and there are few who find it.

15 "Beware of the false prophets, who come to you in sheep's clothing, but inwardly are ravenous wolves. 16 You will know them by their fruits. Are grapes gathered from thorn bushes or figs from thistles? 17 Even so, every good tree bears good fruit, but the bad tree bears bad fruit. 18 A good tree cannot bear bad fruit, nor can a bad tree bear good fruit. 19 Every tree that does not bear good fruit is cut down and thrown into the fire. 20 So then, you will know them by their fruits.

21 "Not everyone who says to Me, 'Lord, Lord,' will enter the kingdom of heaven, but he who does the will of My Father who is in heaven *will enter*. 22 Many will say to Me on that day, 'Lord, Lord, in Your name did we not prophesy, and in Your name cast out demons, and in Your name do many miracles?' 23 And then I will declare to them, 'I never knew you; DEPART FROM ME, YOU WHO PRACTICE LAWLESSNESS.'

24 "Therefore everyone who hears these words of Mine and does them, may be compared to a wise man who built his house on the rock. 25 And the rain descended, and the rivers came, and the winds blew and fell against that house; and *yet* it did not fall, for it had been founded on the rock. 26 And everyone hearing these words of Mine and not doing them, may be compared to a foolish man who built his house on the sand. 27 And the rain descended, and the rivers came, and the winds blew and slammed against that house; and it fell—and great was its fall."

28 Now it happened that when Jesus had finished these words, the crowds were astonished at His teaching; 29 for He was teaching them as *one* having authority, and not as their scribes.

JANUARY 10

Genesis 19:1–20:18

19 Then the two angels came to Sodom in the evening as Lot was sitting in the gate of Sodom. Lot saw *them* and rose to meet them and bowed down *with his* face to the ground. 2 And he said, "Now behold, my lords, please turn aside into your servant's house, and spend the night, and wash your feet; then you may rise early and go on your way." They said however, "No, but we shall spend the night in the square." 3 Yet he pressed them strongly, so they turned aside to him and entered his house; and he made a feast for them and baked unleavened bread, and they ate. 4 Before they lay down, the men of the city, the men of Sodom, surrounded the house, from young to old, all the people from every quarter; 5 and they called to Lot and said to him, "Where are the men who came to you tonight? Bring them out to us that we may know them." 6 But Lot went out to them at the doorway and shut the door behind him, 7 and said, "Please, my brothers, do not act wickedly. 8 Now behold, I have two daughters who have not known a man; please let me bring them out to you, and do to them what is good in your eyes; only do nothing to these men, inasmuch as they have come under the shelter of my roof." 9 But they said, "Step aside." Furthermore, they said, "This one came to sojourn, and already he is persistently acting like a judge; now we will treat you more wickedly than them." So they pressed hard against Lot and stepped up to break the door. 10 But the men reached out their hands and brought Lot into the house with them and shut the door. 11 And they struck the men who were at the doorway of the house with blindness, from small to great, so that they wearied *themselves trying* to find the doorway.

12 Then the *two* men said to Lot, "Whom else have you here? A son-in-law, and your sons, and your daughters, and everyone you have in the city, bring *them* out of the place; 13 for we are about to destroy this place because their outcry has become great before Yahweh, so Yahweh has sent us to destroy it." 14 And Lot went out and spoke to his sons-in-law, who were to marry his daughters, and said, "Get up, get out of this place, for Yahweh will destroy the city." But he appeared to his sons-in-law to be jesting.

15 Now at the breaking of dawn, the angels urged Lot, saying, "Get up, take your wife and your two daughters who are here, lest you be swept away in the punishment

of the city." 16 But he hesitated. So the men seized his hand and the hand of his wife and the hands of his two daughters, for the compassion of Yahweh *was* upon him; and they brought him out and put him outside the city. 17 Now it happened, as they brought them outside, one said, "Escape for your life! Do not look behind you, and do not stay anywhere in the valley; escape to the mountains, lest you be swept away." 18 But Lot said to them, "Oh no, my lords! 19 Now behold, your servant has found favor in your sight, and you have magnified your lovingkindness, which you have shown me by preserving my life; but I cannot escape to the mountains, lest calamity overtake me and I die; 20 now behold, this town is near *enough* to flee to, and it is small. Please, let me escape there (is it not small?) that my life may be preserved." 21 And he said to him, "Behold, I grant you this request also, that I will not overthrow the city of which you have spoken. 22 Hurry, escape there, for I cannot do anything until you arrive there." Therefore the name of the city was called Zoar.

23 The sun had risen over the earth when Lot came to Zoar. 24 And Yahweh rained on Sodom and Gomorrah brimstone and fire from Yahweh out of heaven, 25 and He overthrew those cities, and all the valley, and all the inhabitants of the cities, and what grew on the ground. 26 Then his wife, from behind him, looked *back*, and she became a pillar of salt.

27 Now Abraham arose early in the morning *and went* to the place where he had stood before Yahweh; 28 and he looked down toward Sodom and Gomorrah, and toward all the land of the valley, and he saw, and behold, the smoke of the land went up like the smoke of a furnace.

29 Thus it happened, when God destroyed the cities of the valley, that God remembered Abraham and sent Lot out of the midst of the overthrow, when He overthrew the cities in which Lot lived.

30 And Lot went up from Zoar and stayed in the mountains, and his two daughters with him; for he was afraid to stay in Zoar; and he stayed in a cave, he and his two daughters. 31 Then the firstborn said to the younger, "Our father is old, and there is not a man on earth to come in to us after the manner of the earth. 32 Come, let us make our father drink wine, and let us lie with him that we may preserve *our* seed through our father." 33 So they made their father drink wine that night, and the firstborn went in and lay with her father; and he did not know when she lay down or when she arose. 34 Now it happened on the following day, that the firstborn said to the younger, "Behold, I lay last night with my father; let us make him drink wine tonight also; and you go in and lie with him, that we may preserve *our* seed through our father." 35 So they made their father drink wine that night also, and the younger arose and lay with him; and he did not know when she lay down or when she arose. 36 Thus both the daughters of Lot conceived by their father. 37 And the firstborn bore a son and called his name Moab; he is the father of the Moabites to this day. 38 As for the younger, she also bore a son and called his name Ben-ammi; he is the father of the sons of Ammon to this day.

20 And Abraham journeyed from there toward the land of the Negev and settled between Kadesh and Shur; then he sojourned in Gerar. 2 And Abraham said of Sarah his wife, "She is my sister." So Abimelech king of Gerar sent and took Sarah. 3 But God came to Abimelech in a dream of the night and said to him, "Behold, you are a dead man because of the woman whom you have taken, for she is married." 4 (Now Abimelech had not come near her.) Then he said, "Lord, will You kill a nation, even *though* righteous? 5 Did he not himself say to me, 'She is my sister'? And she herself also said, 'He is my brother.' In the integrity of my heart and the innocence of my hands I have done this." 6 Then God said to him in the dream, "Indeed, I know that in the integrity of your heart you have done this, and I also held you back from sinning against Me; therefore I did not let you touch her. 7 So now, return the man's wife, for he is a prophet, and he will pray for you, and you will live. But if you do not return *her*, know that you shall surely die, you and all who are yours."

8 So Abimelech arose early in the morning and called all his servants and told all these things in their hearing; and the men were greatly afraid. 9 Then Abimelech called Abraham and said to him, "What have you

done to us? And how have I sinned against
you, that you have brought on me and on
my kingdom a great sin? You have done
to me things that ought not to be done."
10 And Abimelech said to Abraham, "What
have you seen, that you have done this
thing?" 11 And Abraham said, "Because I
said, surely there is no fear of God in this
place, and they will kill me because of my
wife. 12 Besides, she actually is my sister, the
daughter of my father, but not the daughter
of my mother, and she became my wife;
13 and it happened when God caused me to
wander from my father's house, that I said
to her, 'This is the lovingkindness which
you will show to me: everywhere we go, say
of me, "He is my brother."'" 14 Abimelech
then took sheep and oxen and male and
female slaves and gave them to Abraham
and returned his wife Sarah to him. 15 And
Abimelech said, "Behold, my land is before
you; settle wherever it is good in your
sight." 16 To Sarah he said, "Behold, I have
given your brother one thousand pieces of
silver; behold, it is your vindication before
all who are with you, and before all you are
cleared." 17 And Abraham prayed to God,
and God healed Abimelech and his wife
and his maidservants, so that they bore
children. 18 For Yahweh had utterly shut all
the wombs of the household of Abimelech
because of Sarah, Abraham's wife.

Psalm 6:1–5

1 O Yahweh, do not reprove
me in Your anger,
Nor discipline me in Your wrath.
2 Be gracious to me, O Yahweh,
for I *am* pining away;
Heal me, O Yahweh, for my
bones are dismayed.
3 And my soul is greatly dismayed;
But You, O Yahweh—how long?

4 Return, O Yahweh, rescue my soul;
Save me because of Your
lovingkindness.
5 For there is no remembrance
of You in death;
In Sheol who will give You thanks?

Proverbs 3:1–4

3 My son, do not forget my law,
But let your heart guard my
commandments;
2 For length of days and years of life
And peace they will add to you.
3 Do not let lovingkindness
and truth forsake you;
Bind them around your neck,
Write them on the tablet of your heart.
4 So you will find favor and good insight
In the eyes of God and man.

Matthew 8:1–17

8 Now when Jesus came down from the
mountain, large crowds followed Him.
2 And behold, a leper came to Him and
was bowing down before Him, and said,
"Lord, if You are willing, You can make me
clean." 3 And Jesus stretched out His hand
and touched him, saying, "I am willing; be
cleansed." And immediately his leprosy
was cleansed. 4 And Jesus *said to him, "See
that you tell no one; but go, show yourself
to the priest and present the offering that
Moses commanded, as a testimony to
them."
5 And when Jesus entered Capernaum,
a centurion came to Him, pleading *with*
Him, 6 and saying, "Lord, my servant is lying
paralyzed at home, fearfully tormented."
7 And Jesus *said to him, "I will come and
heal him." 8 But the centurion said, "Lord,
I am not good enough for You to come
under my roof, but just say the word, and
my servant will be healed. 9 For I also am a
man under authority, with soldiers under
me; and I say to this man, 'Go!' and he goes,
and to another, 'Come!' and he comes, and
to my slave, 'Do this!' and he does *it.*" 10 Now
when Jesus heard *this,* He marveled and said
to those who were following, "Truly I say to
you, I have not found such great faith with
anyone in Israel. 11 And I say to you that
many will come from east and west, and
recline *at the table* with Abraham, Isaac,
and Jacob in the kingdom of heaven; 12 but
the sons of the kingdom will be cast out into
the outer darkness; in that place there will
be weeping and gnashing of teeth." 13 And
Jesus said to the centurion, "Go; it shall be
done for you as you have believed." And the
servant was healed that *very* moment.
14 When Jesus came into Peter's home,
He saw his mother-in-law lying sick in
bed with a fever. 15 And He touched her
hand, and the fever left her; and she got up
and *began* waiting on Him. 16 Now when
evening came, they brought to Him many

who were demon-possessed; and He cast out the spirits with a word, and healed all who were ill 17 in order to fulfill what was spoken through Isaiah the prophet, saying, "HE HIMSELF TOOK OUR INFIRMITIES AND CARRIED AWAY OUR DISEASES."

JANUARY 11

Genesis 21:1–22:24

21 Now Yahweh visited Sarah as He had said, and Yahweh did for Sarah as He had promised. 2 So Sarah conceived and bore a son to Abraham in his old age, at the appointed time of which God had spoken to him. 3 And Abraham called the name of his son who was born to him, whom Sarah bore to him, Isaac. 4 Then Abraham circumcised his son Isaac when he was eight days old, as God had commanded him. 5 Now Abraham was one hundred years old when his son Isaac was born to him. 6 And Sarah said, "God has made laughter for me; everyone who hears will laugh with me." 7 And she said, "Who would have said to Abraham that Sarah would nurse children? Yet I have borne *him* a son in his old age."

8 And the child grew and was weaned, and Abraham made a great feast on the day that Isaac was weaned. 9 And Sarah saw the son of Hagar the Egyptian, whom she had borne to Abraham, laughing *in jest.* 10 Therefore she said to Abraham, "Drive out this maidservant and her son! The son of this maidservant shall not be an heir with my son, with Isaac." 11 And the matter distressed Abraham greatly because of his son. 12 So God said to Abraham, "Do not be distressed because of the boy and your maidservant; whatever Sarah tells you, listen to her voice, for through Isaac your seed shall be named. 13 And of the son of the maidservant I will make a nation also, because he is your seed." 14 So Abraham rose early in the morning and took bread and a skin of water and gave *them* to Hagar, putting *them* on her shoulder, and *gave her* the child, and sent her away. So she went and wandered about in the wilderness of Beersheba.

15 When the water in the skin was finished, she put the child under one of the bushes. 16 Then she went and sat down opposite him, about a bowshot away, for she said, "Do not let me see when the child dies." And she sat opposite him and lifted up her voice and wept. 17 Then God heard the voice of the boy crying; and the angel of God called to Hagar from heaven and said to her, "What is the matter with you, Hagar? Do not fear, for God has heard the voice of the boy where he is. 18 Arise, lift up the boy, and hold him by the hand, for I will make a great nation of him." 19 Then God opened her eyes, and she saw a well of water; and she went and filled the skin with water and gave the boy a drink.

20 And God was with the boy, and he grew; and he lived in the wilderness and was an archer. 21 And he lived in the wilderness of Paran, and his mother took a wife for him from the land of Egypt.

22 Now it happened at that time, that Abimelech and Phicol, the commander of his army, spoke to Abraham, saying, "God is with you in all that you do; 23 so now, swear to me here by God that you will not deal falsely with me or with my offspring or with my posterity, but according to the lovingkindness that I have shown you, you shall show me and the land in which you have sojourned." 24 And Abraham said, "I swear it." 25 But Abraham reproved Abimelech about the well of water which the servants of Abimelech had seized. 26 And Abimelech said, "I do not know who has done this thing; you did not tell me, nor did I hear of it until today."

27 So Abraham took sheep and oxen and gave them to Abimelech, and the two of them cut a covenant. 28 Then Abraham set seven ewe lambs of the flock by themselves. 29 And Abimelech said to Abraham, "What do these seven ewe lambs mean, which you have set by themselves?" 30 He said, "You shall take these seven ewe lambs from my hand so that it may be a witness to me, that I dug this well." 31 Therefore he called that place Beersheba, because there the two of them swore *an oath.* 32 So they cut a covenant at Beersheba; and Abimelech and Phicol, the commander of his army, arose and returned to the land of the Philistines. 33 And *Abraham* planted a tamarisk tree at Beersheba, and there he called upon

the name of Yahweh, the Everlasting God.
34 And Abraham sojourned in the land of
the Philistines for many days.

22 Now it happened after these things,
that God tested Abraham and said to
him, "Abraham!" And he said, "Here I am."
2 Then He said, "Take now your son, your
only one, whom you love, Isaac, and go forth
to the land of Moriah, and offer him there
as a burnt offering on one of the mountains
of which I will tell you." 3 So Abraham rose
early in the morning and saddled his donkey
and took two of his young men with him
and Isaac his son; and he split wood for the
burnt offering and arose and went to the
place of which God had told him. 4 On the
third day Abraham lifted up his eyes and saw
the place from a distance. 5 And Abraham
said to his young men, "Stay here with the
donkey while I and the boy go over there;
and we will worship, and we will return to
you." 6 Then Abraham took the wood of
the burnt offering and put it on Isaac his
son, and he took in his hand the fire and
the knife. So the two of them walked on
together.

7 Then Isaac spoke to Abraham his father
and said, "My father!" And he said, "Here I
am, my son." And he said, "Behold, the fire
and the wood, but where is the lamb for
the burnt offering?" 8 And Abraham said,
"God will provide for Himself the lamb for
the burnt offering, my son." So the two of
them walked on together.

9 Then they came to the place of which
God had told him; and Abraham built the
altar there and arranged the wood and
bound his son Isaac and put him on the
altar, on top of the wood. 10 And Abraham
stretched out his hand and took the knife
to slay his son. 11 But the angel of Yahweh
called to him from heaven and said, "Abra-
ham, Abraham!" And he said, "Here I am."
12 And He said, "Do not stretch out your
hand against the boy, and do nothing to him;
for now I know that you fear God, since you
have not withheld your son, your only one,
from Me." 13 Then Abraham lifted up his
eyes and saw, and behold, *there was* a ram
after *it had been* caught in the thicket by its
horns; and Abraham went and took the ram
and offered it up for a burnt offering in the
place of his son. 14 And Abraham called the
name of that place Yahweh Will Provide, as
it is said this day, "In the mount of Yahweh
it will be provided."

15 Then the angel of Yahweh called to
Abraham a second time from heaven, 16 and
said, "By Myself I have sworn, declares
Yahweh, because you have done this thing
and have not spared your son, your only
one, 17 indeed I will greatly bless you, and I
will greatly multiply your seed as the stars
of the heavens and as the sand which is on
the seashore; and your seed shall possess
the gate of his enemies. 18 In your seed all
the nations of the earth shall be blessed,
because you have listened to My voice."
19 So Abraham returned to his young men,
and they arose and walked together to
Beersheba; and Abraham lived at Beersheba.

20 Now it happened after these things,
that it was told to Abraham, saying, "Behold,
Milcah also has borne children to your
brother Nahor: 21 Uz his firstborn and Buz
his brother and Kemuel the father of Aram
22 and Chesed and Hazo and Pildash and
Jidlaph and Bethuel." 23 And Bethuel was
the father of Rebekah. These eight Milcah
bore to Nahor, Abraham's brother. 24 And
his concubine, whose name was Reumah,
also bore Tebah and Gaham and Tahash and
Maacah.

Psalm 6:6–10

6 I am weary with my sighing;
Every night I make my bed swim,
I flood my couch with my tears.
7 My eye has wasted away with grief;
It has become old because
of all my adversaries.

8 Depart from me, all you
workers of iniquity,
For Yahweh has heard the
sound of my weeping.
9 Yahweh has heard my supplication,
Yahweh receives my prayer.
10 All my enemies will be ashamed
and greatly dismayed;
They shall turn back, they will
suddenly be ashamed.

Proverbs 3:5–6

5 Trust in Yahweh with all your heart
And do not lean on your
own understanding.
6 In all your ways acknowledge Him,
And He will make your paths straight.

Matthew 8:18–34

18 Now when Jesus saw a crowd around
Him, He gave orders to depart to the other
side *of the sea.* 19 Then a scribe came and
said to Him, "Teacher, I will follow You
wherever You go." 20 And Jesus *said to
him, "The foxes have holes and the birds of
the air *have* nests, but the Son of Man has
nowhere to lay His head." 21 And another of
the disciples said to Him, "Lord, permit me
first to go and bury my father." 22 But Jesus
*said to him, "Follow Me, and allow the dead
to bury their own dead."

23 And when He got into the boat, His
disciples followed Him. 24 And behold,
there arose a great storm on the sea, so
that the boat was being covered with the
waves; but Jesus Himself was sleeping.
25 And they came to *Him* and got Him up,
saying, "Save *us*, Lord; we are perishing!"
26 And He *said to them, "Why are you *so*
cowardly, you men of little faith?" Then He
got up and rebuked the winds and the sea,
and it became perfectly calm. 27 And the
men marveled, and said, "What kind of a
man is this, that even the winds and the
sea obey Him?"

28 And when He came to the other side,
into the region of the Gadarenes, two men
who were demon-possessed met Him as
they were coming out of the tombs. *They
were* so extremely violent that no one could
pass by that way. 29 And behold, they cried
out, saying, "What do we have to do with
You, Son of God? Have You come here to
torment us before the time?" 30 Now there
was a herd of many swine feeding at a
distance from them. 31 And the demons
began to plead with Him, saying, "If You *are
going to* cast us out, send us into the herd of
swine." 32 And He said to them, "Go!" And
coming out, they went into the swine; and
behold, the whole herd rushed down the
steep bank into the sea and perished in the
waters. 33 Now the herdsmen ran away, and
went to the city and reported everything,
including what had happened to the demo-
niacs. 34 And behold, the whole city came
out to meet Jesus; and when they saw Him,
they pleaded with Him to leave their region.

JANUARY 12

Genesis 23:1–24:67

23 And Sarah lived 127 years; *these were*
the years of the life of Sarah. 2 Sarah
died in Kiriath-arba (that is, Hebron) in
the land of Canaan; and Abraham came to
mourn for Sarah and to weep for her. 3 Then
Abraham rose from before his dead and
spoke to the sons of Heth, saying, 4 "I am
a sojourner and a foreign resident among
you; give me a possession for a burial site
among you that I may bury my dead out of
my sight." 5 And the sons of Heth answered
Abraham, saying to him, 6 "Hear us, my lord,
you are a mighty prince among us; bury
your dead in the choicest of our burial sites;
none of us will refuse you his burial sites for
burying your dead." 7 So Abraham rose and
bowed to the people of the land, the sons
of Heth. 8 And he spoke with them, saying,
"If it is your desire *for me* to bury my dead
out of my sight, hear me, and meet with
Ephron the son of Zohar for me, 9 that he
may give me the cave of Machpelah which
belongs to him, which is at the end of his
field; for the full price let him give it to me
in your presence as a possession for a burial
site." 10 Now Ephron was sitting among
the sons of Heth; and Ephron the Hittite
answered Abraham in the hearing of the
sons of Heth, *even* of all who went in at the
gate of his city, saying, 11 "No, my lord, hear
me; I give you the field, and I give you the
cave that is in it. In the sight of the sons of
my people I give it to you; bury your dead."
12 And Abraham bowed before the people
of the land. 13 And he spoke to Ephron
in the hearing of the people of the land,
saying, "If you will only please hear me; I
will give the silver for the field, accept *it*
from me that I may bury my dead there."
14 Then Ephron answered Abraham, saying
to him, 15 "My lord, hear me; a piece of land
worth four hundred shekels of silver, what
is that between me and you? So bury your
dead." 16 So Abraham heard Ephron; and
Abraham weighed out for Ephron the silver
which he had named in the hearing of the
sons of Heth, four hundred shekels of silver,
commercial standard.

17 So Ephron's field, which was in Mach-
pelah, which faced Mamre, the field and the
cave which was in it, and all the trees which

were in the field, that were within all the confines of its border, were deeded over 18 to Abraham as purchased in the sight of the sons of Heth, before all who came in at the gate of his city. 19 After this, Abraham buried Sarah his wife in the cave of the field at Machpelah facing Mamre (that is, Hebron) in the land of Canaan. 20 So the field and the cave that is in it were deeded over to Abraham for a possession for a burial site by the sons of Heth.

24 Now Abraham was old, advanced in age; and Yahweh had blessed Abraham in every way. 2 And Abraham said to his servant, the oldest of his household, who ruled over all that he owned, "Please place your hand under my thigh, 3 and I will make you swear by Yahweh, the God of heaven and the God of earth, that you shall not take a wife for my son from the daughters of the Canaanites, among whom I live, 4 but you will go to my land and to my kin, and take a wife for my son Isaac." 5 And the servant said to him, "Suppose the woman is not willing to follow me to this land; should I indeed take your son back to the land from where you came?" 6 Then Abraham said to him, "Beware lest you take my son back there! 7 Yahweh, the God of heaven, who took me from my father's house and from the land of my kin, and who spoke to me and who swore to me, saying, 'To your seed I will give this land,' He will send His angel before you, and you will take a wife for my son from there. 8 But if the woman is not willing to follow you, then you will be free from this oath of mine; only do not take my son back there." 9 So the servant placed his hand under the thigh of Abraham his master and swore to him concerning this matter.

10 Then the servant took ten camels from the camels of his master, and he went with all kinds of good things of his master's in his hand. So he arose and went to Mesopotamia, to the city of Nahor. 11 And he made the camels kneel down outside the city by the well of water at evening time, the time when the women go out to draw water. 12 And he said, "O Yahweh, the God of my master Abraham, please cause *this* to happen before me today, and show lovingkindness to my master Abraham. 13 Behold, I am standing by the spring of water, and the daughters of the men of the city are coming out to draw water; 14 now may it be that the young woman to whom I say, 'Please let down your jar so that I may drink,' and she says, 'Drink, and I will give *water* to your camels to drink also'—*may* she *be the one* whom You have decided for Your servant Isaac; and by this I will know that You have shown lovingkindness to my master."

15 And before he had finished speaking, behold, Rebekah who was born to Bethuel the son of Milcah, the wife of Abraham's brother Nahor, was coming out with her jar on her shoulder. 16 Now the young woman was very beautiful in appearance, a virgin, and no man had known her; and she went down to the spring and filled her jar and came up. 17 Then the servant ran to meet her and said, "Please give me a little water to drink from your jar." 18 And she said, "Drink, my lord"; and she quickly lowered her jar to her hand and gave him a drink. 19 Now when she had finished giving him a drink, she said, "I will draw also for your camels until they have finished drinking." 20 So she hurried and emptied her jar into the watering channel and ran again to the well to draw, and she drew for all his camels. 21 Meanwhile, the man was gazing at her in silence, to know whether Yahweh had made his journey successful or not.

22 Now it happened that when the camels had finished drinking, the man took a gold ring weighing a half-shekel and two bracelets for her wrists weighing ten shekels in gold, 23 and said, "Whose daughter are you? Please tell me, is there a place for us to lodge in your father's house?" 24 And she said to him, "I am the daughter of Bethuel, the son of Milcah, whom she bore to Nahor." 25 And she said to him, "We have plenty of both straw and feed, and a place to lodge in." 26 Then the man bowed low and worshiped Yahweh. 27 And he said, "Blessed be Yahweh, the God of my master Abraham, who has not forsaken His lovingkindness and His truth toward my master; as for me, Yahweh has guided me in the way to the house of my master's brothers."

28 Then the young woman ran and told her mother's household about these things. 29 Now Rebekah had a brother whose name was Laban; and Laban ran outside to the man at the spring. 30 Now it happened, when he saw the ring and the bracelets on his sister's wrists, and when he heard the

words of Rebekah his sister, saying, "This
is what the man said to me," he came out to
the man; and behold, he was standing by the
camels at the spring. 31 And he said, "Come
in, blessed of Yahweh! Why do you stand
outside since I have prepared the house
and a place for the camels?" 32 So the man
came into the house. Then Laban unloaded
the camels, and he gave straw and feed to
the camels, and water to wash his feet and
the feet of the men who were with him.
33 Then *food* was set before him to eat, but
he said, "I will not eat until I have spoken
my words." And he said, "Speak!" 34 So
he said, "I am Abraham's servant. 35 And
Yahweh has greatly blessed my master, so
he has become great; and He has given him
flocks and herds, and silver and gold, and
male slaves and female slaves, and camels
and donkeys. 36 Now Sarah my master's wife
bore a son to my master in her old age, and
he has given him all that he has. 37 And my
master made me swear, saying, 'You shall
not take a wife for my son from the daugh-
ters of the Canaanites, in whose land I live;
38 but you shall go to my father's house and
to my family, and take a wife for my son.'
39 Then I said to my master, 'Suppose the
woman does not follow me.' 40 And he said
to me, 'Yahweh, before whom I have walked,
will send His angel with you and will make
your journey successful, and you will take a
wife for my son from my family and from my
father's house. 41 Then you will be free from
my oath, when you come to my relatives.
Now if they do not give her to you, you will
be free from my oath.'

42 "So I came today to the spring and said,
'O Yahweh, the God of my master Abraham,
if now You will make my journey on which
I go successful; 43 behold, I am standing
by the spring of water, and may it be that
the maiden who comes out to draw, and to
whom I say, "Please let me drink a little water
from your jar"; 44 and she will say to me, "You
drink, and I will draw for your camels also";
she is the woman whom Yahweh has decided
upon for my master's son.'

45 "Before I had finished speaking in my
heart, behold, Rebekah was coming out with
her jar on her shoulder, and she went down
to the spring and drew, and I said to her,
'Please give me a drink.' 46 Then she hurried
and lowered her jar from her *shoulder* and
said, 'Drink, and I will also give *water* to
your camels to drink'; so I drank, and she
also gave *water* to the camels to drink.
47 Then I asked her and said, 'Whose daugh-
ter are you?' And she said, 'The daughter
of Bethuel, Nahor's son, whom Milcah bore
to him'; and I put the ring on her nose and
the bracelets on her wrists. 48 And I bowed
low and worshiped Yahweh; and I blessed
Yahweh, the God of my master Abraham,
who had guided me in the true way to take
the daughter of my master's relative for
his son. 49 So now if you are going to show
lovingkindness and truth with my master,
tell me; and if not, tell me, that I may turn
to the right or to the left."

50 Then Laban and Bethuel answered and
said, "The matter comes from Yahweh; *so* we
cannot speak to you bad or good. 51 Behold,
Rebekah is before you, take *her* and go, and
let her be the wife of your master's son, as
Yahweh has spoken."

52 Now it happened that when Abraham's
servant heard their words, he bowed himself
to the ground before Yahweh. 53 The servant
brought out articles of silver and articles
of gold, and garments, and gave them to
Rebekah; he also gave precious things to her
brother and to her mother. 54 Then he and
the men who were with him ate and drank
and spent the night. And then they arose in
the morning, and he said, "Send me away
to my master." 55 But her brother and her
mother said, "Let the young woman stay
with us *a few* days, or *even* ten; afterward
she will go." 56 And he said to them, "Do
not delay me, since Yahweh has made my
way successful. Send me away that I may
go to my master." 57 And they said, "We
will call the young woman and ask about
her wishes." 58 Then they called Rebekah
and said to her, "Will you go with this man?"
And she said, "I will go." 59 Thus they sent
away their sister Rebekah and her nurse
with Abraham's servant and his men. 60 And
they blessed Rebekah and said to her,

"May you, our sister,
Become thousands of ten thousands,
And may your seed possess
The gate of those who hate him."

61 Then Rebekah arose with her young
women, and they mounted the camels and
went after the man. So the servant took
Rebekah and went.

62 Now Isaac had come from going to
Beer-lahai-roi, for he was living in the land

of the Negev. 63 And Isaac went out to muse
in the field toward evening; and he lifted
up his eyes and looked, and behold, camels
were coming. 64 And Rebekah lifted up her
eyes and saw Isaac and dismounted from
the camel. 65 Then she said to the servant,
"Who is that man walking in the field to
meet us?" And the servant said, "He is my
master." Then she took her veil and cov-
ered herself. 66 And the servant recounted
to Isaac all the things that he had done.
67 Then Isaac brought her into his mother
Sarah's tent, and he took Rebekah, and she
became his wife, and he loved her. Thus,
Isaac was comforted after his mother's
death.

Psalm 7:1–5

1 O Yahweh my God, in You I have
taken refuge;
Save me from all those who
pursue me, and deliver me,
2 Lest he tear my soul like a lion,
Rending me in pieces, while
there is none to deliver.

3 O Yahweh my God, if I have
done this,
If there is injustice in my hands,
4 If I have rewarded evil to him
who is at peace with me,
Or have plundered my
adversary without cause,
5 Let the enemy pursue my
soul and overtake *it*;
And let him trample my life
down to the ground
And cause my glory to dwell
in the dust. Selah.

Proverbs 3:7–8

7 Do not be wise in your own eyes;
Fear Yahweh and turn away from evil.
8 It will be healing to your body
And refreshment to your bones.

Matthew 9:1–17

9 And getting into a boat, Jesus crossed
over *the sea* and came to His own city.
2 And behold, they brought to Him a
paralytic lying on a bed. Seeing their faith,
Jesus said to the paralytic, "Take courage,
son; your sins are forgiven." 3 And behold,
some of the scribes said to themselves, "This
man blasphemes." 4 And Jesus knowing their
thoughts said, "Why are you thinking evil
in your hearts? 5 For which is easier, to say,
'Your sins are forgiven,' or to say, 'Get up and
walk'? 6 But so that you may know that the
Son of Man has authority on earth to forgive
sins"—then He *said to the paralytic, "Get
up, pick up your bed and go home." 7 And he
got up and went home. 8 But when the crowds
saw *this*, they were afraid, and glorified God,
who had given such authority to men.
9 And as Jesus went on from there, He
saw a man called Matthew, sitting in the
tax office; and He *said to him, "Follow Me!"
And he stood up and followed Him.
10 Then it happened that as Jesus was
reclining *at the table* in the house, behold,
many tax collectors and sinners came and
were dining with Jesus and His disciples.
11 And when the Pharisees saw *this*, they
said to His disciples, "Why is your Teacher
eating with the tax collectors and sinners?"
12 But when Jesus heard *this*, He said, "*It is*
not those who are healthy who need a phy-
sician, but those who are sick. 13 But go and
learn what this means: 'I DESIRE COMPASSION,
AND NOT SACRIFICE,' for I did not come to call
the righteous, but sinners."
14 Then the disciples of John *came to
Him, asking, "Why do we and the Pharisees
fast, but Your disciples do not fast?" 15 And
Jesus said to them, "Can the attendants
of the bridegroom mourn as long as the
bridegroom is with them? But the days will
come when the bridegroom is taken away
from them, and then they will fast. 16 But
no one puts a patch of unshrunk cloth on an
old garment; for the patch pulls away from
the garment, and a worse tear results. 17 Nor
do *people* put new wine into old wineskins;
otherwise the wineskins burst, and the wine
pours out and the wineskins are ruined; but
they put new wine into fresh wineskins, and
both are preserved."

JANUARY 13

Genesis 25:1–26:35

25 Now Abraham took another wife,
whose name was Keturah. 2 And she
bore to him Zimran and Jokshan and Medan
and Midian and Ishbak and Shuah. 3 Now
Jokshan was the father of Sheba and Dedan.
And the sons of Dedan were Asshurim and
Letushim and Leummim. 4 And the sons of
Midian *were* Ephah and Epher and Hanoch
and Abida and Eldaah. All these *were* the
sons of Keturah. 5 And Abraham gave all
that he had to Isaac; 6 but to the sons of the
concubines which Abraham had, Abraham
gave gifts while he was still living, and he
sent them away from his son Isaac eastward,
to the land of the east.

7 These are the days of the years of
Abraham's life that he lived, 175 years.
8 And Abraham breathed his last and died
in a good old age, an old man and full *of
days*; and he was gathered to his people.
9 Then his sons Isaac and Ishmael buried
him in the cave of Machpelah, in the field of
Ephron the son of Zohar the Hittite, facing
Mamre, 10 the field which Abraham bought
from the sons of Heth; there Abraham
was buried with Sarah his wife. 11 Now it
happened after the death of Abraham, that
God blessed his son Isaac; and Isaac lived
by Beer-lahai-roi.

12 Now these are the generations of
Ishmael, Abraham's son, whom Hagar the
Egyptian, Sarah's servant-woman, bore to
Abraham; 13 and these are the names of
the sons of Ishmael, by their names, in the
order of their birth: Nebaioth, the firstborn
of Ishmael, and Kedar and Adbeel and
Mibsam 14 and Mishma and Dumah and
Massa, 15 Hadad and Tema, Jetur, Naphish,
and Kedemah. 16 These are the sons of
Ishmael and these are their names, by
their villages, and by their camps; twelve
princes according to their tribes. 17 These
are the years of the life of Ishmael, 137 years;
and he breathed his last and died and was
gathered to his people. 18 And they dwelt
from Havilah to Shur which is east of Egypt
as one goes toward Assyria; he settled in the
face of all his brothers.

19 Now these are the generations of
Isaac, Abraham's son: Abraham became the
father of Isaac; 20 and Isaac was forty years
old when he took Rebekah, the daughter
of Bethuel the Aramean of Paddan-aram,
the sister of Laban the Aramean, to be his
wife. 21 And Isaac entreated Yahweh on
behalf of his wife because she was barren;
and Yahweh was moved by his entreaty.
So Rebekah his wife conceived. 22 But the
children struggled together within her; and
she said, "If it is so, why then am I this *way*?"
So she went to inquire of Yahweh. 23 And
Yahweh said to her,

"Two nations are in your womb;
And two peoples will be
separated from your body;
And one people shall be
stronger than the other;
And the older shall serve the younger."

24 And her days to give birth were fulfilled,
and behold, there were twins in her womb.
25 And the first came forth red, all over like
a hairy garment; and they named him Esau.
26 Afterward his brother came forth with his
hand holding on to Esau's heel, so his name
was called Jacob; and Isaac was sixty years
old when she gave birth to them.

27 And the boys grew up; Esau became a
skillful hunter, a man of the field, but Jacob
was a peaceful man, living in tents. 28 Isaac
loved Esau because he had an appetite for
hunted game, but Rebekah loved Jacob.

29 And Jacob had cooked stew. And Esau
came in from the field, and he was famished.
30 Then Esau said to Jacob, "Please give me a
swallow from the red stuff—this red stuff,
for I am famished." Therefore his name was
called Edom. 31 But Jacob said, "First sell me
your birthright." 32 And Esau said, "Behold,
I am about to die; so of what *use* then is the
birthright to me?" 33 And Jacob said, "First
swear to me"; so he swore to him and sold
his birthright to Jacob. 34 So Jacob gave Esau
bread and lentil stew; and he ate and drank
and rose and went away. Thus Esau despised
his birthright.

26 Now there was a famine in the land,
besides the previous famine that had
occurred in the days of Abraham. So Isaac
went to Gerar, to Abimelech king of the
Philistines. 2 And Yahweh appeared to him
and said, "Do not go down to Egypt; dwell in
the land of which I shall tell you. 3 Sojourn

in this land, and I will be with you and bless
you, for to you and to your seed I will give
all these lands, and I will establish the oath
which I swore to your father Abraham.
4 And I will multiply your seed as the stars
of heaven, and I will give your seed all these
lands; and by your seed all the nations of the
earth shall be blessed; 5 because Abraham
listened to My voice and kept My charge, My
commandments, My statutes, and My laws."
6 So Isaac lived in Gerar. 7 Then the men
of the place asked about his wife. And he
said, "She is my sister," for he was afraid to
say, "my wife," *thinking*, "lest the men of
the place kill me on account of Rebekah,
for she is beautiful in appearance." 8 Now
it happened, when he had been there a long
time, that Abimelech king of the Philistines
looked out through a window and saw,
and behold, Isaac was caressing his wife
Rebekah. 9 Then Abimelech called Isaac and
said, "Behold, surely she is your wife! How
then did you say, 'She is my sister'?" And
Isaac said to him, "Because I said, 'Lest I die
on account of her.'" 10 And Abimelech said,
"What is this you have done to us? One of
the people might easily have lain with your
wife, and you would have brought guilt
upon us." 11 So Abimelech commanded all
the people, saying, "He who touches this
man or his wife shall surely be put to death."
12 And Isaac sowed in that land and
reaped in the same year one hundredfold.
And Yahweh blessed him, 13 and the man
became great and continued to grow greater
until he became very great; 14 and he had
possessions of flocks and possessions
of herds and many servants, so that the
Philistines were jealous of him. 15 Now all
the wells which his father's servants had
dug in the days of Abraham his father, the
Philistines stopped up by filling them with
earth. 16 Then Abimelech said to Isaac, "Go
away from us, for you are too mighty for
us." 17 And Isaac departed from there and
camped in the valley of Gerar and settled
there.

18 Then Isaac dug again the wells of water
which had been dug in the days of his father
Abraham, but the Philistines had stopped
them up after the death of Abraham; and
he called them by the same names by which
his father had called them. 19 Then Isaac's
servants dug in the valley and found there
a well of flowing water. 20 And the herdsmen
of Gerar contended with the herdsmen of
Isaac, saying, "The water is ours!" So he
named the well Esek, because they quar-
reled with him. 21 Then they dug another
well, and they contended over it also, so he
called it Sitnah. 22 Then he moved away from
there and dug another well, and they did not
contend over it; so he named it Rehoboth,
and he said, "At last Yahweh has made room
for us, and we will be fruitful in the land."
23 And he went up from there to Beer-
sheba. 24 And Yahweh appeared to him that
night and said,

"I am the God of your father Abraham;
Do not fear, for I am with you.
I will bless you and multiply your seed,
For the sake of My servant Abraham."

25 So he built an altar there and called upon
the name of Yahweh and pitched his tent
there; and there Isaac's servants dug out a
well.

26 Now Abimelech came to him from
Gerar with his adviser Ahuzzath and Phicol
the commander of his army. 27 And Isaac
said to them, "Why have you come to me,
since you hate me and have sent me away
from you?" 28 Then they said, "We see
plainly that Yahweh has been with you; so
we said, 'Let there now be an oath between
us—between you and us—and let us cut
a covenant with you, 29 that you will do us
no harm, just as we have not touched you
and have done to you nothing but good and
have sent you away in peace. You are now
the blessed of Yahweh.'" 30 Then he made
them a feast, and they ate and drank. 31 In
the morning they arose early, and each
swore to the other; then Isaac sent them
away, and they departed from him in peace.
32 Now it happened on that day, that Isaac's
servants came in and told him about the
well which they had dug and said to him,
"We have found water." 33 So he called it
Shibah; therefore the name of the city is
Beersheba to this day.

34 And Esau was forty years old, and he
took as a wife Judith the daughter of Beeri
the Hittite, and *also* Basemath the daughter
of Elon the Hittite; 35 and they brought
bitterness to Isaac and Rebekah.

Psalm 7:6–8

6 Arise, O Yahweh, in Your anger;
Lift up Yourself against the
fury of my adversaries,

And arouse Yourself for me;
You have appointed judgment.
7 Let the congregation of the
peoples encompass You,
And over them return on high.
8 Yahweh judges the peoples;
Give justice to me, O Yahweh,
according to my righteousness
and my integrity that is in me.

Proverbs 3:9–10

9 Honor Yahweh from your wealth
And from the first of all your
produce;
10 So your barns will be filled with plenty
And your vats will burst
with new wine.

Matthew 9:18–38

18 While He was saying these things to
them, behold, a *synagogue* official came
and was bowing down before Him, and
said, "My daughter has just died; but come
and lay Your hand on her, and she will live."
19 And Jesus got up and *began to* follow him,
and *so did* His disciples.
20 And behold, a woman who had been
suffering from a hemorrhage for twelve
years, came up behind Him and touched
the fringe of His garment; 21 for she was
saying to herself, "If I only touch His gar-
ment, I will be saved *from this*." 22 But Jesus
turning and seeing her said, "Daughter,
take courage; your faith has saved you."
At once the woman was saved *from her
hemorrhage*.
23 And when Jesus came into the official's
house, and saw the flute-players and the
crowd in noisy disorder, 24 He was saying,
"Leave; for the girl has not died, but is
asleep." And they *began* laughing at Him.
25 But when the crowd had been sent out,
coming in, He took her by the hand, and
the girl got up. 26 And this news spread
throughout all that land.
27 And as Jesus went on from there,
two blind men followed Him, crying out,
"Have mercy on us, Son of David!" 28 And
when He entered the house, the blind men
came up to Him, and Jesus *said to them,
"Do you believe that I am able to do this?"
They *said to Him, "Yes, Lord." 29 Then
He touched their eyes, saying, "It shall
be done to you according to your faith."
30 And their eyes were opened. And Jesus
sternly warned them, saying, "See that no
one knows *about this*!" 31 But they went out
and spread the news about Him throughout
all that land.
32 Now as they were going out, behold, a
mute, demon-possessed man was brought
to Him. 33 And after the demon was cast
out, the mute man spoke; and the crowds
marveled, saying, "Nothing like this has ever
been seen in Israel." 34 But the Pharisees
were saying, "He casts out the demons by
the ruler of the demons."
35 And Jesus was going through all the
cities and villages, teaching in their syn-
agogues, and preaching the gospel of the
kingdom, and healing every kind of disease
and every kind of sickness.
36 And seeing the crowds, He felt com-
passion for them, because they were dis-
tressed and downcast like sheep without a
shepherd. 37 Then He *said to His disciples,
"The harvest is plentiful, but the workers
are few. 38 Therefore pray earnestly to the
Lord of the harvest to send out workers into
His harvest."

JANUARY 14

Genesis 27:1–28:22

27 Now it happened that when Isaac was
old and his eyes were too dim to see,
that he called his older son Esau and said to
him, "My son." And he said to him, "Here I
am." 2 And Isaac said, "Behold now, I am old,
and I do not know the day of my death. 3 So
now, please take up your gear, your quiver
and your bow, and go out to the field and
hunt game for me; 4 and prepare a savory
dish for me such as I love, and bring it to
me that I may eat, so that my soul may bless
you before I die."
5 Now Rebekah was listening while Isaac
was speaking to his son Esau. Then Esau went
to the field to hunt for game to bring *to Isaac*.
6 But Rebekah spoke to her son Jacob, saying,
"Behold, I heard your father speaking to your
brother Esau, saying, 7 'Bring me *some* game
and prepare a savory dish for me, that I may
eat and bless you in the presence of Yahweh
before my death.' 8 So now, my son, listen

to my voice as I command you. 9 Go now to
the flock and get for me two choice young
goats from there, that I may prepare them
as a savory dish for your father, such as he
loves. 10 Then you shall bring *it* to your father,
that he may eat, so that he may bless you
before his death." 11 Then Jacob answered his
mother Rebekah, "Behold, Esau my brother is
a hairy man, and I am a smooth man. 12 Per-
haps my father will feel me, then I will be as
a mocker in his sight, and I will bring upon
myself a curse and not a blessing." 13 But his
mother said to him, "Your curse be on me,
my son; only listen to my voice, and go, get
them for me." 14 So he went and got *them* and
brought *them* to his mother; and his mother
made a savory dish such as his father loved.
15 Then Rebekah took the best garments of
Esau her elder son, which were with her in
the house, and she put them on Jacob her
younger son. 16 And she put the skins of the
young goats on his hands and on the smooth
part of his neck. 17 She also gave the savory
dish and the bread, which she had prepared
into the hand of her son Jacob.

18 Then he came to his father and said, "My
father." And he said, "Here I am. Who are you,
my son?" 19 And Jacob said to his father, "I am
Esau your firstborn; I have done as you told
me. Rise up, please, sit and eat of my game,
that your soul may bless me." 20 Then Isaac
said to his son, "How is it that you have found
it so quickly, my son?" And he said, "Because
Yahweh your God caused *it* to happen to me."
21 Then Isaac said to Jacob, "Please come near,
that I may feel you, my son, whether you are
really my son Esau or not." 22 So Jacob came
near to Isaac his father, and he felt him and
said, "The voice is the voice of Jacob, but the
hands are the hands of Esau." 23 And he did
not recognize him because his hands were
hairy like his brother Esau's hands; so he
blessed him. 24 And he said, "Are you really
my son Esau?" And he said, "I am." 25 So he
said, "Bring *it* near to me, and I will eat of my
son's game, that my soul may bless you." And
he brought *it* near to him, and he ate; he also
brought him wine, and he drank. 26 Then his
father Isaac said to him, "Please come near
and kiss me, my son." 27 So he came near and
kissed him; and he smelled the smell of his
garments, and then he blessed him and said,

"See, the smell of my son
Is like the smell of a field which
Yahweh has blessed;
28 Now may God give you of
the dew of heaven,
And of the fatness of the earth,
And an abundance of grain
and new wine;
29 May peoples serve you,
And nations bow down to you;
Be master of your brothers,
And may your mother's sons
bow down to you.
Cursed be those who curse you,
And blessed be those who bless you."

30 Now it happened that as soon as Isaac
had finished blessing Jacob, and Jacob had
hardly gone out from the presence of Isaac
his father, that Esau his brother came in
from his hunting. 31 Then he also made a
savory dish and brought it to his father; and
he said to his father, "Let my father arise
and eat of his son's game, that your soul may
bless me." 32 And Isaac his father said to him,
"Who are you?" And he said, "I am your son,
your firstborn, Esau." 33 Then Isaac trembled
exceedingly violently and said, "Who was
he then that hunted game and brought *it*
to me, so that I ate of all *of it* before you
came and blessed him? Indeed, he shall be
blessed." 34 As Esau heard the words of his
father, he cried out with an exceedingly
great and bitter cry and said to his father,
"Bless me, me also, O my father!" 35 And he
said, "Your brother came deceitfully and
has taken away your blessing." 36 Then he
said, "Is he not rightly named Jacob, for he
has supplanted me these two times? He
took away my birthright, and behold, now
he has taken away my blessing." And he
said, "Have you not reserved a blessing for
me?" 37 But Isaac answered and said to Esau,
"Behold, I have made him your master, and
all his *fellow* brothers I have given to him
as servants; and with grain and new wine
I have sustained him. Now as for you then,
what can I do, my son?" 38 And Esau said to
his father, "Do you have only one blessing,
my father? Bless me, *even* me also, O my
father." So Esau lifted his voice and wept.

39 Then Isaac his father answered and
said to him,

"Behold, away from the fatness of the
earth shall be your habitation,
And away from the dew of
heaven from above.
40 "By your sword you shall live,
And your brother you shall serve;

But it shall be when you
become restless,
That you will break his yoke
from your neck."
41 So Esau bore a grudge against Jacob
because of the blessing with which his
father had blessed him; and Esau said in his
heart, "The days of mourning for my father
are near; then I will kill my brother Jacob."
42 Then the words of her elder son Esau were
told to Rebekah. So she sent and called her
younger son Jacob and said to him, "Behold,
your brother Esau is consoling himself
concerning you *by planning* to kill you. 43 So
now, my son, listen to my voice, and arise,
flee to Haran, to my brother Laban! 44 Stay
with him a few days, until your brother's
wrath subsides, 45 until your brother's anger
against you subsides and he forgets what
you did to him. Then I will send and get you
from there. Why should I be bereaved of you
both in one day?"
46 Then Rebekah said to Isaac, "I am tired
of living because of the daughters of Heth;
if Jacob takes a wife from the daughters of
Heth, like these, from the daughters of the
land, what good will my life be to me?"

28 So Isaac called Jacob and blessed
him and commanded him and said
to him, "You shall not take a wife from the
daughters of Canaan. 2 Arise, go to Paddan-
aram, to the house of Bethuel your mother's
father; and from there take to yourself a wife
from the daughters of Laban your mother's
brother. 3 May God Almighty bless you and
make you fruitful and multiply you, that you
may become an assembly of peoples. 4 May
He also give you the blessing of Abraham, to
you and to your seed with you, that you may
possess the land of your sojournings, which
God gave to Abraham." 5 Then Isaac sent
Jacob away, and he went to Paddan-aram
to Laban, son of Bethuel the Aramean, the
brother of Rebekah, the mother of Jacob
and Esau.
6 And Esau saw that Isaac had blessed
Jacob and sent him away to Paddan-aram to
take for himself a wife from there, *and that*
when he blessed him he commanded him,
saying, "You shall not take a wife from the
daughters of Canaan," 7 and that Jacob had
listened to his father and his mother and
had gone to Paddan-aram. 8 So Esau saw that
the daughters of Canaan were displeasing
in the sight of his father Isaac; 9 and Esau
went to Ishmael and took Mahalath, the
daughter of Ishmael, Abraham's son, the
sister of Nebaioth, to be his wife, besides
the wives that he had.
10 Then Jacob departed from Beersheba
and went toward Haran. 11 And he reached
a certain place and spent the night there
because the sun had set; and he took one of
the stones of the place and put it under his
head and lay down in that place. 12 Then he
had a dream, and behold, a ladder stood on
the earth with its top touching heaven; and
behold, the angels of God were ascending
and descending on it. 13 And behold, Yahweh
stood above it and said, "I am Yahweh, the
God of your father Abraham and the God of
Isaac; the land on which you lie, I will give
it to you and to your seed. 14 And your seed
will also be like the dust of the earth, and
you will spread out to the west and to the
east and to the north and to the south; and
in you and in your seed all the families of
the earth shall be blessed. 15 Behold, I am
with you and will keep you wherever you go.
And I will bring you back to this land; for I
will not forsake you until I have done what
I have promised you." 16 Then Jacob awoke
from his sleep and said, "Surely Yahweh is in
this place, and I did not know it." 17 And he
was afraid and said, "How fearsome is this
place! This is none other than the house of
God, and this is the gate of heaven."
18 So Jacob rose early in the morning and
took the stone that he had put under his
head and set it up as a pillar and poured
oil on its top. 19 And he called the name
of that place Bethel; however, previously
the name of the city had been Luz. 20 Then
Jacob made a vow, saying, "If God will be
with me and will keep me on this journey
on which I am going, and will give me food
to eat and garments to wear, 21 and I return
to my father's house in peace, then Yahweh
will be my God. 22 Now this stone, which I
have set up as a pillar, will be God's house,
and of all that You give me I will surely give
a tenth to You."

Psalm 7:9–17

9 O let the evil of the wicked come to an
end, but establish the righteous;
For the righteous God tests
the hearts and minds.
10 My shield is with God,

Who saves the upright in heart.
11 God is a righteous judge,
And a God who has
indignation every day.

12 If a man does not repent,
He will sharpen His sword;
He has bent His bow and prepared it.
13 He has also prepared for
Himself deadly weapons;
He makes His arrows fiery shafts.
14 Behold, he travails with wickedness,
And he conceives mischief and
gives birth to falsehood.
15 He has dug a pit and hollowed it out,
And has fallen into the hole
which he made.
16 His mischief will return
upon his own head,
And his violence will descend
upon his own skull.

17 I will give thanks to Yahweh
according to His righteousness
And will sing praise to the name
of Yahweh Most High.

Proverbs 3:11–12

11 My son, do not reject the
discipline of Yahweh
Or loathe His reproof,
12 For whom Yahweh loves He reproves,
Even as a father *reproves* the
son in whom he delights.

Matthew 10:1–20

10 And summoning His twelve disci-
ples, *Jesus* gave them authority over
unclean spirits, to cast them out, and to
heal every kind of disease and every kind
of sickness.
2 Now the names of the twelve apostles
are these: The first, Simon, who is called
Peter, and Andrew his brother; and James
the son of Zebedee, and John his brother;
3 Philip and Bartholomew; Thomas and
Matthew the tax collector; James the son
of Alphaeus, and Thaddaeus; 4 Simon the
Zealot, and Judas Iscariot, the one who
betrayed Him.
5 These twelve Jesus sent out after
instructing them, saying, "Do not go in the
way of the Gentiles, and do not enter *any*
city of the Samaritans; 6 but rather go to
the lost sheep of the house of Israel. 7 And
as you go, preach, saying, 'The kingdom of
heaven is at hand.' 8 Heal *the* sick, raise *the*
dead, cleanse *the* lepers, cast out demons.
Freely you received, freely give. 9 Do not
acquire gold, or silver, or copper for your
money belts, 10 or a bag for *your* journey,
or even two tunics, or sandals, or a staff; for
the worker is worthy of his support. 11 And
whatever city or village you enter, inquire
who is worthy in it, and stay there until you
leave. 12 Now as you enter the house, give it
your greeting. 13 And if the house is worthy,
let your peace come upon it. But if it is not
worthy, let your peace return to you. 14 And
whoever does not receive you, nor heed
your words, as you leave that house or that
city, shake the dust off your feet. 15 Truly I
say to you, it will be more tolerable for the
land of Sodom and Gomorrah in the day of
judgment than for that city.
16 "Behold, I send you out as sheep in the
midst of wolves; so be shrewd as serpents
and innocent as doves. 17 But beware of men,
for they will deliver you over to the courts
and flog you in their synagogues; 18 and you
will even be brought before governors and
kings for My sake, as a testimony to them
and to the Gentiles. 19 But when they deliver
you over, do not worry about how or what
you are to say; for it will be given to you in
that hour what you are to say. 20 For it is not
you who speak, but the Spirit of your Father
who speaks in you.

The more you read the Bible and the more you meditate on it,
the more you will be astonished with it.

— CHARLES H. SPURGEON

JANUARY 15

Genesis 29:1–30:43

29 Then Jacob took up his journey and came to the land of the sons of the east. 2 And he looked, and behold, a well in the field, and behold, three flocks of sheep were lying there beside it, for from that well they gave *water* to the flocks to drink. Now the stone on the mouth of the well was large. 3 And all the flocks would be gathered there, and they would roll the stone from the mouth of the well and give *water* to the sheep to drink and return the stone back to its place on the mouth of the well.

4 And Jacob said to them, "My brothers, where are you from?" And they said, "We are from Haran." 5 Then he said to them, "Do you know Laban the son of Nahor?" And they said, "We know *him.*" 6 And he said to them, "Is it well with him?" And they said, "It is well, and here is Rachel his daughter coming with the sheep." 7 And he said, "Behold, it is still high day; it is not time for the livestock to be gathered. Give *water* to the sheep to drink, and go, pasture them." 8 But they said, "We cannot, until all the flocks are gathered, and they roll the stone from the mouth of the well; then we give *water* to the sheep to drink."

9 While he was still speaking with them, Rachel came with her father's sheep, for she was a shepherdess. 10 Now it happened, when Jacob saw Rachel the daughter of Laban his mother's brother and the sheep of Laban his mother's brother, Jacob came near and rolled the stone from the mouth of the well and gave *water* to the flock of Laban his mother's brother to drink. 11 Then Jacob kissed Rachel and lifted his voice and wept. 12 And Jacob told Rachel that he was a relative of her father and that he was Rebekah's son, and she ran and told her father.

13 So it happened that when Laban heard the report of Jacob his sister's son, he ran to meet him, and he embraced him and kissed him and brought him to his house. Then he recounted to Laban all these things. 14 And Laban said to him, "Surely you are my bone and my flesh." And he stayed with him one month.

15 Then Laban said to Jacob, "Because you are my relative, should you therefore serve me for nothing? Tell me, what shall your wages be?" 16 Now Laban had two daughters; the name of the older was Leah, and the name of the younger was Rachel. 17 And Leah's eyes were weak, but Rachel was beautiful in form and beautiful in appearance. 18 Now Jacob loved Rachel, so he said, "I will serve you seven years for your younger daughter Rachel." 19 And Laban said, "It is better that I give her to you than to give her to another man; stay with me." 20 So Jacob served seven years for Rachel, and they were in his sight but a few days because of his love for her.

21 Then Jacob said to Laban, "Give *me* my wife, for my days are fulfilled, that I may go in to her." 22 And Laban gathered all the men of the place and made a feast. 23 Now it happened in the evening that he took his daughter Leah and brought her to him; and *Jacob* went in to her. 24 Laban also gave his servant-woman Zilpah to his daughter Leah as a servant-woman. 25 Now it happened in the morning that, behold, it was Leah! And he said to Laban, "What is this you have done to me? Was it not for Rachel that I served with you? Why then have you deceived me?" 26 But Laban said, "It is not the practice in our place to give the younger before the firstborn. 27 Fulfill the week of this one, and we will give you the other also for the service which you shall serve with me for another seven years." 28 And Jacob did so and fulfilled her week, and he gave him his daughter Rachel as his wife. 29 Laban also gave his servant-woman Bilhah to his daughter Rachel as her servant-woman. 30 So *Jacob* went in to Rachel also, and indeed he loved Rachel more than Leah, and he served with Laban for another seven years.

31 And Yahweh saw that Leah was unloved, and He opened her womb, but Rachel was barren. 32 So Leah conceived and bore a son and named him Reuben, for she said, "Because Yahweh has seen my affliction; surely now my husband will love me." 33 Then she conceived again and bore a son and said, "Because Yahweh has heard that I am unloved, He has therefore given me this *son* also." So she named him Simeon. 34 And she conceived again and bore a son and said, "Now this time my husband will

be joined to me because I have borne him
three sons." Therefore he was named Levi.
35 And she conceived again and bore a son
and said, "This time I will praise Yahweh."
Therefore she named him Judah. Then she
stopped bearing.

30 Then Rachel saw that she bore Jacob
no children, so she became jealous
of her sister; and she said to Jacob, "Give
me children, or else I die." 2 Then Jacob's
anger burned against Rachel, and he said,
"Am I in the place of God, who has withheld
from you the fruit of the womb?" 3 And she
said, "Here is my maidservant Bilhah, go in
to her that she may bear on my knees, that
through her I too may obtain children." 4 So
she gave him her servant-woman Bilhah as a
wife, and Jacob went in to her. 5 And Bilhah
conceived and bore Jacob a son. 6 Then
Rachel said, "God has rendered justice to
me and has indeed listened to my voice and
has given me a son." Therefore she named
him Dan. 7 And Rachel's servant-woman
Bilhah conceived again and bore Jacob a
second son. 8 So Rachel said, "With mighty
wrestlings I have wrestled with my sister,
and I have indeed prevailed." And she
named him Naphtali.

9 Then Leah saw that she had stopped
bearing, so she took her servant-woman
Zilpah and gave her to Jacob as a wife. 10 And
Leah's servant-woman Zilpah bore Jacob a
son. 11 Then Leah said, "How fortunate!"
So she named him Gad. 12 And Leah's
servant-woman Zilpah bore Jacob a second
son. 13 Then Leah said, "Happy am I! For
women will call me happy." So she named
him Asher.

14 And in the days of the wheat harvest,
Reuben went and found mandrakes in the
field and brought them to his mother Leah.
Then Rachel said to Leah, "Please give me
some of your son's mandrakes." 15 But she
said to her, "Is it a small matter for you to
take my husband? And would you take my
son's mandrakes also?" So Rachel said,
"Therefore he will lie with you tonight in
return for your son's mandrakes." 16 Then
Jacob came in from the field in the evening.
And Leah went out to meet him and said,
"You must come in to me, for I have surely
hired you with my son's mandrakes." So he
lay with her that night. 17 And God listened
to Leah, and she conceived and bore Jacob
a fifth son. 18 And Leah said, "God has given
me my wages because I gave my servant-
woman to my husband." So she named him
Issachar. 19 Then Leah conceived again and
bore a sixth son to Jacob. 20 And Leah said,
"God has gifted me a good gift; this time my
husband will honor me because I have borne
him six sons." So she named him Zebulun.
21 Afterward she bore a daughter and named
her Dinah.

22 Then God remembered Rachel, and
God listened to her and opened her womb.
23 So she conceived and bore a son and said,
"God has taken away my reproach." 24 And
she named him Joseph, saying, "May Yahweh
give me another son."

25 Now it happened when Rachel had
borne Joseph, that Jacob said to Laban,
"Send me away, that I may go to my own
place and to my own land. 26 Give *me* my
wives and my children for whom I have
served you, and let me go; for you yourself
know my service which I have rendered
you." 27 But Laban said to him, "If now I
have found favor in your sight, *stay with
me*; I have interpreted an omen that Yahweh
has blessed me on your account." 28 And he
continued to say, "Name me your wages, and
I will give it." 29 But he said to him, "You
yourself know how I have served you and
how your livestock have fared with me.
30 For you had little before I came, but it has
spread out to a multitude, and Yahweh has
blessed you at *every* step of mine. But now,
when shall I provide for my own household
also?" 31 So he said, "What shall I give you?"
And Jacob said, "You shall not give me any-
thing. If you will do this *one* thing for me, I
will again pasture *and* keep your flock: 32 let
me pass through your entire flock today,
removing from there every speckled and
spotted sheep and every black one among
the lambs and the spotted and speckled
among the goats; and *such* shall be my
wages. 33 So my righteousness will answer
for me later, when you come concerning
my wages. Every one that is not speckled
and spotted among the goats and black
among the lambs, *if found* with me, will
be considered stolen." 34 And Laban said,
"Behold, let it be according to your word."
35 So he removed on that day the striped
and spotted male goats and all the speckled
and spotted female goats, every one with
white in it, and all the black ones among

the sheep, and gave them into the care of
his sons. 36 And he put *a distance of* three
days' journey between himself and Jacob,
and Jacob was pasturing the rest of Laban's
flocks.
37 Then Jacob took fresh rods of poplar
and almond and plane trees, and he peeled
white stripes in them, exposing the white
which *was* in the rods. 38 And he set the
rods which he had peeled in front of the
flocks in the trough, *that is*, in the watering
channels, where the flocks came to drink;
and they mated when they came to drink.
39 So the flocks mated by the rods, and the
flocks brought forth striped, speckled, and
spotted. 40 And Jacob separated the lambs,
and he made the flocks face toward the
striped and all the black in the flock of
Laban; and he set his own herds apart and
did not set them with Laban's flock. 41 Now
it would be that, whenever the stronger of
the flock were mating, Jacob would place
the rods in the sight of the flock in the
trough, so that they might mate by the rods;
42 but when the flock was feeble, he did not
put *them* in; so the feebler were Laban's and
the stronger Jacob's. 43 So the man spread
out exceedingly and had large flocks and
female and male servants and camels and
donkeys.

Psalm 8:1–5

1 O Yahweh, our Lord,
How majestic is Your name
in all the earth,
Who displays Your splendor
above the heavens!
2 From the mouth of infants and
nursing babies You have
established strength
Because of Your adversaries,
To make the enemy and the
revengeful cease.

3 When I see Your heavens, the
work of Your fingers,
The moon and the stars, which
You have established;
4 What is man that You remember him,
And the son of man that
You care for him?
5 Yet You have made him a little
lower than *the* angels,
And You crown him with
glory and majesty!

Proverbs 3:13–18

13 How blessed is the man
who finds wisdom
And the man who obtains
discernment.
14 For her profit is better than
the profit of silver
And her produce better than fine gold.
15 She is more precious than pearls;
And nothing you desire
compares with her.
16 Length of days is in her right hand;
In her left hand are riches and glory.
17 Her ways are pleasant ways
And all her pathways are peace.
18 She is a tree of life to those
who seize her,
And all those who hold her
fast are blessed.

Matthew 10:21–42

21 "And brother will betray brother to
death, and a father *his* child; and children
will rise up against parents and cause them
to be put to death. 22 And you will be hated
by all because of My name, but it is the one
who has endured to the end who will be
saved.
23 "But whenever they persecute you in
this city, flee to the next; for truly I say to
you, you will not finish *going through* the
cities of Israel until the Son of Man comes.
24 "A disciple is not above his teacher, nor
a slave above his master. 25 It is enough for
the disciple that he become like his teacher,
and the slave like his master. If they have
called the head of the house Beelzebul, how
much more the members of his household!
26 "Therefore do not fear them, for there is
nothing concealed that will not be revealed,
and hidden that will not be known. 27 What
I tell you in the darkness, speak in the light;
and what you hear *whispered* in *your* ear,
proclaim upon the housetops. 28 And do not
fear those who kill the body but are unable
to kill the soul; but rather fear Him who is
able to destroy both soul and body in hell.
29 Are not two sparrows sold for an assarion?
And *yet* not one of them will fall to the
ground apart from your Father. 30 But the
very hairs of your head are all numbered.
31 So do not fear; you are more valuable than
many sparrows.
32 "Therefore everyone who confesses Me
before men, I will also confess him before

My Father who is in heaven. 33 But whoever denies Me before men, I will also deny him before My Father who is in heaven.

34 "Do not think that I came to bring peace on the earth; I did not come to bring peace, but a sword. 35 For I came to SET A MAN AGAINST HIS FATHER, AND A DAUGHTER AGAINST HER MOTHER, AND A DAUGHTER-IN-LAW AGAINST HER MOTHER-IN-LAW; 36 and A MAN'S ENEMIES WILL BE THE MEMBERS OF HIS HOUSEHOLD.

37 "He who loves father or mother more than Me is not worthy of Me; and he who loves son or daughter more than Me is not worthy of Me. 38 And he who does not take his cross and follow after Me is not worthy of Me. 39 He who has found his life will lose it, and he who has lost his life for My sake will find it.

40 "He who receives you receives Me, and he who receives Me receives Him who sent Me. 41 He who receives a prophet in the name of a prophet shall receive a prophet's reward; and he who receives a righteous man in the name of a righteous man shall receive a righteous man's reward. 42 And whoever in the name of a disciple gives to one of these little ones even a cup of cold water to drink, truly I say to you, he shall not lose his reward."

JANUARY 16

Genesis 31:1–32:32

31 Then Jacob heard the words of Laban's sons, saying, "Jacob has taken away all that belonged to our father, and from what belonged to our father he has made all this wealth." 2 And Jacob saw the face of Laban, and behold, it was not *friendly* toward him as formerly. 3 Then Yahweh said to Jacob, "Return to the land of your fathers and to your kin, and I will be with you." 4 So Jacob sent and called Rachel and Leah to his flock in the field, 5 and he said to them, "I see your father's face, that it is not *friendly* toward me as formerly, but the God of my father has been with me. 6 You also know that I have served your father with all my power. 7 Yet your father has cheated me and changed my wages ten times; however, God did not allow him to harm me. 8 If he spoke thus, 'The speckled shall be your wages,' then all the flock bore speckled; and if he spoke thus, 'The striped shall be your wages,' then all the flock bore striped. 9 Thus God has delivered your father's livestock and given *them* to me. 10 Now it happened at the time when the flock were mating that I lifted up my eyes and saw in a dream, and behold, the male goats which were mating *were* striped, speckled, and mottled. 11 Then the angel of God said to me in the dream, 'Jacob,' and I said, 'Here I am.' 12 He said, 'Lift up now your eyes and see *that* all the male goats which are mating are striped, speckled, and mottled; for I have seen all that Laban has been doing to you. 13 I am the God *of* Bethel, where you anointed a pillar, where you made a vow to Me; now arise, leave this land, and return to the land of your kin.'" 14 Then Rachel and Leah said to him, "Do we still have any portion or inheritance in our father's house? 15 Are we not counted by him as foreigners? For he has sold us and has also entirely consumed our purchase price. 16 Surely all the riches which God has delivered *over to us* from our father belong to us and our children; now then, do whatever God has said to you."

17 Then Jacob arose and put his children and his wives upon camels; 18 and he drove away all his livestock and all his possessions which he had accumulated, his acquired livestock which he had accumulated in Paddan-aram, in order to go to the land of Canaan to his father Isaac. 19 Now Laban had gone to shear his flock. Then Rachel stole the household idols that were her father's. 20 And Jacob deceived Laban the Aramean by not telling him that he was fleeing. 21 So he fled with all that he had; and he arose and crossed the River and set his face toward the hill country of Gilead.

22 Then it was told to Laban on the third day that Jacob had fled; 23 so he took his relatives with him and pursued him *a distance of* seven days' journey, and he overtook him in the hill country of Gilead. 24 And God came to Laban the Aramean in a dream of the night and said to him, "Beware lest you speak to Jacob either good or bad."

25 So Laban caught up with Jacob. Now Jacob had pitched his tent in the hill country, and Laban with his relatives camped in the

hill country of Gilead. 26 Then Laban said to Jacob, "What have you done by deceiving me and carrying away my daughters like captives of the sword? 27 Why did you flee secretly and deceive me and not tell me—so that I might have sent you away with gladness and with songs, with tambourine and with lyre— 28 and not allow me to kiss my sons and my daughters? Now you have acted foolishly. 29 It is in my hand to do evil against you, but the God of your father spoke to me last night, saying, 'Beware of speaking either good or evil to Jacob.' 30 So now you have indeed gone away because you longed greatly for your father's house; *but* why did you steal my gods?" 31 Then Jacob answered and said to Laban, "Because I was afraid, because I said, 'Lest you take your daughters from me by force.' 32 The one with whom you find your gods shall not live; in the presence of our relatives recognize what is yours among my belongings and take *it* for yourself." But Jacob did not know that Rachel had stolen them.

33 So Laban went into Jacob's tent and into Leah's tent and into the tent of the two maidservants, but he did not find *them*. Then he went out of Leah's tent and entered Rachel's tent. 34 Now Rachel had taken the household idols and put them in the camel's saddle, and she sat on them. And Laban felt through all the tent but did not find *them*. 35 And she said to her father, "Let not my lord be angry that I cannot rise before you, for the manner of women is upon me." So he searched but did not find the household idols.

36 Then Jacob became angry and contended with Laban; and Jacob answered and said to Laban, "What is my transgression? What is my sin that you have hotly pursued me? 37 Though you have felt through all my goods, what have you found of all your household goods? Place *it* here before my relatives and your relatives, that they may decide between us two. 38 These twenty years I *have been* with you; your ewes and your female goats have not miscarried, nor have I eaten the rams of your flocks. 39 That which was torn *of beasts* I did not bring to you; I bore the loss of it myself. You required it of my hand *whether* stolen by day or stolen by night. 40 *Thus* I was: by day the heat consumed me and the frost by night, and my sleep fled from my eyes. 41 These twenty years I have been in your house; I served you fourteen years for your two daughters and six years for your flock, and you changed my wages ten times. 42 If the God of my father, the God of Abraham, and the dread of Isaac, had not been for me, surely now you would have sent me away empty. God has seen my affliction and the toil of my hands, so He rendered *the* decision last night."

43 Then Laban answered and said to Jacob, "The daughters are my daughters, and the children are my children, and the flocks are my flocks, and all that you see is mine. But what can I do this day to these daughters of mine or to their children whom they have borne? 44 So now come, let us cut a covenant, you and I, and let it be a witness between you and me." 45 Then Jacob took a stone and raised it up *as* a pillar. 46 And Jacob said to his relatives, "Gather stones." So they took stones and made a heap, and they ate there by the heap. 47 And Laban called it Jegar-sahadutha, but Jacob called it Galeed. 48 Then Laban said, "This heap is a witness between you and me this day." Therefore it was named Galeed, 49 and Mizpah, for he said, "May Yahweh watch between you and me when we are absent one from the other. 50 If you afflict my daughters, or if you take wives besides my daughters, *although* no man is with us, see, God is witness between you and me." 51 And Laban said to Jacob, "Behold this heap and behold the pillar which I have set between you and me. 52 This heap is a witness, and the pillar is a witness, that I will not pass by this heap to you *for harm*, and you will not pass by this heap and this pillar to me for harm. 53 The God of Abraham and the God of Nahor, the God of their father, judge between us." So Jacob swore by the dread of his father Isaac. 54 Then Jacob offered a sacrifice on the mountain and called his relatives to eat a meal; and they ate the meal and spent the night on the mountain. 55 And Laban arose early in the morning and kissed his sons and his daughters and blessed them. Then Laban departed and returned to his place.

32 Now Jacob went on his way, and the angels of God met him. 2 Then Jacob said when he saw them, "This is God's camp." So he named that place Mahanaim.

3 Then Jacob sent messengers before him to his brother Esau in the land of Seir, the country of Edom. 4 He also commanded them saying, "Thus you shall say to my lord,

to Esau: 'Thus says your servant Jacob, "I
have sojourned with Laban and have been
delayed until now; 5 and I have oxen and
donkeys *and* flocks and male and female
slaves; and I have sent to tell my lord, that I
may find favor in your sight."'"

6 Then the messengers returned to Jacob,
saying, "We came to your brother, to Esau,
and furthermore he is coming to meet you,
and four hundred men are with him." 7 Then
Jacob was greatly afraid and distressed;
and he divided the people who were with
him, and the flocks and the herds and the
camels, into two camps. 8 And he said, "If
Esau comes to the one camp and strikes it,
then the camp which remains will escape."

9 And Jacob said, "O God of my father Abra-
ham and God of my father Isaac, O Yahweh,
who said to me, 'Return to your land and
to your kin, and I will prosper you,' 10 I am
unworthy of all the lovingkindness and of all
the truth which You have shown to Your slave;
for with my staff *only* I crossed this Jordan,
and now I have become two camps. 11 Deliver
me, I pray, from the hand of my brother, from
the hand of Esau; for I fear him, lest he come
and strike me down *with* the mothers and the
children. 12 For You said, 'I will surely prosper
you and make your seed as the sand of the
sea, which is too great to be numbered.'"

13 So he spent the night there. Then he
took from what he had with him a present
for his brother Esau: 14 two hundred female
goats and twenty male goats, two hundred
ewes and twenty rams, 15 thirty milking
camels and their colts, forty cows and ten
bulls, twenty female donkeys and ten male
donkeys. 16 And he gave *them* into the hand
of his servants, every flock by itself, and said
to his servants, "Pass on before me and put a
space between flocks." 17 And he commanded
the first one in front, saying, "When my
brother Esau meets you and asks you, saying,
'To whom do you belong, and where are you
going, and to whom do these *animals* in front
of you belong?' 18 then you shall say, '*These*
belong to your servant Jacob; it is a present
sent to my lord, to Esau. And behold, he
also is behind us.'" 19 Then he commanded
also the second and the third and all those
who followed the flocks, saying, "After this
manner you shall speak to Esau when you
find him; 20 and you shall say, 'Behold, your
servant Jacob also is behind us.'" For he said,
"I will appease his face with the present that
goes before me. Then afterward I will see his
face; perhaps he will lift up my face." 21 So
the present passed on before him, while he
himself spent that night in the camp.

22 And he arose that same night and took
his two wives and his two servant-women
and his eleven children and crossed the ford
of the Jabbok. 23 And he took them and sent
them across the stream. And he sent across
whatever he had.

24 Then Jacob was left alone, and a man
wrestled with him until the breaking of
dawn. 25 And he saw that he had not pre-
vailed against him, so he touched the socket
of his thigh; and so the socket of Jacob's thigh
was dislocated while he wrestled with him.
26 Then he said, "Let me go, for the dawn is
breaking." But he said, "I will not let you go
unless you bless me." 27 So he said to him,
"What is your name?" And he said, "Jacob."
28 Then He said, "Your name shall no longer
be Jacob, but Israel; for you have striven with
God and with men and have prevailed."
29 Then Jacob asked him and said, "Please
tell me your name." But he said, "Why is it
that you ask my name?" And he blessed him
there. 30 So Jacob named the place Peniel, for
he said, "I have seen God face to face, yet my
life has been delivered." 31 And the sun rose
upon him just as he crossed over Penuel, and
he was limping on his thigh. 32 Therefore,
to this day the sons of Israel do not eat the
sinew of the hip which is on the socket of
the thigh because he touched the socket of
Jacob's thigh in the sinew of the hip.

Psalm 8:6–9

6 You make him to rule over the
works of Your hands;
You have put all things under his feet,
7 All sheep and oxen,
And also the animals of the field,
8 The birds of the heavens and
the fish of the sea,
Whatever passes through
the paths of the seas.

9 O Yahweh, our Lord,
How majestic is Your name
in all the earth!

Proverbs 3:19–20

19 Yahweh by wisdom founded the earth,
By discernment He established
the heavens.

20 By His knowledge the
deeps were split up
And the skies drip with dew.

Matthew 11:1–30

11 Now it happened that when Jesus had
finished giving instructions to His
twelve disciples, He departed from there
to teach and preach in their cities.
2 Now when John in prison heard of the
works of Christ, he sent *word* by his disciples
3 and said to Him, "Are You the One who is to
come, or shall we look for someone else?"
4 And Jesus answered and said to them, "Go
and report to John what you hear and see:
5 *the* BLIND RECEIVE SIGHT and *the* lame walk,
the lepers are cleansed and *the* deaf hear, *the*
dead are raised up, and *the* POOR HAVE THE
GOSPEL PREACHED TO THEM. 6 And blessed is
he who does not take offense at Me."
7 Now as these men were going *away*,
Jesus began to speak to the crowds about
John, "What did you go out into the wilder-
ness to see? A reed shaken by the wind? 8 But
what did you go out to see? A man dressed in
soft *clothing*? Behold, those who wear soft
clothing are in kings' palaces! 9 But what did
you go out to see? A prophet? Yes, I tell you,
and one who is more than a prophet. 10 This
is the one about whom it is written,

'BEHOLD, I SEND MY MESSENGER
AHEAD OF YOU,
WHO WILL PREPARE YOUR
WAY BEFORE YOU.'

11 "Truly I say to you, among those born of
women there has not arisen *anyone* greater
than John the Baptist! Yet the one who is
least in the kingdom of heaven is greater
than he. 12 And from the days of John the
Baptist until now the kingdom of heaven
suffers violence, and violent men take it by
force. 13 For all the prophets and the Law
prophesied until John. 14 And if you are
willing to accept *it*, John himself is Elijah
who was to come. 15 He who has ears to hear,
let him hear.
16 "But to what shall I compare this
generation? It is like children sitting in the
marketplaces, who call out to the other
children, 17 and say, 'We played the flute for
you, and you did not dance; we sang a dirge,
and you did not mourn.' 18 For John came
neither eating nor drinking, and they say,
'He has a demon!' 19 The Son of Man came
eating and drinking, and they say, 'Behold,
a gluttonous man and a drunkard, a friend
of tax collectors and sinners!' Yet wisdom is
vindicated by her deeds."
20 Then He began to denounce the cities
in which most of His miracles were done,
because they did not repent. 21 "Woe to
you, Chorazin! Woe to you, Bethsaida! For
if the miracles had occurred in Tyre and
Sidon which occurred in you, they would
have repented long ago in sackcloth and
ashes. 22 Nevertheless I say to you, it will
be more tolerable for Tyre and Sidon in
the day of judgment than for you. 23 And
Capernaum, will you be exalted to heaven?
You will descend to Hades; for if the miracles
had occurred in Sodom which occurred in
you, it would have remained to this day.
24 Nevertheless I say to you that it will be
more tolerable for the land of Sodom in the
day of judgment, than for you."
25 At that time Jesus said, "I praise You,
Father, Lord of heaven and earth, that You
have hidden these things from *the* wise
and intelligent and have revealed them
to infants. 26 Yes, Father, for this way was
well-pleasing in Your sight. 27 All things have
been handed over to Me by My Father; and
no one knows the Son except the Father;
nor does anyone know the Father except the
Son, and anyone to whom the Son wills to
reveal *Him*.
28 "Come to Me, all who are weary and
heavy-laden, and I will give you rest. 29 Take
My yoke upon you and learn from Me, for
I am gentle and humble in heart, and YOU
WILL FIND REST FOR YOUR SOULS. 30 For My
yoke is easy and My burden is light."

JANUARY 17

Genesis 33:1–34:31

33 Then Jacob lifted up his eyes and saw,
and behold, Esau was coming, and
four hundred men with him. So he divided
the children among Leah and Rachel and
the two servant-women. 2 And he put the
servant-women and their children first,
and Leah and her children after *them*,
and Rachel and Joseph after *them*. 3 But he
himself passed on ahead of them and bowed

down to the ground seven times, until he came near to his brother.

4 Then Esau ran to meet him and embraced him and fell on his neck and kissed him, and they wept. 5 And he lifted up his eyes and saw the women and the children and said, "Who are these with you?" And he said, "The children whom God has graciously given your servant." 6 Then the servant-women came near with their children, and they bowed down. 7 Leah likewise came near with her children, and they bowed down; and afterward Joseph came near with Rachel, and they bowed down. 8 And he said, "What do you mean by all these camps which I have met?" And he said, "To find favor in the sight of my lord." 9 But Esau said, "I have plenty, my brother; let what you have be your own." 10 And Jacob said, "No, please, if now I have found favor in your sight, then take my present from my hand, for I see your face as one sees the face of God, and you have received me favorably. 11 Please take my blessing which has been brought to you, because God has dealt graciously with me and because I have everything." Thus he urged him, and he took *it*.

12 Then Esau said, "Let us take our journey and go, and I will go before you." 13 But he said to him, "My lord knows that the children are weak and that the flocks and herds which are nursing are a care to me. And if they are driven hard one day, all the flocks will die. 14 Please let my lord pass on before his servant, and I will lead on slowly, according to the pace of the cattle that are before me and according to the pace of the children, until I come to my lord at Seir."

15 Then Esau said, "Please let me leave with you some of the people who are with me." But he said, "Why *do* this? Let me find favor in the sight of my lord." 16 So Esau returned that day on his way to Seir. 17 But Jacob journeyed to Succoth and built for himself a house and made booths for his livestock; therefore the place is named Succoth.

18 Now Jacob came safely to the city of Shechem, which is in the land of Canaan, when he came from Paddan-aram, and he camped before the city. 19 Then he bought a portion of a field where he had pitched his tent from the hand of the sons of Hamor, Shechem's father, for one hundred qesitah. 20 Then he set up there an altar and called it El-Elohe-Israel.

34 Now Dinah the daughter of Leah, whom she had borne to Jacob, went out to see the daughters of the land. 2 Then Shechem the son of Hamor the Hivite, the prince of the land, saw her and took her and lay with her and violated her. 3 And he was deeply attracted to Dinah the daughter of Jacob, and he loved the young woman and spoke to the heart of the young woman. 4 So Shechem spoke to his father Hamor, saying, "Get me this girl as a wife." 5 Now Jacob heard that he had defiled Dinah his daughter; but his sons were with his livestock in the field, so Jacob kept silent until they came in. 6 Then Hamor the father of Shechem went out to Jacob to speak with him. 7 Now the sons of Jacob came in from the field when they heard *it*; and the men were grieved, and they were very angry because he had done a disgraceful thing in Israel by lying with Jacob's daughter, for such a thing ought not to be done.

8 But Hamor spoke with them, saying, "The soul of my son Shechem longs for your daughter; please give her to him as a wife. 9 And intermarry with us; give your daughters to us and take our daughters for yourselves. 10 Thus you shall live with us, and the land shall be *open* before you; live and trade in it and take possession of property in it." 11 And Shechem also said to her father and to her brothers, "If I find favor in your sight, then I will give whatever you say to me. 12 Ask me ever so much bridal payment and gift, and I will give according as you say to me; but give me the girl as a wife."

13 But Jacob's sons answered Shechem and his father Hamor with deceit, and *thus* they spoke, because he had defiled Dinah their sister. 14 And they said to them, "We cannot do this thing, to give our sister to one who is uncircumcised, for that would be a reproach to us. 15 Only on this *condition* will we consent to you: if you will become like us, in that every male among you be circumcised, 16 then we will give our daughters to you, and we will take your daughters for ourselves, and we will live with you and become one people. 17 But if you will not listen to us to be circumcised, then we will take our daughter and go."

18 Now their words seemed good in the
sight of Hamor and Shechem, Hamor's
son. 19 So the young man did not delay
to do the thing because he was delighted
with Jacob's daughter. Now he was more
honored than all the household of his
father. 20 So Hamor and his son Shechem
came to the gate of their city and spoke to
the men of their city, saying, 21 "These men
are peaceful with us; therefore let them live
in the land and trade in it, for behold, the
land is large enough for them. Let us take
their daughters for us as wives and give
our daughters to them. 22 Only on this
condition will the men consent to us to live
with us, to become one people: that every
male among us be circumcised as they are
circumcised. 23 Will not their livestock and
what they acquire and all their cattle be
ours? Only let us consent to them, and they
will live with us." 24 And all who went out
of the gate of his city listened to Hamor
and to his son Shechem, and every male
was circumcised, all who went out of the
gate of his city.

25 Now it happened on the third day,
when they were in pain, that two of Jacob's
sons, Simeon and Levi, Dinah's brothers,
each took his sword and came upon the
unsuspecting city and killed every male.
26 And they killed Hamor and his son
Shechem with the edge of the sword and
took Dinah from Shechem's house and
went away. 27 Jacob's sons came upon the
slain and plundered the city because they
had defiled their sister. 28 They took their
flocks and their herds and their donkeys and
that which was in the city and that which
was in the field; 29 and they captured and
plundered all their wealth and all their little
ones and their wives, even all that *was* in the
houses. 30 Then Jacob said to Simeon and
Levi, "You have brought trouble on me by
making me odious among the inhabitants
of the land, among the Canaanites and the
Perizzites; and my men being few in num-
ber, they will gather together against me and
strike me, and I will be destroyed, I and my
household." 31 But they said, "Should he
treat our sister as a harlot?"

Psalm 9:1–5

1 I will give thanks to Yahweh
with all my heart;
I will recount all Your wondrous deeds.
2 I will be glad and exult in You;
I will sing praise to Your
name, O Most High.

3 When my enemies turn back,
They stumble and perish
before You.
4 For You have maintained my
justice and my cause;
You have sat on the throne
judging righteously.

5 You have rebuked the nations,
You have made the wicked perish;
You have blotted out their
name forever and ever.

Proverbs 3:21–26

21 My son, let them not deviate
from your eyes;
Guard sound wisdom
and discretion,
22 So they will be life for your soul
And grace for your neck.
23 Then you will walk in
your way securely
And your foot will not stumble.
24 When you lie down, you
will not be in dread;
You will lie down, and your
sleep will be pleasant.
25 Do not be afraid of sudden dread
Nor of the storm of the
wicked when it comes;
26 For Yahweh will be your
confidence
And will keep your foot
from being caught.

Matthew 12:1–21

12 At that time Jesus went through the
grainfields on the Sabbath, and His
disciples became hungry and began to pick
the heads of grain and eat. 2 But when the
Pharisees saw *this*, they said to Him, "Look,
Your disciples do what is not lawful to do on
a Sabbath." 3 But He said to them, "Have you
not read what David did when he became
hungry, he and his companions, 4 how he
entered the house of God, and they ate the
consecrated bread, which was not lawful
for him to eat nor for those with him, but
for the priests alone? 5 Or have you not read
in the Law, that on the Sabbath the priests
in the temple break the Sabbath and are

innocent? 6 But I say to you that something
greater than the temple is here. 7 But if you
had known what this means, 'I DESIRE COM-
PASSION, AND NOT A SACRIFICE,' you would
not have condemned the innocent. 8 For the
Son of Man is Lord of the Sabbath."
9 And departing from there, He went into
their synagogue. 10 And behold, a man *was
there* whose hand was withered. And they
questioned Jesus, saying, "Is it lawful to
heal on the Sabbath?"—so that they might
accuse Him. 11 And He said to them, "What
man is there among you who has a sheep,
and if it falls into a pit on the Sabbath, will
not take hold of it and lift it out? 12 How
much more valuable then is a man than a
sheep! So then, it is lawful to do good on
the Sabbath." 13 Then He *said to the man,
"Stretch out your hand!" He stretched it out,
and it was restored to normal, like the other.
14 But going out, the Pharisees took counsel
together against Him, *as to* how they might
destroy Him.
15 But Jesus, aware *of this*, withdrew
from there. Many followed Him, and He
healed them all, 16 and warned them not to
make Him known, 17 in order that what was
spoken through Isaiah the prophet would be
fulfilled, saying,

18 "BEHOLD, MY SERVANT WHOM
I HAVE CHOSEN;
MY BELOVED IN WHOM MY
SOUL IS WELL-PLEASED;
I WILL PUT MY SPIRIT UPON HIM,
AND HE SHALL PROCLAIM
JUSTICE TO THE GENTILES.
19 "HE WILL NOT QUARREL, NOR CRY OUT;
NOR WILL ANYONE HEAR HIS
VOICE IN THE STREETS.
20 "A BATTERED REED HE WILL
NOT BREAK OFF,
AND A SMOLDERING WICK HE
WILL NOT PUT OUT,
UNTIL HE LEADS JUSTICE TO VICTORY.
21 "AND IN HIS NAME THE
GENTILES WILL HOPE."

JANUARY 18

Genesis 35:1–36:43

35 Then God said to Jacob, "Arise, go up
to Bethel and live there, and make
an altar there to God, who appeared to you
when you fled from your brother Esau."
2 So Jacob said to his household and to all
who were with him, "Put away the foreign
gods which are among you and cleanse
yourselves and change your garments; 3 and
let us arise and go up to Bethel, and I will
make an altar there to God, who answered
me in the day of my distress and has been
with me wherever I have gone." 4 So they
gave to Jacob all the foreign gods which they
had and the rings which were in their ears,
and Jacob hid them under the oak which was
near Shechem.
5 Then they journeyed on, and there
was a terror from God upon the cities
which were around them, and they did not
pursue the sons of Jacob. 6 So Jacob came
to Luz (that is, Bethel), which is in the land
of Canaan, he and all the people who were
with him. 7 And he built an altar there and
called the place El-bethel, because there
God had revealed Himself to him when
he fled from his brother. 8 Then Deborah,
Rebekah's nurse, died, and she was buried
below Bethel under the oak; it was named
Allon-bacuth.
9 Then God appeared to Jacob again when
he came from Paddan-aram, and He blessed
him. 10 And God said to him,

"Your name is Jacob;
Your name shall no longer
be called Jacob,
But Israel shall be your name."

Thus He called his name Israel. 11 God
also said to him,

"I am God Almighty;
Be fruitful and multiply;
A nation and an assembly of
nations shall come from you,
And kings shall come forth
from your loins.
12 "And the land which I gave to
Abraham and Isaac,
I will give it to you,
And I will give the land to
your seed after you."

13 Then God went up from him in the place
where He had spoken with him. 14 And
Jacob set up a pillar in the place where
He had spoken with him, a pillar of stone,
and he poured out a drink offering on it;
he also poured oil on it. 15 So Jacob named

the place where God had spoken with him,
Bethel.
16 Then they journeyed from Bethel;
and there was still some distance to go to
Ephrath, and Rachel gave birth, and she
suffered severely in her labor. 17 Now it hap-
pened that when she was in severe labor the
midwife said to her, "Do not fear, for now
you have another son." 18 Now it happened
as her soul was departing (for she died),
that she named him Ben-oni; but his father
called him Benjamin. 19 So Rachel died and
was buried on the way to Ephrath (that is,
Bethlehem). 20 And Jacob set up a pillar over
her grave; that is the pillar of Rachel's grave
to this day. 21 Then Israel journeyed on and
pitched his tent beyond the tower of Eder.
22 Now it happened while Israel was
dwelling in that land, that Reuben went and
lay with Bilhah his father's concubine, and
Israel heard *of it.*

And there were twelve sons of Jacob—
23 the sons of Leah:
Reuben, Jacob's firstborn,
then Simeon and Levi and Judah and
Issachar and Zebulun;
24 the sons of Rachel:
Joseph and Benjamin;
25 and the sons of Bilhah, Rachel's
servant-woman:
Dan and Naphtali;
26 and the sons of Zilpah, Leah's servant-
woman:
Gad and Asher.

These are the sons of Jacob who were
born to him in Paddan-aram.
27 And Jacob came to his father Isaac at
Mamre of Kiriath-arba (that is, Hebron),
where Abraham and Isaac had sojourned.
28 Now the days of Isaac were 180 years.
29 And Isaac breathed his last and died and
was gathered to his people, an old man and
full of days; and his sons Esau and Jacob
buried him.

36 Now these are the generations of
Esau (that is, Edom).
2 Esau took his wives from the daughters
of Canaan: Adah the daughter of Elon the
Hittite, and Oholibamah the daughter of
Anah and the granddaughter of Zibeon the
Hivite; 3 also Basemath, Ishmael's daughter,
the sister of Nebaioth. 4 And Adah bore
Eliphaz to Esau, and Basemath bore Reuel,
5 and Oholibamah bore Jeush and Jalam and
Korah. These are the sons of Esau who were
born to him in the land of Canaan.
6 Then Esau took his wives and his sons
and his daughters and all his household,
and his livestock and all his cattle and all his
acquired goods, which he had accumulated
in the land of Canaan, and he went to a land
away from his brother Jacob. 7 For their
possessions had become too great for them
to live together, and the land where they
sojourned could not sustain them because
of their livestock. 8 So Esau lived in the hill
country of Seir; Esau is Edom.
9 These then are the generations of Esau
the father of the Edomites in the hill country
of Seir. 10 These are the names of Esau's
sons: Eliphaz the son of Esau's wife Adah,
Reuel the son of Esau's wife Basemath.
11 The sons of Eliphaz were Teman, Omar,
Zepho and Gatam and Kenaz. 12 Timna was
a concubine of Esau's son Eliphaz, and she
bore Amalek to Eliphaz. These are the sons
of Esau's wife Adah. 13 These are the sons
of Reuel: Nahath and Zerah, Shammah and
Mizzah. These were the sons of Esau's wife
Basemath. 14 These were the sons of Esau's
wife Oholibamah, the daughter of Anah and
the granddaughter of Zibeon: she bore to
Esau, Jeush and Jalam and Korah.
15 These are the chiefs of the sons of Esau.
The sons of Eliphaz, the firstborn of Esau,
are chief Teman, chief Omar, chief Zepho,
chief Kenaz, 16 chief Korah, chief Gatam,
chief Amalek. These are the chiefs *descended*
from Eliphaz in the land of Edom; these are
the sons of Adah. 17 These are the sons of
Reuel, Esau's son: chief Nahath, chief Zerah,
chief Shammah, chief Mizzah. These are the
chiefs *descended* from Reuel in the land of
Edom; these are the sons of Esau's wife
Basemath. 18 These are the sons of Esau's
wife Oholibamah: chief Jeush, chief Jalam,
chief Korah. These are the chiefs *descended*
from Esau's wife Oholibamah, the daughter
of Anah. 19 These are the sons of Esau (that
is, Edom), and these are their chiefs.
20 These are the sons of Seir the Horite,
the inhabitants of the land: Lotan and
Shobal and Zibeon and Anah, 21 and Dishon
and Ezer and Dishan. These are the chiefs
descended from the Horites, the sons of Seir
in the land of Edom. 22 The sons of Lotan
were Hori and Hemam; and Lotan's sister
was Timna. 23 These are the sons of Shobal:
Alvan and Manahath and Ebal, Shepho and

Onam. 24 These are the sons of Zibeon: Aiah
and Anah—he is the Anah who found the
hot springs in the wilderness when he was
pasturing the donkeys of his father Zibeon.
25 These are the children of Anah: Dishon
and Oholibamah, the daughter of Anah.
26 These are the sons of Dishon: Hemdan
and Eshban and Ithran and Cheran. 27 These
are the sons of Ezer: Bilhan and Zaavan and
Akan. 28 These are the sons of Dishan: Uz
and Aran. 29 These are the chiefs of the
Horites: chief Lotan, chief Shobal, chief
Zibeon, chief Anah, 30 chief Dishon, chief
Ezer, chief Dishan. These are the chiefs
descended from the Horites, according to
their *various* chiefs in the land of Seir.

31 Now these are the kings who reigned
in the land of Edom before *any* king of
the sons of Israel reigned. 32 And Bela the
son of Beor became king in Edom, and the
name of his city was Dinhabah. 33 Then
Bela died, and Jobab the son of Zerah of
Bozrah became king in his place. 34 Then
Jobab died, and Husham of the land of
the Temanites became king in his place.
35 Then Husham died, and Hadad the son
of Bedad, who struck down Midian in the
field of Moab, became king in his place;
and the name of his city was Avith. 36 Then
Hadad died, and Samlah of Masrekah
became king in his place. 37 Then Samlah
died, and Shaul of Rehoboth on the River
became king in his place. 38 Then Shaul
died, and Baal-hanan the son of Achbor
became king in his place. 39 Then Baal-
hanan the son of Achbor died, and Hadar
became king in his place; and the name
of his city was Pau; and his wife's name
was Mehetabel, the daughter of Matred,
daughter of Mezahab.

40 Now these are the names of the chiefs
descended from Esau, according to their
families *and* their places, by their names:
chief Timna, chief Alvah, chief Jetheth,
41 chief Oholibamah, chief Elah, chief
Pinon, 42 chief Kenaz, chief Teman, chief
Mibzar, 43 chief Magdiel, chief Iram. These
are the chiefs of Edom (that is, Esau, the
father of the Edomites), according to their
places of habitation in the land of their
possession.

Psalm 9:6–10

6 The enemy has come to an
  end in perpetual ruins,
And You have uprooted the cities;
  The very memory of them
    has perished.
7 But Yahweh abides forever;
  He has established His
    throne for judgment,
8 And He will judge the world
    in righteousness;
  He will render justice for the
    peoples with equity.
9 Yahweh also will be a stronghold
    for the oppressed,
  A stronghold in times of distress;
10 And those who know Your name
    will put their trust in You,
  For You, O Yahweh, have not
    forsaken those who seek You.

Proverbs 3:27–30

27 Do not withhold good from
    those to whom it is due,
  When it is in your hand to do *it*.
28 Do not say to your neighbor,
    "Go, and come back,
  And tomorrow I will give *it*,"
  When it is there with you.
29 Do not devise harm against
    your neighbor,
  While he lives securely
    beside you.
30 Do not contend with a man
    without cause,
  If he has dealt you no harm.

Matthew 12:22–50

22 Then a demon-possessed man *who was*
blind and mute was brought to Jesus, and He
healed him, so that the mute man spoke and
saw. 23 And all the crowds were astounded,
and were saying, "Can this man *really* be the
Son of David?" 24 But when the Pharisees
heard *this*, they said, "This man does not
cast out demons except by Beelzebul the
ruler of the demons."

25 And knowing their thoughts He said
to them, "Any kingdom divided against
itself is laid waste; and any city or house
divided against itself will not stand. 26 And
if Satan casts out Satan, he is divided against
himself; how then will his kingdom stand?
27 And if I by Beelzebul cast out demons, by

whom do your sons cast *them* out? For this
reason they will be your judges. 28 But if I
cast out demons by the Spirit of God, then
the kingdom of God has come upon you.
29 Or how can anyone enter the strong man's
house and carry off his property, unless he
first binds the strong man? And then he will
plunder his house.

30 "He who is not with Me is against
Me; and he who does not gather with Me
scatters.

31 "Therefore I say to you, any sin and
blasphemy shall be forgiven people, but
the blasphemy against the Spirit shall not
be forgiven. 32 And whoever speaks a word
against the Son of Man, it shall be forgiven
him; but whoever speaks against the Holy
Spirit, it shall not be forgiven him, either in
this age or in the *age* to come.

33 "Either make the tree good and its fruit
good, or make the tree bad and its fruit bad;
for the tree is known by its fruit. 34 You
brood of vipers, how can you, being evil,
speak what is good? For the mouth speaks
out of that which fills the heart. 35 The good
man brings out of *his* good treasure what
is good; and the evil man brings out of *his*
evil treasure what is evil. 36 But I tell you
that every careless word that people speak,
they shall give an accounting for it in the
day of judgment. 37 For by your words you
will be justified, and by your words you will
be condemned."

38 Then some of the scribes and Phari-
sees answered and said to Him, "Teacher,
we want to see a sign from You." 39 But He
answered and said to them, "An evil and
adulterous generation eagerly seeks for a
sign; and *yet* no sign will be given to it but
the sign of Jonah the prophet; 40 for just as
JONAH WAS THREE DAYS AND THREE NIGHTS
IN THE BELLY OF THE SEA MONSTER, so will
the Son of Man be three days and three
nights in the heart of the earth. 41 The men
of Nineveh will stand up with this genera-
tion at the judgment, and will condemn it
because they repented at the preaching of
Jonah; and behold, something greater than
Jonah is here. 42 The Queen of the South will
rise up with this generation at the judgment
and will condemn it, because she came from
the ends of the earth to hear the wisdom
of Solomon; and behold, something greater
than Solomon is here.

43 "Now when the unclean spirit goes
out of a man, it passes through waterless
places seeking rest, and does not find *it*.
44 Then it says, 'I will return to my house
from which I came'; and when it comes, it
finds *it* unoccupied, swept, and put in order.
45 Then it goes and takes along with it seven
other spirits more wicked than itself, and
they go in and live there; and the last state
of that man becomes worse than the first.
That is the way it will also be with this evil
generation."

46 While He was still speaking to the
crowds, behold, His mother and brothers
were standing outside, seeking to speak to
Him. 47 Now someone said to Him, "Behold,
Your mother and Your brothers are stand-
ing outside seeking to speak to You." 48 But
Jesus answered the one who was telling
Him and said, "Who is My mother and
who are My brothers?" 49 And stretching
out His hand toward His disciples, He said,
"Behold My mother and My brothers! 50 For
whoever does the will of My Father who is
in heaven, he is My brother and sister and
mother."

JANUARY 19

Genesis 37:1–38:30

37 Now Jacob lived in the land where his
father had sojourned, in the land of
Canaan. 2 These are the generations of Jacob.

Joseph, when seventeen years of age,
was pasturing the flock with his brothers
while he was *still* a youth, along with the
sons of Bilhah and the sons of Zilpah, his
father's wives. And Joseph brought back an
evil report about them to their father. 3 Now
Israel loved Joseph more than all his sons
because he was the son of his old age; and
he made him a varicolored tunic. 4 And his
brothers saw that their father loved him
more than all his brothers, and *so* they
hated him and could not speak to him in
peace.

5 Then Joseph had a dream, and he told
it to his brothers; so they hated him even
more. 6 And he said to them, "Please listen
to this dream which I have had: 7 Indeed,
behold, we were binding sheaves in the field,

and behold, my sheaf rose up and also stood upright; and behold, your sheaves gathered around and bowed down to my sheaf." 8 Then his brothers said to him, "Are you really going to reign over us? Or are you really going to rule over us?" So they hated him even more for his dreams and for his words.

9 Then he had still another dream and recounted it to his brothers and said, "Behold, I have had still another dream; and behold, the sun and the moon and eleven stars were bowing down to me." 10 And he recounted *it* to his father and to his brothers; and his father rebuked him and said to him, "What is this dream that you have had? Shall I and your mother and your brothers really come to bow ourselves down before you to the ground?" 11 And his brothers were jealous of him, but his father kept the saying *in mind.*

12 Then his brothers went to pasture their father's flock in Shechem. 13 And Israel said to Joseph, "Are not your brothers pasturing *the flock* in Shechem? Come, and I will send you to them." And he said to him, "I will go." 14 Then he said to him, "Go now and see about the welfare of your brothers and the welfare of the flock, and bring word back to me." So he sent him from the valley of Hebron, and he came to Shechem.

15 And a man found him, and behold, he was wandering in the field; and the man asked him, "What are you seeking?" 16 And he said, "I am seeking my brothers; please tell me where they are pasturing *the flock.*" 17 Then the man said, "They have journeyed from here; for I heard *them* saying, 'Let us go to Dothan.'" So Joseph went after his brothers and found them at Dothan.

18 And they saw him from a distance, and before he came close to them, they plotted against him to put him to death. 19 Then they said to one another, "Here comes this dreamer! 20 So now, come and let us kill him and cast him into one of the pits; and we will say, 'A wild beast devoured him.' Then let us see what will become of his dreams!" 21 But Reuben heard *this* and delivered him out of their hands and said, "Let us not strike down his life." 22 Reuben further said to them, "Shed no blood. Cast him into this pit that is in the wilderness, but do not put forth your hands against him"—that he might deliver him out of their hands to return him to his father. 23 Now it happened, when Joseph reached his brothers, that they stripped Joseph of his tunic, the varicolored tunic that was on him; 24 and they took him and cast him into the pit. Now the pit was empty, without any water in it.

25 And they sat down to eat a meal. Then they lifted up their eyes and saw, and behold, a caravan of Ishmaelites was coming from Gilead, with their camels bearing aromatic gum and balm and myrrh, going to bring *them* down to Egypt. 26 And Judah said to his brothers, "What gain is it that we kill our brother and cover up his blood? 27 Come and let us sell him to the Ishmaelites and not lay our hands on him, for he is our brother, our *own* flesh." And his brothers listened. 28 Then some Midianite traders passed by, so they pulled *him* up and lifted Joseph out of the pit and sold Joseph to the Ishmaelites for twenty *shekels* of silver. Thus they brought Joseph into Egypt.

29 Then Reuben returned to the pit, and behold, Joseph was not in the pit; so he tore his garments. 30 Then he returned to his brothers and said, "The boy is not *there*; as for me, where am I to go?" 31 So they took Joseph's tunic and slaughtered a male goat and dipped the tunic in the blood; 32 and they sent the varicolored tunic and brought it to their father and said, "We found this; please recognize *it*—whether it is your son's tunic or not." 33 And he recognized it and said, "It is my son's tunic. A wild beast has devoured him; Joseph has surely been torn to pieces!" 34 So Jacob tore his clothes and put sackcloth on his loins and mourned for his son many days. 35 Then all his sons and all his daughters arose to comfort him, but he refused to be comforted. And he said, "Surely I will go down to Sheol in mourning for my son." So his father wept for him. 36 Meanwhile, the Midianites sold him in Egypt to Potiphar, Pharaoh's officer, the captain of the bodyguard.

38 Now it happened at that time that Judah went down from his brothers and turned aside to a certain Adullamite, whose name was Hirah. 2 And Judah saw there a daughter of a certain Canaanite whose name was Shua; and he took her and went in to her. 3 So she conceived and bore a son, and he named him Er. 4 Then she conceived again and bore a son, and

she named him Onan. 5 And she bore still another son, and she named him Shelah; and it was at Chezib that she bore him.

6 Then Judah took a wife for Er his firstborn, and her name *was* Tamar. 7 But Er, Judah's firstborn, was evil in the sight of Yahweh, so Yahweh put him to death. 8 Then Judah said to Onan, "Go in to your brother's wife, and perform your duty as a brother-in-law to her, and raise up a seed for your brother." 9 And Onan knew that the seed would not be his; and it happened that when he went in to his brother's wife, he wasted it on the ground in order not to give seed to his brother. 10 But what he did was displeasing in the sight of Yahweh; so He put him to death also. 11 Then Judah said to his daughter-in-law Tamar, "Live as a widow in your father's house until my son Shelah grows up"; for he thought, "*I am afraid* lest he also die like his brothers." So Tamar went and lived in her father's house.

12 And after a considerable time, Shua's daughter, the wife of Judah, died. Then Judah was comforted, and he went up to his sheepshearers at Timnah, he and his friend Hirah the Adullamite. 13 Then it was told to Tamar, "Behold, your father-in-law is going up to Timnah to shear his sheep." 14 So she removed her widow's garments from herself and covered *herself* with a veil and wrapped herself. And she sat at the entrance of Enaim, which is on the road to Timnah; for she saw that Shelah had grown up, and she had not been given to him as a wife. 15 Then Judah saw her, and he thought she *was* a harlot, for she had covered her face. 16 So he turned aside to her by the road and said, "Here now, let me come in to you"; for he did not know that she was his daughter-in-law. And she said, "What will you give me, that you may come in to me?" 17 He said, therefore, "I will send you a young goat from the flock." She said, moreover, "Will you give a pledge until you send *it*?" 18 Then he said, "What pledge shall I give you?" And she said, "Your signet and your cord and your staff that is in your hand." So he gave *them* to her and went in to her, and she conceived by him. 19 Then she arose and went. And she removed her veil from herself and put on her widow's garments.

20 Then Judah sent the young goat by his friend the Adullamite to take the pledge from the woman's hand, but he did not find her. 21 So he asked the men of her place, saying, "Where is the cult prostitute who was by the road at Enaim?" But they said, "There has been no cult prostitute here." 22 So he returned to Judah and said, "I did not find her; and furthermore, the men of the place said, 'There has been no cult prostitute here.'" 23 Then Judah said, "Let her keep them, lest we become a laughingstock. Behold, I sent this young goat, but you did not find her."

24 Now it happened about three months later that it was told to Judah saying, "Your daughter-in-law Tamar has played the harlot, and behold, she is also with child by harlotry." Then Judah said, "Bring her out and let her be burned!" 25 It was while she was being brought out that she sent to her father-in-law, saying, "I am with child by the man to whom these things belong." And she said, "Please recognize *this* and see, whose signet ring and cords and staff are these?" 26 And Judah recognized *them* and said, "She is more righteous than I, inasmuch as I did not give her to my son Shelah." And he did not know her again.

27 Now it happened at the time she was giving birth, that behold, there were twins in her womb. 28 And it happened, while she was giving birth, one put out a hand, and the midwife took and tied a scarlet *thread* on his hand, saying, "This one came out first." 29 And then it happened, as he drew back his hand, that behold, his brother came out. So she said, "What a breach you have made for yourself!" So he was named Perez. 30 Afterward his brother came out who had the scarlet *thread* on his hand; and he was named Zerah.

Psalm 9:11–20

11 Sing praises to Yahweh,
 who abides in Zion;
Declare among the peoples His acts.
12 For He who requires blood
 remembers them;
He does not forget the cry
 of the afflicted.

13 Be gracious to me, O Yahweh;
See my affliction from
 those who hate me,
You who lift me up from
 the gates of death,

14 That I may recount all Your praises,
That in the gates of the
daughter of Zion
I may rejoice in Your salvation.

15 The nations have sunk down in
the pit which they have made;
In the net which they hid, their
own foot has been caught.
16 Yahweh has made Himself known;
He has executed judgment.
In the work of his own hands the
wicked is snared. Higgaion Selah.

17 The wicked will return to Sheol,
Even all the nations
who forget God.

18 For the needy will not
always be forgotten,
Nor the hope of the afflicted
perish forever.
19 Arise, O Yahweh, do not
let man prevail;
Let the nations be judged
before You.
20 Put them in fear, O Yahweh;
Let the nations know that
they are but men. Selah.

Proverbs 3:31–35

31 Do not envy a man of violence
And do not choose any of his ways.
32 For the devious one is an
abomination to Yahweh;
But His secret council is
with the upright.
33 The curse of Yahweh is on the
house of the wicked one,
But He blesses the abode
of the righteous.
34 Though He scoffs at the scoffers,
Yet He gives grace to the humble.
35 The wise will inherit glory,
But fools raise up disgrace.

Matthew 13:1–30

13 On that day Jesus went out of the
house and was sitting by the sea. 2 And
large crowds gathered to Him, so He got into
a boat and sat down, and the whole crowd
was standing on the beach.
3 And He spoke many things to them in
parables, saying, "Behold, the sower went
out to sow; 4 and as he sowed, some *seeds*
fell beside the road, and the birds came and
ate them up. 5 And others fell on the rocky
places, where they did not have much soil;
and immediately they sprang up, because
they had no depth of soil. 6 But when the
sun had risen, they were scorched; and
because they had no root, they withered
away. 7 And others fell among the thorns,
and the thorns came up and choked them
out. 8 And others fell on the good soil and
were yielding a crop, some a hundredfold,
some sixty, and some thirty. 9 He who has
ears, let him hear."
10 And the disciples came and said to
Him, "Why do You speak to them in par-
ables?" 11 And Jesus answered and said to
them, "To you it has been given to know the
mysteries of the kingdom of heaven, but to
them it has not been given. 12 For whoever
has, to him *more* shall be given, and he will
have an abundance; but whoever does not
have, even what he has shall be taken away
from him. 13 Therefore I speak to them in
parables; because while seeing they do not
see, and while hearing they do not hear,
nor do they understand. 14 And in them
the prophecy of Isaiah is being fulfilled,
which says,

'YOU WILL KEEP ON HEARING,
BUT WILL NOT UNDERSTAND;
YOU WILL KEEP ON SEEING,
BUT WILL NOT PERCEIVE;
15 FOR THE HEART OF THIS PEOPLE
HAS BECOME DULL,
AND WITH THEIR EARS THEY
SCARCELY HEAR,
AND THEY HAVE CLOSED THEIR EYES,
LEST THEY WOULD SEE WITH THEIR EYES,
HEAR WITH THEIR EARS,
AND UNDERSTAND WITH THEIR
HEART AND RETURN,
AND I WOULD HEAL THEM.'

16 "But blessed are your eyes, because they
see; and your ears, because they hear. 17 For
truly I say to you that many prophets and
righteous men desired to see what you see,
and did not see *it*, and to hear what you
hear, and did not hear *it*.
18 "Hear then the parable of the sower.
19 When anyone hears the word of the
kingdom and does not understand it, the
evil one comes and snatches away what
has been sown in his heart. This is the one
on whom seed was sown beside the road.
20 And the one on whom seed was sown

on the rocky places, this is the man who hears the word and immediately receives it with joy; 21 yet he has no root in himself, but is *only* temporary, and when affliction or persecution arises because of the word, immediately he falls away. 22 And the one on whom seed was sown among the thorns, this is the one who hears the word, and the worry of the world and the deceitfulness of wealth choke the word, and it becomes unfruitful. 23 And the one on whom seed was sown on the good soil, this is the man who hears the word and understands it; who indeed bears fruit and brings forth, some a hundredfold, some sixty, and some thirty."

24 He presented another parable to them, saying, "The kingdom of heaven may be compared to a man who sowed good seed in his field. 25 But while his men were sleeping, his enemy came and sowed tares among the wheat, and went away. 26 But when the wheat sprouted and bore grain, then the tares became evident also. 27 The slaves of the landowner came and said to him, 'Sir, did you not sow good seed in your field? How then does it have tares?' 28 And he said to them, 'An enemy has done this!' The slaves *said to him, 'Do you want us, then, to go and gather them up?' 29 But he *said, 'No; for while you are gathering up the tares, you may uproot the wheat with them. 30 Allow both to grow together until the harvest; and in the time of the harvest I will say to the reapers, "First gather up the tares and bind them in bundles to burn them up; but gather the wheat into my barn."'"

JANUARY 20

Genesis 39:1–40:23

39 Now Joseph was brought down to Egypt; and Potiphar, an Egyptian official of Pharaoh, the captain of the bodyguard, bought him from the Ishmaelites, who had brought him down there. 2 And Yahweh was with Joseph, so he became a successful man. And he was in the house of his master, the Egyptian. 3 Now his master saw that Yahweh was with him and *how* Yahweh caused all that he did to succeed in his hand. 4 So Joseph found favor in his sight and attended on him; and he appointed him overseer over his house, and all that he owned he gave in his hand. 5 Now it happened that from the time he appointed him overseer in his house and over all that he owned, Yahweh blessed the Egyptian's house on account of Joseph; thus the blessing of Yahweh was upon all that he owned, in the house and in the field. 6 So he left everything he owned in Joseph's hand; and with him *there* he did not concern himself with anything except the food which he ate.

Now Joseph was beautiful in form and beautiful in appearance.

7 And it happened after these events that his master's wife set her eyes on Joseph and said, "Lie with me." 8 But he refused and said to his master's wife, "Behold, with me *here*, my master does not concern himself with anything in the house, and he has given all that he owns into my hand. 9 There is no one greater in this house than I, and he has withheld nothing from me except you, because you are his wife. How then could I do this great evil and sin against God?" 10 So it happened that as she spoke to Joseph day after day, he did not listen to her to lie beside her *or* be with her.

11 Now it happened one day that he went into the house to do his work, and none of the men of the household was there inside. 12 Then she seized him by his garment, saying, "Lie with me!" And he left his garment in her hand and fled and went outside. 13 Now it happened, when she saw that he had left his garment in her hand and had fled outside, 14 that she called to the men of her household and spoke to them, saying, "See, he has brought in a Hebrew to us to laugh at us; he came in to me to lie with me, and I screamed. 15 Now it happened that when he heard that I raised my voice and screamed, he left his garment beside me and fled and went outside." 16 And she placed his garment beside her until his master came home. 17 Then she spoke to him with these words, saying, "The Hebrew slave, whom you brought to us, came in to me to laugh at me; 18 and as I raised my voice and screamed, he left his garment beside me and fled outside."

19 Now it happened that when his master heard the words of his wife, which she spoke to him, saying, "This is what your slave did to me," his anger burned. 20 So Joseph's master took him and put him into the jail, the place where the king's prisoners were confined; and he was there in the jail. 21 But Yahweh was with Joseph and extended lovingkindness to him and gave him favor in the sight of the chief jailer. 22 So the chief jailer gave into the hand of Joseph all the prisoners who were in the jail; so that whatever was done there, he was the one who did *it*. 23 The chief jailer did not supervise anything under Joseph's hand because Yahweh was with him; and whatever he did, Yahweh made to succeed.

40 Now it happened that after these things, the cupbearer and the baker for the king of Egypt offended their lord, the king of Egypt. 2 And Pharaoh was furious with his two officials, the chief cupbearer and the chief baker. 3 So he put them in confinement in the house of the captain of the bodyguard, in the jail, the *same* place where Joseph was imprisoned. 4 And the captain of the bodyguard appointed Joseph as overseer over them, and he attended to them; and they were in confinement for some time. 5 Then the cupbearer and the baker for the king of Egypt, who were confined in jail, both had a dream the same night, each man with his *own* dream *and* each dream with its *own* interpretation. 6 Now Joseph came to them in the morning and saw them, and behold, they were dejected. 7 So he asked Pharaoh's officials who were with him in confinement in his master's house, saying, "Why are your faces so sad today?" 8 Then they said to him, "We have had a dream, and there is no one to interpret it." Then Joseph said to them, "Do not interpretations belong to God? Recount *it* to me, please."

9 So the chief cupbearer recounted his dream to Joseph and said to him, "In my dream, behold, *there was* a vine in front of me; 10 and on the vine *were* three branches. And as it was budding, its blossoms came out, *and* its clusters produced ripe grapes. 11 Now Pharaoh's cup was in my hand; so I took the grapes and squeezed them into Pharaoh's cup, and I put the cup into Pharaoh's hand." 12 Then Joseph said to him, "This is the interpretation of it: the three branches are three days; 13 within three more days Pharaoh will lift up your head and restore you to your office; and you will put Pharaoh's cup into his hand according to your former custom when you were his cupbearer. 14 Only remember me when it goes well with you, and please show me lovingkindness by remembering me to Pharaoh and getting me out of this house. 15 For I was in fact stolen from the land of the Hebrews, and even here I have done nothing that they should have put me into the pit."

16 And the chief baker saw that he had interpreted favorably, so he said to Joseph, "I also *saw* in my dream, and behold, *there were* three baskets of white bread on my head; 17 and in the top basket *there were* some of all sorts of baked food for Pharaoh, and the birds were eating them out of the basket on my head." 18 Then Joseph answered and said, "This is its interpretation: the three baskets are three days; 19 within three more days Pharaoh will lift up your head off of you and will hang you on a tree, and the birds will eat your flesh off of you."

20 Thus it happened on the third day, *which was* Pharaoh's birthday, that he made a feast for all his servants; and he lifted up the head of the chief cupbearer and the head of the chief baker among his servants. 21 And he restored the chief cupbearer to his office, and he put the cup into Pharaoh's hand; 22 but he hanged the chief baker, just as Joseph had interpreted to them. 23 Yet the chief cupbearer did not remember Joseph, but forgot him.

Psalm 10:1–11

1 Why do You stand afar off, O Yahweh?
Why do You hide *Yourself*
in times of distress?
2 In *his* lofty pride the wicked
hotly pursues the afflicted;
Let them be caught in the thoughts
which they have devised.

3 For the wicked boasts of
his soul's desire,
And the greedy man curses
and spurns Yahweh.
4 The wicked, in the haughtiness of his
countenance, does not seek *Him*.
All his thoughts are,
"There is no God."

5 His ways prosper at all times;
Your judgments are on high,
out of his sight;
As for all his adversaries,
he snorts at them.
6 He says in his heart,
"I will not be shaken;
From generation to generation
I will not be in adversity."

7 His mouth is full of curses and
deceit and oppression;
Under his tongue is mischief
and wickedness.

8 He sits in the places of the villages
where one lies in wait;
In the hiding places he
kills the innocent;
His eyes stealthily watch
for the unfortunate.
9 He lies in wait in a hiding place
as a lion in his lair;
He lies in wait to catch
the afflicted;
He catches the afflicted when
he draws him into his net.
10 He crouches, he bows down,
And the unfortunate fall
by his mighty ones.
11 He says in his heart,
"God has forgotten;
He has hidden His face;
He will never see it."

Proverbs 4:1–6

4 Hear, O sons, the discipline of a father,
And pay attention that you may
know understanding,
2 For I give you sound learning;
Do not forsake my instruction.
3 When I was a son to my father,
Tender and the only son
before my mother,
4 Then he instructed me
and said to me,
"Let your heart hold fast my words;
Keep my commandments and live;
5 Acquire wisdom! Acquire
understanding!
Do not forget and do not turn away
from the sayings of my mouth.
6 "Do not forsake her, and
she will keep you;
Love her, and she will guard you.

Matthew 13:31–58

31 He presented another parable to them,
saying, "The kingdom of heaven is like a
mustard seed, which a man took and sowed
in his field; 32 and this is the smallest of all
seeds, but when it is fully grown, it is the
largest of the garden plants and becomes a
tree, so that THE BIRDS OF THE AIR come and
NEST IN ITS BRANCHES."
33 He spoke another parable to them,
"The kingdom of heaven is like leaven,
which a woman took and hid in three sata
of flour until it was all leavened."
34 All these things Jesus spoke to the
crowds in parables, and He was not speaking
to them without a parable 35 so that what
was spoken through the prophet might be
fulfilled, saying,

"I WILL OPEN MY MOUTH IN PARABLES;
I WILL UTTER THINGS HIDDEN SINCE
THE FOUNDATION OF THE WORLD."

36 Then He left the crowds and went into
the house. And His disciples came to Him
and said, "Explain to us the parable of the
tares of the field." 37 And He answered and
said, "The one who sows the good seed is
the Son of Man, 38 and the field is the world;
and *as for* the good seed, these are the sons
of the kingdom; and the tares are the sons
of the evil one; 39 and the enemy who sowed
them is the devil, and the harvest is the end
of the age; and the reapers are angels. 40 So
just as the tares are gathered up and burned
with fire, so shall it be at the end of the age.
41 The Son of Man will send forth His angels,
and they will gather out of His kingdom all
stumbling blocks, and those who commit
lawlessness, 42 and will throw them into
the fiery furnace; in that place there will be
weeping and gnashing of teeth. 43 Then THE
RIGHTEOUS WILL SHINE FORTH AS THE SUN in
the kingdom of their Father. He who has
ears, let him hear.
44 "The kingdom of heaven is like a trea-
sure hidden in the field, which a man found
and hid *again*; and from joy over it he goes
and sells all that he has and buys that field.
45 "Again, the kingdom of heaven is like a
merchant seeking fine pearls, 46 and upon
finding one pearl of great value, he went and
sold all that he had and bought it.
47 "Again, the kingdom of heaven is like a
dragnet cast into the sea, and gathering *fish*
of every kind; 48 and when it was filled, they
drew it up on the beach; and they sat down

and gathered the good *fish* into containers, but the bad they threw away. 49 So it will be at the end of the age; the angels will come forth and take out the wicked from among the righteous, 50 and will throw them into the fiery furnace; in that place there will be weeping and gnashing of teeth.

51 "Have you understood all these things?" They *said to Him, "Yes." 52 And He said to them, "Therefore every scribe who has become a disciple of the kingdom of heaven is like a head of a household, who brings out of his treasure things new and old."

53 Now it happened that when Jesus had finished these parables, He departed from there. 54 And He came to His hometown and *began* teaching them in their synagogue, so that they were astonished, and said, "Where *did* this man *get* this wisdom and *these* miraculous powers? 55 Is not this the carpenter's son? Is not His mother called Mary, and His brothers, James and Joseph and Simon and Judas? 56 And His sisters, are they not all with us? Where then *did* this man *get* all these things?" 57 And they were taking offense at Him. But Jesus said to them, "A prophet is not without honor except in his hometown and in his *own* household." 58 And He did not do many miracles there because of their unbelief.

JANUARY 21

Genesis 41:1–42:38

41 Now it happened at the end of two full years that Pharaoh had a dream, and behold, he was standing by the Nile. 2 And behold, from the Nile there came up seven cows, sleek and fat; and they grazed in the reeds. 3 Then behold, seven other cows came up after them from the Nile, ugly and thin, and they stood by the *other* cows on the bank of the Nile. 4 And the ugly and thin cows ate up the seven sleek and fat cows. Then Pharaoh awoke. 5 He again fell asleep and dreamed a second time; and behold, seven ears of grain came up on a single stalk, plump and good. 6 And behold, seven ears, thin and scorched by the east wind, sprouted up after them. 7 And the thin ears swallowed up the seven plump and full ears. Then Pharaoh awoke, and behold, *it was* a dream. 8 Now it happened that in the morning his spirit was troubled, so he sent and called for all the magicians of Egypt and all its wise men. And Pharaoh recounted to them his dream, but there was no one who could interpret them to Pharaoh.

9 Then the chief cupbearer spoke to Pharaoh, saying, "I would bring to remembrance today my *own* offenses. 10 Pharaoh was furious with his servants, and he put me in confinement in the house of the captain of the bodyguard, *both* me and the chief baker. 11 And we had a dream on the same night, he and I; each of us dreamed according to the interpretation of his *own* dream. 12 Now there *was* with us a Hebrew youth, a slave of the captain of the bodyguard, and we recounted *them* to him, and he interpreted our dreams for us. To each one he interpreted according to his *own* dream. 13 And just as he interpreted for us, so it happened; he restored me in my office, but he hanged him."

14 Then Pharaoh sent and called for Joseph, and they rushed him out of the pit; and he shaved himself and changed his clothes, and he came to Pharaoh. 15 And Pharaoh said to Joseph, "I have had a dream, but no one can interpret it; yet I have heard it said about you, that you hear a dream *and that* you can interpret it." 16 Joseph then answered Pharaoh, saying, "It is not in me; God will answer *concerning* the welfare of Pharaoh." 17 So Pharaoh spoke to Joseph, "In my dream, behold, I was standing on the bank of the Nile; 18 and behold, seven cows, fat and sleek came up out of the Nile, and they grazed in the reeds. 19 And behold, seven other cows came up after them, poor and very ugly and lean, such as I had never seen in all the land of Egypt, in regard to ugliness; 20 and the lean and ugly cows ate up the first seven fat cows. 21 But they devoured them, and yet it could not be known that they had devoured them. For they were just as ugly as before. Then I awoke. 22 Then I saw also in my dream, and behold, seven ears, full and good, came up on a single stalk; 23 and behold, seven ears, withered, thin, *and* scorched by the east wind, sprouted up after them; 24 and the

thin ears swallowed the seven good ears. So I told it to the magicians, but there was no one who could declare it to me."

25 Then Joseph said to Pharaoh, "Pharaoh's dreams are one *and the same*; God has declared to Pharaoh what He is about to do. 26 The seven good cows are seven years; and the seven good ears are seven years; the dreams are one *and the same*. 27 And the seven lean and ugly cows that came up after them are seven years, and the seven lean ears scorched by the east wind will be seven years of famine. 28 It is as I have spoken to Pharaoh: God has shown to Pharaoh what He is about to do. 29 Behold, seven years of great abundance are coming in all the land of Egypt; 30 and after them seven years of famine will arise, and all the abundance will be forgotten in the land of Egypt, and the famine will ravage the land, 31 so that the abundance will be unknown in the land because of that subsequent famine; for it *will be* very heavy. 32 Now as for the repeating of the dream to Pharaoh twice, *it means* that the matter is confirmed by God, and God will quickly bring it about. 33 So now let Pharaoh look for a man understanding and wise, and set him over the land of Egypt. 34 Let Pharaoh take action and appoint overseers over the land, and let him exact a fifth *of the produce* of the land of Egypt in the seven years of abundance. 35 Then let them gather all the food of these good years that are coming, and let them store up the grain for food in the cities under Pharaoh's authority, and let them keep watch over *it*. 36 And let the food be appointed for the land for the seven years of famine which will happen in the land of Egypt, so that the land will not be cut off during the famine."

37 And the proposal seemed good to Pharaoh and to all his servants. 38 Then Pharaoh said to his servants, "Can we find a man like this, in whom is a divine spirit?" 39 So Pharaoh said to Joseph, "Since God has made you know all of this, there is no one so understanding and wise as you are. 40 You shall be over my house, and according to your command all my people shall do homage; only in the throne I will be greater than you." 41 And Pharaoh said to Joseph, "See, I have set you over all the land of Egypt." 42 Then Pharaoh removed his signet ring from his hand and put it on Joseph's hand and clothed him in garments of fine linen and put the gold necklace around his neck. 43 And he had him ride in his second chariot; and they called out before him, "Bow the knee!" And he set him over all the land of Egypt. 44 Moreover, Pharaoh said to Joseph, "*Though* I am Pharaoh, yet without your permission no one shall raise his hand or foot in all the land of Egypt." 45 Then Pharaoh named Joseph Zaphenath-paneah; and he gave him Asenath, the daughter of Potiphera priest of On, as a wife. And Joseph went forth over the land of Egypt.

46 Now Joseph was thirty years old when he stood before Pharaoh, king of Egypt. And Joseph went out from the presence of Pharaoh and passed through all the land of Egypt. 47 And during the seven years of plenty the land brought forth abundantly. 48 So he gathered all the food of *these* seven years which happened in the land of Egypt and placed the food in the cities; he placed in every city the food from its own surrounding fields. 49 Thus Joseph stored up grain in great abundance like the sand of the sea, until he stopped measuring *it*, for it was beyond measure.

50 Now before the year of famine came, two sons were born to Joseph, whom Asenath, the daughter of Potiphera priest of On, bore to him. 51 And Joseph named the firstborn Manasseh, "For," *he said*, "God has made me forget all my trouble and all my father's household." 52 And he named the second Ephraim, "For," *he said*, "God has made me fruitful in the land of my affliction."

53 Then the seven years of plenty which had been in the land of Egypt came to an end, 54 and the seven years of famine began to come, just as Joseph had said. So there was famine in all the lands, but in all the land of Egypt there was bread. 55 Then all the land of Egypt was famished, and the people cried out to Pharaoh for bread; and Pharaoh said to all the Egyptians, "Go to Joseph; whatever he says to you, you shall do." 56 Now the famine was over all the face of the land. And Joseph opened all the storehouses and sold to the Egyptians; and the famine was severe in the land of Egypt. 57 Now all the earth *also* came to Egypt to buy grain from Joseph because the famine was severe in all the earth.

42 Now Jacob saw that there was grain in Egypt, and Jacob said to his sons, "Why are you staring at one another?" 2 Then he said, "Behold, I have heard that there is grain in Egypt; go down there and buy *some* for us from there, so that we may live and not die." 3 So ten brothers of Joseph went down to buy grain from Egypt. 4 But Jacob did not send Joseph's brother Benjamin with his brothers, for he said, "Lest *any* harm befall him." 5 So the sons of Israel came to buy grain among those who were coming, for the famine was in the land of Canaan *also.*

6 Now Joseph was the one in power over the land; he was the one who sold to all the people of the land. And Joseph's brothers came and bowed down to him with *their* faces to the ground. 7 And Joseph saw his brothers and recognized them, but he disguised himself to them and spoke to them harshly. And he said to them, "Where have you come from?" And they said, "From the land of Canaan, to buy food."

8 But Joseph recognized his brothers, although they did not recognize him. 9 And Joseph remembered the dreams which he had about them and said to them, "You are spies; you have come to look at the nakedness of the land." 10 Then they said to him, "No, my lord, but your servants have come to buy food. 11 We are all sons of one man; we are honest men; your servants are not spies." 12 And he said to them, "No, but you have come to look at the nakedness of our land!" 13 So they said, "Your servants are twelve brothers *in all*, the sons of one man in the land of Canaan; and behold, the youngest is with our father today, and one is no more." 14 And Joseph said to them, "It is as I said to you, you are spies; 15 by this you will be tested: by the life of Pharaoh, you shall not go from this place unless your youngest brother comes here! 16 Send one of you that he may get your brother, while you remain confined, that your words may be tested, whether there is truth in you. But if not, by the life of Pharaoh, surely you are spies." 17 Then he put them all together in prison for three days.

18 And Joseph said to them on the third day, "Do this and live, for I fear God: 19 if you are honest men, let one of your brothers be confined in your prison; but as for *the rest of* you, go, bring grain for the famine of your households, 20 and bring your youngest brother to me, so your words may be proven true, and you will not die." And they did so. 21 Then they said to one another, "Surely we are guilty concerning our brother because we saw the distress of his soul when he begged us, yet we would not listen; therefore this distress has come upon us." 22 And Reuben answered them, saying, "Did I not tell you, saying, 'Do not sin against the boy'; yet you would not listen? So also his blood, behold, it is required *of us.*" 23 Now they did not know that Joseph was listening, for there was an interpreter between them. 24 And he turned away from them and wept. Then he returned to them and spoke to them. And he took Simeon from them and bound him before their eyes. 25 Then Joseph gave a command to fill their bags with grain and to restore every man's money in his sack and to give them provisions for the journey. And thus it was done for them.

26 So they loaded their donkeys with their grain and went from there. 27 Then one *of them* opened his sack to give his donkey fodder at the lodging place. And he saw his money; and behold, it was in the mouth of his sack. 28 So he said to his brothers, "My money has been returned, and behold, it is even in my sack." And their hearts sank, and they *turned* trembling to one another, saying, "What is this that God has done to us?"

29 Then they came to their father Jacob in the land of Canaan and told him all that had happened to them, saying, 30 "The man, the lord of the land, spoke harshly with us and took us for spies of the country. 31 So we said to him, 'We are honest men; we are not spies. 32 We are twelve brothers, sons of our father; one is no more, and the youngest is with our father today in the land of Canaan.' 33 Then the man, the lord of the land, said to us, 'By this I will know that you are honest men: leave one of your brothers with me and take *grain for* the famine of your households, and go. 34 But bring your youngest brother to me that I may know that you are not spies, but honest men. I will give your brother to you, and you may trade in the land.'"

35 Now it happened that they were emptying their sacks, and behold, every man's bundle of money *was* in his sack; and they and their father saw their bundles of

money, and they feared. [36] And their father
Jacob said to them, "You have bereaved me
of my children: Joseph is no more, and
Simeon is no more, and you would take
Benjamin; all these things are against me."
[37] Then Reuben spoke to his father, saying,
"You may put my two sons to death if I do
not bring him *back* to you; put him in my
hand, and I will return him to you." [38] But
Jacob said, "My son shall not go down with
you; for his brother is dead, and he alone
remains. If harm should befall him on the
journey on which you are going, then you
will bring my gray hair down to Sheol in
sorrow."

Psalm 10:12–18

12 Arise, O Yahweh; O God,
lift up Your hand.
Do not forget the afflicted.
13 Why has the wicked spurned God?
He has said in his heart, "You
will not require *it*."

14 You have seen *it*, for You have
beheld mischief and vexation
to take it into Your hand.
The unfortunate commits
himself to You;
You have been the helper
of the orphan.

15 Break the arm of the wicked
and the evildoer,
Seek out his wickedness
until You find none.

16 Yahweh is King forever and ever;
Nations have perished from His land.

17 O Yahweh, You have heard the
desire of the humble;
You will strengthen their heart,
You will cause Your ear to
give heed
18 To give justice to the orphan
and the oppressed,
So that man who is of the earth
will no longer cause terror.

Proverbs 4:7–9

7 "The beginning of wisdom
is: Acquire wisdom;
And with all your acquiring,
acquire understanding.
8 "Prize her, and she will exalt you;
She will honor you if you
embrace her.
9 "She will give for your head
a garland of grace;
She will present you with
a crown of beauty."

Matthew 14:1–21

14 At that time Herod the tetrarch heard
the news about Jesus, [2] and said to
his servants, "This is John the Baptist; he
has risen from the dead, and that is why
miraculous powers are at work in him."
[3] For when Herod had John arrested, he
bound him and put him in prison because
of Herodias, the wife of his brother Philip.
[4] For John had been saying to him, "It is not
lawful for you to have her." [5] And although
Herod wanted to put him to death, he feared
the crowd, because they were regarding John
as a prophet.
[6] But when Herod's birthday came, the
daughter of Herodias danced before *them*
and pleased Herod, [7] so *much* that he prom-
ised with an oath to give her whatever she
asked. [8] Now having been prompted by her
mother, she *said, "Give me here on a platter
the head of John the Baptist." [9] And although
he was grieved, the king commanded *it* to
be given because of his oaths, and because
of his dinner guests. [10] And he sent and had
John beheaded in the prison. [11] And his head
was brought on a platter and given to the
girl, and she brought it to her mother. [12] And
his disciples came and took away the body
and buried it; and they went and reported
to Jesus.
[13] Now when Jesus heard *about John*, He
withdrew from there in a boat to a desolate
place by Himself; and when the crowds
heard *of this*, they followed Him on foot
from the cities. [14] And when He went ashore,
He saw a large crowd, and felt compassion
for them and healed their sick.
[15] Now when it was evening, the disciples
came to Him and said, "This place is des-
olate and the hour is already late; so send
the crowds away, that they may go into the
villages and buy food for themselves." [16] But
Jesus said to them, "They do not need to
go away; you give them *something* to eat!"
[17] But they *said to Him, "We have here only
five loaves and two fish." [18] And He said,
"Bring them here to Me." [19] And ordering

the crowds to sit down on the grass, He took the five loaves and the two fish, and looking up toward heaven, He blessed *the food.* And breaking the loaves, He gave them to the disciples, and the disciples *gave them* to the crowds, 20 and they all ate and were satisfied. They picked up what was left over of the broken pieces, twelve full baskets. 21 And there were about five thousand men who ate, besides women and children.

Christ is the key which unlocks the golden doors into the temple of Divine truth.

— A. W. PINK

JANUARY 22

Genesis 43:1–44:34

43 Now the famine was heavy in the land. 2 And it happened when they had finished eating the grain which they had brought from Egypt, that their father said to them, "Go back, buy us a little food." 3 Judah spoke to him, however, saying, "The man solemnly warned us, saying, 'You shall not see my face unless your brother is with you.' 4 If you send our brother with us, we will go down and buy you food. 5 But if you do not send *him,* we will not go down; for the man said to us, 'You will not see my face unless your brother is with you.'" 6 Then Israel said, "Why did you treat me so badly by telling the man whether you still had *another* brother?" 7 But they said, "The man questioned particularly about us and our kin, saying, 'Is your father still alive? Have you *another* brother?' So we told him concerning these things. Could we possibly have known that he would say, 'Bring your brother down'?" 8 Then Judah said to his father Israel, "Send the boy with me, and we will arise and go, that we may live and not die, we as well as you and our little ones. 9 I myself will be *the* guarantee for him; from my hand you may require him. If I do not bring him *back* to you and set him before you, then I shall bear the sin before you all *my* days. 10 For if we had not delayed, surely by now we could have returned twice."

11 Then their father Israel said to them, "If *it must be* so, then do this: take some of the best products of the land in your bags, and bring *them* down to the man as a present, a little balm and a little honey, aromatic gum and myrrh, pistachio nuts and almonds. 12 Now take double *the* money in your hand, and take back in your hand the money that was put back in the mouth of your sacks; perhaps it was a mistake. 13 And take your brother also, and arise, return to the man; 14 and may God Almighty grant you compassion before the man, so that he will release to you your other brother and Benjamin. And as for me, if I am bereaved of my children, I am bereaved." 15 So the men took this present, and they took double *the* money in their hand, and Benjamin; and they arose and went down to Egypt and stood before Joseph.

16 Then Joseph saw Benjamin with them and said to his house steward, "Bring the men into the house, and slay an animal and prepare *it;* for the men are to eat with me at noon." 17 So the man did as Joseph said and brought the men to Joseph's house. 18 And the men were afraid because they were brought to Joseph's house; and they said, "*It is* because of the money that was returned in our sacks the first time that we are being brought in, that he may seek occasion against us and fall upon us and take us for slaves with our donkeys." 19 So they came near to Joseph's house steward and spoke to him at the entrance of the house, 20 and they said, "Oh, my lord, we indeed came down the first time to buy food, 21 and it happened when we came to the lodging place, that we opened our sacks, and behold, each man's money was in the mouth of his sack, our money in full. So we have brought it back in our hand. 22 We have also brought down other money in our hand to buy food; we do not know who put our money in our

sacks." 23 And he said, "Be well, do not be afraid. Your God and the God of your father has given you treasure in your sacks; your money has come to me." Then he brought Simeon out to them. 24 Then the man brought the men into Joseph's house and gave them water, and they washed their feet; and he gave their donkeys fodder. 25 So they prepared the present for Joseph's coming at noon; for they had heard that they were to eat a meal there.

26 Then Joseph came home, and they brought into the house to him the present which was in their hand and bowed to the ground before him. 27 And he asked them about their well-being and said, "Is your old father well, of whom you spoke? Is he still alive?" 28 And they said, "Your servant our father is well; he is still alive." They bowed down and prostrated themselves. 29 Then he lifted his eyes and saw his brother Benjamin, his mother's son. And he said, "Is this your youngest brother, of whom you spoke to me?" And he said, "May God be gracious to you, my son." 30 And Joseph hurried *out* for he was deeply stirred with compassion over his brother, and he sought *a place* to weep; and he entered his chamber and wept there. 31 Then he washed his face and came out; and he restrained himself and said, "Set the meal." 32 So they set *the meal* for him by himself, and for them by themselves, and for the Egyptians who ate with him by themselves, because the Egyptians could not eat bread with the Hebrews, for that is an abomination to the Egyptians. 33 And they were seated before him, the firstborn according to his birthright and the youngest according to his youth, and the men looked at one another in astonishment. 34 And he took portions to them from his own table, but Benjamin's portion was five times greater than any of theirs. So they feasted and drank freely with him.

44 Then he commanded his house steward, saying, "Fill the men's sacks with food, as much as they can carry, and put each man's money in the mouth of his sack. 2 Now put my cup, the silver cup, in the mouth of the sack of the youngest, and his money for the grain." And he did as Joseph had told *him*. 3 As the morning light *broke*, the men were sent away, they with their donkeys. 4 Now they had *just* gone out of the city *and* were not far off when Joseph said to his house steward, "Arise, pursue the men; you shall overtake them and say to them, 'Why have you repaid evil for good? 5 Is not this the one from which my lord drinks and which he indeed uses to interpret omens? You have done evil in doing this.'"

6 So he overtook them and spoke these words to them. 7 And they said to him, "Why does my lord speak such words as these? Far be it from your servants to do such a thing. 8 Behold, the money which we found in the mouth of our sacks we have brought back to you from the land of Canaan. How then could we steal silver or gold from your lord's house? 9 With whomever of your servants it is found, let him die, and we also will be my lord's slaves." 10 So he said, "Now let it also be according to your words; he with whom it is found shall be my slave, but *the rest of* you shall be innocent." 11 Then they hurried, each man brought his sack down to the ground, and each man opened his sack. 12 So he searched, beginning with the oldest and ending with the youngest, and the cup was found in Benjamin's sack. 13 Then they tore their clothes, and each man loaded his donkey and returned to the city.

14 Then Judah and his brothers came to Joseph's house, and he was still there. So they fell to the ground before him. 15 And Joseph said to them, "What is this deed that you have done? Do you not know that such a man as I can indeed interpret omens?" 16 So Judah said, "What can we say to my lord? What can we speak? And how can we justify ourselves? God has found out the iniquity of your servants; behold, we are my lord's slaves, both we and the one in whose possession the cup has been found." 17 But he said, "Far be it from me to do this. The man in whose possession the cup has been found, he shall be my slave; but as for you, go up in peace to your father."

18 Then Judah came near to him and said, "O my lord, may your servant please speak a word in my lord's ears, and do not be angry with your servant; for you are equal to Pharaoh. 19 My lord asked his servants, saying, 'Have you a father or a brother?' 20 And we said to my lord, 'We have an old father and a little child of *his* old age. Now his brother is dead, so he alone is left of his mother, and his father loves him.' 21 Then you said to your servants, 'Bring him down to me that I

may set my eyes on him.' 22 And we said to
my lord, 'The boy cannot leave his father; if
he should leave his father, his father would
die.' 23 You said to your servants, however,
'If your youngest brother does not come
down with you, you will not see my face
again.' 24 Thus it happened that when we
went up to your servant my father, we told
him the words of my lord. 25 And our father
said, 'Go back, buy us a little food.' 26 But we
said, 'We cannot go down. If our youngest
brother is with us, then we will go down; for
we cannot see the man's face if our youngest
brother is not with us.' 27 And your servant
my father said to us, 'You know that my wife
bore me two sons; 28 and the one went out
from me, and I said, "Surely he is torn to
pieces," and I have not seen him since. 29 If
you take this one also from me and harm
befalls him, you will bring my gray hair
down to Sheol in evil.' 30 So now, when I
come to your servant my father, and the boy
is not with us—and his life is bound up in
the *boy's* life— 31 so it will be that when he
sees that the boy is not *with us*, he will die.
Thus your servants will bring the gray hair
of your servant our father down to Sheol
in sorrow. 32 For your servant became a
guarantee for the boy to my father, saying,
'If I do not bring him *back* to you, then I
shall bear the sin before my father all *my*
days.' 33 So now, please let your servant
remain instead of the boy as a slave to my
lord, and let the boy go up with his brothers.
34 For how shall I go up to my father if the
boy is not with me, lest I see the evil that
would overtake my father?"

Psalm 11:1–7

1 In Yahweh I take refuge;
How can you say to my soul,
"Flee *as* a bird to your mountain;
2 For, behold, the wicked bend the bow,
They make ready their arrow
upon the string
To shoot in darkness at the
upright in heart.
3 "If the foundations are destroyed,
What can the righteous do?"

4 Yahweh is in His holy temple;
Yahweh's throne is in heaven;
His eyes behold, His eyelids
test the sons of men.
5 Yahweh tests the righteous,
But the wicked and the one who
loves violence His soul hates.
6 May He rain snares upon the wicked;
Fire and brimstone and burning wind
will be the portion of their cup.
7 For Yahweh is righteous,
He loves righteousness;
The upright will behold His face.

Proverbs 4:10–13

10 Hear, my son, and receive my sayings
And the years of your life will be many.
11 I have instructed you in
the way of wisdom;
I have led you in upright tracks.
12 When you walk, your steps
will not be impeded;
And if you run, you will not stumble.
13 Seize discipline; do not let go.
Guard her, for she is your life.

Matthew 14:22–36

22 Immediately He made the disciples get
into the boat and go ahead of Him to the
other side, while He sent the crowds away.
23 And after He had sent the crowds away,
He went up on the mountain by Himself
to pray; and when it was evening, He was
there alone. 24 But the boat was already
many stadia away from the land, being
battered by the waves; for the wind was
against *them*. 25 And in the fourth watch
of the night He came to them, walking on
the sea. 26 Now when the disciples saw Him
walking on the sea, they were terrified, and
said, "It is a ghost!" And they cried out in
fear. 27 But immediately Jesus spoke to
them, saying, "Take courage, it is I; do not
be afraid."

28 And Peter answered and said to Him,
"Lord, if it is You, command me to come to
You on the water." 29 And He said, "Come!"
And getting out of the boat, Peter walked
on the water and came toward Jesus. 30 But
seeing the wind, he became frightened,
and beginning to sink, he cried out, saying,
"Lord, save me!" 31 And immediately Jesus
stretched out His hand and took hold of
him, and *said to him, "You of little faith,
why did you doubt?" 32 And when they got
into the boat, the wind stopped. 33 And
those who were in the boat worshiped Him,
saying, "You are truly God's Son!"

34 And when they had crossed over, they
came to land at Gennesaret. 35 And when

the men of that place recognized Him, they sent *word* into all that surrounding district and brought to Him all who were sick; 36 and they were pleading *with* Him that they might just touch the fringe of His garment; and as many as touched *it* were cured.

JANUARY 23

Genesis 45:1–46:34

45 Then Joseph could not restrain himself before all those who stood by him, and he called out, "Have everyone go out from me." So there was no man with him when Joseph made himself known to his brothers. 2 Then he wept loudly. And the Egyptians heard *it*, and the household of Pharaoh heard *it*. 3 Then Joseph said to his brothers, "I am Joseph! Is my father still alive?" But his brothers could not answer him, for they were terrified at his presence.

4 Then Joseph said to his brothers, "Please come near to me." And they came near. And he said, "I am Joseph, your brother, whom you sold into Egypt. 5 So now do not be grieved or angry with yourselves because you sold me here, for God sent me before you to preserve life. 6 For the famine *has been* in the land these two years, and there are still five years in which there will be neither plowing nor harvesting. 7 So God sent me before you to establish for you a remnant in the earth and to keep you alive for a great *remnant* of survivors. 8 So now, it was not you who sent me here, but God; and He has set me as a father to Pharaoh and lord of all his household and ruler over all the land of Egypt. 9 Hurry and go up to my father, and say to him, 'Thus says your son Joseph, "God has set me as lord of all Egypt; come down to me, do not delay. 10 And you shall live in the land of Goshen, and you shall be near me, you and your children and your children's children and your flocks and your herds and all that you have. 11 There I will also provide for you, for there are still five years of famine *to come*, lest you and your household and all that you have be impoverished."' 12 And behold, your eyes see, and the eyes of my brother Benjamin *see*, that it is my mouth which is speaking to you. 13 So you must tell my father of all my glory in Egypt and all that you have seen; and you must hurry and bring my father down here." 14 Then he fell on his brother Benjamin's neck and wept, and Benjamin wept on his neck. 15 He kissed all his brothers and wept on them, and afterward his brothers talked with him.

16 Now the news was heard in Pharaoh's house, saying, "Joseph's brothers have come." And it was good in the sight of Pharaoh and in the sight of his servants. 17 Then Pharaoh said to Joseph, "Say to your brothers, 'Do this: load your beasts and go to the land of Canaan, 18 and take your father and your households and come to me, and I will give you the best of the land of Egypt, and you will eat the fat of the land.' 19 Now you are commanded, 'Do this: take wagons from the land of Egypt for your little ones and for your wives, and bring your father and come. 20 Now do not concern yourselves with your goods, for the best of all the land of Egypt is yours.'"

21 Then the sons of Israel did so; and Joseph gave them wagons according to the command of Pharaoh, and he gave them provisions for the journey. 22 To each of them he gave changes of garments, but to Benjamin he gave three hundred *pieces of* silver and five changes of garments. 23 Now to his father he sent as follows: ten donkeys loaded with the best things of Egypt and ten female donkeys loaded with grain and bread and sustenance for his father on the journey.

24 So he sent his brothers away, and they departed. And he said to them, "Do not be stirred up on the journey." 25 Then they went up from Egypt, and came to the land of Canaan to their father Jacob. 26 And they told him, saying, "Joseph is still alive, and indeed he is ruler over all the land of Egypt." But his heart was stunned, for he did not believe them. 27 Yet they told him all the words of Joseph that he had spoken to them, and he saw the wagons that Joseph had sent to carry him. Then the spirit of their father Jacob revived. 28 And Israel said, "It is enough! My son Joseph is still alive. I will go and see him before I die."

46 So Israel set out with all that he had and came to Beersheba and offered sacrifices to the God of his father Isaac.

2 And God spoke to Israel in visions of the
night and said, "Jacob, Jacob." And he said,
"Here I am." 3 And He said, "I am God, the
God of your father; do not be afraid to go
down to Egypt, for I will make you a great
nation there. 4 I Myself will go down with
you to Egypt, and I Myself will also bring
you up again; and Joseph will close your eyes
with his hand."

5 Then Jacob arose from Beersheba; and
the sons of Israel carried their father Jacob
and their little ones and their wives in the
wagons which Pharaoh had sent to carry
him. 6 And they took their livestock and
their possessions, which they had accumu-
lated in the land of Canaan, and they came
to Egypt, Jacob and all his seed with him:
7 his sons and his grandsons with him, his
daughters and his granddaughters, and all
his seed he brought with him to Egypt.

8 Now these are the names of the sons of
Israel—of Jacob and his sons—who were
coming to Egypt: Reuben, Jacob's firstborn.
9 The sons of Reuben: Hanoch and Pallu and
Hezron and Carmi. 10 The sons of Simeon:
Jemuel and Jamin and Ohad and Jachin and
Zohar and Shaul the son of a Canaanite
woman. 11 The sons of Levi: Gershon,
Kohath, and Merari. 12 The sons of Judah:
Er and Onan and Shelah and Perez and
Zerah (but Er and Onan died in the land
of Canaan). And the sons of Perez were
Hezron and Hamul. 13 The sons of Issachar:
Tola and Puvvah and Iob and Shimron.
14 The sons of Zebulun: Sered and Elon
and Jahleel. 15 These are the sons of Leah,
whom she bore to Jacob in Paddan-aram,
with his daughter Dinah; all his sons and his
daughters *numbered* thirty-three.

16 The sons of Gad: Ziphion and Haggi,
Shuni and Ezbon, Eri and Arodi and Areli.
17 The sons of Asher: Imnah and Ishvah
and Ishvi and Beriah and their sister Serah.
And the sons of Beriah: Heber and Malchiel.
18 These are the sons of Zilpah, whom Laban
gave to his daughter Leah; and she bore to
Jacob these sixteen persons.

19 The sons of Jacob's wife Rachel: Joseph
and Benjamin. 20 Now to Joseph in the land
of Egypt were born Manasseh and Ephraim,
whom Asenath, the daughter of Potiphera,
priest of On, bore to him. 21 The sons of
Benjamin: Bela and Becher and Ashbel, Gera
and Naaman, Ehi and Rosh, Muppim and
Huppim and Ard. 22 These are the sons of
Rachel, who were born to Jacob; *there were*
fourteen persons in all.

23 The sons of Dan: Hushim. 24 The
sons of Naphtali: Jahzeel and Guni and
Jezer and Shillem. 25 These are the sons of
Bilhah, whom Laban gave to his daughter
Rachel, and she bore these to Jacob; *there*
were seven persons in all. 26 All the persons
belonging to Jacob, who came to Egypt, who
came out of his loins, excluding the wives
of Jacob's sons, *were* sixty-six persons in all,
27 and the sons of Joseph, who were born
to him in Egypt were two; all the persons
of the house of Jacob, who came to Egypt,
were seventy.

28 Now he sent Judah before him to
Joseph, to point out *the way* before him
to Goshen; and they came into the land
of Goshen. 29 And Joseph harnessed his
chariot and went up to Goshen to meet
his father Israel; as soon as he appeared
before him, he fell on his neck and wept
on his neck a long time. 30 Then Israel
said to Joseph, "Now I can die, since I have
seen your face, that you are still alive."
31 And Joseph said to his brothers and to
his father's household, "I will go up and
tell Pharaoh and say to him, 'My brothers
and my father's household, who *were* in the
land of Canaan, have come to me; 32 and
the men are shepherds, for they have been
keepers of livestock; and they have brought
their flocks and their herds and all that they
have.' 33 And it will be when Pharaoh calls
you and says, 'What is your occupation?'
34 then you shall say, 'Your servants have
been keepers of livestock from our youth
and until now, both we and our fathers,'
that you may live in the land of Goshen;
for every shepherd is an abomination to the
Egyptians."

Psalm 12:1–8

1 Save, O Yahweh, for the holy
man ceases to be,
For the faithful disappear from
among the sons of men.
2 They speak worthlessness
to one another;
With a flattering lip and with a
double heart they speak.
3 May Yahweh cut off all flattering lips,
The tongue that speaks great things;
4 Who have said, "With our
tongue we will prevail;

Our lips are our own; who
is lord over us?"
5 "Because of the devastation of
the afflicted, because of the
groaning of the needy,
Now I will arise," says Yahweh;
"I will set him in the safety
for which he longs."

6 The words of Yahweh are pure words;
As silver tried in a furnace on the
ground, refined seven times.
7 You, O Yahweh, will keep them;
You will guard him from this
generation forever.
8 The wicked strut about on every side
When vileness is exalted
among the sons of men.

Proverbs 4:14–17

14 Do not enter the path of wicked men
And do not step into the
way of evil men.
15 Avoid it, do not pass by it;
Stray from it and pass on.
16 For they do not sleep
unless they do evil;
And they are robbed of sleep unless
they make *someone* stumble.
17 For they eat the bread of wickedness
And drink the wine of violence.

Matthew 15:1–20

15 Then some Pharisees and scribes
*came to Jesus from Jerusalem and
said, 2 "Why do Your disciples break the
tradition of the elders? For they do not wash
their hands when they eat bread." 3 And He
answered and said to them, "Why do you
yourselves transgress the commandment of
God for the sake of your tradition? 4 For God
said, 'HONOR YOUR FATHER AND MOTHER,' and,
'HE WHO SPEAKS EVIL OF FATHER OR MOTHER IS
TO BE PUT TO DEATH.' 5 But you say, 'Whoever
says to *his* father or mother, "Whatever you
might benefit from me is given *to God*," 6 he
need not honor his father.' And *by this* you
invalidated the word of God for the sake of
your tradition. 7 You hypocrites, rightly did
Isaiah prophesy of you:
8 'THIS PEOPLE HONORS ME
WITH THEIR LIPS,
BUT THEIR HEART IS FAR AWAY FROM ME.
9 'BUT IN VAIN DO THEY WORSHIP ME,
TEACHING AS DOCTRINES THE
COMMANDS OF MEN.'"
10 After Jesus called the crowd to Him,
He said to them, "Hear and understand.
11 *It is* not what enters into the mouth *that*
defiles the man, but what proceeds out of
the mouth, this defiles the man."
12 Then the disciples *came and *said to
Him, "Do You know that the Pharisees were
offended when they heard this statement?"
13 But He answered and said, "Every plant
which My heavenly Father did not plant
shall be uprooted. 14 Let them alone; they
are blind guides of the blind. And if a blind
man guides a blind man, both will fall into
a pit."
15 Now Peter answered and said to Him,
"Explain the parable to us." 16 And Jesus said,
"Are you still lacking in understanding also?
17 Do you not understand that everything
that goes into the mouth passes into the
stomach, and goes into the sewer? 18 But the
things that proceed out of the mouth come
from the heart, and those defile the man.
19 For out of the heart come evil thoughts,
murders, adulteries, sexual immoralities,
thefts, false witness, slanders. 20 These are
the things which defile the man; but to eat
with unwashed hands does not defile the
man."

JANUARY 24

Genesis 47:1–48:22

47 Then Joseph went in and told Pha-
raoh and said, "My father and my
brothers and their flocks and their herds
and all that they have, have come out of
the land of Canaan; and behold, they are
in the land of Goshen." 2 And he took five
men from among his brothers and set them
before Pharaoh. 3 Then Pharaoh said to his
brothers, "What is your occupation?" So
they said to Pharaoh, "Your servants are
shepherds, both we and our fathers." 4 And
they said to Pharaoh, "We have come to
sojourn in the land, for there is no pasture
for your servants' flocks, for the famine is
heavy in the land of Canaan. So now, please
let your servants live in the land of Goshen."
5 Then Pharaoh said to Joseph, "Your father

and your brothers have come to you. 6 The land of Egypt is at your disposal; have your father and your brothers settle in the best of the land, let them settle in the land of Goshen; and if you know any excellent men among them, then put them in charge of my livestock."

7 Then Joseph brought his father Jacob and stood him before Pharaoh; and Jacob blessed Pharaoh. 8 And Pharaoh said to Jacob, "How many are the days of the years of your life?" 9 So Jacob said to Pharaoh, "The days of the years of my sojourning are 130; few and evil have been the days of the years of my life, and they have not attained to the days of the years that my fathers lived during the days of their sojourning." 10 And Jacob blessed Pharaoh and went out from the presence of Pharaoh. 11 So Joseph settled his father and his brothers and gave them a possession in the land of Egypt, in the best of the land, in the land of Rameses, as Pharaoh had commanded. 12 And Joseph provided his father and his brothers and all his father's household with food, according to their little ones.

13 Now there was no food in all the land because the famine was very heavy, so that the land of Egypt and the land of Canaan languished because of the famine. 14 And Joseph gathered all the money that was found in the land of Egypt and in the land of Canaan for the grain which they bought, and Joseph brought the money into Pharaoh's house. 15 Then the money came to an end in the land of Egypt and in the land of Canaan. So all the Egyptians came to Joseph and said, "Give us food, for why should we die in your presence? For *our* money is gone." 16 Then Joseph said, "Give up your livestock, and I will give you *food* for your livestock, since *your* money is gone." 17 So they brought their livestock to Joseph, and Joseph gave them food in exchange for the horses and the flocks and the herds and the donkeys; and he fed them with food in exchange for all their livestock that year. 18 Then that year came to an end. And they came to him the next year and said to him, "We will not hide from my lord that our money has come to an end, and the livestock are my lord's. There is nothing left for my lord except our bodies and our land. 19 Why should we die before your eyes, both we and our land? Buy us and our land for food, and we and our land will be slaves to Pharaoh. So give us seed, that we may live and not die, and that the land may not be desolate."

20 So Joseph bought all the land of Egypt for Pharaoh, for every Egyptian sold his field because the famine was severe upon them. Thus the land became Pharaoh's. 21 As for the people, he moved them to the cities from one end of Egypt's border to the other end. 22 Only the land of the priests he did not buy, for the priests had an allotment from Pharaoh, and they ate off the allotment which Pharaoh gave them. Therefore, they did not sell their land. 23 Then Joseph said to the people, "Behold, I have today bought you and your land for Pharaoh; now, *here* is seed for you, and you may sow the land. 24 And it will be, at the harvest you shall give a fifth to Pharaoh, and four-fifths shall be your own for seed of the field and for your food and for those of your households and as food for your little ones." 25 So they said, "You have kept us alive! Let us find favor in the sight of my lord, and we will be Pharaoh's slaves." 26 And Joseph made it a statute concerning the land of Egypt *valid* to this day, that Pharaoh should have the fifth; only the land of the priests did not become Pharaoh's.

27 Now Israel lived in the land of Egypt, in Goshen, and they took possession of property in it and were fruitful and became very numerous. 28 And Jacob lived in the land of Egypt seventeen years; so the days of Jacob, the years of his life, were 147 years.

29 Then the days for Israel to die drew near, and he called his son Joseph and said to him, "Please, if I have found favor in your sight, place now your hand under my thigh and deal with me in lovingkindness and truth. Please do not bury me in Egypt. 30 But I will lie down with my fathers, and you will carry me out of Egypt and bury me in their burial place." And he said, "I will do as you have said." 31 Then he said, "Swear to me." So he swore to him. Then Israel bowed *in worship* at the head of the bed.

48 Now it happened after these things that Joseph was told, "Behold, your father is sick." So he took his two sons Manasseh and Ephraim with him. 2 Then it was told to Jacob, "Behold, your son Joseph has come to you," so Israel strengthened himself and sat up in the bed. 3 Then Jacob said to Joseph, "God Almighty appeared to me at Luz in the land of Canaan and blessed me, 4 and He said to me, 'Behold, I will make you fruitful and multiply, and I will make you an assembly of peoples, and I will give this land to your seed after you for an everlasting possession.' 5 So now your two sons, who were born to you in the land of Egypt before I came to you in Egypt, are mine; Ephraim and Manasseh shall be mine, as Reuben and Simeon are. 6 But your kin that have been born after them shall be yours; they shall be called by the names of their brothers in their inheritance. 7 Now as for me, when I came from Paddan, Rachel died, to my sorrow, in the land of Canaan on the journey, when there was still some distance to go to Ephrath; and I buried her there on the way to Ephrath (that is, Bethlehem)."

8 Then Israel saw Joseph's sons and said, "Who are these?" 9 And Joseph said to his father, "They are my sons, whom God has given me here." So he said, "Bring them to me, please, that I may bless them." 10 Now the eyes of Israel were *so* dim from age *that* he could not see. Then Joseph brought them close to him, and he kissed them and embraced them. 11 Then Israel said to Joseph, "I never expected to see your face, and behold, God has let me see your seed as well." 12 Then Joseph took them from his knees and bowed with his face to the ground. 13 And Joseph took them both, Ephraim with his right hand toward Israel's left, and Manasseh with his left hand toward Israel's right, and brought them close to him. 14 But Israel stretched out his right hand and laid it on the head of Ephraim, who was the younger, and his left hand on Manasseh's head, crossing his hands, although Manasseh was the firstborn. 15 And he blessed Joseph and said,

"May the God before whom my fathers
Abraham and Isaac walked,
The God who has been my shepherd
throughout my life to this day,
16 The angel who has redeemed
me from all evil,
Bless *these* boys;
And may my name live on in them,
And the names of my fathers
Abraham and Isaac;
And may they grow into a multitude
in the midst of the earth."

17 But Joseph saw that his father set his right hand on Ephraim's head, and it was displeasing in his sight; so he took hold of his father's hand to remove it from Ephraim's head to Manasseh's head. 18 And Joseph said to his father, "Not so, my father, for this one is the firstborn. Place your right hand on his head." 19 But his father refused and said, "I know, my son, I know; he also will become a people, and he also will be great. However, his younger brother shall be greater than he, and his seed shall become the fullness of nations." 20 And he blessed them that day, saying,

"By you Israel will pronounce
blessing, saying,
'May God make you like Ephraim
and Manasseh!'"

Thus he put Ephraim before Manasseh. 21 Then Israel said to Joseph, "Behold, I am about to die, but God will be with you and will bring you back to the land of your fathers. 22 And I give you one portion more than your brothers, which I took from the hand of the Amorite with my sword and my bow."

Psalm 13:1–6

1 How long, O Yahweh?
Will You forget me forever?
How long will You hide
Your face from me?
2 How long shall I take
counsel in my soul,
Having sorrow in my heart
all the day?
How long will my enemy
be exalted over me?

3 Look *and* answer me,
O Yahweh my God;
Give light to my eyes,
lest I sleep the *sleep of* death,
4 Lest my enemy says,
"I have overcome him,"
And my adversaries rejoice
that I am shaken.

5 But I have trusted in Your
lovingkindness;
My heart shall rejoice in
Your salvation.
6 I will sing to Yahweh,
Because He has dealt
bountifully with me.

Proverbs 4:18–19

18 But the path of the righteous
is like the light of dawn,
That shines brighter and brighter
until the fullness of day.
19 The way of the wicked is
like thick darkness;
They do not know over
what they stumble.

Matthew 15:21–39

21 And going away from there, Jesus
withdrew into the district of Tyre and
Sidon. 22 And behold, a Canaanite woman
from that region came out and *began to* cry
out, saying, "Have mercy on me, Lord, Son
of David; my daughter is cruelly demon-
possessed." 23 But He did not answer her
a word. And His disciples came and were
pleading with Him, saying, "Send her away,
because she keeps shouting at us." 24 But He
answered and said, "I was not sent except to
the lost sheep of the house of Israel." 25 But
she came and was bowing down before Him,
saying, "Lord, help me!" 26 And He answered
and said, "It is not good to take the children's
bread and throw it to the dogs." 27 But she
said, "Yes, Lord; but even the dogs feed on
the crumbs which fall from their masters'
table." 28 Then Jesus answered and said to
her, "O woman, your faith is great; it shall be
done for you as you wish." And her daughter
was healed at once.
29 And departing from there, Jesus went
along by the Sea of Galilee, and having
gone up on the mountain, He was sitting
there. 30 And large crowds came to Him,
bringing with them *those who were* lame,
crippled, blind, mute, and many others,
and they laid them down at His feet; and
He healed them. 31 So the crowd marveled
as they saw the mute speaking, the crip-
pled restored, and the lame walking, and
the blind seeing; and they glorified the
God of Israel.
32 And Jesus called His disciples to Him,
and said, "I feel compassion for the crowd,
because they have remained with Me now
three days and have nothing to eat; and I
do not want to send them away hungry,
lest they faint on the way." 33 And the
disciples *said to Him, "Where would we
get so many loaves in *this* desolate place
to satisfy such a large crowd?" 34 And Jesus
*said to them, "How many loaves do you
have?" And they said, "Seven, and a few
small fish." 35 And He directed the crowd
to sit down on the ground; 36 and He took
the seven loaves and the fish; and giving
thanks, He broke them and kept giving
them to the disciples, and the disciples
gave them to the crowds. 37 And they all
ate and were satisfied, and they picked up
what was left over of the broken pieces,
seven *large* baskets full. 38 And those
who ate were four thousand men, besides
women and children.
39 And sending away the crowds, Jesus
got into the boat and came to the region of
Magadan.

JANUARY 25

Genesis 49:1–50:26

49 Then Jacob summoned his sons
and said, "Gather together that I
may tell you what will befall you in the
last days.

2 "Assemble together and hear,
O sons of Jacob;
And listen to Israel your father.

3 "Reuben, you are my firstborn;
My might and the beginning
of my vigor,
Preeminent in dignity and
preeminent in strength.
4 "Uncontrolled as water, you shall
not have preeminence,
Because you went up to
your father's bed;
Then you defiled *it*—he
went up to my couch.

5 "Simeon and Levi are brothers;
Their swords are implements
of violence.
6 "Let my soul not enter into
their council;
Let not my glory be united
with their assembly;
Because in their anger they
killed men,
And in their self-will they
hamstrung oxen.

7 “Cursed be their anger, for it is strong;
And their wrath, for it is cruel.
I will divide them amongst Jacob,
And scatter them in Israel.

8 “Judah, as for you, your brothers
shall praise you;
Your hand shall be on the
neck of your enemies;
Your father’s sons shall
bow down to you.
9 “Judah is a lion’s whelp;
From the prey, my son,
you have gone up.
He crouches, he lies down as a lion,
And as a lioness, who dares
rouse him up?
10 “The scepter shall not
depart from Judah,
Nor the ruler’s staff from
between his feet,
Until Shiloh comes,
And to him *shall be* the
obedience of the peoples.
11 “He ties *his* foal to the vine,
And his donkey’s colt to
the choice vine;
He washes his garments in wine,
And his robes in the blood of grapes.
12 “His eyes are dark from wine,
And his teeth white from milk.

13 “Zebulun will dwell at the seashore;
And he *shall be* a shore for ships,
And his flank *shall be* toward Sidon.

14 “Issachar is a strong donkey,
Lying down between the sheepfolds.
15 “And he saw that a resting
place was good
And that the land was pleasant,
So he bowed his shoulder
to bear *burdens*,
And became a slave at forced labor.

16 “Dan shall render justice to his people,
As one of the tribes of Israel.
17 “Dan shall be a serpent in the way,
A horned snake in the path,
That bites the horse’s heels,
So that his rider falls backward.
18 “For Your salvation I hope, O Yahweh.

19 “As for Gad, raiders shall raid him,
But he will raid *at* their heels.

20 “As for Asher, his food shall be rich,
And he will yield royal dainties.

21 “Naphtali is a doe let loose,
He gives beautiful words.

22 “Joseph is a fruitful bough,
A fruitful bough by a spring;
Its branches run over a wall.
23 “And the archers bitterly attacked
him and shot *at him*,
And they bore a grudge against him;
24 But his bow remained firm,
And his arms were agile,
From the hands of the
Mighty One of Jacob,
From there is the Shepherd,
the Stone of Israel,
25 From the God of your father
who helps you,
And by the Almighty who blesses you
With blessings of heaven above,
Blessings of the deep that lies beneath,
Blessings of the breasts
and of the womb.
26 “The blessings of your father
Have surpassed the blessings
of my ancestors
Up to the utmost bound of
the everlasting hills;
May they be on the head of Joseph,
And on the top of the head of the one
distinguished among his brothers.

27 “Benjamin is a ravenous wolf;
In the morning he devours the prey,
And in the evening he
divides the spoil.”

28 All these are the twelve tribes of Israel,
and this is what their father spoke to them.
So he blessed them. He blessed them, every
one with the blessing appropriate to him.
29 Then he commanded them and said to
them, “I am about to be gathered to my peo-
ple; bury me with my fathers in the cave that
is in the field of Ephron the Hittite, 30 in the
cave that is in the field of Machpelah, which
is before Mamre, in the land of Canaan,
which Abraham bought along with the field
from Ephron the Hittite as a possession for
a burial site. 31 There they buried Abraham
and his wife Sarah, there they buried Isaac
and his wife Rebekah, and there I buried
Leah— 32 the field and the cave that is in
it, purchased from the sons of Heth.” 33 So

Jacob finished commanding his sons. And he drew his feet into the bed and breathed his last and was gathered to his people.

50 Then Joseph fell on his father's face and wept over him and kissed him. 2 And Joseph commanded his servants the physicians to embalm his father. So the physicians embalmed Israel. 3 Then *the* forty days *to do this* were fulfilled, because in this manner the days of embalming are fulfilled. And the Egyptians wept for him seventy days.

4 Then the days of weeping for him were past, and Joseph spoke to the household of Pharaoh, saying, "If now I have found favor in your sight, please speak in the ears of Pharaoh, saying, 5 'My father made me swear, saying, "Behold, I am about to die; in my grave which I dug for myself in the land of Canaan, there you shall bury me." So now, please let me go up and bury my father; then I will return.'" 6 And Pharaoh said, "Go up and bury your father, as he made you swear."

7 So Joseph went up to bury his father, and with him went up all the servants of Pharaoh, the elders of his household, and all the elders of the land of Egypt, 8 and all the household of Joseph and his brothers and his father's household; they left only their little ones and their flocks and their herds in the land of Goshen. 9 There also went up with him both chariots and horsemen; and it was a very immense camp. 10 And they came to the threshing floor of Atad, which is beyond the Jordan, and they lamented there with a very great and immense lamentation; and he observed seven days of mourning for his father. 11 Now the inhabitants of the land, the Canaanites, saw the mourning at the threshing floor of Atad, and they said, "This is an immense mourning for the Egyptians." Therefore it was named Abel-mizraim, which is beyond the Jordan.

12 Thus his sons did for him as he had commanded them. 13 Indeed, his sons carried him to the land of Canaan and buried him in the cave of the field of Machpelah before Mamre, which Abraham had bought along with the field for *his* possession *as* a burial site from Ephron the Hittite. 14 After he had buried his father, Joseph returned to Egypt, he and his brothers, and all who had gone up with him to bury his father.

15 Then Joseph's brothers saw that their father was dead, and they said, "What if Joseph bears a grudge against us and returns back to us all the evil which we dealt against him!" 16 So they sent *a message* to Joseph, saying, "Your father commanded before he died, saying, 17 'Thus you shall say to Joseph, "Please forgive, I beg you, the transgression of your brothers and their sin, for they dealt evil against you."' So now, please forgive the transgression of the slaves of the God of your father." And Joseph wept when they spoke to him. 18 Then his brothers also came and fell down before him and said, "Behold, we are your slaves." 19 But Joseph said to them, "Do not be afraid, for am I in God's place? 20 As for you, you meant evil against me, *but* God meant it for good in order to do *what has happened on* this day, to keep many people alive. 21 So now, do not be afraid; I will provide for you and your little ones." And he comforted them and spoke to their heart.

22 Now Joseph stayed in Egypt, he and his father's household, and Joseph lived 110 years. 23 And Joseph saw the third generation of Ephraim's sons; also the sons of Machir, the son of Manasseh, were born on Joseph's knees. 24 And Joseph said to his brothers, "I am about to die, but God will surely take care of you and bring you up from this land to the land which He swore to Abraham, to Isaac, and to Jacob." 25 Then Joseph made the sons of Israel swear, saying, "God will surely take care of you, and you shall carry my bones up from here." 26 So Joseph died at the age of 110 years; and they embalmed him, and he was placed in a coffin in Egypt.

Psalm 14:1–7

1 The wicked fool says in his
heart, "There is no God."
They act corruptly, they commit
abominable deeds;
There is no one who does good.
2 Yahweh looks down from heaven
upon the sons of men
To see if there is anyone
who has insight,
Anyone who seeks after God.
3 They have all turned aside, altogether
they have become worthless;
There is no one who does
good, not even one.

4 Do all the workers of
iniquity not know,
Who eat up my people *as*
they eat bread,
And do not call upon Yahweh?
5 There they are in great dread,
For God is with the righteous
generation.
6 You would put to shame the
counsel of the afflicted,
But Yahweh is his refuge.

7 Oh, that the salvation of Israel
would come out of Zion!
When Yahweh restores His
captive people,
May Jacob rejoice, may Israel be glad.

Proverbs 4:20–24

20 My son, pay attention to my words;
Incline your ear to my sayings.
21 Do not let them deviate
from your eyes;
Keep them in the midst of your heart.
22 For they are life to those who find them
And healing to all his flesh.
23 Guard your heart with all diligence,
For from it *flow* the springs of life.
24 Put away from you a perverse mouth
And put devious lips far from you.

Matthew 16:1–28

16 And the Pharisees and Sadducees
came, and testing Him, they asked
Him to show them a sign from heaven. 2 But
He replied to them, "When it is evening, you
say, '*It will be* fair weather, for the sky is red.'
3 And in the morning, '*There will be* a storm
today, for the sky is red and threatening.' Do
you know how to discern the appearance of
the sky, but cannot *discern* the signs of the
times? 4 An evil and adulterous generation
eagerly seeks for a sign; and a sign will not
be given it, except the sign of Jonah." And
He left them and went away.
5 And coming to the other side *of the sea*,
the disciples had forgotten to bring bread.
6 And Jesus said to them, "Watch out and
beware of the leaven of the Pharisees and
Sadducees." 7 Now they *began to* discuss
this among themselves, saying, "*He said
that* because we did not bring bread." 8 But
Jesus, aware of this, said, "You men of little
faith, why do you discuss among your-
selves that you have no bread? 9 Do you
not yet understand or remember the five
loaves of the five thousand, and how many
baskets *full* you picked up? 10 Or the seven
loaves of the four thousand, and how many
large baskets *full* you picked up? 11 How
is it that you do not understand that I did
not speak to you concerning bread? But
beware of the leaven of the Pharisees and
Sadducees." 12 Then they understood that
He did not say to beware of the leaven of
bread, but of the teaching of the Pharisees
and Sadducees.
13 Now when Jesus came into the district
of Caesarea Philippi, He was asking His dis-
ciples, saying, "Who do people say that the
Son of Man is?" 14 And they said, "Some *say*
John the Baptist; and others, Elijah; but still
others, Jeremiah, or one of the prophets."
15 He *said to them, "But who do you say
that I am?" 16 And Simon Peter answered
and said, "You are the Christ, the Son of the
living God." 17 And Jesus answered and said
to him, "Blessed are you, Simon Bar-Jonah,
because flesh and blood did not reveal *this*
to you, but My Father who is in heaven.
18 And I also say to you that you are Peter,
and upon this rock I will build My church;
and the gates of Hades will not overpower
it. 19 I will give you the keys of the kingdom
of heaven; and whatever you bind on earth
shall have been bound in heaven, and
whatever you loose on earth shall have been
loosed in heaven." 20 Then He warned the
disciples that they should tell no one that
He was the Christ.
21 From that time Jesus began to show
His disciples that He must go to Jerusalem,
and suffer many things from the elders and
chief priests and scribes, and be killed, and
be raised up on the third day. 22 And Peter
took Him aside and began to rebuke Him,
saying, "God forbid *it*, Lord! This shall never
happen to You." 23 But He turned and said
to Peter, "Get behind Me, Satan! You are
a stumbling block to Me; for you are not
setting your mind on God's interests, but
man's."
24 Then Jesus said to His disciples, "If
anyone wishes to come after Me, let him
deny himself, and take up his cross and
follow Me. 25 For whoever wishes to save
his life will lose it; but whoever loses his
life for My sake will find it. 26 For what will
it profit a man if he gains the whole world
and forfeits his soul? Or what will a man

give in exchange for his soul? 27 For the Son of Man is going to come in the glory of His Father with His angels, and WILL THEN REPAY EACH ONE ACCORDING TO HIS DEEDS.

28 "Truly I say to you, there are some of those who are standing here who will not taste death until they see the Son of Man coming in His kingdom."

JANUARY 26

Exodus 1:1–2:25

1 Now these are the names of the sons of Israel who came to Egypt with Jacob; they came each one with his household: 2 Reuben, Simeon, Levi, and Judah; 3 Issachar, Zebulun, and Benjamin; 4 Dan and Naphtali, Gad and Asher. 5 And all the persons who came from the loins of Jacob were seventy in number, but Joseph was *already* in Egypt. 6 Then Joseph died, and all his brothers and all that generation. 7 But the sons of Israel were fruitful and increased and multiplied and became exceedingly mighty, so that the land was filled with them.

8 And a new king arose over Egypt, who did not know Joseph. 9 And he said to his people, "Behold, the people of the sons of Israel are more and mightier than we. 10 Come, let us deal wisely with them, lest they multiply and it be in the event of war, that they also join themselves to those who hate us and fight against us and go up from the land." 11 So they appointed taskmasters over them to afflict them with hard labors. And they built for Pharaoh storage cities, Pithom and Raamses. 12 But the more they afflicted them, the more they multiplied and the more they spread out, so that they were in dread of the sons of Israel. 13 So the Egyptians brutally compelled the sons of Israel to slave labor; 14 and they made their lives bitter with hard slave labor in mortar and bricks and in all *kinds* of slave labor in the field, all their slave labor which they brutally compelled them to do.

15 Then the king of Egypt spoke to the Hebrew midwives, one of whom was named Shiphrah and the other was named Puah; 16 and he said, "When you are helping the Hebrew women to give birth and see *them* upon the birthstool, if it is a son, then you shall put him to death; but if it is a daughter, then she shall live." 17 But the midwives feared God and did not do as the king of Egypt had spoken to them, but let the boys live. 18 So the king of Egypt called for the midwives and said to them, "Why have you done this thing, and let the boys live?" 19 Then the midwives said to Pharaoh, "Because the Hebrew women are not as the Egyptian women; for they are vigorous and give birth before the midwife can come to them." 20 So God was good to the midwives, and the people multiplied and became very mighty. 21 Now it happened that because the midwives feared God, He made households for them. 22 And Pharaoh commanded all his people, saying, "Every son who is born you are to cast into the Nile, and every daughter you are to keep alive."

2 And a man from the house of Levi went and took a daughter of Levi *as a wife.* 2 And the woman conceived and bore a son; and she saw that he was beautiful, so she hid him for three months. 3 But she could not hide him any longer. So she took for him an ark of papyrus reeds and covered it over with tar and pitch. Then she put the child into it and put *it* among the reeds by the bank of the Nile. 4 And his sister stood at a distance to know what would be done to him.

5 And the daughter of Pharaoh came down to bathe at the Nile, with her young women walking alongside the Nile; and she saw the ark among the reeds and sent her maidservant, and she took it *to her.* 6 Then she opened *it* and saw the child. And behold, *the* boy was crying. And she had pity on him and said, "This is one of the Hebrews' children." 7 Then his sister said to Pharaoh's daughter, "Shall I go and call a nurse for you from the Hebrew women that she may nurse the child for you?" 8 And Pharaoh's daughter said to her, "Go." So the girl went and called the child's mother. 9 Then Pharaoh's daughter said to her, "Take this child away and nurse him for me, and I will give *you* your wages." So the woman took the child and nursed him. 10 And the child grew, and she brought him to Pharaoh's daughter, and he became her son. And she named him Moses and said, "Because I drew him out of the water."

11 Now it happened in those days, that
Moses had grown up. And he went out to
his brothers and looked on their hard labors.
And he saw an Egyptian striking a Hebrew,
one of his brothers. 12 So he turned this way
and that, and he saw that there was no one
around. So he struck down the Egyptian and
hid him in the sand. 13 Then he went out
the next day, and behold, two Hebrews were
struggling with each other; and he said to
the wicked one, "Why are you striking your
companion?" 14 But he said, "Who made you
a ruler or a judge over us? Are you intending
to kill me as you killed the Egyptian?" Then
Moses was afraid and said, "Surely the
matter has become known." 15 And Pharaoh
heard of this matter, so he sought to kill
Moses. But Moses fled from the presence
of Pharaoh and settled in the land of Midian,
and he sat down by a well. 16 Now the priest
of Midian had seven daughters; and they
came and drew water and filled the troughs
to give *water* to their father's flock to drink.
17 Then the shepherds came and drove them
away, but Moses rose up and saved them and
gave *water* to their flock to drink. 18 Then
they came to Reuel their father, and he said,
"Why have you come *back* so soon today?"
19 So they said, "An Egyptian delivered us
from the hand of the shepherds, and he
actually even drew the water for us and
gave *water* to the flock to drink." 20 And he
said to his daughters, "Where is he then?
Why is it that you have left the man behind?
Call him so that he may eat bread." 21 And
Moses was willing to settle down with the
man, and he gave his daughter Zipporah to
Moses. 22 Then she gave birth to a son, and
he named him Gershom, for he said, "I have
been a sojourner in a foreign land."

23 Now it happened in *the course of* those
many days that the king of Egypt died. And
the sons of Israel sighed because of the
slavery, and they cried out; and their cry for
help because of *their* slavery rose up to God.
24 So God heard their groaning; and God
remembered His covenant with Abraham,
Isaac, and Jacob. 25 And God saw the sons of
Israel, and God knew *them.*

Psalm 15:1–5

1 O Yahweh, who may sojourn
in Your tent?
Who may dwell on Your
holy mountain?
2 He who walks blamelessly, and
works righteousness,
And speaks truth in his heart.
3 He does not slander with his tongue,
Nor does evil to his neighbor,
Nor takes up a reproach
against his friend;
4 In whose eyes a reprobate is despised,
But who honors those
who fear Yahweh;
He swears to his own hurt
and does not change;
5 He does not put out his
money at interest,
Nor does he take a bribe
against the innocent.
He who does these things
will never be shaken.

Proverbs 4:25–27

25 Let your eyes look directly ahead
And *even* let your eyelids be fixed
straight in front of you.
26 Watch the track of your feet
And all your ways will be established.
27 Do not turn to the right nor to the left;
Turn your foot from evil.

Matthew 17:1–27

17 And six days later Jesus *brought with
Him Peter and James and John his
brother, and *led them up on a high moun-
tain by themselves. 2 And He was transfig-
ured before them; and His face shone like
the sun, and His garments became as white
as light. 3 And behold, Moses and Elijah
appeared to them, talking with Him. 4 And
Peter answered and said to Jesus, "Lord, it
is good for us to be here; if You wish, I will
make three booths here, one for You, and
one for Moses, and one for Elijah." 5 While
he was still speaking, behold, a bright cloud
overshadowed them, and behold, a voice
out of the cloud said, "This is My beloved
Son, with whom I am well-pleased; listen to
Him!" 6 And when the disciples heard *this,*
they fell on their faces and were terrified.
7 And Jesus came to *them* and touched them
and said, "Get up, and do not be afraid."
8 And lifting up their eyes, they saw no one
except Jesus Himself alone.

9 And as they were coming down from the
mountain, Jesus commanded them, saying,
"Tell the vision to no one until the Son of
Man has risen from the dead." 10 And His

disciples asked Him, saying, "Why then
do the scribes say that Elijah must come
first?" 11 And He answered and said, "Elijah
is coming and will restore all things; 12 but
I say to you that Elijah already came, and
they did not recognize him, but did to him
whatever they wished. So also the Son
of Man is going to suffer at their hands."
13 Then the disciples understood that He
had spoken to them about John the Baptist.

14 And when they came to the crowd, a
man came up to Jesus, falling on his knees
before Him and saying, 15 "Lord, have mercy
on my son, for he has seizures and suffers
terribly; for he often falls into the fire and
often into the water. 16 And I brought him
to Your disciples, and they could not cure
him." 17 And Jesus answered and said, "O you
unbelieving and perverse generation, how
long shall I be with you? How long shall I put
up with you? Bring him here to Me." 18 And
Jesus rebuked him, and the demon came out
of him, and the boy was cured at once.

19 Then the disciples came to Jesus pri-
vately and said, "Why could we not cast it
out?" 20 And He *said to them, "Because of
your little faith; for truly I say to you, if you
have faith the size of a mustard seed, you
will say to this mountain, 'Move from here
to there,' and it will move; and nothing will
be impossible to you. 21 [But this kind does
not go out except by prayer and fasting."]

22 And while they were gathering together
in Galilee, Jesus said to them, "The Son of
Man is going to be delivered into the hands
of men; 23 and they will kill Him, and He will
be raised on the third day." And they were
deeply grieved.

24 Now when they came to Capernaum,
those who collected the two-drachma *tax*
came to Peter and said, "Does your teacher
not pay the two-drachma *tax*?" 25 He *said,
"Yes." And when he came into the house,
Jesus spoke to him first, saying, "What do
you think, Simon? From whom do the kings
of the earth collect tolls or taxes, from their
sons or from strangers?" 26 And when Peter
said, "From strangers," Jesus said to him,
"Then the sons are exempt. 27 However,
so that we do not offend them, go to the
sea and throw in a hook, and take the first
fish that comes up; and when you open its
mouth, you will find a stater. Take that and
give it to them for Me and you."

JANUARY 27

Exodus 3:1–4:31

3 Now Moses was pasturing the flock of
Jethro his father-in-law, the priest of
Midian; and he led the flock to the west
side of the wilderness and came to Horeb,
the mountain of God. 2 And the angel of
Yahweh appeared to him in a blazing fire
from the midst of the bush; and he looked,
and behold, the bush was burning with
fire, yet the bush was not consumed. 3 So
Moses said, "I must turn aside now and
see this marvelous sight. Why is the bush
not burned up?" 4 And Yahweh saw that
he turned aside to look, so God called to
him from the midst of the bush and said,
"Moses, Moses!" And he said, "Here I am."
5 Then He said, "Do not come near here.
Remove your sandals from your feet, for
the place on which you are standing is
holy ground." 6 He said also, "I am the
God of your father, the God of Abraham,
the God of Isaac, and the God of Jacob."
Then Moses hid his face, for he was afraid
to look at God.

7 And Yahweh said, "I have surely seen
the affliction of My people who are in Egypt,
and I have heard their cry because of their
taskmasters, for I know their sufferings. 8 So
I have come down to deliver them from the
hand of the Egyptians and to bring them up
from that land to a good and spacious land,
to a land flowing with milk and honey, to the
place of the Canaanite and the Hittite and
the Amorite and the Perizzite and the Hivite
and the Jebusite. 9 So now, behold, the cry
of the sons of Israel has come to Me; and I
have also seen the oppression with which
the Egyptians are oppressing them. 10 So
now, come and I will send you to Pharaoh,
and so you shall bring My people, the sons
of Israel, out of Egypt." 11 But Moses said to
God, "Who am I, that I should go to Pharaoh,
and that I should bring the sons of Israel out
of Egypt?" 12 And He said, "Certainly I will
be with you, and this shall be the sign to you
that it is I who have sent you: when you have
brought the people out of Egypt, you shall
serve God at this mountain."

13 Then Moses said to God, "Behold, I am
about to come to the sons of Israel, and I
will say to them, 'The God of your fathers
has sent me to you.' And they will say to
me, 'What is His name?' What shall I say
to them?" 14 And God said to Moses, "I AM
WHO I AM"; and He said, "Thus you shall
say to the sons of Israel, 'I AM has sent me
to you.'" 15 And God furthermore said to
Moses, "Thus you shall say to the sons of
Israel, 'Yahweh, the God of your fathers, the
God of Abraham, the God of Isaac, and the
God of Jacob, has sent me to you.' This is
My name forever, and this is My memorial-
name from generation to generation. 16 Go
and gather the elders of Israel together
and say to them, 'Yahweh, the God of your
fathers, the God of Abraham, Isaac, and
Jacob, has appeared to me, saying, "I indeed
care about you and what has been done to
you in Egypt. 17 So I said, I will bring you up
out of the affliction of Egypt to the land of
the Canaanite and the Hittite and the Amor-
ite and the Perizzite and the Hivite and the
Jebusite, to a land flowing with milk and
honey."' 18 And they will listen to your voice;
and you with the elders of Israel will come
to the king of Egypt, and you *all* will say to
him, 'Yahweh, the God of the Hebrews, has
met with us. So now, please, let us go a three
days' journey into the wilderness, that we
may sacrifice to Yahweh our God.' 19 But I
know that the king of Egypt will not give you
permission to go, except by a strong hand.
20 So I will stretch out My hand and strike
Egypt with all My wondrous deeds which I
shall do in the midst of it; and after that he
will let you go. 21 And I will give this people
favor in the sight of the Egyptians; and it
shall be that when you go, you will not go
empty. 22 But *every* woman shall ask of her
neighbor and of the woman who lives in her
house, for articles of silver and articles of
gold, and clothing; and you will put them
on your sons and daughters. Thus you will
plunder the Egyptians."

4 Then Moses answered and said, "What
if they will not believe me and will
not listen to my voice? For they may say,
'Yahweh has not appeared to you.'" 2 And
Yahweh said to him, "What is this in your
hand?" And he said, "A staff." 3 Then He
said, "Throw it on the ground." So he threw
it on the ground, and it became a serpent;
and Moses fled from it. 4 And Yahweh said
to Moses, "Stretch out your hand and grasp
it by its tail"—so he stretched out his hand
and took hold of it, and it became a staff
in his hand— 5 "that they may believe that
Yahweh, the God of their fathers, the God
of Abraham, the God of Isaac, and the God
of Jacob, has appeared to you."

6 And Yahweh furthermore said to him,
"Now put your hand into your bosom." So
he put his hand into his bosom; then he took
it out, and behold, his hand was leprous like
snow. 7 Then He said, "Return your hand
into your bosom." So he returned his hand
into his bosom, and when he took it out
of his bosom, behold, it returned *to being*
like *the rest of* his flesh. 8 "And so it will be,
if they will not believe you or listen to the
witness of the first sign, they may believe
the witness of this last sign. 9 But if it will
be that they will not believe even these two
signs and that they will not listen to your
voice, then you shall take some water from
the Nile and pour it on the dry land; and
the water which you take from the Nile will
become blood on the dry land."

10 Then Moses said to Yahweh, "Please,
Lord, I have never been a man of words,
neither recently nor in time past, nor since
You have spoken to Your slave; for I am *one*
with a hard mouth and a hard tongue."
11 And Yahweh said to him, "Who has made
man's mouth? Or who makes *him* mute or
deaf, or seeing or blind? Is it not I, Yahweh?
12 So now, go, and I, even I, will be with
your mouth and will instruct you what you
shall speak." 13 But he said, "Please, Lord,
send now *the message* by whomever You
will." 14 Then the anger of Yahweh burned
against Moses, and He said, "Is there not
your brother Aaron the Levite? I know
that he can certainly speak. And moreover,
behold, he is coming out to meet you. And
he will see you and be glad in his heart.
15 And you are to speak to him and put the
words in his mouth; and I, even I, will be
with your mouth and with his mouth, and
I will instruct you in what you shall do.
16 Moreover, he shall speak for you to the
people; and he will become as a mouth for
you, and you will become as God to him.
17 And you shall take in your hand this staff,
with which you shall do the signs."

18 Then Moses went and returned to
Jethro his father-in-law and said to him,

"Please, let me go, that I may return to my
brothers who are in Egypt and see if they
are still alive." And Jethro said to Moses,
"Go in peace." 19 And Yahweh said to Moses
in Midian, "Go, return to Egypt, for all the
men who were seeking your life are dead."
20 So Moses took his wife and his sons and
mounted them on a donkey and returned to
the land of Egypt. Moses also took the staff
of God in his hand.
21 And Yahweh said to Moses, "When
you go to return to Egypt, see *to it* that all
the miraculous wonders which I have put
in your hand, that you do them before
Pharaoh; but as for Me, I will harden his
heart with strength so that he will not
let the people go. 22 Then you shall say to
Pharaoh, 'Thus says Yahweh, "Israel is My
son, My firstborn. 23 So I said to you, 'Let My
son go that he may serve Me'; but you have
refused to let him go. Behold, I will kill your
son, your firstborn."'"
24 Now it happened at the lodging place
on the way that Yahweh encountered him
and sought to put him to death. 25 Then
Zipporah took a flint and cut off her son's
foreskin and touched his feet with it, and
she said, "You are indeed a bridegroom of
blood to me!" 26 So He let him alone. At
that time she said, "*You are* a bridegroom of
blood" with reference to the circumcision.
27 Then Yahweh said to Aaron, "Go to meet
Moses in the wilderness." So he went and
encountered him at the mountain of God
and kissed him. 28 And Moses told Aaron
all the words of Yahweh with which He
had sent him, and all the signs that He had
commanded him *to do*. 29 Then Moses and
Aaron went and gathered all the elders of
the sons of Israel; 30 and Aaron spoke all the
words which Yahweh had spoken to Moses.
He then did the signs in the sight of the
people. 31 So the people believed; and they
heard that Yahweh cared about the sons of
Israel and that He had seen their affliction.
So they bowed low and worshiped.

Psalm 16:1–6

1 Keep me, O God, for I take refuge in You.
2 *O my soul,* you have said to
Yahweh, "You are my Lord;
I have no good without You."
3 As for the saints who are in the earth,
They are the majestic ones in
whom is all my delight.
4 The pains of those who have bartered
for another *god* will be multiplied;
I shall not pour out their drink
offerings of blood,
Nor will I take their names
upon my lips.

5 Yahweh is the portion of my
inheritance and my cup;
You support my lot.
6 The lines have fallen to me
in pleasant places;
Indeed, my inheritance is
beautiful to me.

Proverbs 5:1–6

5 My son, pay attention to my wisdom,
Incline your ear to my discernment;
2 That you may keep discretion
And that your lips may
guard knowledge.
3 For the lips of a strange
woman drip honey
And smoother than oil is
her speech;
4 But her end is bitter as wormwood,
Sharp as a two-edged sword.
5 Her feet go down to death,
Her steps take hold of Sheol,
6 Lest she watch the path of life;
Her tracks are unstable, she
does not know *it*.

Matthew 18:1–20

18 At that time the disciples came to
Jesus and said, "Who then is greatest
in the kingdom of heaven?" 2 And He called
a child to Himself and set him before them,
3 and said, "Truly I say to you, unless you are
converted and become like children, you
will never enter the kingdom of heaven.
4 Whoever therefore will humble himself as
this child, he is the greatest in the kingdom
of heaven. 5 And whoever receives one
such child in My name receives Me; 6 but
whoever causes one of these little ones who
believe in Me to stumble, it is better for him
that a heavy millstone be hung around his
neck, and that he be drowned in the depth
of the sea.
7 "Woe to the world because of *its*
stumbling blocks! For it is inevitable that
stumbling blocks come; nevertheless, woe
to that man through whom the stumbling
block comes!

8 "And if your hand or your foot causes you to stumble, cut it off and throw it from you; it is better for you to enter life crippled or lame, than, having two hands or two feet, to be cast into the eternal fire. 9 And if your eye causes you to stumble, tear it out and throw it from you. It is better for you to enter life with one eye, than, having two eyes, to be cast into the fiery hell.

10 "See that you do not despise one of these little ones, for I say to you that their angels in heaven continually see the face of My Father who is in heaven. 11 [For the Son of Man has come to save that which was lost.]

12 "What do you think? If any man has one hundred sheep, and one of them has gone astray, does he not leave the ninety-nine on the mountains and go and search for the one that is straying? 13 And if it turns out that he finds it, truly I say to you, he rejoices over it more than over the ninety-nine which have not gone astray. 14 In this way, it is not the will of your Father who is in heaven that one of these little ones perish.

15 "Now if your brother sins, go and show him his fault, between you and him alone; if he listens to you, you have won your brother. 16 But if he does not listen *to you*, take one or two more with you, so that BY THE MOUTH OF TWO OR THREE WITNESSES EVERY FACT MAY BE CONFIRMED. 17 And if he refuses to listen to them, tell it to the church; and if he refuses to listen even to the church, let him be to you as the Gentile and the tax collector. 18 Truly I say to you, whatever you bind on earth shall have been bound in heaven; and whatever you loose on earth shall have been loosed in heaven.

19 "Again I say to you, that if two of you agree on earth about anything that they may ask, it shall be done for them by My Father who is in heaven. 20 For where two or three have gathered together in My name, I am there in their midst."

JANUARY 28

Exodus 5:1–6:30

5 And afterward Moses and Aaron came and said to Pharaoh, "Thus says Yahweh, the God of Israel, 'Let My people go that they may celebrate a feast to Me in the wilderness.'" 2 But Pharaoh said, "Who is Yahweh that I should listen to His voice to let Israel go? I do not know Yahweh, and also, I will not let Israel go." 3 Then they said, "The God of the Hebrews has met with us. Please, let us go a three days' journey into the wilderness that we may sacrifice to Yahweh our God, lest He confront us with pestilence or with the sword." 4 But the king of Egypt said to them, "Moses and Aaron, why do you draw the people away from their work? Get *back* to your hard labors!" 5 And Pharaoh said, "Look, the people of the land are now many, and you would have them cease from their hard labors!" 6 So on that day Pharaoh commanded the taskmasters over the people and their foremen, saying, 7 "You are no longer to give the people straw to make brick as previously; let them go and gather straw for themselves. 8 But the quota of bricks which they were making previously, you shall set upon them; you are not to reduce any of it. Because they are lazy, therefore they are crying out, 'Let us go and sacrifice to our God.' 9 Let *their* slavery be hard on the men, and let them work at it so that they will have no regard for false words."

10 So the taskmasters of the people and their foremen went out and spoke to the people, saying, "Thus says Pharaoh, 'I am not going to give you *any* straw. 11 You go *and* get straw for yourselves wherever you can find *it*, but no amount of your slave labor will be reduced.'" 12 So the people scattered through all the land of Egypt to gather stubble for straw. 13 And the taskmasters were pressing them, saying, "Complete your work quota, the daily amount, just as when there was straw." 14 Moreover, the foremen of the sons of Israel, whom Pharaoh's taskmasters had set over them, were beaten and were asked, "Why have you not completed your required amount either yesterday or today in making brick as previously?"

15 Then the foremen of the sons of Israel came and cried out to Pharaoh, saying, "Why do you deal this way with your slaves? 16 There is no straw given to your slaves, yet

they keep saying to us, 'Make bricks!' And
behold, your slaves are being beaten; but it
is the sin of your *own* people." 17 But he said,
"You are lazy—lazy! Therefore you say, 'Let
us go *and* sacrifice to Yahweh.' 18 So now,
go *and* labor; but straw will not be given
to you, yet you must deliver the quota of
bricks." 19 Then the foremen of the sons of
Israel saw that they were in trouble because
they were told, "You must not reduce your
daily amount of bricks." 20 When they left
Pharaoh's presence, they confronted Moses
and Aaron, standing there to meet them.
21 And they said to them, "May Yahweh look
upon you and judge, for you have made us
a foul smell in Pharaoh's sight and in the
sight of his servants, to put a sword in their
hand to kill us."

22 Then Moses returned to Yahweh and
said, "O Lord, why have You brought harm
to this people? Why did You ever send me?
23 Ever since I came to Pharaoh to speak
in Your name, he has done harm to this
people, and You have not delivered Your
people at all."

6 Then Yahweh said to Moses, "Now you
shall see what I will do to Pharaoh; for
by a strong hand he will let them go, and
by a strong hand he will drive them out of
his land."

2 God spoke further to Moses and said
to him, "I am Yahweh; 3 and I appeared
to Abraham, Isaac, and Jacob, as God
Almighty, but *by* My name, Yahweh, I was
not known to them. 4 And I also established
My covenant with them, to give them the
land of Canaan, the land in which they
sojourned. 5 Furthermore I have heard
the groaning of the sons of Israel because
the Egyptians are holding them in slavery,
and I have remembered My covenant.
6 Say, therefore, to the sons of Israel, 'I
am Yahweh, and I will bring you out from
under the hard labors of the Egyptians, and
I will deliver you from their slavery. I will
also redeem you with an outstretched arm
and with great judgments. 7 Then I will take
you for My people, and I will be your God;
and you shall know that I am Yahweh your
God, who brought you out from under the
hard labors of the Egyptians. 8 And I will
bring you to the land which I swore to give
to Abraham, to Isaac, and to Jacob, and I
will give it to you *for* a possession; I am
Yahweh.'" 9 So Moses spoke thus to the sons
of Israel, but they did not listen to Moses
on account of *their* weakness of spirit and
hard slavery.

10 Now Yahweh spoke to Moses, saying,
11 "Come, tell Pharaoh king of Egypt to
let the sons of Israel go out of his land."
12 But Moses spoke before Yahweh, say-
ing, "Behold, the sons of Israel have not
listened to me; how then will Pharaoh
listen to me, for I am of uncircumcised
lips?" 13 Then Yahweh spoke to Moses and
to Aaron and gave them a command for
the sons of Israel and for Pharaoh king of
Egypt, to bring the sons of Israel out of the
land of Egypt.

14 These are the heads of their fathers'
households.

The sons of Reuben, Israel's firstborn:
Hanoch and Pallu, Hezron and Carmi;
these are the families of Reuben.
15 The sons of Simeon:
Jemuel and Jamin and Ohad and
Jachin and Zohar and Shaul the son
of a Canaanite woman; these are the
families of Simeon.
16 These are the names of the sons of
Levi according to their generations:
Gershon and Kohath and Merari;
and the years of Levi's life were 137
years.
17 The sons of Gershon:
Libni and Shimei, according to their
families.
18 The sons of Kohath:
Amram and Izhar and Hebron and
Uzziel; and the years of Kohath's life
were 133 years.
19 The sons of Merari:
Mahli and Mushi.
These are the families of the Levites
according to their generations.
20 And Amram took his father's sister
Jochebed as a wife, and she bore him
Aaron and Moses; and the years of
Amram's life were 137 years.
21 The sons of Izhar:
Korah and Nepheg and Zichri.
22 The sons of Uzziel:
Mishael and Elzaphan and Sithri.
23 And Aaron took Elisheba, the
daughter of Amminadab, the sister
of Nahshon, as a wife, and she bore
him Nadab and Abihu, Eleazar and
Ithamar.

24 The sons of Korah:
Assir and Elkanah and Abiasaph; these are the families of the Korahites.
25 And Aaron's son Eleazar took one of
the daughters of Putiel as a wife, and
she bore him Phinehas. These are the
heads of the fathers' *households* of the
Levites according to their families. 26 It
was *the same* Aaron and Moses to whom
Yahweh said, "Bring out the sons of Israel
from the land of Egypt according to their
hosts." 27 They were the ones who spoke
to Pharaoh king of Egypt to bring out the
sons of Israel from Egypt; it was *the same*
Moses and Aaron.

28 Now it happened on the day when
Yahweh spoke to Moses in the land of Egypt,
29 that Yahweh spoke to Moses, saying,
"I am Yahweh; speak to Pharaoh king of
Egypt all that I am speaking to you." 30 But
Moses said before Yahweh, "Behold, I am of
uncircumcised lips; how then will Pharaoh
listen to me?"

Psalm 16:7–11

7 I will bless Yahweh who
has counseled me;
Indeed, my mind instructs
me in the night.
8 I have set Yahweh continually
before me;
Because He is at my right hand,
I will not be shaken.
9 Therefore my heart is glad
and my glory rejoices;
My flesh also will dwell securely.
10 For You will not forsake
my soul to Sheol;
You will not give Your Holy One
over to see corruption.
11 You will make known to
me the path of life;
In Your presence is fullness of joy;
In Your right hand there are
pleasures forever.

Proverbs 5:7–14

7 So now, *my* sons, listen to me
And do not turn away from
the words of my mouth.
8 Keep your way far from her
And do not go near the
door of her house,
9 Lest you give your splendor to others
And your years to the cruel one;
10 Lest strangers be satisfied
by your strength
And by your painful labor,
those in the house of a foreigner;
11 And you groan at your end,
When your flesh and your
body are consumed;
12 And you say, "How I have
hated discipline!
And my heart spurned reproof!
13 "I have not listened to the voice
of my instructors,
And I have not inclined my
ear to my teachers!
14 "I was almost in utter ruin
In the midst of the assembly
and congregation."

Matthew 18:21–35

21 Then Peter came and said to Him,
"Lord, how often shall my brother sin
against me and I forgive him? Up to seven
times?" 22 Jesus *said to him, "I do not say
to you, up to seven times, but up to seventy
times seven.

23 "For this reason the kingdom of heaven
may be compared to a king who wished to
settle accounts with his slaves. 24 When he
had begun to settle *them*, one who owed
him ten thousand talents was brought to
him. 25 But since he did not have *the means*
to repay, his lord commanded him to be
sold, along with his wife and children and
all that he had, and repayment to be made.
26 Therefore, the slave fell *to the ground* and
was prostrating himself before him, saying,
'Have patience with me and I will repay you
everything.' 27 And feeling compassion, the
lord of that slave released him and forgave
him the debt. 28 But that slave went out and
found one of his fellow slaves who owed
him one hundred denarii; and he seized
him and *began to* choke *him*, saying, 'Pay
back what you owe.' 29 So, his fellow slave
fell *to the ground* and was pleading with
him, saying, 'Have patience with me and
I will repay you.' 30 But he was unwilling
and went and threw him in prison until he
should pay back what was owed. 31 So, when
his fellow slaves saw what had happened,
they were deeply grieved and came and
reported to their lord all that had happened.
32 Then summoning him, his lord *said to
him, 'You wicked slave, I forgave you all
that debt because you pleaded with me.

33 Should you not also have had mercy on your fellow slave, in the same way that I had mercy on you?' 34 And his lord, moved with anger, handed him over to the torturers until he should repay all that was owed him. 35 My heavenly Father will also do the same to you, if each of you does not forgive his brother from your hearts."

Read the Scripture, not only as a history, but as a love-letter sent to you from God.

— THOMAS WATSON

JANUARY 29

Exodus 7:1–8:32

7 Then Yahweh said to Moses, "See, I set you *as* God to Pharaoh, and your brother Aaron shall be your prophet. 2 You shall speak all that I command you, and your brother Aaron shall speak to Pharaoh that he let the sons of Israel go out of his land. 3 But I will harden Pharaoh's heart with stiffness that I may multiply My signs and My wonders in the land of Egypt. 4 But Pharaoh will not listen to you. And I will set My hand upon Egypt and bring out My hosts, My people the sons of Israel, from the land of Egypt by great judgments. 5 Then the Egyptians shall know that I am Yahweh, when I stretch out My hand against Egypt and bring out the sons of Israel from their midst." 6 So Moses and Aaron did *it*; as Yahweh commanded them, thus they did. 7 Now Moses was eighty years old and Aaron eighty-three years old, when they spoke to Pharaoh.

8 And Yahweh spoke to Moses and Aaron, saying, 9 "When Pharaoh speaks to you, saying, 'Work a miraculous wonder,' then you shall say to Aaron, 'Take your staff and throw *it* down before Pharaoh, *that* it may become a serpent.'" 10 So Moses and Aaron came to Pharaoh, and thus they did just as Yahweh had commanded; and Aaron threw his staff down before Pharaoh and his servants, and it became a serpent. 11 Then Pharaoh also called for the wise men and the sorcerers, and they also, the magicians of Egypt, did the same with their secret arts. 12 And each one threw down his staff, and they became serpents. But Aaron's staff swallowed up their staffs. 13 Yet Pharaoh's heart was hardened with strength, and he did not listen to them, as Yahweh had spoken.

14 Then Yahweh said to Moses, "Pharaoh's heart is hard with firmness; he refuses to let the people go. 15 Go to Pharaoh in the morning as he is going out to the water, and station yourself to meet him on the bank of the Nile; and you shall take in your hand the staff that was turned into a serpent. 16 And you shall say to him, 'Yahweh, the God of the Hebrews, sent me to you, saying, "Let My people go, that they may serve Me in the wilderness. But behold, you have not listened until now." 17 Thus says Yahweh, "By this you shall know that I am Yahweh: behold, I am about to strike the water that is in the Nile with the staff that is in my hand, and it will be turned to blood. 18 And the fish that are in the Nile will die, and the Nile will become foul, and the Egyptians will be weary of drinking water from the Nile."'" 19 Then Yahweh said to Moses, "Say to Aaron, 'Take your staff and stretch out your hand over the waters of Egypt, over their rivers, over their streams, and over their pools and over all their reservoirs of water, that they may become blood; and there will be blood throughout all the land of Egypt, both in *vessels of* wood and in *vessels of* stone.'"

20 So Moses and Aaron did thus, as Yahweh had commanded. And he raised up the staff and struck the water that *was* in the Nile, in the sight of Pharaoh and in the sight of his servants, and all the water that *was* in the Nile was turned to blood. 21 And the fish that *were* in the Nile died, and the Nile became foul, so that the Egyptians could not drink water from the Nile. And the blood was through all the land of Egypt. 22 Yet the magicians of Egypt did the same with their secret arts; and Pharaoh's heart

was hardened with strength, and he did not listen to them, as Yahweh had spoken. 23 Then Pharaoh turned and went into his house, and he did not set his heart even on this. 24 So all the Egyptians dug around the Nile for water to drink, for they could not drink of the water of the Nile. 25 And seven full days passed after Yahweh had struck the Nile.

8 Then Yahweh said to Moses, "Come to Pharaoh and say to him, 'Thus says Yahweh, "Let My people go, that they may serve Me. 2 But if you refuse to let *them* go, behold, I will smite your whole territory with frogs. 3 And the Nile will swarm with frogs, and they will go up and come into your house and into your bedroom and on your bed and into the houses of your servants and on your people and into your ovens and into your kneading bowls. 4 So the frogs will come up on you and on your people and on all your servants."'" 5 Then Yahweh said to Moses, "Say to Aaron, 'Stretch out your hand with your staff over the rivers, over the streams and over the pools, and cause the frogs to come up on the land of Egypt.'" 6 So Aaron stretched out his hand over the waters of Egypt, and the frogs came up and covered the land of Egypt. 7 And the magicians did the same with their secret arts; they caused the frogs to come up on the land of Egypt.

8 Then Pharaoh called for Moses and Aaron and said, "Entreat Yahweh that He may cause the frogs to depart from me and from my people; and I will let the people go, that they may sacrifice to Yahweh." 9 And Moses said to Pharaoh, "May the honor be yours to tell me: when shall I entreat for you and for your servants and for your people, that the frogs be cut off from you and your houses, *that* they may remain only in the Nile?"

10 Then he said, "Tomorrow." So he said, "*May it be* according to your word, that you may know that there is no one like Yahweh our God. 11 And the frogs will depart from you and your houses and your servants and your people; they will remain only in the Nile." 12 Then Moses and Aaron went out from Pharaoh, and Moses cried out to Yahweh concerning the frogs which He had set upon Pharaoh. 13 So Yahweh did according to the word of Moses, and the frogs died out of the houses, the courts, and the fields. 14 So they piled them in heaps, and the land became foul. 15 Then Pharaoh saw that there was relief, and he hardened his heart with firmness and did not listen to them, as Yahweh had spoken.

16 Then Yahweh said to Moses, "Say to Aaron, 'Stretch out your staff and strike the dust of the earth, that it may become gnats through all the land of Egypt.'" 17 And they did so; and Aaron stretched out his hand with his staff and struck the dust of the earth, and there were gnats on man and beast. All the dust of the earth became gnats through all the land of Egypt. 18 Then the magicians did the same with their secret arts in order to bring forth gnats, but they could not; so there were gnats on man and beast. 19 And the magicians said to Pharaoh, "This is the finger of God." But Pharaoh's heart was hardened with strength, and he did not listen to them, as Yahweh had spoken.

20 And Yahweh said to Moses, "Rise early in the morning and stand before Pharaoh as he comes out to the water, and you shall say to him, 'Thus says Yahweh, "Let My people go, that they may serve Me. 21 For if you do not let My people go, behold, I will send swarms of flies on you and on your servants and on your people and into your houses; and the houses of the Egyptians will be full of swarms of flies, and also the ground on which they *stand*. 22 But on that day I will make a distinction for the land of Goshen, where My people are living, so that no swarms of flies will be there, that you may know that I, Yahweh, am in the midst of the land. 23 And I will put a division between My people and your people. Tomorrow this sign will happen."'" 24 Then Yahweh did so. And there came heavy swarms of flies into the house of Pharaoh and the houses of his servants, and the land was laid waste because of the swarms of flies in all the land of Egypt.

25 And Pharaoh called for Moses and Aaron and said, "Go, sacrifice to your God within the land." 26 But Moses said, "It is not right to do so, for we will sacrifice to Yahweh our God what is an abomination to the Egyptians. If we sacrifice what is an abomination to the Egyptians before their eyes, will they not then stone us? 27 We must go a three days' journey into the wilderness and sacrifice to Yahweh our God as He says

to us." 28 And Pharaoh said, "I will let you go,
that you may sacrifice to Yahweh your God
in the wilderness; only you shall not go very
far away. Entreat for me." 29 Then Moses
said, "Behold, I am going out from you,
and I shall entreat Yahweh that the swarms
of flies may depart from Pharaoh, from his
servants, and from his people tomorrow;
only may Pharaoh not deal deceitfully again
in not letting the people go to sacrifice to
Yahweh."

30 So Moses went out from Pharaoh
and entreated Yahweh. 31 And Yahweh did
according to the word of Moses and caused
the swarms of flies to depart from Pharaoh,
from his servants, and from his people; not
one remained. 32 Then Pharaoh hardened
his heart with firmness this time also, and
he did not let the people go.

Psalm 17:1–7

1 Hear a righteous cause, O Yahweh,
give heed to my cry of lamentation;
Give ear to my prayer, which is
not from deceitful lips.
2 May my judgment come
from Your presence;
May Your eyes behold what is upright.
3 You have tested my heart;
You have visited *me* by night;
You have tried me and
You find nothing;
I have purposed that my mouth
will not transgress.
4 As for the deeds of men,
by the word of Your lips
I have kept from the paths
of the violent.
5 My steps have held fast to Your paths.
My footsteps have not stumbled.

6 I have called upon You, for You
will answer me, O God;
Incline Your ear to me, hear my speech.
7 Marvelously show Your
lovingkindnesses,
O Savior of those who take
refuge at Your right hand
From those who rise up *against them.*

Proverbs 5:15–20

15 Drink water from your own cistern
And fresh water from your own well.
16 Should your springs be
dispersed abroad,
Streams of water in the streets?
17 Let them be for you alone,
And not for strangers with you.
18 Let your fountain be blessed,
And be glad in the wife of your youth.
19 *As* a loving hind and a graceful doe,
Let her breasts satisfy you at all times;
Be intoxicated always with her love.
20 So why should you, my son, be
intoxicated with a strange woman
And embrace the bosom of
a foreign woman?

Matthew 19:1–30

19 Now it happened that when Jesus had
finished these words, He departed
from Galilee and came into the region of
Judea beyond the Jordan; 2 and large crowds
followed Him, and He healed them there.

3 And *some* Pharisees came to Jesus,
testing Him and saying, "Is it lawful *for a
man* to divorce his wife for any reason at
all?" 4 And He answered and said, "Have
you not read that He who created *them*
from the beginning MADE THEM MALE AND
FEMALE, 5 and said, 'FOR THIS REASON A MAN
SHALL LEAVE HIS FATHER AND MOTHER AND
BE JOINED TO HIS WIFE, AND THE TWO SHALL
BECOME ONE FLESH'? 6 So they are no longer
two, but one flesh. What therefore God
has joined together, let no man separate."
7 They *said to Him, "Why then did Moses
command to GIVE HER A CERTIFICATE OF
DIVORCE AND SEND *her* AWAY?" 8 He *said to
them, "Because of your hardness of heart
Moses permitted you to divorce your wives;
but from the beginning it has not been this
way. 9 And I say to you, whoever divorces
his wife, except for sexual immorality, and
marries another woman commits adultery."

10 The disciples *said to Him, "If the
relationship of the man with his wife is
like this, it is better not to marry." 11 But He
said to them, "Not all men *can* accept this
statement, but *only* those to whom it has
been given. 12 For there are eunuchs who
were born that way from their mother's
womb; and there are eunuchs who were
made eunuchs by men; and there are *also*
eunuchs who made themselves eunuchs for
the sake of the kingdom of heaven. He who
is able to accept *this,* let him accept *it.*"

13 Then *some* children were brought to
Him so that He might lay His hands on them
and pray; and the disciples rebuked them.

14 But Jesus said, "Let the children alone, and do not hinder them from coming to Me; for the kingdom of heaven belongs to such as these." 15 And after laying His hands on them, He departed from there.

16 And behold, someone came to Him and said, "Teacher, what good thing shall I do that I may have eternal life?" 17 And He said to him, "Why are you asking Me about what is good? There is *only* One who is good; but if you wish to enter into life, keep the commandments." 18 *Then* he *said to Him, "Which ones?" And Jesus said, "YOU SHALL NOT MURDER; YOU SHALL NOT COMMIT ADULTERY; YOU SHALL NOT STEAL; YOU SHALL NOT BEAR FALSE WITNESS; 19 HONOR YOUR FATHER AND MOTHER; and YOU SHALL LOVE YOUR NEIGHBOR AS YOURSELF." 20 The young man *said to Him, "All these things I have kept; what am I still lacking?" 21 Jesus said to him, "If you wish to be complete, go *and* sell your possessions and give to the poor, and you will have treasure in heaven; and come, follow Me." 22 But when the young man heard this statement, he went away grieving; for he was one who owned much property.

23 And Jesus said to His disciples, "Truly I say to you, it is hard for a rich man to enter the kingdom of heaven. 24 And again I say to you, it is easier for a camel to go through the eye of a needle, than for a rich man to enter the kingdom of God." 25 And when the disciples heard *this*, they were very astonished and said, "Then who can be saved?" 26 And looking at *them* Jesus said to them, "With people this is impossible, but with God all things are possible."

27 Then Peter answered and said to Him, "Behold, we have left everything and followed You; what then will there be for us?" 28 And Jesus said to them, "Truly I say to you, that you who have followed Me, in the regeneration when the Son of Man will sit on His glorious throne, you also shall sit upon twelve thrones, judging the twelve tribes of Israel. 29 And everyone who has left houses or brothers or sisters or father or mother or children or farms for My name's sake, will receive one hundred times as much, and will inherit eternal life. 30 But many *who are* first will be last; and *the* last, first.

JANUARY 30

Exodus 9:1–10:29

9 Then Yahweh said to Moses, "Come to Pharaoh and speak to him, 'Thus says Yahweh, the God of the Hebrews, "Let My people go, that they may serve Me. 2 For if you refuse to let *them* go and continue to hold them, 3 behold, the hand of Yahweh will come *with* a very heavy pestilence on your livestock which are in the field, on the horses, on the donkeys, on the camels, on the herds, and on the flocks. 4 But Yahweh will make a distinction between the livestock of Israel and the livestock of Egypt, so that nothing will die of all that belongs to the sons of Israel."'" 5 Yahweh also set a definite time, saying, "Tomorrow Yahweh will do this thing in the land." 6 So Yahweh did this thing on the next day, and all the livestock of Egypt died; but of the livestock of the sons of Israel, not one died. 7 And Pharaoh sent, and behold, there was not even one of the livestock of Israel dead. But the heart of Pharaoh was hardened with firmness, and he did not let the people go.

8 Then Yahweh said to Moses and Aaron, "Take for yourselves handfuls of soot from a kiln, and let Moses toss it toward the sky in the sight of Pharaoh. 9 And it will become fine dust over all the land of Egypt, and it will become boils breaking out with sores on man and beast through all the land of Egypt." 10 So they took the soot from the kiln and stood before Pharaoh; and Moses tossed it toward the sky, and it became boils breaking out with sores on man and beast. 11 And the magicians could not stand before Moses because of the boils, for the boils were on the magicians as well as on all the Egyptians. 12 And Yahweh hardened Pharaoh's heart with strength, and he did not listen to them, just as Yahweh had spoken to Moses.

13 And Yahweh said to Moses, "Rise up early in the morning and stand before Pharaoh, and you shall say to him, 'Thus says Yahweh, the God of the Hebrews, "Let My people go, that they may serve Me. 14 For this time I will send all My plagues against your

heart and amongst your servants and your
people, so that you may know that there is
no one like Me in all the earth. 15 For *if by*
now I had sent forth My hand and struck
you and your people with pestilence, you
would then have been wiped out from the
earth. 16 But, indeed, for this reason I have
caused you to stand, in order to show you
My power and in order to recount My name
through all the earth. 17 Still you exalt your-
self against My people by not letting them
go. 18 Behold, about this time tomorrow, I
will rain down very heavy hail, such as has
not been *seen* in Egypt from the day it was
founded until now. 19 So now, send, bring
your livestock and whatever you have in the
field to safety. Every man and beast that is
found in the field and is not brought home,
the hail will come down on them, and they
will die."'" 20 The one among the servants
of Pharaoh who feared the word of Yahweh
made his servants and his livestock flee into
the houses; 21 but he who did not consider
in his heart the word of Yahweh left his
servants and his livestock in the field.

22 Now Yahweh said to Moses, "Stretch
out your hand toward the sky, that there
may be hail on all the land of Egypt, on man
and on beast and on every plant of the field,
throughout the land of Egypt." 23 So Moses
stretched out his staff toward the sky, and
Yahweh gave forth thunder and hail, and
fire went down to the earth. And Yahweh
rained down hail on the land of Egypt. 24 So
there was hail, and fire flashing continually
in the midst of the hail, very heavy, such as
had not been in all the land of Egypt since
it became a nation. 25 And the hail struck
all that was in the field through all the land
of Egypt, from man to beast; the hail also
struck every plant of the field and shattered
every tree of the field. 26 Only in the land of
Goshen, where the sons of Israel *were*, there
was no hail.

27 Then Pharaoh sent and called for
Moses and Aaron and said to them, "I have
sinned this time; Yahweh is the righteous
one, and I and my people are the wicked
ones. 28 Entreat Yahweh, for God's thunder
and hail are too much; and I will let you
go, and you shall stay no longer." 29 And
Moses said to him, "As soon as I go out
of the city, I will spread out my hands to
Yahweh; the thunder will cease, and there
will be hail no longer, that you may know
that the earth is Yahweh's. 30 But as for you
and your servants, I know that you do not
yet fear Yahweh God." 31 (Now the flax and
the barley were struck down, for the barley
was in the ear and the flax was in bud. 32 But
the wheat and the spelt were not struck
down, for they are late-ripening.) 33 And
Moses went out of the city from Pharaoh
and spread out his hands to Yahweh; and
the thunder and the hail ceased, and rain
no longer poured on the earth. 34 But Pha-
raoh saw that the rain and the hail and the
thunder had ceased. So he sinned again and
hardened his heart with firmness, he and
his servants. 35 And Pharaoh's heart was
hardened with strength, and he did not let
the sons of Israel go, just as Yahweh had
spoken by the hand of Moses.

10 Then Yahweh said to Moses, "Come
to Pharaoh, for I have hardened his
heart and the heart of his servants with
firmness, that I may set these signs of Mine
among them, 2 and that you may recount in
the hearing of your son and of your grand-
son, how I dealt severely with the Egyptians,
and how I put My signs among them, that
you may know that I am Yahweh."

3 Then Moses and Aaron came to Pharaoh
and said to him, "Thus says Yahweh, the
God of the Hebrews, 'How long will you
refuse to humble yourself before Me? Let
My people go, that they may serve Me. 4 For
if you refuse to let My people go, behold,
tomorrow I will bring locusts into your
territory. 5 And they shall cover the surface
of the land, so that no one will be able to see
the land. They will also eat the rest of what
has escaped—what remains for you from
the hail—and they will eat every tree which
sprouts for you out of the field. 6 Then your
houses and the houses of all your servants
and the houses of all the Egyptians shall be
filled, *something* which neither your fathers
nor your grandfathers have seen, from the
day that they came upon the earth until this
day.'" And he turned and went out from
Pharaoh. 7 And Pharaoh's servants said to
him, "How long will this man be a snare
to us? Let the men go, that they may serve
Yahweh their God. Do you not yet know that
Egypt is destroyed?" 8 So Moses and Aaron
were brought back to Pharaoh, and he said
to them, "Go, serve Yahweh your God! Who
are the ones that are going?" 9 And Moses

said, "We shall go with our young and our
old; with our sons and our daughters, with
our flocks and our herds we shall go, for it
is a feast of Yahweh for us." 10 Then he said
to them, "Thus may Yahweh be with you, if
ever I let you and your little ones go! See,
for evil is on your faces. 11 Not so! Go now,
the men *among you*, and serve Yahweh, for
that is what you are seeking." So they were
driven out from Pharaoh's presence.

12 Then Yahweh said to Moses, "Stretch
out your hand over the land of Egypt for
the locusts, that they may come up on the
land of Egypt and eat every plant of the
land, all that the hail has left remaining."
13 So Moses stretched out his staff over
the land of Egypt, and Yahweh directed an
east wind on the land all that day and all
that night; *and when* it was morning, the
east wind brought the locusts. 14 And the
locusts came up over all the land of Egypt
and rested on all the territory of Egypt; *they*
were very heavy. There had never been so
many locusts, nor would there be so *many*
again. 15 For they covered the surface of the
whole land, so that the land was darkened;
and they ate every plant of the land and all
the fruit of the trees that the hail had left.
Thus nothing green was left on tree or plant
of the field through all the land of Egypt.
16 Then Pharaoh hurriedly called for Moses
and Aaron, and he said, "I have sinned
against Yahweh your God and against you.
17 So now, please forgive my sin only this
once and entreat Yahweh your God, that He
would only cause this death to depart from
me." 18 And he went out from Pharaoh and
entreated Yahweh. 19 So Yahweh changed
the wind to a very strong west wind which
took up the locusts and drove them into the
Red Sea; not one locust remained in all the
territory of Egypt. 20 But Yahweh hardened
Pharaoh's heart with strength, and he did
not let the sons of Israel go.

21 Then Yahweh said to Moses, "Stretch
out your hand toward the sky, that there
may be darkness over the land of Egypt,
even a darkness which may be felt." 22 So
Moses stretched out his hand toward the
sky, and there was thick darkness in all
the land of Egypt for three days. 23 They
did not see one another, nor did anyone
rise from his place for three days, but all
the sons of Israel had light in their *places of*
habitation. 24 Then Pharaoh called to Moses
and said, "Go, serve Yahweh; only let your
flocks and your herds be detained. Even
your little ones may go with you." 25 But
Moses said, "You must also let us have in
our hand sacrifices and burnt offerings, that
we may sacrifice *them* to Yahweh our God.
26 Therefore, our livestock too shall go with
us; not a hoof shall remain behind, for we
shall take some of them to serve Yahweh
our God. And until we come there, we
ourselves do not know with what we shall
serve Yahweh." 27 But Yahweh hardened
Pharaoh's heart with strength, and he was
not willing to let them go. 28 Then Pharaoh
said to him, "Get away from me! Beware, do
not see my face again, for in the day you see
my face you shall die!" 29 And Moses said,
"As you have spoken; I shall never see your
face again!"

Psalm 17:8–15

8 Keep me as the apple of the eye;
Hide me in the shadow of Your wings
9 From the wicked who devastate me,
My deadly enemies who surround me.
10 They have closed their unfeeling *heart*,
With their mouth they speak proudly.
11 They have now surrounded
us in our steps;
They set their eyes to cast *us*
down to the ground.
12 He is like a lion that is eager to tear,
And as a young lion lurking
in hiding places.

13 Arise, O Yahweh, confront
him, bring him low;
Protect my soul from the
wicked with Your sword,
14 From men with Your hand, O Yahweh,
From men of the world, whose
portion is in *this* life,
And whose belly You fill
with Your treasure;
They are satisfied with children,
And leave their excess to their infants.
15 As for me, I shall behold Your
face in righteousness;
I will be satisfied with Your
likeness when I awake.

Proverbs 5:21–23

21 For the ways of a man are before
the eyes of Yahweh,
And He watches all his tracks.

22 His own iniquities will capture
him *who is* the wicked one,
And with the cords of his sin
he will be held fast.
23 He will die for lack of discipline,
And in the abundance of his folly
he will stumble in intoxication.

Matthew 20:1–16

20 "For the kingdom of heaven is like a landowner who went out early in the morning to hire laborers for his vineyard. 2 Now when he had agreed with the laborers for a denarius for the day, he sent them into his vineyard. 3 And he went out about the third hour and saw others standing idle in the marketplace; 4 and to those he said, 'You also go into the vineyard, and whatever is right I will give you.' And *so* they went. 5 Again he went out about the sixth and the ninth hour, and did the same thing. 6 And about the eleventh *hour* he went out and found others standing *around*; and he *said to them, 'Why have you been standing here idle all day long?' 7 They *said to him, 'Because no one hired us.' He *said to them, 'You go into the vineyard too.'

8 "Now when evening came, the owner of the vineyard *said to his foreman, 'Call the laborers and pay them their wages, beginning with the last *group* to the first.' 9 And when those *hired* about the eleventh hour came, each one received a denarius. 10 And when those *hired* first came, they supposed that they would receive more; but each of them also received a denarius. 11 Now when they received it, they were grumbling at the landowner, 12 saying, 'These last men have worked *only* one hour, and you have made them equal to us who have borne the burden of the day and the scorching heat.' 13 But he answered and said to one of them, 'Friend, I am doing you no wrong; did you not agree with me for a denarius? 14 Take what is yours and go, but I wish to give to this last man the same as to you. 15 Is it not lawful for me to do what I wish with what is my own? Or is your eye envious because I am generous?' 16 So the last shall be first, and the first last."

JANUARY 31

Exodus 11:1–12:51

11 Then Yahweh said to Moses, "One more plague I will bring on Pharaoh and on Egypt; after that he will let you go from here. When he lets you go, he will surely drive you out from here completely. 2 Speak now in the hearing of the people so that each man may ask from his neighbor and each woman from her neighbor for articles of silver and articles of gold." 3 (And Yahweh gave the people favor in the sight of the Egyptians. Moreover, the man Moses *himself* was very great in the land of Egypt, *both* in the sight of Pharaoh's servants and in the sight of the people.)

4 So Moses said, "Thus says Yahweh, 'About midnight I am going out into the midst of Egypt, 5 and all the firstborn in the land of Egypt shall die, from the firstborn of the Pharaoh who sits on his throne, even to the firstborn of the servant-girl who is behind the millstones; and all the firstborn of the cattle. 6 Moreover, there shall be a great cry in all the land of Egypt, such as there has not been *before* and such as shall never be again. 7 But for any of the sons of Israel a dog will not *even* bark, whether against man or beast, that you may know how Yahweh makes a distinction between Egypt and Israel.' 8 Then all these your servants will come down to me and bow themselves before me, saying, 'Go out, you and all the people who follow you,' and after that I will go out." And he went out from Pharaoh in hot anger.

9 Then Yahweh said to Moses, "Pharaoh will not listen to you, so that My miraculous wonders will be multiplied in the land of Egypt." 10 Now Moses and Aaron did all these miraculous wonders before Pharaoh; yet Yahweh hardened Pharaoh's heart with strength, and he did not let the sons of Israel go out of his land.

12 Now Yahweh said to Moses and Aaron in the land of Egypt, 2 "This month shall be the beginning of months for you; it is to be the first month of the year to you. 3 Speak to all the congregation of Israel, saying, 'On the tenth of this month they are each one to take a lamb for themselves, according to their fathers' households,

a lamb for each household. 4 Now if the household is too small for a lamb, then he and his neighbor nearest to his house are to take one according to the number of persons *in them*; according to what each man should eat, you are to apportion the lamb. 5 Your lamb shall be a male, without blemish, a year old; you may take it from the sheep or from the goats. 6 And you shall keep it until the fourteenth day of the same month, then the whole assembly of the congregation of Israel shall slaughter it at twilight. 7 Moreover, they shall take some of the blood and put it on the two doorposts and on the lintel of the houses in which they eat it. 8 And they shall eat the flesh that night, roasted with fire, and they shall eat it with unleavened bread and bitter herbs. 9 Do not eat any of it raw or boiled at all with water, but rather roasted with fire, *both* its head and its legs along with its entrails. 10 And you shall not leave any of it over until morning, but whatever is left of it until morning, you shall burn with fire. 11 Now you shall eat it in this manner: *with* your loins girded, your sandals on your feet, and your staff in your hand; and you shall eat it in haste—it is the Passover of Yahweh. 12 And I will go through the land of Egypt on that night and will strike down all the firstborn in the land of Egypt, both man and beast; and against all the gods of Egypt I will execute judgments—I am Yahweh. 13 And the blood shall be a sign for you on the houses where you are; and I will see the blood, and I will pass over you, and there shall be no plague among you to destroy *you* when I strike the land of Egypt.

14 'Now this day will be a memorial to you, and you shall celebrate it *as* a feast to Yahweh; throughout your generations you are to celebrate it *as* a perpetual statute. 15 Seven days you shall eat unleavened bread, but on the first day you shall remove leaven from your houses; for whoever eats anything leavened from the first day until the seventh day, that person shall be cut off from Israel. 16 Now on the first day there shall be a holy convocation, and on the seventh day there shall be a holy convocation for you; no work at all shall be done on them, except what must be eaten by every person, that alone may be done by you. 17 You shall also keep the *Feast of* Unleavened Bread, for on this very day I brought your hosts out of the land of Egypt; therefore you shall keep this day throughout your generations as a perpetual statute. 18 In the first *month*, on the fourteenth day of the month at evening, you shall eat unleavened bread until the twenty-first day of the month at evening. 19 Seven days there shall be no leaven found in your houses; for whoever eats what is leavened, that person shall be cut off from the congregation of Israel, whether *he is* a sojourner or a native of the land. 20 You shall not eat anything leavened; in all your *places of* habitation you shall eat unleavened bread.'"

21 Then Moses called for all the elders of Israel and said to them, "Bring out and take for yourselves lambs according to your families and slaughter the Passover *lamb*. 22 And you shall take a bunch of hyssop and dip it in the blood which is in the basin, and touch some of the blood that is in the basin to the lintel and the two doorposts; and none of you shall go outside the doorway of his house until morning. 23 And Yahweh will pass through to smite the Egyptians; and He will see the blood on the lintel and on the two doorposts, and Yahweh will pass over the doorway and will not allow the destroyer to come into your houses to smite *you*. 24 And you shall keep this event as a statute for you and your children forever. 25 And it will be, when you enter the land which Yahweh will give you, as He has promised, you shall keep this *new* slavery. 26 And it will be when your children say to you, 'What is the meaning of this *new* slavery to you?' 27 that you shall say, 'It is a Passover sacrifice to Yahweh who passed over the houses of the sons of Israel in Egypt when He smote the Egyptians, but delivered our homes.'" And the people bowed low and worshiped.

28 Then the sons of Israel went and did *so*; just as Yahweh had commanded Moses and Aaron, so they did.

29 Now it happened at midnight that Yahweh struck all the firstborn in the land of Egypt, from the firstborn of Pharaoh who sat on his throne to the firstborn of the captive who was in the dungeon, and all the firstborn of cattle. 30 Then Pharaoh arose in the night, he and all his servants and all the Egyptians, and there was a great cry in Egypt, for there was no home where there was not someone dead. 31 Then he called for Moses and Aaron at night and said, "Rise up,

get out from among my people, both you
and the sons of Israel; and go, serve Yahweh,
as you have spoken. 32 Take both your flocks
and your herds, as you have spoken, and go,
and bless me also."

33 And the Egyptians strongly pressed
the people to send them out of the land in
haste, for they said, "We will all be dead."
34 So the people took up their dough before
it was leavened, *with* their kneading bowls
bound up in the clothes on their shoulders.

35 Now the sons of Israel had done accord-
ing to the word of Moses—they had asked
from the Egyptians for articles of silver and
articles of gold, and clothing; 36 and Yahweh
had given the people favor in the sight of
the Egyptians, so that they let them have
what they asked. Thus they plundered the
Egyptians.

37 And the sons of Israel journeyed from
Rameses to Succoth, about six hundred
thousand men on foot, aside from the little
ones. 38 A foreign multitude also went up
with them, along with flocks and herds, a
very large number of livestock. 39 And they
baked the dough which they had brought
out of Egypt into cakes of unleavened bread.
For it had not become leavened, since they
were driven out of Egypt and could not
delay, nor had they prepared any provisions
for themselves.

40 Now the time that the sons of Israel
lived in Egypt was 430 years. 41 And it hap-
pened at the end of 430 years, to the very
day, that all the hosts of Yahweh went out
from the land of Egypt. 42 It is a night to be
kept for Yahweh for having brought them
out from the land of Egypt; this night is for
Yahweh, to be kept by all the sons of Israel
throughout their generations.

43 And Yahweh said to Moses and Aaron,
"This is the statute of the Passover: no
foreigner shall eat of it; 44 but every man's
slave purchased with money, after you
have circumcised him, then he may eat of
it. 45 A foreign resident or a hired person
shall not eat of it. 46 It shall be eaten in a
single house; you shall not bring forth any
of the flesh outside of the house, and you
shall not break any bone of it. 47 All the
congregation of Israel shall celebrate this.
48 But if a sojourner sojourns with you and
celebrates the Passover to Yahweh, let all
his males be circumcised, and then let him
come near to celebrate it; and he shall be like
a native of the land. But no uncircumcised
person may eat of it. 49 The same law shall
apply to the native as to the sojourner who
sojourns among you."

50 So all the sons of Israel did; as Yahweh
had commanded Moses and Aaron, thus
they did. 51 And on that same day Yahweh
brought the sons of Israel out of the land of
Egypt by their hosts.

Psalm 18:1–12

1 He said, "I love You, O Yahweh,
my strength."
2 Yahweh is my rock and my
fortress and my deliverer,
My God, my rock, in whom
I take refuge;
My shield and the horn of my
salvation, my stronghold.
3 I call upon Yahweh, who is
worthy to be praised,
And I am saved from my enemies.

4 The cords of death encompassed me,
And the torrents of vileness
terrified me.
5 The cords of Sheol surrounded me;
The snares of death confronted me.
6 In my distress I called upon Yahweh,
And cried to my God for help;
He heard my voice out of His temple,
And my cry for help before
Him came into His ears.

7 Then the earth shook and quaked;
And the foundations of the
mountains were trembling
And were shaken, because
He was angry.
8 Smoke went up out of His nostrils,
And fire from His mouth devoured;
Coals were kindled by it.
9 He bowed the heavens
and came down
With thick darkness under His feet.
10 He rode upon a cherub and flew;
And He sped upon the
wings of the wind.
11 He made darkness His hiding place,
His canopy around Him,
Darkness of waters, thick
clouds of the skies.
12 From the brightness before Him
passed His thick clouds,
Hailstones and coals of fire.

Proverbs 6:1–5

6 My son, if you have become a
 guarantor for your neighbor,
Have struck your hands *in*
 pledge for a stranger,
2 *If* you have been snared with
 the words of your mouth,
Have been caught with the
 words of your mouth,
3 Do this then, my son, and
 deliver yourself;
Since you have come into the
 hand of your neighbor,
Go, humble yourself, and
 badger your neighbor.
4 Give no sleep to your eyes,
Nor slumber to your eyelids;
5 Deliver yourself like a gazelle
 from *the hunter's* hand
And like a bird from the
 hand of the fowler.

Matthew 20:17–34

17 And as Jesus was about to go up to Jerusalem, He took the twelve *disciples* aside by themselves, and on the way He said to them, 18 "Behold, we are going up to Jerusalem; and the Son of Man will be betrayed to the chief priests and scribes, and they will condemn Him to death, 19 and will deliver Him over to the Gentiles to mock and flog and crucify *Him*, and on the third day He will be raised up."

20 Then the mother of the sons of Zebedee came to Him with her sons, bowing down and making a request of Him. 21 And He said to her, "What do you wish?" She *said to Him, "Command that in Your kingdom these two sons of mine may sit one on Your right and one on Your left." 22 But Jesus answered and said, "You do not know what you are asking. Are you able to drink the cup that I am about to drink?" They *said to Him, "We are able." 23 He *said to them, "My cup you shall drink; but to sit on My right and on *My* left, this is not Mine to give, but it is for those for whom it has been prepared by My Father."

24 And hearing *this*, the ten became indignant with the two brothers. 25 But Jesus called them to Himself and said, "You know that the rulers of the Gentiles lord it over them, and *their* great men exercise authority over them. 26 It is not this way among you, but whoever wishes to become great among you shall be your servant, 27 and whoever wishes to be first among you shall be your slave; 28 just as the Son of Man did not come to be served, but to serve, and to give His life a ransom for many."

29 And as they were leaving Jericho, a large crowd followed Him. 30 And behold, two blind men sitting by the road, hearing that Jesus *was passing by, cried out, saying, "Lord, have mercy on us, Son of David!" 31 But the crowd sternly told them to be quiet, but they cried out all the more, saying, "Lord, Son of David, have mercy on us!" 32 And Jesus stopped and called them, and said, "What do you want Me to do for you?" 33 They *said to Him, "Lord, that our eyes be opened." 34 And moved with compassion, Jesus touched their eyes; and immediately they regained their sight and followed Him.

FEBRUARY 1

Exodus 13:1–14:31

13 Then Yahweh spoke to Moses, saying, 2 "Sanctify to Me every firstborn, the first offspring of every womb among the sons of Israel, both of man and beast; it belongs to Me."

3 And Moses said to the people, "Remember this day in which you went out from Egypt, from the house of slavery; for by a strong hand Yahweh brought you out from this place. And nothing leavened shall be eaten. 4 This day, in the month of Abib, you are going out. 5 And it shall be when Yahweh brings you to the land of the Canaanite, the Hittite, the Amorite, the Hivite, and the Jebusite, which He swore to your fathers to give you, a land flowing with milk and honey, that you shall do this service in this month. 6 For seven days you shall eat unleavened bread, and on the seventh day *there shall be* a feast to Yahweh. 7 Unleavened bread shall be eaten throughout the seven days; and nothing leavened shall be seen among you, nor shall any leaven be seen among you in all your borders. 8 And you shall tell your son on that day, saying, 'It is because of what Yahweh did for me when I came out of Egypt.' 9 And it will be as a sign to you

on your hand and as a memorial between your eyes, that the law of Yahweh may be in your mouth; for with a strong hand Yahweh brought you out of Egypt. 10 Therefore, you shall keep this statute at its appointed time from year to year.

11 "And it will be when Yahweh brings you to the land of the Canaanite, as He swore to you and to your fathers, and gives it to you, 12 and you shall devote to Yahweh the first offspring of every womb and the first offspring of every beast that you own; the males belong to Yahweh. 13 But every first offspring of a donkey you shall redeem with a lamb, but if you do not redeem *it*, then you shall break its neck; and every firstborn of man among your sons you shall redeem. 14 And it will be when your son asks you in time to come, saying, 'What is this?' then you shall say to him, 'With a strong hand Yahweh brought us out of Egypt, from the house of slavery. 15 And it happened, when Pharaoh hardened *his heart* with stiffness about letting us go, that Yahweh killed every firstborn in the land of Egypt, both the firstborn of man and the firstborn of beast. Therefore, I sacrifice to Yahweh the males, the first offspring of every womb, but every firstborn of my sons I redeem.' 16 So it will be as a sign on your hand and as phylacteries between your eyes, for with a strong hand Yahweh brought us out of Egypt."

17 Now it happened that when Pharaoh had let the people go, God did not guide them by the way of the land of the Philistines, even though it was near; for God said, "Lest the people change their minds when they see war, and return to Egypt." 18 Hence God turned the people to the way of the wilderness to the Red Sea; and the sons of Israel went up in battle array from the land of Egypt. 19 And Moses took the bones of Joseph with him, for he had made the sons of Israel solemnly swear, saying, "God will surely take care of you, and you shall bring up my bones from here with you." 20 Then they set out from Succoth and camped in Etham on the edge of the wilderness. 21 And Yahweh was going before them in a pillar of cloud by day to guide them on the way, and in a pillar of fire by night to give them light, that they might go by day and by night. 22 He did not take away the pillar of cloud by day, nor the pillar of fire by night, from before the people.

14 Now Yahweh spoke to Moses, saying, 2 "Speak to the sons of Israel so that they turn back and camp before Pi-hahiroth, between Migdol and the sea; you shall camp in front of Baal-zephon, opposite it, by the sea. 3 And Pharaoh will say of the sons of Israel, 'They are wandering in confusion in the land; the wilderness has shut them in.' 4 Thus I will harden Pharaoh's heart with strength, and he will pursue them; and I will be glorified through Pharaoh and all his army, so that the Egyptians will know that I am Yahweh." And they did so.

5 Then the king of Egypt was told that the people had fled, and the heart of Pharaoh and his servants was changed toward the people, and they said, "What is this we have done, that we have let Israel go from serving us?" 6 So he made his chariot ready and took his people with him; 7 and he took six hundred choice chariots and all the *other* chariots of Egypt with officers over all of them. 8 And Yahweh hardened the heart of Pharaoh, king of Egypt, with strength, and he pursued the sons of Israel as the sons of Israel were going out with an exalted hand. 9 Then the Egyptians pursued them *with* all the horses *and* chariots of Pharaoh, his horsemen and his army, and they overtook them camping by the sea, beside Pi-hahiroth, in front of Baal-zephon.

10 Now Pharaoh drew near, and the sons of Israel lifted up their eyes, and behold, the Egyptians were marching after them, and they became very afraid; so the sons of Israel cried out to Yahweh. 11 Then they said to Moses, "Is it because there were no graves in Egypt that you have taken us away to die in the wilderness? What is this you have done against us in bringing us out of Egypt? 12 Is this not the word that we spoke to you in Egypt, saying, 'Leave us alone that we may serve the Egyptians'? For it would have been better for us to serve the Egyptians than for us to die in the wilderness." 13 But Moses said to the people, "Do not fear! Stand by and see the salvation of Yahweh which He will accomplish for you today; for the Egyptians whom you have seen today, you will never see them again forever. 14 Yahweh will fight for you, and you will keep silent."

15 Then Yahweh said to Moses, "Why are you crying out to Me? Speak to the sons of Israel so that they go forward. 16 As for you, raise up your staff and stretch out your

hand over the sea and split it, and the sons
of Israel shall go through the midst of the
sea on dry land. 17 As for Me, behold, I will
harden the hearts of the Egyptians with
strength so that they will go in after them;
and I will be glorified through Pharaoh
and all his army, through his chariots and
his horsemen. 18 Then the Egyptians will
know that I am Yahweh, when I am glorified
through Pharaoh, through his chariots and
his horsemen."

19 Then the angel of God, who had been
going before the camp of Israel, moved and
went behind them; and the pillar of cloud
moved from before them and stood behind
them. 20 So it came between the camp of
Egypt and the camp of Israel; and there
was the cloud along with the darkness, yet
it gave light at night. Thus the one did not
come near the other all night.

21 Then Moses stretched out his hand
over the sea; and Yahweh swept the sea *back*
by a strong east wind all night and made
the sea into dry ground, so the waters were
split. 22 So the sons of Israel went through
the midst of the sea on the dry land, and
the waters *were* a wall to them on their
right hand and on their left. 23 Then the
Egyptians pursued *them*, and all Pharaoh's
horses, his chariots and his horsemen
went in after them into the midst of the
sea. 24 Then at the morning watch, Yahweh
looked down on the camp of the Egyptians
through the pillar of fire and cloud and
brought the camp of the Egyptians into
confusion. 25 And He caused their chariot
wheels to swerve, and He made them drive
with difficulty; so the Egyptians said, "Let
us flee from Israel, for Yahweh is fighting
for them against the Egyptians."

26 Then Yahweh said to Moses, "Stretch
out your hand over the sea so that the
waters may come back over the Egyptians,
over their chariots and their horsemen."
27 So Moses stretched out his hand over the
sea, and the sea returned to its normal state
at daybreak while the Egyptians were fleeing
right into it; then Yahweh overthrew the
Egyptians in the midst of the sea. 28 And the
waters returned and covered the chariots
and the horsemen, even Pharaoh's entire
army that had gone into the sea after them;
not even one of them remained. 29 But the
sons of Israel walked on dry land through
the midst of the sea, and the waters *were*
a wall to them on their right hand and on
their left.

30 Thus Yahweh saved Israel that day from
the hand of the Egyptians, and Israel saw
the Egyptians dead on the seashore. 31 Then
Israel saw the great hand which Yahweh had
used against the Egyptians; and the people
feared Yahweh, and they believed in Yahweh
and in His servant Moses.

Psalm 18:13–19

13 Yahweh also thundered in the heavens,
And the Most High gave
forth His voice,
Hailstones and coals of fire.
14 He sent out His arrows,
and scattered them,
And lightning flashes in abundance,
and threw them into confusion.
15 Then the channels of water appeared,
And the foundations of the
world were laid bare
At Your rebuke, O Yahweh,
At the blast of the breath
of Your nostrils.

16 He sent from on high, He took me;
He drew me out of many waters.
17 He delivered me from my
strong enemy,
And from those who hated me,
for they were too mighty for me.
18 They confronted me in the
day of my disaster,
But Yahweh was my support.
19 He brought me forth also
into a broad place;
He rescued me, because
He delighted in me.

Proverbs 6:6–11

6 Go to the ant, O sluggard,
Observe her ways and be wise,
7 Which, having no chief,
Officer or ruler,
8 Prepares her food in the summer
And gathers her provision
in the harvest.
9 How long will you lie down, O sluggard?
When will you arise from your sleep?
10 "A little sleep, a little slumber,
A little folding of the hands to rest"—
11 Your poverty will come in
like a vagabond
And your want like an armed man.

Matthew 21:1–22

21 And when they had approached Jerusalem and came to Bethphage, at the Mount of Olives, then Jesus sent two disciples, 2 saying to them, "Go into the village opposite you, and immediately you will find a donkey tied *there* and a colt with her; untie them and bring them to Me. 3 And if anyone says anything to you, you shall say, 'The Lord has need of them,' and immediately he will send them." 4 And this took place in order that what was spoken through the prophet would be fulfilled, saying,

5 "SAY TO THE DAUGHTER OF ZION,
'BEHOLD YOUR KING IS COMING TO YOU,
LOWLY, AND MOUNTED ON A DONKEY,
AND ON A COLT, THE FOAL
OF A PACK ANIMAL.'"

6 And the disciples went and did just as Jesus had instructed them, 7 and brought the donkey and the colt, and laid their garments on them; and He sat on the garments. 8 And most of the crowd spread their garments in the road, and others were cutting branches from the trees and spreading them in the road. 9 And the crowds going ahead of Him, and those who followed, were crying out, saying,

"Hosanna to the Son of David;
BLESSED IS HE WHO COMES IN
THE NAME OF THE LORD;
Hosanna in the highest!"

10 And when He had entered Jerusalem, all the city was stirred, saying, "Who is this?" 11 And the crowds were saying, "This is the prophet Jesus, from Nazareth in Galilee."

12 And Jesus entered the temple and drove out all those who were buying and selling in the temple, and overturned the tables of the money changers and the seats of those who were selling doves. 13 And He *said to them, "It is written, 'MY HOUSE SHALL BE CALLED A HOUSE OF PRAYER'; but you are making it a ROBBERS' DEN."

14 And the blind and the lame came to Him in the temple, and He healed them. 15 But when the chief priests and the scribes saw the marvelous things which He had done, and the children who were shouting in the temple, saying, "Hosanna to the Son of David," they became indignant 16 and said to Him, "Do You hear what these *children* are saying?" And Jesus *said to them, "Yes; have you never read, 'OUT OF THE MOUTH OF INFANTS AND NURSING BABIES YOU HAVE PREPARED PRAISE FOR YOURSELF'?" 17 And He left them and went out of the city to Bethany, and spent the night there.

18 Now in the morning, when He was returning to the city, He became hungry. 19 And seeing a lone fig tree by the road, He came to it and found nothing on it except leaves only; and He *said to it, "No longer shall there ever be *any* fruit from you." And at once the fig tree withered.

20 And seeing *this*, the disciples marveled, saying, "How did the fig tree wither *all* at once?" 21 And Jesus answered and said to them, "Truly I say to you, if you have faith and do not doubt, you will not only do what was done to the fig tree, but even if you say to this mountain, 'Be taken up and cast into the sea,' it will happen. 22 And all things you ask in prayer, believing, you will receive."

FEBRUARY 2

Exodus 15:1–16:36

15 Then Moses and the sons of Israel sang this song to Yahweh and said,

"I will sing to Yahweh,
for He is highly exalted;
The horse and its rider He
has hurled into the sea.
2 "Yah is my strength and song,
And He has become my salvation;
This is my God, and I will praise Him;
My father's God, and I will
extol Him.
3 "Yahweh is a warrior;
Yahweh is His name.
4 "Pharaoh's chariots and his army
He has cast into the sea;
And the choicest of his officers
are sunk in the Red Sea.
5 "The deeps cover them;
They went down into the
depths like a stone.
6 "Your right hand, O Yahweh,
is majestic in power,
Your right hand, O Yahweh,
shatters the enemy.
7 "And in the greatness of Your
exaltation You pull down those
who rise up against You;

You send forth Your burning anger,
and it devours them as chaff.
8 "And at the blast of Your nostrils
the waters were piled up,
The flowing waters stood
up like a heap;
The deeps were congealed in
the heart of the sea.
9 "The enemy said, 'I will pursue,
I will overtake, I will divide the spoil;
My desire shall be fulfilled
against them;
I will draw out my sword, my
hand will dispossess them.'
10 "You blew with Your wind,
the sea covered them;
They sank like lead in
the mighty waters.
11 "Who is like You among
the gods, O Yahweh?
Who is like You, majestic in holiness,
Fearsome in praises, working wonders?
12 "You stretched out Your right hand,
The earth swallowed them.
13 "In Your lovingkindness You
have guided the people whom
You have redeemed;
In Your strength You have led
them to Your holy habitation.
14 "The peoples have heard, they tremble;
Anguish has seized the
inhabitants of Philistia.
15 "Then the chiefs of Edom
were dismayed;
The leaders of Moab,
trembling seizes them;
All the inhabitants of Canaan
have melted away.
16 "Terror and dread fall upon them;
By the greatness of Your arm
they are still as stone;
Until Your people pass over, O Yahweh,
Until the people pass over whom
You have purchased.
17 "You will bring them and plant them in
the mountain of Your inheritance,
The place, O Yahweh, which You
have made for You to inhabit,
The sanctuary, O Lord, which
Your hands have established.
18 "Yahweh shall reign forever and ever."
19 For the horses of Pharaoh with his
chariots and his horsemen went into the
sea, and Yahweh brought back the waters
of the sea on them, but the sons of Israel
walked on dry land through the midst of
the sea.
20 And Miriam the prophetess, Aaron's
sister, took the tambourine in her hand,
and all the women went out after her with
tambourines and with dancing. 21 And
Miriam answered them,

"Sing to Yahweh, for He is
highly exalted;
The horse and his rider He has
hurled into the sea."

22 Then Moses had Israel set out from
the Red Sea, and they went out into the
wilderness of Shur; and they went three
days in the wilderness and found no water.
23 And they came to Marah, but they could
not drink the waters of Marah, for they
were bitter; therefore it was named Marah.
24 So the people grumbled at Moses, saying,
"What shall we drink?" 25 Then he cried out
to Yahweh, and Yahweh showed him a tree;
and he threw *it* into the waters, and the
waters became sweet.

There He set for them a statute and a
judgment, and there He tested them. 26 And
He said, "If you will earnestly listen to the
voice of Yahweh your God, and do what
is right in His sight, and give ear to His
commandments, and keep all His statutes,
I will put none of the diseases on you which
I have put on the Egyptians; for I, Yahweh,
am your healer."

27 Then they came to Elim where there
were twelve springs of water and seventy
date palms, and they camped there beside
the waters.

16 Then they set out from Elim, and all
the congregation of the sons of Israel
came to the wilderness of Sin, which is
between Elim and Sinai, on the fifteenth day
of the second month after their departure
from the land of Egypt. 2 And the whole
congregation of the sons of Israel grumbled
against Moses and Aaron in the wilderness.
3 And the sons of Israel said to them, "Would
that we had died by the hand of Yahweh in
the land of Egypt, when we sat by the pots
of meat, when we ate bread to the full; for
you have brought us out into this wilderness
to put this whole assembly to death with
hunger."

4 Then Yahweh said to Moses, "Behold,
I will rain bread from heaven for you; and
the people shall go out and gather a day's

portion every day, that I may test them, whether or not they will walk in My law. 5 Now it will be on the sixth day, they shall prepare what they bring in, and it will be twice as much as they gather daily." 6 So Moses and Aaron said to all the sons of Israel, "At evening you will know that Yahweh has brought you out of the land of Egypt; 7 and in the morning you will see the glory of Yahweh, for He hears your grumblings against Yahweh; and what are we, that you grumble against us?"

8 And Moses said, "*This will happen* when Yahweh gives you meat to eat in the evening and bread to the full in the morning; for Yahweh hears your grumblings which you grumble against Him. And what are we? Your grumblings are not against us but against Yahweh."

9 Then Moses said to Aaron, "Say to all the congregation of the sons of Israel, 'Come near before Yahweh, for He has heard your grumblings.'" 10 Now it happened as Aaron spoke to the whole congregation of the sons of Israel, that they turned toward the wilderness, and behold, the glory of Yahweh appeared in the cloud. 11 And Yahweh spoke to Moses, saying, 12 "I have heard the grumblings of the sons of Israel; speak to them, saying, 'At twilight you shall eat meat, and in the morning you shall be filled with bread, so that you shall know that I am Yahweh your God.'"

13 So it happened at evening that the quails came up and covered the camp, and in the morning there was a layer of dew around the camp. 14 Then the layer of dew evaporated, and behold, on the surface of the wilderness there was a fine flake-like thing, fine as the frost on the ground. 15 And the sons of Israel saw *it* and said to one another, "What is it?" For they did not know what it was. And Moses said to them, "It is the bread which Yahweh has given you to eat. 16 This is what Yahweh has commanded, 'Gather of it every man as much as he should eat; you shall take an omer apiece according to the number of persons each of you has in his tent.'" 17 And the sons of Israel did so; *some* gathered much and *some* little. 18 And they measured it with an omer, and he who had gathered much had no excess, and he who had gathered little had no lack; every man gathered as much as he should eat. 19 And Moses said to them, "Let no man leave any of it until morning." 20 But they did not listen to Moses, and some left part of it until morning, and it bred worms and became foul; and Moses was angry with them. 21 So they gathered it morning by morning, every man as much as he should eat; but the sun would grow hot, and it would melt.

22 Now it happened that on the sixth day they gathered twice as much bread, two omers for each one. Then all the leaders of the congregation came and told Moses. 23 And he said to them, "This is what Yahweh has spoken: Tomorrow is a sabbath observance, a holy sabbath to Yahweh. Bake what you will bake and boil what you will boil, and all that is in excess put aside to be kept until morning." 24 So they put it aside until morning, as Moses had commanded, and it did not become foul nor was there any worm in it. 25 And Moses said, "Eat it today, for today is a sabbath to Yahweh; today you will not find it in the field. 26 Six days you shall gather it, but on the seventh day, *the* sabbath, there will be none."

27 Now it happened on the seventh day, that some of the people went out to gather, but they found none. 28 Then Yahweh said to Moses, "How long do you refuse to keep My commandments and My laws? 29 See, Yahweh has given you the sabbath; therefore He gives you bread for two days on the sixth day. Remain every man in his place; let no man go out of his place on the seventh day." 30 So the people rested on the seventh day.

31 And the house of Israel named it manna, and it was like coriander seed, white, and its taste was like wafers with honey. 32 Then Moses said, "This is what Yahweh has commanded, 'Let an omerful of it be kept throughout your generations, that they may see the bread that I fed you in the wilderness, when I brought you out of the land of Egypt.'" 33 And Moses said to Aaron, "Take a jar and put an omerful of manna in it, and place it before Yahweh to be kept throughout your generations." 34 As Yahweh commanded Moses, so Aaron placed it before the Testimony to be kept. 35 And the sons of Israel ate the manna forty years, until they came to an inhabited land; they ate the manna until they came to the border of the land of Canaan. 36 (Now an omer is a tenth of an ephah.)

Psalm 18:20–27

20 Yahweh has rewarded me according
to my righteousness;
According to the cleanness of my
hands He has recompensed me.
21 For I have kept the ways of Yahweh,
And have not wickedly
departed from my God.
22 For all His judgments were before me,
And I did not put away His
statutes from me.
23 I was also blameless with Him,
And I kept myself from my iniquity.
24 Therefore Yahweh has recompensed
me according to my righteousness,
According to the cleanness of
my hands before His eyes.

25 With the kind You show Yourself kind;
With the blameless You show
Yourself blameless;
26 With the pure You show Yourself pure,
And with the crooked You
show Yourself astute.
27 For You save an afflicted people,
But eyes *which are* lifted
up, You bring down.

Proverbs 6:12–15

12 A vile person, a wicked man,
Is the one who walks with
a perverse mouth,
13 Who winks with his eyes, who
signals with his feet,
Who points with his fingers;
14 Who *with* perversity in his heart
continually devises evil,
Who spreads contentions.
15 Therefore his disaster will
come suddenly;
Instantly he will be broken and
there will be no healing.

Matthew 21:23–46

23 And when He entered the temple, the
chief priests and the elders of the people
came to Him while He was teaching, and
said, "By what authority are You doing these
things, and who gave You this authority?"
24 And Jesus answered and said to them,
"I will also ask you one thing, which if
you tell Me, I will also tell you by what
authority I do these things. 25 The baptism
of John was from what *source*, from heaven
or from men?" And they *began* reasoning
among themselves, saying, "If we say, 'From
heaven,' He will say to us, 'Then why did
you not believe him?' 26 But if we say, 'From
men,' we fear the crowd; for they all regard
John as a prophet." 27 And they answered
Jesus and said, "We do not know." He also
said to them, "Neither will I tell you by what
authority I do these things.

28 "But what do you think? A man had two
sons, and he came to the first and said, 'Son,
go work today in the vineyard.' 29 And he
answered and said, 'I will not'; but afterward
he regretted it and went. 30 And the man
came to the second and said the same thing;
and he answered and said, 'I *will*, sir'; but he
did not go. 31 Which of the two did the will
of his father?" They *said, "The first." Jesus
*said to them, "Truly I say to you that the
tax collectors and prostitutes will get into
the kingdom of God before you. 32 For John
came to you in the way of righteousness
and you did not believe him; but the tax
collectors and prostitutes did believe him;
and you, seeing *this*, did not even regret
afterward so as to believe him.

33 "Listen to another parable. There was
a landowner who PLANTED A VINEYARD AND
PUT A WALL AROUND IT AND DUG A WINE PRESS
IN IT, AND BUILT A TOWER, and rented it out
to vine-growers and went on a journey.
34 Now when the harvest time approached,
he sent his slaves to the vine-growers to
receive his fruit. 35 And the vine-growers
took his slaves and beat one, and killed
another, and stoned a third. 36 Again he
sent another group of slaves larger than
the first; and they did the same thing to
them. 37 But afterward he sent his son to
them, saying, 'They will respect my son.'
38 But when the vine-growers saw the son,
they said among themselves, 'This is the
heir; come, let us kill him and seize his
inheritance.' 39 And they took him, and
threw him out of the vineyard and killed
him. 40 Therefore when the owner of the
vineyard comes, what will he do to those
vine-growers?" 41 They *said to Him, "He
will bring those wretches to a wretched
end, and will rent out the vineyard to
other vine-growers who will pay him the
proceeds at the *proper* seasons."

42 Jesus *said to them, "Did you never read
in the Scriptures,

'THE STONE WHICH THE
BUILDERS REJECTED,

THIS HAS BECOME THE CHIEF
CORNER *stone*;
THIS CAME ABOUT FROM THE LORD,
AND IT IS MARVELOUS IN OUR EYES'?

43 "Therefore I say to you, the kingdom of God will be taken away from you and given to a nation, producing the fruit of it. 44 And he who falls on this stone will be broken to pieces; but on whomever it falls, it will scatter him like dust."

45 And when the chief priests and the Pharisees heard His parables, they understood that He *was speaking about them. 46 And although they were seeking to seize Him, they feared the crowds, because they were regarding Him to be a prophet.

FEBRUARY 3

Exodus 17:1–18:27

17 Then all the congregation of the sons of Israel journeyed by stages from the wilderness of Sin, according to the command of Yahweh, and they camped at Rephidim, and there was no water for the people to drink. 2 Therefore the people contended with Moses and said, "Give us water that we may drink." And Moses said to them, "Why do you contend with me? Why do you test Yahweh?" 3 But the people thirsted there for water; and they grumbled against Moses and said, "Why, now, have you brought us up from Egypt, to put us and our children and our livestock to death with thirst?" 4 So Moses cried out to Yahweh, saying, "What shall I do to this people? A little more and they will stone me." 5 Then Yahweh said to Moses, "Pass before the people and take with you some of the elders of Israel; and take in your hand your staff with which you struck the Nile, and go. 6 Behold, I will stand before you there on the rock at Horeb; and you shall strike the rock, and water will come out of it, that the people may drink." And Moses did so in the sight of the elders of Israel. 7 So he named the place Massah and Meribah because of the contending of the sons of Israel, and because they tested Yahweh, saying, "Is Yahweh among us or not?"

8 Then Amalek came and fought against Israel at Rephidim. 9 So Moses said to Joshua, "Choose men for us and go out, fight against Amalek. Tomorrow I will take my stand on the top of the hill with the staff of God in my hand." 10 And Joshua did as Moses told him, to fight against Amalek; and Moses, Aaron, and Hur went up to the top of the hill. 11 So it happened when Moses raised his hand up, that Israel prevailed, and when he let his hand down, Amalek prevailed. 12 But Moses' hands were heavy. Then they took a stone and put it under him, and he sat on it; and Aaron and Hur supported his hands, one on one side and one on the other. Thus his hands were steady until the sun set. 13 So Joshua overwhelmed Amalek and his people with the edge of the sword.

14 Then Yahweh said to Moses, "Write this in a book as a memorial and recite it in Joshua's hearing, that I will utterly blot out the memory of Amalek from under heaven." 15 And Moses built an altar and named it Yahweh is My Banner; 16 and he said, "Because He *has sworn* with a hand upon the throne of Yah, Yahweh will have war against Amalek from generation to generation."

18 Now Jethro, the priest of Midian, Moses' father-in-law, heard of all that God had done for Moses and for Israel His people, how Yahweh had brought Israel out of Egypt. 2 And Jethro, Moses' father-in-law, took Moses' wife Zipporah, after he had sent her away, 3 and her two sons, of whom one was named Gershom, for Moses said, "I have been a sojourner in a foreign land." 4 And the other was named Eliezer, for *he said*, "The God of my father was my help and delivered me from the sword of Pharaoh."

5 Then Jethro, Moses' father-in-law, came with his sons and his wife to Moses in the wilderness where he was camped, at the mount of God. 6 And he sent word to Moses, "I, your father-in-law Jethro, am coming to you with your wife and her two sons with her." 7 Then Moses went out to meet his father-in-law, and he bowed down and kissed him; and they asked each other of their welfare and went into the tent. 8 And Moses recounted to his father-in-law all that Yahweh had done to Pharaoh and to the Egyptians for Israel's

sake, all the hardship that had befallen
them on the journey, and *how* Yahweh
had delivered them. 9 And Jethro rejoiced
over all the goodness which Yahweh had
done to Israel, that He had delivered
them from the hand of the Egyptians.
10 So Jethro said, "Blessed be Yahweh
who delivered you from the hand of the
Egyptians and from the hand of Pharaoh,
and who delivered the people from under
the hand of the Egyptians. 11 Now I know
that Yahweh is greater than all the gods; for
in this matter they acted presumptuously
against the people." 12 Then Jethro, Moses'
father-in-law, took a burnt offering and
sacrifices for God, and Aaron came with
all the elders of Israel to eat a meal with
Moses' father-in-law before God.

13 Now it happened the next day that
Moses sat to judge the people, and the
people stood about Moses from the
morning until the evening. 14 And Moses'
father-in-law saw all that he was doing
for the people, so he said, "What is this
thing that you are doing for the people?
Why do you alone sit *as judge* and all the
people stand about you from morning
until evening?" 15 And Moses said to his
father-in-law, "Because the people come
to me to inquire of God. 16 When they
have a matter, it comes to me, and I judge
between a man and his neighbor and make
known the statutes of God and His laws."
17 And Moses' father-in-law said to him,
"The thing that you are doing is not good.
18 You will surely wear out, both yourself
and these people who are with you, for the
task is too heavy for you; you cannot do
it alone. 19 Now listen to my voice: I will
give you counsel, and God be with you. You
be the people's representative before God,
and you bring the matters to God; 20 then
warn them about the statutes and the laws,
and make known to them the way in which
they shall go and the work they shall do.
21 But you shall select excellent men out of
all the people, those who fear God, men of
truth, those who hate greedy gain; and you
shall place *these men* over them *as* leaders
of thousands, of hundreds, of fifties, and
of tens. 22 And they will judge the people
at all times. And it will be that every major
matter they will bring to you, but every
minor matter they themselves will judge.
So it will be easier for you, and they will
bear *the burden* with you. 23 If you do this
thing and God *so* commands you, then you
will be able to endure, and all these people
also will go to their place in peace."

24 So Moses listened to the voice of his
father-in-law and did all that he had said.
25 And Moses chose excellent men out of all
Israel and made them heads over the people,
leaders of thousands, of hundreds, of fifties,
and of tens. 26 And they judged the people
at all times; the difficult matter they would
bring to Moses, but every minor matter they
themselves would judge. 27 Then Moses let
his father-in-law depart, and he went his
way into his own land.

Psalm 18:28–36

28 For You light my lamp;
Yahweh my God illumines
my darkness.
29 For by You I can run upon a troop;
And by my God I can leap over a wall.

30 As for God, His way is blameless;
The word of Yahweh is tried;
He is a shield to all who
take refuge in Him.
31 For who is God, but Yahweh?
And who is a rock, except our God,
32 The God who girds me with strength
And makes my way blameless?
33 He makes my feet like hinds' *feet*,
And sets me upon my high places.
34 He trains my hands for battle,
So that my arms can bend
a bow of bronze.
35 You have also given me the
shield of Your salvation,
And Your right hand upholds me;
And Your gentleness makes me great.
36 You enlarge my steps under me,
And my ankles have not given way.

Proverbs 6:16–19

16 There are six things which
Yahweh hates,
Even seven which are an
abomination to Him:
17 Haughty eyes, a lying tongue,
And hands that shed innocent blood,
18 A heart that devises wicked thoughts,
Feet that hasten to run to evil,
19 A false witness *who* breathes out lies,
And one who spreads strife
among brothers.

Matthew 22:1–22

22 And Jesus answered and spoke to them again in parables, saying, 2 "The kingdom of heaven may be compared to a king who gave a wedding feast for his son. 3 And he sent out his slaves to call those who had been called to the wedding feast, and they were unwilling to come. 4 Again he sent out other slaves saying, 'Tell those who have been called, "Behold, I have prepared my dinner; my oxen and my fattened livestock are *all* butchered and everything is ready; come to the wedding feast."' 5 But they paid no attention and went their way, one to his own farm, another to his business, 6 and the rest seized his slaves and mistreated them and killed them. 7 But the king was enraged, and he sent his armies and destroyed those murderers and set their city on fire. 8 Then he *said to his slaves, 'The wedding is ready, but those who were called were not worthy. 9 Go therefore to the main highways, and as many as you find *there*, call to the wedding feast.' 10 And those slaves went out into the streets and gathered together all they found, both evil and good; and the wedding hall was filled with dinner guests.

11 "But when the king came in to look over the dinner guests, he saw a man there who was not dressed in wedding clothes, 12 and he *said to him, 'Friend, how did you come in here without wedding clothes?' And the man was speechless. 13 Then the king said to the servants, 'Bind him hand and foot, and throw him into the outer darkness; in that place there will be weeping and gnashing of teeth.' 14 For many are called, but few *are* chosen."

15 Then the Pharisees went and took counsel together about how they might trap Him in what He said. 16 And they *sent their disciples to Him, along with the Herodians, saying, "Teacher, we know that You are truthful and teach the way of God in truth, and defer to no one; for You are not partial to any. 17 Therefore, tell us, what do You think? Is it lawful to give a tax to Caesar, or not?" 18 But Jesus, knowing their wickedness, said, "Why are you testing Me, you hypocrites? 19 Show Me the coin *used* for the tax." And they brought Him a denarius. 20 And He *said to them, "Whose likeness and inscription is this?" 21 They *said to Him, "Caesar's." Then He *said to them, "Therefore, render to Caesar the things that are Caesar's; and to God the things that are God's." 22 And hearing *this*, they marveled, and leaving Him, they went away.

FEBRUARY 4

Exodus 19:1–20:26

19 In the third month after the sons of Israel had gone out of the land of Egypt, on this day they came into the wilderness of Sinai. 2 Then they set out from Rephidim and came to the wilderness of Sinai and camped in the wilderness; and there Israel camped in front of the mountain.

3 Now Moses went up to God, and Yahweh called to him from the mountain, saying, "Thus you shall say to the house of Jacob and tell the sons of Israel: 4 'You yourselves have seen what I did to the Egyptians, and *how* I lifted you up on eagles' wings and brought you to Myself. 5 So now then, if you will indeed listen to My voice and keep My covenant, then you shall be My treasured possession among all the peoples, for all the earth is Mine; 6 and you shall be to Me a kingdom of priests and a holy nation.' These are the words that you shall speak to the sons of Israel."

7 So Moses came and called the elders of the people and set before them all these words which Yahweh had commanded him. 8 And all the people answered together and said, "All that Yahweh has spoken we will do!" And Moses brought back the words of the people to Yahweh. 9 Yahweh said to Moses, "Behold, I will come to you in a thick cloud, so that the people may hear when I speak with you and may also believe in you forever." Then Moses told the words of the people to Yahweh.

10 Yahweh also said to Moses, "Go to the people and set them apart as holy today and tomorrow, and let them wash their garments; 11 and let them be ready for the third day, for on the third day Yahweh will come down on Mount Sinai in the sight of all the people. 12 And you shall set bounds for the people all around, saying, 'Beware that you do not go up on the mountain or touch the border of it; whoever touches the mountain shall

surely be put to death. 13 No hand shall touch
him, but he shall surely be stoned or surely
shot through; whether beast or man, he shall
not live.' When the ram's horn sounds a long
blast, they shall come up to the mountain."
14 So Moses went down from the mountain to
the people and set the people apart as holy,
and they washed their garments. 15 And he
said to the people, "Be ready for the third
day; do not go near a woman."

16 So it happened on the third day, when
it was morning, that there were thunder and
lightning flashes and a thick cloud upon the
mountain and a very loud trumpet sound,
so that all the people who *were* in the camp
trembled. 17 And Moses brought the people
out of the camp to meet God, and they stood
at the foot of the mountain.

18 Now Mount Sinai *was* all in smoke
because Yahweh descended upon it in fire;
and its smoke ascended like the smoke of a
furnace, and the whole mountain trembled
violently. 19 And the sound of the trumpet
grew louder and louder; *then* Moses spoke
and God answered him with thunder. 20 And
Yahweh came down on Mount Sinai, to the
top of the mountain; and Yahweh called
Moses to the top of the mountain, and
Moses went up. 21 Then Yahweh spoke to
Moses, "Go down, warn the people, lest
they break through to Yahweh to see, and
many of them perish. 22 Also let the priests
who come near to Yahweh set themselves
apart as holy, lest Yahweh break out against
them." 23 And Moses said to Yahweh, "The
people cannot come up to Mount Sinai, for
You warned us, saying, 'Set bounds about
the mountain, and set it apart as holy.'"
24 Then Yahweh said to him, "Go down and
come up *again*, you and Aaron with you; but
do not let the priests and the people break
through to come up to Yahweh, lest He break
out against them." 25 So Moses went down
to the people and told them.

20 Then God spoke all these words, saying,

2 "I am Yahweh your God, who brought
you out of the land of Egypt, out of the
house of slavery.

3 "You shall have no other gods before Me.

4 "You shall not make for yourself an
idol, or any likeness of what is in
heaven above or on the earth beneath
or in the water under the earth.
5 "You shall not worship them or serve
them; for I, Yahweh your God, am a
jealous God, visiting the iniquity of the
fathers on the children, on the third
and the fourth generations of those
who hate Me,
6 but showing lovingkindness to
thousands, to those who love Me and
keep My commandments.

7 "You shall not take the name of Yahweh
your God in vain, for Yahweh will not
leave him unpunished who takes His
name in vain.

8 "Remember the sabbath day, to keep it
holy.
9 "Six days you shall labor and do all your
work,
10 but the seventh day is a sabbath of
Yahweh your God; *in it* you shall not
do any work, you or your son or your
daughter, your male or your female
slave or your cattle or your sojourner
who is within your gates.
11 "For in six days Yahweh made the
heavens and the earth, the sea and
all that is in them, and rested on the
seventh day; therefore Yahweh blessed
the sabbath day and made it holy.

12 "Honor your father and your mother,
that your days may be prolonged in the
land which Yahweh your God gives you.

13 "You shall not murder.

14 "You shall not commit adultery.

15 "You shall not steal.

16 "You shall not bear false witness
against your neighbor.

17 "You shall not covet your neighbor's
house; you shall not covet your
neighbor's wife or his male slave or his
female slave or his ox or his donkey
or anything that belongs to your
neighbor."

18 And all the people perceived the thun-
der and the lightning flashes and the sound

of the trumpet and the mountain smoking;
and the people perceived *it*, and they shook
and stood at a distance. 19 Then they said to
Moses, "Speak to us yourself, and we will
listen; but let not God speak to us, lest we
die." 20 And Moses said to the people, "Do not
be afraid; for God has come in order to test
you, and in order that the fear of Him may be
with you, so that you may not sin." 21 So the
people stood at a distance, but Moses came
near the dense gloom where God *was*.

22 Then Yahweh said to Moses, "Thus
you shall say to the sons of Israel, 'You
yourselves have seen that I have spoken
to you from heaven. 23 You shall not make
other gods besides Me; gods of silver or gods
of gold, you shall not make for yourselves.
24 You shall make an altar of earth for Me,
and you shall sacrifice on it your burnt offer-
ings and your peace offerings, your sheep
and your oxen; in every place where I cause
My name to be remembered, I will come to
you and bless you. 25 And if you make an
altar of stone for Me, you shall not build
it of cut stones, for if you wield your tool
on it, you will profane it. 26 And you shall
not go up by steps to My altar, so that your
nakedness will not be exposed on it.'

Psalm 18:37–45

37 I pursued my enemies and
overtook them,
And I did not turn back until
they were consumed.
38 I crushed them, so that they
were not able to rise;
They fell under my feet.
39 For You have girded me with
strength for battle;
You have subdued under me those
who rose up against me.
40 You have also made my enemies
turn their backs to me,
And I destroyed those who hated me.
41 They cried for help, but there
was none to save,
Even to Yahweh, but He did
not answer them.
42 Then I beat them fine as the
dust before the wind;
I emptied them out as the
mire of the streets.

43 You have delivered me from the
contentions of the people;
You have placed me as head
of the nations;
A people whom I have not
known serve me.
44 As soon as they hear, they obey me;
Foreigners cower before me.
45 Foreigners fade away,
And come trembling out
of their fortresses.

Proverbs 6:20–25

20 My son, observe the commandment
of your father
And do not abandon the
law of your mother;
21 Bind them continually on your heart;
Tie them around your neck.
22 When you walk about,
they will lead you;
When you sleep, they will
keep watch over you;
And when you awake,
they will speak to you.
23 For the commandment is a
lamp and the law is light;
And reproofs for discipline
are the way of life
24 To keep you from the evil woman,
From the smooth tongue of
the foreign woman.
25 Do not desire her beauty in your heart,
Nor let her capture you
with her eyelids.

Matthew 22:23–46

23 On that day *some* Sadducees (who say
there is no resurrection) came to Jesus and
asked Him a question, 24 saying, "Teacher,
Moses said, 'IF A MAN DIES HAVING NO CHIL-
DREN, HIS BROTHER AS NEXT OF KIN SHALL
MARRY HIS WIFE AND RAISE UP A SEED FOR HIS
BROTHER.' 25 Now there were seven brothers
with us; and the first married and died, and
having no seed, he left his wife to his brother;
26 so also the second, and the third, down
to the seventh. 27 And last of all, the woman
died. 28 In the resurrection, therefore, whose
wife of the seven will she be? For they all had
married her."

29 But Jesus answered and said to them,
"You are mistaken, not understanding the
Scriptures nor the power of God. 30 For in the
resurrection they neither marry nor are given
in marriage, but are like angels in heaven.
31 But regarding the resurrection of the dead,

have you not read what was spoken to you by God, saying, 32 'I AM THE GOD OF ABRAHAM, AND THE GOD OF ISAAC, AND THE GOD OF JACOB'? He is not the God of the dead but of the living." 33 And when the crowds heard *this,* they were astonished at His teaching.

34 But when the Pharisees heard that Jesus had silenced the Sadducees, they gathered themselves together. 35 And one of them, a scholar of the Law, asked *Him* a question, testing Him, 36 "Teacher, which is the great commandment in the Law?" 37 And He said to him, "'YOU SHALL LOVE THE LORD YOUR GOD WITH ALL YOUR HEART, AND WITH ALL YOUR SOUL, AND WITH ALL YOUR MIND.' 38 This is the great and foremost commandment. 39 And the second is like it, 'YOU SHALL LOVE YOUR NEIGHBOR AS YOURSELF.' 40 On these two commandments hang the whole Law and the Prophets."

41 Now while the Pharisees were gathered together, Jesus asked them a question, 42 saying, "What do you think about the Christ, whose son is He?" They *said to Him, "*The son* of David." 43 He *said to them, "Then how does David in the Spirit call Him 'Lord,' saying,

44 'THE LORD SAID TO MY LORD,
"SIT AT MY RIGHT HAND,
UNTIL I PUT YOUR ENEMIES
BENEATH YOUR FEET"'?

45 "Therefore, if David calls Him 'Lord,' how is He his son?" 46 And no one was able to answer Him a word, nor did anyone dare from that day on to ask Him another question.

The Bible is the greatest of all books; to study it is the noblest of all pursuits; to understand it, the highest of all goals.

— CHARLES RYRIE

FEBRUARY 5

Exodus 21:1–22:31

21 "Now these are the judgments which you are to set before them:

2 "If you buy a Hebrew slave, he shall serve for six years; but on the seventh he shall go out as a free man without payment. 3 If he comes alone, he shall go out alone; if he is the husband of a wife, then his wife shall go out with him. 4 If his master gives him a wife, and she bears him sons or daughters, the wife and her children shall belong to her master, and he shall go out alone. 5 But if the slave plainly says, 'I love my master, my wife, and my children; I will not go out as a free man,' 6 then his master shall bring him to God, and he shall bring him to the door or the doorpost. Then his master shall pierce his ear with an awl; and he shall serve him permanently.

7 "And if a man sells his daughter as a female slave, she is not to go free as the male slaves do. 8 If she is displeasing in the eyes of her master who designated her for himself, then he shall let her be redeemed. He does not have authority to sell her to a foreign people because of his treachery to her. 9 And if he designates her for his son, he shall do to her according to the custom of daughters. 10 If he takes for himself another woman, he may not reduce her food, her clothing, or her conjugal rights. 11 And if he will not do these three *things* for her, then she shall go out for nothing, without *payment of* money.

12 "He who strikes a man so that he dies shall surely be put to death. 13 But if he did not lie in wait *for him,* but God let *him* fall into his hand, then I will appoint you a place to which he may flee. 14 If, however, a man acts presumptuously toward his neighbor, so as to kill him by deceit, you shall take him *even* from My altar, that he may die.

15 "And he who strikes his father or his mother shall surely be put to death.

16 "He who kidnaps a man, whether he sells him or he is found in his hand, shall surely be put to death.

17 "And he who curses his father or his mother shall surely be put to death.

18 "And if men contend *with each other* and one strikes the other with a stone or with *his* fist, and he does not die but remains in bed, 19 if he gets up and walks

around outside on his staff, then he who struck him shall go unpunished; he shall only pay for his loss of time, and he shall take care of him until he is completely healed.

20 "And if a man strikes his male or female slave with a rod and he dies at his hand, he shall surely be punished. 21 But if for a day or two he *is able to* stand, no punishment shall be taken; for he is his property.

22 "And if men struggle with each other and strike a woman with child so that she gives birth prematurely, yet there is no injury, he shall surely be fined as the woman's husband will set for him, and he shall pay as the judges *decide*. 23 But if there is *any further* injury, then you shall pay life for life, 24 eye for eye, tooth for tooth, hand for hand, foot for foot, 25 burn for burn, bruise for bruise, wound for wound.

26 "And if a man strikes the eye of his male or female slave and ruins it, he shall let him go free on account of his eye. 27 And if he knocks out a tooth of his male or female slave, he shall let him go free on account of his tooth.

28 "And if an ox gores a man or a woman to death, the ox shall surely be stoned and its flesh shall not be eaten; but the owner of the ox shall go unpunished. 29 If, however, an ox was previously in the habit of goring and its owner has been warned, yet he does not confine it and it puts a man or a woman to death, the ox shall be stoned and its owner also shall be put to death. 30 If a ransom is demanded of him, then he shall give for the redemption of his life whatever is demanded of him. 31 Whether it gores a son or a daughter, it shall be done to him according to the same judgment. 32 If the ox gores a male or female slave, the owner shall give his *or her* master thirty shekels of silver, and the ox shall be stoned.

33 "And if a man opens a pit, or if a man digs a pit and does not cover it over, and an ox or a donkey falls into it, 34 the owner of the pit shall make restitution; he shall give money to its owner, and the dead *animal* shall become his.

35 "And if one man's ox hurts another's so that it dies, then they shall sell the live ox and divide its price equally; and also they shall divide the dead *ox*. 36 Or *if* it is known that the ox was previously in the habit of goring, yet its owner has not confined it, he shall surely pay ox for ox, and the dead *animal* shall become his.

22 "If a man steals an ox or a sheep and slaughters it or sells it, he shall pay five oxen for the ox and four sheep for the sheep.

2 "If the thief is caught while breaking in and is struck so that he dies, there will be no bloodguiltiness on his account. 3 *But* if the sun has risen on him, there will be bloodguiltiness on his account. He shall surely make restitution; if he owns nothing, then he shall be sold for his theft. 4 If what he stole is actually found alive in his hand, whether an ox or a donkey or a sheep, he shall pay double.

5 "If a man lets a field or vineyard be grazed *bare* and lets his animal loose so that it grazes in another man's field, he shall make restitution from the best of his own field and the best of his own vineyard.

6 "If a fire breaks out and spreads to thorn bushes, so that stacked grain or the standing grain or the field *itself* is consumed, he who started the fire shall surely make restitution.

7 "If a man gives his neighbor money or goods to keep *for him* and it is stolen from the man's house, if the thief is caught, he shall pay double. 8 If the thief is not caught, then the owner of the house shall appear before the judges *to* determine whether he laid his hands on his neighbor's property. 9 For every breach of trust, *whether it is* for ox, for donkey, for sheep, for clothing, *or* for any lost thing about which one says, 'This is it,' the case of both parties shall come before the judges; he whom the judges condemn shall pay double to his neighbor.

10 "If a man gives his neighbor a donkey, an ox, a sheep, or any animal to keep *for him*, and it dies or is injured or is driven away while no one is looking, 11 then an oath before Yahweh shall be made by the two of them that he has not laid hands on his neighbor's property; and its owner shall accept *it*, and he shall not make restitution. 12 But if it is actually stolen from him, he shall make restitution to its owner. 13 Now if it is all torn to pieces, let him bring it as evidence; he shall not make restitution for what has been torn to pieces.

14 "If a man borrows *anything* from his neighbor, and it is injured or dies while its owner is not with it, he shall make full

restitution. 15 But if its owner is with it, he
shall not make restitution; if it is hired, it
came for its hire.
16 "If a man seduces a virgin who is not
engaged and lies with her, he must pay a
dowry for her *to be* his wife. 17 If her father
absolutely refuses to give her to him, he
shall pay money equal to the dowry for
virgins.
18 "You shall not allow a sorceress to live.
19 "Whoever lies with an animal shall
surely be put to death.
20 "And he who sacrifices to any god, other
than to Yahweh alone, shall be devoted to
destruction.
21 "You shall not mistreat a sojourner or
oppress him, for you were sojourners in the
land of Egypt. 22 You shall not afflict any
widow or orphan. 23 And if you indeed afflict
him, *and* if he earnestly cries out to Me, I
will surely hear his cry; 24 and My anger will
burn, and I will kill you with the sword, and
your wives shall become widows and your
children fatherless.
25 "If you lend money to My people, to the
afflicted among you, you are not to act as a
creditor to him; you shall not charge him
interest. 26 If you ever take your neighbor's
cloak as a pledge, you shall return it to him
before the sun sets, 27 for that is his only
covering; it is his cloak for his body. What
else shall he sleep in? And it shall be that
when he cries out to Me, I will hear *him*, for
I am gracious.
28 "You shall not curse God, nor curse a
ruler of your people.
29 "You shall not delay *the offering from*
the fullness of your harvest and the juice of
your wine vat. The firstborn of your sons
you shall give to Me. 30 And you shall do the
same with your oxen *and* with your sheep. It
shall be with its mother seven days; on the
eighth day you shall give it to Me.
31 "You shall be holy men to Me, therefore
you shall not eat *any* flesh torn to pieces in
the field; you shall throw it to the dogs.

Psalm 18:46–50

46 Yahweh lives, and blessed be my rock;
And let the God of my
salvation be lifted high,
47 The God who executes
vengeance for me,
And subdues peoples under me.
48 Who delivers me from my enemies;
Surely You lift me above those
who rise up against me;
You rescue me from the violent man.
49 Therefore I will give thanks to You
among the nations, O Yahweh,
And I will sing praises to Your name.
50 He gives great salvation to His king,
And shows lovingkindness
to His anointed,
To David and his seed forever.

Proverbs 6:26–29

26 For on account of a harlot *one is*
reduced to a loaf of bread,
And an adulteress hunts
for the precious life.
27 Can a man take fire in his bosom
And his clothes not be burned?
28 Or can a man walk on hot coals
And his feet not be scorched?
29 So is the one who goes in to
his neighbor's wife;
Whoever touches her will
not go unpunished.

Matthew 23:1–22

23 Then Jesus spoke to the crowds and
to His disciples, 2 saying: "The scribes
and the Pharisees have seated themselves
in the chair of Moses; 3 therefore all that
they tell you, do and keep, but do not do
according to their deeds; for they say *things*
and do not do *them*. 4 And they tie up heavy
burdens and lay them on men's shoulders,
but they themselves are unwilling to move
them with *so much as* a finger. 5 But they do
all their deeds to be noticed by men; for they
broaden their phylacteries and lengthen the
tassels *of their garments*. 6 And they love the
place of honor at banquets and the best seats
in the synagogues, 7 and respectful greetings
in the marketplaces, and being called Rabbi
by men. 8 But do not be called Rabbi; for One
is your Teacher, and you are all brothers.
9 And do not call *anyone* on earth your
father; for One is your Father, He who is
in heaven. 10 Do not be called instructors;
for One is your Instructor, *that is*, Christ.
11 But the greatest among you shall be your
servant. 12 And whoever exalts himself shall
be humbled; and whoever humbles himself
shall be exalted.
13 "But woe to you, scribes and Pharisees,
hypocrites, because you shut off the king-
dom of heaven from people; for you do not

enter in yourselves, nor do you allow those who are entering to go in. 14 [Woe to you, scribes and Pharisees, hypocrites, because you devour widows' houses, and for a pretense you make long prayers; therefore you will receive greater condemnation.]

15 "Woe to you, scribes and Pharisees, hypocrites, because you travel around on sea and land to make one proselyte; and when he becomes one, you make him twice as much a son of hell as yourselves.

16 "Woe to you, blind guides, who say, 'Whoever swears by the sanctuary, *that* is nothing; but whoever swears by the gold of the sanctuary is obligated.' 17 You fools and blind men! For which is more important, the gold or the sanctuary that sanctified the gold? 18 And, 'Whoever swears by the altar, *that* is nothing, but whoever swears by the offering on it, he is obligated.' 19 You blind men, which is more important, the offering, or the altar that sanctifies the offering? 20 Therefore, whoever swears by the altar, swears *both* by the altar and by everything on it. 21 And whoever swears by the sanctuary, swears *both* by the sanctuary and by Him who dwells within it. 22 And whoever swears by heaven, swears *both* by the throne of God and by Him who sits upon it.

FEBRUARY 6

Exodus 23:1–24:18

23 "You shall not bear a false report; do not join your hand with a wicked man to be a malicious witness. 2 You shall not follow the masses in doing evil, nor shall you testify in a case so as to turn aside after the masses in order to cause *justice* to be turned aside; 3 nor shall you be partial to a poor man in his case.

4 "If you meet your enemy's ox or his donkey wandering away, you shall surely return it to him. 5 If you see the donkey of one who hates you lying *helpless* under its load, you shall refrain from leaving it to him, you shall surely release *it* with him.

6 "You shall not cause the justice *due* to your needy *brother* to be turned aside in his case. 7 Keep far from a false charge, and do not kill the innocent or the righteous, for I will not justify the guilty.

8 "And you shall not take a bribe, for a bribe blinds the clear-sighted and subverts the cause of the just.

9 "And you shall not oppress a sojourner, since you yourselves know the soul of a sojourner, for you *also* were sojourners in the land of Egypt.

10 "Now you shall sow your land for six years and gather in its produce, 11 but *on* the seventh year you shall let it rest and lie fallow, so that the needy of your people may eat; and whatever they leave the beast of the field may eat. Thus you shall do with your vineyard *and* your olive grove.

12 "Six days you are to do your work, but on the seventh day you shall rest so that your ox and your donkey may rest, and the son of your maidservant, as well as your sojourner, may refresh themselves. 13 Now concerning everything which I have said to you, beware; and do not mention the name of other gods, nor let *them* be heard from your mouth.

14 "Three times a year you shall celebrate a feast to Me. 15 You shall keep the Feast of Unleavened Bread; for seven days you are to eat unleavened bread, as I commanded you, at the appointed time in the month Abib, for in it you came out of Egypt. And none shall appear before Me empty-handed. 16 Also *you shall keep* the Feast of the Harvest *of* the first fruits of your labors *from* what you sow in the field; also the Feast of the Ingathering at the end of the year when you gather in *the fruit of* your labors from the field. 17 Three times a year all your males shall appear before the Lord Yahweh.

18 "You shall not offer the blood of My sacrifice with leavened bread; nor is the fat of My feast to remain overnight until morning.

19 "You shall bring the choice first fruits of your ground into the house of Yahweh your God.

"You shall not boil a young goat in the milk of its mother.

20 "Behold, I am going to send an angel before you to keep you along the way and to bring you into the place which I have prepared. 21 Keep watch *of yourself* before him and listen to his voice; do not be rebellious toward him, for he will not pardon

your transgression, since My name is in
him. 22 But if you truly listen to his voice
and do all that I speak, then I will be an
enemy to your enemies and an adversary
to your adversaries. 23 For My angel will go
before you and bring you in to *the land of*
the Amorites, the Hittites, the Perizzites, the
Canaanites, the Hivites, and the Jebusites;
and I will annihilate them. 24 You shall not
worship their gods, you shall not serve
them, and you shall not do according to
their deeds; but you shall utterly pull them
down and shatter their *sacred* pillars in
pieces. 25 But you shall serve Yahweh your
God, and He will bless your bread and your
water; and I will remove sickness from your
midst. 26 There shall be no one miscarrying
or barren in your land; I will fulfill the
number of your days. 27 I will send My terror
ahead of you and throw into confusion all
the people among whom you come, and I
will make all your enemies turn *their* backs
to you. 28 And I will send hornets ahead of
you so that they will drive out the Hivites,
the Canaanites, and the Hittites before you.
29 I will not drive them out before you in a
single year, lest the land become desolate
and the beasts of the field become too
numerous for you. 30 I will drive them out
before you little by little, until you become
fruitful and take the land as an inheritance.
31 And I will set your boundary from the Red
Sea to the sea of the Philistines, and from
the wilderness to the River; for I will give
the inhabitants of the land into your hand,
and you will drive them out from before you.
32 You shall cut no covenant with them or
with their gods. 33 They shall not live in your
land, lest they make you sin against Me; for
if you serve their gods, it will surely be a
snare to you."

24 Then He said to Moses, "Come up to
Yahweh, you and Aaron, Nadab and
Abihu and seventy of the elders of Israel,
and you *all* shall worship at a distance.
2 Moses alone, however, shall come near to
Yahweh, but they shall not come near, and
the people shall not come up with him."

3 Then Moses came and recounted to the
people all the words of Yahweh and all the
judgments; and all the people answered
with one voice and said, "All the words
which Yahweh has spoken we will do!" 4 And
Moses wrote down all the words of Yahweh.
Then he arose early in the morning and built
an altar at the foot of the mountain with
twelve pillars for the twelve tribes of Israel.
5 And he sent young men of the sons of
Israel, and they offered burnt offerings and
sacrificed young bulls as peace offerings to
Yahweh. 6 And Moses took half of the blood
and put *it* in basins, and the *other* half of the
blood he sprinkled on the altar. 7 Then he
took the book of the covenant and read *it* in
the hearing of the people; and they said, "All
that Yahweh has spoken we will do, and we
will be obedient!" 8 So Moses took the blood
and sprinkled *it* on the people and said,
"Behold the blood of the covenant, which
Yahweh has cut with you in accordance with
all these words."

9 Then Moses went up with Aaron, Nadab
and Abihu, and seventy of the elders of
Israel, 10 and they saw the God of Israel;
and under His feet there appeared to be a
pavement of sapphire, as clear as the sky
itself. 11 Yet He did not stretch out His hand
against the nobles of the sons of Israel; and
they beheld God, and they ate and drank.

12 Now Yahweh said to Moses, "Come up
to Me on the mountain and remain there,
and I will give you the stone tablets with
the law and the commandment which I have
written for their instruction." 13 So Moses
arose with Joshua his attendant, and Moses
went up to the mountain of God. 14 But to the
elders he said, "Remain here for us until we
return to you. And behold, Aaron and Hur
are with you; whoever has a *legal* matter, let
him approach them." 15 Then Moses went up
to the mountain, and the cloud covered the
mountain. 16 And the glory of Yahweh dwelt
on Mount Sinai, and the cloud covered it for
six days; and on the seventh day He called
to Moses from the midst of the cloud. 17 And
the appearance of the glory of Yahweh was
like a consuming fire on the mountain top,
in the eyes of the sons of Israel. 18 Then
Moses entered the midst of the cloud as he
went up to the mountain; and Moses was on
the mountain forty days and forty nights.

Psalm 19:1–6

1 The heavens are telling of
the glory of God;
And the expanse is declaring
the work of His hands.
2 Day to day pours forth speech,
And night to night reveals knowledge.

3 There is no speech, nor
are there words;
Their voice is not heard.
4 Their line has gone out
through all the earth,
And their utterances to the
end of the world.
In them He has placed a
tent for the sun,
5 Which is as a bridegroom coming
out of his chamber;
It rejoices as a strong man
to run his course.
6 Its rising is from one end
of the heavens,
And its circuit to the other
end of them;
And there is nothing hidden
from its heat.

Proverbs 6:30–31

30 *Men* do not despise a thief if he steals
To fill himself when he is hungry;
31 But when he is found, he
must repay sevenfold;
He must give all the substance
of his house.

Matthew 23:23–39

23 "Woe to you, scribes and Pharisees, hypocrites! For you tithe mint and dill and cumin, and have neglected the weightier provisions of the Law: justice and mercy and faithfulness; but these are the things you should have done without neglecting the others. 24 You blind guides, who strain out a gnat but swallow a camel!

25 "Woe to you, scribes and Pharisees, hypocrites! For you clean the outside of the cup and of the dish, but inside they are full of robbery and self-indulgence. 26 You blind Pharisee, first clean the inside of the cup and of the dish, so that the outside of it may become clean also.

27 "Woe to you, scribes and Pharisees, hypocrites! For you are like whitewashed tombs which on the outside appear beautiful, but inside they are full of dead men's bones and all uncleanness. 28 In this way, you also outwardly appear righteous to men, but inwardly you are full of hypocrisy and lawlessness.

29 "Woe to you, scribes and Pharisees, hypocrites! For you build the tombs of the prophets and adorn the monuments of the righteous, 30 and say, 'If we had been *living* in the days of our fathers, we would not have been partners with them in *shedding* the blood of the prophets.' 31 So you bear witness against yourselves, that you are sons of those who murdered the prophets. 32 Fill up, then, the measure *of the guilt* of your fathers. 33 You serpents, you brood of vipers, how will you escape the sentence of hell?

34 "On account of this, behold, I am sending you prophets and wise men and scribes; some of them you will kill and crucify, and some of them you will flog in your synagogues, and persecute from city to city, 35 so that upon you may fall *the guilt of* all the righteous blood shed on earth, from the blood of righteous Abel to the blood of Zechariah, the son of Berechiah, whom you murdered between the sanctuary and the altar. 36 Truly I say to you, all these things will come upon this generation.

37 "Jerusalem, Jerusalem, who kills the prophets and stones those who are sent to her! How often I wanted to gather your children together, the way a hen gathers her chicks under her wings, and you did not want *it*. 38 Behold, your house is being left to you desolate! 39 For I say to you, from now on you will not see Me until you say, 'BLESSED IS HE WHO COMES IN THE NAME OF THE LORD!'"

FEBRUARY 7

Exodus 25:1–26:37

25 Then Yahweh spoke to Moses, saying, 2 "Speak with the sons of Israel so that they take a contribution for Me; from every man whose heart is willing you shall take My contribution. 3 And this is the contribution which you shall take from them: gold, silver, and bronze, 4 blue, purple, and scarlet *material*, fine linen, goat *hair*, 5 rams' skins dyed red, porpoise skins, acacia wood, 6 oil for lighting, spices for the anointing oil and for the fragrant incense, 7 onyx stones, and setting stones for the ephod and for the breastpiece. 8 And let them make a

sanctuary for Me, that I may dwell among
them. 9 According to all that I am going to
show you, *as* the pattern of the tabernacle
and the pattern of all its furniture, just so
you shall make *it*.

10 "And they shall make an ark of acacia
wood two and a half cubits long, and one
and a half cubits wide, and one and a half
cubits high. 11 You shall overlay it with pure
gold, inside and out you shall overlay it, and
you shall make a gold molding around it.
12 You shall cast four gold rings for it and
fasten them on its four feet, and two rings
shall be on one side of it and two rings on
the other side of it. 13 You shall make poles
of acacia wood and overlay them with gold.
14 You shall put the poles into the rings on
the sides of the ark, to carry the ark with
them. 15 The poles shall remain in the rings
of the ark; they shall not be removed from
it. 16 You shall put into the ark the testimony
which I shall give you.

17 "You shall make a mercy seat of pure
gold, two and a half cubits long and one
and a half cubits wide. 18 You shall make
two cherubim of gold; make them of ham-
mered work at the two ends of the mercy
seat. 19 Make one cherub at one end and one
cherub at the other end; from *one piece* you
shall make the mercy seat *with* the cheru-
bim at its two ends. 20 The cherubim shall
have *their* wings spread upward, covering
the mercy seat with their wings, with their
faces toward one another; the faces of the
cherubim are to be toward the mercy seat.
21 You shall put the mercy seat on top of
the ark, and in the ark you shall put the
testimony which I will give to you. 22 There
I will meet with you; and from above the
mercy seat, from between the two cherubim
which are upon the ark of the testimony,
I will speak to you about all which I will
command you for the sons of Israel.

23 "You shall make a table of acacia wood,
two cubits long and one cubit wide and one
and a half cubits high. 24 You shall overlay
it with pure gold and make a gold border
around it. 25 You shall make for it a rim of
a handbreadth around *it*; and you shall
make a gold border for the rim around it.
26 You shall make four gold rings for it and
put rings on the four corners which are on
its four feet. 27 The rings shall be close to
the rim as holders for the poles to carry the
table. 28 You shall make the poles of acacia
wood and overlay them with gold, so that
with them the table may be carried. 29 You
shall make its dishes and its pans and its
jars and its offering bowls with which to
pour drink offerings; you shall make them
of pure gold. 30 You shall set the bread of the
Presence on the table before Me at all times.

31 "Then you shall make a lampstand of
pure gold. The lampstand, its base, and its
shaft are to be made of hammered work; its
cups, its bulbs, and its flowers shall be of *the
same piece*. 32 Six branches shall go out from
its sides; three branches of the lampstand
from its one side and three branches of
the lampstand from its other side. 33 Three
cups *shall be* shaped like almond *blossoms*
in the one branch, a bulb and a flower, and
three cups shaped like almond *blossoms* in
the other branch, a bulb and a flower—so
for the six branches going out from the
lampstand; 34 and in the lampstand four
cups shaped like almond *blossoms*, its bulbs
and its flowers. 35 And a bulb shall be under
the *first* pair of branches *coming* out of it,
and a bulb under the *second* pair of branches
coming out of it, and a bulb under the *third*
pair of branches *coming* out of it, for the
six branches coming out of the lampstand.
36 Their bulbs and their branches shall be of
the same piece; all of it shall be one piece of
hammered work of pure gold. 37 Then you
shall make its lamps seven *in number*; and
they shall mount its lamps so as to shed
light on the space in front of it. 38 And its
tongs and their trays *shall be* of pure gold.
39 It shall be made from a talent of pure gold,
with all these utensils. 40 And see that you
make *them* after the pattern for them, which
was shown to you on the mountain.

26 "Moreover you shall make the
tabernacle with ten curtains of fine
twisted linen and blue and purple and
scarlet *material*; you shall make them with
cherubim, the work of a skillful designer.
2 The length of each curtain shall be twenty-
eight cubits, and the width of each curtain
four cubits; all the curtains shall have the
same measurements. 3 Five curtains shall
be joined to one another, and *the other* five
curtains *shall be* joined to one another.
4 And you shall make loops of blue on the
edge of the outermost curtain in the one
set, and likewise you shall make *them* on
the edge of the curtain that is outermost in

the second set. 5 You shall make fifty loops in the one curtain, and you shall make fifty loops on the edge of the curtain that is in the second set; the loops shall be opposite each other. 6 You shall make fifty clasps of gold, and you shall join the curtains to one another with the clasps so that the tabernacle will be a unit.

7 "Then you shall make curtains of goats' *hair* for a tent over the tabernacle; you shall make eleven curtains in all. 8 The length of each curtain *shall be* thirty cubits, and the width of each curtain four cubits; the eleven curtains shall have the same measurements. 9 And you shall join five curtains by themselves and the *other* six curtains by themselves, and you shall double over the sixth curtain at the front of the tent. 10 You shall make fifty loops on the edge of the curtain that is outermost in the one set, and fifty loops on the edge of the curtain *that is outermost in* the second set.

11 "You shall make fifty clasps of bronze, and you shall put the clasps into the loops and join the tent together so that it will be one unit. 12 The overlapping part that is left over in the curtains of the tent, the half curtain that is left over, shall lap over the back of the tabernacle. 13 The cubit on one side and the cubit on the other, of what is left over in the length of the curtains of the tent, shall lap over the sides of the tabernacle on one side and on the other to cover it. 14 You shall make a covering for the tent of rams' skins dyed red and a covering of porpoise skins above.

15 "Then you shall make the boards for the tabernacle of acacia wood, standing upright. 16 Ten cubits *shall be* the length of each board, and one and a half cubits the width of each board. 17 *There shall be* two tenons for each board, fitted to one another; thus you shall do for all the boards of the tabernacle. 18 You shall make the boards for the tabernacle: twenty boards for the south side. 19 You shall make forty bases of silver under the twenty boards, two bases under one board for its two tenons, and two bases under another board for its two tenons; 20 and for the second side of the tabernacle, on the north side, twenty boards, 21 and their forty bases of silver; two bases under one board and two bases under another board. 22 For the rear of the tabernacle, to the west, you shall make six boards. 23 You shall make two boards for the corners of the tabernacle at the rear. 24 They shall be separated beneath, but together at their completion at its top, at the first ring; thus it shall be with both of them: they shall form the two corners. 25 There shall be eight boards with their bases of silver, sixteen bases; two bases under one board and two bases under another board.

26 "Then you shall make bars of acacia wood, five for the boards of one side of the tabernacle, 27 and five bars for the boards of the other side of the tabernacle, and five bars for the boards of the side of the tabernacle for the rear *side* to the west. 28 The middle bar in the center of the boards shall pass through from end to end. 29 You shall overlay the boards with gold and make their rings of gold *as* holders for the bars; and you shall overlay the bars with gold. 30 Then you shall erect the tabernacle according to its plan which you have been shown in the mountain.

31 "You shall make a veil of blue and purple and scarlet *material* and fine twisted linen; it shall be made with cherubim, the work of a skillful designer. 32 You shall hang it on four pillars of acacia overlaid with gold, their hooks *also being of* gold, on four bases of silver. 33 You shall hang up the veil under the clasps, and you shall bring in the ark of the testimony there within the veil; and the veil shall separate for you the holy place and the Holy of Holies. 34 You shall put the mercy seat on the ark of the testimony in the Holy of Holies. 35 You shall set the table outside the veil and the lampstand opposite the table on the side of the tabernacle toward the south; and you shall put the table on the north side.

36 "You shall make a screen for the doorway of the tent of blue and purple and scarlet *material* and fine twisted linen, the work of a weaver. 37 You shall make five pillars of acacia for the screen and overlay them with gold, their hooks *also being of* gold; and you shall cast five bases of bronze for them.

Psalm 19:7–14

7 The law of Yahweh is perfect,
restoring the soul;
The testimony of Yahweh is sure,
making wise the simple.

8 The precepts of Yahweh are
right, rejoicing the heart;
The commandment of Yahweh is
pure, enlightening the eyes.
9 The fear of Yahweh is clean,
enduring forever;
The judgments of Yahweh are true;
they are righteous altogether.
10 *They are* more desirable than gold,
even more than much fine gold;
Sweeter also than honey and the
drippings of the honeycomb.
11 Moreover, by them Your
slave is warned;
In keeping them there
is great reward.
12 Who can discern *his* errors?
Acquit me of hidden *faults*.
13 Also keep back Your slave from
presumptuous *sins*;
Let them not rule over me;
Then I will be blameless,
And I shall be acquitted of
great transgression.
14 Let the words of my mouth and
the meditation of my heart
Be acceptable in Your sight,
O Yahweh, my rock and my Redeemer.

Proverbs 6:32–35

32 The one who commits adultery with a
woman is lacking a heart *of wisdom*;
He who would destroy his soul does it.
33 Wounds and disgrace he will find,
And his reproach will not
be blotted out.
34 For jealousy enrages a man,
And he will not spare in the
day of vengeance.
35 He will not accept any ransom,
He will not be willing though
you give many bribes.

Matthew 24:1–28

24 And coming out from the temple,
Jesus was going along, and His
disciples came up to point out the temple
buildings to Him. 2 And He answered and
said to them, "Do you not see all these
things? Truly I say to you, not one stone
here will be left upon another, which will
not be torn down."
3 Now as He was sitting on the Mount of
Olives, the disciples came to Him privately,
saying, "Tell us, when will these things
happen, and what *will be* the sign of Your
coming and of the end of the age?"
4 And Jesus answered and said to them,
"See to it that no one deceives you. 5 For
many will come in My name, saying, 'I am
the Christ,' and will deceive many. 6 And
you are going to hear of wars and rumors
of wars. See that you are not alarmed, for
those things must take place, but *that* is not
yet the end. 7 For nation will rise against
nation, and kingdom against kingdom, and
in various places there will be famines and
earthquakes. 8 But all these things are *merely*
the beginning of birth pains.
9 "Then they will deliver you to tribula-
tion, and will kill you, and you will be hated
by all nations because of My name. 10 And
at that time many will fall away and will
betray one another and hate one another.
11 Many false prophets will arise and will
deceive many. 12 And because lawlessness
is multiplied, most people's love will grow
cold. 13 But the one who endures to the end,
he will be saved. 14 And this gospel of the
kingdom shall be proclaimed in the whole
world as a witness to all the nations, and
then the end will come.
15 "Therefore when you see the ABOMI-
NATION OF DESOLATION which was spoken
of through Daniel the prophet, standing in
the holy place (let the reader understand),
16 then those who are in Judea must flee
to the mountains. 17 Whoever is on the
housetop must not go down to get the
things out that are in his house. 18 And
whoever is in the field must not turn back
to get his garment. 19 But woe to those who
are pregnant and to those who are nursing
babies in those days! 20 But pray that your
flight will not be in the winter, or on a
Sabbath. 21 For then there will be a great
tribulation, such as has not occurred since
the beginning of the world until now, nor
ever will. 22 And unless those days had
been cut short, no life would have been
saved; but for the sake of the elect those
days will be cut short. 23 Then if anyone
says to you, 'Behold, here is the Christ,'
or 'There *He is*,' do not believe *him*. 24 For
false christs and false prophets will arise
and will show great signs and wonders, so
as to deceive, if possible, even the elect.
25 Behold, I have told you in advance.
26 Therefore, if they say to you, 'Behold,
He is in the wilderness,' do not go out, *or*,

'Behold, He is in the inner rooms,' do not believe *them.* 27 For just as the lightning comes from the east and appears even to the west, so will the coming of the Son of Man be. 28 Wherever the corpse is, there the vultures will gather.

FEBRUARY 8

Exodus 27:1–28:43

27 "And you shall make the altar of acacia wood, five cubits long and five cubits wide; the altar shall be square, and its height shall be three cubits. 2 You shall make its horns on its four corners; its horns shall be of the *same piece,* and you shall overlay it with bronze. 3 You shall make its pots for removing its ashes, and its shovels and its bowls and its flesh hooks and its firepans; you shall make all its utensils of bronze. 4 You shall make for it a grating, a network of bronze, and on the net you shall make four bronze rings at its four corners. 5 You shall put it beneath, under the ledge of the altar, so that the net will reach halfway down the altar. 6 You shall make poles for the altar, poles of acacia wood, and overlay them with bronze. 7 Its poles shall be inserted into the rings, so that the poles shall be on the two sides of the altar when it is carried. 8 You shall make it hollow with planks; as it was shown to you in the mountain, so they shall make *it.*

9 "You shall make the court of the tabernacle. On the south side *there shall be* hangings for the court of fine twisted linen one hundred cubits long for one side; 10 and its pillars *shall be* twenty, with their twenty bases of bronze; the hooks of the pillars and their bands *shall be* of silver. 11 Likewise for the north side in length *there shall be* hangings one hundred *cubits* long, and its twenty pillars with their twenty bases of bronze; the hooks of the pillars and their bands *shall be* of silver. 12 *For* the width of the court on the west side *shall be* hangings of fifty cubits *with* their ten pillars and their ten bases. 13 The width of the court on the east side toward the sunrise *shall be* fifty cubits. 14 The hangings for the *one* side *of the gate shall be* fifteen cubits *with* their three pillars and their three bases. 15 And for the other side *shall be* hangings of fifteen cubits *with* their three pillars and their three bases. 16 And as for the gate of the court *there shall be* a screen of twenty cubits, of blue and purple and scarlet *material* and fine twisted linen, the work of a weaver, *with* their four pillars and their four bases. 17 All the pillars around the court shall be furnished with silver bands *with* their hooks of silver and their bases of bronze. 18 The length of the court *shall be* one hundred cubits, and the width fifty throughout, and the height five cubits of fine twisted linen, and their bases of bronze. 19 All the utensils of the tabernacle *used* in all its service, and all its pegs, and all the pegs of the court, *shall be* of bronze.

20 "And you shall command the sons of Israel, that they bring you clear oil of beaten olives for the light, to make a lamp burn continually. 21 In the tent of meeting, outside the veil which is before the testimony, Aaron and his sons shall keep it in order from evening to morning before Yahweh; *it shall be* a perpetual statute throughout their generations for the sons of Israel.

28 "Now as for you, bring near to yourself Aaron your brother, and his sons with him, from among the sons of Israel, to minister as priests to Me—Aaron, Nadab and Abihu, Eleazar and Ithamar, Aaron's sons. 2 You shall make holy garments for Aaron your brother, for glory and for beauty. 3 You shall speak to all those wise at heart whom I have filled with the spirit of wisdom, that they make Aaron's garments to set him apart as holy, in order for him to minister as priest to Me. 4 These are the garments which they shall make: a breastpiece and an ephod and a robe and a tunic of checkered work, a turban and a sash, and they shall make holy garments for Aaron your brother and his sons, in order for him to minister as priest to Me. 5 They shall take the gold and the blue and the purple and the scarlet *material* and the fine linen.

6 "They shall also make the ephod of gold, of blue and purple *and* scarlet *material* and fine twisted linen, the work of the skillful designer. 7 It shall have two shoulder pieces joined to its two ends, that it may be joined. 8 The skillfully woven band, which is on it,

shall be like its workmanship, of the same material: of gold, of blue and purple and scarlet *material* and fine twisted linen. 9 You shall take two onyx stones and engrave on them the names of the sons of Israel, 10 six of their names on the one stone and the names of the remaining six on the second stone, according to their birth. 11 As a jeweler engraves a signet, you shall engrave the two stones according to the names of the sons of Israel; you shall set them all around in filigree *settings* of gold. 12 You shall put the two stones on the shoulder pieces of the ephod, *as* stones of remembrance for the sons of Israel, and Aaron shall bear their names before Yahweh on his two shoulders for remembrance. 13 You shall make filigree *settings* of gold, 14 and two chains of pure gold; you shall make them a twisted work of cords, and you shall put the chains of cords on the filigree *settings*.

15 "You shall make a breastpiece of judgment, the work of a skillful designer; like the work of the ephod you shall make it: of gold, of blue and purple and scarlet *material* and fine twisted linen you shall make it. 16 It shall be square, *having been* folded double, a span in length and a span in width. 17 You shall mount on it four rows of stones; the first row *shall be* a row of ruby, topaz, and emerald; 18 and the second row a turquoise, a sapphire, and a diamond; 19 and the third row a jacinth, an agate, and an amethyst; 20 and the fourth row a beryl and an onyx and a jasper; they shall be set in gold settings. 21 The stones shall be according to the names of the sons of Israel: twelve, according to their names; they shall be *like* the engravings of a signet, each according to his name for the twelve tribes. 22 You shall make on the breastpiece chains of a twisted work of cords in pure gold. 23 You shall make on the breastpiece two rings of gold, and you shall put the two rings on the two ends of the breastpiece. 24 You shall put the two cords of gold on the two rings at the ends of the breastpiece. 25 You shall put the two ends of the two cords on the two filigree *settings*, and you shall put them on the shoulder pieces of the ephod at the front of it. 26 You shall make two rings of gold and shall place them on the two ends of the breastpiece, on the edge of it, which is toward the inner side of the ephod. 27 You shall make two rings of gold and put them on the bottom of the two shoulder pieces of the ephod, on the front of it close to the place where it is joined, above the skillfully woven band of the ephod. 28 They shall bind the breastpiece by its rings to the rings of the ephod with a blue cord, so that it will be on the skillfully woven band of the ephod, and that the breastpiece will not come loose from the ephod. 29 Aaron shall carry the names of the sons of Israel in the breastpiece of judgment over his heart when he comes into the holy place, for a remembrance before Yahweh continually. 30 You shall put in the breastpiece of judgment the Urim and the Thummim, and they shall be over Aaron's heart when he comes in before Yahweh; and Aaron shall carry the judgment of the sons of Israel over his heart before Yahweh continually.

31 "You shall make the robe of the ephod entirely of blue. 32 There shall be an opening at its top in the middle of it; around the edge of its opening there shall be a binding of woven work, like the opening of a coat of mail, so that it will not be torn. 33 You shall make on its hem pomegranates of blue and purple and scarlet *material*, all around on its hem, and bells of gold between them all around: 34 a golden bell and a pomegranate, a golden bell and a pomegranate, all around on the hem of the robe. 35 It shall be on Aaron when he ministers; and its sound shall be heard when he comes into the holy place before Yahweh and when he goes out, so that he will not die.

36 "You shall also make a plate of pure gold and shall engrave on it, like the engravings of a signet, 'Holy to Yahweh.' 37 You shall fasten it on a blue cord, and it shall be on the turban; it shall be at the front of the turban. 38 It shall be on Aaron's forehead, and Aaron shall take away the iniquity of the holy things which the sons of Israel set apart as holy, with regard to all their holy gifts; and it shall continually be on his forehead, that they may be accepted before Yahweh.

39 "You shall weave the tunic of checkered work of fine linen, and you shall make a turban of fine linen, and you shall make a sash, the work of a weaver.

40 "For Aaron's sons you shall make tunics; you shall also make sashes for them, and you shall make caps for them, for glory and for beauty. 41 You shall put them on Aaron your brother and on his

sons with him; and you shall anoint them and ordain them and set them apart as holy, that they may minister to Me as priests. 42 You shall make for them linen undergarments to cover *their* bare flesh; they shall reach from the loins even to the thighs. 43 They shall be on Aaron and on his sons when they come into the tent of meeting or when they approach the altar to minister in the holy place, so that they do not incur guilt and die. It *shall be* a perpetual statute to him and to his seed after him.

Psalm 20:1–5

1 May Yahweh answer you in
the day of distress!
May the name of the God of Jacob
set you *securely* on high!
2 May He send you help
from the sanctuary
And uphold you from Zion!
3 May He remember all your
meal offerings
And find your burnt offering
acceptable! Selah.
4 May He grant you your heart's desire
And fulfill all your counsel!
5 We will sing for joy over your salvation,
And in the name of our God we
will set up our banners.
May Yahweh fulfill all your petitions.

Proverbs 7:1–5

7 My son, keep my words
And treasure my commandments
within you.
2 Keep my commandments and live,
And my law as the apple of your eye.
3 Bind them on your fingers;
Write them on the tablet of your heart.
4 Say to wisdom, "You are my sister,"
And call understanding
your intimate friend;
5 In order to keep you from
the strange woman,
From the foreign woman who
flatters with her words.

Matthew 24:29–51

29 "But immediately after the tribulation of those days THE SUN WILL BE DARKENED, AND THE MOON WILL NOT GIVE ITS LIGHT, AND THE STARS WILL FALL from the sky, and the POWERS OF THE HEAVENS will be shaken. 30 And then the sign of the Son of Man will appear in the sky, and then all the tribes of the earth will mourn, and they will see the SON OF MAN COMING ON THE CLOUDS OF THE SKY with power and great glory. 31 And He will send forth His angels with A GREAT TRUMPET and THEY WILL GATHER TOGETHER His elect from the four winds, from one end of the sky to the other.

32 "Now learn the parable from the fig tree: when its branch has already become tender and puts forth its leaves, you know that summer is near; 33 so, you too, when you see all these things, recognize that He is near, *right* at the door. 34 Truly I say to you, this generation will not pass away until all these things take place. 35 Heaven and earth will pass away, but My words will not pass away.

36 "But of that day and hour no one knows, not even the angels of heaven, nor the Son, but the Father alone. 37 For just as the days of Noah were, so the coming of the Son of Man will be. 38 For as in those days before the flood they were eating and drinking, marrying and giving in marriage, until the day that Noah entered the ark, 39 and they did not understand until the flood came and took them all away; so will the coming of the Son of Man be. 40 Then there will be two in the field; one will be taken, and one will be left. 41 Two women *will be* grinding *grain* at the mill; one will be taken and one will be left.

42 "Therefore stay awake, for you do not know which day your Lord is coming. 43 But be sure of this, that if the head of the house had known at what time of the night the thief was coming, he would have stayed awake and would not have allowed his house to be broken into. 44 For this reason you also must be ready; for the Son of Man is coming at an hour when you do not think *He will*.

45 "Who then is the faithful and prudent slave whom his master put in charge of his household to give them their food at the proper time? 46 Blessed is that slave whom his master finds so doing when he comes. 47 Truly I say to you that he will put him in charge of all his possessions. 48 But if that evil slave says in his heart, 'My master is not coming for a long time,' 49 and begins to beat his fellow slaves and eat and drink

with drunkards; 50 the master of that slave will come on a day when he does not expect *him* and at an hour which he does not know, 51 and will cut him in pieces and assign him a place with the hypocrites; in that place there will be weeping and gnashing of teeth.

FEBRUARY 9

Exodus 29:1–30:38

29 "Now this is what you shall do to them to set them apart as holy to minister as priests to Me: take one bull from the herd and two rams without blemish, 2 and unleavened bread and unleavened cakes mixed with oil, and unleavened wafers spread with oil; you shall make them of fine wheat flour. 3 And you shall put them in one basket and bring them near in the basket along with the bull and the two rams. 4 Then you shall bring Aaron and his sons near to the doorway of the tent of meeting and wash them with water. 5 And you shall take the garments, and put on Aaron the tunic and the robe of the ephod and the ephod and the breastpiece, and gird him with the skillfully woven band of the ephod; 6 and you shall set the turban on his head and put the holy crown on the turban. 7 Then you shall take the anointing oil and pour it on his head and anoint him. 8 And you shall bring his sons near and put tunics on them. 9 You shall gird them with sashes, Aaron and his sons, and bind caps on them, and they shall have the priesthood by a perpetual statute. So you shall ordain Aaron and his sons.

10 "Then you shall bring the bull near before the tent of meeting, and Aaron and his sons shall lay their hands on the head of the bull. 11 You shall slaughter the bull before Yahweh at the doorway of the tent of meeting. 12 You shall take some of the blood of the bull and put *it* on the horns of the altar with your finger; and you shall pour out all the blood at the base of the altar. 13 You shall take all the fat that covers the entrails and the lobe of the liver and the two kidneys and the fat that is on them, and you shall offer them up in smoke on the altar. 14 But the flesh of the bull and its hide and its refuse, you shall burn with fire outside the camp; it is a sin offering.

15 "You shall also take the one ram, and Aaron and his sons shall lay their hands on the head of the ram; 16 and you shall slaughter the ram, and you shall take its blood and splash it around on the altar. 17 Then you shall cut the ram into its pieces, and wash its entrails and its legs, and put *them* with its pieces and its head. 18 You shall offer up in smoke the whole ram on the altar; it is a burnt offering to Yahweh: it is a soothing aroma, an offering by fire to Yahweh.

19 "Then you shall take the second ram, and Aaron and his sons shall lay their hands on the head of the ram. 20 You shall slaughter the ram, and take some of its blood and put *it* on the lobe of Aaron's right ear and on the lobes of his sons' right ears and on the thumbs of their right hands and on the big toes of their right feet, and splash the *rest of the* blood around on the altar. 21 Then you shall take some of the blood that is on the altar and some of the anointing oil, and sprinkle *it* on Aaron and on his garments and on his sons and on his sons' garments with him; so he and his garments shall be set apart as holy, as well as his sons and his sons' garments with him.

22 "You shall also take the fat from the ram and the fat tail and the fat that covers the entrails and the lobe of the liver and the two kidneys and the fat that is on them and the right thigh (for it is a ram of ordination), 23 and one cake of bread and one cake of bread *mixed with* oil and one wafer from the basket of unleavened bread which is *set* before Yahweh; 24 and you shall put all these in the hands of Aaron and in the hands of his sons, and you shall wave them as a wave offering before Yahweh. 25 You shall take them from their hands and offer them up in smoke on the altar on the burnt offering for a soothing aroma before Yahweh; it is an offering by fire to Yahweh.

26 "Then you shall take the breast of Aaron's ram of ordination and wave it as a wave offering before Yahweh; and it shall be your portion. 27 You shall set apart as holy the breast of the wave offering and the thigh of the contribution offering which was waved and which was raised up *as a contribution* from the ram of ordination, from the one which was for Aaron and from the one which was for his sons. 28 It shall be

for Aaron and his sons as a perpetual statute from the sons of Israel, for it is a contribution offering; and it shall be a contribution offering from the sons of Israel from the sacrifices of their peace offerings, *even* their contribution offering to Yahweh.

29 “The holy garments of Aaron shall be for his sons after him, that in them they may be anointed and ordained. 30 For seven days the one of his sons who is priest in his stead shall put them on when he comes into the tent of meeting to minister in the holy place.

31 “You shall take the ram of ordination and boil its flesh in a holy place. 32 Aaron and his sons shall eat the flesh of the ram and the bread that is in the basket, at the doorway of the tent of meeting. 33 Thus they shall eat those things by which atonement was made to ordain them, to set them apart as holy; but a layman shall not eat *them*, because they are holy. 34 If any of the flesh of ordination or any of the bread remains until morning, then you shall burn the remainder with fire; it shall not be eaten, because it is holy.

35 “Thus you shall do to Aaron and to his sons, according to all that I have commanded you; you shall ordain them through seven days. 36 Each day you shall offer a bull as a sin offering for atonement, and you shall purify the altar when you make atonement for it, and you shall anoint it to set it apart as holy. 37 For seven days you shall make atonement for the altar and set it apart as holy; then the altar shall be most holy, *and* whatever touches the altar shall be holy.

38 “Now this is what you shall offer on the altar: two one year old lambs each day, continuously. 39 The one lamb you shall offer in the morning, and the second lamb you shall offer at twilight; 40 and there *shall be* one-tenth *of an ephah* of fine flour mixed with one-fourth of a hin of beaten oil, and one-fourth of a hin of wine for a drink offering with the one lamb. 41 The second lamb you shall offer at twilight, and you shall offer with it the same grain offering and the same drink offering as in the morning, for a soothing aroma, an offering by fire to Yahweh. 42 It shall be a continual burnt offering throughout your generations at the doorway of the tent of meeting before Yahweh, where I will meet with you, to speak to you there. 43 I will meet there with the sons of Israel, and it shall be set apart as holy by My glory. 44 I will set the tent of meeting and the altar apart as holy; I will also set Aaron and his sons apart as holy to minister as priests to Me. 45 I will dwell among the sons of Israel and will be their God. 46 They shall know that I am Yahweh their God who brought them out of the land of Egypt, that I might dwell among them; I am Yahweh their God.

30 “Moreover, you shall make an altar as a place for burning incense; you shall make it of acacia wood. 2 Its length *shall be* a cubit, and its width a cubit; it shall be square. And its height *shall be* two cubits; its horns *shall be* of the same piece. 3 You shall overlay it with pure gold, its top and its sides all around, and its horns; and you shall make a gold molding all around for it. 4 You shall make two gold rings for it under its molding; you shall make *them* on its two side walls—on opposite sides—and they shall be holders for poles with which to carry it. 5 You shall make the poles of acacia wood and overlay them with gold. 6 You shall put this altar in front of the veil that is near the ark of the testimony, in front of the mercy seat that is over the testimony, where I will meet with you. 7 Aaron shall burn fragrant incense on it; he shall burn it every morning when he trims the lamps. 8 When Aaron trims the lamps at twilight, he shall burn incense. *There shall be* continual incense before Yahweh throughout your generations. 9 You shall not offer any strange incense on this altar or burnt offering or grain offering; and you shall not pour out a drink offering on it. 10 Aaron shall make atonement on its horns once a year; he shall make atonement on it with the blood of the sin offering of atonement once a year throughout your generations. It is most holy to Yahweh.”

11 Yahweh also spoke to Moses, saying, 12 “When you take a census of the sons of Israel to number them, then each one of them shall give a *price of* atonement for himself to Yahweh when you number them, so that there will be no plague among them when you number them. 13 This is what everyone who is numbered shall give: half a shekel according to the shekel of the sanctuary (the shekel is twenty gerahs), half a shekel as a contribution to Yahweh. 14 Everyone who is numbered, from twenty years

old and over, shall give the contribution
to Yahweh. 15 The rich shall not pay more
and the poor shall not pay less than the half
shekel when you give the contribution to
Yahweh to make atonement for your souls.
16 And you shall take the atonement money
from the sons of Israel and shall give it for
the service of the tent of meeting, that it
may be a remembrance for the sons of Israel
before Yahweh, to make atonement for your
souls."
17 And Yahweh spoke to Moses, saying,
18 "You shall also make a laver of bronze,
with its stand of bronze, for washing; and
you shall put it between the tent of meeting
and the altar, and you shall put water in it.
19 And Aaron and his sons shall wash their
hands and their feet from it; 20 when they
come into the tent of meeting, they shall
wash with water, so that they will not die;
or when they approach the altar to minister,
by offering up in smoke a fire *sacrifice* to
Yahweh. 21 So they shall wash their hands
and their feet, so that they will not die;
and it shall be a perpetual statute for them,
for Aaron and his seed throughout their
generations."
22 Moreover, Yahweh spoke to Moses,
saying, 23 "But as for you, take for yourself
the finest of spices: of flowing myrrh 500
shekels, and of fragrant cinnamon half as
much, 250, and of fragrant cane 250, 24 and
of cassia 500, according to the shekel of the
sanctuary, and of olive oil a hin. 25 And you
shall make of these a holy anointing oil, a
perfume mixture, the work of a perfumer;
it shall be a holy anointing oil. 26 And with
it you shall anoint the tent of meeting and
the ark of the testimony, 27 and the table and
all its utensils, and the lampstand and its
utensils, and the altar of incense, 28 and the
altar of burnt offering and all its utensils,
and the laver and its stand. 29 You shall
also set them apart as holy, that they may
be most holy; whatever touches them shall
be holy. 30 And you shall anoint Aaron and
his sons, and you shall set them apart as
holy, that they may minister as priests to
Me. 31 And you shall speak to the sons of
Israel, saying, 'This shall be a holy anointing
oil to Me throughout your generations.
32 It shall not be poured on anyone's body,
nor shall you make *any* like it in the same
specifications; it is holy, *and* it shall be holy
to you. 33 Whoever shall mix *any* like it or
whoever puts any of it on a layman shall be
cut off from his people.'"
34 Then Yahweh said to Moses, "Take
for yourself fragrances, stacte and onycha
and galbanum, fragrances with pure
frankincense; there shall be an equal part
of each. 35 With it you shall make incense,
a perfume, the work of a perfumer, salted,
pure, *and* holy. 36 You shall beat some of it
very fine, and you shall put part of it before
the testimony in the tent of meeting where I
will meet with you; it shall be most holy to
you. 37 The incense which you shall make,
you shall not make in the same specifica-
tions for yourselves; it shall be holy to you
for Yahweh. 38 Whoever shall make *any* like
it, to use as perfume, shall be cut off from
his people."

Psalm 20:6–9

6 Now I know that Yahweh
saves His anointed;
He will answer him from
His holy heaven
With the saving might of
His right hand.
7 Some *boast* in chariots and
some in horses,
But we will boast in the name
of Yahweh, our God.
8 They have bowed down and fallen,
But we have risen and stood upright.
9 Save, O Yahweh;
May the King answer us
in the day we call.

Proverbs 7:6–23

6 For at the window of my house
I looked out through my lattice,
7 And I saw among the simple,
And discerned among the sons
A young man lacking a
heart *of wisdom*,
8 Passing through the street
near her corner;
And he strides along the
way to her house,
9 In the twilight, in the
evening of *that* day,
In the middle of the night, and
in the thick darkness.
10 And behold, a woman
comes to meet him,
Dressed as a harlot and
cunning of heart.

11 She is boisterous and rebellious,
Her feet do not dwell at home;
12 Stepping in the streets,
stepping in the squares,
And near every corner she lies in wait.
13 So she seizes him and kisses him
And with a brazen face she says to him:
14 "The sacrifices of peace
offerings are with me;
Today I paid my vows.
15 "Therefore I have come out to meet you,
To seek your face earnestly,
and I have found you.
16 "I have spread my couch with coverings,
With colored linens of Egypt.
17 "I have sprinkled my bed
With myrrh, aloes, and cinnamon.
18 "Come, then, let us drink our fill
as lovers until morning;
Let us delight ourselves with
the pleasures of love.
19 "For my husband is not at home,
He has gone on a journey far away;
20 He took a bag of silver in his hand,
On the day of the full moon
he will come home."
21 With her abundant persuasions
she entices him;
With her flattering lips she
drives him *to herself*.
22 He suddenly follows her
As an ox goes to the slaughter,
Or as *one in* fetters to the discipline
of an ignorant fool,
23 Until an arrow pierces
through his liver;
As a bird hastens to the snare,
And he does not know that it
will cost him his soul.

Matthew 25:1–30

25 "Then the kingdom of heaven may
be compared to ten virgins, who
took their lamps and went out to meet
the bridegroom. 2 Now five of them were
foolish, and five were prudent. 3 For when
the foolish took their lamps, they took no
oil with them, 4 but the prudent took oil in
flasks along with their lamps. 5 Now while
the bridegroom was delaying, they all got
drowsy and *began to* sleep. 6 But at midnight
there was a shout, 'Behold, the bridegroom!
Come out to meet him.' 7 Then all those vir-
gins rose and trimmed their lamps. 8 And the
foolish said to the prudent, 'Give us some of
your oil, for our lamps are going out.' 9 But
the prudent answered, saying, 'No, there will
not be enough for us and you *too*; go instead
to the dealers and buy *some* for yourselves.'
10 And while they were going away to make
the purchase, the bridegroom came, and
those who were ready went in with him to
the wedding feast; and the door was shut.
11 And later the other virgins also *came,
saying, 'Lord, lord, open up for us.' 12 But
he answered and said, 'Truly I say to you, I
do not know you.' 13 Therefore, stay awake,
for you do not know the day nor the hour.

14 "For *it is* just like a man *about* to go on
a journey, who called his own slaves and
handed over his possessions to them. 15 And
to one he gave five talents, to another, two,
and to another, one, each according to his
own ability; and he went on his journey.
16 Immediately the one who had received
the five talents went and traded with them,
and gained five more talents. 17 In the same
manner the one who *had received* the two
talents gained two more. 18 But he who
received the one *talent* went away, and dug
a hole in the ground and hid his master's
money.

19 "Now after a long time the master of
those slaves *came and *settled accounts
with them. 20 And the one who had received
the five talents came up and brought five
more talents, saying, 'Master, you handed
five talents over to me. See, I have gained
five more talents.' 21 His master said to him,
'Well done, good and faithful slave. You were
faithful with a few things, I will put you in
charge of many things; enter into the joy of
your master.'

22 "Also the one who *had received* the
two talents came up and said, 'Master, you
handed two talents over to me. See, I have
gained two more talents.' 23 His master said
to him, 'Well done, good and faithful slave.
You were faithful with a few things, I will put
you in charge of many things; enter into the
joy of your master.'

24 "And the one also who had received the
one talent came up and said, 'Master, I knew
you to be a hard man, reaping where you did
not sow and gathering where you scattered
no *seed*. 25 And I was afraid, and went away
and hid your talent in the ground. See, you
have what is yours.'

26 "But his master answered and said to
him, 'You wicked, lazy slave, you knew that

I reap where I did not sow and gather where
I scattered no *seed.* 27 Therefore, you ought
to have put my money in the bank, and on
my arrival I would have received my *money*
back with interest. 28 Therefore take away
the talent from him, and give it to the one
who has the ten talents.'

29 "For to everyone who has, *more* shall
be given, and he will have an abundance;
but from the one who does not have, even
what he does have shall be taken away.
30 And throw out the worthless slave into
the outer darkness; in that place there will
be weeping and gnashing of teeth.

FEBRUARY 10

Exodus 31:1–32:35

31 And Yahweh spoke to Moses, saying,
2 "See, I have called by name Bezalel,
the son of Uri, the son of Hur, of the tribe
of Judah. 3 And I have filled him with the
Spirit of God in wisdom, in discernment, in
knowledge, and in all *kinds of* craftsman-
ship, 4 to devise artistic designs for work in
gold, in silver, and in bronze, 5 and in the
cutting of stones for settings, and in the
carving of wood, in order *for him* to work
in all *kinds of* craftsmanship. 6 And behold,
I Myself have appointed with him Oholiab,
the son of Ahisamach, of the tribe of Dan;
and in the hearts of all who are wise at heart
I have put wisdom, that they may make all
that I have commanded you: 7 the tent of
meeting, and the ark of testimony, and the
mercy seat upon it, and all the furniture of
the tent, 8 the table also and its utensils, and
the pure *gold* lampstand with all its utensils,
and the altar of incense, 9 the altar of burnt
offering also with all its utensils, and the
laver and its stand, 10 the woven garments
as well, and the holy garments for Aaron the
priest, and the garments of his sons, *with
which* to minister as priests; 11 the anointing
oil also, and the fragrant incense for the holy
place, they shall make *them* according to all
that I have commanded you."

12 Yahweh spoke to Moses, saying, 13 "But
as for you, speak to the sons of Israel, saying,
'You shall surely keep My sabbaths; for *this*
is a sign between Me and you throughout
your generations, that you may know
that I am Yahweh who makes you holy.
14 Therefore you shall keep the sabbath, for
it is holy to you. Everyone who profanes it
shall surely be put to death; for whoever
does any work on it, that person shall be cut
off from among his people. 15 Six days work
may be done, but on the seventh day there is
a sabbath of complete rest, holy to Yahweh;
whoever does any work on the sabbath day
shall surely be put to death. 16 So the sons
of Israel shall keep the sabbath, to celebrate
the sabbath throughout their generations
as an everlasting covenant.' 17 It is a sign
between Me and the sons of Israel forever;
for in six days Yahweh made heaven and
earth, but on the seventh day He rested and
was refreshed."

18 When He had finished speaking with
him upon Mount Sinai, He gave Moses the
two tablets of the testimony, tablets of
stone, written by the finger of God.

32 Then the people saw that Moses
delayed to come down from the
mountain. So the people assembled about
Aaron and said to him, "Arise, make us gods
who will go before us; as for this Moses, the
man who brought us up from the land of
Egypt, we do not know what has become
of him." 2 And Aaron said to them, "Tear
off the gold rings which are in the ears of
your wives, your sons, and your daughters,
and bring *them* to me." 3 Then all the people
tore off the gold rings which were in their
ears and brought *them* to Aaron. 4 And he
took *this* from their hand and fashioned
it with a graving tool and made it into a
molten calf; and they said, "These are your
gods, O Israel, who brought you up from
the land of Egypt." 5 And Aaron looked and
built an altar before it; and Aaron made a
proclamation and said, "Tomorrow *shall be*
a feast to Yahweh." 6 So the next day they
rose early and offered burnt offerings and
brought peace offerings; and the people sat
down to eat and to drink and rose up to play.

7 Then Yahweh spoke to Moses, "Go! Go
down at once, for your people, whom you
brought up from the land of Egypt, have
corrupted *themselves.* 8 They have quickly
turned aside from the way which I com-
manded them. They have made for them-
selves a molten calf and have worshiped it

and have sacrificed to it and said, 'These are your gods, O Israel, who brought you up from the land of Egypt!'" 9 And Yahweh said to Moses, "I have seen this people, and behold, they are a stiff-necked people. 10 Now then let Me alone, that My anger may burn against them and that I may consume them; and I will make you a great nation."

11 Then Moses entreated the favor of Yahweh his God and said, "O Yahweh, why does Your anger burn against Your people whom You have brought out of the land of Egypt with great power and with a strong hand? 12 Why should the Egyptians speak, saying, 'With evil *intent* He brought them out to kill them in the mountains and to consume them from the face of the earth'? Turn from Your burning anger and relent concerning *doing* harm to Your people. 13 Remember Abraham, Isaac, and Israel, Your servants to whom You swore by Yourself, and You said to them, 'I will multiply your seed as the stars of the heavens, and all this land of which I have spoken I will give to your seed, and they shall inherit *it* forever.'" 14 So Yahweh relented concerning the harm which He said He would do to His people.

15 Then Moses turned and went down from the mountain. And the two tablets of the testimony were in his hand, tablets which were written on both sides; they were written on one *side* and the other. 16 Now the tablets were the work of God, and the writing was the writing of God engraved on the tablets. 17 Then Joshua heard the sound of the people as they shouted. And he said to Moses, "There is a sound of war in the camp." 18 But he said,

"It is not the sound of the
cry of triumph,
Nor is it the sound of the cry of defeat;
But the sound of singing I hear."

19 Now it happened, as soon as Moses came near the camp, that he saw the calf and *the* dancing; and Moses' anger burned, and he threw the tablets from his hands and shattered them at the foot of the mountain. 20 Then he took the calf which they had made and burned *it* with fire and ground it to powder and scattered it over the surface of the water and made the sons of Israel drink *it*.

21 Then Moses said to Aaron, "What did this people do to you, that you have brought *such* great sin upon them?" 22 And Aaron said, "Do not let the anger of my lord burn; you know the people yourself, that they are prone to evil. 23 Indeed they said to me, 'Make gods for us who will go before us; for this Moses, the man who brought us up from the land of Egypt, we do not know what has become of him.' 24 And I said to them, 'Whoever has any gold, let them tear it off.' So they gave *it* to me, and I threw it into the fire, and out came this calf."

25 Now Moses saw that the people were out of control—for Aaron had let them get out of control to be a derision among their enemies— 26 so Moses stood in the gate of the camp and said, "Whoever is for Yahweh, *come* to me!" And all the sons of Levi gathered together to him. 27 And he said to them, "Thus says Yahweh, the God of Israel, 'Every man *among you* put his sword upon his thigh, and go back and forth from gate to gate in the camp, and kill every man his brother and every man his friend and every man his neighbor.'" 28 So the sons of Levi did according to the word of Moses, and about three thousand men of the people fell that day. 29 Then Moses said, "Be ordained today to Yahweh—for every man has been against his son and against his brother—in order that He may bestow a blessing upon you today."

30 Now it happened on the next day, that Moses said to the people, "You yourselves have committed a great sin; but now I am going up to Yahweh, perhaps I can make atonement for your sin." 31 Then Moses returned to Yahweh and said, "Alas, this people has committed a great sin, and they have made gods of gold for themselves. 32 But now, if You will forgive their sin—but if not, please blot me out from Your book which You have written!" 33 And Yahweh said to Moses, "Whoever has sinned against Me, I will blot him out of My book. 34 But now go, guide the people where I told you. Behold, My angel shall go before you; nevertheless in the day when I punish, I will punish them for their sin." 35 Then Yahweh smote the people because of what they did with the calf which Aaron had made.

Psalm 21:1–7

1 O Yahweh, in Your strength
the king will be glad,
And in Your salvation how
greatly he will rejoice!

2 You have given him his heart's desire,
And You have not withheld the request
of his lips. Selah.
3 For You meet him with the
blessings of good things;
You set a crown of fine
gold on his head.
4 He asked life of You,
You gave it to him,
Length of days forever and ever.
5 His glory is great through
Your salvation,
Splendor and majesty You
bestow upon him.
6 For You make him most
blessed forever;
You make him joyful with
gladness in Your presence.

7 For the king trusts in Yahweh,
And through the lovingkindness of the
Most High he will not be shaken.

Proverbs 7:24–27

24 So now, *my* sons, listen to me,
And pay attention to the
words of my mouth.
25 Do not let your heart go
astray into her ways,
Do not wander into her pathways.
26 For many are the slain *whom*
she has cast down,
And numerous are all
those killed by her.
27 The ways to Sheol *are in* her house,
Descending to the chambers of death.

Matthew 25:31–46

31 "But when the Son of Man comes in His
glory, and all the angels with Him, then He
will sit on His glorious throne. 32 And all the
nations will be gathered before Him; and
He will separate them from one another,
as the shepherd separates the sheep from
the goats; 33 and He will put the sheep on
His right, and the goats on the left.
34 "Then the King will say to those on
His right, 'Come, you who are blessed of
My Father, inherit the kingdom, which has
been prepared for you from the foundation
of the world. 35 For I was hungry, and you
gave Me *something* to eat; I was thirsty, and
you gave Me *something* to drink; I was a
stranger, and you invited Me in; 36 naked,
and you clothed Me; I was sick, and you
visited Me; I was in prison, and you came
to Me.' 37 Then the righteous will answer
Him, saying, 'Lord, when did we see You
hungry, and feed You, or thirsty, and give
You *something* to drink? 38 And when did
we see You a stranger, and invite You in, or
naked, and clothe You? 39 And when did we
see You sick, or in prison, and come to You?'
40 And the King will answer and say to them,
'Truly I say to you, to the extent that you did
it to one of these brothers of Mine, *even* the
least *of them*, you did it to Me.'
41 "Then He will also say to those on His
left, 'Depart from Me, accursed ones, into
the eternal fire which has been prepared for
the devil and his angels; 42 for I was hungry,
and you gave Me *nothing* to eat; I was thirsty,
and you gave Me nothing to drink; 43 I was
a stranger, and you did not invite Me in;
naked, and you did not clothe Me; sick,
and in prison, and you did not visit Me.'
44 Then they themselves also will answer,
saying, 'Lord, when did we see You hungry,
or thirsty, or a stranger, or naked, or sick,
or in prison, and did not take care of You?'
45 Then He will answer them, saying, 'Truly
I say to you, to the extent that you did not
do it to one of the least of these, you did not
do it to Me.' 46 And these will go away into
eternal punishment, but the righteous into
eternal life."

FEBRUARY 11

Exodus 33:1–34:35

33 Then Yahweh spoke to Moses, "Go!
Go up from here, you and the people
whom you have brought up from the land
of Egypt, to the land of which I swore to
Abraham, to Isaac, and to Jacob, saying, 'To
your seed I will give it.' 2 And I will send an
angel before you, and I will drive out the
Canaanite, the Amorite, the Hittite, the
Perizzite, the Hivite, and the Jebusite. 3 *Go
up* to a land flowing with milk and honey;
for I will not go up in your midst because
you are a stiff-necked people, lest I consume
you on the way."
4 Then the people heard this sad word
and went into mourning; and none of them

put on his ornaments. 5 So Yahweh said to Moses, "Say to the sons of Israel, 'You are a stiff-necked people; should I go up in your midst for one moment, I would consume you. So now, put off your ornaments from you, that I may know what I shall do with you.'" 6 So the sons of Israel stripped themselves of their ornaments, from Mount Horeb *onward.*

7 Now Moses used to take the tent and pitch it outside the camp, a good distance from the camp, and he called it the tent of meeting. And everyone who sought Yahweh would go out to the tent of meeting which was outside the camp. 8 And it happened whenever Moses went out to the tent, that all the people would arise and stand, each at the entrance of his tent, and gaze after Moses until he entered the tent. 9 And it happened whenever Moses entered the tent, that the pillar of cloud would descend and stand at the entrance of the tent; and Yahweh would speak with Moses. 10 And all the people would see the pillar of cloud standing at the entrance of the tent. And all the people would arise and worship, each at the entrance of his tent. 11 Thus Yahweh used to speak to Moses face to face, just as a man speaks to his friend. Then Moses would return to the camp, and his attendant Joshua the son of Nun, a young man, would not depart from the tent.

12 Then Moses said to Yahweh, "See, You say to me, 'Bring up this people!' But You Yourself have not let me know whom You will send with me. Moreover, You have said, 'I have known you by name, and you have also found favor in My sight.' 13 So now, I pray You, if I have found favor in Your sight, let me know Your ways that I may know You, so that I may find favor in Your sight. See also, that this nation is Your people." 14 And He said, "My presence shall go *with you,* and I will give you rest." 15 Then he said to Him, "If Your presence does not go *with us,* do not lead us up from here. 16 Indeed, how then can it be known that I have found favor in Your sight, I and Your people? Is it not by Your going with us, so that we, I and Your people, may be distinguished from all the *other* people who are upon the face of the earth?"

17 Then Yahweh said to Moses, "I will also do this thing of which you have spoken; for you have found favor in My sight, and I have known you by name." 18 Then Moses said, "I pray You, show me Your glory!" 19 And He said, "I Myself will make all My goodness pass before you, and I will proclaim the name of Yahweh before you; and I will be gracious to whom I will be gracious, and I will show compassion on whom I will show compassion." 20 But He said, "You cannot see My face, for no man can see Me and live!" 21 Then Yahweh said, "Behold, there is a place by Me, and you shall stand *there* on the rock; 22 and it will come about, while My glory is passing by, that I will put you in the cleft of the rock and cover you with My hand until I have passed by. 23 Then I will remove My hand, and you shall see My back, but My face shall not be seen."

34 Now Yahweh said to Moses, "Carve out for yourself two stone tablets like the former ones, and I will write on the tablets the words that were on the former tablets which you shattered. 2 So be prepared by morning, and come up in the morning to Mount Sinai, and present yourself there to Me on the top of the mountain. 3 And no man is to come up with you, nor let any man be seen anywhere on the mountain; even the flocks and the herds may not graze in front of that mountain." 4 So he carved out two stone tablets like the former ones, and Moses rose up early in the morning and went up to Mount Sinai, as Yahweh had commanded him, and he took two stone tablets in his hand. 5 Then Yahweh descended in the cloud and stood there with him, and He called upon the name of Yahweh. 6 Then Yahweh passed by in front of him and called out, "Yahweh, Yahweh God, compassionate and gracious, slow to anger, and abounding in lovingkindness and truth; 7 who keeps lovingkindness for thousands, who forgives iniquity, transgression, and sin; yet He will by no means leave *the guilty* unpunished, visiting the iniquity of fathers on the children and on the grandchildren to the third and fourth generations." 8 And Moses made haste to bow low toward the earth and worship. 9 And he said, "If now I have found favor in Your sight, O Lord, I pray, let the Lord go along in our midst, even though they are a stiff-necked people, and pardon our iniquity and our sin, and take us as Your own inheritance."

10 Then God said, "Behold, I am going to cut a covenant. Before all your people I will

do wondrous deeds which have not been
created in all the earth nor among any of the
nations; and all the people among whom
you live will see the working of Yahweh,
for it is a fearful thing that I am going to
do with you.
11 "Be sure to keep what I am commanding
you this day: behold, I am going to drive out
the Amorite before you, and the Canaanite,
the Hittite, the Perizzite, the Hivite, and the
Jebusite. 12 Beware lest you cut a covenant
with the inhabitants of the land into which
you are going, lest it become a snare in
your midst. 13 But *rather*, you are to tear
down their altars and shatter their *sacred*
pillars and cut down their Asherim 14—for
you shall not worship any other god, for
Yahweh, whose name is Jealous, is a jealous
God— 15 lest you cut a covenant with the
inhabitants of the land, and they play the
harlot with their gods and sacrifice to their
gods, and one *of them* invite you to eat of
his sacrifice, 16 and you take some of his
daughters for your sons, and his daughters
play the harlot with their gods and cause
your sons *also* to play the harlot with their
gods. 17 You shall make for yourself no
molten gods.
18 "You shall keep the Feast of Unleavened
Bread. For seven days you shall eat unleav-
ened bread, which I commanded you, at the
appointed time in the month of Abib, for in
the month of Abib you came out of Egypt.
19 "The first offspring from every womb
belongs to Me, even of all your male live-
stock, the first offspring from cattle and
sheep. 20 And you shall redeem with a lamb
the first offspring from a donkey; and if you
do not redeem *it*, then you shall break its
neck. You shall redeem all the firstborn of
your sons. None shall appear before Me
empty-handed.
21 "You shall work six days, but on the
seventh day you shall rest; *even* during
plowing time and harvest you shall rest.
22 And you shall celebrate the Feast of
Weeks, *that is*, the first fruits of the wheat
harvest, and the Feast of Ingathering at the
turn of the year. 23 Three times a year all
your males are to appear before the Lord
Yahweh, the God of Israel. 24 For I will
dispossess nations before you and enlarge
your borders, and no man shall covet your
land when you go up three times a year to
appear before Yahweh your God.
25 "You shall not offer the blood of My sac-
rifice with leavened bread, and the sacrifice
of the Feast of the Passover shall not be left
over until morning.
26 "You shall bring the very first of the
first fruits of your ground into the house of
Yahweh your God.
"You shall not boil a young goat in its
mother's milk."
27 Then Yahweh said to Moses, "Write
down these words, for in accordance with
these words I have cut a covenant with you
and with Israel." 28 So he was there with
Yahweh forty days and forty nights; he did
not eat bread or drink water. And he wrote
on the tablets the words of the covenant,
the Ten Commandments.
29 Now it happened when Moses was
coming down from Mount Sinai (and the two
tablets of the testimony *were* in Moses' hand
as he was coming down from the mountain),
that Moses did not know that the skin of his
face shone because of his speaking with Him.
30 Then Aaron and all the sons of Israel saw
Moses, and behold, the skin of his face shone,
and they were afraid to come near him.
31 Then Moses called to them, and Aaron and
all the rulers in the congregation returned to
him; and Moses spoke to them. 32 And after-
ward all the sons of Israel came near, and he
commanded them everything that Yahweh
had spoken to him on Mount Sinai. 33 Then
Moses finished speaking with them and put
a veil over his face. 34 But whenever Moses
went in before Yahweh to speak with Him,
he would take off the veil until he came out;
and then he would come out and speak to the
sons of Israel what he had been commanded,
35 and the sons of Israel would see the face of
Moses, that the skin of Moses' face shone.
So Moses would return the veil over his face
until he went in to speak with Him.

Psalm 21:8–13

8 Your hand will find out
all your enemies;
Your right hand will find out
those who hate you.
9 You will make them as a fiery oven
in the time of your anger;
Yahweh will swallow them
up in His wrath,
And fire will devour them.
10 Their offspring You will
destroy from the earth,

And their seed from among
the sons of men.
11 Though they intended evil against You
And devised a scheme,
They will not succeed.
12 For You will make them
turn their back;
You will aim with Your
bowstrings at their faces.
13 Be exalted, O Yahweh, in Your strength;
We will sing and praise Your might.

Proverbs 8:1–5

8 Does not wisdom call,
And discernment give forth her voice?
2 At the top of the heights upon the way,
Where the pathways meet,
she takes her stand;
3 Beside the gates, at the
opening to the city,
At the entrance of the doors,
she makes a shout:
4 "To you, O men, I call,
And my voice is to the sons of men.
5 "O simple ones, understand prudence;
And, O fools, understand
a heart *of wisdom*.

Matthew 26:1–25

26 Now it happened that when Jesus had
finished all these words, He said to
His disciples, 2 "You know that after two
days the Passover is coming, and the Son of
Man is *to be* delivered over for crucifixion."
3 Then the chief priests and the elders of
the people were gathered together in the
court of the high priest, named Caiaphas;
4 and they plotted together to seize Jesus by
stealth and kill Him. 5 But they were saying,
"Not during the festival, lest a riot occur
among the people."
6 Now when Jesus was in Bethany, at the
home of Simon the leper, 7 a woman came
to Him with an alabaster jar of very costly
perfume, and she poured it on His head
as He reclined *at the table*. 8 But when the
disciples saw *this*, they were indignant,
saying, "Why this waste? 9 For this *perfume*
might have been sold for a high price and
the money given to the poor." 10 But Jesus,
aware of this, said to them, "Why do you
bother the woman? For she has done a good
work to Me. 11 For you always have the poor
with you; but you do not always have Me.
12 For when she poured this perfume on
My body, she did it to prepare Me for burial.
13 Truly I say to you, wherever this gospel is
proclaimed in the whole world, what this
woman has done will also be spoken of in
memory of her."
14 Then one of the twelve, named Judas
Iscariot, went to the chief priests 15 and said,
"What are you willing to give me to deliver
Him to you?" And they weighed out thirty
pieces of silver to him. 16 And from then on
he *began* looking for a good opportunity to
betray Jesus.
17 Now on the first *day* of Unleavened
Bread the disciples came to Jesus, saying,
"Where do You want us to prepare for You
to eat the Passover?" 18 And He said, "Go
into the city to a certain man, and say to
him, 'The Teacher says, "My time is near; I
am keeping the Passover at your house with
My disciples."'" 19 And the disciples did as
Jesus had directed them; and they prepared
the Passover.
20 Now when evening came, Jesus was
reclining *at the table* with the twelve dis-
ciples. 21 And as they were eating, He said,
"Truly I say to you that one of you will
betray Me." 22 And being deeply grieved,
they each one began to say to Him, "Surely
not I, Lord?" 23 And He answered and said,
"He who dipped his hand with Me in the
bowl is the one who will betray Me. 24 The
Son of Man is going, just as it is written
of Him; but woe to that man by whom
the Son of Man is betrayed! It would have
been good for that man if he had not been
born." 25 And Judas, who was betraying
Him, answered and said, "Surely not I,
Rabbi?" Jesus *said to him, "You yourself
said *it*."

Gather the riches of God's promises. Nobody can take away from you those texts from the Bible which you have learned by heart.

— CORRIE TEN BOOM

FEBRUARY 12

Exodus 35:1–36:38

35 Then Moses assembled all the congregation of the sons of Israel and said to them, "These are the things that Yahweh has commanded *you* to do:

2 "Six days work may be done, but on the seventh day you shall have a holy *day*, a sabbath of complete rest to Yahweh; whoever does any work on it shall be put to death. 3 You shall not kindle a fire in any of your *places of* habitation on the sabbath day."

4 And Moses spoke to all the congregation of the sons of Israel, saying, "This is the thing which Yahweh has commanded, saying, 5 'Take from among you a contribution to Yahweh; whoever is of a willing heart, let him bring it as a contribution to Yahweh: gold, silver, and bronze, 6 and blue, purple, and scarlet *material*, fine linen, goats' *hair*, 7 and rams' skins dyed red, and porpoise skins, and acacia wood, 8 and oil for lighting, and spices for the anointing oil, and for the fragrant incense, 9 and onyx stones and setting stones for the ephod and for the breastpiece.

10 'And let everyone wise at heart among you come and make all that Yahweh has commanded: 11 the tabernacle, its tent and its covering, its clasps and its boards, its bars, its pillars, and its bases; 12 the ark and its poles, the mercy seat, and the curtain of the screen; 13 the table and its poles, and all its utensils, and the bread of the Presence; 14 the lampstand also for the light and its utensils and its lamps and the oil for the light; 15 and the altar of incense and its poles, and the anointing oil and the fragrant incense, and the screen for the doorway at the entrance of the tabernacle; 16 the altar of burnt offering with its bronze grating, its poles, and all its utensils, the laver and its stand; 17 the hangings of the court, its pillars and its bases, and the screen for the gate of the court; 18 the pegs of the tabernacle and the pegs of the court and their cords; 19 the woven garments for ministering in the holy place, the holy garments for Aaron the priest and the garments of his sons, to minister as priests.'"

20 Then all the congregation of the sons of Israel went out from Moses' presence. 21 And everyone whose heart stirred him and everyone whose spirit was willing came *and* brought the contribution to Yahweh for the work of the tent of meeting and for all its service and for the holy garments. 22 Then all whose hearts were willing, both men and women, came *and* brought brooches and earrings and signet rings and bracelets, all articles of gold; so *did* every man who waved it as a wave offering of gold to Yahweh. 23 And every man, who had in his possession blue and purple and scarlet *material* and fine linen and goats' *hair* and rams' skins dyed red and porpoise skins, brought them. 24 Everyone who could raise up a contribution of silver and bronze brought the contribution to Yahweh; and every man who had in his possession acacia wood for any work of the service brought it. 25 All the women wise at heart spun with their hands and brought what they had spun, *in* blue and purple *and* scarlet *material* and *in* fine linen. 26 And all the women whose heart stirred with wisdom spun the goats' *hair*. 27 And the rulers brought the onyx stones and the stones for setting for the ephod and for the breastpiece; 28 and the spice and the oil for the light and for the anointing oil and for the fragrant incense. 29 The sons of Israel—all the men and women whose heart was willing to bring *material* for all the work, which Yahweh had commanded through the hand of Moses to do—brought a freewill offering to Yahweh.

30 Then Moses said to the sons of Israel, "See, Yahweh has called by name Bezalel the son of Uri, the son of Hur, of the tribe of Judah. 31 And He has filled him with the Spirit of God, in wisdom, in discernment, and in knowledge, and in all craftsmanship; 32 to devise designs for working in gold and in silver and in bronze, 33 and in the cutting of stones for settings and in the carving of wood, so as to do *well* in every work of thoughtful design. 34 He also has put in his heart to teach, both he and Oholiab, the son of Ahisamach, of the tribe of Dan. 35 He has filled them with wisdom *in their* heart to do every work of an engraver and of a designer and of an embroiderer, in blue and in purple *and* in scarlet *material* and in fine linen, and of a weaver, as those who do every work and make designs.

36 "Now Bezalel and Oholiab and every person wise at heart, to whom Yahweh has given wisdom and discernment to know how to do all the work of the service of *constructing* the sanctuary, shall do in accordance with all that Yahweh has commanded."

2 Then Moses called Bezalel and Oholiab and every person wise at heart to whom Yahweh had given wisdom, everyone whose heart stirred him, to come to the work to do it. 3 And they received from Moses the entire contribution which the sons of Israel had brought to do the work in the service of the sanctuary. And they still *continued* bringing to him freewill offerings every morning. 4 And all the wise men who were doing all the work of the sanctuary came, each from the work which he was doing, 5 and they said to Moses, "The people are bringing much more than enough for the service of the work which Yahweh commanded *us* to do." 6 So Moses commanded and a proclamation was passed throughout the camp, saying, "Let no man or woman any longer do the work for the contributions of the sanctuary." Thus the people were restrained from bringing *any more*. 7 Indeed, the material they had was sufficient and more than enough for all the work, to do it.

8 And all those wise at heart among those who were doing the work made the tabernacle with ten curtains; of fine twisted linen and blue and purple and scarlet *material*, with cherubim, the work of a skillful designer, Bezalel made them. 9 The length of each curtain was twenty-eight cubits and the width of each curtain four cubits; all the curtains had the same measurements. 10 He joined five curtains to one another, and *the other* five curtains he joined to one another. 11 He made loops of blue on the edge of the outermost curtain in the first set; he did likewise on the edge of the curtain that was outermost in the second set. 12 He made fifty loops in the one curtain, and he made fifty loops on the edge of the curtain that was in the second set; the loops were opposite each other. 13 He made fifty clasps of gold and joined the curtains to one another with the clasps, so the tabernacle was one unit.

14 Then he made curtains of goats' *hair* for a tent over the tabernacle; he made eleven curtains in all. 15 The length of each curtain *was* thirty cubits and four cubits the width of each curtain; the eleven curtains had the same measurements. 16 He joined five curtains by themselves and *the other* six curtains by themselves. 17 Moreover, he made fifty loops on the edge of the curtain that was outermost in the *first* set, and he made fifty loops on the edge of the curtain *that was outermost in* the second set. 18 He made fifty clasps of bronze to join the tent together so that it would be a unit. 19 He made a covering for the tent of rams' skins dyed red and a covering of porpoise skins above.

20 Then he made the boards for the tabernacle of acacia wood, standing *upright*. 21 Ten cubits *was* the length of each board and one and a half cubits the width of each board. 22 *There were* two tenons for each board, fitted to one another; thus he did for all the boards of the tabernacle. 23 And he made the boards for the tabernacle: twenty boards for the south side; 24 and he made forty bases of silver under the twenty boards; two bases under one board for its two tenons and two bases under another board for its two tenons. 25 Then for the second side of the tabernacle, on the north side, he made twenty boards, 26 and their forty bases of silver; two bases under one board and two bases under another board. 27 For the rear of the tabernacle, to the west, he made six boards. 28 And he made two boards for the corners of the tabernacle at the rear. 29 And they were separated beneath, but were together at their completion at the top, at the first ring; thus he did with both of them for the two corners. 30 And there were eight boards with their bases of silver, sixteen bases, two bases under every board.

31 Then he made bars of acacia wood, five for the boards of one side of the tabernacle, 32 and five bars for the boards of the other side of the tabernacle, and five bars for the boards of the tabernacle for the rear *side* to the west. 33 And he made the middle bar to pass through in the center of the boards from end to end. 34 He also overlaid the boards with gold and made their rings of gold *as* holders for the bars and overlaid the bars with gold.

35 Moreover, he made the veil of blue and purple and scarlet *material* and fine twisted linen; he made it with cherubim, the work of a skillful designer. 36 And he made four

pillars of acacia for it and overlaid them
with gold, with their hooks of gold; and he
cast four bases of silver for them. 37 And he
made a screen for the doorway of the tent,
of blue and purple and scarlet *material* and
fine twisted linen, the work of a weaver;
38 and *he made* its five pillars with their
hooks, and he overlaid their tops and their
bands with gold; but their five bases were
of bronze.

Psalm 22:1–8

1 My God, my God, why have
  You forsaken me?
Far from my salvation are the
  words of my groaning.
2 O my God, I call by day, but
  You do not answer;
And by night, but I have no rest.
3 Yet You are holy,
Enthroned upon the praises of Israel.
4 In You our fathers trusted;
They trusted and You rescued them.
5 To You they cried out and
  were granted escape;
In You they trusted and were
  not disappointed.

6 But I am a worm and not a man,
A reproach of men and
  despised by the people.
7 All who see me mock me;
They smack *their* lip, they
  wag *their* head, *saying,*
8 "Commit *yourself* to Yahweh;
  let Him rescue him;
Let Him deliver him, because
  He delights in him."

Proverbs 8:6–11

6 "Listen, for I will speak noble things;
And the opening of my lips *will*
  reveal upright things.
7 "For my mouth will utter truth;
And wickedness is an
  abomination to my lips.
8 "All the words of my mouth
  are in righteousness;
There is nothing twisted or
  crooked in them.
9 "They are all straightforward to
  him who understands,
And right to those who
  find knowledge.
10 "Take my discipline and not silver,
And knowledge rather than
  choicest fine gold.
11 "For wisdom is better than pearls;
And all desirable things cannot
  compare with her.

Matthew 26:26–50

26 Now while they were eating, Jesus took
some bread, and after a blessing, He broke *it*.
And giving *it* to the disciples, He said, "Take,
eat; this is My body." 27 And when He had
taken a cup and given thanks, He gave *it* to
them, saying, "Drink from it, all of you; 28 for
this is My blood of the covenant, which is
poured out for many for forgiveness of sins.
29 But I say to you, I will not drink of this
fruit of the vine from now on until that day
when I drink it new with you in My Father's
kingdom."
30 And after singing a hymn, they went
out to the Mount of Olives.

31 Then Jesus *said to them, "You will all fall
away because of Me this night, for it is writ-
ten, 'I WILL STRIKE DOWN THE SHEPHERD, AND
THE SHEEP OF THE FLOCK SHALL BE SCATTERED.'
32 But after I have been raised, I will go ahead
of you to Galilee." 33 But Peter answered and
said to Him, "*Even* though all may fall away
because of You, I will never fall away." 34 Jesus
said to him, "Truly I say to you that this *very*
night, before a rooster crows, you will deny
Me three times." 35 Peter *said to Him, "Even
if I have to die with You, I will not deny You."
All the disciples said the same thing too.

36 Then Jesus *came with them to a
place called Gethsemane, and *said to His
disciples, "Sit here while I go over there and
pray." 37 And He took with Him Peter and
the two sons of Zebedee, and began to be
grieved and distressed. 38 Then He *said
to them, "My soul is deeply grieved, to the
point of death; remain here and keep watch
with Me."

39 And He went a little beyond *them,* and
fell on His face and prayed, saying, "My
Father, if it is possible, let this cup pass
from Me; yet not as I will, but as You will."
40 And He *came to the disciples and *found
them sleeping, and *said to Peter, "So, you
men could not keep watch with Me for one
hour? 41 Keep watching and praying that you
may not enter into temptation; the spirit is
willing, but the flesh is weak."

42 He went away again a second time and
prayed, saying, "My Father, if this cannot

pass away unless I drink it, Your will be done." 43 And again He came and found them sleeping, for their eyes were heavy. 44 And He left them again, and went away and prayed a third time, saying the same thing once more. 45 Then He *came to the disciples and *said to them, "Are you still sleeping and resting? Behold, the hour is at hand and the Son of Man is being betrayed into the hands of sinners. 46 Get up, let us go; behold, the one who betrays Me is at hand!"

47 And while He was still speaking, behold, Judas, one of the twelve, came up, and with him *was* a large crowd with swords and clubs, *who came* from the chief priests and elders of the people. 48 Now he who was betraying Him gave them a sign, saying, "Whomever I kiss, He is the one; seize Him." 49 And immediately Judas went to Jesus and said, "Greetings, Rabbi!" and kissed Him. 50 And Jesus said to him, "Friend, *do* what you have come for." Then they came and laid hands on Jesus and seized Him.

FEBRUARY 13

Exodus 37:1–38:31

37 And Bezalel made the ark of acacia wood; its length was two and a half cubits, and its width one and a half cubits, and its height one and a half cubits; 2 and he overlaid it with pure gold inside and out, and made a gold molding for it all around. 3 He cast four rings of gold for it on its four feet; even two rings on one side of it, and two rings on the other side of it. 4 He made poles of acacia wood and overlaid them with gold. 5 He put the poles into the rings on the sides of the ark to carry it. 6 He made a mercy seat of pure gold, two and a half cubits long and one and a half cubits wide. 7 He made two cherubim of gold; he made them of hammered work at the two ends of the mercy seat; 8 one cherub at the one end and one cherub at the other end; from *one piece* he made the mercy seat *with* the cherubim at its two ends. 9 The cherubim had *their* wings spread upward, covering the mercy seat with their wings, with their faces toward each other; the faces of the cherubim were toward the mercy seat.

10 Then he made the table of acacia wood, two cubits long and a cubit wide and one and a half cubits high. 11 He overlaid it with pure gold and made a gold molding for it all around. 12 He made a rim for it of a handbreadth all around and made a gold molding for its rim all around. 13 He cast four gold rings for it and put the rings on the four corners that were on its four feet. 14 Close to the rim were the rings, the holders for the poles to carry the table. 15 He made the poles of acacia wood and overlaid them with gold, to carry the table. 16 He made the utensils which were on the table, its dishes and its pans and its offering bowls and its jars, with which to pour out drink offerings, of pure gold.

17 Then he made the lampstand of pure gold. He made the lampstand of hammered work, its base and its shaft; its cups, its bulbs, and its flowers were of *the same piece.* 18 There were six branches going out of its sides; three branches of the lampstand from the one side of it and three branches of the lampstand from the other side of it; 19 three cups shaped like almond *blossoms,* a bulb and a flower in one branch, and three cups shaped like almond *blossoms,* a bulb and a flower in the other branch—so for the six branches coming out of the lampstand. 20 In the lampstand *there were* four cups shaped like almond *blossoms,* its bulbs and its flowers; 21 and a bulb was under the *first* pair of branches *coming* out of it, and a bulb under the *second* pair of branches *coming* out of it, and a bulb under the *third* pair of branches *coming* out of it, for the six branches coming out of the lampstand. 22 Their bulbs and their branches were *of one piece* with it; the whole of it *was* a single hammered work of pure gold. 23 He made its seven lamps with its tongs and its trays of pure gold. 24 He made it and all its utensils from a talent of pure gold.

25 Then he made the altar of incense of acacia wood: a cubit long and a cubit wide, square, and two cubits high; its horns were *of one piece* with it. 26 He overlaid it with pure gold, its top and its sides all around, and its horns; and he made a gold molding for it all around. 27 He made two golden rings for it under its molding, on its two sides—on opposite sides—as holders for poles with which to carry it. 28 He made the

poles of acacia wood and overlaid them with
gold. 29 And he made the holy anointing oil
and the pure, fragrant incense of spices, the
work of a perfumer.

38 Then he made the altar of burnt
offering of acacia wood, five cubits
long, and five cubits wide, square, and three
cubits high. 2 He made its horns on its four
corners, its horns being *of one piece* with it,
and he overlaid it with bronze. 3 He made
all the utensils of the altar, the pots and
the shovels and the bowls, the flesh hooks
and the firepans; he made all its utensils of
bronze. 4 He made for the altar a grating of a
network of bronze beneath, under its ledge,
reaching halfway down. 5 He cast four rings
on the four ends of the bronze grating *as*
holders for the poles. 6 He made the poles of
acacia wood and overlaid them with bronze.
7 He inserted the poles into the rings on the
sides of the altar, with which to carry it. He
made it hollow with planks.

8 Moreover, he made the laver of bronze
with its base of bronze, from the mirrors
of the serving women who served at the
doorway of the tent of meeting.

9 Then he made the court: for the south
side the hangings of the court were of fine
twisted linen, one hundred cubits; 10 their
twenty pillars, and their twenty bases,
made of bronze; the hooks of the pillars
and their bands *were* of silver. 11 For the
north side *there were* one hundred cubits;
their twenty pillars and their twenty bases
were of bronze, the hooks of the pillars and
their bands *were* of silver. 12 For the west
side *there were* hangings of fifty cubits
with their ten pillars and their ten bases;
the hooks of the pillars and their bands
were of silver. 13 For the east side toward
the sunrise fifty cubits. 14 The hangings for
the *one* side *of the gate were* fifteen cubits,
with their three pillars and their three bases,
15 and so for the other side. On both sides
of the gate of the court *were* hangings of
fifteen cubits, *with* their three pillars and
their three bases. 16 All the hangings of the
court all around *were* of fine twisted linen.
17 The bases for the pillars *were* of bronze,
the hooks of the pillars and their bands
were of silver; and the overlaying of their
tops *were* of silver, and all the pillars of the
court were furnished with silver bands.
18 The screen of the gate of the court was
the work of the weaver, of blue and purple
and scarlet *material* and fine twisted linen.
And the length *was* twenty cubits and the
height *was* five cubits, corresponding to the
hangings of the court. 19 Their four pillars
and their four bases *were* of bronze; their
hooks *were* of silver, and the overlaying of
their tops and their bands *were* of silver.
20 All the pegs of the tabernacle and of the
court all around *were* of bronze.

21 These are the things numbered for the
tabernacle, the tabernacle of the testimony,
as they were numbered according to the com-
mand of Moses, for the service of the Levites,
by the hand of Ithamar the son of Aaron the
priest. 22 Now Bezalel the son of Uri, the son
of Hur, of the tribe of Judah, made all that
Yahweh had commanded Moses. 23 With
him *was* Oholiab the son of Ahisamach, of
the tribe of Dan, a craftsman and a skillful
designer and a weaver in blue and in purple
and in scarlet *material* and fine linen.

24 All the gold that was used for the work,
in all the work of the sanctuary, even the
gold of the wave offering, was 29 talents
and 730 shekels, according to the shekel of
the sanctuary. 25 The silver of those of the
congregation who were numbered was 100
talents and 1,775 shekels, according to the
shekel of the sanctuary; 26 a beka a head
(*that is*, half a shekel according to the shekel
of the sanctuary), for each one who passed
over to those who were numbered, from
twenty years old and upward, for 603,550
men. 27 One hundred talents of silver were
for casting the bases of the sanctuary and
the bases of the veil; one hundred bases
for one hundred talents, a talent for a base.
28 Of the 1,775 *shekels*, he made hooks for
the pillars and overlaid their tops and made
bands for them. 29 The bronze of the wave
offering was 70 talents and 2,400 shekels.
30 With it he made the bases to the doorway
of the tent of meeting, and the bronze altar
and its bronze grating, and all the utensils
of the altar, 31 and the bases of the court
all around and the bases of the gate of the
court, and all the pegs of the tabernacle and
all the pegs of the court all around.

Psalm 22:9–15

9 Yet You are He who brought
me out of the womb;
You made me trust *when* upon
my mother's breasts.

10 Upon You I was cast from birth;
You have been my God from
my mother's womb.
11 Be not far from me, for distress is near;
For there is none to help.
12 Many bulls have surrounded me;
Strong *bulls* of Bashan
have encircled me.
13 They open wide their mouth at me,
As a lion that tears and roars.
14 I am poured out like water,
And all my bones are out of joint;
My heart is like wax;
It is melted within me.
15 My strength is dried up like a potsherd,
And my tongue cleaves to my jaws;
And You lay me in the dust of death.

Proverbs 8:12–21

12 "I, wisdom, dwell with prudence,
And I find knowledge *and* discretion.
13 "The fear of Yahweh is to hate evil;
Pride and arrogance and the evil way
And the mouth of perverted
words, I hate.
14 "Counsel is mine and sound wisdom;
I am understanding, might is mine.
15 "By me kings reign,
And rulers mark out righteousness.
16 "By me princes rule, and nobles,
All who judge rightly.
17 "I love those who love me;
And those who earnestly
seek me will find me.
18 "Riches and glory are with me,
Enduring wealth and righteousness.
19 "My fruit is better than fine
gold, even pure gold,
And my produce *better*
than choice silver.
20 "I walk in the path of righteousness,
In the midst of the pathways of justice,
21 To give those who love me an
inheritance of wealth,
That I may fill their treasuries.

Matthew 26:51–75

51 And behold, one of those who were
with Jesus stretched out his hand and drew
out his sword and struck the slave of the
high priest and cut off his ear. 52 Then Jesus
*said to him, "Put your sword back into its
place; for all those who take up the sword
shall perish by the sword. 53 Or do you think
that I cannot appeal to My Father, and He
will at once put at My disposal more than
twelve legions of angels? 54 Therefore, how
will the Scriptures be fulfilled, *which say*
that it must happen this way?"
55 At that time Jesus said to the crowds,
"Have you come out with swords and clubs
to arrest Me as *you would* against a robber?
Every day I used to sit in the temple teaching
and you did not seize Me. 56 But all this has
taken place in order that the Scriptures of
the prophets would be fulfilled." Then all
the disciples left Him and fled.
57 Now those who had seized Jesus led
Him away to Caiaphas, the high priest,
where the scribes and the elders were
gathered together. 58 But Peter was following
Him at a distance as far as the courtyard of
the high priest, and entered in, and sat down
with the officers to see the outcome.
59 Now the chief priests and the whole
Sanhedrin kept trying to obtain false testi-
mony against Jesus, so that they might put
Him to death. 60 And they did not find *any*,
even though many false witnesses came for-
ward. But later on two came forward, 61 and
said, "This man stated, 'I am able to destroy
the sanctuary of God and to rebuild it in
three days.'" 62 And the high priest stood
up and said to Him, "Do You not answer?
What are these men testifying against You?"
63 But Jesus kept silent. And the high priest
said to Him, "I put You under oath by the
living God, that You tell us whether You are
the Christ, the Son of God." 64 Jesus *said to
him, "You yourself said *it*; nevertheless I tell
you, hereafter you will see THE SON OF MAN
SITTING AT THE RIGHT HAND OF POWER and
COMING ON THE CLOUDS OF HEAVEN."
65 Then the high priest tore his garments
and said, "He has blasphemed! What further
need do we have of witnesses? Behold, you
have now heard the blasphemy; 66 what do
you think?" They answered and said, "He
deserves death!"
67 Then they spat in His face and beat Him
with their fists; and others slapped *Him*,
68 and said, "Prophesy to us, O Christ; who
is the one who hit You?"
69 Now Peter was sitting outside in the
courtyard, and a servant-girl came to him
and said, "You too were with Jesus the Gal-
ilean." 70 But he denied *it* before them all,
saying, "I do not know what you are talking
about." 71 And when he had gone out to the

gateway, another *servant-girl* saw him and *said to those who were there, "This man was with Jesus of Nazareth." 72 And again he denied *it* with an oath, "I do not know the man." 73 A little later the bystanders came up and said to Peter, "Surely you too are *one* of them; for even the way you talk gives you away." 74 Then he began to curse and swear, "I do not know the man!" And immediately a rooster crowed. 75 And Peter remembered the word which Jesus had said, "Before a rooster crows, you will deny Me three times." And he went out and cried bitterly.

FEBRUARY 14

Exodus 39:1–40:38

39 Moreover, from the blue and purple and scarlet *material,* they made finely woven garments for ministering in the holy place as well as the holy garments which were for Aaron, just as Yahweh had commanded Moses.

2 He made the ephod of gold, *and* of blue and purple and scarlet *material,* and fine twisted linen. 3 Then they hammered out gold sheets and cut *them* into threads to be woven in *with* the blue and the purple and the scarlet *material* and the fine linen, the work of a skillful designer. 4 They made joining shoulder pieces for the ephod; it was joined at its two *upper* ends. 5 The skillfully woven band which was on it was like its workmanship, of the same material: of gold, *and* of blue and purple and scarlet *material,* and fine twisted linen, just as Yahweh had commanded Moses.

6 They made the onyx stones, set all around in filigree *settings* of gold; they were engraved *like* the engravings of a signet, according to the names of the sons of Israel. 7 And he placed them on the shoulder pieces of the ephod, *as* stones of remembrance for the sons of Israel, just as Yahweh had commanded Moses.

8 He made the breastpiece, the work of a skillful designer, like the workmanship of the ephod: of gold, *and* of blue and purple and scarlet *material,* and fine twisted linen. 9 It was square; they made the breastpiece, *having been* folded double, a span long and a span wide when folded double. 10 And they mounted four rows of stones on it. The first row *was* a row of ruby, topaz, and emerald; 11 and the second row, a turquoise, a sapphire, and a diamond; 12 and the third row, a jacinth, an agate, and an amethyst; 13 and the fourth row, a beryl, an onyx, and a jasper. They were set in their filigree *settings* with gold filigree. 14 The stones were corresponding to the names of the sons of Israel; they were twelve, corresponding to their names, *engraved with* the engravings of a signet, each with its name for the twelve tribes. 15 They made on the breastpiece chains of a twisted work of cords in pure gold. 16 They made two gold filigree *settings* and two gold rings, and put the two rings on the two ends of the breastpiece. 17 Then they put the two gold cords in the two rings at the ends of the breastpiece. 18 They put the *other* two ends of the two cords on the two filigree *settings* and put them on the shoulder pieces of the ephod at the front of it. 19 They made two gold rings and placed *them* on the two ends of the breastpiece, on its inner edge which was next to the ephod. 20 Furthermore, they made two gold rings and placed them on the bottom of the two shoulder pieces of the ephod, on the front of it, close to the place where it joined, above the skillfully woven band of the ephod. 21 They bound the breastpiece by its rings to the rings of the ephod with a blue cord, so that it would be on the skillfully woven band of the ephod, and that the breastpiece would not come loose from the ephod, just as Yahweh had commanded Moses.

22 Then he made the robe of the ephod of woven work entirely of blue; 23 and the opening of the robe was *at the top* in the center, as the opening of a coat of mail, with a binding all around its opening, so that it would not be torn. 24 They made pomegranates of blue and purple and scarlet *material and* twisted *linen* on the hem of the robe. 25 They also made bells of pure gold and put the bells between the pomegranates all around on the hem of the robe, 26 alternating a bell and a pomegranate all around on the hem of the robe for the ministry, just as Yahweh had commanded Moses.

27 They made the tunics of finely woven linen for Aaron and his sons, 28 and the

turban of fine linen, and the headdresses of the caps of fine linen, and the linen undergarments of fine twisted linen, 29 and the sash of fine twisted linen, and blue and purple and scarlet *material*, the work of the weaver, just as Yahweh had commanded Moses.

30 They made the plate of the holy crown of pure gold and wrote upon it *with* engraved writing *as found on* a signet, "Holy to Yahweh." 31 They fastened a blue cord to it, to fasten it on the turban above, just as Yahweh had commanded Moses.

32 Thus all the service of *constructing* the tabernacle of the tent of meeting was completed; and the sons of Israel did according to all that Yahweh had commanded Moses; so they did. 33 They brought the tabernacle to Moses, the tent and all its furnishings: its clasps, its boards, its bars, and its pillars and its bases; 34 and the covering of rams' skins dyed red, and the covering of porpoise skins, and the screening veil; 35 the ark of the testimony and its poles and the mercy seat; 36 the table, all its utensils, and the bread of the Presence; 37 the pure *gold* lampstand, with its arrangement of lamps and all its utensils, and the oil for the light; 38 and the gold altar, and the anointing oil and the fragrant incense, and the veil for the doorway of the tent; 39 the bronze altar and its bronze grating, its poles and all its utensils, the laver and its stand; 40 the hangings for the court, its pillars and its bases, and the screen for the gate of the court, its cords and its pegs, and all the equipment for the service of the tabernacle, for the tent of meeting; 41 the woven garments for ministering in the holy place and the holy garments for Aaron the priest and the garments of his sons, to minister as priests. 42 Thus, according to all that Yahweh had commanded Moses, so the sons of Israel did in all their service. 43 And Moses saw all the work, and behold, they had done it; just as Yahweh had commanded, so they had done. Then Moses blessed them.

40

Then Yahweh spoke to Moses, saying, 2 "On the first day of the first month you shall set up the tabernacle of the tent of meeting. 3 You shall place the ark of the testimony there, and you shall screen the ark with the veil. 4 You shall bring in the table and arrange what belongs on it; and you shall bring in the lampstand and mount its lamps. 5 Moreover, you shall set the gold altar of incense before the ark of the testimony and set up the veil for the doorway to the tabernacle. 6 You shall set the altar of burnt offering in front of the doorway of the tabernacle of the tent of meeting. 7 You shall set the laver between the tent of meeting and the altar and put water in it. 8 You shall set up the court all around and hang up the screen for the gateway of the court. 9 Then you shall take the anointing oil and anoint the tabernacle and all that is in it and set it apart as holy and all its furnishings; and it shall be holy. 10 You shall anoint the altar of burnt offering and all its utensils, and set the altar apart as holy, and the altar shall be most holy. 11 You shall anoint the laver and its stand, and set it apart as holy. 12 Then you shall bring Aaron and his sons to the doorway of the tent of meeting and wash them with water. 13 You shall put the holy garments on Aaron and anoint him and set him apart as holy, that he may minister as a priest to Me. 14 You shall bring his sons and put tunics on them; 15 and you shall anoint them even as you have anointed their father, that they may minister as priests to Me; and their anointing will be for them for a perpetual priesthood throughout their generations." 16 Thus Moses did; according to all that Yahweh had commanded him, so he did.

17 Now it happened, in the first month of the second year, on the first *day* of the month, the tabernacle was erected. 18 Moses erected the tabernacle and laid its bases and set up its boards and inserted its bars and erected its pillars. 19 He spread the tent over the tabernacle and placed the covering of the tent on top of it, just as Yahweh had commanded Moses. 20 Then he took the testimony and put *it* into the ark and attached the poles to the ark and put the mercy seat on top of the ark. 21 He brought the ark into the tabernacle and placed the veil of the screen and screened off the ark of the testimony, just as Yahweh had commanded Moses. 22 Then he put the table in the tent of meeting on the north side of the tabernacle, outside the veil. 23 He set the arrangement of bread in order on it before Yahweh, just as Yahweh had commanded Moses. 24 Then he placed the lampstand in the tent of meeting, opposite the table,

on the south side of the tabernacle. 25 He
lighted the lamps before Yahweh, just as
Yahweh had commanded Moses. 26 Then
he placed the gold altar in the tent of meet-
ing in front of the veil; 27 and he burned
fragrant incense on it, just as Yahweh had
commanded Moses. 28 Then he placed the
screen at the doorway of the tabernacle.
29 He placed the altar of burnt offering
before the doorway of the tabernacle of
the tent of meeting, and he offered on it
the burnt offering and the meal offering,
just as Yahweh had commanded Moses.
30 He placed the laver between the tent of
meeting and the altar and put water in it for
washing. 31 From it Moses and Aaron and
his sons washed their hands and their feet.
32 When they entered the tent of meeting,
and when they approached the altar, they
washed, just as Yahweh had commanded
Moses. 33 He erected the court all around
the tabernacle and the altar, and he put
up the screen for the gateway of the court.
Thus Moses finished the work.

34 Then the cloud covered the tent of
meeting, and the glory of Yahweh filled the
tabernacle. 35 And Moses was not able to
enter the tent of meeting because the cloud
had dwelt on it, and the glory of Yahweh
filled the tabernacle. 36 Now throughout
all their journeys whenever the cloud was
taken up from over the tabernacle, the sons
of Israel would set out; 37 but if the cloud
was not taken up, then they did not set out
until the day when it was taken up. 38 For
throughout all their journeys, the cloud of
Yahweh was on the tabernacle by day, and
there was fire in it by night, in the sight of
all the house of Israel.

Psalm 22:16–21

16 For dogs have surrounded me;
A band of evildoers has
encompassed me;
They pierced my hands and my feet.
17 I count all my bones.
They look, they stare at me;
18 They divide my garments among them,
And for my clothing they cast lots.

19 But You, O Yahweh, be not far off;
O my Strength, hasten to my help.
20 Deliver my soul from the sword,
My only *life* from the power of the dog.
21 Save me from the mouth of the lion;
From the horns of the wild oxen
You have answered me.

Proverbs 8:22–31

22 "Yahweh possessed me at the
beginning of His way,
Before His deeds of old.
23 "From everlasting I was installed,
From the beginning, from the
earliest times of the earth.
24 "When there were no depths
I was brought forth,
When there were no springs
heavy with water.
25 "Before the mountains were settled,
Before the hills I was brought forth;
26 While He had not yet made the
earth and the *fields* outside,
Nor the first dust of the world.
27 "When He established the
heavens, I was there,
When He marked out a circle
on the face of the deep,
28 When He made firm the skies above,
When the springs of the
deep became strong,
29 When He set for the sea its boundary
So that the water would not
pass over His command,
When He marked out the
foundations of the earth;
30 Then I was beside Him, *as*
a master workman;
And I was a daily delight,
Rejoicing always before Him,
31 Rejoicing in the world, His earth,
My delight *is* in the sons of men.

Matthew 27:1–26

27 Now when morning came, all the
chief priests and the elders of the
people took counsel together against Jesus
to put Him to death; 2 and they bound Him,
and led Him away and delivered Him to
Pilate the governor.

3 Then when Judas, who had betrayed
Him, saw that He had been condemned, he
felt remorse and returned the thirty pieces of
silver to the chief priests and elders, 4 saying,
"I have sinned by betraying innocent blood."
But they said, "What is that to us? See *to
that* yourself!" 5 And he threw the pieces of
silver into the sanctuary and departed; and
he went away and hanged himself. 6 And
the chief priests took the pieces of silver

and said, "It is not lawful to put them into the temple treasury, since it is the price of blood." 7 And taking counsel together, they bought with the money the Potter's Field as a burial place for strangers. 8 For this reason that field has been called the Field of Blood to this day. 9 Then that which was spoken through Jeremiah the prophet was fulfilled, saying, "AND THEY TOOK THE THIRTY PIECES OF SILVER, THE PRICE OF THE ONE WHOSE PRICE HAD BEEN SET by the sons of Israel; 10 AND THEY GAVE THEM FOR THE POTTER'S FIELD, AS THE LORD DIRECTED ME."

11 Now Jesus stood before the governor, and the governor questioned Him, saying, "Are You the King of the Jews?" And Jesus said to him, "You yourself say *it*." 12 And while He was being accused by the chief priests and elders, He did not answer. 13 Then Pilate *said to Him, "Do You not hear how many things they testify against You?" 14 And He did not answer him with regard to even a *single* charge, so the governor marveled greatly.

15 Now at the feast the governor was accustomed to release for the crowd *any* one prisoner whom they wanted. 16 And at that time they were holding a notorious prisoner, called Barabbas. 17 So when the people gathered together, Pilate said to them, "Whom do you want me to release for you? Barabbas, or Jesus who is called Christ?" 18 For he knew that because of envy they had delivered Him over.

19 Now while he was sitting on the judgment seat, his wife sent him *a message*, saying, "Have nothing to do with that righteous Man; for last night I suffered greatly in a dream because of Him." 20 But the chief priests and the elders persuaded the crowds to ask for Barabbas and to put Jesus to death. 21 But the governor answered and said to them, "Which of the two do you want me to release for you?" And they said, "Barabbas." 22 Pilate *said to them, "Then, what shall I do with Jesus who is called Christ?" They all *said, "Let Him be crucified!" 23 And he said, "Why, what evil did He do?" But they were crying out all the more, saying, "Let Him be crucified!"

24 Now when Pilate saw that he was accomplishing nothing, but rather that a riot was starting, he took water and washed his hands in front of the crowd, saying, "I am innocent of this man's blood; see *to that* yourselves." 25 And all the people answered and said, "His blood be on us and on our children!" 26 Then he released Barabbas for them; but after having Jesus scourged, he delivered Him over to be crucified.

FEBRUARY 15

Leviticus 1:1–2:16

1 Then Yahweh called to Moses and spoke to him from the tent of meeting, saying, 2 "Speak to the sons of Israel and say to them, 'When any man from among you brings an offering near to Yahweh, you shall bring your offering of animals from the herd or the flock. 3 If his offering is a burnt offering from the herd, he shall bring it near, a male without blemish; he shall bring it near to the doorway of the tent of meeting, that he may be accepted before Yahweh. 4 And he shall lay his hand on the head of the burnt offering, that it may be accepted for him to make atonement on his behalf. 5 Then he shall slaughter the young bull before Yahweh; and Aaron's sons the priests shall bring near the blood and splash the blood around on the altar that is at the doorway of the tent of meeting. 6 And he shall then skin the burnt offering and cut it into its pieces. 7 And the sons of Aaron the priest shall put fire on the altar and arrange wood on the fire. 8 Then Aaron's sons the priests shall arrange the pieces, the head, and the suet over the wood which is on the fire that is on the altar. 9 Its entrails, however, and its legs he shall wash with water. And the priest shall offer up in smoke all of it on the altar for a burnt offering, an offering by fire of a soothing aroma to Yahweh.

10 'But if his offering is from the flock, of the sheep or of the goats, for a burnt offering, he shall bring near a male without blemish. 11 And he shall slaughter it on the side of the altar northward before Yahweh, and Aaron's sons the priests shall splash its blood around on the altar. 12 He shall then cut it into its pieces with its head and its suet, and the priest shall arrange them on the wood which is on the fire that is on the altar. 13 The entrails, however, and the legs

he shall wash with water. And the priest
shall bring all of it near and offer it up in
smoke on the altar; it is a burnt offering,
an offering by fire of a soothing aroma to
Yahweh.
14 'But if his offering to Yahweh is a burnt
offering of birds, then he shall bring near
his offering from the turtledoves or from
young pigeons. 15 And the priest shall bring
it near to the altar and wring off its head
and offer it up in smoke on the altar; and
its blood is to be drained out on the side of
the altar. 16 He shall also take away its crop
with its feathers and cast it beside the altar
eastward, to the place of the ashes. 17 Then
he shall tear it by its wings, *but* he shall not
separate *it*. And the priest shall offer it up in
smoke on the altar on the wood which is on
the fire; it is a burnt offering, an offering by
fire of a soothing aroma to Yahweh.

2 'Now when anyone brings near a grain
offering as an offering to Yahweh, his
offering shall be of fine flour, and he shall
pour oil on it and put frankincense on it.
2 He shall then bring it to Aaron's sons the
priests; and he shall take from it his handful
of its fine flour and of its oil with all of its
frankincense. And the priest shall offer *it*
up in smoke *as* its memorial portion on the
altar, an offering by fire of a soothing aroma
to Yahweh. 3 And the remainder of the grain
offering belongs to Aaron and his sons: a
thing most holy of the offerings to Yahweh
by fire.
4 'Now when you bring near an offering
of a grain offering baked in an oven, *it shall
be* unleavened cakes of fine flour mixed
with oil or unleavened wafers spread with
oil. 5 And if your offering is a grain offering
made on the griddle, *it shall be* of fine flour,
unleavened, mixed with oil; 6 you shall break
it into bits and pour oil on it; it is a grain
offering. 7 Now if your offering is a grain
offering *made* in a pan, it shall be made of
fine flour with oil. 8 And you will bring in
the grain offering which is made of these
things to Yahweh, and it shall be brought
near to the priest, and he shall bring it to the
altar. 9 The priest then shall raise up from
the grain offering its memorial portion, and
he shall offer *it* up in smoke on the altar *as*
an offering by fire of a soothing aroma to
Yahweh. 10 And the remainder of the grain
offering belongs to Aaron and his sons: a
thing most holy of the offerings to Yahweh
by fire.
11 'No grain offering, which you bring
near to Yahweh, shall be made with leaven,
for you shall not offer up in smoke any
leaven or any honey as an offering by fire
to Yahweh. 12 As an offering of first fruits
you shall bring them near to Yahweh, but
they shall not ascend for a soothing aroma
on the altar. 13 Every grain offering of yours,
moreover, you shall season with salt, so that
the salt of the covenant of your God shall
not be lacking from your grain offering; with
all your offerings you shall bring salt near.
14 'Also if you bring near a grain offering
of early ripened things to Yahweh, you shall
bring near fresh heads of grain roasted in
the fire, grits of new growth, for the grain
offering of your early ripened things. 15 You
shall then put oil on it and place frankin-
cense on it; it is a grain offering. 16 And the
priest shall offer up in smoke its memorial
portion, part of its grits and its oil with all
its frankincense as an offering by fire to
Yahweh.

Psalm 22:22–31

22 I will *surely* recount Your
name to my brothers;
In the midst of the assembly
I will praise You.
23 You who fear Yahweh, praise Him;
All you seed of Jacob, glorify Him,
And stand in awe of Him,
all you seed of Israel.
24 For He has not despised and
He has not abhorred the
affliction of the afflicted;
And He has not hidden
His face from him;
But when he cried to Him
for help, He heard.

25 Of You *is* my praise in the
great assembly;
I shall pay my vows before
those who fear Him.
26 The afflicted will eat and be satisfied;
Those who seek Him will
praise Yahweh.
May your heart live forever!
27 All the ends of the earth will
remember and turn to Yahweh,
And all the families of the nations
will worship before You.

28 For the kingdom is Yahweh's
And He rules over the nations.
29 All the prosperous of the earth
will eat and worship,
All those who go down to the
dust will bow before Him,
Even he who cannot keep
his soul alive.
30 *Their* seed will serve Him;
It will be recounted about the Lord
to the *coming* generation.
31 They will come and will declare
His righteousness
To a people who will be born,
that He has done *it*.

Proverbs 8:32–36

32 "So now, O sons, listen to me,
For blessed are they who
keep my ways.
33 "Hear discipline and be wise,
And do not neglect *it*.
34 "How blessed is the man
who hears me,
To watch daily at my doors,
To keep watch at my doorposts.
35 "For he who finds me finds life
And obtains favor from Yahweh.
36 "But he who sins against me does
violence to his own soul;
All those who hate me love death."

Matthew 27:27–54

27 Then when the soldiers of the governor
took Jesus into the Praetorium, they gath-
ered the whole *Roman* cohort around Him.
28 And they stripped Him and put a scarlet
robe on Him. 29 And after twisting together
a crown of thorns, they put it on His head,
and a reed in His right hand; and they knelt
down before Him and mocked Him, saying,
"Hail, King of the Jews!" 30 And they spat on
Him, and took the reed and *began to* beat
Him on the head. 31 When they had mocked
Him, they took the *scarlet* robe off Him and
put His *own* garments back on Him, and led
Him away to crucify Him.

32 And as they were coming out, they
found a man of Cyrene named Simon, whom
they pressed into service to bear His cross.

33 And when they came to a place called
Golgotha, which means Place of a Skull,
34 they gave Him wine to drink mixed with
gall; and after tasting *it*, He did not want
to drink.

35 And when they had crucified Him, they
divided up His garments among themselves
by casting lots. 36 And sitting down, they
began to keep watch over Him there. 37 And
above His head they put up the charge
against Him which read, "THIS IS JESUS
THE KING OF THE JEWS."

38 At that time two robbers *were cru-
cified with Him, one on the right and one
on the left. 39 And those passing by were
blaspheming Him, shaking their heads
40 and saying, "You who *are going to* destroy
the sanctuary and rebuild it in three days,
save Yourself! If You are the Son of God,
come down from the cross." 41 In the same
way the chief priests also, along with the
scribes and elders, were mocking *Him* and
saying, 42 "He saved others; He cannot save
Himself. He is the King of Israel; let Him
now come down from the cross, and we
will believe in Him. 43 HE TRUSTS IN GOD;
LET GOD RESCUE *Him* now, IF HE DELIGHTS
IN HIM; for He said, 'I am the Son of God.'"
44 And the robbers who had been crucified
with Him were also insulting Him with the
same words.

45 Now from the sixth hour darkness
fell upon all the land until the ninth hour.
46 And about the ninth hour Jesus cried out
with a loud voice, saying, "ELI, ELI, LAMA
SABACHTHANI?" that is, "MY GOD, MY GOD,
WHY HAVE YOU FORSAKEN ME?" 47 And some
of those who were standing there, when
they heard it, *began* saying, "This man is
calling for Elijah." 48 And immediately one
of them ran, and taking a sponge, he filled
it with sour wine and put it on a reed, and
gave Him a drink. 49 But the rest *of them*
were saying, "Let us see whether Elijah
will come to save Him." 50 And Jesus cried
out again with a loud voice, and yielded
up His spirit. 51 And behold, the veil of
the sanctuary was torn in two from top to
bottom; and the earth shook and the rocks
were split. 52 And the tombs were opened,
and many bodies of the saints who had
fallen asleep were raised; 53 and coming
out of the tombs after His resurrection
they entered the holy city and appeared
to many. 54 Now the centurion, and those
who were with him keeping guard over
Jesus, when they saw the earthquake and
the things that were happening, became
very frightened and said, "Truly this was
God's Son!"

FEBRUARY 16

Leviticus 3:1–4:35

3 'Now if his offering is a sacrifice of peace offerings, if he is going to bring near one from the herd, whether male or female, he shall bring it near without blemish before Yahweh. 2 Then he shall lay his hand on the head of his offering and slaughter it at the doorway of the tent of meeting, and Aaron's sons the priests shall splash the blood around on the altar. 3 From the sacrifice of the peace offerings he shall bring an offering by fire near to Yahweh, the fat that covers the entrails and all the fat that is on the entrails, 4 and the two kidneys with the fat that is on them, which is on the loins, and the lobe of the liver, which he shall remove with the kidneys. 5 Then Aaron's sons shall offer *it* up in smoke on the altar on the burnt offering, which is on the wood that is on the fire; it is an offering by fire of a soothing aroma to Yahweh. 6 But if his offering for a sacrifice of peace offerings to Yahweh is from the flock, he shall bring it near, male or female, without blemish. 7 If he is going to bring near a lamb for his offering, then he shall bring it near before Yahweh, 8 and he shall lay his hand on the head of his offering and slaughter it before the tent of meeting, and Aaron's sons shall splash its blood around on the altar. 9 And from the sacrifice of peace offerings he shall bring near as an offering by fire to Yahweh its fat, the entire fat tail which he shall remove close to the backbone, and the fat that covers the entrails and all the fat that is on the entrails, 10 and the two kidneys with the fat that is on them, which is on the loins, and the lobe of the liver, which he shall remove with the kidneys. 11 Then the priest shall offer *it* up in smoke on the altar *as* food, an offering by fire to Yahweh.

12 'Moreover, if his offering is a goat, then he shall bring it near before Yahweh, 13 and he shall lay his hand on its head and slaughter it before the tent of meeting, and the sons of Aaron shall splash its blood around on the altar. 14 And from it he shall bring near his offering as an offering by fire to Yahweh the fat that covers the entrails and all the fat that is on the entrails, 15 and the two kidneys with the fat that is on them, which is on the loins, and the lobe of the liver, which he shall remove with the kidneys. 16 And the priest shall offer them up in smoke on the altar *as* food, an offering by fire for a soothing aroma; all fat is Yahweh's. 17 It is a perpetual statute throughout your generations in all your *places of* habitation: you shall not eat any fat or any blood.'"

4 Then Yahweh spoke to Moses, saying, 2 "Speak to the sons of Israel, saying, 'If a person sins unintentionally in any of the things which Yahweh has commanded not to be done, and he does any one of them, 3 if the anointed priest sins so as to bring guilt on the people, then let him bring near to Yahweh a bull from the herd without blemish as a sin offering for the sin he has committed. 4 Then he shall bring the bull to the doorway of the tent of meeting before Yahweh, and he shall lay his hand on the head of the bull and slaughter the bull before Yahweh. 5 Then the anointed priest shall take some of the blood of the bull and bring it to the tent of meeting, 6 and the priest shall dip his finger in the blood and sprinkle some of the blood seven times before Yahweh in front of the veil of the sanctuary. 7 The priest shall also put some of the blood on the horns of the altar of fragrant incense which is before Yahweh in the tent of meeting; and all the blood of the bull he shall pour out at the base of the altar of burnt offering which is at the doorway of the tent of meeting. 8 Then he shall raise up from it all the fat of the bull of the sin offering: the fat that covers the entrails and all the fat which is on the entrails, 9 and the two kidneys with the fat that is on them, which is on the loins, and the lobe of the liver, which he shall remove with the kidneys 10 (just as it is raised up from the ox of the sacrifice of peace offerings), and the priest shall offer them up in smoke on the altar of burnt offering. 11 But the hide of the bull and all its flesh with its head and its legs and its entrails and its refuse, 12 that is, all *the rest of* the bull, he shall bring out to a clean place outside the camp where the ashes are poured out, and he shall burn it on wood with fire; where the ashes are poured out it shall be burned.

13 'Now if the whole congregation of Israel commits error, and the matter is hidden from the sight of the assembly, and they commit any of the things which Yahweh has commanded not to be done, and they become guilty; 14 when the sin which they have committed becomes known, then the assembly shall bring near a bull from the herd for a sin offering and bring it before the tent of meeting. 15 Then the elders of the congregation shall lay their hands on the head of the bull before Yahweh, and the bull shall be slaughtered before Yahweh. 16 Then the anointed priest shall bring some of the blood of the bull to the tent of meeting; 17 and the priest shall dip his finger in the blood and sprinkle *it* seven times before Yahweh in front of the veil. 18 And he shall put some of the blood on the horns of the altar which is before Yahweh in the tent of meeting; and all the blood he shall pour out at the base of the altar of burnt offering which is at the doorway of the tent of meeting. 19 He shall then raise up all its fat from it and offer it up in smoke on the altar. 20 He shall also do with the bull just as he did with the bull of the sin offering; thus he shall do with it. So the priest shall make atonement for them, and they will be forgiven. 21 Then he shall bring out the bull to *a place* outside the camp and burn it as he burned the first bull; it is the sin offering for the assembly.

22 'When a leader sins and unintentionally does any one of all the things which Yahweh his God has commanded not to be done, and he becomes guilty, 23 or if his sin which he has committed is made known to him, he shall bring for his offering a goat, a male without blemish. 24 Then he shall lay his hand on the head of the male goat and slaughter it in the place where they slaughter the burnt offering before Yahweh; it is a sin offering. 25 Then the priest shall take some of the blood of the sin offering with his finger and put it on the horns of the altar of burnt offering; and *the rest of* its blood he shall pour out at the base of the altar of burnt offering. 26 And all its fat he shall offer up in smoke on the altar as *in the case of* the fat of the sacrifice of peace offerings. Thus the priest shall make atonement for him in regard to his sin, and he will be forgiven.

27 'Now if anyone of the common people sins unintentionally in doing any of the things which Yahweh has commanded not to be done, and becomes guilty, 28 or if his sin which he has committed is made known to him, then he shall bring for his offering a goat, a female without blemish, for his sin which he has committed. 29 And he shall lay his hand on the head of the sin offering and slaughter the sin offering at the place of the burnt offering. 30 And the priest shall take some of its blood with his finger and put it on the horns of the altar of burnt offering; and all *the rest of* its blood he shall pour out at the base of the altar. 31 Then he shall remove all its fat, just as the fat was removed from the sacrifice of peace offerings; and the priest shall offer it up in smoke on the altar for a soothing aroma to Yahweh. Thus the priest shall make atonement for him, and he will be forgiven.

32 'But if he brings a lamb as his offering for a sin offering, he shall bring it, a female without blemish. 33 And he shall lay his hand on the head of the sin offering and slaughter it for a sin offering in the place where they slay the burnt offering. 34 And the priest shall take some of the blood of the sin offering with his finger and put it on the horns of the altar of burnt offering, and all *the rest of* its blood he shall pour out at the base of the altar. 35 Then he shall remove all its fat, just as the fat of the lamb is removed from the sacrifice of the peace offerings, and the priest shall offer them up in smoke on the altar, on the offerings by fire to Yahweh. Thus the priest shall make atonement for him in regard to his sin which he has committed, and he will be forgiven.

Psalm 23:1–6

1 Yahweh is my shepherd,
I shall not want.
2 He makes me lie down in
green pastures;
He leads me beside quiet waters.
3 He restores my soul;
He guides me in the paths
of righteousness
For His name's sake.

4 Even though I walk through the
valley of the shadow of death,
I fear no evil, for You are with me;
Your rod and Your staff,
they comfort me.

5 You prepare a table before me in
the presence of my enemies;
You have anointed my head with oil;
My cup overflows.
6 Surely goodness and lovingkindness
will pursue me all the days of my life,
And I will dwell in the house
of Yahweh forever.

Proverbs 9:1–6

9 Wisdom has built her house,
She has hewn out her seven pillars;
2 She has slaughtered her cattle,
she has mixed her wine;
She has also prepared her table;
3 She has sent out her maidens, she calls
From the tops of the heights of the city:
4 "Whoever is simple, let
him turn in here!"
To him who lacks a heart
of wisdom she says,
5 "Come, eat of my bread
And drink of the wine I have mixed.
6 "Forsake *your* simplicity and live,
And step into the way of
understanding."

Matthew 27:55–66

55 And many women were there looking
on from a distance, who had followed Jesus
from Galilee while ministering to Him.
56 Among them was Mary Magdalene, and
Mary the mother of James and Joseph, and
the mother of the sons of Zebedee.
57 Now when it was evening, there came
a rich man from Arimathea, named Joseph,
who himself had also become a disciple of
Jesus. 58 This man went to Pilate and asked
for the body of Jesus. Then Pilate ordered it
to be given *to him*. 59 And Joseph took the
body and wrapped it in a clean linen cloth,
60 and laid it in his own new tomb, which he
had hewn out in the rock; and he rolled a
large stone against the entrance of the tomb
and went away. 61 And Mary Magdalene was
there, and the other Mary, sitting opposite
the grave.
62 Now on the next day, the day after the
Preparation, the chief priests and the Phar-
isees gathered together with Pilate, 63 and
said, "Sir, we remember that when He was
still alive that deceiver said, 'After three days
I *am to* rise again.' 64 Therefore, order for the
grave to be made secure until the third day,
lest His disciples come and steal Him away
and say to the people, 'He has risen from the
dead,' and the last deception will be worse
than the first." 65 Pilate said to them, "You
have a guard; go, make it *as* secure as you
know how." 66 And they went and made the
grave secure, and along with the guard they
set a seal on the stone.

FEBRUARY 17

Leviticus 5:1–6:30

5 'Now if a person sins after he hears
a public oath *to testify* when he is a
witness, whether he has seen or *otherwise*
known, if he does not tell *it*, then he will
bear his guilt. 2 Or a person who touches
any unclean thing, whether a carcass of
an unclean beast or the carcass of unclean
cattle or a carcass of unclean swarming
things—*though* it is hidden from him, yet he
is unclean—will be guilty. 3 Or if he touches
human uncleanness, of whatever *sort* his
uncleanness *may* be with which he becomes
unclean, and it is hidden from him, and then
he comes to know *it*, he will be guilty. 4 Or if
a person swears thoughtlessly with his lips
to do evil or to do good, in whatever matter
a man may speak thoughtlessly with a *sworn*
oath, and it is hidden from him, and then he
comes to know *it*, he will be guilty in one
of these. 5 So it shall be, when he becomes
guilty in one of these, that he shall confess
that in which he has sinned. 6 He shall also
bring his guilt offering to Yahweh for his
sin which he has committed, a female from
the flock, a lamb or a goat, as a sin offering.
So the priest shall make atonement on his
behalf for his sin.
7 'But if he cannot afford a lamb, then he
shall bring to Yahweh his guilt offering for
that in which he has sinned, two turtledoves
or two young pigeons, one for a sin offering
and the other for a burnt offering. 8 And he
shall bring them to the priest, who shall
bring near first that which is for the sin
offering and shall nip its head at the front
of its neck, but he shall not separate *it*. 9 He
shall also sprinkle some of the blood of the
sin offering on the side of the altar, while the
rest of the blood shall be drained out at the

base of the altar: it is a sin offering. 10 The second he shall then prepare as a burnt offering according to the *legal* judgment. So the priest shall make atonement on his behalf for his sin which he has committed, and it will be forgiven him.

11 'But if his means are insufficient for two turtledoves or two young pigeons, then for his offering for that which he has sinned, he shall bring the tenth of an ephah of fine flour for a sin offering; he shall not place oil on it or put frankincense on it, for it is a sin offering. 12 He shall then bring it to the priest, and the priest shall take his handful of it as its memorial portion and offer *it* up in smoke on the altar, with the offerings of Yahweh by fire: it is a sin offering. 13 So the priest shall make atonement for him concerning his sin which he has committed from one of these, and it will be forgiven him; then *the rest* shall become the priest's, like the grain offering.'"

14 Then Yahweh spoke to Moses, saying, 15 "If a person acts unfaithfully and sins unintentionally against the holy things of Yahweh, then he shall bring his guilt offering to Yahweh: a ram without blemish from the flock, according to your valuation in silver by shekels, in *terms of* the shekel of the sanctuary, for a guilt offering. 16 And he shall make restitution for that which he has sinned against the holy thing, and he shall add to it a fifth part of it and give it to the priest. The priest shall then make atonement for him with the ram of the guilt offering, and it will be forgiven him.

17 "Now if a person sins and does any one of the things which Yahweh has commanded not to be done, but he was unaware, still he is guilty and shall bear his punishment. 18 He is then to bring to the priest a ram without blemish from the flock, according to your valuation, for a guilt offering. So the priest shall make atonement for him concerning his error in which he sinned unintentionally and did not know *it*, and it will be forgiven him. 19 It is a guilt offering; he was certainly guilty before Yahweh."

6 Then Yahweh spoke to Moses, saying, 2 "If a person sins and acts unfaithfully *against Yahweh and deals falsely* with his companion in regard to a deposit or a security entrusted *to him* or through robbery, or *if* he has extorted from his companion, 3 or has found what was lost and dealt falsely about it and sworn falsely, so that he sins in regard to any one of the things a man may do; 4 then it shall be, when he sins and becomes guilty, that he shall return what he took by robbery or what he got by extortion, or the deposit which was entrusted to him or the lost thing which he found, 5 or anything about which he swore falsely; he shall make restitution for it in full and add to it one-fifth more. He shall give it to the one to whom it belongs on the day *he presents* his guilt offering. 6 Then he shall bring to the priest his guilt offering to Yahweh, a ram without blemish from the flock, according to your valuation, for a guilt offering, 7 and the priest shall make atonement for him before Yahweh, and he will be forgiven for any one of the things which he may have done to incur guilt."

8 Then Yahweh spoke to Moses, saying, 9 "Command Aaron and his sons, saying, 'This is the law for the burnt offering: the burnt offering itself *shall remain* on the hearth on the altar all night until the morning, and the fire on the altar shall be kept burning on it. 10 And the priest shall put on his linen robe, and he shall put on undergarments next to his flesh; and he shall raise up the ashes *to* which the fire reduces the burnt offering on the altar and place them beside the altar. 11 Then he shall take off his garments and put on other garments and carry the ashes outside the camp to a clean place. 12 And the fire on the altar shall be kept burning on it. It shall not go out, but the priest shall burn wood on it every morning; and he shall lay out the burnt offering on it and offer up in smoke the fat portions of the peace offerings on it. 13 Fire shall be kept burning continually on the altar; it shall not go out.

14 'Now this is the law of the grain offering: the sons of Aaron shall bring it near before Yahweh in front of the altar. 15 Then one *of them* shall raise up from it a handful of the fine flour of the grain offering, with its oil and all the frankincense that is on the grain offering, and he shall offer *it* up in smoke on the altar, a soothing aroma, as its memorial offering to Yahweh. 16 What is left of it Aaron and his sons shall eat. It shall be eaten as unleavened cakes in a holy place; they shall eat it in the court of the tent of meeting. 17 It shall not be baked with leaven. I have

given it as their share from My offerings by
fire; it is most holy, like the sin offering and
the guilt offering. 18 Every male among the
sons of Aaron may eat it; it is a perpetual
statute throughout your generations, from
the offerings by fire to Yahweh. Whoever
touches them will be set apart as holy.'"
19 Then Yahweh spoke to Moses, saying,
20 "This is the offering which Aaron and his
sons shall bring near to Yahweh on the day
when he is anointed; the tenth of an ephah
of fine flour as a regular grain offering, half
of it in the morning and half of it in the
evening. 21 It shall be prepared with oil on
a griddle. When it is *well* stirred, you shall
bring it. You shall bring near the grain offer-
ing in baked pieces as a soothing aroma to
Yahweh. 22 And the anointed priest, who will
be in his place among his sons, shall offer
it. By a perpetual statute it shall be entirely
offered up in smoke to Yahweh. 23 So every
grain offering of the priest shall be burned
entirely. It shall not be eaten."
24 Then Yahweh spoke to Moses, saying,
25 "Speak to Aaron and to his sons, saying,
'This is the law of the sin offering: in the
place where the burnt offering is slaugh-
tered, the sin offering shall be slaughtered
before Yahweh; it is most holy. 26 The priest
who offers it for sin shall eat it. It shall be
eaten in a holy place, in the court of the
tent of meeting. 27 Anyone who touches its
flesh will be set apart as holy; and when
any of its blood sprinkles on a garment, in
a holy place you shall wash what was sprin-
kled on. 28 Also the earthenware vessel in
which it was boiled shall be broken; and
if it was boiled in a bronze vessel, then it
shall be scoured and rinsed in water. 29 And
every male among the priests may eat of
it; it is most holy. 30 But no sin offering, of
which any of the blood is brought into the
tent of meeting to make atonement in the
holy place, shall be eaten; it shall be burned
with fire.

Psalm 24:1–6

1 The earth is Yahweh's,
as well as its fullness,
The world, and those who dwell in it.
2 For He has founded it upon the seas
And established it upon the rivers.
3 Who may ascend into the
mountain of Yahweh?
And who may rise in His holy place?
4 He who has innocent hands
and a pure heart,
Who has not lifted up his
soul to worthlessness
And has not sworn deceitfully.
5 He shall lift up a blessing
from Yahweh
And righteousness from the
God of his salvation.
6 This is the generation of
those who seek Him,
Who seek Your face—*pay heed*
O Jacob. Selah.

Proverbs 9:7–9

7 He who disciplines a scoffer
receives disgrace for himself,
And he who reproves a wicked man
receives injury for himself.
8 Do not reprove a scoffer,
lest he hate you,
Reprove a wise man and
he will love you.
9 Give *knowledge* to a wise man
and he will be still wiser,
Make a righteous man know *it* and
he will increase *his* learning.

Matthew 28:1–20

28 Now after the Sabbath, as it began
to dawn toward the first *day* of the
week, Mary Magdalene and the other Mary
came to look at the grave. 2 And behold,
there was a great earthquake, for an angel of
the Lord descended from heaven and came
and rolled away the stone and sat upon it.
3 And his appearance was like lightning,
and his clothing as white as snow. 4 And the
guards quaked from fear of him and became
like dead men. 5 And the angel answered and
said to the women, "Do not be afraid; for I
know that you are looking for Jesus who has
been crucified. 6 He is not here, for He has
risen, just as He said. Come, see the place
where He was lying. 7 And go quickly and
tell His disciples that He has risen from the
dead; and behold, He is going ahead of you
into Galilee, there you will see Him; behold,
I have told you."
8 And they left the tomb quickly with
fear and great joy and ran to report it to His
disciples. 9 And behold, Jesus met them
and said, "Greetings!" And they came up
and took hold of His feet and worshiped
Him. 10 Then Jesus *said to them, "Do not

be afraid; go and report to My brothers to leave for Galilee, and there they will see Me."

11 Now while they were on their way, behold, some of the guard came into the city and reported to the chief priests all that had happened. 12 And when they had assembled with the elders and took counsel together, they gave a large sum of money to the soldiers, 13 and said, "You are to say, 'His disciples came by night and stole Him away while we were asleep.' 14 And if this is heard before the governor, we will win him over and keep you out of trouble." 15 And they took the money and did as they had been instructed; and this story was widely spread among the Jews, *and is* to this day.

16 But the eleven disciples proceeded to Galilee, to the mountain which Jesus had designated. 17 And when they saw Him, they worshiped *Him*; but some doubted. 18 And Jesus came up and spoke to them, saying, "All authority has been given to Me in heaven and on earth. 19 Go therefore and make disciples of all the nations, baptizing them in the name of the Father and the Son and the Holy Spirit, 20 teaching them to keep all that I commanded you; and behold, I am with you always, even to the end of the age."

FEBRUARY 18

Leviticus 7:1–8:36

7 'Now this is the law of the guilt offering; it is most holy. 2 In the place where they slaughter the burnt offering they are to slaughter the guilt offering, and he shall splash its blood around on the altar. 3 Then he shall bring near from it all its fat: the fat tail and the fat that covers the entrails, 4 and the two kidneys with the fat that is on them, which is on the loins, and the lobe on the liver he shall remove with the kidneys. 5 And the priest shall offer them up in smoke on the altar as an offering by fire to Yahweh; it is a guilt offering. 6 Every male among the priests may eat of it. It shall be eaten in a holy place; it is most holy. 7 The guilt offering is like the sin offering, there is one law for them; the priest who makes atonement with it shall have it. 8 Also the priest who brings near any man's burnt offering, that priest shall have for himself the skin of the burnt offering which he has brought near. 9 Likewise, every grain offering that is baked in the oven and everything prepared in a pan or on a griddle shall belong to the priest who brings it near. 10 And every grain offering, mixed with oil or dry, shall belong to all the sons of Aaron, to all alike.

11 'Now this is the law of the sacrifice of peace offerings which shall be brought near to Yahweh. 12 If he brings it near for thanksgiving, then along with the sacrifice of thanksgiving he *shall bring near unleavened cakes* mixed with oil and unleavened wafers spread with oil and cakes *of well* stirred fine flour mixed with oil. 13 With the sacrifice of his peace offerings for thanksgiving, he shall bring near his offering with cakes of leavened bread. 14 Of this he shall bring near, one of every offering as a contribution to Yahweh; it shall belong to the priest who splashes the blood of the peace offerings.

15 'Now *as for* the flesh of the sacrifice of his thanksgiving peace offerings, it shall be eaten on the day of his offering; he shall not leave any of it over until morning. 16 But if the sacrifice of his offering is a votive or a freewill offering, it shall be eaten on the day that he brings near his sacrifice, and on the next day what is left of it may be eaten; 17 but what is left over from the flesh of the sacrifice on the third day shall be burned with fire. 18 So if any of the flesh of the sacrifice of his peace offerings should *ever* be eaten on the third day, he who brings it near will not be accepted, *and* it will not be counted to his *benefit*. It shall be an offensive thing, and the person who eats of it will bear his *own* iniquity.

19 'Also the flesh that touches anything unclean shall not be eaten; it shall be burned with fire. As for *other* flesh, anyone who is clean may eat *such* flesh. 20 But the person who eats the flesh of the sacrifice of peace offerings which belong to Yahweh, in his uncleanness, that person shall be cut off from his people. 21 When anyone touches anything unclean, whether human uncleanness or an unclean animal or any unclean detestable thing, and eats of the flesh of the sacrifice of peace offerings which belong to Yahweh, that person shall be cut off from his people.'"

[22] Then Yahweh spoke to Moses, saying,
[23] "Speak to the sons of Israel, saying, 'You
shall not eat any fat *from* an ox, a sheep, or
a goat. [24] Also the fat of *an animal* which
dies and the fat of an animal torn *by beasts*
may be put to any other use, but you must
certainly not eat it. [25] For whoever eats the
fat of the animal from which an offering
by fire is brought near to Yahweh, even the
person who eats shall be cut off from his
people. [26] And you shall not eat any blood,
either of bird or animal, in any of your *places
of* habitation. [27] Any person who eats any
blood, even that person shall be cut off from
his people.'"

[28] Then Yahweh spoke to Moses, saying,
[29] "Speak to the sons of Israel, saying, 'He
who brings the sacrifice of his peace offer-
ings near to Yahweh shall bring his offering
to Yahweh from the sacrifice of his peace
offerings. [30] His own hands are to bring
offerings by fire to Yahweh. He shall bring
the fat with the breast, that the breast may
be waved as a wave offering before Yahweh.
[31] And the priest shall offer up the fat in
smoke on the altar, but the breast shall
belong to Aaron and his sons. [32] And you
shall give the right thigh to the priest as
a contribution from the sacrifices of your
peace offerings. [33] The one among the sons
of Aaron who brings near the blood of the
peace offerings and the fat, the right thigh
shall be his as *his* portion. [34] For I have taken
the breast of the wave offering and the thigh
of the contribution from the sons of Israel
from the sacrifices of their peace offerings,
and I have given them to Aaron the priest
and to his sons as a perpetual statute *taken*
from the sons of Israel.

[35] 'This is the share for Aaron and the
share for his sons from the offerings by fire
to Yahweh, in that day when he brought
them near to minister as priests to Yahweh.
[36] These Yahweh had commanded to be
given them from the sons of Israel in the
day that He anointed them. It is a perpetual
statute throughout their generations.'"

[37] This is the law of the burnt offering,
the grain offering and the sin offering and
the guilt offering and the ordination offering
and the sacrifice of peace offerings, [38] which
Yahweh commanded Moses at Mount Sinai
in the day that He commanded the sons of
Israel to bring their offerings near to Yahweh
in the wilderness of Sinai.

8 Then Yahweh spoke to Moses, saying,
[2] "Take Aaron and his sons with him,
and the garments and the anointing oil and
the bull of the sin offering and the two rams
and the basket of unleavened bread, [3] and
assemble all the congregation at the door-
way of the tent of meeting." [4] So Moses did
just as Yahweh commanded him. Then the
congregation was assembled at the doorway
of the tent of meeting, [5] and Moses said to
the congregation, "This is the thing which
Yahweh has commanded to do."

[6] Then Moses had Aaron and his sons
come near and washed them with water.
[7] And he put the tunic on him and girded
him with the sash and clothed him with
the robe and put the ephod on him; and he
girded him with the skillfully woven band
of the ephod, with which he tied *it* to him.
[8] He then placed the breastpiece on him, and
in the breastpiece he put the Urim and the
Thummim. [9] He also placed the turban on
his head, and on the turban, at its front, he
placed the golden plate, the holy crown, just
as Yahweh had commanded Moses.

[10] Moses then took the anointing oil and
anointed the tabernacle and all that was
in it and set them apart as holy. [11] And he
sprinkled some of it on the altar seven times
and anointed the altar and all its utensils
and the laver and its stand, to set them
apart as holy. [12] Then he poured some of the
anointing oil on Aaron's head and anointed
him, to set him apart as holy. [13] Next Moses
brought Aaron's sons near and clothed them
with tunics and girded them with sashes
and bound caps on them, just as Yahweh
had commanded Moses.

[14] Then he brought the bull of the sin
offering, and Aaron and his sons laid their
hands on the head of the bull of the sin
offering. [15] Next Moses slaughtered *it* and
took the blood and with his finger put *some
of it* around on the horns of the altar and
purified the altar. Then he poured out *the
rest of* the blood at the base of the altar and
set it apart as holy, to make atonement for
it. [16] He also took all the fat that was on
the entrails, and the lobe of the liver, and
the two kidneys and their fat; and Moses
offered it up in smoke on the altar. [17] But
the bull and its hide and its flesh and its
refuse he burned in the fire outside the
camp, just as Yahweh had commanded
Moses.

18 Then he brought near the ram of the
burnt offering, and Aaron and his sons laid
their hands on the head of the ram. 19 Then
Moses slaughtered *it* and splashed the blood
around on the altar. 20 And he cut the ram
into its pieces. Then Moses offered up the
head and the pieces and the suet in smoke.
21 And he washed the entrails and the legs
with water. Then Moses offered up the
whole ram in smoke on the altar. It was a
burnt offering for a soothing aroma; it was
an offering by fire to Yahweh, just as Yahweh
had commanded Moses.

22 Then he brought near the second ram,
the ram of ordination, and Aaron and his
sons laid their hands on the head of the ram.
23 And Moses slaughtered *it* and took some
of its blood and put it on the lobe of Aaron's
right ear and on the thumb of his right hand
and on the big toe of his right foot. 24 He also
brought Aaron's sons near; and Moses put
some of the blood on the lobe of their right
ear and on the thumb of their right hand and
on the big toe of their right foot. Moses then
splashed *the rest of* the blood around on the
altar. 25 And he took the fat, and the fat tail,
and all the fat that was on the entrails, and
the lobe of the liver, and the two kidneys
and their fat, and the right thigh. 26 From the
basket of unleavened bread that was before
Yahweh, he took one unleavened cake and
one cake of bread *mixed with* oil and one
wafer, and he placed *them* on the portions
of fat and on the right thigh. 27 He then put
all *these* on the hands of Aaron and on the
hands of his sons, and waved them as a wave
offering before Yahweh. 28 Then Moses took
them from their hands and offered them up
in smoke on the altar with the burnt offer-
ing. They were an ordination offering for a
soothing aroma; it was an offering by fire to
Yahweh. 29 Moses also took the breast and
waved it as a wave offering before Yahweh; it
was Moses' portion of the ram of ordination,
just as Yahweh had commanded Moses.

30 So Moses took some of the anointing
oil and some of the blood which was on
the altar and sprinkled it on Aaron, on his
garments, on his sons, and on the garments
of his sons with him; and he set Aaron apart
as holy, his garments and his sons and the
garments of his sons with him.

31 Then Moses said to Aaron and to
his sons, "Boil the flesh at the doorway
of the tent of meeting, and eat it there
together with the bread which is in the
basket of the ordination offering, just as
I commanded, saying, 'Aaron and his sons
shall eat it.' 32 And the remainder of the
flesh and of the bread you shall burn in
the fire. 33 And you shall not go outside the
doorway of the tent of meeting for seven
days, until the day that the period of your
ordination is fulfilled; for he will ordain
you through seven days. 34 Yahweh has
commanded to do as has been done this
day, to make atonement on your behalf.
35 At the doorway of the tent of meeting,
moreover, you shall remain day and night
for seven days and keep the charge of
Yahweh, so that you will not die, for so I
have been commanded." 36 Thus Aaron and
his sons did all the things which Yahweh
had commanded through Moses.

Psalm 24:7–10

7 Lift up your heads, O gates,
And be lifted up, O ancient doors,
That the King of glory may come in!
8 Who is this King of glory?
Yahweh strong and mighty,
Yahweh mighty in battle.
9 Lift up your heads, O gates,
And lift *yourselves* up,
O ancient doors,
That the King of glory may come in!
10 Who is He, this King of glory?
Yahweh of hosts,
He is the King of glory. Selah.

Proverbs 9:10–12

10 The fear of Yahweh is the
beginning of wisdom,
And the knowledge of the Holy
One is understanding.
11 For by me your days will become many,
And years of life will be added to you.
12 If you are wise, you are
wise for yourself,
And if you scoff, you alone will bear it.

Mark 1:1–20

1 The beginning of the gospel of Jesus
Christ, the Son of God.
2 As it is written in Isaiah the prophet:
"BEHOLD, I SEND MY MESSENGER
AHEAD OF YOU,
WHO WILL PREPARE YOUR WAY;
3 THE VOICE OF ONE CRYING
IN THE WILDERNESS,

'Make ready the way of the Lord,
Make His paths straight.'"

4 John the Baptist appeared in the wilderness preaching a baptism of repentance for the forgiveness of sins. 5 And all the region of Judea was going out to him, and all the people of Jerusalem; and they were being baptized by him in the Jordan River, confessing their sins. 6 And John was clothed with camel's hair and *wore* a leather belt around his waist and was eating locusts and wild honey. 7 And he was preaching, saying, "After me One is coming who is mightier than I, and I am not fit to stoop down and untie the strap of His sandals. 8 I baptized you with water; but He will baptize you with the Holy Spirit."

9 Now it happened that in those days Jesus came from Nazareth in Galilee and was baptized by John in the Jordan. 10 And immediately coming up out of the water, He saw the heavens opening, and the Spirit like a dove descending upon Him; 11 and a voice came out of the heavens: "You are My beloved Son, in You I am well-pleased."

12 And immediately the Spirit *drove Him *to go* out into the wilderness. 13 And He was in the wilderness forty days being tempted by Satan; and He was with the wild beasts, and the angels were ministering to Him.

14 Now after John had been delivered up *into custody*, Jesus came into Galilee, preaching the gospel of God, 15 and saying, "The time is fulfilled, and the kingdom of God is at hand; repent and believe in the gospel."

16 As He was going along by the Sea of Galilee, He saw Simon and Andrew, the brother of Simon, casting a net in the sea; for they were fishermen. 17 And Jesus said to them, "Follow Me, and I will make you become fishers of men." 18 And immediately they left their nets and followed Him. 19 And going on a little farther, He saw James the son of Zebedee, and John his brother, who were also in the boat mending the nets. 20 And immediately He called them; and they left their father Zebedee in the boat with the hired servants, and went away to follow Him.

The most important thing I had to do was to read the Word of God and to meditate on it. Thus my heart might be comforted, encouraged, warned, reproved, and instructed.

— George Muller

FEBRUARY 19

Leviticus 9:1–10:20

9 Now it happened on the eighth day that Moses called Aaron and his sons and the elders of Israel; 2 and he said to Aaron, "Take for yourself a calf, a bull, for a sin offering, and a ram for a burnt offering, *both* without blemish, and bring *them* near before Yahweh. 3 Then to the sons of Israel you shall speak, saying, 'Take a male goat for a sin offering, and a calf and a lamb, both one year old, without blemish, for a burnt offering, 4 and an ox and a ram for peace offerings, to sacrifice before Yahweh, and a grain offering mixed with oil; for today Yahweh will appear to you.'" 5 So they took what Moses had commanded to the front of the tent of meeting, and the whole congregation came near and stood before Yahweh. 6 And Moses said, "This is the thing which Yahweh has commanded you to do, that the glory of Yahweh may appear to you." 7 Moses then said to Aaron, "Come near to the altar and offer your sin offering and your burnt offering, that you may make atonement for yourself and for the people; then offer the offering for the people, that you may make atonement for them, just as Yahweh has commanded."

8 So Aaron came near to the altar and slaughtered the calf of the sin offering which was for himself. 9 Then Aaron's sons brought the blood near to him; and he dipped his finger in the blood and put *some* on the horns of the altar and poured out *the rest of* the blood at the base of the altar. 10 The fat and the kidneys and the lobe of the liver of

the sin offering he then offered up in smoke
on the altar just as Yahweh had commanded
Moses. 11 The flesh and the skin, however,
he burned with fire outside the camp.
12 Then he slaughtered the burnt offering;
and Aaron's sons handed the blood to him,
and he splashed it around on the altar.
13 And they handed the burnt offering to
him in pieces, with the head, and he offered
them up in smoke on the altar. 14 He also
washed the entrails and the legs and offered
them up in smoke with the burnt offering
on the altar.
15 Then he brought near the people's
offering and took the goat of the sin offering
which was for the people and slaughtered it
and offered it for sin, like the first. 16 He also
brought near the burnt offering and offered
it according to the *legal* judgment. 17 Next
he brought near the grain offering and filled
his hand with some of it and offered *it* up
in smoke on the altar, besides the burnt
offering of the morning.
18 Then he slaughtered the ox and the
ram, the sacrifice of peace offerings which
was for the people; and Aaron's sons handed
the blood to him, and he splashed it around
on the altar. 19 As for the portions of fat from
the ox and from the ram, the fat tail and the
fat covering and the kidneys and the lobe
of the liver, 20 they now placed the portions
of fat on the breasts; and he offered them
up in smoke on the altar. 21 But the breasts
and the right thigh Aaron waved as a wave
offering before Yahweh, just as Moses had
commanded.
22 Then Aaron lifted up his hands toward
the people and blessed them, and he stepped
down after offering the sin offering and
the burnt offering and the peace offerings.
23 And Moses and Aaron went into the
tent of meeting. Then they came out and
blessed the people. And the glory of Yahweh
appeared to all the people. 24 Then fire came
out from before Yahweh and consumed the
burnt offering and the portions of fat on the
altar. And all the people saw *it* and shouted
and fell on their faces.

10 Then Nadab and Abihu, the sons of
Aaron, took their respective firepans
and put fire in them. Then they placed
incense on it and offered strange fire before
Yahweh, which He had not commanded
them. 2 And fire came out from the presence
of Yahweh and consumed them, and they
died before Yahweh. 3 Then Moses said to
Aaron, "It is what Yahweh spoke, saying,
'By those who come near Me
I will be treated as holy,
And before all the people
I will be glorified.'"
So Aaron kept silent.
4 Then Moses called to Mishael and
Elzaphan, the sons of Aaron's uncle Uzziel,
and said to them, "Come near, carry your relatives
away from the front of the sanctuary
to the outside of the camp." 5 So they came
near and carried them still in their tunics to
the outside of the camp, as Moses had said.
6 Then Moses said to Aaron and to his sons
Eleazar and Ithamar, "Do not uncover your
heads nor tear your clothes, so that you will
not die and that He will not become wrathful
against all the congregation. But your relatives,
the whole house of Israel, shall weep
over the burning which Yahweh has brought
about. 7 You shall not even go out from the
doorway of the tent of meeting, lest you die;
for the anointing oil of Yahweh is upon you."
So they did according to the word of Moses.
8 Yahweh then spoke to Aaron, saying,
9 "Do not drink wine or strong drink, neither
you nor your sons with you, when you come
into the tent of meeting, so that you will not
die—it is a perpetual statute throughout
your generations— 10 and so as to separate
between the holy and the profane, and
between the unclean and the clean, 11 and
so as to instruct the sons of Israel in all the
statutes which Yahweh has spoken to them
through Moses."
12 Then Moses spoke to Aaron and to
his remaining sons, Eleazar and Ithamar,
"Take the remaining grain offering from
the offerings to Yahweh by fire and eat it
unleavened beside the altar, for it is most
holy. 13 And you shall eat it in a holy place
because it is a statute for you and a statute
for your sons *taken* out of the offerings of
Yahweh by fire; for thus I have been commanded.
14 The breast of the wave offering,
however, and the thigh of the contribution
offering you may eat in a clean place, you
and your sons and your daughters with
you; for they have been given as a statute
for you and a statute for your sons *taken* out
of the sacrifices of the peace offerings of the
sons of Israel. 15 The thigh contributed by
raising up and the breast offered by waving

they shall bring along with the offerings
by fire of the portions of fat, to wave as a
wave offering before Yahweh; so it shall be
a perpetual statute for you and your sons
with you, just as Yahweh has commanded."
16 But Moses searched carefully for the
goat of the sin offering, and behold, it had
been burned up! So he was angry with Aar-
on's remaining sons Eleazar and Ithamar,
saying, 17 "Why did you not eat the sin offer-
ing at the holy place? For it is most holy, and
He gave it to you to bear away the guilt of the
congregation, to make atonement for them
before Yahweh. 18 Behold, since its blood had
not been brought inside, into the sanctuary,
you should certainly have eaten it in the
sanctuary, just as I commanded." 19 But
Aaron spoke to Moses, "Behold, this very
day they brought near their sin offering and
their burnt offering before Yahweh. Then
things like these happened to me. So if I had
eaten a sin offering today, would it have been
good in the sight of Yahweh?" 20 So Moses
heard *this*, and it was good in his sight.

Psalm 25:1–7

1 To You, O Yahweh, I lift up my soul.

2 O my God, in You I trust,
Do not let me be ashamed;
Do not let my enemies exult over me.

3 Indeed, let none who hope
in You be ashamed;
Let those who deal treacherously
without cause be ashamed.

4 Make me know Your ways, O Yahweh;
Teach me Your paths.

5 Lead me in Your truth and teach me,
For You are the God of my salvation;
In You I hope all the day.

6 Remember, O Yahweh, Your
compassion and Your
lovingkindnesses,
For they have been from of old.

7 Do not remember the sins of my
youth or my transgressions;
According to Your lovingkindness
remember me,
For the sake of Your
goodness, O Yahweh.

Proverbs 9:13–18

13 The woman of foolishness
is boisterous,
A woman of simplicity, and
does not know anything.
14 She sits at the doorway of her house,
On a seat by the high places of the city,
15 To call to those who pass by *that* way,
Who are making their paths straight:
16 "Whoever is simple, let
him turn in here,"
And to him who lacks a heart
of wisdom she says,
17 "Stolen water is sweet;
And bread *eaten* in secret
is pleasant."
18 But he does not know that
the dead are there,
That those she called are in
the depths of Sheol.

Mark 1:21–45

21 And they *went into Capernaum; and
immediately on the Sabbath He entered
the synagogue and *began to* teach. 22 And
they were astonished at His teaching; for He
was teaching them as *one* having authority,
and not as the scribes. 23 And immediately
there was a man in their synagogue with an
unclean spirit; and he cried out, 24 saying,
"What do we have to do with You, Jesus the
Nazarene? Have You come to destroy us? I
know who You are—the Holy One of God!"
25 And Jesus rebuked him, saying, "Be quiet,
and come out of him!" 26 And throwing him
into convulsions, the unclean spirit cried
out with a loud voice and came out of him.
27 And they were all amazed, so that they
were arguing among themselves, saying,
"What is this? A new teaching with author-
ity! He commands even the unclean spirits,
and they obey Him." 28 And immediately the
news about Him spread everywhere into all
the surrounding district of Galilee.
29 And immediately after they came out
of the synagogue, they came into the house
of Simon and Andrew, with James and John.
30 Now Simon's mother-in-law was lying
sick with a fever; and immediately they
*spoke to Jesus about her. 31 And He came
to her and raised her up, taking her by the
hand, and the fever left her, and she *began*
waiting on them.
32 Now when evening came, after the
sun had set, they *began* bringing to Him all

who were ill and those who were demon-possessed. 33 And the whole city had gathered at the door. 34 And He healed many who were ill with various diseases, and cast out many demons; and He was not permitting the demons to speak, because they knew who He was.

35 And in the early morning, while it was still dark, Jesus rose up, went out of *the house*, and went away to a desolate place, and was praying there. 36 And Simon and his companions searched for Him; 37 and they found Him, and *said to Him, "Everyone is looking for You." 38 And He *said to them, "Let us go elsewhere, to the towns nearby, so that I may preach there also; for that is what I came out for." 39 And He went, preaching in their synagogues throughout all Galilee and casting out the demons.

40 And a leper *came to Jesus, pleading with Him and falling on his knees before Him, and saying, "If You are willing, You can make me clean." 41 And moved with compassion, He stretched out His hand and touched him, and *said to him, "I am willing; be cleansed." 42 And immediately the leprosy left him and he was cleansed. 43 And He sternly warned him and immediately sent him away, 44 and He *said to him, "See that you say nothing to anyone; but go, show yourself to the priest and offer for your cleansing what Moses commanded, as a testimony to them." 45 But he went out and began to proclaim it freely and to spread the news around, to such an extent that Jesus could no longer publicly enter a city, but stayed out in desolate areas; and they were coming to Him from everywhere.

FEBRUARY 20

Leviticus 11:1–12:8

11 Yahweh spoke again to Moses and to Aaron, saying to them, 2 "Speak to the sons of Israel, saying, 'These are the creatures which you may eat from all the animals that are on the earth. 3 Whatever divides a hoof, thus making split hoofs, *and* chews the cud, among the animals, that you may eat. 4 Nevertheless, you shall not eat of these, among those which chew the cud or among those which divide the hoof: the camel, for though it chews cud, it does not divide the hoof; it is unclean to you. 5 Likewise, the shaphan, for though it chews cud, it does not divide the hoof; it is unclean to you; 6 the rabbit also, for though it chews cud, it does not divide the hoof; it is unclean to you; 7 and the pig, for though it divides the hoof, thus making a split hoof, it does not chew cud; it is unclean to you. 8 You shall not eat of their flesh, and you shall not touch their carcasses; they are unclean to you.

9 'These you may eat, whatever is in the water: all that have fins and scales, those in the water, in the seas, or in the rivers, you may eat. 10 But whatever is in the seas and in the rivers that does not have fins and scales among all the swarming life of the water, and among all the living creatures that are in the water, they are detestable things to you, 11 and they shall be detestable to you; you may not eat of their flesh, and their carcasses you shall detest. 12 Whatever in the water does not have fins and scales is detestable to you.

13 'These, moreover, you shall detest among the birds; they shall not be eaten; they are detestable: the eagle and the vulture and the buzzard, 14 and the kite and the falcon in its kind, 15 every raven in its kind, 16 and the ostrich and the owl and the gull and the hawk in its kind, 17 and the little owl and the cormorant and the great owl, 18 and the white owl and the pelican and the carrion vulture, 19 and the stork, the heron in its kinds, and the hoopoe, and the bat.

20 'All the swarming things that fly *and* that walk on *all* fours are detestable to you. 21 Yet these you may eat among all the swarming things that fly *and* that walk on *all* fours: those which have above their feet jointed legs with which to jump on the earth. 22 These of them you may eat: the locust in its kinds and the devastating locust in its kinds and the cricket in its kinds and the grasshopper in its kinds. 23 But all other swarming things that fly *and* that are four-footed are detestable to you.

24 'By these, moreover, you will be made unclean: whoever touches their carcasses becomes unclean until evening, 25 and whoever picks up any of their carcasses shall wash his clothes and be unclean until

evening. 26 Concerning all the animals which
divide the hoof but do not make a split *hoof*
or which do not chew cud, they are unclean
to you: whoever touches them becomes
unclean. 27 Also whatever walks on its paws,
among all the creatures that walk on *all* fours,
are unclean to you; whoever touches their
carcasses becomes unclean until evening,
28 and the one who picks up their carcasses
shall wash his clothes and be unclean until
evening; they are unclean to you.

29 'Now these are to you the unclean
among the swarming things which swarm
on the earth: the mole and the mouse and
the great lizard in its kinds, 30 and the gecko
and the crocodile and the lizard and the sand
reptile and the chameleon. 31 These are to
you the unclean among all the swarming
things; whoever touches them when they
are dead becomes unclean until evening.
32 Also anything on which one of them may
fall when they are dead becomes unclean,
including any wooden article or clothing or
a skin or a sack—any article by which work
is done—it shall be put in the water and
be unclean until evening, then it becomes
clean. 33 As for any earthenware vessel into
which one of them may fall, whatever is in
it becomes unclean, and you shall break the
vessel. 34 Any of the food which may be eaten,
on which water comes, shall become unclean,
and any liquid which may be drunk in every
vessel shall become unclean. 35 Everything,
moreover, on which part of their carcass
may fall becomes unclean; an oven or a stove
shall be smashed; they are unclean and shall
continue as unclean to you. 36 Nevertheless
a spring or a cistern collecting water shall
be clean, though the one who touches their
carcass shall be unclean. 37 And if a part of
their carcass falls on any seed for sowing
which is to be sown, it is clean. 38 Though if
water is put on the seed and a part of their
carcass falls on it, it is unclean to you.

39 'Also if one of the animals dies which
you have for food, the one who touches its
carcass becomes unclean until evening.
40 He too, who eats some of its carcass shall
wash his clothes and be unclean until eve-
ning, and the one who picks up its carcass
shall wash his clothes and be unclean until
evening.

41 'Now every swarming thing that
swarms on the earth is detestable; it shall
not be eaten. 42 Whatever goes on its belly,
and whatever goes on *all* fours, whatever
has many feet, in respect to every swarming
thing that swarms on the earth, you shall
not eat them, for they are detestable. 43 Do
not render yourselves detestable through
any of the swarming things that swarm; and
you shall not make yourselves unclean with
them so that you become unclean. 44 For I am
Yahweh your God. Therefore, set yourselves
apart as holy and be holy, for I am holy. And
you shall not make yourselves unclean with
any of the swarming things that move on the
earth. 45 For I am Yahweh who brought you
up from the land of Egypt to be your God;
thus you shall be holy, for I am holy.'"

46 This is the law regarding the animal and
the bird and every living thing that moves
in the waters and everything that swarms
on the earth, 47 to separate between the
unclean and the clean, and between the
edible creature and the creature which is
not to be eaten.

12 Then Yahweh spoke to Moses, saying,
2 "Speak to the sons of Israel, saying:
'When a woman gives birth and bears a
male *child*, then she shall be unclean for
seven days, as in the days of her menstru-
ation she shall be unclean. 3 Now on the
eighth day the flesh of his foreskin shall
be circumcised. 4 Then she shall remain in
the blood of *her* cleansing for thirty-three
days; she shall not touch any holy thing; and
she shall not enter the sanctuary until the
days of her cleansing are fulfilled. 5 But if
she bears a female *child*, then she shall be
unclean for two weeks, as in her menstru-
ation; and she shall remain in the blood of
her cleansing for sixty-six days.

6 'When the days of her cleansing are
fulfilled, for a son or for a daughter, she shall
bring to the priest at the doorway of the tent
of meeting a one year old lamb for a burnt
offering and a young pigeon or a turtledove
for a sin offering. 7 Then he shall bring it
near before Yahweh and make atonement
for her, and she shall be cleansed from the
flow of her blood. This is the law for her who
bears *a child*, whether a male or a female.
8 But if she cannot afford a lamb, then she
shall take two turtledoves or two young
pigeons, the one for a burnt offering and
the other for a sin offering; and the priest
shall make atonement for her, and she will
be clean.'"

Psalm 25:8–15

8 Good and upright is Yahweh;
Therefore He instructs
sinners in the way.

9 May He lead the humble in justice,
And may He teach the humble His way.

10 All the paths of Yahweh are
lovingkindness and truth
To those who guard His covenant
and His testimonies.

11 For Your name's sake, O Yahweh,
Pardon my iniquity, for it is great.

12 Who is the man who fears Yahweh?
He will instruct him in the
way he should choose.

13 His soul will abide in goodness,
And his seed will inherit the land.

14 The secret of Yahweh is for
those who fear Him,
And He will make them
know His covenant.

15 My eyes are continually
toward Yahweh,
For He will bring my feet out of the net.

Proverbs 10:1–3

10 The proverbs of Solomon.
A wise son makes a father glad,
But a foolish son is a grief
to his mother.
2 Treasures *gained* by wickedness
do not profit,
But righteousness delivers from death.
3 Yahweh will not allow the soul
of the righteous to hunger,
But He will push away the
craving of the wicked.

Mark 2:1–28

2 And when He had come back to Capernaum several days afterward, it was
heard that He was at home. 2 And many
were gathered together, so that there was
no longer room, not even near the door; and
He was speaking the word to them. 3 And
they *came, bringing to Him a paralytic,
carried by four men. 4 And being unable
to bring *him* to Jesus because of the crowd,
they removed the roof *over* where He was;
and when they had dug an opening, they
let down the mat where the paralytic was
lying. 5 And Jesus seeing their faith *said to
the paralytic, "Child, your sins are forgiven."
6 But some of the scribes were sitting there
and reasoning in their hearts, 7 "Why does
this man speak that way? He is blaspheming; who can forgive sins but God alone?"
8 Immediately Jesus, aware in His spirit
that they were reasoning that way within
themselves, *said to them, "Why are you
reasoning about these things in your hearts?
9 Which is easier, to say to the paralytic,
'Your sins are forgiven'; or to say, 'Get up,
and pick up your mat and walk'? 10 But so
that you may know that the Son of Man has
authority on earth to forgive sins"—He *said
to the paralytic, 11 "I say to you, get up, pick
up your mat, and go to your home." 12 And
he got up and immediately picked up the
mat and went out before everyone, so that
they were all amazed and were glorifying
God, saying, "We have never seen anything
like this."

13 And He went out again by the seashore;
and the entire crowd was coming to Him,
and He was teaching them.

14 And as He passed by, He saw Levi the
son of Alphaeus sitting in the tax office, and
He *said to him, "Follow Me!" And he stood
up and followed Him.

15 And it *happened that as He was
reclining *at the table* in his house, many
tax collectors and sinners were reclining
with Jesus and His disciples. For there were
many of them, and they were following Him.
16 And when the scribes of the Pharisees
saw that He was eating with the sinners
and tax collectors, they were saying to His
disciples, "He is eating and drinking with
tax collectors and sinners!" 17 And hearing
this, Jesus *said to them, "Those who are
healthy do not have need for a physician,
but *only* those who are sick; I did not come
to call the righteous, but sinners."

18 And John's disciples and the Pharisees
were fasting; and they *came and *said to
Him, "Why do John's disciples and the disciples of the Pharisees fast, but Your disciples
do not fast?" 19 And Jesus said to them, "Can
the attendants of the bridegroom fast when
the bridegroom is with them? So long as
they have the bridegroom with them, they
cannot fast. 20 But the days will come when

the bridegroom is taken away from them, and then they will fast in that day.

21 "No one sews a piece of unshrunk cloth on an old garment; otherwise that patch pulls away from it, the new from the old, and a worse tear results. 22 And no one puts new wine into old wineskins; otherwise the wine will burst the skins, and the wine is lost and the skins *as well*; but *one puts* new wine into fresh wineskins."

23 And it happened that He was passing through the grainfields on the Sabbath, and His disciples began to make their way along while picking the heads *of grain*. 24 And the Pharisees were saying to Him, "Look, why are they doing what is not lawful on the Sabbath?" 25 And He *said to them, "Have you never read what David did when he was in need and he and his companions became hungry; 26 how he entered the house of God around the time of Abiathar the high priest, and ate the consecrated bread, which is not lawful for *anyone* to eat except the priests, and he also gave it to those who were with him?" 27 And Jesus was saying to them, "The Sabbath was made for man, and not man for the Sabbath. 28 Consequently the Son of Man is Lord even of the Sabbath."

FEBRUARY 21

Leviticus 13:1–59

13 Then Yahweh spoke to Moses and to Aaron, saying, 2 "When a man has on the skin of his body a swelling or a scab or a bright spot, and it becomes an infection of leprosy on the skin of his body, then he shall be brought to Aaron the priest or to one of his sons the priests. 3 Then the priest shall look at the mark on the skin of the body, and if the hair in the infection has turned white and the infection appears to be deeper than the skin of his body, it is an infection of leprosy; when the priest has looked at him, he shall pronounce him unclean. 4 But if the bright spot is white on the skin of his body, and it does not appear to be deeper than the skin, and the hair on it has not turned white, then the priest shall isolate *him who has* the infection for seven days. 5 Then the priest shall look at him on the seventh day, and if in his eyes the infection has not changed *and* the infection has not spread on the skin, then the priest shall isolate him for seven more days. 6 And the priest shall look at him again on the seventh day, and if the infection has faded and the mark has not spread on the skin, then the priest shall pronounce him clean; it is *only* a scab. And he shall wash his clothes and be clean.

7 "But if the scab spreads farther on the skin after he has shown himself to the priest for his cleansing, he shall appear again to the priest. 8 And the priest shall look, and if the scab has spread on the skin, then the priest shall pronounce him unclean; it is leprosy.

9 "When the infection of leprosy is on a man, then he shall be brought to the priest. 10 The priest shall then look, and if there is a white swelling in the skin, and it has turned the hair white, and there is raw flesh *still* alive in the swelling, 11 it is a chronic leprosy on the skin of his body, and the priest shall pronounce him unclean; he shall not isolate him, for he is unclean. 12 But if the leprosy breaks out farther on the skin, and the leprosy covers all the skin of *him who has* the infection from his head even to his feet, as far as the priest can see, 13 then the priest shall look, and behold, *if* the leprosy has covered all his body, he shall pronounce clean *him who has* the infection; it has all turned white, *and* he is clean. 14 But whenever raw flesh appears on him, he shall be unclean. 15 And the priest shall look at the raw flesh, and he shall pronounce him unclean; the raw flesh is unclean; it is leprosy. 16 Or if the raw flesh turns again and is changed to white, then he shall come to the priest, 17 and the priest shall look at him, and behold, *if* the infection has turned to white, then the priest shall pronounce clean *him who has* the infection; he is clean.

18 "When the body has a boil on its skin and it is healed, 19 and in the place of the boil there is a white swelling or a reddish-white bright spot, then it shall be shown to the priest; 20 and the priest shall look, and behold, *if* it appears to be lower than the skin, and the hair on it has turned white, then the priest shall pronounce him unclean; it is the infection of leprosy; it has broken out in the boil. 21 But if the priest

looks at it, and behold, there are no white hairs in it, and it is not lower than the skin and is faded, then the priest shall isolate him for seven days; 22 and if it spreads farther on the skin, then the priest shall pronounce him unclean; it is an infection. 23 But if the bright spot remains in its place and does not spread, it is *only* the scar of the boil; and the priest shall pronounce him clean.

24 "Or if the body sustains in its skin a burn by fire, and the raw *flesh* of the burn becomes a bright spot, reddish-white, or white, 25 then the priest shall look at it. And if the hair in the bright spot has turned white and it appears to be deeper than the skin, it is leprosy; it has broken out in the burn. Therefore, the priest shall pronounce him unclean; it is an infection of leprosy. 26 But if the priest looks at it, and behold, there is no white hair in the bright spot, and it is no deeper than the skin but is faded, then the priest shall isolate him for seven days; 27 and the priest shall look at him on the seventh day. If it spreads farther in the skin, then the priest shall pronounce him unclean; it is an infection of leprosy. 28 But if the bright spot remains in its place and has not spread in the skin but is faded, it is the swelling from the burn; and the priest shall pronounce him clean, for it is *only* the scar of the burn.

29 "Now if a man or woman has an infection on the head or on the beard, 30 then the priest shall look at the infection, and if it appears to be deeper than the skin, and there is thin yellowish hair in it, then the priest shall pronounce him unclean; it is a scale; it is leprosy of the head or of the beard. 31 But if the priest looks at the infection of the scale, and behold, it appears to be no deeper than the skin, and there is no black hair in it, then the priest shall isolate *the person* with the scaly infection for seven days. 32 Now on the seventh day the priest shall look at the infection, and if the scale has not spread, and there is no yellowish hair in it, and the appearance of the scale is no deeper than the skin, 33 then he shall shave himself, but he shall not shave the scale; and the priest shall isolate *the person* with the scale seven more days. 34 Then on the seventh day the priest shall look at the scale, and if the scale has not spread in the skin and it appears to be no deeper than the skin, the priest shall pronounce him clean; and he shall wash his clothes and be clean. 35 But if the scale spreads farther in the skin after his cleansing, 36 then the priest shall look at him, and if the scale has spread in the skin, the priest need not seek for the yellowish hair; he is unclean. 37 If in his sight the scale has remained, however, and black hair has grown in it, the scale has healed, he is clean; and the priest shall pronounce him clean.

38 "When a man or a woman has bright spots on the skin of the body, *even* white bright spots, 39 then the priest shall look, and if the bright spots on the skin of their bodies are a faded white, it is eczema that has broken out on the skin; he is clean.

40 "Now if a man loses the hair of his head, he is bald; he is clean. 41 And if his head becomes bald at the front and sides, he is bald on the forehead; he is clean. 42 But if on the bald head or the bald forehead, there occurs a reddish-white infection, it is leprosy breaking out on his bald head or on his bald forehead. 43 Then the priest shall look at him; and if the swelling of the infection is reddish-white on his bald head or on his bald forehead, like the appearance of leprosy in the skin of the body, 44 he is a leprous man; he is unclean. The priest shall surely pronounce him unclean; his infection is on his head.

45 "As for the leper who has the infection, his clothes shall be torn, and the hair of his head shall be uncovered, and he shall cover his mustache and call out, 'Unclean! Unclean!' 46 He shall remain unclean all the days during which he has the infection; he is unclean. He shall live alone; his *place of* habitation shall be outside the camp.

47 "When a garment has a mark of leprosy in it, whether it is a wool garment or a linen garment, 48 whether in warp or woof, of linen or of wool, whether in leather or in any article made of leather, 49 if the mark is greenish or reddish in the garment or in the leather or in the warp or in the woof or in any article of leather, it is a leprous mark and shall be shown to the priest. 50 Then the priest shall look at the mark and shall isolate the article with the mark for seven days. 51 He shall then look at the mark on the seventh day; if the mark has spread in the garment, whether in the warp or in the woof or in the leather, whatever the purpose for which the leather is used, the mark is a leprous malignancy; it

is unclean. 52 So he shall burn the garment,
whether the warp or the woof, in wool or in
linen, or any article of leather in which the
mark occurs, for it is a leprous malignancy;
it shall be burned in the fire.
53 "But if the priest shall look, and indeed
the mark has not spread in the garment,
either in the warp or in the woof or in any
article of leather, 54 then the priest shall
command them to wash the thing in which
the mark occurs, and he shall isolate it for
seven more days. 55 After the article with the
mark has been washed, the priest shall again
look, and if the mark has not changed its
appearance, even though the mark has not
spread, it is unclean; you shall burn it in the
fire, whether an eating away has produced
bareness on the top or on the front of it.
56 "Then if the priest looks, and if the
mark has faded after it has been washed,
then he shall tear it out of the garment or
out of the leather, whether from the warp
or from the woof; 57 and if it appears again
in the garment, whether in the warp or in
the woof or in any article of leather, it is an
outbreak; you shall burn the article with
the mark in the fire. 58 Now the garment,
whether the warp or the woof or any article
of leather from which the mark has departed
when you washed it, shall then be washed a
second time and will be clean."
59 This is the law for the mark of leprosy
in a garment of wool or linen, whether in
the warp or in the woof or in any article of
leather, for pronouncing it clean or unclean.

Psalm 25:16–22

16 Turn to me and be gracious to me,
For I am alone and afflicted.

17 The troubles of my heart are enlarged;
Bring me out of my distresses.

18 See my affliction and my trouble,
And forgive all my sins.

19 See my enemies, for they are many,
And they hate me with violent hatred.

20 Keep my soul and deliver me;
Do not let me be ashamed,
for I take refuge in You.

21 Let integrity and uprightness
guard me,
For I hope in You.
22 Redeem Israel, O God,
Out of all his troubles.

Proverbs 10:4–5

4 Poor is he who works with
a slack hand,
But the hand of the diligent makes rich.
5 He who gathers in summer is a
son who acts insightfully,
But he who sleeps in harvest is
a son who acts shamefully.

Mark 3:1–19

3 And He entered again into a synagogue;
and a man was there with a withered
hand. 2 And they were watching Him *to see*
if He would heal him on the Sabbath, so that
they might accuse Him. 3 And He *said to the
man with the withered hand, "Get up and
come forward!" 4 And He *said to them, "Is
it lawful to do good or to do harm on the
Sabbath, to save a life or to kill?" But they
kept silent. 5 And after looking around at
them with anger, grieved at their hardness
of heart, He *said to the man, "Stretch out
your hand." And he stretched it out, and his
hand was restored. 6 And the Pharisees went
out and immediately *began* taking counsel
together with the Herodians against Him,
as to how they might destroy Him.
7 And Jesus withdrew to the sea with His
disciples; and a great multitude from Galilee
followed; and from Judea, 8 and from Jeru-
salem, and from Idumea, and beyond the
Jordan, and the vicinity of Tyre and Sidon, a
great number of people heard of all that He
was doing and came to Him. 9 And He told
His disciples that a boat should stand ready
for Him because of the crowd, so that they
would not crowd Him; 10 for He had healed
many, with the result that all those who had
afflictions pressed around Him in order to
touch Him. 11 And whenever the unclean
spirits were seeing Him, they would fall
down before Him and cry out, saying, "You
are the Son of God!" 12 And He earnestly
warned them not to tell who He was.
13 And He *went up on the mountain
and *summoned those whom He Himself
wanted, and they came to Him. 14 And He
appointed twelve (whom He also named
apostles) to be with Him and to send them
out to preach, 15 and to have authority to
cast out the demons. 16 And He appointed

the twelve: Simon (to whom He gave the name Peter), 17 and James, the *son* of Zebedee, and John the brother of James (to them He gave the name Boanerges, which means, "Sons of Thunder"); 18 and Andrew, and Philip, and Bartholomew, and Matthew, and Thomas, and James the son of Alphaeus, and Thaddaeus, and Simon the Zealot; 19 and Judas Iscariot, who also betrayed Him.

FEBRUARY 22

Leviticus 14:1–57

14 Then Yahweh spoke to Moses, saying, 2 "This shall be the law of the leper in the day of his cleansing. Now he shall be brought to the priest, 3 and the priest shall go out to the outside of the camp. Thus the priest shall look, and if the infection of leprosy has been healed in the leper, 4 then the priest shall give a command to take two live clean birds and cedar wood and a scarlet string and hyssop for the one who is to be cleansed. 5 The priest shall also give a command to slaughter the one bird in an earthenware vessel over running water. 6 *As for* the live bird, he shall take it together with the cedar wood and the scarlet string and the hyssop, and he shall dip them and the live bird in the blood of the bird that was slaughtered over the running water. 7 He shall then sprinkle seven times the one who is to be cleansed from the leprosy and shall pronounce him clean, and he shall let the live bird go free over the open field. 8 The one to be cleansed shall then wash his clothes and shave off all his hair and bathe in water and be clean. Now afterward, he may enter the camp, but he shall stay outside his tent for seven days. 9 And it will be on the seventh day that he shall shave off all his hair: he shall shave his head and his beard and his eyebrows, even all his hair. He shall then wash his clothes and bathe his body in water and be clean.

10 "Now on the eighth day he shall take two male lambs without blemish, and a yearling ewe lamb without blemish, and three-tenths *of an ephah* of fine flour mixed with oil for a grain offering, and one log of oil; 11 and the priest who pronounces him clean shall present the man to be cleansed as well as these things before Yahweh at the doorway of the tent of meeting. 12 Then the priest shall take the one male lamb and bring it near for a guilt offering, with the log of oil, and wave them as a wave offering before Yahweh. 13 Next he shall slaughter the male lamb in the place where they slaughter the sin offering and the burnt offering, at the place of the sanctuary—for the guilt offering, like the sin offering, belongs to the priest; it is most holy. 14 The priest shall then take some of the blood of the guilt offering, and the priest shall put *it* on the lobe of the right ear of the one to be cleansed and on the thumb of his right hand and on the big toe of his right foot. 15 The priest shall also take some of the log of oil and pour *it* into his left palm; 16 the priest shall then dip his right-hand finger into the oil that is in his left palm, and with his finger sprinkle some of the oil seven times before Yahweh. 17 Of the remaining oil which is in his palm, the priest shall put some on the right ear lobe of the one to be cleansed and on the thumb of his right hand and on the big toe of his right foot, on the blood of the guilt offering; 18 but the rest of the oil that is in the priest's palm, he shall put on the head of the one to be cleansed. So the priest shall make atonement on his behalf before Yahweh. 19 The priest shall next offer the sin offering and make atonement for the one to be cleansed from his uncleanness. Then afterward, he shall slaughter the burnt offering. 20 And the priest shall offer up the burnt offering and the grain offering on the altar. Thus the priest shall make atonement for him, and he will be clean.

21 "But if he is poor and his means are insufficient, then he is to take one male lamb for a guilt offering as a wave offering to make atonement for him, and one-tenth *of an ephah* of fine flour mixed with oil for a grain offering, and a log of oil, 22 and two turtledoves or two young pigeons which are within his means, the one shall be a sin offering and the other a burnt offering. 23 Then the eighth day he shall bring them for his cleansing to the priest, at the doorway of the tent of meeting, before Yahweh. 24 And the priest shall take the lamb of the guilt offering and the log of oil, and the priest

shall wave them as a wave offering before Yahweh. 25 Next he shall slaughter the lamb of the guilt offering; and the priest shall take some of the blood of the guilt offering and put *it* on the lobe of the right ear of the one to be cleansed and on the thumb of his right hand and on the big toe of his right foot. 26 The priest shall also pour some of the oil into his left palm; 27 and with his right-hand finger the priest shall sprinkle some of the oil that is in his left palm seven times before Yahweh. 28 The priest shall then put some of the oil that is in his palm on the lobe of the right ear of the one to be cleansed and on the thumb of his right hand and on the big toe of his right foot, on the place of the blood of the guilt offering. 29 Moreover, the rest of the oil that is in the priest's palm he shall put on the head of the one to be cleansed, to make atonement on his behalf before Yahweh. 30 He shall then offer one of the turtledoves or young pigeons, which are within his means. 31 *He shall offer* what he can afford, the one for a sin offering and the other for a burnt offering, together with the grain offering. So the priest shall make atonement before Yahweh on behalf of the one to be cleansed. 32 This is the law *for him* in whom there is an infection of leprosy, whose means are limited for his cleansing."

33 Yahweh further spoke to Moses and to Aaron, saying:

34 "When you enter the land of Canaan, which I am giving you for a possession, and I put a mark of leprosy on a house in the land of your possession, 35 then the one who owns the house shall come and tell the priest, saying, '*Something* like a mark *of leprosy* has become visible to me in the house.' 36 The priest shall then command that they empty the house before the priest goes in to look at the mark, so that everything in the house need not become unclean; and afterward the priest shall go in to look at the house. 37 So he shall look at the mark, and if the mark on the walls of the house has greenish or reddish depressions and appears deeper than the *surface of* the wall, 38 then the priest shall come out of the house, to the doorway, and put the house under isolation for seven days. 39 And the priest shall return on the seventh day and look *again*. If the mark has indeed spread in the walls of the house, 40 then the priest shall command them to tear out the stones with the mark in them and throw them away at an unclean place outside the city. 41 And he shall have the house scraped all around inside, and they shall pour out the plaster that they scrape off at an unclean place outside the city. 42 Then they shall take other stones and replace *those* stones, and he shall take other plaster and replaster the house.

43 "If, however, the mark breaks out again in the house after he has torn out the stones and scraped the house, and after it has been replastered, 44 then the priest shall come in and look *again*. If he sees that the mark has indeed spread in the house, it is a leprous malignancy in the house; it is unclean. 45 He shall therefore tear down the house, its stones and its timbers and all the plaster of the house, and he shall take *them* outside the city to an unclean place. 46 Moreover, whoever goes into the house during the time that he has put it under isolation becomes unclean until evening. 47 Likewise, whoever lies down in the house shall wash his clothes, and whoever eats in the house shall wash his clothes.

48 "If, on the other hand, the priest comes in and looks *again*, and the mark has not indeed spread in the house after the house has been replastered, then the priest shall pronounce the house clean because the mark has not reappeared. 49 To cleanse the house then, he shall take two birds and cedar wood and a scarlet string and hyssop, 50 and he shall slaughter the one bird in an earthenware vessel over running water. 51 Then he shall take the cedar wood and the hyssop and the scarlet string, with the live bird, and he shall dip them in the blood of the slaughtered bird as well as in the running water, and he shall sprinkle the house seven times. 52 He shall thus cleanse the house with the blood of the bird and with the running water, along with the live bird and with the cedar wood and with the hyssop and with the scarlet string. 53 However, he shall let the live bird go free outside the city into the open field. So he shall make atonement for the house, and it will be clean."

54 This is the law for any mark of leprosy—even for a scale, 55 and for the leprous garment or house, 56 and for a swelling and for a scab and for a bright spot— 57 to instruct when they are unclean and when they are clean. This is the law of leprosy.

Psalm 26:1–5

1 Give justice to me, O Yahweh, for
I have walked in my integrity,
And I have trusted in Yahweh;
I will not waver.
2 Test me, O Yahweh, and try me;
Refine my mind and my heart.
3 For Your lovingkindness
is before my eyes,
And I have walked in Your truth.
4 I do not sit with worthless men,
And I will not go with pretenders.
5 I hate the assembly of evildoers,
And I will not sit with the wicked.

Proverbs 10:6–7

6 Blessings are on the head
of the righteous,
But the mouth of the wicked
covers up violence.
7 The remembrance of the
righteous is blessed,
But the name of the wicked will rot.

Mark 3:20–35

20 And He *came home, and the crowd
*gathered again, so that they could not even
eat a meal. 21 And when His own people
heard *this*, they went out to take custody
of Him; for they were saying, "He has lost
His senses." 22 And the scribes who came
down from Jerusalem were saying, "He is
possessed by Beelzebul," and "He casts out
the demons by the ruler of the demons."
23 And He called them to Himself and *began*
speaking to them in parables, "How can
Satan cast out Satan? 24 And if a kingdom is
divided against itself, that kingdom cannot
stand. 25 And if a house is divided against
itself, that house will not be able to stand.
26 And if Satan has risen up against himself
and is divided, he cannot stand, but he is
finished! 27 But no one can enter the strong
man's house and plunder his property
unless he first binds the strong man, and
then he will plunder his house.

28 "Truly I say to you, all sins shall be
forgiven the sons of men, and whatever
blasphemies they utter; 29 but whoever
blasphemes against the Holy Spirit never
has forgiveness, but is guilty of an eternal
sin"— 30 because they were saying, "He has
an unclean spirit."

31 Then His mother and His brothers
*arrived, and standing outside they sent
word to Him, calling Him. 32 And a crowd
was sitting around Him, and they *said
to Him, "Behold, Your mother and Your
brothers are outside looking for You."
33 And answering them, He *said, "Who
are My mother and My brothers?" 34 And
looking about at those who were sitting
around Him, He *said, "Behold My mother
and My brothers! 35 For whoever does the
will of God, he is My brother and sister and
mother."

FEBRUARY 23

Leviticus 15:1–16:34

15 Yahweh also spoke to Moses and to
Aaron, saying, 2 "Speak to the sons
of Israel and say to them, 'When any man
has a discharge from his body, his dis-
charge is unclean. 3 This, moreover, shall
be his uncleanness in his discharge: it is
his uncleanness whether his body allows
its discharge to flow or whether his body
obstructs its discharge. 4 Every bed on
which the person with the discharge lies
becomes unclean, and everything on which
he sits becomes unclean. 5 Anyone, more-
over, who touches his bed shall wash his
clothes and bathe in water and be unclean
until evening; 6 and whoever sits on the
thing on which the man with the discharge
has been sitting shall wash his clothes and
bathe in water and be unclean until evening.
7 Also whoever touches the person with the
discharge shall wash his clothes and bathe
in water and be unclean until evening. 8 Or
if the man with the discharge spits on one
who is clean, he too shall wash his clothes
and bathe in water and be unclean until
evening. 9 Every saddle on which the person
with the discharge rides becomes unclean.
10 Whoever then touches any of the things
which were under him shall be unclean
until evening, and he who carries them
shall wash his clothes and bathe in water
and be unclean until evening. 11 Likewise,
whomever the one with the discharge
touches without having rinsed his hands
in water shall wash his clothes and bathe
in water and be unclean until evening.

[12] However, an earthenware vessel which the person with the discharge touches shall be broken, and every wooden vessel shall be rinsed in water.

[13] 'Now when the man with the discharge becomes cleansed from his discharge, then he shall count off for himself seven days for his cleansing; he shall then wash his clothes and bathe his body in running water and will become clean. [14] Then on the eighth day he shall take for himself two turtledoves or two young pigeons and come before Yahweh to the doorway of the tent of meeting and give them to the priest; [15] and the priest shall offer them, one for a sin offering and the other for a burnt offering. So the priest shall make atonement on his behalf before Yahweh because of his discharge.

[16] 'Now if a man has a seminal emission, he shall bathe all his body in water and be unclean until evening. [17] As for any garment or any leather on which there is seminal emission, it shall be washed with water and be unclean until evening. [18] If *there is* a woman with whom a man lies *so that* there is a seminal emission, they shall both bathe in water and be unclean until evening.

[19] 'If a woman has a discharge, *and* her discharge in her body is blood, she shall continue in her menstrual impurity for seven days; and whoever touches her shall be unclean until evening. [20] Everything also on which she lies during her menstrual impurity shall be unclean, and everything on which she sits shall be unclean. [21] And anyone who touches her bed shall wash his clothes and bathe in water and be unclean until evening. [22] And whoever touches any thing on which she sits shall wash his clothes and bathe in water and be unclean until evening. [23] Whether it be on the bed or on the thing on which she is sitting, when he touches it, he shall be unclean until evening. [24] If a man actually lies with her so that her menstrual impurity is on him, he shall be unclean seven days, and every bed on which he lies shall be unclean.

[25] 'Now if a woman has a discharge of her blood many days, not at the period of her menstrual impurity, or if she has a discharge beyond that period, all the days of her unclean discharge she shall continue as though in her menstrual impurity; she is unclean. [26] Any bed on which she lies all the days of her discharge shall be to her like her bed at menstruation; and every thing on which she sits shall be unclean, like her uncleanness from her menstrual impurity. [27] Likewise, whoever touches them shall be unclean and shall wash his clothes and bathe in water and be unclean until evening. [28] Now if she becomes clean from her discharge, she shall count off for herself seven days; and afterward she will be clean. [29] Then on the eighth day she shall take for herself two turtledoves or two young pigeons and bring them in to the priest, to the doorway of the tent of meeting. [30] And the priest shall offer the one for a sin offering and the other for a burnt offering. So the priest shall make atonement on her behalf before Yahweh because of her unclean discharge.'

[31] "Thus you shall keep the sons of Israel separated from their uncleanness, so that they will not die in their uncleanness by making My tabernacle that is among them unclean." [32] This is the law for the one with a discharge, and for the man who has a seminal emission so that he is unclean by it, [33] and for the woman who is ill because of menstrual impurity, and for the one who has a discharge, whether a male or a female, or a man who lies with an unclean woman.

16 Now Yahweh spoke to Moses after the death of the two sons of Aaron, when they came near the presence of Yahweh and died. [2] And Yahweh said to Moses:

"Tell your brother Aaron that he shall not enter at any time into the holy place inside the veil, before the mercy seat which is on the ark, so that he will not die; for I will appear in the cloud over the mercy seat. [3] Aaron shall enter the holy place with this: with a bull from the herd for a sin offering and a ram for a burnt offering. [4] He shall put on the holy linen tunic, and the linen undergarments shall be next to his body, and he shall be girded with the linen sash and attired with the linen turban (these are holy garments). Then he shall bathe his body in water and put them on. [5] And he shall take from the congregation of the sons of Israel two male goats for a sin offering and one ram for a burnt offering. [6] Then Aaron shall bring near the bull for the sin offering which is for himself, that he may make atonement for himself and for his household. [7] And he shall take the two goats and present them before Yahweh at the doorway of the tent of meeting. 8 And Aaron shall cast lots for the two goats, one lot for Yahweh and the other lot for the scapegoat. 9 Then Aaron shall bring near the goat on which the lot for Yahweh fell, and he shall offer it as a sin offering. 10 But the goat on which the lot for the scapegoat fell shall be presented alive before Yahweh, to make atonement upon it, to send it out into the wilderness as the scapegoat.

11 "Then Aaron shall bring near the bull of the sin offering, which is for himself, and make atonement for himself and for his household, and he shall slaughter the bull of the sin offering which is for himself. 12 And he shall take a firepan full of coals of fire from upon the altar before Yahweh and two handfuls of finely ground fragrant incense, and bring *it* inside the veil. 13 And he shall put the incense on the fire before Yahweh, that the cloud of incense may cover the mercy seat that is on *the ark of* the testimony, so that he will not die. 14 Moreover, he shall take some of the blood of the bull and sprinkle *it* with his finger on the mercy seat on the east *side*; also in front of the mercy seat he shall sprinkle some of the blood with his finger seven times.

15 "Then he shall slaughter the goat of the sin offering which is for the people and bring its blood inside the veil and do with its blood as he did with the blood of the bull. And he shall sprinkle it on the mercy seat and in front of the mercy seat. 16 So he shall make atonement for the holy place because of the uncleanness of the sons of Israel and because of their transgressions in regard to all their sins; and thus he shall do for the tent of meeting which abides with them in the midst of their uncleanness. 17 Now when he goes in to make atonement in the holy place, no one shall be in the tent of meeting until he comes out, that he may make atonement for himself and for his household and for all the assembly of Israel. 18 Then he shall go out to the altar that is before Yahweh and make atonement for it. And he shall take some of the blood of the bull and of the blood of the goat, and put it on the horns of the altar on all sides. 19 With his finger he shall sprinkle some of the blood on it seven times and cleanse it and set it apart as holy from the uncleanness of the sons of Israel.

20 "And when he finishes making atonement for the holy place and the tent of meeting and the altar, he shall bring near the live goat. 21 Then Aaron shall lay both of his hands on the head of the live goat, and confess over it all the iniquities of the sons of Israel and all their transgressions in regard to all their sins; and he shall lay them on the head of the goat and send *it* out into the wilderness by the hand of a man ready *to do this*. 22 And the goat shall bear on itself all their iniquities to an isolated land; and he shall send out the goat in the wilderness.

23 "Then Aaron shall come into the tent of meeting and take off the linen garments which he put on when he went into the holy place and shall leave them there. 24 And he shall bathe his body with water in a holy place and put on his clothes and come forth, and offer his burnt offering and the burnt offering of the people and make atonement for himself and for the people. 25 Then he shall offer up in smoke the fat of the sin offering on the altar. 26 And the one who sent the goat out as the scapegoat shall wash his clothes and bathe his body with water; then afterward he shall come into the camp. 27 But the bull of the sin offering and the goat of the sin offering, whose blood was brought in to make atonement in the holy place, shall be taken outside the camp, and they shall burn their hides, their flesh, and their refuse in the fire. 28 Then the one who burns them shall wash his clothes and bathe his body with water, and afterward he shall come into the camp.

29 "And *this* shall be a perpetual statute for you: in the seventh month, on the tenth day of the month, you shall humble your souls and not do any work, whether the native or the sojourner who sojourns among you; 30 for it is on this day that atonement shall be made for you to cleanse you; you will be clean from all your sins before Yahweh. 31 It is to be a sabbath of solemn rest for you, that you may humble your souls; it is a perpetual statute. 32 So the priest who is anointed and ordained to minister as a priest in his father's place shall make atonement: he shall thus put on the linen garments, the holy garments, 33 and make atonement for the holy sanctuary, and he shall make atonement for the tent of meeting and for the altar. He shall also make atonement for the priests and for all the people of the assembly. 34 Now you shall have this as a perpetual statute, to make atonement for

the sons of Israel for all their sins once every
year." And just as Yahweh had commanded
Moses, *so* he did.

Psalm 26:6–12

6 I shall wash my hands in innocence,
So I will go around Your
altar, O Yahweh,
7 In order to proclaim with the
voice of thanksgiving
And to recount all Your
wondrous deeds.

8 O Yahweh, I love the habitation
of Your house
And the place where Your glory dwells.
9 Do not take my soul away
along with sinners,
Nor my life with men of bloodshed,
10 In whose hands is a *wicked* scheme,
And whose right hand is full of bribes.
11 But as for me, I shall walk
in my integrity;
Redeem me, and be gracious to me.
12 My foot stands on level ground;
In the congregations I shall
bless Yahweh.

Proverbs 10:8

8 The wise of heart will receive
commandments,
But an ignorant fool of *loose*
lips will be ruined.

Mark 4:1–20

4 And He began to teach again by the sea.
And such a very large crowd gathered to
Him that He got into a boat in the sea and
sat down; and the whole crowd was by the
sea on the land. 2 And He was teaching them
many things in parables, and was saying
to them in His teaching, 3 "Listen *to this*!
Behold, the sower went out to sow; 4 and
it happened that as he was sowing, some
seed fell beside the road, and the birds came
and ate it up. 5 And other *seed* fell on the
rocky *ground* where it did not have much
soil; and immediately it sprang up because
it had no depth of soil. 6 And after the sun
rose, it was scorched; and because it had no
root, it withered away. 7 And other *seed* fell
among the thorns, and the thorns came up
and choked it, and it yielded no crop. 8 And
other *seeds* fell into the good soil, and as
they grew up and increased, they were
yielding a crop and produced thirty, sixty,
and a hundredfold." 9 And He was saying,
"He who has ears to hear, let him hear."
10 And when He was alone, His followers,
along with the twelve, *began* asking Him
about the parables. 11 And He was saying to
them, "To you has been given the mystery
of the kingdom of God, but to those who
are outside, everything comes in parables,
12 so that WHILE SEEING, THEY MAY SEE AND
NOT PERCEIVE, AND WHILE HEARING, THEY
MAY HEAR AND NOT UNDERSTAND, LEST THEY
RETURN AND BE FORGIVEN."
13 And He *said to them, "Do you not
understand this parable? How will you
understand all the parables? 14 The sower
sows the word. 15 And these are the ones
who are beside the road where the word is
sown: when they hear, immediately Satan
comes and takes away the word which has
been sown in them. 16 And in a similar way,
these are the ones being sown on the rocky
places: those who, when hearing the word,
immediately receive it with joy; 17 and they
have no root in themselves, but are *only*
temporary; then, when affliction or persecu-
tion arises because of the word, immediately
they fall away. 18 And others are those being
sown among the thorns; these are the
ones who have heard the word, 19 but the
worries of the world, and the deceitfulness
of riches, and the desires for anything else
enter in and choke the word, and it becomes
unfruitful. 20 And those are the ones which
were sown on the good soil: they who hear
the word and accept it and are bearing fruit,
thirty, sixty, and a hundredfold."

FEBRUARY 24

Leviticus 17:1–18:30

17 Then Yahweh spoke to Moses, saying,
2 "Speak to Aaron and to his sons and
to all the sons of Israel and say to them,
'This is what Yahweh has commanded,
saying, 3 "Any man from the house of Israel
who slaughters an ox or a lamb or a goat
in the camp, or who slaughters it outside
the camp, 4 and has not brought it to the
doorway of the tent of meeting to bring *it*

near as an offering to Yahweh before the tabernacle of Yahweh, it will be counted as bloodguiltiness to that man. He has shed blood, and that man shall be cut off from among his people. 5 *The reason is* so that the sons of Israel may bring their sacrifices which they were sacrificing in the open field, that they may bring them in to Yahweh, at the doorway of the tent of meeting to the priest, and sacrifice them as sacrifices of peace offerings to Yahweh. 6 And the priest shall splash the blood on the altar of Yahweh at the doorway of the tent of meeting and offer up the fat in smoke as a soothing aroma to Yahweh. 7 And they shall no longer sacrifice their sacrifices to the goat demons with which they play the harlot. This shall be a perpetual statute to them throughout their generations."'

8 "Then you shall say to them, 'Any man from the house of Israel, or from the sojourners who sojourn among them, who offers a burnt offering or sacrifice, 9 and does not bring it to the doorway of the tent of meeting to offer it to Yahweh, that man also shall be cut off from his people.

10 'And any man from the house of Israel, or from the sojourners who sojourn among them, who eats any blood, I will set My face against that person who eats blood and will cut him off from among his people. 11 For the life of the flesh is in the blood, and I have given it to you on the altar to make atonement for your souls; for it is the blood that makes atonement by the life.' 12 Therefore I said to the sons of Israel, 'No person among you may eat blood, and no sojourner who sojourns among you may eat blood.' 13 So any man from the sons of Israel, or from the sojourners who sojourn among them, who *in* hunting catches a beast or a bird which may be eaten, shall pour out its blood and cover it with earth.

14 "For *as for the* life of all flesh, its blood is *identified* with its life. Therefore I said to the sons of Israel, 'You are not to eat the blood of any flesh, for the life of all flesh is its blood; whoever eats it shall be cut off.' 15 And when any person eats *an animal* which dies or is torn *by beasts*, whether he is a native or a sojourner, he shall wash his clothes and bathe in water and remain unclean until evening; then he will become clean. 16 But if he does not wash *them* or bathe his body, then he shall bear his guilt."

18 Then Yahweh spoke to Moses, saying, 2 "Speak to the sons of Israel and say to them, 'I am Yahweh your God. 3 You shall not do according to what is done in the land of Egypt where you lived, nor are you to do according to what is done in the land of Canaan where I am bringing you; you shall not walk in their statutes. 4 You are to do My judgments and keep My statutes, to walk in them; I am Yahweh your God. 5 So you shall keep My statutes and My judgments, which if a man does them, he shall live by them; I am Yahweh.

6 'None of you shall approach any blood relative of his to uncover nakedness; I am Yahweh. 7 You shall not uncover the nakedness of your father, that is, the nakedness of your mother. She is your mother; you are not to uncover her nakedness. 8 You shall not uncover the nakedness of your father's wife; it is your father's nakedness. 9 The nakedness of your sister, *either* your father's daughter or your mother's daughter, whether born at home or born outside, their nakedness you shall not uncover. 10 The nakedness of your son's daughter or your daughter's daughter, their nakedness you shall not uncover; for their nakedness is yours. 11 The nakedness of your father's wife's daughter, born to your father, she is your sister; you shall not uncover her nakedness. 12 You shall not uncover the nakedness of your father's sister; she is your father's blood relative. 13 You shall not uncover the nakedness of your mother's sister, for she is your mother's blood relative. 14 You shall not uncover the nakedness of your father's brother; you shall not approach his wife; she is your aunt. 15 You shall not uncover the nakedness of your daughter-in-law; she is your son's wife; you shall not uncover her nakedness. 16 You shall not uncover the nakedness of your brother's wife; it is your brother's nakedness. 17 You shall not uncover the nakedness of a woman and of her daughter, nor shall you take her son's daughter or her daughter's daughter, to uncover her nakedness; they are blood relatives. It is lewdness. 18 And you shall not marry a woman in addition to her sister as a rival while she is alive, to uncover her nakedness.

19 'Also you shall not approach a woman to uncover her nakedness during her menstrual impurity. 20 And you shall not

lie sexually with your neighbor's wife, to
be defiled with her. 21 And you shall not
give any of your seed to pass them over to
Molech, nor shall you profane the name of
your God; I am Yahweh. 22 And you shall not
lie with a male as one lies with a female; it
is an abomination. 23 Also you shall not lie
with any animal to be defiled with it, nor
shall any woman stand before an animal to
mate with it; it is a perversion.
24 'So do not defile yourselves by any of
these things; for by all these the nations
which I am casting out before you have
become defiled. 25 So the land has become
defiled, and I have brought its punishment
upon it. And the land has vomited out its
inhabitants. 26 But as for you, you shall
keep My statutes and My judgments and
shall not do any of these abominations,
neither the native nor the sojourner who
sojourns among you 27 (for the men of the
land who have been before you have done
all these abominations, and the land has
become defiled); 28 so that the land will
not vomit you out, should you defile it, as
it has vomited out the nation which has
been before you. 29 For whoever does any of
these abominations, those persons who do
so shall be cut off from among their people.
30 Thus you are to keep My charge, that you
do not do any of the abominable statutes
which have been done before you, so as not
to defile yourselves with them; I am Yahweh
your God.'"

Psalm 27:1–3

1 Yahweh is my light and my salvation;
Whom shall I fear?
Yahweh is the strong defense
of my life;
Whom shall I dread?
2 When evildoers came upon
me to devour my flesh,
My adversaries and my enemies,
they stumbled and fell.
3 Though a host encamp against me,
My heart will not fear;
Though war arise against me,
In this I trust.

Proverbs 10:9

9 He who walks in integrity
walks securely,
But he who makes his ways
crooked will be found out.

Mark 4:21–41

21 And He was saying to them, "Is a lamp
brought to be put under a basket or under
a bed? Is it not to be put on the lampstand?
22 For nothing is hidden, except to be
revealed; nor has *anything* been secret,
but that it would come to light. 23 If any-
one has ears to hear, let him hear." 24 And
He was saying to them, "Beware what you
listen to. By your standard of measure it
will be measured to you, and more will be
given to you. 25 For whoever has, to him
more shall be given; and whoever does not
have, even what he has shall be taken away
from him."
26 And He was saying, "The kingdom of
God is like a man who casts seed upon the
soil; 27 and he sleeps and rises, night and
day, and the seed sprouts and grows—how,
he himself does not know. 28 The soil pro-
duces crops by itself; first the blade, then
the head, then the mature grain in the head.
29 But when the grain is ripe, he immediately
puts in the sickle, because the harvest has
come."
30 And He was saying, "How shall we
compare the kingdom of God, or by what
parable shall we present it? 31 *It is* like a
mustard seed, which, when sown upon the
soil, though it is smallest of all the seeds
that are upon the soil, 32 yet when it is sown,
it grows up and becomes largest of all the
garden plants and forms large branches; so
that THE BIRDS OF THE AIR can NEST UNDER
ITS SHADE."
33 And with many such parables He was
speaking the word to them, as they were
able to hear *it*; 34 and He was not speaking
to them without a parable; but He was
explaining everything privately to His own
disciples.
35 And on that day, when evening came,
He *said to them, "Let us go over to the
other side." 36 And leaving the crowd, they
*took Him along with them in the boat,
just as He was; and other boats were with
Him. 37 And a great windstorm *arose, and
the waves were breaking into the boat so
that the boat was already filling up. 38 And
Jesus Himself was in the stern, sleeping
on the cushion; and they *got Him up and
*said to Him, "Teacher, do You not care
that we are perishing?" 39 And He woke up
and rebuked the wind and said to the sea,
"Silence! Be still." And the wind died down

and it became perfectly calm. 40 And He said to them, "Why are you *so* cowardly? Do you still have no faith?" 41 And they became very afraid and were saying to one another, "Who then is this, that even the wind and the sea obey Him?"

FEBRUARY 25

Leviticus 19:1–20:27

19 Then Yahweh spoke to Moses, saying: 2 "Speak to all the congregation of the sons of Israel and say to them, 'You shall be holy, for I, Yahweh your God, am holy. 3 Every one of you shall fear his mother and his father, and you shall keep My sabbaths; I am Yahweh your God. 4 Do not turn to idols or make for yourselves molten gods; I am Yahweh your God.

5 'Now when you offer a sacrifice of peace offerings to Yahweh, you shall offer it so that you may be accepted. 6 It shall be eaten the same day you offer *it* and the next day; but what remains until the third day shall be burned with fire. 7 So if it is eaten at all on the third day, it is an offense; it will not be accepted. 8 And everyone who eats it will bear his iniquity, for he has profaned the holy thing of Yahweh; and that person shall be cut off from his people.

9 'Now when you reap the harvest of your land, you shall not reap to the very corners of your field, nor shall you gather the gleanings of your harvest. 10 Nor shall you glean your vineyard, nor shall you gather the fallen fruit of your vineyard; you shall leave them for the afflicted and for the sojourner. I am Yahweh your God.

11 'You shall not steal, nor deal falsely, nor lie to one another. 12 And you shall not swear falsely by My name, so as to profane the name of your God; I am Yahweh.

13 'You shall not oppress your neighbor nor rob *him*. The wages of a hired man shall not remain with you overnight until morning. 14 You shall not curse a deaf man nor place a stumbling block before the blind, but you shall fear your God; I am Yahweh.

15 'You shall do no injustice in judgment; you shall not be partial to the poor nor defer to the great, but you shall judge your neighbor in righteousness. 16 You shall not go about as a slanderer among your people, and you shall not stand against the life of your neighbor; I am Yahweh.

17 'You shall not hate your brother in your heart; you may surely reprove your neighbor, and so not bear sin because of him. 18 You shall not take vengeance, and you shall not keep *your anger* against the sons of your people, but you shall love your neighbor as yourself; I am Yahweh.

19 'You are to keep My statutes. You shall not breed together two kinds of your cattle; you shall not sow your field with two kinds of seed nor wear a garment upon you of two kinds of material mixed together.

20 'Now if a man lies sexually with a woman who is a slave assigned to *another* man, but who has in no way been redeemed nor given her freedom, there shall be punishment; they shall not, *however*, be put to death because she was not free. 21 And he shall bring his guilt offering to Yahweh to the doorway of the tent of meeting, a ram for a guilt offering. 22 The priest shall also make atonement for him with the ram of the guilt offering before Yahweh for his sin which he has committed, and the sin which he has committed will be forgiven him.

23 'When you enter the land and plant all kinds of trees for food, then you shall designate their fruit as forbidden. Three years it shall be forbidden to you; *it* shall not be eaten. 24 But in the fourth year all its fruit shall be holy, an offering of praise to Yahweh. 25 Now in the fifth year you shall eat of its fruit, that its produce may increase for you; I am Yahweh your God.

26 'You shall not eat *anything* with the blood nor interpret omens or soothsaying. 27 You shall not round off the side-growth of your heads nor harm the edges of your beard. 28 And you shall not make any cuts in your body for the dead nor make any tattoo marks on yourselves: I am Yahweh.

29 'Do not profane your daughter by making her a harlot, so that the land will not fall to harlotry and the land become full of lewdness. 30 You shall keep My sabbaths and fear My sanctuary; I am Yahweh.

31 'Do not turn to mediums or spiritists; do not seek them out to be defiled by them. I am Yahweh your God.

32 'You shall rise up before the gray-haired and honor the aged, and you shall fear your God; I am Yahweh.

33 'And when a sojourner sojourns with you in your land, you shall not mistreat him. 34 The sojourner who sojourns with you shall be to you as the native among you, and you shall love him as yourself, for you were sojourners in the land of Egypt; I am Yahweh your God.

35 'You shall do no wrong in judgment, in measurement of weight, or in volume. 36 You shall have just balances, just weights, a just ephah, and a just hin; I am Yahweh your God, who brought you out from the land of Egypt. 37 You shall thus keep all My statutes and all My judgments and do them; I am Yahweh.'"

20 Then Yahweh spoke to Moses, saying, 2 "You shall also say to the sons of Israel:

'Any man from the sons of Israel or from the sojourners sojourning in Israel who gives any of his seed to Molech shall surely be put to death; the people of the land shall stone him with stones. 3 I will also set My face against that man and will cut him off from among his people because he has given some of *those who are* his seed to Molech, so as to defile My sanctuary and to profane My holy name. 4 If the people of the land, however, should ever turn a blind eye to that man when he gives any of *those who are* his seed to Molech, so as not to put him to death, 5 then I Myself will set My face against that man and against his family, and I will cut off from among their people both him and all those who play the harlot after him, in playing the harlot after Molech.

6 'As for the person who turns to mediums and to spiritists, to play the harlot after them, I will also set My face against that person and will cut him off from among his people. 7 Therefore, you shall set yourselves apart as holy and be holy, for I am Yahweh your God. 8 And you shall keep My statutes and do them; I am Yahweh who makes you holy.

9 'If *there is* anyone who curses his father or his mother, he shall surely be put to death; he has cursed his father or his mother. His bloodguiltiness is upon him.

10 'If *there is* a man who commits adultery with another man's wife, one who commits adultery with his friend's wife, the adulterer and the adulteress shall surely be put to death. 11 If *there is* a man who lies with his father's wife, he has uncovered his father's nakedness; both of them shall surely be put to death. Their bloodguiltiness is upon them. 12 If *there is* a man who lies with his daughter-in-law, both of them shall surely be put to death; they have committed perversion. Their bloodguiltiness is upon them. 13 If *there is* a man who lies with a male as those who lie with a woman, both of them have committed an abomination; they shall surely be put to death. Their bloodguiltiness is upon them. 14 If *there is* a man who marries a woman and her mother, it is lewdness; both he and they shall be burned with fire so that there will be no lewdness in your midst. 15 If *there is* a man who lies with an animal, he shall surely be put to death; you shall also kill the animal. 16 If *there is* a woman who approaches any animal to mate with it, you shall kill the woman and the animal; they shall surely be put to death. Their bloodguiltiness is upon them.

17 'If *there is* a man who takes his sister, his father's daughter, or his mother's daughter, so that he sees her nakedness and she sees his nakedness, it is a disgrace; and they shall be cut off in the sight of the sons of their people. He has uncovered his sister's nakedness; he bears his guilt. 18 If *there is* a man who lies with a menstruous woman and uncovers her nakedness, he has laid bare her flow, and she has uncovered the flow of her blood; thus both of them shall be cut off from among their people. 19 You shall also not uncover the nakedness of your mother's sister or of your father's sister, for such a one has made naked his blood relative; they will bear their guilt. 20 If *there is* a man who lies with his aunt, he has uncovered his uncle's nakedness; they will bear their sin. They will die childless. 21 If *there is* a man who takes his brother's wife, it is an impure act; he has uncovered his brother's nakedness. They will be childless.

22 'You shall therefore keep all My statutes and all My judgments and do them, so that the land to which I am bringing you to inhabit will not vomit you out. 23 Moreover, you shall not walk in the statutes of the nation which I will cast out before you, for they did all these things, and therefore I have loathed them. 24 Hence I have said

to you, "You yourselves shall possess their
land, and I Myself will give it to you to pos-
sess it, a land flowing with milk and honey."
I am Yahweh your God, who has separated
you from the peoples. 25 You are therefore
to separate between the clean animal and
the unclean, and between the unclean
bird and the clean; and you shall not make
yourselves detestable by animal or by bird
or by anything that creeps on the ground,
which I have separated for you as unclean.
26 Thus you shall be holy to Me, for I Yahweh
am holy; and I have separated you from the
peoples to be Mine.
27 'Now a man or a woman who is a
medium or a spiritist shall surely be put to
death. They shall be stoned with stones.
Their bloodguiltiness is upon them.'"

Psalm 27:4–10

4 One thing I have asked from
Yahweh, that I shall seek:
That I may dwell in the house of
Yahweh all the days of my life,
To behold the beauty of Yahweh
And to inquire in His temple.
5 For in the day of calamity He will
conceal me in His shelter;
In the secret place of His
tent He will hide me;
He will lift me up on a rock.
6 And now my head will be lifted up
above my enemies around me,
And I will offer in His tent sacrifices
with loud shouts of joy;
I will sing, and I will sing
praises to Yahweh.

7 Hear, O Yahweh, when I
call with my voice,
And be gracious to me
and answer me.
8 On Your *behalf* my heart
says, "Seek My face,"
"Your face, O Yahweh, I shall seek."
9 Do not hide Your face from me,
Do not turn Your slave away
in anger;
You have been my help;
Do not abandon me and
do not forsake me,
O God of my salvation!
10 For my father and my mother
have forsaken me,
But Yahweh will take me up.

Proverbs 10:10–12

10 He who winks the eye causes pain,
And an ignorant fool of *loose*
lips will be ruined.
11 The mouth of the righteous
is a fountain of life,
But the mouth of the wicked
covers up violence.
12 Hatred stirs up strife,
But love covers all transgressions.

Mark 5:1–20

5 Then they came to the other side of
the sea, into the region of the Ger-
asenes. 2 And when He got out of the boat,
immediately a man from the tombs with
an unclean spirit met Him, 3 who had his
dwelling among the tombs. And no one
was able to bind him anymore, even with a
chain; 4 because he had often been bound
with shackles and chains, and the chains
had been torn apart by him and the shackles
broken in pieces, and no one was strong
enough to subdue him. 5 And constantly,
night and day, among the tombs and in the
mountains, he was crying out and gashing
himself with stones. 6 And seeing Jesus
from a distance, he ran up and bowed
down before Him; 7 and crying out with a
loud voice, he *said, "What do I have to do
with You, Jesus, Son of the Most High God?
I implore You by God, do not torment me!"
8 For He had been saying to him, "Come
out of the man, you unclean spirit!" 9 And
He was asking him, "What is your name?"
And he *said to Him, "My name is Legion;
for we are many." 10 And he *began* pleading
with Him earnestly not to send them out
of the region. 11 Now there was a large herd
of swine feeding nearby on the mountain.
12 *And the demons* pleaded with Him, saying,
"Send us into the swine so that we may enter
them." 13 And Jesus gave them permission.
And coming out, the unclean spirits entered
the swine; and the herd rushed down the
steep bank into the sea, about two thousand
of them; and they were drowned in the sea.
14 And their herdsmen ran away and
reported it in the city and in the countryside.
And *the people* came to see what it was that
had happened. 15 And they *came to Jesus
and *observed the demon-possessed man
sitting down, clothed and in his right mind,
the very man who had the "legion"; and they
became frightened. 16 And those who had

seen it recounted to them how *this* had happened to the demon-possessed man, and *all* about the swine. 17 And they began to plead with Him to leave their region. 18 And as He was getting into the boat, the man who had been demon-possessed was pleading with Him that he might accompany Him. 19 And He did not let him, but He *said to him, "Go home to your people and report to them what great things the Lord has done for you, and *how* He had mercy on you." 20 And he went away and began to preach in the Decapolis what great things Jesus had done for him; and everyone was marveling.

There are very few that ever gave this Book of God, the grand charter of salvation, one fair reading through.

— GEORGE WHITEFIELD

FEBRUARY 26

Leviticus 21:1–22:33

21 Then Yahweh said to Moses, "Speak to the priests, the sons of Aaron, and say to them:

'No one shall defile himself for a *dead* person among his people, 2 except for his blood relatives who are nearest to him, his mother and his father and his son and his daughter and his brother, 3 also for his virgin sister, who is near to him because she has had no husband; for her he may defile himself. 4 He shall not defile himself as a relative by marriage among his people, and so profane himself. 5 They shall not make any baldness on their heads nor shave off the edges of their beards nor make any cuts in their flesh. 6 They shall be holy to their God and not profane the name of their God, for they bring near the offerings to Yahweh by fire, the food of their God; so they shall be holy. 7 They shall not take a woman who is profaned by harlotry, nor shall they take a woman divorced from her husband; for he is holy to his God. 8 Therefore, you shall set him apart as holy, for he brings near the food of your God; he shall be holy to you; for I Yahweh, who makes you holy, am holy. 9 Also the daughter of any priest, if she profanes herself by harlotry, she profanes her father; she shall be burned with fire.

10 'And the priest who is the highest among his brothers, on whose head the anointing oil has been poured and who has been ordained to wear the garments, shall not uncover his head nor tear his clothes; 11 nor shall he approach any dead person nor defile himself *even* for his father or his mother; 12 nor shall he go out of the sanctuary nor profane the sanctuary of his God, for the dedication of the anointing oil of his God is on him; I am Yahweh. 13 And he shall take a wife in her virginity. 14 A widow or a divorced woman or one who is profaned by harlotry, these he may not take; but rather he shall take a virgin of his own people as a wife, 15 so that he will not profane his seed among his people; for I am Yahweh who makes him holy.'"

16 Then Yahweh spoke to Moses, saying, 17 "Speak to Aaron, saying, 'No man of your seed throughout their generations who has a defect shall come near to offer the food of his God. 18 For no one who has a defect shall come near: a blind man or a lame man or he who has a disfigured *face* or any deformed *limb*, 19 or a man who has a broken foot or broken hand, 20 or a hunchback or a dwarf, or *one who has* a defect in his eye or eczema or scabs or crushed testicles. 21 No man among the seed of Aaron the priest who has a defect shall approach to bring near the offerings to Yahweh by fire; *since* he has a defect, he shall not approach to bring near the food of his God. 22 He may eat the food of his God, *both* of the most holy and of the holy, 23 only he shall not go in to the veil or approach the altar because he has a defect, so that he will not profane My sanctuaries. For I am Yahweh who makes them holy.'" 24 So Moses spoke to Aaron and to his sons and to all the sons of Israel.

22 Then Yahweh spoke to Moses, saying, 2 "Tell Aaron and his sons to be careful with the holy *gifts* of the sons of Israel,

which they set apart to Me as holy, so as not
to profane My holy name; I am Yahweh. 3 Say
to them, 'If any man among all your seed
throughout your generations comes near
to the holy *gifts* which the sons of Israel
set apart as holy to Yahweh, and he has an
uncleanness, that person shall be cut off
from before Me; I am Yahweh. 4 No man of
the seed of Aaron, who is a leper or who has
a discharge, may eat of the holy *gifts* until
he is clean. And if one touches anything
made unclean by a corpse, or if a man has
a seminal emission, 5 or if a man touches any
teeming things by which he is made unclean
or any man by whom he is made unclean,
whatever his uncleanness, 6 a person who
touches any such thing shall be unclean
until evening and shall not eat of the holy
gifts unless he has bathed his body in water.
7 But the sun will set, and he will be clean.
And afterward he shall eat of the holy *gifts*,
for it is his food. 8 He shall not eat *an animal*
which dies or is torn *by beasts*, becoming
unclean by it; I am Yahweh. 9 They shall
therefore keep My charge so that they will
not bear sin because of it and die thereby
because they profane it; I am Yahweh who
makes them holy.

10 'No layman, however, is to eat the holy
gift; a foreign resident with the priest or a
hired man shall not eat of the holy *gift*. 11 But
if a priest buys a person as *his* property with
his money, that one may eat of it, and those
who are born in his house may eat of his
food. 12 If a priest's daughter is married to a
layman, she shall not eat of the contribution
of the holy *gifts*. 13 But if a priest's daughter
becomes a widow or divorced, and has no
seed, and returns to her father's house as
in her youth, she shall eat of her father's
food; but no layman shall eat of it. 14 But if
a man eats a holy *gift* unintentionally, then
he shall add to it a fifth of it and shall give
the holy *gift* to the priest. 15 They shall not
profane the holy *gifts* of the sons of Israel
which they raise up to Yahweh, 16 and *so*
cause them to bear punishment for guilt
by eating their holy *gifts*; for I am Yahweh
who makes them holy.'"

17 Then Yahweh spoke to Moses, saying,
18 "Speak to Aaron and to his sons and to all
the sons of Israel and say to them, 'Any man
of the house of Israel or of the sojourners in
Israel who brings near his offering, whether
it is any of their votive or any of their
freewill offerings, which they bring near
to Yahweh for a burnt offering— 19 for you
to be accepted—*it must be* a male without
blemish from the cattle, the sheep, or the
goats. 20 Whatever has a defect, you shall
not bring *it* near, for it will not be accepted
for you. 21 And when a man brings a sacrifice
of peace offerings near to Yahweh to fulfill
a special vow or for a freewill offering, of
the herd or of the flock, it must be without
blemish to be accepted; there shall be no
defect in it. 22 Those *that are* blind or frac-
tured or maimed or *have* a running sore or
eczema or scabs, you shall not bring near
to Yahweh nor make of them an offering by
fire on the altar to Yahweh. 23 Now in respect
to an ox or a lamb which has an overgrown
or stunted *member*, you may offer it for a
freewill offering, but for a votive offering it
will not be accepted. 24 Also anything *with
its testicles* bruised or crushed or torn or cut,
you shall not bring near to Yahweh, and you
shall not do *thus* in your land, 25 nor shall you
bring near any such thing from the hand of a
foreigner for offering as the food of your God;
for their corruption is in them, they have a
defect; they shall not be accepted for you.'"

26 Then Yahweh spoke to Moses, saying,
27 "When an ox or a sheep or a goat is born,
it shall remain seven days with its mother,
and from the eighth day on it shall be
accepted as a sacrifice of an offering by fire
to Yahweh. 28 But, *whether* it is an ox or a
sheep, you shall not slaughter *both* it and its
young in one day. 29 And when you sacrifice
a sacrifice of thanksgiving to Yahweh, you
shall sacrifice it so that you may be accepted.
30 It shall be eaten on the same day; you shall
leave none of it until morning; I am Yahweh.
31 So you shall keep My commandments and
do them; I am Yahweh.

32 "And you shall not profane My holy
name, but I will be treated as holy among
the sons of Israel; I am Yahweh who makes
you holy, 33 who brought you out from the
land of Egypt to be your God; I am Yahweh."

Psalm 27:11–14

11 Instruct me in Your way, O Yahweh,
And lead me in a level path
Because of my foes.
12 Do not give me over to the
desire of my adversaries,
For false witnesses have
risen against me,

And such as breathe out violence.
13 *I would have despaired* unless I
had believed that I would see
the goodness of Yahweh
In the land of the living.
14 Hope in Yahweh;
Be strong and let your
heart take courage;
Hope in Yahweh.

Proverbs 10:13–16

13 On the lips of the one who has
understanding, wisdom is found,
But a rod is for the back of him
who lacks a heart *of wisdom.*
14 Wise men store up knowledge,
But the mouth of the ignorant
fool draws ruin near.
15 The rich man's wealth is his strong city,
The ruin of the poor is their poverty.
16 The wages of the righteous is life,
The income of the wicked,
punishment.

Mark 5:21–43

21 And when Jesus had crossed over again
in the boat to the other side, a large crowd
gathered around Him; and so He stayed by
the seashore. 22 And one of the synagogue
officials named Jairus *came up, and on
seeing Him, *fell at His feet 23 and *pleaded
with Him earnestly, saying, "My little daugh-
ter is at the point of death; *please come,* that
by coming, You may lay Your hands on her,
so that she will be saved and live." 24 And
He went off with him; and a large crowd was
following Him and pressing in on Him.
25 And a woman—who had a hemorrhage
for twelve years 26 and had endured much
at the hands of many physicians, and had
spent all that she had and was not helped
at all, but rather had grown worse— 27 after
hearing about Jesus, she came up in the
crowd behind *Him* and touched His gar-
ment. 28 For she was saying, "If I just touch
His garments, I will be saved *from this.*"
29 And immediately the flow of her blood
was dried up; and she knew within her body
that she had been healed of her affliction.
30 And immediately Jesus, perceiving in
Himself that the power *proceeding* from
Him had gone forth, turned around in the
crowd and was saying, "Who touched My
garments?" 31 And His disciples were saying
to Him, "You see the crowd pressing in on
You, and You say, 'Who touched Me?'"
32 And He was looking around to see the
woman who had done this. 33 But the
woman fearing and trembling, aware of
what had happened to her, came and fell
down before Him and told Him the whole
truth. 34 And He said to her, "Daughter,
your faith has saved you; go in peace and
be healed of your affliction."
35 While He was still speaking, they *came
from the *house of* the synagogue official,
saying, "Your daughter has died; why
trouble the Teacher anymore?" 36 But Jesus,
overhearing what had been spoken, *said to
the synagogue official, "Do not be afraid,
only believe." 37 And He allowed no one to
accompany Him, except Peter and James
and John the brother of James. 38 And they
*came to the house of the synagogue offi-
cial; and He *saw a commotion, and *people*
loudly crying and wailing. 39 And entering
in, He *said to them, "Why are you making
a commotion and crying? The child has
not died, but is asleep." 40 And they *began*
laughing at Him. But putting them all out,
He *took along the child's father and mother
and His own companions, and *entered *the
room* where the child was. 41 And taking the
child by the hand, He *said to her, "Talitha
kum!" (which translated means, "Little girl,
I say to you, arise!"). 42 And immediately the
little girl stood up and *began to* walk, for
she was twelve years old. And immediately
they were completely astounded. 43 And He
gave them strict orders that no one should
know about this, and He said that *some food*
should be given to her to eat.

FEBRUARY 27

Leviticus 23:1–24:23

23 And Yahweh spoke again to Moses,
saying, 2 "Speak to the sons of Israel
and say to them, 'The appointed times of
Yahweh which you shall proclaim as holy
convocations—My appointed times are
these:
3 'For six days work may be done, but
on the seventh day there is a sabbath of
complete rest, a holy convocation. You shall

not do any work; it is a sabbath to Yahweh
in all your *places of* habitation.
4 'These are the appointed times of Yah-
weh, holy convocations which you shall
proclaim at the times appointed for them.
5 In the first month, on the fourteenth day
of the month at twilight is the Passover of
Yahweh. 6 Then on the fifteenth day of the
same month there is the Feast of Unleav-
ened Bread to Yahweh; for seven days you
shall eat unleavened bread. 7 On the first
day you shall have a holy convocation; you
shall not do any laborious work. 8 But for
seven days you shall bring near an offering
by fire to Yahweh. On the seventh day is
a holy convocation; you shall not do any
laborious work.'"
9 Then Yahweh spoke to Moses, saying,
10 "Speak to the sons of Israel and say to
them, 'When you enter the land which I am
going to give to you and reap its harvest,
then you shall bring in the sheaf of the first
fruits of your harvest to the priest. 11 And
he shall wave the sheaf before Yahweh for
you to be accepted; on the day after the
sabbath the priest shall wave it. 12 Now
on the day when you wave the sheaf, you
shall offer a male lamb one year old without
blemish for a burnt offering to Yahweh. 13 Its
grain offering shall then be two-tenths *of
an ephah* of fine flour mixed with oil, an
offering by fire to Yahweh *for* a soothing
aroma, with its drink offering, a fourth of
a hin of wine. 14 Until this same day, until
you have brought in the offering of your
God, you shall eat neither bread nor roasted
grain nor new growth. It is to be a perpetual
statute throughout your generations in all
your *places of* habitation.
15 'You shall also count for yourselves
from the day after the sabbath, from the
day when you brought in the sheaf of the
wave offering; there shall be seven complete
sabbaths. 16 You shall count fifty days to the
day after the seventh sabbath; then you shall
bring a new grain offering near to Yahweh.
17 You shall bring in from your *places of*
habitation two *loaves* of bread for a wave
offering, made of two-tenths *of an ephah*;
they shall be of a fine flour, baked with
leaven as first fruits to Yahweh. 18 Along
with the bread you shall bring near seven
one year old male lambs without blemish
and a bull from the herd and two rams;
they shall be a burnt offering to Yahweh,
with their grain offering and their drink
offerings, an offering by fire of a soothing
aroma to Yahweh. 19 You shall also offer one
male goat for a sin offering and two male
lambs one year old for a sacrifice of peace
offerings. 20 The priest shall then wave them
with the bread of the first fruits for a wave
offering with two lambs before Yahweh; they
shall be holy to Yahweh for the priest. 21 On
this same day you shall make a proclamation
as well; it shall be a holy convocation for
you. You shall do no laborious work. It is
to be a perpetual statute in all your *places
of* habitation throughout your generations.
22 'When you reap the harvest of your
land, moreover, you shall not reap to the
very corners of your field nor gather the
gleaning of your harvest; you are to leave
them for the afflicted and the sojourner. I
am Yahweh your God.'"
23 Again Yahweh spoke to Moses, saying,
24 "Speak to the sons of Israel, saying, 'In the
seventh month on the first of the month you
shall have a rest, a memorial by blowing *of
trumpets*, a holy convocation. 25 You shall
not do any laborious work, but you shall
bring an offering by fire near to Yahweh.'"
26 And Yahweh spoke to Moses, saying,
27 "On exactly the tenth day of this seventh
month is the day of atonement; it shall be
a holy convocation for you, and you shall
humble your souls and bring an offering
by fire near to Yahweh. 28 And you shall
not do any work on this same day, for it is
a day of atonement, to make atonement on
your behalf before Yahweh your God. 29 If
there is any person who will not humble
himself on this same day, he shall be cut off
from his people. 30 And as for any person
who does any work on this same day, that
person I will cause to perish from among
his people. 31 You shall do no work at all. It
is to be a perpetual statute throughout your
generations in all your *places of* habitation.
32 It is to be a sabbath of complete rest to
you, and you shall humble your souls; on
the ninth of the month at evening, from
evening until evening you shall keep your
sabbath."
33 Again Yahweh spoke to Moses, saying,
34 "Speak to the sons of Israel, saying, 'On
the fifteenth of this seventh month is the
Feast of Booths for seven days to Yahweh.
35 On the first day is a holy convocation;
you shall do no laborious work of any kind.

36 For seven days you shall bring an offering
by fire near to Yahweh. On the eighth day
you shall have a holy convocation and bring
an offering by fire near to Yahweh; it is a
solemn assembly. You shall do no laborious
work.
37 'These are the appointed times of
Yahweh which you shall proclaim as holy
convocations, to bring offerings by fire near
to Yahweh—burnt offerings and grain offer-
ings, sacrifices and drink offerings, *each*
day's matter on its own day— 38 besides
those of the sabbaths of Yahweh and besides
your gifts and besides all your votive and
freewill offerings, which you give to Yah-
weh.
39 'On exactly the fifteenth day of the
seventh month, when you have gathered in
the produce of the land, you shall celebrate
the feast of Yahweh for seven days, with a
rest on the first day and a rest on the eighth
day. 40 And on the first day you shall take
for yourselves the foliage of beautiful trees,
palm branches and boughs of leafy trees and
willows of the brook, and you shall be glad
before Yahweh your God for seven days.
41 You shall thus celebrate it *as* a feast to
Yahweh for seven days in the year. It *shall
be* a perpetual statute throughout your
generations; you shall celebrate it in the
seventh month. 42 You shall live in booths
for seven days; all the native-born in Israel
shall live in booths, 43 so that your genera-
tions may know that I had the sons of Israel
live in booths when I brought them out from
the land of Egypt. I am Yahweh your God.'"
44 So Moses spoke to the sons of Israel the
appointed times of Yahweh.

24 Then Yahweh spoke to Moses, saying,
2 "Command the sons of Israel that
they bring to you clear oil from beaten
olives for the light, to make a lamp burn
continually. 3 Outside the veil of testimony
in the tent of meeting, Aaron shall keep it
in order from evening to morning before
Yahweh continually; *it shall be* a perpetual
statute throughout your generations. 4 He
shall keep the lamps in order on the pure
gold lampstand before Yahweh continually.
5 "Then you shall take fine flour and bake
twelve cakes with it; two-tenths *of an ephah*
shall be *in* each cake. 6 And you shall set
them *in* two rows, six *to* a row, on the pure
gold table before Yahweh. 7 And you shall
put pure frankincense on each row that it
may be a memorial portion for the bread,
even an offering by fire to Yahweh. 8 Every
sabbath day he shall set it in order before
Yahweh continually; it is an everlasting
covenant for the sons of Israel. 9 And it shall
be for Aaron and his sons, and they shall
eat it in a holy place; for it is most holy to
him from the offerings to Yahweh by fire, *his*
portion forever."
10 Now the son of an Israelite woman,
whose father was an Egyptian, went out
among the sons of Israel; and the Israelite
woman's son and a man of Israel struggled
with each other in the camp. 11 And the
son of the Israelite woman blasphemed the
Name and cursed. So they brought him to
Moses. (Now his mother's name was She-
lomith, the daughter of Dibri, of the tribe
of Dan.) 12 And they put him in custody so
that the command of Yahweh might be made
clear to them.
13 Then Yahweh spoke to Moses, saying,
14 "Bring the one who has cursed outside
the camp, and let all who heard him lay
their hands on his head; then let all the
congregation stone him. 15 And you shall
speak to the sons of Israel, saying, 'If any-
one curses his God, then he will bear his
sin. 16 Moreover, the one who blasphemes
the name of Yahweh shall surely be put to
death; all the congregation shall certainly
stone him. The sojourner as well as the
native, when he blasphemes the Name,
shall be put to death.
17 'If a man strikes down the life of any
human being, he shall surely be put to death.
18 And the one who strikes down the life of
an animal shall make restitution for it, life
for life. 19 If a man injures his neighbor, just
as he has done, so it shall be done to him:
20 fracture for fracture, eye for eye, tooth
for tooth; just as he has injured a man, so
it shall be inflicted on him. 21 Thus the one
who strikes down an animal shall make
restitution for it, but the one who strikes
down a man shall be put to death. 22 There
shall be one *standard of* judgment for you;
it shall be for the sojourner as well as the
native, for I am Yahweh your God.'" 23 Then
Moses spoke to the sons of Israel, and they
brought the one who had cursed outside
the camp and stoned him with stones. Thus
the sons of Israel did, just as Yahweh had
commanded Moses.

Psalm 28:1–5

1 To You, O Yahweh, I call;
My rock, do not be silent to me,
Lest if You are hesitant toward me,
I will become like those who
go down to the pit.
2 Hear the voice of my supplications
when I cry to You for help,
When I lift up my hands toward
Your holy sanctuary.
3 Do not drag me away with the wicked
And with workers of iniquity,
Who speak peace with their neighbors,
While evil is in their hearts.
4 Give to them according to their
work and according to the
evil of their actions;
Give to them according to the
deeds of their hands;
Return their dealings upon them.
5 Because they do not regard
the works of Yahweh
Nor the deeds of His hands,
He will tear them down and
not build them up.

Proverbs 10:17–18

17 He is *on* the path of life who
keeps discipline,
But he who forsakes reproof
makes himself wander about.
18 He who covers up hatred
has lying lips,
And he who spreads a bad
report is a fool.

Mark 6:1–29

6 And Jesus went out from there and
*came into His hometown; and His
disciples *followed Him. 2 And when
the Sabbath came, He began to teach in
the synagogue; and many listeners were
astonished, saying, "Where did this man *get*
these things, and what is *this* wisdom given
to this man, and such miracles as these
performed by His hands? 3 Is this man not
the carpenter, the son of Mary, and brother
of James and Joses and Judas and Simon?
Are not His sisters here with us?" And they
were taking offense at Him. 4 And Jesus was
saying to them, "A prophet is not without
honor except in his hometown and among
his *own* relatives and in his *own* household."
5 And He could do no miracle there except
that He laid His hands on a few sick people
and healed them. 6 And He was marveling
at their unbelief.

And He was going around the villages
teaching.

7 And He *summoned the twelve and
began to send them out in pairs, and was
giving them authority over the unclean
spirits; 8 and He instructed them that they
should take nothing for *their* journey,
except a staff only—no bread, no bag, no
money in their belt— 9 but *to* wear sandals;
and *He added*, "Do not put on two tunics."
10 And He was saying to them, "Wherever
you enter a house, stay there until you leave
town. 11 And any place that does not receive
you or listen to you, as you go out from
there, shake the dust off the soles of your
feet for a testimony against them." 12 And
they went out and preached that *men* should
repent. 13 And they were casting out many
demons and were anointing with oil many
sick people and healing them.

14 And King Herod heard *it*, for His name
had become well known; and *people* were
saying, "John the Baptist has risen from
the dead, and that is why these miraculous
powers are at work in Him." 15 But others
were saying, "He is Elijah." And others were
saying, "*He is* a prophet, like one of the
prophets *of old*." 16 But when Herod heard
it, he kept saying, "John, whom I beheaded,
has risen!"

17 For Herod himself had sent and had
John arrested and bound in prison on
account of Herodias, the wife of his brother
Philip, because he had married her. 18 For
John had been saying to Herod, "It is not
lawful for you to have your brother's wife."
19 Now Herodias was holding a grudge
against him and was wanting to put him
to death and was not able; 20 for Herod
was afraid of John, knowing that he was a
righteous and holy man, and he was keep-
ing him safe. And when he heard him, he
was very perplexed; but he used to enjoy
listening to him. 21 And a strategic day came
when Herod on his birthday gave a banquet
for his great men and military commanders
and the leading men of Galilee; 22 and when
the daughter of Herodias herself came in
and danced, she pleased Herod and his
dinner guests; and the king said to the
girl, "Ask me for whatever you want and I
will give it to you." 23 And he swore to her,
"Whatever you ask of me, I will give it to

you; up to half of my kingdom." 24 And she
went out and said to her mother, "What
shall I ask for?" And she said, "The head
of John the Baptist." 25 And immediately
she came in a hurry to the king and asked,
saying, "I want you to give me at once
the head of John the Baptist on a platter."
26 And although the king was very sorry,
yet because of his oaths and because of his
dinner guests, he did not want to refuse
her. 27 And immediately the king sent an
executioner and commanded *him* to bring
back his head. And he went and beheaded
him in the prison, 28 and brought his head
on a platter, and gave it to the girl; and the
girl gave it to her mother. 29 And when his
disciples heard *this*, they came and took
away his body and laid it in a tomb.

FEBRUARY 28

Leviticus 25:1–55

25 Yahweh then spoke to Moses at
Mount Sinai, saying, 2 "Speak to
the sons of Israel and say to them, 'When
you come into the land which I am giving
to you, then the land shall have a sabbath
to Yahweh. 3 Six years you shall sow your
field, and six years you shall prune your
vineyard and gather in its produce, 4 but
during the seventh year the land shall have
a sabbath rest, a sabbath to Yahweh; you
shall not sow your field nor prune your
vineyard. 5 What grows of its own accord
from your harvest you shall not reap, and
your grapes of untrimmed vines you shall
not gather; the land shall have a sabbatical
year. 6 And the sabbath *produce* of the land
shall be for food; for you and your male and
female slaves and your hired man and your
foreign resident, those who sojourn with
you. 7 Even your cattle and the beasts that
are in your land shall have all its produce
to eat.

8 'You are also to count off seven sabbaths
of years for yourself, seven times seven
years, so that you have the time of the seven
sabbaths of years, *namely*, forty-nine years.
9 You shall then sound a ram's horn abroad
on the tenth day of the seventh month; on
the day of atonement you shall sound a horn
all through your land. 10 You shall thus set
apart as holy the fiftieth year and proclaim
a release through the land to all its inhabi-
tants. It shall be a jubilee for you, and each
of you shall return to his own possession
of land, and each of you shall return to his
family. 11 You shall have the fiftieth year as a
jubilee; you shall not sow; you shall not reap
what grows of its own accord; you shall not
gather in *from* its untrimmed vines. 12 For it
is a jubilee; it shall be holy to you. You shall
eat its produce out of the field.

13 'On this year of jubilee, each of you
shall return to his own possession *of land*.
14 If you make a sale, moreover, to your
companion or buy from your friend's hand,
you shall not mistreat one another. 15 Cor-
responding to the number of years after the
jubilee, you shall buy from your companion;
he is to sell to you according to the number
of years of produce. 16 In proportion to the
extent of the years you shall increase its
price, and in proportion to the fewness of
the years you shall diminish its price, for *it
is the* number of *crops it* produces *that* he
is selling to you. 17 So you shall not mistreat
one another, but you shall fear your God; for
I am Yahweh your God.

18 'You shall thus observe My statutes and
keep My judgments, so as to do them, that
you may live securely on the land. 19 Then
the land will yield its fruit, so that you can
eat your fill and live securely on it. 20 But if
you say, "What are we going to eat on the
seventh year if we do not sow or gather in
our produce?" 21 then I will command My
blessing for you in the sixth year that it will
bring forth the produce for three years.
22 So you shall sow the eighth year and eat
old things from that produce, eating *the
old* until the ninth year when its produce
comes in.

23 'The land, moreover, shall not be sold
permanently, for the land is Mine; for you
are *but* sojourners and foreign residents
with Me. 24 Thus for every piece of land of
your possession, you shall provide for the
redemption of the land.

25 'If a brother of yours becomes so poor
he has to sell part of his possession *of land*,
then his nearest kinsman redeemer is to
come and redeem what his brother has
sold. 26 Or in case a man has no kinsman
redeemer, but recovers his means and finds

sufficient *payment* for its redemption,
27 then he shall calculate the years since
its sale and return the balance to the man
to whom he sold it, and so return to his
possession *of land.* 28 But if he has not found
sufficient means to return it to himself, then
what he has sold shall remain in the hands
of its purchaser until the year of jubilee;
but at the jubilee it shall revert, that he may
return to his possession *of land.*

29 'Likewise, if a man sells a house for hab-
itation in a walled city, then his redemption
right remains valid until a full year from its
sale; his right of redemption lasts a full year.
30 But if it is not redeemed for him within
the space of a full year, then the house that
is in the walled city passes permanently to
its purchaser throughout his generations; it
does not revert in the jubilee. 31 The houses
of the villages, however, which have no
surrounding wall, shall be considered as
open fields; they have redemption rights
and revert in the jubilee. 32 As for cities of
the Levites, the Levites have a permanent
right of redemption for the houses of the
cities which are their possession. 33 What,
therefore, belongs to the Levites may be
redeemed, and a house sale in the city of
their possession reverts in the jubilee, for the
houses of the cities of the Levites are their
possession among the sons of Israel. 34 But
pasture fields of their cities shall not be sold,
for that is their perpetual possession.

35 'Now if a brother of yours becomes
poor and his means with regard to you falter,
then you are to sustain him, like a sojourner
or a foreign resident, that he may live with
you. 36 Do not take usurious interest from
him, but fear your God, that your brother
may live with you. 37 You shall not give him
your silver at interest nor your food for gain.
38 I am Yahweh your God, who brought you
out of the land of Egypt to give you the land
of Canaan *and* to be your God.

39 'If a brother of yours becomes so poor
with regard to you that he sells himself to
you, you shall not subject him to a slave's
service. 40 He shall be with you as a hired
man, as if he were a foreign resident; he shall
serve with you until the year of jubilee. 41 He
shall then go out from you, he and his sons
with him, and shall return to his family,
that he may return to the possession *of the*
land of his fathers. 42 For they are My slaves
whom I brought out from the land of Egypt;
they shall not be sold *in* a slave sale. 43 You
shall not have dominion over him with bru-
tality, but you shall fear your God. 44 As for
your male and female slaves whom you may
have—you may acquire male and female
slaves from the nations that are around
you. 45 And also you may acquire from the
sons of the foreign residents who sojourn
among you, from them and their families
who are with you; as for those whom they
have begotten in your land, they also may
become your possession. 46 You may even
give them as an inheritance to your sons
after you, to receive as a possession; you
can use them as permanent slaves. But in
respect to your brothers, the sons of Israel,
you shall not have dominion over one
another with brutality.

47 'Now if the means of a sojourner or
of a foreign resident with you becomes
sufficient, and a brother of yours becomes
so poor with regard to him as to sell himself
to a sojourner who resides with you or to the
descendants of a sojourner's family, 48 then
he shall have redemption right after he has
been sold. One of his brothers may redeem
him, 49 or his uncle or his uncle's son may
redeem him, or one of his blood relatives
from his family may redeem him; or if he
prospers, he may redeem himself. 50 He then
with his purchaser shall calculate from the
year when he sold himself to him up to the
year of jubilee; and the price of his sale shall
correspond to the number of years. *It is* like
the days of a hired man *that* he shall be with
him. 51 If there are still many years, he shall
return part of his purchase price in propor-
tion to them for his own redemption; 52 and
if few years remain until the year of jubilee,
he shall so calculate with him. In proportion
to his years he shall return *the amount for*
his redemption. 53 Like a man hired year
by year he shall be with him; he shall not
have dominion over him with brutality in
your sight. 54 Even if he is not redeemed by
these *means*, he shall still go out in the year
of jubilee, he and his sons with him. 55 For
the sons of Israel are My slaves; they are My
slaves whom I brought out from the land of
Egypt. I am Yahweh your God.

Psalm 28:6–9

6 Blessed be Yahweh,
Because He has heard the voice
of my supplications.

7 Yahweh is my strength
and my shield;
My heart trusts in Him,
and I am helped;
Therefore my heart exults,
And with my song I shall
thank Him.
8 Yahweh is their strength,
And He is a strong defense of
salvation to His anointed.
9 Save Your people and bless
Your inheritance;
Be their shepherd also, and
carry them forever.

Proverbs 10:19–21

19 When there are many words,
transgression is unavoidable,
But he who holds back his
lips has insight.
20 The tongue of the righteous
is *as* choice silver,
The heart of the wicked is
worth little.
21 The lips of the righteous feed many,
But ignorant fools die for lack
of a heart *of wisdom*.

Mark 6:30–56

30 And the apostles *gathered together
with Jesus; and they reported to Him all
that they had done and taught. 31 And He
*said to them, "Come away by yourselves to
a desolate place and rest a while." (For there
were many *people* coming and going, and
they did not even have time to eat.) 32 And
they went away in the boat to a desolate
place by themselves.

33 And *the people* saw them going, and
many recognized *them* and ran there
together on foot from all the cities, and
got there ahead of them. 34 And when
Jesus went ashore, He saw a large crowd,
and He felt compassion for them because
they were like sheep without a shepherd;
and He began to teach them many things.
35 And when it was already quite late, His
disciples came to Him and *began* saying,
"This place is desolate and it is already
quite late; 36 send them away so that they
may go into the surrounding countryside
and villages and buy themselves something
to eat." 37 But He answered and said to
them, "You give them *something* to eat!"
And they *said to Him, "Shall we go and
spend two hundred denarii on bread and
give them *something* to eat?" 38 And He
*said to them, "How many loaves do you
have? Go look!" And when they found out,
they *said, "Five, and two fish." 39 And He
commanded them all to sit down by groups
on the green grass. 40 And they sat down
in groups of hundreds and of fifties. 41 And
He took the five loaves and the two fish,
and looking up toward heaven, He blessed
the food and broke the loaves. And He kept
giving *them* to the disciples to set before
them, and He divided up the two fish
among them all. 42 And they all ate and
were satisfied, 43 and they picked up twelve
full baskets of the broken pieces, and also
of the fish. 44 And there were five thousand
men who ate the loaves.

45 And immediately Jesus made His
disciples get into the boat and go ahead of
Him to the other side to Bethsaida, while He
Himself was sending the crowd away. 46 And
after bidding them farewell, He left for the
mountain to pray.

47 And when it was evening, the boat was
in the middle of the sea, and He was alone
on the land. 48 And seeing them straining
at the oars, for the wind was against them,
at about the fourth watch of the night He
*came to them, walking on the sea; and He
was intending to pass by them. 49 But when
they saw Him walking on the sea, they
thought that it was a ghost, and cried out;
50 for they all saw Him and were terrified.
But immediately He spoke with them and
*said to them, "Take courage; it is I, do not
be afraid." 51 Then He got into the boat with
them, and the wind stopped; and they were
utterly amazed, 52 for they had not gained
any insight about the loaves, but their heart
was hardened.

53 And when they had crossed over they
came to land at Gennesaret, and moored to
the shore. 54 And when they got out of the
boat, immediately *the people* recognized
Him, 55 and ran about that whole region and
began to carry here and there on their mats
those who were sick, to the place they heard
He was. 56 And wherever He was entering
villages, or cities, or countryside, they
were laying the sick in the marketplaces,
and pleading with Him that they might
just touch the fringe of His garment; and
as many as touched it were being saved *from
their sicknesses.*

MARCH 1

Leviticus 26:1–27:34

26 'You shall not make for yourselves idols, nor shall you set up for yourselves a graven image or a *sacred* pillar, nor shall you place a carved stone in your land to bow down to it; for I am Yahweh your God. 2 You shall keep My sabbaths and fear My sanctuary; I am Yahweh. 3 If you walk in My statutes and keep My commandments so as to do them, 4 then I shall give you rains in their season, so that the land will give forth its produce and the trees of the field will give forth their fruit. 5 Indeed, your threshing will last for you until grape gathering, and grape gathering will last until sowing time. You will thus eat your food to the full and live securely in your land. 6 I shall also give *you* peace in the land so that you may lie down, with no one making *you* tremble. I shall also eliminate wild beasts from the land, and no sword will pass through your land. 7 But you will pursue your enemies, and they will fall before you by the sword; 8 and five of you will pursue one hundred, and one hundred of you will pursue ten thousand, and your enemies will fall before you by the sword. 9 So I will turn toward you and make you fruitful and multiply you, and I will confirm My covenant with you. 10 And you will eat the old supply and clear out the old because of the new. 11 Moreover, I will make My dwelling among you, and My soul will not loathe you. 12 I will also walk among you and be your God, and you shall be My people. 13 I am Yahweh your God, who brought you out of the land of Egypt so that *you* would not be their slaves, and I broke the bars of your yoke and made you walk erect.

14 'But if you do not obey Me and do not do all these commandments, 15 if, instead, you reject My statutes, and if your soul loathes My judgments so as not to do all My commandments *and* so break My covenant, 16 I, in turn, will do this to you: I will appoint over you a sudden terror, consumption and fever that will waste away the eyes and cause the soul to pine away; also, you will sow your seed uselessly, for your enemies will eat it up. 17 And I will set My face against you so that you will be defeated before your enemies; and those who hate you will have dominion over you, and you will flee when no one is pursuing you. 18 If also after these things you do not obey Me, then I will discipline you seven times more for your sins. 19 I will also break down your pride of strength; I will also give your sky over *to become* like iron and your earth like bronze. 20 And your power will be spent uselessly, for your land will not give forth its produce and the trees of the land will not give forth their fruit.

21 'If then, you walk in hostility against Me and are unwilling to obey Me, I will increase the plague on you seven times according to your sins. 22 And I will send out among you the beasts of the field, which will bereave you of your children and cut down your cattle and reduce your number so that your roads lie desolate.

23 'And if by these things you do not accept My discipline, but walk in hostility against Me, 24 then I will walk in hostility against you; and I, even I, will strike you seven times for your sins. 25 I will also bring upon you a sword which will execute vengeance for the covenant; and when you gather together into your cities, I will send pestilence among you so that you shall be given over into enemy hands. 26 When I break your staff of bread, ten women will bake your bread in one oven, and they will bring back your bread by *rationed* weight so that you will eat and not become full.

27 'Yet, if in spite of this you do not obey Me, but walk in hostility against Me, 28 then I will walk in wrathful hostility against you, and I, even I, will discipline you seven times for your sins. 29 Further, you will eat the flesh of your sons, and the flesh of your daughters you will eat. 30 I then will destroy your high places and cut down your incense altars and give your corpses *to lie* on the corpses of your idols, for My soul shall loathe you. 31 And I will give your cities over as a waste and will make your sanctuaries desolate, and I will not smell your soothing aromas. 32 And I will make the land desolate, so that your enemies who inhabit it will *themselves* feel desolate because of it. 33 You, however, I will scatter among the nations and will draw out a sword after you, as your land becomes desolate and your cities become waste.

34 'Then the land will make up for its sabbaths all the days of the desolation, and

you will be in your enemies' land; then the land will rest and make up for its sabbaths. 35 All the days of *its* desolation it will observe the rest which it did not observe on your sabbaths, while you were living on it. 36 As for those of you who may remain, I will also bring weakness into their hearts in the lands of their enemies. And the sound of a driven leaf will pursue them, and even when no one is pursuing they will flee as though from the sword, and they will fall. 37 They will therefore stumble over each other as if *running* from the sword, although no one is pursuing; and you will have *no strength* to stand up before your enemies. 38 But you will perish among the nations, and your enemies' land will consume you. 39 So those of you who may remain will rot away in their iniquity in the lands of your enemies; and also in the iniquities of their fathers they will rot away with them.

40 'If they confess their iniquity and the iniquity of their fathers, in their unfaithfulness which they committed against Me, and also how they walked in hostility against Me— 41 I also was walking in hostility against them, to bring them into the land of their enemies—or if their uncircumcised heart becomes humbled so that they then make up for their iniquity, 42 then I will remember My covenant with Jacob, and I will remember also My covenant with Isaac and My covenant with Abraham as well, and I will remember the land. 43 For the land will be forsaken by them and will make up for its sabbaths while it is made desolate without them. They, meanwhile, will be making up for their iniquity because they rejected My judgments and their soul loathed My statutes. 44 Yet in spite of this, when they are in the land of their enemies, I will not reject them, nor will I so loathe them as to bring an end to them, breaking My covenant with them; for I am Yahweh their God. 45 But I will remember for them the covenant with their ancestors, whom I brought out of the land of Egypt in the sight of the nations, that I might be their God. I am Yahweh.'"

46 These are the statutes and judgments and laws which Yahweh has given *to be* between Himself and the sons of Israel by the hand of Moses at Mount Sinai.

27

Then Yahweh spoke to Moses, saying, 2 "Speak to the sons of Israel and say to them, 'When a man makes a difficult vow, he *shall be valued* according to your valuation of persons belonging to Yahweh. 3 If your valuation is of the male from twenty years even to sixty years old, then your valuation shall be fifty shekels of silver, according to the shekel of the sanctuary. 4 Or if it is a female, then your valuation shall be thirty shekels. 5 If it be from five years even to twenty years old then your valuation for the male shall be twenty shekels and for the female ten shekels. 6 But if *they are* from a month even up to five years old, then your valuation shall be five shekels of silver for the male, and for the female your valuation shall be three shekels of silver. 7 If *they are* from sixty years old and upward, if it is a male, then your valuation shall be fifteen shekels, and for the female ten shekels. 8 But if he is poorer than your valuation, then he shall be presented before the priest, and the priest shall value him; according to the means of the one who vowed, the priest shall value him.

9 'Now if it is an animal of the kind which men can bring near as an offering to Yahweh, any such that one gives to Yahweh shall be holy. 10 He shall not replace it or exchange it, a good for a bad, or a bad for a good; or if he does exchange animal for animal, then both it and its substitute shall become holy. 11 If, however, it is any unclean animal of the kind which men do not bring near as an offering to Yahweh, then he shall present the animal before the priest. 12 And the priest shall value it as either good or bad; as you, the priest, value it, so it shall be. 13 But if he should ever *wish to* redeem it, then he shall add one-fifth of it to your valuation.

14 'Now if a man sets his house apart as holy to Yahweh, then the priest shall value it as either good or bad; as the priest values it, so it shall stand. 15 Yet if the one who sets it apart as holy should *wish to* redeem his house, then he shall add one-fifth of your valuation price to it, so that it may be his.

16 'Again, if a man sets apart as holy to Yahweh a portion of the fields of his own possession, then your valuation shall be proportionate to the seed needed for it: a homer of barley seed at fifty shekels of silver. 17 If he sets apart his field as holy from the year of jubilee, according to your valuation it shall stand. 18 If he sets apart his field as holy after the jubilee, however, then the priest shall calculate the price for

him proportionate to the years that are
left until the year of jubilee; and it shall
be deducted from your valuation. 19 If the
one who sets it apart as holy should ever
wish to redeem the field, then he shall add
one-fifth of your valuation price to it so that
it may stand as his own. 20 Yet if he will not
redeem the field, but has sold the field to
another man, it may no longer be redeemed;
21 and it will be that when it reverts in the
jubilee, the field shall be holy to Yahweh,
like a field *that is* devoted; it shall be for
the priest as his possession. 22 Or if he sets
apart as holy to Yahweh a field which he
has bought, which is not a portion of the
field of his own possession, 23 then the
priest shall calculate for him the amount
of your valuation up to the year of jubilee;
and he shall on that day give your valuation
as holy to Yahweh. 24 In the year of jubilee
the field shall return to the one from whom
he bought it, to whom the possession of the
land belongs. 25 Every valuation of yours,
moreover, shall be according to the shekel
of the sanctuary. The shekel shall be twenty
gerahs.

26 'However, a firstborn among animals,
which as a firstborn belongs to Yahweh, no
man may set it apart as holy; whether ox or
sheep, it is Yahweh's. 27 But if *it is* among
the unclean animals, then he shall ransom
it according to your valuation and add to
it one-fifth of it; and if it is not redeemed,
then it shall be sold according to your
valuation.

28 'Nevertheless, anything which a man
devotes to Yahweh out of all that he has, of
man or animal or of the fields of his own
possession, shall not be sold or redeemed.
Anything devoted to destruction is most
holy to Yahweh. 29 No one who may have
been devoted among men shall be ran-
somed; he shall surely be put to death.

30 'Thus all the tithe of the land, of the
seed of the land or of the fruit of the tree,
belongs to Yahweh; it is holy to Yahweh. 31 If,
therefore, a man wishes to redeem part of
his tithe, he shall add to it one-fifth of it.
32 For every tenth part of herd or flock,
whatever passes under the rod, the tenth
one shall be holy to Yahweh. 33 He shall not
inquire whether *it is* good or bad, nor shall
he exchange it; or if he does exchange it,
then both it and its substitute shall become
holy. It shall not be redeemed.'"

34 These are the commandments which
Yahweh commanded Moses for the sons of
Israel at Mount Sinai.

Psalm 29:1–6

1 Ascribe to Yahweh, O sons
of the mighty,
Ascribe to Yahweh glory and strength.
2 Ascribe to Yahweh the
glory of His name;
Worship Yahweh in the
splendor of holiness.

3 The voice of Yahweh is
upon the waters;
The God of glory thunders,
Yahweh is over many waters.
4 The voice of Yahweh is powerful,
The voice of Yahweh is *full of* splendor.
5 The voice of Yahweh breaks the cedars;
Indeed, Yahweh breaks in pieces
the cedars of Lebanon.
6 He makes Lebanon skip like a calf,
And Sirion like a young wild ox.

Proverbs 10:22–25

22 It is the blessing of Yahweh
that makes rich,
And He adds no pain with it.
23 Doing wickedness is like
laughing to a fool,
And *so is* wisdom to a man
of discernment.
24 What the wicked dreads
will come upon him,
But the desire of the righteous
will be granted.
25 When the whirlwind passes,
the wicked is no more,
But the righteous *has* an
everlasting foundation.

Mark 7:1–13

7 And the Pharisees and some of the
scribes *gathered around Him when they
had come from Jerusalem, 2 and had seen
that some of His disciples were eating their
bread with defiled hands, that is, unwashed.
3 (For the Pharisees and all the Jews do not
eat unless they carefully wash their hands,
thus observing the tradition of the elders;
4 and *when they come* from the marketplace,
they do not eat unless they wash themselves;
and there are many other things which they
have received in order to observe, such as

the washing of cups and pitchers and copper
pots.) 5 And the Pharisees and the scribes
*asked Him, "Why do Your disciples not walk
according to the tradition of the elders, but
eat their bread with defiled hands?" 6 And He
said to them, "Rightly did Isaiah prophesy of
you hypocrites, as it is written:

'THIS PEOPLE HONORS ME
WITH THEIR LIPS,
BUT THEIR HEART IS FAR AWAY FROM ME.
7 'BUT IN VAIN DO THEY WORSHIP ME,
TEACHING AS DOCTRINES THE
COMMANDS OF MEN.'

8 "Leaving the commandment of God, you
hold to the tradition of men."

9 And He was also saying to them,
"You are good at setting aside the com-
mandment of God in order to keep your
tradition. 10 For Moses said, 'HONOR YOUR
FATHER AND YOUR MOTHER'; and, 'HE WHO
SPEAKS EVIL OF FATHER OR MOTHER, IS TO
BE PUT TO DEATH'; 11 but you say, 'If a man
says to *his* father or *his* mother, whatever
you might benefit from me is Corban (that
is to say, given *to God*),' 12 you no longer
leave him to do anything for *his* father or
his mother; 13 *thus* invalidating the word
of God by your tradition which you have
handed down; and you do many things
such as that."

MARCH 2

Numbers 1:1–2:34

1 Then Yahweh spoke to Moses in the wil-
derness of Sinai, in the tent of meeting,
on the first of the second month, in the
second year after they had come out of the
land of Egypt, saying, 2 "Take a census of all
the congregation of the sons of Israel, by
their families, by their fathers' households,
according to the number of names, every
male, head by head 3 from twenty years old
and upward, whoever *is able to* go out to
war in Israel, you and Aaron shall number
them by their armies. 4 With you, moreover,
there shall be a man of each tribe, each one
head of his father's household. 5 These then
are the names of the men who shall stand
with you:

of Reuben, Elizur the son of Shedeur;
6 of Simeon, Shelumiel the son of Zurishaddai;
7 of Judah, Nahshon the son of Amminadab;
8 of Issachar, Nethanel the son of Zuar;
9 of Zebulun, Eliab the son of Helon;
10 of the sons of Joseph:
of Ephraim, Elishama the son of Ammihud;
of Manasseh, Gamaliel the son of Pedahzur;
11 of Benjamin, Abidan the son of Gideoni;
12 of Dan, Ahiezer the son of Ammishaddai;
13 of Asher, Pagiel the son of Ochran;
14 of Gad, Eliasaph the son of Deuel;
15 of Naphtali, Ahira the son of Enan.

16 "These are they who were called *upon*
by the congregation, the leaders of their
fathers' tribes; they were the heads of
divisions of Israel."

17 So Moses and Aaron took these men
who had been designated by name, 18 and
they assembled all the congregation
together on the first of the second month.
Then they registered by genealogy in their
families, by their fathers' households,
according to the number of names, from
twenty years old and upward, head by head,
19 just as Yahweh had commanded Moses.
So he numbered them in the wilderness of
Sinai.

20 Now the sons of Reuben, Israel's
firstborn, their genealogical registration by
their families, by their fathers' households,
according to the number of names, head
by head, every male from twenty years old
and upward, whoever *was able to* go out to
war, 21 their numbered men of the tribe of
Reuben *were* 46,500.

22 Of the sons of Simeon, their genealog-
ical registration by their families, by their
fathers' households, their numbered men,
according to the number of names, head
by head, every male from twenty years old
and upward, whoever *was able to* go out to
war, 23 their numbered men of the tribe of
Simeon *were* 59,300.

24 Of the sons of Gad, their genealogical
registration by their families, by their
fathers' households, according to the
number of names, from twenty years old
and upward, whoever *was able to* go out to

war, 25 their numbered men of the tribe of Gad *were* 45,650.

26 Of the sons of Judah, their genealogical registration by their families, by their fathers' households, according to the number of names, from twenty years old and upward, whoever *was able to* go out to war, 27 their numbered men of the tribe of Judah *were* 74,600.

28 Of the sons of Issachar, their genealogical registration by their families, by their fathers' households, according to the number of names, from twenty years old and upward, whoever *was able to* go out to war, 29 their numbered men of the tribe of Issachar *were* 54,400.

30 Of the sons of Zebulun, their genealogical registration by their families, by their fathers' households, according to the number of names, from twenty years old and upward, whoever *was able to* go out to war, 31 their numbered men of the tribe of Zebulun *were* 57,400.

32 Of the sons of Joseph, *namely*, of the sons of Ephraim, their genealogical registration by their families, by their fathers' households, according to the number of names, from twenty years old and upward, whoever *was able to* go out to war, 33 their numbered men of the tribe of Ephraim *were* 40,500.

34 Of the sons of Manasseh, their genealogical registration by their families, by their fathers' households, according to the number of names, from twenty years old and upward, whoever *was able to* go out to war, 35 their numbered men of the tribe of Manasseh *were* 32,200.

36 Of the sons of Benjamin, their genealogical registration by their families, by their fathers' households, according to the number of names, from twenty years old and upward, whoever *was able to* go out to war, 37 their numbered men of the tribe of Benjamin *were* 35,400.

38 Of the sons of Dan, their genealogical registration by their families, by their fathers' households, according to the number of names, from twenty years old and upward, whoever *was able to* go out to war, 39 their numbered men of the tribe of Dan *were* 62,700.

40 Of the sons of Asher, their genealogical registration by their families, by their fathers' households, according to the number of names, from twenty years old and upward, whoever *was able to* go out to war, 41 their numbered men of the tribe of Asher *were* 41,500.

42 Of the sons of Naphtali, their genealogical registration by their families, by their fathers' households, according to the number of names, from twenty years old and upward, whoever *was able to* go out to war, 43 their numbered men of the tribe of Naphtali *were* 53,400.

44 These are the ones who were numbered, whom Moses and Aaron numbered, with the leaders of Israel, twelve men, each of whom was of his father's household. 45 So all the numbered men of the sons of Israel by their fathers' households, from twenty years old and upward, whoever *was able to* go out to war in Israel, 46 even all the numbered men were 603,550.

47 The Levites, however, were not numbered among them by their fathers' tribe. 48 Yahweh had spoken to Moses, saying, 49 "Only the tribe of Levi you shall not number, nor shall you take their census among the sons of Israel. 50 But you shall appoint the Levites over the tabernacle of the testimony and over all its furnishings and over all that belongs to it. They shall carry the tabernacle and all its furnishings, and they shall attend to it; they shall also camp around the tabernacle. 51 So when the tabernacle is to set out, the Levites shall take it down; and when the tabernacle encamps, the Levites shall set it up. But the layman who comes near shall be put to death. 52 And the sons of Israel shall camp, each man by his own camp, and each man by his own standard, according to their armies. 53 But the Levites shall camp around the tabernacle of the testimony so that there will be no wrath on the congregation of the sons of Israel. So the Levites shall keep charge of the tabernacle of the testimony." 54 Thus the sons of Israel did; according to all which Yahweh had commanded Moses, so they did.

2 Now Yahweh spoke to Moses and to Aaron, saying, 2 "The sons of Israel shall camp, each by his own standard, with the banners of their fathers' households; they shall camp around the tent of meeting at a distance. 3 Now those who camp on the east side toward the sunrise *shall be* of the standard of the camp of Judah, by their

armies, and the leader of the sons of Judah:
Nahshon the son of Amminadab, 4 and his
army, even their numbered men, 74,600.
5 Those who camp next to him *shall be* the
tribe of Issachar, and the leader of the sons
of Issachar: Nethanel the son of Zuar, 6 and
his army, even his numbered men, 54,400.
7 *Then* the tribe of Zebulun, and the leader
of the sons of Zebulun: Eliab the son of
Helon, 8 and his army, even his numbered
men, 57,400. 9 The total of the numbered
men of the camp of Judah: 186,400, by their
armies. They shall set out first.

10 "On the south side *shall be* the standard
of the camp of Reuben by their armies, and
the leader of the sons of Reuben: Elizur the
son of Shedeur, 11 and his army, even his
numbered men, 46,500. 12 And those who
camp next to him *shall be* the tribe of Sim-
eon, and the leader of the sons of Simeon:
Shelumiel the son of Zurishaddai, 13 and his
army, even their numbered men, 59,300.
14 Then the tribe of Gad, and the leader of
the sons of Gad: Eliasaph the son of Deuel,
15 and his army, even their numbered men,
45,650. 16 The total of the numbered men of
the camp of Reuben: 151,450 by their armies.
And they shall set out second.

17 "Then the tent of meeting shall set out
with the camp of the Levites in the midst of
the camps; just as they camp, so they shall
set out, every man in his place by their
standards.

18 "On the west side *shall be* the standard
of the camp of Ephraim by their armies, and
the leader of the sons of Ephraim: Elishama
the son of Ammihud, 19 and his army, even
their numbered men, 40,500. 20 Next to
him *shall be* the tribe of Manasseh, and the
leader of the sons of Manasseh: Gamaliel
the son of Pedahzur, 21 and his army, even
their numbered men, 32,200. 22 Then the
tribe of Benjamin, and the leader of the sons
of Benjamin: Abidan the son of Gideoni,
23 and his army, even their numbered men,
35,400. 24 The total of the numbered men
of the camp of Ephraim: 108,100, by their
armies. And they shall set out third.

25 "On the north side *shall be* the standard
of the camp of Dan by their armies, and the
leader of the sons of Dan: Ahiezer the son
of Ammishaddai, 26 and his army, even their
numbered men, 62,700. 27 Those who camp
next to him *shall be* the tribe of Asher, and
the leader of the sons of Asher: Pagiel the
son of Ochran, 28 and his army, even their
numbered men, 41,500. 29 Then the tribe
of Naphtali, and the leader of the sons of
Naphtali: Ahira the son of Enan, 30 and his
army, even their numbered men, 53,400.
31 The total of the numbered men of the
camp of Dan *was* 157,600. They shall set
out last by their standards."

32 These are the numbered men of the
sons of Israel by their fathers' households;
the total of the numbered men of the
camps by their armies, 603,550. 33 The
Levites, however, were not numbered
among the sons of Israel, just as Yahweh
had commanded Moses. 34 Thus the sons
of Israel did; according to all that Yahweh
commanded Moses, so they camped by
their standards, and so they set out, every
one by his family according to his father's
household.

Psalm 29:7–11

7 The voice of Yahweh hews
out flames of fire.
8 The voice of Yahweh causes the
wilderness to tremble;
Yahweh causes the wilderness
of Kadesh to tremble.
9 The voice of Yahweh makes
the deer to calve
And strips the forests bare;
And in His temple everything
says, "Glory!"

10 Yahweh sat *enthroned over* the flood;
Indeed, Yahweh sits as King forever.
11 Yahweh will give strength
to His people;
Yahweh will bless His
people with peace.

Proverbs 10:26–29

26 Like vinegar to the teeth and
like smoke to the eyes,
So is the sluggard to those
who send him.
27 The fear of Yahweh prolongs life,
But the years of the wicked
will be shortened.
28 The expectation of the
righteous is gladness,
But the hope of the wicked will perish.
29 The way of Yahweh is a stronghold
to the one with integrity,
But ruin to the workers of iniquity.

Mark 7:14–37

14 And after He called the crowd to Him again, He *began* saying to them, “Listen to Me, all of you, and understand: 15 there is nothing outside the man which can defile him if it goes into him; but the things which proceed out of the man are what defile the man. 16 [And if anyone has ears to hear, let him hear.”]

17 And when He had left the crowd *and* entered the house, His disciples were asking Him about the parable. 18 And He *said to them, “Are you lacking understanding in this way as well? Do you not perceive that whatever goes into the man from outside cannot defile him, 19 because it does not go into his heart, but into his stomach, and goes to the sewer?” (*Thus He* declared all foods clean.) 20 And He was saying, “That which proceeds out of the man, that is what defiles the man. 21 For from within, out of the heart of men, proceed the evil thoughts, sexual immoralities, thefts, murders, adulteries, 22 coveting, wickedness, deceit, sensuality, envy, slander, pride, *and* foolishness. 23 All these evil things proceed from within and defile the man.”

24 Now Jesus stood up and went away from there to the region of Tyre. And when He had entered a house, He was wanting no one to know *of it*; yet He could not escape notice. 25 But after hearing of Him, a woman whose little daughter had an unclean spirit immediately came and fell at His feet. 26 Now the woman was a Greek, of Syrophoenician descent. And she kept asking Him to cast the demon out of her daughter. 27 And He was saying to her, “Let the children be satisfied first, for it is not good to take the children’s bread and throw it to the dogs.” 28 But she answered and *said to Him, “Yes, Lord, *but* even the dogs under the table feed on the children’s crumbs.” 29 And He said to her, “Because of this answer go; the demon has gone out of your daughter.” 30 And going back to her home, she found the child lying on the bed, the demon having left.

31 And again He went out from the region of Tyre, and came through Sidon to the Sea of Galilee, within the region of the Decapolis. 32 And they *brought to Him one who was deaf and spoke with difficulty, and they *pleaded with Him to lay His hand on him. 33 And Jesus took him aside from the crowd, by himself, and put His fingers into his ears, and after spitting, He touched his tongue; 34 and looking up to heaven with a sigh, He *said to him, “Ephphatha!” that is, “Be opened!” 35 And his ears were opened, and the impediment of his tongue was removed, and he *began* speaking plainly. 36 And He gave them orders not to tell anyone; but the more He was ordering them, the more widely they continued to proclaim it. 37 And they were utterly astonished, saying, “He has done all things well; He makes even the deaf to hear and the mute to speak.”

MARCH 3

Numbers 3:1–4:49

3 Now these are the generations of Aaron and Moses at the time when Yahweh spoke with Moses on Mount Sinai. 2 These then are the names of the sons of Aaron: Nadab the firstborn, and Abihu, Eleazar and Ithamar. 3 These are the names of the sons of Aaron, the anointed priests, whom he ordained to minister as priests. 4 But Nadab and Abihu died before Yahweh when they offered strange fire before Yahweh in the wilderness of Sinai; and they had no children. So Eleazar and Ithamar ministered as priests in the lifetime of their father Aaron.

5 Then Yahweh spoke to Moses, saying, 6 “Bring the tribe of Levi near and have them stand before Aaron the priest, that they may minister to him. 7 And they shall keep his responsibility and the responsibility for the whole congregation before the tent of meeting, to perform the service of the tabernacle. 8 They shall also keep all the furnishings of the tent of meeting, along with the responsibility of the sons of Israel, to perform the service of the tabernacle. 9 You shall thus give the Levites to Aaron and to his sons; they are wholly given to him from among the sons of Israel. 10 So you shall appoint Aaron and his sons that they may keep their priesthood, but the outsider who comes near shall be put to death.”

11 Then Yahweh spoke to Moses, saying, 12 “Now, behold, I have taken the Levites from among the sons of Israel instead of

every firstborn, the first offspring of the
womb among the sons of Israel. So the Lev-
ites shall be Mine. 13 For all the firstborn are
Mine; on the day that I struck down all the
firstborn in the land of Egypt, I sanctified to
Myself all the firstborn in Israel, from man
to beast. They shall be Mine; I am Yahweh."
14 Then Yahweh spoke to Moses in the
wilderness of Sinai, saying, 15 "Number the
sons of Levi by their fathers' households, by
their families; every male from a month old
and upward you shall number." 16 So Moses
numbered them according to the word of
Yahweh, just as he had been commanded.
17 These then are the sons of Levi by their
names:
Gershon and Kohath and Merari.
18 And these are the names of the sons of
Gershon by their families:
Libni and Shimei;
19 and the sons of Kohath by their
families:
Amram and Izhar, Hebron and Uzziel;
20 and the sons of Merari by their
families:
Mahli and Mushi. These are the
families of the Levites according to
their fathers' households.
21 Of Gershon *was* the family of the
Libnites and the family of the Shimeites;
these *were* the families of the Gershonites.
22 Their numbered men, in the numbering
of every male from a month old and upward,
even their numbered men *were* 7,500. 23 The
families of the Gershonites were to camp
behind the tabernacle westward, 24 and
the leader of the fathers' households of the
Gershonites *was* Eliasaph the son of Lael.
25 Now the responsibility of the sons of
Gershon in the tent of meeting *involved* the
tabernacle and the tent, its covering, and
the screen for the doorway of the tent of
meeting, 26 and the hangings of the court,
and the screen for the doorway of the
court which is around the tabernacle and
the altar, and its cords, according to all the
service concerning them.
27 Of Kohath *was* the family of the
Amramites and the family of the Izharites
and the family of the Hebronites and the
family of the Uzzielites; these were the fam-
ilies of the Kohathites. 28 In the numbering
of every male from a month old and upward,
there were 8,600, keeping the responsibility
of the sanctuary. 29 The families of the sons
of Kohath were to camp on the southward
side of the tabernacle, 30 and the leader of
the fathers' households of the Kohathite
families was Elizaphan the son of Uzziel.
31 Now their responsibility *involved* the ark,
the table, the lampstand, the altars, and the
utensils of the sanctuary with which they
minister, and the screen, and all the service
concerning them; 32 and Eleazar the son of
Aaron the priest *was* the chief of the leaders
of Levi *and had* the oversight of those who
keep the responsibility of the sanctuary.
33 Of Merari *was* the family of the
Mahlites and the family of the Mushites;
these *were* the families of Merari. 34 And
their numbered men, in the numbering of
every male from a month old and upward,
were 6,200. 35 And the leader of the fathers'
households of the families of Merari *was*
Zuriel the son of Abihail. They *were* to camp
on the northward side of the tabernacle.
36 Now the appointed responsibility of the
sons of Merari *involved* the boards of the
tabernacle, its bars, its pillars, its bases, all
its equipment, and the service concerning
them, 37 and the pillars around the court
with their bases and their pegs and their
cords.
38 Now those who were to camp before
the tabernacle eastward, before the tent of
meeting toward the sunrise, are Moses and
Aaron and his sons, keeping the responsibil-
ity of the sanctuary for the responsibility of
the sons of Israel; but the outsider coming
near was to be put to death. 39 All the
numbered men of the Levites, whom Moses
and Aaron numbered at the command of
Yahweh by their families, every male from
a month old and upward, *were* 22,000.
40 Then Yahweh said to Moses, "Number
every firstborn male of the sons of Israel
from a month old and upward, and make
a list of their names. 41 And you shall take
the Levites for Me, I am Yahweh, instead of
all the firstborn among the sons of Israel,
and the cattle of the Levites instead of all
the firstborn among the cattle of the sons
of Israel." 42 So Moses numbered all the
firstborn among the sons of Israel, just as
Yahweh had commanded him; 43 and all the
firstborn males by the number of names
from a month old and upward, for their
numbered men were 22,273.
44 Then Yahweh spoke to Moses, saying,
45 "Take the Levites instead of all the

firstborn among the sons of Israel and the cattle of the Levites. And the Levites shall be Mine; I am Yahweh. [46] For the redemption price of the 273 of the firstborn of the sons of Israel who are in excess beyond the Levites, [47] you shall take five shekels apiece, per head; you shall take *them* in terms of the shekel of the sanctuary (the shekel is twenty gerahs), [48] and give the money, the redemption price of those who are in excess among them, to Aaron and to his sons." [49] So Moses took the money of the redemption price from those who were in excess, beyond those redeemed by the Levites; [50] from the firstborn of the sons of Israel he took the money in terms of the shekel of the sanctuary, 1,365. [51] Then Moses gave the money of the redemption price to Aaron and to his sons, at the command of Yahweh, just as Yahweh had commanded Moses.

4 Then Yahweh spoke to Moses and to Aaron, saying, [2] "Take a census of the descendants of Kohath from among the sons of Levi, by their families, by their fathers' households, [3] from thirty years and upward, even to fifty years old, all who enter the duty of doing the work in the tent of meeting. [4] This is the service of the sons of Kohath in the tent of meeting, *concerning* the most holy things.

[5] "And *when* the camp sets out, Aaron and his sons shall go in and they shall take down the veil of the screen and cover the ark of the testimony with it; [6] and they shall put a covering of porpoise skin on it and shall spread over *it* a cloth of pure blue and shall insert its poles. [7] Over the table of the bread of the Presence they shall also spread a cloth of blue and put on it the dishes and the pans and the offering bowls and the jars for the drink offering, and the continual bread shall be on it. [8] And they shall spread over them a cloth of scarlet *material* and cover the same with a covering of porpoise skin, and they shall insert its poles. [9] Then they shall take a blue cloth and cover the lampstand for the light, along with its lamps and its tongs, and its trays and all its oil vessels, by which they minister in connection to it; [10] and they shall put it and all its utensils in a covering of porpoise skin and shall put it on the carrying bars. [11] And over the golden altar they shall spread a blue cloth and cover it with a covering of porpoise skin and shall insert its poles; [12] and they shall take all the utensils of ministry, with which they minister in the sanctuary, and put them in a blue cloth and cover them with a covering of porpoise skin and put them on the carrying bars. [13] Then they shall take away the ashes from the altar and spread a purple cloth over it. [14] They shall also put on it all its utensils by which they minister in connection with it: the firepans, the flesh hooks and shovels and the bowls, all the utensils of the altar; and they shall spread a cover of porpoise skin over it and insert its poles. [15] When Aaron and his sons have finished covering the holy *objects* and all the furnishings of the sanctuary, when the camp is to set out, after that the sons of Kohath shall come to carry *them*, so that they will not touch the holy *objects* and die. These are the things in the tent of meeting which the sons of Kohath are to carry.

[16] "And the assignment of Eleazar the son of Aaron the priest is the oil for the light and the fragrant incense and the continual grain offering and the anointing oil—the assignment of all the tabernacle and of all that is in it, with the sanctuary and its furnishings."

[17] Then Yahweh spoke to Moses and to Aaron, saying, [18] "Do not let the tribe of the families of the Kohathites be cut off from among the Levites. [19] But do this to them that they may live and not die when they approach the most holy *objects*: Aaron and his sons shall go in and set each of them to his service and to his load; [20] but they shall not go in to see the holy *objects* even for a moment, or they will die."

[21] Then Yahweh spoke to Moses, saying, [22] "Take a census of the sons of Gershon also, by their fathers' households, by their families; [23] from thirty years and upward to fifty years old, you shall number them; all who enter to perform the duty of performing the service in the tent of meeting. [24] This is the service of the families of the Gershonites, in serving and in carrying: [25] they shall carry the curtains of the tabernacle and the tent of meeting *with* its covering and the covering of porpoise skin that is on top of it, and the screen for the doorway of the tent of meeting, [26] and the hangings of the court, and the screen for the doorway of the gate of the court which is around the tabernacle and the altar, and

their cords and all the equipment for their
service; and all that is to be done, they shall
perform. 27 All the service of the sons of the
Gershonites, in all their loads and in all their
service, shall be *performed* at the command
of Aaron and his sons; and you shall assign
to them as a responsibility all their loads.
28 This is the service of the families of
the sons of the Gershonites in the tent of
meeting, and their responsibilities *shall be*
under the direction of Ithamar the son of
Aaron the priest.

29 "*As for* the sons of Merari, you shall
number them by their families, by their
fathers' households; 30 from thirty years
and upward even to fifty years old, you shall
number them, everyone who enters the
duty of performing the service of the tent
of meeting. 31 Now this is the responsibility
of their loads, for all their service in the tent
of meeting: the boards of the tabernacle and
its bars and its pillars and its bases, 32 and
the pillars around the court and their bases
and their pegs and their cords, with all their
equipment and with all their service; and
you shall assign *each man* by name the items
of the responsibility of his load. 33 This is the
service of the families of the sons of Merari,
according to all their service in the tent of
meeting, under the direction of Ithamar the
son of Aaron the priest."

34 So Moses and Aaron and the leaders
of the congregation numbered the sons
of the Kohathites by their families and by
their fathers' households, 35 from thirty
years and upward even to fifty years old,
everyone who entered the duty of service
in the tent of meeting. 36 Their numbered
men by their families were 2,750. 37 These
are the numbered men of the Kohathite
families, everyone who was serving in the
tent of meeting, whom Moses and Aaron
numbered according to the commandment
of Yahweh by the hand of Moses.

38 The numbered men of the sons of
Gershon by their families and by their
fathers' households, 39 from thirty years
and upward even to fifty years old, every-
one who entered the duty of service in
the tent of meeting, 40 their numbered
men by their families, by their fathers'
households, were 2,630. 41 These are the
numbered men of the families of the sons of
Gershon, everyone who was serving in the
tent of meeting, whom Moses and Aaron
numbered according to the commandment
of Yahweh.

42 The numbered men of the families
of the sons of Merari by their families, by
their fathers' households, 43 from thirty
years and upward even to fifty years old,
everyone who entered the duty of service in
the tent of meeting, 44 their numbered men
by their families were 3,200. 45 These are the
numbered men of the families of the sons of
Merari, whom Moses and Aaron numbered
according to the commandment of Yahweh
by the hand of Moses.

46 All the numbered men of the Levites,
whom Moses and Aaron and the leaders of
Israel numbered, by their families and by
their fathers' households, 47 from thirty
years and upward even to fifty years old,
everyone who could enter to perform the
work of service and the service of carrying
in the tent of meeting, 48 their numbered
men were 8,580. 49 According to the word
of Yahweh by the hand of Moses, they were
numbered, everyone by his serving or carry-
ing; thus *these were* his numbered men, just
as Yahweh had commanded Moses.

Psalm 30:1–7

1 I will exalt You, O Yahweh, for
You have lifted me up,
And have not let my enemies
be glad over me.
2 O Yahweh my God,
I cried to You for help, and
You healed me.
3 O Yahweh, You have brought
up my soul from Sheol;
You have kept me alive, that I
would not go down to the pit.
4 Sing praise to Yahweh,
you His holy ones,
And give thanks for the
remembrance of His holy *name*.
5 For His anger is but for
a moment,
His favor is for a lifetime;
Weeping may last for the night,
But a shout of joy *comes*
in the morning.

6 Now as for me, I said in my prosperity,
"I will never be shaken."
7 O Yahweh, by Your favor You have
made my mountain to stand strong;
You hid Your face, I was dismayed.

Proverbs 10:30–32

30 The righteous will never be shaken,
But the wicked will not
dwell in the land.
31 The mouth of the righteous
bears wisdom,
But the tongue of perversions
will be cut out.
32 The lips of the righteous know
what is acceptable,
But the mouth of the wicked
what is perverse.

Mark 8:1–21

8 In those days, when there was again a large crowd and they had nothing to eat, Jesus called His disciples and *said to them, 2 "I feel compassion for the crowd because they have remained with Me now three days and have nothing to eat. 3 And if I send them away hungry to their homes, they will faint on the way; and some of them have come from a great distance." 4 And His disciples answered Him, "Where will anyone be able *to find enough* bread here in *this* desolate place to satisfy these people?" 5 And He was asking them, "How many loaves do you have?" And they said, "Seven." 6 And He *directed the crowd to sit down on the ground; and taking the seven loaves, He gave thanks and broke them. And He kept giving them to His disciples to serve to them, and they served them to the crowd. 7 And they also had a few small fish; and after He blessed them, He ordered these to be served as well. 8 And they ate and were satisfied; and they picked up seven *large* baskets full of what was left over of the broken pieces. 9 Now about four thousand were *there*, and He sent them away. 10 And immediately He entered the boat with His disciples and came to the district of Dalmanutha.

11 And the Pharisees came out and began to argue with Him, seeking from Him a sign from heaven, testing Him. 12 And sighing deeply in His spirit, He *said, "Why does this generation seek a sign? Truly I say to you, no sign will be given to this generation." 13 And leaving them, He again embarked and went away to the other side.

14 And they had forgotten to take bread, and did not have more than one loaf in the boat with them. 15 And He was giving orders to them, saying, "Watch out! Beware of the leaven of the Pharisees and the leaven of Herod." 16 And they *began to* discuss with one another *the fact* that they had no bread. 17 And Jesus, aware of this, *said to them, "Why do you discuss *the fact* that you have no bread? Do you not yet perceive or understand? Do you have a hardened heart? 18 HAVING EYES, DO YOU NOT SEE? AND HAVING EARS, DO YOU NOT HEAR? And do you not remember, 19 when I broke the five loaves for the five thousand, how many baskets full of broken pieces you picked up?" They *said to Him, "Twelve." 20 "When *I broke* the seven for the four thousand, how many *large* baskets full of broken pieces did you pick up?" And they *said to Him, "Seven." 21 And He was saying to them, "Do you not yet understand?"

MARCH 4

Numbers 5:1–6:27

5 Then Yahweh spoke to Moses, saying, 2 "Command the sons of Israel that they send away from the camp every leper and everyone having a discharge and everyone who is unclean because of a *dead* person. 3 You shall send away both male and female; you shall send them outside the camp so that they will not defile their camp where I dwell in their midst." 4 And the sons of Israel did so and sent them outside the camp; just as Yahweh had spoken to Moses, thus the sons of Israel did.

5 Then Yahweh spoke to Moses, saying, 6 "Speak to the sons of Israel, 'When a man or woman commits any of the sins of mankind, acting unfaithfully against Yahweh, and that person is guilty, 7 then he shall confess his sins which he has committed, and he shall make restitution in full for his wrong and add to it one-fifth of it and give *it* to him whom he has wronged. 8 But if the man has no *kinsman* redeemer to whom restitution may be made for the wrong, the restitution which is made for the wrong *must go* to Yahweh for the priest, besides the ram of atonement, by which atonement is made for him. 9 Also every contribution pertaining to all the holy *gifts* of the sons of Israel, which they bring near to the priest,

shall be his. 10 So every man's holy *gifts* shall be his; whatever any man gives to the priest, it becomes his.'"

11 Then Yahweh spoke to Moses, saying, 12 "Speak to the sons of Israel and say to them, 'If any man's wife goes astray and is unfaithful to him, 13 and a man lies sexually with her, and it is hidden from the eyes of her husband, and she is undetected; but she has defiled herself, and there is no witness against her, and she has not been caught in the act, 14 if a spirit of jealousy comes over him and he is jealous of his wife and she has defiled herself, or if a spirit of jealousy comes over him and he is jealous of his wife but she has not defiled herself, 15 the man shall then bring his wife to the priest and shall bring *as* an offering for her one-tenth of an ephah of barley meal; he shall not pour oil on it nor put frankincense on it, for it is a grain offering of jealousy, a grain offering of remembrance, a reminder of iniquity.

16 'Then the priest shall bring her near and have her stand before Yahweh, 17 and the priest shall take holy water in an earthenware vessel; and the priest shall take some of the dust that is on the floor of the tabernacle and put *it* into the water. 18 The priest shall then have the woman stand before Yahweh and let *the hair of* the woman's head go loose, and he shall place the grain offering of remembrance in her hands, which is the grain offering of jealousy; and in the hand of the priest is to be the water of bitterness that brings curses. 19 Then the priest shall have her swear *an oath* and shall say to the woman, "If no man has lain with you, and if you have not gone astray into defilement, *being* under *the authority of* your husband, be free from this water of bitterness that brings curses; 20 if you, however, have gone astray, *being* under *the authority of* your husband, and if you have defiled yourself, and a man other than your husband has lain with you" 21 (then the priest shall have the woman swear with the oath of the curse, and the priest shall say to the woman), "Yahweh make you a curse and an oath among your people by Yahweh making your thigh fall away and your abdomen swell; 22 and this water that brings curses shall go into your stomach and make your abdomen swell and your thigh fall away." And the woman shall say, "Amen. Amen."

23 'The priest shall then write these curses on a scroll, and he shall wash them off into the water of bitterness. 24 Then he shall make the woman drink the water of bitterness that brings curses, so that the water which brings a curse will go into her to cause bitterness. 25 And the priest shall take the grain offering of jealousy from the woman's hand, and he shall wave the grain offering before Yahweh and bring it near to the altar; 26 and the priest shall take a handful of the grain offering as its memorial offering and offer *it* up in smoke on the altar, and afterward he shall make the woman drink the water. 27 So he will have her drink the water, and it will be that, if she has defiled herself and has been unfaithful to her husband, that the water which brings curses will go into her to *cause* bitterness, and her abdomen will swell and her thigh will fall away, and the woman will become a curse among her people. 28 But if the woman has not defiled herself and is clean, she will then be free and conceive a seed.

29 'This is the law of jealousy: when a wife, *being* under *the authority of* her husband, goes astray and defiles herself, 30 or when a spirit of jealousy comes over a man and he is jealous of his wife, he shall then make the woman stand before Yahweh, and the priest shall apply all this law to her. 31 Moreover, the man will be free from guilt, but that woman shall bear her guilt.'"

6 Again Yahweh spoke to Moses, saying, 2 "Speak to the sons of Israel and say to them, 'When a man or woman makes a special vow, the vow of a Nazirite, to dedicate himself as a Nazirite to Yahweh, 3 he shall abstain as a Nazirite from wine and strong drink; he shall drink no vinegar, whether made from wine or strong drink, nor shall he drink any grape juice nor eat fresh or dried grapes. 4 All the days of his Nazirite *vow* he shall not eat anything that is produced by the grape vine, from *the* seeds even to *the* skin.

5 'All the days of his vow as a Nazirite no razor shall pass over his head. He shall be holy until the days are fulfilled for which he dedicated himself as a Nazirite to Yahweh; he shall let the locks of hair on his head grow long.

6 'All the days of his dedication as a Nazirite to Yahweh he shall not go near to a dead

person. 7 He shall not defile himself for his
father or for his mother, for his brother or
for his sister, when they die, because the
Nazirite *vow* to his God is on his head. 8 All
the days of his Nazirite *vow* he is holy to
Yahweh.
9 'But if a man dies very suddenly beside
him and he defiles the head *of hair during*
his Nazirite *vow*, then he shall shave his
head on the day when he becomes clean; he
shall shave it on the seventh day. 10 Then on
the eighth day he shall bring two turtledoves
or two young pigeons to the priest, to the
doorway of the tent of meeting. 11 And the
priest shall offer one for a sin offering and
the other for a burnt offering and make
atonement for him concerning his sin
because of the *dead* person. And that same
day he shall set apart his head as holy, 12 and
shall dedicate to Yahweh the days of his
Nazirite *vow* and shall bring a male lamb a
year old for a guilt offering; but the former
days will be void because his Nazirite *vow*
was defiled.
13 'Now this is the law of the Nazirite
when the days of his Nazirite *vow* are
fulfilled: he shall bring the offering to the
doorway of the tent of meeting. 14 And he
shall bring his offering near to Yahweh:
one male lamb a year old without blemish
for a burnt offering and one ewe-lamb a
year old without blemish for a sin offering
and one ram without blemish for a peace
offering, 15 and a basket of unleavened cakes
of fine flour mixed with oil and unleavened
wafers spread with oil, along with their grain
offering and their drink offering. 16 Then the
priest shall bring *them* near before Yahweh
and shall offer his sin offering and his burnt
offering. 17 He shall also offer with the ram
a sacrifice of peace offerings to Yahweh,
together with the basket of unleavened
cakes; the priest shall likewise offer its grain
offering and its drink offering. 18 The Nazir-
ite shall then shave the head *of hair* for his
Nazirite *vow* at the doorway of the tent of
meeting and take the hair of his head of his
Nazirite *vow* and put *it* on the fire which is
under the sacrifice of peace offerings. 19 And
the priest shall take the ram's shoulder *when*
it has been boiled, and one unleavened cake
out of the basket and one unleavened wafer,
and shall put *them* on the hands of the
Nazirite after he has shaved the *hair* of his
Nazirite *vow*. 20 Then the priest shall wave
them for a wave offering before Yahweh. It is
holy for the priest, together with the breast
offered by waving and the thigh offered by
raising up; and afterward the Nazirite may
drink wine.'
21 "This is the law of the Nazirite who
vows his offering to Yahweh according to
his Nazirite *vow*, in addition to what *else* he
can afford; according to his vow which he
takes, so he shall do according to the law of
his Nazirite *vow*."
22 Then Yahweh spoke to Moses, saying,
23 "Speak to Aaron and to his sons, saying,
'Thus you shall bless the sons of Israel. You
shall say to them:

24 Yahweh bless you, and keep you;

25 Yahweh make His face shine on you,
And be gracious to you;
26 Yahweh lift up His face on you,
And give you peace.'

27 "So they shall invoke My name on the
sons of Israel, and I *then* will bless them."

Psalm 30:8–12

8 To You, O Yahweh, I called,
And to the Lord I made supplication:
9 "What profit is there in my blood,
if I go down to the pit?
Will the dust praise You? Will
it declare Your truth?

10 "Hear, O Yahweh, and be gracious to me;
O Yahweh, be my helper."
11 You have turned for me my
mourning into dancing;
You have loosed my sackcloth and
girded me with gladness,
12 That *my* glory may sing praise
to You and not be silent.
O Yahweh my God, I will give
thanks to You forever.

Proverbs 11:1–3

11 A deceptive balance is an
abomination to Yahweh,
But a just weight is His delight.
2 When arrogance comes,
then comes disgrace,
But with the meek is wisdom.
3 The integrity of the upright
will lead them,
But the crookedness of the
treacherous will destroy them.

Mark 8:22–38

22 And they *came to Bethsaida. And they *brought a blind man to Jesus and *pleaded with Him to touch him. 23 And taking the blind man by the hand, He brought him out of the village; and after spitting on his eyes and laying His hands on him, He was asking him, "Do you see anything?" 24 And he looked up and was saying, "I see men, for I see *them* like trees, walking around." 25 Then again He laid His hands on his eyes; and he looked intently and was restored, and *began to* see everything clearly. 26 And He sent him to his home, saying, "Do not even enter the village."

27 And Jesus went out, along with His disciples, to the villages of Caesarea Philippi; and on the way He was asking His disciples, saying to them, "Who do people say that I am?" 28 And they told Him, saying, "John the Baptist; and others *say* Elijah; but others, one of the prophets." 29 And He *continued* asking them, "But who do you say that I am?" Peter *answered and *said to Him, "You are the Christ." 30 And He warned them to tell no one about Him.

31 And He began to teach them that the Son of Man must suffer many things and be rejected by the elders and the chief priests and the scribes, and be killed, and after three days rise again. 32 And He was stating the matter openly. And Peter took Him aside and began to rebuke Him. 33 But turning around and seeing His disciples, He rebuked Peter and *said, "Get behind Me, Satan! For you are not setting your mind on God's interests, but man's."

34 And He summoned the crowd with His disciples, and said to them, "If anyone wishes to come after Me, he must deny himself, and take up his cross and follow Me. 35 For whoever wishes to save his life will lose it, but whoever loses his life for My sake and the gospel's will save it. 36 For what does it profit a man to gain the whole world, and forfeit his soul? 37 For what will a man give in exchange for his soul? 38 For whoever is ashamed of Me and My words in this adulterous and sinful generation, the Son of Man will also be ashamed of him when He comes in the glory of His Father with the holy angels."

The best evidence of the Bible's being the Word of God is to be found between its covers. It proves itself.

— CHARLES HODGE

MARCH 5

Numbers 7:1–8:26

7 Now it happened on the day that Moses had finished setting up the tabernacle, that he anointed it and set it apart as holy with all its furnishings and the altar and all its utensils; he anointed them and set them apart as holy. 2 Then the leaders of Israel, the heads of their fathers' households, brought an offering near (they were the leaders of the tribes; they were the ones who were over the numbered men). 3 And they brought their offering before Yahweh, six covered carts and twelve oxen, a cart for *every* two of the leaders and an ox for each one, and they brought them near before the tabernacle. 4 Then Yahweh spoke to Moses, saying, 5 "Accept *these things* from them, that they may be used in the service of the tent of meeting, and you shall give them to the Levites, *to* each man according to his service." 6 So Moses took the carts and the oxen and gave them to the Levites. 7 Two carts and four oxen he gave to the sons of Gershon, according to their service, 8 and four carts and eight oxen he gave to the sons of Merari, according to their service, under the direction of Ithamar the son of Aaron the priest. 9 But he did not give *any* to the sons of Kohath because theirs *was* the service of the holy *objects, which* they carried on the shoulder.

10 And the leaders brought near the dedication *offering* for the altar when it was anointed, so the leaders brought their offering near before the altar. 11 Then Yahweh said to Moses, "Let them bring their

offering near, one leader each day, for the dedication of the altar."

12 Now the one who brought his offering near on the first day was Nahshon the son of Amminadab, of the tribe of Judah; 13 and his offering *was* one silver dish whose weight *was* 130 *shekels*, one silver bowl of 70 shekels, according to the shekel of the sanctuary, both of them full of fine flour mixed with oil for a grain offering; 14 one gold pan of 10 *shekels*, full of incense; 15 one bull from the herd, one ram, one male lamb one year old, for a burnt offering; 16 one male goat for a sin offering; 17 and for the sacrifice of peace offerings, two oxen, five rams, five male goats, five male lambs one year old. This *was* the offering of Nahshon the son of Amminadab.

18 On the second day Nethanel the son of Zuar, leader of Issachar, brought *an offering* near; 19 he brought near as his offering one silver dish whose weight *was* 130 *shekels*, one silver bowl of 70 shekels, according to the shekel of the sanctuary, both of them full of fine flour mixed with oil for a grain offering; 20 one gold pan of 10 *shekels*, full of incense; 21 one bull from the herd, one ram, one male lamb one year old, for a burnt offering; 22 one male goat for a sin offering; 23 and for the sacrifice of peace offerings, two oxen, five rams, five male goats, five male lambs one year old. This *was* the offering of Nethanel the son of Zuar.

24 On the third day *it was* Eliab the son of Helon, leader of the sons of Zebulun; 25 his offering *was* one silver dish whose weight *was* 130 *shekels*, one silver bowl of 70 shekels, according to the shekel of the sanctuary, both of them full of fine flour mixed with oil for a grain offering; 26 one gold pan of 10 *shekels*, full of incense; 27 one bull from the herd, one ram, one male lamb one year old, for a burnt offering; 28 one male goat for a sin offering; 29 and for the sacrifice of peace offerings, two oxen, five rams, five male goats, five male lambs one year old. This *was* the offering of Eliab the son of Helon.

30 On the fourth day *it was* Elizur the son of Shedeur, leader of the sons of Reuben; 31 his offering *was* one silver dish whose weight *was* 130 *shekels*, one silver bowl of 70 shekels, according to the shekel of the sanctuary, both of them full of fine flour mixed with oil for a grain offering; 32 one gold pan of 10 *shekels*, full of incense; 33 one bull from the herd, one ram, one male lamb one year old, for a burnt offering; 34 one male goat for a sin offering; 35 and for the sacrifice of peace offerings, two oxen, five rams, five male goats, five male lambs one year old. This *was* the offering of Elizur the son of Shedeur.

36 On the fifth day *it was* Shelumiel the son of Zurishaddai, leader of the sons of Simeon; 37 his offering *was* one silver dish whose weight *was* 130 *shekels*, one silver bowl of 70 shekels, according to the shekel of the sanctuary, both of them full of fine flour mixed with oil for a grain offering; 38 one gold pan of 10 *shekels*, full of incense; 39 one bull from the herd, one ram, one male lamb one year old, for a burnt offering; 40 one male goat for a sin offering; 41 and for the sacrifice of peace offerings, two oxen, five rams, five male goats, five male lambs one year old. This *was* the offering of Shelumiel the son of Zurishaddai.

42 On the sixth day *it was* Eliasaph the son of Deuel, leader of the sons of Gad; 43 his offering *was* one silver dish whose weight *was* 130 *shekels*, one silver bowl of 70 shekels, according to the shekel of the sanctuary, both of them full of fine flour mixed with oil for a grain offering; 44 one gold pan of 10 *shekels*, full of incense; 45 one bull from the herd, one ram, one male lamb one year old, for a burnt offering; 46 one male goat for a sin offering; 47 and for the sacrifice of peace offerings, two oxen, five rams, five male goats, five male lambs one year old. This *was* the offering of Eliasaph the son of Deuel.

48 On the seventh day *it was* Elishama the son of Ammihud, leader of the sons of Ephraim; 49 his offering *was* one silver dish whose weight *was* 130 *shekels*, one silver bowl of 70 shekels, according to the shekel of the sanctuary, both of them full of fine flour mixed with oil for a grain offering; 50 one gold pan of 10 *shekels*, full of incense; 51 one bull from the herd, one ram, one male lamb one year old, for a burnt offering; 52 one male goat for a sin offering; 53 and for the sacrifice of peace offerings, two oxen, five rams, five male goats, five male lambs one year old. This *was* the offering of Elishama the son of Ammihud.

54 On the eighth day *it was* Gamaliel the son of Pedahzur, leader of the sons of

Manasseh; 55 his offering *was* one silver dish whose weight *was* 130 *shekels*, one silver bowl of 70 shekels, according to the shekel of the sanctuary, both of them full of fine flour mixed with oil for a grain offering; 56 one gold pan of 10 *shekels*, full of incense; 57 one bull from the herd, one ram, one male lamb one year old, for a burnt offering; 58 one male goat for a sin offering; 59 and for the sacrifice of peace offerings, two oxen, five rams, five male goats, five male lambs one year old. This *was* the offering of Gamaliel the son of Pedahzur.

60 On the ninth day *it was* Abidan the son of Gideoni, leader of the sons of Benjamin; 61 his offering *was* one silver dish whose weight *was* 130 *shekels*, one silver bowl of 70 shekels, according to the shekel of the sanctuary, both of them full of fine flour mixed with oil for a grain offering; 62 one gold pan of 10 *shekels*, full of incense; 63 one bull from the herd, one ram, one male lamb one year old, for a burnt offering; 64 one male goat for a sin offering; 65 and for the sacrifice of peace offerings, two oxen, five rams, five male goats, five male lambs one year old. This *was* the offering of Abidan the son of Gideoni.

66 On the tenth day *it was* Ahiezer the son of Ammishaddai, leader of the sons of Dan; 67 his offering *was* one silver dish whose weight *was* 130 *shekels*, one silver bowl of 70 shekels, according to the shekel of the sanctuary, both of them full of fine flour mixed with oil for a grain offering; 68 one gold pan of 10 *shekels*, full of incense; 69 one bull from the herd, one ram, one male lamb one year old, for a burnt offering; 70 one male goat for a sin offering; 71 and for the sacrifice of peace offerings, two oxen, five rams, five male goats, five male lambs one year old. This *was* the offering of Ahiezer the son of Ammishaddai.

72 On the eleventh day *it was* Pagiel the son of Ochran, leader of the sons of Asher; 73 his offering *was* one silver dish whose weight *was* 130 *shekels*, one silver bowl of 70 shekels, according to the shekel of the sanctuary, both of them full of fine flour mixed with oil for a grain offering; 74 one gold pan of 10 *shekels*, full of incense; 75 one bull from the herd, one ram, one male lamb one year old, for a burnt offering; 76 one male goat for a sin offering; 77 and for the sacrifice of peace offerings, two oxen, five rams, five male goats, five male lambs one year old. This *was* the offering of Pagiel the son of Ochran.

78 On the twelfth day *it was* Ahira the son of Enan, leader of the sons of Naphtali; 79 his offering *was* one silver dish whose weight *was* 130 *shekels*, one silver bowl of 70 shekels, according to the shekel of the sanctuary, both of them full of fine flour mixed with oil for a grain offering; 80 one gold pan of 10 *shekels*, full of incense; 81 one bull from the herd, one ram, one male lamb one year old, for a burnt offering; 82 one male goat for a sin offering; 83 and for the sacrifice of peace offerings, two oxen, five rams, five male goats, five male lambs one year old. This *was* the offering of Ahira the son of Enan.

84 This *was* the dedication *offering* for the altar from the leaders of Israel when it was anointed: twelve silver dishes, twelve silver bowls, twelve gold pans, 85 each silver dish *weighing* 130 *shekels* and each bowl 70; all the silver of the utensils *was* 2,400 *shekels*, according to the shekel of the sanctuary; 86 the twelve gold pans, full of incense, *weighing* 10 *shekels* apiece, according to the shekel of the sanctuary, all the gold of the pans 120 *shekels*; 87 all the oxen for the burnt offering twelve bulls, *all* the rams twelve, the male lambs one year old with their grain offering twelve, and the male goats for a sin offering twelve; 88 and all the oxen for the sacrifice of peace offerings 24 bulls, *all* the rams 60, the male goats 60, the male lambs one year old 60. This *was* the dedication *offering* for the altar after it was anointed.

89 Now when Moses went into the tent of meeting to speak with Him, he heard the voice speaking to him from above the mercy seat that was on the ark of the testimony, from between the two cherubim, so He spoke to him.

8 Then Yahweh spoke to Moses, saying, 2 "Speak to Aaron and say to him, 'When you mount the lamps, the seven lamps will give light in the front of the lampstand.'" 3 Aaron therefore did so; he mounted its lamps at the front of the lampstand, just as Yahweh had commanded Moses. 4 Now this was the workmanship of the lampstand, hammered work of gold; from its base to its flowers it was hammered work; according to the pattern which Yahweh had shown Moses, so he made the lampstand.

[5] Again Yahweh spoke to Moses, saying,
[6] "Take the Levites from among the sons of
Israel and cleanse them. [7] Thus you shall
do to them, for their cleansing: *sprinkle*
purifying water on them, and let them use
a razor over their whole body and wash
their clothes, and they will be clean. [8] Then
let them take a bull from the herd with its
grain offering, fine flour mixed with oil; and
a second bull from the herd you shall take
for a sin offering. [9] So you shall bring the
Levites near before the tent of meeting. You
shall also assemble the whole congregation
of the sons of Israel, [10] and bring the Levites
near before Yahweh; and the sons of Israel
shall lay their hands on the Levites. [11] Aaron
then shall present the Levites before Yahweh
as a wave offering from the sons of Israel,
that they may be *qualified* to perform the
service of Yahweh. [12] Now the Levites shall
lay their hands on the heads of the bulls;
then offer the one for a sin offering and
the other for a burnt offering to Yahweh, to
make atonement for the Levites. [13] And you
shall have the Levites stand before Aaron
and before his sons so as to present them
as a wave offering to Yahweh.
[14] "Thus you shall separate the Levites
from among the sons of Israel, and the
Levites shall be Mine. [15] Then after that
the Levites may go in to serve the tent of
meeting. But you shall cleanse them and
present them as a wave offering; [16] for they
are wholly given to Me from among the
sons of Israel. I have taken them for Myself
instead of every first issue of the womb, the
firstborn of all the sons of Israel. [17] For every
firstborn among the sons of Israel is Mine,
among the men and among the animals; on
the day that I struck down all the firstborn
in the land of Egypt I sanctified them for
Myself. [18] But I have taken the Levites
instead of every firstborn among the sons
of Israel. [19] And I have given the Levites as
a gift to Aaron and to his sons from among
the sons of Israel, to perform the service of
the sons of Israel at the tent of meeting and
to make atonement on behalf of the sons of
Israel, so that there will be no plague among
the sons of Israel by their coming near to
the sanctuary."
[20] Thus did Moses and Aaron and all
the congregation of the sons of Israel to
the Levites; according to all that Yahweh
had commanded Moses concerning the
Levites, so the sons of Israel did to them.
[21] The Levites, too, purified themselves from
sin and washed their clothes; and Aaron
presented them as a wave offering before
Yahweh. Aaron also made atonement for
them to cleanse them. [22] Then after that the
Levites went in to perform their service in
the tent of meeting before Aaron and before
his sons; just as Yahweh had commanded
Moses concerning the Levites, so they did
to them.
[23] Now Yahweh spoke to Moses, saying,
[24] "This is what *applies* to the Levites: from
twenty-five years old and upward they shall
enter to perform *their* duty in the service
of the tent of meeting. [25] But at the age of
fifty years they shall retire from *their* duty in
the service and not serve anymore. [26] They
may, however, minister to their brothers
in the tent of meeting in order to keep *up*
their responsibility, but they *themselves*
shall perform no service. Thus you shall
deal with the Levites concerning their
responsibilities."

Psalm 31:1–5

1 In You, O Yahweh, I have taken refuge;
Let me never be ashamed;
In Your righteousness protect me.
2 Incline Your ear to me,
deliver me quickly;
Be to me a rock of strength,
A fortress to save me.
3 For You are my high rock
and my fortress;
For Your name's sake You will
lead me and guide me.
4 You will bring me out of the net which
they have secretly laid for me,
For You are my strength.
5 Into Your hand I commit my spirit;
You have ransomed me,
O Yahweh, God of truth.

Proverbs 11:4–6

4 Wealth will not profit in
the day of wrath,
But righteousness will
deliver from death.
5 The righteousness of the blameless
will make his way straight,
But the wicked will fall by
his own wickedness.
6 The righteousness of the
upright will deliver them,

But the treacherous will be
captured by *their own* desire.

Mark 9:1–29

9 And Jesus was saying to them, "Truly I say to you, there are some of those who are standing here who will not taste death until they see the kingdom of God having come in power."

2 And six days later, Jesus *took with Him Peter and James and John, and *brought them up on a high mountain alone by themselves. And He was transfigured before them; 3 and His garments were shining intensely white, as no launderer on earth can whiten them. 4 And Elijah appeared to them along with Moses and they were conversing with Jesus. 5 And Peter answered and *said to Jesus, "Rabbi, it is good for us to be here; let us make three booths, one for You, and one for Moses, and one for Elijah." 6 For he did not know what to answer; for they became terrified. 7 Then a cloud formed, overshadowing them, and a voice came out of the cloud, "This is My beloved Son, listen to Him!" 8 And all at once when they looked around, they saw no one with them anymore, except Jesus alone.

9 And as they were coming down from the mountain, He gave them orders not to recount to anyone what they had seen, until the Son of Man rose from the dead. 10 And they seized upon that statement, arguing with one another what rising from the dead meant. 11 And they *began* asking Him, saying, "*Why is it* that the scribes say that Elijah must come first?" 12 And He said to them, "Elijah does first come and restore all things. And *yet* how is it written of the Son of Man that He will suffer many things and be treated with contempt? 13 But I say to you that Elijah has indeed come, and they did to him whatever they wished, just as it is written of him."

14 And when they came *back* to the disciples, they saw a large crowd around them, and scribes arguing with them. 15 And immediately, when the entire crowd saw Him, they were amazed. And as they ran up, they were greeting Him. 16 And He asked them, "What are you arguing with them?" 17 And one of the crowd answered Him, "Teacher, I brought You my son, possessed with a spirit which makes him mute; 18 and whenever it seizes him, it slams him *to the ground* and he foams *at the mouth*, and grinds his teeth and becomes rigid. I told Your disciples to cast it out, and they could not *do it*." 19 And He *answered them and *said, "O unbelieving generation, how long shall I be with you? How long shall I put up with you? Bring him to Me!" 20 And they brought the boy to Him. When he saw Him, immediately the spirit threw him into a convulsion, and falling to the ground, he *began* rolling around, foaming *at the mouth*. 21 And He asked his father, "How long has this been happening to him?" And he said, "From childhood. 22 And it has often thrown him both into the fire and into the water to destroy him. But if You can do anything, take pity on us and help us!" 23 And Jesus said to him, "'If You can?' All things are possible to him who believes." 24 Immediately the boy's father cried out and was saying, "I do believe; help my unbelief." 25 Now when Jesus saw that a crowd was rapidly gathering, He rebuked the unclean spirit, saying to it, "You mute and deaf spirit, I command you, come out of him and do not enter him again." 26 And after crying out and throwing him into terrible convulsions, it came out; and *the boy* became so much like a corpse that most *of them* said, "He is dead!" 27 But Jesus took him by the hand and raised him; and he stood up. 28 And when He came into the house, His disciples *began* questioning Him privately, "Why could we not cast it out?" 29 And He said to them, "This kind cannot come out by anything but prayer."

MARCH 6

Numbers 9:1–10:36

9 Thus Yahweh spoke to Moses in the wilderness of Sinai, in the first month of the second year after they had come out of the land of Egypt, saying, 2 "Now, let the sons of Israel observe the Passover at its appointed time. 3 On the fourteenth day of this month, at twilight, you shall observe it at its appointed time; you shall observe it according to all its statutes and according to all its judgments." 4 So Moses told the sons of Israel to celebrate the Passover.

5 And they celebrated the Passover in the
first *month*, on the fourteenth day of the
month, at twilight, in the wilderness of
Sinai; according to all that Yahweh had
commanded Moses, so the sons of Israel
did. 6 But there were *some* men who were
unclean because of a dead person, so that
they could not celebrate Passover on that
day; so they came near before Moses and
Aaron on that day. 7 And those men said
to him, "We are unclean because of a dead
person. *But* why are we restrained from
bringing near the offering of Yahweh at its
appointed time among the sons of Israel?"
8 Moses therefore said to them, "Wait, and
I will listen to what Yahweh will command
concerning you."

9 Then Yahweh spoke to Moses, saying,
10 "Speak to the sons of Israel, saying, 'If any
one of you or of your generations becomes
unclean because of a *dead* person, or is
on a distant journey, he may, however,
celebrate the Passover to Yahweh. 11 In the
second month on the fourteenth day at
twilight, they shall observe it; they shall eat
it with unleavened bread and bitter herbs.
12 They shall leave none of it until morning
nor break a bone of it; according to all the
statute of the Passover they shall celebrate
it. 13 But the man who is clean and is not on
a journey, and yet neglects to celebrate the
Passover, that person shall then be cut off
from his people, for he did not bring near
the offering of Yahweh at its appointed time.
That man will bear his sin. 14 If a sojourner
sojourns among you and celebrates the
Passover to Yahweh, according to the
statute of the Passover and according to its
judgment, so he shall do; you shall have one
statute, both for the sojourner and for the
native of the land.'"

15 Now on the day that the tabernacle was
erected the cloud covered the tabernacle,
the tent of the testimony, and in the evening
it was like the appearance of fire over the
tabernacle until morning. 16 So it was con-
tinuously; the cloud would cover it *by day*,
and the appearance of fire by night. 17 Now
whenever the cloud would go up from over
the tent, afterward the sons of Israel would
then set out; and in the place where the
cloud settled down, there the sons of Israel
would camp. 18 At the command of Yahweh
the sons of Israel would set out, and at the
command of Yahweh they would camp; as
long as the cloud settled over the taberna-
cle, they remained camped. 19 Even when
the cloud lingered over the tabernacle for
many days, the sons of Israel would keep the
charge of Yahweh and not set out. 20 If some-
times the cloud remained a few days over
the tabernacle, according to the command
of Yahweh they remained camped. Then
according to the command of Yahweh they
set out. 21 If sometimes the cloud remained
from evening until morning, when the cloud
was lifted in the morning, they would move
out; or *if it remained* in the daytime and at
night, whenever the cloud was lifted, they
would set out. 22 Whether it was two days
or a month or a year that the cloud lingered
over the tabernacle, dwelling above it, the
sons of Israel remained camped and did
not set out; but when it was lifted, they did
set out. 23 At the command of Yahweh they
camped, and at the command of Yahweh
they set out; they kept the charge of Yahweh,
according to the command of Yahweh by the
hand of Moses.

10 Yahweh spoke further to Moses,
saying, 2 "Make yourself two trum-
pets of silver, of hammered work you
shall make them; and you shall use them
for summoning the congregation and for
having the camps set out. 3 So both will be
blown, and all the congregation shall gather
themselves to you at the doorway of the
tent of meeting. 4 Yet if *only* one is blown,
then the leaders, the heads of the divisions
of Israel, shall assemble before you. 5 But
when you blow an alarm, the camps that are
pitched on the east side shall set out. 6 Then
you will blow an alarm the second time, and
the camps that are pitched on the south
side shall set out; an alarm is to be blown
for them to set out. 7 When convening the
assembly, however, you shall blow without
sounding an alarm. 8 The priestly sons of
Aaron, moreover, shall blow the trumpets;
and this shall be for you a perpetual statute
throughout your generations. 9 Now when
you go to war in your land against the adver-
sary who attacks you, then you shall sound
an alarm with the trumpets, that you may be
remembered before Yahweh your God and
be saved from your enemies. 10 Also in the
day of your gladness and in your appointed
feasts, and on the first *days* of your months,
you shall blow the trumpets over your

burnt offerings and over the sacrifices of
your peace offerings; and they shall be as a
remembrance of you before your God. I am
Yahweh your God."

11 Now it happened in the second year,
in the second month, on the twentieth of
the month, *that* the cloud was lifted from
over the tabernacle of the testimony; 12 and
the sons of Israel set out on their journeys
from the wilderness of Sinai. Then the
cloud settled down in the wilderness of
Paran. 13 So they moved out for the first
time according to the command of Yahweh
by the hand of Moses. 14 And the standard
of the camp of the sons of Judah, according
to their armies, set out first, with Nahshon
the son of Amminadab, over its army, 15 and
Nethanel the son of Zuar, over the tribal
army of the sons of Issachar; 16 and Eliab
the son of Helon over the tribal army of the
sons of Zebulun.

17 Then the tabernacle was taken down;
and the sons of Gershon and the sons of
Merari, who were carrying the tabernacle,
set out. 18 Next the standard of the camp of
Reuben, according to their armies, set out
with Elizur the son of Shedeur, over its army,
19 and Shelumiel the son of Zurishaddai
over the tribal army of the sons of Simeon,
20 and Eliasaph the son of Deuel over the
tribal army of the sons of Gad.

21 Then the Kohathites set out, carrying
the holy *objects*; and the tabernacle was set
up before their arrival. 22 Next the standard
of the camp of the sons of Ephraim, accord-
ing to their armies, set out, with Elishama
the son of Ammihud over its army, 23 and
Gamaliel the son of Pedahzur over the
tribal army of the sons of Manasseh; 24 and
Abidan the son of Gideoni over the tribal
army of the sons of Benjamin.

25 Then the standard of the camp of the
sons of Dan, according to their armies,
which formed the rear guard for all the
camps, set out, with Ahiezer the son of
Ammishaddai over its army, 26 and Pagiel
the son of Ochran over the tribal army of the
sons of Asher; 27 and Ahira the son of Enan
over the tribal army of the sons of Naphtali.
28 This was the order of march of the sons of
Israel by their armies as they set out.

29 Then Moses said to Hobab the son of
Reuel the Midianite, Moses' father-in-law,
"We are setting out to the place of which
Yahweh said, 'I will give it to you'; come with
us and we will do you good, for Yahweh has
promised good concerning Israel." 30 But he
said to him, "I will not come, but rather will
go to my *own* land and kin." 31 Then he said,
"Please do not leave us, inasmuch as you
know where we should camp in the wilder-
ness, and you will be as eyes for us. 32 So it
will be, if you go with us, that whatever good
Yahweh does for us, we will do for you."

33 Thus they set out from the mount of
Yahweh three days' journey, with the ark
of the covenant of Yahweh journeying in
front of them for the three days, to spy out
a resting place for them. 34 Now the cloud of
Yahweh was over them by day when they set
out from the camp.

35 Then it happened when the ark set out
that Moses said,

"Rise up, O Yahweh!
And let Your enemies be scattered,
And let those who hate You
flee before You."

36 And when it came to rest, he said,

"Return, O Yahweh,
To the myriad thousands of Israel."

Psalm 31:6–14

6 I hate those who regard
worthless idols,
But I trust in Yahweh.
7 I will rejoice and be glad in
Your lovingkindness,
Because You have seen my affliction;
You have known the
troubles of my soul,
8 And You have not given me over
into the hand of the enemy;
You have set my feet in a large place.

9 Be gracious to me, O Yahweh,
for I am in distress;
My eye is wasted away from grief,
my soul and my body *also*.
10 For my life is worn down with sorrow
And my years with sighing;
My strength fails because
of my iniquity,
And my bones waste away.
11 Among all my adversaries,
I have become a reproach,
Especially to my neighbors,
And an object of dread to
my acquaintances;
Those who see me in the
street flee from me.

12 I am forgotten like a dead
man—out of mind—
I am like a broken vessel.
13 For I have heard the bad
report of many,
Terror is on every side;
While they took counsel
together against me,
They schemed to take my life.

14 But as for me, I trust in You, O Yahweh,
I say, "You are my God."

Proverbs 11:7–11

7 When a wicked man dies,
his hope will perish,
And the expectation of
vigorous men perishes.
8 The righteous is rescued from distress,
But the wicked takes his place.
9 With *his* mouth the godless man
corrupts his neighbor,
But through knowledge the
righteous will be rescued.
10 When it goes well with the
righteous, the city exults,
And when the wicked perish,
there is joyful shouting.
11 By the blessing of the upright
a city is raised up,
But by the mouth of the
wicked it is torn down.

Mark 9:30–50

30 From there they went out and were
going through Galilee, and He was not
wanting anyone to know *about it*. 31 For He
was teaching His disciples and telling them,
"The Son of Man is to be delivered into
the hands of men, and they will kill Him;
and when He has been killed, He will rise
again three days later." 32 But they did not
understand *this* statement, and they were
afraid to ask Him.
33 And they came to Capernaum; and when
He was in the house, He *began to* question
them, "What were you discussing on the
way?" 34 But they kept silent, for on the way
they had discussed with one another which
of them was the greatest. 35 And sitting down,
He called the twelve and *said to them, "If
anyone wants to be first, he shall be last of all
and servant of all." 36 And taking a child, He
set him before them. And taking him in His
arms, He said to them, 37 "Whoever receives
one child like this in My name receives Me;
and whoever receives Me does not receive
Me, but Him who sent Me."
38 John said to Him, "Teacher, we saw
someone casting out demons in Your name,
and we tried to hinder him because he was
not following us." 39 But Jesus said, "Do not
hinder him, for there is no one who will
perform a miracle in My name, and be able
soon afterward to speak evil of Me. 40 For
he who is not against us is for us. 41 For
whoever gives you a cup of water to drink
in *My* name because you are of Christ, truly
I say to you, he will not lose his reward.
42 "And whoever causes one of these little
ones who believe to stumble, it would be
better for him if, with a heavy millstone
hung around his neck, he had been cast into
the sea. 43 And if your hand causes you to
stumble, cut it off; it is better for you to enter
life crippled, than, having your two hands,
to go into hell, into the unquenchable fire,
44 [and where THEIR WORM DOES NOT DIE, AND
THE FIRE IS NOT QUENCHED.] 45 And if your
foot causes you to stumble, cut it off; it is
better for you to enter life lame, than, having
your two feet, to be cast into hell, 46 [and
where THEIR WORM DOES NOT DIE, AND THE
FIRE IS NOT QUENCHED.] 47 And if your eye
causes you to stumble, gouge it out; it is
better for you to enter the kingdom of God
with one eye, than, having two eyes, to be
cast into hell, 48 where THEIR WORM DOES
NOT DIE, AND THE FIRE IS NOT QUENCHED.
49 "For everyone will be salted with
fire. 50 Salt is good; but if the salt becomes
unsalty, with what will you make it salty
again? Have salt in yourselves, and be at
peace with one another."

MARCH 7

Numbers 11:1–12:16

11 Now the people became like those
who complain of calamity in the ears
of Yahweh. And Yahweh heard *it* and His
anger was kindled, and the fire of Yahweh
burned among them and consumed *some*
of the outskirts of the camp. 2 The people
therefore cried out to Moses, and Moses

prayed to Yahweh, and the fire died out. 3 So
the name of that place was called Taberah
because the fire of Yahweh burned among
them.

4 And the rabble who were among them
had greedy desires; and also the sons of
Israel wept again and said, "Who will give
us meat to eat? 5 We remember the fish
which we used to eat free in Egypt, the
cucumbers and the melons and the leeks
and the onions and the garlic, 6 but now our
appetite is dried up. There is nothing at all
to look at except this manna."

7 Now the manna was like coriander seed,
and its appearance like that of bdellium.
8 The people would go about and gather *it*
and grind *it* between two millstones or beat
it in the mortar, and boil *it* in the pot and
make cakes with it; and its taste was as the
taste of cakes baked with oil. 9 And when the
dew fell on the camp at night, the manna
would fall with it.

10 Now Moses heard the people weeping
throughout their families, each man at
the doorway of his tent; and the anger of
Yahweh was kindled greatly, and it was evil
in the sight of Moses. 11 So Moses said to
Yahweh, "Why have You allowed this evil
toward Your slave? And why have I not
found favor in Your sight, that You have laid
the burden of all this people on me? 12 Was
it I who conceived all this people? Was it I
who gave birth to them, that You should say
to me, 'Carry them in your bosom as a nurse
carries a nursing baby, to the land which You
swore to their fathers'? 13 Where am I to
get meat to give to all this people? For they
weep before me, saying, 'Give us meat that
we may eat!' 14 I alone am not able to carry
all this people because it is too heavy for
me. 15 So if You are going to deal thus with
me, please kill me at once, if I have found
favor in Your sight, and do not let me see my
wretchedness."

16 Yahweh therefore said to Moses,
"Gather for Me seventy men from the elders
of Israel, whom you know to be the elders
of the people and their officers, and take
them to the tent of meeting, and let them
take their stand there with you. 17 Then I
will come down and speak with you there,
and I will take of the Spirit who is upon you,
and will put *Him* upon them; and they shall
bear the burden of the people with you, so
that you will not bear *it* all alone. 18 And say
to the people, 'Set yourselves apart as holy
for tomorrow, and you shall eat meat; for
you have wept in the ears of Yahweh, saying,
"Oh that someone would give us meat to eat!
For it was good for us in Egypt." Therefore
Yahweh will give you meat, and you shall
eat. 19 You shall eat, not one day, nor two
days, nor five days, nor ten days, nor twenty
days, 20 but a whole month, until it comes
out of your nostrils and becomes loathsome
to you; because you have rejected Yahweh
who is among you and have wept before
Him, saying, "Why did we ever go out from
Egypt?"'" 21 But Moses said, "The people,
among whom I am, are 600,000 on foot; yet
You have said, 'I will give them meat, so that
they may eat for a whole month.' 22 Should
flocks and herds be slaughtered for them, to
be sufficient for them? Or should all the fish
of the sea be gathered together for them, to
be sufficient for them?" 23 And Yahweh said
to Moses, "Is Yahweh's power limited? Now
you shall see whether My word will happen
for you or not."

24 So Moses went out and told the people
the words of Yahweh. Also, he gathered sev-
enty men of the elders of the people and had
them stand around the tent. 25 Then Yahweh
came down in the cloud and spoke to him;
and He took of the Spirit who was upon him
and placed *Him* upon the seventy elders.
And when the Spirit rested upon them, they
prophesied. But they did not do *it* again.

26 But two men had remained in the camp;
the name of one was Eldad and the name of
the other Medad. And the Spirit rested upon
them (now they were among those who had
been registered, but had not gone out to the
tent), and they prophesied in the camp. 27 So
a young man ran and told Moses and said,
"Eldad and Medad are prophesying in the
camp." 28 Then Joshua the son of Nun, the
attendant of Moses from his youth, said,
"Moses, my lord, restrain them." 29 But
Moses said to him, "Are you jealous for my
sake? Would that all the people of Yahweh
were prophets, that Yahweh would put His
Spirit upon them!" 30 Then Moses returned
to the camp, *both* he and the elders of Israel.

31 Now there went forth a wind from
Yahweh, and it brought quail from the sea,
and let *them* fall beside the camp, about a
day's journey on this side and a day's jour-
ney on the other side, all around the camp
and about two cubits over the surface of the

ground. 32 And the people spent all day and
all night and all the next day, and gathered
the quail (he who gathered least gathered
ten homers), and they spread *them* out for
themselves all around the camp. 33 While
the meat was still between their teeth,
before it was chewed, the anger of Yahweh
was kindled against the people, and Yahweh
struck the people with a very severe plague.
34 So the name of that place was called
Kibroth-hattaavah because there they bur-
ied the people who had been greedy. 35 From
Kibroth-hattaavah the people set out for
Hazeroth, and they remained at Hazeroth.

12 Then Miriam and Aaron spoke against
Moses because of the Cushite woman
whom he had taken *as a wife* (for he had
taken a Cushite woman); 2 and they said,
"Has Yahweh indeed spoken only through
Moses? Has He not spoken through us as
well?" And Yahweh heard it. 3 (Now the
man Moses was very humble, more than
any man who was on the face of the earth.)
4 Suddenly Yahweh said to Moses and Aaron
and to Miriam, "You three come out to the
tent of meeting." So the three of them came
out. 5 Then Yahweh came down in a pillar of
cloud and stood at the doorway of the tent,
and He called Aaron and Miriam. And then
both came forward, 6 and He said,

"Hear now My words:
If there is a prophet among you,
I, Yahweh, shall make Myself
known to him in a vision.
I shall speak with him in a dream.
7 "Not so, with My servant Moses,
He is faithful in all My household;
8 With him I speak mouth to mouth,
Indeed clearly, and not in riddles,
And he beholds the form of Yahweh.
Why then were you not afraid
To speak against My servant,
against Moses?"

9 So the anger of Yahweh burned against
them, and He went away. 10 But the cloud
withdrew from over the tent, and behold,
Miriam *was* leprous, as *white as* snow. And
Aaron turned toward Miriam, and behold,
she *was* leprous. 11 Then Aaron said to Moses,
"Oh, my lord, I beg you, do not place *this* sin
on us, in which we have acted foolishly and in
which we have sinned. 12 Oh, do not let her be
like one dead, whose flesh is half eaten away
when he comes from his mother's womb!"
13 And Moses cried out to Yahweh, saying,
"O God, heal her, I pray!" 14 But Yahweh said
to Moses, "If her father had but spit in her face,
would she not bear her dishonor for seven
days? Let her be shut up for seven days outside
the camp, and afterward she may be received
again." 15 So Miriam was shut up outside the
camp for seven days, and the people did not
set out until Miriam was received again.

16 Afterward, however, the people set out
from Hazeroth and camped in the wilder-
ness of Paran.

Psalm 31:15–18

15 My times are in Your hand;
Deliver me from the hand
of my enemies and from
those who pursue me.
16 Make Your face to shine
upon Your slave;
Save me in Your lovingkindness.
17 O Yahweh, let me not be put to
shame, for I call upon You;
Let the wicked be put to shame,
let them be silent in Sheol.
18 Let the lying lips be mute,
Which speak arrogantly
against the righteous
With lofty pride and contempt.

Proverbs 11:12–14

12 He who despises his neighbor
lacks a heart *of wisdom*,
But a man of discernment keeps silent.
13 He who goes about as a
slanderer reveals secrets,
But he who is faithful in spirit
conceals a matter.
14 Where there is no guidance
the people fall,
But in abundance of counselors
there is salvation.

Mark 10:1–31

10 And standing up, He *went from there
to the region of Judea and beyond the
Jordan; crowds *gathered around Him again,
and, according to His custom, He once more
began to teach them.

2 And *some* Pharisees came up to Jesus,
testing Him, and *began to* question Him
whether it was lawful for a man to divorce
a wife. 3 And He answered and said to them,
"What did Moses command you?" 4 And
they said, "Moses permitted *a man* TO WRITE

A CERTIFICATE OF DIVORCE AND SEND *her*
AWAY." 5 But Jesus said to them, "Because of
your hardness of heart he wrote for you this
commandment. 6 But from the beginning of
creation, *God* MADE THEM MALE AND FEMALE.
7 FOR THIS REASON A MAN SHALL LEAVE HIS
FATHER AND MOTHER, 8 AND THE TWO SHALL
BECOME ONE FLESH; so they are no longer
two, but one flesh. 9 What therefore God
has joined together, let no man separate."

10 And in the house the disciples *began*
questioning Him about this again. 11 And
He *said to them, "Whoever divorces his
wife and marries another woman commits
adultery against her; 12 and if she herself
divorces her husband and marries another
man, she is committing adultery."

13 And they were bringing children to
Him so that He might touch them; but the
disciples rebuked them. 14 But when Jesus
saw this, He was indignant and said to
them, "Permit the children to come to Me;
do not hinder them; for the kingdom of God
belongs to such as these. 15 Truly I say to
you, whoever does not receive the kingdom
of God like a child will not enter it *at all*."
16 And He took them in His arms and *began*
blessing them, laying His hands on them.

17 And as He was setting out on a journey,
a man ran up to Him and knelt before Him,
and *began* asking Him, "Good Teacher,
what shall I do to inherit eternal life?"
18 And Jesus said to him, "Why do you call
Me good? No one is good except God alone.
19 You know the commandments, 'DO NOT
MURDER, DO NOT COMMIT ADULTERY, DO NOT
STEAL, DO NOT BEAR FALSE WITNESS, Do not
defraud, HONOR YOUR FATHER AND MOTHER.'"
20 And he said to Him, "Teacher, I have kept
all these things from my youth up." 21 And
looking at him, Jesus loved him and said to
him, "One thing you lack: go and sell all you
possess and give to the poor, and you will
have treasure in heaven; and come, follow
Me." 22 But at these words he was saddened,
and he went away grieving, for he was one
who owned much property.

23 And Jesus, looking around, *said to
His disciples, "How hard it will be for those
who are wealthy to enter the kingdom of
God!" 24 And the disciples were amazed at
His words. But Jesus *answered again and
*said to them, "Children, how hard it is to
enter the kingdom of God! 25 It is easier for a
camel to go through the eye of a needle than
for a rich man to enter the kingdom of God."
26 And they were even more astonished,
saying to Him, "Then who can be saved?"
27 Looking at them, Jesus *said, "With people
it is impossible, but not with God; for all
things are possible with God."

28 Peter began to say to Him, "Behold,
we have left everything and followed You."
29 Jesus said, "Truly I say to you, there is
no one who has left house or brothers or
sisters or mother or father or children or
farms, for My sake and for the gospel's
sake, 30 except *one who* will receive one
hundred times as much now in the present
age—houses and brothers and sisters and
mothers and children and farms, *along*
with persecutions—and in the age to come,
eternal life. 31 But many *who are* first will be
last, and the last, first."

MARCH 8

Numbers 13:1–14:45

13 Then Yahweh spoke to Moses saying,
2 "Send out for yourself men so that
they may spy out the land of Canaan,
which I am going to give to the sons of
Israel; you shall send a man from each of
their fathers' tribes, every one a leader
among them." 3 So Moses sent them from
the wilderness of Paran at the command of
Yahweh, all of them men who were heads
of the sons of Israel. 4 These then *were*
their names:

from the tribe of Reuben, Shammua
the son of Zaccur;

5 from the tribe of Simeon, Shaphat the
son of Hori;

6 from the tribe of Judah, Caleb the son
of Jephunneh;

7 from the tribe of Issachar, Igal the son
of Joseph;

8 from the tribe of Ephraim, Hoshea the
son of Nun;

9 from the tribe of Benjamin, Palti the
son of Raphu;

10 from the tribe of Zebulun, Gaddiel the
son of Sodi;

11 from the tribe of Joseph, from the tribe
of Manasseh, Gaddi the son of Susi;

12 from the tribe of Dan, Ammiel the son
of Gemalli;
13 from the tribe of Asher, Sethur the son
of Michael;
14 from the tribe of Naphtali, Nahbi the
son of Vophsi;
15 from the tribe of Gad, Geuel the son of
Machi.
16 These are the names of the men whom
Moses sent to spy out the land; but Moses
called Hoshea the son of Nun, Joshua.
17 So Moses sent them to spy out the
land of Canaan and said to them, "Go up
there into the Negev; then go up into the
hill country. 18 And see what the land is
like, and whether the people who live in it
are strong *or* weak, whether they are few
or many. 19 And how is the land in which
they live, is it good or bad? And how are the
cities in which they live, are *they* like *open*
camps or with fortifications? 20 And how is
the land, is it fat or lean? Are there trees in
it or not? Make an effort then to get some
of the fruit of the land." Now the time was
the time of the first ripe grapes.
21 So they went up and spied out the land
from the wilderness of Zin as far as Rehob,
at Lebo-hamath. 22 And they had gone up
into the Negev and came to Hebron where
Ahiman, Sheshai, and Talmai, the descen-
dants of Anak were. (Now Hebron was built
seven years before Zoan in Egypt.)
23 Then they came to the valley of Eshcol
and from there cut down a branch with a
single cluster of grapes; and they carried it
on a pole between two *men* with some of the
pomegranates and the figs. 24 That place was
called the valley of Eshcol, because of the
cluster which the sons of Israel cut down
from there.
25 Then they returned from spying out
the land, at the end of forty days, 26 and
went and came to Moses and Aaron and to
all the congregation of the sons of Israel in
the wilderness of Paran, at Kadesh; and they
brought back word to them and to all the
congregation and showed them the fruit of
the land. 27 Thus they recounted to him and
said, "We went in to the land where you sent
us; and it certainly does flow with milk and
honey, and this is its fruit. 28 Nevertheless,
the people who live in the land are strong,
and the cities are fortified *and* very large;
and moreover, we saw the descendants
of Anak there. 29 Amalek is living in the
land of the Negev and the Hittites and the
Jebusites and the Amorites are living in the
hill country, and the Canaanites are living
by the sea and by the side of the Jordan."
30 Then Caleb quieted the people before
Moses and said, "We should by all means
go up and take possession of it, for we are
surely able to overcome it." 31 But the men
who had gone up with him said, "We are not
able to go up against the people, for they are
too strong for us." 32 So they gave out to the
sons of Israel a bad report of the land which
they had spied out, saying, "The land, which
we have passed through to spy out on, is
a land that devours its inhabitants; and all
the people whom we saw in it are men of
great size. 33 There also we saw the Nephilim
(the sons of Anak are part of the Nephilim);
and we became like grasshoppers in our own
sight, and so we were in their sight."

14 Then all the congregation lifted up
their voices and cried, and the people
wept that night. 2 And all the sons of Israel
grumbled against Moses and Aaron; and the
whole congregation said to them, "Would
that we had died in the land of Egypt! Or
would that we had died in this wilderness!
3 And why is Yahweh bringing us into this
land, to fall by the sword? Our wives and
our little ones will become plunder; would it
not be better for us to return to Egypt?" 4 So
they said to one another, "Let us appoint a
leader and return to Egypt."
5 Then Moses and Aaron fell on their
faces in the presence of all the assembly
of the congregation of the sons of Israel.
6 And Joshua the son of Nun and Caleb the
son of Jephunneh, of those who had spied
out the land, tore their clothes; 7 and they
spoke to all the congregation of the sons of
Israel, saying, "The land which we passed
through to spy out is an exceedingly good
land. 8 If Yahweh is pleased with us, then
He will bring us into this land and give it
to us—a land which flows with milk and
honey. 9 But as for you, only do not rebel
against Yahweh; and do not fear the people
of the land, for they are our bread. Their
protection has been removed from them,
and Yahweh is with us; do not fear them."
10 But all the congregation said to stone
them with stones. Then the glory of Yahweh
appeared in the tent of meeting to all the
sons of Israel.

11 Yahweh said to Moses, "How long will this people spurn Me? And how long will they not believe in Me, despite all the signs which I have done in their midst? 12 I will strike them with pestilence and dispossess them, and I will make you into a nation greater and mightier than they."

13 But Moses said to Yahweh, "Then the Egyptians will hear of it, for by Your power You brought up this people from their midst, 14 and they will tell *it* to the inhabitants of this land. They have heard that You, O Yahweh, are in the midst of this people, for You, O Yahweh, are seen eye to eye, while Your cloud stands over them; and You go before them in a pillar of cloud by day and in a pillar of fire by night. 15 Now if You put this people to death as one man, then the nations who have heard of Your fame will say, 16 'Because Yahweh was not able to bring this people into the land which He swore to them, therefore He slaughtered them in the wilderness.' 17 So now, I pray, let the power of the Lord be great, just as You have declared, 18 'Yahweh is slow to anger and abundant in lovingkindness, forgiving iniquity and transgression; but He will by no means clear *the guilty*, visiting the iniquity of the fathers on the children to the third and the fourth *generations*.' 19 Pardon, I pray, the iniquity of this people according to the greatness of Your lovingkindness, just as You also have forgiven this people, from Egypt even until now."

20 So Yahweh said, "I have pardoned *them* according to your word; 21 but indeed, as I live, all the earth will be filled with the glory of Yahweh. 22 Surely all the men who have seen My glory and My signs which I have done in Egypt and in the wilderness, yet have put Me to the test these ten times and have not listened to My voice, 23 shall by no means see the land which I swore to their fathers, nor shall any of those who spurned Me see it. 24 But My servant Caleb, because he has had a different spirit and has followed Me fully, I will bring into the land which he entered, and his seed shall take possession of it. 25 Now the Amalekites and the Canaanites live in the valleys; turn tomorrow and set out to the wilderness by the way of the Red Sea."

26 Yahweh spoke to Moses and Aaron, saying, 27 "How long *shall I bear* with this evil congregation who are grumbling against Me? I have heard the complaints of the sons of Israel, which they are making against Me. 28 Say to them, 'As I live,' declares Yahweh, 'just as you have spoken in My hearing, so I will surely do to you; 29 your corpses will fall in this wilderness, even all your numbered men, according to your complete number from twenty years old and upward, who have grumbled against Me. 30 Surely you shall not come into the land in which I swore to make you dwell, except Caleb the son of Jephunneh and Joshua the son of Nun. 31 Your little ones, however, who you said would become plunder—I will bring them in, so that they will know the land which you have rejected. 32 But as for you, your corpses will fall in this wilderness. 33 And your sons shall be shepherds for forty years in the wilderness, and they will suffer *for* your unfaithfulness, until your corpses come to an end in the wilderness. 34 According to the number of days which you spied out the land, forty days, for every day you shall bear your guilt a year, *even* forty years, and you will know My opposition. 35 I, Yahweh, have spoken, surely this I will do to all this evil congregation who are gathered together against Me. In this wilderness they shall come to an end, and there they will die.'"

36 As for the men whom Moses sent to spy out the land and who returned and made all the congregation grumble against him by bringing out a bad report concerning the land, 37 even those men who brought out the very bad report of the land died by a plague before Yahweh. 38 But Joshua the son of Nun and Caleb the son of Jephunneh remained alive out of those men who went to spy out the land.

39 Then Moses spoke these words to all the sons of Israel, and the people mourned greatly. 40 In the morning, however, they rose up early and went up to the ridge of the hill country, saying, "Here we are; we will go up to the place which Yahweh has promised because we have indeed sinned." 41 But Moses said, "Why then do you trespass against the command of Yahweh, when it will not succeed? 42 Do not go up, for Yahweh is not among you, so that you are not defeated before your enemies. 43 For the Amalekites and the Canaanites will be there in front of you, and you will fall by the sword, inasmuch as you have turned back from following Yahweh. And Yahweh will not be

with you." 44 But they went up heedlessly to
the ridge of the hill country; neither the ark
of the covenant of Yahweh nor Moses moved
from the camp. 45 Then the Amalekites and
the Canaanites who lived in that hill country
came down, and struck them and beat them
down as far as Hormah.

Psalm 31:19–24

19 How great is Your goodness,
Which You have stored up for
those who fear You,
Which You have worked for those
who take refuge in You,
Before the sons of men!
20 You hide them in the secret
place of Your presence from
the conspiracies of man;
You keep them secretly in a shelter
from the strife of tongues.
21 Blessed be Yahweh,
For He has made marvelous
His lovingkindness to me
in a besieged city.
22 As for me, I said in my alarm,
"I am cut off from before Your eyes";
Nevertheless, You heard the
voice of my supplications
When I cried to You for help.

23 Oh, love Yahweh, all you His holy ones!
Yahweh guards the faithful
But repays fully the one who
acts in lofty pride.
24 Be strong and let your
heart take courage,
All you who wait for Yahweh.

Proverbs 11:15

15 If one becomes a guarantor for a
stranger, he will surely suffer,
But he who hates striking
hands *in pledge* is secure.

Mark 10:32–52

32 And they were on the road going up
to Jerusalem, and Jesus was walking on
ahead of them; and they were amazed, and
those who followed were fearful. And again
He took the twelve aside and began to tell
them what was going to happen to Him:
33 "Behold, we are going up to Jerusalem,
and the Son of Man will be betrayed to the
chief priests and the scribes; and they will
condemn Him to death and will deliver Him
over to the Gentiles. 34 And they will mock
Him and spit on Him, and flog Him and kill
Him, and three days later He will rise again."
35 Then James and John, the two sons
of Zebedee, *came up to Jesus, saying to
Him, "Teacher, we want You to do for us
whatever we ask of You." 36 And He said to
them, "What do you want Me to do for you?"
37 And they said to Him, "Grant that we may
sit, one on Your right and one on *Your* left,
in Your glory." 38 But Jesus said to them, "You
do not know what you are asking. Are you
able to drink the cup that I drink, or to be
baptized with the baptism with which I am
baptized?" 39 And they said to Him, "We
are able." And Jesus said to them, "The cup
that I drink you shall drink; and you shall
be baptized with the baptism with which I
am baptized. 40 But to sit on My right or on
My left, *this* is not Mine to give; but it is for
those for whom it has been prepared."
41 And hearing *this*, the ten began to
feel indignant with James and John. 42 And
calling them to Himself, Jesus *said to them,
"You know that those who are recognized
as rulers of the Gentiles lord it over them;
and their great men exercise authority over
them. 43 But it is not this way among you,
but whoever wishes to become great among
you shall be your servant; 44 and whoever
wishes to be first among you shall be slave
of all. 45 For even the Son of Man did not
come to be served, but to serve, and to give
His life a ransom for many."
46 Then they *came to Jericho. And as He
was leaving Jericho with His disciples and
a large crowd, a blind beggar *named* Barti-
maeus, the son of Timaeus, was sitting by
the road. 47 And when he heard that it was
Jesus the Nazarene, he began to cry out and
say, "Jesus, Son of David, have mercy on me!"
48 And many were sternly telling him to be
quiet, but he kept crying out all the more,
"Son of David, have mercy on me!" 49 And
Jesus stopped and said, "Call him *here*." So
they *called the blind man, saying to him,
"Take courage, get up! He is calling for you."
50 And throwing off his *outer* garment, he
jumped up and came to Jesus. 51 And Jesus
answered him and said, "What do you want
Me to do for you?" And the blind man said to
Him, "Rabboni, *I want* to regain my sight!"
52 And Jesus said to him, "Go; your faith has
saved you." Immediately he regained his
sight and *began* following Him on the road.

MARCH 9

Numbers 15:1–16:50

15 Now Yahweh spoke to Moses, saying, 2 "Speak to the sons of Israel and say to them, 'When you enter the land of your places of habitation, which I am going to give you, 3 then make an offering by fire to Yahweh, a burnt offering or a sacrifice to fulfill a special vow, or as a freewill offering or in your appointed times, to make a soothing aroma to Yahweh, from the herd or from the flock. 4 And the one who brings his offering near shall bring near to Yahweh a grain offering of one-tenth *of an ephah* of fine flour mixed with one-fourth of a hin of oil, 5 and you shall prepare wine for the drink offering, one-fourth of a hin, with the burnt offering or for the sacrifice, for each lamb. 6 Or for a ram you shall prepare as a grain offering two-tenths *of an ephah* of fine flour mixed with one-third of a hin of oil; 7 and for the drink offering you shall bring near one-third of a hin of wine as a soothing aroma to Yahweh. 8 And when you prepare a *bull* from the herd as a burnt offering or a sacrifice, to fulfill a special vow, or for peace offerings to Yahweh, 9 then you shall bring near with the *bull* from the herd a grain offering of three-tenths *of an ephah* of fine flour mixed with one-half a hin of oil; 10 and you shall bring near as the drink offering one-half a hin of wine as an offering by fire, as a soothing aroma to Yahweh.

11 'Thus it shall be done for each ox, or for each ram, or for each of the male lambs, or of the goats. 12 According to the number that you prepare, so you shall do for everyone according to their number. 13 All who are native shall do these things in this manner, in bringing near an offering by fire, as a soothing aroma to Yahweh.

14 'And if a sojourner sojourns with you, or one who may be among you throughout your generations, and he offers an offering by fire as a soothing aroma to Yahweh, just as you do so he shall do. 15 *As for* the assembly, there shall be one statute for you and for the sojourner who sojourns *with you*, a perpetual statute throughout your generations; as you are, so shall the sojourner be before Yahweh. 16 There shall be one law and one judgment for you and for the sojourner who sojourns with you.'"

17 Then Yahweh spoke to Moses, saying, 18 "Speak to the sons of Israel and say to them, 'When you enter the land where I am going to bring you, 19 then it shall be, that when you eat of the food of the land, you shall raise up a contribution offering to Yahweh. 20 Of the first of your dough you shall raise up a cake as a contribution offering; as the contribution offering of the threshing floor, so you shall raise it up. 21 From the first of your dough you shall give to Yahweh a contribution offering throughout your generations.

22 'But when you unintentionally fail and do not observe all these commandments, which Yahweh has spoken to Moses, 23 *even* all that Yahweh has commanded you by the hand of Moses, from the day when Yahweh commanded and onward throughout your generations, 24 then it will be, if it is done unintentionally, *hidden* from the sight of the congregation, that all the congregation shall offer one bull from the herd for a burnt offering as a soothing aroma to Yahweh, with its grain offering and its drink offering, according to the *legal* judgment, and one male goat for a sin offering. 25 Then the priest shall make atonement for all the congregation of the sons of Israel, and they will be pardoned; for it was an error, and they have brought their offering, an offering by fire to Yahweh, and their sin offering before Yahweh, for their error. 26 So all the congregation of the sons of Israel will be pardoned, with the sojourner who sojourns among them, for *it happened* to all the people through error.

27 'Also if one person sins unintentionally, then he shall bring near a one year old female goat for a sin offering. 28 And the priest shall make atonement before Yahweh for the person who goes astray when he sins unintentionally, making atonement for him that he may be pardoned. 29 You shall have one law for him who does *anything* unintentionally, for him who is native among the sons of Israel and for the sojourner who sojourns among them. 30 But the person who does *anything* with a high hand, whether he is native or a sojourner, that one is blaspheming Yahweh; and that person shall be cut off from among his people. 31 Because

he has despised the word of Yahweh and has broken His commandment, that person shall be completely cut off; his guilt *will be* on him.'"

32 Now the sons of Israel were in the wilderness, and they found a man gathering wood on the sabbath day. 33 And those who found him gathering wood brought him near to Moses and Aaron and to all the congregation; 34 and they put him in custody because it had not been declared what should be done to him. 35 Then Yahweh said to Moses, "The man shall surely be put to death; all the congregation shall stone him with stones outside the camp." 36 So all the congregation brought him outside the camp and stoned him to death with stones, just as Yahweh had commanded Moses.

37 Yahweh also spoke to Moses, saying, 38 "Speak to the sons of Israel, and tell them that they shall make for themselves tassels on the corners of their garments throughout their generations, and that they shall put on the tassel of each corner a cord of blue. 39 And it shall be a tassel for you to look at and remember all the commandments of Yahweh, so as to do them and not follow after your own heart and your own eyes, after which you played the harlot, 40 so that you may remember to do all My commandments and be holy to your God. 41 I am Yahweh your God who brought you out from the land of Egypt to be your God; I am Yahweh your God."

16 Now Korah the son of Izhar, the son of Kohath, the son of Levi, with Dathan and Abiram, the sons of Eliab, and On the son of Peleth, sons of Reuben, took *others*, 2 and they rose up before Moses, together with some of the sons of Israel, 250 leaders of the congregation, *those* called *upon* by the assembly, men of renown. 3 Then they assembled together against Moses and Aaron, and said to them, "You have gone far enough, for all the congregation are holy, every one of them, and Yahweh is in their midst; so why do you exalt yourselves above the assembly of Yahweh?"

4 And Moses heard *this* and fell on his face; 5 and he spoke to Korah and all his congregation, saying, "Tomorrow morning Yahweh will show who is His, and who is holy, and will bring *him* near to Himself; even the one whom He will choose, He will bring near to Himself. 6 Do this: take censers for yourselves, Korah and all your congregation, 7 and put fire in them, and lay incense upon them in the presence of Yahweh tomorrow; and the man whom Yahweh chooses *shall be* the one who is holy. You have gone far enough, you sons of Levi!"

8 Then Moses said to Korah, "Hear now, you sons of Levi, 9 is it not enough for you that the God of Israel has separated you from the *rest of* the congregation of Israel, to bring you near to Himself, to perform the service of the tabernacle of Yahweh, and to stand before the congregation to minister to them; 10 and that He has brought you near, *Korah*, and all your brothers, sons of Levi, with you? And are you seeking for the priesthood also? 11 Therefore you and all your congregation are gathered together against Yahweh; but as for Aaron, who is he that you grumble against him?"

12 Then Moses sent a summons to Dathan and Abiram, the sons of Eliab; but they said, "We will not come up. 13 Is it not enough that you have brought us up out of a land flowing with milk and honey to put us to death in the wilderness, but you would also lord it over us? 14 Indeed, you have not brought us into a land flowing with milk and honey, nor have you given us an inheritance of fields and vineyards. Would you put out the eyes of these men? We will not come up!"

15 Then Moses became very angry and said to Yahweh, "Do not regard their offering! I have not taken a single donkey from them, nor have I done harm to any of them." 16 And Moses said to Korah, "You and all your congregation be present before Yahweh tomorrow, both you and they along with Aaron. 17 And each of you take his firepan and put incense on it, and each of you bring his censer near before Yahweh, 250 firepans; also you and Aaron *shall* each *bring* his firepan." 18 So they each took his *own* censer and put fire on it, and laid incense on it; and they stood at the doorway of the tent of meeting, with Moses and Aaron. 19 Thus Korah assembled all the congregation against them at the doorway of the tent of meeting. And the glory of Yahweh appeared to all the congregation.

20 Then Yahweh spoke to Moses and Aaron, saying, 21 "Separate yourselves from among this congregation, that I may

consume them instantly." 22 But they fell on their faces and said, "O God, God of the spirits of all flesh, when one man sins, will You be angry with the entire congregation?"

23 Then Yahweh spoke to Moses, saying, 24 "Speak to the congregation, saying, 'Get back from around the dwellings of Korah, Dathan and Abiram.'"

25 Then Moses arose and went to Dathan and Abiram, with the elders of Israel following him, 26 and he spoke to the congregation, saying, "Turn aside now from the tents of these wicked men, and touch nothing that belongs to them, lest you be swept away in all their sin." 27 So they got back from around the dwellings of Korah, Dathan and Abiram; but Dathan and Abiram came out *and* stood at the doorway of their tents, along with their wives and their sons and their little ones. 28 And Moses said, "By this you shall know that Yahweh has sent me to do all these deeds; for this is not from my heart. 29 If these men die the death of all men or if they suffer the fate of all men, *then* Yahweh has not sent me. 30 But if Yahweh creates an entirely new thing and the ground opens its mouth and swallows them up with all that is theirs, and they go down to Sheol alive, then you will know that these men have spurned Yahweh."

31 And it happened that as he finished speaking all these words, the ground that was under them split open; 32 and the earth opened its mouth and swallowed them up, and their households, and all the men who belonged to Korah with *their* possessions. 33 So they and all that belonged to them went down to Sheol alive; and the earth closed over them, and they perished from the midst of the assembly. 34 Then all Israel who *were* around them fled at their outcry, for they said, "Lest the earth swallow us up!" 35 Fire also came forth from Yahweh and consumed the 250 men who were bringing near the incense.

36 Then Yahweh spoke to Moses, saying, 37 "Say to Eleazar, the son of Aaron the priest, that he shall take up the censers out of the midst of the blaze, and *you* scatter the burning coals abroad; for they are holy. 38 As for the censers of these men who have sinned at the cost of their lives, make them into hammered sheets for a plating of the altar, since they brought them near before Yahweh, and they are holy; and they shall be for a sign to the sons of Israel." 39 So Eleazar the priest took the bronze censers which the men who were burned had brought near, and they hammered them out as a plating for the altar, 40 as a memorial to the sons of Israel that no outsider who is not of the seed of Aaron should come near to burn incense before Yahweh; so that he will not become like Korah and his congregation—just as Yahweh had spoken to him by the hand of Moses.

41 But on the next day all the congregation of the sons of Israel grumbled against Moses and Aaron, saying, "You are the ones who have caused the death of the people of Yahweh." 42 It came about, however, when the congregation had assembled against Moses and Aaron, that they turned toward the tent of meeting, and behold, the cloud covered it and the glory of Yahweh appeared. 43 Then Moses and Aaron came to the front of the tent of meeting, 44 and Yahweh spoke to Moses, saying, 45 "Get away from among this congregation, that I may consume them instantly." Then they fell on their faces. 46 And Moses said to Aaron, "Take your censer and put in it fire from the altar, and lay incense *on it*; then bring it quickly to the congregation and make atonement for them, for wrath has gone forth from Yahweh, the plague has begun!" 47 Then Aaron took *it* as Moses had spoken, and ran into the midst of the assembly, for behold, the plague had begun among the people. So he put *on* the incense and made atonement for the people. 48 And he took his stand between the dead and the living, so that the plague was checked. 49 But those who died by the plague were 14,700, besides those who died on account of Korah. 50 Then Aaron returned to Moses at the doorway of the tent of meeting, for the plague had been checked.

Psalm 32:1–5

1 How blessed is he whose
  transgression is forgiven,
Whose sin is covered!
2 How blessed is the man whose iniquity
  Yahweh will not take into account,
And in whose spirit there is no deceit!

3 When I kept silent *about my sin*,
  my bones wasted away
Through my groaning all day long.

4 For day and night Your hand
was heavy upon me;
My vitality was drained away *as* with
the heat of summer. Selah.
5 I acknowledged my sin to You,
And my iniquity I did not cover up;
I said, "I will confess my
transgressions to Yahweh;"
And You forgave the iniquity of my
sin. Selah.

Proverbs 11:16–18

16 A gracious woman holds fast to glory,
But ruthless men hold fast to riches.
17 The man of lovingkindness deals
bountifully with his soul,
But the cruel man brings
trouble on his flesh.
18 The wicked earns deceptive wages,
But he who sows righteousness
gets a true reward.

Mark 11:1–19

11 And as they *approached Jerusalem,
at Bethphage and Bethany, near the
Mount of Olives, He *sent two of His disci-
ples, 2 and *said to them, "Go into the village
opposite you, and immediately as you enter
it, you will find a colt tied *there*, on which
no one yet has ever sat; untie it and bring it
here. 3 And if anyone says to you, 'Why are
you doing this?' you say, 'The Lord has need
of it'; and immediately he will send it back
here." 4 And they went away and found a colt
tied at the door, outside in the street; and
they *untied it. 5 And some of the bystanders
were saying to them, "What are you doing,
untying the colt?" 6 And they spoke to them
just as Jesus had told *them*, and they gave
them permission. 7 And they *brought the
colt to Jesus and put their garments on it;
and He sat on it. 8 And many spread their
garments in the road, and others *spread*
leafy branches, having cut *them* from the
fields. 9 And those who went in front and
those who followed were shouting:

"Hosanna!
BLESSED IS HE WHO COMES IN
THE NAME OF THE LORD;
10 Blessed *is* the coming kingdom
of our father David;
Hosanna in the highest!"

11 And Jesus entered Jerusalem *and came*
into the temple; and after looking around
at everything, He left for Bethany with the
twelve, since it was already late.
12 And on the next day, when they had
left Bethany, He became hungry. 13 And
seeing at a distance a fig tree that had
leaves, He went *to see* if perhaps He would
find anything on it; and when He came to
it, He found nothing but leaves, for it was
not the season for figs. 14 And He answered
and said to it, "May no one ever eat fruit
from you again!" And His disciples were
listening.
15 Then they *came to Jerusalem. And
He entered the temple and began to drive
out those who were buying and selling in
the temple, and overturned the tables of
the money changers and the seats of those
who were selling doves; 16 and He was not
permitting anyone to carry merchandise
through the temple. 17 And He *began to*
teach and say to them, "Is it not written, 'MY
HOUSE SHALL BE CALLED A HOUSE OF PRAYER
FOR ALL THE NATIONS'? But you have made it
A ROBBERS' DEN." 18 And the chief priests and
the scribes heard *this*, and *began* seeking
how to destroy Him; for they were afraid of
Him, for the whole crowd was astonished
at His teaching.
19 And when evening came, they were
going out of the city.

MARCH 10

Numbers 17:1–18:32

17 Then Yahweh spoke to Moses, saying,
2 "Speak to the sons of Israel, and get
from them a rod for each father's household:
twelve rods from all their leaders according
to their fathers' households. You shall write
each name on his rod, 3 and write Aaron's
name on the rod of Levi; for there is one
rod for the head *of each* of their fathers'
households. 4 You shall then deposit them
in the tent of meeting in front of the testi-
mony, where I meet with you. 5 And it will
come about that the rod of the man whom I
choose will sprout. Thus I will rid Myself of
the grumblings of the sons of Israel, who are
grumbling against you." 6 Moses therefore
spoke to the sons of Israel, and all their lead-
ers gave him a rod apiece, for each leader

according to their fathers' households,
twelve rods, with the rod of Aaron among
their rods. 7 So Moses deposited the rods
before Yahweh in the tent of the testimony.

8 Now it happened on the next day Moses
went into the tent of the testimony; and
behold, the rod of Aaron for the house of
Levi had sprouted and put forth buds and
produced flowers, and it bore ripe almonds.
9 Moses then brought out all the rods from
the presence of Yahweh to all the sons of
Israel; and they looked, and each man took
his rod. 10 But Yahweh said to Moses, "Put
back the rod of Aaron before the testimony
to be kept as a sign against the rebels, that
you may put an end to their grumblings
against Me, so that they will not die." 11 Thus
Moses did; just as Yahweh had commanded
him, so he did.

12 Then the sons of Israel spoke to Moses,
saying, "Behold, we are breathing our last
breath, we are perishing, we are all per-
ishing! 13 Everyone who comes near, who
comes near to the tabernacle of Yahweh,
must die. Are we to breathe our utter last?"

18 So Yahweh said to Aaron, "You
and your sons and your father's
household with you shall bear the guilt in
connection with the sanctuary, and you
and your sons with you shall bear the guilt
in connection with your priesthood. 2 But
bring near with you also your brothers, the
tribe of Levi, the tribe of your father, that
they may be joined with you and minister
to you, while you and your sons with you
are before the tent of the testimony. 3 And
they shall thus keep your responsibility and
the responsibility of all the tent, but they
shall not come near to the furnishings of
the sanctuary and the altar, so that neither
they nor you will die. 4 And they shall be
joined with you and keep the responsibility
of the tent of meeting, for all the service of
the tent; but an outsider may not come near
you. 5 So you shall keep the responsibility of
the sanctuary and the responsibility of the
altar, so that there will no longer be wrath
on the sons of Israel. 6 And behold, I Myself
have taken your brothers the Levites from
among the sons of Israel; they are a gift to
you, given to Yahweh, to perform the service
for the tent of meeting. 7 But you and your
sons with you shall keep your priesthood
in everything that concerns the altar and
inside the veil, and you are to perform
service. I am giving you the priesthood as
a bestowed service, but the outsider who
comes near shall be put to death."

8 Then Yahweh spoke to Aaron, "Now
behold, I Myself have given you the respon-
sibility of My contributions, even all the
holy gifts of the sons of Israel I have given
them to you as a portion and to your sons
as a perpetual statute. 9 This shall be yours
from the most holy *gifts reserved* from the
fire; every offering of theirs, even every grain
offering and every sin offering and every guilt
offering, which they shall render to Me, shall
be most holy for you and for your sons. 10 As
the most holy *gifts* you shall eat it; every male
shall eat it. It shall be holy to you. 11 This also
is yours, the contribution from their gift,
even all the wave offerings of the sons of
Israel; I have given them to you and to your
sons and daughters with you as a perpetual
statute. Everyone of your household who is
clean may eat it. 12 All the best of the fresh oil
and all the best of the fresh wine and of the
grain, the first fruits of those which they give
to Yahweh, I give them to you. 13 The first ripe
fruits of all that is in their land, which they
bring to Yahweh, shall be yours; everyone
of your household who is clean may eat
it. 14 Every devoted thing in Israel shall be
yours. 15 Every first issue of the womb of
all flesh, whether man or animal, which
they bring near to Yahweh, shall be yours;
nevertheless the firstborn of man you shall
surely redeem, and the firstborn of unclean
animals you shall redeem. 16 Now as to their
redemption price, from a month old you
shall redeem them, by your valuation, five
shekels in silver, according to the shekel of
the sanctuary, which is twenty gerahs. 17 But
the firstborn of an ox or the firstborn of a
sheep or the firstborn of a goat, you shall not
redeem; they are holy. You shall splash their
blood on the altar and shall offer up their fat
in smoke *as* an offering by fire, for a soothing
aroma to Yahweh. 18 And their meat shall be
yours; it shall be yours like the breast of a
wave offering and like the right thigh. 19 All
the contributions of the holy *gifts*, which the
sons of Israel raise up to Yahweh, I have given
to you and your sons and your daughters with
you, as a perpetual statute. It is an everlasting
covenant of salt before Yahweh to you and
your seed with you." 20 Then Yahweh said to
Aaron, "You shall have no inheritance in their

land nor own any portion among them; I am
your portion and your inheritance among the
sons of Israel.
21 "Now to the sons of Levi, behold, I have
given all the tithe in Israel for an inheritance,
in return for their service which they per-
form, the service of the tent of meeting.
22 And the sons of Israel shall not come
near the tent of meeting again, or they will
bear sin and die. 23 Only the Levites shall
perform the service of the tent of meeting,
and they shall bear their iniquity; it shall be
a perpetual statute throughout your gener-
ations, and among the sons of Israel they
shall have no inheritance. 24 For the tithe of
the sons of Israel, which they raise up as a
contribution offering to Yahweh, I have given
to the Levites for an inheritance; therefore I
have said concerning them, 'They shall have
no inheritance among the sons of Israel.'"
25 Then Yahweh spoke to Moses, saying,
26 "Moreover, you shall speak to the Levites
and say to them, 'When you take from the
sons of Israel the tithe which I have given
you from them for your inheritance, then
you shall raise up a contribution offering
from it to Yahweh, a tithe of the tithe. 27 And
your contribution offering shall be reckoned
to you as the grain from the threshing floor
or the full produce from the wine vat. 28 So
you shall also raise up a contribution offer-
ing to Yahweh from all your tithes, which
you receive from the sons of Israel; and from
it you shall give the contribution offering of
Yahweh to Aaron the priest. 29 Out of all your
gifts you shall raise up every contribution
offering due to Yahweh, from all the best of
them, the sacred part from them.' 30 And
you shall say to them, 'When you have
raised up from it the best of it, then *the rest*
shall be accounted to the Levites as the
product of the threshing floor and as the
product of the wine vat. 31 And you may eat
it anywhere, you and your households, for
it is your compensation in return for your
service in the tent of meeting. 32 And you
will bear no sin by reason of it when you
have raised up the best of it. But you shall
not profane the sacred gifts of the sons of
Israel, so that you will not die.'"

Psalm 32:6–11

6 Therefore, let every holy one
pray to You at a time when
You may be found;
Surely in a flood of great waters
they will not reach him.
7 You are my hiding place; You
guard me from trouble;
You surround me with songs of
deliverance. Selah.
8 I will give you insight and teach you
in the way which you should go;
I will counsel you with
My eye upon you.
9 Do not be as the horse or as the mule
which have no understanding,
Whose harness are bit and
bridle to control them,
Otherwise they will not come near you.
10 Many are the sorrows of the wicked,
But he who trusts in Yahweh,
lovingkindness shall surround him.
11 Be glad in Yahweh and rejoice,
you righteous ones;
And shout for joy, all you who
are upright in heart.

Proverbs 11:19–21

19 He who is steadfast in righteousness
will attain to life,
And he who pursues evil *will
bring about* his own death.
20 Those with a crooked heart are
an abomination to Yahweh,
But those of a blameless
way are His delight.
21 Assuredly, the evil man will
not go unpunished,
But the seed of the righteous
will escape.

Mark 11:20–33

20 And as they were passing by in the
morning, they saw the fig tree withered
from the roots. 21 And being reminded,
Peter *said to Him, "Rabbi, look, the fig tree
which You cursed has withered." 22 And
Jesus answered and *said to them, "Have
faith in God. 23 Truly I say to you, whoever
says to this mountain, 'Be taken up and
cast into the sea,' and does not doubt in
his heart, but believes that what he says
is going to happen, it will be *granted* him.
24 For this reason I say to you, all things
for which you pray and ask, believe that
you have received them, and they will
be *granted* to you. 25 And whenever you
stand praying, forgive, if you have anything

against anyone, so that your Father who is in heaven will also forgive you your transgressions. 26 [But if you do not forgive, neither will your Father who is in heaven forgive your transgressions."]

27 Then they *came again to Jerusalem. And as He was walking in the temple, the chief priests and the scribes and the elders *came to Him, 28 and *began* saying to Him, "By what authority are You doing these things, or who gave You this authority to do these things?" 29 And Jesus said to them, "I will ask you one question, and you answer Me, and *then* I will tell you by what authority I do these things. 30 Was the baptism of John from heaven, or from men? Answer Me." 31 And they *began* reasoning among themselves, saying, "If we say, 'From heaven,' He will say, 'Then why did you not believe him?' 32 But if we say, 'From men'?"—they were afraid of the crowd, for everyone was regarding John to have been a real prophet. 33 And answering Jesus, they *said, "We do not know." And Jesus *said to them, "Neither will I tell you by what authority I do these things."

MARCH 11

Numbers 19:1–20:29

19 Then Yahweh spoke to Moses and Aaron, saying, 2 "This is the statute of the law which Yahweh has commanded, saying, 'Speak to the sons of Israel that they take to you a red heifer without blemish, in which is no defect *and* on which a yoke has never been placed. 3 And you shall give it to Eleazar the priest, and it shall be brought outside the camp and be slaughtered in his presence. 4 Next Eleazar the priest shall take some of its blood with his finger and sprinkle some of its blood toward the front of the tent of meeting seven times. 5 Then the heifer shall be burned in his sight; its hide and its flesh and its blood, with its refuse, shall be burned. 6 And the priest shall take cedar wood and hyssop and scarlet *material* and cast it into the midst of the burning heifer. 7 The priest shall then wash his clothes and bathe his body in water and afterward come into the camp, but the priest shall be unclean until evening. 8 The one who burns it shall also wash his clothes in water and bathe his body in water and shall be unclean until evening. 9 Now a man who is clean shall gather up the ashes of the heifer and deposit them outside the camp in a clean place, and the congregation of the sons of Israel shall keep it as water to remove impurity; it is purification from sin. 10 And the one who gathers the ashes of the heifer shall wash his clothes and be unclean until evening; and it shall be a perpetual statute to the sons of Israel and to the sojourner who sojourns among them.

11 'The one who touches the corpse of any person shall be unclean for seven days. 12 That one shall purify himself from uncleanness with the water on the third day and on the seventh day, *and then* he will be clean; but if he does not purify himself on the third day and on the seventh day, he will not be clean. 13 Anyone who touches a corpse, the body of a man who has died, and does not purify himself, makes the tabernacle of Yahweh unclean; and that person shall be cut off from Israel. Because the water for impurity was not splashed on him, he shall be unclean; his uncleanness is still on him.

14 'This is the law when a man dies in a tent: everyone who comes into the tent and everyone who is in the tent shall be unclean for seven days. 15 And every open vessel, which has no covering tied down on it, shall be unclean. 16 Also, anyone who in the open field touches one who has been slain with a sword or who has died *naturally*, or a human bone or a grave, shall be unclean for seven days. 17 Then for the unclean *person* they shall take some of the ashes of the burnt purification from sin and flowing water shall be added to them in a vessel. 18 And a clean person shall take hyssop and dip *it* in the water and sprinkle *it* on the tent and on all the furnishings and on the persons who were there and on the one who touched the bone or the one slain or the one dying *naturally* or the grave. 19 Then the clean *person* shall sprinkle on the unclean on the third day and on the seventh day; and on the seventh day he shall purify him from uncleanness, and he shall wash his clothes and bathe *himself* in water and shall be clean by evening.

20 'But the man who is unclean and does
not purify himself from uncleanness, that
person shall be cut off from the midst of
the assembly because he has made the
sanctuary of Yahweh unclean; the water for
impurity has not been splashed on him; he is
unclean. 21 So it shall be a perpetual statute
for them. And he who sprinkles the water
for impurity shall wash his clothes, and he
who touches the water for impurity shall be
unclean until evening. 22 Furthermore, any-
thing that the unclean *person* touches shall
be unclean; and the person who touches *it*
shall be unclean until evening.'"

20 Then the sons of Israel, the whole
congregation, came to the wilderness
of Zin in the first month; and the people
stayed at Kadesh. And Miriam died there
and was buried there.

2 Now there was no water for the con-
gregation, and they assembled themselves
against Moses and Aaron. 3 The people thus
contended with Moses and spoke, saying,
"If only we had breathed our last when our
brothers breathed their last before Yahweh!
4 Why then have you brought the assembly
of Yahweh into this wilderness, for us and
our beasts to die here? 5 And why have you
made us come up from Egypt, to bring us
into this evil place? It is not a place of grain
or figs or vines or pomegranates, nor is there
water to drink." 6 Then Moses and Aaron
came in from the presence of the assembly
to the doorway of the tent of meeting and
fell on their faces. Then the glory of Yahweh
appeared to them; 7 and Yahweh spoke to
Moses, saying, 8 "Take the rod; and you and
your brother Aaron assemble the congrega-
tion and speak to the rock before their eyes,
that it may yield its water. You shall thus
bring forth water for them out of the rock
and let the congregation and their beasts
drink."

9 So Moses took the rod from before Yah-
weh, just as He had commanded him; 10 and
Moses and Aaron gathered the assembly
before the rock. And he said to them, "Listen
now, you rebels; shall we bring forth water
for you out of this rock?" 11 Then Moses
raised high his hand and struck the rock
twice with his rod; and water came forth
abundantly, and the congregation and their
beasts drank. 12 But Yahweh said to Moses
and Aaron, "Because you did not believe Me,
to treat Me as holy in the sight of the sons
of Israel, therefore you shall not bring this
assembly into the land which I have given
them." 13 Those *were* the waters of Meribah
because the sons of Israel contended with
Yahweh, and He proved Himself holy among
them.

14 From Kadesh Moses then sent messen-
gers to the king of Edom: "Thus your brother
Israel has said, 'You know all the hardship
that has befallen us, 15 that our fathers went
down to Egypt, and we stayed in Egypt a
long time, and the Egyptians treated us
and our fathers badly. 16 So we cried out to
Yahweh, and He heard our voice and sent
an angel and brought us out from Egypt;
now behold, we are at Kadesh, a town on
the edge of your territory. 17 Please let us
pass through your land. We will not pass
through field or through vineyard; we will
not even drink water from a well. We will go
along the king's highway; we will not turn to
the right or to the left until we pass through
your territory.'"

18 Edom, however, said to him, "You shall
not pass through us, lest I come out to meet
you with the sword." 19 Again, the sons of
Israel said to him, "We will go up by the
highway, and if I and my livestock do drink
any of your water, then I will pay its price.
Let me only pass through on my feet, noth-
ing *else*." 20 But he said, "You shall not pass
through." And Edom came out to meet him
with a heavy force and with a strong hand.
21 Thus Edom refused to allow Israel to pass
through his territory; so Israel turned away
from him.

22 Then they set out from Kadesh, and the
sons of Israel, the whole congregation, came
to Mount Hor.

23 And Yahweh spoke to Moses and Aaron
at Mount Hor by the border of the land of
Edom, saying, 24 "Aaron will be gathered to
his people, for he shall not enter the land
which I have given to the sons of Israel
because you rebelled against My command
at the waters of Meribah. 25 Take Aaron and
his son Eleazar and bring them up to Mount
Hor; 26 and strip Aaron of his garments and
put them on his son Eleazar. So Aaron will
be gathered *to his people* and will die there."
27 So Moses did just as Yahweh had com-
manded, and they went up to Mount Hor
in the sight of all the congregation. 28 And
Moses stripped Aaron of his garments and

put them on his son Eleazar, and Aaron died
there on the mountain top. Then Moses and
Eleazar came down from the mountain.
29 So all the congregation saw that Aaron
breathed his last, and all the house of Israel
wept for Aaron thirty days.

Psalm 33:1–9

1 Sing for joy in Yahweh,
O righteous ones;
Praise is becoming to the upright.
2 Give thanks to Yahweh with the lyre;
Sing praises to Him with a
harp of ten strings.
3 Sing to Him a new song;
Play skillfully with a loud shout.
4 For the word of Yahweh is upright,
And all His work is *done*
in faithfulness.
5 He loves righteousness and justice;
The earth is full of the
lovingkindness of Yahweh.

6 By the word of Yahweh the
heavens were made,
And by the breath of His
mouth all their host.
7 He gathers the waters of
the sea as a heap;
He lays up the deeps in storehouses.
8 Let all the earth fear Yahweh;
Let all the inhabitants of the
world stand in awe of Him.
9 For He spoke, and it was;
He commanded, and it stood.

Proverbs 11:22–24

22 *As* a ring of gold in a swine's snout
So is a beautiful woman who
turns away from discretion.
23 The desire of the righteous
is only good,
But the hope of the wicked is wrath.
24 There is one who scatters, and
yet increases all the more,
And there is one who holds
back what is rightly due, *and*
yet results only in want.

Mark 12:1–27

12 And He began to speak to them in
parables: "A man PLANTED A VINEYARD
AND PUT A WALL AROUND IT, AND DUG A VAT
UNDER THE WINE PRESS AND BUILT A TOWER,
and rented it out to vine-growers and went
on a journey. 2 And at the *harvest* time he
sent a slave to the vine-growers, in order to
receive *some* of the fruit of the vineyard from
the vine-growers. 3 And they took him, and
beat him and sent him away empty-handed.
4 And again he sent them another slave, and
they wounded him in the head, and treated
him shamefully. 5 And he sent another,
and that one they killed; and *so with* many
others, beating some and killing others.
6 He had one more, a beloved son; he sent
him last *of all* to them, saying, 'They will
respect my son.' 7 But those vine-growers
said to one another, 'This is the heir; come,
let us kill him, and the inheritance will be
ours!' 8 And they took him, and killed him
and threw him out of the vineyard. 9 What
will the owner of the vineyard do? He will
come and destroy the vine-growers, and will
give the vineyard to others. 10 Have you not
even read this Scripture:

'THE STONE WHICH THE
BUILDERS REJECTED,
THIS HAS BECOME THE CHIEF
CORNER *stone*;
11 THIS CAME ABOUT FROM THE LORD,
AND IT IS MARVELOUS IN OUR EYES'?"

12 And they were seeking to seize Him,
and *yet* they feared the crowd, for they
understood that He spoke the parable
against them. And *so* they left Him and
went away.

13 Then they *sent some of the Pharisees
and Herodians to Him in order to trap Him
in a statement. 14 And they *came and *said
to Him, "Teacher, we know that You are
truthful and defer to no one; for You are
not partial to any, but teach the way of God
in truth. Is it lawful to pay a tax to Caesar,
or not? 15 Shall we pay or shall we not pay?"
But He, knowing their hypocrisy, said to
them, "Why are you testing Me? Bring Me
a denarius to look at." 16 And they brought
one. And He *said to them, "Whose likeness
and inscription is this?" And they said to
Him, "Caesar's." 17 And Jesus said to them,
"Render to Caesar the things that are Cae-
sar's, and to God the things that are God's."
And they were amazed at Him.

18 Then *some* Sadducees (who say that
there is no resurrection) *came to Jesus, and
began questioning Him, saying, 19 "Teacher,
Moses wrote for us that IF A MAN'S BROTHER
DIES and leaves behind a wife AND LEAVES
NO CHILD, HIS BROTHER SHOULD MARRY THE

WIFE AND RAISE UP A SEED FOR HIS BROTHER.
20 There were seven brothers; and the first
married a wife, and died leaving no seed.
21 And the second one married her, and
died leaving behind no seed; and the third
likewise; 22 and *so* all seven left no seed. Last
of all the woman died also. 23 In the resur-
rection, when they rise again, whose wife
will she be? For all seven had married her."
24 Jesus said to them, "Is this not the reason
you are mistaken, that you do not under-
stand the Scriptures nor the power of God?
25 For when they rise from the dead, they
neither marry nor are given in marriage, but
are like angels in heaven. 26 But regarding the
fact that the dead are raised, have you not
read in the book of Moses, in the *passage*
about *the burning* bush, how God spoke to
him, saying, 'I AM THE GOD OF ABRAHAM, AND
THE GOD OF ISAAC, AND THE GOD OF JACOB'?
27 He is not the God of the dead, but of the
living; you are greatly mistaken."

Men get wisdom by books, but wisdom toward God is to be gotten out of God's Book—and that by digging.

— MATTHEW HENRY

MARCH 12

Numbers 21:1–22:41

21 Then the Canaanite, the king of Arad,
who lived in the Negev, heard that
Israel was coming by the way of Atharim,
and he fought against Israel and took some
of them captive. 2 So Israel made a vow to
Yahweh and said, "If You will indeed give this
people into my hand, then I will devote their
cities to destruction." 3 Then Yahweh heard
the voice of Israel and gave the Canaanites
over; so they devoted them and their cities
to destruction. Thus the name of the place
was called Hormah.

4 Then they set out from Mount Hor by
the way to the Red Sea, to go around the
land of Edom; and the people became
impatient on the way. 5 And the people
spoke against God and against Moses, "Why
have you brought us up out of Egypt to die in
the wilderness? For there is no food and no
water, and we loathe this miserable food."

6 So Yahweh sent fiery serpents among
the people, and they bit the people so that
many people of Israel died. 7 Then the people
came to Moses and said, "We have sinned
because we have spoken against Yahweh and
against you; pray to Yahweh, that He may
remove the serpents from us." And Moses
prayed for the people. 8 Then Yahweh said
to Moses, "Make a fiery *serpent* and set it
on a standard; and it will be that everyone
who is bitten and looks at it, will live." 9 And
Moses made a bronze serpent and set it on
the standard; and it happened, that if a
serpent bit any man, when he looked to the
bronze serpent, he lived.

10 Then the sons of Israel set out and
camped in Oboth. 11 They then set out from
Oboth and camped at Iye-abarim, in the wil-
derness which is opposite Moab, *east* toward
the sunrise. 12 From there they set out and
camped in Wadi Zered. 13 From there they
set out and camped on the other side of
the Arnon, which is in the wilderness that
comes out of the border of the Amorites, for
the Arnon is the border of Moab, between
Moab and the Amorites. 14 Therefore it is
said in the Book of the Wars of Yahweh,

"Waheb in Suphah,
And the wadis of the Arnon,
15 And the slope of the wadis
That extends to the site of Ar,
And leans to the border of Moab."

16 And from there *they continued* to Beer,
that is the well where Yahweh said to Moses,
"Assemble the people, that I may give them
water."

17 Then Israel sang this song:
"Spring up, O well! Sing to it!
18 "The well, which the leaders dug,
Which the nobles of the
people carved out,
With the scepter *and* with their staffs."
And from the wilderness *they continued*
to Mattanah, 19 and from Mattanah to
Nahaliel, and from Nahaliel to Bamoth,

20 and from Bamoth to the valley that is in
the land of Moab, at the top of Pisgah which
overlooks the wasteland.
21 Then Israel sent messengers to Sihon,
king of the Amorites, saying, 22 "Let me pass
through your land. We will not turn off into
field or vineyard; we will not drink water
from wells. We will go by the king's highway
until we have passed through your border."
23 But Sihon would not allow Israel to pass
through his border. So Sihon gathered all
his people and went out to meet Israel in
the wilderness and came to Jahaz and fought
against Israel. 24 Then Israel struck him with
the edge of the sword and took possession
of his land from the Arnon to the Jabbok, as
far as the sons of Ammon; for the border of
the sons of Ammon *was* Jazer. 25 And Israel
took all these cities, and Israel lived in all
the cities of the Amorites, in Heshbon, and
in all her towns. 26 For Heshbon was the city
of Sihon, king of the Amorites. Now it was
he who had fought against the former king
of Moab and had taken all his land out of
his hand, as far as the Arnon. 27 Therefore
those who use proverbs say,

"Come to Heshbon! Let it be built!
So let the city of Sihon be established.
28 "For a fire went forth from Heshbon,
A flame from the town of Sihon;
It devoured Ar of Moab,
The dominant heights of the Arnon.
29 "Woe to you, O Moab!
You perish, O people of Chemosh!
He has given his sons as fugitives,
And his daughters into captivity,
To an Amorite king, Sihon.
30 "But we have cast them down,
Heshbon perishes as far as Dibon,
And we have made desolate
even to Nophah,
Which *reaches* to Medeba."

31 Thus Israel lived in the land of the
Amorites. 32 And Moses sent to spy out
Jazer, and they captured its towns and
dispossessed the Amorites who *were* there.
33 Then they turned and went up by the
way of Bashan, and Og the king of Bashan
went out to meet them, he and all his people
for battle at Edrei. 34 But Yahweh said to
Moses, "Do not fear him, for I have given
him into your hand, and all his people and
his land; and you shall do to him as you did
to Sihon, king of the Amorites, who lived
at Heshbon." 35 So they struck down him
and his sons and all his people, until there
was no survivor remaining for him; and they
possessed his land.

22 Then the sons of Israel set out and
camped in the plains of Moab beyond
the Jordan *opposite* Jericho.
2 And Balak the son of Zippor saw all that
Israel had done to the Amorites. 3 So Moab
was in great fear because of the people, for
they were numerous; and Moab was in dread
of the sons of Israel. 4 Then Moab said to
the elders of Midian, "Now this assembly
will lick up all that is around us, as the ox
licks up the grass of the field." And Balak the
son of Zippor was king of Moab at that time.
5 So he sent messengers to Balaam the son
of Beor, at Pethor, which is near the River,
in the land of the sons of his people, to call
him, saying, "Behold, a people came out of
Egypt; behold, they cover the surface of the
land, and they are settled opposite me. 6 So
now, please come, curse this people for me
since they are too mighty for me; perhaps I
may be able to strike them down and drive
them out of the land. For I know that he
whom you bless is blessed, and he whom
you curse is cursed."
7 So the elders of Moab and the elders
of Midian went away with the *fees for*
divination in their hand; and they came
to Balaam and spoke Balak's words to him.
8 And he said to them, "Spend the night
here, and I will bring word back to you as
Yahweh may speak to me." And the leaders
of Moab stayed with Balaam. 9 Then God
came to Balaam and said, "Who are these
men with you?" 10 And Balaam said to God,
"Balak the son of Zippor, king of Moab, has
sent *word* to me, 11 'Behold, there is a people
who came out of Egypt, and they cover the
surface of the land; now come, curse them
for me; perhaps I may be able to fight against
them and drive them out.'" 12 And God said
to Balaam, "Do not go with them; you shall
not curse the people, for they are blessed."
13 So Balaam arose in the morning and said
to Balak's leaders, "Go back to your land, for
Yahweh has refused to allow me to go with
you." 14 And the leaders of Moab arose and
came to Balak and said, "Balaam refused to
go with us."
15 Then Balak again sent leaders, more
numerous and more honorable than the
former. 16 And they came to Balaam and said

to him, "Thus says Balak the son of Zippor, 'Let nothing, I beg you, withhold you from coming to me; 17 for I will indeed honor you richly, and I will do whatever you say to me. Please come then, curse this people for me.'" 18 And Balaam replied to the servants of Balak, "Though Balak were to give me his house full of silver and gold, I could not do anything, either small or great, to trespass the command of Yahweh my God. 19 So now, please, you also stay here tonight, and I will know what else Yahweh will speak to me." 20 And God came to Balaam at night and said to him, "If the men have come to call you, rise up *and* go with them; but only the word which I speak to you shall you do."

21 So Balaam arose in the morning and saddled his donkey and went with the leaders of Moab.

22 But God was angry because he was going, so the angel of Yahweh took his stand in the way as an adversary against him. Now he was riding on his donkey, and his two young men were with him. 23 Then the donkey saw the angel of Yahweh standing in the way with his drawn sword in his hand, and the donkey turned off from the way and went into the field; so Balaam struck the donkey to turn it back into the way. 24 Then the angel of Yahweh stood in a narrow path of the vineyards, *with* a wall on this side and a wall on that side. 25 And the donkey saw the angel of Yahweh, and it pressed itself to the wall and pressed Balaam's foot against the wall, so he struck it again. 26 And the angel of Yahweh passed on ahead and stood in a narrow place where there was no way to turn to the right hand or the left. 27 Then the donkey saw the angel of Yahweh and lay down under Balaam; so Balaam was angry and struck the donkey with his stick. 28 And Yahweh opened the mouth of the donkey, and it said to Balaam, "What have I done to you, that you have struck me these three times?" 29 Then Balaam said to the donkey, "Because you have made a mockery of me! If there had been a sword in my hand, I would have killed you by now." 30 And the donkey said to Balaam, "Am I not your donkey on which you have ridden all your life to this day? Have I ever been accustomed to do so to you?" And he said, "No."

31 Then Yahweh opened the eyes of Balaam, and he saw the angel of Yahweh standing in the way with his drawn sword in his hand; and he bowed his head down and prostrated himself to the ground. 32 And the angel of Yahweh said to him, "Why have you struck your donkey these three times? Behold, I have come out as an adversary because your way was contrary to me. 33 And the donkey saw me and turned aside from me these three times. If it had not turned aside from me, I would surely have killed you just now, and let it live." 34 And Balaam said to the angel of Yahweh, "I have sinned, for I did not know that you were standing in the way against me. So now, if it is evil in your sight, I will turn back." 35 But the angel of Yahweh said to Balaam, "Go with the men, but you shall speak only the word which I tell you." So Balaam went along with the leaders of Balak.

36 Then Balak heard that Balaam was coming and went out to meet him at the city of Moab, which is on the Arnon border, at the end of the border. 37 Then Balak said to Balaam, "Did I not urgently send to you to call you? Why did you not come to me? Am I indeed unable to honor you?" 38 So Balaam said to Balak, "Behold, I have come now to you! Am I able to speak anything at all? The word that God puts in my mouth, that I shall speak." 39 And Balaam went with Balak, and they came to Kiriath-huzoth. 40 And Balak sacrificed oxen and sheep, and sent *some* to Balaam and the leaders who were with him.

41 Then it happened in the morning that Balak took Balaam and brought him up to the high places of Baal, and he saw from there the end of *the camp* of the people.

Psalm 33:10–17

10 Yahweh nullifies the counsel
of the nations;
He frustrates the thoughts
of the peoples.
11 The counsel of Yahweh stands forever,
The thoughts of His heart from
generation to generation.
12 Blessed is the nation whose
God is Yahweh,
The people whom He has chosen
for His own inheritance.

13 Yahweh looks from heaven;
He sees all the sons of men;
14 From the place of His
habitation He gazes
On all the inhabitants of the earth,

15 He who forms the hearts of them all,
He who understands all their works.
16 The king is not saved by
a mighty army;
A warrior is not delivered
by great strength.
17 A horse is a false hope for salvation;
Nor does it provide escape to
anyone by its great strength.

Proverbs 11:25–26

25 The soul that blesses will be enriched,
And he who waters will
himself be watered.
26 He who withholds grain, the
people will curse him,
But blessing will be on the
head of him who sells *it*.

Mark 12:28–44

28 And when one of the scribes came and
heard them arguing, he recognized that He
had answered them well and asked Him,
"What commandment is the foremost of
all?" 29 Jesus answered, "The foremost is,
'HEAR, O ISRAEL! THE LORD OUR GOD IS ONE
LORD; 30 AND YOU SHALL LOVE THE LORD YOUR
GOD WITH ALL YOUR HEART, AND WITH ALL
YOUR SOUL, AND WITH ALL YOUR MIND, AND
WITH ALL YOUR STRENGTH.' 31 The second
is this, 'YOU SHALL LOVE YOUR NEIGHBOR AS
YOURSELF.' There is no other commandment
greater than these." 32 And the scribe said to
Him, "Right, Teacher; You have truly stated
that HE IS ONE, AND THERE IS NO ONE ELSE
BESIDES HIM; 33 AND TO LOVE HIM WITH ALL
THE HEART AND WITH ALL THE UNDERSTAND-
ING AND WITH ALL THE STRENGTH, AND TO
LOVE ONE'S NEIGHBOR AS HIMSELF, is much
more than all burnt offerings and sacrifices."
34 And when Jesus saw that he had answered
thoughtfully, He said to him, "You are not far
from the kingdom of God." After that, no one
would dare to ask Him any more questions.
35 And Jesus *began to* say, as He taught in
the temple, "How *is it that* the scribes say
that the Christ is the son of David? 36 David
himself said in the Holy Spirit,

'THE LORD SAID TO MY LORD,
"SIT AT MY RIGHT HAND,
UNTIL I PUT YOUR ENEMIES
BENEATH YOUR FEET."'

37 "David himself calls Him 'Lord'; so in what
sense is He his son?" And the large crowd
enjoyed listening to Him.
38 And in His teaching He was saying:
"Beware of the scribes who want to walk
around in long robes, and *want* respectful
greetings in the marketplaces, 39 and best
seats in the synagogues and places of honor
at banquets, 40 who devour widows' houses,
and for appearance's sake offer long prayers;
these will receive greater condemnation."
41 And He sat down opposite the treasury,
and *began* observing how the crowd was
putting money into the treasury; and many
rich people were putting in large sums.
42 And a poor widow came and put in two
lepta, which amount to a quadrans. 43 And
calling His disciples to Him, He said to them,
"Truly I say to you, this poor widow put in
more than all those putting *money* into the
treasury; 44 for they all put in out of their
surplus, but she, out of her poverty, put in
all she owned, all she had to live on."

MARCH 13

Numbers 23:1–24:25

23 Then Balaam said to Balak, "Build
seven altars for me here, and prepare
seven bulls and seven rams for me here."
2 So Balak did just as Balaam had spoken,
and Balak and Balaam offered up a bull and
a ram on each altar. 3 Then Balaam said to
Balak, "Stand beside your burnt offering,
and I will go; perhaps Yahweh will come to
meet me, and whatever He shows me I will
tell you." So he went to a bare hill.
4 Now God met Balaam, and he said to
Him, "I have set up the seven altars, and I
have offered up a bull and a ram on each
altar." 5 Then Yahweh put a word in Balaam's
mouth and said, "Return to Balak, and you
shall speak thus." 6 So he returned to him,
and behold, he was standing beside his
burnt offering, he and all the leaders of
Moab. 7 Then he took up his discourse and
said,

"From Aram Balak has brought me,
Moab's king from the
mountains of the East,
'Come curse Jacob for me,
And come, denounce Israel!'

8 "How shall I curse whom
God has not cursed?
And how can I denounce whom
Yahweh has not denounced?
9 "For I see him from the top of the rocks,
And I look at him from the hills;
Behold, a people *who* dwells alone,
And will not be reckoned
among the nations.
10 "Who can number the dust of Jacob,
Or count the fourth part of Israel?
Let me die the death of the upright,
And let my end be like his!"

11 Then Balak said to Balaam, "What
have you done to me? I took you to curse
my enemies, but behold, you have blessed
them repeatedly!" 12 And he replied, "Must
I not be careful to speak what Yahweh puts
in my mouth?"

13 Then Balak said to him, "Please come
with me to another place from where you
may see them, but you will only see the
end of them and will not see all of them;
and curse them for me from there." 14 So he
took him to the field of Zophim, to the top of
Pisgah, and built seven altars and offered a
bull and a ram on *each* altar. 15 And he said
to Balak, "Stand here beside your burnt
offering while I myself meet *Yahweh* over
there." 16 Then Yahweh met Balaam and put
a word in his mouth and said, "Return to
Balak, and thus you shall speak." 17 So he
came to him, and behold, he was standing
beside his burnt offering, and the leaders
of Moab with him. And Balak said to him,
"What has Yahweh spoken?" 18 Then he took
up his discourse and said,

"Arise, O Balak, and hear;
Give ear to me, O son of Zippor!
19 "God is not a man, that He should lie,
Nor a son of man, that He
should repent;
Has He said, and will He not do it?
Or has He spoken, and will
He not establish it?
20 "Behold, I have received *a
command* to bless;
When He has blessed, then
I cannot revoke it.
21 "He has not observed
misfortune in Jacob;
Nor has He seen trouble in Israel;
Yahweh his God is with him,
And the shout of a king is among them.
22 "God brings them out of Egypt,
He is for them like the
horns of the wild ox.
23 "For there is no omen against Jacob,
Nor is there any divination
against Israel;
At the proper time it shall
be said to Jacob
And to Israel, what God has done!
24 "Behold, a people rises like a lioness,
And as a lion it lifts itself;
It will not lie down until it
devours the prey,
And drinks the blood of the slain."

25 Then Balak said to Balaam, "Do not
curse them at all nor bless them at all!"
26 But Balaam replied to Balak, "Did I not
tell you, saying, 'Whatever Yahweh speaks,
that I must do'?"

27 Then Balak said to Balaam, "Please
come, I will take you to another place; per-
haps it will be right in the eyes of God that
you curse them for me from there." 28 So
Balak took Balaam to the top of Peor which
overlooks the wasteland. 29 And Balaam said
to Balak, "Build seven altars for me here and
prepare seven bulls and seven rams for me
here." 30 And Balak did just as Balaam had
said and offered up a bull and a ram on *each*
altar.

24 And Balaam saw that it was good in
the eyes of Yahweh to bless Israel, so
he did not go as at other times to encoun-
ter omens, but he set his face toward the
wilderness. 2 And Balaam lifted up his eyes
and saw Israel dwelling tribe by tribe; and
the Spirit of God came upon him. 3 Then he
took up his discourse and said,

"The oracle of Balaam the son of Beor,
And the oracle of the man
whose eye is uncovered;
4 The oracle of him who hears
the words of God,
Who beholds the vision
of the Almighty,
Falling down, yet having
his eyes opened,
5 How fair are your tents, O Jacob,
Your dwellings, O Israel!
6 "Like valleys that stretch out,
Like gardens beside the river,
Like aloes planted by Yahweh,
Like cedars beside the waters.
7 "Water will flow from his buckets,
And his seed *will be* by many waters,

And his king shall be lifted
up higher than Agag,
And his kingdom shall be exalted.
8 "God brings him out of Egypt,
He is for him like the horns
of the wild ox.
He will devour the nations
who are his adversaries,
And will gnaw their bones in pieces,
And shatter *them* with his arrows.
9 "He crouches, he lies down as a lion,
And as a lion, who dares rouse him?
Blessed is everyone who blesses you,
And cursed is everyone
who curses you."

10 Then Balak's anger burned against
Balaam, and he struck his hands together;
and Balak said to Balaam, "I called you to
curse my enemies, but behold, you have
blessed them repeatedly these three times!
11 So now, flee to your place. I said I would
honor you greatly, but behold, Yahweh has
held you back from honor." 12 And Balaam
said to Balak, "Did I not tell your messen-
gers whom you had sent to me, saying,
13 'Though Balak were to give me his house
full of silver and gold, I could not do any-
thing to trespass the command of Yahweh,
either good or bad, of my own accord. What
Yahweh speaks, that I will speak'? 14 So now,
behold, I am going to my people; come, *and*
I will advise you what this people will do to
your people in the last days."

15 Then he took up his discourse and said,
"The oracle of Balaam the son of Beor,
And the oracle of the man
whose eye is uncovered,
16 The oracle of him who hears
the words of God,
And knows the knowledge
of the Most High,
Who beholds the vision
of the Almighty,
Falling down, yet having
his eyes opened.
17 "I see him, but not now;
I behold him, but not near;
A star shall come forth from Jacob,
A scepter shall rise from Israel,
And shall crush through the
forehead of Moab,
And tear down all the sons of Sheth.
18 "And Edom shall be a possession,
Seir, its enemies, also will
be a possession,
While Israel performs valiantly.
19 "And one from Jacob shall
have dominion,
And will make the survivor
perish from the city."

20 Then he looked at Amalek and took up
his discourse and said,
"Amalek was the first of the nations,
But his end *shall be* destruction."

21 Then he looked at the Kenite and took
up his discourse and said,
"Your habitation is enduring,
And your nest is set in the cliff.
22 "Nevertheless Kain will be consumed;
How long will Asshur keep
you captive?"

23 Then he took up his discourse and said,
"Woe, who can live except when
God has ordained it?
24 "But ships *shall come* from
the coast of Kittim,
And they shall afflict Asshur
and will afflict Eber;
So they also *will come* to destruction."

25 Then Balaam arose and went and
returned to his place, and Balak also went
his way.

Psalm 33:18–22

18 Behold, the eye of Yahweh is
on those who fear Him,
On those who wait for His
lovingkindness,
19 To deliver their soul from death
And to keep them alive in famine.
20 Our soul is patient for Yahweh;
He is our help and our shield.
21 For our heart is glad in Him,
Because we trust in His holy name.
22 Let Your lovingkindness,
O Yahweh, be upon us,
As we wait for You.

Proverbs 11:27

27 He who earnestly seeks
good seeks favor,
But he who searches for evil,
evil will come to him.

Mark 13:1–23

13 And as He was going out of the temple,
one of His disciples *said to Him,
"Teacher, behold what wonderful stones
and what wonderful buildings!" 2 And
Jesus said to him, "Do you see these great

buildings? Not one stone will be left upon another which will not be torn down."

3 And as He was sitting on the Mount of Olives opposite the temple, Peter and James and John and Andrew were questioning Him privately, 4 "Tell us, when will these things be, and what *will be* the sign when all these things are going to be fulfilled?" 5 And Jesus began to say to them, "See to it that no one deceives you. 6 Many will come in My name, saying, 'I am *He!*' and will mislead many. 7 And when you hear of wars and rumors of wars, do not be alarmed; *those things* must take place; but *that is* not yet the end. 8 For nation will rise up against nation, and kingdom against kingdom; there will be earthquakes in various places; there will *also* be famines. These things are *merely* the beginning of birth pains.

9 "But see to yourselves; for they will deliver you to *the* courts, and you will be beaten in *the* synagogues, and you will stand before governors and kings for My sake, as a witness to them. 10 And the gospel must first be proclaimed to all the nations. 11 And when they lead you away, delivering you up, do not worry beforehand about what you are to say, but say whatever is given to you in that hour; for it is not you who speak, but *it is* the Holy Spirit. 12 And brother will betray brother to death, and a father *his* child; and children will rise up against parents and have them put to death. 13 And you will be hated by all because of My name, but the one who endures to the end, he will be saved.

14 "But when you see the ABOMINATION OF DESOLATION standing where it should not be (let the reader understand), then those who are in Judea must flee to the mountains. 15 And the one who is on the housetop must not go down, or go in to get anything out of his house; 16 and the one who is in the field must not turn back to get his garment. 17 But woe to those who are pregnant and to those who are nursing babies in those days! 18 But pray that it may not happen in the winter. 19 For those days will be a *time of* tribulation such as has not occurred since the beginning of the creation which God created until now, and never will. 20 And unless the Lord had shortened *those* days, no life would have been saved; but for the sake of the elect, whom He chose, He shortened the days. 21 And then if anyone says to you, 'Behold, here is the Christ'; or, 'Behold, *He is* there'; do not believe *him*; 22 for false christs and false prophets will arise, and will show signs and wonders, in order to lead astray, if possible, the elect. 23 But as for you, see! I have told you everything in advance.

MARCH 14

Numbers 25:1–26:65

25 And Israel remained at Shittim, and the people began to play the harlot with the daughters of Moab. 2 Indeed they called the people to the sacrifices of their gods, and the people ate and bowed down to their gods. 3 So Israel joined themselves to Baal of Peor, and the anger of Yahweh burned against Israel. 4 And Yahweh said to Moses, "Take all *who are* the heads of the people and execute them in broad daylight before Yahweh, so that the burning anger of Yahweh may turn away from Israel." 5 So Moses said to the judges of Israel, "Each of you kill his men who have joined themselves to Baal of Peor."

6 Then behold, one of the sons of Israel came and brought near to his brothers a Midianite woman, in the sight of Moses and in the sight of all the congregation of the sons of Israel, while they were weeping at the doorway of the tent of meeting. 7 And Phinehas the son of Eleazar, the son of Aaron the priest, saw it, so he arose from the midst of the congregation and took a spear in his hand, 8 and he went after the man of Israel into the tent and pierced both of them through, the man of Israel and the woman, through the body. Then the plague on the sons of Israel was checked. 9 So those who died by the plague were 24,000.

10 Then Yahweh spoke to Moses, saying, 11 "Phinehas the son of Eleazar, the son of Aaron the priest, has turned away My wrath from the sons of Israel in that he was jealous with My jealousy among them, so that I did not consume the sons of Israel in My jealousy. 12 Therefore say, 'Behold, I give him My covenant of peace; 13 and it shall be for him and his seed after him, a covenant of

a perpetual priesthood, because he was
jealous for his God and made atonement
for the sons of Israel.'"
14 Now the name of the slain man of Israel
who was slain with the Midianite woman,
was Zimri the son of Salu, a leader of a
father's household among the Simeonites.
15 And the name of the Midianite woman,
who was struck down, was Cozbi the daugh-
ter of Zur, who was head of the people of a
father's household in Midian.
16 Then Yahweh spoke to Moses, saying,
17 "Be hostile to the Midianites and strike
them, 18 for they have been hostile to you
with their deceptive tricks, with which
they have deceived you in the affair of Peor
and in the affair of Cozbi, the daughter of
the leader of Midian, their sister who was
slain on the day of the plague because of
Peor."

26 Then it happened after the plague,
that Yahweh spoke to Moses and to
Eleazar the son of Aaron the priest, saying,
2 "Take a census of all the congregation of
the sons of Israel from twenty years old
and upward, by their fathers' households,
whoever is able to go out to war in Israel."
3 So Moses and Eleazar the priest spoke with
them in the plains of Moab by the Jordan
at Jericho, saying, 4 "*Take a census of the
people* from twenty years old and upward,
as Yahweh has commanded Moses."
Now the sons of Israel who came out of
the land of Egypt *were*:

5 Reuben, Israel's firstborn, the sons of
Reuben:
of Hanoch, the family of the
Hanochites;
of Pallu, the family of the Palluites;
6 of Hezron, the family of the
Hezronites;
of Carmi, the family of the Carmites.
7 These are the families of the
Reubenites, and those who were
numbered of them were 43,730.
8 And the son of Pallu: Eliab.
9 And the sons of Eliab:
Nemuel and Dathan and Abiram.
These are the Dathan and Abiram who
were called *upon* by the congregation,
who contended against Moses and
against Aaron in the congregation of
Korah, when they contended against
Yahweh,
10 and the earth opened its mouth and
swallowed them up along with Korah,
when that congregation died, when
the fire consumed 250 men, so that
they became a warning.
11 The sons of Korah, however, did not
die.

12 The sons of Simeon according to their
families:
of Nemuel, the family of the
Nemuelites;
of Jamin, the family of the Jaminites;
of Jachin, the family of the Jachinites;
13 of Zerah, the family of the Zerahites;
of Shaul, the family of the Shaulites.
14 These are the families of the
Simeonites, 22,200.

15 The sons of Gad according to their
families:
of Zephon, the family of the
Zephonites;
of Haggi, the family of the Haggites;
of Shuni, the family of the Shunites;
16 of Ozni, the family of the Oznites;
of Eri, the family of the Erites;
17 of Arod, the family of the Arodites;
of Areli, the family of the Arelites.
18 These are the families of the sons
of Gad according to those who were
numbered of them, 40,500.

19 The sons of Judah *were* Er and Onan,
but Er and Onan died in the land of
Canaan.
20 And the sons of Judah according to
their families were:
of Shelah, the family of the Shelanites;
of Perez, the family of the Perezites;
of Zerah, the family of the Zerahites.
21 And the sons of Perez were:
of Hezron, the family of the
Hezronites;
of Hamul, the family of the Hamulites.
22 These are the families of Judah
according to those who were
numbered of them, 76,500.

23 The sons of Issachar according to their
families:
of Tola, the family of the Tolaites;
of Puvah, the family of the Punites;
24 of Jashub, the family of the
Jashubites;

of Shimron, the family of the Shimronites.
25 These are the families of Issachar according to those who were numbered of them, 64,300.

26 The sons of Zebulun according to their families:
of Sered, the family of the Seredites;
of Elon, the family of the Elonites;
of Jahleel, the family of the Jahleelites.
27 These are the families of the Zebulunites according to those who were numbered of them, 60,500.

28 The sons of Joseph according to their families: Manasseh and Ephraim.
29 The sons of Manasseh:
of Machir, the family of the Machirites; and Machir became the father of Gilead:
of Gilead, the family of the Gileadites.
30 These are the sons of Gilead:
of Iezer, the family of the Iezerites;
of Helek, the family of the Helekites;
31 and *of* Asriel, the family of the Asrielites;
and *of* Shechem, the family of the Shechemites;
32 and *of* Shemida, the family of the Shemidaites;
and *of* Hepher, the family of the Hepherites.
33 Now Zelophehad the son of Hepher had no sons, but only daughters; and the names of the daughters of Zelophehad were Mahlah, Noah, Hoglah, Milcah and Tirzah.
34 These are the families of Manasseh; and those who were numbered of them were 52,700.

35 These are the sons of Ephraim according to their families:
of Shuthelah, the family of the Shuthelahites;
of Becher, the family of the Becherites;
of Tahan, the family of the Tahanites.
36 And these are the sons of Shuthelah:
of Eran, the family of the Eranites.
37 These are the families of the sons of Ephraim according to those who were numbered of them, 32,500.
These are the sons of Joseph according to their families.

38 The sons of Benjamin according to their families:
of Bela, the family of the Belaites;
of Ashbel, the family of the Ashbelites;
of Ahiram, the family of the Ahiramites;
39 of Shephupham, the family of the Shuphamites;
of Hupham, the family of the Huphamites.
40 And the sons of Bela were Ard and Naaman:
of Ard, the family of the Ardites;
of Naaman, the family of the Naamites.
41 These are the sons of Benjamin according to their families; and those who were numbered of them were 45,600.

42 These are the sons of Dan according to their families:
of Shuham, the family of the Shuhamites.
These are the families of Dan according to their families.
43 All the families of the Shuhamites, according to those who were numbered of them, were 64,400.
44 The sons of Asher according to their families:
of Imnah, the family of the Imnites;
of Ishvi, the family of the Ishvites;
of Beriah, the family of the Beriites.
45 Of the sons of Beriah:
of Heber, the family of the Heberites;
of Malchiel, the family of the Malchielites.
46 And the name of the daughter of Asher *was* Serah.
47 These are the families of the sons of Asher according to those who were numbered of them, 53,400.

48 The sons of Naphtali according to their families:
of Jahzeel, the family of the Jahzeelites;
of Guni, the family of the Gunites;
49 of Jezer, the family of the Jezerites;
of Shillem, the family of the Shillemites.
50 These are the families of Naphtali according to their families; and those

who were numbered of them were
45,400.

51 These are those who were numbered
of the sons of Israel, 601,730.

52 Then Yahweh spoke to Moses, saying,
53 "Among these the land shall be divided
for an inheritance according to the number
of names. 54 To the larger *group* you shall
increase their inheritance, and to the
smaller *group* you shall diminish their
inheritance; each shall be given their
inheritance according to those who were
numbered of them. 55 But the land shall
be divided by lot. They shall receive their
inheritance according to the names of the
tribes of their fathers. 56 According to the
selection by lot, their inheritance shall be
divided between the larger and the smaller
groups."

57 And these are those who were num-
bered of the Levites according to their
families:

of Gershon, the family of the
Gershonites;
of Kohath, the family of the
Kohathites;
of Merari, the family of the Merarites.

58 These are the families of Levi:
the family of the Libnites,
the family of the Hebronites,
the family of the Mahlites,
the family of the Mushites,
the family of the Korahites. Kohath
became the father of Amram.

59 And the name of Amram's wife was
Jochebed, the daughter of Levi, who was
born to Levi in Egypt; and she bore to
Amram: Aaron and Moses and their sister
Miriam. 60 And to Aaron were born Nadab
and Abihu, Eleazar and Ithamar. 61 But
Nadab and Abihu died when they offered
strange fire before Yahweh. 62 And those
who were numbered of them were 23,000,
every male from a month old and upward,
for they were not numbered among the sons
of Israel since no inheritance was given to
them among the sons of Israel.

63 These are those who were numbered
by Moses and Eleazar the priest, who
numbered the sons of Israel in the plains
of Moab by the Jordan at Jericho. 64 But
among these there was not a man of those
who were numbered by Moses and Aaron
the priest, who numbered the sons of Israel
in the wilderness of Sinai. 65 For Yahweh
had said of them, "They shall surely die in
the wilderness." And not a man was left of
them, except Caleb the son of Jephunneh
and Joshua the son of Nun.

Psalm 34:1–7

1 I will bless Yahweh at all times;
His praise shall continually
be in my mouth.

2 My soul will make its boast in Yahweh;
The humble will hear it and rejoice.

3 O magnify Yahweh with me,
And let us exalt His name together.

4 I inquired of Yahweh, and
He answered me,
And delivered me from all that I dread.

5 They looked to Him and were radiant,
And their faces will never
be humiliated.

6 This poor man called out,
and Yahweh heard him
And saved him out of all his troubles.

7 The angel of Yahweh encamps
around those who fear Him,
And rescues them.

Proverbs 11:28

28 He who trusts in his riches will fall,
But the righteous will flourish
like the *green* leaf.

Mark 13:24–37

24 "But in those days, after that tribula-
tion, THE SUN WILL BE DARKENED AND THE
MOON WILL NOT GIVE ITS LIGHT, 25 AND THE
STARS WILL BE FALLING from heaven, AND
THE POWERS THAT ARE IN THE HEAVENS will
be shaken. 26 And then they will see THE SON
OF MAN COMING IN CLOUDS with great power
and glory. 27 And then He will send forth the
angels, and will gather together His elect
from the four winds, from the farthest end
of the earth to the farthest end of heaven.

28 "Now learn the parable from the fig
tree: when its branch has already become
tender and puts forth its leaves, you know
that summer is near. 29 Even so, you too,
when you see these things happening,
recognize that He is near, *right* at the door.

30 Truly I say to you, this generation will not pass away until all these things take place. 31 Heaven and earth will pass away, but My words will not pass away. 32 But of that day or hour no one knows, not even the angels in heaven, nor the Son, but the Father *alone*.

33 "See to it, keep on the alert; for you do not know when the *appointed* time will come. 34 *It is* like a man away on a journey, *who*, leaving his house and giving authority to his slaves—each one his task, also commanded the doorkeeper to stay awake. 35 Therefore, stay awake—for you do not know when the master of the house is coming, whether in the evening, at midnight, or when the rooster crows, or in the morning— 36 lest he come suddenly and find you sleeping. 37 And what I say to you I say to all, 'Stay awake!'"

MARCH 15

Numbers 27:1–28:31

27 Then the daughters of Zelophehad, the son of Hepher, the son of Gilead, the son of Machir, the son of Manasseh, of the families of Manasseh the son of Joseph, came near; and these are the names of his daughters: Mahlah, Noah and Hoglah and Milcah and Tirzah. 2 And they stood before Moses and before Eleazar the priest and before the leaders and all the congregation, at the doorway of the tent of meeting, saying, 3 "Our father died in the wilderness, yet he was not among the congregation of those who gathered themselves together against Yahweh in the congregation of Korah; but he died in his own sin, and he had no sons. 4 Why should the name of our father be withdrawn from among his family because he had no son? Give us a possession among our father's brothers." 5 So Moses brought their case near before Yahweh.

6 Then Yahweh spoke to Moses, saying, 7 "The daughters of Zelophehad are right in *their* statements. You shall surely give them a possession for an inheritance among their father's brothers, and you shall have the inheritance of their father pass on to them. 8 Further, you shall speak to the sons of Israel, saying, 'If a man dies and has no son, then you shall have his inheritance pass on to his daughter. 9 And if he has no daughter, then you shall give his inheritance to his brothers. 10 And if he has no brothers, then you shall give his inheritance to his father's brothers. 11 And if his father has no brothers, then you shall give his inheritance to his blood relative in his own family, and he shall possess it; and it shall be a statutory judgment to the sons of Israel, just as Yahweh commanded Moses.'"

12 Then Yahweh said to Moses, "Go up to this mountain of Abarim, and see the land which I have given to the sons of Israel. 13 So *when* you have seen it, you too will be gathered to your people, as Aaron your brother was, 14 for in the wilderness of Zin, during the strife of the congregation, you rebelled against My command to treat Me as holy before their eyes at the water." (These are the waters of Meribah of Kadesh in the wilderness of Zin.)

15 Then Moses spoke to Yahweh, saying, 16 "May Yahweh, the God of the spirits of all flesh, appoint a man over the congregation, 17 who will go out and come in before them, and who will lead them out and bring them in, so that the congregation of Yahweh will not be like sheep which have no shepherd." 18 So Yahweh said to Moses, "Take Joshua the son of Nun, a man in whom is the Spirit, and lay your hand on him; 19 and have him stand before Eleazar the priest and before all the congregation, and commission him in their sight. 20 And you shall put some of your splendor on him, in order that all the congregation of the sons of Israel may obey *him*. 21 Moreover, he shall stand before Eleazar the priest, who shall inquire for him by the judgment of the Urim before Yahweh. At his command they shall go out, and at his command they shall come in, *both* he and the sons of Israel with him, even all the congregation." 22 So Moses did just as Yahweh commanded him; and he took Joshua and had him stand before Eleazar the priest and before all the congregation. 23 Then he laid his hands on him and commissioned him, just as Yahweh had spoken by the hand of Moses.

28 Then Yahweh spoke to Moses, saying, 2 "Command the sons of Israel and say to them, 'You shall be careful to

bring near My offering, My food for My
offerings by fire, of a soothing aroma to
Me, at their appointed time.' 3 And you
shall say to them, 'This is the offering by
fire which you shall bring near to Yahweh:
two male lambs one year old without
blemish *as* a continual burnt offering
every day. 4 You shall offer the one lamb
in the morning, and the other lamb you
shall offer at twilight, 5 also a tenth of an
ephah of fine flour for a grain offering,
mixed with a fourth of a hin of beaten oil.
6 It is a continual burnt offering which
was ordained in Mount Sinai as a sooth-
ing aroma, an offering by fire to Yahweh.
7 Then the drink offering with it *shall be* a
fourth of a hin for each lamb, in the holy
place you shall pour out a drink offering
of strong drink to Yahweh. 8 And the other
lamb you shall offer at twilight; as the grain
offering of the morning and as its drink
offering, you shall offer it, an offering by
fire, a soothing aroma to Yahweh.

9 'Then on the sabbath day two male
lambs one year old without blemish, and
two-tenths *of an ephah* of fine flour mixed
with oil as a grain offering, and its drink
offering: 10 *This is* the burnt offering of every
sabbath in addition to the continual burnt
offering and its drink offering.

11 'Then at the beginning of each of your
months you shall bring near a burnt offering
to Yahweh: two bulls from the herd and one
ram, seven male lambs one year old without
blemish; 12 and three-tenths *of an ephah* of
fine flour mixed with oil for a grain offering,
for each bull; and two-tenths of fine flour
mixed with oil for a grain offering, for the
one ram; 13 and a tenth *of an ephah* of fine
flour mixed with oil for a grain offering for
each lamb, for a burnt offering of a soothing
aroma, an offering by fire to Yahweh. 14 And
their drink offerings shall be half a hin of
wine for a bull and a third of a hin for the
ram and a fourth of a hin for a lamb; this is
the burnt offering of each month through-
out the months of the year. 15 And one male
goat for a sin offering to Yahweh; it shall be
offered with its drink offering in addition to
the continual burnt offering.

16 'Then on the fourteenth day of the first
month shall be the Passover of Yahweh.
17 And on the fifteenth day of this month
shall be a feast; unleavened bread *shall be*
eaten for seven days. 18 On the first day *shall*
be a holy convocation; you shall do no labo-
rious work. 19 And you shall bring near an
offering by fire, a burnt offering to Yahweh:
two bulls from the herd and one ram and
seven male lambs one year old; they shall
be for you without blemish. 20 Now as for
their grain offering, you shall offer fine flour
mixed with oil: three-tenths *of an ephah* for
a bull and two-tenths for the ram. 21 A tenth
of an ephah you shall offer for each of the
seven lambs; 22 and one male goat for a sin
offering to make atonement for you. 23 You
shall offer these besides the burnt offering
of the morning, which is for a continual
burnt offering. 24 After this manner you
shall offer daily, for seven days, the food
of the offering by fire, of a soothing aroma
to Yahweh; it shall be offered with its drink
offering in addition to the continual burnt
offering. 25 Now on the seventh day you
shall have a holy convocation; you shall do
no laborious work.

26 'Also on the day of the first fruits, when
you bring near a new grain offering to Yah-
weh in your *Feast of* Weeks, you shall have a
holy convocation; you shall do no laborious
work. 27 And you shall bring near a burnt
offering for a soothing aroma to Yahweh:
two bulls from the herd, one ram, seven
male lambs one year old; 28 and their grain
offering, fine flour mixed with oil: three-
tenths *of an ephah* for each bull, two-tenths
for the one ram, 29 a tenth for each of the
seven lambs; 30 *also* one male goat to make
atonement for you. 31 Besides the continual
burnt offering and its grain offering, you
shall offer *them* with their drink offerings.
They shall be without blemish.

Psalm 34:8–14

8 O taste and see that Yahweh is good;
How blessed is the man who
takes refuge in Him!

9 Oh, fear Yahweh, you His saints;
For there is no want to
those who fear Him.

10 The young lions do lack
and suffer hunger;
But they who inquire of Yahweh shall
not be in want of any good thing.

11 Come, you children, listen to me;
I will teach you the fear of Yahweh.

12 Who is the man who delights in life
And loves *many* days that
he may see good?

13 Guard your tongue from evil
And your lips from speaking deceit.

14 Depart from evil and do good;
Seek peace and pursue it.

Proverbs 11:29

29 He who troubles his own
house will inherit wind,
And the ignorant fool will be a
slave to the wise of heart.

Mark 14:1–26

14 Now the Passover and Unleavened
Bread were two days away; and the
chief priests and the scribes were seeking
how, after seizing Him in secret, they
might kill *Him*; 2 for they were saying, "Not
during the festival, lest there be a riot of the
people."
3 And while He was in Bethany at the home
of Simon the leper, and reclining *at the table*,
there came a woman with an alabaster jar of
perfume of very costly pure nard; *and* she
broke the jar and poured it over His head.
4 But some were indignantly *remarking* to
one another, "Why has this perfume been
wasted? 5 For this perfume might have been
sold for over three hundred denarii and
given to the poor." And they were scolding
her. 6 But Jesus said, "Let her alone; why do
you bother her? She did a good work to Me.
7 For you always have the poor with you,
and whenever you wish you can do good to
them; but you do not always have Me. 8 She
has done what she could; she anointed My
body beforehand for the burial. 9 And truly I
say to you, wherever the gospel is proclaimed
in the whole world, what this woman did will
also be spoken of in memory of her."
10 Then Judas Iscariot, who was one of
the twelve, went away to the chief priests
in order to betray Him to them. 11 And
when they heard *this*, they were glad and
promised to give him money. And he *began*
seeking how to betray Him at an opportune
time.
12 And on the first day of Unleavened
Bread, when the Passover lamb was being
sacrificed, His disciples *said to Him,
"Where do You want us to go and prepare
for You to eat the Passover?" 13 And He *sent
two of His disciples and *said to them, "Go
into the city, and a man will meet you car-
rying a pitcher of water; follow him; 14 and
wherever he enters, say to the owner of the
house, 'The Teacher says, "Where is My
guest room in which I may eat the Passover
with My disciples?"' 15 And he himself will
show you a large upper room furnished
and ready; prepare for us there." 16 And the
disciples went out and came to the city, and
found *it* just as He had told them; and they
prepared the Passover.
17 And when it was evening He *came with
the twelve. 18 And as they were reclining *at
the table* and eating, Jesus said, "Truly I say
to you that one of you will betray Me—the
one who is eating with Me." 19 They began
to be grieved and to say to Him one by one,
"Surely not I?" 20 And He said to them, "*It
is* one of the twelve, the one who dips with
Me in the bowl. 21 For the Son of Man *is to* go
just as it is written of Him; but woe to that
man by whom the Son of Man is betrayed!
It would have been good for that man if he
had not been born."
22 And while they were eating, He took
some bread, and after a blessing, He broke
it, and gave *it* to them, and said, "Take *it*;
this is My body." 23 And when He had taken
a cup *and* given thanks, He gave *it* to them,
and they all drank from it. 24 And He said
to them, "This is My blood of the covenant,
which is poured out for many. 25 Truly I say
to you, I will never again drink of the fruit of
the vine until that day when I drink it new
in the kingdom of God."
26 And after singing a hymn, they went
out to the Mount of Olives.

MARCH 16

Numbers 29:1–30:16

29 'Now in the seventh month, on the
first day of the month, you shall also
have a holy convocation; you shall do no
laborious work. It will be to you a day for
blowing trumpets. 2 And you shall offer
a burnt offering as a soothing aroma to
Yahweh: one bull from the herd, one ram,

and seven male lambs one year old without blemish; 3 also their grain offering, fine flour mixed with oil: three-tenths *of an ephah* for the bull, two-tenths for the ram, 4 and one-tenth for each of the seven lambs. 5 And *offer* one male goat for a sin offering, to make atonement for you, 6 besides the burnt offering of the new moon and its grain offering, and the continual burnt offering and its grain offering, and their drink offerings, according to their *legal* judgment, for a soothing aroma, an offering by fire to Yahweh.

7 'Then on the tenth day of this seventh month you shall have a holy convocation, and you shall humble yourselves; you shall not do any work. 8 And you shall bring near a burnt offering to Yahweh *as* a soothing aroma: one bull from the herd, one ram, seven male lambs one year old, having them without blemish; 9 and their grain offering, fine flour mixed with oil: three-tenths *of an ephah* for the bull, two-tenths for the one ram, 10 a tenth for each of the seven lambs; 11 one male goat for a sin offering, besides the sin offering of atonement and the continual burnt offering and its grain offering and their drink offerings.

12 'Then on the fifteenth day of the seventh month you shall have a holy convocation; you shall do no laborious work, and you shall celebrate a feast to Yahweh for seven days. 13 And you shall bring near a burnt offering, an offering by fire as a soothing aroma to Yahweh: thirteen bulls from the herd, two rams, fourteen male lambs one year old, which are without blemish; 14 and their grain offering, fine flour mixed with oil: three-tenths *of an ephah* for each of the thirteen bulls, two-tenths for each of the two rams, 15 and a tenth for each of the fourteen lambs; 16 and one male goat for a sin offering, besides the continual burnt offering, its grain offering, and its drink offering.

17 'Then on the second day: twelve bulls from the herd, two rams, fourteen male lambs one year old without blemish; 18 and their grain offering and their drink offerings for the bulls, for the rams and for the lambs, by their number according to the *legal* judgment; 19 and one male goat for a sin offering, besides the continual burnt offering and its grain offering and their drink offerings.

20 'Then on the third day: eleven bulls, two rams, fourteen male lambs one year old without blemish; 21 and their grain offering and their drink offerings for the bulls, for the rams and for the lambs, by their number according to the *legal* judgment; 22 and one male goat for a sin offering, besides the continual burnt offering and its grain offering and its drink offering.

23 'Then on the fourth day: ten bulls, two rams, fourteen male lambs one year old without blemish; 24 their grain offering and their drink offerings for the bulls, for the rams and for the lambs, by their number according to the *legal* judgment; 25 and one male goat for a sin offering, besides the continual burnt offering, its grain offering and its drink offering.

26 'Then on the fifth day: nine bulls, two rams, fourteen male lambs one year old without blemish; 27 and their grain offering and their drink offerings for the bulls, for the rams and for the lambs, by their number according to the *legal* judgment; 28 and one male goat for a sin offering, besides the continual burnt offering and its grain offering and its drink offering.

29 'Then on the sixth day: eight bulls, two rams, fourteen male lambs one year old without blemish; 30 and their grain offering and their drink offerings for the bulls, for the rams and for the lambs, by their number according to the *legal* judgment; 31 and one male goat for a sin offering, besides the continual burnt offering, its grain offering and its drink offerings.

32 'Then on the seventh day: seven bulls, two rams, fourteen male lambs one year old without blemish; 33 and their grain offering and their drink offerings for the bulls, for the rams and for the lambs, by their number according to the *legal* judgment; 34 and one male goat for a sin offering, besides the continual burnt offering, its grain offering and its drink offering.

35 'On the eighth day you shall have a solemn assembly; you shall do no laborious work. 36 But you shall bring near a burnt offering, an offering by fire, as a soothing aroma to Yahweh: one bull, one ram, seven male lambs one year old without blemish; 37 their grain offering and their drink offerings for the bull, for the ram and for the lambs, by their number according to the *legal* judgment; 38 and one male goat for a sin offering, besides the continual burnt offering and its grain offering and its drink offering.

39 'You shall offer these to Yahweh at your
appointed times, besides your votive offer-
ings and your freewill offerings, for your
burnt offerings and for your grain offerings
and for your drink offerings and for your
peace offerings.'" 40 And Moses spoke to the
sons of Israel according to all that Yahweh
had commanded Moses.

30 Then Moses spoke to the heads
of the tribes of the sons of Israel,
saying, "This is the word which Yahweh
has commanded. 2 If a man makes a vow to
Yahweh or swears an oath to bind himself
with a binding obligation, he shall not
violate his word; he shall do according to
all that proceeds out of his mouth.
3 "Also if a woman makes a vow to Yah-
weh and binds herself by an obligation in
her father's house in her youth, 4 and her
father hears her vow and her obligation by
which she has bound herself, and her father
says nothing to her, then all her vows shall
stand, and every obligation by which she
has bound herself shall stand. 5 But if her
father should forbid her on the day he hears
of it, none of her vows or her obligations by
which she has bound herself shall stand;
and Yahweh will pardon her because her
father had forbidden her.
6 "However, if she should marry while
under her vows or the rash statement of her
lips by which she has bound herself, 7 and
her husband hears of it and says nothing
to her on the day he hears *it*, then her vows
shall stand, and her obligations by which
she has bound herself shall stand. 8 But
if, on the day her husband hears *of it*, he
forbids her, then he shall annul her vow
which she is under and the rash statement
of her lips by which she has bound herself;
and Yahweh will pardon her.
9 "But the vow of a widow or of a divorced
woman, everything by which she has bound
herself, shall stand against her. 10 However,
if she vowed in her husband's house or
bound herself by an obligation with an oath,
11 and her husband heard *it* but said nothing
to her *and* did not forbid her, then all her
vows shall stand, and every obligation by
which she bound herself shall stand. 12 But
if her husband indeed annuls them on the
day he hears *them*, then whatever proceeds
out of her lips concerning her vows or
concerning the obligation of herself shall
not stand; her husband has annulled them,
and Yahweh will pardon her.
13 "Every vow and every binding oath to
humble herself, her husband may cause it
to stand, or her husband may annul it. 14 But
if her husband indeed says nothing to her
from day to day, then he causes all her vows
or all her obligations which are on her to
stand; he has caused them to stand because
he said nothing to her on the day he heard
them. 15 But if he indeed annuls them after
he has heard them, then he shall bear her
guilt."
16 These are the statutes which Yahweh
commanded Moses, *as* between a man and
his wife, *and as* between a father and his
daughter, *while she is* in her youth in her
father's house.

Psalm 34:15–22

15 The eyes of Yahweh are
toward the righteous
And His ears are *open* to
their cry for help.

16 The face of Yahweh is against evildoers,
To cut off the memory of
them from the earth.

17 *The righteous* cry, and Yahweh hears
And delivers them out of
all their troubles.

18 Yahweh is near to the brokenhearted
And saves those who are
crushed in spirit.

19 Many are the evils *against*
the righteous,
But Yahweh delivers him
out of them all.

20 He keeps all his bones,
Not one of them is broken.

21 Evil shall slay the wicked,
And those who hate the righteous
will be condemned.

22 Yahweh redeems the soul of His slaves,
And all those who take refuge in
Him will not be condemned.

Proverbs 11:30–31

30 The fruit of the righteous
is a tree of life,

And he who is wise wins souls.
31 If the righteous will be
repaid in the earth,
How much more the wicked
and the sinner!

Mark 14:27–52

27 And Jesus *said to them, “You will all fall away, because it is written, ‘I WILL STRIKE DOWN THE SHEPHERD, AND THE SHEEP SHALL BE SCATTERED.’ 28 But after I have been raised, I will go ahead of you to Galilee.” 29 But Peter said to Him, “_Even_ though all may fall away, yet I will not.” 30 And Jesus *said to him, “Truly I say to you, that today, this _very_ night, before a rooster crows twice, you yourself will deny Me three times.” 31 But _Peter_ kept saying insistently, “If I have to die with You, I will not deny You!” And they all were saying the same thing also.

32 Then they *came to a place named Gethsemane; and He *said to His disciples, “Sit here until I have prayed.” 33 And He *took with Him Peter and James and John, and began to be very distressed and troubled. 34 And He *said to them, “My soul is deeply grieved to the point of death; remain here and keep watch.” 35 And He went a little beyond _them_, and fell to the ground and _began to_ pray that if it were possible, the hour might pass from Him. 36 And He was saying, “Abba! Father! All things are possible for You; remove this cup from Me; yet not what I will, but what You will.” 37 And He *came and *found them sleeping, and *said to Peter, “Simon, are you sleeping? Could you not keep watch for one hour? 38 Keep watching and praying that you may not come into temptation; the spirit is willing, but the flesh is weak.” 39 And again He went away and prayed, saying the same words. 40 And again He came and found them sleeping, for their eyes were very heavy; and they did not know what to answer Him. 41 And He *came the third time, and *said to them, “Are you still sleeping and resting? It is enough; the hour has come; behold, the Son of Man is being betrayed into the hands of sinners. 42 Get up, let us go; behold, the one who betrays Me is at hand!”

43 And immediately while He was still speaking, Judas, one of the twelve, *came up, and with him _was_ a crowd with swords and clubs, _who were_ from the chief priests and the scribes and the elders. 44 Now he who was betraying Him had given them a signal, saying, “Whomever I kiss, He is the one; seize Him and lead Him away under guard.” 45 And after coming, _Judas_, having immediately gone to Him, *said, “Rabbi!” and kissed Him. 46 And they laid hands on Him and seized Him. 47 But one of those who stood by drew his sword, and struck the slave of the high priest and cut off his ear. 48 And Jesus answered and said to them, “Have you come out with swords and clubs to arrest Me, as _you would_ against a robber? 49 Every day I was with you in the temple teaching, and you did not seize Me; but _this has taken place_ in order that the Scriptures would be fulfilled.” 50 And they all left Him and fled.

51 And a young man was following Him, wearing _nothing but_ a linen sheet over _his_ naked _body_; and they *seized him. 52 But he pulled free of the linen sheet and escaped naked.

MARCH 17

Numbers 31:1–32:42

31 Then Yahweh spoke to Moses, saying, 2 “Take full vengeance for the sons of Israel on the Midianites; afterward you will be gathered to your people.” 3 And Moses spoke to the people, saying, “Arm men from among you for the war, that they may go against Midian to execute Yahweh’s vengeance on Midian. 4 One thousand from each tribe of all the tribes of Israel you shall send to the war.” 5 So there were furnished from the thousands of Israel, one thousand from each tribe, twelve thousand armed for war. 6 And Moses sent them, one thousand from each tribe, to the war, and Phinehas the son of Eleazar the priest, to the war with them, and the holy vessels and the trumpets for the alarm in his hand. 7 So they made war against Midian, just as Yahweh had commanded Moses, and they killed every male. 8 They killed the kings of Midian along with the _rest of_ their slain: Evi and Rekem and Zur and Hur and Reba, the five kings of Midian; they also killed Balaam the son of Beor with the sword. 9 And the sons of Israel captured the women of Midian and their

little ones; and all their cattle and all their
flocks and all their goods they plundered.
10 Then they burned all their cities where
they lived and all their camps with fire.
11 And they took all the spoil and all the
loot, both of man and of beast. 12 And they
brought the captives and the loot and the
spoil to Moses and to Eleazar the priest and
to the congregation of the sons of Israel, to
the camp at the plains of Moab, which are
by the Jordan *opposite* Jericho.

13 And Moses and Eleazar the priest and
all the leaders of the congregation went
out to meet them outside the camp. 14 And
Moses was angry with the officers of the
army, the commanders of thousands and
the commanders of hundreds, who had
come from service in the war. 15 So Moses
said to them, "Have you spared all the
women? 16 Behold, these caused the sons
of Israel, through the word of Balaam, to act
unfaithfully against Yahweh in the matter
of Peor, so the plague was among the con-
gregation of Yahweh. 17 So now, kill every
male among the little ones, and kill every
woman who has known man intimately.
18 But all the girls who have not known man
intimately, spare for yourselves. 19 And you,
camp outside the camp seven days; whoever
has killed any person and whoever has
touched any slain, purify yourselves, you
and your captives, on the third day and on
the seventh day. 20 And you shall purify for
yourselves every garment and every article
of leather and all the work of goats' *hair* and
all articles of wood."

21 Then Eleazar the priest said to the
men of war who had gone to battle, "This
is the statute of the law which Yahweh has
commanded Moses: 22 only the gold and the
silver, the bronze, the iron, the tin and the
lead, 23 everything that can stand the fire,
you shall pass through the fire, and it shall
be clean, but it shall be purified with water
for impurity. But whatever cannot stand the
fire you shall pass through the water. 24 And
you shall wash your clothes on the seventh
day and be clean, and afterward you may
enter the camp."

25 Then Yahweh spoke to Moses, saying,
26 "You and Eleazar the priest and the
heads of the fathers' *households* of the
congregation take a count of the loot that
was captured, both of man and of animal;
27 and divide the loot between the warriors
who went out to battle and all the congre-
gation. 28 And you shall exact a levy for
Yahweh from the men of war who went out
to battle, one in five hundred of the persons
and of the cattle and of the donkeys and of
the sheep; 29 take it from their half and give
it to Eleazar the priest, as a contribution to
Yahweh. 30 And from the sons of Israel's half,
you shall take one drawn out of every fifty
of the persons, of the cattle, of the donkeys,
and of the sheep, from all the animals, and
give them to the Levites who keep charge
of the tabernacle of Yahweh." 31 Moses and
Eleazar the priest did just as Yahweh had
commanded Moses.

32 Now the loot that remained from
the plunder which the men of war had
plundered was 675,000 sheep, 33 and 72,000
cattle, 34 and 61,000 donkeys, 35 and of
human beings, of the women who had not
known man intimately, all the persons were
32,000.

36 And the half, the portion of those who
went out to war, was *as follows*: the number
of sheep was 337,500; 37 and the levy of
Yahweh from the sheep was 675; 38 and the
cattle were 36,000, from which the levy of
Yahweh was 72; 39 and the donkeys were
30,500, from which the levy of Yahweh was
61; 40 and the human beings were 16,000,
from whom the levy of Yahweh was 32
persons. 41 And Moses gave the levy, *which
was* the contribution to Yahweh, to Eleazar
the priest, just as Yahweh had commanded
Moses.

42 As for the sons of Israel's half, which
Moses separated from the men who had
gone to war— 43 now the congregation's
half was 337,500 sheep, 44 and 36,000 cattle,
45 and 30,500 donkeys, 46 and the human
beings were 16,000— 47 and from the sons
of Israel's half, Moses took one drawn out
of every fifty, both of man and of animals,
and gave them to the Levites, who kept the
responsibility of the tabernacle of Yahweh,
just as Yahweh had commanded Moses.

48 Then the officers who were over the
thousands of the army, the commanders
of thousands and the commanders of
hundreds, came near to Moses, 49 and they
said to Moses, "Your servants have taken a
census of men of war who are in our charge,
and no man of us is missing. 50 So we have
brought near as an offering to Yahweh what
each man found—articles of gold, armlets

and bracelets, signet rings, earrings and
necklaces—to make atonement for our-
selves before Yahweh." 51 And Moses and
Eleazar the priest took the gold from them,
all *kinds of* crafted articles. 52 And all the
gold from the contribution offering which
they raised up *in offering* to Yahweh, from
the commanders of thousands and the com-
manders of hundreds, was 16,750 shekels.
53 The men of war had taken plunder, every
man for himself. 54 So Moses and Eleazar the
priest took the gold from the commanders
of thousands and of hundreds, and they
brought it to the tent of meeting as a memo-
rial for the sons of Israel before Yahweh.

32 Now the sons of Reuben and the
sons of Gad had an exceedingly large
number of livestock. And they saw the land
of Jazer and the land of Gilead, that it was
indeed a place suitable for livestock, 2 so the
sons of Gad and the sons of Reuben came
and spoke to Moses and to Eleazar the priest
and to the leaders of the congregation,
saying, 3 "Ataroth, Dibon, Jazer, Nimrah,
Heshbon, Elealeh, Sebam, Nebo, and Beon,
4 the land, which Yahweh struck before the
congregation of Israel, is a land for livestock,
and your servants have livestock." 5 And
they said, "If we have found favor in your
sight, let this land be given to your servants
as a possession; do not take us across the
Jordan."

6 But Moses said to the sons of Gad and
to the sons of Reuben, "Shall your brothers
go to war while you yourselves sit here?
7 Now why are you discouraging the sons
of Israel from crossing over into the land
which Yahweh has given them? 8 This is
what your fathers did when I sent them from
Kadesh-barnea to see the land. 9 Indeed they
went up to the valley of Eshcol and saw the
land, and they discouraged the sons of Israel
so that they did not go into the land which
Yahweh had given them. 10 So Yahweh's
anger burned in that day, and He swore *an
oath*, saying, 11 'None of the men who came
up from Egypt, from twenty years old and
upward, shall see the land which I swore to
Abraham, to Isaac, and to Jacob; for they did
not follow Me fully, 12 except Caleb the son
of Jephunneh the Kenizzite and Joshua the
son of Nun, for they have followed Yahweh
fully.' 13 So Yahweh's anger burned against
Israel, and He made them wander in the
wilderness forty years, until the entire
generation of those who had done evil in
the sight of Yahweh was brought to an end.
14 Now behold, you have risen up in your
fathers' place, a brood of sinful men, to add
still more to the burning anger of Yahweh
against Israel. 15 For if you turn away from
following Him, He will once more abandon
them in the wilderness, and you will destroy
all these people."

16 Then they came near to him and
said, "We will build here sheepfolds for
our livestock and cities for our little ones;
17 but we ourselves will be armed ready *to
go* before the sons of Israel, until we have
brought them to their place, and our little
ones live in the fortified cities because of the
inhabitants of the land. 18 We will not return
to our homes until every one of the sons of
Israel has possessed his inheritance. 19 For
we will not have an inheritance with them
on the other side of the Jordan and beyond
because our inheritance has fallen to us on
this side of the Jordan east."

20 So Moses said to them, "If you will
do this, if you will arm yourselves before
Yahweh for the war, 21 and all of you armed
men cross over the Jordan before Yahweh
until He has dispossessed His enemies
from before Him, 22 and the land is subdued
before Yahweh, then afterward you shall
return and be free of obligation toward Yah-
weh and toward Israel, and this land shall
be yours for a possession before Yahweh.
23 But if you will not do so, behold, you have
sinned against Yahweh, and be sure your sin
will find you out. 24 Build yourselves cities
for your little ones and sheepfolds for your
sheep, and do what you have promised."

25 And the sons of Gad and the sons
of Reuben spoke to Moses, saying, "Your
servants will do just as my lord commands.
26 Our little ones, our wives, our livestock,
and all our cattle shall remain there in
the cities of Gilead; 27 but your servants,
everyone who is armed for war, will cross
over in the presence of Yahweh to battle, just
as my lord says."

28 So Moses gave a command concerning
them to Eleazar the priest and to Joshua the
son of Nun and to the heads of the fathers'
households of the tribes of the sons of Israel.
29 And Moses said to them, "If the sons of
Gad and the sons of Reuben, everyone who
is armed for battle, will cross with you over

the Jordan in the presence of Yahweh, and
the land is subdued before you, then you
shall give them the land of Gilead for a
possession; 30 but if they will not cross over
with you armed, they shall have possessions
among you in the land of Canaan." 31 And
the sons of Gad and the sons of Reuben
answered, saying, "As Yahweh has said to
your servants, so we will do. 32 We ourselves
will cross over armed in the presence of
Yahweh into the land of Canaan, and the
possession of our inheritance *shall remain*
with us across the Jordan."

33 So Moses gave to them, to the sons
of Gad and to the sons of Reuben and to
the half-tribe of Joseph's son Manasseh,
the kingdom of Sihon, king of the Amor-
ites and the kingdom of Og, the king of
Bashan, the land with its cities with *their*
territories, the cities of the surrounding
land. 34 And the sons of Gad built Dibon
and Ataroth and Aroer, 35 and Atroth-
shophan and Jazer and Jogbehah, 36 and
Beth-nimrah and Beth-haran as fortified
cities, and sheepfolds for sheep. 37 And the
sons of Reuben built Heshbon and Elealeh
and Kiriathaim, 38 and Nebo and Baal-
meon—*their* names being changed—and
Sibmah, and they gave *other* names to the
cities which they built. 39 And the sons of
Machir the son of Manasseh went to Gilead
and took it and dispossessed the Amorites
who were in it. 40 So Moses gave Gilead
to Machir the son of Manasseh, and he
lived in it. 41 And Jair the son of Manasseh
went and took its towns and called them
Havvoth-jair. 42 And Nobah went and took
Kenath and its towns and called it Nobah
after his own name.

Psalm 35:1–8

1 Contend, O Yahweh, with those
who contend with me;
Fight against those who
fight against me.
2 Take hold of shield and large shield
And rise up for my help.
3 Draw also the spear and the battle-
axe to meet those who pursue me;
Say to my soul, "I am your salvation."
4 Let those be ashamed and
dishonored who seek my life;
Let those who devise evil against me
be turned back and humiliated.
5 Let them be like chaff before the wind,
With the angel of Yahweh
driving *them* on.
6 Let their way be dark and slippery,
With the angel of Yahweh
pursuing them.
7 For without cause they hid
their net for me;
Without cause they dug
a pit for my soul.
8 Let destruction, which he does
not know, come upon him,
And let the net, which he
hid, catch him;
Let him fall into it in destruction.

Proverbs 12:1

12 Whoever loves discipline
loves knowledge,
But he who hates reproof is senseless.

Mark 14:53–72

53 Then they led Jesus away to the high
priest; and all the chief priests and the elders
and the scribes *gathered together. 54 And
Peter followed Him at a distance, right into
the courtyard of the high priest; and he was
sitting with the officers and warming him-
self at the fire. 55 Now the chief priests and
the whole Sanhedrin were seeking to obtain
testimony against Jesus to put Him to death,
and they were not finding any. 56 For many
were giving false testimony against Him, but
their testimony was not consistent. 57 And
some, standing up, were giving false testi-
mony against Him, saying, 58 "We ourselves
heard Him say, 'I will destroy this sanctuary
made with hands, and in three days I will
build another made without hands.'" 59 And
not even in this way was their testimony
consistent. 60 And the high priest stood up
in *their* midst and questioned Jesus, saying,
"You answer nothing? What are these men
testifying against You?" 61 But He kept silent
and did not answer. Again the high priest
was questioning Him and *said to Him, "Are
You the Christ, the Son of the Blessed *One*?"
62 And Jesus said, "I am; and you shall see
THE SON OF MAN SITTING AT THE RIGHT HAND
OF THE POWER, and COMING WITH THE CLOUDS
OF HEAVEN." 63 And tearing his tunics, the
high priest *said, "What further need do
we have of witnesses? 64 You have heard the
blasphemy; how does it seem to you?" And
they all condemned Him to be deserving of
death. 65 And some began to spit at Him, and

to blindfold Him, and to beat Him with their
fists, and to say to Him, "Prophesy!" And the
officers received Him with slaps *in the face*.
66 And as Peter was below in the court-
yard, one of the servant-girls of the high
priest *came, 67 and seeing Peter warming
himself, she looked at him and *said, "You
also were with the Nazarene, Jesus." 68 But
he denied *it*, saying, "I neither know nor
understand what you are talking about."
And he went out into the entryway. 69 And
when the servant-girl saw him, she began
once more to say to the bystanders, "This is
one of them!" 70 But again he was denying it.
And after a little while the bystanders were
again saying to Peter, "Surely you are *one* of
them, for you are also a Galilean." 71 But he
began to curse and swear, "I do not know
this man you are talking about!" 72 And
immediately a rooster crowed a second time.
And Peter remembered how Jesus had said
the statement to him, "Before a rooster crows
twice, you will deny Me three times." And
throwing himself down, he *began to* cry.

MARCH 18

Numbers 33:1–34:29

33 These are the journeys of the sons of Israel, by which they came out from the land of Egypt by their armies, by
the hand of Moses and Aaron. 2 And Moses
wrote down their starting places according to their journeys by the command of Yahweh, and these are their journeys according to their starting places.

3 They journeyed from Rameses in the first month, on the fifteenth day of the first month; on the next day after the Passover the sons of Israel started out with a high hand in the sight of all the Egyptians,
4 but the Egyptians were burying all their firstborn whom Yahweh had struck down among them. Yahweh had also executed judgments on their gods.

5 Then the sons of Israel journeyed from Rameses and camped in Succoth.
6 They journeyed from Succoth and camped in Etham, which is on the edge of the wilderness.
7 They journeyed from Etham and turned back to Pi-hahiroth, which faces Baal-zephon, and they camped before Migdol.
8 They journeyed from before Hahiroth and passed through the midst of the sea into the wilderness; and they went three days' journey in the wilderness of Etham and camped at Marah.
9 They journeyed from Marah and came to Elim; and in Elim there were twelve springs of water and seventy palm trees, and they camped there.
10 They journeyed from Elim and camped by the Red Sea.
11 They journeyed from the Red Sea and camped in the wilderness of Sin.
12 They journeyed from the wilderness of Sin and camped at Dophkah.
13 They journeyed from Dophkah and camped at Alush.
14 They journeyed from Alush and camped at Rephidim; now it was there that the people had no water to drink.
15 They journeyed from Rephidim and camped in the wilderness of Sinai.
16 They journeyed from the wilderness of Sinai and camped at Kibroth-hattaavah.

17 They journeyed from Kibroth-hattaavah and camped at Hazeroth.
18 They journeyed from Hazeroth and camped at Rithmah.
19 They journeyed from Rithmah and camped at Rimmon-perez.
20 They journeyed from Rimmon-perez and camped at Libnah.
21 They journeyed from Libnah and camped at Rissah.
22 They journeyed from Rissah and camped in Kehelathah.
23 They journeyed from Kehelathah and camped at Mount Shepher.
24 They journeyed from Mount Shepher and camped at Haradah.
25 They journeyed from Haradah and camped at Makheloth.
26 They journeyed from Makheloth and camped at Tahath.
27 They journeyed from Tahath and camped at Terah.

28 They journeyed from Terah and camped at Mithkah.
29 They journeyed from Mithkah and camped at Hashmonah.
30 They journeyed from Hashmonah and camped at Moseroth.
31 They journeyed from Moseroth and camped at Bene-jaakan.
32 They journeyed from Bene-jaakan and camped at Hor-haggidgad.
33 They journeyed from Hor-haggidgad and camped at Jotbathah.
34 They journeyed from Jotbathah and camped at Abronah.
35 They journeyed from Abronah and camped at Ezion-geber.
36 They journeyed from Ezion-geber and camped in the wilderness of Zin, that is, Kadesh.
37 They journeyed from Kadesh and camped at Mount Hor, at the edge of the land of Edom.
38 Then Aaron the priest went up to Mount Hor at the command of Yahweh, and he died there in the fortieth year after the sons of Israel had come from the land of Egypt, on the first *day* in the fifth month.
39 Now Aaron was 123 years old when he died on Mount Hor.

40 Now the Canaanite, the king of Arad who lived in the Negev in the land of Canaan, heard when the sons of Israel were coming.

41 Then they journeyed from Mount Hor and camped at Zalmonah.
42 They journeyed from Zalmonah and camped at Punon.
43 They journeyed from Punon and camped at Oboth.
44 They journeyed from Oboth and camped at Iye-abarim, at the border of Moab.
45 They journeyed from Iyim and camped at Dibon-gad.
46 They journeyed from Dibon-gad and camped at Almon-diblathaim.
47 They journeyed from Almon-diblathaim and camped in the mountains of Abarim, before Nebo.
48 They journeyed from the mountains of Abarim and camped in the plains of Moab by the Jordan *opposite* Jericho.
49 They camped by the Jordan, from Beth-jeshimoth as far as Abel-shittim in the plains of Moab.

50 Then Yahweh spoke to Moses in the
plains of Moab by the Jordan *opposite* Jer-
icho, saying, 51 "Speak to the sons of Israel
and say to them, 'When you cross over the
Jordan into the land of Canaan, 52 then you
shall dispossess all the inhabitants of the
land from before you and destroy all their
carved stones and destroy all their molten
images and demolish all their high places;
53 and you shall take possession of the land
and inhabit it, for I have given the land to
you to possess it. 54 And you shall inherit
the land by lot according to your families;
to the larger you shall give a larger inher-
itance, and to the smaller you shall give a
smaller inheritance. Wherever the lot falls
to anyone, that shall be his. You shall inherit
according to the tribes of your fathers. 55 But
if you do not dispossess the inhabitants of
the land from before you, then it will be
that those whom you let remain of them
will become as pricks in your eyes and as
thorns in your sides, and they will trouble
you in the land which you inhabit. 56 And
it will be as I plan to do to them, so I will
do to you.'"

34 Then Yahweh spoke to Moses, saying,
2 "Command the sons of Israel and
say to them, 'When you enter the land of
Canaan, this is the land that shall fall to you
as an inheritance, *even the* land of Canaan
according to its borders. 3 And your south-
ern sector shall extend from the wilderness
of Zin along the side of Edom, and your
southern border shall extend from the end
of the Salt Sea eastward. 4 Then your border
shall turn from the south to the ascent of
Akrabbim and continue to Zin, and its
termination shall be to the south of Kadesh-
barnea; and it shall reach Hazaraddar and
continue to Azmon. 5 And the border shall
turn from Azmon to the brook of Egypt, and
its termination shall be at the sea.

6 'And as for the west border, you shall
have the Great Sea, that is, *its* coastline; this
shall be your west border.

7 'And this shall be your north border: you
shall draw your *border* line from the Great
Sea to Mount Hor. 8 You shall draw a line
from Mount Hor to Lebo-hamath, and the
termination of the border shall be at Zedad;

9 and the border shall proceed to Ziphron,
and its termination shall be at Hazar-enan.
This shall be your north border.
10 'For your east border you shall also
draw a line from Hazar-enan to Shepham,
11 and the border shall go down from
Shepham to Riblah on the east side of Ain;
and the border shall go down and reach
to the slope on the east side of the Sea of
Chinnereth. 12 And the border shall go down
to the Jordan, and its termination shall be
at the Salt Sea. This shall be your land
according to its borders all around.'"
13 So Moses commanded the sons of
Israel, saying, "This is the land that you shall
inherit by lot among you as a possession,
which Yahweh has commanded to give to
the nine and a half tribes. 14 For the tribe
of the sons of Reuben have received *theirs*
according to their fathers' households, and
the tribe of the sons of Gad according to their
fathers' households, and the half-tribe of
Manasseh have received their inheritance.
15 The two and a half tribes have received
their inheritance across the Jordan opposite
Jericho to the east toward the sunrise."
16 Then Yahweh spoke to Moses, say-
ing, 17 "These are the names of the men
who shall apportion the land to you for
inheritance: Eleazar the priest and Joshua
the son of Nun. 18 And you shall take one
leader of every tribe to apportion the land
for inheritance. 19 Now these are the names
of the men:

Of the tribe of Judah, Caleb the son of
Jephunneh.
20 "Of the tribe of the sons of Simeon,
Samuel the son of Ammihud.
21 "Of the tribe of Benjamin, Elidad the
son of Chislon.
22 "Of the tribe of the sons of Dan a
leader, Bukki the son of Jogli.
23 "Of the sons of Joseph: of the tribe
of the sons of Manasseh a leader,
Hanniel the son of Ephod.
24 "Of the tribe of the sons of Ephraim a
leader, Kemuel the son of Shiphtan.
25 "Of the tribe of the sons of Zebulun a
leader, Elizaphan the son of Parnach.
26 "Of the tribe of the sons of Issachar a
leader, Paltiel the son of Azzan.
27 "Of the tribe of the sons of Asher a
leader, Ahihud the son of Shelomi.
28 "Of the tribe of the sons of Naphtali a
leader, Pedahel the son of Ammihud."

29 These are those whom Yahweh com-
manded to apportion the inheritance to the
sons of Israel in the land of Canaan.

Psalm 35:9–16

9 And my soul shall rejoice in Yahweh;
It shall be joyful in His salvation.
10 All my bones will say,
"Yahweh, who is like You,
Who delivers the afflicted from
him who is too strong for him,
And the afflicted and the needy
from him who robs him?"
11 Malicious witnesses rise up,
Who ask me of things that
I do not know.
12 They repay me evil for good,
It is bereavement to my soul.
13 But as for me, when they were sick,
my clothing was sackcloth;
I humbled my soul with fasting,
And my prayer kept returning
to my bosom.
14 I walked about as though it were
my friend or brother;
I bowed down mourning, as one
who sorrows for a mother.
15 But at my stumbling they were glad
and gathered themselves together;
The smiters whom I did not know
gathered together against me,
They tore at me and never
were silent.
16 Amongst the godless jesters
at a feast,
They gnashed at me with their teeth.

Proverbs 12:2

2 A good man will obtain
favor from Yahweh,
But a man of evil schemes
He will condemn.

Mark 15:1–26

15 And early in the morning the chief
priests with the elders and scribes
and the whole Sanhedrin, immediately
held council; and binding Jesus, led Him
away and delivered *Him* to Pilate. 2 And
Pilate questioned Him, "Are You the King
of the Jews?" And He answered him and
*said, "You yourself say *it*." 3 And the chief
priests *began to* accuse Him of many things.
4 Then Pilate was questioning Him again,
saying, "You answer nothing? See how many

accusations they bring against You!" 5 But Jesus made no further answer; so Pilate marveled.

6 Now at the feast he used to release for them *any* one prisoner whom they requested. 7 And the man named Barabbas had been imprisoned with the insurrectionists who had committed murder in the insurrection. 8 And the crowd went up and began asking him *to do* as he had been accustomed to do for them. 9 And Pilate answered them, saying, "Do you want me to release for you the King of the Jews?" 10 For he was aware that the chief priests had delivered Him over because of envy. 11 But the chief priests stirred up the crowd *to ask* him to release Barabbas for them instead. 12 And answering again, Pilate was saying to them, "Then what shall I do with Him whom you call the King of the Jews?" 13 And they shouted again, "Crucify Him!" 14 But Pilate was saying to them, "Why? What evil did He do?" But they shouted all the more, "Crucify Him!" 15 And wishing to satisfy the crowd, Pilate released Barabbas for them, and after having Jesus scourged, he delivered Him over to be crucified.

16 So the soldiers took Him away into the palace (that is, the Praetorium), and they *called together the whole *Roman* cohort. 17 And they *dressed Him up in purple, and after twisting a crown of thorns, they *put it on Him; 18 and they began to greet Him, "Hail, King of the Jews!" 19 And they kept beating His head with a reed, and spitting on Him; and kneeling, they were bowing down before Him. 20 And after they had mocked Him, they took the purple robe off Him and put His *own* garments on Him. And they *led Him out to crucify Him.

21 And they *pressed into service a passer-by coming from the countryside, Simon of Cyrene (the father of Alexander and Rufus), to carry His cross.

22 Then they *brought Him to the place Golgotha, which is translated, Place of a Skull. 23 And they tried to give Him wine mixed with myrrh; but He did not take it. 24 And they *crucified Him, and *divided up His garments among themselves, casting lots for them *to decide* who should take what. 25 Now it was the third hour, and they crucified Him. 26 And the inscription of the charge against Him read, "THE KING OF THE JEWS."

This Book, when we open it, opens to us the mind and the heart of God.

— WARREN WIERSBE

MARCH 19

Numbers 35:1–36:13

35 Now Yahweh spoke to Moses in the plains of Moab by the Jordan *opposite* Jericho, saying, 2 "Command the sons of Israel that they give to the Levites from the inheritance of their possession cities to live in; and you shall give to the Levites pasture lands around the cities. 3 And the cities shall be theirs to live in; and their pasture lands shall be for their cattle and for their herds and for all their beasts.

4 "And the pasture lands of the cities which you shall give to the Levites *shall extend* from the wall of the city outward one thousand cubits around. 5 You shall also measure outside the city on the east side two thousand cubits, and on the south side two thousand cubits, and on the west side two thousand cubits, and on the north side two thousand cubits, with the city in the center. This shall become theirs as pasture lands for the cities.

6 "And the cities which you shall give to the Levites *shall be* the six cities of refuge, which you shall give for the manslayer to flee to; and in addition to them you shall give forty-two cities. 7 All the cities which you shall give to the Levites *shall be* forty-eight cities, together with their pasture lands. 8 Now as for the cities which you shall give from the possession of the sons of Israel, you shall take more from the larger, and you shall take less from the smaller; each shall give some of his cities to the Levites

in proportion to his possession which he inherits."

9 Then Yahweh spoke to Moses, saying, 10 "Speak to the sons of Israel and say to them, 'When you cross the Jordan into the land of Canaan, 11 then you shall select for yourselves cities to be your cities of refuge, that the manslayer who has struck down any person unintentionally may flee there. 12 And the cities shall be for you as a refuge from the avenger, so that the manslayer will not die until he stands before the congregation for judgment. 13 And the cities which you are to give shall be your six cities of refuge. 14 You shall give three cities across the Jordan and three cities in the land of Canaan; they are to be cities of refuge. 15 These six cities shall be for refuge for the sons of Israel and for the sojourner and for the foreign resident among them; that anyone who strikes a person down unintentionally may flee there.

16 'But if he struck him down with an iron object, so that he died, he is a murderer; the murderer shall surely be put to death. 17 And if he struck him down with a stone in the hand, by which he would die, and *as a result* he died, he is a murderer; the murderer shall surely be put to death. 18 Or if he struck him with a wooden object in the hand, by which he would die, and *as a result* he died, he is a murderer; the murderer shall surely be put to death. 19 The blood avenger himself shall put the murderer to death; he shall put him to death when he meets him. 20 And if he pushed him of hatred or threw something at him lying in wait and *as a result* he died, 21 or if he struck him down with his hand in enmity, and *as a result* he died, the one who struck him shall surely be put to death; he is a murderer; the blood avenger shall put the murderer to death when he meets him.

22 'But if he pushed him suddenly without enmity or threw something at him without lying in wait, 23 or with any stone—by which one might die, *yet* without seeing—and it fell upon him, and he died, but he was not his enemy nor seeking his injury, 24 then the congregation shall judge between the slayer and the blood avenger according to these *legal* judgments. 25 And the congregation shall deliver the manslayer from the hand of the blood avenger, and the congregation shall restore him to his city of refuge to which he fled; and he shall live in it until the death of the high priest who was anointed with the holy oil. 26 But if the manslayer at any time goes beyond the border of his city of refuge to which he may flee, 27 and the blood avenger finds him outside the border of his city of refuge, and the blood avenger kills the manslayer, he will not be guilty of blood 28 because he should have remained in his city of refuge until the death of the high priest. But after the death of the high priest the manslayer shall return to the land of his possession.

29 'And these things shall be for a statutory judgment to you throughout your generations in all your *places of* habitation.

30 'If anyone strikes down a person, the murderer shall be put to death at the mouth of witnesses, but no person shall be put to death on the testimony of one witness. 31 Moreover, you shall not take ransom for the life of a murderer who is guilty of death, but he shall surely be put to death. 32 And you shall not take ransom for him who has fled to his city of refuge, that he may return to live in the land before the death of the priest. 33 So you shall not pollute the land in which you are; for blood pollutes the land, and no propitiation can be made for the land for the blood that is shed on it, except by the blood of him who shed it. 34 And you shall not defile the land in which you live, in the midst of which I dwell; for I Yahweh am dwelling in the midst of the sons of Israel.'"

36 And the heads of the fathers' *households* of the family of the sons of Gilead, the son of Machir, the son of Manasseh, of the families of the sons of Joseph, came near and spoke before Moses and before the leaders, the heads of the fathers' *households* of the sons of Israel, 2 and they said, "Yahweh commanded my lord to give the land by lot to the sons of Israel as an inheritance, and my lord was commanded by Yahweh to give the inheritance of Zelophehad our brother to his daughters. 3 But if they marry one of the sons of the *other* tribes of the sons of Israel, their inheritance will be withdrawn from the inheritance of our fathers and will be added to the inheritance of the tribe to which they belong; thus it will be withdrawn from our allotted inheritance. 4 And when the jubilee of the sons of Israel comes, then their inheritance will be added to the inheritance of the tribe to which they belong; so

their inheritance will be withdrawn from
the inheritance of the tribe of our fathers."
5 Then Moses commanded the sons of
Israel according to the word of Yahweh,
saying, "The tribe of the sons of Joseph
are right in *their* statements. 6 This is what
Yahweh has commanded concerning the
daughters of Zelophehad, saying, 'Let them
marry whoever is good in their sight; only
they must marry within the family of the
tribe of their father.' 7 Thus no inheritance
of the sons of Israel shall be transferred
from tribe to tribe, for the sons of Israel shall
each hold to the inheritance of the tribe of
his fathers. 8 And every daughter who comes
into possession of an inheritance of any
tribe of the sons of Israel shall be wife to
one of the family of the tribe of her father,
so that the sons of Israel each may possess
the inheritance of his fathers. 9 Thus no
inheritance shall be transferred from one
tribe to another tribe, for the tribes of the
sons of Israel shall each hold to his own
inheritance."
10 Just as Yahweh had commanded Moses,
so the daughters of Zelophehad did: 11 And
Mahlah, Tirzah, Hoglah, Milcah, and Noah,
the daughters of Zelophehad married their
uncles' sons. 12 They married *those* from the
families of the sons of Manasseh the son of
Joseph, and their inheritance remained with
the tribe of the family of their father.
13 These are the commandments and the
judgments which Yahweh commanded to
the sons of Israel by the hand of Moses in
the plains of Moab by the Jordan *opposite*
Jericho.

Psalm 35:17–28

17 Lord, how long will You look on?
Bring back my soul from their ravages,
My only *life* from the lions.
18 I will give You thanks in
the great assembly;
I will praise You among a
mighty people.
19 Let those who are wrongfully my
enemies not be glad over me;
Nor let those who hate me without
cause wink maliciously.
20 For they do not speak peace,
But they devise deceitful words against
those who are quiet in the land.
21 They opened their mouth
wide against me;
They said, "Aha, aha, our
eyes have seen it!"
22 You have seen it, O Yahweh,
do not keep silent;
O Lord, do not be far from me.
23 Stir up Yourself, and awake
to my justice
And to my cause, my God and my Lord.
24 Judge me, O Yahweh my God,
according to Your righteousness,
And do not let them be glad over me.
25 Do not let them say in their
heart, "Aha, our desire!"
Do not let them say, "We have
swallowed him up!"
26 Let those be ashamed and
humiliated altogether who are
glad at the evil *done to* me;
Let those be clothed with shame
and dishonor who magnify
themselves over me.

27 Let them shout for joy and be glad,
who delight in my righteousness;
And let them say continually,
"Yahweh be magnified,
Who delights in the peace of
His slave."
28 And my tongue shall utter
Your righteousness
And Your praise all day long.

Proverbs 12:3

3 A man will not be established
by wickedness,
But the root of the righteous
will not be shaken.

Mark 15:27–47

27 And they *crucified two robbers with
Him, one on His right and one on His left.
28 [And the Scripture was fulfilled which
says, "And He was numbered with trans-
gressors."] 29 And those passing by were
blaspheming Him, shaking their heads, and
saying, "Ha! You who *are going to* destroy
the sanctuary and rebuild it in three days,
30 save Yourself by coming down from the
cross!" 31 In the same way, mocking *Him* to
one another, the chief priests also, along
with the scribes, were saying, "He saved
others; He cannot save Himself. 32 Let *this*
Christ, the King of Israel, now come down
from the cross, so that we may see and

believe!" Those who were crucified with Him were also insulting Him.

33 And when the sixth hour came, darkness fell over the whole land until the ninth hour. 34 And at the ninth hour Jesus cried out with a loud voice, "ELOI, ELOI, LAMA SABACHTHANI?" which is translated, "MY GOD, MY GOD, WHY HAVE YOU FORSAKEN ME?" 35 And when some of the bystanders heard it, they *began* saying, "Look, He is calling for Elijah." 36 And someone ran and filled a sponge with sour wine, put it on a reed, and gave Him a drink, saying, "Let us see whether Elijah will come to take Him down." 37 And Jesus, uttering a loud cry, breathed His last. 38 And the veil of the sanctuary was torn in two from top to bottom. 39 And when the centurion, who was standing right in front of Him, saw the way He breathed His last, he said, "Truly this man was God's Son!"

40 And there were also *some* women looking on from a distance, among whom *were* Mary Magdalene, and Mary the mother of James the Less and Joses, and Salome, 41 who, when He was in Galilee, were following Him and serving Him; and *there were* many other women who came up with Him to Jerusalem.

42 And when evening had already come, because it was Preparation day, that is, the day before the Sabbath, 43 Joseph of Arimathea came, a prominent Council member, who himself was waiting for the kingdom of God; and he gathered up courage and went in before Pilate, and asked for the body of Jesus. 44 And Pilate wondered if He had died by this time, and summoning the centurion, he questioned him as to whether He already died. 45 And ascertaining this from the centurion, he granted the body to Joseph. 46 And when Joseph had bought a linen cloth and took Him down, he wrapped Him in the linen cloth and laid Him in a tomb which had been hewn out in the rock. And he rolled a stone against the entrance of the tomb. 47 And Mary Magdalene and Mary the *mother* of Joses were looking on *to see* where He had been laid.

MARCH 20

Deuteronomy 1:1–2:37

1 These are the words which Moses spoke to all Israel across the Jordan in the wilderness, in the Arabah opposite Suph, between Paran and Tophel and Laban and Hazeroth and Dizahab. 2 It is eleven days' *journey* from Horeb by the way of Mount Seir to Kadesh-barnea. 3 Now it happened, in the fortieth year, on the first *day* of the eleventh month, Moses spoke to the children of Israel, according to all that Yahweh had commanded him *to give* to them, 4 after he had struck down Sihon the king of the Amorites, who lived in Heshbon, and Og the king of Bashan, who lived in Ashtaroth and Edrei. 5 Across the Jordan in the land of Moab, Moses undertook to expound this law, saying,

6 "Yahweh our God spoke to us at Horeb, saying, 'You have stayed long enough at this mountain. 7 Turn and set out, and go to the hill country of the Amorites, and to all their neighbors in the Arabah, in the hill country and in the Shephelah and in the Negev and by the seacoast, the land of the Canaanites, and Lebanon, as far as the great river, the river Euphrates. 8 See, I have given over the land before you; go in and possess the land which Yahweh swore to give to your fathers, to Abraham, to Isaac, and to Jacob, to them and to their seed after them.'

9 "And I spoke to you at that time, saying, 'I am not able to bear *the burden* of you alone. 10 Yahweh your God has multiplied you, and behold, you are this day like the stars of heaven in number. 11 May Yahweh, the God of your fathers, increase you a thousand-fold more than you are and bless you, just as He has promised you! 12 How can I alone bear the load and burden of you and your strife? 13 Choose wise and understanding and experienced men from your tribes, and I will appoint them as your heads.' 14 Then you answered me and said, 'The thing which you have said to do is good.' 15 So I took the heads of your tribes, wise and experienced men, and gave them as heads over you, leaders of thousands and of hundreds, of fifties and of tens, and officers for your tribes.

16 "Then I commanded your judges at that time, saying, 'Hear *the cases* between your brothers, and judge righteously between a man and his brother or the sojourner who is

with him. 17 You shall not show partiality in judgment; you shall hear the small and the great alike. You shall not fear man, for the judgment is God's. The case that is too hard for you, you shall bring to me, and I will hear it.' 18 And I commanded you at that time all the things that you should do.

19 "Then we set out from Horeb and went through all that great and fearsome wilderness which you saw on the way to the hill country of the Amorites, just as Yahweh our God had commanded us; and we came to Kadesh-barnea. 20 And I said to you, 'You have come to the hill country of the Amorites which Yahweh our God is about to give us. 21 See, Yahweh your God has given over the land before you; go up, take possession, as Yahweh, the God of your fathers, has spoken to you. Do not fear or be dismayed.'

22 "Then all of you came near to me and said, 'Let us send men before us, that they may search out the land for us and bring back to us word of the way by which we should go up and the cities which we shall enter.' 23 And the thing was good in my sight, and I took twelve of your men, one man for each tribe. 24 Then they turned and went up into the hill country and came to the valley of Eshcol and spied it out. 25 Then they took *some* of the fruit of the land in their hands and brought it down to us; and they brought word back to us and said, 'It is a good land which Yahweh our God is about to give us.'

26 "Yet you were not willing to go up, but rebelled against the command of Yahweh your God; 27 and you grumbled in your tents and said, 'Because Yahweh hates us, He has brought us out of the land of Egypt to give us into the hand of the Amorites to destroy us. 28 Where can we go up? Our brothers have made our hearts melt, saying, "The people are bigger and taller than we; the cities are large and fortified to heaven. And moreover, we saw the sons of the Anakim there."' 29 Then I said to you, 'Do not be in dread, nor fear them. 30 Yahweh your God, who goes before you, will Himself fight on your behalf, just as He did for you in Egypt before your eyes, 31 and in the wilderness where you saw how Yahweh your God carried you, just as a man carries his son, in all the way which you have walked until you came to this place.' 32 But for all this, you did not believe Yahweh your God, 33 who goes before you on *your* way, to spy out a place for you to encamp, in fire by night and cloud by day, to show you the way in which you should go.

34 "Then Yahweh heard the sound of your words, and He was angry and swore *an oath*, saying, 35 'Not one of these men, this evil generation, shall see the good land which I swore to give your fathers, 36 except Caleb the son of Jephunneh; he shall see it, and to him and to his sons I will give the land on which he has set foot, because he has followed Yahweh fully.' 37 Yahweh was angry with me also on your account, saying, 'Not even you shall enter there. 38 Joshua the son of Nun, who stands before you, he shall enter there; strengthen him, for he will cause Israel to inherit it. 39 Moreover, your little ones who you said would become plunder, and your sons, who this day have no knowledge of good or evil, shall enter there, and I will give it to them, and they shall possess it. 40 But as for you, turn around and set out for the wilderness by the way to the Red Sea.'

41 "Then you said to me, 'We have sinned against Yahweh; we will indeed go up and fight, just as Yahweh our God commanded us.' And every man of you girded on his weapons of war and regarded it as easy to go up into the hill country. 42 And Yahweh said to me, 'Say to them, "Do not go up and do not fight—for I am not among you—so that you are not defeated before your enemies."' 43 So I spoke to you, but you would not listen. Instead you rebelled against the command of Yahweh and acted presumptuously and went up into the hill country. 44 And the Amorites who lived in that hill country came out to meet you and pursued you as bees do and crushed you from Seir to Hormah. 45 Then you returned and wept before Yahweh; but Yahweh did not listen to your voice nor give ear to you. 46 So you remained in Kadesh many days, according to the days that you remained *there*.

2 "Then we turned and set out for the wilderness by the way to the Red Sea, as Yahweh spoke to me, and circled Mount Seir for many days. 2 And Yahweh spoke to me, saying, 3 'You have circled this mountain long enough. *Now* turn north, 4 and command the people, saying, "You are going to pass through the territory of your brothers

the sons of Esau who live in Seir; and they
will be afraid of you. So be very careful; 5 do
not provoke them, for I will not give you any
of their land, even *as little as* a footstep
because I have given Mount Seir to Esau as
a possession. 6 You shall buy food from them
with money so that you may eat, and you
shall also bargain with them for water with
money so that you may drink. 7 For Yahweh
your God has blessed you in all the work of
your hand; He has known your wanderings
through this great wilderness. These forty
years Yahweh your God has been with you;
you have not lacked a thing."'

8 "So we passed beyond our brothers the
sons of Esau, who live in Seir, away from
the Arabah road, away from Elath and from
Ezion-geber. And we turned and passed
through by the way of the wilderness of
Moab. 9 Then Yahweh said to me, 'Do not
harass Moab, nor provoke them to war,
for I will not give you any of their land as
a possession because I have given Ar to the
sons of Lot as a possession.' 10 (The Emim
lived there formerly, a people as great,
numerous, and tall as the Anakim. 11 Like the
Anakim, they are also regarded as Rephaim,
but the Moabites call them Emim. 12 Now the
Horites formerly lived in Seir, but the sons of
Esau dispossessed them and destroyed them
from before them and settled in their place,
just as Israel would do to the land of their
possession which Yahweh gave to them.)
13 'Now arise and cross over the brook Zered
yourselves.' So we crossed over the brook
Zered. 14 Now the time that it took for us to
come from Kadesh-barnea until we crossed
over the brook Zered was thirty-eight years,
until all the generation of the men of war
came to an end from within the camp, as
Yahweh had sworn to them. 15 Moreover the
hand of Yahweh was against them, to bring
them into confusion from within the camp
until they all came to an end.

16 "So it happened when all the men
of war had come to an end in death from
among the people, 17 that Yahweh spoke
to me, saying, 18 'Today you are about to
cross over Ar, the border of Moab. 19 And
you will come opposite the sons of Ammon.
Do not harass them nor provoke them, for I
will not give you any of the land of the sons
of Ammon as a possession because I have
given it to the sons of Lot as a possession.'
20 (It is also regarded as the land of the
Rephaim, *for* Rephaim formerly lived in it,
but the Ammonites call them Zamzummin,
21 a people as great, numerous, and tall as
the Anakim, but Yahweh destroyed them
before them. And they dispossessed them
and settled in their place, 22 just as He
did for the sons of Esau, who live in Seir,
when He destroyed the Horites from before
them; they dispossessed them and settled
in their place even to this day. 23 And the
Avvim, who lived in villages as far as Gaza,
the Caphtorim who came from Caphtor,
destroyed them and lived in their place.)
24 'Arise, set out, and pass through the
valley of Arnon. Look! I have given Sihon
the Amorite, king of Heshbon, and his land
into your hand; begin to take possession
and provoke him to battle. 25 This day I will
begin to put the dread and fear of you upon
the peoples everywhere under the heavens,
who, when they hear the report of you, will
tremble and be in anguish because of you.'

26 "So I sent messengers from the wilder-
ness of Kedemoth to Sihon king of Heshbon
with words of peace, saying, 27 'Let me pass
through your land, I will go only on the high-
way; I will not turn aside to the right or to
the left. 28 You will sell me food for money so
that I may eat, and give me water for money
so that I may drink; only let me pass through
on foot, 29 just as the sons of Esau who live in
Seir and the Moabites who live in Ar did for
me, until I cross over the Jordan into the land
which Yahweh our God is giving to us.' 30 But
Sihon king of Heshbon was not willing for
us to pass through his land, for Yahweh your
God stiffened his spirit and made his heart
obstinate, in order to give him over into your
hand, as *he is* today. 31 And Yahweh said to
me, 'See, I have begun to give Sihon and his
land over to you. Begin to possess, so that
you may *fully* possess his land.'

32 "Then Sihon with all his people came
out to meet us in battle at Jahaz. 33 But
Yahweh our God gave him over to us, and
we struck him down with his sons and all
his people. 34 So we captured all his cities
at that time and devoted to destruction the
men, women, and little ones of every city.
We left no survivor remaining. 35 We took
only the animals as our plunder and the
spoil of the cities which we had captured.
36 From Aroer which is on the edge of the
valley of Arnon and *from* the city which is
in the valley, even to Gilead, there was not

a town that was too high for us; Yahweh our
God gave all over to us. 37 Only you did not
go near to the land of the sons of Ammon,
all along the river Jabbok and the cities of
the hill country, and wherever Yahweh our
God had commanded us.

Psalm 36:1–6

1 Transgression declares to the
ungodly within his heart;
There is no dread of God
before his eyes.
2 For it flatters him in his eyes
For one to discover his
iniquity *and* hate *it*.
3 The words of his mouth are
wickedness and deceit;
He has ceased to consider to do good.
4 He devises wickedness upon his bed;
He sets himself on a path
that is not good;
He does not despise evil.

5 Your lovingkindness, O Yahweh,
is in the heavens,
Your faithfulness *reaches* to the skies.
6 Your righteousness is like the
mountains of God;
Your judgments are *like* a great deep.
O Yahweh, You save man and beast.

Proverbs 12:4–6

4 An excellent wife is the
crown of her husband,
But she who causes shame is like
rottenness in his bones.
5 The thoughts of the righteous are just,
But the guidance of the
wicked is deceitful.
6 The words of the wicked lie
in wait for blood,
But the mouth of the upright
will deliver them.

Mark 16:1–20

16 And when the Sabbath passed, Mary
Magdalene, and Mary the *mother* of
James, and Salome, bought spices, so that
they might come and anoint Him. 2 And very
early on the first day of the week, they *came
to the tomb when the sun had risen. 3 And
they were saying to one another, "Who will
roll away the stone for us from the entrance
of the tomb?" 4 And looking up, they *saw
that the stone had been rolled away, although
it was very large. 5 And entering the tomb,
they saw a young man sitting on the right
side, wearing a white robe; and they were
amazed. 6 And he *said to them, "Do not be
amazed; you are looking for Jesus the Naza-
rene, who has been crucified. He has risen;
He is not here; behold, the place where they
laid Him. 7 But go, tell His disciples and Peter,
'He is going ahead of you to Galilee; there
you will see Him, just as He told you.'" 8 And
they went out and fled from the tomb, for
trembling and astonishment were gripping
them; and they said nothing to anyone, for
they were afraid.

9 [Now after He had risen early on the
first day of the week, He first appeared to
Mary Magdalene, from whom He had cast
out seven demons. 10 She went and reported
to those who had been with Him, while they
were mourning and crying. 11 And when
they heard that He was alive and had been
seen by her, they refused to believe it.

12 After that, He appeared in a different
form to two of them while they were walk-
ing along on their way to the countryside.
13 And they went away and reported it to the
others, but they did not believe them either.

14 Afterward He appeared to the eleven
themselves as they were reclining *at the
table*; and He reproached them for their
unbelief and hardness of heart, because
they had not believed those who had seen
Him after He had risen. 15 And He said to
them, "Go into all the world and preach the
gospel to all creation. 16 He who has believed
and has been baptized shall be saved; but he
who has disbelieved shall be condemned.
17 And these signs will accompany those
who have believed: in My name they will
cast out demons, they will speak with new
tongues; 18 and they will pick up serpents,
and if they drink any deadly *poison*, it will
not hurt them; they will lay hands on the
sick, and they will recover."

19 So then, the Lord Jesus, after He had
spoken to them, was taken up into heaven
and sat down at the right hand of God. 20 And
they went out and preached everywhere,
while the Lord worked with them, and con-
firmed the word by the signs that followed.]

[*And they promptly reported all these
instructions to Peter and his companions.
And after that, Jesus Himself sent out through
them from east to west the sacred and imper-
ishable preaching of eternal salvation.*]

MARCH 21

Deuteronomy 3:1–4:49

3 "Then we turned and went up the road to Bashan, and Og king of Bashan, with all his people, came out to meet us in battle at Edrei. 2 But Yahweh said to me, 'Do not fear him, for I have given him and all his people and his land over into your hand; and you shall do to him just as you did to Sihon king of the Amorites, who lived at Heshbon.' 3 So Yahweh our God also gave Og, king of Bashan, with all his people over into our hand, and we struck them until there was no survivor remaining for him. 4 And we captured all his cities at that time; there was not a town which we did not take from them: sixty cities, all the region of Argob, the kingdom of Og in Bashan. 5 All these were cities fortified with high walls, gates and bars, besides a great many unwalled towns. 6 And we devoted them to destruction, as we did to Sihon king of Heshbon, devoting to destruction the men, women, and little ones of every city. 7 But all the animals and the spoil of the cities we took as our plunder.

8 "Thus we took the land at that time from the hand of the two kings of the Amorites who were beyond the Jordan, from the valley of Arnon to Mount Hermon 9 (Sidonians call Hermon Sirion, and the Amorites call it Senir): 10 all the cities of the plateau and all Gilead and all Bashan, as far as Salecah and Edrei, cities of the kingdom of Og in Bashan. 11 (For only Og king of Bashan remained of the remnant of the Rephaim. Behold, his bedstead was an iron bedstead; it is in Rabbah of the sons of Ammon. Its length was nine cubits, and its width four cubits by ordinary cubit.)

12 "So we took possession of this land at that time. From Aroer, which is by the valley of Arnon, and half the hill country of Gilead and its cities I gave to the Reubenites and to the Gadites. 13 And the rest of Gilead and all Bashan, the kingdom of Og, I gave to the half-tribe of Manasseh, all the region of Argob. (Concerning all Bashan, it is called the land of Rephaim. 14 Jair the son of Manasseh took all the region of Argob as far as the border of the Geshurites and the Maacathites and called it—*that is,* Bashan—after his own name, Havvoth-jair, *as it is* to this day.) 15 And to Machir I gave Gilead. 16 And to the Reubenites and to the Gadites I gave from Gilead even as far as the valley of Arnon, the middle of the valley as a border and as far as the river Jabbok, the border of the sons of Ammon; 17 the Arabah also, with the Jordan as *a* border, from Chinnereth even as far as the sea of the Arabah, the Salt Sea, at the foot of the slopes of Pisgah on the east.

18 "Then I commanded you at that time, saying, 'Yahweh your God has given you this land to possess it; all you men of valor shall cross over armed before your brothers, the sons of Israel. 19 But your wives and your little ones and your livestock (I know that you have much livestock) shall remain in your cities which I have given you, 20 until Yahweh gives rest to your brothers as to you, and they also possess the land which Yahweh your God will give them beyond the Jordan. Then you may return, every man to his possession which I have given you.' 21 And I commanded Joshua at that time, saying, 'Your eyes have seen all that Yahweh your God has done to these two kings; so Yahweh shall do to all the kingdoms into which you are about to cross. 22 Do not fear them, for Yahweh your God is the one fighting for you.'

23 "I also pleaded with Yahweh at that time, saying, 24 'O Lord Yahweh, You have begun to show Your slave Your greatness and Your strong hand; for what god is there in heaven or on earth who can do such works and mighty acts as Yours? 25 Let me, I pray, cross over and see the good land that is beyond the Jordan, that good hill country and Lebanon.' 26 But Yahweh was angry with me on your account and would not listen to me; and Yahweh said to me, 'Enough! Speak to Me no more of this matter. 27 Go up to the top of Pisgah and lift up your eyes to the west and north and south and east, and see *it* with your eyes, for you shall not cross over this Jordan. 28 But command Joshua and strengthen him and encourage him, for he shall go across at the head of this people, and he will cause them to inherit the land which you will see.' 29 So we remained in the valley opposite Beth-peor.

4 "So now, O Israel, listen to the statutes and the judgments which I am teaching you to do, so that you may live and go in and take possession of the land which Yahweh, the God of your fathers, is giving you. 2 You shall not add to the word which I am commanding you, nor take away from it, that you may keep the commandments of Yahweh your God which I am commanding you. 3 Your eyes have seen what Yahweh has done in the case of Baal-peor, for all the men who walked after Baal-peor, Yahweh your God has destroyed them from among you. 4 But you who clung to Yahweh your God are alive today, every one of you.

5 "See, I have taught you statutes and judgments just as Yahweh my God commanded me, that you should do thus in the land where you are entering to possess it. 6 You shall keep and do *them*, for that is your wisdom and your understanding in the sight of the peoples who will hear all these statutes and say, 'Surely this great nation is a wise and understanding people.' 7 For what great nation is there that has a god so near to it as is Yahweh our God whenever we call on Him? 8 Or what great nation is there that has statutes and judgments as righteous as this whole law which I am setting before you today?

9 "Only keep yourself and keep your soul very carefully, lest you forget the things which your eyes have seen and lest they depart from your heart all the days of your life. But make them known to your sons and to your grandsons. 10 *Remember* the day you stood before Yahweh your God at Horeb, when Yahweh said to me, 'Assemble the people to Me, that I may cause them to hear My words so they may learn to fear Me all the days they live on the earth, and that they may teach their children.' 11 And you came near and stood at the foot of the mountain, and the mountain burned with fire to the *very* heart of the heavens: darkness, cloud, and dense gloom. 12 Then Yahweh spoke to you from the midst of the fire; you heard the sound of words, but you saw no form—only a voice. 13 So He declared to you His covenant which He commanded you to do, *that is*, the Ten Commandments; and He wrote them on two tablets of stone. 14 And Yahweh commanded me at that time to teach you statutes and judgments, that you might do them in the land where you are going over to possess it.

15 "So keep your souls very carefully, since you did not see any form on the day Yahweh spoke to you at Horeb from the midst of the fire, 16 lest you act corruptly and make a graven image for yourselves in the form of any figure, the likeness of male or female, 17 the likeness of any animal that is on the earth, the likeness of any winged bird that flies in the sky, 18 the likeness of anything that creeps on the ground, the likeness of any fish that is in the water below the earth, 19 and lest you lift up your eyes to heaven and see the sun and the moon and the stars, all the host of heaven, and be drawn away and worship them and serve them, those which Yahweh your God has apportioned for all the peoples under the whole heaven. 20 But Yahweh has taken you and brought you out of the iron furnace, from Egypt, to be a people for His own inheritance, as today.

21 "Now Yahweh was angry with me on your account and swore that I would not cross the Jordan, and that I would not enter the good land which Yahweh your God is giving you as an inheritance. 22 For I will die in this land, I shall not cross the Jordan, but you shall cross and take possession of this good land. 23 So keep yourselves, lest you forget the covenant of Yahweh your God which He cut with you and make for yourselves a graven image in the form of anything *against* which Yahweh your God has commanded you. 24 For Yahweh your God is a consuming fire, a jealous God.

25 "When you become the father of children and children's children and remain long in the land and act corruptly and make a graven image in the form of anything and do that which is evil in the sight of Yahweh your God *so as* to provoke Him to anger, 26 I call heaven and earth to witness against you today, that you will surely perish quickly from the land where you are going over the Jordan to possess it. You shall not prolong your days on it, but will be utterly destroyed. 27 And Yahweh will scatter you among the peoples, and you will remain few in number among the nations where Yahweh drives you. 28 And there you will serve gods, the work of man's hands, wood and stone, which neither see nor hear nor eat nor smell. 29 But from there you will seek Yahweh your God, and you will find *Him*, for you will search for Him with all your heart

and all your soul. 30 When you are in distress
and all these things have come upon you, in
the last days you will return to Yahweh your
God and listen to His voice. 31 For Yahweh
your God is a compassionate God; He will
not fail you nor destroy you nor forget the
covenant with your fathers which He swore
to them.

32 "Indeed, ask now concerning the
former days which were before you, since
the day that God created man on the earth,
and *inquire* from one end of the heavens
to the other. Has *anything* been done like
this great thing, or has *anything* been heard
like it? 33 Has *any* people heard the voice of
God speaking from the midst of the fire,
as you have heard *it*, and lived? 34 Or has a
god tried to go to take for himself a nation
from within *another* nation with trials, with
signs and wonders and with war and with a
mighty hand and with an outstretched arm
and with great terrors, as Yahweh your God
did for you in Egypt before your eyes? 35 To
you it was shown that you might know that
Yahweh, He is God; there is no other besides
Him. 36 Out of the heavens He caused you to
hear His voice to discipline you; and on earth
He caused you to see His great fire, and you
heard His words from the midst of the fire.
37 Because He loved your fathers, therefore
He chose their seed after them. And He
personally brought you from Egypt by His
great power, 38 dispossessing before you
nations greater and mightier than you, to
bring you in *and* to give you their land for an
inheritance, as it is today. 39 Know therefore
today, and take it to your heart, that Yahweh,
He is God in heaven above and on the earth
below; there is no other. 40 So you shall keep
His statutes and His commandments which
I am commanding you today, that it may go
well with you and with your children after
you, and that you may prolong *your* days on
the land which Yahweh your God is giving
you for all the days."

41 Then Moses set apart three cities across
the Jordan to the *east* toward the sunrise,
42 that a manslayer might flee there, who
slew his neighbor without premeditation,
not hating him previously; so he shall flee
to one of these cities that he might live:
43 Bezer in the wilderness on the plateau
for the Reubenites, and Ramoth in Gilead
for the Gadites, and Golan in Bashan for the
Manassites.

44 Now this is the law which Moses
set before the sons of Israel; 45 these are
the testimonies and the statutes and the
judgments which Moses spoke to the sons
of Israel when they came out from Egypt,
46 across the Jordan, in the valley opposite
Beth-peor, in the land of Sihon king of the
Amorites who lived at Heshbon, whom
Moses and the sons of Israel struck down
when they came out from Egypt. 47 And
they took possession of his land and the
land of Og king of Bashan, the two kings of
the Amorites, *who were* across the Jordan to
the *east* toward the sunrise, 48 from Aroer,
which is on the edge of the valley of Arnon,
even as far as Mount Sion (that is, Hermon),
49 with all the Arabah across the Jordan to
the east, even as far as the sea of the Arabah,
at the foot of the slopes of Pisgah.

Psalm 36:7–12

7 How precious is Your
lovingkindness, O God!
And the sons of men take refuge
in the shadow of Your wings.
8 They are satisfied from the
richness of Your house;
And You give them to drink of
the river of Your delights.
9 For with You is the fountain of life;
In Your light we see light.

10 Continue Your lovingkindness
to those who know You,
And Your righteousness to
the upright in heart.
11 Let not the foot of pride
come upon me,
And let not the hand of the
ungodly drive me away.
12 There the workers of
wickedness have fallen;
They have been thrust down
and cannot rise.

Proverbs 12:7

7 The wicked are overthrown
and are no more,
But the house of the
righteous will stand.

Luke 1:1–20

1 Inasmuch as many have undertaken to
compile an account of the things that
have been fulfilled among us, 2 just as those,

who from the beginning were eyewitnesses
and servants of the word, handed *them*
down to us, 3 it seemed fitting for me as well,
having investigated everything carefully
from the beginning, to write *it* out for you
in orderly sequence, most excellent Theoph-
ilus, 4 so that you may know the certainty
about the things you have been taught.
5 In the days of Herod, king of Judea,
there was a priest named Zechariah, of the
division of Abijah, and he had a wife from
the daughters of Aaron, and her name was
Elizabeth. 6 And they were both righteous
in the sight of God, walking blamelessly
in all the commandments and righteous
requirements of the Lord. 7 But they had
no child, because Elizabeth was barren, and
they were both advanced in years.
8 Now it happened that while he was
performing his priestly service before God
in the order of his division, 9 according
to the custom of the priestly office, he
was chosen by lot to enter the sanctuary
of the Lord and burn incense. 10 And the
whole multitude of the people were praying
outside at the hour of the incense offering.
11 And an angel of the Lord appeared to
him, standing to the right of the altar of
incense. 12 And Zechariah was troubled
when he saw *the angel*, and fear fell upon
him. 13 But the angel said to him, "Do not
be afraid, Zechariah, for your prayer has
been heard, and your wife Elizabeth will
bear you a son, and you will call his name
John. 14 And you will have joy and gladness,
and many will rejoice at his birth. 15 For he
will be great in the sight of the Lord; and HE
WILL NOT DRINK ANY WINE OR STRONG DRINK,
and he will be filled with the Holy Spirit
while yet in his mother's womb. 16 And he
will turn many of the sons of Israel back to
the Lord their God. 17 And he will go before
Him in the spirit and power of Elijah, TO
TURN THE HEARTS OF THE FATHERS BACK TO
THE CHILDREN, and the disobedient to the
attitude of the righteous, to make ready a
people prepared for the Lord."
18 And Zechariah said to the angel, "How
will I know this? For I am an old man and my
wife is advanced in years." 19 And the angel
answered and said to him, "I am Gabriel,
who stands before God, and I was sent to
speak to you and to bring you this good
news. 20 And behold, you shall be silent
and unable to speak until the day when
these things take place, because you did not
believe my words, which will be fulfilled in
their proper time."

MARCH 22

Deuteronomy 5:1–6:25

5 Then Moses summoned all Israel and
said to them:
"Hear, O Israel, the statutes and the
judgments which I am speaking today in
your hearing, that you may learn them and
be careful to do them. 2 Yahweh our God cut
a covenant with us at Horeb. 3 Yahweh did
not cut this covenant with our fathers, but
with us, *with* all those of us alive here today.
4 Yahweh spoke to you face to face at the
mountain from the midst of the fire. 5 I was
standing between Yahweh and you at that
time, to declare to you the word of Yahweh;
for you were afraid because of the fire and
did not go up the mountain. He said,

6 'I am Yahweh your God who brought
you out of the land of Egypt, out of the
house of slavery.

7 'You shall have no other gods
before Me.

8 'You shall not make for yourself an
idol—any likeness *of* what is in heaven
above or on the earth beneath or in
the water under the earth.
9 'You shall not worship them or serve
them; for I, Yahweh your God, am a
jealous God, visiting the iniquity of
the fathers on the children and on the
third and the fourth *generations* of
those who hate Me,
10 but showing lovingkindness to
thousands, to those who love Me and
keep My commandments.

11 'You shall not take the name of Yahweh
your God in vain, for Yahweh will not
leave him unpunished who takes His
name in vain.

12 'Observe the sabbath day to keep it
holy, as Yahweh your God commanded
you.

13 'Six days you shall labor and do all
your work,
14 but the seventh day is a sabbath of
Yahweh your God; *in it* you shall not
do any work, you or your son or your
daughter or your male slave or your
female slave or your ox or your donkey
or any of your cattle or your sojourner
who is within your gates, so that your
male slave and your female slave may
rest as well as you.
15 'You shall remember that you were a
slave in the land of Egypt, and Yahweh
your God brought you out of there
with a mighty hand and with an
outstretched arm; therefore Yahweh
your God commanded you to observe
the sabbath day.

16 'Honor your father and your mother,
as Yahweh your God has commanded
you, that your days may be prolonged
and that it may go well with you on
the land which Yahweh your God gives
you.

17 'You shall not murder.

18 'You shall not commit adultery.

19 'You shall not steal.

20 'You shall not bear false witness
against your neighbor.

21 'You shall not covet your neighbor's
wife, and you shall not desire your
neighbor's house, his field, or his male
slave or his female slave, his ox or his
donkey or anything that belongs to
your neighbor.'

22 "These words Yahweh spoke to all your
assembly at the mountain from the midst of
the fire, *of* the cloud and *of* the dense gloom,
with a great voice, and He added no more.
He wrote them on two tablets of stone and
gave them to me. 23 Now it happened that
when you heard the voice from the midst
of the darkness, while the mountain was
burning with fire, you came near to me, all
the heads of your tribes and your elders.
24 And you said, 'Behold, Yahweh our God
has shown us His glory and His greatness,
and we have heard His voice from the midst
of the fire; we have seen today that God
speaks with man, yet he lives. 25 So now
then why should we die? For this great fire
will consume us; if we hear the voice of
Yahweh our God any longer, then we will
die. 26 For who is there of all flesh who has
heard the voice of the living God speaking
from the midst of the fire, as we *have*, and
lived? 27 As for you, go near and hear all that
Yahweh our God says; then speak to us all
that Yahweh our God speaks to you, and we
will hear and do *it*.'

28 "And Yahweh heard the voice of your
words when you spoke to me, and Yahweh
said to me, 'I have heard the voice of the
words of this people which they have
spoken to you. They have done well in all
that they have spoken. 29 Oh that they had
such a heart in them, that they would fear
Me and keep all My commandments all the
days, that it may be well with them and
with their sons forever! 30 Go, say to them,
"Return to your tents." 31 But as for you,
stand here by Me, that I may speak to you
all the commandments and the statutes and
the judgments which you shall teach them,
that they may do *them* in the land which
I give them to possess.' 32 So you shall be
careful to do just as Yahweh your God has
commanded you; you shall not turn aside
to the right or to the left. 33 In all the way
which Yahweh your God has commanded
you, you shall walk, that you may live and
that it may be well with you and that you
may prolong *your* days in the land which
you will possess.

6 "Now this is the commandment, the
statutes and the judgments, which
Yahweh your God has commanded *me* to
teach you, that you might do *it* in the land
where you are going over to possess it, 2 so
that you and your son and your grandson
might fear Yahweh your God, to keep all His
statutes and His commandments which I
am commanding you, all the days of your
life, and that your days may be prolonged.
3 O Israel, you shall listen and be careful to
do *it*, that it may be well with you and that
you may multiply greatly, just as Yahweh,
the God of your fathers, has promised you,
in a land flowing with milk and honey.

4 "Hear, O Israel! Yahweh is our God,
Yahweh is one! 5 You shall love Yahweh your
God with all your heart and with all your

soul and with all your might. 6 These words,
which I am commanding you today, shall
be on your heart. 7 You shall teach them
diligently to your sons and shall speak of
them when you sit in your house and when
you walk by the way and when you lie down
and when you rise up. 8 You shall bind them
as a sign on your hand, and they shall be as
phylacteries between your eyes. 9 You shall
write them on the doorposts of your house
and on your gates.
10 "Then it will be, when Yahweh your
God brings you into the land which He
swore to your fathers, to Abraham, to
Isaac, and to Jacob, to give you, great and
good cities which you did not build, 11 and
houses full of all good things which you did
not fill, and hewn cisterns which you did not
dig, vineyards and olive trees which you did
not plant, and you will eat and be satisfied,
12 then beware, lest you forget Yahweh who
brought you from the land of Egypt, out of
the house of slavery. 13 Yahweh your God
you shall fear; and Him you shall serve; and
by His name you shall swear. 14 You shall not
walk after other gods, any of the gods of the
peoples who surround you, 15 for Yahweh
your God in the midst of you is a jealous
God—lest the anger of Yahweh your God
be kindled against you, and He destroy you
from the face of the earth.
16 "You shall not put Yahweh your God to
the test, as you tested *Him* at Massah. 17 You
should diligently keep the commandments
of Yahweh your God and His testimonies
and His statutes which He has commanded
you. 18 And you shall do what is right and
good in the sight of Yahweh, that it may be
well with you and that you may go in and
possess the good land which Yahweh swore
to *give* your fathers, 19 by driving out all your
enemies from before you, as Yahweh has
spoken.
20 "When your son asks you in time to
come, saying, 'What *do* the testimonies and
the statutes and the judgments *mean* which
Yahweh our God commanded you?' 21 then
you shall say to your son, 'We were slaves to
Pharaoh in Egypt, and Yahweh brought us
from Egypt with a strong hand. 22 Moreover,
Yahweh showed great and calamitous signs
and wonders before our eyes against Egypt,
Pharaoh, and all his household; 23 but He
brought us out from there in order to bring
us in, to give us the land which He had sworn
to our fathers.' 24 So Yahweh commanded
us to do all these statutes, to fear Yahweh
our God for our good all *our* days and for
our survival, as *it is* today. 25 And it will be
righteousness for us if we are careful to do
all this commandment before Yahweh our
God, just as He commanded us.

Psalm 37:1–4

1 Do not fret because of evildoers,
Be not envious toward doers
of unrighteousness.
2 For they will wither quickly
like the grass
And fade like the green herb.

3 Trust in Yahweh and do good;
Dwell in the land and
cultivate faithfulness.
4 Delight yourself in Yahweh;
And He will give you the
desires of your heart.

Proverbs 12:8

8 A man will be praised
according to his insight,
But one of perverse heart
will be despised.

Luke 1:21–38

21 And the people were waiting for Zecha-
riah, and were wondering at his delay in the
sanctuary. 22 But when he came out, he was
unable to speak to them, and they realized
that he had seen a vision in the sanctuary.
And he kept making signs to them, and
remained mute. 23 And it happened that
when the days of his priestly service were
fulfilled, he went back home.
24 After these days Elizabeth his wife
conceived, and she kept herself in seclusion
for five months, saying, 25 "This is the way
the Lord has dealt with me in the days when
He looked upon *me* to take away my disgrace
among men."
26 Now in the sixth month the angel
Gabriel was sent from God to a city in Galilee
called Nazareth, 27 to a virgin betrothed to a
man whose name was Joseph, of the house
of David, and the virgin's name was Mary.
28 And coming in, he said to her, "Greetings,
favored one! The Lord *is* with you." 29 But
she was very perplexed at *this* statement,
and was pondering what kind of greeting
this was. 30 And the angel said to her, "Do

not be afraid, Mary, for you have found favor with God. 31 And behold, you will conceive in *your* womb and bear a son, and you shall name Him Jesus. 32 He will be great and will be called the Son of the Most High, and the Lord God will give Him the throne of His father David, 33 and He will reign over the house of Jacob forever, and there will be no end of His kingdom." 34 But Mary said to the angel, "How will this be, since I am a virgin?" 35 The angel answered and said to her, "The Holy Spirit will come upon you, and the power of the Most High will overshadow you; and for that reason the holy Child shall be called the Son of God. 36 And behold, your relative Elizabeth has also conceived a son in her old age; and this is the sixth month for her who was called barren. 37 For nothing will be impossible with God." 38 And Mary said, "Behold, the slave of the Lord; may it be done to me according to your word." And the angel departed from her.

MARCH 23

Deuteronomy 7:1–8:20

7 "When Yahweh your God brings you into the land where you are entering to possess it, and He clears away many nations before you, the Hittites and the Girgashites and the Amorites and the Canaanites and the Perizzites and the Hivites and the Jebusites, seven nations more numerous and stronger than you, 2 and when Yahweh your God gives them over before you and you strike them down, then you shall devote them to destruction. You shall cut no covenant with them and show no favor to them. 3 Furthermore, you shall not intermarry with them; you shall not give your daughters to their sons, nor shall you take their daughters for your sons. 4 For they will turn your sons away from following Me, and they will serve other gods; then the anger of Yahweh will be kindled against you, and He will quickly destroy you. 5 But thus you shall do to them: you shall tear down their altars and shatter their *sacred* pillars and cut their Asherim in pieces and burn their graven images with fire. 6 For you are a holy people to Yahweh your God; Yahweh your God has chosen you to be a people for His own treasured possession out of all the peoples who are on the face of the earth.

7 "Yahweh did not set His affection on you nor choose you because you were more in number than any of the peoples, for you were the fewest of all peoples, 8 but because Yahweh loved you and kept the oath which He swore to your fathers, Yahweh brought you out with a strong hand and redeemed you from the house of slavery, from the hand of Pharaoh king of Egypt. 9 You shall know therefore that Yahweh your God, He is God, the faithful God, who keeps His covenant and His lovingkindness to a thousand generations with those who love Him and keep His commandments; 10 but repays those who hate Him to their faces, to make them perish; He will not delay with him who hates Him, He will repay him to his face. 11 Therefore, you shall keep the commandment and the statutes and the judgments which I am commanding you today, to do them.

12 "Then it will be, because you listen to these judgments and keep and do them, that Yahweh your God will keep with you His covenant and His lovingkindness which He swore to your fathers. 13 And He will love you and bless you and multiply you; He will also bless the fruit of your womb and the fruit of your ground, your grain and your new wine and your oil, the increase of your herd and the young of your flock, in the land which He swore to your fathers to give you. 14 You shall be blessed above all peoples; there will be no male or female barren among you or among your cattle. 15 And Yahweh will take away from you all sickness; and He will not put on you any of the harmful diseases of Egypt which you have known, but He will give them to all who hate you. 16 And you shall consume all the peoples whom Yahweh your God will give over to you; your eye shall not pity them, nor shall you serve their gods, for that *would be* a snare to you.

17 "If you should say in your heart, 'These nations are more numerous than I; how can I dispossess them?' 18 you shall not be afraid of them; you shall well remember what Yahweh your God did to Pharaoh and to all Egypt: 19 the great trials which your eyes saw and the signs and the wonders

and the mighty hand and the outstretched arm by which Yahweh your God brought you out. So shall Yahweh your God do to all the peoples of whom you are afraid. 20 Moreover, Yahweh your God will send the hornet against them until those who remain and hide themselves from you perish. 21 You shall not dread them, for Yahweh your God is in your midst, a great and fearsome God. 22 And Yahweh your God will clear away these nations before you little by little; you will not be able to put an end to them quickly, lest the wild beasts become too numerous for you. 23 But Yahweh your God will give them over before you and will throw them into great confusion until they are destroyed. 24 And He will give their kings into your hand so that you will make their name perish from under heaven; no man will be able to stand before you until you have destroyed them. 25 The graven images of their gods you are to burn with fire; you shall not covet the silver or the gold that is on them, nor take it for yourselves, lest you be snared by it, for it is an abomination to Yahweh your God. 26 And you shall not bring an abomination into your house and become devoted to destruction like it; you shall utterly detest it, and you shall utterly abhor it, for it is devoted to destruction.

8 "The entire commandment that I am commanding you today you shall be careful to do, that you may live and multiply, and go in and possess the land which Yahweh swore *to give* to your fathers. 2 And you shall remember all the way which Yahweh your God has led you in the wilderness these forty years, that He might humble you, testing you, to know what was in your heart, whether you would keep His commandments or not. 3 And He humbled you and let you be hungry and fed you with manna which you did not know, nor did your fathers know, that He might make you know that man does not live by bread alone, but by everything that proceeds out of the mouth of Yahweh. 4 Your clothing did not wear out on you, nor did your foot swell these forty years. 5 Thus you shall know in your heart that Yahweh your God was disciplining you just as a man disciplines his son. 6 So you shall keep the commandments of Yahweh your God, to walk in His ways and to fear Him. 7 For Yahweh your God is bringing you into a good land, a land of brooks of water, of fountains and springs, flowing forth in valleys and hills; 8 a land of wheat and barley, of vines and fig trees and pomegranates, a land of olive oil and honey; 9 a land where you will eat food without scarcity, in which you will not lack anything; a land whose stones are iron, and out of whose hills you can dig copper. 10 And so you will eat and be satisfied, and you shall bless Yahweh your God for the good land which He has given you.

11 "Beware lest you forget Yahweh your God by not keeping His commandments and His judgments and His statutes which I am commanding you today; 12 lest you eat and are satisfied and build good houses and live *in them*, 13 and your herds and your flocks multiply, and your silver and gold multiply, and all that you have multiplies, 14 and your heart becomes lifted up and you forget Yahweh your God who brought you out from the land of Egypt, out of the house of slavery. 15 He led you through the great and fearsome wilderness, *with its* fiery serpents and scorpions and thirsty ground where there was no water; He brought water for you out of the rock of flint. 16 In the wilderness He fed you manna which your fathers did not know, that He might humble you and that He might test you, to do good for you in the end, 17 lest you say in your heart, 'My power and the might of my hand made me this wealth.' 18 But you shall remember Yahweh your God, for it is He who is giving you power to make wealth, that He may confirm His covenant which He swore to your fathers, as *it is* this day. 19 Now it will be, if you ever forget Yahweh your God and walk after other gods and serve them and worship them, I testify against you today that you will surely perish. 20 Like the nations that Yahweh makes to perish before you, so you shall perish, because you would not listen to the voice of Yahweh your God.

Psalm 37:5–11

5 Commit your way to Yahweh,
Trust in Him, and He will do it.
6 He will bring forth your
righteousness as the light
And your judgment as the noonday.

7 Be still in Yahweh and wait
patiently for Him;

Do not fret because of him
who prospers in his way,
Because of the man who carries
out schemes of wickedness.

8 Cease from anger and forsake wrath;
Do not fret; *it leads* only to evildoing.
9 For evildoers will be cut off,
But those who hope for Yahweh,
they will inherit the land.

10 Yet a little while and the wicked
man will be no more;
You will look carefully at his place,
and he will not be *there*.
11 But the lowly will inherit the land
And will delight themselves
in abundant peace.

Proverbs 12:9–10

9 Better is he who is lightly
esteemed and has a servant
Than he who honors himself
and lacks bread.
10 A righteous man knows *the value of* the life of his animal,
But *even* the compassion of
the wicked is cruel.

Luke 1:39–56

39 Now at this time Mary arose and went in
a hurry to the hill country, to a city of Judah,
40 and entered the house of Zechariah and
greeted Elizabeth. 41 And it happened that
when Elizabeth heard Mary's greeting, the
baby leaped in her womb, and Elizabeth was
filled with the Holy Spirit. 42 And she cried
out with a loud voice and said, "Blessed *are*
you among women, and blessed *is* the fruit
of your womb! 43 And how has it *happened*
to me, that the mother of my Lord would
come to me? 44 For behold, when the sound
of your greeting reached my ears, the baby
leaped in my womb for joy. 45 And blessed
is she who believed that there would be a
fulfillment of what had been spoken to her
by the Lord."

46 And Mary said:
"My soul magnifies the Lord,
47 And my spirit has rejoiced
in God my Savior.
48 "For He has looked upon the
humble state of His slave,
For behold, from this time on, all
generations will count me blessed.
49 "For the Mighty One has done
great things for me,
And holy is His name.
50 "AND HIS MERCY IS UPON GENERATION
AFTER GENERATION
TOWARD THOSE WHO FEAR HIM.
51 "He has done a mighty deed
with His arm;
He has scattered *those who were* proud
in the thoughts of their heart.
52 "He has brought down rulers
from *their* thrones,
And has exalted those
who were humble.
53 "HE HAS FILLED THE HUNGRY
WITH GOOD THINGS,
And sent away the rich empty-handed.
54 "He has given help to Israel His servant,
In remembrance of His mercy,
55 As He spoke to our fathers,
To Abraham and his seed forever."

56 And Mary stayed with her about three
months, and *then* returned to her home.

MARCH 24

Deuteronomy 9:1–10:22

9 "Hear, O Israel! You are crossing over
the Jordan today to go in to dispossess
nations greater and mightier than you, great
cities fortified to heaven, 2 a people great
and tall, the sons of the Anakim, whom you
know and of whom you have heard *it said*,
'Who can stand before the sons of Anak?'
3 So you shall know today that it is Yahweh
your God who is crossing over before you as
a consuming fire. He will destroy them, and
He will subdue them before you, so that you
may dispossess them and make them perish
quickly, just as Yahweh has spoken to you.

4 "Do not say in your heart when Yahweh
your God has driven them out before you,
saying, 'Because of my righteousness Yah-
weh has brought me in to possess this land,'
but *it is* because of the wickedness of these
nations *that* Yahweh is dispossessing them
before you. 5 It is not for your righteousness
or for the uprightness of your heart that
you are going to possess their land, but *it is*
because of the wickedness of these nations

that Yahweh your God is dispossessing them before you, in order to confirm the oath which Yahweh swore to your fathers, to Abraham, to Isaac, and to Jacob.

6 "So you shall know *it is* not because of your righteousness *that* Yahweh your God is giving you this good land to possess, for you are a stiff-necked people. 7 Remember, do not forget how you provoked Yahweh your God to wrath in the wilderness; from the day that you went out of the land of Egypt until you came to this place, you have been rebellious against Yahweh. 8 Even at Horeb you provoked Yahweh to wrath, and Yahweh was so angry with you that He would have destroyed you. 9 When I went up to the mountain to receive the tablets of stone, the tablets of the covenant which Yahweh had cut with you, then I remained on the mountain forty days and nights; I neither ate bread nor drank water. 10 And Yahweh gave me the two tablets of stone written by the finger of God; and on them *were* all the words which Yahweh had spoken with you at the mountain from the midst of the fire on the day of the assembly. 11 Now it happened at the end of forty days and nights, that Yahweh gave me the two tablets of stone, the tablets of the covenant. 12 Then Yahweh said to me, 'Arise, go down from here quickly, for your people whom you brought out of Egypt have acted corruptly. They have quickly turned aside from the way which I commanded them; they have made a molten image for themselves.' 13 Yahweh spoke further to me, saying, 'I have seen this people, and indeed, they are a stiff-necked people. 14 Let Me alone, that I may destroy them and blot out their name from under heaven; and I will make of you a nation mightier and more numerous than they.'

15 "So I turned and came down from the mountain while the mountain was burning with fire, and the two tablets of the covenant were in my two hands. 16 And I saw that you had indeed sinned against Yahweh your God. You had made for yourselves a molten calf; you had turned aside quickly from the way which Yahweh had commanded you. 17 And I took hold of the two tablets and threw them from my hands and shattered them before your eyes. 18 And I fell down before Yahweh, as at the first, forty days and nights; I neither ate bread nor drank water because of all your sin which you had committed in doing what was evil in the sight of Yahweh to provoke Him to anger. 19 For I was afraid of the anger and the wrath with which Yahweh was provoked against you in order to destroy you, but Yahweh listened to me that time also. 20 And Yahweh was angry enough with Aaron to destroy him; so I also prayed for Aaron at the same time. 21 Now I took your sinful *thing*, the calf which you had made, and burned it with fire and crushed it, grinding it very small until it was as fine as dust; and I threw its dust into the brook that came down from the mountain.

22 "Again at Taberah and at Massah and at Kibroth-hattaavah you provoked Yahweh to wrath. 23 When Yahweh sent you from Kadesh-barnea, saying, 'Go up and possess the land which I have given you,' then you rebelled against the command of Yahweh your God; you did not believe Him, and you did not listen to His voice. 24 You have been rebellious against Yahweh from the day I knew you.

25 "So I fell down before Yahweh the forty days and the forty nights, which I did because Yahweh had said He would destroy you. 26 And I prayed to Yahweh and said, 'O Lord Yahweh, do not destroy Your people, even Your inheritance, whom You have redeemed through Your greatness, whom You have brought out of Egypt with a strong hand. 27 Remember Your servants, Abraham, Isaac, and Jacob; do not look at the stiff-*neck* of this people or at their wickedness or their sin, 28 lest the land from which You brought us say, "Because Yahweh was not able to bring them into the land which He had promised them and because He hated them He has brought them out to put them to death in the wilderness." 29 Yet they are Your people, even Your inheritance, whom You have brought out by Your great power and Your outstretched arm.'

10 "At that time Yahweh said to me, 'Carve out for yourself two tablets of stone like the former ones, and come up to Me on the mountain, and make an ark of wood for yourself. 2 And I will write on the tablets the words that were on the former tablets which you shattered, and you shall put them in the ark.' 3 So I made an ark of acacia wood and carved out two tablets of stone like the former ones and went up on

the mountain with the two tablets in my
hand. 4 And He wrote on the tablets, like
the former writing, the Ten Commandments
which Yahweh had spoken to you on the
mountain from the midst of the fire on the
day of the assembly; and Yahweh gave them
to me. 5 Then I turned and came down from
the mountain and put the tablets in the ark
which I had made; and there they are, as
Yahweh commanded me."

6 (Now the sons of Israel set out from
Beeroth Bene-jaakan to Moserah. There
Aaron died, and there he was buried, and
Eleazar his son ministered as priest in his
place. 7 From there they set out to Gudgodah,
and from Gudgodah to Jotbathah, a land of
brooks of water. 8 At that time Yahweh set
apart the tribe of Levi to carry the ark of the
covenant of Yahweh, to stand before Yahweh
to minister for Him and to bless in His name
to this day. 9 Therefore, Levi does not have
a portion or inheritance with his brothers;
Yahweh is his inheritance, just as Yahweh
your God spoke to him.)

10 "I, moreover, stayed on the mountain
forty days and forty nights like the first
time, and Yahweh listened to me that time
also; Yahweh was not willing to destroy
you. 11 Then Yahweh said to me, 'Arise, go
on your journey ahead of the people, that
they may go in and possess the land which
I swore to their fathers to give them.'

12 "So now, Israel, what does Yahweh
your God ask from you, but to fear Yahweh
your God, to walk in all His ways and love
Him, and to serve Yahweh your God with
all your heart and with all your soul, 13 *and*
to keep the commandments of Yahweh and
His statutes which I am commanding you
today for your good? 14 Behold, to Yahweh
your God belong heaven and the highest
heavens, the earth and all that is in it. 15 Yet
on your fathers did Yahweh set His affection
to love them, and He chose their seed after
them, *even* you above all peoples, as *it is*
this day. 16 So circumcise your heart, and
stiffen your neck no longer. 17 For Yahweh
your God is the God of gods and the Lord
of lords, the great, the mighty, and the
fearsome God who does not show partiality
nor take a bribe. 18 He executes justice for
the orphan and the widow, and shows love
for the sojourner by giving him food and
clothing. 19 So show love for the sojourner,
for you were sojourners in the land of Egypt.
20 Yahweh your God you shall fear; Him you
shall serve, and to Him you shall cling, and
by His name you shall swear. 21 He is your
praise, and He is your God, who has done
these great and fearsome things for you
which your eyes have seen. 22 Your fathers
went down to Egypt seventy persons *in all*,
and now Yahweh your God has made you as
numerous as the stars of heaven.

Psalm 37:12–17

12 The wicked schemes against
the righteous
And gnashes at him with his teeth.
13 The Lord laughs at him,
For He sees that his day is coming.

14 The wicked have drawn the
sword and bent their bow
To cast down the afflicted
and the needy,
To slay those who are
upright in conduct.
15 Their sword will enter their own heart,
And their bows will be broken.

16 Better is the little of the righteous
Than the abundance of many wicked.
17 For the arms of the wicked
will be broken,
But Yahweh sustains the righteous.

Proverbs 12:11

11 He who cultivates his land will
be satisfied with bread,
But he who pursues empty *things*
lacks a heart *of wisdom*.

Luke 1:57–80

57 Now the time was fulfilled for Elizabeth
to give birth, and she gave birth to a son.
58 And her neighbors and her relatives heard
that the Lord had magnified His great mercy
toward her, and they were rejoicing with her.

59 And it happened that on the eighth
day they came to circumcise the child, and
they were going to call him Zechariah, after
the name of his father. 60 But his mother
answered and said, "No, but he shall be
called John." 61 And they said to her, "There
is no one among your relatives who is called
by this name." 62 And they were making
signs to his father, as to what he wanted
him called. 63 And he asked for a tablet and
wrote as follows, "His name is John." And

they all marveled. 64 And at once his mouth was opened and his tongue *loosed,* and he *began to* speak, blessing God. 65 And fear came on all those living around them, and all these matters were being talked about in all the hill country of Judea. 66 And all who heard *these things* put *them* in their heart, saying, "What then will this child be?" For the hand of the Lord was indeed with him.

67 And his father Zechariah was filled with the Holy Spirit, and prophesied, saying:

68 "Blessed *be* the Lord God of Israel,
For He visited and accomplished
redemption for His people,
69 And raised up a horn of salvation for us
In the house of David His servant—
70 As He spoke by the mouth of His
holy prophets from of old—
71 Salvation FROM OUR ENEMIES,
And FROM THE HAND OF
ALL WHO HATE US,
72 To show mercy toward our fathers,
And to remember His holy covenant,
73 The oath which He swore to
Abraham our father,
74 To grant us that we, being rescued
from the hand of our enemies,
Might serve Him without fear,
75 In holiness and righteousness
before Him all our days.
76 "And you, child, will be called the
prophet of the Most High,
For you will go on BEFORE THE LORD
TO MAKE READY HIS WAYS,
77 To give to His people *the*
knowledge of salvation
By the forgiveness of their sins,
78 Because of the tender
mercy of our God,
With which the Sunrise from
on high will visit us,
79 TO SHINE UPON THOSE WHO
SIT IN DARKNESS AND THE
SHADOW OF DEATH,
To direct our feet into the
way of peace."

80 And the child continued to grow and to become strong in spirit, and he lived in the desolate regions until the day of his public appearance to Israel.

MARCH 25

Deuteronomy 11:1–12:32

11 "You shall therefore love Yahweh your God, and keep His charge, His statutes, His judgments, and His commandments all *your* days. 2 So know this day that I *am* not *speaking* with your sons who have not known and who have not seen the discipline of Yahweh your God—His greatness, His strong hand and His outstretched arm, 3 and His signs and His works which He did in the midst of Egypt to Pharaoh the king of Egypt and to all his land; 4 and what He did to Egypt's army, to its horses and its chariots, when He made the water of the Red Sea to engulf them while they were pursuing you, and Yahweh made them perish utterly; 5 and what He did to you in the wilderness until you came to this place; 6 and what He did to Dathan and Abiram, the sons of Eliab, the son of Reuben, when the earth opened its mouth and swallowed them, their households, their tents, and *every living thing* that followed them, among all Israel— 7 but your own eyes have seen all the great work of Yahweh which He did.

8 "You shall therefore keep every commandment which I am commanding you today, so that you may be strong and go in and possess the land into which you are about to cross to possess it; 9 so that you may prolong *your* days on the land which Yahweh swore to your fathers to give to them and to their seed, a land flowing with milk and honey. 10 For the land, into which you are entering to possess it, is not like the land of Egypt from which you came out, where you used to sow your seed and water it with your foot like a vegetable garden. 11 But the land into which you are about to cross to possess it, a land of hills and valleys, drinks water from the rain of heaven, 12 a land for which Yahweh your God cares; the eyes of Yahweh your God are always on it, from the beginning even to the end of the year.

13 "And it will be that, if you listen obediently to my commandments which I am commanding you today, to love Yahweh your God and to serve Him with all your heart and all your soul, 14 that I, *Yahweh,* will give the rain for your land in its season, the early and late rains, that you may gather

in your grain and your new wine and your oil. 15 And I will give grass in your fields for your cattle, and you will eat and be satisfied. 16 Beware lest your hearts be deceived, and you turn away and serve other gods and worship them, 17 and the anger of Yahweh will be kindled against you, and He will shut up the heavens so that there will be no rain and the ground will not yield its fruit; and you will perish quickly from the good land which Yahweh is giving you.

18 "You shall therefore place these words of mine on your heart and on your soul; and you shall bind them as a sign on your hand, and they shall be as phylacteries between your eyes. 19 And you shall teach them to your sons, speaking of them when you sit in your house and when you walk along the road and when you lie down and when you rise up. 20 And you shall write them on the doorposts of your house and on your gates, 21 so that your days and the days of your sons may be multiplied on the land which Yahweh swore to your fathers to give them, as long as the heavens *remain* above the earth. 22 For if you are careful to keep this entire commandment which I am commanding you to do, to love Yahweh your God, to walk in all His ways, and to cling to Him, 23 then Yahweh will dispossess all these nations from before you, and you will dispossess nations greater and mightier than you. 24 Every place on which the sole of your foot treads shall be yours; your border will be from the wilderness to Lebanon, *and* from the river, the river Euphrates, as far as the western sea. 25 No man will be able to stand before you; Yahweh your God will put the dread of you and the fear of you on all the land on which you set foot, as He has spoken to you.

26 "See, I am setting before you today a blessing and a curse: 27 the blessing, if you listen to the commandments of Yahweh your God, which I am commanding you today; 28 and the curse, if you do not listen to the commandments of Yahweh your God, but turn aside from the way which I am commanding you today, by walking after other gods which you have not known.

29 "And it will be, when Yahweh your God brings you into the land where you are entering to possess it, that you shall set the blessing on Mount Gerizim and the curse on Mount Ebal. 30 Are they not across the Jordan, west of the way toward the sunset, in the land of the Canaanites who live in the Arabah, opposite Gilgal, beside the oaks of Moreh? 31 For you are about to cross the Jordan to go in to possess the land which Yahweh your God is giving you, and you shall possess it and live in it, 32 and you shall be careful to do all the statutes and the judgments which I am setting before you today.

12 "These are the statutes and the judgments which you shall be careful to do in the land which Yahweh, the God of your fathers, has given you to possess all the days you live on the earth. 2 You shall utterly destroy all the places where the nations whom you shall dispossess serve their gods, on the high mountains and on the hills and under every green tree. 3 And you shall tear down their altars and shatter their *sacred* pillars and burn their Asherim with fire, and you shall cut the graven images of their gods in pieces and destroy their name from that place. 4 You shall not do thus toward Yahweh your God. 5 But you shall seek *Yahweh* at the place which Yahweh your God will choose from all your tribes, to establish His name there for His dwelling, and there you shall come. 6 And there you shall bring your burnt offerings, your sacrifices, your tithes, the contribution of your hand, your votive offerings, your freewill offerings, and the firstborn of your herd and of your flock. 7 There also you and your households shall eat before Yahweh your God, and be glad in all that you send forth your hand *to do*, in which Yahweh your God has blessed you.

8 "You shall not do at all what we are doing here today, every man *doing* whatever is right in his own eyes; 9 for you have not as yet come to the resting place and the inheritance which Yahweh your God is giving you. 10 Now you will cross the Jordan and live in the land which Yahweh your God is giving you to inherit. And He will give you rest from all your enemies around *you* so that you live in security. 11 Then it will be that the place in which Yahweh your God will choose for His name to dwell, there you shall bring all that I am commanding you: your burnt offerings and your sacrifices, your tithes and the contribution of your hand, and all your choice votive offerings which you will vow to Yahweh. 12 And you shall be glad before

Yahweh your God, you and your sons and
daughters, your male and female slaves, and
the Levite who is within your gates, since
he has no portion or inheritance with you.
13 "Beware, lest you offer your burnt
offerings in every *cultic* place you see, 14 but
in the place which Yahweh chooses in one of
your tribes, there you shall offer your burnt
offerings, and there you shall do all that I am
commanding you.
15 "However, you may sacrifice and eat
meat within any of your gates, whatever
you desire, according to the blessing of
Yahweh your God which He has given you;
the unclean and the clean may eat of it, as of
the gazelle and the deer. 16 Only you shall not
eat the blood; you are to pour it out on the
ground like water. 17 You are not allowed to
eat within your gates the tithe of your grain
or new wine or oil, or the firstborn of your
herd or flock, or any of your votive offerings
which you vow, or your freewill offerings,
or the contribution of your hand. 18 But you
shall eat them before Yahweh your God in the
place which Yahweh your God will choose,
you and your son and daughter, and your
male and female slaves, and the Levite who
is within your gates; and you shall be glad
before Yahweh your God in all that you send
forth your hand *to do*. 19 Beware lest you for-
sake the Levite all your days upon your land.
20 "When Yahweh your God enlarges your
territory as He has promised you, and you
say, 'I will eat meat,' because you desire to
eat meat, *then* you may eat meat, whatever
you desire. 21 If the place where Yahweh
your God chooses to set His name is too far
away from you, then you may sacrifice of
your herd and flock which Yahweh has given
you, as I have commanded you; and you may
eat within your gates whatever you desire.
22 Just as a gazelle or a deer is eaten, so you
will eat it; the unclean and the clean alike
may eat of it. 23 Only be strong *in yourselves*
not to eat the blood, for the blood is the life,
and you shall not eat the life with the flesh.
24 You shall not eat it; you shall pour it out
on the ground like water. 25 You shall not eat
it, so that it may be well with you and your
sons after you, for you will be doing what
is right in the sight of Yahweh. 26 Only your
holy things which you may have and your
votive offerings, you shall take and go to the
place which Yahweh chooses. 27 And you
shall offer your burnt offerings, the flesh
and the blood, on the altar of Yahweh your
God; and the blood of your sacrifices shall
be poured out on the altar of Yahweh your
God, and you shall eat the flesh.
28 "Be careful to listen to all these words
which I command you, so that it may be well
with you and your sons after you forever, for
you will be doing what is good and right in
the sight of Yahweh your God.
29 "When Yahweh your God cuts off
before you the nations which you are going
in to dispossess, and you dispossess them
and inhabit their land, 30 beware lest you
be ensnared to follow them, after they are
destroyed before you, and lest you inquire
after their gods, saying, 'How do these
nations serve their gods, that I also may do
likewise?' 31 You shall not do thus toward
Yahweh your God, for every abominable
act which Yahweh hates they have done for
their gods; for they even burn their sons and
daughters in the fire to their gods.
32 "Whatever I am commanding you, you
shall be careful to do; you shall not add to
nor take away from it.

Psalm 37:18–22

18 Yahweh knows the days
  of the blameless,
And their inheritance will be forever.
19 They will not be ashamed
  in the time of evil,
And in the days of famine
  they will be satisfied.

20 But the wicked will perish;
And the enemies of Yahweh will be
  like the glory of the pastures,
They vanish—in smoke
  they vanish away.

21 The wicked borrows and
  does not pay back,
But the righteous is gracious and gives.
22 For those blessed by Him
  will inherit the land,
But those cursed by Him will be cut off.

Proverbs 12:12–14

12 The wicked man desires a
  stronghold of evil men,
But the root of the righteous
  gives *fruit*.
13 The snare of an evil man is in the
  transgression of his lips,

But the righteous *man* will
come out from distress.
14 A man will be satisfied with good
by the fruit of his mouth,
And the good deed of a man's
hands will return to him.

Luke 2:1–24

2 Now it happened that in those days a
decree went out from Caesar Augustus
for a census to be taken of all the inhabited
earth. 2 This was the first census taken
while Quirinius was governor of Syria.
3 And everyone was going to be registered
for the census, each to his own city. 4 And
Joseph also went up from Galilee, from the
city of Nazareth, to Judea, to the city of
David, which is called Bethlehem, because
he was of the house and family of David, 5 in
order to register along with Mary, who was
betrothed to him, *and* was with child. 6 Now
it happened that while they were there, the
days were fulfilled for her to give birth. 7 And
she gave birth to her firstborn son; and she
wrapped Him in cloths, and laid Him in
a manger, because there was no place for
them in the guest room.

8 In the same region there were *some*
shepherds staying out in the fields and keep-
ing watch over their flock by night. 9 And an
angel of the Lord stood before them, and
the glory of the Lord shone around them;
and they were terribly frightened. 10 But the
angel said to them, "Do not be afraid; for
behold, I bring you good news of great joy
which will be for all the people. 11 For today
in the city of David there has been born for
you a Savior, who is Christ the Lord. 12 And
this *will be* the sign for you: you will find
a baby wrapped in cloths and lying in a
manger." 13 And suddenly there appeared
with the angel a multitude of the heavenly
host praising God and saying,
14 "Glory to God in the highest,
And on earth peace among men
with whom He is pleased."

15 And it happened that when the angels
had gone away from them into heaven, the
shepherds *began* saying to one another,
"Let us go to Bethlehem then, and see this
thing that has happened which the Lord
has made known to us." 16 So they went in
a hurry and found their way to Mary and
Joseph, and the baby lying in the manger.
17 And when they had seen this, they made
known the statement which had been told
them about this Child. 18 And all who heard
it marveled at the things which were told
them by the shepherds. 19 But Mary was
treasuring all these things, pondering
them in her heart. 20 And the shepherds
went back, glorifying and praising God for
all that they had heard and seen, just as
was told them.

21 And when eight days were fulfilled so
that *they* could circumcise Him, His name
was called Jesus, the name given by the
angel before He was conceived in the womb.

22 And when the days for their cleansing
according to the Law of Moses were fulfilled,
they brought Him up to Jerusalem to present
Him to the Lord 23 (as it is written in the Law
of the Lord, "EVERY *firstborn* MALE THAT
OPENS THE WOMB SHALL BE CALLED HOLY
TO THE LORD"), 24 and to offer a sacrifice
according to what was said in the Law of
the Lord, "A PAIR OF TURTLEDOVES OR TWO
YOUNG PIGEONS."

Day after day, week after week, month after month, year after year, we study one Book, the Bible. Everything we need to know from God is contained in this one Book.

— JOHN MACARTHUR

MARCH 26

Deuteronomy 13:1–14:29

13 "If a prophet or a dreamer of dreams
arises among you and gives you a sign
or a wonder, 2 and the sign or the wonder
comes true, concerning which he spoke to
you, saying, 'Let us walk after other gods
(whom you have not known) and let us serve
them,' 3 you shall not listen to the words of

that prophet or that dreamer of dreams; for Yahweh your God is testing you to find out if you love Yahweh your God with all your heart and with all your soul. 4 You shall walk after Yahweh your God and fear Him; and you shall keep His commandments, listen to His voice, serve Him, and cling to Him. 5 But that prophet or that dreamer of dreams shall be put to death because he has counseled rebellion against Yahweh your God who brought you from the land of Egypt and redeemed you from the house of slavery, to drive you from the way in which Yahweh your God commanded you to walk. So you shall purge the evil from among you.

6 "If your brother, your mother's son, or your son or daughter, or the wife you cherish, or your friend who is as your own soul, entices you secretly, saying, 'Let us go and serve other gods' (whom neither you nor your fathers have known, 7 of the gods of the peoples who are around you, near you or far from you, from one end of the earth to the other end), 8 you shall not be willing to accept him or listen to him; and your eye shall not pity him; and you shall not spare him or conceal him. 9 But you shall surely kill him; your hand shall be first against him to put him to death, and afterwards the hand of all the people. 10 So you shall stone him to death because he has sought to drive you from Yahweh your God who brought you out from the land of Egypt, out of the house of slavery. 11 Thus all Israel will hear and be afraid and will never again do such an evil thing among you.

12 "If you hear in one of your cities, which Yahweh your God is giving you to live in, *anyone* saying *that* 13 some vile men have gone out from among you and have driven the inhabitants of their city *astray*, saying, 'Let us go and serve other gods' (whom you have not known), 14 then you shall inquire and search out and ask thoroughly. Behold, if it is true *and* the matter is confirmed, that this abomination has been done among you, 15 you shall surely strike the inhabitants of that city with the edge of the sword, devoting it to destruction and all that is in it and its cattle with the edge of the sword. 16 Then you shall gather all its spoil into the middle of its open square and burn the city and all its spoil with fire as a whole burnt offering to Yahweh your God; and it shall be a ruin forever. It shall never be rebuilt. 17 Now nothing from that which is devoted to destruction shall cling to your hand, in order that Yahweh may turn from His burning anger and grant compassion to you and show compassion to you and make you multiply, just as He has sworn to your fathers, 18 if you will listen to the voice of Yahweh your God, keeping all His commandments which I am commanding you today, and doing what is right in the sight of Yahweh your God.

14 "You are the sons of Yahweh your God; you shall not gash yourselves nor shave your forehead for the sake of the dead. 2 For you are a holy people to Yahweh your God, and Yahweh has chosen you to be a people for His treasured possession out of all the peoples who are on the face of the earth.

3 "You shall not eat any abominable thing. 4 These are the animals which you may eat: the ox, the sheep, the goat, 5 the deer, the gazelle, the roebuck, the wild goat, the ibex, the antelope, and the mountain sheep. 6 And any animal that divides the hoof and has the hoof split in two *and* chews the cud, among the animals, that *one* you may eat. 7 Nevertheless, you are not to eat of these among those which chew the cud or among those that divide the hoof in two: the camel and the rabbit and the shaphan, for though they chew the cud, they do not divide the hoof; they are unclean for you. 8 And the pig, because it divides the hoof but *does* not *chew* the cud, it is unclean for you. You shall not eat any of their flesh nor touch their carcasses.

9 "These you may eat of all that are in water: anything that has fins and scales you may eat, 10 but anything that does not have fins and scales you shall not eat; it is unclean for you.

11 "You may eat any clean bird. 12 But these are the ones which you shall not eat: the eagle and the vulture and the buzzard, 13 and the red kite, the falcon, and the kite in their kinds, 14 and every raven in its kind, 15 and the ostrich, the owl, the gull, and the hawk in their kinds, 16 the little owl, the great owl, the white owl, 17 the pelican, the carrion vulture, the cormorant, 18 the stork, and the heron in their kinds, and the hoopoe and the bat. 19 And all the teeming life with wings are unclean to you; they shall not be eaten. 20 You may eat any clean bird.

21 “You shall not eat anything which dies
of itself. You may give it to the sojourner
who is within your gates, so that he may eat
it, or you may sell it to a foreigner, for you
are a holy people to Yahweh your God. You
shall not boil a young goat in its mother’s
milk.
22 “You shall surely tithe all the produce
from what you sow, which comes out of the
field every year. 23 And you shall eat in the
presence of Yahweh your God, at the place
where He chooses for His name to dwell,
the tithe of your grain, your new wine, your
oil, and the firstborn of your herd and your
flock, so that you may learn to fear Yahweh
your God all *your* days. 24 And if the distance
is so great for you that you are not able to
bring *the tithe*, since the place where Yah-
weh your God chooses to set His name is
too far away from you when Yahweh your
God blesses you, 25 then you shall exchange
it for money and bind the money in your
hand and go to the place which Yahweh
your God chooses. 26 And you may spend
the money for whatever your heart desires:
for oxen or sheep or wine or strong drink
or whatever your heart desires; and there
you shall eat in the presence of Yahweh your
God and be glad, you and your household.
27 Also you shall not forsake the Levite who
is within your gates, for he has no portion
or inheritance among you.
28 “At the end of every third year you shall
bring out all the tithe of your produce in
that year and shall deposit *it* within your
gates. 29 And the Levite, because he has no
portion or inheritance among you, and the
sojourner, the orphan, and the widow who
are within your gates, shall come and eat
and be satisfied, in order that Yahweh your
God may bless you in all the work of your
hand which you do.

Psalm 37:23–29

23 The footsteps of a man are
established by Yahweh,
And He delights in his way.
24 When he falls, he will not
be hurled headlong,
Because Yahweh is the One
who sustains his hand.

25 I was young and now I am old,
Yet I have not seen the
righteous forsaken
Or his seed begging bread.
26 All day long he is gracious and lends,
And his seed is a blessing.

27 Depart from evil and do good,
So you will dwell forever.

28 For Yahweh loves justice
And will not forsake
His holy ones;
They are kept forever,
But the seed of the wicked
will be cut off.
29 The righteous will inherit the land
And dwell in it forever.

Proverbs 12:15–16

15 The way of an ignorant fool is
right in his own eyes,
But a wise man is he who
listens to counsel.
16 An ignorant fool’s anger
is known at once,
But a prudent man conceals disgrace.

Luke 2:25–52

25 And behold, there was a man in Jeru-
salem whose name was Simeon, and this
man was righteous and devout, waiting for
the comfort of Israel, and the Holy Spirit
was upon him. 26 And it had been revealed to
him by the Holy Spirit that he would not see
death before he had seen the Lord’s Christ.
27 And he came in the Spirit into the temple,
and when the parents brought in the child
Jesus to carry out for Him the custom of the
Law, 28 then he took Him into his arms and
blessed God, and said,
29 “Now Master, You are releasing
Your slave in peace,
According to Your word.
30 For my eyes have seen Your salvation,
31 Which You prepared in the
presence of all peoples,
32 A LIGHT FOR REVELATION
TO THE GENTILES,
And for the glory of Your
people Israel.”
33 And His father and mother were mar-
veling at the things which were being said
about Him. 34 And Simeon blessed them and
said to Mary His mother, “Behold, this *Child*
is appointed for the fall and rise of many in
Israel, and for a sign to be opposed— 35 and
a sword will pierce through your own soul as

well—that the thoughts from many hearts may be revealed."

36 And there was a prophetess, Anna the daughter of Phanuel, of the tribe of Asher. She was advanced in years having lived with *her* husband seven years from *when she was* a virgin, 37 and then as a widow to the age of eighty-four. She never left the temple, serving night and day with fastings and prayers. 38 And at that very moment she came up and *began* giving thanks to God, and continued to speak of Him to all those who were waiting for the redemption of Jerusalem.

39 And when they had finished everything according to the Law of the Lord, they returned to Galilee, to their own city of Nazareth. 40 Now the Child continued to grow and become strong, being filled with wisdom; and the grace of God was upon Him.

41 And His parents would go to Jerusalem every year at the Feast of the Passover. 42 And when He became twelve years *old*, they went up *there* according to the custom of the Feast; 43 and as they were returning, after finishing the days *of the Feast*, the boy Jesus stayed behind in Jerusalem. But His parents did not know. 44 But supposing Him to be in the caravan, they went a day's journey, and they *began* searching for Him among their relatives and acquaintances. 45 When they did not find Him, they returned to Jerusalem searching for Him. 46 And it happened that after three days they found Him in the temple, sitting in the midst of the teachers, both listening to them and asking them questions. 47 And all who heard Him were astounded at His understanding and His answers. 48 When they saw Him, they were astonished, and His mother said to Him, "Child, why have You treated us this way? Behold, Your father and I have been anxiously searching for You." 49 And He said to them, "Why is it that you were searching for Me? Did you not know that I had to be in My Father's *house*?" 50 But they did not understand the statement which He had spoken to them. 51 And He went down with them and came to Nazareth, and He continued in subjection to them, and His mother was treasuring all *these* things in her heart.

52 And Jesus was advancing in wisdom and stature, and in favor with God and men.

MARCH 27

Deuteronomy 15:1–16:22

15 "At the end of *every* seven years you shall grant a remission *of debts*. 2 And this is the manner of remission: every creditor shall release what he has loaned to his neighbor; he shall not exact it of his neighbor and his brother because the remission from Yahweh has been proclaimed. 3 From a foreigner you may exact *it*, but your hand shall release whatever of yours is with your brother. 4 However, there will be no needy one among you, since Yahweh will surely bless you in the land which Yahweh your God is giving you as an inheritance to possess, 5 if only you listen obediently to the voice of Yahweh your God, to be careful to do all this commandment which I am commanding you today. 6 For Yahweh your God will bless you as He has promised you, and you will lend to many nations, but you will not borrow; and you will rule over many nations, but they will not rule over you.

7 "If there is a needy one among you, one of your brothers, in any of your gates *of the towns* in your land which Yahweh your God is giving you, you shall not harden your heart nor close your hand from your needy brother; 8 but you shall freely open your hand to him and shall generously lend him sufficient for his need *in* whatever he lacks. 9 Beware lest there be a vile thought in your heart, saying, 'The seventh year, the year of the remission of debts, is near,' and your eye is hostile toward your needy brother, and you give him nothing; then he may cry to Yahweh against you, and it will be a sin in you. 10 You shall generously give to him, and your heart shall not be grieved when you give to him, because for this thing Yahweh your God will bless you in all your work and in all that you send forth your hand *to do*. 11 For the needy will never cease *to be* in the land; therefore I am commanding you, saying, 'You shall freely open your hand to your brother, to your afflicted and needy in your land.'

12 "If your brother, a Hebrew man or woman, is sold to you, then he shall serve

you six years, but in the seventh year you
shall let him go *to be* free from you. 13 When
you let him go *to be* free from you, you shall
not let him go empty-handed. 14 You shall
furnish him generously from your flock and
from your threshing floor and from your
wine vat; you shall give to him as Yahweh
your God has blessed you. 15 And you shall
remember that you were a slave in the land
of Egypt, and Yahweh your God redeemed
you; therefore I am commanding you this
today. 16 And it will be that, if he says to you,
'I will not go out from you,' because he loves
you and your household, since he fares well
with you; 17 then you shall take an awl and
pierce it through his ear into the door, and
he shall be your servant forever. Also you
shall do likewise to your maidservant.

18 "It shall not seem hard in your sight
when you let him go *to be* free from you,
for he has given you six years *with* double
the service of a hired man; so Yahweh your
God will bless you in whatever you do.

19 "You shall set apart as holy to Yahweh
your God all the firstborn males that are
born of your herd and of your flock; you
shall not work with the firstborn of your
herd nor shear the firstborn of your flock.
20 You and your household shall eat it every
year before Yahweh your God in the place
which Yahweh chooses. 21 But if it has any
defect, *such as* lameness or blindness, *or* any
serious defect, you shall not sacrifice it to
Yahweh your God. 22 You shall eat it within
your gates; the unclean and the clean alike
may eat it, as a gazelle or a deer. 23 Only you
shall not eat its blood; you are to pour it out
on the ground like water.

16 "Keep the month of Abib and celebrate
the Passover to Yahweh your God, for
in the month of Abib Yahweh your God
brought you out of Egypt by night. 2 And
you shall sacrifice the Passover to Yahweh
your God from the flock and the herd, in
the place where Yahweh chooses for His
name to dwell. 3 You shall not eat leavened
bread with it; seven days you shall eat with it
unleavened bread, the bread of affliction (for
you came out of the land of Egypt in haste),
so that you may remember the day when you
came out of the land of Egypt all the days
of your life. 4 For seven days no leaven shall
be seen with you in all your territory, and
none of the flesh which you sacrifice on the
evening of the first day shall remain over-
night until morning. 5 You are not allowed
to sacrifice the Passover in any of your gates
of the towns which Yahweh your God is
giving you; 6 but at the place where Yahweh
your God chooses for His name to dwell,
there you shall sacrifice the Passover in the
evening at sunset, at the appointed time
that you came out of Egypt. 7 And you shall
cook and eat *it* in the place which Yahweh
your God chooses. In the morning you are to
return to your tents. 8 Six days you shall eat
unleavened bread, and on the seventh day
there shall be a solemn assembly to Yahweh
your God; you shall do no work *on it*.

9 "You shall count seven weeks for your-
self; you shall begin to count seven weeks
from the time you begin to put the sickle
to the standing grain. 10 Then you shall
celebrate the Feast of Weeks to Yahweh
your God with a tribute of a freewill offering
of your hand, which you shall give just as
Yahweh your God blesses you; 11 and you
shall be glad before Yahweh your God, you
and your son and your daughter and your
male and female slaves and the Levite who
is within your gates and the sojourner and
the orphan and the widow who are in your
midst, in the place where Yahweh your God
chooses for His name to dwell. 12 And you
shall remember that you were a slave in
Egypt, and you shall be careful to observe
these statutes.

13 "You shall celebrate the Feast of Booths
seven days after you have gathered in from
your threshing floor and your wine vat;
14 and you shall be glad in your feast, you
and your son and your daughter and your
male and female slaves and the Levite and
the sojourner and the orphan and the widow
who are within your gates. 15 Seven days you
shall celebrate a feast to Yahweh your God
in the place which Yahweh chooses, because
Yahweh your God will bless you in all your
produce and in all the work of your hands,
so that you will be altogether glad.

16 "Three times in a year all your males
shall appear before Yahweh your God in
the place which He chooses, at the Feast of
Unleavened Bread and at the Feast of Weeks
and at the Feast of Booths, and they shall
not appear before Yahweh empty-handed.
17 Every man shall give as he is able,
according to the blessing of Yahweh your
God which He has given you.

18 "You shall appoint for yourself judges
and officers in all your gates *of the towns*
which Yahweh your God is giving you,
according to your tribes, and they shall
judge the people with righteous judgment.
19 You shall not distort justice; you shall not
be partial, and you shall not take a bribe,
for a bribe blinds the eyes of the wise
and perverts the words of the righteous.
20 Righteousness! Righteousness, you shall
pursue, that you may live and possess the
land which Yahweh your God is giving you.

21 "You shall not plant for yourself an
Asherah of any kind of tree beside the altar
of Yahweh your God, which you shall make
for yourself. 22 And you shall not set up for
yourself a *sacred* pillar which Yahweh your
God hates.

Psalm 37:30–36

30 The mouth of the righteous
utters wisdom,
And his tongue speaks justice.
31 The law of his God is in his heart;
His steps do not slip.

32 The wicked spies upon the righteous
And seeks to put him to death.
33 Yahweh will not forsake
him in his hand;
He will not condemn him
when he is judged.

34 Hope for Yahweh and keep His way,
And He will exalt you to
inherit the land;
When the wicked are cut
off, you will see it.

35 I have seen a wicked, ruthless man
Spreading himself like a luxuriant
tree in its native soil.
36 Then he passed away, and
behold, he was no more;
I sought for him, but he
could not be found.

Proverbs 12:17–19

17 He who breathes out truth
declares what is right,
But a false witness, deceit.
18 There is one who speaks rashly
like the thrusts of a sword,
But the tongue of the wise
brings healing.
19 Truthful lips will be
established forever,
But a lying tongue is only
for a moment.

Luke 3:1–38

3 Now in the fifteenth year of the reign
of Tiberius Caesar, when Pontius Pilate
was governor of Judea, and Herod was
tetrarch of Galilee, and his brother Philip
was tetrarch of the region of Ituraea and
Trachonitis, and Lysanias was tetrarch of
Abilene, 2 during the high priesthood of
Annas and Caiaphas, the word of God came
to John, the son of Zechariah, in the wil-
derness. 3 And he came into all the district
around the Jordan, preaching a baptism of
repentance for the forgiveness of sins; 4 as it
is written in the book of the words of Isaiah
the prophet,

"THE VOICE OF ONE CRYING
IN THE WILDERNESS,
'MAKE READY THE WAY OF THE LORD,
MAKE HIS PATHS STRAIGHT.
5 'EVERY RAVINE WILL BE FILLED,
AND EVERY MOUNTAIN AND HILL
WILL BE BROUGHT LOW;
THE CROOKED WILL BE STRAIGHT,
AND THE ROUGH ROADS SMOOTH.
6 AND ALL FLESH WILL SEE THE
SALVATION OF GOD.'"

7 So he was saying to the crowds who were
going out to be baptized by him, "You brood
of vipers, who warned you to flee from the
wrath to come? 8 Therefore bear fruits in
keeping with repentance, and do not begin
to say to yourselves, 'We have Abraham for
our father,' for I say to you that from these
stones God is able to raise up children to
Abraham. 9 But indeed the axe is already laid
at the root of the trees; therefore, every tree
that does not bear good fruit is cut down
and thrown into the fire."

10 And the crowds were questioning him,
saying, "Then what should we do?" 11 And
he would answer and say to them, "The
man who has two tunics is to share with
him who has none; and he who has food
is to do likewise." 12 And tax collectors also
came to be baptized, and they said to him,
"Teacher, what should we do?" 13 And he
said to them, "Collect no more than what
you have been ordered to." 14 And soldiers
were also questioning him, saying, "What
should we also do?" And he said to them,

"Do not take money from anyone by force,
or extort *anyone*, and be content with your
wages."
15 Now while the people were in a state of
expectation and all were reasoning in their
hearts about John, as to whether he was the
Christ, 16 John answered, saying to them all,
"As for me, I baptize you with water, but One
is coming who is mightier than I, and I am
not fit to untie the strap of His sandals; He
will baptize you with the Holy Spirit and
fire. 17 His winnowing fork is in His hand to
thoroughly clear His threshing floor and to
gather the wheat into His barn, but He will
burn up the chaff with unquenchable fire."
18 So with many other exhortations he
proclaimed the gospel to the people. 19 But
when Herod the tetrarch was reproved by
him because of Herodias, his brother's wife,
and because of all the wicked things which
Herod had done, 20 Herod also added this to
them all: he locked John up in prison.
21 Now it happened that when all the
people were being baptized, Jesus was
also baptized, and while He was praying,
heaven was opened, 22 and the Holy Spirit
descended upon Him in bodily form like
a dove, and a voice came out of heaven,
"You are My beloved Son, in You I am well-
pleased."
23 When He began His ministry, Jesus
Himself was about thirty years of age, being,
as was supposed,

the son of Joseph,
the son of Eli,
24 the son of Matthat,
the son of Levi,
the son of Melchi,
the son of Jannai,
the son of Joseph,
25 the son of Mattathias,
the son of Amos,
the son of Nahum,
the son of Hesli,
the son of Naggai,
26 the son of Maath,
the son of Mattathias,
the son of Semein,
the son of Josech,
the son of Joda,
27 the son of Joanan,
the son of Rhesa,
the son of Zerubbabel,
the son of Shealtiel,
the son of Neri,
28 the son of Melchi,
the son of Addi,
the son of Cosam,
the son of Elmadam,
the son of Er,
29 the son of Joshua,
the son of Eliezer,
the son of Jorim,
the son of Matthat,
the son of Levi,
30 the son of Simeon,
the son of Judah,
the son of Joseph,
the son of Jonam,
the son of Eliakim,
31 the son of Melea,
the son of Menna,
the son of Mattatha,
the son of Nathan,
the son of David,
32 the son of Jesse,
the son of Obed,
the son of Boaz,
the son of Salmon,
the son of Nahshon,
33 the son of Amminadab,
the son of Admin,
the son of Ram,
the son of Hezron,
the son of Perez,
the son of Judah,
34 the son of Jacob,
the son of Isaac,
the son of Abraham,
the son of Terah,
the son of Nahor,
35 the son of Serug,
the son of Reu,
the son of Peleg,
the son of Heber,
the son of Shelah,
36 the son of Cainan,
the son of Arphaxad,
the son of Shem,
the son of Noah,
the son of Lamech,
37 the son of Methuselah,
the son of Enoch,
the son of Jared,
the son of Mahalaleel,
the son of Cainan,
38 the son of Enosh,
the son of Seth,
the son of Adam,
the son of God.

MARCH 28

Deuteronomy 17:1–18:22

17 "You shall not sacrifice to Yahweh your God an ox or a sheep which has a defect *or* any blemish, for that is an abominable thing to Yahweh your God.

2 "If there is found in your midst, in any of your gates *of the towns* which Yahweh your God is giving you, a man or a woman who does what is evil in the sight of Yahweh your God, by trespassing against His covenant, 3 and has gone and served other gods and worshiped them, or the sun or the moon or any of the heavenly host, which I have not commanded, 4 and if it is told to you and you have heard of it, then you shall inquire thoroughly. Behold, if it is true and the matter is confirmed that this abomination has been done in Israel, 5 then you shall bring out that man or that woman who has done this evil deed to your gates, *that is,* the man or the woman, and you shall stone them, and they will die. 6 On the mouth of two witnesses or three witnesses, he who is to die shall be put to death; he shall not be put to death on the mouth of one witness. 7 The hand of the witnesses shall be first against him to put him to death, and afterward the hand of all the people. So you shall purge the evil from your midst.

8 "If any case is too difficult for you to judge, between one kind of homicide or another, between one kind of lawsuit or another, and between one kind of assault or another, being cases of dispute in your gates, then you shall arise and go up to the place which Yahweh your God chooses. 9 So you shall come to the Levitical priest or the judge who is *in office* in those days, and you shall inquire *of them,* and they will declare to you the judgment in the case. 10 And you shall do according to the terms of the judgment which they declare to you from that place which Yahweh chooses; and you shall be careful to do according to all that they teach you. 11 According to the terms of the law which they teach you, and according to the judgment which they tell you, you shall do; you shall not turn aside from the word which they declare to you, to the right or the left. 12 And the man who acts presumptuously by not listening to the priest who stands there to minister to Yahweh your God, or to the judge, that man shall die; thus you shall purge the evil from Israel. 13 Then all the people will hear and be afraid and will not act presumptuously again.

14 "When you enter the land which Yahweh your God gives you, and you possess it and live in it, and you say, 'I will set a king over me like all the nations who are around me,' 15 you shall surely set a king over you whom Yahweh your God chooses, *one* from among your brothers you shall set as king over yourselves; you may not put a foreigner over yourselves who is not your brother. 16 Moreover, he shall not multiply horses for himself, nor shall he cause the people to return to Egypt to multiply horses. Yahweh has said to you, 'You shall never again return that way.' 17 And he shall not multiply wives for himself, or else his heart will turn away; nor shall he greatly increase silver and gold for himself.

18 "Now it will be when he sits on the throne of his kingdom, that he shall write for himself a copy of this law on a scroll in the presence of the Levitical priests. 19 And it shall be with him, and he shall read it all the days of his life, that he may learn to fear Yahweh his God, to carefully observe all the words of this law and these statutes, 20 that his heart may not be lifted up above his brothers and that he may not turn aside from the commandment, to the right or the left, so that he may prolong *his* days in his kingdom, he and his sons in the midst of Israel.

18 "The Levitical priests, the whole tribe of Levi, shall have no portion or inheritance with Israel; they shall eat of the offerings to Yahweh by fire and of His inheritance. 2 And they shall have no inheritance among their brothers; Yahweh is their inheritance, as He promised them.

3 "Now this shall be the *legal* judgment for the priests *taken* from the people, from those who offer a sacrifice, either an ox or a sheep: they shall give to the priest the shoulder and the two cheeks and the stomach. 4 You shall give him the first fruits of your grain, your new wine and your oil and the

first shearing of your sheep. 5 For Yahweh
your God has chosen him and his sons from
all your tribes, to stand to minister in the
name of Yahweh all the days.

6 "Now if a Levite comes from any of your
gates *of the towns* throughout Israel where
he sojourns and comes whenever he desires
to the place which Yahweh chooses, 7 then
he shall minister in the name of Yahweh his
God like all his brothers the Levites who
stand there before Yahweh. 8 They shall eat
equal portions, except *what they receive*
from the sale of their fathers' *estates*.

9 "When you enter the land which Yahweh
your God gives you, you shall not learn to
imitate the abominations of those nations.
10 There shall not be found among you any-
one who makes his son or his daughter pass
through the fire, one who uses divination,
one who practices soothsaying or one who
interprets omens or a sorcerer, 11 or one who
is an enchanter or a medium or a spiritist or
one who inquires of the dead. 12 For who-
ever does these things is an abomination to
Yahweh; and because of these abominations
Yahweh your God will dispossess them from
before you. 13 You shall be blameless before
Yahweh your God. 14 For those nations,
which you shall dispossess, listen to those
who practice soothsaying and to diviners,
but as for you, Yahweh your God has not
allowed you *to do* so.

15 "Yahweh your God will raise up for you a
prophet like me from among you, from your
brothers; you shall listen to him. 16 This is
according to all that you asked of Yahweh
your God in Horeb on the day of the assem-
bly, saying, 'Let me not hear again the voice
of Yahweh my God; let me not see this great
fire anymore, or I will die.' 17 And Yahweh
said to me, 'They have spoken well. 18 I will
raise up a prophet from among their broth-
ers like you, and I will put My words in his
mouth, and he shall speak to them all that I
command him. 19 And it will be that whoever
will not listen to My words which he shall
speak in My name, I Myself will require *it* of
him. 20 But the prophet who speaks a word
presumptuously in My name which I have
not commanded him to speak, or which
he speaks in the name of other gods, that
prophet shall die.' 21 Now you may say in
your heart, 'How will we know the word
which Yahweh has not spoken?' 22 When a
prophet speaks in the name of Yahweh, if the
thing does not come about or come true, that
is the thing which Yahweh has not spoken.
The prophet has spoken it presumptuously;
you shall not be afraid of him.

Psalm 37:37–40

37 Observe the blameless man,
and behold the upright;
For the man of peace will
have a posterity.
38 But transgressors will be
altogether destroyed;
The posterity of the wicked
will be cut off.

39 But the salvation of the
righteous is from Yahweh;
He is their strength in time of distress.
40 Yahweh helps them and protects them;
He protects them from the
wicked and saves them,
Because they take refuge in Him.

Proverbs 12:20–22

20 Deceit is in the heart of those
who devise evil,
But counselors of peace have gladness.
21 No misfortune befalls the righteous,
But the wicked are filled with calamity.
22 Lying lips are an abomination
to Yahweh,
But doers of faithfulness
are His delight.

Luke 4:1–30

4 Now Jesus, full of the Holy Spirit,
returned from the Jordan and was being
led around by the Spirit in the wilderness
2 for forty days, being tempted by the devil.
And He ate nothing during those days, and
when they had finished, He was hungry.
3 And the devil said to Him, "If You are the
Son of God, tell this stone to become bread."
4 And Jesus answered him, "It is written,
'MAN SHALL NOT LIVE ON BREAD ALONE.'"

5 And he led Him up and showed Him
all the kingdoms of the world in a moment
of time. 6 And the devil said to Him, "I will
give You all this dominion and its glory, for
it has been handed over to me, and I give
it to whomever I wish. 7 Therefore if You
worship before me, it shall all be Yours."
8 And Jesus answered and said to him, "It is
written, 'YOU SHALL WORSHIP THE LORD YOUR
GOD AND SERVE HIM ONLY.'"

9 And he led Him to Jerusalem and had
Him stand on the pinnacle of the temple,
and said to Him, "If You are the Son of God,
throw Yourself down from here, 10 for it is
written,

'HE WILL COMMAND HIS ANGELS
CONCERNING YOU TO GUARD YOU,'

11 and,

'ON *their* HANDS THEY WILL BEAR YOU UP,
LEST YOU STRIKE YOUR FOOT
AGAINST A STONE.'"

12 And Jesus answered and said to him, "It
is said, 'YOU SHALL NOT PUT THE LORD YOUR
GOD TO THE TEST.'"

13 And when the devil had finished every
temptation, he left Him until an opportune
time.

14 And Jesus returned to Galilee in the
power of the Spirit, and news about Him
spread through all the surrounding district.
15 And He was teaching in their synagogues,
being glorified by all.

16 And He came to Nazareth, where
He had been brought up, and as was His
custom, He entered the synagogue on the
Sabbath and stood up to read. 17 And the
scroll of the prophet Isaiah was handed to
Him. And He opened the scroll and found
the place where it was written,

18 "THE SPIRIT OF THE LORD IS UPON ME,
BECAUSE HE ANOINTED ME TO PREACH
THE GOSPEL TO THE POOR.
HE HAS SENT ME TO PROCLAIM
RELEASE TO THE CAPTIVES,
AND RECOVERY OF SIGHT TO THE BLIND,
TO SET FREE THOSE WHO ARE OPPRESSED,
19 TO PROCLAIM THE FAVORABLE
YEAR OF THE LORD."

20 And He closed the scroll, gave it back to
the attendant and sat down, and the eyes
of all in the synagogue were fixed on Him.
21 And He began to say to them, "Today
this Scripture has been fulfilled in your
hearing." 22 And all were speaking well of
Him and marveling at the gracious words
which were coming forth from His lips, and
they were saying, "Is this not Joseph's son?"
23 And He said to them, "No doubt you will
quote this proverb to Me, 'Physician, heal
yourself! Whatever we heard took place at
Capernaum, do also here in your home-
town.'" 24 And He said, "Truly I say to you,
no prophet is welcome in his hometown.
25 But I say to you in truth, there were many
widows in Israel in the days of Elijah, when
the sky was shut up for three years and six
months, when a great famine came over all
the land, 26 and yet Elijah was sent to none of
them, but only to Zarephath, *in the land* of
Sidon, to a woman who was a widow. 27 And
there were many lepers in Israel in the time
of Elisha the prophet, and none of them
was cleansed, but only Naaman the Syrian."
28 And all *the people* in the synagogue were
filled with rage as they heard these things,
29 and they stood up and drove Him out of
the city, and led Him to the edge of the hill
on which their city had been built, in order
to throw Him down the cliff. 30 But passing
through their midst, He went on His way.

MARCH 29

Deuteronomy 19:1–20:20

19 "When Yahweh your God cuts off
the nations, whose land Yahweh
your God gives you, and you dispossess
them and settle in their cities and in their
houses, 2 you shall set apart three cities for
yourself in the midst of your land, which
Yahweh your God gives you to possess.
3 You shall prepare the roads for yourself,
and divide into three parts the territory of
your land which Yahweh your God will give
you to inherit, so that any manslayer may
flee there.

4 "Now this is the case of the manslayer
who may flee there and live: when he strikes
down his friend without premeditation, not
hating him previously— 5 as when *a man*
goes into the forest with his friend to cut
wood, and his hand swings the axe to cut
down the tree, and the iron *head* slips off
the handle and strikes his friend so that
he dies—he may flee to one of these cities
and live; 6 lest the avenger of blood pursue
the manslayer when his heart is angry, and
overtake him, because the way is long, and
strike down his life, though he was not
deserving of death, since he had not hated
him previously. 7 Therefore, I am command-
ing you, saying, 'You shall set apart three
cities for yourself.'

8 "Now if Yahweh your God enlarges
your territory, just as He has sworn to your

fathers, and gives you all the land which
He promised to give to your fathers— 9 if
you be careful to do all this commandment
which I am commanding you today, to love
Yahweh your God and to walk in His ways all
your days—then you shall add three more
cities for yourself, besides these three. 10 So
innocent blood will not be shed in the midst
of your land which Yahweh your God gives
you as an inheritance, and bloodguiltiness
be on you.

11 “But if there is a man who hates his
neighbor and lies in wait for him and rises
up against him and strikes down his life so
that he dies, and he flees to one of these
cities, 12 then the elders of his city shall
send and take him from there and give
him over into the hand of the avenger of
blood, that he may die. 13 You shall not pity
him, but you shall purge the blood of the
innocent from Israel, that it may go well
with you.

14 “You shall not move your neighbor’s
boundary mark, which the ancestors have
set, in your inheritance which you will
inherit in the land that Yahweh your God
gives you to possess.

15 “A single witness shall not rise up
against a man on account of any iniquity
or any sin which he has committed; at the
mouth of two or three witnesses a matter
shall be established. 16 If a malicious wit-
ness rises up against a man to accuse him
of wrongdoing, 17 then both the men who
have the dispute shall stand before Yahweh,
before the priests and the judges who will
be *in office* in those days. 18 And the judges
shall inquire thoroughly, and behold, *if* the
witness is a false witness *and* he has accused
his brother falsely, 19 then you shall do to
him just as he had intended to do to his
brother. Thus you shall purge the evil from
among you. 20 And the rest will hear and be
afraid and will never again do such an evil
thing among you. 21 Thus your eye shall not
show pity: life for life, eye for eye, tooth for
tooth, hand for hand, foot for foot.

20 “If you go out to battle against your
enemies and see horses and chariots
and people more numerous than you, do
not be afraid of them; for Yahweh your God,
who brought you up from the land of Egypt,
is with you. 2 Now it will be, when you are
drawing near to the battle, the priest shall
approach and speak to the people. 3 And
he shall say to them, ‘Hear, O Israel, you
are drawing near to the battle against your
enemies today. Do not let your heart be
faint. Do not be afraid, nor be alarmed, nor
be in dread before them, 4 for Yahweh your
God is the one who goes with you, to fight
for you against your enemies, to save you.’
5 The officers also shall speak to the people,
saying, ‘Who is the man that has built a new
house and has not dedicated it? Let him go
and return to his house, lest he die in the
battle and another man dedicate it. 6 Who
is the man that has planted a vineyard and
has not begun to use its fruit? Let him go
and return to his house, lest he die in the
battle and another man begin to use its fruit.
7 And who is the man that is engaged to a
woman and has not married her? Let him
go and return to his house, lest he die in the
battle and another man marry her.’ 8 Then
the officers shall speak further to the people
and say, ‘Who is the man that is afraid and
whose heart is faint? Let him go and return
to his house, so that he might not make his
brothers’ hearts melt like his heart.’ 9 Now it
will be that when the officers have finished
speaking to the people, they shall appoint
commanders of armies at the head of the
people.

10 “If you come near a city to fight against
it, you shall call for *terms* of peace. 11 Now it
will be that if it agrees to make peace with
you and opens to you, then all the people
who are found in it shall become your forced
labor and shall serve you. 12 However, if it
does not make peace with you, but makes
war against you, then you shall besiege it.
13 And Yahweh your God shall give it into
your hand, and you shall strike all the males
in it with the edge of the sword. 14 Only the
women and the little ones and the animals
and all that is in the city, all its spoil, you
shall plunder for yourself; and you shall
consume the spoil of your enemies which
Yahweh your God has given you. 15 Thus
you shall do to all the cities that are very
far from you, which are not of the cities of
these nations nearby. 16 Only in the cities
of these peoples that Yahweh your God is
giving you as an inheritance, you shall not
leave alive anything that breathes. 17 But
you shall devote them to destruction, the
Hittite and the Amorite, the Canaanite and
the Perizzite, the Hivite and the Jebusite, as

Yahweh your God has commanded you, 18 so
that they may not teach you to do according
to all their abominations which they have
done for their gods, so that you would sin
against Yahweh your God.
19 "If you besiege a city for many days, to
make war against it in order to capture it,
you shall not destroy its trees by swinging
an axe against them; for you may eat from
them, and you shall not cut them down. For
is the tree of the field a man, that it should
be besieged by you? 20 Only the trees which
you know are not trees for food you shall
destroy and cut down, that you may build
siegeworks against the city that is making
war with you until it falls.

Psalm 38:1–8

1 O Yahweh, reprove me not
in Your wrath,
And discipline me not in
Your burning anger.
2 For Your arrows have pressed
deep into me,
And Your hand has pressed
down upon me.
3 There is no soundness in my flesh
because of Your indignation;
There is no health in my bones
because of my sin.
4 For my iniquities go over
my head;
As a heavy burden they weigh
too much for me.
5 My wounds stink *and* rot
Because of my folly.
6 I am bent over and greatly
bowed down;
I go mourning all day long.
7 For my loins are filled
with burning,
And there is no soundness
in my flesh.
8 I am faint and badly crushed;
I groan because of the
agitation of my heart.

Proverbs 12:23–25

23 A prudent man conceals knowledge,
But the heart of fools proclaims folly.
24 The hand of the diligent will rule,
But the slack *hand* will be
put to forced labor.
25 Anxiety in a man's heart
weighs it down,
But a good word makes it glad.

Luke 4:31–44

31 And He came down to Capernaum, a
city of Galilee, and He was teaching them
on the Sabbath; 32 and they were amazed
at His teaching, for His message was with
authority. 33 And in the synagogue there
was a man possessed by the spirit of an
unclean demon, and he cried out with a
loud voice, 34 "Let us alone! What do we
have to do with You, Jesus the Nazarene?
Have You come to destroy us? I know who
You are—the Holy One of God!" 35 But Jesus
rebuked it, saying, "Be quiet and come out
of him!" And when the demon had thrown
him down in the midst *of the people*, it came
out of him without doing him any harm.
36 And amazement came upon them all, and
they were talking with one another saying,
"What is this message? For with authority
and power He commands the unclean
spirits and they come out." 37 And the report
about Him was spreading into every place
in the surrounding district.
38 Then He stood up and *left* the syna-
gogue, and entered Simon's home. Now
Simon's mother-in-law was suffering from
a high fever, and they asked Him to help her.
39 And standing over her, He rebuked the
fever, and it left her. Immediately she stood
up and *began* waiting on them.
40 And while the sun was setting, all those
who had any *who were* sick with various dis-
eases brought them to Him, and laying His
hands on each one of them, He was healing
them. 41 And demons also were coming out
of many, shouting and saying, "You are the
Son of God!" But rebuking *them*, He was not
allowing them to speak, because they knew
Him to be the Christ.
42 When day came, Jesus left and went
to a secluded place; and the crowds were
eagerly seeking for Him, and came to Him
and tried to keep Him from going away
from them. 43 But He said to them, "I must
proclaim the good news of the kingdom of
God to the other cities also, for I was sent
for this purpose."
44 So He kept on preaching in the syna-
gogues of Judea.

MARCH 30

Deuteronomy 21:1–22:30

21 "If a slain person is found fallen in
the open country in the land which
Yahweh your God gives you to possess, *and*
it is not known who has struck him, 2 then
your elders and your judges shall go out and
measure *the distance* to the cities which are
around the slain one. 3 And it shall be that
the city which is nearest to the slain man,
that is, the elders of that city, shall take
a heifer of the herd, which has not been
worked and which has not pulled in a yoke;
4 and the elders of that city shall bring the
heifer down to a valley with running water,
which has not been plowed or sown, and
they shall break the heifer's neck there in
the valley. 5 Then the priests, the sons of
Levi, shall come near, for Yahweh your God
has chosen them to minister for Him and
to bless in the name of Yahweh; and every
dispute and every assault shall be settled by
them. 6 And all the elders of that city who
are nearest to the slain man shall wash their
hands over the heifer whose neck was bro-
ken in the valley; 7 and they shall answer and
say, 'Our hands did not shed this blood, nor
did our eyes see *it.* 8 Atone for Your people
Israel whom You have redeemed, O Yahweh,
and do not place the guilt of innocent blood
in the midst of Your people Israel.' And the
bloodguiltiness shall be atoned for them.
9 So you shall purge the guilt of innocent
blood from your midst, when you do what
is right in the eyes of Yahweh.

10 "If you go out to battle against your
enemies, and Yahweh your God gives them
over into your hands and you take them
away captive, 11 and see among the captives
a beautiful woman and set your affection on
her and would take her as a wife for yourself,
12 then you shall bring her home to your
house, and she shall shave her head and trim
her nails. 13 She shall also remove the clothes
of her captivity and shall remain in your
house and weep for her father and mother
a full month; and after that you may go in
to her and be her husband, and she shall be
your wife. 14 And it will be that, if you do not
desire her, then you shall let her go wherever
she wishes; but you shall certainly not sell
her for money; you shall not mistreat her
because you have humbled her.

15 "If a man has two wives, the one loved
and the other unloved, and *both* the loved
and the unloved have borne him sons, if
the firstborn son belongs to the unloved,
16 then it shall be in the day he wills what
he has to his sons, he cannot make the son
of the loved the firstborn before the son of
the unloved, who is the firstborn. 17 But he
shall recognize the firstborn, the son of the
unloved, by giving him a double portion of
all that he has, for he is the first of his vigor;
the *legal* judgment for the firstborn belongs
to him.

18 "If any man has a stubborn and rebel-
lious son who will not obey his father or
his mother, and when they discipline him,
he will not even listen to them, 19 then
his father and mother shall seize him and
bring him out to the elders of his city at the
gateway of his hometown. 20 Then they shall
say to the elders of his city, 'This son of ours
is stubborn and rebellious; he will not listen
to our voice; he is a glutton and a drunkard.'
21 Then all the men of his city shall stone
him, and he will die; so you shall purge the
evil from your midst, and all Israel will hear
of it and fear.

22 "And if a man has committed a sin,
the judgment of which is death, and he is
put to death, and you hang him on a tree,
23 his corpse shall not hang all night on the
tree, but you shall surely bury him on the
same day (because cursed of God is he who
is hanged), so that you do not make unclean
your land which Yahweh your God gives you
as an inheritance.

22 "You shall not see your brother's ox
or his sheep straying away and ignore
them; you shall certainly bring them back
to your brother. 2 And if your brother is
not near you, or if you do not know him,
then you shall bring it home to your house,
and it shall be with you until your brother
searches for it; then you shall give it back
to him. 3 Thus you shall do with his donkey,
and you shall do likewise with his garment,
and you shall do likewise with anything lost
by your brother, which he has lost and you
have found. You are not allowed to ignore
them. 4 You shall not see your brother's
donkey or his ox fallen down on the way

and ignore them; you shall certainly help
him to raise *them* up.
5 “A woman shall not wear man’s clothing,
nor shall a man put on a woman’s clothing;
for whoever does these things is an abomi-
nation to Yahweh your God.
6 “If you happen to come upon a bird’s
nest along the way, in any tree or on the
ground, with young ones or eggs, and the
mother sitting on the young or on the eggs,
you shall not take the mother with the
young; 7 you shall certainly let the mother
go, but the young you may take for yourself,
in order that it may be well with you and
that you may prolong your days.
8 “When you build a new house, you shall
make a parapet for your roof, so that you
will not bring bloodguilt on your house if
anyone falls from it.
9 “You shall not sow your vineyard with
two kinds of seed, lest all the produce of the
seed which you have sown and the increase
of the vineyard become defiled.
10 “You shall not plow with an ox and a
donkey together.
11 “You shall not wear a material mixed of
wool and flax together.
12 “You shall make yourself tassels on the
four corners of your garment with which
you cover yourself.
13 “If any man takes a wife and goes in
to her and *then* turns against her, 14 and
charges her with shameful deeds and brings
forth against her a bad name and says, ‘I took
this woman, *but* when I came near her, I did
not find her a virgin,’ 15 then the girl’s father
and her mother shall take and bring out the
evidence of the girl’s virginity to the elders of
the city at the gate. 16 Then the girl’s father
shall say to the elders, ‘I gave my daughter
to this man as a wife, but he turned against
her; 17 and behold, he has charged her with
shameful deeds, saying, “I did not find your
daughter a virgin.” But this is the evidence
of my daughter’s virginity.’ And they shall
spread the garment before the elders of the
city. 18 So the elders of that city shall take
the man and chastise him, 19 and they shall
fine him one hundred *shekels* of silver and
give it to the girl’s father because he brought
forth a bad name against a virgin of Israel.
And she shall be his wife; he cannot divorce
her all his days.
20 “But if this charge is true, that the
girl was not found a virgin, 21 then they
shall bring out the girl to the doorway of
her father’s house, and the men of her city
shall stone her, and she will die because she
has committed a disgraceful act in Israel by
playing the harlot in her father’s house; thus
you shall purge the evil from among you.
22 “If a man is found lying with a married
woman, then both of them shall die, the
man who lay with the woman, and the
woman; thus you shall purge the evil from
Israel.
23 “If there is a girl who is a virgin engaged
to a man, and *another* man finds her in the
city and lies with her, 24 then you shall bring
them both out to the gate of that city, and
you shall stone them, and they will die; the
girl, because she did not cry out in the city,
and the man, because he has violated his
neighbor’s wife. Thus you shall purge the
evil from among you.
25 “But if in the field the man finds the
girl who is engaged, and the man forces her
and lies with her, then only the man who
lies with her shall die. 26 But you shall do
nothing to the girl; there is no sin in the
girl worthy of death, for just as a man rises
against his neighbor and murders him, so is
this case. 27 When he found her in the field,
the engaged girl cried out, but there was no
one to save her.
28 “If a man finds a girl who is a virgin,
who is not engaged, and seizes her and lies
with her and they are found, 29 then the man
who lay with her shall give to the girl’s father
fifty *shekels* of silver, and she shall become
his wife because he has violated her; he
cannot divorce her all his days.
30 “A man shall not take his father’s wife
so that he will not uncover his father’s skirt.

Psalm 38:9–22

9 Lord, all my desire is before You;
And my sighing is not
hidden from You.
10 My heart throbs, my strength
forsakes me;
And the light of my eyes, even
that has gone from me.
11 My loved ones and my friends
stand aloof from my plague;
And my kinsmen stand afar off.
12 Those who search for my
life lay snares *for me*;
And those who seek *to do* me evil
have threatened destruction,

And they meditate on
deception all day long.
13 But I, like a deaf man, do not hear;
And *I am* like a mute man who
does not open his mouth.
14 And I am like a man who does not hear,
And in whose mouth are no reproofs.
15 For I wait on You, O Yahweh;
You will answer, O Lord my God.
16 For I said, "*Save*, lest they
be glad over me,
Who, when my foot stumbles,
magnify themselves against me."
17 For I am ready to fall,
And my sorrow is continually before me.
18 For I confess my iniquity;
I am full of anxiety because of my sin.
19 But my enemies are vigorous
and strong,
And those who wrongfully
hate me abound.
20 And those who repay evil for good,
They accuse me, for I
pursue what is good.
21 Do not forsake me, O Yahweh;
O my God, do not be far from me!
22 Make haste to help me,
O Lord, my salvation!

Proverbs 12:26–28

26 The righteous is a guide
to his neighbor,
But the way of the wicked makes
them wander about.
27 A slack *handed* man does
not roast his prey,
But the wealth of a man is
precious for the diligent.
28 In the path of righteousness is life,
And in *its* pathway there is no death.

Luke 5:1–16

5 Now it happened that while the crowd
was pressing around Him and listening
to the word of God, He was standing at the
edge of the lake of Gennesaret; 2 and He saw
two boats lying at the edge of the lake, and
the fishermen, having gotten out of them,
were washing their nets. 3 And He got into
one of the boats, which was Simon's, and
asked him to put out a little way from the
land. And He sat down and *began* teaching
the crowds from the boat. 4 And when He
had finished speaking, He said to Simon,
"Put out into the deep water and let down
your nets for a catch." 5 Simon answered
and said, "Master, we labored all night and
caught nothing, but at Your word, I will let
down the nets." 6 And when they had done
this, they enclosed a great quantity of fish.
And their nets *began to* break; 7 so they
signaled to their partners in the other boat
for them to come and help them. And they
came and filled both of the boats, so that
they began to sink. 8 But when Simon Peter
saw *this*, he fell down at Jesus' knees, saying,
"Go away from me Lord, for I am a sinful
man!" 9 For amazement had seized him and
all his companions because of the catch of
fish which they had taken, 10 and James and
John, sons of Zebedee, who were partners
with Simon, *were* also likewise *amazed*. And
Jesus said to Simon, "Do not fear, from now
on you will be catching men." 11 And when
they had brought their boats to land, they
left everything and followed Him.
12 And it happened that while He was in
one of the cities, behold, *there was* a man
covered with leprosy; and when he saw Jesus,
he fell on his face and begged Him, saying,
"Lord, if You are willing, You can make me
clean." 13 And He stretched out His hand
and touched him, saying, "I am willing; be
cleansed." And immediately the leprosy left
him. 14 And He directed him to tell no one,
"But go and show yourself to the priest and
make an offering for your cleansing, just as
Moses commanded, as a testimony to them."
15 But the news about Him was spreading
even farther, and large crowds were gath-
ering to hear *Him* and to be healed of their
sicknesses. 16 But He Himself would *often*
slip away to the desolate regions and pray.

MARCH 31

Deuteronomy 23:1–24:22

23 "No one who is emasculated or has
his male organ cut off shall enter the
assembly of Yahweh. 2 No one of illegitimate
birth shall enter the assembly of Yahweh;
even to the tenth generation, none of his
seed shall enter the assembly of Yahweh.
3 No Ammonite or Moabite shall enter the

assembly of Yahweh; even to the tenth
generation, none of their *seed* shall ever
enter the assembly of Yahweh, 4 because
they did not meet you with food and water
on the way when you came out of Egypt, and
because they hired against you Balaam the
son of Beor from Pethor of Mesopotamia,
to curse you. 5 Nevertheless, Yahweh your
God was not willing to listen to Balaam, but
Yahweh your God turned the curse into a
blessing for you because Yahweh your God
loves you. 6 You shall never seek their peace
or their prosperity all your days.

7 "You shall not abhor an Edomite, for
he is your brother; you shall not abhor an
Egyptian, for you were a sojourner in his
land. 8 The sons of the third generation who
are born to them may enter the assembly
of Yahweh.

9 "When you go out as an army against
your enemies, you shall keep yourself from
every evil thing.

10 "If there is among you any man who is
unclean because of a nocturnal emission,
then he must go outside the camp; he may
not reenter the camp. 11 But it shall be when
evening approaches, he shall bathe himself
with water, and at sundown he may reenter
the camp.

12 "You shall also have a place outside
the camp and go out there, 13 and you shall
have a spade among your tools, and it shall
be when you sit down outside, you shall
dig with it and shall turn to cover up your
excrement. 14 Since Yahweh your God walks
in the midst of your camp to deliver you and
to give your enemies over to you, therefore
your camp must be holy; and He must not
see anything indecent among you, or He will
turn away from you.

15 "You shall not hand over to his master
a slave who has escaped from his master to
you. 16 He shall live with you in your midst,
in the place which he shall choose in one
of your gates *of the towns* where it pleases
him; you shall not mistreat him.

17 "None of the daughters of Israel shall
be a cult prostitute, nor shall any of the sons
of Israel be a cult prostitute. 18 You shall not
bring the hire of a harlot or the wages of a
dog into the house of Yahweh your God for
any votive offering, for both of these are an
abomination to Yahweh your God.

19 "You shall not charge interest to your
brother: interest on money, food, *or* any-
thing that may be loaned at interest. 20 You
may charge interest to a foreigner, but to
your brother you shall not charge interest,
so that Yahweh your God may bless you in
all that you send forth your hand *to do* in
the land which you are about to enter to
possess.

21 "When you make a vow to Yahweh your
God, you shall not delay to pay it, for Yahweh
your God will surely require it of you; and it
will be a sin in you. 22 However, if you refrain
from vowing, it will not be a sin in you.
23 You shall be careful and do what goes out
from your lips, just as you have voluntarily
vowed to Yahweh your God that which you
spoke with your mouth.

24 "When you enter your neighbor's
vineyard, then you may eat grapes until you
are fully satisfied, but you shall not put any
in your basket.

25 "When you enter your neighbor's
standing grain, then you may pluck the
heads with your hand, but you shall not
wield a sickle in your neighbor's standing
grain.

24 "If a man takes a wife and marries
her, and it happens that she finds
no favor in his eyes because he has found
some indecency in her, and he writes her
a certificate of divorce and puts *it* in her
hand and sends her out from his house,
2 and she goes out of his house and goes
and becomes another man's *wife*, 3 and if
the latter husband turns against her and
writes her a certificate of divorce and puts *it*
in her hand and sends her out of his house,
or if the latter husband dies who took her
to be his wife, 4 *then* her former husband
who sent her away is not allowed to take
her again to be his wife, since she has been
defiled; for that is an abomination before
Yahweh, and you shall not bring sin on the
land which Yahweh your God gives you as
an inheritance.

5 "When a man takes a new wife, he shall
not go out with the army nor be charged
with any duty; he shall be free at home
one year and shall give gladness to his wife
whom he has taken.

6 "No one shall take a handmill or an
upper millstone in pledge, for he would be
taking a life in pledge.

7 "If a man is caught kidnapping any of
his brothers of the sons of Israel, and he

mistreats him or sells him, then that thief
shall die; so you shall purge the evil from
among you.
8 “Take care against an infection of lep-
rosy, to be very careful and to do according
to all that the Levitical priests instruct you;
as I have commanded them, so you shall
be careful to do. 9 Remember what Yahweh
your God did to Miriam on the way as you
came out of Egypt.
10 “When you make your neighbor a loan
of any sort, you shall not enter his house to
take his deposit. 11 You shall stand outside,
and the man to whom you make the loan
shall bring the deposit out to you. 12 Now
if he is an afflicted man, you shall not sleep
with his deposit. 13 When the sun goes down
you shall surely return the deposit to him,
that he may sleep in his cloak and bless you;
and it will be righteousness for you before
Yahweh your God.
14 “You shall not oppress a hired person
who is afflicted and needy, whether *he is* one
of your brothers or one of your sojourners
who is in your land within your gates. 15 You
shall give him his wages on his day before
the sun goes down, for he is afflicted and
sets his soul on it, so that he will not cry
against you to Yahweh and it become sin in
you.
16 “Fathers shall not be put to death for
their sons, nor shall sons be put to death
for *their* fathers; each shall be put to death
for his own sin.
17 “You shall not pervert the justice
due a sojourner *or* an orphan, nor take a
widow’s garment in pledge. 18 But you shall
remember that you were a slave in Egypt and
that Yahweh your God redeemed you from
there; therefore I am commanding you to
do this thing.
19 “When you reap your harvest in your
field and have forgotten a sheaf in the field,
you shall not go back to get it; it shall be
for the sojourner, for the orphan, and for
the widow, in order that Yahweh your God
may bless you in all the work of your hands.
20 When you beat your olive tree, you shall
not go over the boughs after you *finish*; it
shall be for the sojourner, for the orphan,
and for the widow.
21 “When you gather the grapes of your
vineyard, you shall not glean it after you
finish; it shall be for the sojourner, for the
orphan, and for the widow. 22 And you shall
remember that you were a slave in the land
of Egypt; therefore I am commanding you
to do this thing.

Psalm 39:1–6

1 I said, “I will keep watch *over* my ways
That I may not sin with my tongue;
I will keep watch *over* my
mouth as with a muzzle
While the wicked are in my presence.”
2 I was mute with silence,
I *even* kept silent from *speaking* good,
And my anguish grew worse.
3 My heart was hot within me,
While I meditated the fire was burning;
Then I spoke with my tongue:
4 “Yahweh, cause me to know my end
And what is the extent of my days;
Let me know how transient I am.
5 “Behold, You have made my
days *as* handbreadths,
And my lifetime as nothing before You;
Surely every man, *even* standing firm,
is altogether vanity. Selah.
6 “Surely every man walks
about as a shadow;
Surely they make an uproar in vain;
He piles up *riches* and does not
know who will gather them.

Proverbs 13:1–3

13 A wise son *accepts his*
father’s discipline,
But a scoffer does not listen to rebuke.
2 From the fruit of a man’s mouth
he eats what is good,
But the soul of the treacherous
desires violence.
3 The one who guards his
mouth keeps his soul;
The one who opens wide his
lips *comes* to ruin.

Luke 5:17–39

17 And it happened that one day He was
teaching; and there were *some* Pharisees and
teachers of the law sitting *there*, who had
come from every village of Galilee and Judea
and *from* Jerusalem, and the power of the
Lord was *present* for Him to perform healing.
18 And behold, *some* men *were* carrying on
a stretcher a man who was paralyzed; and
they were trying to bring him in and to set
him down before Him. 19 But not finding any
way to bring him in because of the crowd,

they went up on the roof and let him down
through the tiles with his stretcher, into
the middle *of the crowd*, in front of Jesus.
20 And seeing their faith, He said, "Friend,
your sins are forgiven you." 21 The scribes
and the Pharisees began to reason, saying,
"Who is this who speaks blasphemies? Who
can forgive sins, but God alone?" 22 But
Jesus, knowing their reasonings, answered
and said to them, "Why are you reasoning
in your hearts? 23 Which is easier, to say,
'Your sins have been forgiven you,' or to
say, 'Get up and walk'? 24 But, so that you
may know that the Son of Man has authority
on earth to forgive sins,"—He said to the
paralytic—"I say to you, get up, and, picking
up your stretcher, go home." 25 And immedi-
ately he rose up before them, and picked up
what he had been lying on, and went home
glorifying God. 26 And astonishment seized
them all and they *began* glorifying God; and
they were filled with fear, saying, "We have
seen remarkable things today."

27 And after that He went out and noticed
a tax collector named Levi sitting in the tax
office, and He said to him, "Follow Me."
28 And he left everything behind, and rose
up and *began to* follow Him.

29 And Levi gave a big reception for Him
in his house; and there was a great crowd
of tax collectors and other *people* who were
reclining *at the table* with them. 30 And the
Pharisees and their scribes *began* grumbling
at His disciples, saying, "Why do you eat and
drink with the tax collectors and sinners?"
31 And Jesus answered and said to them,
"*It is* not those who are well who need a
physician, but those who are sick. 32 I have
not come to call the righteous but sinners
to repentance."

33 And they said to Him, "The disciples
of John often fast and offer prayers, the
disciples of the Pharisees also do likewise,
but Yours eat and drink." 34 And Jesus said
to them, "Can you make the attendants of
the bridegroom fast while the bridegroom
is with them? 35 But *the* days will come; and
when the bridegroom is taken away from
them, then they will fast in those days."
36 And He was also telling them a parable:
"No one tears a piece of cloth from a new
garment and puts it on an old garment;
otherwise he will both tear the new and
the piece from the new will not match the
old. 37 And no one puts new wine into old
wineskins; otherwise the new wine will
burst the skins and it will be spilled out,
and the skins will be ruined. 38 But new
wine must be put into fresh wineskins.
39 And no one, after drinking old *wine*
wishes for new; for he says, 'The old is
good enough.'"

APRIL 1

Deuteronomy 25:1–26:19

25 "If there is a dispute between men
and they go to court *for judgment*,
and the judges judge their case, and they
justify the righteous and condemn the
wicked, 2 then it shall be if the wicked man
deserves to be struck, the judge shall then
make him lie down and be struck in his pres-
ence with the number of stripes according
to his guilt. 3 He may strike him forty times
but no more, lest he strike him with many
more stripes than these and your brother
be dishonored in your eyes.

4 "You shall not muzzle the ox while it is
threshing.

5 "If brothers live together and one of
them dies and has no son, then the wife
of the one who died shall not be *married*
outside *the family* to a strange man. Her
husband's brother shall go in to her and
take her to himself as wife and perform the
duty of a husband's brother to her. 6 And it
will be that the firstborn whom she bears
shall assume the name of his dead brother,
so that his name will not be blotted out
from Israel. 7 But if the man does not desire
to take his brother's wife, then his brother's
wife shall go up to the gate to the elders and
say, 'My husband's brother refuses to raise
up a name for his brother in Israel; he is not
willing to perform the duty of a husband's
brother to me.' 8 Then the elders of his city
shall summon him and speak to him. And *if*
he stands and says, 'I do not desire to take
her,' 9 then his brother's wife shall come to
him in the sight of the elders and pull his
sandal off his foot and spit in his face; and
she shall answer and say, 'Thus it is done to
the man who does not build up his brother's
house.' 10 And in Israel his name shall be

called, 'The house of him whose sandal is
removed.'
11 "If *two* men, a man and his brother,
are struggling together, and the wife of one
comes near to deliver her husband from the
hand of the one who is striking him, and she
puts out her hand and seizes his genitals,
12 then you shall cut off her hand; you shall
not show pity.
13 "You shall not have in your bag differing
weights, a large and a small. 14 You shall
not have in your house differing measures,
a large and a small. 15 You shall have a full
and just weight; you shall have a full and just
measure, that your days may be prolonged
in the land which Yahweh your God gives
you. 16 For everyone who does these things,
everyone who acts unjustly, is an abomina-
tion to Yahweh your God.
17 "Remember what Amalek did to you
along the way when you came out from
Egypt, 18 how he met you along the way
and attacked among you all the stragglers at
your rear, but you were faint and weary; and
he did not fear God. 19 Therefore it will be,
when Yahweh your God has given you rest
from all your surrounding enemies, in the
land which Yahweh your God gives you as
an inheritance to possess, you shall blot out
the memory of Amalek from under heaven;
you must not forget.

26 "Then it will be, when you enter the
land which Yahweh your God gives
you as an inheritance and you possess it
and live in it, 2 that you shall take some
of the first of all the fruit of the ground
which you bring in from your land that
Yahweh your God gives you, and you shall
put *it* in a basket and go to the place where
Yahweh your God chooses for His name to
dwell. 3 And you shall go to the priest who
is in office in those days and say to him, 'I
declare this day to Yahweh my God that I
have entered the land which Yahweh swore
to our fathers to give us.' 4 Then the priest
shall take the basket from your hand and set
it down before the altar of Yahweh your God.
5 And you shall answer and say before Yah-
weh your God, 'My father was a wandering
Aramean, and he went down to Egypt and
sojourned there, few in number; but there
he became a great, mighty, and populous
nation. 6 And the Egyptians treated us
harshly and afflicted us and imposed hard
slave labor on us. 7 Then we cried out to
Yahweh, the God of our fathers, and Yahweh
heard our voice and saw our affliction and
our toil and our oppression; 8 and Yahweh
brought us out of Egypt with a strong hand
and an outstretched arm and with great
terror and with signs and wonders; 9 and He
has brought us to this place and has given
us this land, a land flowing with milk and
honey. 10 So now behold, I have brought the
first of the fruit of the ground which You,
O Yahweh, have given me.' And you shall
set it down before Yahweh your God and
worship before Yahweh your God; 11 and
you and the Levite and the sojourner who
is among you shall be glad in all the good
which Yahweh your God has given you and
your household.
12 "When you have finished paying all the
tithe of your produce in the third year, the
year of tithing, then you shall give it to the
Levite, to the sojourner, to the orphan, and
to the widow, that they may eat within your
gates and be satisfied. 13 Then you shall say
before Yahweh your God, 'I have purged the
sacred *portion* from *my* house, and I also
have given it to the Levite and the sojourner,
the orphan and the widow, according to all
Your commandments which You have com-
manded me; I have not trespassed against
or forgotten any of Your commandments.
14 I have not eaten of it while mourning, nor
have I purged any of it while I was unclean,
nor have I given any of it to the dead. I have
listened to the voice of Yahweh my God; I
have done according to all that You have
commanded me. 15 Look down from Your
holy habitation, from heaven, and bless
Your people Israel and the ground which
You have given to us, a land flowing with
milk and honey, as You swore to our fathers.'
16 "This day Yahweh your God commands
you to do these statutes and judgments. You
shall therefore be careful to do them with
all your heart and with all your soul. 17 You
have today declared Yahweh to be your God,
and that you would walk in His ways and
keep His statutes, His commandments,
and His judgments, and listen to His voice.
18 And Yahweh has today declared you to be
His people, a treasured possession, as He
promised you, and that you should keep all
His commandments; 19 and that He will set
you high above all nations which He has
made, for praise, a name, and beauty; and

that you shall be a holy people to Yahweh
your God, as He has spoken."

Psalm 39:7–11

7 "And now, Lord, what do I hope in?
My expectation is in You.
8 "Deliver me from all my transgressions;
Make me not the reproach
of the wicked fool.
9 "I have become mute,
I do not open my mouth,
Because it is You who have done *it*.
10 "Remove Your plague from me;
Because of the opposition of Your
hand I am wasting away.
11 "With reproofs You chasten
a man for iniquity;
You consume as a moth what
is precious to him;
Surely every man is vanity. Selah.

Proverbs 13:4–6

4 The soul of the sluggard craves
and *gets* nothing,
But the soul of the diligent is enriched.
5 A righteous man hates a lying word,
But a wicked man acts odiously
and is humiliated.
6 Righteousness guards the one
whose way is blameless,
But wickedness subverts the sinner.

Luke 6:1–26

6 Now it happened that on a Sabbath He
was passing through *some* grainfields,
and His disciples were picking and eating
the heads of grain, rubbing them in their
hands. 2 But some of the Pharisees said,
"Why do you do what is not lawful on the
Sabbath?" 3 And Jesus answered and said
to them, "Have you never read what David
did when he was hungry, he and those who
were with him, 4 how he entered the house
of God, and took and ate the consecrated
bread which is not lawful for any to eat
except the priests alone, and gave it to
his companions?" 5 And He was saying
to them, "The Son of Man is Lord of the
Sabbath."

6 Now it happened that on another
Sabbath He entered the synagogue and was
teaching; and there was a man there whose
right hand was withered. 7 And the scribes
and the Pharisees were watching Him
closely *to see* if He heals on the Sabbath, so
that they might find *reason* to accuse Him.
8 But He knew what they were thinking, and
He said to the man with the withered hand,
"Get up and come forward!" And he stood
up and came forward. 9 And Jesus said to
them, "I ask you, is it lawful to do good or
to do harm on the Sabbath, to save a life or
to destroy it?" 10 And after looking around
at them all, He said to him, "Stretch out
your hand!" And he did *so*, and his hand was
restored. 11 But they themselves were filled
with rage, and were discussing together
what they might do to Jesus.

12 Now it happened that at this time He
went off to the mountain to pray, and He
was spending the whole night in prayer to
God. 13 And when day came, He called His
disciples to Him and chose twelve of them,
whom He also named as apostles: 14 Simon,
whom He also named Peter, and Andrew his
brother; and James and John; and Philip and
Bartholomew; 15 and Matthew and Thomas;
James *the son* of Alphaeus, and Simon who
was called the Zealot; 16 Judas *the son* of
James, and Judas Iscariot, who became a
traitor.

17 And Jesus came down with them and
stood on a level place; and *there was* a large
crowd of His disciples, and a great multitude
of people from all Judea and Jerusalem and
the coastal region of Tyre and Sidon, 18 who
had come to hear Him and to be healed of
their diseases; and those who were troubled
with unclean spirits were being cured.
19 And all the crowd was trying to touch
Him, for power was coming from Him and
healing *them* all.

20 And turning His gaze toward His
disciples, He *began to* say,

"Blessed *are* the poor, for yours is the
kingdom of God.
21 Blessed *are* those who hunger now, for
you shall be satisfied.
Blessed *are* those who cry now, for you
shall laugh.
22 Blessed are you when men hate you,
and exclude you, and insult you, and
scorn your name as evil, for the sake
of the Son of Man.

23 "Be glad in that day and leap *for joy*, for
behold, your reward is great in heaven. For
their fathers were doing the same things to
the prophets.

24 "But woe to you who are rich, for you
are receiving your comfort in full.

25 Woe to you who are well-fed now, for
you shall be hungry.
Woe *to you* who laugh now, for you
shall mourn and cry.

26 Woe *to you* when all men speak well
of you, for their fathers were doing the
same things to the false prophets.

The importance of reading the Bible is not reading,
but fellowship with the Author.

— A. W. TOZER

APRIL 2

Deuteronomy 27:1–28:68

27 Then Moses and the elders of Israel commanded the people, saying, "Keep the entire commandment which I am commanding you today. 2 So it will be on the day when you cross the Jordan to the land which Yahweh your God gives you, that you shall set up for yourself large stones and coat them with lime 3 and write on them all the words of this law when you cross over, so that you may enter the land which Yahweh your God gives you, a land flowing with milk and honey, as Yahweh, the God of your fathers, promised you. 4 So it will be when you cross the Jordan, you shall set up on Mount Ebal, these stones, as I am commanding you today, and you shall coat them with lime. 5 Moreover, you shall build there an altar to Yahweh your God, an altar of stones; you shall not wield an iron *tool* on them. 6 You shall build the altar of Yahweh your God of uncut stones, and you shall offer on it burnt offerings to Yahweh your God; 7 and you shall sacrifice peace offerings and eat there and be glad before Yahweh your God. 8 And you shall write on the stones all the words of this law very distinctly."

9 Then Moses and the Levitical priests spoke to all Israel, saying, "Be silent and listen, O Israel! This day you have become a people for Yahweh your God. 10 You shall therefore listen to the voice of Yahweh your God and do His commandments and His statutes which I am commanding you today."

11 Moses also commanded the people on that day, saying, 12 "When you cross the Jordan, these shall stand on Mount Gerizim to bless the people: Simeon, Levi, Judah, Issachar, Joseph, and Benjamin. 13 For the curse, these shall stand on Mount Ebal: Reuben, Gad, Asher, Zebulun, Dan, and Naphtali. 14 The Levites shall then answer and say to all the men of Israel with a loud voice,

15 'Cursed is the man who makes a graven image or a molten image, an abomination to Yahweh, the work of the hands of the craftsman, and sets *it* up in secret.' And all the people shall answer and say, 'Amen.'

16 'Cursed is he who dishonors his father or mother.' And all the people shall say, 'Amen.'

17 'Cursed is he who moves his neighbor's boundary mark.' And all the people shall say, 'Amen.'

18 'Cursed is he who leads a blind *person* astray on the road.' And all the people shall say, 'Amen.'

19 'Cursed is he who perverts the justice due a sojourner, orphan, and widow.' And all the people shall say, 'Amen.'

20 'Cursed is he who lies with his father's wife because he has uncovered his father's skirt.' And all the people shall say, 'Amen.'

21 'Cursed is he who lies with any animal.' And all the people shall say, 'Amen.'

22 'Cursed is he who lies with his sister, the daughter of his father or the daughter of his mother.' And all the people shall say, 'Amen.'

23 'Cursed is he who lies with his mother-in-law.' And all the people shall say, 'Amen.'

24 'Cursed is he who strikes his neighbor in secret.' And all the people shall say, 'Amen.'

25 'Cursed is he who takes a bribe to strike down innocent blood.' And all the people shall say, 'Amen.'

26 'Cursed is he who does not confirm the words of this law by doing them.' And all the people shall say, 'Amen.'

28 "Now it will be, if you diligently listen to the voice of Yahweh your God, being careful to do all His commandments which I am commanding you today, Yahweh your God will set you high above all the nations of the earth. 2 And all these blessings will come upon you and overtake you if you listen to the voice of Yahweh your God:

3 "Blessed *shall* you *be* in the city, and blessed *shall* you *be* in the field.

4 "Blessed *shall be* the offspring of your body and the produce of your ground and the offspring of your beasts, the increase of your herd and the young of your flock.

5 "Blessed *shall be* your basket and your kneading bowl.

6 "Blessed *shall* you *be* when you come in, and blessed *shall* you *be* when you go out.

7 "Yahweh shall cause your enemies who rise up against you to be defeated before you; they will come out against you one way and will flee before you seven ways. 8 Yahweh will command the blessing upon you in your barns and in all that *you* send forth your hand *to do*, and He will bless you in the land which Yahweh your God gives you. 9 Yahweh will establish you as a holy people to Himself, as He swore to you, if you keep the commandments of Yahweh your God and walk in His ways. 10 So all the peoples of the earth will see that you are called by the name of Yahweh, and they will be afraid of you. 11 And Yahweh will make you abound in prosperity, in the offspring of your body and in the offspring of your beast and in the produce of your ground, in the land which Yahweh swore to your fathers to give you. 12 Yahweh will open for you His good storehouse, the heavens, to give rain to your land in its season and to bless all the work of your hand; and you shall lend to many nations, but you shall not borrow. 13 And Yahweh will make you the head and not the tail, and you only will be above, and you will not be underneath, if you listen to the commandments of Yahweh your God, which I am commanding you today, to keep and to do, 14 and do not turn aside from any of the words which I am commanding you today, to the right or to the left, to walk after other gods to serve them.

15 "But it will be, if you do not listen to the voice of Yahweh your God, to keep *and* to do all His commandments and His statutes with which I am commanding you today, that all these curses will come upon you and overtake you:

16 "Cursed *shall* you *be* in the city, and cursed *shall* you *be* in the field.

17 "Cursed *shall be* your basket and your kneading bowl.

18 "Cursed *shall be* the offspring of your body and the produce of your ground, the increase of your herd and the young of your flock.

19 "Cursed *shall* you *be* when you come in, and cursed *shall* you *be* when you go out.

20 "Yahweh will send upon you the curse, confusion, and rebuke, in all that you send forth your hand to do, until you are destroyed and until you perish quickly, on account of the evil of your deeds, because you have forsaken Me. 21 Yahweh will make the pestilence cling to you until He has consumed you from the land where you are entering to possess it. 22 Yahweh will strike you with consumption and with fever and with inflammation and with fiery heat and with the sword and with scorching wind and with mildew, and they will pursue you until you perish. 23 And the heaven which is over your head shall be bronze, and the earth which is under you, iron. 24 Yahweh will make the rain of your land powder and dust; from heaven it shall come down on you until you are destroyed.

25 "Yahweh shall cause you to be defeated before your enemies; you will go out one way against them, but you will flee seven ways before them, and you will become *an example of* terror to all the kingdoms of the earth. 26 And your carcasses will be food to all birds of the sky and to the beasts of the earth, and there will be no one to frighten *them* away.

27 "Yahweh will strike you with the boils of Egypt and with tumors and with the scab and with the itch, from which you cannot be healed. 28 Yahweh will strike you with madness and with blindness and with bewilderment of heart; 29 and you will grope at noon, as the blind man gropes in darkness, and you will not succeed in your ways; but you shall only be oppressed

and robbed all *your* days, with none to save you. 30 You shall betroth a wife, but another man will violate her; you shall build a house, but you will not live in it; you shall plant a vineyard, but you will not use its fruit. 31 Your ox shall be slaughtered before your eyes, but you will not eat of it; your donkey shall be torn away from you and will not be returned to you; your sheep shall be given to your enemies, and you will have none to save you. 32 Your sons and your daughters shall be given to another people, while your eyes look on and yearn for them all the day *long*; but there will be nothing you can do. 33 A people whom you do not know shall eat up the produce of your ground and all your labors, and you will never be anything but oppressed and crushed all *your* days. 34 And you shall be driven mad by the sight of what your eyes see. 35 Yahweh will strike you on the knees and legs with sore boils, from which you cannot be healed, from the sole of your foot to the top of your head. 36 Yahweh will lead you and your king, whom you set over you, to a nation which neither you nor your fathers have known, and there you shall serve other gods, wood and stone. 37 You shall become an object of horror, a proverb, and a byword among all the people where Yahweh drives you.

38 "You shall bring out much seed to the field, but you will gather in little, for the locust will consume it. 39 You shall plant and cultivate vineyards, but you will neither drink of the wine nor gather *the grapes*, for the worm will devour them. 40 You shall have olive trees throughout your territory, but you will not anoint yourself with the oil, for your olives will drop off. 41 You shall become the father of sons and daughters, but they will not be yours, for they will go into captivity. 42 The cricket shall possess all your trees and the produce of your ground. 43 The sojourner who is among you shall rise above you higher and higher, but you will go down lower and lower. 44 He shall lend to you, but you will not lend to him; he shall be the head, and you will be the tail.

45 "So all these curses shall come on you and pursue you and overtake you until you are destroyed, because you would not listen to the voice of Yahweh your God to keep His commandments and His statutes which He commanded you. 46 And they shall become a sign and a wonder on you and your seed forever.

47 "Because you did not serve Yahweh your God with gladness and a merry heart—because of the abundance of all things, 48 therefore you shall serve your enemies whom Yahweh will send against you, in hunger, in thirst, in nakedness, and in the lack of all things; and He will put an iron yoke on your neck until He has destroyed you.

49 "Yahweh will bring a nation against you from afar, from the end of the earth, as the eagle swoops down, a nation whose tongue you shall not understand, 50 a nation of fierce countenance who will have no respect for the old, nor show favor to the young. 51 Moreover, it shall eat the offspring of your herd and the produce of your ground until you are destroyed, who also will not allow grain, new wine, or oil, *and* the increase of your herd or the young of your flock to remain for you until they have caused you to perish. 52 And it shall besiege you in all your gates until your high and fortified walls in which you trusted come down throughout your land, and it shall besiege you in all your gates throughout your land which Yahweh your God has given you. 53 Then you shall eat the offspring of your own body, the flesh of your sons and of your daughters whom Yahweh your God has given you, during the siege and the distress by which your enemy will oppress you. 54 The man who is refined and very delicate among you shall be hostile toward his brother and toward the wife he cherishes and toward the rest of his children who remain, 55 so that he will not give *even* one of them any of the flesh of his children which he will eat, since he has nothing *else* remaining, during the siege and the distress by which your enemy will oppress you in all your gates. 56 The refined and delicate woman among you, who would not venture to set the sole of her foot on the ground for delicateness and refinement, shall be hostile toward the husband she cherishes and toward her son and daughter, 57 and toward her afterbirth which issues from between her legs and toward her children whom she bears; for she will eat them secretly for lack of anything *else*, during the siege and the distress by which your enemy will oppress you in your gates.

58 "If you are not careful to do all the words of this law which are written in this

book, to fear this glorious and fearsome
name, Yahweh your God, 59 then Yahweh
will bring wondrous plagues on you and
plagues on *those who are* your seed, even
great and enduring plagues, and miserable
and enduring sicknesses. 60 And He will
bring back on you all the diseases of Egypt
of which you were afraid, and they will
cling to you. 61 Also every sickness and
every plague, which is not written in the
book of this law, Yahweh will bring on you
until you are destroyed. 62 Then you shall
remain few in number, whereas you were as
numerous as the stars of heaven, because
you did not listen to the voice of Yahweh
your God. 63 And it will be that as Yahweh
delighted over you to prosper you and
multiply you, so Yahweh will delight over
you to make you perish and destroy you;
and you will be torn from the land where
you are entering to possess it. 64 Moreover,
Yahweh will scatter you among all peoples,
from one end of the earth to the other end
of the earth; and there you shall serve
other gods, wood and stone, which you or
your fathers have not known. 65 Moreover,
among those nations you shall find no
relief, and there will be no resting place
for the sole of your foot; but there Yahweh
will give you a trembling heart, failing of
eyes, and despair of soul. 66 So your life
shall hang in doubt before you; and you
will be in dread night and day and shall not
have *any* faith in your life. 67 In the morning
you shall say, 'Would that it were evening!'
And at evening you shall say, 'Would that
it were morning!' because of the dread of
your heart which you dread, and because
of the sight of your eyes which you will see.
68 And Yahweh will bring you back to Egypt
in ships, by the way about which I spoke
to you, 'You will never see it again!' And
there you will offer yourselves for sale to
your enemies as male and female slaves,
but there will be no buyer."

Psalm 39:12–13

12 "Hear my prayer, O Yahweh, and
give ear to my cry for help;
Do not be silent at my tears;
For I am a sojourner with You,
A foreign resident like all my fathers.
13 "Turn Your gaze away from me,
that I may smile *again*
Before I go and am no more."

Proverbs 13:7–8

7 There is one who pretends to
be rich, but has nothing;
Another pretends to be poor,
but has great wealth.
8 The ransom of a man's
life is his wealth,
But the poor hears no rebuke.

Luke 6:27–49

27 "But I say to you who hear, love your
enemies, do good to those who hate you,
28 bless those who curse you, pray for
those who disparage you. 29 Whoever hits
you on the cheek, offer him the other also;
and whoever takes away your garment, do
not withhold your tunic from him either.
30 Give to everyone who asks of you, and
whoever takes away what is yours, do not
demand it back. 31 And treat others the
same way you want them to treat you.
32 And if you love those who love you,
what credit is *that* to you? For even sinners
love those who love them. 33 And if you do
good to those who do good to you, what
credit is *that* to you? For even sinners do
the same. 34 And if you lend to those from
whom you expect to receive, what credit is
that to you? Even sinners lend to sinners
in order to receive back the same *amount*.
35 But love your enemies, and do good, and
lend, expecting nothing in return; and your
reward will be great, and you will be sons
of the Most High; for He Himself is kind to
the ungrateful and evil. 36 Be merciful, just
as your Father is merciful.

37 "And do not judge, and you will not be
judged; and do not condemn, and you will
not be condemned; pardon, and you will
be pardoned. 38 Give, and it will be given
to you. They will pour into your lap a good
measure—pressed down, shaken together,
running over. For by your standard of measure
it will be measured to you in return."

39 And He also spoke a parable to them:
"Can a blind man guide a blind man? Will
they not both fall into a pit? 40 A student
is not above his teacher; but everyone,
after he has been fully trained, will be like
his teacher. 41 And why do you look at the
speck that is in your brother's eye, but do
not notice the log that is in your own eye?
42 How can you say to your brother, 'Brother,
let me take out the speck that is in your eye,'
when you yourself do not see the log that

is in your own eye? You hypocrite, first take the log out of your own eye, and then you will see clearly to take out the speck that is in your brother's eye. 43 For there is no good tree which produces bad fruit, nor, on the other hand, a bad tree which produces good fruit. 44 For each tree is known by its own fruit. For men do not gather figs from thorns, nor do they pick grapes from a bramble bush. 45 The good man out of the good treasure of his heart brings forth what is good; and the evil *man* out of the evil *treasure* brings forth what is evil. For his mouth speaks from the abundance of his heart.

46 "Now why do you call Me, 'Lord, Lord,' and do not do what I say? 47 Everyone who comes to Me and hears My words and does them, I will show you whom he is like: 48 he is like a man building a house, who dug and went deep, and laid a foundation on the rock; and when a flood occurred, the river burst against that house and could not shake it, because it had been well built. 49 But the one who heard and did not do *accordingly*, is like a man who built a house on the ground without any foundation; and the river burst against it and immediately it collapsed, and the ruin of that house was great."

APRIL 3

Deuteronomy 29:1–30:20

29 These are the words of the covenant which Yahweh commanded Moses to cut with the sons of Israel in the land of Moab, besides the covenant which He had cut with them at Horeb.

2 And Moses summoned all Israel and said to them, "You have seen all that Yahweh did before your eyes in the land of Egypt to Pharaoh and all his servants and all his land; 3 the great trials which your eyes have seen, those great signs and wonders. 4 Yet to this day Yahweh has not given you a heart to know, nor eyes to see, nor ears to hear. 5 And I have led you forty years in the wilderness; your clothes have not worn out on you, and your sandal has not worn out on your foot. 6 You have not eaten bread, nor have you drunk wine or strong drink, in order that you might know that I am Yahweh your God. 7 Then you came to this place, and Sihon the king of Heshbon and Og the king of Bashan came out to meet us for battle, but we struck them down; 8 and we took their land and gave it as an inheritance to the Reubenites, the Gadites, and the half-tribe of the Manassites. 9 So you shall keep the words of this covenant to do them, that you may prosper in all that you do.

10 "You stand today, all of you, before Yahweh your God: your heads, your tribes, your elders, and your officers, *even* all the men of Israel, 11 your little ones, your wives, and the sojourner who is within your camps, from the one who chops your wood to the one who draws your water, 12 that you may enter into the covenant with Yahweh your God and into His oath, which Yahweh your God is cutting with you today, 13 in order that He may establish you today as His people and that He may be your God, just as He spoke to you and as He swore to your fathers, to Abraham, to Isaac, and to Jacob.

14 "Now not with you alone am I cutting this covenant and this oath, 15 but both with those who stand here with us today in the presence of Yahweh our God and with those who are not with us here today— 16 for you know how we lived in the land of Egypt, and how we came through the midst of the nations through which you passed; 17 moreover, you have seen their detestable things and their idols *of* wood, stone, silver, and gold, which *they had* with them— 18 lest there be among you a man or woman, or family or tribe, whose heart turns away today from Yahweh our God, to go to serve the gods of those nations; lest there be among you a root bearing poisonous fruit and wormwood. 19 And it will be when he hears the words of this curse, that he will bless himself in his heart, saying, 'I have peace though I walk in the stubbornness of my heart in order to sweep away the watered *land* with the dry.' 20 Yahweh shall not be willing to pardon him, but rather the anger of Yahweh and His jealousy will burn against that man, and every curse which is written in this book will rest on him, and Yahweh will blot out his name from under heaven. 21 Then Yahweh will separate him out for adversity from all the tribes of Israel,

according to all the curses of the covenant
which are written in this book of the law.
22 “And the generation to come, your sons
who rise up after you and the foreigner who
comes from a distant land, shall see the
plagues of the land and the diseases with
which Yahweh has afflicted it, and they
will say, 23 ‘All its land is brimstone and
salt, a burning waste, unsown and nothing
sprouting, and no grass grows in it, like the
overthrow of Sodom and Gomorrah, Admah
and Zeboiim, which Yahweh overthrew in
His anger and in His wrath.’ 24 And all the
nations will say, ‘Why has Yahweh done
thus to this land? Why this great burning
anger?’ 25 Then *men* will say, ‘Because they
forsook the covenant of Yahweh, the God of
their fathers, which He cut with them when
He brought them out of the land of Egypt.
26 And they went and served other gods and
worshiped them, gods whom they have not
known and whom He had not apportioned
to them. 27 Therefore, the anger of Yahweh
was kindled against that land, to bring
upon it every curse which is written in this
book; 28 and Yahweh uprooted them from
their land in anger and in fury and in great
wrath, and He cast them into another land,
as *it is* this day.’
29 “The secret things belong to Yahweh
our God, but the things revealed belong to
us and to our sons forever, that we may do
all the words of this law.

30 “So it will be, when all of these things
have come upon you, the blessing
and the curse which I have set before you,
and you cause *these things* to return to your
heart in all the nations where Yahweh your
God has banished you, 2 and you return to
Yahweh your God and listen to His voice
with all your heart and soul according to
all that I am commanding you today, you
and your sons, 3 then Yahweh your God will
return you from captivity and return *His*
compassion on you, and He will gather you
again from all the peoples where Yahweh
your God has scattered you. 4 If those of you
who are banished are at the ends of the sky,
from there Yahweh your God will gather
you, and from there He will take you *back*.
5 And *Yahweh your God will bring* you into
the land which your fathers possessed, and
you shall possess it; and He will prosper you
and multiply you more than your fathers.
6 “Moreover Yahweh your God will circum-
cise your heart and the heart of your seed, to
love Yahweh your God with all your heart and
with all your soul, so that you may live. 7 And
Yahweh your God will inflict all these curses
on your enemies and on those who hate you,
who persecuted you. 8 And you shall return
and listen to the voice of Yahweh, and you
shall do all His commandments which I am
commanding you today. 9 Then Yahweh your
God will prosper you abundantly in all the
work of your hand, in the offspring of your
body and in the offspring of your cattle and
in the produce of your ground, for Yahweh
will return to rejoice over you for good, just
as He rejoiced over your fathers, 10 when
you listen to the voice of Yahweh your God
to keep His commandments and His statutes
which are written in this book of the law,
when you return to Yahweh your God with
all your heart and soul.
11 “For this commandment which I am
commanding you today is not too difficult
for you, nor is it far *from you*. 12 It is not in
heaven, that you should say, ‘Who will go up
to heaven for us and get it for us and make
us hear it, that we may do it?’ 13 Nor is it
beyond the sea, that you should say, ‘Who
will cross the sea for us and get it for us and
make us hear it, that we may do it?’ 14 But the
word is very near you, in your mouth and in
your heart, that you may do it.
15 “See, I have set before you today life
and prosperity, and death and calamity; 16 in
that I am commanding you today to love
Yahweh your God, to walk in His ways, and
to keep His commandments and His statutes
and His judgments, that you may live and
multiply, and that Yahweh your God may
bless you in the land where you are entering
to possess it. 17 But if your heart turns away
and you will not listen, but are drawn away
and worship other gods and serve them, 18 I
declare to you today that you shall surely
perish. You will not prolong *your* days in
the land where you are crossing the Jordan
to enter and possess it. 19 I call heaven and
earth to witness against you today, that
I have set before you life and death, the
blessing and the curse. So choose life in
order that you may live, you and your seed,
20 by loving Yahweh your God, by listening
to His voice, and by holding fast to Him; for
this is your life and the length of your days,
that you may live in the land which Yahweh

swore to your fathers, to Abraham, to Isaac,
and to Jacob, to give them."

Psalm 40:1–5

1 I hoped earnestly for Yahweh;
And He inclined to me and
heard my cry for help.
2 He brought me up out of the pit of
destruction, out of the miry clay,
And He set my feet upon a high
rock, He established my steps.
3 He put a new song in my mouth,
a song of praise to our God;
Many will see and fear
And will trust in Yahweh.

4 How blessed is the man who has
made Yahweh his trust,
And has not turned to the proud, nor
to those who stray into falsehood.
5 Many, O Yahweh my God, are the
wondrous deeds You have done,
And Your thoughts toward us;
There is none to compare with You.
I would declare and speak of them,
But they are too numerous to recount.

Proverbs 13:9–10

9 The light of the righteous is glad,
But the lamp of the wicked goes out.
10 With arrogance comes only quarreling,
But with those who receive
counsel is wisdom.

Luke 7:1–30

7 When He had completed all His words
in the hearing of the people, He went to
Capernaum.
2 And a centurion's slave, who was highly
regarded by him, was sick and about to die.
3 Now when he heard about Jesus, he sent
some Jewish elders asking Him to come
and save the life of his slave. 4 And when
they came to Jesus, they were earnestly
pleading with Him, saying, "He is worthy
for You to grant this to him; 5 for he loves
our nation and it was he who built us our
synagogue." 6 Now Jesus was going on His
way with them; and when He was not far
from the house, the centurion sent friends,
saying to Him, "Lord, do not trouble Yourself
further, for I am not good enough for You to
come under my roof. 7 For this reason I did
not even consider myself worthy to come to
You, but *just* say the word, and my servant
will be healed. 8 For I also am a man placed
under authority, with soldiers under me;
and I say to this one, 'Go!' and he goes, and
to another, 'Come!' and he comes, and to my
slave, 'Do this!' and he does it." 9 Now when
Jesus heard this, He marveled at him. And
He turned to the crowd that was following
Him and said, "I say to you, not even in Israel
have I found such great faith." 10 And when
those who had been sent returned to the
house, they found the slave in good health.
11 And it happened that soon afterwards
He went to a city called Nain, and His disci-
ples were going along with Him, accompanied
by a large crowd. 12 Now as He approached
the gate of the city, behold, a dead man was
being carried out, the only son of his mother,
and she was a widow. And a sizeable crowd
from the city was with her. 13 And when the
Lord saw her, He felt compassion for her and
said to her, "Do not cry." 14 And He came up
and touched the coffin, and the bearers came
to a halt. And He said, "Young man, I say to
you, arise!" 15 And the dead man sat up and
began to speak. And *Jesus* gave him back to
his mother. 16 And fear gripped them all, and
they *began* glorifying God, saying, "A great
prophet has arisen among us!" and, "God
has visited His people!" 17 And this report
concerning Him went out all over Judea and
in all the surrounding district.
18 And the disciples of John reported to
him about all these things. 19 Summoning
two of his disciples, John sent them to the
Lord, saying, "Are You the One who is to
come, or should we look for someone else?"
20 When the men came to Him, they said,
"John the Baptist has sent us to You, saying,
'Are You the One who is to come, or should
we look for someone else?'" 21 At that very
time He cured many *people* of diseases and
afflictions and evil spirits, and He granted
sight to many *who were* blind. 22 And He
answered and said to them, "Go and report
to John what you have seen and heard:
the BLIND RECEIVE SIGHT, *the* lame walk,
the lepers are cleansed, and *the* deaf hear,
the dead are raised up, *the* POOR HAVE THE
GOSPEL PREACHED TO THEM. 23 Blessed is he
who does not take offense at Me."
24 And when the messengers of John
had left, He began to speak to the crowds
about John, "What did you go out into the
wilderness to behold? A reed shaken by the
wind? 25 But what did you go out to see?

A man dressed in soft garments? Behold,
those who are splendidly clothed and live
in luxury are *found* in royal palaces! 26 But
what did you go out to see? A prophet? Yes,
I say to you, and even more than a prophet.
27 This is *the one* about whom it is written,

'BEHOLD, I SEND MY MESSENGER
AHEAD OF YOU,
WHO WILL PREPARE YOUR
WAY BEFORE YOU.'

28 "I say to you, among those born of women
there is no one greater than John; yet he who
is least in the kingdom of God is greater than
he." 29 And when all the people and the tax
collectors heard *this*, they acknowledged
God's justice, having been baptized with the
baptism of John. 30 But the Pharisees and the
scholars of the Law rejected God's purpose
for themselves, not having been baptized
by John.

APRIL 4

Deuteronomy 31:1–32:52

31 So Moses went and spoke these words
to all Israel. 2 And he said to them, "I
am 120 years old today; I am no longer able
to come and go, and Yahweh has said to
me, 'You shall not cross this Jordan.' 3 It is
Yahweh your God who will cross ahead of
you; He will destroy these nations before
you, and you shall dispossess them. Joshua
is the one who will cross ahead of you, just
as Yahweh has spoken. 4 And Yahweh will
do to them just as He did to Sihon and Og,
the kings of the Amorites, and to their land,
when He destroyed them. 5 And Yahweh will
give them over before you, and you shall do
to them according to all the commandments
which I have commanded you. 6 Be strong
and courageous. Do not be afraid or be in
dread of them, for Yahweh your God is the
one who goes with you. He will not fail you
or forsake you."

7 Then Moses called to Joshua and said to
him in the sight of all Israel, "Be strong and
courageous, for you shall go with this people
into the land which Yahweh has sworn to
their fathers to give them, and you shall give
it to them as an inheritance. 8 And Yahweh
is the one who goes ahead of you; He will
be with you. He will not fail you or forsake
you. Do not fear or be dismayed."

9 So Moses wrote this law and gave it to
the priests, the sons of Levi who carried
the ark of the covenant of Yahweh, and to
all the elders of Israel. 10 Then Moses com-
manded them, saying, "At the end of *every*
seven years, at the time of the year of the
remission of debts, at the Feast of Booths,
11 when all Israel comes *to appear* before
Yahweh your God at the place which He will
choose, you shall read this law in front of
all Israel in their hearing. 12 Assemble the
people, the men and the women and little
ones and the sojourner who is within your
gates, so that they may hear and so that they
may learn and fear Yahweh your God and be
careful to do all the words of this law. 13 And
their children, who have not known, will
hear and learn to fear Yahweh your God, all
the days you live on the land which you are
about to cross the Jordan to possess."

14 Then Yahweh said to Moses, "Behold,
the time for you to die is near; call Joshua
and present yourselves at the tent of
meeting, that I may commission him."
So Moses and Joshua went and presented
themselves at the tent of meeting. 15 And
Yahweh appeared in the tent in a pillar of
cloud, and the pillar of cloud stood at the
doorway of the tent. 16 And Yahweh said to
Moses, "Behold, you are about to lie down
with your fathers; and this people will arise
and play the harlot with the foreign gods of
the land, into the midst of which they are
going, and they will forsake Me and break
My covenant which I have cut with them.
17 Then My anger will be kindled against
them in that day, and I will forsake them
and hide My face from them, and they will
be consumed, and many evils and troubles
will find them, so that they will say in that
day, 'Is it not because our God is not among
us that these evils have found us?' 18 But I
will surely hide My face in that day because
of all the evil which they will do, for they
will turn to other gods.

19 "So now, write this song for yourselves
and teach it to the sons of Israel; put it in
their mouths, so that this song may be a
witness for Me against the sons of Israel.
20 For when I bring them into the land
flowing with milk and honey, which I swore
to their fathers, and they have eaten and are

satisfied and become fat, then they will turn
to other gods and serve them and spurn Me
and break My covenant. 21 Then it will be,
when many evils and troubles have found
them, that this song will answer them as a
witness (for it shall not be forgotten from
the mouths of their seed); for I know their
intent which they are developing today,
before I have brought them into the land
which I swore." 22 So Moses wrote this song
the same day and taught it to the sons of
Israel.

23 Then He commissioned Joshua the son
of Nun and said, "Be strong and courageous,
for you shall bring the sons of Israel into
the land which I swore to them, and I will
be with you."

24 And it happened, when Moses finished
writing the words of this law in a book
until they were complete, 25 that Moses
commanded the Levites who carried the ark
of the covenant of Yahweh, saying, 26 "Take
this book of the law and place it beside the
ark of the covenant of Yahweh your God,
that it may be there as a witness against
you. 27 For I know your rebellion and your
stiff-neck; behold, while I am still alive with
you today, you have been rebellious against
Yahweh; how much more, then, after my
death? 28 Assemble to me all the elders of
your tribes and your officers, that I may
speak these words in their hearing and call
the heavens and the earth to witness against
them. 29 For I know that after my death you
will act corruptly and turn away from the
way which I have commanded you; and evil
will befall you in the last days, for you will
do that which is evil in the sight of Yahweh,
provoking Him to anger with the work of
your hands."

30 Then Moses spoke in the hearing of
all the assembly of Israel the words of this
song, until they were complete:

32 "Give ear, O heavens,
and let me speak;
And let the earth hear the
words of my mouth.
2 "Let what I have learned
drop as the rain,
My speech distill as the dew,
As the droplets on the fresh grass
And as the showers on the herb.
3 "For I proclaim the name of Yahweh;
Ascribe greatness to our God!
4 "The Rock! His work is perfect,
For all His ways are just;
A God of faithfulness and
without injustice,
Righteous and upright is He.
5 "They have acted corruptly toward Him,
They are not His children
because of their defect;
But are a perverse and
crooked generation.
6 "Do you thus repay Yahweh,
O people who are wickedly foolish
and without wisdom?
Is not He your Father who
has bought you?
He has made you and established you.
7 "Remember the ancient days,
Consider the years from
generation to generation.
Ask your father, and he
will declare to you,
Your elders, and they will speak to you.
8 "When the Most High gave the
nations their inheritance,
When He separated the sons of man,
He set the boundaries of the peoples
According to the number
of the sons of Israel.
9 "For Yahweh's portion is His people;
Jacob is the allotment of
His inheritance.
10 "He found him in a desert land,
And in the howling waste
of a wilderness;
He encircled him; He cared for him;
He guarded him as the pupil of His eye.
11 "Like an eagle that stirs up its nest,
That hovers over its young,
He spread His wings and
caught them;
He carried them on His pinions.
12 "Yahweh alone guided him,
And there was no foreign
god with him.
13 "He made him ride on the high
places of the earth,
And he ate the produce of the field;
And He made him suck
honey from the rock,
And oil from the flinty rock,
14 Curds of cows, and milk of the flock,
With fat of lambs,
And rams, the breed of
Bashan, and goats,
With the finest of the wheat—

And of the blood of grapes
you drank wine.

15 "But Jeshurun grew fat and kicked—
You grew fat, thick, and sleek—
Then he abandoned God
who made him,
And treated the Rock of his salvation
with wicked foolishness.
16 "They made Him jealous
with strange *gods*;
With abominations they
provoked Him to anger.
17 "They sacrificed to demons
who were not God,
To gods whom they have not known,
New *gods* who came lately,
Whom your fathers did not dread.
18 "You neglected the Rock who begot you,
And forgot the God who
brought you forth.

19 "And Yahweh saw *this* and spurned *them*
Because of the provocation of
His sons and daughters.
20 "Then He said, 'I will hide
My face from them;
I will see what their end *shall be*;
For they are a perverse generation,
Sons in whom is no faithfulness.
21 'They have made Me jealous
with *what* is not God;
They have provoked Me to
anger with their idols.
So I will make them jealous with
those who are not a people;
I will provoke them to anger with
a wickedly foolish nation,
22 For a fire is kindled in My anger,
And it burns to the lowest
part of Sheol,
And it consumes the earth
with its produce,
And it sets on fire the foundations
of the mountains.

23 'I will heap calamities on them;
I will exhaust My arrows on them.
24 '*They will be* wasted by famine,
and consumed by plague
And bitter destruction;
And the teeth of beasts I
will *send upon* them,
With the venom of crawling
things of the dust.
25 'Outside the sword will bereave,
And inside terror—
Both choice man and virgin,
The nursing baby with the
man of gray hair.
26 'I would have said, "I will
cut them to pieces;
I will cause the memory of
them to cease from men,"
27 Had I not feared the provocation
by the enemy,
Lest their adversaries misjudge,
Lest they say, "Our hand is triumphant,
And Yahweh has not done all this."'

28 "For they are a nation where
counsel perishes,
And there is no discernment in them.
29 "Would that they were wise, that
they had insight into this,
That they would understand
their future!
30 "How could one pursue one thousand,
And two put ten thousand to flight,
Unless their Rock had sold them,
And Yahweh had handed them over?
31 "Indeed their rock is not like our Rock,
Even our enemies themselves
judge this.
32 "For their vine is from the
vine of Sodom,
And from the fields of Gomorrah;
Their grapes are grapes of poison,
Their clusters, bitter.
33 "Their wine is the venom of serpents,
And the deadly poison of cobras.

34 'Is it not laid up in store with Me,
Sealed up in My treasuries?
35 'Vengeance is Mine, and retribution,
In due time their foot will stumble;
For the day of their disaster is near,
And the impending things are
hastening upon them.'
36 "For Yahweh will render
justice to His people,
And will have compassion
on His slaves,
When He sees that *their*
strength is gone,
And there is none *remaining*,
bond or free.
37 "And He will say, 'Where are their gods,
The rock in which they sought refuge?
38 'Who ate the fat of their sacrifices,

And drank the wine of their
drink offering?
Let them rise up and help you,
Let them be your hiding place!
39 'See now that I, I am He,
And there is no god besides Me;
It is I who put to death and give life.
I have wounded, and it is I who heal,
And there is no one who can
deliver from My hand.
40 'Indeed, I lift up My hand to heaven,
And say, as I live forever,
41 If I sharpen My flashing sword,
And My hand takes hold on judgment,
I will render vengeance on
My adversaries,
And I will repay those who hate Me.
42 'I will make My arrows
drunk with blood,
And My sword will devour flesh,
With the blood of the slain
and the captives,
From the long-haired leaders
of the enemy.'
43 "O nations, cause His people
to shout for joy;
For He will avenge the
blood of His slaves,
And He will render vengeance
on His adversaries,
And He will atone for His
land *and* His people."

44 Then Moses came and spoke all the
words of this song in the hearing of the
people, he and Joshua the son of Nun.
45 Then Moses finished speaking all these
words to all Israel, 46 and he said to them,
"Place in your heart all the words with
which I am warning you today, which you
shall command your sons to be careful to do,
even all the words of this law. 47 For it is not
an idle word for you; indeed it is your life.
And by this word you will prolong your days
in the land, which you are about to cross the
Jordan to possess."

48 And Yahweh spoke to Moses that very
same day, saying, 49 "Go up to this mountain
of the Abarim, Mount Nebo, which is in the
land of Moab opposite Jericho, and look at
the land of Canaan, which I am giving to
the sons of Israel for a possession. 50 Then
die on the mountain where you ascend, and
be gathered to your people, as Aaron your
brother died on Mount Hor and was gath-
ered to his people, 51 because you *both* acted
unfaithfully with Me in the midst of the sons
of Israel at the waters of Meribah-kadesh, in
the wilderness of Zin, because you *both* did
not treat Me as holy in the midst of the sons
of Israel. 52 For you shall see the land at a
distance, but you shall not go there, into the
land which I am giving the sons of Israel."

Psalm 40:6–12

6 Sacrifice and meal offering
You have not desired;
My ears You have opened;
Burnt offering and sin offering
You have not required.
7 Then I said, "Behold, I come;
In the scroll of the book it
is written of me.
8 "I desire to do Your will, O my God;
Your law is within my inner being."

9 I proclaim good news of righteousness
in the great assembly;
Behold, I do not restrain my lips,
O Yahweh, You know.
10 I do not conceal Your righteousness
within my heart;
I speak of Your faithfulness
and Your salvation;
I do not hide Your lovingkindness and
Your truth from the great assembly.

11 You, O Yahweh, will not withhold
Your compassion from me;
Your lovingkindness and Your truth
will continually guard me.
12 For evils beyond number
have surrounded me;
My iniquities have overtaken me,
so that I am not able to see;
They are more numerous than
the hairs of my head,
And my heart has failed me.

Proverbs 13:11–12

11 Wealth *obtained* from empty
effort dwindles,
But the one who gathers with
his hand abounds.
12 Hope deferred makes the heart sick,
But desire fulfilled is a tree of life.

Luke 7:31–50

31 "To what then shall I compare the
men of this generation, and what are they
like? 32 They are like children, sitting in the

marketplace and calling to one another, who
say, 'We played the flute for you, and you
did not dance; we sang a dirge, and you did
not cry.' 33 For John the Baptist has come
eating no bread and drinking no wine, and
you say, 'He has a demon!' 34 The Son of Man
has come eating and drinking, and you say,
'Behold, a gluttonous man and a drunkard,
a friend of tax collectors and sinners!' 35 Yet
wisdom is vindicated by all her children."

36 Now one of the Pharisees was asking
Him to eat with him, and He entered the
Pharisee's house and reclined *at the table.*
37 And behold, there was a woman in the
city who was a sinner. And when she
learned that He was reclining *at the table*
in the Pharisee's house, she brought an
alabaster jar of perfume. 38 And standing
behind *Him* at His feet, crying, she began
to wet His feet with her tears. And she kept
wiping them with the hair of her head, and
kissing His feet and anointing them with
the perfume. 39 Now when the Pharisee,
who had invited Him, saw this, he said to
himself, saying, "If this man were a prophet
He would know who and what sort of per-
son this woman is who is touching Him,
that she is a sinner."

40 And Jesus answered and said to him,
"Simon, I have something to say to you."
And he replied, "Say it, Teacher." 41 "A
moneylender had two debtors: one owed
five hundred denarii, and the other fifty.
42 When they were unable to repay, he gra-
ciously forgave them both. So which of them
will love him more?" 43 Simon answered and
said, "I suppose the one whom he graciously
forgave more." And He said to him, "You have
judged correctly." 44 And turning toward the
woman, He said to Simon, "Do you see this
woman? I entered your house; you gave Me
no water for My feet, but she has wet My
feet with her tears and wiped them with her
hair. 45 You gave Me no kiss; but she, since
the time I came in, has not ceased to kiss
My feet. 46 You did not anoint My head with
oil, but she anointed My feet with perfume.
47 For this reason I say to you, her sins, which
are many, have been forgiven, for she loved
much. But he who is forgiven little, loves
little." 48 Then He said to her, "Your sins
have been forgiven." 49 And those who were
reclining *at the table* with Him began to say
to themselves, "Who is this *man* who even
forgives sins?" 50 And He said to the woman,
"Your faith has saved you; go in peace."

APRIL 5

Deuteronomy 33:1–34:12

33 Now this is the blessing with which
Moses the man of God blessed the
sons of Israel before his death. 2 And he said,

"Yahweh came from Sinai,
And He dawned on them from Seir;
He shone forth from Mount Paran,
And He came from the midst of
ten thousand holy ones;
At His right hand there was
flashing lightning for them.
3 "Indeed, He loves the people;
All Your holy ones are in
Your hand,
And they followed in Your steps;
Everyone is bearing up Your words.
4 "Moses commanded us with a law,
A possession for the assembly
of Jacob.
5 "And He was king in Jeshurun,
When the heads of the
people were gathered,
The tribes of Israel together.
6 "May Reuben live and not die,
Nor his men be few."

7 And this regarding Judah; so he said,
"Hear, O Yahweh, the voice of Judah,
And bring him to his people.
With his hands he contended for them,
And may You be a help against
his adversaries."

8 Of Levi he said,
"*Let* Your Thummim and Your Urim
belong to Your holy one,
Whom You tested at Massah,
With whom You contended at
the waters of Meribah;
9 Who said of his father and
his mother,
'I did not consider them';
And he did not recognize his brothers,
Nor did he know his own sons,
For they kept Your word,
And they observed Your covenant.

10 "They shall teach Your
judgments to Jacob,
And Your law to Israel.
They shall put incense before You,
And whole burnt offerings
on Your altar.
11 "O Yahweh, bless his substance,
And accept the work of his hands;
Crush the loins of those who
rise up against him,
And those who hate him, so that
they will not rise *again*."

12 Of Benjamin he said,
"May the beloved of Yahweh
dwell in security by Him,
Who shields him all the day,
And he dwells between
His shoulders."

13 Of Joseph he said,
"Blessed of Yahweh *be* his land,
With the choice things of
heaven, with the dew,
And from the deep lying beneath,
14 And with the choice
produce of the sun,
And with the choice yield
of the months,
15 And with the best things of
the ancient mountains,
And with the choice things
of the everlasting hills,
16 And with the choice things of
the earth and its fullness,
And the favor of Him who
dwelt in the bush.
Let it come to the head of Joseph,
And to the top of the head of the one
distinguished among his brothers.
17 "As the firstborn of his ox,
splendor is his,
And his horns are the horns
of the wild ox;
With them he will push the peoples,
All at once, *to* the ends of the earth.
And those are the ten
thousands of Ephraim,
And those are the thousands
of Manasseh."

18 Of Zebulun he said,
"Be glad, Zebulun, in your going forth,
And, Issachar, in your tents.
19 "They will call peoples *to* the mountain;
There they will offer
righteous sacrifices;
For they will draw out the
abundance of the seas,
And the hidden treasures of the sand."

20 Of Gad he said,
"Blessed is the one who enlarges Gad;
He lies down as a lion,
And tears the arm, also the
top of the head.
21 "Then he provided the first
part for himself,
For there the ruler's portion
was reserved;
And he came *with* the
heads of the people;
He did the righteousness of Yahweh,
And His judgments with Israel."

22 Of Dan he said,
"Dan is a lion's whelp,
That leaps forth from Bashan."

23 Of Naphtali he said,
"O Naphtali, satisfied with favor,
And full of the blessing of Yahweh,
Take possession of the sea
and the south."

24 Of Asher he said,
"More blessed than sons is Asher;
May he be favored by his brothers,
And may he dip his foot in oil.
25 "Your locks will be iron and bronze,
And according to your days, so
your fortitude will be.

26 "There is none like the God of Jeshurun,
Who rides the heavens to your help,
And through the skies in His majesty.
27 "The eternal God is a dwelling place,
And underneath are the
everlasting arms;
And He drove out the enemy
from before you,
And said, 'Destroy!'
28 "So Israel dwells in security,
The fountain of Jacob secluded,
In a land of grain and new wine;
His heavens also drop down dew.
29 "Blessed are you, O Israel;
Who is like you, a people
saved by Yahweh,
Who is the shield of your help

And the sword of your majesty!
So your enemies will cower before you,
And you will tread upon
their high places."

34 Then Moses went up from the plains
of Moab to Mount Nebo, to the top
of Pisgah, which is opposite Jericho. And
Yahweh showed him all the land, Gilead as
far as Dan, 2 and all Naphtali and the land
of Ephraim and Manasseh, and all the land
of Judah as far as the western sea, 3 and the
Negev and the plain in the valley of Jericho,
the city of palm trees, as far as Zoar. 4 Then
Yahweh said to him, "This is the land which
I swore to Abraham, to Isaac, and to Jacob,
saying, 'I will give it to your seed'; I have
let you see *it* with your eyes, but you shall
not go over there." 5 So Moses the servant
of Yahweh died there in the land of Moab,
according to the command of Yahweh. 6 And
He buried him in the valley in the land of
Moab, opposite Beth-peor; but no man
knows his burial place to this day. 7 Now
Moses was 120 years old when he died; his
eye was not dim, nor his vigor abated. 8 So
the sons of Israel wept for Moses in the
plains of Moab thirty days. Then the days
of weeping *and* mourning for Moses came
to an end.

9 Now Joshua the son of Nun was filled
with the spirit of wisdom, for Moses had
laid his hands on him; and the sons of
Israel listened to him and did as Yahweh
had commanded Moses. 10 And there has
not yet arisen a prophet in Israel like Moses,
whom Yahweh knew face to face, 11 in regard
to all the signs and wonders which Yahweh
sent him to do in the land of Egypt against
Pharaoh, all his servants, and all his land,
12 and in regard to all the mighty power and
in regard to all the great terror which Moses
did in the sight of all Israel.

Psalm 40:13–17

13 Be pleased, O Yahweh, to deliver me;
Make haste, O Yahweh, to help me.
14 Let those be ashamed and
humiliated together
Who seek my life to sweep it away;
Let those be turned back
and dishonored
Who delight in evil *against* me.
15 Let those be appalled because
of their shame
Who say to me, "Aha, aha!"
16 Let all who seek You rejoice
and be glad in You;
Let those who love Your
salvation say continually,
"Yahweh be magnified!"
17 As for me, I am afflicted and needy,
May the Lord think of me.
You are my help and the One
who rescues me;
Do not delay, O my God.

Proverbs 13:13–14

13 The one who despises the
word will be in debt to it,
But the one who fears the
commandment will be rewarded.
14 The instruction of the wise
is a fountain of life,
To turn aside from the snares of death.

Luke 8:1–25

8 And it happened that soon afterward
He was going around from one city
and village to another, preaching and pro-
claiming the good news of the kingdom of
God. The twelve were with Him, 2 and *also*
some women who had been healed of evil
spirits and sicknesses: Mary who was called
Magdalene, from whom seven demons had
gone out, 3 and Joanna the wife of Chuza,
Herod's manager, and Susanna, and many
others who were ministering to them from
their possessions.

4 Now when a large crowd was coming
together, and those from the various cities
were journeying to Him, He spoke by way
of a parable: 5 "The sower went out to sow
his seed. And as he sowed, some fell beside
the road, and it was trampled under foot
and the birds of the air ate it up. 6 And other
seed fell on rock and as soon as it grew up, it
withered away, because it had no moisture.
7 And other *seed* fell among the thorns,
and when the thorns grew up with it, they
choked it out. 8 And other *seed* fell into the
good soil; and growing up, it produced a
crop one hundred times as great." As He said
these things, He would call out, "He who has
ears to hear, let him hear."

9 And His disciples *began* questioning
Him as to what this parable meant. 10 And
He said, "To you it has been granted to know
the mysteries of the kingdom of God, but
to the rest *it is* in parables, so that SEEING

THEY MAY NOT SEE, AND HEARING THEY MAY NOT UNDERSTAND.

11 “Now the parable is this: the seed is the word of God. 12 And those beside the road are those who have heard; then the devil comes and takes away the word from their heart, so that they will not believe and be saved. 13 And those on the rock are those who, when they hear, receive the word with joy, and these have no root; they believe for a while, and in time of temptation fall away. 14 And the *seed* which fell among the thorns, these are the ones who have heard, and as they go on their way they are choked with worries and riches and pleasures of life, and do not bear ripe fruit. 15 But the *seed* in the good soil, these are the ones who have heard the word in an honest and good heart, and hold it fast, and bear fruit with perseverance.

16 “Now no one after lighting a lamp covers it with a container or puts it under a bed, but he puts it on a lampstand, so that those who come in may see the light. 17 For nothing is hidden that will not become evident, nor *anything* secret that will not be known and come to light. 18 So beware how you listen, for whoever has, to him *more* shall be given; and whoever does not have, even what he thinks he has shall be taken away from him.”

19 And His mother and brothers came to Him, and they were unable to get to Him because of the crowd. 20 And it was reported to Him, “Your mother and Your brothers are standing outside, wishing to see You.” 21 But He answered and said to them, “My mother and My brothers are these who hear the word of God and do it.”

22 Now it happened that on one of *those* days He and His disciples got into a boat, and He said to them, “Let us go over to the other side of the lake.” So they set sail. 23 But as they were sailing along, He fell asleep, and a windstorm descended on the lake, and they *began to* be swamped and in danger. 24 And they came to Him and woke Him up, saying, “Master, Master, we are perishing!” And He woke up and rebuked the wind and the surging waves, and they stopped, and it became calm. 25 And He said to them, “Where is your faith?” They were fearful and marveled, saying to one another, “Who then is this, that He commands even the winds and the water, and they obey Him?”

APRIL 6

Joshua 1:1–2:24

1 Now it came about after the death of Moses the servant of Yahweh, that Yahweh spoke to Joshua the son of Nun, Moses’ attendant, saying, 2 “Moses My servant is dead; so now arise, cross this Jordan, you and all this people, to the land which I am giving to them, to the sons of Israel. 3 Every place on which the sole of your foot treads, I have given it to you, just as I spoke to Moses. 4 From the wilderness and this Lebanon, even as far as the great river, the river Euphrates, all the land of the Hittites, and as far as the Great Sea toward the setting of the sun will be your territory. 5 No man will *be able to* stand before you all the days of your life. Just as I have been with Moses, I will be with you; I will not fail you or forsake you. 6 Be strong and courageous, for you shall cause this people to inherit the land which I swore to their fathers to give them. 7 Only be strong and very courageous to be careful to do according to all the law which Moses My servant commanded you; do not turn aside from it to the right or to the left, so that you may be prosperous wherever you go. 8 This book of the law shall not depart from your mouth, but you shall meditate on it day and night, so that you may be careful to do according to all that is written in it; for then you will make your way successful, and then you will be prosperous. 9 Have I not commanded you? Be strong and courageous! Do not be in dread or be dismayed, for Yahweh your God is with you wherever you go.”

10 Then Joshua commanded the officers of the people, saying, 11 “Pass through the midst of the camp and command the people, saying, ‘Prepare provisions for yourselves, for within three days you are to cross this Jordan, to go in to possess the land which Yahweh your God is giving you, to possess it.’ ”

12 To the Reubenites and to the Gadites and to the half-tribe of Manasseh, Joshua

said, 13 “Remember the word which Moses
the servant of Yahweh commanded you,
saying, ‘Yahweh your God gives you rest
and will give you this land.’ 14 Your wives,
your little ones, and your cattle shall remain
in the land which Moses gave you beyond
the Jordan, but you shall cross before your
brothers in battle array, all your valiant
warriors, and shall help them 15 until
Yahweh gives your brothers rest as *He gives*
you, and they also possess the land which
Yahweh your God is giving them. Then you
shall return to the land of your possession
and possess it, which Moses the servant of
Yahweh gave you beyond the Jordan *to the
east* toward the sunrise.”

16 And they answered Joshua, saying, “All
that you have commanded us we will do, and
wherever you send us we will go. 17 Just as
we listened to Moses in all things, so we will
listen to you; only may Yahweh your God be
with you as He was with Moses. 18 Anyone
who rebels against your command and does
not listen to your words, in all that you
command him, shall be put to death; only
be strong and courageous.”

2 Then Joshua the son of Nun sent two
men as spies secretly from Shittim,
saying, “Go, see the land, especially Jericho.”
So they went and came into the house of a
harlot whose name was Rahab and lodged
there. 2 And it was told to the king of Jericho,
saying, “Behold, men from the sons of Israel
have come here tonight to search out the
land.” 3 And the king of Jericho sent *word* to
Rahab, saying, “Bring out the men who have
come to you, who have entered your house,
for they have come to search out all the
land.” 4 But the woman had taken the two
men and hidden them, and she said, “Yes,
the men came to me, but I did not know
where they were from. 5 Now it happened
when *it was time* to shut the gate at dark,
that the men went out; I do not know where
the men went. Pursue them quickly, for you
may overtake them.” 6 But she had brought
them up to the roof and concealed them in
the stalks of flax which she had laid in order
on the roof. 7 So the men pursued them on
the road to the Jordan to the fords; and as
soon as those who were pursuing them had
gone out, they shut the gate.

8 Now before they lay down, she came up
to them on the roof 9 and said to the men,
“I know that Yahweh has given you the
land, and that the terror of you has fallen
on us, and that all the inhabitants of the
land have melted away before you. 10 For we
have heard how Yahweh dried up the water
of the Red Sea before you when you came
out of Egypt and what you did to the two
kings of the Amorites who were beyond the
Jordan, to Sihon and Og, whom you devoted
to destruction. 11 Indeed we heard *it*, and
our hearts melted, and a *courageous* spirit
no longer rose up in *any* man because of
you; for Yahweh your God, He is God in
heaven above and on earth beneath. 12 So
now, please swear to me by Yahweh, since I
have shown lovingkindness to you, that you
also will show lovingkindness to my father’s
household and give me a pledge of truth,
13 and preserve my father and my mother
and my brothers and my sisters alive, with
all who belong to them, and deliver our lives
from death.” 14 So the men said to her, “Our
life for yours if you do not tell this business
of ours; and it will be when Yahweh gives us
the land that we will show lovingkindness
and truth to you.”

15 Then she let them down by a rope
through the window, for her house was on
the city wall, so that she was living on the
wall. 16 And she said to them, “Go to the
hill country, lest the pursuers reach you.
And hide yourselves there for three days
until the pursuers return. Then afterward
you may go on your way.” 17 And the men
said to her, “We *shall be* free from this oath
to you which you have made us swear,
18 unless, when we come into the land, you
tie this cord of scarlet thread in the window
through which you let us down, and gather
to yourself into the house your father and
your mother and your brothers and all
your father’s household. 19 And it will be
that anyone who goes out of the doors of
your house into the street, his blood *shall
be* on his own head, and we *shall be* free;
but anyone who is with you in the house,
his blood *shall be* on our head if a hand is
laid on him. 20 But if you tell this business
of ours, then we shall be free from the oath
which you have made us swear.” 21 And she
said, “According to your words, so be it.” So
she sent them away, and they went; and she
tied the scarlet cord in the window.

22 And they went and came to the hill
country and remained there for three days

until the pursuers returned. The pursuers had sought *them* all along the road but had not found *them.* 23 Then the two men returned and came down from the hill country and crossed over and came to Joshua the son of Nun, and they recounted to him all that had happened to them. 24 And they said to Joshua, "Surely Yahweh has given all the land into our hands; moreover, all the inhabitants of the land have melted away before us."

Psalm 41:1–13

1 How blessed is he who
considers the poor;
Yahweh will provide him escape
in a day of calamity.
2 Yahweh will keep him and
keep him alive,
And he shall be blessed upon the earth;
And do not give him over to
the desire of his enemies.
3 Yahweh will sustain him
upon his sickbed;
In his illness, You restore him to health.

4 As for me, I said, "O Yahweh,
be gracious to me;
Heal my soul, for I have
sinned against You."
5 My enemies speak evil against me,
"When will he die, and his
name perish?"
6 And when he comes to see *me*,
he speaks worthlessness;
His heart gathers wickedness to itself;
When he goes outside, he speaks it.
7 All who hate me whisper
together against me;
Against me, they devise for
me calamity, *saying*,
8 "A vile thing is poured out upon him,
That when he lies down, he
will not rise up again."
9 Even my close friend in
whom I trusted,
Who ate my bread,
Has lifted up his heel against me.

10 But You, O Yahweh, be gracious
to me and raise me up,
That I may repay them.
11 By this I know that You delight in me,
Because my enemy makes no
shout in triumph over me.
12 As for me, You uphold me
in my integrity,
And You make me stand firm
in Your presence forever.

13 Blessed be Yahweh, the God of Israel,
From everlasting to everlasting.
Amen and Amen.

Proverbs 13:15–16

15 Good insight gives grace,
But the way of the treacherous
is unrelenting.
16 Every prudent man acts
with knowledge,
But a fool spreads out folly.

Luke 8:26–56

26 Then they sailed to the region of the
Gerasenes, which is opposite Galilee. 27 And
when He came out onto the land, a man
from the city met Him, one who was possessed with demons and had not put on any
garment for a long time, and was not living
in a house, but in the tombs. 28 Now seeing
Jesus, he cried out and fell before Him, and
said in a loud voice, "What do I have to do
with You, Jesus, Son of the Most High God?
I beg You, do not torment me." 29 For He
had commanded the unclean spirit to come
out of the man. For it had seized him many
times, and he was bound with chains and
shackles, being kept under guard. And *yet*
breaking his bonds, he was driven by the
demon into the desolate regions. 30 And
Jesus asked him, "What is your name?"
And he said, "Legion," for many demons
had entered him. 31 And they were pleading
with Him not to command them to go away
into the abyss.

32 Now there was a herd of many swine
feeding there on the mountain, and *the
demons* pleaded with Him to permit them
to enter the swine. And He gave them permission. 33 And when the demons came out
of the man, they entered the swine, and the
herd rushed down the steep bank into the
lake and was drowned.

34 And when the herdsmen saw what had
happened, they ran away and reported it in
the city and in the countryside. 35 And *the
people* went out to see what had happened,
and they came to Jesus, and found the man
from whom the demons had gone out, sitting down at the feet of Jesus, clothed and in

his right mind. And they were afraid. 36 And those who had seen *it* reported to them how the man who was demon-possessed had been saved. 37 And all the people of the country of the Gerasenes and the surrounding district asked Him to leave them, for they were gripped with great fear. And He got into a boat and returned. 38 But the man from whom the demons had gone out was begging Him that he might accompany Him. But He sent him away, saying, 39 "Return to your house and recount what great things God has done for you." So he went away, proclaiming throughout the whole city what great things Jesus had done for him.

40 And as Jesus returned, the crowd welcomed Him, for they had all been waiting for Him. 41 And behold, there came a man named Jairus, and he was an official of the synagogue. And falling at Jesus' feet, he *began to* plead with Him to come to his house, 42 for he had an only daughter, about twelve years old, and she was dying. But as He went, the crowds were pressing against Him.

43 And a woman who had a hemorrhage for twelve years, and could not be healed by anyone, 44 came up behind Him and touched the fringe of His garment, and immediately her hemorrhage stopped. 45 And Jesus said, "Who is the one who touched Me?" And while they were all denying it, Peter said, "Master, the crowds are surrounding and pressing in on You." 46 But Jesus said, "Someone did touch Me, for I knew that power had gone out of Me." 47 And when the woman saw that she had not escaped notice, she came trembling. And falling down before Him, she declared in the presence of all the people the reason why she had touched Him and how she had been immediately healed. 48 And He said to her, "Daughter, your faith has saved you; go in peace."

49 While He was still speaking, someone *came from *the house of* the synagogue official, saying, "Your daughter has died; do not trouble the Teacher anymore." 50 But when Jesus heard *this,* He answered him, "Do not be afraid *any longer*; only believe, and she will be saved." 51 So when He came to the house, He did not allow anyone to enter with Him, except Peter and John and James, and the girl's father and mother. 52 Now they were all crying and lamenting for her, but He said, "Stop crying, for she has not died, but is asleep." 53 And they *began* laughing at Him, knowing that she had died. 54 He, however, took her by the hand and called, saying, "Child, arise!" 55 And her spirit returned, and she stood up immediately. And He gave orders for *something* to be given her to eat. 56 And her parents were astounded, but He directed them to tell no one what had happened.

APRIL 7

Joshua 3:1–4:24

3 Then Joshua rose early in the morning; and he and all the sons of Israel set out from Shittim and came to the Jordan, and they lodged there before they crossed. 2 Now it happened that at the end of three days the officers went through the midst of the camp; 3 and they commanded the people, saying, "When you see the ark of the covenant of Yahweh your God with the Levitical priests carrying it, then you shall set out from your place and go after it. 4 However, there shall be between you and it a distance of about 2,000 cubits by measure. Do not come near it, that you may know the way by which you shall go, for you have not passed this way before."

5 Then Joshua said to the people, "Set yourselves apart as holy, for tomorrow Yahweh will do wondrous deeds among you." 6 And Joshua spoke to the priests, saying, "Carry the ark of the covenant and cross over ahead of the people." So they carried the ark of the covenant and went ahead of the people.

7 Then Yahweh said to Joshua, "This day I will begin to magnify you in the sight of all Israel, that they may know that just as I have been with Moses, I will be with you. 8 Moreover, you shall command the priests who are carrying the ark of the covenant, saying, 'When you come to the edge of the waters of the Jordan, you shall stand *still* in the Jordan.'" 9 Then Joshua said to the sons of Israel, "Come near, and hear the words of Yahweh your God." 10 And Joshua said, "By this you shall know that the living God is among you, and that He will assuredly

dispossess from before you the Canaanite,
the Hittite, the Hivite, the Perizzite, the
Girgashite, the Amorite, and the Jebusite.
11 Behold, the ark of the covenant of the
Lord of all the earth is crossing over ahead
of you into the Jordan. 12 So now, take for
yourselves twelve men from the tribes of
Israel, one man for each tribe. 13 And it will
be that when the soles of the feet of the
priests who carry the ark of Yahweh, the
Lord of all the earth, rest in the waters of
the Jordan, the waters of the Jordan will be
cut off, *and* the waters which are flowing
down from above will stand in one heap."

14 So it happened that when the people
set out from their tents to cross the Jordan
with the priests carrying the ark of the cov-
enant before the people, 15 and when those
who carried the ark came into the Jordan,
and the feet of the priests carrying the ark
were dipped in the edge of the water (for the
Jordan overflows all its banks all the days of
harvest), 16 the waters which were flowing
down from above stood *and* rose up in one
heap, a great distance away at Adam, the city
that is beside Zarethan; and those which
were flowing down toward the sea of the
Arabah, the Salt Sea, were completely cut
off. So the people crossed opposite Jericho.
17 And the priests who carried the ark of
the covenant of Yahweh stood firm on dry
ground in the middle of the Jordan while
all Israel crossed on dry ground until all the
nation had completed crossing the Jordan.

4 Now it happened when all the nation
had completed crossing the Jordan, that
Yahweh spoke to Joshua, saying, 2 "Take for
yourselves twelve men from the people,
one man from each tribe, 3 and command
them, saying, 'Carry for yourselves twelve
stones from here out of the middle of the
Jordan, from the place where the priests'
feet are standing firm, and carry them over
with you and lay them down in the lodging
place where you will lodge tonight.'" 4 So
Joshua called the twelve men whom he had
appointed from the sons of Israel, one man
from each tribe; 5 and Joshua said to them,
"Cross again before the ark of Yahweh your
God into the middle of the Jordan, and each
of you carry a stone on his shoulder, accord-
ing to the number of the tribes of the sons
of Israel, 6 in order that this would be a sign
among you, so that when your children ask
later, saying, 'What do these stones mean to
you?' 7 then you shall say to them, 'Because
the waters of the Jordan were cut off before
the ark of the covenant of Yahweh; when it
crossed the Jordan, the waters of the Jordan
were cut off.' So these stones shall become
a memorial to the sons of Israel forever."

8 Thus the sons of Israel did as Joshua
commanded and carried twelve stones from
the middle of the Jordan, just as Yahweh
spoke to Joshua, according to the number
of the tribes of the sons of Israel; and they
carried them over with them to the lodging
place and laid them down there. 9 But Joshua
set up twelve stones in the middle of the
Jordan at the place where the feet of the
priests who carried the ark of the covenant
were standing, and they are there to this day.
10 Now the priests who carried the ark were
standing in the middle of the Jordan until
everything was completed that Yahweh had
commanded Joshua to speak to the people,
according to all that Moses had commanded
Joshua. And the people hurried and crossed.
11 And it happened when all the people
had completed crossing, that the ark of
Yahweh and the priests crossed before the
people. 12 And the sons of Reuben and the
sons of Gad and the half-tribe of Manasseh
crossed over in battle array before the sons
of Israel, just as Moses had spoken to them;
13 about 40,000 equipped for war crossed
for battle before Yahweh to the desert plains
of Jericho.

14 On that day, Yahweh magnified Joshua
in the sight of all Israel, so that they feared
him, just as they had feared Moses all the
days of his life.

15 Then Yahweh said to Joshua, 16 "Com-
mand the priests who carry the ark of the
testimony that they come up from the Jor-
dan." 17 So Joshua commanded the priests,
saying, "Come up from the Jordan." 18 So
it happened when the priests who carried
the ark of the covenant of Yahweh had come
up from the middle of the Jordan, and the
soles of the priests' feet were lifted up to the
dry ground, that the waters of the Jordan
returned to their place and went over all its
banks as before.

19 Now the people came up from the
Jordan on the tenth of the first month and
camped at Gilgal on the eastern edge of
Jericho. 20 And those twelve stones which
they had taken from the Jordan, Joshua

set up at Gilgal. 21 Then he said to the sons
of Israel, "When your children ask their
fathers in time to come, saying, 'What do
these stones mean?' 22 then you shall make
your children know, saying, 'Israel crossed
this Jordan on dry land.' 23 For Yahweh your
God dried up the waters of the Jordan before
you until you had crossed, just as Yahweh
your God had done to the Red Sea, which
He dried up before us until we had crossed,
24 that all the peoples of the earth may know
that the hand of Yahweh is strong, so that
you may fear Yahweh your God forever."

Psalm 42:1–5

1 As the deer pants for the water brooks,
So my soul pants for You, O God.
2 My soul thirsts for God,
for the living God;
When shall I come and
appear before God?
3 My tears have been my
food day and night,
While *they* say to me all day
long, "Where is your God?"
4 These things I remember and I
pour out my soul within me.
For I used to go along with the
throng *and* lead them in
procession to the house of God,
With the sound of a shout
of joy and thanksgiving, a
multitude keeping festival.

5 Why are you in despair, O my soul?
And *why* are you disturbed within me?
Wait for God, for I shall
still praise Him,
For the salvation of His presence.

Proverbs 13:17–18

17 A wicked messenger falls into evil,
But a faithful envoy *brings* healing.
18 Poverty and disgrace *come* to him
who neglects discipline,
But he who keeps reproof
will be honored.

Luke 9:1–17

9 And calling the twelve together, He gave
them power and authority over all the
demons and to heal diseases. 2 And He sent
them out to preach the kingdom of God and
to heal the sick. 3 And He said to them, "Take
nothing for *your* journey, neither a staff, nor
a bag, nor bread, nor money; nor have two
tunics apiece. 4 And whatever house you
enter, stay there until you leave that city.
5 And as for those who do not receive you,
as you go out from that city, shake the dust
off your feet as a testimony against them."
6 And departing, they were going through-
out the villages, proclaiming the gospel and
healing everywhere.

7 Now Herod the tetrarch heard of all
that was happening, and he was greatly
perplexed, because it was said by some
that John had risen from the dead, 8 and
by some that Elijah had appeared, and by
others that one of the prophets of old had
risen again. 9 And Herod said, "I myself had
John beheaded, but who is this man about
whom I hear such things?" And he kept
trying to see Him.

10 And when the apostles returned, they
recounted to Him all that they had done.
Taking them with Him, He slipped away by
Himself to a city called Bethsaida. 11 But
when the crowds became aware of this, they
followed Him; and welcoming them, He
began speaking to them about the kingdom
of God and curing those who had need of
healing.

12 Now the day was ending, and the
twelve came and said to Him, "Send the
crowd away, that they may go into the
surrounding villages and countryside and
obtain lodging and find provisions, for here
we are in a desolate place." 13 But He said to
them, "You give them *something* to eat!" And
they said, "We have no more than five loaves
and two fish, unless perhaps we go and buy
food for all these people." 14 (For there were
about five thousand men.) And He said to
His disciples, "Have them sit down in groups
of about fifty each." 15 And they did so, and
had them all sit down. 16 Then He took the
five loaves and the two fish, and looking up
to heaven, He blessed them. And He broke
them and kept giving *them* to the disciples
to set before the crowd. 17 And they all ate
and were satisfied; and the broken pieces
which they had left over were picked up,
twelve baskets *full*.

APRIL 8

Joshua 5:1–6:27

5 Now it happened when all the kings of the Amorites who *were* beyond the Jordan to the west, and all the kings of the Canaanites who *were* by the sea, heard how Yahweh had dried up the waters of the Jordan before the sons of Israel until they had crossed, that their hearts melted, and there was no spirit in them any longer because of the sons of Israel.

2 At that time Yahweh said to Joshua, "Make for yourself flint knives and circumcise again the sons of Israel the second time." 3 So Joshua made himself flint knives and circumcised the sons of Israel at Gibeath-haaraloth. 4 Now this is the reason why Joshua circumcised them: all the people who came out of Egypt who were males, all the men of war, died in the wilderness along the way when they came out of Egypt. 5 For all the people who came out were circumcised, but all the people who were born in the wilderness along the way as they came out of Egypt had not been circumcised. 6 For the sons of Israel had walked forty years in the wilderness, until all the nation, *that is*, the men of war who came out of Egypt, were completely *destroyed* because they did not listen to the voice of Yahweh, to whom Yahweh had sworn that He would not let them see the land which Yahweh had sworn to their fathers to give us, a land flowing with milk and honey. 7 And their sons whom He raised up in their place, Joshua circumcised; for they were uncircumcised because they had not circumcised them along the way.

8 Now it happened that when they had completed circumcising all the nation, they remained in their places in the camp until they were healed. 9 Then Yahweh said to Joshua, "Today I have rolled away the reproach of Egypt from you." So the name of that place is called Gilgal to this day.

10 Then the sons of Israel camped at Gilgal and celebrated the Passover on the evening of the fourteenth day of the month on the desert plains of Jericho. 11 And on the day after the Passover, on that very day, they ate some of the yield of the land, unleavened cakes and roasted *grain*. 12 Then the manna ceased on the day after they had eaten some of the produce of the land, so that the sons of Israel no longer had manna, but they ate some of the produce of the land of Canaan during that year.

13 Now it happened when Joshua was by Jericho, that he lifted up his eyes and looked, and behold, a man was standing opposite him with his sword drawn in his hand, and Joshua went to him and said to him, "Are you for us or for our adversaries?" 14 He said, "No! Rather I indeed come now *as* commander of the host of Yahweh." And Joshua fell on his face to the earth and bowed down and said to him, "What has my lord to say to his slave?" 15 The commander of the host of Yahweh said to Joshua, "Remove your sandals from your feet, for the place where you are standing is holy." And Joshua did so.

6 Now Jericho was tightly shut because of the sons of Israel; no one went out, and no one came in. 2 And Yahweh said to Joshua, "See, I have given Jericho into your hand, with its king *and* the valiant warriors. 3 And you shall march around the city, all the men of war circling the city once. You shall do so for six days. 4 Also seven priests shall carry seven trumpets of rams' horns before the ark; then on the seventh day you shall march around the city seven times, and the priests shall blow the trumpets. 5 And it will be that when they make a long blast with the ram's horn, and when you hear the sound of the trumpet, all the people shall shout with a great shout; and the wall of the city will fall down beneath itself, and the people will go up every man straight ahead."

6 So Joshua the son of Nun called the priests and said to them, "Carry the ark of the covenant, and let seven priests carry seven trumpets of rams' horns before the ark of Yahweh." 7 Then he said to the people, "Go forward, and march around the city, and let the armed men go on before the ark of Yahweh." 8 And so it happened that, when Joshua had spoken to the people, the seven priests carrying the seven trumpets of rams' horns before Yahweh passed on *forward* and blew the trumpets; and the ark of the covenant of Yahweh came after them. 9 And the armed men went before the priests who blew the trumpets, and the rear guard came after the ark, while they continued to blow

the trumpets. 10 But Joshua commanded the people, saying, "You shall not shout nor let your voice be heard nor let a word proceed out of your mouth, until the day I tell you, 'Shout!' Then you shall shout!" 11 So he had the ark of Yahweh taken around the city, circling *it* once; then they came into the camp and spent the night in the camp.

12 Then Joshua rose early in the morning, and the priests carried the ark of Yahweh. 13 And the seven priests carrying the seven trumpets of rams' horns before the ark of Yahweh went on continually and blew the trumpets; and the armed men went before them, and the rear guard came after the ark of Yahweh, and they continued to blow the trumpets. 14 Thus the second day they marched around the city once and returned to the camp; they did so for six days.

15 Then it happened that on the seventh day they rose early at the breaking of dawn and marched around the city in the same manner seven times; only on that day they marched around the city seven times. 16 Now it happened that on the seventh time, the priests blew the trumpets, and Joshua said to the people, "Shout! For Yahweh has given you the city. 17 And the city shall be devoted to destruction, it and all that is in it belongs to Yahweh; only Rahab the harlot and all who are with her in the house shall live because she hid the messengers whom we sent. 18 But as for you, only keep yourselves from the things devoted to destruction, lest *as* you are devoting *them* to destruction, you also take some of the things devoted to destruction and make the camp of Israel devoted to destruction and bring trouble on it. 19 But all the silver and gold and articles of bronze and iron are holy to Yahweh; they shall go into the treasury of Yahweh." 20 So the people shouted, and *the priests* blew the trumpets; and when the people heard the sound of the trumpet, the people shouted with a great shout, and the wall fell down beneath itself, so that the people went up into the city, every man straight ahead, and they took the city. 21 And they devoted to destruction everything in the city, both man and woman, young and old, and ox and sheep and donkey, with the edge of the sword.

22 Now to the two men who had spied out the land, Joshua said, "Go into the harlot's house and bring the woman and all she has out of there, as you have sworn to her." 23 So the young men who were spies went in and brought out Rahab and her father and her mother and her brothers and all she had; they also brought out all her relatives and placed them outside the camp of Israel. 24 But they burned the city with fire, and all that was in it. Only the silver and gold, and articles of bronze and iron, they put into the treasury of the house of Yahweh. 25 However, Rahab the harlot and her father's household and all she had, Joshua preserved alive; and she has lived in the midst of Israel to this day, for she hid the messengers whom Joshua sent to spy out Jericho.

26 Then Joshua made them swear *an oath* at that time, saying, "Cursed before Yahweh is the man who rises up and builds this city Jericho; with *the loss of* his firstborn he shall lay its foundation, and with *the loss of* his youngest son he shall set up its gates." 27 So Yahweh was with Joshua, and the report about him was in all the land.

Psalm 42:6–11

6 O my God, my soul is in
despair within me;
Therefore I remember You from
the land of the Jordan
And the peaks of Hermon,
from Mount Mizar.
7 Deep calls to deep at the sound
of Your waterfalls;
All Your breakers and Your
waves have rolled over me.
8 By day, Yahweh will command
His lovingkindness;
And by night, His song will be with me,
A prayer to the God of my life.

9 I say to God my rock, "Why
have You forgotten me?
Why do I go mourning because of
the oppression of the enemy?"
10 As a shattering of my bones, my
adversaries reproach me,
While they say to me all day
long, "Where is your God?"
11 Why are you in despair, O my soul?
And why are you disturbed within me?
Wait for God, for I shall
still praise Him,
The salvation of my presence
and my God.

Proverbs 13:19–21

19 Desire realized is pleasant to the soul,
But it is an abomination to fools
to turn away from evil.
20 He who walks with the
wise will be wise,
But the friend of fools will suffer harm.
21 Evil pursues sinners,
But the righteous are repaid with good.

Luke 9:18–36

18 And it happened that while He was
praying alone, the disciples were with Him,
and He questioned them, saying, “Who
do the crowds say that I am?” 19 And they
answered and said, “John the Baptist, and
others *say* Elijah, but others, that one of
the prophets of old has risen again.” 20 And
He said to them, “But who do you say that
I am?” And Peter answered and said, “The
Christ of God.” 21 But He warned them and
directed *them* not to tell this to anyone,
22 saying, “The Son of Man must suffer
many things and be rejected by the elders
and chief priests and scribes, and be killed
and be raised up on the third day.”
23 And He was saying to *them* all, “If
anyone wishes to come after Me, let him
deny himself, and take up his cross daily and
follow Me. 24 For whoever wishes to save his
life will lose it, but whoever loses his life
for My sake, he is the one who will save it.
25 For what is a man profited if he gains the
whole world, and loses or forfeits himself?
26 For whoever is ashamed of Me and My
words, the Son of Man will be ashamed of
him when He comes in His glory, and *the
glory* of the Father and of the holy angels.
27 But I say to you truthfully, there are some
of those standing here who will not taste
death until they see the kingdom of God.”
28 Now it happened some eight days
after these words, that taking along Peter
and John and James, He went up on the
mountain to pray. 29 And it happened that
while He was praying, the appearance of
His face became different, and His clothing
became white *and* gleaming. 30 And behold,
two men were talking with Him, and they
were Moses and Elijah, 31 who, appearing
in glory, were speaking of His departure
which He was about to fulfill at Jerusalem.
32 Now Peter and his companions had been
overcome with sleep, but when they were
fully awake, they saw His glory and the two
men standing with Him. 33 And it happened
that as they were leaving Him, Peter said to
Jesus, “Master, it is good for us to be here;
let us make three booths: one for You, and
one for Moses, and one for Elijah”—not
realizing what he was saying. 34 While he
was saying this, a cloud formed and *began
to* overshadow them; and they were afraid
as they entered the cloud. 35 Then a voice
came out of the cloud, saying, “This is My
Son, *My* Chosen One; listen to Him!” 36 And
when the voice had spoken, Jesus was found
alone. And they kept silent, and reported to
no one in those days any of the things which
they had seen.

---

*The Bible does not explain everything for our intellectual satisfaction,
but it explains everything necessary for our obedience
and hence for God’s satisfaction.*

— ELIZABETH ELLIOT

APRIL 9

Joshua 7:1–8:35

7 But the sons of Israel acted unfaithfully
in regard to the things devoted to
destruction. Achan, the son of Carmi, the
son of Zabdi, the son of Zerah, from the
tribe of Judah, took some of the devoted
things; therefore the anger of Yahweh
burned against the sons of Israel.
2 Now Joshua sent men from Jericho to
Ai, which is near Beth-aven, east of Bethel,
and said to them, “Go up and spy out the
land.” So the men went up and spied out
Ai. 3 Then they returned to Joshua and said
to him, “Do not have all the people go up;
only about two or three thousand men need
go up to strike down Ai; do not have all the

people toil up there, for they are few." 4 So
about three thousand men from the people
went up there, but they fled from the men of
Ai. 5 And the men of Ai struck down about
thirty-six of their men and pursued them
from the gate as far as Shebarim and struck
them down on the descent, so the hearts
of the people melted and became as water.
6 Then Joshua tore his clothes and fell
to the earth on his face before the ark of
Yahweh until the evening, *both* he and the
elders of Israel; and they put dust on their
heads. 7 Joshua said, "Alas, O Lord Yahweh,
why did You ever bring this people over
the Jordan, *only* to give us into the hand
of the Amorites, to make us perish? If
only we had been willing to live beyond
the Jordan! 8 O Lord, what can I say since
Israel has turned *their* back before their
enemies? 9 And the Canaanites and all the
inhabitants of the land will hear of it, and
they will surround us and cut off our name
from the earth. And what will You do for
Your great name?"
10 So Yahweh said to Joshua, "Rise up!
Why is it that you have fallen on your
face? 11 Israel has sinned, and they have
also trespassed against My covenant
which I commanded them. And they have
even taken some of the things devoted
to destruction and have both stolen and
dealt falsely. Moreover, they have also put
them among their own things. 12 Therefore
the sons of Israel cannot rise before their
enemies; they turn *their* backs before their
enemies, for they have become devoted to
destruction. I will not be with you anymore
unless you destroy the things devoted to
destruction from your midst. 13 Rise up! Set
the people apart as holy and say, 'Set your-
selves apart as holy for tomorrow, for thus
Yahweh, the God of Israel, has said, "There
are things devoted to destruction in your
midst, O Israel. You cannot rise before your
enemies until you have removed the things
devoted to destruction from your midst."
14 In the morning then you shall come near
by your tribes. And it will be that the tribe
which Yahweh takes *by lot* shall come near
by families, and the family which Yahweh
takes shall come near by households, and
the household which Yahweh takes shall
come near man by man. 15 And it will be
that the one who is taken with the things
devoted to destruction shall be burned with
fire, he and all that belongs to him, because
he has trespassed against the covenant of
Yahweh, and because he has committed a
disgraceful thing in Israel.'"
16 So Joshua arose early in the morning
and brought Israel near by tribes, and the
tribe of Judah was taken. 17 And he brought
the family of Judah near, and he took the
family of the Zerahites; and he brought the
family of the Zerahites near man by man,
and Zabdi was taken. 18 And he brought his
household near man by man; and Achan,
son of Carmi, son of Zabdi, son of Zerah,
from the tribe of Judah, was taken. 19 Then
Joshua said to Achan, "My son, I implore
you, give glory to Yahweh, the God of Israel,
and give praise to Him; and declare to me
now what you have done. Do not hide it
from me." 20 So Achan answered Joshua and
said, "Truly, I have sinned against Yahweh,
the God of Israel, and this is what I did: 21 I
saw among the spoil a beautiful mantle from
Shinar and two hundred shekels of silver
and a bar of gold fifty shekels in weight; then
I coveted them and took them; and behold,
they are concealed in the earth inside my
tent with the silver underneath it."
22 So Joshua sent messengers, and they
ran to the tent; and behold, it was concealed
in his tent with the silver underneath it.
23 And they took them from inside the tent
and brought them to Joshua and to all the
sons of Israel, and they poured them out
before Yahweh. 24 Then Joshua and all Israel
with him, took Achan the son of Zerah, the
silver, the mantle, the bar of gold, his sons,
his daughters, his oxen, his donkeys, his
sheep, his tent, and all that belonged to him;
and they brought them up to the valley of
Achor. 25 And Joshua said, "Why have you
troubled us? Yahweh will trouble you this
day." And all Israel stoned him with stones;
and they burned them with fire after they
had stoned them with stones. 26 Then they
raised over him a great heap of stones that
stands to this day, and Yahweh turned from
His burning anger. Therefore the name of
that place has been called the valley of
Achor to this day.

8 Now Yahweh said to Joshua, "Do not fear
or be dismayed. Take all the people of
war with you and arise, go up to Ai; see, I
have given into your hand the king of Ai,
his people, his city, and his land. 2 So you

shall do to Ai and its king just as you did to
Jericho and its king; you shall take only its
spoil and its cattle as plunder for yourselves.
Set an ambush for the city behind it."
3 So Joshua rose with all the people of
war to go up to Ai; and Joshua chose 30,000
men, valiant warriors, and sent them out at
night. 4 And he commanded them, saying,
"See, you are going to ambush the city from
behind it. Do not go very far from the city,
but all of you be ready. 5 Then I and all the
people who are with me will come near the
city. And it will be that when they come out
to meet us as at the first, we will flee before
them. 6 And they will come out after us until
we have drawn them away from the city, for
they will say, '*They* are fleeing before us as at
the first.' So we will flee before them. 7 And
you shall rise from *your* ambush and take
possession of the city, for Yahweh your God
will give it into your hand. 8 Then it will be
that when you have seized the city, that
you shall set the city on fire. You shall do
it according to the word of Yahweh. See, I
have commanded you." 9 So Joshua sent
them away, and they went to the place of
ambush and remained between Bethel and
Ai, on the west side of Ai; but Joshua spent
that night among the people.
10 Now Joshua rose early in the morning
and mustered the people, and he went up
with the elders of Israel before the people
to Ai. 11 Then all the people of war who *were*
with him went up and drew near and arrived
in front of the city and camped on the north
side of Ai. Now *there was* a valley between
him and Ai. 12 And he took about 5,000 men
and set them in ambush between Bethel and
Ai, on the west side of the city. 13 So they
set the people, all the army that was on the
north side of the city, and its rear guard on
the west side of the city, and Joshua went
that night into the midst of the valley. 14 Now
it happened that when the king of Ai saw *it*,
the men of the city hurried and rose up early
and went out to meet Israel in battle, he and
all his people at the appointed place before
the desert plain. But he did not know that
there was an ambush against him behind the
city. 15 And Joshua and all Israel pretended
to be beaten before them and fled by the
way of the wilderness. 16 And all the people
who were in the city were called together to
pursue them, and they pursued Joshua and
were drawn away from the city. 17 So not a
man remained in Ai or Bethel who had not
gone out after Israel, and they forsook the
city, *leaving it* open, and pursued Israel.
18 Then Yahweh said to Joshua, "Stretch
out the javelin that is in your hand toward Ai,
for I will give it into your hand." So Joshua
stretched out the javelin that was in his hand
toward the city. 19 Then the *men in* ambush
rose quickly from their place, and when he
had stretched out his hand, they ran and
entered the city and captured it, and they
quickly set the city on fire. 20 Then the men
of Ai turned back and looked, and behold,
the smoke of the city ascended to the sky,
and they had no place to flee this way or
that, for the people who had been fleeing to
the wilderness turned against the pursuers.
21 But Joshua and all Israel saw that the *men
in* ambush had captured the city and that
the smoke of the city ascended. So they
turned back and struck down the men of
Ai. 22 And the others came out from the city
to meet them, so that they were *trapped* in
the midst of Israel, some on this side and
some on that side; and they struck them
down until there was no one remaining for
him who survived or escaped. 23 But they
seized the king of Ai alive and brought him
to Joshua.
24 Now it happened that when Israel had
finished killing all the inhabitants of Ai in
the field in the wilderness where they pur-
sued them, and all of them fell by the edge
of the sword until they were completely
destroyed, then all Israel turned back to Ai
and struck it with the edge of the sword.
25 So all who fell that day, both men and
women, were 12,000—all the people of Ai.
26 For Joshua did not withdraw his hand
with which he stretched out the javelin
until he had devoted to destruction all the
inhabitants of Ai. 27 Israel took only the
cattle and the spoil of that city as plunder
for themselves, according to the word of
Yahweh which He had commanded Joshua.
28 So Joshua burned Ai and made it a heap
forever, a desolation until this day. 29 And
he hanged the king of Ai on a tree until eve-
ning; and at sunset Joshua gave a command,
and they took his body down from the tree
and threw it at the entrance of the city gate
and raised over it a great heap of stones *that
stands* to this day.
30 Then Joshua built an altar to Yahweh,
the God of Israel, on Mount Ebal, 31 just

as Moses the servant of Yahweh had com-
manded the sons of Israel, as it is written
in the book of the law of Moses, an altar of
uncut stones on which no man had wielded
an iron *tool*; and they offered burnt offer-
ings on it to Yahweh and sacrificed peace
offerings. 32 And he wrote there on the
stones a copy of the law of Moses, which
he had written, in the presence of the sons
of Israel. 33 And all Israel with their elders
and officers and their judges were standing
on both sides of the ark before the Levitical
priests who carried the ark of the covenant
of Yahweh, the sojourner as well as the
native. Half of them *stood* in front of Mount
Gerizim and half of them in front of Mount
Ebal, just as Moses the servant of Yahweh
had given a command at first to bless the
people of Israel. 34 Then afterward he read
all the words of the law, the blessing and
the curse, according to all that is written in
the book of the law. 35 There was not a word
of all that Moses had commanded which
Joshua did not read before all the assembly
of Israel with the women and the little ones
and the sojourners who were going among
them.

Psalm 43:1–5

1 Give justice to me, O God, and plead
my case against an unholy nation;
Oh protect me from the deceitful
and unrighteous man!
2 For You are the God of my strength;
why have You rejected me?
Why do I go mourning because of
the oppression of the enemy?

3 Oh send out Your light and Your
truth, let them lead me;
Let them bring me to Your
holy mountain
And to Your dwelling places.
4 Then I will go to the altar of God,
To God my exceeding joy;
And upon the lyre I shall praise
You, O God, my God.

5 Why are you in despair, O my soul?
And why are you disturbed
within me?
Wait for God, for I shall
still praise Him,
The salvation of my presence
and my God.

Proverbs 13:22–23

22 A good man leaves an inheritance
to his children's children,
And the wealth of the sinner is
stored up for the righteous.
23 Abundant food *is in* the fallow
ground of the poor,
But it is swept away by injustice.

Luke 9:37–62

37 Now it happened on the next day, that
when they came down from the mountain, a
large crowd met Him. 38 And behold, a man
from the crowd shouted, saying, "Teacher, I
beg You to look at my son, for he is my only
one, 39 and behold, a spirit seizes him, and
he suddenly screams, and it throws him into
a convulsion with foaming *at the mouth*,
and only with difficulty does it leave him,
mauling him *as it leaves*. 40 And I begged
Your disciples to cast it out, and they could
not." 41 And Jesus answered and said, "You
unbelieving and perverse generation, how
long shall I be with you and put up with
you? Bring your son here." 42 Now while he
was still approaching, the demon slammed
him *to the ground* and threw him into a
convulsion. But Jesus rebuked the unclean
spirit and healed the boy and gave him back
to his father. 43 And they were all astonished
at the majesty of God.

But while everyone was marveling at all
that He was doing, He said to His disciples,
44 "Put these words into your ears; for the
Son of Man is going to be delivered into the
hands of men." 45 But they did not under-
stand this statement, and it was concealed
from them so that they would not perceive
it, and they were afraid to ask Him about
this statement.

46 Now an argument started among them
as to which of them might be the greatest.
47 But Jesus, knowing what they were think-
ing in their heart, took a child and stood him
by His side, 48 and said to them, "Whoever
receives this child in My name receives Me,
and whoever receives Me receives Him who
sent Me; for the one who is least among all
of you, this is the one who is great."

49 And John answered and said, "Master,
we saw someone casting out demons in Your
name, and we tried to hinder him because
he does not follow along with us." 50 But
Jesus said to him, "Do not hinder *him*, for
he who is not against you is for you."

51 Now it happened that when the days for Him to be taken up were soon to be fulfilled, He set His face to go to Jerusalem; 52 and He sent messengers on ahead of Him, and they went and entered a village of the Samaritans to make arrangements for Him. 53 But they did not receive Him, because He was journeying with His face toward Jerusalem. 54 And when His disciples James and John saw *this*, they said, "Lord, do You want us to command fire to come down from heaven and consume them?" 55 But He turned and rebuked them, [and said, "You do not know what kind of spirit you are of, 56 for the Son of Man did not come to destroy men's lives, but to save them."] And they went on to another village.

57 And as they were going along the road, someone said to Him, "I will follow You wherever You go." 58 And Jesus said to him, "The foxes have holes and the birds of the air *have* nests, but the Son of Man has nowhere to lay His head." 59 And He said to another, "Follow Me." But he said, "Lord, permit me first to go and bury my father." 60 But He said to him, "Allow the dead to bury their own dead; but as for you, go and proclaim everywhere the kingdom of God." 61 Another also said, "I will follow You, Lord, but first permit me to say farewell to those at home." 62 But Jesus said to him, "No one, after putting his hand to the plow and looking back, is fit for the kingdom of God."

APRIL 10

Joshua 9:1–10:43

9 Now it happened when all the kings who were beyond the Jordan, in the hill country and in the Shephelah and on all the coast of the Great Sea toward Lebanon, the Hittite and the Amorite, the Canaanite, the Perizzite, the Hivite and the Jebusite, heard of it, 2 that they gathered themselves together with one accord to fight with Joshua and with Israel.

3 Now the inhabitants of Gibeon heard what Joshua had done to Jericho and to Ai. 4 So they also acted craftily and went and traveled as envoys and took worn-out sacks on their donkeys, and wineskins worn-out and torn and mended, 5 and worn-out and patched sandals on their feet, and worn-out clothes on themselves; and all the bread of their provision *was* dry *and* was crumbled. 6 And they went to Joshua to the camp at Gilgal and said to him and to the men of Israel, "We have come from a far country; so now, cut a covenant with us." 7 Then the men of Israel said to the Hivites, "Perhaps you are living within our land; how then shall we cut a covenant with you?" 8 But they said to Joshua, "We are your servants." Then Joshua said to them, "Who are you and where do you come from?" 9 They said to him, "Your servants have come from a very far country because of the fame of Yahweh your God; for we have heard the report of Him and all that He did in Egypt, 10 and all that He did to the two kings of the Amorites who were beyond the Jordan, to Sihon king of Heshbon and to Og king of Bashan who was at Ashtaroth. 11 So our elders and all the inhabitants of our country spoke to us, saying, 'Take provisions in your hand for the journey, and go to meet them and say to them, "We are your servants; now then, cut a covenant with us."' 12 This bread of ours *was* warm *when* we took it for our provisions out of our houses on the day that we left to come to you; but now behold, it is dry and has become crumbled. 13 And these wineskins which we filled were new, and behold, they are torn; and these clothes of ours and our sandals are worn out because of the very long journey." 14 So the men *of Israel* took some of their provisions, but they did not ask for the command of Yahweh. 15 And Joshua made peace with them and cut a covenant with them, to let them live; and the leaders of the congregation swore *an oath* to them.

16 Now it happened at the end of three days after they had cut a covenant with them, that they heard that they were near them and that they were living nearly among them. 17 Then the sons of Israel set out and came to their cities on the third day. Now their cities *were* Gibeon and Chephirah and Beeroth and Kiriath-jearim. 18 But the sons of Israel did not strike them down because the leaders of the congregation had sworn to them by Yahweh the God of Israel. And the whole congregation grumbled against

the leaders. 19 Then all the leaders said to
the whole congregation, "We have sworn to
them by Yahweh, the God of Israel, so now
we cannot touch them. 20 This we will do
to them, even let them live, so that wrath
will not be upon us for the oath which we
swore to them." 21 So the leaders said to
them, "Let them live." Thus they became
hewers of wood and drawers of water for
the whole congregation, just as the leaders
had spoken to them.

22 Then Joshua called for them and spoke
to them, saying, "Why have you deceived
us, saying, 'We are very far from you,' when
you are living nearly in the midst of us?
23 So now, you are cursed, and you shall
never be cut loose from being slaves, both
hewers of wood and drawers of water for
the house of my God." 24 So they answered
Joshua and said, "Because it was certainly
told to your slaves that Yahweh your God
had commanded His servant Moses to
give you all the land and to destroy all the
inhabitants of the land before you; therefore
we feared greatly for our lives because of you
and have done this thing. 25 So now, behold,
we are in your hands; do as it seems good
and right in your sight to do to us." 26 Thus
he did to them and delivered them from the
hands of the sons of Israel, and they did not
kill them. 27 But Joshua made them that day
hewers of wood and drawers of water for the
congregation and for the altar of Yahweh,
to this day, in the place which He would
choose.

10 Now it happened that when Adoni-
zedek king of Jerusalem heard that
Joshua had captured Ai and had devoted it
to destruction (just as he had done to Jericho
and its king, so he had done to Ai and its
king), and that the inhabitants of Gibeon
had made peace with Israel and were within
their land, 2 they feared exceedingly because
Gibeon *was* a great city, like one of the royal
cities, and because it was greater than Ai, and
all its men *were* mighty. 3 Therefore Adoni-
zedek king of Jerusalem sent *word* to Hoham
king of Hebron and to Piram king of Jarmuth
and to Japhia king of Lachish and to Debir
king of Eglon, saying, 4 "Come up to me and
help me, and let us strike Gibeon, for it has
made peace with Joshua and with the sons
of Israel." 5 So the five kings of the Amorites,
the king of Jerusalem, the king of Hebron, the
king of Jarmuth, the king of Lachish, *and* the
king of Eglon, gathered together and went
up, they with all their armies, and camped
by Gibeon and fought against it.

6 Then the men of Gibeon sent *word* to
Joshua to the camp at Gilgal, saying, "Do not
abandon your slaves; come up to us quickly
and save us and help us, for all the kings
of the Amorites that live in the hill country
have assembled against us." 7 So Joshua
went up from Gilgal, he and all the people
of war with him and all the valiant warriors.
8 And Yahweh said to Joshua, "Do not fear
them, for I have given them into your hands;
not one of them shall stand before you." 9 So
Joshua came upon them suddenly—he had
gone up, *marching* all night from Gilgal.
10 And Yahweh threw them into confusion
before Israel, and He struck them with a
great slaughter at Gibeon and pursued them
by the way of the ascent of Beth-horon and
struck them as far as Azekah and Makkedah.
11 Now it happened as they fled from before
Israel, *while* they were at the descent of
Beth-horon, that Yahweh threw down
large stones from heaven on them as far as
Azekah, and they died; *there were* more who
died from the hailstones than those whom
the sons of Israel killed with the sword.

12 Then Joshua spoke to Yahweh in the
day when Yahweh gave over the Amorites
before the sons of Israel, and he said in the
sight of Israel,

"O sun, stand still at Gibeon,
And O moon in the valley of Aijalon."
13 So the sun stood still, and
the moon stopped,
Until the nation avenged
themselves of their enemies.

Is it not written in the book of Jashar?
And the sun stood in the middle of the sky
and did not hasten to go *down* for about a
whole day. 14 And there was no day like that
before it or after it, when Yahweh listened
to the voice of a man; for Yahweh fought for
Israel.

15 Then Joshua and all Israel with him
returned to the camp to Gilgal.

16 And these five kings fled and hid
themselves in the cave at Makkedah. 17 Then
it was told Joshua, saying, "The five kings
have been found hidden in the cave at
Makkedah." 18 And Joshua said, "Roll large
stones against the mouth of the cave and
assign men by it to keep watch over them,

19 but as for you, do not stand *there*; pursue
your enemies and attack them in the rear.
Do not allow them to enter their cities, for
Yahweh your God has given them into your
hand." 20 Now it happened when Joshua and
the sons of Israel had finished striking them
with a very great slaughter until they were
completely *destroyed*, and the survivors—
those of them *who* survived—had entered
the fortified cities, 21 that all the people
returned to the camp to Joshua at Makkedah
in peace. No one *so much as* lifted his tongue
against any of the sons of Israel.

22 Then Joshua said, "Open the mouth of
the cave and bring these five kings out to me
from the cave." 23 And they did so and brought
these five kings out to him from the cave: the
king of Jerusalem, the king of Hebron, the
king of Jarmuth, the king of Lachish, *and*
the king of Eglon. 24 Now it happened that
when they brought these kings out to Joshua,
Joshua called for all the men of Israel and said
to the chiefs of the men of war who had gone
with him, "Come near, put your feet on the
necks of these kings." So they came near and
put their feet on their necks. 25 Joshua then
said to them, "Do not fear or be dismayed!
Be strong and courageous, for thus Yahweh
will do to all your enemies with whom you
fight." 26 So afterward Joshua struck them and
put them to death, and he hanged them on
five trees; and they hung on the trees until
evening. 27 Now it happened that at sunset
Joshua gave a command, and they took
them down from the trees and threw them
down into the cave where they had hidden
themselves, and they put large stones over
the mouth of the cave, to this very day.

28 Now Joshua captured Makkedah on
that day and struck it and its king with
the edge of the sword; he devoted it to
destruction and every person who was in
it. He left no survivor. Thus he did to the
king of Makkedah just as he had done to
the king of Jericho.

29 Then Joshua and all Israel with him
passed on from Makkedah to Libnah and
fought against Libnah. 30 And Yahweh gave
it also with its king into the hands of Israel,
and he struck it and every person who was
in it with the edge of the sword. He left no
survivor remaining in it. Thus he did to its
king just as he had done to the king of Jericho.

31 And Joshua and all Israel with him
passed on from Libnah to Lachish, and
they camped by it and fought against it.
32 And Yahweh gave Lachish into the hands
of Israel; and he captured it on the second
day and struck it and every person who was
in it with the edge of the sword, according
to all that he had done to Libnah.

33 Then Horam king of Gezer came up to
help Lachish, and Joshua struck him and his
people down until there was no survivor
remaining for him.

34 And Joshua and all Israel with him
passed on from Lachish to Eglon, and they
camped by it and fought against it. 35 And
they captured it on that day and struck it
with the edge of the sword; and every per-
son who was in it, he devoted to destruction
on that day according to all that he had done
to Lachish.

36 Then Joshua and all Israel with him
went up from Eglon to Hebron, and they
fought against it. 37 And they captured it and
struck it and its king and all its cities and all
the persons who *were* in it with the edge of
the sword. He left no survivor remaining,
according to all that he had done to Eglon.
And he devoted it and every person who
was in it to destruction.

38 Then Joshua and all Israel with him
returned to Debir, and they fought against it.
39 And he captured it and its king and all its
cities, and they struck them with the edge
of the sword and devoted every person who
was in it to destruction. He left no survivor
remaining. Just as he had done to Hebron,
so he did to Debir and its king, as he had
also done to Libnah and its king.

40 Thus Joshua struck all the land—the hill
country and the Negev and the Shephelah
and the slopes—as well as all their kings. He
left no survivor remaining, but he devoted to
destruction all who breathed, just as Yahweh,
the God of Israel, had commanded. 41 And
Joshua struck them from Kadesh-barnea
even as far as Gaza, and all the country of
Goshen even as far as Gibeon. 42 And Joshua
captured all these kings and their lands at
one time because Yahweh, the God of Israel,
fought for Israel. 43 So Joshua and all Israel
with him returned to the camp at Gilgal.

Psalm 44:1–3

1 O God, we have heard with our ears,
Our fathers have recounted to us
The work that You did in their days,
In the days of old.

2 You with Your own hand
dispossessed the nations;
Then You planted them;
You afflicted the peoples,
Then You cast them out.
3 For by their own sword they
did not possess the land,
And their own arm did not save them,
But Your right hand and Your arm
and the light of Your presence,
For You favored them.

Proverbs 13:24–25

24 He who holds back his
rod hates his son,
But he who loves him disciplines
him diligently.
25 The righteous eats to the
satisfaction of his soul,
But the stomach of the wicked lacks.

Luke 10:1–24

10 Now after this the Lord appointed
seventy others, and sent them in pairs
ahead of Him to every city and place where
He Himself was going to come. 2 And He was
saying to them, "The harvest is plentiful,
but the laborers are few; therefore pray
earnestly to the Lord of the harvest to send
out laborers into His harvest. 3 Go! Behold, I
send you out as lambs in the midst of wolves.
4 Carry no money belt, no bag, no sandals,
and greet no one on the way. 5 Whatever
house you enter, first say, 'Peace *be* to this
house.' 6 And if a man of peace is there,
your peace will rest on him, but if not, it will
return to you. 7 Stay in that house, eating and
drinking what they give you; for the laborer
is worthy of his wages. Do not keep moving
from house to house. 8 And whatever city
you enter and they receive you, eat what is
set before you; 9 and heal those in it who are
sick, and say to them, 'The kingdom of God
has come near to you.' 10 But in whatever city
you enter and they do not receive you, go out
into its streets and say, 11 'Even the dust of
your city which clings to our feet we wipe off
against you; yet know this, that the kingdom
of God is at hand.' 12 I say to you, it will be
more tolerable in that day for Sodom than
for that city.
13 "Woe to you, Chorazin! Woe to you,
Bethsaida! For if the miracles had been per-
formed in Tyre and Sidon which occurred
in you, they would have repented long
ago, sitting in sackcloth and ashes. 14 But it
will be more tolerable for Tyre and Sidon
in the judgment than for you. 15 And you,
Capernaum, will you be exalted to heaven?
You will be brought down to Hades!
16 "The one who listens to you listens to
Me, and the one who rejects you rejects Me.
And he who rejects Me rejects the One who
sent Me."
17 Now the seventy returned with joy,
saying, "Lord, even the demons are subject
to us in Your name." 18 And He said to them,
"I was watching Satan fall from heaven
like lightning. 19 Behold, I have given you
authority to tread on serpents and scorpi-
ons, and over all the power of the enemy,
and nothing will injure you. 20 Nevertheless
do not rejoice in this, that the spirits are
subject to you, but rejoice that your names
are recorded in heaven."
21 At that very time He rejoiced greatly
in the Holy Spirit, and said, "I praise You,
O Father, Lord of heaven and earth, that
You have hidden these things from *the* wise
and intelligent and have revealed them to
infants. Yes, Father, for this way was well-
pleasing in Your sight. 22 All things have
been handed over to Me by My Father, and
no one knows who the Son is except the
Father, and who the Father is except the
Son, and anyone to whom the Son wills to
reveal *Him*."
23 And turning to the disciples, He said
privately, "Blessed *are* the eyes which see
the things you see, 24 for I say to you, that
many prophets and kings wished to see the
things which you see, and did not see *them*,
and to hear the things which you hear, and
did not hear *them*."

APRIL 11

Joshua 11:1–12:24

11 Now it happened, when Jabin king
of Hazor heard *of it*, that he sent to
Jobab king of Madon and to the king of
Shimron and to the king of Achshaph, 2 and
to the kings who were of the north in the
hill country and in the Arabah—south of
Chinneroth and in the Shephelah and on

the heights of Dor on the west— 3 to the Canaanite on the east and on the west, and the Amorite and the Hittite and the Perizzite and the Jebusite in the hill country, and the Hivite at the foot of Hermon in the land of Mizpeh. 4 Then they came out, they and all their armies with them, *as* many people as the sand that is on the seashore, with very many horses and chariots. 5 So all of these kings agreed to meet, and they came and encamped together at the waters of Merom, to fight against Israel.

6 Then Yahweh said to Joshua, "Do not be afraid because of them, for tomorrow at this time I will give all of them over, slain, before Israel; you shall hamstring their horses and burn their chariots with fire." 7 So Joshua and all the people of war with him came upon them suddenly by the waters of Merom, and they fell upon them. 8 And Yahweh gave them into the hand of Israel, so that they struck them down, and they pursued them as far as Great Sidon and Misrephoth-maim and the valley of Mizpeh to the east; and they struck them until there was no survivor remaining for them. 9 And Joshua did to them as Yahweh had said to him; he hamstrung their horses and burned their chariots with fire.

10 Then Joshua turned back at that time and captured Hazor and struck its king with the sword; for Hazor formerly was the head of all these kingdoms. 11 And they struck every person who was in it with the edge of the sword, devoting *them* to destruction; there was no one left who breathed. And he burned Hazor with fire. 12 And Joshua captured all the cities of these kings and all their kings, and he struck them with the edge of the sword, *and* he devoted them to destruction, just as Moses the servant of Yahweh had commanded. 13 However, Israel did not burn any cities that stood on their mounds, except Hazor alone, *which* Joshua burned. 14 Now all the spoil of these cities and the cattle, the sons of Israel took as their plunder; but *they struck* every man with the edge of the sword until they had destroyed them. They left no one remaining who breathed. 15 Just as Yahweh had commanded Moses His servant, so Moses commanded Joshua, and so Joshua did; he left nothing undone of all that Yahweh had commanded Moses.

16 Thus Joshua took all that land: the hill country and all the Negev, all that land of Goshen, the Shephelah, the Arabah, the hill country of Israel and its Shephelah 17 from Mount Halak, that rises toward Seir, even as far as Baal-gad in the valley of Lebanon at the foot of Mount Hermon. And he captured all their kings and struck them down and put them to death. 18 Joshua waged war a long time with all these kings. 19 There was not a city which made peace with the sons of Israel except the Hivites living in Gibeon; they took them all in battle. 20 For it was of Yahweh to strengthen their hearts, to meet Israel in battle in order that he might devote them to destruction, that they might receive no mercy, but that he might destroy them, just as Yahweh had commanded Moses.

21 Then Joshua came at that time and cut off the Anakim from the hill country, from Hebron, from Debir, from Anab and from all the hill country of Judah and from all the hill country of Israel. Joshua devoted them to destruction with their cities. 22 There were no Anakim left in the land of the sons of Israel; only in Gaza, in Gath, and in Ashdod some remained. 23 So Joshua took the whole land, according to all that Yahweh had spoken to Moses, and Joshua gave it for an inheritance to Israel according to their divisions by their tribes. Thus the land was quiet from war.

12 Now these are the kings of the land whom the sons of Israel struck down, and whose land they possessed beyond the Jordan *to the east* toward the sunrise, from the valley of the Arnon as far as Mount Hermon, and all the Arabah to the east: 2 Sihon king of the Amorites, who lived in Heshbon *and* ruled from Aroer, which is on the edge of the valley of the Arnon, both the middle of the valley and half of Gilead, even as far as the brook Jabbok, the border of the sons of Ammon; 3 and the Arabah as far as the Sea of Chinneroth toward the east, and as far as the sea of the Arabah, *even* the Salt Sea, eastward toward Beth-jeshimoth, and on the south, at the foot of the slopes of Pisgah; 4 and the territory of Og king of Bashan, one of the remnant of the Rephaim, who lived at Ashtaroth and at Edrei 5 and ruled over Mount Hermon and Salecah and all Bashan, as far as the border of the Geshurites and the Maacathites, and half of Gilead, *as far as* the border of Sihon king

of Heshbon. 6 Moses the servant of Yahweh
and the sons of Israel struck them down;
and Moses the servant of Yahweh gave it
to the Reubenites and the Gadites and the
half-tribe of Manasseh as a possession.
7 Now these are the kings of the land
whom Joshua and the sons of Israel struck
down beyond the Jordan toward the west,
from Baal-gad in the valley of Lebanon even
as far as Mount Halak, which rises toward
Seir; and Joshua gave it to the tribes of Israel
as a possession according to their divisions,
8 in the hill country and in the Shephelah
and in the Arabah and on the slopes and
in the wilderness and in the Negev; the
Hittite, the Amorite and the Canaanite, the
Perizzite, the Hivite and the Jebusite:

9 the king of Jericho, one;
the king of Ai, which is beside Bethel, one;
10 the king of Jerusalem, one;
the king of Hebron, one;
11 the king of Jarmuth, one;
the king of Lachish, one;
12 the king of Eglon, one;
the king of Gezer, one;
13 the king of Debir, one;
the king of Geder, one;
14 the king of Hormah, one;
the king of Arad, one;
15 the king of Libnah, one;
the king of Adullam, one;
16 the king of Makkedah, one;
the king of Bethel, one;
17 the king of Tappuah, one;
the king of Hepher, one;
18 the king of Aphek, one;
the king of Lasharon, one;
19 the king of Madon, one;
the king of Hazor, one;
20 the king of Shimron-meron, one;
the king of Achshaph, one;
21 the king of Taanach, one;
the king of Megiddo, one;
22 the king of Kedesh, one;
the king of Jokneam in Carmel, one;
23 the king of Dor in the heights of Dor, one;
the king of Goiim in Gilgal, one;
24 the king of Tirzah, one:
in all, thirty-one kings.

Psalm 44:4–19

4 You are my King, O God;
Command salvation for Jacob.
5 Through You we will push back our adversaries;
Through Your name we will tread down those who rise up against us.
6 For I will not trust in my bow,
And my sword will not save me.
7 But You have saved us from our adversaries,
And You have put to shame those who hate us.
8 In God we have boasted all day long,
And we will give thanks to Your name forever. Selah.

9 Yet You have rejected *us* and brought us to dishonor,
And do not go out with our armies.
10 You cause us to turn back from the adversary;
And those who hate us have plundered *us* for themselves.
11 You give us as sheep to be eaten
And have scattered us among the nations.
12 You sell Your people for no amount,
And You have not profited from their price.
13 You make us a reproach to our neighbors,
A mockery and a derision to those around us.
14 You make us a byword among the nations,
A laughingstock among the peoples.
15 All day long my dishonor is before me
And the shame of my face has covered me,
16 Because of the voice of him who reproaches and reviles,
Because of the presence of the enemy and the avenger.

17 All this has come upon us, but we have not forgotten You,
And we have not dealt falsely with Your covenant.
18 Our heart has not turned back,
Nor have our steps deviated from Your path,
19 Yet You have crushed us in a place of jackals
And covered us with the shadow of death.

Proverbs 14:1–2

14 The wise woman builds her house,
But the woman of folly tears it
down with her own hands.
2 He who walks in his uprightness
fears Yahweh,
But he who is devious in his
ways despises Him.

Luke 10:25–42

25 And behold, a scholar of the Law stood
up and was putting Him to the test, saying,
“Teacher, what shall I do to inherit eternal
life?” 26 And He said to him, “What is written
in the Law? How do you read *it*?” 27 And he
answered and said, “YOU SHALL LOVE THE
LORD YOUR GOD WITH ALL YOUR HEART, AND
WITH ALL YOUR SOUL, AND WITH ALL YOUR
STRENGTH, AND WITH ALL YOUR MIND; AND
YOUR NEIGHBOR AS YOURSELF.” 28 And He said
to him, “You have answered correctly; DO
THIS AND YOU WILL LIVE.” 29 But wishing to
justify himself, he said to Jesus, “And who
is my neighbor?” 30 Jesus replied and said,
“A man was going down from Jerusalem to
Jericho, and fell among robbers, and they
stripped him and beat him, and went away
leaving him half dead. 31 And a priest hap-
pened to be going down on that road, and
when he saw him, he passed by on the other
side. 32 Likewise a Levite also, when he came
to the place and saw him, passed by on the
other side. 33 But a Samaritan, who was on a
journey, came upon him, and when he saw
him, he felt compassion. 34 And he came to
him and bandaged up his wounds, pouring
oil and wine on *them*, and he put him on his
own animal, and brought him to an inn and
took care of him. 35 And on the next day he
took out two denarii and gave them to the
innkeeper and said, ‘Take care of him, and
whatever more you spend, when I return I
will repay you.’ 36 Which of these three do
you think proved to be a neighbor to the
man who fell into the robbers’ *hands*?”
37 And he said, “The one who showed mercy
toward him.” Then Jesus said to him, “Go
and do the same.”

38 Now as they were traveling along, He
entered a village; and a woman named
Martha welcomed Him into her home.
39 And she had a sister called Mary, who
was also seated at the Lord’s feet, listening
to His word. 40 But Martha was distracted
with all her preparations; and she came
up *to Him* and said, “Lord, do You not care
that my sister has left me to do all the
preparations alone? Then tell her to help
me.” 41 But the Lord answered and said to
her, “Martha, Martha, you are worried and
bothered about so many things, 42 but *only*
one thing is necessary, for Mary has chosen
the good part, which shall not be taken away
from her.”

APRIL 12

Joshua 13:1–14:15

13 Now Joshua was old, advanced in
years, and Yahweh said to him, “You
are old, advanced in years, and very much
of the land remains to be possessed. 2 This is
the land that remains: all the regions *of* the
Philistines and all *those of* the Geshurites;
3 from the Shihor which is east of Egypt,
even as far as the border of Ekron to the
north (it is counted as Canaanite); the five
lords of the Philistines: the Gazite, the
Ashdodite, the Ashkelonite, the Gittite, the
Ekronite; and the Avvite 4 to the south, all
the land of the Canaanite, and Mearah that
belongs to the Sidonians, as far as Aphek, to
the border of the Amorite; 5 and the land of
the Gebalite, and all of Lebanon, *to the east*
toward the sunrise, from Baal-gad below
Mount Hermon as far as Lebo-hamath.
6 All the inhabitants of the hill country
from Lebanon as far as Misrephoth-maim,
all the Sidonians, I will dispossess them
from before the sons of Israel; only allot it
to Israel for an inheritance as I have com-
manded you. 7 So now, apportion this land
for an inheritance to the nine tribes and the
half-tribe of Manasseh.”

8 With the other half-tribe, the Reubenites
and the Gadites received their inheritance
which Moses gave them beyond the Jordan
to the east, just as Moses the servant of
Yahweh gave to them; 9 from Aroer, which is
on the edge of the valley of the Arnon, with
the city which is in the middle of the valley,
and all the plain of Medeba, as far as Dibon;
10 and all the cities of Sihon king of the
Amorites, who reigned in Heshbon, as far
as the border of the sons of Ammon; 11 and

Gilead, and the territory of the Geshurites
and Maacathites, and all Mount Hermon,
and all Bashan as far as Salecah; 12 all the
kingdom of Og in Bashan, who reigned in
Ashtaroth and in Edrei (he alone remained
of the remnant of the Rephaim); for Moses
struck them and dispossessed them. 13 But
the sons of Israel did not dispossess the
Geshurites or the Maacathites; so Geshur
and Maacath live among Israel until this day.
14 Only to the tribe of Levi he did not give an
inheritance; the offerings by fire to Yahweh,
the God of Israel, are their inheritance, as
He spoke to him.

15 So Moses gave *an inheritance* to the
tribe of the sons of Reuben according to
their families. 16 And their territory was
from Aroer, which is on the edge of the
valley of the Arnon, with the city which is
in the middle of the valley and all the plain
by Medeba; 17 Heshbon, and all its cities
which are on the plain: Dibon and Bamoth-
baal and Beth-baal-meon, 18 and Jahaz and
Kedemoth and Mephaath, 19 and Kiriathaim
and Sibmah and Zereth-shahar on the hill of
the valley, 20 and Beth-peor and the slopes
of Pisgah and Beth-jeshimoth, 21 even all
the cities of the plain and all the kingdom
of Sihon king of the Amorites who reigned
in Heshbon, whom Moses struck with the
leaders of Midian, Evi and Rekem and Zur
and Hur and Reba, the princes of Sihon, who
lived in the land. 22 The sons of Israel also
killed Balaam the son of Beor, the diviner,
with the sword among *the rest of* their slain.
23 And the border of the sons of Reuben was
the Jordan. This was the inheritance of the
sons of Reuben according to their families,
the cities and their villages.

24 Moses also gave *an inheritance* to the
tribe of Gad, to the sons of Gad, according
to their families. 25 And their territory was
Jazer, and all the cities of Gilead, and half the
land of the sons of Ammon, as far as Aroer
which is before Rabbah; 26 and from Hesh-
bon as far as Ramath-mizpeh and Betonim,
and from Mahanaim as far as the border of
Debir; 27 and in the valley, Beth-haram and
Beth-nimrah and Succoth and Zaphon,
the rest of the kingdom of Sihon king of
Heshbon, with the Jordan as a border, as far
as the lower end of the Sea of Chinnereth
beyond the Jordan to the east. 28 This is the
inheritance of the sons of Gad according to
their families, the cities and their villages.

29 Moses also gave *an inheritance* to the
half-tribe of Manasseh; and it was for the
half-tribe of the sons of Manasseh according
to their families. 30 And their territory was
from Mahanaim, all Bashan, all the kingdom
of Og king of Bashan, and all of Havvoth-jair,
which are in Bashan, sixty cities; 31 also half
of Gilead, with Ashtaroth and Edrei, the
cities of the kingdom of Og in Bashan, *were*
for the sons of Machir the son of Manasseh,
for half of the sons of Machir according to
their families.

32 These are *the territories* which Moses
apportioned for an inheritance in the plains
of Moab, beyond the Jordan at Jericho to the
east. 33 But to the tribe of Levi, Moses did
not give an inheritance; Yahweh, the God
of Israel, is their inheritance, as He had
promised to them.

14 Now these are *the territories* which
the sons of Israel inherited in the land
of Canaan, which Eleazar the priest and
Joshua the son of Nun and the heads of the
households of the tribes of the sons of Israel
apportioned to them for an inheritance,
2 by the lot of their inheritance, as Yahweh
commanded by the hand of Moses, for the
nine tribes and the half-tribe. 3 For Moses
had given the inheritance of the two tribes
and the half-tribe beyond the Jordan; but
he did not give an inheritance to the Levites
among them. 4 For the sons of Joseph were
two tribes, Manasseh and Ephraim, and
they did not give a portion to the Levites in
the land, except cities to live in, with their
pasture lands for their livestock and for
their property. 5 Thus the sons of Israel did
just as Yahweh had commanded Moses, and
they divided the land.

6 Then the sons of Judah drew near
to Joshua in Gilgal, and Caleb the son of
Jephunneh the Kenizzite said to him, "You
know the word which Yahweh spoke to
Moses the man of God concerning you and
me in Kadesh-barnea. 7 I was forty years
old when Moses the servant of Yahweh
sent me from Kadesh-barnea to spy out
the land, and I brought word back to him
as *it was* in my heart. 8 Nevertheless, my
brothers who went up with me made the
heart of the people melt *with fear*; but I
followed Yahweh my God fully. 9 So Moses
swore on that day, saying, 'Surely the land
on which your foot has trodden will be an

inheritance to you and to your children
forever because you have followed Yahweh
my God fully.' 10 So now behold, Yahweh has
let me live, just as He spoke, these forty-five
years, from the time that Yahweh spoke this
word to Moses, when Israel walked in the
wilderness; so now behold, I am eighty-five
years old today. 11 I am still as strong today
as I was in the day Moses sent me; as my
strength was then, so my strength is now,
for war and for going out and coming in.
12 So now, give me this hill country about
which Yahweh spoke on that day, for you
heard on that day that Anakim *were* there,
with great fortified cities; perhaps Yahweh
will be with me, and I will dispossess them
as Yahweh has spoken."
13 So Joshua blessed him and gave Hebron
to Caleb the son of Jephunneh for an inher-
itance. 14 Therefore, Hebron became the
inheritance of Caleb the son of Jephunneh
the Kenizzite until this day because he fully
followed Yahweh, the God of Israel. 15 Now
the name of Hebron was formerly Kiriath-
arba; *for Arba* was the greatest man among
the Anakim. Then the land was quiet from
war.

Psalm 44:20–26

20 If we had forgotten the
name of our God
Or spread our hands to a strange god,
21 Would not God find this out?
For He knows the secrets of the heart.
22 But for Your sake we are
killed all day long;
We are counted as sheep
for the slaughter.
23 Arouse Yourself, why do
You sleep, O Lord?
Awake, do not reject us forever.
24 Why do You hide Your face
And forget our affliction
and our oppression?
25 For our soul has sunk
down into the dust;
Our body cleaves to the earth.
26 Rise up, be our help,
And redeem us for the sake of
Your lovingkindness.

Proverbs 14:3

3 In the mouth of the ignorant
fool is a rod of lofty pride,
But the lips of the wise will keep them.

Luke 11:1–28

11 And it happened that while Jesus was
praying in a certain place, after He had
finished, one of His disciples said to Him,
"Lord, teach us to pray just as John also
taught his disciples." 2 And He said to them,
"When you pray, say:
'Father, hallowed be Your name.
Your kingdom come.
3 'Give us each day our daily bread.
4 'And forgive us our sins,
For we ourselves also forgive
everyone who is indebted to us.
And lead us not into temptation.'"
5 Then He said to them, "Which of you has
a friend and will go to him at midnight and
say to him, 'Friend, lend me three loaves,
6 for a friend of mine has come to me from
a journey, and I have nothing to set before
him'; 7 and from inside he answers and says,
'Do not bother me; the door has already
been shut and my children and I are in bed;
I cannot rise up and give you *anything.*' 8 I
tell you, even though he will not arise and
give him *anything* because he is his friend,
yet because of his persistence he will get up
and give him as much as he needs.
9 "So I say to you, ask, and it will be given
to you; seek, and you will find; knock, and it
will be opened to you. 10 For everyone who
asks, receives; and he who seeks, finds; and
to him who knocks, it will be opened. 11 But
what father among you, *if* his son asks for a
fish, will give him a snake instead of a fish?
12 Or, *if his son* asks for an egg, will give him
a scorpion? 13 If you then, being evil, know
how to give good gifts to your children, how
much more will *your* heavenly Father give
the Holy Spirit to those who ask Him?"
14 And He was casting out a demon, and
it was mute. Now it happened that when
the demon had gone out, the mute man
spoke, and the crowds marveled. 15 But
some of them said, "He casts out demons
by Beelzebul, the ruler of the demons."
16 And others, testing *Him,* were seeking
from Him a sign from heaven. 17 But He
knew their thoughts and said to them,
"Any kingdom divided against itself is laid
waste, and a house *divided* against itself
falls. 18 But if Satan also is divided against
himself, how will his kingdom stand? For
you say that I cast out demons by Beelzebul.
19 And if I by Beelzebul cast out demons,
by whom do your sons cast them out? For

this reason, they will be your judges. 20 But if I cast out demons by the finger of God, then the kingdom of God has come upon you. 21 When a strong *man,* fully armed, guards his own house, his possessions are undisturbed. 22 But when someone stronger than he attacks him and overpowers him, he takes away from him all his armor on which he had relied and distributes his plunder. 23 He who is not with Me is against Me and he who does not gather with Me, scatters.

24 "When the unclean spirit goes out of a man, it passes through waterless places seeking rest, and not finding any, it says, 'I will return to my house from which I came.' 25 And when it comes, it finds it swept and put in order. 26 Then it goes and takes along seven other spirits more evil than itself, and they go in and live there, and the last state of that man becomes worse than the first."

27 Now it happened that while Jesus was saying these things, one of the women in the crowd raised her voice and said to Him, "Blessed is the womb that bore You and the breasts at which You nursed." 28 But He said, "On the contrary, blessed are those who hear the word of God and keep it."

APRIL 13

Joshua 15:1–16:10

15 Now the lot for the tribe of the sons of Judah according to their families reached the border of Edom, southward to the wilderness of Zin at the *far* end *toward the* south. 2 And their south border was from the *lower* end of the Salt Sea, from the bay that turns to the south. 3 Then it went out southward to the ascent of Akrabbim and passed on to Zin and went up by the south of Kadesh-barnea and continued to Hezron and went up to Addar and turned about to Karka. 4 And it passed on to Azmon and went out to the brook of Egypt, and the border ended at the sea. This shall be your south border. 5 And the east border *was* the Salt Sea, as far as the mouth of the Jordan. And the border of the north side was from the bay of the sea at the mouth of the Jordan. 6 Then the border went up to Beth-hoglah and passed by on the north of Beth-arabah; and the border went up to the stone of Bohan the son of Reuben. 7 Then the border went up to Debir from the valley of Achor and turned northward toward Gilgal which is opposite the ascent of Adummim, which is on the south of the valley; and the border continued to the waters of En-shemesh and it ended at En-rogel. 8 Then the border went up the valley of Ben-hinnom to the slope of the Jebusite on the south (that is, Jerusalem); and the border went up to the top of the mountain which is before the valley of Hinnom to the west, which is at the end of the valley of Rephaim toward the north. 9 From the top of the mountain the border curved to the spring of the waters of Nephtoah and proceeded to the cities of Mount Ephron; then the border curved to Baalah (that is, Kiriath-jearim). 10 Then the border turned about from Baalah westward to Mount Seir and continued to the slope of Mount Jearim on the north (that is, Chesalon) and went down to Beth-shemesh and continued through Timnah. 11 Then the border went out to the side of Ekron northward. Then the border curved to Shikkeron and passed on to Mount Baalah and went out to Jabneel, and the border ended at the sea. 12 And the west border *was* at the Great Sea, even *its* coastline. This is the border around the sons of Judah according to their families.

13 Now he gave to Caleb the son of Jephunneh a portion among the sons of Judah, according to the command of Yahweh to Joshua, *namely,* Kiriath-arba, *Arba being* the father of Anak (that is, Hebron). 14 And Caleb dispossessed from there the three sons of Anak: Sheshai and Ahiman and Talmai, the children of Anak. 15 Then he went up from there against the inhabitants of Debir; now the name of Debir formerly was Kiriath-sepher. 16 And Caleb said, "The one who strikes down Kiriath-sepher and captures it, I will give him Achsah my daughter as a wife." 17 And Othniel the son of Kenaz, the brother of Caleb, captured it; so he gave him Achsah his daughter as a wife. 18 Now it happened that when she came *to him,* she enticed him to ask her father for a field. So she alighted from the donkey, and Caleb said to her, "What do you want?" 19 Then she said, "Give me a blessing; since you have given me the land

of the Negev, give me also springs of water." So he gave her the upper springs and the lower springs.

20 This is the inheritance of the tribe of the sons of Judah according to their families.

21 Now the cities at the *far* end of the tribe of the sons of Judah toward the border of Edom in the south were Kabzeel and Eder and Jagur, 22 and Kinah and Dimonah and Adadah, 23 and Kedesh and Hazor and Ithnan, 24 Ziph and Telem and Bealoth, 25 and Hazor-hadattah and Kerioth-hezron (that is, Hazor), 26 Amam and Shema and Moladah, 27 and Hazar-gaddah and Heshmon and Beth-pelet, 28 and Hazar-shual and Beersheba and Biziothiah, 29 Baalah and Iim and Ezem, 30 and Eltolad and Chesil and Hormah, 31 and Ziklag and Madmannah and Sansannah, 32 and Lebaoth and Shilhim and Ain and Rimmon; in all, twenty-nine cities with their villages.

33 In the Shephelah: Eshtaol and Zorah and Ashnah, 34 and Zanoah and En-gannim, Tappuah and Enam, 35 Jarmuth and Adullam, Socoh and Azekah, 36 and Shaaraim and Adithaim and Gederah and Gederothaim; fourteen cities with their villages.

37 Zenan and Hadashah and Migdal-gad, 38 and Dilean and Mizpeh and Joktheel, 39 Lachish and Bozkath and Eglon, 40 and Cabbon and Lahmas and Chitlish, 41 and Gederoth, Beth-dagon and Naamah and Makkedah; sixteen cities with their villages.

42 Libnah and Ether and Ashan, 43 and Iphtah and Ashnah and Nezib, 44 and Keilah and Achzib and Mareshah; nine cities with their villages.

45 Ekron, with its towns and its villages; 46 from Ekron even to the sea, all that were by the side of Ashdod, with their villages.

47 Ashdod, its towns and its villages; Gaza, its towns and its villages; as far as the brook of Egypt and the Great Sea, even *its* coastline.

48 And in the hill country: Shamir and Jattir and Socoh, 49 and Dannah and Kiriath-sannah (that is, Debir), 50 and Anab and Eshtemoh and Anim, 51 and Goshen and Holon and Giloh; eleven cities with their villages.

52 Arab and Dumah and Eshan, 53 and Janum and Beth-tappuah and Aphekah, 54 and Humtah and Kiriath-arba (that is, Hebron) and Zior; nine cities with their villages.

55 Maon, Carmel and Ziph and Juttah, 56 and Jezreel and Jokdeam and Zanoah, 57 Kain, Gibeah and Timnah; ten cities with their villages.

58 Halhul, Beth-zur and Gedor, 59 and Maarath and Beth-anoth and Eltekon; six cities with their villages.

60 Kiriath-baal (that is, Kiriath-jearim) and Rabbah; two cities with their villages.

61 In the wilderness: Beth-arabah, Middin and Secacah, 62 and Nibshan and the City of Salt and Engedi; six cities with their villages.

63 Now as for the Jebusites, the inhabitants of Jerusalem, the sons of Judah could not dispossess them; so the Jebusites live with the sons of Judah at Jerusalem until this day.

16 Then the lot for the sons of Joseph went out from the Jordan at Jericho to the waters of Jericho on the east into the wilderness, going up from Jericho through the hill country to Bethel. 2 And it went out from Bethel to Luz and passed on to the border of the Archites at Ataroth. 3 Then it went down westward to the territory of the Japhletites, as far as the territory of lower Beth-horon even to Gezer, and it ended at the sea.

4 So the sons of Joseph, Manasseh and Ephraim, received their inheritance. 5 Now *this* was the territory of the sons of Ephraim according to their families: the border of their inheritance eastward was Ataroth-addar, as far as upper Beth-horon. 6 Then the border went westward at Michmethath on the north, and the border turned about eastward to Taanath-shiloh and passed on *beyond* it to the east of Janoah. 7 And it went down from Janoah to Ataroth and to Naarah and reached Jericho and came out at the Jordan. 8 From Tappuah the border continued westward to the brook of Kanah, and it ended at the sea. This is the inheritance of the tribe of the sons of Ephraim according to their families, 9 *together* with the cities which were set apart for the sons of Ephraim in the midst of the inheritance of the sons of Manasseh, all the cities with their villages. 10 But they did not dispossess the Canaanites who lived in Gezer, so the Canaanites live in the midst of Ephraim to this day, and they became forced laborers.

Psalm 45:1–5

1 My heart overflows with a good theme;
I address my verses to the King;
My tongue is the pen of
a skillful scribe.
2 You are fairer than the sons of men;
Grace is poured upon Your lips;
Therefore God has blessed You forever.

3 Gird Your sword on *Your*
thigh, O Mighty One,
In Your splendor and Your majesty!
4 And in Your majesty ride
on victoriously,
For the cause of truth and
meekness *and* righteousness;
Let Your right hand teach
You awesome things.
5 Your arrows are sharp;
The peoples fall under You;
Your arrows are in the heart
of the King's enemies.

Proverbs 14:4–5

4 Where no oxen are, the
manger is clean,
But much revenue *comes* by
the strength of the ox.
5 A faithful witness will not lie,
But a false witness breathes out lies.

Luke 11:29–54

29 Now as the crowds were increasing,
He began to say, "This generation is a
wicked generation; it seeks a sign, and *yet*
no sign will be given to it but the sign of
Jonah. 30 For just as Jonah became a sign
to the Ninevites, so will the Son of Man
be to this generation. 31 The Queen of the
South will rise up at the judgment with the
men of this generation and condemn them,
because she came from the ends of the
earth to hear the wisdom of Solomon. And
behold, something greater than Solomon is
here. 32 The men of Nineveh will stand up
at the judgment with this generation and
condemn it, because they repented at the
preaching of Jonah. And behold, something
greater than Jonah is here.

33 "No one, after lighting a lamp, puts
it away in a cellar nor under a basket, but
on the lampstand, so that those who enter
may see the light. 34 The eye is the lamp
of your body; when your eye is clear, your
whole body also is full of light, but when it
is bad, your body also is full of darkness.
35 Therefore watch out that the light in you
is not darkness. 36 If therefore your whole
body is full of light, with no dark part in it, it
will be wholly illumined, as when the lamp
illumines you with its rays."

37 Now when He had spoken, a Pharisee
*asked Him to have a meal with him. And He
went in and reclined *at the table.* 38 But when
the Pharisee saw it, he marveled that He had
not first ceremonially washed before the
meal. 39 But the Lord said to him, "Now you
Pharisees clean the outside of the cup and of
the platter, but inside of you, you are full of
robbery and wickedness. 40 You foolish ones,
did not He who made the outside make the
inside also? 41 But give that which is within as
charity, and then all things are clean for you.

42 "But woe to you Pharisees! For you
pay tithe of mint and rue and every *kind of*
garden herb, and *yet* disregard justice and
the love of God, but these are the things
you should have done without neglecting
the others. 43 Woe to you Pharisees! For you
love the best seat in the synagogues and the
respectful greetings in the marketplaces.
44 Woe to you! For you are like concealed
tombs, and the people who walk over *them*
are unaware *of it.*"

45 Now one of the scholars of the Law
answered and said to Him, "Teacher, when
You say these things, You insult us too."
46 But He said, "Woe to you scholars of the
Law as well! For you weigh men down with
burdens hard to bear, and you yourselves
will not even touch the burdens with one
of your fingers. 47 Woe to you! For you build
the tombs of the prophets, but your fathers
killed them. 48 So you are witnesses and
approve the deeds of your fathers; because
it was they who killed them, and you build
their tombs. 49 For this reason also the
wisdom of God said, 'I will send to them
prophets and apostles, and *some* of them
they will kill and *some* they will persecute,
50 so that the blood of all the prophets, shed
since the foundation of the world, may be
charged against this generation, 51 from the
blood of Abel to the blood of Zechariah, who
was killed between the altar and the house *of*
God; yes, I tell you, it shall be charged against
this generation.' 52 Woe to you, scholars of
the Law! For you have taken away the key
of knowledge; you yourselves did not enter,
and you hindered those who were entering."

53 And when He left there, the scribes and
the Pharisees began to be very hostile and
to question Him closely on many subjects,
54 plotting to catch Him in something He
might say.

APRIL 14

Joshua 17:1–18:28

17 And *this* was the lot for the tribe of
Manasseh, for he was the firstborn of
Joseph. To Machir the firstborn of Manasseh,
the father of Gilead, were allotted Gilead
and Bashan, because he was a man of war.
2 So *the lot* was *made* for the rest of the sons
of Manasseh according to their families: for
the sons of Abiezer and for the sons of Helek
and for the sons of Asriel and for the sons
of Shechem and for the sons of Hepher and
for the sons of Shemida; these *were* the sons
of Manasseh the son of Joseph, the males
according to their families.

3 However, Zelophehad, the son of Hep-
her, the son of Gilead, the son of Machir,
the son of Manasseh, had no sons, only
daughters; and these are the names of
his daughters: Mahlah and Noah, Hoglah,
Milcah and Tirzah. 4 And they came near
before Eleazar the priest and before Joshua
the son of Nun and before the leaders,
saying, "Yahweh commanded Moses to give
us an inheritance among our brothers." So
according to the word of Yahweh he gave
them an inheritance among their father's
brothers. 5 Thus there fell ten portions
to Manasseh, besides the land of Gilead
and Bashan, which is beyond the Jordan,
6 because the daughters of Manasseh
received an inheritance among his sons.
And the land of Gilead belonged to the rest
of the sons of Manasseh.

7 And the border of Manasseh ran from
Asher to Michmethath which was east of
Shechem; then the border went southward
to the inhabitants of En-tappuah. 8 The
land of Tappuah belonged to Manasseh,
but Tappuah on the border of Manasseh
belonged to the sons of Ephraim. 9 And the
border went down to the brook of Kanah,
southward of the brook (these cities
belonged to Ephraim among the cities of
Manasseh), and the border of Manasseh
was on the north side of the brook, and
it ended at the sea. 10 The south side
belonged to Ephraim and the north side to
Manasseh, and the sea was their border; and
they reached to Asher on the north and to
Issachar on the east. 11 And in Issachar and
in Asher, Manasseh had Beth-shean and its
towns, and Ibleam and its towns, and the
inhabitants of Dor and its towns, and the
inhabitants of En-dor and its towns, and the
inhabitants of Taanach and its towns, and
the inhabitants of Megiddo and its towns,
the third is Napheth. 12 But the sons of
Manasseh could not take possession of these
cities because the Canaanites persisted in
living in that land. 13 Now it happened that
when the sons of Israel became strong, they
put the Canaanites to forced labor, but they
did not dispossess them completely.

14 Then the sons of Joseph spoke to
Joshua, saying, "Why have you given me
only one lot and one portion for an inheri-
tance, since I am a numerous people whom
Yahweh has thus far blessed?" 15 And Joshua
said to them, "If you are a numerous people,
go up to the forest and clear a place for
yourself there in the land of the Perizzites
and of the Rephaim, since the hill country
of Ephraim is too narrow for you." 16 And
the sons of Joseph said, "The hill country
is not enough for us, and all the Canaanites
who live in the valley land have chariots of
iron, both those who are in Beth-shean and
its towns and those who are in the valley of
Jezreel." 17 Then Joshua spoke to the house
of Joseph, to Ephraim and Manasseh, saying,
"You are a numerous people and have great
power; you shall not have one lot *only*,
18 but the hill country shall be yours. For
though it is a forest, you shall clear it, and
to its farthest borders it shall be yours; for
you shall dispossess the Canaanites, even
though they have chariots of iron *and* even
though they are strong."

18 Then the whole congregation of the
sons of Israel assembled themselves
at Shiloh and set up the tent of meeting
there; and the land was subdued before
them.

2 And there remained among the sons of
Israel seven tribes who had not divided their

inheritance. 3 So Joshua said to the sons of
Israel, "How long will you put off entering to
take possession of the land which Yahweh,
the God of your fathers, has given you?
4 Provide for yourselves three men from
each tribe that I may send them, and that
they may arise and walk through the land
and write *a description of* it according to
their inheritance; then they shall return
to me. 5 And they shall divide it into seven
portions; Judah shall stay in its territory on
the south, and the house of Joseph shall
stay in their territory on the north. 6 So
you shall write *a description of* the land in
seven divisions and bring *the description*
here to me. I will cast lots for you here before
Yahweh our God. 7 For the Levites have no
portion among you because the priesthood
of Yahweh is their inheritance. Gad and
Reuben and the half-tribe of Manasseh also
have received their inheritance eastward
beyond the Jordan, which Moses the servant
of Yahweh gave them."

8 Then the men arose and went, and
Joshua commanded those who went to
write *the description of* the land, saying,
"Go and walk through the land and write
a description of it, and return to me; then
I will cast lots for you here before Yahweh
in Shiloh." 9 So the men went and passed
through the land and wrote *a description of*
it by cities in seven divisions in a book; and
they came to Joshua to the camp at Shiloh.
10 And Joshua cast lots for them in Shiloh
before Yahweh, and there Joshua divided
the land to the sons of Israel according to
their divisions.

11 Now the lot of the tribe of the sons
of Benjamin came up according to their
families, and the territory of their lot lay
between the sons of Judah and the sons of
Joseph. 12 And their border on the north side
was from the Jordan; then the border went
up to the side of Jericho on the north and
went up through the hill country westward,
and it ended at the wilderness of Beth-aven.
13 From there the border passed on to Luz, to
the side of Luz (that is, Bethel) southward;
and the border went down to Ataroth-addar,
near the hill which *lies* on the south of lower
Beth-horon. 14 Then the border curved *from*
there and turned round on the west side
southward, from the hill which *lies* before
Beth-horon southward; and it ended at
Kiriath-baal (that is, Kiriath-jearim), a city
of the sons of Judah. This *was* the west side.
15 Then the south side *was* from the edge
of Kiriath-jearim, and the border went out
westward and went out to the fountain of
the waters of Nephtoah. 16 Then the border
went down to the edge of the hill which
is in the valley of Ben-hinnom, which is
in the valley of Rephaim northward; and
it went down to the valley of Hinnom, to
the slope of the Jebusite southward, and
went down to En-rogel. 17 Then it curved
northward and went out to En-shemesh
and went out to Geliloth, which is opposite
the ascent of Adummim, and it went down
to the stone of Bohan the son of Reuben.
18 Then it continued to the side in front of
the Arabah northward and went down to
the Arabah. 19 And the border passed on to
the side of Beth-hoglah northward; and the
border ended at the north bay of the Salt
Sea, at the south end of the Jordan. This *was*
the south border. 20 Moreover, the Jordan
was its border on the east side. This *was*
the inheritance of the sons of Benjamin,
according to their families *and* according
to its borders all around.

21 Now the cities of the tribe of the sons
of Benjamin according to their families
were Jericho and Beth-hoglah and Emek-
keziz, 22 and Beth-arabah and Zemaraim
and Bethel, 23 and Avvim and Parah and
Ophrah, 24 and Chephar-ammoni and
Ophni and Geba; twelve cities with their
villages. 25 Gibeon and Ramah and Beeroth,
26 and Mizpeh and Chephirah and Mozah,
27 and Rekem and Irpeel and Taralah, 28 and
Zelah, Haeleph and the Jebusite (that is,
Jerusalem), Gibeah, Kiriath; fourteen cities
with their villages. This is the inheritance
of the sons of Benjamin according to their
families.

Psalm 45:6–17

6 Your throne, O God,
  is forever and ever;
A scepter of uprightness is the
  scepter of Your kingdom.
7 You have loved righteousness
  and hated wickedness;
Therefore God, Your God,
  has anointed You
With the oil of joy above
  Your companions.
8 All Your garments are *fragrant with*
  myrrh and aloes *and* cassia;

Out of ivory palaces stringed
instruments have made You glad.
9 Kings' daughters are among
Your noble ladies;
At Your right hand stands the
queen in gold from Ophir.

10 Listen, O daughter, give attention
and incline your ear:
Forget your people and
your father's house;
11 Then the King will desire your beauty.
Because He is your Lord,
bow down to Him.
12 The daughter of Tyre *will*
come with a present;
The rich among the people
will seek your favor.

13 The King's daughter is all glorious
within *her chamber*;
Her clothing is interwoven with gold.
14 She will be led to the King in
embroidered work;
The virgins, her companions
who follow her,
Will be brought to You.
15 They will be led forth with
gladness and rejoicing;
They will enter into the King's palace.

16 In place of your fathers
will be your sons;
You shall set them up as
princes in all the earth.
17 I will cause Your name to be
remembered from generation
to every generation;
Therefore the peoples will give
You thanks forever and ever.

Proverbs 14:6

6 A scoffer seeks wisdom and *finds* none,
But knowledge is easy to one
who has understanding.

Luke 12:1–32

12 At this time, after so many thousands
of the crowd had gathered together
that they were trampling on one another,
He began saying to His disciples first, "Be on
your guard for the leaven of the Pharisees,
which is hypocrisy. 2 But there is nothing
covered up that will not be revealed, and
hidden that will not be known. 3 Accord-
ingly, whatever you have said in the dark
will be heard in the light, and what you
have whispered in the inner rooms will be
proclaimed upon the housetops.
4 "But I say to you, My friends, do not
fear those who kill the body and after that
have no more that they can do. 5 But I will
show you whom to fear: fear the One who,
after He has killed, has authority to cast into
hell; yes, I tell you, fear Him! 6 Are not five
sparrows sold for two assaria? *Yet* not one of
them is forgotten before God. 7 Indeed, the
very hairs of your head are all numbered. Do
not fear; you are more valuable than many
sparrows.
8 "And I say to you, everyone who con-
fesses Me before men, the Son of Man will
confess him also before the angels of God,
9 but he who denies Me before men will be
denied before the angels of God. 10 And
everyone who speaks a word against the Son
of Man, it will be forgiven him, but he who
blasphemes against the Holy Spirit, it will
not be forgiven him. 11 Now when they bring
you before the synagogues and the rulers
and the authorities, do not worry about how
or what you are to speak in your defense,
or what you are to say, 12 for the Holy Spirit
will teach you in that very hour what you
ought to say."
13 And someone from the crowd said to
Him, "Teacher, tell my brother to divide
the *family* inheritance with me." 14 But
He said to him, "Man, who appointed Me
a judge or arbitrator over you?" 15 Then He
said to them, "Watch out and be on your
guard against every form of greed, for not
even when one has an abundance does his
life consist of his possessions." 16 And He
told them a parable, saying, "The land of
a rich man was very productive. 17 And he
began reasoning to himself, saying, 'What
shall I do, since I have no place to store
my crops?' 18 Then he said, 'This is what
I will do: I will tear down my barns and
build larger ones, and there I will store all
my grain and my goods. 19 And I will say to
my soul, "Soul, you have many goods laid
up for many years *to come*; take your ease,
eat, drink *and* be merry."' 20 But God said
to him, 'You fool! This *very* night your soul
is required of you; and *now* who will own
what you prepared?' 21 So is the one who
stores up treasure for himself, and is not
rich toward God."

22 And He said to His disciples, "For this reason I say to you, do not worry about *your* life, *as to* what you will eat; nor for your body, *as to* what you will put on. 23 For life is more than food, and the body more than clothing. 24 Consider the ravens, for they neither sow nor reap; they have no storeroom nor barn, and *yet* God feeds them; how much more valuable you are than the birds! 25 And which of you by worrying can add a *single* cubit to his life span? 26 Therefore, if you cannot do even a very little thing, why do you worry about other matters? 27 Consider the lilies, how they grow: they neither toil nor spin, but I tell you, not even Solomon in all his glory clothed himself like one of these. 28 But if God so clothes the grass in the field, which is *alive* today and tomorrow is thrown into the furnace, how much more *will He clothe* you? You of little faith! 29 And do not seek what you will eat and what you will drink, and do not keep worrying. 30 For all these things the nations of the world eagerly seek, but your Father knows that you need these things. 31 But seek His kingdom, and these things will be added to you. 32 Do not fear, little flock, for your Father is well pleased to give you the kingdom.

APRIL 15

Joshua 19:1–20:9

19 Then the second lot came out for Simeon, for the tribe of the sons of Simeon according to their families, and their inheritance was in the midst of the inheritance of the sons of Judah. 2 So they had as their inheritance Beersheba or Sheba and Moladah, 3 and Hazar-shual and Balah and Ezem, 4 and Eltolad and Bethul and Hormah, 5 and Ziklag and Beth-marcaboth and Hazar-susah, 6 and Beth-lebaoth and Sharuhen; thirteen cities with their villages; 7 Ain, Rimmon and Ether and Ashan; four cities with their villages; 8 and all the villages which *were* around these cities as far as Baalath-beer, Ramah of the Negev. This *was* the inheritance of the tribe of the sons of Simeon according to their families. 9 The inheritance of the sons of Simeon *was taken* from the portion of the sons of Judah, for the share of the sons of Judah was too large for them; so the sons of Simeon received *an* inheritance in the midst of Judah's inheritance.

10 Now the third lot came up for the sons of Zebulun according to their families. And the territory of their inheritance was as far as Sarid. 11 Then their border went up to the west and to Maralah; it then reached Dabbesheth and reached the brook that is before Jokneam. 12 Then it turned from Sarid to the east toward the sunrise as far as the border of Chisloth-tabor, and it went out *to* Daberath and up to Japhia. 13 From there it passed on to the east toward the sunrise to Gath-hepher, to Eth-kazin, and it went out to Rimmon which curves to Neah. 14 And the border circled around it on the north to Hannathon, and it ended at the valley of Iphtahel. 15 *Included* also *were* Kattah and Nahalal and Shimron and Idalah and Bethlehem; twelve cities with their villages. 16 This *was* the inheritance of the sons of Zebulun according to their families, these cities with their villages.

17 The fourth lot came out for Issachar, for the sons of Issachar according to their families. 18 And their territory *included* Jezreel and Chesulloth and Shunem, 19 and Hapharaim and Shion and Anaharath, 20 and Rabbith and Kishion and Ebez, 21 and Remeth and En-gannim and En-haddah and Beth-pazzez. 22 And the border reached to Tabor and Shahazumah and Beth-shemesh, and their border ended at the Jordan; sixteen cities with their villages. 23 This *was* the inheritance of the tribe of the sons of Issachar according to their families, the cities with their villages.

24 Now the fifth lot came out for the tribe of the sons of Asher according to their families. 25 And their territory was Helkath and Hali and Beten and Achshaph, 26 and Allammelech and Amad and Mishal; and it reached to Carmel on the west and to Shihor-libnath. 27 Then it turned *east* toward the sunrise to Beth-dagon and reached to Zebulun and to the valley of Iphtahel northward to Beth-emek and Neiel; then it went out to the north to Cabul, 28 and Ebron and Rehob and Hammon and Kanah, as far as Great Sidon. 29 Then the border turned to Ramah and to the fortified city of Tyre; then the border turned to Hosah, and it ended at

the sea by the region of Achzib. 30 *Included*
also *were* Ummah and Aphek and Rehob;
twenty-two cities with their villages. 31 This
was the inheritance of the tribe of the sons
of Asher according to their families, these
cities with their villages.
32 The sixth lot came out for the sons of
Naphtali, for the sons of Naphtali according
to their families. 33 And their border was
from Heleph, from the oak in Zaanannim
and Adami-nekeb and Jabneel, as far as Lak-
kum, and it ended at the Jordan. 34 Then the
border turned westward to Aznoth-tabor
and went out from there to Hukkok; and
it reached to Zebulun on the south and
reached to Asher on the west and to Judah
at the Jordan *to the east* toward the sunrise.
35 Now the fortified cities *were* Ziddim, Zer
and Hammath, Rakkath and Chinnereth,
36 and Adamah and Ramah and Hazor, 37 and
Kedesh and Edrei and En-hazor, 38 and Yiron
and Migdal-el, Horem and Beth-anath and
Beth-shemesh; nineteen cities with their
villages. 39 This *was* the inheritance of the
tribe of the sons of Naphtali according to
their families, the cities with their villages.
40 The seventh lot came out for the tribe of
the sons of Dan according to their families.
41 And the territory of their inheritance was
Zorah and Eshtaol and Ir-shemesh, 42 and
Shaalabbin and Aijalon and Ithlah, 43 and
Elon and Timnah and Ekron, 44 and Eltekeh
and Gibbethon and Baalath, 45 and Jehud
and Bene-berak and Gath-rimmon, 46 and
Me-jarkon and Rakkon, with the territory
over against Joppa. 47 And the territory of
the sons of Dan went out from them; for
the sons of Dan went up and fought with
Leshem and captured it. Then they struck
it with the edge of the sword and possessed
it and settled in it; and they called Leshem
Dan after the name of Dan their father.
48 This *was* the inheritance of the tribe of
the sons of Dan according to their families,
these cities with their villages.
49 So they finished *apportioning* the land
for inheritance by its borders. Then the sons
of Israel gave an inheritance in their midst
to Joshua the son of Nun. 50 In accordance
with the command of Yahweh they gave him
the city for which he asked, Timnath-serah
in the hill country of Ephraim. So he built
the city and settled in it.
51 These are the inheritances which Elea-
zar the priest and Joshua the son of Nun and
the heads of the households of the tribes of
the sons of Israel distributed by lot in Shiloh
before Yahweh at the doorway of the tent of
meeting. So they finished dividing the land.

20 Then Yahweh spoke to Joshua, saying,
2 "Speak to the sons of Israel, saying,
'Designate the cities of refuge, of which I
spoke to you by the hand of Moses, 3 that
the manslayer who strikes down any person
unintentionally, without premeditation,
may flee there, and they shall become for
you as a refuge from the avenger of blood.
4 And he shall flee to one of these cities and
shall stand at the entrance of the gate of the
city and speak his case in the hearing of the
elders of that city; and they shall take him
into the city to them and give him a place,
so that he may live among them. 5 Now if the
avenger of blood pursues him, then they shall
not surrender the manslayer into his hand
because he struck his neighbor without pre-
meditation and did not hate him beforehand.
6 And he shall live in that city until he stands
before the congregation for judgment, until
the death of the one who is high priest in
those days. Then the manslayer shall return
and come to his own city and to his own
house, to the city from which he fled.'"
7 So they set apart Kedesh in Galilee in
the hill country of Naphtali and Shechem in
the hill country of Ephraim and Kiriath-arba
(that is, Hebron) in the hill country of Judah.
8 Now beyond the Jordan east of Jericho, they
designated Bezer in the wilderness on the
plain from the tribe of Reuben and Ramoth
in Gilead from the tribe of Gad and Golan in
Bashan from the tribe of Manasseh. 9 These
were the appointed cities for all the sons of
Israel and for the sojourner who sojourns
among them, that whoever strikes down any
person unintentionally may flee there and
not die by the hand of the avenger of blood
until he stands before the congregation.

Psalm 46:1–6

1 God is our refuge and strength,
A very present help in trouble.
2 Therefore we will not fear, though
the earth should change
And though the mountains shake
into the heart of the sea;
3 Though its waters roar *and* foam,
Though the mountains quake
at its lofty pride. Selah.

4 There is a river whose streams
make glad the city of God,
The holy dwelling places
of the Most High.
5 God is in the midst of her,
she will not be shaken;
God will help her when
morning dawns.
6 The nations roar, the kingdoms shake;
He gives His voice, the earth melts.

Proverbs 14:7–11

7 Leave the presence of a fool,
As you have not known lips
of knowledge *there.*
8 The wisdom of the prudent is
to understand his way,
But the folly of fools is deceit.
9 Ignorant fools scoff at guilt,
But among the upright there is favor.
10 The heart knows its own bitterness,
And a stranger does not
share its gladness.
11 The house of the wicked
will be destroyed,
But the tent of the upright will flourish.

Luke 12:33–59

33 "Sell your possessions and give *it*
as charity; make yourselves money belts
which do not wear out, an unfailing treasure
in heaven, where no thief comes near nor
moth destroys. 34 For where your treasure
is, there your heart will be also.
35 "GIRD UP YOUR LOINS, and *keep* your lamps
lit. 36 And be like men who are waiting for their
master when he returns from the wedding
feast, so that they may immediately open
the door to him when he comes and knocks.
37 Blessed are those slaves whom the master
will find awake when he comes; truly I say to
you, that he will gird himself *to serve,* and have
them recline *at the table,* and will come up
and wait on them. 38 Whether he comes in the
second watch, or even in the third, and finds
them so, blessed are those *slaves.*
39 "But be sure of this, that if the head of
the house had known at what hour the thief
was coming, he would not have allowed his
house to be broken into. 40 You too, be ready,
for the Son of Man is coming at an hour that
you do not expect."
41 Now Peter said, "Lord, are You addressing
this parable to us, or to everyone *else* as well?"
42 And the Lord said, "Who then is the faithful
and prudent steward, whom his master will
put in charge of his servants, to give them
their rations at the proper time? 43 Blessed
is that slave whom his master finds so doing
when he comes. 44 Truly I say to you that he
will put him in charge of all his possessions.
45 But if that slave says in his heart, 'My master
will be a long time in coming,' and begins to
beat the male and female servants, and to eat
and drink and get drunk, 46 the master of that
slave will come on a day when he does not
expect and at an hour he does not know, and
will cut him in pieces, and assign him a place
with the unbelievers. 47 And that slave who
knew his master's will and did not get ready or
act in accord with his will, will receive many
beatings, 48 but the one who did not know *it,*
and committed deeds worthy of a beating,
will receive but a few. From everyone who has
been given much, much will be required, and
to whom they entrusted much, of him they
will ask all the more.
49 "I have come to cast fire upon the earth,
and how I wish it were already kindled!
50 But I have a baptism to undergo, and how
distressed I am until it is finished! 51 Do you
think that I came to grant peace on earth? I
tell you, no, but rather division; 52 for from
now on five *members* in one household
will be divided, three against two and
two against three. 53 They will be divided,
father against son and son against father,
mother against daughter and daughter
against mother, mother-in-law against
her daughter-in-law and daughter-in-law
against mother-in-law."
54 And He was also saying to the crowds,
"When you see a cloud rising in the west,
immediately you say, 'A shower is coming,'
and so it happens. 55 And when *you see* a
south wind blowing, you say, 'It will be a
hot day,' and it happens. 56 You hypocrites!
You know how to examine the appearance
of the earth and the sky, but why do you not
examine this present time?
57 "And why do you not even judge for
yourselves what is right? 58 For while you
are going with your opponent to appear
before the magistrate, on *your* way *there*
make an effort to settle with him, so that
he may not drag you before the judge, and
the judge turn you over to the officer, and
the officer throw you into prison. 59 I say to
you, you will not get out of there until you
have paid the last lepton."

There can be no authority save that which is infallible and Divine,
that is, God speaking to us directly in His Word.

— HORATIUS BONAR

APRIL 16

Joshua 21:1–22:34

21 Then the heads of households of the Levites came near to Eleazar the priest and to Joshua the son of Nun and to the heads of households of the tribes of the sons of Israel. 2 And they spoke to them at Shiloh in the land of Canaan, saying, "Yahweh commanded by the hand of Moses to give us cities to live in, with their pasture lands for our cattle." 3 So the sons of Israel gave the Levites from their inheritance these cities with their pasture lands, according to the command of Yahweh. 4 Then the lot came out for the families of the Kohathites. And the sons of Aaron the priest, who were of the Levites, received thirteen cities by lot from the tribe of Judah and from the tribe of the Simeonites and from the tribe of Benjamin.

5 Now the rest of the sons of Kohath received ten cities by lot from the families of the tribe of Ephraim and from the tribe of Dan and from the half-tribe of Manasseh.

6 And the sons of Gershon received thirteen cities by lot from the families of the tribe of Issachar and from the tribe of Asher and from the tribe of Naphtali, and from the half-tribe of Manasseh in Bashan.

7 The sons of Merari according to their families received twelve cities from the tribe of Reuben and from the tribe of Gad and from the tribe of Zebulun.

8 So the sons of Israel gave by lot to the Levites these cities with their pasture lands, as Yahweh had commanded by the hand of Moses.

9 They also gave from the tribe of the sons of Judah and from the tribe of the sons of Simeon these cities which are *here* mentioned by name; 10 and they were for the sons of Aaron, one of the families of the Kohathites, of the sons of Levi, for the lot was theirs first. 11 So they gave them Kiriath-arba (*Arba being* the father of Anak), that is, Hebron, in the hill country of Judah, with its pasture lands all around it. 12 But the fields of the city and its villages they gave to Caleb the son of Jephunneh as his possession.

13 Thus to the sons of Aaron the priest they gave Hebron, the city of refuge for the manslayer, with its pasture lands, Libnah also with its pasture lands, 14 Jattir with its pasture lands, Eshtemoa with its pasture lands, 15 Holon with its pasture lands, and Debir with its pasture lands, 16 and Ain with its pasture lands, and Juttah with its pasture lands, *and* Beth-shemesh with its pasture lands; nine cities from these two tribes. 17 From the tribe of Benjamin, Gibeon with its pasture lands, Geba with its pasture lands, 18 Anathoth with its pasture lands and Almon with its pasture lands; four cities. 19 All the cities of the sons of Aaron, the priests, were thirteen cities with their pasture lands.

20 Then the cities from the tribe of Ephraim were allotted to the families of the sons of Kohath, the Levites, *even to* the rest of the sons of Kohath. 21 And they gave them Shechem, the city of refuge for the manslayer, with its pasture lands, in the hill country of Ephraim, and Gezer with its pasture lands, 22 and Kibzaim with its pasture lands, and Beth-horon with its pasture lands; four cities. 23 From the tribe of Dan, Elteke with its pasture lands, Gibbethon with its pasture lands, 24 Aijalon with its pasture lands, and Gath-rimmon with its pasture lands; four cities. 25 From the half-tribe of Manasseh, *they gave* Taanach with its pasture lands and Gath-rimmon with its pasture lands; two cities. 26 All the cities with their pasture lands for the families of the rest of the sons of Kohath were ten.

27 Now to the sons of Gershon, one of the families of the Levites, from the half-tribe of Manasseh, *they gave* Golan in Bashan, the city of refuge for the manslayer, with its pasture lands, and Be-eshterah with its pasture lands; two cities. 28 From the tribe of

Issachar, *they gave* Kishion with its pasture
lands, Daberath with its pasture lands,
29 Jarmuth with its pasture lands, En-gannim
with its pasture lands; four cities. 30 From
the tribe of Asher, *they gave* Mishal with its
pasture lands, Abdon with its pasture lands,
31 Helkath with its pasture lands and Rehob
with its pasture lands; four cities. 32 From
the tribe of Naphtali, *they gave* Kedesh in
Galilee, the city of refuge for the manslayer,
with its pasture lands and Hammoth-dor
with its pasture lands and Kartan with its
pasture lands; three cities. 33 All the cities of
the Gershonites according to their families
were thirteen cities with their pasture lands.
34 Now to the families of the sons of
Merari, the rest of the Levites, *they gave*
from the tribe of Zebulun, Jokneam with
its pasture lands *and* Kartah with its
pasture lands. 35 Dimnah with its pasture
lands, Nahalal with its pasture lands; four
cities. 36 From the tribe of Reuben, *they
gave* Bezer with its pasture lands and Jahaz
with its pasture lands, 37 Kedemoth with
its pasture lands and Mephaath with its
pasture lands; four cities. 38 From the tribe
of Gad, *they gave* Ramoth in Gilead, the city
of refuge for the manslayer, with its pasture
lands and Mahanaim with its pasture lands,
39 Heshbon with its pasture lands, Jazer with
its pasture lands; four cities in all. 40 All
these were the cities of the sons of Merari
according to their families, the rest of the
families of the Levites; and their lot was
twelve cities.

41 All the cities of the Levites in the midst
of the possession of the sons of Israel were
forty-eight cities with their pasture lands.
42 These cities each had its surrounding
pasture lands; thus *it was* with all these
cities.

43 So Yahweh gave Israel all the land which
He had sworn to give to their fathers, and
they possessed it and lived in it. 44 And Yah-
weh gave them rest on every side, according
to all that He had sworn to their fathers, and
no one of all their enemies stood before
them; Yahweh gave all their enemies into
their hand. 45 Not *one* promise of the good
promises which Yahweh had promised to
the house of Israel failed; all came to pass.

22 Then Joshua summoned the Reu-
benites and the Gadites and the
half-tribe of Manasseh, 2 and said to them,
"You have kept all that Moses the servant of
Yahweh commanded you and have listened
to my voice in all that I commanded you.
3 You have not forsaken your brothers these
many days to this day, but have kept the
responsibility of the commandment of Yah-
weh your God. 4 And now Yahweh your God
has given rest to your brothers, as He spoke
to them; so now turn and go to your tents,
to the land of your possession, which Moses
the servant of Yahweh gave you beyond the
Jordan. 5 Only keep yourselves very carefully
to do the commandment and the law which
Moses the servant of Yahweh commanded
you, to love Yahweh your God and walk in
all His ways and keep His commandments
and cling to Him and serve Him with all your
heart and with all your soul." 6 Then Joshua
blessed them and sent them away, and they
went to their tents.

7 Now to the one half-tribe of Manasseh
Moses had given *a possession* in Bashan, but
to the other half Joshua gave *a possession*
among their brothers westward beyond the
Jordan. So when Joshua sent them away to
their tents, he blessed them, 8 and spoke to
them, saying, "Return to your tents with
great riches and with very much livestock,
with silver, gold, bronze, iron, and with
very many clothes; divide the spoil of
your enemies with your brothers." 9 Then
the sons of Reuben and the sons of Gad
and the half-tribe of Manasseh returned
home and departed from the sons of Israel
at Shiloh which is in the land of Canaan,
to go to the land of Gilead, to the land of
their possession which they had possessed,
according to the command of Yahweh by the
hand of Moses.

10 And they came to the region of the Jor-
dan which is in the land of Canaan, and the
sons of Reuben and the sons of Gad and the
half-tribe of Manasseh built an altar there by
the Jordan, a large altar in appearance. 11 And
the sons of Israel heard *it* said, "Behold, the
sons of Reuben and the sons of Gad and the
half-tribe of Manasseh have built an altar at
the entrance of the land of Canaan, in the
region of the Jordan, on the side *belonging to*
the sons of Israel." 12 Then the sons of Israel
heard *of it,* and the whole congregation of
the sons of Israel assembled themselves at
Shiloh to go up against them in war.

13 Then the sons of Israel sent to the sons
of Reuben and to the sons of Gad and to the

half-tribe of Manasseh, into the land of Gil-
ead, Phinehas the son of Eleazar the priest,
14 and with him ten leaders, one leader for
each father's household from each of the
tribes of Israel; and each one of them *was*
the head of his father's household among
the thousands of Israel. 15 So they came to
the sons of Reuben and to the sons of Gad
and to the half-tribe of Manasseh, to the
land of Gilead, and they spoke with them
saying, 16 "Thus says the whole congrega-
tion of Yahweh, 'What is this unfaithful
act which you have committed against the
God of Israel, turning away from following
Yahweh this day, by building yourselves
an altar, to rebel against Yahweh this day?
17 Is the iniquity of Peor too small *a thing*
for us, from which we have not cleansed
ourselves to this day, although there was
a plague on the congregation of Yahweh?
18 Yet you are turning away this day from
following Yahweh. Now it will be that, if
you rebel against Yahweh today, He will be
angry with the whole congregation of Israel
tomorrow. 19 If, however, the land of your
possession is unclean, then cross into the
land of the possession of Yahweh, where the
tabernacle of Yahweh dwells, and take pos-
session among us. But do not rebel against
Yahweh, nor rebel against us by building
an altar for yourselves, besides the altar
of Yahweh our God. 20 Did not Achan the
son of Zerah act unfaithfully in the things
devoted to destruction, and indignation fall
on all the congregation of Israel? But he was
not the only man to breathe his last in his
iniquity.'"

21 Then the sons of Reuben and the sons
of Gad and the half-tribe of Manasseh
answered and spoke to the heads of the
thousands of Israel. 22 "The Mighty One,
God, Yahweh, the Mighty One, God, Yahweh!
He knows, and may Israel itself know. If *it*
was in rebellion or if in an unfaithful act
against Yahweh, do not save us this day!
23 If we have built for ourselves an altar to
turn away from following Yahweh, or if to
perform a burnt offering or grain offering on
it, or if to offer sacrifices of peace offerings
on it, may Yahweh Himself require it. 24 But
truly we have done this out of concern, for
a reason, saying, 'In time to come your sons
may say to our sons, "What have you to do
with Yahweh, the God of Israel? 25 And Yah-
weh has made the Jordan a border between
us and you, *you* sons of Reuben and sons
of Gad; you have no portion in Yahweh." So
your sons may make our sons stop fearing
Yahweh.'

26 "Therefore we said, 'Let us build an
altar, not for burnt offering or for sacrifice;
27 rather it shall be a witness between us
and you and between our generations after
us, that we are to perform the service of
Yahweh before Him with our burnt offerings
and with our sacrifices and with our peace
offerings, so that your sons will not say to
our sons in time to come, "You have no
portion in Yahweh."' 28 Therefore we said,
'It will also be that if they say *this* to us or
to our generations in time to come, then
we shall say, "See the copy of the altar of
Yahweh which our fathers made, not for
burnt offering or for sacrifice; rather it is
a witness between us and you."' 29 Far be it
from us to rebel against Yahweh and turn
away from following Yahweh this day, by
building an altar for burnt offering, for
grain offering or for sacrifice, besides the
altar of Yahweh our God which is before His
tabernacle."

30 So Phinehas the priest and the leaders
of the congregation, even the heads of
the thousands of Israel who *were* with
him, heard the words which the sons of
Reuben and the sons of Gad and the sons
of Manasseh spoke. And it was good in their
sight. 31 And Phinehas the son of Eleazar the
priest said to the sons of Reuben and to the
sons of Gad and to the sons of Manasseh,
"Today we know that Yahweh is in our
midst because you have not committed this
unfaithful act against Yahweh; so then you
have delivered the sons of Israel from the
hand of Yahweh."

32 Then Phinehas the son of Eleazar
the priest and the leaders returned from
the sons of Reuben and from the sons of
Gad, from the land of Gilead to the land of
Canaan, to the sons of Israel, and brought
back word to them. 33 And the word was
good in the sight of the sons of Israel, and
the sons of Israel blessed God; and they
did not speak of going up against them in
war to destroy the land in which the sons
of Reuben and the sons of Gad were living.
34 And the sons of Reuben and the sons of
Gad called the altar *Witness*; "For," *they said*,
"it is a witness between us that Yahweh is
God."

Psalm 46:7–11

7 Yahweh of hosts is with us;
The God of Jacob is our
stronghold. Selah.

8 Come, behold the works of Yahweh,
Who has appointed desolations
in the earth.
9 He makes wars to cease to
the end of the earth;
He breaks the bow and
cuts up the spear;
He burns the chariots with fire.
10 "Cease *striving* and know that I am God;
I will be exalted among the nations,
I will be exalted in the earth."
11 Yahweh of hosts is with us;
The God of Jacob is our
stronghold. Selah.

Proverbs 14:12–13

12 There is a way *which seems*
right to a man,
But its end is the way of death.
13 Even in laughter the heart
may be in pain,
And the end of joy may be grief.

Luke 13:1–21

13 Now at that same time there were
some present who were reporting to
Him about the Galileans whose blood Pilate
had mixed with their sacrifices. 2 And Jesus
answered and said to them, "Do you think
that these Galileans were *greater* sinners
than all *other* Galileans because they suf-
fered these things? 3 I tell you, no, but unless
you repent, you will all likewise perish. 4 Or
do you think that those eighteen on whom
the tower in Siloam fell and killed them were
worse offenders than all the men who live
in Jerusalem? 5 I tell you, no, but unless you
repent, you will all likewise perish."
6 And He was telling this parable: "A man
had a fig tree which had been planted in his
vineyard; and he came seeking fruit on it
and did not find any. 7 And he said to the
vineyard-keeper, 'Behold, for three years
I have come seeking fruit on this fig tree
without finding any. Cut it down! Why
does it even use up the ground?' 8 And he
answered and said to him, 'Let it alone, sir,
for this year too, until I dig around it and put
in manure, 9 and if it bears fruit next year,
fine, but if not, cut it down.'"
10 And He was teaching in one of the
synagogues on the Sabbath. 11 And behold,
there was a woman who for eighteen years
had a sickness caused by a spirit, and she
was bent double, and could not straighten
up at all. 12 But when Jesus saw her, He called
her over and said to her, "Woman, you are
freed from your sickness." 13 And He laid
His hands on her, and immediately she
was made erect again and *began* glorifying
God. 14 But the synagogue official, indig-
nant because Jesus healed on the Sabbath,
answered and was saying to the crowd,
"There are six days in which work should be
done; so come during them and get healed,
and not on the Sabbath day." 15 But the Lord
answered him and said, "You hypocrites,
does not each of you on the Sabbath release
his ox or his donkey from the stall and lead
it away to water *it*? 16 And this woman, being
a daughter of Abraham, whom Satan has
bound for—behold—eighteen years, should
she not have been released from this bond
on the Sabbath day?" 17 And as He said this,
all His opponents were being put to shame;
and the entire crowd was rejoicing over all
the glorious things being done by Him.
18 Therefore, He was saying, "What is
the kingdom of God like, and to what shall
I compare it? 19 It is like a mustard seed,
which a man took and threw into his own
garden, and it grew and became a tree,
and THE BIRDS OF THE AIR NESTED IN ITS
BRANCHES."
20 And again He said, "To what shall I
compare the kingdom of God? 21 It is like
leaven, which a woman took and hid in
three sata of flour until it was all leavened."

APRIL 17

Joshua 23:1–24:33

23 Now it happened after many days,
after Yahweh had given rest to Israel
from all their enemies on every side, and
Joshua was old, advanced in years, 2 that
Joshua called for all Israel, for their elders
and their heads and their judges and
their officers, and said to them, "I am old,

advanced in years. 3 And you have seen all that Yahweh your God has done to all these nations because of you, for Yahweh your God is He who has been fighting for you. 4 See, I have allotted to you these nations which remain as an inheritance for your tribes, with all the nations which I have cut off, from the Jordan even to the Great Sea toward the setting of the sun. 5 And Yahweh your God, He will thrust them out from before you and dispossess them before you; and you will possess their land, just as Yahweh your God promised you. 6 Be very strong, then, to keep and to do all that is written in the book of the law of Moses, so that you may not turn aside from it to the right hand or to the left, 7 so that you will not go *along* with these nations, these which remain among you, and you will not mention the name of their gods, and you will not make *anyone* swear *by them*, and you will not serve them, and you will not bow down to them. 8 But you are to cling to Yahweh your God, as you have done to this day. 9 For Yahweh has dispossessed great and mighty nations from before you; and as for you, no man has stood before you to this day. 10 One of your men will pursue one thousand, for Yahweh your God is He who fights for you, just as He promised you. 11 So keep your souls very carefully to love Yahweh your God. 12 For if you ever turn back and cling to the rest of these nations, these which remain among you, and intermarry with them, so that you go *along* with them and they with you, 13 know with certainty that Yahweh your God will not continue to dispossess these nations from before you; but they will be a snare and a trap to you and a whip on your sides and thorns in your eyes, until you perish from off this good land which Yahweh your God has given you.

14 "Now behold, today I am going the way of all the earth, and you know in all your hearts and in all your souls that not one word of all the good words which Yahweh *your God spoke concerning* you has failed; all have come to pass for you; not one word of them has failed. 15 And it will be that just as all the good words which Yahweh your God spoke to you have come upon you, so Yahweh will bring upon you all the calamitous words, until He has destroyed you from off this good land which Yahweh your God has given you. 16 When you trespass against the covenant of Yahweh your God, which He commanded you, and go and serve other gods and bow down to them, then the anger of Yahweh will burn against you, and you will perish quickly from off the good land which He has given you."

24 Then Joshua gathered all the tribes of Israel to Shechem and called for the elders of Israel and for their heads and their judges and their officers; and they presented themselves before God. 2 And Joshua said to all the people, "Thus says Yahweh, the God of Israel, 'From ancient times your fathers lived beyond the River, *namely*, Terah, the father of Abraham and the father of Nahor, and they served other gods. 3 Then I took your father Abraham from beyond the River and led him through all the land of Canaan and multiplied his seed and gave him Isaac. 4 To Isaac I gave Jacob and Esau, and to Esau I gave Mount Seir to possess it; but Jacob and his sons went down to Egypt. 5 Then I sent Moses and Aaron, and I smote Egypt by what I did in its midst; and afterward I brought you out. 6 And I brought your fathers out of Egypt, and you came to the sea; and Egypt pursued your fathers with chariots and horsemen to the Red Sea. 7 Then they cried out to Yahweh; He put darkness between you and the Egyptians and brought the sea upon them and covered them; and your own eyes saw what I did in Egypt. And you lived in the wilderness for many days. 8 Then I brought you into the land of the Amorites who lived beyond the Jordan, and they fought with you; and I gave them into your hand, and you took possession of their land, and I destroyed them before you. 9 Then Balak the son of Zippor, king of Moab, arose and fought against Israel, and he sent and summoned Balaam the son of Beor to curse you. 10 But I was not willing to listen to Balaam. So he blessed you repeatedly, and I delivered you from his hand. 11 And you crossed the Jordan and came to Jericho; and the citizens of Jericho fought against you, *and* the Amorite and the Perizzite and the Canaanite and the Hittite and the Girgashite, the Hivite and the Jebusite. Thus I gave them into your hand. 12 Then I sent the hornet before you, and it drove out the two kings of the Amorites from before you, *but* not by your sword or your bow. 13 And I gave you a land on which

you had not labored and cities which you
had not built, and you have lived in them;
you are eating of vineyards and olive groves
which you did not plant.’
14 “So now, fear Yahweh and serve Him in
integrity and truth; and put away the gods
which your fathers served beyond the River
and in Egypt, and serve Yahweh. 15 If it is
evil in your sight to serve Yahweh, choose
for yourselves today whom you will serve:
whether the gods which your fathers served
which were beyond the River or the gods of
the Amorites in whose land you are living;
but as for me and my house, we will serve
Yahweh.”
16 And the people answered and said, “Far
be it from us that we should forsake Yahweh
to serve other gods; 17 for Yahweh our God
is He who brought us and our fathers up
out of the land of Egypt, from the house
of slavery, and who did these great signs
in our sight and kept us through all the
way in which we went and among all the
peoples through whose midst we passed.
18 And Yahweh drove out from before us all
the peoples, even the Amorites who lived
in the land. We also will serve Yahweh, for
He is our God.”
19 Then Joshua said to the people, “You
will not be able to serve Yahweh, for He
is a holy God. He is a jealous God; He will
not forgive your transgression or your
sins. 20 If you forsake Yahweh and serve
foreign gods, then He will turn and do
you harm and consume you after He has
done good to you.” 21 And the people said
to Joshua, “No, but we will serve Yahweh.”
22 And Joshua said to the people, “You are
witnesses against yourselves that you have
chosen for yourselves Yahweh, to serve
Him.” And they said, “We are witnesses.”
23 “So now, put away the foreign gods
which are in your midst, and incline your
hearts to Yahweh, the God of Israel.” 24 And
the people said to Joshua, “We will serve
Yahweh our God, and we will listen to His
voice.” 25 So Joshua cut a covenant with
the people that day and made for them a
statute and a judgment in Shechem. 26 And
Joshua wrote these words in the book of
the law of God; and he took a large stone
and set it up there under the oak that was
by the sanctuary of Yahweh. 27 And Joshua
said to all the people, “Behold, this stone
shall be for a witness against us, for it has
heard all the words of Yahweh which He
spoke to us; thus it shall be for a witness
against you, lest you deny your God.”
28 Then Joshua dismissed the people, each
to his inheritance.
29 Now it happened that after these
things, Joshua the son of Nun, the servant
of Yahweh, died, being 110 years old. 30 And
they buried him in the territory of his
inheritance in Timnath-serah, which is in
the hill country of Ephraim, on the north
of Mount Gaash.
31 And Israel served Yahweh all the days
of Joshua and all the days of the elders who
survived Joshua, who knew all the work of
Yahweh which He had done for Israel.
32 Now they buried the bones of Joseph,
which the sons of Israel brought up from
Egypt, at Shechem, in the portion of the
field which Jacob had bought from the
sons of Hamor the father of Shechem for
one hundred qesitah; and they became
the inheritance of Joseph’s sons. 33 And
Eleazar the son of Aaron died; and they
buried him at Gibeah of Phinehas his son,
which was given him in the hill country
of Ephraim.

Psalm 47:1–9

1 O clap your hands, all peoples;
Make a loud shout to God with
the sound of a shout of joy.
2 For Yahweh Most High is fearsome,
A great King over all the earth.
3 He subdues peoples under us
And nations under our feet.
4 He chooses our inheritance for us,
The pride of Jacob whom He
loves. Selah.

5 God has ascended with a loud shout,
Yahweh, with the sound of a trumpet.
6 Sing praises to God, sing praises;
Sing praises to our King,
sing praises.
7 For God is the King of all the earth;
Sing praises with a skillful psalm.
8 God reigns over the nations,
God sits on His holy throne.
9 The nobles of the peoples have
assembled themselves *with* the
people of the God of Abraham,
For the shields of the earth
belong to God;
He is highly exalted.

Proverbs 14:14

14 The one who turns back in *his* heart
will be satisfied with his ways,
But a good man will *be*
satisfied with his.

Luke 13:22–35

22 And He was passing through from one city and village to another, teaching, and proceeding on His way to Jerusalem. 23 And someone said to Him, "Lord, are there *just* a few who are being saved?" And He said to them, 24 "Strive to enter through the narrow door, for many, I tell you, will seek to enter and will not be able. 25 Once the head of the house gets up and shuts the door, and you begin to stand outside and knock on the door, saying, 'Lord, open up to us!' then He will answer and say to you, 'I do not know where you are from.' 26 Then you will begin to say, 'We ate and drank in Your presence, and You taught in our streets.' 27 And He will say, 'I tell you, I do not know where you are from; DEPART FROM ME, ALL YOU WORKERS OF UNRIGHTEOUSNESS.' 28 In that place there will be weeping and gnashing of teeth when you see Abraham and Isaac and Jacob and all the prophets in the kingdom of God, but yourselves being cast out. 29 And they will come from east and west and from north and south, and will recline *at the table* in the kingdom of God. 30 And behold, *some* are last who will be first and *some* are first who will be last."

31 Just at that time some Pharisees approached, saying to Him, "Leave and go from here, for Herod wants to kill You." 32 And He said to them, "Go and tell that fox, 'Behold, I cast out demons and perform cures today and tomorrow, and on the third *day* I finish.' 33 Nevertheless I must journey on today and tomorrow and the next *day*, for it is not possible that a prophet would perish outside of Jerusalem. 34 O Jerusalem, Jerusalem, *the city* that kills the prophets and stones those sent to her! How often I wanted to gather your children together, just as a hen *gathers* her brood under her wings, and you did not want *it*! 35 Behold, your house is left to you *desolate*, and I say to you, you will not see Me until *the time* comes when you say, 'BLESSED IS HE WHO COMES IN THE NAME OF THE LORD!'"

APRIL 18

Judges 1:1–2:23

1 Now it happened after the death of Joshua that the sons of Israel asked of Yahweh, saying, "Who shall go up first for us against the Canaanites, to fight against them?" 2 And Yahweh said, "Judah shall go up; behold, I have given the land into his hand." 3 Then Judah said to Simeon his brother, "Come up with me into the territory allotted me, that we may fight against the Canaanites; and I in turn will go with you into the territory allotted you." So Simeon went with him. 4 So Judah went up, and Yahweh gave the Canaanites and the Perizzites into their hands, and they struck down 10,000 men at Bezek. 5 *Then they found* Adoni-bezek in Bezek and fought against him, and they struck down the Canaanites and the Perizzites. 6 But Adoni-bezek fled; and they pursued him and seized him and cut off his thumbs and big toes. 7 And Adoni-bezek said, "Seventy kings with their thumbs and their big toes cut off used to gather up *scraps* under my table; as I have done, so God has repaid me." So they brought him to Jerusalem, and he died there.

8 Then the sons of Judah fought against Jerusalem and captured it and struck it with the edge of the sword and set the city on fire. 9 And afterward the sons of Judah went down to fight against the Canaanites living in the hill country and in the Negev and in the Shephelah. 10 So Judah went against the Canaanites who lived in Hebron (now the name of Hebron formerly *was* Kiriath-arba); and they struck Sheshai and Ahiman and Talmai.

11 Then from there he went against the inhabitants of Debir (now the name of Debir formerly *was* Kiriath-sepher). 12 And Caleb said, "The one who strikes Kiriath-sepher and captures it, I will even give him my daughter Achsah as a wife." 13 Then Othniel the son of Kenaz, Caleb's younger brother, captured it; so he gave him his daughter Achsah as a wife. 14 Now it happened that when she came *to him*, she enticed him to ask her father for the field. Then she

alighted from her donkey, and Caleb said
to her, "What do you want?" 15 And she said
to him, "Give me a blessing, since you have
given me the land of the Negev, so you shall
give me also springs of water." So Caleb gave
her the upper springs and the lower springs.

16 Now the sons of the Kenite, Moses'
father-in-law, went up from the city of palms
with the sons of Judah, to the wilderness
of Judah which is in the south of Arad; and
they went and lived with the people. 17 Then
Judah went with Simeon his brother, and
they struck the Canaanites living in Zephath
and devoted it to destruction. So the name
of the city was called Hormah. 18 And
Judah captured Gaza with its territory
and Ashkelon with its territory and Ekron
with its territory. 19 Now Yahweh was with
Judah, and they took possession of the hill
country; but they *could* not dispossess the
inhabitants of the valley because they had
iron chariots. 20 Then they gave Hebron
to Caleb, as Moses had promised; and he
dispossessed from there the three sons of
Anak. 21 But the sons of Benjamin did not
dispossess the Jebusites who lived in Jeru-
salem; so the Jebusites have lived with the
sons of Benjamin in Jerusalem to this day.

22 Likewise the house of Joseph went up
against Bethel, and Yahweh was with them.
23 And the house of Joseph spied out Bethel
(now the name of the city was formerly Luz).
24 Then the spies saw a man coming out of
the city, and they said to him, "Please show
us the entrance to the city, and we will treat
you with lovingkindness." 25 So he showed
them the entrance to the city, and they
struck the city with the edge of the sword,
but they let the man and all his family go
free. 26 So the man went into the land of the
Hittites and built a city and named it Luz
which is its name to this day.

27 But Manasseh did not take possession
of Beth-shean and its towns or Taanach and
its towns or the inhabitants of Dor and its
towns or the inhabitants of Ibleam and its
towns or the inhabitants of Megiddo and its
towns; so the Canaanites persisted to live in
that land. 28 And it happened when Israel
became strong, that they put the Canaanites
to forced labor, but they did not dispossess
them completely.

29 Also Ephraim did not dispossess the
Canaanites who were living in Gezer; so
the Canaanites lived in Gezer among them.

30 Zebulun did not dispossess the inhabi-
tants of Kitron or the inhabitants of Nahalol;
so the Canaanites lived among them and
became subject to forced labor.

31 Asher did not dispossess the inhabi-
tants of Acco or the inhabitants of Sidon,
or of Ahlab or of Achzib or of Helbah or of
Aphik or of Rehob. 32 So the Asherites lived
among the Canaanites, the inhabitants of
the land; for they did not dispossess them.

33 Naphtali did not dispossess the
inhabitants of Beth-shemesh or the inhab-
itants of Beth-anath, but lived among the
Canaanites, the inhabitants of the land;
and the inhabitants of Beth-shemesh and
Beth-anath became forced labor for them.

34 Then the Amorites pressed the sons of
Dan into the hill country, for they did not
allow them to come down to the valley;
35 and the Amorites persisted in living in
Mount Heres, in Aijalon, and in Shaalbim;
but the hand of the house of Joseph became
heavy, and they became forced labor. 36 Now
the border of the Amorites ran from the
ascent of Akrabbim, from Sela and upward.

2 Then the angel of Yahweh came up from
Gilgal to Bochim. And he said, "I brought
you up out of Egypt and led you into the
land which I have sworn to your fathers;
and I said, 'I will never break My covenant
with you, 2 and as for you, you shall cut no
covenant with the inhabitants of this land;
you shall tear down their altars.' But you
have not listened to My voice; what is this
you have done? 3 Therefore I also said, 'I will
not drive them out before you; but they will
become *as thorns* in your sides, and their
gods will become a snare to you.'" 4 So it
happened that when the angel of Yahweh
spoke these words to all the sons of Israel,
the people lifted up their voices and wept.
5 So they named that place Bochim; and
there they sacrificed to Yahweh.

6 Then Joshua sent the people away, and
the sons of Israel went each to his inheri-
tance to possess the land. 7 And the people
served Yahweh all the days of Joshua and all
the days of the elders who survived Joshua,
who saw all the great work of Yahweh which
He had done for Israel. 8 Then Joshua the
son of Nun, the servant of Yahweh, died
at the age of 110. 9 And they buried him in
the territory of his inheritance in Timnath-
heres, in the hill country of Ephraim, north

of Mount Gaash. 10 And all that generation
also were gathered to their fathers; and
there arose another generation after them
who did not know Yahweh or even the work
which He had done for Israel.

11 Then the sons of Israel did what was
evil in the eyes of Yahweh and served the
Baals, 12 and they forsook Yahweh, the God
of their fathers, who had brought them out
of the land of Egypt, and followed other gods
from *among* the gods of the peoples who
were around them and bowed themselves
down to them; thus they provoked Yahweh
to anger. 13 So they forsook Yahweh and
served Baal and the Ashtaroth. 14 And the
anger of Yahweh burned against Israel, and
He gave them into the hands of plunderers
who plundered them; and He sold them into
the hands of their enemies around *them*,
so that they could no longer stand before
their enemies. 15 Wherever they went, the
hand of Yahweh was against them for evil,
as Yahweh had spoken and as Yahweh had
sworn to them, so that they were severely
distressed.

16 Then Yahweh raised up judges who
saved them from the hands of those who
plundered them. 17 Yet they did not listen to
their judges either, for they played the harlot
after other gods and bowed themselves
down to them. They turned aside quickly
from the way in which their fathers had
walked in obeying the commandments of
Yahweh; they did not do as *their fathers*.
18 Now when Yahweh raised up judges
for them, Yahweh was with the judge and
saved them from the hand of their enemies
all the days of the judge; for Yahweh was
moved to pity by their groaning because of
those who oppressed and suppressed them.
19 But it happened when the judge died,
that they would turn back and act more
corruptly than their fathers, in following
other gods to serve them and bow down to
them; they did not abandon their practices
or their stubborn ways. 20 So the anger of
Yahweh burned against Israel, and He said,
"Because this nation has trespassed against
My covenant which I commanded their
fathers and has not listened to My voice, 21 I
also will no longer dispossess before them
any of the nations which Joshua left when
he died, 22 in order to test Israel by them,
whether they will keep the way of Yahweh
to walk in it as their fathers did, or not." 23 So
Yahweh allowed those nations to rest, not
dispossessing them quickly; and He did not
give them into the hand of Joshua.

Psalm 48:1–8

1 Great is Yahweh, and greatly
to be praised,
In the city of our God, His
holy mountain.
2 Beautiful in elevation, the joy
of the whole earth,
Is Mount Zion *in* the far north,
The city of the great King.
3 God, in her palaces,
Has made Himself known
as a stronghold.

4 For, behold, the kings
assembled themselves,
They passed by together.
5 They saw *it*, then they
were astonished;
They were dismayed, they
fled in alarm.
6 Panic seized them there,
Anguish, as of a woman in childbirth.
7 With the east wind
You break the ships of Tarshish.
8 As we have heard, so have we seen
In the city of Yahweh of hosts,
in the city of our God;
God will establish her forever. Selah.

Proverbs 14:15–17

15 The simple believes everything,
But the prudent one discerns his steps.
16 A wise man fears and turns
away from evil,
But a fool gets angry and *feels* secure.
17 A quick-tempered man acts in folly,
And a man of evil schemes is hated.

Luke 14:1–24

14 And it happened that when He went
into the house of one of the leaders
of the Pharisees on *the* Sabbath to eat
bread, they were watching Him closely.
2 And behold, in front of Him was a man
suffering from dropsy. 3 And Jesus answered
and spoke to the scholars of the Law and
Pharisees, saying, "Is it lawful to heal on the
Sabbath, or not?" 4 But they were silent. And
He took hold of him, healed him, and sent
him away. 5 And He said to them, "Which
one of you will have a son or an ox fall into a

well, and will not immediately pull him out
on a Sabbath day?" 6 And they could make
no reply to this.

7 And He was telling a parable to the
invited guests when He noticed how they
were picking out the places of honor *at
the table*, saying to them, 8 "When you are
invited by someone to a wedding feast, do not
recline at the place of honor, lest someone
more highly regarded than you be invited by
him, 9 and he who invited you both will come
and say to you, 'Give *your* place to this man,'
and then in shame you proceed to occupy
the last place. 10 But when you are invited,
go and recline at the last place, so that when
the one who has invited you comes, he may
say to you, 'Friend, move up higher'; then you
will have honor in the sight of all who recline
at the table with you. 11 For everyone who
exalts himself will be humbled, and he who
humbles himself will be exalted."

12 And He also went on to say to the one
who had invited Him, "When you give a
luncheon or a dinner, do not invite your
friends or your brothers or your relatives
or rich neighbors, lest they also invite you
in return and *that* will be your repayment.
13 But when you give a reception, invite *the*
poor, *the* crippled, *the* lame, *the* blind, 14 and
you will be blessed, since they do not have
the means to repay you; for it will be repaid
to you at the resurrection of the righteous."

15 But when one of those who were reclin-
ing *at the table* with Him heard this, he said
to Him, "Blessed is everyone who will eat
bread in the kingdom of God!"

16 And He said to him, "A man was giving
a big dinner, and he invited many. 17 And
at the dinner hour he sent his slave to say
to those who had been invited, 'Come,
for everything is ready now.' 18 But they
all alike began to make excuses. The first
one said to him, 'I have bought a piece of
land and I need to go out and look at it.
I ask you, consider me excused.' 19 And
another one said, 'I have bought five yoke
of oxen, and I am going to try them out.
I ask you, consider me excused.' 20 And
another one said, 'I have married a wife,
and for that reason I cannot come.' 21 And
when the slave came *back*, he reported
these things to his master. Then the
head of the household became angry and
said to his slave, 'Go out at once into the
streets and lanes of the city and bring in
here the poor and crippled and blind and
lame.' 22 And the slave said, 'Master, what
you commanded has been done, and still
there is room.' 23 And the master said to the
slave, 'Go out into the highways and along
the fences, and compel *them* to come in,
so that my house may be filled. 24 For I tell
you, none of those men who were invited
shall taste of my dinner.'"

APRIL 19

Judges 3:1–4:24

3 Now these are the nations which Yah-
weh *allowed to* remain, to test Israel by
them (*that is*, all who had not known any of
the wars of Canaan; 2 however, *God tested
them* in order that the generations of the
sons of Israel would know *war*, by learning
war, especially those who had not known it
formerly). 3 *These nations are:* the five lords
of the Philistines and all the Canaanites and
the Sidonians and the Hivites who lived in
Mount Lebanon, from Mount Baal-hermon
as far as Lebo-hamath. 4 And they were for
testing Israel, to know if they would obey
the commandments of Yahweh, which He
had commanded their fathers by the hand
of Moses. 5 Now the sons of Israel lived
among the Canaanites, the Hittites, the
Amorites, the Perizzites, the Hivites, and the
Jebusites; 6 and they took their daughters
for themselves as wives and gave their own
daughters to their sons and served their
gods.

7 Thus the sons of Israel did what was evil
in the eyes of Yahweh and forgot Yahweh
their God and served the Baals and the
Asheroth. 8 Then the anger of Yahweh
burned against Israel, so that He sold them
into the hands of Cushan-rishathaim king
of Mesopotamia; and the sons of Israel
served Cushan-rishathaim eight years.
9 Then the sons of Israel cried to Yahweh,
and Yahweh raised up a savior for the sons
of Israel to save them, Othniel the son of
Kenaz, Caleb's younger brother. 10 And
the Spirit of Yahweh came upon him, and
he judged Israel. And he went out to war,
and Yahweh gave Cushan-rishathaim king

of Mesopotamia into his hand. So his hand
was strong against Cushan-rishathaim.
11 Then the land was quiet for forty years.
And Othniel the son of Kenaz died.

12 Then the sons of Israel again did what
was evil in the eyes of Yahweh. So Yahweh
strengthened Eglon the king of Moab
against Israel because they had done what
was evil in the eyes of Yahweh. 13 And he
gathered to himself the sons of Ammon and
Amalek; and he went and struck Israel, and
they possessed the city of the palm trees.
14 So the sons of Israel served Eglon the king
of Moab eighteen years.

15 Then the sons of Israel cried to Yah-
weh, and Yahweh raised up a savior for
them, Ehud the son of Gera, the Benjamite,
a left-handed man. And the sons of Israel
sent tribute by his hand to Eglon the king
of Moab. 16 And Ehud made himself a sword
which had two edges, a cubit in length, and
he bound it on his right thigh under his
cloak. 17 Then he brought the tribute near
to Eglon king of Moab. Now Eglon was a
very fat man. 18 And it happened when he
had finished bringing the tribute near, that
he sent away the people who had carried
the tribute. 19 But he himself turned back
from the graven images which were at
Gilgal and said, "I have a secret message for
you, O king." And he said, "Keep silence."
And all who stood by him left him. 20 But
Ehud came to him while he was sitting
alone in his cool roof chamber. And Ehud
said, "I have a message from God for you."
And he arose from his seat. 21 Then Ehud
sent forth his left hand, took the sword
from his right thigh, and thrust it into his
belly. 22 The handle also went in after the
blade, and the fat closed over the blade,
for he did not draw the sword out of his
belly; and the refuse came out. 23 Then
Ehud went out into the vestibule and shut
the doors of the roof chamber behind him
and locked *them*.

24 Now he went out, and his servants
came in and looked, and behold, the doors
of the roof chamber were locked; and they
said, "He is surely relieving himself in the
cool room." 25 Then they waited until they
were ashamed; but behold, he did not open
the doors of the roof chamber. Therefore
they took the key and opened them, and
behold, their master had fallen to the floor
dead.

26 Now Ehud escaped while they were
delaying, and he passed by the graven
images and escaped to Seirah. 27 And it
happened when he had arrived, that he blew
the trumpet in the hill country of Ephraim;
and the sons of Israel went down with him
from the hill country, and he *was* in front
of them. 28 Then he said to them, "Pursue
them, for Yahweh has given your enemies
the Moabites into your hands." So they went
down after him and captured the fords of
the Jordan opposite Moab and did not allow
anyone to cross. 29 And they struck down at
that time about 10,000 Moabites, all robust
and valiant men; and no one escaped. 30 So
Moab was subdued that day under the hand
of Israel. And the land was quiet for eighty
years.

31 Now after him was Shamgar the son of
Anath. And he struck down 600 Philistines
with an oxgoad; and he also saved Israel.

4 Then the sons of Israel again did what
was evil in the eyes of Yahweh. Now
Ehud had died. 2 And Yahweh sold them
into the hand of Jabin king of Canaan, who
reigned in Hazor; and the commander of his
army was Sisera, who lived in Harosheth-
hagoyim. 3 Then the sons of Israel cried to
Yahweh; for he had 900 iron chariots, and
he oppressed the sons of Israel severely for
twenty years.

4 Now Deborah, a prophetess, the wife of
Lappidoth, was judging Israel at that time.
5 And she used to sit under the palm tree
of Deborah between Ramah and Bethel in
the hill country of Ephraim; and the sons of
Israel came up to her for judgment. 6 Then
she sent and summoned Barak the son of
Abinoam from Kedesh-naphtali and said
to him, "Has not Yahweh, the God of Israel,
commanded, 'Go and march to Mount
Tabor, and take with you 10,000 men from
the sons of Naphtali and from the sons of
Zebulun? 7 And I will draw out to you Sisera,
the commander of Jabin's army, with his
chariots and his many troops to the river
Kishon, and I will give him into your hand.'"
8 Then Barak said to her, "If you will go with
me, then I will go; but if you will not go with
me, I will not go." 9 So she said, "I will surely
go with you; nevertheless, the honor shall
not be yours on the journey that you are
about to take, for Yahweh will sell Sisera into
the hand of a woman." Then Deborah arose

and went with Barak to Kedesh. 10 Then
Barak called Zebulun and Naphtali together
to Kedesh, and 10,000 men went up with
him; Deborah also went up with him.

11 Now Heber the Kenite had separated
himself from the Kenites, from the sons of
Hobab the father-in-law of Moses, and had
pitched his tent as far away as the oak in
Zaanannim, which is near Kedesh.

12 Then they told Sisera that Barak the son
of Abinoam had gone up to Mount Tabor.
13 So Sisera called together all his chariots,
900 iron chariots, and all the people who
were with him, from Harosheth-hagoyim
to the river Kishon. 14 And Deborah said to
Barak, “Arise! For this is the day in which
Yahweh has given Sisera into your hand;
has not Yahweh gone out before you?” So
Barak went down from Mount Tabor with
10,000 men following him. 15 And Yahweh
threw Sisera and all *his* chariots and all *his*
camp into confusion with the edge of the
sword before Barak; and Sisera came down
from *his* chariot and fled away on foot. 16 But
Barak pursued the chariots and *all those in*
the camp as far as Harosheth-hagoyim, and
all the camp of Sisera fell by the edge of the
sword; not even one remained.

17 Now Sisera fled away on foot to the tent
of Jael the wife of Heber the Kenite, for *there*
was peace between Jabin the king of Hazor
and the house of Heber the Kenite. 18 And
Jael went out to meet Sisera and said to him,
“Turn aside, my master, turn aside to me!
Do not be afraid.” And he turned aside to
her into the tent, and she covered him with
a rug. 19 Then he said to her, “Please give me
a little water to drink, for I am thirsty.” So
she opened a bottle of milk and gave him
a drink; then she covered him. 20 And he
said to her, “Stand in the doorway of the
tent, and it shall be if anyone comes and
asks of you and says, ‘Is there a man here?’
that you shall say, ‘No.’” 21 Then Jael, Heber’s
wife, took a tent peg and placed a hammer
in her hand and went secretly to him and
drove the peg into his temple, and it went
through into the ground; for he was sound
asleep and exhausted. So he died. 22 Now
behold, Barak was pursuing Sisera, and
Jael came out to meet him and said to him,
“Come, and I will show you the man whom
you are seeking.” And he entered with her,
and behold, Sisera was lying dead with the
tent peg in his temple.

23 So God subdued on that day Jabin the
king of Canaan before the sons of Israel.
24 And the hand of the sons of Israel went
forth heavier and heavier against Jabin the
king of Canaan, until they had cut off Jabin
the king of Canaan.

Psalm 48:9–14

9 We have thought on Your
lovingkindness, O God,
In the midst of Your temple.
10 As is Your name, O God,
So is Your praise to the
ends of the earth;
Your right hand is full of
righteousness.
11 Let Mount Zion be glad,
Let the daughters of Judah rejoice
Because of Your judgments.
12 Walk about Zion and go around her;
Count her towers;
13 Consider her ramparts;
Go through her palaces,
That you may recount *it* to
the next generation.
14 For this is God,
Our God forever and ever;
He will guide us over death.

Proverbs 14:18–19

18 The simple inherit folly,
But the prudent are crowned
with knowledge.
19 The evil will bow down
before the good,
And the wicked at the gates
of the righteous.

Luke 14:25–35

25 Now many crowds were going along
with Him, and He turned and said to them,
26 “If anyone comes to Me, and does not hate
his own father and mother and wife and
children and brothers and sisters, yes, and
even his own life, he cannot be My disciple.
27 Whoever does not carry his own cross and
come after Me cannot be My disciple. 28 For
which one of you, when he wants to build a
tower, does not first sit down and calculate
the cost to see if he has enough to complete
it? 29 Lest, when he has laid a foundation
and is not able to finish, all who observe it
begin to ridicule him, 30 saying, ‘This man
began to build and was not able to finish.’
31 Or what king, when he sets out to meet

another king in battle, will not first sit down and consider whether he is strong enough with ten thousand *men* to encounter the one coming against him with twenty thousand?
32 Or else, while the other is still far away, he sends a delegation and asks for terms of peace.
33 So then, none of you can be My disciple who does not give up all his own possessions.

34 "Therefore, salt is good, but if even salt has become tasteless, with what will it be seasoned?
35 It is useless either for the soil or for the manure pile; it is thrown out. He who has ears to hear, let him hear."

APRIL 20

Judges 5:1–6:40

5 Then Deborah and Barak the son of Abinoam sang on that day, saying,
2 "When the leaders led in Israel,
When the people volunteered,
Bless Yahweh!
3 "Hear, O kings; give ear, O rulers!
As for me, to Yahweh, I will sing;
I will sing praise to Yahweh,
the God of Israel.
4 "O Yahweh, when You went
out from Seir,
When You marched from
the field of Edom,
The earth quaked, the
heavens also dripped,
Even the clouds dripped water.
5 "The mountains flowed at the
presence of Yahweh,
This Sinai, at the presence of
Yahweh, the God of Israel.

6 "In the days of Shamgar
the son of Anath,
In the days of Jael, the
paths had ceased,
So travelers went by roundabout
paths.
7 "The peasantry ceased; they
ceased in Israel,
Until I, Deborah, arose,
Until I arose, a mother in Israel.
8 "God chose new *leaders*;
Then war *was* in the gates.
Not a shield or a spear was seen
Among forty thousand in Israel.
9 "My heart *goes out* to the
commanders of Israel,
The volunteers among the people;
Bless Yahweh!
10 "You who ride on white donkeys,
You who sit on *rich* carpets,
And you who travel on the
road—muse *aloud*!
11 "At the sound of those who divide
flocks among the watering places,
There they shall commemorate the
righteous deeds of Yahweh,
The righteous deeds for His
peasantry in Israel.
Then the people of Yahweh
went down to the gates.

12 "Awake, awake, Deborah;
Awake, awake, utter a song!
Arise, Barak, and take away your
captives, O son of Abinoam.
13 "Then survivors came down
to the mighty ones;
The people of Yahweh came
down to me as warriors.
14 "From Ephraim those whose root
is in Amalek *came down*,
Following you, Benjamin,
with your peoples;
From Machir commanders
came down,
And from Zebulun those who
wield the staff of a scribe.
15 "And the princes of Issachar
were with Deborah;
As *was* Issachar, so *was* Barak;
Into the valley they rushed at his heels;
Among the divisions of Reuben
There was great persistence
of *the* heart.
16 "Why did you sit among the sheepfolds,
To hear the whistling for the flocks?
Among the divisions of Reuben
There were great probings of *the* heart.
17 "Gilead dwelt across the Jordan;
And why did Dan stay in ships?
Asher sat at the seashore,
And dwelt by its landings.
18 "Zebulun *was* a people who despised
their lives *even* to death,
And Naphtali also, on the
high places of the field.

19 “The kings came *and* fought;
Then fought the kings of Canaan
At Taanach near the waters
of Megiddo;
They took no gain of silver.
20 “The stars fought from heaven;
From their courses they
fought against Sisera.
21 “The river of Kishon swept them away,
The ancient river, the river Kishon.
O my soul, march on with strength.
22 “Then the horses’ hoofs beat
From the dashing, the dashing
of his valiant steeds.
23 ‘Curse Meroz,’ said the
angel of Yahweh,
‘Utterly curse its inhabitants,
Because they did not come
to the help of Yahweh,
To the help of Yahweh
against the warriors.’

24 “Most blessed of women is Jael,
The wife of Heber the Kenite;
Most blessed is she of
women in the tent.
25 “He asked for water, *and*
she gave him milk;
In a mighty bowl she
brought him curds.
26 “She sent forth her hand
for the tent peg,
And her right hand for the
workmen’s hammer.
Then she beat Sisera; she
smashed his head,
And she crushed and
pierced his temple.
27 “Between her feet he bowed,
he fell, he lay;
Between her feet he bowed, he fell;
Where he bowed, there he fell
violently devastated.

28 “Out of the window she
looked and lamented,
The mother of Sisera
through the lattice,
‘Why does his chariot delay
in coming?
Why do the hoofbeats of
his chariots tarry?’
29 “Her wise princesses would answer her,
Indeed she repeats her
words to herself,
30 ‘Are they not finding, are they
not dividing the spoil?
A maiden, two maidens for
every mighty man;
To Sisera a spoil of dyed work,
A spoil of dyed work embroidered,
Dyed work of double embroidery
on the neck of the spoil?’
31 “Thus let all Your enemies
perish, O Yahweh;
But let those who love Him be like
the rising of the sun in its might.”
And the land was quiet for forty years.

6 Then the sons of Israel did what was
evil in the eyes of Yahweh; and Yahweh
gave them into the hands of Midian seven
years. 2 And the power of Midian prevailed
against Israel. Because of Midian the sons of
Israel made for themselves the dens which
were in the mountains and the caves and the
strongholds. 3 And it was when Israel had
sown, that the Midianites would go up with
the Amalekites and the sons of the east and
go up against them. 4 So they would camp
against them and ruin the produce of the
earth as far as Gaza and leave no sustenance
in Israel as well as no sheep, ox, or donkey.
5 For they would go up with their livestock
and their tents; they would come in like
locusts for number, both they and their
camels were innumerable; and they came
into the land to make it a ruin. 6 So Israel
was brought very low because of Midian,
and the sons of Israel cried out to Yahweh.
7 Now it happened when the sons of Israel
cried out to Yahweh on account of Midian,
8 that Yahweh sent a prophet to the sons
of Israel, and he said to them, “Thus says
Yahweh, the God of Israel, ‘It was I who
brought you up from Egypt and brought you
out from the house of slavery. 9 I delivered
you from the hands of the Egyptians and
from the hands of all your oppressors and
drove them out before you and gave you
their land, 10 and I said to you, “I am Yahweh
your God; you shall not fear the gods of the
Amorites in whose land you live. But you
have not listened to My voice.”’”
11 Then the angel of Yahweh came and
sat under the oak that was in Ophrah,
which belonged to Joash the Abiezrite as
his son Gideon was beating out wheat in
the wine press in order to preserve *it* from
the Midianites. 12 And the angel of Yahweh

appeared to him and said to him, "Yahweh is with you, O mighty man of valor." 13 Then Gideon said to him, "O my lord, if Yahweh is with us, why then has all this happened to us? And where are all His wondrous deeds which our fathers recounted to us, saying, 'Did not Yahweh bring us up from Egypt?' But now Yahweh has abandoned us and given us into the hand of Midian." 14 Then Yahweh turned to him and said, "Go in this strength of yours and save Israel from the hand of Midian. Have I not sent you?" 15 But he said to Him, "O Lord, with what shall I save Israel? Behold, my clan is the least in Manasseh, and I am the youngest in my father's house." 16 But Yahweh said to him, "Surely I will be with you, and you shall strike down Midian as one man." 17 So Gideon said to Him, "If now I have found favor in Your eyes, then do a sign for me that it is You who speak with me. 18 Please do not depart from here until I come *back* to You, and I bring out my offering and lay it before You." And He said, "I will remain until you return."

19 So Gideon went in and prepared a young goat and unleavened bread from an ephah of flour; he put the meat in a basket and the broth in a pot and brought *them* out to him under the oak and presented *them*. 20 And the angel of God said to him, "Take the meat and the unleavened bread and lay them on this rock and pour out the broth." And he did so. 21 Then the angel of Yahweh put out the end of the staff that was in his hand and touched the meat and the unleavened bread; and fire sprang up from the rock and consumed the meat and the unleavened bread. Then the angel of Yahweh went away from *before* his eyes. 22 And Gideon saw that he was the angel of Yahweh, so he said, "Alas, O Lord Yahweh! For now I have seen the angel of Yahweh face to face." 23 And Yahweh said to him, "Peace to you. Do not fear; you shall not die." 24 So Gideon built an altar there to Yahweh and named *it Yahweh is Peace*. To this day it is still in Ophrah of the Abiezrites.

25 Now it happened on the same night that Yahweh said to him, "Take your father's bull and a second bull seven years old, and pull down the altar of Baal which belongs to your father, and cut down the Asherah that is beside it, 26 and build an altar to Yahweh your God on the top of this stronghold in an orderly manner, and take the second bull and offer a burnt offering with the wood of the Asherah which you shall cut down." 27 So Gideon took ten men of his servants and did as Yahweh had spoken to him; and now it happened that because he was too afraid of his father's household and the men of the city to do it by day, he did it by night.

28 Then the men of the city arose early in the morning, and behold, the altar of Baal was torn down, and the Asherah which was beside it was cut down, and the second bull was offered on the altar which had been built. 29 And they said to one another, "Who did this thing?" And when they searched about and inquired, they said, "Gideon the son of Joash did this thing." 30 Then the men of the city said to Joash, "Bring out your son, that he may die, for he has torn down the altar of Baal, and indeed, he has cut down the Asherah which was beside it." 31 But Joash said to all who stood against him, "Will you contend for Baal, or will you save him? Whoever will contend for him shall be put to death by morning. If he is a god, let him contend for himself, because someone has torn down his altar." 32 Therefore on that day he named him Jerubbaal, that is to say, "Let Baal contend against him," because he had torn down his altar.

33 Now all the Midianites and the Amalekites and the sons of the east assembled themselves; and they crossed over and camped in the valley of Jezreel. 34 But the Spirit of Yahweh clothed Gideon; and he blew a trumpet, and the Abiezrites were called together to follow him. 35 And he sent messengers throughout Manasseh, and they also were called together to follow him; and he sent messengers to Asher, Zebulun, and Naphtali, and they came up to meet them.

36 Then Gideon said to God, "If You will save Israel by my hand, as You have spoken, 37 behold, I will put a fleece of wool on the threshing floor. If there is dew on the fleece only, and it is dry on all the ground, then I will know that You will save Israel by my hand, as You have spoken." 38 And it was so. Indeed he arose early the next morning and squeezed the fleece. And he drained the dew from the fleece, a bowl full of water. 39 Then Gideon said to God, "Do not let Your anger burn against me that I may speak once more; please let me make a test once more with the fleece; let it now be dry only on the fleece, and let

there be dew on all the ground." 40 And God
did so that night. So it was dry only on the
fleece, but dew was on all the ground.

Psalm 49:1–9

1 Hear this, all peoples;
Give ear, all inhabitants of the world,
2 Both low and high,
Rich and poor together.
3 My mouth will speak wisdom,
And the meditation of my heart
will be discernment.
4 I will incline my ear to a proverb;
I will express my riddle on the harp.

5 Why should I fear in days of evil,
When the iniquity of my
supplanters surrounds me,
6 Even those who trust in their wealth
And boast in the abundance
of their riches?
7 Truly, no man can redeem *his* brother;
He cannot give to God a
ransom for him—
8 For the redemption price for
their soul is costly,
And *it* ceases forever—
9 That he should live on eternally,
That he should not see corruption.

Proverbs 14:20–21

20 The poor is hated even by his neighbor,
But those who love the rich are many.
21 He who despises his neighbor sins,
But how blessed is he who is
gracious to the poor.

Luke 15:1–10

15 Now all the tax collectors and the
sinners were coming near Him to
listen to Him. 2 And both the Pharisees and
the scribes were grumbling, saying, "This
man receives sinners and eats with them."
3 So He told them this parable, saying,
4 "What man among you, if he has one
hundred sheep and has lost one of them,
does not leave the ninety-nine in the open
pasture and go after the one which is lost
until he finds it? 5 And when he has found
it, he lays it on his shoulders, rejoicing. 6 And
when he comes home, he calls together
his friends and his neighbors, saying to
them, 'Rejoice with me, for I have found
my sheep which was lost!' 7 I tell you that
in the same way, there will be *more* joy in
heaven over one sinner who repents than
over ninety-nine righteous persons who
need no repentance.
8 "Or what woman, if she has ten drach-
mas and loses one drachma, does not light
a lamp and sweep the house and search
carefully until she finds it? 9 And when she
has found it, she calls together her friends
and neighbors, saying, 'Rejoice with me, for
I have found the drachma which I had lost!'
10 In the same way, I tell you, there is joy in
the presence of the angels of God over one
sinner who repents."

APRIL 21

Judges 7:1–8:35

7 Then Jerubbaal (that is, Gideon) and all
the people who were with him rose early
and camped beside the spring of Harod; and
the camp of Midian was on the north side
of them by the hill of Moreh in the valley.
2 And Yahweh said to Gideon, "The people
who are with you are too many for Me to
give Midian into their hands, lest Israel
honor themselves, saying, 'My own hand
has saved me.' 3 So now, come, call out in
the hearing of the people, saying, 'Whoever
is afraid and trembling, let him return and
depart from Mount Gilead.'" So 22,000
people returned, but 10,000 remained.
4 Then Yahweh said to Gideon, "The
people are still too many; bring them down
to the water, and I will test them for you
there. And it will be that he of whom I say
to you, 'This one shall go with you,' he
shall go with you; but everyone of whom
I say to you, 'This one shall not go with
you,' he shall not go." 5 So he brought the
people down to the water. And Yahweh said
to Gideon, "Everyone who laps the water
with his tongue as a dog laps, you shall set
him aside by himself, and *so also* everyone
who kneels to drink." 6 Now the number
of those who lapped, putting their hand to
their mouth, was 300 men; but all the rest
of the people kneeled to drink water. 7 And
Yahweh said to Gideon, "I will save you with
the 300 men who lapped and will give the
Midianites into your hands; so let all the

other people go, each man to his place." 8 So
the 300 men took the people's provisions
and their trumpets into their hands. And
Gideon sent all the *other* men of Israel, each
to his tent, but retained the 300 men; and
the camp of Midian was below him in the
valley.

9 Now it happened the same night that
Yahweh said to him, "Arise, go down against
the camp, for I have given it into your
hands. 10 But if you are afraid to go down,
then both you and Purah your young man,
go down to the camp, 11 and you will hear
what they say; and afterward your hands
will be strengthened, that you may go down
against the camp." So he went with Purah
his young man down to the outskirts of the
armed men that were in the camp. 12 Now
the Midianites and the Amalekites and all
the sons of the east were lying in the valley
as numerous as locusts; and their camels
were without number, as numerous as the
sand on the seashore. 13 Then Gideon came,
and behold, a man was recounting a dream
to his friend. And he said, "Behold, I had a
dream; a loaf of barley bread was tumbling
into the camp of Midian, and it came to the
tent and struck it so that it fell and turned
it upside down so that the tent lay flat."
14 And his friend answered and said, "This
is nothing less than the sword of Gideon the
son of Joash, a man of Israel; God has given
Midian and all the camp into his hand."

15 Now it happened that when Gideon
heard the account of the dream and its
interpretation, he bowed in worship. Then
he returned to the camp of Israel and said,
"Arise, for Yahweh has given the camp of
Midian into your hands." 16 And he divided
the 300 men into three companies, and he
put trumpets and empty pitchers into the
hands of all of them, with torches inside
the pitchers. 17 Then he said to them, "Look
at me and do likewise. And behold, I will
come to the outskirts of the camp, and it
will be that just as I do so you do likewise.
18 And I and all who are with me will blow
the trumpet. Then you also shall blow the
trumpets all around the camp and say, 'For
Yahweh and for Gideon.'"

19 So Gideon and the hundred men who
were with him came to the outskirts of the
camp at the beginning of the middle watch,
when they had just set up the watch; and
they blew the trumpets and smashed the
pitchers that were in their hands. 20 Then
the three companies blew the trumpets
and broke the pitchers, and they held the
torches in their left hands and the trumpets
in their right hands for blowing and called
out, "A sword for Yahweh and for Gideon!"
21 And each stood in his place around the
camp. Then all of the camp ran, and they
made a loud shout and fled. 22 So they blew
300 trumpets. And Yahweh set the sword of
one against another even throughout the
whole camp. And the camp fled as far as
Beth-shittah toward Zererah, as far as the
edge of Abel-meholah, by Tabbath. 23 And
the men of Israel were summoned from
Naphtali and Asher and all Manasseh, and
they pursued Midian.

24 Now Gideon had sent messengers
throughout all the hill country of Ephraim,
saying, "Come down to meet Midian and
capture the waters before them, as far as
Beth-barah and the Jordan." So all the men
of Ephraim were summoned, and they
captured the waters as far as Beth-barah
and the Jordan. 25 Then they captured the
two princes of Midian, Oreb and Zeeb, and
they killed Oreb at the rock of Oreb, and
they killed Zeeb at the wine press of Zeeb.
Then they pursued Midian and brought the
heads of Oreb and Zeeb to Gideon from
across the Jordan.

8 Then the men of Ephraim said to him,
"What is this thing you have done to us,
not calling us when you went to fight against
Midian?" And they strongly contended with
him. 2 But he said to them, "What have I
done now in comparison with you? Is not
the gleaning *of the grapes* of Ephraim better
than the grape harvest of Abiezer? 3 God has
given the princes of Midian, Oreb and Zeeb,
into your hands; and what was I able to do
in comparison with you?" Then their anger
toward him subsided when he spoke this
word.

4 Then Gideon and the 300 men who were
with him came to the Jordan *and* crossed
over, weary yet pursuing. 5 And he said to
the men of Succoth, "Please give loaves of
bread to the people who are following me,
for they are weary, and I am pursuing Zebah
and Zalmunna, the kings of Midian." 6 But
the princes of Succoth said, "Are the hands
of Zebah and Zalmunna already in your
hands, that we should give bread to your

army?" 7 And Gideon said, "Thus, when
Yahweh has given Zebah and Zalmunna
into my hand, then I will thrash your bodies
with the thorns of the wilderness and with
briers." 8 So he went up from there to Penuel
and spoke similarly to them; and the men
of Penuel answered him just as the men of
Succoth had answered. 9 So he spoke also to
the men of Penuel, saying, "When I return
safely, I will tear down this tower."
10 Now Zebah and Zalmunna were in
Karkor, and their camps with them, about
15,000 men, all who were left of the entire
camp of the sons of the east; for the fallen
were 120,000 men who drew the sword.
11 And Gideon went up by the way of those
who dwelt in tents on the east of Nobah and
Jogbehah and struck the camp when the
camp was unsuspecting. 12 Then Zebah and
Zalmunna fled. And he pursued them and
captured the two kings of Midian, Zebah
and Zalmunna, and he threw the whole
camp into *utter* fright.
13 Then Gideon the son of Joash returned
from the battle by the ascent of Heres.
14 And he captured a youth from the men of
Succoth and questioned him. So *the youth*
wrote down for him the princes of Succoth
and its elders, seventy-seven men. 15 Then
he came to the men of Succoth and said,
"Behold Zebah and Zalmunna, about whom
you reproached me, saying, 'Are the hands of
Zebah and Zalmunna already in your hand,
that we should give bread to your men who
are weary?'" 16 Then he took the elders of the
city as well as thorns of the wilderness and
briers, and with them he taught the men of
Succoth a lesson. 17 And he tore down the
tower of Penuel and killed the men of the city.
18 Then he said to Zebah and Zalmunna,
"What kind of men *were* they whom you
killed at Tabor?" And they said, "They were
like you, each one resembling the son of a
king." 19 And he said, "They *were* my broth-
ers, the sons of my mother. *As* Yahweh lives,
if only you had let them live, I would not kill
you." 20 So he said to Jether his firstborn,
"Rise, kill them." But the youth did not draw
his sword, for he was afraid because he was
still a youth. 21 Then Zebah and Zalmunna
said, "Rise up yourself, and smite us; for as
the man, so is his might." So Gideon arose
and killed Zebah and Zalmunna and took
the crescent ornaments which were on their
camels' necks.
22 Then the men of Israel said to Gideon,
"Rule over us, both you and your son, also
your son's son, for you have saved us from
the hand of Midian." 23 But Gideon said to
them, "I will not rule over you, nor shall my
son rule over you; Yahweh shall rule over
you." 24 Yet Gideon said to them, "I would
make one request of you, that each of you
give me an earring from his spoil." (For they
had gold earrings because they were Ishma-
elites.) 25 And they said, "We will surely give
them." So they spread out a garment, and
every one of them threw an earring there
from his spoil. 26 And the weight of the gold
earrings that he requested was 1,700 *shekels*
of gold, besides the crescent ornaments and
the pendants and the purple robes which
were on the kings of Midian, and besides the
neck bands that *were* on their camels' necks.
27 Then Gideon made it into an ephod and
placed it in his city, Ophrah, and all Israel
played the harlot with it there, so that it
became a snare to Gideon and his house-
hold. 28 So Midian was subdued before the
sons of Israel, and they did not lift up their
heads anymore. And the land was quiet for
forty years in the days of Gideon.
29 Then Jerubbaal the son of Joash went
and lived in his own house. 30 Now Gideon
had seventy sons who were his direct
descendants, for he had many wives.
31 And his concubine who was in Shechem
also bore him a son, and he named him
Abimelech. 32 Then Gideon the son of Joash
died at a good old age and was buried in the
tomb of his father Joash, in Ophrah of the
Abiezrites.
33 Then it happened, as soon as Gideon
was dead, that the sons of Israel turned
back and played the harlot with the Baals
and made Baal-berith their god. 34 Thus the
sons of Israel did not remember Yahweh
their God, who had delivered them from
the hands of all their enemies on every side;
35 nor did they show lovingkindness to the
household of Jerubbaal (*that is,* Gideon) in
accord with all the good that he had done
to Israel.

Psalm 49:10–20

10 For he sees *that even* wise men die;
The fool and the senseless alike perish
And leave their wealth to others.
11 Their inner thought is *that*
their houses are forever

And their dwelling places from
generation to generation;
They have called *their* lands
after their own names.
12 But man in *his* honor will not endure;
He is like the animals that perish.

13 This is the way of those
who are foolish,
And of those after them who are
pleased with their words. Selah.
14 As sheep they are appointed for Sheol;
Death will shepherd them;
And the upright shall have dominion
over them in the morning,
And their form shall be for
Sheol to consume,
Far away from his habitation.
15 But God will redeem my soul
from the power of Sheol,
For He will receive me. Selah.

16 Do not be afraid when a
man becomes rich,
When the glory of his house increases;
17 For when he dies he will
not take any of it;
His glory will not descend after him.
18 For while he lives he blesses his soul—
And *men* will praise you when
you do well for yourself—
19 *But his soul* shall go to the
generation of his fathers;
They will eternally not see light.
20 Man in *his* honor, but *who*
does not understand,
Is like the animals that perish.

Proverbs 14:22–24

22 Will they not wander in error
who devise evil?
But lovingkindness and truth *will
be to* those who devise good.
23 In all painful labor there is profit,
But *mere* words from the lips
lead only to want.
24 The crown of the wise is their riches,
But the folly of fools is folly.

Luke 15:11–32

11 And He said, "A man had two sons.
12 And the younger of them said to his
father, 'Father, give me the share of the
estate that falls *to me.*' So he divided his
wealth between them. 13 And not many days
later, the younger son gathered everything
together and went on a journey into a
distant country, and there he squandered
his estate living recklessly. 14 Now when
he had spent everything, a severe famine
occurred in that country, and he began to
be impoverished. 15 So he went and hired
himself out to one of the citizens of that
country, and he sent him into his fields to
feed swine. 16 And he was desiring to be fed
with the pods that the swine were eating,
and no one was giving *anything* to him.
17 But when he came to himself, he said,
'How many of my father's hired men have
more than enough bread, but I am dying
here with hunger! 18 I will rise up and go to
my father, and will say to him, "Father, I have
sinned against heaven, and before you. 19 I
am no longer worthy to be called your son;
make me as one of your hired men."' 20 So
he rose up and came to his father. But while
he was still a long way off, his father saw him
and felt compassion, and ran and embraced
him and kissed him. 21 And the son said to
him, 'Father, I have sinned against heaven
and before you. I am no longer worthy to
be called your son.' 22 But the father said
to his slaves, 'Quickly bring out the best
robe and put it on him, and put a ring on
his hand and sandals on his feet, 23 and
bring the fattened calf, slaughter it, and let
us eat and celebrate, 24 for this son of mine
was dead and has come to life again; he was
lost and has been found.' And they began
to celebrate.

25 "Now his older son was in the field,
and when he came and approached the
house, he heard music and dancing. 26 And
summoning one of the servants, he *began*
inquiring what these things could be. 27 And
he said to him, 'Your brother has come,
and your father has killed the fattened calf
because he has received him back safe and
sound.' 28 But he became angry and was
not wanting to go in, and his father came
out and *began* pleading with him. 29 But
he answered and said to his father, 'Look!
For so many years I have been serving you
and never have I neglected a command of
yours. And *yet* never have you given me a
young goat, so that I might celebrate with
my friends. 30 But when this son of yours
came, who has devoured your wealth with
prostitutes, you killed the fattened calf for
him.' 31 And he said to him, 'Child, you are

always with me, and all that is mine is yours.
32 But we had to celebrate and rejoice, for
this brother of yours was dead and is alive,
and *was* lost and has been found.'"

APRIL 22

Judges 9:1–10:18

9 And Abimelech the son of Jerubbaal
went to Shechem to his mother's rela-
tives and spoke to them and to the whole
family of the household of his mother's
father, saying, 2 "Speak, now, in the hear-
ing of all the lords of Shechem, 'Which is
better for you, that seventy men, all the
sons of Jerubbaal, rule over you, or that
one man rule over you?' Also, remember
that I am your bone and your flesh." 3 And
his mother's relatives spoke all these words
on his behalf in the hearing of all the lords
of Shechem; and they were inclined to
follow Abimelech, for they said, "He is our
relative." 4 So they gave him seventy *pieces*
of silver from the house of Baal-berith with
which Abimelech hired worthless and reck-
less fellows, and they followed him. 5 Then
he came to his father's house at Ophrah and
killed his brothers the sons of Jerubbaal,
seventy men, on one stone. But Jotham the
youngest son of Jerubbaal was left, for he
hid himself. 6 Then all the lords of Shechem
and all Beth-millo assembled together, and
they went and made Abimelech king, by the
oak of the pillar which was in Shechem.

7 Then they told Jotham, so he went and
stood on the top of Mount Gerizim and
lifted his voice and called out. Thus he said
to them, "Listen to me, O lords of Shechem,
that God may listen to you. 8 The trees surely
went forth to anoint a king over them, and
they said to the olive tree, 'Reign over us!'
9 But the olive tree said to them, 'Shall I leave
my fatness, with which God and men are
honored, and go to wave over the trees?'
10 Then the trees said to the fig tree, 'You
come, reign over us!' 11 But the fig tree said
to them, 'Shall I leave my sweetness and my
good produce and go to wave over the trees?'
12 Then the trees said to the vine, 'You come,
reign over us!' 13 But the vine said to them,
'Shall I leave my new wine, which makes
God and men glad, and go to wave over
the trees?' 14 Then all the trees said to the
bramble, 'You come, reign over us!' 15 And
the bramble said to the trees, 'If in truth you
are anointing me as king over you, come and
take refuge in my shade; but if not, may fire
come out from the bramble and consume
the cedars of Lebanon.'

16 "So now, if you have dealt in truth and
integrity and made Abimelech king, and if
you have dealt well with Jerubbaal and his
house and have dealt with him according
to the bountiful works of his hands— 17 for
my father fought for you and risked his life
and delivered you from the hand of Midian;
18 but you have risen against my father's
house today and have killed his sons,
seventy men, on one stone, and have made
Abimelech, the son of his maidservant, king
over the lords of Shechem, because he is
your relative— 19 if then you have dealt in
truth and integrity with Jerubbaal and his
house this day, be glad in Abimelech, and
let him also be glad in you. 20 But if not, let
fire come out from Abimelech and consume
the lords of Shechem and Beth-millo; and let
fire come out from the lords of Shechem and
from Beth-millo and consume Abimelech."
21 Then Jotham escaped and fled and went
to Beer and remained there because of
Abimelech his brother.

22 And Abimelech governed over Israel
three years. 23 Then God sent an evil spirit
between Abimelech and the lords of
Shechem; and the lords of Shechem dealt
treacherously with Abimelech, 24 so that the
violence done to the seventy sons of Jerub-
baal might come, and their blood might be
laid on Abimelech their brother, who killed
them, and on the lords of Shechem, who
strengthened his hands to kill his brothers.
25 And the lords of Shechem set men in
ambush against him on the tops of the
mountains, and they robbed all who might
pass by them along the road; and it was told
to Abimelech.

26 Then Gaal the son of Ebed came with
his relatives, and they crossed over into
Shechem; and the lords of Shechem put
their trust in him. 27 And they went out
into the field and gathered *the grapes of*
their vineyards and trod *them* and cele-
brated a festival; and they came into the
house of their god and ate and drank and

cursed Abimelech. 28 Then Gaal the son of
Ebed said, "Who is Abimelech, and who is
Shechem, that we should serve him? Is he
not the son of Jerubbaal, and *is* Zebul *not*
his officer? Serve the men of Hamor the
father of Shechem; but why should we serve
him? 29 Would, therefore, that this people
were under my hand! Then I would remove
Abimelech." And he said to Abimelech,
"Increase your army and come out."

30 Then Zebul the ruler of the city heard
the words of Gaal the son of Ebed, and his
anger burned. 31 And he sent messengers to
Abimelech deceitfully, saying, "Behold, Gaal
the son of Ebed and his relatives have come
to Shechem; and behold, they are stirring
up the city against you. 32 So now, arise by
night, you and the people who are with you,
and lie in wait in the field. 33 And it will be
in the morning, as soon as the sun is up,
that you shall rise early and rush upon the
city; and behold, he and the people who are
with him will come out against you, and you
shall do to them whatever your hand finds
pleasing."

34 So Abimelech and all the people who
were with him arose by night and lay in
wait against Shechem in four companies.
35 And Gaal the son of Ebed went out and
stood in the entrance of the city gate; and
Abimelech and the people who *were* with
him arose from the ambush. 36 Then Gaal
saw the people and said to Zebul, "Behold,
people are coming down from the tops of
the mountains." But Zebul said to him, "You
are seeing the shadow of the mountains as
if they were men." 37 Yet Gaal spoke again
and said, "Behold, people are coming
down from the highest part of the land,
and one company comes by the way of the
soothsayers' oak." 38 Then Zebul said to him,
"Where is your boasting now with which
you said, 'Who is Abimelech that we should
serve him?' Is this not the people whom
you rejected? Go out now and fight with
them!" 39 So Gaal went out before the lords
of Shechem and fought with Abimelech.
40 And Abimelech pursued him, and he
fled before him; and many fell slain up to
the entrance of the gate. 41 Then Abimelech
remained at Arumah, but Zebul drove out
Gaal and his relatives so that they could not
remain in Shechem.

42 Now it happened the next day, that
the people went out to the field, and it was
told to Abimelech. 43 So he took his people
and divided them into three companies and
lay in wait in the field; then he looked, and
behold, the people were coming out from
the city. So he arose against them and struck
them down. 44 Then Abimelech and the
company who was with him rushed forward
and stood in the entrance of the city gate;
but the other two companies rushed upon
all who *were* in the field and struck them
down. 45 So Abimelech fought against the
city all that day, and he captured the city
and killed the people who *were* in it; then
he tore the city down and sowed it with salt.

46 Then all the lords of the tower of
Shechem heard of *it*, and they entered the
inner chamber of the temple of El-berith.
47 And it was told to Abimelech that all the
lords of the tower of Shechem were gathered
together. 48 So Abimelech went up to Mount
Zalmon, he and all the people who *were*
with him; and Abimelech took an axe in
his hand and cut down a branch from the
trees and lifted it and laid *it* on his shoulder.
Then he said to the people who *were* with
him, "What you have seen me do, hurry *and*
do likewise." 49 And all the people also cut
down each one his branch and followed Abi-
melech and put *them* on the inner chamber
and set the inner chamber on fire over those
inside, so that all the men of the tower of
Shechem also died, about one thousand
men and women.

50 Then Abimelech went to Thebez, and
he camped against Thebez and captured it.
51 But there was a strong tower in the center
of the city, and all the men and women with
all the lords of the city fled there and shut
themselves in; and they went up on the roof
of the tower. 52 So Abimelech came to the
tower and fought against it and approached
the entrance of the tower to burn it with
fire. 53 But a certain woman threw an
upper millstone on Abimelech's head, and
she smashed his skull. 54 Then he called
quickly to the young man, his armor bearer,
and said to him, "Draw your sword and put
me to death, lest they say of me, 'A woman
killed him.'" So the young man pierced him
through, and he died. 55 Then the men of
Israel saw that Abimelech was dead, so
each went *away* to his home. 56 Thus God
returned the evil of Abimelech, which he
had done to his father in killing his seventy
brothers. 57 God also returned all the evil of

the men of Shechem on their own heads, and the curse of Jotham the son of Jerubbaal came upon them.

10 Then after Abimelech died, Tola the son of Puah, the son of Dodo, a man of Issachar, arose to save Israel; and he lived in Shamir in the hill country of Ephraim. 2 And he judged Israel twenty-three years. Then he died and was buried in Shamir.

3 After him, Jair the Gileadite arose and judged Israel twenty-two years. 4 And he had thirty sons who rode on thirty donkeys, and they had thirty cities in the land of Gilead that are called Havvoth-jair to this day. 5 And Jair died and was buried in Kamon.

6 Then the sons of Israel again did what was evil in the eyes of Yahweh and served the Baals and the Ashtaroth, the gods of Aram, the gods of Sidon, the gods of Moab, the gods of the sons of Ammon, and the gods of the Philistines; thus they forsook Yahweh and did not serve Him. 7 So the anger of Yahweh burned against Israel, and He sold them into the hands of the Philistines and into the hands of the sons of Ammon. 8 And they shattered and smashed the sons of Israel that year; for eighteen years they *did this to* all the sons of Israel who were beyond the Jordan in Gilead in the land of the Amorites. 9 Then the sons of Ammon crossed the Jordan to fight also against Judah, Benjamin, and the house of Ephraim, so that Israel was greatly distressed.

10 And the sons of Israel cried out to Yahweh, saying, "We have sinned against You, for indeed, we have forsaken our God and served the Baals." 11 Then Yahweh said to the sons of Israel, "*Did I* not *save you* from the Egyptians, the Amorites, the sons of Ammon, and the Philistines? 12 Also the Sidonians, the Amalekites, and the Maonites oppressed you. And you cried out to Me, and I saved you from their hand. 13 Yet you have forsaken Me and served other gods; therefore I will no longer save you. 14 Go and cry out to the gods which you have chosen; let them save you in the time of your distress." 15 Then the sons of Israel said to Yahweh, "We have sinned, so You, do to us whatever seems good in Your eyes; only please deliver us this day." 16 So they removed the foreign gods from among them and served Yahweh; and He could bear the trouble of Israel no longer.

17 Then the sons of Ammon were summoned, and they camped in Gilead. And the sons of Israel gathered together and camped in Mizpah. 18 And the people, the princes of Gilead, said to one another, "Who is the man who will begin to fight against the sons of Ammon? He shall become head over all the inhabitants of Gilead."

Psalm 50:1–6

1 The Mighty One, God,
Yahweh, has spoken,
And called the earth from the
rising of the sun to its setting.
2 Out of Zion, the perfection of beauty,
God has shone forth.
3 May our God come and not be silent;
Fire devours before Him,
And a *storm* whirls around Him.
4 He calls the heavens above,
And the earth, to render
justice to His people:
5 "Gather My holy ones to Me,
Those who have cut a covenant
with Me by sacrifice."
6 And the heavens declare
His righteousness,
For God Himself is judge. Selah.

Proverbs 14:25–27

25 A truthful witness delivers souls,
But he who breathes out
lies is deceitful.
26 In the fear of Yahweh there
is strong security,
And his children will have refuge.
27 The fear of Yahweh is a fountain of life,
To turn aside from the snares of death.

Luke 16:1–31

16 Now He was also saying to the disciples, "There was a rich man who had a steward, and this *steward* was reported to him as squandering his possessions. 2 And he called for him and said to him, 'What is this I hear about you? Give an accounting of your stewardship, for you can no longer be steward.' 3 And the steward said to himself, 'What shall I do, since my master is taking the stewardship away from me? I am not strong enough to dig; I am ashamed to beg. 4 I know what I shall do, so that when I am removed from the stewardship people will take me into their homes.' 5 And he summoned each one of his master's debtors, and

he *began* saying to the first, 'How much do
you owe my master?' 6 And he said, 'One
hundred baths of oil.' And he said to him,
'Take your bill, and sit down quickly and
write fifty.' 7 Then he said to another, 'And
how much do you owe?' And he said, 'One
hundred kors of wheat.' He *said to him,
'Take your bill, and write eighty.' 8 And his
master praised the unrighteous steward
because he had acted shrewdly, for the sons
of this age are more shrewd in relation to
their own kind than the sons of light. 9 And I
say to you, make friends for yourselves from
the wealth of unrighteousness, so that when
it fails, they will take you into the eternal
dwellings.

10 "He who is faithful in a very little
thing is faithful also in much, and he who
is unrighteous in a very little thing is unrigh-
teous also in much. 11 Therefore if you have
not been faithful in the *use of* unrighteous
wealth, who will entrust the true *riches* to
you? 12 And if you have not been faithful
in *the use of* that which is another's, who
will give you that which is your own? 13 No
servant can serve two masters; for either he
will hate the one and love the other, or else
he will be devoted to one and despise the
other. You cannot serve God and wealth."

14 Now the Pharisees, who were lovers
of money, were listening to all these things
and were scoffing at Him. 15 And He said to
them, "You are those who justify yourselves
in the sight of men, but God knows your
hearts, for that which is highly esteemed
among men is detestable in the sight of God.

16 "The Law and the Prophets were
until John; since that time the good news
of the kingdom of God is proclaimed, and
everyone is forcing his way into it. 17 But it
is easier for heaven and earth to pass away
than for one stroke of a letter of the Law
to fail.

18 "Everyone who divorces his wife and
marries another commits adultery, and he
who marries a woman who is divorced from
a husband commits adultery.

19 "Now there was a rich man, and he
habitually dressed in purple and fine linen,
joyously living in splendor every day. 20 But
a poor man named Lazarus was laid at his
gate, covered with sores, 21 and desiring
to be fed with the *crumbs* which were
falling from the rich man's table; besides,
even the dogs were coming and licking his
sores. 22 Now it happened that the poor man
died and was carried away by the angels to
Abraham's bosom, and the rich man also
died and was buried. 23 And in Hades he
lifted up his eyes, being in torment, and
*saw Abraham far away and Lazarus in his
bosom. 24 And he cried out and said, 'Father
Abraham, have mercy on me, and send
Lazarus so that he may dip the tip of his
finger in water and cool off my tongue, for
I am in agony in this flame.' 25 But Abraham
said, 'Child, remember that during your life
you received your good things, and likewise
Lazarus bad things. But now he is being
comforted here, and you are in agony. 26 And
besides all this, between us and you there
is a great chasm fixed, so that those who
wish to come over from here to you are not
able, and none may cross over from there to
us.' 27 And he said, 'Then I am asking you,
father, that you send him to my father's
house— 28 for I have five brothers—in order
that he may warn them, so that they will not
also come to this place of torment.' 29 But
Abraham *said, 'They have Moses and the
Prophets; let them hear them.' 30 But he said,
'No, father Abraham, but if someone goes to
them from the dead, they will repent!' 31 But
he said to him, 'If they do not listen to Moses
and the Prophets, they will not be persuaded
even if someone rises from the dead.'"

Go to God by prayer for a key to unlock the mysteries of His Word. It is not the plodding but the praying soul, that will get this treasure of Scripture knowledge.

— WILLIAM GURNALL

APRIL 23

Judges 11:1–12:15

11 Now Jephthah the Gileadite was a
mighty man of valor, but he was the
son of a harlot. And Gilead became the
father of Jephthah. 2 And Gilead's wife bore
him sons; and when his wife's sons grew
up, they drove Jephthah out and said to
him, "You shall not have an inheritance in
our father's house, for you are the son of
another woman." 3 So Jephthah fled from
his brothers and lived in the land of Tob;
and worthless fellows gathered themselves
about Jephthah, and they went out with him.
4 Now it happened after a while that the
sons of Ammon fought against Israel. 5 So it
happened that as the sons of Ammon fought
against Israel, the elders of Gilead went to
get Jephthah from the land of Tob; 6 and
they said to Jephthah, "Come and be our
chief that we may fight against the sons of
Ammon." 7 Then Jephthah said to the elders
of Gilead, "Did you not hate me and drive me
from my father's house? So why have you
come to me now when you are in distress?"
8 And the elders of Gilead said to Jephthah,
"For this reason we have now returned to
you, that you may go with us and fight with
the sons of Ammon and become head over
all the inhabitants of Gilead." 9 So Jephthah
said to the elders of Gilead, "If you take me
back to fight against the sons of Ammon and
Yahweh gives them up to me, will I become
your head?" 10 And the elders of Gilead said
to Jephthah, "Yahweh is witness between us;
surely we will do as you have said." 11 Then
Jephthah went with the elders of Gilead,
and the people made him head and chief
over them; and Jephthah spoke all his words
before Yahweh at Mizpah.
12 And Jephthah sent messengers to the
king of the sons of Ammon, saying, "What
is between you and me, that you have come
to me to fight against my land?" 13 Then
the king of the sons of Ammon said to the
messengers of Jephthah, "Because Israel
took away my land when they came up
from Egypt, from the Arnon as far as the
Jabbok and the Jordan; so now, return them
peaceably." 14 But Jephthah sent messengers
again to the king of the sons of Ammon,
15 and they said to him, "Thus says Jephthah,
'Israel did not take away the land of Moab
nor the land of the sons of Ammon. 16 For
when they came up from Egypt, and Israel
went through the wilderness to the Red
Sea and came to Kadesh, 17 then Israel sent
messengers to the king of Edom, saying,
"Please let us pass through your land," but
the king of Edom would not listen. And they
also sent to the king of Moab, but he was
not willing. So Israel remained at Kadesh.
18 Then they went through the wilderness
and around the land of Edom and the
land of Moab and came to the *east* toward
the sunrise of the land of Moab, and they
camped beyond the Arnon; but they did not
enter the territory of Moab, for the Arnon
was the border of Moab. 19 And Israel sent
messengers to Sihon king of the Amorites,
the king of Heshbon, and Israel said to him,
"Please let us pass through your land to our
place." 20 But Sihon did not believe Israel *to
allow* them to pass through his territory; so
Sihon gathered all his people and camped
in Jahaz and fought with Israel. 21 Then
Yahweh, the God of Israel, gave Sihon and
all his people into the hand of Israel, and
they struck them down; so Israel possessed
all the land of the Amorites, the inhabitants
of that country. 22 So they possessed all the
territory of the Amorites, from the Arnon as
far as the Jabbok, and from the wilderness
as far as the Jordan. 23 So now Yahweh, the
God of Israel, dispossessed the Amorites
from before His people Israel. Are you then
to possess it? 24 Do you not possess what
Chemosh your god gives you to possess?
So whatever Yahweh our God has taken
possession of before us, we will possess it.
25 So now are you any better than Balak the
son of Zippor, king of Moab? Did he ever
strive with Israel, or did he ever fight against
them? 26 While Israel lived in Heshbon
and its towns and in Aroer and its towns
and in all the cities that are on the banks
of the Arnon, 300 years, why did you not
deliver them *for yourself* within that time?
27 I therefore have not sinned against you,
but you are doing me evil by making war
against me; may Yahweh, the Judge, judge
today between the sons of Israel and the
sons of Ammon.'" 28 But the king of the sons
of Ammon did not listen to the words which
Jephthah sent him.

29 Now the Spirit of Yahweh came upon Jephthah, so that he passed through Gilead and Manasseh; then he passed through Mizpah of Gilead, and from Mizpah of Gilead he went on to the sons of Ammon. 30 Then Jephthah made a vow to Yahweh and said, "If You will indeed give the sons of Ammon into my hand, 31 then it shall be that whatever comes out of the doors of my house to meet me when I return in peace from the sons of Ammon, it shall be Yahweh's, and I will offer it up as a burnt offering." 32 So Jephthah crossed over to the sons of Ammon to fight against them; and Yahweh gave them into his hand. 33 And he struck them with a very great slaughter from Aroer to the entrance of Minnith, twenty cities, and as far as Abel-keramim. So the sons of Ammon were subdued before the sons of Israel.

34 Then Jephthah came to his house at Mizpah. And behold, his daughter was coming out to meet him with tambourines and with dancing. Now she was his one *and* only child; besides her he had no son or daughter. 35 So it happened that when he saw her, he tore his clothes and said, "Alas, my daughter! You have brought me very low, and you are among those who trouble me. But I have opened my mouth *to vow* to Yahweh, and I cannot take *it* back." 36 So she said to him, "My father, you have opened your mouth *to vow* to Yahweh; do to me according to what has gone out from your mouth, since Yahweh has avenged you of your enemies, the sons of Ammon." 37 Then she said to her father, "Let this thing be done for me; let me alone two months, that I may go to the mountains and weep because of my virginity, I and my companions." 38 Then he said, "Go." So he sent her away for two months; and she went with her companions and wept on the mountains because of her virginity. 39 And it happened at the end of two months that she returned to her father, and he did to her according to the vow *which he had made;* and she did not know a man. Thus it became a custom in Israel, 40 that the daughters of Israel went yearly to commemorate the daughter of Jephthah the Gileadite four days in the year.

12 Then the men of Ephraim were summoned, and they crossed to Zaphon and said to Jephthah, "Why did you cross over to fight against the sons of Ammon, but did not call us to go with you? We will burn your house down on you." 2 Then Jephthah said to them, "I and my people were at great strife with the sons of Ammon. And I cried out to you, but you did not save me from their hand. 3 And I saw that you would not save *me,* so I took my life in my hands and crossed over against the sons of Ammon, and Yahweh gave them into my hand. Why then have you come up to me this day to fight against me?" 4 Then Jephthah gathered all the men of Gilead and fought Ephraim; and the men of Gilead struck Ephraim down because they said, "You are fugitives of Ephraim, O Gileadites, in the midst of Ephraim *and* in the midst of Manasseh." 5 And the Gileadites captured the fords of the Jordan opposite Ephraim. And it happened when *any of* the fugitives of Ephraim said, "Let me cross over," the men of Gilead would say to him, "Are you an Ephraimite?" If he said, "No," 6 then they would say to him, "Say now, 'Shibboleth.'" But he said, "Sibboleth," for he could not pronounce it correctly. Then they seized him and slaughtered him at the fords of the Jordan. Thus there fell at that time 42,000 of Ephraim.

7 And Jephthah judged Israel six years. Then Jephthah the Gileadite died and was buried in *one of* the cities of Gilead.

8 Then Ibzan of Bethlehem judged Israel after him. 9 And he had thirty sons, and thirty daughters *whom* he gave in marriage outside *the family,* and he brought in thirty daughters from outside for his sons. And he judged Israel seven years. 10 Then Ibzan died and was buried in Bethlehem.

11 Then Elon the Zebulunite judged Israel after him; and he judged Israel ten years. 12 And Elon the Zebulunite died and was buried at Aijalon in the land of Zebulun.

13 Then Abdon the son of Hillel the Pirathonite judged Israel after him. 14 And he had forty sons and thirty grandsons who rode on seventy donkeys; and he judged Israel eight years. 15 Then Abdon the son of Hillel the Pirathonite died and was buried at Pirathon in the land of Ephraim, in the hill country of the Amalekites.

Psalm 50:7–15

7 "Hear, O My people, and I will speak;
O Israel, I will testify against you;
I am God, your God.

8 "I do not reprove you for your sacrifices,
And your burnt offerings are
continually before Me.
9 "I shall take no young bull
out of your house
Nor male goats out of your folds.
10 "For every beast of the forest is Mine,
The cattle on a thousand hills.
11 "I know every bird of the mountains,
And everything that moves
in the field is Mine.
12 "If I were hungry I would not tell you,
For the world is Mine, as
well as its fullness.
13 "Shall I eat the flesh of bulls
Or drink the blood of male goats?
14 "Offer to God a sacrifice of thanksgiving
And pay your vows to the Most High;
15 Call upon Me in the day of distress;
I shall rescue you, and you
will glorify Me."

Proverbs 14:28

28 In a multitude of people is
a king's splendor,
But in the dearth of people
is a prince's ruin.

Luke 17:1–19

17 Now He said to His disciples, "It is
inevitable that stumbling blocks
come, but woe to him through whom
they come! 2 It would be better for him if a
millstone were hung around his neck and he
were thrown into the sea, than that he would
cause one of these little ones to stumble. 3 Be
on your guard! If your brother sins, rebuke
him; and if he repents, forgive him. 4 And if
he sins against you seven times a day, and
returns to you seven times, saying, 'I repent,'
forgive him."
5 And the apostles said to the Lord,
"Increase our faith!" 6 And the Lord said,
"If you have faith like a mustard seed,
you would say to this mulberry tree, 'Be
uprooted and be planted in the sea'; and it
would obey you.
7 "But which of you, having a slave
plowing or tending sheep, will say to him
when he has come in from the field, 'Come
immediately and sit down to eat'? 8 But will
he not say to him, 'Prepare something for me
to eat, and, clothing yourself *properly,* serve
me while I eat and drink; and afterward you
may eat and drink'? 9 Is he grateful to the
slave because he did the things which were
commanded? 10 In this way, you also, when
you do all the things which are commanded
of you, say, 'We are unworthy slaves; we
have done *only* that which we ought to have
done.'"
11 And it happened that while He was
on the way to Jerusalem, He was passing
through Samaria and Galilee. 12 And as He
entered a village, ten leprous men who stood
at a distance met Him. 13 And they raised
their voices, saying, "Jesus, Master, have
mercy on us!" 14 When He saw them, He
said to them, "Go and show yourselves to
the priests." And it happened that as they
were going, they were cleansed. 15 Now
one of them, when he saw that he had
been healed, turned back, glorifying God
with a loud voice, 16 and he fell on his face
at His feet, giving thanks to Him. And he
was a Samaritan. 17 Then Jesus answered
and said, "Were there not ten cleansed? But
the nine—where are they? 18 Was there no
one found who turned back to give glory
to God, except this foreigner?" 19 And He
said to him, "Stand up and go; your faith
has saved you."

APRIL 24

Judges 13:1–14:20

13 Then the sons of Israel again did
what was evil in the eyes of Yahweh,
so that Yahweh gave them into the hand of
the Philistines forty years.
2 And there was a certain man of Zorah, of
the family of the Danites, whose name was
Manoah; and his wife was barren and had
borne no *children.* 3 Then the angel of Yah-
weh appeared to the woman and said to her,
"Behold now, you are barren and have borne
no *children,* but you shall be with child and
give birth to a son. 4 So now, be careful not
to drink wine or strong drink, nor eat any
unclean thing. 5 For behold, you shall be
with child and give birth to a son, and no
razor shall come upon his head, for the boy
shall be a Nazirite to God from the womb;
and he shall begin to save Israel from the
hand of the Philistines." 6 Then the woman

came and told her husband, saying, "A man
of God came to me, and his appearance was
like the appearance of the angel of God, very
awesome. And I did not ask him where he
came from, nor did he tell me his name.
7 And he said to me, 'Behold, you shall be
with child and give birth to a son, so now
you shall not drink wine or strong drink,
and you shall not eat any unclean thing, for
the boy shall be a Nazirite to God from the
womb to the day of his death.'"
8 Then Manoah entreated Yahweh and
said, "O Lord, please let the man of God
whom You have sent come to us again that
he may instruct us what to do for the boy
who is to be born." 9 And God listened to the
voice of Manoah; and the angel of God came
again to the woman as she was sitting in the
field, but Manoah her husband was not with
her. 10 So the woman ran quickly and told
her husband, and she said to him, "Behold,
the man who came the *other* day to me has
appeared to me." 11 Then Manoah arose and
followed his wife, and when he came to the
man he said to him, "Are you the man who
spoke to the woman?" And he said, "I am."
12 So Manoah said, "Now your words will
come *to pass*. What shall be the judgment
governing the boy and his work?" 13 So the
angel of Yahweh said to Manoah, "Let the
woman be careful in all that I said. 14 She
should not eat anything that comes from
the vine, nor drink wine or strong drink, nor
eat any unclean thing; let her keep all that
I commanded."
15 Then Manoah said to the angel of Yah-
weh, "Please let us delay you so that we may
prepare a young goat for you." 16 And the
angel of Yahweh said to Manoah, "Though
you delay me, I will not eat your food, but if
you prepare a burnt offering, *then* offer it to
Yahweh." For Manoah did not know that he
was the angel of Yahweh. 17 Then Manoah
said to the angel of Yahweh, "What is your
name, so that when your words come *to*
pass, we may honor you?" 18 But the angel
of Yahweh said to him, "Why do you ask my
name, seeing it is wonderful?" 19 So Manoah
took the young goat with the grain offering
and offered it on the rock to Yahweh, and He
did a wondrous thing while Manoah and his
wife looked on. 20 Indeed, it happened when
the flame went up from the altar toward
heaven, that the angel of Yahweh went up
in the flame of the altar. And Manoah and
his wife saw *this*, so they fell on their faces
to the ground.
21 Now the angel of Yahweh did not
appear to Manoah or his wife again. Then
Manoah knew that he was the angel of Yah-
weh. 22 So Manoah said to his wife, "We will
surely die, for we have seen God." 23 But his
wife said to him, "If Yahweh had desired to
put us to death, He would not have accepted
a burnt offering and a grain offering from
our hands, nor would He have shown us all
these things, nor would He have let us hear
things like this at this time."
24 Then the woman gave birth to a son
and named him Samson; and the child
grew up, and Yahweh blessed him. 25 And
the Spirit of Yahweh began to stir him in
Mahaneh-dan, between Zorah and Eshtaol.

14 Then Samson went down to Timnah
and saw a woman in Timnah, *one*
of the daughters of the Philistines. 2 So
he came *back* up and told his father and
mother, "I saw a woman in Timnah, *one*
of the daughters of the Philistines; so
now, take her for me as a wife." 3 But his
father and his mother said to him, "Is there
no woman among the daughters of your
relatives, or among all our people, that you
go to take a wife from the uncircumcised
Philistines?" But Samson said to his father,
"Take her for me, for she is right in my
eyes." 4 However, his father and mother did
not know that it was of Yahweh, for He was
seeking an occasion against the Philistines.
Now at that time the Philistines were ruling
over Israel.
5 Then Samson went down to Timnah
with his father and mother, and they came
as far as the vineyards of Timnah; and
behold, a young lion *came* roaring toward
him. 6 And the Spirit of Yahweh came upon
him mightily, so that he tore it as one tears
a young goat, though he had nothing in his
hand; but he did not tell his father or mother
what he had done. 7 So he went down and
spoke to the woman; and she was right in
the eyes of Samson. 8 Then he returned later
to take her, and he turned aside to see the
carcass of the lion; and behold, a swarm of
bees and honey were in the body of the lion.
9 So he scraped the honey into his hands and
went on, eating as he went. Then he went
to his father and mother, and he gave *some*
to them, and they ate *it*; but he did not tell

them that he had scraped the honey out of
the body of the lion.
10 Then his father went down to the
woman; and Samson made a feast there,
for the young men customarily did this.
11 Now it happened that when they saw
him, they took thirty companions to be with
him. 12 Then Samson said to them, "Let me
now propound a riddle to you; if you will
indeed tell it to me within the seven days
of the feast and find it out, then I will give
you thirty linen wraps and thirty changes of
clothes. 13 But if you are unable to tell me,
then you shall give me thirty linen wraps
and thirty changes of clothes." And they
said to him, "Propound your riddle, that we
may hear it." 14 So he said to them,

"Out of the eater came something to eat,
And out of the strong came
something sweet."

But they could not tell the riddle in three
days.
15 Then it happened on the fourth day
that they said to Samson's wife, "Entice
your husband, so that he will tell us
the riddle, or we will burn you and your
father's house with fire. Have you invited
us to impoverish us? Is this not *so*?" 16 So
Samson's wife wept before him and said,
"You only hate me, and you do not love me;
you have propounded a riddle to the sons of
my people and have not told *it* to me." And
he said to her, "Behold, I have not told *it* to
my father or mother; so should I tell you?"
17 However she wept before him seven days
while their feast lasted. And on the seventh
day he told her because she pressed him so
hard. She then told the riddle to the sons
of her people. 18 So the men of the city said
to him on the seventh day before the sun
went down,

"What is sweeter than honey?
And what is stronger than a lion?"

And he said to them,

"If you had not plowed with my heifer,
You would not have found
out my riddle."

19 Then the Spirit of Yahweh came upon him
mightily, and he went down to Ashkelon
and struck down thirty of them and took
their spoil and gave the changes *of clothes*
to those who told the riddle. And his anger
burned, and he went up to his father's
house. 20 But Samson's wife was *given* to his
companion who had been his friend.

Psalm 50:16–23

16 But to the wicked God says,
"What right have you to
recount My statutes
And to take My covenant
in your mouth?
17 "For you hate discipline,
And you cast My words behind you.
18 "When you see a thief, you
are pleased with him,
And you associate with adulterers.
19 "You let your mouth loose in evil
And you harness your
tongue for deceit.
20 "You sit and speak against your brother;
You slander your own mother's son.
21 "These things you have done
and I kept silent;
You thought that I was just like you;
I will reprove you and state *the
case* in order before your eyes.

22 "Now consider this, you
who forget God,
Lest I tear *you* in pieces, and there
will be none to deliver.
23 "He who offers a sacrifice of
thanksgiving glorifies Me;
And he who orders *his* way,
I shall show the salvation of God."

Proverbs 14:29–30

29 He who is slow to anger has
great discernment,
But he who is quick-tempered
raises up folly.
30 A tranquil heart is life to the body,
But jealousy is rottenness to the bones.

Luke 17:20–37

20 Now having been questioned by the
Pharisees as to when the kingdom of God
was coming, He answered them and said,
"The kingdom of God is not coming with
signs to be observed, 21 nor will they say,
'Look, here!' or, 'There!' For behold, the
kingdom of God is in your midst."
22 And He said to the disciples, "The
days will come when you will long to see
one of the days of the Son of Man, and you
will not see it. 23 And they will say to you,
'Look there! Look here!' Do not go away, and
do not run after *them*. 24 For just like the
lightning, when it flashes out of one part
of the sky, shines to the other part of the

sky, so will the Son of Man be in His day. 25 But first He must suffer many things and be rejected by this generation. 26 And just as it was in the days of Noah, so it will be also in the days of the Son of Man: 27 they were eating, they were drinking, they were marrying, they were being given in marriage, until the day that Noah entered the ark, and the flood came and destroyed them all. 28 It was the same as in the days of Lot—they were eating, they were drinking, they were buying, they were selling, they were planting, they were building; 29 but on the day that Lot went out from Sodom it rained fire and brimstone from heaven and destroyed them all. 30 It will be just the same on the day that the Son of Man is revealed. 31 On that day, the one who is on the housetop and whose goods are in the house must not go down to take them out, and likewise the one who is in the field must not turn back. 32 Remember Lot's wife. 33 Whoever seeks to keep his life will lose it, and whoever loses *his life* will preserve it. 34 I tell you, on that night there will be two in one bed; one will be taken and the other will be left. 35 There will be two women grinding *grain* at the same place; one will be taken and the other will be left. 36 [Two men will be in the field; one will be taken and the other will be left."] 37 And answering they *said to Him, "Where, Lord?" And He said to them, "Where the body *is*, there also the vultures will be gathered."

APRIL 25

Judges 15:1–16:31

15 Now it happened that after a while, in the time of the wheat harvest, Samson visited his wife with a young goat and said, "I will go in to my wife in *her* room." But her father did not let him enter. 2 And her father said, "I really thought that you hated her intensely; so I gave her to your companion. Is not her younger sister better than she? Please let her be yours instead." 3 Samson then said to them, "This time I shall be innocent in regard to the Philistines when I do them harm." 4 So Samson went and caught 300 foxes and took torches and turned *the foxes* tail to tail and put one torch in the middle between two tails. 5 Then he set fire to the torches and sent the foxes into the standing grain of the Philistines. So he caused both the shocks and the standing grain, along with the vineyards *and* groves, to burn. 6 Then the Philistines said, "Who did this?" And they said, "Samson, the son-in-law of the Timnite, because he took his wife and gave her to his companion." So the Philistines came up and burned her and her father with fire. 7 Then Samson said to them, "If you act like this, then I will surely take revenge on you, but after that I will cease." 8 And he struck them ruthlessly with a great slaughter; and he went down and lived in the cleft of the rock of Etam.

9 Then the Philistines went up and camped in Judah and spread out in Lehi. 10 So the men of Judah said, "Why have you come up against us?" And they said, "We have come up to bind Samson in order to do to him as he did to us." 11 Then 3,000 men of Judah went down to the cleft of the rock of Etam and said to Samson, "Do you not know that the Philistines are rulers over us? What then is this that you have done to us?" And he said to them, "As they did to me, so I have done to them." 12 And they said to him, "We have come down to bind you so that we may give you into the hand of the Philistines." And Samson said to them, "Swear to me that you yourselves will not kill me." 13 So they said to him, "No, but we will bind you fast and give you into their hands; yet surely we will not put you to death." Then they bound him with two new ropes and brought him up from the rock.

14 *When* he came to Lehi, the Philistines shouted as they met him. And the Spirit of Yahweh came upon him mightily so that the ropes that were on his arms were as flax that is burned with fire, and his bonds dropped from his hands. 15 And he found a fresh jawbone of a donkey, so he sent forth his hand and took it and struck down 1,000 men with it. 16 Then Samson said,

"With the jawbone of a donkey,
Heaps upon heaps,
With the jawbone of a donkey
I have struck down 1,000 men."

17 Now it happened that when he had finished speaking, he threw the jawbone from his hand; and he named that place

Ramath-lehi. 18 Then he became very
thirsty, and he called to Yahweh and said,
"You have given this great salvation by
the hand of Your slave, but now shall I
die of thirst and fall into the hands of the
uncircumcised?" 19 So God split the hollow
place that is in Lehi and water came out of
it. Then he drank, and his spirit returned,
and he revived. Therefore he named it En-
hakkore, which is in Lehi to this day. 20 And
he judged Israel twenty years in the days of
the Philistines.

16 Then Samson went to Gaza and saw a
harlot there and went in to her. 2 *And
it was told* to the Gazites, saying, "Samson
has come here," so they surrounded *the
place* and lay in wait for him all night at
the gate of the city. And they kept silent all
night, saying, "*Let us wait* until the morning
light; then we will kill him." 3 But Samson
lay until midnight, and at midnight he arose
and seized the doors of the city gate and the
two posts and pulled them up along with the
bars; then he put them on his shoulders and
brought them up to the top of the mountain
which is opposite Hebron.

4 Now it happened afterwards that he
loved a woman in the valley of Sorek, and
her name was Delilah. 5 And the lords of
the Philistines came up to her and said to
her, "Entice him, and see where his great
strength *lies* and how we may overpower
him that we may bind him to afflict him.
Then we will each give you 1,100 *pieces* of
silver." 6 So Delilah said to Samson, "Please
tell me where your great strength is and how
you may be bound to afflict you." 7 Samson
said to her, "If they bind me with seven fresh
cords that have not been dried, then I will
become weak and be like any *other* man."
8 Then the lords of the Philistines brought
up to her seven fresh cords that had not
been dried, and she bound him with them.
9 Now she had *men* lying in wait, sitting in
an inner room. And she said to him, "The
Philistines are upon you, Samson!" But he
snapped the cords as a string of tinder snaps
when it touches fire. So his strength was *still*
not known.

10 Then Delilah said to Samson, "Behold,
you have deceived me and told me lies; now
please tell me how you may be bound."
11 And he said to her, "If they bind me tightly
with new ropes which have not been used
for work, then I will become weak and be
like any *other* man." 12 So Delilah took
new ropes and bound him with them and
said to him, "The Philistines are upon you,
Samson!" Now the *men* lying in wait were
sitting in the inner room. But he snapped
the ropes from his arms like a thread.

13 Then Delilah said to Samson, "Up to
now you have deceived me and told me
lies; tell me how you may be bound." And
he said to her, "If you weave the seven locks
of my head with the web [and fasten it with
a pin, then I will become weak and be like
any other man." 14 So while he slept, Delilah
took the seven locks of his hair and wove
them into the web]. And she fastened *it* with
the pin and said to him, "The Philistines are
upon you, Samson!" But he awoke from his
sleep and pulled out the pin of the loom and
the web.

15 Then she said to him, "How can you
say, 'I love you,' when your heart is not
with me? You have deceived me these
three times and have not told me where
your great strength is." 16 Now it happened
when she pressed him daily with her words
and urged him, that his soul was annoyed
to death. 17 So he told her all *that was*
in his heart and said to her, "A razor has
never come on my head, for I have been a
Nazirite to God from my mother's womb. If
I am shaved, then my strength will leave me
and I will become weak and be like every
other man."

18 And Delilah saw that he had told her all
that was in his heart, so she sent and called
the lords of the Philistines, saying, "Come up
once more, for he has told me all *that is* in
his heart." Then the lords of the Philistines
came up to her and brought up the silver in
their hands. 19 Then she made him sleep on
her knees and called for a man and had him
shave off the seven locks of his head. Then
she began to afflict him, and his strength
left him. 20 And she said, "The Philistines
are upon you, Samson!" And he awoke from
his sleep and said, "I will go out as at other
times and shake myself free." But he did not
know that Yahweh had left him. 21 Then the
Philistines seized him and gouged out his
eyes; and they brought him down to Gaza
and bound him with bronze chains, and he
was a grinder in the prison. 22 However, the
hair of his head began to grow again after it
was shaved off.

23 Now the lords of the Philistines assem-
bled to offer a great sacrifice to Dagon their
god and to be glad; and they said,
"Our god has given Samson our
enemy into our hands."
24 Then the people saw him and praised
their god, for they said,
"Our god has given our enemy
into our hands,
Even the destroyer of our country,
Who has slain many of us."
25 So it happened when their hearts were
merry, that they said, "Call for Samson,
that he may amuse us." So they called for
Samson from the prison, and he entertained
them. And they made him stand between the
pillars. 26 Then Samson said to the boy who
was holding his hand, "Let me feel the pillars
on which the house is established, that I may
lean against them." 27 Now the house was
full of men and women, and all the lords of
the Philistines were there. And about 3,000
men and women were on the roof looking
on while Samson was amusing *them*.
28 Then Samson called to Yahweh and
said, "O Lord Yahweh, please remember
me and please strengthen me just this time,
O God, that I may at once be avenged of the
Philistines for my two eyes." 29 Samson
grasped the two middle pillars on which
the house was established and supported
himself against them, the one with his right
hand and the other with his left. 30 And
Samson said, "Let me die with the Philis-
tines!" And he bent with his strength so that
the house fell on the lords and all the people
who were in it. So the dead whom he put to
death by his death were more than those
whom he put to death in his life. 31 Then
his brothers and all his father's household
came down, carried him, brought him up,
and buried him between Zorah and Eshtaol,
in the tomb of Manoah his father. Thus he
had judged Israel twenty years.

Psalm 51:1–6

1 *Be gracious to me*, O God, according
to Your lovingkindness;
According to the abundance
of Your compassion blot
out my transgressions.
2 Wash me thoroughly from my iniquity
And cleanse me from my sin.
3 For I know my transgressions,
And my sin is ever before me.
4 Against You, You only, I have sinned
And done what is evil in Your sight,
So that You are justified
when You speak
And pure when You judge.

5 Behold, I was brought forth
in iniquity,
And in sin my mother conceived me.
6 Behold, You delight in truth
in the innermost being,
And in the hidden part You will
make me know wisdom.

Proverbs 14:31–32

31 He who oppresses the poor
reproaches his Maker,
But he who is gracious to the
needy honors Him.
32 The wicked is thrust down
by his own evil,
But the righteous takes refuge
even in his death.

Luke 18:1–27

18 Now He was telling them a parable
to show that at all times they ought
to pray and not to lose heart, 2 saying, "In a
certain city there was a certain judge who
did not fear God and did not respect man.
3 Now there was a widow in that city, and
she kept coming to him, saying, 'Give me
justice from my opponent.' 4 And for a while
he was unwilling; but afterward he said to
himself, 'Even though I do not fear God
nor respect man, 5 yet because this widow
is bothering me, I will give her justice, lest
by continually coming she wears me out.'"
6 And the Lord said, "Hear what the unjust
judge *said. 7 Now, will God not bring about
justice for His elect who cry to Him day and
night, and will He delay long over them? 8 I
tell you that He will bring about justice for
them quickly. However, when the Son of
Man comes, will He find that faith on the
earth?"
9 And He also told this parable to some
people who trusted in themselves that they
were righteous, and viewed others with
contempt: 10 "Two men went up into the
temple to pray, one a Pharisee and the other
a tax collector. 11 The Pharisee stood and
was praying these things to himself: 'God,
I thank You that I am not like other people:
swindlers, unjust, adulterers, or even like

this tax collector. 12 I fast twice a week;
I pay tithes of all that I get.' 13 But the tax
collector, standing some distance away, was
even unwilling to lift up his eyes to heaven,
but was beating his chest, saying, 'God, be
merciful to me, the sinner!' 14 I tell you,
this man went down to his house justified
rather than the other, for everyone who
exalts himself will be humbled, but he who
humbles himself will be exalted."

15 And they were bringing even their
babies to Him so that He would touch them,
but when the disciples saw it, they were
rebuking them. 16 But Jesus called for them,
saying, "Permit the children to come to Me,
and do not hinder them, for the kingdom of
God belongs to such as these. 17 Truly I say
to you, whoever does not receive the king-
dom of God like a child will never enter it."

18 And a ruler questioned Him, saying,
"Good Teacher, what shall I do to inherit
eternal life?" 19 And Jesus said to him,
"Why do you call Me good? No one is good
except God alone. 20 You know the com-
mandments, 'DO NOT COMMIT ADULTERY,
DO NOT MURDER, DO NOT STEAL, DO NOT
BEAR FALSE WITNESS, HONOR YOUR FATHER
AND MOTHER.'" 21 And he said, "All these
things I have kept from *my* youth." 22 And
when Jesus heard *this*, He said to him, "One
thing you still lack: sell all that you possess
and distribute it to the poor, and you shall
have treasure in heaven. And come, follow
Me." 23 But when he heard these things, he
became very sad, for he was extremely rich.
24 And Jesus looked at him and said, "How
hard it is for those who are wealthy to enter
the kingdom of God! 25 For it is easier for a
camel to go through the eye of a needle than
for a rich man to enter the kingdom of God."
26 And those who heard it said, "Then who
can be saved?" 27 But He said, "The things
that are impossible with people are possible
with God."

APRIL 26

Judges 17:1–19:30

17 Now there was a man of the hill
country of Ephraim whose name was
Micah. 2 He said to his mother, "The 1,100
pieces of silver which were taken from you,
about which you uttered a curse and spoke
of it in my hearing, behold, the silver is with
me; it was I who took it." And his mother
said, "Blessed be my son by Yahweh." 3 And
he then returned the 1,100 *pieces* of silver to
his mother, and his mother said, "I wholly
set apart the silver from my hand as holy to
Yahweh for my son to make a graven image
and a molten image; so now I will return
them to you." 4 So he returned the silver to
his mother, and his mother took 200 *pieces*
of silver and gave them to the silversmith.
And he made them into a graven image and
a molten image, and they were in the house
of Micah. 5 And the man Micah had a shrine,
and he made an ephod and household
idols and ordained one of his sons, and he
became his priest. 6 In those days there was
no king in Israel; every man did what was
right in his own eyes.

7 *And* there was a young man from Beth-
lehem in Judah, of the family of Judah, who
was a Levite; and he was sojourning there.
8 Then the man went from the city, from
Bethlehem in Judah, to sojourn wherever
he might find *a place*; and as he made
his journey, he came to the hill country
of Ephraim to the house of Micah. 9 And
Micah said to him, "Where do you come
from?" And he said to him, "I am a Levite
from Bethlehem in Judah, and I am going
to sojourn wherever I may find *a place*."
10 Micah then said to him, "Remain with
me and be a father and a priest to me, and
I will give you ten *pieces* of silver a year, a
suit of clothes, and your sustenance." So
the Levite went *in*. 11 And the Levite was
willing to remain with the man, and the
young man became to him like one of his
sons. 12 So Micah ordained the Levite, and
the young man became his priest and lived
in the house of Micah. 13 Then Micah said,
"Now I know that Yahweh will prosper me
because I have a Levite as priest."

18 In those days there was no king of
Israel; and in those days the tribe
of the Danites was seeking an inheritance
for themselves to live in, for until that day
the land among the tribes of Israel had
not fallen to them as an inheritance. 2 So
the sons of Dan sent from their family five
men out of their whole number, men of

valor from Zorah and Eshtaol, to spy out the land and to search it; and they said to them, "Go, search the land." And they came to the hill country of Ephraim, to the house of Micah, and lodged there. 3 They were near the house of Micah, and they recognized the voice of the young man, the Levite. So they turned aside there and said to him, "Who brought you here? And what are you doing in this *place*? And what do you have here?" 4 And he said to them, "Thus and so has Micah done to me, and he has hired me, and I have become his priest." 5 And they said to him, "Ask of God, please, that we may know whether our way on which we are going will be successful." 6 So the priest said to them, "Go in peace; your way in which you are going is before Yahweh."

7 Then the five men went *forth* and came to Laish and saw the people who were in it living in security, after the manner of the Sidonians, quiet and secure; for there was no oppressive conqueror dishonoring *them* for anything in the land, and they were far from the Sidonians and had no dealings with anyone. 8 So they came back to their brothers at Zorah and Eshtaol, and their brothers said to them, "What *do* you *report*?" 9 And they said, "Arise, and let us go up against them; for we have seen the land, and behold, it is very good. And will you be silent? Do not delay to go, to enter, to possess the land. 10 When you enter, you will come to a secure people and a spacious land; for God has given it into your hand, a place where there is no lack of anything that is on the earth."

11 Then from the family of the Danites, from Zorah and from Eshtaol, 600 men armed with weapons of war set out. 12 And they went up and camped at Kiriath-jearim in Judah. Therefore they called that place Mahaneh-dan to this day; behold, it is west of Kiriath-jearim. 13 Then they passed from there to the hill country of Ephraim and came to the house of Micah.

14 *And the five men* who went to spy out the country of Laish answered and said to their relatives, "Do you know that there are in these houses an ephod and household idols and a graven image and a molten image? So now, know what you should do." 15 Then they turned aside there and came to the house of the young man, the Levite, to the house of Micah, and asked him of his welfare. 16 Now the 600 men armed with their weapons of war, who were of the sons of Dan, were standing by the entrance of the gate. 17 Then the five men who went to spy out the land went up *and* entered there, *and* took the graven image and the ephod and household idols and the molten image. And the priest was standing by the entrance of the gate with the 600 men armed with weapons of war. 18 Now these had entered into Micah's house and took the graven image, the ephod and household idols and the molten image. Then the priest said to them, "What are you doing?" 19 And they said to him, "Be silent; put your hand over your mouth and come with us and be to us a father and a priest. Is it better for you to be a priest to the house of one man or to be priest to a tribe and a family in Israel?" 20 And the priest's heart was merry, and he took the ephod and household idols and the graven image and entered among the people.

21 Then they turned and went *away* and put the little ones and the livestock and the valuables in front of them. 22 They had gone some distance from the house of Micah, and the men who *were* in the houses near Micah's house were summoned and then overtook the sons of Dan. 23 And they called out to the sons of Dan, who turned around and said to Micah, "What is *the matter* with you, that you were summoned together?" 24 And he said, "You have taken away my gods which I made, and the priest, and have gone away, and what do I have besides? So how can you say to me, 'What is *the matter* with you?'" 25 Then the sons of Dan said to him, "Do not let your voice be heard among us, lest men, bitter of soul, fall upon you and you lose your life, with the lives of your household." 26 So the sons of Dan went on their way; and when Micah saw that they were too strong for him, he turned and went back to his house.

27 Now they took what Micah had made and the priest who had belonged to him, and they came to Laish, to a people quiet and secure, and struck them with the edge of the sword; and they burned the city with fire. 28 And there was no one to deliver *them* because it was far from Sidon and they had no dealings with anyone, and it was in the valley which is near Beth-rehob. And they rebuilt the city and lived in it. 29 And they called the name of the city Dan, after the

name of Dan their father who was born in
Israel; however, the name of the city for-
merly was Laish. 30 Then the sons of Dan
set up for themselves the graven image; and
Jonathan, the son of Gershom, the son of
Moses, he and his sons were priests to the
tribe of the Danites until the day of the exile
of the land. 31 So they set up for themselves
Micah's graven image which he had made,
all the time that the house of God was at
Shiloh.

19 Now it happened in those days, when
there was no king in Israel, that there
was a certain Levite sojourning in the
remote part of the hill country of Ephraim,
who took a concubine for himself from
Bethlehem in Judah. 2 But his concubine
played the harlot against him, and she went
away from him to her father's house in Beth-
lehem in Judah and was there for a period
of four months. 3 Then her husband arose
and went after her to speak to her heart in
order to bring her back, and his young man
was with him as well as a pair of donkeys.
So she brought him into her father's house,
and the girl's father saw him and was glad
to meet him. 4 And his father-in-law, the
girl's father, prevailed upon him; and he
remained with him three days. So they ate
and drank and spent the night there. 5 Now
it happened on the fourth day that they got
up early in the morning, and he arose to go;
and the girl's father said to his son-in-law,
"Sustain yourself with a piece of bread, and
afterward you may go." 6 So both of them
sat down and ate and drank together; and
the girl's father said to the man, "Please
be willing to spend the night, and let your
heart be merry." 7 Then the man arose to
go, but his father-in-law pressed him so
that he turned back and spent the night
there. 8 And on the fifth day he arose to go
early in the morning, and the girl's father
said, "Please sustain yourself and wait until
afternoon"; so both of them ate. 9 Then the
man arose to go along with his concubine
and young man, and his father-in-law, the
girl's father, said to him, "Behold now, the
day has drawn to a close; please spend the
night. Behold, the day is coming to an end;
spend the night here that your heart may
be merry. Then tomorrow you may arise
early for your journey so that you may go
to your tent."

10 But the man was not willing to spend
the night, so he arose and went and came
to *a place* before Jebus (that is, Jerusalem).
And there were with him a pair of saddled
donkeys; his concubine also was with him.
11 They *were* alongside of Jebus, and the
day was almost gone. And the young man
said to his master, "Come, please, and let
us turn aside into this city of the Jebusites
and spend the night in it." 12 However, his
master said to him, "We will not turn aside
into the city of foreigners who are not of
the sons of Israel; but we will pass on by
until Gibeah." 13 Then he said to his young
man, "Come and let us draw near to one of
these places; and we will spend the night in
Gibeah or Ramah." 14 So they passed along
and went their way, and the sun set on them
near Gibeah which belongs to Benjamin.
15 Then they turned aside there in order
to enter *and* to spend the night in Gibeah.
So they entered and sat down in the open
square of the city. Now no one was taking
them into *his* house to spend the night.

16 But behold, an old man was coming
from his work, from the field, at evening.
Now the man was from the hill country of
Ephraim, and he was sojourning in Gibeah,
but the men of the place were Benjamites.
17 And he lifted up his eyes and saw the
traveler in the open square of the city; and
the old man said, "Where are you going, and
where do you come from?" 18 And he said
to him, "We are passing from Bethlehem in
Judah to the remote part of the hill country
of Ephraim. I am from there, and I went to
Bethlehem in Judah. But I am *now* going to
the house of Yahweh, and no man is taking
me into his house. 19 Yet there is both straw
and fodder for our donkeys, and also bread
and wine for me, your maidservant, and
the young man who is with your servants;
there is no lack of anything." 20 Then the old
man said, "Peace be to you. Only let me *take
care of* all that you lack; however, do not
spend the night in the open square." 21 So
he brought him into his house and gave the
donkeys fodder, and they washed their feet
and ate and drank.

22 They were making their hearts merry,
and behold, the men of the city, certain vile
fellows, surrounded the house, pounding
the door; and they spoke to the owner of
the house, the old man, saying, "Bring out
the man who came into your house that

we may know him." 23 Then the man, the
owner of the house, went out to them and
said to them, "No, my brothers, please do
not do evil. Since this man has come into my
house, do not commit this disgraceful act.
24 Behold, my daughter who is a virgin, and
his concubine—please let me bring them
out that you may violate them and do to
them whatever is good in your eyes. But do
not commit such a disgraceful act against
this man." 25 But the men were not willing
to listen to him. So the man took hold of his
concubine and brought *her* out to them; and
they knew her and abused her all night until
morning, and they let her go at the breaking
of dawn. 26 As the day began to dawn, the
woman came and fell down at the doorway
of the man's house where her master was,
until *full* daylight.

27 Then her master arose in the morning
and opened the doors of the house and
went out to go on his way, and behold, the
woman, his concubine, was lying at the
doorway of the house with her hands on
the threshold. 28 And he said to her, "Get
up and let us go," but there was no answer.
Then he took her on the donkey; and the
man arose and went to his home. 29 Then
he entered his house and took a knife and
took hold of his concubine and cut her in
twelve pieces, limb by limb, and sent her
throughout the territory of Israel. 30 And all
who saw *it* said, "Nothing like this has *ever*
happened or been seen from the day when
the sons of Israel came up from the land of
Egypt to this day. Consider it; take counsel
and speak up!"

Psalm 51:7–11

7 Purify me with hyssop, and
I shall be clean;
Wash me, and I shall be
whiter than snow.
8 Make me to hear joy and gladness,
Let the bones which You
have crushed rejoice.
9 Hide Your face from my sins
And blot out all my iniquities.

10 Create in me a clean heart, O God,
And renew a steadfast spirit within me.
11 Do not cast me away from
Your presence
And do not take Your Holy
Spirit from me.

Proverbs 14:33–35

33 Wisdom rests in the heart of one
who has understanding,
But in the midst of fools it is
merely made known.
34 Righteousness exalts a nation,
But sin is a disgrace to *any* people.
35 The king's favor is toward a
servant who acts insightfully,
But his fury is toward him
who acts shamefully.

Luke 18:28–43

28 And Peter said, "Behold, we have left *all*
that is our own and followed You." 29 And He
said to them, "Truly I say to you, there is no
one who has left house or wife or brothers
or parents or children, for the sake of the
kingdom of God, 30 who will not receive
many times more at this time and in the
age to come, eternal life."

31 But when He took the twelve aside, He
said to them, "Behold, we are going up to
Jerusalem, and all things which are written
through the prophets about the Son of Man
will be completed. 32 For He will be delivered
over to the Gentiles, and will be mocked and
mistreated and spit upon, 33 and after they
have flogged Him, they will kill Him, and
the third day He will rise again." 34 But the
disciples understood none of these things,
and this statement was hidden from them,
and they did not comprehend the things
that were said.

35 Now it happened that as Jesus was
approaching Jericho, a blind man was
sitting by the road begging. 36 Now hear-
ing a crowd going by, he *began to* inquire
what this was. 37 They reported to him,
"Jesus of Nazareth is passing by." 38 And
he called out, saying, "Jesus, Son of David,
have mercy on me!" 39 And those who went
ahead were rebuking him so that he would
be quiet, but he kept crying out all the more,
"Son of David, have mercy on me!" 40 And
Jesus stopped and commanded that he be
brought to Him, and when he came near, He
questioned him, 41 "What do you want Me
to do for you?" And he said, "Lord, *I want* to
regain my sight!" 42 And Jesus said to him,
"Receive your sight; your faith has saved
you." 43 Immediately he regained his sight
and *began* following Him, glorifying God.
And when all the people saw it, they gave
praise to God.

APRIL 27

Judges 20:1–21:25

20 Then all the sons of Israel from Dan to Beersheba, including the land of Gilead, came out, and the congregation assembled as one man to Yahweh at Mizpah. 2 And the chiefs of all the people, *even* of all the tribes of Israel, took their stand in the assembly of the people of God, 400,000 foot soldiers who draw the sword. 3 (Then the sons of Benjamin heard that the sons of Israel had gone up to Mizpah.) And the sons of Israel said, "Tell *us*, how did this evil take place?" 4 So the Levite, the husband of the woman who was murdered, answered and said, "I came with my concubine to spend the night at Gibeah which belongs to Benjamin. 5 Then the men of Gibeah rose up against me and surrounded the house at night because of me. They intended to kill me; instead, they violated my concubine, and she died. 6 And I seized my concubine and cut her in pieces and sent her throughout the land of Israel's inheritance; for they have committed a lewd and disgraceful act in Israel. 7 Behold, all you sons of Israel, give your advice and counsel here."

8 Then all the people arose as one man, saying, "Not one of us will go to his tent, nor will any of us turn aside to his house. 9 But now this is the thing which we will do to Gibeah; *we will go up* against it by lot. 10 And we will take 10 men out of 100 throughout the tribes of Israel, and 100 out of 1,000, and 1,000 out of 10,000 in order to take up provisions for the people, that when they come to Gibeah of Benjamin, they may do to *them* according to all the disgraceful acts that they have done in Israel." 11 Thus all the men of Israel were gathered against the city, united as one man.

12 Then the tribes of Israel sent men through the entire tribe of Benjamin, saying, "What is this evil that has taken place among you? 13 So now, give up the men, the vile fellows in Gibeah, that we may put them to death and purge *this* evil from Israel." But the sons of Benjamin were not willing to listen to the voice of their brothers, the sons of Israel. 14 Then the sons of Benjamin gathered from the cities to Gibeah, to go out to battle against the sons of Israel. 15 And from the cities on that day the sons of Benjamin were numbered, 26,000 men who draw the sword, besides the inhabitants of Gibeah who were numbered, 700 choice men. 16 Out of all these people 700 choice men were left-handed; each one could sling a stone at a hair and not miss.

17 And the men of Israel besides Benjamin were numbered, 400,000 men who draw the sword; all these were men of war.

18 Then the sons of Israel arose, went up to Bethel, and asked of God and said, "Who shall go up for us to begin the battle against the sons of Benjamin?" Then Yahweh said, "Judah shall begin *it*."

19 So the sons of Israel arose in the morning and camped against Gibeah. 20 And the men of Israel went out to battle against Benjamin, and the men of Israel arranged *themselves* for battle against them at Gibeah. 21 Then the sons of Benjamin came out of Gibeah and destroyed to the ground on that day 22,000 men of Israel. 22 But the people, the men of Israel, strengthened themselves and arranged themselves for battle again in the place where they had arranged *themselves* the first day. 23 And the sons of Israel went up and wept before Yahweh until evening and asked of Yahweh, saying, "Shall we again approach for battle against the sons of my brother Benjamin?" And Yahweh said, "Go up against him."

24 Then the sons of Israel drew near to the sons of Benjamin the second day. 25 And Benjamin went out to meet them from Gibeah the second day and destroyed to the ground again 18,000 men of the sons of Israel; all these drew the sword. 26 Then all the sons of Israel and all the people went up and came to Bethel and wept; thus they remained there before Yahweh and fasted that day until evening. And they offered burnt offerings and peace offerings before Yahweh. 27 Then the sons of Israel asked of Yahweh (now the ark of the covenant of God *was* there in those days, 28 and Phinehas the son of Eleazar, Aaron's son, stood before it *to minister* in those days), saying, "Shall I yet again go out to battle against the sons of my brother Benjamin, or shall I cease?" And Yahweh said, "Go up, for tomorrow I will give them into your hand."

29 So Israel set men in ambush around Gibeah. 30 And the sons of Israel went up against the sons of Benjamin on the third day and arrayed themselves against Gibeah as at other times. 31 So the sons of Benjamin went out to meet the people and were drawn away from the city, and they began to strike and slay some of the people as at other times, on the highways, one of which goes up to Bethel and the other to Gibeah, *and* in the field, about thirty men of Israel. 32 The sons of Benjamin said, "They are defeated before us, as at the first." But the sons of Israel said, "Let us flee that we may draw them away from the city to the highways." 33 Then all the men of Israel arose from their place and arrayed themselves at Baal-tamar; and the men of Israel in ambush burst forth of their place, even out of Maareh-geba. 34 Then 10,000 choice men from all Israel came against Gibeah, and the battle became heavy; but Benjamin did not know that calamity was about to reach them. 35 Then Yahweh defeated Benjamin before Israel, so that the sons of Israel destroyed 25,100 men of Benjamin that day, all who drew the sword.

36 So the sons of Benjamin saw that they were defeated. Now the men of Israel had given ground to Benjamin because they relied on the men in ambush whom they had set against Gibeah. 37 So the men in ambush hurried and rushed against Gibeah. Then the men in ambush deployed and struck all the city with the edge of the sword. 38 Now the appointed sign between the men of Israel and the men in ambush was that they would make a great cloud of smoke rise from the city. 39 So the men of Israel *had* turned around in the battle, and Benjamin *had* begun to strike and slay about thirty men of Israel, for they said, "Surely they are defeated before us, as in the first battle." 40 But the cloud began to rise from the city in a column of smoke, and Benjamin turned behind them; and behold, the whole city was going up *in smoke* to heaven. 41 Then the men of Israel turned around *again*, and the men of Benjamin were dismayed; for they saw that calamity had reached them. 42 Therefore, they turned their backs before the men of Israel toward the direction of the wilderness, but the battle overtook them, and those who came out of the cities destroyed them in the midst of them. 43 They surrounded Benjamin, pursued them without rest, *and* trod them down opposite Gibeah to the *east* toward the sunrise. 44 Thus 18,000 men of Benjamin fell; all these were valiant men. 45 And the rest turned and fled toward the wilderness to the rock of Rimmon, but they caught 5,000 of them on the highways and overtook them at Gidom and struck down 2,000 of them. 46 So all of Benjamin who fell that day were 25,000 men who drew the sword; all these were valiant men. 47 But 600 men turned and fled toward the wilderness to the rock of Rimmon, and they remained at the rock of Rimmon four months. 48 Now the men of Israel returned to the sons of Benjamin and struck them with the edge of the sword, both the entire city with the cattle and all that they found; they also set on fire all the cities which they found.

21

Now the men of Israel had sworn in Mizpah, saying, "None of us shall give his daughter to Benjamin as a wife." 2 So the people came to Bethel and sat there before God until evening and lifted up their voices and wept bitterly. 3 And they said, "Why, O Yahweh, God of Israel, has this come about in Israel, so that one tribe should be missing today from Israel?" 4 Now it happened the next day that the people arose early and built an altar there and offered burnt offerings and peace offerings.

5 Then the sons of Israel said, "Who is there among all the tribes of Israel who did not come up in the assembly to Yahweh?" For they had taken a great oath concerning him who did not come up to Yahweh at Mizpah, saying, "He shall surely be put to death." 6 And the sons of Israel were sorry for their brother Benjamin and said, "One tribe is cut off from Israel today. 7 What shall we do for wives for those who are left? But we have sworn by Yahweh not to give them any of our daughters in marriage."

8 So they said, "What one is there of the tribes of Israel who did not come up to Yahweh at Mizpah?" And behold, no one had come to the camp from Jabesh-gilead to the assembly. 9 Indeed the people were numbered, but behold, not one of the inhabitants of Jabesh-gilead was there. 10 And the congregation sent 12,000 of the men of valor there and commanded them, saying, "Go and strike the inhabitants of

Jabesh-gilead with the edge of the sword,
with the women and the little ones. 11 Now
this is the thing that you shall do: you shall
devote to destruction every man and every
woman who has known, *that is* lain with, a
man." 12 And they found among the inhab-
itants of Jabesh-gilead 400 young virgins
who had not known a man by lying with
him; and they brought them to the camp
at Shiloh, which is in the land of Canaan.

13 Then the whole congregation sent *word*
and spoke to the sons of Benjamin who were
at the rock of Rimmon and called out peace
to them. 14 Then Benjamin returned at that
time, and they gave them the women whom
they had kept alive from the women of
Jabesh-gilead; yet they did not find enough
for them. 15 And the people were sorry for
Benjamin because Yahweh had made a
breach in the tribes of Israel.

16 Then the elders of the congregation
said, "What shall we do for wives for those
who are left, since the women are destroyed
out of Benjamin?" 17 And they said, "*There
must be* a possession for the survivors of
Benjamin, so that a tribe will not be blotted
out from Israel. 18 But we cannot give them
wives of our daughters." For the sons of
Israel had sworn, saying, "Cursed is he who
gives a wife to Benjamin."

19 So they said, "Behold, there is a feast
of Yahweh from year to year in Shiloh,
which is on the north side of Bethel, on the
east side of the highway that goes up from
Bethel to Shechem, and on the south side
of Lebonah." 20 And they commanded the
sons of Benjamin, saying, "Go and lie in wait
in the vineyards, 21 and watch; and behold,
if the daughters of Shiloh come out to take
part in the dances, then you shall come out
of the vineyards, and each of you shall catch
his wife from the daughters of Shiloh and
go to the land of Benjamin. 22 And it will be
when their fathers or their brothers come
to contend with us, that we shall say to
them, 'Be gracious to us concerning them
because we did not take for each man *of
Benjamin* a wife in the battle, and you did
not give *your daughters* to them; *otherwise*
you would now be guilty.'" 23 And the sons
of Benjamin did so and carried away wives
according to their number from those who
danced, whom they stole away. And they
went and returned to their inheritance and
rebuilt the cities and lived in them. 24 Then
the sons of Israel went *away* from there at
that time, every man to his tribe and family,
and each one of them went out from there
to his inheritance.

25 In those days there was no king in
Israel; everyone did what was right in his
own eyes.

Psalm 51:12–19

12 Restore to me the joy of Your salvation
And sustain me with a willing spirit.
13 *Then* I will teach transgressors
Your ways,
And sinners will be converted to You.

14 Deliver me from bloodguiltiness,
O God, the God of my salvation;
Then my tongue will joyfully
sing of Your righteousness.
15 O Lord, open my lips,
That my mouth may
declare Your praise.
16 For You do not delight in sacrifice,
otherwise I would give it;
You are not pleased with
burnt offering.
17 The sacrifices of God are
a broken spirit;
A broken and a contrite heart,
O God, You will not despise.

18 By Your favor do good to Zion;
Build the walls of Jerusalem.
19 Then You will delight in
righteous sacrifices,
In burnt offering and whole
burnt offering;
Then young bulls will be
offered on Your altar.

Proverbs 15:1–3

15 A gentle answer turns away wrath,
But a harsh word stirs up anger.
2 The tongue of the wise makes
knowledge *look* good,
But the mouth of fools
pours forth folly.
3 The eyes of Yahweh are in every place,
Watching the evil and the good.

Luke 19:1–27

19 And He entered Jericho and was
passing through. 2 And behold, there
was a man called by the name of Zaccheus;
he was a chief tax collector and he was rich.

3 And Zaccheus was trying to see who Jesus was, and was unable because of the crowd, for he was small in stature. 4 So he ran on before and climbed up into a sycamore tree in order to see Him, for He was about to pass through that way. 5 And when Jesus came to the place, He looked up and said to him, "Zaccheus, hurry and come down, for today I must stay at your house." 6 And he hurried and came down and received Him gladly. 7 And when they saw it, they all *began to* grumble, saying, "He has gone to be the guest of a man who is a sinner." 8 But Zaccheus stopped and said to the Lord, "Behold, half of my possessions, Lord, I will give to the poor, and if I have extorted anyone of anything, I will give back four times as much." 9 And Jesus said to him, "Today salvation has come to this house, because he, too, is a son of Abraham. 10 For the Son of Man has come to seek and to save the lost."

11 Now while they were listening to these things, Jesus went on to tell a parable, because He was near Jerusalem, and they thought that the kingdom of God was going to appear immediately. 12 So He said, "A nobleman went to a distant country to receive a kingdom for himself, and *then* return. 13 And he called ten of his slaves, and gave them ten minas and said to them, 'Engage in business until I come *back*.' 14 But his citizens hated him and sent a delegation after him, saying, 'We do not want this man to reign over us.' 15 And it happened that when he returned, after receiving the kingdom, he ordered that these slaves, to whom he had given the money, be called to him so that he might know how much they had made in business. 16 So the first appeared, saying, 'Master, your mina has made ten minas more.' 17 And he said to him, 'Well done, good slave, because you have been faithful in a very little thing, you are to be in authority over ten cities.' 18 Then the second came, saying, 'Your mina, master, has made five minas.' 19 And he said to him also, 'And you are to be over five cities.' 20 Then another came, saying, 'Master, here is your mina, which I kept put away in a cloth; 21 for I was afraid of you, because you are a strict man; you take up what you did not lay down and reap what you did not sow.' 22 He *said to him, 'From your own mouth I will judge you, you worthless slave. Did you know that I am a strict man, taking up what I did not lay down and reaping what I did not sow? 23 Then why did you not put my money in the bank, and having come, I would have collected it with interest?' 24 Then he said to the bystanders, 'Take the mina away from him and give it to the one who has the ten minas.' 25 And they said to him, 'Master, he has ten minas *already*.' 26 'I tell you that to everyone who has, more shall be given, but from the one who does not have, even what he does have shall be taken away. 27 But these enemies of mine, who did not want me to reign over them, bring them here and slay them in my presence.'"

APRIL 28

Ruth 1:1–2:23

1 Now it happened in the days when the judges judged, that there was a famine in the land. And a certain man of Bethlehem in Judah went to sojourn in the fields of Moab with his wife and his two sons. 2 The name of the man *was* Elimelech, and the name of his *wife, Naomi; and the names* of his two sons *were* Mahlon and Chilion, Ephrathites of Bethlehem in Judah. Now they came to the fields of Moab and remained there. 3 Then Elimelech, Naomi's husband, died; and she was left with her two sons. 4 They took for themselves Moabite women *as* wives; the name of the one was Orpah and the name of the other Ruth. And they lived there about ten years. 5 Then both Mahlon and Chilion also died, and the woman was left without her two children and her husband.

6 Then she arose with her daughters-in-law and returned from the fields of Moab, for she had heard in the fields of Moab that Yahweh had visited His people to give them food. 7 So she went forth from the place where she was, and her two daughters-in-law with her; and they went on the way to return to the land of Judah. 8 And Naomi said to her two daughters-in-law, "Go, return each of you to her mother's house. May Yahweh show lovingkindness with you as you have shown with the dead and with me. 9 May Yahweh grant that you may find

rest, each in the house of her husband."
Then she kissed them, and they lifted up
their voices and wept. 10 And they said to
her, "*No*, but we will return with you to
your people." 11 But Naomi said, "Return,
my daughters. Why should you go with me?
Have I yet sons in my womb, that they may
be your husbands? 12 Return, my daughters!
Go, for I am too old to have a husband. If
I said I have hope, if I should even have
a husband tonight and also bear sons,
13 would you therefore wait until they were
grown? Would you therefore refrain from
marrying? No, my daughters; for it is more
bitter for me than for you, for the hand of
Yahweh has gone forth against me." 14 And
they lifted up their voices and wept again;
and Orpah kissed her mother-in-law, but
Ruth clung to her.

15 Then she said, "Behold, your sister-
in-law has returned to her people and her
gods; return after your sister-in-law." 16 But
Ruth said, "Do not press me to forsake you in
turning back from following you; for where
you go, I will go, and where you lodge, I will
lodge. Your people *shall be* my people, and
your God, my God. 17 Where you die, I will
die, and there I will be buried. Thus may
Yahweh do to me, and more, if *anything but*
death separates you and me." 18 So she saw
that she was determined to go with her, and
she said no more to her.

19 Then they both went until they came
to Bethlehem. Now it happened, when they
had come to Bethlehem, all the city was
stirred because of them, and the women
said, "Is this Naomi?" 20 She said to them,
"Do not call me Naomi; call me Mara, for the
Almighty has dealt very bitterly with me. 21 I
went out full, but Yahweh has caused me to
return empty. Why do you call me Naomi?
Yahweh has answered against me, and the
Almighty has brought calamity against me."

22 So Naomi returned, and with her Ruth
the Moabitess, her daughter-in-law, who
returned from the fields of Moab. Now
they came to Bethlehem at the beginning
of barley harvest.

2 Now Naomi had a kinsman of her
husband, a mighty man of excellence,
of the family of Elimelech, whose name
was Boaz. 2 And Ruth the Moabitess said
to Naomi, "Please let me go to the field and
glean among the ears of grain after one
whom I may find favor in his eyes." And
she said to her, "Go, my daughter." 3 So she
went. And she came and gleaned in the
field after the reapers. And it so happened
that she happened *to come* to the portion
of the field belonging to Boaz, who was
of the family of Elimelech. 4 Now behold,
Boaz came from Bethlehem and said to
the reapers, "May Yahweh be with you."
And they said to him, "May Yahweh bless
you." 5 Then Boaz said to his young man
who was in charge of the reapers, "Whose
young woman is this?" 6 The young man in
charge of the reapers replied, "She is the
young Moabite woman who returned with
Naomi from the fields of Moab. 7 And she
said, 'Please let me glean and gather after
the reapers among the sheaves.' Thus she
came and has remained from the morning
until now; she has been sitting in the house
for a little while."

8 Then Boaz said to Ruth, "Have you not
heard, my daughter? Do not go to glean
in another field; furthermore, do not go
on from this one, but stay here with my
young women. 9 Let your eyes be on the
field which they reap, and go after them.
Indeed, I have commanded the young men
not to touch you. And *if* you are thirsty,
go to the water jars and drink from what
the young men draw." 10 Then she fell on
her face, bowing to the ground and said to
him, "Why have I found favor in your sight
that you should take notice of me, though I
am a foreigner?" 11 Boaz replied to her, "All
that you have done for your mother-in-law
after the death of your husband has been
fully told to me, and how you forsook your
father and your mother and the land of your
birth, and came to a people that you did
not previously know. 12 May Yahweh fully
repay your work, and may your wages be
full from Yahweh, the God of Israel, under
whose wings you have come to seek refuge."
13 Then she said, "May I find favor in your
eyes, my lord, for you have comforted me
and indeed have spoken to the heart of your
servant-woman, though I am not like one of
your servant-women."

14 At mealtime Boaz said to her, "Come
here, that you may eat of the bread and dip
your piece of bread in the vinegar." So she
sat beside the reapers; and he served her
roasted grain, and she ate and was satisfied
and had some left. 15 Then she rose to glean,

and Boaz commanded his young men, say-
ing, "Let her glean even among the sheaves,
and do not dishonor her. 16 Also you shall
purposely pull out for her *some grain* from
the bundles and leave *it* that she may glean,
and do not rebuke her."
17 So she gleaned in the field until evening.
Then she beat out what she had gleaned,
and it was about an ephah of barley. 18 She
took *it* up and went into the city, and her
mother-in-law saw what she had gleaned.
She also took *it* out and gave Naomi what
she had left after she was satisfied. 19 Her
mother-in-law then said to her, "Where did
you glean today and where did you work?
May he who took notice of you be blessed."
So she told her mother-in-law with whom
she had worked and said, "The name of the
man with whom I worked today is Boaz."
20 Naomi said to her daughter-in-law, "May
he be blessed of Yahweh who has not for-
saken his lovingkindness to the living and
to the dead." Then Naomi said to her, "The
man is our relative; he is one of our *kinsman*
redeemers." 21 Then Ruth the Moabitess
said, "Furthermore, he said to me, 'You
should stay close to my young men until
they have finished all my harvest.'" 22 Naomi
said to Ruth her daughter-in-law, "It is good,
my daughter, that you go out with his young
women, so that *others* do not oppress you
in another field." 23 So she stayed close by
the young women of Boaz in order to glean
until the end of the barley harvest and
the wheat harvest. And she lived with her
mother-in-law.

Psalm 52:1–5

1 Why do you boast in evil,
O mighty man?
The lovingkindness of God
endures all day long.
2 Your tongue devises destruction,
Like a sharp razor, O worker of deceit.
3 You love evil more than good,
Falsehood more than speaking
what is right. Selah.
4 You love all words that devour,
O deceitful tongue.

5 But God will break you down forever;
He will snatch you up and tear
you away from *your* tent,
And uproot you from the
land of the living, Selah.

Proverbs 15:4–5

4 A tongue that brings healing
is a tree of life,
But perversion in it breaks the spirit.
5 An ignorant fool spurns his
father's discipline,
But he who keeps reproof is prudent.

Luke 19:28–48

28 And after He had said these things, He
was going on ahead, going up to Jerusalem.
29 And it happened that when He
approached Bethphage and Bethany, near
the mount called "of Olives," He sent two of
the disciples, 30 saying, "Go into the village
ahead of *you*; in which, as you enter, you
will find a colt tied, on which no one yet
has ever sat; untie it and bring it *here*. 31 And
if anyone asks you, 'Why are you untying
it?' you shall say this: 'Because the Lord
has need of it.'" 32 So when those who were
sent departed, they found it just as He had
told them. 33 And as they were untying the
colt, its owners said to them, "Why are you
untying the colt?" 34 And they said, "The
Lord has need of it." 35 And they brought it
to Jesus, and after they threw their garments
on the colt, they put Jesus *on it*. 36 And as
He was going, they were spreading their
garments on the road. 37 Now as soon as He
was approaching, near the descent of the
Mount of Olives, the whole multitude of the
disciples began to praise God, rejoicing with
a loud voice for all the miracles which they
had seen, 38 saying,
"BLESSED IS THE KING WHO COMES
IN THE NAME OF THE LORD.
Peace in heaven and glory
in the highest!"
39 And some of the Pharisees in the crowd
said to Him, "Teacher, rebuke Your disci-
ples." 40 But Jesus answered and said, "I tell
you, if these were silent, the stones will cry
out!"
41 And as He approached *Jerusalem* and
saw the city, He cried over it, 42 saying, "If
you knew in this day, even you, the things
which make for peace! But now they have
been hidden from your eyes. 43 For the days
will come upon you when your enemies
will throw up a barricade against you, and
surround you and hem you in on every side,
44 and they will level you to the ground and
your children within you, and they will
not leave in you one stone upon another,

because you did not recognize the time of your visitation."

45 And Jesus entered the temple and began to drive out those who were selling, 46 saying to them, "It is written, 'AND MY HOUSE SHALL BE A HOUSE OF PRAYER,' but you have made it a ROBBERS' DEN."

47 And He was teaching daily in the temple, but the chief priests and the scribes and the leading men among the people were trying to destroy Him, 48 and they could not find anything that they might do, for all the people hung upon every word He said.

APRIL 29

Ruth 3:1–4:22

3 Then Naomi her mother-in-law said to her, "My daughter, shall I not seek *a state of* rest for you, that it may be well with you? 2 And now, is not Boaz our kinsman, with whose young women you were? Behold, he is winnowing barley at the threshing floor tonight. 3 So you shall wash yourself and anoint yourself and put on your *best* clothes, and you shall go down to the threshing floor; *but* do not make yourself known to the man until he has finished eating and drinking. 4 Let it be that when he lies down, you shall know the place where he lies, and you shall go and uncover his feet and lie down; then he will tell you what you shall do." 5 She said to her, "All that you say I will do."

6 So she went down to the threshing floor and did according to all that her mother-in-law had commanded her. 7 And Boaz ate and drank and his heart was merry, and he went to lie down at the end of the heap of grain; and she came secretly and uncovered his feet and lay down. 8 Then it happened in the middle of the night that the man was startled and bent forward; and behold, a woman was lying at his feet. 9 And he said, "Who are you?" And she answered, "I am Ruth your maidservant. So spread your wing over your maidservant, for you are a *kinsman* redeemer." 10 Then he said, "May you be blessed of Yahweh, my daughter. You have shown your last lovingkindness to be better than the first by not going after young men, whether poor or rich. 11 So now, my daughter, do not fear. All that you say, I will do for you; for all my people within the gates *of the city* know that you are a woman of excellence. 12 But now it is true I am a *kinsman* redeemer; however, there is a *kinsman* redeemer closer than I. 13 Stay this night, and it will be in the morning that, if he will redeem you, good; let him redeem you. But if he does not desire to redeem you, then I will redeem you, as Yahweh lives. Lie down until morning."

14 So she lay at his feet until morning and rose before one could recognize another; and he said, "Let it not be known that the woman came to the threshing floor." 15 And he said, "Give me the cloak that is on you and hold it." So she held it, and he measured six *measures* of barley and placed *it* on her. Then she went into the city. 16 Then she came to her mother-in-law, and she said, "How did it go, my daughter?" And she told her all that the man had done for her. 17 She said, "These six *measures* of barley he gave to me, for he said, 'Do not go to your mother-in-law empty.'" 18 Then she said, "Sit, *then*, my daughter, until you know how the matter falls *into place*; for the man will not remain quiet until he has finished the matter today."

4 Now Boaz went up to the gate and sat down there, and behold, the *kinsman* redeemer of whom Boaz spoke was passing by, so he said, "Turn aside, my fellow, sit down here." And he turned aside and sat down. 2 Then he took ten men of the elders of the city and said, "Sit down here." So they sat down. 3 Then he said to the *kinsman* redeemer, "Naomi, who has come back from the fields of Moab, has to sell the portion of the field which belonged to our brother Elimelech. 4 So I thought to uncover *this matter* in your hearing, saying, 'Acquire *it* before those who are sitting *here* and before the elders of my people. If you will redeem *it*, redeem *it*; but if no one redeems *it*, tell me that I may know; for there is no one but you to redeem *it*, and I am after you.'" And he said, "I will redeem *it*." 5 Then Boaz said, "On the day you acquire the field from the hand of Naomi, you must also acquire Ruth the Moabitess, the widow of the one who had died, in order to raise up the name

of the one who had died, on behalf of his
inheritance." 6 So the *kinsman* redeemer
said, "I cannot redeem *it* for myself, lest I
ruin my own inheritance. You redeem my
right of redemption for yourself, for I cannot
redeem *it*."
7 Now this was *the custom* in former times
in Israel concerning the right of redemption
and the exchange *of land* to establish any
matter: a man removed his sandal and gave
it to another; and this was the *manner*
of attestation in Israel. 8 So the *kinsman*
redeemer said to Boaz, "Acquire *this* for
yourself." And he removed his sandal.
9 Then Boaz said to the elders and all the
people, "You are witnesses today that I have
acquired all that belonged to Elimelech and
all that belonged to Chilion and Mahlon
from the hand of Naomi. 10 And also, I have
acquired Ruth the Moabitess, the widow of
Mahlon, to be my wife in order to raise up
the name of the one who had died, on behalf
of his inheritance, so that the name of the
one who had died will not be cut off from
his brothers or from the gate of his *birth*
place; you are witnesses today." 11 And all
the people who were in the gate, and the
elders, said, "*We are* witnesses. May Yahweh
grant the woman who is coming into your
home *to be* like Rachel and Leah, both of
whom built the house of Israel, and so you
shall achieve excellence in Ephrathah and
shall proclaim *your* name in Bethlehem.
12 Moreover, may your house be like the
house of Perez whom Tamar bore to Judah,
through the seed which Yahweh will grant
you by this young woman."
13 So Boaz took Ruth, and she became his
wife, and he went in to her. And Yahweh
granted her conception, and she gave birth
to a son. 14 Then the women said to Naomi,
"Blessed is Yahweh who has not left you
without a *kinsman* redeemer today, and
may his name be proclaimed in Israel.
15 May he also be to you a restorer of *your*
soul and a sustainer of your old age; for
your daughter-in-law, who loves you and
is better to you than seven sons, has given
birth to him."
16 Then Naomi took the child and put him
on her bosom and became his nurse. 17 The
neighbor women gave him a name, saying,
"A son has been born to Naomi!" So they
named him Obed. He is the father of Jesse,
the father of David.

18 Now these are the generations of Perez:
Perez became the father of Hezron,
19 and Hezron became the father of Ram,
and Ram became the father of
Amminadab,
20 and Amminadab became the father of
Nahshon,
and Nahshon became the father of
Salmah,
21 and Salmon became the father of
Boaz,
and Boaz became the father of Obed,
22 and Obed became the father of Jesse,
and Jesse became the father of David.

Psalm 52:6–9

6 So that the righteous will see and fear,
And will laugh at him, *saying*,
7 "Behold, the man who would not
set God as his strength,
But trusted in the abundance
of his riches
And was strong in his destruction."

8 But as for me, I am like a green
olive tree in the house of God;
I trust in the lovingkindness
of God forever and ever.
9 I will give You thanks forever,
because You have done *it*,
And I will hope on Your name,
for *it is* good, in the presence
of Your holy ones.

Proverbs 15:6–7

6 The house of the righteous
has much treasure,
But in the income of the
wicked *there is* trouble.
7 The lips of the wise disperse knowledge,
But the hearts of fools are not so.

Luke 20:1–26

20 And it happened that on one of
the days while He was teaching the
people in the temple and proclaiming the
gospel, the chief priests and the scribes with
the elders came up to *Him*, 2 and they spoke,
saying to Him, "Tell us by what authority
You are doing these things, or who is the one
who gave You this authority?" 3 And Jesus
answered and said to them, "I will also ask
you a question, and you tell Me: 4 Was the
baptism of John from heaven or from men?"
5 And they reasoned among themselves,

saying, "If we say, 'From heaven,' He will say, 'Why did you not believe him?' 6 But if we say, 'From men,' all the people will stone us to death, for they are convinced that John was a prophet." 7 So they answered that they did not know where *it came* from. 8 And Jesus said to them, "Neither will I tell you by what authority I do these things."

9 And He began to tell the people this parable: "A man planted a vineyard and rented it out to vine-growers, and went on a journey for a long time. 10 And at the *harvest* time he sent a slave to the vine-growers, so that they would give him *some* of the fruit of the vineyard. But the vine-growers sent him away empty-handed having beaten him. 11 And he proceeded to send another slave; and when they beat him also and treated him shamefully, they sent him away empty-handed. 12 And he proceeded to send a third; and this one also they wounded and cast out. 13 Now the owner of the vineyard said, 'What shall I do? I will send my beloved son; perhaps they will respect him.' 14 But when the vine-growers saw him, they were reasoning with one another, saying, 'This is the heir; let us kill him so that the inheritance will be ours.' 15 So they threw him out of the vineyard and killed him. What, then, will the owner of the vineyard do to them? 16 He will come and destroy these vine-growers and will give the vineyard to others." When they heard *this*, they said, "May it never be!" 17 But when Jesus looked at them, He said, "What then is this that is written:

'THE STONE WHICH THE
BUILDERS REJECTED,
THIS HAS BECOME THE CHIEF
CORNER *stone*'?

18 "Everyone who falls on that stone will be broken to pieces, but on whomever it falls, it will scatter him like dust."

19 And the scribes and the chief priests tried to lay hands on Him that very hour, but they feared the people. For they understood that He spoke this parable against them. 20 So they watched Him, and sent spies who pretended to be righteous, so that they might catch Him in some statement, in order to deliver Him to the rule and the authority of the governor. 21 And they questioned Him, saying, "Teacher, we know that You speak and teach correctly, and You are not partial to any, but teach the way of God in truth. 22 Is it lawful for us to pay taxes to Caesar, or not?" 23 But He perceived their craftiness and said to them, 24 "Show Me a denarius. Whose likeness and inscription does it have?" They said, "Caesar's." 25 And He said to them, "Then render to Caesar the things that are Caesar's, and to God the things that are God's." 26 And they were unable to catch Him in a word in the presence of the people; and marveling at His answer, they became silent.

We must not read the Holy Scripture in order to support our own notions and favorite sentiments, but submit ourselves unto the doctrine contained therein.

— JOHN CALVIN

APRIL 30

1 Samuel 1:1–3:21

1 Now there was a certain man from Ramathaim-zophim from the hill country of Ephraim, and his name was Elkanah the son of Jeroham, the son of Elihu, the son of Tohu, the son of Zuph, an Ephraimite. 2 Now he had two wives: the name of one was Hannah and the name of the other Peninnah; and Peninnah had children, but Hannah had no children.

3 Now that man would go up from his city yearly to worship and to sacrifice to Yahweh of hosts in Shiloh. And the two sons of Eli, Hophni and Phinehas, were priests to Yahweh there. 4 And the day came that Elkanah sacrificed, and he would give portions to Peninnah his wife and to all her sons and her daughters; 5 but to Hannah he would give a double portion, for he loved Hannah, but Yahweh had closed her womb.

6 Her rival, however, would provoke her
bitterly to irritate her because Yahweh had
closed her womb. 7 And so it would happen
year after year, as often as she went up to
the house of Yahweh, she would provoke
her; so she wept and would not eat. 8 Then
Elkanah her husband said to her, "Hannah,
why do you weep and why do you not eat
and why is your heart sad? Am I not better
to you than ten sons?"

9 Then Hannah rose after eating and
drinking in Shiloh. Now Eli the priest was
sitting on the seat by the doorpost of the
temple of Yahweh. 10 And she, bitter of soul,
prayed to Yahweh and wept despondently.
11 And she made a vow and said, "O Yahweh
of hosts, if You will indeed look on the afflic-
tion of Your maidservant and remember me
and not forget Your maidservant, but will
give Your maidservant a seed amongst men,
then I will give him to Yahweh all the days
of his life, and a razor shall never come on
his head."

12 Now it happened, as she multiplied
her praying before Yahweh, that Eli was
watching her mouth. 13 As for Hannah, she
was speaking in her heart; only her lips were
moving, but her voice was not heard. So Eli
thought she was drunk. 14 Then Eli said
to her, "How long will you make yourself
drunk? Put away your wine from you." 15 But
Hannah answered and said, "No, my lord,
I am a woman oppressed in spirit; I have
drunk neither wine nor strong drink, but
I have poured out my soul before Yahweh.
16 Do not consider your maidservant as a
vile woman, for I have spoken until now out
of my great complaint and provocation."
17 Then Eli answered and said, "Go in peace;
and may the God of Israel grant your peti-
tion that you have asked of Him." 18 And she
said, "Let your servant-woman find favor in
your sight." So the woman went her way and
ate, and her face was no longer *sad*.

19 Then they arose early in the morning
and worshiped before Yahweh and turned
back and came to their house in Ramah. And
Elkanah knew Hannah his wife, and Yahweh
remembered her. 20 Now it happened in due
time that Hannah conceived and gave birth
to a son; and she named him Samuel, *saying*,
"Because I have asked him of Yahweh."

21 Then the man Elkanah went up with
all his household to offer to Yahweh the
yearly sacrifice and *pay* his vow. 22 But
Hannah did not go up, for she said to her
husband, "*I will not go up* until the young
boy is weaned; then I will bring him, that
he may appear before Yahweh and stay
there forever." 23 And Elkanah her husband
said to her, "Do what is good in your eyes.
Remain until you have weaned him; only
may Yahweh establish His word." So the
woman remained and nursed her son until
she weaned him. 24 Now when she had
weaned him, she took him up with her,
with a three-year-old bull and one ephah
of flour and a jug of wine and brought him
to the house of Yahweh in Shiloh, although
the boy was young. 25 Then they slaughtered
the bull and brought the young boy to Eli.
26 And she said, "Oh, my lord! As your soul
lives, my lord, I am the woman who stood
here beside you, praying to Yahweh. 27 For
this young boy I prayed, and Yahweh has
given me my petition which I asked of Him.
28 So I have also dedicated him to Yahweh; as
long as he lives, he is dedicated to Yahweh."
So he worshiped Yahweh there.

2 Then Hannah prayed and said,
"My heart exults in Yahweh;
My horn is exalted in Yahweh;
My mouth speaks boldly
against my enemies,
Because I am glad in Your salvation.
2 "There is no one holy like Yahweh;
Indeed, there is no one besides You,
Nor is there any rock like our God.
3 "Do not multiply speaking
so very proudly;
Let arrogance not come
out of your mouth;
For Yahweh is a God of knowledge,
And with Him actions are weighed.
4 "The bows of the mighty are shattered,
But those who stumble
gird on strength.
5 "Those who were full hire
themselves out for bread,
But those who were hungry
cease *to hunger*.
Even the barren gives birth to seven,
But she who has many
children languishes.
6 "Yahweh puts to death and makes alive;
He brings down to Sheol and raises up.
7 "Yahweh makes poor and rich;
He brings low; He also exalts.
8 "He raises the poor from the dust;

He exalts the needy from the ash heap
To make them sit with nobles,
And inherit a seat of glory;
For the pillars of the earth
are Yahweh's,
And He set the world on them.
9 "He keeps the feet of His holy ones,
But the wicked ones are
silenced in darkness,
For not by power shall a man prevail.
10 "Those who contend with
Yahweh will be dismayed;
Against them He will thunder
in the heavens;
Yahweh will render justice to
the ends of the earth,
And He will give strength to His king,
And He will exalt the horn
of His anointed."

11 Then Elkanah went to his home at
Ramah. But the young boy ministered to
Yahweh before Eli the priest.

12 Now the sons of Eli were vile men; they
did not know Yahweh. 13 And *this was* the
legal judgment for the priests with the peo-
ple: when any man was offering a sacrifice,
the priest's young man would come while
the meat was boiling, with a three-pronged
fork in his hand. 14 Then he would thrust
it into the pan or kettle or caldron or pot;
all that the fork would bring up the priest
would take for himself. Thus they would
do in Shiloh to all the Israelites who came
there. 15 Also, before they offered up the
fat in smoke, the priest's young man would
come and say to the man who was sacrific-
ing, "Give the priest meat for roasting; he
will not take boiled meat from you, only
raw." 16 Then the man *would* say to him,
"They must surely offer up the fat in smoke
first, and then take as much as your soul
desires," then he would say, "No, you shall
give *it* now; and if not, I will take it by force."
17 Thus the sin of the young men was very
great before Yahweh, for the men spurned
the offering of Yahweh.

18 Now Samuel was ministering before
Yahweh, *as* a young boy girded with a linen
ephod. 19 And his mother would make him
a little robe and bring it to him from year
to year when she would come up with her
husband to offer the yearly sacrifice. 20 Then
Eli would bless Elkanah and his wife and
say, "May Yahweh establish for you a seed
from this woman in place of the one she
dedicated to Yahweh." And they went to
their own home.

21 Yahweh indeed visited Hannah; and
she conceived and gave birth to three sons
and two daughters. And the young boy
Samuel grew before Yahweh.

22 Now Eli was very old; and he heard all
that his sons were doing to all Israel, and
how they lay with the women who served at
the doorway of the tent of meeting. 23 So he
said to them, "Why do you do such things,
the evil things that I hear from all these
people? 24 No, my sons; for the report is
not good which I hear the people of Yahweh
passing about. 25 If one man sins against
another, God will mediate for him; but if
a man sins against Yahweh, who can pray
for him?" But they would not listen to the
voice of their father, for Yahweh desired to
put them to death.

26 Now the young boy Samuel was grow-
ing in stature and in favor both with Yahweh
and with men.

27 Then a man of God came to Eli and
said to him, "Thus says Yahweh, 'Did I *not*
indeed reveal Myself to the house of your
father when they were in Egypt, *enslaved*
to Pharaoh's house? 28 And did I *not* choose
them from all the tribes of Israel to be My
priests, to go up to My altar, to burn incense,
to carry an ephod before Me; and did I *not*
give to the house of your father all the fire
offerings of the sons of Israel? 29 Why do
you kick at My sacrifice and at My offering
which I have commanded *in My* habitation,
and honor your sons above Me, by making
yourselves fat with the choicest of every
offering of My people Israel?' 30 Therefore
Yahweh, the God of Israel, declares, 'I did
indeed say that your house and the house of
your father should walk before Me forever';
but now Yahweh declares, 'Far be it from
Me—for those who honor Me I will honor,
and those who despise Me will be cursed.
31 Behold, the days are coming, and I will
break your strength and the strength of your
father's house so that there will not be an
old man in your house. 32 And you will look
upon the distress of *My* habitation, in *spite
of* all the good that I do for Israel; and an old
man will not be in your house all the days.
33 Yet I will not cut off every man of yours
from My altar so that your eyes will fail *from
weeping* and your soul grieve, and all the
increase of your house will be put to death in

the prime of life. 34 Now this will be the sign to you which will come concerning your two sons, Hophni and Phinehas: on the same day both of them will be put to death. 35 But I will raise up for Myself a faithful priest who will do according to what is in My heart and in My soul; and I will build him a faithful house, and he will walk before My anointed always. 36 And it will be that everyone who is left in your house will come and bow down to him for a piece of silver or a loaf of bread and say, "Please assign me to one of the priest's offices so that I may eat a piece of bread."'"

3 Now the young boy Samuel was ministering to Yahweh before Eli. And word from Yahweh was rare in those days; visions were infrequent.

2 And it happened at that time as Eli was lying down in his place (now his eyesight had begun to fade, *and* he could not see *well*), 3 and the lamp of God had not yet gone out, and Samuel was lying down in the temple of Yahweh where the ark of God *was*, 4 that Yahweh called Samuel; and he said, "Here I am." 5 Then he ran to Eli and said, "Here I am, for you called me." But he said, "I did not call; go back, lie down." So he went and lay down. 6 Then Yahweh called yet again, "Samuel!" So Samuel arose and went to Eli and said, "Here I am, for you called me." But he answered, "I did not call, my son; go back, lie down." 7 Now Samuel did not yet know Yahweh, nor had the word of Yahweh yet been revealed to him. 8 So Yahweh called Samuel again for the third time. And he arose and went to Eli and said, "Here I am, for you called me." Then Eli discerned that Yahweh was calling the young boy. 9 And Eli said to Samuel, "Go lie down, and it shall be if He calls you, that you shall say, 'Speak, Yahweh, for Your slave is listening.'" So Samuel went and lay down in his place.

10 Then Yahweh came and stood and called as at other times, "Samuel! Samuel!" *And Samuel said, "Speak, for Your slave is listening."* 11 And Yahweh said to Samuel, "Behold, I am about to do a thing in Israel at which both ears of everyone who hears it will tingle. 12 In that day I will establish against Eli all that I have spoken concerning his house, from beginning to end. 13 And I have told him that I am about to judge his house forever for the iniquity which he knew because his sons have been bringing a curse on themselves, but he did not rebuke them. 14 Now therefore I have sworn to the house of Eli that the iniquity of Eli's house shall not be atoned for by sacrifice or offering forever."

15 So Samuel lay down until morning. Then he opened the doors of the house of Yahweh. But Samuel was afraid to tell the vision to Eli. 16 Then Eli called Samuel and said, "Samuel, my son." And he said, "Here I am." 17 And he said, "What is the word that He spoke to you? Please do not hide it from me. May God do so to you, and more also, if you hide anything from me of all the words that He spoke to you." 18 So Samuel told him everything and hid nothing from him. And he said, "It is Yahweh; let Him do what seems good in His eyes."

19 Thus Samuel grew, and Yahweh was with him and let none of his words fall to the ground. 20 So all Israel from Dan even to Beersheba knew that Samuel was confirmed as a prophet of Yahweh. 21 And Yahweh appeared again at Shiloh, because Yahweh revealed Himself to Samuel at Shiloh by the word of Yahweh.

Psalm 53:1–6

1 The wicked fool says in his
heart, "There is no God,"
They act corruptly, and commit
abominable injustice;
There is no one who does good.
2 God looks down from heaven
upon the sons of men
To see if there is anyone
who has insight,
Anyone who seeks after God.
3 Every one of them has turned
back; together they have
become worthless;
There is no one who does
good, not even one.

4 Do the workers of iniquity not know,
Who eat up my people *as*
they eat bread
And do not call upon God?
5 There they were in great dread
where no dread had been;
For God scattered the bones of him
who encamped against you;
You put *them* to shame, because
God had rejected them.

6 Oh, that the salvation of Israel
would come out of Zion!
When God restores His captive people,
May Jacob rejoice, may Israel be glad.

Proverbs 15:8–11

8 The sacrifice of the wicked is an
abomination to Yahweh,
But the prayer of the upright
is His delight.
9 The way of the wicked is an
abomination to Yahweh,
But He loves one who pursues
righteousness.
10 Grievous discipline is for him
who forsakes the way;
He who hates reproof will die.
11 Sheol and Abaddon *lie open*
before Yahweh,
How much more the hearts
of the sons of men!

Luke 20:27–47

27 Now some of the Sadducees (who say that there is no resurrection) came to Him, 28 and they questioned Him, saying, "Teacher, Moses wrote for us that IF A MAN'S BROTHER DIES, having a wife, AND HE IS CHILDLESS, HIS BROTHER SHOULD MARRY THE WIFE AND RAISE UP SEED FOR HIS BROTHER. 29 Now there were seven brothers; and the first married a wife and died childless, 30 and the second 31 and the third married her; and in the same way, all seven died, leaving no children. 32 Finally the woman died also. 33 Therefore, this woman—in the resurrection—whose wife will she be? For all seven had her as a wife."

34 And Jesus said to them, "The sons of this age marry and are given in marriage, 35 but those who are considered worthy to attain to that age and the resurrection from the dead, neither marry nor are given in marriage. 36 For they cannot even die anymore, because they are like angels and are sons of God, being sons of the resurrection. 37 But that the dead are raised, even Moses showed in the *passage about the burning* bush, where he calls the Lord THE GOD OF ABRAHAM, AND THE GOD OF ISAAC, AND THE GOD OF JACOB. 38 Now He is not the God of the dead but of the living; for all live to Him." 39 And some of the scribes answered and said, "Teacher, You have spoken well." 40 For they did not dare to question Him any longer about anything.

41 Then He said to them, "How *is it that* they say the Christ is David's son? 42 For David himself says in the book of Psalms,

'THE LORD SAID TO MY LORD,
"SIT AT MY RIGHT HAND,
43 UNTIL I PUT YOUR ENEMIES AS A
FOOTSTOOL FOR YOUR FEET."'

44 "Therefore David calls Him 'Lord,' so how is He his son?"

45 And while all the people were listening, He said to the disciples, 46 "Beware of the scribes, who want to walk around in long robes, and love greetings in the market-places, and best seats in the synagogues and places of honor at banquets, 47 who devour widows' houses, and for appearance's sake offer long prayers. These will receive greater condemnation."

MAY 1

1 Samuel 4:1–5:12

4 Thus the word of Samuel came to all Israel. Now Israel went out to meet the Philistines in battle and camped beside Ebenezer, and the Philistines camped in Aphek. 2 And the Philistines arranged *themselves* to meet Israel. Then the battle spread, and Israel was defeated before the Philistines who struck down about 4,000 men on the battlefield. 3 Then the people came into the camp, and the elders of Israel said, "Why has Yahweh defeated us today before the Philistines? Let us take to ourselves from Shiloh the ark of the covenant of Yahweh, that it may come among us and save us from the power of our enemies." 4 So the people sent to Shiloh, and from there they carried the ark of the covenant of Yahweh of hosts who sits *above* the cherubim; and the two sons of Eli, Hophni and Phinehas, *were* there with the ark of the covenant of God.

5 And it happened that as the ark of the covenant of Yahweh came into the camp, all Israel shouted with a great shout, so that the earth was thrown into confusion. 6 Then the Philistines heard the noise of the shout and said, "What *does* the noise of this great shout in the camp of the Hebrews *mean*?"

Then they knew that the ark of Yahweh had come into the camp. 7 And the Philistines were afraid, for they said, "God has come into the camp." And they said, "Woe to us! For nothing like this has happened before. 8 Woe to us! Who shall deliver us from the hand of these mighty gods? These are the gods who struck the Egyptians with all *kinds of* plagues in the wilderness. 9 Be strong and become men, O Philistines, lest you become slaves to the Hebrews, as they have been slaves to you; therefore, become men and fight."

10 So the Philistines fought, and Israel was defeated, and every man fled to his tent; and the slaughter was very great, for there fell of Israel 30,000 foot soldiers. 11 And the ark of God was taken; and the two sons of Eli, Hophni and Phinehas, died.

12 Now a man of Benjamin ran from the battle line and came to Shiloh the same day with his robes torn and dust on his head. 13 And he came, and behold, Eli was sitting on *his* seat by the road eagerly watching because his heart was trembling for the ark of God. Now the man came to tell *it* in the city, and all the city cried out. 14 Then Eli heard the noise of the outcry, and he said, "What *does* the noise of this commotion *mean*?" So the man came hurriedly and told Eli. 15 Now Eli was ninety-eight years old, and his eyes had set so that he could not see. 16 And the man said to Eli, "I am the one who came from the battle line. Indeed, I fled from the battle line today." And he said, "How did things go, my son?" 17 Then the one who brought the news answered and said, "Israel has fled before the Philistines, and there has also been a great slaughter among the people, and your two sons also, Hophni and Phinehas, are dead, and the ark of God has been taken." 18 And it happened that when he mentioned the ark of God, Eli fell off the seat backward beside the gate, and his neck was broken, and he died, for the man was old and heavy. Thus he judged Israel forty years.

19 Now his daughter-in-law, Phinehas's wife, was with child and about to give birth. And she heard the report that the ark of God was taken and that her father-in-law and her husband had died, so she kneeled down and gave birth, for her pains came upon her. 20 And about the time of her death the women who stood by her said to her, "Do not be afraid, for you have given birth to a son." But she did not answer or pay attention. 21 And she called the boy Ichabod, saying, "The glory has departed from Israel," because the ark of God was taken and because of her father-in-law and her husband. 22 And she said, "The glory has departed from Israel, for the ark of God was taken."

5 Now the Philistines took the ark of God and brought it from Ebenezer to Ashdod. 2 Then the Philistines took the ark of God and brought it to the house of Dagon and set it by Dagon. 3 Then the Ashdodites arose early the next morning, and behold, Dagon had fallen on his face to the ground before the ark of Yahweh. So they took Dagon and set him in his place again. 4 But they arose early the next morning, and behold, Dagon had fallen on his face to the ground before the ark of Yahweh. And the head of Dagon and both the palms of his hands *were* cut off on the threshold; only the trunk of Dagon was left to him. 5 Therefore neither the priests of Dagon nor all who enter Dagon's house tread on the threshold of Dagon in Ashdod to this day.

6 Now the hand of Yahweh was glorious against the Ashdodites, and He made them desolate and struck them with tumors, both Ashdod and its territories. 7 Thus the men of Ashdod saw that it was so and said, "The ark of the God of Israel must not remain with us, for His hand is severe on us and on Dagon our god." 8 So they sent and gathered all the lords of the Philistines to them and said, "What shall we do with the ark of the God of Israel?" And they said, "Let the ark of the God of Israel be brought around to Gath." And they brought the ark of the God of Israel *around*. 9 Now it happened after they had brought it around, that the hand of Yahweh was against the city with very great confusion; and He struck the men of the city, both young and old, so that tumors broke out on them. 10 So they sent the ark of God to Ekron. And as the ark of God came to Ekron the Ekronites cried out, saying, "They have brought the ark of the God of Israel around to us, to put us and our people to death." 11 They sent therefore and gathered all the lords of the Philistines and said, "Send away the ark of the God of Israel, and let it return to its own place, so that it will not put us and

our people to death." For there was a deadly
confusion throughout the city; the hand of
God was very glorious there. 12 Now the men
who did not die were struck with tumors and
the cry of the city went up to heaven.

Psalm 54:1–7

1 O God, save me by Your name,
And render justice to me
by Your might.
2 O God, hear my prayer;
Give ear to the words of my mouth.
3 For strangers have risen against me
And ruthless men have sought my life;
They have not set God
before them. Selah.
4 Behold, God is my helper;
The Lord is among those
who sustain my soul.
5 He will return the evil to my foes;
Destroy them in Your truth.
6 With a freewill offering I
will sacrifice to You;
I will give thanks to Your name,
O Yahweh, for it is good.
7 For He has delivered me
from all distress,
And my eye has looked *in
triumph* upon my enemies.

Proverbs 15:12–13

12 A scoffer does not love one
who reproves him,
He will not go to the wise.
13 A glad heart makes a face *look* good,
But when the heart is pained,
the spirit is broken.

Luke 21:1–19

21 And He looked up and saw the rich
putting their gifts into the treasury.
2 And He saw a poor widow putting in two
lepta. 3 And He said, "Truly I say to you, this
poor widow put in more than all *of them*.
4 For they all put in their gifts out of their
abundance; but she, out of what she lacked,
put in all that she had for living."
5 And while some were talking about
the temple, that it had been adorned with
beautiful stones and dedicated gifts, He
said, 6 "*As for* these things which you are
looking at, the days will come in which there
will not be left one stone upon another
which will not be torn down."
7 So they questioned Him, saying,
"Teacher, when therefore will these things
happen? And what *will be* the sign when
these things are about to take place?" 8 And
He said, "See to it that you are not deceived;
for many will come in My name, saying, 'I
am *He*,' and, 'The time is at hand.' Do not go
after them. 9 And when you hear of wars and
disturbances, do not be terrified; for these
things must take place first, but the end *does*
not *follow* immediately."
10 Then He continued saying to them,
"Nation will rise against nation and kingdom
against kingdom, 11 and there will be great
earthquakes, and in various places famines
and plagues; and there will be terrors and
great signs from heaven.
12 "But before all these things, they will
lay their hands on you and will persecute
you, delivering you to the synagogues and
prisons, bringing you before kings and gov-
ernors for My name's sake. 13 It will result in
an opportunity for your testimony. 14 So set
in your hearts not to prepare beforehand
to defend yourselves; 15 for I will give you
a mouth and wisdom which none of your
opponents will be able to resist or refute.
16 But you will be betrayed even by parents
and brothers and relatives and friends, and
they will put *some* of you to death, 17 and
you will be hated by all because of My name.
18 Yet not a hair of your head will perish.
19 By your perseverance you will gain your
lives.

MAY 2

1 Samuel 6:1–7:17

6 Now the ark of Yahweh had been in the
fields of the Philistines seven months.
2 And the Philistines called for the priests
and the diviners, saying, "What shall we
do with the ark of Yahweh? Make us know
how we shall send it to its place." 3 So they
said, "If you send away the ark of the God
of Israel, do not send it empty; but you
shall surely return to Him a guilt offering.
Then you will be healed, and it will be
known to you why His hand is not turned

away from you." 4 Then they said, "What shall be the guilt offering which we shall return to Him?" And they said, "Five golden tumors and five golden mice *according to* the number of the lords of the Philistines, for one plague was on all of you and on your lords. 5 So you shall make likenesses of your tumors and likenesses of your mice that bring the land to ruin, and you shall give glory to the God of Israel; perhaps He will ease His hand from you, your gods, and your land. 6 Why then do you harden your hearts as the Egyptians and Pharaoh hardened their hearts? When He had abused them, did they not allow the people to go, and they went? 7 So now, take and make a new cart and two milch cows on which there has never been a yoke; and hitch the cows to the cart and take their calves home, away from them. 8 And take the ark of Yahweh and place it on the cart; and put the articles of gold which you return to Him as a guilt offering in a box by its side. Then send it away that it may go. 9 See, if it goes up by the way of its own territory to Beth-shemesh, then He has done us this great evil. But if not, then we will know that it was not His hand that smote us; it happened to us by chance."

10 Then the men did so and took two milch cows and hitched them to the cart and shut up their calves at home. 11 And they put the ark of Yahweh on the cart, as well as the box with the golden mice and the likenesses of their tumors. 12 And the cows took the straight way in the direction of Beth-shemesh; they went along the highway, lowing as they went, and did not turn aside to the right or to the left. And the lords of the Philistines went after them to the border of Beth-shemesh.

13 Now *the people of* Beth-shemesh were reaping their wheat harvest in the valley, and they raised their eyes and saw the ark and were glad to see *it*. 14 And the cart came into the field of Joshua the Beth-shemite *and stood* there, and a large stone *was* there; and they split the wood of the cart and offered the cows as a burnt offering to Yahweh. 15 And the Levites took down the ark of Yahweh and the box that was with it, in which were the articles of gold, and put them on the large stone; and the men of Beth-shemesh offered burnt offerings and sacrificed sacrifices that day to Yahweh. 16 So the five lords of the Philistines saw it and returned to Ekron that day.

17 Now these are the golden tumors which the Philistines returned for a guilt offering to Yahweh: one for Ashdod, one for Gaza, one for Ashkelon, one for Gath, one for Ekron; 18 and the golden mice, *according* to the number of all the cities of the Philistines belonging to the five lords, both of fortified cities and of country villages. The large stone on which they set the ark of Yahweh *is a witness* to this day in the field of Joshua the Beth-shemite.

19 Then He struck down some of the men of Beth-shemesh because they had looked into the ark of Yahweh. He struck down of all the people, 50,070 men, and the people mourned because Yahweh had struck the people with a great slaughter. 20 And the men of Beth-shemesh said, "Who is able to stand before Yahweh, this holy God? And to whom shall He go up from us?" 21 So they sent messengers to the inhabitants of Kiriath-jearim, saying, "The Philistines have brought back the ark of Yahweh; come down and take it up to you."

7 And the men of Kiriath-jearim came and brought the ark of Yahweh up and brought it into the house of Abinadab on the hill and set apart Eleazar his son as holy in order to keep the ark of Yahweh. 2 Now it happened from the day when the ark remained at Kiriath-jearim, that the time was long; it was twenty years. And all the house of Israel lamented after Yahweh.

3 Then Samuel spoke to all the house of Israel, saying, "If you are to return to Yahweh with all your heart, *then* remove the foreign gods and the Ashtaroth from among you and set your hearts toward Yahweh and serve Him alone; and He will deliver you from the hand of the Philistines." 4 So the sons of Israel removed the Baals and the Ashtaroth and served Yahweh alone.

5 Then Samuel said, "Gather all Israel to Mizpah, and I will pray to Yahweh for you." 6 And they gathered to Mizpah and drew water and poured it out before Yahweh and fasted on that day and said there, "We have sinned against Yahweh." And Samuel judged the sons of Israel at Mizpah.

7 Then the Philistines heard that the sons of Israel had gathered to Mizpah. And the lords of the Philistines went up against

Israel. Then the sons of Israel heard it and
were afraid of the Philistines. 8 So the sons of
Israel said to Samuel, "Do not cease to cry out
to Yahweh our God for us, that He may save
us from the hand of the Philistines." 9 And
Samuel took a suckling lamb and offered
it for a whole burnt offering to Yahweh;
and Samuel cried out to Yahweh for Israel,
and Yahweh answered him. 10 Now Samuel
was offering up the burnt offering, and the
Philistines drew near to battle against Israel.
But Yahweh thundered with a great thunder
on that day against the Philistines and
confused them, so that they were defeated
before Israel. 11 So the men of Israel went out
of Mizpah and pursued the Philistines and
struck them down as far as below Beth-car.

12 Then Samuel took a stone and set it
between Mizpah and Shen, and he named
it Ebenezer. And he said, "Thus far Yahweh
has helped us." 13 So the Philistines were
subdued, and they did not come anymore
within the border of Israel. And the hand
of Yahweh was against the Philistines all
the days of Samuel. 14 And the cities which
the Philistines had taken from Israel were
restored to Israel, from Ekron even to Gath;
and Israel delivered their territory from the
hand of the Philistines. So there was peace
between Israel and the Amorites.

15 Thus Samuel judged Israel all the days
of his life. 16 And he used to go annually on
circuit to Bethel and Gilgal and Mizpah, and
he judged Israel in all these places. 17 But his
return *would be* to Ramah, for his house *was*
there, and there he judged Israel; and he
built there an altar to Yahweh.

Psalm 55:1–8

1 Give ear to my prayer, O God;
And do not hide Yourself
from my supplication.
2 Give heed to me and answer me;
I am restless in my complaint
and am surely distracted,
3 Because of the voice of the enemy,
Because of the pressure of the wicked;
For they shake wickedness
down upon me
And in anger they bear a
grudge against me.

4 My heart is in anguish within me,
And the terrors of death
have fallen upon me.
5 Fear and trembling come upon me,
And horror has covered me.
6 I said, "Oh, that I had wings like a dove!
I would fly away and be at rest.
7 "Behold, I would wander far away,
I would lodge in the wilderness. Selah.
8 "I would hasten to my place of refuge
From the stormy wind *and* tempest."

Proverbs 15:14

14 The heart of the one who has
understanding seeks knowledge,
But the mouth of fools feeds on folly.

Luke 21:20–38

20 "But when you see Jerusalem sur-
rounded by armies, then know that its des-
olation is at hand. 21 Then those who are in
Judea must flee to the mountains, and those
who are in the midst of the city must leave,
and those who are in the countryside must
not enter the city; 22 because these are days
of vengeance, so that all things which are
written will be fulfilled. 23 Woe to those who
are pregnant and to those who are nursing
babies in those days; for there will be great
distress upon the land and wrath against
this people, 24 and they will fall by the edge
of the sword, and will be led captive into all
the nations, and Jerusalem will be trampled
under foot by the Gentiles until the times of
the Gentiles are fulfilled.

25 "And there will be signs in sun and
moon and stars, and on the earth anguish
among nations, in perplexity at the roaring
of the sea and the waves, 26 men fainting
from fear and the expectation of the things
which are coming upon the world; for the
POWERS OF THE HEAVENS will be shaken.
27 And then they will see THE SON OF MAN
COMING IN A CLOUD with power and great
glory. 28 But when these things begin
to take place, straighten up and lift up
your heads, because your redemption is
drawing near."

29 Then He told them a parable: "Behold
the fig tree and all the trees; 30 as soon as
they put forth *leaves* and you see it for
yourselves, know that summer is now near.
31 So you also, when you see these things
happening, know that the kingdom of God
is near. 32 Truly I say to you, this generation
will not pass away until all things take place.
33 Heaven and earth will pass away, but My
words will never pass away.

34 "But be on guard, so that your hearts will not be overcome with dissipation and drunkenness and the worries of life, and that day will not come on you suddenly like a trap; 35 for it will come upon all those who inhabit the face of all the earth. 36 But keep on the alert at all times, praying earnestly that you may have strength to escape all these things that are about to take place, and to stand before the Son of Man."

37 Now during the day He was teaching in the temple, but during the night He would go out and spend it on the mount called "of Olives." 38 And all the people would get up early in the morning *to come* to Him in the temple to listen to Him.

MAY 3

1 Samuel 8:1–9:27

8 And it happened when Samuel was old that he appointed his sons judges over Israel. 2 The name of his firstborn was Joel, and the name of his second, Abijah; *they* were judging in Beersheba. 3 But his sons did not walk in his ways, but turned aside after greedy gain and took bribes and caused justice to turn aside.

4 Then all the elders of Israel gathered together and came to Samuel at Ramah; 5 and they said to him, "Behold, you have grown old, and your sons do not walk in your ways. Now appoint a king for us to judge us like all the nations." 6 But the thing was evil in the sight of Samuel when they said, "Give us a king to judge us." And Samuel prayed to Yahweh. 7 Then Yahweh said to Samuel, "Listen to the voice of the people in regard to all that they say to you, for they have not rejected you, but they have rejected Me from being king over them. 8 Like all the deeds which they have done since the day that I brought them up from Egypt even to this day—in that they have forsaken Me and served other gods—so they are doing to you also. 9 So now, listen to their voice; however, you shall solemnly testify to them and tell them of the custom of the king who will reign over them."

10 So Samuel spoke all the words of Yahweh to the people who had asked of him a king. 11 And he said, "This will be the custom of the king who will reign over you: he will take your sons and appoint *them* for himself in his chariots and among his horsemen, and they will run before his chariots. 12 And he will appoint for himself commanders of thousands and of fifties, and *some* to do his plowing and to reap his harvest and to make his weapons of war and equipment for his chariots. 13 He will also take your daughters for perfumers and cooks and bakers. 14 He will take the best of your fields and your vineyards and your olive groves and give *them* to his servants. 15 He will take a tenth of your seed and of your vineyards and give *it* to his officers and to his servants. 16 He will also take your male slaves and your female slaves and your best young men and your donkeys and use *them* for his work. 17 He will take a tenth of your flocks, and you yourselves will become his slaves. 18 Then you will cry out in that day because of your king whom you have chosen for yourselves, but Yahweh will not answer you in that day."

19 Nevertheless, the people refused to listen to the voice of Samuel, and they said, "No, but there shall be a king over us, 20 that we also may be like all the nations, that our king may judge us and go out before us and fight our battles." 21 So Samuel heard all the words of the people, and he repeated them in the hearing of Yahweh. 22 Then Yahweh said to Samuel, "Listen to their voice and appoint them a king." So Samuel said to the men of Israel, "Go every man to his city."

9 Now there was a man of Benjamin whose name was Kish the son of Abiel, the son of Zeror, the son of Becorath, the son of Aphiah, the son of a Benjamite, a mighty man of valor. 2 Now he had a son whose name was Saul, a choice and handsome *man*, and there was not a more handsome person than he among the sons of Israel; from his shoulders and up he was taller than any of the people.

3 Now the donkeys of Kish, Saul's father, were lost. So Kish said to his son Saul, "Take now with you one of the young men, and arise, go search for the donkeys." 4 Thus he passed through the hill country of Ephraim and passed through the land of Shalishah, but they did not find *them*. Then they passed through the land of Shaalim, but

they were not *there*. Then he passed through
the land of the Benjamites, but they did not
find *them*.
5 They came to the land of Zuph. And
Saul said to his young man who was with
him, "Come, and let us return, lest my father
cease *to be concerned* about the donkeys
and become anxious for us." 6 But he said
to him, "Behold now, there is a man of God
in this city, and the man is held in honor; all
that he says surely comes true. Now let us
go there, perhaps he can tell us about our
journey on which we have gone." 7 Then
Saul said to his young man, "But behold, if
we go, what shall we bring the man? For the
bread is gone from our sack, and there is no
present to bring to the man of God. What do
we have?" 8 And the young man answered
Saul again and said, "Behold, I have in my
hand a fourth of a shekel of silver; I will give
it to the man of God, and he will tell us our
way." 9 (Formerly in Israel, when a man went
to inquire of God, he used to say, "Come, and
let us go to the seer"; for *he who is called*
a prophet now was formerly called a seer.)
10 Then Saul said to his young man, "Your
word is good; come, let us go." So they went
to the city where the man of God was.
11 *As* they were going up the slope to the
city, they found young women going out to
draw water and said to them, "Is the seer
here?" 12 And they answered them and said,
"He is! Behold, *he is* ahead of you. Hurry
now, for he has come into the city today,
for the people have a sacrifice on the high
place today. 13 As soon as you enter the city
you will find him before he goes up to the
high place to eat, for the people will not eat
until he comes because he must bless the
sacrifice; afterward those who are invited
will eat. So now, go up for you will find him
at once." 14 So they went up to the city. As
they came into the city, behold, Samuel was
coming out to meet them to go up to the
high place.
15 Now a day before Saul's coming, Yah-
weh had revealed *this* in Samuel's hearing,
saying, 16 "About this time tomorrow I will
send you a man from the land of Benjamin,
and you shall anoint him to be ruler over
My people Israel; and he will save My people
from the hand of the Philistines. For I have
regarded My people because their cry has
come to Me." 17 Now Samuel saw Saul, and
Yahweh answered him, "Behold, the man of
whom I spoke to you! This one shall restrict
My people." 18 Then Saul approached
Samuel in the gate and said, "Please tell me
where the seer's house is." 19 And Samuel
answered Saul and said, "I am the seer. Go
up before me to the high place, for you shall
eat with me today; and in the morning I will
let you go and will tell you all that is on your
heart. 20 As for your donkeys which were
lost three days ago, do not set your heart
on them, for they have been found. And for
whom is all that is desirable in Israel? Is it
not for you and for all your father's house-
hold?" 21 And Saul answered and said, "Am I
not a Benjamite, of the smallest of the tribes
of Israel, and my family the least of all the
families of the tribe of Benjamin? Why then
do you speak to me in this way?"
22 Then Samuel took Saul and his young
man and brought them into the chamber and
gave them a place at the head of those who
were invited, who were about thirty men.
23 And Samuel said to the cook, "Bring the
portion that I gave you, concerning which I
said to you, 'Set it aside.'" 24 Then the cook
took up the leg with what was on it and set *it*
before Saul. And *Samuel* said, "Here is what
has been reserved! Set *it* before you *and* eat,
because it has been kept for you until the
appointed time, since I said I have invited the
people." So Saul ate with Samuel that day.
25 Then they came down from the high
place into the city, and *Samuel* spoke with
Saul on the roof. 26 And they arose early; and
at the breaking of dawn Samuel called to
Saul on the roof, saying, "Get up, that I may
send you away." So Saul arose, and both he
and Samuel went out into the street. 27 *As*
they were going down to the edge of the
city, Samuel said to Saul, "Say to the young
man that he might pass before us and pass
onwards, but you remain standing now, that
I may cause you to hear the word of God."

Psalm 55:9–15

9 Confuse, O Lord, divide their tongues,
For I have seen violence
and strife in the city.
10 Day and night they go around
her upon her walls,
And wickedness and mischief
are in her midst.
11 Destruction is in her midst;
Oppression and deceit do not
depart from her streets.

12 For it is not an enemy who
reproaches me,
Then I could bear *it*;
Nor is it one who hates me who has
magnified himself against me,
Then I could hide myself from him.
13 But it is you, a man my equal,
My close companion and
my familiar friend;
14 We who had sweet counsel together
Walked in the house of
God in the throng.
15 Let death come deceitfully upon them;
Let them go down alive to Sheol,
For evil is in their dwelling,
in their midst.

Proverbs 15:15–17

15 All the days of the afflicted are evil,
But a good heart *has* a continual feast.
16 Better is a little with the fear of Yahweh
Than great treasure and
turmoil with it.
17 Better is a dish of vegetables
where there is love
Than a fattened ox and hatred in it.

Luke 22:1–23

22 Now the Feast of Unleavened Bread,
which is called the Passover, was
drawing near. 2 And the chief priests and
the scribes were seeking how they might
put Him to death; for they were afraid of
the people.
3 And Satan entered into Judas who
was called Iscariot, who belonged to the
number of the twelve. 4 And he went away
and discussed with the chief priests and
officers how he might betray Him to them.
5 And they were glad and agreed to give
him money. 6 So he consented, and *began*
seeking a good opportunity to betray Him
to them apart from the crowd.
7 Then came the *first* day of Unleavened
Bread on which the Passover lamb had to be
sacrificed. 8 And *Jesus* sent Peter and John,
saying, "Go and prepare the Passover for us,
so that we may eat it." 9 And they said to
Him, "Where do You want us to prepare it?"
10 And He said to them, "Behold, after you
have entered the city, a man will meet you
carrying a pitcher of water; follow him into
the house that he enters. 11 And you shall say
to the owner of the house, 'The Teacher says
to you, "Where is the guest room in which
I may eat the Passover with My disciples?"'
12 And he will show you a large, furnished
upper room; prepare it there." 13 And they
left and found *everything* just as He had told
them; and they prepared the Passover.
14 And when the hour had come, He
reclined *at the table*, and the apostles
with Him. 15 And He said to them, "I have
earnestly desired to eat this Passover with
you before I suffer; 16 for I say to you, I shall
never again eat it until it is fulfilled in the
kingdom of God." 17 And when He had taken
a cup *and* given thanks, He said, "Take this
and share it among yourselves. 18 For I say
to you, I will not drink of the fruit of the
vine from now on until the kingdom of God
comes." 19 And when He had taken *some*
bread *and* given thanks, He broke it and gave
it to them, saying, "This is My body which
is given for you. Do this in remembrance
of Me." 20 And in the same way *He took* the
cup after they had eaten, saying, "This cup
which is poured out for you is the new cov-
enant in My blood. 21 But behold, the hand
of the one betraying Me is with Me on the
table. 22 For indeed, the Son of Man is going
as it has been determined; but woe to that
man by whom He is betrayed!" 23 And they
began to argue among themselves which
one of them it might be who was going to
do this thing.

MAY 4

1 Samuel 10:1–11:15

10 Then Samuel took the flask of oil,
poured it on his head, kissed him, and
said, "Has not Yahweh anointed you a ruler
over His inheritance? 2 When you go from
me today, then you will find two men close
to Rachel's tomb in the territory of Benjamin
at Zelzah; and they will say to you, 'The
donkeys which you went to search for have
been found. Now behold, your father has
ceased to be concerned about the donkeys
and is anxious for you, saying, "What shall
I do about my son?"' 3 Then you will go on
further from there, and you will come as far
as the oak of Tabor, and there three men
going up to God at Bethel will meet you, one

carrying three young goats, another carrying three loaves of bread, and another carrying a jug of wine; 4 and they will greet you and give you two *loaves* of bread. And you will take *them* from their hand. 5 Afterward you will come to the hill of God where the Philistine garrison is; and it shall be as soon as you have come there to the city, that you will meet a group of prophets coming down from the high place with harp, tambourine, flute, and a lyre before them, and they will be prophesying. 6 Then the Spirit of Yahweh will come upon you mightily, and you shall prophesy with them and be changed into another man. 7 Now it will be when these signs come to you, do for yourself whatever your hand finds *to do*, for God is with you. 8 And you shall go down before me to Gilgal; and behold, I will come down to you to offer burnt offerings and sacrifice peace offerings. You shall wait seven days until I come to you and make you know what you should do."

9 Then it happened when he turned his back to leave Samuel, God changed his heart; and all those signs came about on that day. 10 And they came to the hill there, and behold, a group of prophets met him; and the Spirit of God came upon him mightily, so that he prophesied among them. 11 Now it happened that all who knew him previously saw, and behold, he was prophesying with the prophets, so the people said to one another, "What has happened to the son of Kish? Is Saul also among the prophets?" 12 And a man there answered and said, "Now, who is their father?" Therefore it became a proverb: "Is Saul also among the prophets?" 13 Then he finished prophesying and came to the high place.

14 Now Saul's uncle said to him and his young man, "Where did you go?" And he said, "To look for the donkeys. And we saw that they were not *anywhere*, so we went to Samuel." 15 And Saul's uncle said, "Please tell me what Samuel said to you." 16 So Saul said to his uncle, "He told us plainly that the donkeys had been found." But he did not tell him about the matter of the kingdom which Samuel had said.

17 Then Samuel called the people together to Yahweh at Mizpah; 18 and he said to the sons of Israel, "Thus says Yahweh, the God of Israel, 'I brought Israel up from Egypt, and I delivered you from the hand of the Egyptians and from the hand of all the kingdoms that were oppressing you.' 19 But you have today rejected your God, who saves you from all your calamities and your distresses; yet you have said, 'No, but set a king over us!' So now, take your stand before Yahweh by your tribes and by your clans."

20 Thus Samuel brought all the tribes of Israel near, and the tribe of Benjamin was taken *by lot*. 21 Then he brought the tribe of Benjamin near by its families, and the Matrite family was taken. And Saul the son of Kish was taken; but they looked for him, and he could not be found. 22 Therefore they inquired further of Yahweh, "Has the man come here yet?" So Yahweh said, "Behold, he is hiding himself by the baggage." 23 So they ran and took him from there, and he stood among the people. And he was taller than any of the people from his shoulders upward. 24 And Samuel said to all the people, "Do you see him whom Yahweh has chosen? Surely there is no one like him among all the people." So all the people shouted and said, "*Long* live the king!"

25 Then Samuel spoke with the people about the *legal* judgments of the kingdom and wrote *them* in the book and placed *it* before Yahweh. And Samuel sent all the people away, each one to his house. 26 Saul also went to his house at Gibeah; and the valiant *men* whose hearts God had touched went with him. 27 But certain vile men said, "How can this one save us?" And they despised him and did not bring him any present. But he kept silent.

11 And Nahash the Ammonite came up and besieged Jabesh-gilead; and all the men of Jabesh said to Nahash, "Cut a covenant with us, and we will serve you." 2 But Nahash the Ammonite said to them, "I will cut *it* with you on this condition, that I will gouge out the right eye of every one of you, thus I will make it a reproach on all Israel." 3 Then the elders of Jabesh said to him, "Let us alone for seven days, that we may send messengers throughout the territory of Israel. Then, if there is no one to save us, we will come out to you." 4 Then the messengers came to Gibeah of Saul and spoke these words in the hearing of the people, and all the people lifted up their voices and wept.

5 Now behold, Saul was coming from the field behind the oxen, and he said, "What is

the matter with the people that they weep?"
So they recounted to him the words of the
men of Jabesh. 6 Then the Spirit of God came
upon Saul mightily when he heard these
words, and he burned with anger exceed-
ingly. 7 Then he took a pair of oxen and cut
them in pieces and sent *them* throughout
the territory of Israel by the hand of mes-
sengers, saying, "Whoever does not come
out after Saul and after Samuel, so shall it be
done to his oxen." Then the dread of Yahweh
fell on the people, and they came out as one
man. 8 And he numbered them in Bezek;
and the sons of Israel were 300,000, and
the men of Judah 30,000. 9 And they said
to the messengers who had come, "Thus
you shall say to the men of Jabesh-gilead,
'Tomorrow, by the time the sun is hot, you
will have salvation.'" So the messengers
went and told the men of Jabesh; and they
were glad. 10 Then the men of Jabesh said,
"Tomorrow we will come out to you, and
you may do to us whatever seems good in
your eyes." 11 Then the next morning Saul
put the people in three companies; and
they came into the midst of the camp at
the morning watch and struck down the
Ammonites until the heat of the day. Those
who survived were scattered, so that no two
of them were left together.

12 Then the people said to Samuel, "Who
is he that said, 'Shall Saul reign over us?'
Bring the men, that we may put them to
death." 13 But Saul said, "Not a man shall be
put to death this day, for today Yahweh has
accomplished salvation in Israel."

14 Then Samuel said to the people, "Come
and let us go to Gilgal and renew the king-
dom there." 15 So all the people went to
Gilgal, and there they made Saul king before
Yahweh in Gilgal. There they also offered
sacrifices of peace offerings before Yahweh;
and there Saul and all the men of Israel were
exceedingly glad.

Psalm 55:16–23

16 As for me, I shall call upon God,
And Yahweh will save me.
17 Evening and morning and at noon, I
will bring my complaint and moan,
And He will hear my voice.
18 He will redeem my soul in peace from
the battle *which is* against me,
For they are many *who strive* with me.
19 God will hear and answer them—
Even the one who sits
enthroned from of old— Selah.
Because they do not change,
And do not fear God.
20 *My companion* has put forth
his hands against those who
were at peace with him;
He has violated his covenant.
21 His speech was smoother than butter,
But his heart was war;
His words were softer than oil,
Yet they were drawn swords.

22 Cast your burden upon Yahweh
and He will sustain you;
He will never allow the
righteous to be shaken.
23 But You, O God, will bring them
down to the pit of corruption;
Men of bloodshed and deceit will
not live out half their days.
But I will trust in You.

Proverbs 15:18–20

18 A hot-tempered man stirs up strife,
But the slow to anger quiets a dispute.
19 The way of the sluggard is
as a hedge of thorns,
But the path of the upright
is a highway.
20 A wise son makes a father glad,
But a foolish man despises his mother.

Luke 22:24–46

24 And there arose also a dispute among
them *as to* which one of them was regarded
to be greatest. 25 And He said to them, "The
kings of the Gentiles lord it over them, and
those who have authority over them are
called 'Benefactors.' 26 But not so with you;
rather the one who is the greatest among
you must become like the youngest, and the
leader like the servant. 27 For who is greater,
the one who reclines *at the table* or the one
who serves? Is it not the one who reclines?
But I am among you as the one who serves.

28 "Now you are those who have stood
by Me in My trials, 29 and I grant you a
kingdom, just as My Father granted *one* to
Me, 30 that you may eat and drink at My table
in My kingdom, and you will sit on thrones
judging the twelve tribes of Israel.

31 "Simon, Simon, behold, Satan has
demanded to sift *all of* you like wheat. 32 But
I have prayed earnestly for you, that your

faith may not fail; and you, once you have returned, strengthen your brothers." 33 But he said to Him, "Lord, with You I am ready to go both to prison and to death!" 34 And He said, "I say to you, Peter, the rooster will not crow today until you have denied three times that you know Me."

35 And He said to them, "When I sent you out without money belt and bag and sandals, did you lack anything?" They said, "Not a thing." 36 And He said to them, "But now, whoever has a money belt is to take it along, likewise also a bag, and whoever has no sword should sell his garment and buy one. 37 For I tell you that this which is written must be completed in Me, 'AND HE WAS NUMBERED WITH TRANSGRESSORS'; for that which refers to Me has *its* completion." 38 And they said, "Lord, look, here are two swords." And He said to them, "It is enough."

39 And He came out and went as was His custom to the Mount of Olives; and the disciples also followed Him. 40 Now when He arrived at the place, He said to them, "Pray that you may not enter into temptation." 41 And He withdrew from them about a stone's throw, and He knelt down and *began to* pray, 42 saying, "Father, if You are willing, remove this cup from Me, yet not My will, but Yours be done." 43 Now an angel from heaven appeared to Him, strengthening Him. 44 And being in agony He was praying very fervently, and His sweat became like drops of blood, falling down upon the ground. 45 And when He rose from prayer, He came to the disciples and found them sleeping from sorrow, 46 and said to them, "Why are you sleeping? Rise up and pray that you may not enter into temptation."

MAY 5

1 Samuel 12:1–13:23

12 Then Samuel said to all Israel, "Behold, I have listened to your voice in all that you said to me, and I have appointed a king over you. 2 So now, here is the king walking before you, but I am old and gray, and behold, my sons are with you. And I have walked before you from my youth even to this day. 3 Here I am; bear witness against me before Yahweh and His anointed. Whose ox have I taken, or whose donkey have I taken, or whom have I defrauded? Whom have I oppressed, or from whose hand have I taken a bribe to blind my eyes with it? I will restore *it* to you." 4 And they said, "You have not extorted us or oppressed us or taken anything from any man's hand." 5 So he said to them, "Yahweh is witness against you, and His anointed is witness this day that you have found nothing in my hand." And they said, "*He is* witness."

6 Then Samuel said to the people, "It is Yahweh who appointed Moses and Aaron and who brought your fathers up from the land of Egypt. 7 So now, take your stand, that I may judge you before Yahweh concerning all the righteous acts of Yahweh which He did for you and your fathers. 8 When Jacob went into Egypt and your fathers cried out to Yahweh, then Yahweh sent Moses and Aaron who brought your fathers out of Egypt and settled them in this place. 9 But they forgot Yahweh their God, so He sold them into the hand of Sisera, commander of the army of Hazor, and into the hand of the Philistines and into the hand of the king of Moab, and they fought against them. 10 And they cried out to Yahweh and said, 'We have sinned because we have forsaken Yahweh and have served the Baals and the Ashtaroth; but now deliver us from the hands of our enemies, and we will serve You.' 11 Then Yahweh sent Jerubbaal and Bedan and Jephthah and Samuel, and He delivered you from the hands of your enemies all around, so that you lived in security. 12 But you saw that Nahash the king of the sons of Ammon came against you, and you said to me, 'No, but a king shall reign over us,' although Yahweh your God *was* your king. 13 So now, behold, the king whom you have chosen, whom you have asked for, and behold, Yahweh has set a king over you. 14 If you will fear Yahweh and serve Him and listen to His voice and not rebel against the command of Yahweh, then both you and also the king who reigns over you will follow Yahweh your God. 15 But if you will not listen to the voice of Yahweh, but rebel against the command of Yahweh, then the hand of Yahweh will be against you, *as it was* against your fathers. 16 Even now, take your stand and see this great thing

which Yahweh will do before your eyes. 17 Is
it not the wheat harvest today? I will call
to Yahweh, that He may send thunder and
rain. Then you will know and see that your
wickedness is great which you have done in
the eyes of Yahweh by asking for yourselves
a king." 18 So Samuel called to Yahweh, and
Yahweh sent thunder and rain that day;
and all the people greatly feared Yahweh
and Samuel.

19 Then all the people said to Samuel,
"Pray for your servants to Yahweh your God,
so that we may not die, for we have added to
all our sins *this* evil by asking for ourselves
a king." 20 And Samuel said to the people,
"Do not fear. You have committed all this
evil, yet do not turn aside from following
Yahweh, but serve Yahweh with all your
heart. 21 And you must not turn aside, for
then you would go after meaningless things
which cannot profit and cannot deliver,
because they are meaningless. 22 For Yahweh
will not abandon His people on account of
His great name, because Yahweh has been
pleased to make you a people for Himself.
23 Moreover, as for me, far be it from me that
I should sin against Yahweh by ceasing to
pray for you; but I will instruct you in the
good and upright way. 24 Only fear Yahweh
and serve Him in truth with all your heart;
for see what great things He has done for
you. 25 But if you still do wickedly, both you
and your king will be swept away."

13 Saul was *thirty* years old when he
began to reign, and he reigned *forty-*
two years over Israel.

2 And Saul chose for himself 3,000 men
of Israel, of which 2,000 were with Saul in
Michmash and in the hill country of Bethel,
while 1,000 were with Jonathan at Gibeah
of Benjamin. But he sent away the rest of
the people, each to his tent. 3 And Jonathan
struck the garrison of the Philistines that
was in Geba, and the Philistines heard of *it*.
Then Saul blew the trumpet throughout the
land, saying, "Let the Hebrews hear." 4 Then
all Israel heard the news that Saul had struck
the garrison of the Philistines, and also that
Israel had become odious to the Philistines.
The people were then summoned to Saul
at Gilgal.

5 Now the Philistines assembled to fight
with Israel, 30,000 chariots and 6,000
horsemen and people like the sand which
is on the seashore in abundance; and they
came up and camped in Michmash, east
of Beth-aven. 6 Now the men of Israel saw
that they were in a strait (for the people
were hard-pressed). Then the people hid
themselves in caves, in thickets, in cliffs,
in cellars, and in pits. 7 Also *some of* the
Hebrews crossed the Jordan into the land
of Gad and Gilead. But as for Saul, he *was*
still in Gilgal, and all the people followed
him trembling.

8 So he waited seven days, according
to the appointed time set by Samuel, but
Samuel did not come to Gilgal; and the
people were scattering from him. 9 So Saul
said, "Bring near to me the burnt offering
and the peace offerings." And he offered the
burnt offering. 10 And as soon as he finished
offering the burnt offering, behold, Samuel
came; and Saul went out to meet him *and*
to greet him. 11 But Samuel said, "What
have you done?" And Saul said, "Because
I saw that the people were scattering from
me, and that you did not come within the
appointed days, and that the Philistines
were assembling at Michmash, 12 therefore
I said, 'Now the Philistines will come down
against me at Gilgal, and I have not entreated
the favor of Yahweh.' So I forced myself and
offered the burnt offering." 13 And Samuel
said to Saul, "You have acted foolishly; you
have not kept the commandment of Yahweh
your God, which He commanded you, for
now Yahweh would have established your
kingdom over Israel forever. 14 But now
your kingdom shall not endure. Yahweh
has sought out for Himself a man after His
own heart, and Yahweh has appointed him
as ruler over His people because you have
not kept what Yahweh commanded you."

15 Then Samuel arose and went up from
Gilgal to Gibeah of Benjamin. And Saul
numbered the people who were present
with him, about six hundred men. 16 Now
Saul and his son Jonathan and the people
who were present with them were staying
in Geba of Benjamin, and the Philistines
camped at Michmash. 17 And the raiders
came from the camp of the Philistines in
three companies: one company turned
toward Ophrah, to the land of Shual, 18 and
another company turned to the way of
Beth-horon, and another company turned
to the way of the border which overlooks
the valley of Zeboim toward the wilderness.

19 Now no blacksmith could be found in
all the land of Israel, for the Philistines said,
"Lest the Hebrews make swords or spears."
20 So all Israel went down to the Philistines,
each to sharpen his plowshare, his mattock,
his axe, and his goad. 21 And the charge was
two-thirds of a shekel for the plowshares,
the mattocks, the forks, and the axes, and
to fix the goad. 22 So it happened on the day
of battle that neither sword nor spear was
found in the hands of any of the people
who *were* with Saul and Jonathan, but they
were found with Saul and his son Jonathan.
23 And the garrison of the Philistines went
out to the pass of Michmash.

Psalm 56:1–13

1 Be gracious to me, O God, for
man has trampled upon me;
All day long, an attacker oppresses me.
2 My foes have trampled upon
me all day long,
For many attack me proudly.
3 When I am afraid,
I will trust in You.
4 In God, whose word I praise,
In God I trust;
I shall not be afraid.
What can *mere* man do to me?
5 All day long they distort my words;
All their thoughts are
against me for evil.
6 They attack, they lurk,
They watch my heels,
As they have hoped *to take* my life.
7 On account of *their* wickedness,
will they have an escape?
In anger, bring down the
peoples, O God!

8 You have taken account of
my wanderings;
Put my tears in Your bottle.
Are *they* not in Your book?
9 Then my enemies will turn back
in the day when I call;
This I know, that God is for me.
10 In God, *whose* word I praise,
In Yahweh, *whose* word I praise,
11 In God I trust, I shall not be afraid.
What can man do to me?
12 Your vows are *binding*
upon me, O God;
I will fulfill thank offerings to You.
13 For You have delivered my
soul from death,
Indeed my feet from stumbling,
So that I may walk before God
In the light of the living.

Proverbs 15:21–23

21 Folly is gladness to him who
lacks a heart *of wisdom*,
But a man of discernment
walks straight.
22 Without consultation,
plans are frustrated,
But with many counselors
they succeed.
23 A man has gladness in an apt answer,
And how good is a timely word!

Luke 22:47–71

47 While He was still speaking, behold, a
crowd *came*, and the one called Judas, one
of the twelve, was coming ahead of them,
and he approached Jesus to kiss Him. 48 But
Jesus said to him, "Judas, are you betraying
the Son of Man with a kiss?" 49 And when
those around Him saw what was going to
happen, they said, "Lord, shall we strike
with the sword?" 50 And one of them struck
the slave of the high priest and cut off his
right ear. 51 But Jesus answered and said,
"Stop! No more of this." And He touched
his ear and healed him. 52 Then Jesus said to
the chief priests and officers of the temple
and elders who had come against Him,
"Have you come out with swords and clubs
as against a robber? 53 While I was with you
daily in the temple, you did not stretch out
your hands against Me, but this hour and
the authority of darkness are yours."
54 Now having arrested Him, they led
Him *away* and brought Him to the house
of the high priest, but Peter was following
at a distance. 55 And after they had kindled
a fire in the middle of the courtyard and had
sat down together, Peter was sitting among
them. 56 And a servant-girl, seeing him as
he sat in the firelight and looking intently
at him, said, "This man was with Him too."
57 But he denied *it*, saying, "Woman, I do
not know Him." 58 A little later, another
saw him and said, "You are *one* of them too!"
But Peter said, "Man, I am not!" 59 And after
about an hour had passed, another man
began to insist, saying, "Certainly this man
was with Him too, for he also is a Galilean."

60 But Peter said, "Man, I do not know what
you are talking about." Immediately, while
he was still speaking, a rooster crowed.
61 And the Lord turned and looked at Peter.
And Peter remembered the word of the
Lord, how He had told him, "Before a rooster
crows today, you will deny Me three times."
62 And he went out and cried bitterly.

63 Now the men who were holding Jesus
in custody were mocking Him while they
beat Him, 64 and they blindfolded Him and
were asking Him, saying, "Prophesy, who
is the one who hit You?" 65 And they were
saying many other things against Him,
blaspheming.

66 And as the day came, the Council of
elders of the people assembled, both chief
priests and scribes, and they led Him away
to their Sanhedrin, saying, 67 "If You are the
Christ, tell us." But He said to them, "If I tell
you, you will not believe, 68 and if I ask a
question, you will not answer. 69 But from
now on THE SON OF MAN WILL BE SEATED
AT THE RIGHT HAND of the power OF GOD."
70 And they all said, "Are You the Son of God,
then?" And He said to them, "You yourselves
say that I am." 71 Then they said, "What
further need do we have of testimony? For
we have heard it ourselves from His own
mouth."

MAY 6

1 Samuel 14:1–15:35

14 Now the day came that Jonathan, the
son of Saul, said to the young man
who was carrying his armor, "Come and
let us cross over to the Philistines' garrison
that is on the other side." But he did not
tell his father. 2 And Saul was staying in the
outskirts of Gibeah under the pomegranate
tree which is in Migron. And the people who
were with him *were* about six hundred men,
3 and Ahijah, the son of Ahitub, Ichabod's
brother, the son of Phinehas, the son of Eli,
the priest of Yahweh at Shiloh, was wearing
an ephod. And the people did not know that
Jonathan had gone. 4 Now between the
passes by which Jonathan sought to cross
over to the Philistines' garrison, there was
a sharp crag on the one side and a sharp
crag on the other side, and the name of the
one was Bozez, and the name of the other
Seneh. 5 The one crag rose on the north
opposite Michmash, and the other on the
south opposite Geba.

6 Then Jonathan said to the young man
who was carrying his armor, "Come and
let us cross over to the garrison of these
uncircumcised; perhaps Yahweh will work
for us, for Yahweh is not restrained to
save by many or by few." 7 And his armor
bearer said to him, "Do all that is in your
heart; turn yourself, *and* here I am with you
according to your heart." 8 Then Jonathan
said, "Behold, we will cross over to the men
and reveal ourselves to them. 9 If they say to
us, 'Wait until we come to you,' then we will
stand in our place and not go up to them.
10 But if they say, 'Come up to us,' then we
will go up, for Yahweh has given them into
our hands; and this shall be the sign to us."
11 So both of them revealed themselves to
the garrison of the Philistines, and the Phi-
listines said, "Behold, Hebrews are coming
out of the holes where they have hidden
themselves." 12 So the men of the garrison
hailed Jonathan and his armor bearer and
said, "Come up to us, and we will make you
know something." And Jonathan said to
his armor bearer, "Come up after me, for
Yahweh has given them into the hands of
Israel." 13 Then Jonathan climbed up on
his hands and feet, with his armor bearer
behind him; and they fell before Jonathan,
and his armor bearer put some to death after
him. 14 And that first slaughter which Jona-
than and his armor bearer made was about
twenty men within about half a furrow in
an acre of land. 15 And there was a trembling
in the camp, in the field, and among all the
people. Even the garrison and the raiders
trembled, and the earth quaked so that it
became a great trembling.

16 Then Saul's watchmen in Gibeah of
Benjamin looked, and behold, the multitude
melted away; and they went here and *there*.
17 So Saul said to the people who *were* with
him, "Number now and see who has gone
from us." And when they had numbered,
behold, Jonathan and his armor bearer were
not *there*. 18 Then Saul said to Ahijah, "Bring
the ark of God here." For the ark of God was
at that time with the sons of Israel. 19 And
it happened that while Saul talked to the

priest, the commotion in the camp of the
Philistines continued and increased; so Saul
said to the priest, "Withdraw your hand."
20 Then Saul and all the people who *were*
with him rallied and came to the battle; and
behold, every man's sword was against his
fellow, *and there was* very great confusion.
21 Now the Hebrews *who* were with the
Philistines previously, who went up with
them all around in the camp, even they
also *turned* to be with the Israelites who
were with Saul and Jonathan. 22 Now all the
men of Israel who had hidden themselves
in the hill country of Ephraim heard that
the Philistines had fled, and they pursued
them closely in the battle. 23 So Yahweh
saved Israel that day, and the battle spread
beyond Beth-aven.

24 Now the men of Israel were hard-
pressed on that day. And Saul had put the
people under oath, saying, "Cursed be the
man who eats food before evening and until
I have avenged myself on my enemies." So
none of the people tasted food. 25 Now all
the people of the land entered the forest,
and there was honey on the ground. 26 So
the people entered the forest, and behold,
there was a flow of honey; but no man put
his hand to his mouth, for the people feared
the sworn oath. 27 But Jonathan had not
heard when his father put the people under
a sworn oath; therefore, he put out the end
of the staff that *was* in his hand and dipped
it in the honeycomb and put his hand to his
mouth, and his eyes brightened. 28 Then
one of the people answered and said,
"Your father strictly put the people under
a sworn oath, saying, 'Cursed be the man
who eats food today.'" And the people were
weary. 29 Then Jonathan said, "My father has
troubled the land. See now, how my eyes
have brightened because I tasted a little of
this honey. 30 How much more, if only the
people had eaten freely today of the spoil of
their enemies which they found! For now
the slaughter among the Philistines has not
been great."

31 Then they struck among the Philistines
that day from Michmash to Aijalon. And the
people were very weary. 32 So the people
rushed greedily upon the spoil, and they
took sheep and oxen and calves and slaugh-
tered *them* on the ground; and the people
ate *them* with the blood. 33 Then they told
Saul, saying, "Behold, the people are sinning
against Yahweh by eating with the blood."
And he said, "You have acted treacherously;
roll a great stone to me today." 34 And Saul
said, "Scatter yourselves among the people
and say to them, 'Each one of you bring me
his ox or his sheep, and slaughter *it* here
and eat; and do not sin against Yahweh by
eating with the blood.'" So all the people
that night brought each one his ox with him
and slaughtered *it* there. 35 And Saul built an
altar to Yahweh; it was the first altar that he
built to Yahweh.

36 Then Saul said, "Let us go down after
the Philistines by night and take spoil
among them until the morning light, and
let us not leave a man of them." And they
said, "Do whatever seems good in your
eyes." So the priest said, "Let us draw near
to God here." 37 And Saul asked of God,
"Shall I go down after the Philistines? Will
You give them into the hand of Israel?" But
He did not answer him on that day. 38 And
Saul said, "Draw near here, all you chiefs of
the people, and know and see how this sin
has happened today. 39 For as Yahweh lives,
who saves Israel, though it is in Jonathan my
son, he shall surely die." But not one of all
the people answered him. 40 Then he said to
all Israel, "You shall be on one side, and I and
Jonathan my son will be on the other side."
And the people said to Saul, "Do what seems
good in your eyes." 41 Therefore, Saul said
to Yahweh, the God of Israel, "Give a perfect
lot." And Jonathan and Saul were taken, but
the people escaped. 42 And Saul said, "Cast
lots between me and Jonathan my son." And
Jonathan was taken.

43 Then Saul said to Jonathan, "Tell me
what you have done." So Jonathan told him
and said, "I indeed tasted a little honey with
the end of the staff that was in my hand.
Here I am; I must die!" 44 And Saul said,
"May God do this *to me* and more also, for
you shall surely die, Jonathan." 45 But the
people said to Saul, "Must Jonathan die,
who has brought about this great salvation
in Israel? Far from it! As Yahweh lives, not
one hair of his head shall fall to the ground,
for he has worked with God this day." So
the people redeemed Jonathan, and he did
not die. 46 Then Saul went up from pursuing
the Philistines, and the Philistines went to
their own place.

47 Now Saul had taken the kingdom over
Israel, and he fought against all his enemies

on every side, against Moab, the sons of
Ammon, Edom, the kings of Zobah, and
the Philistines; and wherever he turned,
he inflicted punishment. 48 And he acted
valiantly and struck down the Amalekites
and delivered Israel from the hands of those
who plundered them.

49 Now the sons of Saul were Jonathan
and Ishvi and Malchi-shua; and the names
of his two daughters *were these*: the name
of the firstborn Merab and the name of the
younger Michal. 50 And the name of Saul's
wife was Ahinoam the daughter of Ahimaaz.
And the name of the commander of his
army was Abner the son of Ner, Saul's uncle.
51 And Kish *was* the father of Saul, and Ner
the father of Abner *was* the son of Abiel.

52 Now the war against the Philistines was
severe all the days of Saul; and Saul would
see any mighty man or any man of valor and
would gather him to his staff.

15 Then Samuel said to Saul, "Yahweh
sent me to anoint you as king over
His people, over Israel; so now, obey the
voice of the words of Yahweh. 2 Thus says
Yahweh of hosts, 'I will punish Amalek *for*
what he did to Israel, how he set himself
against him on the way while he was coming
up from Egypt. 3 Now go and strike Amalek
and devote to destruction all that he has,
and do not spare him; but put to death both
man and woman, infant and nursing baby,
ox and sheep, camel and donkey.'"

4 Then Saul summoned the people and
numbered them in Telaim, 200,000 foot
soldiers and 10,000 men of Judah. 5 And
Saul came to the city of Amalek and set an
ambush in the valley. 6 And Saul said to the
Kenites, "Go, depart; go down from among
the Amalekites, lest I destroy you with them;
you showed lovingkindness to all the sons
of Israel when they came up from Egypt."
So the Kenites departed from among the
Amalekites. 7 So Saul struck the Amalekites,
from Havilah as you go to Shur, which is
east of Egypt. 8 And he seized Agag the
king of the Amalekites alive and devoted to
destruction all the people with the edge of
the sword. 9 But Saul and the people spared
Agag and the best of the sheep, the oxen, the
fatlings, the lambs, and all that was good,
and they were not willing to devote them
to destruction; but everything despised and
worthless, that they utterly destroyed.

10 Then the word of Yahweh came to Sam-
uel, saying, 11 "I regret that I have made Saul
king, for he has turned back from following
Me and has not established My words." And
Samuel became angry and cried out to Yah-
weh all night. 12 Then Samuel rose early in
the morning to meet Saul; and it was told to
Samuel, saying, "Saul came to Carmel, and
behold, he set up a monument for himself,
then turned and proceeded on down to Gil-
gal." 13 And Samuel came to Saul, and Saul
said to him, "Blessed are you of Yahweh! I
have established the word of Yahweh." 14 But
Samuel said, "What then is this sound of the
sheep in my ears and the sound of the oxen
which I am hearing?" 15 And Saul said, "They
have brought them from the Amalekites, for
the people spared the best of the sheep and
oxen, to sacrifice to Yahweh your God; but
the rest we have devoted to destruction."
16 Then Samuel said to Saul, "Wait, and let
me tell you what Yahweh spoke to me last
night." And he said to him, "Speak!"

17 And Samuel said, "Is it not true, though
you were little in your own eyes, you were
made the head of the tribes of Israel? And
Yahweh anointed you king over Israel, 18 and
Yahweh sent you on a mission and said, 'Go
and devote to destruction the sinners, the
Amalekites, and fight against them until
they are consumed.' 19 Why then did you
not obey the voice of Yahweh, but rushed
upon the spoil and did what was evil in the
eyes of Yahweh?"

20 Then Saul said to Samuel, "I did obey
the voice of Yahweh and went on the way
on which Yahweh sent me and have brought
back Agag the king of Amalek and have
devoted the Amalekites to destruction.
21 But the people took *some* of the spoil,
sheep and oxen, the choicest of the things
devoted to destruction, to sacrifice to Yah-
weh your God at Gilgal." 22 And Samuel said,

"Has Yahweh as much delight in
burnt offerings and sacrifices
As in obeying the voice of Yahweh?
Behold, to obey is better than sacrifice,
And to heed than the fat of rams.
23 "For rebellion is as the sin of divination,
And insubordination is as
wickedness and idolatry.
Because you have rejected
the word of Yahweh,
He has also rejected you
from *being* king."

24 Then Saul said to Samuel, "I have
sinned; I have indeed trespassed against
the command of Yahweh and your words
because I feared the people and obeyed
their voice. 25 So now, please forgive my sin
and return with me, that I may worship Yah-
weh." 26 But Samuel said to Saul, "I will not
return with you; for you have rejected the
word of Yahweh, and Yahweh has rejected
you from being king over Israel." 27 Then
Samuel turned to go, but *Saul* seized the
edge of his robe, and it tore. 28 So Samuel
said to him, "Yahweh has torn the kingdom
of Israel from you today and has given it
to your neighbor, who is better than you.
29 Also the Eternal One of Israel will not lie
or have regret; for He is not a man that He
should have regret." 30 Then he said, "I have
sinned; *but* please honor me now before
the elders of my people and before Israel,
and return with me, that I may worship
Yahweh your God." 31 So Samuel returned,
following after Saul, and Saul worshiped
Yahweh.

32 Then Samuel said, "Bring Agag near
to me, the king of the Amalekites." And
Agag came to him in chains. And Agag
said, "Surely the bitterness of death has
departed." 33 But Samuel said, "As your
sword has made women childless, so shall
your mother be childless among women."
And Samuel hacked Agag to pieces before
Yahweh at Gilgal.

34 Then Samuel went to Ramah, but Saul
went up to his house at Gibeah of Saul. 35 So
Samuel did not see Saul again until the day
of his death; for Samuel grieved over Saul.
And Yahweh regretted that He had made
Saul king over Israel.

Psalm 57:1–3

1 Be gracious to me, O God,
  be gracious to me,
For my soul takes refuge in You;
And in the shadow of Your
  wings I will take refuge
Until destruction passes by.
2 I will call to God Most High,
To God who accomplishes
  all things for me.
3 He will send from heaven and save me;
He reproaches him who
  tramples upon me. Selah.
God will send His lovingkindness
  and His truth.

Proverbs 15:24–25

24 The path of life *leads* upward for
  the one who has insight
That he may turn away
  from Sheol below.
25 Yahweh will tear down the
  house of the proud,
But He will cause the boundary
  of the widow to stand.

Luke 23:1–25

23 Then their whole assembly rose
up and brought Him before Pilate.
2 And they began to accuse Him, saying,
"We found this man misleading our nation
and forbidding to pay taxes to Caesar, and
saying that He Himself is Christ, a King."
3 So Pilate asked Him, saying, "Are You the
King of the Jews?" And He answered him
and said, "You yourself say *it*." 4 Then Pilate
said to the chief priests and the crowds, "I
find no guilt in this man." 5 But they kept
on insisting, saying, "He stirs up the people,
teaching all over Judea, starting from Galilee
even as far as this place."

6 Now when Pilate heard *this*, he asked
whether the man was a Galilean. 7 And when
he learned that He belonged to Herod's
jurisdiction, he sent Him to Herod, who
himself also was in Jerusalem in those days.

8 Now when Herod saw Jesus, he rejoiced
greatly; for he had wanted to see Him for
a long time, because he had been hearing
about Him and was hoping to see some sign
performed by Him. 9 And he questioned Him
at some length, but He answered him noth-
ing. 10 And the chief priests and the scribes
were standing there, vehemently accusing
Him. 11 And Herod with his soldiers, after
treating Him with contempt and mocking
Him, dressed Him in a bright robe and sent
Him back to Pilate. 12 Now Herod and Pilate
became friends with one another that very
day; for before they had been at enmity with
each other.

13 And Pilate summoned the chief priests
and the rulers and the people, 14 and said
to them, "You brought this man to me as
one who incites the people to rebellion, and
behold, having examined Him before you, I
have found in this man no guilt of what you
are accusing Him. 15 No, nor has Herod, for
he sent Him back to us; and behold, nothing
deserving death has been done by Him.
16 Therefore I will punish Him and release

Him." 17 [Now he was obliged to release to them at the feast one prisoner.]

18 But they cried out all together, saying, "Away with this man, and release for us Barabbas!" 19 (He had been thrown into prison for an insurrection made in the city and for murder.) 20 But again Pilate addressed them, wanting to release Jesus, 21 but they kept on calling out, saying, "Crucify, crucify Him!" 22 And he said to them a third time, "Why, what evil has this man done? I have found in Him no guilt *worthy of* death; therefore I will punish Him and release Him." 23 But they were insistent, with loud voices asking that He be crucified. And their voices were prevailing. 24 And Pilate pronounced sentence that their demand be granted. 25 And he released the man they were asking for who had been thrown into prison for insurrection and murder, but he delivered Jesus to their will.

He that would be conformed to Christ's image, and become a Christlike man, must be constantly studying Christ Himself.

— J. C. RYLE

MAY 7

1 Samuel 16:1–17:58

16 Then Yahweh said to Samuel, "How long will you be grieving over Saul? I have rejected him from being king over Israel. Fill your horn with oil and go; I will send you to Jesse the Bethlehemite, for I see among his sons a king for Me." 2 But Samuel said, "How can I go? Saul will hear *of it* and will kill me." Then Yahweh said, "Take a heifer with you and say, 'I have come to sacrifice to Yahweh.' 3 And you shall invite Jesse to the sacrifice, and I will make you know what you shall do; and you shall anoint for Me the one whom I say to you." 4 So Samuel did what Yahweh said and came to Bethlehem. And the elders of the city came trembling to meet him and said, "Do you come in peace?" 5 And he said, "In peace; I have come to sacrifice to Yahweh. Set yourselves apart as holy and come with me to the sacrifice." He also set apart Jesse and his sons as holy and invited them to the sacrifice.

6 Now it happened, when they entered, he looked at Eliab and thought, "Surely the anointed of Yahweh is before Him." 7 But Yahweh said to Samuel, "Do not look at his appearance or at the height of his stature, because I have rejected him; for God *sees* not as man sees, for man looks at the outward appearance, but Yahweh looks at the heart." 8 Then Jesse called Abinadab and made him pass before Samuel. And he said, "Yahweh has not chosen this one either." 9 Next Jesse made Shammah pass by. And he said, "Yahweh has not chosen this one either." 10 Thus Jesse made seven of his sons pass before Samuel. But Samuel said to Jesse, "Yahweh has not chosen these." 11 And Samuel said to Jesse, "Are these all the young men?" And he said, "There remains yet the youngest, and behold, he is shepherding the sheep." Then Samuel said to Jesse, "Send and bring him, for we will not turn around until he comes here." 12 So he sent and brought him in. Now he was ruddy, with beautiful eyes and a handsome appearance. And Yahweh said, "Arise, anoint him, for this is he." 13 Then Samuel took the horn of oil and anointed him in the midst of his brothers; and the Spirit of Yahweh came mightily upon David from that day forward. And Samuel arose and went to Ramah.

14 Now the Spirit of Yahweh departed from Saul, and an evil spirit from Yahweh terrorized him. 15 Saul's servants then said to him, "Behold now, an evil spirit from God is terrorizing you. 16 Let our lord now speak to your servants who are before you. Let them seek a man who is a skillful musician on the harp; and it shall be that when the evil spirit from God is on you, he shall play *the harp* with his hand, and you will be well." 17 So Saul said to his servants, "Provide for me now a man who can play well and bring *him* to me." 18 Then one of

the young men answered and said, "Behold, I have seen a son of Jesse the Bethlehemite who is a skillful musician, a mighty man of valor, a warrior, one who is understanding in speech, and man of fine form; and Yahweh is with him." 19 So Saul sent messengers to Jesse and said, "Send me your son David who is with the flock." 20 And Jesse took a donkey *loaded with* bread and a wineskin of wine and a young goat and sent *them* to Saul by David his son. 21 Then David came to Saul and stood before him; and Saul loved him greatly, and he became his armor bearer. 22 So Saul sent to Jesse, saying, "Let David now stand before me, for he has found favor in my sight." 23 Thus it happened that whenever the *evil* spirit from God came to Saul, David would take the harp and play *it* with his hand; and Saul would be refreshed and be well, and the evil spirit would depart from him.

17 Now the Philistines gathered their camps for battle; and they were gathered at Socoh which belongs to Judah, and they camped between Socoh and Azekah, in Ephes-dammim. 2 But Saul and the men of Israel were gathered and camped in the valley of Elah and arranged *themselves* for battle to meet the Philistines. 3 Now the Philistines stood on the mountain on one side while Israel stood on the mountain on the other side, with the valley between them. 4 Then a champion came out from the camps of the Philistines named Goliath, from Gath, whose height was six cubits and a span. 5 *And he had* a bronze helmet on his head, and he was clothed with scale-armor, and the weight of that scale-armor was five thousand shekels of bronze. 6 *He* also *had* bronze greaves on his legs and a bronze javelin *slung* between his shoulders. 7 And the shaft of his spear was like a weaver's beam, and the head of his spear *weighed* six hundred shekels of iron; his shield-carrier also walked before him. 8 And he stood and called out to the battle lines of Israel and said to them, "Why do you come out to arrange *yourselves* for battle? Am I not the Philistine and you slaves of Saul? Choose a man for yourselves and let him come down to me. 9 If he is able to fight with me and strike me down, then we will become your slaves; but if I prevail against him and strike him down, then you shall become our slaves and serve us." 10 Again the Philistine said, "I *openly* reproach the battle lines of Israel this day; give me a man that we may fight together." 11 When Saul and all Israel heard these words of the Philistine, they were dismayed and greatly afraid.

12 Now David was the son of the Ephrathite of Bethlehem in Judah, whose name was Jesse, and he had eight sons. And Jesse was old in the days of Saul, advanced *in years* among men. 13 And the three older sons of Jesse had gone. They had gone after Saul to the battle. And the names of his three sons who went to the battle were Eliab the firstborn, and the second to him Abinadab, and the third Shammah. 14 But David was the youngest. Now the three oldest had gone after Saul, 15 but David went back and forth from Saul to shepherd his father's flock at Bethlehem.

16 Then the Philistine approached, morning and evening, for forty days and took his stand.

17 Then Jesse said to David his son, "Take now for your brothers an ephah of this roasted grain and these ten loaves and run to the camp to your brothers. 18 You shall also bring these ten cuts of cheese to the commander of *their* thousand, and look into the welfare of your brothers, and bring back a token from them. 19 And Saul and they and all the men of Israel are in the valley of Elah, fighting with the Philistines."

20 So David arose early in the morning and left the flock with a keeper and carried *the supplies* and went as Jesse had commanded him. And he came to the circle of the camp while the military force was going out in battle lines shouting the war cry. 21 And Israel and the Philistines arranged themselves in battle lines, battle line against battle line. 22 Then David left his baggage in the care of the baggage keeper and ran to the battle line and entered in order to greet his brothers. 23 As he was speaking with them, behold, the champion, the Philistine from Gath named Goliath, was coming up from the battle lines of the Philistines, and he spoke these same words; and David heard *them*.

24 Now all the men of Israel saw the man, and they fled from him and were greatly afraid. 25 And the men of Israel said, "Have you seen this man who is coming up? Surely he is coming up to reproach Israel. And it will be that the king will enrich the man who

strikes him down with great riches and will
give him his daughter and make his father's
house free in Israel."
26 Then David spoke to the men who were
standing by him, saying, "What will be done
for the man who strikes down this Philistine
and takes away the reproach from Israel?
For who is this uncircumcised Philistine,
that he should reproach the battle lines of
the living God?" 27 And the people spoke to
him in accord with this word, saying, "Thus
it will be done for the man who strikes him
down."
28 Then Eliab his oldest brother heard
when he spoke to the men; and Eliab's
anger burned against David, and he said,
"Why have you come down? And with
whom have you left those few sheep in the
wilderness? I myself know your arrogance
and the wickedness of your heart, for you
have come down in order to see the battle."
29 But David said, "What have I done now?
Was it not just a word?" 30 Then he turned
away from him to another and said the same
word; and the people responded to him *with*
the same word as before.
31 Then the words which David spoke
were heard. And they told *them* to Saul,
and he sent for him. 32 And David said to
Saul, "Let no man's heart fail on account
of him; your servant will go and fight with
this Philistine." 33 Then Saul said to David,
"You are not able to go against this Philistine
to fight with him; for you are *but* a youth
while he has been a warrior from his youth."
34 But David said to Saul, "Your servant was
shepherding his father's sheep. And a lion
and a bear would come and take a lamb from
the flock, 35 and I would go out after it and
strike it and rescue *the lamb* from its mouth.
Then it rose up against me, and I would
seize *it* by its beard and strike it down and
put it to death. 36 Your servant has struck
down both the lion and the bear; and this
uncircumcised Philistine will be like one
of them, since he has reproached the battle
lines of the living God." 37 And David said,
"Yahweh, who delivered me from the hand
of the lion and from the hand of the bear, He
will deliver me from the hand of this Philis-
tine." And Saul said to David, "Go, and may
Yahweh be with you." 38 Then Saul clothed
David with his robes and put a bronze hel-
met on his head, and he clothed him with
armor. 39 And David girded his sword over
his armor and tried to walk, for he had not
tested *them*. So David said to Saul, "I cannot
go with these, for I have not tested *them*."
And David took them off. 40 Then he took his
stick in his hand and chose for himself five
smooth stones from the brook and put them
in the shepherd's bag which he had, even in
his pouch, and his sling was in his hand; and
he approached the Philistine.
41 Then the Philistine came on and drew
near to David, with the shield-bearer in
front of him. 42 And the Philistine looked
and saw David. And he despised him;
for he was *but* a youth and ruddy, with a
handsome appearance. 43 And the Philistine
said to David, "Am I a dog, that you come to
me with sticks?" And the Philistine cursed
David by his gods. 44 The Philistine also
said to David, "Come to me, and I will give
your flesh to the birds of the sky and the
beasts of the field." 45 Then David said to the
Philistine, "You come to me with a sword,
a spear, and a javelin, but I come to you in
the name of Yahweh of hosts, the God of
the battle lines of Israel, whom you have
reproached. 46 This day Yahweh will deliver
you up into my hands, and I will strike you
down and remove your head from you. And
I will give the dead bodies of the camp of
the Philistines this day to the birds of the
sky and the beasts of the earth, that all the
earth may know that there is a God in Israel,
47 and that all this assembly may know that
Yahweh does not save by sword or by spear;
for the battle is Yahweh's, and He will give
you into our hands."
48 Then it happened when the Philistine
rose and came and drew near to meet David,
that David ran quickly toward the battle line
to meet the Philistine. 49 And David sent his
hand down into his bag and took from it a
stone and slung *it* and struck the Philistine
on his forehead. And the stone sank into his
forehead, so that he fell on his face to the
ground.
50 Thus David prevailed over the Philis-
tine with a sling and a stone, and he struck
the Philistine and put him to death; but
there was no sword in David's hand. 51 Then
David ran and stood over the Philistine and
took his sword and drew it out of its sheath
and put him to death and cut off his head
with it. Then the Philistines saw that their
champion was dead, so they fled. 52 But the
men of Israel and Judah arose and shouted

and pursued the Philistines as far as the
valley and to the gates of Ekron. And the
slain Philistines *lay* fallen along the way to
Shaaraim, even to Gath and Ekron. 53 Then
the sons of Israel returned from hotly pur-
suing the Philistines and plundered their
camps. 54 And David took the Philistine's
head and brought it to Jerusalem, but he
put his weapons in his tent.

55 Now when Saul saw David going out
to meet the Philistine, he said to Abner the
commander of the army, "Abner, whose
son is this young man?" And Abner said,
"By your life, O king, I do not know." 56 And
the king said, "You inquire whose son the
youth is." 57 So when David returned from
striking down the Philistine, Abner took
him and brought him before Saul with the
Philistine's head in his hand. 58 And Saul
said to him, "Whose son are you, young
man?" And David answered, "*I am* the son
of your servant Jesse the Bethlehemite."

Psalm 57:4–11

4 My soul is among lions;
I am lying down among those
who breathe forth fire,
Sons of men whose teeth are
spears and arrows
And their tongue a sharp sword.
5 Be exalted above the heavens,
O God;
Let Your glory *be* above all the earth.
6 They have set a net for my steps;
My soul is bowed down;
They dug a pit before me;
They *themselves* have fallen
into the midst of it. Selah.

7 My heart is set, O God,
my heart is set;
I will sing, yes, I will sing praises!
8 Awake, my glory!
Awake, harp and lyre!
I will awaken the dawn.
9 I will give thanks to You, O Lord,
among the peoples;
I will sing praises to You
among the nations.
10 For Your lovingkindness is
great to the heavens
And Your truth to the skies.
11 Be exalted above the heavens,
O God;
Let Your glory *be* above all the earth.

Proverbs 15:26

26 Evil thoughts are an
abomination to Yahweh,
But pleasant words are pure.

Luke 23:26–56

26 And when they led Him away, they took
hold of a man, Simon of Cyrene, coming in
from the country, and placed on him the
cross to carry behind Jesus.

27 And following Him was a large multitude
of the people, and of women who were
mourning and lamenting Him. 28 But Jesus,
turning to them, said, "Daughters of Jerusa-
lem, stop crying for Me, but cry for yourselves
and for your children. 29 For behold, the days
are coming when they will say, 'Blessed are
the barren, and the wombs that never bore,
and the breasts that never nursed.' 30 Then
they will begin TO SAY TO THE MOUNTAINS,
'FALL ON US,' AND TO THE HILLS, 'COVER US.'
31 For if they do these things when the tree
is green, what will happen when it is dry?"

32 Now two others also, who were crimi-
nals, were being led away to be put to death
with Him.

33 And when they came to the place called
The Skull, there they crucified Him and the
criminals, one on the right and the other
on the left. 34 But Jesus was saying, "Father,
forgive them; for they do not know what they
are doing." AND THEY CAST LOTS, DIVIDING UP
HIS GARMENTS AMONG THEMSELVES. 35 And the
people stood by, looking on. And even the
rulers were scoffing at Him, saying, "He saved
others; let Him save Himself if this is the
Christ of God, His Chosen One." 36 And the
soldiers also mocked Him, coming up to Him,
offering Him sour wine, 37 and saying, "If
You are the King of the Jews, save Yourself!"
38 Now there was also an inscription above
Him, "THIS IS THE KING OF THE JEWS."

39 And one of the criminals hanging *there*
was blaspheming Him, saying, "Are You not
the Christ? Save Yourself and us!" 40 But the
other answered, and rebuking him said, "Do
you not even fear God, since you are under
the same sentence of condemnation? 41 And
we indeed *are suffering* justly, for we are
receiving what we deserve for what we have
done; but this man has done nothing wrong."
42 And he was saying, "Jesus, remember me
when You come in Your kingdom!" 43 And
He said to him, "Truly I say to you, today you
shall be with Me in Paradise."

44 And it was now about the sixth hour, and darkness fell over the whole land until the ninth hour, 45 because the sun was obscured. And the veil of the sanctuary was torn in two. 46 And Jesus, crying out with a loud voice, said, "Father, INTO YOUR HANDS I COMMIT MY SPIRIT." Having said this, He breathed His last. 47 Now when the centurion saw what had happened, he *began* praising God, saying, "Certainly this man was righteous." 48 And all the crowds who came together for this spectacle, when they observed what had happened, were returning, beating their chests. 49 And all His acquaintances and the women who accompanied Him from Galilee were standing at a distance, watching these things.

50 And behold, a man named Joseph, who was a Council member, a good and righteous man 51 (he had not consented to their counsel and action), *a man* from Arimathea, a city of the Jews, who was waiting for the kingdom of God; 52 this man went to Pilate and asked for the body of Jesus. 53 And he took it down and wrapped it in a linen cloth, and laid Him in a tomb cut into the rock, where no one had ever lain. 54 It was Preparation day, and the Sabbath was about to begin. 55 Now the women, who had come with Him from Galilee, followed and beheld the tomb and how His body was laid. 56 Then after they returned, they prepared spices and perfumes.

And on the Sabbath they rested according to the commandment.

MAY 8

1 Samuel 18:1–19:24

18 Now it happened when he had finished speaking to Saul, that the soul of Jonathan was knit to the soul of David, and Jonathan loved him as his own soul. 2 And Saul took him that day and did not let him return to his father's house. 3 Then Jonathan cut a covenant with David because he loved him as his own soul. 4 And Jonathan stripped himself of the robe that was on him and gave it to David, with his armor, even his sword and his bow and his belt. 5 So David went out wherever Saul sent him *and* prospered; and Saul set him over the men of war. And it was pleasing in the eyes of all the people and also in the eyes of Saul's servants.

6 And it happened as they were coming, when David returned from striking down the Philistine, that the women came out of all the cities of Israel, singing and dancing, to meet King Saul, with tambourines, with gladness, and with musical instruments. 7 And the women sang as they were merry and said,

"Saul has struck his thousands,
And David his ten thousands."

8 Then Saul became very angry, for this saying was displeasing in his eyes; and he said, "They have ascribed to David ten thousands, but to me they have ascribed thousands. Now what more can he have but the kingdom?" 9 So Saul looked at David with suspicion from that day on.

10 Now it happened on the next day that an evil spirit from God came mightily upon Saul, and he raved in the midst of the house. Now David was playing *the harp* with his hand, as usual; and a spear *was* in Saul's hand. 11 Then Saul hurled the spear for he thought, "I will pin David to the wall." But David escaped from his presence twice.

12 And Saul was afraid of David, for Yahweh was with him but had turned away from Saul. 13 Therefore Saul turned him away from his presence and appointed him as his commander of one thousand; and he went out and came in before the people. 14 And David was prospering in all his ways, and Yahweh *was* with him. 15 Then Saul saw that he was prospering greatly, so he dreaded him. 16 But all Israel and Judah loved David, for he went out and came in before them.

17 Then Saul said to David, "Here is my older daughter Merab; I will give her to you as a wife; only be a man of valor for me and fight Yahweh's battles." For Saul thought, "My hand shall not be against him, but let the hand of the Philistines be against him." 18 But David said to Saul, "Who am I, and what is my life *or* my father's family in Israel, that I should be the king's son-in-law?" 19 So it happened at the time when Merab, Saul's daughter, should have been given to David, that she was given to Adriel the Meholathite as a wife.

20 And Michal, Saul's daughter, loved David. So they told Saul, and the thing

was right in his eyes. 21 And Saul said, "I
will give her to him that she may become
a snare to him, and that the hand of the
Philistines may be against him." Therefore
Saul said to David, "For a second time you
may be my son-in-law today." 22 Then Saul
commanded his servants, "Speak to David
secretly, saying, 'Behold, the king delights
in you, and all his servants love you; so
now, become the king's son-in-law.'" 23 So
Saul's servants spoke these words in David's
hearing. But David said, "Is it trivial in your
eyes to become the king's son-in-law, since
I am a poor man and lightly esteemed?"
24 And the servants of Saul told to him
according to these words *which* David
spoke. 25 Saul then said, "Thus you shall
say to David, 'The king does not desire any
dowry except one hundred foreskins of the
Philistines, to take vengeance on the king's
enemies.'" Now Saul planned to make David
fall by the hand of the Philistines. 26 Then
his servants told David these words, and it
was right in the eyes of David to become the
king's son-in-law. So before the days had
expired, 27 David rose up and went, he and
his men, and struck down two hundred men
among the Philistines. Then David brought
their foreskins, and they gave them in full
number to the king, that he might become
the king's son-in-law. So Saul gave him
Michal his daughter as a wife. 28 Then Saul
saw and knew that Yahweh was with David,
and *that* Michal, Saul's daughter, loved him,
29 so Saul was even more afraid of David. So
Saul was David's enemy continually.

30 Then the commanders of the Philis-
tines went out *to battle*, and it happened as
often as they went out, that David behaved
himself more insightfully than all the
servants of Saul. So his name was highly
esteemed.

19 Then Saul spoke with Jonathan his
son and all his servants to put David
to death. But Jonathan, Saul's son, greatly
delighted in David. 2 So Jonathan told David
saying, "Saul my father is seeking to put you
to death. So now, please be careful in the
morning, and stay in a secret place and hide
yourself. 3 And I will go out and stand beside
my father in the field where you are, and I
will speak with my father about you; what
I perceive, I will tell you." 4 Then Jonathan
spoke well of David to Saul his father and
said to him, "Do not let the king sin against
his servant David, since he has not sinned
against you, and since his works *have been*
very good for you. 5 For he took his life in his
hand and struck the Philistine, and Yahweh
brought about a great salvation for all Israel;
you saw *it* and were glad. Why then will
you sin against innocent blood by putting
David to death without a cause?" 6 And Saul
listened to the voice of Jonathan, and Saul
swore, "As Yahweh lives, he shall not be put
to death." 7 Then Jonathan called David, and
Jonathan told him all these words. And
Jonathan brought David to Saul, and he was
in his presence as formerly.

8 Then there was war again. And David
went out and fought with the Philistines and
struck them with a great slaughter, so that
they fled before him. 9 Now there was an evil
spirit from Yahweh on Saul as he was sitting
in his house with his spear in his hand, and
David was playing *the harp* with *his* hand.
10 And Saul tried to pin David to the wall
with the spear, but he slipped away out of
Saul's presence, so that he stuck the spear
into the wall. And David fled and escaped
that night.

11 Then Saul sent messengers to David's
house to keep watch over him, in order to
put him to death in the morning. But Michal,
David's wife, told him, saying, "If you do
not make an escape for your life tonight,
tomorrow you will be put to death." 12 So
Michal let David down through a window,
and he went out and fled and escaped.
13 Then Michal took the household idol
and laid *it* on the bed and put a quilt of
goats' *hair* at its head and covered *it* with
clothes. 14 Then Saul sent messengers to
take David, but she said, "He is sick." 15 So
Saul sent messengers to see David, saying,
"Bring him up to me on his bed, that I may
put him to death." 16 The messengers came,
and behold, the household idol *was* on the
bed with the quilt of goats' *hair* at its head.
17 So Saul said to Michal, "Why have you
deceived me like this and let my enemy go,
so that he has escaped?" And Michal said to
Saul, "He said to me, 'Let me go! Why should
I put you to death?'"

18 Now David fled and escaped and came
to Samuel at Ramah and told him all that
Saul had done to him. And he and Samuel
went and stayed in Naioth. 19 And it was told
to Saul, saying, "Behold, David is at Naioth

in Ramah." [20] Then Saul sent messengers
to take David, but they saw the company
of the prophets prophesying, with Samuel
standing *and* presiding over them. And the
Spirit of God came upon the messengers of
Saul; and they also prophesied. [21] This was
told to Saul, and he sent other messengers,
and they also prophesied. So Saul sent
messengers again the third time, and they
also prophesied. [22] Then he himself went to
Ramah and came as far as the large well that
is in Secu; and he asked and said, "Where
are Samuel and David?" And *someone* said,
"Behold, they are at Naioth in Ramah." [23] So
he went there, to Naioth in Ramah; and the
Spirit of God came upon him also, so that he
went along prophesying continually until he
came to Naioth in Ramah. [24] He also stripped
off his clothes, and he too prophesied before
Samuel and lay down naked all that day and
all that night. Therefore they say, "Is Saul
also among the prophets?"

Psalm 58:1–11

1 Do you indeed speak
righteousness, O gods?
Do you judge with equity,
O sons of men?
2 No, in heart you work
unrighteousness;
On earth you prepare a path for
the violence of your hands.
3 The wicked are estranged
from the womb;
These who speak falsehood
wander in error from birth.
4 They have venom like the
venom of a serpent;
Like a deaf cobra that stops up its ear,
5 So that it does not hear the
voice of charmers,
Or a skillful caster of spells.

6 O God, shatter their teeth
in their mouth;
Break out the fangs of the
young lions, O Yahweh.
7 Let them flow away like
water that runs off;
When he aims his arrows, let
them be as headless shafts.
8 *Let them be* as a snail which
melts away as it goes along,
Like the miscarriages of a woman
which never behold the sun.
9 Before your pots can feel
the fire of thorns
He will sweep them away
with a whirlwind, the living
and the burning alike.

10 The righteous will be glad when
he beholds the vengeance;
He will wash his feet in the
blood of the wicked.
11 And men will say, "Surely there is
a reward for the righteous;
Surely there is a God who
judges on earth!"

Proverbs 15:27–30

27 He who is greedy for gain
troubles his own house,
But he who hates gifts *of*
bribery will live.
28 The heart of the righteous
ponders how to answer,
But the mouth of the wicked
pours forth evil things.
29 Yahweh is far from the wicked,
But He hears the prayer
of the righteous.
30 Bright eyes gladden the heart;
A good report puts fat on the bones.

Luke 24:1–35

24 Now on the first day of the week, at
early dawn, they came to the tomb
bringing the spices which they had prepared.
[2] And they found the stone rolled away from
the tomb, [3] but when they entered, they did
not find the body of the Lord Jesus. [4] And it
happened that while they were perplexed
about this, behold, two men suddenly stood
near them in dazzling clothing, [5] and when
the women were terrified and bowed their
faces to the ground, *the men* said to them,
"Why do you seek the living One among
the dead? [6] He is not here, but He has risen.
Remember how He spoke to you while He
was still in Galilee, [7] saying that the Son of
Man must be delivered into the hands of
sinful men, and be crucified, and the third
day rise again." [8] And they remembered His
words, [9] and when they returned from the
tomb, they reported all these things to the
eleven and to all the rest. [10] Now Mary Mag-
dalene and Joanna and Mary the *mother* of
James and the rest of the women with them
were *there*; they were telling these things to

the apostles. 11 But these words appeared to them as nonsense, and they were not believing them. 12 But Peter stood up and ran to the tomb; and stooping to look in, he *saw the linen wrappings only. And he went away by himself, marveling at what had happened.

13 And behold, two of them were going that same day to a village named Emmaus, which was sixty stadia from Jerusalem. 14 And they were conversing with each other about all these things which had happened. 15 And it happened that while they were conversing and debating, Jesus Himself approached and was going with them. 16 But their eyes were prevented from recognizing Him. 17 And He said to them, "What are these words that you are discussing with one another as you are walking?" And they stood still, looking sad. 18 And one *of them*, named Cleopas, answered and said to Him, "Are You the only one visiting Jerusalem and unaware of the things which have happened here in these days?" 19 And He said to them, "What things?" And they said to Him, "The things about Jesus the Nazarene, who was a mighty prophet in deed and word in the sight of God and all the people, 20 and how the chief priests and our rulers delivered Him to the sentence of death, and crucified Him. 21 But we were hoping that it was He who was going to redeem Israel. Indeed, besides all this, it is the third day since these things happened. 22 But also some women among us astounded us. When they were at the tomb early in the morning, 23 and not finding His body, they came, saying that they had also seen a vision of angels who said that He was alive. 24 Some of those who were with us went to the tomb and found it just exactly as the women also said, but Him they did not see." 25 And He said to them, "O foolish ones and slow of heart to believe in all that the prophets have spoken! 26 Was it not necessary for the Christ to suffer these things and to enter into His glory?" 27 Then beginning with Moses and with all the prophets, He interpreted to them the things concerning Himself in all the Scriptures.

28 And they approached the village where they were going, and He acted as though He were going farther. 29 But they urged Him strongly, saying, "Stay with us, for it is toward evening, and the day is now nearly over." So He went in to stay with them. 30 And it happened that when He had reclined *at the table* with them, He took the bread and blessed *it*, and after breaking *it*, He was giving *it* to them. 31 Then their eyes were opened and they recognized Him. And He vanished from their sight. 32 And they said to one another, "Were not our hearts burning within us while He was speaking to us on the road, while He was opening the Scriptures to us?" 33 And they stood up that very hour and returned to Jerusalem, and found gathered together the eleven and those with them, 34 who were saying, "The Lord has really risen and has appeared to Simon." 35 And they were relating their experiences on the road and how He was recognized by them in the breaking of the bread.

MAY 9

1 Samuel 20:1–21:15

20 Then David fled from Naioth in Ramah and came and said before Jonathan, "What have I done? What is my iniquity? And what is my sin before your father, that he is seeking my life?" 2 And he said to him, "Far from it, you shall not die. Behold, my father does nothing either great or small without revealing it in my ear. So why should my father hide this thing from me? It is not so!" 3 Yet David swore again, saying, "Your father knows well that I have found favor in your sight, and he has said, 'Do not let Jonathan know this, lest he be grieved.' But truly as Yahweh lives and as your soul lives, there is hardly a step between me and death." 4 Then Jonathan said to David, "Whatever your soul says, I will do for you." 5 So David said to Jonathan, "Behold, tomorrow is the new moon, and I ought to sit down to eat with the king. But let me go, that I may hide myself in the field until the third evening. 6 If your father misses me at all, then say, 'David earnestly asked *leave* of me to run to Bethlehem his city because it is the yearly sacrifice there for the whole family.' 7 If he says, 'It is good,' your servant will have peace; but if he is very angry, know that he has decided on evil. 8 Therefore show lovingkindness to your

servant, for you have brought your servant into a covenant of Yahweh with you. But if there is iniquity in me, put me to death yourself; for why then should you bring me to your father?" 9 And Jonathan said, "Far be it from you! For if I should indeed come to know that evil has been decided by my father to come upon you, then would I not tell you about it?" 10 Then David said to Jonathan, "Who will tell me if your father answers you harshly?" 11 And Jonathan said to David, "Come, and let us go out into the field." So both of them went out to the field.

12 Then Jonathan said to David, "Yahweh, the God of Israel, *be witness*! When I have examined my father about this time tomorrow, *or* the third day, behold, if there is good *feeling* toward David, shall I not then send to you and reveal it in your ear? 13 If it please my father *to do* you harm, may Yahweh do so to Jonathan and more also, if I do not reveal it in your ear and send you away, that you may go in peace. And may Yahweh be with you as He has been with my father. 14 And if I am still alive, will you not show me the lovingkindness of Yahweh, that I may not die? 15 You shall not cut off your lovingkindness from my house forever, not even when Yahweh cuts off every one of the enemies of David from the face of the earth." 16 So Jonathan cut a *covenant* with the house of David, *saying*, "May Yahweh require *it* at the hands of David's enemies." 17 And Jonathan made David swear again because of his love for him, because he loved him as he loved his own soul.

18 Then Jonathan said to him, "Tomorrow is the new moon, and you will be missed because your seat will be missing. 19 When you have stayed for three days, you shall go down quickly and come to the place where you hid yourself on that eventful day, and you shall remain by the stone Ezel. 20 And I will shoot three arrows to the side, as though I sent them towards a target. 21 And behold, I will send the young man, *saying*, 'Go, find the arrows.' If I specifically say to the young man, 'Behold, the arrows are on this side of you, get them,' then come, for there is peace for you and no harm, as Yahweh lives. 22 But if I say to the youth, 'Behold, the arrows are beyond you,' go, for Yahweh has sent you away. 23 As for the agreement of which you and I have spoken, behold, Yahweh is between you and me forever."

24 So David hid in the field; and when the new moon came, the king sat down to eat food. 25 And the king sat on his seat as usual, the seat by the wall; then Jonathan rose up, and Abner sat down by Saul's side, but David's place was missing. 26 Nevertheless Saul did not speak anything that day, for he said, "It is an accident; he is not clean; surely *he is* not clean." 27 Now it happened the next day, the second *day* of the new moon, that David's place was missing; so Saul said to Jonathan his son, "Why has the son of Jesse not come to the meal, either yesterday or today?" 28 Jonathan then answered Saul, "David earnestly asked leave of me *to go* to Bethlehem, 29 and he said, 'Please send me *on my way*, since our family has a sacrifice in the city, and my brother has commanded me to attend. So now, if I have found favor in your sight, please let me get away that I may see my brothers.' For this reason he has not come to the king's table."

30 Then Saul's anger burned against Jonathan, and he said to him, "You son of a perverse, rebellious woman! Do I not know that you are choosing the son of Jesse to your own shame and to the shame of your mother's nakedness? 31 For as long as the son of Jesse lives on the earth, neither you nor your kingdom will be established. So now, send and bring him to me, for he must surely die." 32 But Jonathan answered Saul his father and said to him, "Why should he be put to death? What has he done?" 33 Then Saul hurled his spear at him to strike him down; so Jonathan knew that his father had decided to put David to death. 34 Then Jonathan arose from the table in burning anger and did not eat food on the second day of the new moon, for he was grieved over David because his father had dishonored him.

35 Now it happened in the morning that Jonathan went out into the field for the appointment with David, and a very young man *was* with him. 36 And he said to his young man, "Run, find now the arrows which I am about to shoot." As the young man was running, he shot an arrow past him. 37 When the young man reached the place of the arrow which Jonathan had shot, Jonathan called after the lad and said, "Is not the arrow beyond you?" 38 And Jonathan called after the young man, "Hurry, be quick, do not stay!" And Jonathan's young

man gathered up the arrow and came to his
master. 39 But the young man did not know
of anything; only Jonathan and David knew
about the matter. 40 Then Jonathan gave his
weapons to his young man and said to him,
"Go, bring *them* to the city." 41 When the
young man was gone, David rose from the
south side and fell on his face to the ground
and bowed three times. And they kissed
each other and wept together, but David
wept more. 42 And Jonathan said to David,
"Go in peace, inasmuch as we have sworn to
each other in the name of Yahweh, saying,
'Yahweh will be between me and you, and
between my seed and your seed forever.'"
Then he rose and departed, while Jonathan
went into the city.

21 Then David came to Nob to Ahimel-
ech the priest; and Ahimelech came
trembling to meet David and said to him,
"Why are you alone, and no one is with
you?" 2 And David said to Ahimelech the
priest, "The king has commanded me with a
matter and has said to me, 'Let no one know
anything about the matter on which I am
sending you and with which I have com-
manded you; and I have directed the young
men to a certain place.' 3 So now, what do
you have on hand? Give five loaves of bread
into my hand, or whatever can be found."
4 And the priest answered David and said,
"There is no ordinary bread on hand, but
there is consecrated bread; if only the young
men have kept themselves from women."
5 And David answered the priest and said to
him, "Surely women have been kept from us
as previously when I set out and the vessels
of the young men were holy, though it was
an ordinary journey; how much more then
today will their vessels be holy?" 6 So the
priest gave him consecrated *bread*; for there
was no bread there but the bread of the
Presence which was removed from before
Yahweh, in order to put hot bread *in its place*
when it was taken away.

7 Now one of the servants of Saul was
there that day, detained before Yahweh; and
his name was Doeg the Edomite, the chief
of Saul's shepherds.

8 And David said to Ahimelech, "Now is
there not a spear or a sword on hand? For I
brought neither my sword nor my weapons
in my hand because the king's matter was
urgent." 9 Then the priest said, "The sword
of Goliath the Philistine, whom you struck
down in the valley of Elah, behold, it is
wrapped in a cloth behind the ephod; if you
would take it for yourself, take *it*. For there
is no other except it here." And David said,
"There is none like it; give it to me."

10 Then David arose and fled that day
from Saul and went to Achish king of Gath.
11 But the servants of Achish said to him, "Is
this not David the king of the land? Did they
not sing of this one as they danced, saying,

'Saul has struck his thousands,
And David his ten thousands'?"

12 And David took these words to heart and
greatly feared Achish king of Gath. 13 So he
disguised his sanity in their sight and acted
insanely in their hands and scribbled on the
doors of the gate and let his saliva run down
into his beard. 14 Then Achish said to his ser-
vants, "Behold, you see the man behaving
as a madman. Why do you bring him to me?
15 Do I lack madmen, that you have brought
this one to act the madman before me? Shall
this one come into my house?"

Psalm 59:1–5

1 Deliver me from my
  enemies, O my God;
Set me *securely* on high away from
  those who rise up against me.
2 Deliver me from workers of iniquity
And save me from men of bloodshed.
3 For behold, they have lain
  in wait for my soul;
Fierce men launch an
  attack against me,
Not for my transgression nor
  for my sin, O Yahweh,
4 For no guilt of *mine*, they run and
  set themselves against me.
Arouse Yourself to meet me, and see!
5 You, O Yahweh God of hosts,
  the God of Israel,
Awake to punish all the nations;
Do not be gracious to any *who are*
  treacherous in iniquity. Selah.

Proverbs 15:31–33

31 He whose ear listens to the
  life-giving reproof
Will lodge among the wise.
32 He who neglects discipline
  despises his soul,
But he who listens to reproof
  acquires a heart *of wisdom*.

33 The fear of Yahweh is the
discipline leading to wisdom,
And before glory *comes* humility.

Luke 24:36–53

36 Now while they were telling these
things, He Himself stood in their midst and
*said to them, "Peace to you." 37 But being
startled and frightened, they were thinking
that they were seeing a spirit. 38 And He said
to them, "Why are you troubled, and why do
doubts arise in your hearts? 39 See My hands
and My feet, that it is I Myself; touch Me and
see, for a spirit does not have flesh and bones
as you see that I have." 40 And when He had
said this, He showed them His hands and His
feet. 41 And while they still were not believing
because of their joy and were *still* marveling,
He said to them, "Have you anything here to
eat?" 42 They gave Him a piece of a broiled
fish, 43 and He took it and ate *it* before them.
44 Now He said to them, "These are My
words which I spoke to you while I was
still with you, that all things which are
written about Me in the Law of Moses
and the Prophets and the Psalms must be
fulfilled." 45 Then He opened their minds
to understand the Scriptures, 46 and He
said to them, "Thus it is written, that the
Christ would suffer and rise again from the
dead the third day, 47 and that repentance
for forgiveness of sins would be proclaimed
in His name to all the nations, beginning
from Jerusalem. 48 You are witnesses of
these things. 49 And behold, I am sending
the promise of My Father upon you, but you
are to stay in the city until you are clothed
with power from on high."
50 And He led them out as far as Bethany,
and lifting up His hands, He blessed them.
51 And it happened that while He was
blessing them, He parted from them and
was carried up into heaven. 52 And they,
after worshiping Him, returned to Jerusalem
with great joy, 53 and were continually in the
temple blessing God.

MAY 10

1 Samuel 22:1–23:29

22 So David departed from there and
escaped to the cave of Adullam; and
his brothers and all his father's household
heard *of it* and went down there to him.
2 Then everyone who was in distress, and
everyone who was in debt, and everyone
who was bitter of soul, gathered to him; and
he became a commander over them. Now
there were about four hundred men with
him.
3 And David went from there to Mizpah
of Moab; and he said to the king of Moab,
"Please let my father and my mother come
and stay with you until I know what God
will do for me." 4 Then he left them with the
king of Moab; and they stayed with him all
the time that David was in the fortress. 5 And
the prophet Gad said to David, "Do not stay
in the fortress; go, and enter into the land
of Judah." So David went and entered into
the forest of Hereth.
6 Then Saul heard that David and the men
who were with him had been discovered.
Now Saul was sitting in Gibeah, under the
tamarisk tree on the height with his spear in
his hand, and all his servants were standing
around him. 7 And Saul said to his servants
who were standing around him, "Hear now,
O Benjamites! Will the son of Jesse also give
to all of you fields and vineyards? Will he
make you all commanders of thousands and
commanders of hundreds? 8 For all of you
have conspired against me so that there is
no one who reveals in my ear when my son
cuts *a covenant* with the son of Jesse, and
there is none of you who is sorry for me or
reveals in my ear that my son has caused
my servant to rise up against me to lie in
ambush, as *it is* this day." 9 Then Doeg the
Edomite, who was standing by the servants
of Saul, said, "I saw the son of Jesse coming
to Nob, to Ahimelech the son of Ahitub.
10 And he asked of Yahweh for him, gave
him provisions, and gave him the sword of
Goliath the Philistine."
11 Then the king sent someone to summon
Ahimelech the priest, the son of Ahitub, and
all his father's household, the priests who
were in Nob; and all of them came to the
king. 12 And Saul said, "Listen now, son of
Ahitub." And he answered, "Here I am, my
lord." 13 Saul then said to him, "Why have
you and the son of Jesse conspired against
me, in that you have given him bread and a
sword and have asked of God on his behalf,

so that he would rise up against me by lying
in ambush as *it is* this day?"
14 Then Ahimelech answered the king and
said, "And who among all your servants is as
faithful as David, even the king's son-in-law,
who is captain over your guard, and is hon-
ored in your house? 15 Did I *just* begin to ask
of God on his behalf today? Far be it from
me! Do not let the king impute anything to
his servant *or* to any of the household of my
father, for your servant knows nothing small
or great of this whole affair." 16 But the king
said, "You shall surely die, Ahimelech, you
and all your father's household!" 17 And the
king said to the guards who were standing
by him, "Turn around and put the priests
of Yahweh to death because their hand
also is with David and because they knew
that he was fleeing and did not reveal it in
my ears." But the servants of the king were
not willing to send forth their hands to fall
upon the priests of Yahweh. 18 Then the king
said to Doeg, "You turn around and attack
the priests." And Doeg the Edomite turned
around and attacked the priests, and he put
to death that day eighty-five men who wore
the linen ephod. 19 So he struck Nob the city
of the priests with the edge of the sword,
both men and women, infants and nursing
babies; also oxen, donkeys, and sheep *he*
struck with the edge of the sword.
20 But one son of Ahimelech the son of
Ahitub, named Abiathar, escaped and fled
after David. 21 And Abiathar told David
that Saul had killed the priests of Yahweh.
22 Then David said to Abiathar, "I knew on
that day, when Doeg the Edomite was there,
that he would surely tell Saul. It is I who
have turned against every person in your
father's household. 23 Stay with me; do not
be afraid, for he who seeks my life seeks
your life, for you are safe with me."

23 Then they told David, saying, "Behold,
the Philistines are fighting against
Keilah and are pillaging the threshing
floors." 2 So David asked of Yahweh, saying,
"Shall I go and strike these Philistines?" And
Yahweh said to David, "Go and strike the
Philistines and save Keilah." 3 But David's
men said to him, "Behold, we are afraid here
in Judah. How much more then if we go to
Keilah against the battle lines of the Philis-
tines?" 4 Then David asked of Yahweh once
more. And Yahweh answered him and said,
"Arise, go down to Keilah, for I will give the
Philistines into your hand." 5 So David and
his men went to Keilah and fought with the
Philistines; and he led away their livestock
and struck them with a great slaughter. Thus
David saved the inhabitants of Keilah.
6 Now it happened when Abiathar the
son of Ahimelech fled to David at Keilah,
that he came down *with* an ephod in his
hand. 7 Then it was told to Saul that David
had come to Keilah, so Saul said, "God has
delivered him into my hand, for he shut
himself in by entering a city with double
gates and bars." 8 Then Saul summoned all
the people for battle, to go down to Keilah
to besiege David and his men. 9 But David
knew that Saul was plotting evil against him;
so he said to Abiathar the priest, "Bring the
ephod here." 10 Then David said, "O Yahweh,
the God of Israel, Your slave has heard for
certain that Saul is seeking to come to Kei-
lah to make the city a ruin on my account.
11 Will the men of Keilah surrender me into
his hand? Will Saul come down just as Your
slave has heard? O Yahweh, the God of Israel,
I pray, tell Your slave." And Yahweh said, "He
will come down." 12 Then David said, "Will
the men of Keilah surrender me and my men
into the hand of Saul?" And Yahweh said,
"They will surrender you." 13 Then David
and his men, about six hundred, arose
and departed from Keilah, and they went
wherever they could go. Now it was told to
Saul that David had escaped from Keilah, so
he ceased going out *in pursuit*. 14 And David
stayed in the wilderness in the strongholds
and remained in the hill country in the wil-
derness of Ziph. And Saul sought him every
day, but God did not give him into his hand.
15 Then David saw that Saul had come out
to seek his life. Now David was in the wilder-
ness of Ziph at Horesh. 16 So Jonathan, Saul's
son, arose and went to David at Horesh and
strengthened his hand in God. 17 And he said
to him, "Do not be afraid, because the hand
of Saul my father will not find you, and you
will be king over Israel, and I will be second
to you; and Saul my father knows that also."
18 So the two of them cut a covenant before
Yahweh; and David stayed at Horesh while
Jonathan went to his house.
19 Then Ziphites came up to Saul at
Gibeah, saying, "Is David not hiding with
us in the strongholds at Horesh, on the
hill of Hachilah, which is on the south of

Jeshimon? 20 So now, O king, according to
all the desire of your soul to come down,
come down *here*; and our part *shall be* to
surrender him into the king's hand." 21 And
Saul said, "May you be blessed of Yahweh,
for you have had compassion on me. 22 Go
now, make more sure, and know and see
his place—where his *very* foot is—*and*
who has seen him there; for I am told that
he is very crafty. 23 So see and know about
all the hiding places where he hides himself
and return to me with certainty, and I will
go with you; and if he is in the land, I will
search him out among all the thousands of
Judah."

24 Then they arose and went to Ziph
before Saul. Now David and his men were
in the wilderness of Maon, in the Arabah
to the south of Jeshimon. 25 So Saul and his
men went to seek *him*, and they told David,
and he came down to the rock and stayed
in the wilderness of Maon. And Saul heard
it and pursued David in the wilderness of
Maon. 26 And Saul went on one side of the
mountain, and David and his men on the
other side of the mountain; and David was
hurrying to get away from Saul, but Saul and
his men were surrounding David and his
men to seize them. 27 But a messenger came
to Saul, saying, "Hurry and come, for the
Philistines have made a raid on the land."
28 So Saul returned from pursuing David and
went to meet the Philistines; therefore they
called that place the Rock of Escape. 29 Then
David went up from there and stayed in the
strongholds of Engedi.

Psalm 59:6–17

6 They return at evening,
they howl like a dog,
And go around the city.
7 Behold, they pour forth *speech*
with their mouth;
Swords are in their lips,
For, *they say*, "Who hears?"
8 But You, O Yahweh, laugh at them;
You mock all the nations.

9 *Because of* his strength I
will watch for You,
For God is my stronghold.
10 My God in His lovingkindness
will approach me;
God will let me look *triumphantly*
upon my foes.
11 Do not slay them, or my
people will forget;
Make them wander about by Your
power, and bring them down,
O Lord, our shield.
12 *On account of* the sin of their mouth
and the word of their lips,
Let them even be caught in their pride,
And on account of curses and
lies which they utter.
13 Destroy *them* in wrath, destroy
them that they may be no more;
That *men* may know that
God rules in Jacob
To the ends of the earth. Selah.
14 They return at evening,
they howl like a dog,
And go around the city.
15 They wander about for food
And growl if they are not satisfied.

16 But as for me, I shall sing
of Your strength;
And I shall joyfully sing of Your
lovingkindness in the morning,
For You have been my stronghold
And a refuge in the day of my distress.
17 O my strength, I will sing
praises to You;
For God is my stronghold, the God
who shows me lovingkindness.

Proverbs 16:1–2

16 The plans of the heart
belong to man,
But the answer of the tongue
is from Yahweh.
2 All the ways of a man are
pure in his own sight,
But Yahweh weighs the motives.

John 1:1–28

1 In the beginning was the Word, and the
Word was with God, and the Word was
God. 2 He was in the beginning with God.
3 All things came into being through Him,
and apart from Him nothing came into
being that has come into being. 4 In Him
was life, and the life was the Light of men.
5 And the Light shines in the darkness, and
the darkness did not overtake it.

6 There was a man having been sent from
God, whose name was John. 7 He came as a
witness, to bear witness about the Light, so
that all might believe through him. 8 He was

not the Light, but *he came* to bear witness about the Light.

9 There was the true Light which, coming into the world, enlightens everyone. 10 He was in the world, and the world was made through Him, and the world did not know Him. 11 He came to what was His own, and those who were His own did not receive Him. 12 But as many as received Him, to them He gave the right to become children of God, *even* to those who believe in His name, 13 who were born, not of blood nor of the will of the flesh nor of the will of man, but of God.

14 And the Word became flesh, and dwelt among us, and we beheld His glory, glory as of the only begotten from the Father, full of grace and truth. 15 John *bore witness about Him and cried out, saying, "This was He of whom I said, 'He who comes after me has been ahead of me, for He existed before me.'" 16 For of His fullness we have all received, and grace upon grace. 17 For the Law was given through Moses; grace and truth came through Jesus Christ. 18 No one has seen God at any time; the only begotten God who is in the bosom of the Father, He has explained *Him.*

19 And this is the witness of John, when the Jews sent to him priests and Levites from Jerusalem to ask him, "Who are you?" 20 And he confessed and did not deny, but confessed, "I am not the Christ." 21 And they asked him, "What then? Are you Elijah?" And he *said, "I am not." "Are you the Prophet?" And he answered, "No." 22 Therefore, they said to him, "Who are you, so that we may give an answer to those who sent us? What do you say about yourself?" 23 He said, "I am A VOICE OF ONE CRYING IN THE WILDERNESS, 'MAKE STRAIGHT THE WAY OF THE LORD,' as Isaiah the prophet said."

24 Now they had been sent from the Pharisees. 25 And they asked him, and said to him, "Why then are you baptizing, if you are not the Christ, nor Elijah, nor the Prophet?" 26 John answered them, saying, "I baptize with water, *but* among you stands One whom you do not know. 27 *This One is* He who comes after me, of whom I am not worthy to untie the strap of His sandal." 28 These things took place in Bethany beyond the Jordan, where John was baptizing.

MAY 11

1 Samuel 24:1–25:44

24 Now when Saul returned from pursuing the Philistines, he was told, saying, "Behold, David is in the wilderness of Engedi." 2 Then Saul took three thousand chosen men from all Israel and went to seek David and his men in front of the Rocks of the Wild Goats. 3 And he came to the sheepfolds on the way, where there *was* a cave; and Saul went in to relieve himself. Now David and his men were sitting in the inner recesses of the cave. 4 Then the men of David said to him, "Behold, *this is* the day of which Yahweh said to you, 'Behold, I am about to give your enemy into your hand, and you shall do to him as it seems good in your eyes.'" Then David arose and cut off the edge of Saul's robe secretly. 5 And it happened afterward that David's heart struck him because he had cut off the edge of Saul's *robe.* 6 So he said to his men, "Far be it from me because of Yahweh that I should do this thing to my lord, the anointed of Yahweh, to send forth my hand against him, since he is the anointed of Yahweh." 7 And David tore his men to pieces with *these* words and did not allow them to rise up against Saul. And Saul arose, left the cave, and went on *his* way.

8 Now afterward David arose and went out of the cave and called after Saul, saying, "My lord the king!" And when Saul looked behind him, David bowed with his face to the ground and prostrated himself. 9 And David said to Saul, "Why do you listen to the words of men, saying, 'Behold, David seeks to do you evil'? 10 Behold, this day your eyes have seen that Yahweh had given you today into my hand in the cave, and some said to kill you, but *my eye* had pity on you; and I said, 'I will not send forth my hand against my lord, for he is the anointed of Yahweh.' 11 Now, my father, see! Indeed, see the edge of your robe in my hand! For in that I cut off the edge of your robe and did not kill you, know and see that there is no evil or transgression in my hand, and I have not sinned against you, though you are lying

in wait for my life to take it. 12 May Yahweh
judge between you and me, and may Yahweh
avenge me on you; but my hand shall not
be against you. 13 As the proverb of the
ancients says, 'Out of the wicked comes
forth wickedness'; but my hand shall not
be against you. 14 After whom has the king
of Israel come out? Whom are you pursu-
ing? After a dead dog, after a single flea?
15 Therefore Yahweh be judge and execute
justice between you and me; and may He
see and plead my cause and execute justice
for me *to escape* from your hand."

16 Now it happened that when David
had finished speaking these words to
Saul, Saul said, "Is this your voice, my son
David?" Then Saul lifted up his voice and
wept. 17 And he said to David, "You are more
righteous than I; for you have dealt well with
me, while I have dealt evil with you. 18 And
you have declared today that you have done
good to me, that Yahweh surrendered me
into your hand, and *yet* you did not kill me.
19 For if a man finds his enemy, will he let
him go away safely? May Yahweh therefore
reward you with good in return for what you
have done to me this day. 20 So now, behold,
I know that you will surely be king, and that
the kingdom of Israel will be established in
your hand. 21 So now swear to me by Yahweh
that you will not cut off my seed after me
and that you will not destroy my name from
my father's household." 22 So David swore to
Saul. And Saul went to his home, but David
and his men went up to the fortress.

25 Then Samuel died; and all Israel
gathered together and lamented for
him and buried him at his house in Ramah.
And David arose and went down to the
wilderness of Paran.

2 Now *there was* a man in Maon whose
work was in Carmel; and the man was very
great, and he had three thousand sheep and
one thousand goats. And it happened, while
he was shearing his sheep in Carmel 3 (now
the man's name was Nabal, and his wife's
name was Abigail. And the woman was good
in insight and beautiful in appearance, but
the man was harsh and evil in *his* dealings,
and he was a Calebite), 4 that David heard
in the wilderness that Nabal was shearing
his sheep. 5 So David sent ten young men;
and David said to the young men, "Go up to
Carmel, come to Nabal, and greet him in my
name; 6 and thus you shall say, 'Have a long
life; peace be to you, and peace be to your
house, and peace be to all that you have. 7 So
now I have heard that you have shearers;
now your shepherds have been with us; and
we have not dishonored them, nor have they
missed anything all the days they were in
Carmel. 8 Ask your young men, and they
will tell you. Therefore let *my* young men
find favor in your eyes, for we have come
on a festive day. Please give whatever you
find at hand to your servants and to your
son, to David.'"

9 Then David's young men came and
spoke to Nabal according to all these words
in David's name. Then they waited. 10 But
Nabal answered David's servants and said,
"Who is David? And who is the son of Jesse?
There are many servants today who are each
breaking away from his master. 11 Shall I
then take my bread and my water and my
meat that I have slaughtered for my shear-
ers, and give it to men whose origin I do not
know?" 12 So David's young men went back
on their way and returned; and they came
and told him according to all these words.
13 Then David said to his men, "Each *of you*
gird on his sword." So each man girded on
his sword. And David also girded on his
sword, and about four hundred men went
up behind David, and two hundred stayed
with the baggage.

14 But one of the young men told Abigail,
Nabal's wife, saying, "Behold, David sent
messengers from the wilderness to greet our
master, and he rushed at them *angrily*. 15 Yet
the men were very good to us, and we were
not dishonored, nor did we miss anything
as long as we went about with them, while
we were in the field. 16 They were a wall to
us both by night and by day, all the time
we were with them shepherding the sheep.
17 So now, know and see what you should
do, for evil is decided against our master and
against all his household; and he is such a
vile man that no one can speak to him."

18 Then Abigail hurried and took two
hundred *loaves* of bread and two jugs of
wine and five sheep already prepared and
five seahs of roasted grain and one hundred
clusters of raisins and two hundred cakes of
figs, and loaded *them* on donkeys. 19 Then
she said to her young men, "Go on before
me; behold, I am coming after you." But she
did not tell her husband Nabal. 20 So it was

happening, as she was riding on her donkey and coming down by the hidden part of the mountain, that behold, David and his men were coming down toward her; and she met them. 21 Now David had said, "Surely for a lie I have guarded all that this *man* has in the wilderness, so that nothing was missed of all that belonged to him; and he has returned me evil for good. 22 May God do so to the enemies of David, and more also, if by morning I leave *as much as* one male of any who belong to him."

23 Then Abigail saw David; so she hurried and dismounted from her donkey and fell on her face before David and bowed herself to the ground. 24 And she fell at his feet and said, "On me alone, my lord, be the blame. And please let your maidservant speak in your ears, and listen to the words of your maidservant. 25 Please do not let my lord pay attention to this vile man, Nabal, for as his name is, so is he. Nabal is his name, and wicked foolishness is with him; but I your maidservant did not see the young men of my lord whom you sent.

26 "So now, my lord, as Yahweh lives and as your soul lives, since Yahweh has restrained you from shedding blood, and from saving yourself by your own hand, so now, let your enemies and those who seek evil against my lord, be as Nabal. 27 So now let this gift which your servant-woman has brought to my lord be given to the young men who went about with my lord. 28 Please forgive the transgression of your maidservant; for Yahweh will certainly make for my lord an enduring house because my lord is fighting the battles of Yahweh, and evil will not be found in you all your days. 29 And should anyone rise up to pursue you and to seek your life, then the life of my lord shall be bound in the bundle of the living with Yahweh your God; but the lives of your enemies He will sling out as from the hollow of a sling. 30 And it will be that when Yahweh does for my lord according to all the good that He has spoken concerning you, and appoints you ruler over Israel, 31 then this will not cause stumbling or a troubled heart to my lord, both by having shed blood without cause and by my lord having saved himself. When Yahweh deals well with my lord, then remember your maidservant."

32 Then David said to Abigail, "Blessed be Yahweh, the God of Israel, who sent you this day to meet me, 33 and blessed be your discernment, and blessed be you, who have kept me this day from bloodshed and from saving myself by my own hand. 34 Nevertheless, as Yahweh, the God of Israel, lives, who has restrained me from harming you, unless you had hurried and come to meet me, surely there would not have been left to Nabal until the morning light *as much as* one male." 35 So David received from her hand what she had brought him and said to her, "Go up to your house in peace. See, I have listened to your voice and granted your request."

36 Then Abigail came to Nabal, and behold, he was holding a feast in his house, like the feast of a king. And Nabal's heart was merry within him, for he was very drunk; so she did not tell him anything small or great until the morning light. 37 But in the morning, when the wine had gone out of Nabal, his wife told him these things, and his heart died within him so that he became *as* a stone. 38 Now it happened that about ten days later, Yahweh smote Nabal, and he died.

39 Then David heard that Nabal was dead, so he said, "Blessed be Yahweh, who has pleaded the cause of my reproach from the hand of Nabal and has kept back His servant from evil. Yahweh has also returned the evil of Nabal on his own head." Then David sent a proposal to Abigail, to take her as his wife. 40 Then the servants of David came to Abigail at Carmel and spoke to her, saying, "David has sent us to you to take you as his wife." 41 And she arose and bowed with her face to the ground and said, "Behold, your maidservant is a servant-woman to wash the feet of my lord's servants." 42 Then Abigail hurried and arose, and she rode on a donkey, with her five young women who went about with her; and she went after the messengers of David and became his wife.

43 David had also taken Ahinoam of Jezreel, and they both became his wives.

44 Now Saul had given Michal his daughter, David's wife, to Palti the son of Laish, who was from Gallim.

Psalm 60:1–5

1 O God, You have rejected us.
  You have broken us;
 You have been angry; Oh, restore us.

2 You have made the land quake,
You have split it open;
Heal its breaches, for it shakes.
3 You have caused Your people
to see hardship;
You have given us wine to drink
that causes reeling.
4 You have given a banner to
those who fear You,
In order to flee *to it* from
the bow. Selah.
5 That Your beloved may be rescued,
Save with Your right hand,
and answer us!

Proverbs 16:3

3 Commit your works to Yahweh
And your plans will be established.

John 1:29–51

29 On the next day, he *saw Jesus coming
to him and *said, "Behold, the Lamb of God
who takes away the sin of the world! 30 This
is He of whom I said, 'After me comes a man
who has been ahead of me, for He existed
before me.' 31 I did not know Him, but so
that He might be manifested to Israel, I came
baptizing with water." 32 And John bore
witness saying, "I have beheld the Spirit
descending as a dove out of heaven, and He
abided on Him. 33 And I did not know Him,
but He who sent me to baptize with water
said to me, 'The One upon whom you see
the Spirit descending and abiding on Him,
this is the One who baptizes with the Holy
Spirit.' 34 And I myself have seen, and have
borne witness that this is the Son of God."
35 On the next day, John again was
standing with two of his disciples, 36 and
he looked at Jesus as He walked, and *said,
"Behold, the Lamb of God!" 37 And the two
disciples heard him speak and followed
Jesus. 38 And when Jesus turned and noticed
them following, He *said to them, "What do
you seek?" They said to Him, "Rabbi (which
translated means Teacher), where are You
staying?" 39 He *said to them, "Come, and
you will see." So they came and saw where
He was staying; and they stayed with Him
that day. It was about the tenth hour.
40 One of the two who heard John *speak*
and followed Him, was Andrew, Simon
Peter's brother. 41 He first *found his own
brother Simon and *said to him, "We have
found the Messiah" (which translated means
Christ). 42 He brought him to Jesus. When
Jesus looked at him, He said, "You are Simon
the son of John; you shall be called Cephas"
(which is translated Peter).
43 On the next day, He desired to go into
Galilee, and He *found Philip. And Jesus
*said to him, "Follow Me." 44 Now Philip
was from Bethsaida, the city of Andrew and
Peter. 45 Philip *found Nathanael and *said
to him, "We have found Him of whom Moses
in the Law and *also* the Prophets wrote—
Jesus of Nazareth, the son of Joseph." 46 And
Nathanael said to him, "Can any good thing
come out of Nazareth?" Philip *said to him,
"Come and see." 47 Jesus saw Nathanael
coming to Him, and *said about him,
"Behold, truly an Israelite in whom there is
no deceit!" 48 Nathanael *said to Him, "From
where do You know me?" Jesus answered
and said to him, "Before Philip called you,
when you were under the fig tree, I saw
you." 49 Nathanael answered Him, "Rabbi,
You are the Son of God; You are the King of
Israel." 50 Jesus answered and said to him,
"Because I said to you that I saw you under
the fig tree, do you believe? You will see
greater things than these." 51 And He *said
to him, "Truly, truly, I say to you, you will
see THE HEAVENS OPENED AND THE ANGELS
OF GOD ASCENDING AND DESCENDING on the
Son of Man."

MAY 12

1 Samuel 26:1–27:12

26 Then the Ziphites came to Saul at
Gibeah, saying, "Is not David hiding
on the hill of Hachilah, *which is* before
Jeshimon?" 2 So Saul arose and went down
to the wilderness of Ziph, having with him
three thousand chosen men of Israel, to
search for David in the wilderness of Ziph.
3 And Saul camped in the hill of Hachilah,
which is before Jeshimon, beside the road.
Now David was staying in the wilderness,
and he saw that Saul came after him into
the wilderness. 4 So David sent out spies
and knew that Saul was certainly coming.
5 David then arose and came to the place
where Saul had camped. And David saw

the place where Saul lay, as well as Abner
the son of Ner, the commander of his army;
and Saul was lying in the circle of the camp,
and the people were camped around him.
6 Then David answered and said to
Ahimelech the Hittite and to Abishai the
son of Zeruiah, Joab's brother, saying,
"Who will go down with me to Saul in the
camp?" And Abishai said, "I will go down
with you." 7 So David and Abishai came to
the people by night, and behold, Saul lay
sleeping inside the circle of the camp with
his spear stuck in the ground at his head;
and Abner and the people were lying around
him. 8 Then Abishai said to David, "Today
God has surrendered your enemy into your
hand; so now, please let me strike him with
the spear to the ground with one stroke, and
I will not strike him the second time." 9 But
David said to Abishai, "Do not destroy him,
for who can send forth his hand against the
anointed of Yahweh and be without guilt?"
10 David also said, "As Yahweh lives, surely
Yahweh will smite him, or his day will come
that he dies, or he will go down into battle
and be swept away. 11 Yahweh forbid that
I should send forth my hand against the
anointed of Yahweh; but now please take
the spear that is at his head and the jug of
water, and let us go." 12 So David took the
spear and the jug of water from *beside* Saul's
head, and they went away, but no one saw or
knew *it*, nor did any awake, for they were all
asleep, because a sound sleep from Yahweh
had fallen on them.
13 Then David crossed over to the other
side and stood on top of the mountain at
a distance *with* a large area between them.
14 And David called to the people and to
Abner the son of Ner, saying, "Will you not
answer, Abner?" Then Abner answered and
said, "Who are you who calls to the king?"
15 So David said to Abner, "Are you not a
man? And who is like you in Israel? Why
then have you not guarded your lord the
king? For one of the people came to destroy
the king your lord. 16 This thing that you
have done is not good. As Yahweh lives, *all*
of you must surely die because you did not
keep watch over your lord, the anointed of
Yahweh. So now, see where the king's spear
is and the jug of water that was at his head."
17 Then Saul recognized David's voice and
said, "Is this your voice, my son David?"
And David said, "It is my voice, my lord the
king." 18 He also said, "Why then is my lord
pursuing his servant? For what have I done?
Or what evil is in my hand? 19 So now, please
let my lord the king listen to the words of
his servant. If Yahweh has incited you up
against me, let Him accept an offering; but
if it is men, cursed are they before Yahweh,
for they have driven me out today so that
I would have no attachment with the
inheritance of Yahweh, saying, 'Go, serve
other gods.' 20 So now, do not let my blood
fall to the ground away from the presence of
Yahweh; for the king of Israel has come out
to search for a single flea, just as one pursues
a partridge in the mountains."
21 Then Saul said, "I have sinned. Return,
my son David, for I will not harm you again
because my life was precious in your sight
this day. Behold, I have played the fool and
have committed a serious error." 22 And
David replied, "Behold the spear of the
king! Now let one of the young men come
over and take it. 23 Now Yahweh will repay
each man *for* his righteousness and his
faithfulness; for Yahweh gave you into *my*
hand today, but I was not willing to send
forth my hand against the anointed of Yah-
weh. 24 Now behold, as your life was highly
valued in my sight this day, so may my life
be highly valued in the sight of Yahweh, and
may He deliver me from all distress." 25 Then
Saul said to David, "Blessed are you, my son
David; you will both accomplish much and
surely prevail." So David went on his way,
and Saul returned to his place.

27 Then David said in his heart, "Now
I will be swept away one day by the
hand of Saul. There is nothing better for
me than that I should utterly escape into
the land of the Philistines. Saul then will
despair of searching for me anymore in all
the territory of Israel, and I will escape from
his hand." 2 So David arose and crossed over,
he and the six hundred men who were with
him, to Achish the son of Maoch, king of
Gath. 3 And David lived with Achish at Gath,
he and his men, each with his household,
even David with his two wives, Ahinoam
the Jezreelitess, and Abigail the Carmelitess,
Nabal's wife. 4 And it was told to Saul that
David had fled to Gath, so he no longer
searched for him.
5 Then David said to Achish, "If now I
have found favor in your sight, let them give

me a place in one of the cities in the country, that I may live there; for why should your servant live in the royal city with you?" 6 So Achish gave him Ziklag that day; therefore Ziklag has belonged to the kings of Judah to this day. 7 And the number of days that David lived in the country of the Philistines was a year and four months.

8 Now David and his men went up and raided the Geshurites and the Girzites and the Amalekites; for they were the inhabitants of the land from ancient times, as you come to Shur even as far as the land of Egypt. 9 And David struck the land and did not leave a man or a woman alive, and he took away the sheep, the cattle, the donkeys, the camels, and the clothing. Then he returned and came to Achish. 10 And Achish said, "Where have you made a raid today?" And David said, "Against the Negev of Judah and against the Negev of the Jerahmeelites and against the Negev of the Kenites." 11 And David did not leave a man or a woman alive to bring to Gath, saying, "Lest they tell about us, saying, 'So has David done and so *has been* his custom all the time he has lived in the country of the Philistines.'" 12 So Achish believed David, saying, "He has surely made himself odious among his people Israel; therefore he will become my servant forever."

Psalm 60:6–12

6 God has spoken in His holiness:
"I will exult, I will portion out
Shechem and measure out
the valley of Succoth.
7 "Gilead is Mine, and Manasseh is Mine;
Ephraim also is the helmet of My head;
Judah is My scepter.
8 "Moab is My washbowl;
Over Edom I shall throw My shoe;
Make a loud shout, O Philistia,
because of Me!"

9 Who will bring me into
the fortified city?
Who will lead me to Edom?
10 Have You Yourself, O God,
not rejected us?
And will You, O God, not go
forth with our armies?
11 Oh give us help against the adversary,
For salvation by man is worthless.
12 Through God we shall do valiantly,
And it is He who will tread
down our adversaries.

Proverbs 16:4–5

4 Yahweh has made everything
for its own purpose,
Even the wicked for the day of evil.
5 Everyone who is proud in heart is
an abomination to Yahweh;
Assuredly, he will not be unpunished.

John 2:1–25

2 And on the third day there was a wedding in Cana of Galilee, and the mother of Jesus was there; 2 and both Jesus and His disciples were invited to the wedding. 3 And when the wine ran out, the mother of Jesus *said to Him, "They have no wine." 4 And Jesus *said to her, "Woman, what do I have to do with you? My hour has not yet come." 5 His mother *said to the servants, "Whatever He says to you, do *it*." 6 Now there were six stone water jars set there for the Jewish custom of purification, containing two or three measures each. 7 Jesus *said to them, "Fill the water jars with water." So they filled them up to the brim. 8 And He *said to them, "Draw *some* out now and take it to the headwaiter." So they took it *to him*. 9 Now when the headwaiter tasted the water which had become wine, and did not know where it came from (but the servants who had drawn the water knew), the headwaiter *called the bridegroom, 10 and *said to him, "Every man serves the good wine first, and when *the people* have drunk freely, *then* the inferior *wine*; *but* you have kept the good wine until now." 11 Jesus did this in Cana of Galilee as the beginning of *His* signs, and manifested His glory, and His disciples believed in Him.

12 After this He went down to Capernaum, He and His mother and *His* brothers and His disciples; and they stayed there a few days.

13 And the Passover of the Jews was near, and Jesus went up to Jerusalem. 14 And He found in the temple those who were selling oxen and sheep and doves, and the money changers seated *at their tables*. 15 And He made a scourge of cords, and drove *them* all out of the temple, with the sheep and the oxen; and He poured out the coins of the money changers and overturned their tables; 16 and to those who were selling the doves He said, "Take these things away;

stop making My Father's house a place of
business." 17 His disciples remembered
that it was written, "ZEAL FOR YOUR HOUSE
WILL CONSUME ME." 18 The Jews then said to
Him, "What sign do You show us as your
authority for doing these things?" 19 Jesus
answered them, "Destroy this sanctuary,
and in three days I will raise it up." 20 The
Jews then said, "It took forty-six years to
build this sanctuary, and will You raise it
up in three days?" 21 But He was speaking
about the sanctuary of His body. 22 So when
He was raised from the dead, His disciples
remembered that He said this; and they
believed the Scripture and the word which
Jesus had spoken.

23 Now when He was in Jerusalem at the
Passover, during the feast, many believed in
His name, when they saw His signs which
He was doing. 24 But Jesus, on His part, was
not entrusting Himself to them, for He knew
all men, 25 and because He had no need that
anyone bear witness concerning man, for
He Himself knew what was in man.

MAY 13

1 Samuel 28:1–25

28 Now it happened in those days that
the Philistines gathered their armed
camps for war, to fight against Israel. And
Achish said to David, "Know assuredly that
you will go out with me in the camp, you and
your men." 2 And David said to Achish, "Very
well, you shall know what your servant can
do." So Achish said to David, "Very well, I
will make you my bodyguard for life."

3 Now Samuel was dead, and all Israel had
lamented for him and buried him in Ramah,
his own city. And Saul had removed from
the land those who were mediums and spir-
itists. 4 So the Philistines gathered together
and came and camped in Shunem; and
Saul gathered all Israel together, and they
camped in Gilboa. 5 Saul saw the camp of
the Philistines and was afraid and his heart
trembled greatly. 6 So Saul asked of Yahweh,
but Yahweh did not answer him, either by
dreams or by Urim or by prophets. 7 So Saul
said to his servants, "Seek for me a woman
who is a medium, that I may go to her and
inquire of her." And his servants said to him,
"Behold, there is a woman who is a medium
at En-dor."

8 Then Saul disguised himself and put on
other clothes, and he went, he and two men
with him, and they came to the woman by
night; and he said, "Divine for me, please,
and bring up for me whom I shall say to
you." 9 But the woman said to him, "Behold,
you know what Saul has done, how he has
cut off those who are mediums and spiritists
from *the land*. Why are you then laying a
snare for my life to bring about my death?"
10 Then Saul swore to her by Yahweh, saying,
"As Yahweh lives, no punishment shall come
upon you for this thing." 11 Then the woman
said, "Whom shall I bring up for you?" And
he said, "Bring up Samuel for me." 12 And
the woman saw Samuel and cried out with
a loud voice; and the woman spoke to Saul,
saying, "Why have you deceived me? For
you are Saul." 13 And the king said to her,
"Do not be afraid; but what do you see?"
And the woman said to Saul, "I see a divine
being coming up out of the earth." 14 And
he said to her, "What is his form?" And she
said, "An old man is coming up, and he is
wrapped with a robe." And Saul knew that
it was Samuel, and he bowed with his face
to the ground and prostrated himself.

15 Then Samuel said to Saul, "Why have
you disturbed me by bringing me up?" And
Saul answered, "I am greatly distressed, for
the Philistines are waging war against me,
and God has turned away from me and no
longer answers me, either by the hand of
the prophets or by dreams; therefore I have
called you, that you may make known to
me what I should do." 16 And Samuel said,
"Why then do you ask me, since Yahweh has
turned away from you and has become your
adversary? 17 So Yahweh has done accord-
ingly as He spoke by my hand, for Yahweh
has torn the kingdom out of your hand and
given it to your neighbor, to David. 18 As you
did not listen to the voice of Yahweh and did
not execute His burning anger on Amalek,
so Yahweh has done this thing to you this
day. 19 Moreover Yahweh will also give over
Israel along with you into the hands of the
Philistines, therefore tomorrow you and
your sons will be with me. Indeed Yahweh
will give over the camp of Israel into the
hands of the Philistines!"

20 Then Saul quickly fell full length upon
the ground and was very afraid because
of the words of Samuel; also there was no
strength in him, for he had eaten no food all
day and all night. 21 And the woman came to
Saul and saw that he was terrified and said to
him, "Behold, your servant-woman has lis-
tened to your voice, and I have taken my life
in my hand and have listened to your words
which you spoke to me. 22 So now also, please
listen to the voice of your servant-woman,
and let me set a piece of bread before you that
you may eat and have strength when you go
on *your* way." 23 But he refused and said, "I
will not eat." However, his servants together
with the woman urged him, and he listened
to them. So he arose from the ground and sat
on the bed. 24 And the woman had a fattened
calf in the house, and she quickly sacrificed
it; and she took flour, kneaded it, and baked
unleavened bread from it. 25 And she brought
it before Saul and his servants, and they ate.
Then they arose and went away that night.

Psalm 61:1–4

1 Hear my cry of lamentation, O God;
Give heed to my prayer.
2 From the end of the earth I call to
You when my heart is faint;
Lead me to the rock that
is higher than I.
3 For You have been a refuge for me,
A tower of strength before the enemy.
4 Let me sojourn in Your tent forever;
Let me take refuge in the shelter of
Your wings. Selah.

Proverbs 16:6

6 By lovingkindness and truth
iniquity is atoned for,
And by the fear of Yahweh one
turns away from evil.

John 3:1–15

3 Now there was a man of the Pharisees,
named Nicodemus, a ruler of the Jews;
2 this man came to Jesus by night and said
to Him, "Rabbi, we know that You have
come from God *as* a teacher; for no one
can do these signs that You do unless God
is with him." 3 Jesus answered and said to
him, "Truly, truly, I say to you, unless one
is born again he cannot see the kingdom
of God."

4 Nicodemus *said to Him, "How can a
man be born when he is old? Can he enter
a second time into his mother's womb and
be born?" 5 Jesus answered, "Truly, truly,
I say to you, unless one is born of water
and the Spirit he cannot enter into the
kingdom of God. 6 That which has been
born of the flesh is flesh, and that which
has been born of the Spirit is spirit. 7 Do
not marvel that I said to you, 'You must
be born again.' 8 The wind blows where it
wishes and you hear its sound, but do not
know where it comes from and where it is
going; so is everyone who has been born
of the Spirit."

9 Nicodemus answered and said to
Him, "How can these things be?" 10 Jesus
answered and said to him, "Are you the
teacher of Israel and do not understand
these things? 11 Truly, truly, I say to you, we
speak of what we know and bear witness of
what we have seen, and you do not accept
our witness. 12 If I told you earthly things
and you do not believe, how will you believe
if I tell you heavenly things? 13 And no one
has ascended into heaven, but He who
descended from heaven, the Son of Man.
14 And as Moses lifted up the serpent in the
wilderness, even so must the Son of Man be
lifted up; 15 so that whoever believes will in
Him have eternal life.

The shortest road to an understanding of the Bible is the acceptance of the fact that God is speaking in every line.

— DONALD GREY BARNHOUSE

MAY 14

1 Samuel 29:1–31:13

29 Then the Philistines gathered
together all their camps to Aphek,
while the Israelites were camping by the
spring which is in Jezreel. 2 And the lords
of the Philistines were proceeding on by
hundreds and by thousands, and David
and his men were proceeding on in the
rear with Achish. 3 Then the commanders
of the Philistines said, "What *are* these
Hebrews *doing here*?" And Achish said to
the commanders of the Philistines, "Is this
not David, the servant of Saul the king of
Israel, who has been with me these days,
or *rather* these years, and I have found no
fault in him from the day he deserted *to me*
to this day?" 4 But the commanders of the
Philistines were angry with him, and the
commanders of the Philistines said to him,
"Make the man return, that he may return to
his place where you have assigned him, and
do not let him go down to battle with us, or
in the battle he may become an adversary
to us. For with what could this *man* make
himself acceptable to his lord? *Would it* not
be with the heads of these men? 5 Is this not
David, of whom they sing in the dances,
saying,

'Saul has struck his thousands,
And David his ten thousands'?"

6 Then Achish called David and said
to him, "*As* Yahweh lives, you *have been*
upright, and your going out and your com-
ing in with me in the camp are pleasing in
my sight; for I have not found evil in you
from the day of your coming to me to this
day. Nevertheless, you are not pleasing in
the sight of the lords. 7 So now, return and
go in peace, that you may not do evil in the
sight of the lords of the Philistines." 8 And
David said to Achish, "But what have I done?
And what have you found in your servant
from the day when I came before you to this
day, that I may not go and fight against the
enemies of my lord the king?" 9 But Achish
answered and said to David, "I know that
you are pleasing in my sight, like an angel
of God; nevertheless the commanders of
the Philistines have said, 'He must not go up
with us to the battle.' 10 So now, arise early in
the morning with the servants of your lord
who have come with you, and as soon as you
have arisen early in the morning and have
light, go." 11 So David arose early, he and his
men, to go in the morning to return to the
land of the Philistines. And the Philistines
went up to Jezreel.

30 Then it happened when David and
his men came to Ziklag on the third
day, that the Amalekites had made a raid
on the Negev and on Ziklag and had struck
Ziklag and burned it with fire; 2 and they
took captive the women *and all* who were
in it, both small and great—they did not put
anyone to death—and carried *them* off and
went their way. 3 Then David and his men
came to the city, and behold, it was burned
with fire, and their wives and their sons and
their daughters had been taken captive. 4 So
David and the people who were with him
lifted their voices and wept until there was
no strength in them to weep. 5 Now David's
two wives had been taken captive, Ahinoam
the Jezreelitess and Abigail the widow of
Nabal the Carmelite. 6 Moreover David
was greatly distressed because the people
said to stone him, for all the people were
embittered, each one because of his sons
and his daughters. But David strengthened
himself in Yahweh his God.

7 Then David said to Abiathar the priest,
the son of Ahimelech, "Please bring the
ephod near to me." So Abiathar brought the
ephod near to David. 8 And David asked of
Yahweh, saying, "Shall I pursue this band?
Shall I overtake them?" And He said to him,
"Pursue, for you will surely overtake them,
and you will surely deliver *all*." 9 So David
went, he and the six hundred men who were
with him, and they came to the brook Besor,
where those left behind remained. 10 But
David pursued, he and four hundred men,
for two hundred who were too exhausted
to cross the brook Besor remained *behind*.

11 Then they found an Egyptian in the
field and brought him to David and gave
him bread, and he ate, and they provided
him water to drink. 12 And they gave him a
piece of fig cake and two clusters of raisins,
and he ate; then his spirit revived. For he
had not eaten bread or drunk water for three
days and three nights. 13 And David said to
him, "To whom do you belong? And where

are you from?" And he said, "I am a young man of Egypt, a slave of an Amalekite; and my master forsook me when I fell sick three days ago. 14 We made a raid on the Negev of the Cherethites and on that which belongs to Judah and on the Negev of Caleb, and we burned Ziklag with fire." 15 Then David said to him, "Will you bring me down to this band?" And he said, "Swear to me by God that you will not put me to death or surrender me into the hands of my master, and I will bring you down to this band."

16 So he brought him down, and behold, they were spread over all the land, eating and drinking and celebrating because of all the great spoil that they had taken from the land of the Philistines and from the land of Judah. 17 Then David struck them down from the twilight until the evening of the next day; and not a man of them escaped, except four hundred young men who rode on camels and fled. 18 So David delivered all that the Amalekites had taken and delivered his two wives. 19 Indeed nothing of theirs was missing, whether small or great, sons or daughters, spoil or anything that they had taken for themselves; David brought *it* all back. 20 And David took all the sheep and the cattle *which the people* drove ahead of the *other* livestock, and they said, "This is David's spoil."

21 Then David came to the two hundred men who were too exhausted to follow David, who had also remained at the brook Besor, and they went out to meet David and to meet the people who were with him, and David approached the people and greeted them. 22 Then all the evil and vile men among those who went with David said, "Because they did not go with us, we will not give them any of the spoil that we have delivered, except to every man his wife and his children, that they may lead *them* away and depart." 23 Then David said, "You must not do so, my brothers, with what Yahweh has given us, who has kept us and given into our hand the band that came against us. 24 And who will listen to you in this matter? For as is the portion of the one who goes down to the battle, so shall the portion be of the one who remains by the baggage; they shall be apportioned together." 25 So it has been from that day forward, that he made it a statute and a judgment for Israel to this day.

26 Then David came to Ziklag and sent *some* of the spoil to the elders of Judah, to his friends, saying, "Behold, a gift for you from the spoil of the enemies of Yahweh: 27 to those who were in Bethel, and to those who were in Ramoth of the Negev, and to those who were in Jattir, 28 and to those who were in Aroer, and to those who were in Siphmoth, and to those who were in Eshtemoa, 29 and to those who were in Racal, and to those who were in the cities of the Jerahmeelites, and to those who were in the cities of the Kenites, 30 and to those who were in Hormah, and to those who were in Bor-ashan, and to those who were in Athach, 31 and to those who were in Hebron, and to all the places where David himself and his men went about."

31 Now the Philistines were fighting against Israel, and the men of Israel fled from before the Philistines and fell slain on Mount Gilboa. 2 And the Philistines closely pursued Saul and his sons; and the Philistines struck down Jonathan and Abinadab and Malchi-shua, the sons of Saul. 3 And the battle became heavy against Saul, and the archers hit him; and he was badly wounded by the archers. 4 Then Saul said to his armor bearer, "Draw your sword and pierce me through with it, lest these uncircumcised come and pierce me through and abuse me." But his armor bearer was not willing, for he was greatly afraid. So Saul took his sword and fell on it. 5 Then his armor bearer saw that Saul was dead, so he also fell on his sword and died with him. 6 Thus Saul died with his three sons, his armor bearer, and all his men on that day together.

7 Then the men of Israel who were on the other side of the valley, with those who were beyond the Jordan, saw that the men of Israel had fled and that Saul and his sons were dead. So they forsook the cities and fled; and the Philistines came and lived in them.

8 Now it happened on the next day, that the Philistines came to strip the slain, and they found Saul and his three sons fallen on Mount Gilboa. 9 Then they cut off his head and stripped off his weapons and sent *them* all around the land of the Philistines, to proclaim the good news to the house of their idols and to the people. 10 And they placed

his weapons in the house of Ashtaroth and
fastened his body to the wall of Beth-shan.
11 Then the inhabitants of Jabesh-gilead
heard what the Philistines had done to Saul,
12 so all the valiant men arose and walked
all night, and took the body of Saul and the
bodies of his sons from the wall of Beth-
shan, and they came to Jabesh and burned
them there. 13 And they took their bones
and buried them under the tamarisk tree
at Jabesh, and fasted seven days.

Psalm 61:5–8

5 For You, O God, have heard
  my vows;
You have given *me* the inheritance
  of those who fear Your name.
6 You will add days to the king's life;
His years will be from
  generation to generation.
7 He will sit enthroned
  before God forever;
Appoint lovingkindness and truth
  that they may guard him.
8 So I will sing praise to Your
  name forever,
As I pay my vows day by day.

Proverbs 16:7–9

7 When a man's ways are
  pleasing to Yahweh,
He makes even his enemies to
  be at peace with him.
8 Better is a little with righteousness
Than great produce with injustice.
9 The heart of man plans his way,
But Yahweh directs his steps.

John 3:16–36

16 "For God so loved the world, that He
gave His only begotten Son, that whoever
believes in Him shall not perish, but have
eternal life. 17 For God did not send the Son
into the world to judge the world, but that
the world might be saved through Him. 18 He
who believes in Him is not judged; he who
does not believe has been judged already,
because he has not believed in the name of
the only begotten Son of God. 19 And this is
the judgment, that the Light has come into
the world, and men loved the darkness
rather than the Light, for their deeds were
evil. 20 For everyone who does evil hates the
Light, and does not come to the Light lest his
deeds be exposed. 21 But he who practices
the truth comes to the Light, so that his
deeds may be manifested as having been
done by God."

22 After these things Jesus and His
disciples came into the land of Judea, and
there He was spending time with them and
baptizing. 23 And John also was baptizing in
Aenon near Salim, because there was much
water there; and *people* were coming and
were being baptized— 24 for John had not
yet been thrown into prison.

25 Therefore there arose a debate between
John's disciples and a Jew about purification.
26 And they came to John and said to him,
"Rabbi, He who was with you beyond the
Jordan, to whom you have borne witness,
behold, He is baptizing and all are coming
to Him." 27 John answered and said, "A man
can receive nothing unless it has been given
him from heaven. 28 You yourselves are my
witnesses that I said, 'I am not the Christ,'
but, 'I have been sent ahead of Him.' 29 He
who has the bride is the bridegroom; but
the friend of the bridegroom, who stands
and hears him, rejoices greatly because of
the bridegroom's voice. So this joy of mine
has been made full. 30 He must increase, but
I must decrease.

31 "He who comes from above is above
all, he who is of the earth is from the earth
and speaks of the earth. He who comes from
heaven is above all. 32 What He has seen
and heard, of that He bears witness; and
no one receives His witness. 33 He who has
received His witness has set his seal to *this*,
that God is true. 34 For He whom God has
sent speaks the words of God; for He gives
the Spirit without measure. 35 The Father
loves the Son and has given all things into
His hand. 36 He who believes in the Son has
eternal life; but he who does not obey the
Son will not see life, but the wrath of God
abides on him."

MAY 15

2 Samuel 1:1–2:32

1 Now it happened after the death of Saul,
that David returned from striking down
the Amalekites. Then David remained two
days in Ziklag. 2 Now it happened that on
the third day, behold, a man came out of the
camp from Saul. And his clothes were torn
and dust was on his head. And it happened
when he came to David, that he fell to the
ground and prostrated himself. 3 Then David
said to him, "From where do you come?"
And he said to him, "I have escaped from
the camp of Israel." 4 And David said to him,
"How did things go? Tell me now." And he
said, "The people have fled from the battle,
and also many of the people have fallen and
are dead; and Saul and Jonathan his son are
dead also." 5 So David said to the young man
who told him, "How do you know that Saul
and his son Jonathan are dead?" 6 And the
young man who told him said, "By chance
I happened to be on Mount Gilboa, and
behold, Saul was leaning on his spear. And
behold, the chariots and the horsemen
pursued him closely. 7 Then he turned *to
look* behind him, and he saw me and called
to me. And I said, 'Here I am.' 8 And he said
to me, 'Who are you?' And I answered him,
'I am an Amalekite.' 9 Then he said to me,
'Please stand beside me and put me to death,
for agony has seized me because my life still
lingers in me.' 10 So I stood beside him and
put him to death, because I knew that he
could not live after he had fallen. And I took
the crown which *was* on his head and the
bracelet which *was* on his arm, and I have
brought them here to my lord."

11 Then David took hold of his clothes and
tore them, and *so* also *did* all the men who
were with him. 12 And they lamented and
wept and fasted until evening for Saul and
his son Jonathan and for the people of Yah-
weh and the house of Israel, because they
had fallen by the sword. 13 And David said
to the young man who told him, "Where
are you from?" And he answered, "I am the
son of a sojourner, an Amalekite." 14 Then
David said to him, "How is it you were not
afraid to send forth your hand to destroy the
anointed of Yahweh?" 15 And David called
one of the young men and said, "Approach
and fall upon him." So he struck him and
he died. 16 And David said to him, "Your
blood is on your head, for your mouth has
answered against you, saying, 'I have put the
anointed of Yahweh to death.'"

17 Then David chanted with this *funeral*
lament over Saul and Jonathan his son,
18 and he told *them* to teach the sons of
Judah *the song of* the bow; behold, it is
written in the book of Jashar.

19 "Your beauty, O Israel, is slain
on your high places!
How have the mighty fallen!
20 "Tell *it* not in Gath,
Proclaim it not in the
streets of Ashkelon,
Lest the daughters of the
Philistines be glad,
Lest the daughters of the
uncircumcised exult.
21 "O mountains of Gilboa,
Let not dew or rain be on you,
nor fields of offerings;
For there the shield of the
mighty was defiled,
The shield of Saul, not
anointed with oil.
22 "From the blood of the slain,
from the fat of the mighty,
The bow of Jonathan did not turn back,
And the sword of Saul did
not return empty.
23 "Saul and Jonathan, beloved
and pleasant in their life,
And in their death they
were not separated;
They were swifter than eagles,
They were mightier than lions.
24 "O daughters of Israel, weep over Saul,
Who clothed you luxuriously
in scarlet,
Who put ornaments of gold
on your clothing.
25 "How have the mighty fallen in
the midst of the battle!
Jonathan is slain on your high places.
26 "I am distressed for you, my
brother Jonathan;
You have been very pleasant to me.
Your love to me was more wonderful
Than the love of women.
27 "How have the mighty fallen,
And the weapons of war perished!"

2 Now it happened afterwards that David asked of Yahweh, saying, "Shall I go up to one of the cities of Judah?" And Yahweh said to him, "Go up." So David said, "Where shall I go up?" And He said, "To Hebron." 2 So David went up there, and his two wives also, Ahinoam the Jezreelitess and Abigail the wife of Nabal the Carmelite. 3 And David brought up his men who *were* with him, each with his household; and they lived in the cities of Hebron. 4 Then the men of Judah came and there anointed David king over the house of Judah.

And they told David, saying, "It was the men of Jabesh-gilead who buried Saul." 5 And David sent messengers to the men of Jabesh-gilead, and said to them, "May you be blessed of Yahweh because you have shown this lovingkindness with your lord, with Saul, and have buried him. 6 So now, may Yahweh show lovingkindness and truth to you; and I also will show this goodness to you, because you have done this thing. 7 So now, let your hands be strong and be valiant; for Saul your lord is dead, and also the house of Judah has anointed me king over them."

8 Now Abner the son of Ner, commander of Saul's army, had taken Ish-bosheth the son of Saul and brought him over to Mahanaim. 9 And he made him king over Gilead, over the Ashurites, over Jezreel, over Ephraim, and over Benjamin, even over all Israel. 10 Ish-bosheth, Saul's son, was forty years old when he became king over Israel, and he was king for two years. The house of Judah, however, followed David. 11 And the time that David was king in Hebron over the house of Judah was seven years and six months.

12 Now Abner the son of Ner, went out from Mahanaim to Gibeon with the servants of Ish-bosheth the son of Saul. 13 And Joab the son of Zeruiah and the servants of David went out and met them by the pool of Gibeon; and they sat down, one on the one side of the pool and the other on the other side of the pool. 14 Then Abner said to Joab, "Now let the young men arise and hold a contest before us." And Joab said, "Let them arise." 15 So they arose and went over by count, twelve for Benjamin and Ish-bosheth the son of Saul, and twelve of the servants of David. 16 And each one of them seized his opponent by the head and *thrust* his sword in his opponent's side; so they fell down together. Therefore that place was called Helkath-hazzurim, which is in Gibeon. 17 And that day the battle was very severe, and Abner and the men of Israel were defeated before the servants of David.

18 Now the three sons of Zeruiah were there, Joab and Abishai and Asahel; and Asahel *was as* swift-footed as one of the gazelles which is in the field. 19 And Asahel pursued Abner and did not turn to the right or to the left from following Abner. 20 Then Abner turned *to look* behind him and said, "Is that you, Asahel?" And he answered, "It is I." 21 So Abner said to him, "Turn to your right or to your left, and seize one of the young men for yourself, and take for yourself his spoil." But Asahel was not willing to turn aside from following him. 22 And Abner repeated again to Asahel, "Turn aside from following me. Why should I strike you to the ground? How then could I lift up my face to your brother Joab?" 23 However, he refused to turn aside; therefore Abner struck him in the belly with the butt end of the spear, so that the spear came out at his back. And he fell there and died on the spot. And it happened that all who came to the place where Asahel had fallen and died, stood still.

24 But Joab and Abishai pursued Abner. Now the sun was going down, and they came to the hill of Ammah, which is in front of Giah by the way of the wilderness of Gibeon. 25 And the sons of Benjamin gathered together behind Abner and became one band, and they stood on the top of a certain hill. 26 Then Abner called to Joab and said, "Shall the sword devour forever? Do you not know that it will be bitter in the end? How long will you refrain from telling the people to turn back from following their brothers?" 27 And Joab said, "As God lives, if you had not spoken, surely then the people would have *only* gone away in the morning, each from following his brother." 28 So Joab blew the trumpet; and all the people stood still and pursued Israel no longer, nor did they continue to fight anymore. 29 But Abner and his men then went through the Arabah all that night; so they crossed the Jordan, walked all morning, and came to Mahanaim.

30 Now Joab returned from following Abner. And he had gathered all the people together, and nineteen of David's servants besides Asahel were missing. 31 But the

servants of David had struck down many
of Benjamin and Abner's men, *so that* 360
men died. 32 And they took up Asahel and
buried him in his father's tomb which was
in Bethlehem. Then Joab and his men went
all night until the day dawned at Hebron.

Psalm 62:1–4

1 Surely my soul *waits* in silence for God;
From Him is my salvation.
2 Surely He is my rock and my salvation,
My stronghold; I shall not
be greatly shaken.

3 How long will you assail a man,
That you may murder *him*, all of you,
Like a leaning wall, like a
fence thrust down?
4 Surely they have counseled to thrust
him down from his high position;
They find pleasure in falsehood;
They bless with their mouth,
But inwardly they curse. Selah.

Proverbs 16:10–12

10 A divine decision is in the
lips of the king;
His mouth should not err in judgment.
11 A just balance and scales
belong to Yahweh;
All the weights of the bag are His work.
12 It is an abomination for kings
to commit wickedness,
For in righteousness a
throne is established.

John 4:1–30

4 Therefore when Jesus knew that the
Pharisees had heard that Jesus was mak-
ing and baptizing more disciples than John
2 (although Jesus Himself was not baptizing,
but His disciples *were*), 3 He left Judea and
went away again into Galilee. 4 And He had
to pass through Samaria. 5 So He *came to
a city of Samaria called Sychar, near the
field that Jacob gave to his son Joseph;
6 and Jacob's well was there. So Jesus, being
wearied from His journey, was sitting thus
by the well. It was about the sixth hour.
7 A woman of Samaria *came to draw water.
Jesus *said to her, "Give Me a drink." 8 For His
disciples had gone away into the city to buy
food. 9 Therefore the Samaritan woman *said
to Him, "How do You, being a Jew, ask for a
drink from me, being a Samaritan woman?"
(For Jews have no dealings with Samaritans.)
10 Jesus answered and said to her, "If you knew
the gift of God, and who it is who says to you,
'Give Me a drink,' you would have asked Him,
and He would have given you living water."
11 She *said to Him, "Sir, You have nothing
to draw with and the well is deep. Where
then do You get that living water? 12 Are You
greater than our father Jacob, who gave us this
well, and drank of it himself and his sons and
his cattle?" 13 Jesus answered and said to her,
"Everyone who drinks of this water will thirst
again; 14 but whoever drinks of the water that
I will give him will never thirst—ever; but the
water that I will give him will become in him
a well of water springing up to eternal life."
15 The woman *said to Him, "Sir, give
me this water, so I will not be thirsty nor
come *back* here to draw." 16 He *said to
her, "Go, call your husband and come *back*
here." 17 The woman answered and said, "I
have no husband." Jesus *said to her, "You
have correctly said, 'I have no husband';
18 for you had five husbands, and the one
you now have is not your husband; this
you have said truly." 19 The woman *said
to Him, "Sir, I see that You are a prophet.
20 Our fathers worshiped on this mountain,
and you *people* say that in Jerusalem is the
place where men ought to worship." 21 Jesus
*said to her, "Woman, believe Me, an hour is
coming when neither in this mountain nor
in Jerusalem will you worship the Father.
22 You worship what you do not know; we
worship what we know, for salvation is from
the Jews. 23 But an hour is coming, and now
is, when the true worshipers will worship
the Father in spirit and truth; for such people
the Father seeks to be His worshipers. 24 God
is spirit, and those who worship Him must
worship in spirit and truth." 25 The woman
*said to Him, "I know that Messiah is coming
(He who is called Christ); when He comes,
He will declare all things to us." 26 Jesus *said
to her, "I who speak to you am *He*."
27 And at this point His disciples came,
and they were marveling that He was speak-
ing with a woman, yet no one said, "What
do You seek?" or, "Why are You speaking
with her?" 28 So the woman left her water
jar, and went into the city and *said to the
men, 29 "Come, see a man who told me all
the things that I *have* done; is this not the
Christ?" 30 They went out of the city, and
were coming to Him.

MAY 16

2 Samuel 3:1–4:12

3 Now the war between the house of Saul and the house of David was long; and David grew steadily stronger, but the house of Saul grew weaker continually.

2 And sons were born to David at Hebron: his firstborn was Amnon, by Ahinoam the Jezreelitess; 3 and his second, Chileab, by Abigail the wife of Nabal the Carmelite; and the third, Absalom the son of Maacah, the daughter of Talmai king of Geshur; 4 and the fourth, Adonijah the son of Haggith; and the fifth, Shephatiah the son of Abital; 5 and the sixth, Ithream, by David's wife Eglah. These were born to David at Hebron.

6 Now it happened, while there was war between the house of Saul and the house of David that Abner was making himself strong in the house of Saul. 7 Now Saul had a concubine whose name was Rizpah, the daughter of Aiah; and Ish-bosheth said to Abner, "Why have you gone in to my father's concubine?" 8 Then Abner was very angry over the words of Ish-bosheth and said, "Am I a dog's head that belongs to Judah? Today I show lovingkindness to the house of Saul your father, to his brothers and to his friends, and have not delivered you into the hands of David; and yet today you charge me with a guilt concerning the woman. 9 May God do so to Abner, and more also, if as Yahweh has sworn to David, I do not do this for him, 10 to transfer the kingdom from the house of Saul and to establish the throne of David over Israel and over Judah, from Dan even to Beersheba." 11 And he could no longer respond a word to Abner, because he was afraid of him.

12 Then Abner sent messengers to David in his place, saying, "Whose is the land? Cut your covenant with me, and behold, my hand shall be with you to turn all Israel over to you." 13 And he said, "Good! I will cut a covenant with you, but I ask one thing of you, namely, you shall not see my face unless you first bring Michal, Saul's daughter, when you come to see my face." 14 So David sent messengers to Ish-bosheth, Saul's son, saying, "Give me my wife Michal, to whom I was betrothed for one hundred foreskins of the Philistines." 15 And Ish-bosheth sent and took her from *her* husband, from Paltiel the son of Laish. 16 But her husband went with her, weeping as he went, and followed her as far as Bahurim. Then Abner said to him, "Go, return." So he returned.

17 Now Abner had consultation with the elders of Israel, saying, "In times past you were seeking for David to be king over you. 18 So now, do *it*! For Yahweh has spoken of David, saying, 'By the hand of My servant David I will save My people Israel from the hand of the Philistines and from the hand of all their enemies.'" 19 Abner also spoke in the hearing of Benjamin; and in addition Abner went to speak in the hearing of David in Hebron all that was good in the sight of Israel and in the sight of the whole house of Benjamin.

20 Then Abner and twenty men with him came to David at Hebron. And David made a feast for Abner and the men who were with him. 21 And Abner said to David, "Let me arise and go and gather all Israel to my lord the king, that they may cut a covenant with you, and that you may be king over all that your soul desires." So David sent Abner away, and he went in peace.

22 And behold, the servants of David and Joab came from a raid and brought much spoil with them; but Abner was not with David in Hebron, for he had sent him away, and he had gone in peace. 23 Now Joab and all the army that was with him arrived, and they told Joab, saying, "Abner the son of Ner came to the king, and he has sent him away, and he has gone in peace." 24 Then Joab came to the king and said, "What have you done? Behold, Abner came to you; why then have you sent him away and he is already gone? 25 You know Abner the son of Ner, that he came to deceive you and to know of your going out and your coming in and to know all that you are doing."

26 Then Joab came out from David and sent messengers after Abner, and they brought him back from the well of Sirah; but David did not know *it*. 27 So when Abner returned to Hebron, Joab took him aside into the middle of the gate to speak with him privately, and there he struck him in the belly so that he died on account of the blood of Asahel his brother. 28 Afterward David heard it, so he said, "I and my kingdom are innocent before Yahweh forever of the blood of Abner the son

of Ner. 29 May it whirl on the head of Joab and on all his father's house; and may one who has a discharge, or who is a leper, or who takes hold of a spindle, or who falls by the sword, or who lacks bread not be cut off from the house of Joab." 30 So Joab and Abishai his brother killed Abner because he had put their brother Asahel to death in the battle at Gibeon.

31 Then David said to Joab and to all the people who were with him, "Tear your clothes and gird on sackcloth and lament before Abner." And King David walked behind the bier. 32 Thus they buried Abner in Hebron; and the king lifted up his voice and wept at the grave of Abner, and all the people wept. 33 And the king chanted a *lament* for Abner and said,

"Should Abner die as a wicked fool dies?
34 "Your hands were not bound, nor
your feet put in fetters;
As one falls before the unrighteous,
you have fallen."

And all the people continued to weep over him. 35 Then all the people came to persuade David to eat bread while it was still day; but David swore *an oath*, saying, "May God do so to me, and more also, if I taste bread or anything else before the sun goes down." 36 Now all the people took note *of it*, and it was good in their sight, just as everything the king did was good in the sight of all the people. 37 So all the people and all Israel knew that day that it had not been *the will* of the king to put Abner the son of Ner to death. 38 Then the king said to his servants, "Do you not know that a prince and a great man has fallen this day in Israel? 39 Thus I am weak today, though anointed king; and these men the sons of Zeruiah are too difficult for me. May Yahweh repay the evildoer according to his evil."

4 Then Ish-bosheth, Saul's son heard that Abner had died in Hebron. And he lost courage, and all Israel was dismayed. 2 Now Saul's son *had* two men who were commanders of bands: the name of the one was Baanah and the name of the other Rechab, sons of Rimmon the Beerothite, of the sons of Benjamin (for Beeroth is also considered *part* of Benjamin, 3 and the Beerothites fled to Gittaim and have been sojourners there until this day).

4 Now Jonathan, Saul's son, had a son crippled in his feet. He was five years old when the report of Saul and Jonathan came from Jezreel, and his nurse took him up and fled. And it happened that in her hurry to flee, he fell and became lame. And his name was Mephibosheth.

5 So the sons of Rimmon the Beerothite, Rechab and Baanah, went forth and came to the house of Ish-bosheth in the heat of the day while he was taking his midday rest. 6 They came to the middle of the house as if to get wheat, and they struck him in the belly; and Rechab and Baanah his brother escaped. 7 Thus they came into the house, as he was lying on his bed in his bedroom, and they struck him and put him to death and beheaded him. And they took his head and went on the way *leading* to the Arabah all night. 8 Then they brought the head of Ish-bosheth to David at Hebron and said to the king, "Behold, the head of Ish-bosheth the son of Saul, your enemy, who sought your life; thus Yahweh has given my lord the king vengeance this day on Saul and his seed."

9 And David answered Rechab and Baanah his brother, sons of Rimmon the Beerothite, and said to them, "As Yahweh lives, who has redeemed my life from all distress, 10 when one told me, saying, 'Behold, Saul is dead,' and thought he was bringing good news, I seized him and killed him in Ziklag, which was the reward I gave him for *his* news. 11 How much more, when wicked men have killed a righteous man in his own house on his bed, shall I not now require his blood from your hand and purge you from the earth?" 12 Then David commanded the young men, and they killed them and cut off their hands and feet and hung them up beside the pool in Hebron. But they took the head of Ish-bosheth and buried it in the grave of Abner in Hebron.

Psalm 62:5–12

5 Surely wait in silence for
God, O my soul,
For my hope is from Him.
6 Surely He is my rock and my salvation,
My stronghold; I shall not be shaken.
7 On God my salvation and my glory *rest*;
The rock of my strength,
my refuge is in God.
8 Trust in Him at all times, O people;
Pour out your heart before Him;
God is a refuge for us. Selah.

9 Surely men of low degree are *merely*
vanity and men of rank are a lie;
In the balances they go up;
They are together lighter than
a breath of vanity.
10 Do not trust in oppression
And do not put vain hope in robbery;
If riches increase, do not set
your heart *upon them.*

11 Once God has spoken;
Twice I have heard this:
That strength belongs to God;
12 And that to You, O Lord,
belongs lovingkindness,
For You repay a man
according to his work.

Proverbs 16:13–15

13 Righteous lips are the delight of kings,
And he who speaks uprightly is loved.
14 The wrath of a king is *like*
messengers of death,
But a wise man will atone for it.
15 In the light of a king's face is life,
And his favor is like a cloud
with the late rain.

John 4:31–54

31 Meanwhile the disciples were urging
Him, saying, "Rabbi, eat." 32 But He said to
them, "I have food to eat that you do not
know about." 33 So the disciples were saying
to one another, "Has anyone brought Him
anything to eat?" 34 Jesus *said to them, "My
food is to do the will of Him who sent Me
and to finish His work. 35 Do you not say,
'There are yet four months, and *then* comes
the harvest'? Behold, I say to you, lift up
your eyes and look on the fields, that they
are white for harvest. 36 Even now he who
reaps is receiving wages and is gathering
fruit for life eternal; so that he who sows
and he who reaps may rejoice together.
37 For in this *case* the saying is true, 'One
sows and another reaps.' 38 I sent you to
reap that for which you have not labored;
others have labored and you have entered
into their labor."
39 From that city many of the Samaritans
believed in Him because of the word of the
woman who bore witness, "He told me all
the things that I *have* done." 40 So when
the Samaritans came to Jesus, they were
asking Him to stay with them; and He stayed
there two days. 41 And many more believed
because of His word; 42 and they were saying
to the woman, "It is no longer because of
what you said that we believe, for we have
heard for ourselves and know that this One
is truly the Savior of the world."
43 And after the two days He went from
there into Galilee. 44 For Jesus Himself bore
witness that a prophet has no honor in his
own country. 45 So when He came to Galilee,
the Galileans received Him, having seen all the
things that He did in Jerusalem at the feast; for
they themselves also went to the feast.
46 Then He came again to Cana of Galilee
where He had made the water wine. And
there was a royal official whose son was sick
at Capernaum. 47 When he heard that Jesus
had come out of Judea into Galilee, he went
to Him and was asking *Him* to come down
and heal his son; for he was about to die. 48 So
Jesus said to him, "Unless you *people* see
signs and wonders, you will never believe."
49 The royal official *said to Him, "Sir, come
down before my child dies." 50 Jesus *said to
him, "Go; your son lives." The man believed
the word that Jesus spoke to him and started
on his way. 51 And while he was still going
down, his slaves met him, saying that his son
was alive. 52 So he inquired of them the hour
when he began to get better. Then they said
to him, "Yesterday at the seventh hour the
fever left him." 53 So the father knew that *it
was* at that hour in which Jesus said to him,
"Your son lives"; and he himself believed
and his whole household. 54 This is again a
second sign that Jesus did when He had come
out of Judea into Galilee.

MAY 17

2 Samuel 5:1–6:23

5 Then all the tribes of Israel came to
David at Hebron and said, "Behold, we
are your bone and your flesh. 2 Previously,
when Saul was king over us, you were the
one who led out and brought in Israel; and
Yahweh said to you, 'You will shepherd My
people Israel, and you will be a ruler over
Israel.'" 3 So all the elders of Israel came
to the king at Hebron, and King David cut

a covenant with them in Hebron before
Yahweh; then they anointed David king
over Israel. 4 Now David was thirty years
old when he became king, *and* he reigned
forty years. 5 At Hebron he reigned over
Judah seven years and six months, and in
Jerusalem he reigned thirty-three years over
all Israel and Judah.

6 Then the king and his men went to Jeru-
salem against the Jebusites, the inhabitants
of the land, and they said to David, "You
shall not come in here, but the blind and
lame will turn you away"; thinking, "David
cannot enter here." 7 Nevertheless, David
captured the fortress of Zion, that is the
city of David. 8 And David said on that day,
"Whoever would strike down the Jebusites,
let him reach the lame and the blind, who
are hated by David's soul, through the
water tunnel." Therefore they say, "The
blind or the lame shall not come into the
house." 9 Then David lived in the fortress
and called it the city of David. And David
built all around from the Millo and inward.
10 And David became greater and greater,
and Yahweh, the God of hosts, was with him.

11 Then Hiram king of Tyre sent messen-
gers to David with cedar trees and craftsmen
of wood and craftsmen of stone walls; and
they built a house for David. 12 Thus David
knew that Yahweh had established him as
king over Israel, and that He had lifted up
his kingdom for the sake of His people Israel.

13 And David took more concubines and
wives from Jerusalem, after he came from
Hebron; and more sons and daughters
were born to David. 14 Now these are the
names of those who were born to him in
Jerusalem: Shammua, Shobab, Nathan,
Solomon, 15 Ibhar, Elishua, Nepheg, Japhia,
16 Elishama, Eliada and Eliphelet.

17 Then the Philistines heard that they
had anointed David king over Israel, so all
the Philistines went up to seek out David.
And David heard *of it* and went down to the
fortress. 18 Now the Philistines had come
and spread themselves out in the valley of
Rephaim. 19 Then David asked of Yahweh,
saying, "Shall I go up against the Philis-
tines? Will You give them into my hand?"
And Yahweh said to David, "Go up, for I
will certainly give the Philistines into your
hand." 20 So David came to Baal-perazim,
and there David struck them down; and
he said, "Yahweh has broken through my
enemies before me, like the breakthrough
of waters." Therefore he named that place
Baal-perazim. 21 And they forsook their
idols there; so David and his men carried
them away.

22 Then the Philistines yet again came up
and spread themselves out in the valley of
Rephaim. 23 So David asked of Yahweh, and
He said, "You shall not go *directly* up; circle
around behind them and come at them in
front of the balsam trees. 24 And it will be
that when you hear the sound of marching
in the tops of the balsam trees, then you
shall act promptly, for then Yahweh will
have gone out before you to strike the camp
of the Philistines." 25 Then David did so,
just as Yahweh had commanded him, and
struck down the Philistines from Geba as
far as Gezer.

6 Then David again gathered all the cho-
sen men of Israel, thirty thousand. 2 And
David arose and went with all the people
who were with him from Baale-judah, to
bring up from there the ark of God which
is called by the Name, the very name of
Yahweh of hosts who is enthroned *above*
the cherubim. 3 And they drove the ark of
God on a new cart that they might bring it
from the house of Abinadab which was on
the hill; and Uzzah and Ahio, the sons of
Abinadab, were leading the new cart. 4 So
they brought it with the ark of God from
the house of Abinadab, which was on the
hill; and Ahio was walking ahead of the ark.
5 Now David and all the house of Israel were
celebrating before Yahweh with all kinds
of *instruments made of* fir wood, and with
lyres, harps, tambourines, castanets, and
cymbals.

6 Then they came to the threshing floor
of Nacon. And Uzzah reached out toward
the ark of God and took hold of it, because
the oxen nearly upset *it*. 7 And the anger
of Yahweh burned against Uzzah, and God
struck him down there for his irreverence;
and he died there by the ark of God. 8 And
David became angry because of Yahweh's
breaking out against Uzzah; and that place
is called Perez-uzzah to this day. 9 So David
was afraid of Yahweh that day; and he said,
"How can the ark of Yahweh come to me?"
10 And David was unwilling to move the
ark of Yahweh into the city of David with
him; but David took it aside to the house

of Obed-edom the Gittite. 11 Thus the ark
of Yahweh remained in the house of Obed-
edom the Gittite three months, and Yahweh
blessed Obed-edom and all his household.
12 Then it was told to King David, saying,
"Yahweh has blessed the house of Obed-
edom and all that belongs to him, on account
of the ark of God." So David went and
brought up the ark of God from the house
of Obed-edom into the city of David with
gladness. 13 And so it happened, that when
those who were carrying the ark of Yahweh
had gone six paces, he sacrificed an ox and
a fatling. 14 And David was dancing before
Yahweh with all *his* strength, and David was
girded with a linen ephod. 15 So David and
all the house of Israel were bringing up the
ark of Yahweh with shouting and the sound
of the trumpet.
16 Then it happened *as* the ark of Yahweh
came into the city of David, that Michal the
daughter of Saul looked out of the window
and saw King David leaping and dancing
before Yahweh; and she despised him in
her heart.
17 And they brought in the ark of Yahweh
and placed it in its place inside the tent which
David had pitched for it; and David offered
burnt offerings and peace offerings before
Yahweh. 18 Then David completed offering
the burnt offerings and the peace offerings.
And he blessed the people in the name of
Yahweh of hosts. 19 And he apportioned to
all the people, to all the multitude of Israel,
both to men and women, a cake of bread and
one of dates and one of raisins to each one.
Then all the people went each to his house.
20 But David returned to bless his house-
hold, and Michal the daughter of Saul came
out to meet David and said, "How the king
of Israel has glorified himself today! He
uncovered himself today in the eyes of his
servants' maids as one of the worthless
ones shamelessly uncovers himself!" 21 So
David said to Michal, "*It was* before Yahweh,
who chose me above your father and above
all his house, to appoint me ruler over the
people of Yahweh, over Israel; therefore I
will celebrate before Yahweh. 22 And I will
be esteemed even more lightly than this and
will be humble in my own eyes, but with
the maids of whom you have spoken, with
them I will be glorified." 23 And Michal the
daughter of Saul had no child to the day of
her death.

Psalm 63:1–11

1 O God, You are my God; I shall
  seek You earnestly;
My soul thirsts for You, my
  flesh yearns for You,
In a dry and weary land without water.
2 Thus I have beheld You
  in the sanctuary,
To see Your power and Your glory.
3 Because Your lovingkindness
  is better than life,
My lips will laud You.
4 Thus I will bless You as long as I live;
I will lift up my hands in Your name.
5 My soul is satisfied as with
  fatness and richness,
And my mouth offers praises
  with lips of joyful songs.

6 When I remember You on my bed,
I meditate on You in the night watches,
7 For You have been my help,
And in the shadow of Your
  wings I sing for joy.
8 My soul clings to You;
Your right hand upholds me.

9 But those who seek my
  life to destroy it,
Will go into the depths of the earth.
10 They will be delivered over to
  the power of the sword;
They will be a portion for foxes.
11 But the king will be glad in God;
Everyone who swears by
  Him will boast,
For the mouths of those who
  speak lies will be closed.

Proverbs 16:16–17

16 How much better it is to acquire
  wisdom than fine gold!
And to acquire understanding is
  to be chosen above silver.
17 The highway of the upright is
  to turn away from evil;
He who guards his way keeps his soul.

John 5:1–23

5 After these things there was a feast of
the Jews, and Jesus went up to Jerusalem.
2 Now there is in Jerusalem by the sheep
gate a pool, which is called in Hebrew
Bethesda, having five porticoes. 3 In these lay
a multitude of those who were sick, blind,

lame, and withered, [waiting for the moving of the waters; 4 for an angel of the Lord went down at certain seasons into the pool and stirred up the water; whoever then first, after the stirring up of the water, stepped in was made well from whatever sickness with which he was afflicted.] 5 And a man was there who had been sick for thirty-eight years. 6 When Jesus saw him lying *there* and knew that he had already been *sick* a long time, He *said to him, "Do you wish to get well?" 7 The sick man answered Him, "Sir, I have no man to put me into the pool when the water is stirred up, but while I am coming, another steps down before me." 8 Jesus *said to him, "Get up, pick up your mat and walk." 9 And immediately the man became well, and picked up his mat and *began to* walk.

Now it was the Sabbath on that day. 10 So the Jews were saying to the man who had been healed, "It is the Sabbath, and it is not lawful for you to carry your mat." 11 But he answered them, "He who made me well was the one who said to me, 'Pick up your mat and walk.'" 12 They asked him, "Who is the man who said to you, 'Pick up *your mat* and walk'?" 13 But the man who was healed did not know who it was, for Jesus had slipped away while there was a crowd in *that* place. 14 Afterward Jesus *found him in the temple and said to him, "Behold, you have become well; do not sin anymore, so that nothing worse happens to you." 15 The man went away, and disclosed to the Jews that it was Jesus who had made him well. 16 And for this reason the Jews were persecuting Jesus, because He was doing these things on the Sabbath. 17 But He answered them, "My Father is working until now, and I Myself am working."

18 For this reason therefore the Jews were seeking all the more to kill Him, because He not only was breaking the Sabbath, but also was calling God His own Father, making Himself equal with God.

19 Therefore Jesus answered and was saying to them, "Truly, truly, I say to you, the Son can do nothing from Himself, unless *it is* something He sees the Father doing; for whatever the Father does, these things the Son also does in the same manner. 20 For the Father loves the Son, and shows Him all things that He Himself is doing; and *the Father* will show Him greater works than these, so that you will marvel. 21 For just as the Father raises the dead and gives *them* life, even so the Son also gives life to whom He wishes. 22 For not even the Father judges anyone, but He has given all judgment to the Son, 23 so that all will honor the Son even as they honor the Father. He who does not honor the Son does not honor the Father who sent Him.

MAY 18

2 Samuel 7:1–8:18

7 Now it happened when the king inhabited his house, and Yahweh had given him rest on every side from all his enemies, 2 that the king said to Nathan the prophet, "See now, I inhabit a house of cedar, but the ark of God inhabits *tent* curtains." 3 So Nathan said to the king, "Go, do all that is in your heart, for Yahweh is with you."

4 Now it happened in the same night, that the word of Yahweh came to Nathan, saying, 5 "Go and say to My servant David, 'Thus says Yahweh, "Are you the one who would build Me a house to inhabit? 6 For I have not inhabited a house since the day I brought up the sons of Israel from Egypt, even to this day; but I have been going about in a tent, even in a tabernacle. 7 Wherever I have gone about with all the sons of Israel, did I speak a word with one of the tribes of Israel, which I commanded to shepherd My people Israel, saying, 'Why have you not built Me a house of cedar?'"'

8 "So now, thus you shall say to My servant David, 'Thus says Yahweh of hosts, "I Myself took you from the pasture, from following the sheep, to be ruler over My people Israel. 9 And I have been with you wherever you have gone and have cut off all your enemies from before you; and I will make you a great name, like the name of the great men who are on the earth. 10 And I will appoint a place for My people Israel and will plant them, that they may dwell in their own place and not be disturbed again; and the unrighteous will not afflict them any more as formerly, 11 even from the day that I commanded judges *to be* over My

people Israel; and I will give you rest from all your enemies. Yahweh also declares to you that Yahweh will make a house for you. 12 When your days are fulfilled and you lie down with your fathers, I will raise up *one of* your seed after you, who will come forth from your own body, and I will establish his kingdom. 13 He shall build a house for My name, and I will establish the throne of his kingdom forever. 14 I will be a father to him and he will be a son to Me; when he commits iniquity, I will reprove him with the rod of men and the strikes from the sons of men, 15 but My lovingkindness shall not be removed from him, as I removed *it* from Saul, whom I removed from before you. 16 And your house and your kingdom shall endure before Me forever; your throne shall be established forever."'" 17 According to all these words and according to all this vision, so Nathan spoke to David.

18 Then David the king went in and sat before Yahweh, and he said, "Who am I, O Lord Yahweh, and what is my house, that You have brought me this far? 19 And yet this was a small thing in Your eyes, O Lord Yahweh, for You have spoken also of the house of Your slave concerning the distant future. And this is the law of man, O Lord Yahweh. 20 And again what more can David say to You? And You know Your slave, O Lord Yahweh! 21 For the sake of Your word, and according to Your own heart, You have done all this greatness to let Your slave know. 22 For this reason You are great, O Lord Yahweh; for there is none like You, and there is no God besides You, according to all that we have heard with our ears. 23 And what one nation on the earth is like Your people Israel, whom God went to redeem for Himself as a people and to make a name for Himself, and to do a great thing for You and awesome things for Your land, before Your people whom You have redeemed for Yourself from Egypt, *from* nations and their gods? 24 Yet You have established for Yourself Your people Israel as Your own people forever, and You, O Yahweh, have become their God. 25 So now, O Yahweh God, the word that You have spoken concerning Your slave and concerning his house, establish *it* forever, and do as You have spoken, 26 that Your name may be magnified forever, by saying, 'Yahweh of hosts is God over Israel'; and the house of Your servant David shall be established before You. 27 For You, O Yahweh of hosts, the God of Israel, have revealed in the hearing of Your slave, saying, 'I will build you a house'; therefore Your slave has found *courage* in his heart to pray this prayer to You. 28 So now, O Lord Yahweh, You are God, and Your words are truth, and You have promised this good thing to Your slave. 29 So now, be pleased and bless the house of Your slave, that it may be forever before You. For You, O Lord Yahweh, have spoken; and with Your blessing may the house of Your slave be blessed forever."

8 Now it happened afterwards, that David struck the Philistines and subdued them; and David took control of the chief city from the hand of the Philistines.

2 He also struck Moab, and measured them with the line, making them lie down on the ground; and he measured two lines to put to death and one full line to keep alive. And the Moabites became servants to David, bringing tribute.

3 Then David struck Hadadezer, the son of Rehob king of Zobah, as he went to restore his power at the River. 4 And David captured from him 1,700 horsemen and 20,000 foot soldiers; and David hamstrung all the chariot horses, but left *enough* of them for 100 chariots. 5 Then the Arameans of Damascus came to help Hadadezer, king of Zobah. And David struck down 22,000 Arameans. 6 Then David placed garrisons among the Arameans of Damascus; and the Arameans became servants to David, bringing tribute. And Yahweh granted salvation to David wherever he went. 7 And David took the small shields of gold which were carried by the servants of Hadadezer and brought them to Jerusalem. 8 Also from Betah and from Berothai, cities of Hadadezer, King David took a very large amount of bronze.

9 Then Toi king of Hamath heard that David had struck down all the military force of Hadadezer, 10 so Toi sent Joram his son to King David to greet him and to bless him, because he had fought against Hadadezer and struck him down; for Hadadezer had been at war with Toi. And in Joram's hand were articles of silver, of gold, and of bronze. 11 King David also set these apart as holy to Yahweh, with the silver and the gold that he had set apart as holy from all the nations which he had subdued: 12 from Aram, Moab,

the sons of Ammon, the Philistines, Amalek,
and from the spoil of Hadadezer, son of
Rehob, king of Zobah.
13 So David made a name *for himself* when
he returned from striking down 18,000
Arameans in the Valley of Salt. 14 Then
he placed garrisons in Edom. In all Edom
he placed garrisons, and all the Edomites
became servants to David. And Yahweh
granted salvation to David wherever he
went.
15 So David reigned over all Israel; and
David was doing justice and righteousness
for all his people. 16 Now Joab the son of
Zeruiah *was* over the army, and Jehoshaphat
the son of Ahilud *was* recorder; 17 and Zadok
the son of Ahitub and Ahimelech the son
of Abiathar *were* priests, and Seraiah *was*
scribe; 18 and Benaiah the son of Jehoiada
was over the Cherethites and the Pelethites;
and the sons of David were priests.

Psalm 64:1–10

1 Hear my voice, O God,
in my complaint;
Guard my life from dread of the enemy.
2 Hide me from the secret
counsel of evildoers,
From the tumult of the
workers of iniquity,
3 Who have sharpened their
tongue like a sword.
They aimed bitter speech
as their arrow,
4 To shoot from places of hiding
at the blameless;
Suddenly they shoot at him,
and do not fear.
5 They hold fast to themselves
an evil purpose;
They talk of laying snares secretly;
They say, "Who can see them?"
6 They searched out
unrighteousness, *saying*,
"We have completed a diligent search";
For the inward thought of a man
and *his* heart are deep.

7 But God will shoot them with an arrow;
Suddenly they will be wounded.
8 So they will cause their own
tongue to turn against them;
All who see them will shake *their* head.
9 Then all men will fear,
And they will declare the work of God,
And will consider what He has done.
10 The righteous man will be glad in
Yahweh and will take refuge in Him;
And all the upright in heart will boast.

Proverbs 16:18–19

18 Pride *goes* before destruction,
And a haughty spirit before stumbling.
19 It is better to be humble in
spirit with the lowly
Than to divide the spoil
with the proud.

John 5:24–47

24 "Truly, truly, I say to you, he who hears
My word, and believes Him who sent Me,
has eternal life, and does not come into
judgment, but has passed out of death into
life.
25 "Truly, truly, I say to you, an hour is
coming and now is, when the dead will hear
the voice of the Son of God, and those who
hear will live. 26 For just as the Father has life
in Himself, even so He gave to the Son also
to have life in Himself; 27 and He gave Him
authority to execute judgment, because He
is the Son of Man. 28 Do not marvel at this;
for an hour is coming, in which all who are
in the tombs will hear His voice, 29 and will
come forth; those who did the good deeds to
a resurrection of life, those who committed
the evil deeds to a resurrection of judgment.
30 "I can do nothing from Myself. As I
hear, I judge; and My judgment is righteous,
because I do not seek My own will, but the
will of Him who sent Me.
31 "If I *alone* bear witness about Myself,
My witness is not true. 32 There is another
who bears witness about Me, and I know
that the witness which He gives about Me
is true.
33 "You have sent to John, and he has
borne witness to the truth. 34 But the
witness I receive is not from man, but I
say these things so that you may be saved.
35 He was the lamp that was burning and
shining and you were willing to rejoice
for a while in his light. 36 But the witness
I have is greater than *the witness of* John;
for the works which the Father has given
Me to finish—the very works that I do—
bear witness about Me, that the Father has
sent Me. 37 And the Father who sent Me,
He has borne witness about Me. You have
neither heard His voice at any time nor

seen His form. 38 And you do not have His word abiding in you, for you do not believe Him whom He sent. 39 You search the Scriptures because you think that in them you have eternal life; it is these that bear witness about Me; 40 and you are unwilling to come to Me so that you may have life. 41 I do not receive glory from men; 42 but I know you, that you do not have the love of God in yourselves. 43 I have come in My Father's name, and you do not receive Me; if another comes in his own name, you will receive him. 44 How can you believe, when you receive glory from one another and you do not seek the glory that is from the only God? 45 Do not think that I will accuse you to the Father; the one who accuses you is Moses, in whom you have set your hope. 46 For if you believed Moses, you would believe Me, for he wrote about Me. 47 But if you do not believe his writings, how will you believe My words?"

MAY 19

2 Samuel 9:1–10:19

9 Then David said, "Is there yet anyone left of the house of Saul, that I may show him lovingkindness for Jonathan's sake?" 2 Now there was a servant of the house of Saul whose name was Ziba, and they called him to David; and the king said to him, "Are you Ziba?" And he said, "*I am* your servant." 3 And the king said, "Is there not yet anyone of the house of Saul to whom I may show the lovingkindness of God?" And Ziba said to the king, "There is still a son of Jonathan who is crippled in both feet." 4 So the king said to him, "Where is he?" And Ziba said to the king, "Behold, he is in the house of Machir the son of Ammiel in Lo-debar." 5 Then King David sent and took him from the house of Machir the son of Ammiel, from Lo-debar. 6 So Mephibosheth, the son of Jonathan the son of Saul, came to David and fell on his face and prostrated himself. And David said, "Mephibosheth." And he said, "Here is your servant!" 7 And David said to him, "Do not fear, for I will surely show lovingkindness to you for the sake of your father Jonathan, and will restore to you all the land of your grandfather Saul; and you shall eat at my table continually." 8 So he prostrated himself and said, "What is your servant, that you should regard a dead dog like me?"

9 Then the king called Saul's young man Ziba and said to him, "All that belonged to Saul and to all his house I have given to your master's grandson. 10 And you and your sons and your servants shall cultivate the land for him, and you shall bring in *the produce* so *that your master's* grandson may have food and eat of it; nevertheless Mephibosheth your master's grandson shall eat at my table continually." Now Ziba had fifteen sons and twenty servants. 11 Then Ziba said to the king, "According to all that my lord the king commands his servant so your servant will do." So Mephibosheth ate at David's table as one of the king's sons. 12 Now Mephibosheth had a young son whose name was Mica. And all who lived in the house of Ziba were servants to Mephibosheth. 13 So Mephibosheth lived in Jerusalem, for he ate at the king's table continually. Now he was lame in both feet.

10 Now it happened afterwards, that the king of the sons of Ammon died, and Hanun his son became king in his place. 2 So David said, "I will show lovingkindness to Hanun the son of Nahash, just as his father showed lovingkindness to me." So David sent to comfort him concerning his father by the hand of his servants. And David's servants came to the land of the sons of Ammon. 3 But the princes of the sons of Ammon said to Hanun their lord, "In your eyes, is David honoring your father because he has sent comforters to you? Has David not sent his servants to you in order to search the city, to spy it out and overthrow it?" 4 So Hanun took David's servants and shaved off half of their beards, and cut off their garments in the middle as far as their hips, and sent them away. 5 Then they told *it* to David. And he sent to meet them, for the men were greatly dishonored. And the king said, "Stay at Jericho until your beards grow, and *then* return."

6 Then the sons of Ammon saw that they had become odious to David. So the sons of Ammon sent and hired the Arameans of Beth-rehob and the Arameans of Zobah, 20,000 foot soldiers, and the king of Maacah

with 1,000 men, and the men of Tob with
12,000 men. 7 Then David heard *of it* and
sent Joab and all the army, the mighty men.
8 And the sons of Ammon came out and
arranged *themselves* for battle at the entrance
of the gate *of the city*. But the Arameans of
Zobah and of Rehob and the men of Tob and
Maacah were by themselves in the field.
9 Then Joab saw that the battle was set
against him from *the* front and from *the*
rear. So he chose from all the choice men
of Israel, and they arranged *themselves* to
meet the Arameans. 10 But the remainder
of the people he put in the hand of Abishai
his brother; and he arranged them to meet
the sons of Ammon. 11 And he said, "If the
Arameans are too strong for me, then you
shall save me, but if the sons of Ammon are
too strong for you, then I will come to save
you. 12 Be strong, and let us show strength
for the sake of our people and for the cities
of our God; and may Yahweh do what is
good in His sight." 13 So Joab and the people
who were with him drew near for the battle
against the Arameans, and they fled before
him. 14 Now the sons of Ammon saw that
the Arameans fled. So they *also* fled before
Abishai and came into the city. Then Joab
returned from *fighting* against the sons of
Ammon and came to Jerusalem.
15 Then the Arameans saw that they had
been defeated by Israel. So they gathered
themselves together. 16 And Hadadezer sent
and brought out the Arameans who were
beyond the River, and they came to Helam;
and Shobach the commander of the army
of Hadadezer led them. 17 And it was told
to David, so he gathered all Israel together
and crossed the Jordan, and came to Helam.
And the Arameans arranged themselves to
meet David and fought against him. 18 But
the Arameans fled before Israel, and David
killed of the Arameans 700 charioteers and
40,000 horsemen and struck down Shobach
the commander of their army, and he died
there. 19 Then all the kings, the servants of
Hadadezer, saw that they were defeated by
Israel. So they made peace with Israel and
served them. And the Arameans were afraid
to save the sons of Ammon anymore.

Psalm 65:1–8

1 To You, there will be silence *and*
praise in Zion, O God,
And to You the vow will be paid.
2 O You who hear prayer,
To You all flesh comes.
3 Words of iniquity prevail against me;
As for our transgressions,
You atone for them.
4 How blessed is the one whom You
choose and bring near *to You*
That he would dwell in Your courts.
We will be satisfied with the
goodness of Your house,
Your holy temple.

5 By fearsome *deeds* You answer
us in righteousness, O God
of our salvation,
You who are the trust of all the ends of
the earth and of the farthest sea;
6 Who establishes the mountains
by His strength,
Being girded with might;
7 Who stills the rumbling of the seas,
The rumbling of their waves,
And the tumult of the peoples.
8 They who inhabit the ends *of the earth*
are in fear on account of Your signs;
You make the dawn and the
sunset shout for joy.

Proverbs 16:20–21

20 He who considers the word
will find good,
And how blessed is he who
trusts in Yahweh.
21 The wise in heart will be
called understanding,
And sweetness of lips
increases learning.

John 6:1–21

6 After these things Jesus went away to
the other side of the Sea of Galilee (or
Tiberias). 2 Now a large crowd was following
Him, because they were seeing the signs
which He was doing on those who were
sick. 3 Then Jesus went up on the mountain,
and there He was sitting down with His
disciples. 4 Now the Passover, the feast of
the Jews, was near. 5 Therefore Jesus, lifting
up His eyes and seeing that a large crowd
was coming to Him, *said to Philip, "Where
should we buy bread, so that these people
may eat?" 6 And this He was saying to test
him, for He Himself knew what He was
going to do. 7 Philip answered Him, "Two
hundred denarii worth of bread is not

sufficient for them, for everyone to receive a little." 8 One of His disciples, Andrew, Simon Peter's brother, *said to Him, 9 "There is a boy here who has five barley loaves and two fish, but what are these for so many people?" 10 Jesus said, "Have the people sit down." Now there was much grass in the place. So the men sat down, in number about five thousand. 11 Jesus then took the loaves, and having given thanks, He distributed *them* to those who were seated; likewise also of the fish, as much as they wanted. 12 And when they were filled, He *said to His disciples, "Gather up the leftover pieces so that nothing will be lost." 13 So they gathered them up, and filled twelve baskets with pieces of the five barley loaves left over by those who had eaten. 14 Therefore when the people saw the sign which He had done, they were saying, "This is truly the Prophet who is to come into the world."

15 So Jesus, knowing that they were going to come and take Him by force to make Him king, withdrew again to the mountain by Himself alone.

16 Now when evening came, His disciples went down to the sea, 17 and after getting into a boat, they *began to* cross the sea to Capernaum. It had already become dark, and Jesus had not yet come to them. 18 And the sea *was stirred up because a strong wind was blowing. 19 Then, when they had rowed about twenty-five or thirty stadia, they *saw Jesus walking on the sea and drawing near to the boat; and they were frightened. 20 But He *said to them, "It is I; do not be afraid." 21 So they were willing to receive Him into the boat, and immediately the boat was at the land to which they were going.

MAY 20

2 Samuel 11:1–12:31

11 Now it happened in the spring, at the time when kings go out *to battle*, that David sent Joab and his servants with him and all Israel, and they destroyed the sons of Ammon and besieged Rabbah. But David stayed at Jerusalem.

2 Now when evening came David arose from his bed and walked around on the roof of the king's house, and from the roof he saw a woman bathing; and the woman was very beautiful in appearance. 3 So David sent and inquired about the woman. And one said, "Is this not Bathsheba, the daughter of Eliam, the wife of Uriah the Hittite?" 4 Then David sent messengers and took her, and she came to him, and he lay with her; and when she had purified herself from her uncleanness, she returned to her house. 5 And the woman became pregnant; and she sent and told David, and said, "I am pregnant."

6 Then David sent to Joab, *saying*, "Send me Uriah the Hittite." So Joab sent Uriah to David. 7 When Uriah came to him, David asked concerning the state of Joab and the state of the people and the state of the war. 8 Then David said to Uriah, "Go down to your house, and wash your feet." And Uriah went out of the king's house, and a present from the king went out after him. 9 But Uriah lay down at the door of the king's house with all the servants of his lord, and did not go down to his house. 10 Then they told David, saying, "Uriah did not go down to his house." And David said to Uriah, "Have you not come from a journey? Why did you not go down to your house?" 11 And Uriah said to David, "The ark and Israel and Judah are staying in booths, and my lord Joab and the servants of my lord are camping in the open field. Shall I then go to my house to eat and to drink and to lie with my wife? By your life and the life of your soul, I will not do this thing." 12 Then David said to Uriah, "Stay here today also, and tomorrow I will send you out." So Uriah remained in Jerusalem that day and the next. 13 Now David called him, and he ate and drank before him, and he made him drunk; and in the evening he went out to lie on his bed with his lord's servants, but he did not go down to his house.

14 Now it happened in the morning that David wrote a letter to Joab and sent *it* by the hand of Uriah. 15 And he had written in the letter, saying, "Place Uriah in the front line of the fiercest battle and withdraw from him, so that he may be struck down and die." 16 So it was as Joab kept watch on the city, that he put Uriah at the place where he knew there *were* valiant men. 17 And the men of the city went out and fought against Joab, and some of the people

among David's servants fell; and Uriah the
Hittite also died. 18 Then Joab sent and told
David all the events of the war. 19 And he
commanded the messenger, saying, "When
you have finished telling all the events of the
war to the king, 20 and if it happens that the
king's wrath rises and he says to you, 'Why
did you approach the city to fight? Did you
not know that they would shoot from the
wall? 21 Who struck down Abimelech the
son of Jerubbesheth? Did not a woman cast
an upper millstone on him from the wall so
he died at Thebez? Why did you approach
the wall?'—then you shall say, 'Your servant
Uriah the Hittite is dead also.'"

22 So the messenger went and came and
told David all that Joab had sent him *to tell.*
23 And the messenger said to David, "The
men prevailed against us and came out
against us in the field, but we pressed them
as far as the entrance of the gate. 24 And the
archers shot at your servants from the wall;
so some of the king's servants died, and your
servant Uriah the Hittite also died." 25 Then
David said to the messenger, "Thus you shall
say to Joab, 'Do not let this thing be evil in
your sight, for the sword devours one as
well as another; make your battle against
the city stronger and tear it down'; and *so*
strengthen him."

26 Then the wife of Uriah heard that Uriah
her husband had died, so she lamented over
her husband. 27 Then the *time of* mourning
passed by, and David sent and gathered her
to his house and she became his wife; then
she bore him a son. But the thing that David
had done was evil in the sight of Yahweh.

12 Then Yahweh sent Nathan to David.
And he came to him and said,
"There were two men in one city, the
one rich and the other poor.
2 "The rich man had a great
many flocks and herds.
3 "But the poor man had nothing
except one little ewe lamb
Which he bought and nourished;
And it grew up together with
him and his children.
It would eat his morsel *of bread* and
drink of his cup and lie in his bosom,
And was like a daughter to him.
4 "Now a visitor came to the rich man,
And he was unwilling to take from
his own flock or his own herd,
To prepare for the traveler
who had come to him;
Rather he took the poor man's ewe
lamb and prepared it for the
man who had come to him."
5 Then David's anger burned greatly against
the man, and he said to Nathan, "As Yah-
weh lives, surely the man who has done
this deserves to die. 6 And he must make
restitution for the lamb fourfold, because
he did this thing and had no compassion."

7 Nathan then said to David, "You are the
man! Thus says Yahweh, the God of Israel,
'It is I who anointed you king over Israel and
it is I who delivered you from the hand of
Saul. 8 I also gave you your master's house
and your master's wives into your care, and
I gave you the house of Israel and Judah;
and if *that had been* too little, I would
have added to you many more things like
these! 9 Why have you despised the word
of Yahweh by doing evil in His sight? You
have struck down Uriah the Hittite with
the sword, have taken his wife to be your
wife, and have killed him with the sword of
the sons of Ammon. 10 So now, the sword
shall never depart from your house, because
you have despised Me and have taken the
wife of Uriah the Hittite to be your wife.'
11 Thus says Yahweh, 'Behold, I will raise up
evil against you from your own household; I
will even take your wives from before your
sight and give *them* to your companion, and
he will lie with your wives in the sight of this
sun. 12 Indeed you did it secretly, but I will
do this thing before all Israel, and before the
sun.'" 13 Then David said to Nathan, "I have
sinned against Yahweh." And Nathan said to
David, "Yahweh also has taken away your
sin; you shall not die. 14 However, because
by this deed you have given occasion to the
enemies of Yahweh to blaspheme, the son
also that is born to you shall surely die."
15 And Nathan went to his house.

Then Yahweh smote the child that Uriah's
wife bore to David, so that he was *very* sick.
16 David therefore sought God about the boy;
and David fasted and went and spent the
night lying on the ground. 17 And the elders
of his household stood beside him in order
to raise him up from the ground, but he was
unwilling and would not eat food with them.
18 Then it happened on the seventh day that
the child died. And the servants of David
were afraid to tell him that the child was

dead, for they said, "Behold, while the child
was *still* alive, we spoke to him and he did
not listen to our voice. How then can we
tell him that the child has died? He might
do *himself* harm!" 19 And David saw that
his servants were whispering together, so
David discerned that the child had died; so
David said to his servants, "Has the child
died?" And they said, "He has died." 20 So
David arose from the ground, washed,
anointed *himself*, and changed his clothes;
and he came into the house of Yahweh and
worshiped. Then he came to his own house,
and he asked, and they set food before him,
and he ate.

21 Then his servants said to him, "What
is this thing that you have done? While
the child was alive, you fasted and wept;
but when the child died, you arose and ate
food." 22 Then he said, "While the child
was *still* alive, I fasted and wept; for I said,
'Who knows, Yahweh may be gracious to
me, that the child may live.' 23 But now he
has died; why should I fast? Can I bring him
back again? I will go to him, but he will not
return to me."

24 Then David comforted his wife Bath-
sheba, and went in to her and lay with her;
and she gave birth to a son, and he named
him Solomon. Now Yahweh loved him
25 and sent *word* by the hand of Nathan the
prophet, and he named him Jedidiah for the
sake of Yahweh.

26 Then Joab fought against Rabbah of the
sons of Ammon and captured the royal city.
27 And Joab sent messengers to David and
said, "I have fought against Rabbah, I have
even captured the city of waters. 28 So now,
gather the rest of the people together and
camp against the city and capture it, lest
I capture the city myself and it be named
after me." 29 So David gathered all the people
and went to Rabbah, fought against it and
captured it. 30 Then he took the crown of
their king from his head; and its weight *was*
a talent of gold, and *in it was* a precious
stone; and it was *placed* on David's head.
And he brought out the spoil of the city
in a very great amount. 31 He also brought
out the people who were in it and set *them*
up with saws, sharp iron instruments, and
iron axes, and made them pass through the
brickkiln. And thus he used to do to all the
cities of the sons of Ammon. Then David
and all the people returned *to* Jerusalem.

Psalm 65:9–13

9 You visit the earth and
cause it to overflow;
You greatly enrich it;
The stream of God is full of water;
You establish their grain, for thus
You establish the earth.
10 You water its furrows abundantly,
You smooth its ridges,
You soften it with showers,
You bless its growth.
11 You crown the year with
Your goodness,
And Your paths drip *with* richness.
12 The pastures of the wilderness drip,
And the hills gird themselves
with rejoicing.
13 The meadows are clothed with flocks
And the valleys are covered with grain;
They make a loud shout,
indeed, they sing.

Proverbs 16:22–24

22 Insight is a fountain of life
to one who has it,
But the discipline of ignorant
fools is folly.
23 The heart of the wise gives
insight to his mouth
And increases learning to his lips.
24 Pleasant words are a honeycomb,
Sweet to the soul and
healing to the bones.

John 6:22–51

22 On the next day, the crowd which stood
on the other side of the sea saw that there
was no other small boat there, except one,
and that Jesus had not entered with His
disciples into the boat, but *that* His disciples
had gone away alone. 23 Other small boats
came from Tiberias near to the place where
they ate the bread after the Lord had given
thanks. 24 So when the crowd saw that
Jesus was not there, nor His disciples, they
themselves got into the small boats, and
came to Capernaum seeking Jesus. 25 And
when they found Him on the other side of
the sea, they said to Him, "Rabbi, when did
You come here?"

26 Jesus answered them and said, "Truly,
truly, I say to you, you seek Me, not because
you saw signs, but because you ate of the
loaves and were filled. 27 Do not work for
the food which perishes, but for the food

which endures to eternal life, which the Son of Man will give to you, for on Him the Father, God, set His seal." 28 Therefore they said to Him, "What should we do, so that we may work the works of God?" 29 Jesus answered and said to them, "This is the work of God, that you believe in Him whom He has sent." 30 So they said to Him, "What then do You do for a sign so that we may see, and believe You? What work do You perform? 31 Our fathers ate the manna in the wilderness; as it is written, 'HE GAVE THEM BREAD FROM HEAVEN TO EAT.'" 32 Jesus then said to them, "Truly, truly, I say to you, Moses has not given you the bread from heaven, but My Father gives you the true bread from heaven. 33 For the bread of God is that which comes down from heaven and gives life to the world." 34 Then they said to Him, "Lord, always give us this bread."

35 Jesus said to them, "I am the bread of life. He who comes to Me will never hunger, and he who believes in Me will never thirst. 36 But I said to you that you have seen Me, and yet do not believe. 37 All that the Father gives Me will come to Me, and the one who comes to Me I will never cast out. 38 For I have come down from heaven, not to do My own will, but the will of Him who sent Me. 39 Now this is the will of Him who sent Me, that of all that He has given Me I lose nothing, but raise it up on the last day. 40 For this is the will of My Father, that everyone who sees the Son and believes in Him will have eternal life, and I Myself will raise him up on the last day."

41 Therefore the Jews were grumbling about Him, because He said, "I am the bread that came down from heaven." 42 They were saying, "Is not this Jesus, the son of Joseph, whose father and mother we know? How does He now say, 'I have come down from heaven'?" 43 Jesus answered and said to them, "Stop grumbling among yourselves. 44 No one can come to Me unless the Father who sent Me draws him; and I will raise him up on the last day. 45 It is written in the prophets, 'AND THEY SHALL ALL BE TAUGHT BY GOD.' Everyone who has heard and learned from the Father comes to Me. 46 Not that anyone has seen the Father, except the One who is from God; He has seen the Father. 47 Truly, truly, I say to you, he who believes has eternal life. 48 I am the bread of life. 49 Your fathers ate the manna in the wilderness, and they died. 50 This is the bread which comes down from heaven, so that one may eat of it and not die. 51 I am the living bread that came down from heaven; if anyone eats of this bread, he will live forever; and also the bread which I will give for the life of the world is My flesh."

The Bible was not given to increase our knowledge but to change our lives.

— D. L. MOODY

MAY 21

2 Samuel 13:1–14:33

13 Now it happened afterwards that Absalom the son of David had a beautiful sister whose name was Tamar, and *Amnon the son of David* loved her. 2 And Amnon was so distressed because of his sister Tamar that he made himself ill, for she was a virgin. So it was hard in Amnon's sight to do anything to her. 3 But Amnon had a friend whose name was Jonadab, the son of Shimeah, David's brother; and Jonadab was a very shrewd man. 4 And he said to him, "O son of the king, why are you so depressed morning after morning? Will you not tell me?" Then Amnon said to him, "I am in love with Tamar, the sister of my brother Absalom." 5 Jonadab then said to him, "Lie down on your bed and pretend to be ill; and your father will come to see you, and you will say to him, 'Please let my sister Tamar come and give me *some* food to eat, and let her prepare the food in my sight, that I may see *it* and eat from her hand.'" 6 So Amnon lay down and pretended to be ill; and the king came to see him, and Amnon said to the king, "Please let my sister Tamar come

and make me a couple of cakes in my sight, that I may eat from her hand."

7 Then David sent to the house for Tamar, saying, "Go now to your brother Amnon's house, and prepare food for him." 8 So Tamar went to her brother Amnon's house, and he was lying down. And she took dough, kneaded *it*, made cakes in his sight, and baked the cakes. 9 And she took the pan and dished *them* out before him, but he refused to eat. And Amnon said, "Have everyone go out from me." So everyone went out from him. 10 Then Amnon said to Tamar, "Bring the food into the bedroom, that I may eat from your hand." So Tamar took the cakes which she had made and brought them into the bedroom to her brother Amnon. 11 Then she brought *them* near to him to eat, but he took hold of her and said to her, "Come, lie with me, my sister." 12 But she said to him, "No, my brother, do not violate me, for such a thing is not done in Israel; do not do this disgraceful thing! 13 As for me, where could I get rid of my reproach? And as for you, you will be like one of the wicked fools in Israel. So now, please speak to the king, for he will not withhold me from you." 14 But he was not willing to listen to her voice. Now he was stronger than she, so he violated her and lay with her.

15 Then Amnon hated her with a very great hatred; for the hatred with which he hated her was greater than the love with which he had loved her. And Amnon said to her, "Get up, go away!" 16 But she said to him, "No, because this wrong in sending me away is greater than the other that you have done to me!" But he was not willing to listen to her. 17 Then he called his young man who attended him and said, "Now cast this woman out of my *presence*, and lock the door behind her." 18 Now she had on a long-sleeved garment; for in this manner the virgin daughters of the king dressed themselves in robes. Then his attendant took her out and locked the door behind her. 19 Then Tamar put ashes on her head and tore her long-sleeved garment which *was* on her; and she put her hand on her head and went away, crying aloud as she went.

20 So Absalom her brother said to her, "Has Amnon your brother been with you? But now keep silent, my sister, he is your brother; do not take this matter to heart." So Tamar remained and was desolate in her brother Absalom's house. 21 Now when King David heard of all these matters, he was very angry. 22 But Absalom did not speak to Amnon either good or bad; for Absalom hated Amnon because he had violated his sister Tamar.

23 Now it happened after two full years that Absalom had sheepshearers in Baalhazor, which is near Ephraim, and Absalom invited all the king's sons.

24 And Absalom came to the king and said, "Behold now, your servant has sheepshearers; please let the king and his servants go with your servant." 25 But the king said to Absalom, "No, my son, we should not all go, for we will be burdensome to you." Although he urged him, he was not willing to go, but blessed him. 26 Then Absalom said, "If not, please let my brother Amnon go with us." And the king said to him, "Why should he go with you?" 27 But Absalom urged him, so he sent Amnon and all the king's sons with him.

28 Then Absalom commanded his young men, saying, "See now, when Amnon's heart is merry with wine, and when I say to you, 'Strike Amnon,' then put him to death. Do not fear; have not I myself commanded you? Be strong and be valiant." 29 Thus the young men of Absalom did to Amnon just as Absalom had commanded. Then all the king's sons arose and each mounted his mule and fled.

30 Now it was while they were on the way that the report came to David, saying, "Absalom has struck down all the king's sons, and not one of them is left." 31 Then the king arose, tore his clothes and lay on the ground; and all his servants were standing by with clothes torn. 32 But Jonadab, the son of Shimeah, David's brother, answered and said, "Do not let my lord suppose they have put to death all the young men, the king's sons, for Amnon alone has died; because by the intent of Absalom this has been set since the day that he violated his sister Tamar. 33 So now, do not let my lord the king take the report to heart, saying, 'all the king's sons have died,' for only Amnon has died."

34 Then Absalom fled. And the young man who was the watchman raised his eyes and looked, and behold, many people were coming from the road behind him by the side of the mountain. 35 And Jonadab said to the king, "Behold, the king's sons have

come; according to your servant's word, so it happened." 36 As soon as he had finished speaking, behold, the king's sons came and lifted their voices and wept; and also the king and all his servants wept very bitterly.

37 Now Absalom had fled and went to Talmai the son of Ammihud, the king of Geshur. And *David* mourned for his son every day. 38 So Absalom had fled and gone to Geshur, and was there three years. 39 *And the heart of* King David was consumed with going out to Absalom; for he was comforted concerning Amnon, since he had died.

14 Now Joab the son of Zeruiah knew that the king's heart *was inclined* toward Absalom. 2 So Joab sent to Tekoa and brought a wise woman from there and said to her, "Please pretend to be a mourner, and put on mourning garments now, and do not anoint yourself with oil, but be like a woman who has been mourning for the dead many days; 3 then you shall go to the king and speak to him in this manner." So Joab put the words in her mouth.

4 So the woman of Tekoa spoke to the king, and she fell on her face to the ground and prostrated herself and said, "Save, O king." 5 And the king said to her, "What is your trouble?" And she answered, "Truly I am a widow; my husband has died. 6 And your servant-woman had two sons, but the two of them struggled together in the field, and there was no one to deliver between them, so one struck the other and put him to death. 7 And behold, the whole family has risen against your servant-woman, and they say, 'Hand over the one who struck his brother, that we may put him to death for the life of his brother whom he killed, and destroy the heir also.' Thus they will extinguish my coal which remains, so as to leave my husband neither name nor remnant on the face of the earth."

8 Then the king said to the woman, "Go to your house, and I will give a command concerning you." 9 And the woman of Tekoa said to the king, "O my lord, the king, the iniquity is on me and my father's house, but the king and his throne are guiltless." 10 So the king said, "Whoever speaks to you, bring him to me, and he will not touch you anymore." 11 Then she said, "Please let the king remember Yahweh your God, *so that* the avenger of blood will not continue to bring about ruin, so that they would not destroy my son." And he said, "As Yahweh lives, not one hair of your son shall fall to the ground."

12 Then the woman said, "Please let your servant-woman speak a word to my lord the king." And he said, "Speak." 13 Then the woman said, "Why then have you thought up such a thing against the people of God? For in speaking this word the king is as one who is guilty, *in that* the king does not bring back his banished one. 14 For we will surely die and are like water spilled on the ground which cannot be gathered up again. Yet God does not take away life, but thinks up ways so that the banished one will not be cast out from him. 15 So now, the reason I have come to speak this word to my lord the king is that the people have made me afraid; so your servant-woman said, 'Let me now speak to the king, perhaps the king will perform the word of his maidservant. 16 For the king will listen and deliver his maidservant from the hand of the man who would destroy both me and my son from the inheritance of God.' 17 Then your servant-woman said, 'Please let the word of my lord the king be a resting place, for as the angel of God, so is my lord the king to listen *with discernment* through the good and evil. And may Yahweh your God be with you.'"

18 Then the king answered and said to the woman, "Please do not hide anything from me that I am about to ask you." And the woman said, "Let my lord the king please speak." 19 So the king said, "Is the hand of Joab with you in all this?" And the woman answered and said, "As your soul lives, my lord the king, no one can turn to the right or to the left from anything that my lord the king has spoken. Indeed, it was your servant Joab who commanded me, and it was he who put all these words in the mouth of your servant-woman; 20 in order to change the appearance of things your servant Joab has done this thing. But my lord is wise, like the wisdom of the angel of God, to know all that is in the earth."

21 Then the king said to Joab, "Behold now, I have done this thing; go therefore, bring back the young man Absalom." 22 And Joab fell on his face to the ground, prostrated himself and blessed the king; then Joab said, "Today your servant knows that I have found favor in your sight, O my lord, the king, in

that the king has performed the word of
his servant." 23 So Joab arose and went to
Geshur and brought Absalom to Jerusalem.
24 However the king said, "Let him turn to
his own house, and let him not see my face."
So Absalom turned to his own house and did
not see the king's face.
25 Now in all Israel was no one as hand-
some as Absalom, so highly praised; from
the sole of his foot to the top of his head
there was no defect in him. 26 When he
shaved the hair of his head (and it was at the
end of every year that he shaved *it*, for it was
heavy on him so he shaved it), he weighed
the hair of his head at 200 shekels by the
king's weight. 27 And to Absalom there were
born three sons, and one daughter whose
name was Tamar; she was a woman of
beautiful appearance.
28 Now Absalom lived two full years in
Jerusalem, and did not see the king's face.
29 Then Absalom sent for Joab, to send him
to the king, but he was not willing to come to
him. So he sent again a second time, but he
was not willing to come. 30 Therefore he said
to his servants, "See, Joab's portion *of land*
is next to mine, and he has barley there; go
and set it on fire." So Absalom's servants
set the portion *of land* on fire. 31 Then Joab
arose, came to Absalom at his house and
said to him, "Why have your servants set
my portion *of land* on fire?" 32 And Absalom
answered Joab, "Behold, I sent for you,
saying, 'Come here, that I may send you
to the king, to say, "Why have I come from
Geshur? It would be better for me still to be
there."' So now, let me see the king's face,
and if there is iniquity in me, let him put me
to death." 33 So Joab came to the king and
told him, and he called for Absalom. Thus
he came to the king and prostrated himself
on his face to the ground before the king,
and the king kissed Absalom.

Psalm 66:1–7

1 Make a loud shout to God, all the earth;
2 Sing praise for the glory of His name;
Establish His praise as glorious.
3 Say to God, "How fearsome
are Your works!
Because of the abundance of
Your strength Your enemies
will cower before You.
4 "All the earth will worship You,
And will sing praises to You;
They will sing praises to Your
name." Selah.
5 Come and see the works of God,
Who is fearsome in *His* deeds
toward the sons of men.
6 He turned the sea into dry land;
They passed through the river on foot;
There let us be glad in Him!
7 He rules by His might forever;
His eyes keep watch on the nations;
Let not the rebellious exalt
themselves. Selah.

Proverbs 16:25–26

25 There is a way *which seems*
right to a man,
But its end is the way of death.
26 A worker's appetite works for him,
For his mouth urges him *on*.

John 6:52–71

52 Then the Jews *began to* argue with one
another, saying, "How can this man give us
His flesh to eat?" 53 So Jesus said to them,
"Truly, truly, I say to you, unless you eat
the flesh of the Son of Man and drink His
blood, you have no life in yourselves. 54 He
who eats My flesh and drinks My blood has
eternal life, and I will raise him up on the
last day. 55 For My flesh is true food, and My
blood is true drink. 56 He who eats My flesh
and drinks My blood abides in Me, and I in
him. 57 As the living Father sent Me, and I
live because of the Father, so he who eats
Me, he also will live because of Me. 58 This is
the bread which came down out of heaven,
not as the fathers ate and died. He who eats
this bread will live forever."
59 These things He said in the synagogue
as He taught in Capernaum.
60 Therefore many of His disciples, when
they heard *this* said, "This is a difficult
statement; who can listen to it?" 61 But Jesus,
knowing in Himself that His disciples were
grumbling at this, said to them, "Does this
cause you to stumble? 62 *What* then if you
see the Son of Man ascending to where He
was before? 63 The Spirit is the One who
gives life; the flesh profits nothing; the words
that I have spoken to you are spirit and are
life. 64 But there are some of you who do not
believe." For Jesus knew from the beginning
who they were who did not believe, and who
it was that would betray Him. 65 And He was

saying, "For this reason I have said to you,
that no one can come to Me unless it has
been granted him from the Father."
66 As a result of this many of His disciples
went away and were not walking with Him
anymore. 67 So Jesus said to the twelve,
"Do you also want to go?" 68 Simon Peter
answered Him, "Lord, to whom shall we
go? You have words of eternal life. 69 And
we have believed and have come to know
that You are the Holy One of God." 70 Jesus
answered them, "Did I Myself not choose
you, the twelve, and *yet* one of you is a
devil?" 71 Now He was speaking of Judas
the son of Simon Iscariot, for he, one of the
twelve, was going to betray Him.

MAY 22

2 Samuel 15:1–16:23

15 Now it happened afterwards, that
Absalom prepared for himself a
chariot and horses and fifty men as runners
before him. 2 And Absalom used to rise early
and stand beside the way to the gate; and
when any man had a case to come to the
king for judgment, Absalom would call to
him and say, "From what city are you?" And
he would say, "Your servant is from one of
the tribes of Israel." 3 Then Absalom would
say to him, "See, your words are good and
right, but no man listens to you on the part
of the king." 4 Then Absalom would say,
"Oh that one would appoint me judge in
the land, then every man who has any case
or judgment could come to me and I would
justify him." 5 And when a man came near to
prostrate himself before him, he would send
forth his hand and take hold of him and kiss
him. 6 In this manner Absalom dealt with all
Israel who came to the king for judgment; so
Absalom stole away the hearts of the men
of Israel.
7 Now it happened at the end of forty
years that Absalom said to the king, "Please
let me go and pay my vow which I have
vowed to Yahweh, in Hebron. 8 For your
servant vowed a vow while I was living at
Geshur in Aram, saying, 'If Yahweh shall
indeed bring me back to Jerusalem, then I
will serve Yahweh.'" 9 And the king said to
him, "Go in peace." So he arose and went
to Hebron. 10 Then Absalom sent spies
throughout all the tribes of Israel, saying,
"As soon as you hear the sound of the trum-
pet, then you shall say, 'Absalom is king in
Hebron.'" 11 Now two hundred men went
with Absalom from Jerusalem, who were
invited and went innocently, and they did
not know anything. 12 And Absalom sent for
Ahithophel the Gilonite, David's counselor,
from his city Giloh, while he was offering
the sacrifices. And the conspiracy was
strong, for the people increased continually
with Absalom.
13 Then an informant came to David,
saying, "The hearts of the men of Israel have
followed Absalom." 14 So David said to all his
servants who were with him at Jerusalem,
"Arise and let us flee, for *otherwise* there
will be no escape for us from Absalom. Go
in haste, lest he overtake us hastily and
drive calamity on us and strike the city
with the edge of the sword." 15 Then the
king's servants said to the king, "Behold,
your servants *are ready to do* whatever my
lord the king chooses." 16 So the king went
out and all his household with him. But
the king left ten concubines to keep the
house. 17 And the king went out and all the
people with him, and they stopped at the
last house. 18 Now all his servants passed
on beside him, all the Cherethites, all the
Pelethites, and all the Gittites, six hundred
men who had come with him from Gath,
passed on before the king.
19 Then the king said to Ittai the Gittite,
"Why will you also go with us? Return and
remain with the king, for you are a foreigner
and also an exile; *return* to your own place.
20 You came *only* yesterday, and shall I today
make you wander with us, going about,
while I go where I go? Return and cause your
brothers to return; lovingkindness and truth
be with you." 21 But Ittai answered the king
and said, "As Yahweh lives, and as my lord
the king lives, surely wherever my lord the
king may be, whether for death or for life,
there also your servant will be." 22 So David
said to Ittai, "Go and pass over." So Ittai the
Gittite passed over with all his men and all
the little ones who *were* with him. 23 While
all the country was weeping with a loud
voice, all the people passed over. The king
also passed over the brook Kidron, and all

the people passed over toward the way of
the wilderness.
24 Now behold, Zadok also *came*, and
all the Levites with him carrying the ark
of the covenant of God. And they set down
the ark of God, and Abiathar came up until
all the people had finished passing from
the city. 25 Then the king said to Zadok,
"Return the ark of God to the city. If I find
favor in the sight of Yahweh, then He will
cause me to return and show me both it
and His habitation. 26 But if He should say
thus, 'I have no delight in you,' behold, here
I am, let Him do to me as seems good in
His sight." 27 The king said also to Zadok
the priest, "Are you *not* a seer? Return to
the city in peace and your two sons with
you, your son Ahimaaz and Jonathan the
son of Abiathar. 28 See, I am going to wait
at the fords of the wilderness until word
comes from you to inform me." 29 So Zadok
and Abiathar returned the ark of God to
Jerusalem and remained there.
30 But David went up the ascent of the
Mount of Olives, and wept as he went, and
his head was covered and he was walking
barefoot. And all the people who were
with him each covered his head and went
up weeping as they went. 31 Now David
informed *them*, saying, "Ahithophel is
among the conspirators with Absalom."
And David said, "O Yahweh, I pray, make the
counsel of Ahithophel foolishness."
32 Then it happened that as David was
coming to the summit, where he used to
worship God, that behold, Hushai the
Archite met him with his coat torn and
dust on his head. 33 And David said to him,
"If you pass over with me, then you will
be a burden to me. 34 But if you return to
the city, and say to Absalom, 'I will be your
servant, O king; as I have been your father's
servant in time past, so I will now be your
servant,' then you can thwart the counsel
of Ahithophel for me. 35 Are not Zadok and
Abiathar the priests with you there? So it
shall be that whatever you hear from the
king's house, you shall inform Zadok and
Abiathar the priests. 36 Behold, their two
sons are with them there, Ahimaaz, Zadok's
son and Jonathan, Abiathar's son; and by
their hand you shall send me everything
that you hear." 37 So Hushai, David's friend,
came into the city, and Absalom came into
Jerusalem.

16 Now David had passed a little beyond
the summit, and behold, Ziba the
young man of Mephibosheth met him with
a couple of saddled donkeys, and on them
were two hundred loaves of bread, one
hundred clusters of raisins, one hundred
summer fruits, and a jug of wine. 2 And
the king said to Ziba, "Why do you have
these?" And Ziba said, "The donkeys are
for the king's household to ride, and the
bread and summer fruit for the young men
to eat, and the wine, for whoever is faint
in the wilderness to drink." 3 Then the king
said, "And where is your master's son?" And
Ziba said to the king, "Behold, he is staying
in Jerusalem, for he said, 'Today the house of
Israel will return the kingdom of my father
to me.'" 4 So the king said to Ziba, "Behold,
all that belongs to Mephibosheth is yours."
And Ziba said, "I prostrate myself; let me
find favor in your sight, O my lord, the king!"
5 And King David came to Bahurim, and
behold, there came out from there a man of
the family of the house of Saul whose name
was Shimei, the son of Gera; he came out
cursing continually as he came. 6 He also
threw stones at David and at all the servants
of King David; and all the people and all the
mighty men were at his right hand and at his
left. 7 And thus Shimei said when he cursed,
"Get out, get out, you man of bloodshed, and
vile fellow! 8 Yahweh has returned upon you
all the bloodshed of the house of Saul, in
whose place you have reigned; and Yahweh
has given the kingdom into the hand of
your son Absalom. And behold, you are
taken in your own evil, for you are a man
of bloodshed!"
9 Then Abishai the son of Zeruiah said
to the king, "Why should this dead dog
curse my lord the king? Let me pass over
now and remove his head." 10 But the king
said, "What have I to do with you, O sons of
Zeruiah? If he curses, and if Yahweh has told
him, 'Curse David,' then who shall say, 'Why
have you done so?'" 11 Then David said to
Abishai and to all his servants, "Behold, my
son who came forth from my body seeks my
life; how much more now this Benjamite?
Let him alone and let him curse, for Yahweh
has told him. 12 Perhaps Yahweh will look on
my affliction and return good to me instead
of his cursing this day." 13 So David and his
men went on the way; and Shimei went
along on the hillside parallel with him and

as he went he cursed and cast stones and threw dust at him. 14 Then the king and all the people who were with him arrived weary and he refreshed himself there.

15 Now Absalom and all the people, the men of Israel, had entered Jerusalem, and Ahithophel with him. 16 And it happened that when Hushai the Archite, David's friend, came to Absalom, that Hushai said to Absalom, "*Long* live the king! *Long* live the king!" 17 And Absalom said to Hushai, "Is this your lovingkindness to your friend? Why did you not go with your friend?" 18 Then Hushai said to Absalom, "No! For whom Yahweh, this people, and all the men of Israel have chosen, his I will be, and with him I will remain. 19 Besides, whom should I serve? *Should I* not *serve* in the presence of his son? As I have served in your father's presence, so I will be in your presence."

20 Then Absalom said to Ahithophel, "Give your advice. What shall we do?" 21 And Ahithophel said to Absalom, "Go in to your father's concubines, whom he has left to keep the house; then all Israel will hear that you have made yourself odious to your father. The hands of all who are with you will also be strengthened." 22 So they pitched a tent for Absalom on the roof, and Absalom went in to his father's concubines in the sight of all Israel. 23 Now the counsel of Ahithophel, which he counseled in those days, *was* as if one asked of the word of God; so was all the counsel of Ahithophel *regarded* by both David and Absalom.

Psalm 66:8–15

8 Bless our God, O peoples,
And make the sound of
His praise heard,
9 Who establishes us among the living
And does not allow our feet to stumble.
10 For You have tested us, O God;
You have refined us as silver is refined.
11 You brought us into the net;
You established an oppressive
burden upon our loins.
12 You made men ride over our heads;
We went through fire and
through water,
Yet You brought us out into
a place of abundance.
13 I shall come into Your house
with burnt offerings;
I shall pay You my vows,
14 Which my lips uttered
And my mouth spoke when
I was in distress.
15 I shall offer to You burnt
offerings of fat beasts,
With the smoke of rams;
I shall make *an offering of*
bulls with male goats. Selah.

Proverbs 16:27–30

27 A vile man digs up evil,
And *the words* on his lips are
like scorching fire.
28 A perverse man spreads strife,
And a whisperer separates
close companions.
29 A man of violence entices his neighbor
And leads him in a way
that is not good.
30 He who winks his eyes *does so*
to devise perverse things;
He who compresses his lips
brings evil to pass.

John 7:1–24

7 And after these things Jesus was walking in Galilee, for He was unwilling to walk in Judea because the Jews were seeking to kill Him. 2 Now the feast of the Jews, the Feast of Booths, was near. 3 Therefore His brothers said to Him, "Leave here and go into Judea, so that Your disciples also may see Your works which You are doing. 4 For no one does anything in secret when he himself seeks to be *known* openly. If You do these things, show Yourself publicly to the world." 5 For not even His brothers were believing in Him. 6 So Jesus *said to them, "My time is not yet here, but your time is always here. 7 The world cannot hate you, but it hates Me because I bear witness about it, that its deeds are evil. 8 Go up to the feast yourselves; I am not yet going up to this feast because My time has not yet been fulfilled." 9 Having said these things to them, He stayed in Galilee.

10 But when His brothers had gone up to the feast, then He Himself also went up, not publicly, but as in secret. 11 So the Jews were seeking Him at the feast and saying, "Where is He?" 12 And there was much grumbling among the crowds concerning Him; some were saying, "He is a good man"; others were saying, "No, on the contrary, He leads the crowd astray." 13 Yet no one was speaking openly about Him for fear of the Jews.

14 But when it was now the middle of the feast Jesus went up into the temple, and *began to* teach. 15 The Jews then were marveling, saying, "How has this man become learned, not having been educated?" 16 So Jesus answered them and said, "My teaching is not Mine, but from Him who sent Me. 17 If anyone is willing to do His will, he will know about the teaching, whether it is of God or I speak from Myself. 18 He who speaks from himself seeks his own glory; but He who is seeking the glory of the One who sent Him, He is true, and there is no unrighteousness in Him.

19 "Did not Moses give you the Law? And *yet* none of you does the Law. Why do you seek to kill Me?" 20 The crowd answered, "You have a demon! Who seeks to kill You?" 21 Jesus answered them, "I did one work, and you all marvel. 22 For this reason Moses has given you circumcision (not because it is from Moses, but from the fathers), and on *the* Sabbath you circumcise a man. 23 If a man receives circumcision on the Sabbath so that the Law of Moses will not be broken, are you angry with Me because I made an entire man well on *the* Sabbath? 24 Do not judge according to appearance, but judge with righteous judgment."

MAY 23

2 Samuel 17:1–18:33

17 Then Ahithophel said to Absalom, "Please let me choose 12,000 men that I may arise and pursue David tonight. 2 And I will come upon him while he is weary with *his* hands falling limp and throw him into *utter* fright, so that all the people who are with him will flee. Then I will strike down the king alone, 3 and I will cause all the people to return to you. The return of everyone depends on the man you seek; *then* all the people will be at peace." 4 And the word was right in the eyes of Absalom and all the elders of Israel.

5 Then Absalom said, "Call now Hushai the Archite also, and let us hear what is also in his mouth." 6 Then Hushai came to Absalom. And Absalom spoke to him, saying, "Ahithophel has spoken thus. Shall we carry out his word? If not, you speak." 7 And Hushai said to Absalom, "This time the counsel that Ahithophel has counseled is not good." 8 Then Hushai said, "You know your father and his men, that they are mighty men and they are bitter of soul, like a bear robbed of her cubs in the field. And your father is a man of war, and will not spend the night with the people. 9 Behold, he has now hidden himself in one of the caves or in another place; and it will be when he falls on them at the first *attack*, that whoever hears *it* will say, 'There has been *a slaughter among the people* who follow Absalom.' 10 And even the one who is a man of valor, whose heart is like the heart of a lion, will utterly melt; for all Israel knows that your father is a mighty man and those who are with him are men of valor. 11 But I counsel that all Israel be utterly gathered to you, from Dan even to Beersheba, as the sand that is by the sea in abundance, and that you personally go into battle. 12 So we shall come to him in one of the places where he can be found, and we will set down on him as the dew falls on the ground; and of him and of all the men who are with him, not even one will be left. 13 If he withdraws into a city, then all Israel shall carry ropes to that city, and we will drag it into the valley until not even a small stone is found there." 14 Then Absalom and all the men of Israel said, "The counsel of Hushai the Archite is better than the counsel of Ahithophel." For Yahweh had ordained to thwart the good counsel of Ahithophel, so that Yahweh might bring calamity on Absalom.

15 Then Hushai said to Zadok and to Abiathar the priests, "This is what Ahithophel counseled Absalom and the elders of Israel, and this is what I have counseled. 16 So now, send quickly and inform David, saying, 'Do not spend the night at the fords of the wilderness, but by all means cross over, lest the king and all the people who are with him be swallowed up.'" 17 Now Jonathan and Ahimaaz were staying at En-rogel, and a servant-woman would go and inform them, and they would go and inform King David, for they could not be seen entering the city. 18 But a boy did see them and informed Absalom; so the two of them went quickly and came to the house of a man in Bahurim,

who had a well in his courtyard, and they
went down into it. 19 And the woman took a
covering and spread it over the well's mouth
and scattered crushed grain on it, so that
nothing was known. 20 Then Absalom's ser-
vants came to the woman at the house and
said, "Where are Ahimaaz and Jonathan?"
And the woman said to them, "They have
crossed the brook of water." And when they
searched and could not find *them*, they
returned to Jerusalem.

21 Now it happened after they went away,
that they came up out of the well and went
and informed King David; and they said
to David, "Arise and cross over the water
quickly for thus Ahithophel has counseled
against you." 22 Then David and all the peo-
ple who *were* with him arose and crossed the
Jordan; and by dawn not even one remained
who had not crossed the Jordan.

23 Now Ahithophel saw that his counsel
was not followed. So he saddled *his* donkey
and arose and went to his home, to his city,
and set his house in order, and strangled
himself; thus he died and was buried in the
grave of his father.

24 Now David came to Mahanaim. And
Absalom crossed the Jordan, he and all the
men of Israel with him. 25 And Absalom
set Amasa over the army in place of Joab.
Now Amasa was the son of a man whose
name was Ithra the Israelite, who went in
to Abigail the daughter of Nahash, sister of
Zeruiah, Joab's mother. 26 And Israel and
Absalom camped in the land of Gilead.

27 Now it happened that when David
had come to Mahanaim, Shobi the son of
Nahash from Rabbah of the sons of Ammon,
Machir the son of Ammiel from Lo-debar,
and Barzillai the Gileadite from Rogelim,
28 brought beds, basins, pottery, wheat,
barley, flour, roasted *grain*, beans, lentils,
roasted *seeds*, 29 honey, curds, sheep, and
cheese of the herd, for David and for the
people who *were* with him, to eat; for they
said, "The people are hungry and weary and
thirsty in the wilderness."

18 Then David numbered the people
who were with him and set over
them commanders of thousands and
commanders of hundreds. 2 And David
sent the people out, one-third under the
hand of Joab, one-third under the hand of
Abishai the son of Zeruiah, Joab's brother,
and one-third under the hand of Ittai the
Gittite. And the king said to the people, "I
myself will surely go out with you also." 3 But
the people said, "You should not go out; for
if we indeed flee, they will not set their heart
on us; even if half of us die, they will not set
their heart on us. But now you are worth ten
thousand of us; so now it is better that you
be ready to help us from the city." 4 Then
the king said to them, "Whatever is good
in your sight I will do." So the king stood
beside the gate, and all the people went out
by hundreds and thousands. 5 Then the king
commanded Joab and Abishai and Ittai,
saying, "*Deal* gently for my sake with the
young man Absalom." And all the people
heard when the king commanded all the
commanders concerning Absalom.

6 Then the people went out into the field
to meet Israel, and the battle took place
in the forest of Ephraim. 7 And the people
of Israel were defeated there before the
servants of David, and the slaughter there
that day was great, 20,000 men. 8 And the
battle there was scattered over the whole
countryside, and the forest devoured more
people that day than the sword devoured.

9 Then Absalom happened to meet the
servants of David. Now Absalom was riding
on *his* mule, and the mule went under the
thick branches of a great oak. And his head
caught fast in the oak, so he was left hanging
between heaven and earth, while the mule
that was under him passed onward. 10 Then
a certain man saw *it*, he told Joab and said,
"Behold, I saw Absalom hanging in an oak."
11 Then Joab said to the man who had told
him, "Now behold, you saw *him*! Why then
did you not strike him there to the ground?
And I would have given you ten *pieces* of
silver and a belt." 12 So the man said to
Joab, "Even if I should receive one thousand
pieces of silver in my hand, I would not send
forth my hand against the king's son; for in
our hearing the king commanded you and
Abishai and Ittai, saying, 'Keep for me the
young man Absalom!' 13 Otherwise, if I had
dealt treacherously against his life (and
there is nothing hidden from the king),
then you yourself would have stood aloof."
14 Then Joab said, "I will not wait around
here before you." So he took three spears
in his hand and thrust them through the
heart of Absalom while he was yet alive in
the midst of the oak. 15 And ten young men

who carried Joab's armor gathered around
and struck Absalom and put him to death.
16 Then Joab blew the trumpet, and the
people returned from pursuing Israel, for
Joab restrained the people. 17 And they took
Absalom and cast him into a deep pit in the
forest and set over him a very great heap of
stones. And all Israel fled, each to his tent.
18 Now Absalom in his lifetime had taken
and set up for himself a pillar which is in
the King's Valley, for he had said, "I have no
son to preserve my name." So he named the
pillar after his own name, and it is called
Absalom's Monument to this day.
19 Then Ahimaaz the son of Zadok said,
"Please let me run and proclaim the good
news to the king that Yahweh has judged
to save him from the hand of his enemies."
20 But Joab said to him, "You are not the man
for the good news this day, but you shall pro-
claim the good news another day; however,
you shall not proclaim the good news today
because the king's son has died." 21 Then
Joab said to the Cushite, "Go, tell the king
what you have seen." So the Cushite bowed
to Joab and ran. 22 Now Ahimaaz the son of
Zadok said once more to Joab, "But whatever
happens, please let me also run after the
Cushite." And Joab said, "Why would you
run, my son, since you will have no reward
for going?" 23 "But whatever happens," *he
said*, "I will run." So he said to him, "Run."
Then Ahimaaz ran by way of the plain and
passed the Cushite.
24 Now David was sitting between the two
gates; and the watchman went up to the roof
of the gate by the wall, and raised his eyes
and looked, and behold, a man running by
himself. 25 And the watchman called and
told the king. And the king said, "If he is by
himself there is good news in his mouth."
And he came nearer and nearer. 26 Then
the watchman saw another man running;
and the watchman called to the gatekeeper
and said, "Behold, *another* man running by
himself." And the king said, "This one also is
bringing good news." 27 And the watchman
said, "I see that the running of the first one
is like the running of Ahimaaz the son of
Zadok." And the king said, "This is a good
man and comes with good news."
28 And Ahimaaz called and said to the
king, "Peace!" And he prostrated himself
before the king with his face to the ground.
And he said, "Blessed is Yahweh your God,
who has delivered up the men who lifted
their hands against my lord the king."
29 Then the king said, "Is there peace with
the young man Absalom?" And Ahimaaz
said, "When Joab sent the king's servant,
and your servant, I saw a great tumult, but
I did not know what *it was*." 30 Then the
king said, "Turn aside and stand here." So
he turned aside and stood still.
31 Behold, the Cushite arrived, and the
Cushite said, "Let my lord the king receive
good news, for Yahweh has judged *to save*
you this day from the hand of all those who
rose up against you." 32 Then the king said to
the Cushite, "Is there peace with the young
man Absalom?" And the Cushite answered,
"Let the enemies of my lord the king, and all
who rise up against you for evil, be as that
young man!"
33 Then the king trembled and went up
to the chamber over the gate and wept.
And thus he said as he walked, "O my son
Absalom, my son, my son Absalom! Would
I had died instead of you, O Absalom, my
son, my son!"

Psalm 66:16–20

16 Come *and* hear, all who fear God,
And I will recount what He
has done for my soul.
17 I called out to Him with my mouth,
And He was exalted with my tongue.
18 If I see wickedness in my heart,
The Lord will not hear;
19 But certainly God has heard;
He has given heed to the
voice of my prayer.
20 Blessed be God,
Who has not turned away my prayer
Nor His lovingkindness from me.

Proverbs 16:31–32

31 Gray hair is a crown of beauty;
It is found in the way of righteousness.
32 He who is slow to anger is
better than the mighty,
And he who rules his own spirit,
than he who captures a city.

John 7:25–53

25 So some of the people of Jerusalem were
saying, "Is this not the man whom they are
seeking to kill? 26 And look, He is speaking
openly, and they are saying nothing to Him.
Do the rulers truly know that this is the

Christ? 27 However, we know where this man
is from; but whenever the Christ comes, no
one knows where He is from." 28 Then Jesus
cried out in the temple, teaching and saying,
"You both know Me and know where I am
from; and I have not come of Myself, but
He who sent Me is true, whom you do not
know. 29 I know Him, because I am from Him,
and He sent Me." 30 So they were seeking to
seize Him; yet no man laid his hand on Him,
because His hour had not yet come. 31 But
many of the crowd believed in Him; and they
were saying, "When the Christ comes, will
He do more signs than this man did?"
32 The Pharisees heard the crowd whis-
pering these things about Him, and the
chief priests and the Pharisees sent officers
to seize Him. 33 Therefore Jesus said, "For a
little while longer I am with you, then I go to
Him who sent Me. 34 You will seek Me, and
will not find Me; and where I am, you cannot
come." 35 The Jews then said to one another,
"Where does this man intend to go that we
will not find Him? Is He intending to go to
the Dispersion among the Greeks and teach
the Greeks? 36 What is this statement that
He said, 'You will seek Me, and will not find
Me; and where I am, you cannot come'?"
37 Now on the last day, the great *day* of
the feast, Jesus stood and cried out, saying,
"If anyone is thirsty, let him come to Me
and drink. 38 He who believes in Me, as the
Scripture said, 'From his innermost being
will flow rivers of living water.'" 39 But this
He spoke of the Spirit, whom those who
believed in Him were going to receive; for
the Spirit was not yet *given*, because Jesus
was not yet glorified.
40 *Some* of the crowd therefore, when
they heard these words, were saying, "This
truly is the Prophet." 41 Others were saying,
"This is the Christ." Still others were saying,
"*No*, for is the Christ going to come from
Galilee? 42 Has not the Scripture said that
the Christ comes from the seed of David
and from Bethlehem, the village where
David was?" 43 So a division occurred in
the crowd because of Him. 44 Some of them
were wanting to seize Him, but no one laid
hands on Him.
45 The officers then came to the chief
priests and Pharisees, and they said to them,
"Why did you not bring Him?" 46 The offi-
cers answered, "Never has a man spoken like
this!" 47 The Pharisees then answered them,
"Have you also been led astray? 48 Have any
of the rulers or Pharisees believed in Him?
49 But this crowd which does not know the
Law is accursed." 50 Nicodemus (he who
came to Him before), being one of them,
*said to them, 51 "Does our Law judge a man
unless it first hears from him and knows
what he is doing?" 52 They answered him,
"Are you also from Galilee? Search and
see that no prophet arises out of Galilee."
53 [Everyone went to his home.

MAY 24

2 Samuel 19:1–20:26

19 Then it was told to Joab, "Behold,
the king is weeping and mourns for
Absalom." 2 And the salvation that day
was turned to mourning for all the people,
for the people heard *it* said that day, "The
king is grieved for his son." 3 So the people
stole away to enter into the city that day, as
people who are dishonored steal away when
they flee in battle. 4 But as for the king, he
wrapped his face up. Then the king cried
out with a loud voice, "O my son Absalom,
O Absalom, my son, my son!" 5 Then Joab
came into the house to the king and said,
"Today you have shamed the faces of all
your servants, who today have provided
escape for your life and the lives of your
sons and daughters, the lives of your wives,
and the lives of your concubines, 6 by loving
those who hate you, and by hating those
who love you. For you have informed *all
of us* today that princes and servants are
nothing to you; for I know this day that if
Absalom were alive and all of us were dead
today, surely then it would be right in your
eyes. 7 So now, arise, go out and speak to
the heart of your servants, for I swear by
Yahweh, if you do not go out, surely not a
man will pass the night with you, and this
will be of greater evil for you than all the
evil that has come upon you from your
youth until now."
8 So the king arose and sat in the gate. And
they told all the people, saying, "Behold,
the king is sitting in the gate." Then all the
people came before the king.

Now Israel had fled, each to his tent. 9 And it happened that all the people were disputing throughout all the tribes of Israel, saying, "The king delivered us from the hand of our enemies and provided us escape from the hand of the Philistines, but now he has fled out of the land from Absalom. 10 However, Absalom, whom we anointed over us, has died in battle. So now, why are you silent about having the king return?"

11 Now King David had sent to Zadok and Abiathar the priests, saying, "Speak to the elders of Judah, saying, 'Why are you the last to have the king return to his house, while the word of all Israel has come to the king, *even* to his house? 12 You are my brothers; you are my bone and my flesh. Why then should you be the last to have the king return?' 13 And say to Amasa, 'Are you not my bone and my flesh? May God do so to me, and more also, if you will not be commander of the army before me continually in place of Joab.'" 14 Thus he inclined the hearts of all the men of Judah as one man, so they sent *word* to the king, *saying*, "Return, you and all your servants." 15 The king then returned and came as far as the Jordan. And Judah came to Gilgal in order to go to meet the king, to cause the king to pass over across the Jordan.

16 Then Shimei the son of Gera, the Benjamite who was from Bahurim, hurried and came down with the men of Judah to meet King David. 17 Now there were one thousand men of Benjamin with him, with Ziba the young man of the house of Saul, and his fifteen sons and his twenty servants with him; and they rushed to the Jordan before the king. 18 Then they kept passing over the ford to cause the king's household to pass over, and to do what was good in his sight. And Shimei the son of Gera fell down before the king as he was about to pass over the Jordan. 19 So he said to the king, "Let not my lord consider me guilty, nor remember what your servant did wrong on the day when my lord the king went out from Jerusalem, so that the king would take *it* to heart. 20 For your servant knows that I have sinned; therefore behold, I have come today, the first of all the house of Joseph to go down to meet my lord the king." 21 But Abishai the son of Zeruiah said, "Should not Shimei be put to death for this, because he cursed the anointed of Yahweh?" 22 David then said, "What have I to do with you, O sons of Zeruiah, that you should this day be an adversary to me? Should any man be put to death in Israel today? For do I not know that I am king over Israel today?" 23 And the king said to Shimei, "You shall not die." Thus the king swore to him.

24 Now Mephibosheth the son of Saul had come down to meet the king; and he had not done *anything* for his feet, nor done *anything* for his mustache, nor washed his clothes, from the day the king departed until the day he came *home* in peace. 25 Now it happened when he came from Jerusalem to meet the king, that the king said to him, "Why did you not go with me, Mephibosheth?" 26 So he answered, "O my lord, the king, my servant deceived me; for your servant said, 'I will saddle a donkey for myself that I may ride on it and go with the king,' because your servant is lame. 27 Moreover, he has slandered your servant to my lord the king; but my lord the king is like the angel of God, therefore do what is good in your sight. 28 For all my father's household was nothing but men *worthy of* death before my lord the king; yet you set your servant among those who ate at your own table. What right do I have yet that I should complain anymore to the king?" 29 So the king said to him, "Why do you still speak of your affairs? I have decided, 'You and Ziba shall divide the land.'" 30 And Mephibosheth said to the king, "Let him even take it all, since my lord the king has come in peace to his own house."

31 Now Barzillai the Gileadite had come down from Rogelim; and he passed over the Jordan with the king in order to send him off over the Jordan. 32 Now Barzillai was very old, being eighty years old; and he had sustained the king while he stayed at Mahanaim, for he was a very great man. 33 And the king said to Barzillai, "You pass over with me and I will sustain you in Jerusalem with me." 34 But Barzillai said to the king, "How long have I yet to live, that I should go up with the king to Jerusalem? 35 I am now eighty years old. Can I know between good and bad? Or can your servant taste what I eat or what I drink? Or can I hear anymore the voice of singing men and women? Why then should your servant be an added burden to my lord the king? 36 Your servant would merely pass over the

Jordan with the king. Why should the king
compensate me *with* this reward? 37 Please
let your servant return, that I may die in
my own city near the grave of my father
and my mother. However, here is your
servant Chimham, let him pass over with
my lord the king, and do for him what is
good in your sight." 38 So the king answered,
"Chimham shall pass over with me, and I
will do for him what is good in your sight;
and whatever you require of me, I will do
for you." 39 Then all the people passed over
the Jordan and the king passed over too. The
king then kissed Barzillai and blessed him,
and he returned to his place.

40 Now the king went on to Gilgal, and
Chimham went on with him; and all the
people of Judah and also half the people of
Israel accompanied the king. 41 And behold,
all the men of Israel came to the king and
said to the king, "Why had our brothers the
men of Judah stolen you away, and caused
the king and his household and all David's
men with him to pass over the Jordan?"
42 Then all the men of Judah answered the
men of Israel, "Because the king is a close
relative to us. Why then are you angry about
this matter? Have we eaten at all at the king's
expense, or has anything been taken for us?"
43 But the men of Israel answered the men
of Judah and said, "We have ten parts in the
king, therefore we also have more *claim* on
David than you. Why then did you treat us
with contempt? Was it not our word first to
have our king return?" Yet the words of the
men of Judah were harsher than the words
of the men of Israel.

20 Now a vile fellow happened to be
there whose name was Sheba, the
son of Bichri, a Benjamite; and he blew the
trumpet and said,

"We have no portion in David,
Nor do we have inheritance
in the son of Jesse;
Every man to his tents, O Israel!"

2 So all the men of Israel went up from fol-
lowing David *and* followed Sheba the son of
Bichri; but the men of Judah clung to their
king, from the Jordan even to Jerusalem.

3 Then David came to his house at Jerusa-
lem, and the king took the ten women, the
concubines whom he had left to keep the
house, and placed them under guard and
provided them with sustenance, but did not
go in to them. So they were shut up until the
day of their death, living as widows.

4 Then the king said to Amasa, "Call out
the men of Judah for me within three days,
and you yourself stand here." 5 So Amasa
went to call out *the men of* Judah, but he
delayed longer than the set time which
he had appointed him. 6 And David said
to Abishai, "Now Sheba the son of Bichri
will do us more harm than Absalom; take
your lord's servants and pursue him, lest he
find for himself fortified cities and deliver
himself from our sight." 7 So Joab's men
pursued him, along with the Cherethites
and the Pelethites and all the mighty men;
and they went out from Jerusalem to pursue
Sheba the son of Bichri. 8 They were at the
large stone which is in Gibeon, and Amasa
came to meet them. Now Joab was dressed
in his military attire, and over it was a belt
with a sword in its sheath fastened at his
waist; and as he came out, it fell out. 9 Then
Joab said to Amasa, "Is it well with you, my
brother?" And Joab took Amasa by the beard
with his right hand to kiss him.

10 But Amasa was not on guard against
the sword which was in Joab's hand so he
struck him in the belly with it and poured
out his inward parts on the ground, and did
not *strike* him again, and he died. Then Joab
and Abishai his brother pursued Sheba the
son of Bichri. 11 Now there stood by him one
of Joab's young men, and said, "Whoever
delights in Joab and whoever is for David, *let
him* follow Joab." 12 But Amasa lay wallowing
in *his* blood in the middle of the highway.
And the man saw that all the people stood
still. So he removed Amasa from the high-
way into the field and threw a garment over
him when he saw that everyone who came
by him stood still.

13 As soon as he was removed from the
highway, all the men passed on after Joab
to pursue Sheba the son of Bichri.

14 Now he went through all the tribes of
Israel to Abel, even Beth-maacah, and all
the Berites; and they were assembled and
also came after him. 15 So they came and
besieged him in Abel Beth-maacah, and
they cast up a siege ramp against the city,
and it stood by the rampart; and all the
people who were with Joab were wreaking
destruction in order to cause the wall to
fall. 16 Then a wise woman called from the
city, "Hear, hear! Please tell Joab, 'Draw

near that I may speak with you.'" 17 So he
drew near to her, and the woman said, "Are
you Joab?" And he answered, "I am." Then
she said to him, "Listen to the words of
your maidservant." And he answered, "I
am listening." 18 Then she spoke, saying,
"Formerly they used to speak *in this way*,
saying, 'They will surely ask *advice* at Abel,'
and thus they ended *the dispute*. 19 I am of
those who are peaceable *and* faithful in
Israel. You are seeking to put to death a
city, even a mother in Israel. Why would
you swallow up the inheritance of Yahweh?"
20 And Joab answered and said, "Far be it, far
be it from me that I should swallow up or
destroy! 21 Such is not the case. But a man
from the hill country of Ephraim, Sheba
the son of Bichri by name, has lifted up his
hand against King David. Give him over
alone, and I will go from the city." And the
woman said to Joab, "Behold, his head will
be thrown to you over the wall." 22 Then
the woman came to all the people in her
wisdom. And they cut off the head of Sheba
the son of Bichri and threw it to Joab. So he
blew the trumpet, and they were scattered
from the city, each to his tent. Joab also
returned to the king at Jerusalem.
23 Now Joab *was* over the whole army
of Israel, and Benaiah the son of Jehoiada
was over the Cherethites and the Pelethites;
24 and Adoram *was* over the forced labor,
and Jehoshaphat the son of Ahilud was
the recorder; 25 and Sheva *was* scribe, and
Zadok and Abiathar *were* priests; 26 and Ira
the Jairite was also a priest to David.

Psalm 67:1–7

1 God be gracious to us and bless us,
And cause His face to
shine upon us— Selah.
2 That Your way may be
known on the earth,
Your salvation among all nations.
3 Let the peoples praise You, O God;
Let all the peoples praise You.
4 Let the nations be glad and sing for joy;
For You will judge the peoples
with uprightness
And lead the nations
on the earth. Selah.
5 Let the peoples praise You, O God;
Let all the peoples praise You.
6 The earth has yielded its produce;
God, our God, blesses us.
7 God blesses us,
That all the ends of the
earth may fear Him.

Proverbs 16:33–17:1

33 The lot is cast into the lap,
But its every judgment is from Yahweh.

17 Better is a dry morsel and
tranquility with it
Than a house full of
feasting with strife.

John 8:1–30

8 But Jesus went to the Mount of Olives.
2 Early in the morning He came again
into the temple, and all the people were
coming to Him; and He sat down and *began*
to teach them. 3 The scribes and the Phari-
sees *brought a woman caught in adultery,
and having set her in the center *of the court*,
4 they *said to Him, "Teacher, this woman
has been caught in adultery, in the very
act. 5 Now in the Law Moses commanded
us to stone such women; what then do You
say?" 6 They were saying this, testing Him,
so that they might have *evidence* to accuse
Him. But Jesus stooped down and with His
finger wrote on the ground. 7 But when they
persisted in asking Him, He straightened up
and said to them, "Let him who is without
sin among you *be the* first to throw a stone
at her." 8 Again He stooped down and wrote
on the ground. 9 When they heard it, they
began *to* go out one by one, beginning with
the older ones, and He was left alone, and
the woman, where she was, in the center *of*
the court. 10 Straightening up, Jesus said to
her, "Woman, where are they? Did no one
condemn you?" 11 She said, "No one, Lord."
And Jesus said, "I do not condemn you,
either. Go, and from now on sin no more."]
12 Then Jesus again spoke to them, saying,
"I am the Light of the world; he who follows
Me will never walk in the darkness, but will
have the Light of life." 13 So the Pharisees
said to Him, "You are bearing witness about
Yourself; Your witness is not true." 14 Jesus
answered and said to them, "Even if I bear
witness about Myself, My witness is true,
for I know where I came from and where
I am going; but you do not know where I
come from or where I am going. 15 You judge
according to the flesh; I am not judging any-
one. 16 But even if I do judge, My judgment

is true; for I am not alone *in it*, but I and the Father who sent Me. 17 Even in your law it has been written that the witness of two men is true. 18 I am He who bears witness about Myself, and the Father who sent Me bears witness about Me." 19 So they were saying to Him, "Where is Your Father?" Jesus answered, "You know neither Me nor My Father; if you knew Me, you would know My Father also." 20 These words He spoke in the treasury, as He was teaching in the temple; and no one seized Him, because His hour had not yet come.

21 Then He said again to them, "I am going away, and you will seek Me, and will die in your sin. Where I am going, you cannot come." 22 So the Jews were saying, "Surely He will not kill Himself, since He says, 'Where I am going, you cannot come'?" 23 And He was saying to them, "You are from below, I am from above. You are of this world, I am not of this world. 24 Therefore I said to you that you will die in your sins. For unless you believe that I am *He*, you will die in your sins." 25 So they were saying to Him, "Who are You?" Jesus said to them, "What have I been saying to you *from* the beginning? 26 I have many things to say and to judge concerning you, but He who sent Me is true; and the things which I heard from Him, these I am saying to the world." 27 They did not know that He had been speaking to them about the Father. 28 So Jesus said, "When you lift up the Son of Man, then you will know that I am *He*, and I do nothing from Myself, but I speak these things as the Father taught Me. 29 And He who sent Me is with Me; He has not left Me alone, for I always do the things that are pleasing to Him." 30 As He was speaking these things, many believed in Him.

MAY 25

2 Samuel 21:1–22:51

21 And there was a famine in the days of David for three years, year after year; and David sought the presence of Yahweh. And Yahweh said, "It is for Saul and his bloody house, because he put the Gibeonites to death." 2 So the king called the Gibeonites and spoke to them (now the Gibeonites were not of the sons of Israel but of the remnant of the Amorites, and the sons of Israel made a covenant with them, but Saul had sought to strike them down in his zeal for the sons of Israel and Judah). 3 Thus David said to the Gibeonites, "What should I do for you? And how can I make atonement that you may bless the inheritance of Yahweh?" 4 Then the Gibeonites said to him, "We have no *concern* of silver or gold with Saul or his house, nor is it for us to put any man to death in Israel." And he said, "I will do for you whatever you say." 5 So they said to the king, "The man who consumed us and who planned to eradicate us from standing within any border of Israel, 6 let seven men from his sons be given to us, and we will hang them before Yahweh in Gibeah of Saul, the chosen of Yahweh." And the king said, "I will give *them*."

7 But the king spared Mephibosheth, the son of Jonathan the son of Saul, because of the oath of Yahweh which was between them, between David and Saul's son Jonathan. 8 So the king took the two sons of Rizpah the daughter of Aiah, Armoni and Mephibosheth whom she had borne to Saul, and the five sons of Merab the daughter of Saul, whom she had borne to Adriel the son of Barzillai the Meholathite. 9 Then he gave them into the hand of the Gibeonites, and they hanged them in the mountain before Yahweh, so that the seven of them fell together; and they were put to death in the first days of harvest at the beginning of barley harvest.

10 And Rizpah the daughter of Aiah took sackcloth and spread it for herself on the rock, from the beginning of harvest until it rained on them from the sky; and she allowed neither the birds of the sky to rest on them by day nor the beasts of the field by night. 11 Then it was told to David what Rizpah the daughter of Aiah, the concubine of Saul, had done. 12 So David went and took the bones of Saul and the bones of Jonathan his son from the men of Jabesh-gilead, who had stolen them from the open square of Beth-shan, where the Philistines had hanged them on the day the Philistines struck down Saul in Gilboa. 13 And he brought up the bones of Saul and the bones of Jonathan his son from there, and they gathered the bones of those who had been hanged. 14 Then they buried the bones of Saul and Jonathan his

son in the land of Benjamin in Zela, in the
grave of Kish his father; thus they did all that
the king commanded, and afterwards God
was moved by the entreaty for the land.
15 And the Philistines were at war again
with Israel, so David went down and his
servants with him; and as they fought
against the Philistines, David became weary.
16 Then Ishbi-benob, who was among those
born to the giants, the weight of whose
spear was three hundred *shekels* of bronze in
weight, was girded with a new *sword*, and he
intended to strike down David. 17 But Abishai
the son of Zeruiah helped him, and struck
the Philistine and put him to death. Then the
men of David swore to him, saying, "You shall
not go out again with us to battle, so that you
do not extinguish the lamp of Israel."
18 Now it happened afterwards that there
was war again with the Philistines at Gob;
then Sibbecai the Hushathite struck down
Saph, who was among those born to the
giants. 19 There was war with the Philis-
tines again at Gob, and Elhanan the son of
Jaare-oregim the Bethlehemite struck down
Goliath the Gittite, the shaft of whose spear
was like a weaver's beam. 20 Then there was
war at Gath again, and there was a man of
great stature who had six fingers on each
hand and six toes on each foot, twenty-four
in number; and he also had been born to
the giants. 21 And he reproached Israel, so
Jonathan the son of Shimei, David's brother,
struck him down. 22 These four were born to
the giants in Gath, and they fell by the hand
of David and by the hand of his servants.

22 And David spoke to Yahweh the
words of this song in the day that
Yahweh delivered him from the hand of all
his enemies and from the hand of Saul. 2 He
said,

"Yahweh is my rock and my
fortress and my deliverer;
3 My God, my rock, in whom
I take refuge,
My shield and the horn of my
salvation, my stronghold
and my refuge;
My savior, You save me from violence.
4 "I call upon Yahweh, who is
worthy to be praised,
And I am saved from my enemies.
5 "For the waves of death
encompassed me;
The torrents of vileness terrorized me;
6 The cords of Sheol surrounded me;
The snares of death confronted me.
7 "In my distress I called upon Yahweh,
And I called to my God;
And out of His temple He
heard my voice,
And my cry for help *came* into His ears.
8 "Then the earth shook and quaked;
The foundations of heaven
were trembling
And were shaken, because
He was angry.
9 "Smoke went up out of His nostrils,
And fire from His mouth devoured;
Coals were kindled by it.
10 "He bowed the heavens and came down
With thick darkness under His feet.
11 "He rode on a cherub and flew;
And He appeared upon the
wings of the wind.
12 "And He made darkness
canopies around Him,
A mass of waters, thick
clouds of the skies.
13 "From the brightness before Him
Coals of fire were kindled.
14 "Yahweh thundered from heaven,
And the Most High gave
forth His voice.
15 "And He sent out arrows,
and scattered them,
Lightning, and threw them
into confusion.
16 "Then the channels of the sea appeared,
The foundations of the
world were laid bare
By the rebuke of Yahweh,
At the blast of the breath
of His nostrils.
17 "He sent from on high, He took me;
He drew me out of many waters.
18 "He delivered me from my
strong enemy,
From those who hated me, for
they were too mighty for me.
19 "They confronted me in the
day of my disaster,
But Yahweh was my support.
20 "He brought me forth also
into a broad place;
He rescued me, because
He delighted in me.
21 "Yahweh has rewarded me according
to my righteousness;

According to the cleanness of my
hands He has recompensed me.
22 "For I have kept the ways of Yahweh,
And have not wickedly
departed from my God.
23 "For all His judgments were before me,
And *as for* His statutes, I did
not depart from them.
24 "I was also blameless toward Him,
And I kept myself from my iniquity.
25 "Therefore Yahweh has recompensed
me according to my righteousness,
According to my cleanness
before His eyes.
26 "With the kind You show Yourself kind,
With the blameless You show
Yourself blameless;
27 With the pure You show
Yourself pure,
And with the crooked You
show Yourself astute.
28 "And You save an afflicted people;
But Your eyes are on the haughty
whom You bring down.
29 "For You are my lamp, O Yahweh;
And Yahweh illumines my darkness.
30 "For by You I can run upon a troop;
By my God I can leap over a wall.
31 "As for God, His way is blameless;
The word of Yahweh is tried;
He is a shield to all who
take refuge in Him.
32 "For who is God, but Yahweh?
And who is a rock, but our God?
33 "God is my strong fortress;
And He sets the blameless in His way.
34 "He makes my feet like hinds' *feet*,
And sets me on my high places.
35 "He trains my hands for battle,
So that my arms can bend
a bow of bronze.
36 "You have also given me the
shield of Your salvation,
And Your answer *to me*
makes me great.
37 "You enlarge my steps under me,
And my ankles have not given way.
38 "I pursued my enemies and
destroyed them,
And I did not turn back until
they were consumed.
39 "And I have consumed them
and crushed them, so that
they did not rise;
And they fell under my feet.
40 "For You have girded me with
strength for battle;
You have subdued under me those
who rose up against me.
41 "You have also made my enemies
turn their backs to me,
And I destroyed those who hated me.
42 "They looked, but there
was none to save;
Even to Yahweh, but He did
not answer them.
43 "Then I beat them fine as the
dust of the earth;
I pulverized *and* stamped them
as the mire of the streets.
44 "You have also delivered me from
the contentions of my people;
You have kept me as head
of the nations;
A people whom I have not
known serve me.
45 "Foreigners cower before me;
As soon as they hear, they obey me.
46 "Foreigners fade away,
And come trembling out
of their fortresses.
47 "Yahweh lives, and blessed
be my rock;
And let God, the rock of my
salvation, be lifted high,
48 The God who executes
vengeance for me,
And brings down peoples under me,
49 Who also brings me out
from my enemies;
You even lift me above those
who rise up against me;
You rescue me from the violent man.
50 "Therefore I will give thanks to You,
O Yahweh, among the nations,
And I will sing praises to Your name.
51 "*He* gives great salvation to His king,
And shows lovingkindness
to His anointed,
To David and his seed forever."

Psalm 68:1–6

1 Let God arise, let His
enemies be scattered,
And let those who hate Him
flee before Him.
2 As smoke is driven away,
so drive *them* away;
As wax melts before the fire,
So let the wicked perish before God.

3 But let the righteous be glad; let
them exult before God;
And let them rejoice with gladness.
4 Sing to God, sing praises to His name;
Lift up *a song* for Him who
rides through the deserts,
Whose name is Yah, and
exult before Him.

5 A father of the fatherless and
a judge for the widows,
Is God in His holy habitation.
6 God causes the lonely to
inhabit a home;
He leads out the prisoners
into prosperity,
Only the rebellious dwell
in a parched land.

Proverbs 17:2–4

2 A slave who acts insightfully will rule
over a son who acts shamefully,
And will share in the inheritance
among brothers.
3 The refining pot is for silver
and the furnace for gold,
But Yahweh tests hearts.
4 An evildoer gives heed to
lips of wickedness;
A liar gives ear to a destructive tongue.

John 8:31–59

31 So Jesus was saying to those Jews who
had believed Him, "If you abide in My word,
then you are truly My disciples; 32 and you
will know the truth, and the truth will make
you free." 33 They answered Him, "We are
Abraham's seed and have never yet been
enslaved to anyone. How is it that You say,
'You will become free'?"

34 Jesus answered them, "Truly, truly, I
say to you, everyone who commits sin is
the slave of sin. 35 And the slave does not
remain in the house forever; the son does
remain forever. 36 So if the Son makes you
free, you will be free indeed. 37 I know that
you are Abraham's seed; yet you are seeking
to kill Me, because My word has no place in
you. 38 I speak the things which I have seen
with *My* Father; therefore you also do the
things which you heard from *your* father."

39 They answered and said to Him, "Abra-
ham is our father." Jesus *said to them, "If
you are Abraham's children, you would do
the deeds of Abraham. 40 But now you are
seeking to kill Me, a man who has told you
the truth, which I heard from God. This
Abraham did not do. 41 You are doing the
deeds of your father." They said to Him,
"We were not born of sexual immorality;
we have one Father: God." 42 Jesus said to
them, "If God were your Father, you would
love Me, for I proceeded forth and have
come from God, for I have not even come
of Myself, but He sent Me. 43 Why do you
not understand what I am saying? *It is*
because you cannot hear My word. 44 You
are of *your* father the devil, and you want
to do the desires of your father. He was a
murderer from the beginning, and does not
stand in the truth because there is no truth
in him. Whenever he speaks a lie, he speaks
from his own *nature*, for he is a liar and
the father of lies. 45 But because I speak the
truth, you do not believe Me. 46 Which one
of you convicts Me of sin? If I speak truth,
why do you not believe Me? 47 He who is of
God hears the words of God; for this reason
you do not hear *them*, because you are not
of God."

48 The Jews answered and said to Him,
"Do we not say rightly that You are a Samari-
tan and have a demon?" 49 Jesus answered, "I
do not have a demon, but I honor My Father,
and you dishonor Me. 50 But I do not seek
My glory; there is One who seeks and judges.
51 Truly, truly, I say to you, if anyone keeps
My word he will never see death—ever."
52 The Jews said to Him, "Now we know that
You have a demon. Abraham died, and the
prophets *also*; and You say, 'If anyone keeps
My word, he will never taste of death—ever.'
53 Surely You are not greater than our father
Abraham who died? The prophets died too;
whom do You make Yourself out *to be*?"
54 Jesus answered, "If I glorify Myself, My
glory is nothing; it is My Father who glorifies
Me, of whom you say, 'He is our God'; 55 and
you have not known Him, but I know Him;
and if I say that I do not know Him, I will
be a liar like you, but I do know Him and
keep His word. 56 Your father Abraham
rejoiced to see My day, and he saw *it* and
was glad." 57 So the Jews said to Him, "You
are not yet fifty years old, and have You seen
Abraham?" 58 Jesus said to them, "Truly,
truly, I say to you, before Abraham was, I
am." 59 Therefore they picked up stones to
throw at Him, but Jesus hid Himself and
went out of the temple.

MAY 26

2 Samuel 23:1–24:25

23 Now these are the last words of David.
David the son of Jesse declares,
The man who raised
on high declares,
The anointed of the God of Jacob,
And the sweet psalmist of Israel,
2 "The Spirit of Yahweh spoke by me,
And His word was on my tongue.
3 "The God of Israel said,
The Rock of Israel spoke to me,
'He who rules over men *as*
a righteous one,
Who rules in the fear of God,
4 Is as the light of the morning
when the sun rises,
A morning without clouds,
From brightness *of the sun* after rain.'
With the tender grass *springing*
from the earth,
5 Truly is not my house so with God?
For He has made an everlasting
covenant with me,
Ordered in all things, and secured;
For all my salvation and all *my* desire,
Will He not indeed make *it* grow?
6 "But the vile *men*, every one of them
will be thrust away like thorns,
Because they cannot be taken in hand;
7 But the man who touches them
Must be armed with iron and
the shaft of a spear,
And they will be completely burned
with fire where *they* sit."

8 These are the names of the mighty men
whom David had: Josheb-basshebeth a
Tahchemonite, chief of the captains, he was
called Adino the Eznite, because of eight
hundred slain *by him* at one time; 9 and after
him was Eleazar the son of Dodo the son of
Ahohi, one of the three mighty men with
David when they reproached the Philistines
who were gathered together there to battle
and the men of Israel had gone up to retreat.
10 He arose and struck the Philistines until
his hand was weary and clung to the sword,
and Yahweh brought about a great salvation
that day; and the people returned after him
only to strip *the slain.*

11 Now after him was Shammah the son
of Agee a Hararite. And the Philistines were
gathered into a troop where there was a
portion of the field full of lentils; and the
people fled from before the Philistines.
12 But he took his stand in the midst of that
portion and delivered it and struck down
the Philistines. So Yahweh brought about a
great salvation.

13 Then three of the thirty chief men went
down and came to David in the harvest time
to the cave of Adullam, while the troop of
the Philistines was camping in the valley
of Rephaim. 14 And David was then in the
fortress, while the garrison of the Philistines
was then in Bethlehem. 15 Then David had a
craving and said, "Oh that someone would
give me water to drink from the well of
Bethlehem, which is by the gate!" 16 So the
three mighty men broke through the camp
of the Philistines and drew water from the
well of Bethlehem which was by the gate,
and carried *it* and brought *it* to David. Nev-
ertheless, he was not willing to drink it, but
poured it out to Yahweh; 17 and he said, "Be
it far from me, O Yahweh, that I should do
this. *Shall I drink* the blood of the men who
went at the risk of their lives?" Therefore he
was not willing to drink it. These things the
three mighty men did.

18 Now Abishai, the brother of Joab, the
son of Zeruiah, was chief of the thirty. And
he swung his spear against three hundred
who were slain *by him*; and he had a name as
well as the three. 19 Of the thirty he was most
honored and became their commander;
however, he did not attain to the three.

20 Then Benaiah the son of Jehoiada, the
son of a valiant man of Kabzeel, mighty in
deeds, struck down the two *sons of* Ariel of
Moab. He also went down and struck down
a lion in the midst of a pit on a snowy day.
21 He had also struck down an Egyptian,
an impressive man. Now in the Egyptian's
hand was a spear, but he went down to him
with a club and snatched the spear from
the Egyptian's hand and killed him with his
own spear. 22 These *things* Benaiah the son
of Jehoiada did, and had a name as well as
the three mighty men. 23 He was honored
among the thirty, but he did not attain to
the three. And David appointed him over
his guard.

24 Asahel the brother of Joab was among
the thirty; Elhanan the son of Dodo of

Bethlehem, 25 Shammah the Harodite, Elika the Harodite, 26 Helez the Paltite, Ira the son of Ikkesh the Tekoite, 27 Abiezer the Anathothite, Mebunnai the Hushathite, 28 Zalmon the Ahohite, Maharai the Netophathite, 29 Heleb the son of Baanah the Netophathite, Ittai the son of Ribai of Gibeah of the sons of Benjamin, 30 Benaiah a Pirathonite, Hiddai of the brooks of Gaash, 31 Abi-albon the Arbathite, Azmaveth the Barhumite, 32 Eliahba the Shaalbonite, the sons of Jashen, Jonathan, 33 Shammah the Hararite, Ahiam the son of Sharar the Ararite, 34 Eliphelet the son of Ahasbai, the son of the Maacathite, Eliam the son of Ahithophel the Gilonite, 35 Hezro the Carmelite, Paarai the Arbite, 36 Igal the son of Nathan of Zobah, Bani the Gadite, 37 Zelek the Ammonite, Naharai the Beerothite, armor bearers of Joab the son of Zeruiah, 38 Ira the Ithrite, Gareb the Ithrite, 39 Uriah the Hittite; thirty-seven in all.

24 And again the anger of Yahweh burned against Israel, and it incited David against them to say, “Go, number Israel and Judah.” 2 So the king said to Joab the commander of the military force who was with him, “Go about now through all the tribes of Israel, from Dan to Beersheba, and take a census of the people, that I may know the *total* count of the people.” 3 But Joab said to the king, “Now may Yahweh your God add to the people a hundred times as many as they are, while the eyes of my lord the king *still* see; but why does my lord the king delight in this thing?” 4 Nevertheless, the king’s word *stood* strong against Joab and against the commanders of the military force. So Joab and the commanders of the military force went out from the presence of the king to take a census of the people of Israel. 5 And they crossed the Jordan and camped in Aroer, on the right side of the city that is in the middle of the valley of Gad and toward Jazer. 6 Then they came to Gilead and to the land of Tahtim-hodshi, and they came to Dan-jaan and around to Sidon, 7 and came to the fortified *city* of Tyre and to all the cities of the Hivites and of the Canaanites, and they went out to the south of Judah, *to* Beersheba. 8 So they had gone about through the whole land, and they came to Jerusalem at the end of nine months and twenty days. 9 And Joab gave the *total* count of the census of the people to the king; and there were in Israel 800,000 valiant men who drew the sword, and the men of Judah were 500,000 men.

10 Then David’s heart struck him after he had counted the people. So David said to Yahweh, “I have sinned greatly in what I have done. But now, O Yahweh, please take away the iniquity of Your slave, for I have acted very foolishly.” 11 Then David arose in the morning, and the word of Yahweh came to the prophet Gad, David’s seer, saying, 12 “Go and speak to David, ‘Thus says Yahweh, “I am offering you three things; choose for yourself one of them, and I will do *that* to you.”’” 13 So Gad came to David and told him, and said to him, “Shall seven years of famine come to you in your land? Or will you flee three months before your adversaries while they pursue you? Or shall there be three days’ pestilence in your land? Now, know and see what word I should return to Him who sent me.” 14 Then David said to Gad, “I am in great distress. Let us now fall into the hand of Yahweh, for His compassions are abundant. But do not let me fall into the hand of man.”

15 So Yahweh sent a pestilence against Israel from the morning until the appointed time, and 70,000 men of the people from Dan to Beersheba died. 16 Then the angel sent forth his hand toward Jerusalem to destroy it, and Yahweh relented of the calamity and said to the angel who destroyed the people, “It is enough! Now relax your hand!” And the angel of Yahweh was by the threshing floor of Araunah the Jebusite. 17 Then David spoke to Yahweh when he saw the angel who was striking down the people, and said, “Behold, it is I who have sinned, and it is I who have done unrighteousness; but these sheep, what have they done? Please let Your hand be against me and my father’s house.”

18 So Gad came to David that day and said to him, “Go up, erect an altar to Yahweh on the threshing floor of Araunah the Jebusite.” 19 So David went up according to the word of Gad, just as Yahweh had commanded. 20 And Araunah looked down and saw the king and his servants crossing over toward him; and Araunah went out and bowed his face to the ground before the king. 21 Then Araunah said, “Why has my lord the king come to his servant?” And David said, “To buy the threshing

floor from you, in order to build an altar to
Yahweh, that the plague may be checked from
being upon the people." 22 And Araunah said
to David, "Let my lord the king take and offer
up what is good in his sight. Look, the oxen
for the burnt offering, the threshing sledges
and the yokes of the oxen for the wood.
23 Everything, O king, Araunah gives to the
king." And Araunah said to the king, "May
Yahweh your God accept you." 24 However,
the king said to Araunah, "No, but I will
surely buy *it* from you for a price, for I will
not offer burnt offerings to Yahweh my God
which cost me nothing." So David bought the
threshing floor and the oxen for fifty shekels
of silver. 25 Then David built there an altar
to Yahweh and offered burnt offerings and
peace offerings. Thus Yahweh was moved by
the entreaty for the land, and the plague was
checked from *being* upon Israel.

Psalm 68:7–10

7 O God, when You went forth
    before Your people,
  When You marched through
    the wasteland, Selah.
8 The earth quaked;
  The heavens also dripped *rain*
    at the presence of God;
  Sinai itself *quaked* at the presence
    of God, the God of Israel.
9 You caused abundant rain to
    sprinkle down, O God;
  You established Your inheritance
    when it was parched.
10 Your creatures inhabited it;
  You established it in Your goodness
    for the poor, O God.

Proverbs 17:5–6

5 He who mocks the poor
    reproaches his Maker;
  He who is glad at disaster will
    not go unpunished.
6 Grandchildren are the
    crown of old men,
  And the beauty of sons is their fathers.

John 9:1–23

9 As He passed by, He saw a man blind from
birth. 2 And His disciples asked Him,
saying, "Rabbi, who sinned, this man or his
parents, that he would be born blind?" 3 Jesus
answered, "Neither this man nor his parents
sinned, but *this was* so that the works of God
might be manifested in him. 4 We must work
the works of Him who sent Me as long as
it is day; night is coming when no one can
work. 5 While I am in the world, I am the light
of the world." 6 When He had said this, He
spat on the ground, made clay of the saliva,
and rubbed the clay on his eyes, 7 and said to
him, "Go, wash in the pool of Siloam" (which
is translated, Sent). So he went away and
washed, and came *back* seeing. 8 Therefore
the neighbors, and those who previously saw
him as a beggar, were saying, "Is not this the
one who used to sit and beg?" 9 Others were
saying, "This is he," *still* others were saying,
"No, but he is like him." He kept saying, "I
am the one." 10 So they were saying to him,
"How then were your eyes opened?" 11 He
answered, "The man who is called Jesus
made clay, and rubbed my eyes, and said to
me, 'Go to Siloam and wash'; so when I went
away and washed, I received sight." 12 And
they said to him, "Where is He?" He *said,
"I do not know."

13 They *brought to the Pharisees the
man who was formerly blind. 14 Now it was
a Sabbath on the day when Jesus made the
clay and opened his eyes. 15 So the Pharisees
also were asking him again how he received
his sight. And he said to them, "He applied
clay to my eyes, and I washed, and I see." 16 So
then some of the Pharisees were saying, "This
man is not from God, because He does not
keep the Sabbath." But others were saying,
"How can a sinful man do such signs?" And
there was a division among them. 17 There-
fore, they *said to the blind man again, "What
do you say about Him, since He opened your
eyes?" And he said, "He is a prophet."

18 Then, the Jews did not believe *it* of
him that he was blind and had received
sight, until they called the parents of the
very one who had received his sight, 19 and
questioned them, saying, "Is this your son,
who you say was born blind? Then how does
he now see?" 20 So his parents answered and
said, "We know that this is our son, and that
he was born blind; 21 but how he now sees,
we do not know; or who opened his eyes,
we do not know. Ask him; he is of age, he
will speak for himself." 22 His parents said
this because they were afraid of the Jews; for
the Jews had already agreed that if anyone
confessed Him to be Christ, he was to be put
out of the synagogue. 23 For this reason his
parents said, "He is of age; ask him."

MAY 27

1 Kings 1:1–2:46

1 Now King David was old, advanced in age; and they covered him with clothes, but he could not keep warm. 2 So his servants said to him, "Let them seek a young virgin for my lord the king, and let her stand before the king and become his nurse; and let her lie in your bosom, that my lord the king may keep warm." 3 So they sought for a beautiful young woman throughout all the territory of Israel, and found Abishag the Shunammite, and brought her to the king. 4 Now the young woman was very beautiful; and she became the king's nurse and attended him, but the king did not know her.

5 Now Adonijah the son of Haggith exalted himself, saying, "I will be king." So he prepared for himself a chariot and horsemen and fifty men as runners before him. 6 But his father had never grieved him at any time by asking, "Why have you done so?" And he was also a very handsome man in form, and he was born after Absalom. 7 And he had conferred with Joab the son of Zeruiah and with Abiathar the priest; and following Adonijah, they helped him. 8 But Zadok the priest, Benaiah the son of Jehoiada, Nathan the prophet, Shimei, Rei, and the mighty men who belonged to David, were not with Adonijah.

9 And Adonijah sacrificed sheep and oxen and fatlings by the stone of Zoheleth, which is beside En-rogel; and he invited all his brothers, the king's sons, and all the men of Judah, the king's servants. 10 But he did not invite Nathan the prophet, Benaiah, the mighty men, and Solomon his brother.

11 Then Nathan spoke to Bathsheba the mother of Solomon, saying, "Have you not heard that Adonijah the son of Haggith has become king, and David our lord does not know *it*? 12 So now come, please let me give you counsel and provide escape for your life and the life of your son Solomon. 13 Go at once to King David and say to him, 'Have you not, my lord, O king, sworn to your maidservant, saying, "Surely Solomon your son shall be king after me, and he shall sit on my throne"? Why then has Adonijah become king?' 14 Behold, while you are still there speaking with the king, I will come in after you and fully confirm your words."

15 So Bathsheba went in to the king in the bedroom. Now the king was very old, and Abishag the Shunammite was ministering to the king. 16 Then Bathsheba bowed and prostrated herself before the king. And the king said, "What do you wish?" 17 And she said to him, "My lord, you swore to your maidservant by Yahweh your God, *saying*, 'Surely your son Solomon shall be king after me and he shall sit on my throne.' 18 But now, behold, Adonijah is king; and now, my lord the king, you do not know *it*. 19 And he has sacrificed oxen and fatlings and sheep in abundance, and has invited all the sons of the king and Abiathar the priest and Joab the commander of the army, but he has not invited Solomon your servant. 20 As for you now, my lord the king, the eyes of all Israel are on you, to tell them who shall sit on the throne of my lord the king after him. 21 Otherwise it will be, as soon as my lord the king sleeps with his fathers, that I and my son Solomon will be considered offenders."

22 Behold, while she was still speaking with the king, Nathan the prophet came in. 23 Then they told the king, saying, "Here is Nathan the prophet." And then he came in before the king and prostrated himself before the king with his face to the ground. 24 Then Nathan said, "My lord the king, have you said, 'Adonijah shall be king after me, and he shall sit on my throne'? 25 For he has gone down today and has sacrificed oxen and fatlings and sheep in abundance, and has invited all the king's sons and the commanders of the army and Abiathar the priest, and behold, they are eating and drinking before him; and they say, '*Long* live King Adonijah!' 26 But me, *even* me your servant, and Zadok the priest and Benaiah the son of Jehoiada and your servant Solomon, he has not invited. 27 Has this thing happened by my lord the king, and you have not made known to your servants who should sit on the throne of my lord the king after him?"

28 Then King David answered and said, "Call Bathsheba to me." And she came into the king's presence and stood before the king. 29 And the king swore and said, "As Yahweh lives, who has redeemed my life

from all distress, 30 surely as I swore to you
by Yahweh, the God of Israel, saying, 'Surely
your son Solomon shall be king after me,
and he shall sit on my throne in my place';
I will surely do so this day." 31 Then Bath-
sheba bowed with her face to the ground,
and prostrated herself before the king and
said, "May my lord King David live forever."

32 Then King David said, "Call to me Zadok
the priest, Nathan the prophet, and Benaiah
the son of Jehoiada." And they came into
the king's presence. 33 And the king said
to them, "Take with you the servants of
your lord, and have my son Solomon ride
on my own mule, and bring him down to
Gihon. 34 And Zadok the priest and Nathan
the prophet shall anoint him there as king
over Israel and blow the trumpet and say,
'*Long* live King Solomon!' 35 Then you shall
come up after him, and he shall come and
sit on my throne. And he shall be king in
my place; for I have commanded him to be
ruler over Israel and Judah." 36 Then Benaiah
the son of Jehoiada answered the king and
said, "Amen! Thus may Yahweh, the God of
my lord the king, say. 37 As Yahweh has been
with my lord the king, so may He be with
Solomon, and make his throne greater than
the throne of my lord King David!"

38 So Zadok the priest, Nathan the
prophet, Benaiah the son of Jehoiada, the
Cherethites, and the Pelethites went down
and had Solomon ride on King David's mule,
and brought him to Gihon. 39 Zadok the
priest then took the horn of oil from the tent
and anointed Solomon. Then they blew the
trumpet, and all the people said, "*Long* live
King Solomon!" 40 And all the people went
up after him, and the people were playing on
flutes and were glad with great gladness, so
that the earth shook at their sound.

41 And Adonijah and all the guests who
were with him heard *it* as they finished
eating. Then Joab heard the sound of the
trumpet and said, "Why is the sound of
the city such an uproar?" 42 While he was
still speaking, behold, Jonathan the son of
Abiathar the priest came. Then Adonijah
said, "Come in, for you are a valiant man
and bring good news." 43 But Jonathan
answered and said to Adonijah, "No! Our
lord King David has made Solomon king.
44 The king has also sent with him Zadok
the priest, Nathan the prophet, Benaiah the
son of Jehoiada, the Cherethites, and the
Pelethites; and they have made him ride
on the king's mule. 45 And Zadok the priest
and Nathan the prophet have anointed
him king in Gihon, and they have come up
from there with gladness, so that the city is
in an uproar. This is the sound which you
have heard. 46 And also, Solomon has even
taken his seat on the throne of the kingdom.
47 And also, the king's servants came to bless
our lord King David, saying, 'May your God
make the name of Solomon better than
your name and his throne greater than
your throne!' And the king bowed himself
on the bed. 48 And also, the king said thus,
'Blessed be Yahweh, the God of Israel, who
has granted one to sit on my throne today
while my own eyes see *it*.'"

49 Then all the guests of Adonijah
trembled; and they arose and each went
on his way. 50 And Adonijah was afraid of
Solomon, and he arose, went, and took hold
of the horns of the altar. 51 Then it was told
to Solomon, saying, "Behold, Adonijah is
afraid of King Solomon, and behold, he has
taken hold of the horns of the altar, saying,
'Let King Solomon swear to me today that
he will not put his servant to death with
the sword.'" 52 And Solomon said, "If he is
a worthy man, not one of his hairs will fall
to the ground; but if evil is found in him,
he will die." 53 So King Solomon sent, and
they brought him down from the altar. And
he came and prostrated himself before King
Solomon, and Solomon said to him, "Go to
your house."

2 Then David's time to die drew near, so
he commanded Solomon his son, saying,
2 "I am going the way of all the earth. So
you shall be strong, and be a man. 3 And
you shall keep the responsibility *given by*
Yahweh your God, to walk in His ways, to
keep His statutes, His commandments, His
judgments, and His testimonies, according
to what is written in the Law of Moses, that
you may be prosperous in all that you do
and wherever you turn, 4 so that Yahweh
may establish His promise which He spoke
concerning me, saying, 'If your sons keep
their way, to walk before Me in truth with all
their heart and with all their soul, He said,
you shall not have a man cut off from the
throne of Israel.'

5 "Now you also know what Joab the son
of Zeruiah did to me, what he did to the

two commanders of the armies of Israel, to
Abner the son of Ner, and to Amasa the son
of Jether, whom he killed; he also shed the
blood of war in peace. And he put the blood
of war on his belt about his waist, and on
his sandals on his feet. 6 So act according
to your wisdom, and do not let his gray
hair go down to Sheol in peace. 7 But show
lovingkindness to the sons of Barzillai the
Gileadite, and let them be among those who
eat at your table; for they assisted me when
I fled from Absalom your brother. 8 Behold,
there is with you Shimei the son of Gera the
Benjamite, of Bahurim; now it was he who
cursed me with a violent curse on the day
I went to Mahanaim. But when he came
down to me at the Jordan, I swore to him
by Yahweh, saying, 'I will not put you to
death with the sword.' 9 So now, do not let
him go unpunished, for you are a wise man;
and you will know what you ought to do to
him, and you will bring his gray hair down
to Sheol with blood."

10 Then David slept with his fathers and
was buried in the city of David. 11 And the
time which David reigned over Israel *was*
forty years; in Hebron he reigned seven
years and in Jerusalem he reigned thirty-
three years. 12 And Solomon sat on the
throne of David his father, and his kingdom
was firmly established.

13 Then Adonijah the son of Haggith
came to Bathsheba the mother of Solomon.
And she said, "Do you come peacefully?"
And he said, "Peacefully." 14 Then he said,
"I have something *to say* to you." And she
said, "Speak." 15 So he said, "You know that
the kingdom was mine and that all Israel
expected me to be king; however, the
kingdom has turned about and become my
brother's, for it was his from Yahweh. 16 So
now, I am making one request of you; do not
turn me away." And she said to him, "Speak."
17 Then he said, "Please speak to Solomon
the king, for he will not turn you away, that
he may give me Abishag the Shunammite as
a wife." 18 And Bathsheba said, "Very well; I
will speak to the king for you."

19 So Bathsheba went to King Solomon
to speak to him for Adonijah. And the king
arose to meet her, bowed before her, and
sat on his throne; then he had a throne set
for the king's mother, and she sat on his
right. 20 Then she said, "I am making one
small request of you; do not turn me away."
And the king said to her, "Ask, my mother,
for I will not turn you away." 21 So she said,
"Let Abishag the Shunammite be given to
Adonijah your brother as a wife." 22 Then
King Solomon answered and said to his
mother, "And why are you asking Abishag
the Shunammite for Adonijah? Ask for
him also the kingdom—for he is my older
brother—even for him, for Abiathar the
priest, and for Joab the son of Zeruiah!"
23 Then King Solomon swore by Yahweh,
saying, "May God do so to me and more also,
if Adonijah has not spoken this word against
his own life. 24 So now, as Yahweh lives, who
has established me and set me on the throne
of David my father and who has made me a
house as He promised, surely Adonijah shall
be put to death today." 25 So King Solomon
sent Benaiah the son of Jehoiada; and he fell
upon him so that he died.

26 Then to Abiathar the priest the king
said, "Go to Anathoth to your own field, for
you deserve to die; but I will not put you to
death at this time, because you carried the
ark of Lord Yahweh before my father David,
and because you were afflicted in everything
with which my father was afflicted." 27 So
Solomon drove Abiathar away from being
priest to Yahweh, in order to fulfill the word
of Yahweh, which He had spoken concern-
ing the house of Eli in Shiloh.

28 Now the news came to Joab, for Joab
had followed Adonijah, although he had
not followed Absalom. And Joab fled to the
tent of Yahweh and took hold of the horns of
the altar. 29 And it was told to King Solomon
that Joab had fled to the tent of Yahweh,
and behold, he is beside the altar. Then
Solomon sent Benaiah the son of Jehoiada,
saying, "Go, fall upon him." 30 So Benaiah
came to the tent of Yahweh and said to him,
"Thus the king has said, 'Come out.'" But he
said, "No, for I will die here." And Benaiah
brought the king word again, saying, "Thus
spoke Joab, and thus he answered me."
31 And the king said to him, "Do as he has
spoken and fall upon him and bury him,
that you may remove from me and from my
father's house the blood which Joab shed
without cause. 32 And Yahweh will return
his blood on his own head, because he fell
upon two men more righteous and better
than he and killed them with the sword, but
my father David did not know *it*: Abner the
son of Ner, commander of the army of Israel,

and Amasa the son of Jether, commander
of the army of Judah. 33 So shall their blood
return on the head of Joab and on the head
of his seed forever; but to David and his seed
and his house and his throne, may there
be peace from Yahweh forever." 34 Then
Benaiah the son of Jehoiada went up and fell
upon him and put him to death, and he was
buried at his own house in the wilderness.
35 And the king appointed Benaiah the son
of Jehoiada over the army in his place, and
the king appointed Zadok the priest in the
place of Abiathar.

36 Then the king sent and called for Shimei
and said to him, "Build for yourself a house
in Jerusalem and live there, and do not go out
from there to any place. 37 Now it will be on
the day you go out and cross over the brook
Kidron, that you will know for certain that
you shall surely die; your blood shall be on
your own head." 38 Shimei then said to the
king, "The word is good. As my lord the king
has said, so your servant will do." So Shimei
lived in Jerusalem many days.

39 But it happened at the end of three
years, that two of the slaves of Shimei ran
away to Achish son of Maacah, king of Gath.
And they told Shimei, saying, "Behold, your
slaves are in Gath." 40 Then Shimei arose and
saddled his donkey, and went to Gath to
Achish to search for his slaves. And Shimei
went and brought his slaves from Gath.
41 And it was told to Solomon that Shimei
had gone from Jerusalem to Gath, and had
returned. 42 So the king sent and called for
Shimei and said to him, "Did I not make you
swear by Yahweh and solemnly warn you,
saying, 'You will know for certain that on
the day you go out and go anywhere, you
shall surely die'? And you said to me, 'The
word which I have heard is good.' 43 Why
then have you not kept the oath of Yahweh,
and the command which I have commanded
you?" 44 The king also said to Shimei, "You
know all the evil which you acknowledge
in your heart, which you did to my father
David; *therefore Yahweh shall* return your
evil on your own head. 45 But King Solomon
shall be blessed, and the throne of David
shall be established before Yahweh forever."
46 So the king commanded Benaiah the son
of Jehoiada, and he went out and fell upon
him so that he died.

Thus the kingdom was established in the hands of Solomon.

Psalm 68:11–14

11 The Lord gives the word;
The women who proclaim the
good news are a great host:
12 "Kings of armies retreat, they retreat,
And she who remains at home
will divide the spoil!"
13 If you *men* lie down among
the sheepfolds,
You all would be like the wings of
a dove covered with silver,
And its pinions with glistening gold.
14 When the Almighty dispersed
the kings there,
It was snowing in Zalmon.

Proverbs 17:7–9

7 Excellent lips are not fitting
for a wicked fool,
Even less are lying lips for a noble man.
8 A bribe is a charm in the
eyes of its owner;
Wherever he turns, he prospers.
9 He who covers a transgression
seeks love,
But he who repeats a matter
separates close companions.

John 9:24–41

24 Therefore, a second time they called
the man who had been blind, and said to
him, "Give glory to God; we know that
this man is a sinner." 25 He then answered,
"Whether He is a sinner, I do not know; one
thing I do know, that though I was blind,
now I see." 26 So they said to him, "What did
He do to you? How did He open your eyes?"
27 He answered them, "I told you already and
you did not listen. Why do you want to listen
again? Do you want to become His disciples
too?" 28 And they reviled him and said, "You
are His disciple, but we are disciples of
Moses. 29 We know that God has spoken to
Moses, but as for this man, we do not know
where He is from." 30 The man answered and
said to them, "Well, here is a marvelous
thing, that you do not know where He is
from, and He opened my eyes. 31 We know
that God does not listen to sinners; but if
anyone is God-fearing and does His will,
He listens to him. 32 Since the beginning of
time it has never been heard that anyone
opened the eyes of a person born blind. 33 If
this man were not from God, He could do
nothing." 34 They answered and said to him,

"You were born entirely in sins, and are you teaching us?" So they put him out.

35 Jesus heard that they had put him out, and after finding him, He said, "Do you believe in the Son of Man?" 36 He answered and said, "Who is He, Lord, that I may believe in Him?" 37 Jesus said to him, "You have both seen Him, and He is the one who is talking with you." 38 And he said, "Lord, I believe." And he worshiped Him. 39 And Jesus said, "For judgment I came into this world, so that those who do not see may see, and that those who see may become blind." 40 Some of the Pharisees who were with Him heard these things and said to Him, "Are we blind too?" 41 Jesus said to them, "If you were blind, you would have no sin; but now *that* you say, 'We see,' your sin remains.

Is it not wonderful to think that this Book, which is such a mighty power if it gets a chance to work in an honest heart, is in our hands today?

— AMY CARMICHAEL

MAY 28

1 Kings 3:1–4:34

3 Then Solomon formed a marriage alliance with Pharaoh king of Egypt, and took Pharaoh's daughter and brought her to the city of David until he had completed building his own house and the house of Yahweh and the wall around Jerusalem. 2 The people were still sacrificing on the high places because there was no house built for the name of Yahweh until those days.

3 And Solomon loved Yahweh, walking in the statutes of his father David, except he sacrificed and burned incense on the high places. 4 And the king went to Gibeon to sacrifice there, for that was the great high place; Solomon offered one thousand burnt offerings on that altar. 5 In Gibeon, Yahweh appeared to Solomon in a dream at night; and God said, "Ask what I should give to you."

6 Then Solomon said, "You have shown great lovingkindness to Your slave David my father, according to how he walked before You in truth and righteousness and uprightness of heart toward You; and You have kept for him this great lovingkindness, that You have given him a son to sit on his throne, as *it is* this day. 7 So now, O Yahweh my God, You have made Your slave king in place of my father David, yet I am but a little child; I do not know how to go out or come in. 8 And Your slave is in the midst of Your people which You have chosen, a numerous people who are too many to be numbered or counted. 9 So give Your slave a listening heart to judge Your people to discern between good and evil. For who is able to judge this glorious people of Yours?"

10 And it was pleasing in the sight of the Lord that Solomon had asked this thing. 11 And God said to him, "Because you have asked this thing and have not asked for yourself long life, nor have asked riches for yourself, nor have you asked for the life of your enemies, but have asked for yourself discernment to listen to justice, 12 behold, I have done according to your words. Behold, I have given you a wise and discerning heart, so that there has been no one like you before you, nor shall one like you arise after you. 13 I have also given you what you have not asked, both riches and honor, so that there will not be any among the kings like you all your days. 14 Now if you walk in My ways, keeping My statutes and commandments, as your father David walked, then I will prolong your days."

15 Then Solomon awoke, and behold, it was a dream. And he came to Jerusalem and stood before the ark of the covenant of the Lord, and offered burnt offerings and made peace offerings, and made a feast for all his servants.

16 Then two women who were harlots came to the king and stood before him. 17 And the one woman said, "Oh, my lord,

this woman and I live in the same house;
and I gave birth to a child while she *was* in
the house. 18 And it happened on the third
day after I gave birth, that this woman also
gave birth to a child, and we were together.
There was no stranger with us in the house,
only the two of us in the house. 19 And this
woman's son died in the night because she
lay on him. 20 So she arose in the middle
of the night and took my son from beside
me while your maidservant slept, and laid
him in her bosom, and laid her dead son in
my bosom. 21 When I rose in the morning
to nurse my son, behold, he was dead;
but when I looked at him carefully in the
morning, behold, he was not my son, whom
I had borne." 22 Then the other woman said,
"No! For the living one is my son, and the
dead one is your son." But the first woman
said, "No! For the dead one is your son, and
the living one is my son." Thus they spoke
before the king.

23 Then the king said, "The one says,
'This is my son who is living, and your son
is the dead one'; and the other says, 'No! For
your son is the dead one, and my son is the
living one.'" 24 And the king said, "Get me
a sword." So they brought a sword before
the king. 25 Then the king said, "Divide the
living child in two, and give half to the one
and half to the other." 26 Then the woman
whose son *was* the living one spoke to the
king, for she was deeply stirred with com-
passion over her son and said, "Oh, my lord,
give her the living child, and by no means
put him to death." But the other said, "He
shall be neither mine nor yours; divide *him*!"
27 Then the king said, "Give the first woman
the living child, and by no means put him to
death. She is his mother." 28 Then all Israel
heard of the judgment which the king had
handed down, and they feared the king, for
they saw that the wisdom of God was in him
to do justice.

4

So King Solomon was king over all
Israel. 2 These were his officials:
Azariah the son of Zadok *was* the
priest;
3 Elihoreph and Ahijah, the sons of
Shisha *were* scribes;
Jehoshaphat the son of Ahilud *was* the
recorder;
4 and Benaiah the son of Jehoiada *was*
over the army;
and Zadok and Abiathar *were* priests;
5 and Azariah the son of Nathan *was*
over the deputies;
and Zabud the son of Nathan, a priest,
was the king's friend;
6 and Ahishar *was* over the household;
and Adoniram the son of Abda *was*
over the men subject to forced labor.
7 Now Solomon had twelve deputies over
all Israel, who sustained the king and his
household; each man had to sustain *them*
for a month in the year. 8 These are their
names:
Ben-hur, in the hill country of
Ephraim;
9 Ben-deker in Makaz and Shaalbim and
Beth-shemesh and Elonbeth-hanan;
10 Ben-hesed, in Arubboth (Socoh *was*
his and all the land of Hepher);
11 Ben-abinadab, *in* all the height of Dor
(Taphath the daughter of Solomon was
his wife);
12 Baana the son of Ahilud, *in* Taanach
and Megiddo, and all Beth-shean
which is beside Zarethan below
Jezreel, from Beth-shean to Abel-
meholah as far as the other side of
Jokmeam;
13 Ben-geber, in Ramoth-gilead (*now*
Havvoth-Jair—*Jair being* the son of
Manasseh—which is in Gilead was
his: the region of Argob, which is in
Bashan, sixty great cities with walls
and bronze bars *were* his);
14 Ahinadab the son of Iddo, *in*
Mahanaim;
15 Ahimaaz, in Naphtali (he also married
Basemath the daughter of Solomon);
16 Baana the son of Hushai, in Asher and
Bealoth;
17 Jehoshaphat the son of Paruah,
in Issachar;
18 Shimei the son of Ela, in Benjamin;
19 Geber the son of Uri, in the land of
Gilead, the country of Sihon king
of the Amorites and of Og king of
Bashan; and *he was* the only deputy
who *was* in the land.

20 Judah and Israel *were* as numerous as
the sand that is on the seashore in abun-
dance; *they* were eating and drinking and
being glad.

21 Now Solomon ruled over all the
kingdoms from the River *to* the land of the
Philistines and to the border of Egypt; *they*

brought tribute and served Solomon all the
days of his life.
22 And Solomon's provision for one day
was thirty kors of fine flour and sixty kors
of meal, 23 ten fat oxen, twenty pasture-fed
oxen, one hundred sheep besides deer,
gazelles, roebucks, and fattened fowl. 24 For
he had dominion over everything west of
the River, from Tiphsah even to Gaza, over
all the kings west of the River; and he had
peace on all sides around about him. 25 So
Judah and Israel lived in security, every man
under his vine and his fig tree, from Dan
even to Beersheba, all the days of Solomon.
26 Solomon had 40,000 stalls of horses for
his chariots, and 12,000 horsemen. 27 And
these deputies sustained King Solomon
and all who came to King Solomon's table,
each in his month; they left nothing lacking.
28 They also brought barley and straw for the
horses and swift steeds to the place where
it should be, each according to the *legal*
judgment for him.
29 And God gave Solomon wisdom and
very great discernment and breadth of
understanding in *his* heart, like the sand
that is on the seashore. 30 And Solomon's
wisdom surpassed the wisdom of all the
sons of the east and all the wisdom of Egypt.
31 And he was wiser than all men, than Ethan
the Ezrahite, Heman, Calcol, and Darda, the
sons of Mahol; and *the renown of* his name
was in all the surrounding nations. 32 He
also spoke 3,000 proverbs, and his songs
were 1,005. 33 And he spoke of trees, from
the cedar that is in Lebanon even to the
hyssop that grows on the wall; he spoke also
of animals and birds and creeping things
and fish. 34 And men came from all peoples
to hear the wisdom of Solomon, from all
the kings of the earth who had heard of his
wisdom.

Psalm 68:15–20

15 A mountain of God is the
mountain of Bashan;
A mountain *of many* peaks is
the mountain of Bashan.
16 Why do you look with envy,
O mountains with *many* peaks,
At the mountain which God has
prized for His habitation?
Surely Yahweh will dwell *there* forever.
17 The chariots of God are myriads,
thousands upon thousands;
The Lord is among them *as*
at Sinai, in holiness.
18 You have ascended on high, You
have led captive *Your* captives;
You have received gifts among men,
Even *among* the rebellious also, that
Yah—God—may dwell *there*.
19 Blessed be the Lord, who
daily bears our burden,
The God *who* is our salvation. Selah.
20 God is to us a God of salvation;
And to Yahweh the Lord belong
escapes from death.

Proverbs 17:10–12

10 A rebuke goes deeper into
one who understands
Than a hundred blows into a fool.
11 A rebellious man seeks only evil,
So a cruel messenger will
be sent against him.
12 Let a man meet a bear
robbed of her cubs,
Rather than a fool in his folly.

John 10:1–21

10 "Truly, truly, I say to you, he who does
not enter by the door into the fold of
the sheep, but climbs up some other way, he
is a thief and a robber. 2 But he who enters
by the door is a shepherd of the sheep. 3 To
him the doorkeeper opens, and the sheep
hear his voice, and he calls his own sheep by
name and leads them out. 4 When he brings
all his own out, he goes ahead of them, and
the sheep follow him because they know his
voice. 5 A stranger they will never follow,
but will flee from him, because they do not
know the voice of strangers." 6 This figure of
speech Jesus spoke to them, but they did not
understand what those things were which
He had been saying to them.
7 So Jesus said to them again, "Truly, truly,
I say to you, I am the door of the sheep.
8 All who came before Me are thieves and
robbers, but the sheep did not hear them. 9 I
am the door; if anyone enters through Me,
he will be saved, and will go in and out and
find pasture. 10 The thief comes only to steal
and kill and destroy; I came that they may
have life, and have *it* abundantly.
11 "I am the good shepherd; the good shep-
herd lays down His life for the sheep. 12 He
who is a hired hand, and not a shepherd,

who is not the owner of the sheep, sees the wolf coming, and leaves the sheep and flees—and the wolf snatches and scatters them— [13] because he is a hired hand and is not concerned about the sheep. [14] I am the good shepherd, and I know My own and My own know Me, [15] even as the Father knows Me and I know the Father; and I lay down My life for the sheep. [16] And I have other sheep, which are not from this fold; I must bring them also, and they will hear My voice; and they will become one flock *with* one shepherd. [17] For this reason the Father loves Me, because I lay down My life so that I may take it again. [18] No one takes it away from Me, but from Myself, I lay it down. I have authority to lay it down, and I have authority to take it up again. This commandment I received from My Father."

[19] A division occurred again among the Jews because of these words. [20] And many of them were saying, "He has a demon and is insane. Why do you listen to Him?" [21] Others were saying, "These are not the words of someone demon-possessed. Can a demon open the eyes of the blind?"

MAY 29

1 Kings 5:1–6:38

5 Then Hiram king of Tyre sent his servants to Solomon, when he heard that they had anointed him king in place of his father, for Hiram had always been one who loved David. [2] And Solomon sent *word* to Hiram, saying, [3] "You know that David my father was unable to build a house for the name of Yahweh his God because of the wars which surrounded him, until Yahweh put them under the soles of his feet. [4] But now Yahweh my God has given me rest on every side; there is neither adversary nor calamity. [5] So behold, I intend to build a house for the name of Yahweh my God, as Yahweh spoke to David my father, saying, 'Your son, whom I will set on your throne in your place, he will build the house for My name.' [6] So now, command that they cut for me cedars from Lebanon, and my servants will be with your servants; and I will give you wages for your servants according to all that you say, for you know that there is no one among us who knows how to cut timber like the Sidonians."

[7] Now it happened, when Hiram heard the words of Solomon, he was very glad and said, "Blessed be Yahweh today, who has given to David a wise son over this great people." [8] So Hiram sent *word* to Solomon, saying, "I have heard *the message* which you have sent me; I will do what you desire concerning the cedar and cypress timber. [9] My servants will bring *them* down from Lebanon to the sea; and I will make them into rafts *to go* by sea to the place where you direct me, and I will have them broken up there, and you shall carry *them* away. Then you shall accomplish my desire by giving food to my household." [10] So Hiram gave Solomon as much as he desired of the cedar and cypress timber. [11] Solomon then gave Hiram 20,000 kors of wheat as food for his household, and 20 kors of beaten oil; thus Solomon would give Hiram year by year. [12] Now Yahweh gave wisdom to Solomon, just as He promised him; and there was peace between Hiram and Solomon, and the two of them cut a covenant.

[13] And King Solomon raised up forced laborers from all Israel; and the forced laborers numbered 30,000 men. [14] And he sent them to Lebanon, 10,000 a month in shifts; they were in Lebanon a month *and* two months at home. And Adoniram *was* over the forced laborers. [15] And Solomon had 70,000 who carried loads, and 80,000 hewers *of stone* in the mountains, [16] besides Solomon's 3,300 chief deputies who *were* over the project *and* who ruled over the people who were doing the work. [17] Then the king commanded, and they quarried great stones, precious stones, to lay the foundation of the house with cut stones. [18] So Solomon's builders and Hiram's builders and the Gebalites carved them out, and prepared the timbers and the stones to build the house.

6 Now it happened in the four hundred and eightieth year after the sons of Israel came out of the land of Egypt, in the fourth year of Solomon's reign over Israel, in the month of Ziv which is the second month, that he began to build the house of Yahweh. [2] As for the house which King

Solomon built for Yahweh, its length *was*
sixty cubits and its width twenty *cubits* and
its height thirty cubits. 3 And the porch in
front of the nave of the house *was* twenty
cubits in length, corresponding to the
width of the house, *and* its depth along the
front of the house *was* ten cubits. 4 Also for
the house he made windows with *artistic*
frames. 5 And he built, against the wall of the
house, stories encompassing the walls of the
house around both the nave and the inner
sanctuary; thus he made side chambers all
around. 6 The lowest story *was* five cubits
wide, and the middle *was* six cubits wide,
and the third *was* seven cubits wide; for on
the outside he made offsets *in the wall* of
the house all around in order that *the beams*
would not be inserted in the walls of the
house.

7 The house, while it was being built, was
built of stone prepared at the quarry, and
there was neither hammer nor axe nor any
iron tool heard in the house while it was
being built.

8 The doorway for the lowest side cham-
ber *was* on the right side of the house; and
they would go up by winding stairs to the
middle *story*, and from the middle to the
third. 9 So he built the house and completed
it; and he paneled the house with beams and
planks of cedar. 10 He also built the stories
against the whole house, each five cubits
high; and they were fastened to the house
with timbers of cedar.

11 And the word of Yahweh came to
Solomon saying, 12 "*Concerning* this house
which you are building, if you will walk
in My statutes and do My judgments and
keep all My commandments by walking in
them, then I will establish My word with you
which I spoke to David your father. 13 And I
will dwell among the sons of Israel, and will
not forsake My people Israel."

14 So Solomon built the house and com-
pleted it. 15 Then he built the walls of the
house on the inside with boards of cedar;
from the floor of the house to the ceiling he
overlaid *the walls* on the inside with wood,
and he overlaid the floor of the house with
boards of cypress. 16 And he built twenty
cubits on the rear part of the house with
boards of cedar from the floor to the ceiling;
he built *them* for it on the inside as an inner
sanctuary, as the Holy of Holies. 17 And the
house, that is, the nave in front of *the inner*
sanctuary, was forty cubits *long*. 18 And
there was cedar on the house within, carved
in the shape of gourds and open flowers; all
was cedar, there was no stone seen. 19 Then
he prepared an inner sanctuary within the
house in order to place there the ark of
the covenant of Yahweh. 20 Now the inner
sanctuary *was* twenty cubits in length,
twenty cubits in width, and twenty cubits
in height, and he overlaid it with pure gold.
He also overlaid the altar with cedar. 21 So
Solomon overlaid the inside of the house
with pure gold. And he drew chains of gold
across the front of the inner sanctuary, and
he overlaid it with gold. 22 So he overlaid the
whole house with gold, until all the house
was finished. Also the whole altar which
was by the inner sanctuary he overlaid
with gold.

23 Also in the inner sanctuary he made
two cherubim of olive wood, each ten cubits
high. 24 And five cubits *was* the one wing of
the cherub and five cubits the other wing
of the cherub; from the end of one wing to
the end of the other wing *were* ten cubits.
25 The other cherub *was* also ten cubits;
both the cherubim were of the same mea-
sure and the same form. 26 The height of the
one cherub *was* ten cubits, and so *was* the
other cherub. 27 And he put the cherubim in
the midst of the inner house, and the wings
of the cherubim were spread out, so that
the wing of the one was touching the *one*
wall, and the wing of the other cherub was
touching the other wall. And their wings
were touching each other in the center of
the house. 28 He also overlaid the cherubim
with gold.

29 Then he carved all the walls of the
house round about with carved engravings
of cherubim, palm trees, and open flowers,
from *within* the inner and outer *sanctuaries*.
30 And he overlaid the floor of the house
with gold, in the inner and outer *sanctu-*
aries.

31 For the entrance of the inner sanctuary
he made doors of olive wood, the lintel, *and*
five-sided doorposts. 32 So *he made* two
doors of olive wood, and he carved on them
carvings of cherubim, palm trees, and open
flowers, and overlaid them with gold; and
he spread the gold on the cherubim and on
the palm trees.

33 So also he made for the entrance of the
nave four-sided doorposts of olive wood

34 and two doors of cypress wood; the two
leaves of the one door turned on pivots, and
the two leaves of the other door turned on
pivots. 35 And he carved *on it* cherubim,
palm trees, and open flowers; and he over-
laid *them* with gold evenly applied on the
engraved work. 36 And he built the inner
court with three rows of cut stone and a
row of cedar beams.
37 In the fourth year the foundation of
the house of Yahweh was laid, in the month
of Ziv. 38 Now in the eleventh year, in the
month of Bul, which is the eighth month,
the house was completed throughout all its
parts and according to all its plans. So he
built it in seven years.

Psalm 68:21–27

21 Surely God will crush the
head of His enemies,
The hairy skull of him who goes
on in his guilty deeds.
22 The Lord said, "I will bring
them back from Bashan.
I will bring *them* back from
the depths of the sea;
23 That your foot may crush
them in blood,
The tongue of your dogs
may have its portion
from *your* enemies."

24 They have seen Your
procession, O God,
The procession of my God,
my King, into the sanctuary.
25 The singers went on,
the musicians after *them*,
In the midst of the maidens
beating tambourines.
26 Bless God in the congregations,
Yahweh, the fountain of Israel.
27 There is Benjamin, the youngest,
having dominion over them,
The princes of Judah *in* their throng,
The princes of Zebulun,
the princes of Naphtali.

Proverbs 17:13–15

13 He who returns evil for good,
Evil will not depart from his house.
14 The beginning of strife is
like letting out water,
So abandon the dispute
before it breaks out.
15 He who justifies the wicked and he
who condemns the righteous,
Both of them alike are an
abomination to Yahweh.

John 10:22–42

22 At that time the Feast of the Dedication
took place at Jerusalem; 23 it was winter, and
Jesus was walking in the temple in the Por-
tico of Solomon. 24 The Jews then gathered
around Him, and were saying to Him, "How
long will You keep us in suspense? If You are
the Christ, tell us openly." 25 Jesus answered
them, "I told you, and you do not believe;
the works that I do in My Father's name,
these bear witness of Me. 26 But you do not
believe because you are not of My sheep.
27 My sheep hear My voice, and I know them,
and they follow Me; 28 and I give eternal life
to them, and they will never perish—ever;
and no one will snatch them out of My hand.
29 My Father, who has given *them* to Me, is
greater than all; and no one is able to snatch
them out of the Father's hand. 30 I and the
Father are one."
31 The Jews picked up stones again
to stone Him. 32 Jesus answered them,
"I showed you many good works from
the Father; for which of them are you
stoning Me?" 33 The Jews answered Him,
"For a good work we do not stone You,
but for blasphemy; and because You,
being a man, make Yourself God." 34 Jesus
answered them, "Has it not been written
in your Law, 'I SAID, YOU ARE GODS'? 35 If
he called them gods, to whom the word
of God came (and the Scripture cannot be
broken), 36 do you say of Him, whom the
Father sanctified and sent into the world,
'You are blaspheming,' because I said, 'I am
the Son of God'? 37 If I do not do the works
of My Father, do not believe Me; 38 but if
I do them, though you do not believe Me,
believe the works, so that you may know
and continue knowing that the Father is in
Me, and I in the Father." 39 Therefore they
were seeking again to seize Him, and He
eluded their grasp.
40 And He went away again beyond the
Jordan to the place where John was first
baptizing, and He was staying there. 41 And
many came to Him and were saying, "While
John did no sign, yet everything John said
about this man was true." 42 And many
believed in Him there.

MAY 30

1 Kings 7:1–8:66

7 Now Solomon built his own house
thirteen years, and he completed all his
house. 2 And he built the house of the forest
of Lebanon; its length was 100 cubits and its
width 50 cubits and its height 30 cubits, on
four rows of cedar pillars with cedar beams
on the pillars. 3 And it was paneled with
cedar above the side chambers which were
on the 45 pillars, 15 in each row. 4 *Now there
were artistic window* frames in three rows,
and window was opposite window in three
ranks. 5 And all the doorways and doorposts
had squared *artistic* frames, and window
was opposite window in three ranks.

6 Then he made the hall of pillars; its
length was 50 cubits and its width 30 cubits,
and a porch *was* in front of them and pillars
and a threshold in front of them.

7 And he made the hall of the throne
where he was to judge, the hall of judgment,
and it was paneled with cedar from floor
to floor.

8 Now his house where he was to live, the
other court inward from the hall, was of the
same workmanship. He also made a house
like this hall for Pharaoh's daughter, whom
Solomon had married.

9 All these were of precious stones, of
stone cut according to measure, sawed
with saws, inside and outside; even from
the foundation to the coping, and so on the
outside to the great court.

10 And the foundation was of precious
stones, *even* large stones, stones of ten
cubits and stones of eight cubits. 11 And
above were precious stones, stone cut
according to measure, and cedar. 12 So the
great court all around *had* three rows of cut
stone and a row of cedar beams even as the
inner court of the house of Yahweh, and the
porch of the house.

13 Then King Solomon sent and brought
Hiram from Tyre. 14 He was a widow's son
from the tribe of Naphtali, and his father
was a man of Tyre, a worker in bronze; and
he was filled with wisdom and discernment
and knowledge to do any work in bronze.
So he came to King Solomon and did all his
work.

15 And he fashioned the two pillars of
bronze; eighteen cubits was the height of
one pillar, and a line of twelve cubits mea-
sured the circumference of both. 16 He also
made two capitals of molten bronze to set
on the tops of the pillars; the height of the
one capital was five cubits and the height
of the other capital was five cubits. 17 *There
were* nets of network and twisted threads
of chainwork for the capitals which were
on the top of the pillars; seven for the one
capital and seven for the other capital. 18 So
he made the pillars, and two rows around
on the one network to cover the capitals
which were on the top of the pomegranates;
and so he did for the other capital. 19 Now
the capitals which *were* on the top of the
pillars in the porch were of lily design, four
cubits. 20 *And there were* capitals on the
two pillars, even right above the rounded
projection which was on the one side of the
network; and the pomegranates *numbered*
two hundred in rows around both capitals.
21 Thus he set up the pillars at the porch of
the nave; and he set up the right pillar and
named it Jachin, and he set up the left pillar
and named it Boaz. 22 And on the top of the
pillars was lily design. So the work of the
pillars was finished.

23 And he made the sea of cast *metal* ten
cubits from brim to brim, circular in form,
and its height was five cubits, and thirty
cubits in its circumference. 24 Now under
its brim gourds went around encircling it
ten to a cubit, entirely encircling the sea;
the gourds were in two rows, cast *with the
Sea* when it was cast. 25 It stood on twelve
oxen, three facing north, three facing west,
three facing south, and three facing east;
and the sea *was set* on top of them, and all
their rear parts *turned* inward. 26 And it was
a handbreadth thick, and its brim was made
like the brim of a cup, *as* a lily blossom; it
could hold two thousand baths.

27 Then he made the ten stands of bronze;
the length of each stand was four cubits and
its width four cubits and its height three
cubits. 28 Now this was the workmanship
of the stands: they had borders, even
borders between the frames, 29 and on the
borders which were between the frames
were lions, oxen, and cherubim; and on
the frames there *was* a pedestal above, and
beneath the lions and oxen *were* wreaths of

hanging work. 30 Now each stand had four
bronze wheels with bronze axles, and its
four feet had supports; beneath the laver
were cast supports with wreaths at each
side. 31 And its opening inside the capital
at the top *was* a cubit, and its opening *was*
round like the workmanship of a pedestal,
a cubit and a half; and also on its opening
there were engravings, and their borders
were square, not round. 32 And the four
wheels *were* underneath the borders, and
the axles of the wheels *were* on the stand.
And the height of a wheel *was* a cubit and
a half. 33 Now the workmanship of the
wheels *was* like the workmanship of a
chariot wheel. Their axles, their rims, their
spokes, and their hubs *were* all cast. 34 Now
there were four supports at the four corners
of each stand; its supports *were* part of the
stand itself. 35 And on the top of the stand
there was a circular form half a cubit high,
and on the top of the stand its stays and its
borders *were* part of it. 36 And he engraved
on the plates of its stays and on its borders,
cherubim, lions, and palm trees, according
to the clear space on each, with wreaths *all*
around. 37 He made the ten stands like this:
all of them had one casting, one measure
and one form.

38 He also made ten lavers of bronze, one
laver held forty baths; each laver *was* four
cubits, *and* on each of the ten stands *was*
one laver. 39 Then he set the stands, five on
the right side of the house and five on the
left side of the house; and he set the sea *of
cast metal* on the right side of the house
eastward toward the south.

40 And Hiram made the lavers and the
shovels and the bowls. So Hiram com-
pleted doing all the work that he did for
King Solomon *in* the house of Yahweh:
41 the two pillars and the *two* bowls of the
capitals which *were* on the top of the two
pillars, and the two networks to cover the
two bowls of the capitals which were on the
top of the pillars, 42 and the four hundred
pomegranates for the two networks, two
rows of pomegranates for each network to
cover the two bowls of the capitals which
were on the tops of the pillars; 43 and
the ten stands with the ten lavers on the
stands; 44 and the one sea and the twelve
oxen under the sea; 45 and the pots and the
shovels and the bowls; and all these utensils
which Hiram made for King Solomon *in* the
house of Yahweh *were* of polished bronze.
46 On the plain of the Jordan the king cast
them, in the clay ground between Succoth
and Zarethan. 47 And Solomon left all the
utensils *unweighed*, because *they were* too
many; the weight of the bronze could not
be found out.

48 Solomon also made all the furniture
which *was in* the house of Yahweh: the
golden altar and the golden table on which
was the bread of the Presence; 49 and the
lampstands, five on the right side and five
on the left, in front of the inner sanctuary,
of pure gold; and the flowers and the lamps
and the tongs, of gold; 50 and the cups and
the snuffers and the bowls and the spoons
and the firepans, of pure gold; and the
hinges both for the doors of the inner house,
the Holy of Holies, *and* for the doors of the
house, *that is*, of the nave, of gold.

51 Thus all the work that King Solomon
did *in* the house of Yahweh was finished.
And Solomon brought in the things set apart
as holy by his father David, the silver and
the gold and the utensils, *and* he put *them*
in the treasuries of the house of Yahweh.

8 Then Solomon assembled the elders of
Israel and all the heads of the tribes, the
leaders of the fathers' *households* of the sons
of Israel, to King Solomon in Jerusalem, to
bring up the ark of the covenant of Yahweh
from the city of David, which is Zion. 2 And
all the men of Israel assembled themselves
to King Solomon at the feast, in the month
Ethanim, which is the seventh month.
3 Then all the elders of Israel came, and the
priests carried the ark. 4 And they brought
up the ark of Yahweh and the tent of meeting
and all the holy utensils, which were in the
tent, and the priests and the Levites brought
them up. 5 And King Solomon and all the
congregation of Israel, who congregated to
him being with him before the ark, were
sacrificing so many sheep and oxen that
they could not be counted or numbered.
6 Then the priests brought the ark of the
covenant of Yahweh to its place, into the
inner sanctuary of the house, to the Holy
of Holies, under the wings of the cherubim.
7 For the cherubim spread *their* wings over
the place of the ark, and the cherubim made
a covering over the ark and its poles from
above. 8 But the poles were so long that the
ends of the poles could be seen from the

holy place before the inner sanctuary, but
they could not be seen outside; and they are
there to this day. 9 There was nothing in the
ark except the two tablets of stone which
Moses laid there at Horeb, where Yahweh
cut a covenant with the sons of Israel, when
they came out of the land of Egypt. 10 Now
it happened that when the priests came
out of the holy place, the cloud filled the
house of Yahweh, 11 so that the priests could
not stand to minister because of the cloud,
for the glory of Yahweh filled the house of
Yahweh.

12 Then Solomon said,

"Yahweh has said that He would dwell
in the *cloud of* dense gloom.
13 "I have surely built You a lofty house,
A place for Your dwelling forever."

14 Then the king turned his face around
and blessed all the assembly of Israel, while
all the assembly of Israel was standing.
15 And he said, "Blessed be Yahweh, the God
of Israel, who spoke with His mouth to my
father David and has fulfilled *it* by His hand,
saying, 16 'Since the day that I brought My
people Israel from Egypt, I did not choose
a city out of all the tribes of Israel *in which*
to build a house that My name might be
there, but I have chosen David to be over
My people Israel.' 17 And it was in the heart
of my father David to build a house for the
name of Yahweh, the God of Israel. 18 But
Yahweh said to my father David, 'Because
it was in your heart to build a house for
My name, you did well that it was in your
heart. 19 Nevertheless you shall not build
the house, but your son who will come forth
from your loins, he shall build the house for
My name.' 20 And Yahweh has established
His word which He spoke; and I have been
established in place of my father David and
sit on the throne of Israel, as Yahweh prom-
ised, and have built the house for the name
of Yahweh, the God of Israel. 21 And there
I have set a place for the ark, in which is
the covenant of Yahweh, which He cut with
our fathers when He brought them from the
land of Egypt."

22 Then Solomon stood before the altar
of Yahweh before all the assembly of Israel
and spread out his hands toward heaven.
23 *And he said,* "O Yahweh, the God of Israel,
there is no god like You in heaven above or
upon earth beneath, keeping covenant and
lovingkindness to Your slaves who walk
before You with all their heart, 24 who have
kept with Your servant, my father David,
that which You have promised him; indeed,
You have promised with Your mouth and
have fulfilled it by Your hand as it is this
day. 25 So now, O Yahweh, the God of Israel,
keep with Your servant David my father that
which You have promised him, saying, 'You
shall not have a man cut off from before Me
who is to sit on the throne of Israel, if only
your sons keep their way to walk as you
have walked before Me.' 26 So now, O God
of Israel, let Your word truly endure which
You have spoken to Your servant, my father
David.

27 "But will God truly dwell on the earth?
Behold, heaven and the highest heaven can-
not contain You; how much less this house
which I have built! 28 Yet have regard to the
prayer of Your slave and to his supplication,
O Yahweh my God, to listen to the cry and to
the prayer which Your slave prays before You
today; 29 that Your eyes may be open toward
this house night and day, toward the place
of which You have said, 'My name shall be
there,' to listen to the prayer which Your
slave shall pray toward this place. 30 And
listen to the supplication of Your slave and
of Your people Israel, when they pray toward
this place; listen in heaven Your dwelling
place; listen and forgive.

31 "If a man sins against his neighbor
and is made to take an oath, and he comes
and takes an oath before Your altar in this
house, 32 then listen in heaven and act and
judge Your slaves, condemning the wicked
by bringing his way on his own head and
justifying the righteous by bringing him
reward according to his righteousness.

33 "When Your people Israel are defeated
before an enemy, because they have sinned
against You, if they turn to You again and
confess Your name and pray and make
supplication to You in this house, 34 then
listen in heaven, and forgive the sin of Your
people Israel, and bring them back to the
land which You gave to their fathers.

35 "When the heavens are shut up and
there is no rain, because they have sinned
against You, and they pray toward this place
and confess Your name and turn from their
sin when You afflict them, 36 then listen in
heaven and forgive the sin of Your slaves and
of Your people Israel; indeed, teach them the
good way in which they should walk. And

give rain on Your land, which You have given
to Your people for an inheritance.
37 “If there is famine in the land, if there
is pestilence, if there is scorching wind
or mildew, locust *or* grasshopper, if their
enemy besieges them in the land of their
cities, whatever plague, whatever sickness
there is, 38 whatever prayer or supplication
is made by any man *or* by all Your people
Israel, each of whom knows the affliction
of his own heart, and spreads his hands
toward this house; 39 then listen in heaven
Your dwelling place, and forgive and act
and give to each according to all his ways,
whose heart You know, for You alone know
the hearts of all the sons of men, 40 that they
may fear You all the days that they live upon
the face of the land which You have given
to our fathers.
41 “Also concerning the foreigner who is
not of Your people Israel, if he comes from
a far country for Your name’s sake 42 (for
they will hear of Your great name and Your
strong hand, and of Your outstretched arm);
so if he comes and prays toward this house,
43 listen in heaven Your dwelling place, and
do according to all for which the foreigner
calls to You, in order that all the peoples of
the earth may know Your name to fear You,
as *do* Your people Israel, and to know that
Your name is called upon this house which
I have built.
44 “When Your people go out to battle
against their enemy, by whatever way You
shall send them, and they pray to Yahweh
toward the city which You have chosen and
the house which I have built for Your name,
45 then listen in heaven to their prayer and
their supplication, and do justice.
46 “When they sin against You (for there
is no man who does not sin) and You are
angry with them and give them over to an
enemy, so that they take them away captive
to the land of the enemy, far off or near;
47 and if they cause *these things* to return
to their heart in the land where they have
been taken captive, and return and make
supplication to You in the land of those who
have taken them captive, saying, ‘We have
sinned and have committed iniquity, we
have acted wickedly’; 48 and if they return
to You with all their heart and with all their
soul in the land of their enemies who have
taken them captive, and pray to You toward
their land which You have given to their
fathers, the city which You have chosen,
and the house which I have built for Your
name; 49 then listen in heaven Your dwelling
place to their prayer and their supplication,
and do justice for them, 50 and forgive Your
people who have sinned against You and
all their transgressions which they have
transgressed against You, and give them
over as *objects of* compassion before those
who have taken them captive, that they may
have compassion on them 51 (for they are
Your people and Your inheritance which
You have brought forth from Egypt, from
the midst of the iron furnace), 52 that Your
eyes may be open to the supplication of Your
slave and to the supplication of Your people
Israel, to listen to them whenever they call
to You. 53 For You have separated them from
all the peoples of the earth as Your inheri-
tance, as You spoke by the hand of Moses
Your servant, when You brought our fathers
forth from Egypt, O Lord Yahweh.”
54 Now it happened that when Solomon
had finished praying this entire prayer and
supplication to Yahweh, he arose from
before the altar of Yahweh, from kneeling
on his knees with his hands spread toward
heaven. 55 And he stood and blessed all the
assembly of Israel with a loud voice, saying:
56 “Blessed be Yahweh, who has given
rest to His people Israel, according to all
that He promised; not one promise has
failed of all His good promises, which He
promised by the hand of Moses His servant.
57 May Yahweh our God be with us, as He
was with our fathers; may He not forsake
us or abandon us, 58 that He may incline our
hearts to Himself, to walk in all His ways and
to keep His commandments and His statutes
and His judgments, which He commanded
our fathers. 59 And may these words of mine,
with which I have made supplication before
Yahweh, be near to Yahweh our God day and
night, that He may do justice for His slave
and justice for His people Israel, as each day
requires, 60 so that all the peoples of the
earth may know that Yahweh is God; there
is no one else. 61 Let your heart therefore be
wholly devoted to Yahweh our God, to walk
in His statutes and to keep His command-
ments, as at this day.”
62 Now the king and all Israel with him
were offering sacrifices before Yahweh.
63 And Solomon offered for the sacrifice of
peace offerings, which he offered to Yahweh,

22,000 oxen and 120,000 sheep. So the
king and all the sons of Israel dedicated
the house of Yahweh. 64 On the same day
the king set apart as holy the middle of the
court that *was* before the house of Yahweh,
because there he offered the burnt offering
and the grain offering and the fat of the
peace offerings; for the bronze altar that
was before Yahweh *was* too small to hold
the burnt offering and the grain offering and
the fat of the peace offerings.
65 So Solomon celebrated the feast at
that time, and all Israel with him, a great
assembly from Lebo-hamath to the brook
of Egypt, before Yahweh our God, for seven
days and seven *more* days, *even* fourteen
days. 66 On the eighth day he sent the people
away and they blessed the king. Then they
went to their tents with gladness and good-
ness of heart because of all the goodness
that Yahweh had shown to David His servant
and to Israel His people.

Psalm 68:28–35

28 Your God has commanded
your strength;
Show Yourself strong, O God,
who has worked on our behalf.
29 Because of Your temple
at Jerusalem
Kings will bring gifts to You.
30 Rebuke the beast in the reeds,
The herd of bulls with the
calves of the peoples,
Trampling under foot the
pieces of silver;
He has cast out the peoples
who delight in war.
31 Envoys will come out of Egypt;
Ethiopia will quickly stretch
out her hands to God.

32 Sing to God, O kingdoms of
the earth,
Sing praises to the Lord, Selah.
33 To Him who rides upon the
highest heavens, which are
from ancient times;
Behold, He gives forth His voice,
a voice *that is* strong.
34 Ascribe strength to God;
His majesty *is* over Israel
And His strength is in the skies.
35 O God, *You are* awesome
from Your sanctuary.
The God of Israel Himself gives
strength and might to the people.
Blessed be God!

Proverbs 17:16–17

16 Why is there a price in the hand
of a fool to acquire wisdom,
When he has no heart *of wisdom*?
17 A friend loves at all times,
And a brother is born for adversity.

John 11:1–27

11 Now a certain man was sick, Lazarus
from Bethany, the village of Mary and
her sister Martha. 2 And it was *the* Mary
who anointed the Lord with perfume, and
wiped His feet with her hair, whose brother
Lazarus was sick. 3 So the sisters sent to
Him, saying, "Lord, behold, he whom You
love is sick." 4 But when Jesus heard *this*, He
said, "This sickness is not to end in death,
but is for the glory of God, so that the Son
of God may be glorified by it." 5 Now Jesus
loved Martha and her sister and Lazarus.
6 So when He heard that he was sick, He then
stayed two days in the place where He was.
7 Then after this He *said to the disciples,
"Let us go to Judea again." 8 The disciples
*said to Him, "Rabbi, the Jews were just now
seeking to stone You, and are You going
there again?" 9 Jesus answered, "Are there
not twelve hours in the day? If anyone walks
in the day, he does not stumble, because he
sees the light of this world. 10 But if anyone
walks in the night, he stumbles, because the
light is not in him." 11 He said these things,
and after that He *said to them, "Our friend
Lazarus has fallen asleep; but I go, so that I
may awaken him." 12 The disciples then said
to Him, "Lord, if he has fallen asleep, he will
be saved *from his sickness*." 13 Now Jesus had
spoken of his death, but they thought that
He was speaking of actual sleep. 14 So Jesus
then said to them plainly, "Lazarus is dead,
15 and I am glad for your sakes that I was not
there, so that you may believe; but let us go
to him." 16 Therefore Thomas, who is called
Didymus, said to *his* fellow disciples, "Let
us also go, so that we may die with Him."
17 So when Jesus came, He found that
he had already been in the tomb four days.
18 Now Bethany was near Jerusalem, about
fifteen stadia away; 19 and many of the Jews
had come to Martha and Mary, to console
them about their brother. 20 Martha

therefore, when she heard that Jesus was
coming, went to meet Him, but Mary was
sitting in the house. 21 Martha then said
to Jesus, "Lord, if You had been here, my
brother would not have died. 22 But even
now I know that whatever You ask from
God, God will give You." 23 Jesus *said to
her, "Your brother will rise again." 24 Mar-
tha *said to Him, "I know that he will rise
again in the resurrection on the last day."
25 Jesus said to her, "I am the resurrection
and the life; he who believes in Me will live
even if he dies, 26 and everyone who lives
and believes in Me will never die—ever.
Do you believe this?" 27 She *said to Him,
"Yes, Lord; I have believed that You are the
Christ, the Son of God, the One who comes
into the world."

MAY 31

1 Kings 9:1–10:29

9 Now it happened when Solomon
had completed building the house
of Yahweh, and the king's house, and all
that Solomon desired to do, 2 that Yahweh
appeared to Solomon a second time, as
He had appeared to him at Gibeon. 3 And
Yahweh said to him, "I have heard your
prayer and your supplication, which you
have made before Me; I have set apart as
holy this house which you have built by
putting My name there forever, and My eyes
and My heart will be there perpetually. 4 As
for you, if you will walk before Me as your
father David walked, in integrity of heart
and uprightness, to do according to all that
I have commanded you *and* will keep My
statutes and My judgments, 5 then I will
establish the throne of your kingdom over
Israel forever, just as I promised to your
father David, saying, 'You shall not have a
man cut off from the throne of Israel.'

6 "But if you or your sons indeed turn
away from following Me, and do not keep
My commandments *and* My statutes which
I have given before you, and go and serve
other gods and worship them, 7 then I will
cut off Israel from the land which I have
given them, and the house which I have
set apart as holy for My name, I will cast
out of My presence. So Israel will become
a proverb and a byword among all peoples.
8 And this house will become a heap of
ruins; everyone who passes by will *feel*
desolate and hiss and say, 'Why has Yahweh
done thus to this land and to this house?'
9 And they will say, 'Because they forsook
Yahweh their God, who brought their fathers
out of the land of Egypt, and took hold of
other gods and worshiped them and served
them, therefore Yahweh has brought all this
calamity on them.'"

10 Now it happened that at the end of
twenty years in which Solomon had built
the two houses, the house of Yahweh and
the king's house 11 (Hiram king of Tyre had
supplied Solomon with cedar and cypress
timber and gold according to all his desire),
that King Solomon then gave Hiram twenty
cities in the land of Galilee. 12 So Hiram
came out from Tyre to see the cities which
Solomon had given him, and they were not
right in his eyes. 13 And he said, "What are
these cities which you have given me, my
brother?" So they were called the land of
Cabul to this day. 14 And Hiram sent to the
king 120 talents of gold.

15 Now this is the account of the forced
labor which King Solomon raised up to
build the house of Yahweh, his own house,
the Millo, the wall of Jerusalem, Hazor,
Megiddo, and Gezer. 16 *For* Pharaoh king of
Egypt had gone up and captured Gezer and
burned it with fire, and killed the Canaan-
ites who lived in the city, and had given it
as a dowry to his daughter, Solomon's wife.
17 So Solomon rebuilt Gezer and the lower
Beth-horon 18 and Baalath and Tamar in the
wilderness, in the land *of Judah*, 19 and all
the storage cities which Solomon had, and
the cities for his chariots, and the cities for
his horsemen, and all that Solomon desired
to build in Jerusalem, in Lebanon, and in
all the land under his rule. 20 *As for* all the
people who were left of the Amorites, the
Hittites, the Perizzites, the Hivites and the
Jebusites, who were not of the sons of Israel,
21 *namely*, their sons who were left after
them in the land whom the sons of Israel
were unable to devote to destruction, *from*
them Solomon raised up forced laborers to
this day. 22 But Solomon did not make slaves
of the sons of Israel; for they were men of

war, his servants, his princes, his captains,
his chariot commanders, and his horsemen.
23 These *were* the chief deputies who
were over Solomon's work, 550, who had
dominion over the people doing the work.
24 As soon as Pharaoh's daughter came up
from the city of David to her house which
Solomon had built for her, then he built the
Millo.

25 And three times in a year Solomon
offered burnt offerings and peace offerings
on the altar which he built to Yahweh,
burning incense with them *on the altar*
which *was* before Yahweh. So he finished
the house.
26 King Solomon also made a fleet of ships
in Ezion-geber, which is near Eloth on the
shore of the Red Sea, in the land of Edom.
27 And Hiram sent his servants with the fleet
of ships, sailors who knew the sea, along
with the servants of Solomon. 28 And they
went to Ophir and took from there 420 tal-
ents of gold and brought *it* to King Solomon.

10 Now the queen of Sheba heard the
report about Solomon concerning the
name of Yahweh. So she came to test him
with riddles. 2 She came to Jerusalem with a
very glorious retinue, with camels carrying
spices and very much gold and precious
stones. And she came to Solomon and spoke
to him about all that was in her heart. 3 And
Solomon declared to her *the answer* to all
her matters; there was not a matter which
was hidden from the king which he did not
declare to her. 4 Then the queen of Sheba
saw all the wisdom of Solomon, the house
that he had built, 5 the food of his table, the
seating of his servants, the disposition of his
attendants and their attire, his cupbearers,
and his stairway by which he went up to the
house of Yahweh, so that there was no more
spirit in her. 6 Then she said to the king,
"The word is true which I heard in my own
land about your words and your wisdom.
7 Nevertheless I did not believe *those* words,
until I came and my eyes had seen it. And
behold, the half was not declared to me. You
exceed, *in* wisdom and prosperity, the report
which I heard. 8 How blessed are your men,
how blessed are these your servants who
stand before you continually *and* hear your
wisdom. 9 Blessed be Yahweh your God who
delighted in you, to set you on the throne of
Israel; because Yahweh loved Israel forever,
therefore He made you king, to do justice
and righteousness." 10 Then she gave the
king 120 talents of gold and a very great
amount of spices and precious stones. Never
again did such abundance of spices come
in as that which the queen of Sheba gave
King Solomon.
11 Also, the ships of Hiram, which carried
gold from Ophir, brought in from Ophir
a very great *number of* almug trees and
precious stones. 12 And the king made of
the almug trees supports for the house of
Yahweh and for the king's house, also lyres
and harps for the singers; such almug trees
have not come in *again* nor have they been
seen to this day.
13 Thus King Solomon gave to the queen
of Sheba all her desire which she asked,
besides what he gave her according to his
royal bounty. Then she turned and went to
her own land, she and her servants.
14 Now the weight of gold which came
to Solomon in one year was 666 talents
of gold, 15 besides *that* from the traders
and the wares of the merchants and all
the kings of the Arabs and the governors
of the country. 16 And King Solomon made
200 large shields of beaten gold, using 600
shekels of gold on each large shield. 17 And
he made 300 shields of beaten gold, using
three minas of gold on each shield, and the
king put them in the house of the forest of
Lebanon. 18 Moreover, the king made a great
throne of ivory and overlaid it with refined
gold. 19 *There were* six steps to the throne
and a round top to the throne at its rear, and
arms on each side of the seat, and two lions
standing beside the arms. 20 Twelve lions
were also standing there on the six steps on
the one side and on the other; nothing like *it*
was made for all the *other* kingdoms. 21 Now
all King Solomon's drinking vessels *were* of
gold, and all the vessels of the house of the
forest of Lebanon *were* of pure gold. None
was of silver; it was not considered valuable
in the days of Solomon. 22 For the king had
at sea the ships of Tarshish with the ships
of Hiram; once every three years the ships
of Tarshish came carrying gold and silver,
ivory and apes and peacocks.
23 So King Solomon became greater than
all the kings of the earth in riches and in
wisdom. 24 And all the earth was seeking the
presence of Solomon, to hear his wisdom
which God had put in his heart. 25 And they

brought every man his present, articles of
silver and gold, garments, weapons, spices,
horses, and mules, a set amount year by year.
26 And Solomon gathered chariots and
horsemen. And he had 1,400 chariots and
12,000 horsemen and stationed them in the
chariot cities and with the king in Jerusalem.
27 The king also made silver *as plentiful* as
stones in Jerusalem, and he made cedars as
plentiful as sycamore trees that are in the
Shephelah. 28 Solomon's import of horses
was from Egypt and Kue; the king's mer-
chants procured *them* from Kue for a price.
29 And a chariot was imported from Egypt
for 600 *shekels* of silver, and a horse for
150; and by the same means they exported
them to all the kings of the Hittites and to
the kings of Aram.

Psalm 69:1–4

1 Save me, O God,
For the waters have threatened my life.
2 I have sunk in deep clay, and
there is no foothold;
I have come into deep waters,
and a flood overflows me.
3 I am weary with my calling out;
my throat is parched;
My eyes fail while I wait for my God.
4 Those who hate me without cause are
more than the hairs of my head;
Those who would destroy
me are powerful, being
wrongfully my enemies;
What I did not steal, I then
have to restore.

Proverbs 17:18–19

18 A man lacking a heart *of wisdom*
strikes his hands *in pledge*
And becomes guarantor in the
presence of his neighbor.
19 He who loves transgression
loves quarreling;
He who makes his doorway
high seeks destruction.

John 11:28–57

28 And when she had said this, she went
away and called Mary her sister, saying
secretly, "The Teacher is here and is calling
for you." 29 And when she heard it, she *got
up quickly and was coming to Him.
30 Now Jesus had not yet come into the
village, but was still in the place where
Martha met Him. 31 Then the Jews—who
were with her in the house and consoling
her—when they saw that Mary rose up
quickly and went out, they followed her,
thinking that she was going to the tomb to
cry there. 32 Therefore, when Mary came
where Jesus was, she saw Him, and fell at
His feet, saying to Him, "Lord, if You had
been here, my brother would not have died."
33 When Jesus therefore saw her crying, and
the Jews who came with her *also* crying,
He was deeply moved in spirit and was
troubled, 34 and said, "Where have you laid
him?" They *said to Him, "Lord, come and
see." 35 Jesus wept. 36 So the Jews were say-
ing, "See how He loved him!" 37 But some of
them said, "Could not this man, who opened
the eyes of the blind man, have kept this
man also from dying?"
38 So Jesus, again being deeply moved
within, *came to the tomb. Now it was a
cave, and a stone was lying against it. 39 Jesus
*said, "Remove the stone." Martha, the sister
of the deceased, *said to Him, "Lord, by this
time he smells, for he has been *dead* four
days." 40 Jesus *said to her, "Did I not say
to you that if you believe, you will see the
glory of God?" 41 So they removed the stone.
Then Jesus raised His eyes, and said, "Father,
I thank You that You have heard Me. 42 And I
knew that You always hear Me; but because
of the crowd standing around I said this, so
that they may believe that You sent Me."
43 And when He had said these things, He
cried out with a loud voice, "Lazarus, come
forth." 44 The man who had died came forth,
bound hand and foot with wrappings, and
his face was wrapped around with a cloth.
Jesus *said to them, "Unbind him, and let
him go."
45 Therefore many of the Jews who
came to Mary, and saw what He had done,
believed in Him. 46 But some of them went
to the Pharisees and told them the things
which Jesus had done.
47 Therefore the chief priests and the
Pharisees gathered the Sanhedrin together,
and were saying, "What are we doing? For
this man is doing many signs. 48 If we let
Him *go on* like this, all will believe in Him,
and the Romans will come and take away
both our place and our nation." 49 But one
of them, Caiaphas, who was high priest that
year, said to them, "You know nothing at
all, 50 nor do you take into account that it

is better for you that one man should die for the people, and that the whole nation not perish." 51 Now he did not say this from himself, but being high priest that year, he prophesied that Jesus was going to die for the nation, 52 and not for the nation only, but in order that He might also gather together into one the children of God who are scattered abroad. 53 So from that day on they planned together to kill Him.

54 Therefore Jesus no longer continued to walk openly among the Jews, but went away from there to the region near the wilderness, into a city called Ephraim; and there He stayed with the disciples.

55 Now the Passover of the Jews was near, and many went up to Jerusalem from the region before the Passover to purify themselves. 56 So they were seeking Jesus, and were saying to one another as they stood in the temple, "What do you think? That He will not come to the feast at all?" 57 Now the chief priests and the Pharisees had given orders that if anyone knew where He was, he was to report it, so that they might seize Him.

JUNE 1

1 Kings 11:1–12:33

11 Now King Solomon loved many foreign women along with the daughter of Pharaoh: Moabite, Ammonite, Edomite, Sidonian, and Hittite women, 2 from the nations concerning which Yahweh had said to the sons of Israel, "You shall not go along with them, nor shall they go along with you, *for* they will surely turn your heart away after their gods." Solomon clung to these in love. 3 And he had 700 wives—princesses—and 300 concubines, and his wives turned his heart away. 4 Now it happened at the time that Solomon was old, his wives turned his heart away after other gods; and his heart was not wholly devoted to Yahweh his God, as the heart of David his father *had been.* 5 For Solomon went after Ashtoreth the goddess of the Sidonians and after Milcom the detestable idol of the Ammonites. 6 And Solomon did what was evil in the sight of Yahweh, and did not follow Yahweh fully, as David his father *had done.* 7 Then Solomon built a high place for Chemosh the detestable idol of Moab, on the mountain which is east of Jerusalem, and for Molech the detestable idol of the sons of Ammon. 8 Thus also he did for all his foreign wives, who burned incense and sacrificed to their gods.

9 Now Yahweh was angry with Solomon because his heart was turned away from Yahweh, the God of Israel, who had appeared to him twice, 10 and had commanded him *concerning this thing,* that he should not walk after other gods; but he did not keep what Yahweh had commanded. 11 So Yahweh said to Solomon, "Because this has happened with you: you have not kept My covenant and My statutes, which I have commanded you, *so* I will surely tear the kingdom from you, and will give it to your servant. 12 Nevertheless I will not do it in your days for the sake of your father David, *but* I will tear it out of the hand of your son. 13 However, I will not tear away all the kingdom, *but* I will give one tribe to your son for the sake of My servant David and for the sake of Jerusalem which I have chosen."

14 Then Yahweh raised up an adversary to Solomon, Hadad the Edomite; he was of the seed of the king in Edom.

15 Now it happened that when David was in Edom, and Joab the commander of the army had gone up to bury the slain, and had struck down every male in Edom 16 (for Joab and all Israel stayed there six months, until he had cut off every male in Edom), 17 that Hadad fled to Egypt, he and certain Edomites of his father's servants with him, while Hadad *was* a young boy. 18 Then they arose from Midian and came to Paran; and they took men with them from Paran and came to Egypt, to Pharaoh king of Egypt. And he gave him a house and assigned him food and gave him land. 19 And Hadad found great favor in the sight of Pharaoh. So he gave him as a wife the sister of his own wife, the sister of Tahpenes the queen. 20 And the sister of Tahpenes bore his son Genubath. And Tahpenes weaned him in Pharaoh's house; and Genubath was in Pharaoh's house among the sons of Pharaoh.

21 But Hadad heard in Egypt that David slept with his fathers and that Joab the commander of the army had died. So Hadad

said to Pharaoh, "Send me away, that I may go to my own country." 22 Then Pharaoh said to him, "But what have you lacked with me, that behold, you are seeking to go to your own country?" And he answered, "Nothing; nevertheless you must surely let me go."

23 And God raised up *another* adversary to him, Rezon the son of Eliada, who had fled from his lord Hadadezer king of Zobah. 24 And he gathered men to himself and became commander of a marauding band, after David killed *some of* them; and they went to Damascus and stayed there, and reigned in Damascus. 25 So he was an adversary to Israel all the days of Solomon, along with the evil that Hadad *did*; and he abhorred Israel and reigned over Aram.

26 Now Jeroboam the son of Nebat, an Ephraimite of Zeredah, Solomon's servant, whose mother's name was Zeruah, a widow, also raised his hand against the king. 27 Now this was the reason why he raised his hand against the king: Solomon built the Millo, *and* closed up the breach of the city of his father David. 28 Now the man Jeroboam was a mighty man of valor. And Solomon saw that the young man was industrious and appointed him over all the load-bearers of the house of Joseph. 29 Now it happened at that time, that Jeroboam went out of Jerusalem, and that the prophet Ahijah the Shilonite found him on the road. Now he had covered himself with a new cloak; and both of them were alone in the field. 30 Then Ahijah took hold of the new cloak which was on him and tore it into twelve pieces. 31 And he said to Jeroboam, "Take for yourself ten pieces; for thus says Yahweh, the God of Israel, 'Behold, I will tear the kingdom out of the hand of Solomon and give you ten tribes, 32 but he will have one tribe, for the sake of My servant David and for the sake of Jerusalem, the city which I have chosen from all the tribes of Israel, 33 because they have forsaken Me, and have worshiped Ashtoreth the goddess of the Sidonians, Chemosh the god of Moab, and Milcom the god of the sons of Ammon; and they have not walked in My ways to do what is right in My sight and *to keep* My statutes and My judgments, as his father David *did*. 34 Nevertheless I will not take the whole kingdom out of his hand, but I will make him ruler all the days of his life, for the sake of My servant David whom I chose, who kept My commandments and My statutes; 35 but I will take the kingdom from his son's hand and give it to you—the ten tribes. 36 But to his son I will give one tribe, that My servant David may have a lamp always before Me in Jerusalem, the city where I have chosen for Myself to put My name. 37 And I will take you, and you shall reign over whatever your soul desires, and you shall be king over Israel. 38 Then it will be, that if you listen to all that I command you and walk in My ways, and do what is right in My sight to keep My statutes and My commandments, as My servant David did, then I will be with you and build you an enduring house as I built for David, and I will give Israel to you. 39 Thus I will afflict the seed of David for this, but not always.'" 40 Solomon sought therefore to put Jeroboam to death; but Jeroboam arose and fled to Egypt to Shishak king of Egypt, and he was in Egypt until the death of Solomon.

41 Now the rest of the acts of Solomon and whatever he did, and his wisdom, are they not written in the book of the acts of Solomon? 42 Thus the time that Solomon reigned in Jerusalem over all Israel was forty years. 43 And Solomon slept with his fathers and was buried in the city of his father David, and his son Rehoboam became king in his place.

12 Then Rehoboam went to Shechem, for all Israel had come to Shechem to make him king. 2 And it happened, when Jeroboam the son of Nebat heard *of it*, he was living in Egypt (for he was yet in Egypt, where he had fled from the presence of King Solomon). 3 Then they sent and called for him. And Jeroboam and all the assembly of Israel came and spoke to Rehoboam, saying, 4 "Your father made our yoke harsh; but you, now, lighten the harsh service of your father and his heavy yoke which he put on us, and we will serve you." 5 Then he said to them, "Go for three days, then return to me." So the people went away.

6 Then King Rehoboam took counsel with the elders who had stood before his father Solomon while he was still alive, saying, "How do you counsel *me* to respond to this people?" 7 And they spoke to him, saying, "If you will be a servant to this people today, and will serve them and grant them their petition, and speak good words to them,

then they will be your servants forever."
8 But he forsook the counsel of the elders
which they had counseled him, and took
counsel with the young men who grew up
with him and stood before him. 9 So he said
to them, "What counsel do you give that we
may respond to this people who have spoken
to me, saying, 'Lighten the yoke which your
father put on us'?" 10 Then the young men
who grew up with him spoke to him, saying,
"Thus you shall say to this people who spoke
to you, saying, 'Your father made our yoke
heavy, now you make it lighter for us!' Thus
you shall speak to them, 'My little finger is
thicker than my father's loins! 11 So now, my
father loaded you with a heavy yoke, but I
will add to your yoke; my father disciplined
you with whips, but I will discipline you
with scorpions.'"

12 So Jeroboam and all the people came to
Rehoboam on the third day as the king had
spoken, saying, "Return to me on the third
day." 13 And the king answered the people
harshly, and he forsook the counsel of the
elders which they had given him, 14 and he
spoke to them according to the counsel of
the young men, saying, "My father made
your yoke heavy, but I will add to your yoke;
my father disciplined you with whips, but I
will discipline you with scorpions." 15 So the
king did not listen to the people; for it was a
turn *of events* from Yahweh, that He might
establish His word, which Yahweh spoke
through Ahijah the Shilonite to Jeroboam
the son of Nebat.

16 Then all Israel saw that the king did not
listen to them. So the people responded to
the king *with this* word, saying,

"What portion do we have in David?
We have no inheritance in
the son of Jesse;
To your tents, O Israel!
Now see to your own house, David!"

So Israel went to their tents. 17 But as for
the sons of Israel who lived in the cities
of Judah, Rehoboam reigned over them.
18 Then King Rehoboam sent Adoram,
who *was* over the forced labor, and all
Israel stoned him and he died. And King
Rehoboam made haste to mount his chariot
to flee to Jerusalem. 19 So Israel has been
in rebellion against the house of David to
this day.

20 Now it happened when all Israel
heard that Jeroboam had returned, that
they sent and called him to the congre-
gation and made him king over all Israel.
None but the tribe of Judah followed the
house of David.

21 Then Rehoboam came to Jerusalem and
assembled all the house of Judah and the
tribe of Benjamin, 180,000 chosen men who
could wage war, to fight against the house of
Israel to return the kingdom to Rehoboam
the son of Solomon. 22 But the word of God
came to Shemaiah the man of God, saying,
23 "Speak to Rehoboam the son of Solomon,
king of Judah, and to all the house of Judah
and Benjamin and to the rest of the people,
saying, 24 'Thus says Yahweh, "You shall
not go up and fight against your brothers,
the sons of Israel; return every man to
his house, for this thing is from Me."'" So
they listened to the word of Yahweh, and
returned to go *their way* according to the
word of Yahweh.

25 Then Jeroboam built Shechem in the
hill country of Ephraim, and lived there. And
he went out from there and built Penuel.
26 And Jeroboam said in his heart, "Now the
kingdom will return to the house of David.
27 If this people go up to offer sacrifices in
the house of Yahweh at Jerusalem, then
the heart of this people will return to their
lord, *even* to Rehoboam king of Judah; and
they will kill me and return to Rehoboam
king of Judah." 28 So the king took counsel,
and made two golden calves, and he said
to them, "It is too much for you to go up to
Jerusalem; behold your gods, O Israel, that
brought you up from the land of Egypt."
29 And he set one in Bethel, and one he put
in Dan. 30 Now this thing became a sin, for
the people went *to worship* before the one
as far as Dan. 31 And he made houses on
high places, and made priests from among
all the people who were not of the sons of
Levi. 32 And Jeroboam made a feast in the
eighth month on the fifteenth day of the
month, like the feast which is in Judah,
and he went up to the altar; thus he did in
Bethel, to sacrifice to the calves which he
had made. And he had the priests of the high
places, which he had made, stand in Bethel.
33 Then he went up to the altar which he had
made in Bethel on the fifteenth day in the
eighth month, even in the month which he
had devised in his own heart; and he made
a feast for the sons of Israel and went up to
the altar to burn incense.

Psalm 69:5–15

5 O God, it is You who knows my folly,
And all my guilt is not
hidden from You.
6 May those who hope for You
not be ashamed through me,
O Lord Yahweh of hosts;
May those who seek You not
be dishonored through
me, O God of Israel,
7 Because for Your sake I have
borne reproach;
Dishonor has covered my face.
8 I have become estranged
from my brothers
And a foreigner to my mother's sons.
9 For zeal for Your house
has consumed me,
And the reproaches of those who
reproach You have fallen on me.
10 When I wept in my soul with fasting,
It became my reproach.
11 When I made sackcloth my clothing,
I became a byword to them.
12 Those who dwell at the gate
moan about me,
And I *am* the drunkards' songs.

13 But as for me, my prayer is to You,
O Yahweh, at an acceptable time;
O God, in the abundance of
Your lovingkindness,
Answer me with the truth
of Your salvation.
14 Deliver me from the mire and
do not let me sink;
May I be delivered from my foes
and from the deep waters.
15 May the flood of water
not overflow me
Nor the deep swallow me up,
Nor the pit shut its mouth on me.

Proverbs 17:20–22

20 He who has a crooked heart
finds no good,
And he who is perverted in his
tongue falls into evil.
21 He who begets a fool *does*
so to his grief,
And the father of a wicked
fool is not glad.
22 A glad heart is good medicine,
But a broken spirit dries up
the bones.

John 12:1–26

12 Jesus, therefore, six days before the
Passover, came to Bethany where
Lazarus was, whom Jesus had raised from
the dead. 2 So they made Him a supper there,
and Martha was serving; and Lazarus was
one of those reclining *at the table* with Him.
3 Mary then took a litra of perfume of very
costly pure nard, and anointed the feet of
Jesus and wiped His feet with her hair; and
the house was filled with the fragrance of
the perfume. 4 But Judas Iscariot, one of
His disciples, who was going to betray Him,
*said, 5 "Why was this perfume not sold for
three hundred denarii and given to the
poor?" 6 Now he said this, not because he
was concerned about the poor, but because
he was a thief, and as he had the money box,
he used to take from what was put into it.
7 Therefore Jesus said, "Let her alone, so that
she may keep it for the day of My burial. 8 For
you always have the poor with you, but you
do not always have Me."
9 Then the large crowd from the Jews
learned that He was there. And they came,
not because of Jesus only, but that they might
also see Lazarus, whom He raised from the
dead. 10 But the chief priests planned to put
Lazarus to death also; 11 because on account
of him many of the Jews were going away
and were believing in Jesus.
12 On the next day the large crowd who
had come to the feast, when they heard that
Jesus was coming to Jerusalem, 13 took the
branches of the palm trees and went out to
meet Him, and *began to* shout, "Hosanna!
BLESSED IS HE WHO COMES IN THE NAME OF
THE LORD, even the King of Israel." 14 And
Jesus, finding a young donkey, sat on it; as it
is written, 15 "FEAR NOT, DAUGHTER OF ZION;
BEHOLD, YOUR KING IS COMING, SEATED ON A
DONKEY'S COLT." 16 These things His disciples
did not understand at the first; but when
Jesus was glorified, then they remembered
that these things were written about Him,
and that they had done these things to Him.
17 So the crowd, who was with Him when He
called Lazarus out of the tomb and raised
him from the dead, continued to bear
witness *about Him*. 18 For this reason also
the crowd went and met Him, because they
heard that He had done this sign. 19 So the
Pharisees said to one another, "You see that
you are gaining nothing; look, the world has
gone after Him."

20 Now there were some Greeks among
those who were going up to worship at the
feast; 21 these then came to Philip, who was
from Bethsaida of Galilee, and *began to*
ask him, saying, "Sir, we wish to see Jesus."
22 Philip *came and *told Andrew; Andrew
and Philip *came and *told Jesus. 23 And
Jesus *answered them, saying, "The hour
has come for the Son of Man to be glorified.
24 Truly, truly, I say to you, unless a grain
of wheat falls into the earth and dies, it
remains alone; but if it dies, it bears much
fruit. 25 He who loves his life loses it, and
he who hates his life in this world will keep
it to life eternal. 26 If anyone serves Me, he
must follow Me; and where I am, there My
servant will be also; if anyone serves Me,
the Father will honor him.

JUNE 2

1 Kings 13:1–14:31

13 Now behold, there came a man of God
from Judah to Bethel by the word of
Yahweh, while Jeroboam was standing by
the altar to burn incense. 2 And he cried
against the altar by the word of Yahweh,
and said, "O altar, altar, thus says Yahweh,
'Behold, a son shall be born to the house
of David, Josiah is his name; and on you he
shall sacrifice the priests of the high places
who burn incense on you, and human bones
shall be burned on you.'" 3 Then he gave a
miraculous sign the same day, saying, "This
is the miraculous sign which Yahweh has
spoken, 'Behold, the altar shall be torn apart
and the ashes which are on it shall be poured
out.'" 4 Now it happened that when the king
heard the word of the man of God, which he
cried against the altar in Bethel, Jeroboam
stretched out his hand from the altar, saying,
"Seize him." But his hand which he stretched
out against him dried up, so that he could not
draw it back to himself. 5 The altar also was
torn apart and the ashes were poured out
from the altar, according to the miraculous
sign which the man of God had given by the
word of Yahweh. 6 Then the king answered
and said to the man of God, "Please entreat
Yahweh your God, and pray for me, that my
hand may be restored to me." So the man
of God entreated Yahweh, and the king's
hand was restored to him, and it became as
it was before. 7 Then the king said to the man
of God, "Come home with me and refresh
yourself, and I will give you a gift." 8 But the
man of God said to the king, "If you were to
give me half your house, I would not go with
you, nor would I eat bread or drink water in
this place. 9 *For so it was* commanded me
by the word of Yahweh, saying, 'You shall
eat no bread, nor drink water, nor return
by the way which you came.'" 10 So he went
another way and did not return by the way
which he came to Bethel.

11 Now an old prophet was living in
Bethel; and his sons came and recounted to
him all the work which the man of God had
done that day in Bethel; the words which
he had spoken to the king, these also they
recounted to their father. 12 And their father
said to them, "Which way did he go?" And
his sons had seen the way which the man
of God who came from Judah had gone.
13 Then he said to his sons, "Saddle the
donkey for me." So they saddled the donkey
for him and he rode away on it. 14 So he went
after the man of God and found him sitting
under an oak; and he said to him, "Are you
the man of God who came from Judah?"
And he said, "I am." 15 Then he said to him,
"Come home with me and eat bread." 16 And
he said, "I cannot return with you, nor go
with you, nor will I eat bread or drink water
with you in this place. 17 For a word *came* to
me by the word of Yahweh, 'You shall eat no
bread, nor drink water there; do not return
by going the way which you came.'" 18 And
he said to him, "I also am a prophet like you,
and an angel spoke to me by the word of
Yahweh, saying, 'Bring him back with you
to your house, that he may eat bread and
drink water.'" *But* he dealt falsely with him.
19 So he went back with him, and ate bread
in his house and drank water.

20 Now it happened as they were sitting
down at the table, that the word of Yahweh
came to the prophet who had brought him
back; 21 and he called out to the man of God
who came from Judah, saying, "Thus says
Yahweh, 'Because you have rebelled against
the word of Yahweh, and have not kept the
commandment which Yahweh your God
commanded you, 22 but have returned and
eaten bread and drunk water in the place

of which He said to you, "Eat no bread and drink no water"; your body shall not come to the grave of your fathers.'" 23 Now it happened after he had eaten bread and after he had drunk, that he saddled the donkey for him, for the prophet whom he had brought back. 24 Then he went and on the way a lion met him and put him to death, and his body was thrown on the road, with the donkey standing beside it; the lion also was standing beside the body. 25 And behold, men passed by and saw the body thrown on the road, and the lion standing beside the body; so they came and spoke *about it* in the city where the old prophet lived.

26 Then the prophet, who brought him back from the way, heard *it* and said, "It is the man of God, who rebelled against the command of Yahweh; therefore Yahweh has given him to the lion, which has mauled him and put him to death, according to the word of Yahweh which He spoke to him." 27 Then he spoke to his sons, saying, "Saddle the donkey for me." And they saddled *it*. 28 And he went and found his body thrown on the road with the donkey and the lion standing beside the body; the lion had not eaten the body nor mauled the donkey. 29 So the prophet took up the body of the man of God and laid it on the donkey and brought it back, and he came to the city of the old prophet to mourn and to bury him. 30 He laid his body in his own grave, and they mourned over him, *saying*, "Alas, my brother!" 31 Now it happened after he had buried him, that he spoke to his sons, saying, "When I die, you shall bury me in the grave in which the man of God is buried; lay my bones beside his bones. 32 For the word shall surely happen which he cried by the word of Yahweh against the altar in Bethel and against all the houses of the high places which are in the cities of Samaria."

33 After this event Jeroboam did not return from his evil way, but he returned and made priests of the high places from among *all the people*; any who delighted *to be so*, he ordained. So they became priests of the high places. 34 And this event became sin to the house of Jeroboam, even to blot *it* out and destroy *it* from off the face of the earth.

14 At that time Abijah the son of Jeroboam became sick. 2 And Jeroboam said to his wife, "Arise now, and disguise yourself so that they will not know that you are the wife of Jeroboam, and go to Shiloh; behold, Ahijah the prophet is there, who spoke concerning me *that I would be* king over this people. 3 And take ten loaves with you, *some* cakes, and a jar of honey, and go to him. He will tell you what will happen to the boy."

4 Then Jeroboam's wife did so, and arose and went to Shiloh, and came to the house of Ahijah. Now Ahijah could not see, for his eyes had set because of his old age. 5 Now Yahweh had said to Ahijah, "Behold, the wife of Jeroboam is coming to inquire of you concerning her son, for he is sick. You shall say thus and thus to her, for it will be when she arrives that she will pretend to be another woman."

6 Now it happened as Ahijah heard the sound of her feet coming in the doorway, that he said, "Come in, wife of Jeroboam, why do you pretend to be another woman? For I am sent to you *with* a harsh *message*. 7 Go, say to Jeroboam, 'Thus says Yahweh, the God of Israel, "Because I exalted you from among the people and made you ruler over My people Israel, 8 and tore the kingdom away from the house of David and gave it to you—yet you have not been like My servant David, who kept My commandments and who walked after Me with all his heart, to do only that which was right in My sight; 9 you also have done more evil than all who were before you, and have gone and made for yourself other gods and molten images to provoke Me to anger, and have cast Me behind your back— 10 therefore behold, I am bringing evil on the house of Jeroboam: I will cut off from Jeroboam every male person, both bond and free in Israel, and I will make a clean sweep of the house of Jeroboam, as one sweeps away dung until it is all gone. 11 Anyone belonging to Jeroboam who dies in the city the dogs will eat. And he who dies in the field the birds of the sky will eat; for Yahweh has spoken *it*."' 12 But you, arise, go to your house. When your feet enter the city the child will die. 13 And all Israel shall mourn for him and bury him, for he alone of Jeroboam's *family* will come to the grave, because in him something good was found toward Yahweh, the God of Israel, in the house of Jeroboam. 14 Moreover, Yahweh will raise up for Himself a king over Israel who will cut off the house of Jeroboam this day and from now on.

15 "So Yahweh will strike Israel, as a reed
is shaken in the water; and He will uproot
Israel from this good land which He gave to
their fathers, and will scatter them beyond
the River, because they have made their
Asherim, provoking Yahweh to anger. 16 And
He will give Israel over on account of the
sins of Jeroboam, which he sinned and with
which he made Israel to sin."
17 Then Jeroboam's wife arose and went
away and came to Tirzah. As she was
entering the threshold of the house, the
child died. 18 And all Israel buried him and
mourned for him, according to the word
of Yahweh which He spoke through His
servant Ahijah the prophet.
19 Now the rest of the acts of Jeroboam,
how he made war and how he reigned,
behold, they are written in the Book of the
Chronicles of the Kings of Israel. 20 Now the
time that Jeroboam reigned *was* twenty-two
years; and he slept with his fathers, and
Nadab his son became king in his place.
21 Now Rehoboam the son of Solomon
became king in Judah. Rehoboam was
forty-one years old when he became
king, and he reigned seventeen years in
Jerusalem, the city which Yahweh had
chosen from all the tribes of Israel to put
His name there. And his mother's name was
Naamah the Ammonitess. 22 And Judah did
what was evil in the sight of Yahweh, and
they provoked Him to jealousy more than
all that their fathers had done, with the sins
which they sinned. 23 They also built for
themselves high places and *sacred* pillars
and Asherim on every high hill and beneath
every green tree. 24 There were also male
cult prostitutes in the land. They did
according to all the abominations of the
nations which Yahweh dispossessed before
the sons of Israel.
25 Now it happened in the fifth year of
King Rehoboam, that Shishak king of Egypt
came up against Jerusalem. 26 And he took
the treasures of the house of Yahweh and
the treasures of the king's house. And he
took everything; he even took all the shields
of gold which Solomon had made. 27 Then
King Rehoboam made shields of bronze in
their place and committed them into the
hand of the commanders of the guard who
kept the door of the king's house. 28 Now it
happened as often as the king entered the
house of Yahweh, that the guards would
carry them and would bring them back into
the guards' room.
29 Now the rest of the acts of Rehoboam
and all that he did, are they not written in
the Book of the Chronicles of the Kings
of Judah? 30 Now there was war between
Rehoboam and Jeroboam all *their* days.
31 And Rehoboam slept with his fathers
and was buried with his fathers in the
city of David; and his mother's name was
Naamah the Ammonitess. And Abijam his
son became king in his place.

Psalm 69:16–21

16 Answer me, O Yahweh, for Your
 lovingkindness is good;
According to the abundance of
 Your compassion, turn to me,
17 And do not hide Your face
 from Your slave,
For I am in distress; answer me quickly.
18 Oh draw near to my soul *and* redeem it;
Ransom me because of my enemies!
19 You know my reproach and my
 shame and my dishonor;
All my adversaries are before You.

20 Reproach has broken my
 heart and I am so sick.
And I hoped for sympathy,
 but there was none,
And for comforters, but I found none.
21 They also gave *me* gall for my food
And for my thirst they gave
 me vinegar to drink.

Proverbs 17:23–24

23 A wicked man receives a
 bribe from the bosom
To thrust aside the paths of justice.
24 Wisdom is in the presence of
 the one who understands,
But the eyes of a fool are on
 the ends of the earth.

John 12:27–50

27 "Now MY SOUL HAS BECOME DISMAYED;
and what shall I say, 'Father, SAVE ME from
this hour'? But for this purpose I came to
this hour. 28 Father, glorify Your name."
Then a voice came from heaven: "I have
both glorified it, and will glorify it again."
29 So the crowd *of people* who stood by and
heard it were saying that it had thundered;
others were saying, "An angel has spoken

to Him." 30 Jesus answered and said, "This
voice has not come for My sake, but for your
sake. 31 Now judgment is upon this world;
now the ruler of this world will be cast out.
32 And I, if I am lifted up from the earth,
will draw all men to Myself." 33 But He was
saying this to indicate the kind of death by
which He was about to die. 34 The crowd
then answered Him, "We have heard from
the Law that the Christ is to remain forever;
and how do You say, 'The Son of Man must
be lifted up'? Who is this Son of Man?" 35 So
Jesus said to them, "For a little while longer
the Light is among you. Walk while you have
the Light, so that darkness will not overtake
you; he who walks in the darkness does not
know where he goes. 36 While you have the
Light, believe in the Light, so that you may
become sons of Light."
These things Jesus spoke, and He went
away and hid Himself from them. 37 But
though He had done so many signs before
them, they *still* were not believing in Him,
38 so that the word of Isaiah the prophet
might be fulfilled, which he spoke: "LORD,
WHO HAS BELIEVED OUR REPORT? AND TO
WHOM HAS THE ARM OF THE LORD BEEN
REVEALED?" 39 For this reason they could
not believe, for Isaiah said again, 40 "HE
HAS BLINDED THEIR EYES AND HE HARDENED
THEIR HEART, LEST THEY SEE WITH THEIR
EYES AND UNDERSTAND WITH THEIR HEART,
AND RETURN AND I HEAL THEM." 41 These
things Isaiah said because he saw His
glory, and he spoke about Him. 42 Never-
theless many even of the rulers believed
in Him, but because of the Pharisees they
were not confessing *Him*, for fear that they
would be put out of the synagogue; 43 for
they loved the glory of men rather than
the glory of God.
44 And Jesus cried out and said, "He who
believes in Me, does not believe in Me but
in Him who sent Me. 45 And he who sees Me
sees the One who sent Me. 46 I have come *as*
Light into the world, so that everyone who
believes in Me will not remain in darkness.
47 And if anyone hears My words and does
not keep them, I do not judge him; for I did
not come to judge the world, but to save
the world. 48 He who rejects Me and does
not receive My words, has one who judges
him; the word I spoke is what will judge him
on the last day. 49 For I did not speak from
Myself, but the Father Himself who sent Me
has given Me a commandment—what to say
and what to speak. 50 And I know that His
commandment is eternal life; therefore the
things I speak, I speak just as the Father has
told Me."

JUNE 3

1 Kings 15:1–16:34

15 Now in the eighteenth year of King
Jeroboam, the son of Nebat, Abijam
became king over Judah. 2 He reigned three
years in Jerusalem; and his mother's name
was Maacah the daughter of Abishalom.
3 And he walked in all the sins of his father
which he had committed before him; and his
heart was not wholly devoted to Yahweh his
God, like the heart of his father David. 4 But
for David's sake Yahweh his God gave him a
lamp in Jerusalem, to raise up his son after
him and to establish Jerusalem; 5 because
David did what was right in the sight of Yah-
weh, and had not turned aside from anything
that He commanded him all the days of his
life, except in the case of Uriah the Hittite.
6 Now there was war between Rehoboam and
Jeroboam all the days of his life.
7 Now the rest of the acts of Abijam and
all that he did, are they not written in the
Book of the Chronicles of the Kings of
Judah? And there was war between Abijam
and Jeroboam. 8 And Abijam slept with his
fathers, and they buried him in the city of
David; and Asa his son became king in his
place.
9 Now in the twentieth year of Jeroboam
the king of Israel, Asa began to reign as
king of Judah. 10 And he reigned forty-one
years in Jerusalem; and his mother's name
was Maacah the daughter of Abishalom.
11 And Asa did what was right in the sight of
Yahweh, like David his father. 12 He also put
away the male cult prostitutes from the land
and removed all the idols which his fathers
had made. 13 He also removed Maacah his
mother from *being* queen mother, because
she had made a horrid image for Asherah;
and Asa cut down her horrid image and
burned *it* at the brook Kidron. 14 But the high
places were not removed; nevertheless the

heart of Asa was wholly devoted to Yahweh
all his days. 15 And he brought into the house
of Yahweh the holy things of his father and
his own holy things: silver and gold and
utensils.

16 Now there was war between Asa and
Baasha king of Israel all their days. 17 And
Baasha king of Israel went up against Judah
and built up Ramah in order to prevent
anyone from going out or coming in to Asa
king of Judah. 18 Then Asa took all the silver
and the gold which were left in the treasuries
of the house of Yahweh and the treasuries of
the king's house, and delivered them into
the hand of his servants. And King Asa sent
them to Ben-hadad the son of Tabrimmon,
the son of Hezion, king of Aram, who lived in
Damascus, saying, 19 "*Let there be* a covenant
between you and me, *as* between my father
and your father. Behold, I have sent you a gift
of silver and gold; go, break your covenant
with Baasha king of Israel so that he will
withdraw from me." 20 So Ben-hadad listened
to King Asa and sent the commanders of his
military force against the cities of Israel, and
struck down Ijon, Dan, Abel-beth-maacah
and all Chinneroth, besides all the land of
Naphtali. 21 Now it happened that when
Baasha heard *of it*, he ceased building up
Ramah and remained in Tirzah. 22 Then King
Asa caused *an announcement* to be heard
throughout all Judah—none was exempt—
and they carried away the stones of Ramah
and its timber with which Baasha had been
building. And King Asa built with them Geba
of Benjamin and Mizpah.

23 Now the rest of all the acts of Asa and
all his might and all that he did and the
cities which he built, are they not written
in the Book of the Chronicles of the Kings of
Judah? But in the time of his old age he was
diseased in his feet. 24 And Asa slept with his
fathers and was buried with his fathers in
the city of David his father; and Jehoshaphat
his son reigned in his place.

25 Now Nadab the son of Jeroboam
became king over Israel in the second year
of Asa king of Judah, and he reigned over
Israel two years. 26 And he did what was evil
in the sight of Yahweh, and walked in the
way of his father and in his sin which he
made Israel sin. 27 Then Baasha the son of
Ahijah of the house of Issachar conspired
against him, and Baasha struck him down
at Gibbethon, which belonged to the Philistines, while Nadab and all Israel were laying
siege to Gibbethon.

28 So Baasha put him to death in the
third year of Asa king of Judah and became
king in his place. 29 Now it happened that
as soon as he was king, he struck down
all the household of Jeroboam. He did
not leave to Jeroboam anyone *who drew*
breath, until he had destroyed them,
according to the word of Yahweh, which
He spoke by the hand of His servant Ahijah
the Shilonite, 30 *and* because of the sins of
Jeroboam which he sinned, and which he
made Israel sin, because of his provocation
with which he provoked Yahweh, the God
of Israel, to anger.

31 Now the rest of the acts of Nadab and
all that he did, are they not written in the
Book of the Chronicles of the Kings of
Israel? 32 Now there was war between Asa
and Baasha king of Israel all their days.

33 In the third year of Asa king of Judah,
Baasha the son of Ahijah became king over
all Israel at Tirzah, *and reigned* twenty-four
years. 34 And he did what was evil in the
sight of Yahweh, and walked in the way
of Jeroboam and in his sin which he made
Israel sin.

16 Now the word of Yahweh came to Jehu
the son of Hanani against Baasha,
saying, 2 "Inasmuch as I exalted you from
the dust and made you ruler over My people
Israel, and you have walked in the way of
Jeroboam and have made My people Israel
sin, provoking Me to anger with their sins,
3 behold, I am going to sweep away Baasha
and his house, and I will make your house
like the house of Jeroboam the son of Nebat.
4 Anyone of Baasha who dies in the city the
dogs will eat, and anyone of his who dies in
the field the birds of the sky will eat."

5 Now the rest of the acts of Baasha and
what he did and his might, are they not
written in the Book of the Chronicles of the
Kings of Israel? 6 And Baasha slept with his
fathers and was buried in Tirzah, and Elah
his son became king in his place. 7 Moreover,
the word of Yahweh through the hand of the
prophet Jehu the son of Hanani also came
about against Baasha and his household,
both because of all the evil which he did in
the sight of Yahweh, provoking Him to anger
with the work of his hands, in being like the
house of Jeroboam, and because he struck it.

8 In the twenty-sixth year of Asa king of
Judah, Elah the son of Baasha became king
over Israel at Tirzah, *and reigned* two years.
9 And his servant Zimri, commander of half
his chariots, conspired against him. Now
he *was* at Tirzah drinking himself drunk
in the house of Arza, who *was* over the
household at Tirzah. 10 Then Zimri went in
and struck him and put him to death in the
twenty-seventh year of Asa king of Judah,
and became king in his place. 11 Now it
happened when he became king, as soon
as he sat on his throne, that he struck down
all the household of Baasha; he did not leave
a single male—not *even any of* his kinsman
redeemers or his friends.

12 Thus Zimri destroyed all the household
of Baasha, according to the word of Yahweh,
which He spoke against Baasha by the hand
of Jehu the prophet, 13 for all the sins of
Baasha and the sins of Elah his son, which
they sinned and which they made Israel
sin, provoking Yahweh, the God of Israel,
to anger with their idols. 14 Now the rest of
the acts of Elah and all that he did, are they
not written in the Book of the Chronicles of
the Kings of Israel?

15 In the twenty-seventh year of Asa king
of Judah, Zimri reigned seven days at Tir-
zah. Now the people were camped against
Gibbethon, which belonged to the Philis-
tines. 16 And the people who were camped
heard it said, "Zimri has conspired and has
also struck down the king." Therefore all
Israel made Omri, the commander of the
army, king over Israel that day in the camp.
17 Then Omri and all Israel with him went
up from Gibbethon and besieged Tirzah.
18 Now it happened that when Zimri saw
that the city was captured, he went into the
citadel of the king's house and burned the
king's house over him with fire, and died,
19 because of his sins which he sinned,
doing what is evil in the sight of Yahweh,
walking in the way of Jeroboam, and in
his sin which he did, making Israel sin.
20 Now the rest of the acts of Zimri and his
conspiracy which he carried out, are they
not written in the Book of the Chronicles
of the Kings of Israel?

21 Then the people of Israel were divided
into two parts: half of the people followed
Tibni the son of Ginath, to make him king;
the *other* half followed Omri. 22 But the
people who followed Omri prevailed over
the people who followed Tibni the son of
Ginath. And Tibni died and Omri became
king. 23 In the thirty-first year of Asa king
of Judah, Omri became king over Israel *and*
reigned twelve years; he reigned six years at
Tirzah. 24 And he bought the hill Samaria
from Shemer for two talents of silver; and he
built on the hill, and named the city which
he built Samaria, after the name of Shemer,
the owner of the hill.

25 And Omri did what was evil in the sight
of Yahweh, and acted more wickedly than all
who *were* before him. 26 For he walked in all
the way of Jeroboam the son of Nebat and in
his sins which he made Israel sin, provoking
Yahweh, the God of Israel, to anger with
their idols. 27 Now the rest of the acts of
Omri which he did and his might which he
showed, are they not written in the Book of
the Chronicles of the Kings of Israel? 28 So
Omri slept with his fathers and was buried
in Samaria; and Ahab his son became king
in his place.

29 Now Ahab the son of Omri became king
over Israel in the thirty-eighth year of Asa
king of Judah, and Ahab the son of Omri
reigned over Israel in Samaria twenty-two
years. 30 And Ahab the son of Omri did what
was evil in the sight of Yahweh more than
all who were before him.

31 Now it happened, as though it had been
a trivial thing for him to walk in the sins
of Jeroboam the son of Nebat, that he took
Jezebel the daughter of Ethbaal king of the
Sidonians as a wife, and went and served
Baal and worshiped him. 32 So he erected
an altar for Baal in the house of Baal which
he built in Samaria. 33 Ahab also made the
Asherah. Thus Ahab did more to provoke
Yahweh, the God of Israel, to anger than all
the kings of Israel who were before him. 34 In
his days Hiel the Bethelite built Jericho; he
laid its foundations with the *loss of* Abiram
his firstborn, and set up its gates with the
loss of his youngest son Segub, according
to the word of Yahweh, which He spoke by
the hand of Joshua the son of Nun.

Psalm 69:22–28

22 May their table before them
become a snare;
And when they are in peace,
may it become a trap.
23 May their eyes darken so
that they cannot see,

And make their loins
quake continually.
24 Pour out Your indignation on them,
And may Your burning anger
overtake them.
25 May their camp be desolate;
May none dwell in their tents.
26 For they have persecuted him whom
You Yourself have struck down,
And they recount the pain of those
whom You have wounded.
27 Add iniquity to their iniquity,
And may they not come into
Your righteousness.
28 May they be blotted out
of the book of life
And may they not be recorded
with the righteous.

Proverbs 17:25–26

25 A foolish son is a vexation to his father
And bitterness to her who
gave birth to him.
26 It is also not good to punish
the righteous,
Nor to strike the noble for
their uprightness.

John 13:1–20

13 Now before the Feast of the Passover,
Jesus knowing that His hour had
come that He would depart out of this
world to the Father, having loved His own
who were in the world, He loved them to
the end. 2 And during supper, the devil
having already put into the heart of Judas
Iscariot, *the son* of Simon, to betray Him,
3 *Jesus,* knowing that the Father had given
all things into His hands, and that He had
come forth from God and was going back to
God, 4 *got up from supper, and *laid aside
His garments; and taking a towel, He tied
it around Himself.
5 Then He *poured water into the wash-
basin, and began to wash the disciples' feet
and to wipe them with the towel which He
had tied around *Himself.* 6 So He *came
to Simon Peter. He *said to Him, "Lord,
are You going to wash my feet?" 7 Jesus
answered and said to him, "What I am
doing you do not realize now, but you will
understand afterwards." 8 Peter *said to
Him, "You will never wash my feet—ever!"
Jesus answered him, "If I do not wash you,
you have no part with Me." 9 Simon Peter
*said to Him, "Lord, not only my feet, but
also my hands and my head." 10 Jesus *said
to him, "He who has bathed needs only to
wash his feet, but is completely clean; and
you are clean, but not all *of you.*" 11 For He
knew the one who was betraying Him; for
this reason He said, "Not all of you are
clean."
12 So when He had washed their feet,
and taken His garments and reclined *at
the table* again, He said to them, "Do you
know what I have done to you? 13 You call
Me Teacher and Lord; and you are right,
for *so* I am. 14 If I then, the Lord and the
Teacher, washed your feet, you also ought
to wash one another's feet. 15 For I gave you
an example that you also should do as I did
to you. 16 Truly, truly, I say to you, a slave is
not greater than his master, nor *is* one who
is sent greater than the one who sent him.
17 If you know these things, you are blessed
if you do them. 18 I do not speak about all of
you. I know the ones I have chosen; but that
the Scripture may be fulfilled, 'HE WHO EATS
MY BREAD HAS LIFTED UP HIS HEEL AGAINST
ME.' 19 From now on I am telling you before
it occurs, so that when it does occur, you
may believe that I am *He.* 20 Truly, truly,
I say to you, he who receives anyone I
send receives Me; and he who receives Me
receives Him who sent Me."

The Bible is alive; it speaks to me. It has feet; it runs after me.
It has hands; it lays hold of me!

— MARTIN LUTHER

JUNE 4

1 Kings 17:1–18:46

17 Now Elijah the Tishbite, who was of
the settlers of Gilead, said to Ahab,
"As Yahweh, the God of Israel, lives, before
whom I stand, surely there shall be neither
dew nor rain these years, except by my
word." 2 Then the word of Yahweh came to
him, saying, 3 "Go away from here and turn
eastward, and hide yourself by the brook
Cherith, which is east of the Jordan. 4 And
it will be that you will drink of the brook,
and I have commanded the ravens to sustain
you there." 5 So he went and did according to
the word of Yahweh, for he went and lived
by the brook Cherith, which is east of the
Jordan. 6 And the ravens were bringing him
bread and meat in the morning and bread
and meat in the evening, and he would drink
from the brook. 7 Now it happened after a
while that the brook dried up, because there
was no rain in the land.

8 Then the word of Yahweh came to him,
saying, 9 "Arise, go to Zarephath, which
belongs to Sidon, and remain there; behold,
I have commanded a widow there to sustain
you." 10 So he arose and went to Zarephath,
and when he came to the gate of the city,
behold, a widow was there gathering sticks;
and he called to her and said, "Please get me a
little water in a jar, that I may drink." 11 So she
went to get *it*, and he called to her and said,
"Please get me a piece of bread in your hand."
12 But she said, "As Yahweh your God lives, I
have no bread, only a handful of flour in the
bowl and a little oil in the jar; and behold, I
am gathering a few sticks that I may go in
and prepare for me and my son, that we may
eat it and die." 13 Then Elijah said to her, "Do
not fear; go, do as you have said, but make
me a little bread cake from it first and bring
it out to me, and afterward you may make
one for yourself and for your son. 14 For thus
says Yahweh, the God of Israel, '*The bowl of
flour shall not be exhausted*, nor shall the
jar of oil be empty, until the day that Yahweh
sends rain on the face of the earth.'" 15 So
she went and did according to the word of
Elijah, and she and he and her household
ate for *many* days. 16 The bowl of flour was
not exhausted nor did the jar of oil become
empty, according to the word of Yahweh
which He spoke by the hand of Elijah.

17 Now it happened after these things that
the son of the woman, the mistress of the
house, became sick; and his sickness was so
severe that there was no breath left in him.
18 So she said to Elijah, "What do I have to
do with you, O man of God? You have come
to me to bring my iniquity to remembrance
and to put my son to death!" 19 And he said
to her, "Give me your son." Then he took
him from her bosom and carried him up to
the upper room where he was living, and
laid him on his own bed. 20 Then he called
to Yahweh and said, "O Yahweh my God, have
You also brought calamity to the widow with
whom I am sojourning, by causing her son
to die?" 21 Then he stretched himself upon
the child three times, and called to Yahweh
and said, "O Yahweh my God, I pray You, let
this child's life return to him." 22 And Yahweh
heard the voice of Elijah, and the life of the
child returned to him and he became alive.
23 Then Elijah took the child and brought
him down from the upper room into the
house and gave him to his mother; and
Elijah said, "See, your son is alive." 24 Then
the woman said to Elijah, "Now I know this:
that you are a man of God and that the word
of Yahweh in your mouth is truth."

18 Now it happened *after* many days that
the word of Yahweh came to Elijah in
the third year, saying, "Go, show yourself to
Ahab, and I will send rain on the face of the
earth." 2 So Elijah went to show himself to
Ahab. Now the famine *was* severe in Samaria.
3 And Ahab called Obadiah who *was* over the
household. (Now Obadiah feared Yahweh
greatly. 4 And it happened that when Jezebel
was cutting down the prophets of Yahweh,
Obadiah took one hundred prophets and
hid them by fifties in a cave, and sustained
them with bread and water.) 5 Then Ahab
said to Obadiah, "Go through the land to all
the springs of water and to all the valleys;
perhaps we will find grass and keep the
horses and mules alive, and not have to cut
down some of the cattle." 6 So they divided
the land between them to pass through it;
Ahab went one way by himself and Obadiah
went another way by himself.

7 Now it happened that as Obadiah was
on the way, behold, Elijah met him, and

he recognized him and fell on his face and
said, "Is this you, Elijah my master?" 8 And
he said to him, "It is I. Go, say to your master,
'Behold, Elijah *is here*.'" 9 And he said, "What
sin have I committed, that you are giving
your servant into the hand of Ahab to put me
to death? 10 As Yahweh your God lives, there
is no nation or kingdom where my master
has not sent to search for you; and if they
said, 'He is not *here*,' he made the kingdom
or nation swear that they could not find you.
11 And now you are saying, 'Go, say to your
master, "Behold, Elijah *is here*."' 12 And it
will be that *when* I leave you, the Spirit of
Yahweh will carry you where I do not know;
and I will come and tell Ahab, and he will
not find you, and he will kill me, although
I your servant have feared Yahweh from my
youth. 13 Has it not been told to my master
what I did when Jezebel killed the prophets
of Yahweh, that I hid one hundred prophets
of Yahweh by fifties in a cave, and sustained
them with bread and water? 14 So now you
are saying, 'Go, say to your master, "Behold,
Elijah *is here*"'; he will then kill me." 15 And
Elijah said, "As Yahweh of hosts lives, before
whom I stand, I will surely show myself to
him today." 16 So Obadiah went to meet Ahab
and told him; and Ahab went to meet Elijah.

17 Now it happened when Ahab saw
Elijah, that Ahab said to him, "Is this you,
you troubler of Israel?" 18 And he said, "I
have not troubled Israel, but you and your
father's house *have*, because you have for-
saken the commandments of Yahweh and
you have followed the Baals. 19 So now then
send *and* gather to me all Israel at Mount
Carmel, *together* with 450 prophets of Baal
and 400 prophets of the Asherah, who eat
at Jezebel's table."

20 So Ahab sent *a message* among all the
sons of Israel and gathered the prophets
together at Mount Carmel. 21 And Elijah
came near to all the people and said, "How
long *will* you be limping between two
opinions? If Yahweh is God, follow Him;
but if Baal, follow him." But the people did
not answer him a word. 22 Then Elijah said
to the people, "I alone am left a prophet of
Yahweh, but Baal's prophets are 450 men.
23 Now let them give us two oxen; and let
them choose one ox for themselves and cut
it up, and place it on the wood, but place no
fire *under it*; and I will prepare the other ox
and put it on the wood, and I will not place
fire *under it*. 24 Then you call on the name
of your god, and I will call on the name of
Yahweh, and the God who answers by fire,
He is God." And all the people answered and
said, "That is a good word."

25 So Elijah said to the prophets of
Baal, "Choose one ox for yourselves and
prepare it first for you are many, and call
on the name of your god, but place no fire
under it." 26 Then they took the ox which
was given them and they prepared it and
called on the name of Baal from morning
until noon saying, "O Baal, answer us." But
there was no voice and no one answered.
And they limped about the altar which they
had made. 27 Now it happened at noon, that
Elijah mocked them and said, "Call out
with a loud voice, for he is a god; either he
is occupied or relieving himself, or is on a
journey, or perhaps he is asleep and needs
to be awakened." 28 So they cried with a loud
voice and gashed themselves according to
their custom with swords and lances until
the blood gushed out on them. 29 Now it
happened when noon had passed, that they
prophesied until the time of the offering of
the *evening* sacrifice; but there was no voice,
no one answered, and no one paid attention.

30 Then Elijah said to all the people, "Come
near to me." So all the people came near to
him. And he repaired the altar of Yahweh
which had been pulled down. 31 Then Elijah
took twelve stones according to the number
of the tribes of the sons of Jacob, to whom
the word of Yahweh had come, saying, "Israel
shall be your name." 32 And with the stones
he built an altar in the name of Yahweh, and
he made a trench around the altar, large
enough to hold two seahs of seed. 33 Then he
arranged the wood and cut the ox in pieces
and placed *it* on the wood. 34 And he said,
"Fill four pitchers with water and pour *it* on
the burnt offering and on the wood." And
he said, "Do it a second time," and they did
it a second time. And he said, "Do it a third
time," and they did it a third time. 35 And the
water flowed around the altar and he also
filled the trench with water.

36 Now it happened at the time of the
offering of the *evening* sacrifice, that Elijah
the prophet came near and said, "O Yahweh,
the God of Abraham, Isaac and Israel, today
let it be known that You are God in Israel
and that I am Your slave and I have done
all these things at Your word. 37 Answer

me, O Yahweh, answer me, that this people
may know that You, O Yahweh, are God,
and *that* You have turned their heart back
again." 38 Then the fire of Yahweh fell and
consumed the burnt offering and the wood
and the stones and the dust, and licked up
the water that was in the trench. 39 And
all the people saw it and fell on their faces
and said, "Yahweh, He is God; Yahweh, He
is God." 40 Then Elijah said to them, "Seize
the prophets of Baal; do not let one of them
escape." So they seized them; and Elijah
brought them down to the brook Kishon,
and slaughtered them there.

41 Now Elijah said to Ahab, "Go up, eat and
drink; for there is the sound of the tumult of
rain." 42 So Ahab went up to eat and drink.
But Elijah went up to the top of Carmel;
and he stretched himself down toward the
ground and put his face between his knees.
43 And he said to his young man, "Go up
now, look toward the sea." So he went up
and looked and said, "There is nothing."
And he said, "Go back" seven times. 44 Now
it happened at the seventh *time*, that he said,
"Behold, a cloud as small as a man's hand is
coming up from the sea." And he said, "Go
up, say to Ahab, 'Prepare *your chariot* and go
down, so that the rain does not stop you.'"
45 Now it happened that in a little while the
sky grew dark with clouds and wind, and
there was a heavy rain. And Ahab rode and
went to Jezreel. 46 But the hand of Yahweh
was on Elijah, and he girded up his loins and
outran Ahab unto *where* you enter Jezreel.

Psalm 69:29–36

29 But I am afflicted and in pain;
May Your salvation, O God,
set me *securely* on high.
30 I will praise the name of God with song
And magnify Him with thanksgiving.
31 And this will please Yahweh
better than an ox
Or a young bull with horns and hoofs.
32 The humble see *it and* are glad;
You who seek God, let
your heart revive.
33 For Yahweh hears the needy
And does not despise His
who are prisoners.

34 Let heaven and earth praise Him,
The seas and everything
that moves in them.
35 For God will save Zion and
build the cities of Judah,
That they may dwell there
and possess it.
36 The seed of His slaves will inherit it,
And those who love His
name will dwell in it.

Proverbs 17:27–28

27 He who holds back his words
has knowledge,
And he who has a cool spirit is
a man of discernment.
28 Even an ignorant fool, when he
keeps silent, is considered wise;
When he closes his lips, he is
considered understanding.

John 13:21–38

21 When Jesus had said these things, He
became troubled in spirit, and bore witness
and said, "Truly, truly, I say to you, that one
of you will betray Me." 22 The disciples *began*
looking at one another, perplexed about
whom He *spoke. 23 There was reclining
on Jesus' bosom one of His disciples, whom
Jesus loved. 24 So Simon Peter *gestured to
him to inquire, "Who is the one of whom
He is speaking?" 25 He, leaning back thus
on Jesus' bosom, *said to Him, "Lord, who
is it?" 26 Jesus *answered, "He is the one for
whom I shall dip the piece of bread and give
it to him." So when He had dipped the piece
of bread, He *took and *gave it to Judas,
the son of Simon Iscariot. 27 And after the
piece of bread, Satan then entered into
him. Therefore Jesus *said to him, "What
you do, do quickly." 28 Now no one of those
reclining *at the table* knew for what purpose
He had said this to him. 29 For some were
thinking, because Judas had the money box,
that Jesus was saying to him, "Buy the things
we have need of for the feast"; or else, that
he should give something to the poor. 30 So
after receiving the piece of bread, he went
out immediately. And it was night.

31 Therefore when he had gone out, Jesus
*said, "Now is the Son of Man glorified, and
God is glorified in Him; 32 if God is glorified
in Him, God will also glorify Him in Himself,
and will glorify Him immediately. 33 Little
children, I am with you a little while longer.
You will seek Me; and as I said to the Jews,
now I also say to you, 'Where I am going,
you cannot come.' 34 A new commandment I

give to you, that you love one another, even
as I have loved you, that you also love one
another. 35 By this all will know that you
are My disciples, if you have love for one
another."
36 Simon Peter *said to Him, "Lord, where
are You going?" Jesus answered, "Where I
go, you cannot follow Me now; but you will
follow later." 37 Peter *said to Him, "Lord,
why can I not follow You right now? I will lay
down my life for You." 38 Jesus *answered,
"Will you lay down your life for Me? Truly,
truly, I say to you, a rooster will not crow
until you deny Me three times.

JUNE 5

1 Kings 19:1–20:43

19 Now Ahab told Jezebel all that Elijah
had done, and how he had killed all
the prophets with the sword. 2 Then Jezebel
sent a messenger to Elijah, saying, "So
may the gods do to me and even more, if
I do not make your life as the life of one of
them by about this time tomorrow." 3 And
he was afraid and arose and ran for his life
and came to Beersheba, which belongs to
Judah, and left his young man there. 4 But
he himself went a day's journey into the
wilderness, and came and sat down under
a broom tree; and he asked for himself that
he might die, and said, "It is enough; now,
O Yahweh, take my life, for I am not better
than my fathers." 5 Then he lay down and
slept under a broom tree; and behold, there
was an angel touching him, and he said
to him, "Arise, eat." 6 Then he looked and
behold, there was at his head a bread cake
baked on hot stones, and a jar of water. So
he ate and drank and lay down again. 7 And
the angel of Yahweh came again a second
time and touched him and said, "Arise, eat,
because the journey is too great for you."
8 So he arose and ate and drank, and went
in the strength of that food forty days and
forty nights to Horeb, the mountain of God.
9 Then he came there to a cave and lodged
there; and behold, the word of Yahweh *came*
to him, and He said to him, "What are you
doing here, Elijah?" 10 And he said, "I have
been very zealous for Yahweh, the God of
hosts; for the sons of Israel have forsaken
Your covenant, pulled down Your altars and
killed Your prophets with the sword. And I
alone am left; and they seek my life, to take
it away."
11 So He said, "Go forth and stand on the
mountain before Yahweh." And behold,
Yahweh was passing by! And a great and
strong wind was tearing up the mountains
and breaking in pieces the rocks before
Yahweh; *but* Yahweh *was* not in the wind.
And after the wind an earthquake, *but*
Yahweh *was* not in the earthquake. 12 Then
after the earthquake a fire, *but* Yahweh *was*
not in the fire; and after the fire a sound of
a thin gentle whisper. 13 Now it happened
that when Elijah heard *it*, he wrapped his
face in his mantle and went out and stood
in the entrance of the cave. And behold, a
voice *came* to him and said, "What are you
doing here, Elijah?" 14 Then he said, "I have
been very zealous for Yahweh, the God of
hosts; for the sons of Israel have forsaken
Your covenant, pulled down Your altars and
killed Your prophets with the sword. And I
alone am left; and they seek my life, to take
it away."
15 And Yahweh said to him, "Go, return
on your way to the wilderness of Damascus,
and you will arrive and anoint Hazael king
over Aram; 16 and Jehu the son of Nimshi
you shall anoint king over Israel; and Elisha
the son of Shaphat of Abel-meholah you
shall anoint as prophet in your place. 17 And
it will be that the one who escapes from the
sword of Hazael, Jehu shall put to death, and
the one who escapes from the sword of Jehu,
Elisha shall put to death. 18 Yet I will leave
7,000 in Israel, all the knees that have not
bowed to Baal and every mouth that has not
kissed him."
19 So he went from there and found Elisha
the son of Shaphat, while he was plowing
with twelve pairs *of oxen* before him, and
he with the twelfth. And Elijah passed over
to him and threw his mantle on him. 20 So
he forsook the oxen and ran after Elijah and
said, "Please let me kiss my father and my
mother, then I will follow you." And he said
to him, "Go back again, for what have I done
to you?" 21 So he returned from following
him, and took the pair of oxen and sacrificed
them and boiled their flesh with the imple-
ments of the oxen, and gave *it* to the people

and they ate. Then he arose and followed
Elijah and ministered to him.

20 Now Ben-hadad king of Aram gath-
ered all his military force, and there
were thirty-two kings with him, and horses
and chariots. And he went up and besieged
Samaria and fought against it. 2 Then he sent
messengers to the city to Ahab king of Israel
and said to him, "Thus says Ben-hadad,
3 'Your silver and your gold are mine; your
most beautiful wives and children are also
mine.'" 4 Then the king of Israel answered
and said, "It is according to your word, my
lord, O king; I am yours, and all that I have."
5 Then the messengers returned and said,
"Thus says Ben-hadad, 'Surely, I sent to
you saying, "You shall give me your silver
and your gold and your wives and your
children," 6 but about this time tomorrow I
will send my servants to you, and they will
search your house and the houses of your
servants; and whatever is desirable in your
eyes, they will put in their hand and carry
away.'"

7 Then the king of Israel called all the
elders of the land and said, "Please know
and see how this man is looking for trou-
ble; for he sent to me for my wives and my
children and my silver and my gold, and I
withheld nothing from him." 8 And all the
elders and all the people said to him, "Do not
listen or consent." 9 So he said to the mes-
sengers of Ben-hadad, "Say to my lord the
king, 'All that you sent for to your servant at
the first I will do, but this thing I cannot do.'"
And the messengers departed and brought
him word again. 10 Then Ben-hadad sent to
him and said, "May the gods do so to me
and more also, if the dust of Samaria will
be sufficient for a handful for all the people
who follow me." 11 Then the king of Israel
answered and said, "Speak *to him*, 'Let not
him who girds on *his armor* boast like him
who takes *it* off.'" 12 Now it happened that
when *Ben-hadad* heard this message, as he
was drinking with the kings in the booths,
he said to his servants, "Station *yourselves*."
So they stationed *themselves* against the
city.

13 Now behold, a prophet approached
Ahab king of Israel and said, "Thus says
Yahweh, 'Have you seen all this great mul-
titude? Behold, I will deliver them into your
hand today, and you shall know that I am
Yahweh.'" 14 And Ahab said, "By whom?" So
he said, "Thus says Yahweh, 'By the young
men of the rulers of the provinces.'" Then he
said, "Who shall begin the battle?" And he
said, "You." 15 Then he mustered the young
men of the rulers of the provinces, and there
were 232; and after them he mustered all
the people, *even* all the sons of Israel, 7,000.

16 And they went out at noon, while
Ben-hadad was drinking himself drunk in
the booths with the thirty-two kings who
helped him. 17 And the young men of the
rulers of the provinces went out first; and
Ben-hadad sent out and they told him,
saying, "Men have come out from Samaria."
18 Then he said, "If they have come out for
peace, take them alive; or if they have come
out for war, take them alive."

19 So these went out from the city, the
young men of the rulers of the provinces,
and the military force which followed them.
20 And they each struck his man; and the
Arameans fled and Israel pursued them,
and Ben-hadad king of Aram escaped on
a horse with horsemen. 21 And the king of
Israel went out and struck down the horses
and chariots, and struck the Arameans with
a great slaughter.

22 Then the prophet came near to the king
of Israel and said to him, "Go, strengthen
yourself and know and see what you have
to do; for at the turn of the year the king of
Aram will come up against you."

23 Now the servants of the king of Aram
said to him, "Their gods are gods of the
mountains, therefore they were stronger
than we; but rather let us fight against them
in the plain, *and* surely we will be stronger
than they. 24 Do this thing: remove the kings,
each from his place, and put captains in their
place, 25 and you shall number a military
force like the military force that you have
lost, horse for horse, and chariot for chariot.
Then we will fight against them in the plain,
and surely we will be stronger than they."
And he listened to their voice and did so.

26 Now it happened at the turn of the year,
that Ben-hadad mustered the Arameans and
went up to Aphek to fight against Israel.
27 Now the sons of Israel were mustered
and were provided for and went to meet
them; and the sons of Israel camped before
them like two little flocks of goats, but the
Arameans filled the land. 28 Then a man
of God came near and spoke to the king of

Israel and said, "Thus says Yahweh, 'Because
the Arameans have said, "Yahweh is a god
of *the* mountains, but He is not a god of *the*
valleys," therefore I will give all this great
multitude into your hand, and you shall
know that I am Yahweh.'" 29 So they camped
one opposite the other seven days. Now it
happened that on the seventh day the battle
was joined, and the sons of Israel struck
down *of* the Arameans 100,000 foot soldiers
in one day. 30 But the rest fled to Aphek into
the city, and the wall fell on 27,000 men who
were left. And Ben-hadad fled and came into
the city into an inner chamber.

31 Then his servants said to him, "Behold
now, we have heard that the kings of the
house of Israel are kings of lovingkindness,
please let us put sackcloth on our loins and
ropes on our heads, and go out to the king
of Israel; perhaps he will preserve your life."
32 So they girded sackcloth on their loins
and *put* ropes on their heads, and came to
the king of Israel and said, "Your servant
Ben-hadad says, 'Please let me live.'" And
he said, "Is he still alive? He is my brother."
33 Now the men interpreted this as an omen,
and hastily catching his word said, "Your
brother Ben-hadad." Then he said, "Go,
bring him." Then Ben-hadad came out to
him, and he took him up into the chariot.
34 And *Ben-hadad* said to him, "The cities
which my father took from your father I
will return, and you shall make streets for
yourself in Damascus, as my father made in
Samaria." *Ahab said,* "And I will let you go
with this covenant." So he cut a covenant
with him and let him go.

35 Now a certain man of the sons of the
prophets said to another by the word of
Yahweh, "Please strike me." But the man
refused to strike him. 36 Then he said to
him, "Because you have not listened to
the voice of Yahweh, behold, as soon as
you walk away from me, a lion will strike
you down." And as soon as he had walked
away from him, a lion found him and struck
him down. 37 Then he found another man
and said, "Please strike me." And the man
struck him, wounding him. 38 So the prophet
walked away and stood by, for the king,
by the way, and disguised himself with a
bandage over his eyes. 39 Now it happened
that as the king was passing by, he cried out
to the king and said, "Your servant went out
into the midst of the battle; and behold, a
man turned aside and brought a man to me
and said, 'Guard this man; if for any reason
he is missing, then your life shall be for his
life, or else you shall pay a talent of silver.'
40 Now it happened that while your servant
was busy here and there, he was gone." And
the king of Israel said to him, "So shall your
judgment be; you yourself have decided
it." 41 Then he hastily took the bandage
away from his eyes, and the king of Israel
recognized him, that he was of the prophets.
42 And he said to him, "Thus says Yahweh,
'Because you have let go out of *your* hand
the man whom I had devoted to destruction,
therefore your life shall go for his life, and
your people for his people.'" 43 So the king of
Israel went to his house sullen and enraged,
and came to Samaria.

Psalm 70:1–5

1 O God, *hasten* to deliver me;
O Yahweh, hasten to my help!
2 Let those be ashamed and humiliated
Who seek my life;
Let those be turned back
and dishonored
Who delight in evil *against* me.
3 Let those turn back because
of their shame
Who say, "Aha, aha!"

4 Let those be joyful and glad in You
All who seek You
And let them say continually,
"Let God be magnified,"
Those who love Your salvation.
5 But I am afflicted and needy;
Hasten to me, O God!
You are my help and my protector;
O Yahweh, do not delay.

Proverbs 18:1–2

18 He who separates himself
seeks *his own* desire,
He breaks out *in dispute* against
all sound wisdom.
2 A fool does not delight in discernment,
But only in revealing his own heart.

John 14:1–31

14 "Do not let your heart be troubled;
believe in God, believe also in Me. 2 In
My Father's house are many dwelling places;
if it were not so, I would have told you; for
I go to prepare a place for you. 3 And if I go

and prepare a place for you, I will come again and receive you to Myself, that where I am, *there* you may be also. 4 And you know the way where I am going." 5 Thomas *said to Him, "Lord, we do not know where You are going. How do we know the way?" 6 Jesus *said to him, "I am the way, and the truth, and the life. No one comes to the Father but through Me.

7 "If you have come to know Me, you will know My Father also; from now on you know Him, and have seen Him."

8 Philip *said to Him, "Lord, show us the Father, and it is enough for us." 9 Jesus *said to him, "Have I been with you all so long and have you not come to know Me, Philip? He who has seen Me has seen the Father; how *can* you say, 'Show us the Father'? 10 Do you not believe that I am in the Father, and the Father is in Me? The words that I say to you I do not speak from Myself, but the Father abiding in Me does His works. 11 Believe Me that I am in the Father and the Father is in Me; otherwise believe because of the works themselves. 12 Truly, truly, I say to you, he who believes in Me, the works that I do, he will do also; and greater *works* than these he will do because I go to the Father. 13 Whatever you ask in My name, this will I do, so that the Father may be glorified in the Son. 14 If you ask Me anything in My name, I will do *it*.

15 "If you love Me, you will keep My commandments.

16 "And I will ask the Father, and He will give you another Advocate, that He may be with you forever; 17 the Spirit of truth, whom the world cannot receive, because it does not see Him or know Him. You know Him because He abides with you and will be in you.

18 "I will not leave you as orphans; I will come to you. 19 After a little while the world will no longer see Me, but you *will* see Me; because I live, you will live also. 20 On that day you will know that I am in My Father, and you in Me, and I in you. 21 He who has My commandments and keeps them is the one who loves Me; and he who loves Me will be loved by My Father, and I will love him and will disclose Myself to him." 22 Judas (not Iscariot) *said to Him, "Lord, what then has happened that You are going to disclose Yourself to us and not to the world?" 23 Jesus answered and said to him, "If anyone loves Me, he will keep My word; and My Father will love him, and We will come to him and make Our dwelling with him. 24 He who does not love Me does not keep My words; and the word which you hear is not Mine, but the Father's who sent Me.

25 "These things I have spoken to you while abiding with you. 26 But the Advocate, the Holy Spirit, whom the Father will send in My name, He will teach you all things, and bring to your remembrance all that I said to you. 27 Peace I leave with you; My peace I give to you; not as the world gives do I give to you. Do not let your heart be troubled, nor let it be fearful. 28 You heard that I said to you, 'I go away, and I will come to you.' If you loved Me, you would have rejoiced because I go to the Father, for the Father is greater than I. 29 And now I have told you before it happens, so that when it happens, you may believe. 30 I will not speak much more with you, for the ruler of the world is coming, and he has nothing in Me; 31 but so that the world may know that I love the Father, I do exactly as the Father commanded Me. Get up, let us go from here.

JUNE 6

1 Kings 21:1–22:53

21 Now it happened after these things that Naboth the Jezreelite had a vineyard which *was* in Jezreel beside the palace of Ahab king of Samaria. 2 And Ahab spoke to Naboth, saying, "Give me your vineyard, that I may have it for a vegetable garden because it is close beside my house, and I will give you a better vineyard than it in its place; if it is good in your sight, I will give you the price of it in money." 3 But Naboth said to Ahab, "Yahweh forbid me that I should give you the inheritance of my fathers." 4 So Ahab came into his house sullen and enraged because of the word which Naboth the Jezreelite had spoken to him; for he said, "I will not give you the inheritance of my fathers." And he lay down on his bed and turned away his face and ate no food.

5 But Jezebel his wife came to him and said to him, "How is it that your spirit is so sullen that you are not eating food?" 6 So

he said to her, "Because I spoke to Naboth
the Jezreelite and said to him, 'Give me your
vineyard for money; or else, if it pleases you,
I will give you a vineyard in its place.' But
he said, 'I will not give you my vineyard.'"
7 And Jezebel his wife said to him, "Do you
now exercise kingship over Israel? Arise, eat
bread, and let your heart be merry; I will give
you the vineyard of Naboth the Jezreelite."
8 So she wrote letters in Ahab's name and
sealed them with his seal, and sent letters to
the elders and to the nobles who were living
with Naboth in his city. 9 And she wrote in
the letters, saying, "Call for a fast and seat
Naboth at the head of the people; 10 and
seat two vile men before him, and let them
testify against him, saying, 'You cursed God
and the king.' Then take him out and stone
him so that he will die."

11 So the men of his city, the elders and
the nobles who lived in his city, did as
Jezebel had sent *word* to them, just as it
was written in the letters which she had sent
them. 12 They called for a fast and seated
Naboth at the head of the people. 13 Then
the two vile men came in and sat before
him; and the vile men testified against him,
against Naboth, before the people, saying,
"Naboth cursed God and the king." So they
took him outside the city and stoned him
with stones and he died. 14 Then they sent
word to Jezebel, saying, "Naboth has been
stoned and is dead."

15 Now it happened that when Jezebel
heard that Naboth had been stoned and
was dead, Jezebel said to Ahab, "Arise, take
possession of the vineyard of Naboth the
Jezreelite, which he refused to give you
for money; for Naboth is not alive, but
dead." 16 Now it happened that when Ahab
heard that Naboth was dead, Ahab arose
to go down to the vineyard of Naboth the
Jezreelite, to take possession of it.

17 Then the word of Yahweh came to
Elijah the Tishbite, saying, 18 "Arise, go
down to meet Ahab king of Israel, who is
in Samaria; behold, he is in the vineyard
of Naboth where he has gone down to take
possession of it. 19 And you shall speak to
him, saying, 'Thus says Yahweh, "Have you
murdered and also taken possession?"' And
you shall speak to him, saying, 'Thus says
Yahweh, "In the place where the dogs licked
up the blood of Naboth the dogs will lick up
your blood, even yours."'"

20 And Ahab said to Elijah, "Have you
found me, O my enemy?" And he answered,
"I have found *you*, because you have sold
yourself to do what is evil in the sight of
Yahweh. 21 Behold, I will bring evil upon you,
and will utterly sweep you away, and will
cut off from Ahab every male, both bond
and free in Israel; 22 and I will make your
house like the house of Jeroboam the son
of Nebat, and like the house of Baasha the
son of Ahijah, because of the provocation
with which you have provoked *Me* to anger,
and *because* you have made Israel sin. 23 Of
Jezebel also has Yahweh spoken, saying,
'The dogs will eat Jezebel in the district of
Jezreel.' 24 The one belonging to Ahab, who
dies in the city, the dogs will eat, and the
one who dies in the field the birds of the
sky will eat."

25 Surely there was no one who sold
himself to do what is evil in the sight of
Yahweh like Ahab, whom Jezebel his wife
incited. 26 And he acted very abominably
in following idols, according to all that the
Amorites had done, whom Yahweh dispos-
sessed before the sons of Israel.

27 Now it happened when Ahab heard
these words, that he tore his clothes and
put on sackcloth and fasted, and he lay in
sackcloth and went about despondently.
28 Then the word of Yahweh came to Elijah
the Tishbite, saying, 29 "Do you see how
Ahab has humbled himself before Me?
Because he has humbled himself before
Me, I will not bring the evil in his days, *but*
I will bring the evil upon his house in his
son's days."

22 So they lived for three years without
war between Aram and Israel. 2 Now it
happened in the third year, that Jehoshaphat
the king of Judah came down to the king of
Israel. 3 Then the king of Israel said to his
servants, "Do you know that Ramoth-gilead
belongs to us, but we are *sitting* still so as
not to take it out of the hand of the king of
Aram?" 4 So he said to Jehoshaphat, "Will
you go with me to battle at Ramoth-gilead?"
And Jehoshaphat said to the king of Israel,
"I am as you are, my people as your people,
my horses as your horses."
5 Moreover, Jehoshaphat said to the king
of Israel, "Please inquire first for the word of
Yahweh." 6 Then the king of Israel gathered
the prophets together, about four hundred

men, and said to them, "Shall I go against
Ramoth-gilead to battle or shall I refrain?"
And they said, "Go up, for the Lord will give *it*
into the hand of the king." 7 But Jehoshaphat
said, "Is there not yet a prophet of Yahweh
here that we may inquire of him?" 8 And the
king of Israel said to Jehoshaphat, "There
is yet one man by whom we may inquire of
Yahweh, but I hate him, because he does not
prophesy good concerning me, but evil. *He
is* Micaiah son of Imlah." But Jehoshaphat
said, "Let not the king say so." 9 Then the
king of Israel called an officer and said,
"Hasten *to bring* Micaiah son of Imlah."
10 Now the king of Israel and Jehoshaphat
king of Judah were sitting each on his
throne, clothed in *their royal* garments, at
the threshing floor at the entrance of the
gate of Samaria; and all the prophets were
prophesying before them. 11 And Zedekiah
the son of Chenaanah made horns of iron
for himself and said, "Thus says Yahweh,
'With these you will gore the Arameans until
they are consumed.'" 12 All the prophets
were also prophesying thus, saying, "Go up
to Ramoth-gilead and succeed, and Yahweh
will give *it* into the hand of the king."

13 Now the messenger who went to sum-
mon Micaiah spoke to him saying, "Behold
now, the words of the prophets, *as if* from
one mouth, are good towards the king.
Please let your word be like the word of
one of them, and speak *that which is* good."
14 But Micaiah said, "As Yahweh lives, what
Yahweh says to me, that I shall speak."

15 Then he came to the king, and the
king said to him, "Micaiah, shall we go to
Ramoth-gilead to battle, or shall we refrain?"
And he said to him, "Go up and succeed,
and Yahweh will give *it* into the hand of the
king." 16 Then the king said to him, "How
many times must I make you swear that you
will speak to me nothing but the truth in the
name of Yahweh?" 17 So he said,

"I saw all Israel
Scattered on the mountains,
Like sheep which have no shepherd.
And Yahweh said,
'These have no master.
Let each of them return to
his house in peace.'"

18 Then the king of Israel said to
Jehoshaphat, "Did I not say to you that he
would not prophesy good concerning me,
but evil?"

19 Then Micaiah said, "Therefore, hear the
word of Yahweh. I saw Yahweh sitting on His
throne, and all the host of heaven standing
by Him on His right and on His left. 20 And
Yahweh said, 'Who will entice Ahab so that
he will go up and fall at Ramoth-gilead?'
And one said this while another said that.
21 Then a spirit came forward and stood
before Yahweh and said, 'I will entice him.'
22 And Yahweh said to him, 'How?' And he
said, 'I will go out and be a lying spirit in the
mouth of all his prophets.' Then He said,
'You shall entice *him* and also prevail. Go
out and do so.' 23 So now, behold, Yahweh
has put a lying spirit in the mouth of all
these your prophets; but Yahweh has spoken
calamity against you."

24 Then Zedekiah the son of Chenaanah
came near and struck Micaiah on the cheek
and said, "How did the Spirit of Yahweh pass
from me to speak to you?" 25 And Micaiah
said, "Behold, you will see on that day when
you enter an inner room to hide." 26 Then
the king of Israel said, "Take Micaiah and
return him to Amon the commander of the
city and to Joash the king's son; 27 and say,
'Thus says the king, "Put this *man* in prison
and feed him sparingly with bread and water
until I come *back* safely."'" 28 And Micaiah
said, "If you indeed return safely, Yahweh
has not spoken by me." And he said, "Listen,
all you people."

29 So the king of Israel and Jehoshaphat
king of Judah went up *against* Ramoth-
gilead. 30 And the king of Israel said to
Jehoshaphat, "I will disguise myself and
go into the battle, but you put on your
garments." So the king of Israel disguised
himself and went into the battle. 31 Now the
king of Aram had commanded the thirty-
two commanders of his chariots, saying,
"Do not fight with small or great, but with
the king of Israel alone." 32 Now it happened
that when the commanders of the chariots
saw Jehoshaphat, they said, "Surely it is the
king of Israel," and they turned aside to fight
against him, and Jehoshaphat cried out. 33 So
it happened that when the commanders of
the chariots saw that it was not the king of
Israel, they turned back from pursuing him.

34 Now a certain man drew his bow at
random and struck the king of Israel in a
joint of the armor. So he said to the driver
of his chariot, "Turn around and take me
out of the fight, for I am severely wounded."

35 Now the battle raged that day, and the
king was propped up in his chariot in front
of the Arameans, and died at evening, and
the blood from the wound ran into the
bottom of the chariot. 36 Then a shout of
lament passed throughout the camp close
to sunset, saying, "Every man to his city and
every man to his land."

37 So the king died and was brought
to Samaria, and they buried the king in
Samaria. 38 And they washed the chariot
by the pool of Samaria, and the dogs licked
up his blood (now the harlots bathed
themselves *there*), according to the word
of Yahweh which He spoke. 39 Now the rest
of the acts of Ahab and all that he did and
the ivory house which he built and all the
cities which he built, are they not written in
the Book of the Chronicles of the Kings of
Israel? 40 So Ahab slept with his fathers, and
Ahaziah his son became king in his place.

41 Now Jehoshaphat the son of Asa became
king over Judah in the fourth year of Ahab
king of Israel. 42 Jehoshaphat was thirty-five
years old when he became king, and he
reigned twenty-five years in Jerusalem. And
his mother's name was Azubah the daughter
of Shilhi. 43 And he walked in all the way of
Asa his father; he did not turn away from it,
doing what is right in the sight of Yahweh.
However, the high places were not taken
away; the people still sacrificed and burnt
incense on the high places. 44 Jehoshaphat
also made peace with the king of Israel.

45 Now the rest of the acts of Jehoshaphat,
and his might which he showed and how he
warred, are they not written in the Book of
the Chronicles of the Kings of Judah? 46 And
the remnant of the male cult prostitutes
who remained in the days of his father Asa,
he purged from the land.

47 Now there was no king in Edom; a dep-
uty was king. 48 Jehoshaphat made ships of
Tarshish to go to Ophir for gold, but they did
not go for the ships were broken at Ezion-
geber. 49 Then Ahaziah the son of Ahab said
to Jehoshaphat, "Let my servants go with
your servants in the ships." But Jehoshaphat
was not willing. 50 And Jehoshaphat slept
with his fathers and was buried with his
fathers in the city of his father David, and
Jehoram his son became king in his place.

51 Ahaziah the son of Ahab became king
over Israel in Samaria in the seventeenth
year of Jehoshaphat king of Judah, and he
reigned two years over Israel. 52 And he did
what was evil in the sight of Yahweh and
walked in the way of his father and in the way
of his mother and in the way of Jeroboam
the son of Nebat, who caused Israel to sin.
53 So he served Baal and worshiped him and
provoked Yahweh, the God of Israel, to anger,
according to all that his father had done.

Psalm 71:1–8

1 In You, O Yahweh, I have taken refuge;
Let me never be ashamed.
2 In Your righteousness deliver
me and protect me;
Incline Your ear to me and save me.
3 Be to me a rock of habitation to
which I may continually come;
You have given the command
to save me,
For You are my rock and my fortress.
4 Protect me, O my God, out of
the hand of the wicked,
Out of the grasp of the unrighteous
and ruthless man,
5 For You are my hope;
O Lord Yahweh, *You are* my
trust from my youth.
6 By You I have been sustained
from *my* birth;
You are He who took me from
my mother's womb;
My praise is continually of You.

7 I have become a marvel to many,
For You are my strong refuge.
8 My mouth is filled with Your praise
And with Your beauty all day long.

Proverbs 18:3–5

3 When a wicked man comes,
despising also comes,
And with disgrace *comes* reproach.
4 The words of a man's mouth
are deep waters;
The fountain of wisdom
is a flowing brook.
5 To show partiality to the
wicked is not good,
Nor to thrust aside the
righteous in judgment.

John 15:1–27

15 "I am the true vine, and My Father is
the vine-grower. 2 Every branch in Me
that does not bear fruit, He takes away; and

every *branch* that bears fruit, He cleans it so that it may bear more fruit. 3 You are already clean because of the word which I have spoken to you. 4 Abide in Me, and I in you. As the branch cannot bear fruit from itself unless it abides in the vine, so neither *can* you unless you abide in Me. 5 I am the vine, you are the branches; he who abides in Me and I in him, he bears much fruit, for apart from Me you can do nothing. 6 If anyone does not abide in Me, he is thrown away as a branch and dries up; and they gather them, and cast them into the fire and they are burned. 7 If you abide in Me, and My words abide in you, ask whatever you wish, and it will be done for you. 8 My Father is glorified by this, that you bear much fruit, and *so* prove to be My disciples. 9 Just as the Father has loved Me, I have also loved you; abide in My love. 10 If you keep My commandments, you will abide in My love; just as I have kept My Father's commandments and abide in His love. 11 These things I have spoken to you so that My joy may be in you, and *that* your joy may be complete.

12 "This is My commandment, that you love one another, just as I have loved you. 13 Greater love has no one than this, that one lay down his life for his friends. 14 You are My friends if you do what I command you. 15 No longer do I call you slaves, for the slave does not know what his master is doing; but I have called you friends, for all things that I have heard from My Father I have made known to you. 16 You did not choose Me but I chose you, and appointed you that you would go and bear fruit, and *that* your fruit would abide, so that whatever you ask of the Father in My name He may give to you. 17 This I command you, that you love one another.

18 "If the world hates you, know that it has hated Me before *it hated* you. 19 If you were of the world, the world would love its own; but because you are not of the world, but I chose you out of the world, because of this the world hates you. 20 Remember the word that I said to you, 'A slave is not greater than his master.' If they persecuted Me, they will also persecute you; if they kept My word, they will keep yours also. 21 But all these things they will do to you for My name's sake, because they do not know the One who sent Me. 22 If I had not come and spoken to them, they would not have sin, but now they have no excuse for their sin. 23 He who hates Me hates My Father also. 24 If I had not done among them the works which no one else did, they would not have sin; but now they have both seen and hated Me and My Father as well. 25 But *this happened* to fulfill the word that is written in their Law, 'THEY HATED ME WITHOUT CAUSE.'

26 "When the Advocate comes, whom I will send to you from the Father, the Spirit of truth who proceeds from the Father, He will bear witness about Me, 27 and you *will* bear witness also, because you have been with Me from the beginning.

JUNE 7

2 Kings 1:1–2:25

1 Now Moab revolted against Israel after the death of Ahab. 2 And Ahaziah fell through the lattice in his upper chamber, which *was* in Samaria, and became ill. So he sent messengers and said to them, "Go, inquire of Baal-zebub, the god of Ekron, whether I will live from this sickness." 3 But the angel of Yahweh said to Elijah the Tishbite, "Arise, go up to meet the messengers of the king of Samaria and say to them, 'Is it because there is no God in Israel *that* you are going to inquire of Baal-zebub, the god of Ekron?' 4 Now therefore thus says Yahweh, 'You shall not come down from the bed where you have gone up, but you shall surely die.'" Then Elijah departed.

5 So the messengers returned to him, and he said to them, "Why have you returned?" 6 And they said to him, "A man came up to meet us and said to us, 'Go, return to the king who sent you and say to him, "Thus says Yahweh, 'Is it because there is no God in Israel *that* you are sending to inquire of Baal-zebub, the god of Ekron? Therefore you shall not come down from the bed where you have gone up, but shall surely die.'"'" 7 And he said to them, "What kind of man was he who came up to meet you and spoke these words to you?" 8 And they said to him, "*He was* a hairy man with a leather girdle

girded about his loins." And he said, "It is Elijah the Tishbite."

9 Then *the king* sent to him a commander of fifty with his fifty. And he went up to him, and behold, he was sitting on the top of the hill. And he said to him, "O man of God, the king says, 'Come down.'" 10 And Elijah answered and spoke to the commander of fifty, "If I am a man of God, let fire come down from heaven and consume you and your fifty." Then fire came down from heaven and consumed him and his fifty.

11 So he again sent to him another commander of fifty with his fifty. And he answered and spoke to him, "O man of God, thus says the king, 'Come down quickly.'" 12 And Elijah answered and spoke to them, "If I am a man of God, let fire come down from heaven and consume you and your fifty." Then the fire of God came down from heaven and consumed him and his fifty.

13 So he again sent the commander of a third fifty with his fifty. Then the third commander of fifty went up and came and bowed down on his knees before Elijah, and he begged him and said to him, "O man of God, please let my life and the lives of these fifty servants of yours be precious in your sight. 14 Behold, fire came down from heaven and consumed the first two commanders of fifty with their fifties; but now let my life be precious in your sight." 15 Then the angel of Yahweh spoke to Elijah, "Go down with him; do not be afraid of him." So he arose and went down with him to the king. 16 Then he spoke to him, "Thus says Yahweh, 'Because you have sent messengers to inquire of Baal-zebub, the god of Ekron—is it because there is no God in Israel to inquire of His word?—therefore you shall not come down from the bed where you have gone up, but shall surely die.'"

17 So Ahaziah died according to the word of Yahweh which Elijah had spoken. And because he had no son, Jehoram became king in his place in the second year of Jehoram the son of Jehoshaphat, king of Judah. 18 Now the rest of the acts of Ahaziah which he did, are they not written in the Book of the Chronicles of the Kings of Israel?

2 Now it happened when Yahweh was about to take up Elijah by a whirlwind to heaven, that Elijah went with Elisha from Gilgal. 2 And Elijah said to Elisha, "Stay here please, for Yahweh has sent me as far as Bethel." But Elisha said, "As Yahweh lives and as your soul lives, I will not forsake you." So they went down to Bethel. 3 Then the sons of the prophets who *were at* Bethel came out to Elisha and said to him, "Do you know that Yahweh will take away your master from over you today?" And he said, "Yes, I know; be silent."

4 And Elijah said to him, "Elisha, please stay here, for Yahweh has sent me to Jericho." But he said, "As Yahweh lives and as your soul lives, I will not forsake you." So they came to Jericho. 5 Then the sons of the prophets who *were* at Jericho approached Elisha and said to him, "Do you know that Yahweh will take away your master from over you today?" And he answered, "Yes, I know; be silent." 6 Then Elijah said to him, "Please stay here, for Yahweh has sent me to the Jordan." And he said, "As Yahweh lives and as your soul lives, I will not forsake you." So the two of them went on.

7 Now fifty men of the sons of the prophets went and stood opposite *them* at a distance, but the two of them stood by the Jordan. 8 And Elijah took his mantle and folded it together and struck the waters, and they were divided here and there, so that the two of them crossed over on dry ground.

9 Now it happened when they crossed over, that Elijah said to Elisha, "Ask what I shall do for you before I am taken from you." And Elisha said, "Please, let a double portion of your spirit be upon me." 10 And he said, "You have asked a hard thing. *Nevertheless,* if you see me when I am taken from you, it shall be so for you; but if not, it shall not be *so.*" 11 As they were going along and talking, behold, *there appeared* a chariot of fire and horses of fire, and it separated the two of them. And Elijah went up by a whirlwind to heaven. 12 And Elisha was seeing *this* and he was crying out, "My father, my father, the chariots of Israel and its horsemen!" And he saw Elijah no more. Then he took hold of his own clothes and tore them in two pieces. 13 He also took up the mantle of Elijah that fell from him and returned and stood by the bank of the Jordan. 14 And he took the mantle of Elijah that fell from him and struck the waters and said, "Where is Yahweh, the God of Elijah?" Indeed, he himself also struck the waters, and they were divided here and there! And Elisha crossed over.

15 Then the sons of the prophets who
were at Jericho opposite *him* saw him and
said, "The spirit of Elijah rests on Elisha."
And they came to meet him and bowed
themselves to the ground before him.
16 Then they said to him, "Behold now,
there are with your servants fifty excellent
men, please let them go and search for your
master, lest the Spirit of Yahweh has taken
him up and cast him on some mountain or
into some valley." And he said, "You shall
not send." 17 But when they urged him until
he was ashamed, he said, "Send." They sent
therefore fifty men; and they searched
three days but did not find him. 18 So they
returned to him while he was staying at
Jericho; and he said to them, "Did I not say
to you, 'Do not go'?"

19 Then the men of the city said to Elisha,
"Behold now, the habitat of this city is
pleasant, as my lord sees; but the water is
bad and the land is unfruitful." 20 And he
said, "Bring me a new jar, and put salt in it."
So they brought *it* to him. 21 And he went
out to the spring of water and threw salt
in it and said, "Thus says Yahweh, 'I have
purified these waters; there shall not be
from there death or barrenness any longer.'"
22 So the waters have been purified to this
day, according to the word of Elisha which
he spoke.

23 Then he went up from there to Bethel;
and as he was going up by the way, young
boys came out from the city and mocked
him and said to him, "Go up, you baldhead;
go up, you baldhead!" 24 Then he looked
behind him and saw them. And he cursed
them in the name of Yahweh. Then two
female bears came out of the woods and tore
up forty-two lads of their number. 25 And he
went from there to Mount Carmel, and from
there he returned to Samaria.

Psalm 71:9–16

9 Do not cast me off in the
time of old age;
Do not forsake me when
my strength fails.
10 For my enemies have
spoken against me;
And those who watch my life
have counseled together,
11 Saying, "God has forsaken him;
Pursue and seize him, for there
is no one to deliver."
12 O God, do not be far from me;
O my God, hasten to my help!
13 Let those who accuse my soul be
ashamed *and* consumed;
Let them be wrapped up with
reproach and dishonor,
who seek *to do* me evil.
14 But as for me, I will wait continually,
And will praise You yet more and more.
15 My mouth shall recount
Your righteousness
And Your salvation all day long;
For I do not know the sum *of them*.
16 I will come with the mighty
deeds of Lord Yahweh;
I will bring to remembrance Your
righteousness, Yours alone.

Proverbs 18:6–8

6 A fool's lips come with strife,
And his mouth calls for beatings.
7 A fool's mouth is his ruin,
And his lips are the snare of his soul.
8 The words of a whisperer are
like dainty morsels,
And they go down into the
innermost parts of the stomach.

John 16:1–33

16 "These things I have spoken to you so
that you may be kept from stumbling.
2 They will put you out of the synagogue, but
an hour is coming for everyone who kills you
to think that he is offering service to God.
3 These things they will do because they did
not know the Father or Me. 4 But these things
I have spoken to you, so that when their hour
comes, you may remember that I told you of
them. These things I did not say to you at the
beginning, because I was with you.

5 "But now I am going to Him who sent
Me; and none of you asks Me, 'Where are
You going?' 6 But because I have said these
things to you, sorrow has filled your heart.
7 But I tell you the truth, it is to your advan-
tage that I go away; for if I do not go away, the
Advocate will not come to you; but if I go,
I will send Him to you. 8 And He, when He
comes, will convict the world concerning sin
and righteousness and judgment; 9 concern-
ing sin, because they do not believe in Me;
10 and concerning righteousness, because I
go to the Father and you no longer see Me;
11 and concerning judgment, because the
ruler of this world has been judged.

12 "I still have many more things to say to
you, but you cannot bear *them* now. 13 But
when He, the Spirit of truth, comes, He will
guide you into all the truth; for He will not
speak from Himself, but whatever He hears,
He will speak; and He will disclose to you
what is to come. 14 He will glorify Me, for He
will take of Mine and will disclose *it* to you.
15 All things that the Father has are Mine;
therefore I said that He takes of Mine and
will disclose *it* to you.

16 "A little while, and you will no longer
see Me; and again a little while, and you will
see Me." 17 *Some* of His disciples then said
to one another, "What is this He is telling
us, 'A little while, and you will not see Me;
and again a little while, and you will see
Me'; and, 'because I go to the Father'?" 18 So
they were saying, "What is this that He says,
'A little while'? We do not know what He is
talking about." 19 Jesus knew that they were
wishing to question Him, and He said to
them, "Are you deliberating together about
this, that I said, 'A little while, and you will
not see Me, and again a little while, and
you will see Me'? 20 Truly, truly, I say to
you, that you will cry and lament, but the
world will rejoice; you will be sorrowful,
but your sorrow will be turned into joy.
21 Whenever a woman is in labor she has
sorrow, because her hour has come; but
when she gives birth to the child, she no
longer remembers the suffering because
of the joy that a child has been born into
the world. 22 Therefore you too have sorrow
now; but I will see you again, and your heart
will rejoice, and no one *will* take your joy
away from you.

23 "And on that day you will not question
Me about anything. Truly, truly, I say to
you, if you ask the Father for anything in
My name, He will give it to you. 24 Until now
you have asked for nothing in My name; ask
and you will receive, so that your joy may be
made complete.

25 "These things I have spoken to you in
figures of speech; an hour is coming when
I will no longer speak to you in figures of
speech, but will tell you openly of the Father.
26 On that day you will ask in My name, and
I do not say to you that I will request of the
Father on your behalf; 27 for the Father
Himself loves you, because you have loved
Me and have believed that I came forth from
the Father. 28 I came forth from the Father
and have come into the world; I am leaving
the world again and going to the Father."

29 His disciples *said, "Behold, now You
are speaking openly and are not using a
figure of speech. 30 Now we know that
You know all things, and have no need for
anyone to question You; by this we believe
that You came from God." 31 Jesus answered
them, "Do you now believe? 32 Behold, an
hour is coming, and has *already* come,
for you to be scattered, each to his own
home, and to leave Me alone; and *yet* I am
not alone, because the Father is with Me.
33 These things I have spoken to you, so that
in Me you may have peace. In the world you
have tribulation, but take courage; I have
overcome the world."

JUNE 8

2 Kings 3:1–4:44

3 Now Jehoram the son of Ahab became
king over Israel at Samaria in the eigh-
teenth year of Jehoshaphat king of Judah,
and reigned twelve years. 2 And he did what
was evil in the sight of Yahweh, though not
like his father and his mother; and he took
away the *sacred* pillar of Baal which his
father had made. 3 Nevertheless, he clung
to the sins of Jeroboam the son of Nebat,
which he made Israel sin; he did not turn
away from them.

4 Now Mesha king of Moab was a sheep
breeder and used to pay the king of Israel
100,000 lambs and the wool of 100,000
rams. 5 But it happened that when Ahab
died, the king of Moab rebelled against the
king of Israel. 6 And King Jehoram went
out of Samaria at that time and mustered
all Israel. 7 Then he went and sent *word* to
Jehoshaphat the king of Judah, saying, "The
king of Moab has rebelled against me. Will
you go with me to fight against Moab?" And
he said, "I will go up; I am as you are, my
people as your people, my horses as your
horses." 8 And he said, "Which way shall we
go up?" And he answered, "The way of the
wilderness of Edom."

9 So the king of Israel went with the king
of Judah and the king of Edom; and they

went around on a seven days' journey, and there was no water for the camp or for the cattle that followed them. 10 Then the king of Israel said, "Alas! For Yahweh has called these three kings to give them into the hand of Moab." 11 But Jehoshaphat said, "Is there not a prophet of Yahweh here, that we may inquire of Yahweh by him?" And one of the king of Israel's servants answered and said, "Elisha the son of Shaphat is here, who used to pour water on the hands of Elijah." 12 And Jehoshaphat said, "The word of Yahweh is with him." So the king of Israel and Jehoshaphat and the king of Edom went down to him.

13 Now Elisha said to the king of Israel, "What do I have to do with you? Go to the prophets of your father and to the prophets of your mother." And the king of Israel said to him, "No, for Yahweh has called these three kings *together* to give them into the hand of Moab." 14 And Elisha said, "As Yahweh of hosts lives, before whom I stand, were it not that I regard the presence of Jehoshaphat the king of Judah, I would not look at you nor see you. 15 So now bring me a musician." And it came about, when the musician played, that the hand of Yahweh came upon him. 16 And he said, "Thus says Yahweh, 'Make this valley full of trenches.' 17 For thus says Yahweh, 'You shall not see wind nor shall you see rain; yet that valley shall be filled with water, so that you shall drink, both you and your livestock and your cattle. 18 And this is but a light thing in the sight of Yahweh; He will also give the Moabites into your hand. 19 Then you shall strike every fortified city and every choice city, and fell every good tree and stop all springs of water, and mar every good piece of land with stones.'" 20 Then it happened in the morning about the time of offering the sacrifice, that behold, water came by the way of Edom, and the country was filled with water.

21 Now all the Moabites heard that the kings had come up to fight against them. And they summoned all who were able to put on armor and older, and they stood on the border. 22 Then they rose early in the morning, and the sun shone on the water, and the Moabites saw the water opposite *them* as red as blood. 23 Then they said, "This is blood; the kings have surely fought together, and they have struck down one another. So now, Moab, to the spoil!" 24 So they came to the camp of Israel. And the Israelites arose and struck the Moabites. So they fled before them; and they went forward into the land, striking down the Moabites. 25 Thus they tore down the cities; and each one threw a stone on every piece of good land and filled it. And they stopped all the springs of water and felled all the good trees, until in Kir-hareseth they let its stones remain; however, the slingers went about *it* and struck it. 26 Then the king of Moab saw that the battle was too strong for him, so he took with him 700 men who drew swords, to break through to the king of Edom; but they could not. 27 So he took his oldest son, who was to reign in his place, and offered him as a burnt offering on the wall. And there came great wrath against Israel, and they set out from him and returned to their own land.

4 Now a certain woman of the wives of the sons of the prophets cried out to Elisha, "Your servant my husband is dead, and you know that your servant feared Yahweh; and the creditor has come to take my two children to be his slaves." 2 And Elisha said to her, "What shall I do for you? Tell me, what do you have in the house?" And she said, "Your servant-woman has nothing in the house except a jar of oil." 3 Then he said, "Go, ask for vessels for yourself, from *those* outside, from all your neighbors, *even* empty vessels; do not get a few. 4 And you shall go in and shut the door behind you and your sons, and pour out into all these vessels, and you shall set aside what is full." 5 So she went from him and shut the door behind her and her sons; they were bringing *the vessels* to her and she poured. 6 Now it happened that when the vessels were full, she said to her son, "Bring me another vessel." And he said to her, "There is not one vessel more." And the oil stopped. 7 Then she came and told the man of God. And he said, "Go, sell the oil and pay your debt, and you *and* your sons can live on the rest."

8 Now there came a day when Elisha passed over to Shunem, where there was a prominent woman, and she prevailed upon him to eat food. Now it happened, as often as he passed by, that he turned in there to eat food. 9 And she said to her husband, "Behold now, I know that this is a holy man of God passing by us continually. 10 Please, let us

make a little walled upper chamber and let
us set a bed for him there, and a table and a
chair and a lampstand; and it will be, when
he comes to us, *that* he can turn in there."
11 Now it happened that one day he came
there and turned in to the upper chamber,
and there he lay down. 12 Then he said
to Gehazi his young man, "Call this Shu-
nammite." So he called her, and she stood
before him. 13 And he said to him, "Say now
to her, 'Behold, you have been careful for
us with all this care; what can I do for you?
Would you be spoken for to the king or to
the commander of the army?'" And she
answered, "I live among my own people."
14 So he said, "What then is to be done for
her?" And Gehazi answered, "Truly she has
no son, and her husband is old." 15 And he
said, "Call her." So he called her, and she
stood in the doorway. 16 Then he said, "At
this season next year you will embrace a
son." And she said, "No, my lord, O man of
God, do not lie to your servant-woman."
17 Then the woman conceived and bore
a son at that season the next year, as Elisha
had said to her.
18 Then the child was grown. And the day
came that he went out to his father to the
reapers. 19 And he said to his father, "My
head, my head." And he said to his young
man, "Carry him to his mother." 20 Then he
carried him and brought him to his mother,
and he sat on her knees until noon, and *then*
died. 21 Then she went up and laid him on
the bed of the man of God and shut *the
door* behind him and went out. 22 And she
called to her husband and said, "Please send
me one of the young men and one of the
donkeys, that I may run to the man of God
and return." 23 And he said, "Why will you
go to him today? It is neither new moon nor
sabbath." And she said, "*It is* well." 24 Then
she saddled a donkey and said to her young
man, "Drive and go; do not hold back *the
pace of* the ride for me unless I tell you."
25 So she went and came to the man of God
to Mount Carmel.
Now it happened that when the man of
God saw her at a distance, he said to Gehazi
his young man, "Behold, there is the Shu-
nammite. 26 Please run now to meet her and
say to her, 'Is it well with you? Is it well with
your husband? Is it well with the child?'"
And she answered, "It is well." 27 Then she
came to the man of God to the hill and took
hold of his feet. And Gehazi came near to
push her away; but the man of God said, "Let
her alone, for her soul is bitter within her;
and Yahweh has hidden it from me and has
not told me." 28 Then she said, "Did I ask for
a son from my lord? Did I not say, 'Do not
deceive me'?"
29 Then he said to Gehazi, "Gird up your
loins and take my staff in your hand, and go;
if you meet anyone, do not greet him, and
if anyone greets you, do not answer him;
and lay my staff on the boy's face." 30 But the
mother of the boy said, "As Yahweh lives and
as your soul lives, I will not forsake you."
And he arose and followed her. 31 Now
Gehazi passed on before them and laid the
staff on the boy's face, but there was no
sound or response. So he returned to meet
him and told him, saying, "The boy has not
awakened."
32 Then Elisha came into the house, and
behold, the boy was dead and laid on his
bed. 33 So he entered and shut the door
behind them both and prayed to Yahweh.
34 And he went up and lay on the child and
put his mouth on his mouth and his eyes on
his eyes and his hands on his hands, and he
stretched himself on him; and the flesh of
the child became warm. 35 Then he returned
and walked in the house once back and
forth, and went up and stretched himself on
him; and the boy sneezed seven times and
the boy opened his eyes. 36 Then he called
Gehazi and said, "Call this Shunammite."
So he called her. Then she came in to him,
and he said, "Take up your son." 37 Then
she came in and fell at his feet and bowed
herself to the ground, and she took up her
son and went out.
38 Now Elisha returned to Gilgal, and
there was a famine in the land. As the sons
of the prophets were sitting before him, he
said to his young man, "Put on the large pot
and boil stew for the sons of the prophets."
39 Then one went out into the field to gather
herbs and found a wild vine and gathered
from it wild gourds filling his cloak and
came and sliced them into the pot of stew,
for they did not know *what they were.* 40 So
they poured *it* out for the men to eat. And
it happened that as they were eating of the
stew, they cried out and said, "O man of
God, there is death in the pot." And they
were unable to eat. 41 But he said, "Now
bring flour." He threw it into the pot and

said, "Pour *it* out for the people that they may eat." Then there was no harm in the pot.
42 Now a man came from Baal-shalishah, and brought the man of God bread of the first fruits, twenty loaves of barley and fresh ears of grain in his sack. And he said, "Give *them* to the people that they may eat."
43 And his attendant said, "What, will I give this before one hundred men?" But he said, "Give *them* to the people that they may eat, for thus says Yahweh, 'They shall eat and have *some* left over.'" 44 So he gave *it* before them, and they ate and had *some* left over, according to the word of Yahweh.

Psalm 71:17–24

17 O God, You have taught
me from my youth,
And I still declare Your
wondrous deeds.
18 And even when *I am* old and gray,
O God, do not forsake me,
Until I declare Your strength
to *this* generation,
Your might to all who are to come.
19 For Your righteousness, O God,
reaches to the heavens,
You who have done great things;
O God, who is like You?
20 You, who have shown me
many troubles and evils,
Will revive me again,
And will bring me up again from
the depths of the earth.
21 May You increase my greatness
And turn *to* comfort me.

22 I will also praise You with a harp,
Even Your truth, O my God;
To You I will sing praises with
the lyre,
O Holy One of Israel.
23 My lips will sing for joy when
I sing praises to You;
And my soul, which You
have redeemed.
24 My tongue also will utter Your
righteousness all day long;
For they are ashamed, for they are
humiliated who seek *to do* me evil.

Proverbs 18:9

9 He also who is slack in his work
Is brother to him who destroys.

John 17:1–26

17 Jesus spoke these things; and lifting up
His eyes to heaven, He said, "Father,
the hour has come; glorify Your Son, that the
Son may glorify You, 2 even as You gave Him
authority over all flesh, that to all whom You
have given Him, He may give eternal life.
3 And this is eternal life, that they may know
You, the only true God, and Jesus Christ
whom You have sent. 4 I glorified You on the
earth, having finished the work which You
have given Me to do. 5 Now, Father, glorify
Me together with Yourself, with the glory
which I had with You before the world was.
6 "I have manifested Your name to the
men whom You gave Me out of the world;
they were Yours and You gave them to Me,
and they have kept Your word. 7 Now they
have come to know that everything You have
given Me is from You; 8 for the words which
You gave Me I have given to them; and they
received *them* and truly understood that
I came forth from You, and they believed
that You sent Me. 9 I ask on their behalf; I do
not ask on behalf of the world but of those
whom You have given Me; for they are Yours;
10 and all things that are Mine are Yours, and
Yours are Mine; and I have been glorified in
them. 11 And I am no longer in the world;
and *yet* they themselves are in the world,
and I come to You. Holy Father, keep them
in Your name, *the name* which You have
given Me, that they may be one even as We
are. 12 While I was with them, I was keeping
them in Your name which You have given
Me; and I guarded them and not one of
them perished but the son of perdition, so
that the Scripture would be fulfilled. 13 But
now I come to You; and these things I speak
in the world so that they may have My joy
made full in themselves. 14 I have given them
Your word; and the world has hated them,
because they are not of the world, even as
I am not of the world. 15 I do not ask You
to take them out of the world, but to keep
them from the evil one. 16 They are not of
the world, even as I am not of the world.
17 Sanctify them by the truth; Your word is
truth. 18 As You sent Me into the world, I also
sent them into the world. 19 For their sake I
sanctify Myself, that they themselves also
may be sanctified in truth.
20 "I do not ask on behalf of these alone,
but for those also who believe in Me through
their word; 21 that they may all be one; even

as You, Father, *are* in Me and I in You, that
they also may be in Us, so that the world
may believe that You sent Me. 22 The glory
which You have given Me I have given to
them, that they may be one, just as We are
one; 23 I in them and You in Me, that they
may be perfected in unity, so that the world
may know that You sent Me, and loved them,
even as You have loved Me. 24 Father, I desire
that they also, whom You have given Me, be
with Me where I am, so that they may see
My glory which You have given Me, for You
loved Me before the foundation of the world.

25 "O righteous Father, although the world
has not known You, yet I have known You;
and these have known that You sent Me;
26 and I have made Your name known to
them, and will make it known, so that the
love with which You loved Me may be in
them, and I in them."

JUNE 9

2 Kings 5:1–6:33

5 Now Naaman, commander of the army
of the king of Aram, was a great man
with his master, and highly respected,
because by him Yahweh had given salva-
tion to Aram. The man was also a mighty
man of valor, *but he was* a leper. 2 Now the
Arameans had gone out in marauding bands
and had taken captive a little girl from the
land of Israel; and she waited on Naaman's
wife. 3 And she said to her mistress, "I wish
that my master were before the prophet who
is in Samaria! Then he would cure him of his
leprosy." 4 Then Naaman went in and told
his master, saying, "Thus and thus spoke the
girl who is from the land of Israel." 5 Then
the king of Aram said, "Go now, and I will
send a letter to the king of Israel." So he
went and took in his hand ten talents of
silver and six thousand *shekels* of gold and
ten changes of clothes.

6 And he brought the letter to the king of
Israel, saying,

> "So now as this letter comes to you,
> behold, I have sent Naaman my
> servant to you, that you may cure him
> of his leprosy."

7 Now it happened that when the king of
Israel read the letter, he tore his clothes
and said, "Am I God, to put to death and to
make alive, that this man is sending *word* to
me to cure a man of his leprosy? But know
now, and see how he is seeking a quarrel
against me."

8 Now it happened when Elisha the man
of God heard that the king of Israel had
torn his clothes, that he sent *word* to the
king, saying, "Why have you torn your
clothes? Now let him come to me, and
he shall know that there is a prophet in
Israel." 9 So Naaman came with his horses
and his chariots and stood at the doorway
of the house of Elisha. 10 And Elisha sent a
messenger to him, saying, "Go and wash in
the Jordan seven times, and your flesh will
be restored to you and *you will* be clean."
11 But Naaman was furious and went away
and said, "Behold, I said *to myself*, 'He will
surely come out to me and stand and call
on the name of Yahweh his God, and wave
his hand over the place and cure the leper.'
12 Are not Abanah and Pharpar, the rivers
of Damascus, better than all the waters
of Israel? Could I not wash in them and
be clean?" So he turned and went away
in wrath. 13 Then his servants approached
and spoke to him and said, "My father, had
the prophet spoken with you *to do some*
great thing, would you not have done *it*?
How much more *then*, when he says to
you, 'Wash, and be clean'?" 14 So he went
down and dipped *himself* seven times in the
Jordan, according to the word of the man of
God; and his flesh was restored like the flesh
of a young boy and he was clean.

15 Then he returned to the man of God
with all his camp, and came and stood
before him, and said, "Behold now, I know
that there is no God in all the earth, but in
Israel; so now please take a blessing from
your servant." 16 But he said, "As Yahweh
lives, before whom I stand, I will take
nothing." And he urged him to take *it*, but he
refused. 17 So Naaman said, "If not, please
let your servant at least be given two mules'
load of earth; for your servant will no longer
offer burnt offering nor will he sacrifice to
other gods, but to Yahweh. 18 In this matter
may Yahweh pardon your servant: when
my master goes into the house of Rimmon
to worship there, and he leans on my hand
and I bow myself in the house of Rimmon,

when I bow myself in the house of Rimmon,
Yahweh pardon your servant in this matter."
19 And he said to him, "Go in peace." So he
went from him some distance.

20 Then Gehazi, the young man of Elisha
the man of God, said *to himself*, "Behold,
my master has spared this Naaman the
Aramean, by not receiving from his hands
what he brought. As Yahweh lives, I will run
after him and take something from him."
21 So Gehazi pursued Naaman. And Naaman
saw one running after him, so he came
down from the chariot to meet him and
said, "Is *all* at peace?" 22 And he said, "*All*
is at peace. My master has sent me, saying,
'Behold, just now two young men of the sons
of the prophets have come to me from the
hill country of Ephraim. Please give them a
talent of silver and two changes of clothes.'"
23 Then Naaman said, "Be pleased to take
two talents." And he urged him and bound
two talents of silver in two bags with two
changes of clothes and gave *them* to two of
his young men; and they carried *them* before
him. 24 So he came to the hill, and he took
them from their hand and deposited them
in the house. Then he sent the men away,
and they departed. 25 But he came in and
stood before his master. And Elisha said to
him, "Where have you been, Gehazi?" And
he said, "Your servant went nowhere."

26 Then he said to him, "Did not my heart
go *with you*, when the man turned from his
chariot to meet you? Is it a time to receive
money and to receive clothes and olive
groves and vineyards and sheep and oxen
and male and female slaves? 27 Thus the
leprosy of Naaman shall cling to you and
to your seed forever." So he went out from
his presence a leper *as white* as snow.

6 And the sons of the prophets said to
Elisha, "Behold now, the place before
you where we are living is too limited for
us. 2 Please let us go to the Jordan and each
of us take from there a beam, and let us
make a place there for ourselves where we
may live." So he said, "Go." 3 Then one said,
"Please be willing to go with your servants."
And he answered, "I shall go." 4 So he went
with them; and they came to the Jordan and
cut down trees. 5 Now it happened that as
one was felling a beam, the axe head fell into
the water; and he cried out and said, "Alas,
my master! For it was borrowed." 6 Then the
man of God said, "Where did it fall?" And
when he showed him the place, he cut off a
stick and threw *it* in there and made the iron
float. 7 And he said, "Take it up for yourself."
So he sent forth his hand and took it.

8 Now the king of Aram was warring
against Israel; and he counseled with his
servants saying, "In such and such a place
shall be my camp." 9 And the man of God
sent *word* to the king of Israel saying,
"Beware that you do not pass this place,
for the Arameans are coming down there."
10 And the king of Israel sent to the place
about which the man of God had told him;
thus he warned him, so that he guarded
himself there, more than once or twice.

11 Then the heart of the king of Aram was
enraged over this thing; and he called his
servants and said to them, "Will you not tell
me which of us is for the king of Israel?"
12 And one of his servants said, "No, my
lord, O king; but Elisha, the prophet who
is in Israel, tells the king of Israel the words
that you speak in your bedroom." 13 So he
said, "Go and see where he is, that I may
send and take him." And it was told to him,
saying, "Behold, he is in Dothan." 14 So he
sent horses and chariots and a heavy mili-
tary force there, and they came by night and
surrounded the city.

15 Then the attendant of the man of God
arose early and went out, and behold, a
military force with horses and chariots
was all around the city. And his young man
said to him, "Alas, my master! What shall
we do?" 16 So he said, "Do not fear, for those
who are with us are more than those who
are with them." 17 Then Elisha prayed and
said, "O Yahweh, I pray, open his eyes that
he may see." And Yahweh opened the eyes
of the young man and he saw; and behold,
the mountain was full of horses and chariots
of fire all around Elisha. 18 And they came
down to him, and Elisha prayed to Yahweh
and said, "Strike this people with blindness,
I pray." So He struck them with blindness
according to the word of Elisha. 19 Then
Elisha said to them, "This is not the way,
and this is not the city; walk after me and
I will walk you over to the man whom you
seek." And he walked them over to Samaria.

20 Now it happened that when they had
come into Samaria, Elisha said, "O Yahweh,
open the eyes of these *men*, that they may
see." So Yahweh opened their eyes and they

saw; and behold, they were in the midst of
Samaria. 21 Then the king of Israel when he
saw them, said to Elisha, "My father, shall
I strike *them* down? Shall I strike *them*
down?" 22 And he said, "You shall not strike
them down. Would you strike down those
you have taken captive with your sword
and with your bow? Set bread and water
before them, that they may eat and drink
and walk *back* to their master." 23 So he
prepared a great feast for them; and when
they had eaten and drunk, he sent them
away, and they went to their master. And
the marauding bands of Arameans did not
come again into the land of Israel.

24 Now it happened afterwards, that
Ben-hadad king of Aram gathered all his
military camp and went up and besieged
Samaria. 25 Now there was a great famine
in Samaria. And behold, they besieged it,
until a donkey's head was sold for eighty
shekels of silver, and a fourth of a kab of
dove's dung for five *shekels* of silver. 26 As
the king of Israel was passing by on the wall,
a woman cried out to him, saying, "Save,
my lord, O king!" 27 He said, "If Yahweh
does not save you, from where shall I save
you? From the threshing floor, or from the
wine press?" 28 And the king said to her,
"What is the matter with you?" And she
said, "This woman said to me, 'Give your
son that we may eat him today, and we will
eat my son tomorrow.' 29 So we boiled my
son and ate him; and I said to her on the
next day, 'Give your son, that we may eat
him'; but she has hidden her son." 30 Now
it happened that when the king heard the
words of the woman, he tore his clothes—
now he was passing by on the wall—and the
people looked, and behold, he had sackcloth
beneath on his body. 31 Then he said, "May
God do so to me and more also, if the head
of Elisha the son of Shaphat remains on him
today."

32 Now Elisha was sitting in his house,
and the elders were sitting with him. And
the king sent a man from his presence; but
before the messenger came to him, he said
to the elders, "Do you see how this son of
a murderer has sent to take away my head?
Look, when the messenger comes, shut the
door and hold the door shut against him. Is
not the sound of his master's feet behind
him?" 33 While he was still speaking with
them, behold, the messenger came down to
him and he said, "Behold, this evil is from
Yahweh; why should I wait for Yahweh any
longer?"

Psalm 72:1–7

1 O God, give the king Your judgments,
And Your righteousness
to the king's son.
2 May he render judgment to Your
people with righteousness
And Your afflicted with justice.
3 Let the mountains lift up
peace to the people,
And the hills, in righteousness.
4 May he give justice to the
afflicted of the people,
Save the children of the needy,
And crush the oppressor.

5 Let them fear You while
the sun *endures*,
And as long as the moon, *from*
generation to *all* generations.
6 May he come down like rain
upon the mown grass,
Like showers that water the earth.
7 May the righteous flourish in his days,
And abundance of peace until
the moon is no more.

Proverbs 18:10–11

10 The name of Yahweh is a strong tower;
The righteous runs into it and
is set securely on high.
11 A rich man's wealth is his strong city,
And like a high wall in his
own delusion.

John 18:1–18

18 When Jesus had spoken these words,
He went forth with His disciples to
the other side of the Kidron Valley, where
there was a garden, into which He entered
with His disciples. 2 Now Judas also, who
was betraying Him, knew the place, for
Jesus had often gathered there with His
disciples. 3 Judas then, having received the
Roman cohort and officers from the chief
priests and the Pharisees, *came there
with lanterns and torches and weapons.
4 So Jesus, knowing all the things that were
coming upon Him, went forth and *said
to them, "Whom do you seek?" 5 They
answered Him, "Jesus the Nazarene." He
*said to them, "I am *He*." And Judas also,

who was betraying Him, was standing with them. 6 So when He said to them, "I am *He*," they drew back and fell to the ground. 7 Therefore He again asked them, "Whom do you seek?" And they said, "Jesus the Nazarene." 8 Jesus answered, "I told you that I am *He*; so if you seek Me, let these go their way," 9 in order that the word which He spoke would be fulfilled, "Of those whom You have given Me, I lost not one." 10 Simon Peter then, having a sword, drew it and struck the high priest's slave, and cut off his right ear; and the slave's name was Malchus. 11 So Jesus said to Peter, "Put the sword into the sheath; the cup which the Father has given Me, shall I not drink it?"

12 So the *Roman* cohort and the commander and the officers of the Jews, arrested Jesus and bound Him, 13 and led Him to Annas first; for he was father-in-law of Caiaphas, who was high priest that year. 14 Now Caiaphas was the one who had advised the Jews that it was better for one man to die on behalf of the people.

15 And Simon Peter was following Jesus, and *so was* another disciple. Now that disciple was known to the high priest, and entered with Jesus into the court of the high priest, 16 but Peter was standing at the door outside. So the other disciple, who was known to the high priest, went out and spoke to the doorkeeper, and brought Peter in. 17 Then the servant-girl who kept the door *said to Peter, "Are you not also *one* of this man's disciples?" He *said, "I am not." 18 Now the slaves and the officers were standing *there*, having made a charcoal fire, for it was cold and they were warming themselves; and Peter was also with them, standing and warming himself.

JUNE 10

2 Kings 7:1–8:29

7 Then Elisha said, "Listen to the word of Yahweh; thus says Yahweh, 'About this time tomorrow a seah of fine flour will be *sold* for a shekel, and two seahs of barley for a shekel, in the gate of Samaria.'" 2 And the royal officer on whose hand the king was leaning answered the man of God and said, "Behold, if Yahweh should make windows in heaven, could this thing be?" Then he said, "Behold, you will see it with your own eyes, but you will not eat of it."

3 Now there were four leprous men at the entrance of the gate; and they said to one another, "Why do we sit here until we die? 4 If we say, 'We will enter the city,' then the famine is in the city and we will die there; and if we sit here, we die also. So now come, and let us go over to the camp of the Arameans. If they spare us, we will live; and if they put us to death, we will die." 5 So they arose at twilight to go to the camp of the Arameans. Then they came to the outskirts of the camp of the Arameans, but behold, there was no one there. 6 Now the Lord had caused the camp of the Arameans to hear a sound of chariots and a sound of horses, *even* the sound of a great military force, so that they said to one another, "Behold, the king of Israel has hired against us the kings of the Hittites and the kings of the Egyptians, to come upon us." 7 Therefore they arose and fled in the twilight, and forsook their tents and their horses and their donkeys, *even* the camp just as it was, and fled for their life. 8 So these lepers came to the outskirts of the camp and entered one tent and ate and drank. Then they carried from there silver and gold and clothes, and they went and hid *them*; and they returned and entered another tent and carried from there *also* and went and hid *them*.

9 Then they said to one another, "We are not doing right. This day is a day of good news, but we are keeping silent; if we wait until morning light, punishment will overtake us. So now, come, let us go and tell the king's household." 10 So they came and called to the gatekeepers of the city, and they told them, saying, "We came to the camp of the Arameans, and behold, there was no one there, nor the voice of man, only the horses tied and the donkeys tied, and the tents just as they were." 11 And the gatekeepers called and told *it* within the king's household. 12 Then the king arose in the night and said to his servants, "I will now tell you what the Arameans have done to us. They know that we are hungry; therefore they have gone from the camp to hide themselves in the field, saying, 'When they

come out of the city, we will capture them alive and get into the city.'" 13 And one of his servants answered and said, "Please, let some *men* take five of the remaining horses, which remain in the city. Behold, they *will be in any case* like all the multitude of Israel who remain in it; behold, they *will be in any case* like all the multitude of Israel who have already come to an end, so let us send and see." 14 They took therefore two chariots with horses, and the king sent after the camp of the Arameans, saying, "Go and see."

15 Then they went after them to the Jordan, and behold, all the way was full of clothes and equipment which the Arameans had thrown away in their haste. Then the messengers returned and told the king.

16 So the people went out and plundered the camp of the Arameans. Then a seah of fine flour *was sold* for a shekel and two seahs of barley for a shekel, according to the word of Yahweh. 17 Now the king appointed the royal officer on whose hand he leaned to have charge of the gate; but the people trampled on him at the gate, and he died just as the man of God had spoken, who spoke when the king came down to him. 18 So it happened just as the man of God had spoken to the king, saying, "Two seahs of barley for a shekel and a seah of fine flour for a shekel will be *sold* tomorrow about this time at the gate of Samaria." 19 And the royal officer had answered the man of God and said, "Now behold, if Yahweh should make windows in heaven, could such a thing be?" And he had said, "Behold, you will see it with your own eyes, but you will not eat of it." 20 And so it happened to him, for the people trampled on him at the gate and he died.

8 Now Elisha spoke to the woman whose son he had restored to life, saying, "Arise and go with your household, and sojourn wherever you can sojourn; for Yahweh has called for a famine, and it will even come on the land for seven years." 2 So the woman arose and did according to the word of the man of God, and she went with her household and sojourned in the land of the Philistines seven years. 3 Now it happened at the end of seven years, that the woman returned from the land of the Philistines; and she went out to cry out to the king for her house and for her field. 4 Now the king was speaking with Gehazi, the young man of the man of God, saying, "Please recount to me all the great things that Elisha has done." 5 Now it happened as he was recounting to the king how he had restored to life the one who was dead, that behold, the woman whose son he had restored to life was crying out to the king for her house and for her field. And Gehazi said, "My lord, O king, this is the woman, and this is her son, whom Elisha restored to life." 6 Then the king asked the woman, and she recounted *it* to him. So the king appointed for her a certain officer, saying, "Restore all that was hers and all the produce of the field from the day that she left the land even until now."

7 Then Elisha came to Damascus. Now Ben-hadad king of Aram was sick, and it was told to him, saying, "The man of God has come here." 8 And the king said to Hazael, "Take a present in your hand and go to meet the man of God, and inquire of Yahweh by him, saying, 'Will I be restored to life from this sickness?'" 9 So Hazael went to meet him and took a present in his hand, even every kind of good thing of Damascus, forty camels' loads; and he came and stood before him and said, "Your son Ben-hadad king of Aram has sent me to you, saying, 'Will I be restored to life from this sickness?'" 10 Then Elisha said to him, "Go, say to him, 'You will surely be restored to life,' but Yahweh has shown me that he will certainly die." 11 And he fixed his gaze steadily *on him* until he was ashamed, and the man of God wept. 12 Then Hazael said, "Why does my lord weep?" Then he said, "Because I know the evil that you will do to the sons of Israel: their fortifications you will set on fire, and their young men you will kill with the sword, and their infants you will dash in pieces, and their pregnant women you will rip up." 13 Then Hazael said, "But what is your servant, *who is but* a dog, that he should do this great thing?" And Elisha answered, "Yahweh has shown me that you will be king over Aram." 14 So he went from Elisha and came to his master. And he said to him, "What did Elisha say to you?" And he said, "He said to me that you would surely be restored to life." 15 Now it happened that on the following day, he took the cover and dipped it in water and spread it on his face; so he died. And Hazael became king in his place.

16 Now in the fifth year of Joram the son of Ahab king of Israel, Jehoshaphat being

then the king of Judah, Jehoram the son of
Jehoshaphat king of Judah became king.
17 He was thirty-two years old when he
became king, and he reigned eight years in
Jerusalem. 18 And he walked in the way of the
kings of Israel, just as the house of Ahab had
done, for the daughter of Ahab became his
wife; and he did what was evil in the sight of
Yahweh. 19 However, Yahweh was not willing
to make Judah a ruin, for the sake of David
His servant, since He had promised him to
give a lamp to him through his sons always.
20 In his days Edom revolted from under
the hand of Judah and made a king over
themselves. 21 Then Joram crossed over to
Zair, and all his chariots with him. And he
arose by night and struck the Edomites who
were surrounding him and the commanders
of the chariots; but *his* army fled to their
tents. 22 So Edom revolted against Judah to
this day. Then Libnah revolted at the same
time. 23 Now the rest of the acts of Joram
and all that he did, are they not written in
the Book of the Chronicles of the Kings of
Judah?
24 So Joram slept with his fathers and was
buried with his fathers in the city of David;
and Ahaziah his son became king in his
place.
25 In the twelfth year of Joram the son
of Ahab king of Israel, Ahaziah the son
of Jehoram king of Judah became king.
26 Ahaziah *was* twenty-two years old when
he became king, and he reigned one year
in Jerusalem. And his mother's name was
Athaliah the granddaughter of Omri king
of Israel. 27 He also walked in the way of the
house of Ahab and did what was evil in the
sight of Yahweh, like the house of Ahab *had
done*, because he was a son-in-law of the
house of Ahab.
28 Then he went with Joram the son of
Ahab to war with Hazael king of Aram at
Ramoth-gilead, and the Arameans struck
Joram. 29 So King Joram returned to be
healed in Jezreel of the wounds which the
Arameans had caused by striking him at
Ramah when he fought against Hazael king
of Aram. Then Ahaziah the son of Jehoram
king of Judah went down to see Joram the
son of Ahab in Jezreel because he was sick.

Psalm 72:8–16

8 May he also have dominion
from sea to sea
And from the River to the
ends of the earth.
9 Let the desert creatures
kneel before him,
And his enemies lick the dust.
10 Let the kings of Tarshish and of the
coastlands bring a present;
The kings of Sheba and
Seba offer tribute.
11 And let all kings bow down to him,
All nations serve him.

12 For he will deliver the needy
when he cries for help,
The afflicted also, and him
who has no helper.
13 He will have compassion on
the poor and needy,
And the lives of the needy he will save.
14 He will redeem their life from
oppression and violence,
And their blood will be
precious in his sight;
15 So may he live! And may they give
to him the gold of Sheba;
And let each pray for him continually;
Let each bless him all day long.

16 May there be abundance of grain in
the earth on top of the mountains;
May its fruit wave like *the
cedars of* Lebanon;
And may those from the city blossom
like vegetation of the earth.

Proverbs 18:12–13

12 Before destruction the heart
of man is haughty,
But humility *goes* before glory.
13 He who responds with a
word before he hears,
It is folly and shame to him.

John 18:19–40

19 The high priest then questioned
Jesus about His disciples, and about His
teaching. 20 Jesus answered him, "I have
spoken openly to the world; I always taught
in synagogues and in the temple, where
all the Jews come together; and I spoke
nothing in secret. 21 Why do you question
Me? Question those who have heard what
I spoke to them; behold, they know what
I said." 22 And when He had said this, one
of the officers standing nearby gave Jesus

a slap, saying, "Is that the way You answer the high priest?" 23 Jesus answered him, "If I have spoken wrongly, bear witness of the wrong; but if rightly, why do you strike Me?" 24 So Annas sent Him bound to Caiaphas the high priest.

25 Now Simon Peter was standing and warming himself. So they said to him, "You are not also *one* of His disciples, are you?" He denied *it*, and said, "I am not." 26 One of the slaves of the high priest, being a relative of the one whose ear Peter cut off, *said, "Did I not see you in the garden with Him?" 27 Peter then denied *it* again, and immediately a rooster crowed.

28 Then they *led Jesus from Caiaphas into the Praetorium, and it was early; and they themselves did not enter into the Praetorium so that they would not be defiled, but might eat the Passover. 29 Therefore Pilate went out to them and *said, "What accusation do you bring against this man?" 30 They answered and said to him, "If this man were not an evildoer, we would not have delivered Him to you." 31 So Pilate said to them, "Take Him yourselves, and judge Him according to your law." The Jews said to him, "It is not lawful for us to put anyone to death," 32 in order that the word of Jesus which He spoke would be fulfilled, signifying by what kind of death He was about to die.

33 Therefore Pilate entered again into the Praetorium, and summoned Jesus and said to Him, "Are You the King of the Jews?" 34 Jesus answered, "Are you saying this from yourself, or did others tell you about Me?" 35 Pilate answered, "Am I a Jew? Your own nation and the chief priests delivered You to me; what did You do?" 36 Jesus answered, "My kingdom is not of this world. If My kingdom were of this world, then My servants would be fighting so that I would not be delivered over to the Jews; but as it is, My kingdom is not from here." 37 Therefore Pilate said to Him, "So You are a king?" Jesus answered, "You yourself said I am a king. For this I have been born, and for this I have come into the world, to bear witness to the truth. Everyone who is of the truth hears My voice." 38 Pilate *said to Him, "What is truth?"

And when he had said this, he went out again to the Jews and *said to them, "I find no guilt in Him. 39 But you have a custom that I release someone for you at the Passover; do you wish then that I release for you the King of the Jews?" 40 So they cried out again, saying, "Not this man, but Barabbas." Now Barabbas was a robber.

He has his back to the world, his face toward heaven and a Book in his hand.

— JOHN BUNYAN

JUNE 11

2 Kings 9:1–10:36

9 Now Elisha the prophet called one of the sons of the prophets and said to him, "Gird up your loins, and take this flask of oil in your hand and go to Ramoth-gilead. 2 And you will come there and look there for Jehu the son of Jehoshaphat the son of Nimshi. And you will come in and bid him arise from among his brothers. And you will cause him to come in to an inner room. 3 Then you will *take the flask of oil and pour it* on his head and say, 'Thus says Yahweh, "I have anointed you king over Israel."' Then open the door and flee and do not wait."

4 So the young man—the young man of the prophet—went to Ramoth-gilead. 5 Then he came, and behold, the commanders of the military were sitting, and he said, "I have a word for you, O commander." And Jehu said, "For which *one* of us?" And he said, "For you, O commander." 6 And he arose and came into the house, and he poured the oil on his head and said to him, "Thus says Yahweh, the God of Israel, 'I have anointed you king over the people of Yahweh, *even* over Israel. 7 And you shall strike the house of Ahab your master, that I may avenge the blood of My slaves the prophets, and the

blood of all the slaves of Yahweh, at the
hand of Jezebel. 8 For the whole house of
Ahab shall perish, and I will cut off from
Ahab every male person both bond and
free in Israel. 9 And I will make the house of
Ahab like the house of Jeroboam the son of
Nebat, and like the house of Baasha the son
of Ahijah. 10 And the dogs shall eat Jezebel in
the property of Jezreel, and none shall bury
her.'" Then he opened the door and fled.
11 Now Jehu came out to the servants of
his master, and one said to him, "Is all well?
Why did this mad fellow come to you?" And
he said to them, "You know the man and his
talk." 12 And they said, "It is a lie, declare
it to us now." And he said, "Thus and thus
he said to me, 'Thus says Yahweh, "I have
anointed you king over Israel."'" 13 Then
they hurried and each man took his garment
and placed it under him on the bare steps,
and blew the trumpet, saying, "Jehu is king!"
14 So Jehu the son of Jehoshaphat the son
of Nimshi conspired against Joram. Now
Joram with all Israel was guarding Ramoth-
gilead against Hazael king of Aram, 15 but
King Joram had returned to be healed in
Jezreel of the wounds which the Arameans
had struck him with when he fought with
Hazael king of Aram. So Jehu said, "If this is
your mind, *then* let no one escape *or* leave
the city to go declare *it* in Jezreel." 16 Then
Jehu rode in a chariot and went to Jezreel,
for Joram was lying there. Ahaziah king of
Judah had come down to see Joram.
17 Now the watchman was standing on the
tower in Jezreel and he saw the company of
Jehu as he came, and said, "I see a company."
And Joram said, "Take a horseman and send
him to meet them and let him say, 'Is it
peace?'" 18 So a horseman went to meet him
and said, "Thus says the king, 'Is it peace?'"
And Jehu said, "What have you to do with
peace? Turn behind me." And the watchman
declared saying, "The messenger came to
them, but he did not return." 19 Then he
sent out a second horseman. And he came
to them and said, "*Thus says* the king, 'Is it
peace?'" And Jehu answered, "What have
you to do with peace? Turn behind me."
20 And the watchman declared saying, "He
came up to them, but he did not return; and
the driving is like the driving of Jehu the son
of Nimshi, for he drives in madness."
21 Then Joram said, "Get ready." And they
made his chariot ready. Joram king of Israel
and Ahaziah king of Judah went out, each in
his chariot, and they went out to meet Jehu
and found him in the property of Naboth
the Jezreelite. 22 Now it happened that when
Joram saw Jehu, he said, "Is it peace, Jehu?"
And he answered, "What peace, so long as
the harlotries of your mother Jezebel and
her sorceries are so many?" 23 So Joram
turned about and fled and said to Ahaziah,
"*There is* deception, O Ahaziah!" 24 And
Jehu drew his bow with his full strength
and struck Joram between his arms; and
the arrow went through his heart and he
crouched down in his chariot. 25 Then *Jehu*
said to Bidkar his officer, "Lift *him* up and
cast him into the property of the field of
Naboth the Jezreelite, for I remember when
you and I were riding together after Ahab
his father, that Yahweh lifted up this oracle
against him: 26 'Surely I have seen yesterday
the blood of Naboth and the blood of his
sons,' says Yahweh, 'and I will repay you in
this property,' says Yahweh. So now, lift *him*
up and cast him into the property, according
to the word of Yahweh."
27 And Ahaziah the king of Judah saw *this*
and fled by the way of the garden house.
And Jehu pursued him and said, "Strike him
down too, in the chariot." *So they struck
him down* at the ascent of Gur, which is at
Ibleam. But he fled to Megiddo and died
there. 28 Then his servants carried him in a
chariot to Jerusalem and buried him in his
grave with his fathers in the city of David.
29 Now in the eleventh year of Joram, the
son of Ahab, Ahaziah became king over
Judah.
30 Then Jehu came to Jezreel, and Jezebel
heard *of it* and she painted her eyes and
adorned her head and looked out the win-
dow. 31 As Jehu entered the gate, she said,
"Is it peace, Zimri, your master's killer?"
32 Then he lifted up his face to the window
and said, "Who is on my side? Who?" And
two or three officials looked down at him.
33 And he said, "Throw her down." So they
threw her down, and some of her blood was
sprinkled on the wall and on the horses, and
he trampled her under foot. 34 Then he came
in and ate and drank. And he said, "Take
care now of this cursed woman and bury
her, for she is a king's daughter." 35 They
went to bury her, but they found nothing
more of her than the skull and the feet and
the palms of her hands. 36 Therefore they

returned and declared *it* to him. And he said, "This is the word of Yahweh, which He spoke by His servant Elijah the Tishbite, saying, 'In the property of Jezreel the dogs shall eat the flesh of Jezebel; 37 and the corpse of Jezebel will be as dung on the face of the field in the property of Jezreel, so they cannot say, "This is Jezebel."'"

10 Now Ahab had seventy sons in Samaria. And Jehu wrote letters and sent *them* to Samaria, to the rulers of Jezreel, the elders, and to the guardians of *the children of* Ahab, saying, 2 "So now, when this letter comes to you, since your master's sons are with you, as well as the chariots and horses and a fortified city and the weapons, 3 look for the best and fittest of your master's sons, and set *him* on his father's throne, and fight for your master's house." 4 But they feared exceedingly greatly and said, "Behold, the two kings did not stand before him; how then can we stand?" 5 And the one who *was* over the household, and he who *was* over the city, the elders, and the guardians of *the children*, sent *word* to Jehu, saying, "We are your servants, all that you say to us we will do, we will not make any man king; do what is good in your sight." 6 Then he wrote a letter to them a second time saying, "If you are on my side, and you will listen to my voice, take the heads of the men, your master's sons, and come to me about this time tomorrow at Jezreel." Now the king's sons, seventy persons, *were* with the great men of the city, *who* were rearing them. 7 Now it happened that when the letter came to them, they took the king's sons and slaughtered *them*, seventy persons, and put their heads in baskets, and sent *them* to him at Jezreel. 8 Then the messenger came and told him, saying, "They have brought the heads of the king's sons." So he said, "Put them in two heaps at the entrance of the gate until morning." 9 Now it happened in the morning that he went out and stood and said to all the people, "You are righteous; behold, I conspired against my master and killed him, but who struck down all these? 10 Know then that nothing from the word of Yahweh, which Yahweh spoke concerning *the house of Ahab, shall fall* to the earth. Indeed, Yahweh has done what He spoke by the hand of His servant Elijah." 11 So Jehu struck down all who remained of the house of Ahab in Jezreel, and all his great men and his acquaintances and his priests, until there was no survivor remaining for him.

12 Then he arose and came out and went to Samaria. On the way, *while* he was at Beth-eked of the shepherds, 13 Jehu found the relatives of Ahaziah king of Judah and said, "Who are you?" And they said, "We are the relatives of Ahaziah; and we have come down to greet the sons of the king and the sons of the queen mother." 14 Then he said, "Take them alive." So they took them alive and slaughtered them at the pit of Beth-eked, forty-two men; and he left none of them.

15 Then he went from there and found Jehonadab the son of Rechab *coming* to meet him; and he blessed him and said to him, "Is your heart right, as my heart is with your heart?" And Jehonadab answered, "It is." *Jehu said*, "If it is, give *me* your hand." And he gave him his hand, and he took him up to him into the chariot. 16 Then he said, "Come with me and see my zeal for Yahweh." So he made him ride in his chariot. 17 And he came to Samaria and struck down all who were left to Ahab in Samaria, until he had destroyed him, according to the word of Yahweh which He spoke to Elijah.

18 Then Jehu gathered all the people and said to them, "Ahab served Baal a little; Jehu will serve him much. 19 So now, summon to me all the prophets of Baal, all his slaves and all his priests; let no one be missing, for I have a great sacrifice for Baal; whoever is missing shall not live." But Jehu did it in cunning, so that he might cause the slaves of Baal to perish. 20 And Jehu said, "Sanctify a solemn assembly for Baal." And they summoned *them*. 21 Then Jehu sent throughout Israel, and all the slaves of Baal came, so that there was not a man left who did not come. So they came into the house of Baal, and the house of Baal was filled from one end to the other. 22 Then he said to the one who *was* in charge of the wardrobe, "Bring out garments for all the slaves of Baal." So he brought out garments for them. 23 And Jehu came into the house of Baal with Jehonadab the son of Rechab; and he said to the slaves of Baal, "Search and see lest there be here with you *any* of the slaves of Yahweh, but only the slaves of Baal." 24 Then they came in to offer sacrifices and burnt offerings.

Now Jehu had placed for himself eighty
men outside, and he had said, "The one
who permits *any* of the men whom I cause
to come into your hands to escape, shall give
up his life in exchange."
25 Now it happened that as soon as he had
finished offering the burnt offering, Jehu
said to the guard and to the royal officers,
"Come in, strike them down; let none come
out." And they struck them down with the
edge of the sword; and the guard and the
royal officers threw *them* out and went to
the inner room of the house of Baal. 26 And
they brought out the *sacred* pillars of the
house of Baal and burned them. 27 They also
broke down the *sacred* pillar of Baal and
broke down the house of Baal and made it
a latrine to this day.
28 Thus Jehu destroyed Baal out of Israel.
29 However, *as for* the sins of Jeroboam the
son of Nebat, which he made Israel sin, from
these Jehu did not depart, *even* the golden
calves that *were* at Bethel and that *were* at
Dan. 30 And Yahweh said to Jehu, "Because
you have done well in doing what is right
in My eyes, *and* have done to the house of
Ahab according to all that *was* in My heart,
your sons of the fourth generation shall sit
on the throne of Israel." 31 But Jehu was not
careful to walk in the law of Yahweh, the
God of Israel, with all his heart; he did not
depart from the sins of Jeroboam, which he
made Israel sin.
32 In those days Yahweh began to cut off
portions from Israel; and Hazael struck them
throughout the territory of Israel: 33 from
the Jordan *to the east* toward the sunrise,
all the land of Gilead, the Gadites and the
Reubenites and the Manassites, from Aroer,
which is by the valley of the Arnon, even
Gilead and Bashan.
34 Now the rest of the acts of Jehu and all
that he did and all his might, are they not
written in the Book of the Chronicles of the
Kings of Israel? 35 And Jehu slept with his
fathers, and they buried him in Samaria.
And Jehoahaz his son became king in his
place. 36 Now the time which Jehu reigned
over Israel in Samaria *was* twenty-eight
years.

Psalm 72:17–20

17 May his name endure forever;
May his name increase as
long as the sun *shines*;
Let *all nations* be blessed in him;
Let all nations call him blessed.

18 Blessed be Yahweh God,
the God of Israel,
Who alone works wondrous deeds.
19 And blessed be His glorious
name forever;
And may the whole earth be
filled with His glory.
Amen, and Amen.

20 The prayers of David, the son
of Jesse, are completed.

Proverbs 18:14–15

14 The spirit of a man can
endure his sickness,
But *as for* a broken spirit,
who can bear it?
15 The heart of the understanding
acquires knowledge,
And the ear of the wise
seeks knowledge.

John 19:1–22

19 Pilate then took Jesus and flogged
Him. 2 And when the soldiers twisted
together a crown of thorns, they put it on
His head, and put a purple robe on Him;
3 and they were coming to Him and saying,
"Hail, King of the Jews!" and were giving Him
slaps *in the face*. 4 And Pilate came out again
and *said to them, "Behold, I am bringing
Him out to you so that you may know that
I find no guilt in Him." 5 Jesus then came
out, wearing the crown of thorns and the
purple robe. *Pilate* *said to them, "Behold,
the man!" 6 So when the chief priests and
the officers saw Him, they cried out saying,
"Crucify, crucify!" Pilate *said to them,
"Take Him yourselves and crucify Him, for
I find no guilt in Him." 7 The Jews answered
him, "We have a law, and by that law He
ought to die because He made Himself out
to be the Son of God."
8 Therefore when Pilate heard this
statement, he became more afraid; 9 and
he entered into the Praetorium again and
*said to Jesus, "Where are You from?" But
Jesus gave him no answer. 10 So Pilate *said
to Him, "You do not speak to me? Do You not
know that I have authority to release You,
and I have authority to crucify You?" 11 Jesus
answered, "You would have no authority

over Me, unless it had been given you from above; for this reason he who delivered Me to you has *the* greater sin." 12 As a result of this Pilate kept seeking to release Him, but the Jews cried out saying, "If you release this man, you are no friend of Caesar; everyone who makes himself *to be* a king opposes Caesar."

13 Therefore when Pilate heard these words, he brought Jesus out, and sat down on the judgment seat at a place called The Stone Pavement, but in Hebrew, Gabbatha. 14 Now it was the day of Preparation for the Passover; it was about the sixth hour. And he *said to the Jews, "Behold, your King!" 15 So they cried out, "Away with *Him*! Away with *Him*! Crucify Him!" Pilate *said to them, "Shall I crucify your King?" The chief priests answered, "We have no king but Caesar."

16 So he then delivered Him over to them to be crucified.

17 They took Jesus, therefore, and He went out, bearing His own cross, to the place called the Place of a Skull, which is called in Hebrew, Golgotha. 18 There they crucified Him, and with Him two other men, one on either side, and Jesus in between. 19 And Pilate also wrote an inscription and put it on the cross. It was written, "JESUS THE NAZARENE, THE KING OF THE JEWS." 20 Therefore many of the Jews read this inscription, for the place where Jesus was crucified was near the city; and it was written in Hebrew, Latin, *and* in Greek. 21 So the chief priests of the Jews were saying to Pilate, "Do not write, 'The King of the Jews;' but that He said, 'I am King of the Jews.'" 22 Pilate answered, "What I have written I have written."

JUNE 12

2 Kings 11:1–13:25

11 Now Athaliah the mother of Ahaziah saw that her son had died. So she rose and caused all the royal seed to perish. 2 But Jehosheba, the daughter of King Joram, sister of Ahaziah, took Joash the son of Ahaziah and stole him from among the king's sons who were being put to death, *and put* him and his nurse in the bedroom. So they hid him from Athaliah, and he was not put to death. 3 So he was hidden away with her in the house of Yahweh six years, while Athaliah was reigning over the land.

4 Now in the seventh year Jehoiada sent for and took the commanders of hundreds of the Carites and of the guard, and brought them to him in the house of Yahweh. Then he cut a covenant with them and had them swear in the house of Yahweh, and showed them the king's son. 5 And he commanded them, saying, "This is the thing that you shall do: one-third of you, who come in on the sabbath and keep watch over the king's house 6 (one-third also *shall be* at the gate Sur, and one-third at the gate behind the guards), shall keep watch over the house for defense. 7 And two parts of you, *even* all who go out on the sabbath, shall also keep watch over the house of Yahweh for the king. 8 And you shall surround the king, each with his weapons in his hand; and whoever comes within the ranks shall be put to death. And be with the king when he goes out and when he comes in."

9 So the commanders of hundreds did according to all that Jehoiada the priest commanded. And each one of them took his men who were to come in on the sabbath, with those who were to go out on the sabbath, and came to Jehoiada the priest. 10 Then the priest gave to the commanders of hundreds the spears and small shields that *had been* King David's, which *were* in the house of Yahweh. 11 And the guards stood each with his weapons in his hand, from the right side of the house to the left side of the house, by the altar and by the house, around the king. 12 Then he brought the king's son out and put the crown on him and *gave him* the testimony; and they made him king and anointed him, and they clapped their hands and said, "*Long* live the king!"

13 Then Athaliah heard the noise of the guard *and of* the people, and she came to the people in the house of Yahweh. 14 And she looked, and behold, the king was standing by the pillar, according to the custom, with the commanders and the trumpeters beside the king; and all the people of the land were glad and blew trumpets. Then Athaliah tore her clothes and cried, "Treason! Treason!"

15 And Jehoiada the priest commanded
the commanders of hundreds who were
appointed over the military force and said
to them, "Bring her out between the ranks,
and whoever follows her put to death with
the sword." For the priest said, "Let her not
be put to death in the house of Yahweh."
16 So they laid hands on her, and she arrived
at the horses' entrance of the king's house
and was put to death there.

17 Then Jehoiada cut a covenant between
Yahweh and the king and the people, that
they would be the people of Yahweh, also
between the king and the people. 18 And all
the people of the land came to the house
of Baal and tore it down; his altars and his
images they broke in pieces thoroughly,
and they killed Mattan the priest of Baal
before the altars. And the priest appointed
overseers over the house of Yahweh. 19 And
he took the commanders of hundreds and
the Carites and the guards and all the people
of the land; and they brought the king down
from the house of Yahweh, and came by the
way of the gate of the guards to the king's
house. And he sat on the throne of the
kings. 20 So all the people of the land were
glad, and the city was quiet. For they had
put Athaliah to death with the sword at the
king's house.

21 Jehoash was seven years old when he
became king.

12 In the seventh year of Jehu, Jehoash
became king, and he reigned forty
years in Jerusalem; and his mother's name
was Zibiah of Beersheba. 2 And Jehoash did
what was right in the sight of Yahweh all his
days in which Jehoiada the priest instructed
him. 3 Only the high places were not taken
away; the people still sacrificed and burned
incense on the high places.

4 Then Jehoash said to the priests, "All
the money of the sacred things which is
brought into the house of Yahweh, *both*
the money for each numbered man—the
*money from each person's assessment in
the census—and* all the money which any
man's heart prompts him to bring into the
house of Yahweh, 5 let the priests take it for
themselves, each from his acquaintance;
and they shall repair the damages of the
house wherever any damage may be found."

6 Now it happened that in the twenty-
third year of King Jehoash the priests had
not repaired the damages of the house.
7 Then King Jehoash called for Jehoiada the
priest, and for the *other* priests and said to
them, "Why do you not repair the damages
of the house? So now, take no *more* money
from your acquaintances, but give it over
to pay for the damages of the house." 8 So
the priests agreed that they would take no
more money from the people, nor repair the
damages of the house.

9 But Jehoiada the priest took a chest and
bored a hole in its lid and put it beside the
altar, on the right side as one comes into the
house of Yahweh; and the priests who kept
watch over the threshold put in it all the
money which was brought into the house
of Yahweh. 10 Now it happened that when
they saw that there was much money in the
chest, the king's scribe and the high priest
came up and tied *it* in bags and counted the
money which was found in the house of
Yahweh. 11 And they gave the money, which
was weighed out, into the hands of those
who did the work, who had the oversight of
the house of Yahweh; and they paid it out to
the craftsmen of wood and the builders who
worked on the house of Yahweh; 12 and to
the masons and the hewers of stone, and for
buying timber and hewn stone to repair the
damages to the house of Yahweh, and for all
that was laid out for the house to repair it.
13 But there were not made for the house of
Yahweh silver cups, snuffers, bowls, trum-
pets, any vessels of gold, or vessels of silver
from the money which was brought into
the house of Yahweh; 14 for they gave that
to those who did the work, and with it they
repaired the house of Yahweh. 15 Moreover,
they did not require an accounting from the
men into whose hand they paid the money
in order to pay those who did the work, for
they were doing it faithfully. 16 The money
from the guilt offerings and the money from
the sin offerings was not brought into the
house of Yahweh; it was for the priests.

17 Then Hazael king of Aram went up and
fought against Gath and captured it, and
Hazael set his face to go up to Jerusalem.
18 And Jehoash king of Judah took all the
holy things that Jehoshaphat and Jehoram
and Ahaziah, his fathers, kings of Judah, had
set apart as holy, and his own holy things
and all the gold that was found among the
treasuries of the house of Yahweh and of
the king's house, and sent *them* to Hazael

king of Aram. Then he went away from
Jerusalem.
19 Now the rest of the acts of Joash and
all that he did, are they not written in the
Book of the Chronicles of the Kings of
Judah? 20 And his servants arose and made
a conspiracy and struck down Joash at the
house of Millo *as he was* going down to Silla.
21 Now Jozacar the son of Shimeath and
Jehozabad the son of Shomer, his servants,
struck *him* and he died; and they buried him
with his fathers in the city of David, and
Amaziah his son became king in his place.

13 In the twenty-third year of Joash the
son of Ahaziah, king of Judah, Jehoa-
haz the son of Jehu became king over Israel
at Samaria, *and he reigned* seventeen years.
2 And he did what was evil in the sight of
Yahweh and followed the sins of Jeroboam
the son of Nebat, with which he made Israel
sin; he did not depart from them. 3 So the
anger of Yahweh burned against Israel, and
He gave them continually into the hand of
Hazael king of Aram, and into the hand
of Ben-hadad the son of Hazael. 4 Then
Jehoahaz entreated the face of Yahweh,
and Yahweh listened to him; for He saw the
oppression of Israel, how the king of Aram
oppressed them. 5 And Yahweh gave Israel
a savior, so that they came out from under
the hand of the Arameans; and the sons
of Israel lived in their tents as formerly.
6 Nevertheless they did not depart from the
sins of the house of Jeroboam, with which
he made Israel sin, but walked in them;
and the Asherah also remained standing in
Samaria. 7 For he did not leave to Jehoahaz
any people *for the army* except 50 horsemen
and 10 chariots and 10,000 foot soldiers, for
the king of Aram had caused them to perish
and made them like the dust at threshing.
8 Now the rest of the acts of Jehoahaz, and
all that he did and his might, are they not
written in the Book of the Chronicles of the
Kings of Israel? 9 And Jehoahaz slept with
his fathers, and they buried him in Samaria;
and Joash his son became king in his place.
10 In the thirty-seventh year of Joash
king of Judah, Jehoash the son of Jehoahaz
became king over Israel in Samaria *and
reigned* sixteen years. 11 And he did what
was evil in the sight of Yahweh; he did not
depart from all the sins of Jeroboam the
son of Nebat, with which he made Israel
sin, but he walked in them. 12 Now the rest
of the acts of Joash and all that he did and
his might with which he fought against
Amaziah king of Judah, are they not written
in the Book of the Chronicles of the Kings
of Israel? 13 So Joash slept with his fathers,
and Jeroboam sat on his throne; and Joash
was buried in Samaria with the kings of
Israel.
14 Now Elisha became sick with the
illness of which he was to die. So Joash the
king of Israel came down to him and wept
over him and said, "My father, my father,
the chariots of Israel and its horsemen!"
15 And Elisha said to him, "Take a bow and
arrows." So he took a bow and arrows.
16 Then he said to the king of Israel, "Put
your hand on the bow." And he put his hand
on it, then Elisha placed his hands on the
king's hands. 17 And he said, "Open the
window toward the east," and he opened
it. Then Elisha said, "Shoot!" And he shot.
And he said, "Yahweh's arrow of salvation,
even the arrow of salvation over Aram;
for you will strike the Arameans at Aphek
until you have consumed *them*." 18 Then he
said, "Take the arrows," and he took them.
And he said to the king of Israel, "Strike
the ground," and he struck *it* three times
and stood *still*. 19 So the man of God was
angry with him and said, "You should have
struck five or six times, then you would
have struck Aram until you would have
consumed *it*. But now you shall strike Aram
only three times."
20 And Elisha died, and they buried him.
Now the marauding bands of the Moabites
would enter into the land in the spring
of the year. 21 Now it happened that they
were burying a man, and behold, they saw
a marauding band; and they cast the man
into the grave of Elisha. And when the man
touched the bones of Elisha he became alive
and stood up on his feet.
22 Now Hazael king of Aram had
oppressed Israel all the days of Jehoahaz.
23 But Yahweh was gracious to them and had
compassion on them and turned to them
because of His covenant with Abraham,
Isaac, and Jacob, and would not bring them
to ruin or cast them from His presence until
now.
24 Then Hazael king of Aram died, and
Ben-hadad his son became king in his place.
25 Then Jehoash the son of Jehoahaz took

again from the hand of Ben-hadad the son of Hazael the cities which he had taken in war from the hand of Jehoahaz his father. Three times Joash struck him and recovered the cities of Israel.

Psalm 73:1–9

1 Surely God is good to Israel,
To those who are pure in heart!
2 But as for me, my feet had
almost stumbled,
My steps had almost slipped.
3 For I was envious of the boastful,
I saw the peace of the wicked.
4 For there are no pains in their death,
And their body is fat.
5 They are not in trouble *as other* men,
And they are not stricken along
with *the rest of* mankind.
6 Therefore lofty pride is their necklace;
The garment of violence covers them.
7 Their eye bulges from fatness;
The delusions of *their* heart overflow.
8 They scoff and wickedly
speak of oppression;
They speak from on high.
9 They have set their mouth
against the heavens,
And their tongue goes
through the earth.

Proverbs 18:16–17

16 A man's gift makes room for him
And leads him into the
presence of great men.
17 The first to plead his case *seems* right,
Until another comes and
examines him.

John 19:23–42

23 Then the soldiers, when they had
crucified Jesus, took His garments and
made four parts, a part to each soldier and
also His tunic; now that tunic was seamless,
woven in one piece from the top. 24 So they
said to one another, "Let us not tear it, but
cast lots for it, *to decide* whose it shall be;"
this was in order that the Scripture would
be fulfilled: "THEY DIVIDED MY GARMENTS
AMONG THEM, AND FOR MY CLOTHING THEY
CAST LOTS." 25 Therefore the soldiers did
these things.

But standing by the cross of Jesus were
His mother, and His mother's sister, Mary
the *wife* of Clopas, and Mary Magdalene.
26 When Jesus then saw His mother, and the
disciple whom He loved standing nearby,
He *said to His mother, "Woman, behold,
your son!" 27 Then He *said to the disciple,
"Behold, your mother!" From that hour the
disciple took her into his *home*.

28 After this, Jesus, knowing that all
things had already been finished, in order
to finish the Scripture, *said, "I am thirsty."
29 A jar full of sour wine was standing there;
so they put a sponge full of the sour wine
upon *a branch of* hyssop and brought it
up to His mouth. 30 Therefore when Jesus
had received the sour wine, He said, "It is
finished!" And bowing His head, He gave
up His spirit.

31 Then the Jews, because it was the day
of Preparation, so that the bodies would not
remain on the cross on the Sabbath (for that
Sabbath was a high day), asked Pilate that
their legs might be broken, and *that* they
might be taken away. 32 So the soldiers came,
and broke the legs of the first man and of the
other who was crucified with Him; 33 but
coming to Jesus, when they saw that He
was already dead, they did not break His
legs. 34 But one of the soldiers pierced His
side with a spear, and immediately blood
and water came out. 35 And he who has
seen has borne witness, and his witness
is true; and he knows that he is telling the
truth, so that you also may believe. 36 For
these things came to pass in order that the
Scripture would be fulfilled, "NOT A BONE OF
HIM SHALL BE BROKEN." 37 And again another
Scripture says, "THEY SHALL LOOK ON HIM
WHOM THEY PIERCED."

38 Now after these things Joseph of Ari-
mathea, being a disciple of Jesus, but secretly
because of his fear of the Jews, asked Pilate
that he might take away the body of Jesus;
and Pilate granted permission. So he came
and took away His body. 39 And Nicodemus,
who had first come to Him by night, also
came, bringing a mixture of myrrh and
aloes, *weighing* about one hundred litras.
40 So they took the body of Jesus and bound
it in linen wrappings with the spices, as is
the burial custom of the Jews. 41 Now in the
place where He was crucified there was a
garden, and in the garden a new tomb in
which no one had yet been laid. 42 Therefore
because of the Jewish day of Preparation,
since the tomb was nearby, they laid Jesus
there.

JUNE 13

2 Kings 14:1–29

14 In the second year of Joash son of Joahaz king of Israel, Amaziah the son of Joash king of Judah became king. 2 He was twenty-five years old when he became king, and he reigned twenty-nine years in Jerusalem. And his mother's name was Jehoaddin of Jerusalem. 3 And he did what was right in the sight of Yahweh, yet not like David his father; he did according to all that Joash his father had done. 4 Only the high places were not taken away; the people still sacrificed and burned incense on the high places. 5 Now it happened as soon as the kingdom was strong in his hand, that he struck down his servants who had struck down the king his father. 6 But the sons of those who struck *him* down he did not put to death, according to what is written in the book of the Law of Moses, which Yahweh commanded, saying, "Fathers shall not be put to death for *their* sons, nor sons be put to death for *their* fathers; but each shall be put to death for his own sin."

7 He struck down 10,000 *of* Edom in the Valley of Salt and seized Sela by war and named it Joktheel to this day.

8 Then Amaziah sent messengers to Jehoash, the son of Jehoahaz son of Jehu, king of Israel, saying, "Come, let us face each other." 9 And Jehoash king of Israel sent to Amaziah king of Judah, saying, "The thorn bush which was in Lebanon sent to the cedar which was in Lebanon, saying, 'Give your daughter to my son as a wife.' But a beast of the field that was in Lebanon passed by and trampled the thorn bush. 10 You have indeed struck down Edom, and your heart has lifted you up. Enjoy your glory and stay at home; for why should you provoke calamity so that you, even you, would fall, and Judah with you?"

11 But Amaziah would not listen. So Jehoash king of Israel went up; and he and Amaziah king of Judah faced each other at Beth-shemesh, which belongs to Judah. 12 And Judah was defeated by Israel, and they fled each to his tent. 13 Then Jehoash king of Israel seized Amaziah king of Judah, the son of Jehoash the son of Ahaziah, at Beth-shemesh, and came to Jerusalem and broke down the wall of Jerusalem from the Gate of Ephraim to the Corner Gate, 400 cubits. 14 And he took all the gold and silver and all the utensils which were found in the house of Yahweh, and in the treasuries of the king's house, the hostages also, and returned to Samaria.

15 Now the rest of the acts of Jehoash which he did, and his might and how he fought with Amaziah king of Judah, are they not written in the Book of the Chronicles of the Kings of Israel? 16 So Jehoash slept with his fathers and was buried in Samaria with the kings of Israel; and Jeroboam his son became king in his place.

17 And Amaziah the son of Joash king of Judah lived fifteen years after the death of Jehoash son of Jehoahaz king of Israel. 18 Now the rest of the acts of Amaziah, are they not written in the Book of the Chronicles of the Kings of Judah? 19 And they conspired against him in Jerusalem, and he fled to Lachish; but they sent after him to Lachish and put him to death there. 20 Then they carried him on horses, and he was buried at Jerusalem with his fathers in the city of David. 21 And all the people of Judah took Azariah, who *was* sixteen years old, and made him king in the place of his father Amaziah. 22 He built Elath and restored it to Judah after the king slept with his fathers.

23 In the fifteenth year of Amaziah the son of Joash king of Judah, Jeroboam the son of Joash king of Israel became king in Samaria *and reigned* forty-one years. 24 And he did what was evil in the sight of Yahweh; he did not depart from all the sins of Jeroboam the son of Nebat, which he made Israel sin. 25 He restored the border of Israel from Lebo-hamath as far as the Sea of the Arabah, according to the word of Yahweh, the God of Israel, which He spoke through His servant Jonah the son of Amittai, the prophet, who was of Gath-hepher. 26 For Yahweh saw the affliction of Israel, *which was* very bitter; for there was neither bond nor free, nor was there any helper for Israel. 27 But Yahweh did not say that He would blot out the name of Israel from under heaven, so He saved them by the hand of Jeroboam the son of Joash.

28 Now the rest of the acts of Jeroboam and all that he did and his might, how he fought and how he restored Damascus and

Hamath to Judah in Israel, are they not written in the Book of the Chronicles of the Kings of Israel? 29 And Jeroboam slept with his fathers, even with the kings of Israel, and Zechariah his son became king in his place.

Psalm 73:10–20

10 Therefore his people return
    here, *to his place*,
  And waters of fullness are
    drunk by them.
11 They say, "How does God know?
  And is there knowledge with
    the Most High?"
12 Behold, these are the wicked;
  And always at ease, they have
    increased *in* wealth.
13 Surely in vain I have kept
    my heart pure
  And washed my hands in innocence;
14 For I have been stricken all day long
  And reproved every morning.

15 If I had said, "I will recount thus,"
  Behold, I would have betrayed the
    generation of Your children.
16 When I gave thought to know this,
  It was trouble in my sight
17 Until I came into the sanctuary of God;
  Then I understood their end.
18 Surely You set them in slippery places;
  You cause them to fall to destruction.
19 How they become desolate
    in a moment!
  They are completely swept
    away by terrors!
20 Like a dream when one awakes,
  O Lord, when aroused, You
    will despise their form.

Proverbs 18:18–19

18 The *cast* lot puts an end to contentions
  And decides between the mighty ones.
19 A brother offended *is harder to*
    win over than a strong city,
  And contentions are like
    the bars of a citadel.

John 20:1–31

20 Now on the first *day* of the week, Mary Magdalene *came early to the tomb, while it *was still dark, and *saw the stone *already* taken away from the tomb. 2 So she *ran and *came to Simon Peter and to the other disciple whom Jesus loved, and *said to them, "They have taken away the Lord out of the tomb, and we do not know where they have laid Him." 3 So Peter and the other disciple went forth, and they were going to the tomb. 4 And the two were running together; and the other disciple ran ahead faster than Peter and came to the tomb first; 5 and stooping and looking in, he *saw the linen wrappings lying *there*; but he did not go in. 6 And so Simon Peter also *came, following him, and entered the tomb; and he *saw the linen wrappings lying there, 7 and the face-cloth which had been on His head, not lying with the linen wrappings, but folded up in a place by itself. 8 So the other disciple who had first come to the tomb then also entered, and he saw and believed. 9 For as yet they did not understand the Scripture, that He must rise again from the dead. 10 So the disciples went away again to where they were staying.

11 But Mary was standing outside the tomb crying; and so, as she was crying, she stooped to look into the tomb; 12 and she *saw two angels in white sitting, one at the head and one at the feet, where the body of Jesus had been lying. 13 And they *said to her, "Woman, why are you crying?" She *said to them, "Because they have taken away my Lord, and I do not know where they have laid Him." 14 When she had said this, she turned around and *saw Jesus standing *there*, and did not know that it was Jesus. 15 Jesus *said to her, "Woman, why are you crying? Whom are you seeking?" Thinking Him to be the gardener, she *said to Him, "Sir, if you have carried Him away, tell me where you have laid Him, and I will take Him away." 16 Jesus *said to her, "Mary!" She turned and *said to Him in Hebrew, "Rabboni!" (which means, Teacher). 17 Jesus *said to her, "Stop clinging to Me, for I have not yet ascended to the Father; but go to My brothers and say to them, 'I ascend to My Father and your Father, and My God and your God.'" 18 Mary Magdalene *came, announcing to the disciples, "I have seen the Lord," and *that* He had said these things to her.

19 So while it was evening on that day, the first *day* of the week, and while the doors were shut where the disciples were, for fear of the Jews, Jesus came and stood in their midst and *said to them, "Peace *be* with you." 20 And when He had said this,

He showed them both His hands and His
side. The disciples then rejoiced when they
saw the Lord. 21 So Jesus said to them again,
"Peace *be* with you; as the Father has sent
Me, I also send you." 22 And when He had
said this, He breathed on *them* and *said
to them, "Receive the Holy Spirit. 23 If you
forgive the sins of any, *their sins* have been
forgiven them; if you retain the *sins* of any,
they have been retained."

24 But Thomas, one of the twelve, called
Didymus, was not with them when Jesus
came. 25 So the other disciples were saying
to him, "We have seen the Lord!" But he
said to them, "Unless I see in His hands the
imprint of the nails, and put my finger into
the place of the nails, and put my hand into
His side, I will not believe."

26 And after eight days His disciples were
again inside, and Thomas with them. Jesus
*came, the doors having been shut, and stood
in their midst and said, "Peace *be* with you."
27 Then He *said to Thomas, "Bring your
finger here, and see My hands; and bring
your hand *here* and put it into My side; and do
not be unbelieving, but believing." 28 Thomas
answered and said to Him, "My Lord and my
God!" 29 Jesus *said to him, "Because you
have seen Me, have you believed? Blessed
are those who did not see, and *yet* believed."

30 Therefore many other signs Jesus also
did in the presence of the disciples, which
are not written in this book; 31 but these
have been written so that you may believe
that Jesus is the Christ, the Son of God; and
that believing you may have life in His name.

JUNE 14

2 Kings 15:1–16:20

15 In the twenty-seventh year of
Jeroboam king of Israel, Azariah son
of Amaziah king of Judah became king. 2 He
was sixteen years old when he became king,
and he reigned fifty-two years in Jerusalem;
and his mother's name was Jecoliah of
Jerusalem. 3 And he did what was right in
the sight of Yahweh, according to all that his
father Amaziah had done. 4 Only the high
places were not taken away; the people still
sacrificed and burned incense on the high
places. 5 Then Yahweh smote the king, so
that he was a leper to the day of his death.
And he lived in a separate house, while
Jotham the king's son *was* over the house,
judging the people of the land. 6 Now the
rest of the acts of Azariah and all that he
did, are they not written in the Book of the
Chronicles of the Kings of Judah? 7 And
Azariah slept with his fathers, and they
buried him with his fathers in the city of
David, and Jotham his son became king in
his place.

8 In the thirty-eighth year of Azariah king
of Judah, Zechariah the son of Jeroboam
became king over Israel in Samaria *for* six
months. 9 And he did what was evil in the
sight of Yahweh, as his fathers had done; he
did not depart from the sins of Jeroboam
the son of Nebat, which he made Israel sin.
10 Then Shallum the son of Jabesh conspired
against him and struck him before the
people and put him to death and became
king in his place. 11 Now the rest of the acts
of Zechariah, behold, they are written in
the Book of the Chronicles of the Kings of
Israel. 12 This is the word of Yahweh which
He spoke to Jehu, saying, "Your sons to the
fourth generation shall sit on the throne of
Israel." And so it was.

13 Shallum son of Jabesh became king
in the thirty-ninth year of Uzziah king
of Judah, and he reigned one month in
Samaria. 14 Then Menahem son of Gadi went
up from Tirzah and came to Samaria, and
struck Shallum son of Jabesh in Samaria,
and put him to death and became king in his
place. 15 Now the rest of the acts of Shallum
and his conspiracy which he made, behold,
they are written in the Book of the Chroni-
cles of the Kings of Israel. 16 Then Menahem
struck Tiphsah and all who were in it and
its borders from Tirzah, because they did
not open *to him*; therefore he struck *it* and
ripped up all its pregnant women.

17 In the thirty-ninth year of Azariah king
of Judah, Menahem son of Gadi became king
over Israel *and reigned* ten years in Samaria.
18 And he did what was evil in the sight of
Yahweh; he did not depart all his days from
the sins of Jeroboam the son of Nebat, which
he made Israel sin.

19 Pul, king of Assyria, came against the
land, and Menahem gave Pul one thousand
talents of silver so that his hand might be

with him to strengthen the kingdom in his hand. 20 Then Menahem exacted the money from Israel, even from all the mighty men of valor, from each man fifty shekels of silver to pay the king of Assyria. So the king of Assyria returned and did not stay there in the land. 21 Now the rest of the acts of Menahem and all that he did, are they not written in the Book of the Chronicles of the Kings of Israel? 22 And Menahem slept with his fathers, and Pekahiah his son became king in his place.

23 In the fiftieth year of Azariah king of Judah, Pekahiah son of Menahem became king over Israel in Samaria *and reigned* two years. 24 And he did what was evil in the sight of Yahweh; he did not depart from the sins of Jeroboam son of Nebat, which he made Israel sin. 25 Then Pekah son of Remaliah, his officer, conspired against him and struck him in Samaria, in the castle of the king's house with Argob and Arieh; and with him were fifty men of the Gileadites, and he put him to death and became king in his place. 26 Now the rest of the acts of Pekahiah and all that he did, behold, they are written in the Book of the Chronicles of the Kings of Israel.

27 In the fifty-second year of Azariah king of Judah, Pekah son of Remaliah became king over Israel in Samaria *and reigned* twenty years. 28 And he did what was evil in the sight of Yahweh; he did not depart from the sins of Jeroboam son of Nebat, which he made Israel sin.

29 In the days of Pekah king of Israel, Tiglath-pileser king of Assyria came and took Ijon and Abel-beth-maacah and Janoah and Kedesh and Hazor and Gilead and Galilee, all the land of Naphtali; and he took them away into exile to Assyria. 30 And Hoshea the son of Elah made a conspiracy against Pekah the son of Remaliah and struck him and put him to death and became king in his place, in the twentieth year of Jotham the son of Uzziah. 31 Now the *rest of the acts of* Pekah and all that he did, behold, they are written in the Book of the Chronicles of the Kings of Israel.

32 In the second year of Pekah the son of Remaliah king of Israel, Jotham the son of Uzziah king of Judah became king. 33 He was twenty-five years old when he became king, and he reigned sixteen years in Jerusalem. And his mother's name was Jerusha the daughter of Zadok. 34 And he did what was right in the sight of Yahweh; he did according to all that his father Uzziah had done. 35 Only the high places were not taken away; the people still sacrificed and burned incense on the high places. He built the upper gate of the house of Yahweh. 36 Now the rest of the acts of Jotham and all that he did, are they not written in the Book of the Chronicles of the Kings of Judah? 37 In those days Yahweh began to send Rezin king of Aram and Pekah the son of Remaliah against Judah. 38 And Jotham slept with his fathers, and he was buried with his fathers in the city of David his father; and Ahaz his son became king in his place.

16 In the seventeenth year of Pekah the son of Remaliah, Ahaz the son of Jotham, king of Judah, became king. 2 Ahaz *was* twenty years old when he became king, and he reigned sixteen years in Jerusalem; and he did not do what was right in the sight of Yahweh his God, as David his father *had done*. 3 But he walked in the way of the kings of Israel, and even made his son pass through the fire, according to the abominations of the nations whom Yahweh had dispossessed from before the sons of Israel. 4 He also sacrificed and burned incense on the high places and on the hills and under every green tree.

5 Then Rezin king of Aram and Pekah son of Remaliah, king of Israel, went up to Jerusalem to *wage* war; and they besieged Ahaz, but could not overcome him. 6 At that time Rezin king of Aram restored Elath for Aram and cleared the Judeans out of Elath entirely; and the Arameans came to Elath and have lived there to this day.

7 So Ahaz sent messengers to Tiglath-pileser king of Assyria, saying, "I am your servant and your son; come up and save me from the hand of the king of Aram and from the hand of the king of Israel, who are rising up against me." 8 Ahaz also took the silver and gold that was found in the house of Yahweh and in the treasuries of the king's house, and sent a gift to the king of Assyria. 9 So the king of Assyria listened to him; and the king of Assyria went up against Damascus and seized it and took *the people of* it away into exile to Kir, and put Rezin to death.

10 Now King Ahaz went to Damascus to meet Tiglath-pileser king of Assyria and saw

the altar which *was* at Damascus; and King
Ahaz sent to Urijah the priest the likeness
of the altar and its pattern, according to
all its workmanship. 11 So Urijah the priest
built an altar; according to all that King
Ahaz had sent from Damascus, thus Urijah
the priest made *it*, before the coming of
King Ahaz from Damascus. 12 So the king
came from Damascus, and the king saw
the altar; then the king drew near the altar
and made offerings on it, 13 and offered his
burnt offering and his meal offering up in
smoke, and poured his drink offering and
splashed the blood of his peace offerings
on the altar. 14 Now *as for* the bronze altar,
which *was* before Yahweh, he drew *it* away
from the front of the house, from between
his altar and the house of Yahweh, and he
put it on the north side of *his* altar. 15 Then
King Ahaz commanded Urijah the priest,
saying, "Upon the great altar offer up in
smoke the morning burnt offering and
the evening grain offering and the king's
burnt offering and his grain offering, with
the burnt offering of all the people of the
land and their grain offering and their drink
offerings; and splash on it all the blood of
the burnt offering and all the blood of the
sacrifice. But the bronze altar shall be for
me to inquire *by*." 16 So Urijah the priest did
according to all that King Ahaz commanded.

17 Then King Ahaz cut off the borders
of the stands and removed the laver from
them; he also took down the sea from the
bronze oxen which were under it and put it
on a pavement of stone. 18 And the covered
way for the sabbath which they had built in
the house, and the outer entry of the king,
he removed from the house of Yahweh
because of the king of Assyria.

19 Now the rest of the acts of Ahaz which
he did, are they not written in the Book of
the Chronicles of the Kings of Judah? 20 So
Ahaz slept with his fathers and was buried
with his fathers in the city of David; and
Hezekiah his son became king in his place.

Psalm 73:21–28

21 When my heart was embittered
And I was pierced within,
22 Then I was senseless and ignorant;
I was like an animal before You.
23 Nevertheless I am
continually with You;
You have taken hold of my right hand.
24 With Your counsel You will lead me,
And afterward take me in glory.
25 Whom have I in heaven *but You*?
And besides You, I desire
nothing on earth.
26 My flesh and my heart fail,
But God is the rock of my heart
and my portion forever.
27 For, behold, those who are far
from You will perish;
You have destroyed everyone
who is unfaithful to You.
28 But as for me, the nearness
of God is my good;
I have set Lord Yahweh as my refuge,
That I may recount all Your works.

Proverbs 18:20–21

20 From the fruit of a man's mouth
his stomach will be satisfied;
With the produce of his lips
he will be satisfied.
21 Death and life are in the
power of the tongue,
And those who love it will eat its fruit.

John 21:1–25

21 After these things Jesus manifested
Himself again to the disciples at the
Sea of Tiberias, and He manifested *Himself*
in this way. 2 Simon Peter, and Thomas called
Didymus, and Nathanael of Cana in Galilee,
and the *sons* of Zebedee, and two others of
His disciples were together. 3 Simon Peter
*said to them, "I am going fishing." They
*said to him, "We will also come with you."
They went out and got into the boat; and
that night they caught nothing.

4 But when the day was now breaking,
Jesus stood on the beach; yet the disciples
did not know that it was Jesus. 5 So Jesus
*said to them, "Children, do you have any
fish?" They answered Him, "No." 6 And
He said to them, "Cast the net on the right
side of the boat and you will find *some*." So
they cast, and then they were not able to
haul it in because of the great number of
fish. 7 Therefore that disciple whom Jesus
loved *said to Peter, "It is the Lord." So
when Simon Peter heard that it was the
Lord, he put his outer garment on (for he
was stripped *for work*), and cast himself into
the sea. 8 But the other disciples came in the
little boat, for they were not far from the

land, but about two hundred cubits away,
dragging the net *full* of fish.
9 So when they got out on the land, they
*saw a charcoal fire in place and fish placed
on it, and bread. 10 Jesus *said to them,
"Bring some of the fish which you have now
caught." 11 Simon Peter went up and drew
the net to land, full of large fish, 153; and
although there were so many, the net was
not torn.
12 Jesus *said to them, "Come, have
breakfast." None of the disciples dared to
question Him, "Who are You?" knowing that
it was the Lord. 13 Jesus *came and *took
the bread and *gave *it* to them, and the fish
likewise. 14 This is now the third time that
Jesus was manifested to the disciples, after
He was raised from the dead.
15 So when they had finished breakfast,
Jesus *said to Simon Peter, "Simon, *son* of
John, do you love Me more than these?"
He *said to Him, "Yes, Lord; You know
that I love You." He *said to him, "Tend My
lambs." 16 He *said to him again a second
time, "Simon, *son* of John, do you love Me?"
He *said to Him, "Yes, Lord; You know that
I love You." He *said to him, "Shepherd My
sheep." 17 He *said to him the third time,
"Simon, *son* of John, do you love Me?"
Peter was grieved because He said to him
the third time, "Do you love Me?" And he
said to Him, "Lord, You know all things; You
know that I love You." Jesus *said to him,
"Tend My sheep. 18 Truly, truly, I say to you,
when you were younger, you used to gird
yourself and walk wherever you wished;
but when you grow old, you will stretch
out your hands and someone else will gird
you, and bring you where you do not wish
to *go*." 19 Now this He said, signifying by
what kind of death he would glorify God.
And when He had spoken this, He *said to
him, "Follow Me!"
20 Peter, turning around, *saw the disciple
whom Jesus loved following *them*; the one
who also had leaned back on His bosom at
the supper and said, "Lord, who is the one
who betrays You?" 21 So Peter seeing him
*said to Jesus, "Lord, and what about this
man?" 22 Jesus *said to him, "If I want him to
remain until I come, what *is that* to you? You
follow Me!" 23 Therefore this saying went out
among the brothers that this disciple would
not die; yet Jesus did not say to him that he
would not die, but *only*, "If I want him to
remain until I come, what *is that* to you?"
24 This is the disciple who is bearing
witness to these things and wrote these
things, and we know that his witness is true.
25 And there are also many other things
which Jesus did, which if they *were written
one after the other, I suppose that even the
world itself *could not contain the books
that *would be written.

JUNE 15

2 Kings 17:1–18:37

17 In the twelfth year of Ahaz king
of Judah, Hoshea the son of Elah
became king over Israel in Samaria *and
reigned* nine years. 2 And he did what was
evil in the sight of Yahweh, only not as the
kings of Israel who were before him. 3 Shal-
maneser king of Assyria went up against
him, and Hoshea became his servant and
paid him tribute. 4 But the king of Assyria
found conspiracy in Hoshea, who had sent
messengers to So king of Egypt and had
offered no tribute to the king of Assyria,
as *he had done* year by year; therefore the
king of Assyria shut him up and bound him
in prison.
5 Then the king of Assyria went up against
the whole land and he went up to Samaria
and besieged it three years.
6 In the ninth year of Hoshea, the king of
Assyria captured Samaria and took Israel
away into exile to Assyria, and settled them
in Halah and Habor, *on* the river of Gozan,
and in the cities of the Medes.
7 Now *this* happened because the sons of
Israel had sinned against Yahweh their God—
who had brought them up from the land of
Egypt from under the hand of Pharaoh, king
of Egypt—and they had feared other gods
8 and walked in the statutes of the nations
whom Yahweh had dispossessed from before
the sons of Israel, and *in the statutes* of the
kings of Israel which they had made. 9 And
the sons of Israel did things secretly which
were not right against Yahweh their God.
Moreover, they built for themselves high
places in all their cities, from watchtower to
fortified city. 10 And they set for themselves

sacred pillars and Asherim on every high hill and under every green tree, 11 and there they burned incense on all the high places as the nations *did* which Yahweh had taken away into exile before them; and they did evil things provoking Yahweh to anger. 12 And they served idols, concerning which Yahweh had said to them, "You shall not do this thing." 13 Yet Yahweh warned Israel and Judah by the hand of all His prophets *and* every seer, saying, "Turn from your evil ways and keep My commandments, My statutes according to all the law which I commanded your fathers, and which I sent to you by the hand of My slaves the prophets." 14 However, they did not listen, but stiffened their neck like their fathers, who did not believe in Yahweh their God. 15 They also rejected His statutes and His covenant which He cut with their fathers and His warnings with which He warned them. And they followed vanity and became vain, and *went* after the nations which surrounded them, concerning which Yahweh had commanded them not to do like them. 16 And they forsook all the commandments of Yahweh their God and made for themselves molten images, *even* two calves, and made an Asherah and worshiped all the host of heaven and served Baal. 17 Then they made their sons and their daughters pass through the fire, and practiced divination and omens, and sold themselves to do what is evil in the sight of Yahweh, provoking Him to anger. 18 So Yahweh was very angry with Israel and caused them to depart from His presence; none was left except the tribe of Judah alone.

19 Also Judah did not keep the commandments of Yahweh their God, but walked in the statutes which Israel had made. 20 So Yahweh rejected all the seed of Israel and afflicted them and gave them into the hand of plunderers, until He had cast them from His presence.

21 When He had torn Israel from the house of David, they made Jeroboam the son of Nebat king. Then Jeroboam drove Israel away from following Yahweh and made them sin a great sin. 22 And the sons of Israel walked in all the sins of Jeroboam which he did; they did not depart from them 23 until Yahweh caused Israel to depart from His presence, as He spoke through all His slaves the prophets. So Israel went into exile from their own land to Assyria until this day.

24 And the king of Assyria brought *men* from Babylon and from Cuthah and from Avva and from Hamath and Sepharvaim, and settled *them* in the cities of Samaria in place of the sons of Israel. So they possessed Samaria and lived in its cities. 25 Now it happened at the beginning of their settlement there, that they did not fear Yahweh; therefore Yahweh sent lions among them which were killing them. 26 So they spoke to the king of Assyria, saying, "The nations whom you have taken away into exile and settled in the cities of Samaria do not know the custom of the god of the land; so he has sent lions among them, and behold, they are putting them to death because they do not know the custom of the god of the land."

27 Then the king of Assyria commanded, saying, "Take there one of the priests whom you took away into exile and let him go and live there; and let him instruct them the custom of the god of the land." 28 So one of the priests whom they had taken away into exile from Samaria came and settled at Bethel, and instructed them how they should fear Yahweh.

29 But each nation was still making gods of its own and put them in the houses of the high places which the people of Samaria had made, each nation in their cities in which they lived. 30 And the men of Babylon made Succoth-benoth, the men of Cuth made Nergal, the men of Hamath made Ashima, 31 and the Avvites made Nibhaz and Tartak; and the Sepharvites burned their children in the fire to Adrammelech and Anammelech, the gods of *the* Sepharvaim. 32 They were also fearing Yahweh and appointed from among all of themselves priests of the high places, and they were acting for them in the houses of the high places. 33 They were fearing Yahweh and serving their own gods according to the custom of the nations from among whom they had been taken away into exile.

34 To this day they are acting according to the earlier customs: they are not fearing Yahweh; they are not acting according to their statutes or their judgments or the law, or the commandment which Yahweh commanded the sons of Jacob, whom He named Israel; 35 with whom Yahweh cut a covenant and commanded them, saying, "You shall not fear other gods, nor worship them nor serve them nor sacrifice to them.

36 But Yahweh, who brought you up from the land of Egypt with great power and with an outstretched arm, Him you shall fear, and to Him you shall worship, and to Him you shall sacrifice. 37 And the statutes and the judgments and the law and the commandment which He wrote for you, you shall be careful to do forever; and you shall not fear other gods. 38 And the covenant that I have cut with you, you shall not forget, nor shall you fear other gods. 39 But Yahweh your God you shall fear; and He will deliver you from the hand of all your enemies." 40 However, they did not listen, but they were acting according to their earlier custom. 41 So while these nations were fearing Yahweh, they also were serving their graven images; their children likewise and their grandchildren, as their fathers acted, so they are acting *this way* to this day.

18 Now it happened in the third year of Hoshea, the son of Elah king of Israel, that Hezekiah the son of Ahaz king of Judah became king. 2 He was twenty-five years old when he became king; and he reigned twenty-nine years in Jerusalem. And his mother's name was Abi, the daughter of Zechariah. 3 And he did what was right in the sight of Yahweh, according to all that David his father had done. 4 He took away the high places and shattered the *sacred* pillars and cut down the Asherah. And he broke in pieces the bronze serpent that Moses had made, for until those days the sons of Israel were burning incense to it; and it was called Nehushtan. 5 He trusted in Yahweh, the God of Israel; so that after him there was none like him among all the kings of Judah, nor *among those* who were before him. 6 So he clung to Yahweh; he did not turn away from following Him, but kept His commandments, which Yahweh had commanded Moses.

7 And Yahweh was with him; wherever he went he prospered. And he rebelled against the king of Assyria and did not serve him. 8 He struck the Philistines as far as Gaza and its territory, from watchtower to fortified city.

9 Now in the fourth year of King Hezekiah, which was the seventh year of Hoshea son of Elah king of Israel, Shalmaneser king of Assyria came up against Samaria and besieged it. 10 And at the end of three years they captured it; in the sixth year of Hezekiah, which was the ninth year of Hoshea king of Israel, Samaria was captured. 11 Then the king of Assyria took Israel away into exile to Assyria, and put them in Halah and on the Habor, the river of Gozan, and in the cities of the Medes, 12 because they did not listen to the voice of Yahweh their God, but trespassed against His covenant, *even* all that Moses the servant of Yahweh commanded; they would neither listen nor do *it*.

13 Now in the fourteenth year of King Hezekiah, Sennacherib king of Assyria came up against all the fortified cities of Judah and seized them. 14 Then Hezekiah king of Judah sent to the king of Assyria at Lachish, saying, "I have done wrong. Turn away from me; whatever *penalty* you give to me I will bear." So the king of Assyria set *a penalty* on Hezekiah king of Judah three hundred talents of silver and thirty talents of gold. 15 Thus Hezekiah gave *him* all the silver which was found in the house of Yahweh and in the treasuries of the king's house. 16 At that time Hezekiah cut off *the gold from* the doors of the temple of Yahweh and *from* the doorposts, which Hezekiah king of Judah had overlaid, and gave it to the king of Assyria.

17 Then the king of Assyria sent Tartan and Rab-saris and Rabshakeh from Lachish to King Hezekiah with a heavy military force to Jerusalem. So they went up and came to Jerusalem. And when they went up, they came and stood by the conduit of the upper pool, which is on the highway of the fuller's field. 18 Then they called to the king, and Eliakim the son of Hilkiah, who *was* over the household, and Shebnah the scribe and Joah the son of Asaph the recorder, came out to them.

19 Then Rabshakeh said to them, "Say now to Hezekiah, 'Thus says the great king, the king of Assyria, "What is this trust that you have? 20 You say (but *they are* only empty words), '*I have* counsel and might for the war.' Now on whom do you trust, that you have rebelled against me? 21 Now behold, you trust in the staff of this crushed reed, *even* on Egypt; on which if a man leans, it will go into his hand and pierce it. So is Pharaoh king of Egypt to all who trust in him. 22 But if you say to me, 'We trust in Yahweh our God,' is it not He whose high places

and whose altars Hezekiah has taken away,
and has said to Judah and to Jerusalem, 'You
shall worship before this altar in Jerusalem'?
23 So now, come, make a bargain with my
master the king of Assyria, and I will give
you two thousand horses, if you are able
on your part to give riders for them. 24 How
then can you turn away one official of the
least of my master's servants, and trust in
Egypt for chariots and for horsemen? 25 So
now, have I come up without the approval of
Yahweh against this place to make it a ruin?
Yahweh said to me, 'Go up against this land
and make it a ruin.'""
26 Then Eliakim the son of Hilkiah, and
Shebnah and Joah, said to Rabshakeh,
"Speak now to your servants in Aramaic, for
we understand *it*; and do not speak with us
in Judean in the hearing of the people who
are on the wall." 27 But Rabshakeh said to
them, "Has my master sent me only to your
master and to you to speak these words, *and*
not to the men who sit on the wall, *doomed*
to eat their own dung and drink their own
urine with you?"
28 Then Rabshakeh stood and cried with a
loud voice in Judean, saying, "Hear the word
of the great king, the king of Assyria. 29 Thus
says the king, 'Do not let Hezekiah deceive
you, for he will not be able to deliver you
from his hand; 30 and do not let Hezekiah
make you trust in Yahweh, saying, "Yahweh
will surely deliver us, and this city will
not be given into the hand of the king of
Assyria." 31 Do not listen to Hezekiah, for
thus says the king of Assyria, "Make your
peace with me and come out to me, and eat
each of his vine and each of his fig tree and
drink each of the waters of his own cistern,
32 until I come and take you away to a land
like your own land, a land of grain and new
wine, a land of bread and vineyards, a land
of olive oil and honey, that you may live
and not die." But do not listen to Hezekiah
when he misleads you, saying, "Yahweh
will deliver us." 33 Has any one of the gods
of the nations delivered his land from the
hand of the king of Assyria? 34 Where are
the gods of Hamath and Arpad? Where are
the gods of Sepharvaim, Hena, and Ivvah?
When have they delivered Samaria from
my hand? 35 Who among all the gods of the
lands have delivered their land from my
hand, that Yahweh would deliver Jerusalem
from my hand?'"
36 But the people were silent and
answered him not a word, for the king's
commandment was, "Do not answer him."
37 Then Eliakim the son of Hilkiah, who *was*
over the household, and Shebna the scribe
and Joah the son of Asaph, the recorder,
came to Hezekiah with their clothes torn
and told him the words of Rabshakeh.

Psalm 74:1–8

1 Why, O God? Have You
rejected *us* forever?
Why does Your anger smoke against
the sheep of Your pasture?
2 Remember Your congregation, which
You have purchased of old,
Which You have redeemed to be
the tribe of Your inheritance;
And this Mount Zion, where
You have dwelt.
3 Lift up Your steps toward
the perpetual ruins;
The enemy has damaged everything
within the sanctuary.
4 Your adversaries have roared in the
midst of Your meeting place;
They have set up their own
signs for signs.
5 Each seems like one who lifts up
An axe against the
undergrowth of trees.
6 And now its carved work altogether
They smash with hatchet
and hammers.
7 They have set Your sanctuary on fire;
By bringing it to the ground,
they have defiled the dwelling
place of Your name.
8 They said in their heart, "Let us
completely subdue them."
They have burned all the meeting
places of God in the land.

Proverbs 18:22–24

22 He who finds a wife finds a good thing
And obtains favor from Yahweh.
23 The poor man speaks supplications,
But the rich man answers
with strong *words*.
24 A man of *too many* friends
comes to ruin,
But there is a friend who sticks
closer than a brother.

Acts 1:1–26

1 The first account, O Theophilus, I composed, about all that Jesus began to do and teach, 2 until the day when He was taken up *to heaven*, after He had by the Holy Spirit given orders to the apostles whom He had chosen, 3 to whom He also presented Himself alive after His suffering by many convincing proofs, appearing to them over forty days and speaking about the things concerning the kingdom of God. 4 And gathering them together, He commanded them not to leave Jerusalem, but to wait for the promise of the Father, "Which," *He said*, "you heard of from Me; 5 for John baptized with water, but you will be baptized with the Holy Spirit not many days from now."

6 So when they had come together, they were asking Him, saying, "Lord, is it at this time You are restoring the kingdom to Israel?" 7 But He said to them, "It is not for you to know times or seasons which the Father has set by His own authority; 8 but you will receive power when the Holy Spirit has come upon you; and you shall be My witnesses both in Jerusalem, and in all Judea and Samaria, and even to THE END OF THE EARTH."

9 And after He had said these things, He was lifted up while they were looking on, and a cloud received Him out of their sight. 10 And as they were gazing intently into the sky while He was going, behold, two men in white clothing stood beside them. 11 They also said, "Men of Galilee, why do you stand looking toward heaven? This Jesus, who has been taken up from you into heaven, will come in just the same way as you have watched Him go into heaven."

12 Then they returned to Jerusalem from the mount called Olivet, which is near Jerusalem, a Sabbath day's journey away. 13 And when they had entered *the city*, they went up to the upper room where they were staying; that is, Peter and John and James and Andrew, Philip and Thomas, Bartholomew and Matthew, James *the son* of Alphaeus, and Simon the Zealot, and Judas *the son* of James. 14 These all with one accord were continually devoting themselves to prayer, along with *the* women, and Mary the mother of Jesus, and His brothers.

15 And in those days, Peter stood up in the midst of the brothers (a crowd of about 120 persons was there together), and said, 16 "Men, brothers, the Scripture had to be fulfilled, which the Holy Spirit foretold by the mouth of David concerning Judas, who became a guide to those who arrested Jesus. 17 For he was counted among us and received his share in this ministry." 18 (Now this man acquired a field with the price of his unrighteousness, and falling headlong, he burst open in the middle and all his intestines gushed out. 19 And it became known to all who were living in Jerusalem; so that in their own language that field was called Hakeldama, that is, Field of Blood.) 20 "For it is written in the book of Psalms,

'LET HIS RESIDENCE BE MADE DESOLATE,
AND LET NO ONE DWELL IN IT';

and,

'LET ANOTHER MAN TAKE HIS OFFICE.'

21 "Therefore it is necessary that of the men who have accompanied us all the time that the Lord Jesus went in and out among us— 22 beginning with the baptism of John until the day that He was taken up from us—one of these *must* become a witness with us of His resurrection." 23 And they put forward two men, Joseph called Barsabbas (who was also called Justus), and Matthias. 24 And they prayed and said, "You, Lord, who know the hearts of all men, show which one of these two You have chosen 25 to take the place of this ministry and apostleship from which Judas turned aside to go to his own place." 26 And they cast lots for them, and the lot fell to Matthias; and he was added to the eleven apostles.

JUNE 16

2 Kings 19:1–21:26

19 Now it happened that when King Hezekiah heard *it*, he tore his clothes, covered himself with sackcloth, and entered the house of Yahweh. 2 Then he sent Eliakim who *was* over the household with Shebna the scribe and the elders of the priests, covered with sackcloth, to Isaiah the prophet the son of Amoz. 3 And they said to him, "Thus says Hezekiah, 'This day is a day of distress, reproof, and rejection; for children have come to the point of breaking forth, but

there is no strength to give birth. 4 Perhaps
Yahweh your God will hear all the words of
Rabshakeh, whom his master the king of
Assyria has sent to reproach the living God,
and will reprove the words which Yahweh
your God has heard. Therefore, lift up a
prayer for the remnant that is left.'" 5 So the
servants of King Hezekiah came to Isaiah.
6 And Isaiah said to them, "Thus you shall
say to your master, 'Thus says Yahweh, "Do
not be afraid because of the words that you
have heard, with which the young men of
the king of Assyria have blasphemed Me.
7 Behold, I will put a spirit in him so that
he will hear a report and return to his own
land. And I will make him fall by the sword
in his own land."'"

8 Then Rabshakeh returned and found
the king of Assyria fighting against Libnah,
for he had heard that the king had set out
from Lachish. 9 Then he heard *them* say con-
cerning Tirhakah king of Ethiopia, "Behold,
he has come out to fight against you." So he
sent messengers again to Hezekiah saying,
10 "Thus you shall say to Hezekiah king of
Judah, 'Do not let your God in whom you
trust deceive you, saying, "Jerusalem will
not be given into the hand of the king of
Assyria." 11 Behold, you have heard what the
kings of Assyria have done to all the lands,
devoting them to destruction. So will you be
delivered? 12 Did the gods of those nations
which my fathers brought to ruin deliver
them, *even* Gozan and Haran and Rezeph
and the sons of Eden who *were* in Telassar?
13 Where is the king of Hamath, the king of
Arpad, the king of the city of Sepharvaim,
and *of* Hena and Ivvah?'"

14 Then Hezekiah took the letter from the
hand of the messengers and read it, and he
went up to the house of Yahweh and spread
it out before Yahweh. 15 And Hezekiah
prayed before Yahweh and said, "O Yahweh,
the God of Israel, who is enthroned *above*
the cherubim, You are the God, You alone,
of all the kingdoms of the earth. You have
made heaven and earth. 16 Incline Your
ear, O Yahweh, and hear; open Your eyes,
O Yahweh, and see; and listen to the words
of Sennacherib, who sent them to reproach
the living God. 17 Truly, O Yahweh, the kings
of Assyria have laid waste the nations and
their lands 18 and have put their gods into
the fire, for they were not gods but the work
of men's hands, wood and stone. So they
have destroyed them. 19 But now, O Yahweh
our God, I pray, save us from his hand that
all the kingdoms of the earth may know that
You alone, O Yahweh, are God."

20 Then Isaiah the son of Amoz sent *word*
to Hezekiah saying, "Thus says Yahweh, the
God of Israel, 'Because you have prayed to
Me about Sennacherib king of Assyria, I
have heard *you*.' 21 This is the word that
Yahweh has spoken against him:

'She has despised you and mocked you,
The virgin daughter of Zion;
She has shaken *her* head behind you,
The daughter of Jerusalem!
22 'Whom have you reproached
and blasphemed?
And against whom have you
heightened *your* voice,
And haughtily lifted up your eyes?
Against the Holy One of Israel!
23 'Through your messengers you
have reproached the Lord,
And you have said, "With
my many chariots
I came up to the heights
of the mountains,
To the remotest parts of Lebanon;
And I cut down its tall cedars
and its choice cypresses.
And I entered its farthest lodging
place, its thickest forest.
24 "I dug *wells* and drank foreign waters,
And with the sole of my feet I dried up
All the rivers of Egypt."

25 'Have you not heard?
Long ago I did it;
From days of old I formed it.
Now I have brought it to pass,
That you should devastate fortified
cities into ruinous heaps.
26 'So their inhabitants were
short of power,
They were dismayed and put to shame;
They were as the plant of the
field and as the green herb,
As grass on the rooftops is
scorched before it rises.
27 'But I know your sitting down,
And your going out and
your coming in,
And your raging against Me.
28 'Because of your raging against Me,
And because your presumptuousness
has come up to My ears,

Therefore I will put My
hook in your nose,
And My bridle in your lips,
And I will turn you back by the
way which you came.

29 'Then this shall be the sign for you: you will eat this year what grows of its own accord, in the second year what springs from the same, and in the third year sow, reap, plant vineyards, and eat their fruit. 30 And the surviving remnant of the house of Judah will again take root downward and bear fruit upward. 31 For out of Jerusalem will go forth a remnant, and out of Mount Zion survivors. The zeal of Yahweh will do this.

32 'Therefore thus says Yahweh concerning the king of Assyria, "He will not come to this city or shoot an arrow there; and he will not come before it with a shield or throw up a siege ramp against it. 33 By the way that he came, by the same he will return, and he shall not come to this city,"' declares Yahweh. 34 'Indeed I will defend this city to save it for My own sake and for My servant David's sake.'"

35 Now it happened that night, that the angel of Yahweh went out and struck 185,000 in the camp of the Assyrians. And the men arose early in the morning, and behold, all of them were dead bodies. 36 So Sennacherib king of Assyria set out and went away and returned *home* and lived at Nineveh. 37 Now it happened that as he was worshiping in the house of Nisroch his god, Adrammelech and Sharezer struck him down with the sword; and they escaped into the land of Ararat. And Esarhaddon his son became king in his place.

20 In those days Hezekiah became ill to the point of death. And Isaiah the prophet the son of Amoz came to him and said to him, "Thus says Yahweh, 'Set your house in order, for you shall die and not live.'" 2 Then he turned his face to the wall and prayed to Yahweh, saying, 3 "Remember now, *O Yahweh, I beseech You,* how I have walked before You in truth and with a whole heart and have done what is good in Your sight." And Hezekiah wept greatly. 4 Now it happened that Isaiah had not gone out of the middle court, and the word of Yahweh came to him, saying, 5 "Return and say to Hezekiah the ruler of My people, 'Thus says Yahweh, the God of your father David, "I have heard your prayer, I have seen your tears; behold, I will heal you. On the third day you shall go up to the house of Yahweh. 6 And I will add fifteen years to your life, and I will deliver you and this city from the hand of the king of Assyria; and I will defend this city for My own sake and for My servant David's sake."'" 7 Then Isaiah said, "Take a cake of figs." And they took and laid *it* on the boil, and he was restored to life.

8 Now Hezekiah said to Isaiah, "What will be the sign that Yahweh will heal me, and that I shall go up to the house of Yahweh the third day?" 9 And Isaiah said, "This shall be the sign to you from Yahweh, that Yahweh will do the thing that He has spoken: shall the shadow go forward ten steps or turn back ten steps?" 10 So Hezekiah answered, "It is easy for the shadow to stretch forward ten steps; no, but let the shadow turn backward ten steps." 11 Isaiah the prophet cried to Yahweh, and He turned the shadow on the stairway back ten steps by which it had gone down on the stairway of Ahaz.

12 At that time Berodach-baladan a son of Baladan, king of Babylon, sent letters and a present to Hezekiah, for he heard that Hezekiah had been sick. 13 And Hezekiah listened to them, and showed them all his treasure house, the silver and the gold and the spices and the good oil and the house of his armor and all that was found in his treasuries. There was nothing in his house nor in all his dominion that Hezekiah did not show them. 14 Then Isaiah the prophet came to King Hezekiah and said to him, "What did these men say, and from where have they come to you?" And Hezekiah said, "They have come from a far country, from Babylon." 15 And he said, "What have they seen in your house?" So Hezekiah said, "They have seen all that is in my house; there is nothing among my treasuries that I have not shown them."

16 Then Isaiah said to Hezekiah, "Hear the word of Yahweh. 17 'Behold, the days are coming when all that is in your house, and all that your fathers have treasured up to this day will be carried to Babylon; nothing shall be left,' says Yahweh. 18 'And some of your sons who will issue from you, whom you will beget, will be taken away; and they will become officials in the palace of the king of Babylon.'" 19 Then Hezekiah said to Isaiah, "The word of Yahweh which you

have spoken is good." For he said, "Will it
not be *good*, if there will be peace and truth
in my days?"

20 Now the rest of the acts of Hezekiah
and all his might, and how he made the pool
and the conduit and brought water into
the city, are they not written in the Book
of the Chronicles of the Kings of Judah?
21 So Hezekiah slept with his fathers, and
Manasseh his son became king in his place.

21

Manasseh was twelve years old when
he became king, and he reigned fifty-
five years in Jerusalem; and his mother's
name was Hephzibah. 2 And he did what
was evil in the sight of Yahweh, according
to the abominations of the nations whom
Yahweh dispossessed before the sons of
Israel. 3 Indeed, he rebuilt the high places
which Hezekiah his father had destroyed;
and he erected altars for Baal and made an
Asherah, as Ahab king of Israel had done,
and worshiped all the host of heaven and
served them. 4 And he built altars in the
house of Yahweh, of which Yahweh had
said, "In Jerusalem I will put My name."
5 Indeed, he built altars for all the host
of heaven in the two courts of the house
of Yahweh. 6 He even made his son pass
through the fire, practiced soothsaying and
interpreted omens, and dealt with mediums
and spiritists. He did much that was evil in
the sight of Yahweh provoking *Him to anger*.
7 Then he put the graven image of Asherah,
which he had made, in the house of which
Yahweh had said to David and to Solomon
his son, "In this house and in Jerusalem,
which I have chosen from all the tribes of
Israel, I will put My name forever. 8 And I will
not make the foot of Israel wander anymore
from the land which I gave their fathers, if
only they will be careful to do according
to all that I have commanded them, and
according to all the law that My servant
Moses commanded them." 9 But they did
not listen, and Manasseh led them astray
in order to do more evil than the nations
whom Yahweh destroyed before the sons
of Israel.

10 Then Yahweh spoke by the hand of
His slaves the prophets, saying, 11 "Because
Manasseh king of Judah has done these
abominations—he has done evil more than
all the Amorites did who *were* before him—
and has also made Judah sin with his idols,
12 therefore thus says Yahweh, the God of
Israel, 'Behold, I am bringing *such* calamity
on Jerusalem and Judah, that whoever hears
of it, both his ears will tingle. 13 And I will
stretch over Jerusalem the line of Samaria
and the level of the house of Ahab, and I
will wipe Jerusalem as one wipes a dish—he
wipes it and turns it upside down. 14 And I
will abandon the remnant of My inheritance
and give them into the hand of their enemies,
and they will become as plunder and spoil
to all their enemies; 15 because they have
done what is evil in My sight, and have been
provoking Me to anger since the day their
fathers came out of Egypt, even to this day.'"

16 Moreover, Manasseh shed very much
innocent blood until he had filled Jerusalem
from one end to another; besides his sin
with which he made Judah sin, in doing
what is evil in the sight of Yahweh. 17 Now
the rest of the acts of Manasseh and all that
he did and his sin which he sinned, are they
not written in the Book of the Chronicles
of the Kings of Judah? 18 And Manasseh
slept with his fathers and was buried in the
garden of his own house, in the garden of
Uzza. And Amon his son became king in
his place.

19 Amon was twenty-two years old when
he became king, and he reigned two years
in Jerusalem; and his mother's name was
Meshullemeth the daughter of Haruz of
Jotbah. 20 And he did what was evil in the
sight of Yahweh, as Manasseh his father had
done. 21 And he walked in all the way that
his father had walked and served the idols
that his father had served and worshiped
them. 22 So he forsook Yahweh, the God
of his fathers, and did not walk in the way
of Yahweh. 23 Then the servants of Amon
conspired against him and put the king to
death in his own house. 24 Then the people
of the land struck down all those who had
conspired against King Amon, and the
people of the land made Josiah his son king
in his place. 25 Now the rest of the acts of
Amon which he did, are they not written
in the Book of the Chronicles of the Kings
of Judah? 26 And he was buried in his grave
in the garden of Uzza, and Josiah his son
became king in his place.

Psalm 74:9–17

9 We do not see our signs;
There is no longer any prophet,

Nor is there any among us
who knows how long.
10 How long, O God, will the
adversary reproach?
Will the enemy spurn Your
name forever?
11 Why do You turn back Your hand,
even Your right hand?
From within Your bosom,
destroy *them*!

12 Yet God is my King from of old,
Who works deeds of salvation
in the midst of the earth.
13 You divided the sea by Your strength;
You broke the heads of the sea
monsters in the waters.
14 You crushed the heads of Leviathan;
You gave him as food for the
creatures of the desert.
15 You split open spring and river;
You dried up ever-flowing rivers.
16 Yours is the day, Yours also is
the night;
You have established the
light and the sun.
17 You have caused all the boundaries
of the earth to stand firm;
You have formed summer and winter.

Proverbs 19:1–2

19 Better is a poor man who
walks in his integrity
Than he who is crooked in
lips and is a fool.
2 Also it is not good for a person
to be without knowledge,
And he who hurries his footsteps sins.

Acts 2:1–21

2 And when the day of Pentecost had
fully come, they were all together in
one place. 2 And suddenly there came from
heaven a noise like a violent rushing wind,
and it filled the whole house where they
were sitting. 3 And there appeared to them
tongues like fire distributing themselves,
and they rested on each one of them. 4 And
they were all filled with the Holy Spirit and
began to speak with other tongues, as the
Spirit was giving them utterance.
5 Now there were Jews living in Jerusa-
lem, devout men from every nation under
heaven. 6 And when this sound occurred,
the multitude came together, and were
bewildered because each one of them was
hearing them speak in his own language.
7 So they were astounded and marveling,
saying, "Behold, are not all these who are
speaking Galileans? 8 And how is it that
we each hear *them* in our own language
in which we were born? 9 Parthians and
Medes and Elamites, and residents of Mes-
opotamia, Judea and Cappadocia, Pontus
and Asia, 10 Phrygia and Pamphylia, Egypt
and the district of Libya around Cyrene, and
visitors from Rome, both Jews and prose-
lytes, 11 Cretans and Arabs—we hear them
in our *own* tongues speaking of the mighty
deeds of God." 12 And they all continued in
astonishment and great perplexity, saying to
one another, "What does this mean?" 13 But
others, mocking, were saying, "They are full
of new wine."
14 But Peter, taking his stand with the
eleven, raised his voice and declared to
them: "Men of Judea and all you who live
in Jerusalem, let this be known to you and
give heed to my words. 15 For these men
are not drunk, as you suppose, for it is the
third hour of the day; 16 but this is what was
spoken through the prophet Joel:
17 'And it shall be in the last
days,' God says,
'That I will pour out My
Spirit on all mankind;
And your sons and your
daughters shall prophesy,
And your young men
shall see visions,
And your old men shall
dream dreams;
18 Even on My male slaves
and female slaves,
I will in those days pour
out My Spirit
And they shall prophesy.
19 'And I will put wonders
in the sky above
And signs on the earth below,
Blood, and fire, and vapor
of smoke.
20 'The sun will be turned
into darkness
And the moon into blood,
Before the great and awesome
day of the Lord comes.
21 'And it will be that everyone
who calls on the name of
the Lord will be saved.'

JUNE 17

2 Kings 22:1–24:20

22 Josiah was eight years old when he became king, and he reigned thirty-one years in Jerusalem; and his mother's name was Jedidah the daughter of Adaiah of Bozkath. 2 And he did what was right in the sight of Yahweh and walked in all the way of his father David and did not turn aside to the right or to the left.

3 Now it happened in the eighteenth year of King Josiah, that the king sent Shaphan, the son of Azaliah the son of Meshullam the scribe, to the house of Yahweh saying, 4 "Go up to Hilkiah the high priest that he may count the money brought into the house of Yahweh which the doorkeepers have gathered from the people. 5 And let them give it into the hand of those who do the work, who have the oversight of the house of Yahweh, and let them give it to those who do the work, who are in the house of Yahweh, to repair the damages of the house, 6 to the craftsmen and the builders and the masons and for buying timber and hewn stone to repair the house. 7 Only no accounting shall be made with them for the money given into their hands, for they deal faithfully."

8 Then Hilkiah the high priest said to Shaphan the scribe, "I have found the book of the law in the house of Yahweh." And Hilkiah gave the book to Shaphan and he read it. 9 Then Shaphan the scribe came to the king and responded to the king with a word and said, "Your servants have poured out the money that was found in the house and have given it into the hand of those who do the work, who have the oversight of the house of Yahweh." 10 Moreover, Shaphan the scribe told the king saying, "Hilkiah the priest has given me a book." And Shaphan read it in the presence of the king.

11 Now it happened that when the king heard the words of the book of the law, he tore his clothes. 12 Then the king commanded Hilkiah the priest, Ahikam the son of Shaphan, Achbor the son of Micaiah, Shaphan the scribe, and Asaiah the king's servant, saying, 13 "Go, inquire of Yahweh for me and the people and all Judah, concerning the words of this book that has been found, for great is the wrath of Yahweh which is set aflame against us, because our fathers have not listened to the words of this book, to do according to all that is written concerning us."

14 So Hilkiah the priest, Ahikam, Achbor, Shaphan, and Asaiah went to Huldah the prophetess, the wife of Shallum the son of Tikvah, the son of Harhas, keeper of the wardrobe (now she lived in Jerusalem in the Second Quarter); and they spoke to her. 15 And she said to them, "Thus says Yahweh, the God of Israel, 'Say to the man who sent you to me, 16 thus says Yahweh, "Behold, I am bringing evil on this place and on its inhabitants, *even* all the words of the book which the king of Judah has read. 17 Because they have forsaken Me and have burned incense to other gods that they might provoke Me to anger with all the work of their hands, therefore My wrath is set aflame against this place, and it shall not be quenched."' 18 But to the king of Judah who sent you to inquire of Yahweh thus you shall say to him, 'Thus says Yahweh, the God of Israel, "*Regarding* the words which you have heard, 19 because your heart was soft and you humbled yourself before Yahweh when you heard what I spoke against this place and against its inhabitants that they should become an object of horror, and a curse, and you have torn your clothes and wept before Me, I truly have heard you," declares Yahweh. 20 "Therefore, behold, I will gather you to your fathers, and you will be gathered to your grave in peace, so your eyes will not see all the evil which I will bring on this place."'" So they brought back word to the king.

23 Then the king sent, and they gathered to him all the elders of Judah and Jerusalem. 2 And the king went up to the house of Yahweh and all the men of Judah and all the inhabitants of Jerusalem with him, and the priests and the prophets and all the people, both small and great; and he read in their hearing all the words of the book of the covenant which was found in the house of Yahweh. 3 Then the king stood by the pillar and cut a covenant before Yahweh, to walk after Yahweh, and to keep His commandments and His testimonies and

His statutes with all *his* heart and all *his*
soul, to establish the words of this covenant
that were written in this book. And all the
people entered into the covenant.
4 Then the king commanded Hilkiah the
high priest and the priests of the second
order and the doorkeepers, to bring out
of the temple of Yahweh all the vessels
that were made for Baal, for Asherah, and
for all the host of heaven; and he burned
them outside Jerusalem in the fields of the
Kidron, and carried their ashes to Bethel.
5 And he did away with the idolatrous priests
whom the kings of Judah had appointed and
who burn incense in the high places in the
cities of Judah and in the surrounding area
of Jerusalem, as well as those who burned
incense to Baal, to the sun and to the moon
and to the constellations and to all the host
of heaven. 6 And he brought out the Asherah
from the house of Yahweh outside Jerusalem
to the brook Kidron, and burned it at the
brook Kidron, and ground *it* to dust, and
threw its dust on the graves of the common
people. 7 He also tore down the houses of
the *male* cult prostitutes which *were* in the
house of Yahweh, where the women were
weaving hangings for the Asherah. 8 Then
he brought all the priests from the cities of
Judah and defiled the high places where the
priests had burned incense, from Geba to
Beersheba; and he tore down the high places
of the gates which *were* at the entrance of
the gate of Joshua the ruler of the city, which
were on one's left at the city gate. 9 Never-
theless the priests of the high places did not
go up to the altar of Yahweh in Jerusalem,
but they ate unleavened bread among their
brothers. 10 He also defiled Topheth, which
is in the valley of the son of Hinnom, that
no man might make his son or his daughter
pass through the fire for Molech. 11 And he
did away with the horses which the kings of
Judah had given to the sun, at the entrance
of the house of Yahweh, by the chamber of
Nathan-melech the official, which *was* in
the precincts; and he burned the chariots
of the sun with fire. 12 Also, the altars which
were on the roof, the upper chamber of
Ahaz, which the kings of Judah had made,
and the altars which Manasseh had made
in the two courts of the house of Yahweh,
the king tore down; and he crushed them
there and threw their dust into the brook
Kidron. 13 And the high places which *were*
before Jerusalem, which *were* on the right
of the mount of destruction which Solomon
the king of Israel had built for Ashtoreth the
detestable idol of the Sidonians, and for
Chemosh the detestable idol of Moab, and
for Milcom the abomination of the sons of
Ammon, the king defiled. 14 And he broke in
pieces the *sacred* pillars and cut down the
Asherim and filled their places with human
bones.

15 Furthermore, the altar that *was* at Bethel
and the high place which Jeroboam the son of
Nebat, who made Israel sin, had made, even
that altar and the high place he tore down.
Then he demolished its stones, ground them
to dust, and burned the Asherah. 16 Then
Josiah turned, and he saw the graves that
were there on the mountain, and he sent and
took the bones from the graves and burned
them on the altar and defiled it according to
the word of Yahweh which the man of God
proclaimed, who proclaimed these things.
17 Then he said, "What is this monument that
I see?" And the men of the city told him, "It is
the grave of the man of God who came from
Judah and proclaimed these things which
you have done against the altar of Bethel."
18 And he said, "Let him alone; let no one
move his bones." So they left his bones
undisturbed with the bones of the prophet
who came from Samaria. 19 And also all the
houses of the high places which *were* in the
cities of Samaria, which the kings of Israel
had made provoking Yahweh to anger, Josiah
removed; and he did to them just as he had
done in Bethel. 20 And all the priests of the
high places who *were* there he slaughtered
on the altars and burned human bones on
them. Then he returned to Jerusalem.

21 Then the king commanded all the
people saying, "Celebrate the Passover to
Yahweh your God as it is written in this book
of the covenant." 22 For such a Passover
had not been celebrated from the days of
the judges who judged Israel, nor in all the
days of the kings of Israel and of the kings
of Judah. 23 But in the eighteenth year of
King Josiah, this Passover was celebrated
to Yahweh in Jerusalem.

24 Moreover, the mediums and the spir-
itists and the teraphim and the idols and
all the detestable things that were seen in
the land of Judah and in Jerusalem, Josiah
purged in order that he might establish the
words of the law which were written in the

book that Hilkiah the priest found in the house of Yahweh. 25 And before him there was no king like him who turned to Yahweh with all his heart and with all his soul and with all his might, according to all the law of Moses; nor did any like him arise after him.

26 However, Yahweh did not turn from His great burning anger, His anger which burned against Judah, because of all the provocations with which Manasseh had provoked Him to anger. 27 And Yahweh said, "I will remove Judah also from My presence, as I have removed Israel. And I will reject Jerusalem, this city which I have chosen, and the house of which I said, 'My name shall be there.'"

28 Now the rest of the acts of Josiah and all that he did, are they not written in the Book of the Chronicles of the Kings of Judah? 29 In his days Pharaoh Neco king of Egypt went up to the king of Assyria to the river Euphrates. And King Josiah went to meet him, and when *Pharaoh Neco* saw him he put him to death at Megiddo. 30 And his servants drove his body in a chariot from Megiddo and brought him to Jerusalem and buried him in his own tomb. Then the people of the land took Jehoahaz the son of Josiah and anointed him and made him king in place of his father.

31 Jehoahaz was twenty-three years old when he became king, and he reigned three months in Jerusalem; and his mother's name was Hamutal the daughter of Jeremiah of Libnah. 32 And he did what was evil in the sight of Yahweh, according to all that his fathers had done. 33 And Pharaoh Neco imprisoned him at Riblah in the land of Hamath, that he might not reign in Jerusalem; and he imposed on the land a fine of one hundred talents of silver and one talent of gold.

34 Then Pharaoh Neco made Eliakim the son of Josiah king in the place of Josiah his father and changed his name to Jehoiakim. But he took Jehoahaz and brought *him* to Egypt, and he died there. 35 So Jehoiakim gave the silver and gold to Pharaoh, but he taxed the land in order to give the money at the command of Pharaoh. He exacted the silver and gold from the people of the land, each according to his valuation, to give it to Pharaoh Neco.

36 Jehoiakim was twenty-five years old when he became king, and he reigned eleven years in Jerusalem; and his mother's name was Zebidah the daughter of Pedaiah of Rumah. 37 And he did what was evil in the sight of Yahweh, according to all that his fathers had done.

24 In his days Nebuchadnezzar king of Babylon came up, and Jehoiakim became his servant *for* three years; then he turned and rebelled against him. 2 And Yahweh sent against him marauding bands of Chaldeans, marauding bands of Arameans, marauding bands of Moabites, and marauding bands of Ammonites. So He sent them against Judah to destroy it, according to the word of Yahweh which He had spoken by the hand of His slaves the prophets. 3 Surely at the command of Yahweh it came upon Judah, to remove *them* from His presence because of the sins of Manasseh, according to all that he had done, 4 and also for the innocent blood which he shed, for he filled Jerusalem with innocent blood; and Yahweh was not willing to pardon. 5 Now the rest of the acts of Jehoiakim and all that he did, are they not written in the Book of the Chronicles of the Kings of Judah?

6 So Jehoiakim slept with his fathers, and Jehoiachin his son became king in his place. 7 And the king of Egypt did not go out of his land again, for the king of Babylon had taken all that belonged to the king of Egypt from the brook of Egypt to the river Euphrates.

8 Jehoiachin was eighteen years old when he became king, and he reigned three months in Jerusalem; and his mother's name was Nehushta the daughter of Elnathan of Jerusalem. 9 And he did what was evil in the sight of Yahweh, according to all that his father had done.

10 At that time the servants of Nebuchadnezzar king of Babylon went up to Jerusalem, and the city came under siege. 11 And Nebuchadnezzar the king of Babylon came to the city, while his servants were besieging it. 12 Then Jehoiachin the king of Judah went out to the king of Babylon, he and his mother and his servants and his commanders and his officials. So the king of Babylon took him captive in the eighth year of his reign. 13 And he brought out from there all the treasures of the house of Yahweh, and the treasures of the king's house, and cut in pieces all the vessels of

gold which Solomon king of Israel had made
in the temple of Yahweh, just as Yahweh had
spoken. 14 Then he took away into exile all
Jerusalem and all the commanders and all
the mighty men of valor, 10,000 captives,
and all the craftsmen and the smiths. None
was left except the poorest people of the
land.
15 So he took Jehoiachin away into exile
to Babylon; also the king's mother and the
king's wives and his officials and the leading
men of the land, he led away into exile from
Jerusalem to Babylon. 16 Now all the valiant
men, seven thousand, and the craftsmen
and the smiths, one thousand, all mighty
men who could wage war, and these the king
of Babylon brought into exile to Babylon.
17 Then the king of Babylon made his
uncle Mattaniah king in his place and
changed his name to Zedekiah.
18 Zedekiah was twenty-one years old
when he became king, and he reigned
eleven years in Jerusalem; and his mother's
name was Hamutal the daughter of Jeremiah
of Libnah. 19 And he did what was evil in
the sight of Yahweh, according to all that
Jehoiakim had done. 20 For through the
anger of Yahweh *this* came about in Jerusa-
lem and Judah until He cast them out from
His presence. And Zedekiah rebelled against
the king of Babylon.

Psalm 74:18–23

18 Remember this, O Yahweh, that
the enemy has reproached,
And a wickedly foolish people
has spurned Your name.
19 Do not deliver the soul of Your
turtledove to the wild beast;
Do not forget the life of Your
afflicted forever.
20 Look to the covenant;
For the dark places of the land are
full of the haunts of violence.
21 Let not the oppressed
return dishonored;
Let the afflicted and needy
praise Your name.

22 Arise, O God, *and* plead
Your own cause;
Remember how the wicked fool
reproaches You all day long.
23 Do not forget the voice of
Your adversaries,
The rumbling of those who rise against
You which ascends continually.

Proverbs 19:3

3 The folly of man subverts his way,
But his heart rages against Yahweh.

Acts 2:22–47

22 "Men of Israel, listen to these words:
Jesus the Nazarene, a man attested to you
by God with miracles and wonders and signs
which God did through Him in your midst,
just as you yourselves know— 23 this *Man*,
delivered over by the predetermined plan
and foreknowledge of God, you nailed to
a cross by the hands of lawless men and
put *Him* to death. 24 But God raised Him up
again, putting an end to the agony of death,
since it was impossible for Him to be held in
its power. 25 For David says of Him,
'I SAW THE LORD CONTINUALLY
BEFORE ME;
BECAUSE HE IS AT MY RIGHT HAND,
SO THAT I WILL NOT BE SHAKEN.
26 'THEREFORE MY HEART WAS GLAD
AND MY TONGUE EXULTED;
MOREOVER MY FLESH ALSO
WILL LIVE IN HOPE;
27 BECAUSE YOU WILL NOT FORSAKE
MY SOUL TO HADES,
NOR GIVE YOUR HOLY ONE OVER
TO SEE CORRUPTION.
28 'YOU HAVE MADE KNOWN TO
ME THE WAYS OF LIFE;
YOU WILL MAKE ME FULL OF GLADNESS
WITH YOUR PRESENCE.'
29 "Men, brothers, I may confidently say
to you regarding the patriarch David that he
both died and was buried, and his tomb is
with us to this day. 30 And so, because he was
a prophet and knew that GOD HAD SWORN TO
HIM WITH AN OATH TO SET *one* OF THE FRUIT OF
HIS BODY ON HIS THRONE, 31 he looked ahead
and spoke of the resurrection of the Christ,
that HE WAS NEITHER FORSAKEN TO HADES,
NOR DID His flesh SEE CORRUPTION. 32 This
Jesus God raised up again, to which we
are all witnesses. 33 Therefore having been
exalted to the right hand of God, and having
received from the Father the promise of the
Holy Spirit, He has poured out this which
you both see and hear. 34 For David did not
ascend into the heavens, but he himself says:
'THE LORD SAID TO MY LORD,
"SIT AT MY RIGHT HAND,

35 UNTIL I PUT YOUR ENEMIES AS A
FOOTSTOOL FOR YOUR FEET."'
36 "Therefore let all the house of Israel
know for certain that God has made Him
both Lord and Christ—this Jesus whom you
crucified."
37 Now when they heard *this*, they were
pierced to the heart, and said to Peter and
the rest of the apostles, "Men, brothers,
what should we do?" 38 And Peter *said*
to them, "Repent, and each of you be
baptized in the name of Jesus Christ for
the forgiveness of your sins; and you will
receive the gift of the Holy Spirit. 39 For the
promise is for you and your children and
for all who are far off, as many as the Lord
our God will call to Himself." 40 And with
many other words he solemnly bore wit-
ness and kept on exhorting them, saying,
"Be saved from this crooked generation!"
41 So then, those who had received his
word were baptized; and that day there
were added about three thousand souls.
42 And they were continually devoting
themselves to the apostles' teaching and
to the fellowship, to the breaking of bread
and to the prayers.
43 And fear came upon every soul; and
many wonders and signs were taking place
through the apostles. 44 And all those
who had believed were together and had
all things in common; 45 and they *began*
selling their property and possessions and
were dividing them up with all, as anyone
might have need. 46 And daily devoting
themselves with one accord in the temple
and breaking bread from house to house,
they were taking their meals together with
gladness and sincerity of heart, 47 praising
God and having favor with all the people.
And the Lord was adding to their number
daily those who were being saved.

Therefore Faithful Christian, Seek the truth, listen to the truth, learn the truth, love the truth, defend the truth even to death.

— JAN HUS

JUNE 18

2 Kings 25:1–30

25 Now in the ninth year of his reign,
on the tenth day of the tenth month,
Nebuchadnezzar king of Babylon came, he
and all his military force, against Jerusa-
lem, and he camped against it and built a
siege wall all around it. 2 So the city came
under siege until the eleventh year of King
Zedekiah. 3 On the ninth day of the *fourth*
month the famine was so strong in the city
that there was no food for the people of the
land. 4 Then the city was broken into, and
all the men of war *fled* by night by way of
the gate between the two walls beside the
king's garden, though the Chaldeans were
all around the city. And they went by way
of the Arabah. 5 But the military force of the
Chaldeans pursued the king and overtook
him in the plains of Jericho and all his mil-
itary force was scattered from him. 6 Then
they seized the king and brought him up
to the king of Babylon at Riblah, and they
spoke *their* judgment on him. 7 And they
slaughtered the sons of Zedekiah before his
eyes; then he blinded the eyes of Zedekiah
and bound him with bronze fetters and
brought him to Babylon.
8 Now on the seventh day of the fifth
month, which was the nineteenth year of
King Nebuchadnezzar, king of Babylon,
Nebuzaradan the captain of the guard, a
servant of the king of Babylon, came to
Jerusalem. 9 And he burned the house of
Yahweh, the king's house, and all the houses
of Jerusalem; even every great house he
burned with fire. 10 So all the military force
of the Chaldeans who *were with* the captain
of the guard tore down the walls around
Jerusalem. 11 Then the rest of the people
who were left in the city and the defectors
who had defected to the king of Babylon and
the rest of the multitude, Nebuzaradan the
captain of the guard took away into exile.
12 But the captain of the guard left some of
the poorest of the land to be vinedressers
and plowmen.

13 Now the bronze pillars which were in the house of Yahweh, and the stands and the bronze sea which were in the house of Yahweh, the Chaldeans shattered and carried the bronze to Babylon. 14 They also took away the pots, the shovels, the snuffers, the spoons, and all the bronze vessels which were used to minister. 15 The captain of the guard also took away the firepans and the bowls, what was fine gold and what was fine silver. 16 The two pillars, the one sea, and the stands which Solomon had made for the house of Yahweh—the bronze of all these vessels was beyond weight. 17 The height of the one pillar was eighteen cubits, and a bronze capital was on it; the height of the capital was three cubits, with a network and pomegranates on the capital all around, all of bronze. And the second pillar was like these with network.

18 Then the captain of the guard took Seraiah the chief priest and Zephaniah the second priest, with the three doorkeepers of the temple. 19 And from the city he took one official who was overseer of the men of war, and five of the king's advisers who were found in the city; and the scribe of the commander of the army who mustered the people of the land; and sixty men of the people of the land who were found in the city. 20 And Nebuzaradan the captain of the guard took them and led them to the king of Babylon at Riblah. 21 Then the king of Babylon struck them down and put them to death at Riblah in the land of Hamath. So Judah went into exile from its land.

22 Now *as for* the people who were left in the land of Judah, whom Nebuchadnezzar king of Babylon had left, he appointed Gedaliah the son of Ahikam, the son of Shaphan over them. 23 Then all the commanders of the military forces, they and *their* men, heard that the king of Babylon had appointed Gedaliah *governor*. So they came to Gedaliah to Mizpah, namely, Ishmael the son of Nethaniah, and Johanan the son of Kareah, and Seraiah the son of Tanhumeth the Netophathite, and Jaazaniah the son of the Maacathite, they and their men. 24 Then Gedaliah swore to them and their men and said to them, "Do not be afraid of the servants of the Chaldeans; live in the land and serve the king of Babylon, and it will be well with you."

25 But it happened in the seventh month, that Ishmael the son of Nethaniah, the son of Elishama, of the royal seed, came with ten men and struck Gedaliah down so that he died, along with the Jews and the Chaldeans who were with him at Mizpah. 26 Then all the people, both small and great, and the commanders of the military forces arose and went to Egypt; for they were afraid of the Chaldeans.

27 Now it happened in the thirty-seventh year of the exile of Jehoiachin king of Judah, in the twelfth month, on the twenty-seventh *day* of the month, that Evil-merodach king of Babylon, in the year that he became king, lifted up the head of Jehoiachin king of Judah from prison; 28 and he spoke to him good *words*, and he set his throne above the throne of the kings who *were* with him in Babylon. 29 So Jehoiachin changed his prison clothes and had his meals in the king's presence continually all the days of his life; 30 and for his allowance, a continual allowance was given him by the king, a portion for each day, all the days of his life.

Psalm 75:1–10

1 We give thanks to You, O God,
we give thanks,
For Your name is near;
Men recount Your wondrous deeds.
2 "For I select an appointed time,
It is I who judge with equity.
3 "The earth and all who
dwell in it melt;
It is I who have firmly set
its pillars. Selah.
4 "I said to the boastful, 'Do not boast,'
And to the wicked, 'Do not
raise up the horn;
5 Do not raise up your horn on high,
Nor speak with insolent pride.'"

6 For *one's* rising up does not
come from the east,
nor from the west,
And not from the desert;
7 But God is the Judge;
He puts down one and
raises up another.
8 For a cup is in the hand of Yahweh,
and the wine foams;
It is full of *His* mixture, and
He pours from this;

Surely all the wicked of the earth must
drain *and* drink down its dregs.

9 But as for me, I will declare *it* forever;
I will sing praises to the God of Jacob.
10 And all the horns of the
wicked I will cut off,
But the horns of the righteous
will be raised up.

Proverbs 19:4–5

4 Wealth adds many friends,
But a poor man is separated
from his friend.
5 A false witness will not go unpunished,
And he who breathes out
lies will not escape.

Acts 3:1–26

3 Now Peter and John were going up to
the temple at the ninth *hour*, the hour
of prayer. 2 And a man who had been lame
from his mother's womb was being carried,
whom they used to set down daily at the
gate of the temple which is called Beautiful,
in order to beg alms of those who were
entering the temple. 3 When he saw Peter
and John about to go into the temple, he
began asking to receive alms. 4 But when
Peter, along with John, fixed his gaze on
him, he said, "Look at us!" 5 And he *began to*
give them his attention, expecting to receive
something from them. 6 But Peter said, "I
do not possess silver and gold, but what I
do have I give to you: In the name of Jesus
Christ the Nazarene—walk!" 7 And seizing
him by the right hand, he raised him up; and
immediately his feet and his ankles were
strengthened. 8 And leaping up, he stood
upright and *began to* walk; and he entered
the temple with them, walking and leaping
and praising God. 9 And all the people saw
him walking and praising God; 10 and they
were recognizing him, that he was the one
who used to sit at the Beautiful Gate of the
temple to *beg* alms, and they were filled
with wonder and amazement at what had
happened to him.
11 And while he was clinging to Peter and
John, all the people ran together to them at
the portico called Solomon's, full of wonder.
12 But when Peter saw *this*, he replied to the
people, "Men of Israel, why do you marvel
at this, or why do you gaze at us, as if by our
own power or piety we had made him walk?
13 The God of Abraham, Isaac, and Jacob, the
God of our fathers, has glorified His Servant
Jesus, whom you delivered and denied in the
presence of Pilate, when he had decided to
release Him. 14 But you denied the Holy and
Righteous One and asked for a murderer to
be granted to you, 15 but put to death the
Author of life, whom God raised from the
dead, *a fact* to which we are witnesses.
16 And on the basis of faith in His name, *it*
is the name of Jesus which has strengthened
this man whom you see and know; and the
faith which *is* through Him has given him
this perfect health in the presence of you all.
17 "And now, brothers, I know that you
acted in ignorance, just as your rulers did
also. 18 But the things which God announced
beforehand by the mouth of all the proph-
ets, that His Christ would suffer, He has thus
fulfilled. 19 Therefore repent and return, so
that your sins may be wiped away, in order
that times of refreshing may come from
the presence of the Lord; 20 and that He
may send Jesus, the Christ appointed for
you, 21 whom heaven must receive until
the period of restoration of all things about
which God spoke by the mouth of His holy
prophets from ancient time. 22 Moses said,
'THE LORD GOD WILL RAISE UP FOR YOU A
PROPHET LIKE ME FROM YOUR BROTHERS; TO
HIM YOU SHALL LISTEN to everything He says
to you. 23 AND IT WILL BE THAT EVERY SOUL
THAT DOES NOT HEED THAT PROPHET SHALL
BE UTTERLY DESTROYED FROM AMONG THE
PEOPLE.' 24 And likewise, all the prophets
who have spoken, from Samuel and *his*
successors onward, also proclaimed these
days. 25 It is you who are the sons of the
prophets and of the covenant which God
made with your fathers, saying to Abraham,
'AND IN YOUR SEED ALL THE FAMILIES OF THE
EARTH SHALL BE BLESSED.' 26 For you first, God
raised up His Servant and sent Him to bless
you by turning every one *of you* from your
wicked ways."

JUNE 19

1 Chronicles 1:1–2:55

1 Adam, Seth, Enosh,
2 Kenan, Mahalalel, Jared,
3 Enoch, Methuselah, Lamech,
4 Noah, Shem, Ham, and Japheth.

5 The sons of Japheth *were* Gomer,
Magog, Madai, Javan, Tubal, Meshech,
and Tiras.
6 The sons of Gomer *were* Ashkenaz,
Diphath, and Togarmah.
7 The sons of Javan *were* Elishah,
Tarshish, Kittim, and Rodanim.

8 The sons of Ham *were* Cush, Mizraim,
Put, and Canaan.
9 The sons of Cush *were* Seba, Havilah,
Sabta, Raama, and Sabteca;
and the sons of Raama *were* Sheba and
Dedan.
10 Cush was the father of Nimrod;
he began to be a mighty one on the
earth.

11 Mizraim was the father of the people
of Lud, Anam, Lehab, Naphtuh,
12 Pathrus, Casluh (from which came the
Philistines), and Caphtor.

13 Canaan was the father of Sidon, his
firstborn, Heth,
14 and the Jebusites, the Amorites, the
Girgashites,
15 the Hivites, the Arkites, the Sinites,
16 the Arvadites, the Zemarites, and the
Hamathites.

17 The sons of Shem *were* Elam, Asshur,
Arpachshad, Lud, Aram, Uz, Hul,
Gether, and Meshech.
18 Arpachshad was the father of Shelah,
and Shelah was the father of Eber.
19 Two sons were born to Eber, the
name of the one was Peleg, for in his
days the earth was divided, and his
brother's name was Joktan.
20 Joktan was the father of Almodad,
Sheleph, Hazarmaveth, Jerah,
21 Hadoram, Uzal, Diklah,
22 Ebal, Abimael, Sheba,
23 Ophir, Havilah, and Jobab; all these
were the sons of Joktan.

24 Shem, Arpachshad, Shelah,
25 Eber, Peleg, Reu,
26 Serug, Nahor, Terah,
27 Abram, that is Abraham.
28 The sons of Abraham *were* Isaac and
Ishmael. 29 These are their generations:
the firstborn of Ishmael *was* Nebaioth,
then Kedar, Adbeel, Mibsam,
30 Mishma, Dumah, Massa, Hadad,
Tema,
31 Jetur, Naphish, and Kedemah; these
were the sons of Ishmael.
32 The sons of Keturah, Abraham's
concubine, *whom* she bore, *were*
Zimran, Jokshan, Medan, Midian,
Ishbak, and Shuah.
And the sons of Jokshan *were* Sheba
and Dedan.
33 The sons of Midian were Ephah,
Epher, Hanoch, Abida, and Eldaah. All
these were the sons of Keturah.
34 Abraham became the father of Isaac.
The sons of Isaac *were* Esau
and Israel.
35 The sons of Esau *were* Eliphaz, Reuel,
Jeush, Jalam, and Korah.
36 The sons of Eliphaz *were* Teman,
Omar, Zephi, Gatam, Kenaz, Timna,
and Amalek.
37 The sons of Reuel *were* Nahath, Zerah,
Shammah, and Mizzah.
38 The sons of Seir *were* Lotan, Shobal,
Zibeon, Anah, Dishon, Ezer, and
Dishan.
39 The sons of Lotan *were* Hori and
Homam; and Lotan's sister *was* Timna.
40 The sons of Shobal *were* Alian,
Manahath, Ebal, Shephi, and Onam.
And the sons of Zibeon *were* Aiah and
Anah.
41 The son of Anah *was* Dishon.
And the sons of Dishon *were* Hamran,
Eshban, Ithran, and Cheran.
42 The sons of Ezer *were* Bilhan, Zaavan,
and Jaakan.
The sons of Dishon *were* Uz and Aran.

43 Now these are the kings who reigned
in the land of Edom before *any* king of
the sons of Israel reigned. Bela was the
son of Beor, and the name of his city
was Dinhabah.

44 Then Bela died, and Jobab the son of
Zerah of Bozrah became king in his
place.
45 Then Jobab died, and Husham of the
land of the Temanites became king in
his place.
46 Then Husham died, and Hadad the
son of Bedad, who struck down
Midian in the field of Moab, became
king in his place; and the name of his
city *was* Avith.
47 Then Hadad died, and Samlah of
Masrekah became king in his place.
48 Then Samlah died, and Shaul of
Rehoboth by the River became king in
his place.
49 Then Shaul died, and Baal-hanan the
son of Achbor became king in his place.
50 Then Baal-hanan died, and Hadad
became king in his place; and the
name of his city was Pai, and his wife's
name was Mehetabel, the daughter of
Matred, daughter of Mezahab.
51 Then Hadad died.
Now the chiefs of Edom were:
chief Timna, chief Aliah, chief Jetheth,
52 chief Oholibamah, chief Elah, chief
Pinon,
53 chief Kenaz, chief Teman, chief Mibzar,
54 chief Magdiel, chief Iram.
These *were* the chiefs of Edom.

2 These are the sons of Israel:
Reuben, Simeon, Levi, Judah, Issachar,
Zebulun,
2 Dan, Joseph, Benjamin, Naphtali, Gad,
and Asher.

3 The sons of Judah *were* Er, Onan, and
Shelah; *these* three were born to him
by Bath-shua the Canaanitess. And Er,
Judah's firstborn, was evil in the sight
of Yahweh, so He put him to death.
4 Tamar his daughter-in-law bore him
Perez and Zerah.
Judah had five sons in all.
5 The sons of Perez *were* Hezron and
Hamul.
6 The sons of Zerah *were* Zimri, Ethan,
Heman, Calcol, and Dara;
five of them in all.
7 The son of Carmi *was* Achar, the
troubler of Israel, who violated what
was devoted to destruction.
8 The son of Ethan *was* Azariah.
9 Now the sons of Hezron, who were
born to him *were* Jerahmeel, Ram, and
Chelubai.
10 Ram became the father of Amminadab,
and Amminadab became the father of
Nahshon, leader of the sons of Judah;
11 Nahshon became the father of Salma,
Salma became the father of Boaz,
12 Boaz became the father of Obed,
and Obed became the father of Jesse;
13 and Jesse became the father of Eliab
his firstborn, then Abinadab the
second, Shimea the third,
14 Nethanel the fourth, Raddai the fifth,
15 Ozem the sixth, David the seventh;
16 and their sisters *were* Zeruiah and
Abigail.
And the three sons of Zeruiah *were*
Abshai, Joab, and Asahel.
17 Abigail bore Amasa, and the father of
Amasa was Jether the Ishmaelite.

18 Now Caleb the son of Hezron became
a father by Azubah *his* wife, and by
Jerioth; and these were her sons:
Jesher, Shobab, and Ardon.
19 Then Azubah died, and Caleb took
for himself Ephrath *as a wife*, and she
bore him Hur.
20 Hur became the father of Uri,
and Uri became the father of Bezalel.
21 Afterward Hezron went in to the
daughter of Machir the father of
Gilead, whom he took *as a wife* when
he was sixty years old; and she bore
him Segub.
22 Segub became the father of Jair, and
he had twenty-three cities in the land
of Gilead.
23 But Geshur and Aram took Havvoth-
jair from them, with Kenath and its
villages, *even* sixty cities. All these
were the sons of Machir, the father of
Gilead.
24 After the death of Hezron in Caleb-
ephrathah, Abijah, Hezron's wife, bore
him Ashhur the father of Tekoa.

25 And the sons of Jerahmeel the
firstborn of Hezron *were* Ram the
firstborn, then Bunah, Oren, Ozem,
and Ahijah.
26 Jerahmeel had another wife, whose
name was Atarah; she was the mother
of Onam.

27 The sons of Ram, the firstborn of
Jerahmeel, were Maaz, Jamin, and
Eker.
28 The sons of Onam were Shammai and
Jada.
And the sons of Shammai *were* Nadab
and Abishur.
29 The name of Abishur's wife *was*
Abihail, and she bore him Ahban and
Molid.
30 The sons of Nadab *were* Seled and
Appaim, and Seled died without sons.
31 The son of Appaim *was* Ishi.
And the son of Ishi *was* Sheshan.
And the son of Sheshan *was* Ahlai.
32 The sons of Jada the brother of
Shammai *were* Jether and Jonathan,
and Jether died without sons.
33 The sons of Jonathan *were* Peleth and
Zaza.
These were the sons of Jerahmeel.
34 Now Sheshan had no sons, only
daughters. And Sheshan had an
Egyptian slave whose name was Jarha.
35 Sheshan gave his daughter to Jarha his
servant as a wife, and she bore him
Attai.
36 Attai became the father of Nathan,
and Nathan became the father of
Zabad,
37 and Zabad became the father of
Ephlal,
and Ephlal became the father of Obed,
38 and Obed became the father of Jehu,
and Jehu became the father of Azariah,
39 and Azariah became the father of
Helez,
and Helez became the father of
Eleasah,
40 and Eleasah became the father of
Sismai,
and Sismai became the father of
Shallum,
41 and Shallum became the father of
Jekamiah,
and Jekamiah became the father of
Elishama.
42 Now the sons of Caleb, the brother of
Jerahmeel, *were* Mesha his firstborn,
who was the father of Ziph; and his
son was Mareshah, the father of
Hebron.
43 The sons of Hebron *were* Korah and
Tappuah and Rekem and Shema.
44 Shema became the father of Raham,
the father of Jorkeam;
and Rekem became the father of
Shammai.
45 The son of Shammai was Maon,
and Maon *was* the father of Bethzur.
46 Ephah, Caleb's concubine, bore Haran,
Moza, and Gazez;
and Haran became the father of Gazez.
47 The sons of Jahdai *were* Regem,
Jotham, Geshan, Pelet, Ephah, and
Shaaph.
48 Maacah, Caleb's concubine, bore
Sheber and Tirhanah.
49 She also bore Shaaph the father of
Madmannah, Sheva the father of
Machbena and the father of Gibea;
and the daughter of Caleb *was* Achsah.
50 These were the sons of Caleb.

The sons of Hur, the firstborn of
Ephrathah, *were* Shobal the father of
Kiriath-jearim,
51 Salma the father of Bethlehem *and*
Hareph the father of Beth-gader.
52 Shobal the father of Kiriath-jearim had
sons:
Haroeh, half of the Manahathites,
53 and the families of Kiriath-jearim:
the Ithrites, the Puthites, the
Shumathites, and the Mishraites; from
these came the Zorathites and the
Eshtaolites.
54 The sons of Salma *were* Bethlehem
and the Netophathites, Atroth-beth-
joab and half of the Manahathites, the
Zorites.
55 The families of scribes who lived
at Jabez *were* the Tirathites, the
Shimeathites, *and* the Sucathites.
Those are the Kenites who came from
Hammath, the father of the house of
Rechab.

Psalm 76:1–6

1 God is known in Judah;
His name is great in Israel.
2 So His tabernacle is in Salem;
His dwelling place is in Zion.
3 There He broke the flaming arrows,
The shield and the sword and the
battle. Selah.

4 You are shining,
Majestic from the mountains of prey.

5 The stouthearted were plundered,
They sank into sleep;
And none of the warriors
could use his hands.
6 At Your rebuke, O God of Jacob,
Both chariot rider and horse
slumbered *into* a deep sleep.

Proverbs 19:6–7

6 Many will seek the favor
of a noble man,
And everyone is a friend to a
man who gives gifts.
7 All the brothers of a poor
man hate him;
How much more do his friends
distance *themselves* from him!
He pursues *them with* words,
but they are no more.

Acts 4:1–22

4 Now as they were speaking to the people, the priests and the captain of the temple *guard* and the Sadducees came up to them, 2 being greatly agitated because they were teaching the people and proclaiming in Jesus the resurrection from the dead. 3 And they laid hands on them and put them in jail until the next day, for it was already evening. 4 But many of those who had heard the message believed, and the number of the men came to be about five thousand.

5 Now it happened that on the next day, their rulers and elders and scribes were gathered together in Jerusalem; 6 and Annas the high priest *was there*, and Caiaphas and John and Alexander, and all who were of high-priestly descent. 7 And when they had placed them in their midst, they *began to* inquire, "By what power, or in what name, have you done this?" 8 Then Peter, filled with the Holy Spirit, said to them, "Rulers and elders of the people, 9 if we are being examined today for a good deed *done* to a sick man, as to how this man has been saved *from his sickness*, 10 let it be known to all of you and to all the people of Israel, that by the name of Jesus Christ the Nazarene, whom you crucified, whom God raised from the dead—by this *name* this man stands here before you in good health. 11 He is the STONE WHICH WAS REJECTED by you, THE BUILDERS, *but* WHICH BECAME THE CHIEF CORNER *stone*. 12 And there is salvation in no one else, for there is no other name under heaven that has been given among men by which we must be saved."

13 Now as they observed the confidence of Peter and John and comprehended that they were uneducated and ordinary men, they were marveling, and *began to* recognize them as having been with Jesus. 14 And seeing the man who had been healed standing with them, they had nothing to say in reply. 15 But when they had ordered them to leave the Sanhedrin, they *began to* confer with one another, 16 saying, "What should we do with these men? For the fact that a noteworthy sign has happened through them is apparent to all who live in Jerusalem, and we cannot deny it. 17 But lest it spread any further among the people, let us warn them to speak no longer to any man in this name." 18 And when they had summoned them, they commanded them not to speak or teach at all in the name of Jesus. 19 But Peter and John answered and said to them, "Whether it is right in the sight of God to hear you rather than God, you be the judge; 20 for we cannot stop speaking about what we have seen and heard." 21 And when they had threatened them further, they let them go (finding no basis on which to punish them) on account of the people, because they were all glorifying God for what had happened; 22 for the man was more than forty years old on whom this sign of healing had occurred.

JUNE 20

1 Chronicles 3:1–4:43

3 Now these were the sons of David who were born to him in Hebron:
the firstborn was Amnon, by Ahinoam
the Jezreelitess;
the second *was* Daniel, by Abigail the
Carmelitess;
2 the third *was* Absalom the son of
Maacah, the daughter of Talmai king
of Geshur;
the fourth *was* Adonijah the son of
Haggith;
3 the fifth *was* Shephatiah,
by Abital;

the sixth *was* Ithream, by his wife Eglah.
4 Six were born to him in Hebron, and there he reigned seven years and six months. And in Jerusalem he reigned thirty-three years.
5 These were born to him in Jerusalem: Shimea, Shobab, Nathan, and Solomon, four, by Bath-shua the daughter of Ammiel;
6 and Ibhar, Elishama, Eliphelet,
7 Nogah, Nepheg, and Japhia,
8 Elishama, Eliada, and Eliphelet, nine.
9 All *these were* the sons of David, besides the sons of the concubines; and Tamar *was* their sister.

10 Now Solomon's son *was* Rehoboam, Abijah *was* his son, Asa his son, Jehoshaphat his son,
11 Joram his son, Ahaziah his son, Joash his son,
12 Amaziah his son, Azariah his son, Jotham his son,
13 Ahaz his son, Hezekiah his son, Manasseh his son,
14 Amon his son, Josiah his son.
15 The sons of Josiah *were* Johanan the firstborn, and the second *was* Jehoiakim, the third Zedekiah, the fourth Shallum.
16 The sons of Jehoiakim *were* Jeconiah his son, Zedekiah his son.
17 The sons of Jeconiah, the prisoner, *were* Shealtiel his son,
18 and Malchiram, Pedaiah, Shenazzar, Jekamiah, Hoshama, and Nedabiah.
19 The sons of Pedaiah *were* Zerubbabel and Shimei.
And the sons of Zerubbabel *were* Meshullam and Hananiah, and Shelomith *was* their sister;
20 and Hashubah, Ohel, Berechiah, Hasadiah, and Jushab-hesed, five.
21 The sons of Hananiah *were* Pelatiah and Jeshaiah, the sons of Rephaiah, the sons of Arnan, the sons of Obadiah, the sons of Shecaniah.
22 The sons of Shecaniah *were* Shemaiah, and the sons of Shemaiah: Hattush, Igal, Bariah, Neariah, and Shaphat, six.
23 The sons of Neariah *were* Elioenai, Hizkiah, and Azrikam, three.
24 The sons of Elioenai *were* Hodaviah, Eliashib, Pelaiah, Akkub, Johanan, Delaiah, and Anani, seven.

4 The sons of Judah *were* Perez, Hezron, Carmi, Hur, and Shobal.
2 Reaiah the son of Shobal became the father of Jahath,
and Jahath became the father of Ahumai and Lahad. These *were* the families of the Zorathites.
3 These *were* the sons of Etam: Jezreel, Ishma, and Idbash; and the name of their sister *was* Hazzelelponi.
4 Penuel *was* the father of Gedor, and Ezer the father of Hushah. These *were* the sons of Hur, the firstborn of Ephrathah, the father of Bethlehem.
5 Ashhur, the father of Tekoa, had two wives, Helah and Naarah.
6 Naarah bore him Ahuzzam, Hepher, Temeni, and Haahashtari. These were the sons of Naarah.
7 The sons of Helah *were* Zereth, Izhar, and Ethnan.
8 Koz became the father of Anub and Zobebah, and the families of Aharhel the son of Harum.
9 Now Jabez was more honorable than his brothers, and his mother named him Jabez saying, "Because I bore *him* with pain."
10 Then Jabez called on the God of Israel, saying, "Oh that You would bless me indeed and enlarge my border, and that Your hand might be with me, and that You would keep *me* from harm that *it* may not pain me!" And God brought about what he asked.

11 Chelub the brother of Shuhah became the father of Mehir, who was the father of Eshton.
12 Eshton became the father of Beth-rapha and Paseah, and Tehinnah the father of Ir-nahash.
These are the men of Recah.

13 Now the sons of Kenaz *were* Othniel and Seraiah.
And the sons of Othniel *were* Hathath and Meonothai.
14 Meonothai became the father of Ophrah,

and Seraiah became the father of Joab
the father of Ge-harashim, for they
were craftsmen.
15 The sons of Caleb the son of
Jephunneh *were* Iru, Elah, and Naam;
and the son of Elah *was* Kenaz.
16 The sons of Jehallelel *were* Ziph and
Ziphah, Tiria and Asarel.
17 The sons of Ezrah *were* Jether, Mered,
Epher, and Jalon. (And these are
the sons of Bithia the daughter of
Pharaoh, whom Mered took) and she
conceived *and bore* Miriam, Shammai,
and Ishbah the father of Eshtemoa.
18 His Jewish wife bore Jered the father of
Gedor, and Heber the father of Soco,
and Jekuthiel the father of Zanoah.
19 The sons of the wife of Hodiah, the
sister of Naham, *were* the fathers of
Keilah the Garmite and Eshtemoa the
Maacathite.
20 The sons of Shimon *were* Amnon and
Rinnah, Benhanan and Tilon.
And the sons of Ishi *were* Zoheth and
Ben-zoheth.
21 The sons of Shelah the son of Judah
were Er the father of Lecah and
Laadah the father of Mareshah, and
the families of the house of the fine
linen workers at Beth-ashbea;
22 and Jokim, the men of Cozeba, Joash,
Saraph, who ruled in Moab, and
Jashubi-lehem. And the records are
ancient.
23 These were the potters and the
inhabitants of Netaim and Gederah;
they lived there with the king for his
work.
24 The sons of Simeon *were* Nemuel and
Jamin, Jarib, Zerah, Shaul;
25 Shallum his son, Mibsam his son,
Mishma his son.
26 The sons of Mishma *were* Hammuel
his son, Zaccur his son, Shimei his
son.

27 Now Shimei had sixteen sons and six
daughters; but his brothers did not have
many sons, nor did all their family multi-
ply like the sons of Judah. 28 They lived at
Beersheba, Moladah, and Hazar-shual, 29 at
Bilhah, Ezem, Tolad, 30 Bethuel, Hormah,
Ziklag, 31 Beth-marcaboth, Hazar-susim,
Beth-biri, and Shaaraim. These *were* their
cities until the reign of David. 32 Their vil-
lages *were* Etam, Ain, Rimmon, Tochen, and
Ashan, five cities; 33 and all their villages
that *were* all around these cities as far as
Baal. These *were* their settlements, and they
have their genealogy.
34 Meshobab and Jamlech and Joshah the
son of Amaziah,
35 and Joel and Jehu the son of Joshibiah,
the son of Seraiah, the son of Asiel,
36 and Elioenai, Jaakobah, Jeshohaiah,
Asaiah, Adiel, Jesimiel, Benaiah,
37 Ziza the son of Shiphi, the son of
Allon, the son of Jedaiah, the son of
Shimri, the son of Shemaiah;
38 these, who came *into the record* by
name, *were* leaders in their families;
and their fathers' houses increased
greatly.

39 They went to the entrance of Gedor, even
to the east side of the valley, to seek pasture
for their flocks. 40 They found rich and good
pasture, and the land was broad and quiet
and peaceful; for those who lived there for-
merly *were* Hamites. 41 And these, recorded
by name, came in the days of Hezekiah king
of Judah, and struck down their tents and
the Meunites who were found there, and
devoted them to destruction to this day,
and lived in their place, because there was
pasture there for their flocks. 42 From them,
from the sons of Simeon, five hundred men
went to Mount Seir, with Pelatiah, Neariah,
Rephaiah, and Uzziel, the sons of Ishi, as
their chiefs. 43 They struck down the rem-
nant of the Amalekites who escaped, and
have lived there to this day.

Psalm 76:7–12

7 But You, You are fearsome;
And who can stand in Your presence
when once You are angry?

8 You made *Your* cause to be
heard from heaven;
The earth feared and was quiet
9 When God arose to judgment,
To save all the humble of
the earth. Selah.
10 For the wrath of man shall praise You;
With a remnant of wrath
You will gird Yourself.

11 Make vows to Yahweh your
God and pay *them*;
Let all who are around Him bring
gifts to the Fearsome One.

12 He will cut off the spirit of princes;
He is feared by the kings of the earth.

Proverbs 19:8–9

8 He who acquires a heart *of*
wisdom loves his own soul;
He who keeps discernment
will find good.
9 A false witness will not go unpunished,
And he who breathes out
lies will perish.

Acts 4:23–37

23 So when they were released, they went
to their own *companions* and reported all
that the chief priests and the elders had said
to them. 24 And when they heard *this*, they
lifted their voices to God with one accord
and said, "O Master, it is You who MADE THE
HEAVEN AND THE EARTH AND THE SEA, AND ALL
THAT IS IN THEM, 25 who by the Holy Spirit,
through the mouth of our father David Your
servant, said,

'WHY DID THE GENTILES RAGE,
AND THE PEOPLES DEVISE VAIN THINGS?
26 'THE KINGS OF THE EARTH
TOOK THEIR STAND,
AND THE RULERS WERE
GATHERED TOGETHER
AGAINST THE LORD AND
AGAINST HIS CHRIST.'

27 "For truly in this city there were gath-
ered together against Your holy Servant
Jesus, whom You anointed, both Herod
and Pontius Pilate, along with the Gentiles
and the peoples of Israel, 28 to do whatever
Your hand and Your purpose predestined
to occur. 29 And now, Lord, take note of
their threats, and grant that Your slaves
may speak Your word with all confidence,
30 while You extend Your hand to heal, and
signs and wonders happen through the
name of Your holy Servant Jesus." 31 And
when they had prayed earnestly, the place
where they had gathered together was
shaken, and they were all filled with the
Holy Spirit and *began to* speak the word of
God with confidence.

32 And the congregation of those who
believed were of one heart and soul,
and not one was saying that any of his
possessions was his own, but, for them,
everything was common. 33 And with great
power the apostles were bearing witness
to the resurrection of the Lord Jesus, and
great grace was upon them all. 34 For there
was not a needy person among them, for all
who were owners of land or houses would
sell them and bring the proceeds of the
sales 35 and lay them at the apostles' feet,
and they would be distributed to each as
any had need.

36 Now Joseph, a Levite of Cyprian
birth, who was also called Barnabas by the
apostles (which translated means Son of
Encouragement), 37 and who owned a field,
sold it and brought the money and laid it at
the apostles' feet.

JUNE 21

1 Chronicles 5:1–6:81

5 Now the sons of Reuben the firstborn
of Israel (for he was the firstborn, but
because he profaned his father's bed, his
birthright was given to the sons of Joseph
the son of Israel; so that he is not recorded
in the genealogy according to the birthright.
2 Though Judah prevailed over his brothers,
and from him came the ruler, yet the birth-
right belonged to Joseph),

3 the sons of Reuben the firstborn of
Israel *were* Hanoch and Pallu, Hezron
and Carmi.
4 The sons of Joel *were* Shemaiah his
son, Gog his son, Shimei his son,
5 Micah his son, Reaiah his son, Baal his
son,
6 Beerah his son, whom Tilgath-pilneser
king of Assyria took away into exile; he
was leader of the Reubenites.

7 His relatives by their families, in the gene-
alogy of their generations, *were* Jeiel the
chief, then Zechariah, 8 and Bela the son of
Azaz, the son of Shema, the son of Joel, who
lived in Aroer, even to Nebo and Baal-meon.
9 To the east he lived as far as the entrance
of the wilderness from the river Euphrates,
because their cattle had increased in the
land of Gilead. 10 In the days of Saul they
made war with the Hagrites, and they fell
by their hand. So they lived in their tents
throughout all the land east of Gilead.

11 Now the sons of Gad lived opposite
them in the land of Bashan as far as Salecah.

12 Joel *was* the chief and Shapham the
second, then Janai and Shaphat in Bashan.
13 Their relatives of their fathers' house-
holds *were* Michael, Meshullam, Sheba,
Jorai, Jacan, Zia, and Eber, seven. 14 These
were the sons of Abihail, the son of Huri,
the son of Jaroah, the son of Gilead,
the son of Michael, the son of
Jeshishai,
the son of Jahdo, the son of Buz;
15 Ahi the son of Abdiel, the son of Guni, *was*
head of their fathers' households. 16 They
lived in Gilead, in Bashan and in its towns,
and in all the pasture lands of Sharon, as
far as their borders. 17 All of these were
recorded in the genealogies in the days of
Jotham king of Judah and in the days of
Jeroboam king of Israel.

18 The sons of Reuben and the Gadites
and the half-tribe of Manasseh, *consisting*
of men of valor, men who bore shield and
sword and shot with bow and *were* learned
in *the ways of* battle, *were* 44,760, who went
out for *military* duty. 19 They made war
against the Hagrites, Jetur, Naphish, and
Nodab. 20 They were helped against them,
and the Hagrites and all who *were* with them
were given into their hand; for they cried
out to God in the battle, and He was moved
by their entreaty because they trusted
in Him. 21 They took captive their cattle:
their 50,000 camels, 250,000 sheep, 2,000
donkeys; and 100,000 men. 22 For many fell
slain, because the war *was* of God. And they
lived in their place until the exile.

23 Now the sons of the half-tribe of
Manasseh lived in the land; from Bashan
to Baal-hermon and Senir and Mount
Hermon they were numerous. 24 These
were the heads of their fathers' households,
even Epher, Ishi, Eliel, Azriel, Jeremiah,
Hodaviah, and Jahdiel, mighty men of
valor, men of renown, heads of their fathers'
households.

25 But they acted unfaithfully against the
God of their fathers and played the harlot
after the gods of the peoples of the land,
whom God had destroyed before them. 26 So
the God of Israel stirred up the spirit of Pul,
king of Assyria, even the spirit of Tilgath-
pilneser, king of Assyria, and he took them
away into exile, namely the Reubenites, the
Gadites, and the half-tribe of Manasseh, and
brought them to Halah, Habor, Hara, and to
the river of Gozan, to this day.

6 The sons of Levi *were* Gershon,
Kohath, and Merari.
2 The sons of Kohath *were* Amram,
Izhar, Hebron, and Uzziel.
3 The children of Amram *were* Aaron,
Moses, and Miriam.
And the sons of Aaron *were* Nadab,
Abihu, Eleazar, and Ithamar.
4 Eleazar became the father of
Phinehas,
and Phinehas became the father of
Abishua,
5 and Abishua became the father of
Bukki,
and Bukki became the father of Uzzi,
6 and Uzzi became the father of
Zerahiah,
and Zerahiah became the father of
Meraioth,
7 Meraioth became the father of
Amariah,
and Amariah became the father of
Ahitub,
8 and Ahitub became the father of
Zadok,
and Zadok became the father of
Ahimaaz,
9 and Ahimaaz became the father of
Azariah,
and Azariah became the father of
Johanan,
10 and Johanan became the father of
Azariah (it was he who ministered as
the priest in the house which Solomon
built in Jerusalem),
11 and Azariah became the father of
Amariah,
and Amariah became the father of
Ahitub,
12 and Ahitub became the father of
Zadok,
and Zadok became the father of
Shallum,
13 and Shallum became the father of
Hilkiah,
and Hilkiah became the father of
Azariah,
14 and Azariah became the father of
Seraiah,
and Seraiah became the father of
Jehozadak;
15 and Jehozadak went *along* when
Yahweh took Judah and Jerusalem
away into exile by the hand of
Nebuchadnezzar.

16 The sons of Levi *were* Gershom,
Kohath, and Merari.
17 These are the names of the sons of
Gershom: Libni and Shimei.
18 The sons of Kohath *were* Amram,
Izhar, Hebron, and Uzziel.
19 The sons of Merari *were* Mahli and
Mushi.
And these are the families of the
Levites according to their fathers'
households.
20 Of Gershom: Libni his son, Jahath his
son, Zimmah his son,
21 Joah his son, Iddo his son, Zerah his
son, Jeatherai his son.
22 The sons of Kohath *were* Amminadab
his son, Korah his son, Assir his son,
23 Elkanah his son, Ebiasaph his son, and
Assir his son,
24 Tahath his son, Uriel his son, Uzziah
his son, and Shaul his son.
25 The sons of Elkanah *were* Amasai and
Ahimoth.
26 *As for* Elkanah, the sons of Elkanah
were Zophai his son and Nahath his
son,
27 Eliab his son, Jeroham his son,
Elkanah his son.
28 The sons of Samuel *were* Joel the
firstborn, and Abijah the second.
29 The sons of Merari *were* Mahli, Libni
his son, Shimei his son, Uzzah his son,
30 Shimea his son, Haggiah his son,
Asaiah his son.

31 Now these are those whom David
caused to stand over the service of song in
the house of Yahweh, after the ark rested
there. 32 And they ministered with song
before the tabernacle of the tent of meeting,
until Solomon had built the house of Yahweh
in Jerusalem; and they stood for their service
according to their custom. 33 These are those
who stood *for service* with their sons:

From the sons of the Kohathites *were*
Heman the singer, the son of Joel, the
son of Samuel,
34 the son of Elkanah, the son of
Jeroham, the son of Eliel, the son of
Toah,
35 the son of Zuph, the son of Elkanah,
the son of Mahath, the son of Amasai,
36 the son of Elkanah, the son of Joel, the
son of Azariah, the son of Zephaniah,
37 the son of Tahath, the son of Assir, the
son of Ebiasaph, the son of Korah,
38 the son of Izhar, the son of Kohath,
the son of Levi, the son of Israel.
39 *Heman's* brother Asaph stood at his
right hand, even Asaph the son of
Berechiah, the son of Shimea,
40 the son of Michael, the son of
Baaseiah, the son of Malchijah,
41 the son of Ethni, the son of Zerah, the
son of Adaiah,
42 the son of Ethan, the son of Zimmah,
the son of Shimei,
43 the son of Jahath, the son of Gershom,
the son of Levi.
44 On the left hand *were* their relatives
the sons of Merari:
Ethan the son of Kishi, the son of
Abdi, the son of Malluch,
45 the son of Hashabiah, the son of
Amaziah, the son of Hilkiah,
46 the son of Amzi, the son of Bani, the
son of Shemer,
47 the son of Mahli, the son of Mushi, the
son of Merari, the son of Levi.

48 Their relatives the Levites were given over
unto all the service of the tabernacle of the
house of God.

49 But Aaron and his sons offered *offer-
ings* up in smoke on the altar of burnt
offering and on the altar of incense, for all
the work of the Holy of Holies, and to make
atonement for Israel, according to all that
Moses the servant of God had commanded.
50 These are the sons of Aaron:

Eleazar his son, Phinehas his son,
Abishua his son,
51 Bukki his son, Uzzi his son, Zerahiah
his son,
52 Meraioth his son, Amariah his son,
Ahitub his son,
53 Zadok his son, Ahimaaz his son.

54 Now these are their settlements accord-
ing to their camps within their borders. To
the sons of Aaron of the families of the
Kohathites (for the lot was theirs *first*), 55 to
them they gave Hebron in the land of Judah,
with its pasture lands all around it; 56 but
the fields of the city and its villages, they
gave to Caleb the son of Jephunneh. 57 To
the sons of Aaron they gave the *following*
cities of refuge:

Hebron, Libnah also with its pasture
lands, Jattir, Eshtemoa with its pasture
lands,
58 Hilen with its pasture lands, Debir
with its pasture lands,

59 Ashan with its pasture lands, and
Beth-shemesh with its pasture lands;
60 from the tribe of Benjamin:
Geba with its pasture lands, Allemeth
with its pasture lands, and Anathoth
with its pasture lands.
All their cities throughout their
families were thirteen cities.

61 Now to the rest of the sons of Kohath
were given by lot, from the family of
the tribe, from the half-tribe, the half
of Manasseh, ten cities.
62 And to the sons of Gershom, according
to their families, *were given* from the
tribe of Issachar and from the tribe of
Asher, the tribe of Naphtali, and the
tribe of Manasseh, thirteen cities in
Bashan.
63 To the sons of Merari *were given* by
lot, according to their families, from
the tribe of Reuben, the tribe of Gad,
and the tribe of Zebulun, twelve cities.
64 So the sons of Israel gave to the Levites
the cities with their pasture lands. 65 They
also gave by lot from the tribe of the sons
of Judah, the tribe of the sons of Simeon,
and the tribe of the sons of Benjamin, these
cities which are mentioned *here* by name.
66 Now some of the families of the sons of
Kohath had cities of their territory from the
tribe of Ephraim. 67 And they gave to them
the *following* cities of refuge:
Shechem, with its pasture lands, in
the hill country of Ephraim, and Gezer
with its pasture lands,
68 Jokmeam with its pasture lands,
Beth-horon with its pasture lands,
69 Aijalon with its pasture lands, and
Gath-rimmon with its pasture lands;
70 and from the half-tribe of Manasseh:
Aner with its pasture lands and Bileam
with its pasture lands, for the family of
the rest of the sons of Kohath.
71 To the sons of Gershom *were given*,
from the family of the half-tribe of
Manasseh:
Golan in Bashan with its pasture lands
and Ashtaroth with its pasture lands;
72 and from the tribe of Issachar:
Kedesh with its pasture lands,
Daberath with its pasture lands,
73 and Ramoth with its pasture lands,
Anem with its pasture lands;
74 and from the tribe of Asher:
Mashal with its pasture lands, Abdon
with its pasture lands,
75 Hukok with its pasture lands, and
Rehob with its pasture lands;
76 and from the tribe of Naphtali:
Kedesh in Galilee with its pasture
lands, Hammon with its pasture lands,
and Kiriathaim with its pasture lands.
77 To the sons of Merari, the rest *of the
Levites, were given*, from the tribe of Zeb-
ulun:
Rimmono with its pasture lands,
Tabor with its pasture lands;
78 and beyond the Jordan at Jericho, on
the east side of the Jordan, *were given
them*, from the tribe of Reuben:
Bezer in the wilderness with its
pasture lands, Jahzah with its pasture
lands,
79 Kedemoth with its pasture lands, and
Mephaath with its pasture lands;
80 and from the tribe of Gad:
Ramoth in Gilead with its pasture
lands, Mahanaim with its pasture
lands,
81 Heshbon with its pasture lands, and
Jazer with its pasture lands.

Psalm 77:1–3

1 My voice *rises* to God, and
I must cry aloud;
My voice *rises* to God, and
He will hear me.
2 In the day of my distress I
sought the Lord;
In the night my hand was stretched
out without weariness;
My soul refused to be comforted.
3 I remember God and I am disturbed;
I muse and my spirit faints. Selah.

Proverbs 19:10–12

10 Luxury is not fitting for a fool;
Much less for a slave to
rule over princes.
11 A man's insight makes
him slow to anger,
And it is his honor to overlook
a transgression.
12 The king's wrath is like the
roaring of a lion,
But his favor is like dew on the grass.

Acts 5:1–21

5 But a man named Ananias, with his wife
Sapphira, sold a piece of property, 2 and
kept back *some* of the price for himself, with
his wife's full knowledge. And bringing a
portion of it, he laid it at the apostles' feet.
3 But Peter said, "Ananias, why has Satan filled
your heart to lie to the Holy Spirit and to keep
back *some* of the price of the land? 4 While
it remained *unsold*, did it not remain your
own? And after it was sold, was it not under
your authority? Why is it that you laid this
deed in your heart? You have not lied to men
but to God." 5 And as he heard these words,
Ananias fell down and breathed his last; and
great fear came over all who heard. 6 And the
young men rose up and wrapped him up, and
after carrying him out, they buried him.

7 Now there was an interval of about three
hours, and his wife came in, not knowing
what had happened. 8 And Peter responded
to her, "Tell me whether you were paid this
much for the land?" And she said, "Yes,
that much." 9 Then Peter *said* to her, "Why
is it that you have agreed together to put
the Spirit of the Lord to the test? Behold,
the feet of those who buried your husband
are at the door, and they will carry you out
as well." 10 And immediately she fell at his
feet and breathed her last, and the young
men came in and found her dead, and they
carried her out and buried her beside her
husband. 11 And great fear came over the
whole church, and over all who heard these
things.

12 Now at the hands of the apostles many
signs and wonders were happening among
the people, and they were all with one
accord in Solomon's Portico. 13 But none
of the rest dared to associate with them;
however, the people were holding them in
high esteem. 14 And more than ever believ-
ers in the Lord were added to *their number*,
multitudes of men and women, 15 to such an
extent that they even carried the sick out
into the streets and laid them on cots and
mats, so that when Peter came by at least
his shadow might fall on any one of them.
16 Also the multitude from the cities in the
vicinity of Jerusalem were coming together,
bringing people who were sick or afflicted
with unclean spirits, and they were all being
healed.

17 But the high priest rose up and those
with him (that is the sect of the Saddu-
cees), and they were filled with jealousy.
18 And they laid hands on the apostles and
put them in a public jail. 19 But during the
night an angel of the Lord opened the
doors of the prison, and taking them out,
he said, 20 "Go, stand and speak to the
people in the temple the whole message
of this Life." 21 Upon hearing *this*, they
entered into the temple about daybreak
and *began to* teach.

Now when the high priest and those
with him came, they called the Sanhedrin
together, even all the Council of the sons of
Israel, and sent *orders* to the jailhouse for
them to be brought.

JUNE 22

1 Chronicles 7:1–8:40

7 Now the sons of Issachar: Tola, Puah,
Jashub, and Shimron, four.

2 The sons of Tola *were* Uzzi, Rephaiah,
Jeriel, Jahmai, Ibsam, and Samuel,
heads of their fathers' households. *The
sons* of Tola *were* mighty men of valor
in their generations; their number in
the days of David was 22,600.

3 The son of Uzzi *was* Izrahiah.
And the sons of Izrahiah *were*
Michael, Obadiah, Joel, Isshiah; all five
of them *were* chief men.

4 With them by their generations according
to their fathers' households were 36,000
troops of the army for war, for they had
many wives and sons. 5 Their relatives
among all the families of Issachar *were*
mighty men of valor, recorded by genealogy,
in all 87,000.

6 *The sons of* Benjamin: Bela and Becher
and Jediael, three.

7 The sons of Bela: Ezbon, Uzzi,
Uzziel, Jerimoth, and Iri, five. They
were heads of fathers' households,
mighty men of valor, and were 22,034
recorded by genealogy.

8 The sons of Becher *were* Zemirah,
Joash, Eliezer, Elioenai, Omri,
Jeremoth, Abijah, Anathoth, and
Alemeth. All these *were* the sons of
Becher.

9 They were recorded by genealogy, accord-
ing to their generations, heads of their
fathers' households, 20,200 mighty men
of valor.

10 The son of Jediael *was* Bilhan.
And the sons of Bilhan *were* Jeush,
Benjamin, Ehud, Chenaanah, Zethan,
Tarshish, and Ahishahar.

11 All these *were* sons of Jediael, according
to the heads of their fathers' *households*,
17,200 mighty men of valor, who went
out with the army to war. 12 Shuppim and
Huppim *were* the sons of Ir; Hushim *was*
the son of Aher.

13 The sons of Naphtali *were* Jahziel, Guni,
Jezer, and Shallum, the sons of Bilhah.

14 The sons of Manasseh *were* Asriel,
whom his Aramean concubine bore; she
bore Machir the father of Gilead. 15 Now
Machir took a wife for Huppim and Shup-
pim, whose sister's name was Maacah. And
the name of the second was Zelophehad,
and Zelophehad had daughters. 16 And
Maacah the wife of Machir bore a son, and
she named him Peresh; and the name of
his brother *was* Sheresh, and his sons *were*
Ulam and Rakem. 17 The son of Ulam *was*
Bedan. These *were* the sons of Gilead the
son of Machir, the son of Manasseh. 18 And
his sister Hammolecheth bore Ishhod and
Abiezer and Mahlah. 19 The sons of Shemida
were Ahian and Shechem and Likhi and
Aniam.

20 The sons of Ephraim *were* Shuthelah
and Bered his son, Tahath his son, Eleadah
his son, Tahath his son, 21 Zabad his son,
Shuthelah his son, and Ezer and Elead
whom the men of Gath who were born in the
land killed, because they came down to take
their livestock. 22 And their father Ephraim
mourned many days, and his relatives came
to comfort him. 23 Then he went in to his
wife, and she conceived and bore a son, and
he named him Beriah, because calamity had
come upon his house. 24 And his daughter
was Sheerah, and she built lower and upper
Beth-horon, also Uzzen-sheerah. 25 Rephah
was his son *along* with Resheph, Telah his
son, Tahan his son, 26 Ladan his son, Ammi-
hud his son, Elishama his son, 27 Non his son
and Joshua his son.

28 Now their possessions and settlements
were Bethel with its towns, and to the east
Naaran, and to the west Gezer with its towns,
and Shechem with its towns as far as Ayyah
with its towns, 29 and along the borders of
the sons of Manasseh, Beth-shean with its
towns, Taanach with its towns, Megiddo
with its towns, Dor with its towns. In these
lived the sons of Joseph the son of Israel.

30 The sons of Asher *were* Imnah, Ishvah,
Ishvi, and Beriah, and Serah their
sister.
31 The sons of Beriah *were* Heber and
Malchiel, who was the father of
Birzaith.
32 Heber became the father of Japhlet,
Shomer, and Hotham, and Shua their
sister.
33 The sons of Japhlet *were* Pasach,
Bimhal, and Ashvath.
These were the sons of Japhlet.
34 The sons of Shemer *were* Ahi and
Rohgah, Jehubbah and Aram.
35 The sons of his brother Helem *were*
Zophah, Imna, Shelesh, and Amal.
36 The sons of Zophah *were* Suah,
Harnepher, Shual, Beri, and Imrah,
37 Bezer, Hod, Shamma, Shilshah, Ithran,
and Beera.
38 The sons of Jether *were* Jephunneh,
Pispa, and Ara.
39 The sons of Ulla *were* Arah, Hanniel,
and Rizia.
40 All these *were* the sons of Asher,
heads of the fathers' houses, choice
and mighty men of valor, heads of
the princes. And the number of them
recorded by genealogy for the army in
war was 26,000 men.

8 And Benjamin became the father of
Bela his firstborn, Ashbel the second,
Aharah the third,
2 Nohah the fourth, and Rapha the fifth.
3 Bela had sons: Addar, Gera, Abihud,
4 Abishua, Naaman, Ahoah,
5 Gera, Shephuphan, and Huram.
6 These are the sons of Ehud: these are
the heads of fathers' *households* of the
inhabitants of Geba, and they took
them away into exile to Manahath,
7 namely, Naaman, Ahijah, and
Gera—he took them away into exile;
and he became the father of Uzza and
Ahihud.
8 Shaharaim became the father of
children in the country of Moab after
he had sent away Hushim and Baara
his wives.

9 By Hodesh his wife he became the
father of Jobab, Zibia, Mesha, Malcam,
10 Jeuz, Sachia, Mirmah. These were his
sons, heads of fathers' *households*.
11 By Hushim he became the father of
Abitub and Elpaal.
12 The sons of Elpaal *were* Eber, Misham,
and Shemed, who built Ono and Lod,
with its towns;
13 and Beriah and Shema, who were
heads of fathers' *households* of the
inhabitants of Aijalon, who made the
inhabitants of Gath flee;
14 and Ahio, Shashak, and Jeremoth.
15 Zebadiah, Arad, Eder,
16 Michael, Ishpah, and Joha *were* the
sons of Beriah.
17 Zebadiah, Meshullam, Hizki, Heber,
18 Ishmerai, Izliah, and Jobab *were* the
sons of Elpaal.
19 Jakim, Zichri, Zabdi,
20 Elienai, Zillethai, Eliel,
21 Adaiah, Beraiah, and Shimrath *were*
the sons of Shimei.
22 Ishpan, Eber, Eliel,
23 Abdon, Zichri, Hanan,
24 Hananiah, Elam, Anthothijah,
25 Iphdeiah and Penuel *were* the sons of
Shashak.
26 Shamsherai, Shehariah, Athaliah,
27 Jaareshiah, Elijah, and Zichri *were* the
sons of Jeroham.
28 These were heads of the fathers'
households according to their
generations, *the* heads who lived in
Jerusalem.

29 Now in Gibeon, *Jeiel* the father of
Gibeon lived, and his wife's name was
Maacah;
30 and his firstborn son *was* Abdon, then
Zur, Kish, Baal, Nadab,
31 Gedor, Ahio, and Zecher.
32 Mikloth became the father of
Shimeah. And they also lived with
their relatives in Jerusalem opposite
their *other* relatives.
33 Ner became the father of Kish,
and Kish became the father of Saul,
and Saul became the father of
Jonathan, Malchi-shua, Abinadab, and
Eshbaal.
34 The son of Jonathan *was* Merib-baal,
and Merib-baal became the father of
Micah.
35 The sons of Micah *were* Pithon,
Melech, Tarea, and Ahaz.
36 Ahaz became the father of Jehoaddah,
and Jehoaddah became the father of
Alemeth, Azmaveth, and Zimri;
and Zimri became the father of Moza.
37 Moza became the father of Binea;
Raphah *was* his son, Eleasah his son,
Azel his son.
38 Azel had six sons, and these *were* their
names: Azrikam, Bocheru, Ishmael,
Sheariah, Obadiah, and Hanan.
All these *were* the sons of Azel.
39 The sons of Eshek his brother *were*
Ulam his firstborn, Jeush the second,
and Eliphelet the third.
40 The sons of Ulam were mighty men of
valor, archers, and had many sons and
grandsons, 150 *of them*.
All these *were* of the sons of Benjamin.

Psalm 77:4–9

4 You have held my eyelids *open*;
I am so troubled that I cannot speak.
5 I give thought to the days of old,
The years of long ago.
6 I remember my music in the night;
I am musing with my heart,
And my spirit is searching:

7 Will the Lord reject evermore?
And will He not be favorable again?
8 Has His lovingkindness
ceased forever?
Has *His* word ended from
generation to generation?
9 Has God forgotten to be gracious,
Or has He in anger shut up His
compassion? Selah.

Proverbs 19:13–14

13 A foolish son is destruction
to his father,
And the contentions of a wife
are a constant dripping.
14 House and wealth are an
inheritance from fathers,
But a wife who has insight
is from Yahweh.

Acts 5:22–42

22 But the officers who came did not find
them in the prison, and they returned and
reported back, 23 saying, "We found the
jailhouse locked quite securely and the

guards standing at the doors, but we opened it and found no one inside." 24 Now when the captain of the temple *guard* and the chief priests heard these words, they were greatly perplexed about them as to what would come of this. 25 But someone came and reported to them, "The men whom you put in prison are standing in the temple and teaching the people!" 26 Then the captain went along with the officers and *proceeded* to bring them *back* without violence (for they were afraid of the people, that they might be stoned).

27 And when they had brought them, they stood them before the Sanhedrin. And the high priest questioned them, 28 saying, "We strictly commanded you not to continue teaching in this name, and yet, you have filled Jerusalem with your teaching and intend to bring this man's blood upon us." 29 But Peter and the apostles answered and said, "We must obey God rather than men. 30 The God of our fathers raised up Jesus, whom you put to death by hanging Him on a tree. 31 This One God exalted to His right hand as a Leader and a Savior, to grant repentance to Israel, and forgiveness of sins. 32 And we are witnesses of these things, and *so is* the Holy Spirit, whom God gave to those who obey Him."

33 But when they heard this, they became furious and intended to kill them. 34 But a Pharisee named Gamaliel, a teacher of the Law, respected by all the people, stood up in the Sanhedrin and gave orders to put the men outside for a short time. 35 And he said to them, "Men of Israel, take care what you propose to do with these men. 36 For some time ago Theudas rose up, claiming to be somebody, and a group of about four hundred men joined up with him. But he was killed, and all who were following him were dispersed and came to nothing. 37 After this man, Judas the Galilean rose up in the days of the census and drew away people after him. He too perished, and all those who were following him were scattered. 38 So in the present case, I also say to you, stay away from these men and let them alone, for if this plan or action is of men, it will be overthrown; 39 but if it is of God, you will not be able to overthrow them; or you may even be found fighting against God."

40 So they followed his advice. And after calling the apostles in *and* beating them, they commanded them not to speak in the name of Jesus, and *then* released them. 41 So they went on their way from the presence of the Sanhedrin, rejoicing that they had been considered worthy to suffer shame for the Name. 42 And every day, in the temple and from house to house, they did not cease teaching and proclaiming the good news that Jesus *is* the Christ.

JUNE 23

1 Chronicles 9:1–10:14

9 So all Israel was recorded by genealogies; and behold, they are written in the Book of the Kings of Israel. And Judah was taken away into exile to Babylon for their unfaithfulness.

2 Now the first who lived in their possessions in their cities *were* Israel, the priests, the Levites, and the temple servants. 3 And some of the sons of Judah, of the sons of Benjamin and of the sons of Ephraim and Manasseh lived in Jerusalem:

4 Uthai the son of Ammihud, the son of
Omri, the son of Imri, the son of Bani,
from the sons of Perez the son of Judah.
5 From the Shilonites *were* Asaiah the
firstborn and his sons.
6 From the sons of Zerah *were* Jeuel and
their relatives, 690 *of them.*
7 From the sons of Benjamin *were* Sallu
the son of Meshullam, the son of
Hodaviah, the son of Hassenuah,
8 and Ibneiah the son of Jeroham, and
Elah the son of Uzzi, the son of Michri,
and Meshullam the son of Shephatiah,
the son of Reuel, the son of Ibnijah;
9 and their relatives according to their
generations, 956.
All these *were* heads of fathers'
households according to their fathers'
houses.

10 From the priests *were* Jedaiah,
Jehoiarib, Jachin,
11 and Azariah the son of Hilkiah, the
son of Meshullam, the son of Zadok,
the son of Meraioth, the son of Ahitub,
the leader of the house of God;

12 and Adaiah the son of Jeroham, the
son of Pashhur, the son of Malchijah,
and Maasai the son of Adiel, the son
of Jahzerah, the son of Meshullam,
the son of Meshillemith, the son of
Immer;
13 and their relatives, heads of their
fathers' households, 1,760 mighty men
of valor for the work of the service of
the house of God.

14 Of the Levites *were* Shemaiah the
son of Hasshub, the son of Azrikam,
the son of Hashabiah, of the sons of
Merari;
15 and Bakbakkar, Heresh, and Galal and
Mattaniah the son of Mica, the son of
Zichri, the son of Asaph,
16 and Obadiah the son of Shemaiah, the
son of Galal, the son of Jeduthun, and
Berechiah the son of Asa, the son of
Elkanah, who lived in the villages of
the Netophathites.

17 Now the gatekeepers *were* Shallum
and Akkub and Talmon and Ahiman
and their relatives (Shallum the chief
18 *being stationed* until now at the king's
gate to the east).
These *were* the gatekeepers for the
camp of the sons of Levi.

[19] Shallum the son of Kore, the son of
Ebiasaph, the son of Korah, and his rela-
tives of his father's house, the Korahites,
were over the work of the service, keepers
of the thresholds of the tent; and their
fathers had been over the camp of Yahweh,
keepers of the entrance. [20] And Phinehas
the son of Eleazar was ruler over them
previously, *and* Yahweh was with him.
[21] Zechariah the son of Meshelemiah was
gatekeeper of the entrance of the tent of
meeting. [22] All these who were chosen to
be gatekeepers at the thresholds were 212.
These were recorded by genealogy in their
villages, whom David and Samuel the seer
established in their office of trust. [23] So
they and their sons were over the gates of
the house of Yahweh, *even* the house of
the tent, as those who kept watch. [24] The
gatekeepers were on the four sides, to the
east, west, north, and south. [25] And their
relatives in their villages *were* to come in
every seven days from time to time *to be*
with them; [26] for the four chief gatekeepers
who *were* Levites, were in an office of trust,
and were over the chambers and over the
treasuries in the house of God. [27] And they
spent the night all around the house of God,
because the watch was committed to them;
and they *were* over opening *it* morning by
morning.

[28] Now some of them were over the
utensils of service, for they counted them
when they brought them in and when they
took them out. [29] Some of them also were
appointed over the furniture and over all
the utensils of the sanctuary and over the
fine flour and the wine and the oil and the
frankincense and the spices. [30] Some of the
sons of the priests prepared the mixing of
the spices. [31] And Mattithiah, one of the
Levites, who was the firstborn of Shallum
the Korahite, had the office of trust over the
things which were baked in pans. [32] Some of
their relatives of the sons of the Kohathites
were over the showbread to prepare it every
sabbath.

[33] Now these are the singers, heads of
fathers' *households* of the Levites, *who
lived* in the chambers *of the temple* free
from other service; for they were over them
in their work day and night. [34] These were
heads of fathers' *households* of the Levites
according to their generations, the heads
who lived in Jerusalem.

35 Now in Gibeon, Jeiel the father of
Gibeon lived, and his wife's name was
Maacah,
36 and his firstborn son *was* Abdon, then
Zur, Kish, Baal, Ner, Nadab,
37 Gedor, Ahio, Zechariah, and Mikloth.
38 Mikloth became the father of
Shimeam. And they also lived with
their relatives in Jerusalem opposite
their *other* relatives.
39 Ner became the father of Kish,
and Kish became the father of Saul,
and Saul became the father of
Jonathan, Malchi-shua, Abinadab, and
Eshbaal.
40 The son of Jonathan *was* Merib-baal,
and Merib-baal became the father of
Micah.
41 The sons of Micah *were* Pithon,
Melech, Tahrea, *and Ahaz*.
42 Ahaz became the father of Jarah,
and Jarah became the father of
Alemeth, Azmaveth, and Zimri;
and Zimri became the father of Moza.

43 Moza became the father of Binea and
Rephaiah his son, Eleasah his son,
Azel his son.
44 Azel had six sons, and these *were* their
names: Azrikam, Bocheru, Ishmael,
Sheariah, Obadiah, and Hanan.
These *were* the sons of Azel.

10 Now the Philistines fought against
Israel; and the men of Israel fled
from before the Philistines and fell slain on
Mount Gilboa. 2 And the Philistines closely
pursued Saul and his sons, and the Philis-
tines struck down Jonathan and Abinadab
and Malchi-shua, the sons of Saul. 3 And the
battle became heavy against Saul, and the
archers hit him; and he was wounded by
the archers. 4 Then Saul said to his armor
bearer, "Draw your sword and pierce me
through with it, lest these uncircumcised
come and abuse me." But his armor bearer
was not willing, for he was greatly afraid. So
Saul took his sword and fell on it. 5 Then his
armor bearer saw that Saul was dead, so he
also fell on his sword and died. 6 Thus Saul
died with his three sons, and all *those* of his
house died together.

7 Then all the men of Israel who were in
the valley saw that they had fled, and that
Saul and his sons were dead. So they forsook
their cities and fled; and the Philistines
came and lived in them.

8 Now it happened on the next day, that
the Philistines came to strip the slain, and
they found Saul and his sons fallen on
Mount Gilboa. 9 So they stripped him and
took his head and his weapons and sent
them all around the land of the Philistines,
to proclaim the good news to their idols
and to the people. 10 And they placed his
weapons in the house of their gods and
fastened his head in the house of Dagon.

11 Then all Jabesh-gilead heard all that
the Philistines had done to Saul, 12 so all the
valiant men arose and took away the body of
Saul and the bodies of his sons and brought
them to Jabesh, and they buried their bones
under the oak in Jabesh and fasted seven
days.

13 Thus Saul died for his unfaithfulness,
which he committed against Yahweh,
because of the word of Yahweh which he did
not keep; and also because he asked counsel
of a medium, making inquiry *of it*, 14 and
did not inquire of Yahweh. Therefore He
put him to death and turned the kingdom
to David the son of Jesse.

Psalm 77:10–15

10 Then I said, "It is my grief,
That the right hand of
the Most High has changed."

11 I shall remember the deeds of Yah;
Surely I will remember Your
wonders of old.
12 I will meditate on all Your work
And muse on Your deeds.
13 O God, Your way is holy;
What god is great like God?
14 You are the God who works wonders;
You have made known Your
strength among the peoples.
15 You have by *Your* arm
redeemed Your people,
The sons of Jacob and Joseph. Selah.

Proverbs 19:15–16

15 Laziness casts into a deep sleep,
And a slack-handed soul
will suffer hunger.
16 He who keeps the commandment
keeps his soul,
But he who despises his way will die.

Acts 6:1–15

6 Now in those days, while the disciples
were multiplying *in number*, there was
grumbling from the Hellenists against the
Hebrews, because their widows were being
overlooked in the daily serving *of food*. 2 So
the twelve summoned the congregation of
the disciples and said, "It is not pleasing *to
God* for us to neglect the word of God in
order to serve tables. 3 Therefore, brothers,
select from among you seven men of good
reputation, full of the Spirit and of wisdom,
whom we may put in charge of this need.
4 But we will devote ourselves to prayer and
to the service of the word." 5 And this word
pleased the whole congregation, and they
chose Stephen, a man full of faith and of the
Holy Spirit, and Philip, Prochorus, Nicanor,
Timon, Parmenas, and Nicolas, a proselyte
from Antioch. 6 And these they stood before
the apostles, and after praying, they laid
their hands on them.

7 And the word of God kept on spreading,
and the number of the disciples continued
to multiply greatly in Jerusalem, and a great

many of the priests were becoming obedient to the faith.

8 And Stephen, full of grace and power, was doing great wonders and signs among the people. 9 But some men from what was called the Synagogue of the Freedmen, *including* both Cyrenians and Alexandrians, and some from Cilicia and Asia, rose up and were arguing with Stephen. 10 But they were unable to oppose the wisdom and the Spirit by whom he was speaking. 11 Then they secretly induced men to say, "We have heard him speak blasphemous words against Moses and God." 12 And they stirred up the people, the elders, and the scribes, and they came up to him, dragged him away, and brought him to the Sanhedrin. 13 And they put forward false witnesses who said, "This man never ceases speaking words against this holy place and the Law; 14 for we have heard him say that this Jesus the Nazarene will destroy this place and alter the customs which Moses handed down to us." 15 And fixing their gaze on him, all who were sitting in the Sanhedrin saw his face like the face of an angel.

JUNE 24

1 Chronicles 11:1–12:40

11 Then all Israel gathered to David at Hebron and said, "Behold, we are your bone and your flesh. 2 Previously, even when Saul was king, you *were* the one who led out and brought in Israel; and Yahweh your God said to you, 'You will shepherd My people Israel, and you will be a ruler over My people Israel.'" 3 So all the elders of Israel came to the king at Hebron, and David cut a covenant with them in Hebron before Yahweh; then they anointed David king over Israel, according to the word of Yahweh through Samuel.

4 Then David and all Israel went to Jerusalem (that is, Jebus); and the Jebusites, the inhabitants of the land, *were* there. 5 Then the inhabitants of Jebus said to David, "You shall not come in here." Nevertheless, David captured the fortress of Zion, that is, the city of David. 6 And David said, "Whoever strikes down a Jebusite first shall be chief and commander." Joab the son of Zeruiah went up first, so he became chief. 7 Then David lived in the stronghold; therefore it was called the city of David. 8 And he built the city all around, from the Millo even to the surrounding area; and Joab repaired the rest of the city. 9 And David became greater and greater, and Yahweh of hosts *was* with him.

10 Now these are the heads of the mighty men whom David had, who gave him strong support in his kingdom, together with all Israel, to make him king, according to the word of Yahweh concerning Israel. 11 These *constitute* the list of the mighty men whom David had: Jashobeam, the son of a Hachmonite, the chief of the thirty; he lifted up his spear against three hundred slain *by him* at one time.

12 And after him was Eleazar the son of Dodo, the Ahohite, who *was* one of the three mighty men. 13 He was with David at Pasdammim. Now the Philistines had gathered together there to battle, and there was a portion of the field full of barley; and the people fled from before the Philistines. 14 But they took their stand in the midst of that portion and delivered it, and struck down the Philistines. So Yahweh saved them by a great salvation.

15 Then three of the thirty chief men went down to the rock to David, to the cave of Adullam, while the camp of the Philistines was camping in the valley of Rephaim. 16 And David was then in the fortress, while the garrison of the Philistines was then in Bethlehem. 17 Then David had a craving and said, "Oh that someone would give me water to drink from the well of Bethlehem, which is by the gate!" 18 So the three broke through the camp of the Philistines and drew water from the well of Bethlehem which was by the gate, and carried *it* and brought *it* to David. Nevertheless, David was not willing to drink it, but poured it out to Yahweh; 19 and he said, "Be it far from me before my God that I should do this. Shall I drink the blood of these men *who went* at the risk of their lives? For at the risk of their lives they brought it." Therefore he was not willing to drink it. These things the three mighty men did.

20 Now Abshai, the brother of Joab, was chief of the thirty. And he swung his spear

against three hundred *who were* slain
by him; and he had a name as well as the
thirty. 21 Of the three in the second *rank* he
was the most honored and became their
commander; however, he did not attain to
the *first* three.
22 Benaiah the son of Jehoiada, the son of
a valiant man of Kabzeel, mighty in deeds,
struck down the two *sons of* Ariel of Moab.
He also went down and struck down a lion in
the midst of a pit on a snowy day. 23 He had
also struck down an Egyptian, an impressive
man, five cubits tall. Now in the Egyptian's
hand was a spear like a weaver's beam,
but he went down to him with a club and
snatched the spear from the Egyptian's hand
and killed him with his own spear. 24 These
things Benaiah the son of Jehoiada did, and
had a name as well as the three mighty men.
25 Behold, he was honored among the thirty,
but he did not attain to the three. And David
appointed him over his guard.
26 Now the mighty men of the military
forces *were*

Asahel the brother of Joab,
Elhanan the son of Dodo of
Bethlehem,
27 Shammoth the Harorite,
Helez the Pelonite,
28 Ira the son of Ikkesh the Tekoite,
Abiezer the Anathothite,
29 Sibbecai the Hushathite,
Ilai the Ahohite,
30 Maharai the Netophathite,
Heled the son of Baanah the
Netophathite,
31 Ithai the son of Ribai of Gibeah of the
sons of Benjamin,
Benaiah the Pirathonite,
32 Hurai of the brooks of Gaash,
Abiel the Arbathite,
33 Azmaveth the Baharumite,
Eliahba the Shaalbonite,
34 the sons of Hashem the Gizonite,
Jonathan the son of Shagee the
Hararite,
35 Ahiam the son of Sacar the Hararite,
Eliphal the son of Ur,
36 Hepher the Mecherathite,
Ahijah the Pelonite,
37 Hezro the Carmelite,
Naarai the son of Ezbai,
38 Joel the brother of Nathan,
Mibhar the son of Hagri,
39 Zelek the Ammonite,
Naharai the Berothite, the armor
bearer of Joab the son of Zeruiah,
40 Ira the Ithrite,
Gareb the Ithrite,
41 Uriah the Hittite,
Zabad the son of Ahlai,
42 Adina the son of Shiza the Reubenite,
a chief of the Reubenites, and thirty
with him,
43 Hanan the son of Maacah
and Joshaphat the Mithnite,
44 Uzzia the Ashterathite,
Shama and Jeiel the sons of Hotham
the Aroerite,
45 Jediael the son of Shimri
and Joha his brother, the Tizite,
46 Eliel the Mahavite
and Jeribai and Joshaviah, the sons of
Elnaam,
and Ithmah the Moabite,
47 Eliel and Obed and Jaasiel the
Mezobaite.

12 Now these are the ones who came
to David at Ziklag, while he was still
restricted because of Saul the son of Kish; and
they were among the mighty men who helped
him in war. 2 They were equipped with bows,
using both the right hand and the left *to sling*
stones and *to shoot* arrows from the bow; *they
were* Saul's relatives from Benjamin.

3 The chief was Ahiezer, then Joash, the
sons of Shemaah the Gibeathite; and
Jeziel and Pelet, the sons of Azmaveth,
and Beracah and Jehu the Anathothite,
4 and Ishmaiah the Gibeonite, a mighty
man among the thirty, and over
the thirty. Then Jeremiah, Jahaziel,
Johanan, Jozabad the Gederathite,
5 Eluzai, Jerimoth, Bealiah, Shemariah,
Shephatiah the Haruphite,
6 Elkanah, Isshiah, Azarel, Joezer,
Jashobeam, the Korahites,
7 and Joelah and Zebadiah, the sons of
Jeroham of Gedor.
8 From the Gadites, mighty men of valor
separated themselves to David in the
stronghold in the wilderness, men
of war *who had gone out for military*
duty, who could handle large shield
and spear, and whose faces were like
the faces of lions, and *they were* as
swift as the gazelles on the mountains.
9 Ezer *was* the first, Obadiah the second,
Eliab the third,

10 Mishmannah the fourth, Jeremiah the fifth,
11 Attai the sixth, Eliel the seventh,
12 Johanan the eighth, Elzabad the ninth,
13 Jeremiah the tenth, Machbannai the eleventh.

14 These of the sons of Gad were chiefs of
the army; he who was least was equal to one
hundred and the greatest to one thousand.
15 These are the ones who crossed the Jordan
in the first month when it was overflowing
all its banks and they made all those in the
valleys flee, both to the east and to the west.

16 Then some of the sons of Benjamin
and Judah came to the stronghold to David.
17 David went out before them, and he
answered and said to them, "If you come
peacefully to me to help me, my heart shall
be united with you; but if to betray me to
my adversaries, since there is no violence in
my hands, may the God of our fathers look
on *it* and reprove." 18 And the Spirit clothed
Amasai, who was the chief of the thirty, *and
he said,*

"*We* are yours, O David,
And with you, O son of Jesse!
Peace, peace to you,
And peace to him who helps you;
Indeed, your God helps you!"

Then David received them and made them chiefs of the band.

19 Now from Manasseh also some
defected to David when he was about to
go to battle with the Philistines against
Saul. But they did not help them, for the
lords of the Philistines after counsel sent
him away, saying, "At *the cost of* our heads
he may defect to his master Saul." 20 As he
went to Ziklag there defected to him from
Manasseh: Adnah, Jozabad, Jediael, Michael,
Jozabad, Elihu and Zillethai, chiefs of thou-
sands who belonged to Manasseh. 21 They
helped David against the marauding band,
for they were all mighty men of valor, and
were commanders in the army. 22 For day
by day *men* came to David to help him, until
there was a great camp like the camp of God.

23 Now these are the numbers of the
companies equipped for *military* duty,
who came to David at Hebron, to turn the
kingdom of Saul to him, according to the
command of Yahweh.

24 The sons of Judah who bore shield and spear *were* 6,800, equipped for *military* duty.
25 Of the sons of Simeon, mighty men of valor for *military* duty, 7,100.
26 Of the sons of Levi 4,600.
27 Now Jehoiada was the leader of *the house of* Aaron, and with him were 3,700,
28 also Zadok, a young man mighty of valor, and of his father's house 22 commanders.
29 Of the sons of Benjamin, Saul's relatives, 3,000; for until now the greatest part of them had kept their allegiance to the house of Saul.
30 Of the sons of Ephraim 20,800, mighty men of valor, men who had a name in their fathers' households.
31 Of the half-tribe of Manasseh 18,000, who were designated by name to come and make David king.
32 Of the sons of Issachar, men who knew *how to* discern the times, to know what Israel should do, their chiefs *were* two hundred; and all their relatives *were* at their command.
33 Of Zebulun, there were 50,000 who went out in the army, who could arrange *themselves* for battle with all kinds of weapons of war and helped *David* with an undivided heart.
34 Of Naphtali *there were* 1,000 commanders, and with them 37,000 with large shield and spear.
35 Of the Danites who could arrange *themselves* for battle, *there were* 28,600.
36 Of Asher *there were* 40,000 who went out in the army to arrange *themselves* for battle.
37 From the other side of the Jordan, of the Reubenites and the Gadites and of the half-tribe of Manasseh, *there were* 120,000 with all *kinds* of weapons for the army for battle.

38 All these, being men of war who could
draw up in battle lines, came to Hebron
with *their* whole heart to make David king
over all Israel; and all the rest also of Israel
were of one heart to make David king.
39 They were there with David three days,
eating and drinking, for their relatives had
prepared for them. 40 Moreover those who
were near to them, *even* as far as Issachar
and Zebulun and Naphtali, brought food on
donkeys, camels, mules, and on oxen, great
provisions *of* flour, fig cakes and bunches

of raisins, wine, oil, oxen, and sheep. There was gladness indeed in Israel.

Psalm 77:16–20

16 The waters saw You, O God;
The waters saw You, they
were in anguish;
The deeps also trembled.
17 The clouds poured out water;
The skies gave forth a sound;
Your arrows went here and there.
18 The sound of Your thunder
was in the whirlwind;
The lightnings lit up the world;
The earth trembled and shook.
19 Your way was in the sea
And Your paths in the mighty waters,
But Your footprints were not known.
20 You led Your people like a flock
By the hand of Moses and Aaron.

Proverbs 19:17–19

17 He who is gracious to a poor
man lends to Yahweh,
And He will repay him for
his bountiful deed.
18 Discipline your son while
there is hope,
And do not direct your soul
to put him to death.
19 *A man of* great wrath will
bear the penalty,
For if you deliver *him*, you will
only have to do it again.

Acts 7:1–16

7 And the high priest said, "Are these
things so?"
2 And he said, "Hear me, brothers and
fathers! The God of glory appeared to our
father Abraham when he was in Mesopo-
tamia, before he lived in Haran, 3 and said
to him, 'LEAVE YOUR COUNTRY AND YOUR
RELATIVES, AND COME INTO THE LAND THAT
I WILL SHOW YOU.' 4 Then he left the land of
the Chaldeans and settled in Haran. From
there, after his father died, *God* had him
move to this country in which you are now
living. 5 But He gave him no inheritance
in it, not even a foot of ground, and He
promised that HE WOULD GIVE IT TO HIM
AS A POSSESSION, AND TO HIS SEED AFTER
HIM, even when he had no child. 6 But God
spoke in this way, that his SEED WOULD BE
SOJOURNERS IN A FOREIGN LAND, AND THAT
THEY WOULD BE ENSLAVED AND MISTREATED
FOR FOUR HUNDRED YEARS. 7 'AND I MYSELF
WILL JUDGE THE NATION TO WHICH THEY
WILL BE ENSLAVED,' said God, 'AND AFTER
THAT THEY WILL COME OUT AND SERVE ME IN
THIS PLACE.' 8 And He gave him the covenant
of circumcision; and so *Abraham* was the
father of Isaac, and circumcised him on the
eighth day; and Isaac *was the father of* Jacob,
and Jacob *of* the twelve patriarchs.
9 "And the patriarchs, becoming jealous
of Joseph, sold him into Egypt. *Yet* God was
with him, 10 and rescued him from all his
afflictions, and granted him favor and wis-
dom in the sight of Pharaoh, king of Egypt,
and he appointed him governor over Egypt
and all his household.
11 "Now a famine came over all Egypt and
Canaan, and great affliction *with it*, and our
fathers could find no food. 12 But when Jacob
heard that there was grain in Egypt, he sent
our fathers *there* the first time. 13 And on
the second *visit* Joseph made himself known
to his brothers, and Joseph's family was
disclosed to Pharaoh. 14 Then Joseph sent
word and invited Jacob his father and all his
relatives to come to him, seventy-five per-
sons *in all*. 15 And Jacob went down to Egypt
and *there* he and our fathers died. 16 *And
from there* they were removed to Shechem
and placed in the tomb which Abraham had
purchased for a sum of money from the sons
of Hamor in Shechem.

This one thing I have proved to myself beyond all question; I shall never, never exhaust this precious book.

— CHARLES H. SPURGEON

JUNE 25

1 Chronicles 13:1–14:17

13 Then David took counsel with the commanders of the thousands and the hundreds, even with every leader. 2 And David said to all the assembly of Israel, "If it seems good to you, and if it is from Yahweh our God, let us send everywhere to our relatives who remain in all the lands of Israel, also to the priests and Levites who are with them in their cities with pasture lands, that they may gather with us; 3 and let us bring back the ark of our God to us, for we did not seek it in the days of Saul." 4 Then all the assembly said that they would do so, for the thing was right in the eyes of all the people.

5 So David assembled all Israel together, from the Shihor of Egypt even to Lebo-hamath, to bring the ark of God from Kiriath-jearim. 6 And David and all Israel went up to Baalah, *that is*, to Kiriath-jearim, which belongs to Judah, to bring up from there the ark of God, Yahweh, who is enthroned *above* the cherubim, where His name is called. 7 And they drove the ark of God on a new cart from the house of Abinadab, and Uzza and Ahio were leading the cart. 8 Now David and all Israel were celebrating before God with all *their* strength, even with songs and with lyres, harps, tambourines, cymbals, and with trumpets.

9 Then they came to the threshing floor of Chidon. And Uzza reached out with his hand to take hold of the ark, because the oxen nearly upset *it*. 10 And the anger of Yahweh burned against Uzza, and He struck him down because he reached out with his hand to the ark; and he died there before God. 11 And David became angry because of Yahweh's breaking out against Uzza; and that place is called Perez-uzza to this day. 12 So David was afraid of God that day, saying, "How can I bring the ark of God *back* to me?" 13 And David did not move the ark with him to the city of David, but took it aside to the house of Obed-edom the Gittite. 14 Thus the ark of God remained with the household of Obed-edom in his house three months; and Yahweh blessed the household of Obed-edom with all that he had.

14 Then Hiram king of Tyre sent messengers to David with cedar trees and craftsmen of walls and craftsmen of wood, to build a house for him. 2 Thus David knew that Yahweh had established him as king over Israel, *and* that his kingdom was lifted up, for the sake of His people Israel.

3 Then David took more wives at Jerusalem, and David became the father of more sons and daughters. 4 These are the names of the children born to him in Jerusalem:

Shammua, Shobab, Nathan, Solomon,
5 Ibhar, Elishua, Elpelet,
6 Nogah, Nepheg, Japhia,
7 Elishama, Beeliada, and Eliphelet.

8 Then the Philistines heard that David had been anointed king over all Israel, so all the Philistines went up to seek out David. And David heard *of it* and went out against them. 9 Now the Philistines had come and made a raid in the valley of Rephaim. 10 Then David asked of God, saying, "Shall I go up against the Philistines? And will You give them into my hand?" And Yahweh said to him, "Go up, for I will give them into your hand." 11 So they came up to Baal-perazim, and there David struck them down; and David said, "God has broken through my enemies by my hand, like the breakthrough of waters." Therefore they named that place Baal-perazim. 12 And they forsook their gods there; so David said *the word*, and they were burned with fire.

13 Then the Philistines yet again made a raid in the valley. 14 So David again asked of God, and God said to him, "You shall not go *directly* up after them; circle around from behind them and come at them in front of the balsam trees. 15 And it will be that when you hear the sound of marching in the tops of the balsam trees, then you shall go out to battle, for God will have gone out before you to strike the camp of the Philistines." 16 Then David did just as God had commanded him, and they struck down the camp of the Philistines from Gibeon even as far as Gezer. 17 Then the name of David went out into all the lands; and Yahweh brought the dread of him on all the nations.

Psalm 78:1–11

1 Give ear, O my people, to
   my instruction;
Incline your ears to the
   words of my mouth.

2 I will open my mouth in a parable;
I will pour forth dark sayings of old,
3 Which we have heard and known,
And our fathers have recounted to us.
4 We will not conceal them
from their children,
But recount to the generation to
come the praises of Yahweh,
And His strength and His wondrous
deeds that He has done.

5 For He established a testimony in Jacob
And set a law in Israel,
Which He commanded our fathers
That they should teach them
to their children,
6 That the generation to come
might know, *even* the
children *yet* to be born,
That they may arise and recount
them to their children,
7 That they should set their
confidence in God
And not forget the deeds of God,
But observe His commandments,
8 And not be like their fathers,
A stubborn and rebellious generation,
A generation that did not
prepare its heart
And whose spirit was not
faithful to God.

9 The sons of Ephraim were archers
equipped with bows,
Yet they turned back in
the day of battle.
10 They did not keep the covenant of God
And refused to walk in His law;
11 So they forgot His acts
And His wondrous deeds that
He had shown them.

Proverbs 19:20–21

20 Listen to counsel and
receive discipline,
That you may be wise in the
end of your *days*.
21 Many thoughts are in a man's heart,
But it is the counsel of Yahweh
that will stand.

Acts 7:17–43

17 "But as the time of the promise was
drawing near which God had assured
to Abraham, the people increased and
multiplied in Egypt, 18 until ANOTHER KING
AROSE OVER EGYPT WHO DID NOT KNOW ABOUT
JOSEPH. 19 It was he who deceitfully took
advantage of our family and mistreated
our fathers to set their infants outside so
that they would not survive. 20 It was at this
time that Moses was born, and he was lovely
in the sight of God, and he was nurtured
three months in his father's home. 21 And
after he had been set outside, Pharaoh's
daughter took him away and nurtured him
as her own son. 22 And Moses was educated
in all the wisdom of the Egyptians, and he
was powerful in words and deeds. 23 But
when he was approaching the age of forty,
it entered his heart to visit his brothers, the
sons of Israel. 24 And when he saw one *of*
them being treated unjustly, he defended
him and took justice for the oppressed
by striking down the Egyptian. 25 And he
supposed that his brothers understood that
God was granting them salvation through
him, but they did not understand. 26 On
the following day he appeared to them as
they were fighting together, and he tried
to reconcile them in peace, saying, 'Men,
you are brothers, why are you treating one
another unjustly?' 27 But the one who was
treating his neighbor unjustly pushed him
away, saying, 'WHO MADE YOU A RULER AND
JUDGE OVER US? 28 DO YOU INTEND TO KILL ME
AS YOU KILLED THE EGYPTIAN YESTERDAY?'
29 At this remark, MOSES FLED AND BECAME
A SOJOURNER IN THE LAND OF MIDIAN, where
he was the father of two sons.

30 "And after forty years had passed, AN
ANGEL APPEARED TO HIM IN THE WILDERNESS
OF MOUNT Sinai, IN THE FLAME OF A BURNING
BUSH. 31 When Moses saw it, he was mar-
veling at the sight; and as he approached to
look *more* closely, there came the voice of
the Lord: 32 'I AM THE GOD OF YOUR FATHERS,
THE GOD OF ABRAHAM AND ISAAC AND JACOB.'
Moses trembled with fear and would not
dare to look. 33 BUT THE LORD SAID TO HIM,
'REMOVE THE SANDALS FROM YOUR FEET, FOR
THE PLACE ON WHICH YOU ARE STANDING IS
HOLY GROUND. 34 I HAVE SURELY SEEN THE
OPPRESSION OF MY PEOPLE IN EGYPT AND
HAVE HEARD THEIR GROANS, AND I HAVE COME
DOWN TO DELIVER THEM; COME NOW, AND I
WILL SEND YOU TO EGYPT.'

35 "This Moses whom they disowned,
saying, 'WHO MADE YOU A RULER AND A
JUDGE?' is the one whom God sent *to be*

both a ruler and a deliverer with the help
of the angel who appeared to him in the
bush. 36 This man led them out, doing
wonders and signs in the land of Egypt
and in the Red Sea and in the wilderness
for forty years. 37 This is the Moses who
said to the sons of Israel, 'God will raise
up for you a prophet like me from your
brothers.' 38 This is the one who, in the
congregation in the wilderness, was with
the angel who was speaking to him on
Mount Sinai and with our fathers; the one
who received living oracles to pass on to
you. 39 Our fathers were unwilling to be
obedient to him, but rejected him and in
their hearts turned back to Egypt, 40 saying
to Aaron, 'Make for us gods who will go
before us; for this Moses who led us out
of the land of Egypt—we do not know
what has become of him.' 41 At that time
they made a calf and brought a sacrifice to
the idol, and were rejoicing in the works
of their hands. 42 But God turned away
and delivered them up to serve the host
of heaven; as it is written in the book of
the prophets, 'Did you present Me with
slain beasts and sacrifices forty years
in the wilderness, O house of Israel?
43 You also took along the tabernacle of
Moloch and the star of the god Rompha,
the images which you made to worship.
I also will remove you beyond Babylon.'

JUNE 26

1 Chronicles 15:1–16:43

15 Then *David* made houses for himself
in the city of David; and he prepared
a place for the ark of God and pitched a tent
for it. 2 And David said, "No one is to carry
the ark of God but the Levites; for Yahweh
chose them to carry the ark of God and
to minister to Him forever." 3 Then David
assembled all Israel at Jerusalem to bring
up the ark of Yahweh to its place which he
had prepared for it. 4 And David gathered
together the sons of Aaron and the Levites:
5 of the sons of Kohath, Uriel the chief,
and 120 of his relatives;
6 of the sons of Merari, Asaiah the chief,
and 220 of his relatives;
7 of the sons of Gershom, Joel the chief,
and 130 of his relatives;
8 of the sons of Elizaphan, Shemaiah
the chief, and 200 of his relatives;
9 of the sons of Hebron, Eliel the chief,
and 80 of his relatives;
10 of the sons of Uzziel, Amminadab the
chief, and 112 of his relatives.

11 Then David called for Zadok and
Abiathar the priests, and for the Levites,
for Uriel, Asaiah, Joel, Shemaiah, Eliel and
Amminadab, 12 and said to them, "You are
the heads of the fathers' *households* of the
Levites; set yourselves apart as holy, both
you and your relatives, that you may bring
up the ark of Yahweh, the God of Israel,
to *the place* that I have prepared for it.
13 Because you did not *carry it* at the first,
Yahweh our God broke out against us, for
we did not seek Him according to the *legal*
judgment." 14 So the priests and the Levites
set themselves apart as holy to bring up the
ark of Yahweh, the God of Israel. 15 And the
sons of the Levites carried the ark of God
on their shoulders with the poles thereon,
as Moses had commanded according to the
word of Yahweh.

16 Then David said to the chiefs of the
Levites to appoint their relatives the singers,
with instruments of music, harps, lyres,
loud-sounding cymbals, to raise a sound
of gladness. 17 So the Levites appointed
Heman the son of Joel, and from his rela-
tives, Asaph the son of Berechiah; and from
the sons of Merari their relatives, Ethan the
son of Kushaiah, 18 and with them their
relatives of the second rank, Zechariah,
Ben, Jaaziel, Shemiramoth, Jehiel, Unni,
Eliab, Benaiah, Maaseiah, Mattithiah, Eliph-
elehu, Mikneiah, Obed-edom, and Jeiel,
the gatekeepers. 19 So the singers, Heman,
Asaph and Ethan *were appointed* to sound
aloud cymbals of bronze; 20 and Zechariah,
Aziel, Shemiramoth, Jehiel, Unni, Eliab,
Maaseiah, and Benaiah, with harps *set*
according to alamoth; 21 and Mattithiah,
Eliphelehu, Mikneiah, Obed-edom, Jeiel,
and Azaziah, to lead with lyres *set* according
to the sheminith. 22 Chenaniah, chief of the
Levites, was *in charge of* the singing; he
gave instruction in singing because he had
understanding. 23 Berechiah and Elkanah
were gatekeepers for the ark. 24 Shebaniah,
Joshaphat, Nethanel, Amasai, Zechariah,

Benaiah, and Eliezer, the priests, blew the
trumpets before the ark of God. Obed-edom
and Jehiah also *were* gatekeepers for the ark.
25 So *it was* David, with the elders of Israel
and the commanders over thousands, who
went to bring up the ark of the covenant of
Yahweh from the house of Obed-edom with
gladness. 26 Now this happened because God
was helping the Levites who were carrying
the ark of the covenant of Yahweh. And they
sacrificed seven bulls and seven rams. 27 Now
David was clothed with a robe of fine linen
with all the Levites who were carrying the
ark, as well as the singers and Chenaniah the
leader of the singing *with* the singers. David
also wore a linen ephod. 28 Thus all Israel
was bringing up the ark of the covenant of
Yahweh with shouting, and with sound of
the horn, with trumpets, with loud-sounding
cymbals, with harps, and lyres.
29 Now it happened *as* the ark of the cov-
enant of Yahweh came to the city of David,
that Michal the daughter of Saul looked out
of the window and saw King David leaping
and celebrating; and she despised him in
her heart.

16 And they brought in the ark of God
and placed it inside the tent which
David had pitched for it, and they brought
burnt offerings and peace offerings near
before God. 2 Then David completed offering
the burnt offerings and the peace offerings.
And he blessed the people in the name of
Yahweh. 3 And he apportioned to everyone
of Israel, both men and women, to everyone
a loaf of bread and a portion *of meat* and a
raisin cake.
4 And he made some of the Levites
ministers before the ark of Yahweh, even
to bring remembrance and to thank and
praise Yahweh, the God of Israel: 5 Asaph
the chief, and second to him Zechariah,
then Jeiel, Shemiramoth, Jehiel, Mattithiah,
Eliab, Benaiah, Obed-edom, and Jeiel, with
musical instruments, harps, lyres; also
Asaph *played* loud-sounding cymbals,
6 and Benaiah and Jahaziel the priests *blew*
trumpets continually before the ark of the
covenant of God.
7 Then on that day David first assigned
Asaph and his relatives to give thanks to
Yahweh.

8 Oh give thanks to Yahweh,
call upon His name;
Make known His acts
among the peoples.
9 Sing to Him, sing praises to Him;
Muse on all His wondrous deeds.
10 Boast in His holy name;
Let the heart of those who
seek Yahweh be glad.
11 Inquire of Yahweh and His strength;
Seek His face continually.
12 Remember His wondrous deeds
which He has done,
His miraculous signs and the
judgments uttered by His mouth,
13 O seed of Israel His servant,
O sons of Jacob, His chosen ones!
14 He is Yahweh our God;
His judgments are in all the earth.
15 Remember His covenant forever,
The word which He commanded
for a thousand generations,
16 Which He cut with Abraham,
And His oath to Isaac.
17 Then He also confirmed it
to Jacob for a statute,
To Israel as an everlasting covenant,
18 Saying, "To you I will give
the land of Canaan,
As the portion of your inheritance,"
19 When you were only a few
men in number,
Of little account, and sojourners in it,
20 And they wandered about
from nation to nation,
And from *one* kingdom to
another people,
21 He permitted no man to oppress them,
And He reproved kings for their sakes,
22 "Do not touch My anointed ones,
And against My prophets do no evil."
23 Sing to Yahweh, all the earth;
Proclaim good news of His
salvation from day to day.
24 Recount His glory among the nations,
His wondrous deeds among
all the peoples.
25 For great is Yahweh, and
greatly to be praised;
And He is more fearsome than all gods.
26 For all the gods of the peoples are idols,
But Yahweh made the heavens.
27 Splendor and majesty are before Him,
Strength and joy are in His place.
28 Ascribe to Yahweh, O families
of the peoples,
Ascribe to Yahweh glory and strength.

29 Ascribe to Yahweh the
glory of His name;
Lift up an offering, and
come before Him;
Worship Yahweh in the
splendor of holiness.
30 Tremble before Him, all the earth;
Indeed, the world is established,
it will not be shaken.
31 Let the heavens be glad, and
let the earth rejoice;
And let them say among the
nations, "Yahweh reigns."
32 Let the sea roar, as well as its fullness;
Let the field exult, and all that is in it.
33 Then the trees of the forest will
sing for joy before Yahweh;
For He is coming to judge the earth.
34 Oh give thanks to Yahweh,
for He is good,
For His lovingkindness
endures forever.
35 Then say, "Save us, O God
of our salvation,
And gather us and deliver us
from among the nations,
To give thanks to Your holy name
And revel in Your praise."
36 Blessed be Yahweh, the God of Israel,
From everlasting to everlasting.

Then all the people said, "Amen," and
praised Yahweh.
37 So he left behind Asaph and his rela-
tives there before the ark of the covenant
of Yahweh to minister before the ark
continually, as every day's work required;
38 and Obed-edom with his 68 relatives;
Obed-edom, also the son of Jeduthun, and
Hosah as gatekeepers. 39 Now *he left behind*
Zadok the priest and his relatives the priests
before the tabernacle of Yahweh in the high
place, which *was* at Gibeon, 40 to offer burnt
offerings to Yahweh on the altar of burnt
offering continually morning and evening,
even according to all that is written in the
law of Yahweh, which He commanded
Israel. 41 And with them *were* Heman and
Jeduthun, and the rest who were chosen,
who were designated by name, to give
thanks to Yahweh, because His lovingk-
indness endures forever. 42 And with them
were Heman and Jeduthun *with* trumpets
and cymbals for those who should sound
aloud, and *with* instruments *for* the songs of
God, and the sons of Jeduthun for the gate.
43 Then all the people went each to his
house, and David returned to bless his
household.

Psalm 78:12–16

12 He did wonders before their fathers
In the land of Egypt, in
the field of Zoan.
13 He split the sea and caused
them to pass through,
And He made the waters
stand up like a heap.
14 Then He led them with
the cloud by day
And all the night with a light of fire.
15 He was splitting the rocks
in the wilderness
And so gave *them* abundant
drink like the ocean depths.
16 He brought forth streams
also from the cliff face
And caused waters to run
down like rivers.

Proverbs 19:22–24

22 What is desirable in a man
is his lovingkindness,
And better is a poor man than
a man of falsehood.
23 The fear of Yahweh *leads* to life,
So that one may sleep satisfied,
not visited by evil.
24 The sluggard buries his
hand in the dish,
But will not even bring it
back to his mouth.

Acts 7:44–60

44 "Our fathers had the tabernacle of
testimony in the wilderness, just as He,
who spoke to Moses, directed *him* to make
it according to the pattern which he had
seen. 45 And having received it in their turn,
our fathers brought it in with Joshua when
they dispossessed the nations whom God
drove out before our fathers, until the time
of David. 46 *David* found favor in the sight of
God, and asked that he might find a dwelling
place for the God of Jacob. 47 But Solomon
built a house for Him. 48 However, the Most
High does not dwell in *houses* made by
human hands, as the prophet says:
49 'HEAVEN IS MY THRONE,
AND EARTH IS THE FOOTSTOOL
OF MY FEET.

WHAT KIND OF HOUSE WILL YOU
BUILD FOR ME?' says the Lord,
'OR WHAT PLACE IS THERE FOR MY REST?
50 'WAS IT NOT MY HAND WHICH
MADE ALL THESE THINGS?'

51 "You men—stiff-necked and uncircumcised in heart and ears—are always resisting the Holy Spirit. As your fathers did, so do you. 52 And which one of the prophets did your fathers not persecute? They killed those who had previously announced the coming of the Righteous One, whose betrayers and murderers you have now become; 53 you who received the Law as ordained by angels, and *yet* did not observe it."

54 Now when they heard this, they became furious in their hearts, and they *began* gnashing their teeth at him. 55 But being full of the Holy Spirit, he gazed intently into heaven and saw the glory of God, and Jesus standing at the right hand of God; 56 and he said, "Behold, I see the heavens opened up and the Son of Man standing at the right hand of God." 57 But crying out with a loud voice, they covered their ears and rushed at him with one accord. 58 And when they had driven him out of the city, they *began* stoning *him*; and the witnesses laid aside their garments at the feet of a young man named Saul. 59 They went on stoning Stephen as he was calling out and saying, "Lord Jesus, receive my spirit!" 60 Then falling on his knees, he cried out with a loud voice, "Lord, do not hold this sin against them!" And having said this, he fell asleep.

JUNE 27

1 Chronicles 17:1–18:17

17 Now it happened when David inhabited his house, that David said to Nathan the prophet, "Behold, I inhabit a house of cedar, but the ark of the covenant of Yahweh is under *tent* curtains." 2 So Nathan said to David, "Do all that is in your heart, for God is with you."

3 Now it happened in the same night, that the word of God came to Nathan, saying, 4 "Go and say to David My servant, 'Thus says Yahweh, "You shall not build Me a house to inhabit; 5 for I have not inhabited a house since the day that I brought up Israel to this day, but I have been from tent to tent and from *one* dwelling place *to another*. 6 Wherever I have gone about with all Israel, did I speak a word with *even* one of the judges of Israel, whom I commanded to shepherd My people, saying, 'Why have you not built Me a house of cedar?'"'

7 "So now, thus shall you say to My servant David, 'Thus says Yahweh of hosts, "I Myself took you from the pasture, from following the sheep, to be ruler over My people Israel. 8 And I have been with you wherever you have gone, and have cut off all your enemies from before you; and I will make you a name like the name of the great men who are on the earth. 9 And I will appoint a place for My people Israel and will plant them, that they may dwell in their own place and not be disturbed again; and the unrighteous will not waste them anymore as formerly, 10 even from the day that I commanded judges *to be* over My people Israel. And I will subdue all your enemies.

And I tell you that Yahweh will build a house for you. 11 And it will be that when your days are fulfilled to go *to be* with your fathers, I will raise up *one of* your seed after you, who will be of your sons; and I will establish his kingdom. 12 He shall build for Me a house, and I will establish his throne forever. 13 I will be a father to him and he will be a son to Me; and I will not remove My lovingkindness from him, as I removed *it* from him who was before you. 14 But I will cause him to stand in My house and in My kingdom forever, and his throne shall be established forever."'" 15 According to all these words and according to all this vision, so Nathan spoke to David.

16 Then David the king went in and sat before Yahweh and said, "Who am I, O Yahweh God, and what is my house that You have brought me this far? 17 And this was a small thing in Your eyes, O God; but You have spoken of the house of Your slave concerning the distant future, and have regarded me according to the standard of a man of high degree, O Yahweh God. 18 Again what more can David *say* to You concerning the glory *bestowed* on Your slave? You know Your slave. 19 O Yahweh, for the sake of Your slave, and according to Your own heart, You

have done all this greatness, to make known
all these great things. 20 O Yahweh, there is
none like You, and there is no God besides
You, according to all that we have heard with
our ears. 21 And what one nation in the earth
is like Your people Israel, whom God went
to redeem for Himself *as* a people, to make
You a name by great and awesome things, in
driving out nations from before Your people,
whom You redeemed out of Egypt? 22 Yet
You gave Your people Israel *to be* Your own
people forever, and You, O Yahweh, have
become their God.

23 "So now, O Yahweh, let the word that
You have spoken concerning Your slave
and concerning his house endure forever,
and do as You have spoken, 24 that Your
name endure and be magnified forever,
by saying, 'Yahweh of hosts is the God of
Israel, *even* a God to Israel; and the house
of David Your servant is established before
You.' 25 For You, O my God, have revealed
in the hearing of Your slave that You will
build for him a house; therefore Your slave
has found *courage* to pray before You. 26 So
now, O Yahweh, You are God, and You have
promised this good thing to Your slave. 27 So
now, You have been pleased to bless the
house of Your slave, that it may be forever
before You. For You, O Yahweh, have blessed,
and it is blessed forever."

18 Now it happened afterwards, that
David struck the Philistines and
subdued them and took Gath and its towns
from the hand of the Philistines. 2 He also
struck Moab, and the Moabites became
servants to David, bringing tribute.

3 Then David struck Hadadezer king of
Zobah *as far as* Hamath, as he went to set
up his power at the Euphrates River. 4 And
David captured from him 1,000 chariots and
7,000 horsemen and 20,000 foot soldiers,
and David hamstrung all the chariot horses,
but left *enough* of them for 100 chariots.

5 Then the Arameans of Damascus came
to help Hadadezer king of Zobah. And David
struck down 22,000 men of the Arameans.
6 Then David placed *garrisons* among the
Arameans of Damascus; and the Arameans
became servants to David, bringing tribute.
And Yahweh granted salvation to David
wherever he went. 7 And David took the
small shields of gold which were carried
by the servants of Hadadezer and brought
them to Jerusalem. 8 Also from Tibhath
and from Cun, cities of Hadadezer, David
took a very large amount of bronze, with
which Solomon made the bronze sea and
the pillars and the bronze utensils.

9 Then Tou king of Hamath heard that
David had struck down all the military
force of Hadadezer king of Zobah, 10 so he
sent Hadoram his son to King David to greet
him and to bless him, because he had fought
against Hadadezer and struck him down; for
Hadadezer had been at war with Tou. And
Hadoram brought all kinds of articles of gold
and silver and bronze. 11 King David also set
these apart as holy to Yahweh with the silver
and the gold which he had carried away from
all the nations: from Edom, Moab, the sons of
Ammon, the Philistines, and from Amalek.

12 Moreover, Abishai the son of Zeruiah
smote 18,000 of Edom in the Valley of Salt.
13 Then he placed garrisons in Edom, and all
the Edomites became servants to David. And
Yahweh granted salvation to David wherever
he went.

14 So David reigned over all Israel; and he
was doing justice and righteousness for all
his people. 15 Now Joab the son of Zeruiah
was over the army, and Jehoshaphat the son
of Ahilud *was* recorder; 16 and Zadok the son
of Ahitub and Abimelech the son of Abia-
thar *were* priests, and Shavsha *was* scribe;
17 and Benaiah the son of Jehoiada *was* over
the Cherethites and the Pelethites, and the
sons of David *were* chiefs at the king's side.

Psalm 78:17–25

17 Yet they still continued to
sin against Him,
To rebel against the Most
High in the desert.
18 And in their heart they
put God to the test
By asking for food according
to their desire.
19 Then they spoke against God;
They said, "Can God prepare a
table in the wilderness?
20 "Behold, He struck the rock so
that waters gushed out,
And streams were overflowing;
Can He give bread also?
Will He prepare meat for His people?"

21 Therefore Yahweh heard and
was full of wrath;

And a fire was kindled against Jacob
And anger also mounted against Israel,
22 Because they did not believe in God
And did not trust in His salvation.
23 Yet He commanded the skies above
And opened the doors of heaven;
24 He rained down manna
upon them to eat
And gave them grain from heaven.
25 Man ate the bread of angels;
He sent them provision to satisfy.

Proverbs 19:25–26

25 Strike a scoffer and the simple
may become prudent,
But reprove one who has
understanding and he will
understand knowledge.
26 He who assaults *his* father *and*
causes *his* mother to flee
Is a son who brings shame
and humiliation.

Acts 8:1–25

8 Now Saul was in hearty agreement with
putting him to death.
And on that day a great persecution began
against the church in Jerusalem, and they
were all scattered throughout the regions
of Judea and Samaria, except the apostles.
2 And *some* devout men buried Stephen
and made loud lamentation over him. 3 But
Saul *began* ravaging the church, entering
house after house, and dragging off men and
women, he was delivering them into prison.
4 Therefore, those who had been scattered
went about, proclaiming the good news of
the word. 5 Now Philip went down to the city
of Samaria and *began* preaching Christ to
them. 6 And the crowds with one accord
were giving attention to what was being
said by Philip, as they heard and saw the
signs which he was doing. 7 For *in the case*
of many who had unclean spirits, they were
coming out *of them* shouting with a loud
voice; and many who had been paralyzed
and lame were healed. 8 So there was great
joy in that city.
9 Now there was a man named Simon,
who formerly was practicing magic in the
city and astounding the people of Samaria,
claiming to be someone great; 10 and they
all, from smallest to greatest, were giving
attention to him, saying, "This man is what
is called the Great Power of God." 11 And
they were giving him attention because he
had for a long time astounded them with
his magic arts. 12 But when they believed
Philip proclaiming the good news about
the kingdom of God and the name of Jesus
Christ, they were being baptized, both
men and women. 13 Even Simon himself
believed; and after being baptized, he con-
tinued on with Philip, and as he observed
signs and great miracles taking place, he was
constantly astounded.
14 Now when the apostles in Jerusalem
heard that Samaria had received the word of
God, they sent them Peter and John, 15 who
came down and prayed for them that they
might receive the Holy Spirit. 16 For He had
not yet fallen upon any of them; they had
simply been baptized in the name of the
Lord Jesus. 17 Then they *began* laying their
hands on them, and they were receiving the
Holy Spirit. 18 Now when Simon saw that
the Spirit had been bestowed through the
laying on of the apostles' hands, he offered
them money, 19 saying, "Give this authority
to me as well, so that everyone on whom I
lay my hands may receive the Holy Spirit."
20 But Peter said to him, "May your silver
perish with you, because you supposed you
could obtain the gift of God with money!
21 You have no part or portion in this mat-
ter, for your heart is not right before God.
22 Therefore repent of this wickedness of
yours, and pray earnestly to the Lord that,
if possible, the intention of your heart may
be forgiven you. 23 For I see that you are in
the gall of bitterness and in the bondage of
unrighteousness." 24 But Simon answered
and said, "Pray earnestly to the Lord for me
yourselves, so that nothing of what you have
said may come upon me."
25 So, when they had solemnly borne
witness and spoken the word of the Lord,
they started back to Jerusalem, and were
proclaiming the gospel to many villages of
the Samaritans.

JUNE 28

1 Chronicles 19:1–20:8

19 Now it happened afterwards, that
Nahash the king of the sons of
Ammon died, and his son became king
in his place. 2 So David said, "I will show
lovingkindness to Hanun the son of Nahash,
because his father showed lovingkindness
to me." So David sent messengers to comfort
him concerning his father. And David's
servants came into the land of the sons of
Ammon to Hanun to comfort him. 3 But
the princes of the sons of Ammon said to
Hanun, "In your eyes, is David honoring
your father because he has sent comforters
to you? Have not his servants come to you to
search and to overthrow and to spy out the
land?" 4 So Hanun took David's servants and
shaved them and cut off their garments in
the middle as far as their hips, and sent them
away. 5 Then *certain persons* went and told
David about the men. And he sent to meet
them, for the men were greatly dishonored.
And the king said, "Stay at Jericho until your
beards grow, and *then* return."

6 Then the sons of Ammon saw that they
had made themselves odious to David. So
Hanun and the sons of Ammon sent 1,000
talents of silver to hire for themselves
chariots and horsemen from Mesopotamia,
from Aram-maacah, and from Zobah. 7 So
they hired for themselves 32,000 chariots,
and the king of Maacah and his people, who
came and camped before Medeba. And the
sons of Ammon gathered together from
their cities and came to battle. 8 Then David
heard *of it*, and he sent Joab and all the army,
the mighty men. 9 And the sons of Ammon
came out and arranged *themselves* for battle
at the entrance of the city. But the kings who
had come were by themselves in the field.

10 Then Joab saw that the battle was set
against him in front and in the rear. So he
chose from all the choice men of Israel
and they arranged *themselves* to meet the
Arameans. 11 But the remainder of the
people he put in the hand of Abshai his
brother; and they arranged themselves to
meet the sons of Ammon. 12 And he said,
"If the Arameans are too strong for me, then
you shall save me; but if the sons of Ammon
are too strong for you, then I will save you.
13 Be strong, and let us show strength for the
sake of our people and for the cities of our
God; and may Yahweh do what is good in His
sight." 14 So Joab and the people who were
with him drew near before the Arameans for
the battle, and they fled before him. 15 Now
the sons of Ammon saw that the Arameans
fled. So they themselves also fled before
Abshai his brother and came into the city.
Then Joab came to Jerusalem.

16 Then the Arameans saw that they
had been defeated by Israel. So they sent
messengers and brought out the Arameans
who were beyond the River, and Shophach
the commander of the army of Hadadezer
led them. 17 And it was told to David, so he
gathered all Israel together and crossed the
Jordan, and came upon them and arranged
for battle against them. So David arranged
them in battle to meet the Arameans. And
they fought against him. 18 But the Arameans
fled before Israel, and David killed of the
Arameans 7,000 charioteers and 40,000
foot soldiers, and put to death Shophach
the commander of the army. 19 Then the
servants of Hadadezer saw that they were
defeated by Israel. So they made peace with
David and served him. And the Arameans
were not willing to save the sons of Ammon
anymore.

20 Now it happened in the spring, at the
time when kings go out *to battle*, that
Joab led out the force of the military and
brought the land of the sons of Ammon to
ruin, and came and besieged Rabbah. But
David stayed at Jerusalem. And Joab struck
Rabbah and tore it down. 2 Then David took
the crown of their king from his head; and
he found it to weigh a talent of gold, and in
it *was* a precious stone; and it was *placed* on
David's head. And he brought out the spoil
of the city *in* a very great amount. 3 He also
brought out the people who were in it and
made *them* work with saws and with sharp
iron instruments and with axes. And thus
David used to do to all the cities of the sons
of Ammon. Then David and all the people
returned *to* Jerusalem.

4 Now it happened afterwards, that war
broke out at Gezer with the Philistines;
then Sibbecai the Hushathite struck
down Sippai, *one* among those born of

the giants, and they were subdued. 5 And
there was war with the Philistines again,
and Elhanan the son of Jair struck down
Lahmi the brother of Goliath the Gittite,
the shaft of whose spear was like a weaver's
beam. 6 Then there was war at Gath again,
and there was a man of *great* stature who
had twenty-four fingers and toes, six *fingers
on each hand* and six *toes on each foot*; and
he also had been born to the giants. 7 And
he reproached Israel, so Jonathan the son of
Shimea, David's brother, struck him down.
8 These were born to the giants in Gath, and
they fell by the hand of David and by the
hand of his servants.

Psalm 78:26–33

26 He led forth the east wind
in the heavens
And by His strength He
guided the south wind.
27 Then He rained meat upon
them like the dust,
Even winged fowl like the
sand of the seas,
28 He caused *them* to fall in the
midst of His camp,
All around His dwelling places.
29 So they ate and were very satisfied,
And their desire He brought to them.
30 Before they had satisfied their desire,
While their food was in their mouths,
31 The anger of God rose against them
And killed some of their stoutest ones,
And subdued the choice men of Israel.
32 In spite of all this they still sinned
And did not believe in His
wondrous deeds.
33 So He brought their days
to an end in futility
And their years in sudden terror.

Proverbs 19:27–29

27 Cease listening, my son, to discipline,
And you will stray from the
words of knowledge.
28 A vile witness scoffs at justice,
And the mouth of the wicked
swallows up iniquity.
29 Judgments are established for scoffers,
And beatings for the back of fools.

Acts 8:26–40

26 But an angel of the Lord spoke to Philip
saying, "Rise up and go south to the road
that descends from Jerusalem to Gaza."
(This is a desert *road*.) 27 So he rose up and
went; and behold, there was an Ethiopian
eunuch, a court official of Candace, queen of
the Ethiopians, who was in charge of all her
treasure; and he had come to Jerusalem to
worship, 28 and he was returning and sitting
in his chariot, and was reading the prophet
Isaiah. 29 Then the Spirit said to Philip, "Go
over and join this chariot." 30 And Philip
ran up and heard him reading Isaiah the
prophet, and said, "Do you understand what
you are reading?" 31 And he said, "Well, how
could I, unless someone guides me?" And he
invited Philip to come up and sit with him.
32 Now the passage of Scripture which he
was reading was this:

"AS A SHEEP IS LED TO SLAUGHTER;
AND AS A LAMB BEFORE ITS
SHEARER IS SILENT,
SO HE DOES NOT OPEN HIS MOUTH.
33 "IN HUMILIATION HIS JUDGMENT
WAS TAKEN AWAY;
WHO WILL RECOUNT HIS GENERATION?
FOR HIS LIFE IS REMOVED
FROM THE EARTH."

34 And the eunuch answered Philip and
said, "I ask you earnestly, of whom does the
prophet say this? Of himself or of someone
else?" 35 Then Philip opened his mouth, and
beginning from this Scripture he proclaimed
the good news about Jesus to him. 36 And as
they went along the road they came to some
water; and the eunuch *said, "Look! Water!
What prevents me from being baptized?"
37 [And Philip said, "If you believe with all
your heart, you may." And he answered and
said, "I believe that Jesus Christ is the Son of
God."] 38 And he ordered the chariot to stop,
and they both went down into the water,
Philip as well as the eunuch, and he bap-
tized him. 39 When they came up out of the
water, the Spirit of the Lord snatched Philip
away, and the eunuch no longer saw him,
but went on his way rejoicing. 40 But Philip
found himself at Azotus, and as he passed
through he kept proclaiming the gospel to
all the cities until he came to Caesarea.

JUNE 29

1 Chronicles 21:1–22:19

21 Then Satan stood up against Israel and incited David to number Israel. 2 So David said to Joab and to the princes of the people, "Go, count Israel from Beersheba even to Dan, and bring me *word* that I may know their *total* count." 3 But Joab said, "May Yahweh add to His people a hundred times as many as they are! But, my lord the king, are they not all my lord's servants? Why does my lord seek this thing? Why should he be a cause of guilt to Israel?" 4 Nevertheless, the king's word *stood* strong against Joab. So, Joab went out and went throughout all Israel, and came to Jerusalem. 5 And Joab gave the *total* count of the census of the people to David. And all Israel were 1,100,000 men who drew the sword; and Judah *was* 470,000 men who drew the sword. 6 But he did not number Levi and Benjamin among them, for the king's command was abominable to Joab.

7 And this thing was displeasing in the sight of God, so He struck Israel. 8 Then David said to God, "I have sinned greatly, in that I have done this thing. But now, please take away the iniquity of Your slave, for I have acted very foolishly."

9 And Yahweh spoke to Gad, David's seer, saying, 10 "Go and speak to David, saying, 'Thus says Yahweh, "I am offering you three things; choose for yourself one of them, and I will do *that* to you."'" 11 So Gad came to David and said to him, "Thus says Yahweh, 'Take for yourself 12 either three years of famine, or three months to be swept away before your adversaries, while the sword of your enemies overtakes *you*, or else three days of the sword of Yahweh, even pestilence in the land, and the angel of Yahweh destroying throughout all the territory of Israel.' So now, see what word I should return to Him who sent me." 13 Then David said to Gad, "I am in great distress. Let me now fall into the hand of Yahweh, for His compassions are exceedingly abundant. But do not let me fall into the hand of man."

14 So Yahweh sent a pestilence against Israel; and 70,000 men of Israel fell. 15 And God sent an angel to Jerusalem to destroy it; but as he was about to destroy *it*, Yahweh saw and relented concerning the calamity, and said to the destroying angel, "It is enough! Now relax your hand." And the angel of Yahweh was standing by the threshing floor of Ornan the Jebusite. 16 Then David lifted up his eyes and saw the angel of Yahweh standing between earth and heaven, with his drawn sword in his hand stretched out over Jerusalem. Then David and the elders, covered with sackcloth, fell on their faces. 17 And David said to God, "Is it not I who commanded to number the people? Indeed, I am the one who has sinned and done a great evil; but these sheep, what have they done? O Yahweh my God, please let Your hand be against me and my father's household, but not against Your people that they should be plagued."

18 Then the angel of Yahweh said to Gad to say to David, that David should go up and erect an altar to Yahweh on the threshing floor of Ornan the Jebusite. 19 So David went up at the word of Gad, which he spoke in the name of Yahweh. 20 Now Ornan turned back and saw the angel, and his four sons *who were* with him hid themselves. And Ornan was threshing wheat. 21 Then David came to Ornan, and Ornan looked and saw David, and went out from the threshing floor and bowed his face to the ground before David. 22 Then David said to Ornan, "Give me the site of *this* threshing floor, that I may build on it an altar to Yahweh; for the full price you shall give it to me, that the plague may be checked from *being* upon the people." 23 And Ornan said to David, "Take *it* for yourself; and let my lord the king do what is good in his sight. See, I will give the oxen for the burnt offerings and the threshing sledges for the wood and the wheat for the grain offering; I will give everything." 24 However, King David said to Ornan, "No, but I will surely buy *it* for the full price; for I will not lift up what is yours to Yahweh, or offer a burnt offering which costs me nothing." 25 So David gave Ornan 600 shekels of gold by weight for the site. 26 Then David built there an altar to Yahweh and offered burnt offerings and peace offerings. And he called to Yahweh and He answered him with fire from heaven on the altar of burnt offering. 27 Then Yahweh spoke to the angel, and he returned his sword to its sheath.

28 At that time, when David saw that Yah-
weh had answered him on the threshing floor
of Ornan the Jebusite, he sacrificed there.
29 Now the tabernacle of Yahweh, which
Moses had made in the wilderness, and the
altar of burnt offering *were* in the high place
at Gibeon at that time. 30 But David could
not go before it to inquire of God, for he was
terrified by the sword of the angel of Yahweh.

22 Then David said, "This is the house
of Yahweh God, and this is the altar
of burnt offering for Israel."
2 So David said to gather the sojourners
who were in the land of Israel, and he
appointed stonecutters to hew out stones
to build the house of God. 3 And David
prepared large quantities of iron to make
the nails for the doors of the gates and for
the clamps, and more bronze than could
be weighed; 4 and timbers of cedar logs
beyond number, for the Sidonians and
Tyrians brought large quantities of cedar
timber to David. 5 And David said, "My son
Solomon is young and inexperienced, and
the house that is to be built for Yahweh shall
be highly exalted, for a name and beauty
throughout all lands. *Therefore* now I will
make preparation for it." So David made
ample preparations before his death.
6 Then he called for his son Solomon,
and commanded him to build a house for
Yahweh, the God of Israel. 7 And David said to
Solomon, "My son, I had it within my heart to
build a house to the name of Yahweh my God.
8 But the word of Yahweh came to me, saying,
'You have shed much blood and have waged
great wars; you shall not build a house for My
name, because you have shed *so* much blood
on the earth before Me. 9 Behold, a son will
be born to you, who shall be a man of rest;
and I will give him rest from all his enemies
on every side; for his name shall be Solomon,
and I will give peace and quiet to Israel in his
days. 10 He shall build a house for My name,
and he shall be a son to Me and I will be a
father to him; and I will establish the throne
of his kingdom over Israel forever.' 11 Now,
my son, Yahweh be with you that you may
be successful, and build the house of Yahweh
your God just as He has spoken concerning
you. 12 Only Yahweh give you insight and
understanding, and give you command
over Israel, so that you may keep the law of
Yahweh your God. 13 Then you will succeed,
if you are careful to do the statutes and
the judgments which Yahweh commanded
Moses concerning Israel. Be strong and cou-
rageous, do not fear nor be dismayed. 14 Now
behold, with great pains I have prepared for
the house of Yahweh 100,000 talents of
gold and 1,000,000 talents of silver, and
bronze and iron beyond weight, for they
are in great quantity; also timber and stone
I have prepared, and you may add to them.
15 Moreover, there are many of those who
do the work with you, hewers *of stone* and
craftsmen of stone and wood, and all men
who are wise in every kind of work. 16 Of the
gold, the silver and the bronze and the iron
there is no number. Arise and work, and may
Yahweh be with you."
17 David also commanded all the officials
of Israel to help his son Solomon, *saying*,
18 "Is not Yahweh your God with you? And
has He not given you rest on every side? For
He has given the inhabitants of the land into
my hand, and the land is subdued before
Yahweh and before His people. 19 Now give
your heart and your soul to seek Yahweh
your God; arise, therefore, and build the
sanctuary of Yahweh God, so that you may
bring the ark of the covenant of Yahweh and
the holy vessels of God into the house that is
to be built for the name of Yahweh."

Psalm 78:34–39

34 When He killed them, then
they sought Him,
And returned and sought
earnestly for God;
35 And they remembered that
God was their rock,
And the Most High God
their Redeemer.
36 But they deceived Him
with their mouth
And lied to Him with their tongue.
37 For their heart was not prepared
to remain with Him,
Nor were they faithful in His covenant.
38 But He, being compassionate,
atoned for *their* iniquity and
did not destroy *them*;
And He abounded in turning
back His anger
And did not arouse all His wrath.
39 Thus He remembered that
they were but flesh,
A wind that goes and does not return.

Proverbs 20:1–2

20 Wine is a mocker, strong
drink a brawler,
And whoever is led astray
by it is not wise.
2 The terror of a king is like
the roar of a lion;
He who provokes him to anger
sins against his own soul.

Acts 9:1–22

9 Now Saul, still breathing threats and
murder against the disciples of the
Lord, went to the high priest, 2 and asked
for letters from him to the synagogues at
Damascus, so that if he found any belonging
to the Way, both men and women, he might
bring them bound to Jerusalem. 3 And as
he was traveling, it happened that when
he was approaching Damascus, suddenly a
light from heaven flashed around him; 4 and
falling to the ground, he heard a voice saying
to him, "Saul, Saul, why are you persecuting
Me?" 5 And he said, "Who are You, Lord?"
And He *said*, "I am Jesus whom you are
persecuting, 6 but rise up and enter the
city, and it will be told you what you must
do." 7 And the men who traveled with him
stood speechless, hearing the voice but
seeing no one. 8 And Saul got up from the
ground, and though his eyes were open, he
could see nothing. Leading him by the hand,
they brought him into Damascus. 9 And he
was three days without sight, and neither
ate nor drank.

10 Now there was a disciple at Damascus
named Ananias, and the Lord said to him
in a vision, "Ananias." And he said, "Here
I am, Lord." 11 And the Lord *said* to him,
"Rise up and go to the street called Straight,
and inquire at the house of Judas for a man
from Tarsus named Saul, for behold, he is
praying, 12 and he has seen in a vision a man
named Ananias come in and lay his hands
on him, so that he might regain his sight."
13 But Ananias answered, "Lord, I have heard
from many about this man, how much harm
he did to Your saints at Jerusalem. 14 And
here he has authority from the chief priests
to bind all who call on Your name." 15 But
the Lord said to him, "Go, for he is a cho-
sen instrument of Mine, to bear My name
before the Gentiles and kings and the sons
of Israel; 16 for I will show him how much
he must suffer for My name." 17 So Ananias
departed and entered the house. And he
laid his hands on him and said, "Brother
Saul, the Lord sent me—*that is* Jesus who
appeared to you on the road by which you
were coming—so that you may regain your
sight and be filled with the Holy Spirit."
18 And immediately there fell from his eyes
something like scales, and he regained his
sight, and he rose up and was baptized;
19 and he took food and was strengthened.

Now for several days he was with the
disciples who were at Damascus, 20 and
immediately he *began to* proclaim Jesus in
the synagogues, saying, "He is the Son of
God." 21 And all those hearing him contin-
ued to be astounded, and were saying, "Is
this not the one who in Jerusalem destroyed
those that called on this name, and *who* had
come here for the purpose of bringing them
bound before the chief priests?" 22 But Saul
kept increasing in strength and confounding
the Jews who lived at Damascus by proving
that this One is the Christ.

JUNE 30

1 Chronicles 23:1–25:31

23 Now David became old and full of
days, and he made his son Solomon
king over Israel. 2 And he gathered together
all the leaders of Israel with the priests and
the Levites.

3 And the Levites were numbered from
thirty years old and upward, and their
number by census of men was 38,000. 4 Of
these, 24,000 were to direct the work of the
house of Yahweh; and 6,000 *were* officers
and judges, 5 and 4,000 *were* gatekeepers,
and 4,000 *were* praising Yahweh with the
instruments which David made for giving
praise. 6 And David divided them into divi-
sions according to the sons of Levi: Gershon,
Kohath, and Merari.

7 Of the Gershonites *were* Ladan and
Shimei.
8 The sons of Ladan *were* Jehiel the first
and Zetham and Joel, three.
9 The sons of Shimei *were* Shelomoth
and Haziel and Haran, three.

These were the heads of the fathers' *households* of Ladan.

10 The sons of Shimei *were* Jahath, Zina, Jeush, and Beriah.
These four *were* the sons of Shimei.

11 Jahath was the first and Zizah the second; but Jeush and Beriah did not have many sons, so they became a father's household, one unit.

12 The sons of Kohath: Amram, Izhar, Hebron, and Uzziel, four.

13 The sons of Amram were Aaron and Moses. And Aaron was separated in order to sanctify him as most holy, he and his sons forever, to offer *offerings* up in smoke before Yahweh, to minister to Him and to bless in His name forever.

14 But *as for* Moses the man of God, his sons were named among the tribe of Levi.

15 The sons of Moses *were* Gershom and Eliezer.

16 The son of Gershom *was* Shebuel the chief.

17 The son of Eliezer was Rehabiah the chief; and Eliezer had no other sons, but the sons of Rehabiah were very many.

18 The son of Izhar was Shelomith the chief.

19 The sons of Hebron *were* Jeriah the first, Amariah the second, Jahaziel the third and Jekameam the fourth.

20 The sons of Uzziel *were* Micah the first and Isshiah the second.

21 The sons of Merari were Mahli and Mushi. The sons of Mahli *were* Eleazar and Kish.

22 And Eleazar died and had no sons, but daughters only, so their brothers, the sons of Kish, took them up *as wives.*

23 The sons of Mushi: Mahli, Eder, and Jeremoth, three.

24 These were the sons of Levi according
to their fathers' households, *even* the
heads of the fathers' *households* of those
of them who were counted, in the number
of names by their census, doing the work
for the service of the house of Yahweh,
from twenty years old and upward. 25 For
David said, "Yahweh, the God of Israel, has
given rest to His people, and He dwells in
Jerusalem forever. 26 Also, the Levites will
no longer need to carry the tabernacle and
all its furnishings for its service." 27 For by
the last words of David the sons of Levi
were numbered from twenty years old and
upward. 28 For their station is to be on hand
for the sons of Aaron with the service of the
house of Yahweh, in the courts and in the
chambers and in the cleansing of all holy
things, even the work of the service of the
house of God, 29 and with the showbread,
and the fine flour for a grain offering, and
unleavened wafers, or *what is made on* the
griddle, or what is *well* stirred, and all measures of volume and size. 30 And they are to
stand every morning to thank and to praise
Yahweh, and likewise at evening, 31 and to
offer all burnt offerings to Yahweh, on the
sabbaths, the new moons and the appointed
times in the number *set* by the judgments
concerning them, continually before Yahweh. 32 Thus they shall keep responsibility
of the tent of meeting, and responsibility
of the holy place, and responsibility of the
sons of Aaron their relatives, for the service
of the house of Yahweh.

24 Now the divisions of the sons of
Aaron *were these*: the sons of Aaron
were Nadab, Abihu, Eleazar, and Ithamar.
2 But Nadab and Abihu died before their
father and had no sons. So Eleazar and
Ithamar ministered as priests. 3 And David,
with Zadok of the sons of Eleazar and
Ahimelech of the sons of Ithamar, divided
them according to their assignments for
their service. 4 And more chief men were
found from the sons of Eleazar than the
sons of Ithamar, so they divided them
thus: *there were* sixteen heads of fathers'
households of the sons of Eleazar and
eight of the sons of Ithamar, according to
their fathers' households. 5 Thus they were
divided by lot, the one as the other; for they
were leaders for the sanctuary and leaders
for God, both from the sons of Eleazar and
the sons of Ithamar. 6 Shemaiah, the son of
Nethanel the scribe, from the Levites, wrote
them down in the presence of the king,
the princes, Zadok the priest, Ahimelech
the son of Abiathar, and the heads of the
fathers' *households* of the priests and of
the Levites; one father's household taken
for Eleazar and one taken for Ithamar.

7 Now the first lot came out for
Jehoiarib,
the second for Jedaiah,

8 the third for Harim,
the fourth for Seorim,
9 the fifth for Malchijah,
the sixth for Mijamin,
10 the seventh for Hakkoz,
the eighth for Abijah,
11 the ninth for Jeshua,
the tenth for Shecaniah,
12 the eleventh for Eliashib,
the twelfth for Jakim,
13 the thirteenth for Huppah,
the fourteenth for Jeshebeab,
14 the fifteenth for Bilgah,
the sixteenth for Immer,
15 the seventeenth for Hezir,
the eighteenth for Happizzez,
16 the nineteenth for Pethahiah,
the twentieth for Jehezkel,
17 the twenty-first for Jachin,
the twenty-second for Gamul,
18 the twenty-third for Delaiah,
the twenty-fourth for Maaziah.
19 These were their assignments for their
service when *they* came in to the house of
Yahweh according to the *legal* judgment
rendered to them by the hand of Aaron their
father, just as Yahweh, the God of Israel, had
commanded him.
20 Now for the rest of the sons of Levi:
of the sons of Amram, Shubael;
of the sons of Shubael, Jehdeiah.
21 Of Rehabiah: of the sons of Rehabiah,
Isshiah the first.
22 Of the Izharites, Shelomoth; of the
sons of Shelomoth, Jahath.
23 The sons *of Hebron:* Jeriah *the first,*
Amariah the second, Jahaziel the
third, Jekameam the fourth.
24 The sons of Uzziel, Micah; of the sons
of Micah, Shamir.
25 The brother of Micah, Isshiah; of the
sons of Isshiah, Zechariah.
26 The sons of Merari, Mahli and Mushi;
the sons of Jaaziah, Beno.
27 The sons of Merari: by Jaaziah *were*
Beno, Shoham, Zaccur, and Ibri.
28 *By Mahli: Eleazar, who had no sons.*
29 By Kish: the sons of Kish, Jerahmeel.
30 The sons of Mushi: Mahli, Eder and
Jerimoth.
These *were* the sons of the Levites
according to their fathers' households.
31 These also cast lots alongside their
relatives the sons of Aaron in the presence
of David the king, Zadok, Ahimelech, and
the heads of the fathers' *households* of the
priests and of the Levites—the head of
fathers' *households* alongside those of his
younger brother.

25 Moreover, David and the commanders of the army separated for
the service *some* of the sons of Asaph and
of Heman and of Jeduthun, who *were* to
prophesy with lyres, harps, and cymbals;
and the number of those who performed
their service was:
2 Of the sons of Asaph:
Zaccur, Joseph, Nethaniah, and
Asharelah; the sons of Asaph *were*
under the direction of Asaph, who
prophesied under the direction of the
king.
3 Of Jeduthun, the sons of Jeduthun:
Gedaliah, Zeri, Jeshaiah, Shimei,
Hashabiah, and Mattithiah, six, under
the direction of their father Jeduthun
with the harp, who prophesied in
giving thanks and praising Yahweh.
4 Of Heman, the sons of Heman:
Bukkiah, Mattaniah, Uzziel, Shebuel
and Jerimoth, Hananiah, Hanani,
Eliathah, Giddalti and Romamti-ezer,
Joshbekashah, Mallothi, Hothir,
Mahazioth.
5 All these *were* the sons of Heman the
king's seer to exalt him according to the
words of God. So God gave fourteen sons
and three daughters to Heman. 6 All these
were under the direction of their father to
sing in the house of Yahweh, with cymbals,
harps, and lyres, for the service of the house
of God. Asaph, Jeduthun, and Heman *were*
under the direction of the king. 7 And their
number who were trained in singing to
Yahweh, with their relatives, all who were
skillful, *was* 288.
8 They cast lots for their responsibilities,
each alongside *the other*, the small as well
as the great, the teacher *as well* as the pupil.
9 Now the first lot came out for Asaph to
Joseph,
the second for Gedaliah, he with his
relatives and sons *were* twelve;
10 the third to Zaccur, his sons and his
relatives, twelve;
11 the fourth to Izri, his sons and his
relatives, twelve;
12 the fifth to Nethaniah, his sons and
his relatives, twelve;

13 the sixth to Bukkiah, his sons and his relatives, twelve;
14 the seventh to Jesharelah, his sons and his relatives, twelve;
15 the eighth to Jeshaiah, his sons and his relatives, twelve;
16 the ninth to Mattaniah, his sons and his relatives, twelve;
17 the tenth to Shimei, his sons and his relatives, twelve;
18 the eleventh to Azarel, his sons and his relatives, twelve;
19 the twelfth to Hashabiah, his sons and his relatives, twelve;
20 for the thirteenth, Shubael, his sons and his relatives, twelve;
21 for the fourteenth, Mattithiah, his sons and his relatives, twelve;
22 for the fifteenth to Jeremoth, his sons and his relatives, twelve;
23 for the sixteenth to Hananiah, his sons and his relatives, twelve;
24 for the seventeenth to Joshbekashah, his sons and his relatives, twelve;
25 for the eighteenth to Hanani, his sons and his relatives, twelve;
26 for the nineteenth to Mallothi, his sons and his relatives, twelve;
27 for the twentieth to Eliathah, his sons and his relatives, twelve;
28 for the twenty-first to Hothir, his sons and his relatives, twelve;
29 for the twenty-second to Giddalti, his sons and his relatives, twelve;
30 for the twenty-third to Mahazioth, his sons and his relatives, twelve;
31 for the twenty-fourth to Romamti-ezer, his sons and his relatives, twelve.

Psalm 78:40–55

40 How often they rebelled against
Him in the wilderness
And grieved Him in the wasteland!
41 Again and again they tested God,
And pained the Holy One of Israel.
42 They did not remember His power,
The day when He redeemed
them from the adversary,
43 When He performed His signs in Egypt
And His miracles in the field of Zoan,
44 And turned their rivers to blood,
And their streams, they
could not drink.
45 He sent among them swarms of
flies which devoured them,
And frogs which destroyed them.
46 He gave also their crops to
the grasshopper
And the fruit of their labor
to the locust.
47 He killed their vines with hailstones
And their sycamore trees with frost.
48 He gave over their cattle
also to the hailstones
And their herds to bolts of lightning.
49 He sent upon them His burning anger,
Fury and indignation and distress,
A band of destroying angels.
50 He leveled a path for His anger;
He did not hold back their
soul from death,
But gave over their life to the plague,
51 So He struck all the firstborn in Egypt,
The first of their vigor in
the tents of Ham.
52 But He led forth His own
people like sheep
And guided them in the
wilderness like a flock;
53 He led them safely, so that
they did not fear;
But the sea covered their enemies.

54 So He brought them to His holy land,
To this hill country which His
right hand had acquired.
55 He also drove out the
nations before them
And apportioned them for an
inheritance by measurement,
And made the tribes of Israel
dwell in their tents.

Proverbs 20:3

3 It is a glory for a man to
cease quarreling,
But any ignorant fool will
break out *in dispute*.

Acts 9:23–43

23 And when many days had elapsed, the
Jews plotted together to put him to death,
24 but their plot became known to Saul.
They were also watching the gates day and
night so that they might put him to death;
25 but his disciples took him by night and let
him down through the wall, lowering him
in a *large* basket.
26 And when he came to Jerusalem, he
was trying to associate with the disciples,

but they were all afraid of him, not believing
that he was a disciple. 27 But Barnabas took
him and brought him to the apostles and
recounted to them how he had seen the
Lord on the road, and that He had talked
to him, and how at Damascus he had spo-
ken out boldly in the name of Jesus. 28 So
he was with them, moving about freely
in Jerusalem, speaking out boldly in the
name of the Lord. 29 And he was talking
and arguing with the Hellenistic *Jews*, but
they were attempting to put him to death.
30 But when the brothers learned *of it*, they
brought him down to Caesarea and sent him
away to Tarsus.

31 So the church throughout all Judea and
Galilee and Samaria was having peace, being
built up. And going on in the fear of the Lord
and in the encouragement of the Holy Spirit,
it continued to multiply.

32 Now it happened that as Peter was
traveling through all *those regions*, he
came down also to the saints who lived at
Lydda. 33 And there he found a man named
Aeneas, who had been bedridden eight
years, for he was paralyzed. 34 And Peter
said to him, "Aeneas, Jesus Christ heals you.
Rise up and make your bed." Immediately
he rose up. 35 And all who lived at Lydda
and Sharon saw him, and they turned to
the Lord.

36 Now in Joppa there was a disciple
named Tabitha (which translated is called
Dorcas). This woman was full of good
works and charity which she continually
did. 37 And it happened at that time that
she fell sick and died; and when they had
washed her body, they laid it in an upper
room. 38 Now since Lydda was near Joppa,
the disciples, having heard that Peter was
there, sent two men to him, pleading with
him, "Do not delay in coming to us." 39 So
Peter arose and went with them. When he
arrived, they brought him into the upper
room; and all the widows stood beside him,
crying and showing all the tunics and gar-
ments that Dorcas used to make while she
was with them. 40 But Peter sent them all out
and knelt down and prayed, and turning to
the body, he said, "Tabitha, arise." And she
opened her eyes, and when she saw Peter,
she sat up. 41 And he gave her his hand and
raised her up. And calling the saints and
widows, he presented her alive. 42 And it
became known all over Joppa, and many
believed in the Lord. 43 And it happened
that he stayed many days in Joppa with a
tanner *named* Simon.

JULY 1

1 Chronicles 26:1–27:34

26 For the divisions of the gatekeepers *there were* of the Korahites,
Meshelemiah the son of Kore, of the sons of Asaph.

2 Meshelemiah had sons:
Zechariah the firstborn, Jediael the second, Zebadiah the third, Jathniel the fourth,

3 Elam the fifth, Johanan the sixth, Eliehoenai the seventh.

4 Obed-edom had sons:
Shemaiah the firstborn, Jehozabad *the second*, Joah the third, Sacar the fourth, Nethanel the fifth,

5 Ammiel the sixth, Issachar the seventh *and* Peullethai the eighth; God had indeed blessed him.

6 Also to his son Shemaiah sons were born who ruled over the house of their father, for they were mighty men of valor.

7 The sons of Shemaiah *were* Othni, Rephael, Obed, and Elzabad, whose brothers, Elihu and Semachiah, were men of valor.

8 All these *were* of the sons of Obed-edom; they and their sons and their relatives *were* valiant men with strength for the service, sixty-two from Obed-edom.

9 Meshelemiah had sons and relatives, eighteen men of valor.

10 Also Hosah, *one* of the sons of Merari had sons:
Shimri the first (although he was not the firstborn, his father made him first),

11 Hilkiah the second, Tebaliah the third, Zechariah the fourth; all the sons and relatives of Hosah *were* thirteen.

12 To these divisions of the gatekeepers,
the chief men, *were given* responsibilities
like their relatives to minister in the house of

Yahweh. 13 And they cast lots, the small and
the great alike, according to their fathers'
households, for every gate. 14 And the lot
to the east fell to Shelemiah. Then they cast
lots *for* his son Zechariah, a counselor with
insight, and his lot came out to the north.
15 For Obed-edom *it fell* to the south, and
to his sons went the house of storerooms.
16 For Shuppim and Hosah *it was* to the
west, by the gate of Shallecheth, on the
ascending highway. Guard corresponded to
guard. 17 On the east there were six Levites,
on the north four daily, on the south four
daily, and at the storerooms two by two. 18 At
the Parbar on the west *there were* four at
the highway and two at the Parbar. 19 These
were the divisions of the gatekeepers of the
sons of Korah and of the sons of Merari.

20 As for the Levites, Ahijhah was over
the treasures of the house of God and of
the treasures of the holy gifts. 21 The sons
of Ladan, the sons of the Gershonites
belonging to Ladan, *namely*, the Jehielites,
were the heads of the fathers' *households*,
belonging to Ladan the Gershonite.

22 The sons of Jehieli, Zetham, and Joel his
brother, were over the treasures of the house
of Yahweh. 23 As for the Amramites, the
Izharites, the Hebronites and the Uzzielites,
24 Shebuel the son of Gershom, the son of
Moses, was officer over the treasures. 25 And
his relatives by Eliezer *were* Rehabiah his
son, Jeshaiah his son, Joram his son, Zichri
his son, and Shelomoth his son. 26 This Shelomoth
and his relatives were over all the
treasures of the holy gifts which King David
and the heads of the fathers' *households*, the
commanders of thousands and hundreds,
and the commanders of the army, had set
apart as holy. 27 They set apart as holy part
of what was won in battles and part of the
spoil to repair the house of Yahweh. 28 And
all that Samuel the seer had set apart as holy
and Saul the son of Kish, Abner the son of
Ner, and Joab the son of Zeruiah, everyone
who had set apart *anything* as holy, *all of
this* was in the care of Shelomoth and his
relatives.

29 As for the Izharites, Chenaniah and his
sons were *assigned* to the outside work for
Israel, as officers and judges. 30 As for the
Hebronites, Hashabiah and his relatives,
1,700 men of valor, were over the administration
of Israel across the Jordan to the
west, for all the work of Yahweh and the
service of the king. 31 As for the Hebronites,
Jerijah the chief (these Hebronites were
investigated according to their generations
and fathers' *households*, in the fortieth year
of David's reign, and mighty men of valor
were found among them at Jazer of Gilead)
32 and his relatives, men of valor, *were* 2,700
in number, heads of fathers' *households*.
And King David made them overseers of the
Reubenites, the Gadites and the half-tribe
of the Manassites concerning all the affairs
of God and of the king.

27 Now *this is* the *total* count of the
sons of Israel, the heads of fathers'
households, the commanders of thousands
and of hundreds, and their officers who
ministered to the king in each matter of
the divisions which came in and went out
month by month throughout all the months
of the year, each division *numbering* 24,000:

2 Jashobeam the son of Zabdiel *was* over
the first division for the first month;
and in his division *were* 24,000.
3 *He was* from the sons of Perez, *and
was* chief of all the commanders of the
army for the first month.
4 Dodai the Ahohite and his division
were over the division for the second
month, Mikloth *being* the chief officer;
and in his division *were* 24,000.
5 The third commander of the army for
the third month *was* Benaiah, the son
of Jehoiada the priest, *as* chief; and in
his division *were* 24,000.
6 This Benaiah *was* the mighty man of
the thirty, and *was* over thirty; and
over his division was Ammizabad his
son.
7 The fourth for the fourth month
was Asahel the brother of Joab, and
Zebadiah his son after him; and in his
division *were* 24,000.
8 The fifth for the fifth month *was* the
commander Shamhuth the Izrahite;
and in his division *were* 24,000.
9 The sixth for the sixth month *was* Ira
the son of Ikkesh the Tekoite; and in
his division *were* 24,000.
10 The seventh for the seventh month
was Helez the Pelonite of the sons
of Ephraim; and in his division *were*
24,000.
11 The eighth for the eighth month
was Sibbecai the Hushathite of the

Zerahites; and in his division *were* 24,000.
12 The ninth for the ninth month *was* Abiezer the Anathothite of the Benjamites; and in his division *were* 24,000.
13 The tenth for the tenth month *was* Maharai the Netophathite of the Zerahites; and in his division *were* 24,000.
14 The eleventh for the eleventh month *was* Benaiah the Pirathonite of the sons of Ephraim; and in his division *were* 24,000.
15 The twelfth for the twelfth month *was* Heldai the Netophathite of Othniel; and in his division *were* 24,000.
16 Now *those* over the tribes of Israel: chief officer for the Reubenites was Eliezer the son of Zichri;
for the Simeonites, Shephatiah the son of Maacah;
17 for Levi, Hashabiah the son of Kemuel;
for Aaron, Zadok;
18 for Judah, Elihu, *one* of David's brothers;
for Issachar, Omri the son of Michael;
19 for Zebulun, Ishmaiah the son of Obadiah;
for Naphtali, Jeremoth the son of Azriel;
20 for the sons of Ephraim, Hoshea the son of Azaziah;
for the half-tribe of Manasseh, Joel the son of Pedaiah;
21 for the half-tribe of Manasseh in Gilead, Iddo the son of Zechariah;
for Benjamin, Jaasiel the son of Abner;
22 for Dan, Azarel the son of Jeroham.
These *were* the princes of the tribes of Israel.

23 But David did not take up a count of those
twenty years of age and under, because Yah-
weh had said He would multiply Israel as the
stars of heaven. 24 Joab the son of Zeruiah
had begun to number *them*, but did not
finish; and because of this, wrath came upon
Israel, and this count was not included in the
total count of the chronicles of King David.

25 Now Azmaveth the son of Adiel *was* over the king's storehouses.
And Jonathan the son of Uzziah *was* over the storehouses in the country, in the cities, in the villages and in the towers.
26 Ezri the son of Chelub *was* over the workers of the field who cultivated the soil.
27 Shimei the Ramathite *was* over the vineyards;
and Zabdi the Shiphmite *was* over the produce of the vineyards *stored* in the wine cellars.
28 Baal-hanan the Gederite *was* over the olive and sycamore trees in the Shephelah;
and Joash had charge of the stores of oil.
29 Shitrai the Sharonite *was* over the cattle which were grazing in Sharon;
and Shaphat the son of Adlai *was* over the cattle in the valleys.
30 Obil the Ishmaelite *was* over the camels;
and Jehdeiah the Meronothite *was* over the donkeys.
31 Jaziz the Hagrite *was* over the flocks.
All these were officials over the possessions which belonged to King David.
32 Also Jonathan, David's uncle, *was* a counselor, a man of understanding, and a scribe;
and Jehiel the son of Hachmoni was with the king's sons.
33 Ahithophel *was* counselor to the king;
and Hushai the Archite *was* the king's friend.
34 Jehoiada the son of Benaiah, and Abiathar succeeded Ahithophel;
and Joab was the commander of the king's army.

Psalm 78:56–66

56 Yet they tested and rebelled
against the Most High God
And did not keep His testimonies,
57 But turned back and acted
treacherously like their fathers;
They turned aside like a
treacherous bow.
58 For they provoked Him with
their high places
And aroused His jealousy with
their graven images.
59 God heard and was filled with wrath
And greatly rejected Israel;
60 So that He abandoned the
dwelling place at Shiloh,

The tent which He caused
to dwell among men,
61 And gave up His strength to captivity
And His beauty into the hand
of the adversary.
62 He also gave over His
people to the sword,
And was filled with wrath
at His inheritance.
63 Fire devoured His choice men,
And His virgins had no wedding songs.
64 His priests fell by the sword,
And His widows could not weep.

65 Then the Lord awoke as *if from* sleep,
As *if He were a* warrior
overcome by wine.
66 He struck His adversaries backward;
He put on them an
everlasting reproach.

Proverbs 20:4–5

4 The sluggard does not plow
from winter *on*,
So he begs during the harvest
and has nothing.
5 Counsel in the heart of a man
is *like* deep water,
But a man of discernment draws it out.

Acts 10:1–23

10 Now *there was* a man at Caesarea named Cornelius, a centurion of what was called the Italian cohort, 2 a devout man and one who feared God with all his household, and gave many alms to the people and prayed to God continually. 3 About the ninth hour of the day he clearly saw in a vision an angel of God who had come in and said to him, "Cornelius!" 4 And looking intently on him and becoming afraid, he said, "What is it, Lord?" And he said to him, "Your prayers and alms have ascended as a memorial before God. 5 Now send *some* men to Joppa and summon a man *named* Simon, who is also called Peter; 6 he is lodging with a tanner *named* Simon, whose house is by the sea." 7 And when the angel who was speaking to him had left, he called two of his servants and a devout soldier of those who were his personal attendants, 8 and after he explained everything to them, he sent them to Joppa.

9 And on the next day, as they were on their way and approaching the city, Peter went up on the housetop about the sixth hour to pray. 10 But he became hungry and was desiring to eat. And while they were making preparations, he fell into a trance 11 and *saw heaven opened up, and an object like a great sheet coming down, lowered by four corners to the ground, 12 and there were in it all *kinds of* four-footed animals and crawling creatures of the earth and birds of the sky. 13 And a voice came to him, "Rise up, Peter, slaughter and eat!" 14 But Peter said, "By no means, Lord, for I have never eaten anything defiled and unclean." 15 Again a voice *came* to him a second time, "What God has cleansed, no *longer* consider defiled." 16 And this happened three times and immediately the object was taken up into heaven.

17 Now while Peter was greatly perplexed in mind as to what the vision which he had seen might be, behold, the men who had been sent by Cornelius, having asked directions for Simon's house, appeared at the gate; 18 and calling out, they were asking whether Simon, who was also called Peter, was lodging there. 19 And while Peter was reflecting on the vision, the Spirit said to him, "Behold, three men are looking for you. 20 But rise up, go down and accompany them without taking issue at all, for I have sent them Myself." 21 And Peter went down to the men and said, "Behold, I am the one you are looking for; what is the reason for which you have come?" 22 And they said, "Cornelius, a centurion, a righteous and God-fearing man well spoken of by the entire nation of the Jews, was directed by a holy angel to summon you to his house and hear a message from you." 23 So he invited them in and gave them lodging. And on the next day he rose up and went away with them, and some of the brothers from Joppa went with him.

The chief means for attaining wisdom, and suitable gifts for the ministry, are the Holy Scriptures, and prayer.

— JOHN NEWTON

JULY 2

1 Chronicles 28:1–29:30

28 And David assembled at Jerusalem all the commanders of Israel, the commanders of the tribes, and the commanders of the divisions that ministered to the king, and the commanders of thousands, and the commanders of hundreds, and the commanders over all the property and livestock belonging to the king and his sons, with the officials and the mighty men, even all the mighty men of valor. 2 Then King David rose to his feet and said, "Listen to me, my brothers and my people; I *had it* within my heart to build a house of rest for the ark of the covenant of Yahweh and for the footstool of the feet of our God. So I had made preparations to build *it*. 3 But God said to me, 'You shall not build a house for My name because you are a man of war and have shed blood.' 4 Yet, Yahweh, the God of Israel, chose me from all the house of my father to be king over Israel forever. For He has chosen Judah to be a ruler; and in the house of Judah, my father's house, and among the sons of my father He took pleasure in me to make *me* king over all Israel. 5 Now of all my sons (for Yahweh has given me many sons), He has chosen my son Solomon to sit on the throne of the kingdom of Yahweh over Israel. 6 And He said to me, 'Your son Solomon is the one who shall build My house and My courts; for I have chosen him to be a son to Me, and I will be a father to him. 7 And I will establish his kingdom forever if he will be strong to do My commandments and My judgments, as is done now.' 8 So now, in the sight of all Israel, the assembly of Yahweh, and in the hearing of our God, keep and seek after all the commandments of Yahweh your God so that you may possess the good land and cause your sons after you to inherit *it* forever.

9 "As for you, my son Solomon, know the God of your father, and serve Him with a whole heart and a delighted soul; for Yahweh searches all hearts, and understands every intent of the thoughts. If you seek Him, He will be found; but if you forsake Him, He will reject you forever. 10 See now, for Yahweh has chosen you to build a house for the sanctuary; be strong and act."

11 Then David gave to his son Solomon the pattern of the porch *of the temple*, its buildings, its storehouses, its upper rooms, its inner rooms, and the room for the mercy seat; 12 and the pattern of all that he had in mind, for the courts of the house of Yahweh, and for all the surrounding chambers, for the treasuries of the house of God, and for the treasuries of the holy things; 13 also for the divisions of the priests and the Levites and for all the work of the service of the house of Yahweh and for all the utensils of service in the house of Yahweh; 14 for the golden *utensils*, the weight of gold for all utensils for every kind of service; for the silver utensils, the weight *of silver* for all utensils for every kind of service; 15 and the weight *of gold* for the golden lampstands and their golden lamps, with the weight of each lampstand and its lamps; and *the weight of silver* for the silver lampstands, with the weight of each lampstand and its lamps according to the service of each lampstand; 16 and the gold by weight for the tables of showbread, for each table; and silver for the silver tables; 17 and the flesh hooks, the bowls, and the jars of pure gold; and for the golden bowls with the weight for each bowl; and for the silver bowls with the weight for each bowl; 18 and for the altar of incense refined gold by weight; and gold for the pattern of the chariot, *even* the cherubim that spread out *their wings* and covered the ark of the covenant of Yahweh.

19 "All *this*," *said David*, "has been granted to me as insight in writing by the hand of Yahweh, all the details of this pattern."

20 Then David said to his son Solomon, "Be strong and courageous, and act; do not fear nor be dismayed, for Yahweh God, my God, is with you. He will not fail you nor forsake you until all the work for the service of the house of Yahweh is completed. 21 Now behold, *there are* the divisions of the priests and the Levites for all the service of the house of God, and every willing man with wisdom will be with you in all the work for all the service. The officials also and all the people will be entirely at your command."

29 Then King David said to the entire assembly, "My son Solomon, whom alone God has chosen, is still young and inexperienced and the work is great; for the

temple is not for man, but for Yahweh God. 2 Now with all my power I have prepared for the house of my God the gold for the *things of* gold, and the silver for the *things of* silver, and the bronze for the *things of* bronze, the iron for the *things of* iron, and wood for the *things of* wood, onyx stones and inlaid *stones*, stones of antimony and stones of various colors, and all kinds of precious stones and alabaster in abundance. 3 Moreover, in my pleasure in the house of my God, the treasure I have of gold and silver, I give to the house of my God, over and above all that I have already prepared for the holy house, 4 *namely*, 3,000 talents of gold, of the gold of Ophir, and 7,000 talents of refined silver, to overlay the walls of the buildings; 5 of gold for the *things of* gold and of silver for the *things of* silver, that is, for all the work *done* by the hand of craftsmen. Who then would offer willingly to ordain himself this day to Yahweh?"

6 Then the commanders of the fathers' *households*, and the commanders of the tribes of Israel, and the commanders of thousands and of hundreds, with the commanders of the king's work, offered willingly; 7 and for the service for the house of God they gave 5,000 talents and 10,000 darics of gold, and 10,000 talents of silver, and 18,000 talents of brass, and 100,000 talents of iron. 8 And whoever possessed *precious* stones gave them to the treasury of the house of Yahweh, in the care of Jehiel the Gershonite. 9 Then the people were glad because they had offered so willingly, for they made their freewill offering to Yahweh with a whole heart, and King David also was exceedingly glad.

10 So David blessed Yahweh in the sight of all the assembly; and David said, "Blessed are You, O Yahweh, the God of Israel our father, from everlasting to everlasting. 11 Yours, O Yahweh, is the greatness and the power and the glory and the victory and the majesty, indeed everything that is in the heavens and the earth; Yours is the kingdom, O Yahweh, and You exalt Yourself as head over all. 12 Both riches and honor *come* from You, and You rule over all, and in Your hand is power and might; and it lies in Your hand to make great and to strengthen everyone. 13 So now, our God, we are thanking You and praising Your glorious name.

14 "But who am I and who are my people that we should be able to offer as willingly as this? For all things come from You, and from Your hand we have given You. 15 For we are sojourners before You, and foreign residents, like all our fathers were; our days on the earth are like a shadow, and there is no hope. 16 O Yahweh our God, all this abundance that we have prepared to build You a house for Your holy name, it is from Your hand, and all is Yours. 17 And I know, O my God, that You try the heart and delight in uprightness. I, in the uprightness of my heart, have willingly offered all these *things*. So now with gladness I have seen Your people, who are present here, make *their* offerings willingly to You. 18 O Yahweh, the God of Abraham, Isaac, and Israel, our fathers, keep this forever in the intentions of the heart of Your people, and prepare their heart to You; 19 and give to my son Solomon a whole heart to keep Your commandments, Your testimonies and Your statutes, and to do *them* all, and to build the temple, for which I have made preparation."

20 Then David said to all the assembly, "Now bless Yahweh your God." And all the assembly blessed Yahweh, the God of their fathers, and bowed low and prostrated themselves to Yahweh and to the king.

21 And on the next day they made sacrifices to Yahweh and offered burnt offerings to Yahweh, 1,000 bulls, 1,000 rams, *and* 1,000 lambs, with their drink offerings and sacrifices in abundance for all Israel. 22 So they ate and drank that day before Yahweh with great gladness.

And they made Solomon the son of David king a second time, and they anointed *him* as ruler for Yahweh and Zadok as priest. 23 Then Solomon sat on the throne of Yahweh as king instead of David his father; and he succeeded, and all Israel obeyed him. 24 And all the officials, the mighty men, and also all the sons of King David pledged allegiance to King Solomon. 25 And Yahweh highly exalted Solomon in the sight of all Israel, and granted to him royal majesty which had not been on any king before him in Israel.

26 Now David the son of Jesse reigned over all Israel. 27 And the time which he reigned over Israel *was* forty years; in Hebron he reigned seven years and in Jerusalem thirty-three *years*.

28 Then he died in a good old age, full of days, riches and glory; and his son Solomon

became king in his place. 29 Now the acts of
King David, from first to last, behold, they
are written in the chronicles of Samuel
the seer, in the chronicles of Nathan the
prophet and in the chronicles of Gad the
seer, 30 with all his reign, his might, and
the circumstances which came on him, on
Israel, and on all the kingdoms of the lands.

Psalm 78:67–72

67 He also rejected the tent of Joseph,
And did not choose the
tribe of Ephraim,
68 But chose the tribe of Judah,
Mount Zion which He loved.
69 And He built His sanctuary
like the heights,
Like the earth which He has
founded forever.
70 He also chose David His servant
And took him from the sheepfolds;
71 From following the nursing
ewes He brought him
To shepherd Jacob His people,
And Israel His inheritance.
72 So he shepherded them according
to the integrity of his heart,
And led them with his skillful hands.

Proverbs 20:6–7

6 Many a man will call out his
own lovingkindness,
But a faithful man, who can find?
7 A righteous man who walks
in his integrity—
How blessed are his sons after him.

Acts 10:24–48

24 And on the following day he entered
Caesarea. Now Cornelius was waiting for
them and had called together his relatives
and close friends. 25 And when Peter
entered, Cornelius met him, and fell at his
feet and worshiped *him.* 26 But Peter raised
him up, saying, "Stand up; I too am *just* a
man." 27 As he talked with him, he entered
and *found many people assembled. 28 And
he said to them, "You yourselves know how
unlawful it is for a man who is a Jew to asso-
ciate with a foreigner or to visit him; and
yet God has shown me that I should not call
any man defiled or unclean. 29 That is why
I came without even raising any objection
when I was summoned. So I ask for what
reason you have summoned me."

30 And Cornelius said, "Four days ago
to this hour, I was praying in my house
during the ninth hour; and behold, a man
stood before me in shining garments, 31 and
he *said, 'Cornelius, your prayer has been
heard and your alms have been remembered
before God. 32 Therefore send to Joppa and
invite Simon, who is also called Peter, to
come to you; he is lodging at the house of
Simon *the* tanner by the sea.' 33 So I sent for
you immediately, and you have been kind
enough to come. Now then, we are all here
present before God to hear all that you have
been ordered by the Lord."

34 And opening his mouth, Peter said:

"I most truly comprehend *now* that God
is not one to show partiality, 35 but in every
nation the one who fears Him and does
righteousness is welcome to Him. 36 As for
the word which He sent to the sons of Israel,
proclaiming the good news of peace through
Jesus Christ—He is Lord of all— 37 you
yourselves know the thing which happened
throughout all Judea, starting from Galilee,
after the baptism which John proclaimed.
38 *You know of* Jesus of Nazareth, how God
anointed Him with the Holy Spirit and with
power, and *how* He went about doing good
and healing all who were oppressed by the
devil, for God was with Him. 39 And we are
witnesses of all the things He did both in
the land of the Jews and in Jerusalem. They
also put Him to death by hanging Him on a
tree. 40 God raised Him up on the third day
and granted that He appear, 41 not to all the
people, but to witnesses who were chosen
beforehand by God, *that is,* to us who ate
and drank with Him after He arose from the
dead. 42 And He commanded us to preach to
the people, and solemnly to bear witness
that this is the One who has been designated
by God as Judge of the living and the dead.
43 Of Him all the prophets bear witness that
through His name everyone who believes in
Him receives forgiveness of sins."

44 While Peter was still speaking these
things, the Holy Spirit fell upon all those
who were listening to the word. 45 And all
the circumcised believers who came with
Peter were astounded that the gift of the
Holy Spirit had been poured out on the
Gentiles also. 46 For they were hearing them
speaking with tongues and magnifying God.
Then Peter answered, 47 "Can anyone refuse
water for these to be baptized who have

received the Holy Spirit just as we *did*?" 48 And he ordered them to be baptized in the name of Jesus Christ. Then they asked him to remain for a few days.

JULY 3

2 Chronicles 1:1–2:18

1 Now Solomon the son of David strengthened himself over his kingdom, and Yahweh his God *was* with him and highly exalted him.

2 And Solomon spoke to all Israel, to the commanders of thousands and of hundreds and to the judges and to every leader in all Israel, the heads of the fathers' *households*. 3 Then Solomon and all the assembly with him went to the high place which was at Gibeon, for God's tent of meeting was there, which Moses the servant of Yahweh had made in the wilderness. 4 However, David had brought up the ark of God from Kiriath-jearim to the place he had prepared for it, for he had pitched a tent for it in Jerusalem. 5 Now the bronze altar, which Bezalel the son of Uri, the son of Hur, had made, was there before the tabernacle of Yahweh, and Solomon and the assembly sought it out. 6 And Solomon went up there before Yahweh to the bronze altar which *was* at the tent of meeting, and offered one thousand burnt offerings on it.

7 In that night God appeared to Solomon and said to him, "Ask what I should give to you."

8 Then Solomon said to God, "You have shown great lovingkindness to my father David, and have made me king in his place. 9 Now, O Yahweh God, let Your promise to my father David endure, for You have made me king over a people as numerous as the dust of the earth. 10 Give me now wisdom and knowledge, that I may go out and come in before this people, for who can do justice for this great people of Yours?" 11 And God said to Solomon, "Because you had this in your heart, and did not ask for riches, wealth, or glory, or the life of those who hate you, nor have you even asked for long life, but you have asked for yourself wisdom and knowledge that you may do justice for My people over whom I have made you king, 12 wisdom and knowledge have been given to you. And I will give you riches and wealth and glory, such as none of the kings who were before you had nor those who will come after you." 13 So Solomon went from the high place which was at Gibeon, from the tent of meeting, to Jerusalem, and he reigned over Israel.

14 And Solomon gathered chariots and horsemen. And he had 1,400 chariots and 12,000 horsemen, and he stationed them in the chariot cities and with the king in Jerusalem. 15 The king also made silver and gold *as plentiful* as stones in Jerusalem, and he made cedars as plentiful as sycamore trees that are in the Shephelah. 16 Solomon's import of horses was from Egypt and from Kue; the king's merchants procured *them* from Kue for a price. 17 And they imported a chariot from Egypt for 600 *shekels* of silver and a horse for 150; and by the same means they exported them to all the kings of the Hittites and the kings of Aram.

2 Then Solomon decided to build a house for the name of Yahweh and a royal palace for himself. 2 So Solomon numbered 70,000 men to carry loads and 80,000 men to hew *stone* in the mountains and 3,600 to direct them.

3 Then Solomon sent *word* to Huram the king of Tyre, saying, "As you dealt with David my father and sent him cedars to build him a house to live in, *so do for me.* 4 Behold, I am about to build a house for the name of Yahweh my God, setting it apart to Him as holy, to burn fragrant incense before Him and *to set out* the showbread continually, and to offer burnt offerings morning and evening, on sabbaths and on new moons and on the appointed feasts of Yahweh our God, this *being required* forever in Israel. 5 Now the house which I am about to build *will be* great, for greater is our God than all the gods. 6 But who is able to build a house for Him, for the heavens and the highest heavens cannot contain Him? So who am I, that I should build a house for Him, except to burn *incense* before Him? 7 So now, send me a wise man to work in gold, silver, brass, and iron, and in purple, crimson, and blue *fabrics,* and who knows how to make engravings, to *work* with the wise men whom

I have in Judah and Jerusalem, whom David
my father prepared. 8 Send me also cedar,
cypress and algum timber from Lebanon, for
I know that your servants know how to cut
timber of Lebanon; and behold, my servants
will work with your servants, 9 to prepare
timber in abundance for me, for the house
which I am about to build *will be* great and
wonderful. 10 And behold, I will give to your
servants, the woodsmen who cut the timber,
20,000 kors of crushed wheat and 20,000
kors of barley, and 20,000 baths of wine and
20,000 baths of oil."

11 Then Huram king of Tyre said in a letter
sent to Solomon: "Because Yahweh loves His
people, He has given you *to be* king over
them." 12 Then Huram said, "Blessed be
Yahweh, the God of Israel, who has made
heaven and earth, who has given King David
a wise son, knowledgeable in insight and
understanding, who will build a house for
Yahweh and a royal palace for himself.

13 "So now, I am sending Huram-abi, a
wise man, who is knowledgeable in under-
standing, 14 the son of a Danite woman and
a Tyrian father, who knows how to work in
gold, silver, bronze, iron, stone, and wood,
and in purple, blue, linen, and crimson fab-
rics, and *who knows how* to make all kinds of
engravings and to devise any design which
may be given to him, *to work* with your wise
men and with the wise men of my lord David
your father. 15 So now, let my lord send to
his servants wheat and barley, oil and wine,
of which he has spoken. 16 And we will cut
whatever timber you need from Lebanon
and bring it to you on rafts by sea to Joppa,
so that you may carry it up to Jerusalem."

17 Then Solomon numbered all the
sojourners who *were* in the land of Israel,
following the census which his father David
had taken; and 153,600 were found. 18 And
he made 70,000 of them to carry loads and
80,000 as hewers *of stone* in the mountains
and 3,600 directors to make the people
work.

Psalm 79:1–4

1 O God, the nations have come
  into Your inheritance;
They have defiled Your holy temple;
They have laid Jerusalem in ruins.
2 They have given the dead bodies
  of Your slaves for food to
  the birds of the heavens,
The flesh of Your holy ones to
  the beasts of the earth.
3 They have poured out their blood
  like water round about Jerusalem;
And there was no one to bury them.
4 We have become a reproach
  to our neighbors,
A mockery and derision to
  those around us.

Proverbs 20:8–9

8 A king who sits on the throne of justice
Disperses all evil with his eyes.
9 Who can say, "I have kept
  my heart pure,
I am clean from my sin"?

Acts 11:1–30

11 Now the apostles and the brothers who
were throughout Judea heard that the
Gentiles also had received the word of God.
2 And when Peter came up to Jerusalem,
those who were circumcised took issue with
him, 3 saying, "You went to uncircumcised
men and ate with them." 4 But Peter began
speaking and *proceeded* to explain to them
in orderly sequence, saying, 5 "I was in the
city of Joppa praying; and in a trance I saw
a vision, an object coming down like a great
sheet lowered by four corners from heaven,
and it came right down to me, 6 and when
looking closely at it, I was observing it and
saw the four-footed animals of the earth and
the wild beasts and the crawling creatures
and the birds of the sky. 7 And I also heard a
voice saying to me, 'Rise up, Peter; slaughter
and eat.' 8 But I said, 'By no means, Lord, for
nothing defiled or unclean has ever entered
my mouth.' 9 But a voice from heaven
answered a second time, 'What God has
cleansed, no longer consider defiled.' 10 And
this happened three times, and everything
was drawn back up into heaven. 11 And
behold, immediately three men appeared
at the house in which we were, having been
sent to me from Caesarea. 12 And the Spirit
told me to go with them without taking issue
at all. These six brothers also went with me
and we entered the man's house. 13 And he
reported to us how he had seen the angel
standing in his house, and saying, 'Send to
Joppa and summon Simon, who is also called
Peter; 14 and he will speak words to you by
which you will be saved, you and all your
household.' 15 And as I began to speak, the

Holy Spirit fell upon them just as *He did* upon us at the beginning. 16 And I remembered the word of the Lord, how He used to say, 'John baptized with water, but you will be baptized with the Holy Spirit.' 17 Therefore if God gave to them the same gift as *He gave* to us also after believing in the Lord Jesus Christ, who was I that I could prevent God's way?" 18 And when they heard this, they quieted down and glorified God, saying, "Well then, God has granted to the Gentiles also the repentance *that leads* to life."

19 So then those who were scattered because of the persecution that occurred in connection with Stephen made their way to Phoenicia and Cyprus and Antioch, speaking the word to no one except to Jews alone. 20 But there were some of them, men of Cyprus and Cyrene, who came to Antioch and *began* speaking to the Greeks also, proclaiming the good news of the Lord Jesus. 21 And the hand of the Lord was with them, and a large number who believed turned to the Lord. 22 Now the news about them reached the ears of the church at Jerusalem, and they sent Barnabas off to Antioch, 23 who, when he arrived and saw the grace of God, rejoiced and *began to* encourage them all with a purposeful heart to remain *true* to the Lord; 24 for he was a good man, and full of the Holy Spirit and of faith. And a considerable crowd was brought to the Lord. 25 And he left for Tarsus to search for Saul; 26 and when he found him, he brought him to Antioch. And it happened that for an entire year they met with the church and taught a considerable crowd. And the disciples were first called Christians in Antioch.

27 Now in those days, some prophets came down from Jerusalem to Antioch. 28 And one of them named Agabus stood up and indicated by the Spirit that there was going to be a great famine all over the world. And this took place in the *reign* of Claudius. 29 And as any of the disciples had means, each of them determined to send *a contribution* for the service of the brothers living in Judea. 30 And this they did, sending it in charge of Barnabas and Saul to the elders.

JULY 4

2 Chronicles 3:1–4:22

3 Then Solomon began to build the house of Yahweh in Jerusalem on Mount Moriah, where *Yahweh* had appeared to his father David, at the place that David had prepared on the threshing floor of Ornan the Jebusite. 2 Then he began to build on the second *day* in the second month of the fourth year of his reign. 3 Now these are the foundations which Solomon laid for building the house of God. The length in cubits, according to the old standard *was* sixty cubits, and the width twenty cubits. 4 And the porch which was in front of the house was as long as the width of the house, 20 cubits, and the height 120; and inside he overlaid it with pure gold. 5 Now he overlaid the main room with cypress wood and overlaid it with fine gold, and ornamented it with palm trees and chains. 6 Further, he overlaid the house with precious stones for beauty; and the gold was gold from Parvaim. 7 He also covered the house with gold—the beams, the thresholds and its walls and its doors; and he carved cherubim on the walls.

8 And he made the room of the Holy of Holies: its length across the width of the house *was* twenty cubits, and its width *was* twenty cubits; and he covered it with fine gold, *amounting* to 600 talents. 9 Now the weight of the nails was fifty shekels of gold. He also covered the upper rooms with gold.

10 Then in the room of the Holy of Holies he made two cherubim of fashioned work and overlaid them with gold. 11 Now the wingspan of the cherubim *was* twenty cubits; the wing of one, of five cubits, touched the wall of the house, and *its* other wing, of five cubits, touched the wing of the other cherub. 12 And the wing of the other cherub, of five cubits, touched the wall of the house; and *its* other wing of five cubits was attached to the wing of the first cherub. 13 The wings of these cherubim extended twenty cubits, and they stood on their feet facing the *main* room. 14 And he made the veil of blue, purple, crimson, and fine linen, and he ornamented cherubim on it.

15 He also made two pillars for the front of the house, thirty-five cubits high, and the capital on the top of each *was* five cubits.

16 And he made chains in the inner sanctuary and put *them* on the top of the pillars; and he made one hundred pomegranates and put *them* on the chains. 17 Thus he set up the pillars in front of the temple, one on the right and one on the left, and named the one on the right Jachin and the one on the left Boaz.

4 Then he made a bronze altar, twenty cubits in length and twenty cubits in width and ten cubits in height. 2 And he made the sea of cast *metal* ten cubits from brim to brim, circular in form, and its height was five cubits, and thirty cubits in its circumference. 3 Now figures like oxen *were* under it *and* encircling it, ten cubits, entirely encircling the sea. The oxen *were* in two rows, cast in one piece. 4 It stood on twelve oxen, three facing the north, three facing west, three facing south, and three facing east; and the sea *was set* on top of them, and all their rear parts *turned* inward. 5 And it was a handbreadth thick, and its brim was made like the brim of a cup, *as* a lily blossom; it could hold 3,000 baths. 6 He also made ten lavers and set five on the right side and five on the left, in which to wash *things, that is,* in which they would rinse things for the burnt offering; but the sea *was* for the priests to wash in.

7 Then he made the ten golden lampstands in the way prescribed for them and he put them in the temple, five on the right side and five on the left. 8 He also made ten tables and placed them in the temple, five on the right side and five on the left. And he made one hundred golden bowls. 9 Then he made the court of the priests and the great court and doors for the court, and overlaid their doors with bronze. 10 And he put the sea on the right side *of the house* toward the southeast.

11 And Huram made the pots and the shovels and the bowls. So Huram completed doing the work which he did for King Solomon in the house of God: 12 the two pillars and the *two* bowls and the two capitals on top of the pillars, and the two networks to cover the two bowls of the capitals which were on top of the pillars, 13 and the four hundred pomegranates for the two networks, two rows of pomegranates for each network to cover the two bowls of the capitals which were on the pillars. 14 He also made the stands and he made the lavers on the stands, 15 *and* the one sea with the twelve oxen under it. 16 And the pots and the shovels and the flesh hooks and all its utensils, Huram-abi made of polished bronze for King Solomon for the house of Yahweh. 17 On the plain of the Jordan the king cast them, in the clay ground between Succoth and Zeredah. 18 Thus Solomon made all these utensils in great quantities, for the weight of the bronze could not be found out.

19 Solomon also made all the furniture which *was in* the house of God: even the golden altar and the tables with the bread of the Presence on them, 20 and the lampstands with their lamps of pure gold, to burn in front of the inner sanctuary in the way prescribed; 21 and the flowers and the lamps and the tongs of gold, of purest gold; 22 and the snuffers and the bowls and the spoons and the firepans, of pure gold; and the entrance of the house, its inner doors for the Holy of Holies and the doors of the house, *that is,* of the nave, of gold.

Psalm 79:5–10

5 How long, O Yahweh? Will
You be angry forever?
Will Your jealousy burn like fire?
6 Pour out Your wrath upon the
nations which do not know You,
And upon the kingdoms which
do not call upon Your name.
7 For they have devoured Jacob
And laid waste his abode.

8 Do not remember *our* former
iniquities against us;
Let Your compassion
quickly approach us,
For we are brought very low.
9 Help us, O God of our salvation,
for the glory of Your name;
And deliver us and atone for our
sins for Your name's sake.
10 Why should the nations say,
"Where is their God?"
Let it be known among the
nations before our eyes:
Vengeance for the blood of Your
slaves which has been poured out.

Proverbs 20:10–12

10 Differing weights and
differing measures,

Both of them are an
abomination to Yahweh.
11 It is by his deeds that a young
man makes himself known
If his conduct is pure and right.
12 The hearing ear and the seeing eye,
Yahweh has made both of them.

Acts 12:1–25

12 Now about that time Herod the king laid hands on some who belonged to the church in order to harm them. 2 And he had James the brother of John put to death with a sword. 3 And when he saw that it pleased the Jews, he proceeded to arrest Peter also. Now it was during the days of Unleavened Bread. 4 When he had seized him, he put him in prison, delivering him to four squads of soldiers to guard him, intending after the Passover to bring him out before the people. 5 So Peter was kept in the prison, but prayer for him was being made fervently by the church to God.

6 Now on the very night when Herod was about to bring him forward, Peter was sleeping between two soldiers, bound with two chains, and guards in front of the door were watching over the prison. 7 And behold, an angel of the Lord suddenly appeared and a light shone in the cell; and he struck Peter's side and woke him up, saying, "Rise up quickly." And his chains fell off his hands. 8 And the angel said to him, "Gird yourself and put on your sandals." And he did so. And he *said to him, "Wrap your garment around yourself and follow me." 9 And he went out and continued to follow, and he did not know that what was being done by the angel was real, but was thinking he was seeing a vision. 10 And when they had passed the first and second guard posts, they came to the iron gate that leads into the city, which opened for them by itself; and they went out and went along one street, and immediately the angel departed from him. 11 When Peter came to himself, he said, "Now truly I know that the Lord has sent His angel and rescued me from the hand of Herod and from all that the Jewish people were expecting." 12 And when he realized *this,* he went to the house of Mary, the mother of John who was also called Mark, where many were gathered together and were praying. 13 And when he knocked at the door of the gate, a servant-girl named Rhoda came to answer. 14 And when she recognized Peter's voice, because of her joy she did not open the gate. But she ran in and reported that Peter was standing in front of the gate. 15 And they said to her, "You are out of your mind!" But she kept insisting that it was so. They kept saying, "It is his angel." 16 But Peter continued knocking, and when they opened *the door,* they saw him and were astounded. 17 But motioning to them with his hand to be silent, he recounted to them how the Lord had led him out of the prison. And he said, "Report these things to James and the brothers." Then he left and went to another place.

18 Now when day came, there was no small disturbance among the soldiers *as to* what had become of Peter. 19 And when Herod had searched for him and had not found him, he examined the guards and ordered that they be led away *to execution.* Then he went down from Judea to Caesarea and was spending time there.

20 Now he was very angry with the people of Tyre and Sidon; and with one accord they came to him, and having won over Blastus the king's chamberlain, they were asking for peace, because their country was fed by the king's country. 21 And on an appointed day Herod, having put on his royal apparel and sitting on the judgment seat, *began* delivering an address to them. 22 And the assembly kept crying out, "The voice of a god and not of a man!" 23 And immediately an angel of the Lord struck him because he did not give God the glory, and he was eaten by worms and breathed his last.

24 But the word of the Lord continued to grow and to be multiplied.

25 And Barnabas and Saul returned to Jerusalem, fulfilling their ministry, taking along with *them* John, who was also called Mark.

JULY 5

2 Chronicles 5:1–6:42

5 Thus all the work that Solomon did for the house of Yahweh was finished. And Solomon brought in the things set apart as holy by his father David, even the silver and the gold and all the utensils, *and* he put *them* in the treasuries of the house of God.

2 Then Solomon assembled the elders of Israel and all the heads of the tribes, the leaders of the fathers' *households* of the sons of Israel to Jerusalem, to bring up the ark of the covenant of Yahweh from the city of David, which is Zion. 3 And all the men of Israel assembled themselves to the king at the feast, that is *in* the seventh month. 4 Then all the elders of Israel came, and the Levites carried the ark. 5 And they brought up the ark and the tent of meeting and all the holy utensils which were in the tent; the Levitical priests brought them up. 6 And King Solomon and all the congregation of Israel who congregated with him before the ark, were sacrificing so many sheep and oxen that they could not be counted or numbered. 7 Then the priests brought the ark of the covenant of Yahweh to its place, into the inner sanctuary of the house, to the Holy of Holies, under the wings of the cherubim. 8 And the cherubim spread *their* wings over the place of the ark, and the cherubim made a covering over the ark and its poles from above. 9 But the poles were so long that the ends of the poles of the ark could be seen before the inner sanctuary, but they could not be seen outside; and they are there to this day. 10 There was nothing in the ark except the two tablets which Moses put *there* at Horeb, where Yahweh cut a covenant with the sons of Israel, when they came out of Egypt.

11 Now it happened that when the priests came out of the holy place (for all the priests who were present had sanctified themselves, *without regard to divisions*), 12 and all the Levitical singers, Asaph, Heman, Jeduthun, and their sons and relatives, clothed in fine linen, with cymbals, harps, and lyres, standing east of the altar, and with them 120 priests blowing trumpets 13 in unison when the trumpeters and the singers were to make themselves heard with one voice to praise and to give thanks to Yahweh, and when they lifted up their voice accompanied by trumpets and cymbals and instruments of music, and when they praised Yahweh *saying*, "*He* indeed is good for His lovingkindness endures forever," then the house, the house of Yahweh, was filled with a cloud, 14 so that the priests could not stand to minister because of the cloud, for the glory of Yahweh filled the house of God.

6 Then Solomon said,
"Yahweh has said that He would
dwell in the *cloud of* dense gloom.
2 "Now I have built You a lofty house,
And a place for Your dwelling forever."

3 Then the king turned his face around and blessed all the assembly of Israel, while all the assembly of Israel was standing. 4 And he said, "Blessed be Yahweh, the God of Israel, who spoke with His mouth to my father David and has fulfilled *it* by His hands, saying, 5 'Since the day that I brought My people from the land of Egypt, I did not choose a city out of all the tribes of Israel *in which* to build a house that My name might be there, nor did I choose any man for a ruler over My people Israel; 6 but I have chosen Jerusalem that My name might be there, and I have chosen David to be over My people Israel.' 7 And it was in the heart of my father David to build a house for the name of Yahweh, the God of Israel. 8 But Yahweh said to my father David, 'Because it was in your heart to build a house for My name, you did well that it was in your heart. 9 Nevertheless you shall not build the house, but your son who will come forth from your loins, he shall build the house for My name.' 10 And Yahweh has established His word which He spoke; and I have been established in place of my father David and sit on the throne of Israel, as Yahweh promised, and have built the house for the name of Yahweh, the God of Israel. 11 And there I have set the ark in which is the covenant of Yahweh, which He cut with the sons of Israel."

12 Then he stood before the altar of Yahweh before all the assembly of Israel and spread out his hands. 13 Now Solomon had made a bronze platform, five cubits long, five cubits wide and three cubits high, and had put it in the midst of the court; and he

stood on it, knelt on his knees in the pres-
ence of all the assembly of Israel, and spread
out his hands toward heaven. 14 And he said,
"O Yahweh, the God of Israel, there is no
god like You in heaven or on earth, keeping
covenant and lovingkindness to Your slaves
who walk before You with all their heart;
15 who have kept with Your servant David,
my father, that which You have promised
him; indeed You have promised with Your
mouth and have fulfilled it by Your hand, as
it is this day. 16 So now, O Yahweh, the God
of Israel, keep with Your servant David my
father, that which You have promised him,
saying, 'You shall not have a man cut off
from before Me who is to sit on the throne
of Israel, if only your sons keep their way to
walk in My law as you have walked before
Me.' 17 So now, O Yahweh, the God of Israel,
let Your word *truly* endure which You have
spoken to Your servant David.

18 "But will God truly dwell with mankind
on the earth? Behold, heaven and the high-
est heaven cannot contain You; how much
less this house which I have built. 19 Yet have
regard to the prayer of Your slave and to his
supplication, O Yahweh my God, to listen to
the cry and to the prayer which Your slave
prays before You; 20 that Your eyes may
be open toward this house day and night,
toward the place of which You have said
that *You would* place Your name there, to
listen to the prayer which Your slave shall
pray toward this place. 21 And listen to the
supplications of Your slave and of Your
people Israel, when they pray toward this
place; listen from Your dwelling place, from
heaven; listen and forgive.

22 "If a man sins against his neighbor
and is made to take an oath, and he comes
and takes an oath before Your altar in this
house, 23 then listen from heaven and act
and judge Your slaves, punishing the wicked
by bringing his way on his own head and
justifying the righteous by bringing him
reward according to his righteousness.

24 "And if Your people Israel are defeated
before an enemy because they have sinned
against You, and they turn *to You* and
confess Your name, and pray and make
supplication before You in this house,
25 then listen from heaven and forgive the
sin of Your people Israel, and bring them
back to the land which You have given to
them and to their fathers.

26 "When the heavens are shut up and
there is no rain because they have sinned
against You, and they pray toward this place
and confess Your name, *and* turn from their
sin when You afflict them; 27 then listen in
heaven and forgive the sin of Your slaves and
of Your people Israel; indeed, teach them the
good way in which they should walk. And
give rain on Your land, which You have given
to Your people for an inheritance.

28 "If there is famine in the land, if there is
pestilence, if there is scorching wind or mil-
dew, if there is locust or grasshopper, if their
enemies besiege them in the land of their
cities, whatever plague or whatever sickness
there is, 29 whatever prayer or supplication
is made by any man or by all Your people
Israel, who know his own affliction and
his own pain, and spread his hands toward
this house, 30 then listen from heaven Your
dwelling place, and forgive, and give to each
according to all his ways, whose heart You
know, for You alone know the hearts of the
sons of men, 31 that they may fear You, to
walk in Your ways all the days they live upon
the face of the land which You have given
to our fathers.

32 "Also concerning the foreigner who is
not of Your people Israel, if he comes from
a far country for Your great name's sake and
Your strong hand and Your outstretched
arm, so if they come and pray toward this
house, 33 then listen from heaven, from
Your dwelling place, and do according to
all for which the foreigner calls to You, in
order that all the peoples of the earth may
know Your name even to fear You, as *do* Your
people Israel, and to know that Your name
is called upon this house which I have built.

34 "When Your people go out to battle
against their enemies, by whatever way
You shall send them, and they pray to You
toward this city which You have chosen and
the house which I have built for Your name,
35 then listen from heaven to their prayer
and their supplication, and do justice.

36 "When they sin against You (for there
is no man who does not sin) and You are
angry with them and give them over to an
enemy, so that they take them away captive
to a land far off or near, 37 and if they cause
these things to return to their heart in the
land where they have been taken captive,
and return and make supplication to You
in the land of their captivity, saying, 'We

have sinned, we have committed iniquity
and have acted wickedly'; 38 and if they
return to You with all their heart and with
all their soul in the land of their captivity,
where they have been taken captive, and
pray toward their land which You have
given to their fathers and the city which You
have chosen, and toward the house which I
have built for Your name, 39 then listen from
heaven, from Your dwelling place, to their
prayer and supplications, and do justice
for them and forgive Your people who have
sinned against You.

40 "Now, O my God, I pray, let Your eyes be
open and Your ears attentive to the prayer
offered in this place.

41 "So now, arise, O Yahweh God, to
Your resting place, You and the ark of Your
strength; let Your priests, O Yahweh God,
be clothed with salvation and let Your holy
ones be glad in what is good.

42 "O Yahweh God, do not turn away
the face of Your anointed; remember *Your*
lovingkindness to Your servant David."

Psalm 79:11–13

11 Let the groaning of the prisoner
come before You;
According to the greatness of
Your power preserve those
who are doomed to die.
12 And return to our neighbors
sevenfold into their bosom
The reproach with which they
have reproached You, O Lord.
13 But as for us, as Your people and
the sheep of Your pasture,
We will give thanks to You forever;
From generation to generation
we will recount Your praise.

Proverbs 20:13–14

13 Do not love sleep, lest you
become poor;
Open your eyes, *and* you will
be satisfied with food.
14 "Bad, bad," says the buyer,
But when he goes his way,
then he boasts.

Acts 13:1–25

13 Now there were at Antioch, in the
church that was *there*, prophets and
teachers: Barnabas, and Simeon who was
called Niger, and Lucius of Cyrene, and
Manaen who had been brought up with
Herod the tetrarch, and Saul. 2 And while
they were ministering to the Lord and
fasting, the Holy Spirit said, "Set apart for
Me Barnabas and Saul for the work to which
I have called them." 3 Then, when they had
fasted and prayed and laid their hands on
them, they sent them away.

4 So, being sent out by the Holy Spirit,
they went down to Seleucia and from there
they sailed to Cyprus. 5 And when they
reached Salamis, they *began to* proclaim
the word of God in the synagogues of the
Jews, and they also had John as their helper.
6 And when they had gone through the
whole island as far as Paphos, they found
a magician, a Jewish false prophet whose
name was Bar-Jesus, 7 who was with the
proconsul, Sergius Paulus, a man of intelli-
gence. This man summoned Barnabas and
Saul and sought to hear the word of God.
8 But Elymas the magician (for so his name
is translated) was opposing them, seeking
to turn the proconsul away from the faith.
9 But Saul, who was also *known as* Paul,
filled with the Holy Spirit, fixed his gaze
on him, 10 and said, "You who are full of all
deceit and fraud, you son of the devil, you
enemy of all righteousness, will you not
cease to make crooked the straight ways of
the Lord? 11 Now, behold, the hand of the
Lord is upon you, and you will be blind and
not see the sun for a time." And immediately
a mist and a darkness fell upon him, and he
went about seeking those who would lead
him by the hand. 12 Then the proconsul
believed when he saw what had happened,
being astonished at the teaching of the Lord.

13 Now after Paul and his companions
set sail from Paphos, they came to Perga in
Pamphylia, but John left them and returned
to Jerusalem. 14 But going on from Perga,
they arrived at Pisidian Antioch. And on the
Sabbath day, they went into the synagogue
and sat down. 15 And after the reading of
the Law and the Prophets the synagogue
officials sent to them, saying, "Brothers, if
you have any word of exhortation for the
people, say it." 16 So Paul stood up, and
motioning with his hand said,

"Men of Israel, and you who fear God,
listen: 17 The God of this people Israel chose
our fathers and lifted up the people during
their stay in the land of Egypt, and with an
uplifted arm He led them out from it. 18 And

for a period of about forty years He put up with them in the wilderness. 19 And when He destroyed seven nations in the land of Canaan, He distributed their land as an inheritance—*all of which took* about 450 years. 20 After these things He gave *them* judges until Samuel the prophet. 21 Then they asked for a king, and God gave them Saul the son of Kish, a man of the tribe of Benjamin, for forty years. 22 And after He had removed him, He raised up David to be their king, about whom He also said, bearing witness, 'I HAVE FOUND DAVID the son of Jesse, A MAN AFTER MY HEART, who will do all My will.' 23 From the seed of this man, according to promise, God has brought to Israel a Savior, Jesus, 24 after John had preached before His coming a baptism of repentance to all the people of Israel. 25 And as John was fulfilling his course, he kept saying, 'What do you suppose that I am? I am not *He*. But behold, one is coming after me of whom I am not worthy to untie the sandals of His feet.'

JULY 6

2 Chronicles 7:1–8:18

7 Now when Solomon had finished praying, fire came down from heaven and consumed the burnt offering and the sacrifices, and the glory of Yahweh filled the house. 2 And the priests could not enter into the house of Yahweh because the glory of Yahweh filled the house of Yahweh. 3 And all the sons of Israel, seeing the fire come down and the glory of Yahweh upon the house, bowed down on the pavement with their faces to the ground, and they worshiped and gave praise to Yahweh, *saying*, "For He is good, for His lovingkindness endures forever."

4 Now the king and all the people were offering sacrifices before Yahweh. 5 And King Solomon offered a sacrifice of 22,000 oxen and 120,000 sheep. So the king and all the people dedicated the house of God. 6 And the priests stood at their posts, and the Levites also, with the instruments of music to Yahweh, which King David had made for giving thanks to Yahweh—"for His lovingkindness endures forever"—whenever he gave praise by their hand, while the priests on the other side blew trumpets; and all Israel was standing.

7 Then Solomon set apart as holy the middle of the court that *was* before the house of Yahweh, because there he offered the burnt offerings and the fat of the peace offerings; for the bronze altar which Solomon had made was not able to hold the burnt offering and the grain offering and the fat.

8 So Solomon celebrated the feast at that time for seven days, and all Israel with him, a very great assembly from Lebo-hamath to the brook of Egypt. 9 And on the eighth day they celebrated a solemn assembly; for the dedication of the altar they celebrated seven days and the feast seven days. 10 And on the twenty-third day of the seventh month he sent the people to their tents, with gladness and goodness of heart because of the goodness that Yahweh had shown to David and to Solomon and to Israel His people.

11 Thus Solomon completed the house of Yahweh and the king's house; and all that had come into Solomon's heart to do in the house of Yahweh and in his house, he did successfully.

12 Then Yahweh appeared to Solomon at night and said to him, "I have heard your prayer and have chosen this place for Myself as a house of sacrifice. 13 If I shut up the heavens so that there is no rain, or if I command the grasshopper to devour the land, or if I send pestilence among My people, 14 and My people who are called by My name humble themselves and pray and seek My face and turn from their evil ways, then I will listen from heaven, I will forgive their sin, and I will heal their land. 15 Now My eyes will be open and My ears attentive to the prayer *offered* in this place. 16 So now I have chosen and set this house apart as holy that My name may be there forever, and My eyes and My heart will be there perpetually. 17 As for you, if you will walk before Me as your father David walked, even to do according to all that I have commanded you, and will keep My statutes and My judgments, 18 then I will establish your royal throne as I cut *a covenant* with your father David, saying, 'You shall not have a man cut off as ruler in Israel.'

19 "But if you turn away and forsake My statutes and My commandments which I

have set before you, and go and serve other
gods and worship them, 20 then I will uproot
you from My land which I have given you,
and this house which I have set apart as holy
for My name I will cast out of My presence
and I will make it a proverb and a byword
among all peoples. 21 As for this house,
which was exalted, everyone who passes
by it will *feel* desolate and say, 'Why has
Yahweh done thus to this land and to this
house?' 22 And they will say, 'Because they
forsook Yahweh, the God of their fathers,
who brought them out of the land of Egypt
and took hold of other gods and worshiped
them and served them, therefore He has
brought all this calamity on them.'"

8 Now it happened at the end of the twenty
years in which Solomon had built the
house of Yahweh and his own house 2 that
he built the cities which Huram had given
to him, and settled the sons of Israel there.
3 Then Solomon went to Hamath-zobah
and overpowered it. 4 And he built Tadmor
in the wilderness and all the storage cities
which he had built in Hamath. 5 He also
built upper Beth-horon and lower Beth-
horon, fortified cities *with* walls, gates and
bars; 6 and Baalath and all the storage cities
which Solomon had, and all the cities for his
chariots, and the cities for his horsemen,
and all that Solomon desired to build in
Jerusalem, in Lebanon, and in all the land
under his rule.
7 *As for* all the people who were left of
the Hittites, the Amorites, the Perizzites, the
Hivites, and the Jebusites, who were not of
Israel, 8 *namely*, from their sons who were
left after them in the land whom the sons
of Israel had not consumed, *from* them
Solomon raised up forced laborers to this
day. 9 But Solomon did not make slaves for
his work from the sons of Israel; for they
were men of war, his chief captains and his
chariot commanders and his horsemen.
10 These were the chief deputies of King
Solomon, 250 who ruled over the people.
11 Then Solomon brought Pharaoh's
daughter up from the city of David to the
house which he had built for her, for he said,
"My wife shall not live in the house of David
king of Israel, because the places are holy
where the ark of Yahweh has entered."
12 Then Solomon offered burnt offerings
to Yahweh on the altar of Yahweh which
he had built before the porch; 13 and *did so*
according to the daily rule, offering *them*
up according to the commandment of
Moses, for the sabbaths, the new moons
and the three annual feasts—the Feast of
Unleavened Bread, the Feast of Weeks and
the Feast of Booths.
14 And according to the judgment of his
father David, he caused the divisions of the
priests to stand for their service, and the
Levites for their responsibilities to praise
and minister before the priests according to
the daily rule, and the gatekeepers by their
divisions at every gate; for David the man
of God had so commanded. 15 And they did
not turn away from the commandment of
the king to the priests and Levites in any
manner or concerning the treasuries.
16 Thus all the work of Solomon was
carried out from the day of the foundation
of the house of Yahweh, and until it was
completed. So the house of Yahweh was
finished.
17 Then Solomon went to Ezion-geber and
to Eloth on the shore of the sea in the land
of Edom. 18 And Huram by the hand of his
servants sent him ships and servants who
knew the sea; and they went with Solomon's
servants to Ophir, and took from there 450
talents of gold and brought *them* to King
Solomon.

Psalm 80:1–6

1 O Shepherd of Israel, give ear,
You who guide Joseph like a flock;
You who are enthroned *above*
the cherubim, shine forth!
2 Before Ephraim and Benjamin and
Manasseh, stir up Your might
And come to save us!
3 O God, restore us
And cause Your face to shine *upon*
us, that we would be saved.

4 O Yahweh God *of* hosts,
How long will You smolder against
the prayer of Your people?
5 You have fed them with
the bread of tears,
And You have made them to
drink tears in large measure.
6 You set us as an object of
strife to our neighbors,
And our enemies mock *us*
among themselves.

Proverbs 20:15

15 There is gold, and an
abundance of pearls;
But the lips of knowledge are
a more precious vessel.

Acts 13:26–52

26 "Brothers, sons of Abraham's family,
and those among you who fear God, to us
the word of this salvation was sent. 27 For
those who live in Jerusalem, and their rulers,
recognizing neither Him nor the utterances
of the prophets which are read every Sab-
bath, fulfilled *them* by condemning *Him*.
28 And though they found no ground for
death, they asked Pilate that He be executed.
29 And when they had finished all that was
written concerning Him, they took Him
down from the tree and laid Him in a tomb.
30 But God raised Him from the dead; 31 and
for many days He appeared to those who
came up with Him from Galilee to Jerusalem,
the very ones who are now His witnesses
to the people. 32 And we proclaim to you
the good news of the promise made to the
fathers, 33 that God has fulfilled this *promise*
to our children in that He raised up Jesus, as
it is also written in the second Psalm, 'YOU
ARE MY SON; TODAY I HAVE BEGOTTEN YOU.'
34 *But* that He raised Him up from the dead,
no longer to return to corruption, He has
spoken in this way: 'I WILL GIVE YOU THE HOLY
and FAITHFUL *lovingkindnesses* OF DAVID.'
35 Therefore He also says in another *Psalm*,
'YOU WILL NOT GIVE YOUR HOLY ONE OVER
TO SEE CORRUPTION.' 36 For David, after he
had served the purpose of God in his own
generation, fell asleep and was laid among
his fathers and saw corruption; 37 but He
whom God raised did not see corruption.
38 Therefore let it be known to you, broth-
ers, that through Him forgiveness of sins
is proclaimed to you, 39 and *that* in Him,
everyone who believes is justified from
all things which you could not be justified
from through the Law of Moses. 40 Therefore
watch out, so that the thing spoken of in the
Prophets may not come upon *you*:

41 'LOOK, YOU SCOFFERS, AND
MARVEL, AND PERISH;
FOR I AM ACCOMPLISHING A
WORK IN YOUR DAYS,
A WORK WHICH YOU WILL NEVER
BELIEVE, THOUGH SOMEONE
SHOULD RECOUNT IT TO YOU.'"

42 And as Paul and Barnabas were leaving,
the people kept pleading that these words
might be spoken to them the next Sabbath.
43 Now when *the meeting of* the synagogue
had broken up, many of the Jews and of the
God-fearing proselytes followed Paul and
Barnabas, who, speaking to them, were
urging them to continue in the grace of God.

44 And the next Sabbath, nearly the whole
city assembled to hear the word of the Lord.
45 But when the Jews saw the crowds, they
were filled with jealousy and *began* contra-
dicting the things spoken by Paul, blasphem-
ing. 46 Paul and Barnabas spoke out boldly
and said, "It was necessary that the word of
God be spoken to you first. Since you reject
it and judge yourselves unworthy of eternal
life, behold, we are turning to the Gentiles.
47 For so the Lord has commanded us,

'I HAVE PLACED YOU AS A LIGHT
FOR THE GENTILES,
THAT YOU MAY BRING SALVATION
TO THE END OF THE EARTH.'"

48 And when the Gentiles heard this,
they *began* rejoicing and glorifying the
word of the Lord, and as many as had been
appointed to eternal life believed. 49 And the
word of the Lord was being spread through
the whole region. 50 But the Jews incited
the God-fearing women of prominence and
the leading men of the city, and instigated
a persecution against Paul and Barnabas,
and drove them out of their district. 51 But
having shaken off the dust of their feet
against them, they went to Iconium. 52 And
the disciples were continually filled with joy
and with the Holy Spirit.

JULY 7

2 Chronicles 9:1–10:19

9 Now the queen of Sheba heard the
report about Solomon. So she came to
Jerusalem to test Solomon with riddles. She
had a very glorious retinue, with camels car-
rying spices and a large amount of gold and
precious stones. And she came to Solomon
and spoke with him about all that was in her
heart. 2 And Solomon declared to her *the
answer* to all her matters; and not a matter

was hidden from Solomon which he did not declare to her. 3 Then the queen of Sheba saw the wisdom of Solomon, the house which he had built, 4 the food at his table, the seating of his servants, the disposition of his attendants and their attire, his cupbearers and their attire, and his stairway by which he went up to the house of Yahweh, so that there was no more spirit in her. 5 Then she said to the king, "The word is true which I heard in my own land about your words and your wisdom. 6 Nevertheless I did not believe their words until I came and my eyes had seen it. And behold, the half of the greatness of your wisdom was not declared to me. You exceed the report which I heard. 7 How blessed are your men, how blessed are these your servants who stand before you continually and hear your wisdom. 8 Blessed be Yahweh your God who delighted in you, to set you on His throne as king for Yahweh your God; because your God loved Israel to cause them to stand forever, therefore He gave you as king over them, to do justice and righteousness." 9 Then she gave the king 120 talents of gold and a very great *amount of* spices and precious stones. There had never been spice like that which the queen of Sheba gave to King Solomon.

10 Also, the servants of Huram and the servants of Solomon, who brought gold from Ophir, brought algum trees and precious stones. 11 And the king made of the algum trees steps for the house of Yahweh and for the king's house, and lyres and harps for the singers; and none like that was seen before in the land of Judah.

12 Thus King Solomon gave to the queen of Sheba all her desire which she asked, besides *a return for* what she had brought to the king. Then she turned around and went to her own land together with her servants.

13 Now the weight of gold which came to Solomon in one year was 666 talents of gold, 14 besides that which the traders and merchants brought; and all the kings of Arabia and the governors of the country brought gold and silver to Solomon. 15 And King Solomon made 200 large shields of beaten gold, using 600 *shekels of* beaten gold on each large shield. 16 And *he made* 300 shields of beaten gold, using 300 shekels of gold on each shield, and the king put them in the house of the forest of Lebanon.

17 Moreover, the king made a great throne of ivory and overlaid it with pure gold. 18 *And there were* six steps to the throne and a footstool in gold attached to the throne, and arms on each side of the seat, and two lions standing beside the arms. 19 Twelve lions were also standing there on the six steps on the one side and on the other; nothing like *it* was made for any *other* kingdom. 20 Now all King Solomon's drinking vessels *were* of gold, and all the vessels of the house of the forest of Lebanon *were* of pure gold; silver was not considered valuable in the days of Solomon. 21 For the king had ships which went to Tarshish with the servants of Huram; once every three years the ships of Tarshish came carrying gold and silver, ivory and apes and peacocks.

22 So King Solomon became greater than all the kings of the earth in riches and wisdom. 23 And all the kings of the earth were seeking the presence of Solomon, to hear his wisdom which God had put in his heart. 24 And they brought every man his present, articles of silver and gold, garments, weapons, spices, horses and mules, a set amount year by year.

25 And Solomon had 4,000 stalls for horses and chariots and 12,000 horsemen, and he stationed them in the chariot cities and with the king in Jerusalem. 26 And he was the ruler over all the kings from the River even to the land of the Philistines, and to the border of Egypt. 27 The king also made silver *as plentiful* as stones in Jerusalem, and he made cedars as plentiful as sycamore trees that are in the Shephelah. 28 And they were importing horses for Solomon from Egypt and from all countries.

29 Now the rest of the acts of Solomon, from first to last, are they not written in the chronicles of Nathan the prophet, and in the prophecy of Ahijah the Shilonite, and in the visions of Iddo the seer concerning Jeroboam the son of Nebat? 30 Thus Solomon reigned forty years in Jerusalem over all Israel. 31 And Solomon slept with his fathers and was buried in the city of his father David; and his son Rehoboam became king in his place.

10 Then Rehoboam went to Shechem, for all Israel had come to Shechem to make him king. 2 And it happened, when Jeroboam the son of Nebat heard *of it* (for

he was in Egypt where he had fled from
the presence of King Solomon), Jeroboam
returned from Egypt. 3 Then they sent and
called for him. And Jeroboam and all Israel
came and spoke to Rehoboam, saying,
4 "Your father made our yoke harsh; but
now, lighten the harsh service of your father
and his heavy yoke which he put on us, and
we will serve you." 5 Then he said to them,
"Return to me again in three days." So the
people went away.
6 Then King Rehoboam took counsel with
the elders who had stood before his father
Solomon while he was still alive, saying,
"How do you counsel *me* to respond to this
people?" 7 And they spoke to him, saying, "If
you will be good to this people and please
them and speak good words to them, then
they will be your servants forever." 8 But he
forsook the counsel of the elders which they
had counseled him, and took counsel with
the young men who grew up with him and
stood before him. 9 So he said to them, "What
counsel do you give that we may respond to
this people, who have spoken to me, saying,
'Lighten the yoke which your father put on
us'?" 10 Then the young men who grew up
with him spoke with him, saying, "Thus you
shall say to the people who spoke to you,
saying, 'Your father made our yoke heavy,
but you make it lighter for us.' Thus you shall
say to them, 'My little finger is thicker than
my father's loins! 11 So now my father loaded
you with a heavy yoke, but I will add to your
yoke; my father disciplined you with whips,
but I *will discipline you* with scorpions.'"
12 So Jeroboam and all the people came
to Rehoboam on the third day as the king
had spoken, saying, "Return to me on the
third day." 13 And the king answered them
harshly, and King Rehoboam forsook the
counsel of the elders, 14 and he spoke
to them according to the counsel of the
young men, saying, "My father made your
yoke heavy, but I will add to it; my father
disciplined you with whips, but I *will
discipline you* with scorpions." 15 So the
king did not listen to the people, for it was
a turn *of events* from God, that Yahweh
might establish His word, which He spoke
through Ahijah the Shilonite to Jeroboam
the son of Nebat.
16 Now all Israel *saw* that the king did not
listen to them. So the people responded to
the king, saying,

"What portion do we have in David?
We have no inheritance in
the son of Jesse.
Every man to your tents, O Israel;
Now see to your own house, David."

So all Israel went to their tents. 17 But as
for the sons of Israel who lived in the cities
of Judah, Rehoboam reigned over them.
18 Then King Rehoboam sent Hadoram,
who was over the forced labor, and the
sons of Israel stoned him and he died. And
King Rehoboam made haste to mount his
chariot to flee to Jerusalem. 19 So Israel has
been in rebellion against the house of David
to this day.

Psalm 80:7–13

7 O God *of* hosts, restore us
And cause Your face to shine *upon
us,* that we might be saved.

8 You removed a vine from Egypt;
You drove out the nations and
then You planted it.
9 You cleared *the ground* before it,
And it took deep root and
filled the land.
10 The mountains were covered
with its shadow,
And the cedars of God with its boughs.
11 It sent out its branches to the sea
And its shoots to the River.
12 Why have You broken down its hedges,
So that all who pass *that*
way pick its *fruit*?
13 A boar from the forest devours it
And whatever moves in the
field feeds on it.

Proverbs 20:16–18

16 Take his garment when he becomes
a guarantor for a stranger;
And for foreigners, hold him in pledge.
17 Bread obtained by lying
is sweet to a man,
But afterward his mouth will
be filled with gravel.
18 Thoughts are established by counsel,
So make war by guidance.

Acts 14:1–28

14 Now it happened that in Iconium they
entered the synagogue of the Jews
together and spoke in such a manner that
a large number of people believed, both of

Jews and of Greeks. 2 But the unbelieving Jews instigated and embittered the minds of the Gentiles against the brothers. 3 Therefore they spent a long time *there* speaking boldly *with reliance* upon the Lord, who was testifying to the word of His grace, granting that signs and wonders be done through their hands. 4 But the multitude of the city was divided; and some sided with the Jews, and some with the apostles. 5 And when an attempt was made by both the Gentiles and the Jews with their rulers to mistreat and to stone them, 6 they became aware of it and fled to the cities of Lycaonia, Lystra and Derbe, and the surrounding region; 7 and there they continued to proclaim the gospel.

8 And at Lystra a man was sitting who had no strength in his feet, lame from his mother's womb, who had never walked. 9 This man listened to Paul as he spoke, who, when he fixed his gaze on him and saw that he had faith to be saved *from being lame,* 10 said with a loud voice, "Stand upright on your feet." And he leaped up and *began to* walk. 11 And when the crowds saw what Paul had done, they raised their voice, saying in the Lycaonian language, "The gods have become like men and have come down to us." 12 And they *began* calling Barnabas, Zeus, and Paul, Hermes, because he was the chief speaker. 13 And the priest of Zeus, whose *temple* was just outside the city, brought oxen and garlands to the gates, and was wanting to offer sacrifice with the crowds. 14 But when the apostles Barnabas and Paul heard of it, they tore their garments and rushed out into the crowd, crying out 15 and saying, "Men, why are you doing these things? We are also men of the same nature as you, proclaiming the gospel to you that you should turn from these vain things to a living God, WHO MADE THE HEAVEN AND THE EARTH AND THE SEA AND ALL THAT IS IN THEM. 16 In the generations gone by He permitted all the nations to go their own ways; 17 and yet He did not leave Himself without witness, in that He did good and gave you rains from heaven and fruitful seasons, filling your hearts with food and gladness." 18 And saying these things, with difficulty they restrained the crowds from offering sacrifice to them.

19 But Jews came from Antioch and Iconium, and after winning over the crowds and stoning Paul, they were dragging him out of the city, supposing him to be dead. 20 But while the disciples stood around him, he rose up and entered the city. The next day he went away with Barnabas to Derbe. 21 And after they had proclaimed the gospel to that city and had made many disciples, they returned to Lystra and to Iconium and to Antioch, 22 strengthening the souls of the disciples, encouraging them to continue in the faith, and *saying,* "Through many afflictions we must enter the kingdom of God." 23 And when they had appointed elders for them in every church, having prayed with fasting, they commended them to the Lord in whom they had believed.

24 And when they passed through Pisidia, they came into Pamphylia. 25 And when they had spoken the word in Perga, they went down to Attalia. 26 And from there they sailed to Antioch, from where they had been committed to the grace of God for the work that they had fulfilled. 27 And when they had arrived and gathered the church together, they *began to* report all things that God had done with them and how He had opened a door of faith to the Gentiles. 28 And they spent not a little time with the disciples.

JULY 8

2 Chronicles 11:1–12:16

11 Then Rehoboam came to Jerusalem and assembled the house of Judah and Benjamin, 180,000 chosen men who could wage war, to fight against Israel to return the kingdom to Rehoboam. 2 But the word of Yahweh came to Shemaiah the man of God, saying, 3 "Speak to Rehoboam the son of Solomon, king of Judah, and to all Israel in Judah and Benjamin, saying, 4 'Thus says Yahweh, "You shall not go up and fight against your brothers; return every man to his house, for this thing is from Me."'" So they listened to the words of Yahweh and returned from going against Jeroboam.

5 Rehoboam lived in Jerusalem and built cities for fortifications in Judah. 6 Thus he built Bethlehem, Etam, Tekoa, 7 Beth-zur, Soco, Adullam, 8 Gath, Mareshah, Ziph, 9 Adoraim, Lachish, Azekah, 10 Zorah,

Aijalon and Hebron, which are fortified cities in Judah and in Benjamin. 11 He also strengthened the fortresses and put officers in them and stores of food, oil and wine. 12 And *he put* large shields and spears in every city and strengthened them greatly. So he held Judah and Benjamin.

13 Moreover, the priests and the Levites who were in all Israel took their stand with him from all their territories.

14 For the Levites left their pasture lands and their possession *of land* and went to Judah and Jerusalem, for Jeroboam and his sons had rejected them from ministering as priests to Yahweh— 15 And he set up priests of his own for the high places, for the goat demons and for the calves which he had made— 16 Now those from all the tribes of Israel who gave their hearts to seek Yahweh, the God of Israel, followed them to Jerusalem, to sacrifice to Yahweh, the God of their fathers. 17 They strengthened the kingdom of Judah and gave courage to Rehoboam the son of Solomon for three years, for they walked in the way of David and Solomon for three years.

18 Then Rehoboam took as a wife Mahalath the daughter of Jerimoth the son of David *and of* Abihail the daughter of Eliab the son of Jesse, 19 and she bore him sons: Jeush, Shemariah, and Zaham. 20 And after her he took Maacah the daughter of Absalom, and she bore him Abijah, Attai, Ziza, and Shelomith. 21 And Rehoboam loved Maacah the daughter of Absalom more than all his *other* wives and concubines. For he had taken eighteen wives and sixty concubines and became the father of twenty-eight sons and sixty daughters. 22 And Rehoboam set up Abijah the son of Maacah *to be* head and ruler among his brothers, for he *intended* to make him king. 23 And he acted with discernment and distributed some of his sons through all the lands of Judah and Benjamin to all the fortified cities, and he gave them sustenance in abundance. And he sought a multitude of wives *for them*.

12 Now it happened that when the kingdom of Rehoboam was established and strong, he and all Israel with him forsook the law of Yahweh. 2 Now it happened in the fifth year of King Rehoboam, because they had been unfaithful to Yahweh, that Shishak king of Egypt came up against Jerusalem 3 with 1,200 chariots and 60,000 horsemen. And the people who came with him from Egypt were without number: the Lubim, the Sukkiim and the Ethiopians. 4 And he captured the fortified cities of Judah and came as far as Jerusalem. 5 Now Shemaiah the prophet came to Rehoboam and the princes of Judah who had gathered at Jerusalem because of Shishak, and he said to them, "Thus says Yahweh, 'You have forsaken Me, so I also have forsaken you to Shishak.'" 6 So the princes of Israel and the king humbled themselves and said, "Yahweh is righteous."

7 When Yahweh saw that they humbled themselves, the word of Yahweh came to Shemaiah, saying, "They have humbled themselves *so* I will not bring them to ruin, but I will grant them some *measure* of escape, and My wrath shall not be poured out on Jerusalem by the hand of Shishak. 8 But they will become his slaves so that they may know *the difference between* My slavery and the slavery of the kingdoms of the countries."

9 So Shishak king of Egypt came up against Jerusalem, and took the treasures of the house of Yahweh and the treasures of the king's house. He took everything; he even took the shields of gold which Solomon had made. 10 Then King Rehoboam made shields of bronze in their place and committed them to the hand of the commanders of the guard who kept the door of the king's house. 11 Now it happened that as often as the king entered the house of Yahweh, the guards would come and carry them and *then* bring them back into the guards' room. 12 And when he humbled himself, the anger of Yahweh turned away from him, so as not to ruin *him* completely; and also conditions were good in Judah.

13 So King Rehoboam strengthened himself in Jerusalem and reigned. Now Rehoboam was forty-one years old when he became king, and he reigned seventeen years in Jerusalem, the city which Yahweh had chosen from all the tribes of Israel to put His name there. And his mother's name was Naamah the Ammonitess. 14 And he did evil because he did not set his heart to seek Yahweh.

15 Now the acts of Rehoboam, from first to last, are they not written in the records

of Shemaiah the prophet and of Iddo the
seer, according to genealogical record? Now
there were wars between Rehoboam and
Jeroboam all *their* days. 16 And Rehoboam
slept with his fathers and was buried in the
city of David; and Abijah his son became
king in his place.

Psalm 80:14–19

14 O God *of* hosts, return now,
we beseech You;
Look down from heaven and
see, and visit this vine,
15 Even the sapling which Your
right hand has planted,
And on the son whom You have
strengthened for Yourself.
16 It is burned with fire, it is cut down;
They perish at the rebuke of Your face.
17 Let Your hand be upon the
man of Your right hand,
Upon the son of man whom You
made strong for Yourself.
18 Then we shall not turn back from You;
Revive us, and we will call
upon Your name.
19 O Yahweh God of hosts, restore us;
Cause Your face to shine *upon*
us, that we might be saved.

Proverbs 20:19–21

19 He who goes about as a
slanderer reveals secrets,
Therefore do not associate
with one of loose lips.
20 He who curses his father
or his mother,
His lamp will go out in the
midst of darkness.
21 An inheritance gained hurriedly
at the beginning
In the end will not be blessed.

Acts 15:1–21

15 Some men came down from Judea and
began teaching the brothers, "Unless
you are circumcised according to the custom
of Moses, you cannot be saved." 2 And when
Paul and Barnabas had not a little dissension
and debate with them, *the brothers* deter-
mined that Paul and Barnabas and some
others of them should go up to Jerusalem
to the apostles and elders concerning this
issue. 3 Therefore, being sent on their way
by the church, they were passing through
both Phoenicia and Samaria, recounting in
detail the conversion of the Gentiles, and
were bringing great joy to all the brothers.
4 When they arrived at Jerusalem, they were
received by the church and the apostles and
the elders, and they reported all that God
had done with them. 5 But some of the sect
of the Pharisees who had believed stood up,
saying, "It is necessary to circumcise them
and to command them to keep the Law of
Moses."

6 Both the apostles and the elders came
together to look into this matter. 7 And after
there had been much debate, Peter stood up
and said to them, "Brothers, you know that
in the early days God made a choice among
you, that by my mouth the Gentiles would
hear the word of the gospel and believe.
8 And God, who knows the heart, testified to
them giving them the Holy Spirit, just as He
also did to us; 9 and He made no distinction
between us and them, cleansing their hearts
by faith. 10 Now therefore why do you put
God to the test by placing upon the neck
of the disciples a yoke which neither our
fathers nor we have been able to bear? 11 But
we believe that we are saved through the
grace of the Lord Jesus, in the same way as
they also are."

12 And all the multitude kept silent, and
they were listening to Barnabas and Paul as
they were relating what signs and wonders
God had done through them among the
Gentiles.

13 Now after they had stopped speaking,
James answered, saying, "Brothers, listen
to me. 14 Simeon has related how God first
concerned Himself about taking from
among the Gentiles a people for His name.
15 And with this the words of the Prophets
agree, just as it is written,

16 'After these things I will return,
And I will rebuild the fallen
booth of David,
And I will rebuild its ruins,
And I will restore it,
17 So that the rest of mankind
may seek the Lord,
And all the Gentiles who
are called by My name,'
18 Says the Lord, who makes these
things known from long ago.

19 "Therefore I judge that we do not trouble
those who are turning to God from among
the Gentiles, 20 but that we write to them

that they abstain from things contaminated by idols and from sexual immorality and from what is strangled and from blood. [21] For from ancient generations, Moses has those who preach him in every city, since he is read in the synagogues every Sabbath."

It is well to remember that reading books about the Bible is a vey different thing to searching the Word for oneself.

— H. A. IRONSIDE

JULY 9

2 Chronicles 13:1–14:15

13 In the eighteenth year of King Jeroboam, Abijah became king over Judah. [2] He reigned three years in Jerusalem; and his mother's name was Micaiah the daughter of Uriel of Gibeah.

Now there was war between Abijah and Jeroboam. [3] And Abijah began the battle with a military force of mighty men, 400,000 chosen men, while Jeroboam arranged *them* all for battle against him with 800,000 chosen men *who were* mighty men of valor.

[4] Then Abijah rose up on Mount Zemaraim, which is in the hill country of Ephraim, and said, "Listen to me, Jeroboam and all Israel: [5] Do you not know that Yahweh, the God of Israel, gave the rule over Israel forever to David and his sons by a covenant of salt? [6] Yet Jeroboam the son of Nebat, the servant of Solomon the son of David, rose up and rebelled against his master, [7] and worthless men gathered about him, vile men, who proved too strong for Rehoboam, the son of Solomon; he was young and timid and could not exert his strength before them.

[8] "So now you intend to exert your strength before the kingdom of Yahweh by the hand of the sons of David, being a great multitude and *having* with you the golden calves which Jeroboam made for gods for you. [9] Have you not driven out the priests of Yahweh, the sons of Aaron and the Levites, and made for yourselves priests like the peoples of *other* lands? Whoever comes to ordain himself with a bull from the herd and seven rams, even he may become a priest of *what are* no gods. [10] But as for us, Yahweh is our God, and we have not forsaken Him; and the sons of Aaron are ministering to Yahweh as priests, and the Levites are in their work. [11] And every morning and evening they burn to Yahweh burnt offerings and fragrant incense, and the showbread is *set* on the clean table, and the golden lampstand with its lamps is *ready* to light every evening; for we keep the responsibility *given by* Yahweh our God, but you have forsaken Him. [12] And behold, God is with us at *our* head and His priests with the signal trumpets to raise the shout *of war* against you. O sons of Israel, do not fight against Yahweh, the God of your fathers, for you will not succeed."

[13] But Jeroboam had encircled an ambush to come from the rear, so that *Israel* was in front of Judah and the ambush was behind them. [14] So Judah turned around, and behold, they were attacked both front and rear; so they cried to Yahweh, and the priests blew the trumpets. [15] Then the men of Judah raised a shout *of war*, and when the men of Judah raised the shout *of war*, then it was that God smote Jeroboam and all Israel before Abijah and Judah. [16] So the sons of Israel fled before Judah, and God gave them into their hand. [17] And Abijah and his people struck them down with a great slaughter, and 500,000 chosen men of Israel fell slain. [18] Thus the sons of Israel were subdued at that time, and the sons of Judah were strong because they leaned upon Yahweh, the God of their fathers. [19] And Abijah pursued Jeroboam and captured from him *several* cities, Bethel with its towns, Jeshanah with its towns, and Ephron with its towns.

[20] Now Jeroboam did not again recover power in the days of Abijah; and Yahweh smote him and he died.

[21] But Abijah became stronger; and he took fourteen wives to himself, and became the father of twenty-two sons and sixteen daughters. [22] Now the rest of the acts of

Abijah, and his ways and his words are
written in the treatise of the prophet Iddo.

14 So Abijah slept with his fathers, and
they buried him in the city of David;
and Asa his son became king in his place.
The land was quiet for ten years during his
days.
2 And Asa did what was good and right in
the sight of Yahweh his God, 3 for he removed
the foreign altars and high places, shattered
the *sacred* pillars, cut the Asherim in pieces,
4 and said for Judah to seek Yahweh, the God
of their fathers, and to do the law and the
commandment. 5 He also removed the high
places and the incense altars from all the
cities of Judah. And the kingdom was quiet
before him. 6 And he built fortified cities in
Judah, since the land was quiet, and there
was no one at war with him during those
years, because Yahweh had given him rest.
7 And he said to Judah, "Let us build these
cities and surround *them* with walls and
towers, gates and bars. The land is still ours
because we have sought Yahweh our God;
we have sought Him, and He has given us
rest on every side." So they built and suc-
ceeded. 8 Now Asa had a military force of
300,000 from Judah, bearing large shields
and spears, and 280,000 from Benjamin,
bearing shields and wielding bows; all of
them were mighty men of valor.
9 Then Zerah the Ethiopian went out
against them with a military force of one
million men and 300 chariots, and he came
to Mareshah. 10 So Asa went out to meet
him, and they arranged *themselves* for battle
in the valley of Zephathah at Mareshah.
11 Then Asa called to Yahweh his God and
said, "Yahweh, there is no one besides You
to help *in the battle* between those of abun-
dant *power* and those who have no power;
so help us, O Yahweh our God, for we lean
on You, and in Your name have come against
this multitude. O Yahweh, You are our God;
let not mortal man prevail against You."
12 So Yahweh smote the Ethiopians before
Asa and before Judah, and the Ethiopians
fled. 13 And Asa and the people who *were*
with him pursued them as far as Gerar; and
so many Ethiopians fell that they could not
recover, for they were shattered before
Yahweh and before His army. And they
carried away very much spoil. 14 And they
struck down all the cities around Gerar, for
the dread of Yahweh had fallen on them; and
they plundered all the cities, for there was
much plunder in them. 15 They also struck
down those who owned livestock, and they
carried away large numbers of sheep and
camels. Then they returned to Jerusalem.

Psalm 81:1–5

1 Sing for joy to God our strength;
Make a loud shout to the God of Jacob.
2 Lift up a song of praise, strike
the tambourine,
The sweet sounding lyre with the harp.
3 Blow the trumpet at the new moon,
At the full moon, on our feast day.
4 For it is a statute for Israel,
A judgment of the God of Jacob.
5 He established it for a
testimony in Joseph
When he went forth over
the land of Egypt.
I heard a language that I did not know:

Proverbs 20:22–23

22 Do not say, "I will repay evil";
Hope in Yahweh, and He will save you.
23 Differing weights are an
abomination to Yahweh,
And a deceitful balance is not good.

Acts 15:22–41

22 Then it seemed good to the apostles
and the elders, with the whole church, to
choose men from among them—Judas
called Barsabbas, and Silas, leading men
among the brothers—to send to Antioch
with Paul and Barnabas, 23 and they sent
this letter by them,
"The apostles and the brothers who
are elders, to the brothers in Antioch
and Syria and Cilicia who are from
the Gentiles, greetings. 24 Since we
have heard that some of us, to whom
we gave no instruction, have gone out
and disturbed you with *their* words,
unsettling your souls, 25 it seemed
good to us, having come to one
accord, to select men to send to you
with our beloved Barnabas and Paul,
26 men who have risked their lives for
the name of our Lord Jesus Christ.
27 Therefore we have sent Judas and
Silas, and they themselves will report
the same things by word *of mouth*.
28 For it seemed good to the Holy Spirit

and to us to lay upon you no greater
burden than these essentials: 29 that
you abstain from things sacrificed to
idols and from blood and from things
strangled and from sexual immorality,
from which if you keep yourselves,
you will do well. Farewell."

30 So when they were sent away, they went down to Antioch; and having gathered the congregation together, they delivered the letter. 31 And when they had read it, they rejoiced because of its encouragement. 32 And both Judas and Silas, also being prophets themselves, encouraged and strengthened the brothers with a lengthy message. 33 And after they had spent time *there*, they were sent away from the brothers in peace to those who had sent them. 34 [But it seemed good to Silas to remain there.] 35 But Paul and Barnabas spent a long time in Antioch, teaching and preaching with many others also, the word of the Lord.

36 Now after some days Paul said to Barnabas, "Let us return and visit the brothers in every city in which we proclaimed the word of the Lord, *and see* how they are." 37 And Barnabas wanted to take John, called Mark, along with them also. 38 But Paul kept insisting that they should not take him along who had deserted them in Pamphylia and had not gone with them to the work. 39 And there was such a sharp disagreement that they separated from one another, and Barnabas took Mark with him and sailed away to Cyprus. 40 But Paul chose Silas and left, being committed by the brothers to the grace of the Lord. 41 And he was traveling through Syria and Cilicia, strengthening the churches.

JULY 10

2 Chronicles 15:1–16:14

15 Now the Spirit of God came on Azariah the son of Oded, 2 and he went out to meet Asa and said to him, "Listen to me, Asa, and all Judah and Benjamin: Yahweh is with you when you are with Him. And if you seek Him, He will be found; but if you forsake Him, He will forsake you. 3 Now for many days Israel was without the true God and without a teaching priest and without law. 4 But in their distress they turned to Yahweh, the God of Israel, and they searched for Him, and He was found *by them*. 5 Now in those times there was no peace to him who went out or to him who came in, for much confusion was upon all the inhabitants of the lands. 6 And nation was crushed by nation, and city by city, for God threw them into confusion with every kind of distress. 7 But you, be strong and do not let your hands fall limp, for there is reward for your work."

8 Now when Asa heard these words and the prophecy which Azariah the son of Oded the prophet spoke, he strengthened himself and took away the detestable idols from all the land of Judah and Benjamin and from the cities which he had captured in the hill country of Ephraim. He then renewed the altar of Yahweh which was in front of the porch of Yahweh. 9 And he gathered all Judah and Benjamin and those from Ephraim, Manasseh and Simeon who sojourned with them, for many defected to him from Israel when they saw that Yahweh his God was with him. 10 So they assembled at Jerusalem in the third month of the fifteenth year of Asa's reign. 11 And they sacrificed to Yahweh that day 700 oxen and 7,000 sheep from the spoil they had brought. 12 They entered into the covenant to seek Yahweh, the God of their fathers, with all their heart and soul; 13 and whoever would not seek Yahweh, the God of Israel, should be put to death, whether small or great, man or woman. 14 Moreover, they swore *an oath* to Yahweh with a loud voice, with shouting, with trumpets and with horns. 15 All Judah was glad concerning the oath, for they had sworn with their whole heart and had searched for Him with all their desire, and He was found *by them*. So Yahweh gave them rest on every side.

16 He also removed Maacah, the mother of King Asa, from *being* queen mother, because she had made a horrid image as an Asherah; and Asa cut down her horrid image, crushed *it* and burned *it* at the brook Kidron. 17 But the high places were not removed from Israel; nevertheless Asa's heart was wholly devoted all his days. 18 And he brought into the house of God the holy things of his father and his own holy things: silver and

gold and utensils. 19 And there was no more war until the thirty-fifth year of Asa's reign.

16 In the thirty-sixth year of Asa's reign Baasha king of Israel went up against Judah and built up Ramah in order to prevent *anyone* from going out or coming in to Asa king of Judah. 2 Then Asa brought out silver and gold from the treasuries of the house of Yahweh and the king's house, and sent them to Ben-hadad king of Aram, who lived in Damascus, saying, 3 "*Let there be* a covenant between you and me, *as* between my father and your father. Behold, I have sent you silver and gold; go, break your covenant with Baasha king of Israel so that he will withdraw from me." 4 So Ben-hadad listened to King Asa and sent the commanders of his military forces against the cities of Israel, and they struck down Ijon, Dan, Abel-maim, and all the store cities of Naphtali. 5 Now it happened that when Baasha heard *of it*, he ceased building up Ramah and stopped his work. 6 Then King Asa brought all Judah, and they carried away the stones of Ramah and its timber with which Baasha had been building, and with them he built Geba and Mizpah.

7 Now at that time Hanani the seer came to Asa king of Judah and said to him, "Because you have leaned on the king of Aram and have not leaned on Yahweh your God, therefore the military force of the king of Aram has escaped out of your hand. 8 Were not the Ethiopians and the Lubim a vast military force with an exceedingly vast *number* of chariots and horsemen? Yet because you leaned on Yahweh, He gave them into your hand. 9 For the eyes of Yahweh move to and fro throughout the earth that He may strongly support those whose heart is wholly devoted to Him. You have acted foolishly in this. Indeed, from now on you will surely have wars." 10 Then Asa was vexed with the seer and put him in prison, for he was enraged at him for this. And Asa oppressed some of the people at the same time.

11 Now behold, the acts of Asa from first to last, behold, they are written in the Book of the Kings of Judah and Israel. 12 And Asa became diseased in his feet in the thirty-ninth year of his reign. His disease was severe, yet even in his disease he did not seek Yahweh, but the physicians. 13 So Asa slept with his fathers. And he died in the forty-first year of his reign. 14 And they buried him in his own tomb which he had cut out for himself in the city of David, and they laid him in the resting place which he had filled with spices of various kinds blended by the perfumers' art; and they made a very great fire for him.

Psalm 81:6–10

6 "I relieved his shoulder of the burden,
His hands were freed from the basket.
7 "You called in distress and
I rescued you;
I answered you in the hiding
place of thunder;
I tested you at the waters of
Meribah. Selah.
8 "Hear, O My people, and I will
testify against you;
O Israel, if you would listen to Me!
9 "Let there be no strange god among you;
And you shall not worship
a foreign god.
10 "I am Yahweh your God,
Who brought you up from
the land of Egypt;
Open your mouth wide and I will fill it.

Proverbs 20:24–25

24 The steps of a man are from Yahweh,
How then can man
understand his way?
25 It is a trap for a man to say
rashly, "It is holy!"
And after the vows to make inquiry.

Acts 16:1–18

16 Now Paul also arrived at Derbe and at Lystra. And behold, a disciple was there, named Timothy, the son of a Jewish woman who was a believer, but his father was a Greek, 2 and he was well spoken of by the brothers who were in Lystra and Iconium. 3 Paul wanted this man to go with him, and he took him and circumcised him because of the Jews who were in those parts, for they all knew that his father was a Greek. 4 Now while they were passing through the cities, they were delivering the decrees which had been decided upon by the apostles and elders who were in Jerusalem, for them to keep. 5 So the churches were being strengthened in the faith, and were abounding in number daily.

6 And they passed through the Phrygian
and Galatian region, having been forbidden
by the Holy Spirit to speak the word in Asia;
7 and after they came to Mysia, they were
trying to go into Bithynia, and the Spirit of
Jesus did not permit them; 8 and passing by
Mysia, they came down to Troas. 9 And a
vision appeared to Paul in the night: a man
of Macedonia was standing and appealing to
him, and saying, "Come over to Macedonia
and help us." 10 And when he had seen the
vision, immediately we sought to go into
Macedonia, concluding that God had called
us to proclaim the gospel to them.

11 So setting sail from Troas, we ran a
straight course to Samothrace, and on the
day following to Neapolis; 12 and from
there to Philippi, which is a leading city
of the district of Macedonia, a Roman
colony; and we were staying in this city
for some days. 13 And on the Sabbath day
we went outside the gate to a riverside,
where we were supposing that there would
be a place of prayer; and sitting down,
we *began* speaking to the women who
had assembled. 14 And a woman named
Lydia, from the city of Thyatira, a seller
of purple fabrics, a worshiper of God, was
listening, whose heart the Lord opened to
pay attention to the things spoken by Paul.
15 And when she and her household had
been baptized, she urged us, saying, "If
you have judged me to be faithful to the
Lord, come into my house and stay." And
she prevailed upon us.

16 Now it happened that as we were
going to the place of prayer, a servant-girl
having a spirit of divination met us, who
was bringing her masters much profit by
fortune-telling. 17 Following after Paul and
us, she kept crying out, saying, "These men
are slaves of the Most High God, who are
proclaiming to you the way of salvation."
18 And she continued doing this for many
days. But being greatly annoyed, Paul turned
and said to the spirit, "I command you in
the name of Jesus Christ to leave her!" And
it left at that very moment.

JULY 11

2 Chronicles 17:1–18:34

17 Jehoshaphat his son then became king
in his place, and strengthened himself
over Israel. 2 And he put military forces in
all the fortified cities of Judah, and put
garrisons in the land of Judah and in the
cities of Ephraim which Asa his father had
captured.

3 And Yahweh was with Jehoshaphat
because he walked in the ways of his father
David's earlier days and did not seek the Baals,
4 but sought the God of his father, walked in
His commandments, and did not act as Israel
did. 5 So Yahweh established the kingdom in
his hand, and all Judah brought presents to
Jehoshaphat, and he had great riches and
honor. 6 And his heart took great pride in
the ways of Yahweh, and again he took away
the high places and the Asherim from Judah.

7 Then in the third year of his reign
he sent his officials, Ben-hail, Obadiah,
Zechariah, Nethanel and Micaiah, to teach
in the cities of Judah; 8 and with them the
Levites, Shemaiah, Nethaniah, Zebadiah,
Asahel, Shemiramoth, Jehonathan, Adoni-
jah, Tobijah, and Tobadonijah, the Levites;
and with them Elishama and Jehoram, the
priests. 9 And they taught in Judah, *having*
the book of the law of Yahweh with them;
and they went throughout all the cities of
Judah and taught among the people.

10 Now the dread of Yahweh was on all the
kingdoms of the lands which *were* around
Judah, so that they did not make war against
Jehoshaphat. 11 Indeed, some of the Philis-
tines brought presents and silver as *their*
tax burden to Jehoshaphat; the Arabians
also brought him flocks, 7,700 rams and
7,700 male goats. 12 So Jehoshaphat grew
greater and greater, and he built fortresses
and store cities in Judah. 13 And he had large
supplies in the cities of Judah, and men of
war, mighty men of valor, in Jerusalem.
14 This was their muster according to their
fathers' households:

of Judah, commanders of thousands,
Adnah *was* the commander, and with
him 300,000 mighty men of valor;
15 and next to him *was* Johanan the
commander, and with him 280,000;
16 and next to him Amasiah the son of
Zichri, who volunteered for Yahweh,
and with him 200,000 mighty men of
valor;

17 and of Benjamin, Eliada a mighty
man of valor, and with him 200,000
equipped with bow and shield;
18 and next to him Jehozabad, and with
him 180,000 armed for *military* duty.
19 These are they who attended on the king,
apart from those whom the king put in the
fortified cities through all Judah.

18 Now Jehoshaphat had riches and
honor in abundance; and he allied
himself by marriage with Ahab. 2 And
some years later he went down to Ahab at
Samaria. And Ahab sacrificed sheep and
oxen in abundance for him and the people
who were with him, and incited him to go
up against Ramoth-gilead. 3 And Ahab king
of Israel said to Jehoshaphat king of Judah,
"Will you go with me *against* Ramoth-
gilead?" And he said to him, "I am as you
are, and my people as your people, and *we
will be* with you in the battle."
4 Moreover, Jehoshaphat said to the king
of Israel, "Please inquire first for the word of
Yahweh." 5 Then the king of Israel gathered
the prophets, four hundred men, and said
to them, "Shall we go against Ramoth-gilead
to battle, or shall I refrain?" And they said,
"Go up, for God will give *it* into the hand of
the king." 6 But Jehoshaphat said, "Is there
not yet a prophet of Yahweh here that we
may inquire of him?" 7 And the king of Israel
said to Jehoshaphat, "There is yet one man
by whom we may inquire of Yahweh, but
I hate him, because he never prophesies
good concerning me but always evil. He is
Micaiah, son of Imla." But Jehoshaphat said,
"Let not the king say so."
8 Then the king of Israel called an
officer and said, "Hasten to bring Micaiah
son of Imla." 9 Now the king of Israel and
Jehoshaphat the king of Judah were sit-
ting each on his throne, clothed in *their
royal* garments, and *they* were sitting
at the threshing floor at the entrance of
the gate of Samaria; and all the prophets
were prophesying before them. 10 And
Zedekiah the son of Chenaanah made
horns of iron for himself and said, "Thus
says Yahweh, 'With these you shall gore
the Arameans until they are consumed.'"
11 All the prophets were also prophesying
thus, saying, "Go up to Ramoth-gilead and
succeed, and Yahweh will give *it* into the
hand of the king."
12 Now the messenger who went to sum-
mon Micaiah spoke to him saying, "Behold,
the words of the prophets, *as if* from one
mouth, are good to the king. So please let
your word be like one of them and speak
that which is good." 13 But Micaiah said, "As
Yahweh lives, what my God says, that I shall
speak."
14 Then he came to the king, and the
king said to him, "Micaiah, shall we go to
Ramoth-gilead to battle, or shall I refrain?"
And he said, "Go up and succeed, and they
will be given into your hand." 15 Then the
king said to him, "How many times must
I make you swear to speak to me nothing
but the truth in the name of Yahweh?" 16 So
he said,

"I saw all Israel
Scattered on the mountains,
Like sheep which have no shepherd;
And Yahweh said,
'These have no master.
Let each of them return to
his house in peace.'"

17 So the king of Israel said to Jehoshaphat,
"Did I not say to you that he would not
prophesy good concerning me, but evil?"
18 Then Micaiah said, "Therefore, hear the
word of Yahweh. I saw Yahweh sitting on His
throne, and all the host of heaven standing
on His right and on His left. 19 And Yahweh
said, 'Who will entice Ahab king of Israel so
that he will go up and fall at Ramoth-gilead?'
And one said this while another said that.
20 Then a spirit came forward and stood
before Yahweh and said, 'I will entice him.'
And Yahweh said to him, 'How?' 21 And he
said, 'I will go out and be a lying spirit in the
mouth of all his prophets.' Then He said,
'You shall entice *him* and also prevail. Go out
and do so.' 22 So now, behold, Yahweh has
put a lying spirit in the mouth of these your
prophets, but Yahweh has spoken calamity
against you."
23 Then Zedekiah the son of Chenaanah
approached and struck Micaiah on the
cheek and said, "How did the Spirit of Yah-
weh pass from me to speak to you?" 24 And
Micaiah said, "Behold, you will see on that
day when you enter an inner room to hide."
25 Then the king of Israel said, "Take Micaiah
and return him to Amon the ruler of the city
and to Joash the king's son; 26 and say, 'Thus
says the king, "Put this *man* in prison and
feed him sparingly with bread and water

until I return safely.”’” 27 And Micaiah said,
“If you indeed return safely, Yahweh has not
spoken by me.” And he said, “Listen, all you
people.”
28 So the king of Israel and Jehoshaphat
king of Judah went up against Ramoth-
gilead. 29 And the king of Israel said
to Jehoshaphat, “I will disguise myself
and go into battle, but you put on your
garments.” So the king of Israel disguised
himself, and they went into battle. 30 Now
the king of Aram had commanded the
commanders of his chariots, saying, “Do
not fight with small or great, but with the
king of Israel alone.” 31 Now it happened
that when the commanders of the chari-
ots saw Jehoshaphat, they said, “It is the
king of Israel,” and they turned to fight
against him. But Jehoshaphat cried out,
and Yahweh helped him, and God incited
them away from him. 32 So it happened
that when the commanders of the chariots
saw that it was not the king of Israel, they
turned back from pursuing him. 33 Now a
certain man drew his bow at random and
struck the king of Israel in a joint of the
armor. So he said to the driver of the char-
iot, “Turn around and take me out of the
fight, for I am severely wounded.” 34 Now
the battle raged that day, and the king of
Israel propped himself up in his chariot in
front of the Arameans until the evening;
and at sunset he died.

Psalm 81:11–16

11 “But My people did not
listen to My voice,
And Israel was not willing *to obey* Me.
12 “So I released them over to the
stubbornness of their heart,
That they would walk in
their own devices.
13 “Oh that My people would listen to Me,
That Israel would walk in My ways!
14 “I would quickly subdue their enemies
And I would turn My hand
against their adversaries.
15 “Those who hate Yahweh would
cower before Him,
And their time *of punishment*
would be forever.
16 “But I would feed you with the
finest of the wheat,
And with honey from the rock
I would satisfy you.”

Proverbs 20:26–28

26 A wise king winnows the wicked,
And turns the *threshing*
wheel over them.
27 The breath of man is the
lamp of Yahweh,
Searching all the innermost
parts of his body.
28 Lovingkindness and truth
will guard the king,
And he upholds his throne
by lovingkindness.

Acts 16:19–40

19 But when her masters saw that their
hope of profit had left, they seized Paul and
Silas and dragged them into the marketplace
before the authorities, 20 and when they had
brought them to the chief magistrates, they
said, “These men are throwing our city into
confusion, being Jews, 21 and are proclaim-
ing customs that are not lawful for us to
accept or to observe, being Romans.” 22 And
the crowd joined together to attack them,
and the chief magistrates, tearing their
garments off of them, proceeded to order
them to be beaten with rods. 23 And when
they had inflicted them with many wounds,
they threw them into prison, commanding
the jailer to guard them securely, 24 who,
having received such a command, threw
them into the inner prison and fastened
their feet in the stocks.
25 But about midnight Paul and Silas
were praying and singing hymns of praise
to God, and the prisoners were listening to
them. 26 And suddenly there came a great
earthquake, so that the foundations of the
jailhouse were shaken; and immediately
all the doors were opened and everyone’s
chains were unfastened. 27 And when the
jailer awoke and saw the prison doors
opened, he drew his sword and was about
to kill himself, supposing that the prisoners
had escaped. 28 But Paul cried out with a
loud voice, saying, “Do not harm yourself,
for we are all here!” 29 And he called for
lights and rushed in, and trembling with fear
he fell down before Paul and Silas, 30 and
after he brought them out, he said, “Sirs,
what must I do to be saved?” 31 And they
said, “Believe in the Lord Jesus, and you will
be saved, you and your house.” 32 And they
spoke the word of the Lord to him together
with all who were in his household. 33 And

he took them that *very* hour of the night and washed their wounds, and immediately he was baptized, he and all his *household*. 34 And he brought them into his house and set food before them, and rejoiced greatly with his whole household, because he had believed in God.

35 Now when day came, the chief magistrates sent their policemen, saying, "Release those men." 36 And the jailer reported these words to Paul, *saying*, "The chief magistrates have sent to release you. Therefore come out now and go in peace." 37 But Paul said to them, "Having beaten us in public without trial, men who are Romans, they have thrown us into prison. And now are they sending us away secretly? No indeed! But let them come themselves and bring us out." 38 And the policemen reported these words to the chief magistrates. They were afraid when they heard that they were Romans, 39 and they came and appealed to them, and when they had brought them out, they kept requesting them to leave the city. 40 And they went out of the prison and entered *the house of* Lydia, and when they saw the brothers, they encouraged them and left.

JULY 12

2 Chronicles 19:1–20:37

19 Then Jehoshaphat the king of Judah returned in peace to his house in Jerusalem. 2 And Jehu the son of Hanani the seer went out *to meet him* to his face and said to King Jehoshaphat, "Should you help the wicked and love those who hate Yahweh and so *bring* wrath on yourself from Yahweh? 3 But *some* good has been found in you, for you have purged the Asheroth from the land and you have set your heart to seek God."

4 So Jehoshaphat lived in Jerusalem. Indeed, he returned and went out among the people from Beersheba to the hill country of Ephraim and caused them to return back to Yahweh, the God of their fathers.

5 And he appointed judges in the land in all the fortified cities of Judah, in each city. 6 And he said to the judges, "Consider what you are doing, for you do not judge for man but for Yahweh who is with you when you render judgment. 7 So now then let the dread of Yahweh be upon you; be careful what you do, because with Yahweh our God there is no unrighteousness or partiality or the taking of a bribe."

8 In Jerusalem also Jehoshaphat appointed *some of the* Levites and priests, and some of the heads of the fathers' *households* of Israel, for the judgment of Yahweh and to judge disputes. So they returned to Jerusalem. 9 Then he commanded them saying, "Thus you shall do in the fear of Yahweh, faithfully and wholeheartedly. 10 Whenever any dispute comes to you from your brothers who live in their cities, between blood and blood, between law and commandment, statutes and judgments, you shall warn them so that they may not be guilty before Yahweh and wrath may *not* come on you and your brothers. Thus you shall do, and you will not be guilty. 11 And behold, Amariah the chief priest will be over you in all that pertains to Yahweh, and Zebadiah the son of Ishmael, the ruler of the house of Judah, in all that pertains to the king. Also the Levites shall be officers before you. Be strong and act, and Yahweh be with the one who is good."

20 Now it happened after this, that the sons of Moab and the sons of Ammon, together with some of the Ammonites, came to make war against Jehoshaphat. 2 Then some came and told Jehoshaphat, saying, "A great multitude is coming against you from beyond the sea, out of Aram and behold, they are in Hazazon-tamar (that is Engedi)." 3 And Jehoshaphat was afraid and set his face to seek Yahweh, and called for a fast throughout all Judah. 4 So Judah gathered together to seek *help* from Yahweh; they even came from all the cities of Judah to seek Yahweh.

5 Then Jehoshaphat stood in the assembly of Judah and Jerusalem, in the house of Yahweh before the new court, 6 and he said, "O Yahweh, the God of our fathers, are You not God in the heavens? And are You not ruler over all the kingdoms of the nations? Power and might are in Your hand so that no one can take their stand against You. 7 Did You not, O our God, dispossess the inhabitants of this land before Your people

Israel and give it to the seed of Abraham Your friend forever? 8 And they have lived in it, and have built You a sanctuary there for Your name, saying, 9 'Should evil come upon us, the sword, *or* judgment, or pestilence, or famine, we will stand before this house and before You (for Your name is in this house) and cry to You in our distress, and You will hear and save *us*.' 10 So now, behold, the sons of Ammon and Moab and Mount Seir, whom You did not let Israel invade when they came out of the land of Egypt (they turned aside from them and did not destroy them), 11 and behold, they are rewarding us by coming to drive us out from Your possession which You have caused us to possess. 12 O our God, will You not judge them? For we are powerless before this great multitude who are coming against us; and we do not know what we should do, but our eyes are on You."

13 Now all Judah was standing before Yahweh, with their little ones, their wives, and their children.

14 Then in the midst of the assembly the Spirit of Yahweh came upon Jahaziel the son of Zechariah, the son of Benaiah, the son of Jeiel, the son of Mattaniah, the Levite of the sons of Asaph; 15 and he said, "Pay attention, all Judah and the inhabitants of Jerusalem and King Jehoshaphat: thus says Yahweh to you, 'Do not fear or be dismayed because of this great multitude, for the battle is not yours but God's. 16 Tomorrow go down against them. Behold, they will come up by the ascent of Ziz, and you will find them at the end of the valley in front of the wilderness of Jeruel. 17 You *need* not fight in this *battle*; take your stand—stand and see the salvation of Yahweh on your behalf, O Judah and Jerusalem.' Do not fear or be dismayed; tomorrow go out to face them, for Yahweh is with you."

18 So Jehoshaphat bowed his head with *his* face to the ground, and all Judah and the inhabitants of Jerusalem fell down before Yahweh, worshiping Yahweh. 19 Then the Levites, from the sons of the Kohathites and of the sons of the Korahites, rose up to praise Yahweh, the God of Israel, with a very loud voice.

20 And they rose early in the morning and went out to the wilderness of Tekoa; and *when they went out*, Jehoshaphat stood and said, "Listen to me, O Judah and inhabitants of Jerusalem, establish your faith in Yahweh your God and you will be established. Establish your faith in His prophets and succeed." 21 When he had taken counsel with the people, he caused those who sang to Yahweh and those who praised *Him* to stand in holy attire, as they went out before the army, saying, "Give thanks to Yahweh, for His lovingkindness endures forever." 22 When they began singing for joy and praising, Yahweh set ambushes against the sons of Ammon, Moab, and Mount Seir, who had come against Judah; so they were defeated. 23 Indeed, the sons of Ammon and Moab stood against the inhabitants of Mount Seir to devote *them* to destruction and to utterly eradicate *them*; and when they had finished with the inhabitants of Seir, they helped to bring one another to ruin.

24 Now Judah came to the lookout of the wilderness, and they turned toward the multitude, and behold, they *were* corpses fallen on the ground, and no one had escaped. 25 So Jehoshaphat and his people came to take their spoil and found much among them, *including* goods, garments, and valuable things which they took for themselves, more than they could carry. And they were three days taking the spoil because there was so much.

26 Then on the fourth day they assembled in the valley of Beracah, for there they blessed Yahweh. Therefore they have named that place "The Valley of Beracah" until today. 27 And every man of Judah and Jerusalem returned with Jehoshaphat at their head, returning to Jerusalem with gladness, for Yahweh had made them glad over their enemies. 28 And they came to Jerusalem with harps, lyres, and trumpets to the house of Yahweh. 29 And the dread of God was on all the kingdoms of the lands when they heard that Yahweh had fought against the enemies of Israel. 30 So the kingdom of Jehoshaphat was quiet, for his God gave him rest all around.

31 Thus Jehoshaphat reigned over Judah. He *was* thirty-five years old when he became king, and he reigned in Jerusalem twenty-five years. And his mother's name was Azubah the daughter of Shilhi. 32 And he walked in the way of his father Asa and did not turn away from it, doing what is right in the sight of Yahweh. 33 The high places, however, were not taken away; the people had not yet set their hearts to the God of their fathers.

34 Now the rest of the acts of Jehoshaphat,
first to last, behold, they are written in the
chronicles of Jehu the son of Hanani, which
is recorded in the Book of the Kings of Israel.
35 Afterwards, Jehoshaphat king of Judah
allied himself with Ahaziah king of Israel.
He acted wickedly in so doing. 36 So he
allied himself with him to make ships to
go to Tarshish, and they made the ships
in Ezion-geber. 37 Then Eliezer the son of
Dodavahu of Mareshah prophesied against
Jehoshaphat saying, "Because you have
allied yourself with Ahaziah, Yahweh has
destroyed your works." So the ships were
broken and could not go to Tarshish.

Psalm 82:1–8

1 God takes His stand in the
congregation of God;
He judges in the midst of gods.
2 How long will you judge unrighteously
And show partiality to the
wicked? Selah.
3 Give justice to the poor
and the orphan;
Justify the afflicted and destitute.
4 Protect the poor and needy;
Deliver *them* out of the
hand of the wicked.

5 They do not know and do
not understand;
They walk about in darkness;
All the foundations of the
earth are shaken.
6 I said, "You are gods,
And all of you are sons of
the Most High.
7 "Nevertheless you will die like men
And you will fall like *any*
one of the princes."
8 Arise, O God, judge the earth!
For it is You who will inherit
all the nations.

Proverbs 20:29–30

29 The honor of young men
is their strength,
And the majesty of old men
is their gray hair.
30 Stripes that wound scour away evil,
And strokes *reach* the innermost
parts of the body.

Acts 17:1–15

17 Now when they had traveled through
Amphipolis and Apollonia, they
came to Thessalonica, where there was a
synagogue of the Jews. 2 And according to
Paul's custom, he went to them, and for
three Sabbaths reasoned with them from
the Scriptures, 3 explaining and setting
before them that the Christ had to suffer
and rise again from the dead, and *saying,*
"This Jesus whom I am proclaiming to you
is that Christ." 4 And some of them were
persuaded and joined Paul and Silas, along
with a great multitude of the God-fearing
Greeks and not a few of the leading women.
5 But the Jews, becoming jealous, taking
along some wicked men from the mar-
ketplace, and forming a mob, set the city
in an uproar. And attacking the house of
Jason, they were seeking to bring them out
to the assembly. 6 And when they did not
find them, they *began* dragging Jason and
some brothers before the city authorities,
shouting, "These men who have upset the
world have come here also; 7 and Jason has
welcomed them, and they all act contrary
to the decrees of Caesar, saying that there is
another king, Jesus." 8 And they disturbed
the crowd and the city authorities who
heard these things. 9 And when they had
received the bond from Jason and the
others, they released them.
10 And the brothers immediately sent
Paul and Silas away by night to Berea, and
when they arrived, they went into the
synagogue of the Jews. 11 Now these were
more noble-minded than those in Thes-
salonica, for they received the word with
great eagerness, examining the Scriptures
daily *to see* whether these things were so.
12 Therefore many of them believed, along
with not a few prominent Greek women and
men. 13 But when the Jews of Thessalonica
found out that the word of God had been
proclaimed by Paul in Berea also, they came
there as well, shaking up and disturbing the
crowds. 14 Then immediately the brothers
sent Paul out to go as far as the sea; and Silas
and Timothy remained there. 15 Now those
who escorted Paul brought him as far as
Athens; and after receiving a command for
Silas and Timothy to come to him as soon
as possible, they left.

JULY 13

2 Chronicles 21:1–22:12

21 And Jehoshaphat slept with his fathers and was buried with his fathers in the city of David, and Jehoram his son became king in his place. 2 Now he had brothers, the sons of Jehoshaphat: Azariah, Jehiel, Zechariah, Azaryahu, Michael, and Shephatiah. All these *were* the sons of Jehoshaphat king of Israel. 3 And their father gave them many gifts of silver, gold, and precious things, with fortified cities in Judah, but he gave the kingdom to Jehoram because he was the firstborn.

4 So Jehoram arose over the kingdom of his father and strengthened himself, and he killed all his brothers with the sword, and some of the commanders of Israel also. 5 Jehoram *was* thirty-two years old when he became king, and he reigned eight years in Jerusalem. 6 And he walked in the way of the kings of Israel, just as the house of Ahab had done, for Ahab's daughter was his wife; and he did what was evil in the sight of Yahweh. 7 However, Yahweh was not willing to make the house of David a ruin because of the covenant which He had cut with David, and since He had promised to give a lamp to him and his sons forever.

8 In his days Edom revolted from under the hand of Judah and made a king over themselves. 9 Then Jehoram crossed over with his commanders and all his chariots with him. And he arose by night and struck down the Edomites who were surrounding him and the commanders of the chariots. 10 So Edom revolted from under the hand of Judah to this day. Then Libnah revolted at the same time from under his hand, because he had forsaken Yahweh, the God of his fathers. 11 Moreover, he made high places in the mountains of Judah, and caused the inhabitants of Jerusalem to play the harlot and drove Judah astray.

12 Then a letter came to him from Elijah the prophet saying, "Thus says Yahweh, the God of your father David, 'Because you have not walked in the ways of Jehoshaphat your father and the ways of Asa king of Judah, 13 *but have walked in the* way of the kings of Israel, and have caused Judah and the inhabitants of Jerusalem to play the harlot as the house of Ahab played the harlot, and you have also killed your brothers, your own family, who were better than you, 14 behold, Yahweh is going to smite your people, your sons, your wives, and all your possessions with a great calamity; 15 and you will suffer severe sickness, a disease of your bowels, until your bowels come out because of the sickness, day by day.'"

16 Then Yahweh stirred up against Jehoram the spirit of the Philistines and the Arabs who bordered the Ethiopians; 17 and they went up against Judah and invaded it, and carried away all the possessions found in the king's house together with his sons and his wives, so that no son was left to him except Jehoahaz, the youngest of his sons.

18 So after all this Yahweh smote him in his bowels with an incurable sickness. 19 Now it happened in the course of time, at the end of two years, that his bowels came out because of his sickness and he died with *this* greatly painful disease. And his people made no fire for him like the fire for his fathers. 20 He was thirty-two years old when he became king, and he reigned in Jerusalem eight years; and he departed with no one's regret, and they buried him in the city of David, but not in the tombs of the kings.

22 Then the inhabitants of Jerusalem made Ahaziah, his youngest son, king in his place, for the band of men who came with the Arabs to the camp had killed all the older *sons*. So Ahaziah the son of Jehoram king of Judah became king. 2 Ahaziah *was* twenty-two years old when he became king, and he reigned one year in Jerusalem. And his mother's name was Athaliah, the granddaughter of Omri. 3 He also walked in the ways of the house of Ahab, for his mother was his counselor to do wickedly. 4 And he did what was evil in the sight of Yahweh like the house of Ahab, for they were his counselors after the death of his father, to his destruction.

5 He also walked according to their counsel, and went with Jehoram the son of Ahab king of Israel to wage war against Hazael king of Aram at Ramoth-gilead. But the Arameans struck Joram. 6 So he returned to be healed in Jezreel of the wounds which

they caused by striking him at Ramah, when he fought against Hazael king of Aram. And Ahaziah, the son of Jehoram king of Judah, went down to see Jehoram the son of Ahab in Jezreel, because he was sick.

7 Now the downfall of Ahaziah was from God, in that he went to Joram. And when he came, he went out with Jehoram against Jehu the son of Nimshi, whom Yahweh had anointed to cut off the house of Ahab.

8 Now it happened when Jehu was executing judgment on the house of Ahab, he found the princes of Judah and the sons of Ahaziah's brothers attending to Ahaziah, and killed them. 9 And he sought Ahaziah, and they caught him while he was hiding himself in Samaria; they brought him to Jehu, put him to death, and buried him. For they said, "He is the son of Jehoshaphat, who sought Yahweh with all his heart." So there was no one of the house of Ahaziah to retain the power of the kingdom.

10 Now Athaliah the mother of Ahaziah saw that her son had died. So she rose and destroyed all the royal seed of the house of Judah. 11 But Jehoshabeath the king's daughter took Joash the son of Ahaziah, and stole him from among the king's sons who were being put to death, and put him and his nurse in the bedroom. So Jehoshabeath, the daughter of King Jehoram, the wife of Jehoiada the priest (for she was the sister of Ahaziah), hid him from Athaliah, so she did not put him to death. 12 So he was hidden with them in the house of God six years while Athaliah was reigning over the land.

Psalm 83:1–8

1 O God, do not remain at rest;
Do not be silent and, O God,
do not be quiet.
2 For behold, Your enemies roar,
And those who hate You have
lifted up their heads.
3 They make shrewd plans
against Your people,
And conspire together against
Your treasured ones.
4 They have said, "Come, and let us
wipe them out as a nation,
That the name of Israel be
remembered no more."
5 For they have conspired
together with one heart;
Against You they cut a covenant:
6 The tents of Edom and the Ishmaelites,
Moab and the Hagrites;
7 Gebal and Ammon and Amalek,
Philistia with the inhabitants of Tyre;
8 Assyria also has joined with them;
They have become the power of the
children of Lot. Selah.

Proverbs 21:1

21 The king's heart is *like* channels of water in the hand of Yahweh;
He turns it wherever He pleases.

Acts 17:16–34

16 Now while Paul was waiting for them at Athens, his spirit was being provoked within him as he was observing the city full of idols. 17 So he was reasoning in the synagogue with the Jews and the God-fearing *Gentiles*, and in the marketplace every day with those who happened to be present. 18 And also some of the Epicurean and Stoic philosophers were conversing with him. Some were saying, "What would this idle babbler wish to say?" Others, "He seems to be a proclaimer of strange deities,"—because he was proclaiming the good news of Jesus and the resurrection. 19 And they took him and brought him to the Areopagus, saying, "May we know what this new teaching is which you are speaking? 20 For you are bringing some strange things to our ears. So we want to know what these things mean." 21 (Now all the Athenians and the strangers visiting there used to spend their time in nothing other than telling or hearing something newer.)

22 So Paul stood in the midst of the Areopagus and said, "Men of Athens, I observe that you are very religious in all respects. 23 For while I was passing through and examining the objects of your worship, I also found an altar with this inscription, 'TO AN UNKNOWN GOD.' Therefore what you worship in ignorance, this I proclaim to you. 24 The God who made the world and all things in it, since He is Lord of heaven and earth, does not dwell in temples made with hands; 25 nor is He served by human hands, as though He needed anything, since He Himself gives to all *people* life and breath and all things; 26 and He made from one *man* every nation of mankind to inhabit all the face of the earth, having determined *their* appointed times and

the boundaries of their habitation, 27 that they would seek God, if perhaps they might grope for Him and find Him, though He is not far from each one of us; 28 for in Him we live and move and exist, as even some of your own poets have said, 'For we also are His offspring.' 29 Being then the offspring of God, we ought not to suppose that the Divine Nature is like gold or silver or stone, an image formed by the craft and thought of man. 30 Therefore having overlooked the times of ignorance, God is now commanding men that everyone everywhere should repent, 31 because He has fixed a day in which He will judge the world in righteousness through a Man whom He determined, having furnished proof to all by raising Him from the dead."

32 Now when they heard about the resurrection of the dead, some *began to* sneer, but others said, "We shall hear you again concerning this." 33 In this way, Paul went out of their midst. 34 But some men joined him and believed, among whom also were Dionysius the Areopagite and a woman named Damaris and others with them.

JULY 14

2 Chronicles 23:1–24:27

23 Now in the seventh year Jehoiada strengthened himself, and took commanders of hundreds: Azariah the son of Jeroham, Ishmael the son of Johanan, Azariah the son of Obed, Maaseiah the son of Adaiah, and Elishaphat the son of Zichri, *and they entered* into a covenant with him. 2 And they went around Judah and gathered the Levites from all the cities of Judah, and the heads of the fathers' *households* of Israel, and they came to Jerusalem. 3 Then all the assembly cut a covenant with the king in the house of God. And Jehoiada said to them, "Behold, the king's son shall reign, as Yahweh has spoken concerning the sons of David. 4 This is the thing which you shall do: one-third of you, of the priests and Levites who come in on the sabbath, *shall be* gatekeepers at the thresholds, 5 and one-third *shall be* at the king's house, and one-third at the Gate of the Foundation; and all the people *shall be* in the courts of the house of Yahweh. 6 But let no one enter the house of Yahweh except the priests and the ministering Levites; they may enter, for they are holy. And let all the people keep the charge of Yahweh. 7 And the Levites will surround the king, each man with his weapons in his hand; and whoever enters the house, let him be put to death. And be with the king when he comes in and when he goes out."

8 So the Levites and all Judah did according to all that Jehoiada the priest commanded. And each one of them took his men who were to come in on the sabbath, with those who were to go out on the sabbath, for Jehoiada the priest did not dismiss *any of* the divisions. 9 Then Jehoiada the priest gave to the commanders of hundreds the spears and the shields and small shields which had been King David's, which were in the house of God. 10 And he caused all the people to stand, each man with his weapon in his hand, from the right side of the house to the left side of the house, by the altar and by the house, around the king. 11 Then they brought out the king's son and put the crown on him, and *gave him* the testimony and made him king. And Jehoiada and his sons anointed him and said, "*Long* live the king!"

12 Then Athaliah heard the noise of the people running and praising the king, so she came into the house of Yahweh to the people. 13 And she looked, and behold, the king was standing by his pillar at the entrance, and the commanders and the trumpeters *were* beside the king. And all the people of the land were glad and blew trumpets, the singers with *their* musical instruments leading the praise. Then Athaliah tore her clothes and said, "Treason! Treason!" 14 Then Jehoiada the priest brought out the commanders of hundreds who were appointed over the military force and said to them, "Bring her out between the ranks; and whoever follows her, let him be put to death with the sword." For the priest said, "You shall not put her to death in the house of Yahweh." 15 So they laid hands on her, and when she arrived at the entrance of the Horse Gate of the king's house, they put her to death there.

16 Then Jehoiada cut a covenant between himself and all the people and the king, that

they would be the people of Yahweh. 17 And all the people came to the house of Baal and tore it down, and his altars and his images they broke in pieces, and they killed Mattan the priest of Baal before the altars. 18 And Jehoiada placed the assignments concerning the house of Yahweh in the hand of the Levitical priests, whom David had divided *by lot to be* over the house of Yahweh, to offer the burnt offerings of Yahweh, as it is written in the law of Moses—with gladness and singing according to the order of David. 19 And he caused the gatekeepers of the house of Yahweh to stand, so that no one would enter *who was* in any way unclean. 20 And he took the commanders of hundreds, the nobles, the rulers of the people, and all the people of the land, and brought the king down from the house of Yahweh, and they came through the upper gate to the king's house. And they sat the king upon the royal throne. 21 So all of the people of the land were glad, and the city was quiet. For they had put Athaliah to death with the sword.

24 Joash was seven years old when he became king, and he reigned forty years in Jerusalem; and his mother's name was Zibiah from Beersheba. 2 And Joash did what was right in the sight of Yahweh all the days of Jehoiada the priest. 3 And Jehoiada took up two wives for him, and he became the father of sons and daughters.

4 Now it happened afterwards, that Joash had in *his* heart to restore the house of Yahweh. 5 And he gathered the priests and Levites and said to them, "Go out to the cities of Judah and gather money from all Israel to repair the house of your God annually, and you shall do the matter quickly." But the Levites did not act quickly. 6 So the king called for Jehoiada the chief *priest* and said to him, "Why have you not required the Levites to bring in from Judah and from Jerusalem the levy *fixed by* Moses the servant of Yahweh on the congregation of Israel for the tent of the testimony?" 7 For the sons of the wicked Athaliah had broken into the house of God and even used the holy things of the house of Yahweh for the Baals.

8 So the king said *the word*, and they made a chest and put it outside by the gate of the house of Yahweh. 9 And they made a proclamation in Judah and Jerusalem to bring to Yahweh the levy *fixed by* Moses the servant of God on Israel in the wilderness. 10 And all the officials and all the people were glad and brought *in their levies* and dropped *them* into the chest until they had finished. 11 Now it happened that whenever the chest was brought in to the king's officer by the hand of the Levites, and when they saw that there was much money, then the king's scribe and the chief priest's officer would come, empty the chest, take it, and return it to its place. Thus they did daily and collected much money. 12 And the king and Jehoiada gave it to those who did the work of the service of the house of Yahweh; and they hired masons and carpenters to restore the house of Yahweh, and also craftsmen in iron and bronze to repair the house of Yahweh. 13 So those who did the work labored, and the repair work progressed in their hands, and they restored the house of God according to its specifications and strengthened it. 14 When they had completed, they brought the rest of the money before the king and Jehoiada; and it was made into utensils for the house of Yahweh, utensils for the ministry and the burnt offering, and pans and utensils of gold and silver. And they were offering burnt offerings in the house of Yahweh continually all the days of Jehoiada.

15 Then Jehoiada became old and full of days, and he died; he was 130 years old at his death. 16 They buried him in the city of David among the kings, because he had done what is good in Israel and to God and His house.

17 But after the death of Jehoiada the officials of Judah came and bowed down to the king, and the king listened to them. 18 And they forsook the house of Yahweh, the God of their fathers, and served the Asherim and the idols; so wrath came upon Judah and Jerusalem for this their guilt. 19 Yet He sent prophets to them to bring them back to Yahweh; though they testified against them, they did not give ear.

20 Now the Spirit of God clothed Zechariah the son of Jehoiada the priest; and he stood above the people and said to them, "Thus says God, 'Why do you trespass against the commandments of Yahweh and do not succeed? Because you have forsaken Yahweh, He has also forsaken you.'" 21 So they conspired against him and at the

command of the king they stoned him to
death in the court of the house of Yahweh.
22 Thus Joash the king did not remember the
lovingkindness which his father Jehoiada
had shown him, but he killed his son. And
as he died he said, “May Yahweh see and
avenge!”
23 Now it happened at the turn of the
year that the military force of the Arameans
came up against him; and they came to
Judah and Jerusalem, destroyed all the
officials of the people from among the
people, and sent all their spoil to the king
of Damascus. 24 Indeed the military force of
the Arameans came with a small number of
men; yet Yahweh gave a very great military
force into their hands, because they had
forsaken Yahweh, the God of their fathers.
Thus they executed judgment on Joash.
25 When they had gone from him (for they
left him very sick), his servants conspired
against him because of the blood of the son
of Jehoiada the priest, and killed him on his
bed. So he died, and they buried him in the
city of David, but they did not bury him in
the tombs of the kings. 26 Now these are
those who conspired against him: Zabad
the son of Shimeath the Ammonitess, and
Jehozabad the son of Shimrith the Moabi-
tess. 27 Now as to his sons and the many
oracles against him and the rebuilding of
the house of God, behold, they are written
in the treatise of the Book of the Kings. Then
Amaziah his son became king in his place.

Psalm 83:9–18

9 Do to them as to Midian,
As to Sisera, *and* Jabin at
the river of Kishon,
10 Who were destroyed at En-dor,
Who were as dung for the ground.
11 Make their nobles like Oreb and Zeeb
And all their princes like
Zebah and Zalmunna,
12 Who said, “Let us possess for ourselves
The pastures of God.”

13 O my God, make them like
the whirling dust,
Like chaff before the wind.
14 Like fire that burns the forest
And like a flame that burns
up the mountains,
15 So pursue them with Your tempest
And dismay them with Your storm.
16 Fill their faces with disgrace,
That they may seek Your
name, O Yahweh.
17 Let them be ashamed and
dismayed forever,
And let them be humiliated and perish,
18 That they may know that You
alone—Your name is Yahweh—
Are the Most High over all the earth.

Proverbs 21:2–3

2 Every man’s way is right
in his own eyes,
But Yahweh weighs the hearts.
3 To do righteousness and justice
Is chosen by Yahweh over sacrifice.

Acts 18:1–28

18 After these things he departed Athens
and went to Corinth. 2 And he found a
Jew named Aquila, a native of Pontus, and
his wife Priscilla, who recently came from
Italy because Claudius had commanded
all the Jews to depart from Rome. He came
to them, 3 and because he was of the same
trade, he was staying with them and they
were working, for by trade they were
tent-makers. 4 And he was reasoning in
the synagogue every Sabbath and trying to
persuade both Jews and Greeks.
5 But when Silas and Timothy came down
from Macedonia, Paul *began* devoting
himself completely to the word, solemnly
bearing witness to the Jews that Jesus is
the Christ. 6 But when they resisted and
blasphemed, he shook out his garments and
said to them, “Your blood *be* on your own
heads! I am clean. From now on I will go to
the Gentiles.” 7 Then he left there and went
to the house of a man named Titius Justus,
a God-fearer, whose house was next to the
synagogue. 8 And Crispus, the leader of the
synagogue, believed in the Lord with all his
household, and many of the Corinthians
when they heard were believing and being
baptized. 9 And the Lord said to Paul in the
night by a vision, “Do not be afraid, but go
on speaking and do not be silent; 10 for I am
with you, and no man will lay *a hand* on
you in order to harm you, for I have many
people in this city.” 11 And he stayed *there* a
year and six months, teaching the word of
God among them.
12 But while Gallio was proconsul of
Achaia, the Jews with one accord rose

up against Paul and brought him before the judgment seat, 13 saying, "This man persuades men to worship God contrary to the law." 14 But when Paul was about to open his mouth, Gallio said to the Jews, "If it were a wrongdoing or vicious crime, O Jews, it would be reasonable for me to put up with you; 15 but if there are questions about words and names and your own law, see to it yourselves; I am not willing to be a judge of these matters." 16 And he drove them away from the judgment seat. 17 And they all took hold of Sosthenes, the leader of the synagogue, and *began* beating him in front of the judgment seat. But Gallio was not concerned about any of these things.

18 And Paul, having remained many days longer, took leave of the brothers and put out to sea for Syria, and with him were Priscilla and Aquila. In Cenchreae he had his hair cut, for he was keeping a vow. 19 And they arrived at Ephesus, and he left them there. Now he himself entered the synagogue and reasoned with the Jews. 20 When they asked him to stay for a longer time, he did not consent, 21 but taking leave of them and saying, "I will return to you again if God wills," he set sail from Ephesus.

22 And when he had landed at Caesarea, he went up and greeted the church, and went down to Antioch. 23 And having spent some time *there*, he left and passed successively through the Galatian region and Phrygia, strengthening all the disciples.

24 Now a Jew named Apollos, an Alexandrian by birth, an eloquent man, arrived at Ephesus; and he was mighty in the Scriptures. 25 This man had been instructed in the way of the Lord; and being fervent in spirit, he was speaking and teaching accurately the things concerning Jesus, being acquainted only with the baptism of John; 26 and he began to speak out boldly in the synagogue. But when Priscilla and Aquila heard him, they took him aside and explained to him the way of God more accurately. 27 And when he wanted to go across to Achaia, the brothers encouraged him and wrote to the disciples to welcome him; and when he had arrived, he greatly helped those who had believed through grace, 28 for he powerfully refuted the Jews in public, demonstrating by the Scriptures that Jesus is the Christ.

JULY 15

2 Chronicles 25:1–27:9

25 Amaziah was twenty-five years old when he became king, and he reigned twenty-nine years in Jerusalem. And his mother's name was Jehoaddan of Jerusalem. 2 And he did what was right in the sight of Yahweh, yet not with a whole heart. 3 Now it happened as soon as the kingdom was strong in his grasp, that he killed his servants who had struck down the king his father. 4 But he did not put their sons to death, but *did* as it is written in the law in the book of Moses, which Yahweh commanded, saying, "Fathers shall not be put to death for *their* sons, nor sons be put to death for *their* fathers, but each shall be put to death for his own sin."

5 Moreover, Amaziah assembled Judah and appointed them according to *their* fathers' households under commanders of thousands and commanders of hundreds throughout Judah and Benjamin; and he took a census of those from twenty years old and upward and found them to be 300,000 choice men, *able* to go out for *military* duty, *able to* handle spear and large shield. 6 And he hired also 100,000 mighty men of valor out of Israel for one hundred talents of silver. 7 But a man of God came to him saying, "O king, do not let the army of Israel go with you, for Yahweh is not with Israel *nor with* any of the sons of Ephraim. 8 But if you do go, do *it*, be strong for the battle; *yet* God will cause you to stumble before the enemy, for God has power to help and to cause to stumble." 9 Then Amaziah said to the man of God, "But what *shall we* do for the hundred talents which I have given to the troops of Israel?" And the man of God answered, "Yahweh has much more to give you than this." 10 Then Amaziah dismissed them, the troops which came to him from Ephraim, to go home; so their anger burned against Judah and they returned home in burning anger.

11 Now Amaziah strengthened himself and led his people forth, and went to the Valley of Salt and struck down 10,000 of

the sons of Seir. 12 The sons of Judah also
captured 10,000 alive and brought them to
the top of the cliff and threw them down
from the top of the cliff, so that they were all
split open. 13 But the troops whom Amaziah
sent back from going with him to battle,
raided the cities of Judah, from Samaria to
Beth-horon, and struck down 3,000 of them
and plundered much plunder.

14 Now it happened that after Amaziah
came from striking down the Edomites,
he brought the gods of the sons of Seir, set
them up as his gods, worshiped them, and
burned incense to them. 15 Then the anger
of Yahweh burned against Amaziah, and He
sent him a prophet who said to him, "Why
have you sought the gods of the people
who have not delivered their own people
from your hand?" 16 Now it happened that
as he was talking with him, the king said
to him, "Have we given you *to be* a royal
counselor? Stop! Why should you be struck
down?" Then the prophet stopped and said,
"I know that God has counseled to destroy
you, because you have done this and have
not listened to my counsel."

17 Then Amaziah king of Judah took
counsel and sent to Joash the son of Jehoahaz
the son of Jehu, the king of Israel, saying,
"Come, let us face each other." 18 And Joash
the king of Israel sent to Amaziah king of
Judah, saying, "The thorn bush which was
in Lebanon sent to the cedar which was in
Lebanon, saying, 'Give your daughter to my
son as a wife.' But a beast of the field that
was in Lebanon passed by and trampled the
thorn bush. 19 You said, 'Behold, you have
struck down Edom.' And your heart has lifted
you up to boast. Now stay at home; for why
should you provoke calamity so that you,
even you, would fall and Judah with you?"

20 But Amaziah would not listen, for it
was from God, that He might give them
into the hand *of Joash* because they had
sought the gods of Edom. 21 So Joash king
of Israel went up, and he and Amaziah king
of Judah faced each other at Beth-shemesh,
which belonged to Judah. 22 And Judah was
defeated by Israel, and they fled each to
his tent. 23 Then Joash king of Israel seized
Amaziah king of Judah, the son of Joash
the son of Jehoahaz, at Beth-shemesh,
and brought him to Jerusalem and broke
down the wall of Jerusalem from the Gate
of Ephraim to the Corner Gate, 400 cubits.
24 And *he took* all the gold and silver and all
the utensils which were found in the house
of God with Obed-edom, and the treasures
of the king's house, the hostages also, and
returned to Samaria.

25 And Amaziah the son of Joash king of
Judah lived fifteen years after the death of
Joash son of Jehoahaz king of Israel. 26 Now
the rest of the acts of Amaziah, from first to
last, behold, are they not written in the Book
of the Kings of Judah and Israel? 27 Now from
the time that Amaziah turned away from
following Yahweh they conspired against
him in Jerusalem, and he fled to Lachish;
but they sent after him to Lachish and put
him to death there. 28 Then they carried him
on horses and buried him with his fathers
in the city of Judah.

26 And all the people of Judah took
Uzziah, who *was* sixteen years old,
and made him king in the place of his father
Amaziah. 2 He built Eloth and restored it to
Judah after the king slept with his fathers.
3 Uzziah was sixteen years old when he
became king, and he reigned fifty-two years
in Jerusalem; and his mother's name was
Jechiliah of Jerusalem. 4 And he did what
was right in the sight of Yahweh, according
to all that his father Amaziah had done.
5 And he continued to seek God in the
days of Zechariah, who had understanding
through the vision of God; and as long as
he sought Yahweh, God made him succeed.

6 Then he went out and fought against
the Philistines, and broke down the wall of
Gath and the wall of Jabneh and the wall of
Ashdod; and he built cities in *the area of*
Ashdod and among the Philistines. 7 And
God helped him against the Philistines,
and against the Arabians who lived in Gur-
baal, and the Meunites. 8 The Ammonites
also gave tribute to Uzziah, and his fame
extended to the border of Egypt, for he
became very strong. 9 Moreover, Uzziah
built towers in Jerusalem at the Corner Gate
and at the Valley Gate and at the corner but-
tress and strengthened them. 10 He also built
towers in the wilderness and hewed many
cisterns, for he had much livestock, both
in the Shephelah and in the plain. *He also
had* plowmen and vinedressers in the hill
country and the fertile fields, for he loved
the soil. 11 Moreover, Uzziah had a military
force which could wage war, which went out

for *military* duty by divisions according to
the number of their muster, *prepared* by the
hand of Jeiel the scribe and Maaseiah the
officer, under the hand of Hananiah, one
of the king's officials. 12 The total number of
the heads of the households, of mighty men
of valor, was 2,600. 13 And under their hand
was a mighty army of 307,500, who could
wage war with mighty power, to help the
king against the enemy. 14 Moreover, Uzziah
prepared for all the army shields, spears,
helmets, body armor, bows, and stones for
slings. 15 In Jerusalem he also made devices
of war devised by skillful designers to be
on the towers and on the corners for the
purpose of shooting arrows and great
stones. Hence his fame spread afar, for he
was marvelously helped until he *was* strong.

16 But when he became strong, his heart
was so proud that he acted corruptly, and
he was unfaithful to Yahweh his God. And
he entered the temple of Yahweh to burn
incense on the altar of incense. 17 Then
Azariah the priest entered after him and
with him eighty priests of Yahweh, men
of valor. 18 And they stood against Uzziah
the king and said to him, "It is not for you,
Uzziah, to burn incense to Yahweh, but for
the priests, the sons of Aaron who are set
apart as holy to burn incense. Get out of
the sanctuary, for you have been unfaithful
and will have no honor from Yahweh God."
19 But Uzziah, with a censer in his hand for
burning incense, was enraged; and while he
was enraged with the priests, the leprosy
broke out on his forehead before the priests
in the house of Yahweh, beside the altar of
incense. 20 And Azariah the chief priest and
all the priests looked at him, and behold,
he *was* leprous on his forehead; and they
hurried him out of there, and he himself
also hastened to get out because Yahweh
had smitten him. 21 So King Uzziah was a
leper to the day of his death; and he lived
in a separate house, being a leper, for he
was cut off from the house of Yahweh. And
Jotham his son was over the king's house,
judging the people of the land.

22 Now the rest of the acts of Uzziah, first
to last, the prophet Isaiah, the son of Amoz,
has written. 23 So Uzziah slept with his
fathers, and they buried him with his fathers
in the field of the grave which belonged to
the kings, for they said, "He is a leper." And
Jotham his son became king in his place.

27 Jotham was twenty-five years old
when he became king, and he
reigned sixteen years in Jerusalem. And his
mother's name was Jerushah the daughter
of Zadok. 2 And he did what was right in
the sight of Yahweh, according to all that
his father Uzziah had done; however he
did not enter the temple of Yahweh. But
the people continued acting corruptly. 3 He
built the upper gate of the house of Yah-
weh, and he built extensively the wall of
Ophel. 4 Moreover, he built cities in the hill
country of Judah, and he built fortresses
and towers on the wooded *hills*. 5 He fought
also with the king of the sons of Ammon
and prevailed over them. So the sons of
Ammon gave him during that year 100
talents of silver, 10,000 kors of wheat, and
10,000 of barley. The sons of Ammon also
brought back to him this *amount* in the
second and in the third year. 6 So Jotham
became strong because he established his
ways before Yahweh his God. 7 Now the
rest of the acts of Jotham, even all his wars
and his ways, behold, they are written in
the Book of the Kings of Israel and Judah.
8 He was twenty-five years old when he
became king, and he reigned sixteen years
in Jerusalem. 9 And Jotham slept with his
fathers, and they buried him in the city of
David; and Ahaz his son became king in
his place.

Psalm 84:1–7

1 How lovely are Your dwelling places,
O Yahweh of hosts!
2 My soul has longed and even fainted
for the courts of Yahweh;
My heart and my flesh sing for
joy to the living God.
3 Even the bird has found a home,
And the swallow a nest for herself,
where she sets her young,
At Your altars, O Yahweh of hosts,
My King and my God.
4 How blessed are those who
dwell in Your house!
They are ever praising You. Selah.

5 How blessed is the man whose
strength is in You,
In whose heart are the
highways *to Zion*!
6 Passing through the valley of
Baca they make it a spring;

The early rain also wraps it
up with blessings.
7 They go from strength to strength,
Each one of them appears
before God in Zion.

Proverbs 21:4–5

4 Haughty eyes and a proud heart—
The fallow ground of the
wicked—are sin.
5 The thoughts of the diligent
lead surely to profit,
But everyone who is hasty
comes surely to poverty.

Acts 19:1–20

19 Now it happened that while Apollos
was at Corinth, Paul passed through
the upper regions and came to Ephesus
and found some disciples. 2 And he said to
them, "Did you receive the Holy Spirit when
you believed?" And they *said* to him, "No,
we have not even heard if the Holy Spirit
is *being received*." 3 And he said, "Into
what then were you baptized?" And they
said, "Into John's baptism." 4 Then Paul
said, "John baptized with the baptism of
repentance, telling the people to believe
in Him who was coming after him, that
is, in Jesus." 5 And when they heard this,
they were baptized in the name of the Lord
Jesus. 6 And when Paul had laid his hands
upon them, the Holy Spirit came on them,
and they *began* speaking with tongues and
prophesying. 7 Now there were in all about
twelve men.

8 And after he entered the synagogue,
he continued speaking out boldly for three
months, reasoning and persuading *them*
about the kingdom of God. 9 But when some
were becoming hardened and were not
believing, speaking evil of the Way before
the multitude, he left them and took away
the disciples, reasoning daily in the school
of Tyrannus. 10 This took place for two years,
so that all who lived in Asia heard the word
of the Lord, both Jews and Greeks.

11 And God was doing extraordinary mir-
acles by the hands of Paul, 12 so that cloths
or aprons were even carried from his body
to the sick, and the diseases left them and
the evil spirits went out. 13 But also some of
the Jewish exorcists, who went from place
to place, attempted to invoke over those
who had the evil spirits the name of the
Lord Jesus, saying, "I implore you by Jesus
whom Paul preaches." 14 Now seven sons of
one *named* Sceva, a Jewish chief priest, were
doing this. 15 And the evil spirit answered
and said to them, "I recognize Jesus, and I
know about Paul, but who are you?" 16 And
the man, in whom was the evil spirit, leaped
on them, subdued all of them, and utterly
prevailed against them, so that they fled out
of that house naked and wounded. 17 And
this became known to all, both Jews and
Greeks, who lived in Ephesus; and fear fell
upon them all and the name of the Lord
Jesus was being magnified. 18 Also, many
of those who had believed kept coming,
confessing and disclosing their practices.
19 And many of those who practiced magic
brought their books together and were
burning them in the sight of everyone; and
they counted up the price of them and found
it fifty thousand pieces of silver. 20 So the
word of the Lord was growing mightily and
prevailing.

The Spirit never loosens where the Word binds; the Spirit never justifies where the Word condemns; the Spirit never approves where the Word disapproves; the Spirit never blesses where the Word curses.

— THOMAS BROOKS

JULY 16

2 Chronicles 28:1–29:36

28 Ahaz *was* twenty years old when he became king, and he reigned sixteen years in Jerusalem; and he did not do what was right in the sight of Yahweh, as David his father *had done.* 2 But he walked in the ways of the kings of Israel; he also made molten images for the Baals. 3 Moreover, he offered *offerings* in smoke in the valley of Ben-hinnom and burned his sons in the fire, according to the abominations of the nations whom Yahweh had dispossessed from before the sons of Israel. 4 He also sacrificed and offered *offerings* in smoke on the high places and on the hills and under every green tree.

5 So, Yahweh his God gave him into the hand of the king of Aram; and they struck him and carried away from him a great number of captives and brought *them* to Damascus. And he was also given into the hand of the king of Israel, who struck him with a great slaughter. 6 Indeed, Pekah the son of Remaliah killed in Judah 120,000 in one day, all men of valor, because they had forsaken Yahweh, the God of their fathers. 7 And Zichri, a mighty man of Ephraim, killed Maaseiah the king's son and Azrikam the ruler of the house and Elkanah the second to the king.

8 Then the sons of Israel carried away captive of their brothers 200,000 women, sons, and daughters; and they plundered also a great deal of spoil from them and brought the spoil to Samaria. 9 But a prophet of Yahweh was there, whose name *was* Oded; and he went out before the army which came to Samaria and said to them, "Behold, because of the wrath of Yahweh, the God of your fathers, against Judah, He has given them into your hand, and you have killed them in a rage *which* has even reached heaven. 10 So now you are intending *to subdue for yourselves* the people of Judah and Jerusalem for male and female slaves. Surely, *do* you not *have* your own *matters of* guilt against Yahweh your God? 11 So now, listen to me and return the captives whom you carried away from your brothers, for the burning anger of Yahweh is against you." 12 Then some of the heads of the sons of Ephraim—Azariah the son of Johanan, Berechiah the son of Meshillemoth, Jehizkiah the son of Shallum, and Amasa the son of Hadlai—arose against those who were coming from the *engagement of* the army, 13 and said to them, "You must not bring the captives in here, for you are intending *to bring* upon us guilt against Yahweh adding to our sins and our guilt; for our guilt is great so that *His* burning anger is against Israel." 14 So the armed men left the captives and the plunder before the commanders and all the assembly. 15 Then the men who were designated by name arose, took hold of the captives, and they clothed all their naked ones from the spoil; and they gave them clothes and sandals, fed them and gave them drink, anointed them *with oil,* led all their feeble ones on donkeys, and brought them to Jericho, the city of palm trees, to their brothers; then they returned to Samaria.

16 At that time King Ahaz sent to the kings of Assyria for help. 17 Indeed, again the Edomites had come and struck Judah and carried away captives. 18 And the Philistines also had raided the cities of the Shephelah and of the Negev of Judah, and had captured Beth-shemesh, Aijalon, Gederoth, and Soco with its towns, Timnah with its towns, and Gimzo with its towns, and they settled there. 19 For Yahweh humbled Judah because of Ahaz king of Israel, for he had caused *it* to be out of control in Judah and was very unfaithful to Yahweh. 20 So Tilgath-pilneser king of Assyria came against him and distressed him instead of strengthening him. 21 Although Ahaz took a portion out of the house of Yahweh and out of the house of the king and of the princes, and gave *it* to the king of Assyria, it did not help him.

22 Now in the time of his distress this same King Ahaz became yet more unfaithful to Yahweh. 23 Indeed, he sacrificed to the gods of Damascus which had struck him, and said, "Because the gods of the kings of Aram helped them, I will sacrifice to them that they may help me." But they became the stumbling of him and all Israel. 24 Ahaz gathered together the utensils of the house of God. Then he cut the utensils of the house of God in pieces; and he closed the doors of the house of Yahweh and made altars for himself in every corner of Jerusalem. 25 Now

in each and every city of Judah he made high
places to offer *offerings* in smoke to other
gods, and provoked Yahweh, the God of his
fathers, to anger. 26 Now the rest of his acts
and all his ways, from first to last, behold,
they are written in the Book of the Kings
of Judah and Israel. 27 So Ahaz slept with
his fathers, and they buried him in the city,
in Jerusalem, for they did not bring him
into the tombs of the kings of Israel; and
Hezekiah his son became king in his place.

29 Hezekiah became king *when he was*
twenty-five years old; and he reigned
twenty-nine years in Jerusalem. And his
mother's name was Abijah, the daughter of
Zechariah. 2 And he did what was right in
the sight of Yahweh, according to all that
David his father had done.
3 In the first year of his reign, in the first
month, he opened the doors of the house
of Yahweh and repaired them. 4 And he
brought in the priests and the Levites and
gathered them into the square on the east.
5 Then he said to them, "Listen to me,
O Levites. Set yourselves apart now as
holy, and set apart as holy the house of
Yahweh, the God of your fathers, and bring
out the impurity from the holy place. 6 For
our fathers have been unfaithful and have
done what is evil in the sight of Yahweh our
God, and have forsaken Him and turned
their faces away from the dwelling place of
Yahweh, and have turned *their* backs. 7 They
have also shut the doors of the porch and
put out the lamps, and have not burned
incense or offered burnt offerings in the
holy place to the God of Israel. 8 Therefore
the wrath of Yahweh was against Judah and
Jerusalem, and He has made them an object
of terror, of horror, and of hissing, as you
see with your own eyes. 9 And behold, our
fathers have fallen by the sword, and our
sons and our daughters and our wives are
in captivity for this. 10 Now it is in my heart
to cut a covenant with Yahweh, the God of
Israel, that His burning anger may turn away
from us. 11 My sons, do not be at ease now,
for Yahweh has chosen you to stand before
Him, to minister to Him, and to be His
ministers and offer *offerings* up in smoke."
12 Then the Levites arose:
Mahath, the son of Amasai and Joel
the son of Azariah, from the sons of
the Kohathites;
and from the sons of Merari, Kish the
son of Abdi and Azariah the son of
Jehallelel;
and from the Gershonites, Joah the
son of Zimmah and Eden the son of
Joah;
13 and from the sons of Elizaphan,
Shimri and Jeiel;
and from the sons of Asaph, Zechariah
and Mattaniah;
14 and from the sons of Heman, Jehiel
and Shimei;
and from the sons of Jeduthun,
Shemaiah and Uzziel.
15 And they gathered their brothers, set
themselves apart as holy, and went in to
cleanse the house of Yahweh, according to
the commandment of the king by the words
of Yahweh. 16 So the priests went in to the
inner part of the house of Yahweh to cleanse
it, and every unclean thing which they
found in the temple of Yahweh they brought
out to the court of the house of Yahweh.
Then the Levites received *it* to bring out to
the Kidron valley, to an outer area. 17 Then
they began to set *it* apart as holy on the first
day of the first month, and on the eighth
day of the month they entered the porch of
Yahweh. Then they set apart the house of
Yahweh as holy in eight days, and completed
it on the sixteenth day of the first month.
18 Then they went in to King Hezekiah and
said, "We have cleansed the whole house of
Yahweh, the altar of burnt offering with all
of its utensils, and the table of showbread
with all of its utensils. 19 Moreover, all the
utensils which King Ahaz had rejected
during his reign in his unfaithfulness, we
have prepared and set apart as holy; and
behold, they are before the altar of Yahweh."
20 Then King Hezekiah arose early and
gathered the princes of the city and went up
to the house of Yahweh. 21 And they brought
seven bulls, seven rams, seven lambs, and
seven male goats for a sin offering for the
kingdom, the sanctuary, and Judah. And he
ordered the priests, the sons of Aaron, to
offer *them* on the altar of Yahweh. 22 So they
slaughtered the bulls, and the priests took
the blood and splashed it on the altar. They
also slaughtered the rams and splashed the
blood on the altar; they slaughtered the
lambs also and splashed the blood on the
altar. 23 Then they had the male goats of the
sin offering approach before the king and

the assembly, and they laid their hands on
them. 24 And the priests slaughtered them
and purged the altar with their blood to
atone for all Israel, for the king ordered the
burnt offering and the sin offering for all
Israel.
25 He then caused the Levites to stand in
the house of Yahweh with cymbals, with
harps, and with lyres, according to the
command of David and of Gad the king's
seer, and of Nathan the prophet; for the
command was from Yahweh by the hand of
His prophets. 26 And the Levites stood with
the *musical* instruments of David, and the
priests with the trumpets. 27 Then Hezekiah
said to offer the burnt offering on the altar.
When the burnt offering began, the song
to Yahweh also began with the trumpets,
accompanied by the instruments of David,
king of Israel. 28 While the whole assembly
worshiped, the singers also sang and the
trumpets sounded; all this *continued* until
the burnt offering was completed.
29 Now at the completion of the burnt
offerings, the king and all who were pres-
ent with him bowed down and worshiped.
30 Moreover, King Hezekiah and the officials
ordered the Levites to sing praises to Yah-
weh with the words of David and Asaph the
seer. So they sang praises with gladness, and
bowed down and worshiped.
31 Then Hezekiah answered and said,
"Now *that* you have become ordained to
Yahweh, approach and bring sacrifices and
thank offerings to the house of Yahweh."
And the assembly brought sacrifices and
thank offerings, and all those who were
willing of heart *brought* burnt offerings.
32 And the number of the burnt offerings
which the assembly brought was 70 bulls,
100 rams, and 200 lambs; all these were
for a burnt offering to Yahweh. 33 And the
holy things were 600 bulls and 3,000 sheep.
34 But the priests were too few, so that they
were unable to skin all the burnt offerings;
therefore their brothers the Levites helped
them until the work was completed and
until the *other* priests had set themselves
apart as holy. For the Levites were more
upright of heart to set themselves apart
as holy than the priests. 35 There *were* also
many burnt offerings with the fat of the
peace offerings and with the drink offerings
for the burnt offerings. Thus the service
of the house of Yahweh was established
again. 36 Then Hezekiah and all the people
were glad over what God had prepared for
the people, because the thing came about
suddenly.

Psalm 84:8–12

8 O Yahweh God of hosts,
hear my prayer;
Give ear, O God of Jacob! Selah.
9 See our shield, O God,
And look upon the face
of Your anointed.
10 For better is a day in Your courts
than a thousand *elsewhere.*
I would choose to stand at the
threshold of the house of my God
Than dwell in the tents of wickedness.
11 For Yahweh God is a sun and shield;
Yahweh gives grace and glory;
No good thing does He withhold
from those who walk blamelessly.
12 O Yahweh of hosts,
How blessed is the man
who trusts in You!

Proverbs 21:6–8

6 Working for treasures by a lying tongue
Is a fleeting breath, by those
who pursue death.
7 The destruction of the wicked
will drag them away,
Because they refuse to do justice.
8 The way of a guilty man is perverse,
But as for the pure, his work is upright.

Acts 19:21–41

21 Now after these things were finished,
Paul purposed in the Spirit to go to Jerusalem
after he had passed through Macedonia and
Achaia, saying, "After I have been there, I
must also see Rome." 22 And having sent into
Macedonia two of those who ministered to
him, Timothy and Erastus, he himself stayed
in Asia for a while.
23 Now about that time there occurred
no small disturbance concerning the Way.
24 For a man named Demetrius, a silver-
smith, who made silver shrines of Artemis,
was bringing no little business to the crafts-
men; 25 these he gathered together with the
workers of similar *trades,* and said, "Men,
you know that our prosperity is from this
business. 26 And you see and hear that not
only in Ephesus, but in almost all of Asia,
this Paul has persuaded and turned away

a considerable crowd, saying that things made with hands are not gods. 27 And not only is there danger that this trade of ours fall into disrepute, but also that the temple of the great goddess Artemis be considered as worthless and that she, whom all of Asia and the world worship, is even about to be brought down from her majesty."

28 When they heard *this* and were filled with rage, they *began* crying out, saying, "Great is Artemis of the Ephesians!" 29 And the city was filled with the confusion, and they rushed with one accord into the theater, dragging along Gaius and Aristarchus, Paul's traveling companions from Macedonia. 30 And when Paul wanted to go into the assembly, the disciples would not let him. 31 Also some of the Asiarchs who were friends of his sent to him and repeatedly urged him not to venture into the theater. 32 So then, some were shouting one thing and some another, for the meeting was in confusion and the majority did not know for what reason they had come together. 33 And some of the crowd concluded *it was* Alexander, since the Jews had put him forward; and having motioned with his hand, Alexander was intending to make a defense to the assembly. 34 But when they recognized that he was a Jew, a single cry arose from them all as they shouted for about two hours, "Great is Artemis of the Ephesians!" 35 Now after calming the crowd, the city clerk *said, "Men of Ephesus, what man is there after all who does not know that the city of the Ephesians is guardian of the temple of the great Artemis and of the *image* which fell down from heaven? 36 So, since these are undeniable facts, you ought to keep calm and to do nothing rash. 37 For you have brought these men *here* who are neither robbers of temples nor blasphemers of our goddess. 38 So then, if Demetrius and the craftsmen who are with him have a complaint against anyone, the courts are in session and proconsuls are *available*; let them bring charges against one another. 39 But if you want anything beyond this, it shall be settled in the lawful meeting. 40 For indeed we are in danger of being accused of a riot in connection with today's events, since there is no cause for which we can give as an account for this disorderly gathering." 41 After saying this he dismissed the meeting.

JULY 17

2 Chronicles 30:1–31:21

30 And Hezekiah sent to all Israel and Judah and wrote letters also to Ephraim and Manasseh, that they should come to the house of Yahweh at Jerusalem to celebrate the Passover to Yahweh, the God of Israel. 2 And the king and his princes and all the assembly in Jerusalem had taken counsel to celebrate the Passover in the second month, 3 since they could not celebrate it at that time, because the priests had not set themselves apart as holy in sufficient numbers, nor had the people been gathered to Jerusalem. 4 Thus the thing was right in the eyes of the king and in the eyes of all the assembly. 5 So they established a decree to make a proclamation pass throughout all Israel from Beersheba even to Dan, that they should come to celebrate the Passover to Yahweh, the God of Israel, at Jerusalem. For they had not celebrated *it* in great numbers as it was written. 6 And the couriers went throughout all Israel and Judah with the letters from the hand of the king and his princes, even according to the commandment of the king, saying, "O sons of Israel, return to Yahweh, the God of Abraham, Isaac, and Israel, that He may return to those of you who escaped *and* remain from the hand of the kings of Assyria. 7 Now do not be like your fathers and your brothers, who were unfaithful to Yahweh, the God of their fathers, so that He made them an object of horror, as you see. 8 Now do not stiffen your neck like your fathers, but give your hand to Yahweh and enter His sanctuary which He has set apart as holy forever, and serve Yahweh your God, that His burning anger may turn away from you. 9 For when you return to Yahweh, your brothers and your sons *will find* compassion before those who led them captive and will return to this land. For Yahweh your God is gracious and compassionate, and will not turn *His* face away from you if you return to Him."

10 So the couriers passed from city to city through the country of Ephraim and Manasseh, and as far as Zebulun, but they were laughing at them to scorn and mocking them. 11 Nevertheless some men of Asher, Manasseh and Zebulun humbled themselves and came to Jerusalem. 12 The hand of God was also on Judah to give them one heart to do what the king and the princes commanded by the word of Yahweh.

13 Now many people were gathered at Jerusalem to celebrate the Feast of Unleavened Bread in the second month, a very large assembly. 14 And they arose and took away the altars which *were* in Jerusalem; they also took away all the incense altars and cast *them* into the brook Kidron. 15 Then they slaughtered the Passover *lambs* on the fourteenth of the second month. And the priests and Levites were ashamed of themselves, and set themselves apart as holy and brought burnt offerings to the house of Yahweh. 16 And they stood at their stations according to the *legal* judgment for them, according to the law of Moses the man of God; the priests splashed the blood *which they received* from the hand of the Levites. 17 For *there were* many in the assembly who had not set themselves apart as holy; therefore, the Levites *were* over the slaughter of the Passover *lambs* for everyone who *was* unclean, in order to set *them* apart as holy to Yahweh. 18 For a multitude of the people, *even* many from Ephraim and Manasseh, Issachar, and Zebulun, had not cleansed themselves, yet they ate the Passover otherwise than what was written. For Hezekiah prayed for them, saying, "May Yahweh, *who is* good, atone 19 for everyone who prepares his heart to seek God, Yahweh, the God of his fathers, though not according to the *rules* of cleansing of the sanctuary." 20 So Yahweh heard Hezekiah and healed the people. 21 And the sons of Israel present in Jerusalem celebrated the Feast of Unleavened Bread *for* seven days with great gladness, and the Levites and the priests praised Yahweh day after day with loud instruments to Yahweh. 22 Then Hezekiah spoke to the hearts of all the Levites who showed good insight *in the things* of Yahweh. So they ate for the appointed seven days, sacrificing peace offerings and giving thanks to Yahweh, the God of their fathers.

23 Then the whole assembly took counsel *to determine* to celebrate *the feast* another seven days, so they celebrated the seven days with gladness. 24 For Hezekiah king of Judah had contributed to the assembly 1,000 bulls and 7,000 sheep, and the princes had contributed to the assembly 1,000 bulls and 10,000 sheep; and a large number of priests set themselves apart as holy. 25 And all the assembly of Judah were glad, with the priests and the Levites and all the assembly that came from Israel, both the sojourners who came from the land of Israel and those living in Judah. 26 So there was great gladness in Jerusalem, because there was nothing like this in Jerusalem since the days of Solomon the son of David, king of Israel. 27 Then the Levitical priests arose and blessed the people; and their voice was heard and their prayer came to His holy habitation, to heaven.

31 Now when all this was completed, all Israel who were present went out to the cities of Judah, shattered the pillars, cut the Asherim in pieces, and tore down the high places and the altars throughout all Judah and Benjamin, as well as in Ephraim and Manasseh, until *the destruction* was completed. Then all the sons of Israel returned to their cities, each to his possession.

2 And Hezekiah set up the divisions of the priests and the Levites by their divisions, each according to his service, *both* the priests and the Levites, for burnt offerings and for peace offerings, to minister and to give thanks and to praise in the gates of the camp of Yahweh. 3 *He* also *appointed* the king's portion of his goods for the burnt offerings, *namely*, for the morning and evening burnt offerings, and the burnt offerings for the sabbaths and for the new moons and for the appointed times, as it is written in the law of Yahweh. 4 Also he said to the people who lived in Jerusalem to give the portion due to the priests and the Levites, that they might be strong in the law of Yahweh. 5 As soon as the word spread forth, the sons of Israel provided in abundance the first fruits of grain, new wine, oil, honey, and of all the produce of the field; and they brought in abundantly the tithe of all. 6 Now the sons of Israel and Judah who lived in the cities of Judah also brought in the tithe of

oxen and sheep, and the tithe of the holy gifts which were made holy to Yahweh their God, and put *them* in heaps. 7 In the third month they began to make the heaps, and completed *them* by the seventh month. 8 Then Hezekiah and the rulers came and saw the heaps, and they blessed Yahweh and His people Israel. 9 Then Hezekiah inquired of the priests and the Levites concerning the heaps. 10 And Azariah the chief priest of the house of Zadok said to him, "Since the contributions began to be brought into the house of Yahweh, *there has been* much to eat and be satisfied with and have left over, for Yahweh has blessed His people, and this great quantity is left over."

11 Then Hezekiah ordered *them* to prepare rooms in the house of Yahweh, and they prepared *them*. 12 And they faithfully brought in the contribution and the tithe and the holy things; and Conaniah the Levite *was* the officer over them and his brother Shimei *was* second. 13 Now Jehiel, Azaziah, Nahath, Asahel, Jerimoth, Jozabad, Eliel, Ismachiah, Mahath, and Benaiah *were* overseers *assisting* at the hand of Conaniah and Shimei his brother by the appointment of King Hezekiah, and Azariah *was* the *chief* officer of the house of God. 14 And Kore the son of Imnah the Levite, the keeper of the eastern *gate, was* over the freewill offerings of God, to distribute the contributions for Yahweh and the most holy things. 15 Now *assisting* by his hand *were* Eden, Miniamin, Jeshua, Shemaiah, Amariah, and Shecaniah in the cities of the priests, to distribute faithfully *their portions* to their brothers by divisions, whether great or small, 16 without regard to their genealogical record, to the males from thirty years old and upward—everyone who entered the house of Yahweh for his daily obligations—for their service in their responsibilities according to their divisions; 17 as well as the priests who were recorded genealogically according to their fathers' households, and the Levites from twenty years old and upwards, by their responsibilities *and* their divisions. 18 The genealogical record *included* all their little ones, their wives, their sons, and their daughters, for the whole assembly, for they set themselves apart faithfully in holiness. 19 Also for the sons of Aaron the priests *who were* in the pasture lands of their cities, or in each and every city, *there were* men who were designated by name to distribute portions to every male among the priests and to everyone genealogically recorded among the Levites.

20 Thus Hezekiah did throughout all Judah; and he did what *was* good, right, and true before Yahweh his God. 21 And every work which he began in the service of the house of God in law and in commandment—to seek his God—he did with all his heart and succeeded.

Psalm 85:1–7

1 O Yahweh, You showed
favor to Your land;
You returned the fortunes of Jacob.
2 You forgave the iniquity of Your people;
You covered all their sin. Selah.
3 You withdrew all Your fury;
You turned back from Your
burning anger.

4 Turn us back, O God of our salvation,
And cause Your vexation
toward us to cease.
5 Will You be angry with us forever?
Will You prolong Your anger from
generation to generation?
6 Will You not Yourself
return to revive us,
That Your people may be glad in You?
7 Show us, O Yahweh, Your
lovingkindness,
And give us Your salvation.

Proverbs 21:9–11

9 It is better to live in a corner of a roof
Than in a house shared with
a contentious woman.
10 The soul of the wicked craves evil;
His neighbor finds no favor in his eyes.
11 When the scoffer is punished,
the simple becomes wise;
And when one considers wisdom,
he receives knowledge.

Acts 20:1–16

20 Now after the uproar had ceased, Paul having summoned and exhorted the disciples, said farewell and left to go to Macedonia. 2 And when he had gone through those districts and had given them much exhortation, he came to Greece. 3 And *there* he spent three months, and when a plot was formed against him

by the Jews as he was about to set sail for Syria, he decided to return through Macedonia. 4 And he was accompanied by Sopater of Berea, *the son* of Pyrrhus, and by Aristarchus and Secundus of the Thessalonians, and Gaius of Derbe, and Timothy, and Tychicus and Trophimus of Asia. 5 But these had gone on ahead and were waiting for us at Troas. 6 And we sailed from Philippi after the days of Unleavened Bread, and came to them at Troas within five days; and there we stayed seven days.

7 And on the first day of the week, when we were gathered together to break bread, Paul *began* speaking to them, intending to leave the next day, and he prolonged his message until midnight. 8 Now there were many lamps in the upper room where we were gathered together. 9 And there was a young man named Eutychus sitting on the windowsill, sinking into a deep sleep. And as Paul kept on talking, he sunk into that sleep and fell down from the third floor and was picked up dead. 10 But Paul went down and fell upon him, and after embracing him, he said, "Do not be troubled, for his life is in him." 11 And when he had gone *back* up and had broken the bread and eaten, he talked with them a long while until daybreak, and then left. 12 And they took away the boy alive, and were not a little comforted.

13 But we, going ahead to the ship, set sail for Assos, intending from there to take Paul on board; for so he had arranged it, intending himself to go by land. 14 And when he met us at Assos, we took him on board and came to Mitylene. 15 And sailing from there, we arrived the following day opposite Chios; and the next day we crossed over to Samos; and the day following we came to Miletus. 16 For Paul had decided to sail past Ephesus so that he would not have to spend time in Asia; for he was hurrying to be in Jerusalem, if possible, on the day of Pentecost.

JULY 18

2 Chronicles 32:1–33:25

32 After these acts of faithfulness Sennacherib king of Assyria came and invaded Judah and encamped against the fortified cities, and thought to break into them for himself. 2 Then Hezekiah saw that Sennacherib had come and that *he had set* his face to make war on Jerusalem, 3 and he took counsel with his commanders and his warriors to stop up the *supply of* water from the springs which *were* outside the city, and they helped him. 4 So many people gathered and stopped up all the springs and the stream which flowed in the midst of the land, saying, "Why should the kings of Assyria come and find abundant water?" 5 And he strengthened himself and rebuilt all the wall that had been broken down and erected towers on it, and *built* another outside wall and strengthened the Millo *in* the city of David, and made weapons and shields in great number. 6 He also put military commanders over the people and gathered them to him in the square at the city gate, and spoke to their hearts, saying, 7 "Be strong and courageous. Do not fear or be dismayed because of the king of Assyria nor because of all the multitude that is with him; for the one with us is greater than the one with him. 8 With him is *only* an arm of flesh, but with us is Yahweh our God to help us and to fight our battles." And the people were sustained by the words of Hezekiah king of Judah.

9 After this Sennacherib king of Assyria sent his servants to Jerusalem while he *was* besieging Lachish with all his forces with him, against Hezekiah king of Judah and against all Judah who *were* at Jerusalem, saying, 10 "Thus says Sennacherib king of Assyria, 'On what are you trusting that you are remaining in Jerusalem under siege? 11 Is not Hezekiah inciting you to give yourselves over to die by hunger and by thirst, saying, "Yahweh our God will deliver us from the hand of the king of Assyria"? 12 Has not the same Hezekiah taken away His high places and His altars, and said to Judah and Jerusalem, "You shall worship before one altar, and on it you shall offer *offerings* up in smoke"? 13 Do you not know what I and my fathers have done to all the peoples of the lands? Were the gods of the nations of the lands able at all to deliver their land from my hand? 14 Who *was there* among all the gods of these nations which my fathers devoted to destruction, who could deliver his people from my hand, that your God should be able

to deliver you from my hand? 15 So now, do not let Hezekiah deceive you or incite you like this, and do not believe him, for no god of any nation or kingdom was able to deliver his people from my hand or from the hand of my fathers. How much less will your God deliver you from my hand?'"

16 His servants spoke further against Yahweh God and against His servant Hezekiah. 17 He also wrote letters to reproach Yahweh, the God of Israel, and to speak against Him, saying, "As the gods of the nations of the lands have not delivered their people from my hand, so the God of Hezekiah will not deliver His people from my hand." 18 And they called this out with a loud voice in the language of Judah to the people of Jerusalem who were on the wall, to instill fear and terrify them, so that they might capture the city. 19 And they spoke of the God of Jerusalem as of the gods of the peoples of the earth, the work of men's hands.

20 But King Hezekiah and Isaiah the prophet, the son of Amoz, prayed about this and cried out to heaven. 21 And Yahweh sent an angel who wiped out every mighty man of valor, ruler, and commander in the camp of the king of Assyria. So he returned in shame to his own land. And he entered the house of his god, and some of his own children caused him to fall there by the sword. 22 So Yahweh saved Hezekiah and the inhabitants of Jerusalem from the hand of Sennacherib the king of Assyria and from the hand of all *others*, and He guided them on every side. 23 And many were bringing presents to Yahweh at Jerusalem and precious things to Hezekiah king of Judah, so that he was lifted up in the sight of all nations thereafter.

24 In those days Hezekiah became sick to the point of death; and he prayed to Yahweh, and Yahweh spoke to him and gave him a miraculous sign. 25 But Hezekiah gave no return for the benefit he received, because his heart was proud; therefore wrath came on him and on Judah and Jerusalem. 26 However, Hezekiah humbled the pride of his heart, both he and the inhabitants of Jerusalem, so that the wrath of Yahweh did not come on them in the days of Hezekiah.

27 Now Hezekiah had abundant riches and honor; and he made for himself treasuries for silver, gold, precious stones, spices, shields, and all kinds of desirable articles, 28 storehouses also for the produce of grain, wine, and oil, stalls for all kinds of cattle, and sheepfolds for the flocks. 29 He also made cities for himself and acquired flocks and herds in abundance, for God had given him exceedingly abundant wealth. 30 And it was Hezekiah who stopped the upper outlet of the waters of Gihon and directed them to the west side of the city of David. And Hezekiah succeeded in all that he did. 31 Even *in the matter of* the envoys of the rulers of Babylon, who sent to him to inquire of the miraculous sign that had happened in the land, God left him *alone only* to test him, that He might know all that was in his heart.

32 Now the rest of the acts of Hezekiah and his deeds of lovingkindness, behold, they are written in the vision of Isaiah the prophet, the son of Amoz, in the Book of the Kings of Judah and Israel. 33 So Hezekiah slept with his fathers, and they buried him in the upper section of the tombs of the sons of David; and all Judah and the inhabitants of Jerusalem honored him at his death. And Manasseh his son became king in his place.

33 Manasseh was twelve years old when he became king, and he reigned fifty-five years in Jerusalem. 2 And he did what was evil in the sight of Yahweh, according to the abominations of the nations whom Yahweh dispossessed before the sons of Israel. 3 Indeed, he rebuilt the high places which Hezekiah his father had torn down; and he erected altars for the Baals and made Asherim, and worshiped all the host of heaven and served them. 4 And he built altars in the house of Yahweh, of which Yahweh had said, "In Jerusalem My name shall be forever." 5 Indeed, he built altars for all the host of heaven in the two courts of the house of Yahweh. 6 He even made his sons pass through the fire in the valley of Ben-hinnom; and he practiced soothsaying, interpreted omens, practiced sorcery, and dealt with mediums and spiritists. He did much that was evil in the sight of Yahweh, provoking Him *to anger*. 7 Then he put the graven image of the idol, which he had made, in the house of God, of which God had said to David and to Solomon his son, "In this house and in Jerusalem, which I have chosen from all the tribes of Israel, I will put My name forever. 8 And I will not again remove the foot of Israel from the land which I have set up for your fathers, if

only they will be careful to do all that I have
commanded them according to all the law,
the statutes and the judgments *given* by the
hand of Moses." 9 Thus Manasseh led Judah
and the inhabitants of Jerusalem astray in
order to do more evil than the nations whom
Yahweh destroyed before the sons of Israel.
10 Then Yahweh spoke to Manasseh and
his people, but they paid no attention.
11 Therefore Yahweh brought the command-
ers of the army of the king of Assyria against
them, and they captured Manasseh with
hooks, bound him with bronze *chains*, and
took him to Babylon. 12 And when he was in
distress, he entreated Yahweh his God and
humbled himself greatly before the God of
his fathers. 13 Then he prayed to Him, and
He was moved by his entreaty and heard
his supplication, and returned him back to
Jerusalem to his kingdom. Then Manasseh
knew that Yahweh *was* God.
14 Afterwards, he built the outer wall of
the city of David on the west side of Gihon,
in the valley, even to the entrance of the
Fish Gate; and he encircled the Ophel *with it*
and made it very high. Then he put military
commanders in all the fortified cities of
Judah. 15 He also removed the foreign gods
and the idol from the house of Yahweh, as
well as all the altars which he had built on
the mountain of the house of Yahweh and
in Jerusalem, and he threw *them* outside the
city. 16 And he set up the altar of Yahweh
and sacrificed peace offerings and thank
offerings on it; and he said for Judah to serve
Yahweh, the God of Israel. 17 Nevertheless
the people still sacrificed in the high places,
although only to Yahweh their God.
18 Now the rest of the acts of Manasseh,
even his prayer to his God, and the words of
the seers who spoke to him in the name of
Yahweh, the God of Israel, behold, they are
among the chronicles of the kings of Israel.
19 His prayer also and *how God* was entreated
by him, and all his sin, his unfaithfulness, and
the sites on which he built high places and
erected *the Asherim* and the graven images,
before he humbled himself, behold, they are
written in the chronicles of the Hozai. 20 And
Manasseh slept with his fathers, and they
buried him in his own house. And Amon his
son became king in his place.
21 Amon *was* twenty-two years old when
he became king, and he reigned two years
in Jerusalem. 22 And he did what was evil in
the sight of Yahweh, as Manasseh his father
had done, and Amon sacrificed to all the
graven images which his father Manasseh
had made, and he served them. 23 Moreover,
he did not humble himself before Yahweh as
his father Manasseh had humbled himself,
but Amon multiplied guilt. 24 Then his
servants conspired against him and put
him to death in his own house. 25 Then the
people of the land struck down all those
who had conspired against King Amon, and
the people of the land made Josiah his son
king in his place.

Psalm 85:8–13

8 Let me hear what the God,
Yahweh, will speak;
For He will speak peace to His
people, to His holy ones;
But let them not turn back to folly.
9 Surely His salvation is near
to those who fear Him,
That glory may dwell in our land.
10 Lovingkindness and truth
have met together;
Righteousness and peace
have kissed each other.
11 Truth springs up from the earth,
And righteousness looks
down from heaven.
12 Indeed, Yahweh will give what is good,
And our land will yield its produce.
13 Righteousness will go before Him
And will establish the way of His steps.

Proverbs 21:12

12 The righteous one considers
the house of the wicked,
Turning the wicked to ruin.

Acts 20:17–38

17 Now from Miletus he sent to Ephesus
and called to him the elders of the church.
18 And when they had come to him, he said
to them,
"You yourselves know, from the first day
that I set foot in Asia, how I was with you
the whole time, 19 serving the Lord with
all humility and with tears and with trials
which came upon me through the plots of
the Jews; 20 how I did not shrink from declar-
ing to you anything that was profitable, and
teaching you publicly and from house to
house, 21 solemnly testifying to both Jews
and Greeks about repentance toward God

and faith in our Lord Jesus Christ. 22 And now, behold, bound by the Spirit, I am on my way to Jerusalem, not knowing what will happen to me there, 23 except that the Holy Spirit solemnly testifies to me in every city, saying that chains and afflictions await me. 24 But I do not make my life of any account nor dear to myself, so that I may finish my course and the ministry which I received from the Lord Jesus, to testify solemnly of the gospel of the grace of God.

25 "And now, behold, I know that all of you, among whom I went about preaching the kingdom, will no longer see my face. 26 Therefore, I testify to you this day that I am innocent of the blood of all. 27 For I did not shrink from declaring to you the whole purpose of God. 28 Be on guard for yourselves and for all the flock, among which the Holy Spirit has made you overseers, to shepherd the church of God which He purchased with His own blood. 29 I know that after my departure savage wolves will come in among you, not sparing the flock; 30 and from among your own selves men will arise, speaking perverse things, to draw away the disciples after them. 31 Therefore be watchful, remembering that night and day for a period of three years I did not cease to admonish each one with tears. 32 And now I commend you to God and to the word of His grace, which is able to build *you* up and to give *you* the inheritance among all those who have been sanctified. 33 I have coveted no one's silver or gold or clothes. 34 You yourselves know that these hands ministered to my *own* needs and to those who were with me. 35 In everything I showed you that by laboring in this manner you must help the weak and remember the words of the Lord Jesus, that He Himself said, 'It is more blessed to give than to receive.'"

36 And when he had said these things, he knelt down and prayed with them all. 37 And they *began* to weep aloud and falling on Paul's neck, they were kissing him, 38 being in agony especially over the word which he had spoken, that they would not see his face again. And they were accompanying him to the ship.

JULY 19

2 Chronicles 34:1–36:23

34 Josiah was eight years old when he became king, and he reigned thirty-one years in Jerusalem. 2 And he did what was right in the sight of Yahweh and walked in the ways of his father David and did not turn aside to the right or to the left. 3 Now in the eighth year of his reign while he was still a youth, he began to seek the God of his father David; and in the twelfth year he began to cleanse Judah and Jerusalem of the high places, the Asherim, the graven images, and the molten images. 4 And they tore down the altars of the Baals in his presence, and the incense altars that were high above them he cut in pieces; also the Asherim, the graven images, and the molten images he broke in pieces and ground to powder and scattered *it* on the graves of those who had sacrificed to them. 5 Then he burned the bones of the priests on their altars and cleansed Judah and Jerusalem. 6 And in the cities of Manasseh, Ephraim, Simeon, even as far as Naphtali, in their surrounding ruins, 7 he also tore down the altars and beat the Asherim and the graven images into powder, and cut in pieces all the incense altars throughout the land of Israel. Then he returned to Jerusalem.

8 Now in the eighteenth year of his reign, when he had cleansed the land and the house, he sent Shaphan the son of Azaliah, and Maaseiah an official of the city, and Joah the son of Joahaz the recorder, to repair the house of Yahweh his God. 9 And they came to Hilkiah the high priest and gave him the money that was brought into the house of God, which the Levites, the doorkeepers, had gathered from the hand of Manasseh and Ephraim, and from all the remnant of Israel, and from all Judah and Benjamin and the inhabitants of Jerusalem. 10 Then they gave *it* into the hand of those who did the work, who had the oversight of the house of Yahweh; and those who did the work, who were doing *this* in the house of Yahweh, used it to restore and repair the house. 11 They in turn gave *it* to the craftsmen and to the builders to buy hewn stone and timber for clamps and to make beams for the houses which the kings of Judah had let go to ruin. 12 And the men did the work faithfully with

foremen over them to direct: Jahath and Obadiah, the Levites of the sons of Merari, Zechariah and Meshullam of the sons of the Kohathites, and the Levites, all who were skillful with musical instruments. 13 *They were* also over those who carried loads, and directed all those who did the work from service to service; and *some* of the Levites *were* scribes and officials and gatekeepers.

14 When they were taking out the money which had been brought into the house of Yahweh, Hilkiah the priest found the book of the law of Yahweh *given* by the hand of Moses. 15 So Hilkiah answered and said to Shaphan the scribe, "I have found the book of the law in the house of Yahweh." And Hilkiah gave the book to Shaphan. 16 Then Shaphan brought the book to the king and furthermore responded to the king with a word, saying, "Everything that was given to the hand of your servants they are doing. 17 They have also poured out the money that was found in the house of Yahweh, and have given it into the hand of the supervisors and those who did the work." 18 Moreover, Shaphan the scribe told the king saying, "Hilkiah the priest gave me a book." And Shaphan read from it in the presence of the king.

19 Now it happened that when the king heard the words of the law, he tore his clothes. 20 Then the king commanded Hilkiah, Ahikam the son of Shaphan, Abdon the son of Micah, Shaphan the scribe, and Asaiah the king's servant, saying, 21 "Go, inquire of Yahweh for me and those who are left in Israel and in Judah, concerning the words of the book which has been found, for great is the wrath of Yahweh which is poured out against us, because our fathers have not kept the word of Yahweh, to do according to all that is written in this book."

22 So Hilkiah and *those* whom the king had told went to Huldah the prophetess, the wife of Shallum the son of Tokhath, the son of Hasrah, keeper of the wardrobe (now she lived in Jerusalem in the Second Quarter); and they spoke to her regarding this. 23 And she said to them, "Thus says Yahweh, the God of Israel, 'Say to the man who sent you to Me, 24 thus says Yahweh, "Behold, I am bringing evil on this place and on its inhabitants, *even* all the curses written in the book which they have read in the presence of the king of Judah. 25 Because they have forsaken Me and have burned incense to other gods that they might provoke Me to anger with all the works of their hands, therefore My wrath will be poured out against this place, and it shall not be quenched."' 26 But to the king of Judah who sent you to inquire of Yahweh, thus you shall say to him, 'Thus says Yahweh, the God of Israel, "*Regarding* the words which you have heard, 27 because your heart was soft and you humbled yourself before God when you heard His words against this place and against its inhabitants, and *because* you humbled yourself before Me, tore your clothes and wept before Me, I truly have heard you," declares Yahweh. 28 "Behold, I will gather you to your fathers, and you will be gathered to your grave in peace, so your eyes will not see all the evil which I will bring on this place and on its inhabitants."'" So they brought back word to the king.

29 Then the king sent and gathered all the elders of Judah and Jerusalem. 30 And the king went up to the house of Yahweh and all the men of Judah, and the inhabitants of Jerusalem, and the priests and the Levites and all the people, from the greatest to the least; and he read in their hearing all the words of the book of the covenant which was found in the house of Yahweh.

31 Then the king stood in his place and cut a covenant before Yahweh, to walk after Yahweh, and to keep His commandments and His testimonies and His statutes with all his heart and with all his soul, to do the words of the covenant that were written in this book. 32 Moreover, he made all who were present in Jerusalem and Benjamin to stand *with him*. So the inhabitants of Jerusalem did according to the covenant of God, the God of their fathers. 33 And Josiah took away all the abominations from all the lands belonging to the sons of Israel, and made all who were present in Israel to serve Yahweh their God. Throughout his lifetime they did not turn away from following Yahweh, the God of their fathers.

35 Then Josiah celebrated the Passover to Yahweh in Jerusalem, and they slaughtered the Passover *animals* on the fourteenth *day* of the first month. 2 And he caused the priests to stand in their responsibilities and strengthened them in the service of the house of Yahweh. 3 He also said to the

Levites who provided understanding to all
Israel *and* who were holy to Yahweh, "Put
the holy ark in the house which Solomon
the son of David king of Israel built; it will
be a burden on *your* shoulders no longer.
Now serve Yahweh your God and His
people Israel. 4 So prepare *yourselves* by
your fathers' households in your divisions,
according to the writing of David king of
Israel and according to the writing of his son
Solomon. 5 Moreover, stand in the holy place
according to the sections of the fathers'
households of your brothers the lay people,
and according to the Levites, by division of
a father's household. 6 Now slaughter the
Passover *animals*, sanctify yourselves and
prepare for your brothers to do according to
the word of Yahweh by the hand of Moses."

7 And Josiah contributed to the lay people,
to all who were present, flocks of lambs and
young goats, all for the Passover offerings,
numbering 30,000 plus 3,000 bulls; these
were from the king's possessions. 8 His
officials also contributed a freewill offering
to the people, the priests, and the Levites.
Hilkiah and Zechariah and Jehiel, the offi-
cers of the house of God, gave to the priests
for the Passover offerings 2,600 *from the
flocks* and 300 bulls. 9 Conaniah also, and
Shemaiah and Nethanel, his brothers,
and Hashabiah and Jeiel and Jozabad, the
officials of the Levites, contributed to the
Levites for the Passover offerings 5,000
from the flocks and 500 bulls.

10 So the service was prepared, and the
priests stood at their stations and the Levites
by their divisions according to the king's
commandment. 11 And they slaughtered
the Passover *animals*, and while the priests
splashed the blood *received* from their
hand, the Levites skinned *them*. 12 Then
they took away *the portions for* the burnt
offerings that *they* might give them to the
sections of the fathers' households of the
lay people to bring near to Yahweh, as it
is written in the book of Moses. *They did*
this also with the bulls. 13 So they roasted
the Passover *animals* on the fire according
to the *legal* judgment, and they boiled the
holy things in pots, in kettles, in pans, and
carried *them* speedily to all the lay people.
14 Afterwards they prepared for themselves
and for the priests, because the priests,
the sons of Aaron, *were* offering the burnt
offerings and the fat until night; therefore
the Levites prepared for themselves and for
the priests, the sons of Aaron. 15 The singers,
the sons of Asaph, *were* also at their stations
according to the commandment of David,
Asaph, Heman, and Jeduthun the king's seer;
and the gatekeepers at each gate did not have
to turn aside from their service, because the
Levites their brothers prepared for them.

16 So all the service of Yahweh was pre-
pared on that day to celebrate the Passover,
and to offer burnt offerings on the altar of
Yahweh according to the commandment
of King Josiah. 17 Thus the sons of Israel
who were present celebrated the Passover
at that time, and the Feast of Unleavened
Bread seven days. 18 And there had not been
celebrated a Passover like it in Israel from
the days of Samuel the prophet; nor had any
of the kings of Israel celebrated such a Pass-
over as Josiah celebrated with the priests,
the Levites, all Judah and Israel who were
present, and the inhabitants of Jerusalem.
19 In the eighteenth year of Josiah's reign,
this Passover was celebrated.

20 After all this, when Josiah had set the
house in order, Neco king of Egypt went up
to make war at Carchemish on the Euphra-
tes, and Josiah went out to meet him. 21 But
Neco sent messengers to him, saying, "What
have I to do with you, O King of Judah? *I am*
not *coming* against you today but against
the house with which I am at war, and God
has said for me to hurry. Stop for your own
sake from *interfering with* God who is with
me, so that He will not bring you to ruin."
22 However, Josiah would not turn away
from him, but disguised himself in order to
make war with him; nor did he listen to the
words of Neco from the mouth of God, but
came to make war on the plain of Megiddo.
23 Then the archers shot King Josiah, and the
king said to his servants, "Take me away, for
I am badly wounded." 24 So his servants took
him out of the chariot and drove him in the
second chariot which he had, and brought
him to Jerusalem where he died, and he was
buried in the tombs of his fathers. And all
Judah and Jerusalem mourned for Josiah.
25 Then Jeremiah chanted a *lament* for
Josiah. And all the male and female singers
speak about Josiah in their lamentations to
this day. And they made them a statute in
Israel; behold, they are also written in the
lamentations. 26 Now the rest of the acts
of Josiah and his deeds of lovingkindness

according to what was written in the law of Yahweh, 27 and his acts, first to last, behold, they are written in the Book of the Kings of Israel and Judah.

36 Then the people of the land took Joahaz the son of Josiah, and made him king in place of his father in Jerusalem. 2 Joahaz was twenty-three years old when he became king, and he reigned three months in Jerusalem. 3 Then the king of Egypt had him removed in Jerusalem and imposed on the land a fine of one hundred talents of silver and one talent of gold. 4 Then the king of Egypt made Eliakim his brother king over Judah and Jerusalem, and changed his name to Jehoiakim. But Neco took Joahaz his brother and brought him to Egypt.

5 Jehoiakim was twenty-five years old when he became king, and he reigned eleven years in Jerusalem; and he did what was evil in the sight of Yahweh his God. 6 Nebuchadnezzar king of Babylon came up against him and bound him with bronze *chains* to lead him off to Babylon. 7 Nebuchadnezzar also brought *some* of the articles of the house of Yahweh to Babylon and put them in his temple at Babylon. 8 Now the rest of the acts of Jehoiakim and the abominations which he did, and what was found against him, behold, they are written in the Book of the Kings of Israel and Judah. And Jehoiachin his son became king in his place.

9 Jehoiachin was eight years old when he became king, and he reigned three months and ten days in Jerusalem, and he did what was evil in the sight of Yahweh. 10 And at the turn of the year King Nebuchadnezzar sent and brought him to Babylon with the valuable articles of the house of Yahweh, and he made his relative Zedekiah king over Judah and Jerusalem.

11 Zedekiah was twenty-one years old when he became king, and he reigned eleven years in Jerusalem. 12 And he did what was evil in the sight of Yahweh his God; *he did not humble himself before* Jeremiah the prophet *who spoke* from the mouth of Yahweh. 13 He also rebelled against King Nebuchadnezzar who had made him swear *allegiance* by God. But he stiffened his neck and hardened his heart against turning to Yahweh, the God of Israel. 14 Furthermore, all the leaders of the priests and the people were very unfaithful *following* all the abominations of the nations; and they defiled the house of Yahweh which He had set apart as holy in Jerusalem.

15 And Yahweh, the God of their fathers, sent *word* to them again and again by the hand of His messengers, because He had compassion on His people and on His habitation; 16 but they *continually* mocked the messengers of God, despised His words and scoffed at His prophets, until the wrath of Yahweh arose against His people, until there was no remedy. 17 Therefore He brought up against them the king of the Chaldeans who killed their choice men with the sword in the house of their sanctuary, and had no compassion on choice man or virgin, old man or infirm; He gave *them* all into his hand. 18 And all the articles of the house of God, great and small, and the treasures of the house of Yahweh, and the treasures of the king and of his officials, he brought *them* all to Babylon. 19 Then they burned the house of God and tore down the wall of Jerusalem, and burned all its palaces with fire and destroyed all its valuable articles. 20 And those who had escaped from the sword he took away into exile to Babylon; and they were slaves to him and to his sons until the rule of the kingdom of Persia, 21 to fulfill the word of Yahweh by the mouth of Jeremiah, until the land had made up for its sabbaths. All the days of its desolation it kept sabbath until seventy years were fulfilled.

22 Now in the first year of Cyrus king of Persia—in order to complete the word of Yahweh by the mouth of Jeremiah—Yahweh stirred up the spirit of Cyrus king of Persia, so that he had a proclamation pass throughout all his kingdom, and also *put it* in writing, saying, 23 "Thus says Cyrus king of Persia,

> 'Yahweh, the God of heaven, has given
> me all the kingdoms of the earth, and
> He has appointed me to build Him a
> house in Jerusalem, which is in Judah.
> Whoever there is among you of all His
> people, may Yahweh his God be with
> him, and let him go up!'"

Psalm 86:1–5

1 Incline Your ear, O Yahweh,
    and answer me;
  For I am afflicted and needy.
2 Keep my soul, for I am a holy one;
  O You my God, save Your slave
    who trusts in You.

3 Be gracious to me, O Lord,
For to You I call all day long.
4 Make glad the soul of Your slave,
For to You, O Lord, I lift up my soul.
5 For You, Lord, are good, and
by nature forgiving,
And abundant in lovingkindness
to all who call upon You.

Proverbs 21:13–14

13 He who shuts his ear to the
outcry of the poor
Will himself also call and
not be answered.
14 A gift in secret subdues anger,
And a bribe in the bosom,
strong wrath.

Acts 21:1–16

21 Now when we had parted from them
and had set sail, we came by a straight
course to Cos and the next day to Rhodes
and from there to Patara; 2 and having
found a ship crossing over to Phoenicia,
we went aboard and set sail. 3 And when
we came in sight of Cyprus, leaving it on
the left, we kept sailing to Syria and landed
at Tyre; for there the ship was to unload its
cargo. 4 And after looking up the disciples,
we stayed there seven days; and they kept
telling Paul through the Spirit not to set
foot in Jerusalem. 5 And when our days
there were ended, we left and started on
our journey, while they all, with wives and
children, escorted us until *we were* out of
the city. After kneeling down on the beach
and praying, we said farewell to one another.
6 Then we went on board the ship, and they
returned home again.
7 And when we had finished the voyage
from Tyre, we arrived at Ptolemais, and after
greeting the brothers, we stayed with them
for a day. 8 And on the next day we left and
came to Caesarea, and entering the house
of Philip the evangelist, who was one of the
seven, we stayed with him. 9 Now this man
had four virgin daughters who prophesied.
10 And as we were staying there for some
days, a prophet named Agabus came down
from Judea. 11 And coming to us, he took
Paul's belt and bound his own feet and
hands, and said, "This is what the Holy
Spirit says: 'In this way the Jews at Jerusalem
will bind the man who owns this belt and
deliver him into the hands of the Gentiles.'"
12 And when we had heard this, we as well as
the local residents *began* begging him not to
go up to Jerusalem. 13 Then Paul answered,
"What are you doing, crying and breaking
my heart? For I am ready not only to be
bound, but even to die at Jerusalem for
the name of the Lord Jesus." 14 And since
he would not be persuaded, we fell silent,
saying, "The will of the Lord be done!"
15 Now after these days we got ready
and started on our way up to Jerusalem.
16 And *some* of the disciples from Caesarea
also came with us, taking us to Mnason of
Cyprus, an early disciple with whom we
were to lodge.

JULY 20

Ezra 1:1–2:70

1 Now in the first year of Cyrus king of
Persia—in order to complete the word
of Yahweh from the mouth of Jeremiah—
Yahweh stirred up the spirit of Cyrus king
of Persia, so that he had a proclamation pass
throughout all his kingdom, and also *put it*
in writing, saying:
2 "Thus says Cyrus king of Persia,
'Yahweh, the God of heaven, has given
me all the kingdoms of the earth, and
He has appointed me to build Him a
house in Jerusalem, which is in Judah.
3 Whoever there is among you of all
His people, may his God be with him!
Let him go up to Jerusalem which
is in Judah and rebuild the house of
Yahweh, the God of Israel; He is the
God who is in Jerusalem. 4 So everyone
who remains, at whatever place he
may sojourn, let the men of that place
support him with silver and gold,
with goods and cattle, together with a
freewill offering for the house of God
which is in Jerusalem.'"
5 Then the heads of fathers' *households*
of Judah and Benjamin and the priests and
the Levites arose, *that is* of everyone whose
spirit God had stirred to go up to rebuild the
house of Yahweh which is in Jerusalem.
6 All those around them strengthened
them with articles of silver, with gold, with

possessions, with cattle, and with precious
things, aside from all that was given as a
freewill offering. 7 Also King Cyrus brought
out the articles of the house of Yahweh,
which Nebuchadnezzar had brought out
from Jerusalem and put in the house of his
gods; 8 and Cyrus, king of Persia, had them
brought out by the hand of Mithredath
the treasurer, and he counted them out to
Sheshbazzar, the prince of Judah. 9 Now
this *was* their number: 30 gold dishes,
1,000 silver dishes, 29 duplicates; 10 30 gold
bowls, 410 silver bowls of a second *kind and*
1,000 other articles. 11 All the articles of gold
and silver *numbered* 5,400. Sheshbazzar
brought them all up with the exiles who
went up from Babylon to Jerusalem.

2 Now these are the people of the province who came up out of the captivity of the exiles whom Nebuchadnezzar the king of Babylon had taken away into exile to Babylon, and who returned to Jerusalem and
Judah, each to his city. 2 These came with
Zerubbabel, Jeshua, Nehemiah, Seraiah, Reelaiah, Mordecai, Bilshan, Mispar, Bigvai, Rehum, *and* Baanah.

The number of the men of the people of Israel:

3 the sons of Parosh, 2,172;
4 the sons of Shephatiah, 372;
5 the sons of Arah, 775;
6 the sons of Pahath-moab of the sons of Jeshua *and* Joab, 2,812;
7 the sons of Elam, 1,254;
8 the sons of Zattu, 945;
9 the sons of Zaccai, 760;
10 the sons of Bani, 642;
11 the sons of Bebai, 623;
12 the sons of Azgad, 1,222;
13 the sons of Adonikam, 666;
14 the sons of Bigvai, 2,056;
15 the sons of Adin, 454;
16 the sons of Ater of Hezekiah, 98;
17 the sons of Bezai, 323;
18 the sons of Jorah, 112;
19 the sons of Hashum, 223;
20 the sons of Gibbar, 95;
21 the sons of Bethlehem, 123;
22 the men of Netophah, 56;
23 the men of Anathoth, 128;
24 the sons of Azmaveth, 42;
25 the sons of Kiriath-arim, Chephirah and Beeroth, 743;
26 the sons of Ramah and Geba, 621;
27 the men of Michmas, 122;
28 the men of Bethel and Ai, 223;
29 the sons of Nebo, 52;
30 the sons of Magbish, 156;
31 the sons of the other Elam, 1,254;
32 the sons of Harim, 320;
33 the sons of Lod, Hadid and Ono, 725;
34 the men of Jericho, 345;
35 the sons of Senaah, 3,630.

36 The priests:
the sons of Jedaiah of the house of Jeshua, 973;
37 the sons of Immer, 1,052;
38 the sons of Pashhur, 1,247;
39 the sons of Harim, 1,017.

40 The Levites:
the sons of Jeshua and Kadmiel, of the sons of Hodaviah, 74.

41 The singers:
the sons of Asaph, 128.

42 The sons of the gatekeepers:
the sons of Shallum, the sons of Ater, the sons of Talmon, the sons of Akkub, the sons of Hatita, the sons of Shobai, in all 139.

43 The temple servants:
the sons of Ziha, the sons of Hasupha, the sons of Tabbaoth,
44 the sons of Keros, the sons of Siaha, the sons of Padon,
45 the sons of Lebanah, the sons of Hagabah, the sons of Akkub,
46 the sons of Hagab, the sons of Shalmai, the sons of Hanan,
47 the sons of Giddel, the sons of Gahar, the sons of Reaiah,
48 the sons of Rezin, the sons of Nekoda, the sons of Gazzam,
49 the sons of Uzza, the sons of Paseah, the sons of Besai,
50 the sons of Asnah, the sons of Meunim, the sons of Nephisim,
51 the sons of Bakbuk, the sons of Hakupha, the sons of Harhur,
52 the sons of Bazluth, the sons of Mehida, the sons of Harsha,
53 the sons of Barkos, the sons of Sisera, the sons of Temah,
54 the sons of Neziah, the sons of Hatipha.

55 The sons of Solomon's servants:
the sons of Sotai, the sons of Hassophereth, the sons of Peruda,
56 the sons of Jaalah, the sons of Darkon, the sons of Giddel,

57 the sons of Shephatiah, the sons
of Hattil, the sons of Pochereth-
hazzebaim, the sons of Ami.

58 All the temple servants and the sons of
Solomon's servants were 392.

59 Now these are those who came up from
Tel-melah, Tel-harsha, Cherub, Addan, *and*
Immer, but they were not able to declare
their fathers' households and their *fathers'*
seed, whether they were of Israel: 60 the sons
of Delaiah, the sons of Tobiah, the sons of
Nekoda, 652. 61 Of the sons of the priests:
the sons of Hobaiah, the sons of Hakkoz,
the sons of Barzillai, who took a wife from
the daughters of Barzillai the Gileadite,
and he was called by their name. 62 These
searched *in* their genealogical records, but
they could not be found; therefore they were
considered unclean *and excluded* from the
priesthood. 63 The governor said to them
that they should not eat from the most holy
things until a priest stood with Urim and
Thummim.

64 The whole assembly together *was*
42,360,
65 besides their male and female slaves of
whom *there were* 7,337;
and they had 200 male and female
singers.
66 Their horses were 736; their mules,
245;
67 their camels, 435; *their* donkeys,
6,720.

68 Some of the heads of fathers' *households*,
when they arrived at the house of Yahweh
which is in Jerusalem, gave a freewill offer-
ing for the house of God to restore it on its
foundation. 69 According to their ability,
they gave to the treasury for the work 61,000
gold drachmas and 5,000 silver minas and
100 priestly tunics.

70 So the priests and the Levites, some of
the people, the singers, the gatekeepers, and
the temple servants lived in their cities, and
all Israel in their cities.

Psalm 86:6–10

6 Give ear, O Yahweh, to my prayer;
And give heed to the voice
of my supplications!
7 In the day of my distress I
shall call upon You,
For You will answer me.
8 There is no one like You among
the gods, O Lord,
Nor are there any works like Yours.
9 All nations whom You have
made shall come and worship
before You, O Lord,
And they shall glorify Your name.
10 For You are great and do
wondrous deeds;
You alone are God.

Proverbs 21:15–16

15 To do justice is pleasure
for the righteous,
But is ruin to the workers of iniquity.
16 A man who wanders from
the way of insight
Will rest in the assembly of the dead.

Acts 21:17–40

17 And after we arrived in Jerusalem, the
brothers welcomed us gladly. 18 And the
following day Paul went in with us to James,
and all the elders were present. 19 And after
he had greeted them, he *began to* relate one
by one the things which God did among the
Gentiles through his ministry. 20 And when
they heard it they *began* glorifying God;
and they said to him, "You see, brother,
how many thousands there are among
the Jews of those who have believed, and
they are all zealous for the Law; 21 and
they have been told about you, that you
are teaching all the Jews who are among
the Gentiles to forsake Moses, telling them
not to circumcise their children nor to walk
according to the customs. 22 What, then, is
to be done? They will certainly hear that
you have come. 23 Therefore do this that we
tell you. We have four men who are under a
vow; 24 take them and purify yourself along
with them, and pay their expenses so that
they may shave their heads. Then all will
know that there is nothing to the things
which they have been told about you, but
that you yourself also walk orderly, keeping
the Law. 25 But concerning the Gentiles who
have believed, we wrote, having decided
that they should keep from meat sacrificed
to idols and from blood and from what is
strangled and from sexual immorality."
26 Then Paul took the men, and the next
day, purifying himself along with them,
went into the temple giving notice of the
completion of the days of purification,
until the sacrifice was offered for each one
of them.

27 Now when the seven days were almost over, the Jews from Asia, upon noticing him in the temple, *began to* throw all the crowd into confusion and laid hands on him, 28 crying out, "Men of Israel, help! This is the man who teaches to everyone everywhere against our people and the Law and this place; and besides, he has even brought Greeks into the temple and has defiled this holy place." 29 For they had previously seen Trophimus the Ephesian in the city with him, and they supposed that Paul had brought him into the temple. 30 Then all the city was stirred, and the people rushed together, and taking hold of Paul they dragged him out of the temple, and immediately the doors were shut. 31 While they were seeking to kill him, a report came up to the commander of the *Roman* cohort that all Jerusalem was in confusion. 32 At once he took along soldiers and centurions and ran down to them; and when they saw the commander and the soldiers, they stopped beating Paul. 33 Then the commander came up and took hold of him, and ordered him to be bound with two chains; and he *began* asking who he was and what he had done. 34 But among the crowd some were shouting one thing *and* some another, and when he could not find out the facts because of the uproar, he ordered him to be brought into the barracks. 35 And when he got to the stairs, he actually was carried by the soldiers because of the violence of the crowd; 36 for the multitude of the people kept following them, shouting, "Away with him!"

37 As Paul was about to be brought into the barracks, he said to the commander, "May I say something to you?" And he *said, "Do you know Greek? 38 Then you are not the Egyptian who some time ago raised a revolt and led the four thousand men of the Assassins out into the wilderness?" 39 But Paul said, "I am a Jew of Tarsus in Cilicia, a citizen of no insignificant city; and I beg you, allow me to speak to the people." 40 And when he had given him permission, Paul, standing on the stairs, motioned to the people with his hand; and when there was a great hush, he spoke to them in the Hebrew language, saying,

JULY 21

Ezra 3:1–4:24

3 Then the seventh month came, and the sons of Israel *were* in the cities. And the people gathered together as one man to Jerusalem. 2 Then Jeshua the son of Jozadak and his brothers the priests, and Zerubbabel the son of Shealtiel and his brothers arose and built the altar of the God of Israel to offer burnt offerings on it, as it is written in the law of Moses, the man of God. 3 So they set up the altar on its foundation, for they were terrified because of the peoples of the lands; and they offered burnt offerings on it to Yahweh, burnt offerings morning and evening. 4 They celebrated the Feast of Booths, as it is written, and *offered* the fixed *number of burnt offerings* daily, according to the *legal* judgment, as each day required; 5 and afterward *there was* a continual burnt offering, also for the new moons and for all the appointed times of Yahweh that were set apart as holy, and from everyone who offered a freewill offering to Yahweh. 6 From the first day of the seventh month they began to offer burnt offerings to Yahweh, but the foundation of the temple of Yahweh had not been laid. 7 Then they gave money to the masons and carpenters, and food, drink, and oil to the Sidonians and to the Tyrians, to bring cedar wood from Lebanon to the sea at Joppa, according to the permission they had from Cyrus king of Persia.

8 Now in the second year of their coming to the house of God at Jerusalem in the second month, Zerubbabel the son of Shealtiel and Jeshua the son of Jozadak and the rest of their brothers the priests and the Levites, and all who came from the captivity to Jerusalem, began *the work* and appointed the Levites from twenty years and older to direct the work of the house of Yahweh. 9 Then Jeshua *with* his sons and brothers stood united *with* Kadmiel and his sons, the sons of Judah *and* the sons of Henadad *with* their sons and brothers the Levites, to direct those who do the work in the house of God.

10 So the builders laid the foundation of the temple of Yahweh. Then the priests stood in their apparel with trumpets, and the Levites, the sons of Asaph, with

cymbals, to praise Yahweh according to the
directions of King David of Israel. 11 And
they sang, praising and giving thanks to
Yahweh, *saying*, "For He is good, for His lov-
ingkindness endures forever upon Israel."
And all the people shouted with a great
shout when they praised Yahweh because
the foundation of the house of Yahweh was
laid. 12 Yet many of the priests and Levites
and heads of fathers' *households*, the old
men who had seen the first house *of Yah-
weh*, were weeping with a loud voice when
the foundation of this house was laid before
their eyes, while many in loud shouts with
gladness *were* raising *their* voice, 13 so that
the people could not distinguish the voices
of the shouting of gladness from the voices
of the weeping of the people, for the people
were shouting with a loud shout, and those
voices were heard far away.

4 Then the adversaries of Judah and Ben-
jamin heard that the people of the exile
were building a temple to Yahweh, the God
of Israel, 2 so they approached Zerubbabel
and the heads of fathers' *households* and
said to them, "Let us build with you, for
we, like you, seek your God; and we have
been sacrificing to Him since the days of
Esarhaddon king of Assyria, who brought us
up here." 3 But Zerubbabel and Jeshua and
the rest of the heads of fathers' *households*
of Israel said to them, "You have nothing in
common with us in building a house to our
God; but we ourselves will together build to
Yahweh, the God of Israel, as King Cyrus, the
king of Persia has commanded us."
4 So the people of the land discouraged
the people of Judah and dismayed them
from building, 5 and hired counselors
against them to frustrate their counsel all
the days of Cyrus king of Persia, even until
the reign of Darius king of Persia.
6 Now in the reign of Ahasuerus, in
the beginning of his reign, they wrote an
accusation against the inhabitants of Judah
and Jerusalem.
7 And in the days of Artaxerxes, Bishlam,
Mithredath, Tabeel, and the rest of his col-
leagues wrote to Artaxerxes king of Persia;
and the text of the letter was written in
Aramaic and translated *from* Aramaic.
8 Rehum the commander and Shimshai
the scribe wrote a letter against Jerusalem
to King Artaxerxes, as follows—

9 then *wrote* Rehum the commander
and Shimshai the scribe and the rest
of their colleagues, the judges and
the lesser governors, the officials,
the secretaries, the men of Erech,
the Babylonians, the men of Susa,
that is, the Elamites, 10 and the rest
of the nations, which the great and
honorable Osnappar took away into
exile and settled in the city of Samaria
and in the rest of the region beyond
the River. And now—
11 this is the copy of the letter which they
sent to him:
"To King Artaxerxes: Your servants, the
men in the region beyond the River,
and now— 12 let it be known to the
king that the Jews who came up from
you have come to us at Jerusalem; they
are rebuilding the rebellious and evil
city and are completing the walls and
repairing the foundations. 13 Now let it
be known to the king, that if that city
is rebuilt and the walls are completed,
they will not give tribute, custom, or
toll, and it will damage the revenue
of the kings. 14 Now because we are
in the service of the palace, and it
is not fitting for us to see the king's
dishonor, therefore we have sent and
made known to the king, 15 that a
search be made in the record books
of your fathers. And you will find in
the record books and come to know
that that city is a rebellious city and
damaging to kings and provinces, and
that they have incited revolt within it
in past days; therefore that city was
laid waste. 16 We make known to the
king that if that city is rebuilt and
the walls completed, as a result you
will have no portion in *the province*
beyond the River."
17 *Then* the king sent an edict to Rehum
the commander, to Shimshai the scribe,
and to the rest of their colleagues who live
in Samaria and in the rest of *the provinces*
beyond the River: "Peace. And now— 18 the
document which you sent to us has been
plainly read before me.
19 "So a decree has been issued by me,
and a search has been made and it has
been found that that city has lifted
itself up against the kings in past days,
that rebellion and revolt have been

perpetrated in it, 20 that strong kings
have been over Jerusalem, even rulers
in all *the provinces* beyond the River,
and that tribute, custom, and toll were
given to them. 21 Now issue a decree
to make those men stop, that this city
may not be rebuilt until a decree is
issued by me. 22 And beware of being
negligent in doing this *matter*; why
should harm increase to damage the
kings?"

23 Then as soon as the copy of King
Artaxerxes' document was read before
Rehum and Shimshai the scribe and their
colleagues, they went in haste to Jerusalem
to the Jews and stopped them by force and
military.

24 Then the work on the house of God in
Jerusalem stopped, and it was stopped until
the second year of the reign of Darius king
of Persia.

Psalm 86:11–17

11 Teach me Your way, O Yahweh;
I will walk in Your truth;
Unite my heart to fear Your name.
12 I will give thanks to You, O Lord
my God, with all my heart,
And will glorify Your name forever.
13 For Your lovingkindness
toward me is great,
And You have delivered my
soul from Sheol below.

14 O God, arrogant men have
risen up against me,
And a band of ruthless men
have sought my life,
And they have not set You before them.
15 But You, O Lord, are a God
compassionate and gracious,
Slow to anger and abundant in
lovingkindness and truth.
16 Turn to me, and be gracious to me;
Oh grant Your strength to Your slave,
And save the son of Your maidservant.
17 Show me a sign for good,
That those who hate me may
see *it* and be ashamed,
Because You, O Yahweh,
have helped me and comforted me.

Proverbs 21:17–18

17 He who loves pleasure *will
become* a poor man;
He who loves wine and oil
will not become rich.
18 The wicked is a ransom
for the righteous,
And the treacherous is in the
place of the upright.

Acts 22:1–30

22 "Men, brothers, and fathers, hear my
defense which I now *offer* to you."
2 And when they heard that he was
addressing them in the Hebrew language,
they became even quieter; and he *said,
3 "I am a Jew, born in Tarsus of Cilicia, but
having been brought up in this city, having
been instructed at the feet of Gamaliel
according to the strictness of the law of
our fathers, being zealous for God just as
you all are today, 4 I persecuted this Way to
the death, binding and delivering both men
and women into prisons, 5 as also the high
priest and all the Council of the elders can
testify. From them I also received letters to
the brothers, and started off for Damascus
in order to bring even those who were there
to Jerusalem as prisoners to be punished.
6 "But it happened that as I was on my
way, approaching Damascus about noon-
time, a very bright light suddenly flashed
from heaven all around me, 7 and I fell to the
ground and heard a voice saying to me, 'Saul,
Saul, why are you persecuting Me?' 8 And I
answered, 'Who are You, Lord?' And He said
to me, 'I am Jesus the Nazarene, whom you
are persecuting.' 9 And those who were with
me beheld the light, to be sure, but did not
understand the voice of the One who was
speaking to me. 10 And I said, 'What should
I do, Lord?' And the Lord said to me, 'Rise
up and go on into Damascus, and there you
will be told of all that has been determined
for you to do.' 11 But since I could not see
because of the glory of that light, being led
by the hand by those who were with me, I
came into Damascus.
12 "Now a certain Ananias, a man who was
devout by the standard of the Law, *and* well
spoken of by all the Jews who lived there,
13 came to me, and standing near, said to me,
'Brother Saul, regain your sight!' And at that
very hour I regained my sight and *saw* him.
14 And he said, 'The God of our fathers has
appointed you to know His will and to see
the Righteous One and to hear a voice from
His mouth. 15 For you will be a witness for

Him to all men of what you have seen and heard. 16 Now why do you delay? Rise up and be baptized, and wash away your sins, calling on His name.'

17 "Now it happened when I returned to Jerusalem and was praying in the temple, that I fell into a trance, 18 and I saw Him saying to me, 'Hurry and get out of Jerusalem quickly, because they will not accept your witness about Me.' 19 And I said, 'Lord, they themselves understand that in one synagogue after another I used to imprison and beat those who believed in You. 20 And when the blood of Your witness Stephen was being shed, I also was standing by approving, and guarding the garments of those who were slaying him.' 21 And He said to me, 'Go! For I will send you far away to the Gentiles.'"

22 And they were listening to him up to this statement, and *then* they raised their voices and said, "Away with such a fellow from the earth, for he should not be allowed to live!" 23 And as they were crying out and throwing off their garments and tossing dust into the air, 24 the commander ordered him to be brought into the barracks, stating that he should be examined by flogging so that he might find out the reason why they were shouting against him that way. 25 But when they stretched him out with leather straps, Paul said to the centurion who was standing by, "Is it lawful for you to flog a man who is a Roman and uncondemned?" 26 And when the centurion heard *this*, he went to the commander and reported to him, saying, "What are you about to do? For this man is a Roman." 27 And the commander came and said to him, "Tell me, are you a Roman?" And he said, "Yes." 28 And the commander answered, "I acquired this citizenship with a large sum of money." And Paul said, "But I have been born *a citizen.*" 29 Therefore those who were about to examine him immediately withdrew from him; and the commander also was afraid when he learned that he was a Roman, and because he had bound him.

30 But on the next day, wishing to know for certain why he had been accused by the Jews, he released him and ordered the chief priests and all the Sanhedrin to come together, and brought Paul down and set him before them.

JULY 22

Ezra 5:1–6:22

5 And the prophets, Haggai the prophet and Zechariah the son of Iddo, prophesied to the Jews who were in Judah and Jerusalem in the name of the God of Israel, who was over them. 2 Then Zerubbabel the son of Shealtiel and Jeshua the son of Jozadak arose and began to rebuild the house of God which is in Jerusalem; and the prophets of God were with them supporting them.

3 At that time Tattenai, the governor of *the province* beyond the River, and Shethar-bozenai and their colleagues came to them and spoke to them thus, "Who issued you a decree to rebuild this house and to complete this structure?" 4 Then we told them accordingly what the names of the men were who were rebuilding this building. 5 But the eye of their God was on the elders of the Jews, and they did not stop them until a report could come to Darius, and then a document be returned concerning this.

6 *This is* the copy of the letter which Tattenai, the governor of *the province* beyond the River, and Shethar-bozenai and his colleagues the officials, who were beyond the River, sent to Darius the king. 7 They sent word to him in which it was written thus:

"To Darius the king, all peace. 8 Let it be known to the king that we have gone to the province of Judah, to the house of the great God, and it is being built with huge stones, and timber is being put within the walls; and that work is going on with all diligence and is succeeding in their hands. 9 Then we asked those elders and said to them thus, 'Who issued you a decree to rebuild this house and to complete this structure?' 10 And we also asked them their names in order to make known to you, *and* that we might write down the names of the men who were at their head.

11 "Thus they responded with a word to us, saying,

'We are the servants of the God of heaven and earth, and are rebuilding

the house that was built many years
ago, which a great king of Israel built
and completed. 12 But because our
fathers had provoked the God of
heaven to wrath, He gave them into
the hand of Nebuchadnezzar king of
Babylon, the Chaldean, *who* destroyed
this house and took the people away
into exile in Babylon. 13 However, in
the first year of Cyrus king of Babylon,
King Cyrus issued a decree to rebuild
this house of God. 14 Also the gold
and silver utensils of the house of
God, which Nebuchadnezzar had
taken from the temple in Jerusalem
and brought them to the temple of
Babylon, these King Cyrus took out
from the temple of Babylon, and they
were given to one whose name was
Sheshbazzar, whom he had appointed
governor. 15 He said to him, "Take
these articles, go *and* deposit them in
the temple in Jerusalem, and let the
house of God be rebuilt in its place."
16 Then that Sheshbazzar came *and*
laid the foundations of the house of
God in Jerusalem; and from then until
now it is being rebuilt, and it is not *yet*
finished.' 17 So now if it seems good to
the king, let a search be made in the
king's treasure house, which is there
in Babylon, if it be that a decree was
issued by King Cyrus to rebuild that
house of God in Jerusalem; and let the
king send to us his will concerning
this *matter*."

6 Then King Darius issued a decree, and a
search was made in the archives, where
the treasures were deposited in Babylon.
2 And in Ecbatana in the fortress, which is
in the province of Media, a scroll was found
and there was written in it as follows:
"Memorandum— 3 In the first year of
King Cyrus, Cyrus the king issued a
decree:
'*Concerning* the house of God in
Jerusalem, let that house, the place
where sacrifices are offered, be rebuilt
and let its foundations be retained, its
height being 60 cubits and its width
60 cubits; 4 with three layers of huge
stones and one layer of timbers. And
let the cost be given from the royal
treasury. 5 And also let the gold and
silver articles of the house of God,
which Nebuchadnezzar took out from
the temple in Jerusalem and brought
to Babylon, be returned and brought
to their places in the temple in
Jerusalem; and you shall deposit *them*
in the house of God.'

6 "Now Tattenai, governor of *the province*
beyond the River, Shethar-bozenai
and their colleagues, the officials of
the provinces beyond the River, keep
away from there. 7 Leave that work
on the house of God alone; let the
governor of the Jews and the elders
of the Jews rebuild that house of God
in its *designated* place. 8 Moreover, I
issue a decree concerning what you
shall do for those elders of Judah in
the rebuilding of that house of God:
the full cost is to be given to those
people from the royal treasury out of
the tribute of *the provinces* beyond the
River, and that without negligence.
9 Whatever is needed, both young
bulls, rams, and lambs for a burnt
offering to the God of heaven, and
wheat, salt, wine, and anointing
oil, according to what the priests in
Jerusalem say, *it* is to be given to them
daily without negligence, 10 that they
may bring sweet-smelling sacrifices
near to the God of heaven and pray for
the life of the king and his sons. 11 And
I issued a decree that any man who
violates this edict, a timber shall be
pulled out from his house and he shall
be impaled on it and his house shall
be made a refuse heap on account of
this. 12 May the God who has caused
His name to dwell there overthrow any
king or people who stretches out his
hand to change *it*, so as to destroy that
house of God in Jerusalem. I, Darius,
have issued *this* decree, let *it* be done
with all diligence!"
13 Then Tattenai, the governor of *the prov-
ince* beyond the River, Shethar-bozenai and
their colleagues carried out *the decree* with
all diligence, just as King Darius had sent.
14 And the elders of the Jews were building
and succeeding through the prophesying
of Haggai the prophet and Zechariah the
son of Iddo. So they built and completed
it according to the decree of the God of

Israel and the decree of Cyrus, Darius, and Artaxerxes king of Persia. 15 And this house was brought to completion on the third day of the month Adar; it was the sixth year of the reign of King Darius.

16 And the sons of Israel, the priests, the Levites and the rest of the exiles, celebrated the dedication of this house of God with joy. 17 They brought near for the dedication of this house of God 100 bulls, 200 rams, 400 lambs, and as a sin offering for all Israel 12 male goats, corresponding to the number of the tribes of Israel. 18 Then they appointed the priests to their sections and the Levites in their divisions for the service of God in Jerusalem, as it is written in the book of Moses.

19 And the exiles celebrated the Passover on the fourteenth of the first month. 20 For the priests and the Levites had cleansed themselves together; all of them were clean. Then they slaughtered the Passover *lamb* for all the exiles, both for their brothers the priests and for themselves. 21 Then the sons of Israel who returned from exile and all those who had separated themselves from the uncleanness of the nations of the land to *join* them, to seek Yahweh, the God of Israel, ate *the Passover*. 22 And they celebrated the Feast of Unleavened Bread seven days with gladness, for Yahweh had caused them to be glad and had turned the heart of the king of Assyria toward them to strengthen them in the work of the house of God, the God of Israel.

Psalm 87:1–7

1 His foundation is in the
holy mountains.
2 Yahweh loves the gates of Zion
More than all the dwelling
places of Jacob.
3 Glorious things are spoken of you,
O city of God. Selah.
4 "I shall mention Rahab and Babylon
among those who know Me;
Behold, Philistia and Tyre
with Ethiopia:
'This one was born there.'"
5 But of Zion it shall be said, "This one
and that one were born in her";
And the Most High Himself
will establish her.
6 Yahweh will count when He
registers the peoples,
"This one was born there." Selah.
7 And singers, just like the
dancers, *will all say*,
"All my springs are in you."

Proverbs 21:19–20

19 It is better to live in a desert land
Than with a contentious
and vexing woman.
20 There is desirable treasure and
oil in the abode of the wise,
But a foolish man swallows it up.

Acts 23:1–15

23 Now Paul, looking intently at the Sanhedrin, said, "Brothers, I have lived my life in all good conscience before God up to this day." 2 And the high priest Ananias commanded those standing beside him to strike him on the mouth. 3 Then Paul said to him, "God is going to strike you, you whitewashed wall! Do you sit to try me according to the Law, and in violation of the Law order me to be struck?" 4 But those standing nearby said, "Do you revile the high priest of God?" 5 And Paul said, "I was not aware, brothers, that he was high priest; for it is written, 'YOU SHALL NOT SPEAK EVIL OF A RULER OF YOUR PEOPLE.'"

6 But knowing that one group were Sadducees and the other Pharisees, Paul *began* crying out in the Sanhedrin, "Brothers, I am a Pharisee, a son of Pharisees; I am on trial for the hope and resurrection of the dead!" 7 As he said this, there was dissension between the Pharisees and Sadducees, and the assembly was divided. 8 For the Sadducees say that there is no resurrection, nor an angel, nor a spirit, but the Pharisees acknowledge them all. 9 And there occurred a great outcry; and some of the scribes of the Pharisaic party stood up and *began to* argue heatedly, saying, "We find nothing wrong with this man. Suppose a spirit or an angel has spoken to him?" 10 And as a great dissension was developing, because the commander was afraid Paul would be torn to pieces by them, he ordered the troops to go down and take him away from them by force, and bring him into the barracks.

11 But on that very night, the Lord stood at his side and said, "Take courage; for as you have solemnly borne witness to My cause at Jerusalem, so you must bear witness at Rome also."

12 Now when it was day, the Jews formed
a conspiracy and bound themselves under
a curse, saying that they would neither eat
nor drink until they had killed Paul. 13 And
there were more than forty who formed this
scheme. 14 They came to the chief priests
and the elders and said, "We have bound
ourselves under a curse to taste nothing
until we have killed Paul. 15 So now you,
along with the Sanhedrin, notify the com-
mander to bring him down to you, as though
you were going to determine his case more
carefully; and we for our part are ready to
slay him before he comes near."

We shall not benefit from reading the Old Testament unless we look for and meditate on the glory of Christ in its pages.

— JOHN OWEN

JULY 23

Ezra 7:1–8:36

7 Now after these things, in the reign of
Artaxerxes king of Persia, *there went up*
Ezra son of Seraiah, son of Azariah, son of
Hilkiah, 2 son of Shallum, son of Zadok, son
of Ahitub, 3 son of Amariah, son of Azariah,
son of Meraioth, 4 son of Zerahiah, son of
Uzzi, son of Bukki, 5 son of Abishua, son
of Phinehas, son of Eleazar, son of Aaron
the chief priest. 6 This Ezra went up from
Babylon, and he was a scribe skilled in the
law of Moses, which Yahweh, the God of
Israel had given; and the king granted him
all he requested because the hand of Yahweh
his God *was* upon him. 7 And some of the
sons of Israel and some of the priests, the
Levites, the singers, the gatekeepers, and the
temple servants went up to Jerusalem in the
seventh year of King Artaxerxes.

8 He came to Jerusalem in the fifth month,
which was in the seventh year of the king.
9 For on the first of the first month he began
to go up from Babylon; and on the first of the
fifth month he came to Jerusalem, because
the good hand of his God *was* upon him.
10 For Ezra had set his heart to study the law
of Yahweh and to practice *it*, and to teach *His*
statute and judgment in Israel.

11 *Now this is the copy of the* letter which
King Artaxerxes gave to Ezra the priest, the
scribe, learned in the words of the com-
mandments of Yahweh and His statutes to
Israel:

12 "Artaxerxes, king of kings, to Ezra the
priest, the scribe of the law of the God
of heaven, perfect *peace*. And now—
13 I have issued a decree that any of
the people of Israel and their priests
and the Levites in my kingdom who
freely offer to go to Jerusalem, may go
with you. 14 Forasmuch as you are sent
from before the king and his seven
counselors to inquire concerning Judah
and Jerusalem according to the law of
your God which is in your hand, 15 and
to bring the silver and gold, which the
king and his counselors have freely
offered to the God of Israel, whose
dwelling is in Jerusalem, 16 and all the
silver and gold which you find in the
whole province of Babylon, along with
the freewill offering of the people and
of the priests, who offered willingly
for the house of their God which
is in Jerusalem; 17 with this money,
therefore, you shall with all diligence
buy bulls, rams, and lambs, with
their grain offerings and their drink
offerings, and bring them near to the
altar of the house of your God which
is in Jerusalem. 18 And whatever seems
good to you and to your brothers to
do with the rest of the silver and gold,
you may do according to the will of
your God. 19 Also the utensils which
are given to you for the service of
the house of your God, deliver in full
before the God of Jerusalem. 20 The rest
of the needs for the house of your God,
which may fall upon you to provide,
provide *for it* from the royal treasury.

21 "So I, even I, King Artaxerxes, issue a
decree to all the treasurers who are *in*

the provinces beyond the River, that
whatever Ezra the priest, the scribe
of the law of the God of heaven, may
ask of you, it shall be done with all
diligence, 22 *even* up to 100 talents of
silver, 100 kors of wheat, 100 baths of
wine, 100 baths of oil, and salt without
written order. 23 Whatever is decreed
by the God of heaven, let it be done
with zeal for the house of the God of
heaven, so that there will not be wrath
against the kingdom of the king and
his sons. 24 We also make known to
you that it is not allowed to impose
tribute, custom, or toll *on* any of the
priests, Levites, singers, doorkeepers,
temple servants, or *other* servants of
this house of God.

25 "And you, Ezra, according to the
wisdom of your God which is in your
hand, appoint magistrates and judges
that they may judge all the people who
are in *the province* beyond the River,
even all those who know the laws of
your God; and to anyone who does not
know *the laws*, you shall make *them*
known. 26 Whoever will not do the law
of your God and the law of the king,
let judgment be done to him with all
diligence, whether for death or for
banishment or for confiscation of
goods or for imprisonment."

27 Blessed be Yahweh, the God of our
fathers, who has put *such a thing* as this in
the king's heart, to beautify the house of
Yahweh which is in Jerusalem, 28 and has
extended lovingkindness to me before the
king and his counselors and before all the
king's mighty princes. Thus I was strength-
ened according to the hand of Yahweh my
God upon me, and I gathered chief men
from Israel to go up with me.

8 Now these are the heads of their fathers'
households and the genealogical records
of those who went up with me from Babylon
in the reign of King Artaxerxes:
2 of the sons of Phinehas, Gershom;
of the sons of Ithamar, Daniel;
of the sons of David, Hattush;
3 of the sons of Shecaniah *who was* of
the sons of Parosh, Zechariah and
with him 150 males *who were in* the
genealogical records;
4 of the sons of Pahath-moab,
Eliehoenai the son of Zerahiah and
200 males with him;
5 of the sons of Zattu, Shecaniah, the
son of Jahaziel and 300 males with
him;
6 and of the sons of Adin, Ebed the son
of Jonathan and 50 males with him;
7 and of the sons of Elam, Jeshaiah the
son of Athaliah and 70 males with
him;
8 and of the sons of Shephatiah,
Zebadiah the son of Michael and 80
males with him;
9 of the sons of Joab, Obadiah the son of
Jehiel and 218 males with him;
10 and of the sons of Bani, Shelomith, the
son of Josiphiah and 160 males with
him;
11 and of the sons of Bebai, Zechariah
the son of Bebai and 28 males with
him;
12 and of the sons of Azgad, Johanan the
son of Hakkatan and 110 males with
him;
13 and of the sons of Adonikam, the
last ones, these being their names,
Eliphelet, Jeiel, and Shemaiah, and 60
males with them;
14 and of the sons of Bigvai, Uthai, and
Zabbud, and 70 males with them.

15 Now I gathered them at the river that
runs to Ahava, where we camped for three
days. And I observed the people and the
priests, but I did not find any Levites there.
16 So I sent for Eliezer, Ariel, Shemaiah,
Elnathan, Jarib, Elnathan, Nathan, Zech-
ariah, and Meshullam, chief men, and for
Joiarib and Elnathan, teachers. 17 I sent
them out to Iddo the chief man at the place
Casiphia; and I put words in their mouths
to say to Iddo *and* his brothers, the temple
servants at the place Casiphia, *that is*, to
bring ministers to us for the house of our
God. 18 So, according to the good hand of
our God upon us, they brought us a man
of insight of the sons of Mahli, the son of
Levi, the son of Israel, namely Sherebiah,
and his sons and brothers, 18 men; 19 and
Hashabiah and Jeshaiah of the sons of
Merari, with his brothers and their sons,
20 men; 20 and 220 of the temple servants,
whom David and the princes had given
for the service of the Levites, all of them
designated by name.

21 Then I called for a fast there at the river
of Ahava, that we might humble ourselves
before our God to seek from Him a direct
journey for us, our little ones, and all our
possessions. 22 For I was ashamed to ask
from the king for a military force and horse-
men to help us against the enemy on the
way, because we had said to the king, "The
hand of our God is upon all those who seek
Him, for *their* good, but His strength and
His anger are against all those who forsake
Him." 23 So we fasted and sought our God
concerning this *matter*, and He was moved
by our entreaty.

24 Then I set apart twelve of the leading
priests, Sherebiah, Hashabiah, and with
them ten of their brothers; 25 and I weighed
out to them the silver, the gold, and the
utensils, the contribution for the house of
our God which the king and his counselors
and his princes and all Israel present *there*
had offered. 26 Thus I weighed into their
hands 650 talents of silver, and silver uten-
sils *worth* 100 talents, *and* 100 gold talents,
27 and 20 gold bowls *worth* 1,000 darics, and
two utensils of fine shiny bronze, precious
as gold. 28 Then I said to them, "You are holy
to Yahweh, and the utensils are holy; and the
silver and the gold are a freewill offering to
Yahweh, the God of your fathers. 29 Watch
and keep *them* until you weigh *them* before
the officials of the priests, the Levites and
the officials of the fathers' *households* of
Israel at Jerusalem, *in* the chambers of the
house of Yahweh." 30 So the priests and the
Levites accepted the weighed out silver
and gold and the utensils, to bring *them* to
Jerusalem to the house of our God.

31 Then we set out from the river Ahava
on the twelfth of the first month to go to
Jerusalem; and the hand of our God was
upon us, and He delivered us from the hand
of the enemy and the ambushes by the way.
32 Thus we came to Jerusalem and remained
there three days.

33 On the fourth day the silver and the
gold and the utensils were weighed out
in the house of our God into the hand of
Meremoth the son of Uriah the priest, and
with him *was* Eleazar the son of Phinehas;
and with them *were* the Levites, Jozabad
the son of Jeshua and Noadiah the son of
Binnui. 34 Everything *was* numbered *and*
weighed, and all the weight was written
down at that time.

35 The exiles who had come from the
captivity brought burnt offerings near to the
God of Israel: 12 bulls for all Israel, 96 rams,
77 lambs, 12 male goats for a sin offering,
all as a burnt offering to Yahweh. 36 Then
they gave the king's edicts to the king's
satraps and to the governors *in the provinces*
beyond the River, and they supported the
people and the house of God.

Psalm 88:1–5

1 O Yahweh, the God of my salvation,
I have cried out by day and
throughout the night before You.
2 Let my prayer come before You;
Incline Your ear to my cry
of lamentation!
3 For my soul has been saturated
with calamities,
And my life has reached Sheol.
4 I am counted among those
who go down to the pit;
I am like a man without strength,
5 Released among the dead,
Like the slain who lie in the grave,
Whom You remember no more,
And they are cut off from Your hand.

Proverbs 21:21–22

21 He who pursues righteousness
and lovingkindness
Finds life, righteousness, and glory.
22 A wise man goes up to the
city of the mighty
And brings down the stronghold
in which they trust.

Acts 23:16–35

16 But when the son of Paul's sister heard
of their ambush, he came and entered the
barracks and reported *it* to Paul. 17 And Paul
called one of the centurions to him and said,
"Lead this young man to the commander,
for he has something to report to him." 18 So
he took him and led him to the commander
and *said, "Paul the prisoner called me to
him and asked me to lead this young man
to you since he has something to tell you."
19 And the commander took him by the
hand and stepping aside, *began to* inquire
of him privately, "What is it that you have
to report to me?" 20 And he said, "The Jews
have agreed to ask you to bring Paul down
tomorrow to the Sanhedrin, as though
they were going to inquire somewhat

more carefully about him. 21 So do not be persuaded by them, for more than forty of them—who have bound themselves under a curse not to eat or drink until they slay him—are lying in wait for him and now they are ready and waiting for the promise from you." 22 So the commander let the young man go, instructing him, "Tell no one that you have notified me of these things."

23 And when he called to him two of the centurions, he said, "Make ready two hundred soldiers, seventy horsemen, and two hundred spearmen to proceed to Caesarea by the third hour of the night, 24 and provide mounts to put Paul on and bring him safely to Felix the governor." 25 And he wrote a letter having this form:

26 "Claudius Lysias, to the most excellent governor Felix, greetings.

27 "When this man was arrested by the Jews and was about to be slain by them, I came up to them with the troops and rescued him, having learned that he was a Roman. 28 And wanting to ascertain the charge for which they were accusing him, I brought him down to their Sanhedrin; 29 and I found him to be accused over questions about their Law, but under no accusation deserving death or imprisonment.

30 "And when I was informed that there would be a plot against the man, I sent him to you at once, also instructing his accusers to speak against him before you."

31 So the soldiers, according to their orders, took Paul and brought him by night to Antipatris. 32 But the next day, leaving the horsemen to go on with him, they returned to the barracks. 33 When these had come to Caesarea and delivered the letter to the governor, they also presented Paul to him. 34 And when he had read it, he asked from what province he was, and when he learned that he was from Cilicia, 35 he said, "I will give you a hearing after your accusers arrive also," giving orders for him to be kept in Herod's Praetorium.

JULY 24

Ezra 9:1–10:44

9 Now when these things had been completed, the princes approached me, saying, "The people of Israel and the priests and the Levites have not separated themselves from the peoples of the lands, according to their abominations, *those* of the Canaanites, the Hittites, the Perizzites, the Jebusites, the Ammonites, the Moabites, the Egyptians and the Amorites. 2 For they have taken some of their daughters *as wives* for themselves and for their sons, so that the holy seed has intermingled with the peoples of the lands; indeed, the hands of the princes and the officials have been foremost in this unfaithfulness." 3 When I heard about this matter, I tore my garment and my robe, and pulled some of the hair from my head and my beard, and sat down in consternation. 4 Then everyone who trembled at the words of the God of Israel on account of the unfaithfulness of the exiles gathered to me, and I sat appalled until the evening offering.

5 But at the evening offering I arose from my affliction, even with my garment and my robe torn, and I fell on my knees and stretched out my hands to Yahweh my God; 6 and I said, "O my God, I am ashamed and humiliated to lift up my face to You, my God, for our iniquities have multiplied above our heads and our guilt has become great even to the heavens. 7 Since the days of our fathers to this day we *have been* in great guilt, and on account of our iniquities we, our kings *and* our priests have been given into the hand of the kings of the lands, to the sword, to captivity, and to plunder and to open shame, as *it is* this day. 8 But now for a brief moment grace has been *shown* from Yahweh our God, to leave us an escaped remnant and to give us a peg in His holy place, that our God may enlighten our eyes and give us a little reviving in our slavery. 9 For we are slaves; yet in our slavery our God has not forsaken us, but has extended lovingkindness to us before the kings of Persia, to give us reviving to raise up the house of our God, to restore its

waste places, and to give us a wall in Judah and Jerusalem.

10 “So now, our God, what shall we say after this? For we have forsaken Your commandments, 11 which You have commanded by the hand of Your slaves the prophets, saying, ‘The land which you are entering to possess is an impure land with the impurity of the peoples of the lands, with their abominations which have filled it from end to end, *and* with their uncleanness. 12 So now do not give your daughters to their sons nor take their daughters to your sons, and never seek their peace or their prosperity, that you may be strong and eat the good *things* of the land and leave *it* as a possession to your sons forever.’ 13 After all that has come upon us for our evil deeds and our great guilt, since You our God have requited *us* less than our iniquities *deserve,* and have given us an escaped remnant as this, 14 shall we again break Your commandments and intermarry with the peoples who commit these abominations? Would You not be angry with us to the point of destruction, until there is no remnant nor any who escape? 15 O Yahweh, the God of Israel, You are righteous, for we have been left an escaped remnant, as *it is* this day; behold, we are before You in our guilt, for no one can stand before You because of this.”

10 Now while Ezra was praying and making confession, weeping and prostrating himself before the house of God, a very large assembly, men, women, and children, gathered to him from Israel; for the people wept bitterly. 2 And Shecaniah the son of Jehiel, one of the sons of Elam, answered and said to Ezra, “We have been unfaithful to our God and have married foreign women from the peoples of the land; yet now there is hope for Israel in spite of this. 3 So now let us cut a covenant with our God to put away all the wives and their children, according to the counsel of *my lord and of those* who tremble at the commandment of our God; and let it be done according to the law. 4 Arise! For *this* matter is your responsibility, but we will be with you; be strong and act.”

5 Then Ezra arose and made the leading priests, the Levites and all Israel, swear *an oath* that they would do according to this word; so they swore *an oath.* 6 Then Ezra arose from before the house of God and went into the chamber of Jehohanan the son of Eliashib. He went there, *but* he did not eat bread nor drink water, for he was mourning over the unfaithfulness of the exiles. 7 And they made a proclamation throughout Judah and Jerusalem to all the exiles, that they should gather at Jerusalem, 8 and that whoever would not come within three days, according to the counsel of the prince and the elders, all his possessions should be devoted to destruction and he himself separated from the assembly of the exiles.

9 So all the men of Judah and Benjamin gathered at Jerusalem within the three days. It was the ninth month on the twentieth of the month, and all the people sat in the open square *before* the house of God, trembling because of this matter and the heavy rain. 10 Then Ezra the priest arose and said to them, “You have been unfaithful and have married foreign wives adding to the guilt of Israel. 11 So now, make confession to Yahweh, the God of your fathers, and do His will; and separate yourselves from the peoples of the land and from the foreign wives.” 12 Then all the assembly answered and said with a loud voice, “This is so! As you have said, so it is our duty to do. 13 But there are many people; it is the rainy season, and we are not able to stand outside. Nor *can* the task *be done* in one or two days, for we have transgressed greatly in this matter. 14 Let our princes stand in for the whole assembly, and let all those in our cities who have married foreign wives come at set times, together with the elders and judges of each city, until the burning anger of our God on account of this matter is turned away from us.” 15 However, Jonathan the son of Asahel and Jahzeiah the son of Tikvah stood against this, with Meshullam and Shabbethai the Levite helping them.

16 But the exiles did so. And Ezra the priest separated out men *who were* heads of fathers’ *households* for *each of* their father’s households, all of them by name. So they convened on the first day of the tenth month to investigate the matter. 17 And they completed *investigating* all the men who had married foreign wives by the first day of the first month.

18 Among the sons of the priests who had married foreign wives were found of

the sons of Jeshua the son of Jozadak, and
his brothers: Maaseiah, Eliezer, Jarib and
Gedaliah. 19 They gave their hand *in pledge*
to put away their wives, and being guilty,
they offered a ram of the flock for their guilt.

20 Of the sons of Immer *there were*
Hanani and Zebadiah;
21 and of the sons of Harim: Maaseiah,
Elijah, Shemaiah, Jehiel and Uzziah;
22 and of the sons of Pashhur: Elioenai,
Maaseiah, Ishmael, Nethanel, Jozabad
and Elasah.

23 Of Levites *there were* Jozabad, Shimei,
Kelaiah (that is, Kelita), Pethahiah,
Judah and Eliezer.

24 Of the singers *there was* Eliashib; and
of the gatekeepers: Shallum, Telem
and Uri.

25 Of Israel, of the sons of Parosh *there*
were Ramiah, Izziah, Malchijah,
Mijamin, Eleazar, Malchijah and
Benaiah;
26 and of the sons of Elam: Mattaniah,
Zechariah, Jehiel, Abdi, Jeremoth and
Elijah;
27 and of the sons of Zattu: Elioenai,
Eliashib, Mattaniah, Jeremoth, Zabad
and Aziza;
28 and of the sons of Bebai: Jehohanan,
Hananiah, Zabbai *and* Athlai;
29 and of the sons of Bani: Meshullam,
Malluch and Adaiah, Jashub, Sheal
and Jeremoth;
30 and of the sons of Pahath-moab: Adna,
Chelal, Benaiah, Maaseiah, Mattaniah,
Bezalel, Binnui and Manasseh;
31 and *of* the sons of Harim: Eliezer,
Isshijah, Malchijah, Shemaiah,
Shimeon,
32 Benjamin, Malluch *and* Shemariah;
33 of the sons of Hashum: Mattenai,
Mattattah, Zabad, Eliphelet, Jeremai,
Manasseh *and* Shimei;
34 of the sons of Bani: Maadai, Amram,
Uel,
35 Benaiah, Bedeiah, Cheluhi,
36 Vaniah, Meremoth, Eliashib,
37 Mattaniah, Mattenai, Jaasu,
38 Bani, Binnui, Shimei,
39 Shelemiah, Nathan, Adaiah,
40 Machnadebai, Shashai, Sharai,
41 Azarel, Shelemiah, Shemariah,
42 Shallum, Amariah *and* Joseph.
43 Of the sons of Nebo *there were* Jeiel,
Mattithiah, Zabad, Zebina, Jaddai, Joel
and Benaiah.

44 All these had taken up foreign women *as*
wives, and some of them had wives *by whom*
they had children.

Psalm 88:6–10

6 You have put me in the pit far below,
In dark places, in the depths.
7 Your wrath lies upon me,
And You afflict me with all Your
breaking waves. Selah.
8 You have removed my
acquaintances far from me;
You have set me as an
abomination to them;
I am shut up and cannot go out.
9 My eye has wasted away
because of affliction;
I have called upon You every
day, O Yahweh;
I have spread out my hands to You.

10 Will You do wonders for the dead?
Will the departed spirits rise *and*
praise You? Selah.

Proverbs 21:23–24

23 He who keeps his mouth
and his tongue,
Keeps his soul from troubles.
24 "Arrogant," "Haughty,"
"Scoffer," are his names,
Who acts with arrogant fury.

Acts 24:1–27

24 Now after five days the high priest
Ananias came down with some
elders, with an attorney *named* Tertullus,
and they brought charges to the governor
against Paul. 2 And after *Paul* had been
summoned, Tertullus began to accuse him,
saying,
"As we have attained much peace
through you—and because by your pro-
vision reforms are being carried out for
this nation— 3 we welcome *this* in every
way and everywhere, most excellent Felix,
with all thankfulness. 4 But, that I may not
weary you any further, I plead with you by
your forbearance to hear us briefly. 5 For
we have found this man a real pest and
a fellow who stirs up dissension among

all the Jews throughout the world, and a ringleader of the sect of the Nazarenes. 6 And he even tried to desecrate the temple; and then we arrested him. [We wanted to judge him according to our own Law. 7 But Lysias the commander came along, and with much violence took him out of our hands, 8 ordering his accusers to come before you.] By examining him yourself concerning all these matters you will be able to ascertain the things of which we accuse him." 9 And the Jews also joined in the attack, asserting that these things were so.

10 And when the governor had nodded for him to speak, Paul answered:

"Knowing that for many years you have been a judge to this nation, I cheerfully make my defense, 11 since you are able to ascertain the fact that no more than twelve days ago I went up to Jerusalem to worship. 12 And neither in the temple, nor in the synagogues, nor across the city did they find me carrying on a discussion with anyone or causing a riot. 13 Nor are they able to prove to you of what they are now accusing me. 14 But this I confess to you, that according to the Way, which they call a sect, I do serve the God of our fathers, believing everything that is in accordance with the Law and that is written in the Prophets; 15 having a hope in God, for which these men are waiting, that there shall certainly be a resurrection of both the righteous and the unrighteous. 16 In view of this, I also do my best to maintain always a conscience without fault *both* before God and before men. 17 Now after several years I came to bring alms to my nation and offerings; 18 in which they found me, having been purified in the temple, without *any* crowd or uproar. But *there were* some Jews from Asia— 19 who ought to have been present before you and to make accusation, if they should have anything against me. 20 Or else let these men themselves tell what wrongdoing they found when I stood before the Sanhedrin, 21 other than for this one statement which I shouted out while standing among them, 'For the resurrection of the dead I am on trial before you today.'"

22 But Felix, having a more accurate knowledge about the Way, put them off, saying, "When Lysias the commander comes down, I will decide your case." 23 Then he gave orders to the centurion for him to be kept in custody and *yet* have *some* rest, and not to prevent any of his friends from ministering to him.

24 But some days later Felix arrived with Drusilla, his wife who was a Jewess, and summoned Paul and heard him *speak* about faith in Christ Jesus. 25 But as he was discussing righteousness, self-control, and the judgment to come, Felix became frightened and answered, "Go away for the present, and when I find time I will call for you." 26 At the same time, he was also hoping that money would be given him by Paul; therefore he also used to summon for him quite often and converse with him. 27 But after two years had passed, Felix was succeeded by Porcius Festus, and wishing to do the Jews a favor, Felix left Paul imprisoned.

JULY 25

Nehemiah 1:1–2:20

1 The words of Nehemiah the son of Hacaliah.

Now it happened in the month Chislev, *in* the twentieth year—and I was in Susa the *capitol*— 2 *that* Hanani, one of my brothers, and some men from Judah came; and I asked them concerning the Jews who had escaped and remain from the captivity, and about Jerusalem. 3 They said to me, "The remnant there in the province who remain from the captivity are in great calamity and reproach, and the wall of Jerusalem is broken down and its gates are burned with fire."

4 Now it happened that when I heard these words, I sat down and wept and mourned for days; and I was fasting and praying before the God of heaven. 5 I said, "I beseech You, O Yahweh, the God of heaven, the great and fearsome God, who keeps the covenant and lovingkindness for those who love Him and keep His commandments, 6 let Your ear now be attentive and Your eyes open to hear the prayer of Your slave which I am praying before You today, day and night, on behalf of the sons of Israel Your slaves, confessing the sins of the sons of Israel which we have sinned against You; I and my father's

house have sinned. 7 We have worked *in* utter destruction against You and have not kept the commandments, nor the statutes, nor the judgments which You commanded Your servant Moses. 8 Remember the word which You commanded Your servant Moses, saying, '*If* you are unfaithful, I will scatter you among the peoples; 9 but *if* you return to Me and keep My commandments and do them, though those of you who have been banished were at the ends of the sky, I will gather them from there and will bring them to the place where I have chosen to cause My name to dwell.' 10 They are Your slaves and Your people whom You redeemed by Your great power and by Your strong hand. 11 O Lord, I beseech You, may Your ear be attentive to the prayer of Your slave and the prayer of Your slaves who delight to fear Your name, and make Your slave successful today and grant him compassion before this man."

Now I was the cupbearer to the king.

2 Now it happened in the month Nisan, in the twentieth year of King Artaxerxes, that wine *was* before him, and I took up the wine and gave it to the king. Now I had not been sad in his presence. 2 So the king said to me, "Why is your face sad though you are not sick? This is nothing but sadness of heart." Then I was very much afraid. 3 I said to the king, "Let the king live forever. Why should my face not be sad when the city, the place of my fathers' tombs, lies waste and its gates have been consumed by fire?" 4 Then the king said to me, "What would you request?" So I prayed to the God of heaven. 5 I said to the king, "If it is good for the king, and if your servant is good before you, send me to Judah, to the city of my fathers' tombs, that I may rebuild it." 6 Then the king said to me, the queen sitting beside him, "How long will your journey be, and when will you return?" So it was good to the king to send me, and I gave him a set time. 7 And I said to the king, "If it is good to the king, let letters be given me for the governors *of the provinces* beyond the River, that they may allow me to pass through until I come to Judah, 8 and a letter to Asaph the keeper of the king's forest, that he may give me timber to make beams for the gates of the fortress which is by the house *of God*, for the wall of the city and for the house to which I will go." And the king granted *them* to me because the good hand of my God *was* on me.

9 Then I came to the governors *of the provinces* beyond the River and gave them the king's letters. Now the king had sent with me commanders of the military force and horsemen. 10 Then Sanballat the Horonite and Tobiah the Ammonite official heard *about it*, and it was a very great evil to them that someone had come to seek the good of the sons of Israel.

11 So I came to Jerusalem and was there three days. 12 And I arose in the night, I and a few men with me. I did not tell anyone what my God was putting into my heart to do for Jerusalem; and there was no animal with me except the animal on which I was riding. 13 So I went out at night by the Valley Gate in the direction of the Dragon's Spring and *on* to the Dung Gate, inspecting the walls of Jerusalem which were broken down and its gates which were consumed by fire. 14 Then I passed on to the Spring Gate and the King's Pool, but there was no place for my animal to pass. 15 So I went up at night by the ravine and inspected the wall. Then I turned and entered the Valley Gate and turned around. 16 Now the officials did not know where I had gone or what I was doing; nor had I as yet told the Jews, the priests, the nobles, the officials, or the rest who were doing the work.

17 Then I said to them, "You see the calamity we are in, that Jerusalem lies waste and its gates burned by fire. Come, let us rebuild the wall of Jerusalem so that we will no longer be a reproach." 18 And I told them how the hand of my God had been good to me and also about the king's words which he had said to me. Then they said, "Let us arise and build." So they strengthened their hands for the good *work*. 19 But Sanballat the Horonite and Tobiah the Ammonite official and Geshem the Arab heard *it*. And they mocked us and despised us and said, "What is this thing you are doing? Are you rebelling against the king?" 20 So I responded to them with a word and said to them, "The God of heaven will give us success; therefore we His slaves will arise and build, but you have no portion, right, or remembrance in Jerusalem."

Psalm 88:11–18

11 Will Your lovingkindness be
recounted in the grave,

Your faithfulness in Abaddon?
12 Will Your wonders be known
in the darkness?
And Your righteousness in the
land of forgetfulness?

13 But as for me, O Yahweh, I have
cried out to You for help,
And in the morning my prayer
comes before You.
14 O Yahweh, why do You reject my soul?
Why do You hide Your face from me?
15 I *have been* afflicted and about to
breathe my last from *my* youth on;
I bear Your terrors; I am overcome.
16 Your burning anger has
passed over me;
Your horrors have destroyed me.
17 They have surrounded me
like water all day long;
They have encompassed me altogether.
18 You have removed lover and
friend far from me;
My acquaintances are *in* darkness.

Proverbs 21:25–26

25 The desire of the sluggard
puts him to death,
For his hands refuse to work;
26 All day long he is insatiably craving,
While the righteous gives and
does not hold back.

Acts 25:1–27

25 Festus then, having arrived in the
province, after three days went
up to Jerusalem from Caesarea. 2 And the
chief priests and the leading men of the
Jews brought charges against Paul, and
they were pleading with him, 3 requesting
a favor against Paul, that he might have
him brought to Jerusalem (while they set
an ambush to kill him on the way). 4 Festus
then answered that Paul was being kept in
custody at Caesarea and that he himself
was about to leave shortly. 5 "Therefore," he
*said, "let the influential men among you go
down there with me, and if there is anything
wrong about the man, let them accuse him."
6 And after he had spent not more than
eight or ten days among them, he went
down to Caesarea, and on the next day
he took his seat on the judgment seat and
ordered Paul to be brought. 7 And after Paul
arrived, the Jews who had come down from
Jerusalem stood around him, bringing many
and serious charges against him which
they could not prove, 8 while Paul said in
his own defense, "I have committed no sin
either against the Law of the Jews or against
the temple or against Caesar." 9 But Festus,
wishing to do the Jews a favor, answered
Paul and said, "Are you willing to go up to
Jerusalem and to be tried before me on these
matters?" 10 But Paul said, "I am standing
before Caesar's judgment seat, where I ought
to be tried. I have done no wrong to *the* Jews,
as you also very well know. 11 If, then, I am
a wrongdoer and have committed anything
worthy of death, I do not refuse to die; but if
none of those things is *true* of which these
men accuse me, no one can hand me over
to them. I appeal to Caesar." 12 Then when
Festus had conferred with his council, he
answered, "You have appealed to Caesar, to
Caesar you shall go."
13 Now when several days had passed,
King Agrippa and Bernice arrived at Cae-
sarea and greeted Festus. 14 And while they
were spending many days there, Festus laid
Paul's case before the king, saying, "There
is a man who was left as a prisoner by Felix;
15 and when I was at Jerusalem, the chief
priests and the elders of the Jews brought
charges against him, asking for a sentence
of condemnation against him. 16 I answered
them that it is not the custom of the Romans
to hand over any man before the accused
meets his accusers face to face and has an
opportunity to make his defense against
the charges. 17 So after they had assembled
here, I did not delay, but on the next day
took my seat on the judgment seat and
ordered the man to be brought before me.
18 When the accusers stood up, they were
not bringing any charges against him for
the evil deeds I was expecting, 19 but they
had some points of disagreement with him
about their own religion and about a certain
Jesus, a dead man whom Paul asserted to
be alive. 20 And being perplexed about how
to investigate such matters, I was asking
whether he was willing to go to Jerusalem
and there to be tried on these matters. 21 But
when Paul appealed to be held in custody for
the Emperor's decision, I ordered him to be
kept in custody until I send him to Caesar."
22 Then Agrippa *said* to Festus, "I also would
like to hear the man myself." "Tomorrow,"
he *said, "you shall hear him."

23 So, on the next day when Agrippa came together with Bernice amid great pomp, and entered the hall accompanied by the commanders and the prominent men of the city, at the order of Festus, Paul was brought in. 24 And Festus *said, "King Agrippa, and all you gentlemen here present with us, you see this man about whom all the people of the Jews appealed to me, both at Jerusalem and here, loudly declaring that he ought not to live any longer. 25 But I found that he had committed nothing worthy of death, and since he himself appealed to the Emperor, I decided to send him. 26 Yet I have nothing definite about him to write to my lord. Therefore I have brought him before you *all* and especially before you, King Agrippa, so that after the investigation has taken place, I may have something to write. 27 For it seems absurd to me in sending a prisoner, not to indicate also the charges against him."

JULY 26

Nehemiah 3:1–5:19

3 Then Eliashib the high priest arose with his brothers the priests and built the Sheep Gate; they set it apart as holy and made its doors stand. And they set apart as holy the wall to the Tower of the Hundred *and* the Tower of Hananel. 2 Next to him the men of Jericho built, and next to them Zaccur the son of Imri built.

3 Now the sons of Hassenaah built the Fish Gate; they laid its beams and made its doors stand with its bolts and bars. 4 Next to them Meremoth the son of Uriah the son of Hakkoz made repairs. And next to them Meshullam the son of Berechiah the son of Meshezabel made repairs. And next to them Zadok the son of Baana *also* made repairs. 5 Moreover, next to them the Tekoites made repairs, but their nobles did not support the service of their masters.

6 Joiada the son of Paseah and Meshullam the son of Besodeiah repaired the Old Gate; they laid its beams and made its doors stand with its bolts and its bars. 7 Next to them Melatiah the Gibeonite and Jadon the Meronothite, the men of Gibeon and of Mizpah, also made repairs for the official seat of the governor *of the province* beyond the River. 8 Next to him Uzziel the son of Harhaiah of the goldsmiths made repairs. And next to him Hananiah, one of the perfumers, made repairs, and they restored Jerusalem as far as the Broad Wall. 9 Next to them Rephaiah the son of Hur, the official of half the district of Jerusalem, made repairs. 10 Next to them Jedaiah the son of Harumaph made repairs opposite *his house*. And next to him Hattush the son of Hashabneiah made repairs. 11 Malchijah the son of Harim and Hasshub the son of Pahath-moab repaired another section and the Tower of Furnaces. 12 Next to him Shallum the son of Hallohesh, the official of half the district of Jerusalem, made repairs, he and his daughters.

13 Hanun and the inhabitants of Zanoah repaired the Valley Gate. They built it and made its doors stand with its bolts and its bars, and one thousand cubits of the wall to the Dung Gate.

14 Malchijah the son of Rechab, the official of the district of Beth-haccherem, repaired the Dung Gate. He built it and made its doors stand with its bolts and its bars.

15 Shallum the son of Col-hozeh, the official of the district of Mizpah, repaired the Spring Gate. He built it, covered it and made its doors stand with its bolts and its bars, and the wall of the Pool of Shelah at the king's garden as far as the steps that descend from the city of David. 16 After him Nehemiah the son of Azbuk, official of half the district of Beth-zur, made repairs as far as *a point* opposite the tombs of David, and as far as the artificial pool and the house of the mighty men. 17 After him the Levites made repairs *under* Rehum the son of Bani. Next to him Hashabiah, the official of half the district of Keilah, made repairs for his district. 18 After him their brothers made repairs *under* Bavvai the son of Henadad, the official of *the other* half of the district of Keilah. 19 Next to him Ezer the son of Jeshua, the official of Mizpah, repaired another section in front of the ascent of the armory at the Angle. 20 After him Baruch the son of Zabbai zealously repaired another section, from the Angle to the doorway of the house of Eliashib the high priest. 21 After him Meremoth the son of Uriah the son of Hakkoz repaired another section, from the

doorway of Eliashib's house even as far as the end of Eliashib's house. 22 After him the priests, the men of the valley, made repairs. 23 After them Benjamin and Hasshub made repairs in front of their house. After them Azariah the son of Maaseiah, son of Ananiah, made repairs beside his house. 24 After him Binnui the son of Henadad repaired another section, from the house of Azariah as far as the Angle and as far as the corner. 25 Palal the son of Uzai *made repairs* in front of the Angle and the tower projecting from the upper house of the king, which is by the court of the guard. After him Pedaiah the son of Parosh *made repairs.* 26 The temple servants living in Ophel *made repairs* as far as the front of the Water Gate toward the east and the projecting tower. 27 After them the Tekoites repaired another section in front of the great projecting tower and as far as the wall of Ophel.

28 Above the Horse Gate the priests made repairs, each in front of his house. 29 After them Zadok the son of Immer made repairs in front of his house. And after him Shemaiah the son of Shecaniah, the keeper of the East Gate, made repairs. 30 After him Hananiah the son of Shelemiah, and Hanun the sixth son of Zalaph, repaired another section. After him Meshullam the son of Berechiah made repairs in front of his own quarters. 31 After him Malchijah, one of the goldsmiths, made repairs as far as the house of the temple servants and of the merchants, in front of the Inspection Gate, and as far as the upper room of the corner. 32 Between the upper room of the corner and the Sheep Gate, the goldsmiths and the merchants made repairs.

4 Now it happened that when Sanballat heard that we were rebuilding the wall, he became angry and very vexed and mocked the Jews. 2 He spoke in the presence of his brothers and the wealthy *men* of Samaria and said, "What are these feeble Jews doing? *Are they going to restore it* for themselves? Can they offer sacrifices? Can they complete *it* in a day? Can they bring the stones to life from the dusty rubble, though they are burned?" 3 Now Tobiah the Ammonite *was* near him and he said, "Even what they are building—if a fox should jump on *it*, he would break their stone wall down!"

4 Hear, O our God, for we are despised! Return their reproach on their own heads and give them up for plunder in a land of captivity. 5 Do not forgive their iniquity and let not their sin be blotted out before You, for they have vexed the builders.

6 So we built the wall and the whole wall was joined together to half its *height*, and the people had a heart to work.

7 Now it happened that when Sanballat, Tobiah, the Arabs, the Ammonites, and the Ashdodites heard that the repair of the walls of Jerusalem went on, *and* that the *places* broken down began to be closed, they were very angry. 8 All of them joined together to come *and* fight against Jerusalem and to cause a disturbance in it. 9 But we prayed to our God, and because of them we stood a guard against them day and night.

10 Then Judah said,

"The strength of the burden
bearers is failing,
Yet there is much rubbish;
And we ourselves are unable
To rebuild the wall."

11 Our adversaries said, "They will not know or see until we come among them, kill them, and put a stop to the work." 12 Now it happened when the Jews who lived near them came and said to us ten times, "They will come up against us from every place where you may turn," 13 that I had *men* stand in the lowest parts of the space behind the wall, the exposed places, and I had the people stand by families with their swords, spears, and bows. 14 Then I saw *their fear*. And I arose and said to the nobles, the officials, and the rest of the people: "Do not fear them; remember the Lord who is great and fearsome, and fight for your brothers, your sons, your daughters, your wives, and your houses."

15 Now it happened that when our enemies heard that it was known to us, and that God had thwarted their counsel, then all of us returned to the wall, each one to his work. 16 And it happened that from that day on, half of my young men carried on the work while half of them took hold of the spears, the shields, the bows, and the breastplates; and the commanders *were* behind the whole house of Judah. 17 Those who were rebuilding the wall and those who carried burdens took *their* load with one hand doing the work and the other

holding a weapon. 18 As for the builders,
each *wore* his sword girded at his side as he
built, while the trumpeter *stood* near me.
19 I said to the nobles, the officials and the
rest of the people, "The work is great and
extensive, and we are separated on the wall
far from one another. 20 At whatever place
you hear the sound of the trumpet, there
gather together to us. Our God will fight for
us."
21 So we kept doing the work with half of
them holding spears from dawn until the
stars came out. 22 At that time I also said to
the people, "Let each man with his young
man spend the night within Jerusalem so
that they may be a guard for us by night
and a worker by day." 23 So neither I, my
brothers, my young men, nor the men of the
guard who followed me, none of us removed
our clothes, each *took* his weapon *even to*
the water.

5 Then there was a great outcry of the
people and of their wives against their
Jewish brothers. 2 Now there were those
who were saying, "We, *with* our sons and
our daughters, are many; therefore let us get
grain that we may eat and live." 3 There were
others who were saying, "We are mortgaging
our fields, our vineyards, and our houses,
that we might get grain because of the
famine." 4 Also there were those who were
saying, "We have borrowed money for the
king's tax *on* our fields and our vineyards.
5 But now our flesh is like the flesh of our
brothers, our children like their children.
Yet behold, we are forcing our sons and
our daughters to be slaves, and some of our
daughters are forced into subjugation, and
we have no power in our hands *to help*, and
our fields and vineyards belong to others."
6 Then I was very angry when I had heard
their outcry and these words. 7 I consulted
within my own heart and contended with
the nobles and the officials and said to
them, "You are exacting usury, each from his
brother!" Therefore, I held a great assembly
against them. 8 I said to them, "We, according
to our ability, have bought *back* our Jewish
brothers who were sold to the nations; and
now would you also sell your brothers that
they may be sold to us?" Then they were
silent and could not find a word *to say*. 9 And
I said, "The thing which you are doing is not
good; should you not walk in the fear of our
God because of the reproach of the nations,
our enemies? 10 And likewise I, my brothers,
and my young men are lending them money
and grain. Please, let us forsake this usury.
11 Please, give back to them this very day
their fields, their vineyards, their olive groves
and their houses, also the hundredth *part* of
the money and of the grain, the new wine
and the oil that you are exacting from them."
12 Then they said, "We will give *it* back and
will require nothing from them; we will do
exactly as you are saying." So I called the
priests and made them swear that they would
do according to this word. 13 I also shook out
the front of my garment and said, "Thus may
God shake out every man from his house and
from his possessions who does not establish
this word; even thus may he be shaken out
and emptied." And all the assembly said,
"Amen!" And they praised Yahweh. Then the
people did according to this word.
14 Moreover, from the day that I was put in
command to be their governor in the land of
Judah, from the twentieth year to the thirty-
second year of King Artaxerxes, *for* twelve
years, neither I nor my relatives have eaten
the governor's food *allowance*. 15 But the
former governors who were before me laid
heavy burdens on the people and took from
them bread and wine besides forty shekels
of silver; even their young men exerted *their*
power over the people. But I did not do so
because of the fear of God. 16 I also took hold
of the work on this wall; we did not buy any
land, and all my young men were gathered
there for the work. 17 Moreover, *there were*
at my table 150 Jews and officials, besides
those who came to us from the nations
that were around us. 18 Now that which was
prepared for each day was one ox *and* six
choice sheep, also birds were prepared for
me; and once in ten days all sorts of wine
were furnished in abundance. Yet for all
this I did not require the governor's food
allowance, because the slavery was heavy
on this people. 19 Remember me, O my God,
for good, *according to* all that I have done
for this people.

Psalm 89:1–4

1 I will sing of the lovingkindnesses
  of Yahweh forever;
From generation to generation
  I will make known Your
  faithfulness with my mouth.

2 For I have said, "Lovingkindness
will be built up forever;
In the heavens You will establish
Your faithfulness."
3 "I have cut a covenant with My chosen;
I have sworn to David My servant,
4 I will establish your seed forever
And build up your throne from
generation to generation." Selah.

Proverbs 21:27

27 The sacrifice of the wicked
is an abomination,
How much more when he brings
it with a wicked scheme!

Acts 26:1–32

26 Now Agrippa said to Paul, "You are
permitted to speak for yourself."
Then Paul, stretching out his hand, *began*
to make his defense:
2 "Concerning all the things of which I am
accused by the Jews, I regard myself blessed,
King Agrippa, that I am about to make
my defense before you today; 3 especially
because you are an expert in all customs and
questions among *the* Jews; therefore I beg
you to listen to me patiently.
4 "So then, all Jews know my manner
of life from my youth, which from the
beginning was spent among my *own* nation
and at Jerusalem; 5 since they have known
about me for a long time, if they are willing
to testify, that I lived *as* a Pharisee according
to the strictest sect of our religion. 6 And
now I am standing here being tried for the
hope of the promise made by God to our
fathers; 7 *the promise* to which our twelve
tribes hope to attain, as they earnestly
serve *God* night and day. And for this hope,
O King, I am being accused by Jews. 8 Why
is it considered unbelievable among all of
you if God does raise the dead?
9 "So then, I thought to myself that I had
to do many things hostile to the name of
Jesus the Nazarene. 10 And this is just what I
did in Jerusalem; not only did I lock up many
of the saints in prisons, having received
authority from the chief priests, but also
when they were being put to death I cast
my vote against them. 11 And as I punished
them often in all the synagogues, I tried
to force them to blaspheme; and being
furiously enraged at them, I kept pursuing
them even to foreign cities.
12 "While so engaged as I was journeying
to Damascus with the authority and com-
mission of the chief priests, 13 at midday,
O King, I saw on the way a light from
heaven, brighter than the sun, shining all
around me and those who were journeying
with me. 14 And when we had all fallen to
the ground, I heard a voice saying to me in
the Hebrew language, 'Saul, Saul, why are
you persecuting Me? It is hard for you to
kick against the goads.' 15 And I said, 'Who
are You, Lord?' And the Lord said, 'I am
Jesus whom you are persecuting. 16 But rise
up and stand on your feet; for this purpose
I have appeared to you, to appoint you a
servant and a witness not only to the things
which you have seen, but also to the things
in which I will appear to you; 17 rescuing
you from the *Jewish* people and from the
Gentiles, to whom I am sending you, 18 to
open their eyes so that they may turn from
darkness to light and from the authority
of Satan to God, that they may receive
forgiveness of sins and an inheritance
among those who have been sanctified by
faith in Me.'
19 "So, King Agrippa, I did not prove dis-
obedient to the heavenly vision, 20 but *kept*
declaring both to those of Damascus first,
and *also* at Jerusalem and *then* throughout
all the region of Judea, and *even* to the
Gentiles, that they should repent and turn to
God, practicing deeds appropriate to repen-
tance. 21 For this reason *some* Jews seized me
in the temple and were trying to put me to
death. 22 Therefore, having obtained help
from God to this day, I stand here bearing
witness both to small and great, stating
nothing but what the Prophets and Moses
said was going to take place; 23 that the
Christ was to suffer, *and* that as first of the
resurrection from the dead, He was going
to proclaim light both to the *Jewish* people
and to the Gentiles."
24 Now while Paul was saying this in
his defense, Festus *said in a loud voice,
"Paul, you are out of your mind! Great
learning is driving you out of your mind."
25 But Paul *said, "I am not out of my mind,
most excellent Festus, but I utter words of
sober truth. 26 For the king knows about
these matters, and I speak to him also with
confidence, since I am persuaded that none
of these things escape his notice; for this has
not been done in a corner. 27 King Agrippa,

do you believe the Prophets? I know you
believe." 28 But Agrippa *replied* to Paul, "In
such short time are you persuading me to
become a Christian?" 29 And Paul *said*, "I
would pray to God, that whether in a short
or long time, not only you, but also all who
hear me this day, might become such as I
am, except for these chains."

30 And the king stood up and the governor
and Bernice, and those who were sitting
with them, 31 and when they had gone aside,
they *began* talking to one another, saying,
"This man is not doing anything worthy of
death or imprisonment." 32 And Agrippa
said to Festus, "This man could have been
set free if he had not appealed to Caesar."

JULY 27

Nehemiah 6:1–7:73

6 Now it happened when it was heard by
Sanballat, Tobiah, Geshem the Arab,
and the rest of our enemies that I had rebuilt
the wall, and *that* no breach remained in it,
although at that time I had not made the
doors to stand in the gates, 2 that Sanballat
and Geshem sent *a message* to me, saying,
"Come, let us meet together at Chephirim in
the plain of Ono." But they were planning
to do me harm. 3 So I sent messengers to
them, saying, "I am doing a great work and
I cannot come down. Why should the work
stop while I leave it and come down to you?"
4 And they sent *messages* to me four times
in this manner, and I responded to them in
the same manner. 5 Then Sanballat sent his
young man to me in the same manner a fifth
time with an open letter in his hand. 6 In it
was written,

"It is heard among the nations, and
Gashmu says, that you and the Jews
are planning to rebel; therefore you
are rebuilding the wall. And you are
to be their king, according to these
words. 7 You have also set up prophets
to call out in Jerusalem concerning
you, 'A king is in Judah!' So now it
will be heard by the king according to
these words. So now, come, let us take
counsel together."

8 Then I sent *a message* to him, saying,

"Such words as you are saying have not
been done, but you are devising them
in your own heart."

9 For all of them were *trying* to frighten us,
thinking, "Their hands will become limp in
doing the work, and it will not be done." But
now, *O God*, strengthen my hands.

10 Now I entered the house of Shemaiah
the son of Delaiah, son of Mehetabel, who
was confined at home, and he said, "Let us
meet together in the house of God, within
the temple, and let us close the doors of the
temple, for they are coming to kill you, and
they are coming to kill you at night." 11 But I
said, "Should a man like me flee? And could
one such as I go into the temple *just* to live?
I will not go in." 12 Then I recognized that
surely God had not sent him, but he spoke
his prophecy against me because Tobiah
and Sanballat had hired him. 13 He was
hired for this reason, that I might become
afraid and act accordingly and sin, so that
they could give *me* a bad name in order
that they could reproach me. 14 Remember,
O my God, Tobiah and Sanballat according
to these works of theirs, and also Noadiah
the prophetess and the rest of the prophets
who were *trying* to make me afraid.

15 So the wall was finished on the
twenty-fifth of *the month* Elul, in fifty-two
days. 16 Now it happened that when all our
enemies heard *of it*, and all the nations
surrounding us saw *it*, their confidence fell.
And they knew that it was from our God that
this work had been accomplished. 17 Also
in those days many letters went from the
nobles of Judah to Tobiah, and Tobiah's
letters came to them. 18 For many in Judah
were sworn by oath to him because he was
the son-in-law of Shecaniah the son of
Arah, and his son Jehohanan had taken the
daughter of Meshullam the son of Berechiah
as a wife. 19 Moreover, they were speaking
about his good deeds in my presence and
bringing my words to him. Then Tobiah sent
letters to make me afraid.

7 Now it happened when the wall was
rebuilt and I had made the doors to
stand, and the gatekeepers and the singers
and the Levites were appointed, 2 that I com-
manded Hanani my brother and Hananiah
the commander of the fortress, *to be* over
Jerusalem, for he was a faithful man and

lives." 11 But the centurion was being more persuaded by the pilot and the captain of the ship than by what was being said by Paul. 12 And because the harbor was not suitable for wintering, the majority reached a decision to set sail from there, if somehow they could arrive at Phoenix, a harbor of Crete facing southwest and northwest, to spend the winter *there.*

13 And when a moderate south wind came up, thinking that they had attained their purpose, they weighed anchor and *began* sailing along the shore of Crete.

14 But before very long there rushed down from the land a violent wind, called Euraquilo; 15 and when the ship was caught *in it* and could not face the wind, we gave way *to it* and let ourselves be carried along. 16 And running under the shelter of a small island called Clauda, we were scarcely able to get the *ship's* boat under control. 17 After they had hoisted it up, they used supporting cables in undergirding the ship. Fearing that they might run aground on *the shallows* of Syrtis, they let down the sea anchor and in this way let themselves be carried along. 18 And the next day as we were being violently storm-tossed, they *began to* jettison the cargo; 19 and on the third day they cast the ship's tackle overboard with their own hands. 20 And since neither sun nor stars appeared for many days, and no small storm was assailing *us,* from then on all hope of our being saved was gradually abandoned.

21 And when they had gone a long time without food, then Paul stood up in their midst and said, "Men, you ought to have followed my advice to not set sail from Crete and to avoid this damage and loss. 22 And now I advise you to be cheerful, for there will be no loss of life among you, but *only* of the ship. 23 For this very night an angel of the God to whom I belong and whom I serve stood before me, 24 saying, 'Do not be afraid, Paul; you must stand before Caesar; and behold, God has granted you all those who are sailing with you.' 25 Therefore, be cheerful, men, for I believe God that it will turn out exactly as I have been told. 26 But we must run aground on some island."

JULY 28

Nehemiah 8:1–9:38

8 And all the people gathered as one man at the square which was in front of the Water Gate, and they said to Ezra the scribe to bring the book of the law of Moses which Yahweh had commanded to Israel. 2 Then Ezra the priest brought the law before the assembly of men, women, and all who *could* understand when listening, on the first day of the seventh month. 3 And he read from it before the square which was in front of the Water Gate from early morning until midday, in the presence of men and women, those who could understand; and all the ears of the people were attentive to the book of the law. 4 Ezra the scribe stood on a wooden podium which they had made for the purpose. And beside him stood Mattithiah, Shema, Anaiah, Uriah, Hilkiah, and Maaseiah on his right hand; and Pedaiah, Mishael, Malchijah, Hashum, Hashbaddanah, Zechariah, *and* Meshullam on his left hand. 5 And Ezra opened the book in the sight of all the people for he was above all the people; and when he opened it, all the people stood up. 6 Then Ezra blessed Yahweh the great God. And all the people answered, "Amen, Amen!" while lifting up their hands; then they bowed low and worshiped Yahweh with *their* faces to the ground. 7 Also Jeshua, Bani, Sherebiah, Jamin, Akkub, Shabbethai, Hodiah, Maaseiah, Kelita, Azariah, Jozabad, Hanan, Pelaiah, the Levites, were providing understanding of the law to the people while the people *stood* in their place. 8 They read from the book, from the law of God, explaining and giving insight, and they provided understanding of the reading.

9 Then Nehemiah, who was the governor, and Ezra the priest *and* scribe, and the Levites, who provided the people with understanding, said to all the people, "This day is holy to Yahweh your God; do not mourn or weep." For all the people were weeping when they heard the words of the law. 10 Then he said to them, "Go, eat of the fat, drink of the sweet, and send portions to him who has nothing prepared; for this day is holy to our Lord. Do not be grieved, for the joy of Yahweh is your strength." 11 So

the Levites quieted all the people, saying,
"Be still, for the day is holy; do not be
grieved." 12 Then all the people went away
to eat, to drink, to send portions, and to
celebrate with great gladness, because they
understood the words which had been made
known to them.

13 Then on the second day the heads of
fathers' *households* of all the people, the
priests and the Levites were gathered to
Ezra the scribe that they might gain insight
into the words of the law. 14 They found
written in the law how Yahweh had com-
manded by the hand of Moses that the sons
of Israel should live in booths during the
feast of the seventh month, 15 and that they
should make the report heard and make
a proclamation *of it* pass throughout all
their cities and in Jerusalem, saying, "Go
out to the hills, and bring olive branches
and wild olive branches, myrtle branches,
palm branches, and branches of *other* leafy
trees, to make booths, as it is written." 16 So
the people went out and brought *them* and
made booths for themselves, each on his
roof, and in their courts and in the courts
of the house of God, and in the square at
the Water Gate and in the square at the
Gate of Ephraim. 17 The entire assembly of
those who had returned from the captivity
made booths and lived in the booths. The
sons of Israel had indeed not done so
from the days of Joshua the son of Nun to
that day. And there was exceedingly great
gladness. 18 And he read from the book of
the law of God daily, from the first day to
the last day. And they celebrated the feast
seven days, and on the eighth day *there
was* a solemn assembly according to the
legal judgment.

9 Now on the twenty-fourth day of this
month the sons of Israel gathered
with fasting, in sackcloth and with dirt
upon them. 2 The seed of Israel separated
themselves from all foreigners, and stood
and confessed their sins and the iniquities
of their fathers. 3 And they rose up in their
place and read from the book of the law of
Yahweh their God for a fourth of the day;
and for *another* fourth they were confessing
and worshiping Yahweh their God. 4 Then
Jeshua rose up on the Levites' platform,
along with Bani, Kadmiel, Shebaniah,
Bunni, Sherebiah, Bani, *and* Chenani, and
they cried out with a loud voice to Yahweh
their God.

5 And the Levites, Jeshua, Kadmiel,
Bani, Hashabneiah, Sherebiah, Hodiah,
Shebaniah, *and* Pethahiah, said, "Rise up,
bless Yahweh your God from everlasting to
everlasting!

O may Your glorious name be blessed
And exalted above all
blessing and praise!

6 "You alone are Yahweh.
You have made the heavens,
The heaven of heavens
with all their host,
The earth and all that is on it,
The seas and all that is in them.
You give life to all of them
And the heavenly host
bows down to You.

7 "You are Yahweh God,
Who chose Abram
And brought him out from
Ur of the Chaldees,
And gave him the name Abraham.

8 "You found his heart faithful before You,
And cut a covenant with him
To give *him* the land of the Canaanite,
Of the Hittite and the Amorite,
Of the Perizzite, the Jebusite,
and the Girgashite—
To give *it* to his seed.
And You have established
Your promise,
For You are righteous.

9 "You saw the affliction of
our fathers in Egypt,
And heard their cry by the Red Sea.

10 "Then You performed signs and
wonders against Pharaoh,
Against all his servants and all
the people of his land;
For You knew that they acted
presumptuously toward them,
And made a name for Yourself
as *it is* this day.

11 "You split the sea before them,
So they passed through the midst
of the sea on dry land;
And their pursuers You cast
into the depths,
Like a stone into mighty waters.

12 "And with a pillar of cloud
You led them by day,
And with a pillar of fire by night

To light for them the way
In which they were to go.
13 "Then You came down on Mount Sinai,
And spoke with them from heaven;
You gave them upright
judgments and true laws,
Good statutes and commandments.
14 "So You made known to them
Your holy sabbath,
And commanded to them
commandments, statutes and law,
By the hand of Your servant Moses.
15 "You gave bread from heaven for
them for their hunger,
You brought forth water from a
rock for them for their thirst,
And You said to them to enter
in order to possess
The land which You swore
to give them.

16 "But they, our fathers, acted
presumptuously;
They became stiff-necked and would
not listen to Your commandments.
17 "They refused to listen,
And did not remember Your wondrous
deeds which You did among them;
So they became stiff-necked and
gave *themselves* a chief to return
to their slavery in Egypt.
But You are a God of lavish forgiveness,
Gracious and compassionate,
Slow to anger and abounding
in lovingkindness;
And You did not forsake them.
18 "Even when they made for themselves
A molten calf
And said, 'This is your God
Who brought you up from Egypt,'
And committed great blasphemies,
19 But You, in Your abundant compassion,
Did not forsake them in the wilderness;
The pillar of cloud did not
depart from them by day,
To lead them on their way,
Nor the pillar of fire by night,
To light for them the way in
which they were to go.
20 "You gave Your good Spirit
to give them insight,
Your manna You did not withhold
from their mouth,
And You gave them water
for their thirst.
21 "Indeed, forty years You sustained
them in the wilderness,
and they did not lack;
Their clothes did not wear out,
nor did their feet swell.
22 "You also gave them kingdoms
and peoples,
And apportioned *them* to
them as a boundary.
They took possession of the land
of Sihon the king of Heshbon
And the land of Og the king of Bashan.
23 "You made their sons numerous
as the stars of heaven,
And You brought them into the land
Which You had said for their
fathers to enter and possess.
24 "So their sons entered and
possessed the land.
And You subdued before
them the inhabitants of the
land, the Canaanites,
And You gave them into their
hand, with their kings and
the peoples of the land,
To do with them according
to their desire.
25 "They captured fortified
cities and a rich land.
They took possession of houses
full of every good thing,
Hewn cisterns, vineyards,
olive groves,
Trees for food in abundance.
So they ate, were filled,
and grew fat,
And reveled in Your great goodness.

26 "But they became disobedient
and rebelled against You,
And cast Your law behind their backs
And killed Your prophets who
had testified to them
So that they might return to You,
And they committed great
blasphemies.
27 "Therefore You gave them into
the hand of the ones who
distressed them, and they
afflicted them with distress,
But at the time of their distress
they cried to You,
And You listened from heaven,
and according to Your
abundant compassion

You gave them saviors and they
saved them from the hand of
the ones that distressed them.
28 "But as soon as they had rest, they
returned to do evil before You;
Therefore You forsook them in the
hand of their enemies, so they
had dominion over them.
Then they returned and cried to You.
And You listened from heaven,
And many times You delivered them
according to Your compassion,
29 And testified to them in order to
turn them back to Your law.
Yet they acted presumptuously and did
not listen to Your commandments
but sinned against Your judgments,
By which if a man does
them, he shall live.
And they gave a stubborn
shoulder and stiffened their
neck, and would not listen.
30 "However, You bore with
them for many years,
And testified to them by Your Spirit
by the hand of Your prophets,
Yet they would not give ear.
So You gave them into the hand
of the peoples of the lands.
31 "Nevertheless, in Your abundant
compassion You did not make
a complete destruction of
them or forsake them,
For You are a gracious and
compassionate God.

32 "So now, our God, the great, the mighty,
and the awesome God, who keeps
covenant and lovingkindness,
Do not let all the hardship seem
insignificant before You,
Which has found us, our kings, our
princes, our priests, our prophets,
our fathers, and all Your people,
From the days of the kings
of Assyria to this day.
33 "However, You are righteous in
all that has come upon us;
For You have dealt in truth, but
we have acted wickedly.
34 "Now our kings, our princes,
our priests, and our fathers
did not do Your law
Or pay attention to Your
commandments and Your
testimonies with which You
testified against them.
35 "But they, in their own kingdom,
With Your abundant goodness
which You gave them,
With the broad and rich land
which You set before them,
Did not serve You or turn
from their evil deeds.
36 "Behold, we are slaves today,
And as to the land which You
gave to our fathers to eat of
its fruit and its goodness,
Behold, we are slaves in it.
37 "Its abundant produce is for
the kings
Whom You have put over us
because of our sins;
They also rule over our bodies
And over our cattle according
to their desire,
So we are in great distress.
38 "Now because of all this
We are cutting an agreement
in writing;
And on the sealed document *are
the names of* our princes, our
Levites, *and* our priests."

Psalm 89:11–18

11 The heavens are Yours, the
earth also is Yours;
The world and its fullness,
You have founded them.
12 The north and the south, You
have created them;
Tabor and Hermon sing with
joy at Your name.
13 You have a mighty arm;
Your hand is strong, Your
right hand is exalted.
14 Righteousness and justice are the
foundation of Your throne;
Lovingkindness and truth
go before You.
15 How blessed are the people who
know the loud shout of joy!
O Yahweh, they walk in the
light of Your face.
16 In Your name they rejoice all the day,
And by Your righteousness
they are exalted.
17 For You are the beauty of
their strength,
And by Your favor our horn is exalted.

18 For our shield belongs to Yahweh,
And our king to the Holy One of Israel.

Proverbs 21:29–31

29 A wicked man displays a brazen face,
But as for the upright, he
establishes his way.
30 There is no wisdom, there
is no discernment
And there is no counsel
against Yahweh.
31 The horse is set for the day of battle,
But salvation belongs to Yahweh.

Acts 27:27–44

27 But when the fourteenth night came, as
we were being carried about in the Adriatic
Sea, about midnight the sailors *began to*
suspect that some land was approaching
them. 28 And when they took soundings, they
found *it to be* twenty fathoms; and a little
farther on they took another sounding and
found *it to be* fifteen fathoms. 29 And fearing
that we might run aground somewhere on
the rocks, they cast four anchors from the
stern and were praying for daybreak. 30 But
as the sailors were trying to escape from the
ship and had let down the *ship's* boat into
the sea, on the pretense of intending to lay
out anchors from the bow, 31 Paul said to the
centurion and to the soldiers, "Unless these
men remain in the ship, you yourselves can-
not be saved." 32 Then the soldiers cut away
the ropes of the *ship's* boat and let it fall away.
33 Until the day was about to dawn, Paul
was encouraging them all to take some
food, saying, "Today is the fourteenth day
that you have been constantly watching and
going without eating, having taken nothing.
34 Therefore I encourage you to take some
food, for this is for your salvation, for not
a hair from the head of any of you will
perish." 35 And having said these things, he
took bread and gave thanks to God in the
presence of all. And he broke it and began
to eat. 36 And all of them became cheerful
and they themselves also took food. 37 And
all of us in the ship were 276 persons. 38 And
when they had eaten enough, they *began to*
lighten the ship by throwing out the wheat
into the sea.
39 Now when day came, they could not
recognize the land; but they were noticing
a bay with a beach, and they were resolving
to drive the ship onto it if they could. 40 And
casting off the anchors, they left them in the
sea while at the same time they were loos-
ening the ropes of the rudders. And hoisting
the foresail to the wind, they were heading
for the beach. 41 But striking a reef where two
seas met, they ran the vessel aground; and
the bow stuck fast and remained immovable,
but the stern *began to* be broken up by the
force *of the waves*. 42 Now the soldiers' plan
was to kill the prisoners, so that none *of*
them would swim away and escape; 43 but
the centurion, wanting to bring Paul safely
through, kept them from their intention, and
ordered that those who could swim should
jump overboard first and get to land, 44 and
the rest *should follow*, some on planks, and
others on various things from the ship. And
so it happened that they all were brought
safely to land.

JULY 29

Nehemiah 10:1–11:36

10 Now on the sealed document *were the following names*:
Nehemiah the governor, the son of
Hacaliah, and Zedekiah,
2 Seraiah, Azariah, Jeremiah,
3 Pashhur, Amariah, Malchijah,
4 Hattush, Shebaniah, Malluch,
5 Harim, Meremoth, Obadiah,
6 Daniel, Ginnethon, Baruch,
7 Meshullam, Abijah, Mijamin,
8 Maaziah, Bilgai, Shemaiah.
These *were* the priests.
9 And the Levites:
Jeshua the son of Azaniah,
Binnui of the sons of Henadad,
Kadmiel;
10 also their brothers Shebaniah, Hodiah,
Kelita, Pelaiah, Hanan,
11 Mica, Rehob, Hashabiah,
12 Zaccur, Sherebiah, Shebaniah,
13 Hodiah, Bani, Beninu.
14 The heads of the people:
Parosh, Pahath-moab, Elam, Zattu, Bani,
15 Bunni, Azgad, Bebai,
16 Adonijah, Bigvai, Adin,
17 Ater, Hezekiah, Azzur,
18 Hodiah, Hashum, Bezai,

19 Hariph, Anathoth, Nebai,
20 Magpiash, Meshullam, Hezir,
21 Meshezabel, Zadok, Jaddua,
22 Pelatiah, Hanan, Anaiah,
23 Hoshea, Hananiah, Hasshub,
24 Hallohesh, Pilha, Shobek,
25 Rehum, Hashabnah, Maaseiah,
26 Ahiah, Hanan, Anan,
27 Malluch, Harim, Baanah.

28 Now the rest of the people—the priests,
the Levites, the gatekeepers, the singers,
the temple servants, and all those who had
separated themselves from the peoples of
the lands to the law of God, their wives, their
sons and their daughters—all those who
had knowledge *and* understanding, 29 are
joining with their relatives, their nobles, and
are entering into a curse and an oath to walk
in God's law, which was given by the hand of
Moses, God's servant, and to keep and to do
all the commandments of Yahweh our Lord
and His judgments and His statutes; 30 and
that we will not give our daughters to the
peoples of the land or take their daughters
for our sons. 31 As for the peoples of the land
who bring wares or any grain on the sabbath
day to sell, we will not receive from them on
the sabbath or a holy day; and we will forego
the crops the seventh year and the exaction
of every debt.

32 We also set ourselves under *the*
commandments to give yearly one-third
of a shekel for the service of the house
of our God: 33 for the showbread, for the
continual grain offering, for the continual
burnt offering, the sabbaths, the new moon,
for the appointed times, for the holy things
and for the sin offerings to make atonement
for Israel, and all the work of the house of
our God.

34 Likewise we cast lots for the supply of
wood *among* the priests, the Levites, and
the people, in order to bring it to the house
of our God, according to our fathers' house-
holds, at fixed times annually, to burn on the
altar of Yahweh our God, as it is written in
the law; 35 and to bring the first fruits of our
ground and the first fruits of all the fruit of
every tree to the house of Yahweh annually,
36 and to bring to the house of our God the
firstborn of our sons and of our cattle, and
the firstborn of our herds and our flocks as
it is written in the law, for the priests who
are ministering in the house of our God.
37 We will also bring the first of our dough,
our contributions, the fruit of every tree,
the new wine and the oil to the priests at
the chambers of the house of our God, and
the tithe of our ground to the Levites, for
the Levites are they who receive the tithes
in all the towns *where we* serve. 38 And the
priest, the son of Aaron, shall be with the
Levites when the Levites receive tithes,
and the Levites shall bring up the tenth of
the tithes to the house of our God, to the
chambers of the storehouse. 39 For the sons
of Israel and the sons of Levi shall bring the
contribution of the grain, the new wine and
the oil to the chambers; the utensils of the
sanctuary are there, as well as the priests
who are ministering and the gatekeepers
and the singers. Thus we will not forsake
the house of our God.

11 And the officials of the people lived in
Jerusalem, but the rest of the people
cast lots to bring one out of ten to live in
Jerusalem, the holy city, while nine-tenths
remained in the *other* cities. 2 And the peo-
ple blessed all the men who freely offered
to live in Jerusalem.

3 Now these are the heads of the provinces
who lived in Jerusalem, but in the cities of
Judah each lived in his own possession in
their cities—the Israelites, the priests, the
Levites, the temple servants, and the sons of
Solomon's servants. 4 And some of the sons
of Judah and some of the sons of Benjamin
lived in Jerusalem. From the sons of Judah:

Athaiah the son of Uzziah, the son
of Zechariah, the son of Amariah,
the son of Shephatiah, the son of
Mahalalel, from the sons of Perez;

5 and Maaseiah the son of Baruch, the
son of Col-hozeh, the son of Hazaiah,
the son of Adaiah, the son of Joiarib,
the son of Zechariah, the son of the
Shilonite.

6 All the sons of Perez who lived in
Jerusalem were 468 valiant men.

7 Now these are the sons of Benjamin:

Sallu the son of Meshullam, the son
of Joed, the son of Pedaiah, the son of
Kolaiah, the son of Maaseiah, the son
of Ithiel, the son of Jeshaiah;

8 and after him Gabbai *and* Sallai, 928.

9 Joel the son of Zichri was their
overseer,
and Judah the son of Hassenuah was
second in command of the city.

10 From the priests:
Jedaiah the son of Joiarib, Jachin,
11 Seraiah the son of Hilkiah, the son of
Meshullam, the son of Zadok, the son
of Meraioth, the son of Ahitub, the
leader of the house of God,
12 and their relatives who did the work of
the house, 822;
and Adaiah the son of Jeroham, the
son of Pelaliah, the son of Amzi, the
son of Zechariah, the son of Pashhur,
the son of Malchijah,
13 and his relatives, heads of fathers'
households, 242; and Amashsai the son
of Azarel, the son of Ahzai, the son of
Meshillemoth, the son of Immer,
14 and their relatives, mighty men of
valor, 128.
And their overseer was Zabdiel, the
son of Haggedolim.
15 Now from the Levites:
Shemaiah the son of Hasshub, the son
of Azrikam, the son of Hashabiah, the
son of Bunni;
16 and Shabbethai and Jozabad, from the
chiefs of the Levites, who were over
the outside work of the house of God;
17 and Mattaniah the son of Mica,
the son of Zabdi, the son of Asaph,
who was the chief in beginning the
thanksgiving in prayer,
and Bakbukiah, the second among his
relatives;
and Abda the son of Shammua, the
son of Galal, the son of Jeduthun.
18 All the Levites in the holy city *were* 284.
19 Now the gatekeepers, Akkub, Talmon,
and their relatives who kept watch at the
gates, *were* 172.
20 The rest of Israel, of the priests *and* of
the Levites, *were* in all the cities of Judah,
each on his own inheritance. 21 But the tem-
ple servants were living in Ophel, and Ziha
and Gishpa were over the temple servants.
22 Now the overseer of the Levites in Jeru-
salem was Uzzi the son of Bani, the son of
Hashabiah, the son of Mattaniah, the son of
Mica, from the sons of Asaph, who were the
singers over the work of the house of God.
23 For *there was* a commandment from the
king concerning them and a firm regulation
for the song leaders day by day. 24 Pethahiah
the son of Meshezabel, of the sons of Zerah
the son of Judah, was the king's representa-
tive in all matters concerning the people.
25 Now as for the villages with their fields,
some of the sons of Judah lived in
Kiriath-arba and its towns, in Dibon
and its towns, and in Jekabzeel and its
villages,
26 and in Jeshua, in Moladah and Beth-
pelet,
27 and in Hazar-shual, in Beersheba and
its towns,
28 and in Ziklag, in Meconah and in its
towns,
29 and in En-rimmon, in Zorah and in
Jarmuth,
30 Zanoah, Adullam, and their villages,
Lachish and its fields, Azekah and
its towns. So they encamped from
Beersheba as far as the valley of
Hinnom.
31 The sons of Benjamin also *lived* from
Geba *onward*, at Michmash and Aija,
at Bethel and its towns,
32 at Anathoth, Nob, Ananiah,
33 Hazor, Ramah, Gittaim,
34 Hadid, Zeboim, Neballat,
35 Lod and Ono, the valley of craftsmen.
36 From the Levites, *some* divisions in
Judah belonged to Benjamin.

Psalm 89:19–29

19 Formerly You spoke in vision
to Your holy ones,
And said, "I have bestowed
help to a mighty one;
I have exalted one chosen
from the people.
20 "I have found David My servant;
With My holy oil I have anointed him,
21 With whom My hand will
be established;
My arm also will strengthen him.
22 "The enemy will not deceive him,
Nor the son of unrighteousness
afflict him.
23 "But I shall crush his
adversaries before him,
And strike those who hate him.
24 "My faithfulness and My
lovingkindness will be with him,
And in My name his horn
will be exalted.
25 "I shall also set his hand on the sea
And his right hand on the rivers.
26 "He will call to Me, 'You are my Father,
My God, and the rock of my salvation.'
27 "I also shall make him *My* firstborn,

The highest of the kings of the earth.
28 "My lovingkindness I will
keep for him forever,
And My covenant shall be
confirmed to him.
29 "So I will set up his seed
to endure forever
And his throne as the days of heaven.

Proverbs 22:1–2

22 A *good* name is to be chosen
over great wealth,
Favor is better than silver and gold.
2 The rich and the poor meet
together *in this*—
Yahweh is the Maker of them all.

Acts 28:1–31

28 And when they had been brought safely
through *to shore*, then we learned
that the island was called Malta. 2 And the
natives showed us extraordinary affection; for
because of the rain that had set in and because
of the cold, they kindled a fire and received us
all. 3 But when Paul had gathered a bundle of
sticks and laid them on the fire, a viper came
out because of the heat and fastened itself
on his hand. 4 And when the natives saw the
creature hanging from his hand, they *began*
saying to one another, "Undoubtedly this man
is a murderer, and though he has been saved
from the sea, Justice has not allowed him to
live." 5 However he shook the creature off into
the fire and suffered no harm. 6 But they were
waiting for him to soon swell up or suddenly
fall down dead. But after they had waited a
long time and had seen nothing unusual
happen to him, changing their minds, they
began to say that he was a god.

7 Now in the areas around that place were
lands belonging to the leading man of the
island, named Publius, who welcomed
us and entertained us courteously three
days. 8 And it happened that the father of
Publius was lying afflicted with fever and
dysentery; and Paul, going *to see* him and
having prayed, laid his hands on him and
healed him. 9 And after this had happened,
the rest of the people on the island who
had diseases were coming to him and being
healed. 10 They also bestowed on us many
honors of respect; and when we were setting
sail, they supplied *us* with all we needed.

11 Now at the end of three months we
set sail on an Alexandrian ship which had
wintered at the island, and which had the
Twin Brothers for its figurehead. 12 After we
put into Syracuse, we stayed there for three
days. 13 From there we sailed around and
arrived at Rhegium, and after a day when
a south wind sprang up, on the second day
we came to Puteoli. 14 There we found *some*
brothers, and were invited to stay with them
for seven days; and thus we came to Rome.
15 And the brothers, when they heard about
us, came from there as far as the Market of
Appius and Three Inns to meet us. When
Paul saw them, he thanked God and took
courage.

16 And when we entered Rome, Paul was
allowed to stay by himself, with the soldier
who was guarding him.

17 And it happened that after three days
Paul called together those who were the
leading men of the Jews, and when they
came together, he *began* saying to them,
"Brothers, though I had done nothing
against our people or the customs of our
fathers, yet I was delivered as a prisoner
from Jerusalem into the hands of the
Romans. 18 And when they had examined
me, they were willing to release me because
there was no ground for putting me to death.
19 But when the Jews objected, I was forced
to appeal to Caesar, not that I had any accu-
sation against my nation. 20 For this reason,
therefore, I requested to see you and to
speak with you, for I am wearing this chain
for the sake of the hope of Israel." 21 And
they said to him, "We have neither received
letters from Judea concerning you, nor have
any of the brothers come here and reported
or spoken anything bad about you. 22 But we
desire to hear from you what you think; for
concerning this sect, it is known to us that
it is spoken against everywhere."

23 And when they had set a day for Paul,
they came to him at his lodging in large
numbers; and he was explaining to them
by solemnly bearing witness about the
kingdom of God and trying to persuade
them concerning Jesus, from both the Law
of Moses and from the Prophets, from
morning until evening. 24 And some were
being persuaded by the things spoken, but
others were not believing. 25 And when they
disagreed with one another, they *began*
leaving after Paul had spoken one word,
"The Holy Spirit rightly spoke through
Isaiah the prophet to your fathers, 26 saying,

'Go to this people and say,
"You will keep on hearing,
but will not understand;
And you will keep on seeing,
but will not perceive;
27 For the heart of this people
has become dull,
And with their ears they
scarcely hear,
And they have closed their eyes;
Lest they might see with
their eyes,
And hear with their ears,
And understand with their
heart and return,
And I heal them."'
28 "Therefore let it be known to you that this
salvation of God was sent to the Gentiles—
they will also hear." 29 [When he had spoken
these words, the Jews departed, having a
great dispute among themselves.]
30 And he stayed two full years in his own
rented quarters and was welcoming all who
came to him, 31 preaching the kingdom of
God and teaching concerning the Lord Jesus
Christ with all confidence, unhindered.

Meditation upon the Word of God is one of the most important of all the means of grace and growth in spirituality, yea there can be no true progress in vital and practical godliness without it.

— A. W. PINK

JULY 30

Nehemiah 12:1–13:31

12 Now these are the priests and the
Levites who came up with Zerubbabel
the son of Shealtiel, and Jeshua:
Seraiah, Jeremiah, Ezra,
2 Amariah, Malluch, Hattush,
3 Shecaniah, Rehum, Meremoth,
4 Iddo, Ginnethoi, Abijah,
5 Mijamin, Maadiah, Bilgah,
6 Shemaiah and Joiarib, Jedaiah,
7 Sallu, Amok, Hilkiah, and Jedaiah.
These were the heads of the priests
and their relatives in the days of
Jeshua.
8 The Levites *were*
Jeshua, Binnui, Kadmiel, Sherebiah,
Judah, *and* Mattaniah *who was* over of
the songs of thanksgiving, he and his
brothers.
9 Also Bakbukiah and Unni, their
brothers, stood opposite them in
keeping their responsibilities.
10 Jeshua became the father of
Joiakim,
and Joiakim became the father of
Eliashib,
and Eliashib became the father of
Joiada,
11 and Joiada became the father of
Jonathan,
and Jonathan became the father of
Jaddua.
12 Now in the days of Joiakim, the priests,
the heads of fathers' *households* were:
of Seraiah, Meraiah; of Jeremiah,
Hananiah;
13 of Ezra, Meshullam; of Amariah,
Jehohanan;
14 of Malluchi, Jonathan; of Shebaniah,
Joseph;
15 of Harim, Adna; of Meraioth, Helkai;
16 of Iddo, Zechariah; of Ginnethon,
Meshullam;
17 of Abijah, Zichri; of Miniamin, of
Moadiah, Piltai;
18 of Bilgah, Shammua; of Shemaiah,
Jehonathan;
19 of Joiarib, Mattenai; of Jedaiah, Uzzi;
20 of Sallai, Kallai; of Amok, Eber;
21 of Hilkiah, Hashabiah; of Jedaiah,
Nethanel.
22 As for the Levites, in the days of
Eliashib, Joiada, and Johanan and Jaddua,
the heads of fathers' *households* were
written down; the priests *were* also in the
reign of Darius the Persian. 23 The sons
of Levi, the heads of fathers' *households*,
were written down in the Book of the
Chronicles up to the days of Johanan the
son of Eliashib.

24 The heads of the Levites *were*
Hashabiah, Sherebiah, and Jeshua the
son of Kadmiel, with their brothers
opposite them, to praise *and* give
thanks, by the commandment of
David the man of God, watch by
watch.
25 Mattaniah, Bakbukiah, Obadiah,
Meshullam, Talmon, *and* Akkub *were*
gatekeepers keeping watch at the
storerooms of the gates.

26 These *served* in the days of Joiakim the
son of Jeshua, the son of Jozadak, and in the
days of Nehemiah the governor and of Ezra
the priest *and* scribe.

27 Now at the dedication of the wall of
Jerusalem they sought out the Levites from
all their places, to bring them to Jerusalem
so that they might celebrate the dedication
with gladness, with hymns of thanksgiving
and with songs *to the accompaniment* of
cymbals, harps and lyres. 28 So the sons of
the singers were gathered from the district
around Jerusalem and from the villages of
the Netophathites, 29 from Beth-gilgal and
from *their* fields in Geba and Azmaveth, for
the singers had built themselves villages
around Jerusalem. 30 The priests and the
Levites cleansed themselves; they also
cleansed the people, the gates, and the wall.

31 Then I had the leaders of Judah come
up on top of the wall, and I had two great
choirs of thanksgiving stand, the first
proceeding to the right on top of the wall
toward the Dung Gate.

32 Hoshaiah and half of the leaders of
Judah followed them,
33 with Azariah, Ezra, Meshullam,
34 Judah, Benjamin, Shemaiah, Jeremiah,
35 and some of the sons of the priests
with trumpets; *and* Zechariah the son
of Jonathan, the son of Shemaiah, the
son of Mattaniah, the son of Micaiah,
the son of Zaccur, the son of Asaph,
36 and his relatives, Shemaiah, Azarel,
Milalai, Gilalai, Maai, Nethanel,
Judah, *and* Hanani, with the musical
instruments of David the man of God.
And Ezra the scribe *went* before them.

37 At the Spring Gate they went directly up
the steps of the city of David by the stairway
of the wall above the house of David to the
Water Gate on the east.

38 The second choir proceeded to the left,
while I followed them with half of the people
on the wall, above the Tower of Furnaces,
to the Broad Wall, 39 and above the Gate of
Ephraim, by the Old Gate, by the Fish Gate,
the Tower of Hananel, and the Tower of the
Hundred, as far as the Sheep Gate; and they
stood at the Gate of the Guard. 40 Then the
two choirs took their stand in the house of
God. So did I and half of the officials with
me; 41 and the priests:

Eliakim, Maaseiah, Miniamin,
Micaiah, Elioenai, Zechariah and
Hananiah, with the trumpets;
42 and Maaseiah, Shemaiah, Eleazar,
Uzzi, Jehohanan, Malchijah, Elam, and
Ezer.

And the singers made *their voices* heard,
with Jezrahiah *their* overseer, 43 and on that
day they offered great sacrifices and were
glad because God had given them great
gladness, even the women and children
were glad, so that the gladness of Jerusalem
was heard from afar.

44 On that day men were also appointed
over the chambers for the stores, the con-
tributions, the first fruits, and the tithes,
to gather into them from the fields of the
cities the portions required by the law for the
priests and Levites; for Judah was glad over
the priests and Levites who stood *to min-
ister*. 45 And they kept *their* responsibility
given by their God and the responsibility of
cleansing, together with the singers and the
gatekeepers, according to the commandment
of David *and* his son Solomon. 46 For in the
days of David and Asaph, in ancient times,
there were chiefs of the singers, songs of
praise and hymns of thanksgiving to God.
47 So all Israel in the days of Zerubbabel and
Nehemiah were giving the portions due the
singers and the gatekeepers as each day
required, and set apart the holy *portion* for
the Levites, and the Levites set apart the holy
portion for the sons of Aaron.

13 On that day they read from the book
of Moses in the hearing of the people;
and there was found written in it that no
Ammonite or Moabite should ever enter
the assembly of God, 2 because they did
not meet the sons of Israel with bread and
water, but hired Balaam against them to
curse them. However, our God turned the
curse into a blessing. 3 So when they heard
the law, they separated all foreigners from
Israel.

4 Now prior to this, Eliashib the priest, who was put in *charge* over the chambers of the house of our God, being related to Tobiah, 5 had prepared a large room for him, where formerly they put the grain offerings, the frankincense, the utensils, and the tithes of grain, *also* new wine and oil commanded for the Levites, the singers, and the gatekeepers, as well as the contributions for the priests. 6 But during all this *time* I was not in Jerusalem, for in the thirty-second year of Artaxerxes king of Babylon I had gone to the king. After some time, however, I asked *leave* from the king, 7 and I came to Jerusalem and discerned the evil that Eliashib had done for Tobiah, by preparing a chamber for him in the courts of the house of God. 8 It was very evil to me, so I threw all of Tobiah's household goods out of the chamber. 9 Then I said *the word*, and they cleansed the chambers; and I returned there the utensils of the house of God with the grain offerings and the frankincense.

10 I also came to know that the portions of the Levites had not been given *them*, so the Levites and the singers who did the work had fled, each to his own field. 11 So I contended against the officials and said, "Why is the house of God forsaken?" Then I gathered them together and had them stand in their posts. 12 All Judah then brought the tithe of the grain, new wine, and oil into the storehouses. 13 In charge of the storehouses I appointed Shelemiah the priest, Zadok the scribe, and Pedaiah of the Levites, and in addition to them was Hanan the son of Zaccur, the son of Mattaniah; for they were counted as faithful, and it was their task to apportion *everything* to their relatives. 14 Remember me for this, O my God, and do not blot out my lovingkindnesses which I have shown for the house of my God and its responsibilities.

15 In those days I saw in Judah some who were treading wine presses on the sabbath, and bringing in sacks of grain and loading *them* on donkeys, as well as wine, grapes, figs and all kinds of loads, and they brought *them* into Jerusalem on the sabbath day. So I testified against *them* on the day they sold food. 16 Also men of Tyre were living there *who* brought in fish and all kinds of merchandise, and sold *them* to the sons of Judah on the sabbath, even in Jerusalem. 17 Then I contended with the nobles of Judah and said to them, "What is this evil thing you are doing, even profaning the sabbath day? 18 Did not your fathers do the same, so our God brought on us and on this city all this calamity? Yet you are adding to *His* anger on Israel by profaning the sabbath."

19 Now it happened that just as it grew dark at the gates of Jerusalem before the sabbath, I said *the word*, and the doors were shut. Then I said that they should not open them until after the sabbath. Then I had some of my young men stand at the gates *so that* no load would enter on the sabbath day. 20 Once or twice the traders and merchants of every kind of merchandise spent the night outside Jerusalem. 21 Then I warned them and said to them, "Why do you spend the night in front of the wall? If you do so again, I will send forth *my* hand against you." From that time on they did not come on the sabbath. 22 And I said to the Levites that they should cleanse themselves and come as gatekeepers to keep the sabbath day holy. *For* this also remember me, O my God, and have compassion on me according to the greatness of Your lovingkindness.

23 In those days I also saw that the Jews had married women from Ashdod, Ammon, *and* Moab. 24 As for their children, half spoke in the language of Ashdod, and none of them was able to speak the language of Judah, but only the tongue of his own people. 25 So I contended with them and cursed them and struck some of them and pulled out their hair and made them swear by God, "You shall not give your daughters to their sons, nor take up their daughters for your sons or for yourselves. 26 Did not Solomon king of Israel sin regarding these things? Yet among the many nations there was no king like him, and he was loved by his God, and God gave him *to be* king over all Israel; nevertheless the foreign women caused even him to sin. 27 Do we then hear about you that you have done all this great evil by acting unfaithfully against our God by marrying foreign women?" 28 And even one of the sons of Joiada, the son of Eliashib the high priest, was a son-in-law of Sanballat the Horonite, so I made him flee away from me. 29 Remember them, O my God, because they have defiled the priesthood and the covenant of the priesthood and the Levites.

30 Thus I cleansed them from everything foreign and *ensured* that the responsibilities

stood for the priests and the Levites, each
in his work, 31 and *I arranged* for the supply
of wood at fixed times and for the first
fruits. Remember me, O my God, for good.

Psalm 89:30–37

30 "If his sons forsake My law
And do not walk in
My judgments,
31 If they profane My statutes
And do not keep My commandments,
32 Then I will punish their
transgression with the rod
And their iniquity with striking.
33 "But I will not break off My
lovingkindness from him,
Nor deal falsely in My faithfulness.
34 "My covenant I will not profane,
Nor will I alter what comes
forth from My lips.
35 "Once I have sworn by My holiness;
I will not lie to David.
36 "His seed shall endure forever
And his throne as the sun before Me.
37 "It shall be established forever
like the moon,
And the witness in the sky is
faithful." Selah.

Proverbs 22:3–4

3 A prudent man sees evil and hides,
But the simple pass on,
and are punished.
4 The reward of humility—
the fear of Yahweh—
Is riches, glory, and life.

Romans 1:1–32

1 Paul, a slave of Christ Jesus, called *as*
an apostle, having been set apart for
the gospel of God, 2 which He promised
beforehand through His prophets in the
holy Scriptures, 3 concerning His Son, who
was born of the seed of David according to
the flesh, 4 who was designated as the Son
of God in power, according to the Spirit of
holiness, by the resurrection from the dead,
Jesus Christ our Lord, 5 through whom we
received grace and apostleship for *the*
obedience of faith among all the Gentiles
for the sake of His name, 6 among whom you
also are the called of Jesus Christ;
7 to all who are beloved of God in Rome,
called *as* saints: Grace to you and peace from
God our Father and the Lord Jesus Christ.
8 First, I thank my God through Jesus
Christ for you all, because your faith is
being proclaimed throughout the whole
world. 9 For God, whom I serve in my spirit
in the gospel of His Son, is my witness *as to*
how without ceasing I make mention of you,
10 always in my prayers earnestly asking, if
perhaps now at last by the will of God I may
succeed in coming to you. 11 For I long to see
you so that I may impart some spiritual gift
to you, that you may be strengthened; 12 that
is, to be mutually encouraged, *while* among
you, by each other's faith, both yours and
mine. 13 I do not want you to be unaware,
brothers, that often I have planned to come
to you (and have been prevented so far) so
that I may have some fruit among you also,
even as among the rest of the Gentiles. 14 I
am under obligation both to Greeks and
to barbarians, both to the wise and to the
foolish. 15 In this way, for my part, I am eager
to proclaim the gospel to you also who are
in Rome.
16 For I am not ashamed of the gospel,
for it is the power of God for salvation to
everyone who believes, to the Jew first and
also to the Greek. 17 For in it *the* righteous-
ness of God is revealed from faith to faith;
as it is written, "BUT THE RIGHTEOUS WILL
LIVE BY FAITH."
18 For the wrath of God is revealed from
heaven against all ungodliness and unrigh-
teousness of men who suppress the truth in
unrighteousness, 19 because that which is
known about God is evident within them;
for God made it evident to them. 20 For
since the creation of the world His invisi-
ble attributes, both His eternal power and
divine nature, have been clearly seen, being
understood through what has been made,
so that they are without excuse. 21 For even
though they knew God, they did not glorify
Him as God or give thanks, but they became
futile in their thoughts, and their foolish
heart was darkened. 22 Professing to be
wise, they became fools, 23 and exchanged
the glory of the incorruptible God for an
image in the likeness of corruptible man
and of birds and four-footed animals and
crawling creatures.
24 Therefore God gave them over in the
lusts of their hearts to impurity, so that their
bodies would be dishonored among them.
25 For they exchanged the truth of God for a
lie, and worshiped and served the creature

rather than the Creator, who is blessed
forever. Amen.
26 For this reason God gave them over to
dishonorable passions; for their females
exchanged the natural function for that
which is unnatural, 27 and in the same
way also the males abandoned the natural
function of the female and burned in their
desire toward one another, males with males
committing indecent acts and receiving in
their own persons the due penalty of their
error.
28 And just as they did not see fit to
acknowledge God, God gave them over to
an unfit mind, to do those things which are
not proper, 29 having been filled with all
unrighteousness, wickedness, greed, evil;
full of envy, murder, strife, deceit, malice;
they are gossips, 30 slanderers, haters of
God, violent, arrogant, boastful, inventors
of evil, disobedient to parents, 31 without
understanding, untrustworthy, unloving,
unmerciful; 32 and although they know the
righteous requirement of God, that those
who practice such things are worthy of
death, they not only do the same, but also
give hearty approval to those who practice
them.

JULY 31

Esther 1:1–2:23

1 Now it happened in the days of Aha-
suerus, the Ahasuerus who reigned
from India to Ethiopia over 127 provinces,
2 in those days as King Ahasuerus sat on
his royal throne which *was* at the citadel
in Susa, 3 in the third year of his reign, he
held a feast for all his princes and servants,
the military *officers* of Persia and Media,
the nobles and the princes of his provinces
being in his presence, 4 while he displayed
the riches of his royal glory and the splendor
of his great majesty for many days, 180 days.
5 And when these days were fulfilled, the
king held a feast lasting seven days for all
the people who were present at the citadel
in Susa, from the greatest to the least, in
the court of the garden of the king's palace.
6 *There were hangings of* fine white and blue
linen held by cords of fine purple linen on
silver rings and marble pillars, *and* couches
of gold and silver on a mosaic pavement of
porphyry, marble, mother-of-pearl, and
precious stones. 7 And drinks were served
in golden vessels of various kinds, and the
royal wine was plentiful according to the
king's hand. 8 And the drinking was *done*
according to the law; there was no com-
pulsion, for so the king had established *it*
for each official of his household—that he
should do according to what pleased each
person. 9 Queen Vashti also held a feast
for the women in the royal house which
belonged to King Ahasuerus.
10 On the seventh day, when the heart
of the king was merry with wine, he said
for Mehuman, Biztha, Harbona, Bigtha,
Abagtha, Zethar, and Carkas, the seven
eunuchs who attended to the presence of
King Ahasuerus, 11 to bring Queen Vashti
before the king with *her* royal crown in
order to display her beauty to the people
and the princes, for she was beautiful in
appearance. 12 But Queen Vashti refused
to come at the word of the king which *was*
delivered by the hand of the eunuchs. Then
the king became exceedingly furious, and
his wrath burned within him.
13 Then the king said to the wise men who
knew the times—for it was the custom of
the king thus *to speak* before all who knew
law and justice 14 and were close to him: Car-
shena, Shethar, Admatha, Tarshish, Meres,
Marsena, and Memucan, the seven princes
of Persia and Media who had access to the
king's presence and sat in the first place in
the kingdom— 15 "According to law, what is
to be done with Queen Vashti, because she
did not do the declaration of King Ahasuerus
delivered by the hand of the eunuchs?"
16 Then in the presence of the king and the
princes, Memucan said, "Queen Vashti has
committed iniquity against not only the
king but *also* against all the princes and all
the peoples who are in all the provinces of
King Ahasuerus. 17 For the word about the
queen will get out to all the women causing
them to despise their husbands in their eyes
by saying, 'King Ahasuerus said for Queen
Vashti to be brought in to his presence, but
she did not come.' 18 This day the ladies of
Persia and Media who have heard of the
word about the queen will speak in *the same*
way to all the king's princes, and there will

be plenty of spite and indignation. 19 If it
seems good to the king, let a royal word go
forth from him, and let it be written in the
laws of Persia and Media so that it cannot
be repealed, that Vashti may no longer
come into the presence of King Ahasuerus,
and let the king give her royal position to
another who is better than she. 20 And the
king's sentence, which he will make, will be
heard throughout all his kingdom, for it is
vast, and all women will give respect to their
husbands, great and small."

21 And *this* word was good in the eyes of
the king and the princes, and the king did
according to the word of Memucan. 22 So
he sent letters to all the king's provinces,
to each province according to its script and
to every people according to their tongue,
that every man should be the ruler in his
own house and the one who speaks in the
tongue of his own people.

2 After these things when the wrath
of King Ahasuerus had subsided, he
remembered Vashti and what she had
done and what had been decided against
her. 2 Then the young men of the king, who
attended to him, said, "Let young virgins,
beautiful in appearance, be sought for the
king. 3 And let the king appoint overseers in
all the provinces of his kingdom that they
may gather every young virgin, beautiful
in appearance, to the citadel of Susa, to the
harem, into the hand of Hegai, the king's
eunuch, who keeps *charge of* the women;
and let their cosmetics be given *to them.*
4 Then let the young lady who is good in the
eyes of the king be queen in place of Vashti."
And the word was good in the eyes of the
king, and he did so.

5 *Now* there was at the citadel in Susa a
Jew. And his name was Mordecai, the son
of Jair, the son of Shimei, the son of Kish, a
Benjamite, 6 who had been taken away into
exile from Jerusalem with the exiles who
had been taken away into exile with Jeco-
niah king of Judah, whom Nebuchadnezzar
the king of Babylon had taken away into
exile. 7 And he was bringing up Hadassah,
that is Esther, his uncle's daughter, for she
had no father or mother. Now the young
lady was beautiful in form and beautiful in
appearance, and when her father and her
mother died, Mordecai took her as his own
daughter.

8 Now it happened that when the word
and law of the king were heard and many
young ladies were gathered to the citadel
of Susa into the hand of Hegai, that Esther
was taken to the king's house into the
hand of Hegai, who kept *charge of* the
women. 9 And the young lady was good
in his eyes, and she advanced in lovingk-
indness before him. So he hurried to give
her cosmetics and portions *of food* to her,
and to give to her seven choice young
women from the king's house. And he
transferred her and her young women to
the best place in the harem. 10 Esther did
not tell *anyone* about her people or her
kinsmen, for Mordecai had commanded
her that she should not tell *anyone* about
them. 11 And every day Mordecai walked
back and forth in front of the court of the
harem to know the well-being of Esther
and how she fared.

12 Now when it reached the turn of each
young lady to go in to King Ahasuerus, after
the end of her twelve months under the
regulations for the women—for the days
of their cosmetic treatment were fulfilled
as follows: six months with oil of myrrh and
six months with spices and the cosmetics
for women— 13 then the young lady would
go in to the king in this way: anything that
she said *she desired* was given to her to
come with her from the harem to the king's
house. 14 In the evening she would go in,
and in the morning she would return to the
second harem, to the hand of Shaashgaz,
the king's eunuch who kept *charge of* the
concubines. She would not again go in to
the king unless the king delighted in her and
she was summoned by name.

15 Now when it reached the turn of
Esther, the daughter of Abihail the uncle
of Mordecai who had taken her as his
daughter, to go in to the king, she did not
seek anything except what Hegai, the king's
eunuch who kept *charge of* the women, said.
And Esther advanced in favor in the eyes
of all who saw her. 16 So Esther was taken
to King Ahasuerus to his royal house in the
tenth month which is the month Tebeth, in
the seventh year of his reign.

17 And the king loved Esther more than
all the women, and she advanced in favor
and lovingkindness before him more than
all the virgins, so that he set the royal crown
on her head and made her queen in place of

Vashti. 18 Then the king held a great feast,
Esther's feast, for all his princes and his
servants; he also held a remission of taxes
for the provinces and gave gifts according
to the king's hand.
19 And when the virgins were gathered
together the second time, then Mordecai
was sitting at the king's gate. 20 Esther had
not yet told *anyone* about her kinsmen
or her people, just as Mordecai had com-
manded her; indeed Esther was doing what
Mordecai declared *that she do*, just as she
had done when she was being brought up
by him.
21 In those days, while Mordecai was
sitting at the king's gate, Bigthan and Teresh,
two of the king's eunuchs from those who
were doorkeepers, became furious and
sought to send forth *their* hand against King
Ahasuerus. 22 But the matter became known
to Mordecai, and he told *it* to Queen Esther,
and Esther said *it* to the king in Mordecai's
name. 23 Then the matter was sought out
and found *to be true*, so they were both
hanged on a gallows; and it was written
in the book of the chronicles in the king's
presence.

Psalm 89:38–45

38 But You have cast off and rejected,
You have been full of wrath
against Your anointed.
39 You have spurned the
covenant of Your slave;
You have profaned his
crown to the ground.
40 You have broken down all his walls;
You have beset his
strongholds with ruin.
41 All who pass along the
way plunder him;
He has become a reproach
to his neighbors.
42 You have exalted the right
hand of his adversaries;
You have made all his enemies be glad.
43 You also turn back the
edge of his sword
And have not made him arise in battle.
44 You have made his splendor to cease
And cast his throne to the ground.
45 You have shortened the
days of his youth;
You have wrapped him up with
shame. Selah.

Proverbs 22:5–6

5 Thorns *and* snares are in the
way of the crooked;
He who keeps his soul will
be far from them.
6 Train up a child according to his way,
Even when he is old he will
not depart from it.

Romans 2:1–29

2 Therefore you are without excuse,
O man, everyone who passes judgment,
for in that which you judge another, you
condemn yourself; for you who judge
practice the same things. 2 And we know
that the judgment of God rightly falls
upon those who practice such things.
3 But do you presume this, O man—who
passes judgment on those who practice
such things and does the same—that you
will escape the judgment of God? 4 Or
do you think lightly of the riches of His
kindness and forbearance and patience,
not knowing that the kindness of God
leads you to repentance? 5 But because of
your stubbornness and unrepentant heart
you are storing up wrath for yourself in the
day of wrath and revelation of the righteous
judgment of God, 6 who WILL REPAY TO EACH
ACCORDING TO HIS WORKS: 7 to those who by
perseverance in doing good seek for glory
and honor and immortality, eternal life;
8 but to those who are selfishly ambitious
and do not obey the truth, but obey unrigh-
teousness, wrath and anger. 9 *There will be*
affliction and turmoil for every soul of man
who works out evil, of the Jew first and also
of the Greek, 10 but glory and honor and
peace to everyone who works good, to the
Jew first and also to the Greek. 11 For there
is no partiality with God.
12 For all who have sinned without the
Law will also perish without the Law, and
all who have sinned under the Law will be
judged by the Law. 13 For *it is* not the hearers
of the Law *who* are just before God, but the
doers of the Law will be justified. 14 For
when Gentiles who do not have the Law
naturally do the things of the Law, these,
not having the Law, are a law to themselves,
15 in that they demonstrate the work of the
Law written in their hearts, their conscience
bearing witness and their thoughts alter-
nately accusing or else defending them,
16 on the day when, according to my gospel,

God will judge the secrets of men through Christ Jesus.

17 But if you bear the name "Jew" and rely upon the Law and boast in God, 18 and know *His* will and approve the things that are essential, being instructed out of the Law, 19 and are confident that you yourself are a guide to the blind, a light to those who are in darkness, 20 a corrector of the foolish, a teacher of the immature, having in the Law the embodiment of knowledge and of the truth, 21 you, therefore, who teach another, do you not teach yourself? You who preach that one shall not steal, do you steal? 22 You who say that one should not commit adultery, do you commit adultery? You who abhor idols, do you rob temples? 23 You who boast in the Law, through your transgression of the Law, do you dishonor God? 24 For "THE NAME OF GOD IS BLASPHEMED AMONG THE GENTILES BECAUSE OF YOU," just as it is written.

25 For indeed circumcision is of value if you practice the Law, but if you are a transgressor of the Law, your circumcision has become uncircumcision. 26 So if the uncircumcised man observes the righteous requirements of the Law, will not his uncircumcision be counted as circumcision? 27 And he who is physically uncircumcised, if he fulfills the Law, will he not judge you who, through the letter *of the Law* and circumcision, are a transgressor of the Law? 28 For he is not a Jew who is one outwardly, nor is circumcision that which is outward in the flesh. 29 But he is a Jew who is one inwardly; and circumcision is that which is of the heart, by the Spirit, not by the letter; and his praise is not from men, but from God.

AUGUST 1

Esther 3:1–4:17

3 After these things, King Ahasuerus magnified Haman, the son of Hammedatha the Agagite, and advanced him and set his seat above all the princes who *were* with him. 2 And all the king's servants who were at the king's gate were bowing down and prostrating themselves before Haman, for so the king had commanded concerning him. But Mordecai would not bow down or prostrate himself. 3 So the king's servants who were at the king's gate said to Mordecai, "Why do you trespass against the king's command?" 4 Now it happened when they had spoken daily to him and he would not listen to them, that they told Haman to see whether Mordecai's words would stand; for he had told them that he was a Jew. 5 Then Haman saw that Mordecai was not bowing down or prostrating himself before him. So Haman was filled with wrath. 6 But he despised in his eyes to send forth *his* hand against Mordecai alone, for they had told him *who* the people of Mordecai *were*; therefore Haman sought to destroy all the Jews, the people of Mordecai, who *were* throughout the whole kingdom of Ahasuerus.

7 In the first month, which is the month Nisan, in the twelfth year of King Ahasuerus, Pur, that is the lot, was cast before Haman from day to day and from month *to month*, until the twelfth month, that is the month Adar. 8 Then Haman said to King Ahasuerus, "There is a certain people scattered and separated among the peoples in all the provinces of your kingdom; their laws are different from *those* of all *other* people, and they do not do the king's laws, so it is not worth it for the king to let them remain. 9 If it *seems* good to the king, let it be written down that they should perish, and I will pay 10,000 talents of silver into the hands of those who do this work, to bring into the king's treasuries." 10 Then the king removed his signet ring from his hand and gave it to Haman, the son of Hammedatha the Agagite, the adversary of the Jews. 11 And the king said to Haman, "The silver is yours, and the people *also*, to do with them according to what is good in your eyes."

12 Then the king's scribes were summoned on the thirteenth day of the first month, and it was written just as Haman commanded to the king's satraps, to the governors who were over each province, and to the princes of each people, each province according to its script, each people according to its tongue, being written in the name of King Ahasuerus and sealed with the king's signet ring. 13 And letters were sent by the hand of couriers to all the king's provinces to

destroy, to kill, and to cause all the Jews
to perish, both young and old, little ones
and women, in one day, the thirteenth *day*
of the twelfth month, which is the month
Adar, and to plunder their spoil. 14 A copy
of that which was written down to be given
as law in every province was revealed to all
the peoples so that they should be ready for
this day. 15 The couriers went out, hastened
by the word of the king. And the law was
given at the citadel in Susa. Now the king
and Haman sat down to drink, but the city
of Susa was in confusion.

4 Now Mordecai came to know of all that
had been done. And he tore his clothes,
put on sackcloth and ashes, and went out
into the midst of the city and cried out
loudly and bitterly. 2 And he went as far as
the king's gate, for no one was to enter the
king's gate clothed in sackcloth. 3 Now in
each and every province where the word
and law of the king reached, there was great
mourning among the Jews, with fasting,
weeping, and wailing; and many made their
bed in sackcloth and ashes.

4 Then Esther's young women and her
eunuchs came and told her, and the queen
writhed in great anguish. And she sent
garments to clothe Mordecai and to remove
his sackcloth from upon him, but he did
not accept *them*. 5 Then Esther summoned
Hathach from the king's eunuchs, whom
the king had appointed to attend her, and
commanded him *to go* to Mordecai to know
what this *was* and why it *was*. 6 So Hathach
went out to Mordecai to the city square
in front of the king's gate. 7 And Mordecai
told him all that had happened to him, and
the exact amount of silver that Haman had
promised to pay to the king's treasuries
to cause the Jews to perish. 8 He also gave
him a copy of the written law which had
been given in Susa for their destruction, in
order to show Esther and to tell her and to
command her to go in to the king to implore
his favor and to seek him out for her people.

9 Then Hathach came back and told
Mordecai's words to Esther. 10 Then Esther
spoke to Hathach and commanded him *to
reply* to Mordecai: 11 "All the king's servants
and the people of the king's provinces know
that for any man or woman who comes to
the king to the inner court who is not sum-
moned, he has but one law, that he be put
to death, unless the king holds out to him
the golden scepter so that he may live. And
I have not been summoned to come to the
king for these thirty days." 12 So they told
Esther's words to Mordecai.

13 Then Mordecai said *for them* to respond
to Esther, "Do not imagine that you in the
king's house can escape any more than all
the Jews. 14 For if you remain silent at this
time, relief and deliverance will arise for the
Jews from another place, and you and your
father's house will perish. And who knows
whether you have not reached royalty for
such a time as this?"

15 Then Esther said *for them* to respond
to Mordecai, 16 "Go, gather all the Jews who
are found in Susa, and fast for me; do not eat
or drink for three days, night or day. I and
my young women also will fast in the same
way. And thus I will go in to the king, which
is not according to the law; and if I perish, I
perish." 17 So Mordecai went away and did
just as Esther had commanded him.

Psalm 89:46–52

46 How long, O Yahweh?
Will You hide Yourself forever?
Will Your wrath burn like fire?
47 Remember what my span of life is;
For what vanity You have created
all the sons of men!
48 What man can live and not see death?
Can he provide his soul escape from
the power of Sheol? Selah.

49 Where are Your former
lovingkindnesses, O Lord,
Which You swore to David
in Your faithfulness?
50 Remember, O Lord, the
reproach of Your slaves;
How I bear in my bosom *the reproach
of* all the many peoples,
51 With which Your enemies have
reproached, O Yahweh,
With which they have reproached
the footsteps of Your anointed.

52 Blessed be Yahweh forever!
Amen and Amen.

Proverbs 22:7–8

7 The rich rules over the poor,
And the borrower is the
slave of the lender.

8 He who sows unrighteousness
will reap iniquity,
And the rod of his fury will end.

Romans 3:1–31

3 Then what advantage has the Jew?
Or what is the value of circumcision?
2 Great in every respect. First of all, that
they were entrusted with the oracles of
God. 3 What then? If some did not believe,
does their unbelief abolish the faithfulness
of God? 4 May it never be! Rather, let God be
true and every man a liar, as it is written,

"THAT YOU MAY BE JUSTIFIED
IN YOUR WORDS,
AND OVERCOME WHEN YOU ARE JUDGED."

5 But if our unrighteousness demonstrates
the righteousness of God, what shall we say?
Is the God who inflicts wrath unrighteous?
(I am speaking in human terms.) 6 May it
never be! For otherwise, how will God judge
the world? 7 But if through my lie the truth of
God abounded to His glory, why am I also still
being judged as a sinner? 8 And why not *say*
(as we are slanderously reported and as some
claim that we say), "Let us do evil that good
may come"? Their condemnation is just.

9 What then? Are we better? Not at all; for
we have already charged that both Jews and
Greeks are all under sin; 10 as it is written,

"THERE IS NONE RIGHTEOUS, NOT EVEN ONE;
11 THERE IS NONE WHO UNDERSTANDS,
THERE IS NONE WHO SEEKS FOR GOD;
12 ALL HAVE TURNED ASIDE, TOGETHER
THEY HAVE BECOME WORTHLESS;
THERE IS NONE WHO DOES GOOD,
THERE IS NOT EVEN ONE."
13 "THEIR THROAT IS AN OPEN TOMB,
WITH THEIR TONGUES THEY
KEEP DECEIVING,"
"THE POISON OF ASPS IS
UNDER THEIR LIPS";
14 "WHOSE MOUTH IS FULL OF
CURSING AND BITTERNESS";
15 "THEIR FEET ARE SWIFT TO SHED BLOOD,
16 DESTRUCTION AND MISERY
ARE IN THEIR PATHS,
17 AND THE PATH OF PEACE THEY
HAVE NOT KNOWN."
18 "THERE IS NO FEAR OF GOD
BEFORE THEIR EYES."

19 Now we know that whatever the Law
says, it speaks to those who are in the Law,
so that every mouth may be shut and all
the world may become accountable to God;
20 because by the works of the Law NO FLESH
WILL BE JUSTIFIED IN HIS SIGHT, for through
the Law *comes* the knowledge of sin.

21 But now apart from the Law *the* righ-
teousness of God has been manifested,
being witnessed by the Law and the
Prophets, 22 even *the* righteousness of God
through faith in Jesus Christ for all those
who believe; for there is no distinction;
23 for all have sinned and fall short of the
glory of God, 24 being justified as a gift by
His grace through the redemption which
is in Christ Jesus; 25 whom God displayed
publicly as a propitiation in His blood
through faith, for a demonstration of His
righteousness, because in the forbearance
of God He passed over the sins previously
committed; 26 for the demonstration of His
righteousness at the present time, so that
He would be just and the justifier of the one
who has faith in Jesus.

27 Where then is boasting? It is excluded.
By what kind of law? Of works? No, but by a
law of faith. 28 For we maintain that a man
is justified by faith apart from works of the
Law. 29 Or is God *the God* of Jews only? Is He
not *the God* of Gentiles also? Yes, of Gentiles
also, 30 since indeed God, who will justify
the circumcised by faith and the uncircum-
cised through that faith, is one.

31 Do we then abolish the Law through
faith? May it never be! On the contrary, we
establish the Law.

AUGUST 2

Esther 5:1–6:14

5 Now it happened on the third day,
that Esther put on her royal robes and
stood in the inner court of the king's house
in front of the king's rooms, and the king
was sitting on his royal throne in the throne
room, opposite the entrance to *his* house.
2 Now it happened that when the king saw
Esther the queen standing in the court,
she advanced in favor in his eyes; and the
king extended to Esther the golden scepter
which *was* in his hand. So Esther came near
and *reached out* and touched the top of the
scepter. 3 Then the king said to her, "What

is *troubling* you, Queen Esther? And what
is your request? Even to half of the kingdom
it shall be given to you." 4 And Esther said,
"If it *seems* good to the king, may the king
and Haman come this day to the feast that
I have prepared for him."

5 Then the king said, "Bring Haman
quickly that we may do the word of Esther."
So the king and Haman came to the feast
which Esther had prepared. 6 Then, as they
drank their wine at the feast, the king said to
Esther, "What is your petition? For it shall be
given to you. And what is your request? Even
to half of the kingdom it shall be done." 7 So
Esther answered and said, "My petition and
my request is: 8 if I have found favor in the
eyes of the king, and if it *seems* good to the
king to give *heed to* my petition and to do my
request, may the king and Haman come to
the feast which I will prepare for them, and
tomorrow I will do according to the word
of the king."

9 Then Haman went out that day glad
and merry of heart; but when Haman saw
Mordecai in the king's gate and that he did
not stand up or tremble before him, Haman
was filled with wrath against Mordecai.
10 But Haman controlled himself, went to
his house, and sent for and brought his
friends and his wife Zeresh. 11 Then Haman
recounted to them the glory of his riches
and the number of his sons and every
instance where the king had magnified him
and how he had advanced him above the
princes and servants of the king. 12 Haman
also said, "Even Esther the queen let no
one but me come with the king to the feast
which she had prepared; and tomorrow also
I am called *to come* to her with the king.
13 Yet all of this is worth nothing to me every
time I see Mordecai the Jew sitting at the
king's gate." 14 Then Zeresh his wife and all
his friends said to him, "Have a gallows fifty
cubits high made and in the morning say to
the king that Mordecai should be hanged on
it; then go gladly with the king to the feast."
And the word was good to Haman, so he had
the gallows made.

6 During that night, sleep had fled from
the king, so he said *for them* to bring
the book of memoranda, the chronicles,
and they were read before the king. 2 And
it was found written what Mordecai had
told concerning Bigthana and Teresh, two
of the king's eunuchs from those who were
doorkeepers, that they had sought to send
forth *their* hand against King Ahasuerus.
3 And the king said, "What honor or great-
ness has been done to Mordecai for this?"
Then the king's young men who attended
him said, "Nothing has been done for him."
4 So the king said, "Who is in the court?"
Now Haman had entered the outer court
of the king's house in order to speak to
the king about hanging Mordecai on the
gallows which he had set up for him. 5 And
the king's young men said to him, "Behold,
Haman is standing in the court." And the
king said, "Let him come in." 6 So Haman
came in, and the king said to him, "What
is to be done for the man whom the king
delights to honor?" And Haman said in his
heart, "Whom would the king delight to
honor more than me?" 7 Then Haman said
to the king, "For the man whom the king
delights to honor, 8 let them bring a royal
robe which the king clothes himself in, and
the horse on which the king has ridden,
and on whose head a royal crown has been
placed; 9 and let the robe and the horse be
given over to the hand of one of the king's
most noble princes, and let them clothe
the man whom the king delights to honor
and lead him on horseback through the city
square and call out before him, 'Thus it shall
be done to the man whom the king delights
to honor.'"

10 Then the king said to Haman, "Take
quickly the robes and the horse as you have
said, and do so for Mordecai the Jew, who
is sitting at the king's gate; do not fall short
in anything of all that you have spoken."
11 So Haman took the robe and the horse
and clothed Mordecai and led him *on horse-*
back through the city square and called out
before him, "Thus it shall be done to the
man whom the king delights to honor."

12 Then Mordecai returned to the king's
gate. But Haman hastened home, mourn-
ing, with *his* head covered. 13 And Haman
recounted to Zeresh his wife and all his
friends everything that had happened to
him. Then his wise men and Zeresh his wife
said to him, "If Mordecai, before whom you
have begun to fall, is of the seed of the Jews,
you will not overcome him, but will surely
fall before him."

14 While they were still speaking with
him, the king's eunuchs reached *Haman's*

home and hastily brought Haman to the
feast which Esther had prepared.

Psalm 90:1–6

1 Lord, You have been our dwelling place
from generation to generation.
2 Before the mountains were born
Or You brought forth the
earth and the world,
Even from everlasting to
everlasting, You are God.

3 You turn man back into dust
And say, "Return, O sons of men."
4 For a thousand years in Your sight
Are like yesterday when it passes by,
Or *as* a watch in the night.
5 You have swept them away like
a flood, they fall asleep;
In the morning they are like
grass which sprouts anew.
6 In the morning it blossoms
and sprouts anew;
Toward evening it withers
away and dries up.

Proverbs 22:9

9 He who is generous will be blessed,
For he gives from his food to the poor.

Romans 4:1–25

4 What then shall we say that Abraham,
our forefather according to the flesh,
has found? 2 For if Abraham was justified by
works, he has something to boast about—
but not before God! 3 For what does the
Scripture say? "ABRAHAM BELIEVED GOD, AND
IT WAS COUNTED TO HIM AS RIGHTEOUSNESS."
4 Now to the one who works, his wage is not
counted according to grace, but according
to what is due. 5 But to the one who does
not work, but believes upon Him who
justifies the ungodly, his faith is counted as
righteousness, 6 just as David also speaks
of the blessing on the man to whom God
counts righteousness apart from works:
7 "BLESSED ARE THOSE WHOSE LAWLESS
DEEDS HAVE BEEN FORGIVEN,
AND WHOSE SINS HAVE BEEN COVERED.
8 "BLESSED IS THE MAN WHOSE SIN THE
LORD WILL NOT TAKE INTO ACCOUNT."
9 Therefore, is this blessing on the
circumcised, or on the uncircumcised
also? For we say, "FAITH WAS COUNTED
TO ABRAHAM AS RIGHTEOUSNESS." 10 How
then was it counted? While he was cir-
cumcised, or uncircumcised? Not while
circumcised, but while uncircumcised;
11 and he received the sign of circumci-
sion, a seal of the righteousness of the
faith which he had while uncircumcised,
so that he might be the father of all who
believe without being circumcised, that
righteousness might be counted to them,
12 and the father of circumcision to those
who not only are of the circumcision, but
who also follow in the steps of the faith of
our father Abraham which he had while
uncircumcised.
13 For the promise to Abraham or to his
seed that he would be heir of the world
was not through the Law, but through the
righteousness of faith. 14 For if those who
are of the Law are heirs, faith has been
made empty and the promise has been
abolished; 15 for the Law brings about
wrath, but where there is no law, there also
is no trespass.
16 For this reason *it is* by faith, in order
that *it may be* according to grace, so that
the promise will be guaranteed to all the
seed, not only to those who are of the Law,
but also to those who are of the faith of
Abraham, who is the father of us all— 17 as
it is written, "A FATHER OF MANY NATIONS
HAVE I MADE YOU"—in the presence of Him
whom he believed, *even* God, who gives life
to the dead and calls into being that which
does not exist. 18 In hope against hope he
believed, so that he might become a father
of many nations according to that which
had been spoken, "SO SHALL YOUR SEED BE."
19 And without becoming weak in faith he
contemplated his own body, now as good
as dead since he was about a hundred
years old, and the deadness of Sarah's
womb; 20 yet, with respect to the promise
of God, he did not waver in unbelief but
grew strong in faith, giving glory to God,
21 and being fully assured that what God
had promised, He was able also to do.
22 Therefore IT WAS ALSO COUNTED TO HIM
AS RIGHTEOUSNESS. 23 Now not for his sake
only was it written THAT IT WAS COUNTED TO
HIM, 24 but for our sake also, to whom it will
be counted, as those who believe upon Him
who raised Jesus our Lord from the dead,
25 *He* who was delivered over on account
of our transgressions, and was raised on
account of our justification.

AUGUST 3

Esther 7:1–8:17

7 Then the king and Haman came to drink
wine with Esther the queen. 2 And the
king said to Esther on the second day also
as they drank their wine at the feast, "What
is your petition, Queen Esther? It shall be
given you. And what is your request? Even to
half of the kingdom it shall be done." 3 Then
Queen Esther answered and said, "If I have
found favor in your eyes, O king, and if it
seems good to the king, let my life be given
to me as my petition, and my people as my
request; 4 for we have been sold, I and my
people, to be destroyed, to be killed, and
to be caused to perish. Now if we had only
been sold as slaves, men and women, I
would have remained silent, for the adver-
sity would not be worth the annoyance to
the king." 5 Then King Ahasuerus said—he
said to Esther the Queen, "Who is this one,
and where is this one, who fills his heart to
do thus?" 6 So Esther said, "An adversary and
an enemy is this evil Haman!" Then Haman
became terrified before the king and queen.
7 And the king arose in his wrath from
drinking wine *and went* into the garden
of *his* palace; but Haman stayed to seek
for his life from Queen Esther, for he saw
that calamity had been determined against
him by the king. 8 Now the king returned
from the garden of *his* palace into the place
where they were drinking wine. And Haman
was falling on the couch where Esther was.
So the king said, "Will he even assault the
queen with me in the house?" *As* the word
went out of the king's mouth, they covered
Haman's face. 9 Then Harbonah, one of
the eunuchs who *were* before the king,
said, "Behold indeed, the gallows—which
Haman made for Mordecai who spoke
good on behalf of the king—are standing
at Haman's house fifty cubits high!" And
the king said, "Hang him on it." 10 So they
hanged Haman on the gallows which he had
set up for Mordecai, and the king's wrath
subsided.

8 On that day King Ahasuerus gave the
house of Haman, the adversary of the
Jews, to Queen Esther; and Mordecai came
before the king, for Esther had told what
he was to her. 2 And the king removed his
signet ring, which he had taken away from
Haman, and gave it to Mordecai. And Esther
set Mordecai over the house of Haman.
3 Then Esther spoke again to the king, fell
at his feet, wept, and implored him to repeal
the evil *scheme* of Haman the Agagite and
his scheme which he had devised against
the Jews. 4 And the king extended the golden
scepter to Esther. So Esther arose and stood
before the king. 5 Then she said, "If it *seems*
good to the king, and if I have found favor
before him and the matter *seems* proper
to the king and I am good in his eyes, let it
be written to turn back the letters devised
by Haman, the son of Hammedatha the
Agagite, which he wrote to cause the Jews
who are in all the king's provinces to perish.
6 For how can I endure to see the calamity
which will befall my people, and how can I
endure to see the perishing of my kinsmen?"
7 So King Ahasuerus said to Queen
Esther and to Mordecai the Jew, "Behold, I
have given the house of Haman to Esther,
and him they have hanged on the gallows
because he had sent forth his hand against
the Jews. 8 Now you write to the Jews,
according to what is good in your eyes, in
the king's name, and seal *it* with the king's
signet ring; for a written *decree* which is
written in the name of the king and sealed
with the king's signet ring may not be turned
back."
9 So the king's scribes were called at that
time in the third month (that is, the month
Sivan), on the twenty-third day; and it
was written according to all that Mordecai
commanded to the Jews, the satraps, the
governors, and the princes of the provinces
which *extended* from India to Ethiopia, 127
provinces, to every province according to its
script, and to every people according to their
tongue as well as to the Jews according to
their script and their tongue. 10 And he wrote
in the name of King Ahasuerus and sealed it
with the king's signet ring and sent letters
by the hand of couriers on horses, riding
on steeds sired by the royal stud. 11 In them
the king gave the Jews who were in each and
every city *the right* to assemble and to make
a stand for their lives, to destroy, to kill, and
to cause to perish the entire military force of
any people or province which would act as

their adversaries, including little ones and
women, and to plunder their spoil, 12 on one
day in all the provinces of King Ahasuerus,
the thirteenth *day* of the twelfth month
(that is, the month Adar). 13 A copy of that
which was written down to be given as law
in each and every province was revealed
to all the peoples, so that the Jews would
be ready for this day to avenge themselves
on their enemies. 14 The couriers, hurried
and hastened by the king's word, went out,
riding on the royal steeds; and the law was
given out at the citadel in Susa.

15 Then Mordecai went out from the
presence of the king in royal robes of blue
and fine white, with a large crown of gold
and a garment of fine linen and purple;
and the city of Susa cried aloud and was
glad. 16 For the Jews there was light and
gladness and joy and honor. 17 And in each
and every province and in each and every
city, wherever the king's word and his law
reached, there was gladness and joy for the
Jews, a feast and a holiday. And many among
the peoples of the land became Jews, for the
dread of the Jews had fallen on them.

Psalm 90:7–17

7 For we have been consumed
by Your anger
And by Your wrath we have
been dismayed.
8 You have set our iniquities before You,
Our secret *sins* in the light
of Your presence.
9 For all our days have declined
in Your fury;
We have finished our years like a sigh.
10 As for the days of our life, they
contain seventy years,
Or if due to might, eighty years,
Yet their pride is *but* labor
and wickedness;
For soon it is gone and we fly away.
11 Who knows the power of Your anger
And Your fury, according to
the fear that is due You?
12 So teach us to number our days,
That we may present *to You*
a heart of wisdom.

13 Return, O Yahweh; how long *will it be*?
And be sorry for Your slaves.
14 O satisfy us in the morning with
Your lovingkindness,
That we may sing for joy and
be glad all our days.
15 Make us glad according to the
days You have afflicted us,
And the years we have seen evil.
16 Let Your work appear to
Your slaves
And Your majesty to their sons.
17 Let the favor of the Lord
our God be upon us;
And establish for us the
work of our hands;
Establish the work of our hands.

Proverbs 22:10–11

10 Drive out the scoffer, and
strife will go out,
Even contention and
disgrace will cease.
11 He who loves purity of heart
And grace on his lips, the
king is his friend.

Romans 5:1–21

5 Therefore, having been justified by
faith, we have peace with God through
our Lord Jesus Christ, 2 through whom
also we have obtained our introduction
by faith into this grace in which we stand;
and we boast in hope of the glory of God.
3 And not only this, but we also boast in our
afflictions, knowing that affliction brings
about perseverance; 4 and perseverance,
proven character; and proven character,
hope; 5 and hope does not put to shame,
because the love of God has been poured
out within our hearts through the Holy
Spirit who was given to us.

6 For while we were still weak, at the right
time Christ died for the ungodly. 7 For one
will hardly die for a righteous man, though
perhaps for the good man someone would
dare even to die. 8 But God demonstrates
His own love toward us, in that while we
were yet sinners, Christ died for us. 9 Much
more then, having now been justified by His
blood, we shall be saved from the wrath *of
God* through Him. 10 For if while we were
enemies we were reconciled to God through
the death of His Son, much more, having
been reconciled, we shall be saved by His
life. 11 And not only this, but we also boast
in God through our Lord Jesus Christ,
through whom we have now received the
reconciliation.

12 Therefore, just as through one man sin
entered into the world, and death through
sin, and so death spread to all men, because
all sinned— 13 for until the Law sin was in
the world, but sin is not imputed when there
is no law. 14 Nevertheless death reigned from
Adam until Moses, even over those who had
not sinned in the likeness of the trespass
of Adam, who is a type of Him who was to
come.

15 But the gracious gift is not like the
transgression. For if by the transgression
of the one the many died, much more did
the grace of God and the gift by the grace
of the one Man, Jesus Christ, abound to the
many. 16 And the gift is not like *that which
came* through the one who sinned; for on
the one hand the judgment *arose* from one
transgression resulting in condemnation,
but on the other hand the gracious gift *arose*
from many transgressions resulting in justi-
fication. 17 For if by the transgression of the
one, death reigned through the one, much
more those who receive the abundance of
grace and of the gift of righteousness will
reign in life through the One, Jesus Christ.

18 So then as through one transgression
there resulted condemnation to all men,
even so through one act of righteousness
there resulted justification of life to all men.
19 For as through the one man's disobedi-
ence the many were appointed sinners, even
so through the obedience of the One the
many will be appointed righteous. 20 Now
the Law came in so that the transgression
would increase, but where sin increased,
grace abounded all the more, 21 so that, as
sin reigned in death, even so grace would
reign through righteousness to eternal life
through Jesus Christ our Lord.

AUGUST 4

Esther 9:1–10:3

9 Now in the twelfth month (that is, the
month Adar), on the thirteenth day
when the king's word and law had reached
the point for them to be done, on the day
when the enemies of the Jews hoped to gain
power over them, it was turned around so
that the Jews themselves gained power over
those who hated them. 2 The Jews assembled
in their cities throughout all the provinces
of King Ahasuerus to send forth *their* hand
against those who sought their calamity;
and no one could stand before them, for the
dread of them had fallen on all the peoples.
3 Even all the princes of the provinces, the
satraps, the governors, and those who were
doing the king's work advanced the Jews,
because the dread of Mordecai had fallen
on them. 4 Indeed, Mordecai was great in the
king's house, and the report about him went
throughout all the provinces; for the man
Mordecai became greater and greater. 5 Thus
the Jews struck all their enemies with the
sword, killing and causing *them* to perish;
and they did what they pleased to those who
hated them. 6 And at the citadel in Susa the
Jews killed and caused to perish 500 men,
7 and Parshandatha, Dalphon, Aspatha,
8 Poratha, Adalia, Aridatha, 9 Parmashta,
Arisai, Aridai, and Vaizatha, 10 the 10 sons
of Haman the son of Hammedatha, the Jews'
adversary; but they did not send forth their
hand for the plunder.

11 On that day the number of those who
were killed at the citadel in Susa came to the
king. 12 So the king said to Queen Esther,
"The Jews have killed and caused to perish
500 men and the 10 sons of Haman at the
citadel in Susa. *Now* in the rest of the king's
provinces, what have they done? So what is
your petition? It shall even be given to you.
And what is your further request? It shall
also be done." 13 Then Esther said, "If it is
good to the king, let tomorrow also be given
to the Jews who are in Susa to do according
to the law for today; and let Haman's 10 sons
be hanged on the gallows." 14 So the king
said that it should be done so; and a law was
given in Susa, and Haman's 10 sons were
hanged. 15 And the Jews who were in Susa
assembled also on the fourteenth day of the
month Adar and killed 300 men in Susa, but
they did not send forth their hand for the
plunder.

16 Now the rest of the Jews who *were* in
the king's provinces assembled, to make
a stand for their lives and obtain rest for
themselves from their enemies, and to kill
75,000 of those who hated them; but they
did not send forth their hand for the plun-
der. 17 *This was done* on the thirteenth day
of the month Adar, and on the fourteenth

day they rested and made it a day of feasting
and gladness.
18 But the Jews who were in Susa assem-
bled on the thirteenth and the fourteenth
of the same month, and they rested on the
fifteenth day and made it a day of feasting
and gladness. 19 Therefore the Jews of the
rural areas, who live in the rural towns,
make the fourteenth day of the month
Adar *a* holiday for gladness and feasting
and sending portions *of food* to one another.
20 Then Mordecai wrote down these
events, and he sent letters to all the Jews who
were in all the provinces of King Ahasuerus,
both near and far, 21 to establish among
them to celebrate the fourteenth day of the
month Adar, and the fifteenth day of the
same month, annually, 22 because on those
days the Jews obtained rest for themselves
from their enemies, and *it was a* month
which was turned around for them from
sorrow into gladness and from mourning
into a holiday; that they should make them
days of feasting and gladness and sending
portions *of food* to one another and gifts
to the poor.
23 Thus the Jews *fully* accepted what they
had started to do and what Mordecai had
written to them. 24 For Haman the son of
Hammedatha, the Agagite, the adversary of
all the Jews, had devised against the Jews to
cause them to perish and had cast Pur, that
is the lot, to throw them into confusion and
cause them to perish. 25 But when it came
before the king, he said by letter that his evil
scheme, which he had devised against the
Jews, should return on his own head and
that he and his sons should be hanged on
the gallows. 26 Therefore they called these
days Purim after the name of Pur. Therefore,
because of the words in this letter, both
what they had seen in this regard and what
had reached them, 27 the Jews established
and accepted a custom for themselves and
for their seed and for all those who joined
themselves to them, so that celebrating
these two days according to what was
written down and according to their fixed
time from year to year would not pass away.
28 So these days were to be remembered and
celebrated throughout every generation,
every family, every province, and every
city; thus these days of Purim were not to
pass away from among the Jews, nor their
memory come to an end from their seed.
29 Then Queen Esther, daughter of
Abihail, with Mordecai the Jew, wrote
with full authority to establish this second
letter about Purim. 30 And he sent letters
to all the Jews, to the 127 provinces of the
kingdom of Ahasuerus, *namely,* words of
peace and truth, 31 to establish these days
of Purim at their appointed times, just as
Mordecai the Jew and Queen Esther had
established for them, and just as they had
established for themselves and for their
seed with words concerning their times
of fasting and their crying out. 32 And the
declaration of Esther established these
words concerning Purim, and it was
written in the book.

10 Then King Ahasuerus set forced labor
upon the land and the coastlands of
the sea. 2 And the entire work of his author-
ity and his might, and the full account of
the greatness of Mordecai, whom the king
had made *so* great, are they not written in
the book of the chronicles of the kings of
Media and Persia? 3 For Mordecai the Jew
was second *only* to King Ahasuerus and
was great among the Jews and pleasing to
his many *fellow* brothers, one who sought
the good of his people and one who spoke
for the peace of all his seed.

Psalm 91:1–6

1 He who abides in the shelter
of the Most High
Will abide in the shadow
of the Almighty.
2 I will say to Yahweh,
"My refuge and my fortress,
My God, in whom I trust!"
3 For it is He who delivers you from
the snare of the trapper
And from the destructive pestilence.
4 He will cover you with His pinions,
And under His wings you
will take refuge;
His truth is a large shield
and bulwark.
5 You will not be afraid of
terror by night,
Or arrow that flies by day;
6 Of pestilence that moves
in darkness,
Or of destruction that
devastates at noon.

Proverbs 22:12

12 The eyes of Yahweh guard knowledge,
But He subverts the words of
the treacherous one.

Romans 6:1–23

6 What shall we say then? Are we to con-
tinue in sin so that grace may increase?
2 May it never be! How shall we who died to
sin still live in it? 3 Or do you not know that
all of us who were baptized into Christ Jesus
were baptized into His death? 4 Therefore we
were buried with Him through baptism into
death, so that as Christ was raised from the
dead through the glory of the Father, so we too
might walk in newness of life. 5 For if we have
become united with *Him* in the likeness of His
death, certainly we shall also be *in the likeness*
of His resurrection, 6 knowing this, that our
old man was crucified with *Him*, in order that
our body of sin might be done away with, so
that we would no longer be slaves to sin; 7 for
he who has died has been justified from sin.
8 Now if we died with Christ, we believe
that we shall also live with Him, 9 knowing
that Christ, having been raised from the
dead, is never to die again; death no longer
is master over Him. 10 For the death that
He died, He died to sin once for all, but the
life that He lives, He lives to God. 11 Even so
consider yourselves to be dead to sin, but
alive to God in Christ Jesus.
12 Therefore do not let sin reign in your
mortal body so that you obey its lusts, 13 and
do not go on presenting your members to
sin *as* instruments of unrighteousness,
but present yourselves to God as those
alive from the dead, and your members *as*
instruments of righteousness to God. 14 For
sin shall not be master over you, for you are
not under law but under grace.
15 What then? Shall we sin because we are
not under law but under grace? May it never
be! 16 Do you not know that when you go on
presenting yourselves to someone *as* slaves
for obedience, you are slaves of the one whom
you obey, either of sin leading to death, or of
obedience leading to righteousness? 17 But
thanks be to God that *though* you were
slaves of sin, you obeyed from the heart that
pattern of teaching to which you were given
over, 18 and having been freed from sin, you
became slaves of righteousness. 19 I am speak-
ing in human terms because of the weakness
of your flesh. For just as you presented
your members as slaves to impurity and to
lawlessness, leading to *further* lawlessness,
so now present your members as slaves to
righteousness, leading to sanctification.
20 For when you were slaves of sin,
you were free in regard to righteousness.
21 Therefore what benefit were you then
having from the things of which you are
now ashamed? For the end of those things
is death. 22 But now having been freed from
sin and enslaved to God, you have your
benefit, leading to sanctification, and the
end, eternal life. 23 For the wages of sin is
death, but the gracious gift of God is eternal
life in Christ Jesus our Lord.

AUGUST 5

Job 1:1–2:13

1 There was a man in the land of Uz whose
name was Job; and that man was blame-
less, upright, fearing God, and turning away
from evil. 2 Seven sons and three daughters
were born to him. 3 His possessions also
were 7,000 sheep, 3,000 camels, 500 pairs
of oxen, 500 female donkeys, and very many
servants; and that man was the greatest of
all the sons of the east. 4 His sons used to
go and hold a feast in the house of each one
on his day, and they would send and invite
their three sisters to eat and drink with
them. 5 Now it happened when the days
of feasting had completed their cycle, that
Job would send and set them apart as holy.
And he would rise up early in the morning
and offer burnt offerings *according to* the
number of them all; for Job said, "Perhaps
my sons have sinned and cursed God in their
hearts." Thus Job did continually.
6 Now it was the day that the sons of God
came to stand before Yahweh, and Satan
also came among them. 7 And Yahweh said
to Satan, "From where do you come?" Then
Satan answered Yahweh and said, "From
roaming about on the earth and walking
around on it." 8 Then Yahweh said to Satan,
"Have you set your heart upon My servant
Job? For there is no one like him on the earth,
a blameless and upright man, fearing God and
turning away from evil." 9 And Satan answered

Yahweh and said, "Does Job fear God without
cause? 10 Have You not made a hedge about
him and his house and all that he has, on
every side? You have blessed the work of his
hands, and his possessions have increased in
the land. 11 But send forth Your hand now and
touch all that he has; he will surely curse You
to Your face." 12 Then Yahweh said to Satan,
"Behold, all that he has is in your hand, only
do not send forth your hand toward him." So
Satan went out from the presence of Yahweh.
13 Now it happened that on the day when
his sons and his daughters were eating and
drinking wine in the house of their brother,
the firstborn, 14 a messenger came to Job and
said, "The oxen were plowing and the don-
keys feeding beside them, 15 and the Sabeans
fell *upon them* and took them. They also
struck down the young men with the edge
of the sword, and I alone have escaped to
tell you." 16 While this one was still speaking,
another also came and said, "The fire of God
fell from heaven and burned up the sheep
and the young men and consumed them, and
I alone have escaped to tell you." 17 While
this one was still speaking, another also
came and said, "The Chaldeans set up three
companies and made a raid on the camels
and took them and struck down the young
men with the edge of the sword, and I alone
have escaped to tell you." 18 While this one
was still speaking, another also came and
said, "Your sons and your daughters were
eating and drinking wine in the house of
their brother, the firstborn, 19 and behold, a
great wind came from across the wilderness
and touched the four corners of the house,
and it fell on the young people, and they
died, and I alone have escaped to tell you."
20 Then Job arose and tore his robe and
shaved his head, and he fell to the ground
and worshiped. 21 And he said,

"Naked I came from my mother's womb,
And naked I shall return there.
Yahweh gave, and Yahweh
has taken away.
Blessed be the name of Yahweh."

22 Through all this Job did not sin, nor did
he give offense to God.

2 Again it was the day that the sons of God
came to stand before Yahweh, and Satan
also came among them to stand himself before
Yahweh. 2 And Yahweh said to Satan, "Where
do you come from?" Then Satan answered
Yahweh and said, "From roaming about on the
earth and walking around on it." 3 And Yahweh
said to Satan, "Have you set your heart upon
My servant Job? For there is no one like him
on the earth, a blameless and upright man,
fearing God and turning away from evil. And
he still holds fast his integrity. So you incited
Me against him to swallow him up in vain."
4 Satan answered Yahweh and said, "Skin for
skin! Yes, all that a man has he will give for
his life. 5 However, send forth Your hand now,
and touch his bone and his flesh; he will curse
You in Your face." 6 So Yahweh said to Satan,
"Behold, he is in your hand, only spare his life."
7 Then Satan went out from the presence
of Yahweh and struck Job with terrible boils
from the sole of his foot to the top of his head.
8 And he took a potsherd to scrape himself
while he was sitting among the ashes.
9 Then his wife said to him, "Do you still
hold fast your integrity? Curse God and die!"
10 But he said to her, "You speak as one of
the wickedly foolish women speaks. Shall
we indeed accept good from God and not
accept calamity?" In all this Job did not sin
with his lips.
11 Then Job's three friends heard of all
this calamity that had come upon him. So
they came each one from his own place,
Eliphaz the Temanite, Bildad the Shuhite,
and Zophar the Naamathite; and they
made an appointment together to come
to console him and comfort him. 12 Then
they lifted up their eyes at a distance and did
not recognize him, and they lifted up their
voices and wept. And each of them tore his
robe, and they threw dust over their heads
toward the sky. 13 Then they sat down on the
ground with him for seven days and seven
nights with no one speaking a word to him,
for they saw that *his* pain was very great.

Psalm 91:7–13

7 A thousand may fall at your side
And ten thousand at your right hand,
But it shall not approach you.
8 You will only look on with your eyes
And see the recompense of the wicked.
9 For you have made Yahweh—my refuge,
The Most High—your dwelling place.
10 No evil will befall you,
And no plague will come near your tent.
11 For He will command His
angels concerning you,

To guard you in all your ways.
12 On their hands they will bear you up,
Lest you strike your foot against a stone.
13 You will tread upon the
fierce lion and cobra,
The young lion and the serpent
you will trample down.

Proverbs 22:13–14

13 The sluggard says,
"There is a lion outside;
I will be killed in the streets!"
14 The mouth of strange
women is a deep pit;
He who is cursed of Yahweh
will fall into it.

Romans 7:1–25

7 Or do you not know, brothers—for I am
speaking to those who know the law—
that the law is master over a person as long as
he lives? 2 For the married woman has been
bound by law to her husband while he is
living, but if her husband dies, she is released
from the law concerning the husband. 3 So
then, if while her husband is living she is
joined to another man, she shall be called an
adulteress. But if her husband dies, she is free
from the law, so that she is not an adulteress
though she is joined to another man.
4 So, my brothers, you also were made to
die to the Law through the body of Christ, so
that you might be joined to another, to Him
who was raised from the dead, in order that
we might bear fruit for God. 5 For while we
were in the flesh, the sinful passions, which
were *aroused* by the Law, were at work in our
members to bear fruit for death. 6 But now
we have been released from the Law, having
died to that by which we were constrained,
so that we serve in newness of the Spirit and
not in oldness of the letter.
7 What shall we say then? Is the Law sin?
May it never be! Rather, I would not have
come to know sin except through the Law.
For I would not have known about coveting
if the Law had not said, "YOU SHALL NOT
COVET." 8 But sin, taking opportunity through
the commandment, worked out in me cov-
eting of every kind. For apart from the Law
sin *is* dead. 9 Now I was once alive apart from
the Law, but when the commandment came,
sin revived and I died; 10 and this command-
ment, which was to lead to life, was found
to lead to death for me. 11 For sin, taking an
opportunity through the commandment,
deceived me and through it killed me. 12 So,
the Law is holy, and the commandment is
holy and righteous and good.
13 Therefore did that which is good
become *a cause of* death for me? May it
never be! Rather it was sin, in order that it
might be shown to be sin by working out
my death through that which is good, so
that through the commandment sin would
become utterly sinful.
14 For we know that the Law is spiritual,
but I am fleshly, having been sold into bond-
age under sin. 15 For what I am working out,
I do not understand; for I am not practicing
what I *would* like to *do*, but I am doing the
very thing I hate. 16 But if I do the very thing
I do not want, I agree with the Law, that it
is good. 17 So now, no longer am I the one
working it out, but sin which dwells in me.
18 For I know that nothing good dwells in
me, that is, in my flesh; for the willing is
present in me, but the working out of the
good *is* not. 19 For the good that I want, I
do not do, but I practice the very evil that
I do not want. 20 But if I am doing the very
thing I do not want, I am no longer the one
working it out, but sin which dwells in me.
21 I find then the principle that in me evil
is present—in me who wants to do good.
22 For I joyfully concur with the law of God
in the inner man, 23 but I see a different law
in my members, waging war against the
law of my mind and making me a captive
to the law of sin which is in my members.
24 Wretched man that I am! Who will deliver
me from the body of this death? 25 Thanks
be to God through Jesus Christ our Lord!
So then, on the one hand I myself with my
mind am serving the law of God, but on the
other, with my flesh the law of sin.

Through His Word, our Father speaks to us, encourages us, comforts us, instructs us, humbles us, and reproves us.

— GEORGE MULLER

AUGUST 6

Job 3:1–4:21

3 Afterward Job opened his mouth and
cursed the day of his *birth.* 2 And Job
answered and said,

3 "Let the day perish on which
I was to be born,
And the night *which* said, 'A
man is conceived.'
4 "May that day be darkness;
Let not God seek it from above,
Nor light shine on it.
5 "Let darkness and shadow
of death redeem it;
Let a cloud dwell upon it;
Let the blackness of the day terrify it.
6 "*As for* that night, let thick
darkness take it;
Let it not rejoice among the
days of the year;
Let it not come into the
number of the months.
7 "Behold, let that night be barren;
Let no joyful shout enter it.
8 "Let those curse it who curse the day,
Who are ready to rouse Leviathan.
9 "Let the stars of its twilight
be darkened;
Let it hope for light but have none,
And let it not see the breaking dawn,
10 Because it did not shut the
opening of my *mother's* body,
Or hide trouble from my eyes.

11 "Why did I not die from the womb,
Come forth from the womb
and breathe my last?
12 "Why did the knees receive me,
And why the breasts, that
I should suck?
13 "For now I would have lain
down and been quiet;
I would have slept then; it would
have been rest to me,
14 With kings and *with*
counselors of the earth,
Who rebuilt waste places
for themselves,
15 Or with princes who had gold,
Who were filling their
houses *with* silver.
16 "Or *why* was I not like a
miscarriage hidden away,
As infants that never saw light?
17 "There the wicked cease from raging,
And there the weary of
strength are at rest.
18 "The prisoners are at ease together;
They do not hear the voice
of the taskmaster.
19 "The small and the great are there,
And the slave is free from his master.

20 "Why is light given to him
who is troubled,
And life to the bitter of soul,
21 Who long for death, but there is none,
And dig for it more than for
hidden treasures,
22 Who are glad with joy,
And rejoice when they find the grave?
23 "*Why is light given* to a man
whose way is hidden,
And whom God has hedged in?
24 "For my groaning comes at
the sight of my food,
And my roaring pours out like water.
25 "For the dread that I dread
comes upon me,
And what I am afraid of befalls me.
26 "I am not complacent, nor am I quiet,
And I am not at rest, and
raging comes."

4 Then Eliphaz the Temanite answered
and said,

2 "If one tries a word with you,
will you become weary?
But who can hold back from speaking?
3 "Behold, you have disciplined many,
And you have strengthened
limp hands.
4 "Your words have helped the
stumbling to stand,
And you have encouraged feeble knees.
5 "But now it has come to you,
and you are impatient;
It touches you, and you are dismayed.
6 "Is not your fear *of God*
your confidence,
And the integrity of your
ways your hope?

7 "Remember now, who *ever*
perished being innocent?

Or where were the upright wiped out?
8 "According to what I have seen,
those who plow wickedness
And those who sow trouble harvest it.
9 "By the breath of God they perish,
And by the wind of His anger
they come to an end.
10 "The roaring of the lion and the
voice of the *fierce* lion,
And the teeth of the young
lions are broken.
11 "The lion perishes for lack of prey,
And the whelps of the
lioness are scattered.

12 "Now a word was brought
to me stealthily,
And my ear received a whisper of it.
13 "Amid disquieting thoughts from
the visions of the night,
When deep sleep falls on men,
14 Dread came upon me, and trembling,
And made the multitude of my
bones shake in dread.
15 "Then a spirit swept by my face;
The hair of my flesh bristled up.
16 "It stood still, but I could not
recognize its appearance;
A form *was* before my eyes;
There was silence, then I heard a voice:
17 'Can mankind be right before God?
Can a man be pure before his Maker?
18 'He puts no trust even in His slaves;
And against His angels
He charges error.
19 'How much more those who
dwell in houses of clay,
Whose foundation is in the dust,
Who are crushed before the moth!
20 'Between morning and evening
they are broken in pieces;
Unobserved, they perish forever.
21 'Is not their tent-cord pulled
up within them?
They die, yet without wisdom.'

Psalm 91:14–16

14 "Because he has loved Me,
therefore I will protect him;
I will set him *securely* on high,
because he has known My name.
15 "He will call upon Me, and
I will answer him;
I will be with him in *his* distress;
I will rescue him and honor him.
16 "With a long life I will satisfy him
And I will show him My salvation."

Proverbs 22:15

15 Folly is bound up in the
heart of a child;
The rod of discipline will
remove it far from him.

Romans 8:1–17

8 Therefore there is now no condemnation
for those who are in Christ Jesus. 2 For
the law of the Spirit of life in Christ Jesus has
set you free from the law of sin and of death.
3 For what the Law could not do, weak as it
was through the flesh, God *did*: sending His
own Son in the likeness of sinful flesh and *as*
an offering for sin, He condemned sin in the
flesh, 4 so that the righteous requirement of
the Law might be fulfilled in us, who do not
walk according to the flesh but according to
the Spirit. 5 For those who are according to
the flesh set their minds on the things of
the flesh, but those who are according to
the Spirit, the things of the Spirit. 6 For the
mind set on the flesh is death, but the mind
set on the Spirit is life and peace, 7 because
the mind set on the flesh is *at* enmity toward
God, for it does not subject itself to the law
of God, for it is not even able *to do so*, 8 and
those who are in the flesh are not able to
please God.
9 However, you are not in the flesh but in
the Spirit, if indeed the Spirit of God dwells
in you. But if anyone does not have the Spirit
of Christ, he does not belong to Him. 10 But
if Christ is in you, though the body is dead
because of sin, yet the spirit is alive because
of righteousness. 11 But if the Spirit of Him
who raised Jesus from the dead dwells in
you, He who raised Christ Jesus from the
dead will also give life to your mortal bodies
through His Spirit who dwells in you.
12 So then, brothers, we are under obliga-
tion, not to the flesh, to live according to the
flesh— 13 for if you are living according to
the flesh, you must die, but if by the Spirit
you are putting to death the practices of
the body, you will live. 14 For as many as are
being led by the Spirit of God, these are sons
of God. 15 For you have not received a spirit
of slavery leading to fear again, but you have
received *the* Spirit of adoption as sons by
whom we cry out, "Abba! Father!" 16 The
Spirit Himself testifies with our spirit that

we are children of God, [17] and if children, also heirs, heirs of God and fellow heirs with Christ, if indeed we suffer with *Him* so that we may also be glorified with *Him*.

AUGUST 7

Job 5:1–6:30

5 "Call now, is there anyone
who will answer you?
And to which of the holy
ones will you turn?
2 "For vexation kills the ignorant fool,
And jealousy puts to death the simple.
3 "I have seen the ignorant
fool taking root,
And I cursed his abode suddenly.
4 "His sons are far from salvation,
They are even crushed in the gate,
And there is no deliverer.
5 "His harvest the hungry devour
And take it to a *place of* thorns,
And the schemer pants
after their wealth.
6 "For wickedness does not come
out from the dust,
Nor does trouble sprout
from the ground,
7 For man is born for trouble,
As sparks fly upward.

8 "But as for me, I would seek God,
And I would set my cause before God,
9 Who does great and
unsearchable things,
Wonders without number.
10 "He gives rain on the earth
And sends water on the *fields* outside,
11 So that He sets on high
those who are lowly,
And those who mourn are
lifted to salvation.
12 "He frustrates the thoughts
of the crafty,
So that their hands cannot attain
success of sound wisdom.
13 "He catches the wise by their
own craftiness,
And the counsel of the twisted
is quickly thwarted.
14 "By day they meet with darkness
And grope at noon as in the night.
15 "But He saves from the sword
of their mouth,
And the needy from the
hand of the strong.
16 "So the poor has hope,
And unrighteousness must
shut its mouth.

17 "Behold, how blessed is the man
whom God reproves,
So do not reject the discipline
of the Almighty.
18 "For He inflicts pain and gives relief;
He wounds, and His hands *also* heal.
19 "From six distresses He will deliver you,
Even in seven evil will not touch you.
20 "In famine He will redeem
you from death,
And in war from hands with swords.
21 "You will be hidden from the
scourge of the tongue,
And you will not be afraid of
devastation when it comes.
22 "You will laugh at devastation
and starvation,
And you will not be afraid of
the beasts of the earth.
23 "For your covenant will be with
the stones of the field,
And the beasts of the field will
be at peace with you.
24 "You will know that your
tent is at peace,
For you will visit your abode
and fear no loss.
25 "You will know also that your
seed will be many,
And your offspring as the
vegetation of the land.
26 "You will come to the grave in full vigor,
Like the stacking of grain in its season.
27 "Behold this; we have investigated
it, *and* so it is.
Hear it, and know for yourself."

6 Then Job answered and said,
2 "Oh that my vexation were
actually weighed
And laid in the balances together
with my destruction!
3 "For then it would be heavier
than the sand of the seas;
Therefore my words have been rash.

4 “For the arrows of the Almighty
are within me,
Their poison my spirit drinks;
The horrors of God are
arranged against me.
5 “Does the wild donkey bray
over *his* grass,
Or does the ox low over his fodder?
6 “Can something tasteless be
eaten without salt,
Or is there any taste in the
slime of a yolk?
7 “My soul refuses to touch *them*;
They are like loathsome food to me.

8 “Oh that my request might
come to pass,
And that God would grant my hope!
9 “Would that God were
willing to crush me,
That He would release His
hand and cut me off!
10 “But it is still my comfort,
And I rejoice in unsparing pain,
That I have not *at all* hidden away
the words of the Holy One.
11 “What is my strength, that
I should wait?
And what is my end, that
I should endure?
12 “Is my strength the strength of stones,
Or is my flesh bronze?
13 “Is it that there is no help within me,
And that the *success* of sound
wisdom is driven from me?

14 “For the despairing man lovingkindness
should be from his friend;
But he forsakes the fear
of the Almighty.
15 “My brothers have betrayed
me like a wadi,
Like the torrents of wadis
which pass away,
16 Which grow dark because of ice
And upon which the snow hides itself.
17 “When they become waterless,
they are silent;
When it is hot, they vanish
from their place.
18 “The paths of their course wind along;
They go up into a formless
place and perish.
19 “The caravans of Tema looked;
The travelers of Sheba hoped for them.
20 “They were ashamed for
they had trusted;
They came there and were humiliated.
21 “Indeed, you have now become such;
You see a terror and are afraid.
22 “Have I said, ‘Give me *something*,’
Or, ‘Offer a bribe for me
from your wealth,’
23 Or, ‘Give me escape from the
hand of the adversary,’
Or, ‘Redeem me from the hand
of the ruthless men’?

24 “Instruct me, and I will be silent;
And cause me to understand
how I have erred.
25 “How painful are upright words!
But what does your reproof prove?
26 “Do you think to reprove *my* words,
Or *think* of the words of one
in despair as wind?
27 “You would even cast *lots*
for the orphans
And bargain over your friend.
28 “So now be willing to face me,
And *see* if I lie to your face.
29 “Now turn *from this*, let there
be no unrighteousness;
Even turn *from this*, my
righteousness is yet in it.
30 “Is there unrighteousness
on my tongue?
Cannot my palate discern destruction?

Psalm 92:1–7

1 It is good to give thanks to Yahweh
And to sing praises to Your
name, O Most High;
2 To declare Your lovingkindness
in the morning
And Your faithfulness by night,
3 With the ten-stringed lute
and with the harp,
With resounding music upon the lyre.
4 For You, O Yahweh, have made me
glad by what You have done,
I will sing for joy at the
works of Your hands.

5 How great are Your works, O Yahweh!
Your thoughts are very deep.
6 A senseless man does not know,
And a fool does not understand this:
7 That when the wicked
flourished like grass

And all *the* workers of
iniquity blossomed,
It *was only* that they might be
destroyed forevermore.

Proverbs 22:16

16 He who oppresses the poor to
make more for himself
Or who gives to the rich *will*
only *come to* lack.

Romans 8:18–39

18 For I consider that the sufferings of this present time are not worthy to be compared with the glory that is to be revealed to us. 19 For the anxious longing of the creation eagerly waits for the revealing of the sons of God. 20 For the creation was subjected to futility, not willingly, but because of Him who subjected it, in hope 21 that the creation itself also will be set free from its slavery to corruption into the freedom of the glory of the children of God. 22 For we know that the whole creation groans and suffers the pains of childbirth together until now. 23 And not only this, but also we ourselves, having the first fruits of the Spirit, even we ourselves groan within ourselves, eagerly waiting for *our* adoption as sons, the redemption of our body. 24 For in hope we were saved, but hope that is seen is not hope, for who hopes for what he *already* sees? 25 But if we hope for what we do not see, with perseverance we eagerly wait for it.

26 And in the same way the Spirit also helps our weakness, for we do not know how to pray as we should, but the Spirit Himself intercedes for *us* with groanings too deep for words; 27 and He who searches the hearts knows what the mind of the Spirit is, because He intercedes for the saints according to *the will of* God.

28 And we know that for those who love God all things work together for good, for those who are called according to *His* purpose. 29 Because those whom He foreknew, He also predestined *to become* conformed to the image of His Son, so that He would be the firstborn among many brothers; 30 and those whom He predestined, He also called; and those whom He called, He also justified; and those whom He justified, He also glorified.

31 What then shall we say to these things? If God *is* for us, who *is* against us? 32 He who indeed did not spare His own Son, but delivered Him over for us all, how will He not also with Him graciously give us all things? 33 Who will bring a charge against God's elect? God is the one who justifies; 34 who is the one who condemns? Christ Jesus is He who died, yes, rather who was raised, who is at the right hand of God, who also intercedes for us. 35 Who will separate us from the love of Christ? Will affliction, or turmoil, or persecution, or famine, or nakedness, or peril, or sword? 36 Just as it is written,

"FOR YOUR SAKE WE ARE BEING PUT
TO DEATH ALL DAY LONG;
WE WERE COUNTED AS SHEEP
FOR *the* SLAUGHTER."

37 But in all these things we overwhelmingly conquer through Him who loved us. 38 For I am convinced that neither death, nor life, nor angels, nor rulers, nor things present, nor things to come, nor powers, 39 nor height, nor depth, nor any other created thing, will be able to separate us from the love of God, which is in Christ Jesus our Lord.

AUGUST 8

Job 7:1–8:22

7 "Is not man conscripted
to labor on earth,
And *are not* his days like the
days of a hired man?
2 "As a slave who pants for
the shade,
And as a hired man who eagerly
hopes for his wages,
3 So am I apportioned months
of worthlessness,
And nights of trouble are
appointed me.
4 "If I lie down I say,
'When shall I arise?'
But the twilight continues,
And I am saturated with
tossing until dawn.
5 "My flesh is clothed with worms
and a crust of dirt;
My skin scabs over and
flows *out again.*

6 “My days are swifter than
a weaver’s shuttle,
And come to an end without hope.
7 “Remember that my life is
but wind;
My eye will not again see good.
8 “The eye of him who sees me
will behold me no longer;
Your eyes *will be* on me,
but I will not be.
9 “A cloud vanishes, and it is gone,
So he who goes down to Sheol
does not come up.
10 “He will not return again to his house,
Nor will his place recognize
him anymore.

11 “Indeed I will not hold back my mouth;
I will speak in the distress of
my spirit;
I will muse on the bitterness
of my soul.
12 “Am I the sea or the sea monster,
That You set a guard over me?
13 “If I say, ‘My bed will comfort me;
My couch will ease my *bitter* musing,’
14 Then You frighten me with dreams
And terrify me by visions,
15 So that my soul would
choose suffocation,
Death rather than my pains.
16 “I have rejected *everything*; I
will not live forever.
Leave me alone, for my days
are *but* a breath.
17 “What is man that You magnify him,
And that You set Your heart on him,
18 That You examine him every morning
And test him every moment?
19 “Will You never turn Your
gaze away from me,
Nor let me alone until I
swallow my spit?
20 “Have I sinned? What have
I done to You,
O watcher of men?
Why have You set me as Your target,
So that I am a burden to myself?
21 “Why then do You not forgive
my transgression
And take away my iniquity?
For now I will lie down in the dust;
And You will seek me earnestly,
but I will not be.”

8 Then Bildad the Shuhite answered and
said,
2 “How long will you say these things,
And the words of your mouth
be a mighty wind?
3 “Does God pervert justice?
Or does the Almighty
pervert what is right?
4 “If your sons sinned against Him,
Then He sent them into the power
of their transgression.
5 “If you would seek God earnestly
And plead for the grace
of the Almighty,
6 If you are pure and upright,
Indeed now He would rouse
Himself for you
And make your righteous
abode at peace.
7 “Though your beginning
was insignificant,
Yet your end will increase greatly.

8 “Please ask of past generations,
And establish the things searched
out by their fathers.
9 “For we are *only* of yesterday
and know nothing,
Because our days on earth
are *but* a shadow.
10 “Will they not instruct you *and* tell you,
And bring forth words
from their hearts?

11 “Can the papyrus grow up
without a marsh?
Can the rushes grow without water?
12 “While it is still green *and*
not cut down,
Yet it dries up before any *other* plant.
13 “So are the paths of all who forget God;
And the hope of the
godless will perish,
14 Whose confidence is fragile,
And whose trust a spider’s web.
15 “He relies on his house, but
it does not stand;
He holds fast to it, but it
is not established.
16 “He thrives before the sun,
And his shoots go forth
over his garden.
17 “His roots wrap around a rock pile;
He looks upon a house of stones.
18 “If He swallows him up from his place,

Then it will deny him, *saying*,
'I never saw you.'
19 "Behold, this is the joy of His way;
And out of the dust others will spring.
20 "Behold, God will not reject
a blameless *man*,
Nor will He strengthen the
hand of the evildoers.
21 "He will yet fill your mouth with laughter
And your lips with shouting.
22 "Those who hate you will be
clothed with shame,
And the tent of the wicked
will be no longer."

Psalm 92:8–15

8 But You are on high forever, O Yahweh.
9 For, behold, Your enemies, O Yahweh,
For, behold, Your enemies will perish;
All *the* workers of iniquity
will be scattered.

10 But You have raised up my horn
like *that of* the wild ox;
I have been anointed with fresh oil.
11 And my eye has looked
exultantly upon my foes,
My ears hear of the evildoers
who rise up against me.
12 The righteous man will flourish
like the palm tree,
He will grow like a cedar in Lebanon.
13 Planted in the house of Yahweh,
They will flourish in the
courts of our God.
14 They will still yield fruit in old age;
They shall be rich and fresh,
15 To declare that Yahweh is upright;
He is my rock, and there is no
unrighteousness in Him.

Proverbs 22:17–21

17 Incline your ear and hear the
words of the wise,
And set your heart on my knowledge;
18 For it will be pleasant if you
keep them within you,
That they may be established
on your lips.
19 So that your trust may be in Yahweh,
I have made you know today, even you.
20 Have I not written to you
excellent things
Of counsels and knowledge,
21 To make you know the veracity
of the words of truth
That you may respond with the words
of truth to him who sent you?

Romans 9:1–13

9 I am telling the truth in Christ, I am not
lying, my conscience testifies with me
in the Holy Spirit, 2 that I have great sorrow
and unceasing grief in my heart. 3 For I could
wish that I myself were accursed, *separated*
from Christ for the sake of my brothers, my
kinsmen according to the flesh, 4 who are
Israelites, to whom belongs the adoption as
sons, and the glory and the covenants and
the giving of the Law and the *temple* service
and the promises, 5 whose are the fathers,
and from whom is the Christ according
to the flesh, who is God over all, blessed
forever. Amen.
6 But *it is* not as though the word of God
has failed. For they are not all Israel who
are *descended* from Israel; 7 nor are they all
children because they are Abraham's seed,
but: "THROUGH ISAAC YOUR SEED WILL BE
NAMED." 8 That is, the children of the flesh
are not the children of God, but the children
of the promise are considered as seed. 9 For
this is the word of promise: "AT THIS TIME I
WILL COME, AND SARAH SHALL HAVE A SON."
10 And not only this, but there was Rebekah
also, when she had conceived *twins* by one
man, our father Isaac; 11 for though *the*
twins were not yet born and had not done
anything good or bad, so that the purpose
of God according to *His* choice would stand,
not because of works but because of Him
who calls, 12 it was said to her, "THE OLDER
SHALL SERVE THE YOUNGER." 13 Just as it is
written, "JACOB I LOVED, BUT ESAU I HATED."

AUGUST 9

Job 9:1–10:22

9 Then Job answered and said,
2 "In truth I know that
this is so;
But how can a man be in the
right before God?
3 "If one desired to contend
with Him,

He could not answer Him once
in a thousand *times*.
4 "Wise in heart and mighty in power,
Who has stiffened *his neck* against
Him and been at peace?
5 "*God* is the One who removes the
mountains, they know not *how*,
When He overturns them in His anger;
6 The One who shakes the
earth out of its place,
And its pillars tremble;
7 The One who says for the
sun not to shine,
And sets a seal upon the stars;
8 Who alone stretches out the heavens,
And tramples down the
waves of the sea;
9 Who makes the Bear, Orion,
and the Pleiades,
And the chambers of the south;
10 Who does great things,
unsearchable,
And wondrous works, innumerable.
11 "Were He to sweep by me,
I would not see Him;
Were He to move past *me*,
I would not perceive Him.
12 "Were He to snatch away, who
could turn Him back?
Who could say to Him,
'What are You doing?'

13 "God will not turn back His anger;
Beneath Him crouch the
helpers of Rahab.
14 "How then can I answer Him,
And choose my words before Him?
15 "For though I were right, I
could not answer;
I would have to plead for the
grace of my judge.
16 "If I called and He answered me,
I could not believe that He was
giving ear to my voice.
17 "For He bruises me with a tempest
And multiplies my wounds
without cause.
18 "He will not allow me to get my breath,
But saturates me with bitterness.
19 "If *it is a matter* of power, behold,
He is the mighty one!
And if *it is a matter* of justice,
who can make Him testify?
20 "Though I am righteous, my
mouth will condemn me;
Though I am blameless, He
will declare me perverse.
21 "I am blameless;
I do not know my soul;
I reject my life.
22 "It is *all* one; therefore I say,
'He consumes the blameless
and the wicked.'
23 "If the scourge puts to death suddenly,
He mocks the despair of the innocent.
24 "The earth is given into the
hand of the wicked;
He covers the faces of its judges.
If *it is* not *He*, then who is it?

25 "Now my days are swifter than a runner;
They flee away; they do not see good.
26 "They sweep by like reed boats,
Like an eagle that swoops on its food.
27 "Though I say, 'I will forget my musing,
I will forsake my *sad* countenance
and be cheerful,'
28 I am afraid of all my pains;
I know that You will not acquit me.
29 "I am accounted wicked;
Why then should I toil in vain?
30 "If I should wash myself with snow
And cleanse my hands with lye,
31 Yet You would plunge me into the pit,
And my own clothes would abhor me.
32 "For *He is* not a man as I am
that I may answer Him,
That we may go to court *for
judgment* together.
33 "There is no adjudicator between us,
Who may lay his hand upon us both.
34 "Let Him remove His rod from me,
And let not dread of Him terrify me.
35 "*Then* I would speak and not fear Him;
But I am not like that in myself.

10 "My soul is loathed by my life;
I will abandon *all restraint* in
myself to my complaint;
I will speak in the bitterness
of my soul.
2 "I will say to God, 'Do not
account me as wicked;
Let me know why You
contend with me.
3 'Is it good to You that You oppress,
That You reject the labor
of Your hands,
And cause the counsel of the
wicked to shine forth?

4 'Have You eyes of flesh?
Or do You see as a mortal man sees?
5 'Are Your days as the days
of a mortal man,
Or Your years as man's years,
6 That You should seek for my guilt
And search after my sin?
7 'According to Your knowledge
I am indeed not wicked,
Yet there is no deliverer
from Your hand.

8 'Your hands fashioned and
made me altogether,
And would You swallow me up?
9 'Remember now, that You
have made me as clay;
And would You turn me
into dust again?
10 'Did You not pour me out like milk
And curdle me like cheese,
11 Clothe me with skin and flesh,
And knit me together with
bones and sinews?
12 'You have made alongside me
life and lovingkindness;
And Your care has kept my spirit.
13 'Yet these things You have
concealed in Your heart;
I know that this is within You:
14 If I sin, then You would take
note of me
And would not acquit me of my guilt.
15 'If I am wicked, woe to me!
And if I am righteous, I dare
not lift up my head.
I am sated with disgrace—so
see my misery!
16 'Should *my head* be set on high,
You would hunt me like a lion;
And again You would show
Your wonders against me.
17 'You renew Your witnesses against me
And increase Your vexation toward me;
Hardship after hardship is with me.

18 'Why then have You brought
me out of the womb?
Would that I had breathed my last
and no eye had seen me!
19 'I should have been as though
I had not been,
Carried from womb to tomb.'
20 "Would He not cease for a
few of my days?
Withdraw from me that I
may have a little cheer
21 Before I go—and I shall not return—
To the land of darkness and
shadow of death,
22 The land of utter gloom as *the*
thick darkness *itself*,
Of the shadow of death, without order,
And which shines as the
thick darkness."

Psalm 93:1–5

1 Yahweh reigns, He is clothed
with majesty;
Yahweh has clothed and girded
Himself with strength;
Indeed, the world is established,
it will not be shaken.
2 Your throne is established from of old;
You are from everlasting.

3 The rivers have lifted up, O Yahweh,
The rivers have lifted up their voice,
The rivers lift up their pounding waves.
4 More than the voices of many waters,
Than the mighty breakers of the sea,
Yahweh on high is mighty.
5 Your testimonies are very faithful;
Holiness befits Your house,
O Yahweh, forevermore.

Proverbs 22:22–23

22 Do not rob the poor because he is poor,
And do not crush the afflicted at the gate;
23 For Yahweh will plead their case
And rob the soul of those
who rob them.

Romans 9:14–33

14 What shall we say then? Is there any
unrighteousness with God? May it never be!
15 For He says to Moses, "I WILL HAVE MERCY
ON WHOM I HAVE MERCY, AND I WILL HAVE
COMPASSION ON WHOM I HAVE COMPASSION."
16 So then it *does* not *depend* on the one
who wills or the one who runs, but on God
who has mercy. 17 For the Scripture says to
Pharaoh, "FOR THIS VERY PURPOSE I RAISED YOU
UP, IN ORDER TO DEMONSTRATE MY POWER IN
YOU, AND IN ORDER THAT MY NAME MIGHT BE
PROCLAIMED THROUGHOUT THE WHOLE EARTH."
18 So then He has mercy on whom He desires,
and He hardens whom He desires.
19 You will say to me then, "Why does He
still find fault? For who resists His will?"

20 On the contrary, who are you, O man,
who answers back to God? WILL THE THING
MOLDED SAY TO THE MOLDER, "WHY DID YOU
MAKE ME LIKE THIS"? 21 Or does not the potter
have authority over the clay, to make from
the same lump one vessel for honorable use
and another for dishonorable use? 22 And
what if God, wanting to demonstrate His
wrath and to make His power known,
endured with much patience vessels of
wrath having been prepared for destruction,
23 and in order that He might make known
the riches of His glory upon vessels of
mercy, which He prepared beforehand for
glory— 24 *even* us, whom He also called, not
from among Jews only, but also from among
Gentiles? 25 As He says also in Hosea,

"I WILL CALL THOSE WHO WERE NOT
MY PEOPLE, 'MY PEOPLE,'
AND HER WHO WAS NOT
BELOVED, 'BELOVED.'"

26 "AND IT SHALL BE THAT IN THE PLACE
WHERE IT WAS SAID TO THEM,
'YOU ARE NOT MY PEOPLE,'
THERE THEY SHALL BE CALLED
SONS OF THE LIVING GOD."

27 And Isaiah cries out concerning
Israel, "THOUGH THE NUMBER OF THE SONS
OF ISRAEL BE LIKE THE SAND OF THE SEA, IT
IS THE REMNANT THAT WILL BE SAVED; 28 FOR
THE LORD WILL EXECUTE HIS WORD ON THE
LAND, THOROUGHLY AND QUICKLY." 29 And just
as Isaiah foretold,

"UNLESS THE LORD OF SABAOTH
HAD LEFT TO US A SEED,
WE WOULD HAVE BECOME LIKE
SODOM, AND WOULD HAVE
RESEMBLED GOMORRAH."

30 What shall we say then? That Gentiles,
who did not pursue righteousness, laid hold
of righteousness, even the righteousness
which is by faith; 31 but Israel, pursuing a
law of righteousness, did not attain *that* law.
32 Why? Because *they did* not *pursue it* by
faith, but as though *it were* by works. They
stumbled over the stumbling stone, 33 just
as it is written,

"BEHOLD, I AM LAYING IN ZION
A STONE OF STUMBLING AND
A ROCK OF OFFENSE,
AND THE ONE WHO BELIEVES UPON
HIM WILL NOT BE PUT TO SHAME."

AUGUST 10

Job 11:1–12:25

11 Then Zophar the Naamathite answered
and said,

2 "Shall a multitude of words
go unanswered,
And a man of lips be in the right?
3 "Shall your boasts silence men?
And shall you mock and none rebuke?
4 "You have said, 'My learning is pure,
And I am innocent in your eyes.'
5 "But would that God might speak,
And open His lips against you,
6 And tell you the secrets of wisdom!
For sound wisdom has two sides.
Know then that God forgets
a part of your iniquity.

7 "Can you find the depths of God?
Can you find the limits
of the Almighty?
8 "*They are* high as the heavens,
what can you do?
Deeper than Sheol, what
can you know?
9 "Its measure is longer than the earth
And broader than the sea.
10 "If He sweeps by or shuts up,
Or calls an assembly, who
can turn Him around?
11 "For He knows worthless men,
And He sees wickedness, so will
He not carefully consider *it*?
12 "Yet an empty *headed* man will
obtain a heart *of wisdom*,
And the foal of a wild donkey
is born a man.

13 "If you would set your heart right
And spread out your hand to Him,
14 If wickedness is in your
hand, put it far away,
And do not let unrighteousness
dwell in your tents;
15 Then, indeed, you could lift up your
face without *moral* defect,
And you would be steadfast
and not fear.
16 "For you would forget *your* trouble,
As waters that pass by, so you
would remember *it*.

17 "And your lifetime would arise
brighter than noonday;
Darkness would be like the morning.
18 "Then you would trust,
because there is hope;
And you would search around
and rest securely.
19 "You would lie down and none
would make *you* tremble,
And many would entreat your favor.
20 "But the eyes of the wicked
will come to an end,
And escape will perish from them;
And their hope is the expiring
of their soul."

12 Then Job answered and said,
2 "Truly then you are the people,
And with you wisdom will die!
3 "But I have a heart *of wisdom*
as well as you;
I do not fall *short* of you.
And who does not know
such things as these?
4 "I am a laughingstock to my friends,
The one who called on God
and He answered him;
The righteous *and* blameless
man is a laughingstock.
5 "As for upheaval, *there is only* contempt
by the one who acts at ease,
But it is prepared for those
whose feet slip.
6 "The tents of the destroyers
are complacent,
And those who provoke God are secure,
Whom God brings into their power.

7 "But now ask the beasts, and
let them instruct you;
And the birds of the sky, and
let them tell you.
8 "Or muse to the earth, and
let it instruct you;
And let the fish of the sea
recount *it* to you.
9 "Who among all these does not know
That the hand of Yahweh has done this,
10 In whose hand is the life of
every living thing,
And the breath of all the flesh of man?
11 "Does not the ear test words,
As the palate tastes its food?
12 "Wisdom is with aged men,
With long life is discernment.
13 "With Him are wisdom and might;
To Him belong counsel
and discernment.
14 "Behold, He pulls down,
and it cannot be rebuilt;
He closes a man in, and it
cannot be opened.
15 "Behold, He restrains the
waters, and they dry up;
And He sends them out, and
they overturn the earth.
16 "With Him are strength and
sound wisdom;
The misled and the misleader
belong to Him.
17 "He makes counselors walk barefoot
And makes fools of judges.
18 "He opens the bond of kings
And binds their loins with a belt.
19 "He makes priests walk barefoot
And subverts the enduring ones.
20 "He removes speech from the faithful
And takes away the *discerning*
taste of the elders.
21 "He pours contempt on nobles
And loosens the belt of the strong.
22 "He reveals mysteries from the darkness
And brings out the shadows
of death into light.
23 "He makes the nations great,
then makes them perish;
He enlarges the nations,
then leads them away.
24 "He removes the heart *of wisdom* from
the heads of the earth's people
And makes them wander
in a pathless waste.
25 "They grope in darkness with no light,
And He makes them wander
about like a drunken man.

Psalm 94:1–11

1 O Yahweh, God of vengeance,
God of vengeance, shine forth!
2 Be lifted up, O Judge of the earth,
Render recompense to the proud.
3 How long shall the wicked, O Yahweh,
How long shall the wicked exult?
4 They pour forth *words*,
they speak arrogantly;
All workers of iniquity vaunt themselves.
5 They crush Your people, O Yahweh,
And afflict Your inheritance.
6 They slay the widow and the sojourner
And murder the orphans.

7 They have said, "Yah does not see,
Nor does the God of Jacob discern."

8 Discern, you senseless
among the people;
And when will you have
insight, *you* fools?
9 He who planted the ear,
does He not hear?
He who formed the eye,
does He not see?
10 He who disciplines the nations,
will He not rebuke,
Even He who teaches man knowledge?
11 Yahweh knows the thoughts of man,
That they are vanity.

Proverbs 22:24–25

24 Do not befriend a man of anger;
And do not come along with
a man of great wrath,
25 Lest you learn his ways
And take *on* a snare against your soul.

Romans 10:1–21

10 Brothers, my heart's desire and my
prayer to God for them is for *their*
salvation. 2 For I testify about them that
they have a zeal for God, but not according
to knowledge. 3 For not knowing about
the righteousness of God and seeking to
establish their own, they did not subject
themselves to the righteousness of God.
4 For Christ is the end of the law for righ-
teousness to everyone who believes.
5 For Moses writes about the righteous-
ness which is of law: "THE MAN WHO DOES
THESE THINGS SHALL LIVE BY THEM." 6 But the
righteousness of faith speaks in this way:
"DO NOT SAY IN YOUR HEART, 'WHO WILL GO
UP INTO HEAVEN?' (that is, to bring Christ
down), 7 or 'WHO WILL GO DOWN INTO THE
ABYSS?' (that is, to bring Christ up from the
dead)." 8 But what does it say? "THE WORD
IS NEAR YOU, IN YOUR MOUTH AND IN YOUR
HEART"—that is, the word of faith which
we are preaching, 9 that if you confess with
your mouth Jesus *as* Lord, and believe in
your heart that God raised Him from the
dead, you will be saved; 10 for with the heart
a person believes, leading to righteousness,
and with the mouth he confesses, leading
to salvation. 11 For the Scripture says,
"WHOEVER BELIEVES UPON HIM WILL NOT BE
PUT TO SHAME." 12 For there is no distinction
between Jew and Greek, for the same *Lord* is
Lord of all, abounding in riches for all who
call on Him, 13 for "WHOEVER CALLS ON THE
NAME OF THE LORD WILL BE SAVED."
14 How then will they call on Him in
whom they have not believed? How will
they believe in Him whom they have not
heard? And how will they hear without
a preacher? 15 And how will they preach
unless they are sent? Just as it is written,
"HOW BEAUTIFUL ARE THE FEET OF THOSE WHO
PROCLAIM GOOD NEWS OF GOOD THINGS!"
16 However, they did not all heed the
good news, for Isaiah says, "LORD, WHO HAS
BELIEVED OUR REPORT?" 17 So faith *comes*
from hearing, and hearing by the word of
Christ.
18 But I say, have they never heard? On the
contrary, they have;

"THEIR VOICE HAS GONE OUT
INTO ALL THE EARTH,
AND THEIR WORDS TO THE
ENDS OF THE WORLD."

19 But I say, did Israel not know? First Moses
says,

"I WILL MAKE YOU JEALOUS BY THAT
WHICH IS NOT A NATION,
BY A NATION WITHOUT UNDERSTANDING
WILL I ANGER YOU."

20 And Isaiah is very bold and says,

"I WAS FOUND BY THOSE WHO
DID NOT SEEK ME,
I BECAME MANIFEST TO THOSE
WHO DID NOT ASK FOR ME."

21 But as for Israel He says, "ALL DAY LONG
I HAVE STRETCHED OUT MY HANDS TO A
DISOBEDIENT AND OBSTINATE PEOPLE."

AUGUST 11

Job 13:1–14:22

13 "Behold, my eye has seen all *this*;
My ear has heard and understood it.
2 "What you know I also know;
I have not fallen *short* of you.
3 "But I would speak to the Almighty,
And I desire to argue with God.
4 "But you cover me with lies;
You are all worthless physicians.
5 "O that you would be completely silent,

And that it would become
your wisdom!
6 "Please hear my argument
And give heed to the
contentions of my lips.
7 "Will you speak what is
unrighteous for God,
And speak what is deceitful for Him?
8 "Will you show partiality for Him?
Will you contend for God?
9 "Will it be well when He examines you?
Or will you deceive Him as
one deceives a man?
10 "He will surely reprove you
If you secretly show partiality.
11 "Will not His exaltedness terrify you,
And the dread of Him fall on you?
12 "Your memorable sayings are
proverbs of ashes;
Your defenses are defenses of clay.

13 "Be silent before me so that I may speak;
Then let come on me what may.
14 "Why should I take my flesh in my teeth
And put my life in my hands?
15 "Though He slay me,
I will hope in Him.
Nevertheless I will argue
my ways before Him.
16 "This also will be my salvation,
For a godless man may not
come before His presence.
17 "Listen carefully to my words,
And let my declaration *fill* your ears.
18 "Behold now, I have arranged
my *case for* justice;
I know that I will be
declared righteous.
19 "Who will contend with me?
For now I am silent and will
breathe my last.

20 "Only two things do not do to me,
Then I will not hide from Your face:
21 Move Your hand far from me,
And let not the dread of You terrify me.
22 "Then call, and I will answer;
Or let me speak, then respond to me.
23 "How many are my iniquities and sins?
Make known to me my
transgression and my sin.
24 "Why do You hide Your face
And think of me as Your enemy?
25 "Will You cause a driven leaf to tremble?
Or will You pursue the dry chaff?
26 "For You write bitter things against me
And make me to possess the
iniquities of my youth.
27 "You put my feet in the stocks
And kept watch over all my paths;
You set a limit for the soles of my feet,
28 While I am decaying like a rotten thing,
Like a garment that is moth-eaten.

14 "Man, who is born of woman,
Is short-lived and full of turmoil.
2 "Like a flower he comes
forth and withers.
He also flees like a shadow
and does not stand.
3 "You also open Your eyes on him
And bring me into judgment
with Yourself.
4 "Who can make the clean
out of the unclean?
No one!
5 "Since his days are determined,
The number of his months is with You;
And his limits You have set
so that he cannot pass.
6 "Turn Your gaze from him that
he may cease *from toil*,
Until he accepts his day
like a hired man.

7 "For there is hope for a tree,
When it is cut down, that it will
change back *sprouting* again,
And its shoots will not cease.
8 "Though its roots grow
old in the ground
And its stump dies in the dry soil,
9 At the scent of water it will flourish
And put forth sprigs like a plant.
10 "But man dies and lies prostrate.
Man breathes his last, and where is he?
11 "*As* water evaporates from the sea,
And a river becomes parched
and dried up,
12 So man lies down and does not rise.
Until the heavens are no longer,
He will not awake nor be
aroused out of his sleep.

13 "Oh that You would conceal
me in Sheol,
That You would hide me until
Your anger returns *to You*,
That You would set a limit for
me and remember me!

14 "If a man dies, will he live *again*?
All the days of my labor I will wait
Until my change comes.
15 "You will call, and I will answer You;
You will long for the work of Your hands.
16 "For now You number my steps,
You do not keep watch over my sin.
17 "My transgression is sealed up in a bag,
And You cover up my iniquity.

18 "But the falling mountain
crumbles away,
And the rock moves from its place;
19 Water wears away stones;
Its torrents wash away the
dust of the earth;
So You make man's hope perish.
20 "You forever overpower him
and he goes *away*;
You alter his appearance
and send him away.
21 "His sons achieve honor, but
he does not know *it*;
Or they become insignificant,
but he does not perceive it.
22 "But his flesh pains him,
And he mourns only for himself."

Psalm 94:12–19

12 Blessed is the man whom
You discipline, O Yah,
And whom You teach out of Your law;
13 That You may grant him calm
from the days of calamity,
Until a pit is dug for the wicked.
14 For Yahweh will not
abandon His people,
Nor will He forsake His inheritance.
15 For judgment will again be righteous,
And all the upright in
heart will follow it.
16 Who will arise for me
against evildoers?
Who will take his stand for me
against workers of iniquity?

17 If Yahweh had not been my help,
My soul would soon have dwelt
in *the abode of* silence.
18 If I should say, "My foot has stumbled,"
Your lovingkindness, O Yahweh,
will hold me up.
19 When my anxious thoughts
multiply within me,
Your consolations delight my soul.

Proverbs 22:26–27

26 Do not be among those who
strike hands *in pledge*,
Among those who become
guarantors for debts.
27 If you have nothing with which to pay,
Why should he take your
bed from under you?

Romans 11:1–16

11 I say then, has God rejected His peo-
ple? May it never be! For I too am an
Israelite, a seed of Abraham, of the tribe of
Benjamin. 2 GOD HAS NOT REJECTED HIS PEO-
PLE whom He foreknew. Or do you not know
what the Scripture says in *the passage about*
Elijah, how he appeals to God against Israel?
3 "Lord, THEY HAVE KILLED YOUR PROPHETS,
THEY HAVE TORN DOWN YOUR ALTARS, AND I
ALONE AM LEFT, AND THEY ARE SEEKING MY
LIFE." 4 But what does the divine response
say to him? "I HAVE LEFT for Myself SEVEN
THOUSAND MEN WHO HAVE NOT BOWED THE
KNEE TO BAAL." 5 In this way then, at the
present time, a remnant according to *God's*
gracious choice has also come to be. 6 But
if it is by grace, it is no longer of works,
otherwise grace is no longer grace.
7 What then? What Israel is seeking, it
has not obtained, but the chosen obtained
it, and the rest were hardened; 8 just as it
is written,

"GOD GAVE THEM A SPIRIT OF STUPOR,
EYES TO SEE NOT AND EARS TO HEAR NOT,
DOWN TO THIS VERY DAY."

9 And David says,

"LET THEIR TABLE BECOME A
SNARE AND A TRAP,
AND A STUMBLING BLOCK AND
A RETRIBUTION TO THEM.
10 "LET THEIR EYES BE DARKENED TO SEE NOT,
AND BEND THEIR BACKS FOREVER."

11 I say then, did they stumble so as to
fall? May it never be! But by their trans-
gression salvation *has come* to the Gentiles,
to make them jealous. 12 Now if their
transgression is riches for the world and
their failure is riches for the Gentiles, how
much more will their fullness be! 13 But I
am speaking to you who are Gentiles. Inas-
much then as I am an apostle of Gentiles, I
magnify my ministry, 14 if somehow I might
move to jealousy my fellow countrymen
and save some of them. 15 For if their
rejection is the reconciliation of the world,

what will *their* acceptance be but life from the dead? [16] And if the first piece *of dough* is holy, the lump is also; and if the root is holy, the branches are too.

AUGUST 12

Job 15:1–16:22

15 Then Eliphaz the Temanite answered and said,

2 "Should a wise man answer
with windy knowledge
And fill his belly with the east wind?
3 "Should he argue with a word
that cannot be used,
Or with speech which is not profitable?
4 "Indeed, you annul *reverent* fear
And cut off musing before God.
5 "For your iniquity teaches your mouth,
And you choose the tongue
of the crafty.
6 "Your own mouth condemns
you, and not I;
And your own lips answer against you.
7 "Were you the first man to be born,
Or were you brought forth
before the hills?
8 "Do you hear the secret counsel of God,
And cut down wisdom
only unto yourself?
9 "What do you know that
we do not know?
What do you understand
that is not with us?
10 "Both the gray-haired and the
aged are among us,
Older than your father.
11 "Are the consolations of God
too small for you,
Even the word *spoken* gently with you?
12 "Why does your heart take you away?
And why do your eyes flash,
13 That you should turn your
spirit against God
And allow *such* words to go
out of your mouth?
14 "What is man, that he should be pure,
Or he who is born of a woman,
that he should be righteous?
15 "Behold, He puts no faith
in His holy ones,
And the heavens are not
pure in His sight;
16 How much less one who is
abominable and corrupt,
Man, who drinks unrighteousness
like water!
17 "I will tell you, listen to me;
And what I have beheld I
will also recount;
18 What wise men have told,
And have not concealed
from their fathers,
19 To whom alone the land was given,
And no stranger passed among them.
20 "The wicked man writhes
in pain all *his* days,
And numbered are the years
stored up for the ruthless.
21 "Sounds of dread are in his ears;
While at peace the destroyer
comes upon him.
22 "He does not believe that he will
return from darkness,
And he is destined for the sword.
23 "He wanders about for food,
saying, 'Where is it?'
He knows that a day of darkness
is ready at his hand.
24 "Distress and anguish terrify him;
They overpower him like a
king ready for the attack,
25 Because he has stretched out
his hand against God
And magnifies himself
against the Almighty.
26 "He rushes headlong at Him
With his massive shield.
27 "For he has covered his face
with his fat
And made his thighs heavy with flesh.
28 "He has dwelt in desolate cities,
In houses no one would inhabit,
Which are destined to become ruins.
29 "He will not become rich, nor
will his wealth endure;
And his grain will not stretch
out over the land.
30 "He will not be able to depart
from darkness;
The flame will wither his shoots,
And by the breath of His
mouth he will depart.

31 "Let him not believe in emptiness,
deceiving himself;
For emptiness will be his reward,
32 When his days are not *yet* fulfilled,
And his palm branch is not green.
33 "He will drop off his unripe
grape like the vine,
And will cast off his flower
like the olive tree.
34 "For the company of the
godless is barren,
And fire consumes the
tents of the corrupt.
35 "They conceive trouble and give
birth to wickedness,
And their belly prepares deception."

16 Then Job answered and said,
2 "I have heard many such things;
Troublesome comforters are you all.
3 "Is there *no* end to windy words?
Or what pains you that you answer?
4 "I too could speak like you,
If your soul were in the place
of my soul.
I could compose words against you
And shake my head at you.
5 "I could encourage you with my mouth,
And the solace of my lips
could lessen *your pain*.

6 "If I speak, my pain is not lessened,
And if I cease, what will
go forth from me?
7 "But now He has exhausted me;
You have made desolate
all my company.
8 "You have shriveled me up,
It has become a witness;
And my leanness rises up against me,
It answers to my face.
9 "His anger has torn me and
hunted me down;
He has gnashed at me with His teeth;
My adversary sharpens his
eyes *to look* at me.
10 "They have opened their
mouth wide at me;
They have struck me on the
cheek in reproach;
They have massed themselves
against me.
11 "God hands me over to ruffians
And tosses me into the
hands of the wicked.
12 "I was at ease, but He shattered me,
And He has grasped me by the
neck and shaken me to pieces;
He has also set me up as His target.
13 "His arrows surround me.
Without mercy He splits
my kidneys open;
He pours out my gall on the ground.
14 "He breaks through me with
breach after breach;
He runs at me like a warrior.
15 "I have sewed sackcloth over my skin
And thrust my horn in the dust.
16 "My face is flushed from weeping,
And the shadow of death
is on my eyelids,
17 *Why?*—because there is no
violence in my hands,
And my prayer is pure.

18 "O earth, do not cover my blood,
And let there be no *resting*
place for my cry.
19 "Even now, behold, my
witness is in heaven,
And my advocate is on high.
20 "My friends are my scoffers;
My eye weeps to God.
21 "O that a man might argue with God
As a man with his neighbor!
22 "For when a few years are past,
I shall go the way of no return.

Psalm 94:20–23

20 Can a throne of destruction
be allied with You,
One which forms trouble by statute?
21 They band themselves together
against the life of the righteous
And condemn the innocent to death.
22 But Yahweh has been my stronghold,
And my God the rock of my refuge.
23 He has brought back their
iniquity upon them
And will destroy them in their evil;
Yahweh our God will destroy them.

Proverbs 22:28–29

28 Do not move the ancient boundary
Which your fathers made.

29 Do you see a man skilled in his work?
He will stand before kings;
He will not stand before
obscure men.

Romans 11:17–36

17 But if some of the branches were broken
off, and you, being a wild olive, were grafted
in among them and became a partaker with
them of the rich root of the olive tree, 18 do
not boast against the branches. But if you
do boast against *them, remember that* it is
not you who supports the root, but the root
supports you. 19 You will say then, "Branches
were broken off so that I might be grafted
in." 20 Quite right! They were broken off for
their unbelief, but you stand by your faith.
Do not be haughty, but fear, 21 for if God
did not spare the natural branches, He will
not spare you, either. 22 Behold then the
kindness and severity of God; to those who
fell, severity, but to you, God's kindness, if
you continue in His kindness; otherwise
you also will be cut off. 23 And they also,
if they do not continue in their unbelief,
will be grafted in, for God is able to graft
them in again. 24 For if you were cut off from
what is by nature a wild olive tree, and were
grafted contrary to nature into a cultivated
olive tree, how much more will these who
are the natural *branches* be grafted into their
own olive tree?

25 For I do not want you, brothers, to be
uninformed of this mystery—so that you
will not be wise in your own estimation—
that a partial hardening has happened to
Israel until the fullness of the Gentiles has
come in; 26 and so all Israel will be saved;
just as it is written,

"The Deliverer will come from Zion,
He will remove ungodliness
from Jacob."
27 "And this is My covenant with them,
When I take away their sins."

28 From the standpoint of the gospel they
are enemies for your sake, but from the
standpoint of *God's* choice they are beloved
for the sake of the fathers; 29 for the gifts and
the calling of God are irrevocable. 30 For just
as you once were disobedient to God, but
now have been shown mercy because of their
disobedience, 31 so these also now have been
disobedient, that because of the mercy shown
to you they also may now be shown mercy.
32 For God has shut up all in disobedience so
that He may show mercy to all.

33 Oh, the depth of the riches and wisdom
and knowledge of God! How unsearchable
are His judgments and unfathomable His
ways! 34 For who has known the mind of
the Lord, or who became His counselor?
35 Or who has first given to Him that it
might be repaid to him? 36 For from Him
and through Him and to Him are all things.
To Him *be* the glory forever. Amen.

There are four things that we ought to do with the Word of God—admit it as the Word of God, commit it to our hearts and minds, submit to it, and transmit it to the world.

— William Wilberforce

AUGUST 13

Job 17:1–18:21

17 "My spirit is broken; my
days are extinguished;
The grave is *ready* for me.
2 "Surely mockers are with me,
And my eye gazes on their provocation.

3 "Establish, now, a pledge for
me with Yourself;
Who is there that will clap
my hand *in pledge*?
4 "For You have hidden their
heart from insight,
Therefore You will not exalt *them*.
5 "He who informs against friends
for a share *of the spoil*,
The eyes of his children also
will come to an end.

6 "But He has made me a
byword of the people,
And I am one at whom men spit.
7 "My eye has also grown dim
because of grief,
And all my members are as a shadow.
8 "The upright will be appalled at this,

And the innocent will stir up
himself against the godless.
9 "Nevertheless the righteous
will hold to his way,
And he who has clean hands will
grow mightier and mightier.
10 "But come again all of you now,
For I do not find a wise
man among you.
11 "My days are past; my plans
are torn apart,
Even the wishes of my heart.
12 "They make night into day, *saying*,
'The light is near,' in the
presence of darkness.
13 "If I hope for Sheol as my home,
I make my bed in the darkness;
14 If I call to the pit, 'You are my father';
To the worm, 'my mother
and my sister';
15 Where now is my hope?
And who beholds my hope?
16 "Will it go down with me to Sheol?
Shall we together go down
into the dust?"

18 Then Bildad the Shuhite answered
and said,
2 "How long until you put an
end to *your* words?
Show understanding and
then we can talk.
3 "Why are we regarded as beasts,
As dense in your eyes?
4 "O you who tear yourself
in your anger—
For your sake is the earth
to be forsaken,
Or the rock to be moved from its place?

5 "Indeed, the light of the
wicked goes out,
And the flame of his fire gives no light.
6 "The light in his tent is darkened,
And his lamp goes out above him.
7 "His vigorous stride is shortened,
And his own counsel brings him down.
8 "For he is thrown into the
net by his own feet,
And he steps on the netting.
9 "A snare seizes *him* by the heel,
And a device snaps shut on him.
10 "A rope for him is hidden in the ground,
And a trap for him on the path.
11 "All around terrors frighten him,
And harass him at every step.
12 "His vigor is famished,
And disaster is ready at his side.
13 "The firstborn of death eats
parts of his skin;
It eats parts of him.
14 "He is torn from the security of his tent,
And they march him in step
before the king of terrors.
15 "There dwells in his tent nothing of his;
Brimstone is scattered on his abode.
16 "His roots are dried below,
And his branch is cut off above.
17 "Memory of him perishes
from the earth,
And he has no name abroad.
18 "He is driven from light into darkness,
And chased from the inhabited world.
19 "He has neither offspring nor
posterity among his people,
Nor any survivor where he sojourned.
20 "Those in the west are
appalled at his fate,
And those in the east are
seized with horror.
21 "Surely such are the dwellings
of the unjust,
And this is the place of him
who does not know God."

Psalm 95:1–5

1 Oh come, let us sing for joy to Yahweh,
Let us make a loud shout to the
rock of our salvation.
2 Let us come before His presence
with thanksgiving,
Let us make a loud shout to
Him with songs of praise.
3 For Yahweh is a great God
And a great King above all gods,
4 In whose hand are the
depths of the earth,
The peaks of the mountains
are His also.
5 The sea is His, for it was
He who made it,
And His hands formed the dry land.

Proverbs 23:1–3

23 When you sit down to
dine with a ruler,
Understand well what is before you,
2 So you should put a knife
to your throat
If you are a man of appetite.

3 Do not desire his delicacies,
For it is bread of falsehood.

Romans 12:1–21

12 Therefore I exhort you, brothers, by
the mercies of God, to present your
bodies as a sacrifice—living, holy, *and* pleas-
ing to God, *which is* your spiritual service of
worship. 2 And do not be conformed to this
world, but be transformed by the renewing
of your mind, so that you may approve what
the will of God is, that which is good and
pleasing and perfect.
3 For through the grace given to me I say
to each one among you not to think more
highly of himself than he ought to think; but
to think so as to have sound thinking, as God
has allotted to each a measure of faith. 4 For
just as we have many members in one body
and all the members do not have the same
function, 5 so we, who are many, are one
body in Christ, and individually members
one of another, 6 but having gifts that differ
according to the grace given to us: whether
prophecy, in agreement with the faith; 7 or
service, in his serving; or he who teaches,
in his teaching; 8 or he who exhorts, in his
exhortation; he who gives, with generosity;
he who leads, with diligence; he who shows
mercy, with cheerfulness.
9 *Let* love *be* without hypocrisy—by
abhorring what is evil, clinging to what is
good, 10 *being* devoted to one another in
brotherly love, giving preference to one
another in honor, 11 not lagging behind in
diligence, being fervent in spirit, serving
the Lord, 12 rejoicing in hope, persevering
in affliction, being devoted to prayer,
13 contributing to the needs of the saints,
pursuing hospitality.
14 Bless those who persecute you; bless,
and do not curse. 15 Rejoice with those
who rejoice; weep with those who weep,
16 by being of the same mind toward one
another, not being haughty in mind, but
associating with the humble. Do not be
wise in your own mind. 17 Never paying
back evil for evil to anyone, respecting
what is good in the sight of all men, 18 if
possible, so far as it depends on you, being
at peace with all men, 19 never taking your
own revenge, beloved—instead leave room
for the wrath *of God*. For it is written,
"VENGEANCE IS MINE, I WILL REPAY," says
the Lord. 20 "BUT IF YOUR ENEMY IS HUNGRY,
FEED HIM, AND IF HE IS THIRSTY, GIVE HIM
A DRINK; FOR IN SO DOING YOU WILL HEAP
BURNING COALS ON HIS HEAD." 21 Do not be
overcome by evil, but overcome evil with
good.

AUGUST 14

Job 19:1–20:29

19 Then Job answered and said,
2 "How long will you
torment my soul
And crush me with words?
3 "These ten times you have
dishonored me;
You are not ashamed *that*
you wrong me.
4 "Even if I have truly erred,
My error lodges with me.
5 "If truly you magnify
yourselves against me
And argue my disgrace to me,
6 Know then that God has wronged me
And has closed His net around me.

7 "Behold, I cry, 'Violence!'
but I get no answer;
I shout for help, but there is
no justice.
8 "He has walled up my way so
that I cannot pass,
And He has put darkness on my paths.
9 "He has stripped my honor from me
And removed the crown from my head.
10 "He breaks me down on every
side, and I am gone;
And He has uprooted my
hope like a tree.
11 "He has also kindled His
anger against me
And counted me as His adversary.
12 "His troops come together,
And build up their way against me
And camp around my tent.

13 "He has removed my brothers
far from me,
And my acquaintances are
completely estranged from me.
14 "My relatives have failed,

And my familiar friends
have forgotten me.
15 "Those who sojourn in my
house and my maidservants
count me a stranger.
I am a foreigner in their sight.
16 "I call to my servant, but he
does not answer;
I have to implore him with my mouth.
17 "My breath is offensive to my wife,
And I am loathsome to
my own brothers.
18 "Even young children reject me;
I rise up, and they speak against me.
19 "All the men of my counsel abhor me,
And those I love have
turned against me.
20 "My bone clings to my skin and my flesh,
And I have escaped *only* by
the skin of my teeth.
21 "Pity me, pity me, O you my friends,
For the hand of God has smitten me.
22 "Why do you persecute me as God *does*,
And are not satisfied with my flesh?

23 "Oh that my words were written!
Oh that they were inscribed in a book!
24 "That with an iron stylus and lead
They were engraved in
the rock forever!
25 "As for me, I know that my
Redeemer lives,
And at the last He will rise up
over the dust *of this world*.
26 "Even after my skin is destroyed,
Yet from my flesh I shall behold God,
27 Whom I myself shall behold,
And whom my eyes will see
and not another.
My heart faints within me!
28 "If you say, 'How shall we
persecute him?'
'And the root of the matter
is found in him?'
29 "*Then* be afraid of the sword
for yourselves,
For wrath *brings* the
punishment of the sword,
So that you may know
there is judgment."

20 Then Zophar the Naamathite answered and said,
2 "Therefore my disquieting
thoughts make me respond,
Even because of my haste
within me.
3 "I listened to the discipline
which dishonors me,
And the spirit of my understanding
makes me answer.
4 "Do you know this from of old,
From the establishment
of man on earth,
5 That the shouts of joy of the
wicked are short,
And the gladness of the
godless momentary?
6 "Though his loftiness goes
up to the heavens,
And his head touches the clouds,
7 He perishes forever like his refuse;
Those who have seen him
will say, 'Where is he?'
8 "He flies away like a dream, and
they cannot find him;
Even like a vision of the night
he is chased away.
9 "The eye which saw him
sees him no longer,
And his place no longer beholds him.
10 "His sons seek the favor of the poor,
And his hands give back his wealth.
11 "His bones are full of his
youthful vigor,
But it lies down with him in the dust.

12 "Though evil is sweet in his mouth
And he hides it under his tongue,
13 *Though* he desires it and
will not forsake it,
And holds it to his palate,
14 *Yet* his food in his stomach is changed
To the venom of cobras within him.
15 "He swallows up wealth,
But will vomit it up;
God will expel it from his belly.
16 "He sucks the poison of cobras;
The viper's tongue kills him.
17 "He does not look at the streams,
The rivers flowing with
honey and curds.
18 "He returns what he has attained
And cannot swallow *it*;
As to the wealth of his trading,
He cannot even enjoy *it*.
19 "For he has crushed *and*
forsaken the poor;
He has seized a house which
he has not built.

20 "Because he knew no ease
within his belly,
In his covetousness, he does
not let *anything* escape.
21 "Nothing remains for him to devour;
Therefore his prosperity
does not endure.
22 "In the fullness of his plenty
he will be confined;
The hand of everyone who is
troubled will come *against* him.
23 "So it will be that he fills his belly,
And God will send His
burning anger on him
And will rain *it* on him
while he is eating.
24 "He may flee from the iron weapon,
But the bronze bow will pierce him.
25 "It is drawn forth and comes
out of his back,
Even the glittering point from his gall;
Bouts of dread come upon him.
26 Complete darkness is held in
reserve for his treasures;
A fire unfanned will devour him;
It will consume the survivor in his tent.
27 "The heavens will reveal his iniquity,
And the earth will rise up against him.
28 "The increase of his house will depart;
His possessions will flow away
in the day of His anger.
29 "This is the wicked man's
portion from God,
Even the inheritance decreed
to him by God."

Psalm 95:6–11

6 Come, let us worship and bow down,
Let us kneel before Yahweh our Maker.
7 For He is our God,
And we are the people of His pasture
and the sheep of His hand.
Today, if you hear His voice,
8 Do not harden your hearts,
as at Meribah,
As in the day of Massah
in the wilderness,
9 "When your fathers tried Me,
They tested Me, though they
had seen My work.
10 "For forty years I loathed
that generation,
And said they are a people who
wander in their heart,
And they do not know My ways.
11 "Therefore I swore in My anger,
They shall never enter into My rest."

Proverbs 23:4–5

4 Do not weary yourself to gain wealth,
Because of your understanding, cease!
5 Do you make your eyes fly *up to*
see it? But it is not there!
Because it certainly makes itself wings
Like an eagle that flies
toward the heavens.

Romans 13:1–14

13 Every person is to be in subjection to
the governing authorities. For there
is no authority except from God, and those
which exist have been appointed by God.
2 Therefore whoever resists that authority
has opposed the ordinance of God; and they
who have opposed will receive condemna-
tion upon themselves. 3 For rulers are not *a*
cause of fear for good behavior, but for evil.
Do you want to have no fear of that author-
ity? Do what is good, and you will have
praise from the same; 4 for it is a minister
of God to you for good. But if you do what
is evil, be afraid; for it does not bear the
sword in vain, for it is a minister of God, an
avenger who brings wrath on the one who
practices evil. 5 Therefore it is necessary to
be in subjection, not only because of that
wrath, but also because of conscience. 6 For
because of this you also pay taxes, for *rulers*
are servants of God, devoting themselves
to this very thing. 7 Render to all what is
due them: tax to whom tax *is due*; custom
to whom custom; fear to whom fear; honor
to whom honor.
8 Owe nothing to anyone except to love
one another; for he who loves his neigh-
bor has fulfilled *the* law. 9 For this, "YOU
SHALL NOT COMMIT ADULTERY, YOU SHALL
NOT MURDER, YOU SHALL NOT STEAL, YOU
SHALL NOT COVET," and if there is any other
commandment, it is summed up in this
word, "YOU SHALL LOVE YOUR NEIGHBOR AS
YOURSELF." 10 Love does not work evil against
a neighbor; therefore love is the fulfillment
of *the* Law.
11 And *do* this, knowing the time, that it
is already the hour for you to awaken from
sleep; for now salvation is nearer to us than
when we believed. 12 The night is almost
gone, and the day is at hand. Therefore
let us lay aside the deeds of darkness and

put on the armor of light. 13 Let us walk properly as in the day, not in carousing and drunkenness, not in sexual promiscuity and sensuality, not in strife and jealousy. 14 But put on the Lord Jesus Christ, and make no provision for the flesh in regard to *its* lusts.

AUGUST 15

Job 21:1–22:30

21 Then Job answered and said,
2 "Listen carefully to my speech,
And let this be your *way*
of consolation.
3 "Bear with me that I may speak;
Then after I have spoken,
you may mock.
4 "As for me, is my musing to man?
And why should I not be impatient?
5 "Look at me, and be appalled,
And put *your* hand over *your* mouth.
6 "Even when I remember, I am dismayed,
And horror seizes my flesh.
7 "Why do the wicked *still* live,
Continue on, also become
very powerful?
8 "Their seed is established with
them in their presence,
And their offspring before their eyes,
9 Their houses are safe from dread,
And the rod of God is not on them.
10 "His ox mates and does not fail;
His cow calves and does not miscarry.
11 "They send forth their little
ones like the flock,
And their children skip about.
12 "They lift up the tambourine and harp
And are glad at the sound of the pipe.
13 "They spend their days in prosperity,
And suddenly they go down to Sheol.
14 "They say to God, 'Depart from us!
We do not even desire the
knowledge of Your ways.
15 'Who is the Almighty, that
we should serve Him,
And what would we profit
if we entreat Him?'
16 "Behold, their prosperity is
not in their hand;
The counsel of the wicked
is far from me.

17 "How often is the lamp of
the wicked put out,
Or does their disaster fall on them?
Does God apportion destruction
in His anger?
18 "Are they as straw before the wind,
And like chaff which the
storm steals away?
19 "*You say*, 'God stores away a man's
wickedness for his sons.'
Let God repay him so that
he may know *it*.
20 "Let his own eyes see his decay,
And let him drink of the
wrath of the Almighty.
21 "For what desire does he have for
his household after him,
When the number of his
months is cut off?
22 "Can anyone teach God knowledge,
In that He judges those on high?
23 "One dies in his full strength,
Being wholly carefree and at ease;
24 His sides are filled out with fat,
And the marrow of his bones is moist,
25 But another dies with a bitter soul,
Never even eats *anything* good.
26 "Together they lie down in the dust,
And worms cover them.

27 "Behold, I know your thoughts,
And the plans by which you
do violence against me.
28 "For you say, 'Where is the
house of the nobleman,
And where is the tent, the dwelling
places of the wicked?'
29 "Have you not asked those who
pass by along the way,
And do you not recognize
their witness?
30 "That the wicked is reserved
for the day of disaster;
They will be led forth at
the day of fury.
31 "Who will declare to his face
about his actions,
And who will repay him for
what he has done?
32 "While he is led forth to the grave,
Men will keep watch over *his* tomb.
33 "The clods of the valley will
gently cover him;

Moreover, all men will
draw up after him,
While countless ones *go* before him.
34 "How then will you vainly comfort me,
Indeed *when* your answers
remain *full of* falsehood?"

22 Then Eliphaz the Temanite answered
and said,
2 "Can a mighty man be of use to God,
Or an insightful man be
useful to himself?
3 "Is there any pleasure to the
Almighty if you are righteous,
Or profit if you make your
ways perfect?
4 "Is it because of your *reverent*
fear that He reproves you,
That He enters into judgment
against you?
5 "Is not your evil great,
And your iniquities without end?
6 "For you have taken pledges of
your brothers without cause,
And stripped the clothing of the naked.
7 "To the weary you have given
no water to drink,
And from the hungry you
have withheld bread.
8 "But the earth belongs to
the mighty man,
And the highly respected
man inhabits it.
9 "You have sent widows away empty,
And the might of the orphans
has been crushed.
10 "Therefore snares surround you,
And sudden dread terrifies you,
11 Or darkness, so that you cannot see,
And an abundance of water
covers you.

12 "Is not God *in* the height of heaven?
Look also at the distant stars,
how high they are!
13 "You say, 'What does God know?
Can He judge through the
dense gloom?
14 'Clouds are a hiding place for
Him, so that He cannot see;
And He walks on the vault of heaven.'
15 "Will you keep to the ancient path
Which wicked men have trod,
16 Who were snatched away
before their time,
Whose foundations were
washed away by a river?
17 "They said to God, 'Depart from us!'
And 'What can the Almighty
do to them?'
18 "Yet He filled their houses
with good *things*,
But the counsel of the wicked
is far from me.
19 "The righteous see and are glad,
And the innocent mock them,
20 *Saying*, 'Truly those who rise
against us are wiped out,
And their abundance the
fire has consumed.'

21 "Yield now and be at peace with Him;
Thereby good will come to you.
22 "Please receive instruction
from His mouth
And set His words in your heart.
23 "If you return to the Almighty,
you will be restored;
If you remove unrighteousness
far from your tent,
24 And put *your* gold in the dust,
And *the gold of* Ophir among
the stones of the brooks,
25 Then the Almighty will be your gold
And choice silver to you.
26 "For then you will delight
in the Almighty
And lift up your face to God.
27 "You will entreat Him, and
He will hear you;
And you will pay your vows.
28 "You will also decree a thing, and
it will be established for you;
And light will shine on your ways.
29 "When some are cast down, you
will speak with confidence,
And the humble person He will save.
30 "He will provide escape for one
who is not innocent,
And he will escape through the
cleanness of your hands."

Psalm 96:1–6

1 Sing to Yahweh a new song;
Sing to Yahweh, all the earth.
2 Sing to Yahweh, bless His name;
Proclaim good news of His
salvation from day to day.
3 Recount His glory among
the nations,

His wondrous deeds among
all the peoples.
4 For great is Yahweh and
greatly to be praised;
He is more fearsome than all gods.
5 For all the gods of the peoples are idols,
But Yahweh made the heavens.
6 Splendor and majesty are before Him,
Strength and beauty are
in His sanctuary.

Proverbs 23:6–8

6 Do not eat the bread of a selfish man,
And do not desire his delicacies;
7 For as he calculates in his soul, so he is.
"Eat and drink!" he says to you,
But his heart is not with you.
8 You will vomit up the morsel
you have eaten,
And you will corrupt your
pleasant words.

Romans 14:1–23

14 Now accept the one who is weak in
faith, *but* not for *the purpose of* pass-
ing judgment on opinions. 2 One person has
faith that he may eat all things, but he who
is weak eats vegetables *only*. 3 The one who
eats must not view the one who does not
eat with contempt, and the one who does
not eat must not judge the one who eats, for
God accepted him. 4 Who are you to judge
the servant of another? To his own master
he stands or falls; and he will stand, for the
Lord is able to make him stand.
5 One person judges one day above
another, another judges every day *alike*.
Each person must be fully convinced in his
own mind. 6 He who regards the day, regards
it for the Lord, and he who eats, eats for the
Lord, for he gives thanks to God; and he who
does not eat, for the Lord he does not eat
and gives thanks to God. 7 For not one of
us lives for himself, and not one dies for
himself; 8 for if we live, we live for the Lord,
or if we die, we die for the Lord; therefore
whether we live or die, we are the Lord's.
9 For to this end Christ died and lived again,
that He might be Lord both of the dead and
of the living.
10 But you, why do you judge your
brother? Or you again, why do you view
your brother with contempt? For we will
all stand before the judgment seat of God.
11 For it is written,
"As I live, says the Lord, to Me
every knee shall bow,
And every tongue shall
confess to God."
12 So then each one of us will give an account
of himself to God.
13 Therefore let us not judge one another
anymore, but rather judge this—not to put a
stumbling block or offense before a brother.
14 I know and am convinced in the Lord Jesus
that nothing is defiled in itself; but to him
who considers anything to be defiled, to him
it is defiled. 15 For if because of food your
brother is grieved, you are no longer walking
according to love. Do not destroy with your
food him for whom Christ died. 16 Therefore
do not let what is for you a good thing be slan-
dered; 17 for the kingdom of God is not eating
and drinking, but righteousness and peace
and joy in the Holy Spirit. 18 For he who in
this *way* serves Christ is pleasing to God and
approved by men. 19 So then let us pursue the
things which make for peace and the building
up of one another. 20 Do not tear down the
work of God for the sake of food. All things
indeed are clean, but they are evil for the man
who eats and gives offense. 21 It is good not to
eat meat or to drink wine, or *to do anything*
by which your brother stumbles. 22 The faith
which you have, have as your own conviction
before God. Blessed is he who does not judge
himself in what he approves. 23 But he who
doubts is condemned if he eats, because *his
eating is* not from faith; and whatever is not
from faith is sin.

AUGUST 16

Job 23:1–25:6

23 Then Job answered and said,
2 "Even today my musing
is rebellion;
His hand is heavy despite my groaning.
3 "Oh that I knew where I might find Him,
That I might come to His seat!
4 "I would arrange *my case for*
justice before Him
And fill my mouth with arguments.
5 "I would know the words *which*
He would answer,

And discern what He would say to me.
6 "Would He contend with me by
the greatness of *His* power?
No, surely He would pay
attention to me.
7 "There the upright would
argue with Him;
And I would have escaped
forever from my Judge.

8 "Behold, I go forward but
He is not *there*,
And backward, but I cannot
discern Him;
9 When He acts on the left,
I cannot behold *Him*;
He turns on the right,
I cannot see Him.
10 "But He knows the way I take;
When He has tested me, I shall
come forth as gold.
11 "My foot has held fast to His path;
I have kept His way and
not turned aside.
12 "I have not departed from the
command of His lips;
I have treasured the words
of His mouth more than
my portion *of food*.
13 "But He is unique and who
can turn Him?
And *what* His soul desires,
that He does.
14 "For He performs what is
apportioned for me,
And many such *decrees* are with Him.
15 "Therefore, I would be dismayed
at His presence;
I carefully consider, and I
am in dread of Him.
16 "*It is* God *who* has made my heart faint,
And the Almighty *who*
has dismayed me,
17 But I am not silenced by the darkness,
Nor thick darkness *which* covers me.

24 "Why are times not stored
up by the Almighty,
And why do those who know
Him not behold His days?
2 "Some move the boundaries;
They seize and devour flocks.
3 "They drive away the donkeys
of the orphans;
They take the widow's ox for a pledge.
4 "They push the needy aside
from the road;
The afflicted of the land are made
to hide themselves altogether.
5 "Behold, as wild donkeys
in the wilderness
They go forth seeking food
earnestly in their work,
The desert becomes for him a *place*
of bread for *his* young ones.
6 "They harvest their fodder in the field
And glean the vineyard of the wicked.
7 "They spend the night naked,
without clothing,
And have no covering against the cold.
8 "They are wet with the mountain rains
And hug the rock for want of a shelter.
9 "Others snatch the orphan
from the breast,
And against the afflicted
they take a pledge.
10 "Those *poor* ones walk about
naked without clothing,
And hungry ones carry the sheaves.
11 "Within the walls they produce oil;
They tread wine presses but thirst.
12 "From the city men groan,
And the souls of the wounded cry out;
Yet God does not pay attention
to *such* offense.

13 "Others have been with those
who rebel against the light;
They do not want to
recognize its ways
Nor abide in its paths.
14 "The murderer arises at dawn;
He kills the afflicted and the needy,
And at night he is as a thief.
15 "The eye of the adulterer keeps
watch for the twilight,
Saying, 'No eye will see me.'
And he keeps his face hidden.
16 "In the dark they dig into houses;
They shut themselves up by day;
They do not know the light.
17 "For the morning is the same to
him as the shadow of death,
For he recognizes the terrors
of the shadow of death.

18 "They are insignificant on the
surface of the water;
Their portion is cursed on the earth.
They do not turn toward the vineyards.

19 "Drought and heat seize
the snow waters,
So does Sheol *those who* have sinned.
20 "A mother will forget him;
The worm feasts sweetly till he
is no longer remembered.
And unrighteousness will
be broken like a tree.
21 "He feeds on the barren woman
who does not give birth
And does no good for the widow.

22 "But He drags off the mighty
by His power;
He rises, but no one believes in his life.
23 "He provides them with security,
and they are supported;
And His eyes are on their ways.
24 "They are exalted a little while,
then they are gone;
Moreover, they are brought low and
like everything gathered up;
Even like the heads of grain
they are cut off.
25 "Now if it is not so, who can
prove me a liar,
And make my speech worthless?"

25 Then Bildad the Shuhite answered
and said,
2 "Rule and dread belong to Him
Who makes peace in His heights.
3 "Is there any number to His troops?
And upon whom does His
light not rise?
4 "How then can mortal man
be right with God?
Or how can he be pure who
is born of woman?
5 "Behold even the moon
has no brightness,
And the stars are not pure in
His sight;
6 How much less mortal
man, *that* maggot,
And the son of man, *that* worm!"

Psalm 96:7–10

7 Ascribe to Yahweh, O families
of the peoples,
Ascribe to Yahweh glory and strength.
8 Ascribe to Yahweh the
glory of His name;
Lift up an offering and come
into His courts.
9 Worship Yahweh in the
splendor of holiness;
Tremble before Him, all the earth.
10 Say among the nations,
"Yahweh reigns;
Indeed, the world is established,
it will not be shaken;
He will render justice to the
peoples with equity."

Proverbs 23:9

9 Do not speak in the hearing of a fool,
For he will despise the insight
of your speech.

Romans 15:1–21

15 Now we who are strong ought to bear
the weaknesses of those without
strength and not *just* please ourselves.
2 Each of us is to please his neighbor for his
good, to his building up. 3 For even Christ
did not please Himself; but as it is written,
"The reproaches of those who reproached
You fell on Me." 4 For whatever was written
in earlier times was written for our instruc-
tion, so that through the perseverance and
the encouragement of the Scriptures we
might have hope. 5 Now may the God of
perseverance and encouragement grant you
to be of the same mind with one another
according to Christ Jesus, 6 so that with one
accord you may with one voice glorify the
God and Father of our Lord Jesus Christ.
7 Therefore, accept one another, just as
Christ also accepted us to the glory of God.
8 For I say that Christ has become a servant
to the circumcision on behalf of the truth
of God to confirm the promises *given* to the
fathers, 9 and for the Gentiles to glorify God
for His mercy; as it is written,
"Therefore I will give praise to
You among the Gentiles,
And I will sing to Your name."
10 And again he says,
"Rejoice, O Gentiles, with His people."
11 And again,
"Praise the Lord all you Gentiles,
And let all the peoples praise Him."
12 And again Isaiah says,
"There shall come the root of Jesse,
And He who arises to rule
over the Gentiles,
In Him shall the Gentiles hope."
13 Now may the God of hope fill you with all
joy and peace in believing, so that you will

abound in hope by the power of the Holy
Spirit.
14 But I myself am also convinced about
you, my brothers, that you yourselves are
full of goodness, having been filled with all
knowledge and being able also to admonish
one another. 15 But I have written very boldly
to you on some points so as to remind you
again, because of the grace that was given
me by God 16 for me to be a minister of
Christ Jesus to the Gentiles, ministering as a
priest the gospel of God, so that *my* offering
of the Gentiles may become acceptable,
having been sanctified by the Holy Spirit.
17 Therefore in Christ Jesus I have reason for
boasting in things pertaining to God. 18 For I
will not be bold to speak of anything except
what Christ has brought about through me,
leading to the obedience of the Gentiles by
word and deed, 19 in the power of signs and
wonders, in the power of the Spirit; so that
from Jerusalem and all around as far as
Illyricum I have fully preached the gospel
of Christ. 20 And in this way I make it my
ambition to proclaim the gospel, not where
Christ was *already* named, so that I would
not build on another man's foundation;
21 but as it is written,

"THEY WHO HAD NO DECLARATION
OF HIM SHALL SEE,
AND THEY WHO HAVE NOT HEARD
SHALL UNDERSTAND."

AUGUST 17

Job 26:1–14

26 Then Job answered and said,
2 "What a help you are to
the one without power!
How you have saved the arm
without strength!
3 "What counsel you have given
to *one* without wisdom!
What sound wisdom you have
abundantly made known!
4 "To whom have you declared words?
And whose breath comes
out from you?

5 "The departed spirits tremble
Under the waters and
their inhabitants.
6 "Naked is Sheol before Him,
And Abaddon has no covering.
7 "He stretches out the north
over what is formless
And hangs the earth on nothing.
8 "He wraps up the waters in His clouds,
And the cloud does not break
out under them.
9 "He obscures the face of *His* throne
And spreads His cloud over it.
10 "He has marked a circle on the
surface of the waters
At the boundary of light and darkness.
11 "The pillars of heaven tremble
And are astonished at His rebuke.
12 "He quieted the sea with His power,
And by His understanding
He crushed Rahab.
13 "By His breath the heavens
are *made* beautiful;
His hand has pierced the
fleeing serpent.
14 "Behold, these are the
fringes of His ways;
And how *only with* a whisper of
a word do we hear of Him!
But His mighty thunder, who
can understand?"

Psalm 96:11–13

11 Let the heavens be glad, and
let the earth rejoice;
Let the sea roar, as well as
its fullness;
12 Let the field exult, and all that is in it.
Then all the trees of the
forest will sing for joy
13 Before Yahweh, for He is coming,
For He is coming to judge the earth.
He will judge the world
in righteousness
And the peoples in His faithfulness.

Proverbs 23:10–12

10 Do not move the ancient
boundary
And do not come into the
fields of the orphans,
11 For their Redeemer is strong;
He will plead their case against you.
12 Bring your heart to discipline
And your ears to words
of knowledge.

Romans 15:22–33

22 For this reason I have often been pre-
vented from coming to you; 23 but now, with
no further place for me in these regions, and
since I have had for many years a longing to
come to you 24 whenever I go to Spain—for
I hope, passing through, to see you, and to
be helped on my way there by you, when
I have first enjoyed your company for a
while. 25 But now I am going to Jerusalem
to serve the saints. 26 For Macedonia and
Achaia were pleased to share with the poor
among the saints in Jerusalem. 27 Yes, they
were pleased *to do so*, and they are indebted
to them. For if the Gentiles have shared in
their spiritual things, they are indebted to
minister to them also in material things.
28 Therefore, when I have completed this
and have put my seal on this fruit of theirs,
I will go on by way of you to Spain. 29 And I
know that when I come to you, I will come
in the fullness of the blessing of Christ.

30 Now I urge you, brothers, by our Lord
Jesus Christ and by the love of the Spirit, to
strive together with me in your prayers to
God for me, 31 that I may be rescued from
those who are disobedient in Judea, and
that my service for Jerusalem may prove
acceptable to the saints; 32 so that I may
come to you in joy by the will of God and
find rest in your company. 33 Now may the
God of peace be with you all. Amen.

AUGUST 18

Job 27:1–28:28

27 Then Job continued to lift up his discourse and said,

2 "As God lives, who has
removed my justice,
And the Almighty, who has
embittered my soul,
3 For as long as breath is in me,
And the spirit from God
is in my nostrils,
4 My lips certainly will not
speak unrighteousness,
Nor will my tongue utter deceit.
5 "Far be it from me that I should
declare you right;
Till I breathe my last I will not
remove my integrity from me.
6 "I hold fast my righteousness
and will not let it go.
My heart does not reproach
any of my days.

7 "May my enemy be as the wicked
And the one who rises against
me as the unjust.
8 "For what is the hope of the
godless when he is cut off,
When God requires his soul?
9 "Will God hear his cry
When distress comes upon him?
10 "Will he take delight in the Almighty?
Will he call on God at all times?
11 "I will instruct you in the power of God;
What is with the Almighty
I will not conceal.
12 "Behold, all of you have seen *it*;
Why then do you speak
with utter vanity?

13 "This is the portion of a
wicked man from God,
And the inheritance *which* the ruthless
receive from the Almighty.
14 "Though his sons are many, they
are destined for the sword;
And his offspring will not be
satisfied with bread.
15 "His survivors will be buried
because of the plague,
And their widows will not
be able to weep.
16 "Though he piles up silver like dust
And prepares garments as
plentiful as the clay,
17 He may prepare *it*, but the
righteous will wear *it*,
And the innocent will divide the silver.
18 "He has built his house like the moth,
Or as a hut *which* the
watchman has made.
19 "He lies down rich, but never again;
He opens his eyes, and it is no longer.
20 "Terrors overtake him like *many* waters;
A tempest steals him away in the night.
21 "The east wind carries him
away, and he goes,
And it whirls him away from his place.
22 "For it will hurl at him without sparing;
He will surely try to flee
from its power.

[23] "*Men* will clap their hands at him
And will hiss him from his place.

28

"Surely there is a mine for silver,
And a place where they
refine for gold.
[2] "Iron is taken from the dust,
And copper is smelted from rock.
[3] "*Man* puts an end to darkness,
And to the farthest limit
he searches out
The rock in thick darkness
and shadow of death.
[4] "He sinks a shaft far from habitation,
Forgotten by the foot;
They hang and swing to and
fro far from men.
[5] "The earth, from it comes food,
And underneath it is
overturned as fire.
[6] "Its rocks are the source of sapphires,
And its dust *contains* gold.
[7] "The path no bird of prey knows,
Nor has the falcon's eye
caught sight of it.
[8] "The proud beasts have not trodden it,
Nor has the *fierce* lion passed over it.
[9] "He sends his hand forth to the flint;
He overturns the mountains
at the base.
[10] "He breaks out channels
through the rocks,
And his eye sees anything precious.
[11] "He dams up the streams from flowing,
And what is hidden he brings
out to the light.

[12] "But where can wisdom be found?
And where is the place of
understanding?
[13] "Man does not know its worth,
And it is not found in the
land of the living.
[14] "The deep says, 'It is not in me';
And the sea says, 'It is not with me.'
[15] "Pure gold cannot be given in place of it,
Nor can silver be weighed as its price.
[16] "It cannot be valued in the
gold of Ophir,
In precious onyx or sapphire.
[17] "Gold or glass cannot meet its worth,
Nor can it be exchanged for
articles of fine gold.
[18] "Coral and crystal are not
to be mentioned;
And the acquisition of wisdom
is above *that of* pearls.
[19] "The topaz of Ethiopia cannot
meet its worth,
Nor can it be valued in pure gold.
[20] "Where then does wisdom come from?
And where is the place of
understanding?
[21] "Thus it is hidden from the
eyes of all living
And concealed from the
birds of the sky.
[22] "Abaddon and Death say,
'With our ears we have
heard a report of it.'
[23] "God understands its way,
And He knows its place.
[24] "For He looks to the ends of the earth
And sees everything under
the heavens.
[25] "When He set weight to the wind
And meted out the waters by measure,
[26] When He set a limit for the rain
And a course for the thunderbolt,
[27] Then He saw it and recounted it;
He established it and also
searched it out.
[28] "So He said to man, 'Behold, the fear
of the Lord, that is wisdom;
And to turn away from evil
is understanding.'"

Psalm 97:1–6

[1] Yahweh reigns, let the earth rejoice;
Let the many coastlands be glad.
[2] Clouds and thick darkness
are all around Him;
Righteousness and justice are the
foundation of His throne.
[3] Fire goes before Him
And burns up His adversaries
all around.
[4] His lightnings light up the world;
The earth sees and trembles.
[5] The mountains melt like wax at
the presence of Yahweh,
At the presence of the Lord
of all the earth.
[6] The heavens declare His righteousness,
And all the peoples see His glory.

Proverbs 23:13–14

[13] Do not withhold discipline
from the child,

Although you strike him with
the rod, he will not die.
14 You shall strike him with the rod
And deliver his soul from Sheol.

Romans 16:1–27

16 Now I commend to you our sister
Phoebe, who is a servant of the church
which is at Cenchrea; 2 that you receive her in
the Lord in a manner worthy of the saints, and
that you help her in whatever matter she may
have need of you; for she herself has also been
a benefactor of many, and of myself as well.
3 Greet Prisca and Aquila, my fellow
workers in Christ Jesus,
4 who for my life risked their own necks,
to whom not only do I give thanks, but
also all the churches of the Gentiles;
5 also *greet* the church that is in their
house.
Greet Epaenetus, my beloved, who is
the first convert to Christ from Asia.
6 Greet Mary, who has labored much for
you.
7 Greet Andronicus and Junia, my
kinsmen and my fellow prisoners, who
are outstanding to the apostles, who
also were in Christ before me.
8 Greet Ampliatus, my beloved in the
Lord.
9 Greet Urbanus, our fellow worker in
Christ, and Stachys my beloved.
10 Greet Apelles, the approved in Christ.
Greet those who are of the *household*
of Aristobulus.
11 Greet Herodion, my kinsman.
Greet those of the *household* of
Narcissus, who are in the Lord.
12 Greet Tryphaena and Tryphosa,
laborers in the Lord.
Greet Persis the beloved, who labored
much in the Lord.
13 Greet Rufus, a choice man in the Lord,
also his mother and mine.
14 Greet Asyncritus, Phlegon, Hermes,
Patrobas, Hermas and the brothers
with them.
15 Greet Philologus and Julia, Nereus and
his sister, and Olympas, and all the
saints who are with them.
16 Greet one another with a holy kiss.
All the churches of Christ greet you.
17 Now I urge you, brothers, to keep
your eye on those who cause dissensions
and stumblings contrary to the teaching
which you learned, and turn away from
them. 18 For such men are slaves, not of
our Lord Christ but of their own stomach,
and by their smooth and flattering speech
they deceive the hearts of the unsuspecting.
19 For the report of your obedience has
reached to all. Therefore I am rejoicing over
you, but I want you to be wise in what is
good and innocent in what is evil. 20 And the
God of peace will soon crush Satan under
your feet.
The grace of our Lord Jesus be with you.
21 Timothy my fellow worker greets you,
and *so do* Lucius and Jason and Sosipater,
my kinsmen.
22 I, Tertius, who wrote this letter, greet
you in the Lord.
23 Gaius, host to me and to the whole
church, greets you. Erastus, the city trea-
surer greets you, and Quartus, the brother.
24 [The grace of our Lord Jesus Christ be with
you all. Amen.]
25 Now to Him who is able to strengthen
you according to my gospel and the
preaching of Jesus Christ, according to the
revelation of the mystery which has been
kept secret for long ages past, 26 but now
is manifested, and by the Scriptures of the
prophets, according to the commandment
of the eternal God, has been made known
to all the Gentiles, *leading* to obedience of
faith; 27 to the only wise God, through Jesus
Christ, be the glory forever. Amen.

AUGUST 19

Job 29:1–30:31

29 And Job continued to lift up his
discourse and said,
2 "Oh that I were as in months gone by,
As in the days when God kept me,
3 When His lamp shone
over my head,
And by His light I walked
through darkness,
4 As I was in the prime of my days,
When the *intimate* counsel with
God *was* over my tent,
5 When the Almighty was yet with me,
And my children were around me,

6 When my steps were bathed in butter,
And the rock poured out for
me streams of oil!
7 "When I went out to the gate of the city,
When I took my seat in the square,
8 The young men saw me and hid,
And the old men arose *and* stood.
9 "The princes stopped talking
And put *their* hands on their mouths;
10 The voice of the nobles
was hidden *away*,
And their tongue clung to their palate.
11 "For the ear heard, and it
called me blessed,
And the eye saw, and it
gave witness of me,
12 Because I provided escape for the
afflicted who cried for help,
And the orphan who had no helper.
13 "The blessing of the one ready
to perish came upon me,
And I made the widow's
heart sing for joy.
14 "I clothed *myself* with righteousness,
and it clothed me;
My justice was like a robe and a turban.
15 "I was eyes to the blind
And feet to the lame.
16 "I was a father to the needy,
And I searched out the case
which I did not know.
17 "I broke the fangs of the unjust
And snatched the prey from his teeth.
18 "Then I said, 'I will breathe
my last in my nest,
And I shall multiply *my*
days as the sand.
19 'My root is spread out to the waters,
And dew lies all night on my branch.
20 'My glory is *ever* new with me,
And my bow is renewed in my hand.'

21 "To me they listened and waited,
And kept silent for my counsel.
22 "After my words they did
not speak again,
And my speech dropped on them.
23 "They waited for me as for the rain,
And opened their mouth
as for the late rain.
24 "I laughed with them *as* they
could not believe *it*,
And the light of my face they
did not cast down.
25 "I chose a way for them and sat as chief,
And dwelt as *their* head
among the troops,
As one who comforted the mourners.

30 "But now those younger
than I laugh at me,
Whose fathers I rejected *even* to
put with the dogs of my flock.
2 "Indeed, what *good was* the strength
of their hands to me?
Vigor had perished from them.
3 "From want and famine they
are gaunt,
Who gnaw the dry ground by night
in destruction and desolation,
4 Who pluck mallow by the bushes,
And whose food is the root
of the broom tree.
5 "They are driven from the community;
They shout against them
as *against* a thief,
6 So that they dwell in the
slopes of the valleys,
In holes of the dust and of the rocks.
7 "Among the bushes they cry out;
Under the nettles they are
gathered together.
8 "Wicked fools, even those
without a name,
They were scourged from the land.

9 "And now I have become
their *mocking* song;
I have even become a *taunting*
word to them.
10 "They abhor me *and* keep a
distance from me,
And they do not hold back
from spitting at my face.
11 "Because He has loosed His
bowstring and afflicted me,
They have thrust aside *their*
bridle before me.
12 "On the right hand their brood arises;
They thrust aside my feet and build up
against me their ways to disaster.
13 "They break up my path;
They profit from my destruction;
They have no helper.
14 "As *through* a wide breach they come,
Amid the storm they roll on.
15 "Terrors are turned against me;
They pursue my nobility as the wind,
And my *hope for* salvation has
passed away like a cloud.

16 "And now my soul is poured
out within me;
Days of affliction have seized me.
17 "At night it pierces my bones within me,
And my gnawing *pains* take no rest.
18 "By a great force my garment
is distorted;
It seizes me about as the
collar of my tunic.
19 "He has cast me into the mire,
And I have become like dust and ashes.
20 "I cry out to You for help, but
You do not answer me;
I stand up, and You carefully
consider *how to be* against me.
21 "You have become cruel to me;
With the might of Your hand
You hunted me down.
22 "You lift me up to the wind
and cause me to ride;
And You melt me away in a storm.
23 "For I know that You will
bring me to death
And to the house of meeting
for all living.

24 "Yet does not one in a heap of
ruins stretch out *his* hand,
Or, in his upheaval, is there a cry
for help because of them?
25 "Have I not wept for the one
whose life is hard?
Was not my soul grieved for the needy?
26 "When I hoped for good, then evil came;
When I waited for light, then
thick darkness came.
27 "I am boiling within and
cannot be silent;
Days of affliction confront me.
28 "I go about darkened *but* not by the sun;
I stand up in the assembly
and cry out for help.
29 "I have become a brother to jackals
And a companion of ostriches.
30 "My skin turns black on me,
And my bones burn with fever.
31 "Therefore my harp is turned
to mourning,
And my flute to the sound
of those who weep.

Psalm 97:7–12

7 Let all those be ashamed who
serve graven images,
Who boast of idols;
Worship Him, all you gods!
8 Zion heard *this* and was glad,
And the daughters of Judah
have rejoiced
Because of Your judgments, O Yahweh.
9 For You are Yahweh Most
High over all the earth;
You are exalted far above all gods.

10 Hate evil, you who love Yahweh,
Who keeps the souls of His holy ones;
He delivers them from the
hand of the wicked.
11 Light is sown for the righteous
And gladness for the upright in heart.
12 Be glad in Yahweh, you righteous ones,
And give thanks for the
remembrance of His holy *name*.

Proverbs 23:15–16

15 My son, if your heart is wise,
My own heart also will be glad;
16 And my inmost being will exult
When your lips speak upright things.

1 Corinthians 1:1–31

1 Paul, called *as* an apostle of Jesus Christ
by the will of God, and Sosthenes our
brother,
2 To the church of God which is at
Corinth, to those who have been sanctified
in Christ Jesus, called as saints, with all who
in every place call on the name of our Lord
Jesus Christ, their *Lord* and ours:
3 Grace to you and peace from God our
Father and the Lord Jesus Christ.
4 I thank my God always concerning you
for the grace of God which was given you
in Christ Jesus, 5 that in everything you
were enriched in Him, in all word and all
knowledge, 6 even as the witness about
Christ was confirmed in you, 7 so that you
are not lacking in any gift, eagerly awaiting
the revelation of our Lord Jesus Christ, 8 who
will also confirm you to the end, beyond
reproach in the day of our Lord Jesus Christ.
9 God is faithful, through whom you were
called into fellowship with His Son, Jesus
Christ our Lord.
10 Now I exhort you, brothers, by the
name of our Lord Jesus Christ, that you all
agree and that there be no divisions among
you, but that you be made complete in the
same mind and in the same judgment. 11 For
I have been informed concerning you, my

brothers, by Chloe's *people*, that there are
quarrels among you. 12 Now I mean this, that
each one of you is saying, "I am of Paul,"
and "I of Apollos," and "I of Cephas," and "I
of Christ." 13 Has Christ been divided? Was
Paul crucified for you? Or were you baptized
in the name of Paul? 14 I thank God that I
baptized none of you except Crispus and
Gaius, 15 so that no one would say you were
baptized in my name. 16 Now I did baptize
also the household of Stephanas; beyond
that, I do not know whether I baptized
any other. 17 For Christ did not send me to
baptize, but to proclaim the gospel, not in
wisdom of word, so that the cross of Christ
will not be made empty.

18 For the word of the cross is foolishness
to those who are perishing, but to us who
are being saved, it is the power of God. 19 For
it is written,

"I WILL DESTROY THE WISDOM
OF THE WISE,
AND THE CLEVERNESS OF THE
CLEVER I WILL SET ASIDE."

20 Where is the wise man? Where is the
scribe? Where is the debater of this age?
Has not God made foolish the wisdom of the
world? 21 For since, in the wisdom of God,
the world through its wisdom did not *come*
to know God, God was well-pleased, through
the foolishness of the message preached, to
save those who believe. 22 For indeed Jews
ask for signs and Greeks search for wisdom,
23 but we preach Christ crucified, to Jews a
stumbling block and to Gentiles foolishness,
24 but to those who are the called, both Jews
and Greeks, Christ the power of God and the
wisdom of God. 25 Because the foolishness
of God is wiser than men, and the weakness
of God is stronger than men.

26 For consider your calling, brothers, that
there were not many wise according to the
flesh, not many mighty, not many noble.
27 But God has chosen the foolish things
of the world to shame the wise, and God
has chosen the weak things of the world
to shame the things which are strong,
28 and the base things of the world and the
despised God has chosen, the things that
are not, so that He may abolish the things
that are, 29 so that no flesh may boast before
God. 30 But by His doing you are in Christ
Jesus, who became to us wisdom from God,
and righteousness and sanctification, and
redemption, 31 so that, just as it is written,
"LET HIM WHO BOASTS, BOAST IN THE LORD."

In every land, in every language, it is the same tale: where that Book is read, not with the eyes only, but with the mind and heart, the life is changed.

— AMY CARMICHAEL

AUGUST 20

Job 31:1–32:22

31 "I have cut a covenant with my eyes;
How then could I gaze at a virgin?
2 "And what is the portion of
God from above
Or the inheritance of the
Almighty from on high?
3 "Is it not disaster to the unjust
And misfortune to those
who work iniquity?
4 "Does He not see my ways
And number all my steps?

5 "If I have walked with worthlessness,
And my foot has hastened after deceit,
6 Let Him weigh me with just scales,
And let God know my integrity.
7 "If my step has turned from the way,
Or my heart followed my eyes,
Or if any spot has stuck to my hands,
8 Let me sow and another eat,
And let my crops be uprooted.

9 "If my heart has been enticed
by a woman,
Or I have lain in wait at my
neighbor's doorway,
10 May my wife grind for another,
And let others kneel down over her.
11 "For that would be lewdness;
Moreover, it would be an iniquity
punishable by judges.

12 "For it would be fire that
consumes to Abaddon,
And would uproot all my produce.

13 "If I have rejected the justice of
my male or female slaves
When they filed a complaint
against me,
14 What then could I do when God arises?
And when He calls me to account,
with what will I respond to Him?
15 "Did not He who made me in
the womb make him,
And the same one fashion
us in the womb?

16 "If I have held back the poor
from *their* desire,
Or have caused the eyes of
the widow to fail,
17 Or have eaten my morsel alone,
And the orphan has not eaten from it
18 (But from my youth he grew up
with me as *with* a father,
And from the womb of my
mother I guided her),
19 If I have seen anyone perish
for lack of clothing,
Or that the needy had no covering,
20 If his loins have not blessed me,
And if he has not been warmed
with the fleece of my sheep,
21 If I have waved my hand
against the orphan
Because I saw my help in the gate,
22 Let my shoulder fall from the socket,
And my arm be broken off at the elbow.
23 "For disaster from God is a dread to me,
And because of His exaltedness
I can do nothing.

24 "If I have put my confidence *in* gold,
And called fine gold my trust,
25 If I have been glad because
my wealth was great,
And because my hand had
found *so* much,
26 If I have looked at the sun when it shone
Or the moon going in splendor,
27 And my heart became secretly enticed,
And my hand threw a kiss
from my mouth,
28 That too would have been an
iniquity *calling for* judgment,
For I would have denied God above.
29 "If I have been glad at the upheaval
of the one who hated me,
Or exulted when evil found him—
30 "But I have not given over
my mouth to sin
By asking for his life in a curse—
31 "If the men of my tent have not said,
'Who can find one who has not
been satisfied with his meat'—
32 "The sojourner has not lodged outside,
For I have opened my doors
to the traveler—
33 "If I have covered my
transgressions like Adam,
By hiding my iniquity in my bosom,
34 Because I feared the great multitude,
And the contempt of
families terrified me,
And I kept silent and did not
go out of doors—
35 "Oh that I had one to hear me!
Behold, here is my signature;
Let the Almighty answer me!
And the indictment which my
accuser has written,
36 Surely I would carry it
on my shoulder;
I would bind it to myself like a crown.
37 "I would declare to Him the
number of my steps;
Like a prince I would approach Him—

38 "If my land cries out against me,
And its furrows weep together,
39 If I have eaten its fruit without money,
Or have caused its owners
to lose their lives,
40 Let briars come out instead of wheat,
And stinkweed instead of barley."
The words of Job are ended.

32 Then these three men ceased answer-
ing Job because he was righteous in
his own eyes. 2 But the anger of Elihu the
son of Barachel the Buzite, of the family of
Ram, burned; against Job his anger burned
because he was proving himself righteous
before God. 3 And his anger burned against
his three friends because they had found
no answer, and yet had condemned Job.
4 Now Elihu had waited with *his* words for
Job because they were years older than he.
5 Then Elihu saw that there was no answer
in the mouth of the three men, so his anger
burned.

[6] So Elihu the son of Barachel the Buzite
answered and said,

7 "I am young in years and you are old;
Therefore I was shy and afraid
to tell you my knowledge.
7 "I thought age should speak,
And increased years should
make wisdom known.
8 "But it is a spirit in man,
And the breath of the Almighty
gives them understanding.
9 "The abundant *in years*
may not be wise,
Nor may elders understand justice.
10 "So I say, 'Listen to me,
I too will tell my knowledge.'

11 "Behold, I waited for your words,
I gave ear to your reasonings,
While you searched out what to say.
12 "I even carefully considered you;
And behold, there was no
one who reproved Job,
Not one of you who
answered his words.
13 "Lest you say,
'We have found wisdom;
God will drive him away, not man.'
14 "Now he has not arranged *his*
words against me,
Nor will I respond to him
with your words.

15 "They are dismayed; they
no longer answer;
Words have moved away from them.
16 "Shall I wait, because they
do not speak,
Because they stand *still and*
no longer answer?
17 "I myself will also answer my share;
I also will tell my knowledge.
18 "For I am full of words;
The spirit within my belly presses me.
19 "Behold, my belly is like *unvented*
wine, not opened;
Like new wineskins it is about
to burst.
20 "Let me speak that I may get relief;
Let me open my lips and answer.
21 "Let me now be partial to no one,
Nor flatter *any* man.
22 "For I do not know how to flatter,
Else my Maker would soon
carry me away.

Psalm 98:1–3

1 Sing to Yahweh a new song,
For He has done wondrous deeds,
His right hand and His holy arm
have worked out His salvation.
2 Yahweh has made known His salvation;
He has revealed His righteousness
in the eyes of the nations.
3 He has remembered His
lovingkindness and His faithfulness
to the house of Israel;
All the ends of the earth have seen
the salvation of our God.

Proverbs 23:17–18

17 Do not let your heart be
jealous of sinners,
But *be zealous* in the fear
of Yahweh always.
18 Surely there is a future,
And your hope will not be cut off.

1 Corinthians 2:1–16

2 And when I came to you, brothers, I did
not come with superiority of word or of
wisdom, proclaiming to you the witness of
God. [2] For I determined to know nothing
among you except Jesus Christ, and Him
crucified. [3] And I was with you in weakness
and in fear and in much trembling, [4] and my
word and my preaching were not in persua-
sive words of wisdom, but in demonstration
of the Spirit and of power, [5] so that your
faith would not be in the wisdom of men,
but in the power of God.

[6] Yet we do speak wisdom among those
who are mature, a wisdom, however, not of
this age nor of the rulers of this age, who are
being abolished. [7] But we speak God's wisdom
in a mystery, the *wisdom* which has been
hidden, which God predestined before the
ages to our glory, [8] which none of the rulers
of this age has understood; for if they had
understood it, they would not have crucified
the Lord of glory. [9] But just as it is written,

"THINGS WHICH EYE HAS NOT SEEN
AND EAR HAS NOT HEARD,
AND *which* HAVE NOT ENTERED
THE HEART OF MAN,
ALL THAT GOD HAS PREPARED FOR
THOSE WHO LOVE HIM."

[10] But to us God revealed *them* through the
Spirit, for the Spirit searches all things, even
the depths of God. [11] For who among men
knows the *depths* of a man except the spirit of

the man which is in him? Even so the *depths*
of God no one knows except the Spirit of God.
12 Now we have received, not the spirit of the
world, but the Spirit who is from God, so that
we may know the *depths* graciously given to
us by God, 13 of which *depths* we also speak,
not in words taught by human wisdom, but
in those taught by the Spirit, combining
spiritual *depths* with spiritual *words*.
14 But a natural man does not accept the
depths of the Spirit of God, for they are fool-
ishness to him, and he cannot understand
them, because they are spiritually exam-
ined. 15 But he who is spiritual examines
all things, yet he himself is examined by no
one. 16 For WHO HAS KNOWN THE MIND OF THE
LORD, THAT HE WILL DIRECT HIM? But we have
the mind of Christ.

AUGUST 21

Job 33:1–34:37

33 "However now, Job, please
hear my speech,
And give ear to all my words.
2 "Behold now, I open my mouth;
My tongue in my mouth speaks.
3 "My words are *from* the
uprightness of my heart,
And my lips speak
knowledge sincerely.
4 "The Spirit of God has made me,
And the breath of the
Almighty gives me life.
5 "Respond to me if you can;
Arrange yourselves before
me, take your stand.
6 "Behold, I belong to God like you;
I too have been formed out of the clay.
7 "Behold, no dread of me
should terrify you,
Nor should my pressure
weigh heavily on you.

8 "Surely you have spoken in my hearing,
And I have heard the sound
of *your* speech:
9 'I am pure, without transgression;
I am innocent, and there
is no guilt in me.
10 'Behold, He finds *reasons for*
opposition against me;
He counts me as His enemy.
11 'He puts my feet in the stocks;
He keeps watch over all my paths.'
12 "Behold, let me answer you;
you are not right in this,
For God is greater than mortal man.

13 "Why do you contend against Him?
For He does not give an answer
for all His doings.
14 "Indeed God speaks once,
Or twice, *yet* no one perceives it.
15 "In a dream, a vision of the night,
When deep sleep falls on men,
While they slumber in their beds,
16 Then He opens the ears of men,
And seals in their discipline,
17 That He may turn man aside
from his conduct,
And keep man from pride;
18 He holds back his soul from the pit,
And his life from passing over
to death by a weapon.

19 "Man is also reproved with
pain on his bed,
And with unceasing contention
in his bones,
20 So that his life loathes bread,
And his soul favorite food.
21 "His flesh wastes away from sight,
And his bones which were
not seen stick out.
22 "Then his soul draws near to the pit,
And his life to those who bring death.

23 "If there is an angel *as* mediator for him,
One out of a thousand,
To declare to a man what
is right for him,
24 Then let him be gracious
to him, and say,
'Deliver him from going
down to the pit;
I have found atonement';
25 Let his flesh become fresher
than in youth,
Let him return to the days
of his youthful vigor;
26 Then he will entreat God, and
He will accept him,
And he will see His face
with joyful shouts,

And He may restore His
righteousness to man.
27 "He will sing to men and say,
'I have sinned and perverted
what is right,
But He has not done what is due to me.
28 'He has redeemed my soul from
passing into the pit,
And my life shall see the light.'

29 "Behold, God does all these *things*
twice, three times with men,
30 To bring back his soul from the pit,
That he may be enlightened
with the light of life.
31 "Pay attention, O Job, listen to me;
Keep silent, and I will speak.
32 "*Then* if you have any speech,
respond to me;
Speak, for I desire to prove
you righteous.
33 "If not, listen to me;
Keep silent, and I will teach
you wisdom."

34 Then Elihu answered and said,
2 "Hear my speech, you wise men,
And give ear to me, you who know.
3 "For the ear tests words
As the palate tastes food.
4 "Let us choose for ourselves
what is just;
Let us know among ourselves
what is good.
5 "For Job has said, 'I am righteous,
But God has removed my justice;
6 Should I lie concerning my justice?
My wound is incurable, *though I
am* without transgression.'
7 "What man is like Job,
Who drinks up mocking like water,
8 But he travels in company with
the workers of iniquity,
And walks with wicked men?
9 "For he has said, 'It is of no use to a man
When he is pleased with God.'

10 "Therefore, listen to me, you men
with a heart *of wisdom*.
Far be it from God to do injustice,
And from the Almighty to do wrong.
11 "For He pays a man according
to his work,
And makes him find it
according to his way.
12 "Truly, God will not act wickedly,
And the Almighty will not
pervert justice.
13 "Who appointed Him with
authority over the earth?
And who has laid *on Him*
the whole world?
14 "If He should set His heart on it,
If He should gather to Himself
His spirit and His breath,
15 All flesh would breathe
its last together,
And man would return to dust.

16 "But if *you have* understanding,
hear this;
Give ear to the sound of my speech.
17 "Shall one who hates justice rule?
And will you condemn the
righteous mighty One,
18 Who says to a king, 'Vile one,'
To nobles, 'Wicked ones';
19 Who shows no partiality to princes
Nor recognizes the rich above the poor,
For they all are the work of His hands?
20 "In a moment they die, and at midnight
People are shaken and pass away,
And the mighty are taken
away without a hand.

21 "For His eyes are upon the
ways of a man,
And He sees all his steps.
22 "There is no darkness or
shadow of death
Where the workers of iniquity
may hide themselves.
23 "For He does not *need to*
consider a man further,
That he should go before
God in judgment.
24 "He breaks in pieces mighty men
without searching *anything* out,
And sets others in their place.
25 "Therefore He recognizes their labors,
And He overthrows *them* in the night,
And they are crushed.
26 "He strikes them like the wicked
In a public place,
27 Because they turned aside
from following Him,
And had no insight from
any of His ways;
28 So that they caused the cry of
the poor to come to Him,

And that He might hear the
cry of the afflicted.
29 So *if* He keeps quiet, who
then can condemn?
So *if* He hides His face, who
then can perceive Him?
He is above both nation
and man altogether,
30 So that godless men would not rule
Nor be snares of the people.

31 "For has anyone said to God,
'I have borne *chastisement*;
I will not work destructively
anymore;
32 Instruct me what I do not behold;
If I have done injustice,
I will not do it again'?
33 "Shall He repay on your terms,
because you have rejected *it*?
For you must choose, and not I;
Therefore say what you know.
34 "Men with a heart *of wisdom*
will say to me,
And a wise man who hears me,
35 'Job speaks without knowledge,
And his words are without insight.
36 'Job ought to be tested to the limit
Because he answers like wicked men.
37 'For he adds transgression to his sin;
He strikes his hands
together among us,
And multiplies his words
against God.'"

Psalm 98:4–9

4 Make a loud shout to
Yahweh, all the earth;
Break forth and sing for joy
and sing praises.
5 Sing praises to Yahweh with the lyre,
With the lyre and the sound of singing.
6 With trumpets and the
sound of the horn
Make a loud shout before King Yahweh.

7 Let the sea roar, as well as its fullness,
The world and those who dwell in it.
8 Let the rivers clap their hands,
Let the mountains sing together for joy
9 Before Yahweh, for He is coming
to judge the earth;
He will judge the world
with righteousness
And the peoples with equity.

Proverbs 23:19–21

19 You, my son, listen and be wise,
And direct your heart in the way.
20 Do not be with heavy
drinkers of wine,
Or with gluttonous eaters of meat;
21 For the heavy drinker and the
glutton will come to poverty,
And drowsiness will clothe
them with rags.

1 Corinthians 3:1–23

3 And I, brothers, was not able to speak to
you as to spiritual men, but as to fleshly
men, as to infants in Christ. 2 I gave you milk
to drink, not solid food, for you were not yet
able *to receive it*. Indeed, even now you are
still not able, 3 for you are still fleshly. For
since there is jealousy and strife among you,
are you not fleshly, and are you not walking
like mere men? 4 For when one says, "I am
of Paul," and another, "I am of Apollos," are
you not *mere* men?
5 What then is Apollos? And what is Paul?
Servants through whom you believed, even
as the Lord gave to each one. 6 I planted,
Apollos watered, but God was causing the
growth. 7 So then neither the one who plants
nor the one who waters is anything, but God
who causes the growth. 8 Now he who plants
and he who waters are one, but each will
receive his own reward according to his own
labor. 9 For we are God's fellow workers; you
are God's field, God's building.
10 According to the grace of God which
was given to me, like a wise master builder
I laid a foundation, and another is building
on it. But each man must be careful how
he builds on it. 11 For no one can lay a
foundation other than the one which is
laid, which is Jesus Christ. 12 Now if anyone
builds on the foundation with gold, silver,
precious stones, wood, hay, straw, 13 each
man's work will become evident, for the day
will indicate it because it is revealed with
fire, and the fire itself will test the quality of
each man's work. 14 If any man's work which
he has built on it remains, he will receive a
reward. 15 If any man's work is burned up, he
will suffer loss, but he himself will be saved,
yet so as through fire.
16 Do you not know that you are a sanc-
tuary of God and *that* the Spirit of God
dwells in you? 17 If any man destroys the
sanctuary of God, God will destroy him,

for the sanctuary of God is holy, and that is
what you are.
18 Let no man deceive himself. If any man
among you thinks that he is wise in this age,
he must become foolish, so that he may
become wise. 19 For the wisdom of this world
is foolishness before God. For it is written, "*He
is* THE ONE WHO CATCHES THE WISE IN THEIR
CRAFTINESS"; 20 and again, "THE LORD KNOWS
THE REASONINGS of the wise, THAT THEY ARE
USELESS." 21 So then let no one boast in men.
For all things belong to you, 22 whether Paul
or Apollos or Cephas or the world or life or
death or things present or things to come;
all things belong to you, 23 and you belong
to Christ, and Christ belongs to God.

AUGUST 22

Job 35:1–36:33

35 Then Elihu answered and said,
2 "Do you think this is
according to justice?
Do you say, 'My righteousness
is more than God's'?
3 "For you say, 'What use will it be to You?
What profit will I have, more
than if I had sinned?'
4 "I will respond to you,
And your friends with you.
5 "Look at the heavens and see;
And perceive the clouds—
they are higher than you.
6 "If you have sinned, what do you
accomplish against Him?
And if your transgressions are
many, what do you do to Him?
7 "If you are righteous, what
do you give to Him,
Or what does He receive
from your hand?
8 "Your wickedness is for a
man like yourself,
And your righteousness is
for a son of man.

9 "Because of many oppressions
they cry out;
They cry for help because of the
arm of many *oppressors*.
10 "But no one says, 'Where
is God my Maker,
Who gives songs of praise in the night,
11 Who teaches us more than
the beasts of the earth
And makes us wiser than the
birds of the heavens?'
12 "There they cry out, but He
does not answer
Because of the pride of evil men.
13 "Surely God will not listen
to an empty *cry*,
Nor will the Almighty perceive it.
14 "How much less when you say
you do not perceive Him,
The case is before Him, and
you must wait for Him!
15 "And now, because He has not
visited *in* His anger,
Nor has He acknowledged
transgression well,
16 So Job opens his mouth vainly;
He multiplies words without
knowledge."

36 Then Elihu continued and said,
2 "Wait for me a little,
and I will show you
That there is yet more to be
said in God's behalf.
3 "I will take up my knowledge from afar,
And I will ascribe righteousness
to my Maker.
4 "For truly my words are not a lie;
One who is perfect in
knowledge is with you.
5 "Behold, God is mighty but
does not reject;
He is mighty in the power of *His* heart.
6 "He does not keep the wicked alive,
But gives justice to the afflicted.
7 "He does not withdraw His eyes
from the righteous;
But with kings on the throne
He has seated them forever,
and they are exalted.
8 "And if they are bound in fetters,
And are caught in the
cords of affliction,
9 Then He declares to them their work
And their transgressions, that they
have magnified themselves.
10 "He opens their ear to discipline,
And says that they return
from wickedness.

11 "If they hear and serve *Him*,
They will end their days in prosperity
And their years in pleasures.
12 "But if they do not hear, they shall
pass away by a weapon
And they will breathe their
last without knowledge.
13 "But the godless in heart lay up anger;
They do not cry for help
when He binds them.
14 "They die in youth,
And their life *perishes* among
the cult prostitutes.
15 "He delivers the afflicted
in their affliction,
And opens their ear in
time of oppression.
16 "Then indeed, He enticed you
from the mouth of distress,
Instead of it, a broad place
with no constraint;
And the comfort of your
table full of fatness.

17 "But you were full of judgment
on the wicked;
Judgment and justice take hold *of you*.
18 "*Beware* lest wrath entice
you to scoffing;
And do not let the greatness of the
atonement turn you aside.
19 "Will your cries keep you from distress,
Or all the forces of *your* power?
20 "Do not long for the night,
When people vanish in their place.
21 "Be careful, do not turn to wickedness,
For you have chosen this to affliction.
22 "Behold, God is exalted in His power;
Who is a teacher like Him?
23 "Who has appointed Him His way,
And who has said, 'You have
worked *out* unrighteousness'?

24 "Remember that you should
exalt His work,
Of which men have sung.
25 "All men have beheld it;
Man looks from afar.
26 "Behold, God is exalted, and
we do not know *Him*;
The number of His years
is unsearchable.
27 "For He draws up the drops of water,
They distill rain for His stream,
28 Which the clouds pour down,
They drip upon man abundantly.
29 "Can anyone discern the
spreading of the clouds,
The thundering of His pavilion?
30 "Behold, He spreads His
lightning about Him,
And He covers the depths of the sea.
31 "For by these He judges peoples;
He gives food in abundance.
32 "He covers *His* hands with the lightning,
And commands it to strike the mark.
33 "Its thundering declares about Him;
The cattle also, concerning
what is coming up.

Psalm 99:1–9

1 Yahweh reigns, let the peoples tremble;
He sits enthroned *above* the
cherubim, let the earth quake!
2 Yahweh is great in Zion,
And He is exalted above
all the peoples.
3 Let them praise Your great
and awesome name;
Holy is He.
4 The strength of the King loves justice;
You have established equity;
You have done justice and
righteousness in Jacob.
5 Exalt Yahweh our God
And worship at the footstool of His feet;
Holy is He.

6 Moses and Aaron were
among His priests,
And Samuel was among those
who called on His name;
They would call upon Yahweh
and He would answer them.
7 He would speak to them in
the pillar of cloud;
They kept His testimonies
And the statute that He gave them.
8 O Yahweh our God, You
answered them;
You were a forgiving God to them,
And *yet* an avenger of their *evil* deeds.
9 Exalt Yahweh our God
And worship at His holy mountain,
For holy is Yahweh our God.

Proverbs 23:22–25

22 Listen to your father who begot you,
And do not despise your
mother when she is old.

23 Buy truth, and do not sell *it*,
Get wisdom and discipline
and understanding.
24 The father of the righteous
will greatly rejoice,
And he who begets a wise
son will be glad in him.
25 Let your father and your
mother be glad,
And let her rejoice who
gave birth to you.

1 Corinthians 4:1–21

4 Let a man consider us in this manner,
as servants of Christ and stewards of
the mysteries of God. 2 In this case, more-
over, it is required of stewards that one be
found faithful. 3 But to me it is a very small
thing that I may be examined by you, or
by *any* human court. In fact, I do not even
examine myself. 4 For I am conscious of
nothing against myself, yet I am not by this
acquitted. But the one who examines me is
the Lord. 5 Therefore do not go on passing
judgment before the time, *but wait* until the
Lord comes who will both bring to light the
things hidden in the darkness and make
manifest the motives of hearts. And then
each one's praise will come to him from God.

6 Now these things, brothers, I have
applied to myself and Apollos for your
sakes, so that in us you may learn not to go
beyond what is written, so that no one of
you will become puffed up on behalf of one
against the other. 7 For who regards you as
superior? What do you have that you did
not receive? And if you did receive it, why
do you boast as if you had not received it?
8 You are already filled, you have already
become rich, you have ruled without us—
and *how I* wish that you had ruled indeed
so that we also might rule with you. 9 For, I
think that God has exhibited us apostles last
of all, as men condemned to death, because
we have become a spectacle to the world,
and to angels, and to men. 10 We are fools
for the sake of Christ, but you are prudent in
Christ! We are weak, but you are strong! You
are glorious, but we are without honor! 11 To
this present hour we hunger and thirst, and
are poorly clothed, and roughly treated, and
homeless; 12 and we labor, working with our
own hands; when we are reviled, we bless;
when we are persecuted, we endure; 13 when
we are slandered, we try to plead; we have
become as the scum of the world, the grime
of all things, *even* until now.

14 I do not write these things to shame
you, but to admonish you as my beloved
children. 15 For if you were to have countless
tutors in Christ, yet *you would* not *have*
many fathers, for in Christ Jesus I became
your father through the gospel. 16 Therefore
I exhort you, be imitators of me. 17 For this
reason I have sent to you Timothy, who is
my beloved and faithful child in the Lord,
and who will remind you of my ways which
are in Christ, just as I teach everywhere in
every church. 18 Now some have become
puffed up, as though I were not coming to
you. 19 But I will come to you soon, if the
Lord wills, and I shall know, not the words
of those who are puffed up but their power.
20 For the kingdom of God does not consist
in words but in power. 21 What do you
desire? Shall I come to you with a rod, or
with love and a spirit of gentleness?

AUGUST 23

Job 37:1–38:41

37 "At this also my heart trembles,
And leaps from its place.
2 "Listen closely to the thunder
of His voice,
And the rumbling that goes
out from His mouth.
3 "Under the whole heaven
He lets it loose,
And His lightning to the
ends of the earth.
4 "After it, a voice roars;
He thunders with His majestic voice,
And He does not restrain the
lightnings when His voice is heard.
5 "God thunders with His
voice marvelously,
Doing great things which
we do not know.
6 "For to the snow He says,
'Fall on the earth,'
And to the downpour of rain
and the downpour of rains,
'Be strong.'

7 "He seals the hand of every man,
That all men may know His work.
8 "Then the beast goes into its lair
And dwells in its den.
9 "Out of the south comes the storm,
And out of the north the cold.
10 "From the breath of God ice is made,
And the expanse of the
waters is frozen.
11 "Also with moisture He loads
the thick cloud;
He scatters the cloud of His lightning.
12 "It changes direction, turning
around by His guidance,
That it may do whatever
He commands it
On the face of the inhabited earth.
13 "Whether for correction,
or for His world,
Or for lovingkindness,
He causes it to happen.

14 "Give ear to this, O Job,
Stand and carefully consider the
wondrous deeds of God.
15 "Do you know how God
establishes them,
And makes the lightning of
His cloud to shine?
16 "Do you know about the layers
of the thick clouds,
The wonders of one perfect
in knowledge,
17 You whose garments are hot,
When the land is quiet because
of the south wind?
18 "Can you, with Him, spread
out the skies,
Strong as a molten mirror?
19 "Make us know what we
shall say to Him;
We cannot arrange *our case*
because of darkness.
20 "Shall it be recounted to Him
that I would speak?
If a man says *a word*, will He
indeed be swallowed up?

21 "So now men do not see the light
which is bright in the skies;
But the wind has passed
and cleared them.
22 "Out of the north comes
golden *splendor*;
Around God is fearsome majesty.
23 "The Almighty—we cannot find Him;
He is exalted in power
And He will not afflict justice and
abundant righteousness.
24 "Therefore men fear Him;
He does not regard any who
are wise of heart."

38 Then Yahweh answered Job out of the
whirlwind and said,
2 "Who is this that darkens counsel
By words without knowledge?
3 "Now gird up your loins like a man,
And I will ask you, and you
make Me know!
4 "Where were you when I laid the
foundation of the earth?
Tell *Me*, if you know understanding,
5 Who set its measurements?
Since you know.
Or who stretched the line on it?
6 "On what were its bases sunk?
Or who laid its cornerstone,
7 When the morning stars sang together
And all the sons of God
shouted for joy?

8 "Or *who* enclosed the sea with doors
When, bursting forth, it went
out from the womb,
9 When I made a cloud its garment
And dense gloom its swaddling band,
10 And I placed boundaries on it
And set a bolt and doors,
11 And I said, 'Thus far you shall
come, but no farther;
And here shall your proud waves stop'?
12 "Have you ever in your life
commanded the morning,
And caused the dawn to know its place,
13 That it might seize the
ends of the earth,
And the wicked be shaken out of it?
14 "It is changed like clay *under* the seal;
And they stand forth like clothing.
15 "From the wicked their light is withheld,
And the arm raised high is broken.

16 "Have you entered into the
springs of the sea
Or walked in the recesses of the deep?
17 "Have the gates of death been
revealed to you,
Or have you seen the gates of
the shadow of death?

18 "Have you carefully considered
the expanse of the earth?
Tell *Me*, if you know all this.

19 "Where is the way to *where*
the light dwells?
And darkness, where is its place,
20 That you may take it to its territory
And that you may discern
the paths to its home?
21 "You know, for you were born then,
And the number of your days is great!

22 "Have you entered the
storehouses of the snow,
Or have you seen the
storehouses of the hail,
23 Which I have reserved for
the time of distress,
For the day of war and battle?
24 "Where is the way that the
light is divided,
Or the east wind scattered
on the earth?

25 "Who has cleft a conduit for the flood,
Or a way for the thunderbolt,
26 To bring rain on a land without people,
On a desert without a man in it,
27 To satisfy the waste and desolate land
And to make the growth
of grass to sprout?
28 "Has the rain a father?
Or who has begotten the drops of dew?
29 "From whose womb has come the ice?
And the frost of heaven, who
has given it birth?
30 "Water becomes hard like stone,
And the surface of the deep
is interlocked.

31 "Can you bind the chains
of the Pleiades,
Or loose the cords of Orion?
32 "Can you lead forth a constellation
in its season,
And guide the Bear with her satellites?
33 "Do you know the statutes
of the heavens,
Or fix their rule over the earth?

34 "Can you raise your voice
up to the clouds,
So that an abundance of
water will cover you?
35 "Can you send forth lightnings
that they may go
And say to you, 'Here we are'?
36 "Who has given wisdom in
the innermost being
Or given understanding to the mind?
37 "Who can count the clouds by wisdom,
Or tip the water jars of the heavens,
38 When the dust hardens into a mass
And the clods stick together?
39 "Can you hunt the prey for the lion,
Or fulfill the appetite of
the young lions,
40 When they crouch in *their* dens
And lie in wait in *their* lair?
41 "Who prepares for the
raven its provision
When its young cry for help to God
And wander about without food?

Psalm 100:1–5

1 Make a loud shout to Yahweh,
all the earth.
2 Serve Yahweh with gladness;
Come before Him with joyful songs.
3 Know that Yahweh, He is God;
It is He who has made us,
and not we ourselves;
We are His people and the
sheep of His pasture.

4 Enter His gates with thanksgiving
And His courts with praise.
Give thanks to Him, bless His name.
5 For Yahweh is good;
His lovingkindness endures forever
And His faithfulness, generation
unto generation.

Proverbs 23:26–28

26 Give your heart to me, my son,
And let your eyes delight in my ways.
27 For a harlot is a deep pit
And a foreign woman is a narrow well.
28 Surely she lies in wait as a robber,
And adds to the treacherous
among men.

1 Corinthians 5:1–13

5 It is actually reported that there is sexual
immorality among you, and sexual
immorality of such a kind as does not exist
even among the Gentiles, that someone has
his father's wife. 2 And you have become
puffed up and have not mourned instead, so

that the one who had done this deed would be removed from your midst.

3 For I, on my part, though absent in body but present in spirit, have already judged him who has so committed this, as though I were present: 4 in the name of our Lord Jesus, when you are assembled, and I with you in spirit, with the power of our Lord Jesus, 5 deliver such a one to Satan for the destruction of his flesh, so that his spirit may be saved in the day of the Lord.

6 Your boasting is not good. Do you not know that a little leaven leavens the whole lump? 7 Clean out the old leaven so that you may be a new lump, just as you are *in fact* unleavened. For Christ, our Passover lamb, also was sacrificed. 8 Therefore let us celebrate the feast, not with old leaven, nor with the leaven of malice and wickedness, but with the unleavened bread of sincerity and truth.

9 I wrote you in my letter not to associate with sexually immoral people; 10 I *did* not at all *mean* with the sexually immoral people of this world, or with the greedy and swindlers, or with idolaters, for then you would have to go out of the world. 11 But now I am writing to you not to associate with any so-called brother if he is a sexually immoral person, or greedy, or an idolater, or a reviler, or a drunkard, or a swindler—not even to eat with such a one. 12 For what have I to do with judging outsiders? Are you not to judge those who are within *the church*? 13 But those who are outside, God will judge. REMOVE THE WICKED MAN FROM AMONG YOURSELVES.

AUGUST 24

Job 39:1–40:24

39 "Do you know the time the
mountain goats give birth?
Do you keep watch over the
calving of the deer?
2 "Can you count the months they fulfill,
Or do you know the time
they give birth?
3 "They kneel down; they bring
forth their young;
They send out their labor pains.
4 "Their children become strong; they
grow up in the open field;
They leave and do not return to them.

5 "Who sent out the wild donkey free?
And who loosed the bonds
of the swift donkey,
6 For whom I have set the
desert plain as a home
And the salt land as his dwelling place?
7 "He laughs at the tumult of the city;
The shoutings of the driver
he does not hear.
8 "He explores the mountains
for his pasture
And searches after every green thing.
9 "Will the wild ox consent to serve you,
Or will he spend the night
at your manger?
10 "Can you bind the wild ox in
a furrow with ropes,
Or will he harrow the valleys after you?
11 "Will you trust him because
his power is great
And leave your labor to him?
12 "Will you believe him that he will
return your seed *of grain*
And gather *it from* your
threshing floor?

13 "The ostriches' wings flap joyously
But are they the pinion and
plumage of a stork?
14 For she leaves her eggs to the earth
And warms them in the dust,
15 And she forgets that a foot
may crush them,
Or that a beast of the field
may trample them.
16 "She treats her children cruelly,
as if *they* were not hers;
Though her labor be empty,
she is without dread,
17 Because God has made her
forget wisdom,
And has not given her a share
of understanding.
18 "When she raises herself up high,
She laughs at the horse and his rider.

19 "Do you give the horse *his* might?
Do you clothe his neck with a mane?
20 "Do you make him leap like
the locust?
His splendid snorting is terrible.

21 “He paws in the valley and
rejoices in *his* power;
He goes out to meet the weapons.
22 “He laughs at dread and
is not dismayed;
And he does not turn back
from the sword.
23 “The quiver rattles against him,
The flashing spear and javelin.
24 “With shaking and rage he
races over the ground,
And he does not stand still at
the sound of the trumpet.
25 “As often as the trumpet
sounds he says, ‘Aha!’
And he scents the battle from afar,
And the thunder of the commanders
and the shout *of war*.

26 “Is it by your understanding
that the hawk soars,
Stretching his wings toward the south?
27 “Is it at your command that
the eagle goes on high
And raises his nest high?
28 “On the cliff he dwells and lodges,
Upon the rocky crag, a fortress.
29 “From there he spies out food;
His eyes see *it* from afar.
30 “His young ones also suck up blood;
And where the slain are, there is he.”

40 Then Yahweh answered Job and said,
2 “Will the faultfinder
contend with the Almighty?
Let him who reproves God answer it.”

3 Then Job answered Yahweh and said,
4 “Behold, I am insignificant; what
can I respond to You?
I place my hand over my mouth.
5 “Once I have spoken, and
I will not answer;
Even twice, and I will add
nothing more.”
6 Then Yahweh answered Job out of the
whirlwind and said,
7 “Now gird up your loins like a man;
I will ask you, and you make Me know.
8 “Will you really annul My judgment?
Will you condemn Me that
you may be justified?
9 “Or do you have an arm like God,
And can you thunder with
a voice like His?
10 “Adorn yourself with exaltation
and loftiness,
And clothe yourself with
splendor and majesty.
11 “Pour out the overflowings
of your anger,
And look on everyone who is
proud, and make him low.
12 “Look on everyone who is
proud, *and* humble him,
And tread down the wicked
in their place.
13 “Hide them in the dust together;
Bind their faces in the hidden *place*.
14 “Then I will also praise you,
That your own right hand can save you.
15 “Behold now, Behemoth, which
I made along with you;
It eats grass like an ox.
16 “Behold now, its power in its loins
And its vigor in the muscles of its belly.
17 “It hangs its tail like a cedar;
The sinews of its thighs
are knit together.
18 “Its bones are tubes of bronze;
Its limbs are like bars of iron.

19 “It is the first of the ways of God;
Let its Maker bring near its sword.
20 “Surely the mountains bring it food,
And all the beasts of the
field play there.
21 “Under the lotus plants it lies down,
In the hidden place of the
reeds and the marsh.
22 “The lotus plants cover it with shade;
The willows of the brook surround it.
23 “If a river oppresses, it is not alarmed;
It is secure, though the Jordan
bursts forth to its mouth.
24 “Can anyone capture it before its eyes,
With snares can anyone
pierce *its* nose?

Psalm 101:1–4

1 I will sing of lovingkindness
and justice,
To You, O Yahweh, I will sing praises.
2 I will consider the way of
the blameless.
When will You come to me?
I will walk within my house in
the integrity of my heart.
3 I will set no vile thing before my eyes;
I hate the work of those who fall away;

It shall not cling to me.
4 A crooked heart shall depart from me;
I will know no evil.

Proverbs 23:29–30

29 Who has woe? Who has sorrow?
Who has contentions? Who
has complaining?
Who has wounds without cause?
Who has redness of eyes?
30 Those who linger long over wine,
Those who go to search
out mixed wine.

1 Corinthians 6:1–20

6 Does any one of you, when he has a case
against another, dare to be tried before
the unrighteous and not before the saints?
2 Or do you not know that the saints will
judge the world? If the world is judged by
you, are you not worthy *to constitute* the
smallest law courts? 3 Do you not know
that we will judge angels? How much more
matters of this life? 4 So if you have law
courts dealing with matters of this life, do
you appoint those who are of no account
in the church as judges? 5 I say *this* to your
shame. *Is it really* this way: there is not one
wise man among you who will be able to
pass judgment between his brothers? 6 On
the contrary, brother is tried with brother,
and that before unbelievers!
7 Actually, then, it is already a failure
for you, that you have lawsuits with one
another. Why not rather be wronged? Why
not rather be defrauded? 8 On the contrary,
you yourselves wrong and defraud. *You do*
this even to *your* brothers.
9 Or do you not know that the unrigh-
teous will not inherit the kingdom of God?
Do not be deceived; neither *the* sexually
immoral, nor idolaters, nor adulterers, nor
effeminate, nor homosexuals, 10 nor thieves,
nor *the* greedy, nor drunkards, nor revilers,
nor swindlers, will inherit the kingdom of
God. 11 And such were some of you; but you
were washed, but you were sanctified, but
you were justified in the name of the Lord
Jesus Christ and in the Spirit of our God.
12 All things are lawful for me, but not
all things are profitable. All things are
lawful for me, but I will not be mastered by
anything. 13 Food is for the stomach and the
stomach is for food, but God will do away
with both of them. Yet the body is not for
sexual immorality, but for the Lord, and the
Lord is for the body. 14 Now God has not only
raised the Lord, but will also raise us up
through His power. 15 Do you not know that
your bodies are members of Christ? Shall I
then take away the members of Christ and
make them members of a prostitute? May
it never be! 16 Or do you not know that the
one who joins himself to a prostitute is one
body *with her*? For He says, "THE TWO SHALL
BECOME ONE FLESH." 17 But the one who joins
himself to the Lord is one spirit *with Him*.
18 Flee sexual immorality. Every *other* sin
that a man commits is outside the body, but
the sexually immoral man sins against his
own body. 19 Or do you not know that your
body is a sanctuary of the Holy Spirit who
is in you, whom you have from God, and
that you are not your own? 20 For you were
bought with a price: therefore glorify God
in your body.

AUGUST 25

Job 41:1–42:17

41 "Can you draw out Leviathan
with a fishhook?
Or press down its tongue
with a cord?
2 "Can you put a rope in its nose
Or pierce its jaw with a hook?
3 "Will it make many
supplications to you,
Or will he speak to you soft words?
4 "Will it cut a covenant with you?
Will you take it for a slave forever?
5 "Will you play with it as with a bird,
Or will you bind it for your
young women?
6 "Will the traders bargain over it?
Will they divide it among
the merchants?
7 "Can you fill its skin with harpoons,
Or its head with fishing spears?
8 "Place your hand on it;
Remember the battle; you
will not do that again!
9 "Behold, his expectation is a lie;
Will he be laid low even
at the sight of it?

10 “No one is so fierce that he
dares to arouse it;
Who then is he that can
stand before Me?
11 “Who has given to Me that I
should repay *him*?
Whatever is under the whole
heaven is Mine.
12 “I will not keep silence
concerning its limbs,
Or its mighty strength or
its graceful frame.
13 “Who can strip off its outer armor?
Who can come with its
doubled bridle?
14 “Who can open the doors of its face?
Around its teeth there is
dreadful terror.
15 “*Its* strong scales are *its* pride,
Shut up *as with* a tight seal.
16 “One is so near to another
That no air can come between them.
17 “They cling one to another;
They are interlocked and
cannot be separated.
18 “Its sneezes flash forth light,
And its eyes are like the
eyelids of the morning.
19 “Out of its mouth go burning torches;
Sparks of fire leap forth.
20 “Out of its nostrils smoke goes forth
As *from* a boiling pot and
burning reeds.
21 “Its breath kindles coals,
And a flame goes forth from its mouth.
22 “In its neck lodges strength,
And dismay leaps before it.
23 “The folds of its flesh cling together,
Hardened upon it and is not shaken.
24 “Its heart is as hard as a stone,
Even as hard as a lower millstone.
25 “When it raises itself up,
the mighty fear,
Because of the crashing
they are bewildered.
26 “The sword that reaches it cannot avail,
Nor the spear, the dart, or the javelin.
27 “It regards iron as straw,
Bronze as rotten wood.
28 “The arrow cannot make it flee;
Slingstones are turned
into stubble for it.
29 “Clubs are regarded as stubble;
It laughs at the rattling of the javelin.
30 “Its underparts are *like* sharp potsherds;
It spreads out *like* a threshing
sledge on the mire.
31 “It makes the depths boil like a pot;
It makes the sea like a jar of ointment.
32 “Behind it, it makes a wake to shine;
One would think the deep
to be gray-haired.
33 “There is nothing upon the dust like it,
One made without terror.
34 “It looks on everything that is high;
It is king over all the sons of pride.”

42 Then Job answered Yahweh and said,
2 “I know that You can do all things,
And that no purpose of Yours
can be thwarted.
3 ‘Who is this that hides counsel
without knowledge?’
Therefore I have declared that
which I did not understand,
Things too marvelous for me,
which I did not know.
4 ‘Hear, now, and I will speak;
I will ask You, and You make
me know.’
5 “I have heard of You by the
hearing of the ear;
But now my eye sees You;
6 Therefore I reject *myself*,
And I repent in dust and ashes.”

7 Now it happened after Yahweh had
spoken these words to Job, that Yahweh said
to Eliphaz the Temanite, “My anger burns
against you and against your two friends
because you have not spoken of Me what
is right as My servant Job has. 8 So now,
take for yourselves seven bulls and seven
rams, and go to My servant Job, and offer
up a burnt offering for yourselves, and My
servant Job will pray for you. For I will accept
him so that I may not do with you *according
to your* folly, because you have not spoken
of Me what is right, as My servant Job has.”
9 So Eliphaz the Temanite and Bildad the
Shuhite *and* Zophar the Naamathite went
and did as Yahweh told them; and Yahweh
accepted Job.

10 And Yahweh restored the fortunes of
Job when he prayed for his friends, and
Yahweh increased all that Job had twofold.
11 Then all his brothers and all his sisters
and all who had known him before came
to him, and they ate bread with him in
his house; and they consoled him and

comforted him for all the calamity that Yah-
weh had brought on him. And each one gave
him one qesitah, and each a ring of gold.
12 And Yahweh blessed the latter *days* of Job
more than his beginning; and he had 14,000
sheep and 6,000 camels and 1,000 pairs of
oxen and 1,000 female donkeys. 13 He also
had seven sons and three daughters. 14 And
he named the first Jemimah and the sec-
ond Keziah and the third Keren-happuch.
15 Now in all the land no women were found
so beautiful as Job's daughters; and their
father gave them inheritance among their
brothers. 16 And after this, Job lived 140
years and saw his sons and his grandsons,
four generations. 17 Then Job died, an old
man and full of days.

Psalm 101:5–8

5 Whoever secretly slanders his
neighbor, him I will destroy;
Whoever has a haughty look and an
arrogant heart, I will not endure.

6 My eyes shall be upon the
faithful of the land, that
they may abide with me;
He who walks in the way of
the blameless is the one
who will minister to me.
7 He who practices deceit shall
not dwell within my house;
He who speaks lies shall not be
established before my eyes.
8 Every morning I will destroy all
the wicked of the land,
To cut off from the city of Yahweh
all the workers of iniquity.

Proverbs 23:31–35

31 Do not look on the wine
when it glistens red,
When it sparkles in the cup,
When it goes down smoothly;
32 At the end—like a serpent it bites,
And like a viper it stings.
33 Your eyes will see strange things
And your heart will speak
perverse things.
34 And you will be like one who lies
down in the heart of the sea,
Or like one who lies down
on the top of a mast.
35 "They struck me, *but* I did
not become ill;
They beat me, *but* I did not know *it*.
When shall I awake?
I will seek yet another."

1 Corinthians 7:1–16

7 Now concerning the things about which
you wrote, it is good for a man not to
touch a woman. 2 But because of sexual
immoralities, each man is to have his own
wife, and each woman is to have her own
husband. 3 The husband must fulfill his duty
to his wife, and likewise also the wife to her
husband. 4 The wife does not have authority
over her own body, but the husband *does*;
and likewise also the husband does not have
authority over his own body, but the wife
does. 5 Stop depriving one another, except
by agreement for a time, so that you may
devote yourselves to prayer, and come
together again so that Satan will not tempt
you because of your lack of self-control.
6 But this I say as a concession, not as a
command. 7 Yet I wish that all men were
even as I myself am. However, each man
has his own gift from God, one this way,
and another that.

8 But I say to the unmarried and to widows
that it is good for them if they remain even
as I. 9 But if they do not have self-control, let
them marry, for it is better to marry than to
burn *with passion*.

10 But to the married I give instructions,
not I, but the Lord, that the wife should
not leave her husband 11 (but if she does
leave, she must remain unmarried, or else
be reconciled to her husband), and that the
husband should not divorce his wife.

12 But to the rest I say, not the Lord, that if
any brother has a wife who is an unbeliever,
and she consents to live with him, he must
not divorce her. 13 And a woman who has
an unbelieving husband, and he consents
to live with her, she must not divorce her
husband. 14 For the unbelieving husband
is sanctified through his wife, and the
unbelieving wife is sanctified through her
believing husband. For otherwise your
children are unclean, but now they are
holy. 15 Yet if the unbelieving one leaves,
let him leave. The brother or the sister is
not enslaved in such *cases*, but God has
called us to peace. 16 For how do you know,
O wife, whether you will save your husband?
Or how do you know, O husband, whether
you will save your wife?

AUGUST 26

Ecclesiastes 1:1–2:26

1 The words of the Preacher, the son of
David, king in Jerusalem.
2 "Vanity of vanities," says the Preacher,
"Vanity of vanities! All is vanity."

3 What advantage does man
have in all his labor
In which he labors under the sun?
4 A generation goes and a
generation comes,
But the earth stands forever.
5 Also, the sun rises and the sun sets;
And hastening to its place
it rises there *again.*
6 Going toward the south,
Then circling toward the north,
The wind goes circling along;
And on its circular courses
the wind returns.
7 All the rivers go into the sea,
Yet the sea is not full.
To the place where the rivers go,
There they continually go.
8 All things are wearisome;
Man is not able to speak *of it.*
The eye is not satisfied with seeing,
Nor is the ear filled with hearing.
9 That which has been is
that which will be,
And that which has been done
is that which will be done.
So there is nothing new under the sun.
10 Is there anything of which
one might say,
"See this, it is new"?
Already it has been for ages
Which were before us.
11 There is no remembrance
of earlier things;
And also of the later things
which will be,
There will be for them no
remembrance
Among those who will come later *still.*

12 I, the Preacher, have been king over
Israel in Jerusalem. 13 And I gave my heart
to seek and explore by wisdom concerning
all that has been done under heaven. *It*
is a grievous endeavor *which* God has
given to the sons of men with which to
occupy *themselves.* 14 I have seen all the
works which have been done under the
sun, and behold, all is vanity and striving
after wind. 15 What is bent cannot be
straightened, and what is lacking cannot
be counted.

16 I spoke within my heart, saying,
"Behold, I have magnified and increased
wisdom more than all who were over Jeru-
salem before me; and my heart has seen
an abundance of wisdom and knowledge."
17 And I gave my heart to know wisdom and
to know madness and simpleminded folly; I
came to know that this also is striving after
wind. 18 Because in much wisdom there
is much vexation, and *whoever* increases
knowledge increases pain.

2 I said in my heart, "Come now, I will test
you with gladness, so that you shall see
good things." And behold, it too was vanity.
2 I said of laughter, "It is madness," and of
gladness, "What does it do?" 3 I explored
with my heart *how* to stimulate my body
with wine—while my heart was guiding
me wisely—and how to seize simpleminded
folly, until I could see where is this good
for the sons of men *in* what they do under
heaven the few days of their lives. 4 I made
my works great: I built houses for myself; I
planted vineyards for myself; 5 I made for
myself gardens and parks, and I planted in
them all kinds of fruit trees; 6 I made for
myself pools of water from which to water
a forest of growing trees. 7 I bought male and
female slaves, and I had homeborn slaves.
Also I possessed flocks and herds larger
than all who preceded me in Jerusalem.
8 Also, I collected for myself silver and gold
and the treasure of kings and provinces. I
provided for myself male and female singers
and the pleasures of the sons of men—many
concubines.

9 Then I became great and increased more
than all who preceded me in Jerusalem. My
wisdom also stood by me. 10 All that my eyes
asked for I did not refuse them. I did not
withhold my heart from any gladness, for
my heart was glad because of all my labor,
and this was my reward for all my labor.
11 Thus I turned to all my works which my
hands had done and the labor which I had
labored to do, and behold, all was vanity

and striving after wind, and there was no
advantage under the sun.
12 So I turned to see wisdom, madness,
and simpleminded folly. What *will* the
man *do* who will come after the king *except*
what has already been done? 13 And I saw
that there is an advantage in wisdom over
simpleminded folly as light has an advantage
over darkness. 14 The wise man's eyes are in
his head, but the fool walks in darkness. And
yet I know that the fate of one becomes the
fate of all of them. 15 Then I said in my heart,
"As is the fate of the fool, so will my fate be
also. Why then have I been extremely wise?"
So I said in my heart, "This too is vanity."
16 For there is no remembrance of the wise
man along with the fool forever, inasmuch as
in the coming days all will be forgotten. And
how the wise man dies with the fool! 17 So I
hated life, for the work which had been done
under the sun was grievous to me; because
everything is vanity and striving after wind.
18 Thus I hated all the fruit of my labor
for which I had labored under the sun, for I
must leave it to the man who will come after
me. 19 And who knows whether he will be a
wise man or a *man of* simpleminded folly?
Yet he will have power over all the fruit of
my labor for which I have labored and for
which I have acted wisely under the sun.
This too is vanity. 20 Therefore I turned my
heart to despair of all my labor for which I
had labored under the sun. 21 When there
is a man who has labored with wisdom,
knowledge, and skill, then he gives his
portion to one who has not labored with
them. This too is vanity and a great evil.
22 For what does a man get in all his labor
and in the striving of his heart with which
he labors under the sun? 23 Because all his
days his endeavor is painful and vexing;
even at night his heart does not lie down.
This too is vanity.
24 There is nothing better for a man *than*
to eat and drink and have his soul see good
in his labor. This also I have seen that it is
from the hand of God. 25 For who can eat and
who can have enjoyment outside of Him?
26 For to a man who is good before Him,
He has given wisdom and knowledge and
gladness, while to the sinner He has given
the endeavor of gathering and collecting so
that he may give to one who is good before
God. This too is vanity and striving after
wind.

Psalm 102:1–11

1 O Yahweh, hear my prayer!
And let my cry for help come to You.
2 Do not hide Your face from me
in the day of my distress;
Incline Your ear to me;
In the day when I call
answer me quickly.
3 For my days have vanished in smoke,
And my bones have been
scorched like a hearth.
4 My heart has been stricken like
grass and it has dried up,
Indeed, I forget to eat my bread.
5 Because of the sound of my groaning
My bones cling to my flesh.
6 I resemble a pelican of the wilderness;
I have become like an owl
of the waste places.
7 I lie awake,
I have become like a lonely
bird on a roof.
8 My enemies have reproached
me all day long;
Those who ridicule me
swear against me.
9 For I have eaten ashes like bread
And mixed my drinks with weeping
10 Because of Your indignation
and Your wrath,
For You have lifted me up
and cast me away.
11 My days are like an
outstretched shadow,
And as for me, I dry up like grass.

Proverbs 24:1–2

24 Do not be jealous of evil men,
And do not desire to be with them;
2 For their heart meditates
on destruction,
And their lips talk of mischief.

1 Corinthians 7:17–40

17 Only, as the Lord has assigned to
each one, as God has called each, in this
manner let him walk. And so I direct in all
the churches. 18 Was any man called *when
he was already* circumcised? He is not to
become uncircumcised. Has anyone been
called in uncircumcision? He is not to be
circumcised. 19 Circumcision is nothing, and
uncircumcision is nothing, but *what mat-
ters is* the keeping of the commandments

of God. 20 Each man must remain in that condition in which he was called.

21 Were you called while a slave? Do not worry about it. But if you are able also to become free, rather do that. 22 For he who was called in the Lord while a slave, is the Lord's freedman. Likewise he who was called while free, is Christ's slave. 23 You were bought with a price; do not become slaves of men. 24 Brothers, each one is to remain with God in that *condition* in which he was called.

25 Now concerning virgins I have no command of the Lord, but I give an opinion as one who by the mercy of the Lord is trustworthy. 26 I think then that this is good because of the present distress, that it is good for a man to remain as he is. 27 Are you bound to a wife? Do not seek to be released. Are you released from a wife? Do not seek a wife. 28 But if you marry, you have not sinned. And if a virgin marries, she has not sinned. Yet such will have trouble in this life, and I am trying to spare you. 29 But this I say, brothers, the time has been shortened, so that from now on those who have wives should be as though they had none; 30 and those who cry, as though they did not cry; and those who rejoice, as though they did not rejoice; and those who buy, as though they did not possess; 31 and those who use the world, as though they did not make full use of it. For the form of this world is passing away.

32 But I want you to be free from concern. One who is unmarried is concerned about the things of the Lord, how he may please the Lord. 33 But one who is married is concerned about the things of the world, how he may please his wife, 34 and *his interests* have been divided. The woman who is unmarried, and the virgin, is concerned about the things of the Lord, that she may be holy both in body and spirit. But one who is married is concerned about the things of the world, how she may please her husband. 35 Now this I say for your own benefit, not to put a restraint upon you, but to promote propriety and undistracted devotion to the Lord.

36 But if any man thinks that he is acting unbecomingly toward his virgin *daughter*, if she is past her youth, and if it must be so, let him do what he wishes, he does not sin; let her marry. 37 But he who stands firm in his heart, being under no compulsion, but has authority over his own will, and has decided this in his own heart, to keep his own virgin *daughter*, he will do well. 38 So then both he who gives his own virgin *daughter* in marriage does well, and he who does not give her in marriage will do better.

39 A wife is bound as long as her husband lives; but if her husband has fallen asleep, she is free to be married to whom she wishes, only in the Lord. 40 But in my opinion she is happier if she remains as she is. And I think that I also have the Spirit of God.

The true Christian was intended by Christ to prove all things by the Word of God, all churches, all ministers, all teaching, all preaching, all doctrines, all sermons, all writings, all opinions, all practices.

— JOHN WYCLIFFE

AUGUST 27

Ecclesiastes 3:1–22

3 There is an appointed time for everything. And there is a time for every matter under heaven—

2 A time to give birth and
a time to die;
A time to plant and a time to
uproot what is planted.
3 A time to kill and a time to heal;
A time to tear down and a
time to build up.
4 A time to weep and a time to laugh;
A time to mourn and a time to dance.
5 A time to throw stones and a
time to gather stones;
A time to embrace and a time
to shun embracing.
6 A time to search and a time to lose;

A time to keep and a time
to throw away.
7 A time to tear apart and a
time to sew together;
A time to be silent and a time to speak.
8 A time to love and a time to hate;
A time for war and a time for peace.

9 What advantage is there to the worker
from that in which he labors? 10 I have seen
the endeavor which God has given the sons
of men with which to occupy themselves.

11 He has made everything beautiful in its
time. He has also set eternity in their heart,
yet so that man will not find out the work
which God has done from the beginning
even to the end.

12 I know that there is nothing better
for them than to be glad and to do good in
one's lifetime; 13 moreover, that every man
who eats and drinks and sees good in all his
labor—it is the gift of God. 14 I know that
everything God does will be forever; there is
nothing to add to it and there is nothing to
take from it—God has *so* worked that men
should fear Him. 15 That which is has been
already and that which will be has already
been, yet God seeks what is pursued.

16 Furthermore, I have seen under the sun
that in the place of justice there is wicked-
ness, and in the place of righteousness there
is wickedness. 17 I said in my heart, "God
will judge both the righteous man and the
wicked man," for a time for every matter and
for every work is there. 18 I said in my heart
concerning the sons of men, "God is testing
them in order for them to see that they are
but beasts." 19 For the fate of the sons of men
and the fate of beasts is the same fate for
each of them. As one dies so dies the other,
and they all have the same breath. So there
is no advantage for man over beast, for all
is vanity. 20 All go to the same place. All
came from the dust, and all return to the
dust. 21 Who knows that the breath of man
ascends upward and the breath of the beast
descends downward to the earth? 22 I have
seen that nothing is better than that man
should be glad in his works, for that is his
portion. For who will bring him to see what
will occur after him?

Psalm 102:12–17

12 But You, O Yahweh, abide forever,
And the remembrance of Your *name*
from generation to generation.
13 You will arise *and* have
compassion on Zion—
For it is time to be gracious to it,
For the appointed time has come.
14 For Your slaves find pleasure
in its stones
And show grace to its dust—
15 So the nations will fear the
name of Yahweh
And all the kings of the
earth Your glory.
16 For Yahweh has built up Zion;
He has appeared in His glory.
17 He has turned toward the
prayer of the destitute
And has not despised their prayer.

Proverbs 24:3–4

3 By wisdom a house is built,
And by discernment it is
firmly established;
4 And by knowledge the rooms are filled
With all precious and pleasant riches.

1 Corinthians 8:1–13

8 Now concerning things sacrificed to
idols, we know that we all have knowl-
edge. Knowledge puffs up, but love builds
up. 2 If anyone thinks that he has known
anything, he has not yet known as he ought
to know; 3 but if anyone loves God, he has
been known by Him.

4 Therefore, concerning the eating of
things sacrificed to idols, we know that an
idol is nothing in the world, and that there
is no God but one. 5 For even if there are
so-called gods whether in heaven or on
earth, as indeed there are many gods and
many lords, 6 yet for us there is one God,
the Father, from whom are all things and we
exist for Him, and one Lord, Jesus Christ, by
whom are all things, and we *exist* through
Him.

7 However, not all men have this
knowledge; but some, being accustomed
to the idol until now, eat *food* as if it were
sacrificed to an idol; and their conscience,
being weak, is defiled. 8 But food will not
commend us to God. We neither lack if we
do not eat, nor abound if we do eat. 9 But see
to it that this authority of yours does not
somehow become a stumbling block to the
weak. 10 For if someone sees you, who have
knowledge, dining in an idol's temple, will
not his conscience, if he is weak, be built

up to eat things sacrificed to idols? 11 For through your knowledge he who is weak is ruined, the brother for whose sake Christ died. 12 And in that way, by sinning against the brothers and wounding their conscience when it is weak, you sin against Christ. 13 Therefore, if food causes my brother to stumble, I will never eat meat again—ever, so that I will not cause my brother to stumble.

AUGUST 28

Ecclesiastes 4:1–6:12

4 Then I looked again at all the acts of oppression which were being done under the sun. And behold, *I saw* the tears of the oppressed and *that* they had no one to comfort *them*; and on the side of their oppressors was power, but they had no one to comfort *them*. 2 So I lauded the dead who are already dead more than the living who are still living. 3 But better *off* than both of them is the one who never has been, who has never seen the evil work that is done under the sun.

4 I have seen that every labor and every success of the work is *the result of* jealousy between a man and his neighbor. This too is vanity and striving after wind. 5 The fool folds his hands in embrace and consumes his own flesh. 6 One hand full of rest is better than two fists full of labor and striving after wind.

7 Then I looked again at vanity under the sun. 8 There was a certain man without a second man, having neither a son nor a brother, yet there was no end to all his labor. Indeed, his eyes were not satisfied with riches—"And for whom am I laboring and depriving myself of good?" This too is vanity, and it is a grievous endeavor.

9 Two are better than one because they have good wages for their labor. 10 For if either of them falls, the one will lift up his companion. But woe to the one who falls when there is not a second one to lift him up. 11 Furthermore, if two lie down together they keep warm, but how can one be warm *alone*? 12 And if one can overpower him who is alone, two can stand against him. A cord of three *strands* is not quickly torn apart.

13 A poor yet wise lad is better than an old and foolish king who no longer knows *how* to receive warning. 14 For he has come out of prison to become king, even though he was born poor in his kingdom. 15 I have seen all the living who walk about under the sun *go along* with the second lad who stands in place of him. 16 There is no end to all the people, to all who were before them, and even the ones who will come later will not be glad with him, for this too is vanity and striving after wind.

5 Guard your steps as you go to the house of God and draw near to listen rather than to offer the sacrifice of fools; for they do not know they are doing evil. 2 Do not be hasty with your mouth or impulsive in your heart to bring up a matter in the presence of God. For God is in heaven but you are on the earth; therefore let your words be few. 3 For the dream comes through abundant endeavor and the voice of a fool through abundant words.

4 When you make a vow to God, do not be late in paying it; for *He takes* no delight in fools. Pay what you vow! 5 It is better that you should not vow than that you should vow and not pay. 6 Do not allow your mouth to cause your flesh to sin, and do not say in the presence of the messenger *of God* that it was a mistake. Why should God be angry on account of your voice and wreak destruction on the work of your hands? 7 For in many dreams and vanities are many words. Rather, fear God.

8 If you see oppression of the poor and robbery of justice and righteousness in the province, do not be astonished over the matter; for a lofty one keeps watch over another lofty one, and there are loftier ones over them. 9 But *the* advantage of the land in everything is this—a king *committed* to a cultivated field.

10 He who loves money will not be satisfied with money, nor he who loves abundance *with its* produce. This too is vanity. 11 When good things increase, those who consume them increase. So what is the success to their masters except to look on *with* their eyes? 12 The sleep of the laboring man is sweet, whether he eats little or much; but the satisfaction of the rich man does not allow him to sleep.

13 There is a sickening evil *which* I have
seen under the sun: riches being hoarded
by their master to his own evil *demise.*
14 And those riches were lost through a bad
endeavor; and he became the father of a son,
but there was nothing in his hand *for him.*
15 As he had come naked from his mother's
womb, so will he return as he came. He will
carry nothing from the fruit of his labor that
he can bring in his hand. 16 This also is a
sickening evil—exactly as a man came, so
will he go. So what is the advantage to him
who labors for the wind? 17 Also, all his days
he eats in darkness with much vexation, and
his sickness and anger.

18 Here is what I have seen to be good,
which is beautiful: to eat, to drink, and to
see good in all one's labor in which he labors
under the sun *during* the few days of his
life which God has given him; for this is his
portion. 19 Furthermore, as for every man to
whom God has given riches and wealth, He
has also empowered him to eat from them
and to take up his portion and be glad in
his labor; this is the gift of God. 20 For he
will not remember much the days of his life
because God allows him to occupy himself
with the gladness of his heart.

6 There is an evil which I have seen
under the sun and it is prevalent among
men— 2 a man to whom God gives riches
and wealth and honor so that his soul lacks
nothing of all that he desires; yet God does
not empower him to eat from them, for a
foreigner eats from them. This is vanity
and a sickening evil. 3 If a man becomes
the father of one hundred *children* and lives
many years, however many the days of his
years may be, but his soul is not satisfied
with good things, and he does not even
have a *proper* burial, *then* I say, "Better the
miscarriage than he, 4 for *that* one comes
in vanity and goes into darkness; and *that*
one's name is covered in darkness. 5 Indeed,
that one never sees the sun and never
knows *anything*; *that* one has more rest
than he. 6 Even if the *other* man lives one
thousand years twice and does not see good
things—do not all go to the same place?"

7 All a man's labor is for his mouth, and
yet the soul is not fulfilled. 8 For what
advantage does the wise man have over
the fool? What *advantage* does the afflicted
man have, knowing *how* to walk before the
living? 9 What the eyes see is better than
what the soul goes after. This too is vanity
and striving after wind.

10 Whatever exists has already been
named, and it is known what man is; and
he cannot dispute with him who is stronger
than he is. 11 For there are many words
which increase vanity. What *then* is the
advantage to a man? 12 For who knows what
is good for a man during *his* lifetime, *during*
the few days of his vain life? He will make do
with them like a shadow. For who can tell a
man what will be after him under the sun?

Psalm 102:18–28

18 This will be written for the
generation to come,
And a people yet to be created
will praise Yah.
19 For He looked down from
His holy height;
From heaven Yahweh gazed
upon the earth,
20 To hear the groaning of the prisoner,
To set free those who were
doomed to death,
21 To recount the name of Yahweh in Zion
And His praise in Jerusalem,
22 When the peoples are
gathered together,
And the kingdoms, to serve Yahweh.

23 He has afflicted my strength
in the way;
He has shortened my days.
24 I say, "O my God, do not take me
away in the midst of my days,
Your years are from generation
to *all* generations.
25 "Of old You founded the earth,
And the heavens are the
work of Your hands.
26 "Even they will perish, but
You will remain;
And all of them will wear
out like a garment;
Like clothing You will change them
and they will be changed.
27 "But You are the same,
And Your years will not
come to an end.
28 "The children of Your slaves
will dwell *securely*,
And their seed will be
established before You."

Proverbs 24:5–6

5 A wise man is strong,
And a man of knowledge
strengthens his power.
6 For by guidance you will make war,
And in abundance of counselors
there is salvation.

1 Corinthians 9:1–27

9 Am I not free? Am I not an apostle? Have I not seen Jesus our Lord? Are you not my work in the Lord? 2 If to others I am not an apostle, at least I am to you, for you are the seal of my apostleship in the Lord.

3 My defense to those who examine me is this: 4 Do we not have authority to eat and drink? 5 Do we not have authority to take along a believing wife, even as the rest of the apostles and the brothers of the Lord and Cephas? 6 Or do only Barnabas and I not have authority to refrain from working? 7 Who at any time serves as a soldier at his own expense? Who plants a vineyard and does not consume the fruit of it? Or who shepherds a flock and does not consume the milk of the flock?

8 Am I speaking these things according to human judgment? Or does not the Law also say these things? 9 For it is written in the Law of Moses, "YOU SHALL NOT MUZZLE THE OX WHILE IT IS THRESHING." Is God *merely* concerned about oxen? 10 Or is He speaking altogether for our sake? Yes, for our sake it was written, because the plowman ought to plow in hope, and the thresher *to thresh* in hope of sharing *the crops.* 11 If we sowed spiritual things in you, is it too much if we reap material things from you? 12 If others share this authority over you, do we not more? Nevertheless, we did not use this authority, but we endure all things so that we will cause no hindrance to the gospel of Christ. 13 Do you not know that those who perform sacred services eat the *food* of the temple, *and* those who attend regularly to the altar have their share from the altar? 14 So also the Lord directed those who proclaim the gospel to get their living from the gospel.

15 But I have used none of these things. And I am not writing these things so that it will be done so in my case, for it would be better for me to die than have anyone make my boast an empty one. 16 For if I proclaim the gospel, I have nothing to boast, for I am under compulsion. For woe is me if I do not proclaim the gospel. 17 For if I do this voluntarily, I have a reward; but if against my will, I have a stewardship entrusted to me. 18 What then is my reward? That, when I proclaim the gospel, I may offer the gospel without charge, so as not to make full use of my authority in the gospel.

19 For though I am free from all, I have made myself a slave to all, so that I may win more. 20 And to the Jews I became as a Jew, so that I might win Jews. To those who are under the Law, as under the Law though not being myself under the Law, so that I might win those who are under the Law. 21 To those who are without law, as without law, though not being without the law of God but under the law of Christ, so that I might win those who are without law. 22 To the weak I became weak, that I might win the weak. I have become all things to all men, so that I may by all means save some. 23 So I do all things for the sake of the gospel, so that I may become a fellow partaker of it.

24 Do you not know that those who run in a race all run, but *only* one receives the prize? Run in such a way that you may win. 25 Now everyone who competes in the games exercises self-control in all things. They then *do it* to receive a corruptible crown, but we an incorruptible. 26 Therefore I run in such a way, as not without aim; I box in such a way, as not beating the air; 27 but I discipline my body and make it my slave, so that, after I have preached to others, I myself will not be disqualified.

AUGUST 29

Ecclesiastes 7:1–29

7 Better is a good name than good oil,
And better is the day of *one's* death
than the day of one's birth.
2 Better to go to a house of mourning
Than to go to a house of feasting
Because that is the end of
all mankind,
And the living puts *this* in his heart.
3 Better is vexation than laughter,
For when a face is sad a
heart may be merry.

4 The heart of the wise is in the
house of mourning,
While the heart of fools is in
the house of gladness.
5 Better to listen to the rebuke
of a wise man
Than for one to listen to
the song of fools.
6 For as the *crackling* sound of
thorn bushes under a pot,
So is the laughter of the fool;
And this too is vanity.
7 For oppression gives a wise
man over to madness,
And a bribe destroys the heart.
8 Better is the end of a matter
than its beginning;
Better is patience of spirit than
haughtiness of spirit.
9 Do not be eager in your
spirit to be vexed,
For vexation rests in the
bosom of fools.
10 Do not say, "Why is it that the former
days were better than these?"
For it is not from wisdom that
you ask about this.
11 Wisdom along with an
inheritance is good
And an advantage to those
who see the sun.
12 For wisdom is a shadow *of protection*
as money is a shadow *of protection*,
And the advantage of knowledge
is that wisdom preserves
the lives of its masters.
13 See the work of God,
For who is able to straighten
what He has bent?
14 In the day *when there is* good
be of good cheer,
But in the day *when there is* evil see—
God has made the one as
well as the other
So that man will not find out
anything *that will be* after him.

15 I have seen everything during my days
of vanity; there is a righteous man who
perishes in his righteousness, and there
is a wicked man who prolongs *his life* in
his evildoing. 16 Do not be excessively
righteous, and do not be overly wise. Why
should you make yourself desolate? 17 Do
not be excessively wicked, and do not be
a simpleminded fool. Why should you die
before your time? 18 It is good that you seize
one thing and also not let go of the other;
for the one who fears God comes forth with
both of them.

19 Wisdom strengthens a wise man more
than ten *men with* power who are in a city.
20 Indeed, there is not a righteous man on
earth who *continually* does good and who
never sins. 21 Also, do not give your heart to
all words which are spoken, so that you will
not hear your slave cursing you. 22 For your
heart also knows that you likewise have
many times cursed others.

23 I tested all this with wisdom, *and* I
said, "I will be wise," but it was far from me.
24 What has been is far away and exceedingly
deep. Who can find it? 25 I turned my heart
to know, to explore, and to seek wisdom and
an explanation, and to know the wickedness
of foolishness and the simpleminded folly
of madness. 26 And I found more bitter than
death the woman whose heart is snares and
nets, whose hands are chains. One who is
good before God will escape from her, but
the sinner will be captured by her.

27 "See, I have found this," says the
Preacher, "*adding* one thing to another to
find an explanation, 28 which my soul still
seeks but has not found. I have found one
man out of a thousand, but I have not found
a woman among all these. 29 See, I have
found only this, that God made men upright,
but they have sought out many devices."

Psalm 103:1–5

1 Bless Yahweh, O my soul,
And all that is within me,
bless His holy name.
2 Bless Yahweh, O my soul,
And forget none of His benefits;
3 Who pardons all your iniquities,
Who heals all your diseases;
4 Who redeems your life from the pit,
Who crowns you with lovingkindness
and compassion;
5 Who satisfies your years
with good things,
So that your youth is renewed
like the eagle.

Proverbs 24:7–9

7 Wisdom is *too* exalted for
an ignorant fool,
He does not open his
mouth in the gate.

8 One who deliberately thinks to do evil,
Men will call a schemer.
9 The scheming of folly is sin,
And the scoffer is an
abomination to men.

1 Corinthians 10:1–13

10 For I do not want you to be unaware,
brothers, that our fathers were all
under the cloud and all passed through the
sea; 2 and all were baptized into Moses in
the cloud and in the sea; 3 and all ate the
same spiritual food; 4 and all drank the same
spiritual drink, for they were drinking from
a spiritual rock which followed them, and
the rock was Christ. 5 Nevertheless, with
most of them God was not well-pleased. For
THEY WERE STRUCK DOWN IN THE WILDERNESS.
6 Now these things happened as examples
for us, so that we would not crave evil things
as they also craved.
7 Do not be idolaters, as some of them
were. As it is written, "THE PEOPLE SAT DOWN
TO EAT AND DRINK, AND STOOD UP TO PLAY."
8 Nor let us act in sexual immorality, as some
of them did, and twenty-three thousand fell
in one day. 9 Nor let us put Christ to the test,
as some of them did, and were destroyed
by the serpents. 10 Nor grumble, as some
of them did, and were destroyed by the
destroyer. 11 Now these things happened to
them as an example, and they were written
for our instruction, upon whom the ends of
the ages have arrived. 12 Therefore let him
who thinks he stands take heed that he does
not fall. 13 No temptation has overtaken
you but such as is common to man, but
God is faithful, who will not allow you to
be tempted beyond what you are able, but
with the temptation will provide the way
of escape also, so that you will be able to
endure it.

AUGUST 30

Ecclesiastes 8:1–10:20

8 Who is like the wise man and who knows
the interpretation of a matter? A man's
wisdom illumines his face and causes his
stern face to beam.
2 I *say*, "Keep the command of the king
because of the sworn oath before God. 3 Do
not be in a hurry to go from his presence.
Do not stand in an evil matter, for he will
do whatever he pleases." 4 Since the word
of the king is powerful, who will say to him,
"What are you doing?"
5 He who keeps a *royal* command experi-
ences no evil thing, for a wise heart knows
the *proper* time and custom. 6 For there is a
proper time and custom for every matter,
though a man's trouble is multiplied upon
him. 7 If no one knows what will happen,
who can tell him when it will happen?
8 There is no man who has power to restrain
the wind with the wind, and there is none
who has power over the day of death; and
there is no discharge in the time of war,
and wickedness will not provide escape to
its masters. 9 All this I have seen and given
my heart to every work that has been done
under the sun wherein a man has power
over *another* man to his calamity.
10 So then, I have seen the wicked buried,
those who used to go in and out from the
holy place, and they are *soon* forgotten in the
city where they did thus. This too is vanity.
11 Because the sentence against an evil work
is not executed quickly, therefore the hearts
of the sons of men among them are given
fully to do evil. 12 Although a sinner does
evil a hundred *times* and may prolong his
life, still I know that it will be well for those
who fear God, who fear Him openly. 13 But
it will not be well for the wicked man, and
he will not prolong his days like a shadow,
because he does not fear God openly.
14 There is vanity which is done on the
earth, that is, there are righteous men to
whom it happens according to the works
of the wicked. On the other hand, there are
wicked men to whom it happens according
to the works of the righteous. I say that this
too is vanity. 15 So I laud gladness, for there
is nothing good for a man under the sun
except to eat and to drink and to be merry,
and this will join with him in his labor
throughout the days of his life which God
has given him under the sun.
16 When I gave my heart to know wisdom
and to see the endeavor which has been
done on the earth (even though one never
sees sleep with his eyes day or night), 17 and
I saw every work of God, *I concluded* that
man cannot find out the work which has

been done under the sun. Even though man
should seek laboriously, he will not find *it*
out; and though the wise man should say,
"I know," he cannot find *it* out.

9 For I have given all this to my heart
and explain it that righteous men, wise
men, and their service are in the hand of
God. Man does not know whether *it will be*
love or hatred; anything may be before him.
2 It is the same for all. There is one fate
for the righteous and for the wicked; for the
good, for the clean and for the unclean; for
the man who offers a sacrifice and for the
one who does not sacrifice. As the good man
is, so is the sinner; as the swearer is, so is
the one who is afraid to swear. 3 This is an
evil in all that is done under the sun, that
there is one fate for all. Furthermore, the
hearts of the sons of men are full of evil, and
madness is in their hearts throughout their
lives. Afterwards they *go* to the dead. 4 For
whoever is joined with all the living, there
is confidence; surely a live dog is better than
a dead lion. 5 For the living know they will
die; but the dead do not know anything,
nor have they any longer a reward, for the
memory of them is forgotten. 6 Indeed their
love, their hate, and their zeal have already
perished, and they will never again have a
portion in all that is done under the sun.
7 Go *then*, eat your bread in gladness and
drink your wine with a merry heart; for God
has already accepted your works. 8 Let your
clothes be white all the time, and let not oil
be lacking on your head. 9 See life with the
woman whom you love all the days of your
vain life, which He has given to you under
the sun—all the days of your vanity; for this
is your portion in life and in your labor in
which you have labored under the sun.
10 Whatever your hand finds to do, do *it*
with *all* your might; for there is no working
or explaining or knowledge or wisdom in
Sheol where you are going.
11 I again saw under the sun that the
race is not to the swift and the battle is not
to the mighty, and neither is bread to the
wise nor riches to the discerning nor favor
to men who know; for time and misfortune
overtake them all. 12 Moreover, man does
not know his time: like fish seized in an evil
net and birds seized in a trap, so the sons
of men are ensnared at an evil time when it
suddenly falls on them.
13 Also this I came to see as wisdom under
the sun, and it was great to me. 14 There was
a small city with few men in it, and a great
king came to it, surrounded it, and built
large siegeworks against it. 15 But there was
found in it a poor wise man, and he provided
a way of escape for the city by his wisdom.
Yet no one remembered that poor man. 16 So
I said, "Wisdom is better than strength." But
the wisdom of the poor man is despised,
and his words are not heard. 17 The words
of the wise heard in restfulness are *better*
than the shouting of a ruler among fools.
18 Wisdom is better than weapons of war,
but one sinner destroys much good.

10 Dead flies make a perfumer's oil
stink, so a little simpleminded folly is
weightier than wisdom *and* honor. 2 A wise
man's heart *directs him* toward the right, but
the foolish man's heart *directs him* toward
the left. 3 Even when the simpleminded
fool walks along the road, his heart lacks
wisdom, and he says to all *that* he is a sim-
pleminded fool. 4 If the ruler's temper rises
against you, do not abandon your position,
because calmness causes great offenses to
be abandoned.
5 There is an evil I have seen under the
sun, like a mistake which goes forth from
the one in power— 6 folly is set in many
exalted places while rich men sit in humble
places. 7 I have seen slaves *riding* on horses
and princes walking like slaves on the land.
8 He who digs a pit may fall into it, and a
serpent may bite him who breaks through
a wall. 9 He who quarries stones may be
hurt by them, and he who splits logs may
be endangered by them. 10 If the axe is dull
and he does not sharpen *its* edge, then he
must exert more strength. Wisdom has
the advantage of giving success. 11 If the
serpent bites before being charmed, there
is no advantage for the charmer. 12 Words
from the mouth of a wise man are gracious,
but the lips of a fool swallow him up; 13 the
beginning of the words of his mouth is
simpleminded folly, and the end of *what
comes from* his mouth is evil madness. 14 Yet
the simpleminded fool multiplies words. No
man knows what will happen, and who can
tell him what will come after him? 15 The
labor of a fool *so* wearies him that he does
not *even* know how to go to a city. 16 Woe to
you, O land, whose king is a young man and

whose princes eat in the morning. 17 Blessed
are you, O land, whose king is of nobility
and whose princes eat at the appropriate
time—for might and not for drinking.
18 Through indolence the beams sag, and
through slack hands the house leaks. 19 *Men*
prepare bread for laughter, and wine makes
life glad, and money is the answer to every-
thing. 20 Furthermore, in your bedchamber
do not curse a king, and in your sleeping
rooms do not curse a rich man, for a bird of
the sky will bring the sound and the winged
creature will tell the matter.

Psalm 103:6–14

6 Yahweh performs righteous deeds
And judgments for all who
are oppressed.
7 He made known His ways to Moses,
His acts to the sons of Israel.
8 Yahweh is compassionate and gracious,
Slow to anger and abounding
in lovingkindness.
9 He will not always contend *with us,*
And He will not keep *His anger* forever.
10 He has not dealt with us
according to our sins,
And He has not rewarded us
according to our iniquities.
11 For as high as the heavens
are above the earth,
So great is His lovingkindness
toward those who fear Him.
12 As far as the east is from the west,
So far has He removed our
transgressions from us.
13 As a father has compassion
on *his* children,
So Yahweh has compassion
on those who fear Him.
14 For He Himself knows our form;
He remembers that we are *but* dust.

Proverbs 24:10–12

10 If you are slack in the day of trouble,
Your strength is in trouble.

11 Deliver those who are being
taken away to death,
And those who are stumbling to the
slaughter, Oh hold *them* back.
12 If you say, "Behold, we did
not know this,"
Does not He who weighs the
hearts understand?
And *does not* He who guards
your soul know?
And will not He render to man
according to his work?

1 Corinthians 10:14–33

14 Therefore, my beloved, flee from
idolatry. 15 I speak as to prudent people. You
judge what I say. 16 Is not the cup of blessing
which we bless a sharing in the blood of
Christ? Is not the bread which we break a
sharing in the body of Christ? 17 Since there
is one bread, we who are many are one body,
for we all partake of the one bread. 18 Look
at the nation Israel. Are not those who eat
the sacrifices sharers in the altar? 19 What
do I mean then? That a thing sacrificed to
idols is anything, or that an idol is anything?
20 *No,* but *I say* that the things which the
Gentiles sacrifice, they SACRIFICE TO DEMONS
AND NOT TO GOD. And I do not want you to
become sharers in demons. 21 You cannot
drink the cup of the Lord and the cup of
demons. You cannot partake of the table of
the Lord and the table of demons. 22 Or do
WE PROVOKE THE LORD TO JEALOUSY? Are we
stronger than He?

23 All things are lawful, but not all
things are profitable. All things are lawful,
but not all things build up. 24 Let no one
seek his own *good,* but that of the other
person. 25 Eat anything that is sold in the
meat market without asking questions
for conscience' sake. 26 FOR THE EARTH IS
THE LORD'S, AS WELL AS ITS FULLNESS. 27 If
one of the unbelievers invites you and
you want to go, eat anything that is set
before you without asking questions for
conscience' sake. 28 But if anyone says to
you, "This is meat consecrated to idols,"
do not eat *it,* for the sake of the one who
informed *you,* and for conscience' sake.
29 I do not mean your own conscience,
but the other *person's.* For why is my
freedom judged by another's conscience?
30 If I partake with gratefulness, why am
I slandered concerning that for which I
give thanks?

31 Whether, then, you eat or drink or
whatever you do, do all to the glory of
God. 32 Give no offense either to Jews or to
Greeks or to the church of God; 33 just as I
also please all men in all things, not seeking
my own profit but the *profit* of the many, so
that they may be saved.

AUGUST 31

Ecclesiastes 11:1–12:14

11 Cast your bread on the surface of the
waters, for you will find it after many
days. 2 Divide your portion to seven, or even
to eight, for you do not know what calamity
may occur on the earth. 3 If the clouds are
full, they empty *the* rain upon the earth;
and whether a tree falls toward the south
or toward the north, wherever the tree falls,
there it lies. 4 He who watches the wind will
not sow, and he who looks at the clouds will
not reap. 5 Just as you do not know the path
of the wind and how bones *are formed* in the
womb of the pregnant woman, so you do not
know the work of God who works all things.
6 Sow your seed in the morning and do
not put your hands down in the evening,
for you do not know whether morning or
evening sowing will succeed, or whether
both of them alike will be good.
7 The light is sweet, and *it is* good for the
eyes to see the sun. 8 Indeed, if a man should
live many years, let him be glad in them all,
and let him remember the days of darkness,
for they will be many. Everything that is to
come *will be* vanity.
9 Be glad, young man, during your child-
hood, and let your heart be merry during
the days of young manhood. And walk in the
ways of your heart and in the sights of your
eyes. Yet know that God will bring you to
judgment for all these things. 10 So, remove
vexation from your heart and put away evil
from your flesh because childhood and the
prime of life are vanity.

12 Remember also your Creator in the
days of your youth, before the evil
days happen and the years draw near in
which you will say, "I have no delight in
them"; 2 before the sun and the light, the
moon and the stars are darkened, and
clouds return after the rain; 3 in the day
that the watchmen of the house tremble,
and valiant men bend down, the grinding
ones stand idle because they are few, and
those who look through windows grow
dark; 4 and the doors on the street are shut
as the sound of the grinding mill is low, and
one will arise at the sound of the bird, and
all the daughters of song will sing softly.
5 Furthermore, men are afraid of a high place
and of terrors on the road; the almond tree
blooms, the grasshopper drags itself along,
and the caperberry is ineffective. For man
goes to his eternal home, but the mourners
go about in the street. 6 *Remember Him*
before the silver cord is snapped and the
golden bowl is crushed, the pitcher by the
spring is broken and the wheel at the cistern
is crushed; 7 then the dust will return to the
earth as it was, and the spirit will return to
God who gave it. 8 "Vanity of vanities," says
the Preacher, "all is vanity!"
9 In addition to being a wise man, the
Preacher also taught the people knowl-
edge; and he pondered, searched out, and
arranged many proverbs. 10 The Preacher
sought to find delightful words and words
of truth written uprightly.
11 The words of wise men are like goads,
and masters of *these* collections are like
well-driven nails; they are given by one
Shepherd. 12 But in addition to this, my
son, be warned: the making of many books
is endless, and much devotion *to books* is
wearying to the flesh.
13 The end of the matter, all *that* has
been heard: fear God and keep His com-
mandments, because this is *the end of the*
matter for all mankind. 14 For God will bring
every work to judgment, everything which
is hidden, whether it is good or evil.

Psalm 103:15–22

15 As for man, his days are like grass;
As a flower of the field, so he flowers.
16 When the wind has passed
over it, it is no more,
And its place acknowledges
it no longer.
17 But the lovingkindness of Yahweh
is from everlasting to everlasting
on those who fear Him,
And His righteousness to
children's children,
18 To those who keep His covenant
And remember His precepts
to do them.

19 Yahweh has established His
throne in the heavens,
And His kingdom rules over all.
20 Bless Yahweh, you His angels,

Mighty in strength, who
perform His word,
Obeying the voice of His word!
21 Bless Yahweh, all *you* His hosts,
You who serve Him, doing His will.
22 Bless Yahweh, all you works of His,
In all places of His rule;
Bless Yahweh, O my soul!

Proverbs 24:13–14

13 Eat honey, my son, for it is good,
Indeed, the honey from the
comb is sweet to your taste;
14 Know *that* wisdom is thus
for your soul;
If you find *it*, then there
will be a future,
And your hope will not be cut off.

1 Corinthians 11:1–16

11 Be imitators of me, just as I also am
of Christ.
2 Now I praise you because you remember
me in everything and hold firmly to the
traditions, just as I delivered them to you.
3 But I want you to understand that Christ
is the head of every man, and the man is
the head of a woman, and God is the head
of Christ. 4 Every man who has *something*
on his head while praying or prophesying,
shames his head. 5 But every woman who
has her head uncovered while praying or
prophesying, shames her head, for she is
one and the same as the woman whose
head is shaved. 6 For if a woman does not
cover her head, let her also have her hair
cut short. But if it is disgraceful for a woman
to have her hair cut short or her head
shaved, let her cover her head. 7 For a man
ought not to have his head covered, since
he is the image and glory of God, but the
woman is the glory of man. 8 For man does
not originate from woman, but woman from
man. 9 For indeed man was not created for
the woman's sake, but woman for the man's
sake. 10 Therefore the woman ought to have
a symbol of authority on her head, because
of the angels. 11 Nevertheless, in the Lord,
neither is woman independent of man, nor
is man independent of woman. 12 For as the
woman originates from the man, so also
the man *has his birth* through the woman,
but all things originate from God. 13 Judge
for yourselves: is it proper for a woman
to pray to God *with her head* uncovered?
14 Does not even nature itself teach you that
if a man has long hair, it is a dishonor to
him, 15 but if a woman has long hair, it is
a glory to her? For her hair is given to her
for a covering. 16 But if one is inclined to be
contentious, we have no other practice, nor
have the churches of God.

SEPTEMBER 1

Song of Songs 1:1–2:17

1 The Song of Songs, which is Solomon's.
2 "May he kiss me with the
kisses of his mouth!
For your love is better than wine.
3 "Your oils have a pleasing fragrance,
Your name is *like* purified oil;
Therefore the maidens love you.
4 "Draw me after you *and* let
us run *together*!
The king has brought me
into his chambers."

"We will rejoice in you and be glad;
We will extol your love
more than wine.
Rightly do they love you."

5 "I am black but lovely,
O daughters of Jerusalem,
Like the tents of Kedar,
Like the curtains of Solomon.
6 "Do not look at me because
I am swarthy,
For the sun has burned me.
My mother's sons were angry with me;
They made me caretaker
of the vineyards,
But I have not taken care of
my own vineyard.
7 "Tell me, O you whom my soul loves,
Where do you shepherd *your flock*,
Where do you make *it* lie
down at noon?
For why should I be like one
who veils herself
Beside the flocks of your companions?"
8 "If you yourself do not know,
Most beautiful among women,
Go forth on the trail of the flock

And pasture your young goats
By the dwellings of the shepherds.

9 "To a mare of mine among the
chariots of Pharaoh
I compare you, O my darling.
10 "Your cheeks are lovely with ornaments,
Your neck with strings of beads."

11 "We will make for you
ornaments of gold
With beads of silver."

12 "While the king was at his
banqueting table,
My perfume gave forth its fragrance.
13 "My beloved is to me a pouch of myrrh
Which lies all night between
my breasts.
14 "My beloved is to me a cluster
of henna blossoms
In the vineyards of Engedi."

15 "Behold, you are beautiful,
my darling,
Behold, you are beautiful!
Your eyes are *like* doves."

16 "Behold, you are handsome,
my beloved,
Indeed, *so* pleasant!
Indeed, our couch is luxuriant!
17 "The beams of our houses are cedars,
Our rafters, cypresses.

2 "I am the rose of Sharon,
The lily of the valleys."

2 "Like a lily among the thorns,
So is my darling among the daughters."

3 "Like an apple tree among the
trees of the forest,
So is my beloved among the sons.
In his shade I had great
desire and sat down,
And his fruit was sweet to my taste.
4 "He has brought me to *his*
house of banqueting,
And his banner over me is love.
5 "Sustain me with raisin cakes,
Refresh me with apples,
Because I am lovesick.
6 "Let his left hand be under my head
And his right hand embrace me."

7 "I call you to *solemnly* swear,
O daughters of Jerusalem,
By the gazelles or by the
hinds of the field,
That you do not arouse or
awaken *my* love
Until she pleases."
8 "The voice of my beloved!
Behold, he is coming,
Leaping on the mountains,
Jumping on the hills!
9 "My beloved is like a gazelle
or a young stag.
Behold, he is standing behind
our wall;
He gazes through the windows;
He is peering through the lattice.

10 "My beloved answered and said to me,
'Arise, my darling, my beautiful one,
And come along.
11 'For behold, the winter is past,
The rain is over; it is gone.
12 'The flowers have appeared in the land;
The time for pruning has arrived;
And the voice of the turtledove
has been heard in our land.
13 'The fig tree has ripened its figs,
And the vines in blossom have
given forth *their* fragrance.
Arise, my darling, my beautiful one,
And come along!'"

14 "O my dove, in the clefts of the rock,
In the secret place of the
steep pathway,
Let me see your appearance,
Let me hear your voice;
For your voice is sweet,
And your appearance is lovely."

15 "Seize the foxes for us,
The little foxes that are wreaking
destruction on the vineyards,
While our vineyards are in blossom."

16 "My beloved is mine, and I am his,
He who shepherds *his flock*
among the lilies.
17 "Until the day breathes and
the shadows flee,
Turn, my beloved, and be like
a gazelle
Or a young stag on the
mountains of Bether."

Psalm 104:1–9

1 Bless Yahweh, O my soul!
O Yahweh my God, You are very great;
You are clothed with
splendor and majesty,
2 Wrapping Yourself with
light as with a cloak,
Stretching out the heavens
like a *tent* curtain.
3 He lays the beams of His upper
chambers in the waters;
He sets up the clouds *to be* His chariot;
He walks upon the wings of the wind;
4 He makes His angels the winds,
His ministers flaming fire.

5 He founded the earth upon its place,
So that it will not shake
forever and ever.
6 You covered it with the deep
as with a garment;
The waters were standing
above the mountains.
7 At Your rebuke they fled,
At the sound of Your thunder
they hurried away in alarm.
8 The mountains went up; the
valleys went down
To the place which You
founded for them.
9 You set a boundary that they
may not pass over,
So that they will not return
to cover the earth.

Proverbs 24:15–16

15 Do not lie in wait, O wicked man,
against the abode of the righteous;
Do not destroy his resting place;
16 For a righteous man falls seven
times, and rises again,
But the wicked will stumble in calamity.

1 Corinthians 11:17–34

17 But in giving this instruction, I do not
praise you, because you come together not
for the better but for the worse. 18 For, in
the first place, when you come together as a
church, I hear that divisions exist among you,
and in part I believe it. 19 For there must also
be factions among you, so that those who are
approved may become evident among you.
20 Therefore when you meet together in the
same *place*, it is not to eat the Lord's Supper,
21 for in your eating each one takes his own
supper first, and one is hungry and another
is drunk. 22 For do you not have houses in
which to eat and drink? Or do you despise
the church of God and shame those who
have nothing? What shall I say to you? Shall
I praise you? In this I will not praise you.

23 For I received from the Lord that which
I also delivered to you, that the Lord Jesus
in the night in which He was being betrayed
took bread, 24 and when He had given
thanks, He broke it and said, "This is My
body, which is for you. Do this in remem-
brance of Me." 25 In the same way *He took*
the cup also after supper, saying, "This cup
is the new covenant in My blood; do this,
as often as you drink *it*, in remembrance of
Me." 26 For as often as you eat this bread and
drink the cup, you proclaim the death of the
Lord until He comes.

27 Therefore whoever eats the bread or
drinks the cup of the Lord in an unworthy
manner, shall be guilty of the body and the
blood of the Lord. 28 But a man must test
himself, and in so doing he is to eat of the
bread and drink of the cup. 29 For he who
eats and drinks, eats and drinks judgment to
himself if he does not judge the body rightly.
30 For this reason many among you are weak
and sick, and a number sleep. 31 But if we
judged ourselves rightly, we would not be
judged. 32 But when we are judged, we are
disciplined by the Lord so that we will not
be condemned along with the world.

33 So then, my brothers, when you come
together to eat, wait for one another. 34 If
anyone is hungry, let him eat at home, so
that you will not come together for judg-
ment. The remaining matters I will direct
when I come.

SEPTEMBER 2

Song of Songs 3:1–4:16

3 "On my bed night after
night I sought him
Whom my soul loves;
I sought him but did not find him.
2 'I must arise now and go about the city;
In the streets and in the squares
I must seek him whom my soul loves.'

I sought him but did not find him.
3 "The watchmen who go about
the city found me,
And I said, 'Have you seen him
whom my soul loves?'
4 "Scarcely had I passed them by
When I found him whom
my soul loves;
I seized him and would not
let him go
Until I had brought him to
my mother's house,
And into the chamber of her
who conceived me."

5 "I call you to *solemnly* swear,
O daughters of Jerusalem,
By the gazelles or by the
hinds of the field,
That you do not arouse or
awaken *my* love
Until she pleases."
6 "Who is this coming up from
the wilderness
Like columns of smoke,
As rising incense of myrrh
and frankincense,
With all scented powders
of the merchant?
7 "Behold, it is the *traveling*
couch of Solomon;
Sixty mighty men around it,
Of the mighty men of Israel.
8 "All of them are those who
seize the sword,
Learned in war;
Each man has his sword at his side,
Guarding against the dreadful
things of the night.
9 "King Solomon has made for
himself a sedan chair
From the timber of Lebanon.
10 "He made its posts of silver,
Its back of gold
And its seat of purple fabric,
With its interior inlaid with love
By the daughters of Jerusalem.
11 "Go forth and see,
O daughters of Zion,
King Solomon with the crown
With which his mother
has crowned him
On the day of his wedding,
And on the day of his
gladness of heart."

4 "Behold, you are beautiful, my darling,
Behold, you are beautiful!
Your eyes are *like* doves
behind your veil;
Your hair is like a flock of goats
That have leapt down from
Mount Gilead.
2 "Your teeth are like a flock
of *newly* shorn ewes
Which have come up from
their washing,
All of which bear twins,
And not one among them
has lost her young.
3 "Your lips are like a scarlet thread,
And your mouth is lovely.
Your temples are like a slice
of a pomegranate
Behind your veil.
4 "Your neck is like the tower of David,
Built with rows of stones
On which are hung one
thousand shields,
All the small shields of
the mighty men.
5 "Your two breasts are like two fawns,
Twins of a gazelle
Which feed among the lilies.
6 "Until the day breathes
And the shadows flee,
I will go my way to the
mountain of myrrh
And to the hill of frankincense.

7 "You are altogether beautiful,
my darling,
And there is no blemish in you.
8 "*Come* with me from
Lebanon, *my* bride,
May you come with me from Lebanon.
Journey down from the top of Amana,
From the top of Senir and Hermon,
From the dens of lions,
From the mountains of leopards.
9 "You have made my heart beat
faster, my sister, *my* bride;
You have made my heart beat faster
with a single *glance* of your eyes,
With a single strand of your necklace.
10 "How beautiful is your love,
my sister, *my* bride!
How much better is your
love than wine,
And the fragrance of your oils
Than all *kinds* of spices!

11 "Your lips, *my* bride, drip
honey from the comb;
Honey and milk are under
your tongue,
And the fragrance of your garments
is like the fragrance of Lebanon.
12 "A garden locked is my sister, *my* bride,
A rock garden locked,
a spring sealed up.
13 "Your shoots are an orchard
of pomegranates
With choice fruits, henna
with nard plants,
14 Nard and saffron, calamus
and cinnamon,
With all the trees of frankincense,
Myrrh and aloes, along with
all the finest spices.
15 "*You are* a garden spring,
A well of fresh water,
And streams *flowing* from Lebanon."

16 "Awake, O north *wind*,
And come, *wind of* the south;
Make my garden breathe out *fragrance*,
Let its spices flow forth.
May my beloved come into his garden
And eat its choice fruits!"

Psalm 104:10–23

10 He sends forth springs in the valleys;
They flow between the mountains;
11 They give water to every
beast of the field;
The wild donkeys quench their thirst.
12 Above them the birds of
the heavens dwell;
They give forth *their* voices
among the branches.
13 He gives water to the mountains
from His upper chambers;
The earth is satisfied with
the fruit of His works.

14 He causes the grass to
grow for the cattle,
And vegetation for man's cultivation,
To bring forth food from the earth,
15 And wine which makes
man's heart glad,
To make *his* face glisten more than oil,
And food which sustains man's heart.
16 The trees of Yahweh are satisfied,
The cedars of Lebanon
which He planted,
17 Where the birds build their nests,
The stork's home is in the fir trees.

18 The high mountains are
for the wild goats;
The cliffs are a refuge for
the shephanim.
19 He made the moon for the seasons;
The sun knows the place of its setting.
20 You appoint darkness so that
it becomes night,
In which all the beasts of the
forest creep about.
21 The young lions roar *to*
go after their prey
And to seek their food from God.
22 *When* the sun rises they
gather together
And lie down in their dens.
23 Man goes forth to his work
And to his labor until evening.

Proverbs 24:17–18

17 When your enemy falls, do not be glad,
And when he stumbles, do not
let your heart rejoice;
18 Lest Yahweh see *it* and it
be evil in His eyes,
And turn His anger away from him.

1 Corinthians 12:1–31

12 Now concerning spiritual *gifts*, broth-
ers, I do not want you to be ignorant.
2 You know that when you were pagans,
you were being led astray to the mute idols,
however you were led. 3 Therefore I make
known to you that no one speaking by the
Spirit of God says, "Jesus is accursed," and
no one can say, "Jesus is Lord," except by
the Holy Spirit.
4 Now there are varieties of gifts, but the
same Spirit. 5 And there are varieties of min-
istries, and the same Lord. 6 And there are
varieties of workings, but the same God who
works everything in everyone. 7 But to each
one is given the manifestation of the Spirit
for what is profitable. 8 For to one is given
the word of wisdom through the Spirit, and
to another the word of knowledge according
to the same Spirit; 9 to someone else faith
by the same Spirit, and to another gifts of
healing by the one Spirit, 10 and to another
the workings of miracles, and to another
prophecy, and to another the distinguishing
of spirits, to someone else *various* kinds of

tongues, and to another the translation
of tongues. 11 But one and the same Spirit
works all these things, distributing to each
one individually just as He wills.

12 For even as the body is one and *yet* has
many members, and all the members of the
body, though they are many, are one body,
so also is Christ. 13 For also by one Spirit we
were all baptized into one body, whether
Jews or Greeks, whether slaves or free, and
we were all made to drink of one Spirit.

14 For also the body is not one member,
but many. 15 If the foot says, "Because I am
not a hand, I am not *a part* of the body," it
is not for this reason any the less *a part* of
the body. 16 And if the ear says, "Because I
am not an eye, I am not *a part* of the body,"
it is not for this reason any the less *a part* of
the body. 17 If the whole body were an eye,
where would the hearing be? If the whole
were hearing, where would the sense of
smell be? 18 But now God has appointed the
members, each one of them, in the body,
just as He desired. 19 And if they were all
one member, where would the body be?
20 But now there are many members, but
one body. 21 And the eye cannot say to the
hand, "I have no need of you"; or again the
head to the feet, "I have no need of you."
22 On the contrary, *how* much more is it
that the members of the body which seem
to be weaker are necessary, 23 and those
members of the body which we think as
less honorable, on these we bestow more
abundant honor, and our less presentable
members become much more presentable,
24 whereas our more presentable members
have no *such* need. But God has *so* composed
the body, giving more abundant honor to
that *member* which lacked, 25 so that there
may be no division in the body, but *that* the
members may have the same care for one
another. 26 And if one member suffers, all
the members suffer with it; if *one* member
is honored, all the members rejoice with it.

27 Now you are Christ's body, and indi-
vidually members of it. 28 And God has
appointed in the church, first apostles,
second prophets, third teachers, then
miracles, then gifts of healings, helps,
administrations, *various* kinds of tongues.
29 Are all apostles? Are all prophets? Are
all teachers? Are all *workers of* miracles?
30 Do all have gifts of healings? Do all speak
with tongues? Do all translate? 31 But you
earnestly desire the greater gifts.

And I will yet show you a more excellent
way.

The Bible was given to bear witness to one God, Creator and Sustainer of the universe, through Christ, Redeemer of sinful man. It presents one continuous story—that of human redemption.

— MERRILL UNGER

SEPTEMBER 3

Song of Songs 5:1–6:13

5 "I have come into my garden,
my sister, *my* bride;
I have picked my myrrh along
with my balsam.
I have eaten my honeycomb
with my honey;
I have drunk my wine with my milk.
Eat, friends;
Drink and imbibe deeply, O lovers."

2 "I was asleep, but my heart was awake.
A voice! My beloved was knocking:
'Open to me, my sister, my darling,
My dove, my perfect one!
For my head is full of dew,
My locks with the damp of the night.'
3 "I have taken off my long-
sleeved garment,
How can I put it on *again*?
I have washed my feet,
How can I dirty them *again*?
4 "My beloved sent forth his hand
through the opening,
And my feelings moaned for him.
5 "I arose to open to my beloved;
And my hands dripped with myrrh,
And my fingers with liquid myrrh,

On the handles of the lock.
6 "I opened to my beloved,
But my beloved had turned
away *and* passed by!
My soul went out *to him* as
he spoke.
I searched for him,
but I did not find him;
I called him, but he did not
answer me.
7 "The watchmen who go about
in the city found me,
They struck me *and* wounded me;
The guardsmen of the walls took
away my shawl from me.
8 "I call you to *solemnly* swear,
O daughters of Jerusalem,
If you find my beloved,
What will you tell him?
Tell him that I am sick with love."

9 "What is your beloved *that he is*
more than *any other* beloved,
O most beautiful among women?
What is your beloved *that he is*
more than *any other* beloved,
That thus you call us to
solemnly swear?"
10 "My beloved is dazzling and ruddy,
Lifted up as a banner among
ten thousand.
11 "His head is *like* gold, fine gold;
His locks are *like* clusters of dates
And black as a raven.
12 "His eyes are like doves
Beside streams of water,
Washed in milk,
And sitting in *their* setting.
13 "His cheeks are like a bed of spices,
Towers of sweet-scented herbs;
His lips are lilies
Dripping with liquid myrrh.
14 "His hands are rods of gold
Set with beryl;
His abdomen is a plate of ivory
Inlaid with sapphires.
15 "His legs are pillars of marble
Set on bases of fine gold;
His appearance is like Lebanon
Choice as the cedars.
16 "His mouth is *full of* sweetness.
And he is wholly desirable.
This is my beloved and
this is my friend,
O daughters of Jerusalem."

6 "Where has your beloved gone,
O most beautiful among women?
Where has your beloved turned,
That we may seek him with you?"

2 "My beloved has gone down
to his garden,
To the beds of spices,
To shepherd *his flock* in the gardens
And gather lilies.
3 "I am my beloved's and my
beloved is mine,
He who shepherds *his flock*
among the lilies."

4 "You are as beautiful as
Tirzah, my darling,
As lovely as Jerusalem,
As majestic as an army with banners.
5 "Turn your eyes away from me,
For they have overwhelmed me;
Your hair is like a flock of goats
That have leapt down from Gilead.
6 "Your teeth are like a flock of ewes
Which have come up from
their washing,
All of which bear twins,
And not one among them
has lost her young.
7 "Your temples are like a slice
of a pomegranate
Behind your veil.
8 "There are sixty queens and
eighty concubines,
And maidens without number;
9 She is the only one—my
dove, my perfect one;
She is the only one of her mother;
She is the pure one of her
who bore her.
The daughters saw her and
called her blessed,
The queens and the concubines *also*,
and they praised her, *saying*,
10 'Who is this that looks down
like the dawn,
As beautiful as the full moon,
As pure as the sun,
As majestic as an army with banners?'

11 "I went down to the garden of nut trees
To see the blossoms of the valley,
To see whether the vine had
flourished
Or the pomegranates had bloomed.

12 "I did not know *it*, *but* my soul set me
Among the chariots of my
noble people."

13 "Come back, come back,
O Shulammite;
Come back, come back,
that we may behold you!"

"Why should you behold
the Shulammite,
As at the dance of the two companies?

Psalm 104:24–30

24 How numerous are Your
works, O Yahweh!
In wisdom You have made them all;
The earth is full of Your possessions.
25 This is the sea, great and broad,
There *the* creeping things
are without number,
Creatures both small and great.
26 There the ships move along,
And Leviathan, which You
have formed to play in it.

27 They all wait for You
To give them their food in
due season.
28 You give to them, they gather *it* up;
You open Your hand, they are
satisfied with good.
29 You hide Your face,
they are dismayed;
You take away their spirit,
they breathe their last
And return to their dust.
30 You send forth Your Spirit,
they are created;
And You renew the face
of the ground.

Proverbs 24:19–20

19 Do not fret because of evildoers
Do not be jealous of the wicked;
20 For there will be no future
for the evil one;
The lamp of the wicked will go out.

1 Corinthians 13:1–13

13 If I speak with the tongues of men and
of angels, but do not have love, I have
become a noisy gong or a clanging cymbal.
2 And if I have *the gift of* prophecy, and
know all mysteries and all knowledge; and
if I have all faith, so as to remove mountains,
but do not have love, I am nothing. 3 And if I
give all my possessions to feed *the poor*, and
if I surrender my body to be burned, but do
not have love, it profits me nothing.
4 Love is patient, love is kind, is not
jealous, does not brag, is not puffed up; 5 it
does not act unbecomingly, does not seek
its own, is not provoked, does not take
into account a wrong *suffered*; 6 it does not
rejoice in unrighteousness, but rejoices with
the truth; 7 it bears all things, believes all
things, hopes all things, endures all things.
8 Love never fails, but if *there are gifts*
of prophecy, they will be done away; if
there are tongues, they will cease; if *there*
is knowledge, it will be done away. 9 For
we know in part and we prophesy in part,
10 but when the perfect comes, the partial
will be done away. 11 When I was a child, I
used to speak like a child, think like a child,
reason like a child. When I became a man, I
did away with childish things. 12 For now we
see in a mirror dimly, but then face to face.
Now I know in part, but then I will know
fully just as I also have been fully known.
13 But now abide faith, hope, love—these
three; but the greatest of these is love.

SEPTEMBER 4

Song of Songs 7:1–8:14

7 "How beautiful are your feet in sandals,
O noble's daughter!
The curves of your thighs
are like ornaments,
The work of the hands of an artist.
2 "Your navel is *like* a round basin
Which never lacks mixed wine;
Your belly is like a heap of wheat
Encircled with lilies.
3 "Your two breasts are like two fawns,
Twins of a gazelle.
4 "Your neck is like a tower of ivory,
Your eyes *like* the pools in Heshbon
By the gate of Bath-rabbim;
Your nose is like the tower of Lebanon,
Which faces toward Damascus.
5 "Your head crowns you like Carmel,
And the flowing locks of your
head are like purple threads;

The king is captivated by *your* tresses.
6 "How beautiful and how
pleasant you are,
My love, with *all* your pleasures!
7 "Your stature is like a palm tree,
And your breasts are *like its* clusters.
8 "I said, 'I will climb the palm tree;
I will seize its fruit stalks.'
Oh, may your breasts be like
clusters of the vine,
And the fragrance of your
breath like apples,
9 And your mouth like the best wine!"

"It goes *down* smoothly for my beloved,
Flowing gently *through* the lips
of those who fall asleep.
10 "I am my beloved's,
And his desire is for me.
11 "Come, my beloved, let us go
out into the fields,
Let us spend the night in the villages.
12 "Let us rise early *and go*
to the vineyards;
Let us see whether the
vine has flourished
And its blossoms have opened,
And whether the pomegranates
have bloomed.
There I will give you my love.
13 "The mandrakes have given
forth fragrance;
And over our doors are all choice *fruits*,
Both new and old,
Which I have treasured up
for you, my beloved.

8 "Oh that you were like a brother to me
Who nursed at my mother's breasts.
If I found you outside, I would kiss you;
No one would despise me, either.
2 "I would lead you *and* bring you
Into the house of my mother,
who used to teach me;
I would give you spiced wine to
drink from the sweet wine
of my pomegranates.
3 "Let his left hand be under my head
And his right hand embrace me."

4 "I call you to *solemnly* swear,
O daughters of Jerusalem,
Why should you arouse or
awaken *my* love
Until she pleases?"

5 "Who is this coming up from
the wilderness
Leaning on her beloved?"

"Beneath the apple tree I awakened you;
There your mother was
in labor with you;
There she was in labor *and*
gave you birth.
6 "Put me like a seal over your heart,
Like a seal on your arm.
For love is as strong as death,
Jealousy is as severe as Sheol;
Its flashes are flashes of fire,
The *very* flame of Yah.
7 "Many waters cannot quench love,
Nor will rivers overflow it;
If a man were to give all the
riches of his house for love,
It would be utterly despised."

8 "We have a little sister,
And she has no breasts;
What shall we do for our sister
On the day when she is spoken for?
9 "If she is a wall,
We will build on her a
battlement of silver;
But if she is a door,
We will barricade her with
planks of cedar."

10 "I was a wall, and my breasts
were like towers;
Then I became in his eyes as
one who finds peace.
11 "Solomon had a vineyard
at Baal-hamon;
He gave the vineyard to caretakers.
Each one was to bring one thousand
shekels of silver for its fruit.
12 "My very own vineyard is before me;
The thousand *shekels* are
for you, Solomon,
And two hundred are for those
who take care of its fruit."

13 "O you who sit in the gardens,
My companions are giving
heed to your voice—
Let me hear it!"

14 "Hurry, my beloved,
And be like a gazelle or a young stag
On the mountains of spices."

Psalm 104:31–35

31 Let the glory of Yahweh
endure forever;
Let Yahweh be glad in His works;
32 He looks at the earth,
and it trembles;
He touches the mountains,
and they smoke.
33 I will sing to Yahweh
throughout my life;
I will sing praise to my God
while I have *my* being.
34 Let my musing be pleasing to Him;
As for me, I shall be glad in Yahweh.
35 Let sinners be consumed
from the earth
And let the wicked be no more.
Bless Yahweh, O my soul.
Praise Yah!

Proverbs 24:21–22

21 My son, fear Yahweh and the king;
Do not associate with
those who change,
22 For suddenly their disaster will rise,
And who knows the upheaval *that*
comes from both of them?

1 Corinthians 14:1–19

14 Pursue love, yet earnestly desire
spiritual *gifts*, but especially that
you may prophesy. 2 For one who speaks
in a tongue does not speak to men but to
God, for no one understands, but in *his*
spirit he speaks mysteries. 3 But one who
prophesies speaks to men for edification
and exhortation and encouragement. 4 One
who speaks in a tongue edifies himself; but
one who prophesies edifies the church. 5 But
I wish that you all spoke in tongues, but *even*
more that you would prophesy. And greater
is one who prophesies than one who speaks
in tongues, unless he translates, so that the
church may receive edification.
6 But now, brothers, if I come to you
speaking in tongues, what will I profit
you unless I speak to you either by way of
revelation or of knowledge or of prophecy or
of teaching? 7 Yet *even* lifeless things, either
flute or harp, in producing a sound, if they
do not produce a distinction in the tones,
how will it be known what is played on the
flute or on the harp? 8 For if the trumpet
produces an indistinct sound, who will
prepare himself for battle? 9 So also you,
unless you utter by the tongue a word that is
clear, how will it be known what is spoken?
For you will be speaking into the air. 10 There
are, perhaps, a great many kinds of sounds
in the world, and none is without meaning.
11 If then I do not know the meaning of the
sound, I will be to the one who speaks a
barbarian, and the one who speaks will be a
barbarian to me. 12 So also you, since you are
zealous for spiritual *gifts*, seek to abound for
the edification of the church.
13 Therefore let one who speaks in a
tongue pray that he may translate. 14 For if
I pray in a tongue, my spirit prays, but my
mind is unfruitful. 15 What is *the outcome*
then? I will pray with the spirit and I will
pray with the mind also; I will sing with
the spirit and I will sing with the mind also.
16 Otherwise if you bless in the spirit *only*,
how will the one who fills the place of the
uninformed say the "Amen" at your giving
of thanks, since he does not know what you
are saying? 17 For you are giving thanks well
enough, but the other person is not edified.
18 I thank God that I speak in tongues more
than you all; 19 however, in the church I
desire to speak five words with my mind so
that I may instruct others also, rather than
ten thousand words in a tongue.

SEPTEMBER 5

Isaiah 1:1–2:22

1 The vision of Isaiah the son of Amoz
concerning Judah and Jerusalem, which
he beheld in the days of Uzziah, Jotham,
Ahaz, *and* Hezekiah, kings of Judah.
2 Hear, O heavens, and give ear, O earth;
For Yahweh speaks,
"Sons I have reared and raised up,
But they have transgressed against Me.
3 "An ox knows its owner,
And a donkey its master's manger,
But Israel does not know;
My people do not perceive."

4 Alas, sinful nation,
People heavy with iniquity,
Seed of evildoers,
Sons who act corruptly!

They have forsaken Yahweh;
They have spurned the
Holy One of Israel;
They have become estranged
from Him.

5 Where will you be stricken again,
As you continue in *your* rebellion?
The whole head is sick,
And the whole heart is faint.
6 From the sole of the foot
even to the head
There is nothing sound in it,
Only bruises, wounds,
and raw wounds,
Not pressed out, not bandaged,
Not softened with oil.

7 Your land is desolate;
Your cities are burned with fire;
Your fields—strangers are devouring
them in your presence;
It is desolate, as overthrown
by strangers.
8 The daughter of Zion is left like
a shelter in a vineyard,
Like a watchman's hut in a cucumber
field, like a besieged city.
9 Unless Yahweh of hosts
Had left us a few survivors,
We would be like Sodom,
We would be like Gomorrah.

10 Hear the word of Yahweh,
You rulers of Sodom;
Give ear to the law of our God,
You people of Gomorrah.
11 "What are your multiplied
sacrifices to Me?"
Says Yahweh.
"I have had enough of burnt
offerings of rams
And the fat of fed cattle;
And in the blood of bulls, lambs,
or goats I take no pleasure.
12 "When you come to appear before Me,
Who requires of you this
trampling of My courts?
13 "Bring your worthless
offerings no longer,
Incense is an abomination to Me.
New moon and sabbath, the
calling of convocation—
I cannot endure wickedness
and the solemn assembly.
14 "My soul hates your new moon *festivals*
and your appointed times,
They have become a burden to Me;
I am weary of bearing *them.*
15 "So when you spread out
your hands *in prayer*,
I will hide My eyes from you;
Indeed, even though you
multiply prayers,
I will not listen.
Your hands are full of blood.

16 "Wash yourselves, purify yourselves;
Remove the evil of your deeds
from before My eyes.
Cease to do evil,
17 Learn to do good;
Seek justice,
Reprove the ruthless,
Execute justice for the orphan,
Plead for the widow.

18 "Come now, and let us reason together,"
Says Yahweh,
"Though your sins are as scarlet,
They will be as white as snow;
Though they are red like crimson,
They will be like wool.
19 "If you are willing and obey,
You will eat the best of the land;
20 But if you refuse and rebel,
You will be eaten by the sword."
For the mouth of Yahweh has spoken.
21 How the faithful city has
become a harlot,
She *who* was full of justice!
Righteousness once lodged in her,
But now murderers.
22 Your silver has become dross,
Your drink diluted with water.
23 Your rulers are rebels
And companions of thieves;
Everyone loves a bribe
And pursues rewards.
They do not execute justice
for the orphan,
Nor does the widow's plea
come before them.

24 Therefore the Lord, Yahweh of hosts,
The Mighty One of Israel, declares,
"Ah, I will be comforted
concerning My adversaries,
And I will avenge Myself
on My enemies.

25 “I will also turn My hand against you,
And will smelt away your
dross as with lye
And will remove all your alloy.
26 “Then I will have your judges
return as at the first,
And your counselors as
at the beginning;
Afterwards you will be called
the city of righteousness,
A faithful town.”

27 Zion will be redeemed with justice
And her repentant ones
with righteousness.
28 But transgressors and sinners
will be broken together,
And those who forsake Yahweh
will come to an end.
29 For you will be ashamed of the
oaks which you have desired,
And you will be humiliated
because of the gardens
which you have chosen.
30 For you will be like an oak
whose leaf withers away
Or as a garden that has no water.
31 And the strong man will
become tinder,
His work also a spark.
Thus they shall both burn together,
And there will be none
to quench *them.*

2 The word which Isaiah the son of Amoz
beheld concerning Judah and Jerusalem.
2 Now it will be that
In the last days
The mountain of the house of Yahweh
Will be established as the
head of the mountains,
And will be lifted up above the hills;
And all the nations will stream to it.
3 And many peoples will come and say,
“Come, let us go up to the
mountain of Yahweh,
To the house of the God of Jacob,
That He may instruct us from His ways
And that we may walk in His paths.”
For from Zion the law will go forth
And the word of Yahweh
from Jerusalem.
4 And He will judge between the nations,
And will render decisions
for many peoples;
And they will hammer their swords
into plowshares and their
spears into pruning hooks.
Nation will not lift up sword
against nation,
And never again will they learn war.
5 Come, house of Jacob, and let us
walk in the light of Yahweh.
6 For You have abandoned Your
people, the house of Jacob,
Because they are filled *with
influences* from the east,
And *they are* soothsayers
like the Philistines,
And they strike *bargains* with
the children of foreigners.
7 Their land has also been filled
with silver and gold,
And there is no end to their treasures;
Their land has also been
filled with horses,
And there is no end to their chariots.
8 Their land has also been
filled with idols;
They worship the work of their hands,
That which their fingers have made.
9 So the *common* man has
been bowed down,
And the man *of importance*
has been made low,
But do not forgive them.
10 Enter the rock and hide in the dust
From the dread of Yahweh and from
the splendor of His majesty.
11 The lofty look of man will be made low,
And the men made high
will be bowed down,
And Yahweh alone will be
exalted in that day.

12 For Yahweh of hosts will have
a day *of reckoning*
Against everyone who is
proud and high
And against everyone who is lifted up,
That he may be made low.
13 And *it will be* against all the cedars of
Lebanon that are high and lifted up,
Against all the oaks of Bashan,
14 Against all the high mountains,
Against all the hills that are lifted up,
15 Against every lofty tower,
Against every fortified wall,
16 Against all the ships of Tarshish
And against all the desirable craft.

17 The loftiness of man will
be bowed down,
And the men who are high
will be made low;
And Yahweh alone will be
exalted in that day,
18 But the idols will completely vanish.
19 *Men* will go into caves of the rocks
And into holes of the ground
Before the dread of Yahweh
And the splendor of His majesty,
When He arises to make
the earth tremble.
20 In that day men will cast away
to the moles and the bats
Their idols of silver and
their idols of gold,
Which they made for
themselves to worship,
21 In order to go into the caverns
of the rocks and the
clefts of the cliffs
Before the dread of Yahweh and
the splendor of His majesty,
When He arises to make
the earth tremble.
22 Stop regarding man, whose breath
of life is in his nostrils;
For why should he be esteemed?

Psalm 105:1–6

1 Oh give thanks to Yahweh,
call upon His name;
Make known His acts
among the peoples.
2 Sing to Him, sing praises to Him;
Muse on all His wondrous deeds.
3 Boast in His holy name;
Let the heart of those who
seek Yahweh be glad.
4 Inquire of Yahweh and His strength;
Seek His face continually.
5 Remember His wondrous deeds
which He has done,
His miracles and the judgments
uttered by His mouth,
6 O seed of Abraham, His servant,
O sons of Jacob, His chosen ones!

Proverbs 24:23–25

23 These also are *sayings* of the wise.
To show partiality in
judgment is not good.
24 He who says to the wicked,
"You are righteous,"
Peoples will curse him, nations
will be indignant with him;
25 But to those who reprove the
wicked, it will be pleasant,
And a good blessing will
come upon them.

1 Corinthians 14:20–40

20 Brothers, do not be children in your
thinking; rather in evil be infants, but in
your thinking be mature. 21 In the Law it is
written, "BY MEN OF STRANGE TONGUES AND BY
THE LIPS OF STRANGERS I WILL SPEAK TO THIS
PEOPLE, AND EVEN SO THEY WILL NOT LISTEN
TO ME," says the Lord. 22 So then tongues are
for a sign, not to those who believe but to
unbelievers; but prophecy *is for a sign* not
to unbelievers but to those who believe.
23 Therefore if the whole church assembles
together and all speak in tongues, and
uninformed men or unbelievers enter, will
they not say that you are out of your mind?
24 But if all prophesy, and an unbeliever or
an uninformed man enters, he is convicted
by all, he is called to account by all; 25 the
secrets of his heart are disclosed; and so
he will fall on his face and worship God,
declaring that SURELY GOD IS AMONG YOU.

26 What is *the outcome* then, brothers?
When you assemble, each one has a psalm,
has a teaching, has a revelation, has a tongue,
has a translation. Let all things be done for
edification. 27 If anyone speaks in a tongue,
it should be by two or at the most three, and
each in turn, and one must translate; 28 but
if there is no translator, he must keep silent
in the church, and let him speak to himself
and to God. 29 And let two or three prophets
speak, and let the others pass judgment.
30 But if a revelation is made to another who
is seated, the first one must keep silent. 31 For
you can all prophesy one by one, so that all
may learn and all may be exhorted. 32 And
the spirits of prophets are subject to proph-
ets; 33 for God is not *a God* of confusion but
of peace, as in all the churches of the saints.

34 The women are to keep silent in the
churches, for they are not permitted to
speak, but are to subject themselves, just
as the Law also says. 35 But if they desire
to learn anything, let them ask their own
husbands at home, for it is disgraceful for
a woman to speak in church. 36 Was it from
you that the word of God *first* went forth?
Or has it arrived to you only?

[37] If anyone thinks he is a prophet or spiritual, let him recognize that the things which I write to you are the Lord's commandment. [38] But if anyone remains ignorant about *this,* he is ignored *by God.*

[39] Therefore, my brothers, earnestly desire to prophesy, and do not forbid to speak in tongues. [40] But all things must be done properly and in an orderly manner.

SEPTEMBER 6

Isaiah 3:1–4:6

3 For behold, the Lord, Yahweh
of hosts, is going to remove
from Jerusalem and Judah
Both supply and support, the
whole supply of bread
And the whole supply of water,
2 The mighty man and the man of war,
The judge and the prophet,
The diviner and the elder,
3 The commander of fifty and
the highly respected man,
The counselor and the
wise craftsman,
And the experienced enchanter.
4 And I will make young
men their princes,
And capricious children
will rule over them,
5 And the people will be oppressed,
Each one by another, and each
one by his neighbor;
The youth will overwhelm the elder
And the dishonorable,
the honorable.
6 When a man grasps his brother
in his father's house, *saying,*
"You have a cloak, you shall be our ruler,
And these ruins will be
under your hand,"
7 He will protest on that day, saying,
"I will not be *your* healer,
For in my house there is
neither bread nor cloak;
You should not appoint me
ruler of the people."
8 For Jerusalem has stumbled
and Judah has fallen,
Because their tongue and their
deeds are against Yahweh,
To rebel against His glorious presence.
9 The expression of their faces
answers against them,
And they declare their sin like Sodom;
They do not *even* conceal *it.*
Woe to their soul!
For they have dealt out evil
on themselves.
10 Say to the righteous that *it
will go* well *with them,*
For they will eat the fruit
of their deeds.
11 Woe to the wicked! *It will
go* badly *with him,*
For what he has dealt out
will be done to him.
12 O My people! Their
taskmasters are infants,
And women rule over them.
O My people! Those who guide
you lead *you* astray
And swallow up the way of your paths.

13 Yahweh takes His stand to contend,
And stands to judge the peoples.
14 Yahweh enters into judgment with the
elders of His people and His princes,
"It is you who have consumed
the vineyard;
The *plunder* robbed of the
afflicted is in your houses.
15 "What do you mean by
crushing My people
And grinding the face of the afflicted?"
Declares Lord Yahweh of hosts.
16 Moreover, Yahweh said,
"Because the daughters of
Zion are haughty
And walk with outstretched
necks and seductive eyes,
And go along with mincing steps
And tinkle the bangles on their feet,
17 Therefore the Lord will smite the skull
of the daughters of Zion with scabs,
And Yahweh will make their
foreheads bare."

[18] In that day the Lord will remove the
beauty of *their* anklets, headbands, crescent
ornaments, [19] dangling earrings, bracelets,
veils, [20] headdresses, ankle chains, sashes,
perfume boxes, enchanted charms, [21] fin-
ger rings, nose rings, [22] festal robes, outer

tunics, cloaks, money purses, [23] hand mirrors, undergarments, turbans, and shawls.
24 Now it will be that instead of
sweet perfume there will
be *the smell of* rot;
Instead of a belt, a rope;
Instead of well-set hair, a
plucked-out scalp;
Instead of fine clothes, a
donning of sackcloth;
And branding instead of beauty.
25 Your men will fall by the sword
And your mighty ones in battle.
26 And her gates will lament and mourn,
And deserted she will sit
on the ground.

4 And seven women will take hold of one man in that day, saying, "We will eat our own bread and wear our own clothes, only let us be called by your name; take away our reproach!"

[2] In that day the Branch of Yahweh will be beautiful and glorious, and the fruit of the earth *will be* the pride and the honor of those of Israel who escape. [3] It will be that he who remains in Zion and is left in Jerusalem will be called holy—everyone who is written down for life in Jerusalem. [4] When the Lord has washed away the filth of the daughters of Zion and rinsed away the bloodshed of Jerusalem from her midst, by the spirit of judgment and the spirit of burning, [5] then Yahweh will create over the whole area of Mount Zion and over her convocation a cloud by day, even smoke, and the brightness of a flaming fire by night; for over all the glory will be a canopy. [6] And there will be a booth to *give* shade from the heat by day, and refuge and a hiding place from the storm and the rain.

Psalm 105:7–22

7 He is Yahweh our God;
His judgments are in all the earth.

8 He has remembered His
covenant forever,
The word which He commanded
for a thousand generations,
9 Which He cut with Abraham,
And His oath to Isaac.
10 Then He confirmed it to
Jacob for a statute,
To Israel as an everlasting covenant,
11 Saying, "To you I will give
the land of Canaan
As the portion of your inheritance,"
12 When they were only a few
men in number,
Of little account, and sojourners in it.
13 And they wandered about
from nation to nation,
From *one* kingdom to another people.
14 He permitted no man to oppress them,
And He reproved kings for their sakes:
15 "Do not touch My anointed ones,
And to My prophets do no evil."

16 And He called for a famine
upon the land;
He broke the whole staff of bread.
17 He sent a man before them,
Joseph, *who* was sold as a slave.
18 They afflicted his feet with fetters,
He himself was laid in irons;
19 Until the time that his
word came to pass,
The word of Yahweh refined him.
20 The king sent and released him,
The ruler of peoples *sent*
and set him free.
21 He set him up as lord of his house
And ruler over all his possessions,
22 To imprison his princes at will,
And that he might teach
his elders wisdom.

Proverbs 24:26–27

26 He kisses the lips
Who responds with right words.

27 Establish your work outside
And make it ready for
yourself in the field;
And afterwards, you shall
build your house.

1 Corinthians 15:1–28

15 Now I make known to you, brothers, the gospel which I proclaimed as good news to you, which also you received, in which also you stand, [2] by which also you are saved, if you hold fast the word which I proclaimed to you as good news, unless you believed for nothing.

[3] For I delivered to you as of first importance what I also received, that Christ died for our sins according to the Scriptures, [4] and that He was buried, and that He

was raised on the third day according to
the Scriptures, 5 and that He appeared to
Cephas, then to the twelve. 6 After that He
appeared to more than five hundred broth-
ers at one time, most of whom remain until
now, but some have fallen asleep. 7 After
that, He appeared to James, then to all the
apostles, 8 and last of all, as to one untimely
born, He appeared to me also. 9 For I am the
least of the apostles, and not worthy to be
called an apostle, because I persecuted the
church of God. 10 But by the grace of God I
am what I am, and His grace toward me did
not prove vain; but I labored even more than
all of them, yet not I, but the grace of God
with me. 11 Whether then *it was* I or they, so
we preach and so you believed.

12 Now if Christ is preached, that He has
been raised from the dead, how do some
among you say that there is no resurrection
of the dead? 13 But if there is no resurrection
of the dead, not even Christ has been raised.
14 And if Christ has not been raised, then
our preaching is vain, your faith also is vain.
15 Moreover we are even found *to be* false
witnesses of God, because we bore witness
against God that He raised Christ, whom
He did not raise, if in fact the dead are not
raised. 16 For if the dead are not raised, not
even Christ has been raised. 17 And if Christ
has not been raised, your faith is worthless;
you are still in your sins. 18 Then those also
who have fallen asleep in Christ have per-
ished. 19 If we have hoped in Christ in this
life only, we are of all men most to be pitied.

20 But now Christ has been raised from
the dead, the first fruits of those who have
fallen asleep. 21 For since by a man *came*
death, by a man also *came* the resurrection
of the dead. 22 For as in Adam all die, so also
in Christ all will be made alive. 23 But each
in his own order: Christ the first fruits, after
that those who are Christ's at His coming.
24 Then *comes* the end, when He hands
over the kingdom to the God and Father,
when He has abolished all rule and all
authority and power. 25 For He must reign
UNTIL HE HAS PUT ALL HIS ENEMIES UNDER
HIS FEET. 26 The last enemy to be abolished
is death. 27 For HE HAS PUT ALL THINGS IN
SUBJECTION UNDER HIS FEET. But when He
says, "All things are put in subjection," it
is evident that He is excepted who put all
things in subjection to Him. 28 And when all
things are subjected to Him, then the Son
Himself also will be subjected to the One
who subjected all things to Him, so that God
may be all in all.

SEPTEMBER 7

Isaiah 5:1–6:13

5 Let me sing now for my well-beloved
A song of my beloved
concerning His vineyard.
My well-beloved had a
vineyard on a fertile hill.
2 He dug it all around,
removed its stones,
And planted it with the choicest vine.
And He built a tower in
the middle of it
And also hewed out a wine vat in it;
Then He hoped for *it* to
produce *good* grapes,
But it produced *only* worthless ones.

3 "So now, O inhabitants of
Jerusalem and men of Judah,
Please judge between Me
and My vineyard.
4 "What more was there to do for My
vineyard that I have not done in it?
Why, *when* I hoped for *it* to
produce *good* grapes did it
produce worthless ones?
5 "So now let Me tell you what I am
going to do to My vineyard:
I will remove its hedge, and
it will be consumed;
I will break down its wall, and it
will become trampled ground.
6 "I will lay it waste;
It will not be pruned or hoed,
But briars and thorns
will come up.
I will also command the clouds
to rain no rain on it."

7 For the vineyard of Yahweh of
hosts is the house of Israel
And the men of Judah His
delightful plant.
Thus He hoped for justice,
but behold, bloodshed;

For righteousness, but behold,
a cry of distress.
8 Woe to those who add house to
house *and* join field to field,
Until there is no more room,
So that you have to live alone
in the midst of the land!
9 In my ears Yahweh of hosts *has
sworn,* "Surely, many houses
shall become desolate,
Even great and good ones,
without inhabitants.
10 "For ten acres of vineyard will
yield *only* one bath *of wine,*
And a homer of seed will yield
but an ephah *of grain.*"

11 Woe to those who rise early in
the morning that they may
pursue strong drink,
Who stay up late in the evening
that wine may inflame them!
12 And their banquets are *accompanied*
by lyre and harp, by tambourine
and flute, and by wine;
But they do not look upon
the deeds of Yahweh,
Nor do they see the work of
His hands.

13 Therefore My people go into exile
for their lack of knowledge;
And their honorable men
are famished,
And their multitude is
parched with thirst.
14 Therefore Sheol has enlarged its throat
and opened its mouth without limit;
And Jerusalem's majesty, her
multitude, her rumbling,
and the exultant within
her, descend *into it.*
15 So the *common* man will be
bowed down and the man of
importance will be made low,
The eyes of the lofty also
will be made low.
16 But Yahweh of hosts will be
lofty in judgment,
And the holy God will show
Himself holy in righteousness.
17 Then the lambs will graze
as in their pasture,
And sojourners will eat in the
waste places of the wealthy.

18 Woe to those who drag iniquity with
the cords of worthlessness,
And sin as if with cart ropes,
19 Who say, "Let Him hurry, let Him
hasten His work, that we may see *it;*
And let the counsel of the Holy
One of Israel draw near
And come to pass, that
we may know *it!*"
20 Woe to those who call evil
good and good evil,
Who substitute darkness for
light and light for darkness,
Who substitute bitter for sweet
and sweet for bitter!
21 Woe to those who are wise
in their own eyes
And understanding in their own sight!
22 Woe to those who are mighty
men in drinking wine
And valiant men in mixing
strong drink,
23 Who declare the wicked
righteous for a bribe,
And remove the righteous standing
of the ones who are righteous!
24 Therefore, as a tongue of fire
consumes stubble
And dry grass collapses into the flame,
So their root will become like rot and
their blossom blow away as dust;
For they have rejected the
law of Yahweh of hosts
And the word of the Holy One of
Israel they have spurned.
25 On this account, the anger of Yahweh
has burned against His people,
And He has stretched out His hand
against them and struck them down.
And the mountains trembled, and
their corpses lay like refuse in
the middle of the streets.
For all this His anger is
not turned back,
But His hand is still stretched out.

26 He will also lift up a standard
to the distant nations,
And will whistle for it from
the ends of the earth;
And behold, it will come
with speed swiftly.
27 No one in it is weary or stumbles,

None slumbers or sleeps;
Nor is the belt at its waist undone,
Nor its sandal strap broken.
28 Its arrows are sharp and all
its bows are bent;
The hoofs of its horses seem
like flint and its *chariot*
wheels like a whirlwind.
29 Its roaring is like a lioness, and
it roars like young lions;
It growls and seizes the prey
And carries *it* off with no
one to deliver *it*.
30 And it will growl over it in that day
like the roaring of the sea.
If one looks to the land, behold,
there is darkness *and* distress;
Even the light is darkened
by its clouds.

6 In the year of King Uzziah's death I saw
the Lord sitting on a throne, high and
lifted up, with the train of His robe filling
the temple. 2 Seraphim stood above Him,
each having six wings: with two he covered
his face, and with two he covered his feet,
and with two he flew. 3 And one called out
to another and said,
"Holy, Holy, Holy, is Yahweh of hosts;
The whole earth is full of His glory."
4 And the foundations of the thresholds
shook at the voice of him who called out,
while the house *of God* was filling with
smoke. 5 Then I said,
"Woe is me, for I am ruined!
For I am a man of unclean lips,
And I live among a people
of unclean lips;
For my eyes have seen the
King, Yahweh of hosts."
6 Then one of the seraphim flew to me
with a burning coal in his hand, which he
had taken from the altar with tongs. 7 And he
touched my mouth *with it* and said, "Behold,
this has touched your lips; and your iniquity
is taken away, and your sin is atoned for."
8 Then I heard the voice of the Lord,
saying, "Whom shall I send, and who will
go for Us?" Then I said, "Here am I. Send
me!" 9 He said, "Go, and tell this people:
'Keep on hearing, but do
not understand;
Keep on seeing, but do not know.'
10 "Render the hearts of this
people insensitive,
Their ears dull,
And their eyes dim,
Lest they see with their eyes,
And hear with their ears,
And understand with their hearts,
And return and be healed."
11 Then I said, "Lord, how long?" And He
said,
"Until cities are devastated *and*
without inhabitant,
Houses are without people,
And the land is devastated
to desolation,
12 And Yahweh has removed
men far away,
And the forsaken places are many
in the midst of the land.
13 "Yet there will be a tenth portion in it,
And it will again be *subject* to burning,
Like a terebinth or like an oak
Whose stump remains
when it is felled.
The holy seed is its stump."

Psalm 105:23–36

23 Then Israel came to Egypt;
And Jacob sojourned in
the land of Ham.
24 And He caused His people
to be very fruitful,
And He caused them to be stronger
than their adversaries.
25 He turned their heart to
hate His people,
To deal craftily with His slaves.
26 He sent Moses His servant,
And Aaron, whom He had chosen.
27 They set forth the words of
His signs among them,
And miracles in the land of Ham.
28 He sent darkness and made *it* dark;
And they did not rebel
against His words.
29 He turned their waters into blood
And caused their fish to die.
30 Their land swarmed with frogs
Even in the chambers of their kings.
31 He spoke, and there came
a swarm of flies
And gnats in all their territory.
32 He gave them hail for rain,
And flaming fire in their land.
33 He also struck down their
vines and their fig trees,

And He shattered the trees
of their territory.
34 He spoke, and locusts came,
And creeping locusts, without number,
35 And they ate up all vegetation
in their land,
And they ate up the fruit of their ground.
36 He also struck down all the
firstborn in their land,
The first of all their vigor.

Proverbs 24:28–29

28 Do not be a witness against your
neighbor without cause,
Nor deceive with your lips.
29 Do not say, "As he did to me
so I shall do to him;
I will render to the man
according to his work."

1 Corinthians 15:29–58

29 Otherwise, what will those do who are
baptized for the dead? If the dead are not
raised at all, why then are they baptized for
them? 30 Why are we also in danger every
hour? 31 I affirm, brothers, by the boasting
in you which I have in Christ Jesus our Lord,
I die daily. 32 If from human motives I fought
with wild beasts at Ephesus, what does it
profit me? If the dead are not raised, LET US
EAT AND DRINK, FOR TOMORROW WE DIE. 33 Do
not be deceived: "Bad company corrupts
good morals." 34 Become righteously sober-
minded, and stop sinning; for some have no
knowledge of God. I speak *this* to your shame.
35 But someone will say, "How are the dead
raised? And with what kind of body do they
come?" 36 You fool! That which you sow does
not come to life unless it dies; 37 and that which
you sow, you do not sow the body which is to
be, but a bare grain, perhaps of wheat or of
something else. 38 But God gives it a body just
as He wished, and to each of the seeds a body
of its own. 39 All flesh is not the same flesh, but
there is one *flesh* of men, and another flesh of
beasts, and another flesh of birds, and another
of fish. 40 There are also heavenly bodies and
earthly bodies, but the glory of the heavenly
is one, and the *glory* of the earthly is another.
41 There is one glory of the sun, and another
glory of the moon, and another glory of the
stars; for star differs from star in glory.
42 So also is the resurrection of the dead.
It is sown a corruptible *body*, it is raised an
incorruptible *body*; 43 it is sown in dishonor,
it is raised in glory; it is sown in weakness,
it is raised in power; 44 it is sown a natural
body, it is raised a spiritual body. If there is
a natural body, there is also a spiritual *body*.
45 So also it is written, "The first MAN, Adam,
BECAME A LIVING SOUL." The last Adam
became a life-giving spirit. 46 However, the
spiritual is not first, but the natural; then the
spiritual. 47 The first man is from the earth,
earthy; the second man is from heaven.
48 As is the earthy, so also are those who are
earthy; and as is the heavenly, so also are
those who are heavenly. 49 And just as we
have borne the image of the earthy, we will
also bear the image of the heavenly.
50 Now I say this, brothers, that flesh and
blood cannot inherit the kingdom of God,
nor does the corruptible inherit the incor-
ruptible. 51 Behold, I tell you a mystery: we
will not all sleep, but we will all be changed,
52 in a moment, in the twinkling of an eye,
at the last trumpet. For the trumpet will
sound, and the dead will be raised incor-
ruptible, and we will be changed. 53 For this
corruptible must put on the incorruptible,
and this mortal must put on immortality.
54 But when this corruptible puts on the
incorruptible, and this mortal puts on
immortality, then will come about the word
that is written, "DEATH IS SWALLOWED UP in
victory. 55 O DEATH, WHERE IS YOUR VICTORY?
O DEATH, WHERE IS YOUR STING?" 56 Now the
sting of death is sin, and the power of sin is
the law; 57 but thanks be to God, who gives
us the victory through our Lord Jesus Christ!
58 Therefore, my beloved brothers, be
steadfast, immovable, always abounding
in the work of the Lord, knowing that your
labor is not *in* vain in the Lord.

SEPTEMBER 8

Isaiah 7:1–8:22

7 Now it happened in the days of Ahaz, the
son of Jotham, the son of Uzziah, king
of Judah, that Rezin the king of Aram and
Pekah the son of Remaliah, king of Israel,
went up to Jerusalem to *wage* war against
it, but could not conquer it. 2 When it was
told to the house of David, saying, "The

Arameans have camped in Ephraim," his
heart and the hearts of his people shook as
the trees of the forest shake before the wind.
3 Then Yahweh said to Isaiah, "Go out
now to meet Ahaz, you and your son Shear-
jashub, at the end of the conduit of the upper
pool, to the highway of the fuller's field,
4 and say to him, 'Take care and stay quiet,
have no fear and do not be fainthearted
because of these two stubs of smoldering
firebrands, on account of the burning anger
of Rezin and Aram and the son of Remaliah.
5 Because Aram, *with* Ephraim and the son
of Remaliah, has counseled evil against you,
saying, 6 "Let us go up against Judah and ter-
rorize it, and make for ourselves a breach in
its walls and set up the son of Tabeel as king
in the midst of it," 7 thus says Lord Yahweh:
"It shall not stand, nor shall it happen. 8 For
the head of Aram is Damascus and the head
of Damascus is Rezin (now within another
sixty-five years Ephraim will be shattered,
so that it is no longer a people), 9 and the
head of Ephraim is Samaria and the head
of Samaria is the son of Remaliah. If you
do not establish your faith *in Yahweh*, you
surely shall not be established."'"
10 Then Yahweh spoke again to Ahaz,
saying, 11 "Ask a sign for yourself from
Yahweh your God; make *it* deep as Sheol or
high as heaven." 12 But Ahaz said, "I will not
ask, and I will not test Yahweh!" 13 Then he
said, "Listen now, O house of David! Is it too
slight a thing for you to try the patience of
men, that you will try the patience of my
God as well? 14 Therefore the Lord Himself
will give you a sign: Behold, the virgin will be
with child and bear a son, and she will call
His name Immanuel. 15 He will eat curds and
honey in order that He will know to refuse
evil and choose good. 16 For before the boy
will know to refuse evil and choose good,
the land whose two kings you dread will be
forsaken. 17 Yahweh will bring on you, on
your people, and on your father's house days
which have never come since the day that
Ephraim separated from Judah—the king
of Assyria!"
18 And it will be in that day, *that* Yahweh
will whistle for the fly that is in the remotest
part of the rivers of Egypt and for the bee
that is in the land of Assyria. 19 And they will
all come and rest upon the steep ravines, on
the crevices of the cliffs, on all the thorn
bushes, and on all the watering places.
20 In that day, the Lord will shave with
a razor—*one* hired from regions beyond
the River (*that is*, the king of Assyria)—the
head and the hair of the legs; and it will also
remove the beard.
21 And it will be in that day, *that* a man
may keep alive a heifer and a pair of sheep;
22 and because of the abundance of the milk
produced, he will eat curds, for everyone
that is left within the land will eat curds and
honey.
23 And it will be in that day, *that* every
place where there used to be one thousand
vines, *valued* at one thousand *shekels*
of silver, will become briars and thorns.
24 *People* will come there with bows and
arrows because all the land will be briars
and thorns. 25 As for all the hills which used
to be cultivated with the hoe, you will not go
there for fear of briars and thorns; but they
will become a place for pasturing oxen and
for sheep to trample.

8 Then Yahweh said to me, "Take for
yourself a large tablet and write on it in
ordinary letters: Concerning Maher-shalal-
hash-baz. 2 And I will take to Myself faithful
witnesses for testimony, Uriah the priest
and Zechariah the son of Jeberechiah."
3 Then I drew near to the prophetess, and
she conceived and bore a son. Then Yahweh
said to me, "Call his name Maher-shalal-
hash-baz, 4 for before the boy knows how
to cry out 'My father' or 'My mother,'
the wealth of Damascus and the spoil of
Samaria will be carried away before the
king of Assyria."
5 Again Yahweh spoke to me further,
saying,

6 "Inasmuch as these people
have rejected the gently
flowing waters of Shiloah
And rejoice in Rezin and
the son of Remaliah;
7 Now therefore, behold, the Lord is
about to bring on them the mighty
and abundant waters of the River—
The king of Assyria and all his glory;
And it will rise up over all its channels
and go over all its banks.
8 "Then it will sweep on into Judah; it
will overflow and pass through;
It will reach even to the neck;
And the spread of its wings will fill the
breadth of Your land, O Immanuel.

9 "Be broken, O peoples,
and be shattered;
And give ear, all remote
places of the earth.
Gird yourselves, yet be shattered;
Gird yourselves, yet be shattered.
10 "Devise counsel, but it will be thwarted;
Speak a word, but it will not stand,
For God is with us."
11 For thus Yahweh spoke to me with a
strong hand and disciplined me not to walk
in the way of this people, saying,
12 "You are not to say, '*It is* a conspiracy!'
In regard to all that this people
call a conspiracy;
And you are not to fear what they
fear, and you shall not tremble.
13 "It is Yahweh of hosts whom you
should regard as holy.
And He shall be your fear,
And He shall be your cause
of trembling.
14 "Then He shall become a sanctuary;
But to both the houses of Israel,
a stone to strike and a
rock to stumble over,
And a snare and a trap for the
inhabitants of Jerusalem.
15 "And many will stumble over them;
Then they will fall and be broken;
They will even be snared and caught."
16 Bind up the testimony, seal the law
among my disciples. 17 And I will wait for
Yahweh who is hiding His face from the
house of Jacob; and I will hope for Him.
18 Behold, I and the children whom Yahweh
has given me are for signs and wonders in
Israel from Yahweh of hosts, who dwells on
Mount Zion.
19 Now when they say to you, "Inquire
of the mediums and the spiritists who
whisper and mutter," should not a people
inquire of their God? *Should they inquire
of* the dead on behalf of the living? 20 To
the law and to the testimony! If they do not
speak according to this word, it is because
they have no dawn. 21 And they will
pass through the land hard-pressed and
hungry, and it will be that when they are
hungry, they will be angry and curse their
king and their God as they face upward.
22 Then they will look to the earth, and
behold, distress and darkness, the gloom
of anguish; and *they will be* banished into
thick darkness.

Psalm 105:37–45

37 Then He brought them out
with silver and gold,
And there was none among
His tribes who stumbled.
38 Egypt was glad when they went out,
For the dread of them had
fallen upon them.
39 He spread a cloud for a covering,
And fire to give light by night.
40 They asked, and He brought quail,
And He satisfied them with
the bread of heaven.
41 He opened the rock and
water flowed out;
It ran in the dry places *like* a river.
42 For He remembered His holy word
With Abraham His servant;
43 And He brought His people
out with joy,
His chosen ones with a shout of joy.
44 He gave them also the lands
of the nations,
That they might take possession of
the fruit of the peoples' labor,
45 So that they might keep His statutes
And observe His laws,
Praise Yah!

Proverbs 24:30–34

30 I passed by the field of the sluggard
And by the vineyard of the man
lacking a heart *of wisdom,*
31 And behold, it was completely
overgrown with thistles;
Nettles have covered its surface,
And its stone wall has been
torn down.
32 And I beheld, I set my heart upon it;
I saw, I received discipline.
33 "A little sleep, a little slumber,
A little folding of the hands to rest,"
34 Then your poverty will
come *as* a robber
And your want like an armed man.

1 Corinthians 16:1–24

16 Now concerning the collection for
the saints, as I directed the churches
of Galatia, so do you also. 2 On the first
day of every week each one of you is to
set *something* aside, saving whatever he
has prospered, so that no collections be
made when I come. 3 And when I arrive,
whomever you may approve, I will send

them with letters to carry your gracious gift to Jerusalem, 4 and if it is fitting for me to go also, they will go with me.

5 But I will come to you after I go through Macedonia, for I am going through Macedonia; 6 and perhaps I will stay with you, or even spend the winter, so that you may send me on my way wherever I may go. 7 For I do not wish to see you now *just* in passing, for I hope to remain with you for some time, if the Lord permits. 8 But I will remain in Ephesus until Pentecost, 9 for a wide and effective door has opened to me, and there are many adversaries.

10 Now if Timothy comes, take care that he is with you without fear, for he is doing the Lord's work, as I also am. 11 So let no one despise him. But send him on his way in peace, so that he may come to me, for I expect him with the brothers.

12 Now concerning Apollos our brother, I encouraged him greatly to come to you with the brothers, and it was not at all *his* desire to come now, but he will come when he has opportunity.

13 Be watchful, stand firm in the faith, act like men, be strong. 14 Let all that you do be done in love.

15 Now I exhort you, brothers (you know the household of Stephanas, that they were the first fruits of Achaia, and that they have devoted themselves for service to the saints), 16 that you also be in subjection to such men and to everyone who helps in the work and labors. 17 And I rejoice over the coming of Stephanas and Fortunatus and Achaicus, because they have supplied what was lacking on your part. 18 For they have refreshed my spirit and yours. Therefore recognize such men.

19 The churches of Asia greet you. Aquila and Prisca greet you heartily in the Lord, with the church that is in their house. 20 All the brothers greet you. Greet one another with a holy kiss.

21 The greeting is in my own hand—Paul. 22 If anyone does not love the Lord, he is to be accursed. Maranatha. 23 The grace of the Lord Jesus be with you. 24 My love be with you all in Christ Jesus. Amen.

SEPTEMBER 9

Isaiah 9:1–10:34

9 But there will be no *more* gloom for her who was in anguish; in earlier times He treated the land of Zebulun and the land of Naphtali with contempt, but later on He shall make *it* glorious, by the way of the sea, on the other side of Jordan, Galilee of the Gentiles.

2 The people who walk in darkness
Will see a great light;
Those who live in the land of
the shadow of death,
The light will shine on them.
3 You shall multiply the nation,
You shall make great their gladness;
They will be glad in Your presence
As with the gladness of harvest,
As men rejoice when they
divide the spoil.
4 For You shall shatter the yoke
of their burden and the
staff on their shoulders,
The rod of their taskmaster, as
at the battle of Midian.
5 For every boot of the booted warrior
in the rumbling *of battle*,
And cloak rolled in blood, will be
for burning, fuel for the fire.
6 For a child will be born to us,
a son will be given to us;
And the government will
rest on His shoulders;
And His name will be called Wonderful
Counselor, Mighty God,
Eternal Father, Prince of Peace.
7 There will be no end to the increase
of *His* government or of peace,
On the throne of David and
over his kingdom,
To establish it and to uphold it
with justice and righteousness
From then on and forevermore.
The zeal of Yahweh of hosts
will accomplish this.
8 The Lord sends a message
against Jacob,
And it falls on Israel.
9 And all the people know *it*,
That is, Ephraim and the
inhabitants of Samaria,
Saying in lofty pride and in
arrogance of heart:

10 "The bricks have fallen down,
But we will rebuild with cut stones;
The sycamores have been cut in pieces,
But we will replace *them* with cedars."
11 Therefore Yahweh exalts against
them adversaries from Rezin
And incites their enemies,
12 The Arameans on the east and
the Philistines on the west;
And they devour Israel
with gaping jaws.
In *spite of* all this, His anger
does not turn back,
And His hand is still stretched out.

13 Yet the people do not turn back
to Him who struck them,
Nor do they seek Yahweh of hosts.
14 So Yahweh cuts off head
and tail from Israel,
Both palm branch and
bulrush in a single day.
15 The head is the elder and the
highly respected man,
And the prophet who teaches
falsehood is the tail.
16 For those who guide this people
are leading *them* astray;
And those who are guided by them
are brought to confusion.
17 Therefore the Lord is not glad
in their choice men,
Nor does He have compassion on
their orphans or their widows;
For every one of them is
godless and an evildoer,
And every mouth is speaking
wicked foolishness.
In *spite of* all this, His anger
does not turn back,
And His hand is still stretched out.

18 For wickedness burns like a fire;
It consumes briars and thorns;
It even sets the thickets of
the forest aflame,
And they roll upward in a
column of smoke.
19 By the fury of Yahweh of hosts
the land is burned up,
And the people are like fuel
for the fire;
No man spares his brother.
20 They slice off *what is* on the right
hand but *still* are hungry,
And they eat *what is* on the left
hand but they are not satisfied;
Each of them eats the flesh
of his own arm.
21 Manasseh *devours* Ephraim,
and Ephraim Manasseh,
And together they are against Judah.
In *spite of* all this, His anger
does not turn back,
And His hand is still stretched out.

10 Woe to those who enact evil statutes
And to those who constantly
record mischief,
2 So as to turn the poor away
from *their* cause
And rob the afflicted of My
people of *their* justice,
So that widows may be their spoil
And that they may plunder
the orphans.
3 Now what will you do in
the day of visitation,
And in the devastation which
will come from afar?
To whom will you flee for help?
And where will you leave your glory?
4 Nothing *remains* but to crouch
among the captives
Or fall among those killed.
In *spite of* all this, His anger
does not turn back
And His hand is still stretched out.
5 Woe to Assyria, the rod of My anger
And the staff in whose hands
is My indignation,
6 I send it against a godless nation
And command it against the
people of My fury
To capture spoil and to seize plunder,
And to trample them down
like mud in the streets.
7 But it does not intend *to*
act in this way,
And it does not think in its
heart in this way,
Rather, *what is* in its heart is to destroy
And to cut off many nations.
8 For it says, "Are not my
princes all kings?
9 "Is not Calno like Carchemish,
Or Hamath like Arpad,
Or Samaria like Damascus?
10 "As my hand has reached to the
kingdoms of the idols,

Whose graven images *were*
greater than those of
Jerusalem and Samaria,
11 Shall I not do to Jerusalem
and her images
Just as I have done to Samaria
and her idols?"

12 So it will be that when the Lord has
completed all His work on Mount Zion and
on Jerusalem, *He will say*, "I will punish
the fruit of the arrogant heart of the king
of Assyria and the pomp of his eyes *which
are* raised high." 13 For he has said,

"By the power of my hand and
by my wisdom I did *this*,
For I have understanding;
And I removed the boundaries
of the peoples
And plundered their treasures,
And like a mighty man I brought
down *their* inhabitants,
14 And my hand reached for the wealth
of the peoples like a nest,
And as one gathers abandoned
eggs, I gathered all the earth;
And there was not one that flapped its
wing or opened *its* beak or chirped."

15 Is the axe to boast itself over the
one who chops with it?
Is the saw to magnify itself over
the one who wields it?
That would be like a rod
wielding those who lift it,
Or like a staff lifting *him
who* is not wood.
16 Therefore the Lord, Yahweh of
hosts, will send a wasting disease
among his stout warriors;
And under his glory a fire will be
kindled like a burning flame.
17 And the light of Israel will become
a fire and his Holy One a flame,
And it will burn and devour his thorns
and his briars in a single day.
18 And He will bring to an end the glory
of his forest and of his fruitful
orchard, both soul and body,
And it will be as when a sick
man wastes away.
19 And the rest of the trees of his forest
will be so small in number
That a child could write them down.

20 Now it will be in that day, *that* the
remnant of Israel and those of the house of
Jacob who have escaped, will never again
rely on the one who struck them, but will
truly rely on Yahweh, the Holy One of Israel.

21 A remnant will return, the remnant
of Jacob, to the mighty God.
22 For though your people, O Israel,
may be like the sand of the sea,
Only a remnant within
them will return;
A *destructive* end is decreed,
overflowing with righteousness.

23 For a complete destruction, one that is
decreed, Lord Yahweh of hosts will do in the
midst of the whole land.

24 Therefore thus says Lord Yahweh of
hosts, "O My people who inhabit Zion,
do not fear the Assyrian who strikes you
with the rod and lifts up his staff against
you, the way Egypt *did*. 25 For in a very
little while My indignation *against you*
will end and My anger *will be directed* to
their destruction." 26 And Yahweh of hosts
will waken a scourge against him like the
slaughter of Midian at the rock of Oreb;
and His staff will be over the sea and He
will lift it up the way *He did* in Egypt. 27 So
it will be in that day, *that* his burden will
be removed from your shoulders and his
yoke from your neck, and the yoke will be
broken because of fatness.

28 He has come against Aiath,
He has passed through Migron;
At Michmash he deposited his baggage.
29 They have gone through
the pass, *saying*,
"Geba will be our lodging place."
Ramah trembles, and Gibeah
of Saul has fled away.
30 Cry aloud with your voice,
O daughter of Gallim!
Pay attention, Laishah *and*
afflicted Anathoth!
31 Madmenah has fled.
The inhabitants of Gebim
have sought refuge.
32 Yet today he will stand at Nob;
He shakes his fist at the mountain
of the daughter of Zion,
the hill of Jerusalem.

33 Behold, the Lord, Yahweh of
hosts, will lop off the boughs
with a terrible crash;
Those also who are high in
stature will be cut in pieces

And those who are lofty
will be made low.
34 He will cut down the thickets of
the forest with an iron *axe,*
And Lebanon will fall by
the Mighty One.

Psalm 106:1–5

1 Praise Yah!
Oh give thanks to Yahweh,
for He is good;
For His lovingkindness
endures forever.
2 Who can speak of the mighty
deeds of Yahweh,
Or can make all His praise to be heard?
3 How blessed are those
who keep justice,
And he who does righteousness
at all times!

4 Remember me, O Yahweh, in *Your*
favor toward Your people;
Visit me with Your salvation,
5 That I may see the goodness
of Your chosen ones,
That I may rejoice in the
gladness of Your nation,
That I may boast with
Your inheritance.

Proverbs 25:1–2

25 These also are proverbs of Solomon
which the men of Hezekiah, king of
Judah, transcribed.
2 It is the glory of God to
conceal a matter,
But the glory of kings is to
search out a matter.

2 Corinthians 1:1–24

1 Paul, an apostle of Christ Jesus by the will
of God, and Timothy *our* brother,
To the church of God which is at Corinth
with all the saints who are throughout
Achaia:
2 Grace to you and peace from God our
Father and the Lord Jesus Christ.
3 Blessed *be* the God and Father of our
Lord Jesus Christ, the Father of mercies
and God of all comfort, 4 who comforts us
in all our affliction so that we will be able
to comfort those who are in any affliction
with the comfort with which we ourselves
are comforted by God. 5 For just as the
sufferings of Christ abound to us, so also
our comfort abounds through Christ. 6 But
whether we are afflicted, it is for your
comfort and salvation; or whether we are
comforted, it is for your comfort, which is
working in *your* perseverance in the same
sufferings which we also suffer. 7 And our
hope for you is firmly grounded, knowing
that as you are sharers of our sufferings, so
also you are *sharers* of our comfort.
8 For we do not want you to be unaware,
brothers, of our affliction which came *to us*
in Asia, that we were burdened excessively,
beyond our strength, so that we despaired
even to live. 9 Indeed, we had the sentence
of death within ourselves so that we would
not have confidence in ourselves, but in
God who raises the dead; 10 who rescued
us from so great a *peril of* death, and will
rescue *us,* He on whom we have set our
hope. And He will yet rescue us, 11 you also
joining in helping *us* through your prayers
on our behalf, so that thanks may be given
on our behalf by many persons for the
gracious gift bestowed on us through *the*
prayers of many.
12 For our boasting is this: the testimony
of our conscience, that in holiness and godly
sincerity, not in fleshly wisdom but in the
grace of God, we have conducted ourselves
in the world, and especially toward you.
13 For we write nothing else to you than
what you read and understand, and I hope
you will understand until the end, 14 just as
you also partially did understand us, that we
are your reason for boasting as you also are
ours, in the day of our Lord Jesus.
15 And in this confidence I intended
at first to come to you, so that you might
receive grace twice; 16 that is, to pass
your way into Macedonia, and again
from Macedonia to come to you, and by
you to be helped on my journey to Judea.
17 Therefore, was I vacillating when I
intended to do this? Or what I purpose,
do I purpose according to the flesh, so that
with me there will be yes, yes and no, no
at the same time? 18 But as God is faithful,
our word to you is not yes and no. 19 For
the Son of God, Jesus Christ, who was
preached among you by us—by me and
Silvanus and Timothy—was not yes and
no, but has become yes in Him. 20 For as
many as are the promises of God, in Him
they are yes. Therefore also through Him is

our Amen to the glory of God through us. 21 Now He who establishes us with you in Christ and anointed us is God, 22 who also sealed us and gave the pledge of the Spirit in our hearts.

23 But I call God as witness to my soul, that to spare you I did not come again to Corinth. 24 Not that we lord it over your faith, but are workers with you for your joy; for in your faith you are standing firm.

The Word is both a glass to show us the spots of our soul and a laver to wash them away.

— THOMAS WATSON

SEPTEMBER 10

Isaiah 11:1–12:6

11 Then a shoot will spring
from the stem of Jesse,
And a branch from his
roots will bear fruit.
2 The Spirit of Yahweh will rest on Him,
The spirit of wisdom and
understanding,
The spirit of counsel and might,
The spirit of knowledge and
the fear of Yahweh.
3 And He will delight in the
fear of Yahweh,
And He will not judge by
what His eyes see,
Nor render a decision by
what His ears hear;
4 But with righteousness He
will judge the poor,
And decide with uprightness for
the afflicted of the earth;
And He will strike the earth
with the rod of His mouth,
And with the breath of His lips He
will put the wicked to death.
5 Also righteousness will be the
belt about His loins,
And faithfulness the belt
about His waist.

6 And the wolf will dwell with the lamb,
And the leopard will lie down
with the young goat,
And the calf and the young lion
and the fatling together;
And a young boy will lead them.
7 Also the cow and the bear will graze,
Their young will lie down together,
And the lion will eat straw like the ox.
8 And the nursing baby will play
by the hole of the cobra,
And the weaned child will put
his hand on the viper's den.
9 They will do no evil nor act corruptly
in all My holy mountain,
For the earth will be full of the
knowledge of Yahweh
As the waters cover the sea.
10 Then it will be in that day,
That the nations will seek
the root of Jesse,
Who will stand as a standard
for the peoples;
And His resting place will be glorious.

11 Then it will be in that day,
that the Lord
Will again acquire the second
time with His hand
The remnant of His people,
who will remain,
From Assyria, Egypt, Pathros,
Ethiopia, Elam, Shinar, Hamath,
And from the coastlands of the sea.
12 And He will lift up a standard
for the nations
And assemble the banished
ones of Israel,
And will gather the scattered of Judah
From the four corners of the earth.
13 Then the jealousy of
Ephraim will depart,
And those who assail Judah
will be cut off;
Ephraim will not be jealous of Judah,
And Judah will not assail Ephraim.
14 And they will swoop down on the
slopes of the Philistines on the west;

Together they will plunder
the sons of the east;
They will stretch out their hands
over Edom and Moab,
And the sons of Ammon
will obey them.
15 And Yahweh will devote to destruction
The tongue of the Sea of Egypt;
And He will wave His hand
over the River
With His scorching wind;
And He will strike it into seven streams
And make *men* walk over dry-shod.
16 And there will be a highway
from Assyria
For the remnant of His people
who will remain,
Just as there was for Israel
In the day that they came up
out of the land of Egypt.

12 Then you will say in that day,
"I will give thanks to You, O Yahweh;
For although You were angry with me,
Your anger is turned away,
And You comfort me.
2 "Behold, God is my salvation,
I will trust and not dread;
For Yah—Yahweh *Himself*—is
my strength and song,
And He has become my salvation."
3 Therefore you will joyously draw water
From the springs of salvation.
4 And in that day you will say,
"Give thanks to Yahweh,
call on His name.
Make known His deeds
among the peoples;
Make *them* remember that
His name is exalted."
5 Praise Yahweh in song, for He
has done majestic things;
Let this be known throughout
the earth.
6 Cry aloud and shout for joy,
O inhabitant of Zion,
For great in your midst is the
Holy One of Israel.

Psalm 106:6–18

6 We have sinned with our fathers,
We have committed iniquity,
we have acted wickedly.
7 Our fathers in Egypt did not
consider Your wondrous deeds;
They did not remember Your
abundant lovingkindnesses,
But they rebelled by the
sea, at the Red Sea.
8 Yet He saved them for the
sake of His name,
That He might make His might known.
9 Thus He rebuked the Red
Sea and it dried up,
And He led them through the deeps,
as through the wilderness.
10 So He saved them from the hand
of the one who hated *them*,
And redeemed them from the
hand of the enemy.
11 The waters covered their adversaries;
Not one of them was left.
12 Then they believed His words;
They sang His praise.

13 They quickly forgot His works;
They did not wait for His counsel,
14 But craved intensely in the wilderness,
And put God to the test
in the wasteland.
15 So He gave them their request,
But sent a wasting disease
against their lives.

16 Then they became envious
of Moses in the camp,
And of Aaron, the holy one of Yahweh,
17 The earth opened and
swallowed up Dathan,
And covered up the
company of Abiram.
18 And a fire burned up in their company;
The flame consumed the wicked.

Proverbs 25:3–5

3 *As* the heavens for height and
the earth for depth,
So the heart of kings is unsearchable.
4 Take away the dross from the silver,
And there comes out a
vessel for the smith;
5 Take away the wicked before the king,
And his throne will be established
in righteousness.

2 Corinthians 2:1–17

2 But I determined this for my own sake,
that I would not come to you again in
sorrow. 2 For if I cause you sorrow, who then
makes me glad but the one whom I made

sorrowful? 3 And this is the very thing I wrote
you, so that when I came, I would not have
sorrow from those who ought to make me
rejoice; having confidence in you all that my
joy would be *the joy* of you all. 4 For out of
much affliction and anguish of heart I wrote
to you with many tears; not so that you would
be made sorrowful, but that you might know
the love which I have abundantly for you.

5 But if any has caused sorrow, he has
caused sorrow not to me, but in some
degree—in order not to say too much—to
all of you. 6 Sufficient for such a one is
this punishment which *was inflicted* by
the majority, 7 so that on the contrary you
should rather graciously forgive and com-
fort *him*, lest such a one be swallowed up by
excessive sorrow. 8 Therefore I encourage
you to reaffirm *your* love for him. 9 For to this
end also I wrote, so that I might know your
proven character, whether you are obedient
in all things. 10 But one whom you graciously
forgive anything, I *graciously forgive* also.
For indeed what I have graciously forgiven,
if I have graciously forgiven anything, *I did
it* for your sakes in the presence of Christ,
11 so that no advantage would be taken of
us by Satan, for we are not ignorant of his
schemes.

12 Now when I came to Troas for the
gospel of Christ and when a door was
opened for me in the Lord, 13 I had no rest
for my spirit, not finding Titus my brother.
But saying farewell to them, I went on to
Macedonia.

14 But thanks be to God, who always
leads us in triumphal procession in Christ,
and manifests through us the aroma of the
knowledge of Him in every place. 15 For we
are a fragrance of Christ to God among those
who are being saved and among those who
are perishing; 16 to the one an aroma from
death to death, to the other an aroma from
life to life. And who is sufficient for these
things? 17 For we are not like many, peddling
the word of God, but as from sincerity, but
as from God, in the sight of God, we speak
in Christ.

SEPTEMBER 11

Isaiah 13:1–14:32

13 The oracle concerning Babylon which
Isaiah the son of Amoz beheld.

2 Lift up a standard on the bare hill,
Heighten your voice at them,
Wave the hand that they may
enter the doors of the nobles.
3 I have commanded My set
apart ones,
I have even called My mighty warriors,
My proudly exulting ones,
To *execute* My anger.
4 A sound of tumult on the mountains,
Like that of many people!
A sound of the rumbling of kingdoms,
Of nations gathered together!
Yahweh of hosts is mustering
the host for battle.
5 They are coming from a far country,
From the end of the sky,
Yahweh and His instruments
of indignation,
To wreak destruction *on*
the whole land.
6 Wail, for the day of Yahweh is near!
It will come as destruction
from the Almighty.
7 Therefore all hands will fall limp,
And every man's heart will melt.
8 They will be terrified,
Pains and labor pangs will
take hold of *them*;
They will writhe like a woman in labor,
They will look at one another
in astonishment,
Their faces aflame.
9 Behold, the day of Yahweh is coming,
Cruel, with fury and burning anger,
To make the land a desolation;
And He will exterminate
its sinners from it.
10 For the stars of heaven and
their constellations
Will not flash forth their light;
The sun will be dark when it rises
And the moon will not shed its light.
11 Thus I will punish the world for its evil
And the wicked for their iniquity;
I will also put an end to the
pride of the arrogant
And bring low the lofty
pride of the ruthless.
12 I will make mortal man
scarcer than fine gold

And mankind than the gold of Ophir.
13 Therefore I will make the
heavens tremble,
And the earth will be shaken
from its place
At the fury of Yahweh of hosts
In the day of His burning anger.
14 And it will be that like a hunted gazelle,
Or like sheep with none
to gather *them,*
They will each turn to his own people,
And each one flee to his own land.
15 Anyone who is found will
be pierced through,
And anyone who is captured
will fall by the sword.
16 Their infants also will be
dashed to pieces
Before their eyes;
Their houses will be plundered
And their wives ravished.

17 Behold, I am going to awaken
the Medes against them,
Who will not think about silver
or take pleasure in gold.
18 And *their* bows will dash the
young men to pieces,
They will not even have compassion
on the fruit of the womb,
Nor will their eye pity children.
19 And it will be that Babylon, the
beauty of kingdoms, the honor
of the Chaldeans' pride,
Will be as when God overthrew
Sodom and Gomorrah.
20 It will never be inhabited or dwelt in
from generation to generation;
Nor will the Arab pitch *his* tent there,
Nor will shepherds make *their*
flocks lie down there.
21 But desert creatures will
lie down there,
And their houses will be full of owls;
Ostriches also will dwell there, and
shaggy goats will leap there.
22 And hyenas will howl in
their fortified towers
And jackals in their luxurious palaces.
Her *fateful* time also will soon come
And her days will not be prolonged.

14 When Yahweh will have compassion
on Jacob and again choose Israel, and
put them in their own land, then sojourners
will join them and attach themselves to the
house of Jacob. 2 And the peoples will take
them along and bring them to their place,
and the house of Israel will possess them
as an inheritance in the land of Yahweh
for *their* male and female slaves; and they
will take their captors captive and will have
dominion over their taskmasters.
3 And it will be in the day when Yahweh
gives you rest from your pain and turmoil
and harsh slavery in which you have been
enslaved, 4 that you will take up this taunt
against the king of Babylon, and say,
"How the taskmaster has ceased,
And how fury has ceased!
5 "Yahweh has broken the
staff of the wicked,
The scepter of rulers
6 Which used to strike the peoples in
fury with unceasing strokes,
Which had dominion over
the nations in anger with
unrestrained persecution.
7 "The whole earth is at rest *and* is quiet;
They break forth into shouts of joy.
8 "Even the cypress trees are glad
over you, *and* the cedars
of Lebanon, *saying,*
'Since you were laid low, no *tree*
cutter comes up against us.'
9 "Sheol from beneath trembles
excitedly over you to meet
you when you come;
It wakens for you the spirits of the
dead, all the leaders of the earth;
It raises all the kings of the
nations from their thrones.
10 "They will all answer and say to you,
'Even you have been made weak as we,
You have become like us.
11 'Your pride *and* the music of your harps
Have been brought down to Sheol;
Maggots are spread out *as*
your bed beneath you
And worms are your covering.'
12 "How you have fallen from heaven,
O star of the morning, son of the dawn!
You have been cut down to the earth,
You who have weakened the nations!
13 "But you said in your heart,
'I will ascend to heaven;
I will raise my throne above
the stars of God,
And I will sit on the mount of assembly
In the recesses of the north.

14 ‘I will ascend above the
heights of the clouds;
I will make myself like the Most High.’
15 “Nevertheless you will be
brought down to Sheol,
To the recesses of the pit.
16 “Those who see you will gaze at you,
They will carefully consider
you, *saying*,
‘Is this the man who made
the earth tremble,
Who caused kingdoms to quake,
17 Who made the world like a wilderness
And pulled down its cities,
Who did not allow his
prisoners to *go* home?’
18 “All the kings of the nations lie in glory,
Each in his own place.
19 “But you have been cast
out of your grave
Like an abhorred branch,
Clothed with those killed who
are pierced with a sword,
Who go down to the stones of the pit
Like a trampled corpse.
20 “You will not be united with
them in burial,
Because you have ruined your country,
You have killed your people.
May the seed of evildoers not
be called upon forever.
21 “Prepare for his sons a
place of slaughter
Because of the iniquity of their fathers.
They must not arise and take
possession of the earth
And fill the face of the
world with cities.”

22 “I will rise up against them,” declares
Yahweh of hosts, “and will cut off from
Babylon name and remnant, offspring and
posterity,” declares Yahweh. 23 “I will also
make it a possession for the hedgehog and
swamps of water, and I will sweep it with
the broom of destruction,” declares Yahweh
of hosts.

24 Yahweh of hosts has sworn saying,
“Surely, just as I have intended so it has hap-
pened, and just as I have counseled so it will
stand, 25 to break Assyria in My land, and I
will trod him down on My mountains. Then
his yoke will be removed from them and his
burden removed from their shoulder. 26 This
is the counsel that is counseled against the
whole earth; and this is the hand that is
stretched out against all the nations. 27 For
Yahweh of hosts has counseled, and who
can thwart *it*? And as for His stretched-out
hand, who can turn it back?”

28 In the year that King Ahaz died this
oracle came:

29 “Do not be glad, O Philistia, all of you,
Because the rod that struck
you is broken;
For from the serpent’s root a
viper will come out,
And its fruit will be a flying
fiery serpent.
30 “And the foremost of the poor will eat,
And the needy will lie
down in security;
I will put to death your
root with famine,
And it will kill off your remnant.
31 “Wail, O gate; cry, O city;
Melt away, O Philistia, all of you;
For smoke comes from the north,
And there is no straggler in his ranks.
32 “How then will one answer the
messengers of the nation?
That Yahweh has founded Zion,
And the afflicted of His people
will take refuge in it.”

Psalm 106:19–23

19 They made a calf in Horeb
And worshiped a molten image.
20 Thus they exchanged their glory
For the image of an ox that eats grass.
21 They forgot God their Savior,
Who had done great things in Egypt,
22 Wondrous deeds in the land of Ham
And awesome things by the Red Sea.
23 Therefore He said that He
would destroy them,
Had not Moses His chosen one
stood in the breach before Him,
To turn away His wrath from
eradicating *them*.

Proverbs 25:6–7

6 Do not promote your majesty in
the presence of the king,
And in the place of great
men do not stand;
7 For it is better that it be said
to you, “Come up here,”
Than for you to be placed lower
in the presence of a noble,
Whom your eyes have seen.

2 Corinthians 3:1–18

3 Are we beginning to commend ourselves
again? Or do we need, as some, letters
of commendation to you or from you? 2 You
are our letter, having been written in our
hearts, known and read by all men, 3 being
manifested that you are a letter of Christ,
ministered to by us, having been written
not with ink but with the Spirit of the living
God, not on tablets of stone but on tablets
of hearts of flesh.

4 And such confidence we have through
Christ toward God. 5 Not that we are suffi-
cient in ourselves to consider anything as
coming from ourselves, but our sufficiency
is from God, 6 who also made us sufficient
as ministers of a new covenant, not of the
letter but of the Spirit; for the letter kills,
but the Spirit gives life.

7 But if the ministry of death, in letters
having been engraved on stones, came with
glory, so that the sons of Israel could not
look intently at the face of Moses because
of the glory of his face, which was being
brought to an end, 8 how will the ministry
of the Spirit not be even more in glory?
9 For if the ministry of condemnation has
glory, much more does the ministry of
righteousness abound in glory. 10 For indeed
what had been glorious, in this case has no
glory because of the glory that surpasses *it*.
11 For if that which was being brought to an
end *was* with glory, much more that which
remains *is* in glory.

12 Therefore having such a hope, we use
great boldness, 13 and *are* not like Moses,
who used to put a veil over his face so that
the sons of Israel would not look intently at
the consequence of what was being brought
to an end. 14 But their minds were hardened;
for until this very day at the reading of the
old covenant the same veil remains unlifted,
because it is brought to an end in Christ.
15 But to this day whenever Moses is read, a
veil lies over their heart, 16 but WHENEVER a
person TURNS TO THE LORD, THE VEIL IS TAKEN
AWAY. 17 Now the Lord is the Spirit, and where
the Spirit of the Lord is, *there* is freedom.
18 But we all, with unveiled face, beholding
as in a mirror the glory of the Lord, are being
transformed into the same image from glory
to glory, just as from the Lord, the Spirit.

SEPTEMBER 12

Isaiah 15:1–16:14

15 The oracle concerning Moab.
Surely in a night Ar of Moab
is destroyed *and* ruined;
Surely in a night Kir of Moab
is destroyed *and* ruined.

2 They have gone up to the
temple and *to* Dibon, *even* to
the high places to weep.
Moab wails over Nebo and Medeba;
Everyone's head is bald *and*
every beard is cut off.

3 In their streets they have girded
themselves with sackcloth;
On their rooftops and in
their squares
Everyone is wailing,
dissolved in weeping.

4 Heshbon and Elealeh also
cry out,
Their voice is heard all
the way to Jahaz;
Therefore the armed men of
Moab make a loud shout;
His soul trembles within him.

5 My heart cries out for Moab;
Those who flee *from* her are as far
as Zoar *and* Eglath-shelishiyah,
For they go up the ascent
of Luhith weeping;
Surely on the road to Horonaim
they keep awake with crying in
distress over *their* destruction.

6 For the waters of Nimrim
are desolate.
Surely the grass is dried up, the tender
grass has completely ceased,
There is no green thing.

7 Therefore the abundance they
have made and stored up
They carry off over the
brook of Arabim.

8 For the cry has gone around
the territory of Moab,
Its wailing *goes* as far as Eglaim and
its wailing even to Beer-elim.

9 For the waters of Dimon
are full of blood;
Surely I will put added
woes upon Dimon,

A lion upon those of Moab who
have escaped and upon the
remnant of the land.

16 Send the *tribute* lamb to
the ruler of the land,
From Sela by way of the
wilderness to the mountain
of the daughter of Zion.
2 Then, like fleeing birds *or*
scattered nestlings,
The daughters of Moab will be
at the fords of the Arnon.
3 "Bring *us* counsel, make a decision;
Cast your shadow like
night at high noon;
Hide those banished, do not
reveal the one who flees.
4 "Let the banished of Moab
sojourn with you;
Be a hiding place to them
from the destroyer."
For the extortioner has come to an
end, destruction has ceased,
Oppressors have completely
disappeared from the land.
5 And a throne will be established
in lovingkindness,
And a judge will sit on it in
truth in the tent of David;
Moreover, he will seek justice
And be prompt in righteousness.

6 We have heard of the pride of
Moab, an excessive pride;
Even of his lofty pride, pride, and fury;
His idle boasts are false.
7 Therefore Moab will wail;
everyone of Moab will wail.
You will moan for the raisin
cakes of Kir-hareseth
As those who are utterly stricken.
8 For the fields of Heshbon
have languished, the vines
of Sibmah *as well*;
The lords of the nations have
trampled down its choice clusters
Which reached as far as Jazer *and*
wandered to the deserts;
Its tendrils spread themselves
out *and* passed over the sea.
9 Therefore I will weep bitterly for
Jazer, for the vine of Sibmah;
I will drench you with my tears,
O Heshbon and Elealeh;
For the shouting over your
summer fruits and your
harvest has fallen away.
10 Gladness and joy are taken away
from the fruitful orchard;
In the vineyards also there will be no
cries of joy or shouts of jubilation,
No treader treads out wine
in the presses,
For I have made the shouting to cease.
11 Therefore my inner being moans
like a harp for Moab
And my inward feelings
for Kir-hareseth.
12 So it will be when Moab appears,
When he wearies himself
upon *his* high place
And comes to his sanctuary to pray,
That he will not prevail.

13 This is the word which Yahweh spoke
earlier concerning Moab. 14 But now Yahweh
speaks, saying, "Within three years, as a
hired man would count them, the glory of
Moab will be dishonored along with all *his*
great population, and *his* remnant will be
very small *and* not mighty."

Psalm 106:24–31

24 Then they despised the pleasant land;
They did not believe in His word,
25 But grumbled in their tents;
They did not listen to the
voice of Yahweh.
26 So He swore to them
To make them fall in the wilderness,
27 And to make their seed fall
among the nations
And to scatter them in the lands.

28 They then joined themselves
to Baal-peor,
And ate sacrifices *offered to* the dead.
29 Thus they provoked *Him* to
anger with their actions,
And the plague broke out among them.
30 Then Phinehas stood up
and interceded,
And so the plague was checked.
31 And it was counted to him
for righteousness,
From generation to generation forever.

Proverbs 25:8–10

8 Do not go out hastily to
plead *your case*;

Lest, what will you do in the end,
When your neighbor humiliates you?
9 Plead your case with your neighbor,
And do not reveal the
secret of another,
10 Lest he who hears *it* bring
disgrace upon you,
And the bad report about you
will not turn away.

2 Corinthians 4:1–18

4 Therefore, since we have this ministry, as we received mercy, we do not lose heart, 2 but we have renounced the hidden things of shame, not walking in craftiness or adulterating the word of God, but by the manifestation of truth commending ourselves to every man's conscience in the sight of God. 3 And even if our gospel is veiled, it is veiled to those who are perishing, 4 in whose case the god of this age has blinded the minds of the unbelieving so that they might not see the light of the gospel of the glory of Christ, who is the image of God. 5 For we do not preach ourselves but Jesus Christ as Lord, and ourselves as your slaves for the sake of Jesus. 6 For God, who said, "Light shall shine out of darkness," is the One who has shone in our hearts to give the Light of the knowledge of the glory of God in the face of Christ.

7 But we have this treasure in earthen vessels, so that the surpassing greatness of the power will be of God and not from ourselves; 8 in every way afflicted, but not crushed; perplexed, but not despairing; 9 persecuted, but not forsaken; struck down, but not destroyed; 10 always carrying about in the body the dying of Jesus, so that the life of Jesus also may be manifested in our body. 11 For we who live are constantly being delivered over to death for Jesus' sake, so that the life of Jesus also may be manifested in our mortal flesh. 12 So death works in us, but life in you.

13 But having the same spirit of faith, according to what is written, "I BELIEVED, THEREFORE I SPOKE," we also believe, therefore we also speak, 14 knowing that He who raised the Lord Jesus will raise us also with Jesus and will present us with you. 15 For all things *are* for your sakes, so that the grace which is spreading to more and more people may cause the giving of thanks to abound to the glory of God.

16 Therefore we do not lose heart, but though our outer man is decaying, yet our inner man is being renewed day by day. 17 For our momentary, light affliction is working out for us an eternal weight of glory far beyond all comparison, 18 while we look not at the things which are seen, but at the things which are not seen; for the things which are seen are temporal, but the things which are not seen are eternal.

SEPTEMBER 13

Isaiah 17:1–18:7

17 The oracle concerning Damascus.
"Behold, Damascus is about to
be removed from being
a city
And will become a fallen ruin.
2 "The cities of Aroer are forsaken;
They will be for flocks, and they
will lie down in *them*;
And there will be no one to
cause *them* to tremble.
3 "And the fortified city will
cease from Ephraim,
And sovereignty from
Damascus
And the remnant of Aram;
They will be like the glory
of the sons of Israel,"
Declares Yahweh of hosts.
4 Now it will be in that day, *that*
the glory of Jacob will wane,
And the fatness of his flesh
will become lean.
5 And it will be even like the reaper
gathering the standing grain,
As his arm harvests the ears of grain,
Or it will be like one gleaning
ears of grain
In the valley of Rephaim.
6 Yet gleanings will remain in it like
the shaking of an olive tree,
Two *or* three olives on the
topmost branch,
Four *or* five on the twigs
of a fruitful tree,
Declares Yahweh, the God of Israel.
7 In that day man will have
regard for his Maker

And his eyes will look to the
Holy One of Israel.
8 He will not have regard for the
altars, the work of his hands,
Nor will he look to that which
his fingers have made,
Even the Asherim and incense stands.
9 In that day their strong cities will be
like forsaken places in the forest,
Or like branches which they forsook
before the sons of Israel;
And the land will be a desolation.
10 For you have forgotten the
God of your salvation
And have not remembered the
rock of your strong defense.
Therefore you plant delightful plants
And set them with vine
branches of a strange *god*.
11 In the day that you plant *it*
you carefully fence *it* in,
And in the morning you cause
your seed to flourish;
But the harvest will *be* a heap
In a day of sickliness and
incurable pain.

12 Alas, the uproar of many peoples
Who roar like the roaring of the seas,
And the rumbling of nations
Who rumble on like the rumbling
of mighty waters!
13 The nations rumble on like the
rumbling of many waters,
But He will rebuke them, and
they will flee far away,
And be pursued like chaff in the
mountains before the wind,
Or like whirling dust before
a whirlwind.
14 At evening time, behold, *there is* terror!
Before morning they are no more.
Such *will be* the portion of
those who pillage us
And the lot of those who plunder us.

18 Alas, O land of whirring wings
Which lies beyond the
rivers of Ethiopia,
2 Which sends envoys by the sea,
Even in papyrus vessels on the
surface of the waters.
Go, swift messengers,
to a nation tall and smooth,
To a people feared far and wide,
A powerful and oppressive nation
Whose land the rivers divide.
3 All you inhabitants of the world
and dwellers on earth,
As soon as a standard is raised on
the mountains, you will see *it*,
And as soon as the trumpet is
blown, you will hear *it*.
4 For thus Yahweh has told me,
"I will look from My dwelling
place quietly
Like dazzling heat in
the sunshine,
Like a cloud of dew in the
heat of harvest."
5 For before the harvest, as soon
as the bud blossoms
And the flower becomes
a ripening grape,
Then He will cut off the sprigs
with pruning knives
And remove *and* cut away the
spreading branches.
6 They will be left together for
mountain birds of prey,
And for the beasts of the earth;
And the birds of prey will spend
the summer *feeding* on them,
And all the beasts of the earth will
spend harvest time on them.
7 At that time a gift of homage will
be brought to Yahweh of hosts
From a people tall and smooth,
Even from a people feared
far and wide,
A powerful and oppressive nation,
Whose land the rivers divide—
To the place of the name of Yahweh
of hosts, *even* Mount Zion.

Psalm 106:32–39

32 They also provoked *Him* to wrath
at the waters of Meribah,
So that it went badly with
Moses on their account;
33 Because they were rebellious
against His Spirit,
He spoke rashly with his lips.

34 They did not destroy the peoples,
As Yahweh commanded them,
35 But they mingled with the nations
And learned their works,
36 And served their idols,
Which became a snare to them.

37 They sacrificed their sons and their
daughters to the demons,
38 And they shed innocent blood,
The blood of their sons and
their daughters,
Whom they sacrificed to
the idols of Canaan;
And the land was polluted
with the blood.
39 Thus they became unclean
in their works,
And played the harlot in their actions.

Proverbs 25:11–12

11 *Like* apples of gold in settings of silver
Is a word spoken in right
circumstances.
12 *Like* an earring of gold and an
ornament of fine gold
Is a wise reprover to a listening ear.

2 Corinthians 5:1–21

5 For we know that if the earthly tent which
is our house is torn down, we have a
building from God, a house not made with
hands, eternal in the heavens. 2 For indeed
in this we groan, longing to be clothed with
our dwelling from heaven, 3 inasmuch as we,
having put it on, will not be found naked. 4 For
indeed while we are in this tent, we groan,
being burdened, because we do not want to
be unclothed but to be clothed, so that what
is mortal will be swallowed up by life. 5 Now
He who prepared us for this very purpose is
God, who gave to us the Spirit as a pledge.
6 Therefore, being always of good courage,
and knowing that while we are at home in
the body we are absent from the Lord—
7 for we walk by faith, not by sight— 8 we
are of good courage and prefer rather to be
absent from the body and to be at home
with the Lord. 9 Therefore we also have as
our ambition, whether at home or absent, to
be pleasing to Him. 10 For we must all appear
before the judgment seat of Christ, so that
each one may be recompensed for his deeds
in the body, according to what he has done,
whether good or bad.
11 So then, knowing the fear of the Lord,
we persuade men, but we have been made
manifest to God; and I hope that we have
been made manifest also in your con-
sciences. 12 We are not again commending
ourselves to you but *are* giving you an oppor-
tunity to boast of us, so that you will have *an*
answer for those who boast in appearance
and not in heart. 13 For if we are out of our
mind, it is for God, or if we are of right mind,
it is for you. 14 For the love of Christ controls
us, having concluded this, that one died for
all, therefore all died. 15 And He died for all,
so that they who live would no longer live
for themselves, but for Him who died and
rose again on their behalf.
16 Therefore from now on we recognize
no one according to the flesh; even though
we have known Christ according to the flesh,
yet now we know *Him in this way* no longer.
17 Therefore if anyone is in Christ, *he is* a
new creation; the old things passed away;
behold, new things have come. 18 Now all
these things are from God, who reconciled
us to Himself through Christ and gave us the
ministry of reconciliation, 19 namely, that
God was in Christ reconciling the world to
Himself, not counting their transgressions
against them, and He has committed to us
the word of reconciliation.
20 So then, we are ambassadors for Christ,
as God is pleading through us. We beg you
on behalf of Christ, be reconciled to God.
21 He made Him who knew no sin *to be* sin
on our behalf, so that we might become the
righteousness of God in Him.

SEPTEMBER 14

Isaiah 19:1–20:6

19 The oracle concerning Egypt.
Behold, Yahweh is riding on a swift
cloud and is about to
come to Egypt;
The idols of Egypt will shake
at His presence,
And the heart of the Egyptians
will melt within them.
2 "So I will incite Egyptians
against Egyptians;
And they will each fight
against his brother and each
against his neighbor,
City against city *and* kingdom
against kingdom.
3 "Then the spirit of the Egyptians will be
emptied to destruction within them;

And I will confuse their counsel,
So that they will seek idols
and ghosts of the dead
And to mediums and spiritists.
4 "Moreover, I will deliver the Egyptians
into the hand of a cruel master,
And a strong king will rule over them,"
declares the Lord, Yahweh of hosts.

5 The waters from the sea will dry up,
And the river will be
parched and dry.
6 The rivers will emit a stench,
The streams of Egypt will
thin out and dry up;
The reeds and rushes will rot away.
7 The bulrushes by the Nile,
by the edge of the Nile
And all the sown fields by the Nile
Will become dry, be driven
away, and be no more.
8 And the fishermen will lament,
And all those who cast a line
into the Nile will mourn,
And those who spread nets on
the waters will languish.
9 Moreover, the manufacturers of
linen made from combed flax
And the weavers of white
cloth will be ashamed.
10 And the pillars *of Egypt*
will be crushed;
All the hired laborers will
be grieved in soul.

11 The princes of Zoan are
merely ignorant fools;
The counsel of Pharaoh's wisest
counselors has become senseless.
How can you *men* say to Pharaoh,
"I am a son of the wise, a son
of the kings of old"?
12 Well then, where are your wise men?
Please let them tell you,
And let them understand
what Yahweh of hosts
Has counseled against Egypt.
13 The princes of Zoan have
acted as ignorant fools,
The princes of Memphis are deluded;
Those who are the cornerstone
of her tribes
Have led Egypt astray.
14 Yahweh has mixed within her
a spirit of distortion;
They have led Egypt astray
in all that it does,
As a drunken man strays
into his vomit.
15 There will be no work for Egypt
Which *its* head or tail, *its* palm
branch or bulrush, may do.

16 In that day the Egyptians will become
like women, and they will tremble and be
in dread because of the waving of the hand
of Yahweh of hosts, which He is going to
wave over them. 17 And the land of Judah
will become a terror to Egypt; everyone to
whom it is mentioned will be in dread of it
because of the counsel of Yahweh of hosts
which He is counseling against them.

18 In that day five cities in the land of
Egypt will be speaking the language of
Canaan and swearing *allegiance* to Yah-
weh of hosts; one will be called the City of
Destruction.

19 In that day there will be an altar to Yah-
weh in the midst of the land of Egypt, and
a pillar to Yahweh near its border. 20 And it
will become a sign and a witness to Yahweh
of hosts in the land of Egypt; for they will
cry to Yahweh because of oppressors, and
He will send them a Savior and a Champion,
and He will deliver them. 21 Thus Yahweh
will make Himself known to Egypt, and
the Egyptians will know Yahweh in that
day. They will even worship with sacrifice
and offering, and they will make a vow
to Yahweh and pay it. 22 And Yahweh will
smite Egypt, smiting but healing; so they
will return to Yahweh, and He will be moved
by their entreaty and will heal them.

23 In that day there will be a highway
from Egypt to Assyria, and the Assyrians
will come into Egypt and the Egyptians into
Assyria, and the Egyptians will worship with
the Assyrians.

24 In that day Israel will be the third *party*
with Egypt and Assyria, a blessing in the
midst of the earth, 25 whom Yahweh of hosts
has blessed, saying, "Blessed is Egypt My
people, and Assyria the work of My hands,
and Israel My inheritance."

20 In the year that the commander
came to Ashdod, when Sargon the
king of Assyria sent him and he fought
against Ashdod and captured it, 2 at that
time Yahweh spoke by the hand of Isaiah
the son of Amoz, saying, "Go and loosen

the sackcloth from your hips and take
your shoes off your feet." And he did so,
going naked and barefoot. 3 And Yahweh
said, "Even as My servant Isaiah has gone
naked and barefoot three years as a sign and
wonder against Egypt and Ethiopia, 4 so the
king of Assyria will lead away the captives
of Egypt and the exiles of Ethiopia, young
and old, naked and barefoot with buttocks
uncovered, to the shame of Egypt. 5 Then
they will be dismayed and ashamed because
of Ethiopia their hope and Egypt their boast.
6 So the inhabitants of this coastland will
say in that day, 'Behold, such is our hope,
where we fled for help to be delivered from
the king of Assyria; and we, how shall we
escape?'"

Psalm 106:40–48

40 So the anger of Yahweh was
kindled against His people
And He abhorred His inheritance.
41 Then He gave them into the
hand of the nations,
And those who hated them
ruled over them.
42 Their enemies oppressed them,
And they were subdued
under their hand.
43 Many times He would deliver them;
But they were rebellious
in their counsel,
And *so* they sank down
in their iniquity.
44 Nevertheless He looked
upon their distress
When He heard their cry
of lamentation;
45 And He remembered for
them His covenant,
And relented according to the
abundance of His lovingkindness.
46 He also made them *objects*
of compassion
In the presence of all their captors.

47 Save us, O Yahweh our God,
And gather us from among the nations,
To give thanks to Your holy name
And revel in Your praise.
48 Blessed be Yahweh, the God of Israel,
From everlasting to everlasting.
And let all the people say, "Amen."
Praise Yah!

Proverbs 25:13

13 Like the cold of snow in
the time of harvest
Is a faithful envoy to those
who send him,
For he refreshes the soul
of his masters.

2 Corinthians 6:1–18

6 And working together *with Him,* we also
plead with you not to receive the grace
of God in vain— 2 for He says,

"AT THE ACCEPTABLE TIME I
LISTENED TO YOU,
AND ON THE DAY OF SALVATION
I HELPED YOU."

Behold, now is "THE ACCEPTABLE TIME,"
behold, now is "THE DAY OF SALVATION"—
3 giving no cause for offense in anything,
so that the ministry will not be discredited,
4 but in everything commending ourselves
as ministers of God, in much perseverance,
in afflictions, in distresses, in hardships,
5 in beatings, in imprisonments, in dis-
turbances, in labors, in sleeplessness,
in hunger, 6 in purity, in knowledge, in
patience, in kindness, in the Holy Spirit, in
unhypocritical love, 7 in the word of truth,
in the power of God; by the weapons of righ-
teousness for the right hand and the left,
8 by glory and dishonor, by evil report and
good report; *regarded* as deceivers and *yet*
true; 9 as unknown and *yet* well-known, as
dying and *yet* behold, we live; as punished
and *yet* not put to death, 10 as sorrowful but
always rejoicing, as poor but making many
rich, as having nothing and *yet* possessing
all things.

11 Our mouth has spoken freely to you,
O Corinthians, our heart is opened wide.
12 You are not restrained by us, but you are
restrained in your own affections. 13 Now in
a like exchange—I speak as to children—
open wide *to us* also.

14 Do not be unequally yoked with unbe-
lievers; for what partnership have righteous-
ness and lawlessness, or what fellowship has
light with darkness? 15 Or what harmony has
Christ with Belial, or what has a believer in
common with an unbeliever? 16 Or what
agreement has a sanctuary of God with
idols? For we are a sanctuary of the living
God; just as God said,

"I WILL DWELL IN THEM AND
WALK AMONG THEM;

AND I WILL BE THEIR GOD, AND
THEY SHALL BE MY PEOPLE.
17 "Therefore, COME OUT FROM THEIR MIDST
AND BE SEPARATE," says the Lord.
"AND DO NOT TOUCH WHAT IS UNCLEAN,
And I will welcome you.
18 "AND I WILL BE A FATHER TO YOU,
And you shall be sons and
daughters to Me,"
SAYS THE LORD ALMIGHTY.

SEPTEMBER 15

Isaiah 21:1–22:25

21 The oracle concerning the wilderness
of the sea.
As whirlwinds in the Negev sweep on,
It comes from the wilderness,
from a fearsome land.
2 A harsh vision has been
declared to me;
The treacherous one *still*
deals treacherously, and the
destroyer *still* destroys.
Go up, Elam, lay siege, Media;
I have made an end of all the
groaning she has caused.
3 For this reason my loins
are full of anguish;
Pains have seized me like the
pains of a woman in labor.
I am so bewildered I cannot hear,
so terrified I cannot see.
4 My heart reels; horror terrorizes me;
The twilight I longed for has been
turned for me into trembling.
5 They set the table, they spread out
the cloth, they eat, they drink;
"Rise up, commanders,
oil the shields,"
6 For thus the Lord says to me,
"Go, station the lookout, let him
declare what he sees.
7 "Indeed, he shall see riders,
horsemen in pairs,
Riders of donkeys, riders of camels,
So let him pay close attention,
very close attention."
8 Then the lookout called,
"O Lord, I stand continually by
day on the watchtower,
And I am stationed every
night at my guard post.
9 "Now behold, here comes a troop
of riders, horsemen in pairs."
And one answered and said,
"Fallen, fallen is Babylon;
And all the graven images of her gods
are shattered on the ground."
10 O my trampled *people* and my
afflicted of the threshing floor!
What I have heard from
Yahweh of hosts,
The God of Israel, I have
declared to you.
11 The oracle concerning Dumah.
One keeps calling to me from Seir,
"Watchman, how far gone is the night?
Watchman, how far gone is the night?"
12 The watchman says,
"Morning comes but also night.
If you would inquire, inquire;
Come back again."

13 The oracle about Arabia.
In the thickets of Arabia you
must spend the night,
O caravans of Dedanites.
14 Bring water to meet the thirsty,
O inhabitants of the land of Tema,
Meet with bread the one who has fled.
15 For they have fled from the swords,
From the drawn sword, and
from the bent bow
And from the heaviness of battle.
16 For thus the Lord said to me, "In a year,
as a hired man would count it, all the glory
of Kedar will end; 17 and the remainder of
the number of bowmen, the mighty men of
the sons of Kedar, will be few; for Yahweh,
the God of Israel, has spoken."

22 The oracle concerning the valley of
vision.
What is the matter with you
now, that you have all gone
up to the housetops?
2 You who were full of noise,
You roaring city, you exultant town;
Your slain were not slain
with the sword,
Nor did they die in battle.
3 All your rulers have fled together,
And have been captured
without the bow;

All of you who were found
were captured together,
Though they had fled far away.
4 Therefore I say, "Turn your
gaze away from me,
Let me weep bitterly,
Do not insist on comforting me
concerning the destruction of
the daughter of my people."
5 For Lord Yahweh of hosts has
a day of confusion,
oppression, and panic
In the valley of vision,
A breaking down of walls
And a crying to the mountain.
6 Now Elam took up the quiver
With the chariots, infantry,
and horsemen;
And Kir uncovered the shield.
7 Then your choicest valleys
were full of chariots,
And the horsemen took up fixed
positions at the gate.
8 And He revealed the defense of Judah.
In that day you looked to the weapons
of the house of the forest,
9 And you saw that the breaches
In the *wall* of the city of
David were many;
And you collected the waters
of the lower pool.
10 Then you counted the
houses of Jerusalem
And tore down houses to
fortify the wall.
11 And you made a reservoir
between the two walls
For the waters of the old pool.
But you did not look to
Him who made it,
Nor did you see Him who
formed it long ago.

12 Therefore in that day Lord
Yahweh of hosts called *you*
to weeping, to wailing,
To shaving the head, and to
wearing sackcloth.
13 Instead, behold, *there is*
joy and gladness,
Killing of cattle and
slaughtering of sheep,
Eating of meat and drinking of wine:
"Let us eat and drink, for
tomorrow we may die."
14 But Yahweh of hosts revealed
Himself in my ears,
"Surely this iniquity shall not
be atoned for you
Until you die," says Lord
Yahweh of hosts.

15 Thus says Lord Yahweh of hosts,
"Come, go to this steward,
To Shebna, who is in charge
of the *royal* household,
16 'What right do you have here,
And whom do you have here,
That you have hewn a tomb
for yourself here,
You who hew a tomb on the height,
You who carve a dwelling place
for yourself in the cliff?
17 'Behold, Yahweh is about to hurl
you headlong, O man.
And He is about to grasp you firmly
18 *And* He will surely roll you
tightly like a ball,
To be cast into a vast country;
There you will die,
And there your glorious
chariots will be,
You disgrace of your
master's house.'
19 "I will push you out of your office,
And I will pull you down
from your station.
20 "Then it will be in that day,
That I will summon My servant
Eliakim the son of Hilkiah,
21 And I will clothe him with your tunic
And tie your sash securely about him.
I will give your authority into
his hand,
And he will become a father to
the inhabitants of Jerusalem
and to the house of Judah.
22 "Then I will set the key of the house
of David on his shoulder,
When he opens no one will shut,
When he shuts no one will open.
23 "I will drive him *like* a peg
in a firm place,
And he will become a throne of
glory to his father's house.
24 "So they will hang on him all the glory
of his father's house, offspring and issue,
all the least of vessels, from bowls to all
the jars. 25 In that day," declares Yahweh of
hosts, "the peg driven in a firm place will

give way; it will even break off and fall, and the load hanging on it will be cut off, for Yahweh has spoken."

Psalm 107:1–9

1 Oh give thanks to Yahweh,
for He is good,
For His lovingkindness
endures forever.
2 Let the redeemed of Yahweh say *so*,
Whom He has redeemed from
the hand of the adversary
3 And gathered from the lands,
From the east and from the west,
From the north and from
the south.

4 They wandered in the wilderness
along the way of the wasteland;
They did not find an inhabited city.
5 Hungry and thirsty,
Their soul fainted within them.
6 Then they cried out to Yahweh
in their trouble;
He delivered them out of
their distresses.
7 He led them by a straight way,
To go to an inhabited city.
8 Let them give thanks to Yahweh
for His lovingkindness,
And for His wondrous deeds
to the sons of men!
9 For He has satisfied the thirsty soul,
And the hungry soul He has
filled with what is good.

Proverbs 25:14–16

14 *Like* clouds and wind without rain
Is a man who boasts of his
gifts falsely.
15 When one is slow to anger,
a ruler may be persuaded,
And a soft tongue breaks the bone.
16 Have you found honey?
Eat *only* enough for you,
Lest you have more than
your fill and vomit it.

2 Corinthians 7:1–16

7 Therefore, having these promises,
beloved, let us cleanse ourselves from
all defilement of flesh and spirit, perfecting
holiness in the fear of God.
2 Make room for us *in your hearts*. We
wronged no one, we corrupted no one,
we took advantage of no one. 3 I do not
speak to condemn you, for I have said
before that you are in our hearts to die
together and to live together. 4 Great is my
boldness toward you; great is my boasting
on your behalf. I have been filled with
comfort; I am overflowing with joy in all
our affliction.
5 For even when we came into Mace-
donia our flesh had no rest, but we were
afflicted on every side—conflicts without,
fears within. 6 But God, who comforts the
humbled, comforted us by the coming of
Titus; 7 and not only by his coming, but
also by the comfort with which he was
comforted in you, as he reported to us your
longing, your mourning, your zeal for me,
so that I rejoiced even more. 8 For though
I caused you sorrow by my letter, I do not
regret it, though I did regret it—*for* I see
that that letter caused you sorrow, though
only for a while— 9 I now rejoice, not that
you were made sorrowful, but that you
were made sorrowful to repentance. For
you were made to have godly sorrow, so
that you might not suffer loss in anything
through us. 10 For godly sorrow produces a
repentance without regret, *leading* to sal-
vation, but the sorrow of the world brings
about death. 11 For behold what earnestness
this very thing—this godly sorrow—has
brought about in you: what vindication of
yourselves, what indignation, what fear,
what longing, what zeal, what avenging of
wrong! In everything you demonstrated
yourselves to be innocent in the matter.
12 So although I wrote to you, *it was* not for
the sake of the offender nor for the sake of
the one offended, but that your earnestness
on our behalf might be manifested to you in
the sight of God. 13 For this reason we have
been comforted.
And besides our comfort, we rejoiced
even much more for the joy of Titus,
because his spirit has been refreshed by
you all. 14 For if in anything I have boasted
to him about you, I was not put to shame,
but as we spoke all things to you in truth,
so also our boasting before Titus proved to
be *the* truth. 15 And his affection abounds
all the more toward you, as he remembers
the obedience of you all, how you received
him with fear and trembling. 16 I rejoice
that in everything I am encouraged about
you.

SEPTEMBER 16

Isaiah 23:1–24:23

23 The oracle concerning Tyre.
Wail, O ships of Tarshish,
For *Tyre* is destroyed, without
house *or* harbor;
It is revealed to them from
the land of Cyprus.
2 Be silent, you inhabitants
of the coastland,
You merchants of Sidon;
Your messengers crossed the sea
3 And *were* on many waters.
The grain of Shihor, the harvest
of the Nile was her revenue;
And she was the nations' gain.
4 Be ashamed, O Sidon;
For the sea speaks, the strong
defense of the sea, saying,
"I have neither travailed nor given birth;
I have neither brought up choice
men *nor* reared virgins."
5 When the report *reaches* Egypt,
They will be in travail at
the report of Tyre.
6 Pass over to Tarshish;
Wail, O inhabitants of the coastland.
7 Is this your exultant *city*,
Whose origin is from days of old,
Whose feet used to lead her to
sojourn in distant places?
8 Who has counseled this against
Tyre, the bestower of crowns,
Whose merchants were princes,
whose traders were the
honored of the earth?
9 Yahweh of hosts has counseled it,
to defile the pride of all beauty,
To make contemptuous all the
honored of the earth.
10 Overflow your land like the Nile,
O daughter of Tarshish;
There is no more restraint.
11 He has stretched His hand
out over the sea;
He has made the kingdoms tremble;
Yahweh has given a command
concerning Canaan to demolish
its strong defenses.
12 So He said, "You shall exult no more,
O crushed virgin daughter of Sidon.
Arise, pass over to Cyprus; even
there you will find no rest."

13 Behold, the land of the Chaldeans—
this is the people *which* was not; Assyria
established it for desert creatures—they
erected their siege towers, they stripped its
palaces, they made it a ruin.

14 Wail, O ships of Tarshish,
For your strong defense is destroyed.

15 Now it will be in that day, that Tyre will be
forgotten for seventy years like the days of
one king. At the end of seventy years it will
happen to Tyre as *in* the song of the harlot:

16 Take *your* harp, walk about the city,
O forgotten harlot;
Pluck the strings skillfully,
sing many songs,
That you may be remembered.

17 And it will be at the end of seventy years
that Yahweh will visit Tyre. Then she will go
back to her harlot's wages and will play the
harlot with all the kingdoms on the face of
the earth. 18 And her gain and her harlot's
wages will be set apart to Yahweh; it will not
be treasured up or hoarded, but her gain will
become sufficient food and choice attire for
those who inhabit the presence of Yahweh.

24 Behold, Yahweh empties the earth to
destruction, eviscerates it, distorts its
surface, and scatters its inhabitants. 2 And
the people will be like the priest, the male
slave like his master, the female slave like
her mistress, the buyer like the seller, the
lender like the borrower, the creditor like
the debtor. 3 The earth will be completely
emptied to destruction and completely
plundered, for Yahweh has spoken this
word. 4 The earth mourns *and* withers; the
world languishes *and* withers; the exalted of
the people of the earth languish. 5 The earth
is also polluted by its inhabitants, for they
trespassed laws, violated statutes, broke the
everlasting covenant. 6 Therefore, a curse
devours the earth, and those who inhabit it
are held guilty. Therefore, the inhabitants of
the earth are burned, and few men remain.

7 The new wine mourns;
The vine languishes;
All the glad of heart sigh.
8 The joy of tambourines ceases;
The rumbling of those exulting stops;

The joy of the harp ceases.
9 They do not drink wine with song;
Strong drink is bitter to
those who drink it.
10 The city of chaos is broken down;
Every house is shut up so
that none may enter.
11 There is an outcry in the streets
concerning the wine;
All gladness turns to gloom.
The joy of the earth is taken
away into exile.
12 Desolation remains in the city,
And the gate is struck down to ruins.
13 For thus it will be in the midst of
the earth among the peoples,
As the shaking of an olive tree,
As the gleanings when the
grape harvest is over.
14 They lift up their voices,
they shout for joy;
They cry out from the west concerning
the majesty of Yahweh.
15 Therefore glorify Yahweh in the east,
The name of Yahweh, the God of Israel,
In the coastlands of the sea.
16 From the ends of the earth we hear
songs, "Glory to the Righteous One,"
But I say, "I waste away!
I waste away! Woe is me!
The treacherous deal treacherously,
And the treacherous deal
very treacherously."
17 Panic and pit and pitfall
Are upon you, O inhabitant
of the earth.
18 Then it will be that he who flees the
sound of panic will fall into the pit,
And he who climbs out of the pit
will be caught in the pitfall;
For the windows above are
opened, and the foundations
of the earth quake.
19 The earth is broken asunder;
The earth is split through;
The earth is shaken violently.
20 The earth reels to and fro
like a drunkard
And it totters like a shack,
For its transgression is heavy upon it,
And it will fall, never to rise again.
21 So it will be in that day,
That Yahweh will punish the
host of heights on high,
And the kings of the earth on earth.
22 They will be gathered together
Like prisoners in the pit,
And will be confined in prison;
And after many days they
will be punished.
23 Then the moon will be humiliated
and the sun ashamed,
For Yahweh of hosts will reign on
Mount Zion and in Jerusalem,
And *His* glory will be before
His elders.

Psalm 107:10–22

10 There were those who inhabited
darkness and the shadow of death,
Prisoners in affliction and irons,
11 Because they had rebelled
against the words of God
And spurned the counsel
of the Most High.
12 So He subdued their heart with labor;
They stumbled and there
was none to help.
13 Then they cried out to Yahweh
in their trouble;
He saved them out of their distresses.
14 He brought them out of darkness
and the shadow of death
And broke their bands apart.
15 Let them give thanks to Yahweh
for His lovingkindness,
And for His wondrous deeds
to the sons of men!
16 For He has shattered the
doors of bronze
And cut through the bars of iron.
17 Ignorant fools, because of their
way of transgression,
And because of their iniquities,
were afflicted.
18 Their soul abhorred all kinds of food,
And they reached the gates of death.
19 Then they cried out to Yahweh
in their trouble;
He saved them out of their distresses.
20 He sent His word and healed them,
And provided *them* escape
from their destructions.
21 Let them give thanks to Yahweh
for His lovingkindness,
And for His wondrous deeds
to the sons of men!
22 Let them also offer sacrifices
of thanksgiving,

And recount His works
with joyful singing.

Proverbs 25:17

17 Let your foot rarely be in your
neighbor's house,
Lest he have more than his fill
of you and hate you.

2 Corinthians 8:1–24

8 Now brothers, we make known to you
the grace of God which has been given in
the churches of Macedonia, 2 that in a great
testing by affliction their abundance of joy
and their deep poverty abounded unto the
richness of their generosity. 3 For I testify
that according to their ability, and beyond
their ability, *they gave* of their own accord,
4 begging us with much urging for the grace
of sharing in the ministry to the saints, 5 and
this, not as we had expected, but they first
gave themselves to the Lord and to us by the
will of God. 6 So we encouraged Titus that
as he had previously made a beginning, so
he would also complete in you this gracious
work as well.

7 But just as you abound in everything, in
faith and word and knowledge and in all ear-
nestness and in the love we inspired in you,
see that you abound in this gracious work
also. 8 I am not speaking *this* as a command,
but as proving through the earnestness of
others the sincerity of your love also. 9 For
you know the grace of our Lord Jesus Christ,
that though being rich, yet for your sake
He became poor, so that you through His
poverty might become rich. 10 And I give *my*
opinion in this matter, for this is profitable
for you, who were the first to begin a year
ago not only to do *this*, but also to desire *to*
do it. 11 But now complete doing it also, so
that just as *there was* the readiness to desire
it, so *there may be* also the completion of it
from what you have. 12 For if the readiness
is present, it is acceptable according to what
a person has, not according to what he does
not have. 13 For *this* is not for the relief of
others *and* for your affliction, but by way
of equality— 14 at this present time your
abundance *being a supply* for their need,
so that their abundance also may become
a supply for your need, that there may be
equality. 15 As it is written, "HE WHO *gath-*
ered MUCH DID NOT HAVE TOO MUCH, AND HE
WHO *gathered* LITTLE HAD NO LACK."

16 But thanks be to God who puts the
same earnestness on your behalf in the
heart of Titus. 17 For he not only accepted
our plea, but being himself very earnest,
he has gone out to you of his own accord.
18 And we have sent along with him the
brother whose praise in *the things of* the
gospel is throughout all the churches. 19 And
not only *this*, but he has also been appointed
by the churches to travel with us in this
gracious work that is being ministered by
us for the glory of the Lord Himself, and *to*
show our readiness, 20 taking precaution lest
anyone discredits us in our ministering of
this generous gift, 21 for we respect what is
good, not only in the sight of the Lord, but
also in the sight of men. 22 And we have sent
with them our brother, whom we have often
tested and found earnest in many things,
but now even more earnest because of *his*
great confidence in you. 23 As for Titus, *he is*
my partner and fellow worker among you;
as for our brothers, *they are* messengers of
the churches, a glory to Christ. 24 Therefore
openly before the churches, show them the
proof of your love and of our reason for
boasting about you.

The Holy Scriptures tell us what we could never learn any other way: they tell us what we are, who we are, how we got here, why we are here and what we are required to do while we remain here.

— A. W. TOZER

SEPTEMBER 17

Isaiah 25:1–26:21

25 O Yahweh, You are my God;
I will exalt You, I will give
thanks to Your name;
For You have worked wonders,
Counsels *formed* long ago, with
perfect faithfulness.
2 For You have made a city into a heap,
A fortified town into a ruin;
A palace of strangers is a city no more,
It will never be rebuilt.
3 Therefore a strong people
will glorify You;
Towns of ruthless nations will fear You.
4 For You have been a strong
defense for the poor,
A strong defense for the
needy in his distress,
A refuge from the storm, a
shade from the heat;
For the breath of the ruthless
Is like a *rain* storm *against* a wall.
5 Like heat in a dry land, You subdue
the rumbling of strangers;
Like heat by the shadow of a cloud,
the song of the ruthless is silenced.

6 And Yahweh of hosts will
prepare a lavish banquet for all
peoples on this mountain;
A banquet of aged wine, choice
pieces with marrow,
And refined, aged wine.
7 And on this mountain He will
swallow up the covering
which is over all peoples,
Even the veil which is stretched
over all nations.
8 He will swallow up death for all time,
And Lord Yahweh will wipe
tears away from all faces,
And He will remove the reproach of
His people from all the earth;
For Yahweh has spoken.
9 And it will be said in that day,
"Behold, this is our God in whom we
have hoped that He would
save us.
This is Yahweh in whom
we have hoped;
Let us rejoice and be glad
in His salvation."
10 For the hand of Yahweh will
rest on this mountain,
And Moab will be trodden
down in his place
As straw is trodden down in
the water of a manure pile.
11 And he will spread out his
hands in the middle of it
As a swimmer spreads out
his hands to swim,
But *Yahweh* will lay low his
lofty pride together with the
trickery of his hands.
12 The unassailable fortifications of
your walls He will bring down,
Lay low, *and* cast to the ground,
even to the dust.

26 In that day this song will be sung in
the land of Judah:
"We have a strong city;
He sets up walls and ramparts
for salvation.
2 "Open the gates, that the righteous
nation may enter,
The one that keeps faithfulness.
3 "The steadfast of mind You will
keep in perfect peace
Because he trusts in You.
4 "Trust in Yahweh forever,
For in Yah—Yahweh *Himself—we*
have an everlasting Rock.
5 "For He has laid low those who
settle on high, the exalted city;
He brings it low, He brings it low to
the ground, He casts it to the dust.
6 "The foot will trample it,
The feet of the afflicted, the
steps of the poor."

7 The way of the righteous
is upright;
O Upright One, make the path
of the righteous level.
8 Indeed, *while following* the way of
Your judgments, O Yahweh,
We have hoped for You eagerly;
Your name—the memory of
You—is the desire of *our* souls.
9 At night my soul longs for You,
Indeed, my spirit within me
seeks You earnestly;

For when the earth experiences
Your judgments,
The inhabitants of the world
learn righteousness.
10 *Though* the wicked is shown favor,
He does not learn righteousness;
He deals unjustly in the
land of uprightness,
And does not perceive the
majesty of Yahweh.

11 O Yahweh, Your hand is raised up
high, yet they do not behold it.
They behold *Your* zeal for the
people and are put to shame;
Indeed, fire will devour
Your adversaries.
12 Yahweh, You will establish
peace for us,
Since You have also performed
for us all our works.
13 O Yahweh our God, other masters
besides You have ruled us;
But through You alone we bring
Your name to remembrance.
14 The dead will not live; the
departed spirits will not rise;
Therefore You have visited
and destroyed them,
And You have made all
remembrance of them perish.
15 You have increased the nation,
O Yahweh;
You have increased the nation,
You are glorified;
You have extended all the
borders of the land.
16 O Yahweh, they visited You in distress;
They could only whisper a prayer;
Your chastening was upon them.
17 As the woman with child draws
near to *the time* to give birth,
She writhes *and* cries out in
her pangs of labor,
Thus were we before You, O Yahweh.
18 We were with child,
we writhed *in labor*;
We gave birth, as it seems,
only to wind.
We could not accomplish
salvation for the earth,
And the inhabitants of
the world were not born.
19 Your dead will live;
Their corpses will rise.
You who dwell in the dust,
awake and shout for joy,
For your dew *is as* the dew of the dawn,
And the earth will give birth
to the departed spirits.

20 Come, my people, enter
into your rooms
And close your doors behind you;
Hide for a little while
Until indignation passes by.
21 For behold, Yahweh is about to
come out from His place
To visit the iniquity of the
inhabitants of the earth;
And the earth will reveal
her bloodshed
And will no longer cover those
of hers who were killed.

Psalm 107:23–32

23 Those who go down to the sea in ships,
Who do business on many waters;
24 They have seen the works of Yahweh,
And His wondrous deeds in the deep.
25 He spoke and set up a stormy wind,
Which raised up the waves of the sea.
26 They went up to the heavens, they
went down to the depths;
Their soul melted away in *the* calamity.
27 They staggered and swayed
like a drunken man,
And all their wisdom was
swallowed up.
28 Then they cried to Yahweh
in their trouble,
And He brought them out
of their distresses.
29 He caused the storm to stand still,
So that its waves were hushed.
30 Then they were glad because
they were quiet,
So He led them to their desired haven.
31 Let them give thanks to Yahweh
for His lovingkindness,
And for His wondrous deeds
to the sons of men!
32 Let them exalt Him also in the
assembly of the people,
And praise Him at the
seat of the elders.

Proverbs 25:18–19

18 *Like* a club and a sword
and a sharp arrow

Is a man who bears false witness
against his neighbor.
19 *Like* an aching tooth and a slipping foot
Is trust in a treacherous man
in a day of distress.

2 Corinthians 9:1–15

9 For it is superfluous for me to write to
you about this ministry to the saints;
2 for I know your readiness, of which I boast
about you to the Macedonians, that Achaia
has been prepared since last year, and your
zeal stirred up most of them. 3 But I have
sent the brothers, in order that our boasting
about you may not be made empty in this
case, so that, as I was saying, you may be
prepared; 4 lest if any Macedonians come
with me and find you unprepared, we—not
to speak of you—be put to shame in this
certainty *of ours*. 5 So I regarded it necessary
to encourage the brothers that they would
go on ahead to you and arrange beforehand
your previously promised blessing, so that
the same would be ready as a blessing and
not as a begrudging obligation.

6 Now this *I say*, he who sows sparingly
will also reap sparingly, and he who sows
with blessing will also reap with blessing.
7 Each one *must do* just as he has purposed
in his heart, not grudgingly or under com-
pulsion, for God loves a cheerful giver. 8 And
God is able to make every grace abound to
you, so that in everything at every time
having every sufficiency, you may have an
abundance for every good deed; 9 as it is
written,

"HE SCATTERED ABROAD,
HE GAVE TO THE NEEDY,
HIS RIGHTEOUSNESS STANDS FOREVER."

10 Now He who supplies SEED TO THE SOWER
AND BREAD FOR FOOD will supply and multi-
ply your seed and increase the harvest of
your righteousness; 11 you will be enriched
in everything for all generosity, which
through us is bringing about thanksgiving
to God. 12 For the ministry of this service
is not only fully supplying the needs of
the saints, but is also abounding through
many thanksgivings to God. 13 Because of
the proven character given by this ministry,
they will glorify God for *your* obedience to
your confession of the gospel of Christ and
for the generosity of your fellowship toward
them and toward all, 14 while they also, by
prayer on your behalf, long for you because
of the surpassing grace of God on you.
15 Thanks be to God for His indescribable
gift!

SEPTEMBER 18

Isaiah 27:1–28:29

27 In that day Yahweh will punish
Leviathan the fleeing serpent,
With His fierce and great
and mighty sword,
Even Leviathan the twisted serpent;
And He will kill the dragon
who *lives* in the sea.

2 In that day,
"A vineyard of delight, sing of it!
3 "I, Yahweh, am its keeper;
I water it every moment.
Lest anyone damage it,
I keep it night and day.
4 "I have no wrath.
Who would *ever* give Me briars
and thorns in the battle?
I would step on them, I would
burn them completely.
5 "Or let him rely on My strong defense,
Let him make peace with Me,
Let him make peace with Me."
6 In the days to come Jacob
will take root,
Israel will blossom and bud,
And they will fill the whole
world with produce.

7 Like the striking of Him who has
struck them, has He struck them?
Or like the slaughter of those
of His who were killed,
have they been killed?
8 You contended with them by driving
them away, by making them forlorn.
With His fierce wind He has expelled
them on the day of the east wind.
9 Therefore through this, Jacob's
iniquity will be atoned for;
And this will be the whole fruit of
the turning away of his sin:
When he makes all the altar stones
like pulverized chalk stones,

When Asherim and incense
altars will not stand.
10 For the fortified city is isolated,
A haunt forlorn and forsaken
like the desert;
There the calf will graze,
And there it will lie down
and feed on its twigs.
11 When its limbs are dry,
they are broken off;
Women come *and* light
a fire with them,
For they are not a people
of discernment,
Therefore their Maker will not
have compassion on them.
And their Creator will not
be gracious to them.

12 And it will be in that day, *that* Yahweh
will start *His* threshing from the flowing
stream of the River to the brook of Egypt,
and you will be gathered up one by one,
O sons of Israel. 13 And it will be in that
day, *that* a great trumpet will be blown,
and those who were perishing in the land
of Assyria and who were banished in the
land of Egypt will come and worship Yahweh
in the holy mountain at Jerusalem.

28

Woe to the proud crown of
the drunkards of Ephraim,
And to the fading flower of
its glorious beauty,
Which is at the head of
the fertile valley
Of those who are overcome with wine!
2 Behold, the Lord has a strong
and courageous *agent*;
As a storm of hail, a tempest
of destruction,
Like a storm of mighty
overflowing waters,
He has set *it* down to the
earth with *His* hand.
3 The proud crown of the drunkards of
Ephraim is trodden under foot.
4 And the fading flower of
its glorious beauty,
Which is at the head of
the fertile valley,
Will be like the first-ripe fig
prior to summer,
Which one sees,
And as soon as it is in his hand,
He swallows it.

5 In that day Yahweh of hosts will
become a beautiful crown
And a glorious diadem to the remnant
of His people;
6 A spirit of *just* judgment for
him who sits in judgment,
A might to those who turn back
the onslaught at the gate.
7 And these also reel with wine
and stagger from strong drink:
The priest and the prophet
reel with strong drink;
They are swallowed up by wine,
they stagger from strong drink;
They reel while having visions;
They totter *when rendering* a verdict.
8 For all the tables are full of filthy
vomit, without a *single clean* place.

9 "Whom would He instruct
in knowledge,
And whom would He provide
understanding about the report?
Those *just* weaned from milk?
Those *just* taken from the breast?
10 "For *He says*,
'Order on order, order on order,
Line on line, line on line,
A little here, a little there.'"
11 Indeed, He will speak to this people
Through stammering lips
and a foreign tongue,
12 He who said to them, "Here is
rest, give rest to the weary,"
And, "Here is repose," but
they would not listen.
13 So the word of Yahweh to them will be,
"Order on order, order on order,
Line on line, line on line,
A little here, a little there,"
That they may go and stumble
backward, be broken, snared,
and taken captive.
14 Therefore, hear the word of
Yahweh, O scoffers,
Who rule this people who
are in Jerusalem,
15 Because you have said, "We have
cut a covenant with death,
And with Sheol we have made a pact.
The overflowing scourge will not
reach us when it passes by,
For we have made falsehood our
refuge and we have hidden
ourselves with lying."

16 Therefore thus says Lord Yahweh,
"Behold, I am laying in Zion
a stone, a tested stone,
A costly cornerstone *for* the
foundation, firmly placed.
He who believes *in it* will
not be disturbed.
17 "I will make justice the measuring line
And righteousness the level;
Then hail will sweep away the
refuge of falsehood,
And the waters will overflow
the secret place.
18 "Your covenant with death
will be canceled,
And your pact with Sheol
will not stand;
When the overflowing scourge
passes through,
Then you will become its
trampling *place*.
19 "As often as it passes through,
it will take you;
For morning after morning it
will pass through, *anytime*
during the day or night,
And it will be sheer terror to
understand the report."
20 The bed is too short on
which to stretch out,
And the blanket is too narrow
to wrap oneself in.
21 For Yahweh will rise up as
at Mount Perazim;
He will be stirred up as in
the valley of Gibeon,
To work His work, His unusual work,
And to labor in His labor,
His exceptional labor.
22 So now do not carry on as scoffers,
Lest your fetters be made stronger;
For I have heard from Lord
Yahweh of hosts
Of complete destruction, one that
is decreed, on all the earth.

23 Give ear and hear my voice,
Pay attention and hear my words.
24 Does the farmer plow
continually to plant seed?
Does he *continually* turn and
harrow his ground?
25 Does he not level its surface
And sow dill and scatter cumin
And plant wheat in rows,
Barley in its place and rye
within its area?
26 For his God disciplines and teaches
him *proper* judgment.
27 For dill is not threshed with
a threshing sledge,
Nor is the wheel of a cart
driven over cumin;
But dill is beaten out with a staff,
and cumin with a rod.
28 *Grain for* bread is crushed,
But he does not continue
to thresh it forever.
Because the wheel of *his* cart and
his horses *eventually* disturb *it*,
He does not crush it longer.
29 This also comes from Yahweh of hosts,
Who has made *His* counsel wonderful
and *His* wisdom great.

Psalm 107:33–43

33 He makes rivers into a wilderness
And springs of water into
a thirsty ground;
34 A fruitful land into a salt waste,
Because of the evil of those
who inhabited it.
35 He makes a wilderness
into a pool of water
And a dry land into springs of water;
36 And there He causes the
hungry to inhabit,
So that they may establish
an inhabited city,
37 And sow fields and plant vineyards,
And produce a fruitful harvest.
38 Also He blesses them and
they multiply greatly,
And He does not let their
cattle decrease.

39 But when they decrease and
are bowed down
Through oppression, evil, and sorrow,
40 He pours contempt upon nobles
And makes them wander
in a pathless void.
41 But He sets the needy securely on
high away from affliction,
And makes *his* families like a flock.
42 The upright see it and are glad;
But all unrighteousness
shuts its mouth.
43 Who is wise?
Let him keep these things,

And carefully consider the
lovingkindnesses of Yahweh.

Proverbs 25:20

20 *Like* one who takes off a garment on
a cold day, *or like* vinegar on soda,
Is he who sings songs to
an aching heart.

2 Corinthians 10:1–18

10 Now I, Paul, myself plead with you
by the gentleness and forbearance
of Christ—I who am humble when face-
to-face with you, but courageous toward
you when absent! 2 But I beg that when I
am present I *need* not act *so* courageously
with the confidence that I consider to
daringly *use* against some, who consider
us as if we walked according to the flesh.
3 For though we walk in the flesh, we do not
war according to the flesh, 4 for the weapons
of our warfare are not of the flesh, but
divinely powerful for the tearing down of
strongholds, 5 as we tear down speculations
and every lofty thing raised up against the
knowledge of God, and take every thought
captive to the obedience of Christ, 6 and are
ready to punish all disobedience, whenever
your obedience is fulfilled.
7 You are looking at things as they are
outwardly. If anyone is confident in himself
that he is Christ's, let him consider this again
within himself, that just as he is Christ's, so
also are we. 8 For even if I boast somewhat
further about our authority, which the Lord
gave for building you up and not for tearing
you down, I will not be put to shame, 9 for I
do not wish to seem as if I would terrify you
by my letters. 10 For they say, "His letters are
weighty and strong, but his personal pres-
ence is weak and his words contemptible."
11 Let such a person consider this, that what
we are in word by letters when absent, such
persons we are also in deed when present.
12 For we do not dare to classify or
compare ourselves with some of those
who commend themselves, but when they
measure themselves by themselves and
compare themselves with themselves, they
are without understanding. 13 But we will
not boast beyond *our* measure, but within
the measure of the area of influence which
God apportioned to us as a measure, to
reach even as far as you. 14 For we are not
overextending ourselves, as if we did not
reach you, (for we were the first to come
even as far as you in the gospel of Christ),
15 not boasting beyond *our* measure in other
men's labors, but having the hope—that as
your faith grows—to be enlarged even more
by you within our area of influence, 16 so as
to proclaim the gospel even to the regions
beyond you, *and* not to boast in what has
been accomplished in the area of influence
of another. 17 But HE WHO BOASTS IS TO BOAST
IN THE LORD. 18 For it is not the one who
commends himself that is approved, but
the one whom the Lord commends.

SEPTEMBER 19

Isaiah 29:1–24

29 Woe, O Ariel, Ariel the city
where David *once* camped!
Add year to year, observe *your*
feasts on schedule.
2 I will bring distress to Ariel,
And she will be *a city of*
mourning and moaning;
And she will be like an Ariel to me.
3 And I will camp against
you encircling *you*,
And I will fortify siegeworks
against you,
And I will raise up fortifications
against you.
4 Then you will be brought low;
From the earth you will speak,
And from the dust *where*
you are prostrate
Your words *will come*.
Your voice will also be like that
of a spirit from the ground,
And your speech will whisper
from the dust.

5 But it will be that the multitude
of your enemies will
become like fine dust,
And the multitude of the ruthless ones
like the chaff which blows away;
And it will happen instantly, suddenly.
6 From Yahweh of hosts you will
be punished with thunder and
earthquake and loud noise,

With whirlwind and tempest and
the flame of a consuming fire.
7 And it will be that the multitude
of all the nations who wage
war against Ariel,
Even all who wage war against
her and her stronghold,
and who distress her,
Will be like a dream,
a vision of the night.
8 And it will be as when a
hungry man dreams—
And behold, he is eating;
But he awakens, and his soul
is empty,
Or as when a thirsty man dreams—
And behold, he is drinking,
But he awakens, and behold, he is faint,
And his soul is not quenched.
Thus the multitude of all
the nations will be
Who wage war against Mount Zion.

9 Astonish yourselves and be astonished,
Blind yourselves and be blind;
They become drunk, but
not with wine;
They stagger, but not with
strong drink.
10 For Yahweh has poured over
you a spirit of deep sleep;
He has shut your eyes, the prophets;
And He has covered your
heads, the seers.
11 The entire vision will be to you like the
words of a sealed book, which when they
give it to the one who is literate, saying,
"Please read this," he will say, "I cannot, for
it is sealed." 12 Then the book will be given
to the one who does not know *how to read*
a book, saying, "Please read this." And he
will say, "I do not know *how to read* a book."
13 Then the Lord said,
"Because this people draw
near with their mouth
And honor Me with their lips,
But they remove their
hearts far from Me,
And their fear of Me is *in the*
command of men learned *by rote*,
14 Therefore behold, I will once again
deal marvelously with this
people, wondrously marvelous;
And the wisdom of their
wise men will perish,
And the discernment of their
discerning men will be hidden."

15 Woe to those who deeply hide
their counsel from Yahweh,
And whose deeds are *done*
in a dark place,
And they say, "Who sees us?"
or "Who knows us?"
16 You turn *things* around!
Shall the potter be considered
as equal with the clay,
That what is made would say to its
maker, "He did not make me";
Or what is formed say to him
who formed it, "He has
no understanding"?
17 Is it not yet just a little while
Before Lebanon will be turned
into a fruitful orchard,
And the fruitful orchard will
be counted as a forest?
18 On that day the deaf will
hear words of a book,
And out of darkness and
thick darkness the eyes
of the blind will see.
19 The afflicted also will increase
their gladness in Yahweh,
And the needy of mankind will
rejoice in the Holy One of Israel.
20 For the ruthless will come to an end
and the scoffer will be finished,
Indeed all who are watching out
to do evil will be cut off;
21 Who cause a person to sin by a word,
And ensnare him who
reproves at the gate,
And defraud the one in the right
with meaningless arguments.

22 Therefore thus says Yahweh, who
redeemed Abraham, concerning the house
of Jacob:
"Jacob shall not now be ashamed, and
now his face shall not turn pale;
23 But when he sees his children, the
work of My hands, in his midst,
They will sanctify My name;
Indeed, they will sanctify
the Holy One of Jacob
And will stand trembling
before the God of Israel.
24 "Those who err in spirit will
know discernment,

And those who criticize
will gain learning.

Psalm 108:1–6

1 My heart is set, O God;
I will sing, I will sing praises,
even with my glory.
2 Awake, harp and lyre;
I will awaken the dawn!
3 I will give thanks to You, O Yahweh,
among the peoples,
And I will sing praises to You
among the nations.
4 For Your lovingkindness is
great above the heavens,
And Your truth *reaches* to the skies.
5 Be exalted above the heavens, O God,
And Your glory above all the earth.
6 That Your beloved may be rescued,
Save with Your right hand,
and answer me!

Proverbs 25:21–22

21 If your enemy is hungry,
give him food to eat;
And if he is thirsty, give
him water to drink;
22 For you will heap burning
coals on his head,
And Yahweh will repay you.

2 Corinthians 11:1–15

11 I wish that you would bear with me
in a little foolishness, but indeed you
are bearing with me. 2 For I am jealous for
you with a godly jealousy, for I betrothed
you to one husband, so that I might present
you *as* a pure virgin to Christ. 3 But I fear
that, as the serpent deceived Eve by his
craftiness, your minds will be corrupted
from the simplicity and purity *of devotion*
to Christ. 4 For if one comes and preaches
another Jesus whom we did not preach, or
you receive a different spirit which you did
not receive, or a different gospel which you
did not accept, you bear *this* beautifully.
5 For I consider myself in no way inferior
to the most-eminent apostles. 6 But even if
I am unskilled in word, yet I am not *so* in
knowledge; in fact, in every way we have
made *this* evident to you in all things.
7 Or did I commit a sin in humbling
myself so that you might be exalted,
because I proclaimed the gospel of God
to you without charge? 8 I robbed other
churches by taking wages *from them* to
minister to you. 9 And when I was present
with you and was in need, I was not a
burden to anyone; for when the brothers
came from Macedonia they fully supplied
my need, and in everything I kept and
will keep myself from being a burden to
you. 10 As the truth of Christ is in me, this
boasting of mine will not be stopped in the
regions of Achaia. 11 Why? Because I do not
love you? God knows *I do*!
12 But what I am doing I will continue
to do, so that I may cut off opportunity
from those who desire an opportunity to
be found just as we are in the matter about
which they are boasting. 13 For such men are
false apostles, deceitful workers, disguising
themselves as apostles of Christ. 14 And no
wonder, for even Satan disguises himself
as an angel of light. 15 Therefore it is not
surprising if his ministers also disguise
themselves as ministers of righteousness,
whose end will be according to their deeds.

SEPTEMBER 20

Isaiah 30:1–32:20

30 "Woe to the rebellious
children," declares Yahweh,
"Who execute counsel,
but not Mine,
And make an alliance,
but not of My Spirit,
In order to add sin to sin,
2 Who go down to Egypt—
But did not ask Me—
To find strength in the strong
defense of Pharaoh
And to take refuge in the
shadow of Egypt!
3 "Therefore the strong defense of
Pharaoh will be your shame
And the refuge in the shadow
of Egypt, your dishonor.
4 "For their princes are at Zoan
And their messengers reach Hanes.
5 "Everyone will be ashamed because of
a people who cannot profit them,
Who are not for help or profit, but
for shame and also for reproach."

6 The oracle concerning the beasts of the Negev.

Through a land of distress
and anguish,
From where *come* lioness and lion,
viper and flying fiery serpent,
They carry their wealth on the
backs of young donkeys
And their treasures on camels' humps,
To a people who cannot profit *them*;
7 Even Egypt, whose help is
vain and empty.
Therefore, I have called her
"Rahab who has ceased."
8 Now go, write it on a tablet
before them
And inscribe it on a scroll,
That it may be in the time to come
As a witness forever.
9 For this is a rebellious
people, false sons,
Sons who are not willing to listen
To the law of Yahweh,
10 Who say to the seers,
"You must not see,"
And to those who have visions,
"You must not behold visions
for us of what is right,
Speak to us pleasant words,
Behold visions of illusions.
11 "Get out of the way, turn
aside from the path,
Cease *speaking* before us about
the Holy One of Israel."

12 Therefore thus says the Holy One of Israel,

"Since you have rejected this word
And have put your trust in
oppression and deviousness
and have relied on them,
13 Therefore this iniquity will be to you
Like a breach about to fall,
A bulge in a high wall,
Whose breaking comes
suddenly in an instant,
14 Whose breaking is like the
breaking of a potter's jar,
So ruthlessly shattered
That a potsherd will not be
found among its pieces
To take fire from a hearth
Or to scoop water from a cistern."

15 For thus Lord Yahweh, the Holy One of Israel, has said,

"In repentance and rest
you will be saved,
In quietness and trust is your might."
But you were not willing,
16 And you said, "No, for we
will flee on horses,"
Therefore you shall flee!
"And we will ride on swift *horses*,"
Therefore those who pursue
you shall be swift.
17 One thousand *will flee* at the
threat of one *man*;
You will flee at the threat of five,
Until you are left as a flag
on a mountain top
And as a standard on a hill.
18 Therefore Yahweh waits *with
longing* to be gracious to you,
And therefore He is on high to
have compassion on you.
For Yahweh is a God of justice;
How blessed are all those
who wait for Him.

19 O people in Zion, inhabitant in Jerusa-
lem, you will weep no longer. He will surely
be gracious to you at the sound of your cry;
when He hears it, He will answer you. 20 The
Lord has given you bread of distress and
water of oppression; *He*, your Teacher will
no longer hide Himself, but your eyes will
see your Teacher. 21 And your ears will hear
a word behind you, "This is the way, walk
in it," whenever you turn to the right or to
the left. 22 And you will defile your graven
images overlaid with your silver, and your
molten images plated with your gold. You
will scatter them as an impure thing *and* say
to them, "Be gone!"

23 Then He will give *you* rain for the seed
which you will sow in the ground, and bread
from the produce of the ground, and it will be
rich and fat; on that day your livestock will
graze in a roomy pasture. 24 Also the oxen
and the donkeys which work the ground will
eat salted fodder, which has been winnowed
with shovel and fork. 25 And it will be that
on every lofty mountain and on every lifted
up hill there will be streams running with
water on the day of the great slaughter, when
the towers fall. 26 And the light of the moon
will be as the light of the sun, and the light
of the sun will be seven times *brighter*, like
the light of seven days, on the day Yahweh
binds up the fracture of His people and heals
the bruise He has inflicted.

27 Behold, the name of Yahweh
comes from afar;

Burning is His anger and
heavy is *His* smoke;
His lips are filled with indignation
And His tongue is like a
consuming fire;
28 His breath is like an
overflowing torrent,
Which reaches to the neck,
To shake the nations back and forth
in a sieve of worthlessness,
And to *put* in the jaws of the
peoples the bridle which
staggers one to ruin.
29 You will have songs as in the
night when you set yourself
apart as holy for the festival,
And gladness of heart as when one
marches to *the sound of* the flute,
To go to the mountain of Yahweh,
to the Rock of Israel.
30 And Yahweh will cause His
splendid voice to be heard,
And the descending of His arm
to be seen in raging anger,
And *in* the flame of a consuming fire
In cloudburst, downpour,
and hailstones.
31 For at the voice of Yahweh
Assyria will be dismayed,
When He strikes with the rod.
32 And every blow of the
appointed staff,
Which Yahweh will cause
to rest upon him,
Will be with *the music of*
tambourines and lyres;
And in battles, waving *weapons*
He will fight them.
33 For Topheth has long been ready,
Indeed, it has been prepared
for the king.
He has made it deep and large,
A pyre of fire with plenty of wood;
The breath of Yahweh, like a torrent
of brimstone, sets it afire.

31 Woe to those who go down
to Egypt for help
And rely on horses,
And trust in chariots because
they are many
And in horsemen because
they are very mighty,
But they do not have regard for the
Holy One of Israel, nor seek Yahweh!
2 Yet He also is wise and will
bring about an evil *demise*
And does not turn His words aside,
But will arise against the
house of evildoers
And against the help of the
workers of iniquity.
3 Now the Egyptians are
men and not God,
And their horses are flesh
and not spirit;
So Yahweh will stretch out His hand,
And he who helps will stumble,
And he who is helped will fall,
And all of them will come
to an end together.

4 For thus says Yahweh to me,
"As the lion or the young lion
growls over its prey,
Against which a multitude of
shepherds is called out,
And it will not be dismayed at their
voice nor afflicted at their noise,
So will Yahweh of hosts come
down to wage war on Mount
Zion and on its hill."
5 Like flying birds so Yahweh of
hosts will defend Jerusalem.
He will defend and deliver *it*;
He will pass over and provide
a way of escape.
6 Return to Him against whom you have
deeply rebelled, O sons of Israel. 7 For in that
day every man will reject his silver idols and
his gold idols, which your hands have made
for you as a sin.
8 And the Assyrian will fall by
a sword not of man,
And a sword not of man
will devour him.
So he will flee from the sword,
And his choice men will
become forced laborers.
9 "His rock will pass away
because of terror,
And his princes will be dismayed
at the standard,"
Declares Yahweh, whose fire is in Zion
and whose furnace is in Jerusalem.

32 Behold, a king will reign righteously
And princes will rule justly.
2 Each will be like a refuge from the wind
And a shelter from the storm,

Like streams of water in a dry country,
Like the shade of a huge
rock in a weary land.
3 Then the eyes of those who
see will not be blinded,
And the ears of those who
hear will pay attention.
4 And the heart of the hasty
will discern knowledge,
And the tongue of the stammerers
will hasten to speak clearly.
5 No longer will the wicked
fool be called noble,
Or the rogue be spoken of *as* generous.
6 For a wicked fool speaks wicked folly,
And his heart does wickedness:
To do ungodliness and to speak
error against Yahweh,
In order to make the hungry
person empty;
He even causes the thirsty
to lack a drink.
7 As for a rogue, his weapons are evil;
He counsels wicked schemes
To wreak destruction *on the*
afflicted with lying words,
Even though *the* needy
one speaks justly.
8 But the noble man counsels noble plans;
And by noble plans he rises up.

9 Rise up, you women who are at ease,
And hear my voice;
Give ear to my word,
You complacent daughters.
10 Within a year and *a few* days
You will quake, O complacent
daughters;
For the grape harvest is ended,
And the *fruit* gathering will not come.
11 Tremble, you *women* who are at ease;
Quake, you complacent *daughters*;
Strip, undress, and put
sackcloth on *your* waist,
12 Beat your breasts for the desirable
fields, for the fruitful vine,
13 For the land of my people *in which*
thorns *and* briars shall come up,
Indeed, against all the joyful
houses *and* the exultant city.
14 Because the palace has been
abandoned, the populated
city forsaken.
Hill and watchtower have
become caves forever,
A joy for wild donkeys,
a pasture for flocks,
15 Until the Spirit is poured out
upon us from on high,
And the wilderness becomes
a fruitful orchard,
And the fruitful orchard is
counted as a forest.
16 Then justice will dwell in
the wilderness,
And righteousness will live
in the fruitful orchard.
17 And the work of righteousness
will be peace,
And the service of righteousness,
quietness and security forever.
18 Then my people will live in
a peaceful abode,
And in secure dwellings and in
undisturbed resting places;
19 And it will hail when the
forest comes down,
And the city will be utterly laid low.
20 How blessed will you be, you
who sow beside all waters,
Who let out freely the ox
and the donkey.

Psalm 108:7–13

7 God has spoken in His holiness:
"I will exult, I will portion out Shechem
And measure out the valley of Succoth.
8 "Gilead is Mine, Manasseh is Mine;
Ephraim also is the helmet of My head;
Judah is My scepter.
9 "Moab is My washbowl;
Over Edom I shall throw My shoe;
Over Philistia I will make a loud shout."

10 Who will bring me into the
well-defended city?
Who will lead me to Edom?
11 Have You, O God, not rejected us?
And will You, O God, not go
forth with our armies?
12 Oh give us help against the adversary,
For salvation by man is worthless.
13 Through God we shall do valiantly,
And it is He who will tread
down our adversaries.

Proverbs 25:23–24

23 The north wind brings forth rain,
And a tongue of secrets,
an indignant face.

24 It is better to live in a corner of the roof
Than in a house shared with
a contentious woman.

2 Corinthians 11:16–33

16 Again I say, let no one think me foolish;
but if *you do*, receive me even as foolish, so
that I also may boast a little. 17 What I am
saying, I am not saying according to the Lord,
but as in foolishness, in this confidence of
boasting. 18 Since many boast according to
the flesh, I will boast also. 19 For you, being
so wise, are bearing the foolish gladly. 20 For
you bear it if anyone enslaves you, anyone
devours you, anyone takes advantage of you,
anyone exalts himself, anyone hits you in
the face. 21 To *my* shame I *must* say that we
have been weak *by comparison*.

But in whatever respect anyone *else* is
daring—I speak in foolishness—I am just as
daring myself. 22 Are they Hebrews? So am I.
Are they Israelites? So am I. Are they Abra-
ham's seed? So am I. 23 Are they ministers of
Christ?—I speak as if insane—I more so; in
far more labors, in far more imprisonments,
in beatings without number, in frequent
danger of death. 24 Five times I received
from the Jews forty *lashes* less one. 25 Three
times I was beaten with rods, once I was
stoned, three times I was shipwrecked—a
night and a day I have spent in the deep. 26 *I
have been* on frequent journeys, in dangers
from rivers, dangers from robbers, dangers
from *my* countrymen, dangers from the
Gentiles, dangers in the city, dangers in the
desolate places, dangers on the sea, dangers
among false brothers. 27 *I have been* in labor
and hardship, in many sleepless nights, in
starvation and thirst, often hungry, in cold
and without enough clothing. 28 Apart
from *such* external things, there is the
daily pressure on me *of* concern for all the
churches. 29 Who is weak without my being
weak? Who is made to stumble without my
burning concern?

30 If I have to boast, I will boast of what
pertains to my weakness. 31 The God and
Father of the Lord Jesus, He who is blessed
forever, knows that I am not lying. 32 In
Damascus the ethnarch under Aretas the
king was guarding the city of the Dama-
scenes in order to seize me, 33 and I was let
down in a basket through a window in the
wall, and *so* escaped his hands.

SEPTEMBER 21

Isaiah 33:1–34:17

33 Woe to you, O destroyer,
While you were not destroyed;
And he who is treacherous,
while *others* did not deal
treacherously with him.
As soon as you finish destroying,
you will be destroyed;
As soon as you cease to deal
treacherously, *others* will deal
treacherously with you.
2 O Yahweh, be gracious to us;
we have hoped in You.
Be their strength every morning,
Our salvation also in the
time of distress.
3 At the sound of the tumult
peoples flee;
At the lifting up of Yourself
nations scatter.
4 Your spoil is gathered *as* the
caterpillar gathers;
As locusts rushing about
men rush about on it.
5 Yahweh is exalted, for He
dwells on high;
He has filled Zion with justice
and righteousness.
6 And He will be the stability
of your times,
A wealth of salvation, wisdom,
and knowledge;
The fear of Yahweh is his treasure.
7 Behold, their brave men
cry in the streets;
The messengers of peace weep bitterly.
8 The highways are desolate,
the traveler has ceased;
He has broken the covenant,
he has rejected the cities;
He has no regard for man.
9 The land mourns *and* languishes,
Lebanon is humiliated *and* withers;
Sharon is like a desert plain,
And Bashan and Carmel
lose *their foliage*.
10 "Now I will be on high,"
says Yahweh,

"Now I will be lifted up, now
I will be lifted up.
11 "You have conceived chaff, you
will give birth to stubble;
My breath will consume you
like a fire.
12 "The peoples will be burned to lime,
Like cut thorns which are
burned in the fire.

13 "You who are far away, hear
what I have done;
And you who are near,
acknowledge My might."
14 Sinners in Zion are in dread;
Trembling has seized the godless.
"Who among us can sojourn
with the consuming fire?
Who among us can sojourn
with continual burning?"
15 He who walks righteously
and speaks uprightly;
He who rejects greedy gain
of oppression,
And shakes his hands so that
they hold no bribe;
He who stops his ears from
hearing about bloodshed
And shuts his eyes from
looking upon evil;
16 He will dwell on the heights,
His refuge will be the
strongholds of the cliffs;
His bread will be given *him*,
His water will be sure.

17 Your eyes will behold the
King in His beauty;
They will see a far-distant land.
18 Your heart will meditate on terror:
"Where is he who counts?
Where is he who weighs?
Where is he who counts the towers?"
19 You will no longer see a fierce people,
A people of unintelligible speech
which no one comprehends,
Of a stammering tongue which
no one understands.
20 Behold Zion, the city of our
appointed times;
Your eyes will see Jerusalem,
an abode at ease,
A tent which will not be folded;
Its stakes will never be pulled up,
Nor any of its cords ever be torn apart.
21 But there the Mighty *One*,
Yahweh, will be for us
A place of rivers *and* wide canals
On which no boat with oars will go,
And on which no mighty
ship will pass—
22 For Yahweh is our judge,
Yahweh is our lawgiver,
Yahweh is our king;
He will save us—
23 Your cords hang slack;
They cannot hold the base
of their mast firmly,
Nor spread out the sail.
Then the prey of an abundant
spoil will be divided;
The lame will take the plunder.
24 And no one who dwells *there*
will say, "I am sick";
The people who inhabit there will
be forgiven *their* iniquity.

34 Draw near, O nations, to hear;
and pay attention, O peoples!
Let the earth hear, as well as
its fullness, the world and
all that springs from it.
2 For the indignation of Yahweh
is against all the nations,
And *His* wrath against all their hosts;
He has devoted them to destruction;
He has given them over to slaughter.
3 So their slain will be cast out,
And their corpses will give
off their stench,
And the mountains will be
drenched with their blood.
4 And all the host of heaven
will rot away,
And the sky will be rolled
up like a scroll;
All their hosts will also wither away
As a leaf withers from the vine,
Or as *one* withers from the fig tree.
5 For My sword is satiated in heaven;
Behold, it shall descend for
judgment upon Edom
And upon the people whom I
have devoted to destruction.
6 The sword of Yahweh is
filled with blood;
It is sated with fat, with the
blood of lambs and goats,
With the fat of the kidneys of rams.
For Yahweh has a sacrifice in Bozrah

And a great slaughter in
the land of Edom.
7 And wild oxen will also fall with them,
And young bulls with strong ones;
Thus their land will be
soaked with blood,
And their dust become greasy with fat.
8 For Yahweh has a day of vengeance,
A year of recompense for
the cause of Zion.
9 And its streams will be
turned into pitch,
And its dust into brimstone,
And its land will become
burning pitch.
10 It will not be quenched night or day;
Its smoke will go up forever.
From generation to generation
it will be laid waste;
None will pass through it
forever and ever.
11 But pelican and hedgehog
will possess it,
And owl and raven will dwell in it;
And He will stretch over it the
line of *utter* formlessness
And the plumb line of *utter* void.
12 Its nobles—there is no one there
Whom they may proclaim king—
And all its princes will be non-existent.
13 And thorns will come up in
its fortified towers,
Weeds and thistles in its fortified cities;
It will also be a haunt of jackals
And an abode of ostriches.
14 And the desert creatures will
meet with the wolves;
The hairy goat also will cry to its kind;
Surely, the night creature
will obtain relief there
And will find itself a resting place.
15 The owl will make its nest and
find its escape there,
And it will hatch *its eggs* and
gather *them* in its shade.
Surely, the falcons will be
gathered there,
Every one with its kind.

16 Seek from the book of Yahweh, and read:
Not one of these will be missing;
None will lack its mate.
For His mouth has commanded,
And His Spirit has gathered them.
17 He has cast the lot for them,
And His hand has divided
it to them by line.
They shall possess it forever;
From generation to generation
they will dwell in it.

Psalm 109:1–5

1 O God of my praise,
Do not be silent!
2 For they have opened a wicked mouth
and a deceitful mouth against me;
They have spoken to me
with a lying tongue.
3 They have also surrounded me
with words of hatred,
And fought against me without cause.
4 In return for my love they accuse me;
But I am *in* prayer.
5 Thus they have set upon
me evil for good
And hatred for my love.

Proverbs 25:25–26

25 *Like* cold water to a weary soul,
So is a good report from a distant land.
26 *Like* a muddied spring and
a corrupted well
Is a righteous man shaking
before the wicked.

2 Corinthians 12:1–21

12 It is necessary to boast, though it is not
profitable, but I will go on to visions
and revelations of the Lord. 2 I know a man
in Christ who fourteen years ago—whether
in the body I do not know, or out of the body
I do not know, God knows—such a man was
caught up to the third heaven. 3 And I know
how such a man—whether in the body or
apart from the body I do not know, God
knows— 4 was caught up into Paradise and
heard inexpressible words, which a man is
not permitted to speak. 5 On behalf of such
a man I will boast, but on my own behalf I
will not boast, except in weaknesses. 6 For if
I do wish to boast I will not be foolish, for I
will be speaking the truth; but I refrain *from*
this, so that no one will consider me beyond
what he sees *in* me or hears from me.
7 Because of the surpassing greatness of
the revelations, for this reason, to keep me
from exalting myself, there was given me
a thorn in the flesh, a messenger of Satan
to torment me—to keep me from exalting
myself! 8 Concerning this I pleaded with the

Lord three times that it might leave me. 9 And
He has said to me, “My grace is sufficient for
you, for power is perfected in weakness.”
Most gladly, therefore, I will rather boast in
my weaknesses, so that the power of Christ
may dwell in me. 10 Therefore I am well
content with weaknesses, with insults, with
distresses, with persecutions and hardships,
for the sake of Christ, for when I am weak,
then I am strong.

11 I have become foolish; you yourselves
compelled me. For I ought to have been
commended by you, for in no respect was I
inferior to the most-eminent apostles, even
if I am nothing. 12 The signs of a true apostle
were worked out among you with all perse-
verance, by signs and wonders and miracles.
13 For in what respect were you treated as
less than the rest of the churches, except
that I myself did not become a burden to
you? Forgive me this wrong!

14 Here for this third time I am ready to
come to you, and I will not be a burden to
you; for I do not seek what is yours, but
you. For children ought not to save up for
their parents, but parents for *their* children.
15 So I will most gladly spend and be fully
spent for your souls. If I love you more, am
I to be loved less? 16 But be that as it may, I
did not burden you myself. Nevertheless,
crafty fellow that I am, I took you in by
deceit. 17 Have I taken advantage of you
through any of those whom I have sent to
you? 18 I encouraged Titus *to go*, and I sent
the brother with him. Did Titus take any
advantage of you? Did we not walk in the
same spirit—in the very same steps?

19 All this time you think we are defending
ourselves to you. We speak in Christ in the
sight of God. And all *these* things, beloved,
are for your building up. 20 For I am afraid
that perhaps when I come I may find you
to be not what I wish and may be found by
you to be not what you wish; that perhaps
there will be strife, jealousy, outbursts of
anger, selfish ambition, slanders, gossip,
arrogance, disturbances. 21 *I am afraid that*
when I come again my God may humiliate
me before you, and I may mourn over many
of those who have sinned in the past and not
repented of the impurity, sexual immorality,
and sensuality which they have practiced.

SEPTEMBER 22

Isaiah 35:1–36:22

35 The wilderness and the
desert will be delighted,
And the Arabah will rejoice
and flourish;
Like the crocus
2 It will flourish profusely
And rejoice with rejoicing
and shout of joy.
The glory of Lebanon will
be given to it,
The majesty of Carmel and Sharon.
They will see the glory of Yahweh,
The majesty of our God.
3 Strengthen limp hands, and
give courage to the knees
of the stumbling.
4 Say to those with an anxious heart,
“Be strong, fear not.
Behold, your God will come
with vengeance;
The recompense of God will come,
But He will save you.”
5 Then the eyes of the blind
will be opened,
And the ears of the deaf
will be unstopped.
6 Then the lame will leap like a deer,
And the tongue of the mute
will shout for joy.
For waters will break forth
in the wilderness
And streams in the Arabah.
7 Then the scorched land
will become a pool
And the thirsty ground
springs of water;
In the haunt of jackals, its resting place,
Grass *becomes* reeds and rushes.
8 And a roadway will be there, a highway,
And it will be called the
Highway of Holiness.
The unclean will not pass by on it,
But it *will* be for him who
walks *in that* way,
And ignorant fools will
not wander *on it*.
9 No lion will be there,
Nor will any vicious beast go up on it;
These will not be found there.

But the redeemed will walk *there*,
10 And the ransomed of
Yahweh will return
And come with joyful shouting to Zion,
With everlasting gladness
upon their heads.
They will attain delight and gladness,
And sorrow and sighing will flee away.

36 Now it happened in the fourteenth
year of King Hezekiah, *that* Sen-
nacherib king of Assyria came up against
all the fortified cities of Judah and seized
them. 2 And the king of Assyria sent Rab-
shakeh from Lachish to Jerusalem to King
Hezekiah with a heavy military force. And
he stood by the conduit of the upper pool
on the highway of the fuller's field. 3 Then
Eliakim the son of Hilkiah, who was over
the household, and Shebna the scribe, and
Joah the son of Asaph, the recorder, came
out to him.

4 Then Rabshakeh said to them, "Say now
to Hezekiah, 'Thus says the great king, the
king of Assyria, "What is this trust that you
have? 5 I say, 'Your counsel and might for the
war are only empty words.' Now in whom
do you trust, that you have rebelled against
me? 6 Behold, you trust in the staff of this
crushed reed, *even* on Egypt, on which if
a man leans, it will go into his hand and
pierce it. So is Pharaoh king of Egypt to all
who trust in him. 7 But if you say to me, 'We
trust in Yahweh our God,' is it not He whose
high places and whose altars Hezekiah has
taken away and has said to Judah and to
Jerusalem, 'You shall worship before this
altar'? 8 So now, come make a bargain with
my master the king of Assyria, and I will give
you two thousand horses, if you are able on
your part to give riders for them. 9 How then
can you turn away one official of the least
of my master's servants and trust in Egypt
for chariots and for horsemen? 10 So now,
have I come up without the approval of
Yahweh against this land to make it a ruin?
Yahweh said to me, 'Go up against this land
and make it a ruin.'""'"

11 Then Eliakim and Shebna and Joah
said to Rabshakeh, "Speak now to your
servants in Aramaic, for we understand *it*;
and do not speak with us in Judean in the
hearing of the people who are on the wall."
12 But Rabshakeh said, "Has my master sent
me only to your master and to you to speak
these words, *and* not to the men who sit on
the wall, *doomed* to eat their own dung and
drink their own urine with you?"

13 Then Rabshakeh stood and cried with
a loud voice in Judean and said, "Hear the
words of the great king, the king of Assyria.
14 Thus says the king, 'Do not let Hezekiah
deceive you, for he will not be able to
deliver you; 15 and do not let Hezekiah
make you trust in Yahweh, saying, "Yahweh
will surely deliver us, this city will not be
given into the hand of the king of Assyria."
16 Do not listen to Hezekiah,' for thus says
the king of Assyria, 'Make your peace with
me and come out to me, and eat each of his
vine and each of his fig tree, and drink each
of the waters of his own cistern, 17 until I
come and take you away to a land like your
own land, a land of grain and new wine,
a land of bread and vineyards. 18 *Beware*
lest Hezekiah mislead you, saying, "Yahweh
will deliver us." Has any one of the gods
of the nations delivered his land from the
hand of the king of Assyria? 19 Where are
the gods of Hamath and Arpad? Where are
the gods of Sepharvaim? And when have
they delivered Samaria from my hand?
20 Who among all the gods of these lands
have delivered their land from my hand,
that Yahweh would deliver Jerusalem from
my hand?'"

21 But they were silent and answered
him not a word, for the king's command-
ment was, "Do not answer him." 22 Then
Eliakim the son of Hilkiah, who was over
the household, and Shebna the scribe, and
Joah the son of Asaph, the recorder, came
to Hezekiah with their clothes torn and told
him the words of Rabshakeh.

Psalm 109:6–13

6 Appoint a wicked man over him,
And let an accuser stand
at his right hand.
7 When he is judged, let him
come forth a wicked man,
And let his prayer become sin.
8 Let his days be few;
Let another take his office.
9 Let his sons be orphans
And his wife a widow.
10 Let his sons wander aimlessly and beg;
And let them search *for food*
from their ruined homes.
11 Let the creditor seize all that he has,

And let strangers plunder
the fruit of his labor.
12 Let there be none to extend
lovingkindness to him,
And let there be none to be
gracious to his orphans.
13 Let *those who* follow him be cut off;
In a following generation let
their name be blotted out.

Proverbs 25:27–28

27 To eat too much honey is not good,
Nor is it glory to search out
one's own glory.
28 *Like* a city that is broken into
and without a wall
Is a man without restraint
over his spirit.

2 Corinthians 13:1–14

13 This is the third time I am coming
to you. BY THE MOUTH OF TWO OR
THREE WITNESSES EVERY MATTER SHALL BE
CONFIRMED. 2 I have previously said when
present the second time, and though now
absent I say in advance to those who have
sinned in the past and to all the rest *as well*,
that if I come again I will not spare *anyone*,
3 since you are seeking proof that Christ
speaks in me; He is not weak toward you,
but mighty in you. 4 For indeed He was
crucified because of weakness, yet He lives
because of the power of God. For we also
are weak in Him, yet we will live with Him
because of the power of God toward you.
5 Test yourselves *to see* if you are in the
faith; examine yourselves! Or do you not
recognize about yourselves that Jesus Christ
is in you—unless indeed you fail the test?
6 But I hope that you will realize that we
ourselves do not fail the test. 7 Now we pray
to God that you do no wrong, not that we
ourselves may appear approved, but that
you may do what is right, even though we
may appear unapproved. 8 For we can do
nothing against the truth, but *only* for the
truth. 9 For we rejoice when we ourselves are
weak but you are strong. This we also pray
for, that you be restored. 10 For this reason
I am writing these things while absent, so
that when present I *need* not use severity,
in accordance with the authority which the
Lord gave me for building up and not for
tearing down.
11 Finally, brothers, rejoice, be restored,
be comforted, be like-minded, live in peace,
and the God of love and peace will be with
you. 12 Greet one another with a holy kiss.
13 All the saints greet you.
14 The grace of the Lord Jesus Christ, and
the love of God, and the fellowship of the
Holy Spirit, be with you all.

SEPTEMBER 23

Isaiah 37:1–38:22

37 Now it happened that when King
Hezekiah heard *it*, he tore his
clothes, covered himself with sackcloth,
and entered the house of Yahweh. 2 Then he
sent Eliakim, who was over the household
with Shebna the scribe, and the elders
of the priests, covered with sackcloth, to
Isaiah the prophet, the son of Amoz. 3 And
they said to him, "Thus says Hezekiah, 'This
day is a day of distress, reproof, and rejec-
tion; for children have come to the point
of breaking forth, but there is no strength
to give birth. 4 Perhaps Yahweh your God
will hear the words of Rabshakeh, whom
his master the king of Assyria has sent to
reproach the living God, and will reprove
the words which Yahweh your God has
heard. Therefore, lift up a prayer for the
remnant that is left.'"
5 So the servants of King Hezekiah came
to Isaiah. 6 And Isaiah said to them, "Thus
you shall say to your master, 'Thus says Yah-
weh, "Do not be afraid because of the words
that you have heard, with which the young
men of the king of Assyria have blasphemed
Me. 7 Behold, I will put a spirit in him so that
he will hear a report and return to his own
land. And I will make him fall by the sword
in his own land."'"
8 Then Rabshakeh returned and found
the king of Assyria fighting against Libnah,
for he had heard that the king had set out
from Lachish. 9 Then he heard *them* say
concerning Tirhakah king of Ethiopia, "He
has come out to fight against you." So he
heard *it* and sent messengers to Hezekiah,
saying, 10 "Thus you shall say to Hezekiah
king of Judah, 'Do not let your God in whom
you trust deceive you, saying, "Jerusalem

will not be given into the hand of the king
of Assyria." 11 Behold, you have heard what
the kings of Assyria have done to all the
lands, devoting them to destruction. So will
you be delivered? 12 Did the gods of those
nations, which my fathers have brought to
ruin, deliver them, *even* Gozan and Haran
and Rezeph and the sons of Eden who *were*
in Telassar? 13 Where is the king of Hamath,
the king of Arpad, the king of the city of
Sepharvaim, *and of* Hena and Ivvah?'"

14 Then Hezekiah took the letter from the
hand of the messengers and read it, and he
went up to the house of Yahweh and spread
it out before Yahweh. 15 And Hezekiah
prayed to Yahweh saying, 16 "O Yahweh of
hosts, the God of Israel, who is enthroned
above the cherubim, You are the God, You
alone, of all the kingdoms of the earth. You
have made heaven and earth. 17 Incline
Your ear, O Yahweh, and hear; open Your
eyes, O Yahweh, and see; and listen to all
the words of Sennacherib, who sent *them* to
reproach the living God. 18 Truly, O Yahweh,
the kings of Assyria have laid waste to all
the countries and their lands 19 and have
cast their gods into the fire, for they were
not gods but the work of men's hands,
wood and stone. So they have destroyed
them. 20 But now, O Yahweh our God, save
us from his hand that all the kingdoms of
the earth may know that You are Yahweh,
You alone."

21 Then Isaiah the son of Amoz sent *word*
to Hezekiah, saying, "Thus says Yahweh,
the God of Israel, 'Because you have prayed
to Me about Sennacherib king of Assyria,
22 this is the word that Yahweh has spoken
against him:

"She has despised you and mocked you,
The virgin daughter of Zion;
She has shaken *her* head behind you,
The daughter of Jerusalem!
23 "Whom have you reproached
and blasphemed?
And against whom have you
heightened *your* voice
And haughtily lifted up your eyes?
Against the Holy One of Israel!
24 "Through your servants you
have reproached the Lord,
And you have said, 'With my
many chariots I came up to the
heights of the mountains,
To the remotest parts of Lebanon;
And I cut down its tall cedars
and its choice cypresses.
And I will go to its highest
peak, its thickest forest.
25 'I dug *wells* and drank waters,
And with the sole of my feet I dried up
All the rivers of Egypt.'
26 "Have you not heard?
Long ago I did it;
From days of old I formed it.
Now I have brought it to pass,
That you should devastate fortified
cities into ruinous heaps.
27 "So their inhabitants were
short of power;
They were dismayed and put to shame;
They were *as* the plant of the
field and *as* the green herb,
As grass on the rooftops is
scorched before it rises.
28 "But I know your sitting down
And your going out and your coming in
And your raging against Me.
29 "Because of your raging against Me
And because your presumptuousness
has come up to My ears,
Therefore I will put My
hook in your nose
And My bridle in your lips,
And I will turn you back by the
way which you came.

30 "Then this shall be the sign for you:
you will eat this year what grows of its own
accord, in the second year what springs from
the same, and in the third year sow, reap,
plant vineyards, and eat their fruit. 31 And
the surviving remnant of the house of Judah
will again take root downward and bear fruit
upward. 32 For out of Jerusalem will go forth
a remnant and out of Mount Zion survivors.
The zeal of Yahweh of hosts will do this."'

33 "Therefore, thus says Yahweh concern-
ing the king of Assyria, 'He will not come to
this city or shoot an arrow there; and he will
not come before it with a shield or throw
up a siege ramp against it. 34 By the way
that he came, by the same he will return,
and he will not come to this city,' declares
Yahweh. 35 'Indeed I will defend this city to
save it for My own sake and for My servant
David's sake.'"

36 Then the angel of Yahweh went out and
struck 185,000 in the camp of the Assyrians.
And the men arose early in the morning,
and behold, all of them were dead bodies.

37 So Sennacherib king of Assyria set out and
returned *home* and lived at Nineveh. 38 Now
it happened that as he was worshiping in
the house of Nisroch his god, Adrammelech
and Sharezer his sons struck him down with
the sword; and they escaped into the land
of Ararat. And Esarhaddon his son became
king in his place.

38 In those days Hezekiah became ill
to the point of death. And Isaiah the
prophet the son of Amoz came to him and
said to him, "Thus says Yahweh, 'Set your
house in order, for you shall die and not live.'"
2 Then Hezekiah turned his face to the wall
and prayed to Yahweh 3 and said, "Remember
now, O Yahweh, I beseech You, how I have
walked before You in truth and with a whole
heart and have done what is good in Your
sight." And Hezekiah wept greatly.

4 Then the word of Yahweh came to
Isaiah, saying, 5 "Go and say to Hezekiah,
'Thus says Yahweh, the God of your father
David, "I have heard your prayer; I have seen
your tears; behold, I will add fifteen years
to your life. 6 And I will deliver you and this
city from the hand of the king of Assyria;
and I will defend this city."'

7 "Now this shall be the sign to you from
Yahweh, that Yahweh will do this word that
He has spoken: 8 Behold, I will cause the
shadow on the stairway, which has gone
down with the sun on the stairway of Ahaz,
to go back ten steps." So the sun's *shadow*
went back ten steps on the stairway on
which it had gone down.

9 A writing of Hezekiah king of Judah
after his illness and recovery:

10 I said, "In the middle of my life
I am to enter the gates of Sheol;
I am to be deprived of the
rest of my years."
11 I said, "I will not see Yah,
Yah in the land of the living;
I will look on man no more among
the inhabitants of the world.
12 "Like a shepherd's tent my dwelling is
pulled up and removed from me;
As a weaver I rolled up my life.
He cuts me off from the loom;
From day until night You
make an end of me.
13 "I soothed *my soul* until morning.
Like a lion—so He shatters
all my bones;
From day until night You
make an end of me.
14 "Like a swallow, *like* a crane,
so I chirped;
I moan like a dove;
My eyes look wistfully to the heights;
O Lord, I am oppressed, be my security.

15 "What shall I say?
Indeed, He has spoken to me,
and He Himself has done it;
I will wander about all my years
because of the bitterness of my soul.
16 "O Lord, by *these* things *men* live,
And in all these is the life of my spirit;
O restore me to health and let me live!

17 "Behold, for *my own* well-being
I had great bitterness;
But it is You who has held back my
soul from the pit of nothingness,
For You have cast all my sins
behind Your back.
18 "For Sheol cannot thank You;
Death cannot praise You;
Those who go down to the pit cannot
keep watch for Your truth.
19 "It is the living, the living who give
thanks to You, as I do today;
A father makes known to his
sons about Your truth.
20 "Yahweh *is here* to save me;
So we will play my songs on
stringed instruments
All *the* days of our life at the
house of Yahweh."

21 Now Isaiah had said, "Let them take up
a cake of figs and apply it to the boil, that he
may live." 22 Then Hezekiah had said, "What
is the sign that I shall go up to the house of
Yahweh?"

Psalm 109:14–20

14 Let the iniquity of his fathers be
remembered before Yahweh,
And let not the sin of his
mother be blotted out.
15 Let them be before Yahweh
continually,
That He may cut off their
memory from the earth;
16 Because he did not remember
to show lovingkindness,
But persecuted the afflicted,
the needy man,

And the disheartened to
put *them* to death.
17 He also loved cursing, so
it came to him;
And he did not delight in blessing,
so it was far from him.
18 But he clothed himself with
cursing as his garment,
And it came into his inward
parts like water
And like oil into his bones.
19 Let it be to him as a garment with
which he wraps himself,
And for a belt with which he
constantly girds himself.
20 This is the reward of my
accusers from Yahweh,
And of those who speak
evil against my soul.

Proverbs 26:1

26 Like snow in summer and
like rain in harvest,
So glory is not fitting for a fool.

Galatians 1:1–24

1 Paul, an apostle—not *sent* from men nor
through man, but through Jesus Christ
and God the Father, who raised Him from
the dead— 2 and all the brothers who are
with me,
To the churches of Galatia:
3 Grace to you and peace from God our
Father and the Lord Jesus Christ, 4 who gave
Himself for our sins so that He might rescue
us from this present evil age, according to
the will of our God and Father, 5 to whom *be*
the glory forever and ever. Amen.
6 I marvel that you are so quickly
deserting Him who called you by the grace
of Christ for a different gospel, 7 which is
really not another, only there are some who
are disturbing you and want to distort the
gospel of Christ. 8 But even if we, or an
angel from heaven, should proclaim to
you a gospel contrary to the gospel we have
proclaimed to you, let him be accursed! 9 As
we have said before, so I say again now, if
any man is proclaiming to you a gospel
contrary to what you received, let him be
accursed!
10 For am I now seeking the favor of men,
or of God? Or am I striving to please men?
If I were still trying to please men, I would
not be a slave of Christ.
11 For I make known to you, brothers, that
the gospel which I am proclaiming as good
news is not according to man. 12 For I nei-
ther received it from man, nor was I taught
it, but *I received it* through a revelation of
Jesus Christ.
13 For you have heard of my former con-
duct in Judaism, how I used to persecute
the church of God beyond measure and
tried to destroy it. 14 And I was advancing in
Judaism beyond many of my contemporar-
ies among my countrymen, being far more
zealous for the traditions of my fathers.
15 But when God, who had set me apart
from my mother's womb and called me
through His grace, was pleased 16 to reveal
His Son in me so that I might proclaim Him
as good news among the Gentiles, I did not
immediately consult with flesh and blood,
17 nor did I go up to Jerusalem to those
who were apostles before me, but I went
away to Arabia, and returned once more
to Damascus.
18 Then three years later I went up to
Jerusalem to become acquainted with
Cephas, and stayed with him fifteen days.
19 But I did not see any other of the apostles
except James, the Lord's brother. 20 (Now in
what I am writing to you, I assure you before
God that I am not lying!) 21 Then I went into
the regions of Syria and Cilicia. 22 And I was
still unknown by sight to the churches of
Judea which are in Christ; 23 but only, they
kept hearing, "He who once persecuted us is
now proclaiming the good news of the faith
which he once tried to destroy." 24 And they
were glorifying God because of me.

It is a very blessed thing to hear the Word of the living God.
It is also a very blessed thing to proclaim that Word to others.

— J. GRESHAM MACHEN

SEPTEMBER 24

Isaiah 39:1–40:31

39 At that time Merodach-baladan
son of Baladan, king of Babylon,
sent letters and a present to Hezekiah, for
he heard that he had been sick and was
growing stronger. 2 And Hezekiah was glad
about these things and showed them *all*
his treasure house, the silver and the gold
and the spices and the good oil and his
whole armory and all that was found in his
treasuries. There was nothing in his house
nor in all his dominion that Hezekiah did
not show them. 3 Then Isaiah the prophet
came to King Hezekiah and said to him,
"What did these men say, and from where
have they come to you?" And Hezekiah said,
"They have come to me from a far country,
from Babylon." 4 And he said, "What have
they seen in your house?" So Hezekiah said,
"They have seen all that is in my house;
there is nothing among my treasuries that
I have not shown them."

5 Then Isaiah said to Hezekiah, "Hear the
word of Yahweh of hosts, 6 'Behold, the days
are coming when all that is in your house
and all that your fathers have treasured
up to this day will be carried to Babylon;
nothing will be left,' says Yahweh. 7 'And
some of your sons who will issue from you,
whom you will beget, will be taken away,
and they will become officials in the palace
of the king of Babylon.'" 8 Then Hezekiah
said to Isaiah, "The word of Yahweh which
you have spoken is good." For he said, "For
there will be peace and truth in my days."

40 "Comfort, O comfort My
people," says your God.
2 "Speak to the heart of Jerusalem;
And call out to her, that her
warfare has been fulfilled,
That her iniquity has been removed,
That she has received from
the hand of Yahweh
Double for all her sins."

3 A voice is calling,
"Prepare the way for Yahweh
in the wilderness;
Make smooth in the desert
a highway for our God.
4 "Let every valley be lifted up,
And every mountain and
hill be made low;
And let the rough ground
become a plain,
And the rugged terrain a broad valley;
5 Then the glory of Yahweh
will be revealed,
And all flesh will see *it* together;
For the mouth of Yahweh has spoken."
6 A voice says, "Call out."
Then he answered, "What
shall I call out?"
All flesh is grass, and all its
lovingkindness is like the
flower of the field.
7 The grass withers, the flower fades,
When the breath of Yahweh
blows upon it;
Surely the people are grass.
8 The grass withers, the flower fades,
But the word of our God stands forever.

9 Get yourself up on a high mountain,
O Zion, bearer of good news,
Raise up your voice powerfully,
O Jerusalem, bearer of good news;
Raise *it* up, do not fear.
Say to the cities of Judah,
"Behold your God!"
10 Behold, Lord Yahweh will
come with strength,
With His arm ruling for Him.
Behold, His reward is with Him
And His recompense before Him.
11 Like a shepherd He will
shepherd His flock;
In His arm He will gather the lambs
And carry *them* in His bosom;
He will gently lead the nursing *ewes*.

12 Who has measured the waters
in the hollow of His hand,
And encompassed the
heavens by the span,
And calculated the dust of the
earth by the measure,
And weighed the mountains
in a balance
And the hills in a pair of scales?
13 Who has encompassed the
Spirit of Yahweh,
Or as His counselor has informed Him?

14 With whom did He take counsel and
who gave Him understanding?
And *who* taught Him in the path of
justice and taught Him knowledge
And made Him know the way
of understanding?
15 Behold, the nations are like
a drop from a bucket,
And are counted as a speck
of dust on the scales;
Behold, He lifts up the
coastlands like fine dust.
16 Even Lebanon is not enough to burn,
Nor its beasts enough for
a burnt offering.
17 All the nations are as
nothing before Him;
They are counted by Him as
non-existent and *utterly* formless.

18 To whom then will you liken God?
Or what likeness will you
compare with Him?
19 *As for* the graven images, a
craftsman casts it,
A goldsmith plates it with gold,
And a silversmith *fashions*
chains of silver.
20 He who is too impoverished *to
make such* a contribution
Chooses a tree that does not rot;
He seeks out for himself
a wise craftsman
To prepare a graven image
that will not be shaken.

21 Do you not know? Have you not heard?
Has it not been declared to
you from the beginning?
Have you not understood from
the foundations of the earth?
22 It is He who inhabits above
the circle of the earth,
And its inhabitants are like grasshoppers;
It is He who stretches out the
heavens like a curtain
And spreads them out like
a tent to inhabit.
23 It is He who reduces rulers to nothing,
Who makes the judges of the
earth *utterly* formless.
24 Scarcely have they been planted;
Scarcely have they been sown;
Scarcely has their stem taken
root in the earth,
But He merely blows on
them, and they wither,
And the storm carries them
away like stubble.
25 "To whom then will you liken Me
That I would be *his* equal?"
says the Holy One.
26 Lift up your eyes on high
And see who has created these *stars*,
The One who leads forth
their host by number,
He calls them all by name;
Because of the greatness of His vigor
and the strength of *His* power,
Not one *of them* is missing.

27 Why do you say, O Jacob,
and assert, O Israel,
"My way is hidden from Yahweh,
And the justice due me
passes by my God"?
28 Do you not know? Have you not heard?
The Everlasting God, Yahweh, the
Creator of the ends of the earth,
Does not become weary or tired.
His understanding is unsearchable.
29 He gives power to the weary,
And to *him who* lacks vigor
He increases might.
30 Though youths grow weary and tired,
And choice young men stumble badly,
31 Yet those who hope in Yahweh
Will gain new power;
They will mount up *with*
wings like eagles;
They will run and not get tired;
They will walk and not
become weary.

Psalm 109:21–25

21 But as for You, O Yahweh, O Lord, deal
with me for Your name's sake;
Because Your lovingkindness
is good, deliver me;
22 For I am afflicted and needy,
And my heart is pierced within me.
23 I am passing like a shadow
when it is stretched out;
I am shaken off like the locust.
24 My knees are feeble from fasting,
And my flesh has grown
lean, without fatness.
25 As for me, I have become a
reproach to them;
They see me, they wag their head.

Proverbs 26:2

2 Like a sparrow in *its* flitting,
like a swallow in flying,
So a curse without cause
does not come *to pass*.

Galatians 2:1–21

2 Then after fourteen years I went up
again to Jerusalem with Barnabas, taking
Titus along also. 2 And I went up because
of a revelation, and I laid out to them the
gospel which I preach among the Gentiles,
but *I did so* in private to those who were
of reputation, lest somehow I might be
running, or had run, in vain. 3 But not even
Titus, who was with me, though he was a
Greek, was compelled to be circumcised.
4 But *this was* because of the false brothers
secretly brought in, who had sneaked in
to spy out our freedom which we have in
Christ Jesus, in order to enslave us. 5 But
we did not yield in subjection to them for
even a moment, so that the truth of the
gospel would remain with you. 6 But from
those who were of high reputation (what
they were makes no difference to me; God
shows no partiality)—well, those who
were of reputation contributed nothing
to me. 7 But on the contrary, seeing that I
had been entrusted with the gospel to the
uncircumcised, just as Peter *had been* to the
circumcised 8 (for He who worked in Peter
unto *his* apostleship to the circumcised
worked in me also unto the Gentiles), 9 and
recognizing the grace that had been given
to me, James and Cephas and John, who
were reputed to be pillars, gave to me and
Barnabas the right hand of fellowship, so
that we *might go* to the Gentiles and they
to the circumcised. 10 Only *they asked* us to
remember the poor—the very thing I also
was eager to do.
11 But when Cephas came to Antioch, I
opposed him to his face, because he stood
condemned. 12 For prior to the coming of
certain men from James, he used to eat with
the Gentiles, but when they came, he *began*
to shrink back and separate himself, fearing
the party of the circumcision. 13 And the rest
of the Jews joined him in hypocrisy, with the
result that even Barnabas was carried away
by their hypocrisy. 14 But when I saw that
they were not straightforward about the
truth of the gospel, I said to Cephas before
everyone, "If you, being a Jew, live like the
Gentiles and not like the Jews, how *is it that*
you compel the Gentiles to live like Jews?
15 "We *are* Jews by nature and not sinners
from among the Gentiles; 16 nevertheless
knowing that a man is not justified by the
works of the Law but through faith in Jesus
Christ, even we have believed in Christ
Jesus, so that we may be justified by faith
in Christ and not by the works of the Law;
since by the works of the Law no flesh will
be justified. 17 But if, while seeking to be
justified in Christ, we ourselves have also
been found sinners, is Christ then a minister
of sin? May it never be! 18 For if I rebuild
what I have *once* destroyed, I prove myself
to be a transgressor. 19 For through the Law
I died to the Law, so that I might live to God.
20 I have been crucified with Christ, and it is
no longer I who live, but Christ lives in me.
And the *life* which I now live in the flesh I
live by faith in the Son of God, who loved me
and gave Himself up for me. 21 I do not set
aside the grace of God, for if righteousness
comes through the Law, then Christ died
needlessly."

SEPTEMBER 25

Isaiah 41:1–42:25

41 "Coastlands, listen to Me in silence,
And let the peoples gain new power;
Let them come forward,
then let them speak;
Let us draw near together
for judgment.
2 "Who has awakened one from the east
Whom He calls in righteousness
to His feet?
He gives up nations before him
And has dominion over kings.
He makes them like dust
with his sword,
As the wind-driven chaff with his bow.
3 "He pursues them, passing on in peace,
By a way he had not come with his feet.
4 "Who has worked and done *it*,
Calling forth the generations
from the beginning?
'I, Yahweh, am the first; and
with the last, I am He.'"

5 The coastlands have seen
and are afraid;
The ends of the earth tremble;
They have drawn near and have come.
6 Each one helps his neighbor
And says to his brother, "Be strong!"
7 So the craftsman strengthens
the smelter,
And he who smooths *metal*
with the hammer *strengthens*
him who beats the anvil,
Saying of the soldering, "It is good";
And he strengthens it with nails,
So that it will not be shaken.
8 "But you, Israel, My servant,
Jacob whom I have chosen,
Seed of Abraham My friend,
9 You whom I have strongly taken hold
of from the ends of the earth,
And called from its remotest parts
And said to you, 'You are My servant,
I have chosen you and
not rejected you.
10 'Do not fear, for I am with you;
Do not anxiously look about
you, for I am your God.
I will make you mighty,
surely I will help you;
Surely I will uphold you with
My righteous right hand.'
11 "Behold, all those who are angered at
you will be shamed and dishonored;
Those who contend with you will
be as nothing and will perish.
12 "You will seek those who quarrel with
you, but will not find them,
Those who war with you will be
as nothing and non-existent.
13 "For I am Yahweh your God,
who strongly takes hold
of your right hand,
Who says to you, 'Do not
fear, I will help you.'
14 "Do not fear, you worm Jacob,
you men of Israel;
I will help you," declares Yahweh,
"and your Redeemer is the
Holy One of Israel.
15 "Behold, I have made you a new, sharp
threshing sledge with double edges;
You will thresh the mountains
and pulverize *them*,
And will make the hills like chaff.
16 "You will winnow them, and the
wind will carry them away,
And the storm will scatter them;
But you will rejoice in Yahweh;
You will boast in the Holy One
of Israel.

17 "The afflicted and needy are seeking
water, but there is none,
And their tongue is parched
with thirst;
I, Yahweh, will answer them Myself,
As the God of Israel I will
not forsake them.
18 "I will open rivers on the bare heights
And springs in the midst of the valleys;
I will make the wilderness
a pool of water
And the dry land fountains of water.
19 "I will put the cedar in the wilderness,
The acacia and the myrtle
and the olive tree;
I will place the juniper in the desert
Together with the box tree
and the cypress,
20 That they may see and know,
And establish and gain insight as well,
That the hand of Yahweh
has done this,
And the Holy One of Israel
has created it.

21 "Bring near your case," Yahweh says.
"Bring forward your mighty *arguments*,"
The King of Jacob says.
22 Let them bring *it* forth and declare
to us what is going to take place;
As for the former *events*,
declare what they *were*,
That we may establish our heart on
them and know their outcome.
Or cause us to hear of what is coming;
23 Declare the things that are
to come afterward,
That we may know that you are gods;
Indeed, do good or evil, that we
may anxiously look about
us and fear together.
24 Behold, you are nothing,
And your work is non-existent;
He who chooses you is
an abomination.

25 "I have awakened one from the
north, and he has come;
From the rising of the sun he
will call on My name;

And he will come upon
officials as *upon* mortar,
Even as the potter treads clay."
26 Who has declared *this* from the
beginning, that we might know?
Or from former times, that we
may say, "*He is* right!"?
Surely there was no one who declared;
Surely there was no one who caused
those words to be heard;
Surely there was no one who
heard your words.
27 "Formerly *I said* to Zion,
'Behold, here they are.'
And to Jerusalem, 'I will give a
messenger of good news.'
28 "But I look, and there is no one,
And there is no counselor
among them
Who, if I ask, can respond *with* a word.
29 "Behold, all of them are false;
Their works are non-existent;
Their molten images are wind
and *utter* formlessness.

42 "Behold, My Servant,
whom I uphold;
My chosen one *in whom* My
soul is well-pleased.
I have put My Spirit upon Him;
He will bring forth justice
to the nations.
2 "He will not cry out or raise *His voice,*
Nor make His voice heard in the street.
3 "A crushed reed He will not break
And a faintly burning wick
He will not extinguish;
He will bring forth justice in truth.
4 "He will not be faint or crushed
Until He has established
justice in the earth;
And the coastlands will wait
expectantly for His law."

5 Thus says the God, Yahweh,
Who created the heavens and
stretched them out,
Who spread out the earth
and its offspring,
Who gives breath to the people on it
And spirit to those who walk in it,
6 "I am Yahweh, I have called
You in righteousness;
I will also take hold of You by
the hand and guard You,
And I will give You as a
covenant to the people,
As a light to the nations,
7 To open blind eyes,
To bring out prisoners
from the dungeon
And those who inhabit darkness
from the prison.
8 "I am Yahweh, that is My name;
I will not give My glory to another,
Nor My praise to graven images.
9 "Behold, the former things
have come to pass;
Now I declare new things;
Before they spring forth I cause
you to hear *them.*"

10 Sing to Yahweh a new song,
Sing His praise from the
end of the earth!
You who go down to the sea,
as well as its fullness.
You coastlands, and those
who inhabit them.
11 Let the wilderness and its
cities lift up *their voices,*
The villages where Kedar inhabits.
Let the inhabitants of Sela sing aloud,
Let them shout for joy from the
tops of the mountains.
12 Let them give glory to Yahweh
And declare His praise in
the coastlands.
13 Yahweh will go forth like a warrior;
He will awaken *His* zeal
like a man of war.
He will make a loud shout, indeed,
He will raise a war cry.
He will prevail against His enemies.
14 "I have kept silent for a long time;
I have kept still and restrained Myself.
Now like a woman in labor I will groan;
I will both gasp and pant.
15 "I will lay waste the mountains and hills
And dry up all their vegetation;
I will make the rivers into coastlands
And dry up the pools *of waters.*
16 "I will lead the blind by a way
they do not know,
In paths they do not know
I will guide them.
I will make darkness into
light before them
And rugged places into plains.
These are the things I will do,

And I will not forsake them."
17 They will be turned back *and*
be utterly put to shame,
Who trust in graven images,
Who say to molten images,
"You are our gods."

18 Hear, you deaf!
And look, you blind, that you may see.
19 Who is blind but My servant,
Or so deaf as My messenger
whom I send?
Who is so blind as he that
is at peace *with Me*,
Or so blind as the servant of Yahweh?
20 You have seen many things,
but you do not keep *them*;
Your ears are open, but none hears.
21 Yahweh was pleased for His
righteousness' sake
That He make the law
great and majestic.
22 But this is a people plundered
and *pillaged* as spoil;
All of them are trapped in caves,
Or are hidden away in prisons;
They have become a plunder
with none to deliver *them*,
And a spoil, with none to say,
"Have *them* return!"

23 Who among you will give ear to this?
Who will give heed and hear hereafter?
24 Who gave Jacob up for spoil,
and Israel to plunderers?
Was it not Yahweh, against
whom we have sinned,
And in whose ways they were
not willing to walk,
And whose law they did not obey?
25 So He poured out on him
the heat of His anger
And the fierceness of battle;
And it set him aflame all around,
Yet he did not know *it*;
And it burned him, but he did
not set it upon his heart.

Psalm 109:26–31

26 Help me, O Yahweh my God;
Save me according to Your
lovingkindness.
27 And let them know that
this is Your hand;
You, O Yahweh, have done it.
28 Let them curse, but You bless;
They arise and will be put to shame,
But Your slave shall be glad.
29 Let my accusers be clothed
with dishonor,
And let them wrap themselves with
their own shame as with a robe.
30 With my mouth I will give thanks
abundantly to Yahweh;
And in the midst of many
I will praise Him.
31 For He stands at the right
hand of the needy,
To save him from those
who judge his soul.

Proverbs 26:3–4

3 A whip is for the horse,
a bridle for the donkey,
And a rod for the back of fools.
4 Do not answer a fool
according to his folly,
Lest you yourself also be like him.

Galatians 3:1–29

3 O foolish Galatians, who bewitched
you, before whose eyes Jesus Christ
was publicly portrayed *as* crucified? 2 This
is the only thing I want to learn from you:
did you receive the Spirit by the works of
the Law, or by hearing with faith? 3 Are you
so foolish? Having begun by the Spirit, are
you now being perfected by the flesh? 4 Did
you suffer so many things for nothing—if
indeed it was for nothing? 5 So then, does He
who provides you with the Spirit and works
miracles among you, do it by the works of
the Law, or by hearing with faith?
6 Just as Abraham BELIEVED GOD AND IT
WAS COUNTED TO HIM AS RIGHTEOUSNESS, 7 SO
know that those who are of faith, those are
sons of Abraham. 8 And the Scripture, fore-
seeing that God would justify the Gentiles
by faith, proclaimed the gospel beforehand
to Abraham, *saying*, "ALL THE NATIONS WILL
BE BLESSED IN YOU." 9 So then those who
are of faith are blessed with Abraham, the
believer.
10 For as many as are of the works of
the Law are under a curse, for it is written,
"CURSED IS EVERYONE WHO DOES NOT ABIDE
BY ALL THINGS WRITTEN IN THE BOOK OF THE
LAW, TO DO THEM." 11 Now that no one is
justified by the Law before God is evident,

for "THE RIGHTEOUS SHALL LIVE BY FAITH." 12 However, the Law is not of faith; rather, "HE WHO DOES THEM SHALL LIVE BY THEM." 13 Christ redeemed us from the curse of the Law, having become a curse for us—for it is written, "CURSED IS EVERYONE WHO HANGS ON A TREE"— 14 in order that in Christ Jesus the blessing of Abraham might come to the Gentiles, so that we would receive the promise of the Spirit through faith.

15 Brothers, I speak in human terms: even though it is *only* a man's covenant, yet when it has been ratified, no one sets it aside or adds conditions to it. 16 Now the promises were spoken to Abraham and to his seed. He does not say, "And to seeds," as *referring* to many, but *rather* to one, "And TO YOUR SEED," that is, Christ. 17 And what I am saying is this: the Law, which came 430 years later, does not invalidate a covenant previously ratified by God, so as to abolish the promise. 18 For if the inheritance is by law, it is no longer by promise, but God has granted it to Abraham through promise.

19 Why the Law then? It was added because of trespasses, having been ordained through angels by the hand of a mediator, until the seed would come to whom the promise had been made. 20 Now a mediator is not for one *person only*, whereas God is one. 21 Is the Law then contrary to the promises of God? May it never be! For if a law had been given which was able to impart life, then righteousness would indeed be by law. 22 But the Scripture has shut up everyone under sin, so that the promise by faith in Jesus Christ might be given to those who believe.

23 But before faith came, we were held in custody under the Law, being shut up for the coming faith to be revealed. 24 Therefore the Law has become our tutor unto Christ, so that we may be justified by faith. 25 But now that faith has come, we are no longer under a tutor. 26 For you are all sons of God through faith in Christ Jesus. 27 For all of you who were baptized into Christ have clothed yourselves with Christ. 28 There is neither Jew nor Greek, there is neither slave nor free man, there is no male and female, for you are all one in Christ Jesus. 29 And if you belong to Christ, then you are Abraham's seed, heirs according to promise.

SEPTEMBER 26

Isaiah 43:1–44:28

43 But now, thus says Yahweh,
your Creator, O Jacob,
And He who formed you, O Israel,
"Do not fear, for I have redeemed you;
I have called you by name;
you are Mine!
2 "When you pass through the
waters, I will be with you;
And through the rivers,
they will not overflow you.
When you walk through the fire,
you will not be scorched,
Nor will the flame burn you.
3 "For I am Yahweh your God,
The Holy One of Israel, your Savior;
I have given Egypt as your ransom,
Ethiopia and Seba in your place.
4 "Since you are precious in My sight,
Since you are honored and I love you,
I will give *other* men in your
place and *other* peoples in
exchange for your life.
5 "Do not fear, for I am with you;
I will bring your seed from the east,
And gather you from the west.
6 "I will say to the north, 'Give *them* up!'
And to the south, 'Do not hold
them back.'
Bring My sons from afar
And My daughters from the
ends of the earth,
7 Everyone who is called by My name,
And whom I have created for My glory,
Whom I have formed, even
whom I have made."
8 Bring out the people who are blind,
even though they have eyes,
And the deaf, even though
they have ears.
9 All the nations have gathered together
So that the peoples may be assembled.
Who among them can declare this
And make us hear the former things?
Let them present their witnesses
that they may be justified,
Or let them hear and say, "It is true."
10 "You are My witnesses,"
declares Yahweh,
"And My servant whom I have chosen,

So that you may know
and believe Me
And understand that I am He.
Before Me there was no god formed,
And there will be none after Me.
11 "I, even I, am Yahweh,
And there is no savior besides Me.
12 "It is I who have declared and saved
and caused *it* to be heard,
And there was no strange
god among you;
So you are My witnesses,"
declares Yahweh,
"And I am God.
13 "Even from eternity I am He,
And there is none who can
deliver out of My hand;
I act and who can reverse it?"
14 Thus says Yahweh your Redeemer, the
Holy One of Israel,
"For your sake I have sent to Babylon,
And will bring down those
who fled—all of them,
Even the Chaldeans—into the ships
in which they shouted for joy.
15 "I am Yahweh, your Holy One,
The Creator of Israel, your King."
16 Thus says Yahweh,
Who makes a way through the sea
And a path through the
mighty waters,
17 Who brings forth the chariot
and the horse,
The military force and the mighty man;
They will lie down together
and not rise again;
They have been extinguished
and quenched like a wick:
18 "Do not remember the former things,
Nor carefully consider
things of the past.
19 "Behold, I will do something new;
Now it will spring forth;
Will you not know it?
I will even make a roadway
in the wilderness,
Rivers in the wasteland.
20 "The beasts of the field will glorify Me,
The jackals and the ostriches,
Because I have given waters
in the wilderness
And rivers in the wasteland,
To give drink to My chosen people.
21 "The people whom I formed for Myself
Will recount My praise.
22 "Yet you have not called on Me, O Jacob;
But you have become weary
of Me, O Israel.
23 "You have not brought to Me the
sheep of your burnt offerings,
Nor have you glorified Me
with your sacrifices.
I have not burdened you with offerings,
Nor wearied you with frankincense.
24 "You have not bought Me sweet
cane with money,
Nor have you satisfied Me with
the fat of your sacrifices;
Rather you have burdened
Me with your sins;
You have wearied Me with
your iniquities.

25 "I, even I, am the one who wipes
out your transgressions
for My own sake,
And I will not remember your sins.
26 "Bring Me to remembrance, let us
enter into judgment together;
Recount your *cause*, that you
may be proved right.
27 "Your first father sinned,
And your spokesmen have
transgressed against Me.
28 "So I will profane the princes
of the sanctuary,
And I will give Jacob to be devoted to
destruction and Israel to revilement.

44 "But now hear, O Jacob, My servant,
And Israel, whom I have chosen:
2 Thus says Yahweh who made you
And formed you from the
womb, who will help you,
'Do not fear, O Jacob My servant,
And you Jeshurun whom
I have chosen.
3 'For I will pour out water on
the thirsty *ground*
And streams on the dry land;
I will pour out My Spirit on your seed
And My blessing on your offspring;
4 And they will spring up
among the grass
Like poplars by streams of water.'
5 "This one will say, 'I am Yahweh's';
And this one will call on
the name of Jacob;
And this one will write *on* his
hand, 'Belonging to Yahweh,'

And will name Israel's
name with honor.

6 "Thus says Yahweh, the King of Israel and
his Redeemer, Yahweh of hosts:
'I am the first, and I am the last,
And there is no God besides Me.
7 'Who is like Me? Let him call
out and declare it;
And let him tell it to Me in order,
From the time that I established
the ancient people.
And let them declare to them
the things that are to come
And the events that are
going to take place.
8 'Do not be in dread and
do not be afraid;
Have I not long since caused *it* to be
heard to you and declared *it*?
And you are My witnesses.
Is there any God besides Me,
Or is there any *other* Rock?
I know of none.'"

9 Those who form a graven image are all
of them futile, and their desirable things
are of no profit; even their own witnesses
fail to see or know, so that they will be put
to shame. 10 Who has formed a god or cast
a graven image to no profit? 11 Behold, all
his companions will be put to shame. The
craftsmen themselves are mere men. Let
them all assemble themselves, let them
stand up, let them be in dread, let them
together be put to shame.

12 The man crafts iron into a cutting tool
and does his work over the coals, forming
it with hammers and working it with his
powerful arm. He also gets hungry and has
no power; he drinks no water and becomes
weary. 13 *Another* crafts wood, he extends a
measuring line; he outlines it with a stylus.
He makes it with planes and outlines it with
a compass and makes it like the form of a
man, like the glory of man, so that it may
sit in a house. 14 In order to cut cedars for
himself, he takes a cypress or an oak and
raises *it* for himself among the trees of the
forest. He plants a fir, and the rain makes
it grow. 15 Then it becomes *something* for
a man to burn, so he takes one of them
and warms himself; he also kindles a fire
to bake bread. He also works *to produce* a
god and worships it; he makes it a graven
image and falls down before it. 16 Half of it
he burns in the fire; over *this* half he eats
meat as he roasts a roast and is satisfied.
He also warms himself and says, "Aha! I am
warm; I have seen the fire." 17 But the rest
of it he makes into a god, his graven image.
He falls down before it and worships; he
also prays to it and says, "Deliver me, for
you are my god."

18 They do not know, nor do they under-
stand, for He has smeared over their eyes
so that they cannot see and their hearts
so that they will have no insight. 19 No one
causes *this* to return to his heart, nor is
there knowledge or understanding to say,
"I have burned half of it in the fire and also
have baked bread over its coals. I roast meat
and eat *it*. Then I make the rest of it into
an abomination; I fall down before a block
of wood!" 20 He feeds on ashes; a deceived
heart has turned him aside. And he cannot
deliver his soul, and he cannot say, "Is there
not a lie in my right hand?"

21 "Remember these things, O Jacob,
And Israel, for you are My servant;
I have formed you, you are My servant;
O Israel, you will not be
forgotten by Me.
22 "I have wiped out your transgressions
like a thick cloud
And your sins like a cloud.
Return to Me, for I have
redeemed you."
23 Shout for joy, O heavens,
for Yahweh has done *it*!
Make a loud shout, you lower
parts of the earth;
Break forth into a shout of
joy, you mountains,
O forest, and every tree in it;
For Yahweh has redeemed Jacob
And in Israel He shows forth
His beautiful glory.

24 Thus says Yahweh, your Redeemer, and
the one who formed you from the womb,
"I, Yahweh, am the maker of all things,
Stretching out the heavens by Myself
And spreading out the earth all alone,
25 Causing the omens of boasters
to be annulled,
And making fools out of diviners,
Causing wise men to turn back,
And making foolishness out
of their knowledge,
26 Confirming the word of His servant—

And the counsel of His messengers
He will complete—
And being the One who says of
Jerusalem, 'She shall be inhabited!'
And of the cities of Judah,
'They shall be built.'
And I will raise up her
waste places *again*.
27 "*It is I* who says to the depth of
the sea, 'Be dried up!'
And I will make your rivers dry.
28 "*It is I* who says of Cyrus,
'*He is* My shepherd!
And all My good pleasure
he will complete.'
And saying of Jerusalem,
'She will be built,'
And of the temple, 'Your
foundation will be laid.'"

Psalm 110:1–7

1 Yahweh says to my Lord:
"Sit at My right hand
Until I put Your enemies as a
footstool for Your feet."
2 Yahweh will stretch forth Your strong
scepter from Zion, *saying*,
"Have dominion in the midst
of Your enemies."
3 Your people will offer themselves
freely in the day of Your power;
In the splendor of holiness, from
the womb of the dawn,
The dew of Your youthfulness
will be Yours.

4 Yahweh has sworn and will
not change His mind,
"You are a priest forever
According to the order of Melchizedek."
5 The Lord is at Your right hand;
He will crush kings in the
day of His anger.
6 He will render justice
among the nations,
He will fill *them* with corpses,
He will crush the head *that*
is over *the* wide earth.
7 He will drink from the brook
by the wayside;
Therefore He will lift up *His* head.

Proverbs 26:5–9

5 Answer a fool according to his folly,
Lest he be wise in his own eyes.
6 He cuts off *his own* feet
and drinks violence
Who sends words by the hand of a fool.
7 *Like* the legs *which* hang
limp on the lame,
So is a proverb in the mouth of fools.
8 Like one who binds a stone in a sling,
So is he who gives glory to a fool.
9 *Like* a thorn *which* goes up into
the hand of a drunkard,
So is a proverb in the mouth of fools.

Galatians 4:1–31

4 Now I say, as long as the heir is a child,
he does not differ at all from a slave
although he is owner of everything, 2 but
he is under guardians and stewards until the
date set by the father. 3 So also we, while
we were children, were enslaved under the
elemental things of the world. 4 But when
the fullness of the time came, God sent forth
His Son, born of a woman, born under the
Law, 5 so that He might redeem those who
were under the Law, that we might receive
the adoption as sons. 6 And because you
are sons, God sent forth the Spirit of His
Son into our hearts, crying, "Abba! Father!"
7 Therefore you are no longer a slave, but a
son; and if a son, then an heir through God.
8 However at that time, when you did not
know God, you were slaves to those which
by nature are no gods. 9 But now, having
known God, or rather having been known
by God, how is it that you turn back again
to the weak and worthless elemental things,
to which you want to be enslaved all over
again? 10 You observe days and months and
seasons and years. 11 I fear for you, that
perhaps I have labored over you for nothing.
12 I beg of you, brothers, become as I
am, for I also *have become* as you *are*. You
have done me no wrong. 13 But you know
that it was because of a bodily illness that
I proclaimed the gospel to you the first
time; 14 and that which was a trial to you
in my bodily condition you did not despise
or loathe, but you received me as an angel
of God, as Christ Jesus *Himself*. 15 Where
then is that sense of blessing you had? For
I testify to you that, if possible, you would
have plucked out your eyes and given them
to me. 16 So have I become your enemy by
telling you the truth? 17 They zealously seek
you, not commendably, but they wish to
shut you out so that you will zealously seek

them. 18 But it is good always to be zeal-
ously sought in a commendable manner,
and not only when I am present with you.
19 My children, with whom I am again in
labor until Christ is formed in you— 20 but I
could wish to be present with you now and
to change my tone, because I am perplexed
about you.
21 Tell me, you who want to be under
law, do you not listen to the Law? 22 For
it is written that Abraham had two sons,
one by the servant-woman and one by the
free woman. 23 But the son by the servant-
woman had been born according to the
flesh, while the son by the free woman
through the promise. 24 This is spoken
with allegory, for these women are two
covenants: one from Mount Sinai bearing
children into slavery; she is Hagar. 25 Now
this Hagar is Mount Sinai in Arabia and
corresponds to the present Jerusalem, for
she is in slavery with her children. 26 But
the Jerusalem above is free; she is our
mother. 27 For it is written,

"REJOICE, BARREN WOMAN WHO
DOES NOT GIVE BIRTH;
BREAK FORTH AND SHOUT,
YOU WHO ARE NOT IN LABOR;
FOR MORE NUMEROUS ARE THE
CHILDREN OF THE DESOLATE ONE
THAN OF THE ONE WHO HAS A HUSBAND."

28 And you brothers, in accordance with
Isaac, are children of promise. 29 But as at
that time he who was born according to the
flesh was persecuting him *who was born*
according to the Spirit, so it is now also.
30 But what does the Scripture say?

"CAST OUT THE SERVANT-
WOMAN AND HER SON,
FOR THE SON OF THE SERVANT-WOMAN
SHALL NOT BE AN HEIR WITH THE
SON OF THE FREE WOMAN."

31 So then, brothers, we are not children of
a servant-woman, but of the free woman.

SEPTEMBER 27

Isaiah 45:1–46:13

45 Thus says Yahweh to
Cyrus His anointed,
Whom I have taken hold of
by his right hand,
To subdue nations before him
And to loose the loins of kings,
To open doors before him so
that gates will not be shut:
2 "I will go before you and make
the rough places smooth;
I will shatter the doors of bronze
and cut through their iron bars.
3 "I will give you the treasures of darkness
And hidden wealth of secret places,
So that you may know that it is I,
Yahweh, the God of Israel, who
calls you by your name.
4 "For the sake of Jacob My servant,
And Israel My chosen *one*,
I have also called you by your name;
I have given you a title of honor
Though you have not known Me.
5 "I am Yahweh, and there is no other;
Besides Me there is no God.
I will gird you, though you
have not known Me,
6 That they may know from the
rising to the setting of the sun
That there is no one besides Me.
I am Yahweh, and there is no other,
7 The One forming light and
creating darkness,
Producing peace and creating calamity;
I am Yahweh who does all these.
8 "Drip down, O heavens, from above,
And let the skies pour down
righteousness;
Let the earth open up and
salvation bear fruit,
And righteousness spring up with it.
I, Yahweh, have created it.

9 "Woe to *the one* who contends
with his Maker—
An earthenware vessel among
the vessels of earth!
Will the clay say to the potter,
'What are you doing?'
Or the thing you are making
say, 'He has no hands'?
10 "Woe to him who says to a father,
'What are you begetting?'
Or to a woman, '*With* what are
you in labor pains?'"

11 Thus says Yahweh, the Holy One of Israel,
and his Maker:

11 "Ask Me about the things that are
to come concerning My sons,
And you shall commit to Me
the work of My hands.
12 "It is I who made the earth and
created man upon it.
I stretched out the heavens
with My hands,
And I commanded all their host.
13 "I have awakened him in
righteousness,
And I will make all his ways smooth;
He will build My city and
will let My exiles go,
Without any payment or reward,"
says Yahweh of hosts.

14 Thus says Yahweh,
"The fruit of the labor of Egypt
and the profit of Ethiopia
And the Sabeans, men of stature,
Will come over to you
and will be yours;
They will walk behind you;
they will come over in chains
And will bow down to you;
They will make supplication to you:
'Surely, God is with you,
and there is none else,
No other God.'"
15 Truly, You are a God who
hides Himself,
O God of Israel, Savior!
16 They will be put to shame and
even dishonored, all of them;
The craftsmen of idols will go
away together in dishonor.
17 Israel has been saved by Yahweh
With an everlasting salvation;
You will not be put to shame
or dishonored
To all eternity.

18 For thus says Yahweh, who created the
heavens (He is the God who formed the
earth and made it; He established it *and* did
not create it a formless place, *but* formed it
to be inhabited),
"I am Yahweh, and there is none else.
19 "I have not spoken in secret,
In some dark land;
I did not say to the seed of Jacob,
'Seek Me in a formless place';
I, Yahweh, speak righteousness,
Declaring things that are upright.
20 "Gather yourselves and come;
Draw near together, you who have
escaped from the nations;
They do not know,
Who carry about their
graven image of wood
And pray to a god who cannot save.
21 "Declare and draw near *with your case*;
Indeed, let them consult together.
Who has made this heard from of old?
Who has long since declared it?
Is it not I, Yahweh?
And there is no other God besides Me,
A righteous God and a Savior;
There is none except Me.
22 "Turn to Me and be saved, all
the ends of the earth;
For I am God, and there is no other.
23 "I have sworn by Myself,
The word has gone forth from
My mouth in righteousness
And will not turn back,
That to Me every knee will bow,
every tongue will swear *allegiance*.
24 "They will say of Me, 'Only in Yahweh
are righteousness and strength.'
Men will come to Him,
And all who were angry at Him
will be put to shame.
25 "In Yahweh all the seed of Israel
Will be justified and will boast."

46

Bel has bowed down,
Nebo stoops over;
Their images are on the
beasts and the cattle.
The things that you carry
are burdensome,
A load for the weary *beast*.
2 They stooped over, they have
bowed down together;
They could not rescue the load,
But have themselves gone
into captivity.

3 "Hear Me, O house of Jacob,
And all the remnant of the
house of Israel,
You who have been burdening
Me from birth
And have been carried from the womb;
4 Even to *your* old age I will be the same,
And even to *your* graying
years I will bear *you*!
I have done *it*, and I will carry *you*;

And I will bear *you*, and
I will rescue *you*.

5 "To whom would you liken Me
And make Me equal and compare Me,
That we would be alike?
6 "Those who lavish gold from the purse
And weigh silver on the scale,
They hire a goldsmith, and
he makes it *into* a god;
They fall down, indeed they worship it.
7 "They carry it upon the
shoulder *and* bear it;
They set it in its place,
and it stands *there*.
It does not move from its place.
Though one may cry to it,
it cannot answer;
It cannot save him from his distress.

8 "Remember this, and be assured;
Cause it to return to your
heart, you transgressors.
9 "Remember the former things
long past,
For I am God, and there is no other;
I am God, and there is no one like Me,
10 Declaring the end from the beginning,
And from ancient times things
which have not been done,
Saying, 'My counsel will be established,
And I will accomplish all
My good pleasure',
11 Calling a bird of prey from the east,
The man of My counsel
from a far country.
Truly I have spoken; truly I
will bring it to pass.
I have formed *it*, surely I will do it.

12 "Hear Me, you stubborn of heart,
Who are far from righteousness.
13 "I bring near My righteousness,
it is not far off;
And My salvation will not delay.
And I will grant salvation in Zion,
And My glory for Israel.

Psalm 111:1–6

1 Praise Yah!
I will give thanks to Yahweh
with all *my* heart,
In the council of the upright
and in the congregation.
2 Great are the works of Yahweh;
They are sought by all who
delight in them.
3 Splendid and majestic is His work,
And His righteousness stands forever.
4 He has made His wondrous
deeds to be remembered;
Yahweh is gracious and compassionate.
5 He has given food to those
who fear Him;
He will remember His
covenant forever.
6 He has declared to His people
the power of His works,
In giving them an inheritance
of the nations.

Proverbs 26:10

10 *Like* an archer who wounds everyone,
So is he who hires a fool or who
hires those who pass by.

Galatians 5:1–26

5 It was for freedom that Christ set us
free. Therefore, stand firm and do not
be subject again to a yoke of slavery.
2 Behold I, Paul, say to you that if you
receive circumcision, Christ will be of no
benefit to you. 3 And I testify again to every
man who receives circumcision, that he is
under obligation to keep the whole Law.
4 You have been severed from Christ, you
who are being justified by law; you have
fallen from grace! 5 For we through the
Spirit, by faith, are eagerly waiting for the
hope of righteousness. 6 For in Christ Jesus
neither circumcision nor uncircumcision
means anything, but faith working through
love.
7 You were running well; who hindered
you from obeying the truth? 8 This per-
suasion *is* not from Him who calls you. 9 A
little leaven leavens the whole lump. 10 I
have confidence in you in the Lord that you
will adopt no other view. But the one who
is disturbing you will bear his judgment,
whoever he is. 11 But I, brothers, if I still
preach circumcision, why am I still per-
secuted? Then the stumbling block of the
cross would have been abolished. 12 I wish
that those who are upsetting you would
even mutilate themselves.
13 For you were called to freedom, broth-
ers; only *do* not *turn* your freedom into an
opportunity for the flesh, but through love
serve one another. 14 For the whole Law is

fulfilled in one word, in this: "YOU SHALL LOVE YOUR NEIGHBOR AS YOURSELF." 15 But if you bite and devour one another, beware that you are not consumed by one another.
16 But I say, walk by the Spirit and you will not carry out the desire of the flesh. 17 For the flesh sets its desire against the Spirit, and the Spirit against the flesh; for these are in opposition to one another, so that you do not do the things that you want. 18 But if you are led by the Spirit, you are not under the Law. 19 Now the deeds of the flesh are evident, which are: sexual immorality, impurity, sensuality, 20 idolatry, sorcery, enmities, strife, jealousy, outbursts of anger, selfish ambition, dissensions, factions, 21 envying, drunkenness, carousing, and things like these, of which I forewarn you, just as I have forewarned you, that those who practice such things will not inherit the kingdom of God. 22 But the fruit of the Spirit is love, joy, peace, patience, kindness, goodness, faithfulness, 23 gentleness, self-control. Against such things there is no law. 24 Now those who belong to Christ Jesus crucified the flesh with its passions and desires.
25 If we live by the Spirit, let us also walk in step with the Spirit. 26 Let us not become *those* with vain glory, challenging one another, envying one another.

SEPTEMBER 28

Isaiah 47:1–48:22

47 "Come down and sit in the dust,
O virgin daughter of Babylon;
Sit on the ground without a throne,
O daughter of the Chaldeans!
For you shall no longer be called
tender and delicate.
2 "Take the millstones and grind flour.
Uncover your veil, strip off the skirt,
Uncover the leg, cross the rivers.
3 "Your nakedness will be uncovered;
Your reproach also will be seen;
I will take vengeance and
will not spare a man."
4 Our Redeemer, Yahweh of
hosts is His name,
The Holy One of Israel.
5 "Sit silently, and go into darkness,
O daughter of the Chaldeans,
For you will no longer be called
The queen of kingdoms.
6 "I was furious with My people;
I profaned My inheritance
And gave them into your hand.
You did not show compassion to them,
On the aged you made your
yoke very heavy.
7 "Yet you said, 'I will be a queen forever.'
These things you did not
put on your heart
Nor remember the outcome of them.

8 "So now, hear this, you sensual one,
Who sits securely,
Who says in your heart,
'I am, and there is no one besides me.
I will not sit as a widow,
Nor know loss of children.'
9 "But these two things will come
on you suddenly in one day:
Loss of children and widowhood.
They will come on you in full measure
In spite of your many sorceries,
In spite of the great might
of your spells.
10 "You felt secure in your evil and said,
'No one sees me,'
Your wisdom and your knowledge
have turned you *astray*;
So you have said in your heart,
'I am, and there is no one besides me.'
11 "But evil will come on you
Which you will not know
how to charm away;
And disaster will fall on you
For which you cannot atone;
And destruction about which
you do not know
Will come on you suddenly.

12 "Stand *fast* now in your spells
And in your many sorceries
With which you have labored
from your youth;
Perhaps you will be able to profit;
Perhaps you may cause trembling.
13 "You are wearied with your
many counsels;
Let now the astrologers,
Those who behold *visions*
by the stars,
Those who predict by the new moons,

Stand up and save you from
what will come upon you.
14 "Behold, they have become
like stubble,
Fire burns them;
They cannot deliver themselves
from the power of the flame;
There will be no coal to warm by
Nor a fire to sit before!
15 "Thus they have become for you, those
among whom you have labored,
Who have traded with you
from your youth;
Each has wandered in his own way;
There is none to save you.

48 "Hear this, O house of Jacob, who
are called by the name Israel
And who came forth from
the loins of Judah,
Who swear by the name of Yahweh
And bring to remembrance
the God of Israel,
But not in truth or in righteousness.
2 "For they call themselves
after the holy city
And are supported by the
God of Israel;
Yahweh of hosts is His name.
3 "I declared the former things long ago,
And they went forth from My mouth,
and I caused them to be heard.
Suddenly I acted, and they
came to pass.
4 "Because I know that you are stiff,
And your neck is an iron sinew
And your forehead bronze,
5 Therefore I declared *them*
to you long ago,
Before they happened I caused
them to be heard by you,
Lest you say, 'My idol has done them,
And my graven image and my molten
image have commanded them.'
6 "You have heard; look at all this.
And you, will you not declare it?
I caused you to hear new
things from this time,
Even hidden things which
you have not known.
7 "They are created now and not
long ago;
And before today you have
not heard them,
Lest you say, 'Behold, I knew them.'
8 "Indeed, you have not heard;
indeed, you have not known.
Indeed, even from long ago your
ear has not been open
Because I knew that you would
deal very treacherously;
And you have been called a
transgressor from the womb.
9 "For the sake of My name
I delay My anger,
And *for* My praise I restrain
it for you,
In order not to cut you off.
10 "Behold, I have refined you,
but not as silver;
I have tested you in the
furnace of affliction.
11 "For My own sake, for My
own sake, I will act;
For how can *My name* be profaned?
And My glory I will not give
to another.
12 "Hear Me, O Jacob, even
Israel whom I called;
I am He, I am the first,
I am also the last.
13 "Also, My hand founded the earth,
And My right hand spread
out the heavens;
When I call to them,
they stand together.
14 "Assemble, all of you, and hear!
Who among them has
declared these things?
Yahweh loves him; he will
carry out His good
pleasure on Babylon,
And His arm *will be against*
the Chaldeans.
15 "I, even I, have spoken; indeed
I have called him,
I have brought him, and He will
make his ways successful.
16 "Draw near to Me, hear this:
From the first I have not
spoken in secret,
From the time it took place,
I was there.
So now Lord Yahweh has sent
Me, and His Spirit."

17 Thus says Yahweh, your Redeemer, the
Holy One of Israel,
"I am Yahweh your God,
who teaches you to profit,

Who leads you in the way
you should go.
18 "If only you had paid attention
to My commandments!
Then your peace would have
been like a river,
And your righteousness like
the waves of the sea.
19 "Your seed would have
been like the sand,
And the offspring from your
loins like its grains;
Their name would never be cut off
or destroyed from My presence."

20 Go forth from Babylon!
Flee from the Chaldeans!
Declare with the sound of joyful
shouting, cause this to be heard,
Bring it forth to the end of
the earth;
Say, "Yahweh has redeemed
His servant Jacob."
21 And they did not thirst when He led
them through the waste places.
He made the water flow out
of the rock for them;
He split the rock, and the
water gushed forth.
22 "There is no peace for the
wicked," says Yahweh.

Psalm 111:7–10

7 The works of His hands are
truth and justice;
All His precepts are faithful.
8 They are upheld forever and ever;
They are done in truth
and uprightness.
9 He has sent redemption to
His people;
He has commanded His
covenant forever;
Holy and fearsome is His name.
10 The fear of Yahweh is the
beginning of wisdom;
Good insight belongs to all those
who do *His commandments*;
His praise stands forever.

Proverbs 26:11–12

11 Like a dog that returns to its vomit
Is a fool who repeats his folly.
12 Do you see a man wise in
his own eyes?
There is more hope for a
fool than for him.

Galatians 6:1–18

6 Brothers, even if anyone is caught
in any transgression, you who are
spiritual, restore such a one in a spirit of
gentleness, *each of you* looking to yourself,
so that you too will not be tempted. 2 Bear
one another's burdens, and so fulfill the
law of Christ. 3 For if anyone thinks he is
something when he is nothing, he deceives
himself. 4 But each one must examine his
own work, and then he will have *reason*
for boasting in regard to himself alone, and
not in regard to another. 5 For each one will
bear his own load.

6 And the one who is instructed in the
word is to share in all good things with
the one who instructs *him*. 7 Do not be
deceived, God is not mocked, for whatever
a man sows, this he will also reap. 8 For the
one who sows to his own flesh will from
the flesh reap corruption, but the one who
sows to the Spirit will from the Spirit reap
eternal life. 9 And let us not lose heart in
doing good, for in due time we will reap
if we do not grow weary. 10 So then, while
we have opportunity, let us do good to all
people, and especially to those who are of
the household of the faith.

11 See with what large letters I am writing
to you with my own hand! 12 As many as
are wanting to make a good showing in the
flesh, these are trying to compel you to be
circumcised, simply so that they will not
be persecuted for the cross of Christ. 13 For
those who are circumcised do not even keep
the Law themselves, but they want to have
you circumcised so that they may boast
in your flesh. 14 But may it never be that I
would boast, except in the cross of our Lord
Jesus Christ, through which the world has
been crucified to me, and I to the world.
15 For neither is circumcision anything, nor
uncircumcision, but a new creation. 16 And
those who will walk in step with this rule,
peace and mercy *be* upon them, and upon
the Israel of God.

17 From now on let no one cause trouble
for me, for I bear on my body the marks of
Jesus.

18 The grace of our Lord Jesus Christ be
with your spirit, brothers. Amen.

SEPTEMBER 29

Isaiah 49:1–50:11

49 Listen to Me, O coastlands,
And pay attention, you
peoples from afar.
Yahweh called Me from the womb;
From the body of My mother He made
My name to be remembered.
2 He has set My mouth like
a sharp sword;
In the shadow of His hand
He has concealed Me;
And He has also set Me
as a select arrow;
He has hidden Me in His quiver.
3 He said to Me, "You are
My Servant, Israel,
In Whom I will show forth
My beautiful glory."
4 But I said, "I have toiled in vain;
I have spent My might for
nothing and vanity;
Yet surely the justice *due* to
Me is with Yahweh,
And My reward with My God."

5 So now says Yahweh,
who formed Me from the
womb to be His Servant,
To return Jacob back to Him, so that
Israel might be gathered to Him
(For I am glorified in the
sight of Yahweh,
And My God is My strength),
6 He says, "It is too small a thing that
You should be My Servant
To raise up the tribes of Jacob
and to cause the preserved
ones of Israel to return;
I will also give You as a
light of the nations
So that My salvation may reach
to the end of the earth."
7 Thus says Yahweh, the Redeemer
of Israel *and* its Holy One,
To the despised One,
To the One abhorred by the nation,
To the Servant of rulers,
"Kings will see and arise,
Princes will also bow down,
Because of Yahweh who is
faithful, the Holy One of Israel
who has chosen You."

8 Thus says Yahweh,
"In an acceptable time I
have answered You,
And in a day of salvation I
have helped You;
And I will guard You and give You
for a covenant of the people,
To establish the land, to make *them*
inherit the desolate inheritance;
9 Saying to those who are
bound, 'Go forth,'
To those who are in darkness,
'Show yourselves.'
Along the roads they will feed,
And their pasture *will be*
on all bare heights.
10 "They will not hunger or thirst,
Nor will the scorching heat or
sun strike them down;
For He who has compassion
on them will guide them
And will lead them to springs of water.
11 "I will set all My mountains as a road,
And My highways will be raised up.
12 "Behold, these will come from afar;
And behold, these *will come* from
the north and from the west,
And these from the land of Sinim."
13 Shout for joy, O heavens!
And rejoice, O earth!
Break forth into joyful
shouting, O mountains!
For Yahweh has comforted His people
And will have compassion
on His afflicted.
14 But Zion said, "Yahweh
has forsaken me,
And the Lord has forgotten me."
15 "Can a woman forget her infant
And have no compassion on
the son of her womb?
Even these may forget, but
I will not forget you.
16 "Behold, I have inscribed you on
the palms *of My hands*;
Your walls are continually before Me.
17 "Your builders hurry;
Your destroyers and devastators
Will depart from you.
18 "Lift up your eyes and look around;
All of them gather together;
they come to you.

As I live," declares Yahweh,
"You will surely put on all of them as
jewels and bind them on as a bride.
19 "For your devastated and desolate
places and your destroyed land—
Surely now you will be too
cramped for the inhabitants,
And those who swallowed
you will be far away.
20 "The children of whom you were
bereaved will yet say in your ears,
'The place is too cramped for me;
Make room for me that I may live *here.*'
21 "Then you will say in your heart,
'Who has borne these for me?
Indeed, I have been bereaved
of my children
And am barren, an exile
and a wanderer.
And who has reared these?
Behold, I remained alone;
From where did these come?'"

22 Thus says Lord Yahweh,
"Behold, I will lift up My
hand to the nations
And make high My standard
to the peoples;
And they will bring your
sons in *their* bosom,
And your daughters will be lifted
up on *their* shoulders.
23 "Kings will be your guardians,
And their princesses your nurses.
They will bow down to you with
their faces to the earth
And lick the dust of your feet;
And *you* will know that I am Yahweh;
Those who hope in Me will
not be put to shame.

24 "Can the prey be taken from
the mighty man,
Or the captives of *the* righteous
be granted escape?"
25 Surely, thus says Yahweh,
"Even the captives of the mighty
man will be taken away,
And the prey of the tyrant
will be granted escape;
For I will contend with the one
who contends with you,
And I will save your sons.
26 "I will feed those who mistreat
you with their own flesh,
And they will become drunk with their
own blood as with sweet wine;
And all flesh will know that I,
Yahweh, am your Savior
And your Redeemer, the
Mighty One of Jacob."

50 Thus says Yahweh,
"Where is the certificate of divorce
By which I have sent your
mother away?
Or to which of My creditors
did I sell you?
Behold, you were sold for
your iniquities,
And for your transgressions your
mother was sent away.
2 "Why was there no man when I came?
When I called, why was there
none to answer?
Is My hand so short that
it cannot ransom?
Or have I no power to deliver?
Behold, I dry up the sea
with My rebuke;
I make the rivers a wilderness;
Their fish stink for lack of water
And die of thirst.
3 "I clothe the heavens with blackness
And make sackcloth their covering."

4 Lord Yahweh has given Me
the tongue of disciples,
That I may know how to sustain
the weary one with a word.
He awakens *Me* morning by morning;
He awakens My ear to
listen as a disciple.
5 Lord Yahweh has opened My ear;
And I did not rebel
Nor did I turn back.
6 I gave My back to those who strike *Me*,
And My cheeks to those who
pluck out the beard;
I did not hide My face from
dishonor and spitting.
7 Even *now* Lord Yahweh helps Me,
Therefore, I am not dishonored;
Therefore, I have set My face like flint,
And I know that I will not be ashamed.
8 He who vindicates Me is near;
Who will contend with Me?
Let us stand up to each other;
Who has a judgment against Me?
Let him approach Me.

9 Behold, Lord Yahweh helps Me;
Who is he who condemns Me?
Behold, they will all wear
out like a garment;
The moth will eat them.
10 Who is among you that fears Yahweh,
That listens to the voice of His Servant,
That walks in darkness
and has no light?
Let him trust in the name of
Yahweh and rely on his God.
11 Behold, all you who kindle a fire,
Who gird yourselves with firebrands,
Walk in the light of your fire
And among the brands you
have set ablaze.
This you will have from My hand:
You will lie down in torment.

Psalm 112:1–4

1 Praise Yah!
How blessed is the man
who fears Yahweh,
Who greatly delights in His
commandments.
2 His seed will be mighty on earth;
The generation of the upright
will be blessed.
3 Wealth and riches are in his house,
And his righteousness stands forever.
4 Light arises in the darkness
for the upright;
He is gracious and compassionate
and righteous.

Proverbs 26:13–15

13 The sluggard says, "There is a
fierce lion in the road!
A lion is among the streets!"
14 *As* the door turns on its hinges,
So *does* the sluggard on his bed.
15 The sluggard buries his
hand in the dish;
He is *too* weary to return
it to his mouth.

Ephesians 1:1–23

1 Paul, an apostle of Christ Jesus by the
will of God,
To the saints who are at Ephesus and *who*
are faithful in Christ Jesus: 2 Grace to you
and peace from God our Father and the Lord
Jesus Christ.
3 Blessed *be* the God and Father of our
Lord Jesus Christ, who has blessed us with
every spiritual blessing in the heavenly
places in Christ, 4 just as He chose us in Him
before the foundation of the world, that we
would be holy and blameless before Him
in love, 5 by predestining us to adoption
as sons through Jesus Christ to Himself,
according to the good pleasure of His will,
6 to the praise of the glory of His grace,
which He graciously bestowed on us in
the Beloved. 7 In Him we have redemption
through His blood, the forgiveness of our
transgressions, according to the riches of
His grace 8 which He caused to abound to us
in all wisdom and insight, 9 making known
to us the mystery of His will, according to
His good pleasure which He purposed in
Him 10 for an administration of the fullness
of the times, *that is*, the summing up of all
things in Christ, things in the heavens and
things on the earth in Him. 11 In Him, we
also have been made an inheritance, having
been predestined according to the purpose
of Him who works all things according to
the counsel of His will, 12 to the end that
we who first have hoped in Christ would
be to the praise of His glory. 13 In Him, you
also, after listening to the word of truth,
the gospel of your salvation—having also
believed, you were sealed in Him with the
Holy Spirit of promise, 14 who is given
as a pledge of our inheritance, unto the
redemption of *God's own* possession, to
the praise of His glory.
15 For this reason I too, having heard
of the faith in the Lord Jesus which *exists*
among you and your love for all the saints,
16 do not cease giving thanks for you, while
making mention *of you* in my prayers:
17 that the God of our Lord Jesus Christ, the
Father of glory, may give to you *the* Spirit
of wisdom and of revelation in the full
knowledge of Him, 18 so that you—the eyes
of your heart having been enlightened—
will know what is the hope of His calling,
what are the riches of the glory of His
inheritance in the saints, 19 and what is the
surpassing greatness of His power toward
us who believe according to the working
of the might of His strength, 20 which He
worked in Christ, by raising Him from the
dead and seating Him at His right hand in
the heavenly *places*, 21 far above all rule and
authority and power and dominion, and
every name that is named, not only in this
age but also in the one to come. 22 And He

PUT ALL THINGS IN SUBJECTION UNDER HIS FEET, and gave Him as head over all things to the church, 23 which is His body, the fullness of Him who fills all in all.

SEPTEMBER 30

Isaiah 51:1–52:15

51 "Listen to Me, you who
pursue righteousness,
Who seek Yahweh:
Look to the rock from which
you were hewn
And to the quarry from
which you were dug.
2 "Look to Abraham your father
And to Sarah who brought you
forth through labor pains;
When *he was but* one I called him,
Then I blessed him and
multiplied him."
3 Indeed, Yahweh will comfort Zion;
He will comfort all her waste places.
And her wilderness He will
make like Eden,
And her desert like the
garden of Yahweh;
Joy and gladness will be found in her,
Thanksgiving and sound of a melody.

4 "Pay attention to Me, O My people,
And give ear to Me, O My nation;
For a law will go forth from Me,
And I will set My justice for
a light of the peoples.
5 "My righteousness is near, My
salvation has gone forth,
And My arms will judge the peoples;
The coastlands will hope in Me,
And for My arm they will
wait expectantly.
6 "Lift up your eyes to the sky,
Then look to the earth beneath;
For the sky will vanish like smoke,
And the earth will wear
out like a garment,
And its inhabitants will
die in like manner;
But My salvation will be forever,
And My righteousness will
not be dismayed.
7 "Listen to Me, you who know
righteousness,
A people in whose heart is My law;
Do not fear the reproach of man,
Nor be dismayed at their revilings.
8 "For the moth will eat them
like a garment,
And the grub will eat them like wool.
But My righteousness will be forever,
And My salvation to all generations."

9 Awake, awake, put on strength,
O arm of Yahweh;
Awake as in the days of old, the
generations of long ago.
Was it not You who chopped
Rahab in pieces,
Who pierced the dragon?
10 Was it not You who dried up the sea,
The waters of the great deep,
Who made the depths of
the sea a pathway
For the redeemed to cross over?
11 So the ransomed of Yahweh will return
And come with joyful shouting to Zion,
And everlasting gladness
will be on their heads.
They will obtain joy and gladness,
And sorrow and sighing will flee away.

12 "I, even I, am He who comforts you.
Who are you that you are
afraid of man who dies
And of the son of man who
is made like grass,
13 That you have forgotten
Yahweh your Maker,
Who stretched out the heavens
And laid the foundations of the earth,
That you tremble in dread continually
all day long because of the wrath
of the one who brings distress,
As he makes ready to bring ruin?
But where is the wrath of the
one who brings distress?
14 "The one in chains will soon be set free
and will not die in the pit, nor will his bread
be lacking. 15 For I am Yahweh your God,
who stirs up the sea, and its waves roar—
Yahweh of hosts is His name. 16 I have put
My words in your mouth and have covered
you with the shadow of My hand, to estab-
lish the heavens, to found the earth, and to
say to Zion, 'You are My people.'"

17 Awaken yourself! Awaken
yourself! Arise, O Jerusalem,
You who have drunk from the hand
of Yahweh the cup of His wrath;
The chalice of reeling you have
drained to the dregs.
18 There is none to guide her among
all the sons she has borne,
Nor is there one to take hold of
her by the hand among all
the sons she has reared.
19 These two things have befallen you;
Who will console you?
The devastation and destruction,
famine and sword;
How shall I comfort you?
20 Your sons have fainted;
They lie *helpless* at the head
of every street,
Like an antelope in a net,
Full of the wrath of Yahweh,
The rebuke of your God.

21 Therefore, now, listen to
this, you afflicted,
Who are drunk, but not with wine:
22 Thus says your Lord, Yahweh,
even your God
Who contends for His people,
"Behold, I have taken out of your
hand the cup of reeling,
The chalice of My wrath;
You will never drink it again.
23 "I will set it into the hand of
those who cause you grief,
Who have said to you, 'Lie down
that we may walk over *you.*'
You have even set your back
down like the ground
And like the street for those
who walk over *it.*"

52 Awake, awake,
Clothe yourself in your
strength, O Zion;
Clothe yourself in your
glorious garments,
O Jerusalem, the holy city;
For the uncircumcised and the unclean
Will no longer come into you.
2 Shake yourself from the dust, rise up,
O captive Jerusalem;
Loose yourself from the chains
around your neck,
O captive daughter of Zion.

3 For thus says Yahweh, "You were sold for
nothing, and you will be redeemed without
money." 4 For thus says Lord Yahweh, "My
people went down at the first into Egypt to
sojourn there; then the Assyrian oppressed
them without cause. 5 So now, what do I have
here," declares Yahweh, "since My people
have been taken away for nothing?" Yahweh
declares, "Those who rule over them howl,
and My name is continually blasphemed all
day long. 6 Therefore My people shall know
My name; therefore in that day I am the one
who is speaking, 'Here I am.'"

7 How lovely on the mountains
Are the feet of him who
proclaims good news,
Who announces peace
And proclaims good news
of good things,
Who announces salvation,
And says to Zion, "Your God reigns!"
8 The voice of Your watchmen!
They lift up *their* voices;
They shout joyfully together;
For they will see with their own eyes
When Yahweh returns to Zion.
9 Break forth, shout joyfully together,
You waste places of Jerusalem;
For Yahweh has comforted His people;
He has redeemed Jerusalem.
10 Yahweh has bared His holy arm
In the sight of all the nations,
That all the ends of the earth may see
The salvation of our God.

11 Depart, depart, go out from there,
Touch nothing unclean;
Go out of the midst of her,
purify yourselves,
You who carry the vessels of Yahweh.
12 But you will not go out in haste,
Nor will you go as those who flee;
For Yahweh will go before you,
And the God of Israel *will
be* your rear guard.
13 Behold, My Servant will prosper;
He will be high and lifted up
and greatly exalted.
14 Just as many were appalled
at you, *My people,*
So His appearance was marred
more than any man
And His form more than
the sons of men.
15 Thus He will sprinkle many nations,

Kings will shut their mouths
on account of Him;
For what had not been told
them they will see,
And what they had not heard
they will understand.

Psalm 112:5–10

5 It is well with the man who
is gracious and lends;
Who sustains his works with justice.
6 For he will never be shaken;
The righteous will be
remembered forever.
7 He will not fear an evil report;
His heart is set, trusting in Yahweh.
8 His heart is upheld, he will not fear,
Until he looks *in triumph*
on his adversaries.
9 He has given freely to the needy,
His righteousness stands forever;
His horn will be raised in glory.
10 The wicked will see it and be vexed,
He will gnash his teeth and melt away;
The desire of the wicked will perish.

Proverbs 26:16

16 The sluggard is wiser in his own eyes
Than seven men who can respond
with a discreet answer.

Ephesians 2:1–22

2 And you were dead in your transgres-
sions and sins, 2 in which you formerly
walked according to the course of this
world, according to the ruler of the power
of the air, the spirit that is now working
in the sons of disobedience, 3 among
whom we all also formerly conducted
ourselves in the lusts of our flesh, doing
the desires of the flesh and of the mind,
and were by nature children of wrath, even
as the rest. 4 But God, being rich in mercy
because of His great love with which He
loved us, 5 even when we were dead in our
transgressions, made us alive together with
Christ—by grace you have been saved—
6 and raised us up with Him, and seated us
with Him in the heavenly *places* in Christ
Jesus, 7 so that in the ages to come He
might show the surpassing riches of His
grace in kindness toward us in Christ Jesus.
8 For by grace you have been saved through
faith, and this not of yourselves, *it is* the
gift of God; 9 not of works, so that no one
may boast. 10 For we are His workmanship,
created in Christ Jesus for good works,
which God prepared beforehand so that
we would walk in them.

11 Therefore, remember that formerly
you—the Gentiles in the flesh, who are
called “Uncircumcision” by the so-called
“Circumcision,” *which is* performed in
the flesh by *human* hands— 12 *remember*
that you were at that time without Christ,
alienated from the citizenship of Israel, and
strangers to the covenants of promise, hav-
ing no hope and without God in the world.
13 But now in Christ Jesus you who formerly
were far off have been brought near by the
blood of Christ. 14 For He Himself is our
peace, who made both *groups* one and broke
down the dividing wall of the partition 15 by
abolishing in His flesh the enmity, the Law
of commandments *contained* in ordinances,
so that in Himself He might create the two
into one new man, making peace, 16 and
might reconcile them both in one body to
God through the cross, having in Himself
put to death the enmity. 17 AND HE CAME AND
PREACHED THE GOOD NEWS OF PEACE TO YOU
WHO WERE FAR AWAY, AND PEACE TO THOSE
WHO WERE NEAR; 18 for through Him we both
have our access in one Spirit to the Father.
19 So then you are no longer strangers and
sojourners, but you are fellow citizens with
the saints, and are of God’s household,
20 having been built on the foundation of
the apostles and prophets, Christ Jesus
Himself being the corner *stone*, 21 in whom
the whole building, being joined together,
is growing into a holy sanctuary in the Lord,
22 in whom you also are being built together
into a dwelling of God in the Spirit.

Sanctification means intense concentration on God’s point of view.
It will cause an intense narrowing of all our interests on earth,
and an immense broadening of all our interests in God.

— OSWALD CHAMBERS

OCTOBER 1

Isaiah 53:1–54:17

53 Who has believed our report?
And to whom has the arm of
Yahweh been revealed?
2 For He grew up before Him
like a tender shoot,
And like a root out of parched ground;
He has no *stately* form or majesty
That we should look upon Him,
Nor appearance that we
should desire Him.
3 He was despised and forsaken of men,
A man of sorrows and
acquainted with grief;
And like one from whom
men hide their face
He was despised, and we
did not esteem Him.

4 Surely our griefs He Himself bore,
And our sorrows He carried;
Yet we ourselves esteemed
Him stricken,
Smitten of God, and afflicted.
5 But He was pierced through
for our transgressions,
He was crushed for our iniquities;
The chastening for our
peace *fell* upon Him,
And by His wounds we are healed.
6 All of us like sheep have gone astray,
Each of us has turned to his own way;
But Yahweh has caused the
iniquity of us all
To fall on Him.

7 He was oppressed and He was afflicted,
Yet He did not open His mouth;
Like a lamb that is led to slaughter,
And like a sheep that is silent
before its shearers,
So He did not open His mouth.
8 By oppression and judgment
He was taken away;
And as for His generation,
who considered
That He was cut off out of
the land of the living,
That for the transgression of my
people, striking *was due* to Him?
9 So His grave was assigned
with wicked men,
Yet He was with a rich
man in His death,
Because He had done no violence,
Nor was there any deceit in His mouth.

10 But Yahweh was pleased
To crush Him, putting *Him* to grief;
If You would place His soul
as a guilt offering,
He will see *His* seed,
He will prolong *His* days,
And the good pleasure of Yahweh
will succeed in His hand.
11 As a result of the anguish of His soul,
He will see *it and* be satisfied;
By His knowledge the Righteous One,
My Servant, will justify the many,
As He will bear their iniquities.
12 Therefore, I will divide for Him
a portion with the many,
And He will divide the spoil
with the strong;
Because He poured out
His soul to death,
And was numbered with
the transgressors;
Yet He Himself bore the sin of many,
And interceded for the transgressors.

54 "Shout for joy, O barren woman,
who has not given birth;
Break forth into joyful shouting
and cry aloud, *you* who
have not been in labor;
For more numerous are the
sons of the desolate one
Than the sons of the married
woman," says Yahweh.
2 "Enlarge the place of your tent;
Stretch out the curtains of your
dwellings, do not hold back;
Lengthen your cords
And strengthen your pegs.
3 "For you will spread abroad to
the right and to the left.
And your seed will possess nations
And will resettle the desolate cities.

4 "Do not be afraid, for you will
not be put to shame;
And do not feel dishonored, for
you will not be humiliated;

But you will forget the shame
of your virginity,
And the reproach of your widowhood
you will remember no more.
5 "For your husband is your Maker,
Whose name is Yahweh of hosts;
And your Redeemer is the
Holy One of Israel,
Who is called the God of all the earth.
6 "For Yahweh has called you,
Like a wife forsaken and
grieved in spirit,
Even like a wife of *one's* youth
when she is rejected,"
Says your God.
7 "For a brief moment I forsook you,
But with great compassion
I will gather you.
8 "In a flood of fury
I hid My face from you for a moment,
But with everlasting lovingkindness
I will have compassion on you,"
Says Yahweh your Redeemer.

9 "For this is like the days of Noah to Me,
When I swore that the waters of Noah
Would not overflow the earth again;
So I have sworn that I will not
be furious with you
Nor will I rebuke you.
10 "For the mountains may be removed
and the hills may shake,
But My lovingkindness will not
be removed from you,
And My covenant of peace
will not be shaken,"
Says Yahweh who has
compassion on you.

11 "O afflicted one, storm-tossed,
and not comforted,
Behold, I will lay your
stones in antimony,
And your foundations I will
set in sapphires.
12 "Moreover, I will make your
battlements of rubies,
And your gates of crystal,
And your entire wall of
precious stones.
13 "All your sons will be taught of Yahweh;
And the peace of your
sons will be great.
14 "In righteousness you will
be established;
You will be far from oppression,
for you will not fear,
And from terror, for it will
not come near you.
15 "If anyone fiercely attacks *you*
it will not be from Me.
Whoever attacks you will
fall because of you.
16 "Behold, I Myself have created
the craftsman who blows
the fire of coals
And brings out a weapon for its work;
And I have created the bringer of
ruin to wreak destruction.
17 "No weapon that is formed
against you will succeed;
And every tongue that accuses you
in judgment you will condemn.
This is the inheritance of
the slaves of Yahweh,
And their righteousness is from Me,"
declares Yahweh.

Psalm 113:1–4

1 Praise Yah!
Praise, O slaves of Yahweh,
Praise the name of Yahweh.
2 May the name of Yahweh be blessed
From now until forever.
3 From the rising of the sun to its setting
The name of Yahweh is to be praised.
4 Yahweh is high above all nations;
His glory is above the heavens.

Proverbs 26:17–19

17 *Like* one who seizes a dog by the ears
Is he who passes by *and* becomes
passionate about strife
not belonging to him.
18 Like a madman who shoots
Firebrands, arrows, and death,
19 So is the man who deceives
his neighbor,
And says, "Am I not joking?"

Ephesians 3:1–21

3 For this reason I, Paul, the prisoner of
Christ Jesus on behalf of you Gentiles—
2 if indeed you heard of the stewardship
of God's grace which was given to me for
you; 3 that by revelation there was made
known to me the mystery, as I wrote before
in brief. 4 About which, when you read you
can understand my insight into the mystery
of Christ, 5 which in other generations was

not made known to the sons of men, as it
was now revealed to His holy apostles and
prophets in the Spirit: 6 that the Gentiles
are fellow heirs and fellow members of the
body, and fellow partakers of the promise
in Christ Jesus through the gospel, 7 of
which I was made a minister, according to
the gift of God's grace which was given to
me according to the working of His power.
8 To me, the very least of all saints, this
grace was given, to proclaim to the Gentiles
the good news of the unfathomable riches
of Christ, 9 and to bring to light for all
what is the administration of the mystery
which for ages has been hidden in God who
created all things; 10 so that the manifold
wisdom of God might now be made known
through the church to the rulers and the
authorities in the heavenly *places.* 11 *This
was* in accordance with the eternal purpose
which He carried out in Christ Jesus our
Lord, 12 in whom we have boldness and
confident access through faith in Him.
13 Therefore I ask you not to lose heart at
my afflictions on your behalf, which are
your glory.

14 For this reason I bow my knees before
the Father, 15 from whom every family in
heaven and on earth is named, 16 that He
would give you, according to the riches of
His glory, to be strengthened with power
through His Spirit in the inner man, 17 so
that Christ may dwell in your hearts through
faith; *and* that you, being firmly rooted and
grounded in love, 18 may be able to compre-
hend with all the saints what is the breadth
and length and height and depth, 19 and to
know the love of Christ which surpasses
knowledge, that you may be filled up to all
the fullness of God.

20 Now to Him who is able to do far
more abundantly beyond all that we ask
or understand, according to the power that
works within us, 21 to Him *be* the glory in the
church and in Christ Jesus to all generations
forever and ever. Amen.

OCTOBER 2

Isaiah 55:1–56:12

55 "Ho! Every one who thirsts,
come to the waters;
And you who have no money
come, buy and eat.
Come, buy wine and milk
Without money and without cost.
2 "Why do you spend money
for what is not bread,
And your wages for what
does not satisfy?
Listen carefully to Me, and
eat what is good,
And delight your soul in richness.
3 "Incline your ear and come to Me.
Listen, that your soul may live;
And I will cut an everlasting
covenant with you,
According to the faithful
lovingkindnesses of David.
4 "Behold, I have given him as a
witness to the peoples,
A ruler and commander
for the peoples.
5 "Behold, you will call a nation
you do not know,
And a nation which knows
you not will run to you,
Because of Yahweh your God,
even the Holy One of Israel;
For He has adorned you
with beautiful glory."

6 Seek Yahweh while He may be found;
Call upon Him while He is near.
7 Let the wicked forsake his way
And the unrighteous man
his thoughts;
And let him return to Yahweh,
And He will have compassion on him,
And to our God,
For He will abundantly pardon.
8 "For My thoughts are not your thoughts,
Nor are your ways My ways,"
declares Yahweh.
9 "For *as* the heavens are higher
than the earth,
So are My ways higher than your ways
And My thoughts than your thoughts.
10 "For as the rain and the snow
come down from heaven,
And do not return there without
watering the earth
And making it bear and sprout,
And giving seed to the sower
and bread to the eater,

11 So will My word be which goes
forth from My mouth;
It will not return to Me empty,
Without accomplishing
what pleases Me,
And without succeeding *in the matter* for which I sent it.
12 "For you will go out with gladness
And be led forth with peace;
The mountains and the hills will break
forth into shouts of joy before you,
And all the trees of the field
will clap *their* hands.
13 "Instead of the thorn bush the
cypress will come up,
And instead of the nettle the
myrtle will come up,
And it will be to Yahweh for *His* renown,
For an everlasting sign which
will not be cut off."

56 Thus says Yahweh,
"Keep justice and do righteousness,
For My salvation is about to come
And My righteousness to be revealed.
2 "How blessed is the man who does this,
And the son of man who
takes hold of it,
Who keeps from profaning
the sabbath,
And keeps his hand from
doing any evil."
3 Let not the foreigner who has
joined himself to Yahweh say,
"Yahweh will surely separate
me from His people."
Nor let the eunuch say,
"Behold, I am a dry tree."
4 For thus says Yahweh,
"To the eunuchs who keep My sabbaths,
And choose what pleases Me,
And hold fast My covenant,
5 To them I will give in My house and
within My walls a memorial,
And a name better than that
of sons and daughters;
I will give them an everlasting
name which will not be cut off.

6 "Also the foreigners who join
themselves to Yahweh,
To minister to Him, and to love
the name of Yahweh,
To be His slaves, every one who keeps
from profaning the sabbath
And takes hold of My covenant,
7 Even those I will bring to
My holy mountain
And make them glad in My
house of prayer.
Their burnt offerings and
their sacrifices will be
acceptable on My altar;
For My house will be called a house
of prayer for all the peoples."
8 Lord Yahweh, who gathers the
banished of Israel, declares,
"Yet *others* I will gather to them,
to those *already* gathered."

9 All you beasts of the field,
All you beasts in the forest,
Come to eat.
10 His watchmen are blind;
All of them know nothing.
All of them are mute dogs
unable to bark,
Dreamers lying down, who
love to slumber;
11 And the dogs *have* a strong appetite;
they do not know satisfaction.
And they are shepherds who do
not know understanding;
They have all turned to their own way,
Each one to his greedy gain,
to the last one.
12 "Come," *they say,* "let us take wine, and
let us drink heavily of strong drink;
And tomorrow will be like today—
beyond exceedingly great."

Psalm 113:5–9

5 Who is like Yahweh our God,
The One who sits on high,
6 The One who brings Himself low to see
The things in heaven and on the earth?
7 Who raises the poor from the dust
And lifts high the needy
from the ash heap,
8 To make *them* sit with nobles,
With the nobles of His people.
9 He makes the barren woman
of the house sit
As a glad mother of children.
Praise Yah!

Proverbs 26:20–21

20 With no wood the fire goes out,
And where there is no whisperer,
strife quiets down.

21 *Like* charcoal to hot embers
and wood to fire,
So is a contentious man to kindle strife.

Ephesians 4:1–32

4 Therefore I, the prisoner in the Lord,
exhort you to walk worthy of the calling
with which you have been called, 2 with all
humility and gentleness, with patience,
bearing with one another in love, 3 being
diligent to keep the unity of the Spirit in
the bond of peace. 4 *There is* one body and
one Spirit, just as also you were called in one
hope of your calling; 5 one Lord, one faith,
one baptism; 6 one God and Father of all who
is over all and through all and in all.
7 But to each one of us grace was given
according to the measure of Christ's gift.
8 Therefore it says,

"WHEN HE ASCENDED ON HIGH,
HE LED CAPTIVE A HOST OF CAPTIVES,
And HE GAVE GIFTS TO MEN."

9 (Now this *expression*, "He ascended," what
does it mean except that He also descended
into the lower parts of the earth? 10 He who
descended is Himself also He who ascended
far above all the heavens, so that He might
fill all things.) 11 And He Himself gave some
as apostles, and some *as* prophets, and some
as evangelists, and some *as* pastors and
teachers, 12 for the equipping of the saints
for the work of service, to the building up
of the body of Christ, 13 until we all attain
to the unity of the faith, and of the full
knowledge of the Son of God, to a mature
man, to the measure of the stature which
belongs to the fullness of Christ, 14 so that
we are no longer to be children, tossed here
and there by waves and carried about by
every wind of doctrine, by the trickery of
men, by craftiness in deceitful scheming,
15 but speaking the truth in love, we are
to grow up in all *aspects* into Him who is
the head, *that is* Christ, 16 from whom the
whole body, being joined and held together
by what every joint supplies, according to
the properly measured working of each
individual part, causes the growth of the
body for the building up of itself in love.
17 Therefore this I say, and testify in the
Lord, that you walk no longer just as the
Gentiles also walk, in the futility of their
mind, 18 being darkened in their mind,
alienated from the life of God because of
the ignorance that is in them, because of the
hardness of their heart. 19 *And* they, having
become callous, have given themselves over
to sensuality for the practice of every kind
of impurity with greediness. 20 But you did
not learn Christ in this way— 21 if indeed you
heard Him and were taught in Him, just as
truth is in Jesus, 22 to lay aside, in reference to
your former conduct, the old man, which is
being corrupted in accordance with the lusts
of deceit, 23 and to be renewed in the spirit
of your mind, 24 and to put on the new man,
which in *the likeness of* God has been created
in righteousness and holiness of the truth.
25 Therefore, laying aside falsehood,
SPEAK TRUTH EACH ONE *of you* WITH HIS
NEIGHBOR, for we are members of one
another. 26 BE ANGRY, AND *yet* DO NOT SIN;
do not let the sun go down on your anger,
27 and do not give the devil an opportunity.
28 He who steals must steal no longer, but
rather he must labor, performing with his
own hands what is good, so that he will have
something to share with one who has need.
29 Let no unwholesome word proceed from
your mouth, but only such *a word* as is good
for building up what is needed, so that it
will give grace to those who hear. 30 And do
not grieve the Holy Spirit of God, by whom
you were sealed for the day of redemption.
31 Let all bitterness and anger and wrath and
shouting and slander be put away from you,
along with all malice. 32 Instead, be kind to
one another, tender-hearted, graciously
forgiving each other, just as God in Christ
also has graciously forgiven you.

OCTOBER 3

Isaiah 57:1–58:14

57 The righteous man perishes, and
no man puts it upon his heart;
And men of lovingkindness
are gathered away, while
no one understands.
For the righteous man is
gathered away from evil,
2 He enters into peace;
They rest in their beds,
Each one who walked in
his upright way.

3 "But draw near, you sons
of a soothsayer,
Seed of an adulterer and a prostitute.
4 "Against whom do you jest?
Against whom do you open
wide your mouth
And stick out your tongue?
Are you not children of transgression,
Seed of lying,
5 *Who* inflame yourselves
among the oaks,
Under every green tree,
Who slaughter the children
in the ravines,
Under the clefts of the cliffs?
6 "Among the smooth *stones* of the ravine
Is your portion, they are your lot;
Even to them you have poured
out a drink offering;
You have made a grain offering.
Shall I relent concerning these things?
7 "Upon a mountain lofty and lifted up
You have made your bed.
You also went up there
to offer sacrifice.
8 "Behind the door and the doorpost
You have set up your memorial;
Indeed, far removed from Me,
you have uncovered yourself,
And have gone up and made
your bed wide,
And you have cut *a covenant*
for yourself with them;
You have loved their bed;
You have looked on *their* manhood.
9 "You have journeyed to the king with oil
And increased your perfumes;
You have sent your envoys
a great distance
And made *them* go down to Sheol.
10 "You were tired out by the
length of your road,
Yet you did not say, 'It is hopeless.'
You found renewed strength;
Therefore you did not faint.

11 "Of whom were you anxious and fearful
When you lied and did not
remember Me,
Nor *even* put *Me* upon your heart?
Was I not silent even for a long time
So you do not fear Me?
12 "I will declare your righteousness
and your deeds,
But they will not profit you.
13 "When you cry out, let your
collection *of idols* deliver you.
But the wind will lift all of them up,
And a breath will take *them away*.
But he who takes refuge in Me
will inherit the land
And will possess My holy mountain."
14 And it will be said,
"Build up, build up, prepare the way,
Remove *every* stumbling block
out of the way of My people."
15 For thus says the One
high and lifted up
Who dwells forever, whose
name is Holy,
"I dwell *on* a high and holy place,
And *also* with the crushed
and lowly of spirit
In order to revive the spirit of the lowly
And to revive the heart of the crushed.
16 "For I will not contend forever,
Nor will I always be angry;
For the spirit would grow
faint before Me,
And the breath *of those*
whom I have made.
17 "Because of the iniquity of his greedy
gain I was angry and struck him;
I hid *My face* and was angry,
And he went on turning away,
in the way of his heart.
18 "I have seen his ways, but
I will heal him;
I will lead him and pay him and his
mourners in full *with* comfort,
19 Creating the praise of the lips.
Peace, peace to him who is far
and to him who is near,"
Says Yahweh, "and I will heal him."
20 But the wicked are like the tossing sea,
For it cannot be quiet,
And its waters toss up refuse and mud.
21 "There is no peace," says my
God, "for the wicked."

58 "Call out from your throat,
do not hold back;
Raise your voice like a trumpet,
And declare to My people
their transgression
And to the house of Jacob their sins.
2 "Yet they seek Me day by day and find
pleasure in knowing My ways,
As a nation that has done
righteousness

And has not forsaken the
judgment of their God.
They ask Me *for* righteous judgments;
They find pleasure in the
nearness of God.
3 'Why have we fasted and
You do not see?
Why have we afflicted our souls
and You do not know?'
Behold, on the day of your fast
you find *your* desire,
And oppress all your workers.
4 "Behold, you fast for contention
and quarreling and to strike
with a wicked fist.
You do not fast like *you do* today to
make your voice heard on high.
5 "Is it a fast like this which I choose,
a day for a man to afflict himself?
Is it for bowing one's head like a reed
And for spreading out sackcloth
and ashes as a bed?
Will you call this a fast, even an
acceptable day to Yahweh?
6 "Is this not the fast which I choose,
To loosen the bonds of wickedness,
To release the bands of the yoke,
And to let the oppressed go free
And break every yoke?
7 "Is it not to divide your bread
with the hungry
And bring the afflicted
homeless into the house;
When you see the naked,
you cover him;
And not to hide yourself
from your own flesh?
8 "Then your light will break
out like the dawn,
And your recovery will
speedily spring forth;
And your righteousness
will go before you;
The glory of Yahweh will
be your rear guard.
9 "Then you will call, and
Yahweh will answer;
You will cry, and He will
say, 'Here I am.'
If you remove the yoke
from your midst,
The pointing of the finger and
speaking wickedness,
10 And if you offer your soul
to the hungry
And satisfy the soul of the afflicted,
Then your light will rise in darkness
And your thick darkness *will*
become like midday.
11 "And Yahweh will continually guide you,
And satisfy your soul in
scorched places,
And fortify your bones;
And you will be like a watered garden,
And like a spring of water
whose waters do not fail.
12 "Those from among you will rebuild
the ancient waste places;
You will raise up the foundations of
past generation upon generation;
And you will be called the
repairer of the breach,
The restorer of the paths
for one to inhabit.
13 "If because of the sabbath,
you turn your foot
From doing your *own* desire
on My holy day,
And call the sabbath a delight,
the holy *day* of Yahweh honorable,
And honor it, by not doing
your *own* ways,
By not finding your *own* desire
And speaking *your own* word,
14 Then you will take delight in Yahweh,
And I will make you ride on
the heights of the earth;
And I will feed you *with* the
inheritance of Jacob your father,
For the mouth of Yahweh has spoken."

Psalm 114:1–8

1 When Israel went out from Egypt,
The house of Jacob from a people
of strange language,
2 Judah became His sanctuary,
Israel, His dominion.

3 The sea looked and fled;
The Jordan turned back.
4 The mountains skipped like rams,
The hills, like lambs.
5 What disturbs you, O sea,
that you flee?
O Jordan, that you turn back?
6 O mountains, that you skip like rams?
O hills, like lambs?

7 Tremble, O earth, before the Lord,
Before the God of Jacob,

8 Who turned the rock into
a pool of water,
The flint into a spring of water.

Proverbs 26:22

22 The words of a whisperer are
like dainty morsels,
And they go down into the
innermost parts of the stomach.

Ephesians 5:1–14

5 Therefore be imitators of God, as
beloved children, [2] and walk in love, just
as Christ also loved us and gave Himself up
for us, an offering and a sacrifice to God as
a fragrant aroma.
[3] But sexual immorality or any impurity or
greed must not even be named among you,
as is proper among saints; [4] *nor* filthiness
and foolish talk, or coarse jesting, which
are not fitting, but rather giving of thanks.
[5] For this you know with certainty, that no
one sexually immoral or impure or greedy,
who is an idolater, has an inheritance in the
kingdom of Christ and God.
[6] Let no one deceive you with empty
words, for because of these things the
wrath of God comes upon the sons of
disobedience. [7] Therefore do not be par-
takers with them, [8] for you were formerly
darkness, but now you are light in the
Lord; walk as children of light [9] (for the
fruit of that light *consists* in all goodness
and righteousness and truth), [10] trying to
learn what is pleasing to the Lord. [11] And
do not participate in the unfruitful works
of darkness, but instead even expose them.
[12] For it is disgraceful even to speak of the
things which are done by them in secret.
[13] But all things become visible when they
are exposed by the light, for everything that
becomes visible is light. [14] For this reason
it says,

"Awake, sleeper,
And arise from the dead,
And Christ will shine on you."

OCTOBER 4

Isaiah 59:1–60:22

59 Behold, the hand of
Yahweh is not so short
That it cannot save;
Nor is His ear so dull
That it cannot hear.
2 But your iniquities have made
a separation between
you and your God,
And your sins have hidden *His* face
from you so that He does not hear.
3 For your hands are defiled with blood
And your fingers with iniquity;
Your lips have spoken a lie;
Your tongue mutters unrighteousness.
4 No one calls in righteousness, and
no one seeks justice in truth.
They trust in confusion and
speak worthlessness;
They conceive trouble and give
birth to wickedness.
5 They break open vipers' eggs and
weave the spider's web;
He who eats of their eggs dies,
And *from* that which is crushed
a snake breaks forth.
6 Their webs will not become
a garment,
Nor will they cover themselves
with their works;
Their works are works of wickedness,
And a deed of violence is
in their hands.
7 Their feet run to evil,
And they are quick to shed
innocent blood;
Their thoughts are thoughts
of wickedness;
Devastation and destruction
are in their highways.
8 They do not know the way of peace,
And there is no justice in their tracks;
They have made their paths crooked,
Whoever treads on them
does not know peace.
9 Therefore justice is far from us,
And righteousness does
not overtake us;
We hope for light, but behold,
darkness,
For brightness, but we walk
in thick darkness.
10 We grope along the wall like blind men;
We grope like those who have no eyes;
We stumble at midday as
in the twilight,

Among those who are vigorous
we are like dead men.
11 All of us growl like bears,
And moan sadly like doves;
We hope for justice, but there is none,
For salvation, *but* it is far from us.
12 For our transgressions are
multiplied before You,
And our sins answer against us;
For our transgressions are with us,
And we know our iniquities:
13 Transgressing and denying Yahweh,
And turning back from our God,
Speaking oppression and revolt,
Conceiving *in* and uttering from
the heart lying words.
14 Justice is turned back,
And righteousness stands far away;
For truth has stumbled in the street,
And rightness cannot enter.
15 So it is that truth is missing;
And he who turns aside from
evil makes himself plunder.

Then Yahweh saw,
And it was evil in His eyes that
there was no justice.
16 And He saw that there was no man,
And was astonished that there
was no one to intercede;
Then His own arm brought
salvation to Him,
And His righteousness upheld Him.
17 He put on righteousness
like a breastplate,
And a helmet of salvation
on His head;
And He put on garments of
vengeance for clothing
And wrapped Himself with
zeal as a mantle.
18 According to what they deserve,
so He will pay in full,
Wrath to His adversaries,
what is deserved to His enemies;
To the coastlands He will pay
what they deserve.
19 So they will fear the name of
Yahweh from the west
And His glory from the
rising of the sun,
For He will come like a rushing stream
Which the wind of Yahweh
makes flee.
20 "A Redeemer will come to Zion,
And to those who turn from
transgression in Jacob,"
declares Yahweh.

21 "As for Me, this is My covenant with
them," says Yahweh: "My Spirit which is
upon you, and My words which I have put
in your mouth, shall not depart from your
mouth, nor from the mouth of your seed,
nor from the mouth of your seed's seed,"
says Yahweh, "from now and forever."

60 "Arise, shine, for your
light has come,
And the glory of Yahweh
has risen upon you.
2 "For behold, darkness will
cover the earth
And dense gloom the peoples;
But Yahweh will rise upon you,
And His glory will appear upon you.
3 "Nations will come to your light,
And kings to the brightness
of your rising.

4 "Lift up your eyes round about and see;
They all gather together;
they come to you.
Your sons will come from afar,
And your daughters will be
carried on the nurses' hip.
5 "Then you will see and be radiant,
And your heart will tremble
and be large *with joy*;
Because the abundance of the
sea will be turned to you,
The wealth of the nations
will come to you.
6 "A multitude of camels will cover you,
The young camels of
Midian and Ephah;
All those from Sheba will come;
They will bring gold and frankincense,
And will bear good news of
the praises of Yahweh.
7 "All the flocks of Kedar will be
gathered together to you;
The rams of Nebaioth will
minister to you;
They will go up with
acceptance on My altar,
And I shall adorn My glorious
house with beautiful glory.
8 "Who are these who fly like a cloud
And like the doves to their lattices?
9 "Surely the coastlands will hope in Me;

And the ships of Tarshish
will come first,
To bring your sons from afar,
Their silver and their gold with them,
For the name of Yahweh your God,
And for the Holy One of Israel
because He has adorned
you with beautiful glory.

10 "Foreigners will build up your walls,
And their kings will minister to you;
For in My wrath I struck you,
And in My favor I have had
compassion on you.
11 "Your gates will be open continually;
They will not be closed day or night,
So that *men* may bring to you
the wealth of the nations,
With their kings led in procession.
12 "For the nation and the kingdom which
will not serve you will perish,
And the nations will surely
be laid waste.
13 "The glory of Lebanon will come to you,
The juniper, the box tree, and
the cypress together,
To adorn the place of My sanctuary
with beautiful glory;
And I shall make the place
of My feet glorious.
14 "The sons of those who afflicted
you will come bowing to you,
And all those who spurned
you will bow themselves at
the soles of your feet;
And they will call you the
City of Yahweh,
The Zion of the Holy One of Israel.

15 "Instead of being forsaken and hated
With no one passing through,
I will make you an everlasting pride,
A joy from generation to generation.
16 "You will also suck the milk of nations
And suck the breast of kings;
Then you will know that I,
Yahweh, am your Savior
And your Redeemer, the
Mighty One of Jacob.
17 "Instead of bronze I will bring gold,
And instead of iron I will bring silver,
And instead of wood, bronze,
And instead of stones, iron.
And I will make peace your overseers
And righteousness your taskmasters.
18 "Violence will not be heard
again in your land,
Nor devastation or destruction
within your borders;
But you will call your walls salvation,
and your gates praise.
19 "No longer will you have
the sun for light by day,
Nor for brightness will the
moon give you light;
But you will have Yahweh
for an everlasting light,
And your God for your glory.
20 "Your sun will no longer set,
Nor will your moon wane;
For you will have Yahweh for
an everlasting light,
And the days of your mourning
will be finished.
21 "Then all your people *will
be* righteous;
They will possess the land forever,
The branch of My planting,
The work of My hands,
That I may show forth My
beautiful glory.
22 "The smallest one will become a clan,
And the miniscule one a
mighty nation.
I, Yahweh, will hasten it in its time."

Psalm 115:1–8

1 Not to us, O Yahweh, not to us,
But to Your name give glory
Because of Your lovingkindness,
because of Your truth.
2 Why should the nations say,
"Where, now, is their God?"
3 But our God is in the heavens;
He does whatever He pleases.
4 Their idols are silver and gold,
The work of man's hands.
5 They have mouths,
but they do not speak;
They have eyes, but they do not see;
6 They have ears, but they do not hear;
They have noses, but they
do not smell;
7 As for their hands, they do not feel;
As for their feet, they do not walk;
They do not make a sound
with their throat.
8 Those who make them will
become like them,
Everyone who trusts in them.

Proverbs 26:23

23 *Like* an earthen vessel overlaid
with silver dross
Are fiery lips and an evil heart.

Ephesians 5:15–33

15 Therefore look carefully how you walk,
not as unwise but as wise, 16 redeeming the
time, because the days are evil. 17 On account
of this, do not be foolish, but understand
what the will of the Lord is. 18 And do not get
drunk with wine, for that is dissipation, but
be filled with the Spirit, 19 speaking to one
another in psalms and hymns and spiritual
songs, singing and making melody with
your heart to the Lord; 20 always giving
thanks for all things in the name of our
Lord Jesus Christ to God, even the Father;
21 and being subject to one another in the
fear of Christ.

22 Wives, *be subject* to your own hus-
bands, as to the Lord. 23 For the husband is
the head of the wife, as Christ also is the
head of the church, He Himself *being* the
Savior of the body. 24 But as the church is
subject to Christ, so also the wives *ought to
be* to their husbands in everything.

25 Husbands, love your wives, just as
Christ also loved the church and gave
Himself up for her, 26 so that He might
sanctify her, having cleansed her by the
washing of water with the word, 27 that He
might present to Himself the church in all
her glory, having no spot or wrinkle or any
such thing, but that she would be holy and
blameless. 28 So husbands ought also to love
their own wives as their own bodies. He who
loves his own wife loves himself; 29 for no
one ever hated his own flesh, but nourishes
and cherishes it, just as Christ also *does* the
church, 30 because we are members of His
body. 31 FOR THIS REASON A MAN SHALL LEAVE
HIS FATHER AND MOTHER AND BE JOINED TO HIS
WIFE, AND THE TWO SHALL BECOME ONE FLESH.
32 This mystery is great, but I am speaking
with reference to Christ and the church.
33 Nevertheless, each individual among you
also is to love his own wife even as himself,
and the wife must *see to it* that she respects
her husband.

OCTOBER 5

Isaiah 61:1–62:12

61 The Spirit of Lord
Yahweh is upon me
Because Yahweh has anointed me
To bring good news to the afflicted;
He has sent me to bind up
the brokenhearted,
To proclaim release to captives
And freedom to prisoners,
2 To proclaim the favorable
year of Yahweh
And the day of vengeance of
our God,
To comfort all who mourn,
3 To grant those who mourn *in* Zion,
Giving them a headdress
instead of ashes,
The oil of rejoicing instead
of mourning,
The mantle of praise instead
of a spirit of fainting.
So they will be called oaks
of righteousness,
The planting of Yahweh,
that He may show forth
His beautiful glory.
4 Then they will rebuild the
ancient waste places;
They will raise up the
former desolations;
And they will make new
the ruined cities,
The desolations from
generation to generation.
5 Strangers will stand and
pasture your flocks,
And foreigners will be your farmers
and your vinedressers.
6 But you will be called the
priests of Yahweh;
You will be spoken of *as*
ministers of our God.
You will eat the wealth of nations,
And in their glories you will boast.
7 Instead of your shame *you will
have a* double *portion*,
And *instead of* dishonor they will
shout for joy over their portion.
Therefore they will possess a
double *portion* in their land;
Everlasting gladness will be theirs.
8 For I, Yahweh, love justice,

I hate robbery in the burnt offering;
And in truth I will give them
their recompense
And cut an everlasting
covenant with them.
9 Then their seed will be known
among the nations,
And their offspring in the
midst of the peoples.
All who see them will recognize them
Because they are the seed *whom*
Yahweh has blessed.

10 I will rejoice greatly in Yahweh;
My soul will rejoice in my God,
For He has clothed me with
garments of salvation,
He has wrapped me with a
robe of righteousness,
As a bridegroom decks himself
with a headdress,
And as a bride adorns herself
with her jewels.
11 For as the earth brings
forth its branches,
And as a garden causes the things
sown in it to branch out,
So Lord Yahweh will cause
righteousness and praise
To branch out before all the nations.

62 For Zion's sake I will not keep silent,
And for Jerusalem's sake
I will not keep quiet,
Until her righteousness goes
forth like brightness,
And her salvation like a
torch that is burning.
2 The nations will see your
righteousness,
And all kings your glory;
And you will be called by a new name
Which the mouth of Yahweh
will designate.
3 You will also be a crown of glory
in the hand of Yahweh,
And a turban of royalty in
the hand of your God.
4 It will no longer be said to
you, "Forsaken,"
Nor to your land will it any
longer be said, "Desolate";
But you will be called,
"My delight is in her,"
And your land, "Married";
For Yahweh takes pleasure in you,
And *to Him* your land will be married.
5 For *as* a young man marries a virgin,
So your sons will marry you;
And *as* the bridegroom
rejoices over the bride,
So your God will rejoice over you.

6 On your walls, O Jerusalem,
I have appointed watchmen;
All day and all night they
will never keep silent.
You who remind Yahweh, take
no rest for yourselves;
7 And give Him no rest until
He establishes
And sets Jerusalem as a
praise in the earth.
8 Yahweh has sworn by His right
hand and by His strong arm,
"I will never again give your grain
as food for your enemies;
Nor will foreigners drink your new
wine for which you have labored."
9 But those who collect it will
eat it and praise Yahweh;
And those who gather it will drink
it in the courts of My sanctuary.

10 Go through, go through the gates,
Clear the way for the people;
Build up, build up the highway,
Remove the stones, raise up a
standard over the peoples.
11 Behold, Yahweh has announced
to the end of the earth,
Say to the daughter of Zion,
"Behold, your salvation comes;
Behold, His reward is with Him, and
His recompense before Him."
12 And they will call them,
"The holy people,
The redeemed of Yahweh";
And you will be called, "Sought
out, a city not forsaken."

Psalm 115:9–13

9 O Israel, trust in Yahweh;
He is their help and their shield.
10 O house of Aaron, trust in Yahweh;
He is their help and their shield.
11 You who fear Yahweh, trust in Yahweh;
He is their help and their shield.
12 Yahweh remembered us; He will bless!
He will bless the house of Israel.

He will bless the house of Aaron.
13 He will bless those who fear Yahweh,
The small together with the great.

Proverbs 26:24–26

24 He who hates disguises *it* with his lips,
But he sets up deceit within himself.
25 When he makes his voice
gracious, do not believe him,
For there are seven abominations
in his heart.
26 *Though his* hatred covers
itself with guile,
His evil will be revealed
in the assembly.

Ephesians 6:1–24

6 Children, obey your parents in the Lord,
for this is right. 2 HONOR YOUR FATHER
AND MOTHER (which is the first command-
ment with a promise), 3 SO THAT IT MAY BE
WELL WITH YOU, AND THAT YOU MAY LIVE LONG
IN THE LAND.

4 Fathers, do not provoke your children to
anger, but bring them up in the discipline
and instruction of the Lord.

5 Slaves, be obedient to those who are
your masters according to the flesh, with
fear and trembling, in the integrity of
your heart, as to Christ; 6 not by way of
eyeservice, as men-pleasers, but as slaves of
Christ, doing the will of God from the heart,
7 serving with good will as to the Lord, and
not to men, 8 knowing that whatever good
thing each one does, this he will receive
back from the Lord, whether slave or free.

9 And masters, do the same things to
them, giving up threatening, knowing that
both their Master and yours is in heaven,
and there is no partiality with Him.

10 Finally, be strong in the Lord and in
the might of His strength. 11 Put on the full
armor of God, so that you will be able to
stand firm against the schemes of the devil.
12 For our struggle is not against flesh and
blood, but against the rulers, against the
authorities, against the world forces of
this darkness, against the spiritual *forces*
of wickedness in the heavenly *places*.
13 Therefore, take up the full armor of God,
so that you will be able to resist in the evil
day, and having done everything, to stand
firm. 14 Stand firm therefore, HAVING GIRDED
YOUR LOINS WITH TRUTH, and HAVING PUT ON
THE BREASTPLATE OF RIGHTEOUSNESS, 15 and
having shod YOUR FEET WITH THE PREPARA-
TION OF THE GOSPEL OF PEACE. 16 In addition
to all, having taken up the shield of faith
with which you will be able to extinguish
all the flaming arrows of the evil one, 17 also
receive THE HELMET OF SALVATION, and the
sword of the Spirit, which is the word of
God,

18 praying at all times with all prayer
and petition in the Spirit, and to this end,
being on the alert with all perseverance and
petition for all the saints, 19 as well as on my
behalf, that words may be given to me in the
opening of my mouth, to make known with
boldness the mystery of the gospel— 20 for
which I am an ambassador in chains—so
that in *proclaiming* it I may speak boldly,
as I ought to speak.

21 But that you also may know about
all my affairs, how I am doing, Tychicus,
the beloved brother and faithful servant
in the Lord, will make everything known
to you. 22 I have sent him to you for this
very purpose, so that you may know our
circumstances, and that he may encourage
your hearts.

23 Peace be to the brothers, and love with
faith, from God the Father and the Lord
Jesus Christ. 24 Grace be with all those who
love our Lord Jesus Christ with incorruptible
love.

OCTOBER 6

Isaiah 63:1–64:12

63 Who is this who comes from Edom,
With garments of glowing
colors from Bozrah,
This One who is majestic
in His clothing,
Marching in the greatness
of His power?
"It is I who speak in righteousness,
mighty to save."
2 Why is Your clothing red,
And Your garments like the one
who treads in the wine press?
3 "I have trodden the wine trough alone,
And from the peoples there
was no man with Me.

I also trod them in My anger
And trampled them in My wrath;
And their lifeblood is sprinkled
on My garments,
And I stained all My clothes.
4 "For the day of vengeance
was in My heart,
And My year of redemption has come.
5 "I looked, and there was no
one to help,
And I was astonished, and there
was no one to uphold;
So My own arm brought
salvation to Me,
And My wrath upheld Me.
6 "I trod down the peoples in My anger
And made them drunk in My wrath,
And I brought down their
lifeblood to the earth."
7 I shall bring to remembrance the
lovingkindnesses of Yahweh,
the praises of Yahweh,
According to all *the ways* that Yahweh
has dealt bountifully with us,
And the abundant goodness
toward the house of Israel,
Which He has dealt bountifully to
them according to His compassion
And according to the abundance
of His lovingkindnesses.
8 And He said, "Surely, they
are My people,
Sons who will not deal falsely."
So He became their Savior.
9 In all their distress He was distressed,
And the angel of His
presence saved them;
In His love and in His mercy
He redeemed them,
And He lifted them and carried
them all the ancient days.
10 But they rebelled
And grieved His Holy Spirit;
Therefore He turned Himself
to become their enemy;
He fought against them.
11 Then His people remembered
the ancient days, of Moses.
Where is He who brought them
up out of the sea with the
shepherds of His flock?
Where is He who put His Holy
Spirit in the midst of them,
12 Who caused His glorious arm to
go at the right hand of Moses,
Who split the waters before
them to make for Himself
an everlasting name,
13 Who led them through the depths?
Like the horse in the wilderness,
they did not stumble;
14 As the cattle which go down
into the valley,
The Spirit of Yahweh gave them rest.
So You led Your people,
To make for Yourself a glorious name.
15 Look down from heaven and see from
Your holy and glorious habitation;
Where are Your zeal and
Your mighty deeds?
The tumults within You
and Your compassion are
restrained toward me.
16 For You are our Father, though
Abraham does not know us
And Israel does not recognize us.
You, O Yahweh, are our Father,
Our Redeemer from everlasting
is Your name.
17 Why, O Yahweh, do You cause
us to stray from Your ways
And stiffen our heart from fearing You?
Return for the sake of Your slaves,
the tribes of Your inheritance.
18 Your holy people possessed Your
sanctuary for a little while;
Our adversaries have trodden *it* down.
19 We have become *like* those over
whom You have never ruled,
Like those who were not
called by Your name.

64 Oh, that You would rend the
heavens *and* come down,
That the mountains might
quake at Your presence—
2 As fire kindles the brushwood,
as fire causes water to boil—
To make Your name known
to Your adversaries,
That the nations may tremble
at Your presence!
3 When You did awesome things
for which we did not hope,
You came down; the mountains
quaked at Your presence.
4 For from ancient *times* they have
not heard or given ear,
Nor has the eye seen a
God besides You,

Who acts in behalf of the one
who waits for Him.
5 You meet him who rejoices
and does righteousness,
Who remembers You in Your ways.
Behold, You were angry; indeed
we have sinned—
We continued in them a long time—
And shall we be saved?
6 For all of us have become like
one who is unclean,
And all our righteous deeds
are like a filthy garment;
And all of us wither like a leaf,
And our iniquities, like the
wind, carry us away.
7 There is no one who calls
on Your name,
Who awakens himself to
take hold of You,
For You have hidden Your face from us
And have melted us into the
hand of our iniquities.

8 But now, O Yahweh, You are our Father;
We are the clay, and You our potter;
And all of us are the work
of Your hand.
9 Do not be angry beyond
measure, O Yahweh,
Nor remember iniquity forever;
Behold, look now, all of us
are Your people.
10 Your holy cities have become
a wilderness;
Zion has become a wilderness,
Jerusalem a desolation.
11 Our holy and glorious house,
Where our fathers praised You,
Has been burned *by* fire;
And all our precious things have
become a waste place.
12 Will You restrain Yourself at
these things, O Yahweh?
Will You keep silent and afflict
us beyond measure?

Psalm 115:14–18

14 May Yahweh give you increase,
You and your children.
15 May you be blessed of Yahweh,
Who made heaven and earth.

16 The heavens are the
heavens of Yahweh,
But the earth He has given
to the sons of men.
17 It is not the dead that praise Yah,
And it is none of those who
go down to silence;
18 But as for us, we will bless Yah
From now until forever.
Praise Yah!

Proverbs 26:27

27 He who digs a pit will fall into it,
And he who rolls a stone,
it will turn back on him.

Philippians 1:1–30

1 Paul and Timothy, slaves of Christ Jesus,
To all the saints in Christ Jesus who are
in Philippi, with the overseers and deacons:
2 Grace to you and peace from God our
Father and the Lord Jesus Christ.
3 I thank my God in all my remembrance
of you, 4 always offering prayer with joy in
my every prayer for you all, 5 because of
your fellowship in the gospel from the first
day until now. 6 *For I am* confident of this
very thing, that He who began a good work
in you will perfect it until the day of Christ
Jesus. 7 For it is only right for me to think
this way about you all, because I have you
in my heart, since both in my chains and in
the defense and confirmation of the gospel,
you all are fellow partakers with me in this
grace. 8 For God is my witness, how I long
for you all with the affection of Christ Jesus.
9 And this I pray, that your love may abound
still more and more in full knowledge and
all discernment, 10 so that you may approve
the things that are excellent, in order to be
sincere and without fault until the day of
Christ, 11 having been filled with the fruit
of righteousness which *comes* through Jesus
Christ, to the glory and praise of God.
12 Now I want you to know, brothers, that
my circumstances have turned out for the
greater progress of the gospel, 13 so that my
chains in Christ have become well known
throughout the whole praetorian guard and
to everyone else, 14 and that most of the
brothers, having become confident in the
Lord because of my chains, have far more
courage to speak the word of God without
fear. 15 Some, to be sure, are preaching
Christ even from envy and strife, but some
also from good will; 16 the latter *do it* out of
love, knowing that I am appointed for the

defense of the gospel; 17 the former proclaim Christ out of selfish ambition rather than from pure motives, thinking to cause me affliction in my chains. 18 What then? Only that in every way, whether in pretense or in truth, Christ is proclaimed, and in this I rejoice.

Yes, and I will rejoice, 19 for I know that THIS WILL TURN OUT FOR MY SALVATION through your prayers and the provision of the Spirit of Jesus Christ, 20 according to my earnest expectation and hope, that I will not be put to shame in anything, but *that* with all boldness, Christ will even now, as always, be magnified in my body, whether by life or by death.

21 For to me, to live is Christ and to die is gain. 22 But if *I am* to live *on* in the flesh, this *will mean* fruitful labor for me; and I do not know what I will choose. 23 But I am hard-pressed between the two, having the desire to depart and be with Christ, for *that* is very much better, 24 yet to remain on in the flesh is more necessary for your sake. 25 And convinced of this, I know that I will remain and continue with you all for your progress and joy in the faith, 26 so that your reason for boasting may abound in Christ Jesus in me, through my coming to you again.

27 Only live your lives in a manner worthy of the gospel of Christ, so that whether I come and see you or remain absent, I will hear about your circumstances, that you are standing firm in one spirit, with one mind contending together for the faith of the gospel, 28 in no way alarmed by *your* opponents—which is a sign of destruction for them, but of salvation for you, and that *too,* from God. 29 For to you it has been granted for Christ's sake, not only to believe in Him, but also to suffer for His sake, 30 having the same struggle which you saw in me, and now hear *to be* in me.

OCTOBER 7

Isaiah 65:1–66:24

65 "I permitted Myself to be sought
by those who did not ask *for Me*;
I permitted Myself to be found by
those who did not seek Me.
I said, 'Here am I, here am I,'
To a nation which did not
call on My name.
2 "I have spread out My hands all day
long to a rebellious people,
Who walk *in* the way which is not
good, following their own
thoughts,
3 A people who continually
provoke Me to My face,
Offering sacrifices in gardens and
burning incense on bricks,
4 Who sit among graves and spend
the night in secret places,
Who eat swine's flesh,
And the broth of offensive
meat is *in* their pots,
5 Who say, 'Keep to yourself,
do not come near me,
For I am holier than you!'
These are smoke in My nostrils,
A fire that burns all the day.
6 "Behold, it is written before Me:
I will not keep silent, but I will repay;
I will even repay into their bosom,
7 Both their own iniquities and
the iniquities of their fathers
together," says Yahweh.
"Because they have burned
incense on the mountains
And reproached Me on the hills,
Therefore I will measure their
former work into their bosom."

8 Thus says Yahweh,
"As the new wine is found in the cluster,
And one says, 'Do not make it a
ruin, for there is benefit in it,'
So I will act on behalf of My slaves
In order not to make all of them a ruin.
9 "I will bring forth a seed from Jacob,
And a possessor of My
mountains from Judah;
Even My chosen ones shall possess it,
And My slaves will dwell there.
10 "Sharon will be a pasture land for flocks,
And the valley of Achor a
resting place for herds,
For My people who seek Me.
11 "But you who forsake Yahweh,
Who forget My holy mountain,
Who set a table for Fortune,
And who fill *cups* with mixed
wine for Destiny,
12 I will destine you for the sword,

And all of you will bow down
to the slaughter,
Because I called, but you
did not answer;
I spoke, but you did not hear.
And you did what was evil in My eyes
And chose that in which I
was not pleased."

13 Therefore, thus says Lord Yahweh,
"Behold, My slaves will eat,
but you will be hungry.
Behold, My slaves will drink,
but you will be thirsty.
Behold, My slaves will be glad, but
you will be put to shame.
14 "Behold, My slaves will shout
joyfully with a merry heart,
But you will cry out with a pained heart,
And you will wail with a broken spirit.
15 "You will leave your name for a
curse to My chosen ones,
And Lord Yahweh will put you to death.
But My slaves will be called
by another name,
16 Because he who is blessed in the earth
Will be blessed by the God of truth,
And he who swears in the earth
Will swear by the God of truth;
Because the former distresses
are forgotten,
And because they are hidden
from My sight!
17 "For behold, I am creating a new
heavens and a new earth;
And the former things will not be
remembered or come upon the heart.
18 "But be joyful and rejoice
forever in what I create;
For behold, I create Jerusalem
for rejoicing
And her people *for* joy.
19 "I will also rejoice in Jerusalem
and be joyful in My people;
And there will no longer be heard in her
The voice of weeping and
the voice of crying.
20 "No longer will there be in it an
infant *who lives but a few* days,
Or an old man who does
not fulfill his days;
For the youth will die at the
age of one hundred,
And the one who does not reach
the age of one hundred
Will be *thought* accursed.
21 "They will build houses
and inhabit *them*;
They will also plant vineyards
and eat their fruit.
22 "They will not build and
another inhabit;
They will not plant and another eat;
For as the lifetime of a tree, *so will
be* the days of My people,
And My chosen ones will wear
out the work of their hands.
23 "They will not labor in vain,
Or bear *children* for terror;
For they are the seed of those
blessed by Yahweh,
And their offspring with them.
24 "And it will be that before they call, I will
answer, and while they are still speaking, I
will hear. 25 The wolf and the lamb will graze
together, and the lion will eat straw like the
ox; and dust will be the serpent's food. They
will do no evil nor act corruptly in all My
holy mountain," says Yahweh.

66 Thus says Yahweh,
"Heaven is My throne, and the
earth is the footstool of My feet.
Where then is a house you
could build for Me?
And where is a place that I may rest?
2 "For My hand made all these things,
Thus all these things came into
being," declares Yahweh.
"But to this one I will look,
To him who is humble and contrite of
spirit, and who trembles at My word.

3 "*But* he who slaughters an ox is the
one who strikes down a man;
He who sacrifices a lamb is the
one who breaks a dog's neck;
He who offers a grain offering *is the
one who offers* swine's blood;
He who offers a memorial offering
of frankincense is the one
who blesses wickedness.
As they have chosen their *own* ways,
And their soul takes pleasure
in their detestable things,
4 So I will choose their punishments
And will bring on them
what they dread,
Because I called, but no one answered;
I spoke, but they did not listen.

And they did what was evil in My eyes
And chose that in which I did
not take pleasure."
5 Hear the word of Yahweh, you
who tremble at His word:
"Your brothers who hate you, who
exclude you for My name's sake,
Have said, 'Let Yahweh be glorified,
that we may see your gladness.'
But they will be put to shame.
6 "A voice of rumbling from the city,
a voice from the temple,
The voice of Yahweh who is paying
recompense to His enemies.

7 "Before she was in labor
pains, she gave birth;
Before her pangs came,
she delivered a male *child*.
8 "Who has heard such a thing?
Who has seen such things?
Can a land be brought forth through
labor pains in one day?
Can a nation be born all at once?
As soon as Zion was in labor pains,
she also gave birth to her sons.
9 "Shall I bring to the point of
breaking forth and not cause
birth?" says Yahweh.
"Or shall I who causes birth shut
the womb?" says your God.
10 "Be glad with Jerusalem and rejoice
for her, all you who love her;
Be exceedingly joyful with her,
all you who mourn over her,
11 That you may nurse and be satisfied
with her comforting breasts,
That you may suck and be delighted
with her bountiful bosom."
12 For thus says Yahweh, "Behold,
I stretch out peace to her like a river,
And the glory of the nations like
an overflowing stream;
And you will be nursed; you
will be carried on the hip and
played with on the knees.
13 "As one whom his mother comforts,
so I will comfort you;
And you will be comforted in Jerusalem."
14 Then you will see *this*, and
your heart will be joyful,
And your bones will flourish
like the new grass;
And the hand of Yahweh will be
made known to His slaves,
But He will be indignant
toward His enemies.
15 For behold, Yahweh will come in fire
And His chariots like the whirlwind,
To return His anger with wrath,
And His rebuke with flames of fire.
16 For Yahweh will execute
judgment by fire
And by His sword on all flesh,
And those slain by Yahweh
will be many.
17 "Those who sanctify and purify
themselves *to go* to the gardens,
Following one in the center,
Who eat swine's flesh, detestable
things, and mice,
Will come to an end altogether,"
declares Yahweh.

18 "And I know their works and their
thoughts; the time is coming to gather all
nations and tongues. And they shall come
and see My glory. 19 I will set a sign among
them and will send those who have escaped
from them to the nations: Tarshish, Put,
Lud, Meshech, Tubal, and Javan, to the
distant coastlands that have neither heard
My report nor seen My glory. And they will
declare My glory among the nations. 20 Then
they shall bring all your brothers from all
the nations as a grain offering to Yahweh, on
horses, in chariots, in litters, on mules, and
on camels, to My holy mountain Jerusalem,"
says Yahweh, "just as the sons of Israel bring
their grain offering in a clean vessel to the
house of Yahweh. 21 I will also take some
of them for priests *and* for Levites," says
Yahweh.

22 "For just as the new heavens
and the new earth
Which I make will endure before
Me," declares Yahweh,
"So your seed and your
name will endure.
23 "And it shall be from new
moon to new moon
And from sabbath to sabbath,
All mankind will come to worship
before Me," says Yahweh.
24 "Then they will go forth and look
On the corpses of the men
Who have transgressed against Me.
For their worm will not die
And their fire will not be quenched;
And they will be an *object of*
contempt to all mankind."

Psalm 116:1–4

1 I love Yahweh, because He hears
My voice *and* my supplications.
2 Because He has inclined His ear to me,
So I shall call *upon Him* in all my days.
3 The cords of death encompassed me
And the distresses of Sheol found me;
I found distress and sorrow.
4 Then I called upon the name of Yahweh:
"O Yahweh, I beseech You,
provide my soul escape!"

Proverbs 26:28

28 A lying tongue hates those it crushes,
And a flattering mouth works ruin.

Philippians 2:1–30

2 Therefore if there is any encouragement
in Christ, if there is any consolation of
love, if there is any fellowship of the Spirit,
if any affection and compassion, 2 fulfill my
joy, that you think the same *way*, by main-
taining the same love, *being* united in spirit,
thinking on one purpose, 3 doing nothing
from selfish ambition or vain glory, but with
humility of mind regarding one another as
more important than yourselves, 4 not *merely*
looking out for your own personal interests,
but also for the interests of others. 5 Have
this *way of* thinking in yourselves which was
also in Christ Jesus, 6 who, although existing
in the form of God, did not regard equality
with God a thing to be grasped, 7 but emptied
Himself, by taking the form of a slave, by
being made in the likeness of men. 8 Being
found in appearance as a man, He humbled
Himself by becoming obedient to the point
of death, even death on a cross. 9 Therefore,
God also highly exalted Him, and bestowed
on Him the name which is above every
name, 10 so that at the name of Jesus EVERY
KNEE WILL BOW, of those who are in heaven
and on earth and under the earth, 11 and that
EVERY TONGUE WILL CONFESS that Jesus Christ
is LORD, to the glory of God the Father.

12 So then, my beloved, just as you have
always obeyed, not as in my presence only,
but now much more in my absence, work
out your salvation with fear and trembling;
13 for it is God who is at work in you, both
to will and to work for *His* good pleasure.

14 Do all things without grumbling or dis-
puting, 15 so that you will be blameless and
innocent, children of God without blemish
in the midst of a crooked and perverse gen-
eration, among whom you shine as lights in
the world, 16 holding fast the word of life, so
that in the day of Christ I will have reason to
boast because I did not run in vain nor labor
in vain. 17 But even if I am being poured out
as a drink offering upon the sacrifice and
service of your faith, I rejoice and share my
joy with you all. 18 And you also, rejoice in
the same way and share your joy with me.

19 But I hope in the Lord Jesus to send
Timothy to you shortly, so that I also may
be in good spirits when I learn of your
circumstances. 20 For I have no one *else*
of kindred spirit who will genuinely be
concerned about your circumstances. 21 For
they all seek after their own interests, not
those of Christ Jesus. 22 But you know of his
proven worth, that he served with me in the
furtherance of the gospel like a child *serving*
his father. 23 Therefore I hope to send him
immediately, as soon as I evaluate my own
circumstances, 24 and I am confident in
the Lord that I myself also will be coming
shortly. 25 But I regarded it necessary to
send to you Epaphroditus, my brother and
fellow worker and fellow soldier, who is
also your messenger and minister to my
need; 26 because he was longing for you all
and was distressed because you had heard
that he was sick. 27 For indeed he was sick
to the point of death, but God had mercy
on him, and not on him only but also on
me, so that I would not have sorrow upon
sorrow. 28 Therefore I have sent him all the
more eagerly so that when you see him again
you may rejoice and I may be less concerned.
29 Receive him then in the Lord with all
joy, and hold men like him in high regard
30 because he came close to death for the
work of Christ, risking his life to fulfill what
was lacking in your service to me.

The Bible. Know it in your head. Stow it in your heart. Show it in your life. Sow it in the world.

— J. VERNON MCGEE

OCTOBER 8

Jeremiah 1:1–2:37

1 The words of Jeremiah the son of Hilkiah,
of the priests who were in Anathoth in
the land of Benjamin, 2 to whom the word of
Yahweh came in the days of Josiah the son
of Amon, king of Judah, in the thirteenth
year of his reign. 3 And it came in the days
of Jehoiakim the son of Josiah, king of
Judah, until the end of the eleventh year of
Zedekiah the son of Josiah, king of Judah,
until the exile of Jerusalem in the fifth
month.

4 Now the word of Yahweh came to me
saying,

5 "Before I formed you in the
innermost parts I knew you,
And before you came out from
the womb I set you apart;
I have given you as a prophet
to the nations."
6 Then I said, "Alas, Lord Yahweh!
Behold, I do not know how to speak
Because I am a youth."
7 But Yahweh said to me,
"Do not say, 'I am a youth,'
Because everywhere I send
you, you shall go,
And all that I command
you, you shall speak.
8 "Do not be afraid of them,
For I am with you to deliver
you," declares Yahweh.

9 Then Yahweh sent forth His hand and
touched my mouth, and Yahweh said to me,

"Behold, I have put My words
in your mouth.
10 "See, I have appointed you this day over
the nations and over the kingdoms,
To uproot and to tear down,
To cause to perish and to pull down,
To build and to plant."

11 Now the word of Yahweh came to me
saying, "What do you see, Jeremiah?" And I
said, "I see a rod of an almond tree." 12 Then
Yahweh said to me, "You have seen well, for
I am watching over My word to do it."

13 The word of Yahweh came to me a
second time saying, "What do you see?"
And I said, "I see a boiling pot, facing away
from the north." 14 Then Yahweh said to
me, "From the north the evil will break
open on all the inhabitants of the land.
15 For, behold, I am calling all the families
of the kingdoms of the north," declares
Yahweh; "and they will come, and each one
of them will put his throne at the opening
of the gates of Jerusalem, and against all its
walls round about and against all the cities
of Judah. 16 I will speak My judgments on
them concerning all their evil, whereby they
have forsaken Me and have burned incense
to other gods and worshiped the works of
their own hands. 17 Now, gird up your loins
and arise and speak to them all which I
command you. Do not be dismayed before
them, lest I dismay you before them. 18 Now
behold, I have given you today as a fortified
city and as a pillar of iron and as walls of
bronze against the whole land, to the kings
of Judah, to its princes, to its priests, and to
the people of the land. 19 And they will fight
against you, but they will not overcome you,
for I am with you to deliver you," declares
Yahweh.

2 Now the word of Yahweh came to me
saying, 2 "Go and call out in the ears of
Jerusalem, saying, 'Thus says Yahweh,

"I remember concerning you the
lovingkindness of your youth,
The love of your betrothals,
Your walking after Me in
the wilderness,
Through a land not sown.
3 "Israel was holy to Yahweh,
The first of His produce.
All who ate of it became guilty;
Evil came upon them,"
declares Yahweh.'"

4 Hear the word of Yahweh, O house of
Jacob and all the families of the house of
Israel. 5 Thus says Yahweh,

"What injustice did your
fathers find in Me,
That they went far from Me
And walked after vanity
and became vain?
6 "They did not say, 'Where is Yahweh
Who brought us up out of
the land of Egypt,
Who led us through the wilderness,
Through a land of deserts and of pits,
Through a land of drought and
of the shadow of death,

Through a land that no one crossed
And where no man inhabited?'
7 "I brought you into the fruitful land
To eat its fruit and its good things.
But you came and defiled My land,
And My inheritance you
made an abomination.
8 "The priests did not say,
'Where is Yahweh?'
And those who handle the
law did not know Me;
The shepherds also
transgressed against Me,
And the prophets prophesied by Baal
And walked after things
that did not profit.

9 "Therefore I will yet contend with
you," declares Yahweh,
"And with your sons' sons
I will contend.
10 "For cross to the coastlands
of Kittim and see,
And send to Kedar and perceive closely
And see if there has been
such *a thing* as this!
11 "Has a nation changed gods
Though they were not gods?
But My people have
changed their glory
For that which does not profit.
12 "Be appalled, O heavens, at this,
And be horribly afraid, be very
devastated," declares Yahweh.
13 "For My people have done two evils:
They have forsaken Me,
The fountain of living waters,
To hew for themselves cisterns,
Broken cisterns
That can hold no water.

14 "Is Israel a slave? Or is he a
homeborn *slave*?
Why has he become plunder?
15 "The young lions have roared at him;
They have given forth their voice.
And they have made his
land a desolation;
His cities have been turned into
ruin, without inhabitant.
16 "Also the men of Memphis
and Tahpanhes
Have shaved the top of your head.
17 "Have you not done this to yourself
By your forsaking Yahweh your God
When He led you in the way?
18 "But now what are you doing
on the road to Egypt,
To drink the waters of the Nile?
Or what are you doing on
the road to Assyria,
To drink the waters of the River?
19 "Your own evil will chastise you,
And your acts of faithlessness
will reprove you;
Know therefore and see that
it is evil and bitter
For you to forsake Yahweh your God,
And the dread of Me is not in you,"
declares Lord Yahweh of hosts.

20 "For long ago I broke your yoke
And tore off your bonds;
But you said, 'I will not serve!'
For on every high hill
And under every green tree
You have lain down as a harlot.
21 "Yet I planted you a choice vine,
A completely true seed.
How then have you turned
yourself before Me
Into the degenerate shoots
of a foreign vine?
22 "Although you wash yourself with lye
And use much soap,
The stain of your iniquity is before
Me," declares Lord Yahweh.
23 "How can you say, 'I am not defiled;
I have not walked after the Baals'?
Look at your way in the valley!
Know what you have done!
You are a swift young camel
entangling her ways,
24 A wild donkey accustomed
to the wilderness,
That sniffs the wind in her passion.
In *the time of* her heat who
can turn her away?
All who seek her will not
become weary;
In her month they will find her.
25 "Keep your feet from being barefoot
And your throat from thirst;
But you said, 'It is hopeless!
No! For I have loved strangers,
And after them I will walk.'

26 "As the thief is shamed
when he is found,
So the house of Israel is shamed;

They, their kings, their princes,
And their priests and their prophets,
27 Who say to a tree, 'You are my father,'
And to a stone, 'You gave me birth.'
For they have turned *their* back to Me
And not *their* face;
But in the time *when* their evil
comes they will say,
'Arise and save us.'
28 "But where are your gods
Which you made for yourself?
Let them arise, if they can save you
In the time *when* your evil *comes*;
For *according to* the number
of your cities
Are your gods, O Judah.

29 "Why do you contend with Me?
You have all transgressed against
Me," declares Yahweh.
30 "In vain I have struck your sons;
They received no discipline.
Your sword has devoured
your prophets
Like a destroying lion.
31 "O generation, behold the
word of Yahweh.
Have I been a wilderness to Israel
Or a land of thick darkness?
Why do My people say,
'We *are free to* roam;
We will no longer come to You'?
32 "Can a virgin forget her ornaments,
Or a bride her attire?
Yet My people have forgotten Me
Days without number.
33 "How well you prepare your way
To seek love!
Therefore even the wicked women
You have taught your ways.
34 "Also on your skirts is found
The lifeblood of the innocent needy;
You did not find them breaking in.
But in spite of all these things,
35 Yet you said, 'I am innocent;
Surely His anger is turned
away from me.'
Behold, I will enter into
judgment with you
Because you say, 'I have not sinned.'
36 "Why do you despise *Him* so much
In changing your way?
Also, you will be put to shame by Egypt
As you were put to shame by Assyria.
37 "From this *place* also you will go out
With your hands on your head;
For Yahweh has rejected those
in whom you trust,
And you will not succeed with them."

Psalm 116:5–14

5 Gracious is Yahweh, and righteous;
And our God is compassionate.
6 Yahweh keeps the simple;
I was brought low, and He saved me.
7 Return to your rest, O my soul,
For Yahweh has dealt
bountifully with you.
8 For You have rescued my
soul from death,
My eyes from tears,
My feet from stumbling.
9 I shall walk before Yahweh
In the land of the living.
10 I believed when I said,
"I am greatly afflicted."
11 I said in my alarm,
"All men are liars."

12 What shall I give to Yahweh in return
For all His bountiful dealings with me?
13 I shall lift up the cup of salvation
And call upon the name of Yahweh.
14 I shall pay my vows to Yahweh,
Oh *may it be* in the presence
of all His people.

Proverbs 27:1

27 Do not boast about tomorrow,
For you do not know what
a day may bring forth.

Philippians 3:1–21

3 Finally, my brothers, rejoice in the Lord.
To write the same things *again* is no
trouble to me, and it is a safeguard for you.
2 Beware of the dogs! Beware of the evil
workers! Beware of the mutilation! 3 For
we are the circumcision, who worship
in the Spirit of God and boast in Christ
Jesus and put no confidence in the flesh,
4 although I myself might have confidence
even in the flesh. If anyone else has a mind
to put confidence in the flesh, I far more:
5 circumcised the eighth day, of the nation
of Israel, of the tribe of Benjamin, a Hebrew
of Hebrews; as to the Law, a Pharisee; 6 as to
zeal, a persecutor of the church; as to the
righteousness which is in the Law, found
blameless.

7 But whatever things were gain to me,
those things I have counted as loss for the
sake of Christ. 8 More than that, I count all
things to be loss because of the surpassing
value of knowing Christ Jesus my Lord, for
whom I have suffered the loss of all things,
and count them but rubbish so that I may
gain Christ 9 and be found in Him, not hav-
ing a righteousness of my own which is from
the Law, but that which is through faith in
Christ, the righteousness which *is* from God
upon faith, 10 that I may know Him and the
power of His resurrection and the fellowship
of His sufferings, being conformed to His
death, 11 in order that I may attain to the
resurrection from the dead.

12 Not that I have already obtained *it* or
have already become perfect, but I press on
so that I may lay hold of that for which also I
was laid hold of by Christ Jesus. 13 Brothers,
I do not consider myself as having laid hold
of *it* yet, but one thing *I do*: forgetting what
lies behind and reaching forward to what
lies ahead, 14 I press on toward the goal for
the prize of the upward call of God in Christ
Jesus. 15 Let us therefore, as many as are
perfect, think this way; and if in anything
you think differently, God will reveal that
also to you. 16 However, *let us* keep walking
in step with the same *standard* to which we
have attained.

17 Brothers, join in following my example,
and look for those who walk according to
the pattern you have in us. 18 For many
walk—of whom I often told you, and now
tell you even crying—as enemies of the
cross of Christ, 19 whose end is destruction,
whose god is *their* stomach and glory is in
their shame, who set their thoughts on
earthly things. 20 For our citizenship is in
heaven, from which also we eagerly wait
for a Savior, the Lord Jesus Christ, 21 who
will transform the body of our humble state
into conformity with the body of His glory,
by His working through which He is able to
even subject all things to Himself.

OCTOBER 9

Jeremiah 3:1–4:31

3 *God* says, "If a husband
divorces his wife
And she goes from him
And belongs to another man,
Will he still return to her?
Will not that land be
completely polluted?
But you are a harlot *with* many lovers;
Yet you turn to Me," declares Yahweh.
2 "Lift up your eyes to the bare
heights and see;
Where have you not been ravished?
By the roads you have sat for them
Like an Arab in the wilderness,
And you have polluted a land
With your harlotry and with your evil.
3 "Therefore the showers have
been withheld,
And the late rain has not come.
Yet you had a harlot's forehead;
You refused to feel dishonor.
4 "Have you not just now called to Me,
'My Father, You are the close
companion of my youth?
5 'Will He be angry forever?
Will He keep *it* to the end?'
Behold, you have spoken
And have done evil things,
And you have had your way."

6 Then Yahweh said to me in the days
of Josiah the king, "Have you seen what
faithless Israel did? She went up on every
high hill and under every green tree, and
she was a harlot there. 7 I said, 'After she has
done all these things, she will return to Me';
but she did not return, and her treacherous
sister Judah saw it. 8 And I saw that for all
the adulteries of faithless Israel, I had sent
her away and given her a certificate of
divorce, yet her treacherous sister Judah
did not fear; but she went and was a harlot
also. 9 So it was, because of the lightness of
her harlotry, that she polluted the land and
committed adultery with stones and trees.
10 Yet in spite of all this, her treacherous
sister Judah did not return to Me with all
her heart, but rather in lying," declares
Yahweh.

11 And Yahweh said to me, "Faithless
Israel has proved herself more righteous
than treacherous Judah. 12 Go and call out
these words toward the north and say,
'Return, faithless Israel,'
declares Yahweh;
'I will not look upon you in anger.

For I am One of lovingkindness,'
declares Yahweh;
'I will not be angry forever.
13 'Only acknowledge your iniquity,
That you have transgressed
against Yahweh your God
And have scattered your ways
of harlotry to the strangers
under every green tree,
And you have not listened to My
voice,' declares Yahweh.
14 'Return, O faithless sons,'
declares Yahweh;
'For I am a master to you,
And I will take you one from a
city and two from a family,
And I will bring you to Zion.'

15 "Then I will give you shepherds after
My own heart, who will shepherd you on
knowledge and understanding. 16 It shall be
in those days when you are multiplied and
fruitful in the land," declares Yahweh, "they
will no longer say, 'The ark of the covenant
of Yahweh.' And it will not come upon the
heart, nor will they remember it, nor will
they miss *it*, nor will it be made again. 17 At
that time they will call Jerusalem 'The
Throne of Yahweh,' and all the nations will
be gathered to it, to Jerusalem, for the name
of Yahweh; nor will they walk anymore
after the stubbornness of their evil heart.
18 In those days the house of Judah will
walk with the house of Israel, and they will
come together from the land of the north
to the land that I gave your fathers as an
inheritance.

19 "Then I said,
'How I would set you among My sons
And give you a pleasant land,
The most beautiful inheritance
of the nations!'
And I said, 'You shall call Me,
"My Father,"
And not turn away from following Me.'
20 "Surely, as a woman treacherously
departs from her lover,
So you have dealt
treacherously with Me,
O house of Israel," declares Yahweh.

21 A voice is heard on the bare heights,
The weeping *and* the supplications
of the sons of Israel;
Because they have perverted their way,
They have forgotten Yahweh their God.
22 "Return, O faithless sons;
I will heal your faithlessness."
"Behold, we come to You,
For You are Yahweh our God.
23 "Surely, the hills are a lie,
A tumult *on* the mountains.
Surely in Yahweh our God
Is the salvation of Israel.
24 "But the shameful thing has devoured
the labor of our fathers since our youth,
their flocks and their herds, their sons and
their daughters. 25 Let us lie down in our
shame, and let our dishonor cover us; for
we have sinned against Yahweh our God, we
and our fathers, from our youth even to this
day. And we have not listened to the voice
of Yahweh our God."

4 "If you will return, O Israel,"
declares Yahweh,
"*Then* you should return to Me.
And if you will put away your detested
things from My presence
And will not waver
2 And you will swear, 'As Yahweh lives,'
In truth, in justice, and in
righteousness;
Then the nations will be
blessed in Him,
And in Him they will boast."

3 For thus says Yahweh to the men of Judah
and to Jerusalem,
"Break up your fallow ground,
And do not sow among thorns.
4 "Circumcise yourselves to Yahweh
And remove the foreskins
of your heart,
Men of Judah and inhabitants
of Jerusalem,
Lest My wrath go forth like fire
And burn with none to quench it
Because of the evil of your deeds."
5 Declare in Judah and make *it*
heard in Jerusalem and say,
"Blow the trumpet in the land;
Call out, make *your voice* full, and say,
'Gather yourselves, and let us go
Into the fortified cities.'
6 "Lift up a standard toward Zion!
Seek safety, do not stand *still*,
For I am bringing evil from the north,
And great destruction.
7 "A lion has gone up from his thicket,
And a destroyer of nations has set out;

He has gone out from his place
To make your land a desolation.
Your cities will be turned into ruins
Without inhabitant.
8 "For this, I gird myself with sackcloth,
Lament and wail;
For the burning anger of Yahweh
Has not turned back from us."
9 "It will be in that day," declares Yahweh,
"*that* the heart of the king and the heart
of the princes will perish; and the priests
will be appalled, and the prophets will be
astonished."
10 Then I said, "Ah, Lord Yahweh! Surely
You have utterly deceived this people and
Jerusalem, saying, 'You will have peace';
whereas a sword touches the throat."
11 In that time it will be said to this people
and to Jerusalem, "A scorching wind from
the bare heights in the wilderness along the
way of the daughter of My people—not to
winnow and not to cleanse, 12 a wind too
full for these things—will come for My
purpose; now I will also speak judgments
against them.
13 "Behold, he goes up like clouds,
And his chariots like the whirlwind;
His horses are swifter than eagles.
Woe to us, for we are devastated!"

14 Wash your heart from
evil, O Jerusalem,
That you may be saved.
How long will your wicked thoughts
Lodge within you?
15 For a voice declares from Dan,
And makes wickedness heard
from Mount Ephraim.
16 "Make mention *of it* to the
nations, *saying,* 'Behold!'
Make *it* heard over Jerusalem,
'Besiegers come from a far country,
And give forth their voices
against the cities of Judah.
17 'Like watchmen of a field they
are against her round about
Because she has rebelled against
Me,' declares Yahweh.
18 "Your ways and your deeds
Have done these things to you.
This is your evil. How bitter!
How it has touched your heart!"
19 My soul, my soul! I am in
anguish! Oh, my heart!
My heart is pounding in me;
I cannot be silent
Because you have heard, O my soul,
The sound of the trumpet,
The shout of war.
20 Destruction upon destruction
is called out,
For the whole land is devastated;
Suddenly my tents are devastated,
My curtains in an instant.
21 How long must I see the standard
And hear the sound of the trumpet?
22 "For My people are ignorant fools,
They know Me not;
They are simpleminded children
And have no understanding.
They are wise to do evil,
But to do good they do not know."

23 I saw on the earth, and behold,
it was formless and void;
And to the heavens, and
they had no light.
24 I saw on the mountains, and
behold, they were quaking,
And all the hills moved to and fro.
25 I saw, and behold, there was no man,
And all the birds of the sky had fled.
26 I saw, and behold, the fruitful
orchard was a wilderness,
And all its cities were torn down
Before Yahweh, before His
burning anger.

27 For thus says Yahweh,
"The whole land shall be
a desolation,
Yet I will not execute a
complete destruction.
28 "For this the earth shall mourn
And the heavens above be dark
Because I have spoken;
I have purposed,
And I will not relent, nor
will I turn from it."
29 At the sound of the horseman and
bowman every city flees;
They go into the thickets and
climb up among the rocks;
Every city is forsaken,
And no man inhabits them.
30 And you, O devastated one,
what will you do?
Although you dress in scarlet,
Although you decorate *yourself*
with ornaments of gold,

Although you enlarge your
eyes with paint,
In vain you make yourself
beautiful.
Your lovers despise you;
They seek your life.
31 For I heard a sound as of a
woman in labor pains,
The distress as of one giving
birth to her first child,
The sound of the daughter of
Zion gasping for breath,
Stretching out her hands, *saying*,
"Ah, woe is me, for my soul
faints before murderers."

Psalm 116:15–19

15 Precious in the sight of Yahweh
Is the death of His holy ones.
16 O Yahweh, surely I am Your slave,
I am Your slave, the son of
Your maidservant,
You have loosed my bonds.
17 To You I shall offer a sacrifice
of thanksgiving,
And call upon the name of Yahweh.
18 I shall pay my vows to Yahweh,
Oh *may it be* in the presence
of all His people,
19 In the courts of the house of Yahweh,
In the midst of you, O Jerusalem.
Praise Yah!

Proverbs 27:2

2 Let a stranger praise you, and
not your own mouth;
A foreigner, and not your own lips.

Philippians 4:1–23

4 Therefore my brothers, loved and
longed for, my joy and crown, in this
way stand firm in the Lord, my beloved.
2 I urge Euodia and I urge Syntyche to
think the same way in the Lord. 3 Indeed,
I ask you also, genuine companion, help
these women who have contended together
alongside of me in the gospel, with also
Clement and the rest of my fellow workers,
whose names are in the book of life.
4 Rejoice in the Lord always; again I will
say, rejoice! 5 Let your considerate *spirit* be
known to all men. The Lord is near. 6 Be
anxious for nothing, but in everything
by prayer and petition with thanksgiving
let your requests be made known to God.
7 And the peace of God, which surpasses all
comprehension, will guard your hearts and
your minds in Christ Jesus.
8 Finally, brothers, whatever is true, what-
ever is dignified, whatever is right, whatever
is pure, whatever is lovely, whatever is
commendable, if there is any excellence and
if anything worthy of praise, consider these
things. 9 The things you have learned and
received and heard and seen in me, practice
these things, and the God of peace will be
with you.
10 But I rejoiced in the Lord greatly, that
now at last you have revived thinking about
me; indeed, you were thinking about me
before, but you lacked opportunity. 11 Not
that I speak from want, for I learned to be
content in whatever circumstances I am. 12 I
know how to get along with humble means,
and I also know how to live in abundance; in
any and all things I have learned the secret
of being filled and going hungry, both of
having abundance and suffering need. 13 I
can do all things through Him who strength-
ens me. 14 Nevertheless, you have done well
to fellowship *with me* in my affliction.
15 And you yourselves also know, Phi-
lippians, that at the first preaching of the
gospel, after I left Macedonia, no church fel-
lowshipped with me in the matter of giving
and receiving but you alone. 16 For even in
Thessalonica you sent *a gift* more than once
for my needs. 17 Not that I seek the gift itself,
but I seek the fruit which increases to your
account. 18 But I have received everything
in full and have an abundance; I have been
filled, having received from Epaphroditus
what you have sent, a fragrant aroma, an
acceptable sacrifice, pleasing to God. 19 And
my God will fulfill all your needs according
to His riches in glory in Christ Jesus. 20 Now
to our God and Father *be* the glory forever
and ever. Amen.
21 Greet every saint in Christ Jesus. The
brothers who are with me greet you. 22 All
the saints greet you, especially those of
Caesar's household.
23 The grace of the Lord Jesus Christ be
with your spirit.

OCTOBER 10

Jeremiah 5:1–6:30

5 "Roam to and fro through the
streets of Jerusalem,
And see now and know,
And seek in her open squares,
If you can find a man,
If there is one who does justice,
who seeks faithfulness,
Then I will pardon her.
2 "And if they say, 'As Yahweh lives,'
Then they swear to a lie."
3 O Yahweh, do not Your eyes
look for faithfulness?
You have struck them,
But they did not weaken;
You have consumed them,
But they refused to receive discipline.
They have made their faces
stronger than rock;
They have refused to repent.

4 Then I said, "They are only the poor;
They are foolish;
For they do not know the
way of Yahweh
Or the *legal* judgment of their God.
5 "Let me go to the great
And let me speak to them,
For they know the way of Yahweh
And the *legal* judgment of their God."
But they too, altogether,
have broken the yoke
And torn apart the bonds.
6 Therefore a lion from the forest
will strike them down;
A wolf of the deserts will
devastate them;
A leopard is watching their cities.
Everyone who goes out of them
will be torn in pieces
Because their transgressions are many;
Their acts of faithlessness are mighty.

7 "Why should I pardon you?
Your sons have forsaken Me
And sworn by those who are not gods.
I had satisfied them to the full,
Then they committed adultery
And trooped to the harlot's house.
8 "They were well-fed lusty horses,
Each one neighing after
his neighbor's wife.
9 "Shall I not punish these *people*,"
declares Yahweh,
"And on a nation such as this
Shall I not avenge Myself?

10 "Go up through her vine rows
and make them a ruin,
But do not make a complete
destruction;
Remove her branches,
For they are not Yahweh's.
11 "For the house of Israel and
the house of Judah
Have dealt very treacherously
with Me," declares Yahweh.
12 They have dealt falsely about Yahweh
And said, "Not He;
Calamity will not come on us,
And we will not see sword or famine.
13 "The prophets are *as* wind,
And the word is not in them.
Thus it will be done to them!"
14 Therefore, thus says Yahweh, the God
of hosts,
"Because you have spoken this word,
Behold, I am making My words
in your mouth fire
And this people wood, and
it will devour them.
15 "Behold, I am bringing a nation
against you from afar, O house
of Israel," declares Yahweh.
"It is an enduring nation;
It is an ancient nation,
A nation whose tongue
you do not know,
Nor can you understand what they say.
16 "Their quiver is like an open grave;
All of them are mighty men.
17 "They will devour your harvest
and your food;
They will devour your sons
and your daughters;
They will devour your flocks
and your herds;
They will devour your vines
and your fig trees;
They will demolish with the
sword your fortified cities
in which you trust.
18 "Yet even in those days," declares
Yahweh, "I will not make you a complete

destruction. [19] It shall come about when
they say, 'Why has Yahweh our God done
all these things to us?' then you shall say to
them, 'As you have forsaken Me and served
foreign gods in your land, so you will serve
strangers in a land that is not yours.'

20 "Declare this in the house of Jacob
And cause *it* to be heard
in Judah, saying,
21 'Now hear this, O people *who*
are simpleminded fools and
without a heart *of wisdom*,
Who have eyes but do not see,
Who have ears but do not hear.
22 'Do you not fear Me?' declares Yahweh.
'Do you not tremble in My presence?
For I have placed the sand
as a boundary for the sea,
A perpetual statute, so it
cannot cross over it.
Though the waves toss,
yet they cannot prevail;
Though they roar, yet they
cannot cross over it.
23 'But this people has a stubborn
and rebellious heart;
They have turned aside
and gone away.
24 'They do not say in their heart,
"Let us now fear Yahweh our God,
Who gives rain in its season,
Both the early rain and the late rain,
Who keeps for us
The appointed weeks of the harvest."
25 'Your iniquities have turned these away,
And your sins have withheld
good from you.
26 'For wicked men are found
among My people;
They watch like fowlers lying in wait;
They set a trap;
They catch men.
27 'Like a cage full of birds,
So their houses are full of deceit;
Therefore they have become
great and rich.
28 'They are fat, they are sleek;
They also excel in deeds of evil;
They do not plead the cause,
The cause of the orphan,
that they may succeed;
And they do not render
justice for the poor.
29 'Shall I not punish these *people*?'
declares Yahweh,
'On a nation such as this
Shall I not avenge Myself?'

30 "A horrible and appalling thing
Has happened in the land:
31 The prophets prophesy with lying,
And the priests have dominion
by their *own* hand;
And My people love it so!
But what will you do at the end of it?

6 "Flee for safety, O sons of Benjamin,
From the midst of Jerusalem!
Now blow a trumpet in Tekoa
And raise a signal over
Beth-haccerem,
For evil looks down from the north,
As well as great destruction.
2 "The comely and delicate one,
the daughter of Zion, I will ruin.
3 "Shepherds and their flocks
will come to her;
They will pitch *their* tents around her;
They will pasture each in his place.
4 "Set *yourselves* apart for
war against her;
Arise, and let us go up at noon.
Woe to us, for the day declines,
For the shadows of the
evening stretch out!
5 "Arise, and let us go up by night
And destroy her palaces!"
6 For thus says Yahweh of hosts,
"Cut down her trees
And cast up a siege against Jerusalem.
This is the city to be punished,
In whose midst there is
only oppression.
7 "Like a well keeps its waters fresh,
So she keeps fresh her evil.
Violence and devastation
are heard in her;
Sickness and wounds are
continually before Me.
8 "Heed discipline, O Jerusalem,
Lest My soul become disgusted at you,
Lest I make you a desolation,
A land not inhabited."

9 Thus says Yahweh of hosts,
"They will thoroughly glean as
the vine the remnant of Israel;
Pass your hand again like
a grape gatherer
Over the branches."

10 To whom shall I speak
and give warning
That they may hear?
Behold, their ears are uncircumcised,
And they cannot give heed.
Behold, the word of Yahweh has
become a reproach to them;
They have no delight in it.
11 But I am full of the wrath of Yahweh;
I am weary of holding *it* in.
"Pour *it* out on the infants in the street
And on the gathering of
choice men together;
For both husband and wife
shall be captured,
The aged with *the one* full of days.
12 "Their houses shall be turned
over to others,
Their fields and their wives together,
For I will stretch out My hand
Against the inhabitants of the
land," declares Yahweh.
13 "For from the least of them even
to the greatest of them,
Everyone is greedy for gain,
And from the prophet
even to the priest
Everyone practices lying.
14 "They have healed the brokenness
of My people superficially,
Saying, 'Peace, peace,'
But there is no peace.
15 "Were they ashamed because of the
abomination they have done?
They were not even ashamed at all;
They did not even know
how to feel dishonor.
Therefore they shall fall
among those who fall;
At the time that I punish them,
They shall be cast down,"
says Yahweh.

16 Thus says Yahweh,
"Stand by the ways and see and
ask for the ancient paths,
Where the good way is, and walk in it;
And you will find rest for your souls.
But they said, 'We will not walk *in it.*'
17 "And I set watchmen over you, *saying,*
'Give heed to the sound of the trumpet!'
But they said, 'We will not give heed.'
18 "Therefore hear, O nations,
And know, O congregation,
what is among them.
19 "Hear, O earth: behold, I am
bringing evil on this people,
The fruit of their plans,
Because they have not given
heed to My words,
And as for My law, they
have rejected it also.
20 "For what purpose does frankincense
come to Me from Sheba
And the sweet cane from
a distant land?
Your burnt offerings are
not acceptable,
And your sacrifices are not
pleasing to Me."
21 Therefore, thus says Yahweh,
"Behold, I am laying stumbling
blocks before this people.
And they will stumble against them,
Fathers and sons together;
Neighbor and friend will perish."
22 Thus says Yahweh,
"Behold, a people is coming from
the land of the north,
And a great nation will be aroused
from the remote parts of the earth.
23 "They take hold of bow and spear;
They are cruel and have
no compassion;
Their voice roars like the sea,
And they ride on horses,
Arranged as a man for the battle
Against you, O daughter of Zion!"
24 We have heard the report of it;
Our hands are limp.
Distress has taken hold of us,
Pain as of a woman in childbirth.
25 Do not go out into the field
And do not walk on the road,
For the enemy has a sword;
Terror is on every side.
26 O daughter of my people, gird
yourself with sackcloth
And roll in ashes;
Mourn as for an only son,
A lamentation most bitter.
For suddenly the destroyer
Will come upon us.

27 "I have made you a tester *of metals*
and an assayer among My people,
That you may know and test their way."
28 All of them are rebelliously stubborn,
Going about as a slanderer.
They are bronze and iron;

They, all of them, are corrupt.
29 The bellows blow fiercely;
The lead is consumed by the fire;
In vain the refining goes on,
But the evil ones are not separated.
30 They call them rejected silver
Because Yahweh has rejected them.

Psalm 117:1–2

1 Praise Yahweh, all nations;
Laud Him, all peoples!
2 For His lovingkindness
prevails over us,
And the truth of Yahweh is everlasting.
Praise Yah!

Proverbs 27:3–4

3 A stone is heavy and the sand weighty,
But the provocation of an ignorant
fool is heavier than both of them.
4 Wrath is cruelty and anger is a flood,
But who can stand before jealousy?

Colossians 1:1–29

1 Paul, an apostle of Christ Jesus by the will
of God, and Timothy our brother,
2 To the saints and faithful brothers in
Christ in Colossae: Grace to you and peace
from God our Father.
3 We give thanks to God, the Father of
our Lord Jesus Christ, praying always for
you, 4 since we heard of your faith in Christ
Jesus and the love which you have for all the
saints, 5 because of the hope laid up for you
in heaven, of which you previously heard
in the word of truth, the gospel 6 which has
come to you, just as in all the world also it
is constantly bearing fruit and multiplying,
just as *it has been doing* in you also since the
day you heard and understood the grace of
God in truth; 7 just as you learned *it* from
Epaphras, our beloved fellow slave, who is
a faithful servant of Christ on our behalf,
8 who also informed us of your love in the
Spirit.
9 For this reason also, since the day we
heard, we have not ceased to pray for you
and to ask that you may be filled with the
full knowledge of His will in all spiritual
wisdom and understanding, 10 so that you
may walk in a manner worthy of the Lord,
to please *Him* in all respects, bearing fruit in
every good work and multiplying in the full
knowledge of God; 11 being strengthened
with all power, according to His glorious
might, for the attaining of all steadfastness
and patience; joyously 12 giving thanks to
the Father, who has qualified us to share in
the inheritance of the saints in light. 13 Who
rescued us from the authority of darkness,
and transferred us to the kingdom of the Son
of His love, 14 in whom we have redemption,
the forgiveness of sins.

15 Who is the image of the invisible
God, the firstborn of all creation.
16 For in Him all things were created,
both in the heavens and on earth,
visible and invisible, whether
thrones or dominions or rulers or
authorities—all things have been
created through Him and for Him.

17 And He is before all things,
And in Him all things hold together.
18 And He is the head of the
body, the church;

Who is the beginning, the firstborn
from the dead, so that He
Himself will come to have
first place in everything.
19 For in Him all the fullness *of
God* was pleased to dwell,
20 And through Him to reconcile all
things to Himself, having made
peace through the blood of His
cross—through Him—whether
things on earth or things in heaven.

21 And although you were formerly
alienated and enemies in mind *and* in evil
deeds, 22 but now He reconciled you in the
body of His flesh through death, in order to
present you before Him holy and blameless
and beyond reproach— 23 if indeed you
continue in the faith firmly grounded and
steadfast, and not moved away from the
hope of the gospel, which you have heard,
which was proclaimed in all creation under
heaven, and of which I, Paul, was made a
minister.
24 Now I rejoice in my sufferings for your
sake, and I fill up what is lacking of Christ's
afflictions in my flesh, on behalf of His body,
which is the church, 25 of which I was made
a minister according to the stewardship
from God given to me for you, so that I
might fully carry out *the preaching of* the
word of God, 26 *that is,* the mystery which
has been hidden from the *past* ages and
generations, but has now been manifested

to His saints, 27 to whom God willed to
make known what is the riches of the glory
of this mystery among the Gentiles, which
is Christ in you, the hope of glory. 28 Him
we proclaim, admonishing every man and
teaching every man with all wisdom, so
that we may present every man complete
in Christ. 29 For this purpose I also labor,
striving according to His working, which
He works in me in power.

OCTOBER 11

Jeremiah 7:1–8:22

7 The word that came to Jeremiah from
Yahweh, saying, 2 "Stand in the gate of
the house of Yahweh, and you shall call out
there this word, and you shall say, 'Hear the
word of Yahweh, all you of Judah, who enter
by these gates to worship Yahweh!'" 3 Thus
says Yahweh of hosts, the God of Israel,
"Make your ways and your deeds good, and I
will let you dwell in this place. 4 Do not trust
in lying words, saying, 'This is the temple of
Yahweh, the temple of Yahweh, the temple
of Yahweh.' 5 For if you truly make your ways
and your deeds good, if you truly do justice
between a man and his neighbor, 6 *if* you do
not oppress the sojourner, the orphan, or
the widow, and do not shed innocent blood
in this place, nor walk after other gods to
your own evil *demise*, 7 then I will let you
dwell in this place, in the land that I gave to
your fathers forever and ever.

8 "Behold, you are trusting in lying words
to no avail. 9 Will you steal, murder, and
commit adultery and swear *while* lying,
and burn incense to Baal and walk after
other gods that you have not known, 10 then
come and stand before Me in this house,
which is called by My name, and say, 'We
are delivered!'—that you may do all these
abominations? 11 Has this house, which is
called by My name, become a robbers' den
in your sight? Behold, I, even I, have seen
it," declares Yahweh.

12 "But go now to My place which was
in Shiloh, where I made My name dwell at
the first, and see what I did to it because
of the evil of My people Israel. 13 And now,
because you have done all these works,"
declares Yahweh, "and I spoke to you,
rising up early and speaking, but you did
not hear, and I called you but you did not
answer, 14 therefore, I will do to the house
which is called by My name, in which you
trust, and to the place which I gave you
and your fathers, as I did to Shiloh. 15 I
will cast you out of My presence, as I have
cast out all your brothers, all the seed of
Ephraim.

16 "As for you, do not pray for this people
and do not lift up a cry of lamentation or
prayer for them and do not intercede with
Me, for I am not hearing you. 17 Are you not
seeing what they are doing in the cities of
Judah and in the streets of Jerusalem? 18 The
children gather wood, and the fathers make
the fire burn, and the women knead dough
to make cakes for the queen of heaven; and
they pour out drink offerings to other gods
in order to provoke Me. 19 Do they provoke
Me?" declares Yahweh. "Is it not themselves
they provoke to the shame of their own
face?" 20 Therefore thus says Lord Yahweh,
"Behold, My anger and My wrath will be
poured out on this place, on man and on
beast and on the trees of the field and on
the fruit of the ground; and it will burn and
not be quenched."

21 Thus says Yahweh of hosts, the God
of Israel, "Add your burnt offerings to your
sacrifices and eat flesh. 22 For I did not
speak to your fathers or command them in
the day that I brought them out of the land
of Egypt concerning burnt offerings and
sacrifices. 23 But this is what I commanded
them, saying, 'Listen to My voice, and I will
be your God, and you will be My people;
and you will walk in the entire way which I
command you, that it may be well with you.'
24 Yet they did not listen or incline their ear,
but walked in *their own* counsels *and* in the
stubbornness of their evil heart and went
backward and not forward. 25 Since the day
that your fathers came out of the land of
Egypt until this day, I have sent you all My
slaves the prophets, daily rising up early and
sending *them*. 26 Yet they did not listen to
Me or incline their ear, but stiffened their
neck; they did more evil than their fathers.

27 "You shall speak all these words to
them, but they will not listen to you; and
you shall call to them, but they will not
answer you. 28 You shall say to them, 'This

is the nation that did not listen to the voice
of Yahweh their God or receive discipline;
truth has perished and has been cut off from
their mouth.
29 'Cut off your hair and cast *it* away,
And lift up a *funeral* lamentation
on the bare heights;
For Yahweh has rejected
and abandoned
The generation of His wrath.'
30 "For the sons of Judah have done that
which is evil in My sight," declares Yahweh,
"they have set their detestable things in
the house, which is called by My name, to
defile it. 31 They have built the high places of
Topheth, which is in the valley of the son of
Hinnom, to burn their sons and their daugh-
ters in the fire, which I did not command,
and it did not come upon My heart.
32 "Therefore, behold, days are coming,"
declares Yahweh, "when it will no longer be
called Topheth or the valley of the son of
Hinnom, but the valley of the Slaughter; for
they will bury in Topheth because there is
no *other* place. 33 The dead bodies of this
people will be food for the birds of the sky
and for the beasts of the earth; and no one
will frighten *them away*. 34 Then I will make
to cease from the cities of Judah and from
the streets of Jerusalem the voice of joy
and the voice of gladness, the voice of the
bridegroom and the voice of the bride, for
the land will become a waste place.

8 "At that time," declares Yahweh, "they
will bring out the bones of the kings of
Judah and the bones of its princes, and the
bones of the priests and the bones of the
prophets, and the bones of the inhabitants
of Jerusalem from their graves. 2 And they
will spread them out to the sun, the moon,
and to all the host of heaven, which they
have loved and which they have served, and
which they have walked after and which
they have sought, and which they have
worshiped. They will not be gathered or bur-
ied; they will be as dung on the face of the
ground. 3 And death will be chosen rather
than life by all the remnant that remains of
this evil family, that remains in all the places
to which I have banished them," declares
Yahweh of hosts. 4 "You shall say to them,
'Thus says Yahweh,
"Do *men* fall and not get up again?
Does one turn away and not turn back?
5 "Why then has this people, Jerusalem,
Turned away in continual
faithlessness?
They hold fast to deceit;
They refuse to return.
6 "I have given heed and heard,
They have spoken what is not right;
No man regretted his evil,
Saying, 'What have I done?'
Everyone turned to his course,
Like a horse charging into the battle.
7 "Even the stork in the sky
Knows her seasons;
And the turtledove and the
swift and the crane
Keep the time of their migration;
But My people do not know
The *legal* judgment of Yahweh.
8 "How can you say, 'We are wise,
And the law of Yahweh is with us'?
But behold, the lying pen of the scribes
Has made *it* into a lie.
9 "The wise men are put to shame;
They are dismayed and captured;
Behold, they have rejected
the word of Yahweh,
And what kind of wisdom
do they have?
10 "Therefore I will give their
wives to others,
Their fields to new possessors,
Because from the least
even to the greatest
Everyone is greedy for gain;
From the prophet even to the priest
Everyone practices lying.
11 "They heal the brokenness of the
daughter of My people superficially,
Saying, 'Peace, peace,'
But there is no peace.
12 "Were they ashamed because of the
abomination they had done?
They certainly were not ashamed,
And they did not know how
to feel dishonor;
Therefore they shall fall
among those who fall;
At the time of their punishment
they shall be brought down,"
Says Yahweh.
13 "I will surely gather them up,"
declares Yahweh;
"There will be no grapes on the vine

And no figs on the fig tree,
And the leaf will wither;
And what I have given them
will pass away.'"'
14 Why are we sitting still?
Gather yourselves, and let us
go into the fortified cities
And let us be silent there
Because Yahweh our God
has silenced us
And given us poisoned water to drink,
For we have sinned against Yahweh.
15 *We* waited for peace, but
there was no good;
For a time of healing, but
behold, terror!
16 From Dan is heard the
snorting of his horses;
At the sound of the neighing
of his valiant steeds
The whole land quakes;
And they come and devour the
land as well as its fullness,
The city and its inhabitants.
17 "For behold, I am sending
serpents against you,
Vipers, for which there is no charm,
And they will bite you,"
declares Yahweh.
18 My sorrow is beyond healing;
My heart is faint within me!
19 Behold, *the* sound! The cry of
the daughter of my people
from a distant land:
"Is Yahweh not in Zion? Is her
King not within her?"
"Why have they provoked Me
to anger with their graven
images, with foreign idols?"
20 "Harvest is past, summer is ended,
And we are not saved."
21 For the brokenness of the daughter
of my people I am broken;
I mourn, desolation has
taken hold of me.
22 Is there no balm in Gilead?
Is there no physician there?
Why then has not the health of the
daughter of my people gone up?

Psalm 118:1–4

1 Give thanks to Yahweh,
for He is good;
For His lovingkindness
endures forever.
2 Oh let Israel say,
"His lovingkindness endures forever."
3 Oh let the house of Aaron say,
"His lovingkindness endures forever."
4 Oh let those who fear Yahweh say,
"His lovingkindness endures forever."

Proverbs 27:5–6

5 Better is reproof that is revealed
Than love that is hidden.
6 Faithful are the wounds of a friend,
But deceitful are the kisses
of an enemy.

Colossians 2:1–23

2 For I want you to understand how great
a struggle I have on your behalf and for
those who are at Laodicea, and for all those
who have not seen my face in the flesh, 2 so
that their hearts may be encouraged, having
been held together in love, even unto all
the wealth of the full assurance of under-
standing, unto the full knowledge of God's
mystery, *that is,* Christ *Himself,* 3 in whom
are hidden all the treasures of wisdom and
knowledge. 4 I say this so that no one will
delude you with persuasive argument. 5 For
even though I am absent in body, neverthe-
less I am with you in spirit, rejoicing to see
your good order and the stability of your
faith in Christ.
6 Therefore as you received Christ Jesus
the Lord, *so* walk in Him, 7 having been
firmly rooted and being built up in Him, and
having been established in your faith—just
as you were instructed—*and* abounding
with thanksgiving.
8 See to it that no one takes you captive
through philosophy and empty deception,
according to the tradition of men, according
to the elementary principles of the world,
and not according to Christ. 9 For in Him all
the fullness of Deity dwells bodily, 10 and in
Him you have been filled, who is the head
over all rule and authority; 11 in whom you
were also circumcised with a circumcision
made without hands, in the removal of the
body of the flesh, in the circumcision of
Christ, 12 having been buried with Him in
baptism, in which you were also raised up
with Him through faith in the working of
God, who raised Him from the dead. 13 And
you being dead in your transgressions and
the uncircumcision of your flesh, He made
you alive with Him, having graciously

forgiven us all our transgressions. 14 Having canceled out the certificate of debt consisting of decrees against us which was hostile to us, He also has taken it out of the way, having nailed it to the cross. 15 Having disarmed the rulers and authorities, He made a public display of them, having triumphed over them in Him.

16 Therefore, no one is to judge you in food and drink, or in respect to a festival or a new moon or a Sabbath day— 17 things which are *only* a shadow of what is to come; but the substance belongs to Christ. 18 Let no one keep defrauding you of your prize by delighting in self-abasement and the worship of the angels, going into detail about *visions* he has seen, being puffed up for nothing by his fleshly mind, 19 and not holding fast to the head, from whom the entire body, being supplied and held together by the joints and ligaments, grows with a growth that is from God.

20 If you have died with Christ to the elementary principles of the world, why, as if you were living in the world, do you submit yourself to decrees: 21 "Do not handle, nor taste, nor touch"? 22 Which deal with everything destined to perish with use, *which are* in accordance with the commands and teachings of men; 23 which are matters having, to be sure, a word of wisdom in self-made religion and self-abasement and severe treatment of the body, *but are* of no value against fleshly indulgence.

OCTOBER 12

Jeremiah 9:1–10:25

9 Oh that my head were waters
And my eyes a fountain of tears,
That I might weep day and night
For the slain of the daughter
of my people!
2 Oh that I had in the desert
A travelers' lodging place,
That I might leave my people
And go from them!
For all of them are adulterers,
A solemn assembly of
treacherous men.
3 "They bend their tongue
like their bow;
Lies and unfaithfulness
prevail in the land,
For they go onward from evil to evil,
And they do not know Me,"
declares Yahweh.
4 "Let everyone beware of his neighbor,
And do not trust any brother,
Because every brother
surely supplants,
And every neighbor goes
about as a slanderer.
5 "Everyone deceives his neighbor
And does not speak the truth;
They have taught their
tongue to speak lies;
They weary themselves
committing iniquity.
6 "Your habitation is in the
midst of deceit;
Through deceit they refuse to
know Me," declares Yahweh.

7 Therefore thus says Yahweh of hosts,
"Behold, I will refine them
and test them;
For what *else* can I do, because of
the daughter of My people?
8 "Their tongue is a slaughtering arrow;
It speaks deceit;
With his mouth one speaks
peace to his neighbor,
But inwardly he sets an
ambush for him.
9 "Shall I not punish them for these
things?" declares Yahweh.
"On a nation such as this
Shall I not avenge Myself?

10 "For the mountains I will take
up a weeping and wailing,
And for the pastures of the wilderness
a *funeral* lamentation,
Because they are turned into ruin
so that no one passes through,
And the lowing of the
cattle is not heard;
Both the birds of the sky and the
beasts have fled; they are gone.
11 "I will make Jerusalem a heap
of ruins,
A haunt of jackals;
And I will make the cities of Judah a
desolation, without inhabitant."

12 Who is the wise man that may under-
stand this? And *who is* he to whom the mouth
of Yahweh has spoken, that he may declare it?
Why has the land perished, turned into ruin
like a desert, so that no one passes through?
13 Yahweh said, "Because they have forsaken
My law, which I set before them, and have not
listened to My voice nor walked according to
it, 14 but have walked after the stubbornness
of their heart and after the Baals, as their
fathers taught them," 15 therefore thus says
Yahweh of hosts, the God of Israel, "behold, I
will feed them, this people, with wormwood
and give them poisoned water to drink. 16 I
will scatter them among the nations, whom
neither they nor their fathers have known;
and I will send the sword after them until I
have consumed them."

17 Thus says Yahweh of hosts,
"Carefully consider and call
for the mourning women,
that they may come;
And send for the skillful women,
that they may come!
18 "Let them make haste and take
up a wailing for us,
That our eyes may shed tears
And our eyelids flow with water.
19 "For a voice of wailing is
heard from Zion,
'How we are destroyed!
We are put to great shame,
For we have left the land
Because they have cast down
our dwellings.'"
20 Indeed, hear the word of
Yahweh, O you women,
And let your ear receive the
word of His mouth;
Teach your daughters wailing,
And everyone her neighbor
a *funeral* lamentation.
21 For death has come up
through our windows;
It has entered our palaces
To cut off the infants from the streets,
The choice men from the
open squares.
22 Speak, "Thus declares Yahweh,
'The corpses of men will fall like
dung on the open field
And like the sheaf after the reaper,
But no one will gather *them*.'"

23 Thus says Yahweh, "Let not a wise
man boast in his wisdom, and let not the
mighty man boast in his might; let not a rich
man boast in his riches, 24 but let him who
boasts boast in this, that he understands
and knows Me, that I am Yahweh who shows
lovingkindness, justice, and righteousness
on earth; for I delight in these things,"
declares Yahweh.

25 "Behold, the days are coming," declares
Yahweh, "that I will punish all who are cir-
cumcised and yet uncircumcised— 26 Egypt
and Judah, and Edom and the sons of
Ammon, and Moab and all those inhabiting
the desert who clip the hair on their tem-
ples; for all the nations are uncircumcised,
and all the house of Israel are uncircumcised
of heart."

10 Hear the word which Yahweh speaks
to you, O house of Israel. 2 Thus says
Yahweh,

"Do not learn the way of the nations,
And do not be terrified by the
signs of the heavens
Although the nations are
terrified by them;
3 For the statutes of the
peoples are vanity
Because it is wood cut from
the forest,
The work of the hands of a
craftsman with a cutting tool.
4 "They make *it* beautiful with
silver and with gold;
They strengthen it with nails
and with hammers
So that it will not totter.
5 "Like a scarecrow in a cucumber
field are they,
And they cannot speak;
They must be carried
Because they cannot take a step!
Do not fear them,
For they can do no harm,
Nor can they do any good."

6 There is none like You, O Yahweh;
You are great, and great is
Your name in might.
7 Who would not fear You,
O King of the nations?
Indeed it is Your due!
For among all the wise
men of the nations
And in all their kingdoms,
There is none like You.

8 But they are altogether
senseless and foolish;
They are in a discipline of
vanities—it is *mere* wood!
9 Beaten silver is brought from Tarshish,
And gold from Uphaz,
The work of a craftsman and of
the hands of a goldsmith;
Blue and purple are their clothing;
They are all the work of
wise *craftsmen.*
10 But Yahweh is the true God;
He is the living God and the
everlasting King.
At His wrath the earth quakes,
And the nations cannot
endure His indignation.

11 Thus you shall say to them, "The gods
that did not make the heavens and the earth
will perish from the earth and from under
the heavens."

12 *It is* He who made the
earth by His power,
Who established the world
by His wisdom;
And by His understanding He has
stretched out the heavens.
13 When He gives forth His voice, *there is*
a tumult of waters in the heavens,
And He causes the clouds to ascend
from the end of the earth;
He makes lightning for the rain,
And brings out the wind
from His storehouses.
14 Every man is senseless,
devoid of knowledge;
Every goldsmith is put to shame
by his graven images;
For his molten images are a lie,
And there is no breath in them.
15 They are vanity, a work of mockery;
In the time of their punishment
they will perish.
16 The portion of Jacob is not like these;
For the Maker of all is He,
And Israel is the tribe of
His inheritance;
Yahweh of hosts is His name.

17 Gather up your bundle
from the ground,
You who inhabit *a land* under siege!
18 For thus says Yahweh,
"Behold, I am slinging out the
inhabitants of the land
At this time,
And will cause them distress,
That they may find *it.*"
19 Woe is me, because of my injury!
My wound is desperately sick.
But I said, "Truly this is a sickness,
And I must bear it."
20 My tent is destroyed,
And all my ropes are torn out;
My sons have gone from me
and are no more.
There is no one to stretch
out my tent again
Or to set up my curtains.
21 For the shepherds have
become senseless
And have not sought Yahweh;
Therefore they have not prospered,
And all their flock is scattered.
22 The sound of a report!
Behold, it comes—
A great quaking out of the
land of the north—
To make the cities of Judah
A desolation, a haunt of jackals.

23 I know, O Yahweh, that a man's
way is not in himself,
Nor is it in a man who walks
to direct his steps.
24 Discipline me, O Yahweh,
but with justice;
Not with Your anger, lest You
bring me to nothing.
25 Pour out Your wrath on the
nations that do not know You
And on the families that do
not call Your name,
For they have devoured Jacob;
They have devoured him
and consumed him
And have made desolate his abode.

Psalm 118:5–9

5 From *my* distress I called upon Yah;
Yah answered me *and set*
me in a large place.
6 Yahweh is for me; I will not fear;
What can man do to me?
7 Yahweh is for me among
those who help me;
Therefore I will look *in triumph*
on those who hate me.
8 It is better to take refuge in Yahweh

Than to trust in man.
9 It is better to take refuge in Yahweh
Than to trust in nobles.

Proverbs 27:7

7 A satisfied soul tramples
the honeycomb,
But to a hungry soul any
bitter thing is sweet.

Colossians 3:1–25

3 Therefore, if you have been raised up
with Christ, keep seeking the things
above, where Christ is, seated at the right
hand of God. 2 Set your mind on the things
above, not on the things that are on earth.
3 For you died and your life has been hidden
with Christ in God. 4 When Christ, who is
our life, is manifested, then you also will be
manifested with Him in glory.
5 Therefore, consider the members of
your earthly body as dead to sexual immo-
rality, impurity, passion, evil desire, and
greed, which is idolatry. 6 On account of
these things, the wrath of God is coming
upon the sons of disobedience, 7 and in
them you also once walked, when you
were living in them. 8 But now you also,
lay them all aside: wrath, anger, malice,
slander, *and* abusive speech from your
mouth. 9 Do not lie to one another, since
you put off the old man with its *evil*
practices, 10 and have put on the new man
who is being renewed to a full knowledge
according to the image of the One who
created him— 11 *a renewal* in which
there is no *distinction between* Greek and
Jew, circumcised and uncircumcised,
barbarian, Scythian, slave, *and* freeman,
but Christ is all and in all.
12 So, as the elect of God, holy and beloved,
put on a heart of compassion, kindness,
humility, gentleness, *and* patience; 13 bearing
with one another, and graciously forgiving
each other, whoever has a complaint against
anyone, just as the Lord graciously forgave
you, so also should you. 14 Above all these
things *put on* love, which is the perfect bond
of unity. 15 And let the peace of Christ rule in
your hearts, to which indeed you were called
in one body, and be thankful. 16 Let the word
of Christ dwell in you richly, with all wisdom
teaching and admonishing one another with
psalms *and* hymns *and* spiritual songs,
singing with gratefulness in your hearts to
God. 17 And whatever you do in word or deed,
do all in the name of the Lord Jesus, giving
thanks to God the Father through Him.
18 Wives, be subject to your husbands,
as is fitting in the Lord. 19 Husbands, love
your wives and do not be embittered against
them. 20 Children, obey your parents in
all things, for this is pleasing to the Lord.
21 Fathers, do not exasperate your children,
so that they will not lose heart.
22 Slaves, in all things obey those who are
your masters according to the flesh, not with
eyeservice, as men-pleasers, but with integ-
rity of heart, fearing the Lord. 23 Whatever
you do, do your work heartily, as for the
Lord rather than for men, 24 knowing that
from the Lord you will receive the reward
of the inheritance. Serve the Lord Christ.
25 For he who does wrong will receive the
consequences of the wrong which he has
done, and that without partiality.

OCTOBER 13

Jeremiah 11:1–12:17

11 The word which came to Jeremiah from
Yahweh, saying, 2 "Hear the words of
this covenant, and you shall speak to the
men of Judah and to the inhabitants of
Jerusalem 3 and say to them, 'Thus says
Yahweh, the God of Israel, "Cursed is the
man who does not hear the words of this
covenant 4 which I commanded your fathers
in the day that I brought them out of the
land of Egypt, from the iron furnace, saying,
'Listen to My voice, and do according to all
which I command you; so you shall be My
people, and I will be your God,' 5 in order
to establish the oath which I swore to your
fathers, to give them a land flowing with
milk and honey, as *it is* this day."'" Then I
answered and said, "Amen, O Yahweh."
6 And Yahweh said to me, "Call out all
these words in the cities of Judah and in the
streets of Jerusalem, saying, 'Hear the words
of this covenant so that you will do them.
7 For I solemnly warned your fathers in the
day that I brought them up from the land
of Egypt, even to this day, rising up early
and warning, saying, "Listen to My voice."

8 Yet they did not listen or incline their ear,
but walked, each one, in the stubbornness
of his evil heart; therefore I brought on
them all the words of this covenant, which
I commanded *them* to do, but they did not.'"
9 Then Yahweh said to me, "A conspiracy
has been found among the men of Judah
and among the inhabitants of Jerusalem.
10 They have turned back to the iniquities
of their ancestors who refused to hear My
words, and they have walked after other
gods to serve them; the house of Israel
and the house of Judah have broken My
covenant which I cut with their fathers."
11 Therefore thus says Yahweh, "Behold, I
am bringing calamity on them which they
will not be able to get out of; and they will
cry to Me, yet I will not listen to them.
12 Then the cities of Judah and the inhab-
itants of Jerusalem will go and cry to the
gods to whom they burn incense, but they
surely will not save them in the time of their
calamity. 13 For your gods are the number
of your cities, O Judah; and the number of
the streets of Jerusalem are the altars you
have set up to the shameful thing, altars to
burn incense to Baal.

14 "But as for you, do not pray for this
people, nor lift up a cry of lamentation or
prayer for them; for I will not listen when
they call to Me because of their calamity.

15 "What *possession* has My
beloved in My house
When she has done many
schemes of wickedness?
Can the flesh, *which is* set
apart as holy, take away
from you your calamity,
So *that* you can exult?"

16 Yahweh called your name,
"A green olive tree, beautiful
in fruit and form";
With the noise of a great tumult
He has kindled fire on it,
And its foliage has an evil *demise*.

17 Yahweh of hosts, who planted you, has
spoken forth evil against you because of the
evil of the house of Israel and of the house of
Judah, which they have done to provoke Me
to anger by burning incense to Baal.

18 Moreover, Yahweh made it
known to me, and I knew it;
Then You showed me their deeds.
19 But I was like a gentle lamb
led to the slaughter;
And I did not know that they had
devised thoughts against me, *saying*,
"Let us make the tree with
its fruit a ruin,
And let us cut him off from
the land of the living,
That his name be remembered
no more."
20 But, O Yahweh of hosts, who
judges righteously,
Who tests the insides and the heart,
Let me see Your vengeance on them,
For to You have I revealed my case.

21 Therefore thus says Yahweh concerning
the men of Anathoth, who seek your life,
saying, "Do not prophesy in the name of
Yahweh, so that you will not die at our
hand"; 22 therefore thus says Yahweh of
hosts, "Behold, I am about to punish them!
The choice men will die by the sword; their
sons and daughters will die by famine;
23 and a remnant will not be left to them,
for I will bring calamity on the men of
Anathoth—the year of their punishment."

12 Righteous are You, O Yahweh, when
I would plead *my* case with You;
Indeed I would speak matters
of justice with You:
Why has the way of the
wicked succeeded?
Why are all those who deal in
treachery complacent?
2 You have planted them; they
have also taken root;
They grow; they have even
produced fruit.
You are near to their lips
But far from their inmost being.
3 But You, O Yahweh, You know me;
You see me;
And You test my heart's
attitude toward You.
Drag them off like sheep
for the slaughter
And set them apart for a
day of carnage!
4 How long is the land to mourn
And the plants of every field to dry up?
Because of the evil of those
who inhabit it,
Animals and birds have
been swept away,
Because *men* have said, "He will
not see our latter ending."

5 “If you have run with footmen
and they have tired you out,
Then how can you compete
with horses?
If you fall down in a land of peace,
How will you do in the
thicket of the Jordan?
6 “For even your brothers and the
household of your father,
Even they have dealt
treacherously with you,
Even they have called aloud
after you.
Do not believe them, although they
may say nice things to you.”

7 “I have forsaken My house;
I have abandoned My inheritance;
I have given the beloved of My soul
Into the hand of her enemies.
8 “My inheritance has become to Me
Like a lion in the forest;
She has given forth its
voice against Me;
Therefore I have come to hate her.
9 “Is My inheritance like a speckled
bird of prey to Me?
Are the birds of prey against
her on every side?
Go, gather all the beasts of the field,
Bring them to devour!
10 “Many shepherds have
ruined My vineyard;
They have trampled down My portion;
They have made My desired portion
A desolate wilderness.
11 “It has been made a desolation;
Desolate, it mourns before Me;
The whole land has been
made desolate
Because no man sets it upon his heart.
12 “On all the bare heights in
the wilderness
Destroyers have come,
For a sword of Yahweh is devouring
From one end of the land
even to the other;
There is no peace for any flesh.
13 “They have sown wheat and
have reaped thorns;
They have strained themselves
to no profit.
But be ashamed of your produce
Because of the burning
anger of Yahweh.”

14 Thus says Yahweh concerning all My
evil neighbors who beat at the inheritance
with which I have caused My people Israel to
inherit, “Behold, I am about to uproot them
from their land and will uproot the house
of Judah from among them. 15 And it will
come about that after I have uprooted them,
I will return and have compassion on them;
and I will cause them to return, each one
to his inheritance and each one to his land.
16 Then if they will really learn the ways of
My people, to swear by My name, ‘As Yahweh
lives,’ even as they taught My people to
swear by Baal, they will be built up in the
midst of My people. 17 But if they will not
listen, then I will uproot that nation, uproot
and make it perish,” declares Yahweh.

Psalm 118:10–14

10 All nations surrounded me;
In the name of Yahweh I will
surely cut them off.
11 They surrounded me, indeed,
they surrounded me;
In the name of Yahweh I will
surely cut them off.
12 They surrounded me like bees;
They were extinguished
as a fire of thorns;
In the name of Yahweh I will
surely cut them off.
13 You pushed me down violently
to *make* me fall,
But Yahweh helped me.
14 Yah is my strength and song,
And He has become my salvation.

Proverbs 27:8

8 Like a bird that wanders from her nest,
So is a man who wanders
from his place.

Colossians 4:1–18

4 Masters, show to your slaves what is
right and fair, knowing that you too
have a Master in heaven.
2 Devote yourselves to prayer, being
watchful in it with thanksgiving; 3 praying
at the same time for us as well, that God will
open up to us a door for the word, so that we
may speak the mystery of Christ, for which
I have also been bound, 4 that I may make it
manifest in the way I ought to speak.
5 Walk in wisdom toward outsiders,
redeeming the time. 6 Let your words always

be with grace, seasoned with salt, so that you will know how you should answer each person.

7 Tychicus, *our* beloved brother and faithful servant and fellow slave in the Lord, will make known to you all my affairs, 8 whom I have sent to you for this very purpose, that you may know about our circumstances and that he may encourage your hearts; 9 and with him Onesimus, *our* faithful and beloved brother, who is one of you. They will inform you about the whole situation here.

10 Aristarchus, my fellow prisoner, sends you his greetings; and *also* Mark, the cousin of Barnabas (about whom you received instructions; if he comes to you, welcome him); 11 and *also* Jesus who is called Justus. These are the only fellow workers for the kingdom of God who are from the circumcision, and they have proved to be a comfort to me. 12 Epaphras, who is one of your number, a slave of Christ Jesus, sends you his greetings, always striving for you in his prayers, that you may stand complete and fully assured in all the will of God. 13 For I testify for him that he has a deep concern for you and for those who are in Laodicea and Hierapolis. 14 Luke, the beloved physician, sends you his greetings, and *also* Demas. 15 Greet the brothers who are in Laodicea and also Nympha and the church that is in her house. 16 And when this letter is read among you, have it also read in the church of the Laodiceans; and you, for your part read my letter *that is coming* from Laodicea. 17 And say to Archippus, "Take heed to the ministry which you have received in the Lord, that you may fulfill it."

18 The greeting is in my own hand—Paul. Remember my chains. Grace be with you.

OCTOBER 14

Jeremiah 13:1–14:22

13 Thus Yahweh said to me, "Go and buy yourself a linen belt and put it around your loins, but do not put it in water." 2 So I bought the belt in accordance with the word of Yahweh and put it around my loins. 3 Then the word of Yahweh came to me a second time, saying, 4 "Take the belt that you have bought, which is around your loins, and arise, go to the Euphrates and hide it there in a crevice of the rock." 5 So I went and hid it by the Euphrates, as Yahweh had commanded me. 6 Now it happened that after many days Yahweh said to me, "Arise, go to the Euphrates and take from there the belt which I commanded you to hide there." 7 Then I went to the Euphrates and dug, and I took the belt from the place where I had hidden it; and behold, the belt was ruined; it was totally worthless.

8 Then the word of Yahweh came to me, saying, 9 "Thus says Yahweh, 'Just so will I ruin the pride of Judah and the great pride of Jerusalem. 10 This evil people, who refuse to listen to My words, who walk in the stubbornness of their hearts and have walked after other gods to serve them and to worship them, let them be just like this belt which is totally worthless. 11 For as the belt clings to the loins of a man, so I made the whole household of Israel and the whole household of Judah cling to Me,' declares Yahweh, 'that they might be for Me a people, for a name, for praise, and for beauty; but they did not listen.'

12 "Therefore you are to say this word to them, 'Thus says Yahweh, the God of Israel, "Every jug is to be filled with wine."' And they will say to you, 'Do we not very well know that every jug is to be filled with wine?' 13 Then you shall say to them, 'Thus says Yahweh, "Behold, I am about to fill all the inhabitants of this land—the kings that sit for David on his throne, the priests, the prophets, and all the inhabitants of Jerusalem—with drunkenness! 14 I will shatter them against each other, both the fathers and the sons together," declares Yahweh. "I will not spare nor show pity nor have compassion so as not to ruin them."'"

15 Listen and give ear, do not be haughty,
For Yahweh has spoken.
16 Give glory to Yahweh your God,
Before He brings darkness
And before your feet stumble
On the dusky mountains;
And while you are hoping for light,
He makes it into the shadow of death
And turns *it* into dense gloom.
17 But if you will not listen to it,
My soul will cry in secret
for *such* pride;

And my eyes will bitterly weep
And flow down with tears
Because the flock of Yahweh
has been taken captive.
18 Say to the king and the
queen mother,
"Take a lowly seat,
For your beautiful crown
Has come down from your head."
19 The cities of the Negev have
been closed up,
And there is no one to open *them*;
All Judah has been taken
away into exile,
Wholly taken away into exile.

20 "Lift up your eyes and see
Those coming from the north.
Where is the flock that was given you,
Your beautiful sheep?
21 "What will you say when He
appoints over you—
And you yourself had taught them—
Former companions to be
head over you?
Will not pangs seize you
Like a woman in childbirth?
22 "If you say in your heart,
'Why have these things
happened to me?'
Because of the magnitude
of your iniquity
Your skirts have been uncovered
And your heels have suffered violence.
23 "Can the Ethiopian change his skin
Or the leopard his spots?
Then you also can do good
Who are accustomed to doing evil.
24 "Therefore I will scatter them
like chaff passing away
Into the wilderness wind.
25 "This is your lot, the portion
measured to you
From Me," declares Yahweh,
"Because you have forgotten Me
And trusted in lies.
26 "So I Myself have also stripped
your skirts off over your face,
That your disgrace may be seen.
27 "As for your adulteries and
your *lustful* neighings,
The lewdness of your prostitution
On the hills in the field,
I have seen your detestable things.
Woe to you, O Jerusalem!
How long will you not
cleanse yourself?"

14 That which came as the word of
Yahweh to Jeremiah in regard to the
drought:
2 "Judah mourns,
And her gates languish;
They sit on the ground in mourning,
And the outcry of Jerusalem
has gone up.
3 "Their mighty ones have sent
their underlings for water;
They have come to the trenches
and found no water.
They have returned with
their vessels empty;
They have been put to shame
and dishonored,
And they cover their heads.
4 "Because the ground is dismayed,
For there has been no rain on the land,
The farmers have been put to shame;
They have covered their heads.
5 "For even the doe in the field has given
birth only to forsake *her young*
Because there is no grass.
6 "The wild donkeys stand on
the bare heights;
They pant for air like jackals;
Their eyes fail
For there is no vegetation.
7 "Although our iniquities
answer against us,
O Yahweh, act for Your name's sake!
Truly our acts of faithlessness
have been many;
We have sinned against You.
8 "O Hope of Israel,
Its Savior in time of distress,
Why are You like a sojourner
in the land
Or like a traveler who has pitched
his *tent* to lodge for the night?
9 "Why are You like a man confused,
Like a mighty man who cannot save?
Yet You are in our midst, O Yahweh,
And we are called by Your name;
Do not leave us!"
10 Thus says Yahweh to this people, "Even
so they have loved to wander; they have not
kept their feet in check. Therefore Yahweh
does not accept them; now He will remem-
ber their iniquity and punish their sins."
11 So Yahweh said to me, "Do not pray for

the good of this people. 12 When they fast, I
am not going to listen to their cry; and when
they offer burnt offering and grain offering,
I am not going to accept them. Rather I am
going to make an end of them by the sword,
famine, and pestilence."
13 But, "Ah, Lord Yahweh!" I said, "Behold,
the prophets are saying to them, 'You will
not see the sword nor will you have famine,
but I will give you true peace in this place.'"
14 Then Yahweh said to me, "The prophets are
prophesying lies in My name. I have neither
sent them nor commanded them nor spoken
to them; they are prophesying to you a vision
of lies, divination, futility, and the deception
of their own hearts. 15 Therefore thus says
Yahweh concerning the prophets who are
prophesying in My name, although it was not I
who sent them—yet they keep saying, 'There
will be no sword or famine in this land'—by
that sword and famine those prophets shall
meet their end! 16 The people also to whom
they are prophesying will be thrown out into
the streets of Jerusalem because of the famine
and the sword; and there will be no one to
bury them—*neither* them, *nor* their wives,
nor their sons, nor their daughters—for I will
pour out their *own* evil on them.

17 "And you will say this word to them,
'Let my eyes flow down with
tears night and day,
And let them not cease,
For the virgin daughter of my
people has been shattered
with a mighty shattering,
With a sorely sick wound.
18 'If I go out to the field,
Behold, those slain with the sword!
Or if I enter the city,
Behold, diseases of famine!
For both prophet and priest
Have gone around as merchants in
the land that they do not know.'"

19 Have You completely rejected Judah?
Or have You loathed Zion?
Why have You stricken us so that
there is no healing for us?
We hoped for peace, but
there was no good;
And for a time of healing,
but behold, terror!
20 We know our wickedness, O Yahweh,
The iniquity of our fathers, for
we have sinned against You.
21 Do not despise *us*, for Your
own name's sake;
Do not disgrace the throne
of Your glory;
Remember *and* do not break
Your covenant with us.
22 Are there any among the idols of
the nations who give rain?
Or can the heavens give showers?
Is it not You, O Yahweh our God?
Therefore we hope in You,
For You are the one who has
done all these things.

Psalm 118:15–20

15 The sound of joyful shouting
and salvation is in the
tents of the righteous;
The right hand of Yahweh
does valiantly.
16 The right hand of Yahweh is exalted;
The right hand of Yahweh
does valiantly.
17 I will not die; indeed I will live,
And recount the works of Yah.
18 Yah has disciplined me severely,
But He has not given me over to death.

19 Open to me the gates of righteousness;
I shall enter through them,
I shall give thanks to Yah.
20 This is the gate of Yahweh;
The righteous will enter through it.

Proverbs 27:9

9 Oil and incense make the heart glad,
So counsel from the soul is
sweet to his friend.

1 Thessalonians 1:1–10

1 Paul and Silvanus and Timothy,
To the church of the Thessalonians in
God the Father and the Lord Jesus Christ:
Grace to you and peace.
2 We give thanks to God always for all of
you, making mention *of you* in our prayers;
3 remembering without ceasing your work
of faith and labor of love and steadfastness
of hope in our Lord Jesus Christ before our
God and Father, 4 knowing, brothers beloved
by God, your election, 5 for our gospel did
not come to you in word only, but also in
power and in the Holy Spirit and with full
assurance; just as you know what kind of
men we proved to be among you for your

sake. 6 You also became imitators of us and
of the Lord, having received the word in
much affliction with the joy of the Holy
Spirit, 7 so that you became a model to all the
believers in Macedonia and in Achaia. 8 For
the word of the Lord has sounded forth from
you, not only in Macedonia and Achaia, but
also in every place your faith toward God
has gone forth, so that we have no need to
say anything. 9 For they themselves report
about us what kind of an entrance we had
with you, and how you turned to God from
idols to serve a living and true God, 10 and
to wait for His Son from heaven, whom He
raised from the dead, Jesus, who rescues us
from the wrath to come.

The Bible is an inexhaustible fountain of all truths. The existence of the Bible is the greatest blessing which humanity ever experienced.

— ROBERT MURRAY M'CHEYNE

OCTOBER 15

Jeremiah 15:1–16:21

15 Then Yahweh said to me, "Even
though Moses and Samuel were to
stand before Me, My soul would not be
with this people; send them away from My
presence and let them go! 2 And it will be
that when they say to you, 'Where should
we go?' then you are to tell them, 'Thus says
Yahweh:

"Those *destined* for death, to death;
And those *destined* for the
sword, to the sword;
And those *destined* for
famine, to famine;
And those *destined* for
captivity, to captivity."'

3 "I will appoint over them four kinds *of
doom*," declares Yahweh: "the sword to kill,
the dogs to drag off, and the birds of the sky
and the beasts of the earth to devour and
bring to ruin. 4 I will give them over *to be* an
example of terror among all the kingdoms
of the earth because of Manasseh, the son
of Hezekiah, the king of Judah, for what he
did in Jerusalem.

5 "Indeed, who will spare
you, O Jerusalem,
Or who will console you,
Or who will turn aside to ask
about your well-being?
6 "You who have abandoned
Me," declares Yahweh,
"You keep going backward.
So I will stretch out My hand against
you and bring you to ruin;
I am tired of relenting!
7 "And I will winnow them with
a winnowing fork
At the gates of the land;
I will bereave *them* of children;
I will make My people perish;
They did not repent of their ways.
8 "Their widows will be more
numerous before Me
Than the sand of the seas;
I will bring against them, against
the mother of a choice man,
A destroyer at noonday;
I will suddenly bring down on her
Anguish and terror.
9 "She who bore seven *sons* languishes;
Her breathing is labored.
Her sun has set while it was yet day;
She has been shamed and
humiliated.
So I will give over their
survivors to the sword
Before their enemies,"
declares Yahweh.
10 Woe to me, my mother, that
you have borne me
As a man of strife and a man of
contention to all the land!
I have not lent, nor have men
lent money to me,
Yet everyone curses me.
11 Yahweh said, "Surely I will set you
free for *purposes of* good;
Surely I will cause the enemy
to intercede with you
In a time of disaster and
a time of distress.

12 "Can anyone smash iron,
Iron from the north, or bronze?
13 "Your wealth and your treasures
I will give for plunder without cost,
Even for all your sins
And within all your borders.
14 "Then I will cause your
enemies to pass *it* over
Into a land you do not know,
For a fire has been kindled in My anger;
It will burn upon you."

15 You who know, O Yahweh,
Remember me, take notice of me,
And take vengeance for me
on my persecutors.
Do not, in view of Your
patience, take me away;
Know that for Your sake I
endure reproach.
16 Your words were found, and I ate them,
And Your words became for me
joy and gladness in my heart,
For I have been called by Your name,
O Yahweh God of hosts.
17 I did not sit in the circle
of merrymakers,
Nor did I exult.
Because of Your hand *upon*
me I sat alone,
For You filled me with indignation.
18 Why has my pain been perpetual
And my wound incurable,
refusing to be healed?
Will You indeed be to me like
a deceptive *stream*
With water that is unreliable?
19 Therefore thus says Yahweh,
"If you return, then I will
cause you to return—
Before Me you will stand;
And if you extract the precious
from the worthless,
You will become My mouthpiece.
They for their part may turn to you,
But as for you, you must
not turn to them.
20 "Then I will make you to this people
A fortified wall of bronze;
And they will fight against you,
But they will not prevail against you,
For I am with you to save you
And deliver you," declares Yahweh.
21 "So I will deliver you from the
hand of the evil ones,
And I will redeem you from the
grasp of the ruthless ones."

16 The word of Yahweh also came to me
saying, 2 "You shall not take a wife for
yourself nor have sons or daughters in this
place." 3 For thus says Yahweh concerning
the sons and daughters born in this place
and concerning their mothers who bear
them and their fathers who beget them in
this land: 4 "They will die of deadly diseases;
they will not be lamented or buried; they
will be as dung on the surface of the ground
and come to an end by sword and famine,
and their carcasses will become food for the
birds of the sky and for the beasts of the
earth."
5 For thus says Yahweh, "Do not enter the
house of the funeral meal, or go to lament
or to console them; for I have withdrawn My
peace from this people," declares Yahweh,
"*My* lovingkindness and compassion. 6 Both
great men and small will die in this land;
they will not be buried; they will not be
lamented, nor will anyone gash himself
or shave his head for them. 7 Men will
not break *bread* in mourning for them, to
comfort anyone for the dead, nor give them
a cup of comforting to drink for anyone's
father or mother. 8 Moreover you shall not
go into a house of feasting to sit with them
to eat and drink." 9 For thus says Yahweh of
hosts, the God of Israel: "Behold, I am going
to cause to cease from this place, before your
eyes and in your days, the voice of rejoicing
and the voice of gladness, the voice of the
groom and the voice of the bride.
10 "Now when you tell this people all these
words, they will say to you, 'For what reason
has Yahweh declared all this great calamity
against us? And what is our iniquity, or
what is our sin which we have committed
against Yahweh our God?' 11 Then you are
to say to them, '*It is* because your fathers
have forsaken Me,' declares Yahweh, 'and
have walked after other gods and served
them and worshiped them; but Me they
have forsaken and have not kept My law.
12 You too have done evil, *even* more than
your fathers; for behold, you are each one
walking according to the stubbornness of
his own evil heart, without listening to Me.
13 So I will hurl you out of this land into the
land which you have not known, neither
you nor your fathers; and there you will

serve other gods day and night, for I will
grant you no favor.'
14 "Therefore behold, days are coming,"
declares Yahweh, "when it will no longer
be said, 'As Yahweh lives, who brought up
the sons of Israel out of the land of Egypt,'
15 but, 'As Yahweh lives, who brought up the
sons of Israel from the land of the north and
from all the lands where He had banished
them.' For I will return them to their own
land which I gave to their fathers.
16 "Behold, I am going to send for many
fishermen," declares Yahweh, "and they will
fish for them; and afterwards I will send for
many hunters, and they will hunt them from
every mountain and every hill and from the
crevices of the rocks. 17 For My eyes are on
all their ways; they are not hidden from My
face, nor is their iniquity concealed from My
eyes. 18 I will first doubly repay their iniquity
and their sin because they have profaned My
land; they have filled My inheritance with
the carcasses of their detestable idols and
with their abominations."

19 O Yahweh, my strength and
my strong defense,
And my refuge in the day of distress,
To You the nations will come
From the ends of the earth and say,
"Our fathers have inherited
nothing but lies,
Futility and things of no profit."
20 Can man make gods for himself?
Yet they are not gods!

21 "Therefore behold, I am going
to make them know—
This time I will make them know
My power and My might;
And they shall know that
My name is Yahweh."

Psalm 118:21–24

21 I shall give thanks to You, for
You have answered me,
And You have become my salvation.

22 The stone which the
builders rejected
Has become the chief corner *stone*.
23 This is from Yahweh;
It is marvelous in our eyes.
24 This is the day which
Yahweh has made;
Let us rejoice and be glad in it.

Proverbs 27:10

10 Do not forsake your friend or
your father's friend,
And do not come to your brother's
house in the day of your disaster;
Better is one who dwells near
than a brother far away.

1 Thessalonians 2:1–20

2 For you yourselves know, brothers, that
our entrance to you was not in vain,
2 but after we had already suffered and
been mistreated in Philippi, as you know,
we had the boldness in our God to speak to
you the gospel of God amid much struggle.
3 For our exhortation does not *come* from
error or impurity or by way of deceit; 4 but
just as we have been approved by God to be
entrusted with the gospel, so we speak, not
as pleasing men, but God who examines our
hearts. 5 For we never came with a flattering
word, as you know, nor with a pretext for
greed—God is witness— 6 nor seeking glory
from men, either from you or from others,
even though as apostles of Christ we could
have been a burden to *you*. 7 But we proved
to be gentle among you, as a nursing *mother*
tenderly cares for her own children. 8 In this
way, having fond affection for you, we were
pleased to impart to you not only the gospel
of God but also our own lives, because you
had become beloved to us.
9 For you remember, brothers, our labor
and hardship, *how* working night and day so
as not to be a burden to any of you, we pro-
claimed to you the gospel of God. 10 You are
witnesses, and *so is* God, of how devoutly
and righteously and blamelessly we behaved
toward you believers; 11 just as you know
how we *were* exhorting and encouraging
and bearing witness to each one of you as
a father *would* his own children, 12 so that
you would walk in a manner worthy of the
God who calls you into His own kingdom
and glory.
13 And for this reason we also thank God
without ceasing that when you received
the word of God which you heard from us,
you accepted *it* not *as* the word of men,
but *for* what it really is, the word of God,
which also is at work in you who believe.
14 For you, brothers, became imitators of
the churches of God in Christ Jesus that
are in Judea, for you also suffered the
same things at the hands of your own

countrymen, even as they *did* from the
Jews, [15] who both killed the Lord Jesus
and the prophets, and drove us out, and
do not please God, and *are* hostile to all
men, [16] hindering us from speaking to
the Gentiles so that they may be saved;
with the result that they always fill up the
measure of their sins. But wrath has come
upon them to the utmost.

[17] But we, brothers, having been taken
away from you for a short while—in face
but not in heart—were all the more eager
with great desire to see your face. [18] For we
wanted to come to you—I, Paul, more than
once—and *yet* Satan hindered us. [19] For who
is our hope or joy or crown of boasting? Is
it not even you, before our Lord Jesus at His
coming? [20] For you are our glory and joy.

OCTOBER 16

Jeremiah 17:1–18:23

17 The sin of Judah is written
down with an iron stylus;
With a diamond point it is engraved
upon the tablet of their heart
And on the horns of their altars,
2 As they remember their children,
So they *remember* their altars
and their Asherim
By green trees on the high hills.
3 O mountain of Mine in
the countryside,
I will give over your wealth and all
your treasures for plunder,
Your high places for sin
throughout your borders.
4 And you will, even of yourself,
let go of your inheritance
That I gave you;
And I will make you serve
your enemies
In the land which you do not know,
For you have kindled a fire in
My anger
Which will burn forever.

5 Thus says Yahweh,
"Cursed is the man who
trusts in mankind
And makes flesh his strength,
And whose heart turns
away from Yahweh.
6 "And he will be like a juniper
in the desert
And will not see when
prosperity comes,
But will dwell in stony wastes
in the wilderness,
A land of salt *which is* not inhabited.
7 "Blessed is the man who
trusts in Yahweh
And whose trust is Yahweh.
8 "And he will be like a tree
planted by the water,
That sends forth its roots by a stream
And will not fear when the heat comes;
But its leaves will be green,
And it will not be anxious
in a year of drought
Nor refrain from yielding fruit.

9 "The heart is more deceitful
than all else
And is desperately sick;
Who can know it?
10 "I, Yahweh, search the heart;
I test the inmost being,
Even to give to each man
according to his ways,
According to the fruit of his deeds.
11 "*As* a partridge that hatches eggs
which it has not laid,
So is he who makes a
fortune, but unjustly;
In the midst of his days it
will forsake him,
And in the end he will be
a wicked fool."

12 A glorious throne on high
from the beginning
Is the place of our sanctuary.
13 O Yahweh, the hope of Israel,
All who forsake You will
be put to shame.
Those who turn away on earth
will be written down
Because they have forsaken
the fountain of living
water, even Yahweh.
14 Heal me, O Yahweh, and
I will be healed;
Save me and I will be saved,
For You are my praise.

15 Behold, they keep saying to me,
“Where is the word of Yahweh?
Let it come now!”
16 But as for me, I have not hurried away
from *being* a shepherd after You,
Nor have I longed for the
sickening day;
You Yourself know that the
utterance of my lips
Was in Your presence.
17 Do not be a terror to me;
You are my refuge in the
day of calamity.
18 Let those who pursue me be put
to shame, but as for me, let
me not be put to shame;
Let them be dismayed, but let
me not be dismayed.
Bring on them a day of calamity,
And crush them with
twofold crushing!

19 Thus Yahweh said to me, “Go and stand
in the public gate, through which the kings
of Judah come in and go out, as well as
in all the gates of Jerusalem, 20 and say to
them, ‘Listen to the word of Yahweh, kings
of Judah and all Judah and all inhabitants
of Jerusalem who come in through these
gates: 21 Thus says Yahweh, “Take care of
yourselves, and do not carry any load on the
sabbath day or bring anything in through
the gates of Jerusalem. 22 You shall not bring
a load out of your houses on the sabbath day
nor do any work, but keep the sabbath day
holy, as I commanded your fathers. 23 Yet
they did not listen or incline their ears, but
stiffened their necks in order not to listen
or receive discipline.

24 “But it will be, if you listen carefully
to Me,” declares Yahweh, “to bring no load
in through the gates of this city on the
sabbath day, but to keep the sabbath day
holy by doing no work on it, 25 then there
will come in through the gates of this city
kings and princes sitting on the throne of
David, riding in chariots and on horses,
they and their princes, the men of Judah
and the inhabitants of Jerusalem, and this
city will be inhabited forever. 26 And they
will come in from the cities of Judah and
from all around Jerusalem, from the land
of Benjamin, from the Shephelah, from the
hill country, and from the Negev, bringing
burnt offerings, sacrifices, grain offerings,
and frankincense, and bringing sacrifices
of thanksgiving to the house of Yahweh.
27 But if you do not listen to Me to keep the
sabbath day holy by not carrying a load and
coming in through the gates of Jerusalem on
the sabbath day, then I will kindle a fire in
its gates, and it will devour the palaces of
Jerusalem and not be quenched.”’”

18

The word which came to Jeremiah
from Yahweh saying, 2 “Arise and go
down to the potter’s house, and there I will
make you hear My words.” 3 Then I went
down to the potter’s house, and behold,
he was making something on the wheel.
4 But the vessel that he was making of clay
was ruined in the hand of the potter, so he
turned around and made it into another
vessel, according to what was right in the
eyes of the potter to make.

5 Then the word of Yahweh came to me
saying, 6 “Can I not, O house of Israel, deal
with you as this potter *does*?” declares
Yahweh. “Behold, like the clay in the pot-
ter’s hand, so are you in My hand, O house
of Israel. 7 At one moment I might speak
concerning a nation or concerning a king-
dom to uproot, to tear down, or to make *it*
perish; 8 but if that nation against which I
have spoken turns from its evil, I will relent
concerning the calamity I planned to do
against it. 9 Or at another moment I might
speak concerning a nation or concerning
a kingdom to build up or to plant *it*; 10 but
if it does evil in My sight by not listening
to My voice, then I will relent concerning
the good which I promised, to do good to it.
11 So now then, speak to the men of Judah
and against the inhabitants of Jerusalem
saying, ‘Thus says Yahweh, “Behold, I am
forming calamity against you and devising
a plan against you. Oh turn back, each of
you from his evil way, and do good in your
ways and your deeds.”’ 12 But they will say,
‘It’s hopeless! For we are going to follow our
own plans, and each of us will act according
to the stubbornness of his evil heart.’

13 “Therefore thus says Yahweh,
‘Ask now among the nations,
Who ever heard the like of this?
The virgin of Israel
Has done a most appalling thing.
14 ‘Does the snow of Lebanon forsake
the rock of the open country?
Or is the cold flowing water *from*
a strange *land* ever uprooted?

15 'For My people have forgotten Me;
They burn incense to worthless gods,
And they have stumbled
from their ways,
From the ancient paths,
To walk in bypaths,
Not on a highway,
16 To make their land an object
of horror,
An object of perpetual hissing;
Everyone who passes by
it will be horrified
And shake his head.
17 'Like an east wind I will scatter them
Before the enemy;
I will show them My back
and not *My* face
In the day of their disaster.'"
18 Then they said, "Come and let us devise
plans against Jeremiah. Surely the law is not
going to perish from the priest, nor counsel
to the wise man, nor the *divine* word to the
prophet! Come on and let us strike at him
with *our* tongue, and let us give no heed to
any of his words."
19 Do give heed to me, O Yahweh,
And listen to the voice of those
who contend against me!
20 Should good be repaid with evil?
For they have dug a pit for me.
Remember how I stood before You
To speak good on their behalf,
So as to turn away Your
wrath from them.
21 Therefore, give their children
over to famine
And deliver them up to the
power of the sword;
And let their wives become
childless and widowed.
Let their men also be smitten to death,
Their young men struck down
by the sword in battle.
22 May an outcry be heard
from their houses,
When You suddenly bring
raiders upon them;
For they have dug a pit to capture me
And hidden snares for my feet.
23 Yet You, O Yahweh, know
All their deadly counsel against me;
Do not atone for their iniquity
Or blot out their sin from before You.
But may they be overthrown
before You;
Deal with them in the time
of Your anger!

Psalm 118:25–29

25 O Yahweh, save!
O Yahweh, succeed!
26 Blessed is the one who comes
in the name of Yahweh;
We have blessed you from
the house of Yahweh.
27 Yahweh is God, and He
has given us light;
Bind the festival sacrifice with
cords to the horns of the altar.
28 You are my God, and I give
thanks to You;
You are my God, I exalt You.
29 Give thanks to Yahweh, for He is good;
For His lovingkindness
endures forever.

Proverbs 27:11–12

11 Be wise, my son, and make
my heart glad,
That I may respond with a word
to him who reproaches me.
12 A prudent man sees evil *and* hides,
The simple pass on *and* are punished.

1 Thessalonians 3:1–13

3 Therefore when we could endure *it* no
longer, we were pleased to be left behind
at Athens alone, 2 and we sent Timothy, our
brother and God's fellow worker in the gos-
pel of Christ, to strengthen and encourage
you as to your faith, 3 so that no one would
be shaken by these afflictions, for you your-
selves know that we have been destined for
this. 4 For indeed when we were with you,
we *kept* telling you in advance that we were
going to suffer affliction, just as it happened
and *as* you know. 5 For this reason, when I
could endure *it* no longer, I also sent to know
about your faith, lest somehow the tempter
has tempted you, and our labor be in vain.
6 But now that Timothy has come to us
from you, and has brought us good news
of your faith and love, and that you always
remember us kindly, longing to see us just
as we also long to see you, 7 for this reason,
brothers, in all our distress and affliction
we were comforted about you through your
faith; 8 for now we *really* live, if you stand
firm in the Lord. 9 For what thanks can we
render to God for you in return for all the

joy with which we rejoice before our God because of you, 10 as we night and day keep praying most earnestly that we may see your face, and may complete what is lacking in your faith?

11 Now may our God and Father Himself and Jesus our Lord direct our way to you, 12 and may the Lord cause you to increase and abound in love for one another, and for all people, just as we also *do* for you, 13 so that He may strengthen your hearts blameless in holiness, before our God and Father, at the coming of our Lord Jesus with all His saints.

OCTOBER 17

Jeremiah 19:1–20:18

19 Thus says Yahweh, "Go and buy a potter's earthenware jar, and *take* some of the elders of the people and some of the elders of the priests. 2 Then go out to the valley of Ben-hinnom, which is by the entrance of the potsherd gate, and there call out the words that I tell you 3 and say, 'Hear the word of Yahweh, O kings of Judah and inhabitants of Jerusalem: thus says Yahweh of hosts, the God of Israel, "Behold, I am about to bring a calamity upon this place, at which the ears of everyone that hears of it will tingle. 4 Because they have forsaken Me and have made this a foreign place and have burned incense in it to other gods, that neither they nor their fathers nor the kings of Judah had *ever* known, and *because* they have filled this place with the blood of the innocent 5 and have built the high places of Baal to burn their sons in the fire as burnt offerings to Baal, a thing which I never commanded or spoke of, nor did it *ever* come upon My heart, 6 therefore, behold, days are coming," declares Yahweh, "when this place will no longer be called Topheth or the valley of Ben-hinnom, but rather the valley of Slaughter. 7 I will empty out the counsel of Judah and Jerusalem to *the point of* destruction in this place, and I will cause them to fall by the sword before their enemies and by the hand of those who seek their life; and I will give over their carcasses as food for the birds of the sky and the beasts of the earth. 8 I will also make this city an object of horror and of hissing; everyone who passes by it will be horrified and hiss because of all its slaughtering. 9 I will make them eat the flesh of their sons and the flesh of their daughters, and they will eat one another's flesh in the siege and in the distress with which their enemies and those who seek their life will distress them."'

10 "Then you are to break the jar in the sight of the men who accompany you, 11 and you shall say to them, 'Thus says Yahweh of hosts, "Just so will I break this people and this city, even as one breaks a potter's vessel, which cannot again be repaired; and they will bury in Topheth because there is no *other* place for burial. 12 This is what I will do to this place and its inhabitants," declares Yahweh, "so as to make this city like Topheth. 13 And the houses of Jerusalem and the houses of the kings of Judah will be defiled like the place Topheth because of all the houses on whose rooftops they burned incense to all the heavenly host and poured out drink offerings to other gods."'"

14 Then Jeremiah came from Topheth, where Yahweh had sent him to prophesy; and he stood in the court of the house of Yahweh and said to all the people: 15 "Thus says Yahweh of hosts, the God of Israel, 'Behold, I am about to bring on this city and all its towns the entire calamity that I have spoken against it because they have stiffened their necks so as not to hear My words.'"

20 Then Pashhur the priest, the son of Immer, who was ruling overseer in the house of Yahweh, heard Jeremiah prophesying these words; 2 and Pashhur had Jeremiah the prophet struck and put him in the stocks that were at the upper Benjamin Gate, which was by the house of Yahweh. 3 Now it happened that on the next day, Pashhur released Jeremiah from the stocks. And Jeremiah said to him, "Pashhur is not the name Yahweh has called you, but rather Magor-missabib. 4 For thus says Yahweh, 'Behold, I am going to make you a terror to yourself and to all your friends; and while your eyes look on, they will fall by the sword of their enemies. So I will give over all Judah to the hand of the king of Babylon, and he

will take them away into exile to Babylon
and will strike them down with the sword. 5 I
will also give over all the wealth of this city,
all the fruit of its labor, and all its precious
things; even all the treasures of the kings
of Judah I will give over to the hand of their
enemies, and they will plunder them, take
them away, and bring them to Babylon.
6 And you, Pashhur, and all who live in your
house will go into captivity; and you will
enter Babylon, and there you will die, and
there you will be buried, you and all your
friends to whom you have prophesied lies.'"

7 O Yahweh, You have enticed
me, and I was enticed;
You were stronger than I,
and You prevailed.
I have become a laughingstock
all day long;
Everyone mocks me.
8 For each time I speak, I cry aloud;
I call out violence and devastation
Because for me the word of
Yahweh has resulted
In reproach and derision all day long.
9 But if I say, "I will not remember Him
Or speak anymore in His name,"
Then in my heart it becomes
like a burning fire
Shut up in my bones;
And I am weary of holding *it* in,
And I cannot prevail.
10 For I have heard the bad
report of many,
"Terror on every side!
Denounce *him*; yes, let us
denounce him!"
All my trusted friends,
Keeping watch for my fall, say:
"Perhaps he will be deceived, so that
we may prevail against him
And take our revenge on him."
11 But Yahweh is with me like a
ruthless mighty one;
Therefore my persecutors will
stumble and not prevail.
They will be utterly ashamed,
because they have not prospered,
With an everlasting dishonor
that will not be forgotten.
12 Yet, O Yahweh of hosts, You
who test the righteous,
Who see the mind and the heart;
Let me see Your vengeance on them,
For to You I have revealed my cause.

13 Sing to Yahweh, praise Yahweh!
For He has delivered the
soul of the needy one
From the hand of evildoers.

14 Cursed be the day when
I was born;
Let the day not be blessed when
my mother bore me!
15 Cursed be the man who
brought the good news
To my father, saying,
"A baby boy has been born to you!"
And made him very glad.
16 But let that man be like the cities
Which Yahweh overthrew
without relenting,
And let him hear an outcry
in the morning
And a shout of war at noon,
17 Because he did not put me to
death from the womb,
So that my mother would
have been my grave,
And her womb ever pregnant.
18 Why did I ever come forth
from the womb
To look on trouble and sorrow,
So that my days have been
spent in shame?

Psalm 119:1–8

1 How blessed are those whose
way is blameless,
Who walk in the law of Yahweh.
2 How blessed are those who
observe His testimonies,
They seek Him with all
their heart.
3 They also do not work
unrighteousness;
They walk in His ways.
4 You have commanded *us*,
To keep Your precepts diligently.
5 Oh may my ways be established
To keep Your statutes!
6 Then I shall not be ashamed
When I look upon all Your
commandments.
7 I shall give thanks to You with
uprightness of heart,
When I learn Your righteous
judgments.
8 I shall keep Your statutes;
Do not forsake me utterly!

Proverbs 27:13

13 Take his garment when he becomes
a guarantor for a stranger;
And for a foreign woman
seize it as a pledge.

1 Thessalonians 4:1–18

4 Finally then, brothers, we ask and
exhort you in the Lord Jesus, that as
you received from us as to how you ought
to walk and please God (just as you actually
do walk), that you excel still more. 2 For you
know what commandments we gave you
through the Lord Jesus. 3 For this is the will
of God, your sanctification: that you abstain
from sexual immorality; 4 that each of you
know how to possess his own vessel in sanc-
tification and honor, 5 not in lustful passion,
like the Gentiles who do not know God;
6 *and* that no man transgress and defraud
his brother in the matter because the Lord
is *the* avenger in all these things, just as we
also told you before and solemnly warned
you. 7 For God did not call us to impurity, but
in sanctification. 8 Consequently, he who
sets *this* aside is not setting aside man but
the God who gives His Holy Spirit to you.
9 Now concerning love of the brothers,
you have no need for *anyone* to write to you,
for you yourselves are taught by God to love
one another, 10 for indeed you do practice it
toward all the brothers who are in all Mace-
donia. But we urge you, brothers, to excel
still more, 11 and to make it your ambition
to lead a quiet life and attend to your own
business and work with your hands, just
as we commanded you, 12 so that you will
walk properly toward outsiders and not be
in any need.
13 But we do not want you to be unin-
formed, brothers, about those who are
asleep, so that you will not grieve as do the
rest who have no hope. 14 For if we believe
that Jesus died and rose again, even so God
will bring with Him those who have fallen
asleep in Jesus. 15 For this we say to you by
the word of the Lord, that we who are alive
and remain until the coming of the Lord,
will not precede those who have fallen
asleep. 16 For the Lord Himself will descend
from heaven with a shout, with the voice of
the archangel and with the trumpet of God,
and the dead in Christ will rise first. 17 Then
we who are alive and remain will be caught
up together with them in the clouds to meet
the Lord in the air, and so we shall always
be with the Lord. 18 Therefore comfort one
another with these words.

OCTOBER 18

Jeremiah 21:1–22:30

21 The word which came to Jeremiah
from Yahweh when King Zedekiah
sent to him Pashhur, the son of Malchijah,
and Zephaniah the priest, the son of Maa-
seiah, saying, 2 "Please inquire of Yahweh
on our behalf, for Nebuchadnezzar king
of Babylon is warring against us; perhaps
Yahweh will deal with us according to all
His wonderful acts, so that *the enemy* will
go up from us."
3 Then Jeremiah said to them, "Thus you
shall say to Zedekiah, 4 'Thus says Yahweh,
the God of Israel, "Behold, I am about to turn
back the weapons of war which are in your
hands, with which you are warring against
the king of Babylon and the Chaldeans who
are besieging you outside the wall; and
I will gather them into the center of this
city. 5 I Myself will war against you with an
outstretched hand and a strong arm, even
in anger and wrath and great indignation.
6 I will also strike down the inhabitants of
this city, both man and beast; they will die
of a great pestilence. 7 Then afterwards,"
declares Yahweh, "I will give over Zedekiah
king of Judah and his servants and the peo-
ple, even those who remain in this city from
the pestilence, the sword, and the famine,
into the hand of Nebuchadnezzar king of
Babylon and into the hand of their enemies
and into the hand of those who seek their
lives; and he will strike them down with the
edge of the sword. He will not show pity on
them nor spare nor have compassion."'
8 "You shall also say to this people, 'Thus
says Yahweh, "Behold, I set before you the
way of life and the way of death. 9 He who
inhabits this city will die by the sword and
by famine and by pestilence; but he who
goes out and falls away to the Chaldeans
who are besieging you will live, and he will
have his own life as spoil. 10 For I have set
My face against this city for evil and not for

good," declares Yahweh. "It will be given into the hand of the king of Babylon, and he will burn it with fire."'

11 "Then *say* to the household of the king of Judah, 'Hear the word of Yahweh,
12 O house of David, thus says Yahweh:

"Render justice every morning;
And deliver the *person* who
has been robbed from the
power of *his* oppressor,
Lest My wrath go forth like fire
And burn with none to extinguish *it*,
Because of the evil of their deeds.

13 "Behold, I am against you,
O inhabitant of the valley,
O rocky plain," declares Yahweh,
"You men who say, 'Who will
come down against us?
Or who will enter into our
dwelling places?'
14 "But I will punish you according
to the results of your deeds,"
declares Yahweh,
"And I will kindle a fire in its forest
That it may devour all its
surroundings."'"

22 Thus says Yahweh, "Go down to
the house of the king of Judah, and
there you shall speak this word 2 and say,
'Hear the word of Yahweh, O king of Judah,
who sits on David's throne, you and your
servants and your people who enter these
gates. 3 Thus says Yahweh, "Do justice and
righteousness, and deliver the one who has
been robbed from the power of *his* oppres-
sor. Also do not mistreat *or* do violence to
the sojourner, the orphan, or the widow;
and do not shed innocent blood in this
place. 4 For if you men will indeed do this
thing, then kings will enter the gates of this
house, sitting for David on his throne, riding
in chariots and on horses, *even the king* him-
self and his servants and his people. 5 But
if you will not obey these words, I swear by
Myself," declares Yahweh, "that this house
will become a waste place."'" 6 For thus says
Yahweh concerning the house of the king
of Judah:

"You are *like* Gilead to Me,
Like the summit of Lebanon;
Yet most assuredly I will make
you like a wilderness,
Like cities which are not inhabited.
7 "For I will set apart destroyers
against you,
Each with his weapons;
And they will cut down
your choicest cedars
And throw *them* on the fire.

8 "Many nations will pass by this city;
and they will say to one another, 'Why has
Yahweh done thus to this great city?' 9 Then
they will say, 'Because they forsook the cov-
enant of Yahweh their God and worshiped
other gods and served them.'"

10 Do not weep for the dead
or console him,
But weep continually for the
one who goes away,
For he will never return
Or see the land of his birth.

11 For thus says Yahweh in regard to
Shallum the son of Josiah, king of Judah,
who became king in the place of Josiah his
father, who went forth from this place, "He
will never return there; 12 but in the place
where they took him away into exile, there
he will die and not see this land again.

13 "Woe to him who builds his house
without righteousness
And his upper rooms
without justice,
Who uses his neighbor's
services without pay
And does not give him his wages,
14 Who says, 'I will build myself
a roomy house
With spacious upper rooms
And cut out its windows,
Paneling *it* with cedar and
painting *it* bright red.'
15 "Do you become a king because
you are competing in cedar?
Did not your father eat and drink
And do justice and righteousness?
Then it was well with him.
16 "He pled the cause of the
afflicted and needy;
Then it was well.
Is not that what it means to
know Me?"
Declares Yahweh.
17 "But your eyes and your heart
Are *set* on nothing except
your own greedy gain
And on shedding innocent blood
And on doing oppression
and extortion."

18 Therefore thus says Yahweh in regard to
Jehoiakim the son of Josiah, king of Judah,
"They will not lament for him:
'Alas, my brother!' or, 'Alas, sister!'
They will not lament for him:
'Alas for the master!' or, 'Alas
for his splendor!'
19 "He will be buried with a
donkey's burial,
Dragged off and thrown out beyond
the gates of Jerusalem.
20 "Go up to Lebanon and cry out,
And lift up your voice in Bashan;
Cry out also from Abarim,
For all your lovers have been broken.
21 "I spoke to you in your prosperity,
But you said, 'I will not listen!'
This has been your way
from your youth,
That you have not listened to My voice.
22 "The wind will sweep away
all your shepherds,
And your lovers will go into captivity;
Then you will surely be ashamed
and feel dishonor
Because of all your evil.
23 "You who inhabit Lebanon,
Nested in the cedars,
How you will groan when
pangs come upon you,
Pain like a woman in childbirth!
24 "As I live," declares Yahweh, "even
though Coniah the son of Jehoiakim king of
Judah were a signet *ring* on My right hand, yet
I would pull you off; 25 and I will give you over
into the hand of those who are seeking your
life, indeed, into the hand of those whom you
dread, even into the hand of Nebuchadnezzar
king of Babylon and into the hand of the
Chaldeans. 26 I will hurl you and your mother
who bore you into another land—there you
were not born, but there you will die. 27 But
as for the land to which their soul desires to
return, they will not return to it.
28 "Is this man Coniah a despised,
shattered jar?
Or is he an undesirable vessel?
Why have he and his seed
been hurled out
And cast into a land that
they had not known?
29 "O land, land, land,
Hear the word of Yahweh!
30 "Thus says Yahweh,
'Write this man down childless,
A man who will not
succeed in his days;
For no man of his seed will succeed
Sitting on the throne of David
Or ruling again in Judah.'"

Psalm 119:9–16

9 How can a young man
keep his way pure?
By keeping *it* according to Your word.
10 With all my heart I have sought You;
Do not let me stray from
Your commandments.
11 Your word I have treasured in my heart,
That I may not sin against You.
12 Blessed are You, O Yahweh;
Teach me Your statutes.
13 With my lips I have recounted
All the judgments of Your mouth.
14 I have rejoiced in the way
of Your testimonies,
As much as in all riches.
15 I will muse upon Your precepts
And look upon Your ways.
16 I shall delight in Your statutes;
I shall not forget Your word.

Proverbs 27:14

14 He who blesses his friend with a
loud voice early in the morning,
It will be counted as a curse to him.

1 Thessalonians 5:1–28

5 Now concerning the times and the
seasons, brothers, you have no need
of anything to be written to you. 2 For you
yourselves know full well that the day of the
Lord will come just like a thief in the night.
3 While they are saying, "Peace and safety!"
then destruction will come upon them sud-
denly like labor pains upon a woman who is
pregnant, and they will never escape. 4 But
you, brothers, are not in darkness, that the
day would overtake you like a thief, 5 for you
are all sons of light and sons of day. We are
not of night nor of darkness; 6 so then let us
not sleep as others do, but let us be awake
and sober. 7 For those who sleep, sleep at
night, and those who get drunk, get drunk
at night. 8 But since we are of *the* day, let us
be sober, having put on the breastplate of
faith and love, and as a helmet, the hope of
salvation. 9 For God has not appointed us for
wrath, but for obtaining salvation through
our Lord Jesus Christ, 10 who died for us, so

that whether we are awake or asleep, we
will live together with Him. 11 Therefore,
comfort one another and build up one
another, just as you also are doing.

12 But we ask of you, brothers, that you
know those who labor among you, and lead
you in the Lord and admonish you, 13 and
that you regard them very highly in love
because of their work. Live in peace with
one another. 14 And we urge you, brothers,
admonish the unruly, encourage the faint-
hearted, help the weak, be patient with
everyone. 15 See that no one repays another
with evil for evil, but always seek after that
which is good for one another and for all
people. 16 Rejoice always; 17 pray without
ceasing; 18 in everything give thanks, for this
is God's will for you in Christ Jesus. 19 Do
not quench the Spirit; 20 do not despise
prophecies, 21 but examine all things; hold
fast to that which is good; 22 abstain from
every form of evil.

23 Now may the God of peace Himself
sanctify you entirely, and may your spirit
and soul and body be preserved complete,
without blame at the coming of our Lord
Jesus Christ. 24 Faithful is He who calls you,
who also will do it.

25 Brothers, pray for us.

26 Greet all the brothers with a holy kiss.
27 I implore you by the Lord to have this
letter read to all the brothers.

28 The grace of our Lord Jesus Christ be
with you.

OCTOBER 19

Jeremiah 23:1–24:10

23 "Woe to the shepherds who are
destroying and scattering the
sheep of My pasture!" declares Yahweh.
2 Therefore thus says Yahweh, the God of
Israel, concerning the shepherds who are
shepherding My people: "You have scattered
My flock and banished them and have not
attended to them; behold, I am about to
attend to you for the evil of your deeds,"
declares Yahweh. 3 "Then I Myself will
gather the remnant of My flock out of all
the land where I have banished them and
cause them to return to their pasture, and
they will be fruitful and multiply. 4 I will also
raise up shepherds over them, and they will
shepherd them; and they will not be afraid
any longer, nor be terrified, nor will any be
left unattended," declares Yahweh.

5 "Behold, *the* days are coming,"
declares Yahweh,
"When I will raise up for David
a righteous Branch;
And He will reign as king and prosper
And do justice and righteousness
in the land.
6 "In His days Judah will be saved,
And Israel will dwell securely;
And this is His name by which
He will be called,
'Yahweh our righteousness.'

7 "Therefore behold, *the* days are com-
ing," declares Yahweh, "when they will no
longer say, 'As Yahweh lives, who brought
up the sons of Israel from the land of Egypt,'
8 but, 'As Yahweh lives, who brought up and
brought back the seed of the household of
Israel from *the* north land and from all the
lands where I had banished them.' Then
they will live on their own soil."

9 As for the prophets:
My heart is broken within me;
All my bones tremble;
I have become like a drunken man,
Even like a man overcome with wine,
Because of Yahweh
And because of His holy words.
10 For the land is full of adulterers;
For the land mourns
because of the curse.
The pastures of the wilderness
have dried up.
Their course also is evil,
And their might is not right.
11 "For both prophet and
priest are polluted;
Even in My house I have found
their evil," declares Yahweh.
12 "Therefore their way will be like
slippery paths to them;
They will be driven away into the
thick darkness and fall down in it;
For I will bring *their* evil upon them,
The year of their punishment,"
declares Yahweh.

13 "Moreover, among the prophets of
Samaria I saw an offensive thing:

They prophesied by Baal and led
My people Israel astray.
14 "Also among the prophets of Jerusalem
I have seen an appalling thing:
The committing of adultery
and walking in lying;
And they strengthen the
hands of evildoers,
So that no one has turned
back from his evil.
All of them have become
to Me like Sodom,
And her inhabitants like Gomorrah.
15 "Therefore thus says Yahweh of hosts
concerning the prophets,
'Behold, I am going to feed
them wormwood
And make them drink poisoned water,
For from the prophets of Jerusalem
Pollution has gone forth
into all the land.'"

16 Thus says Yahweh of hosts,
"Do not listen to the words
of the prophets who are
prophesying to you.
They are leading you into vanity;
They speak a vision of their own heart,
Not from the mouth of Yahweh.
17 "They keep saying to those
who spurn Me,
'Yahweh has said, "You
will have peace"';
And as for everyone who walks in the
stubbornness of his own heart,
They say, 'Evil will not come upon you.'
18 "But who has stood in the
council of Yahweh,
That he should see and hear His word?
Who has given heed to His
word and heard?
19 "Behold, the storm of Yahweh
has gone forth in wrath,
Even a whirling storm;
It will whirl down on the
head of the wicked.
20 "The anger of Yahweh will not turn back
Until He has done and established
the purposes of His heart;
In the last days you will
clearly understand it.
21 "I did not send *these* prophets,
But they ran.
I did not speak to them,
But they prophesied.
22 "But if they had stood in My council,
Then they would have caused My
words to be heard by My people
And would have turned them
back from their evil way
And from the evil of their deeds.

23 "Am I a God who is near,"
declares Yahweh,
"And not a God far off?
24 "Can a man hide himself
in hiding places
So I do not see him?" declares Yahweh.
"Do I not fill the heavens and the
earth?" declares Yahweh.
25 "I have heard what the prophets have
said who prophesy a lie in My name, saying,
'I had a dream, I had a dream!' 26 How long?
Is there *anything* in the hearts of the proph-
ets who prophesy a lie, even *these* prophets
of the deception of their own heart, 27 who
intend to make My people forget My name
by their dreams which they recount to one
another, just as their fathers forgot My
name because of Baal? 28 The prophet who
has a dream may recount *his* dream, but
let him who has My word speak My word
in truth. What does straw have *in common*
with grain?" declares Yahweh. 29 "Is not My
word like fire?" declares Yahweh, "and like a
hammer which shatters a rock? 30 Therefore
behold, I am against the prophets," declares
Yahweh, "who steal My words from each
other. 31 Behold, I am against the prophets,"
declares Yahweh, "who take their tongues
and declare, '*Yahweh* declares.' 32 Behold,
I am against those who have prophesied
lying dreams," declares Yahweh, "and who
recounted them and led My people astray
by their lying and reckless boasting; yet I
did not send them, and I did not command
them, and they do not furnish this people
the slightest benefit," declares Yahweh.
33 "Now when this people or the prophet
or a priest asks you, saying, 'What is the
oracle of Yahweh?' then you shall say to
them, 'What oracle?' Yahweh declares, 'I will
abandon you.' 34 Then as for the prophet or
the priest or the people who say, 'The oracle
of Yahweh,' I will bring punishment upon
that man and his household. 35 Thus will
each of you say to his neighbor and to his
brother, 'What has Yahweh answered?' or,
'What has Yahweh spoken?' 36 For you will
no longer remember the oracle of Yahweh

because every man's own word will become
the oracle, and you have perverted the words
of the living God, Yahweh of hosts, our God.
37 Thus you will say to *that* prophet, 'What
has Yahweh answered you?' and, 'What has
Yahweh spoken?' 38 For if you *all* say, 'The
oracle of Yahweh!' surely thus says Yahweh,
'Because you said this word, "The oracle of
Yahweh!" I have also sent to you, saying,
"You shall not say, 'The oracle of Yahweh!'"'
39 Therefore behold, I will surely forget you
and abandon you, along with the city which
I gave you and your fathers, *so that you are*
out of My presence. 40 I will put an ever-
lasting reproach on you and an everlasting
humiliation which will not be forgotten."

24 After Nebuchadnezzar king of
Babylon had taken away into exile
Jeconiah the son of Jehoiakim, king of Judah,
and the officials of Judah with the crafts-
men and smiths from Jerusalem, and had
brought them to Babylon, Yahweh showed
me: behold, two baskets of figs set before
the temple of Yahweh! 2 One basket had very
good figs, like first-ripe figs, and the other
basket had very rotten figs which could not
be eaten due to rottenness. 3 Then Yahweh
said to me, "What do you see, Jeremiah?"
And I said, "Figs, the good figs, very good;
and the rotten *figs*, very rotten, which
cannot be eaten due to rottenness."
4 Then the word of Yahweh came to me,
saying, 5 "Thus says Yahweh, the God of
Israel, 'Like these good figs, so I will rec-
ognize as good the exiles of Judah, whom
I have sent out of this place *into* the land
of the Chaldeans. 6 For I will set My eyes on
them for good, and I will return them to this
land; and I will build them up and not pull
them down, and I will plant them and not
uproot them. 7 I will give them a heart to
know Me, for I am Yahweh; and they will be
My people, and I will be their God, for they
will return to Me with their whole heart.
8 'But like the rotten figs which cannot be
eaten due to rottenness—indeed, thus says
Yahweh—so I will give over Zedekiah king
of Judah and his officials and the remnant
of Jerusalem who remain in this land and
the ones who inhabit the land of Egypt. 9 I
will give them over *to be* a terror *and an*
evil for all the kingdoms of the earth, as
a reproach and a proverb, a byword and a
curse in all places where I will banish them.
10 I will send the sword, the famine, and the
pestilence upon them until they come to an
end from *being* upon the land which I gave
to them and their fathers.'"

Psalm 119:17–24

17 Deal bountifully with Your slave,
That I may live and keep Your word.
18 Open my eyes, that I may behold
Wonderful things from Your law.
19 I am a sojourner in the earth;
Do not hide Your commandments
from me.
20 My soul is crushed with longing
For Your judgments at all times.
21 You rebuke the arrogant, the cursed,
Who stray from Your commandments.
22 Take away reproach and
contempt from me,
For I observe Your testimonies.
23 Even though princes sit
and talk against me,
Your slave muses on Your statutes.
24 Your testimonies also are my delight;
They are my counselors.

Proverbs 27:15–16

15 A constant dripping on a
day of steady rain
And a contentious woman are alike;
16 He who would restrain her
restrains the wind,
And grasps oil with his right hand.

2 Thessalonians 1:1–12

1 Paul and Silvanus and Timothy,
To the church of the Thessalonians in
God our Father and the Lord Jesus Christ:
2 Grace to you and peace from God the
Father and the Lord Jesus Christ.
3 We ought always to give thanks to God
for you, brothers, as is *only* fitting, because
your faith is growing abundantly, and the
love of each one of you all toward one
another increases *all the more*, 4 so that
we ourselves boast about you among the
churches of God for your perseverance and
faith in the midst of all your persecutions
and afflictions which you endure.
5 *This is* a plain indication of God's
righteous judgment so that you will be
considered worthy of the kingdom of God,
for which indeed you are suffering. 6 Since
it is right for God to repay with affliction
those who afflict you, 7 and *to give* rest

to you who are afflicted and to us as well at the revelation of the Lord Jesus from heaven with His mighty angels in flaming fire, 8 executing vengeance on those who do not know God and to those who do not obey the gospel of our Lord Jesus. 9 These will pay the penalty of eternal destruction, AWAY FROM THE PRESENCE OF THE LORD AND FROM THE GLORY OF HIS MIGHT, 10 when He comes to be glorified in His saints on that day, and to be marveled at among all who have believed—for our witness to you was believed. 11 To this end also we pray for you always, that our God will count you worthy of your calling, and fulfill all *your* good pleasure for goodness and the work of faith with power, 12 so that the name of our Lord Jesus will be glorified in you, and you in Him, according to the grace of our God and *the* Lord Jesus Christ.

OCTOBER 20

Jeremiah 25:1–26:24

25 The word that came to Jeremiah concerning all the people of Judah in the fourth year of Jehoiakim the son of Josiah, king of Judah (that was the first year of Nebuchadnezzar king of Babylon), 2 which Jeremiah the prophet spoke to all the people of Judah and to all the inhabitants of Jerusalem, saying, 3 "From the thirteenth year of Josiah the son of Amon, king of Judah, even to this day, these twenty-three years the word of Yahweh has come to me, and I have spoken to you, rising up early and speaking, but you have not listened. 4 And Yahweh has sent to you all His slaves the prophets, rising up early and sending, but you have not listened nor inclined your ear to hear, 5 saying, 'Turn now everyone from his evil way and from the evil of your deeds, and live on the ground which Yahweh has given to you and your fathers forever and ever; 6 and do not walk after other gods to serve them and to worship them, and do not provoke Me to anger with the work of your hands, and I will bring no evil against you.' 7 Yet you have not listened to Me," declares Yahweh, "in order that you might provoke Me to anger with the work of your hands to your own evil *demise*.

8 "Therefore thus says Yahweh of hosts, 'Because you have not listened to My words, 9 behold, I will send and take all the families of the north,' declares Yahweh, 'and *I will send* to Nebuchadnezzar king of Babylon, My servant, and will bring them against this land and against its inhabitants and against all these surrounding nations; and I will devote them to destruction and make them an object of horror and of hissing and an everlasting waste place. 10 Moreover, I will make the voice of joy and the voice of gladness, the voice of the bridegroom and the voice of the bride, the sound of the millstones and the light of the lamp, to perish from them. 11 This whole land will be a waste place and an object of horror, and these nations will serve the king of Babylon seventy years.

12 'Then it will be when seventy years are fulfilled, *that* I will punish the king of Babylon and that nation,' declares Yahweh, 'for their iniquity, even the land of the Chaldeans; and I will make it an everlasting desolation. 13 I will bring upon that land all My words which I have spoken against it, all that is written in this book which Jeremiah has prophesied against all the nations. 14 —For many nations and great kings will make slaves of them, even them; and I will repay them according to their deeds and according to the work of their hands—'"

15 For thus Yahweh, the God of Israel, says to me, "Take this cup of the wine of wrath from My hand and cause all the nations to whom I send you to drink it. 16 They will drink and stagger and go mad because of the sword that I will send among them."

17 Then I took the cup from the hand of Yahweh and made all the nations to whom Yahweh sent me drink it: 18 Jerusalem and the cities of Judah and its kings *and* its princes, to make them a waste place, an object of horror, an object of hissing, and a curse, as it is this day; 19 Pharaoh king of Egypt, his servants, his princes, and all his people, 20 and all the foreign people, all the kings of the land of Uz, all the kings of the land of the Philistines (even Ashkelon, Gaza, Ekron, and the remnant of Ashdod), 21 Edom, Moab, and the sons of Ammon, 22 and all the kings of Tyre, all the kings of Sidon, and the kings of the coastlands

which are beyond the sea, 23 and Dedan,
Tema, Buz, and all who cut the corners *of*
their hair, 24 and all the kings of Arabia and
all the kings of the foreign people who dwell
in the desert, 25 and all the kings of Zimri,
all the kings of Elam, and all the kings of
Media, 26 and all the kings of the north,
near and far, one with another; and all the
kingdoms of the earth which are upon the
face of the ground, and the king of Sheshach
shall drink after them.

27 "You shall say to them, 'Thus says Yah-
weh of hosts, the God of Israel, "Drink, be
drunk, vomit, fall, and rise no more because
of the sword which I will send among you."'
28 And it will be, if they refuse to take the
cup from your hand to drink, then you will
say to them, 'Thus says Yahweh of hosts:
"You shall surely drink! 29 For behold, I
am beginning to bring evil against *this* city
which is called by My name. But shall you be
completely free from punishment? You will
not be free from punishment, for I am call-
ing for a sword against all the inhabitants of
the earth," declares Yahweh of hosts.'

30 "Therefore you shall prophesy against
them all these words, and you shall say to
them,

'Yahweh will roar from on high
And give forth His voice from
His holy habitation;
He will roar mightily
against His pasture.
He will bellow a shout like those
who tread *the grapes*,
Against all the inhabitants of the earth.
31 'A rumbling has come to the
end of the earth
Because Yahweh has a contention
against the nations.
He is entering into judgment
with all flesh;
As for the wicked, He has given them
to the sword,' declares Yahweh."

32 Thus says Yahweh of hosts,
"Behold, evil is going forth
From nation to nation,
And a great storm is being stirred up
From the remotest parts of the earth.

33 "Those slain by Yahweh on that day will
be from one end of the earth to the other.
They will not be lamented, gathered, or
buried; they will be like dung on the face
of the ground.

34 "Wail, you shepherds, and cry out;
And roll yourselves *in ashes*,
you masters of the flock;
For the days of your slaughter and
your scatterings are being fulfilled,
And you will fall like a desirable vessel.
35 "Refuge will perish from the shepherds
And escape from the mighty
ones of the flock.
36 "*Hear* the sound of the cry
of the shepherds,
And the wailing of the mighty
ones of the flock!
For Yahweh is destroying their pasture,
37 And the peaceful pastures
are made silent
Because of the burning
anger of Yahweh.
38 "He has forsaken His hiding
place like the lion;
For their land has become
an object of horror
Because of the burning *desire*
of the oppressor
And because of His burning anger."

26 In the beginning of the reign of
Jehoiakim the son of Josiah, king of
Judah, this word came from Yahweh, saying,
2 "Thus says Yahweh, 'Stand in the court of
the house of Yahweh, and you shall speak
to all the cities of Judah who have come
to worship *in* the house of Yahweh all the
words that I have commanded you to speak
to them. Do not take away a word! 3 Perhaps
they will listen and everyone will turn from
his evil way, that I may relent of the evil
which I am devising to bring against them
because of the evil of their deeds.' 4 And
you will say to them, 'Thus says Yahweh, "If
you will not listen to Me, to walk in My law
which I have given before you, 5 to listen to
the words of My slaves the prophets, whom
I have been sending to you, rising up early
and sending, but you have not listened,
6 then I will make this house like Shiloh,
and this city I will make a curse to all the
nations of the earth."'"

7 The priests and the prophets and all the
people heard Jeremiah speaking these words
in the house of Yahweh. 8 Now it happened
that when Jeremiah finished speaking
all that Yahweh had commanded *him* to
speak to all the people, the priests and the
prophets and all the people seized him,

saying, "You must surely die! 9 Why have you
prophesied in the name of Yahweh saying,
'This house will be like Shiloh, and this city
will be laid waste, without inhabitant'?" And
all the people gathered about Jeremiah in
the house of Yahweh.

10 When the officials of Judah heard
these things, they came up from the king's
house to the house of Yahweh and sat in
the entrance of the New Gate of *the house*
of Yahweh. 11 Then the priests and the
prophets spoke to the officials and to all the
people, saying, "A judgment of death for this
man! For he has prophesied against this city
as you have heard in your hearing."

12 Then Jeremiah spoke to all the officials
and to all the people, saying, "Yahweh sent
me to prophesy against this house and
against this city all the words that you have
heard. 13 So now, make good your ways
and your deeds and listen to the voice of
Yahweh your God; and Yahweh will relent of
the evil *demise* which He has spoken against
you. 14 But as for me, behold, I am in your
hands; do with me as is good and right in
your eyes. 15 Only know for certain that if
you put me to death, you will bring innocent
blood on yourselves and on this city and on
its inhabitants; for truly Yahweh has sent
me to you to speak all these words in your
hearing."

16 Then the officials and all the people
said to the priests and to the prophets, "No
judgment of death for this man! For he has
spoken to us in the name of Yahweh our
God." 17 Then some of the elders of the land
rose up and spoke to all the assembly of
the people, saying, 18 "Micah of Moresheth
prophesied in the days of Hezekiah king
of Judah; and he spoke to all the people of
Judah, saying, 'Thus Yahweh of hosts has
said,

"Zion will be plowed *as* a field,
And Jerusalem will become
a heap of ruins,
And the mountain of the house *will*
become the high places of a forest."'

19 "Did Hezekiah king of Judah and all Judah
put him to death? Did he not fear Yahweh
and entreat the favor of Yahweh, and
Yahweh relented of the evil *demise* which
He had spoken against them? But we are
committing a great evil against ourselves."

20 Indeed, there was also a man who
prophesied in the name of Yahweh, Uriah
the son of Shemaiah from Kiriath-jearim;
and he prophesied against this city and
against this land words similar to all those
of Jeremiah. 21 And King Jehoiakim and all
his mighty men and all the officials heard
his words. So the king sought to put him
to death; but Uriah heard *it*, and he was
afraid and fled and went to Egypt. 22 Then
King Jehoiakim sent men to Egypt: Elnathan
the son of Achbor and *certain* men with
him *went* into Egypt. 23 And they brought
Uriah out from Egypt and led him to King
Jehoiakim, who struck him down with a
sword and cast his dead body into the burial
place of the common people.

24 But the hand of Ahikam the son of
Shaphan was with Jeremiah, so that he was
not given into the hands of the people to
put him to death.

Psalm 119:25–32

25 My soul clings to the dust;
Revive me according to Your word.
26 I have recounted my ways, and
You have answered me;
Teach me Your statutes.
27 Make me understand the
way of Your precepts,
So I will muse on Your
wondrous deeds.
28 My soul weeps because of grief;
Raise me up according to Your word.
29 Remove the false way from me,
And graciously grant me Your law.
30 I have chosen the faithful way;
I have placed Your judgments
before me.
31 I cling to Your testimonies;
O Yahweh, do not put me to shame!
32 I shall run the way of Your
commandments,
For You will enlarge my heart.

Proverbs 27:17

17 Iron sharpens iron,
So one man sharpens another.

2 Thessalonians 2:1–17

2 Now we ask you, brothers, with regard
to the coming of our Lord Jesus Christ
and our gathering together to Him, 2 that
you not be quickly shaken in your mind or
be alarmed whether by a spirit or a word
or a letter as if from us, to the effect that
the day of the Lord has come. 3 Let no one

in any way deceive you, for *it has not come* unless the apostasy comes first, and the man of lawlessness is revealed, the son of destruction, 4 who opposes and exalts himself above every so-called god or object of worship, so that he takes his seat in the sanctuary of God, exhibiting himself as being God. 5 Do you not remember that while I was still with you, I was telling you these things? 6 And you know what restrains him now, so that in his time he will be revealed. 7 For the mystery of lawlessness is already at work; only he who now restrains *will do so* until he is taken out of the way. 8 And then that lawless one will be revealed—whom the Lord Jesus WILL SLAY WITH THE BREATH OF HIS MOUTH and bring to an end by the appearance of His coming— 9 whose coming is in accord with the working of Satan, with all power and signs and false wonders, 10 and with all the deception of unrighteousness for those who perish, because they did not receive the love of the truth so as to be saved. 11 And for this reason God sends upon them a deluding influence so that they will believe what is false, 12 in order that they all may be judged who did not believe the truth, but took pleasure in unrighteousness.

13 But we should always give thanks to God for you, brothers beloved by the Lord, because God has chosen you as the first fruits for salvation through sanctification by the Spirit and faith in the truth. 14 It was for this He called you through our gospel, that you may obtain the glory of our Lord Jesus Christ. 15 So then, brothers, stand firm and hold to the traditions which you were taught, whether by word *of mouth* or by letter from us.

16 Now may our Lord Jesus Christ Himself and God our Father, who has loved us and given us eternal comfort and good hope by grace, 17 encourage your hearts and strengthen *them* in every good work and word.

OCTOBER 21

Jeremiah 27:1–28:17

27 In the beginning of the reign of Zedekiah the son of Josiah, king of Judah, this word came to Jeremiah from Yahweh, saying— 2 thus says Yahweh to me—"Make for yourself bonds and the bars of a yoke and put them on your neck, 3 and you shall send word to the king of Edom, to the king of Moab, to the king of the sons of Ammon, to the king of Tyre, and to the king of Sidon by the hand of messengers who come to Jerusalem to Zedekiah king of Judah. 4 And you shall command them *to go* to their masters, saying, 'Thus says Yahweh of hosts, the God of Israel, thus you shall say to your masters, 5 "I have made the earth, the men, and the animals which are on the face of the earth by My great power and by My outstretched arm, and I will give it to the one who is right in My eyes. 6 So now, I have given all these lands into the hand of Nebuchadnezzar king of Babylon, My servant, and I have given him even the wild beasts of the field to serve him. 7 All the nations shall serve him and his son and his grandson until the time of his own land comes; then many nations and great kings will make him their servant.

8 "And it will be, *that* the nation or the kingdom which will not serve him, Nebuchadnezzar king of Babylon, and which will not put its neck under the yoke of the king of Babylon, I will punish that nation with the sword, with famine, and with pestilence," declares Yahweh, "until I have brought it to an end by his hand. 9 But as for you, do not listen to your prophets, your diviners, your dreamers, your soothsayers, or your sorcerers who speak to you, saying, 'You will not serve the king of Babylon.' 10 For they prophesy a lie to you in order to remove you far from your land; and I will banish you, and you will perish. 11 But the nation which will bring its neck under the yoke of the king of Babylon and serve him, I will leave *it* on its land," declares Yahweh, "and they will serve it and inhabit it."'"

12 I spoke words like all these to Zedekiah king of Judah, saying, "Bring your necks under the yoke of the king of Babylon and serve him and his people, and live! 13 Why will you die, you and your people, by the sword, famine, and pestilence, as Yahweh has spoken to that nation which will not serve the king of Babylon? 14 So do not listen to the words of the prophets who

speak to you, saying, 'You will not serve the
king of Babylon,' for they prophesy a lie to
you; 15 for I have not sent them," declares
Yahweh, "but they prophesy a lie in My
name, in order that I may banish you and
that you may perish, you and the prophets
who prophesy to you."
16 *Then* I spoke to the priests and to all
this people, saying, "Thus says Yahweh: Do
not listen to the words of your prophets
who prophesy to you, saying, 'Behold, the
vessels of the house of Yahweh will now
shortly be returned from Babylon'; for they
are prophesying a lie to you. 17 Do not listen
to them; serve the king of Babylon, and live!
Why should this city become a waste place?
18 But if they are prophets, and if the word of
Yahweh is with them, let them now intercede
with Yahweh of hosts that the vessels which
are left in the house of Yahweh, in the house
of the king of Judah, and in Jerusalem may
not go to Babylon. 19 For thus says Yahweh of
hosts concerning the pillars, concerning the
sea, concerning the stands, and concerning
the rest of the vessels that are left in this
city, 20 which Nebuchadnezzar king of
Babylon did not take when he carried away
into exile Jeconiah the son of Jehoiakim,
king of Judah, from Jerusalem to Babylon,
and all the nobles of Judah and Jerusalem.
21 Indeed, thus says Yahweh of hosts, the
God of Israel, concerning the vessels that
are left in the house of Yahweh and in the
house of the king of Judah and in Jerusalem,
22 'They will be brought to Babylon, and
they will be there until the day I visit them,'
declares Yahweh. 'Then I will bring them up
and return them to this place.'"

28 Now it happened in the same year,
in the beginning of the reign of
Zedekiah king of Judah, in the fourth year,
in the fifth month, *that* Hananiah the son of
Azzur, the prophet, who was from Gibeon,
spoke to me in the house of Yahweh in the
sight of the priests and all the people, say-
ing, 2 "Thus says Yahweh of hosts, the God
of Israel, 'I have broken the yoke of the king
of Babylon. 3 Within two years I am going
to return to this place all the vessels of the
house of Yahweh, which Nebuchadnezzar
king of Babylon took away from this place
and carried to Babylon. 4 I am also going
to return to this place Jeconiah the son of
Jehoiakim, king of Judah, and all the exiles
of Judah who went to Babylon,' declares
Yahweh, 'for I will break the yoke of the king
of Babylon.'"
5 Then the prophet Jeremiah spoke to the
prophet Hananiah in the sight of the priests
and in the sight of all the people who were
standing in the house of Yahweh, 6 and the
prophet Jeremiah said, "Amen! May Yahweh
do so; may Yahweh establish your words
which you have prophesied to return the
vessels of the house of Yahweh and all the
exiles, from Babylon to this place. 7 Yet hear
now this word which I am about to speak in
your hearing and in the hearing of all the
people! 8 The prophets who were before me
and before you from ancient times proph-
esied against many lands and against great
kingdoms, of war and of calamity and of
pestilence. 9 The prophet who prophesies of
peace, when the word of the prophet comes
to pass, then that prophet will be known *as*
one whom Yahweh has truly sent."
10 Then Hananiah the prophet took the
bar of the yoke from the neck of Jeremiah
the prophet and broke it. 11 And Hananiah
spoke in the sight of all the people, saying,
"Thus says Yahweh, 'Even so will I break
within two full years the yoke of Nebuchad-
nezzar king of Babylon from the neck of all
the nations.'" Then the prophet Jeremiah
went his way.
12 Then the word of Yahweh came to
Jeremiah after Hananiah the prophet had
broken the bar of the yoke from off the
neck of the prophet Jeremiah, saying, 13 "Go
and speak to Hananiah, saying, 'Thus says
Yahweh, "You have broken the bars of a
yoke *made* of wood, but you have made in
their place the bars of a yoke *made* of iron."
14 For thus says Yahweh of hosts, the God of
Israel, "I have put a yoke of iron on the neck
of all these nations, that they may serve
Nebuchadnezzar king of Babylon, and they
will serve him. And I have even given him
the beasts of the field."'" 15 Then Jeremiah
the prophet said to Hananiah the prophet,
"Listen now, Hananiah, Yahweh has not sent
you, and you have made this people trust in
a lie. 16 Therefore thus says Yahweh, 'Behold,
I am about to remove you from the face of
the earth. This year you are going to die
because you have spoken rebellion against
Yahweh.'"
17 So Hananiah the prophet died in the
same year in the seventh month.

Psalm 119:33–40

33 Instruct me, O Yahweh, in the
way of Your statutes,
That I may observe it to the end.
34 Cause me to understand, that
I may observe Your law
And keep it with all *my* heart.
35 Cause me to walk in the path
of Your commandments,
For I delight in it.
36 Cause my heart to incline
to Your testimonies
And not to *dishonest* gain.
37 Cause my eyes to turn away from
looking at worthlessness,
And revive me in Your ways.
38 Cause Your word to be
established for Your slave,
As that which produces fear for You.
39 Cause my reproach which I
dread to pass away,
For Your judgments are good.
40 Behold, I long for Your precepts;
Revive me in Your righteousness.

Proverbs 27:18

18 He who guards the fig tree
will eat its fruit,
And he who keeps *watch for* his
master will be honored.

2 Thessalonians 3:1–18

3 Finally, brothers, pray for us that the
word of the Lord will spread rapidly
and be glorified, just as *it did* also with you;
2 and that we will be rescued from perverse
and evil men, for not all have faith. 3 But the
Lord is faithful, who will strengthen and
guard you from the evil one. 4 And we have
confidence in the Lord about you, that you
are doing and will *continue to* do what we
command. 5 And may the Lord direct your
hearts into the love of God and into the
steadfastness of Christ.
6 Now we command you, brothers, in
the name of our Lord Jesus Christ, that you
keep away from every brother who walks
in an unruly manner and not according to
the tradition which they received from us.
7 For you yourselves know how you ought
to imitate us, because we did not act in an
unruly manner among you, 8 nor did we eat
anyone's bread without paying for it, but
with labor and hardship we *kept* working
night and day so that we would not be a
burden to any of you; 9 not because we do
not have the authority, but in order to offer
ourselves as a model for you, so that you
would imitate us. 10 For even when we were
with you, we used to command this to you: if
anyone is not willing to work, neither let him
eat. 11 For we hear that some among you are
walking in an unruly manner, doing no work
at all, but acting like busybodies. 12 Now such
persons we command and exhort in the Lord
Jesus Christ, that working with quietness,
they eat their own bread. 13 But as for you,
brothers, do not lose heart in doing good.
14 And if anyone does not obey our word
in this letter, take special note of that person
to not associate with him, so that he will be
put to shame. 15 And *yet* do not regard him
as an enemy, but admonish him as a brother.
16 Now may the Lord of peace Himself
continually give you peace in every circum-
stance. The Lord be with you all!
17 The greeting is in my own hand—Paul,
which is a distinguishing mark in every
letter; this is the way I write. 18 The grace
of our Lord Jesus Christ be with you all.

The Scriptures teach us the best way of living, the noblest way of suffering, and the most comfortable way of dying.

— JOHN FLAVEL

OCTOBER 22

Jeremiah 29:1–30:24

29 Now these are the words of the letter
which Jeremiah the prophet sent
from Jerusalem to the rest of the elders of
the exile, the priests, the prophets, and all
the people whom Nebuchadnezzar had
taken away into exile from Jerusalem to
Babylon. 2 (This was after King Jeconiah and

the queen mother, the court officials, the princes of Judah and Jerusalem, the craftsmen, and the smiths had gone out from Jerusalem.) 3 *The letter was sent* by the hand of Elasah the son of Shaphan and Gemariah the son of Hilkiah, whom Zedekiah king of Judah sent to Babylon to Nebuchadnezzar king of Babylon, saying, 4 "Thus says Yahweh of hosts, the God of Israel, to all the exiles whom I have sent into exile from Jerusalem to Babylon, 5 'Build houses and live *in them*; and plant gardens and eat their fruit. 6 Take wives and become the fathers of sons and daughters, and take wives for your sons and give your daughters to husbands, that they may bear sons and daughters; and multiply there and do not decrease. 7 Seek the peace of the city where I have sent you into exile, and pray to Yahweh on its behalf; for in its peace you will have peace.' 8 For thus says Yahweh of hosts, the God of Israel, 'Do not let your prophets who are in your midst and your diviners deceive you, and do not listen to your dreams which you dream. 9 For they prophesy a lie to you in My name; I have not sent them,' declares Yahweh.

10 "For thus says Yahweh, 'When seventy years have been fulfilled for Babylon, I will visit you and establish My good word to you, to return you to this place. 11 For I know the plans that I have for you,' declares Yahweh, 'plans for peace and not for calamity, to give you a future and a hope. 12 Then you will call upon Me and come and pray to Me, and I will listen to you. 13 You will seek Me and find *Me* when you search for Me with all your heart. 14 I will be found by you,' declares Yahweh, 'and I will return your fortunes and will gather you from all the nations and from all the places where I have banished you,' declares Yahweh, 'and I will cause you to return to the place from where I sent you into exile.'

15 "Because you have said, 'Yahweh has raised up prophets for us in Babylon'— 16 for thus says Yahweh concerning the king who sits on the throne of David and concerning all the people who live in this city, your brothers who did not go with you into exile— 17 thus says Yahweh of hosts, 'Behold, I am sending upon them the sword, famine, and pestilence, and I will make them like split-open figs that cannot be eaten due to rottenness. 18 I will pursue them with the sword, with famine, and with pestilence; and I will give them over *to be* a terror to all the kingdoms of the earth, to be a curse and an object of horror and of hissing, and a reproach among all the nations where I have banished them, 19 because they have not listened to My words,' declares Yahweh, 'which I sent to them by My slaves the prophets, rising up early and sending; but you did not listen,' declares Yahweh. 20 You, therefore, hear the word of Yahweh, all you exiles, whom I have sent away from Jerusalem to Babylon.

21 "Thus says Yahweh of hosts, the God of Israel, concerning Ahab the son of Kolaiah and concerning Zedekiah the son of Maaseiah, who are prophesying to you falsely in My name, 'Behold, I will give them into the hand of Nebuchadnezzar king of Babylon, and he will strike them down before your eyes. 22 And because of them a curse will be used by all the exiles from Judah who are in Babylon, saying, "May Yahweh make you like Zedekiah and like Ahab, whom the king of Babylon roasted in the fire 23 because they have acted with wicked foolishness in Israel and have committed adultery with their neighbors' wives and have spoken words in My name falsely, which I did not command them; and I am He who knows and am a witness," declares Yahweh.'"

24 And to Shemaiah the Nehelamite you shall speak, saying, 25 "Thus says Yahweh of hosts, the God of Israel, 'Because you have sent letters in your own name to all the people who are in Jerusalem and to Zephaniah the son of Maaseiah, the priest, and to all the priests, saying, 26 "Yahweh has given you *to be* a priest instead of Jehoiada the priest, to be the overseer in the house of Yahweh over every madman who prophesies, to put him in the stocks and in the iron collar, 27 so now, why have you not rebuked Jeremiah of Anathoth who prophesies to you? 28 For he has sent to us in Babylon, saying, '*The exile* will be long; build houses and live *in them* and plant gardens and eat their fruit.'"'"

29 So Zephaniah the priest read this letter in the hearing of Jeremiah the prophet. 30 Then came the word of Yahweh to Jeremiah, saying, 31 "Send to all the exiles, saying, 'Thus says Yahweh concerning Shemaiah the Nehelamite, "Because Shemaiah has prophesied to you, although I did not send him, and he has made you trust in a lie," 32 therefore thus says Yahweh,

"Behold, I am about to punish Shemaiah the
Nehelamite and his seed; he will not have
anyone living among this people, and he will
not see the good that I am about to do to My
people," declares Yahweh, "because he has
spoken rebellion against Yahweh."'"

30 The word which came to Jeremiah
from Yahweh, saying, 2 "Thus says
Yahweh, the God of Israel, 'Write all the words
which I have spoken to you in a book. 3 For
behold, days are coming,' declares Yahweh,
'when I will return the fortunes of My people
Israel and Judah.' Yahweh says, 'I will also
cause them to return to the land that I gave
to their fathers, and they shall possess it.'"

4 Now these are the words which Yahweh
spoke concerning Israel and concerning
Judah:

5 "For thus says Yahweh,
'We have heard a sound of trembling,
Of dread, and there is no peace.
6 'Ask now, and see
If a male can give birth.
Why do I see every man
With his hands on his loins,
as a woman in childbirth?
And *why* have all faces turned pale?
7 'Alas! For that day is great,
There is none like it;
And it is the time of Jacob's distress,
But he will be saved from it.

8 'And it will be in that day,' declares
Yahweh of hosts, '*that* I will break his yoke
from off your neck and will tear off your
bonds; and strangers will no longer make
them their slaves. 9 But they shall be a slave
to Yahweh their God and David their king,
whom I will raise up for them.

10 'Fear not, O Jacob My servant,'
declares Yahweh,
'And do not be dismayed, O Israel;
For behold, I will save you from afar
And your seed from the land
of their captivity.
And Jacob will return and will
be quiet and at ease,
And no one will make him tremble.
11 'For I am with you,' declares
Yahweh, 'to save you;
For I will make a complete
destruction of all the nations
where I have scattered you,
Only I will not make a complete
destruction of you.
But I will chasten you justly
And will by no means leave
you unpunished.'

12 "For thus says Yahweh,
'Your injury is incurable,
And your wound is desperately sick.
13 'There is no one to plead your cause;
No healing for *your* sore,
No recovery for you.
14 'All your lovers have forgotten you;
They do not seek you;
For I have wounded you with
the wound of an enemy,
With the punishment of a cruel one,
Because your iniquity is numerous
And your sins are mighty.
15 'Why do you cry out over your injury?
Your pain is incurable.
Because your iniquity is numerous
And your sins are mighty,
I have done these things to you.
16 'Therefore all who devour
you will be devoured;
And all your adversaries, every one
of them, will go into captivity;
And those who take you as
spoil will be spoil,
And all who plunder you I
will give as plunder.
17 'For I will restore you to health,
And I will heal you of your
wounds,' declares Yahweh,
'Because they have called you
a banished one, saying:
"It is Zion; no one is seeking her."'

18 "Thus says Yahweh,
'Behold, I will return the fortunes
of the tents of Jacob
And have compassion on
his dwelling places;
And the city will be rebuilt on its ruin,
And the palace will sit on its just place.
19 'From them will come forth
thanksgiving
And the voice of those who celebrate;
And I will multiply them,
and they will not decrease;
I will also honor them, and they
will not be insignificant.
20 'Their children also will be as formerly,
And their congregation shall be
established before Me;
And I will punish all their oppressors.

21 'And their mighty one shall
be one of them,
And their ruler shall come
forth from their midst;
And I will bring Him near, and
He shall approach Me;
For who would *dare* to give his
heart as security to approach
Me?' declares Yahweh.
22 'You shall be My people,
And I will be your God.'"

23 Behold, the storm of Yahweh!
Wrath has gone forth,
A sweeping storm;
It will burst on the head
of the wicked.
24 The burning anger of Yahweh
will not turn back
Until He has done and until
He has established
The intent of His heart;
In the last days you will
understand this.

Psalm 119:41–48

41 May Your lovingkindnesses also
come to me, O Yahweh,
Your salvation according to
Your word;
42 So I will have an answer for
him who reproaches me,
For I trust in Your word.
43 And do not take away the word of
truth utterly from my mouth,
For I wait for Your judgments.
44 So I will keep Your law
continually,
Forever and ever.
45 And I will walk in a wide place,
For I seek Your precepts.
46 I will also speak of Your
testimonies before kings
And I shall not be ashamed.
47 I shall delight in Your
commandments,
Which I love.
48 And I shall lift up my hands to
Your commandments,
Which I love;
And I will muse on Your statutes.

Proverbs 27:19

19 As in water face *reflects* face,
So the heart of man *reflects* man.

1 Timothy 1:1–20

1 Paul, an apostle of Christ Jesus according
to the commandment of God our Savior,
and of Christ Jesus, our hope,
2 To Timothy, *my* genuine child in *the*
faith: Grace, mercy, *and* peace from God the
Father and Christ Jesus our Lord.
3 As I exhorted you when going to Mace-
donia, remain on at Ephesus so that you
may command certain ones not to teach a
different doctrine, 4 nor to pay attention to
myths and endless genealogies, which give
rise to mere speculation rather than *further-
ing* the stewardship from God which is by
faith. 5 But the goal of our command is love
from a pure heart and a good conscience
and an unhypocritical faith. 6 For some,
straying from these things, have turned
aside to fruitless discussion, 7 wanting to
be teachers of the Law, even though they
do not understand either what they are
saying or the matters about which they
make confident assertions.
8 But we know that the Law is good, if
one uses it lawfully, 9 knowing this, that law
is not made for a righteous person, but for
those who are lawless and rebellious, for the
ungodly and sinners, for the unholy and god-
less, for those who kill their fathers or moth-
ers, for murderers, 10 for sexually immoral
persons, for homosexuals, for kidnappers,
for liars, for perjurers, and whatever else is
contrary to sound teaching, 11 according to
the gospel of the glory of the blessed God,
with which I have been entrusted.
12 I am grateful to Christ Jesus our
Lord, who has strengthened me, because
He regarded me faithful, putting me into
service, 13 even though I was formerly a
blasphemer and a persecutor and a violent
aggressor. Yet I was shown mercy because I
acted ignorantly in unbelief; 14 and the grace
of our Lord was more than abundant, with
the faith and love which *are* in Christ Jesus.
15 It is a trustworthy saying and deserving
full acceptance: that Christ Jesus came into
the world to save sinners, among whom I am
foremost. 16 Yet for this reason I was shown
mercy, so that in me as the foremost, Christ
Jesus might demonstrate all His patience
as an example for those who are going to
believe upon Him for eternal life. 17 Now to
the King of the ages, immortal, invisible, the
only God, *be* honor and glory forever and
ever. Amen.

[18] This command I entrust to you, Timothy, *my* child, in accordance with the prophecies previously made concerning you, that by them you may fight the good fight, [19] keeping faith and a good conscience, which some, having rejected, suffered shipwreck in regard to their faith. [20] Among these are Hymenaeus and Alexander, whom I have handed over to Satan, so that they will be taught not to blaspheme.

OCTOBER 23

Jeremiah 31:1–32:44

31 "At that time," declares Yahweh, "I will
be the God of all the families of Israel,
and they shall be My people."

[2] Thus says Yahweh,
"The people who survived the sword
Found grace in the wilderness—
Israel, when it went to find its relief."
3 Yahweh appeared to him
from afar, *saying*,
"I have loved you with an
everlasting love;
Therefore I have drawn you
with lovingkindness.
4 "Again I will build you, and
you will be rebuilt,
O virgin of Israel!
Again you will take up
your tambourines
And go forth to the dances
of those celebrating.
5 "Again you will plant vineyards
On the hills of Samaria;
The planters will plant
And will enjoy *them*.
6 "For there will be a day when watchmen
On the hills of Ephraim call out,
'Arise, and let us go up *to* Zion,
To Yahweh our God.'"

[7] For thus says Yahweh,
"Sing aloud with gladness for Jacob,
And shout among the head
of the nations;
Make *it* heard, give praise, and say,
'O Yahweh, save Your people,
The remnant of Israel.'
8 "Behold, I am bringing them
from the north country,
And I will gather them from the
remote parts of the earth,
Among them the blind and the lame,
The woman with child and she who
is in labor with child, together;
A great assembly, they will return here.
9 "With weeping they will come,
And by supplication I will lead them;
I will make them walk by
streams of waters,
On a straight path in which
they will not stumble;
For I am a father to Israel,
And Ephraim is My firstborn."

10 Hear the word of Yahweh, O nations,
And declare in the coastlands far away,
And say, "He who dispersed
Israel will gather him
And keep him as a shepherd
keeps his flock."
11 For Yahweh has ransomed Jacob
And redeemed him from the hand of
him who was stronger than he.
12 "They will come and sing for joy
on the height of Zion,
And they will be radiant over
the goodness of Yahweh—
Over the grain and the new
wine and the oil,
And over the young of the
flock and the herd;
And their soul will be like
a watered garden,
And they will never waste away again.
13 "Then the virgin will be
glad in the dance,
And the young men and
the old, together,
For I will turn their mourning into joy
And will comfort them and give
them gladness for their sorrow.
14 "I will fill the soul of the
priests with richness,
And My people will be satisfied with
My goodness," declares Yahweh.

[15] Thus says Yahweh,
"A voice is heard in Ramah,
Wailing *and* bitter weeping.
Rachel is weeping for her children;
She refuses to be comforted
for her children

Because they are no more."
16 Thus says Yahweh,
"Restrain your voice from weeping
And your eyes from tears,
For your work will be rewarded,"
declares Yahweh,
"And they will return from the
land of the enemy.
17 "And there is hope for your
future," declares Yahweh,
"And *your* children will return
to their own territory.
18 "I have surely heard Ephraim grieving,
'You have chastised me, and
I was chastised,
Like an untrained calf;
Cause me to return that I may return,
For You are Yahweh my God.
19 'For after I turned away, I repented;
And after I was instructed,
I slapped *my* thigh;
I was ashamed and also dishonored
Because I bore the reproach
of my youth.'
20 "Is Ephraim My dear son?
Is he a delightful child?
Indeed, as often as I have
spoken against him,
I certainly still remember him;
Therefore My inmost being
yearns for him;
I will surely have compassion
on him," declares Yahweh.

21 "Set up roadmarks for yourself,
Place for yourself guideposts;
Set your heart to the highway,
The way by which you went.
Return, O virgin of Israel,
Return to these your cities.
22 "How long will you go here and there,
O faithless daughter?
For Yahweh has created a new
thing in the earth—
A woman will encompass a man."
23 Thus says Yahweh of hosts, the God of
Israel, "Once again they will speak this word
in the land of Judah and in its cities when I
return their fortunes,
'Yahweh bless you, O abode
of righteousness,
O holy hill!'
24 "And Judah and all its cities will inhabit it
together, the farmer and they who go about
with flocks. 25 For I satisfy the weary soul
and fill up every soul who wastes away."
26 At this I awoke and looked, and my sleep
was pleasant to me.
27 "Behold, days are coming," declares
Yahweh, "when I will sow the house of
Israel and the house of Judah with the seed
of man and with the seed of beast. 28 And
it will be that as I have watched over them
to uproot, to tear down, to pull down, to
destroy, and to bring calamity, so I will
watch over them to build and to plant,"
declares Yahweh.
29 "In those days they will not say again,
'The fathers have eaten sour grapes,
And the children's teeth
are set on edge.'
30 "But everyone will die for his own iniq-
uity; each man who eats the sour grapes,
his teeth will be set on edge.
31 "Behold, days are coming," declares
Yahweh, "when I will cut a new covenant
with the house of Israel and with the house
of Judah, 32 not like the covenant which I cut
with their fathers in the day I took them by
the hand to bring them out of the land of
Egypt, My covenant which they broke, but
I was a husband to them," declares Yahweh.
33 "But this is the covenant which I will cut
with the house of Israel after those days,"
declares Yahweh: "I will put My law within
them, and on their heart I will write it; and
I will be their God, and they shall be My
people. 34 And they will not teach again,
each man his neighbor and each man his
brother, saying, 'Know Yahweh,' for they will
all know Me, from the least of them to the
greatest of them," declares Yahweh, "for I
will forgive their iniquity, and their sin I will
remember no more."
35 Thus says Yahweh,
Who gives the sun for light by day
And the statutes for the moon and
the stars for light by night,
Who stirs up the sea so
that its waves roar;
Yahweh of hosts is His name:
36 "If these statutes are removed
From before Me," declares Yahweh,
"Then the seed of Israel also will cease
From being a nation before
Me forever."
37 Thus says Yahweh,
"If the heavens above can be measured
And the foundations of the
earth searched out below,

Then I will also reject all
the seed of Israel
For all that they have done,"
declares Yahweh.

38 "Behold, days are coming," declares Yahweh, "when the city will be rebuilt for Yahweh from the Tower of Hananel to the Corner Gate. 39 The measuring line will go out farther, straight ahead to the hill Gareb; then it will turn to Goah. 40 And the whole valley of the dead bodies and of the ashes, and all the fields as far as the brook Kidron, to the corner of the Horse Gate toward the east, shall be holy to Yahweh; it will not be uprooted or pulled down anymore forever."

32 The word that came to Jeremiah from Yahweh in the tenth year of Zedekiah king of Judah, which was the eighteenth year of Nebuchadnezzar. 2 Now at that time the military force of the king of Babylon was besieging Jerusalem, and Jeremiah the prophet was shut up in the court of the guard, which *was in* the house of the king of Judah, 3 because Zedekiah king of Judah had shut him up, saying, "Why do you prophesy, saying, 'Thus says Yahweh, "Behold, I am about to give this city into the hand of the king of Babylon, and he will capture it; 4 and Zedekiah king of Judah will not escape out of the hand of the Chaldeans, but he will surely be given into the hand of the king of Babylon, and he will speak with him face to face and see him eye to eye; 5 and he will lead Zedekiah to Babylon, and he will be there until I visit him," declares Yahweh. "If you fight against the Chaldeans, you will not succeed"'?"

6 And Jeremiah said, "The word of Yahweh came to me, saying, 7 'Behold, Hanamel the son of Shallum your uncle is coming to you, saying, "Buy for yourself my field which is at Anathoth, for you have the *legal* judgment for redemption to buy *it*."' 8 Then Hanamel my uncle's son came to me in the court of the guard according to the word of Yahweh and said to me, 'Buy my field, please, that is at Anathoth, which is in the land of Benjamin; for you have the *legal* judgment for possession, and the redemption is yours; buy *it* for yourself.' Then I knew that this was the word of Yahweh.

9 "I bought the field which was at Anathoth from Hanamel my uncle's son, and I weighed out the silver for him, seventeen shekels of silver. 10 And I signed and sealed the deed and called in witnesses and weighed out the silver on the scales. 11 Then I took the deeds of purchase, both the sealed *copy containing* the commandment and statutes and the open *copy*, 12 and I gave the deed of purchase to Baruch the son of Neriah, the son of Mahseiah, in the sight of Hanamel my uncle's *son* and in the sight of the witnesses who signed the deed of purchase, in the sight of all the Jews who were sitting in the court of the guard. 13 And I commanded Baruch in their sight, saying, 14 'Thus says Yahweh of hosts, the God of Israel, "Take these deeds—this deed of purchase—that is the sealed one as well as this open deed, and put them in an earthenware jar, that they may last a long time." 15 For thus says Yahweh of hosts, the God of Israel, "Houses and fields and vineyards will again be bought in this land."'

16 "After I had given the deed of purchase to Baruch the son of Neriah, then I prayed to Yahweh, saying, 17 'Ah Lord Yahweh! Behold, You have made the heavens and the earth by Your great power and by Your outstretched arm! Nothing is too difficult for You, 18 who shows lovingkindness to thousands, but repays the iniquity of fathers into the bosom of their children after them, O great *and* mighty God. Yahweh of hosts is His name, 19 great in counsel and abundant in deeds, whose eyes are open to all the ways of the sons of men, giving to everyone according to his ways and according to the fruit of his deeds, 20 who has set signs and wonders in the land of Egypt, *and* even to this day both in Israel and among mankind; and You have made a name for Yourself, as at this day. 21 You brought Your people Israel out of the land of Egypt with signs and with wonders, and with a strong hand and with an outstretched arm and with great terror 22 and gave them this land, which You swore to their fathers to give them, a land flowing with milk and honey. 23 They came in and took possession of it, but they did not listen to Your voice and did not walk in Your law. They have not done anything that You commanded them to do; therefore You have made all this *harmful* evil come upon them. 24 Behold, the siege ramps have come to the city to capture it; and the city is given into the hand of the Chaldeans, who fight against it, because of the sword, the famine, and the pestilence; and what You have spoken has

happened; and behold, You see *it*. 25 And
You have said to me, O Lord Yahweh, "Buy
for yourself the field with money and call
in witnesses"—but the city is given into the
hand of the Chaldeans.'"

26 Then the word of Yahweh came to
Jeremiah, saying, 27 "Behold, I am Yahweh,
the God of all flesh; is anything too difficult
for Me?" 28 Therefore thus says Yahweh,
"Behold, I am about to give this city into the
hand of the Chaldeans and into the hand of
Nebuchadnezzar king of Babylon, and he
will capture it. 29 And the Chaldeans who
are fighting against this city will enter and
set this city on fire and burn it, with the
houses where *people* have burned incense
to Baal on their roofs and poured out drink
offerings to other gods to provoke Me to
anger. 30 Indeed the sons of Israel and the
sons of Judah have been doing only evil in
My sight from their youth; for the sons of
Israel have been only provoking Me to anger
by the work of their hands," declares Yah-
weh. 31 "Indeed this city has been to Me *a
provocation of* My anger and My wrath from
the day that they built it, even to this day,
so that it should be removed from before
My face 32 because of all the evil of the sons
of Israel and the sons of Judah which they
have done to provoke Me to anger—they,
their kings, their princes, their priests, their
prophets, the men of Judah, and the inhab-
itants of Jerusalem. 33 And they have turned
their back to Me and not *their* face; though
I taught them, rising up early and teaching,
they would not listen and receive discipline.
34 But they put their detestable things in
the house which is called by My name, to
defile it. 35 And they built the high places of
Baal that are in the valley of Ben-hinnom to
cause their sons and their daughters to pass
through *the fire* to Molech, which I had not
commanded them, nor had it come upon My
heart that they should do this abomination,
to cause Judah to sin.

36 "So now, therefore thus says Yahweh,
the God of Israel, concerning this city of
which you are saying, 'It is given into the
hand of the king of Babylon by sword, by
famine, and by pestilence.' 37 Behold, I will
gather them out of all the lands to which
I have banished them in My anger, in My
wrath, and in great indignation; and I will
cause them to return to this place and make
them inhabit *it* in safety. 38 And they shall be
My people, and I will be their God; 39 and I
will give them one heart and one way, that
they may fear Me always, for their own good
and for *the good of* their children after them.
40 And I will cut an everlasting covenant with
them that I will not turn away from them, to
do them good; and I will put the fear of Me in
their hearts so that they will not turn away
from Me. 41 And I will rejoice over them to do
them good and will truly plant them in this
land with all My heart and with all My soul.
42 For thus says Yahweh, 'Just as I brought all
this great evil on this people, so I am going to
bring on them all the good that I am prom-
ising them. 43 Thus fields will be bought in
this land of which you *all* are saying, "It is a
desolation, without man or beast; it is given
into the hand of the Chaldeans." 44 Men will
buy fields for money, sign and seal deeds, and
call in witnesses in the land of Benjamin, in
the surroundings of Jerusalem, in the cities
of Judah, in the cities of the hill country, in
the cities of the Shephelah, and in the cities
of the Negev; for I will return their fortunes,'
declares Yahweh."

Psalm 119:49–56

49 Remember the word to Your slave,
In which You have made me wait.
50 This is my comfort in my affliction,
That Your word has revived me.
51 The arrogant utterly scoff at me,
Yet I do not turn aside from Your law.
52 I have remembered Your judgments
from of old, O Yahweh,
And comfort myself.
53 Burning indignation has seized
me because of the wicked,
Who forsake Your law.
54 Your statutes have become my songs
In the house of my sojourning.
55 I remember in the night Your
name, O Yahweh,
So I keep Your law.
56 This has become mine,
That I observe Your precepts.

Proverbs 27:20

20 Sheol and Abaddon are never satisfied,
So the eyes of man are never satisfied.

1 Timothy 2:1–15

2 First of all, then, I exhort that petitions
and prayers, requests *and* thanksgiv-
ings, be made for all men, 2 for kings and

all who are in authority, so that we may lead a tranquil and quiet life in all godliness and dignity. 3 This is good and acceptable in the sight of God our Savior, 4 who desires all men to be saved and to come to the full knowledge of the truth. 5 For there is one God, *and* one mediator also between God and men, *the* man Christ Jesus, 6 who gave Himself as a ransom for all, the witness for this proper time. 7 For this I was appointed a preacher and an apostle (I am telling the truth, I am not lying) as a teacher of the Gentiles in faith and truth.

8 Therefore I want the men in every place to pray, lifting up holy hands, without wrath and dissension.

9 Likewise, *I want* women to adorn themselves with proper clothing, with modesty and self-restraint, not with braided hair and gold or pearls or costly clothing, 10 but rather by means of good works, as is proper for women professing godliness. 11 A woman must learn in quietness, in all submission. 12 But I do not allow a woman to teach or exercise authority over a man, but to remain quiet. 13 For it was Adam who was first formed, *and* then Eve. 14 And *it was* not Adam *who* was deceived, but the woman being deceived, fell into trespass. 15 But she will be saved through the bearing of children, if they continue in faith and love and sanctification with self-restraint.

OCTOBER 24

Jeremiah 33:1–34:22

33 Then the word of Yahweh came to Jeremiah the second time, while he was still confined in the court of the guard, saying, 2 "Thus says Yahweh who made *the earth*, Yahweh who formed it to establish it; Yahweh is His name, 3 'Call to Me and I will answer you, and I will tell you great and mighty things, which you do not know.' 4 For thus says Yahweh, the God of Israel, concerning the houses of this city and concerning the houses of the kings of Judah which are torn down *to make a defense* against the siege ramps and against the sword, 5 'While *they* are coming to fight with the Chaldeans and to fill them with the corpses of men whom I have struck down in My anger and in My wrath, and I have hidden My face from this city because of all their evil: 6 Behold, I will bring to it health and healing, and I will heal them; and I will reveal to them an abundance of peace and truth. 7 I will return the fortunes of Judah and the fortunes of Israel and will rebuild them as they were at first. 8 And I will cleanse them from all their iniquity by which they have sinned against Me, and I will pardon all their iniquities by which they have sinned against Me and by which they have transgressed against Me. 9 And it will be to Me a name of joy, praise, and beauty before all the nations of the earth which will hear of all the good that I do for them, and they will be in dread and tremble because of all the good and all the peace that I make for it.'

10 "Thus says Yahweh, 'Yet again there will be heard in this place, of which you say, "It is a waste, without man and without beast," *that is*, in the cities of Judah and in the streets of Jerusalem that are desolate, without man and without inhabitant and without beast, 11 the voice of joy and the voice of gladness, the voice of the bridegroom and the voice of the bride, the voice of those who say,

"Give thanks to Yahweh of hosts,
For Yahweh is good,
For His lovingkindness
endures forever";

and of those who bring a thank offering into the house of Yahweh. For I will return the fortunes of the land as they were at first,' says Yahweh.

12 "Thus says Yahweh of hosts, 'There will again be in this place which is waste, without man or beast, and in all its cities, an abode of shepherds who cause their flocks to lie down. 13 In the cities of the hill country, in the cities of the Shephelah, in the cities of the Negev, in the land of Benjamin, in the surroundings of Jerusalem, and in the cities of Judah, the flocks will again pass under the hands of the one who numbers them,' says Yahweh.

14 'Behold, days are coming,' declares Yahweh, 'when I will establish the good word which I have spoken concerning the house of Israel and the house of Judah. 15 In those days and at that time I will cause a righteous Branch of David to branch forth;

and He shall do justice and righteousness on the earth. 16 In those days Judah will be saved, and Jerusalem will dwell in security; and this is *the name* by which she will be called: Yahweh is our righteousness.' 17 For thus says Yahweh, 'David shall not have a man cut off from sitting on the throne of the house of Israel; 18 and the Levitical priests shall not have a man cut off from before Me who is to offer burnt offerings, to offer up grain offerings in smoke, and to perform sacrifices continually.'"

19 Then the word of Yahweh came to Jeremiah, saying, 20 "Thus says Yahweh, 'If you can break My covenant for the day and My covenant for the night, so that day and night will not be at their appointed time, 21 then My covenant may also be broken with David My servant so that he will not have a son to reign on his throne, and with the Levitical priests, My ministers. 22 As the host of heaven cannot be counted and the sand of the sea cannot be measured, so I will multiply the seed of David My servant and the Levites who minister to Me.'"

23 And the word of Yahweh came to Jeremiah, saying, 24 "Have you not seen what this people have spoken, saying, 'The two families which Yahweh chose, He has rejected them'? Thus they have spurned My people from being a nation any longer in their sight. 25 Thus says Yahweh, 'If My covenant *for* day and night *stand* not, *and* the statutes for heaven and earth I have not established, 26 then I would reject the seed of Jacob and David My servant, not taking from his seed rulers over the seed of Abraham, Isaac, and Jacob. But I will return their fortunes and will have compassion on them.'"

34 The word which came to Jeremiah from Yahweh, when Nebuchadnezzar king of Babylon and all his military force, with all the kingdoms of the earth that were under his dominion and all the peoples, were fighting against Jerusalem and against all its cities, saying, 2 "Thus says Yahweh, the God of Israel, 'Go and speak to Zedekiah king of Judah and say to him: "Thus says Yahweh, 'Behold, I am giving this city into the hand of the king of Babylon, and he will burn it with fire. 3 And you will not escape from his hand, for you will surely be seized and given into his hand; and you will see the king of Babylon eye to eye, and he will speak with you face to face, and you will go to Babylon.'"' 4 Yet hear the word of Yahweh, O Zedekiah king of Judah! Thus says Yahweh concerning you, 'You will not die by the sword. 5 You will die in peace; and as *spices* were burned for your fathers, the former kings who were before you, so they will burn *spices* for you; and they will lament for you, "Alas, lord!"' For I have spoken the word," declares Yahweh.

6 Then Jeremiah the prophet spoke all these words to Zedekiah king of Judah in Jerusalem 7 when the military force of the king of Babylon was fighting against Jerusalem and against all the cities of Judah that were left, *that is*, Lachish and Azekah, for they *alone* remained as fortified cities among the cities of Judah.

8 The word which came to Jeremiah from Yahweh after King Zedekiah had cut a covenant with all the people who were in Jerusalem to proclaim release to them: 9 that each man should let his male slave go free and each man his female slave, a Hebrew man or a Hebrew woman, so that no one should enslave them, each *being* a Jew, his brother. 10 And all the officials and all the people obeyed who had entered into the covenant that each man should let his male slave go free and each man his female slave, so that no one should enslave them any longer; they obeyed and let *them* go *free*. 11 But afterwards they turned around and returned *to themselves* the male slaves and the female slaves, whom they had let go as free, and subdued them to be male slaves and female slaves.

12 Then the word of Yahweh came to Jeremiah from Yahweh, saying, 13 "Thus says Yahweh, the God of Israel, 'I cut a covenant with your fathers in the day that I brought them out of the land of Egypt, from the house of slavery, saying, 14 "At the end of seven years each of you shall let his Hebrew brother go who has been sold to you and has served you six years, and you shall let him go *to be* free from you; but your fathers did not obey Me or incline their ear to Me. 15 Although recently you *had* turned and done what is right in My sight, each man proclaiming release to his neighbor, and you had cut a covenant before Me in the house which is called by My name. 16 Yet you turned and profaned My name, and

each man returned *to themselves* his male
slave and each man his female slave whom
you had let go as free according to their
desire, and you subdued them to be your
male slaves and female slaves."'
17 "Therefore thus says Yahweh, 'You have
not obeyed Me in proclaiming release each
man to his brother and each man to his
neighbor. Behold, I am proclaiming a release
to you,' declares Yahweh, 'to the sword, to
the pestilence, and to the famine; and I will
make you a terror to all the kingdoms of the
earth. 18 And I will give the men who have
trespassed against My covenant, who have
not established the words of the covenant
which they cut before Me, *when* they cut the
calf in two and passed between its parts—
19 the officials of Judah and the officials of
Jerusalem, the court officers and the priests
and all the people of the land who passed
between the parts of the calf— 20 And I will
give them into the hand of their enemies and
into the hand of those who seek their life.
And their dead bodies will be food for the
birds of the sky and the beasts of the earth.
21 And as for Zedekiah king of Judah and his
officials, I will give *them* into the hand of
their enemies and into the hand of those
who seek their life and into the hand of the
military force of the king of Babylon which
has gone away from you. 22 Behold, I am
going to command,' declares Yahweh, 'and
I will cause them to return to this city; and
they will fight against it and capture it and
burn it with fire; and I will make the cities
of Judah a desolation without inhabitant.'"

Psalm 119:57–64

57 Yahweh is my portion;
I have promised to keep Your words.
58 I have sought to please Your
face with all *my* heart;
Be gracious to me according
to Your word.
59 I thought upon my ways
And I turned my feet to
Your testimonies.
60 I hastened and did not delay
To keep Your commandments.
61 The cords of the wicked
have encircled me,
But I have not forgotten Your law.
62 At midnight I shall rise to
give thanks to You
Because of Your righteous judgments.
63 I am a companion of all
those who fear You,
And of those who keep Your precepts.
64 The earth, O Yahweh, is full of
Your lovingkindness;
Teach me Your statutes.

Proverbs 27:21

21 The refining pot is for silver
and the furnace for gold,
And each *is tested* by the
mouth that praises him.

1 Timothy 3:1–16

3 It is a trustworthy saying: if any man
aspires to the office of overseer, he
desires a good work. 2 An overseer, then,
must be above reproach, the husband of
one wife, temperate, sensible, respectable,
hospitable, able to teach, 3 not addicted
to wine or pugnacious, but considerate,
peaceable, free from the love of money;
4 leading his own household well, having
his children in submission with all dignity
5 (but if a man does not know how to lead his
own household, how will he take care of the
church of God?), 6 *and* not a new convert, so
that he will not become conceited and fall
into the condemnation of the devil. 7 And
he must have a good reputation with those
outside *the church*, so that he will not fall
into reproach and the snare of the devil.
8 Deacons likewise *must be* dignified, not
double-tongued, not indulging in much
wine, not fond of dishonest gain, 9 *but*
holding to the mystery of the faith with a
clear conscience. 10 And these men must
also first be tested; then let them serve
as deacons if they are beyond reproach.
11 Women *must* likewise *be* dignified, not
malicious gossips, but temperate, faithful
in all things. 12 Deacons must be husbands
of *only* one wife, leading *their* children and
their own households well. 13 For those
who have served well as deacons obtain
for themselves a high standing and great
boldness in the faith that is in Christ Jesus.
14 I am writing these things to you,
hoping to come to you soon, 15 but in case
I am delayed, *I write* so that you will know
how one ought to conduct himself in the
household of God, which is the church of
the living God, the pillar and support of the
truth. 16 And by common confession, great
is the mystery of godliness:

He who was manifested in the flesh,
Was vindicated in the Spirit,
Seen by angels,
Proclaimed among the nations,
Believed on in the world,
Taken up in glory.

OCTOBER 25

Jeremiah 35:1–36:32

35 The word which came to Jeremiah from Yahweh in the days of Jehoiakim the son of Josiah, king of Judah, saying, 2 "Go to the house of the Rechabites and speak to them and bring them into the house of Yahweh, into one of the chambers, and give them wine to drink." 3 Then I took Jaazaniah the son of Jeremiah, son of Habazziniah, and his brothers and all his sons and the whole house of the Rechabites, 4 and I brought them into the house of Yahweh, into the chamber of the sons of Hanan the son of Igdaliah, the man of God, which was beside the chamber of the officials, which was above the chamber of Maaseiah the son of Shallum, the doorkeeper. 5 Then I put before the men of the house of the Rechabites pitchers full of wine and cups; and I said to them, "Drink wine!" 6 But they said, "We will not drink wine, for Jonadab the son of Rechab, our father, commanded us, saying, 'You shall not drink wine, you or your sons, forever. 7 And you shall not build a house, and you shall not sow seed, and you shall not plant a vineyard or own one; but tents you shall inhabit all your days, that you may live many days in the land where you sojourn.' 8 So we have listened to the voice of Jonadab the son of Rechab, our father, in all that he commanded us, not to drink wine all our days, we, our wives, our sons, or our daughters, 9 nor to build ourselves houses to inhabit; and we do not have vineyard or field or seed. 10 We have only inhabited tents and have listened and have done according to all that Jonadab our father commanded us. 11 But it happened that when Nebuchadnezzar king of Babylon came up against the land, we said, 'Come, let us come to Jerusalem before the military force of the Chaldeans and before the military force of the Arameans.' So we have inhabited Jerusalem."

12 Then the word of Yahweh came to Jeremiah, saying, 13 "Thus says Yahweh of hosts, the God of Israel, 'Go and say to the men of Judah and the inhabitants of Jerusalem, "Will you not receive discipline by listening to My words?" declares Yahweh. 14 "The words of Jonadab the son of Rechab, which he commanded his sons, not to drink wine, are established. So they do not drink *wine* to this day, for they have listened to their father's command. But I have spoken to you, rising up early and speaking; yet you have not listened to Me. 15 Also I have sent to you all My slaves the prophets, rising up early and sending, saying: 'Turn now every man from his evil way and make good your deeds, and do not walk after other gods to serve them. Then you will inhabit the land which I have given to you and to your fathers; but you have not inclined your ear or listened to Me. 16 Indeed, the sons of Jonadab the son of Rechab have established the command of their father which he commanded them, but this people has not listened to Me.'"' 17 Therefore thus says Yahweh, the God of hosts, the God of Israel, 'Behold, I am bringing on Judah and on all the inhabitants of Jerusalem all the *harmful* evil that I have spoken against them because I spoke to them but they did not listen, and I have called them but they did not answer.'"

18 Then Jeremiah said to the house of the Rechabites, "Thus says Yahweh of hosts, the God of Israel, 'Because you have listened to the command of Jonadab your father, kept all his commands, and done according to all that he commanded you, 19 therefore thus says Yahweh of hosts, the God of Israel, "Jonadab the son of Rechab shall not have a man cut off from standing before Me always."'"

36 Now it happened that in the fourth year of Jehoiakim the son of Josiah, king of Judah, this word came to Jeremiah from Yahweh, saying, 2 "Take a scroll of a book and write on it all the words which I have spoken to you concerning Israel and concerning Judah and concerning all the nations, from the day I *first* spoke to you, from the days of Josiah, even to this day. 3 Perhaps the house of Judah will hear all

the evil which I devise to bring on them, in order that every man will turn from his evil way; then I will forgive their iniquity and their sin."

4 Then Jeremiah called Baruch the son of Neriah, and Baruch wrote on a scroll at the dictation of Jeremiah all the words of Yahweh which He had spoken to him. 5 And Jeremiah commanded Baruch, saying, "I am confined; I cannot go into the house of Yahweh. 6 So you shall go and read from the scroll, which you have written at my dictation, the words of Yahweh in the hearing of the people in the house of Yahweh on a fast day. And also you shall read them in the hearing of all *the people of* Judah who come from their cities. 7 Perhaps their supplication will come before Yahweh, and everyone will turn from his evil way, for great is the anger and the wrath that Yahweh has spoken against this people." 8 So Baruch the son of Neriah did according to all that Jeremiah the prophet commanded him, reading from the book the words of Yahweh in the house of Yahweh.

9 Now it happened in the fifth year of Jehoiakim the son of Josiah, king of Judah, in the ninth month, that all the people in Jerusalem and all the people who came from the cities of Judah to Jerusalem called for a fast before Yahweh. 10 Then Baruch read from the book the words of Jeremiah in the house of Yahweh in the chamber of Gemariah the son of Shaphan the scribe, in the upper court, at the entry of the New Gate of the house of Yahweh, in the hearing of all the people.

11 Then Micaiah the son of Gemariah, the son of Shaphan, heard all the words of Yahweh from the book. 12 And he went down to the king's house, into the scribe's chamber. And behold, all the officials were sitting there—Elishama the scribe, and Delaiah the son of Shemaiah, and Elnathan the son of Achbor, and Gemariah the son of Shaphan, and Zedekiah the son of Hananiah, and all the *other* officials. 13 And Micaiah declared to them all the words that he had heard when Baruch read from the book in the hearing of the people. 14 Then all the officials sent Jehudi the son of Nethaniah, the son of Shelemiah, the son of Cushi, to Baruch, saying, "Take in your hand the scroll from which you have read in the hearing of the people and come." So Baruch the son of Neriah took the scroll in his hand and went to them. 15 And they said to him, "Sit down, please, and read it in our hearing." So Baruch read it in their hearing. 16 Now it happened that when they heard all the words, they turned in dread one to another and said to Baruch, "We will surely declare all these words to the king." 17 And they asked Baruch, saying, "Declare to us, please, how did you write all these words? *Was it* at his dictation?" 18 Then Baruch said to them, "He dictated all these words to me, and I wrote them with ink on the book." 19 Then the officials said to Baruch, "Go, hide yourself, you and Jeremiah, and do not let anyone know where you are."

20 So they went to the king in the court, but they had deposited the scroll in the chamber of Elishama the scribe, and they declared all the words in the hearing of the king. 21 Then the king sent Jehudi to get the scroll, and he took it out of the chamber of Elishama the scribe. And Jehudi read it in the hearing of the king as well as in the hearing of all the officials who stood beside the king. 22 Now the king was sitting in the winter house in the ninth month, with *a fire* burning in the brazier before him. 23 And it happened that when Jehudi had read three or four columns, *the king* cut it with a scribe's knife and threw *it* into the fire that was in the brazier, until all the scroll was consumed in the fire that was in the brazier. 24 Yet the king and all his servants who heard all these words were not in dread, nor did they tear their garments. 25 Even though Elnathan and Delaiah and Gemariah interceded with the king not to burn the scroll, he would not listen to them. 26 And the king commanded Jerahmeel the king's son, Seraiah the son of Azriel, and Shelemiah the son of Abdeel to take Baruch the scribe and Jeremiah the prophet, but Yahweh hid them.

27 Then the word of Yahweh came to Jeremiah after the king had burned the scroll and the words which Baruch had written at the dictation of Jeremiah, saying, 28 "Take again another scroll and write on it all the former words that were on the first scroll which Jehoiakim the king of Judah burned. 29 And concerning Jehoiakim king of Judah you shall say, 'Thus says Yahweh, "You have burned this scroll, saying, 'Why have you written on it that the king of Babylon will certainly come and make this land a ruin and will make man and beast to cease from it?'" 30 Therefore

thus says Yahweh concerning Jehoiakim king of Judah, "He shall have no one to sit on the throne of David, and his dead body shall be cast out to the heat of the day and the frost of the night. 31 And I will also punish him and his seed and his servants for their iniquity, and I will bring on them and the inhabitants of Jerusalem and the men of Judah all the evil that I have spoken about to them—but they did not listen."'"

32 Then Jeremiah took another scroll and gave it to Baruch the son of Neriah, the scribe, and he wrote on it at the dictation of Jeremiah all the words of the book which Jehoiakim king of Judah had burned in the fire; and many similar words were added to them.

Psalm 119:65–72

65 You have dealt well with Your slave,
O Yahweh, according to Your word.
66 Teach me good discernment
and knowledge,
For I believe in Your commandments.
67 Before I was afflicted I went astray,
But now I keep Your word.
68 You are good and do good;
Teach me Your statutes.
69 The arrogant have smeared
me with lying;
With all *my* heart I will
observe Your precepts.
70 Their heart is covered with fat,
But I delight in Your law.
71 It is good for me that I was afflicted,
That I may learn Your statutes.
72 The law of Your mouth is better to me
Than thousands of gold
and silver *pieces*.

Proverbs 27:22

22 Though you pound an ignorant
fool in a mortar with a pestle in
the midst of crushed grain,
His folly will not turn aside from him.

1 Timothy 4:1–16

4 But the Spirit explicitly says that in later times some will fall away from the faith, paying attention to deceitful spirits and doctrines of demons, 2 by the hypocrisy of liars, who have been seared in their own conscience, 3 who forbid marriage *and advocate* abstaining from foods which God created to be shared in with thanksgiving by those who believe and know the truth. 4 For everything created by God is good, and nothing is to be rejected if it is received with thanksgiving, 5 for it is sanctified by the word of God and prayer.

6 In pointing out these things to the brothers, you will be a good servant of Christ Jesus, being nourished on the words of the faith and of the sound doctrine which you have been following. 7 But refuse godless myths fit only for old women. On the other hand, train yourself for the purpose of godliness, 8 for bodily training is only of little profit, but godliness is profitable for all things, since it holds promise for the present life and *also* for the *life* to come. 9 It is a trustworthy saying and deserving full acceptance. 10 For it is for this we labor and strive, because we have fixed our hope on the living God, who is the Savior of all men, especially of believers.

11 Command and teach these things. 12 Let no one look down on your youthfulness, but show yourself as a model to those who believe in word, conduct, love, faith, *and* purity. 13 Until I come, give attention to the public reading *of Scripture*, to exhortation and teaching. 14 Do not neglect the gift within you, which was given to you through prophetic utterance with the laying on of hands by the council of elders. 15 Take pains with these things; be *absorbed* in them, so that your progress will be evident to all. 16 Pay close attention to yourself and to your teaching; persevere in these things, for as you do this you will save both yourself and those who hear you.

OCTOBER 26

Jeremiah 37:1–38:28

37 Now Zedekiah the son of Josiah, whom Nebuchadnezzar king of Babylon had made king in the land of Judah, reigned as king in place of Coniah the son of Jehoiakim. 2 But neither he nor his servants nor the people of the land listened to the words of Yahweh which He spoke through Jeremiah the prophet.

3 Yet King Zedekiah sent Jehucal the son of Shelemiah and Zephaniah the son of Maaseiah, the priest, to Jeremiah the

prophet, saying, "Please pray to Yahweh our God on our behalf." 4 Now Jeremiah was *still* coming in and going out among the people; they had not *yet* put him in the prison. 5 Meanwhile, Pharaoh's military force had come out from Egypt; and the Chaldeans who had been besieging Jerusalem heard the report about them. So they withdrew from Jerusalem.

6 Then the word of Yahweh came to Jeremiah the prophet, saying, 7 "Thus says Yahweh, the God of Israel, 'Thus you are to say to the king of Judah, who sent you to Me to inquire of Me: "Behold, the military force of Pharaoh which has come out for your assistance is going to return to its own land of Egypt. 8 The Chaldeans will also return and fight against this city, and they will capture it and burn it with fire."' 9 Thus says Yahweh, 'Do not deceive yourselves, saying, "The Chaldeans will surely go away from us," for they will not go. 10 For even if you had struck down the entire military force of the Chaldeans who were fighting against you, and there were *only* wounded men remaining among them, each man in his tent, they would rise up and burn this city with fire.'"

11 Now it happened when the military force of the Chaldeans had withdrawn from Jerusalem because of the military force of Pharaoh, 12 that Jeremiah went out from Jerusalem to go to the land of Benjamin in order to obtain his portion of *some* property there among the people. 13 Now it happened that while he was at the Gate of Benjamin, the master of the guard whose name was Irijah the son of Shelemiah the son of Hananiah was there; and he seized Jeremiah the prophet, saying, "You are going over to the Chaldeans!" 14 But Jeremiah said, "A lie! I am not going over to the Chaldeans"; yet he would not listen to him. So Irijah seized Jeremiah and brought him to the officials. 15 Then the officials were angry at Jeremiah and struck him, and they put him in jail in the house of Jonathan the scribe because they had made *that house* into the prison. 16 For Jeremiah had come into the pit, that is, the vaulted cell; and Jeremiah stayed there many days.

17 Then King Zedekiah sent and took him *out*; and in his palace the king secretly asked him and said, "Is there a word from Yahweh?" And Jeremiah said, "There is!" Then he said, "You will be given into the hand of the king of Babylon!" 18 Moreover, Jeremiah said to King Zedekiah, "*In* what *way* have I sinned against you or against your servants or against this people, that you have put me in prison? 19 Where then are your prophets who prophesied to you, saying, 'The king of Babylon will not come against you or against this land'? 20 But now, please listen, O my lord the king; please let my supplication come before you, and do not make me return to the house of Jonathan the scribe, that I may not die there." 21 Then King Zedekiah gave commandment, and they committed Jeremiah to the court of the guard and gave him a loaf of bread daily from the bakers' street, until all the bread in the city had come to an end. So Jeremiah remained in the court of the guard.

38 And Shephatiah the son of Mattan, and Gedaliah the son of Pashhur, and Jucal the son of Shelemiah, and Pashhur the son of Malchijah heard the words that Jeremiah was speaking to all the people, saying, 2 "Thus says Yahweh, 'He who stays in this city will die by the sword and by the famine and by the pestilence, but he who goes out to the Chaldeans will live and have his *own* life as spoil and stay alive.' 3 Thus says Yahweh, 'This city will certainly be given into the hand of the military force of the king of Babylon, and he will capture it.'" 4 Then the officials said to the king, "Now let this man be put to death, inasmuch as he is making the hands of the men of war who remain in this city as well as the hands of all the people limp, by speaking such words to them; for this man is not seeking peace for this people but rather calamity." 5 So King Zedekiah said, "Behold, he is in your hands; for the king can *do* nothing against you." 6 Then they took Jeremiah and cast him into the cistern *of* Malchijah the king's son, which was in the court of the guard; and they let Jeremiah down with ropes. Now in the cistern there was no water but only mire, and Jeremiah sank into the mire. 7 But Ebed-melech the Ethiopian, a eunuch, while he was in the king's palace, heard that they had put Jeremiah into the cistern. Now the king was sitting in the Gate of Benjamin; 8 and Ebed-melech went out from the king's house and spoke to the king, saying, 9 "My lord the king, these men have done evil in all

that they have done to Jeremiah the prophet whom they have cast into the cistern; and he will die right where he is because of the famine, for there is no more bread in the city." 10 Then the king commanded Ebed-melech the Ethiopian, saying, "Take in your hand thirty men from here and bring up Jeremiah the prophet from the cistern before he dies." 11 So Ebed-melech took the men in his hand and went into the king's palace to *a place* beneath the storeroom and took from there worn-out clothes and worn-out rags and let them down by ropes into the cistern to Jeremiah. 12 Then Ebed-melech the Ethiopian said to Jeremiah, "Now put these worn-out clothes and rags under your armpits under the ropes"; and Jeremiah did so. 13 So they pulled Jeremiah up with the ropes and brought him up from the cistern, and Jeremiah stayed in the court of the guard.

14 Then King Zedekiah sent and had Jeremiah the prophet brought to him at the third entrance that is in the house of Yahweh; and the king said to Jeremiah, "I am going to ask you something; do not hide anything from me." 15 Then Jeremiah said to Zedekiah, "If I tell you, will you not certainly put me to death? Besides, if I give you counsel, you will not listen to me." 16 But King Zedekiah swore to Jeremiah in secret saying, "As Yahweh lives, who made this life for us, surely I will not put you to death, nor will I give you over to the hand of these men who are seeking your life."

17 Then Jeremiah said to Zedekiah, "Thus says Yahweh God of hosts, the God of Israel, 'If you will indeed go out to the officers of the king of Babylon, then you will live, this city will not be burned with fire, and you and your household will live. 18 But if you will not go out to the officers of the king of Babylon, then this city will be given over to the hand of the Chaldeans; and they will burn it with fire, and you yourself will not escape from their hand.'" 19 Then King Zedekiah said to Jeremiah, "I am anxious *because of* the Jews who have gone over to the Chaldeans, lest they give me over into their hand and they deal severely with me." 20 But Jeremiah said, "They will not give you over. Please listen to the voice of Yahweh in what I am saying to you, that it may go well with you and you may live. 21 But if you keep refusing to go out, this is the word which Yahweh has shown me: 22 'And behold, all of the women who have remained in the house of the king of Judah are going to be brought out to the officers of the king of Babylon; and behold, those women will say,

"Your close friends
Have misled and overpowered you;
While your feet were sunk in the mud,
They turned back."

23 'And they will also bring out all your wives and your sons to the Chaldeans, and you yourself will not escape from their hand, but will be seized by the hand of the king of Babylon, and this city will be burned with fire.'"

24 Then Zedekiah said to Jeremiah, "Let no man know about these words and you will not die. 25 But if the officials hear that I have talked with you and come to you and say to you, 'Tell us now what you said to the king and what the king said to you; do not hide *it* from us, and we will not put you to death,' 26 then you are to say to them, 'I was presenting my petition before the king, not to make me return to the house of Jonathan to die there.'" 27 Then all the officials came to Jeremiah and questioned him. So he told them in accordance with all these words which the king had commanded; and they ceased speaking with him since the conversation had not been overheard. 28 So Jeremiah stayed in the court of the guard until the day that Jerusalem was captured.

Psalm 119:73–80

73 Your hands made me and
established me;
Give me understanding, that I may
learn Your commandments.
74 May those who fear You
see me and be glad,
Because I wait for Your word.
75 I know, O Yahweh, that Your
judgments are righteous,
And that in faithfulness You
have afflicted me.
76 Oh may Your lovingkindness
comfort me,
According to Your word to Your slave.
77 May Your compassion come
to me that I may live,
For Your law is my delight.
78 May the arrogant be ashamed, for
they wrong me with lying;
But I shall muse on Your precepts.
79 May those who fear You turn to me,
And those who know Your testimonies.

80 May my heart be blameless
in Your statutes,
So that I will not be ashamed.

Proverbs 27:23–27

23 Know well the condition of your flocks,
And pay attention to your herds;
24 For wealth is not forever,
Neither is a crown from
generation to generation.
25 *When* the grass disappears and
the vegetation appears,
And the herbs of the mountains
are gathered in,
26 The lambs *will be* for your clothing,
And the goats *will bring*
the price of a field,
27 And *there will be enough* goats'
milk for your food,
For the food of your household,
And sustenance for your maidens.

1 Timothy 5:1–25

5 Do not sharply rebuke an older man,
but *rather* plead with *him* as a father,
to the younger men as brothers, 2 the older
women as mothers, *and* the younger women
as sisters, in all purity.
3 Honor widows who are widows indeed,
4 but if any widow has children or grand-
children, they must first learn to practice
piety in regard to their own family and to
make some return to their parents; for this
is acceptable in the sight of God. 5 Now she
who is a widow indeed and who has been
left alone, has fixed her hope on God and
continues in petitions and prayers night and
day. 6 But she who lives in self-indulgence is
dead even while she lives. 7 And command
these things as well, so that they may be
above reproach. 8 But if anyone does not
provide for his own, and especially for those
of his household, he has denied the faith
and is worse than an unbeliever.
9 A widow is to be put on the list only if
she is not less than sixty years old, *having
been* the wife of one man, 10 having a rep-
utation for good works; if she has brought
up children, if she has shown hospitality
to strangers, if she has washed the saints'
feet, if she has assisted those in affliction, if
she has devoted herself to every good work.
11 But refuse *to put* younger widows *on the
list*, for when they feel sensual desires in dis-
regard of Christ, they want to get married,
12 *thus* incurring condemnation, because
they have set aside their previous pledge.
13 And at the same time they also learn *to be*
idle, as they go around from house to house.
And not merely idle, but also gossips and
busybodies, talking about things not proper
to mention. 14 Therefore, I want younger
widows to get married, bear children, keep
house, *and* give the enemy no opportunity
for reviling, 15 for some have already turned
aside after Satan. 16 If any believing woman
has widows, she must assist them and the
church must not be burdened, so that it may
assist those who are widows indeed.
17 The elders who lead well are to be con-
sidered worthy of double honor, especially
those who labor at *preaching* the word
and teaching. 18 For the Scripture says,
"YOU SHALL NOT MUZZLE THE OX WHILE IT IS
THRESHING," and "THE LABORER IS WORTHY OF
HIS WAGES." 19 Do not receive an accusation
against an elder except on the basis of two
or three witnesses. 20 Those who continue in
sin, reprove in the presence of all, so that the
rest also will be fearful. 21 I solemnly charge
you in the presence of God and of Christ
Jesus and of *His* elect angels, to observe these
instructions without bias, doing nothing in
partiality. 22 Do not lay hands upon anyone
hastily and thereby share *responsibility for*
the sins of others; keep yourself pure.
23 No longer drink water *only*, but use a
little wine for the sake of your stomach and
your frequent ailments.
24 The sins of some men are quite evident,
going before them to judgment; for others,
their *sins* follow after. 25 So also good works
are quite evident, and those which are
otherwise cannot be concealed.

OCTOBER 27

Jeremiah 39:1–40:16

39 Now when Jerusalem was captured
in the ninth year of Zedekiah king of
Judah, in the tenth month, Nebuchadnezzar
king of Babylon and all his military force
came to Jerusalem and laid siege to it; 2 in
the eleventh year of Zedekiah, in the fourth
month, in the ninth *day* of the month, the

city was breached. 3 Then all the officials of the king of Babylon came in and sat down at the Middle Gate: Nergal-sar-ezer, Samgar-nebu, Sar-sekim the Rab-saris, Nergal-sar-ezer *the* Rab-mag, and all the rest of the officials of the king of Babylon. 4 Now it happened that when Zedekiah the king of Judah and all the men of war saw them, they fled and went out of the city at night by way of the king's garden through the gate between the two walls; and he went out toward the Arabah. 5 But the military force of the Chaldeans pursued them and overtook Zedekiah in the plains of Jericho; and they took him and brought him up to Nebuchadnezzar king of Babylon at Riblah in the land of Hamath, and he spoke judgment on him. 6 Then the king of Babylon slaughtered the sons of Zedekiah before his eyes at Riblah; the king of Babylon also slaughtered all the nobles of Judah. 7 He then blinded Zedekiah's eyes and bound him in fetters of bronze to bring him to Babylon. 8 The Chaldeans also burned with fire the house of the king and the houses of the people, and they tore down the walls of Jerusalem. 9 And as for the rest of the people who remained in the city, the defectors who had gone over to him and the rest of the people who remained, Nebuzaradan the captain of the bodyguard took *them* away into exile in Babylon. 10 But some of the poorest people who had nothing, Nebuzaradan the captain of the bodyguard had *them* remain in the land of Judah and gave them vineyards and fields at that time.

11 Now Nebuchadnezzar king of Babylon gave a command about Jeremiah through Nebuzaradan the captain of the bodyguard, saying, 12 "Take him and set your eyes *to look* after him and do nothing harmful to him, but rather deal with him just as he speaks to you." 13 So Nebuzaradan the captain of the bodyguard sent *word*, along with Nebushazban the Rab-saris and Nergal-sar-ezer the Rab-mag and all the leading officers of the king of Babylon; 14 they even sent and took Jeremiah out of the court of the guard and gave him over to Gedaliah, the son of Ahikam, the son of Shaphan, to take him home. So he stayed among the people.

15 Now the word of Yahweh had come to Jeremiah while he was confined in the court of the guard, saying, 16 "Go and speak to Ebed-melech the Ethiopian, saying, 'Thus says Yahweh of hosts, the God of Israel, "Behold, I am about to bring My words on this city for calamity and not for prosperity; and they will take place before you on that day. 17 But I will deliver you on that day," declares Yahweh, "and you will not be given into the hand of the men of whom you are terrified. 18 For I will certainly provide you escape, and you will not fall by the sword; but you will have your *own* life as spoil because you have trusted in Me," declares Yahweh.'"

40

The word which came to Jeremiah from Yahweh after Nebuzaradan captain of the bodyguard had released him from Ramah, when he had taken him bound in chains among all the exiles of Jerusalem and Judah who were being exiled to Babylon. 2 And the captain of the bodyguard had taken Jeremiah and said to him, "Yahweh your God promised this calamity against this place; 3 and Yahweh has brought *it* on and done just as He promised. Because you *people* sinned against Yahweh and did not listen to His voice, therefore this thing has happened to you. 4 So now, behold, I am freeing you today from the chains which are on your hands. If it is good in your eyes to come with me to Babylon, come *along*, and I will set my eyes *to look* after you; but if it is displeasing in your eyes to come with me to Babylon, never mind. Look, the whole land is before you; go wherever it seems good and right in your eyes to go." 5 But as Jeremiah had not yet *set out to* return, *he said*, "Return then to Gedaliah the son of Ahikam, the son of Shaphan, whom the king of Babylon has appointed over the cities of Judah, and stay with him among the people; or else go anywhere that is right in your eyes to go." So the captain of the bodyguard gave him a ration and a gift and let him go. 6 Then Jeremiah went to Mizpah to Gedaliah the son of Ahikam and stayed with him among the people who remained in the land.

7 Then all the commanders of the military forces that were in the field, they and their men, heard that the king of Babylon had appointed Gedaliah the son of Ahikam over the land and that he had appointed him over the men, women, little ones, and those of the poorest of the land who had not been exiled to Babylon. 8 So they came to Gedaliah at Mizpah, along with Ishmael

the son of Nethaniah, and Johanan and
Jonathan the sons of Kareah, and Seraiah
the son of Tanhumeth, and the sons of
Ephai the Netophathite, and Jezaniah the
son of the Maacathite, *both* they and their
men. 9 Then Gedaliah the son of Ahikam,
the son of Shaphan, swore to them and
to their men, saying, "Do not be afraid of
serving the Chaldeans; stay in the land and
serve the king of Babylon, that it may go
well with you. 10 Now as for me, behold, I
am going to stay at Mizpah to stand *for you*
before the Chaldeans who come to us; but
as for you, gather in wine and summer fruit
and oil and put *them* in your *storage* vessels
and stay in your cities that you have seized."
11 And also all the Jews, who were in Moab
and among the sons of Ammon and in Edom
and who were in all the *other* lands, heard
that the king of Babylon had left a remnant
for Judah and that he had appointed over
them Gedaliah the son of Ahikam, the son
of Shaphan. 12 Then all the Jews returned
from all the places to which they had been
banished and came to the land of Judah, to
Gedaliah at Mizpah, and gathered in wine
and summer fruit in great abundance.

13 Now Johanan the son of Kareah and all
the commanders of the military forces that
were in the field came to Gedaliah at Mizpah
14 and said to him, "Do you indeed know
that Baalis the king of the sons of Ammon
has sent Ishmael the son of Nethaniah
to strike down your life?" But Gedaliah
the son of Ahikam did not believe them.
15 Then Johanan the son of Kareah spoke
secretly to Gedaliah in Mizpah, saying, "Let
me go and strike down Ishmael the son of
Nethaniah, and not a man will know! Why
should he strike down your life, so that all
the Jews who are gathered to you would be
scattered and the remnant of Judah would
perish?" 16 But Gedaliah the son of Ahikam
said to Johanan the son of Kareah, "Do not
do this thing, for you are telling a lie about
Ishmael."

Psalm 119:81–88

81 My soul fails *with longing*
for Your salvation;
I wait for Your word.
82 My eyes fail *with longing*
for Your word,
Saying, "When will You comfort me?"
83 For I am like a wineskin in the smoke,
But I do not forget Your statutes.
84 How many are the days of Your slave?
When will You execute judgment
on those who persecute me?
85 The arrogant have dug pits for me,
Men who are not in accord
with Your law.
86 All Your commandments are faithful;
They have persecuted me
with lying; help me!
87 They almost made an end
of me on the earth,
But as for me, I did not
forsake Your precepts.
88 Revive me according to Your
lovingkindness,
So that I may keep the
testimony of Your mouth.

Proverbs 28:1

28 The wicked flee when there
is no one pursuing,
But the righteous are secure as a lion.

1 Timothy 6:1–21

6 All who are under the yoke as slaves are
to regard their own masters as worthy
of all honor so that the name of God and
our doctrine will not be slandered. 2 But
those who have believers as their masters
must not be disrespectful to them because
they are brothers, but must serve them all
the more, because those who partake of the
benefit are believers and beloved. Teach and
exhort these *things*.

3 If anyone teaches a different doctrine
and does not agree with sound words—
those of our Lord Jesus Christ—and with
the doctrine conforming to godliness, 4 he is
conceited, understanding nothing but having
a morbid interest in controversial questions
and disputes about words, out of which arise
envy, strife, slander, evil suspicions, 5 and
constant friction between men of depraved
mind and deprived of the truth, who sup-
pose that godliness is a means of gain. 6 But
godliness *actually* is a means of great gain,
when accompanied by contentment. 7 For we
have brought nothing into the world, so we
cannot take anything out of it either. 8 And
if we have food and covering, with these
we shall be content. 9 But those who want
to get rich fall into temptation and a snare
and many foolish and harmful desires which
plunge men into ruin and destruction. 10 For

the love of money is a root of all sorts of evils, and some by aspiring to it have wandered away from the faith and pierced themselves with many griefs.

11 But you, O man of God, flee from these things, and pursue righteousness, godliness, faith, love, perseverance, gentleness. 12 Fight the good fight of faith. Take hold of the eternal life to which you were called, and you made the good confession in the presence of many witnesses. 13 I charge you in the presence of God, who gives life to all things, and of Christ Jesus, who testified the good confession before Pontius Pilate, 14 that you keep the commandment without stain or reproach until the appearing of our Lord Jesus Christ, 15 which He will bring about at the proper time—He who is the blessed and only Sovereign, the King of kings and Lord of lords, 16 who alone has immortality and dwells in unapproachable light, whom no man has seen or can see. To Him *be* honor and eternal might! Amen.

17 Command those who are rich in this present age not to be haughty or to set their hope on the uncertainty of riches, but on God, who richly supplies us with all things to enjoy. 18 *Command them* to do good, to be rich in good works, to be generous and ready to share, 19 storing up for themselves the treasure of a good foundation for the future, so that they may take hold of that which is life indeed.

20 O Timothy, guard what has been entrusted to you, turning aside from godless *and* empty chatter *and* the opposing arguments of what is falsely called knowledge— 21 which some, while professing, have gone astray from the faith.

Grace be with you.

OCTOBER 28

Jeremiah 41:1–42:22

41 Now it happened in the seventh month, that Ishmael the son of Nethaniah, the son of Elishama, of the royal seed and *one* of the chief officers of the king, along with ten men, came to Mizpah to Gedaliah the son of Ahikam. And they were eating bread together there in Mizpah. 2 Then Ishmael the son of Nethaniah and the ten men who were with him arose and struck down Gedaliah the son of Ahikam, the son of Shaphan, with the sword and put to death the one whom the king of Babylon had appointed over the land. 3 Ishmael also struck down all the Jews who were with him, *that is* with Gedaliah at Mizpah, as well as the Chaldeans who were found there, the men of war.

4 Now it happened on the next day after putting Gedaliah to death, when no one knew about *it*, 5 that eighty men came from Shechem, from Shiloh, and from Samaria with their beards shaved off and their clothes torn and their bodies gashed, having grain offerings and frankincense in their hands to bring to the house of Yahweh. 6 Then Ishmael the son of Nethaniah went out from Mizpah to meet them, weeping as he went; and it happened that as he encountered them, he said to them, "Come to Gedaliah the son of Ahikam!" 7 But it happened that as soon as they came inside the city, Ishmael the son of Nethaniah and the men that were with him slaughtered them *and cast them* into the cistern. 8 But ten men who were found among them said to Ishmael, "Do not put us to death; for we have stores of wheat, barley, oil, and honey hidden in the field." So he refrained and did not put them to death along with their companions.

9 Now as for the cistern where Ishmael had cast all the corpses of the men whom he had struck down because of Gedaliah, it was the one that King Asa had made on account of Baasha, king of Israel; Ishmael the son of Nethaniah filled it with the slain. 10 Then Ishmael took captive all the remnant of the people who were in Mizpah, the king's daughters and all the people who remained in Mizpah, over whom Nebuzaradan the captain of the bodyguard had appointed Gedaliah the son of Ahikam; thus Ishmael the son of Nethaniah took them captive and went to cross over to the sons of Ammon.

11 But Johanan the son of Kareah and all the commanders of the military forces that were with him heard of all the evil that Ishmael the son of Nethaniah had done. 12 So they took all the men and went to fight with Ishmael the son of Nethaniah, and they found him by the great pool that

is in Gibeon. 13 Now it happened as soon as all the people who were with Ishmael saw Johanan the son of Kareah and all the commanders of the military forces that were with him, they were glad. 14 So all the people whom Ishmael had taken captive from Mizpah turned around and returned and went to Johanan the son of Kareah. 15 But Ishmael the son of Nethaniah escaped from Johanan with eight men and went to the sons of Ammon. 16 Then Johanan the son of Kareah and all the commanders of the military forces that were with him took from Mizpah all the remnant of the people whom he had returned from Ishmael the son of Nethaniah, after he had struck down Gedaliah the son of Ahikam, *that is*, the mighty men who were men of war, *the* women, *the* little ones, and *the* eunuchs, whom he had returned from Gibeon. 17 And they went and stayed in Geruth Chimham, which is beside Bethlehem, in order to proceed into Egypt 18 because of the Chaldeans; for they were afraid of them, since Ishmael the son of Nethaniah had struck down Gedaliah the son of Ahikam, whom the king of Babylon had appointed over the land.

42 Then all the commanders of the military forces, Johanan the son of Kareah, Jezaniah the son of Hoshaiah, and all the people both small and great approached 2 and said to Jeremiah the prophet, "Please let our supplication come before you, and pray for us to Yahweh your God, *that is* for all this remnant, because we remain *but* a few out of many, as your own eyes *now* see us, 3 that Yahweh your God may tell us the way in which we should walk and the thing that we should do." 4 Then Jeremiah the prophet said to them, "I have heard *you*. Behold, I am going to pray to Yahweh your God in accordance with your words; and I will tell you the whole message which Yahweh will answer you. I will not keep back a word from you." 5 And they said to Jeremiah, "May Yahweh be a true and faithful witness against us if we do not act in accordance with the whole message with which Yahweh your God will send you to us. 6 Whether *it* is good or bad, we will listen to the voice of Yahweh our God to whom we are sending you, so that good may come to us when we listen to the voice of Yahweh our God."

7 Now it happened that at the end of ten days the word of Yahweh came to Jeremiah. 8 Then he called for Johanan the son of Kareah and all the commanders of the military forces that were with him, and for all the people both small and great, 9 and said to them, "Thus says Yahweh the God of Israel, to whom you sent me to present your supplication before Him: 10 'If you will indeed stay in this land, then I will build you up and not pull you down, and I will plant you and not uproot you; for I have relented of the calamity that I have done against you. 11 Do not be afraid of the king of Babylon, whom you are *now* fearing; do not be afraid of him,' declares Yahweh, 'for I am with you to save you and deliver you from his hand. 12 I will also show you compassion, so that he will have compassion on you and return you to your own soil. 13 But if you are going to say, "We will not stay in this land," so as not to listen to the voice of Yahweh your God, 14 saying, "No, but we will go to the land of Egypt, where we will not see war or hear the sound of a trumpet or hunger for bread, and we will stay there," 15 then now, listen to the word of Yahweh, O remnant of Judah. Thus says Yahweh of hosts, the God of Israel, "If you really set your face to enter Egypt, and you will enter to sojourn there, 16 then the sword, which you are afraid of, will overtake you there in the land of Egypt; and the famine, about which you are anxious, will follow closely after you there *in* Egypt, and you will die there. 17 So all the men who set their face to go to Egypt to sojourn there will die by the sword, by the famine, and by the pestilence; and they will have no survivors or *any who* escaped from the calamity that I am going to bring on them."'"

18 For thus says Yahweh of hosts, the God of Israel, "As My anger and wrath have been poured out on the inhabitants of Jerusalem, so My wrath will be poured out on you when you enter Egypt. And you will become a curse, an object of horror, an imprecation, and a reproach; and you will see this place no more." 19 Yahweh has spoken to you, O remnant of Judah, "Do not go into Egypt!" You should clearly know that today I have testified against you. 20 For you have *only* led yourselves astray; for it is you who sent me to Yahweh your God, saying, "Pray for us to Yahweh our God; and

according to all that Yahweh our God says,
tell us so, and we will do it." 21 So I have told
you today, but you have not listened to the
voice of Yahweh your God, even according
to all that He has sent me to *tell* you. 22 So
now, you should clearly know that you
will die by the sword, by famine, and by
pestilence, in the place where you desire
to go to sojourn.

Psalm 119:89–96

89 Forever, O Yahweh,
Your word stands firm in heaven.
90 Your faithfulness *endures* from
generation to generation;
You established the earth,
and it stands.
91 They stand this day according
to Your judgments,
For all things are Your slaves.
92 If Your law had not been my delight,
Then I would have perished
in my affliction.
93 I will never forget Your precepts,
For by them You have revived me.
94 I am Yours, save me;
For I have sought Your precepts.
95 The wicked hope for me—
to destroy me;
I shall perceive Your testimonies.
96 I have seen a limit to all perfection;
Your commandment is
exceedingly broad.

Proverbs 28:2

2 By the transgression of a land
many are its princes,
But by a man who understands,
who knows, so it endures.

2 Timothy 1:1–18

1 Paul, an apostle of Christ Jesus by the will
of God, according to the promise of life
in Christ Jesus,
2 To Timothy, my beloved child: Grace,
mercy, *and* peace from God the Father and
Christ Jesus our Lord.
3 I am grateful to God, whom I serve with
a clear conscience the way my forefathers
did, as I unceasingly remember you in my
prayers night and day, 4 longing to see you,
having remembered your tears, so that I may
be filled with joy, 5 being reminded of the
unhypocritical faith within you, which first
dwelt in your grandmother Lois and your
mother Eunice, and I am convinced that *it is*
in you as well. 6 For this reason I remind you
to kindle afresh the gift of God which is in
you through the laying on of my hands. 7 For
God has not given us a spirit of timidity, but
of power and love and self-discipline.
8 Therefore do not be ashamed of either
the witness about our Lord or me His pris-
oner, but join with *me* in suffering for the
gospel according to the power of God, 9 who
has saved us and called us with a holy calling,
not according to our works, but according to
His own purpose and grace which was given
to us in Christ Jesus from all eternity, 10 but
now has been manifested by the appearing
of our Savior Christ Jesus, who abolished
death and brought life and immortality to
light through the gospel, 11 for which I was
appointed a preacher and an apostle and a
teacher. 12 For this reason I also suffer these
things, but I am not ashamed; for I know
whom I have believed and I am convinced
that He is able to guard what I have entrusted
to Him until that day. 13 Hold to the standard
of sound words which you have heard from
me, in the faith and love which are in Christ
Jesus. 14 Guard, through the Holy Spirit who
dwells in us, the treasure which has been
entrusted to *you*.
15 You are aware of this: that all who are
in Asia turned away from me, among whom
are Phygelus and Hermogenes. 16 The Lord
give mercy to the house of Onesiphorus, for
he often refreshed me and was not ashamed
of my chains, 17 but when he was in Rome,
he eagerly searched for me and found me—
18 the Lord grant to him to find mercy from
the Lord on that day—and you know very
well what services he rendered at Ephesus.

Feed on Christ, and then go and live your life, and it is Christ in you that lives your life, that helps the poor, that tells the truth, that fights the battle, and that wins the crown.

— PHILLIPS BROOKS

OCTOBER 29

Jeremiah 43:1–44:30

43 But it happened that as soon as Jer-
emiah, whom Yahweh their God had
sent, had finished speaking to all the people
all the words of Yahweh their God—that
is, all these words— 2 Azariah the son of
Hoshaiah, and Johanan the son of Kareah,
and all the arrogant men said to Jeremiah,
"You are speaking a lie! Yahweh our God
has not sent you to say, 'You are not to enter
Egypt to sojourn there'; 3 but Baruch the
son of Neriah is inciting you against us to
give us over into the hand of the Chaldeans,
so they will put us to death or exile us to
Babylon." 4 So Johanan the son of Kareah
and all the commanders of the military
forces and all the people did not listen to
the voice of Yahweh to stay in the land of
Judah. 5 But Johanan the son of Kareah and
all the commanders of the military forces
took the entire remnant of Judah, who had
returned from all the nations to which they
had been banished, in order to sojourn in
the land of Judah— 6 the men, the women,
the little ones, the king's daughters, and
every person that Nebuzaradan the captain
of the bodyguard had left with Gedaliah the
son of Ahikam and grandson of Shaphan,
together with Jeremiah the prophet and
Baruch the son of Neriah— 7 and they
entered the land of Egypt (for they did not
listen to the voice of Yahweh) and went in
as far as Tahpanhes.

8 Then the word of Yahweh came to Jer-
emiah in Tahpanhes, saying, 9 "Take *some*
large stones in your hands and hide them in
the mortar in the brick *terrace* which is at
the entrance of Pharaoh's house in Tahpan-
hes, in the sight of some *of the* Jews; 10 and
you will say to them, 'Thus says Yahweh of
hosts, the God of Israel, "Behold, I am going
to send and get Nebuchadnezzar the king
of Babylon, My servant, and I am going to
set his throne *right* over these stones that I
have hidden; and he will spread his canopy
over them. 11 He will also come and strike
the land of Egypt; those who are *meant* for
death *will be given over* to death, and those
for captivity to captivity, and those for the
sword to the sword. 12 And I shall set fire
to the houses of the gods of Egypt, and he
will burn them and take them captive. So
he will wrap himself with the land of Egypt
as a shepherd wraps himself with his gar-
ment, and he will depart from there safely.
13 He will also shatter the *sacred* pillars of
Heliopolis, which is in the land of Egypt; and
the houses of the gods of Egypt he will burn
with fire."'"

44 The word that came to Jeremiah
for all the Jews living in the land of
Egypt, those who were living in Migdol, Tah-
panhes, Memphis, and the land of Pathros,
saying, 2 "Thus says Yahweh of hosts, the
God of Israel, 'You yourselves have seen all
the evil that I have brought on Jerusalem
and all the cities of Judah; and behold, this
day they are a waste place and no one lives
in them 3 because of their evil which they
did so as to provoke Me to anger by con-
tinuing to burn incense *and* to serve other
gods whom they had not known, *neither*
they, you, nor your fathers. 4 Yet I sent you
all My slaves the prophets, rising up early
and sending, saying, "Oh, do not do this
abominable thing which I hate." 5 But they
did not listen or incline their ears to turn
from their evil, so as not to burn incense to
other gods. 6 Therefore My wrath and My
anger were poured out and burned in the
cities of Judah and in the streets of Jerusa-
lem, so they have become a waste place and
a desolation as it is this day. 7 So now, thus
says Yahweh, the God of hosts, the God of
Israel, "Why are you doing great evil against
yourselves, so as to cut off from you man
and woman, infant and nursing baby, from
among Judah, leaving yourselves without
remnant, 8 provoking Me to anger with the
works of your hands, burning incense to
other gods in the land of Egypt, where you
are entering to sojourn, so that you might
be cut off and become an imprecation and a
reproach among all the nations of the earth?
9 Have you forgotten the evil of your fathers,
the evil of the kings of Judah, and the evil
of their wives, your own evil, and the evil
of your wives, which they did in the land of
Judah and in the streets of Jerusalem? 10 But
they have not become contrite even to this
day, nor have they feared nor walked in My
law or My statutes, which I have put before
you and before your fathers."'

11 “Therefore thus says Yahweh of hosts,
the God of Israel, ‘Behold, I am going to set
My face against you for *your* evil *demise*,
even to cut off all Judah. 12 And I will take
away the remnant of Judah who have set
their face on entering the land of Egypt to
sojourn there, and they will all meet their
end in the land of Egypt; they will fall by
the sword *and* meet their end by famine.
Both small and great will die by the sword
and famine; and they will become a curse,
an object of horror, an imprecation, and a
reproach. 13 And I will punish those who
live in the land of Egypt, as I have punished
Jerusalem, with the sword, with famine,
and with pestilence. 14 So there will be no
one who escapes or *any* survivors for the
remnant of Judah who have entered the
land of Egypt to sojourn there and then to
return to the land of Judah, to which they
are longing to return to live; for none will
return except *a few* who escape.’”

15 Then all the men who knew that
their wives were burning incense to other
gods, along with all the women who were
standing by, *as* a large assembly, including
all the people who were living in Pathros in
the land of Egypt, answered to Jeremiah,
saying, 16 “As for the message that you have
spoken to us in the name of Yahweh, we
are not going to listen to you! 17 But rather
we will certainly carry out every word
that has proceeded from our mouths, by
burning incense to the queen of heaven and
pouring out drink offerings to her, just as we
ourselves, our fathers, our kings, and our
princes did in the cities of Judah and in the
streets of Jerusalem; for *then* we had plenty
of food and were well off and saw no evil.
18 But since we stopped burning incense to
the queen of heaven and pouring out drink
offerings to her, we have lacked everything
and have met our end by the sword and by
famine.” 19 “And,” *said the women*, “when
we were burning incense to the queen of
heaven and were pouring out drink offerings
to her, was it without our husbands that we
made for her *sacrificial* cakes in her image
and poured out drink offerings to her?”

20 Then Jeremiah said to all the people,
to the men and women—even to all the
people who were answering him with *such*
a word—saying, 21 “As for the smoking sac-
rifices that you offered in the cities of Judah
and in the streets of Jerusalem, you and
your fathers, your kings and your princes,
and the people of the land, did not Yahweh
remember them and did not *all this* come
upon His heart? 22 So Yahweh was no longer
able to bear *it*, because of the evil of your
deeds, because of the abominations which
you have done; thus your land has become
a waste place, an object of horror, and an
imprecation, without an inhabitant, as *it is*
this day. 23 Because you have burned incense
and have sinned against Yahweh and not
listened to the voice of Yahweh or walked
in His law, His statutes, or His testimonies,
therefore this evil has befallen you, as *it has*
this day.”

24 Then Jeremiah said to all the people,
including all the women, “Hear the word
of Yahweh, all Judah who are in the land
of Egypt, 25 thus says Yahweh of hosts, the
God of Israel, saying: ‘As for you and your
wives, you have spoken with your mouths
and fulfilled *it* with your hands, saying, “We
will certainly perform our vows that we have
vowed, to burn incense to the queen of
heaven and pour out drink offerings to her.”
Go ahead and establish your vows, and cer-
tainly perform your vows!’ 26 Nevertheless,
hear the word of Yahweh, all Judah who are
living in the land of Egypt, ‘Behold, I have
sworn by My great name,’ says Yahweh,
‘never shall My name be called upon again
by the mouth of any man of Judah in all
the land of Egypt, saying, “As Lord Yahweh
lives.” 27 Behold, I am watching over them
for evil and not for good, and all the men of
Judah who are in the land of Egypt will meet
their end by the sword and by famine until
they are completely consumed. 28 Those
who escape the sword will return out of
the land of Egypt to the land of Judah few
in number. Then all the remnant of Judah
who have gone to the land of Egypt to
sojourn there will know whose word will
be established, Mine or theirs. 29 This will
be the sign to you,’ declares Yahweh, ‘that
I am going to punish you in this place, so
that you may know that My words will surely
be established against you for evil.’ 30 Thus
says Yahweh, ‘Behold, I am going to give over
Pharaoh Hophra king of Egypt to the hand of
his enemies, to the hand of those who seek
his life, just as I gave over Zedekiah king of
Judah to the hand of Nebuchadnezzar king
of Babylon, *who was* his enemy and was
seeking his life.’”

Psalm 119:97–104

97 Oh how I love Your law!
It is my meditation all the day.
98 Your commandments make me
wiser than my enemies,
For they are mine forever.
99 I have more insight than
all my teachers,
For Your testimonies are
my meditation.
100 I perceive more than the aged,
Because I have observed
Your precepts.
101 I have restrained my feet
from every evil way,
That I may keep Your word.
102 I have not turned aside from
Your judgments,
For You Yourself have taught me.
103 How sweet is Your word to my taste!
Sweeter than honey to my mouth!
104 From Your precepts I get perception;
Therefore I hate every false way.

Proverbs 28:3

3 A poor man who oppresses the lowly
Is a driving rain which leaves no food.

2 Timothy 2:1–26

2 You therefore, my child, be strong in
the grace that is in Christ Jesus. 2 And
the things which you have heard from me
in the presence of many witnesses, entrust
these to faithful men who will be able to
teach others also. 3 Suffer hardship with
me, as a good soldier of Christ Jesus. 4 No
soldier in active service entangles himself
in the affairs of everyday life, so that he
may please the one who enlisted him as
a soldier. 5 And also if anyone competes
as an athlete, he is not crowned unless
he competes according to the rules. 6 The
hard-working farmer ought to be the first to
receive his share of the crops. 7 Understand
what I say, for the Lord will give you insight
in everything.

8 Remember Jesus Christ, risen from the
dead, of the seed of David, according to my
gospel, 9 for which I endure hardship even
to chains as a criminal. But the word of God
has not been chained. 10 For this reason I
endure all things for the sake of the elect,
so that they also may obtain the salvation,
which is in Christ Jesus, with eternal glory.
11 It is a trustworthy saying:

For if we died with Him,
we will also live with Him;
12 If we endure, we will also
reign with Him;
If we will deny Him,
He also will deny us;
13 If we are faithless, He remains faithful,
for He cannot deny Himself.

14 Remind *them* of these things, solemnly
charging *them* in the presence of God not to
dispute about words, which is useless *and
leads* to the ruin of the hearers. 15 Be diligent
to present yourself approved to God as a
workman who does not need to be ashamed,
accurately handling the word of truth. 16 But
avoid godless *and* empty chatter, for it will
lead to further ungodliness, 17 and their
word will spread like gangrene. Among
them are Hymenaeus and Philetus, 18 who
have gone astray from the truth saying that
the resurrection has already taken place,
and they upset the faith of some. 19 Never-
theless, the firm foundation of God stands,
having this seal, "THE LORD KNOWS THOSE
WHO ARE HIS," and, "EVERYONE WHO NAMES
THE NAME OF THE LORD IS TO DEPART FROM
WICKEDNESS."

20 Now in a large house there are not only
gold and silver vessels, but also vessels of
wood and of clay, and some to honor and
some to dishonor. 21 Therefore, if anyone
cleanses himself from these *things*, he will
be a vessel for honor, sanctified, useful to
the Master, having been prepared for every
good work. 22 Now flee from youthful lusts
and pursue righteousness, faith, love, *and*
peace, with those who call on the Lord
from a pure heart. 23 But refuse foolish and
ignorant speculations, knowing that they
produce quarrels. 24 And the Lord's slave
must not be quarrelsome, but be kind to
all, able to teach, patient when wronged,
25 with gentleness correcting those who are
in opposition, if perhaps God may give them
repentance leading to the full knowledge
of the truth, 26 and they may come to their
senses *and escape* from the snare of the
devil, having been held captive by him to
do his will.

OCTOBER 30

Jeremiah 45:1–46:28

45 *This is* the message which Jeremiah
the prophet spoke to Baruch the son
of Neriah, when he had written down these
words in a book at Jeremiah's dictation, in
the fourth year of Jehoiakim the son of
Josiah, king of Judah, saying: 2 "Thus says
Yahweh the God of Israel to you, O Baruch:
3 'You said, "Ah, woe is me! For Yahweh has
added sorrow to my pain; I am weary with
my sighing and have found no rest."' 4 Thus
you are to say to him, 'Thus says Yahweh,
"Behold, what I have built I am about to pull
down, and what I have planted I am about
to uproot, that is, the whole land." 5 But as
for you, are you seeking great things for
yourself? Do not seek *them*; for behold, I am
going to bring calamity on all flesh,' declares
Yahweh, 'but I will give your life to you as
spoil in all the places where you may go.'"

46 That which came as the word of
Yahweh to Jeremiah the prophet
concerning the nations.

2 To Egypt, concerning the military force
of Pharaoh Neco king of Egypt, which was
by the Euphrates River at Carchemish,
which Nebuchadnezzar king of Babylon
struck down in the fourth year of Jehoiakim
the son of Josiah, king of Judah:

3 "Arrange the shield and large shield,
And draw near for the battle!
4 "Harness the horses,
And mount the steeds,
And take your stand with helmets *on*!
Polish the spears,
Put on the scale-armor!
5 "Why have I seen *it*?
They are shattered;
They are drawing back,
And their mighty men are crushed
And have fled to refuge,
Without facing back;
Terror is on every side!"
Declares Yahweh.
6 Let not the swift man flee,
Nor the mighty man escape;
In the north beside the river Euphrates
They have stumbled and fallen.
7 Who is this that rises like the Nile,
Like the rivers whose
waters toss about?
8 Egypt rises like the Nile,
Even like the rivers whose
waters toss about;
And He has said, "I will rise
and cover *that* land;
I will surely cause the city to perish,
as well as its inhabitants."
9 Go up, you horses, and drive
madly, you chariots,
That the mighty men may go forth:
Ethiopia and Put, who seize the shield,
And the Lydians, who seize
and bend the bow.
10 Indeed, that day belongs to
Lord Yahweh of hosts,
A day of vengeance, so as to avenge
Himself on His adversaries;
And the sword will devour
and be satiated
And drink its fill of their blood;
For there will be a sacrifice to
Lord Yahweh of hosts
In the land of the north by
the river Euphrates.
11 Go up to Gilead and obtain balm,
O virgin daughter of Egypt!
In vain have you multiplied remedies;
There is no healing for you.
12 The nations have heard
of your disgrace,
And the earth is full of your outcry;
For one warrior has stumbled
over another,
And both of them have
fallen down together.

13 *This is* the message which Yahweh
spoke to Jeremiah the prophet about the
coming of Nebuchadnezzar king of Babylon
to strike down the land of Egypt:

14 "Declare in Egypt and cause *it*
to be heard in Migdol;
Cause *it* to be heard also in
Memphis and Tahpanhes;
Say, 'Take your stand and
get yourself ready,
For the sword has devoured
those around you.'
15 "Why are your mighty ones
thrown down?
They do not stand because Yahweh
has thrust them down.
16 "They have repeatedly stumbled;

Indeed, they have fallen
one against another.
Then they said, 'Rise up!
And let us return
To our own people and
land of our birth
Away from the sword of the oppressor.'
17 "They called out there, 'Pharaoh
king of Egypt *is but* a rumbling;
He has let the appointed time pass by!'
18 "As I live," declares the King
Whose name is Yahweh of hosts,
"Surely one shall come *who looms up*
like Tabor among the mountains,
Or like Carmel by the sea.
19 "Make your baggage ready for exile,
O inhabitant of the daughter of Egypt,
For Memphis will become a desolation;
It will even be turned into ruin
and without inhabitants.
20 "Egypt is a pretty heifer,
But a horsefly is coming from
the north—it is coming!
21 "Also her mercenaries in her midst
Are like fattened calves,
For even they have turned back
and have fled away together;
They did not stand *their ground.*
For the day of their disaster
has come upon them,
The time of their punishment.
22 "Its sound moves along like a serpent;
For they move on like a military force
And come to her as
woodcutters with axes.
23 "They have cut down her
forest," declares Yahweh;
"Surely it will no *longer* be searched out,
Even though they are *now* more
numerous than locusts
And are without number.
24 "The daughter of Egypt has
been put to shame,
Given over to the hand of the
people of the north."

25 Yahweh of hosts, the God of Israel, says,
"Behold, I am going to punish Amon of The-
bes, and Pharaoh, and Egypt along with her
gods and her kings, even Pharaoh and those
who trust in him. 26 I shall give them into the
hand of those who are seeking their lives,
even into the hand of Nebuchadnezzar king
of Babylon and into the hand of his servants.
Afterwards, however, it will be dwelt in like
in the days of old," declares Yahweh.

27 "But as for you, O Jacob My
servant, do not fear,
Nor be dismayed, O Israel!
For behold, I am going to
save you from afar,
And your seed from the land
of their captivity;
And Jacob will return and have quiet
And be at ease, with no one
making *him* tremble.
28 "O Jacob My servant, do not
fear," declares Yahweh,
"For I am with you.
For I will make a complete
destruction of all the nations
Where I have banished you,
Yet I will not make a complete
destruction of you;
But I will discipline you with justice
And by no means leave
you unpunished."

Psalm 119:105–112

105 Your word is a lamp to my feet
And a light to my path.
106 I have sworn and I have confirmed,
To keep Your righteous judgments.
107 I am exceedingly afflicted;
O Yahweh, revive me according
to Your word.
108 Oh be pleased with the freewill
offerings of my mouth, O Yahweh,
And teach me Your judgments.
109 My soul is continually in my hand,
Yet I do not forget Your law.
110 The wicked have laid a snare for me,
Yet I have not wandered
from Your precepts.
111 I have inherited Your
testimonies forever,
For they are the joy of my heart.
112 I have inclined my heart
to do Your statutes
Forever, to the end.

Proverbs 28:4

4 Those who forsake the law
praise the wicked,
But those who keep the law
strive with them.

2 Timothy 3:1–17

3 But know this, that in the last days
difficult times will come. 2 For men will
be lovers of self, lovers of money, boastful,

arrogant, blasphemers, disobedient to
parents, ungrateful, unholy, 3 unloving,
irreconcilable, malicious gossips, without
self-control, without gentleness, without
love for good, 4 treacherous, reckless, con-
ceited, lovers of pleasure rather than lovers
of God, 5 holding to a form of godliness, but
having denied its power. Keep away from
such men as these. 6 For among them are
those who enter into households and take
captive weak women weighed down with
sins, being led on by various desires, 7 always
learning and never able to come to the full
knowledge of the truth. 8 Just as Jannes and
Jambres opposed Moses, so these *men* also
oppose the truth, men of depraved mind,
disqualified in regard to the faith. 9 But they
will not make further progress, for their folly
will be obvious to all, just as theirs was also.
10 But you followed my teaching, conduct,
purpose, faith, patience, love, perseverance,
11 persecutions, *and* sufferings, such as
happened to me at Antioch, at Iconium,
and at Lystra. What persecutions I endured,
and out of them all the Lord rescued me!
12 Indeed, all who desire to live godly in
Christ Jesus will be persecuted.
13 But evil men and impostors will pro-
ceed *from bad* to worse, deceiving and being
deceived.
14 But you, continue in the things you
learned and became convinced of, knowing
from whom you learned *them*, 15 and that
from childhood you have known the sacred
writings which are able to make you wise
unto salvation through faith which is in
Christ Jesus. 16 All Scripture is God-breathed
and profitable for teaching, for reproof, for
correction, for training in righteousness,
17 so that the man of God may be equipped,
having been thoroughly equipped for every
good work.

OCTOBER 31

Jeremiah 47:1–48:47

47 That which came as the word of
Yahweh to Jeremiah the prophet
concerning the Philistines, before Pharaoh
struck down Gaza. 2 Thus says Yahweh:

“Behold, waters are going to
rise from the north
And become an overflowing torrent,
And overflow the land as
well as its fullness,
The city and those who inhabit it;
And the men will cry out,
And every inhabitant of
the land will wail.

3 “Because of the noise of the galloping
hoofs of his valiant steeds,
The quaking of his chariots, *and*
the tumult of his wheels,
The fathers have not turned
back for *their* children,
Because of the limpness
of *their* hands,

4 On account of the day that is coming
To destroy all the Philistines,
To cut off from Tyre and Sidon
Every ally that is left;
For Yahweh is going to
destroy the Philistines,
The remnant of the
coastland of Caphtor.

5 “Baldness has come upon Gaza;
Ashkelon has been ruined.
O remnant of their valley,
How long will you gash yourself?

6 “Ah, sword of Yahweh,
How long will you not be quiet?
Withdraw into your sheath;
Be at rest and stay still.

7 “How can it be quiet?
Yahweh has given it a command;
Against Ashkelon and against
the seacoast—
There He has assigned it.”

48 Concerning Moab. Thus says Yahweh
of hosts, the God of Israel,

“Woe to Nebo, for it has been destroyed;
Kiriathaim has been put to shame,
it has been captured;
The lofty stronghold has been
put to shame and shattered.

2 “There is praise for Moab no longer;
In Heshbon they have devised
calamity against her:
‘Come and let us cut her off
from *being* a nation!’
You too, Madmen, will be silenced;
The sword will follow after you.

3 “The sound of an outcry
from Horonaim,

'Devastation and great destruction!'
4 "Moab is broken;
Her little ones have made *their*
cry *of distress* heard.
5 "For by the ascent of Luhith
They will ascend with
continual weeping;
For at the descent of Horonaim
They have heard the distressed
cry of destruction.
6 "Flee, escape with your lives,
That you may be like a juniper
in the wilderness.
7 "For because of your trust in your
own works and treasures,
Even you yourself will be captured;
And Chemosh will go off into exile
Together with his priests
and his princes.
8 "A destroyer will come to every city,
So that no city will escape;
The valley also will perish,
And the plateau will be destroyed,
As Yahweh has said.
9 "Give wings to Moab,
For she will flee away;
And her cities will become
a desolation,
Without inhabitants in them.
10 "Cursed be the one who does the work
of Yahweh with a slack *hand*,
And cursed be the one who
restrains his sword from blood.

11 "Moab has been at ease since
his youth;
He has also had quiet, *like*
wine on its dregs,
And he has not been emptied
from vessel to vessel,
Nor has he gone into exile.
Therefore he retains his flavor,
And his aroma has not changed.
12 "Therefore behold, the days are coming,"
declares Yahweh, "when I will send to him
those who tip *vessels*, and they will tip
him over, and they will empty his vessels
and shatter his jars. 13 And Moab will be
ashamed of Chemosh, as the house of Israel
was ashamed of Bethel, their trust.
14 "How can you say, 'We are
mighty warriors,
And men valiant for battle'?
15 "Moab has been destroyed, and men
have gone up to his cities;
His choicest young men have also
gone down to the slaughter,"
Declares the King, whose name
is Yahweh of hosts.
16 "The disaster of Moab will soon come,
And his calamity has quickly hastened.
17 "Mourn for him, all you who
live around him,
Even all of you who know his name;
Say, 'How has the strong
scepter been broken,
A staff of beauty!'
18 "Come down from your glory
And inhabit the parched ground,
O inhabitant of the daughter of Dibon;
For the destroyer of Moab has
come up against you,
He has ruined your strongholds.
19 "Stand by the road and keep watch,
O inhabitant of Aroer;
Ask him who flees and
her who escapes
And say, 'What has happened?'
20 "Moab has been put to shame,
for it has been shattered.
Wail and cry out;
Declare by the Arnon
That Moab has been destroyed.
21 "Judgment has also come upon the
plain, upon Holon, upon Jahzah, and against
Mephaath, 22 and against Dibon, Nebo, and
Beth-diblathaim, 23 and against Kiriathaim,
Beth-gamul, and Beth-meon, 24 and against
Kerioth, Bozrah, and all the cities of the land
of Moab, far and near. 25 The horn of Moab
has been cut in pieces and his arm broken,"
declares Yahweh. 26 "Make him drunk, for he
has magnified *himself* against Yahweh; so
Moab will wallow in his vomit, and he also will
become a laughingstock. 27 Now was not Israel
a laughingstock to you? Or was he caught
among thieves? For each time you speak
about him you shake *your head in scorn*.
28 "Leave the cities and dwell
among the crags,
O inhabitants of Moab,
And be like a dove that nests
Beyond the mouth of the chasm.
29 "We have heard of the pride of
Moab—he *is* very proud—
Of his haughtiness, his pride,
his arrogance, and the
exaltedness of his heart.
30 "I know his fury," declares Yahweh,
"But it is nothing;

His idle boasts have
accomplished nothing.
31 "Therefore I will wail for Moab,
Even for all Moab will I cry out;
I will moan for the men of Kir-heres.
32 "More than the weeping for Jazer
I will weep for you, O vine of Sibmah!
Your branches stretched across the sea,
They reached to the sea of Jazer;
Upon your summer fruits and
your grape harvest
The destroyer has fallen.
33 "So gladness and joy are gathered up
From the fruitful orchard, even
from the land of Moab.
And I have made the wine to
cease from the wine presses;
No one will tread *them* with shouting,
The shouting will not be shouts *of joy*.
34 "From the outcry at Heshbon even to
Elealeh, even to Jahaz they have given forth
their voice, from Zoar even to Horonaim
and to Eglath-shelishiyah; for even the
waters of Nimrim will become desolate. 35 I
will make Moab cease," declares Yahweh,
"the one who offers *offerings* on the high
place and the one who offers *offerings* in
smoke to his gods.
36 "Therefore My heart moans for Moab
like flutes; My heart also moans like flutes
for the men of Kir-heres. Therefore they
have lost the abundance it produced. 37 For
every head is bald and every beard cut
short; there are gashes on all the hands and
sackcloth on the loins. 38 On all the rooftops
of Moab and in its open squares there is
lamentation everywhere; for I have broken
Moab like an undesirable vessel," declares
Yahweh. 39 "How shattered it is! *How* they
have wailed! How Moab has turned his
back—he is ashamed! So Moab will become
a laughingstock and an object of terror to
all around him."

40 For thus says Yahweh:
"Behold, one will swoop like an eagle
And spread out his wings
against Moab.
41 "Kerioth has been captured,
And the strongholds have been seized,
So the hearts of the mighty
men of Moab in that day
Will be like the heart of a
woman in labor.
42 "Moab will be destroyed
from *being* a people
Because he has magnified
himself against Yahweh.
43 "Panic and pit and pitfall are
coming upon you,
O inhabitant of Moab,"
declares Yahweh.
44 "The one who flees from the panic
Will fall into the pit,
And the one who climbs
up out of the pit
Will be caught in the pitfall;
For I shall bring upon her,
even upon Moab,
The year of their punishment,"
declares Yahweh.

45 "In the shadow of Heshbon
Those who flee stand without strength;
For a fire has gone forth from Heshbon
And a flame from the midst of Sihon,
And it has devoured the top
of the head of Moab
And the scalps of those who rumble.
46 "Woe to you, Moab!
The people of Chemosh have perished;
For your sons have been
taken away captive
And your daughters into captivity.
47 "Yet I will return the fortunes of Moab
In the last days," declares Yahweh.
Thus far the judgment on Moab.

Psalm 119:113–120

113 I hate those who are double-minded,
But I love Your law.
114 You are my hiding place and my shield;
I wait for Your word.
115 Depart from me, evildoers,
That I may observe the
commandments of my God.
116 Sustain me according to Your
word, that I may live;
And do not put me to shame
because of my hope.
117 Uphold me that I may be saved,
That I may have regard for Your
statutes continually.
118 You have rejected all those who
stray from Your statutes,
For their deceitfulness is a lie.
119 You remove all the wicked of
the earth *like* dross;
Therefore I love Your testimonies.
120 My flesh quakes for dread of You,
And I am afraid of Your judgments.

Proverbs 28:5

5 Evil men do not understand justice,
But those who seek Yahweh
understand all things.

2 Timothy 4:1–22

4 I solemnly charge *you* in the presence of
God and of Christ Jesus, who is to judge
the living and the dead, and by His appearing
and His kingdom: 2 preach the word; be ready
in season *and* out of season; reprove, rebuke,
exhort, with great patience and teaching.
3 For the time will come when they will not
endure sound doctrine, but *wanting* to have
their ears tickled, they will accumulate for
themselves teachers in accordance to their
own desires, 4 and will turn away their ears
from the truth and will turn aside to myths.
5 But you, be sober in all things, endure
hardship, do the work of an evangelist,
fulfill your ministry.

6 For I am already being poured out as a
drink offering, and the time of my departure
has come. 7 I have fought the good fight, I
have finished the course, I have kept the
faith. 8 In the future there is laid up for me
the crown of righteousness, which the Lord,
the righteous Judge, will award to me on that
day, and not only to me, but also to all who
have loved His appearing.

9 Be diligent to come to me soon, 10 for
Demas, having loved this present age, has
deserted me and gone to Thessalonica;
Crescens *has gone* to Galatia, Titus to
Dalmatia. 11 Only Luke is with me. Pick
up Mark and bring him with you, for he is
useful to me for service. 12 But Tychicus I
sent to Ephesus. 13 When you come bring
the cloak which I left at Troas with Carpus,
and the scrolls, especially the parchments.
14 Alexander the coppersmith showed me
much harm; the Lord will award him accord-
ing to his deeds. 15 Be on guard against him
yourself, for he vigorously opposed our
words.

16 At my first defense no one supported
me, but all deserted me. May it not be
counted against them. 17 But the Lord stood
with me and strengthened me, so that
through me the preaching might be ful-
filled, and that all the Gentiles might hear.
And I was rescued out of the lion's mouth.
18 The Lord will rescue me from every evil
deed, and will save me unto His heavenly
kingdom; to Him *be* the glory forever and
ever. Amen.

19 Greet Prisca and Aquila, and the house-
hold of Onesiphorus. 20 Erastus remained
at Corinth, but Trophimus I left sick at
Miletus. 21 Be diligent to come before winter.
Eubulus greets you, also Pudens and Linus
and Claudia and all the brothers.

22 The Lord be with your spirit. Grace be
with all of you.

NOVEMBER 1

Jeremiah 49:1–50:46

49 Concerning the sons of Ammon.
Thus says Yahweh:
"Does Israel have no sons?
Or has he no one who can
take possession?
Why then has Malcam taken
possession of Gad
And his people settled in its cities?
2 "Therefore behold, the days are
coming," declares Yahweh,
"That I will cause a trumpet
blast of war to be heard
Against Rabbah of the sons of Ammon;
And it will become a desolate heap,
And her towns will be set on fire.
Then Israel will take possession
of his possessors,"
Says Yahweh.
3 "Wail, O Heshbon, for Ai has
been destroyed!
Cry out, O daughters of Rabbah,
Gird yourselves with
sackcloth and lament,
And rush back and forth
inside the walls;
For Malcam will go into exile
Together with his priests
and his princes.
4 "How boastful you are
about the valleys!
Your valley is flowing *away*,
O faithless daughter
Who trusts in her treasures, *saying*,
'Who will come against me?'
5 "Behold, I am going to bring
dread upon you,"
Declares Lord Yahweh of hosts,

"From all around you;
And each of you will be
banished headlong,
With no one to gather the
one who flees.
6 "But afterward I will return
The fortunes of the sons of Ammon,"
Declares Yahweh.
7 Concerning Edom.
Thus says Yahweh of hosts,
"Is there no longer any
wisdom in Teman?
Has counsel been lost to
the understanding?
Has their wisdom decayed?
8 "Flee away, turn back,
inhabit the depths,
O inhabitants of Dedan,
For I will bring the disaster
of Esau upon him
At the time I punish him.
9 "If grape gatherers came to you,
Would they not have
gleanings remain?
If thieves *came* by night,
They would ruin *only* until
they had enough.
10 "But I have stripped Esau bare;
I have uncovered his hiding places,
So that he will not be able
to conceal himself;
His seed has been destroyed
along with his relatives
And his neighbors, and he is no more.
11 "Leave your orphans behind,
I will keep *them* alive;
And let your widows trust in Me."
12 For thus says Yahweh, "Behold, those
who are not *under* judgment to drink the
cup will certainly drink *it*, but are you the
one who will go completely unpunished?
You will not go unpunished, but you will
certainly drink *it*. 13 For I have sworn by
Myself," declares Yahweh, "that Bozrah will
become an object of horror, a reproach, a
ruin, and an imprecation; and all its cities
will become perpetual ruins."
14 I have heard a message from Yahweh,
And an envoy is sent among
the nations, *saying*,
"Gather yourselves together
and come against her,
And rise up for battle!"
15 "For behold, I have made you
small among the nations,
Despised among men.
16 "As for the terror of you,
The arrogance of your heart
has deceived you,
O you who dwell in the
clefts of the rock,
Who seize the height of the hill.
Though you make your nest
as high as an eagle's,
I will bring you down from
there," declares Yahweh.
17 "Edom will become an object of horror;
everyone who passes by it will be horrified
and will hiss at all its wounds. 18 Like the
overthrow of Sodom and Gomorrah with
its neighbors," says Yahweh, "no one will
live there, nor will a son of man sojourn in
it. 19 Behold, one will come up like a lion from
the thickets of the Jordan against an enduring
pasture; for in an instant I will make him run
away from it, and whoever is chosen I shall
appoint over it. For who is like Me, and who
will summon Me *into court*? And who then
is the shepherd who can stand against Me?"
20 Therefore hear the counsel of Yahweh
which He has counseled against Edom, and
His purposes which He has purposed against
the inhabitants of Teman: surely they will
drag them off, *even* the little ones of the
flock; surely He will make their pasture
desolate because of them. 21 The earth has
quaked at the noise of their downfall. There
is an outcry! The noise of it has been heard
at the Red Sea. 22 Behold, He will mount up
and swoop like an eagle and spread out His
wings against Bozrah; and the hearts of the
mighty men of Edom in that day will be like
the heart of a woman in labor.
23 Concerning Damascus.
"Hamath and Arpad are put to shame,
For they have heard a bad report;
They are melting away.
There is anxiety by the sea,
It cannot be quieted.
24 "Damascus has become
limp *in their hands*;
She has turned away to flee,
And panic has taken hold of her;
Distress and pangs have seized her
Like a woman in childbirth.
25 "How the city of praise has
not been forsaken,
The town of My joy!
26 "Therefore, her young men will
fall in her open squares,

And all the men of war will
be silenced in that day,"
declares Yahweh of hosts.
27 "I will set fire to the wall
of Damascus,
And it will devour the fortified
towers of Ben-hadad."
28 Concerning Kedar and the kingdoms
of Hazor, which Nebuchadnezzar king of
Babylon struck down. Thus says Yahweh,
"Arise, go up to Kedar
And destroy the men of the east.
29 "They will take away their
tents and their flocks;
They will carry off for themselves
Their tent curtains, all their
goods, and their camels,
And they will call out to one
another, 'Terror on every side!'
30 "Run away, flee earnestly!
Inhabit the depths,
O inhabitants of Hazor,"
declares Yahweh;
"For Nebuchadnezzar king of Babylon
has taken counsel against you
And purposed a purpose against you.
31 "Arise, go up against a nation
which is at ease,
Which inhabits *its land* securely,"
declares Yahweh.
"It has no gates or bars;
They dwell alone.
32 "Their camels will become plunder,
And their many cattle for spoil,
And I will scatter to all the winds those
who cut the corners *of their hair*;
And I will bring their disaster from
every side," declares Yahweh.
33 "Hazor will become a haunt of jackals,
A desolation forever;
No one will inhabit there,
Nor will a son of man sojourn in it."
34 That which came as the word of Yahweh
to Jeremiah the prophet concerning Elam, in
the beginning of the reign of Zedekiah king
of Judah, saying:
35 "Thus says Yahweh of hosts,
'Behold, I am going to break
the bow of Elam,
The finest of their might.
36 'I will bring upon Elam the four winds
From the four ends of heaven,
And I will scatter them to
all these winds;
And there will be no nation
To which the banished ones
of Elam will not go.
37 'So I will shatter Elam before
their enemies
And before those who seek their lives;
And I will bring calamity upon them,
Even My burning anger,'
declares Yahweh,
'And I will send out the
sword after them
Until I have consumed them.
38 'Then I will set My throne in Elam
And cause king and princes
from there to perish,'
Declares Yahweh.
39 'But it will be in the last days
That I will return the
fortunes of Elam,'"
Declares Yahweh.

50 The word which Yahweh spoke
concerning Babylon, the land of
the Chaldeans, by the hand of Jeremiah
the prophet:
2 "Declare and make *it* heard
among the nations.
Make *it* heard and lift up a standard.
Do not conceal *it but* say,
'Babylon has been captured;
Bel has been put to shame;
Marduk has been shattered;
Her images have been put to shame;
her idols have been shattered.'
3 "For a nation has come up against her out
of the north; it will make her land an object
of horror, and there will be no inhabitant in
it. Both man and beast have wandered off;
they have gone away!
4 "In those days and at that time," declares
Yahweh, "the sons of Israel will come, *both*
they and the sons of Judah as well; they will
go along weeping as they go, and it will be
Yahweh their God they will seek. 5 They will
ask for the way to Zion—*turning* their faces
in its direction *and saying*, 'Come!'—in
order that they may join themselves to
Yahweh *in* an everlasting covenant that will
not be forgotten.
6 "My people have become lost sheep;
Their shepherds have led them astray.
They have made them turn
away *on* the mountains;
They have gone along from
mountain to hill
And have forgotten their resting place.

7 "All who came out against them
have devoured them;
And their adversaries have
said, 'We are not guilty,
Inasmuch as they have sinned
against Yahweh, *who is* the
abode of righteousness,
Even Yahweh, the hope
of their fathers.'

8 "Wander away from the
midst of Babylon
And go forth from the land
of the Chaldeans;
Be also like male goats at
the head of the flock.
9 "For behold, I am going to arouse
and bring up against Babylon
An assembly of great nations
from the land of the north,
And they will arrange *their*
battle lines against her;
From there she will be taken captive.
Their arrows will be like a warrior
who makes *one* childless
Who does not return empty-handed.
10 "Chaldea will become spoil;
All who take her spoil will have
enough," declares Yahweh.

11 "Because you are glad,
because you exult,
O you who plunder My inheritance,
Because you skip about like
a threshing heifer
And neigh like valiant steeds,
12 Your mother will be greatly ashamed;
She who gave you birth
will be humiliated.
Behold, *she will be* the least
of the nations,
A wilderness, a parched
land, and a desert.
13 "Because of the wrath of Yahweh
she will not be inhabited,
But she will be completely desolate;
Everyone who passes by Babylon
will be in desolation
And will hiss because of
all her wounds.
14 "Arrange your battle lines against
Babylon on every side,
All you who bend the bow;
Shoot at her, do not be sparing
with *your* arrows,
For she has sinned against Yahweh.
15 "Raise a loud shout against
her on every side!
She has given herself up, her
pillars have fallen,
Her walls have been pulled down.
For this is the vengeance of Yahweh:
Take vengeance on her;
As she has done *to others, so* do to her.
16 "Cut off the sower from Babylon
And the one who seizes the sickle
at the time of harvest;
From before the sword of the oppressor
They will each turn back
to his own people,
And they will each flee to his own land.

17 "Israel is a scattered flock; the lions
have banished *them* away. The first one *who*
devoured him was the king of Assyria, and
this last one *who* has broken his bones is
Nebuchadnezzar king of Babylon. 18 There-
fore thus says Yahweh of hosts, the God of
Israel: 'Behold, I am going to punish the king
of Babylon and his land, just as I punished the
king of Assyria. 19 And I will return Israel back
to his pasture, and he will graze on Carmel
and Bashan, and his desire will be satisfied
in the hill country of Ephraim and Gilead.
20 In those days and at that time,' declares
Yahweh, 'search will be made for the iniquity
of Israel, but there will be none; and for the
sins of Judah, but they will not be found; for I
will pardon those whom I leave as a remnant.'

21 "Against the land of Merathaim,
go up against it,
And against the inhabitants of Pekod.
Put *them* to the sword and devote them
to destruction," declares Yahweh,
"And do according to all that I
have commanded you.
22 "The noise of battle is in the land,
And great destruction.
23 "How the hammer of the whole earth
Has been cut in pieces and broken!
How Babylon has become
An object of horror among the nations!
24 "I set a snare for you, and you were
also caught, O Babylon,
But you yourself did not know;
You have been found and also seized
Because you have engaged in
conflict with Yahweh."
25 Yahweh has opened His armory
And has brought forth the
weapons of His indignation,

For it is a work of Lord Yahweh of hosts
In the land of the Chaldeans.
26 Come to her from the farthest
border;
Open up her barns;
Pile her up like heaps,
And devote her to destruction;
Let nothing of her remain.
27 Put all her young bulls to the sword;
Let them go down to the slaughter!
Woe be upon them, for
their day has come,
The time of their punishment.

28 There is a sound of those who flee and
escape from the land of Babylon,
To declare in Zion the vengeance
of Yahweh our God,
Vengeance for His temple.

29 "Summon many against Babylon,
All those who bend the bow:
Encamp against her on every side,
Let there be no escape.
Repay her according to her work;
According to all that she has
done, *so* do to her;
For she has become arrogant
against Yahweh,
Against the Holy One of Israel.
30 "Therefore her young men will
fall in her open squares,
And all her men of war will be silenced
in that day," declares Yahweh.
31 "Behold, I am against you,
O arrogant one,"
Declares Lord Yahweh of hosts,
"For your day has come,
The time when I will punish you.
32 "The arrogant one will stumble and fall
With no one to raise him up;
And I will set fire to his cities,
And it will devour him on every side."

33 Thus says Yahweh of hosts,
"The sons of Israel are oppressed,
And the sons of Judah as well;
And all who took them captive
have held them fast;
They have refused to let them go.
34 "Their Redeemer is strong, Yahweh
of hosts is His name;
He will vigorously plead their case
So that He may bring
relief to the earth,
But turmoil to the inhabitants
of Babylon.
35 "A sword against the Chaldeans,"
declares Yahweh,
"And against the inhabitants of Babylon
And against her officials
and her wise men!
36 "A sword against the oracle priests,
and they will become fools!
A sword against her mighty men,
and they will be shattered!
37 "A sword against their horses
and against their chariots
And against all the foreigners
who are in the midst of her,
And they will become women!
A sword against her treasures,
and they will be plundered!
38 "A drought on her waters, and
they will be dried up!
For it is a land of graven images,
And they are mad over terrifying idols.

39 "Therefore the desert creatures will
live *there* along with the jackals;
The ostriches also will live in it,
And it will never again be lived in
Or dwelt in from generation
to generation.
40 "As when God overthrew Sodom
And Gomorrah with its neighbors,"
declares Yahweh,
"No man will live there,
Nor will *any* son of man sojourn in it.

41 "Behold, a people is coming
from the north,
And a great nation and many kings
Will be aroused from the
remote parts of the earth.
42 "They seize *their* bow and javelin;
They are cruel and have
no compassion.
Their voice roars like the sea;
And they ride on horses,
Arranged like a man for the battle
Against you, O daughter of Babylon.
43 "The king of Babylon has heard
the report about them,
And his hands hang limp;
Distress has taken hold of him,
Agony like a woman in childbirth.

44 "Behold, one will come up like a lion
from the thicket of the Jordan to an enduring
pasture; for in an instant I will make them run

away from it, and whoever is chosen I will
appoint over it. For who is like Me, and who
will summon Me *into court*? And who then
is the shepherd who can stand before Me?"
45 Therefore hear the counsel of Yahweh
which He has counseled against Babylon, and
His purposes which He has purposed against
the land of the Chaldeans: surely they will
drag them off, *even* the little ones of the flock;
surely He will make their pasture desolate
because of them. 46 At the sound, "Babylon
has been seized!" the earth is shaken, and an
outcry is heard among the nations.

Psalm 119:121–128

121 I have done justice and righteousness;
Do not leave me to my oppressors.
122 Be for Your slave a guarantee for good;
Do not let the arrogant oppress me.
123 My eyes fail *with longing*
for Your salvation
And for Your righteous word.
124 Deal with Your slave according
to Your lovingkindness
And teach me Your statutes.
125 I am Your slave; give me understanding,
That I may know Your testimonies.
126 It is time for Yahweh to act,
For they have broken Your law.
127 Therefore I love Your commandments
Above gold, even above fine gold.
128 Therefore I deem all *Your* precepts
concerning everything to be right,
I hate every false way.

Proverbs 28:6

6 Better is the poor who walks
in his integrity
Than he who is crooked—double
dealing—though he be rich.

Titus 1:1–16

1 Paul, a slave of God and an apostle of
Jesus Christ, for the faith of God's elect
and the full knowledge of the truth which
is according to godliness, 2 in the hope of
eternal life, which the God who cannot
lie promised from all eternity, 3 but at the
proper time manifested His word in preach-
ing, with which I was entrusted according to
the commandment of God our Savior,

4 To Titus, my genuine child according to
our common faith: Grace and peace from
God the Father and Christ Jesus our Savior.

5 For this reason I left you in Crete, that
you would set in order what remains and
appoint elders in every city as I directed you,
6 *namely*, if any man is beyond reproach,
the husband of one wife, having faithful
children, *who are* not accused of dissipation,
or rebellious. 7 For the overseer must be
beyond reproach as God's steward, not self-
willed, not quick-tempered, not addicted to
wine, not pugnacious, not fond of dishonest
gain, 8 but hospitable, loving what is good,
sensible, righteous, holy, self-controlled,
9 holding fast the faithful word which is in
accordance with the teaching, so that he will
be able both to exhort in sound doctrine and
to reprove those who contradict.

10 For there are many rebellious men,
empty talkers and deceivers, especially
those of the circumcision, 11 who must be
silenced because they are upsetting whole
families, teaching things they should not
teach for the sake of dishonest gain. 12 One
of themselves, a prophet of their own, said,
"Cretans are always liars, evil beasts, lazy
gluttons." 13 This testimony is true. For this
reason reprove them severely so that they
may be sound in the faith, 14 not paying
attention to Jewish myths and command-
ments of men who turn away from the
truth. 15 To the pure, all things are pure, but
to those who are defiled and unbelieving,
nothing is pure, but both their mind and
their conscience are defiled. 16 They profess
to know God, but by *their* works they deny
Him, being detestable and disobedient and
unfit for any good work.

NOVEMBER 2

Jeremiah 51:1–52:34

51 Thus says Yahweh:
"Behold, I am going to
arouse against Babylon
And against the inhabitants
of Leb-kamai
The spirit of a destroyer.
2 "I will send strangers to
Babylon that they may
winnow her
And may empty her land
to destruction;

For on every side they will
be against her
In the day of *her* calamity.
3 "Let not him who bends
his bow bend *it*,
Nor let him rise up in his scale-armor;
So do not spare her young men;
Devote all her army to destruction.
4 "They will fall down slain in the
land of the Chaldeans,
And pierced through in their streets."

5 For neither Israel nor Judah
has been widowed
By his God, by Yahweh of hosts,
Although their land is full of guilt
Before the Holy One of Israel.
6 Flee from the midst of Babylon,
And each of you escape with his life!
Do not be silenced in her iniquity,
For this is Yahweh's time of vengeance;
He is going to render
recompense to her.
7 Babylon has been a golden cup
in the hand of Yahweh,
Intoxicating all the earth.
The nations have drunk of her wine;
Therefore the nations are going mad.
8 Suddenly Babylon has fallen
and been broken;
Wail over her!
Take balm for her pain;
Perhaps she may be healed.
9 We applied healing to Babylon,
but she was not healed;
Forsake her and let us each
go to his own country,
For her judgment has touched heaven
And lifts up to the very skies.
10 Yahweh has brought about
our righteousness;
Come and let us recount in Zion
The work of Yahweh our God!

11 Sharpen the arrows, fill the quivers!
Yahweh has aroused the spirit
of the kings of the Medes
Because His purpose is against
Babylon to destroy it;
For it is the vengeance of Yahweh,
vengeance for His temple.
12 Lift up a standard against
the walls of Babylon;
Make strong the watch;
Raise up watchmen;
Establish men in ambush!
For Yahweh has both purposed
and performed
What He spoke concerning the
inhabitants of Babylon.
13 O you who dwell by abundant waters,
Abundant in treasures,
Your end has come,
The measure of your end.
14 Yahweh of hosts has sworn by Himself:
"Surely I will fill you with a
population like locusts,
And they will cry out with shouts
of victory over you."

15 *It is* He who made the
earth by His power,
Who established the world
by His wisdom,
And by His understanding He
stretched out the heavens.
16 When He gives forth His voice, *there is*
a tumult of waters in the heavens,
And He causes the clouds to ascend
from the end of the earth;
He makes lightning for the rain
And brings forth the wind
from His storehouses.
17 All mankind is senseless,
devoid of knowledge;
Every goldsmith is put to shame
by his graven image,
For his molten images are a lie,
And there is no breath in them.
18 They are vanity, a work of mockery;
In the time of their punishment
they will perish.
19 The portion of Jacob is not like these;
For the Maker of all is He,
And of the tribe of His inheritance;
Yahweh of hosts is His name.
20 *He says,* "You are My *instrument* of
shattering, *My* weapon of war;
And with you I shatter nations,
And with you I destroy kingdoms.
21 "With you I shatter the
horse and his rider,
And with you I shatter the
chariot and its rider,
22 And with you I shatter
man and woman,
And with you I shatter old
man and youth,
And with you I shatter choice
man and virgin,

23 And with you I shatter the
shepherd and his flock,
And with you I shatter the
farmer and his pair *of oxen*,
And with you I shatter
governors and prefects.
24 "But I will repay Babylon and all the
inhabitants of Chaldea for all their evil that
they have done in Zion before your eyes,"
declares Yahweh.
25 "Behold, I am against you,
O destroying mountain,
Who destroys the whole
earth," declares Yahweh,
"And I will stretch out My
hand against you
And roll you down from the crags,
And I will make you a burnt
out mountain.
26 "They will not take from you
even a stone for a corner
Nor a stone for foundations,
But you will be a perpetual
desolation," declares Yahweh.

27 Lift up a standard in the land,
Blow a trumpet among the nations!
Set apart the nations against her;
Summon against her the kingdoms
of Ararat, Minni, and Ashkenaz;
Appoint a marshal against her;
Bring up the horses like bristly locusts.
28 Set apart the nations against her,
The kings of the Medes,
Their governors and all their prefects
And every land of their rule.
29 So the land quakes and writhes,
For the purposes of Yahweh
against Babylon stand,
To make the land of Babylon
A desolation without inhabitants.
30 The mighty men of Babylon
have ceased fighting;
They inhabit the strongholds;
Their might is dried up;
They are becoming *like* women;
Their dwelling places are set on fire;
The bars of her *gates* are broken.
31 One runner runs to meet another,
And one messenger to meet another,
To give a message to the
king of Babylon
That his city has been captured
from end *to end*;
32 The fords also have been seized,
And they have burned the
marshes with fire,
And the men of war are terrified.

33 For thus says Yahweh of hosts, the God
of Israel:
"The daughter of Babylon is
like a threshing floor
At the time it is stamped firm;
Yet in a little while the time of
harvest will come for her."

34 "Nebuchadnezzar king of Babylon
has devoured me *and* brought
me into confusion;
He has set me down *like*
an empty vessel;
He has swallowed me like
a sea monster;
He has filled his stomach
with my delicacies;
He has rinsed me away.
35 "May the violence *done* to me and
to my flesh be upon Babylon,"
The inhabitant of Zion will say;
And, "May my blood be upon the
inhabitants of Chaldea,"
Jerusalem will say.
36 Therefore thus says Yahweh,
"Behold, I am going to plead your case
And exact full vengeance for you;
And I will dry up her sea
And make her fountain dry.
37 "Babylon will become a heap *of
ruins*, a haunt of jackals,
An object of horror and hissing,
without inhabitants.
38 "They will roar together
like young lions;
They will growl like lions' cubs.
39 "When they become heated up, I
will set *before them* their feast
And make them drunk,
that they may exult
And may sleep a perpetual sleep
And not wake up," declares Yahweh.
40 "I will bring them down like
lambs to the slaughter,
Like rams together with male goats.

41 "How Sheshak has been captured,
And the praise of the whole
earth been seized!
How Babylon has become an object
of horror among the nations!

42 “The sea has come up over Babylon;
She has been covered with
its tumultuous waves.
43 “Her cities have become an
object of horror,
A parched land, and a desert,
A land in which no man lives
And through which no
son of man passes.
44 “I will punish Bel in Babylon,
And I will make what he has
swallowed come out of his mouth;
And the nations will no
longer stream to him.
Even the wall of Babylon
has fallen down!

45 “Come forth from her midst,
My people,
And each of you escape with his life
From the burning anger of Yahweh.
46 “Now lest your heart grow faint,
And you fear the report that *will
be* heard in the land—
For the report will come one year,
And after that another report
in another year,
And violence *will be* in the land
With ruler against ruler—
47 Therefore behold, days are coming
When I will punish the graven
images of Babylon;
And her whole land will
be put to shame,
And all her slain will fall in her midst.
48 “Then heaven and earth and
all that is in them
Will shout for joy over Babylon,
For the destroyers will come
to her from the north,”
Declares Yahweh.

49 Indeed Babylon is to fall *for*
the slain of Israel,
As also for Babylon the slain of
all the earth have fallen.
50 You who have escaped the sword,
Go! Do not stand around!
Remember Yahweh from afar,
And let Jerusalem come
upon your heart.
51 We are ashamed because we
have heard reproach;
Dishonor has covered our faces,
For strangers have entered
The holy places of the
house of Yahweh.
52 “Therefore behold, the days are
coming,” declares Yahweh,
“When I will punish her graven images,
And the mortally wounded will
groan throughout her land.
53 “Though Babylon should
ascend to the heavens,
And though she should fortify
her lofty stronghold,
From Me destroyers will come
to her,” declares Yahweh.

54 The sound of an outcry from Babylon,
And of great destruction from
the land of the Chaldeans!
55 For Yahweh is going to
destroy Babylon,
And He will make *her* loud
noise vanish from her.
And their waves will roar
like many waters;
The rumbling of their
voices sounds forth.
56 For the destroyer is coming
against her, against Babylon,
And her mighty men will be captured;
Their bows are shattered;
For Yahweh is a God of recompense,
He will fully repay.
57 “I will make her princes and
her wise men drunk,
Her governors, her prefects,
and her mighty men,
That they may sleep a perpetual
sleep and not wake up,”
Declares the King, whose name
is Yahweh of hosts.
58 Thus says Yahweh of hosts,
“The broad wall of Babylon will
be completely razed,
And her high gates will be set on fire;
So the peoples will toil for nothing,
And the nations become
weary *only* for fire.”

59 The message which Jeremiah the
prophet commanded Seraiah the son of
Neriah, the grandson of Mahseiah, when
he went with Zedekiah the king of Judah to
Babylon in the fourth year of his reign. (Now
Seraiah was quartermaster.) 60 So Jeremiah
wrote in a single scroll all the calamity
which would come upon Babylon, *that is*,

all these words which have been written
concerning Babylon. 61 Then Jeremiah said
to Seraiah, "As soon as you come to Babylon,
then see that you read all these words aloud,
62 and then you will say, 'You, O Yahweh,
have promised concerning this place to
cut it off, so that there will be nothing
inhabiting it, whether man or beast, but
it will be a perpetual desolation.' 63 And as
soon as you finish reading this scroll, you
will tie a stone to it and throw it into the
middle of the Euphrates, 64 and then you
will say, 'Just so shall Babylon sink down
and not rise again because of the calamity
that I am going to bring upon her; and they
will become *utterly* weary.'" Thus far are the
words of Jeremiah.

52 Zedekiah was twenty-one years
old when he became king, and he
reigned eleven years in Jerusalem; and his
mother's name was Hamutal the daughter of
Jeremiah of Libnah. 2 And he did what was
evil in the sight of Yahweh, according to all
that Jehoiakim had done. 3 For through the
anger of Yahweh *this* came about in Jerusa-
lem and Judah until He cast them out from
His presence. And Zedekiah rebelled against
the king of Babylon. 4 Now it happened in
the ninth year of his reign, on the tenth *day*
of the tenth month, that Nebuchadnezzar
king of Babylon came, he and all his military
force, against Jerusalem, and they camped
against it and built a siege wall all around
it. 5 So the city came under siege until the
eleventh year of King Zedekiah. 6 On the
ninth *day* of the fourth month, the famine
was so strong in the city that there was no
food for the people of the land. 7 Then the
city was breached, and all the men of war
fled and went forth from the city at night
by way of the gate between the two walls
which *was* by the king's garden, though the
Chaldeans were all around the city. And they
went by way of the Arabah. 8 But the military
force of the Chaldeans pursued the king and
overtook Zedekiah in the plains of Jericho,
and all his military force was scattered
from him. 9 Then they seized the king and
brought him up to the king of Babylon at
Riblah in the land of Hamath, and he spoke
his judgment on him. 10 Then the king of
Babylon slaughtered the sons of Zedekiah
before his eyes, and he also slaughtered all
the princes of Judah in Riblah. 11 Then he
blinded the eyes of Zedekiah; and the king
of Babylon bound him with bronze fetters
and brought him to Babylon and put him in
prison until the day of his death.

12 Now on the tenth *day* of the fifth
month, which was the nineteenth year of
King Nebuchadnezzar, king of Babylon,
Nebuzaradan the captain of the bodyguard,
who stood before the king of Babylon, came
to Jerusalem. 13 And he burned the house of
Yahweh, the king's house, and all the houses
of Jerusalem; even every large house he
burned with fire. 14 So all the military force
of the Chaldeans who *were* with the captain
of the guard tore down all the walls around
Jerusalem. 15 Then Nebuzaradan the captain
of the guard took away into exile some of the
poorest of the people, the rest of the people
who remained in the city, the defectors who
had defected to the king of Babylon, and the
rest of the artisans. 16 But Nebuzaradan the
captain of the guard had some of the poorest
of the land remain to be vinedressers and
plowmen.

17 Now the bronze pillars which belonged
to the house of Yahweh and the stands and
the bronze sea, which were in the house of
Yahweh, the Chaldeans shattered and car-
ried all their bronze to Babylon. 18 They also
took away the pots, the shovels, the snuffers,
the bowls, the pans, and all the bronze
vessels which were used to minister. 19 And
the captain of the guard also took away
the cups, the firepans, the bowls, the pots,
the lampstands, the pans, and the offering
bowls, what was fine gold and what was fine
silver. 20 The two pillars, the one sea, and the
twelve bronze bulls that were under the sea,
and the stands, which King Solomon had
made for the house of Yahweh—the bronze
of all these vessels was beyond weight. 21 As
for the pillars, the height of each pillar
was eighteen cubits, and it *was* twelve
cubits in circumference and four fingers
in thickness, *and* hollow. 22 Now a capital
of bronze was on it; and the height of each
capital was five cubits, with network and
pomegranates upon the capital all around,
all of bronze. And the second pillar was like
these, including pomegranates. 23 There
were ninety-six exposed pomegranates; all
the pomegranates *numbered* one hundred
on the network all around.

24 Then the captain of the guard took
Seraiah the chief priest and Zephaniah the

second priest, with the three doorkeepers
of the temple. 25 And from the city he took
one official who was overseer of the men of
war, and seven of the king's advisers who
were found in the city, and the scribe of the
commander of the army who mustered the
people of the land, and sixty men of the peo-
ple of the land who were found in the midst
of the city. 26 And Nebuzaradan the captain
of the guard took them and led them to the
king of Babylon at Riblah. 27 Then the king
of Babylon struck them down and put them
to death at Riblah in the land of Hamath. So
Judah went into exile from its land.
28 These are the people whom Nebuchad-
nezzar took away into exile: in the seventh
year 3,023 Jews; 29 in the eighteenth year
of Nebuchadnezzar 832 persons from
Jerusalem; 30 in the twenty-third year of
Nebuchadnezzar, Nebuzaradan the captain
of the guard took away into exile 745 Jewish
people; there were 4,600 persons in all.
31 Now it happened in the thirty-seventh
year of the exile of Jehoiachin king of Judah,
in the twelfth month, on the twenty-fifth
of the month, that Evil-merodach king of
Babylon, in the *first* year of his reign, lifted
up the head of Jehoiachin king of Judah and
brought him out of prison; 32 and he spoke
to him good *words*, and he set his throne
above the throne of the kings who *were* with
him in Babylon. 33 So Jehoiachin changed
his prison clothes and had his meals in the
king's presence continually all the days of
his life. 34 For his allowance, a continual
allowance was given him by the king of
Babylon, a daily portion all the days of his
life until the day of his death.

Psalm 119:129–136

129 Your testimonies are wonderful;
Therefore my soul observes them.
130 The unfolding of Your
words gives light;
It gives understanding to the simple.
131 I opened my mouth wide and panted,
For I longed for Your commandments.
132 Turn to me and be gracious to me,
According to *Your* judgment for
those who love Your name.
133 Establish my steps in Your word,
And do not let any wickedness
overpower me.
134 Redeem me from the
oppression of man,
That I may keep Your precepts.
135 Make Your face shine upon Your slave,
And teach me Your statutes.
136 My eyes shed streams of water,
Because they do not keep Your law.

Proverbs 28:7–8

7 He who observes the law is a
son who understands,
But he who befriends gluttons
humiliates his father.
8 He who increases his wealth
by interest and usury
Gathers it for him who is
gracious to the lowly.

Titus 2:1–15

2 But as for you, speak the things which
are proper for sound doctrine. 2 Older
men are to be temperate, dignified, sensible,
sound in faith, in love, in perseverance.
3 Older women likewise are to be reverent
in their behavior, not malicious gossips nor
enslaved to much wine, teaching what is
good, 4 so that they may instruct the young
women in sensibility: to love their husbands,
to love their children, 5 *to be* sensible, pure,
workers at home, kind, being subject to their
own husbands, so that the word of God will
not be slandered.
6 Likewise urge the younger men to be sen-
sible; 7 in all things show yourself to be a model
of good works, *with* purity in doctrine, digni-
fied, 8 sound *in* word which is irreproachable,
so that the opponent will be put to shame,
having nothing bad to say about us.
9 *Urge* slaves to be subject to their own
masters in everything, to be pleasing, not
contradicting, 10 not pilfering, but demon-
strating all good faith so that they will adorn
the doctrine of God our Savior in everything.
11 For the grace of God has appeared,
bringing salvation to all men, 12 instructing
us that, denying ungodliness and worldly
desires, we should live sensibly, righteously,
and godly in the present age, 13 looking for
the blessed hope and the appearing of the
glory of our great God and Savior, Jesus
Christ, 14 who gave Himself for us that He
might redeem us from all lawlessness, and
purify for Himself a people for His own
possession, zealous for good works.
15 These things speak and exhort and
reprove with all authority. Let no one
disregard you.

NOVEMBER 3

Lamentations 1:1–2:22

1 How lonely sits the city
That was great with people!
She has become like a widow
Who was *once* great among
the nations!
She who was a princess
among the provinces
Has become a forced laborer!

2 She weeps bitterly in the night,
And her tears are on her cheeks;
She has none to comfort her
Among all her lovers.
All her friends have dealt
treacherously with her;
They have become her enemies.

3 Judah has gone into exile
because of affliction
And because of great slavery;
She sits among the nations,
But she has found no rest;
All her pursuers have overtaken her
In the midst of distress.

4 The roads of Zion are in mourning
Because no one comes to
the appointed times.
All her gates are desolate;
Her priests are sighing,
Her virgins are grieving,
And she herself is bitter.

5 Her adversaries have
become her masters;
Her enemies are complacent;
For Yahweh has caused her grief
Because of the greatness of
her transgressions;
Her infants have gone away
As captives before the adversary.

6 So all her majesty
Has gone out from the daughter of Zion;
Her princes have become like deer
That have found no pasture;
So they have fled without strength
Before the pursuer.

7 In the days of her affliction
and homelessness
Jerusalem remembers all
her precious things
That were from the days of old,
When her people fell into the
hand of the adversary
And no one helped her.
The adversaries saw her;
They laughed at her ruin.

8 Jerusalem sinned greatly;
Therefore she has become
an impure thing.
All who honored her despise her
Because they have seen her nakedness;
Even she herself sighs and turns away.

9 Her uncleanness was in her skirts;
She did not remember her future.
Therefore she has gone
down astonishingly;
She has no comforter.
"See, O Yahweh, my affliction,
For the enemy has magnified himself!"

10 The adversary has stretched
out his hand
Over all her desirable things,
For she has seen the nations
enter her sanctuary,
The ones whom You commanded
That they should not enter
into Your assembly.

11 All her people are sighing,
seeking bread;
They have given their desirable
things for food
To restore *their* souls.
"See, O Yahweh, and look,
For I am despised."

12 "Is it nothing to all you who
pass this way?
Look and see if there is any
pain like my pain
Which was dealt severely to me,
Which Yahweh grieved *me* with on
the day of His burning anger.

13 "From on high He sent fire
into my bones,

And it dominated *them*.
He has spread a net for my feet;
He has turned me back;
He has made me desolate,
Faint all day long.

14 "The yoke of my transgressions
is bound;
By His hand they are knit together.
They have come upon my neck;
He has made my strength stumble.
The Lord has given me into the hands
Of *those against whom* I am
not able to stand.

15 "The Lord has rejected all
my mighty men
In my midst;
He has called an appointed
time against me
To break my young men;
The Lord has trodden *as*
in a wine press
The virgin daughter of Judah.

16 "For these things I am weeping;
My eyes run down with water;
Because far from me is a comforter,
One who restores my soul.
My children are desolate
Because the enemy has prevailed."

17 Zion stretches out her hands;
There is no one to comfort her;
Yahweh has commanded
concerning Jacob
That the ones round about him
should be his adversaries;
Jerusalem has become an impure
thing among them.

18 "Yahweh is righteous;
For I have rebelled against
His command;
Hear now, all peoples,
And behold my pain;
My virgins and my young men
Have gone into captivity.

19 "I called to my lovers, *but*
they deceived me;
My priests and my elders breathed
their last in the city
While they sought food for themselves
in order to restore their souls.

20 "See, O Yahweh, for I am in distress;
My inmost being is greatly
disturbed;
My heart is overturned within me,
For I have been very rebellious.
In the street the sword bereaves;
In the house it is like death.

21 "They have heard that I am sighing;
There is no one to comfort me;
All my enemies have heard
of the evil *done to* me;
They rejoice that You have done *it*.
You have brought the day which
You have proclaimed,
So that they will become like me.

22 "Let all their evil come before You;
And deal severely with them as You
have dealt severely with me
For all my transgressions;
For my groans are great and
my heart is faint."

2 How the Lord has covered
the daughter of Zion
With a cloud in His anger!
He has cast from heaven to earth
The beauty of Israel,
And has not remembered the
footstool of His feet
In the day of His anger.

2 The Lord has swallowed up;
He has not spared
All the habitations of Jacob.
In His wrath He has pulled down
The strongholds of the
daughter of Judah;
He has brought *them* down
to the ground;
He has profaned the kingdom
and its princes.

3 In hot anger He has cut in pieces
All the strength of Israel;
He has turned back His right hand
From before the enemy.
And He has burned in Jacob
like a flaming fire
Devouring round about.

4 He has bent His bow like an enemy;
He has set His right hand
like an adversary

And killed all that were
desirable to the eye;
In the tent of the daughter of Zion
He has poured out His wrath like fire.

5 The Lord has become like an enemy.
He has swallowed up Israel;
He has swallowed up all its palaces;
He has brought its strongholds to ruin
And multiplied in the
daughter of Judah
Mourning and moaning.

6 And He has violently treated His
tabernacle like a garden *booth*;
He has brought His appointed
meeting place to ruin.
Yahweh has caused to be forgotten
The appointed time and
sabbath in Zion,
And He has spurned king and priest
In the indignation of His anger.

7 The Lord has rejected His altar;
He has abandoned His sanctuary;
He has delivered into the
hand of the enemy
The walls of her palaces.
They have made a noise in
the house of Yahweh
As in the day of an appointed time.

8 Yahweh determined to bring to ruin
The wall of the daughter of Zion.
He has stretched out a line;
He has not turned His hand
back from swallowing up,
And He has caused rampart
and wall to mourn;
They have languished together.

9 Her gates have sunk into the ground;
He has destroyed and broken her bars.
Her king and her princes are
among the nations;
The law is no more.
Also, her prophets find
No vision from Yahweh.

10 The elders of the daughter of Zion
Sit on the ground; they are silent.
They have thrown dust
up on their heads;
They have girded themselves
with sackcloth.
The virgins of Jerusalem
Have bowed their heads
down to the ground.

11 My eyes fail because of tears;
My inmost being is greatly disturbed;
My heart is poured out on the earth
Because of the destruction of
the daughter of my people,
When infants and nursing babies faint
In the open squares of the city.

12 They say to their mothers,
"Where is grain and wine?"
As they faint like a wounded man
In the open squares of the city,
As their life is poured out
On their mothers' bosom.

13 What shall I testify about you?
To what shall I equate you,
O daughter of Jerusalem?
To what shall I liken you
as I comfort you,
O virgin daughter of Zion?
For your destruction is as vast as the sea;
Who can heal you?

14 Your prophets have beheld for you
Worthless and ineffective *visions*;
And they have not uncovered
your iniquity
So as to return you from captivity,
But they have beheld for you
worthless and misleading oracles.

15 All who pass along the way
Clap their hands *in derision* at you;
They hiss and shake their heads
At the daughter of Jerusalem,
"Is this the city of which they said,
'The perfection of beauty,
The joy of the whole earth'?"

16 All your enemies
Have opened their mouths
wide against you;
They hiss and gnash *their* teeth.
They say, "We have swallowed *her* up!
Surely this is the day for
which we have hoped;
We have found *it*, we have seen *it*."

17 Yahweh has done what He purposed;
He has completed His word

Which He commanded
from days of old.
He has pulled down without sparing,
And He has caused the enemy
to be glad over you;
He has exalted the might
of your adversaries.

18 Their heart cried out to the Lord,
"O wall of the daughter of Zion,
Let *your* tears run down like
a river day and night;
Give yourself no relief;
Let your eyes not be still.

19 "Arise, cry aloud in the night
At the head of the night watches;
Pour out your heart like water
Before the presence of the Lord;
Lift up your hands to Him
For the life of your infants
Who are faint because of hunger
At the head of every street."

20 See, O Yahweh, and look!
With whom have You dealt thus?
Should women eat their offspring,
The infants who were born healthy?
Should priest and prophet be killed
In the sanctuary of the Lord?

21 On the ground in the streets
Lie young and old;
My virgins and my young men
Have fallen by the sword.
You have killed *them* in the
day of Your anger;
You have slaughtered, not sparing.

22 You called as in the day of
an appointed time
My terrors on every side;
And there was no one who
escaped or survived
In the day of Yahweh's anger.
Those whom I gave birth to and reared,
My enemy consumed them.

Psalm 119:137–144

137 Righteous are You, O Yahweh,
And upright are Your judgments.
138 In righteousness, You have
commanded Your testimonies
And in exceeding faithfulness.
139 My zeal has consumed me,
Because my adversaries have
forgotten Your words.
140 Your word is exceedingly refined,
Therefore Your slave loves it.
141 I am small and despised,
Yet I do not forget Your precepts.
142 Your righteousness is an
everlasting righteousness,
And Your law is truth.
143 Trouble and anguish have found me,
Yet Your commandments
are my delight.
144 Righteous are Your testimonies forever;
Give me understanding that I may live.

Proverbs 28:9–10

9 He who turns away his ear
from listening to the law,
Even his prayer is an abomination.
10 He who leads the upright
astray in an evil way
Will himself fall into his own pit,
But the blameless will inherit good.

Titus 3:1–15

3 Remind them to be subject to rulers, to
authorities, to be obedient, to be ready
for every good work, 2 to slander no one, to
be peaceable, considerate, demonstrating
all gentleness to all men. 3 For we ourselves
also once were foolish, disobedient,
deceived, enslaved to various lusts and
pleasures, spending our life in malice and
envy, despicable, hating one another. 4 But
when the kindness and affection of God
our Savior appeared, 5 He saved us, not by
works which we did in righteousness, but
according to His mercy, through the wash-
ing of regeneration and renewing by the
Holy Spirit, 6 whom He poured out upon us
richly through Jesus Christ our Savior, 7 so
that having been justified by His grace, we
would become heirs according to *the* hope
of eternal life. 8 This is a trustworthy saying.
And concerning these things I want you to
speak confidently, so that those who have
believed God will be intent to lead in good
works. These things are good and profitable
for men. 9 But avoid foolish controversies
and genealogies and strife and conflicts
about the Law, for they are unprofitable and
worthless. 10 Reject a factious man after a
first and second warning, 11 knowing that
such a man is perverted and is sinning,
being self-condemned.

[12] When I send Artemas or Tychicus to you, be diligent to come to me at Nicopolis, for I have decided to spend the winter there. [13] Diligently help send Zenas the lawyer and Apollos on their way so that nothing is lacking for them. [14] And our people must also learn to lead in good works to meet pressing needs, so that they will not be unfruitful.

[15] All who are with me greet you. Greet those who love us in *the* faith.

Grace be with you all.

NOVEMBER 4

Lamentations 3:1–5:22

3 I am the man who has seen affliction
Because of the rod of His wrath.
2 He has driven me and made me walk
In darkness and not in light.
3 Surely against me He has turned His hand
Repeatedly all the day.

4 He has caused my flesh and my skin to waste away;
He has broken my bones.
5 He has besieged and encompassed me with gall and hardship.
6 Dark places He has made me inhabit,
Like those who have long been dead.

7 He has walled me in so that I cannot go out;
He has made my chain heavy.
8 Even when I cry out and call for help,
He shuts out my prayer.
9 He has blocked my ways with cut stone;
He has made my paths crooked.

10 He is to me like a bear lying in wait,
Like a lion in secret places.
11 He has turned aside my ways and torn me to pieces;
He has made me desolate.
12 He bent His bow
And set me as a target for the arrow.

13 He made the arrows of His quiver
To enter into my inward parts.
14 I have become a laughingstock to all my people,
Their music of *mockery* all the day.
15 He has saturated me with bitterness;
He has sated me with wormwood.

16 He has broken my teeth with gravel;
He has made me cower in the dust.
17 My soul has been rejected from peace;
I have forgotten goodness.
18 So I say, "My strength has perished,
As well as my hopeful waiting *which comes* from Yahweh."

19 Remember my affliction and my homelessness, the wormwood and gall.
20 Surely my soul remembers
And is bowed down within me.
21 This I will return to my heart;
Therefore I will wait in hope.

22 The lovingkindnesses of Yahweh indeed never cease,
For His compassions never fail.
23 *They* are new every morning;
Great is Your faithfulness.
24 "Yahweh is my portion," says my soul,
"Therefore I wait for Him."

25 Yahweh is good to those who hope in Him,
To the soul who seeks Him.
26 *It is* good that he waits silently
For the salvation of Yahweh.
27 *It is* good for a man that he should bear
The yoke in his youth.

28 Let him sit alone and be silent
Since He has laid *it* on him.
29 Let him put his mouth in the dust;
Perhaps there is hope.
30 Let him give his cheek to the one who strikes him;
Let him be saturated with reproach.

31 For the Lord will not reject forever,
32 For if He causes grief,
Then He will have compassion
According to His abundant lovingkindness.
33 For He does not afflict from His heart
Or grieve the sons of men.

34 To crush under His feet
All the prisoners of the land,
35 To deprive a man of justice
In the presence of the Most High,
36 To defraud a man in his *legal* case—
These things the Lord does
not see *with approval.*

37 Who is there who speaks
and it happens,
Unless the Lord has commanded *it*?
38 *Is it* not from the mouth
of the Most High
That both calamities and
good go forth?
39 Why should *any* living
person or *any* man
Complain because of his sins?

40 Let us search out and
examine our ways,
And let us return to Yahweh.
41 We lift up our heart to *our* hands
Toward God in heaven;
42 We have transgressed and rebelled;
You have not pardoned.

43 You have covered *Yourself* with anger
And pursued us;
You have killed *and* have not spared.
44 You have covered Yourself with a cloud
So that no prayer can pass through.
45 *You have made us mere*
scum and refuse
In the midst of the peoples.

46 All our enemies have opened
their mouths against us.
47 Panic and pitfall have befallen us,
Devastation and destruction;
48 My eyes run down with
streams of water
Because of the destruction of
the daughter of my people.

49 My eyes pour down unceasingly,
Without stopping,
50 Until Yahweh looks down
And sees from heaven.
51 My eyes deal severely with my soul
Because of all the daughters of my city.

52 My enemies without cause
Hunted me down like a bird;
53 They have silenced my life in the pit
And have placed a stone on me.
54 Waters flowed over my head;
I said, "I am cut off!"

55 I called on Your name, O Yahweh,
Out of the lowest pit.
56 You have heard my voice,
"Do not hide Your ear from
my *prayer for* relief,
From my cry for help."
57 You drew near when I called on You;
You said, "Do not fear!"

58 O Lord, You have pleaded
my soul's cause;
You have redeemed my life.
59 O Yahweh, You have seen
my oppression;
Judge my case.
60 You have seen all their vengeance,
All their purposes against me.

61 You have heard their
reproach, O Yahweh,
All their purposes against me.
62 The lips of those who rise against
me and their whispering
Are against me all day long.
63 Look on their sitting and their rising;
I am their mocking song.

64 You will recompense them,
O Yahweh,
According to the work of their hands.
65 You will give them dullness of heart;
Your curse will be on them.
66 You will pursue them in anger
and destroy them
From under the heavens of Yahweh!

4 How dark the gold has become,
How the pure gold has changed!
The sacred stones are poured out
At the head of every street.

2 The precious sons of Zion,
Weighed against fine gold,
How they are regarded as earthen jars,
The work of a potter's hands!

3 Even jackals offer the breast;
They nurse their young;
But the daughter of my people
has become cruel
Like ostriches in the wilderness.

4 The tongue of the nursing baby cleaves
To the roof of its mouth
because of thirst;
The infants ask for bread,
But no one breaks *it* for them.

5 Those who ate delicacies
Are desolate in the streets;
Those reared in crimson
Embrace ash pits.

6 So the iniquity of the
daughter of my people
Is greater than the sin of Sodom,
Which was overthrown
as in a moment,
And no hands whirled toward her.

7 Her Nazirites were purer than snow;
They were whiter than milk;
They were more ruddy *in*
body than corals,
Their polishing *was like* lapis lazuli.

8 Their form is blacker than soot;
They are not recognized in the streets;
Their skin is shriveled on their bones;
It is withered, it has become like wood.

9 Better are those pierced
through with the sword
Than those pierced through
with hunger;
For their *life* flows away, being stricken
For lack of the produce of the field.

10 The hands of compassionate women
Boiled their own children;
They became food for them
Because of the destruction of
the daughter of my people.

11 Yahweh has spent His wrath;
He has poured out His burning anger;
And He has kindled a fire in Zion
Which has devoured its foundations.

12 The kings of the earth did not believe,
Nor *did* any of the inhabitants
of the world,
That the adversary and the enemy
Could enter the gates of Jerusalem.

13 Because of the sins of her prophets
And the iniquities of her priests,
Who have shed in her midst
The blood of the righteous;

14 They wandered, blind, in the streets;
They were defiled with blood
So that no one could touch
their garments.

15 "Depart! Unclean!"
they cried of themselves.
"Depart, depart, do not touch!"
So they fled and wandered;
Men among the nations said,
"They shall not continue to
sojourn *with us*."

16 The presence of Yahweh has
eradicated them;
He will not continue to look at them;
They did not honor the priests;
They did not favor the elders.

17 Yet our eyes were spent,
Looking for help was vanity;
In our watching we have watched
For a nation that could not save.

18 They hunted our steps
So that we could not walk
in our open squares;
Our end drew near,
Our days were finished,
For our end had come.

19 Our pursuers were swifter
Than the eagles of the sky;
They hotly pursued us on
the mountains;
They waited in ambush for
us in the wilderness.

20 The breath of our nostrils, the
anointed of Yahweh,
Was captured in their pits,
Of whom we had said,
"Under his shadow
We shall live among the nations."

21 Rejoice and be glad,
O daughter of Edom,
Who inhabits the land of Uz;
But the cup will pass on to you
as well;
You will become drunk and
make yourself naked.

22 *The punishment* of your iniquity has
come to an end, O daughter of Zion;
He will exile you no longer.
But He will punish your iniquity,
O daughter of Edom;
He will expose your sins!

5 Remember, O Yahweh, what
has happened to us;
Look, and see our reproach!
2 Our inheritance has been
turned over to strangers,
Our houses to foreigners.
3 We have become orphans
without a father;
Our mothers are like widows.
4 We drink our water by means of silver;
Our wood comes *to us* at a price.
5 Our pursuers are at our necks;
We are worn out; there is no rest for us.
6 We have given over *our* hands to Egypt
and Assyria to get enough bread.
7 Our fathers sinned; they are no more;
It is we who have borne
their iniquities.
8 Slaves rule over us;
There is no one to tear us
away from their hand.
9 We get our bread at the risk
of our lives
Because of the sword in the wilderness.
10 Our skin has become as hot as an oven
Because of the burning heat of famine.
11 They violated the women in Zion,
The virgins in the cities of Judah.
12 Princes were hung by their hands;
Elders were not respected.
13 Young men lifted up *the stone*
at the grinding mill,
And youths stumbled down
under *loads* of wood.
14 Elders have ceased from
being at the gate,
Young men from their music.
15 The joy of our hearts has ceased;
Our dancing has been turned
into mourning.
16 The crown has fallen from our head;
Woe to us, for we have sinned!
17 Because of this our heart is faint;
Because of these things
our eyes are dim;
18 Because of Mount Zion
which lies desolate,
Foxes walk about in it.
19 You, O Yahweh, sit enthroned forever;
Your throne is from generation
to generation.
20 Why do You forget us forever?
Why do You forsake us so long?
21 Cause us to return to You, O Yahweh,
that we may be returned;
Renew our days as of old,
22 Even if You have utterly rejected us
And are exceedingly angry with us.

Psalm 119:145–152

145 I called with all my heart;
answer me, O Yahweh!
I will observe Your statutes.
146 I called to You; save me
And I shall keep Your testimonies.
147 I eagerly greet the dawn
and cry for help;
I wait for Your words.
148 My eyes eagerly greet the
night watches,
That I may muse on Your word.
149 Hear my voice according to
Your lovingkindness;
O Yahweh, revive me, according
to Your judgments.
150 Near are those who pursue
wickedness;
They are far from Your law.
151 Near are You, O Yahweh,
And all Your commandments are truth.
152 Of old I have known from
Your testimonies
That You have founded them forever.

Proverbs 28:11

11 The rich man is wise in his own eyes,
But the lowly who understands
searches him.

Philemon 1–25

1 Paul, a prisoner of Christ Jesus, and
Timothy our brother,
To Philemon our beloved *brother* and
fellow worker, 2 and to Apphia our sister,
and to Archippus our fellow soldier, and
to the church in your house: 3 Grace to you
and peace from God our Father and the Lord
Jesus Christ.
4 I thank my God, always making mention
of you in my prayers, 5 because I hear of your
love and of the faith which you have toward
the Lord Jesus and toward all the saints;
6 *and I pray* that the fellowship of your

faith may become effective through the full knowledge of every good thing which is in you for the sake of Christ. 7 For I have come to have much joy and comfort in your love, because the hearts of the saints have been refreshed through you, brother.

8 Therefore, though I have much boldness in Christ to command you *to do* what is proper, 9 yet for love's sake I rather plead with *you*—since I am such a person as Paul, the aged, and now also a prisoner of Christ Jesus—

10 I plead with you for my child Onesimus, of whom I became a father in my chains, 11 who formerly was useless to you, but now is useful both to you and to me. 12 I have sent him back to you in person, that is, my very heart, 13 whom I intended to keep with me, so that on your behalf he might minister to me in my chains for the gospel, 14 but without your consent I did not want to do anything, so that your goodness would not be, in effect, by compulsion but voluntary. 15 For perhaps he was for this reason separated *from you* for a while, that you would have him back forever, 16 no longer as a slave, but more than a slave, a beloved brother, especially to me, but how much more to you, both in the flesh and in the Lord.

17 If then you regard me a partner, accept him as *you would accept* me. 18 But if he has wronged you in any way or owes you anything, charge that to my account. 19 I, Paul, am writing this with my own hand, I will repay it (not to mention to you that you owe to me even your own self as well). 20 Yes, brother, let me benefit from you in the Lord. Refresh my heart in Christ!

21 Having confidence in your obedience, I write to you, since I know that you will do even more than what I say.

22 And at the same time also prepare me a lodging, for I hope that through your prayers I will be graciously given to you.

23 Epaphras, my fellow prisoner in Christ Jesus, greets you, 24 *as do* Mark, Aristarchus, Demas, Luke, my fellow workers.

25 The grace of the Lord Jesus Christ be with your spirit.

The way to understand the Scriptures and all theology is to become holy.
It is to be under the authority of the Spirit.

— D. MARTYN LLOYD-JONES

NOVEMBER 5

Ezekiel 1:1–2:10

1 Now it happened in the thirtieth year, on the fifth *day* of the fourth month, while I was by the river Chebar among the exiles, *that* the heavens were opened, and I saw visions of God. 2 (On the fifth of the month in the fifth year of King Jehoiachin's exile, 3 the word of Yahweh came expressly to Ezekiel the priest, son of Buzi, in the land of the Chaldeans by the river Chebar; and there the hand of Yahweh came upon him.)

4 Then I looked, and behold, a storm wind was coming from the north, a great cloud with fire flashing forth continually and a bright light all around it, and in its midst something like the gleam of glowing metal in the midst of the fire. 5 And within it there were figures with the likeness of four living creatures. And this was their appearance: they had the likeness of a man. 6 And each of them had four faces and four wings. 7 And their legs were straight, and their feet were like a calf's hoof, and they sparkled like the gleam of burnished bronze. 8 And under their wings on their four sides *were* hands of a man. As for the faces and wings of the four of them, 9 their wings touched one another; *their faces* did not turn as they went; each went straight forward. 10 And as for the likeness of their faces, *each* had the face of a man; all four had the face of a lion on the right and the face of a bull on the left, and all four had the face of an eagle. 11 And such were their faces. Their wings were spread out above; each had two touching another *being*, and two covering their bodies. 12 And each went straight forward; wherever the spirit was about to go, they would go,

without turning as they went. 13 As for
the likeness of the living creatures, their
appearance was like burning coals of fire,
like the appearance of torches going back
and forth among the living creatures. The
fire was bright, and lightning was flashing
from the fire. 14 And the living creatures ran
to and fro with the appearance of lightning.
15 Then I looked at the living creatures,
and behold, there was one wheel on the
earth beside the living creatures, for *each
of* the four of them. 16 The appearance of
the wheels and their workmanship *was*
like the gleam of beryl, and all four of them
had the same likeness, their appearance and
workmanship *being* as if one wheel were
within another. 17 Whenever they went,
they went in any of their four directions
without turning as they went. 18 And as for
their rims, they were lofty and awesome,
and the rims of all four of them were full of
eyes all around. 19 And when the living crea-
tures went, the wheels went beside them.
And when the living creatures rose from
the earth, the wheels rose *also*. 20 Wherever
the spirit was about to go, they would go in
that direction, *where* the spirit *was about*
to go. And the wheels rose alongside of
them; for the spirit of the living creatures
was in the wheels. 21 Whenever those went,
these went; and whenever those stood still,
these stood still. And whenever those rose
from the earth, the wheels rose close beside
them; for the spirit of the living creatures
was in the wheels.
22 Now over the heads of the living crea-
tures *there was* something with the likeness
of an expanse, like the awesome gleam of
crystal, spread out over their heads above.
23 And underneath the expanse their wings
were stretched out straight, one toward the
other; each one also had two wings covering
its body on the one side and on the other. 24 I
also heard the sound of their wings like the
sound of many waters as they went, like the
sound of the Almighty, a sound of tumult
like the sound of an army camp; whenever
they stood still, they dropped their wings.
25 And there came a sound from above the
expanse that was over their heads; whenever
they stood still, they dropped their wings.
26 Now above the expanse that was over
their heads there was something in the
likeness of a throne, like sapphire stone in
appearance; and upon the likeness of the
throne, high up, *was* the likeness of one with
the appearance of a man. 27 Then I saw from
the appearance of His loins and upward
something like the gleam of glowing metal
with the appearance of fire all around within
it, and from the appearance of His loins
and downward I saw something with the
appearance of fire; and *there was* a radiance
all around Him. 28 As the appearance of the
rainbow in the clouds on a rainy day, so *was*
the appearance of the radiance all around.
Such *was* the appearance of the likeness of
the glory of Yahweh. And I saw *this*, and I
fell on my face and heard a sound *of a voice*
speaking.

2 Then He said to me, "Son of man, stand
on your feet that I may speak with you!"
2 And as He spoke to me, the Spirit entered
me and caused me to stand on my feet; and
I heard *Him* speaking to me. 3 Then He said
to me, "Son of man, I am sending you to the
sons of Israel, to a rebellious people who
have rebelled against Me; they and their
fathers have transgressed against Me to
this very day. 4 I am sending you to them
who are stiff-faced and strong-hearted
children, and you shall say to them, 'Thus
says Lord Yahweh.' 5 As for them, whether
they listen or whether they refuse—for they
are a rebellious house—they will know that
a prophet has been among them. 6 Now as
for you, son of man, do not fear them and
do not fear their words, though thistles and
briers are with you and you sit on scorpions;
neither fear their words nor be dismayed
at their presence, for they are a rebellious
house. 7 But you shall speak My words to
them whether they listen or whether they
refuse, for they are rebellious.
8 "Now as for you, son of man, listen
to what I am speaking to you; do not be
rebellious like that rebellious house. Open
your mouth and eat what I am giving you."
9 Then I looked, and behold, a hand was
sent forth to me; and behold, a scroll *was*
in it. 10 Then He spread it out before me, and
it was written on the front and back, and
written on it were lamentations, sighing,
and woe.

Psalm 119:153–160

153 See my affliction and rescue me,
For I do not forget Your law.
154 Plead my cause and redeem me;

Revive me according to Your word.
155 Salvation is far from the wicked,
For they do not seek Your statutes.
156 Many are Your compassions,
O Yahweh;
Revive me according to
Your judgments.
157 Many are my persecutors
and my adversaries,
Yet I do not turn aside from
Your testimonies.
158 I see the treacherous and loathe *them*,
Those who do not keep Your word.
159 See how I love Your precepts;
O Yahweh, revive me according
to Your lovingkindness.
160 The sum of Your word is truth,
And every one of Your righteous
judgments is everlasting.

Proverbs 28:12

12 When the righteous exult,
there is great honor,
But when the wicked rise, man
has to be sought out.

Hebrews 1:1–14

1 God, having spoken long ago to the
fathers in the prophets in many portions
and in many ways, 2 in these last days spoke
to us in *His* Son, whom He appointed heir
of all things, through whom also He made
the worlds, 3 who is the radiance of His glory
and the exact representation of His nature,
and upholds all things by the word of His
power; who, having accomplished cleansing
for sins, sat down at the right hand of the
Majesty on high, 4 having become so much
better than the angels, as He has inherited
a more excellent name than they.
5 For to which of the angels did He ever
say,

"You are My Son,
Today I have begotten You"?

And again,

"I will be a Father to Him
And He shall be a Son to Me"?

6 And when He again brings the firstborn
into the world, He says,

"And let all the angels of
God worship Him."

7 And of the angels He says,

"Who makes His angels winds,
And His ministers flaming fire."

8 But of the Son *He says*,

"Your throne, O God, is
forever and ever,
And the scepter of uprightness is
the scepter of Your kingdom.
9 "You have loved righteousness
and hated lawlessness;
Therefore God, Your God,
has anointed You
With the oil of gladness
above Your companions."

10 And,

"You, Lord, in the beginning
founded the earth,
And the heavens are the
works of Your hands;
11 They will perish, but You remain;
And they all will wear
out like a garment,
12 And like a mantle You
will roll them up;
Like a garment they will
also be changed.
But You are the same,
And Your years will not
come to an end."

13 But to which of the angels has He ever
said,

"Sit at My right hand,
Until I put Your enemies
As a footstool for Your feet"?

14 Are they not all ministering spirits, sent
to render service for the sake of those who
will inherit salvation?

NOVEMBER 6

Ezekiel 3:1–4:17

3 Then He said to me, "Son of man, eat
what you find; eat this scroll, and go,
speak to the house of Israel." 2 So I opened
my mouth, and He fed me this scroll. 3 And
He said to me, "Son of man, feed your
stomach and fill your body with this scroll
which I am giving you." Then I ate it, and it
was sweet as honey in my mouth.
4 Then He said to me, "Son of man,
go *now*, come to the house of Israel, and
you shall speak with My words to them.
5 For you are not being sent to a people of
unintelligible lips or a difficult tongue, *but*

to the house of Israel, 6 nor to many peoples
of unintelligible lips or a difficult tongue,
whose words you cannot understand. But
I have sent you to them who should listen
to you; 7 yet the house of Israel will not be
willing to listen to you, since they are not
willing to listen to Me. Surely the whole
house of Israel is *stubborn with* a strong
forehead and stiff heart. 8 Behold, I have
made your face as strong as their faces and
your forehead as strong as their foreheads.
9 Like diamond stronger than flint I have
made your forehead. Do not be afraid of
them or be dismayed before them, though
they are a rebellious house." 10 Moreover, He
said to me, "Son of man, take into your heart
all My words which I will speak to you and
listen with your ears. 11 And go *now*, come
to the exiles, to the sons of your people, and
you shall speak to them and say to them,
whether they listen or whether they refuse,
'Thus says Lord Yahweh.'"

12 Then the Spirit lifted me up, and I heard
a great rumbling sound behind me, "Blessed
be the glory of Yahweh in His place." 13 And
I *heard* the sound of the wings of the living
creatures touching one another and the
sound of the wheels beside them, even
a great rumbling sound. 14 So the Spirit
lifted me up and took me away; and I went
embittered in the wrath of my spirit, and the
hand of Yahweh was strong on me. 15 Then
I came to the exiles who lived beside the
river Chebar at Tel-abib, and I sat there
seven days where they were living, causing
consternation among them.

16 Now it happened at the end of seven
days, that the word of Yahweh came to me,
saying, 17 "Son of man, I have given you as a
watchman to the house of Israel; so you will
hear a word from My mouth, and you shall
warn them from Me. 18 When I say to the
wicked, 'You will surely die,' and you do not
warn him or speak out to warn the wicked
from his wicked way that he may live, that
wicked man shall die in his iniquity, but his
blood I will require at your hand. 19 Yet if
you have warned the wicked and he does
not turn from his wickedness or from his
wicked way, he shall die in his iniquity;
but you have delivered yourself. 20 Again,
when a righteous man turns away from
his righteousness and does evil, and I put
a stumbling block before him, he will die;
since you have not warned him, he shall die
in his sin, and his righteous deeds which he
has done shall not be remembered; but his
blood I will require at your hand. 21 However,
if you have warned the righteous man that
the righteous should not sin and he does
not sin, he shall surely live because he took
warning; and you have delivered yourself."

22 And the hand of Yahweh was on me
there, and He said to me, "Get up, go out
to the plain, and there I will speak to you."
23 So I got up and went out to the plain; and
behold, the glory of Yahweh was standing
there, like the glory which I saw by the river
Chebar, and I fell on my face. 24 The Spirit
then entered me and caused me to stand
on my feet, and He spoke with me and said
to me, "Go, shut yourself up in your house.
25 Now as for you, son of man, they will
put ropes on you and bind you with them
so that you cannot go out among them.
26 Moreover, I will make your tongue cling
to the roof of your mouth so that you will
be mute and cannot be a man who reproves
them, for they are a rebellious house. 27 But
when I speak to you, I will open your mouth,
and you will say to them, 'Thus says Lord
Yahweh.' He who hears, let him hear; and
he who refuses, let him refuse; for they are
a rebellious house.

4 "Now as for you, son of man, get
yourself a brick, set it before you, and
inscribe a city on it, Jerusalem. 2 Then set
a siege against it, build a siege wall against
it, raise up a ramp against it, set up camps
against it, and place battering rams against
it all around. 3 Now as for you, get yourself
an iron plate and set it up as an iron wall
between you and the city, and establish
your face toward it so that it is under siege,
and besiege it. This is a sign to the house
of Israel.

4 "Now as for you, lie down on your left
side and lay the iniquity of the house of
Israel on it; you shall bear their iniquity
for the number of days that you lie on it.
5 Now I have set a number of days for you
corresponding to the years of their iniquity,
390 days; thus you shall bear the iniquity of
the house of Israel. 6 And you shall complete
these, and you shall lie down a second time,
but on your right side and bear the iniquity
of the house of Judah; I have set it for you
for forty days, a day for each year. 7 Then
you shall establish your face toward the

siege of Jerusalem with your arm bared and
prophesy against it. 8 Now behold, I will set
ropes upon you so that you cannot turn
from one side to the other until you have
completed the days of your siege.
9 "Now as for you, take wheat, barley,
beans, lentils, millet, and spelt; set them
in one vessel and make them into bread
for yourself; you shall eat it according to
the number of the days that you lie on your
side, 390 days. 10 And your food which you
eat *shall be* twenty shekels a day by weight;
you shall eat it from time to time. 11 The
water you drink shall be the sixth part of a
hin by measure; you shall drink it from time
to time. 12 You shall eat it as a barley cake,
having baked *it* in their sight over human
dung." 13 Then Yahweh said, "Thus will the
sons of Israel eat their bread unclean among
the nations where I will banish them." 14 But
I said, "Ah, Lord Yahweh! Behold, I have
never been defiled; for from my youth until
now I have never eaten what died of itself
or was torn by beasts, nor has any offensive
meat ever entered my mouth." 15 Then He
said to me, "See, I will set for you cow's dung
in place of human dung over which you will
prepare your bread." 16 Moreover, He said to
me, "Son of man, behold, I am going to break
the staff of bread in Jerusalem, and they will
eat bread by weight and with anxiety, and
they will drink water by measure and in
desolation 17 because bread and water will be
lacking; and they will be in desolation with
one another and rot away in their iniquity.

Psalm 119:161–168

161 Princes persecute me without cause,
But my heart is in dread of Your words.
162 I rejoice at Your word,
As one who finds much spoil.
163 I hate and abhor lying,
But I love Your law.
164 Seven times a day I praise You,
Because of Your righteous judgments.
165 Those who love Your law
have much peace,
And nothing causes them to stumble.
166 I hope for Your salvation, O Yahweh,
And I do Your commandments.
167 My soul keeps Your testimonies,
And I love them exceedingly.
168 I keep Your precepts and
Your testimonies,
For all my ways are before You.

Proverbs 28:13

13 He who conceals his transgressions
will not prosper,
But he who confesses and forsakes
them will receive compassion.

Hebrews 2:1–18

2 For this reason we must pay much
closer attention to what we have heard,
lest we drift away. 2 For if the word spoken
through angels proved unalterable, and
every trespass and disobedience received
a just penalty, 3 how will we escape if we
neglect so great a salvation? That *salvation*,
first spoken by the Lord, was confirmed to
us by those who heard, 4 God also testifying
with them, both by signs and wonders and
by various miracles and by gifts of the Holy
Spirit according to His own will.
5 For He did not subject to angels the
world to come, concerning which we are
speaking. 6 But one has testified somewhere,
saying,

"What is man, that You
remember him?
Or the son of man, that You
are concerned about him?
7 "You have made him for a little
while lower than the angels;
You have crowned him with
glory and honor,
And have appointed him over
the works of Your hands;
8 You have put all things in
subjection under his feet."

For in subjecting all things to him, He left
nothing that is not subject to him. But now
we do not yet see all things subjected to him.
9 But we do see Him who was made for a
little while lower than the angels—Jesus,
because of the suffering of death crowned
with glory and honor, so that by the grace
of God He might taste death for everyone.
10 For it was fitting for Him, for whom
are all things, and through whom are all
things, in bringing many sons to glory, to
perfect the author of their salvation through
sufferings. 11 For both He who sanctifies
and those who are being sanctified are all
of One; for which reason He is not ashamed
to call them brothers, 12 saying,

"I will recount Your name
to My brothers,
In the midst of the assembly
I will sing Your praise."

13 And again,

"I WILL PUT MY TRUST IN HIM."

And again,

"BEHOLD, I AND THE CHILDREN
WHOM GOD HAS GIVEN ME."

14 Therefore, since the children share in flesh and blood, He Himself likewise also partook of the same, that through death He might render powerless him who had the power of death, that is, the devil, 15 and might free those who through fear of death were subject to slavery all their lives. 16 For assuredly He does not give help to angels, but He gives help to the seed of Abraham. 17 Therefore, He had to be made like His brothers in all things, so that He might become a merciful and faithful high priest in things pertaining to God, to make propitiation for the sins of the people. 18 For since He Himself was tempted in that which He has suffered, He is able to come to help those who are tempted.

NOVEMBER 7

Ezekiel 5:1–6:14

5 "Now as for you, son of man, take a sharp sword; take and use it *as* a barber's razor on your head and beard. Then take scales for weighing and divide the hair. 2 One-third you shall burn in the fire at the center of the city when the days of the siege are fulfilled. Then you shall take one-third and strike *it* with the sword all around the city, and one-third you shall scatter to the wind; and I will unsheathe a sword behind them. 3 You shall also take a few in number from them and bind them in the edges of your *robes*. 4 Take again some of them and throw them into the fire and burn them in the fire; from it a fire will spread to all the house of Israel.

5 "Thus says Lord Yahweh, 'This is Jerusalem; I have set her at the center of the nations, with lands all around her. 6 But she has rebelled against My judgments more wickedly than the nations and against My statutes more than the lands which are all around her; for they have rejected My judgments and have not walked in My statutes.' 7 Therefore, thus says Lord Yahweh, 'Because you have more turmoil than the nations which are all around you *and* have not walked in My statutes, nor done My judgments, nor done the judgments of the nations which are all around you,' 8 therefore, thus says Lord Yahweh, 'Behold, I, even I, am against you, and I will execute judgments among you in the sight of the nations. 9 And I will do among you what I have not done and the like of which I will never do again because of all your abominations. 10 Therefore, fathers will eat *their* sons among you, and sons will eat their fathers; for I will execute judgments on you and scatter all your remnant to every wind. 11 So as I live,' declares Lord Yahweh, 'surely, because you have defiled My sanctuary with all your detestable idols and with all your abominations, therefore I will also withdraw, and My eye will have no pity, and I will not spare. 12 One-third of you will die by the plague or be consumed by the famine among you, one-third will fall by the sword around you, and one-third I will scatter to every wind, and I will unsheathe a sword behind them.

13 'Thus My anger will be spent, and I will cause My wrath against them to be at rest, and I will be appeased; then they will know that I, Yahweh, have spoken in My zeal when I have spent My wrath upon them. 14 Moreover, I will make you a ruin and a reproach among the nations which are all around you, in the sight of all who pass by. 15 So it will be a reproach, a reviling, a chastisement, and a desecration to the nations who are all around you when I execute judgments against you in anger, wrath, and wrathful reproofs. I, Yahweh, have spoken. 16 When I send against them the deadly arrows of famine which were for the destruction of those whom I will send to destroy you, then I will also intensify the famine upon you and break the staff of bread. 17 Moreover, I will send on you famine and wild beasts, and they will bereave you of children; plague and bloodshed also will pass through you, and I will bring the sword on you. I, Yahweh, have spoken.'"

6 And the word of Yahweh came to me saying, 2 "Son of man, set your face toward the mountains of Israel, and prophesy against them 3 and say, 'Mountains of

Israel, hear the word of Lord Yahweh! Thus
says Lord Yahweh to the mountains, the
hills, the ravines, and the valleys: "Behold,
I Myself am going to bring a sword on you,
and I will destroy your high places. 4 So
your altars will become desolate, and your
incense altars will be broken; and I will
make your slain fall in front of your idols.
5 I will also put the dead bodies of the sons
of Israel in front of their idols; and I will
scatter your bones all around your altars.
6 In all your *places of* habitation, cities will
become waste, and the high places will be
desolate, that your altars may become waste
and desolate, your idols may be broken and
cease, your incense altars may be cut in
pieces, and your works may be blotted out.
7 The slain will fall among you, and you will
know that I am Yahweh.

8 "However, I will leave a remnant, for
you will have those who escaped the sword
among the nations when you are scattered
among the lands. 9 Then those of you who
escape will remember Me among the nations
to which they will be carried captive, how
I have been broken over their adulterous
hearts which turned away from Me, and
by their eyes which played the harlot after
their idols; and they will loathe themselves
to their own faces for the evils which they
have done, for all their abominations.
10 Then they will know that I am Yahweh;
I have not said in vain that I would do this
calamitous evil against them."'

11 "Thus says Lord Yahweh, 'Strike your
hands *together*, stamp your foot and say,
"Alas, because of all the evil abominations
of the house of Israel, which will fall by the
sword, by the famine, and by the plague!
12 He who is far off will die by the plague,
and he who is near will fall by the sword,
and he who remains and is besieged will
die by the famine. Thus will I spend My
wrath on them. 13 Then you will know that
I am Yahweh when their slain are among
their idols all around their altars, on every
high hill, on all the tops of the mountains,
under every green tree, and under every
leafy oak—the places where they offered
a soothing aroma to all their idols. 14 So
throughout all their habitations I will
stretch out My hand against them and make
the land more desolate and desecrated than
the wilderness toward Diblah; thus they will
know that I am Yahweh."'"

Psalm 119:169–176

169 Let my cry of lamentation come
near before You, O Yahweh;
Give me understanding
according to Your word.
170 Let my supplication come before You;
Deliver me according to Your word.
171 Let my lips pour forth praise,
For You teach me Your statutes.
172 Let my tongue answer with Your word,
For all Your commandments
are righteous.
173 Let Your hand be ready to help me,
For I have chosen Your precepts.
174 I long for Your salvation, O Yahweh,
And Your law is my delight.
175 Let my soul live that it may praise You,
And let Your judgments help me.
176 I have wandered off like a lost
sheep; search for Your slave,
For I have not forgotten Your
commandments.

Proverbs 28:14

14 How blessed is the man who
is always in dread,
But he who hardens his heart
will fall into calamity.

Hebrews 3:1–19

3 Therefore, holy brothers, partakers of a
heavenly calling, consider the Apostle
and High Priest of our confession—Jesus,
2 who was faithful to Him who appointed
Him, as Moses also was in all His house. 3 For
He has been counted worthy of more glory
than Moses, in so much as the builder of
the house has more honor than the house.
4 For every house is built by someone, but
the builder of all things is God. 5 Now Moses
was faithful in all His house as a servant,
for a testimony of those things which were
to be spoken later, 6 but Christ *was faithful*
as a Son over His house—whose house we
are, if we hold fast our confidence and the
boast of our hope.

7 Therefore, just as the Holy Spirit says,
"Today if you hear His voice,
8 Do not harden your hearts as
when they provoked Me,
As in the day of trial in
the wilderness,
9 Where your fathers tried
Me by testing *Me*,
And saw My works for forty years.

10 “THEREFORE I WAS ANGRY WITH
THIS GENERATION,
AND SAID, ‘THEY ALWAYS GO
ASTRAY IN THEIR HEART,
AND THEY DID NOT KNOW MY WAYS’;
11 AS I SWORE IN MY WRATH,
‘THEY SHALL NOT ENTER MY REST.’”

12 See *to it* brothers, that there not be in any one of you an evil, unbelieving heart that falls away from the living God. 13 But encourage one another day after day, as long as it is *still* called “TODAY,” so that none of you will be hardened by the deceitfulness of sin. 14 For we have become partakers of Christ, if we hold fast the beginning of our assurance firm until the end, 15 while it is said,

“TODAY IF YOU HEAR HIS VOICE,
DO NOT HARDEN YOUR HEARTS, AS
WHEN THEY PROVOKED ME.”

16 For who provoked *Him* when they had heard? Indeed, did not all those who came out of Egypt *led* by Moses? 17 And with whom was He angry for forty years? Was it not with those who sinned, whose corpses fell in the wilderness? 18 And to whom did He swear that they would not enter His rest, but to those who were disobedient? 19 *So* we see that they were not able to enter because of unbelief.

NOVEMBER 8

Ezekiel 7:1–8:18

7 Moreover, the word of Yahweh came to me saying, 2 “Now as for you, son of man, thus says Lord Yahweh to the land of Israel, ‘An end! The end is coming on the four corners of the earth. 3 Now the end is upon you, and I will send My anger against you; I will judge you according to your ways and put all your abominations upon you. 4 For My eye will have no pity on you, nor will I spare *you*, but I will put your ways upon you, and your abominations will be among you; then you will know that I am Yahweh!’

5 “Thus says Lord Yahweh, ‘A *calamitous* evil, a unique *calamitous* evil, behold, it is coming! 6 An end has come; the end has come! It has awakened against you; behold, it is coming! 7 Your doom has come to you, O inhabitant of the land. The time has come; the day is near—confusion rather than joyful shouting on the mountains. 8 Now *it is* near *when* I will pour out My wrath on you and spend My anger against you and judge you according to your ways and put on you all your abominations. 9 My eye will show no pity, nor will I spare. I will give to you according to your ways, while your abominations are among you; then you will know that I, Yahweh, do the striking.

10 ‘Behold, the day! Behold, it is coming! *Your* doom has gone forth; the rod has blossomed; arrogance has budded. 11 Violence has grown into a rod of wickedness. None of them *shall remain*, none of their multitude, none of their moaning, nor anything eminent among them. 12 The time has come; the day has arrived. Let not the buyer be glad nor the seller mourn; for wrath is against all their multitude. 13 Indeed, the seller will not return *to himself* what he sold as long as they *both* live; for the vision regarding all their multitude will not return *empty*, nor will any of them strengthen his life by his iniquity.

14 ‘They have blown the trumpet and made everything ready, but no one is going to the battle, for My wrath is against all their multitude. 15 The sword is outside, and the plague and the famine are inside. He who is in the field will die by the sword; famine and the plague will also devour those in the city. 16 Even when their survivors escape, they will be on the mountains like doves of the valleys, all of them moaning, each over his own iniquity. 17 All hands will hang limp, and all knees will become *like* water. 18 They will gird themselves with sackcloth, and horror will cover them; and shame *will be* on all faces and baldness on all their heads. 19 They will throw their silver into the streets, and their gold will become an impure thing; their silver and their gold will not be able to deliver them in the day of the fury of Yahweh. They cannot satisfy their soul, nor can they fill their stomachs, for their iniquity has become an occasion of stumbling.

20 ‘They transformed the beauty of His ornaments into pride, and they made the images of their abominations *and* their detestable things with it; therefore I will make it an impure thing to them. 21 I will give it into the hands of the foreigners as

plunder and to the wicked of the earth as spoil, and they will profane it. 22 I will also turn My face from them, and they will profane My secret place; then robbers will enter and profane it.

23 'Make the chain, for the land is full of judgments *that promote* bloodshed, and the city is full of violence. 24 Therefore, I will bring the *most* evil of the nations, and they will possess their houses. I will also make the pride of the strong ones cease, and their holy places will be profaned. 25 Anguish has come, and they will seek peace, but there will be none. 26 Disaster will come upon disaster, and report will be *added* to report; then they will seek a vision from a prophet, but the law will be lost from the priest and counsel from the elders. 27 The king will mourn, the prince will be clothed with desolation, and the hands of the people of the land will be dismayed. According to their way I will deal with them, and by their judgments I will judge them. And they will know that I am Yahweh.'"

8 Now it happened in the sixth year, on the fifth *day* of the sixth month, as I was sitting in my house with the elders of Judah sitting before me, that the hand of Lord Yahweh fell on me there. 2 Then I looked, and behold, a likeness as the appearance of *one on* fire; from His loins and downward *there was* the appearance of fire, and from His loins and upward the appearance of brightness, like the gleam of glowing metal. 3 He sent forth the form of a hand and took me by a lock of my head; and the Spirit lifted me up between earth and heaven and brought me in the visions of God to Jerusalem, to the entrance of the north gate of the inner *court*, where the seat of the figure of jealousy, which provokes to jealousy, was *located*. 4 And behold, the glory of the God of Israel *was* there, like the appearance which I saw in the plain.

5 Then He said to me, "Son of man, raise your eyes now toward the north." So I raised my eyes toward the north, and behold, to the north of the altar gate *was* this figure of jealousy at the entrance. 6 And He said to me, "Son of man, are you seeing what they are doing, the great abominations which the house of Israel is doing here, so that I would be far from My sanctuary? But yet you will see still greater abominations."

7 Then He brought me to the entrance of the court, and when I looked, behold, a hole in the wall. 8 He said to me, "Son of man, now dig through the wall." So I dug through the wall, and behold, an entrance. 9 And He said to me, "Go in and see the evil abominations that they are doing here." 10 So I entered and looked, and behold, every form of creeping things and beasts *and* detestable things, with all the idols of the house of Israel, were carved on the wall all around. 11 Standing in front of them were seventy elders of the house of Israel, with Jaazaniah the son of Shaphan standing among them, each man with his censer in his hand and the fragrance of the cloud of incense rising. 12 Then He said to me, "Son of man, do you see what the elders of the house of Israel are doing in the dark, each man in the room of his carved images? For they say, 'Yahweh does not see us; Yahweh has forsaken the land.'" 13 And He said to me, "Yet you will see still greater abominations which they are doing."

14 Then He brought me to the entrance of the gate of the house of Yahweh which *was* toward the north; and behold, women were sitting there weeping for Tammuz. 15 He said to me, "Do you see *this*, son of man? Yet you will see still greater abominations than these."

16 Then He brought me into the inner court of the house of Yahweh. And behold, at the entrance to the temple of Yahweh, between the porch and the altar, *were* about twenty-five men with their backs to the temple of Yahweh and their faces toward the east; and they were prostrating themselves eastward toward the sun. 17 He said to me, "Do you see *this*, son of man? Is it too light a thing for the house of Judah to do the abominations which they have done here, that they have filled the land with violence and provoked Me to anger still more? For behold, they are sending forth the twig to their nose. 18 Therefore, I also will do *this* in wrath: My eye will have no pity, nor will I spare; and they will cry in My ears with a loud voice, yet I will not listen to them."

Psalm 120:1–7

1 In my distress I called to Yahweh,
And He answered me.
2 O Yahweh, deliver my soul
from a lying lip,

From a deceitful tongue.
3 What shall He give to you, and
what shall He add to you,
O deceitful tongue?
4 Sharp arrows of the warrior,
With the *burning* coals of
the broom tree.

5 Woe is me, for I sojourn in Meshech,
For I dwell among the tents of Kedar!
6 Too long has my soul had its dwelling
With those who hate peace.
7 I am *for* peace, but when I speak,
They are for war.

Proverbs 28:15

15 *Like* a roaring lion and a rushing bear
Is a wicked ruler over a poor people.

Hebrews 4:1–16

4 Therefore, let us fear, lest, while a
promise remains of entering His rest,
any one of you may seem to have fallen
short of it. 2 For indeed we have had good
news proclaimed to us, just as they also; but
the word that was heard did not profit those
who were not united with faith among those
who heard. 3 For we who have believed enter
that rest, just as He has said,
"AS I SWORE IN MY WRATH,
THEY SHALL NOT ENTER MY REST,"
although His works were finished from
the foundation of the world. 4 For He has
spoken somewhere in this way concerning
the seventh *day*: "AND GOD RESTED ON THE
SEVENTH DAY FROM ALL HIS WORKS"; 5 and
again in this *passage*, "THEY SHALL NOT
ENTER MY REST." 6 Therefore, since it remains
for some to enter it, and those who formerly
had good news proclaimed to them failed to
enter because of disobedience, 7 He again
determines a certain day, "TODAY," saying
through David after so long a time just as
has been said before,
"TODAY IF YOU HEAR HIS VOICE,
DO NOT HARDEN YOUR HEARTS."
8 For if Joshua had given them rest, He would
not have spoken of another day after that.
9 So there remains a Sabbath rest for the peo-
ple of God. 10 For the one who has entered
His rest has himself also rested from his
works, as God did from His. 11 Therefore let
us be diligent to enter that rest, lest anyone
fall into the same example of disobedience.
12 For the word of God is living and active
and sharper than any two-edged sword, and
piercing as far as the division of soul and
spirit, of both joints and marrow, and able
to judge the thoughts and intentions of the
heart. 13 And there is no creature hidden
from His sight, but all things are uncovered
and laid bare to the eyes of Him to whom we
have an account *to give*.
14 Therefore, since we have a great
high priest who has passed through the
heavens, Jesus the Son of God, let us take
hold of our confession. 15 For we do not
have a high priest who cannot sympathize
with our weaknesses, but One who has
been tempted in all things like *we are, yet*
without sin. 16 Therefore let us draw near
with confidence to the throne of grace, so
that we may receive mercy and find grace to
help in time of need.

NOVEMBER 9

Ezekiel 9:1–10:22

9 Then He cried out in my hearing with a
loud voice saying, "Draw near, O execu-
tioners of the city, each with his destroying
weapon in his hand." 2 And behold, six
men were coming from the direction of the
upper gate which faces north, each with his
shattering weapon in his hand; and among
them was a certain man clothed in linen
with a scribe's case at his loins. And they
went in and stood beside the bronze altar.
3 Then the glory of the God of Israel went
up from the cherub on which it had been, to
the threshold of the house *of Yahweh*. And
He called to the man clothed in linen at
whose loins was the scribe's case. 4 Yahweh
said to him, "Go through the midst of the
city, *even* through the midst of Jerusalem,
and put a mark on the foreheads of the men
who sigh and groan over all the abomina-
tions which are being done in its midst."
5 But to the others He said in my hearing,
"Go through the city after him and strike; do
not let your eye have pity and do not spare.
6 Kill to *utter* destruction old men, chosen
men, virgins, little ones, and women, but do
not touch any man on whom is the mark;
and you shall start from My sanctuary." So

they started with the elders who *were* before
the house. 7 And He said to them, "Defile the
house and fill the courts with the slain. Go
out!" Thus they went out and struck down
the people in the city. 8 Now it happened as
they were striking *the people* and I *alone*
remained, that I fell on my face and cried
out and said, "Alas, Lord Yahweh! Are You
destroying the whole remnant of Israel by
pouring out Your wrath on Jerusalem?"

9 Then He said to me, "The iniquity of the
house of Israel and Judah is very, very great,
and the land is filled with bloodshed, and
the city is full of perversion; for they say,
'Yahweh has forsaken the land, and Yahweh
does not see!' 10 But as for Me, My eye will
have no pity, nor will I spare, but I will put
their way upon their heads."

11 Then behold, the man clothed in
linen at whose loins was the *scribe's* case
responded with a word, saying, "I have done
just as You have commanded me."

10 Then I looked, and behold, in the
expanse that was over the heads of
the cherubim something like a sapphire
stone, in appearance in the likeness of a
throne, appeared above them. 2 And He
spoke to the man clothed in linen and said,
"Enter between the whirling wheels under
the cherubim and fill your hands with coals
of fire from between the cherubim and
scatter *them* over the city." And he entered
in my sight.

3 Now the cherubim were standing on
the right side of the house when the man
entered, and the cloud filled the inner court.
4 Then the glory of Yahweh rose up from the
cherub to the threshold of the house, and
the house was filled with the cloud, and
the court was filled with the brightness of
the glory of Yahweh. 5 Moreover, the sound
of the wings of the cherubim was heard as
far as the outer court, like the voice of God
Almighty when He speaks.

6 Now it happened that when He
commanded the man clothed in linen,
saying, "Take fire from between the whirling
wheels, from between the cherubim," he
entered and stood beside a wheel. 7 Then the
cherub sent forth his hand from between
the cherubim to the fire which was between
the cherubim, took *some* up, and put *it* into
the hands of the one clothed in linen, who
took *it* and went out. 8 And the cherubim
appeared to have the form of a man's hand
under their wings.

9 Then I looked, and behold, four wheels
beside the cherubim, one wheel beside each
cherub; and the appearance of the wheels
was like the gleam of a Tarshish stone. 10 As
for their appearance, all four of them had
the same likeness, as if one wheel were
within another wheel. 11 As they went,
they went in *any of* their four directions
without turning as they went; but they went
in the direction which they faced, without
turning as they went. 12 And their whole
body, their backs, their hands, their wings,
and the wheels were full of eyes all around,
the wheels belonging to all four of them.
13 The wheels were called in my hearing, the
whirling wheels. 14 And each one had four
faces. The first face *was* the face of a cherub,
the second face *was* the face of a man, the
third the face of a lion, and the fourth the
face of an eagle.

15 Then the cherubim rose up. They are
the living creatures that I saw by the river
Chebar. 16 Now as the cherubim went, the
wheels went beside them; also when the
cherubim lifted up their wings to rise from
the ground, the wheels would not turn from
beside them. 17 When the cherubim stood
still, the wheels would stand still; and when
they rose up, the wheels would rise with
them, for the spirit of the living creatures
was in them.

18 Then the glory of Yahweh departed
from the threshold of the house and stood
over the cherubim. 19 When the cherubim
departed, they lifted their wings and rose
up from the earth in my sight with the
wheels beside them; and they stood still at
the entrance of the east gate of the house of
Yahweh, and the glory of the God of Israel
hovered over them.

20 These are the living creatures that I
saw beneath the God of Israel by the river
Chebar; so I knew that they *were* cherubim.
21 Each one had four faces and each one
four wings, and beneath their wings *was*
the likeness of human hands. 22 As for the
likeness of their faces, they were the same
faces whose appearance I had seen by the
river Chebar. Each one went straight ahead.

Psalm 121:1–8

1 I will lift up my eyes to the mountains;
From where shall my help come?

2 My help *comes* from Yahweh,
Who made heaven and earth.
3 He will not allow your foot to stumble;
He who keeps you will not slumber.
4 Behold, He who keeps Israel
Will not slumber and will not sleep.

5 Yahweh is your keeper;
Yahweh is your shade on
your right hand.
6 The sun will not strike you by day,
Nor the moon by night.
7 Yahweh will keep you from all evil;
He will keep your soul.
8 Yahweh will keep your going
out and your coming in
From now until forever.

Proverbs 28:16

16 A leader who lacks discernment
abounds in oppressions,
But he who hates greedy gain
will prolong *his* days.

Hebrews 5:1–14

5 For every high priest taken from among
men is appointed on behalf of men in
things pertaining to God, in order to offer
both gifts and sacrifices for sins, 2 being
able to deal gently with the ignorant and
misguided, since he himself also is beset
with weakness; 3 and because of it, he is
obligated, just as for the people, to also
offer *sacrifices* for sins in the same way for
himself. 4 And no one takes this honor to
himself, but *receives it* when he is called by
God, even as Aaron was.
5 In this way also Christ did not glorify
Himself to become a high priest, but He who
said to Him,
"You are My Son,
Today I have begotten You";
6 just as He says also in another *passage*,
"You are a priest forever
According to the order
of Melchizedek."
7 He, in the days of His flesh, offered up
both prayers and supplications with loud
crying and tears to the One able to save Him
from death, and He was heard because of
His reverence. 8 Although He was a Son, He
learned obedience from the things which He
suffered. 9 And having been made perfect,
He became to all those who obey Him the
source of eternal salvation, 10 being desig-
nated by God as a high priest according to
the order of Melchizedek.
11 Concerning him we have much to say,
and *it is* hard to explain, since you have
become dull of hearing. 12 For though by
this time you ought to be teachers, you
have need again for someone to teach you
the elementary principles of the oracles of
God, and you have come to need milk and
not solid food. 13 For everyone who partakes
only of milk is not accustomed to the word
of righteousness, for he is an infant. 14 But
solid food is for the mature, who because of
practice have their senses trained to discern
both good and evil.

NOVEMBER 10

Ezekiel 11:1–12:28

11 Moreover, the Spirit lifted me up and
brought me to the east gate of the
house of Yahweh which faced eastward. And
behold, at the entrance of the gate, *there
were* twenty-five men, and I saw among
them Jaazaniah son of Azzur and Pelatiah
son of Benaiah, officials of the people. 2 He
said to me, "Son of man, these are the men
who devise wickedness and give evil counsel
in this city, 3 who say, '*The time* is not near
to build houses. This *city* is the pot, and we
are the flesh.' 4 Therefore, prophesy against
them, son of man, prophesy!"
5 Then the Spirit of Yahweh fell upon
me, and He said to me, "Say, 'Thus says
Yahweh, "So you say, house of Israel, for I
know what comes up in your spirit. 6 You
have multiplied your slain in this city,
and you have filled its streets with them."
7 Therefore, thus says Lord Yahweh, "Your
slain whom you have laid in the midst of
the city are the flesh, and this *city* is the
pot; but I will bring you out of it. 8 You have
feared a sword; so a sword I will bring upon
you," Lord Yahweh declares. 9 "And I will
bring you out of the midst of the city and
give you into the hands of strangers and
execute judgments against you. 10 You will
fall by the sword. I will judge you to the
border of Israel; so you shall know that I
am Yahweh. 11 This *city* will not be a pot for

you, nor will you be flesh in the midst of it, *but* I will judge you to the border of Israel. 12 Thus you will know that I am Yahweh; for you have not walked in My statutes, nor have you executed My judgments, but have executed according to the judgments of the nations around you."'"

13 Now it happened as I prophesied, that Pelatiah son of Benaiah died. Then I fell on my face and cried out with a loud voice and said, "Alas, Lord Yahweh! Will You bring the remnant of Israel to complete destruction?"

14 Then the word of Yahweh came to me, saying, 15 "Son of man, your brothers, your relatives, your fellow exiles, and the whole house of Israel, all of them, *are those* to whom the inhabitants of Jerusalem have said, 'Go far from Yahweh; this land has been given to us as a possession.' 16 Therefore say, 'Thus says Lord Yahweh, "Though I had removed them far away among the nations, and though I had scattered them among the countries, yet I was a sanctuary for them a little while in the countries where they had gone."' 17 Therefore say, 'Thus says Lord Yahweh, "I will gather you from the peoples and assemble you out of the countries among which you have been scattered, and I will give you the land of Israel."' 18 When they come there, they will remove all its detestable things and all its abominations from it. 19 And I will give them one heart and give within them a new spirit. And I will take the heart of stone out of their flesh and give them a heart of flesh, 20 that they may walk in My statutes and keep My judgments and do them. Then they will be My people, and I shall be their God. 21 But as for those whose hearts walk after their detestable things and abominations, I will give *what is due* for their way on their heads," declares Lord Yahweh.

22 Then the cherubim lifted up their wings with the wheels beside them, and the glory of the God of Israel hovered over them. 23 The glory of Yahweh went up from the midst of the city and stood over the mountain which is east of the city. 24 Now the Spirit lifted me up and brought me in a vision by the Spirit of God to the exiles in Chaldea. So the vision that I had seen went up *and* away from me. 25 Then I told the exiles all the things that Yahweh had shown me.

12 Then the word of Yahweh came to me, saying, 2 "Son of man, you live in the midst of the rebellious house, who have eyes to see but do not see, ears to hear but do not hear; for they are a rebellious house. 3 Now as for you, son of man, prepare for yourself baggage for exile and go into exile by day in their sight; even go into exile from your place to another place in their sight. Perhaps they will see, though they are a rebellious house. 4 Bring your baggage out by day in their sight, as baggage for exile. Then you will go out at evening in their sight, as those going into exile. 5 In their sight, dig a hole through the wall and go out through it. 6 In their sight, carry *the baggage* on *your* shoulder *and* bring *it* out in the dark. You shall cover your face so that you cannot see the land, for I have set you as a wondrous sign to the house of Israel."

7 I did so, as I had been commanded. By day I brought out my baggage like the baggage of an exile. Then in the evening I dug through the wall with my hands; I went out in the dark *and* carried *the baggage* on *my* shoulder in their sight.

8 And in the morning the word of Yahweh came to me, saying, 9 "Son of man, has not the house of Israel, the rebellious house, said to you, 'What are you doing?' 10 Say to them, 'Thus says Lord Yahweh, "This oracle *concerns* the prince in Jerusalem as well as all the house of Israel who are in it."' 11 Say, 'I am a wondrous sign to you. As I have done, so it will be done to them; they will go into exile, into captivity.' 12 The prince who is among them will carry *his baggage* on *his* shoulder in the dark and go out. They will dig a hole through the wall to bring *it* out. He will cover his face so that he cannot see the land with *his* eyes. 13 I will also spread My net over him, and he will be caught in My snare. And I will bring him to Babylon in the land of the Chaldeans; yet he will not see it, though he will die there. 14 And I will scatter to every wind all who are around him, his helpers and all his troops; and I will draw out a sword after them. 15 So they will know that I am Yahweh when I scatter them among the nations and spread them among the countries. 16 But I will spare a few of them from sword, famine, and pestilence that they may recount all their abominations among the nations where they go, and may know that I am Yahweh."

17 Moreover, the word of Yahweh came to
me saying, 18 "Son of man, you shall eat your
bread with trembling and drink your water
with quivering and anxiety. 19 Then you will
say to the people of the land, 'Thus says
Lord Yahweh concerning the inhabitants
of Jerusalem in the land of Israel, "They
will eat their bread with anxiety and drink
their water with desolation because their
very soil will be made desolate of its fullness
on account of the violence of all who inhabit
it. 20 The inhabited cities will be laid waste,
and the land will be a desolation. So you will
know that I am Yahweh."'"

21 Then the word of Yahweh came to me,
saying, 22 "Son of man, what is this proverb
you *people* have concerning the land of
Israel, saying, 'The days are long, and every
vision fails'? 23 Therefore say to them, 'Thus
says Lord Yahweh, "I will make this proverb
cease so that they will no longer use it as a
proverb in Israel." But speak to them, "The
days draw near as well as the fulfillment
of every vision. 24 For there will no longer
be any worthless vision or flattering divi-
nation in the midst of the house of Israel.
25 For I, Yahweh, will speak, and whatever
word I speak will be done. It will no longer
be delayed, for in your days, O rebellious
house, I will speak the word and do it,"
declares Lord Yahweh.'"

26 Furthermore, the word of Yahweh came
to me, saying, 27 "Son of man, behold, the
house of Israel is saying, 'The vision that he
beholds is for many years *from now*, and he
prophesies of times far off.' 28 Therefore say
to them, 'Thus says Lord Yahweh, "None of
My words will be delayed any longer. What-
ever word I speak will be done,"'" declares
Lord Yahweh.

Psalm 122:1–5

1 I was glad when they said to me,
"Let us go to the house of Yahweh."
2 Our feet are standing
Within your gates,
O Jerusalem,
3 Jerusalem, which is built
As a city joined altogether;
4 To which the tribes, the
tribes of Yah, go up—
A testimony for Israel—
To give thanks to the name of Yahweh.
5 For there, thrones sit for judgment,
The thrones of the house of David.

Proverbs 28:17–18

17 A man oppressed with the
bloodguilt of life
Will flee until death; let no
one uphold him.
18 He who walks blamelessly
will be saved,
But he who is crooked—double
dealing—will fall all at once.

Hebrews 6:1–20

6 Therefore leaving the elementary teach-
ing about the Christ, let us press on to
maturity, not laying again a foundation of
repentance from dead works and of faith
toward God, 2 of teaching about washings
and laying on of hands, and the resurrection
of the dead and eternal judgment. 3 And
this we will do, if God permits. 4 For in the
case of those once having been enlightened
and having tasted of the heavenly gift and
having become partakers of the Holy Spirit,
5 and having tasted the good word of God
and the powers of the age to come, 6 and
having fallen away, it is impossible to renew
them again to repentance, since they again
crucify to themselves the Son of God and
put Him to open shame. 7 For ground that
drinks the rain which often falls on it and
brings forth vegetation useful to those
for whose sake it is also tilled, receives a
blessing from God; 8 but if it yields thorns
and thistles, it is unfit and close to being
cursed, and its end is to be burned.

9 But we are convinced about you,
beloved, of things that are better and that
belong to salvation, though we are speaking
in this way. 10 For God is not unrighteous so
as to forget your work and the love which
you have shown toward His name, in having
ministered and continuing to minister to the
saints. 11 And we desire that each one of you
show the same diligence so as to realize the
full assurance of hope until the end, 12 so
that you may not become dull, but imitators
of those who through faith and patience
inherit the promises.

13 For when God made the promise to
Abraham, since He could swear by no one
greater, He swore by Himself, 14 saying, "I
WILL GREATLY BLESS YOU AND I WILL GREATLY
MULTIPLY YOU." 15 And so, having patiently
waited, he obtained the promise. 16 For men
swear by one greater *than themselves*, and
with them an oath *given* as confirmation is

an end of every dispute. 17 In the same way
God, desiring even more to show to the heirs
of the promise the unchangeableness of His
purpose, guaranteed *it* with an oath, 18 so
that by two unchangeable things in which
it is impossible for God to lie, we who have
taken refuge would have strong encourage-
ment to take hold of the hope set before us.
19 This hope we have as an anchor of the
soul, a *hope* both sure and confirmed and
one which enters within the veil, 20 where a
forerunner has entered for us—Jesus, hav-
ing become a high priest forever according
to the order of Melchizedek.

NOVEMBER 11

Ezekiel 13:1–14:23

13 Then the word of Yahweh came to me
saying, 2 "Son of man, prophesy against
the prophets of Israel who prophesy, and say
to those who prophesy from their own heart,
'Hear the word of Yahweh! 3 Thus says Lord
Yahweh, "Woe to the wickedly foolish proph-
ets who are walking after their own spirit and
have seen nothing. 4 O Israel, your prophets
have been like foxes among waste places. 5 You
have not gone up into the breaches, nor did
you build the wall around the house of Israel
to stand in the battle on the day of Yahweh.
6 They behold worthlessness and lying div-
ination who are saying, 'Yahweh declares,'
when Yahweh has not sent them; yet they wait
for the establishing of *their* word. 7 Did you
not see a worthless vision and speak a lying
divination when you said, 'Yahweh declares,'
but it is not I who have spoken?"'"

8 Therefore, thus says Lord Yahweh,
"Because you have spoken worthlessness
and beheld a lie, therefore behold, I am
against you," declares Lord Yahweh. 9 "So My
hand will be against the prophets who see
worthless visions and utter lying divinations.
They will not be in the council of My people,
nor will they be written down in the register
of the house of Israel, nor will they enter the
land of Israel, that you may know that I am
Lord Yahweh. 10 It is definitely because they
have misled My people by saying, 'Peace!'
when there is no peace. And when anyone
builds a wall, behold, they plaster it over with
whitewash; 11 *so* tell those who plaster *it* over
with whitewash that it will fall. A flooding
rain will come, and you, O hailstones, will
fall; and a stormy wind will break out. 12 Now
behold, the wall will fall. Will it *then* not be
said to you, 'Where is the plaster with which
you plastered *it?*'" 13 Therefore, thus says
Lord Yahweh, "I will make a stormy wind
break out in My wrath. There will also be in
My anger a flooding rain and hailstones to
consume *it* in wrath. 14 So I will pull down the
wall which you plastered over with white-
wash and bring it down to the ground, so
that its foundation is laid bare; and it will fall,
and you will be consumed in its midst. And
you will know that I am Yahweh. 15 Thus I
will spend My wrath on the wall and on those
who have plastered it over with whitewash;
and I will say to you, 'The wall is gone, and
its plasterers are gone— 16 the prophets of
Israel who prophesy to Jerusalem and who
see visions of peace for her when there is no
peace,' declares Lord Yahweh.

17 "Now as for you, son of man, set your
face against the daughters of your people
who are prophesying from their own heart.
Prophesy against them 18 and say, 'Thus says
Lord Yahweh, "Woe to the women who sew
magic bands on all wrists and make veils
for the heads of *persons* of every stature to
hunt down souls! Will you hunt down My
people's souls, but preserve your own souls?
19 For handfuls of barley and fragments of
bread, you have profaned Me to My people
to put to death souls who should not die
and to keep *other* souls alive who should
not live, by your lying to My people who
listen to lies."'"

20 Therefore, thus says Lord Yahweh,
"Behold, I am against your *magic* bands by
which you hunt souls there as birds, and I
will tear them from your arms; and I will
let *their* souls go, *the very* souls whom you
hunt as birds. 21 I will also tear off your veils
and deliver My people from your hands,
and they will no longer be in your hands
to be hunted; and you will know that I am
Yahweh. 22 Because you disheartened the
righteous with falsehood when I did not
cause him grief, but have strengthened the
hands of the wicked not to turn from his evil
way *and* preserve his life, 23 therefore, you
women will no longer see worthless visions
or practice divination, and I will deliver My

people out of your hand. Thus you will know that I am Yahweh."

14 Then some elders of Israel came to me and sat down before me. 2 And the word of Yahweh came to me, saying, 3 "Son of man, these men have set up their idols in their hearts and have put right before their faces the stumbling block of their iniquity. Should I be inquired by them at all? 4 Therefore speak to them and tell them, 'Thus says Lord Yahweh, "Any man of the house of Israel who sets up his idols in his heart, puts right before his face the stumbling block of his iniquity, and *then* comes to the prophet, I Yahweh will be brought to give him an answer in light of it, in light of the multitude of his idols, 5 in order to seize the house of Israel by their heart, *those* who are estranged from Me through all their idols."'

6 "Therefore say to the house of Israel, 'Thus says Lord Yahweh, "Turn back and turn away from your idols and turn your faces away from all your abominations. 7 For anyone of the house of Israel or of the sojourners who sojourn in Israel who separates himself from Me, sets up his idols in his heart, puts right before his face the stumbling block of his iniquity, and *then* comes to the prophet to inquire of Me for himself, I, Yahweh, will be brought to answer him in My own person. 8 I will set My face against that man and make him a sign and a proverb, and I will cut him off from among My people. So you will know that I am Yahweh.

9 "But if the prophet is enticed to speak a word, it is I, Yahweh, who have enticed that prophet, and I will stretch out My hand against him and destroy him from among My people Israel. 10 They will bear *the punishment of* their iniquity; as the iniquity of the inquirer is, so the iniquity of the prophet will be, 11 in order that the house of Israel may no longer wander from Me and no longer defile themselves with all their transgressions. Thus they will be My people, and I shall be their God,"' declares Lord Yahweh."

12 Then the word of Yahweh came to me saying, 13 "Son of man, if a country sins against Me by committing unfaithfulness, and I stretch out My hand against it, break its staff of bread, send famine against it, and cut off from it both man and beast, 14 even *though* these three men, Noah, Daniel, and Job were in its midst, by their *own* righteousness they could *only* deliver themselves," declares Lord Yahweh. 15 "If I were to cause wild beasts to pass through the land and they bereaved it of children and it became desolate so that no one would pass through it because of the beasts, 16 *though* these three men were in its midst, as I live," declares Lord Yahweh, "they could not deliver either *their* sons or *their* daughters. They alone would be delivered, but the country would become desolate. 17 Or *if* I should bring a sword on that country and say, 'Let the sword pass through the country and cut off man and beast from it,' 18 even *though* these three men were in its midst, as I live," declares Lord Yahweh, "they could not deliver either *their* sons or *their* daughters, but they alone would be delivered. 19 Or *if* I should send a plague against that country and pour out My wrath in blood on it to cut off man and beast from it, 20 even *though* Noah, Daniel, and Job were in its midst, as I live," declares Lord Yahweh, "they could not deliver either *their* son or *their* daughter. They would deliver only themselves by their righteousness."

21 For thus says Lord Yahweh, "How much more when I send My four calamitous judgments against Jerusalem: sword, famine, wild beasts, and plague to cut off man and beast from it! 22 Yet, behold, survivors will be left in it who will be brought out, *both* sons and daughters. Behold, they are going to come forth to you, and you will see their way and actions; then you will be comforted for the calamity which I have brought against Jerusalem for everything which I have brought upon it. 23 Then they will comfort you when you see their way and actions, so you will know that I have not done in vain all that I did to it," declares Lord Yahweh.

Psalm 122:6–9

6 Pray for the peace of Jerusalem:
"May they prosper who love you.
7 "May peace be within your walls,
And tranquility within your palaces."
8 For the sake of my brothers
and my friends,
I will now say, "May peace
be within you."
9 For the sake of the house
of Yahweh our God,
I will seek your good.

Proverbs 28:19

19 He who cultivates his ground
will be satisfied with food,
But he who pursues empty *things*
will be satisfied with poverty.

Hebrews 7:1–28

7 For this MELCHIZEDEK, KING OF SALEM, PRIEST OF THE MOST HIGH GOD, who met ABRAHAM AS HE WAS RETURNING FROM THE SLAUGHTER OF THE KINGS and BLESSED HIM, 2 TO WHOM ALSO ABRAHAM APPORTIONED A TENTH PART OF ALL, was first of all, by the translation *of his name*, king of righteousness, and then also king of Salem, which is king of peace. 3 Without father, without mother, without genealogy, having neither beginning of days nor end of life, but made like the Son of God, he remains a priest continually.

4 Now observe how great this man was TO WHOM ABRAHAM, the patriarch, GAVE A TENTH of the spoils. 5 And those indeed of the sons of Levi, who receive the priest's office, have a commandment in the Law to collect a tenth from the people, that is, from their brothers, although these are descended from Abraham. 6 But the one whose genealogy is not traced from them had collected a tenth from Abraham and blessed the one who had the promises. 7 But without any dispute the lesser is blessed by the greater. 8 And in this case mortal men receive tithes, but in that case one *receives them*, of whom it is witnessed that he lives on. 9 And, so to speak, through Abraham even Levi, who received tithes, paid tithes, 10 for he was still in the loins of his father when Melchizedek met him.

11 Now if perfection was through the Levitical priesthood (for on the basis of it the people received the Law), what further need *was there* for another priest to arise according to the order of Melchizedek, and not be designated according to the order of Aaron? 12 For when the priesthood is changed, of necessity there takes place a change of law also. 13 For the one concerning whom these things are spoken belongs to another tribe, from which no one has officiated at the altar. 14 For it is evident that our Lord was descended from Judah, a tribe with reference to which Moses spoke nothing concerning priests. 15 And this is clearer still, if another priest arises according to the likeness of Melchizedek, 16 who has become *such* not according to a law of physical requirement, but according to the power of an indestructible life. 17 For it is witnessed *about Him*,

"YOU ARE A PRIEST FOREVER
ACCORDING TO THE ORDER
OF MELCHIZEDEK."

18 For, on the one hand, there is a setting aside of a former commandment because of its weakness and uselessness 19 (for the Law made nothing perfect), and on the other hand there is a bringing in of a better hope, through which we draw near to God. 20 And inasmuch as *it was* not without an oath 21 (for they indeed became priests without an oath, but He with an oath through the One who said to Him,

"THE LORD HAS SWORN
AND WILL NOT CHANGE HIS MIND,
'YOU ARE A PRIEST FOREVER'");

22 so much more Jesus also has become the guarantee of a better covenant.

23 And the *former* priests, on the one hand, existed in greater numbers because they were prevented by death from continuing, 24 but *Jesus*, on the other hand, because He continues forever, holds His priesthood permanently. 25 Therefore He is able also to save forever those who draw near to God through Him, since He always lives to make intercession for them.

26 For it was fitting for us to have such a high priest, holy, innocent, undefiled, separated from sinners and exalted above the heavens; 27 who does not need daily, like those high priests, to offer up sacrifices, first for His own sins and then for the *sins* of the people, because this He did once for all when He offered up Himself. 28 For the Law appoints men as high priests who are weak, but the word of the oath, which came after the Law, *appoints* a Son, who has been made perfect forever.

There are two ways to read Scripture—the way a lawyer reads a will and the way an heir reads a will.

— ALEXANDER WHYTE

NOVEMBER 12

Ezekiel 15:1–16:63

15 Then the word of Yahweh came to me, saying, 2 "Son of man, how is the wood of the vine *better* than any wood of a branch which is among the trees of the forest? 3 Can wood be taken from it to make anything, or can *men* take a peg from it on which to hang any vessel? 4 If it has been put into the fire for fuel, *and* the fire has consumed both of its ends, and its middle part has been charred, is it *then* useful for anything? 5 Behold, while it is intact, it is not made into anything. How much less, when the fire has consumed it and it is charred, can it still be made into anything! 6 Therefore, thus says Lord Yahweh, 'As the wood of the vine among the trees of the forest, which I have given to the fire for fuel, so have I given up the inhabitants of Jerusalem; 7 and I will give My face *to be* against them. *Though* they have come out of the fire, yet the fire will consume them. Then you will know that I am Yahweh, when I set My face against them. 8 Thus I will give over the land *to* desolation because they have acted unfaithfully,'" declares Lord Yahweh.

16 Then the word of Yahweh came to me, saying, 2 "Son of man, make known to Jerusalem her abominations 3 and say, 'Thus says Lord Yahweh to Jerusalem, "Your origin and your birth are from the land of the Canaanite; your father was an Amorite and your mother a Hittite. 4 As for your birth, on the day you were born your navel cord was not cut, nor were you washed with water for cleansing; you were not rubbed with salt or even wrapped in cloths. 5 No eye had pity on you to do any of these things for you, to have compassion on you. Rather you were thrown out into the open field, for your soul was abhorred on the day you were born.

6 "Then I passed by you and saw you squirming in your blood. So I said to you *while you were* in your blood, 'Live!' Indeed I said to you *while you were* in your blood, 'Live!' 7 I made you numerous like plants of the field. Then you grew up, became tall, and came into the age for fine ornaments; *your* breasts were formed, and your hair had grown. Yet you were naked and bare.

8 "Then I passed by you and saw you, and behold, you were at the time for love; so I spread My skirt over you and covered your nakedness. I also swore to you and entered into a covenant with you so that you became Mine," declares Lord Yahweh. 9 "Then I washed you with water, rinsed your blood off from you, and anointed you with oil. 10 I also clothed you with embroidered cloth and put sandals of porpoise skin on your feet; and I wrapped you with fine linen and covered you with silk. 11 I also adorned you with ornaments and put bracelets on your hands and a necklace around your neck. 12 I also put a ring in your nose, earrings in your ears, and a splendid crown on your head. 13 Thus you were adorned with gold and silver, and your clothing was of fine linen, silk, and embroidered cloth. You ate fine flour, honey, and oil; so you were exceedingly beautiful and advanced to royalty. 14 Then your name went forth among the nations on account of your beauty, for it was perfect because of My majesty which I set on you," declares Lord Yahweh.

15 "But you trusted in your beauty and played the harlot because of your name, and you poured out your harlotries on every passer-by who might be *willing*. 16 You took some of your clothes, made for yourself high places of various colors, and played the harlot on them, which should never come about nor happen. 17 You also took your splendid jewelry *made* of My gold and of My silver, which I had given you, and made for yourself male images that you might play the harlot with them. 18 Then you took your embroidered cloth and covered them and gave My oil and My incense before them. 19 Also My bread which I gave you, fine flour, oil, and honey with which I had you eat, you gave before them for a soothing aroma; so it happened," declares Lord Yahweh. 20 "Moreover, you took your sons and daughters, whom you had borne to Me, and sacrificed them to idols to be devoured. Were your harlotries so small a matter? 21 You slaughtered My children and gave them up to idols by causing them to pass through *the fire*. 22 Besides all your abominations and harlotries you did not remember the days of your youth, when you

were naked and bare—you were squirming in your blood!

23 “Now it happened after all your evil—‘Woe, woe to you!’ declares Lord Yahweh— 24 that you built yourself a shrine and made yourself a high place in every square. 25 You built yourself a high place at the head of every street and made your beauty abominable, and you spread your legs to every passer-by to multiply your harlotry. 26 You also played the harlot with the Egyptians, your lustful neighbors, and you multiplied your harlotry to provoke Me to anger. 27 Behold now, I have stretched out My hand against you and cut off your rations. And I gave you up to the desire of those who hate you, the daughters of the Philistines, who are ashamed of your lewd way. 28 Moreover, you played the harlot with the Assyrians because you were not satisfied; you played the harlot with them and still were not satisfied. 29 You also multiplied your harlotry with the land of merchants, Chaldea, yet even with this you were not satisfied.”’”

30 “How languishing is your heart,” declares Lord Yahweh, “while you do all these things, the actions of a bold-faced harlot. 31 When you built your shrine at the head of every way and made your high place in every square, in disdaining *your* earnings, you were not like a harlot. 32 You adulteress wife, who takes strangers instead of her husband! 33 Men give gifts to all harlots, but you give your gifts to all your lovers to bribe them to come to you from all around for your harlotries. 34 Thus you are the opposite of those women in your harlotries, in that no one plays the harlot as you do, because you give away *your* earnings and no earnings are given to you; thus you are the opposite.”

35 Therefore, O harlot, hear the word of Yahweh. 36 Thus says Lord Yahweh, “Because your lewdness was poured out and your nakedness uncovered through your harlotries with your lovers and with all your abominable idols, and because of the blood of your sons which you gave to idols, 37 therefore, behold, I will gather all your lovers with whom you took pleasure, even all those whom you loved *and* all those whom you hated. So I will gather them against you from all around and uncover your nakedness to them that they may see all your nakedness. 38 Thus I will judge you like women who commit adultery or shed blood are judged; and I will bring on you the blood of wrath and jealousy. 39 I will also give you into the hands of your lovers, and they will pull down your shrines, tear down your high places, strip you of your clothing, take away your splendid jewelry, and will leave you naked and bare. 40 They will bring up an assembly against you, and they will stone you and cut you to pieces with their swords. 41 They will burn your houses with fire and execute judgments on you in the sight of many women. Then I will make you cease from playing the harlot, and you will also no longer give *your* earnings *to your lovers.* 42 So I will cause My wrath against you to be at rest, and My jealousy will depart from you, and I will be quiet, and I will not be provoked anymore. 43 Because you have not remembered the days of your youth but have enraged Me by all these things, behold, I in turn will bring your way down on your own head,” declares Lord Yahweh, “so that you will not commit this lewdness on top of all your *other* abominations.

44 “Behold, everyone who quotes proverbs will quote *this* proverb concerning you, saying, ‘Like mother, like daughter.’ 45 You are the daughter of your mother, who loathed her husband and children. You are also the sister of your sisters, who loathed their husbands and children. Your mother was a Hittite and your father an Amorite. 46 Now your older sister is Samaria, who lives north of you with her daughters; and your younger sister, who lives south of you, is Sodom with her daughters. 47 Yet you have not merely walked in their ways or done according to their abominations; but, as if that were too little, you acted more corruptly in all your ways than they. 48 As I live,” declares Lord Yahweh, “Sodom your sister and her daughters have not done as you and your daughters have done. 49 Behold, this was the iniquity of your sister Sodom: she and her daughters had lofty pride, abundant food, and quiet ease, but she did not strengthen the hand of the afflicted and needy. 50 Then they were haughty and committed abominations before Me. So I removed them when I saw *it.* 51 Furthermore, Samaria did not commit half of your sins, for you have multiplied your abominations more than they. Thus you have made your sisters appear

righteous by all your abominations which
you have done. 52 Also bear your dishonor in
that you have made judgment favorable for
your sisters. Because of your sins in which
you acted more abominably than they, they
are more in the right than you. Yes, be also
ashamed and bear your dishonor, in that
you made your sisters appear righteous.

53 "Nevertheless, I will return their
captivity, the captivity of Sodom and her
daughters, the captivity of Samaria and
her daughters, and along with them your
own captivity, 54 in order that you may bear
your dishonor and feel dishonor for all that
you have done when you become a comfort
to them. 55 Your sisters, Sodom with her
daughters and Samaria with her daughters,
will return to their former state, and you
with your daughters will *also* return to your
former state. 56 As *the name of* your sister
Sodom was not heard in your mouth in your
day of lofty pride, 57 before your wickedness
was uncovered, so now you have become the
reproach of the daughters of Edom and of
all who are around her, of the daughters of
the Philistines—those all around *you* who
despise you. 58 You have borne *the penalty of*
your lewdness and abominations," declares
Yahweh. 59 For thus says Lord Yahweh, "I
will also do with you as you have done, you
who have despised the oath by breaking the
covenant.

60 "Nevertheless, I Myself will remember
My covenant with you in the days of your
youth, and I will establish an everlasting
covenant with you. 61 Then you will
remember your ways and feel dishonor
when you receive your sisters, *both* your
older and your younger; and I will give
them to you as daughters, but not because
of your covenant. 62 Thus I will establish My
covenant with you, and you shall know that
I am Yahweh, 63 so that you may remember
and be ashamed and never open your mouth
anymore because of your dishonor, when
I have atoned for you for all that you have
done," declares Lord Yahweh.

Psalm 123:1–4

1 To You I lift up my eyes,
The One enthroned in the heavens!
2 Behold, as the eyes of slaves *look*
to the hand of their master,
As the eyes of a servant-girl to
the hand of her mistress,
So our eyes *look* to Yahweh our God,
Until He is gracious to us.

3 Be gracious to us, O Yahweh,
be gracious to us,
For we are greatly saturated
with contempt.
4 Our soul is greatly saturated
With the mockery of those
who are at ease,
And with the contempt of the proud.

Proverbs 28:20

20 A faithful man will abound
with blessings,
But he who makes haste to be
rich will not go unpunished.

Hebrews 8:1–13

8 Now the main point in what is being said
is this: we have such a high priest, who
sat down at the right hand of the throne of
the Majesty in the heavens, 2 a minister in
the holy places and in the true tabernacle,
which the Lord pitched, not man. 3 For every
high priest is appointed to offer both gifts
and sacrifices; so it is necessary that this
high priest also have something to offer.
4 Now if He were on earth, He would not be
a priest at all, since there are those who offer
the gifts according to the Law; 5 who serve a
copy and shadow of the heavenly things, just
as Moses was warned *by God* when he was
about to erect the tabernacle; for, "SEE," He
says, "THAT YOU MAKE all things ACCORDING
TO THE PATTERN WHICH WAS SHOWN YOU ON
THE MOUNTAIN." 6 But now He has obtained a
more excellent ministry, by as much as He is
also the mediator of a better covenant, which
has been enacted on better promises. 7 For if
that first *covenant* had been faultless, there
would have been no occasion sought for a
second. 8 For finding fault with them, He says,

"BEHOLD, DAYS ARE COMING,
SAYS THE LORD,
WHEN I WILL COMPLETE A
NEW COVENANT
WITH THE HOUSE OF ISRAEL AND
WITH THE HOUSE OF JUDAH;
9 NOT LIKE THE COVENANT WHICH I
MADE WITH THEIR FATHERS
IN THE DAY WHEN I TOOK
THEM BY THE HAND
TO LEAD THEM OUT OF THE
LAND OF EGYPT;

For they did not continue
in My covenant,
And I did not care for
them, says the Lord.
10 "For this is the covenant that I will
make with the house of Israel
After those days, says the Lord:
I will put My laws into their minds,
And upon their hearts I
will write them.
And I will be their God,
And they shall be My people.
11 "And they shall not teach
everyone his fellow citizen,
And everyone his brother,
saying, 'Know the Lord,'
For all will know Me,
From the least to the
greatest of them.
12 "For I will be merciful to
their iniquities,
And I will remember their
sins no more."

13 When He said, "A new *covenant*," He has made the first obsolete. But whatever is becoming obsolete and growing old is ready to disappear.

NOVEMBER 13

Ezekiel 17:1–18:32

17 Now the word of Yahweh came to me saying, 2 "Son of man, propound a riddle and speak a parable to the house of Israel, 3 and you will say, 'Thus says Lord Yahweh, "A great eagle with great wings, long pinions, and a full plumage of many colors came to Lebanon and took away the top of the cedar. 4 He plucked off the topmost of its young twigs and brought it to a land of merchants; he set it in a city of traders. 5 He also took some of the seed of the land and planted it in a field *fit for* seed. He placed *it* beside abundant waters; he set it *like* a willow. 6 Then it sprouted and became a low, spreading vine with its foliage turned toward him, but its roots remained under it. So it became a vine and yielded shoots and sent out branches.

7 "But there was another great eagle with great wings and much plumage; and behold, this vine bent its roots toward him and sent out its foliage toward him from the beds where it was planted, that he might water it. 8 It was planted in a good field beside abundant waters, that it might yield branches and bear fruit *and* become a majestic vine."' 9 Say, 'Thus says Lord Yahweh, "Will it succeed? Will he not pull up its roots and cut off its fruit, so that it dries up—so that all its sprouting leaves dry up? And neither by great strength nor by many people can it be raised from its roots *again*. 10 And behold, though it is planted, will it succeed? Will it not completely dry up as soon as the east wind strikes it—dry up on the beds where it sprouted?"'"

11 Moreover, the word of Yahweh came to me, saying, 12 "Say now to the rebellious house, 'Do you not know what these things *mean*?' Say, 'Behold, the king of Babylon came to Jerusalem, took its king and princes, and brought them to him in Babylon. 13 He took one of the royal seed and cut a covenant with him and brought him under oath. He also took away the dominant one of the land, 14 that the kingdom might become lowly, not lifting itself up, *but* keeping his covenant that it might continue. 15 But he rebelled against him by sending his messengers to Egypt that they might give him horses and many troops. Will he succeed? Will he who does such things escape? Can he indeed break the covenant and escape? 16 As I live,' declares Lord Yahweh, 'Surely in the country of the king who made him king, whose oath he despised and whose covenant he broke, in Babylon he shall die. 17 And Pharaoh with *his* mighty military force and great assembly will not help him in the war, when they cast up ramps and build siege walls to cut off many lives. 18 Now he despised the oath by breaking the covenant, and behold, he pledged his allegiance, yet did all these things; he shall not escape.'" 19 Therefore, thus says Lord Yahweh, "As I live, surely My oath which he despised and My covenant which he broke, I will put on his head. 20 I will spread My net over him, and he will be caught in My snare. Then I will bring him to Babylon and enter into judgment with him there *regarding* the unfaithful act which he has committed against Me. 21 All the choice men in all his troops will fall by the sword,

and the remnant will be scattered to every
wind; and you will know that I, Yahweh,
have spoken."
22 Thus says Lord Yahweh, "I will also take
a sprig from the lofty top of the cedar and
set *it* out; I will pluck from the topmost of its
young twigs a tender one, and I will plant *it*
on an exalted and lofty mountain. 23 On the
high mountain of Israel I will plant it, that it
may lift up boughs and yield fruit and become
a majestic cedar. And birds of every kind will
dwell under it; they will dwell in the shade of
its branches. 24 And all the trees of the field
will know that I am Yahweh; I bring down the
exalted tree, exalt the low tree, dry up the
green tree, and make the dry tree flourish. I
am Yahweh; I have spoken, and I will do *it*."

18 Then the word of Yahweh came to me,
saying, 2 "What do you mean by using
this proverb concerning the land of Israel,
saying,

'The fathers eat the sour grapes,
But the children's teeth
are set on edge'?

3 "As I live," declares Lord Yahweh, "you are
surely not going to use this proverb in Israel
anymore. 4 Behold, all souls are Mine; the
soul of the father as well as the soul of the
son is Mine. The soul who sins will die.
5 "But if a man is righteous and does
justice and righteousness, 6 and does not eat
at the mountain *shrines* or lift up his eyes
to the idols of the house of Israel, or defile
his neighbor's wife or approach a woman
during her menstrual period— 7 if a man
does not mistreat anyone, but returns to the
debtor his pledge, does not commit robbery,
but gives his bread to the hungry and covers
the naked with clothing, 8 if he does not
lend *money* on interest or take increase, *if*
he turns his hand from injustice *and* does
true justice between man and man, 9 *if* he
walks in My statutes and My judgments *and*
is careful to do *the* truth—he is righteous
and will surely live," declares Lord Yahweh.
10 "Then he may have a violent son who
sheds blood and who does any of these
things to a brother 11 (though he himself
did not do any of these things), that is,
he even eats at the mountain *shrines* and
defiles his neighbor's wife; 12 he mistreats
the afflicted and needy, commits robbery,
does not return a pledge, but lifts up his eyes
to the idols *and* does abominations; 13 he
lends *money* on interest and takes increase;
will he live? He will not live! He has done all
these abominations; he will surely be put to
death; his blood will be on himself.
14 "Now behold, he has a son who has
seen all his father's sins which he has done.
And he saw *this* but does not do likewise.
15 He does not eat at the mountain *shrines*
or lift up his eyes to the idols of the house
of Israel, or defile his neighbor's wife 16 or
mistreat anyone, or retain a pledge or com-
mit robbery, *but* he gives his bread to the
hungry and covers the naked with clothing;
17 he turns his hand away from the afflicted,
does not take interest or increase, *but* does
My judgments *and* walks in My statutes; he
will not die for his father's iniquity; he will
surely live. 18 As for his father, because he
practiced extortion, robbed *his* brother, and
did what was not good among his people,
behold, he will die for his iniquity.
19 "Yet you say, 'Why should the son not
bear the punishment for the father's iniquity?'
But the son has done justice and righteous-
ness and has kept all My statutes and done
them. He shall surely live. 20 The soul who sins
will die. The son will not bear the iniquity of
the father, nor will the father bear the iniquity
of the son; the righteousness of the righteous
will be upon himself, and the wickedness of
the wicked will be upon himself.
21 "But if the wicked man turns from all
his sins which he has done and keeps all My
statutes and does justice and righteousness,
he shall surely live; he shall not die. 22 All his
transgressions which he has done will not
be remembered against him; because of his
righteousness which he has done, he will
live. 23 Do I have any pleasure in the death of
the wicked," declares Lord Yahweh, "is it not
that he should turn from his ways and live?
24 "But when a righteous man turns away
from his righteousness, does injustice, and
does according to all the abominations that
a wicked man does, will he live? All his righ-
teous deeds which he has done will not be
remembered for his unfaithfulness which
he has committed and his sin which he
has committed; for them he will die. 25 Yet
you say, 'The way of the Lord is not right.'
Hear now, O house of Israel! Is My way not
right? Is it not your ways that are not right?
26 When a righteous man turns away from
his righteousness, does injustice, and dies
because of it, for his injustice which he has

done he will die. 27 Again, when a wicked
man turns away from his wickedness which
he has done and does justice and righteous-
ness, he will preserve his life. 28 Again, he
considered and turned away from all his
transgressions which he had done; he shall
surely live; he shall not die. 29 But the house
of Israel says, 'The way of the Lord is not
right.' Are My ways not right, O house of
Israel? Is it not your ways that are not right?
30 "Therefore I will judge you, O house of
Israel, each according to his way," declares
Lord Yahweh. "Turn back and turn away
from all your transgressions, so that iniq-
uity may not become a stumbling block to
you. 31 Cast away from yourselves all your
transgressions which you have committed
and make yourselves a new heart and a new
spirit! Now why will you die, O house of
Israel? 32 For I have no pleasure in the death
of anyone who dies," declares Lord Yahweh.
"Therefore, turn back and live."

Psalm 124:1–8

1 "Had it not been Yahweh who
was on our side,"
Let Israel now say,
2 "Had it not been Yahweh
who was on our side
When men rose up against us,
3 Then they would have
swallowed us alive,
When their anger was
kindled against us;
4 Then the waters would
have flowed over us,
The stream would have
swept over our soul;
5 Then the raging waters would
have swept over our soul."

6 Blessed be Yahweh,
Who has not given us to be
prey for their teeth.
7 Our soul has escaped as a bird out
of the snare of the trapper;
The snare is broken and
we have escaped.
8 Our help is in the name of Yahweh,
Who made heaven and earth.

Proverbs 28:21

21 To show partiality is not good,
Even for a piece of bread a
man will transgress.

Hebrews 9:1–28

9 Now even the first *covenant* had require-
ments of divine worship and the earthly
sanctuary. 2 For there was a tabernacle
prepared: the first part, in which *were* the
lampstand and the table and the sacred
bread, which is called the holy place. 3 And
behind the second veil there was a taber-
nacle which is called the Holy of Holies,
4 having a golden altar of incense and the
ark of the covenant covered on all sides with
gold, in which was a golden jar holding the
manna, and Aaron's rod which budded, and
the tablets of the covenant. 5 And above it
were the cherubim of glory overshadowing
the mercy seat. Of these things we cannot
now speak in detail.
6 Now when these things have been
so prepared, the priests are continually
entering the first part *of the* tabernacle
performing the divine worship, 7 but into
the second, only the high priest *enters* once
a year, not without *taking* blood, which he
offers for himself and for the sins of the
people committed in ignorance. 8 The Holy
Spirit *is* indicating this, that the way into
the holy places has not yet been manifested
while that first part *of the* tabernacle is
still standing, 9 which *is* a symbol for the
present time. Accordingly both gifts and
sacrifices are offered which cannot make
the worshiper perfect in conscience, 10 since
they *relate* only to food and drink and var-
ious washings, requirements for the body
imposed until a time of reformation.
11 But when Christ appeared *as* a high
priest of the good things to come, *He entered*
through the greater and more perfect taber-
nacle, not made with hands, that is to say,
not of this creation, 12 and not through the
blood of goats and calves, but through His
own blood, He entered the holy places once
for all, having obtained eternal redemption.
13 For if the blood of goats and bulls and the
ashes of a heifer sprinkling those who have
been defiled sanctify for the cleansing of
the flesh, 14 how much more will the blood
of Christ, who through the eternal Spirit
offered Himself without blemish to God,
cleanse your conscience from dead works
to serve the living God?
15 And for this reason He is the mediator
of a new covenant, so that, since a death
has taken place for the redemption of the
trespasses that were *committed* under the

first covenant, those who have been called
may receive the promise of the eternal
inheritance. 16 For where a covenant is,
there must of necessity be the death of the
one who made it. 17 For a covenant is valid
only when men are dead, for it is never
in force while the one who made it lives.
18 Therefore not even the first *covenant*
was inaugurated without blood. 19 For when
every commandment had been spoken by
Moses to all the people according to the
Law, he took the blood of the calves and
the goats, with water and scarlet wool
and hyssop, and sprinkled both the book
itself and all the people, 20 saying, "THIS IS
THE BLOOD OF THE COVENANT WHICH GOD
COMMANDED YOU." 21 And in the same way,
both the tabernacle and all the vessels of the
ministry he sprinkled with the blood. 22 And
according to the Law, *one may* almost *say*, all
things are cleansed with blood, and without
shedding of blood there is no forgiveness.
23 Therefore it was necessary for the
copies of the things in the heavens to be
cleansed with these, but the heavenly things
themselves with better sacrifices than these.
24 For Christ did not enter holy places made
with hands, *mere* copies of the true ones,
but into heaven itself, now to appear in the
presence of God for us; 25 nor was it that
He would offer Himself often, as the high
priest enters the holy places year by year
with blood that is not his own. 26 Otherwise,
He would have needed to suffer often since
the foundation of the world; but now once at
the consummation of the ages He has been
manifested to put away sin by the sacrifice of
Himself. 27 And inasmuch as it is appointed
for men to die once and after this *comes*
judgment, 28 so Christ also, having been
offered once to bear the sins of many, will
appear a second time for salvation without
reference to sin, to those who eagerly await
Him.

NOVEMBER 14

Ezekiel 19:1–20:49

19 "As for you, take up a lamentation for
the princes of Israel 2 and say,
'What was your mother?
A lioness among lions!
She lay down among young lions;
She reared her cubs.
3 'So she brought up one of her cubs;
He became a lion,
And he learned to tear *his* prey;
He devoured men.
4 'Then nations heard about him;
He was captured in their pit,
And they brought him with hooks
To the land of Egypt.
5 'Then she saw, as she waited,
That her hope was lost,
So she took another of her cubs
And made him a young lion.
6 'And he walked about among the lions;
He became a young lion;
He learned to tear *his* prey;
He devoured men.
7 'He knew *how to destroy*
their fortified towers
And laid waste their cities;
And the land was in desolation,
as well as its fullness
Because of the sound of his roaring.
8 'Then nations put *themselves*
against him
All around from *their* provinces,
And they spread their net over him;
He was captured in their pit.
9 'They put him in a cage with hooks
And brought him to the
king of Babylon;
They brought him in hunting nets
So that his voice would
be heard no more
On the mountains of Israel.
10 'Your mother was like a vine
in your vineyard,
Planted by the waters;
It was fruitful and full of branches
Because of abundant waters.
11 'And it had strong thick branches
fit for scepters of rulers,
And its height was exalted
above the clouds
So that it was seen in its exaltedness
with the mass of its foliage.
12 'But it was uprooted in wrath;
It was cast down to the ground;
And the east wind dried up its fruit.
Its strong thick branch was torn off
So that it dried up;
The fire consumed it.

13 'So now it is planted in the wilderness,
In a dry and thirsty land.
14 'And fire has gone out from
its thick branch;
It has consumed its shoots *and* fruit,
So that there is not in it a
strong thick branch,
A scepter to rule.'"
This is a lamentation and has become a
lamentation.

20 Now it happened in the seventh year,
in the fifth *month*, on the tenth of
the month, *that* some of the elders of Israel
came to inquire of Yahweh and sat before
me. 2 And the word of Yahweh came to me
saying, 3 "Son of man, speak to the elders
of Israel and say to them, 'Thus says Lord
Yahweh, "Do you come to inquire of Me? As
I live," declares Lord Yahweh, "I will not be
inquired of by you."' 4 Will you judge them,
will you judge them, son of man? Make them
know the abominations of their fathers
5 and say to them, 'Thus says Lord Yahweh,
"On the day when I chose Israel and swore
to the seed of the house of Jacob and made
Myself known to them in the land of Egypt,
when I swore to them, saying, I am Yahweh
your God, 6 on that day I swore to them, to
bring them out from the land of Egypt into
a land that I had selected for them, flowing
with milk and honey, which is the glory of
all lands. 7 I said to them, 'Cast away, each
of you, the detestable things of his eyes, and
do not defile yourselves with the idols of
Egypt; I am Yahweh your God.' 8 But they
rebelled against Me and were not willing to
listen to Me; each one did not cast away the
detestable things of their eyes, nor did they
forsake the idols of Egypt.

Then I said *I would* pour out My wrath on
them, to spend My anger against them in the
midst of the land of Egypt. 9 But I acted for
the sake of My name, that it should not be
profaned in the sight of the nations among
whom they *lived*, in whose sight I made
Myself known to them by bringing them out
of the land of Egypt. 10 So I took them out
of the land of Egypt and brought them into
the wilderness. 11 I gave them My statutes
and made them know My judgments, which,
if a man does them, he will live by them.
12 And I also gave them My sabbaths to be
a sign between Me and them, that they
might know that I am Yahweh who sanctifies
them. 13 But the house of Israel rebelled
against Me in the wilderness. They did not
walk in My statutes, and they rejected My
judgments, which, if a man does them, he
will live by them; and My sabbaths they
greatly profaned. Then I said *I would* pour
out My wrath on them in the wilderness, to
completely destroy them. 14 But I acted for
the sake of My name, that it should not be
profaned in the sight of the nations, before
whose sight I had brought them out. 15 Also I
swore to them in the wilderness that I would
not bring them into the land which I had
given them, flowing with milk and honey,
which is the glory of all lands, 16 because
they rejected My judgments, and as for My
statutes, they did not walk in them; they
even profaned My sabbaths, for their heart
continually walked after their idols. 17 Yet
My eye had pity on them rather than bring-
ing them to ruin, and I did not make *of* them
a complete destruction in the wilderness.

18 "I said to their children in the wilder-
ness, 'Do not walk in the statutes of your
fathers and do not keep their judgments and
do not defile yourselves with their idols. 19 I
am Yahweh your God; walk in My statutes
and keep My judgments and do them.
20 Keep My sabbaths holy; and they shall be
a sign between Me and you, that you may
know that I am Yahweh your God.' 21 But the
children rebelled against Me; they did not
walk in My statutes, nor were they careful
to do My judgments, which, *if* a man does
them, he will live by them; they profaned
My sabbaths. So I said *I would* pour out My
wrath on them, to spend My anger against
them in the wilderness. 22 But I turned back
My hand and acted for the sake of My name,
that it should not be profaned in the sight
of the nations in whose sight I had brought
them out. 23 Also I swore to them in the
wilderness that I would scatter them among
the nations and disperse them among the
lands 24 because they had not done My judg-
ments, but had rejected My statutes and had
profaned My sabbaths, and their eyes were
going after the idols of their fathers. 25 And
I also gave them statutes that were not good
and judgments by which they could not live;
26 and I pronounced them unclean because
of their gifts, in that they caused all their
firstborn to pass through *the fire* so that I
might make them desolate, in order that
they might know that I am Yahweh."'

27 "Therefore, son of man, speak to the
house of Israel and say to them, 'Thus says
Lord Yahweh, "Yet in this your fathers have
blasphemed Me by acting unfaithfully
against Me. 28 Indeed, I brought them into
the land which I swore to give to them, and
they saw every high hill and every leafy
tree, and they offered there their sacrifices,
and there they gave the provocation of
their offering. There also they made their
soothing aroma, and there they poured out
their drink offerings. 29 Then I said to them,
'What is the high place to which you are
going?' So its name is called Bamah to this
day."' 30 Therefore, say to the house of Israel,
'Thus says Lord Yahweh, "Will you defile
yourselves in the way of your fathers and
play the harlot after their detestable things?
31 And when you offer your gifts, when you
cause your sons to pass through the fire, you
are defiling yourselves with all your idols to
this day. And shall I be inquired of by you,
O house of Israel? As I live," declares Lord
Yahweh, "I will not be inquired of by you.
32 And what comes upon your spirit will not
happen, when you say: 'We will be like the
nations, like the families of the lands, to
minister to wood and stone.'

33 "As I live," declares Lord Yahweh,
"surely with a strong hand and with an
outstretched arm and with wrath poured
out, I shall be king over you. 34 And I will
bring you out from the peoples and gather
you from the lands where you are scattered,
with a strong hand and with an outstretched
arm and with wrath poured out; 35 and I will
bring you into the wilderness of the peoples,
and there I will enter into judgment with you
face to face. 36 As I entered into judgment
with your fathers in the wilderness of the
land of Egypt, so I will enter into judgment
with you," declares Lord Yahweh. 37 "And
I will make you pass under the rod, and I
will bring you into the bond of the covenant;
38 and I will purge from you the rebels and
those who transgress against Me; I will bring
them out of the land where they sojourn,
but they will not enter the land of Israel.
Thus you will know that I am Yahweh.

39 "As for you, O house of Israel," thus
says Lord Yahweh, "Go, serve everyone his
idols; but after *this* you will surely listen
to Me, and My holy name you will profane
no longer with your gifts and with your
idols. 40 For on My holy mountain, on the
high mountain of Israel," declares Lord
Yahweh, "there the whole house of Israel,
all of them, will serve Me in the land; there
I will accept them, and there I will seek your
contributions and the choicest of your gifts,
with all your holy things. 41 As a soothing
aroma I will accept you when I bring you
out from the peoples and gather you from
the lands where you are scattered; and I will
prove Myself holy among you in the sight of
the nations. 42 And you will know that I am
Yahweh, when I bring you onto the ground
of Israel, into the land which I swore to
give to your fathers. 43 And there you will
remember your ways and all your deeds
with which you have defiled yourselves; and
you will loathe yourselves to your own faces
for all the evil things that you have done.
44 Then you will know that I am Yahweh
when I have dealt with you for My name's
sake, not according to your evil ways or
according to your corrupt deeds, O house
of Israel," declares Lord Yahweh.'"

45 Now the word of Yahweh came to me,
saying, 46 "Son of man, set your face toward
Teman and speak, dripping out *words*,
against the south and prophesy against
the forest land of the Negev 47 and say to
the forest of the Negev, 'Hear the word of
Yahweh: thus says Lord Yahweh, "Behold, I
am about to kindle a fire in you, and it will
consume every green tree in you, as well as
every dry tree; the blazing flame will not
be quenched, and the whole surface from
south to north will be scorched by it. 48 And
all flesh will see that I, Yahweh, have made
it burn; it shall not be quenched."'" 49 Then
I said, "Ah Lord Yahweh! They are saying of
me, 'Is he not *just* speaking parables?'"

Psalm 125:1–5

1 Those who trust in Yahweh
Are as Mount Zion, which will not
be shaken but will abide forever.
2 As the mountains surround Jerusalem,
So Yahweh surrounds His people
From now until forever.
3 For the scepter of wickedness shall not
rest upon the land of the righteous,
So that the righteous would
not send forth their hands
in unrighteousness.

4 Do good, O Yahweh, to
those who are good

And to those who are upright
in their hearts.
5 But as for those who turn aside
to their crooked ways,
Yahweh will lead them away with
the workers of iniquity.
Peace be upon Israel.

Proverbs 28:22

22 A man with an evil eye
hurries after wealth
And does not know that want
will come upon him.

Hebrews 10:1–18

10 For the Law, since it has *only* a shadow
of the good things to come *and* not
the very form of things, can never, by the
same sacrifices which they offer continually
year by year, make perfect those who draw
near. 2 Otherwise, would they not have
ceased to be offered, because the worship-
ers, having once been cleansed, would no
longer have consciousness of sins? 3 But in
those *sacrifices* there is a reminder of sins
year by year. 4 For it is impossible for the
blood of bulls and goats to take away sins.
5 Therefore, when He comes into the world,
He says,

"SACRIFICE AND OFFERING YOU
HAVE NOT DESIRED,
BUT A BODY YOU HAVE PREPARED
FOR ME;
6 IN BURNT OFFERINGS AND *sacrifices* FOR
SIN YOU HAVE TAKEN NO PLEASURE.
7 "THEN I SAID, 'BEHOLD, I HAVE COME,
IN THE SCROLL OF THE BOOK
IT IS WRITTEN OF ME,
TO DO YOUR WILL, O GOD.'"

8 After saying above, "SACRIFICES AND OFFER-
INGS AND BURNT OFFERINGS AND *sacrifices*
FOR SIN YOU HAVE NOT DESIRED, NOR HAVE
YOU TAKEN PLEASURE *in them*" (which are
offered according to the Law), 9 then He said,
"BEHOLD, I HAVE COME TO DO YOUR WILL."
He takes away the first in order to establish
the second. 10 By this will we have been
sanctified through the offering of the body
of Jesus Christ once for all.

11 And every priest stands daily minister-
ing and offering time after time the same
sacrifices, which can never take away sins;
12 but He, having offered one sacrifice for
sins for all time, SAT DOWN AT THE RIGHT
HAND OF GOD, 13 waiting from that time
UNTIL HIS ENEMIES ARE PUT AS A FOOTSTOOL
FOR HIS FEET. 14 For by one offering He has
perfected for all time those who are being
sanctified. 15 And the Holy Spirit also testi-
fies to us, for after saying,

16 "THIS IS THE COVENANT THAT I
WILL MAKE WITH THEM
AFTER THOSE DAYS, SAYS THE LORD:
I WILL PUT MY LAWS UPON THEIR HEART,
AND ON THEIR MIND I WILL
WRITE THEM,"

He then says,

17 "AND THEIR SINS AND THEIR
LAWLESS DEEDS
I WILL REMEMBER NO MORE."

18 Now where there is forgiveness of these
things, there is no longer *any* offering for sin.

NOVEMBER 15

Ezekiel 21:1–22:31

21 And the word of Yahweh came to me,
saying, 2 "Son of man, set your face
toward Jerusalem and speak, dripping out
words against the sanctuaries and prophesy
against the land of Israel 3 and say to the
land of Israel, 'Thus says Yahweh, "Behold,
I am against you; and I will bring out My
sword from its sheath and cut off from you
the righteous and the wicked. 4 Because I
will cut off from you the righteous and the
wicked, therefore My sword will go out
from its sheath against all flesh from south
to north. 5 Thus all flesh will know that I,
Yahweh, have brought out My sword from
its sheath. It will not return *to its sheath*
again."' 6 Now as for you, son of man, groan
with breaking heart and bitter grief, groan
in their sight. 7 And it will be *that* when they
say to you, 'Why do you groan?' you shall
say, 'Because of the report that is coming;
and every heart will melt, all hands will fall
limp, every spirit will faint, and all knees
will be weak as water. Behold, it is coming,
and it will happen,' declares Lord Yahweh."

8 Again the word of Yahweh came to me,
saying, 9 "Son of man, prophesy and say,
'Thus says the Lord.' Say,

'A sword, a sword sharpened
And also polished!

10 'Sharpened to make a slaughter,
Polished to flash like lightning!'
Or shall we rejoice *in* the scepter of My
son? *The sword* despises every tree. 11 It is
given to be polished, that it may be seized
by the hand; the sword is sharpened and
polished, to give it into the hand of the one
who kills. 12 Cry out and wail, son of man;
for it is against My people; it is against all
the princes of Israel. They are delivered over
to the sword with My people; therefore slap
your thigh. 13 For *there is* a testing; and what
if even the scepter which *the sword* despises
will be no more?" declares Lord Yahweh.

14 "You therefore, son of man, prophesy
and strike *your* hands together; and let the
sword be doubled the third time, the sword
for the slain. It is the sword for the great
one slain, which surrounds them, 15 that
their hearts may melt, and many *will be*
stumbling blocks at all their gates. I have
given the glittering sword. Ah! It is made
for striking like lightning, it is wrapped up
in readiness for slaughter. 16 Show yourself
sharp, go to the right; set yourself; go to the
left, wherever your edge is appointed. 17 And
I will also strike My hands together, and I
will cause My wrath to be at rest; I, Yahweh,
have spoken."

18 And the word of Yahweh came to me
saying, 19 "Now as for you, son of man,
make two ways for the sword of the king
of Babylon to come; both of them will go
out of one land. And make a signpost; make
it at the head of the way to the city. 20 You
shall mark a way for the sword to come to
Rabbah of the sons of Ammon and to Judah
into fortified Jerusalem. 21 For the king of
Babylon stands at the parting of the way, at
the head of the two ways, to use divination;
he shakes the arrows; he asks the household
idols; he looks at the liver. 22 Into his right
hand came the divination, 'Jerusalem,' to
set battering rams, to open the mouth for
killing, to lift up the voice with a shout of
war, to set battering rams against the gates,
to cast up ramps, to build a siege wall. 23 And
it will be to them like a worthless divination
in their eyes; they have *sworn* solemn oaths.
But he brings iniquity to remembrance, that
they may be seized.

24 "Therefore, thus says Lord Yahweh,
'Because you have made your iniquity to be
remembered, in that your transgressions are
uncovered, so that in all your deeds your
sins appear—because you have come to
remembrance, you will be seized with the
hand. 25 And you, O slain, wicked one, the
prince of Israel, whose day has come, in
the time of the iniquity of the end,' 26 thus
says Lord Yahweh, 'Remove the turban and
take off the crown; this *will* no longer *be* the
same. Make high that which is low and make
low that which is high. 27 A ruin, a ruin, a
ruin, I will make it. This also will be no more
until He comes to whom the *legal* judgment
belongs, and I will give it *to Him.*'

28 "Now as for you, son of man, prophesy
and say, 'Thus says Lord Yahweh concerning
the sons of Ammon and concerning their
reproach,' and say: 'A sword, a sword is
drawn, polished for the slaughter, to cause
it to consume, that it may be like lightning—
29 while they behold for you worthless
visions, while they divine lies for you—to
place you on the necks of the wicked who
are slain, whose day has come, in the time
of the iniquity of the end. 30 Return *it* to its
sheath. In the place where you were created,
in the land of your origin, I will judge you.
31 And I will pour out My indignation on you;
I will blow on you with the fire of My fury,
and I will give you into the hand of brutal
men, craftsmen of destruction. 32 You will
be fuel for the fire; your blood will be in the
midst of the land. You will not be remem-
bered, for I, Yahweh, have spoken.'"

22 Then the word of Yahweh came to
me, saying, 2 "Now as for you, son of
man, will you judge, will you judge the city
of blood? Then you shall cause her to know
all her abominations. 3 And you shall say,
'Thus says Lord Yahweh, "A city shedding
blood in her midst, so that her time will
come; and she makes idols against herself
for defilement! 4 You have become guilty by
the blood which you have shed, and defiled
by your idols which you have made. Thus
you have brought your day near and have
come to your years; therefore I have made
you a reproach to the nations and a mocking
to all the lands. 5 Those who are near and
those who are far from you will mock you,
you of unclean name, full of turmoil.

6 "Behold, the princes of Israel, each
according to his power, have been in you
for the purpose of shedding blood. 7 They
have treated father and mother with con-
tempt within you. The sojourner they have

oppressed in your midst; the fatherless and
the widow they have mistreated in you. 8 You
have despised My holy things and profaned
My sabbaths. 9 Slanderous men have been
in you for the purpose of shedding blood,
and in you they have eaten at the mountain
shrines. In your midst they have done acts
of lewdness. 10 In you they have uncovered
their fathers' nakedness; in you they have
humbled her who was unclean in her
menstrual impurity. 11 One has also done
what is an abomination with his neighbor's
wife, and another has lewdly defiled his
daughter-in-law. And another in you has
violated his sister, his father's daughter. 12 In
you they have taken bribes for the purpose
of shedding blood; you have taken interest
and profits, and you have injured your
neighbors for gain by oppression, and you
have forgotten Me," declares Lord Yahweh.

13 "Now behold, I have struck My hand at
your greedy gain which you have acquired
and at the bloodshed which is among you.
14 Can your heart stand, or can your hands
be strong in the days that I will act *against*
you? I, Yahweh, have spoken and will act.
15 I will scatter you among the nations, and
I will disperse you through the lands, and I
will put an end to your uncleanness from
you. 16 You will profane yourself in the sight
of the nations, and you will know that I am
Yahweh."'"

17 And the word of Yahweh came to me,
saying, 18 "Son of man, the house of Israel
has become dross to Me; all of them are
bronze and tin and iron and lead in the fur-
nace; they are the dross of silver. 19 There-
fore, thus says Lord Yahweh, 'Because all of
you have become dross, therefore, behold,
I am going to gather you into the midst
of Jerusalem. 20 As they gather silver and
bronze and iron and lead and tin into the
furnace to blow fire on it in order to melt
it, so I will gather *you* in My anger and in
My wrath, and I will lay you *there* and melt
you. 21 And I will collect you *together* and
blow on you with the fire of My fury, and
you will be melted in the midst of it. 22 As
silver is melted in the furnace, so you will
be melted in the midst of it; and you will
know that I, Yahweh, have poured out My
wrath on you.'"

23 And the word of Yahweh came to me,
saying, 24 "Son of man, say to her, 'You are a
land that is not cleansed *or* rained on in the
day of indignation.' 25 There is a conspiracy
of her prophets in her midst like a roaring
lion tearing the prey. They have devoured
lives; they have taken treasure and precious
things; they have made many widows in
the midst of her. 26 Her priests have done
violence to My law and have profaned My
holy things; they have made no separation
between the holy and the profane, and
they have not made known the difference
between the unclean and the clean; and
they hide their eyes from My sabbaths,
and I am profaned among them. 27 Her
princes within her are like wolves tearing
the prey by shedding blood *and* destroying
lives in order to get greedy gain. 28 And her
prophets have smeared whitewash for them,
beholding worthless visions and divining
lies for them, saying, 'Thus says Lord
Yahweh,' when Yahweh has not spoken.
29 The people of the land have practiced
oppression and committed robbery, and
they have mistreated the afflicted and
needy and have oppressed the sojourner
without justice. 30 And I searched for a man
among them who would build up the wall
and stand in the breach before Me for the
land, so that I would not bring it to ruin; but
I found no one. 31 Thus I have poured out
My indignation on them; I have consumed
them with the fire of My fury; their way I
have brought upon their heads," declares
Lord Yahweh.

Psalm 126:1–6

1 When Yahweh returned the
captive ones of Zion,
We were like those who dream.
2 Then our mouth was filled
with laughter
And our tongue with shouts of joy;
Then they said among the nations,
"Yahweh has done great
things for them."
3 Yahweh has done great things for us;
We are glad.

4 Restore our captivity, O Yahweh,
As the streams in the Negev.
5 Those who sow in tears shall
reap with shouts of joy.
6 He who goes to and fro weeping,
carrying *his* bag of seed,
Shall indeed come again with a shout
of joy, carrying his sheaves *with him.*

Proverbs 28:23

23 He who reproves a man will
afterward find *more* favor
Than he who flatters with the tongue.

Hebrews 10:19–39

19 Therefore, brothers, since we have con-
fidence to enter the holy places by the blood
of Jesus, 20 by a new and living way which
He inaugurated for us through the veil, that
is, His flesh, 21 and since *we have* a great
priest over the house of God, 22 let us draw
near with a sincere heart in full assurance
of faith, having our hearts sprinkled from
an evil conscience and our bodies washed
with pure water. 23 Let us hold fast the
confession of our hope without wavering,
for He who promised is faithful. 24 And let
us consider how to stimulate one another
to love and good deeds, 25 not forsaking our
own assembling together, as is the habit of
some, but encouraging *one another*, and all
the more as you see the day drawing near.
26 For if we go on sinning willfully after
receiving the knowledge of the truth, there
no longer remains a sacrifice for sins, 27 but
a terrifying expectation of judgment and
THE FURY OF A FIRE WHICH WILL CONSUME THE
ADVERSARIES. 28 Anyone who has set aside
the Law of Moses dies without mercy by
the mouth of two or three witnesses. 29 How
much worse punishment do you think he
will deserve who has trampled underfoot
the Son of God, and has regarded as defiled
the blood of the covenant by which he was
sanctified, and has insulted the Spirit of
grace? 30 For we know Him who said, "VEN-
GEANCE IS MINE, I WILL REPAY." And again,
"THE LORD WILL JUDGE HIS PEOPLE." 31 It is
a terrifying thing to fall into the hands of
the living God.
32 But remember the former days, when,
after being enlightened, you endured a
great conflict of sufferings, 33 partly by
being made a public spectacle through
reproaches and afflictions, and partly by
becoming sharers with those who were so
treated. 34 For you also showed sympathy
to the prisoners and accepted with joy the
seizure of your possessions, knowing that
you have for yourselves a better and lasting
possession. 35 Therefore, do not throw away
that confidence of yours, which has a great
reward. 36 For you have need of endurance,
so that when you have done the will of God,
you may receive the promise.

37 FOR YET IN A VERY LITTLE WHILE,
HE WHO IS COMING WILL COME,
AND WILL NOT DELAY.
38 BUT MY RIGHTEOUS ONE
SHALL LIVE BY FAITH,
AND IF HE SHRINKS BACK, MY SOUL
HAS NO PLEASURE IN HIM.

39 But we are not of those who shrink back
to destruction, but of those who have faith
to the preserving of the soul.

NOVEMBER 16

Ezekiel 23:1–24:27

23 The word of Yahweh came to me
again, saying, 2 "Son of man, there
were two women, the daughters of one
mother; 3 and they played the harlot in
Egypt. They played the harlot in their youth;
there their breasts were pressed, and there
their virgin bosom was handled. 4 Their
names were Oholah the elder and Oholibah
her sister. And they became Mine, and they
bore sons and daughters. And *as for* their
names, Samaria is Oholah and Jerusalem
is Oholibah.
5 "Oholah played the harlot while she was
Mine; and she lusted after her lovers, after
the Assyrians, *her* neighbors, 6 who were
clothed in purple, governors and officials,
all of them desirable young men, horsemen
riding on horses. 7 She gave her harlotries
to them, all of them the choicest men of
Assyria; and with all whom she lusted after,
with all their idols she defiled herself. 8 She
did not forsake her harlotries from *the time
in* Egypt; for in her youth men had lain with
her, and they handled her virgin bosom and
poured out their harlotry on her. 9 There-
fore, I gave her into the hand of her lovers,
into the hand of the Assyrians, after whom
she lusted. 10 They uncovered her naked-
ness; they took her sons and her daughters,
but they killed her with the sword. Thus she
became a *despised* name among women,
and they executed judgments on her.
11 "Now her sister Oholibah saw *this*,
yet she was more corrupt in her lust than
she, and her harlotries were more than the

harlotries of her sister. 12 She lusted after
the Assyrians, governors and officials,
the ones near, magnificently dressed,
horsemen riding on horses, all of them
desirable choice men. 13 And I saw that
she had defiled herself; they both took the
same way. 14 So she increased her harlotries.
And she saw men portrayed on the wall,
images of the Chaldeans portrayed with
vermilion, 15 girded with belts on their loins,
with flowing turbans on their heads, all of
them looking like officers, in the likeness
of the Babylonians *in* Chaldea, the land of
their birth. 16 And she saw them and lusted
after them and sent messengers to them
in Chaldea. 17 So the Babylonians came to
her to the bed of love and defiled her with
their harlotry. Then she became defiled by
them, and her soul became disgusted with
them. 18 And she uncovered her harlotries
and uncovered her nakedness; then My soul
became disgusted with her, as My soul had
become disgusted with her sister. 19 Yet she
multiplied her harlotries, remembering
the days of her youth, when she played the
harlot in the land of Egypt. 20 She lusted
after their paramours, whose flesh is *like* the
flesh of donkeys and whose issue is *like* the
issue of horses. 21 Thus you longed for the
lewdness of your youth, when the Egyptians
handled your bosom because of the breasts
of your youth.

22 "Therefore, O Oholibah, thus says Lord
Yahweh, 'Behold, I will arouse your lovers
against you, *those* with whom your soul was
disgusted, and I will bring them against you
from every side: 23 the Babylonians and all
the Chaldeans, Pekod and Shoa and Koa,
and all the Assyrians with them; desirable
choice men, governors and officials, all of
them, officers and men of renown, all of
them riding on horses. 24 They will come
against you with weapons, chariots and
wagons, and with an assembly of peoples.
They will set themselves against you on
every side with large shield and shield
and helmet; and I will give the judgment
to them, and they will judge you according
to their judgments. 25 And I will set My
jealousy against you, that they may deal
with you in wrath. They will remove your
nose and your ears; and your survivors will
fall by the sword. They will take your sons
and your daughters; and your survivors will
be consumed by the fire. 26 They will also
strip you of your clothes and take away your
beautiful jewelry. 27 Thus I will make your
lewdness and your harlotry *brought* from
the land of Egypt to cease from you, so that
you will not lift up your eyes to them or
remember Egypt anymore.' 28 For thus says
Lord Yahweh, 'Behold, I will give you into
the hand of those whom you hate, into the
hand of those with whom your soul was dis-
gusted. 29 They will deal with you in hatred,
take all the fruit of your labor, and leave
you naked and bare. And the nakedness
of your harlotries will be uncovered, both
your lewdness and your harlotries. 30 These
things will be done to you because you have
played the harlot with the nations, because
you have defiled yourself with their idols.
31 You have walked in the way of your sister;
therefore I will give her cup into your hand.'
32 Thus says Lord Yahweh,

'You will drink your sister's cup,
Which is deep and wide.
You will be laughed at and
held in derision;
It contains much.

33 'You will be filled with
drunkenness and sorrow,
The cup of horror and desolation,
The cup of your sister Samaria.

34 'You will drink it and drain it.
Then you will gnaw its fragments
And tear your breasts;

for I have spoken,' declares Lord Yah-
weh. 35 Therefore, thus says Lord Yahweh,
'Because you have forgotten Me and cast Me
behind your back, bear now the *punishment*
of your lewdness and your harlotries.'"

36 Moreover, Yahweh said to me, "Son of
man, will you judge Oholah and Oholibah?
Then declare to them their abominations.
37 For they have committed adultery, and
blood is on their hands. Thus they have
committed adultery with their idols and
even caused their sons, whom they bore
to Me, to pass through *the fire* to them as
food. 38 Again, they have done this to Me:
they have defiled My sanctuary on the same
day and have profaned My sabbaths. 39 For
when they had slaughtered their children
for their idols, they entered My sanctuary
on the same day to profane it; and behold,
thus they did within My house.

40 "Furthermore, they have even sent
for men who come from afar, to whom
a messenger was sent; and behold, they

came—for whom you bathed, painted
your eyes, and decorated yourselves with
ornaments; 41 and you sat on a splendid
couch with a table arranged before it on
which you had set My incense and My oil.
42 The sound of a multitude at ease was with
her; and drunkards were brought from the
wilderness with men of the common sort.
And they put bracelets on the hands of the
women and beautiful crowns on their heads.

43 "Then I said concerning her who was
worn out by adulteries, 'Will they now
commit harlotry with her when she is *thus*?'
44 But they went in to her as they would go
in to a harlot. Thus they went in to Oholah
and to Oholibah, the lewd women. 45 But they,
righteous men, will judge them with the judg-
ment of adulteresses and with the judgment
of women who shed blood, because they are
adulteresses and blood is on their hands.

46 "For thus says Lord Yahweh, 'Bring up
an assembly against them and give them
over to terror and plunder. 47 The assembly
will stone them with stones and cut them
down with their swords; they will kill their
sons and their daughters and burn their
houses with fire. 48 Thus I will make lewd-
ness cease from the land, that all women
may be chastised and not commit lewdness
as you have done. 49 Your lewdness will be
requited upon you, and you will bear the
sin of *worshiping* your idols; thus you will
know that I am Lord Yahweh.'"

24

And the word of Yahweh came to me
in the ninth year, in the tenth month,
on the tenth of the month, saying, 2 "Son of
man, write the name of the day, this very
day. The king of Babylon has laid siege to
Jerusalem this very day. 3 Speak a parable
to the rebellious house, and you shall say
to them, 'Thus says Lord Yahweh,

"Put on the pot, put *it* on and
also pour water in it;
4 Put in it the pieces,
Every good piece, the thigh
and the shoulder;
Fill *it* with choice bones.
5 "Take the choicest of the flock,
And also pile wood under the pot.
Make it seethe vigorously.
Also boil its bones in it."

6 'Therefore, thus says Lord Yahweh,
"Woe to the city of blood,
To the pot in which there is rust
And whose rust has not gone out of it!
Take out of it piece after piece,
Without making a choice.
7 "For her blood is in her midst;
She placed it on the bare rock;
She did not pour it on the ground
To cover it with dust.
8 "That it may cause wrath to come
up to take vengeance,
I have put her blood on the bare rock,
That it may not be covered."
9 'Therefore, thus says Lord Yahweh,
"Woe to the city of blood!
I also will make the pile great.
10 "Heap on the wood, kindle the fire,
Completely *cook* the flesh
And mix in the spices
And let the bones be burned.
11 "Then stand it empty on its coals
So that it may be hot
And its bronze may glow
And its uncleanness may
be melted in it,
Its rust brought to a complete end.
12 "She has wearied *Me* with toil,
Yet her great rust has not
gone from her;
Let her rust *be* in the fire!
13 "In your uncleanness is lewdness.
Because I *would* have cleansed you,
Yet you are not clean;
You will not be cleansed from
your uncleanness again
Until I have caused My wrath
against you to be at rest.
14 "I, Yahweh, have spoken; it is coming, and
I will act. I will not regret, and I will not pity,
and I will not relent; according to your ways
and according to your deeds I will judge
you," declares Lord Yahweh.'"

15 And the word of Yahweh came to me
saying, 16 "Son of man, behold, I am about
to take from you the desire of your eyes
with a blow; but you shall not mourn, and
you shall not weep, and your tears shall not
come. 17 Groan silently; make no mourning
for the dead. Bind on your headdress and
put your shoes on your feet and do not
cover *your* mustache and do not eat the
bread of men." 18 So I spoke to the people
in the morning, and in the evening my
wife died. And in the morning I did as I
was commanded. 19 The people said to me,
"Will you not tell us what these things that

you are doing mean for us?" 20 Then I said to them, "The word of Yahweh came to me saying, 21 'Say to the house of Israel, "Thus says Lord Yahweh, 'Behold, I am about to profane My sanctuary, the pride of your strength, the desire of your eyes, and the delight of your soul; and your sons and your daughters whom you have left behind will fall by the sword. 22 And you will do as I have done; you will not cover *your* mustache, and you will not eat the bread of men. 23 And your headdresses will be on your heads and your shoes on your feet. You will not mourn, and you will not weep, but you will rot away in your iniquities, and you will groan to one another. 24 Thus Ezekiel will be a wondrous sign to you; according to all that he has done you will do; when it comes, then you will know that I am Lord Yahweh.'"

25 'Now as for you, son of man, will *it* not be on the day when I take from them their strong defense, the joy of their beauty, the desire of their eyes, and what lifts up their soul, their sons and their daughters, 26 that on that day he who escapes will come to you with a report for *your* ears? 27 On that day your mouth will be opened to him who escaped, and you will speak and be mute no longer. Thus you will be a wondrous sign to them, and they will know that I am Yahweh.'"

Psalm 127:1–5

1 Unless Yahweh builds the house,
They labor in vain who build it;
Unless Yahweh watches the city,
The watchman keeps awake in vain.
2 It is in vain that you rise up early,
That you sit out late,
O you who eat the bread
of painful labors;
For in this manner, He gives
sleep to His beloved.

3 Behold, children are an
inheritance of Yahweh,
The fruit of the womb is a reward.
4 Like arrows in the hand
of a warrior,
So are the children of one's youth.
5 How blessed is the man who
fills his quiver with them;
They will not be ashamed
When they speak with
enemies in the gate.

Proverbs 28:24

24 He who robs his father or his mother
And says, "It is not a transgression,"
Is the companion of a man
who destroys.

Hebrews 11:1–16

11 Now faith is the assurance of *things* hoped for, the conviction of things not seen. 2 For by it the men of old gained approval.

3 By faith we understand that the worlds were prepared by the word of God, so that what is seen was not made out of things which are visible. 4 By faith Abel offered to God a better sacrifice than Cain, through which he was approved as being righteous—God approving his gifts—and through faith, though he is dead, he still speaks. 5 By faith Enoch was taken up so that he would not see death; AND HE WAS NOT FOUND BECAUSE GOD TOOK HIM UP; for prior to being taken up, he was approved as being pleasing to God. 6 And without faith it is impossible to please *Him*, for he who draws near to God must believe that He is and *that* He is a rewarder of those who seek Him. 7 By faith Noah, being warned about things not yet seen, in reverence prepared an ark for the salvation of his household, by which he condemned the world, and became an heir of the righteousness which is according to faith.

8 By faith Abraham, when he was called, obeyed by going out to a place which he was to receive for an inheritance; and he went out, not knowing where he was going. 9 By faith he sojourned in the land of promise, as in a foreign *land*, dwelling in tents with Isaac and Jacob, fellow heirs of the same promise, 10 for he was looking for the city which has foundations, whose architect and builder is God. 11 By faith even Sarah herself received ability to conceive, even beyond the proper time of life, since she regarded Him faithful who had promised. 12 Therefore there were born even of one man, and him as good as dead at that, *as many* AS THE STARS OF HEAVEN IN NUMBER, AND INNUMERABLE AS THE SAND WHICH IS BY THE SEASHORE.

13 All these died in faith, without receiving the promises, but having seen them and having welcomed them from a distance, and having confessed that they were strangers

and exiles on the earth. 14 For those who say such things make it clear that they are seeking a country of their own. 15 And indeed if they had been remembering that *country* from which they went out, they would have had opportunity to return. 16 But now, they aspire to a better *country*, that is, a heavenly one. Therefore God is not ashamed to be called their God, for He prepared a city for them.

NOVEMBER 17

Ezekiel 25:1–26:21

25 And the word of Yahweh came to me saying, 2 "Son of man, set your face toward the sons of Ammon and prophesy against them 3 and say to the sons of Ammon, 'Hear the word of Lord Yahweh! Thus says Lord Yahweh, "Because you said, 'Aha!' against My sanctuary when it was profaned, and against the land of Israel when it was made desolate, and against the house of Judah when they went into exile, 4 therefore, behold, I am going to give you to the sons of the east for a possession, and they will set their encampments among you and make their dwellings among you; they will eat your fruit and drink your milk. 5 I will make Rabbah a pasture for camels and the sons of Ammon a resting place for flocks. Thus you will know that I am Yahweh." 6 For thus says Lord Yahweh, "Because you have clapped your hands and stamped your feet and were glad with all the scorn of your soul against the land of Israel, 7 therefore, behold, I have stretched out My hand against you, and I will give you for plunder to the nations. And I will cut you off from the peoples and make you perish from the lands; I will destroy you. Thus you will know that I am Yahweh."

8 'Thus says Lord Yahweh, "Because Moab and Seir say, 'Behold, the house of Judah is like all the nations,' 9 therefore, behold, I am going to open the flank of Moab by *its* cities, by its cities which are on its frontiers, the glory of the land, Beth-jeshimoth, Baal-meon, and Kiriathaim, 10 and I will give it for a possession along with the sons of Ammon to the sons of the east, so that the sons of Ammon will not be remembered among the nations. 11 Thus I will execute judgments on Moab, and they will know that I am Yahweh."

12 'Thus says Lord Yahweh, "Because Edom has acted against the house of Judah by taking vengeance and has incurred grievous guilt and avenged themselves upon them," 13 therefore thus says Lord Yahweh, "I will also stretch out My hand against Edom and cut off man and beast from it. And I will lay it waste; from Teman even to Dedan they will fall by the sword. 14 I will lay My vengeance on Edom by the hand of My people Israel. Therefore, they will act in Edom according to My anger and according to My wrath; thus they will know My vengeance," declares Lord Yahweh.

15 'Thus says Lord Yahweh, "Because the Philistines have acted in revenge and have taken vengeance with scorn of soul to bring ruin with everlasting enmity," 16 therefore thus says Lord Yahweh, "Behold, I will stretch out My hand against the Philistines and cut off the Cherethites and cause the remnant of the seacoast to perish. 17 So I will execute great vengeance on them with wrathful reproofs; and they will know that I am Yahweh when I lay My vengeance on them."'"

26 Now it happened in the eleventh year, on the first of the month, *that* the word of Yahweh came to me saying, 2 "Son of man, because Tyre has said concerning Jerusalem, 'Aha, the gateway of the peoples is broken; it has opened to me. I shall be filled, *now that* she is laid waste,' 3 therefore thus says Lord Yahweh, 'Behold, I am against you, O Tyre, and I will bring up many nations against you, as the sea brings up its waves. 4 They will make the walls of Tyre a ruin and pull down her towers; and I will scrape her dust from her and make her a bare rock. 5 She will be a place for the spreading of nets in the midst of the sea, for I have spoken,' declares Lord Yahweh, 'and she will become plunder for the nations. 6 Also her daughters who are on the mainland will be killed by the sword, and they will know that I am Yahweh.'"

7 For thus says Lord Yahweh, "Behold, I will bring upon Tyre from the north Nebuchadnezzar king of Babylon, king of kings, with horses, chariots, horsemen, and an

assembly, a great *number of* people. 8 He will
kill your daughters on the mainland with the
sword; and he will make siege walls against
you, cast up a ramp against you, and raise
up a large shield against you. 9 The blow of
his battering rams he will direct against your
walls, and with his swords he will tear down
your towers. 10 Because of the abundance of
his horses, the fine dust *raised by* them will
cover you; your walls will shake at the noise
of horsemen and wagons and chariots when
he enters your gates as men enter a city that
is breached. 11 With the hoofs of his horses
he will trample all your streets. He will
kill your people with the sword; and your
strong pillars will come down to the ground.
12 Also they will make a spoil of your wealth
and a plunder of your merchandise, and
pull down your walls and tear down your
desirable houses, and throw your stones and
your timbers and your debris into the water.
13 So I will cause the tumult of your songs
to cease, and the sound of your harps will
be heard no more. 14 I will make you a bare
rock; you will be a place for the spreading of
nets. You will be built no more, for I Yahweh
have spoken," declares Lord Yahweh.

15 Thus says Lord Yahweh to Tyre, "Shall
not the coastlands shake at the sound of
your downfall when the wounded groan,
when the killing occurs in your midst?
16 Then all the princes of the sea will go
down from their thrones, remove their
robes, and strip off their embroidered
garments. They will clothe themselves
with trembling; they will sit on the ground,
tremble every moment, and be appalled at
you. 17 They will take up a lamentation over
you and say to you,

'How you have perished,
O inhabited one,
From the seas, O city that was praised,
Which was strong on the sea,
She and her inhabitants,
Who imposed her terror
On all her inhabitants!
18 'Now the coastlands will tremble
On the day of your downfall;
Yes, the coastlands which
are by the sea
Will be dismayed at your departure.'"

19 For thus says Lord Yahweh, "When I
make you a city laid waste, like the cities
which are not inhabited, when I bring up
the deep over you and the great waters cover
you, 20 then I will bring you down with those
who go down to the pit, to the people of old,
and I will make you inhabit the lower parts
of the earth, like the ancient waste places,
with those who go down to the pit, so that
you will not be inhabited; but I will set glory
in the land of the living. 21 I will bring terrors
on you, and you will be no more; though
you will be sought, you will never be found
again," declares Lord Yahweh.

Psalm 128:1–6

1 How blessed is everyone
who fears Yahweh,
Who walks in His ways.
2 When you shall eat of the fruit
of the labor of your hands,
How blessed will you be and
how well will it be for you.
3 Your wife shall be like a fruitful vine
In the innermost parts of your house,
Your children like olive plants
All around your table.
4 Behold, for thus shall the
man be blessed
Who fears Yahweh.

5 May Yahweh bless you from Zion,
That you may see the prosperity of
Jerusalem all the days of your life.
6 Indeed, may you see your
children's children.
Peace be upon Israel!

Proverbs 28:25

25 An arrogant man stirs up strife,
But he who trusts in Yahweh
will be enriched.

Hebrews 11:17–40

17 By faith Abraham, when he was tested,
offered up Isaac, and he who had received
the promises was offering up his only *son*,
18 to whom it was said, "IN ISAAC YOUR SEED
SHALL BE CALLED." 19 He considered that God
is able to raise *people* even from the dead,
from which, figuratively speaking, he also
received him back. 20 By faith Isaac blessed
Jacob and Esau, even regarding things to
come. 21 By faith Jacob, as he was dying,
blessed each of the sons of Joseph, and
WORSHIPED, *leaning* ON THE TOP OF HIS STAFF.
22 By faith Joseph, when he was dying, made
mention of the exodus of the sons of Israel,
and gave commands concerning his bones.

23 By faith Moses, when he was born, was
hidden for three months by his parents,
because they saw he was a beautiful child,
and they were not afraid of the king's edict.
24 By faith Moses, when he had grown up,
refused to be called the son of Pharaoh's
daughter, 25 choosing rather to be mistreated
with the people of God than to enjoy the
passing pleasures of sin, 26 regarding the
reproach of Christ greater riches than the
treasures of Egypt; for he was looking to the
reward. 27 By faith he left Egypt, not fearing
the rage of the king; for he endured, as seeing
Him who is unseen. 28 By faith he kept the
Passover and the sprinkling of the blood, so
that he who destroyed the firstborn would
not touch them. 29 By faith they passed
through the Red Sea as though *they were*
passing through dry land, and the Egyptians,
when they attempted it, were drowned.

30 By faith the walls of Jericho fell down
after they had been encircled for seven days.
31 By faith Rahab the harlot did not perish
along with those who were disobedient,
after welcoming the spies in peace.

32 And what more shall I say? For time
will fail me if I recount Gideon, Barak,
Samson, Jephthah, as well as David and
Samuel and the prophets, 33 who through
faith conquered kingdoms, performed
righteousness, obtained promises, shut the
mouths of lions, 34 quenched the power of
fire, escaped the edge of the sword, were
made strong from weakness, became
mighty in war, put foreign armies to flight.
35 Women received *back* their dead by
resurrection; and others were tortured, not
accepting their release, so that they might
obtain a better resurrection; 36 and others
experienced mockings and floggings, yes,
also chains and imprisonment. 37 They
were stoned, they were sawn in two, they
were tempted, they were put to death with
the sword. They went about in sheepskins,
in goatskins, being destitute, afflicted,
mistreated 38 (of whom the world was not
worthy), wandering in desolate places
and mountains and caves and holes in the
ground.

39 And all these, having gained approval
through their faith, did not receive what
was promised, 40 because God had provided
something better for us, so that apart from
us they would not be made perfect.

NOVEMBER 18

Ezekiel 27:1–28:26

27 Moreover, the word of Yahweh came
to me saying, 2 "Now as for you, son of
man, take up a lamentation over Tyre 3 and
say to Tyre, who inhabits the entrance to
the sea, a trader of the peoples to many
coastlands, 'Thus says Lord Yahweh,

"O Tyre, you have said, 'I am
perfect in beauty.'
4 "Your borders are in the
heart of the seas;
Your builders have perfected
your beauty.
5 "They have made all *your* planks
of fir trees from Senir;
They have taken a cedar from
Lebanon to make a mast for you.
6 "Of oaks from Bashan they
have made your oars;
With ivory they have inlaid
your deck of boxwood from
the coastlands of Cyprus.
7 "Your sail was of fine embroidered
linen from Egypt
So that it became your standard;
Your awning was blue and purple
from the coastlands of Elishah.
8 "The inhabitants of Sidon and
Arvad were your rowers;
Your wise men, O Tyre, were
aboard; they were your pilots.
9 "The elders of Gebal and her wise men
were with you repairing your seams;
All the ships of the sea and their
sailors were with you in order
to deal in your merchandise.

10 "Persia and Lud and Put were in your
military force, your men of war. They hung
shield and helmet in you; they set forth
your majesty. 11 The sons of Arvad and
your military force were on your walls, *all*
around, and the Gammadim were in your
towers. They hung their small shields on
your walls *all* around; they perfected your
beauty.

12 "Tarshish was your customer because
of the abundance of all *kinds* of wealth; with
silver, iron, tin, and lead they paid for your

wares. 13 Javan, Tubal, and Meshech, they
were your traders; with the lives of men
and vessels of bronze they paid for your
merchandise. 14 Those from Beth-togarmah
gave horses and war horses and mules for
your wares. 15 The sons of Dedan were your
traders. Many coastlands were customers
at your hand; ivory tusks and ebony they
brought as your payment. 16 Aram was
your customer because of the abundance
of your goods; they paid for your wares
with emeralds, purple, embroidered work,
fine linen, coral, and rubies. 17 Judah and
the land of Israel, they were your traders;
with the wheat of Minnith, cakes, honey, oil,
and balm they paid for your merchandise.
18 Damascus was your customer because
of the abundance of your goods, because
of the abundance of all *kinds* of wealth,
because of the wine of Helbon and white
wool. 19 Also Vedan and Javan paid for your
wares from Uzal; wrought iron, cassia, and
sweet cane were among your merchandise.
20 Dedan traded with you in saddlecloths
for riding. 21 Arabia and all the princes of
Kedar, they were customers at your hand
for lambs, rams, and goats; for these, they
were your customers. 22 The traders of
Sheba and Raamah, they traded with you;
they paid for your wares with the best of all
kinds of spices and with all *kinds* of precious
stones and gold. 23 Haran, Canneh, Eden,
the traders of Sheba, Asshur, *and* Chilmad
traded with you. 24 They traded with you
in choice garments, in clothes of blue and
embroidered work, and in carpets of many
colors *and* tightly wound cords, *which were*
among your merchandise. 25 The ships of
Tarshish were the carriers for your merchandise.

And you were filled and
were very glorious
In the heart of the seas.

26 "Your rowers have brought you
Into great waters;
The east wind has broken you
In the heart of the seas.
27 "Your wealth, your wares,
your merchandise,
Your sailors and your pilots,
Your repairers of seams, your
dealers in merchandise,
And all your men of war
who are in you,
With all your assembly that
is in your midst,
Will fall into the heart of the seas
On the day of your downfall.
28 "At the sound of the cry of your pilots
The pasture lands will shake.
29 "All who handle the oar,
The sailors *and* all the pilots of the sea,
Will come down from their ships;
They will stand on the land,
30 And they will make their
voice heard over you
And will cry bitterly.
They will cast dust on their heads;
They will wallow in ashes.
31 "Also they will make themselves
bald for you
And gird themselves with sackcloth;
And they will weep for you
in bitterness of soul
With bitter mourning.
32 "Moreover, in their wailing they will
take up a lamentation for you
And lament over you:
'Who is like Tyre,
Like her who is silent in the
midst of the sea?
33 'When your wares went
out from the seas,
You satisfied a great
number of peoples;
With the greatness of your wealth
and your merchandise
You enriched the kings of earth.
34 'Now that you are broken by the seas
In the depths of the waters,
Your merchandise and all
your assembly
Have fallen in the midst of you.
35 'All the inhabitants of the coastlands
Are appalled at you,
And their kings are horribly horrified;
They are troubled in countenance.
36 'The merchants among the
peoples hiss at you;
You have become terrified,
And you will cease to be forever.'"'"

28

The word of Yahweh came again to
me, saying, 2 "Son of man, say to the
ruler of Tyre, 'Thus says Lord Yahweh,
"Because your heart is lofty
And you have said, 'I am a god;
I sit enthroned in the seat of gods
In the heart of the seas';

Yet you are a man and not God,
Although you make your heart
like the heart of God—
3 Behold, you are wiser than Daniel;
There is no secret that is
a match for you.
4 "By your wisdom and understanding
You have acquired wealth for yourself
And have acquired gold and
silver for your treasuries.
5 "By your great wisdom, by your trade
You have increased your wealth,
And your heart is lofty because
of your wealth—
6 Therefore thus says Lord Yahweh,
'Because you have made your heart
Like the heart of God,
7 Therefore, behold, I will bring
strangers upon you,
The most ruthless of the nations.
And they will draw their swords
Against the beauty of your wisdom
And defile your splendor.
8 'They will bring you down to the pit,
And you will die the death of
those who are slain
In the heart of the seas.
9 'Will you still say, "I am a god,"
In the presence of the one
who kills you,
Though you are a man and not God,
In the hands of those who slay you?
10 'You will die the death of
the uncircumcised
By the hand of strangers,
For I have spoken!' declares
Lord Yahweh!"'"

11 Again the word of Yahweh came to me
saying, 12 "Son of man, take up a lamenta-
tion over the king of Tyre and say to him,
'Thus says Lord Yahweh,
"You had the seal of perfection,
Full of wisdom and perfect in beauty.
13 "You were in Eden, the garden of God;
Every precious stone was
your covering:
The ruby, the topaz, and the diamond;
The beryl, the onyx, and the jasper;
The lapis lazuli, the turquoise,
and the emerald;
And the gold, the workmanship
of your settings and sockets,
Was in you.
On the day that you were created
They were prepared.
14 "You were the anointed
cherub who covers,
And I placed you *there*.
You were on the holy mountain of God;
You walked in the midst of
the stones of fire.
15 "You were blameless in your ways
From the day you were created
Until unrighteousness
was found in you.
16 "By the abundance of your trade
You were internally filled
with violence,
And you sinned;
Therefore I have cast you as profane
From the mountain of God.
And I have destroyed you,
O covering cherub,
From the midst of the stones of fire.
17 "Your heart was lofty because
of your beauty;
You corrupted your wisdom by
reason of your splendor.
I cast you to the ground;
I put you before kings,
That they may see you.
18 "By the abundance of your iniquities,
In the unrighteousness of your trade
You profaned your sanctuaries.
Therefore I have brought out
fire from the midst of you;
It has consumed you,
And I have turned you to
ashes on the earth
In the eyes of all who see you.
19 "All who know you among the peoples
Are appalled at you;
You have become terrified,
And you will cease to be forever."'"

20 And the word of Yahweh came to me
saying, 21 "Son of man, set your face toward
Sidon, prophesy against her 22 and say, 'Thus
says Lord Yahweh,
"Behold, I am against you, O Sidon,
And I will be glorified in your midst.
Then they will know that I am Yahweh
when I execute judgments in her,
And I will manifest My holiness in her.
23 "For I will send pestilence to her
And blood to her streets,
And the wounded will fall in her midst
By the sword upon her on every side;
Then they will know that I am Yahweh.
24 "And there will be no more for the house
of Israel a prickling brier or a painful thorn

from any round about them who scorned them; then they will know that I am Lord Yahweh."

25 'Thus says Lord Yahweh, "When I gather the house of Israel from the peoples, among whom they are scattered, and will manifest My holiness in them in the sight of the nations, then they will live in their land which I gave to My servant Jacob. 26 They will live in it securely; and they will build houses, plant vineyards, and live securely when I execute judgments upon all who scorn them all around them. Then they will know that I am Yahweh their God."'"

Psalm 129:1–4

1 "Many times they have assailed
me from my youth up,"
Let Israel now say,
2 "Many times they have assailed
me from my youth up;
Yet they have not prevailed
against me.
3 "The plowers plowed upon my back;
They lengthened their furrows."
4 Yahweh is righteous;
He has cut up the cords of the wicked.

Proverbs 28:26

26 He who trusts in his own
heart is a fool,
But he who walks wisely will escape.

Hebrews 12:1–29

12 Therefore, since we have so great a cloud of witnesses surrounding us, laying aside every weight and the sin which so easily entangles us, let us run with endurance the race that is set before us, 2 fixing our eyes on Jesus, the author and perfecter of faith, who for the joy set before Him endured the cross, despising the shame, and has sat down at the right hand of the throne of God.

3 For consider Him who has endured such hostility by sinners against Himself, so that you will not grow weary, fainting in heart. 4 You have not yet resisted to the point of shedding blood in your striving against sin. 5 And you have forgotten the exhortation which is addressed to you as sons,

"MY SON, DO NOT REGARD LIGHTLY
THE DISCIPLINE OF THE LORD,
NOR FAINT WHEN YOU ARE
REPROVED BY HIM;
6 FOR THOSE WHOM THE LORD
LOVES HE DISCIPLINES,
AND HE FLOGS EVERY SON
WHOM HE RECEIVES."

7 It is for discipline that you endure; God deals with you as with sons; for what son is there whom *his* father does not discipline? 8 But if you are without discipline, of which all have become partakers, then you are illegitimate children and not sons. 9 Furthermore, we had earthly fathers to discipline us, and we respected them. Shall we not much rather be subject to the Father of spirits, and live? 10 For they disciplined us for a short time as seemed best to them, but He *disciplines us* for our benefit, so that we may share His holiness. 11 And all discipline for the moment seems not to be joyful, but sorrowful, but to those who have been trained by it, afterwards it yields the peaceful fruit of righteousness.

12 Therefore, STRENGTHEN THE HANDS THAT ARE WEAK AND THE KNEES THAT ARE FEEBLE, 13 and make straight paths for your feet, so that what is lame may not be put out of joint, but rather be healed.

14 Pursue peace with all men, and the sanctification without which no one will see the Lord, 15 seeing to it that no one falls short of the grace of God; that no ROOT OF BITTERNESS SPRINGING UP CAUSES TROUBLE, and by it many be defiled; 16 that *also there be* no sexually immoral or godless person like Esau, who sold his own birthright for a *single* meal. 17 For you know that even afterwards, when he desired to inherit the blessing, he was rejected, for he found no place for repentance, though he sought for it with tears.

18 For you have not come to *a mountain* that can be touched and to a blazing fire, and to darkness and gloom and whirlwind, 19 and to the blast of a trumpet and the sound of words which *was such that* those who heard begged that no further word be spoken to them. 20 For they could not bear what was being commanded, "IF EVEN A BEAST TOUCHES THE MOUNTAIN, IT WILL BE STONED." 21 And so terrible was what appeared, *that* Moses said, "I AM FULL OF FEAR and trembling." 22 But you have come to Mount Zion and to the city of the living God, the heavenly Jerusalem, and to myriads of angels, 23 to the festal gathering and assembly of the firstborn

who are enrolled in heaven, and to God,
the Judge of all, and to the spirits of *the*
righteous made perfect, 24 and to Jesus,
the mediator of a new covenant, and to
the sprinkled blood, which speaks better
than *the blood* of Abel.

25 See to it that you do not refuse Him
who is speaking. For if those did not escape
when they refused him who warned *them*
on earth, much less *will* we *escape* who turn
away from Him who *warns* from heaven.
26 And His voice shook the earth then, but
now He has promised, saying, "YET ONCE
MORE I WILL SHAKE NOT ONLY THE EARTH, BUT
ALSO THE HEAVEN." 27 Now this *expression*,
"Yet once more," indicates the removing
of those things which can be shaken, as of
created things, so that those things which
cannot be shaken may remain. 28 Therefore,
since we are receiving a kingdom which
cannot be shaken, let us show gratitude, by
which we may offer to God an acceptable
service with reverence and awe; 29 for OUR
GOD IS A CONSUMING FIRE.

Blessed Bible, Book of Gold, precious truths Thy pages hold, truths to lead me day by day, all along my pilgrim way.

— FANNY CROSBY

NOVEMBER 19

Ezekiel 29:1–30:26

29 In the tenth year, in the tenth *month*,
on the twelfth of the month, the
word of Yahweh came to me saying, 2 "Son
of man, set your face against Pharaoh king of
Egypt and prophesy against him and against
all Egypt. 3 Speak and say, 'Thus says Lord
Yahweh,

"Behold, I am against you,
Pharaoh king of Egypt,
The great monster that lies in the
midst of his canals of the Nile,
That has said, 'My Nile is mine,
and I myself have made *it*.'

4 "I will put hooks in your jaws
And make the fish of your canals
of the Nile cling to your scales.
And I will bring you up out of the
midst of your canals of the Nile,
And all the fish of your canals of the
Nile will cling to your scales.

5 "I will abandon you to the
wilderness, you and all the fish
of your canals of the Nile;
You will fall on the open field;
you will not be brought
together or gathered.
I have given you for food to
the beasts of the earth and
to the birds of the sky.

6 "Then all the inhabitants of Egypt
will know that I am Yahweh
Because they have been *only* a staff
made of reed to the house of Israel.

7 "When they seized you with the hand,
You tore and split open all
their shoulders;
And when they leaned on you,
You broke and made all
their loins quake."

8 'Therefore thus says Lord Yahweh,
"Behold, I will bring upon you a sword,
and I will cut off from you man and beast.
9 The land of Egypt will become a desolation
and waste. Then they will know that I am
Yahweh.

Because you said, 'The Nile is mine, and
I have made *it*,' 10 therefore, behold, I am
against you and against your canals of the
Nile, and I will make the land of Egypt an
utter waste and desolation, from Migdol *to*
Syene and even to the border of Ethiopia.
11 A man's foot will not pass through it, and
the foot of a beast will not pass through it,
and it will not be inhabited for forty years.
12 So I will make the land of Egypt a deso-
lation in the midst of desolated lands. And
her cities, in the midst of cities that are laid
waste, will be desolate forty years; and I will
scatter the Egyptians among the nations and
disperse them among the lands."

13 'For thus says Lord Yahweh, "At the end
of forty years I will gather the Egyptians
from the peoples among whom they were

scattered. 14 I will return the fortunes of
Egypt and make them return to the land of
Pathros, to the land of their origin, and there
they will be a lowly kingdom. 15 It will be the
lowest of the kingdoms, and it will never
again lift itself up above the nations. And I
will make them so small that they will not
have dominion over the nations. 16 And it
will never again be the security of the house
of Israel, bringing to remembrance the
iniquity of their having turned *to go* after
Egypt. Then they will know that I am Lord
Yahweh."'"

17 Now in the twenty-seventh year, in the
first *month*, on the first of the month, the
word of Yahweh came to me saying, 18 "Son
of man, Nebuchadnezzar king of Babylon
made his military force labor hard against
Tyre; every head was made bald, and every
shoulder was rubbed bare. But he and his
military force had no wages from Tyre
for the labor that he had labored against
it." 19 Therefore thus says Lord Yahweh,
"Behold, I will give the land of Egypt to
Nebuchadnezzar king of Babylon. And he
will carry off her abundance and capture her
spoil and seize her plunder; and it will be
wages for his military force. 20 I have given
him the land of Egypt *for* his work which he
labored because they acted for Me," declares
Lord Yahweh.

21 "On that day I will make a horn sprout
for the house of Israel, and I will open your
mouth in their midst. Then they will know
that I am Yahweh."

30

The word of Yahweh came again to
me saying, 2 "Son of man, prophesy
and say, 'Thus says Lord Yahweh,

"Wail, 'Alas for the day!'
3 "For the day is near,
Even the day of Yahweh is near;
It will be a day of clouds,
A time *of doom* for the nations.
4 "A sword will come upon Egypt,
And anguish will be in Ethiopia;
When the slain fall in Egypt,
They take away her multitude,
And her foundations are pulled down.

5 "Ethiopia, Put, Lud, all Arabia, Libya, and
the people of the land that is in covenant
will fall with them by the sword."

6 'Thus says Yahweh,
"Indeed, those who support
Egypt will fall,
And the pride of her strength
will come down;
From Migdol *to* Syene
They will fall within her by the sword,"
Declares Lord Yahweh.
7 "They will be desolate
In the midst of the desolated lands;
And her cities will be
In the midst of the cities laid waste.
8 "And they will know that I am Yahweh,
When I set a fire in Egypt
And all her helpers are broken.

9 "On that day messengers will go forth from
Me in ships to frighten secure Ethiopia; and
anguish will be on them as on the day of
Egypt; for behold, it is coming!"

10 'Thus says Lord Yahweh,
"I will also make the multitude
of Egypt cease
By the hand of Nebuchadnezzar
king of Babylon.
11 "He and his people with him,
The most ruthless of the nations,
Will be brought in to make
the land a ruin;
And they will draw their
swords against Egypt
And fill the land with the slain.
12 "Moreover, I will make the
canals of the Nile dry
And sell the land into the
hands of evil men.
And I will make the land desolate,
As well as its fullness,
By the hand of strangers;
I, Yahweh, have spoken."

13 'Thus says Lord Yahweh,
"I will also destroy the idols
And make the images cease
from Memphis.
And there will no longer be a
prince in the land of Egypt;
And I will put fear in the land of Egypt.
14 "I will make Pathros desolate,
Set a fire in Zoan,
And execute judgments on Thebes.
15 "I will pour out My wrath on Sin,
The strong defense of Egypt;
I will also cut off the
multitude of Thebes.
16 "I will set a fire in Egypt;
Sin will writhe in anguish;
Thebes will be breached,

And Memphis *will have*
distresses daily.
17 "The choice men of On and of Pi-beseth
Will fall by the sword,
And the women will go into captivity.
18 "In Tehaphnehes the day will be dark
When I break there the bars
of the yoke of Egypt.
Then the pride of her strength
will cease in her;
A cloud will cover her,
And her daughters will
go into captivity.
19 "Thus I will execute
judgments on Egypt,
And they will know that
I am Yahweh."'"

20 In the eleventh year, in the first *month*,
on the seventh of the month, the word of
Yahweh came to me saying, 21 "Son of man,
I have broken the arm of Pharaoh king of
Egypt; and behold, it has not been bound
up to *be* given healing or wrapped with a
bandage, that it may be strong to seize the
sword. 22 Therefore thus says Lord Yahweh,
'Behold, I am against Pharaoh king of Egypt
and will break his arms, both the strong and
the broken; and I will make the sword fall
from his hand. 23 I will scatter the Egyptians
among the nations and disperse them
among the lands. 24 For I will strengthen
the arms of the king of Babylon and put
My sword in his hand; and I will break the
arms of Pharaoh so that he will groan before
him with the groanings of a wounded man.
25 Thus I will strengthen the arms of the
king of Babylon, but the arms of Pharaoh
will fall. Then they will know that I am
Yahweh, when I put My sword into the hand
of the king of Babylon and he stretches it
out against the land of Egypt. 26 When I
scatter the Egyptians among the nations
and disperse them among the lands, then
they will know that I am Yahweh.'"

Psalm 129:5–8

5 Let all who hate Zion
Be put to shame and turned backward;
6 Let them be like grass
upon the rooftops,
Which dries up before it grows up;
7 With which the reaper does
not fill his hand,
Nor the binder of sheaves the
fold of his garment;
8 And those who pass by will not say,
"The blessing of Yahweh be upon you;
We bless you in the name of Yahweh."

Proverbs 28:27

27 He who gives to the poor
will never want,
But he who shuts his eyes
will have many curses.

Hebrews 13:1–25

13 Let love of the brothers continue. 2 Do
not neglect to show hospitality to
strangers, for by this some have entertained
angels without knowing it. 3 Remember the
prisoners, as though in prison with them,
and those who are mistreated, since you
yourselves also are in the body. 4 Marriage
is to be held in honor among all, and the
marriage bed *is to be* undefiled, for the
sexually immoral and adulterers God will
judge. 5 *Make sure that* your way *of life* is
free from the love of money, being content
with what you have; for He Himself has said,
"I WILL NEVER DESERT YOU, NOR WILL I EVER
FORSAKE YOU," 6 so that we confidently say,

"THE LORD IS MY HELPER, I
WILL NOT BE AFRAID.
WHAT WILL MAN DO TO ME?"

7 Remember your leaders, who spoke
the word of God to you; and considering
the result of their conduct, imitate their
faith. 8 Jesus Christ *is* the same yesterday
and today and forever. 9 Do not be carried
away by varied and strange teachings; for it
is good for the heart to be strengthened by
grace, not by foods, through which those
who were so occupied were not benefited.
10 We have an altar from which those who
serve the tabernacle have no authority to
eat. 11 For the bodies of those animals whose
blood is brought into the holy places by the
high priest *as an offering* for sin, are burned
outside the camp. 12 Therefore Jesus also,
that He might sanctify the people through
His own blood, suffered outside the gate.
13 So, let us go out to Him outside the camp,
bearing His reproach. 14 For here we do not
have a lasting city, but we are seeking *the
one* to come. 15 Through Him then, let us
continually offer up a sacrifice of praise to
God, that is, the fruit of lips that confess
His name. 16 And do not neglect doing good
and sharing, for with such sacrifices God is
pleased.

17 Obey your leaders and submit *to them*—
for they keep watch over your souls as those
who will give an account—so that they will
do this with joy and not with groaning, for
this would be unprofitable for you.
18 Pray for us, for we are convinced that
we have a good conscience, desiring to
conduct ourselves well in all things. 19 And
I urge *you* all the more to do this, so that I
may be restored to you the sooner.
20 Now the God of peace, who brought
up from the dead the great Shepherd of
the sheep through the blood of the eternal
covenant, our Lord Jesus, 21 equip you in
every good thing to do His will, by doing
in us what is pleasing in His sight, through
Jesus Christ, to whom *be* the glory forever
and ever. Amen.
22 But I urge you, brothers, bear with
this word of exhortation, for I have written
to you briefly. 23 Know that our brother
Timothy has been released, with whom, if
he comes soon, I will see you. 24 Greet all of
your leaders and all the saints. Those from
Italy greet you.
25 Grace be with you all.

NOVEMBER 20

Ezekiel 31:1–32:32

31 Now it happened in the eleventh year,
in the third *month*, on the first of the
month, *that* the word of Yahweh came to me
saying, 2 "Son of man, say to Pharaoh king
of Egypt and to his multitude,

'To whom do you liken *yourself*
in your greatness?
3 'Behold, Assyria *was* a
cedar in Lebanon
With beautiful branches
and forest shade
And lofty in height,
And its top was among the clouds.
4 'The waters made it grow; the
deep made it high.
With its rivers it was going all
around its planting place
And sent out its conduits to
all the trees of the field.
5 'Therefore its height was loftier
than all the trees of the field,
And its boughs became many
and its branches long
Because of many waters as
it spread them out.
6 'All the birds of the sky
nested in its boughs,
And under its branches all the
beasts of the field gave birth,
And all great nations lived
under its shade.
7 'So it was beautiful in its greatness,
in the length of its foliage;
For its roots extended to
many waters.
8 'The cedars in God's garden
could not match it;
The cypresses could not liken
themselves with its boughs,
And the plane trees were
not like its branches.
No tree in God's garden could liken
itself with it in its beauty.
9 'I made it beautiful with the
multitude of its foliage,
And all the trees of Eden,
which were in the garden of
God, were jealous of it.

10 'Therefore thus says Lord Yahweh,
"Because it is lofty in height and has put
its top among the clouds, and its heart is
high up in its loftiness, 11 therefore I will
give it into the hand of a dominant one of
the nations; he will thoroughly deal with it.
According to its wickedness I have driven
it away. 12 Strangers—ruthless ones of the
nations have cut it down and abandoned it;
on the mountains and in all the valleys its
foliage have fallen, and its boughs have been
broken in all the ravines of the land. And
all the peoples of the earth have gone down
from its shade and abandoned it. 13 On its
downfall all the birds of the sky will dwell,
and all the beasts of the field will be on its
fallen branches 14 so that all the trees by
the waters may not be lofty in their height,
nor put their top among the clouds, nor
their dominant ones—all the well-watered
ones—stand in their loftiness. For they have
all been given over to death, to the earth
beneath, among the sons of men, with those
who go down to the pit."
15 'Thus says Lord Yahweh, "On the
day when it went down to Sheol I caused
mourning; I covered it with the deep over it

and held back its rivers. And *its* many waters
were stopped up, and I made Lebanon
mourn for it, and all the trees of the field
wilted away on account of it. 16 I made the
nations quake at the sound of its downfall
when I made it go down to Sheol with those
who go down to the pit; and all the trees of
Eden, the choicest and best of Lebanon, all
the well-watered ones, were comforted in
the earth beneath. 17 They also went down
with it to Sheol to those who were slain by
the sword; and those who were its strength
lived under its shade among the nations.

18 "To which among the trees of Eden do
you thus liken *yourself* in glory and greatness?
Yet you will be brought down with
the trees of Eden to the earth beneath; you
will lie in the midst of the uncircumcised,
with those who were slain by the sword. So
is Pharaoh and all his multitude!"' declares
Lord Yahweh."

32 And it happened in the twelfth year,
in the twelfth *month*, on the first
of the month, *that* the word of Yahweh
came to me saying, 2 "Son of man, take up
a lamentation over Pharaoh king of Egypt
and say to him,

'You liken yourself to a young
lion of the nations,
Yet you are like the monster in the seas;
And you burst forth in your rivers
And muddied the waters with your feet
And fouled their rivers.'"

3 Thus says Lord Yahweh,
"So I will spread My net over you
With an assembly of many peoples,
And they shall bring you up in My net.
4 "I will abandon you on the land;
I will hurl you on the open field.
And I will cause all the birds of
the sky to dwell on you,
And I will satisfy the beasts of
the whole earth with you.
5 "I will put your flesh on the mountains
And fill the valleys with your refuse.
6 "I will also make the land drink
the discharge of your blood
As far as the mountains,
And the ravines will be full of you.
7 "And when *I* extinguish you,
I will cover the heavens and
darken their stars;
I will cover the sun with a cloud,
And the moon will not give its light.
8 "All the shining lights in the heavens
I will darken over you
And will give darkness on your land,"
Declares Lord Yahweh.

9 "I will also vex the hearts of many peoples
when I bring your destruction among the
nations, into lands which you have not
known. 10 I will make many peoples appalled
at you, and their kings will be horribly afraid
of you when I brandish My sword before
them; and they will tremble every moment,
every man for his own life, on the day of
your downfall."

11 For thus says Lord Yahweh, "The sword
of the king of Babylon will come upon you.
12 By the swords of the mighty ones I will
cause your multitude to fall; all of them are
ruthless ones of the nations,

And they will devastate the
lofty pride of Egypt,
And all its multitude will be destroyed.
13 "I will also make all its cattle perish
from beside many waters;
And the foot of man will not
muddy them anymore,
And the hoofs of beasts will
not muddy them.
14 "Then I will make their waters settle
And will cause their rivers
to run like oil,"
Declares Lord Yahweh.
15 "When I make the land of
Egypt a desolation,
And the land is desolate of its fullness,
When I strike all those who inhabit it,
Then they shall know
that I am Yahweh.

16 "This is a lamentation, and they shall
lament over it. The daughters of the nations
shall lament over it. Over Egypt and over
all her multitude they shall lament over it,"
declares Lord Yahweh.

17 Now it happened in the twelfth year, on
the fifteenth of the month, *that* the word of
Yahweh came to me saying, 18 "Son of man,
wail for the hordes of Egypt and bring it
down, her and the daughters of the powerful
nations, to the nether world, with those who
go down to the pit;

19 'Whom do you surpass in beauty?
Go down and make your bed
with the uncircumcised.'

20 "They shall fall in the midst of those who
are slain by the sword. She is given over to

the sword; they have drawn her and all her
multitude away. 21 The dominant among
the mighty ones shall speak of him *and* his
helpers from the midst of Sheol, 'They have
gone down, they lie still, the uncircumcised,
slain by the sword.'
22 "Assyria is there and all her assembly;
her graves are round about her. All of them
are slain, fallen by the sword, 23 whose
graves are put in the remotest parts of the
pit, and her assembly is all round about
her grave. All of them are slain, fallen by
the sword, who put terror in the land of the
living.
24 "Elam is there and all her multitude all
around her grave; all of them slain, fallen by
the sword, who went down uncircumcised
to the lower parts of the earth, who put their
terror in the land of the living and bore their
dishonor with those who went down to the
pit. 25 They have put a bed for her among the
slain with all her multitude. Her graves are
all around it; all of them are uncircumcised,
slain by the sword (although their terror was
put in the land of the living), and they bore
their dishonor with those who go down to
the pit; they were put in the midst of the
slain.
26 "Meshech, Tubal, and all their multi-
tude are there; their graves are all around
them. All of them were slain by the sword
uncircumcised, though they put their terror
in the land of the living. 27 Nor do they lie
beside the fallen mighty ones of the uncir-
cumcised, who went down to Sheol with
their weapons of war and whose swords
were put under their heads; but the *punish-
ment for* their iniquity rested on their bones,
though the terror of *these* mighty ones *was
once* in the land of the living. 28 But as for
you, in the midst of the uncircumcised you
will be broken and lie with those slain by
the sword.
29 "There also is Edom, its kings, and all
its princes, who for *all* their might are put
with those slain by the sword; they will lie
with the uncircumcised and with those who
go down to the pit.
30 "There also are the chiefs of the north,
all of them, and all the Sidonians, who in
spite of the terror resulting from their
might, in shame went down with the slain.
So they lay down uncircumcised with those
slain by the sword and bore their dishonor
with those who go down to the pit.
31 "These Pharaoh will see, and he will
be comforted for all his multitude slain by
the sword, *even* Pharaoh and all his military
force," declares Lord Yahweh. 32 "Though I
put a terror of him in the land of the living,
yet he will be made to lie down among *the*
uncircumcised *along* with those slain by
the sword, *even* Pharaoh and all his hordes,"
declares Lord Yahweh.

Psalm 130:1–4

1 Out of the depths I called
to You, O Yahweh.
2 O Lord, hear my voice!
Let Your ears be attentive
To the voice of my supplications.
3 If You should keep iniquities, O Yah,
O Lord, who could stand?
4 But with You there is forgiveness,
That You may be feared.

Proverbs 28:28

28 When the wicked rise, men
hide themselves;
But when they perish, the
righteous increase.

James 1:1–27

1 James, a slave of God and of the Lord
Jesus Christ,
To the twelve tribes who are in the Dis-
persion: Greetings.
2 Consider it all joy, my brothers, when
you encounter various trials, 3 knowing
that the testing of your faith brings about
perseverance. 4 And let perseverance have
its perfect work, so that you may be perfect
and complete, lacking in nothing.
5 But if any of you lacks wisdom, let him
ask of God, who gives to all generously and
without reproach, and it will be given to
him. 6 But he must ask in faith, doubting
nothing, for the one who doubts is like the
surf of the sea, driven and tossed by the
wind. 7 For that man ought not to expect
that he will receive anything from the Lord,
8 *being* a double-minded man, unstable in
all his ways.
9 But the brother of humble circumstances
is to boast in his high position; 10 and the
rich man *is to boast* in his humiliation,
because like flowering grass he will pass
away. 11 For the sun rises with a scorching
heat and withers the grass; and its flower
falls off and the beauty of its appearance is

destroyed; so too the rich man in the midst of his pursuits will fade away.

12 Blessed is a man who perseveres under trial; for once he has been approved, he will receive the crown of life which *the Lord* has promised to those who love Him. 13 Let no one say when he is tempted, "I am being tempted by God"; for God cannot be tempted by evil, and He Himself does not tempt anyone. 14 But each one is tempted when he is carried away and enticed by his own lust. 15 Then when lust has conceived, it gives birth to sin, and when sin is fully matured, it brings forth death. 16 Do not be deceived, my beloved brothers. 17 Every good thing given and every perfect gift is from above, coming down from the Father of lights, with whom there is no variation or shifting shadow. 18 In the exercise of His will He brought us forth by the word of truth, so that we would be a kind of first fruits among His creatures.

19 Know *this*, my beloved brothers. But everyone must be quick to hear, slow to speak *and* slow to anger; 20 for the anger of man does not achieve the righteousness of God. 21 Therefore, laying aside all filthiness and *all* that remains of wickedness, in gentleness receive the implanted word, which is able to save your souls. 22 But become doers of the word, and not merely hearers who delude themselves. 23 For if anyone is a hearer of the word and not a doer, he is like a man who looks at his natural face in a mirror; 24 for *once* he looked at himself and has gone away, he immediately forgot what kind of person he was. 25 But one who looks intently at the perfect law, the *law* of freedom, and abides by it, not having become a forgetful hearer but a doer of the work, this man will be blessed in what he does.

26 If anyone thinks himself to be religious while not bridling his tongue but deceiving his *own* heart, this man's religion is worthless. 27 Pure and undefiled religion before *our* God and Father is this: to visit orphans and widows in their affliction, *and* to keep oneself unstained by the world.

NOVEMBER 21

Ezekiel 33:1–34:31

33 And the word of Yahweh came to me, saying, 2 "Son of man, speak to the sons of your people and say to them, 'If I bring a sword upon a land, and the people of the land take one man from among them and make him their watchman, 3 and he sees the sword coming upon the land and blows on the trumpet and warns the people, 4 then he who hears the sound of the trumpet and does not take warning, and a sword comes and takes him away, his blood will be on his *own* head. 5 He heard the sound of the trumpet but did not take warning; his blood will be on himself. But had he taken warning, he would have escaped with his life. 6 But if the watchman sees the sword coming and does not blow the trumpet and the people are not warned, and a sword comes and takes a person from them, he is taken away in his iniquity; but his blood I will require from the watchman's hand.'

7 "Now as for you, son of man, I have given you as a watchman for the house of Israel; so you will hear a word from My mouth and give them warning from Me. 8 When I say to the wicked, 'O wicked man, you will surely die,' and you do not speak to warn the wicked from his way, that wicked man shall die in his iniquity, but his blood I will require from your hand. 9 But as for you, if you on your part warn a wicked man to turn from his way and he does not turn from his way, he will die in his iniquity, but you have delivered your life.

10 "Now as for you, son of man, say to the house of Israel, 'Thus you have spoken, saying, "Surely our transgressions and our sins are upon us, and we are rotting away in them; how then can we live?"' 11 Say to them, 'As I live!' declares Lord Yahweh, 'I take no pleasure in the death of the wicked, but rather that the wicked turn from his way and live. Turn back, turn back from your evil ways! Why then will you die, O house of Israel?' 12 Now as for you, son of man, say to the sons of your people, 'The righteousness of a righteous man will not deliver him in the day of his transgression, and as for the wickedness of the wicked, he will not stumble because of it in the day when he turns from his wickedness; whereas a righteous man will not be able to live by his righteousness on the day when he commits sin.' 13 When

I say to the righteous he will surely live, and
he *so* trusts in his righteousness that he does
iniquity, none of his righteous deeds will be
remembered; but in that same iniquity of his
which he has done he will die. 14 But when I
say to the wicked, 'You will surely die,' and
he turns from his sin and does justice and
righteousness, 15 *if a* wicked man restores
a pledge, pays back what he has taken by
robbery, walks by the statutes of life without
committing iniquity, he shall surely live; he
shall not die. 16 None of his sins that he has
done will be remembered against him. He
has done justice and righteousness; he shall
surely live.

17 "Yet the sons of your people say, 'The
way of the Lord is not right,' when it is
their own way that is not right. 18 When the
righteous turns from his righteousness and
does iniquity, then he shall die in it. 19 But
when the wicked turns from his wickedness
and does justice and righteousness, he will
live by them. 20 Yet you say, 'The way of the
Lord is not right.' O house of Israel, I will
judge each of you according to his ways."

21 Now it happened in the twelfth year of
our exile, on the fifth of the tenth month,
that those who escaped from Jerusalem
came to me, saying, "The city has been
struck down." 22 Now the hand of Yahweh
had been upon me in the evening, before
those who escaped came. And He opened
my mouth at the time *they* came to me in
the morning; so my mouth was opened, and
I was no longer mute.

23 Then the word of Yahweh came to me
saying, 24 "Son of man, they who inhabit
these waste places in the land of Israel
are saying, 'Abraham was *only* one, yet he
possessed the land; so to us who are many
the land has been given as a possession.'
25 Therefore say to them, 'Thus says Lord
Yahweh, "You eat *meat* with the blood *in it*
and lift up your eyes to your idols as you
shed blood. Should you then possess the
land? 26 You stand on account of your sword,
you do abominations, and each of you
defiles his neighbor's wife. Should you then
possess the land?"' 27 Thus you shall say to
them, 'Thus says Lord Yahweh, "As I live,
surely those who are in the waste places will
fall by the sword, and whoever is in the open
field I will give to the beasts to be devoured,
and those who are in the strongholds and in
the caves will die of pestilence. 28 I will make
the land a desolation and a desecration, and
the lofty pride of her strength will cease; and
the mountains of Israel will be desolate so
that no one will pass through. 29 Then they
will know that I am Yahweh, when I make
the land a desolation and a desecration
because of all their abominations which
they have done."'

30 "But as for you, son of man, the sons
of your people who talk about you by the
walls and in the doorways of the houses,
speak to one another, each to his brother,
saying, 'Come now and hear what the word
is which comes forth from Yahweh.' 31 They
come to you as people come and sit before
you *as* My people and hear your words, but
they do not do them, for they do the lustful
desires *expressed* by their mouth, *and* their
heart goes after their greedy gain. 32 Behold,
you are to them like a lustful song by one
who has a beautiful voice and plays well on
an instrument; for they hear your words but
they do not do them. 33 So when it comes to
pass—behold, it is coming—then they will
know that a prophet has been in their midst."

34 Then the word of Yahweh came to
me saying, 2 "Son of man, prophesy
against the shepherds of Israel. Prophesy
and say to those shepherds, 'Thus says Lord
Yahweh, "Woe, shepherds of Israel who have
been shepherding themselves! Should not
the shepherds shepherd the flock? 3 You eat
the fat and clothe yourselves with the wool;
you sacrifice the fat *sheep* without shep-
herding the flock. 4 Those who are sickly you
have not strengthened, and the diseased you
have not healed, and the broken you have
not bound up, and the scattered you have
not brought back, nor have you searched for
the lost; but with strength and with severity
you have dominated them. 5 They were
scattered for lack of a shepherd, and they
became food for every beast of the field and
were scattered. 6 My flock wandered through
all the mountains and on every high hill;
My flock was scattered over all the surface
of the earth, and there was no one to seek
or search *for them.*"'"

7 Therefore, you shepherds, hear the word
of Yahweh: 8 "As I live," declares Lord Yahweh,
"surely because My flock has become plun-
der, My flock has even become food for all the
beasts of the field for lack of a shepherd, and
My shepherds did not seek for My flock, but

rather the shepherds shepherded themselves
and did not shepherd My flock; 9 therefore,
you shepherds, hear the word of Yahweh:
10 'Thus says Lord Yahweh, "Behold, I am
against the shepherds, and I will seek My
flock from their hand and make them cease
from shepherding the flock. So the shepherds
will not shepherd themselves anymore, but I
will deliver My flock from their mouth so that
they will not be food for them."'"
11 For thus says Lord Yahweh, "Behold,
I Myself will seek My sheep and care for
them. 12 As a shepherd cares for his herd in
the day when he is among his sheep which
are spread out, so I will care for My sheep
and will deliver them from all the places to
which they were scattered on a cloudy and
gloomy day. 13 I will bring them out from the
peoples and gather them from the countries
and bring them to their own land; and I will
shepherd them on the mountains of Israel,
by the streams, and in all the inhabited
places of the land. 14 I will shepherd them
in a good pasture, and their grazing ground
will be on the mountain heights of Israel.
There they will lie down on good grazing
ground and *be* shepherded in rich pasture
on the mountains of Israel. 15 I will shepherd
My flock, and I will make them lie down,"
declares Lord Yahweh. 16 "I will search for
the lost, bring back the scattered, bind up
the broken, and strengthen the sick; but
the fat and the strong I will destroy. I will
shepherd them with judgment.
17 "As for you, My flock, thus says Lord
Yahweh, 'Behold, I will judge between one
sheep and another, between the rams and
the male goats. 18 Is it too slight a thing for
you that you should *be* shepherded in the
good pasture, that you must tread down
with your feet the rest of your pastures? Or
that you should drink of the clear waters,
that you must foul the rest with your feet?
19 As for My flock, they must *be* shepherded
on what you tread down with your feet and
drink what you foul with your feet!'"
20 Therefore, thus says Lord Yahweh to
them, "Behold, I, even I, will judge between
the fat sheep and the lean sheep. 21 Because
you push with side and with shoulder, and
thrust at all the sickly with your horns until
you have scattered them abroad, 22 there-
fore, I will save My flock, and they will no
longer be plunder; and I will judge between
one sheep and another.
23 "Then I will establish over them one
shepherd, My servant David, and he will
shepherd them; he will shepherd them
himself and be their shepherd. 24 And I,
Yahweh, will be their God, and My servant
David will be prince among them; I, Yahweh,
have spoken.
25 "I will cut a covenant of peace with
them and cause harmful beasts to cease
from the land so that they may live securely
in the wilderness and sleep in the woods. 26 I
will make them and the places all around
My hill a blessing. And I will cause showers
to come down in their season; they will be
showers of blessing. 27 Also the tree of the
field will yield its fruit, and the earth will
yield its produce, and they will be secure
on their land. Then they will know that I
am Yahweh, when I have broken the bars of
their yoke and have delivered them from the
hand of those who enslaved them. 28 They
will no longer be plunder to the nations, and
the beasts of the earth will not devour them;
but they will live securely, and no one will
make *them* tremble. 29 I will establish for
them a renowned planting place, and they
will not again be victims of famine in the
land, and they will not bear the dishonor
of the nations anymore. 30 Then they will
know that I, Yahweh their God, am with
them, and that they, the house of Israel, are
My people," declares Lord Yahweh. 31 "As for
you, My sheep, the sheep of My pasture, you
are men, and I am your God," declares Lord
Yahweh.

Psalm 130:5–8

5 I hope for Yahweh, my soul does hope,
And for His word do I wait.
6 My soul *waits* for the Lord
More than the watchmen
for the morning,
The watchmen for the morning.
7 O Israel, wait for Yahweh;
For with Yahweh there is
lovingkindness,
And with Him is abundant redemption.
8 And it is He who will redeem Israel
From all his iniquities.

Proverbs 29:1

29 A man who hardens *his*
neck after much reproof
Will suddenly be broken
beyond healing.

James 2:1–26

2 My brothers, do not hold your faith in our glorious Lord Jesus Christ with *an attitude of* personal favoritism. 2 For if a man comes into your assembly with a gold ring and dressed in bright clothes, and there also comes in a poor man in dirty clothes, 3 and you pay special attention to the one who is wearing the bright clothes, and say, "You sit here in a good place," and you say to the poor man, "You stand over there, or sit down by my footstool," 4 have you not made distinctions among yourselves, and become judges with evil thoughts? 5 Listen, my beloved brothers: did not God choose the poor of this world *to be* rich in faith and heirs of the kingdom which He promised to those who love Him? 6 But you have dishonored the poor man. Is it not the rich who oppress you and they themselves drag you into court? 7 Do they not blaspheme the good name by which you have been called?

8 If, however, you are fulfilling the royal law according to the Scripture, "YOU SHALL LOVE YOUR NEIGHBOR AS YOURSELF," you are doing well. 9 But if you show partiality, you are committing sin, being convicted by the law as transgressors. 10 For whoever keeps the whole law and yet stumbles in one *point*, he has become guilty of all. 11 For He who said, "DO NOT COMMIT ADULTERY," also said, "DO NOT MURDER." Now if you do not commit adultery, but murder, you have become a transgressor of the law. 12 So speak and so act as those who are to be judged by *the* law of freedom. 13 For judgment *will be* merciless to one who has shown no mercy. Mercy triumphs over judgment.

14 What use is it, my brothers, if someone says he has faith but he has no works? Can that faith save him? 15 If a brother or sister is without clothing and in need of daily food, 16 and one of you says to them, "Go in peace, be warmed and be filled," and yet you do not give them what is necessary for *their* body, what use is that? 17 Even so faith, if it has no works, is dead by itself.

18 But someone will say, "You have faith; and I have works. Show me your faith without the works, and I will show you my faith by my works." 19 You believe that God is one. You do well; the demons also believe, and shudder. 20 But are you willing to recognize, you foolish fellow, that faith without works is useless? 21 Was not Abraham our father justified by works when he offered up Isaac his son on the altar? 22 You see that faith was working with his works, and as a result of the works, faith was perfected. 23 And the Scripture was fulfilled which says, "AND ABRAHAM BELIEVED GOD, AND IT WAS COUNTED TO HIM AS RIGHTEOUSNESS," and he was called the friend of God. 24 You see that a man is justified by works and not by faith alone. 25 And in the same way, was not Rahab the harlot also justified by works when she received the messengers and sent them out by another way? 26 For just as the body without *the* spirit is dead, so also faith without works is dead.

NOVEMBER 22

Ezekiel 35:1–36:38

35 Moreover, the word of Yahweh came to me saying, 2 "Son of man, set your face against Mount Seir and prophesy against it 3 and say to it, 'Thus says Lord Yahweh,

"Behold, I am against you, Mount Seir,
And I will stretch out My
hand against you
And make you a desolation
and a desecration.
4 "I will lay waste your cities,
And you will become a desolation.
Then you will know that I am Yahweh.

5 "Because you have had everlasting enmity and have delivered the sons of Israel to the power of the sword at the time of their disaster, at the time of the punishment of the end, 6 therefore as I live," declares Lord Yahweh, "I will prepare you for bloodshed, and bloodshed will pursue you; you surely have not hated bloodshed, so bloodshed will pursue you. 7 I will make Mount Seir a waste and a desolation, and I will cut off from it the one who passes through and returns. 8 I will fill its mountains with its slain; on your hills and in your valleys and in all your ravines those slain by the sword will fall. 9 I will make you an everlasting desolation, and your cities will not be inhabited. Then you will know that I am Yahweh.

10 “Because you have said, ‘These two nations and these two lands will be mine, and we will possess them,’ although Yahweh was there, 11 therefore as I live,” declares Lord Yahweh, “I will deal *with you* according to your anger and according to your jealousy which you dealt *with them* because of your hatred against them; so I will make Myself known among them when I judge you. 12 Then you will know that I, Yahweh, have heard all your contempt which you have spoken against the mountains of Israel saying, ‘They are laid desolate; they are given to us for food.’ 13 And you have magnified *yourselves* with your mouth against Me and have multiplied your words against Me; I have heard *it*.” 14 Thus says Lord Yahweh, “As all the earth delights, I will make you a desolation. 15 As you delighted over the inheritance of the house of Israel because it was desolate, so I will do to you. You will be a desolation, O Mount Seir, and all Edom, all of it. Then they will know that I am Yahweh.”’

36 “Now as for you, son of man, prophesy to the mountains of Israel and say, ‘O mountains of Israel, hear the word of Yahweh. 2 Thus says Lord Yahweh, “Because the enemy has spoken against you, ‘Aha!’ and, ‘The everlasting heights have become our possession,’ 3 therefore prophesy and say, ‘Thus says Lord Yahweh, “For good reason they have made you desolate and bruised you from every side, that you would become a possession of the rest of the nations, and you have been taken up in the speech of *their* tongue and the rumors of the people.”’” 4 Therefore, O mountains of Israel, hear the word of Lord Yahweh. Thus says Lord Yahweh to the mountains and to the hills, to the ravines and to the valleys, to the desolate wastes and to the forsaken cities which have become plunder and *objects of* scoffing to the rest of the nations which are round about, 5 therefore thus says Lord Yahweh, “Surely in the fire of My jealousy I have spoken against the rest of the nations and against all Edom, who gave My land to themselves as a possession with wholehearted gladness *and* with scorn of soul, to drive it out for plunder.” 6 Therefore prophesy concerning the land of Israel and say to the mountains and to the hills, to the ravines and to the valleys, “Thus says Lord Yahweh, ‘Behold, I have spoken in My jealousy and in My wrath because you have borne the dishonor of the nations.’ 7 Therefore thus says Lord Yahweh, ‘I have sworn that surely the nations which are around you will themselves bear their dishonor. 8 But you, O mountains of Israel, you will put forth your branches and bear your fruit for My people Israel; for they will soon come. 9 For, behold, I am for you, and I will turn to you, and you will be cultivated and sown. 10 I will multiply men on you, all the house of Israel, all of it; and the cities will be inhabited, and the waste places will be rebuilt. 11 I will multiply on you man and beast; and they will multiply and be fruitful; and I will cause you to be inhabited as you were formerly and will treat you better than at the first. Thus you will know that I am Yahweh. 12 And I will cause men—My people Israel—to walk on you and possess you so that you will become their inheritance and never again bereave them of children.’

13 “Thus says Lord Yahweh, ‘Because they say to you, “You are a devourer of men and have bereaved your nation of children,” 14 therefore you will no longer devour men and no longer bereave your nation of children,’ declares Lord Yahweh. 15 I will not let you hear dishonor from the nations anymore, nor will you bear reproach from the peoples any longer, nor will you cause your nation to stumble any longer,” declares Lord Yahweh.’”

16 Then the word of Yahweh came to me saying, 17 “Son of man, when the house of Israel was living in their own land, they defiled it by their ways and their deeds; their way before Me was like the uncleanness of a woman in her impurity. 18 Therefore I poured out My wrath on them for the blood which they had shed on the land, because they had defiled it with their idols. 19 Also I scattered them among the nations, and they were dispersed throughout the lands. According to their ways and their deeds I judged them. 20 Then they came to the nations to which they came. And they profaned My holy name because it was said of them, ‘These are the people of Yahweh; yet they have come out of His land.’ 21 But I had concern for My holy name, which the house of Israel had profaned among the nations where they went.

22 "Therefore say to the house of Israel,
'Thus says Lord Yahweh, "It is not for your
sake, O house of Israel, that I am about to
act, but for My holy name, which you have
profaned among the nations, to which you
have come. 23 I will prove the holiness of My
great name which has been profaned among
the nations, which you have profaned in
their midst. Then the nations will know that
I am Yahweh," declares Lord Yahweh, "when
I prove Myself holy among you in their sight.
24 And I will take you from the nations,
gather you from all the lands, and bring you
into your own land. 25 Then I will sprinkle
clean water on you, and you will be clean; I
will cleanse you from all your uncleanness
and from all your idols. 26 Moreover, I will
give you a new heart and put a new spirit
within you; and I will remove the heart of
stone from your flesh and give you a heart
of flesh. 27 I will put My Spirit within you and
cause you to walk in My statutes, and you
will be careful to do My judgments. 28 And
you will inhabit the land that I gave to your
fathers; so you will be My people, and I will
be your God. 29 Moreover, I will save you from
all your uncleanness; and I will call for the
grain and multiply it, and I will not bring a
famine on you. 30 I will multiply the fruit of
the tree and the produce of the field so that
you will not receive again the reproach of
famine among the nations. 31 Then you will
remember your evil ways and your deeds that
were not good, and you will loathe yourselves
to your own faces for your iniquities and your
abominations. 32 I am not doing *this* for your
sake," declares Lord Yahweh, "let it be known
to you. Be ashamed and feel dishonor for
your ways, O house of Israel!"

33 'Thus says Lord Yahweh, "On the day
that I cleanse you from all your iniquities,
I will cause the cities to be inhabited, and
the waste places will be rebuilt. 34 The
desolate land will be cultivated instead of
being a desolation in the sight of everyone
who passes by. 35 And they will say, 'This
desolate land has become like the garden
of Eden; and the waste, desolate, and ruined
cities are fortified *and* inhabited.' 36 Then
the nations that remain all around you will
know that I, Yahweh, have rebuilt the ruined
places *and* planted that which was desolate;
I, Yahweh, have spoken and will do it."

37 'Thus says Lord Yahweh, "This also I
will let the house of Israel inquire of Me to
do for them: I will increase their men like a
flock. 38 Like the flock for holy *offerings*, like
the flock at Jerusalem during her appointed
times, so will the waste cities be filled with
flocks of men. Then they will know that I
am Yahweh."'"

Psalm 131:1–3

1 O Yahweh, my heart is not exalted,
   and my eyes are not raised high;
And I do not involve myself
   in great matters,
Or in matters too marvelous for me.
2 Surely I have soothed and
   quieted my soul,
Like a weaned child with his mother,
Like a weaned child is my
   soul within me.
3 O Israel, wait for Yahweh
From now until forever.

Proverbs 29:2–3

2 When the righteous increase,
   the people are glad,
But when a wicked man
   rules, people groan.
3 A man who loves wisdom
   makes his father glad,
But he who befriends harlots
   destroys *his* wealth.

James 3:1–18

3 Do not, many *of you*, become teachers,
my brothers, knowing that we will
receive a stricter judgment. 2 For we all
stumble in many *ways*. If anyone does not
stumble in what he says, he is a perfect man,
able to bridle the entire body as well. 3 Now
if we put the bits into the horses' mouths so
that they will obey us, we direct their entire
body as well. 4 Look at the ships also, though
they are so great and are driven by strong
winds, they are still directed by a very small
rudder wherever the inclination of the pilot
wills. 5 So also the tongue is a small part of
the body, and *yet* it boasts of great things.

Behold how great a forest is set aflame
by such a small fire! 6 And the tongue is a
fire, the *very* world of unrighteousness; the
tongue is set among our members as that
which defiles the entire body, and sets on
fire the course of *our* existence, and is set
on fire by hell. 7 For every kind of beasts and
birds, of reptiles and creatures of the sea,
is tamed and has been tamed by mankind.

8 But no one can tame the tongue; *it is* a restless evil *and* full of deadly poison. 9 With it we bless *our* Lord and Father, and with it we curse men, who have been made in the likeness of God. 10 From the same mouth come blessing and cursing. My brothers, these things ought not to be so. 11 Does a fountain pour forth from the same opening fresh and bitter *water*? 12 Can a fig tree, my brothers, produce olives, or a vine produce figs? Nor *can* saltwater produce fresh.

13 Who among you is wise and understanding? Let him show by his good conduct his works in the gentleness of wisdom. 14 But if you have bitter jealousy and selfish ambition in your heart, do not be arrogant and *so* lie against the truth. 15 This wisdom is not coming down from above, but is earthly, natural, demonic. 16 For where jealousy and selfish ambition exist, there is disorder and every evil practice. 17 But the wisdom from above is first pure, then peaceable, considerate, submissive, full of mercy and good fruits, without doubting, without hypocrisy. 18 And the fruit of righteousness is sown in peace by those who make peace.

NOVEMBER 23

Ezekiel 37:1–38:23

37 The hand of Yahweh was upon me, and He brought me out by the Spirit of Yahweh and caused me to rest in the middle of the valley; and it was full of bones. 2 He caused me to pass among them all around, and behold, *there were* very many on the surface of the valley; and behold, *they were* very dry. 3 He said to me, "Son of man, can these bones live?" And I answered, "O Lord Yahweh, You know." 4 Then He said to me, "Prophesy over these bones and say to them, 'O dry bones, hear the word of Yahweh.' 5 Thus says Lord Yahweh to these bones, 'Behold, I will cause breath to enter you that you may come to life. 6 I will put sinews on you, make flesh come up upon you, cover you with skin, and put breath in you that you may come alive; and you will know that I am Yahweh.'"

7 So I prophesied as I was commanded; and as I prophesied, there was a noise, and behold, a rumbling; and the bones came together, bone to its bone. 8 And I looked, and behold, sinews were on them, and flesh came up *upon them*, and skin covered them; but there was no breath in them. 9 Then He said to me, "Prophesy to the breath, prophesy, son of man, and say to the breath, 'Thus says Lord Yahweh, "Come from the four winds, O breath, and breathe on these *who were* killed, that they may come to life."'" 10 So I prophesied as He commanded me, and the breath came into them, and they came to life and stood on their feet, an exceedingly great military force.

11 Then He said to me, "Son of man, these bones are the whole house of Israel; behold, they say, 'Our bones are dried up, and our hope has perished. We are completely cut off.' 12 Therefore prophesy and say to them, 'Thus says Lord Yahweh, "Behold, I will open your graves and cause you to come up out of your graves, My people; and I will bring you into the land of Israel. 13 Then you will know that I am Yahweh, when I have opened your graves and caused you to come up out of your graves, My people. 14 And I will put My Spirit within you, and you will come to life, and I will place you on your own land. Then you will know that I, Yahweh, have spoken and done it," declares Yahweh.'"

15 The word of Yahweh came again to me saying, 16 "Now as for you, son of man, take for yourself one stick and write on it, 'For Judah and for the sons of Israel, his companions'; then take another stick and write on it, 'For Joseph, the stick of Ephraim and all the house of Israel, his companions.' 17 Then draw them together for yourself one to another into one stick, that they may become one in your hand. 18 And when the sons of your people speak to you saying, 'Will you not declare to us what you mean by these?' 19 say to them, 'Thus says Lord Yahweh, "Behold, I will take the stick of Joseph, which is in the hand of Ephraim, and the tribes of Israel, his companions; and I will put them with it, with the stick of Judah, and make them one stick, and they will be one in My hand."' 20 And the sticks on which you write will be in your hand before their eyes. 21 And speak to them, 'Thus says Lord Yahweh, "Behold, I will take the sons of Israel from among the nations where they have gone, and I will gather them from every

side and bring them into their own land;
22 and I will make them one nation in the
land, on the mountains of Israel; and one
king will be king for all of them; and they
will no longer be two nations and no longer
be divided into two kingdoms. 23 They also
will no longer defile themselves with their
idols or with their detestable things or with
any of their transgressions; but I will save
them from all their *places of* habitation in
which they have sinned, and I will cleanse
them. And they will be My people, and I will
be their God.

24 "And My servant David will be king
over them, and they will all have one shep-
herd; and they will walk in My judgments
and keep My statutes and do them. 25 They
will inhabit the land that I gave to Jacob
My servant, which your fathers inhabited;
and they will inhabit it, they, and their sons
and their sons' sons, forever; and David My
servant will be their prince forever. 26 And
I will cut a covenant of peace with them; it
will be an everlasting covenant with them.
And I will give them *the land* and multiply
them and will set My sanctuary in their
midst forever. 27 My dwelling place also will
be with them; and I will be their God, and
they will be My people. 28 And the nations
will know that I am Yahweh who sanctifies
Israel, when My sanctuary is in their midst
forever."'"

38 And the word of Yahweh came to
me saying, 2 "Son of man, set your
face toward Gog of the land of Magog, the
chief prince of Meshech and Tubal, and
prophesy against him 3 and say, 'Thus says
Lord Yahweh, "Behold, I am against you,
O Gog, chief prince of Meshech and Tubal.
4 I will turn you about and put hooks into
your jaws, and I will bring you out, and all
your military force, horses and horsemen,
all of them magnificently dressed, a great
assembly *with* large shield and shield, all
of them wielding swords; 5 Persia, Ethiopia,
and Put with them, all of them *with* shield
and helmet; 6 Gomer with all its troops;
Beth-togarmah *from* the remote parts of
the north with all its troops—many peoples
with you.

7 "Be prepared, and prepare yourself, you
and all your assembly that are assembled
about you, and be a guard for them. 8 After
many days you will be mustered; in the last
years you will come into the land that is
restored from the sword, *whose inhabitants*
have been gathered from many peoples to
the mountains of Israel which had been
a continual waste; but its people were
brought out from the peoples, and they
are living securely, all of them. 9 And you
will go up; you will come like a storm; you
will be like a cloud covering the land, you
and all your troops and many peoples with
you."

10 'Thus says Lord Yahweh, "It will be in
that day, *that* thoughts will come into your
heart, and you will devise an evil plan,
11 and you will say, 'I will go up against the
land of unwalled villages. I will go against
those who *dwell* quietly, that live securely,
all of them living without walls and having
no bars or gates, 12 to capture spoil and to
seize plunder, to turn your hand against
the waste places, which are *now* inhabited,
and against the people who are gathered
from the nations, who have acquired cattle
and property, who live at the center of the
world.' 13 Sheba and Dedan and the mer-
chants of Tarshish with all its young lions
will say to you, 'Have you come to capture
spoil? Have you assembled your assembly to
seize plunder, to carry away silver and gold,
to take away cattle and goods, to capture
great spoil?'"'

14 "Therefore prophesy, son of man, and
say to Gog, 'Thus says Lord Yahweh, "On
that day when My people Israel are living
securely, will you not know *it*? 15 You will
come from your place out of the remote
parts of the north, you and numerous peo-
ples with you, all of them riding on horses,
a great assembly and a numerous military
force; 16 and you will come up against My
people Israel like a cloud to cover the land.
It will be in the last days that I will bring
you against My land so that the nations may
know Me when I prove Myself holy through
you before their eyes, O Gog."

17 'Thus says Lord Yahweh, "Are you the
one of whom I spoke in former days by the
hand of My slaves the prophets of Israel, who
prophesied in those days for *many* years that
I would bring you against them? 18 And it
will be in that day, when Gog comes against
the land of Israel," declares Lord Yahweh,
"*that* My wrath will mount up in My anger.
19 In My zeal and in My blazing fury I have
spoken *that* on that day there will surely

be a great earthquake in the land of Israel.
20 And the fish of the sea, the birds of the
sky, the beasts of the field, all the creeping
things that creep on the ground, and all the
men who are on the face of the earth will
quake at My presence; the mountains also
will be pulled down, the steep pathways
will fall, and every wall will fall to the earth.
21 And I will call for a sword against him on
all My mountains," declares Lord Yahweh.
"Every man's sword will be against his
brother. 22 With pestilence and with blood
I will enter into judgment with him; and I
will rain on him and on his troops, and on
the numerous peoples who are with him,
a torrential rain, with hailstones, fire, and
brimstone. 23 And I will magnify Myself, I
will manifest Myself as holy, and I will make
Myself known in the sight of many nations;
and they will know that I am Yahweh."'

Psalm 132:1–9

1 Remember, O Yahweh,
on David's behalf,
All his affliction;
2 How he swore to Yahweh
And vowed to the Mighty One of Jacob,
3 "Surely I will not come into my house,
Nor lie in the comfort of my bed;
4 I will not give sleep to my eyes
Or slumber to my eyelids,
5 Until I find a place for Yahweh,
A dwelling place for the
Mighty One of Jacob."

6 Behold, we heard of it in Ephrathah,
We found it in the fields of Jaar.
7 Let us come into His dwelling place;
Let us worship at the
footstool of His feet.
8 Arise, O Yahweh, to Your resting place,
You and the ark of Your strength.
9 Let Your priests be clothed
with righteousness,
And let Your holy ones sing for joy.

Proverbs 29:4

4 By justice the king causes
the land to stand,
But a man of bribes tears it down.

James 4:1–17

4 What is the source of quarrels and con-
flicts among you? Is not the source your
pleasures that wage war in your members?
2 You lust and do not have, *so* you murder.
You are envious and cannot obtain, *so* you
fight and quarrel. You do not have because
you do not ask. 3 You ask and do not receive,
because you ask with wrong motives, so that
you may spend *it* on your pleasures. 4 You
adulteresses, do you not know that friend-
ship with the world is enmity *toward* God?
Therefore, whoever wishes to be a friend of
the world sets himself as an enemy of God.
5 Or do you think that the Scripture speaks
to no purpose: "He jealously desires the
Spirit which He has made to dwell in us"?
6 But He gives a greater grace. Therefore *it*
says, "GOD IS OPPOSED TO THE PROUD, BUT
GIVES GRACE TO THE HUMBLE." 7 Be subject
therefore to God. Resist the devil and he will
flee from you. 8 Draw near to God and He
will draw near to you. Cleanse your hands,
you sinners, and purify your hearts, you
double-minded. 9 Be miserable and mourn
and cry. Let your laughter be turned into
mourning and your joy to gloom. 10 Humble
yourselves in the presence of the Lord, and
He will exalt you.

11 Do not slander one another, brothers.
He who slanders a brother or judges his
brother, slanders the law and judges the
law; but if you judge the law, you are not a
doer of the law but a judge *of it*. 12 There is
only one Lawgiver and Judge, the One who
is able to save and to destroy. But who are
you who judge your neighbor?

13 Come now, you who say, "Today or
tomorrow we will go to such and such a
city, and spend a year there and engage in
business and make a profit." 14 Yet you do
not know what your life will be like tomor-
row. You are a vapor that appears for a little
while and then vanishes away. 15 Instead,
you ought to say, "If the Lord wills, we will
live and also do this or that." 16 But as it
is, you boast in your arrogance. All such
boasting is evil. 17 Therefore, to one who
knows to do *the* right thing and does not
do it, to him it is sin.

NOVEMBER 24

Ezekiel 39:1–40:49

39 "Now as for you, son of man, prophesy against Gog and say, 'Thus says Lord Yahweh, "Behold, I am against you, O Gog, chief prince of Meshech and Tubal; 2 and I will turn you around, drive you on, take you up from the remotest parts of the north, and bring you against the mountains of Israel. 3 And I will strike your bow from your left hand and cause your arrows from your right hand to fall. 4 You will fall on the mountains of Israel, you and all your troops and the peoples who are with you; I will give you as food to every kind of predatory bird and beast of the field. 5 You will fall on the open field; for it is I who have spoken," declares Lord Yahweh. 6 "And I will send fire upon Magog and those who inhabit the coastlands securely; and they will know that I am Yahweh.

7 "And My holy name I will make known in the midst of My people Israel; and I will not let My holy name be profaned anymore. And the nations will know that I am Yahweh, the Holy One in Israel. 8 Behold, it is coming, and it shall be done," declares Lord Yahweh. "That is the day of which I have spoken.

9 "Then those who inhabit the cities of Israel will go out and make fires with the weapons and burn *them*, both shields and large shields, bows and arrows, war clubs and spears; and for seven years they will make fires of them. 10 They will not carry wood from the field or gather firewood from the forests, for they will make fires with the weapons; and they will take the spoil of those who made them into spoil and seize the plunder of those who plundered them," declares Lord Yahweh.

11 "And it will be in that day, *that* I will give Gog a burial ground there in Israel, the valley of those who pass by east of the sea, and it will block off those who would pass by. So they will bury Gog there with all his multitude, and they will call *it* the valley of Hamon-gog. 12 And for seven months the house of Israel will be burying them in order to cleanse the land. 13 Even all the people of the land will bury *them*; and it will be unto their name *on* the day that I glorify Myself," declares Lord Yahweh. 14 "Now they will set apart men who will continually pass through the land, burying those who were passing through, even those left on the surface of the ground, in order to cleanse it. At the end of seven months they will make a search. 15 And those who pass through the land will pass through, and *when* anyone sees a man's bone, he will set up a marker by it until the buriers have buried it in the valley of Hamon-gog. 16 And even *the* name of *the* city will be Hamonah. So they will cleanse the land."'

17 "Now as for you, son of man, thus says Lord Yahweh, 'Say to every kind of bird and to every beast of the field, "Gather and come, assemble from every side to My sacrifice which I am going to sacrifice for you, as a great sacrifice on the mountains of Israel, that you may eat flesh and drink blood. 18 You will eat the flesh of mighty men and drink the blood of the princes of the earth, as *though they were* rams, lambs, goats, and bulls, all of them fatlings of Bashan. 19 So you will eat fat until you are satisfied and drink blood until you are drunk, from My sacrifice which I have sacrificed for you. 20 And you will be satisfied at My table with horses and charioteers, with mighty men and all the men of war," declares Lord Yahweh.

21 "And I will put My glory among the nations; and all the nations will see My judgment which I have executed and My hand which I have placed on them. 22 And the house of Israel will know that I am Yahweh their God from that day onward. 23 And the nations will know that the house of Israel went into exile for their iniquity because they acted unfaithfully against Me, and I hid My face from them; so I gave them into the hand of their adversaries, and all of them fell by the sword. 24 According to their uncleanness and according to their transgressions I dealt with them, and I hid My face from them."'"

25 Therefore thus says Lord Yahweh, "Now I will return the fortunes of Jacob and have compassion on the whole house of Israel; and I will be jealous for My holy name. 26 So they will forget their dishonor and all their unfaithfulness which they perpetrated against Me, when they live securely on their *own* land with no one to make *them* tremble.

27 When I return them from the peoples and
gather them from the lands of their enemies,
then I shall prove Myself holy through them
in the sight of the many nations. 28 Then
they will know that I am Yahweh their God
because I made them go into exile among
the nations, and then collected them *again*
to their own land; and I will leave none of
them there any longer. 29 And I will not hide
My face from them any longer, for I will have
poured out My Spirit on the house of Israel,"
declares Lord Yahweh.

40 In the twenty-fifth year of our exile,
at the beginning of the year, on the
tenth of the month, in the fourteenth year
after the city was struck down, on that same
day the hand of Yahweh was upon me, and
He brought me there. 2 In the visions of God
He brought me into the land of Israel and
caused me to rest on a very high mountain,
and on it to the south *there was* a structure
like a city. 3 So He brought me there; and
behold, there was a man whose appearance
was like the appearance of bronze, with a
line of flax and a measuring rod in his hand;
and he was standing in the gateway. 4 And
the man spoke to me, "Son of man, see with
your eyes, hear with your ears, and set your
heart on all that I am going to show you; for
you have been brought here in order to show
it to you. Declare to the house of Israel all
that you are seeing."

5 And behold, there was a wall on the
outside of the house *of Yahweh* all around,
and in the man's hand was a measuring rod
of six cubits, *each of which was* a cubit and a
handbreadth. So he measured the thickness
of the wall, one rod; and the height, one
rod. 6 Then he went to the gate which faced
east, went up its steps, and measured the
threshold of the gate, one rod in width; and
the other threshold *was* one rod in width.
7 The guardroom *was* one rod long and
one rod wide; and *there were* five cubits
between the guardrooms. And the threshold
of the gate by the porch of the gate facing
inward *was* one rod. 8 Then he measured
the porch of the gate facing inward, one
rod. 9 He measured the porch of the gate,
eight cubits; and its side pillars, two cubits.
And the porch of the gate was faced inward.
10 The guardrooms of the gate toward the
east *numbered* three on each side; the three
of them had the same measurement. The
side pillars also had the same measurement
on each side. 11 And he measured the width
of the entrance of the gate, ten cubits, and
the length of the gate, thirteen cubits.
12 *There was* a barrier *wall* one cubit *wide*
in front of the guardrooms on each side;
and the guardrooms *were* six cubits *square*
on each side. 13 He measured the gate from
the roof of the one guardroom to the roof
of the other, a width of twenty-five cubits
from *one* door to *the* door opposite. 14 He
made the side pillars sixty cubits *high*;
the gate *extended* round about to the side
pillar of the courtyard. 15 *From* the front of
the entrance gate to the front of the inner
porch of the gate *was* fifty cubits. 16 *There
were* shuttered windows *looking* toward the
guardrooms and toward their side pillars
within the gate all around, and likewise for
the porches. And *there were* windows all
around inside; and on *each* side pillar *were*
palm tree ornaments.

17 Then he brought me into the outer
court, and behold, *there were* chambers and
a pavement made for the court all around;
thirty chambers faced the pavement. 18 The
pavement (*that is*, the lower pavement) *was*
by the side of the gates, corresponding to the
length of the gates. 19 Then he measured the
width from the front of the lower gate to the
front of the exterior of the inner court, one
hundred cubits on the east and on the north.

20 *As for* the gate of the outer court which
faced the north, he measured its length and
its width. 21 It had three guardrooms on each
side; and its side pillars and its porches had
the same measurement as the first gate.
Its length *was* fifty cubits and the width
twenty-five cubits. 22 Its windows and its
porches and its palm tree ornaments *had*
the same measurements as the gate which
faced toward the east; and it was reached
by seven steps, and its porch *was* in front of
them. 23 The inner court had a gate opposite
the gate on the north as well as *the gate* on
the east; and he measured one hundred
cubits from gate to gate.

24 Then he led me toward the south,
and behold, there was a gate toward the
south; and he measured its side pillars
and its porches according to those same
measurements. 25 The gate and its porches
had windows all around like those other
windows; the length *was* fifty cubits and
the width twenty-five cubits. 26 *There were*

seven steps going up to it, and its porches
were in front of them; and it had palm tree
ornaments on its side pillars, one on each
side. 27 The inner court had a gate toward
the south; and he measured from gate to
gate toward the south, one hundred cubits.

28 Then he brought me to the inner
court by the south gate; and he measured
the south gate according to those same
measurements. 29 Its guardrooms also, its
side pillars, and its porches *were* according
to those same measurements. And the gate
and its porches had windows all around; it
was fifty cubits long and twenty-five cubits
wide. 30 *There were* porches all around,
twenty-five cubits long and five cubits wide.
31 Its porches *were* toward the outer court;
and palm tree ornaments *were* on its side
pillars, and its stairway *had* eight steps.

32 Then he brought me into the inner
court toward the east. And he measured the
gate according to those same measurements.
33 Its guardrooms also, its side pillars, and its
porches *were* according to those same mea-
surements. And the gate and its porches had
windows all around; it *was* fifty cubits long
and twenty-five cubits wide. 34 Its porches
were toward the outer court; and palm tree
ornaments *were* on its side pillars, on each
side, and its stairway *had* eight steps.

35 Then he brought me to the north gate;
and he measured *it* according to those same
measurements, 36 *with* its guardrooms, its
side pillars, and its porches. And the gate
had windows all around; the length *was*
fifty cubits and the width twenty-five cubits.
37 Its side pillars *were* toward the outer
court; and palm tree ornaments *were* on its
side pillars on each side, and its stairway
had eight steps.

38 A chamber with its doorway was by the
side pillars at the gates; there they rinse the
burnt offering. 39 In the porch of the gate
were two tables on each side, on which to
slaughter the burnt offering, the sin offering
and the guilt offering. 40 On the outer side,
as one went up to the entrance of the gate
toward the north, *were* two tables; and on
the other side of the porch of the gate *were*
two tables. 41 Four tables *were* on each side
next to the gate; *or*, eight tables on which
they slaughter *sacrifices*. 42 For the burnt
offering *there were* four tables of cut stone,
a cubit and a half long, a cubit and a half
wide, and one cubit high, on which they lay
the instruments with which they slaughter
the burnt offering and the sacrifice. 43 The
double hooks, one handbreadth in length,
were installed in the house all around; and
on the tables *was* the flesh of the offering.

44 From the outside to the inner gate
were chambers for the singers in the inner
court, *one of* which was at the side of the
north gate, with its front toward the south,
and one at the side of the south gate facing
toward the north. 45 Then he said to me,
"This is the chamber which faces toward
the south, *intended* for the priests who keep
the responsibility of the house; 46 but the
chamber which faces toward the north is
for the priests who keep the responsibility of
the altar. These are the sons of Zadok, who
from the sons of Levi come near to Yahweh
to minister to Him." 47 He measured the
court, a *perfect* square, one hundred cubits
long and one hundred cubits wide; and the
altar was in front of the house.

48 Then he brought me to the porch of
the house and measured *each* side pillar of
the porch, five cubits on each side; and the
width of the gate was three cubits on each
side. 49 The length of the porch *was* twenty
cubits and the width eleven cubits; and at
the stairway by which it was ascended *were*
columns belonging to the side pillars, one
on each side.

Psalm 132:10–18

10 For the sake of David Your servant,
Do not turn away the face
of Your anointed.
11 Yahweh has sworn to David
A truth from which He
will not turn back:
"Of the fruit of your body I will
set upon your throne.
12 "If your sons keep My covenant
And My testimony which
I will teach them,
Their sons also shall sit upon
your throne forever."

13 For Yahweh has chosen Zion;
He has desired it for His habitation.
14 "This is My resting place forever;
Here I will inhabit, for I have desired it.
15 "I will abundantly bless her provision;
I will satisfy her needy with bread.
16 "Her priests also I will clothe
with salvation,

And her holy ones will
sing loudly for joy.
17 "There I will cause the horn
of David to spring up;
I have prepared a lamp for
Mine anointed.
18 "His enemies I will clothe with shame,
But upon him, his crown
shall blossom."

Proverbs 29:5

5 A man who flatters his neighbor
Is spreading a net for his steps.

James 5:1–20

5 Come now, you rich, cry, howling over
your miseries which are coming upon
you. 2 Your riches have rotted and your
garments have become moth-eaten. 3 Your
gold and your silver have rusted, and their
corrosion will be a witness against you
and will consume your flesh like fire. You
have stored up *such* treasure in the last
days! 4 Behold, the pay of the laborers who
mowed your fields—that which has been
withheld by you—cries out *against you*;
and the outcries of those who did the har-
vesting have reached the ears of the Lord of
Sabaoth. 5 You have lived luxuriously on the
earth and lived in self-indulgence. You have
fattened your hearts in a DAY OF SLAUGHTER.
6 You have condemned and murdered the
righteous *man*; he does not resist you.
7 Therefore be patient, brothers, until
the coming of the Lord. Behold, the farmer
waits for the precious fruit of the soil,
being patient about it, until it receives the
early and late rains. 8 You too be patient;
strengthen your hearts, for the coming of
the Lord is at hand. 9 Do not groan, brothers,
against one another, so that you yourselves
may not be judged. Behold, the Judge is
standing right at the door. 10 As an example,
brothers, of suffering and patience, take
the prophets who spoke in the name of the
Lord. 11 Behold, we count those blessed who
persevere. You have heard of the persever-
ance of Job and have seen the outcome of
the Lord's dealings, that the Lord is full of
compassion and *is* merciful.
12 But above all, my brothers, do not
swear, either by heaven or by earth or with
any other oath. But let your yes be yes, and
your no, no, so that you may not fall under
judgment.
13 Is anyone among you suffering? *Then*
he must pray. Is anyone cheerful? He is
to sing praises. 14 Is anyone among you
sick? *Then* he must call for the elders of
the church and they are to pray over him,
anointing him with oil in the name of the
Lord. 15 And the prayer offered in faith will
save the one who is sick, and the Lord will
raise him up, and if he has committed sins,
they will be forgiven him. 16 Therefore,
confess your sins to one another, and
pray for one another so that you may be
healed. The effective prayer of a righteous
man can accomplish much. 17 Elijah was a
man with a nature like ours, and he prayed
earnestly that it would not rain, and it did
not rain on the earth for three years and
six months. 18 Then he prayed again, and
the sky gave rain and the earth produced
its fruit.
19 My brothers, if any among you strays
from the truth and one turns him back, 20 let
him know that he who turns a sinner from
the error of his way will save his soul from
death and will COVER A MULTITUDE OF SINS.

NOVEMBER 25

Ezekiel 41:1–42:20

41 Then he brought me to the nave and
measured the side pillars; six cubits
wide on each side *was* the width of the side
pillar. 2 The width of the entrance *was* ten
cubits, and the sides of the entrance *were*
five cubits on each side. And he measured
the length of the nave, forty cubits, and the
width, twenty cubits.
3 Then he went inside and measured each
side pillar of the doorway, two cubits, and
the doorway, six cubits *high*; and the width
of the doorway, seven cubits. 4 He measured
its length, twenty cubits, and the width,
twenty cubits, before the nave; and he said
to me, "This is the Holy of Holies."
5 Then he measured the wall of the house
of Yahweh, six cubits; and the width of the
side chambers, four cubits, all around
about the house on every side. 6 The side
chambers were in three stories, one above
another, and thirty in each story; and the

side chambers extended to the wall which
stood on their inward side all around, that
they might be fastened, and not be fastened
into the wall of the house *itself*. 7 The side
chambers surrounding the house were
wider at each successive story. Because
the structure surrounding the house went
upward by stages on all sides of the house,
therefore the width of the house *increased*
as it went higher; and thus one went up from
the lowest *story* to the highest by way of the
second *story*. 8 I saw also that the house had
a raised platform all around; the foundations
of the side chambers were a full rod of six
long cubits *in height*. 9 The thickness of the
outer wall of the side chambers *was* five
cubits. But the free space between the side
chambers belonging to the house 10 and the
outer chambers *was* twenty cubits in width
all around the house on every side. 11 The
doorways of the side chambers toward the
free space *consisted of* one doorway toward
the north and another doorway toward the
south; and the width of the place of the free
space *was* five cubits all around.

12 The building that *was* in front of the
separate area at the side toward the west
was seventy cubits wide; and the wall of
the building *was* five cubits thick all around,
and its length *was* ninety cubits.

13 Then he measured the house, one hun-
dred cubits long; the separate area with the
building and its walls *were* also one hundred
cubits long. 14 Also the width of the front
of the house and *that of* the separate areas
along the east *side totaled* one hundred
cubits.

15 He measured the length of the building
along the front of the separate area behind
it, with a gallery on each side, one hundred
cubits, along with the inner nave and the
porches of the court.

16 The thresholds, the latticed windows,
and the galleries round about their three
stories, opposite the threshold, were pan-
eled with wood all around, and *from* the
ground to the windows (but the windows
were covered), 17 over the entrance, and to
the inner house, and on the outside, and on
all the wall all around inside and outside,
by measurement. 18 It was carved with
cherubim and palm trees; and a palm tree
was between cherub and cherub, and every
cherub had two faces, 19 a man's face toward
the palm tree on one side and a young lion's
face toward the palm tree on the other side;
they were carved on all the house all around.
20 From the ground to above the entrance
cherubim and palm trees were carved, as
well as *on* the wall of the nave.

21 The doorposts of the nave were square;
as for the front of the sanctuary, the appear-
ance of one doorpost was like that of the
other. 22 The altar *was* of wood, three cubits
high and its length two cubits; its corners,
its base, and its sides *were* of wood. And he
said to me, "This is the table that is before
Yahweh." 23 The nave and the sanctuary
each had a double door. 24 Each of the doors
had two leaves, two swinging leaves; two
leaves for one door and two leaves for the
other. 25 Also there were carved on them, on
the doors of the nave, cherubim and palm
trees like those carved on the walls; and
there was a canopy of wood over the front
of the porch outside. 26 *There were* latticed
windows and palm trees on one side and
on the other, on the sides of the porch; thus
were the side chambers of the house and
the canopies.

42 Then he brought me out into the
outer court, the way toward the
north; and he brought me to the chamber
which *was* opposite the separate area and
opposite the building toward the north.
2 Along the length, *which was* one hundred
cubits, *was* the north door; the width *was*
fifty cubits. 3 Opposite the twenty *cubits*
which belonged to the inner court, and
opposite the pavement which belonged to
the outer court, *was* gallery corresponding
to gallery in three stories. 4 Before the
chambers *was* an inner walk ten cubits
wide, a way of one *hundred* cubits; and
their openings *were* on the north. 5 Now the
upper chambers *were* smaller because the
galleries took more *space* away from them
than from the lower and middle ones in the
building. 6 For they *were* in three stories and
had no pillars like the pillars of the courts;
therefore *the upper chambers* were set back
from the ground upward, more than the
lower and middle ones. 7 As for the outer
wall by the side of the chambers, toward the
outer court facing the chambers, its length
was fifty cubits. 8 For the length of the
chambers which *were* in the outer court *was*
fifty cubits; and behold, *the length of those*
facing the temple *was* one hundred cubits.

9 Below these chambers *was* the entrance
on the east side, as one enters them from
the outer court.
10 In the thickness of the wall of the court
toward the east, facing the separate area and
facing the building, *there were* chambers.
11 The way in front of them *was* like the
appearance of the chambers which *were*
on the north, according to their length so
was their width, and all their exits *were* both
according to their arrangements and open-
ings. 12 Corresponding to the openings of
the chambers which were toward the south
was an opening at the head of the way, the
way in front of the wall toward the east, as
one enters them.
13 Then he said to me, "The north cham-
bers *and* the south chambers, which are
opposite the separate area, they are the holy
chambers where the priests who are near to
Yahweh shall eat the most holy things. There
they shall lay the most holy things, the grain
offering, the sin offering, and the guilt
offering; for the place is holy. 14 When the
priests enter, then they shall not go out into
the outer court from the sanctuary without
laying there their garments in which they
minister, for they are holy. They shall put on
other garments; then they shall come near
to that which is for the people."
15 Then he had finished measuring the
inner house; he brought me out by the way
of the gate which faced toward the east and
measured it all around. 16 He measured on
the east side with the measuring reed 500
reeds by the measuring reed. 17 He measured
on the north side 500 reeds by the measur-
ing reed. 18 On the south side he measured
500 reeds with the measuring reed. 19 He
turned to the west side *and* measured 500
reeds with the measuring reed. 20 He mea-
sured it on the four sides; it had a wall all
around, the length 500 and the width 500,
to divide between the holy and the profane.

Psalm 133:1–3

1 Behold, how good and
how pleasant it is
For brothers to dwell together in unity!
2 It is like the good oil upon the head,
Coming down upon the beard,
Aaron's beard,
Coming down upon the
edge of his robes.
3 It is like the dew of Hermon
Coming down upon the
mountains of Zion;
For there, Yahweh commanded
the blessing—life forever.

Proverbs 29:6

6 By transgression an evil
man is ensnared,
But the righteous sings
with joy and is glad.

1 Peter 1:1–25

1 Peter, an apostle of Jesus Christ,
To those who reside as exiles, scat-
tered throughout Pontus, Galatia, Cappa-
docia, Asia, and Bithynia, who are chosen
2 according to the foreknowledge of God
the Father, by the sanctifying work of the
Spirit, to the obedience of Jesus Christ and
the sprinkling of His blood: May grace and
peace be multiplied to you.
3 Blessed be the God and Father of our
Lord Jesus Christ, who according to His
great mercy has caused us to be born again
to a living hope through the resurrection
of Jesus Christ from the dead, 4 to *obtain*
an inheritance incorruptible and undefiled
and unfading, having been kept in heaven
for you, 5 who are protected by the power
of God through faith for a salvation ready
to be revealed in the last time. 6 In this you
greatly rejoice, even though now for a little
while, if necessary, you have been grieved
by various trials, 7 so that the proof of your
faith, *being* more precious than gold which
is perishable, even though tested by fire,
may be found to result in praise and glory
and honor at the revelation of Jesus Christ.
8 And though you have not seen Him, you
love Him, and though you do not see Him
now, but believe in Him, you rejoice with joy
inexpressible and full of glory, 9 receiving
as the outcome of your faith the salvation
of your souls.
10 Concerning this salvation, the proph-
ets, who prophesied of the grace that *would*
come to you, made careful searches and
inquiries, 11 inquiring to know what *time* or
what kind of time the Spirit of Christ within
them was indicating as He was predicting
the sufferings of Christ and the glories to
follow. 12 It was revealed to them that they
were not serving themselves, but you, in
these things which now have been declared
to you through those who proclaimed the

gospel to you by the Holy Spirit sent from heaven—things into which angels long to look.

13 Therefore, having girded your minds for action, being sober *in spirit,* fix your hope completely on the grace to be brought to you at the revelation of Jesus Christ. 14 As obedient children, not being conformed to the former lusts *which were yours* in your ignorance, 15 but like the Holy One who called you, be holy yourselves also in all *your* conduct; 16 because it is written, "YOU SHALL BE HOLY, FOR I AM HOLY."

17 And if you address as Father the One who impartially judges according to each one's work, conduct yourselves in fear during the time of your sojourn, 18 knowing that you were not redeemed with corruptible things like silver or gold from your futile conduct inherited from your forefathers, 19 but with precious blood, as of a lamb unblemished and spotless, *the blood* of Christ. 20 He was foreknown before the foundation of the world, but appeared in these last times for the sake of you 21 who through Him are believers in God, who raised Him from the dead and gave Him glory, so that your faith and hope are in God.

22 Since you have in obedience to the truth purified your souls for a love of the brothers without hypocrisy, fervently love one another from the heart, 23 for you have been born again not of corruptible seed but incorruptible, *that is,* through the living and enduring word of God. 24 For,

"ALL FLESH IS LIKE GRASS,
AND ALL ITS GLORY LIKE THE
FLOWER OF GRASS.
THE GRASS WITHERS,
AND THE FLOWER FALLS OFF,
25 BUT THE WORD OF THE LORD
ENDURES FOREVER."

And this is the word which was proclaimed to you as good news.

There are three great truths, first, that there is a God;
second, that He has spoken to us in the Bible;
third, that He means what He says.

— J. HUDSON TAYLOR

NOVEMBER 26

Ezekiel 43:1–44:31

43 Then he led me to the gate, the gate facing toward the east; 2 and behold, the glory of the God of Israel was coming from the way of the east. And His voice was like the sound of many waters; and the earth shone with His glory. 3 And *it was* like the appearance of the vision which I saw, like the vision which I saw when He came to bring the city to ruin. And the visions *were* like the vision which I saw by the river Chebar; and I fell on my face. 4 And the glory of Yahweh came into the house by the way of the gate facing toward the east. 5 And the Spirit lifted me up and brought me into the inner court; and behold, the glory of Yahweh filled the house.

6 Then I heard one speaking to me from the house, while a man was standing beside me. 7 He said to me, "Son of man, *this is* the place of My throne and the place of the soles of My feet, where I will dwell among the sons of Israel forever. And the house of Israel will not again defile My holy name, neither they nor their kings, by their harlotry and by the corpses of their kings when they die, 8 by putting their threshold by My threshold and their door post beside My door post, with *only* the wall between Me and them. And they have defiled My holy name by their abominations which they have done. So I have consumed them in My anger. 9 Now let them put away their harlotry and the corpses of their kings far from Me; and I will dwell among them forever.

10 "As for you, son of man, describe the house *of Yahweh* to the house of Israel, that they may feel dishonor for their iniquities; and let them measure the plan. 11 If they feel dishonor for all that they have done, make known to them the design of the house, its structure, its exits, its entrances, all its

designs, all its statutes, and all its laws. And write *it* in their sight so that they may keep its whole design and all its statutes and do them. 12 This is the law of the house: *within* its entire boundary, on the top of the mountain all around, *shall be* most holy. Behold, this is the law of the house.

13 "And these are the measurements of the altar by cubits (the cubit being a cubit and a handbreadth): the base *shall be* a cubit and the width a cubit, and its border on its edge round about one span; and this *shall be the height of* the base of the altar. 14 And from the base on the ground to the lower ledge *shall be* two cubits and the width one cubit; and from the smaller ledge to the larger ledge *shall be* four cubits and the width one cubit. 15 And the altar hearth *shall be* four cubits; and from the altar hearth *shall* extend upwards four horns. 16 Now the altar hearth *shall be* twelve *cubits* long by twelve wide, square in its four sides. 17 The ledge *shall be* fourteen *cubits* long by fourteen wide in its four sides; the border around it *shall be* half a cubit, and its base *shall be* a cubit round about; and its steps shall face the east."

18 And He said to me, "Son of man, thus says Lord Yahweh, 'These are the statutes for the altar on the day it is made, to offer burnt offerings on it and to splash blood on it. 19 And you shall give to the Levitical priests who are from the seed of Zadok, who draw near to Me to minister to Me,' declares Lord Yahweh, 'a bull from the herd for a sin offering. 20 You shall also take some of its blood and put it on its four horns and on the four corners of the ledge and on the border round about; thus you shall purify it and make atonement for it. 21 And you shall take the bull for the sin offering, and it shall be burned in the appointed place of the house, outside the sanctuary.

22 'Now on the second day you shall bring near a male goat without blemish for a sin offering, and they shall purify the altar as they purified *it* with the bull. 23 When you have finished purifying *it*, you shall present a bull from the herd without blemish and a ram without blemish from the flock. 24 And you shall bring them near before Yahweh, and the priests shall throw salt on them, and they shall offer them up as a burnt offering to Yahweh. 25 For seven days you shall offer daily a goat for a sin offering; also a bull from the herd and a ram from the flock, without blemish, shall be offered. 26 For seven days they shall make atonement for the altar and purify it; so shall they ordain it. 27 So they will complete the days. And it shall be that on the eighth day and onward, the priests shall offer on the altar your burnt offerings and your peace offerings; and I will accept you,' declares Lord Yahweh."

44 Then He brought me back by the way of the outer gate of the sanctuary, which faces the east; and it was shut. 2 Yahweh said to me, "This gate shall be shut; it shall not be opened, and no one shall enter by it, for Yahweh, the God of Israel, has entered by it; therefore it shall be shut. 3 As for the prince, he shall sit in it as prince to eat bread before Yahweh; he shall enter by way of the porch of the gate and shall go out by the same way."

4 Then He brought me by way of the north gate to the front of the house; and I looked, and behold, the glory of Yahweh filled the house of Yahweh, and I fell on my face. 5 Then Yahweh said to me, "Son of man, set your heart on and see with your eyes and hear with your ears all that I say to you concerning all the statutes of the house of Yahweh and concerning all its laws; and set your heart on the entrance of the house, with all exits of the sanctuary. 6 And you shall say to the rebellious ones, to the house of Israel, 'Thus says Lord Yahweh, "Enough of all your abominations, O house of Israel, 7 when you brought in foreigners, uncircumcised in heart and uncircumcised in flesh, to be in My sanctuary to profane it, *even* My house, when you brought near My food, the fat and the blood. So they made My covenant void—*this* in addition to all your abominations. 8 And you have not kept the responsibility of My holy things yourselves, but you have set *foreigners* as keepers of the responsibility *given by* Me for My sanctuary."

9 'Thus says Lord Yahweh, "No foreigner, uncircumcised in heart and uncircumcised in flesh, of all the foreigners who are among the sons of Israel, shall enter My sanctuary. 10 But the Levites who went far from Me when Israel went astray, who went astray from Me after their idols, shall bear the punishment for their iniquity. 11 Yet they shall be ministers in My sanctuary, having

oversight at the gates of the house and ministering in the house; they shall slaughter the burnt offering and the sacrifice for the people, and they shall stand before them to minister to them. 12 Because they ministered to them before their idols and became a stumbling block of iniquity to the house of Israel, therefore I have sworn against them," declares Lord Yahweh, "that they shall bear *the punishment for* their iniquity. 13 And they shall not approach Me to minister as a priest to Me, nor approach any of My holy things, to the things that are most holy; but they will bear their dishonor and their abominations which they have done. 14 Yet I will appoint them as keepers of the responsibility for the house, of all its service and of all that shall be done in it.

15 "But the Levitical priests, the sons of Zadok, who kept the responsibility of My sanctuary when the sons of Israel went astray from Me, shall come near to Me to minister to Me; and they shall stand before Me to bring near to Me the fat and the blood," declares Lord Yahweh. 16 "They shall enter My sanctuary; they shall come near to My table to minister to Me and keep the responsibility *given by* Me. 17 And it will be that when they enter at the gates of the inner court, they shall be clothed with linen garments; and wool shall not be on them while they are ministering in the gates of the inner court and in the house. 18 Linen headdresses shall be on their heads, and linen undergarments shall be on their loins; they shall not gird themselves with *anything which makes them* sweat. 19 And when they go out into the outer court, into the outer court to the people, they shall put off their garments in which they have been ministering and lay them in the holy chambers; then they shall put on other garments so that they will not transmit holiness to the people with their garments. 20 Also they shall not shave their heads, yet they shall not let their locks grow long; they shall only trim *the hair of* their heads. 21 Nor shall any of the priests drink wine when they enter the inner court. 22 And they shall not take a widow or a divorced woman as a wife but shall take virgins from the seed of the house of Israel or a widow who is the widow of a priest. 23 Moreover, they shall instruct My people *about the difference* between the holy and the profane, and make them know *the difference* between the unclean and the clean. 24 And in a dispute, they shall take their stand to judge; they shall judge it according to My judgments. They shall also keep My laws and My statutes in all My appointed times and keep My sabbaths holy. 25 But they shall not go to a dead person to make *themselves* unclean; however, for father, for mother, for son, for daughter, for brother, or for a sister who has not had a husband, they may make themselves unclean. 26 And after he is cleansed, seven days shall be counted for him. 27 And on the day that he goes into the sanctuary, into the inner court to minister in the sanctuary, he shall bring near his sin offering," declares Lord Yahweh.

28 "And it shall be with regard to an inheritance for them, *that* I am their inheritance; and you shall give them no possession in Israel—I am their possession. 29 They shall eat the grain offering, the sin offering, and the guilt offering; and every devoted thing in Israel shall be theirs. 30 And the first of all the first fruits of every kind and every contribution of every kind, from all your contributions, shall be for the priests; you shall also give to the priest the first of your dough to cause a blessing to rest on your house. 31 The priests shall not eat any bird or beast that has died *of itself* or has been torn to pieces.

Psalm 134:1–3

1 Behold, bless Yahweh, all
you slaves of Yahweh,
Who stand in the house of
Yahweh by night!
2 Lift up your hands to the sanctuary
And bless Yahweh.
3 May Yahweh bless you from Zion,
Who made heaven and earth.

Proverbs 29:7

7 The righteous knows the
cause of the poor,
The wicked does not understand
that knowledge.

1 Peter 2:1–25

2 Therefore, laying aside all malice and all deceit and hypocrisy and envy and all slander, 2 like newborn babies, long for the pure milk of the word, so that by it you may grow in respect to salvation, 3 if you have TASTED THE KINDNESS OF THE LORD.

4 *And* coming to Him as to a living stone which has been rejected by men, but is choice and precious in the sight of God, 5 you also, as living stones, are being built up as a spiritual house for a holy priesthood, to offer up spiritual sacrifices acceptable to God through Jesus Christ. 6 For *this* is contained in Scripture:

"BEHOLD, I LAY IN ZION A CHOICE
STONE, A PRECIOUS CORNER *stone*,
AND HE WHO BELIEVES UPON HIM
WILL NOT BE PUT TO SHAME."

7 This precious value, then, is for you who believe; but for those who disbelieve,

"THE STONE WHICH THE
BUILDERS REJECTED,
THIS HAS BECOME THE CHIEF
CORNER *stone*,"

8 and,

"A STONE OF STUMBLING AND
A ROCK OF OFFENSE."

They stumble because they are disobedient to the word, and to this *stumbling* they were also appointed.

9 But you are A CHOSEN FAMILY, A royal PRIESTHOOD, A HOLY NATION, A PEOPLE FOR *God's* OWN POSSESSION, so that you may proclaim the excellencies of Him who has called you out of darkness into His marvelous light; 10 for you once were NOT A PEOPLE, but now you are THE PEOPLE OF GOD; you had NOT RECEIVED MERCY, but now you have RECEIVED MERCY.

11 Beloved, I urge you as sojourners and exiles to abstain from fleshly lusts which wage war against the soul, 12 by keeping your conduct excellent among the Gentiles, so that in the thing which they slander you as evildoers, they may because of your good works, as they observe *them*, glorify God in the DAY OF VISITATION.

13 Be subject for the sake of the Lord to every human institution, whether to a king as the one in authority, 14 or to governors as sent by him for the punishment of evildoers and the praise of those who do good. 15 For such is the will of God that by doing good you may silence the ignorance of foolish men. 16 *Act* as free people, and do not use your freedom as a covering for evil, but *use it* as slaves of God. 17 Honor all people, love the brethren, fear God, honor the king.

18 Servants, be subject to your masters with all fear, not only to those who are good and considerate, but also to those who are crooked. 19 For this *finds* favor, if for the sake of conscience toward God a person bears up under sorrows when suffering unrighteously. 20 For what credit is there if, when you sin and are harshly treated, you endure? But if when you do good and suffer *for it*, you endure, this *finds* favor with God.

21 For to this you have been called, since Christ also suffered for you, leaving you an example that you should follow in His steps, 22 WHO DID NO SIN, NOR WAS ANY DECEIT FOUND IN HIS MOUTH; 23 who being reviled, was not reviling in return; while suffering, He was uttering no threats, but kept entrusting *Himself* to Him who judges righteously. 24 Who Himself bore our sins in His body on the tree, so that having died to sin, we might live to righteousness; by His WOUNDS YOU WERE HEALED. 25 For you were continually straying like sheep, but now you have returned to the Shepherd and Overseer of your souls.

NOVEMBER 27

Ezekiel 45:1–46:24

45 "And when you divide by lot the land for inheritance, you shall offer a contribution to Yahweh, a holy portion of the land; the length shall be the length of 25,000 *cubits*, and the width shall be 20,000. It shall be holy within all its boundary round about. 2 Out of this there shall be for the holy place a square round about five hundred by five hundred *cubits*, and fifty cubits for its open space round about. 3 And from this area you shall measure a length of 25,000 *cubits* and a width of 10,000 *cubits*; and in it shall be the sanctuary, *the* Holy of Holies. 4 It shall be the holy portion of the land; it shall be for the priests, the ministers of the sanctuary, who come near to minister to Yahweh, and it shall be a place for their houses and a holy place for the sanctuary. 5 *And an area* 25,000 *cubits* in length and 10,000 in width shall be for the Levites, the ministers of the house, *and* for their possession as cities to dwell in.

6 "And you shall give the city possession
of *an area* 5,000 *cubits* wide and 25,000
cubits long, alongside the contribution of
the holy portion; it shall be for the whole
house of Israel.

7 "Now the prince shall have *land* on either
side of the holy contribution and the city's
possession *of land*, adjacent to the holy
contribution and the city's possession *of
land*, on the west side toward the west and on
the east side toward the east, and in length
comparable to one of the portions, from the
west border to the east border. 8 This shall
be his land for a possession in Israel; so My
princes shall no longer mistreat My people,
but they shall give *the rest of* the land to the
house of Israel according to their tribes."

9 'Thus says Lord Yahweh, "Enough, you
princes of Israel; put away violence and dev-
astation, and do justice and righteousness.
Stop your eviction of My people," declares
Lord Yahweh.

10 "You shall have just balances, a just
ephah, and a just bath. 11 The ephah and
the bath shall be the same quantity so that
the bath will contain a tenth of a homer and
the ephah a tenth of a homer; their standard
shall be according to the homer. 12 And
the shekel shall be twenty gerahs; twenty
shekels, twenty-five shekels, *and* fifteen
shekels shall be your maneh.

13 "This is the contribution that you shall
offer: a sixth of an ephah from a homer of
wheat, a sixth of an ephah from a homer of
barley, 14 and the statute for the oil (*namely*,
the bath of oil), a tenth of a bath from *each* kor
(*which is* ten baths *or* a homer, for ten baths
are a homer), 15 and one sheep from *each*
flock of two hundred from the watering places
of Israel—for a grain offering, for a burnt
offering, and for peace offerings, to make
atonement for them," declares Lord Yahweh.
16 "All the people of the land shall give to this
contribution for the prince in Israel. 17 And it
shall be the prince's part *to provide* the burnt
offerings, the grain offerings, and the drink
offerings, at the feasts, on the new moons,
and on the sabbaths, at all the appointed
times of the house of Israel; he shall provide
the sin offering, the grain offering, the burnt
offering, and the peace offerings, to make
atonement for the house of Israel."

18 'Thus says Lord Yahweh, "In the first
month, on the first of the month, you shall
take a bull from the herd without blemish
and purify the sanctuary. 19 The priest
shall take some of the blood from the sin
offering and put *it* on the door posts of the
house, on the four corners of the ledge of
the altar, and on the posts of the gate of the
inner court. 20 And thus you shall do on the
seventh *day* of the month for everyone who
errs or is simpleminded; so you shall make
atonement for the house.

21 "In the first *month*, on the fourteenth
day of the month, you shall have the
Passover, a feast of seven days; unleavened
bread shall be eaten. 22 And on that day the
prince shall provide for himself and all the
people of the land a bull for a sin offering.
23 And *during* the seven days of the feast he
shall provide as a burnt offering to Yahweh
seven bulls and seven rams without blemish
on every day of the seven days, and a male
goat daily for a sin offering. 24 And he shall
provide as a grain offering an ephah with a
bull, an ephah with a ram, and a hin of oil
with an ephah. 25 In the seventh *month*, on
the fifteenth day of the month, at the feast,
he shall provide like this, seven days for the
sin offering, the burnt offering, the grain
offering, and the oil."

46 'Thus says Lord Yahweh, "The gate
of the inner court facing east shall
be shut the six working days; but it shall be
opened on the sabbath day and opened on
the day of the new moon. 2 Then the prince
shall enter by way of the porch of the gate
from outside and stand by the post of the
gate. Then the priests shall provide his
burnt offering and his peace offerings, and
he shall worship at the threshold of the gate
and then go out; but the gate shall not be
shut until the evening. 3 And the people of
the land shall also worship at the entrance
of that gate before Yahweh on the sabbaths
and on the new moons. 4 Now the burnt
offering which the prince shall bring near
to Yahweh on the sabbath day shall be six
lambs without blemish and a ram without
blemish; 5 and the grain offering shall be an
ephah with the ram, and the grain offering
with the lambs shall be a gift from his
hand, as well as a hin of oil with an ephah.
6 And on the day of the new moon *he shall
offer* a bull from the herd without blemish,
also six lambs and a ram, *which* shall be
without blemish. 7 And he shall provide a
grain offering, an ephah with the bull and

an ephah with the ram, and with the lambs
as much as he is able, and a hin of oil with
an ephah. 8 And when the prince enters, he
shall go in by way of the porch of the gate
and go out by the same way. 9 But when the
people of the land come before Yahweh at
the appointed times, he who enters by way
of the north gate to worship shall go out by
way of the south gate. And he who enters by
way of the south gate shall go out by way of
the north gate. No one shall return by way
of the gate by which he entered but shall
go straight out. 10 So when they go in, the
prince shall go in among them; and when
they go out, he shall go out.
11 "Now at the feasts and the appointed
times the grain offering shall be an ephah
with a bull and an ephah with a ram, and
with the lambs shall be a gift from his hand,
as well as a hin of oil with an ephah. 12 And
when the prince provides a freewill offering,
a burnt offering, or peace offerings *as* a
freewill offering to Yahweh, the gate facing
east shall be opened for him. And he shall
provide his burnt offering and his peace
offerings as he does on the sabbath day.
Then he shall go out, and the gate shall be
shut after he goes out.
13 "And you shall provide a lamb a year
old without blemish for a burnt offering to
Yahweh daily; morning by morning you shall
provide it. 14 Also you shall provide a grain
offering with it morning by morning—a
sixth of an ephah as well as a third of a hin of
oil to moisten the fine flour—a grain offering
to Yahweh continually by a perpetual statute.
15 Thus they shall provide the lamb, the grain
offering, and the oil, morning by morning,
for a continual burnt offering."
16 'Thus says Lord Yahweh, "If the prince
gives a gift *out of* his inheritance to any of
his sons, it shall belong to his sons; it is
their possession by inheritance. 17 But if he
gives a gift from his inheritance to one of
his servants, it shall be his until the year of
liberty; then it shall return to the prince. His
inheritance *shall be* only his sons'; it shall
belong to them. 18 Now the prince shall
not take from the people's inheritance,
mistreating them out of their possession;
he shall give his sons inheritance from his
own possession so that My people will not
be scattered, anyone from his possession."'"
19 Then he brought me through the
entrance, which *was* at the side of the gate,
into the holy chambers for the priests,
which faced north; and behold, there *was*
a place at the extreme rear toward the west.
20 Then he said to me, "This is the place
where the priests shall boil the guilt offering
and the sin offering *and* where they shall
bake the grain offering, in order that they
may not bring *them* out into the outer court
to transmit holiness to the people."
21 Then he brought me out into the outer
court and had me pass through to the four
corners of the court; and behold, in every
corner of the court *there was* a *small* court.
22 In the four corners of the court *there*
were enclosed courts, forty *cubits* long
and thirty wide; these four in the corners
were the same size. 23 *Now there was* a row
of masonry round about in them, around
the four of them, and boiling places were
made under the rows round about. 24 Then
he said to me, "These are the boiling places
where the ministers of the house shall boil
the sacrifices of the people."

Psalm 135:1–7

1 Praise Yah!
Praise the name of Yahweh;
Praise *Him*, O slaves of Yahweh,
2 You who stand in the house of Yahweh,
In the courts of the house of our God!
3 Praise Yah, for Yahweh is good;
Sing praises to His name, for it is lovely.
4 For Yah has chosen Jacob for Himself,
Israel for His treasured possession.

5 For I know that Yahweh is great
And that our Lord is *greater*
than all gods.
6 Whatever Yahweh pleases, He does,
In heaven and on earth, in the
seas and in all deeps.
7 The One who causes the clouds to
ascend from the end of the earth;
Who makes lightnings for the rain,
Who brings forth the wind
from His storehouses.

Proverbs 29:8

8 Scoffers set a city aflame,
But wise men turn away anger.

1 Peter 3:1–22

3 In the same way, you wives, be subject to
your own husbands so that even if any
of them are disobedient to the word, they

may be won without a word by the conduct
of their wives, 2 as they observe your pure
conduct with fear. 3 Your adornment must
not be *merely* external—braiding the hair,
and wearing gold jewelry, or putting on
garments; 4 but *let it be* the hidden person of
the heart, with the incorruptible quality of a
lowly and quiet spirit, which is precious in
the sight of God. 5 For in this way in former
times the holy women also, who hoped in
God, used to adorn themselves, being sub-
ject to their own husbands, 6 just as Sarah
obeyed Abraham, calling him lord. You have
become her children if you do good, NOT
FEARING ANY INTIMIDATION.

7 You husbands in the same way, live with
your wives in an understanding way, as
with a weaker vessel, since she is a woman;
and show her honor as a fellow heir of the
grace of life, so that your prayers will not
be hindered.

8 Now to sum up, all of you be like-minded,
sympathetic, brotherly, tender-hearted,
and humble in spirit; 9 not returning evil
for evil or reviling for reviling, but giving
a blessing instead, for you were called for
the very purpose that you might inherit a
blessing. 10 For,

"THE ONE WHO DESIRES LIFE, TO
LOVE AND SEE GOOD DAYS,
MUST KEEP HIS TONGUE FROM EVIL AND
HIS LIPS FROM SPEAKING DECEIT.
11 "HE MUST TURN AWAY FROM
EVIL AND DO GOOD;
HE MUST SEEK PEACE AND PURSUE IT.
12 "FOR THE EYES OF THE LORD ARE
TOWARD THE RIGHTEOUS,
AND HIS EARS ATTEND TO THEIR PRAYER,
BUT THE FACE OF THE LORD IS
AGAINST THOSE WHO DO EVIL."

13 And who is there to harm you if you
prove zealous for what is good? 14 But even if
you should suffer for the sake of righteous-
ness, you are blessed. AND DO NOT FEAR
THEIR FEAR, AND DO NOT BE TROUBLED, 15 but
sanctify Christ as Lord in your hearts, always
being ready to make a defense to everyone
who asks you to give an account for the hope
that is in you, yet with gentleness and fear,
16 having a good conscience so that in the
thing in which you are slandered, those who
disparage your good conduct in Christ will
be put to shame. 17 For it is better, if God
should will it so, that you suffer for doing
good rather than for doing wrong. 18 For
Christ also suffered for sins once for all,
the righteous for *the* unrighteous, so that
He might bring you to God, having been put
to death in the flesh, but made alive in the
spirit; 19 in which also He went and made
proclamation to the spirits *now* in prison,
20 who once were disobedient, when the
patience of God kept waiting in the days
of Noah, during the construction of the
ark, in which a few, that is, eight persons,
were brought safely through *the* water.
21 Corresponding to that, baptism now
saves you—not the removal of dirt from the
flesh, but an appeal of a good conscience
to God—through the resurrection of Jesus
Christ, 22 who is at the right hand of God,
having gone into heaven, after angels and
authorities and powers had been subjected
to Him.

NOVEMBER 28

Ezekiel 47:1–48:35

47 Then he brought me back to the door
of the house; and behold, water was
flowing from under the threshold of the
house toward the east, for the house faced
east. And the water was flowing down from
under, from the right side of the house, from
south of the altar. 2 He brought me out by
way of the north gate and led me around by
way of the outside to the outer gate by way
of *the gate* that faces east. And behold, water
was trickling from the south side.

3 When the man went out toward the
east with a line in his hand, he measured
one thousand cubits, and he had me pass
through the water, water *reaching* the
ankles. 4 Again he measured one thousand
and had me pass through the water, water
reaching the knees. Again he measured
one thousand and had me pass through *the
water*, water *reaching* the loins. 5 Again he
measured one thousand; *and it was* a river
that I could not pass through, for the water
had become high—*enough* water to swim
in, a river that could not be passed through.
6 And he said to me, "Son of man, have you
seen *this*?" Then he led and returned me
back to the bank of the river. 7 When I had

returned, now behold, on the bank of the
river there *were* very many trees on the one
side and on the other. 8 Then he said to me,
"These waters go out toward the eastern
region and go down into the Arabah; then
they go toward the sea, being made to flow
out to the sea, and the waters *of the sea* will
be healed. 9 And it will be that every living
creature, which swarms in every place
where the river goes, will live. And there
will be very many fish, for these waters go
there and *the other waters* are healed; so
everything will live where the river goes.
10 And it will be that fishermen will stand
beside it; from Engedi to Eneglaim there will
be a place for the spreading of nets. Their
fish will be according to their kinds, like the
fish of the Great Sea, very many. 11 But its
marshes and swamps will not be healed;
they will be left for salt. 12 And by the river
on its bank, on one side and on the other,
will grow all *kinds of* trees for food. Their
leaves will not wither, and their fruit will
not fail. They will bear every month because
their water flows out from the sanctuary,
and their fruit will be for food and their
leaves for healing."

13 Thus says Lord Yahweh, "This *shall be*
the boundary by which you shall apportion
the land for an inheritance among the
twelve tribes of Israel; Joseph *shall have*
two portions. 14 You shall then apportion it
for an inheritance, each one equally with
the other; for I swore to give it to your
fathers, and this land shall fall to you as an
inheritance.

15 "This *shall be* the boundary of the land:
on the north side, from the Great Sea *by* the
way of Hethlon, to the entrance of Zedad;
16 Hamath, Berothah, Sibraim, which is
between the border of Damascus and the
border of Hamath; Hazer-hatticon, which is
by the border of Hauran. 17 And the bound-
ary shall be from the sea *to* Hazar-enan *at*
the border of Damascus, and on the north
toward the north is the border of Hamath.
This is the north side.

18 "And the east side, from between
Hauran, Damascus, Gilead, and the land of
Israel, *shall be* the Jordan; from the *north*
border to the eastern sea you shall measure.
This is the east side.

19 "And the south side toward the south
shall extend from Tamar as far as the waters
of Meribath-kadesh, to the brook *of Egypt*
and to the Great Sea. This is the south side
toward the south.

20 "And the west side *shall be* the Great
Sea, from the *south* border to a point oppo-
site Lebo-hamath. This is the west side.

21 "So you shall divide this land among
yourselves according to the tribes of Israel.
22 And it will be that you shall divide it by
lot for an inheritance among yourselves and
among the sojourners who sojourn in your
midst, who bring forth sons in your midst.
And they shall be to you as the native-born
among the sons of Israel. They shall be
allotted an inheritance with you among
the tribes of Israel. 23 And it will be that in
the tribe with which the sojourner sojourns,
there you shall give *him* his inheritance,"
declares Lord Yahweh.

48 "Now these are the names of the
tribes: from the northern extremity,
beside the way of Hethlon to Lebo-hamath,
as far as Hazar-enan *at* the border of
Damascus, toward the north beside Hamath,
running from east to west, Dan, one *por-
tion.* 2 And beside the border of Dan, from
the east side to the west side, Asher, one
portion. 3 And beside the border of Asher,
from the east side to the west side, Naph-
tali, one *portion.* 4 And beside the border
of Naphtali, from the east side to the west
side, Manasseh, one *portion.* 5 And beside
the border of Manasseh, from the east side
to the west side, Ephraim, one *portion.* 6 And
beside the border of Ephraim, from the east
side to the west side, Reuben, one *portion.*
7 And beside the border of Reuben, from
the east side to the west side, Judah, one
portion.

8 "And beside the border of Judah, from
the east side to the west side, shall be the
contribution which you shall contribute,
25,000 *cubits* in width, and in length like
one of the portions, from the east side to
the west side; and the sanctuary shall be in
the middle of it. 9 The contribution that you
shall contribute to Yahweh *shall be* 25,000
cubits in length and 10,000 in width. 10 And
the holy contribution shall be for these,
namely for the priests, toward the north
25,000 *cubits in length,* toward the west
10,000 in width, toward the east 10,000
in width, and toward the south 25,000 in
length; and the sanctuary of Yahweh shall
be in its midst. 11 *It shall be* for the priests

who are sanctified of the sons of Zadok, who have kept the responsibility *given by* Me, who did not go astray when the sons of Israel went astray as the Levites went astray. 12 And it shall be a contribution to them from the contribution of the land, a Holy of Holies, by the border of the Levites. 13 Now alongside the border of the priests, the Levites *shall have* 25,000 *cubits* in length and 10,000 in width. The whole length *shall be* 25,000 *cubits* and the width 10,000. 14 Moreover, they shall not sell or exchange any of it, or let this choice *portion* of land pass over *to another*; for it is holy to Yahweh.

15 "And the remainder, 5,000 *cubits* in width and 25,000 in length, shall be for common use for the city, for *places of* habitation, and for open spaces; and the city shall be in its midst. 16 And these *shall be* its measurements: the north side 4,500 *cubits*, the south side 4,500 *cubits*, the east side 4,500 *cubits*, and the west side 4,500 *cubits*. 17 And the city shall have open spaces: on the north 250 *cubits*, on the south 250 *cubits*, on the east 250 *cubits*, and on the west 250 *cubits*. 18 And the remainder of the length alongside the holy contribution shall be 10,000 *cubits* toward the east and 10,000 toward the west; and it shall be alongside the holy contribution. And its produce shall be food for the workers of the city. 19 The workers of the city, out of all the tribes of Israel, shall cultivate it. 20 The whole contribution *shall be* 25,000 by 25,000 *cubits*; you shall contribute the holy contribution, a square, with the city's possession *of land*.

21 "And the remainder *shall be* for the prince, on the one side and on the other of the holy contribution and of the city's possession *of land*; in front of the 25,000 *cubits* of the contribution toward the east border and westward in front of the 25,000 toward the west border, alongside the portions, *it shall be* for the prince. And the holy contribution and the sanctuary of the house shall be in the middle of it. 22 And apart from the Levites' possession and the city's possession, *which* are in the middle of that which belongs to the prince, *everything* between the border of Judah and the border of Benjamin shall be for the prince.

23 "Now as for the rest of the tribes: from the east side to the west side, Benjamin, one *portion*. 24 And beside the border of Benjamin, from the east side to the west side, Simeon, one *portion*. 25 And beside the border of Simeon, from the east side to the west side, Issachar, one *portion*. 26 And beside the border of Issachar, from the east side to the west side, Zebulun, one *portion*. 27 And beside the border of Zebulun, from the east side to the west side, Gad, one *portion*. 28 And beside the border of Gad, at the south side toward the south, the border shall be from Tamar to the waters of Meribath-kadesh, to the brook *of Egypt*, to the Great Sea. 29 This is the land which you shall divide by lot to the tribes of Israel for an inheritance, and these are their *several* portions," declares Lord Yahweh.

30 "And these are the exits of the city: on the north side, 4,500 *cubits* by measurement. 31 "And the gates of the city *shall be* named for the tribes of Israel, three gates toward the north: the gate of Reuben, one; the gate of Judah, one; the gate of Levi, one. 32 And on the east side, 4,500 *cubits*, shall be three gates: the gate of Joseph, one; the gate of Benjamin, one; the gate of Dan, one. 33 And on the south side, 4,500 *cubits* by measurement, shall be three gates: the gate of Simeon, one; the gate of Issachar, one; the gate of Zebulun, one. 34 *On* the west side, 4,500 *cubits, shall be* three gates: the gate of Gad, one; the gate of Asher, one; the gate of Naphtali, one. 35 *The city shall be* 18,000 *cubits* round about; and the name of the city from *that* day *shall be*, 'Yahweh is there.'"

Psalm 135:8–14

8 He struck the firstborn of Egypt,
From man to beast.
9 He sent signs and wonders into
your midst, O Egypt,
Amongst Pharaoh and all his slaves.
10 He struck many nations
And slew mighty kings,
11 Sihon, king of the Amorites,
And Og, king of Bashan,
And all the kingdoms of Canaan;
12 And He gave their land as
an inheritance,
An inheritance to Israel His people.
13 O Yahweh, Your name is everlasting,
O Yahweh, Your remembrance is
from generation to generation.
14 For Yahweh will render
justice for His people
And will give comfort to His slaves.

Proverbs 29:9

9 When a wise man is brought
into judgment with a man
who is an ignorant fool,
The *ignorant fool* both rages and
laughs, and there is no rest.

1 Peter 4:1–19

4 Therefore, since Christ has suffered in the flesh, arm yourselves also with the same purpose—because he who has suffered in the flesh has ceased from sin— 2 so as to no longer live the rest of the time in the flesh for the lusts of men, but for the will of God. 3 For the time already past is sufficient *for you* to have worked out the desire of the Gentiles, having pursued a course of sensuality, lusts, drunkenness, carousing, drinking parties, and abominable idolatries. 4 In *all* this, they are surprised that you do not run with *them* into the same excesses of dissipation, maligning *you*, 5 but they will give account to Him who is ready to judge the living and the dead. 6 For to this the gospel has been proclaimed even to those who are *now* dead, so that though they were judged in the flesh as men, they live in the spirit according to *the will of* God.

7 The end of all things is at hand; therefore, be of sound thinking and sober *spirit* for the purpose of prayer. 8 Above all, keep fervent in your love for one another, because LOVE COVERS A MULTITUDE OF SINS. 9 Be hospitable to one another without grumbling. 10 As each one has received a gift, employ it in serving one another as good stewards of the manifold grace of God— 11 whoever speaks, as one *speaking* the oracles of God; whoever serves, as one *serving* by the strength which God supplies; so that in all things God may be glorified through Jesus Christ, to whom belongs the glory and might forever and ever. Amen.

12 Beloved, do not be surprised at the fiery trial among you, which comes upon you for your testing, as though some strange thing were happening to you. 13 But to the degree you are sharing the sufferings of Christ, keep on rejoicing, so that also at the revelation of His glory you may rejoice with exultation. 14 If you are insulted for the name of Christ, you are blessed, because the Spirit of glory and of God rests on you. 15 Make sure that none of you suffers as a murderer, or thief, or evildoer, or a troublesome meddler; 16 but if *anyone suffers* as a Christian, he is not to be put to shame, but is to glorify God in this name. 17 For *it is* time for judgment to begin with the house of God; and if *it begins* with us first, what *will be* the outcome for those who do not obey the gospel of God? 18 AND IF IT IS WITH DIFFICULTY THAT THE RIGHTEOUS IS SAVED, WHAT WILL BECOME OF THE GODLESS MAN AND THE SINNER? 19 Therefore, those also who suffer according to the will of God must entrust their souls to a faithful Creator in doing good.

NOVEMBER 29

Daniel 1:1–2:49

1 In the third year of the reign of Jehoiakim king of Judah, Nebuchadnezzar king of Babylon came to Jerusalem and besieged it. 2 And the Lord gave Jehoiakim king of Judah into his hand, along with some of the vessels of the house of God; and he brought them to the land of Shinar, to the house of his god, and he brought the vessels into the treasury of his god.

3 Then the king said for Ashpenaz, the chief of his officials, to bring in some of the sons of Israel, including some of the royal seed and of the nobles, 4 youths in whom was no defect, who were good in appearance, showing insight in every *branch of* wisdom, being thoroughly knowledgeable and discerning knowledge, and who had ability to stand in the king's palace; and *he said for him* to teach them the literature and tongue of the Chaldeans. 5 And the king appointed for them a daily ration from the king's choice food and from the wine which he drank, and *appointed* that they should be educated three years, at the end of which they were to stand before the king. 6 Now among them from the sons of Judah were Daniel, Hananiah, Mishael, and Azariah. 7 Then the commander of the officials set names for them; and for Daniel he set *the name* Belteshazzar, for Hananiah Shadrach, for Mishael Meshach, and for Azariah Abed-nego.

8 But Daniel set in his heart that he would not defile himself with the king's choice

food or with the wine which he drank; so he
sought *permission* from the commander of
the officials that he might not defile himself.
9 Now God granted Daniel lovingkindness
and compassion before the commander
of the officials, 10 and the commander of
the officials said to Daniel, "I am afraid of
my lord the king, who has appointed your
food and your drink; for why should he
see your faces looking more haggard than
the youths who are your own age? Then
you would make me forfeit my head to the
king." 11 But Daniel said to the overseer
whom the commander of the officials had
appointed over Daniel, Hananiah, Mishael,
and Azariah, 12 "Please test your servants
for ten days, and let us be given some veg-
etables to eat and water to drink. 13 Then
let our appearance be observed before you
and the appearance of the youths who are
eating the king's choice food; and deal with
your servants according to what you see."

14 So he listened to them in this matter
and tested them for ten days. 15 At the end
of ten days it was seen that their appearance
was better and that they were fatter than all
the youths who had been eating the king's
choice food. 16 So the overseer continued
to withhold their choice food and the wine
they were to drink, and kept giving them
vegetables.

17 And as for these four youths, God gave
them knowledge and insight in every *branch
of* literature and wisdom; Daniel even
understood all *kinds of* visions and dreams.

18 Then at the end of the days which the
king had spoken of for bringing them in,
the commander of the officials brought
them in before Nebuchadnezzar. 19 And the
king talked with them, and out of them all
not one was found like Daniel, Hananiah,
Mishael, and Azariah; so they stood *in
service* before the king. 20 And as for every
matter of wisdom in understanding which
the king sought from them, he found them
ten times better than all the magicians *and*
conjurers who *were* in all his kingdom.
21 And Daniel continued until the first year
of Cyrus the king.

2 Now in the second year of the reign of
Nebuchadnezzar, Nebuchadnezzar had
dreams; and his spirit was troubled, and his
sleep left him. 2 Then the king said to call
in the magicians, the conjurers, the sorcer-
ers, and the Chaldeans to tell the king his
dreams. So they came in and stood before
the king. 3 Then the king said to them, "I
had a dream, and my spirit is troubled to
know the dream."

4 Then the Chaldeans spoke to the king
in Aramaic: "O king, live forever! Say the
dream to your servants, and we will declare
the interpretation." 5 The king answered and
said to the Chaldeans, "The word from me
is firm: if you do not make known to me
the dream and its interpretation, you will
be torn limb from limb, and your houses
will be made a rubbish heap. 6 But if you
declare the dream and its interpretation,
you will receive from me gifts and a reward
and great glory; therefore declare to me
the dream and its interpretation." 7 They
answered a second time and said, "Let the
king say the dream to his servants, and we
will declare the interpretation." 8 The king
answered and said, "I know for certain that
you are buying time, inasmuch as you have
seen that the word from me is firm, 9 that if
you do not make the dream known to me,
there is only one law for you. Indeed, you
have agreed together to speak lying and
corrupt words before me until the time is
changed; therefore say the dream to me,
that I may know that you can declare to
me its interpretation." 10 The Chaldeans
answered the king and said, "There is not
a man on earth who is able to declare the
matter for the king, inasmuch as no great
king or powerful ruler has *ever* asked *about*
a matter like this of any magician, conjurer,
or Chaldean. 11 Moreover, the matter which
the king asks is difficult, and there is no
one else who could declare it to the king
except gods, whose dwelling place is not
with flesh."

12 Because of this the king became indig-
nant and very furious and said *for them* to
destroy all the wise men of Babylon. 13 So
the law went forth that the wise men were
to be killed; and they sought out Daniel and
his friends to kill *them*.

14 Then Daniel replied with discretion and
discernment to Arioch, the captain of the
king's bodyguard, who had gone forth to
kill the wise men of Babylon; 15 he answered
and said to Arioch, a powerful official for
the king, "For what reason is the law from
the king *so* urgent?" Then Arioch made the
matter known to Daniel. 16 So Daniel went

in and sought from the king that he would
give him time, in order that he might declare
the interpretation to the king.
17 Then Daniel went to his house and
made the matter known to his friends,
to Hananiah, Mishael, and Azariah, 18 so
that they might seek compassion from the
God of heaven concerning this mystery,
so that Daniel and his friends would not
be destroyed with the rest of the wise
men of Babylon. 19 Then the mystery was
revealed to Daniel in a night vision. Then
Daniel blessed the God of heaven; 20 Daniel
answered and said,

"Let the name of God be blessed
forever and ever,
For wisdom and might belong to Him.
21 "And He changes the times
and the seasons;
He removes kings and
establishes kings;
He gives wisdom to wise men
And knowledge to men of
understanding.
22 "He reveals the deep and hidden things;
He knows what is in the darkness,
And the light dwells with Him.
23 "To You, O God of my fathers,
I give thanks and praise,
For You have given me
wisdom and might;
Even now You have made known to
me what we sought from You,
For You have made known to
us the king's matter."

24 Therefore, Daniel went in to Arioch,
whom the king had appointed to destroy
the wise men of Babylon; he went and said
thus to him: "Do not destroy the wise men
of Babylon! Bring me before the king, and I
will declare the interpretation to the king."
25 Then Arioch hurriedly brought Daniel
before the king and said thus to him: "I have
found a man among the exiles from Judah
who can make the interpretation known to
the king!" 26 The king answered and said to
Daniel, whose name was Belteshazzar, "Are
you able to make known to me the dream
which I have seen and its interpretation?"
27 Daniel answered before the king and
said, "As for the mystery about which the
king is asking, neither wise men, conjurers,
magicians, *nor* diviners are able to declare
it to the king. 28 However, there is a God in
heaven who reveals mysteries, and He has
made known to King Nebuchadnezzar what
will take place in the last days. This was your
dream and the visions of your head *while*
on your bed. 29 As for you, O king, *while*
on your bed your thoughts turned to what
would happen in the future; and He who
reveals mysteries has made known to you
what will happen. 30 But as for me, this
mystery has not been revealed to me by
any wisdom which is in me more than *in*
any *other* living man, but for the purpose
of making the interpretation known to the
king, and that you may know the thoughts
of your heart.
31 "You, O king, were looking, and behold,
there was a single great image; that image,
which was large and of extraordinary
splendor, was rising up in front of you, and
its appearance was awesome. 32 The head of
that image *was made* of fine gold, its breast
and its arms of silver, its belly and its thighs
of bronze, 33 its legs of iron, its feet partly
of iron and partly of clay. 34 You continued
looking until a stone was cut out without
hands, and it struck the image on its feet
of iron and clay and crushed them. 35 Then
the iron, the clay, the bronze, the silver, and
the gold were crushed all at the same time
and became like chaff from the summer
threshing floors; and the wind carried them
away so that not a trace of them was found.
But the stone that struck the image became
a great mountain and filled the whole earth.
36 "This *was* the dream; now we will say
its interpretation before the king. 37 You,
O king, are the king of kings, to whom the
God of heaven has given the kingdom, the
power, the strength, and the glory; 38 and
wherever the sons of men inhabit, *or* the
beasts of the field, or the birds of the sky, He
has given *them* into your hand and has made
you rule with power over them all. You are
the head of gold. 39 But after you there will
arise another kingdom inferior to you, then
another third kingdom of bronze, which will
rule with power over all the earth. 40 Then
there will be a fourth kingdom as strong as
iron; inasmuch as iron crushes and shatters
all things, so, like iron that breaks in pieces,
it will crush and break all these in pieces.
41 Now in that you saw the feet and toes,
partly of potter's clay and partly of iron; it
will be a divided kingdom; but it will have
in it the toughness of iron, inasmuch as
you saw the iron mixed with common clay.

42 *And as* the toes of the feet *were* partly
of iron and partly of clay, *so* some of the
kingdom will be strong and part of it will
be brittle. 43 And in that you saw the iron
mixed with common clay; they will combine
with one another in the seed of men; but
they will not cling to one another, even as
iron does not combine with clay. 44 And in
the days of those kings the God of heaven
will cause a kingdom to rise up which will
never be destroyed, and *that* kingdom will
not be left for another people; it will crush
and put an end to all these kingdoms, but
it will itself stand forever. 45 Inasmuch as
you saw that a stone was cut out of the
mountain without hands and that it crushed
the iron, the bronze, the clay, the silver, and
the gold, the great God has made known to
the king what will happen in the future; so
the dream is certain, and its interpretation
is trustworthy."

46 Then King Nebuchadnezzar fell on
his face and did homage to Daniel and
said *for them* to present to him an offering
and fragrant incense. 47 The king answered
Daniel and said, "Truly your God is a God
of gods and a Lord of kings and a revealer
of mysteries since you have been able to
reveal this mystery." 48 Then the king
promoted Daniel and gave him many
great gifts, and he made him rule with
power over the whole province of Babylon
and chief prefect over all the wise men of
Babylon. 49 And Daniel sought of the king,
and he appointed Shadrach, Meshach, and
Abed-nego over the administration of the
province of Babylon, while Daniel *was* at
the king's court.

Psalm 135:15–21

15 The idols of the nations
are silver and gold,
The work of man's hands.
16 They have mouths, but
they do not speak;
They have eyes, but they do not see;
17 They have ears, but they do not hear,
Surely, there is not any breath
in their mouths.
18 Those who make them
will be like them,
All who trust in them.

19 O house of Israel, bless Yahweh;
O house of Aaron, bless Yahweh;
20 O house of Levi, bless Yahweh;
You who fear Yahweh, bless Yahweh.
21 Blessed be Yahweh from Zion,
Who dwells in Jerusalem.
Praise Yah!

Proverbs 29:10

10 Men of bloodshed hate
the blameless,
But the upright seek *the well-being*
of his soul.

1 Peter 5:1–14

5 Therefore, I exhort the elders among
you, as *your* fellow elder and witness
of the sufferings of Christ, and a partaker
also of the glory that is to be revealed,
2 shepherd the flock of God among you,
overseeing not under compulsion, but
willingly, according to God; and not for
dishonest gain, but with eagerness; 3 nor
yet as lording it over those allotted to you,
but being examples to the flock. 4 And
when the Chief Shepherd appears, you will
receive the unfading crown of glory. 5 You
younger men, likewise, be subject to *your*
elders. And all of you, clothe yourselves
with humility toward one another, for GOD
IS OPPOSED TO THE PROUD, BUT GIVES GRACE
TO THE HUMBLE.

6 Therefore humble yourselves under
the mighty hand of God, that He may exalt
you at the proper time, 7 CASTING ALL YOUR
ANXIETY ON HIM, because He cares for
you. 8 Be of sober *spirit*, be watchful. Your
adversary, the devil, prowls around like a
roaring lion, seeking someone to devour.
9 But resist him, firm in the faith, knowing
that the same experiences of suffering are
being accomplished among your brethren
who are in the world. 10 And after you have
suffered for a little while, the God of all
grace, who called you to His eternal glory
in Christ, will Himself restore, strengthen,
confirm, *and* ground you. 11 To Him *be*
might forever and ever. Amen.

12 Through Silvanus, our faithful brother
as I regard *him*, I have written to you briefly,
exhorting and bearing witness that this
is the true grace of God. Stand firm in it!
13 She who is in Babylon, chosen together
with you, sends you greetings, and *so does*
my son, Mark. 14 Greet one another with a
kiss of love.

Peace be to you all who are in Christ.

NOVEMBER 30

Daniel 3:1–4:37

3 Nebuchadnezzar the king made an image of gold, the height of which *was* sixty cubits *and* its width six cubits; he set it up on the plain of Dura in the province of Babylon. 2 Then Nebuchadnezzar the king sent *word* to assemble the satraps, the prefects and the governors, the counselors, the treasurers, the judges, the magistrates and all the rulers of the provinces to come to the dedication of the image that Nebuchadnezzar the king had set up. 3 Then the satraps, the prefects and the governors, the counselors, the treasurers, the judges, the magistrates and all the rulers of the provinces were assembled for the dedication of the image that Nebuchadnezzar the king had set up; and they were standing before the image that Nebuchadnezzar had set up. 4 Then the herald loudly called out: "To you it is said, O peoples, nations, and *men of every* tongue, 5 that at the time you hear the sound of the horn, flute, lyre, trigon, psaltery, bagpipe, and all kinds of music, you are to fall down and worship the golden image that Nebuchadnezzar the king has set up. 6 But whoever does not fall down and worship shall immediately be cast into the midst of a furnace of blazing fire." 7 Therefore at that time, when all the peoples heard the sound of the horn, flute, lyre, trigon, psaltery, bagpipe, and all kinds of music, all the peoples, nations, and *men of every* tongue fell down *and* worshiped the golden image that Nebuchadnezzar the king had set up.

8 For this reason at that time certain Chaldeans came near and brought charges against the Jews. 9 They answered and said to Nebuchadnezzar the king: "O king, live forever! 10 You, O king, have made a decree that every man who hears the sound of the horn, flute, lyre, trigon, psaltery, and bagpipe and all kinds of music, is to fall down and worship the golden image. 11 But whoever does not fall down and worship shall be cast into the midst of a furnace of blazing fire. 12 There are certain Jews whom you have appointed over the administration of the province of Babylon, *namely* Shadrach, Meshach, and Abed-nego. These men, O king, do not pay attention to you; they do not serve your gods and do not worship the golden image which you have set up."

13 Then Nebuchadnezzar in rage and wrath said to bring Shadrach, Meshach, and Abed-nego; then these men were brought before the king. 14 Nebuchadnezzar answered and said to them, "Is it true, Shadrach, Meshach, and Abed-nego, that you are not serving my gods and do not worship the golden image that I have set up? 15 Now if you are ready, at the time you hear the sound of the horn, flute, lyre, trigon, psaltery, and bagpipe and all kinds of music, then you shall fall down and worship the image that I have made. But if you do not worship, you will immediately be cast into the midst of a furnace of blazing fire; and what god is there who can save you out of my hands?"

16 Shadrach, Meshach, and Abed-nego answered and said to the king, "O Nebuchadnezzar, we do not need to respond to you *with* an answer concerning this matter. 17 If it be *so*, our God whom we serve is able to save us from the furnace of blazing fire; and He will save us out of your hand, O king. 18 But if not, let it be known to you, O king, that we are not going to serve your gods, and we will not worship the golden image that you have set up."

19 Then Nebuchadnezzar was filled with wrath, and the image of his face changed toward Shadrach, Meshach, and Abed-nego. He answered and said to heat the furnace seven times more than it was usually heated. 20 And he said to certain mighty men of valor who *were* in his military host to tie up Shadrach, Meshach, and Abed-nego in order to cast *them* into the furnace of blazing fire. 21 Then these men were tied up in their trousers, their coats, their caps, and their *other* clothes and were cast into the midst of the furnace of blazing fire. 22 For this reason, because the king's word *was* urgent and the furnace had been heated to an extraordinary degree, the flame of the fire killed those men who carried up Shadrach, Meshach, and Abed-nego. 23 But these three men, Shadrach, Meshach, and Abed-nego, fell into the midst of the furnace of blazing fire *still* tied up.

[24]Then Nebuchadnezzar the king was
astounded and hurriedly stood up; he
answered and said to his high officials,
"Was it not three men we cast tied up into
the midst of the fire?" They answered and
said to the king, "Certainly, O king." [25]He
answered and said, "Look! I see four men
loosed *and* walking about in the midst of the
fire without harm, and the appearance of
the fourth is like a son of *the* gods!" [26]Then
Nebuchadnezzar came near to the door of
the furnace of blazing fire; he answered
and said, "Shadrach, Meshach, and Abed-
nego, come out, you servants of the Most
High God, and come here!" Then Shadrach,
Meshach, and Abed-nego came out of the
midst of the fire. [27]Then the satraps, the
prefects, the governors, and the king's high
officials gathered around *and* saw in regard
to these men that the fire had no power over
the bodies of these men, nor was the hair of
their head singed, nor were their trousers
damaged, nor had the smell of fire *even*
come upon them.

[28]Nebuchadnezzar answered and said,
"Blessed be the God of Shadrach, Meshach,
and Abed-nego, who has sent His angel and
saved His servants who put their trust in
Him, violating the king's word, and gave
up their bodies so as not to serve and not
to worship any god except their own God.
[29]Therefore I make a decree that any people,
nation, or tongue that says anything offen-
sive against the God of Shadrach, Meshach,
and Abed-nego shall be torn limb from limb
and their houses reduced to a rubbish heap,
inasmuch as there is no other god who is
able to deliver in this way." [30]Then the king
caused Shadrach, Meshach, and Abed-nego
to succeed in the province of Babylon.

4 Nebuchadnezzar the king to all the
peoples, nations, and *men of every*
tongue that inhabit all the earth: "May your
peace abound! [2]It has seemed good to me
to declare the signs and wonders which the
Most High God has done for me.

3 "How great are His signs,
And how strong are His wonders!
His kingdom is an
everlasting kingdom,
And His dominion is from
generation to generation.

[4]"I, Nebuchadnezzar, was at ease in
my house and flourishing in my palace. [5]I
saw a dream, and it made me fearful; and
these fantasies *as I lay* on my bed and the
visions in my head kept alarming me. [6]So I
gave a decree to bring into my presence all
the wise men of Babylon, that they might
make known to me the interpretation of the
dream. [7]Then the magicians, the conjurers,
the Chaldeans, and the diviners came in,
and I said the dream to them, but they could
not make its interpretation known to me.
[8]But at last Daniel came in before me, whose
name is Belteshazzar according to the name
of my god, and in whom is a spirit of the
holy gods; and I said the dream to him:
[9]'O Belteshazzar, chief of the magicians,
since I know that a spirit of the holy gods is
in you, and no mystery is difficult for you,
say to *me* the visions of my dream which
I have seen, along with its interpretation.

[10]'Now *these were* the visions in my
head *as I lay* on my bed: I was looking, and
behold, *there was* a tree in the midst of the
earth, and its height *was* great.

11 'The tree grew large and became strong,
And its height reached to the sky,
And it *was* visible to the end
of the whole earth.

12 'Its foliage *was* beautiful and
its fruit abundant,
And in it *was* food for all.
The beasts of the field found
shade under it,
And the birds of the sky
inhabited its branches,
And all flesh fed itself from it.

[13]'I was looking in the visions in my head
as I lay on my bed, and behold, a watcher, a
holy one, descended from heaven.

14 'He called out loudly and said thus:
"Chop down the tree and
cut off its branches,
Strip off its foliage and scatter its fruit;
Let the beasts flee from under it
And the birds from its branches.

15 "Yet leave the stump with its
roots in the earth,
But with a band of iron and
bronze *around it*
In the new grass of the field;
And let him be drenched with
the dew of heaven,
And let him share with the beasts
in the grass of the earth.

16 "Let his heart be changed
from *that of* a man,

And let the heart of a beast
be given to him,
And let seven periods of
time pass over him.
17 "This edict is by the resolution
of the watchers,
And the decision is a command
of the holy ones,
In order that the living may know
That the Most High is the powerful
ruler over the kingdom of mankind
And gives it to whom He wishes
And sets up over it the
lowliest of men."

18 'This is the dream *which* I, King Nebu-
chadnezzar, have seen. Now you, Belteshaz-
zar, say to *me* its interpretation, inasmuch as
none of the wise men of my kingdom is able
to make known to me the interpretation; but
you are able, for a spirit of the holy gods is
in you.'

19 "Then Daniel, whose name is Belte-
shazzar, was appalled for a while as his
thoughts were alarming him. The king
answered and said, 'Belteshazzar, do not let
the dream or its interpretation alarm you.'
Belteshazzar answered and said, 'My lord,
if only the dream applied to those who hate
you and its interpretation to your adversar-
ies! 20 The tree that you saw, which became
large and grew strong, whose height reached
to the sky and was visible to all the earth,
21 and whose foliage *was* beautiful and its
fruit abundant, and in which *was* food
for all, under which the beasts of the field
inhabited, and in whose branches the birds
of the sky dwelt— 22 it is you, O king; for
you have become great and grown strong,
and your greatness has become *even* greater
and reached to the sky and your dominion
to the end of the earth. 23 But in that the
king saw a watcher, a holy one, descending
from heaven and saying, "Chop down the
tree and destroy it; yet leave the stump with
its roots in the earth, but with a band of iron
and bronze *around it* in the new grass of the
field, and let him be drenched with the dew
of heaven, and let him share with the beasts
of the field until seven periods of time pass
over him," 24 this is the interpretation,
O king, and this is the resolution of the Most
High, which has reached my lord the king:
25 that you be driven away from mankind
and your *place of* habitation be with the
beasts of the field, and you be given grass
to eat like cattle and be drenched with the
dew of heaven; and seven periods of time
will pass over you, until you know that
the Most High is the powerful ruler over
the kingdom of mankind and gives it to
whomever He wishes. 26 And in that they
said to leave the stump with the roots of
the tree, your kingdom will endure for you
after you know that *it is* Heaven *that* rules
with power. 27 Therefore, O king, may my
advice seem good to you: break away now
from your sins by *doing* righteousness and
from your iniquities by showing mercy to
the poor, in case there may be a prolonging
of your prosperity.'

28 "All *this* reached Nebuchadnezzar the
king. 29 At the end of twelve months he was
walking on the *roof of* the royal palace of
Babylon. 30 The king answered and said, 'Is
this not Babylon the great, which I myself
have built as a royal house by the strength
of my power and for the glory of my maj-
esty?' 31 While the word *was* in the king's
mouth, a voice came from heaven, *saying,*
'King Nebuchadnezzar, to you it is said: the
kingdom has been removed from you, 32 and
you will be driven away from mankind,
and your *place of* habitation *will be* with
the beasts of the field. You will be given
grass to eat like cattle, and seven periods
of time will pass over you until you know
that the Most High is the powerful ruler
over the kingdom of mankind and gives it
to whomever He wishes.' 33 Immediately
the word concerning Nebuchadnezzar was
accomplished; and he was driven away from
mankind and began eating grass like cattle,
and his body was drenched with the dew of
heaven until his hair had grown like eagles'
feathers and his nails like birds' *claws*.

34 "But at the end of *those* days, I,
Nebuchadnezzar, lifted up my eyes toward
heaven, and my knowledge returned to me,
and I blessed the Most High and praised and
honored Him who lives forever;

For His dominion is an
everlasting dominion,
And His kingdom *endures* from
generation to generation.
35 "And all the inhabitants of the earth
are accounted as nothing,
But He does according to His
will in the host of heaven
And *among* the inhabitants of earth;
And no one can strike against His hand

Or say to Him, 'What have You done?'
36 "At that time my knowledge returned to
me. And my majesty and splendor were
returned to me for the glory of my kingdom,
and my high officials and my nobles began
seeking me out; so I was reestablished in
my kingdom, and extraordinary greatness
was added to me. 37 Now I, Nebuchadnezzar,
praise, exalt, and honor the King of heaven,
for all His works are true and His ways just,
and He is able to humble those who walk
in pride."

Psalm 136:1–9

1 Give thanks to Yahweh, for He is good,
For His lovingkindness
endures forever.
2 Give thanks to the God of gods,
For His lovingkindness
endures forever.
3 Give thanks to the Lord of lords,
For His lovingkindness
endures forever.

4 To Him who alone does great wonders,
For His lovingkindness
endures forever;
5 To Him who made the
heavens with skill,
For His lovingkindness
endures forever;
6 To Him who spread out the
earth above the waters,
For His lovingkindness
endures forever;
7 To Him who made *the* great lights,
For His lovingkindness
endures forever:
8 The sun to rule by day,
For His lovingkindness
endures forever,
9 The moon and stars to rule by night,
For His lovingkindness
endures forever.

Proverbs 29:11

11 A fool lets out all of his spirit,
But a wise man holds it back.

2 Peter 1:1–21

1 Simeon Peter, a slave and apostle of Jesus
Christ,
To those who have received the same
kind of faith as ours, by the righteousness
of our God and Savior, Jesus Christ: 2 Grace
and peace be multiplied to you in the full
knowledge of God and of Jesus our Lord;
3 seeing that His divine power has granted
to us everything pertaining to life and
godliness, through the full knowledge of
Him who called us by His own glory and
excellence. 4 For by these He has granted to
us His precious and magnificent promises,
so that by them you may become partakers
of *the* divine nature, having escaped the
corruption that is in the world by lust. 5 Now
for this very reason also, applying all dili-
gence, in your faith supply moral excellence,
and in *your* moral excellence, knowledge,
6 and in *your* knowledge, self-control, and
in *your* self-control, perseverance, and in
your perseverance, godliness, 7 and in *your*
godliness, brotherly kindness, and in *your*
brotherly kindness, love. 8 For if these things
are yours and are increasing, they render
you neither useless nor unfruitful in the
full knowledge of our Lord Jesus Christ.
9 For in whom these things are not present,
that one is blind, being nearsighted, having
forgotten the purification from his former
sins. 10 Therefore, brothers, be all the more
diligent to make your calling and choosing
sure; for in doing these things, you will never
stumble; 11 for in this way the entrance into
the eternal kingdom of our Lord and Savior
Jesus Christ will be abundantly supplied to
you.
12 Therefore, I will always be ready to
remind you of these things, even though
you *already* know *them*, and have been
strengthened in the truth which is present
with *you*. 13 I consider it right, as long as I
am in this *earthly* dwelling, to stir you up by
way of reminder, 14 knowing that the laying
aside of my *earthly* dwelling is imminent, as
also our Lord Jesus Christ has indicated to
me. 15 And I will also be diligent that at any
time after my departure you will be able to
call these things to mind.
16 For we did not make known to you
the power and coming of our Lord Jesus
Christ, following cleverly devised myths,
but being eyewitnesses of His majesty.
17 For when He received honor and glory
from God the Father, such an utterance as
this was made to Him by the Majestic Glory,
"This is My beloved Son with whom I am
well-pleased"— 18 and we ourselves heard
this utterance made from heaven when we
were with Him on the holy mountain.

19 And we have as more sure the prophetic word, to which you do well to pay attention as to a lamp shining in a dark place, until the day dawns and the morning star arises in your hearts. 20 Know this first of all, that no prophecy of Scripture comes by one's own interpretation. 21 For no prophecy was ever made by the will of man, but men being moved by the Holy Spirit spoke from God.

DECEMBER 1

Daniel 5:1–6:28

5 Belshazzar the king held a great feast for one thousand of his nobles, and he was drinking wine in the presence of the thousand. 2 When Belshazzar tasted the wine, he said to bring the gold and silver vessels which Nebuchadnezzar his father had taken out of the temple which *was* in Jerusalem, so that the king and his nobles, his wives and his concubines might drink from them. 3 Then they brought the gold vessels that had been taken out of the temple, the house of God which *was* in Jerusalem; and the king and his nobles, his wives and his concubines drank from them. 4 They drank the wine and praised the gods of gold and silver, of bronze, iron, wood and stone.

5 Suddenly the fingers of a man's hand came out and began writing opposite the lampstand on the plaster of the wall of the king's palace, and the king saw the back of the hand that did the writing. 6 Then the splendor of the king's *face* changed, and his thoughts alarmed him, and his hip joints went slack, and his knees were knocking against each other. 7 The king called out loudly to bring in the conjurers, the Chaldeans, and the diviners. The king answered and said to the wise men of Babylon, "Any man who can read this writing and declare its interpretation to me shall be clothed with purple and *have* a necklace of gold around his neck and rule with power as third *ruler* in the kingdom." 8 Then all the king's wise men came in, but they could not read the writing or make known its interpretation to the king. 9 Then King Belshazzar was greatly alarmed, and the splendor of his *face* changed *further*, and his nobles were perplexed.

10 The queen entered the banquet hall because of the words of the king and his nobles; the queen answered and said, "O king, live forever! Do not let your thoughts alarm you or the splendor of your *face* be changed. 11 There is a man in your kingdom in whom is a spirit of the holy gods; and in the days of your father, illumination, insight, and wisdom like the wisdom of the gods were found in him. And King Nebuchadnezzar, your father, your father the king, set him as chief of the magicians, conjurers, Chaldeans, *and* diviners. 12 *This was* because an extraordinary spirit, knowledge and insight, interpretation of dreams, explanation of enigmas, and solving of difficult problems were found in this Daniel, whom the king named Belteshazzar. Let Daniel now be summoned, and he will declare the interpretation."

13 Then Daniel was brought in before the king. The king answered and said to Daniel, "Are you that Daniel who is one of the exiles from Judah, whom my father the king brought from Judah? 14 Now I have heard about you that a spirit of the gods is in you, and that illumination, insight, and extraordinary wisdom have been found in you. 15 Just now the wise men *and* the conjurers were brought in before me that they might read this writing and make its interpretation known to me, but they could not declare the interpretation of the message. 16 But I personally have heard about you, that you are able to give interpretations and solve difficult problems. Now if you are able to read the writing and make its interpretation known to me, you will be clothed with purple and *wear* a necklace of gold around your neck, and you will rule with power as the third *ruler* in the kingdom."

17 Then Daniel answered and said before the king, "Let your gifts *remain* with you or give your rewards to someone else; however, I will read the writing to the king and make the interpretation known to him. 18 O king, the Most High God granted the kingdom, grandeur, glory, and majesty to Nebuchadnezzar your father. 19 And because of the grandeur which He bestowed on him, all the peoples, nations, and *men of every* tongue feared and were

in dread before him; whomever he wished
he killed, and whomever he wished he kept
alive, and whomever he wished he raised
up, and whomever he wished he made low.
20 But when his heart was raised up and his
spirit became so strong that he behaved
arrogantly, he was deposed from his royal
throne, and *his* glory was taken away from
him. 21 He was also driven away from the
sons of men, and his heart was made like
that of beasts, and his *place* of habitation
was with the wild donkeys. He was given
grass to eat like cattle, and his body was
drenched with the dew of the sky until he
knew that the Most High God is the pow-
erful ruler over the kingdom of mankind
and *that* He sets up over it whomever He
wishes. 22 Yet you, his son, Belshazzar, have
not made your heart lowly, even though you
knew all this, 23 but you have raised yourself
up against the Lord of heaven; and they have
brought the vessels of His house before you,
and you and your nobles, your wives and
your concubines have been drinking wine
from them; and you have praised the gods
of silver and gold, of bronze, iron, wood and
stone, which do not see, hear, or know. But
the God in whose hand are your life-breath
and all your ways, you have not honored.
24 Then the hand was sent from Him, and
this writing was inscribed.

25 "Now this is the writing that was
inscribed: 'MENĒ, MENĒ, TEKĒL,
UPHARSIN.' 26 This is the interpretation
of the message: 'MENĒ'—God has num-
bered your kingdom and put an end to it.
27 'TEKĒL'—you have been weighed on the
scales and found lacking. 28 'PERĒS'—your
kingdom has been divided and given over
to the Medes and Persians."

29 Then Belshazzar said *the word*, and
they clothed Daniel with purple and *put* a
necklace of gold around his neck and issued
a proclamation concerning him that he *now*
would be the third powerful ruler in the
kingdom.

30 That same night Belshazzar the Chal-
dean king was killed.

31 So Darius the Mede received the king-
dom at about the age of sixty-two.

6 It seemed good to Darius that he set
120 satraps over the kingdom, that they
would be in charge of the whole kingdom,
2 and over them three commissioners (of
whom Daniel was one), that these satraps
might be accountable to them, and that
the king might not suffer loss. 3 Then this
Daniel began distinguishing himself among
the commissioners and satraps because an
extraordinary spirit was in him, and the king
planned to set him over the entire kingdom.
4 Then the commissioners and satraps began
seeking to find a ground of accusation
against Daniel in regard to *matters of* the
kingdom; but they were not able to find any
ground of accusation or *evidence of* corrup-
tion, inasmuch as he was faithful, and no
negligence or corruption was *to be* found
in him. 5 Then these men said, "We will not
find any ground of accusation against this
Daniel unless we find *it* against him with
regard to the law of his God."

6 Then these commissioners and satraps
came by agreement to the king and said thus
to him: "King Darius, live forever! 7 All the
commissioners of the kingdom, the prefects
and the satraps, the high officials and the
governors have counseled together that the
king should establish a statute and enforce
an injunction that anyone who seeks *to
make* a petition to any god or man besides
you, O king, for thirty days, shall be cast into
the lions' den. 8 Now, O king, establish the
injunction and sign the written *document* so
that it may not be changed, according to the
law of the Medes and Persians, which may
not be revoked." 9 Therefore King Darius
signed the written *document*, that is, the
injunction.

10 Now when Daniel knew that the
written *document* was signed, he entered
his house (now in his roof chamber he had
windows open toward Jerusalem); and he
continued kneeling on his knees three times
a day, praying and giving thanks before
his God, as he had been doing previously.
11 Then these men came by agreement and
found Daniel seeking *to make* a petition and
making supplication before his God. 12 Then
they came near and said before the king
concerning the king's injunction, "Did you
not sign an injunction that any man who
seeks *to make* a petition to any god or man
besides you, O king, for thirty days, is to be
cast into the lions' den?" The king answered
and said, "The word is certain, according to
the law of the Medes and Persians, which
may not be revoked." 13 Then they answered
and said before the king, "Daniel, who is one

of the exiles from Judah, pays no attention
to you, O king, or to the injunction which
you signed, but keeps seeking *to make* his
petition three times a day."
14 Then, as soon as the king heard this
word, he was greatly distressed within
himself and set *his* mind on saving Daniel;
and even until sunset he kept exerting
himself to deliver him. 15 Then these men
came by agreement to the king and said to
the king, "Know, O king, that it is a law of
the Medes and Persians that no injunction
or statute which the king establishes may
be changed."
16 Then the king said *the word,* and Daniel
was brought in and cast into the lions' den.
The king answered and said to Daniel, "Your
God whom you constantly serve will Him-
self save you." 17 And a stone was brought
and placed over the mouth of the den; and
the king sealed it with his own signet ring
and with the signet rings of his nobles so
that nothing would be changed in regard
to Daniel. 18 Then the king went off to his
palace and spent the night fasting, and no
entertainment was brought before him; and
his sleep fled from him.
19 Then the king arose at dawn, at the
break of day, and hurriedly went to the
lions' den. 20 When he had come near the
den to Daniel, he cried out with a troubled
voice. The king answered and said to Daniel,
"Daniel, servant of the living God, has your
God, whom you constantly serve, been able
to save you from the lions?" 21 Then Daniel
spoke to the king, "O king, live forever!
22 My God sent His angel and shut the lions'
mouths, and they have not harmed me,
inasmuch as I was found innocent before
Him; and also toward you, O king, I have
done no harm." 23 Then the king was greatly
pleased and said for Daniel to be taken up
out of the den. So Daniel was taken up out
of the den, and no harm whatsoever was
found on him because he had believed in
his God. 24 The king then said *the word,* and
they brought those men who had brought
charges against Daniel, and they cast them,
their children, and their wives into the lions'
den; and they had not reached the bottom of
the den before the lions overpowered them
and crushed all their bones.
25 Then Darius the king wrote to all the
peoples, nations, and *men of every* tongue
who were inhabiting all the land: "May your
peace abound! 26 I make a decree that in
all the dominion of my kingdom, men are
to fear and be in dread before the God of
Daniel;

For He is the living God and
enduring forever,
And His kingdom is one which
will not be destroyed,
And His dominion *will be* unto
the end.

27 "He saves and delivers and
does signs and wonders
In heaven and on earth,
Who has *also* saved Daniel from
the power of the lions."

28 So this Daniel enjoyed success in the
kingdom of Darius and in the kingdom of
Cyrus the Persian.

Psalm 136:10–26

10 To Him who struck the Egyptians
through their firstborn,
For His lovingkindness
endures forever,
11 Then brought Israel out
from their midst,
For His lovingkindness
endures forever,
12 With a strong hand and an
outstretched arm,
For His lovingkindness
endures forever.

13 To Him who divided the
Red Sea in two,
For His lovingkindness
endures forever,
14 And made Israel pass through
the midst of it,
For His lovingkindness
endures forever,
15 But He overthrew Pharaoh and
his army in the Red Sea,
For His lovingkindness
endures forever.

16 To Him who led His people
through the wilderness,
For His lovingkindness
endures forever;

17 To Him who struck great kings,
For His lovingkindness
endures forever,
18 And killed mighty kings,

For His lovingkindness
endures forever:
19 Sihon, king of the Amorites,
For His lovingkindness
endures forever,
20 And Og, king of Bashan,
For His lovingkindness
endures forever,
21 And gave their land as an inheritance,
For His lovingkindness
endures forever,
22 Even an inheritance to
Israel His servant,
For His lovingkindness
endures forever.

23 Who remembered us in our
low estate,
For His lovingkindness
endures forever,
24 And has snatched us from
our adversaries,
For His lovingkindness
endures forever;
25 Who gives food to all flesh,
For His lovingkindness
endures forever.
26 Give thanks to the God of heaven,
For His lovingkindness
endures forever.

Proverbs 29:12–13

12 *If* a ruler pays attention to a lying word,
All his ministers *become* wicked.
13 The poor man and the oppressor
meet together *in this*—
Yahweh gives light to the eyes of both.

2 Peter 2:1–22

2 But false prophets also arose among the
people, just as there will also be false
teachers among you, who will secretly intro-
duce destructive heresies, even denying the
Master who bought them, bringing swift
destruction upon themselves. 2 And many
will follow their sensuality, and because of
them the way of the truth will be maligned.
3 And in *their* greed they will exploit you
with false words, their judgment from long
ago is not idle, and their destruction is not
asleep.
4 For if God did not spare angels who
sinned, but cast them into the pit and deliv-
ered them to chains of darkness, being kept
for judgment; 5 and did not spare the ancient
world, but preserved Noah, a preacher of
righteousness, with seven others, when
He brought a flood upon the world of the
ungodly; 6 and *if* He condemned the cities
of Sodom and Gomorrah to destruction
by reducing *them* to ashes, having made
them an example to those who would
live ungodly *lives* thereafter; 7 and *if* He
rescued righteous Lot, oppressed by the
sensual conduct of unprincipled men 8 (for
by what he saw and heard *that* righteous
man, while living among them, felt *his*
righteous soul tormented day after day by
their lawless deeds), 9 *then* the Lord knows
how to rescue the godly from trial, and to
keep the unrighteous under punishment for
the day of judgment, 10 and especially those
who go after the flesh in *its* corrupt lust and
despise authority.
Daring, self-willed, they do not tremble
when they blaspheme glorious ones,
11 whereas angels who are greater in strength
and power do not bring a reviling judgment
against them before the Lord. 12 But these,
like unreasoning animals, born as creatures
of instinct to be captured and killed, blas-
pheming where they have no knowledge,
will in the destruction of those creatures
also be destroyed, 13 suffering unrighteous-
ness as the wages of *their* unrighteousness,
considering it a pleasure to revel in the
daytime—*they are* stains and blemishes,
reveling in their deceptions, as they feast
with you, 14 having eyes full of adultery
and unceasing sin, enticing unstable souls,
having a heart trained in greed—*they are*
accursed children. 15 Forsaking the right
way, they have gone astray, having followed
the way of Balaam, the *son* of Beor, who
loved the wages of unrighteousness, 16 but
he received a rebuke for his own lawless-
ness, *for* a mute donkey, speaking out with
a voice of a man, restrained the madness of
the prophet.
17 These are springs without water and
mists driven by a storm, for whom the black
darkness has been kept. 18 For speaking
out arrogant *words* of vanity, they entice
by sensual lusts of the flesh, those who
barely escape from the ones who conducted
themselves in error, 19 promising them
freedom while they themselves are slaves of
corruption; for by what a man is overcome,
by this he is enslaved. 20 For if they are over-
come, having *both* escaped the defilements

of the world by the knowledge of the Lord
and Savior Jesus Christ and having again
been entangled in them, *then* the last state
has become worse for them than the first.
21 For it would be better for them not to
have known the way of righteousness, than
having known it, to turn away from the holy
commandment handed on to them. 22 The
message of the true proverb has happened
to them, "A DOG RETURNS TO ITS OWN VOMIT,"
and, "A sow, after washing, *returns* to wal-
lowing in the mire."

DECEMBER 2

Daniel 7:1–8:27

7 In the first year of Belshazzar king
of Babylon Daniel saw a dream and
visions in his head *as he lay* on his bed;
then he wrote the dream down *and* said the
following summary of the matter. 2 Daniel
answered and said, "I was looking in my
vision by night, and behold, the four winds
of heaven were stirring up the great sea.
3 And four great beasts were coming up
from the sea, different from one another.
4 The first *was* like a lion and had *the* wings
of an eagle. I kept looking until its wings
were plucked, and it was lifted up from the
ground and made to stand on two feet like
a man; and a heart of a man was given to it.
5 And behold, another beast, a second one
in the likeness of a bear. And it was raised
up on one side, and three ribs *were* in its
mouth between its teeth; and thus they said
to it, 'Arise, devour much meat!' 6 After this
I kept looking, and behold, another one,
like a leopard, which had on its back four
wings of a bird; the beast also had four
heads, and dominion was given to it. 7 After
this I kept looking in the night visions,
and behold, a fourth beast, fearsome and
terrifying and extraordinarily strong; and
it had large iron teeth. It devoured and
crushed and trampled down the remainder
with its feet; and it was different from all
the beasts that were before it, and it had
ten horns. 8 While I was contemplating the
horns, behold, another horn, a little one,
came up among them, and three of the first
horns were pulled out by the roots before it;
and behold, this horn possessed eyes like
the eyes of a man and a mouth speaking
great *boasts.*

9 "I kept looking
Until thrones were set up,
And the Ancient of Days was seated;
His clothing *was* like white snow
And the hair of His head
like pure wool.
His throne *was* ablaze with fire,
Its wheels *were* a burning fire.
10 "A river of fire was flowing
And coming out from before Him;
Thousands upon thousands
were attending Him,
And myriads upon myriads were
standing before Him;
The court sat,
And the books were opened.

11 "Then I kept looking because of the sound
of the great *boastful* words which the horn
was speaking; I kept looking until the beast
was killed, and its body was destroyed and
given to the burning fire. 12 As for the rest of
the beasts, their dominion was taken away,
but an extension of life was given to them
for an appointed season of time.

13 "I kept looking in the night visions,
And behold, with the clouds of heaven
One like a Son of Man was coming,
And He came up to the Ancient of Days
And came near before Him.
14 "And to Him was given dominion,
Glory, and a kingdom,
That all the peoples, nations,
and *men of every* tongue
Might serve Him.
His dominion is an
everlasting dominion
Which will not be taken away;
And His kingdom is one
Which will not be destroyed.

15 "As for me, Daniel, my spirit was dis-
tressed within me, and the visions of my
head kept alarming me. 16 I came near to one
of those who were standing by and began
seeking out *from* him the exact meaning of
all this. So he said *it* to me and made known
to me the interpretation of these things:
17 'These great beasts, which are four *in
number*, are four kings *who* will arise from
the earth. 18 But the saints of the Highest
One will receive the kingdom and possess
the kingdom forever, for all ages to come.'

19 "Then I desired to know the exact meaning of the fourth beast, which was different from all the others, extraordinarily fearsome, with its teeth of iron and its claws of bronze, *and which* devoured, crushed, and trampled down the remainder with its feet, 20 and *the meaning* of the ten horns that *were* on its head and the other *horn* which came up and before which three *of them* fell, namely, that horn which had eyes and a mouth speaking great *boasts* and which was larger in appearance than its associates. 21 I kept looking, and that horn was waging war with the saints and overcoming them 22 until the Ancient of Days came and judgment was given in favor of the saints of the Highest One, and the season arrived when the saints took possession of the kingdom.

23 "Thus he said: 'The fourth beast will be a fourth kingdom on the earth, which will be different from all the *other* kingdoms and will devour the whole earth and tread it down and crush it. 24 As for the ten horns, out of this kingdom ten kings will arise; and another will arise after them, and he will be different from the previous ones and will make low three kings. 25 He will speak words against the Most High and wear down the saints of the Highest One, and he will intend to make changes in seasons and in law; and they will be given into his hand for a time, times, and half a time. 26 But the court will sit *for judgment*, and his dominion will be taken away, annihilated and destroyed forever. 27 Then the reign, the dominion, and the greatness of *all* the kingdoms under the whole heaven will be given to the people of the saints of the Highest One; His kingdom *will be* an everlasting kingdom, and all the dominions will serve and obey Him.'

28 "At this point the matter *of this revelation* ended. As for me, Daniel, my thoughts were greatly alarming me, and the splendor of my *face* changed, but I kept the matter in my heart."

8 In the third year of the reign of Belshazzar the king, a vision appeared to me, Daniel, after the one which appeared to me previously. 2 And I looked in the vision. And it happened that while I was looking, I was in the citadel of Susa, which is in the province of Elam; and I looked in the vision, and I myself was beside the Ulai Canal. 3 Then I lifted my eyes and looked, and behold, a ram which had two horns was standing in front of the canal. Now the two horns *were* long, but one *was* longer than the other, with the longer one coming up last. 4 I saw the ram butting westward, northward, and southward, and no *other* beasts could stand before it, nor was there anyone to deliver from its power, but it did as it pleased and magnified *itself*.

5 And while I was considering, behold, a male goat was coming from the west over the surface of the whole earth without touching the ground; and the goat *had* a conspicuous horn between its eyes. 6 Then it came up to the ram that had the two horns, which I had seen standing in front of the canal, and ran at it in his strong wrath. 7 And I saw it reach the side of the ram, and it was enraged at it; and it struck the ram and broke its two horns in pieces, and the ram had no strength to stand in opposition to it. So it threw it down to the ground and trampled on it, and there was none to deliver the ram from its power. 8 Then the male goat magnified *itself* exceedingly. But as soon as it was mighty, the large horn was broken; and in its place there came up four conspicuous *horns* toward the four winds of heaven.

9 And out of one of them came forth a rather small horn. And it grew exceedingly great toward the south, toward the east, and toward the Beautiful *Land*. 10 Then it grew up to the host of heaven and caused some of the host and some of the stars to fall to the earth, and it trampled them down. 11 And it even magnified *itself* to be equal with the Commander of the host; and it removed the regular sacrifice from Him, and the place of His sanctuary was thrown down. 12 And on account of transgression the host will be given over *to the horn* along with the regular sacrifice; and it will throw truth down to the ground and do *its will* and succeed. 13 Then I heard a holy one speaking, and another holy one said to that particular one who was speaking, "How long will the vision *about* the regular sacrifice apply, while the transgression causes desolation, so as to allow both the holy place and the host to be trampled?" 14 He said to me, "For 2,300 evenings *and* mornings; then the holy place will be made righteous."

15 Now it happened when I, Daniel, had seen the vision, that I sought to understand it; and behold, standing before me was one

who had the appearance of a man. 16 And I
heard the voice of a man between *the banks
of* Ulai, and he called out and said, "Gabriel,
give this *man* an understanding of what has
appeared." 17 So he came near to where I was
standing, and when he came I was terrified
and fell on my face; but he said to me, "Son
of man, understand that the vision pertains
to the time of the end."
18 Now while he was talking with me, I
sank into a deep sleep with my face to the
ground; but he touched me and made me
stand upright. 19 Then he said, "Behold, I
am going to let you know what will happen
at the final period of the indignation, for
it pertains to the appointed time of the
end. 20 The ram which you saw with the
two horns is the kings of Media and Persia.
21 Now the shaggy goat is the king of Greece,
and the large horn that is between his eyes
is the first king. 22 And the broken *horn* and
the four *horns that* stood in its place *are* four
kingdoms *which* will *take their* stand from
his nation, although not with his power.

23 "In the latter period of their reign,
When the transgressors have
run *their course*,
A king will stand,
Insolent and skilled in intrigue.
24 "His power will be mighty, but
not by his *own* power,
And he will destroy to an
astonishing degree
And succeed and do *his will*;
He will destroy mighty men
and the holy people.
25 "And through his insight
He will cause deceit to
succeed by his hand;
And he will magnify
himself in his heart,
And he will destroy many
while *they are* at ease.
He will even stand against
the Prince of princes,
But he will be broken without hands.
26 "And what had appeared about
the evenings and mornings
Which has been told is true;
But as for you, conceal the vision,
For *it* pertains to many
days *in the future*."

27 Then I, Daniel, was exhausted and sick
for days. Then I rose up *again* and did the
king's work; but I was appalled at what had
appeared, and there was none to make *me*
understand *it*.

Psalm 137:1–6

1 By the rivers of Babylon,
There we sat and also wept,
When we remembered Zion.
2 Upon the willows in the midst of it
We hung our lyres.
3 For there our captors asked us
about the words of a song,
And our tormentors *asked*
joyfully, *saying*,
"Sing for us one of the songs of Zion."

4 How can we sing a song of Yahweh
In a foreign land?
5 If I forget you, O Jerusalem,
May my right hand forget *her skill*.
6 May my tongue cling to the
roof of my mouth
If I do not remember you,
If I do not exalt Jerusalem
Above my chief joy.

Proverbs 29:14

14 If a king judges the poor with truth,
His throne will be established forever.

2 Peter 3:1–18

3 This is now, beloved, the second letter I
am writing to you in which I am stirring
up your sincere mind by way of reminder,
2 that you should remember the words spo-
ken beforehand by the holy prophets and
the commandment of the Lord and Savior
spoken by your apostles, 3 knowing this
first of all, that in the last days mockers will
come with *their* mocking, following after
their own lusts, 4 and saying, "Where is the
promise of His coming? For since the fathers
fell asleep, all continues just as it was from
the beginning of creation." 5 For when they
maintain this, it escapes their notice that by
the word of God *the* heavens existed long
ago and *the* earth was formed out of water
and by water, 6 through which the world
at that time was destroyed, being deluged
with water. 7 But by His word the present
heavens and earth are being reserved for
fire, being kept for the day of judgment and
destruction of ungodly men.
8 But do not let this one *fact* escape your
notice, beloved, that with the Lord one day
is like a thousand years, and a thousand

years like one day. 9 The Lord is not slow about His promise, as some consider slowness, but is patient toward you, not willing for any to perish but for all to come to repentance. 10 But the day of the Lord will come like a thief, in which the heavens will pass away with a roar and the elements will be destroyed with intense heat, and the earth and its works will be found *out*.

11 Since all these things are to be destroyed in this way, what sort of people ought you to be in holy conduct and godliness, 12 looking for and hastening the coming of the day of God, because of which the heavens burning will be destroyed, and the elements will melt with intense heat! 13 But according to His promise we are looking for NEW HEAVENS AND A NEW EARTH, in which righteousness dwells.

14 Therefore, beloved, since you are looking for these things, be diligent to be found by Him in peace, spotless and blameless, 15 and consider the patience of our Lord *as* salvation, just as also our beloved brother Paul, according to the wisdom given him, wrote to you, 16 as also in all *his* letters, speaking in them of these things, in which are some things hard to understand, which the untaught and unstable distort, as *they do* also the rest of the Scriptures, to their own destruction. 17 You therefore, beloved, knowing this beforehand, be on your guard lest you, having been carried away by the error of unprincipled men, fall from your own steadfastness, 18 but grow in the grace and knowledge of our Lord and Savior Jesus Christ. To Him *be* the glory, both now and to the day of eternity. Amen.

The Holy Scriptures require a humble reader who shows reverence and fear toward the Word of God, and constantly says, "teach me, teach me, teach me."

— MARTIN LUTHER

DECEMBER 3

Daniel 9:1–10:21

9 In the first year of Darius the son of Ahasuerus, from the seed of the Medes, who was made king over the kingdom of the Chaldeans— 2 in the first year of his reign, I, Daniel, discerned in the books the number of the years *concerning* which the word of Yahweh came to Jeremiah the prophet for the fulfillment of the laying waste of Jerusalem, *namely*, seventy years. 3 So I gave my face to the Lord God to seek *Him by* prayer and supplications, with fasting, sackcloth, and ashes. 4 And I prayed to Yahweh my God and confessed and said, "Alas, O Lord, the great and awesome God, who keeps His covenant and lovingkindness for those who love Him and keep His commandments, 5 we have sinned and committed iniquity and acted wickedly and rebelled, even turning aside from Your commandments and judgments. 6 Moreover, we have not listened to Your slaves the prophets, who spoke in Your name to our kings, our princes, our fathers, and all the people of the land.

7 "To You, O Lord, belongs righteousness, but to us open shame, as it is this day—to the men of Judah, the inhabitants of Jerusalem, and all Israel, those who are nearby and those who are far away in all the countries to which You have banished them, because of their unfaithful deeds which they have committed against You. 8 O Yahweh, to us belongs open shame, to our kings, our princes, and our fathers, because we have sinned against You. 9 To the Lord our God *belong* compassion and forgiveness, for we have rebelled against Him; 10 nor have we listened to the voice of Yahweh our God, to walk in His laws which He put before us through His slaves the prophets. 11 Indeed all Israel has trespassed against Your law, even turning aside, not listening to Your voice; so the curse has been poured out on us, along with the oath which is written in the law of Moses the servant of God, for we have sinned against Him. 12 Thus He has established His words which He had spoken against us and against our judges

who judged us, to bring on us great calamity;
for under the whole heaven there has not
been done *anything* like what was done to
Jerusalem. 13 As it is written in the law of
Moses, all this calamity has come on us; yet
we have not entreated the favor of Yahweh
our God by turning from our iniquity and
acting wisely in Your truth. 14 Therefore
Yahweh has watched over the calamity
and brought it on us; for Yahweh our God
is righteous with respect to all His deeds
which He has done, but we have not listened
to His voice.

15 "So now, O Lord our God, who have
brought Your people out of the land of Egypt
with a strong hand and have made a name for
Yourself, as it is this day—we have sinned;
we have acted wickedly. 16 O Lord, in accor-
dance with all Your righteousness, let now
Your anger and Your wrath turn away from
Your city Jerusalem, Your holy mountain;
for because of our sins and the iniquities
of our fathers, Jerusalem and Your people
have become a reproach to all those around
us. 17 So now, our God, listen to the prayer
of Your slave and to his supplications, and
for Your sake, O Lord, let Your face shine on
Your desolate sanctuary. 18 O my God, incline
Your ear and listen! Open Your eyes and see
our desolations and the city which is called
by Your name; for we are not presenting our
supplications before You on account of *any*
righteousness of our own, but on account of
Your abundant compassion. 19 O Lord, listen!
O Lord, forgive! O Lord, give heed and take
action! For Your own sake, O my God, do not
delay, because Your city and Your people are
called by Your name."

20 Now while I was speaking and praying,
and confessing my sin and the sin of my peo-
ple Israel, and presenting my supplication
before Yahweh my God in behalf of the holy
mountain of my God, 21 and while I was still
speaking in prayer, then the man Gabriel,
whom I had seen in the vision previously,
touched me in *my* extreme weariness about
the time of the evening offering. 22 Then he
made *me* understand and spoke with me
and said, "O Daniel, I have now come forth
to give you insight with understanding. 23 At
the beginning of your supplications the
word was issued, so I have come to tell *you*,
for you are highly esteemed; so understand
the message and gain understanding in what
has appeared.

24 "Seventy weeks have been determined
for your people and for your holy city, to
finish the transgression, to make an end
of sin, to make atonement for iniquity, to
bring in everlasting righteousness, to seal
up vision and prophecy, and to anoint *the*
Holy of Holies. 25 So you are to know and
have insight *that* from the going out of a
word to restore and rebuild Jerusalem until
Messiah the Prince, *there will be* seven
weeks and sixty-two weeks; it will be
restored and rebuilt, with plaza and moat,
even in times of distress. 26 Then after the
sixty-two weeks the Messiah will be cut off
and have nothing, and the people of the
prince who is to come will destroy the city
and the sanctuary. And its end *will come*
with a flood; even to the end there will be
war; desolations are decreed. 27 And he will
make a firm covenant with the many for one
week, but in the middle of the week he will
make sacrifice and grain offering cease; and
on the wing of abominations *will come* one
who makes desolate, even until a complete
destruction, one that is decreed, is poured
out on the one who makes desolate."

10 In the third year of Cyrus king of
Persia, a word was revealed to Daniel,
who was named Belteshazzar; and the word
was true and *one of* great conflict, but he
understood the word and had an under-
standing of what had appeared.

2 In those days, I, Daniel, had been
mourning for three entire weeks. 3 I did
not eat any tasty food, nor did meat or
wine enter my mouth, nor did I use any
ointment at all until the entire three weeks
were fulfilled.

4 And on the twenty-fourth day of the first
month, while I was by the bank of the great
river, that is, the Tigris, 5 I lifted my eyes and
looked, and behold, there was a certain man
dressed in linen, whose loins were girded
with *a belt of* pure fine gold of Uphaz. 6 His
body also *was* like beryl, his face had the
appearance of lightning, his eyes were like
flaming torches, his arms and feet like the
gleam of burnished bronze, and the sound of
his words like the sound of a multitude. 7 Now
I, Daniel, alone saw the *vision* that appeared,
but the men who were with me did not see
the *vision* that appeared; nevertheless, a
great terror fell on them, and they ran away
to hide themselves. 8 So I alone remained

and saw this great *vision* that appeared; yet
no might remained in me, for my *outward*
splendor turned to a deathly pallor, and I
retained no might. 9 But I heard the sound of
his words; and as soon as I heard the sound
of his words, I fell into a deep sleep on my
face, with my face to the ground.

10 Then behold, a hand touched me and
set me shaking on my hands and knees.
11 And he said to me, "O Daniel, man of
high esteem, understand the words that I
am about to speak to you and stand upright,
for I have now been sent to you." And when
he had spoken this word to me, I stood up
trembling. 12 Then he said to me, "Do not
be afraid, Daniel, for from the first day that
you gave your heart to understand *this*
and to humble yourself before your God,
your words were heard, and I have come *in*
response to your words. 13 But the prince of
the kingdom of Persia was standing against
me for twenty-one days; then behold,
Michael, one of the chief princes, came to
help me. Now I had been left there with
the kings of Persia. 14 Now I have come to
give you an understanding of what will
happen to your people in the last days, for
the vision pertains to the days yet *future*."
15 Now when he had spoken to me according
to these words, I turned my face toward the
ground and became speechless.

16 And behold, one in the likeness of the
sons of men was touching my lips; then I
opened my mouth and spoke and said to him
who was standing before me, "O my lord, as
a result of the *vision* that appeared, pains
have come upon me, and I have retained no
might. 17 Now how can such a servant of my
lord talk with such as my lord? As for me,
right now no might stands within me, nor
does any breath remain within me."

18 Then *this* one with the appearance of
a man touched me again and strengthened
me. 19 And he said, "O man of high esteem,
do not be afraid. Peace be with you; gather
strength and be strong!" Now as soon as he
spoke to me, I received strength and said,
"May my lord speak, for you have strengthened me."
20 Then he said, "Do you know
why I came to you? But I shall now return
to fight against the prince of Persia; so I
am going forth, and behold, the prince of
Greece is about to come. 21 However, I will
tell you what is inscribed in the writing
of truth. Now there is no one who exerts
strength with me against these *forces* except
Michael your prince.

Psalm 137:7–9

7 Remember, O Yahweh, against
the sons of Edom
The day of Jerusalem,
Who said, "Tear it down! Tear it down
To its very foundation."
8 O daughter of Babylon,
you devastated one,
How blessed will be the
one who repays you
With the recompense with which
you have recompensed us.
9 How blessed will be the one who
seizes and dashes your infants
Against the cliff.

Proverbs 29:15

15 The rod and reproof give wisdom,
But a child left *to himself* brings
shame to his mother.

1 John 1:1–10

1 What was from the beginning, what we
have heard, what we have seen with our
eyes, what we beheld and touched with our
hands, concerning the Word of Life— 2 and
the life was manifested, and we have seen
and bear witness and proclaim to you the
eternal life, which was with the Father and
was manifested to us— 3 what we have seen
and heard we proclaim to you also, so that
you may also have fellowship with us; and
indeed our fellowship is with the Father, and
with His Son Jesus Christ. 4 And these things
we are writing, so that our joy may be made
complete.

5 And this is the message we have heard
from Him and declare to you, that God is
Light, and in Him there is no darkness at
all. 6 If we say that we have fellowship with
Him and *yet* walk in the darkness, we lie and
do not do the truth; 7 but if we walk in the
Light as He Himself is in the Light, we have
fellowship with one another, and the blood
of Jesus His Son cleanses us from all sin.
8 If we say that we have no sin, we deceive
ourselves and the truth is not in us. 9 If we
confess our sins, He is faithful and righteous
to forgive us our sins and to cleanse us from
all unrighteousness. 10 If we say that we have
not sinned, we make Him a liar and His word
is not in us.

DECEMBER 4

Daniel 11:1–12:13

11 “Now I, in the first year of Darius the
Mede, I stood to strengthen and to be
a fortress for him. 2 So now I will tell you the
truth. Behold, three more kings are going
to stand in Persia. Then a fourth will gain
far more riches than all *of them*; as soon as
he becomes strong through his riches, he
will arouse the whole *empire* against the
kingdom of Greece. 3 And a mighty king will
stand, and he will dominate with great dom-
ination and do as he pleases. 4 But as soon
as he stands, his kingdom will be broken up
and parceled out toward the four winds of
heaven, but not to his *own* descendants, nor
according to his domination with which he
dominated, for his kingdom will be uprooted
and *given* to others besides them.
5 “Then the king of the South will grow
strong, along with *one* of his princes who will
grow strong over him and obtain dominion;
indeed, his domain *will be* a great dominion.
6 And after some years they will form an
alliance, and the daughter of the king of the
South will come to the king of the North to
carry out an equitable arrangement. But she
will not retain her position of power, nor
will he *continue to* stand with his power, but
she will be given up, along with those who
brought her in and the one who fathered her
as well as he who strengthened her in *those*
times. 7 But one of the descendants of her
line will stand in his place, and he will come
against *their* military force and enter the
fortress of the king of the North, and he will
deal with them and display strength. 8 And
also their gods with their metal images *and*
their desirable vessels of silver and gold he
will bring into captivity to Egypt, and he on
his part will stand *back* from *attacking* the
king of the North for *some* years. 9 Then the
latter will enter the kingdom of the king of
the South, but will return to his *own* land.
10 “And his sons will wage war. So they will
gather a multitude of great forces; and one
of them will keep on coming and overflow
and pass through, that he may again wage
war up to his *very* fortress. 11 And the king of
the South will be enraged and go forth and
fight with the king of the North. Then the
latter will cause a great multitude to stand,
but *that* multitude will be given into the
hand of the *former*. 12 Then the multitude
will be carried away, his heart will be lifted
up, and he will cause tens of thousands to
fall; yet he will not prevail. 13 And the king
of the North will again cause a much *greater*
multitude than the former to stand, and at
the end of the times of *those* years, he will
keep on coming with a great military force
and much equipment.
14 “Now in those times many will stand
against the king of the South; the violent
ones among your people will also lift
themselves up in order to cause the vision
to stand, but they will fall down. 15 Then the
king of the North will come, cast up a siege
ramp, and capture a well-fortified city; and
the might of the South will not stand, not
even their choicest troops, for there will be
no strength to make a stand. 16 But he who
comes against him will do as he pleases, and
no one will *be able to* stand in opposition
to him; he will also stand *for a time* in the
Beautiful Land, with destruction in his
hand. 17 And he will set his face to come
with the authority of his whole kingdom,
bringing with him an equitable proposal
which he will put into effect; he will also
give him the daughter of women to destroy
it. But she will not take a stand *for him* or
be on his side. 18 Then he will turn his face
to the coastlands and capture many. But a
ruler will make his reproach against him
cease; moreover, he will repay him for his
reproach. 19 So he will turn his face toward
the fortresses of his own land, but he will
stumble and fall and be found no more.
20 “Then in his place one will stand who
will have an oppressor pass through the
Jewel of *his* kingdom; yet within a few days
he will be broken, though not in anger nor
in battle. 21 And in his place a despised
person will stand, to whom the splendor of
the kingdom has not been given, but he will
come in a time of ease and take hold of the
kingdom by intrigue. 22 But the overflowing
might will be flooded away before him and
broken, and also the prince of the covenant.
23 And after an alliance is made with him,
he will practice deception, and he will go
up and gain power with a small *force of*
people. 24 In a time of ease he will enter the
richest *parts* of the province, and he will do

what his fathers never did, nor his fathers' fathers; he will distribute plunder, spoil, and possessions among them, and he will devise his schemes against strongholds, but *only* for a time. 25 And he will stir up his strength and heart against the king of the South with a great military force; so the king of the South will wage war with an extremely large and mighty military force for war; but he will not stand, for schemes will be devised against him. 26 And those who eat his choice food will break him, and his military force will overflow, but many will fall down slain. 27 And as for both kings, their hearts will be *intent* on evil, and they will speak falsehood at the same table; but it will not succeed, for the end is still *to come* at the appointed time. 28 Then he will return to his land with great possessions; but his heart will be *set* against the holy covenant, and he will take action and *then* return to his *own* land.

29 "At the appointed time he will return and come into the South, but this last time it will not happen the way it did before. 30 Indeed, ships of Kittim will come against him; therefore he will be disheartened and will return and become indignant at the holy covenant and take action; so he will come back and show regard for those who forsake the holy covenant. 31 Mighty forces from him will stand, profane the sanctuary fortress, and abolish the regular sacrifice. And they will set up the abomination of desolation. 32 And by smooth *words* he will turn to godlessness those who act wickedly toward the covenant, but the people who know their God will display strength and take action. 33 And those who have insight among the people will give understanding to the many; yet they will fall by sword and by flame, by captivity and by plunder for *many* days. 34 Now when they fall, they will be granted a little help, and many will join with them in intrigue. 35 And some of those who have insight will fall, in order to refine, purge, and make them pure until the time of the end, because *it is* still *to come* at the appointed time.

36 "Then the king will do as he pleases, and he will exalt and magnify himself above every god and will speak astonishing things against the God of gods; and he will succeed until the indignation is finished, for that which is decreed will be done. 37 He will show no regard for the gods of his fathers or for the desire of women, nor will he show regard for any *other* god; for he will magnify himself above *them* all. 38 But instead he will honor a god of fortresses, a god whom his fathers did not know; he will honor *him* with gold, silver, costly stones, and desirable things. 39 And he will take action against the strongest of fortresses with *the help of* a foreign god; he will give great honor to those who recognize *him* and will cause them to rule over the many and will apportion land for a price.

40 "And at the time of the end, the king of the South will collide with him, and the king of the North will storm against him with chariots, with horsemen, and with many ships; and he will enter lands, overflow *them*, and pass through. 41 And he will also enter the Beautiful Land, and many *countries* will fall; but these will be rescued out of his hand: Edom, Moab, and the foremost of the sons of Ammon. 42 Then he will send forth his hand against *other* countries, and the land of Egypt will not escape. 43 But he will rule over the hidden treasures of gold and silver and over all the desirable things of Egypt; and Libyans and Ethiopians *will follow* at his heels. 44 But reports from the East and from the North will dismay him, and he will go forth with great wrath to destroy and devote many to destruction. 45 And he will pitch the tents of his royal pavilion between the seas and the beautiful Holy Mountain; yet he will come to his end, and no one will help him.

12 "Now at that time, Michael, the great prince who stands *guard* over the sons of your people, will stand. And there will be a time of distress such as never happened since there was a nation until that time; and at that time your people, everyone who is found written in the book, will be rescued. 2 And many of those who sleep in the dust of the ground will awake, these to everlasting life, but the others to reproach *and* everlasting contempt. 3 And those who have insight will shine brightly like the brightness of the expanse *of heaven*, and those who lead the many to righteousness, like the stars forever and ever. 4 But as for you, Daniel, conceal these words and seal up the book until the time of the end; many will go to and fro, and knowledge will increase."

5 Then I, Daniel, looked, and behold, two others were standing, one on this bank of

the river and the other on that bank of the river. 6 And one said to the man dressed in linen, who was above the waters of the river, "How long *will it be* until the end of *these* wonders?" 7 And I heard the man dressed in linen, who was above the waters of the river, as he raised his right hand and his left toward heaven, and swore by Him who lives forever that it would be for a time, times, and half *a time*; and as soon as they complete shattering the power of the holy people, all these *events* will be completed. 8 As for me, I heard but could not understand; so I said, "My lord, what *will be* the outcome of these *events*?" 9 Then he said, "Go *your way*, Daniel, for *these* words are concealed and sealed up until the time of the end. 10 Many will be purged, purified, and refined, but the wicked will act wickedly; and none of the wicked will understand, but those who have insight will understand. 11 But from the time that the regular sacrifice is abolished and the abomination of desolation is set up, *there will be* 1,290 days. 12 How blessed is he who keeps waiting and reaches the 1,335 days! 13 But as for you, go *your way* to the end; then you will enter into rest and stand *again* for your allotted portion at the end of the days."

Psalm 138:1–3

1 I will give You thanks with all my heart;
I will sing praises to You
before the gods.
2 I will worship toward Your holy temple
And give thanks to Your name for Your
lovingkindness and Your truth;
For You have magnified Your word
according to all Your name.
3 On the day I called, You answered me;
You made me bold with
strength in my soul.

Proverbs 29:16

16 When the wicked increase,
transgression increases;
But the righteous will see their fall.

1 John 2:1–29

2 My little children, I am writing these things to you so that you may not sin. And if anyone sins, we have an Advocate with the Father, Jesus Christ the righteous; 2 and He Himself is the propitiation for our sins, and not for ours only, but also for *those of* the whole world.

3 And by this we know that we have come to know Him, if we keep His commandments. 4 The one who says, "I have come to know Him," and does not keep His commandments, is a liar, and the truth is not in him; 5 but whoever keeps His word, truly in him the love of God has been perfected. By this we know that we are in Him: 6 the one who says he abides in Him ought himself to walk in the same manner as He walked.

7 Beloved, I am not writing a new commandment to you, but an old commandment which you have had from the beginning; the old commandment is the word which you have heard. 8 On the other hand, I am writing a new commandment to you, which is true in Him and in you, because the darkness is passing away and the true Light is already shining. 9 The one who says he is in the Light and *yet* hates his brother is in the darkness until now. 10 The one who loves his brother abides in the Light and there is no cause for stumbling in him. 11 But the one who hates his brother is in the darkness and walks in the darkness, and does not know where he is going because the darkness blinded his eyes.

12 I am writing to you, little children, because your sins have been forgiven you for His name's sake. 13 I am writing to you, fathers, because you have known Him who has been from the beginning. I am writing to you, young men, because you have overcome the evil one. I have written to you, children, because you have known the Father. 14 I have written to you, fathers, because you have known Him who has been from the beginning. I have written to you, young men, because you are strong, and the word of God abides in you, and you have overcome the evil one.

15 Do not love the world nor the things in the world. If anyone loves the world, the love of the Father is not in him. 16 For all that is in the world, the lust of the flesh and the lust of the eyes and the boastful pride of life, is not from the Father, but is from the world. 17 And the world is passing away, and *also* its lusts, but the one who does the will of God abides forever.

18 Children, it is the last hour; and just as you heard that antichrist is coming, even now many antichrists have appeared. From this we know that it is the last hour. 19 They went out from us, but they were not *really*

of us; for if they were of us, they would have remained with us; but *they went out*, so that it would be manifested that they all are not of us. 20 But you have an anointing from the Holy One, and you all know. 21 I have not written to you because you do not know the truth, but because you do know it, and because no lie is of the truth. 22 Who is the liar but the one who denies that Jesus is the Christ? This is the antichrist, the one who denies the Father and the Son. 23 Everyone who denies the Son does not have the Father; the one who confesses the Son has the Father also. 24 As for you, let that which you heard from the beginning abide in you. If what you heard from the beginning abides in you, you also will abide in the Son and in the Father. 25 And this is the promise which He Himself made to us: eternal life.

26 These things I have written to you about those who are trying to deceive you. 27 And as for you, the anointing whom you received from Him abides in you, and you have no need for anyone to teach you. But as His anointing teaches you about all things, and is true and is not a lie, and just as He has taught you, abide in Him.

28 And now, little children, abide in Him, so that when He is manifested, we may have confidence and not shrink away from Him in shame at His coming. 29 If you know that He is righteous, you know that everyone also who does righteousness has been born of Him.

DECEMBER 5

Hosea 1:1–2:23

1 The word of Yahweh which came to Hosea the son of Beeri, in the days of Uzziah, Jotham, Ahaz, *and* Hezekiah, kings of Judah, and in the days of Jeroboam the son of Joash, king of Israel.

2 When Yahweh first spoke through Hosea, Yahweh said to Hosea, "Go, take for yourself a wife of harlotry and *have* children of harlotry; for the land commits flagrant harlotry, forsaking Yahweh." 3 So he went and took Gomer the daughter of Diblaim, and she conceived and gave birth to a son for him. 4 And Yahweh said to him, "Name him Jezreel; for yet a little while, and I will visit the bloodshed of Jezreel upon the house of Jehu, and I will cause the kingdom of the house of Israel to cease. 5 And it will be in that day, that I will break the bow of Israel in the valley of Jezreel."

6 Then she conceived again and gave birth to a daughter. And Yahweh said to him, "Name her Lo-ruhamah, for I will no longer have compassion on the house of Israel, that I would ever forgive them. 7 But I will have compassion on the house of Judah and save them by Yahweh their God, and I will not save them by bow, sword, battle, horses, or horsemen."

8 Then she weaned Lo-ruhamah. And she conceived and gave birth to a son. 9 And Yahweh said, "Name him Lo-ammi, for you are not My people, and I am not your God."

10 Yet the number of the sons of Israel
Will be like the sand of the sea,
Which cannot be measured
or numbered;
And it will be that in the place
Where it is said to them,
"You are not My people,"
It will be said to them,
"*You are* the sons of the living God."
11 And the sons of Judah and the sons
of Israel will be gathered together,
And they will set for
themselves one head,
And they will go up from the land,
For great will be the day of Jezreel.

2 Say to your brothers, "Ammi," and to your sisters, "Ruhamah."

2 "Contend with your mother, contend,
For she is not my wife,
and I am not her husband;
And let her remove her
harlotry from her face
And her adultery from
between her breasts,
3 Lest I strip her naked
And set her forth as on the
day when she was born
And make her like a wilderness
And make her like dry land
And put her to death with thirst.
4 "Also, I will have no compassion
on her children
Because they are children of harlotry.

5 “For their mother has played the harlot;
She who conceived them
has acted shamefully.
For she said, ‘I will go after my lovers,
Who give *me* my bread and my water,
My wool and my flax, my
oil and my drink.’
6 “Therefore, behold, I will hedge
up her way with thorns,
And I will build a wall against her so
that she cannot find her paths.
7 “So she will pursue her lovers, but
she will not overtake them;
And she will seek them, but
will not find *them*.
Then she will say, ‘I will go, and I
will return to my first husband,
For it was better for me then than now!’

8 “Now she does not know that it
was I who gave her the grain,
the new wine, and the oil,
And multiplied silver and gold for her,
Which they used for Baal.
9 “Therefore, I will take back My
grain at harvest time
And My new wine in its season.
I will also deliver My wool
and My flax *from them*
Given to cover her nakedness.
10 “So now I will uncover her lewdness
In the sight of her lovers,
And no one will deliver her
out of My hand.
11 “I will also cease all her joy,
Her feasts, her new moons,
her sabbaths,
And all her appointed times.
12 “And I will make desolate her
vines and fig trees,
Of which she said, ‘These are my wages
Which my lovers have given me.’
And I will make them a forest,
And the beasts of the field
will devour them.
13 “So I will visit the days of
the Baals upon her
When she used to offer *offerings*
in smoke to them
And adorn herself with her
earrings and jewelry
And go after her lovers, so that she
forgot Me,” declares Yahweh.
14 “Therefore, behold, I will allure her
And bring her into the wilderness
And speak to her heart.
15 “Then I will give her her
vineyards from there
And the valley of Achor
as a door of hope.
And she will sing there as in
the days of her youth,
As in the day when she came up
from the land of Egypt.
16 “And it will be in that day,”
declares Yahweh,
“*That* you will call Me Ishi
And will no longer call Me Baali.
17 “So I will remove the names of
the Baals from her mouth
So that they will be remembered
by their names no more.
18 “And in that day I will cut a
covenant for them
With the beasts of the field,
The birds of the sky,
And the creeping things of the ground.
And I will break the bow, the
sword, and war from the land,
And I will make them lie
down in security.
19 “And I will betroth you to Me forever;
Indeed, I will betroth you to Me in
righteousness and in justice,
In lovingkindness and in compassion,
20 And I will betroth you to
Me in faithfulness.
Then you will know Yahweh.

21 “And it will be in that day, *that* I will
answer,” declares Yahweh.
“I will answer the heavens, and
they will answer the earth,
22 And the earth will answer the grain,
the new wine, and the oil,
And they will answer Jezreel.
23 “And I will sow her for
Myself in the land.
I will also have compassion on her
who had not obtained compassion,
And I will say to those who
were not My people,
‘You are My people!’
And they will say, ‘*You are* my God!’”

Psalm 138:4–6

4 All the kings of the earth, O Yahweh,
will give You thanks,
When they hear the words
of Your mouth.

5 And they will sing of the ways of Yahweh,
For great is the glory of Yahweh.
6 For Yahweh is high,
Yet He sees the lowly,
But the one who exalts *himself*
He knows from afar.

Proverbs 29:17

17 Discipline your son, and he
will give you rest;
And he will give delight to your soul.

1 John 3:1–24

3 See how great a love the Father has given
to us, that we would be called children
of God; and we are. For this reason the world
does not know us, because it did not know
Him. 2 Beloved, now we are children of God,
and it has not been manifested as yet what
we will be. We know that when He is mani-
fested, we will be like Him, because we will
see Him just as He is. 3 And everyone who
has this hope *fixed* on Him purifies himself,
just as He is pure.
4 Everyone who does sin also does law-
lessness; and sin is lawlessness. 5 And you
know that He was manifested in order to
take away sins, and in Him there is no sin.
6 No one who abides in Him sins; no one who
sins has seen Him or has come to know Him.
7 Little children, let no one deceive you. The
one who does righteousness is righteous,
just as He is righteous. 8 The one who does
sin is of the devil, because the devil sins
from the beginning. The Son of God was
manifested for this purpose, to destroy the
works of the devil. 9 Everyone who has been
born of God does not sin, because His seed
abides in him; and he cannot sin, because
he has been born of God. 10 By this the
children of God and the children of the devil
are manifested: everyone who does not do
righteousness is not of God, as well as the
one who does not love his brother.
11 For this is the message which you have
heard from the beginning, that we should
love one another; 12 not as Cain, *who* was
of the evil one and slew his brother. And
for what reason did he slay him? Because
his deeds were evil, and his brother's were
righteous.
13 Do not marvel, brothers, if the world
hates you. 14 We know that we have passed
out of death into life, because we love the
brothers. The one who does not love abides
in death. 15 Everyone who hates his brother
is a murderer, and you know that no mur-
derer has eternal life abiding in him. 16 By
this we have known love, that He laid down
His life for us; and we ought to lay down our
lives for the brothers. 17 But whoever has
the world's goods, and sees his brother in
need and closes his heart against him, how
does the love of God abide in him? 18 Little
children, let us not love with word or with
tongue, but in deed and truth. 19 And by
this we will know that we are of the truth,
and will assure our heart before Him 20 in
whatever our heart condemns us; for God is
greater than our heart and knows all things.
21 Beloved, if our heart does not condemn
us, we have confidence before God; 22 and
whatever we ask we receive from Him,
because we keep His commandments and
do the things that are pleasing in His sight.
23 And this is His commandment, that we
believe in the name of His Son Jesus Christ,
and love one another, just as He gave a com-
mandment to us. 24 And the one who keeps
His commandments abides in Him, and He
in him. We know by this that He abides in
us, by the Spirit whom He gave us.

DECEMBER 6

Hosea 3:1–4:19

3 Then Yahweh said to me, "Go again, love
a woman *who* is loved by *her* compan-
ion and is an adulteress, even as Yahweh
loves the sons of Israel, though they turn
to other gods and love raisin cakes." 2 So
I bargained for her for myself for fifteen
shekels of silver and a homer and a half of
barley. 3 Then I said to her, "You shall stay
with me for many days. You shall not play
the harlot, nor shall you have a man; so I
will also be toward you." 4 For the sons of
Israel will remain for many days without
king or prince, without sacrifice or *sacred*
pillar, and without ephod or household
idols. 5 Afterward the sons of Israel will
return and seek Yahweh their God and
David their king; and they will come in
dread to Yahweh and to His goodness in
the last days.

4 Listen to the word of Yahweh,
O sons of Israel,
For Yahweh has a contention against
the inhabitants of the land,
Because there is no truth
or lovingkindness
Or knowledge of God in the land.
2 *There is* swearing of oaths, deception,
murder, stealing, and adultery.
They break forth *in violence* so that
bloodshed follows bloodshed.
3 Therefore the land mourns,
And everyone who inhabits it languishes
Along with the beasts of the field
and the birds of the sky,
And also the fish of the sea disappear.

4 Yet let no man contend, and
let no man offer reproof;
Indeed, your people are like those
who contend with the priest.
5 So you will stumble by day,
And the prophet also will
stumble with you by night;
And I will destroy your mother.
6 My people are destroyed for
lack of knowledge.
Because you have rejected knowledge,
I also will reject you from
ministering as My priest.
Since you have forgotten
the law of your God,
I Myself also will forget your children.

7 The more they multiplied, the
more they sinned against Me;
I will change their glory into disgrace.
8 They eat the sin of My people
And lift up their soul toward
their iniquity.
9 And it will be like people, like priest;
So I will punish them for their ways
And cause their deeds to
return to them.
10 They will eat, but not be satisfied;
They will play the harlot, but
not break forth *in number*,
Because they have forsaken
Yahweh to keep *harlotry*.

11 Harlotry, wine, and new wine
take away a heart *of wisdom*.
12 My people ask their wooden
idol, and their *diviner's*
wand declares to them;
For a spirit of harlotry has
led *them* astray,
And they have played the harlot,
departing from their God.
13 They offer sacrifices on the
tops of the mountains
And burn incense on the hills,
Under oak, poplar, and terebinth
Because their shade is good.
Therefore your daughters
play the harlot,
And your brides commit adultery.
14 I will not punish your daughters
when they play the harlot
Or your brides when they
commit adultery,
For *the men* themselves go
apart with harlots
And offer sacrifices with
cult prostitutes;
So the people without
understanding are ruined.

15 Though you, Israel, play the harlot,
Do not let Judah become guilty;
Also do not go to Gilgal
Nor go up to Beth-aven
And swear the oath:
"As Yahweh lives!"
16 Since Israel is stubborn
Like a stubborn heifer,
Can Yahweh now feed them
Like a lamb in a large field?
17 Ephraim is joined to idols;
Let him alone.
18 Their drink gone;
They play the harlot continually;
Their rulers dearly love disgrace.
19 The wind binds them up
in its wings,
And they will be ashamed
because of their sacrifices.

Psalm 138:7–8

7 Though I walk in the midst of
distress, You will revive me;
You will stretch forth Your hand
against the wrath of my enemies,
And Your right hand will save me.
8 Yahweh will accomplish
what concerns me;
O Yahweh, Your lovingkindness
endures forever;
Do not fail the works of
Your hands.

Proverbs 29:18

18 Where there is no vision, the
people are out of control,
But how blessed is he who
keeps the law.

1 John 4:1–21

4 Beloved, do not believe every spirit,
but test the spirits to see whether they
are from God, because many false prophets
have gone out into the world. 2 By this you
know the Spirit of God: every spirit that
confesses that Jesus Christ has come in the
flesh is from God, 3 and every spirit that
does not confess Jesus is not from God. This
is the *spirit* of the antichrist, of which you
have heard that it is coming, and now it is
already in the world. 4 You are from God,
little children, and have overcome them;
because greater is He who is in you than
he who is in the world. 5 They are from the
world; therefore they speak *as* from the
world, and the world hears them. 6 We are
from God. The one who knows God hears us;
the one who is not from God does not hear
us. From this we know the spirit of truth and
the spirit of error.

7 Beloved, let us love one another, for
love is from God; and everyone who loves
has been born of God and knows God. 8 The
one who does not love does not know God,
because God is love. 9 By this the love of God
was manifested in us, that God has sent His
only begotten Son into the world so that we
might live through Him. 10 In this is love, not
that we have loved God, but that He loved
us and sent His Son *to be* the propitiation
for our sins. 11 Beloved, if God so loved us,
we also ought to love one another. 12 No one
has beheld God at any time; if we love one
another, God abides in us, and His love is
perfected in us. 13 By this we know that we
abide in Him and He in us, because He has
given us of His Spirit. 14 We have beheld and
bear witness that the Father has sent the
Son *to be* the Savior of the world.

15 Whoever confesses that Jesus is the
Son of God, God abides in him, and he in
God. 16 And we have come to know and
have believed the love which God has in
us. God is love, and the one who abides in
love abides in God, and God abides in him.
17 By this, love has been perfected with us,
so that we may have confidence in the day
of judgment, because as He is, so also are
we in this world. 18 There is no fear in love;
but perfect love casts out fear, because fear
involves punishment, and the one who fears
is not perfected in love. 19 We love, because
He first loved us. 20 If someone says, "I love
God," and hates his brother, he is a liar;
for the one who does not love his brother
whom he has seen, cannot love God whom
he has not seen. 21 And this commandment
we have from Him, that the one who loves
God should love his brother also.

DECEMBER 7

Hosea 5:1–6:11

5 Hear this, O priests!
Give heed, O house of Israel!
Give ear, O house of the king!
For the judgment is for you,
For you have been a snare at Mizpah
And a net spread out on Tabor.
2 And the revolters have dug
deep into slaughtering,
But I will chastise all of them.
3 I know Ephraim, and Israel is
not hidden from Me;
For now, O Ephraim, you
have played the harlot;
Israel has defiled itself.
4 Their deeds will not allow them
To return to their God.
For a spirit of harlotry is within them,
And they do not know Yahweh.
5 Moreover, the pride of Israel
answers against him,
And Israel and Ephraim
stumble in their iniquity;
Judah also has stumbled
with them.
6 They will go with their
flocks and herds
To seek Yahweh, but they
will not find *Him*;
He has withdrawn from them.
7 They have dealt treacherously
against Yahweh,
For they have borne children
of strangers.
Now the new moon will devour
them with their portions.

8 Blow the horn in Gibeah,
The trumpet in Ramah.
Make a loud shout at Beth-aven:
"Behind you, Benjamin!"
9 Ephraim will become a desolation
in the day of reproof;
Among the tribes of Israel I will
make known what is true.
10 The princes of Judah have become
like those who move a boundary;
On them I will pour out My
wrath like water.
11 Ephraim is oppressed,
crushed in judgment,
Because he was determined to
walk after *man's* command.
12 Therefore I am like a moth
to Ephraim
And like rottenness to the
house of Judah.
13 Then Ephraim saw his sickness,
And Judah his sore,
So Ephraim went to Assyria
And sent to King Jareb.
But he is unable to heal you
Or to cure you of your sore.
14 For I *will be* like a lion to Ephraim
And like a young lion to
the house of Judah.
I, even I, will tear to pieces
and go away;
I will carry away, and there
will be none to deliver.
15 I will go away *and* return to My place
Until they acknowledge their
guilt and seek My face;
In their affliction they will
seek Me earnestly.

6 "Come, let us return to Yahweh.
For He has torn *us*, but He will heal us;
He has struck *us*, but He
will bandage us.
2 "He will make us alive after two days;
He will raise us up on the third day,
That we may live before Him.
3 "So let us know, let us pursue
to know Yahweh.
His going forth is established
as the dawn;
And He will come to us like the rain,
Like the late rain watering the earth."

4 What shall I do with you, O Ephraim?
What shall I do with you, O Judah?
For your lovingkindness is
like a morning cloud
And like the dew which
goes away early.
5 Therefore I have hewn *them* in
pieces by the prophets;
I have killed them by the
words of My mouth;
And the judgments on you are
like the light that goes forth.
6 For I delight in lovingkindness
rather than sacrifice,
And in the knowledge of God
rather than burnt offerings.
7 But like Adam they have trespassed
against the covenant;
There they have dealt
treacherously against Me.
8 Gilead is a city of workers
of iniquity,
With a track of blood.
9 And as raiders wait for a man,
So a band of priests murder
on the way to Shechem;
Surely they have committed
lewdness.
10 In the house of Israel I have
seen an appalling thing;
Ephraim's harlotry is there;
Israel has defiled itself.
11 Also, O Judah, there is a
harvest set for you
When I restore the fortunes
of My people,

Psalm 139:1–6

1 O Yahweh, You have searched
me and known *me*.
2 You know when I sit down
and when I rise up;
You understand my thought
from afar.
3 You scrutinize my path and
my lying down,
And are intimately acquainted
with all my ways.
4 Even before there is a word
on my tongue,
Behold, O Yahweh, You know it all.
5 You have enclosed me
behind and before,
And You have put Your hand upon me.
6 *Such* knowledge is too
wonderful for me;
It is *too* high, I cannot attain to it.

Proverbs 29:19

19 A slave will not be corrected
by words *alone*;
For though he understands,
there will be no answer.

1 John 5:1–21

5 Everyone who believes that Jesus is the Christ has been born of God, and everyone who loves the One who gives *new* birth loves also the one who has been born of Him. 2 By this we know that we love the children of God, when we love God and do His commandments. 3 For this is the love of God, that we keep His commandments; and His commandments are not burdensome. 4 For everything that has been born of God overcomes the world; and this is the overcoming that has overcome the world—our faith.

5 Who is the one who overcomes the world, but he who believes that Jesus is the Son of God? 6 This is the One who came by water and blood, Jesus Christ; not with the water only, but with the water and with the blood. It is the Spirit who bears witness, because the Spirit is the truth. 7 For there are three that bear witness: 8 the Spirit and the water and the blood; and the three are in agreement. 9 If we receive the witness of men, the witness of God is greater; for the witness of God is this, that He has borne witness about His Son. 10 The one who believes in the Son of God has this witness in himself. The one who does not believe God has made Him a liar, because he has not believed in the witness which God has borne witness about His Son. 11 And the witness is this, that God gave us eternal life, and this life is in His Son. 12 He who has the Son has the life; he who does not have the Son of God does not have that life.

13 These things I have written to you who believe in the name of the Son of God, so that you may know that you have eternal life. 14 And this is the confidence which we have before Him, that, if we ask anything according to His will, He hears us. 15 And if we know that He hears us *in* whatever we ask, we know that we have the requests which we have asked from Him.

16 If anyone sees his brother committing a sin not *leading* to death, he shall ask and *God* will for him give life to those who commit sin not *leading* to death. There is a sin *leading* to death; I do not say that he should make request for this. 17 All unrighteousness is sin, and there is a sin not *leading* to death.

18 We know that no one who has been born of God sins; but He who was begotten of God keeps him, and the evil one does not touch him. 19 We know that we are of God, and that the whole world lies in *the power of* the evil one. 20 And we know that the Son of God has come, and has given us understanding so that we may know Him who is true; and we are in Him who is true, in His Son Jesus Christ. This is the true God and eternal life.

21 Little children, guard yourselves from idols.

DECEMBER 8

Hosea 7:1–8:14

7 When I would heal Israel,
Then the iniquity of Ephraim
is uncovered,
And the evil deeds of Samaria,
For they work falsehood;
The thief enters in;
Raiders ransack outside,
2 And they do not say to their hearts
That I remember all their evil.
Now their deeds are all around them;
They are before My face.
3 With their evil they make the king glad,
And the princes with their deceptions.
4 They are all adulterers,
Like an oven heated by the baker
Who ceases to stir up *the fire*
From the kneading of the dough
until it is leavened.
5 On the day of our king, the princes
became sick with the heat of wine;
He stretched out his hand
with scoffers,
6 For their hearts are like an oven
As they draw near in their plotting;
Their anger smolders all night;
In the morning it burns
like a flaming fire.
7 All of them are hot like an oven,
And they devour their judges;
All their kings have fallen.
None of them calls on Me.

8 Ephraim mixes himself
with the peoples;
Ephraim has become a
cake not turned.
9 Strangers devour his power,
Yet he does not know *it*;
Gray hairs also are sprinkled on him,
Yet he does not know *it*.
10 So the pride of Israel
answers against him,
Yet they have not returned
to Yahweh their God,
Nor have they sought Him, for all this.
11 So Ephraim has become like a silly
dove, without a heart *of wisdom*;
They call to Egypt; they go to Assyria.
12 When they go, I will spread
My net over them;
I will bring them down like
the birds of the sky.
I will chastise them in accordance with
the report to their congregation.
13 Woe to them, for they
have fled from Me!
Destruction is theirs, for they have
transgressed against Me!
And I would redeem them, but
they speak lies against Me.
14 And they do not cry out to
Me in their heart
When they wail on their beds;
For the sake of grain and new wine
they gather together as sojourners;
They depart from Me.
15 Although I disciplined *and*
strengthened their arms,
Yet they devise evil against Me.
16 They turn, *but* not upward;
They are like a deceitful bow;
Their princes will fall by the sword
Because of the indignation
of their tongue.
This *will be* their scoffing
in the land of Egypt.

8 *Put* the trumpet to your mouth!
Like an eagle *the enemy comes*
against the house of Yahweh
Because they have trespassed
against My covenant
And transgressed against My law.
2 They cry out to Me,
"My God, we of Israel know You!"
3 Israel has rejected the good;
The enemy will pursue him.
4 They have set up kings,
but not by Me;
They have appointed princes,
but I did not know *it*.
With their silver and gold they have
made idols for themselves,
That they might be cut off.
5 He has rejected your calf,
O Samaria, *saying*,
"My anger burns against them!"
How long will they be
incapable of innocence?
6 For from Israel is even this!
A craftsman made it,
so it is not God;
Surely the calf of Samaria will
be smashed to splinters.
7 For they sow the wind,
And they reap the whirlwind.
The standing grain has no growth;
It makes no flour.
Should it make *anything*, strangers
would swallow it up.

8 Israel is swallowed up;
They are now among the nations
Like a vessel in which
no one delights.
9 For they have gone up to Assyria
Like a wild donkey all alone;
Ephraim has hired lovers.
10 Even though they hire *allies*
among the nations,
Now I will gather them up;
And they will begin to diminish
Because of the burden of
the king of princes.

11 Since Ephraim has multiplied
altars for sin,
They have become altars
of sinning for him.
12 Though I wrote for him ten
thousand *precepts* of My law,
They are counted as a strange thing.
13 As for My sacrificial gifts,
They sacrifice the flesh and eat *it*,
But Yahweh has not accepted them.
Now He will remember their iniquity
And punish *them* for their sins;
They will return to Egypt.
14 So Israel has forgotten his
Maker and built palaces;
And Judah has multiplied
fortified cities,

But I will send a fire on its
cities that it may consume
its palatial dwellings.

Psalm 139:7–12

7 Where can I go from Your Spirit?
Or where can I flee from
Your presence?
8 If I ascend to heaven, You are there;
If I make my bed in Sheol,
behold, You are there.
9 If I lift up the wings of the dawn,
If I dwell in the remotest
part of the sea,
10 Even there Your hand will lead me,
And Your right hand will
lay hold of me.
11 If I say, "Surely the darkness
will bruise me,
And the light around me will
be night,"
12 Even the darkness is not
too dark for You,
And the night is as bright as the day.
Darkness and light are alike *to You.*

Proverbs 29:20

20 Do you behold a man who is
hasty in his words?
There is more hope for a
fool than for him.

2 John 1–13

1 The elder to the elect lady and her
children, whom I love in truth, and not
only I, but also all who know the truth, 2 for
the sake of the truth which abides in us and
will be with us forever: 3 Grace, mercy, *and*
peace will be with us, from God the Father
and from Jesus Christ, the Son of the Father,
in truth and love.
4 I rejoiced greatly to find *some* of your
children walking in truth, just as we received
commandment from the Father. 5 Now I
ask you, lady, not as though *I were* writing
to you a new commandment, but the one
which we have had from the beginning, that
we love one another. 6 And this is love, that
we walk according to His commandments.
This is the commandment, just as you have
heard from the beginning, that you should
walk in it.
7 For many deceivers have gone out
into the world, those who do not confess
Jesus Christ *as* coming in the flesh. This
is the deceiver and the antichrist. 8 See to
yourselves, that you do not lose what we
accomplished, but that you may receive a
full reward. 9 Anyone who goes too far and
does not abide in the teaching of Christ,
does not have God. The one who abides in
the teaching, he has both the Father and the
Son. 10 If anyone comes to you and does not
bring this teaching, do not receive him into
your house, and do not give him a greeting,
11 for the one who gives him a greeting
participates in his evil deeds.
12 Though I have many things to write to
you, I do not want to *do so* with paper and
ink; but I hope to come to you and speak
face to face, so that your joy may be made
complete.
13 The children of your elect sister greet
you.

DECEMBER 9

Hosea 9:1–10:15

9 Do not be glad, O Israel, with
rejoicing like the peoples!
For you have played the harlot,
forsaking your God.
You have loved *harlots'* earnings
on every threshing floor.
2 Threshing floor and wine press
will not feed them,
And the new wine will
deceive them.
3 They will not remain in the
land of Yahweh,
But Ephraim will return to Egypt,
And in Assyria they will
eat unclean *food.*
4 They will not pour out drink
offerings of wine to Yahweh;
Their sacrifices will not please Him.
Their bread will be like
mourners' bread;
All who eat of it will be defiled,
For their bread will be for
themselves *alone*;
It will not enter the house of Yahweh.
5 What will you do on the day
of the appointed festival
And on the day of the feast of Yahweh?

6 For behold, they will go
because of destruction;
Egypt will gather them up;
Memphis will bury them.
Weeds will possess their
desirable items of silver;
Thorns *will be* in their tents.
7 The days of punishment have come;
The days of recompense have come;
Let Israel know *this*!
The prophet is an ignorant fool,
The inspired man has madness,
Because of the abundance
of your iniquity
And *because* your hostility
has abounded.
8 Ephraim *was* a watchman with
my God, a prophet;
Yet the snare of a bird catcher
is in all his ways,
And there is *only* hostility in
the house of his God.
9 They have dug deep in corruption
As in the days of Gibeah;
He will remember their iniquity;
He will punish their sins.
10 I found Israel like grapes
in the wilderness;
I saw your fathers as the earliest fruit
on the fig tree in its first *season*.
But they came to Baal-peor and
devoted themselves to shame,
And they became as detestable
as that which they loved.
11 As for Ephraim, their glory will
fly away like a bird—
No birth, no pregnancy,
and no conception!
12 Though they bring up their children,
Yet I will bereave them until
not a man is left.
Surely, woe to them indeed
when I depart from them!
13 Ephraim, as I have seen,
Is planted in a pasture like Tyre;
But Ephraim will bring out
his children for killing.
14 Give them, O Yahweh—
what will You give?
Give them a miscarrying
womb and dry breasts.

15 All their evil is at Gilgal;
Indeed, I came to hate them there!
Because of the evil of their deeds
I will drive them out of My house!
I will love them no more;
All their princes are rebels.
16 Ephraim is stricken; their
root is dried up;
They will bear no fruit.
Even though they bear children,
I will put to death the desirable
ones of their womb.
17 My God will despise them
Because they have not listened
to Him;
And they will be those who
flee among the nations.

10 Israel is a luxuriant vine;
He produces fruit for himself.
The more abundant his fruit,
The more altars he abounded;
The better his land,
The better he made the *sacred* pillars.
2 Their heart is faithless;
Now they must bear their guilt.
Yahweh will break down their altars
And destroy their *sacred* pillars.

3 Surely now they will say,
"We have no king,
For we do not fear Yahweh.
As for the king, what can he do for us?"
4 They speak *mere* words;
With worthless oaths they
cut covenants;
And judgment flourishes like gall
in the furrows of the field.
5 The dweller of Samaria will fear
For the calf of Beth-aven.
Indeed, its people will mourn for it,
And its idolatrous priests
will cry out over it,
Over its glory, since it has gone
into exile from them.
6 The thing itself will be
carried to Assyria
As tribute to King Jareb;
Ephraim will receive shame,
And Israel will be ashamed
of its own counsel.
7 Samaria will be ruined *with* her king
Like a stick on the surface of the water.
8 Also the high places of Aven, the
sin of Israel, will be eradicated;
Thorn and thistle will grow
on their altars;

Then they will say to the mountains,
"Cover us!" And to the hills,
"Fall on us!"
9 From the days of Gibeah you
have sinned, O Israel;
There they stand!
Will not the battle against the sons of
injustice overtake them in Gibeah?
10 When it is My desire, I will
chastise them;
And the peoples will be
gathered against them
When they are bound for
their double guilt.
11 And Ephraim is a trained heifer
that loves to thresh,
But I will come over her fair
neck *with a yoke*;
I will harness Ephraim;
Judah will plow; Jacob will
harrow for himself.
12 Sow with a view to righteousness,
Reap in accordance with
lovingkindness;
Break up your fallow ground,
Indeed, it is time to seek Yahweh
Until He comes and rains
righteousness on you.
13 You have plowed wickedness;
you have reaped injustice;
You have eaten the fruit of deception.
Because you have trusted in your
way, in your abundant warriors,
14 Therefore a rumbling will arise
among your people,
And all your fortifications
will be destroyed,
As Shalman destroyed Beth-
arbel on the day of battle,
When mothers were dashed in
pieces with *their* children.
15 Thus it will be done to you at Bethel
because of your evil of evils.
At dawn the king of Israel will
be completely ruined.

Psalm 139:13–16

13 For You formed my inward parts;
You wove me in my mother's womb.
14 I will give thanks to You, for I am
fearfully and wonderfully made;
Wonderful are Your works,
And my soul knows it very well.
15 My frame was not hidden from You,
When I was made in secret,
And intricately woven in the
depths of the earth;
16 Your eyes have seen my
unshaped substance;
And in Your book all of
them were written
The days that were formed *for me*,
When as yet there was
not one of them.

Proverbs 29:21

21 He who pampers his slave
from childhood
Will in the end find him to
be arrogant.

3 John 1–15

1 The elder to the beloved Gaius, whom I
love in truth.
2 Beloved, I pray that in all respects you
may prosper and be in good health, just as
your soul prospers. 3 For I rejoiced greatly
when brothers came and bore witness to
your truth, *that is*, how you are walking in
truth. 4 I have no greater joy than this, to
hear that my children are walking in the
truth.
5 Beloved, you are acting faithfully in
whatever work you do for the brothers, and
are doing this *though they are* strangers;
6 and they bore witness to your love before
the church. You will do well to send them
on their way in a manner worthy of God.
7 For they went out for the sake of the
Name, receiving nothing from the Gentiles.
8 Therefore we ought to support such men,
so that we may be fellow workers with the
truth.
9 I wrote something to the church, but
Diotrephes, who loves to be first among
them, does not welcome what we say. 10 For
this reason, if I come, I will bring to remem-
brance his deeds which he does, unjustly
disparaging us with wicked words. And
not satisfied with this, he himself does not
welcome the brothers either, and he forbids
those who want *to do so* and puts *them* out
of the church.
11 Beloved, do not imitate what is evil,
but what is good. The one who does good
is of God; the one who does evil has not
seen God. 12 Demetrius has received a *good*
witness from everyone, and from the truth
itself; and we add our witness, and you
know that our witness is true.

[13] I had many things to write to you, but
I am not willing to write *them* to you with
pen and ink; [14] but I hope to see you shortly,
and we will speak face to face.

[15] Peace *be* to you. The friends greet you.
Greet the friends by name.

Nothing can possibly compare with or make up for, daily definite study of and meditation on the Word of God.

— W. H. GRIFFITH THOMAS

DECEMBER 10

Hosea 11:1–12:14

11 When Israel *was* a youth I loved him,
And out of Egypt I called My son.
2 The more they called them,
The more they went from them;
They kept sacrificing to the Baals
And burning incense to graven images.
3 Yet it is I who taught Ephraim to walk;
I took them in My arms;
But they did not know that
I healed them.
4 I led them with cords of a man,
with bonds of love,
And I became to them as one who
lifts the yoke from their jaws;
And I bent down *and* fed them.

5 They will not return to
the land of Egypt;
But Assyria—he will be their king
Because they refused to return *to Me.*
6 And the sword will whirl
against their cities
And will consume their gate bars
And devour *them* because
of their counsels.
7 So My people are hung up
on turning from Me.
Though they call them to
the One on high,
None at all exalts *Him.*

8 How can I give you up, O Ephraim?
How can I surrender you, O Israel?
How can I give you over
to be like Admah?
How can I make you like Zeboiim?
My heart is turned over within Me;
All My compassions are stirred.
9 I will not execute My burning anger;
I will not make Ephraim a ruin again.
For I am God and not man, the
Holy One in your midst,
And I will not come in wrath.
10 They will walk after Yahweh;
He will roar like a lion;
Indeed, He will roar,
And *His* sons will come
trembling from the west.
11 They will come trembling
like birds from Egypt
And like doves from the
land of Assyria;
And I will settle them in their
houses, declares Yahweh.

12 Ephraim surrounds Me with lies
And the house of Israel with deceit;
And Judah is also unruly against God,
Even against the Holy One
who is faithful.

12 Ephraim feeds on wind
And pursues the east
wind continually;
He abounds in falsehood
and destruction.
Moreover, he cuts a covenant
with Assyria,
And oil is carried to Egypt.
2 And Yahweh has a contention
with Judah
And will punish Jacob
according to his ways;
He will cause *everything* to return
to him according to his deeds.
3 In the womb he took his
brother by the heel,
And in his maturity he
wrestled with God.

4 Indeed, he wrestled with the
angel and prevailed;
He wept and sought His favor.
He found Him at Bethel,
And there He spoke with us,
5 Even Yahweh, the God of hosts,
Yahweh is His *name* of remembrance.
6 Therefore, return to your God,
Keep lovingkindness and justice,
And hope in your God continually.
7 A merchant, in whose hands
are deceptive balances,
He loves to oppress.
8 And Ephraim said, "Surely
I have become rich;
I have found wealth for myself;
In all my labors they will find in me
No iniquity, which *would be* sin."
9 But I *have been* Yahweh your God
since the land of Egypt;
I will make you settle in tents again,
As in the days of the appointed festival.
10 And I have spoken to the prophets,
And I made visions abound,
And by the hand of the
prophets I gave parables.
11 Is there wickedness *in* Gilead?
Surely they are worthless.
In Gilgal they sacrifice bulls;
Yes, their altars are like the stone heaps
Beside the furrows of the field.

12 Now Jacob fled to the field of Aram,
And Israel worked for a wife,
And for a wife he kept *sheep*.
13 But by a prophet Yahweh brought
Israel up from Egypt,
And by a prophet he was kept.
14 Ephraim has provoked to bitter anger;
So his Lord will leave his
bloodguilt on him
And cause his reproach
to return to him.

Psalm 139:17–24

17 How precious are Your
thoughts to me, O God!
How vast is the sum of them!
18 If I should count them, they
would outnumber the sand.
When I awake, I am still with You.

19 Oh that You would slay the
wicked, O God!
O men of bloodshed, depart from me.
20 For they speak against You wickedly,
And Your enemies take
Your name in vain.
21 Do I not hate those who
hate You, O Yahweh?
And do I not revile those who
rise up against You?
22 I hate them with the utmost hatred;
They have become my enemies.

23 Search me, O God, and know my heart;
Try me and know my
anxious thoughts;
24 And see if there be any
hurtful way in me,
And lead me in the everlasting way.

Proverbs 29:22

22 An angry man stirs up strife,
And a hot-tempered man
abounds in transgression.

Jude 1–25

1 Jude, a slave of Jesus Christ, and brother of James,
To those who are the called, beloved in God the Father, and kept for Jesus Christ:
2 May mercy and peace and love be multiplied to you.
3 Beloved, while I was making every effort to write you about our common salvation, I felt the necessity to write to you exhorting that you contend earnestly for the faith which was once for all handed down to the saints.
4 For certain persons have crept in unnoticed, those who were long beforehand marked out for this condemnation, ungodly persons who turn the grace of our God into sensuality and deny our only Master and Lord, Jesus Christ.
5 Now I want to remind you, though you know all things, that Jesus, having once saved a people out of the land of Egypt, subsequently destroyed those who did not believe.
6 And angels who did not keep their own domain, but abandoned their proper abode, He has kept in eternal bonds under darkness for the judgment of the great day,
7 just as Sodom and Gomorrah and the cities around them, having indulged in the same way as these in gross sexual immorality and having gone after strange flesh, are exhibited as an example in undergoing the punishment of eternal fire.
8 Yet in the same way these men, also by dreaming, defile the flesh, and reject

authority, and blaspheme glorious ones.
9 But Michael the archangel, when he,
disputing with the devil, was arguing about
the body of Moses, did not dare pronounce
against him a blasphemous judgment, but
said, "The Lord rebuke you!" 10 But these
men blaspheme the things which they do
not understand; and the things which they
know by instinct, like unreasoning animals,
by these things they are destroyed. 11 Woe to
them! For they have gone the way of Cain,
and for pay they have poured themselves
into the error of Balaam, and perished in the
rebellion of Korah. 12 These are the men who
are hidden reefs in your love feasts when
they feast with you without fear, caring for
themselves; clouds without water, carried
along by winds; autumn trees without
fruit, doubly dead, uprooted; 13 wild waves
of the sea, casting up their own shame like
foam; wandering stars, for whom the black
darkness has been reserved forever.

14 But Enoch, *in* the seventh *generation*
from Adam, also prophesied about these
men, saying, "Behold, the Lord came with
many thousands of His holy ones, 15 to
execute judgment upon all, and to convict
all the ungodly of all their ungodly deeds
which they have done in an ungodly way,
and of all the harsh things which ungodly
sinners have spoken against Him." 16 These
are grumblers, finding fault, following after
their *own* lusts; and their mouth speaks
arrogantly, flattering people for the sake of
their own benefit.

17 But you, beloved, must remember the
words that were spoken beforehand by the
apostles of our Lord Jesus Christ, 18 that they
were saying to you, "In the last time there
will be mockers, following after their own
ungodly lusts." 19 These are the ones who
cause divisions, worldly-minded, not having
the Spirit. 20 But you, beloved, building your-
selves up on your most holy faith, praying
in the Holy Spirit, 21 keep yourselves in the
love of God, waiting for the mercy of our
Lord Jesus Christ to eternal life. 22 And on
some, who are doubting, have mercy; 23 and
for others, save, snatching them out of the
fire; and on others have mercy with fear,
hating even the tunic polluted by the flesh.

24 Now to Him who is able to keep you
from stumbling, and to make you stand in
the presence of His glory blameless with
great joy, 25 to the only God our Savior,
through Jesus Christ our Lord, *be* glory,
majesty, might, and authority, before all
time and now and forever. Amen.

DECEMBER 11

Hosea 13:1–14:9

13 When Ephraim spoke,
there was trembling.
He lifted himself up in Israel,
But through Baal he became
guilty and died.
2 And now they sin more and more
And make for themselves
molten images,
Idols *made* from their silver according
to their understanding,
All of them the work of craftsmen.
They are saying of them,
"Let the men who sacrifice
kiss the calves!"
3 Therefore they will be like
the morning cloud
And like dew which soon
disappears,
Like chaff which is blown away
from the threshing floor
And like smoke from a chimney.
4 Yet I *have been* Yahweh your God
Since the land of Egypt;
And you were not to know
any god except Me,
And there is no savior besides Me.
5 I Myself knew you in
the wilderness,
In the land of drought.
6 As *they had* their pasture, then
they became satisfied,
Indeed, they were satisfied, and
their heart became raised up;
Therefore they forgot Me.
7 So I will be like a lion to them;
Like a leopard I will lie in
wait by the wayside.
8 I will encounter them like a
bear robbed of her cubs,
And I will tear open the chest
enclosing their heart;
There I will also devour
them like a lioness,

As a beast of the field would
rip them open.

9 *It is* your ruin, O Israel,
That *you are* against Me,
against your help.
10 Where now is your king,
That he may save you in all your cities,
And your judges of whom you said,
"Give me a king and princes"?
11 I gave you a king in My anger
And took him away in My wrath.

12 The iniquity of Ephraim is bound up;
His sin is stored up.
13 The pains of childbirth
come upon him;
He is not a wise son,
For it is not the time that he should
delay at the opening of the womb.
14 Shall I ransom them from
the power of Sheol?
Shall I redeem them from death?
O Death, where are your thorns?
O Sheol, where is your sting?
Compassion will be hidden
from My sight.
15 Though he is fruitful among the reeds,
An east wind will come,
The wind of Yahweh coming
up from the wilderness;
And his fountain will become dry,
And his spring will be dried up;
It will plunder *his* treasury of
every desirable article.
16 Samaria will be held guilty,
For she has rebelled against her God.
They will fall by the sword;
Their infants will be dashed in pieces,
And their pregnant women
will be ripped open.

14 Return, O Israel, to
Yahweh your God,
For you have stumbled in your iniquity.
2 Take words with you and
return to Yahweh.
Say to Him, "Forgive all iniquity
And take *what is* good,
That we may pay in full the
fruit of our lips.
3 "Assyria will not save us;
We will not ride on horses,
Nor will we say again, 'Our god,'
To the work of our hands;
For in You the orphan
finds compassion."

4 I will heal their turning away
from Me;
I will love them freely,
For My anger has turned
away from them.
5 I will be like the dew to Israel;
He will flourish like the lily,
And he will take root like *the*
cedars of Lebanon.
6 His shoots will go forth,
And his splendor will be
like the olive tree
And his fragrance like *the*
cedars of Lebanon.
7 Those who live in his shadow
Will again raise grain,
And they will flourish like the vine.
His *name of* remembrance *will*
be like the wine of Lebanon.

8 O Ephraim, what more have
I to do with idols?
It is I who answer and look after you.
I am like a luxuriant cypress;
From Me comes your fruit.

9 Whoever is wise, so let him
discern these things;
Whoever is discerning,
let him know them.
For the ways of Yahweh are right,
And the righteous will walk in them,
But transgressors will stumble in them.

Psalm 140:1–5

1 Rescue me, O Yahweh, from evil men;
Guard me from violent men
2 Who think up evil things
in *their* hearts;
They continually stir up wars.
3 They sharpen their tongues
as a serpent;
Poison of an asp is under
their lips. Selah.

4 Keep me, O Yahweh, from the
hands of the wicked;
Guard me from violent men
Who give thought to trip up my steps.
5 The proud have hidden a trap
for me, and cords;

They have spread a net by the wayside;
They have set snares for me. Selah.

Proverbs 29:23

23 A man's lofty pride will bring him low,
But a lowly spirit will take
hold of glory.

Revelation 1:1–20

1 The Revelation of Jesus Christ, which God
gave Him to show to His slaves the things
which must soon happen; and He indicated
this by sending *it* through His angel to His
slave John, 2 who bore witness to the word
of God and to the witness of Jesus Christ,
even to all that he saw. 3 Blessed is he who
reads and those who hear the words of the
prophecy and keep the things which are
written in it, for the time is near.
4 John to the seven churches that are in
Asia: Grace to you and peace, from the One
who is and who was and who is to come, and
from the seven Spirits who are before His
throne, 5 and from Jesus Christ, the faithful
witness, the firstborn of the dead, and the
ruler of the kings of the earth. To Him who
loves us and released us from our sins by
His blood— 6 and He has made us *to be* a
kingdom, priests to His God and Father—to
Him *be* the glory and the might forever and
ever. Amen. 7 BEHOLD, HE IS COMING WITH
THE CLOUDS, and EVERY EYE WILL SEE HIM,
EVEN THOSE WHO PIERCED HIM; and all the
tribes of the earth will MOURN OVER HIM.
Yes, amen.
8 "I am the Alpha and the Omega," says
the Lord God, "who is and who was and who
is to come, the Almighty."
9 I, John, your brother and fellow partaker
in the tribulation and kingdom and perse-
verance *which are* in Jesus, was on the island
called Patmos because of the word of God
and the witness of Jesus. 10 I was in the Spirit
on the Lord's day, and I heard behind me a
loud voice like a trumpet, 11 saying, "Write
in a scroll what you see, and send *it* to the
seven churches: to Ephesus and to Smyrna
and to Pergamum and to Thyatira and to
Sardis and to Philadelphia and to Laodicea."
12 Then I turned to see the voice that
was speaking with me. And having turned
I saw seven golden lampstands; 13 and in the
middle of the lampstands *I saw* one like a
son of man, clothed in a robe reaching to
the feet, and girded across His chest with
a golden sash. 14 And His head and His hair
were white like white wool, like snow; and
His eyes were like a flame of fire. 15 His feet
were like burnished bronze, when it has
been made to glow in a furnace, and His
voice *was* like the sound of many waters,
16 and having in His right hand seven stars,
and a sharp two-edged sword which comes
out of His mouth, and His face was like the
sun shining in its power.
17 And when I saw Him, I fell at His feet
like a dead man. And He placed His right
hand on me, saying, "Do not fear; I am the
first and the last, 18 and the living One; and
I was dead, and behold, I am alive forever
and ever, and I have the keys of death and of
Hades. 19 Therefore write the things which
you have seen, and the things which are,
and the things which will take place after
these things. 20 As for the mystery of the
seven stars which you saw in My right hand,
and the seven golden lampstands: the seven
stars are the angels of the seven churches,
and the seven lampstands are the seven
churches.

DECEMBER 12

Joel 1:1–3:21

1 The word of Yahweh that came to Joel,
the son of Pethuel:

2 Hear this, O elders,
And give ear, all inhabitants of the land.
Has *anything like* this
happened in your days
Or in your fathers' days?
3 Recount about it to your sons,
And *let* your sons *recount*
about it to their sons,
And their sons to the next
generation.

4 What the gnawing locust has left, the
swarming locust has consumed;
And what the swarming locust has left,
the creeping locust has consumed;
And what the creeping locust has left,
the stripping locust has consumed.
5 Awake, drunkards, and weep;
And wail, all you wine drinkers,

On account of the sweet wine
That is cut off from your mouth.
6 For a nation has come up
against my land,
Mighty and without number;
Its teeth are the teeth of a lion,
And it has the fangs of a lioness.
7 It has made my vine a desolation
And my fig tree splinters.
It has stripped them bare
and cast *them* away;
Their branches have become white.

8 Wail like a virgin girded with sackcloth
For the bridegroom of her youth.
9 The grain offering and the
drink offering are cut off
From the house of Yahweh.
The priests mourn,
The ministers of Yahweh.
10 The field is destroyed;
The land mourns,
For the grain is destroyed,
The new wine dries up,
Fresh oil fails.
11 Be ashamed, O farmers,
Wail, O vinedressers,
For the wheat and the barley,
Because the harvest of the field perishes.
12 The vine dries up,
And the fig tree fails;
The pomegranate, the palm
also, and the apple tree,
All the trees of the field dry up.
Indeed, rejoicing dries up
From the sons of men.
13 Gird yourselves *with sackcloth*
And lament, O priests;
Wail, O ministers of the altar!
Come, spend the night in sackcloth,
O ministers of my God;
For the grain offering and
the drink offering
Are withheld from the
house of your God.
14 Set apart a fast as holy,
Call for a solemn assembly;
Gather the elders
And all the inhabitants of the land
To the house of Yahweh your God,
And cry out to Yahweh.
15 Alas for the day!
For the day of Yahweh is near,
And it will come as destruction
from the Almighty.
16 Has not food been cut off
before our eyes,
Gladness and joy from the
house of our God?
17 The seeds shrivel under their clods;
The storehouses are desolate;
The barns are pulled down,
For the grain is dried up.
18 How the beasts groan!
The herds of cattle wander aimlessly
Because there is no pasture for them;
Even the flocks of sheep suffer.
19 To You, O Yahweh, I cry;
For fire has consumed the
pastures of the wilderness,
And the flame has burned up
all the trees of the field.
20 Even the beasts of the
field pant for You;
For the water brooks are dried up,
And fire has consumed the
pastures of the wilderness.

2 Blow a trumpet in Zion,
And make a loud shout on
My holy mountain!
Let all the inhabitants of
the land tremble,
For the day of Yahweh is coming;
Surely it is near,
2 A day of darkness and
thick darkness,
A day of clouds and dense gloom.
As the dawn is spread over
the mountains,
So there is a numerous and
mighty people;
There has never been *anything* like it,
Nor will there be again after it
For the years from generation
to generation.
3 A fire consumes before them,
And behind them a flame burns.
The land is like the garden
of Eden before them
But a desolate wilderness behind them,
And nothing at all escapes them.
4 Their appearance is like the
appearance of horses;
And like war horses, so they run.
5 With a noise as of chariots
They leap on the tops of
the mountains,
Like the crackling of a flame of
fire consumes the stubble,

Like a mighty people
arranged for battle.
6 Before them the peoples are writhing;
All faces turn pale.
7 They run like mighty men;
They climb up the wall like men of war;
And they each march in line,
And they do not deviate
from their paths.
8 They do not crowd each other;
They march everyone in his path;
When they fall against the
defending weapons,
They do not break ranks.
9 They rush on the city;
They run on the wall;
They climb up into the houses;
They enter through the
windows like a thief.
10 Before them the earth trembles;
The heavens quake;
The sun and the moon grow dark,
And the stars lose their brightness.
11 But Yahweh gives forth His voice
before His military force;
Surely His camp is very numerous,
For mighty is he who does His word.
The day of Yahweh is indeed
great and very awesome,
And who can endure it?
12 "Yet even now," declares Yahweh,
"Return to Me with all your heart
And with fasting, weeping,
and wailing;
13 And tear your heart and
not your garments."
Now return to Yahweh your God,
For He is gracious and compassionate,
Slow to anger, abounding
in lovingkindness,
And relenting concerning evil.
14 Who knows whether He will
not turn and relent
And leave a blessing behind Him,
Even a grain offering and
a drink offering
For Yahweh your God?
15 Blow a trumpet in Zion,
Set apart a fast as holy, call
for a solemn assembly,
16 Gather the people, set apart
the congregation as holy,
Assemble the elders,
Gather the infants and the
nursing babies.
Let the bridegroom come
out of his room
And the bride out of her
bridal chamber.
17 Let the priests, the ministers
of Yahweh,
Weep between the porch and the altar,
And let them say, "Pity Your people,
O Yahweh,
And do not make Your
inheritance a reproach,
A byword among the nations.
Why should they among
the peoples say,
'Where is their God?'"
18 Then Yahweh will be
zealous for His land
And will spare His people.
19 Then Yahweh will answer
and say to His people,
"Behold, I am going to send you
grain, new wine, and oil,
And you will be satisfied
in full with them;
And I will never again make you a
reproach among the nations.
20 "But I will remove the northern
military force far from you,
And I will drive it into a parched
and desolate land,
And its vanguard into the eastern sea,
And its rear guard into the western sea.
And its stench will rise up, and
its foul smell will rise up,
For it has done great things."

21 Do not fear, O land, rejoice and be glad,
For Yahweh has done great things.
22 Do not fear, beasts of the field,
For the pastures of the wilderness
have turned green,
For the tree has borne its fruit;
The fig tree and the vine have
yielded their full force.
23 So rejoice, O sons of Zion,
And be glad in Yahweh your God,
For He has given you the early
rain in righteousness.
And He has poured down
for you the rain,
The early and late rains as before.
24 The threshing floors will
be full of grain,
And the vats will overflow with
the new wine and oil.

25 “Then I will pay back to you
in full for the years
That the swarming locust
has consumed,
The creeping locust, the stripping
locust, and the gnawing locust,
My great military force which
I sent among you.
26 “And you will have plenty to
consume and be satisfied
And praise the name of
Yahweh your God,
Who has dealt wondrously
with you;
Then My people will never
be put to shame.
27 “Thus you will know that I am
in the midst of Israel,
And that I am Yahweh your God,
And there is no other;
And My people will never
be put to shame.
28 “And it will be afterwards
That I will pour out My Spirit
on all mankind;
And your sons and your
daughters shall prophesy;
Your old men will dream dreams;
Your young men will see visions.
29 “Even on the male slaves
and female slaves
I will in those days pour out My Spirit.
30 “And I will put wonders in the
sky and on the earth,
Blood, fire, and columns of smoke.
31 “The sun will be turned into darkness
And the moon into blood
Before the great and awesome
day of Yahweh comes.
32 “And it will be that everyone who
calls on the name of Yahweh
Will be delivered;
For on Mount Zion and in Jerusalem
There will be those who escape,
As Yahweh has said,
Even among the survivors
whom Yahweh calls.

3 “For behold, in those days
and at that time,
When I restore the fortunes
of Judah and Jerusalem,
2 I will gather all the nations
And bring them down to the
valley of Jehoshaphat.
Then I will enter into judgment
with them there
On behalf of My people and
My inheritance, Israel,
Whom they have scattered
among the nations;
And they have divided up My land.
3 “They have also cast lots for My people,
Traded a boy for a harlot,
And sold a girl for wine that
they may drink.

4 “Moreover, what are you to Me, O Tyre,
Sidon, and all the regions of Philistia? Are
you rendering Me a recompense? But if you
do recompense Me, swiftly and speedily I
will return your recompense on your head.
5 Since you have taken My silver and My
gold, brought My desirable treasures to
your temples, 6 and sold the sons of Judah
and the sons of Jerusalem to the sons of the
Greeks in order to remove them far from
their borders, 7 behold, I am going to rouse
them from the place where you have sold
them and return your recompense on your
head. 8 Also I will sell your sons and your
daughters into the hand of the sons of Judah,
and they will sell them to the Sabeans, to
a distant nation,” for Yahweh has spoken.

9 Call out this *message*
among the nations:
Set *yourselves* apart for a war;
rouse the mighty men!
Let all the men of war approach,
let them come up!
10 Beat your plowshares into swords
And your pruning hooks into spears;
Let the weak say, “I am a mighty man.”
11 Hasten and come, all you
surrounding nations,
And gather yourselves.
There, bring down, O Yahweh,
Your mighty ones.
12 Let the nations be roused up
And come up to the valley
of Jehoshaphat,
For there I will sit to judge
All the surrounding nations.
13 Send in the sickle, for the
harvest is ripe.
Come, tread, for the wine press is full;
The vats overflow, for their evil is great.
14 Multitudes, multitudes in
the valley of decision!
For the day of Yahweh is near
in the valley of decision.

15 The sun and moon grow dark,
And the stars lose their brightness.
16 And Yahweh roars from Zion
And gives forth His voice
from Jerusalem,
And the heavens and the earth quake.
But Yahweh is a refuge for His people
And a strong defense to
the sons of Israel.
17 Then you will know that I
am Yahweh your God,
Dwelling in Zion, My holy mountain.
So Jerusalem will be holy,
And strangers will pass
through it no more.
18 And it will be in that day,
That the mountains will
drip with sweet wine,
And the hills will flow with milk,
And all the brooks of Judah
will flow with water;
And a spring will go out from
the house of Yahweh
To water the valley of Shittim.
19 Egypt will become a desolation,
And Edom will become a
desolate wilderness,
Because of the violence done
to the sons of Judah,
In whose land they have
shed innocent blood.
20 But Judah will be inhabited forever
And Jerusalem from generation
to generation.
21 And I will avenge their blood
which I have not avenged,
Indeed, Yahweh dwells in Zion.

Psalm 140:6–13

6 I said to Yahweh, "You are my God;
Give ear, O Yahweh, to the voice
of my supplications.
7 "O Yahweh, O Lord, the strength
of my salvation,
You have covered my head
in the day of battle.
8 "Do not grant, O Yahweh,
the desires of the wicked;
Do not promote his *evil* scheme,
that they *not* be exalted. Selah.
9 "As for the head of those
who surround me,
May the trouble *from* their
lips cover them.
10 "May burning coals be shaken
out upon them;
May He cause them to fall into the fire,
Into bottomless pits from which
they can never rise.
11 "May a slanderer not be
established in the earth;
May evil hunt the violent
man speedily."

12 I know that Yahweh will maintain
the cause for the afflicted
And judgment for the needy.
13 Surely the righteous will give
thanks to Your name;
The upright will abide in
Your presence.

Proverbs 29:24

24 He who divides *the spoil* with a
thief hates his own soul;
He hears the oath but declares nothing.

Revelation 2:1–29

2 "To the angel of the church in Ephesus
write:
This is what the One who holds the seven
stars in His right hand, the One who walks
among the seven golden lampstands, says:
2 'I know your deeds and your toil and
perseverance, and that you cannot bear
with those who are evil, and you put to the
test those who call themselves apostles,
and they are not, and you found them *to
be* false; 3 and you have perseverance and
have endured for My name's sake, you also
have not grown weary. 4 But I have *this*
against you, that you have left your first
love. 5 Therefore remember from where
you have fallen, and repent and do the deeds
you did at first. But if not, I am coming to
you and will remove your lampstand out
of its place, unless you repent. 6 Yet this
you do have, that you hate the deeds of the
Nicolaitans, which I also hate. 7 He who has
an ear, let him hear what the Spirit says to
the churches. To him who overcomes, I will
grant to eat of the tree of life which is in the
Paradise of God.'
8 "And to the angel of the church in
Smyrna write:
This is what THE FIRST AND THE LAST, who
was dead, and has come to life, says:
9 'I know your tribulation and your pov-
erty (but you are rich), and the blasphemy by

those who say they are Jews and are not, but
are a synagogue of Satan. 10 Do not fear what
you are about to suffer. Behold, the devil is
about to cast some of you into prison, so that
you will be tested, and you will have tribula-
tion for ten days. Be faithful until death, and I
will give you the crown of life. 11 He who has
an ear, let him hear what the Spirit says to
the churches. He who overcomes will never
be hurt by the second death.'

12 "And to the angel of the church in
Pergamum write:

This is what the One who has the sharp
two-edged sword says:

13 'I know where you dwell, where Satan's
throne is; and you hold fast My name, and
did not deny My faith even in the days of
Antipas, My witness, My faithful one, who
was killed among you, where Satan dwells.
14 But I have a few things against you, that
you have there some who hold the teaching
of Balaam, who kept teaching Balak to put a
stumbling block before the sons of Israel, to
eat things sacrificed to idols and to commit
sexual immorality. 15 So you also have some
who in the same way hold the teaching of
the Nicolaitans. 16 Therefore repent. But if
not, I am coming to you quickly, and I will
make war against them with the sword of My
mouth. 17 He who has an ear, let him hear
what the Spirit says to the churches. To him
who overcomes, to him I will give *some* of the
hidden manna, and I will give him a white
stone, and a new name written on the stone
which no one knows but he who receives it.'

18 "And to the angel of the church in
Thyatira write:

This is what the Son of God, the One who
has eyes like a flame of fire and His feet are
like burnished bronze, says:

19 'I know your deeds, and your love
and faith and service and perseverance,
and that your last deeds are greater than
at first. 20 But I have *this* against you,
that you tolerate the woman Jezebel,
who calls herself a prophetess, and she
teaches and deceives My slaves so that
they commit sexual immorality and eat
things sacrificed to idols. 21 And I gave her
time to repent, and she does not wish to
repent of her sexual immorality. 22 Behold,
I will throw her on a bed *of sickness*, and
those who commit adultery with her into
great tribulation, unless they repent of
her deeds. 23 And I will kill her children
with pestilence, and all the churches will
know that I am He who searches the minds
and hearts; and I will give to each one of
you according to your deeds. 24 But I say
to you, the rest who are in Thyatira, who
do not have this teaching, who have not
known the deep things of Satan, as they
call them—I place no other burden on you.
25 Nevertheless what you have, hold fast
until I come. 26 And he who overcomes,
and he who keeps My deeds until the
end, TO HIM I WILL GIVE AUTHORITY OVER
THE NATIONS; 27 AND HE SHALL RULE THEM
WITH A ROD OF IRON, AS THE VESSELS OF THE
POTTER ARE BROKEN TO PIECES, as I also have
received *authority* from My Father; 28 and
I will give him the morning star. 29 He who
has an ear, let him hear what the Spirit says
to the churches.'

DECEMBER 13

Amos 1:1–3:15

1 The words of Amos, who was among
the sheepherders from Tekoa, which
he beheld *in visions* concerning Israel in
the days of Uzziah king of Judah, and in
the days of Jeroboam son of Joash, king of
Israel, two years before the earthquake.
2 And he said,

"Yahweh roars from Zion
And from Jerusalem He
gives forth His voice;
And the shepherds' pasture
grounds mourn,
And the top of Carmel dries up."

3 Thus says Yahweh,

"For three transgressions of
Damascus and for four
I will not turn back its *punishment*
Because they threshed Gilead with
implements of sharp iron.

4 "So I will send fire upon the
house of Hazael,
And it will consume the
citadels of Ben-hadad.

5 "I will also break the *gate*
bar of Damascus
And cut off the inhabitant
from the valley of Aven

And him who holds the
scepter from Beth-eden;
So the people of Aram will
go into exile to Kir,"
Says Yahweh.

6 Thus says Yahweh,
"For three transgressions of
Gaza and for four
I will not turn back its *punishment*
Because they took away into exile
the whole *community* of exiles
To deliver *it* up to Edom.
7 "So I will send fire upon
the wall of Gaza,
And it will consume her citadels.
8 "I will also cut off the inhabitant
from Ashdod
And him who holds the
scepter from Ashkelon;
I will even turn My hand
against Ekron,
And the remnant of the
Philistines will perish,"
Says Lord Yahweh.

9 Thus says Yahweh,
"For three transgressions of
Tyre and for four
I will not turn back its *punishment*
Because they delivered up the whole
community of exiles to Edom
And did not remember *the*
covenant of brotherhood.
10 "So I will send fire upon
the wall of Tyre,
And it will consume her citadels."

11 Thus says Yahweh,
"For three transgressions of
Edom and for four
I will not turn back its *punishment*
Because he pursued his
brother with the sword
While he corrupted his compassion;
And his anger also tore continually,
And he kept his wrath forever.
12 "So I will send fire upon Teman,
And it will consume the
citadels of Bozrah."

13 Thus says Yahweh,
"For three transgressions of the
sons of Ammon and for four
I will not turn back its *punishment*
Because they ripped open the
pregnant women of Gilead
In order to enlarge their borders.
14 "So I will kindle a fire on
the wall of Rabbah,
And it will consume her citadels
Amid a loud shout on the day of battle
And a storm on the day of tempest.
15 "And their king will go into exile,
He and his princes together,"
Says Yahweh.

2 Thus says Yahweh,
"For three transgressions of
Moab and for four
I will not turn back its *punishment*
Because he burned the bones of
the king of Edom to lime.
2 "So I will send fire upon Moab,
And it will consume the
citadels of Kerioth;
And Moab will die amid
great rumbling,
Amid a loud shout and the
sound of a trumpet.
3 "I will also cut off the judge
from her midst
And kill all her princes with him,"
says Yahweh.

4 Thus says Yahweh,
"For three transgressions of
Judah and for four
I will not turn back its *punishment*
Because they rejected the
law of Yahweh
And have not kept His statutes;
Their falsehood also has
led them astray,
That which their fathers walked after.
5 "So I will send fire upon Judah,
And it will consume the
citadels of Jerusalem."

6 Thus says Yahweh,
"For three transgressions of
Israel and for four
I will not turn back its *punishment*
Because they sell the
righteous for money
And the needy for a pair of sandals.
7 "These who pant after the *very* dust of
the earth on the head of the poor
Also turn aside the way of the humble;
And a man and his father go to
the same young woman
In order to profane My holy name.

8 "On garments taken as pledges they
stretch out beside every altar,
And in the house of their God
they drink the wine of those
who have been fined.

9 "Yet it was I who destroyed the
Amorite before them,
Though his height *was* like
the height of cedars,
And he *was* strong as the oaks;
I even destroyed his fruit above
and his root below.
10 "And it was I who brought you
up from the land of Egypt,
And I led you in the
wilderness forty years
That you might take possession
of the land of the Amorite.
11 "Then I raised up some of your
sons to be prophets
And some of your choice
men to be Nazirites.
Is this not so, O sons of Israel?"
declares Yahweh.
12 "But you made the Nazirites
drink wine,
And you commanded the prophets
saying, 'You shall not prophesy!'
13 "Behold, I am weighted
down beneath you
As a wagon is weighted down
when filled with sheaves.
14 "So flight will perish from the swift,
And the strong will not instill
his power with courage,
Nor will the mighty man
make his life escape.
15 "He who grasps the bow will
not stand *his ground*,
The swift of foot will not escape,
Nor will he who rides the horse
make his life escape.
16 "Even the most courageous of heart
among the mighty men will flee
naked in that day," declares Yahweh.

3 Hear this word which Yahweh has spoken against you, sons of Israel, against
the entire family which He brought up from
the land of Egypt, saying,
2 "You only have I known among
all the families of the earth;
Therefore I will punish you
for all your iniquities."
3 Do two men walk together unless
they have made an appointment?
4 Does a lion roar in the forest
when it has no prey?
Does a young lion give forth its
voice from its den unless it
has captured *something*?
5 Does a bird fall into a trap on the
ground when there is no bait in it?
Does a trap spring up from the earth
when it captures nothing at all?
6 If a trumpet is blown in a city will
not the people tremble?
If a calamity happens in a city
has not Yahweh done it?
7 Surely Lord Yahweh does nothing
Unless He reveals His secret counsel
To His slaves the prophets.
8 A lion has roared! Who will not fear?
Lord Yahweh has spoken!
Who can but prophesy?
9 Make it heard on the citadels in Ashdod
and on the citadels in the land of Egypt and
say, "Gather yourselves on the mountains of
Samaria and see *the* great confusions within
her and *the* oppressions in her midst. 10 But
they do not know how to do what is right,"
declares Yahweh, "these who hoard up
violence and devastation in their citadels."
11 Therefore, thus says Lord Yahweh,
"An adversary, even one
surrounding the land,
Will pull down your strength from you,
And your citadels will be plundered."
12 Thus says Yahweh,
"Just as the shepherd delivers from
the lion's mouth a couple of
legs or a piece of an ear,
So will the sons of Israel inhabiting
Samaria be delivered—
With *the* corner of a bed and
the cover of a couch!
13 "Hear and testify against
the house of Jacob,"
Declares Lord Yahweh,
the God of hosts.
14 "For on the day that I punish
Israel's transgressions,
I will also punish the altars of Bethel;
The horns of the altar will
be cut in pieces,
And they will fall to the ground.
15 "I will also strike the winter house
together with the summer house;
The houses of ivory will also perish,

And the great houses will
come to an end,"
Declares Yahweh.

Psalm 141:1–4

1 O Yahweh, I call upon You;
hasten to me!
Give ear to my voice when I call to You!
2 May my prayer be established
as incense before You;
The lifting up of my hands as
the evening offering.
3 Set a guard, O Yahweh, over my mouth;
Keep watch over the door of my lips.
4 Do not incline my heart
to any evil thing,
To practice deeds in wickedness
With men who are workers of iniquity;
And do not let me eat of
their delicacies.

Proverbs 29:25

25 Trembling before man brings a snare,
But he who trusts in Yahweh will
be set securely on high.

Revelation 3:1–22

3 "And to the angel of the church in Sardis
write:
This is what He who has the seven Spirits
of God and the seven stars, says: 'I know
your deeds, that you have a name that you
are alive, but you are dead. 2 Wake up, and
strengthen the things that remain, which
were about to die, for I have not found your
deeds complete in the sight of My God. 3 So
remember what you have received and heard;
and keep *it*, and repent. Therefore if you do
not wake up, I will come like a thief, and you
will not know at what hour I will come to you.
4 But you have a few names in Sardis who
have not defiled their garments, and they will
walk with Me in white, for they are worthy.
5 He who overcomes will thus be clothed in
white garments, and I will never erase his
name from the book of life, and I will confess
his name before My Father and before His
angels. 6 He who has an ear, let him hear what
the Spirit says to the churches.'
7 "And to the angel of the church in
Philadelphia write:
This is what He who is holy, who is true,
who has the key of David, who opens and
no one will shut, and who shuts and no one
opens, says:
8 'I know your deeds. Behold, I have given
before you an open door which no one can
shut, because you have a little power, and
have kept My word, and have not denied
My name. 9 Behold, I am giving *up those* of
the synagogue of Satan, those who say that
they are Jews and are not, but lie. Behold,
I will make them come and bow down
before your feet, and *make them* know that
I have loved you. 10 Because you have kept
the word of My perseverance, I also will
keep you from the hour of testing, which
is about to come upon the whole world, to
test those who dwell on the earth. 11 I am
coming quickly; hold fast what you have,
so that no one will take your crown. 12 He
who overcomes, I will make him a pillar in
the sanctuary of My God, and he will never
go out from it anymore. And I will write on
him the name of My God, and the name
of the city of My God, the new Jerusalem,
which comes down out of heaven from My
God, and My new name. 13 He who has an
ear, let him hear what the Spirit says to the
churches.'
14 "And to the angel of the church in
Laodicea write:
This is what the Amen, the faithful and
true Witness, the Beginning of the creation
of God, says:
15 'I know your deeds, that you are neither
cold nor hot. I wish that you were cold or
hot. 16 So because you are lukewarm, and
neither hot nor cold, I will spit you out of
My mouth. 17 Because you say, "I am rich,
and have become wealthy, and have need of
nothing," and you do not know that you are
wretched and pitiable and poor and blind
and naked. 18 I advise you to buy from Me
gold refined by fire so that you may become
rich, and white garments so that you may
clothe yourself, and *that* the shame of your
nakedness will not be manifested; and eye
salve to anoint your eyes so that you may
see. 19 Those whom I love, I reprove and
discipline. Therefore be zealous and repent.
20 Behold, I stand at the door and knock. If
anyone hears My voice and opens the door,
I will come in to him and will dine with him,
and he with Me. 21 He who overcomes, I
will grant to him to sit down with Me on
My throne, as I also overcame and sat down
with My Father on His throne. 22 He who has
an ear, let him hear what the Spirit says to
the churches.'"

DECEMBER 14

Amos 4:1–5:27

4 Hear this word, you cows
of Bashan who are on the
mountain of Samaria,
Who oppress the poor, who
crush the needy,
Who say to their husbands,
"Bring now, that we may drink!"
2 Lord Yahweh has sworn by
His holiness that,
"Behold, the days are coming upon you,
And they will take you away
with meat hooks,
And the last of you with fish hooks.
3 "And you will go out *through*
breaches *in the walls*,
Each one straight before her,
And you will be cast to Harmon,"
declares Yahweh.

4 "Enter Bethel and transgress;
In Gilgal multiply transgression!
Bring your sacrifices every morning,
Your tithes every three days.
5 "And offer a thank offering also
from that which is leavened,
And call for freewill offerings;
cause *them* to be heard about.
For so you love *to do*, you
sons of Israel,"
Declares Lord Yahweh.

6 "But I gave you also cleanness
of teeth in all your cities
And lack of bread in all your places,
Yet you have not returned to
Me," declares Yahweh.
7 "And I also withheld the rain from you
While *there were* still three
months until harvest.
Then I would send rain on one city,
And on another city I would
not send rain;
One portion would be rained on,
While the portion not rained
on would dry up.
8 "So two or three cities would
wander around to another
city to drink water,
But would not be satisfied;
Yet you have not returned to Me,"
declares Yahweh.
9 "I struck you with scorching
wind and mildew;
And the gnawing locust was devouring
Your many gardens and vineyards,
fig trees, and olive trees;
Yet you have not returned to
Me," declares Yahweh.
10 "I sent a pestilence among you
after the manner of Egypt;
I killed your choice men by the sword
along with your captured horses,
And I made the stench of your camp
rise up even in your nostrils;
Yet you have not returned to
Me," declares Yahweh.
11 "I overthrew you as God overthrew
Sodom and Gomorrah,
And you were like a firebrand
delivered from a blaze;
Yet you have not returned to Me,"
declares Yahweh.
12 "Therefore thus I will do
to you, O Israel;
Because I will do this to you,
Prepare to meet your God, O Israel."
13 For behold, He who forms mountains
and creates the wind
And declares to man what
are His thoughts,
He who makes dawn into gloom
And treads on the high
places of the earth,
Yahweh God of hosts is His name.

5 Hear this word which I take up
for you as a *funeral* lament,
O house of Israel:
2 She has fallen; she will not rise again—
The virgin Israel.
She *lies* abandoned on her land;
There is none to raise her up.
3 For thus says Lord Yahweh,
"The city which goes forth
one thousand *strong*
Will have one hundred left,
And the one which goes forth
one hundred *strong*
Will have ten left to the
house of Israel."

4 For thus says Yahweh to the house of Israel,
"Seek Me that you may live.

5 “But do not seek Bethel,
And do not come to Gilgal,
Nor cross over to Beersheba;
For Gilgal will certainly go into exile,
And Bethel will become evil.
6 “Seek Yahweh that you may live,
Lest He come mightily like a
fire, O house of Joseph,
And it will consume with none
to quench *it* for Bethel,
7 *For* those who overturn
justice into wormwood
And put righteousness
down to the earth.”

8 He who made the Pleiades and Orion
And overturns the shadow of
death into morning,
Who also darkens day *into* night,
Who calls for the waters of the sea
And pours them out on the
surface of the earth,
Yahweh is His name.
9 It is He who flashes forth *with*
devastation upon the strong
So that devastation comes
upon the fortification.

10 They hate him who
reproves in the gate,
And they abhor him who
speaks *with* integrity.
11 Therefore because you impose
heavy rent on the poor
And take a tribute of grain from them,
Though you have built
houses of cut stone,
Yet you will not live in them;
You have planted desirable vineyards,
yet you will not drink their wine.
12 For I know your transgressions are
many and your sins are mighty,
You who distress the righteous
and take bribes
And turn aside the needy in the gate.
13 Therefore at such a time the
one with insight keeps silent,
for it is an evil time.

14 Seek good and not evil, in
order that you may live;
And thus may Yahweh God
of hosts be with you,
Just as you have said!
15 Hate evil, love good,
And set justice at the gate!
Perhaps Yahweh God of hosts
May be gracious to the
remnant of Joseph.

16 Therefore thus says Yahweh God of hosts,
the Lord,
“There is wailing in all the plazas,
And in all the streets they
say, ‘Alas! Alas!’
They also call the farmer to mourning
And professional weepers to wailing.
17 “And in all the vineyards *there is* wailing
Because I will pass through the
midst of you,” says Yahweh.

18 Woe, you who are longing
for the day of Yahweh,
For what purpose *will* the day
of Yahweh *be* to you?
It *will be* darkness and not light;
19 As when a man flees from a lion
And a bear meets him;
Or he goes home, leans his
hand against the wall,
And a snake bites him.
20 *Will* not the day of Yahweh *be*
darkness instead of light,
Even thick darkness with
no brightness in it?

21 “I hate, I reject your feasts,
Nor do I delight in your
solemn assemblies.
22 “Even though you offer up to Me burnt
offerings and your grain offerings,
I will not accept *them*;
And I will not *even* look at the peace
offerings of your fatlings.
23 “Remove from Me the tumult
of your songs;
I will not even listen to the
melody of your harps.
24 “But let justice roll down like waters
And righteousness like an
ever-flowing stream.

25 “Did you present Me with sacrifices
and grain offerings in the wilderness for
forty years, O house of Israel? 26 You also
carried along Sikkuth your king and Kiyyun,
your images, the star of your gods which
you made for yourselves. 27 Therefore, I will
make you go into exile beyond Damascus,”
says Yahweh, whose name is the God of
hosts.

Psalm 141:5–10

5 Let the righteous smite me in
lovingkindness and reprove me;
It is oil upon the head;
Let not my head refuse it,
For still my prayer is against
their evil deeds.
6 Their judges are thrown down
by the sides of the cliff,
And they hear my words,
for they are pleasant.
7 As when one plows and
splits open the earth,
Our bones have been scattered
at the mouth of Sheol.

8 For my eyes are toward You,
O Yahweh, O Lord;
In You I take refuge; do not pour
out my soul *to death.*
9 Keep me from the jaws of the trap
which they have set for me,
And from the snares of
workers of iniquity.
10 Let the wicked fall into their own nets,
As for myself—meanwhile,
I am passing by.

Proverbs 29:26

26 Many seek the face of a ruler,
But justice for man *comes*
from Yahweh.

Revelation 4:1–11

4 After these things I looked, and behold,
a door *standing* open in heaven, and the
first voice which I had heard, like *the sound*
of a trumpet speaking with me, said, "Come
up here, and I will show you what must take
place after these things." 2 Immediately I
was in the Spirit, and behold, a throne was
standing in heaven, and One sitting on the
throne. 3 And He who was sitting *was* like
a jasper stone and a sardius in appearance;
and *there was* a rainbow around the throne,
like an emerald in appearance. 4 Around
the throne *were* twenty-four thrones, and
upon those thrones *I saw* twenty-four
elders sitting, clothed in white garments,
and golden crowns on their heads. 5 And out
from the throne come flashes of lightning
and sounds and peals of thunder. And *there*
were seven lamps of fire burning before the
throne, which are the seven Spirits of God.
6 And before the throne *there was something*
like a sea of glass, like crystal. And in the
center and around the throne, four living
creatures full of eyes in front and behind.
7 And the first creature *was* like a lion, and
the second creature like a calf, and the third
creature had a face like that of a man, and
the fourth creature *was* like a flying eagle.
8 And the four living creatures, each one
of them having six wings, are full of eyes
around and within, and day and night they
do not cease to say,

"HOLY, HOLY, HOLY *is* THE LORD GOD, THE
ALMIGHTY, WHO WAS AND WHO IS AND
WHO IS TO COME."

9 And when the living creatures give glory
and honor and thanks to Him who sits on
the throne, to Him who lives forever and
ever, 10 the twenty-four elders will fall down
before Him who sits on the throne, and will
worship Him who lives forever and ever, and
will cast their crowns before the throne,
saying,

11 "Worthy are You, our Lord and our God,
to receive glory and honor and power,
for You created all things, and because
of Your will they existed, and were
created."

DECEMBER 15

Amos 6:1–7:17

6 Woe to those who are at ease in Zion
And to those who *feel* secure in
the mountain of Samaria,
The distinguished men of the
first of the nations,
To whom the house of Israel comes.
2 Pass on over to Calneh and look,
And go from there to Hamath
the great,
Then go down to Gath of the Philistines.
Are they better than these kingdoms,
Or are their borders greater
than your borders?
3 Do you put off the day of calamity,
And would you cause the seat
of violence to approach?

4 Those who lay down on beds of ivory
And sprawl on their couches

And eat lambs from the flock
And calves from the midst of the stall,
5 Who improvise to the
sound of the harp,
And like David have composed
songs for themselves,
6 Who drink wine from *sacrificial* bowls
While they anoint themselves
with the first *pick* of the oils,
Yet they have not grieved over
the destruction of Joseph.
7 Therefore, they will now go into exile
among the first of the exiles,
And the sprawlers' banqueting
will turn aside.

8 Lord Yahweh has sworn by Himself,
Yahweh God of hosts has declared:
"I abhor the lofty pride of Jacob
And hate his citadels;
Therefore I will deliver up *the*
city as well as its fullness."
9 And it will be, if ten men are left in one
house, they will die. 10 Then one's uncle, or
the one who burns his *bones*, will lift him
up to bring out *his* bones from the house,
and he will say to the one who is in the
innermost part of the house, "Is anyone else
with you?" And that one will say, "No one."
Then he will answer, "Keep quiet. For the
name of Yahweh is not to be mentioned."
11 For behold, Yahweh is going to command
and will strike the great house to pieces and
the small house to fragments.
12 Do horses run on rocks?
Or does one plow them with oxen?
Yet you have overturned
justice into gall
And the fruit of righteousness
into wormwood,
13 You who are glad in Lo-debar
And say, "Have we not by
our *own* strength taken
Karnaim for ourselves?"
14 "For behold, I am going to raise
up a nation against you,
O house of Israel," declares
Yahweh God of hosts,
"And they will press down on
you from Lebo-hamath
To the brook of the Arabah."

7 Thus Lord Yahweh showed me, and
behold, He was forming a locust-swarm
when the spring crop began to come up.
And behold, the spring crop *was* after the
king's mowing. 2 And it happened when it
had completed eating the vegetation of the
land, that I said,
"Lord Yahweh, please pardon!
How can Jacob rise up,
For he is small?"
3 Yahweh relented concerning this.
"It shall not be," said Yahweh.
4 Thus Lord Yahweh showed me, and
behold, Lord Yahweh was calling to contend
with them by fire, and it consumed the great
deep and began to consume the farm land.
5 Then I said,
"Lord Yahweh, please stop!
How can Jacob rise up, for he is small?"
6 Yahweh relented concerning this.
"This too shall not be,"
said Lord Yahweh.
7 Thus He showed me, and behold, the
Lord was standing by a wall *made with* a
plumb line, and in His hand was a plumb
line. 8 And Yahweh said to me, "What do you
see, Amos?" And I said, "A plumb line." Then
the Lord said,
"Behold, I am about to put a plumb line
In the midst of My people Israel.
I will pass over them no longer.
9 "The high places of Isaac
will be desolated
And the sanctuaries of
Israel laid waste.
Then I will rise up against the house
of Jeroboam with the sword."
10 Then Amaziah, the priest of Bethel,
sent *word* to Jeroboam king of Israel,
saying, "Amos has conspired against you in
the midst of the house of Israel; the land
is unable to endure all his words. 11 For
thus Amos says, 'Jeroboam will die by the
sword, and Israel will certainly go from its
land into exile.'" 12 Then Amaziah said to
Amos, "Go, you seer, flee away to the land
of Judah, and there eat bread, and there do
your prophesying! 13 But no longer prophesy
at Bethel, for it is a sanctuary of the king and
a royal house."
14 Then Amos answered and said to Ama-
ziah, "I am not a prophet, nor am I the son of
a prophet; for I am a herdsman and a grower
of sycamore figs. 15 But Yahweh took me
from following the flock, and Yahweh said
to me, 'Go prophesy to My people Israel.'
16 So now, hear the word of Yahweh: you
are saying, 'You shall not prophesy against

Israel, nor shall you drip out *words* against
the house of Isaac.' 17 Therefore, thus says
Yahweh, 'Your wife will play the harlot in the
city, your sons and your daughters will fall
by the sword, your land will be divided up
by a *measuring* line, and you yourself will
die upon unclean land. Moreover, Israel will
certainly go from its land into exile.'"

Psalm 142:1–7

1 With my voice to Yahweh, I cry aloud;
With my voice to Yahweh, I
make supplication.
2 I pour out my complaint before Him;
I declare my distress before Him.
3 When my spirit was faint within me,
You knew my path.
In the way where I walk
They have hidden a trap for me.
4 Look to the right and see;
That there is no one who regards me;
A *way of* escape has been
destroyed from me;
No one cares for my soul.

5 I cried out to You, O Yahweh;
I said, "You are my refuge,
My portion in the land of the living.
6 "Give heed to my cry of lamentation,
For I am brought very low;
Deliver me from my persecutors,
For they are too strong for me.
7 "Bring my soul out of prison,
To give thanks to Your name;
The righteous will encircle me,
For You will deal bountifully with me."

Proverbs 29:27

27 An unjust man is an abomination
to the righteous,
And he who is upright in the way is
an abomination to the wicked.

Revelation 5:1–14

5 Then I saw in the right hand of Him who
sits on the throne a scroll written inside
and on the back, sealed up with seven seals.
2 Then I saw a strong angel proclaiming with
a loud voice, "Who is worthy to open the
scroll and to break its seals?" 3 And no one
in heaven or on the earth or under the earth
was able to open the scroll or to look into it.
4 Then I was crying greatly because no one
was found worthy to open the scroll or to
look into it. 5 And one of the elders *said to
me, "Stop crying! Behold, the Lion that is
from the tribe of Judah, the Root of David,
has overcome so as to open the scroll and
its seven seals."

6 Then I saw in the midst of the throne
and the four living creatures and in the
midst of the elders a Lamb standing, as if
slain, having seven horns and seven eyes,
which are the seven Spirits of God, sent out
into all the earth. 7 And He came and took
the scroll out of the right hand of Him who
sits on the throne. 8 And when He had taken
the scroll, the four living creatures and the
twenty-four elders fell down before the
Lamb, each one having a harp and golden
bowls full of incense, which are the prayers
of the saints. 9 And they *sang a new song,
saying,

"Worthy are You to take the scroll and
to open its seals, because You were
slain and purchased for God with Your
blood *people* from every tribe and
tongue and people and nation. 10 And
You made them *to be* a kingdom and
priests to our God, and they will reign
upon the earth."

11 Then I looked, and I heard the voice
of many angels around the throne and the
living creatures and the elders; and the
number of them was myriads of myriads,
and thousands of thousands, 12 saying with
a loud voice,

"Worthy is the Lamb that was slain to
receive power and riches and wisdom
and strength and honor and glory and
blessing."

13 And every created thing which is in
heaven and on the earth and under the
earth and on the sea, and all things in them,
I heard saying,

"To Him who sits on the throne, and
to the Lamb, *be* the blessing and the
honor and the glory and the might
forever and ever."

14 And the four living creatures kept saying,
"Amen." And the elders fell down and
worshiped.

DECEMBER 16

Amos 8:1–9:15

8 Thus Lord Yahweh showed me, and
behold, *there was* a basket of summer
fruit. 2 And he said, "What do you see,
Amos?" And I said, "A basket of summer
fruit." Then Yahweh said to me, "The end
has come for My people Israel. I will pass
over them no longer. 3 And they will wail
with the songs of the palace in that day,"
declares Lord Yahweh. "Many *will be* the
corpses; in every place they will cast them
forth in silence."
4 Hear this, you who trample the needy,
even to cause the humble of the land to
cease, 5 saying,

"When will the new moon pass over,
So that we may sell grain,
And the sabbath, that we may
open the wheat *market*,
To make the bushel smaller
and the shekel bigger,
And to cheat with a deceptive balance,
6 So as to buy the poor for money
And the needy for a pair of sandals,
And *that* we may sell the
refuse of the wheat?"

7 Yahweh has sworn by the
lofty pride of Jacob,
"Indeed, I will never forget
any of their works.
8 "Because of this will not
the land tremble
And everyone who inhabits it mourn?
Indeed, all of it will rise
up like the Nile,
And it will be tossed about
And subside like the Nile of Egypt.
9 "And it will be in that day,"
declares Lord Yahweh,
"That I will make the sun
go down at noon
And make the earth dark
in broad daylight.
10 "Then I will overturn your
feasts into mourning
And all your songs into lamentation;
And I will bring up sackcloth
on everyone's loins
And baldness on every head.
And I will make it like *a time of*
mourning for an only son,
And the end of it will be
like a bitter day.
11 "Behold, days are coming,"
declares Lord Yahweh,
"When I will send a famine on the land,
Not a famine for bread or
a thirst for water,
But rather for hearing the
words of Yahweh.
12 "People will wander from sea to sea
And from the north even to the east;
They will go to and fro to seek
the word of Yahweh,
But they will not find *it*.
13 "In that day the beautiful virgins
And the choice men will
faint from thirst.
14 "*As for* those who swear by
the guilt of Samaria,
Who say, 'As your god lives, O Dan,'
And, 'As the way of Beersheba lives,'
They will fall and not rise again."

9 I saw the Lord standing beside the altar,
and He said,
"Strike the capitals so that the
thresholds will quake,
And break them on the
heads of them all!
Then I will kill the rest of
them with the sword;
Not one of them who
can flee will flee,
And not one of them who can
survive will escape.
2 "Though they dig into Sheol,
From there will My hand take them;
And though they ascend to heaven,
From there will I bring them down.
3 "And though they hide on
the top of Carmel,
From there I will search them
out and take them;
And though they conceal themselves
from My eyes on the floor of the sea,
From there I will command the
serpent, and it will bite them.
4 "And though they go into captivity
before their enemies,
From there I will command the
sword that it kill them,

And I will set My eyes against them
for evil and not for good."

5 Now Lord Yahweh of hosts,
The One who touches the
land so that it melts,
And all those who inhabit it mourn,
And all of it rises up like the Nile
And subsides like the Nile of Egypt;
6 The One who builds His upper
chambers in the heavens
And has founded His vaulted
dome over the earth;
The One who calls for the
waters of the sea
And pours them out on the
face of the earth;
Yahweh is His name.

7 "Are you not as the sons of
Ethiopia to Me,
O sons of Israel?" declares Yahweh.
"Have I not brought up Israel
from the land of Egypt,
And the Philistines from Caphtor
and the Arameans from Kir?
8 "Behold, the eyes of Lord Yahweh
are on the sinful kingdom,
And I will destroy it from
the face of the earth;
Nevertheless, I will not totally
destroy the house of Jacob,"
Declares Yahweh.
9 "For behold, I am commanding,
And I will shake the house of
Israel among all nations
As *grain* is shaken in a sieve,
But not a kernel will fall to the ground.
10 "All the sinners of My people
will die by the sword,
Those who say, 'The calamity will
not overtake or confront us.'
11 "In that day I will raise up the
fallen booth of David
And wall up its breaches;
I will also raise up its ruins
And rebuild it as in the ancient days,
12 That they may possess the
remnant of Edom
And all the nations who are
called by My name,"
Declares Yahweh who does this.

13 "Behold, days are coming,"
declares Yahweh,
"When the plowman will
overtake the reaper
And the treader of grapes
him who sows seed;
When the mountains will
drip sweet wine
And all the hills will melt.
14 "Also I will restore the captivity
of My people Israel,
And they will rebuild the desolated
cities and live *in them*;
They will also plant vineyards
and drink their wine
And make gardens and eat their fruit.
15 "I will also plant them on their land,
And they will not again be
uprooted from their land
Which I have given them,"
Says Yahweh your God.

Psalm 143:1–6

1 O Yahweh, hear my prayer,
Give ear to my supplications!
Answer me in Your faithfulness,
in Your righteousness!
2 And do not enter into judgment
with Your slave,
For no one living is righteous
in Your sight.
3 For the enemy has pursued my soul;
He has crushed my life to the ground;
He has made me inhabit dark
places, like those who
have long been dead.
4 Therefore my spirit was
faint within me;
My heart was appalled within me.

5 I remember the days of old;
I meditate on all You have done;
I muse on the work of Your hands.
6 I stretch out my hands to You;
My soul *reaches* for You like
a weary land. Selah.

Proverbs 30:1–4

30 The words of Agur the son of Jakeh,
the oracle.
The man declares to Ithiel, to Ithiel and
Ucal:
2 Surely I am more senseless
than any man,
And I do not have the
understanding of mankind.
3 Neither have I learned wisdom,

Nor do I know the knowledge
of the Holy One.
4 Who has ascended into
heaven and descended?
Who has gathered the
wind in His fists?
Who has wrapped the waters
in His garment?
Who has established all the
ends of the earth?
What is His name? And what
is His Son's name?
Surely you know!

Revelation 6:1–17

6 Then I looked when the Lamb opened
one of the seven seals, and I heard one
of the four living creatures saying as with a
voice of thunder, "Come." 2 Then I looked,
and behold, a white horse, and he who sits
on it had a bow; and a crown was given to
him, and he went out overcoming and to
overcome.
3 And when He opened the second seal,
I heard the second living creature saying,
"Come." 4 And another, a red horse, went
out; and to him who sits on it, it was given
to him to take peace from the earth, and that
men would slay one another; and a great
sword was given to him.
5 And when He opened the third seal,
I heard the third living creature saying,
"Come." Then I looked, and behold, a black
horse; and he who sits on it had a pair of
scales in his hand. 6 And I heard *something*
like a voice in the midst of the four living
creatures saying, "One choinix of wheat for
one denarius, and three choinix of barley
for one denarius, and do not harm the oil
and the wine."
7 And when He opened the fourth seal, I
heard the voice of the fourth living creature
saying, "Come." 8 Then I looked, and behold,
a pale horse; and he who sits on it had the
name Death, and Hades was following with
him. Authority was given to them over a
fourth of the earth, to kill with sword and
with famine and with pestilence and by the
wild beasts of the earth.
9 And when He opened the fifth seal,
I saw underneath the altar the souls of
those who had been slain because of the
word of God, and because of the witness
which they had maintained; 10 and they
cried out with a loud voice, saying, "How
long, O Master, holy and true? Will You not
judge and avenge our blood on those who
dwell on the earth?" 11 And a white robe
was given to each of them; and it was told
to them that they should rest for a little
while longer, until *the number of* their
fellow slaves and their brothers who were
to be killed even as they had been, would
be completed also.
12 Then I looked when He opened the
sixth seal, and there was a great earthquake;
and the sun became black as sackcloth *made*
of hair, and the whole moon became like
blood; 13 and the stars of the sky fell to
the earth, as a fig tree casts its unripe figs
when shaken by a great wind. 14 And the
sky was split apart like a scroll when it is
rolled up, and every mountain and island
were moved out of their places. 15 Then the
kings of the earth and the great men and the
commanders and the rich and the strong
and every slave and free man HID THEM-
SELVES IN THE CAVES and among the rocks
of the mountains; 16 and they *SAID TO THE
MOUNTAINS AND TO THE ROCKS, "FALL ON US
AND HIDE US from the presence of Him who
sits on the throne, and from the wrath of the
Lamb, 17 for the great DAY OF their WRATH has
come, and who is able to stand?"

The Bible teems with promises which are backed up with testimonies of God's faithfulness in answer to the earnest pleadings of His people.

— THOMAS PAYNE

DECEMBER 17

Obadiah 1–21

1 The vision of Obadiah.
Thus says Lord Yahweh concerning Edom—
We have heard a report from Yahweh,
And an envoy has been sent
among the nations *saying*,
"Arise! And let us arise against
her for battle"—
2 "Behold, I will make you small
among the nations;
You are greatly despised.
3 "The arrogance of your heart
has deceived you,
You who dwell in the clefts
of the cliff,
In the height of your habitation,
Who says in his heart,
'Who will bring me down to earth?'
4 "Though you build loftily like the eagle,
Though you set your nest
among the stars,
From there I will bring you
down," declares Yahweh.
5 "If thieves came to you,
If robbers by night—
Oh how you will be ruined!—
Would they not thieve *only*
until they had enough?
If grape gatherers came to you,
Would they not allow some
gleanings to remain?
6 "Oh how Esau will be searched out
And his hidden treasures ransacked!
7 "All the men *who have* a
covenant with you
Will send you forth to the border,
And the men at peace with you
Will deceive you and overpower you.
They who eat your bread
Will set an ambush for you.
(There is no discernment in him.)
8 "Will I not on that day,"
declares Yahweh,
"Cause the wise men to
perish from Edom
And discernment from the
mountain of Esau?
9 "Then your mighty men will
be dismayed, O Teman,
So that each one may be cut off from
the mountain of Esau by slaughter.
10 "Because of violence to
your brother Jacob,
You will be covered *with* shame,
And you will be cut off forever.
11 "On the day that you stood aloof,
On the day that strangers
took his wealth captive
And foreigners entered his gate
And cast lots for Jerusalem—
You too were as one of them.

12 "Now do not look on your
brother's day *with triumph*,
The day of his misfortune.
And do not be glad over
the sons of Judah
In the day *when* they perish;
And do not let your mouth
speak great things
In the day of *their* distress.
13 "Do not enter the gate of My people
In the day of their disaster.
Indeed, you, do not look on their
calamity *with triumph*
In the day of their disaster.
And do not send out for their wealth
In the day of their disaster.
14 "Do not stand at the fork of the road
To cut down those among
them who escape;
And do not deliver over their survivors
In the day of their distress.
15 "For the day of Yahweh draws
near on all the nations.
As you have done, it will
be done to you.
Your dealings will return
on your own head.
16 "Because just as you *all* drank
on My holy mountain,
All the nations will drink continually.
They will drink and swallow,
And they will be as if they never were.
17 "But on Mount Zion there will
be those who escape,
And it will be holy.
And the house of Jacob will
possess their possessions.
18 "Then the house of Jacob will be a fire
And the house of Joseph a flame;
But the house of Esau *will
be* as stubble.

And they will set them on fire
and consume them
So that there will be no survivor
of the house of Esau,"
For Yahweh has spoken.
19 Then *those of* the Negev will
possess the mountain of Esau,
And *those of* the Shephelah,
the Philistine *plain*;
And they will possess the
territory of Ephraim and
the territory of Samaria,
And Benjamin *will possess* Gilead.
20 And the exiles of this military
force of the sons of Israel,
Who are *among* the Canaanites
as far as Zarephath,
And the exiles of Jerusalem
who are in Sepharad,
Will possess the cities of the Negev.
21 And the saviors will ascend
Mount Zion
To judge the mountain of Esau,
And the kingdom will
belong to Yahweh.

Psalm 143:7–12

7 Answer me quickly, O Yahweh,
my spirit wastes away;
Do not hide Your face from me,
Or I will become like those
who go down to the pit.
8 Cause me to hear Your
lovingkindness in the morning;
For I trust in You;
Cause me to know the way in
which I should walk;
For to You I lift up my soul.
9 Deliver me from my
enemies, O Yahweh,
I have concealed *myself* in You.

10 Teach me to do Your will,
For You are my God;
Let Your good Spirit lead
me on level ground.
11 For the sake of Your name,
O Yahweh, revive me.
In Your righteousness bring
my soul out of distress.
12 And in Your lovingkindness,
cut off my enemies
And cause all those who assail
my soul to perish,
For I am Your slave.

Proverbs 30:5

5 Every word of God is tested;
He is a shield to those who
take refuge in Him.

Revelation 7:1–17

7 After this I saw four angels standing at
the four corners of the earth, holding
back the four winds of the earth, so that no
wind would blow on the earth or on the sea
or on any tree. 2 Then I saw another angel
ascending from the rising of the sun, having
the seal of the living God; and he cried out
with a loud voice to the four angels to whom
it was granted to harm the earth and the sea,
3 saying, "Do not harm the earth or the sea
or the trees until we have sealed the slaves
of our God on their foreheads."
4 And I heard the number of those having
been sealed, 144,000 sealed from every tribe
of the sons of Israel:

5 from the tribe of Judah, 12,000 having
been sealed,
from the tribe of Reuben 12,000,
from the tribe of Gad 12,000,
6 from the tribe of Asher 12,000,
from the tribe of Naphtali 12,000,
from the tribe of Manasseh 12,000,
7 from the tribe of Simeon 12,000,
from the tribe of Levi 12,000,
from the tribe of Issachar 12,000,
8 from the tribe of Zebulun 12,000,
from the tribe of Joseph 12,000,
from the tribe of Benjamin, 12,000
having been sealed.

9 After these things I looked, and behold,
a great multitude which no one could count,
from every nation and *all* tribes and peoples
and tongues, standing before the throne and
before the Lamb, clothed in white robes, and
palm branches *were* in their hands; 10 and
they cry out with a loud voice, saying,
"Salvation *belongs* to our God who sits
on the throne, and to the Lamb." 11 And all
the angels were standing around the throne
and the elders and the four living creatures,
and they fell on their faces before the throne
and worshiped God, 12 saying,
"Amen, the blessing and the glory and the
wisdom and the thanksgiving and the honor
and the power and the strength, *be* to our
God forever and ever. Amen."
13 Then one of the elders answered,
saying to me, "These, clothed in the white
robes, who are they, and from where have

they come?" 14 And I said to him, "My lord,
you know." And he said to me, "These are
the ones who come out of the great tribula-
tion, and they washed their robes and made
them white in the blood of the Lamb. 15 For
this reason, they are before the throne of
God; and they serve Him day and night
in His sanctuary; and He who sits on the
throne will dwell over them. 16 THEY WILL
HUNGER NO LONGER, NOR THIRST ANYMORE;
NOR WILL THE SUN BEAT DOWN ON THEM, NOR
ANY HEAT; 17 for the Lamb at the center of
the throne will shepherd them and will
guide them to springs of the water of life.
And God WILL WIPE EVERY TEAR FROM THEIR
EYES."

DECEMBER 18

Jonah 1:1–4:11

1 Now the word of Yahweh came to Jonah
the son of Amittai saying, 2 "Arise, go to
Nineveh, the great city, and call out against
it, for their evil has come up before Me."
3 Yet Jonah arose to flee to Tarshish from
the presence of Yahweh. So he went down
to Joppa, found a ship which was going to
Tarshish, and paid its fare and went down
into it to go with them to Tarshish from the
presence of Yahweh.

4 But Yahweh hurled a great wind on the
sea, and there was a great storm on the sea
so that the ship gave thought to breaking
apart. 5 Then the sailors became fearful, and
every man cried to his god, and they hurled
the cargo which was in the ship into the sea
to lighten *it* for them. But Jonah had gone
down *below* into the innermost part of the
vessel, lain down, and fallen deep asleep.
6 So the captain came near to him and said to
him, "How is it that you are deeply sleeping?
Arise, call on your god. Perhaps *your* god
will be concerned about us so that we will
not perish."

7 Then each man said to the other, "Come,
let us have *the* lots fall so we may know on
whose account this *calamitous* evil *has
struck* us." So they had *the* lots fall, and the
lot fell on Jonah. 8 Then they said to him,
"Tell us, now! On whose account *has* this
calamitous evil *struck* us? What is your
occupation? And where do you come from?
What is your country? From what people are
you?" 9 And he said to them, "I am a Hebrew,
and I fear Yahweh, the God of heaven, who
made the sea and the dry land."

10 Then the men became greatly fearful,
and they said to him, "What is this you
have done?" For the men knew that he
was fleeing from the presence of Yahweh
because he had told them. 11 So they said
to him, "What should we do to you that
the sea may become quiet for us?"—for
the sea was becoming increasingly stormy.
12 So he said to them, "Lift me up and hurl
me into the sea. Then the sea will become
quiet for you, for I know that on account of
me this great storm *has come* upon you."
13 However, the men rowed *desperately* to
return to dry land, but they could not, for
the sea was becoming increasingly stormy
against them. 14 Then they called on Yahweh
and said, "Ah! O Yahweh, we earnestly pray,
do not let us perish on account of this man's
life, and do not put innocent blood on us;
for You, O Yahweh, as You have pleased You
have done."

15 So they lifted Jonah up and hurled him
into the sea, and the sea stood still from its
raging. 16 Then the men greatly feared Yah-
weh, and they offered a sacrifice to Yahweh
and made vows.

17 And Yahweh appointed a great fish to
swallow Jonah, and Jonah was in the stom-
ach of the fish three days and three nights.

2 Then Jonah prayed to Yahweh his God
from the stomach of the fish, 2 and he
said,

"I called out of my distress to Yahweh,
And He answered me.
I cried for help from the belly of Sheol;
You heard my voice.

3 "For You had cast me into the deep,
Into the heart of the seas,
And the current surrounded me.
All Your breakers and waves
passed over me.

4 "So I said, 'I have been driven
away from Your sight.
Nevertheless I will look again
toward Your holy temple.'

5 "Water encompassed me
to *my very* soul.
The great deep surrounded me,

Weeds were wrapped around my head.
6 "I went down to the base
of the mountains.
The earth with its bars *closed*
behind me forever,
But You have brought up my life
from the pit, O Yahweh my God.
7 "While my soul was fainting within me,
I remembered Yahweh,
And my prayer came to You,
To Your holy temple.
8 "Those who regard worthless idols
Forsake their lovingkindness,
9 But as for me, I will sacrifice to You
With the voice of thanksgiving.
That which I have vowed I will pay.
Salvation belongs to Yahweh."
10 Then Yahweh spoke to the fish, and it
vomited Jonah up onto the dry land.

3 Now the word of Yahweh came to Jonah
the second time, saying, 2 "Arise, go to
Nineveh, the great city, and call out to it
this *very* call which I am going to speak to
you." 3 So Jonah arose and went to Nineveh
according to the word of Yahweh. Now
Nineveh was an exceedingly great city, a
three days' walk. 4 Then Jonah began to go
into the city, one day's walk; and he called
out and said, "Yet forty days and Nineveh
will be overthrown."
5 And the people of Nineveh believed
in God; and they called a fast and put on
sackcloth, from the greatest to the least of
them. 6 Then the word reached the king of
Nineveh, and he arose from his throne, laid
aside his mantle from him, covered *himself*
with sackcloth, and sat on the ashes. 7 And
he cried out and said,

"In Nineveh by the decree of the
king and his nobles: Do not let man,
animal, herd, or flock taste a thing.
Do not let them eat, and do not let
them drink water. 8 But both man
and animal must be covered with
sackcloth; and let men call on God
with *their* strength that each may
turn from his evil way and from the
violence which is in his hands. 9 Who
knows, God may turn and relent and
turn away from His burning anger so
that we will not perish."

10 Then God saw their works, that they
turned from their evil way, so God relented
concerning the evil which He had spoken
He would bring upon them. And He did not
bring *it upon them.*

4 But this was a great evil to Jonah, and
he became angry. 2 And he prayed to
Yahweh and said, "Ah! O Yahweh, was not
this my word *to myself* while I was still in my
own land? Therefore I went ahead to flee to
Tarshish, for I knew that You are a gracious
and compassionate God, slow to anger and
abundant in lovingkindness, and one who
relents concerning evil. 3 So now, O Yahweh,
please take my life from me, for death is
better to me than life." 4 And Yahweh said,
"Do you have good reason to be angry?"
5 Then Jonah went out from the city and
sat east of the city. And there he made a
booth for himself and sat under it in the
shade until he could see what would hap-
pen in the city. 6 So Yahweh God appointed
a plant, and it came up over Jonah to be a
shade over his head to deliver him from his
miserable evil. And Jonah was extremely glad
about the plant. 7 But God appointed a worm
at the breaking of dawn the next day, and
it struck the plant, and it dried up. 8 Then
it happened that as the sun rose up, God
appointed a scorching east wind, and the
sun struck down on Jonah's head so that he
became faint and asked with *all* his soul to
die and said, "Death is better to me than life."
9 Then God said to Jonah, "Do you have
good reason to be angry about the plant?"
And he said, "I have good reason to be angry,
even to death." 10 Then Yahweh said, "You
had pity on the plant for which you did not
work and *which* you did not cause to grow,
which came to be overnight and perished
overnight. 11 So should I not have pity on
Nineveh, the great city, in which there are
more than 120,000 persons who do not
know *the difference* between their right and
left hand, as well as many animals?"

Psalm 144:1–8

1 Blessed be Yahweh, my rock,
Who trains my hands for war,
My fingers for battle;
2 My lovingkindness and my fortress,
My stronghold and my deliverer,
My shield and He in whom
I take refuge,
Who subdues my people under me.
3 O Yahweh, what is man,
that You know him?

Or the son of man, that
You think of him?
4 Man is like a breath;
His days are like a passing shadow.

5 O Yahweh, bow Your heavens,
and come down;
Touch the mountains, that
they may smoke.
6 Flash forth lightning and scatter them;
Send out Your arrows and
confuse them.
7 Send forth Your hand from on high;
Set me free and deliver me
out of many waters,
Out of the hand of foreigners
8 Whose mouth speaks worthlessness,
And whose right hand is a
right hand of lying.

Proverbs 30:6–9

6 Do not add to His words
Lest He reprove you, and
you be proved a liar.

7 Two things I asked of You,
Do not withhold from me before I die:
8 Keep worthlessness and *every*
false word far from me,
Give me neither poverty nor riches;
Feed me with the food
that is my portion,
9 Lest I be full and deny *You* and
say, "Who is Yahweh?"
Or lest I be impoverished and steal,
And profane the name of my God.

Revelation 8:1–13

8 When He opened the seventh seal, there
was silence in heaven for about half an
hour. 2 Then I saw the seven angels who
stand before God, and seven trumpets were
given to them.
3 And another angel came and stood at
the altar, having a golden censer; and much
incense was given to him, so that he might
add it to the prayers of all the saints on the
golden altar which was before the throne.
4 And the smoke of the incense went up with
the prayers of the saints, out of the angel's
hand, before God. 5 Then the angel took the
censer and filled it with the fire of the altar,
and threw it to the earth; and there followed
peals of thunder and sounds and flashes of
lightning and an earthquake.
6 And the seven angels who had the seven
trumpets prepared themselves to sound
them.
7 And the first sounded, and there came
hail and fire, mixed with blood, and they
were thrown to the earth; and a third of the
earth was burned up, and a third of the trees
were burned up, and all the green grass was
burned up.
8 And the second angel sounded, and
something like a great mountain burning
with fire was thrown into the sea; and a
third of the sea became blood, 9 and a third
of the creatures which were in the sea—
those which had life—died; and a third of
the ships were destroyed.
10 And the third angel sounded, and a great
star fell from heaven, burning like a torch,
and it fell on a third of the rivers and on the
springs of waters. 11 And the name of the star
is called Wormwood; and a third of the waters
became wormwood, and many men died from
the waters, because they were made bitter.
12 And the fourth angel sounded, and a
third of the sun and a third of the moon and
a third of the stars were struck, so that a
third of them would be darkened and the
day would not shine for a third of it, and the
night in the same way.
13 Then I looked, and I heard an eagle
flying in midheaven, saying with a loud
voice, "Woe, woe, woe to those who dwell on
the earth, because of the remaining blasts
of the trumpet of the three angels who are
about to sound!"

DECEMBER 19

Micah 1:1–3:12

1 The word of Yahweh which came *to*
Micah of Moresheth in the days of
Jotham, Ahaz, *and* Hezekiah, kings of Judah,
which he beheld concerning Samaria and
Jerusalem.

2 Hear, O peoples, all of you;
Give heed, O earth, as well
as its fullness,
And let Lord Yahweh be a
witness against you,
The Lord from His holy temple.

3 For behold, Yahweh is going
forth from His place.
He will come down and tread on
the high places of the earth.
4 The mountains will melt under Him,
And the valleys will be split,
Like wax before the fire,
Like water poured down a steep place.
5 All this is for the transgression
of Jacob
And for the sins of the house of Israel.
What is the transgression of Jacob?
Is it not Samaria?
What is the high place of Judah?
Is it not Jerusalem?
6 So I will make Samaria a heap
of ruins in the field,
Planting places for a vineyard.
And I will pour her stones
down into the valley
And will lay bare her foundations.
7 And all of her graven images
will be smashed,
And all of her earnings will
be burned with fire
And all of her idols I will
make desolate,
For she collected *them* from
a harlot's earnings,
And to the earnings of a
harlot they will return.

8 Because of this I must lament and wail;
I must go barefoot and naked;
I must make a lament like the jackals
And a mourning like the ostriches.
9 For her wound is incurable,
For it has come to Judah;
It has reached the gate of my people,
Even to Jerusalem.
10 Tell it not in Gath,
Weep not at all.
At Beth-le-aphrah roll
yourself in the dust.
11 Pass on by, inhabitant of Shaphir,
in shameful nakedness.
The inhabitant of Zaanan
does not go out.
The lamentation of Beth-ezel:
"He will take from you its support."
12 For the inhabitant of Maroth
Writhes *in waiting* for good
Because a calamity has come
down from Yahweh
To the gate of Jerusalem.
13 Harness the chariot to the
team of horses,
O inhabitant of Lachish—
She was the beginning of sin
To the daughter of Zion—
Because in you were found
The transgressions of Israel.
14 Therefore you will give parting gifts
On behalf of Moresheth-gath;
The houses of Achzib *will*
become a deception
To the kings of Israel.
15 Moreover, I will bring on you
The one who takes possession,
O inhabitant of Mareshah.
The glory of Israel will enter Adullam.
16 Make yourself bald and
cut off your hair,
Because of the children of your delight;
Extend your baldness like the eagle,
For they will go from you into exile.

2 Woe to those who devise wickedness,
Who work out evil on their beds!
When the light of the morning
comes, they do it,
For it is in the power of their hands.
2 And they covet fields and
then tear *them* away,
And houses, and take *them* away.
And they oppress a man and his house,
A man and his inheritance.
3 Therefore thus says Yahweh,
"Behold, I am devising against
this family an evil *demise*
From which you cannot
remove your necks;
And you will not walk haughtily,
For it will be an evil time.
4 "On that day they will take up
against you a taunt
And utter a bitter wailing *and* say,
'We are completely devastated!
He exchanges the portion
of my people;
How He removes it from me!
To the faithless one, He
apportions our fields.'
5 "Therefore you will have no one
stretching a measuring line
For you by lot in the
assembly of Yahweh.
6 'Do not speak, dripping out *words*,'
they say *while* dripping out *words*.

But if they do not drip out *words*
concerning these things,
Dishonor will not be turned back.
7 "Is it being said, O house of Jacob:
'Is the Spirit of Yahweh impatient?
Are these His deeds?'
Do not My words do good
To the one walking uprightly?
8 "And recently My people have
arisen as an enemy—
You strip the robe off the garment
From unsuspecting passers-by,
From those returned from war.
9 "The women of My people
you drive out,
Each *one* from her pleasant house.
From her infants you take
My splendor forever.
10 "Arise and go,
For this is no place of rest
Because of the uncleanness
that wreaks destruction,
A painful destruction.
11 "If a man walking after wind and lying
Had acted falsely *and said,*
'I will speak, dripping out *words* to
you concerning wine and liquor,'
He would be one who drips out *words*
as a spokesman to this people.

12 "I will surely assemble all of you, Jacob;
I will surely gather the
remnant of Israel.
I will put them together like
sheep in the fold;
Like a flock in the midst of its pasture
They will be noisy with men.
13 "The breaker goes up before them;
They break out, pass through
the gate, and go out by it.
So their king goes on before them,
And Yahweh at their head."

3 And I said,
"Hear now, heads of Jacob
And rulers of the house of Israel.
Is it not for you to know justice?
2 "You who hate good and love evil,
Who tear off their skin from them
And their flesh from their bones,
3 And who eat the flesh of my people,
Strip off their skin from them,
Break their bones,
And spread *them* out as for the pot
And as meat in a caldron."
4 Then they will cry out to Yahweh,
But He will not answer them.
Instead, He will hide His face
from them at that time
Because they have practiced evil deeds.

5 Thus says Yahweh concerning the prophets
who lead my people astray;
When they have *something*
to bite with their teeth,
They call out, "Peace,"
But against him who puts
nothing in their mouths,
They set *themselves* apart for war.
6 Therefore *it will be* night for
you—without vision,
And darkness for you—
without divination.
The sun will go down on the prophets,
And the day will grow black over them.
7 The seers will be ashamed,
And the diviners will be humiliated.
Indeed, they will all cover
their mouths
Because there is no answer from God.
8 On the other hand I am
filled with power—
With the Spirit of Yahweh—
And with justice and might
To declare to Jacob his transgression,
Even to Israel his sin.
9 Now hear this, heads of
the house of Jacob
And rulers of the house of Israel,
Who abhor justice
And twist everything that is straight,
10 Who build Zion with bloodshed
And Jerusalem with violent injustice.
11 Her heads pronounce
judgment for a bribe,
And her priests instruct for a price,
And her prophets divine for money.
Yet they lean on Yahweh saying,
"Is not Yahweh in our midst?
Evil will not come upon us."
12 Therefore, on account of you
Zion will be plowed as a field;
Jerusalem will become a heap of ruins,
And the mountain of the house *of God*
will become high places of a forest.

Psalm 144:9–15

9 O God, I will sing a new song to You;
Upon a harp of ten strings I
will sing praises to You,

10 Who gives salvation to kings,
Who sets David His servant
free from the evil sword.
11 Set me free and deliver me out of the
hand of the sons of a foreigner,
Whose mouth speaks worthlessness
And whose right hand is a
right hand of lying.

12 That our sons would be as grown-up
plants in their youth,
And our daughters as corner pillars
fashioned as for a palace;
13 *That* our granaries would be full,
furnishing every kind of produce,
And our flocks would bring forth
thousands and ten thousands
in our *fields* outside;
14 That our cattle would bear
Without mishap and without loss,
And without outcry in our streets!
15 How blessed are the people
for whom this is so;
How blessed are the people for
whom God is Yahweh!

Proverbs 30:10

10 Do not slander a slave to his master,
Lest he curse you and you
be found guilty.

Revelation 9:1–21

9 Then the fifth angel sounded. Then I
saw a star from heaven which had fallen
to the earth, and the key of the pit of the
abyss was given to him. 2 And he opened the
pit of the abyss and smoke went up out of
the pit, like the smoke of a great furnace,
and the sun and the air were darkened
by the smoke of the pit. 3 Then out of the
smoke came locusts upon the earth, and
power was given them, as the scorpions of
the earth have power. 4 And they were told
not to hurt the grass of the earth, nor any
green thing, nor any tree, but only the men
who do not have the seal of God on their
foreheads. 5 And they were not permitted to
kill anyone, but to torment for five months,
and their torment was like the torment of
a scorpion when it stings a man. 6 And in
those days men will seek death and will
never find it; they will long to die, and death
flees from them.

7 And the appearance of the locusts
was like horses prepared for battle. And
on their heads appeared to be crowns like
gold, and their faces were like the faces
of men. 8 And they had hair like the hair
of women, and their teeth were like *the*
teeth of lions. 9 And they had breastplates
like breastplates of iron, and the sound of
their wings was like the sound of chariots,
of many horses running to battle. 10 And
they have tails like scorpions, and stings;
and in their tails is their power to hurt men
for five months. 11 They have as king over
them, the angel of the abyss. His name in
Hebrew is Abaddon, and in the Greek he
has the name Apollyon.

12 One woe is past; behold, two woes are
still coming after these things.

13 Then the sixth angel sounded, and I
heard a voice from the four horns of the
golden altar which is before God, 14 one
saying to the sixth angel who had the
trumpet, "Release the four angels who
have been bound at the great river Euphra-
tes." 15 And the four angels were released,
who had been prepared for the hour and
day and month and year, so that they
would kill a third of mankind. 16 And the
number of the armies of the horsemen was
two hundred million; I heard the number
of them. 17 And this is how I saw in the
vision the horses and those who sit on
them: *the riders* had breastplates *the color*
of fire and of hyacinth and of brimstone;
and the heads of the horses are like the
heads of lions; and out of their mouths
come fire and smoke and brimstone. 18 A
third of mankind was killed by these three
plagues, by the fire and the smoke and
the brimstone which came out of their
mouths. 19 For the power of the horses is
in their mouths and in their tails; for their
tails are like serpents, having heads, and
with them they do harm.

20 And the rest of mankind, who were not
killed by these plagues, did not repent of the
works of their hands, so as not to worship
demons, and the idols of gold and of silver
and of brass and of stone and of wood,
which can neither see nor hear nor walk.
21 And they did not repent of their murders
nor of their sorceries nor of their sexual
immorality nor of their thefts.

DECEMBER 20

Micah 4:1–5:15

4 Now it will be that in the last days
The mountain of the house of Yahweh
Will be established as the
head of the mountains,
And will be lifted up above the hills,
And the peoples will stream to it.
2 And many nations will come and say,
"Come and let us go up to the
mountain of Yahweh
And to the house of the God of Jacob,
That He may instruct us from His ways
And that we may walk in His paths."
For from Zion will go forth the law,
And the word of Yahweh
from Jerusalem.
3 And He will judge between
many peoples
And will render decisions for
mighty, distant nations.
And they will hammer their
swords into plowshares
And their spears into pruning hooks;
Nation will not lift up sword
against nation,
And never again will they learn war.
4 And each of them will sit
under his vine
And under his fig tree,
With no one to make *them* tremble,
For the mouth of Yahweh
of hosts has spoken.
5 Though all the peoples walk
Each in the name of his god,
As for us, we will walk
In the name of Yahweh our
God forever and ever.

6 "In that day," declares Yahweh,
"I will assemble the lame
And gather the banished,
Even those *upon* whom I
have brought calamity.
7 "I will make the lame a remnant
And the outcasts a mighty nation,
And Yahweh will reign over
them in Mount Zion
From now on and forever.
8 "And as for you, tower of the flock,
Hill of the daughter of Zion,
To you it will come—
Even the former dominion will come,
The kingdom of the daughter
of Jerusalem.

9 "Now, why do you make a loud shout?
Is there no king among you,
Or has your counselor perished,
That writhing has taken hold of you
like a woman in childbirth?
10 "Writhe and labor to give birth,
Daughter of Zion,
Like a woman in childbirth;
For now you will go out of the city,
Dwell in the field,
And go to Babylon.
There you will be delivered;
There Yahweh will redeem you
From the hand of your enemies.
11 "But now many nations have been
assembled against you
Who say, 'Let her be polluted,
And let our eyes behold
Zion *in triumph*.'
12 "But they do not know the
thoughts of Yahweh,
And they do not understand
His counsel;
For He has gathered them like
sheaves to the threshing floor.
13 "Arise and thresh, daughter of Zion,
For your horn I will make iron,
And your hoofs I will make bronze,
That you may pulverize
many peoples,
That you may devote to Yahweh their
greedy gain unto destruction
And their wealth to the
Lord of all the earth.

5 "Now muster yourselves in
troops, daughter of troops;
They have laid siege against us;
With a rod they will strike the
judge of Israel on the cheek.
2 "But as for you, Bethlehem Ephrathah,
Too little to be among the
clans of Judah,
From you One will go forth for
Me to be ruler in Israel.
His goings forth are from everlasting,
From the ancient days."
3 Therefore He will give them
up until the time

When she who is in childbirth
has borne a child.
Then the remainder of His brothers
Will return to the sons of Israel.
4 And He will stand and
shepherd *His flock*
In the strength of Yahweh,
In the majesty of the name
of Yahweh His God.
And they will remain
Because at that time He will be great
To the ends of the earth.
5 And this One will be peace.

When the Assyrian enters our land,
When he treads on our citadels,
Then we will raise against him
Seven shepherds and eight
princes of men.
6 And they will shepherd the land
of Assyria with the sword,
The land of Nimrod at its entrances;
And He will deliver *us*
from the Assyrian
When he enters our land
And when he treads within
our borders.

7 Then the remnant of Jacob
Will be among many peoples
Like dew from Yahweh,
Like showers on vegetation
Which do not hope for man
Or wait for the sons of men.
8 Then the remnant of Jacob
Will be among the nations,
Among many peoples
Like a lion among the
beasts of the forest,
Like a young lion among
flocks of sheep,
Which, if it passes through,
Tramples down and tears,
And there is none to deliver.
9 Your hand will be raised up
against your adversaries,
And all your enemies will be cut off.

10 "And it will be in that day,"
declares Yahweh,
"That I will cut off your horses
from among you
And destroy your chariots.
11 "And I will cut off the cities of your land
And pull down all your fortifications.
12 "And I will cut off sorceries
from your hand,
And you will have
soothsaying no more.
13 "And I will cut off your graven images
And your *sacred* pillars
from among you
So that you will no longer worship
The work of your hands.
14 "And I will uproot your Asherim
from among you
And eradicate your cities.
15 "And I will execute vengeance
in anger and wrath
On the nations which have
not listened."

Psalm 145:1–9

1 I will exalt You, my God, O King,
And I will bless Your name
forever and ever.

2 Every day I will bless You,
And I will praise Your name
forever and ever.

3 Great is Yahweh, and highly
to be praised,
And His greatness is unsearchable.

4 One generation shall laud
Your works to another,
And shall declare Your mighty deeds.

5 On the glorious splendor
of Your majesty
And on the words of Your
wondrous deeds, I will muse.

6 Men shall speak of the strength
of Your fearsome acts,
And I will recount Your greatness.

7 They shall pour forth the memory
of Your abundant goodness
And will shout joyfully of
Your righteousness.

8 Yahweh is gracious and compassionate;
Slow to anger and great in
lovingkindness.

9 Yahweh is good to all,
And His compassions are
over all His works.

Proverbs 30:11–14

11 There is a generation that
curses its father
And does not bless its mother.
12 There is a generation that is
clean in its own eyes,
Yet is not washed from its filthiness.
13 There is a generation—oh how
haughty are its eyes!
And its eyelids are lifted up.
14 There is a generation whose
teeth are *like* swords
And its fangs *like* knives,
To devour the afflicted from the earth
And the needy from among men.

Revelation 10:1–11

10 Then I saw another strong angel com-
ing down out of heaven, clothed with
a cloud, and the rainbow was upon his head,
and his face was like the sun, and his feet like
pillars of fire; 2 and he had in his hand a little
scroll which was open. He placed his right
foot on the sea and his left on the earth, 3 and
he cried out with a loud voice, as when a lion
roars. And when he had cried out, the seven
peals of thunder uttered their voices. 4 And
when the seven peals of thunder had spoken,
I was about to write; and I heard a voice from
heaven saying, "Seal up the things which the
seven peals of thunder have spoken and do
not write them." 5 Then the angel, whom I
saw standing on the sea and on the earth,
lifted up his right hand to heaven, 6 and
swore by Him who lives forever and ever,
WHO CREATED HEAVEN AND THE THINGS IN IT,
AND THE EARTH AND THE THINGS IN IT, AND
THE SEA AND THE THINGS IN IT, that there
will be delay no longer, 7 but in the days of
the voice of the seventh angel, when he is
about to sound, then the mystery of God is
finished, as He proclaimed good news to His
slaves, the prophets.
8 Then the voice which I heard from
heaven, *I heard* again speaking with me, and
saying, "Go, take the scroll which is open in
the hand of the angel who stands on the sea
and on the earth." 9 So I went to the angel,
telling him to give me the little scroll. And he
*said to me, "Take it and eat it; it will make
your stomach bitter, but in your mouth it
will be sweet as honey." 10 And I took the
little scroll out of the angel's hand and ate
it, and in my mouth it was sweet as honey;
and when I had eaten it, my stomach was
made bitter. 11 And they *said to me, "You
must prophesy again about many peoples
and nations and tongues and kings."

DECEMBER 21

Micah 6:1–7:20

6 Listen now to what Yahweh is saying,
"Arise, plead your case before
the mountains,
And let the hills listen to your voice.
2 "Listen, you mountains, to
the case of Yahweh,
And you enduring foundations
of the earth,
Because Yahweh has a case
against His people;
Even with Israel He will reprove.
3 "My people, what have I done to you,
And how have I wearied
you? Answer Me.
4 "Indeed, I brought you up
from the land of Egypt
And ransomed you from
the house of slavery,
And I sent before you Moses,
Aaron, and Miriam.
5 "My people, remember now
What Balak king of Moab counseled
And what Balaam son of
Beor answered him,
And from Shittim to Gilgal,
So that you might know the
righteous acts of Yahweh."
6 With what shall I come
before Yahweh
And bow myself before
the God on high?
Shall I come before Him
with burnt offerings,
With yearling calves?
7 Is Yahweh pleased with
thousands of rams,
With ten thousand rivers of oil?
Shall I give my firstborn *for*
my transgression,
The fruit of my body for
the sin of my soul?
8 He has told you, O man, what is good;
And what does Yahweh require of you

But to do justice, to love
lovingkindness,
And to walk humbly with your God?
9 The voice of Yahweh will
call to the city—
And it is sound wisdom to
fear Your name:
"Hear, O tribe. Who even has
appointed its time?
10 "Is there yet a man in the wicked house,
Along with treasures of wickedness,
And a short measure *which is* cursed?
11 "Can I purify wicked scales
And a bag of deceptive weights?
12 "For the rich men of *the* city
are full of violence,
And her inhabitants speak lies,
And their tongue is deceitful
in their mouth.
13 "So also I will make *you* sick,
striking you down,
Desolating *you* because of your sins.
14 "You will eat, but you will
not be satisfied,
And your vileness will be
in your midst.
And you will *try to* remove
something for safekeeping,
But you will not cause
anything to escape,
And that which you do have escape,
I will give to the sword.
15 "You will sow but you will not reap.
You will tread the olive but will
not anoint yourself with oil;
And the grapes, but you
will not drink wine.
16 "The statutes of Omri
And all the works of the house
of Ahab are kept;
And in their counsels you walk.
Therefore I will give you up
as an object of horror
And your inhabitants as an
object of hissing,
And you will bear the reproach
of My people."

7 Woe is me! For I am
Like the fruit pickers, like
the grape gatherers.
There is not a cluster of grapes to eat,
Or a first-ripe fig *which*
my soul desires.
2 The holy one has perished
from the land,
And there is no upright
person among men.
All of them lie in wait for bloodshed;
Each of them hunts the
other with a net.
3 Concerning evil, both hands do it well.
The prince asks, also the
judge, for a payment,
And a great man speaks the
craving of his soul;
So they weave it together.
4 The best of them is like a briar,
The most upright like a thorn hedge.
The day when you post
your watchmen,
Your punishment will come.
At that time their panic will happen.
5 Do not believe in a neighbor;
Do not have confidence in
a close companion.
From her who lies in your bosom
Guard the openings of your mouth.
6 For son treats father as a wicked fool;
Daughter rises up against her mother,
Daughter-in-law against
her mother-in-law;
A man's enemies are the men
of his own household.
7 But as for me, I will watch
expectantly for Yahweh;
I will wait for the God of my salvation.
My God will hear me.
8 Do not be glad over me, O my enemy.
Though I fall I will rise;
Though I inhabit the darkness,
Yahweh is a light for me.

9 I will bear the rage of Yahweh
Because I have sinned against Him,
Until He pleads my case and
does justice for me.
He will bring me out to the light,
And I will see His righteousness.
10 Then my enemy will see,
And shame will cover her
who said to me,
"Where is Yahweh your God?"
My eyes will look on her;
At that time she will be trampled down
Like mire of the streets.
11 *It will be* a day for building your walls.
On that day your boundary
will be extended.

12 It *will be* a day when they
will come to you
From Assyria and the cities of Egypt,
From Egypt even to the River,
Even from sea to sea and
mountain to mountain.
13 And the earth will become desolate
because of her inhabitants,
On account of the fruit of their deeds.

14 Shepherd Your people
with Your scepter,
The flock of Your inheritance
Which dwells by itself in the forest,
In the midst of a fruitful orchard.
Let them feed in Bashan and Gilead
As in the ancient days.
15 "As in the days when you came
out from the land of Egypt,
I will show you wondrous deeds."
16 Nations will see and be ashamed
Of all their might.
They will put *their* hand on *their* mouth;
Their ears will be deaf.
17 They will lick the dust like a serpent,
Like crawling things of the earth.
They will come trembling
out of their fortresses;
To Yahweh our God they
will come in dread,
And they will be afraid before You.
18 Who is a God like You,
who forgives iniquity
And passes over the transgression of
the remnant of His inheritance?
He does not hold fast to
His anger forever
Because He delights in lovingkindness.
19 He will again have compassion on us;
He will subdue our iniquities.
And You will cast all their sins
Into the depths of the sea.
20 You will give truth to Jacob
And lovingkindness to Abraham,
Which You swore to our fathers
From the days of old.

Psalm 145:10–16

10 All Your works, O Yahweh,
shall give thanks to You,
And Your holy ones shall bless You.

11 They shall speak of the glory
of Your kingdom
And talk of Your might;
12 To make known to the sons of
men His mighty deeds
And the glory of the majesty
of His kingdom.

13 Your kingdom is an
everlasting kingdom,
And Your dominion *endures* from
generation to every generation.

14 Yahweh sustains all who fall
And raises up all who
are bowed down.

15 The eyes of all wait on You,
And You give them their
food in due time.

16 You open Your hand
And satisfy the desire of
every living thing.

Proverbs 30:15

15 The leech has two daughters,
"Give," "Give."
There are three things that
will not be satisfied,
Four that will not say, "Enough":

Revelation 11:1–19

11 Then a measuring rod like a staff
was given to me, saying, "Get up and
measure the sanctuary of God and the altar,
and those who worship in it. 2 And leave out
the court which is outside the sanctuary and
do not measure it, for it has been given to
the Gentiles, and they will trample the holy
city under foot for forty-two months. 3 And I
will give *authority* to my two witnesses, and
they will prophesy for 1,260 days, clothed in
sackcloth." 4 These are the two olive trees
and the two lampstands that stand before
the Lord of the earth. 5 And if anyone wishes
to harm them, fire comes out of their mouth
and devours their enemies; so if anyone
wishes to harm them, he must be killed in
this way. 6 These have the authority to shut
up the sky, so that rain will not fall during
the days of their prophesying; they also have
authority over the waters to turn them into
blood, and to strike the earth with every
plague, as often as they wish.
7 And when they have finished their
witness, the beast that comes up out of
the abyss will make war with them and

overcome them and kill them. 8 And their dead bodies *will lie* in the street of the great city which spiritually is called Sodom and Egypt, where also their Lord was crucified. 9 And those from the peoples and tribes and tongues and nations *will* look at their dead bodies for three and a half days, and will not permit their dead bodies to be laid in a tomb. 10 And those who dwell on the earth *will* rejoice over them and celebrate and send gifts to one another, because these two prophets tormented those who dwell on the earth.

11 But after the three and a half days, the breath of life from God came into them, and they stood on their feet, and great fear fell upon those who were watching them. 12 And they heard a loud voice from heaven saying to them, "Come up here." Then they went up into heaven in the cloud, and their enemies watched them. 13 And in that hour there was a great earthquake, and a tenth of the city fell; seven thousand people were killed in the earthquake, and the rest were terrified and gave glory to the God of heaven.

14 The second woe is past; behold, the third woe is coming quickly.

15 Then the seventh angel sounded, and there were loud voices in heaven, saying,

"The kingdom of the world has become *the kingdom* of our Lord and of His Christ, and He will reign forever and ever." 16 And the twenty-four elders, who sit on their thrones before God, fell on their faces and worshiped God, 17 saying,

"We give You thanks, O Lord God, the Almighty, who is and who was, because You have taken Your great power and have begun to reign. 18 And the nations were enraged, and Your rage came, and the time *came* for the dead to be judged, and to give reward to Your slaves—the prophets and the saints and those who fear Your name, the small and the great—and to destroy those who destroy the earth."

19 And the sanctuary of God which is in heaven was opened, and the ark of His covenant appeared in His sanctuary, and there were flashes of lightning and sounds and peals of thunder and an earthquake and a great hailstorm.

DECEMBER 22

Nahum 1:1–3:19

1 The oracle of Nineveh. The book of the vision of Nahum the Elkoshite.

2 A jealous and avenging God is Yahweh;
Yahweh is avenging and wrathful.
Yahweh is avenging against
His adversaries,
And He keeps *His anger* for His enemies.
3 Yahweh is slow to anger
and great in power,
And Yahweh will by no means
leave *the guilty* unpunished.

In whirlwind and storm is His way,
And clouds are the dust
beneath His feet.

4 He rebukes the sea and makes it dry;
He dries up all the rivers.
Bashan and Carmel languish;
The blossoms of Lebanon languish.

5 Mountains quake because of Him,
And the hills melt;
Indeed the earth is upheaved
by His presence,
The world and all the inhabitants in it.

6 Who can stand before His
indignation?
Who can endure the burning
of His anger?

His wrath is poured out like fire,
And the rocks are torn down by Him.

7 Yahweh is good,
A strong defense in the day
of distress,

And He knows those who
take refuge in Him.
8 But with an overflowing flood

He will make a complete
destruction of its place
And will pursue His enemies
into darkness.

9 Whatever you devise against
Yahweh,
He will make a complete
destruction of it.
Distress will not rise up twice.
10 Like tangled thorns,
And like those who are drunken
with their drink,
They are consumed
As stubble fully dried up.
11 From you has gone forth
One who devised evil against
Yahweh,
A vile counselor.
12 Thus says Yahweh,
"Though they are at full *strength*
and likewise many,
Even so, they will be cut
off and pass away.
Though I have afflicted you,
I will afflict you no longer.
13 "So now, I will break his yoke
bar from upon you,
And I will break your bands apart."

14 And Yahweh has commanded
concerning you:
"There will no longer be seed
from your name.
From the house of your gods,
I will cut off graven image
and molten image.
I will prepare your grave,
For you are contemptible."

15 Behold, on the mountains the feet of
him who proclaims good news,
Who announces peace!
Celebrate your feasts, O Judah;
Pay your vows.
For never again will the vile
one pass through you;
He is cut off completely.

2 The one who scatters has
come up against you.
Guard the fortification, watch the road;
Strengthen your loins, instill *your*
power with exceeding courage.
2 For Yahweh will restore the
majesty of Jacob
Like the majesty of Israel,
Even though those who empty *them*
have emptied them to destruction
And ruined their vine branches.
3 The shields of his mighty
men are *colored* red,
The valiant men are dressed in scarlet,
The chariots are *enveloped*
in flashing steel
When he is set up *to march*,
And the cypress *spears*
are brandished.
4 The chariots race madly in the streets;
They rush wildly in the squares;
Their appearance is like torches;
They dash to and fro like
lightning flashes.
5 He remembers his mighty ones;
They stumble in their march;
They hurry to her wall,
And the mantelet is set up.
6 The gates of the rivers are opened,
And the palace is melted away.
7 So it stands fixed:
She is exiled, she is carried away,
And her maidservants are moaning
like the sound of doves,
Beating on their hearts.

8 Though Nineveh *was* like a pool
of water throughout her days,
Now they are fleeing;
"Stand! Stand!"
But no one turns back.
9 Plunder the silver!
Plunder the gold!
And there is no limit to the treasure—
Wealth from every kind of
desirable object.
10 She is emptied! Yes, she is emptied
out and eviscerated!
Hearts are melting and
knees knocking!
Also anguish is in all *their* loins,
And all their faces turn pale!
11 Where is the den of the lions
And the feeding place of
the young lions,
Where the lion, lioness, and
lion's cub prowled,
With nothing to make *them* tremble?
12 The lion tore enough for its cubs
And strangled *enough* for its lionesses
And filled its lairs with torn up prey
And its dens with torn up flesh.
13 "Behold, I am against you," declares
Yahweh of hosts. "And I will burn up her
chariots in smoke, and a sword will devour
your young lions; and I will cut off your prey

from the land, and no longer will the voice of your messengers be heard."

3 Woe to the city of bloodshed,
completely full of
deception *and* pillage;
Her prey never departs.
2 The sound of the whip,
And the sound of the
rumbling of the wheel,
Galloping horses,
And bounding chariots!
3 Horsemen charging,
And swords flaming,
and spears flashing,
Many slain, a mass of corpses,
And there is no end to dead bodies—
They stumble over the dead bodies!
4 *All* because of the many
harlotries of the harlot,
The charming one, the
mistress of sorceries,
Who sells nations by her harlotries
And families by her sorceries.
5 "Behold, I am against you,"
declares Yahweh of hosts;
"And I will uncover your
skirts over your face
And show to the nations your nakedness
And to the kingdoms your disgrace.
6 "I will throw detestable *filth* on you
And display you as a wicked fool
And set you up as a spectacle.
7 "And it will be that all who see you
Will flee from you and say,
'Nineveh is devastated!
Who will console her?'
Where will I seek comforters for you?"

8 Are you better than No-amon,
Which sits along the waters of the Nile,
With water surrounding her,
Whose rampart *was* the sea,
Whose wall *consisted* of the sea?
9 Ethiopia was *her* might,
And Egypt too, without end.
Put and Lubim were among
her helpers.
10 Yet she became an exile;
She went into captivity;
Also her infants were dashed to pieces
At the head of every street;
They cast lots for her honorable men,
And all her great men were
bound with fetters.
11 You too will become drunk;
You will be hidden.
You too will search for a strong
defense from the enemy.
12 All your fortifications are fig
trees with ripe fruit—
When shaken, they fall into
the eater's mouth.
13 Behold, your people are
women in your midst!
The gates of your land are opened
wide to your enemies;
Fire consumes your gate bars.
14 Draw for yourself water for the siege!
Strengthen your fortifications!
Go into the clay and tread the mortar!
Take hold of the brick mold!
15 There, fire will consume you;
The sword will cut you down;
It will consume you as the locust *does*.

Multiply yourself like the
creeping locust,
Multiply yourself like the
swarming locust.
16 You have increased your traders
more than the stars of heaven—
The creeping locust strips
and flies away.
17 Your guardsmen are like the
swarming locust.
Your marshals are like a
locust-swarm
Encamping in the stone
walls on a cold day.
The sun rises, and they flee,
And the place where they
are is not known.
18 Your shepherds are sleeping,
O king of Assyria;
Your mighty ones are lying down.
Your people are scattered
on the mountains,
And there is no one to regather *them*.
19 There is no relief for your
breakdown,
Your wound is incurable.
All who hear the report about you
Will clap *their* hands over you,
For on whom has not your
evil passed continually?

Psalm 145:17–21

17 Yahweh is righteous in all His ways
And holy in all His works.

18 Yahweh is near to all who
call upon Him,
To all who call upon Him in truth.

19 He will work out the desire of
those who fear Him;
He will hear their cry for help
and He will save them.

20 Yahweh keeps all who love Him,
But all the wicked He will destroy.

21 My mouth will speak the
praise of Yahweh,
And all flesh will bless His holy
name forever and ever.

Proverbs 30:16

16 Sheol, and the barren womb,
Earth that is never satisfied with water,
And fire that never says, "Enough."

Revelation 12:1–17

12 And a great sign appeared in heaven: a
woman clothed with the sun, and the
moon under her feet, and on her head a crown
of twelve stars. 2 And she was with child, and
she *cried out, being in labor and in pain to
give birth. 3 Then another sign appeared in
heaven: and behold, a great red dragon having
seven heads and ten horns, and on his heads
were seven diadems. 4 And his tail *swept
away a third of the stars of heaven and threw
them to the earth. And the dragon stood
before the woman who was about to give
birth, so that when she gave birth he might
devour her child. 5 And she gave birth to a son,
a male *child*, who is to rule all the nations with
a rod of iron; and her child was caught up to
God and to His throne. 6 Then the woman fled
into the wilderness where she *had a place
prepared by God, so that there she would be
nourished for 1,260 days.

7 And there was war in heaven, Michael
and his angels waging war with the dragon.
The dragon and his angels waged war, 8 and
they were not strong enough, and there was
no longer a place found for them in heaven.
9 And the great dragon was thrown down,
the serpent of old who is called the devil
and Satan, who deceives the whole world.
He was thrown down to the earth, and his
angels were thrown down with him. 10 Then
I heard a loud voice in heaven, saying,

"Now the salvation, and the power, and
the kingdom of our God and the authority
of His Christ have come, for the accuser of
our brothers has been thrown down, he who
accuses them before our God day and night.
11 And they overcame him because of the
blood of the Lamb and because of the word
of their witness, and they did not love their
life even to death. 12 For this reason, rejoice,
O heavens and you who dwell in them. Woe
to the earth and the sea, because the devil
has come down to you, having great wrath,
knowing that he has *only* a short time."

13 And when the dragon saw that he was
thrown down to the earth, he persecuted
the woman who gave birth to the male *child*.
14 But the two wings of the great eagle were
given to the woman, so that she could fly
into the wilderness to her place, where she
*was nourished for a time and times and
half a time, from the presence of the ser-
pent. 15 And the serpent poured water like
a river out of his mouth after the woman,
so that he might cause her to be swept away
with the flood. 16 But the earth helped the
woman, and the earth opened its mouth
and drank up the river which the dragon
poured out of his mouth. 17 So the dragon
was enraged with the woman and went off
to make war with the rest of her seed, who
keep the commandments of God and have
the witness of Jesus.

DECEMBER 23

Habakkuk 1:1–3:19

1 The oracle which Habakkuk the prophet
beheld.

2 How long, O Yahweh, will
I call for help,
And You will not hear?
I cry out to You, "Violence!"
Yet You do not save.

3 Why do You make me see wickedness
And cause *me* to look on trouble?
Indeed, devastation and
violence are before me;
And there is strife, and
contention is lifted up.

4 Therefore the law is ignored,
And justice never comes forth.

For the wicked surround the righteous;
Therefore justice comes
forth perverted.
5 "See among the nations! And look!
Be also astonished! Be astounded!
Because *I am* doing something
in your days—
You would not believe if it
was recounted *to you.*
6 "For behold, I am raising
up the Chaldeans,
That bitter and hasty nation
Who walks on the breadth of the land
To possess dwelling places
which are not theirs.
7 "They are dreaded and feared;
Their justice and exaltation come
forth from themselves.
8 "Their horses are swifter than leopards
And sharper than wolves
in the evening.
Their horsemen come galloping;
Their horsemen come from afar;
They fly like an eagle swooping
down to devour.
9 "All of them come for violence.
Their horde of faces *moves* forward.
And they gather captives like sand.
10 "And they mock at kings,
And rulers are a laughing
matter to them.
They laugh at every fortress
And heap up dirt and capture it.
11 "Then they will sweep through
like the wind and pass on.
But they will be held guilty,
They whose power is their god."
12 Are You not from everlasting,
O Yahweh, my God, my Holy One?
We will not die.
You, O Yahweh, have placed
them to judge;
And You, O Rock, have established
them to reprove.
13 *Your* eyes are too pure to see evil,
And You cannot look on trouble.
Why do You look
On those who deal treacherously?
Why are You silent when the
wicked swallow up
Those more righteous than they?
14 And You have made men like
the fish of the sea,
Like creeping things without
a ruler over them.
15 *The Chaldeans* bring all of
them up with a hook,
Drag them away with their net,
And gather them together
in their fishing net.
Therefore they are glad and rejoice.
16 Therefore they offer a
sacrifice to their net
And burn incense to their fishing net
Because through these things
their portion is rich
And their food is fat.
17 Will they therefore empty their net
And continually kill nations
without sparing?

2 I will stand on my guard post
And station myself on the fortification;
And I will keep watch to see
what He will speak to me
And how I may respond
when I am reproved.
2 Then Yahweh answered me and said,
"Write down the vision
And write *it* on tablets distinctly,
That the one who reads it may run.
3 "For the vision is yet for the
appointed time;
It pants toward its end,
and it will not lie.
Though it tarries, wait for it;
For it will certainly come;
it will not delay.

4 "Behold, as for the proud one,
His soul is not right within him;
But the righteous will live by
his faith.
5 "And indeed, wine betrays
the haughty man
So that he does not stay at home.
He enlarges his appetite like Sheol,
And he is like death, never satisfied.
He also gathers to himself all nations
And assembles to himself all peoples.

6 "Will not all of these lift up a
taunt-song against him,
Even satire *and* riddles against him
And say, 'Woe to him who
increases what is not his—
For how long—
And makes himself rich with loans?'
7 "Will not your creditors
rise up suddenly,

And those who make you
tremble awaken?
Indeed, you will become
spoil for them.
8 "Because you have taken
many nations as spoil,
All that is left of the peoples
will take you as spoil—
Because of human bloodshed and
violence done to the land,
To the town and all its inhabitants.

9 "Woe to him who is greedy for
evil gain for his house
To put his nest on high,
To be delivered from the hand of evil!
10 "You have counseled a shameful
thing for your house
By cutting off many peoples;
So you are sinning against
your own soul.
11 "Surely the stone will cry
out from the wall,
And the rafter will answer it
from the framework.

12 "Woe to him who builds a
city with bloodshed
And founds a town with injustice!
13 "Is it not, behold,
from Yahweh of hosts
That peoples toil for fire,
And nations grow weary for nothing?
14 "For the earth will be filled
With the knowledge of the
glory of Yahweh,
As the waters cover the sea.

15 "Woe to you who make your
neighbors drink,
Who mix in your venom even
to make *them* drunk
So as to look on their nakedness!
16 "You will be filled with disgrace
rather than glory.
Now you yourself drink and
expose your *own* nakedness.
The cup in Yahweh's right hand
will come around to you,
And utter disgrace *will come*
upon your glory.
17 "For the violence done to
Lebanon will cover you,
And the devastation of *its* beasts
by which you terrified them,
Because of human bloodshed and
violence done to the land,
To the town and all its inhabitants.

18 "What profit is the graven image
when its maker has engraved it,
Or a molten image, a teacher of lies?
For *its* maker trusts in his *own* making
When he fashions speechless idols.
19 "Woe to him who says to a
piece of wood, 'Awake!'
To a mute stone, 'Arise!'
And that is *your* teacher?
Behold, it is overlaid with
gold and silver,
And there is no breath at all inside it.
20 "But Yahweh is in His holy temple.
Let all the earth be silent before Him."

3 A prayer of Habakkuk the prophet,
according to Shigionoth.
2 O Yahweh, I have heard the
report about You, *and* I fear.
O Yahweh, revive Your work in
the midst of the years;
In the midst of the years
make it known;
In rage remember compassion.

3 God comes from Teman,
And the Holy One from
Mount Paran. Selah.
His splendor covers the heavens,
And the earth is full of His praise.
4 *His* brightness is like the sunlight;
He has rays *flashing* from His hand,
And there is the hiding of His strength.
5 Before Him goes pestilence,
And plague comes after Him.
6 He stood and measured out the earth;
He looked and startled the nations.
So the perpetual mountains
were shattered;
The ancient hills collapsed.
His ways are everlasting.
7 I saw the tents of Cushan
under wickedness;
The tent curtains of the land of
Midian were trembling.

8 Did Yahweh's *fury* burn
against the rivers,
Or *was* Your anger against the rivers,
Or *was* Your wrath against the sea,
That You rode on Your horses,

On Your chariots of salvation?
9 Your bow was made bare;
Rods were sworn *unto*
battle by word. Selah.
You split the earth with rivers.
10 The mountains saw You *and* writhed;
The downpour of waters passed by.
The deep gave forth its voice;
It lifted high its hands.
11 Sun *and* moon stood in
their lofty places;
They went away at the light
of Your arrows,
At the brightness of Your
flashing spear.
12 In indignation You marched
through the earth;
In anger You trampled the nations.
13 You went forth for the salvation
of Your people,
For salvation with Your anointed.
You crushed the head of the
house of the wicked
To lay him bare from
thigh to neck. Selah.
14 You pierced with his own
sharpened rods
The head of his throngs.
They stormed in to scatter us;
Their exultation *was* like those
Who devour the afflicted in secret.
15 You tread on the sea with Your horses,
On the surge of many waters.

16 I heard, and my inward parts trembled;
At the sound my lips tingled.
Decay enters my bones,
And in my place I tremble.
Because I must wait quietly
for the day of distress,
For the people to arise *who*
will invade us.
17 Though the fig tree should
not blossom
And there be no produce on the vines,
Though the yield of the
olive should fail
And the fields yield no food,
Though the flock should be
cut off from the fold
And there be no cattle in the stalls,
18 Yet I will exult in Yahweh;
I will rejoice in the God of my salvation.
19 Yahweh, the Lord, is my strength,
And He has set my feet like hinds' *feet*
And makes me tread on
my high places.
For the choir director, on my stringed
instruments.

Psalm 146:1–10

1 Praise Yah!
Praise Yahweh, O my soul!
2 I will praise Yahweh
throughout my life;
I will sing praises to my God
while I have my being.
3 Do not trust in nobles,
In *merely* a son of man, in whom
there is no salvation.
4 His spirit departs, he
returns to the earth;
In that very day his plans perish.
5 How blessed is he whose help
is the God of Jacob,
Whose hope is in Yahweh his God,
6 Who made heaven and earth,
The sea and all that is in them;
Who keeps truth forever;
7 Who does justice for the oppressed;
Who gives food to the hungry.
Yahweh sets the prisoners free.

8 Yahweh opens *the eyes of* the blind;
Yahweh raises up those who
are bowed down;
Yahweh loves the righteous;
9 Yahweh keeps the sojourners;
He helps up the orphan and the widow,
But He bends the way of the wicked.
10 Yahweh will reign forever,
Your God, O Zion, from
generation to generation.
Praise Yah!

Proverbs 30:17

17 The eye that mocks a father
And despises obedience to a mother,
The ravens of the valley will pick it out,
And the young eagles will eat it.

Revelation 13:1–18

13 And the dragon stood on the sand of
the seashore.
Then I saw a beast coming up out of the
sea, having ten horns and seven heads, and
on his horns *were* ten diadems, and on his
heads *were* blasphemous names. 2 And the
beast which I saw was like a leopard, and
his feet were like *those* of a bear, and his

mouth like the mouth of a lion. And the dragon gave him his power and his throne and great authority. 3 And *I saw* one of his heads as if it had been slain fatally, and his fatal wound was healed. And the whole earth marveled *and followed* after the beast. 4 And they worshiped the dragon because he gave his authority to the beast, and they worshiped the beast, saying, "Who is like the beast, and who is able to wage war with him?" 5 And there was given to him a mouth speaking great boasts and blasphemies, and authority to act for forty-two months was given to him. 6 And he opened his mouth in blasphemies against God, to blaspheme His name and His tabernacle, *that is*, those who dwell in heaven.

7 And it was also given to him to make war with the saints and to overcome them, and authority over every tribe and people and tongue and nation was given to him. 8 And all who dwell on the earth will worship him, *everyone* whose name has not been written from the foundation of the world in the book of life of the Lamb who has been slain. 9 If anyone has an ear, let him hear. 10 If anyone *is destined* for captivity, to captivity he goes; if anyone kills with the sword, with the sword he must be killed. Here is the perseverance and the faith of the saints.

11 Then I saw another beast coming up out of the earth, and he had two horns like a lamb and he was speaking as a dragon. 12 And he exercises all the authority of the first beast in his presence. And he makes the earth and those who dwell in it to worship the first beast, whose fatal wound was healed. 13 And he does great signs, so that he even makes fire come down out of heaven to the earth in the presence of men. 14 And he deceives those who dwell on the earth because of the signs which were given to him to do in the presence of the beast, telling those who dwell on the earth to make an image to the beast who *had the wound of the sword and has come to life. 15 And it was given to him to give breath to the image of the beast, so that the image of the beast would even speak and cause as many as do not worship the image of the beast to be killed. 16 And he causes all, the small and the great, and the rich and the poor, and the free men and the slaves, that they be given a mark on their right hand or on their forehead, 17 and that no one will be able to buy or to sell, except the one who has the mark, *either* the name of the beast or the number of his name. 18 Here is wisdom. Let him who has understanding calculate the number of the beast, for it is the number of man; and his number is 666.

Knowledge of the Bible is the best antidote against modern heresies.

— J. C. RYLE

DECEMBER 24

Zephaniah 1:1–3:20

1 The word of Yahweh which came to Zephaniah son of Cushi, son of Gedaliah, son of Amariah, son of Hezekiah, in the days of Josiah son of Amon, king of Judah:

2 "I will completely end all *things*
From the face of the ground,"
declares Yahweh.
3 "I will end man and beast;
I will end the birds of the sky
And the fish of the sea
And the ruins along with the wicked;
And I will cut off man from the face
of the ground," declares Yahweh.
4 "So I will stretch out My
hand against Judah
And against all the inhabitants
of Jerusalem.
And I will cut off the remnant
of Baal from this place,
And the names of the idolatrous
priests along with the priests,
5 And those who worship on the
housetops the host of heaven,
And those who worship *and*
swear to Yahweh and *yet*
swear by Milcom,
6 And those who have turned back
from following Yahweh,

And those who have not sought
Yahweh or inquired of Him."
7 Be silent before Lord Yahweh!
For the day of Yahweh is near,
For Yahweh has prepared a sacrifice;
He has set apart His guests.
8 "Then it will be on the day
of Yahweh's sacrifice
That I will punish the princes,
the king's sons,
And all who clothe themselves
with foreign garments.
9 "And I will punish on that day all who
leap on the *temple* threshold,
Who fill the house of their Lord
with violence and deceit.
10 "And it will be in that day,"
declares Yahweh,
"*That* there will be the sound of
a cry from the Fish Gate
And a wail from the Second Quarter
And a great destruction from the hills.
11 "Wail, O inhabitants of the Mortar,
For all the people of Canaan
will be silenced;
All who weigh out silver will be cut off.
12 "And it will be at that time
That I will search Jerusalem
with lamps,
And I will punish the men
Who are stagnant in spirit,
Who say in their hearts,
'Yahweh will not do good or evil!'
13 "And it will be that their wealth
will become spoil
And their houses desolate;
Indeed, they will build houses
but not inhabit *them*,
And plant vineyards but not
drink their wine."

14 Near is the great day of Yahweh,
Near and coming very quickly;
O the sound, the day of Yahweh!
In it the mighty man cries out bitterly.
15 A day of fury is that day,
A day of trouble and distress,
A day of destruction and desolation,
A day of darkness and thick darkness,
A day of clouds and dense gloom,
16 A day of trumpet and loud shouting
Against the fortified cities
And the high corner towers.
17 I will bring distress on men
So that they will walk like the blind
Because they have sinned
against Yahweh;
And their blood will be
poured out like dust
And their flesh like dung.
18 Neither their silver nor their gold
Will be able to deliver them
On the day of the fury of Yahweh;
And all the earth will be devoured
In the fire of His jealousy,
For He will make a complete
destruction,
Indeed a terrifying one,
Of all the inhabitants of the earth.

2 Gather yourselves together,
indeed, gather,
O nation without shame,
2 Before the decree takes effect—
The day passes like the chaff—
Before the burning anger of
Yahweh comes upon you,
Before the day of Yahweh's
anger comes upon you.
3 Seek Yahweh,
All you humble of the earth
Who have worked His justice;
Seek righteousness, seek humility.
Perhaps you will be hidden
In the day of Yahweh's anger.

4 For Gaza will be forsaken
And Ashkelon a desolation;
Ashdod will be driven out at noon,
And Ekron will be uprooted.
5 Woe to the inhabitants of the seacoast,
The nation of the Cherethites!
The word of Yahweh is against you,
O Canaan, land of the Philistines;
And I will make you perish
So that there will be no inhabitant.
6 So the seacoast will be pastures,
With caves for shepherds
and folds for flocks.
7 And the coast will be
For the remnant of the house of Judah;
They will feed upon it.
In the houses of Ashkelon they
will lie down at evening;
For Yahweh their God will care for them
And restore their fortune.

8 "I have heard the reproach of Moab
And the revilings of the
sons of Ammon,

With which they have
reproached My people
And magnified *themselves*
against their territory.
9 "Therefore, as I live," declares
Yahweh of hosts,
The God of Israel,
"Surely Moab will be like Sodom
And the sons of Ammon
like Gomorrah—
A place possessed by nettles
and salt pits,
And a perpetual desolation.
The remnant of My people
will plunder them,
And the remainder of My
nation will inherit them."
10 This they will have in return for their
pride because they have reproached and
magnified *themselves* against the people of
Yahweh of hosts. 11 Yahweh will be fearsome
to them, for He will starve all the gods of the
earth; and all the coastlands of the nations
will bow down to Him, everyone from his
own place.
12 "You also, O Ethiopians,
will be slain by My sword."
13 And He will stretch out His
hand against the north
And cause Assyria to perish,
And He will make Nineveh
a desolation,
Parched like the wilderness.
14 Flocks will lie down in her midst,
All the beasts of the nation;
Both the pelican and the hedgehog
Will lodge in the tops of her pillars;
Their voice will sing in the window,
Ruin *will be* on the threshold;
For He has laid bare the cedar work.
15 This is the exultant city
Which inhabits securely,
Who says in her heart,
"I am, and there is no one besides me."
How she has become an
object of horror,
A resting place for beasts!
Everyone who passes by her will hiss
And wave his hand *in contempt*.

3 Woe to her who is rebellious
and defiled,
The oppressive city!
2 She did not listen to *any* voice;
She did not receive discipline.
She did not trust in Yahweh;
She did not draw near to her God.
3 Her princes in her midst
are roaring lions;
Her judges are wolves at evening;
They *leave* nothing to gnaw
for the morning.
4 Her prophets are reckless,
treacherous men;
Her priests have profaned
the sanctuary.
They have done violence to the law.
5 Yahweh is righteous in her midst;
He will do no injustice.
Every morning He brings
His justice to light;
He does not fail.
But the unjust knows no shame.
6 "I have cut off nations;
Their corner towers are desolate.
I have made their streets a waste,
With no one passing by;
Their cities are laid waste,
Without a man, without an inhabitant.
7 "I said, 'Surely you will fear Me,
Receive discipline.'
So her abode will not be cut off
According to all that I have
appointed concerning her.
But they were eager to corrupt
all their deeds.
8 "Therefore wait for Me,"
declares Yahweh,
"For the day when I rise up as a witness.
Indeed, My judgment is to
assemble nations,
To gather kingdoms,
To pour out on them My indignation,
All My burning anger;
For all the earth will be devoured
By the fire of My zeal.
9 "For then I will change *them* to
peoples with purified lips,
That all of them may call on
the name of Yahweh,
To serve Him shoulder to shoulder.
10 "From beyond the rivers of Ethiopia
My worshipers, My scattered ones,
Will bring My offerings.
11 "In that day you will feel no shame
Because of all your deeds
By which you have transgressed
against Me;
For then I will remove from your midst
Your proud, exulting ones,

And you will never again be haughty
On My holy mountain.
12 "But I will cause to remain in your midst
A lowly and poor people,
And they will take refuge in
the name of Yahweh.
13 "The remnant of Israel will
do no injustice
And not speak falsehood,
Nor will a deceitful tongue
Be found in their mouths;
For they will feed and lie down
With no one to make them tremble."
14 Sing for joy, O daughter of Zion!
Make a loud shout, O Israel!
Be glad and exult with all *your* heart,
O daughter of Jerusalem!
15 Yahweh has taken away *His*
judgments against you;
He has cleared away your enemies.
The King of Israel, Yahweh,
is in your midst;
You will fear evil no more.
16 In that day it will be said to Jerusalem:
"Do not fear, O Zion;
Do not let your hands fall limp.
17 "Yahweh your God is in your midst,
A mighty one who will save.
He will be joyful over you
with gladness;
He will be quiet in His love;
He will rejoice over you
with joyful singing.
18 "I will assemble those who grieve
about the appointed feasts—
They were from you, *O Zion*;
The reproach *of exile* is a
burden on them.
19 "Behold, I am going to deal
at that time
With all those who afflict you,
And I will save the lame
And gather the banished,
And I will turn them—in their
shame—into praise and a name
In all the earth.
20 "At that time I will bring you in,
Even at the time when I
gather you together;
Indeed, I will give you *to be*
a name and praise
Among all the peoples of the earth,
When I restore your fortunes
before your eyes,"
Says Yahweh.

Psalm 147:1–6

1 Praise Yah!
For it is good to sing praises to our God;
For it is pleasant *and* praise
is becoming.
2 Yahweh builds up Jerusalem;
He gathers the outcasts of Israel.
3 *He is* the One who heals
the brokenhearted
And who binds up their wounds,
4 Who counts the number of the stars;
He gives names to all of them.
5 Great is our Lord and
abundant in power;
His discernment is infinite.
6 Yahweh helps up the afflicted;
He brings down the wicked
to the ground.

Proverbs 30:18–19

18 There are three things which
are too wonderful for me,
Four which I do not understand:
19 The way of an eagle in the sky,
The way of a serpent on a rock,
The way of a ship in the
heart of the sea,
And the way of a man with a virgin.

Revelation 14:1–20

14 Then I looked, and behold, the Lamb
was standing on Mount Zion, and
with Him 144,000, having His name and the
name of His Father written on their fore-
heads. 2 And I heard a voice from heaven,
like the sound of many waters and like the
sound of loud thunder, and the voice which
I heard *was* like *the sound* of harpists playing
on their harps. 3 And they *sang a new song
before the throne and before the four living
creatures and the elders. And no one could
learn that song except the 144,000 who had
been purchased from the earth. 4 These are
the ones who are not defiled with women,
for they are virgins. These *are* the ones who
follow the Lamb wherever He goes. These
have been purchased from among men as
first fruits to God and to the Lamb. 5 And
NO LIE WAS FOUND IN THEIR MOUTH; they are
blameless.

6 Then I saw another angel flying in
midheaven, having an eternal gospel to
proclaim to those who inhabit the earth,
and to every nation and tribe and tongue
and people. 7 And he said with a loud voice,

"Fear God, and give Him glory, because the hour of His judgment has come; worship Him who made the heaven and the earth and sea and springs of waters."

8 And another angel, a second one, followed, saying, "FALLEN, FALLEN IS BABYLON THE GREAT, she who has made all the nations drink of the wine of the wrath of her sexual immorality."

9 Then another angel, a third one, followed them, saying with a loud voice, "If anyone worships the beast and his image, and receives a mark on his forehead or on his hand, 10 and he also will drink of the wine of the wrath of God, which is mixed in full strength in the cup of His rage, and he will be tormented with fire and brimstone in the presence of the holy angels and in the presence of the Lamb. 11 And the smoke of their torment goes up forever and ever; they have no rest day and night, those who worship the beast and his image, and whoever receives the mark of his name." 12 Here is the perseverance of the saints who keep the commandments of God and their faith in Jesus.

13 And I heard a voice from heaven, saying, "Write, 'Blessed are the dead who die in the Lord from now on!'" "Yes," says the Spirit, "so that they may rest from their labors, for their deeds follow with them."

14 Then I looked, and behold, a white cloud, and sitting on the cloud *was* one like a son of man, having a golden crown on His head and a sharp sickle in His hand. 15 And another angel came out of the sanctuary, crying out with a loud voice to Him who sits on the cloud, "Put in Your sickle and reap, for the hour to reap has come, because the harvest of the earth is ripe." 16 Then He who sits on the cloud swung His sickle over the earth, and the earth was reaped.

17 And another angel came out of the sanctuary which is in heaven, and he also had a sharp sickle. 18 Then another angel, the one who has authority over fire, came out from the altar; and he called with a loud voice to him who had the sharp sickle, saying, "Put in your sharp sickle and gather the clusters from the vine of the earth, because her grapes are ripe." 19 So the angel swung his sickle to the earth and gathered *the clusters from* the vine of the earth, and threw them into the great wine press of the wrath of God. 20 And the wine press was trodden outside the city, and blood came out from the wine press, up to the horses' bridles, for a distance of 1,600 stadia.

DECEMBER 25

Haggai 1:1–2:23

1 In the second year of Darius the king, on the first day of the sixth month, the word of Yahweh came by the hand of Haggai the prophet to Zerubbabel the son of Shealtiel, governor of Judah, and to Joshua the son of Jehozadak, the high priest, saying, 2 "Thus says Yahweh of hosts, 'This people says, "The time has not come, *even* the time for the house of Yahweh to be rebuilt."'" 3 Then the word of Yahweh came by the hand of Haggai the prophet, saying, 4 "Is it time for you yourselves to live in your paneled houses while this house *lies* waste?" 5 So now, thus says Yahweh of hosts, "Set your heart *to consider* your ways! 6 You have sown much, but bring in little; *you* eat, but *there is* not *enough* to be satisfied; *you* drink, but *there is* not *enough* to become drunk; *you* put on clothing, but no one is warm *enough*; and he who earns, earns wages *to put* into a bag with holes."

7 Thus says Yahweh of hosts, "Set your heart *to consider* your ways! 8 Go up to the mountains and bring wood and rebuild the house *of God*, that I may be pleased with it and be glorified," says Yahweh. 9 "*You* look for much, but behold, *it comes* to little; and you bring *it* home, and I blow it *away*. Why?" declares Yahweh of hosts, "Because of My house which *lies* waste, while each of you runs to his own house. 10 Therefore, because of you the sky has restrained its dew and the earth has restrained its produce. 11 And I called for a drought on the land, on the mountains, on the grain, on the new wine, on the oil, on what the ground brings forth, on men, on cattle, and on all the labor of your hands."

12 Then Zerubbabel the son of Shealtiel, and Joshua the son of Jehozadak, the high priest, with all the remnant of the people, listened to the voice of Yahweh their God and the words of Haggai the prophet, as

Yahweh their God had sent him. And the people feared Yahweh. 13 Then Haggai, the messenger of Yahweh, spoke by the commissioned message of Yahweh to the people saying, "'I am with you,' declares Yahweh." 14 So Yahweh stirred up the spirit of Zerubbabel the son of Shealtiel, governor of Judah, and the spirit of Joshua the son of Jehozadak, the high priest, and the spirit of all the remnant of the people; and they came and did work on the house of Yahweh of hosts, their God, 15 on the twenty-fourth day of the sixth month in the second year of Darius the king.

2 On the twenty-first of the seventh month, the word of Yahweh came by the hand of Haggai the prophet saying, 2 "Speak now to Zerubbabel the son of Shealtiel, governor of Judah, and to Joshua the son of Jehozadak, the high priest, and to the remnant of the people saying, 3 'Who among you remains who saw this house in its former glory? And how do you see it now? Does it not seem like nothing in your eyes? 4 But now, be strong, Zerubbabel,' declares Yahweh, 'be strong also, Joshua son of Jehozadak, the high priest, and all you people of the land, be strong,' declares Yahweh, 'and work; for I am with you,' declares Yahweh of hosts. 5 'As for the promise which I cut with you when you came out of Egypt, My Spirit is standing in your midst; do not fear!' 6 For thus says Yahweh of hosts, 'Once more—in a little while—I am going to shake the heavens and the earth, the sea also and the dry land. 7 And I will shake all the nations; and they will come with the desirable things of all nations, and I will fill this house with glory,' says Yahweh of hosts. 8 'The silver is Mine, and the gold is Mine,' declares Yahweh of hosts. 9 'The latter glory of this house will be greater than the former,' says Yahweh of hosts, 'and in this place I will give peace,' declares Yahweh of hosts."

10 On the twenty-fourth of the ninth *month*, in the second year of Darius, the word of Yahweh came to Haggai the prophet, saying, 11 "Thus says Yahweh of hosts, 'Ask now the priests *about the* law: 12 If a man carries holy meat in the fold of his garment and touches bread with this fold or cooked food, wine, oil, or any *other* food, will it become holy?'" And the priests answered, "No." 13 Then Haggai said, "If one who is unclean from a corpse touches any of these, will *the latter* become unclean?" And the priests answered, "It will become unclean." 14 Then Haggai answered and said, "'So is this people. And so is this nation before Me,' declares Yahweh, 'and so is every work of their hands; and what they bring near *to Me* there is unclean. 15 But now, oh set your heart *to consider* from this day onward: from before one stone was set on another in the temple of Yahweh, 16 from when it was that one came to a *grain* heap of twenty *measures*, then there would be only ten; and *from when* one came to the wine vat to draw fifty troughs full, then there would be *only* twenty. 17 I struck you *and* every work of your hands with scorching wind, mildew, and hail; yet you *did* not *come back* to Me,' declares Yahweh. 18 'Oh set your heart *to consider* from this day onward, from the twenty-fourth day of the ninth *month*; from the day when the temple of Yahweh was founded, set your heart *to consider*: 19 Is the seed still in the barn? Even including the vine, the fig tree, the pomegranate, and the olive tree, it has not borne *fruit*. Yet from this day on I will bless *you*.'"

20 Then the word of Yahweh came a second time to Haggai on the twenty-fourth *day* of the month, saying, 21 "Speak to Zerubbabel governor of Judah, saying, 'I am going to shake the heavens and the earth. 22 I will overthrow the thrones of kingdoms and destroy the strength of the kingdoms of the nations; and I will overthrow the chariots and their riders, and the horses and their riders will go down, everyone by the sword of another.' 23 'On that day,' declares Yahweh of hosts, 'I will take you, Zerubbabel, son of Shealtiel, My servant,' declares Yahweh, 'and I will make you like a signet *ring*, for I have chosen you,'" declares Yahweh of hosts.

Psalm 147:7–11

7 Sing to Yahweh with thanksgiving;
Sing praises to our God on the lyre.
8 *He is* the One who covers the
heavens with clouds,
The One who provides
rain for the earth,
The One who makes grass to
sprout on the mountains,
9 Who gives to the animal its food,

And to the young ravens
which call out.
10 He does not delight in the
might of the horse;
He does not take pleasure
in the legs of a man.
11 Yahweh is pleased with
those who fear Him,
Those who wait for His
lovingkindness.

Proverbs 30:20

20 This is the way of an
adulterous woman:
She eats and wipes her mouth,
And says, "I have done no wrong."

Revelation 15:1–8

15 Then I saw another sign in heaven,
great and marvelous, seven angels
who have seven plagues, *which are* the
last, because in them the wrath of God is
finished.
2 Then I saw something like a sea of
glass mixed with fire, and those who have
overcome the beast and his image and the
number of his name, standing on the sea of
glass, having harps of God. 3 And they *sang
the song of Moses, the slave of God, and the
song of the Lamb, saying,
"GREAT AND MARVELOUS
ARE YOUR WORKS,
O LORD GOD, THE ALMIGHTY;
RIGHTEOUS AND TRUE ARE YOUR WAYS,
KING OF THE NATIONS!
4 "WHO WILL NOT FEAR, O LORD,
AND GLORIFY YOUR NAME?
For You alone are holy;
For ALL THE NATIONS WILL COME
AND WORSHIP BEFORE YOU,
FOR YOUR RIGHTEOUS ACTS
HAVE BEEN REVEALED."
5 And after these things I looked, and the
sanctuary of the tabernacle of testimony in
heaven was opened, 6 and the seven angels
who have the seven plagues came out of
the sanctuary, clothed in linen, clean *and*
bright, and girded around their chests with
golden sashes. 7 Then one of the four living
creatures gave to the seven angels seven
golden bowls full of the wrath of God, who
lives forever and ever. 8 And the sanctuary
was filled with smoke from the glory of God
and from His power; and no one was able to
enter the sanctuary until the seven plagues
of the seven angels were finished.

DECEMBER 26

Zechariah 1:1–3:10

1 In the eighth month of the second year
of Darius, the word of Yahweh came to
Zechariah the prophet, the son of Bere-
chiah, the son of Iddo, saying, 2 "Yahweh
was very wrathful against your fathers.
3 Therefore say to them, 'Thus says Yahweh
of hosts, "Return to Me," declares Yahweh
of hosts, "that I may return to you," says
Yahweh of hosts. 4 "Do not be like your
fathers, to whom the former prophets called
out, saying, 'Thus says Yahweh of hosts,
"Return now from your evil ways and from
your evil deeds."' But they did not listen or
give heed to Me," declares Yahweh. 5 "Your
fathers, where are they? And the prophets,
do they live forever? 6 But did not My words
and My statutes, which I commanded My
slaves the prophets, overtake your fathers?
Then they returned and said, 'As Yahweh of
hosts purposed to do to us in accordance
with our ways and our deeds, so He has
done with us.'"'"
7 On the twenty-fourth day of the elev-
enth month, which is the month Shebat,
in the second year of Darius, the word of
Yahweh came to Zechariah the prophet, the
son of Berechiah, the son of Iddo, saying,
8 I saw at night, and behold, a man was
riding on a red horse, and he was standing
among the myrtle trees which were in the
ravine, with red, sorrel, and white horses
behind him. 9 Then I said, "My lord, what
are these?" And the angel who was speaking
with me said to me, "I will show you what
these are." 10 And the man who was standing
among the myrtle trees answered and said,
"These are those whom Yahweh has sent to
patrol the earth." 11 So they answered the
angel of Yahweh who was standing among
the myrtle trees and said, "We have patrolled
the earth, and behold, all the earth is sitting
still and quiet."
12 Then the angel of Yahweh answered
and said, "O Yahweh of hosts, how long
will You have no compassion for Jerusalem

and the cities of Judah, with which You have been indignant these seventy years?" 13 Yahweh answered the angel who was speaking with me with good words, comforting words. 14 So the angel who was speaking with me said to me, "Call out, saying, 'Thus says Yahweh of hosts, "I am exceedingly jealous for Jerusalem and Zion. 15 But I am very wrathful with the nations who are at ease; for I was only a little wrathful, but they helped *increase* the calamity." 16 Therefore thus says Yahweh, "I will return to Jerusalem with compassion; My house will be built in it," declares Yahweh of hosts, "and a measuring line will be stretched over Jerusalem."'
17 Again, call out, saying, 'Thus says Yahweh of hosts, "My cities will again overflow with good, and Yahweh will again comfort Zion and again choose Jerusalem."'"

18 Then I lifted up my eyes and saw, and behold, *there were* four horns. 19 So I said to the angel who was speaking with me, "What are these?" And he said to me, "These are the horns which have scattered Judah, Israel, and Jerusalem." 20 Then Yahweh showed me four craftsmen. 21 And I said, "What are these coming to do?" And he said, "These are the horns which have scattered Judah so that no man lifts up his head; but these *craftsmen* have come to cause them to tremble, to throw down the horns of the nations who have lifted up *their* horns against the land of Judah in order to scatter it."

2 Then I lifted up my eyes and saw, and behold, *there was* a man with a measuring cord in his hand. 2 So I said, "Where are you going?" And he said to me, "To measure Jerusalem, to see how wide it is and how long it is." 3 And behold, the angel who was speaking with me was going out, and another angel was coming out to meet him
4 and said to him, "Run, speak to that young man, saying, 'Jerusalem will be inhabited without walls because of the multitude of men and cattle within it. 5 Indeed I,' declares Yahweh, 'will be a wall of fire around her, and I will be the glory in her midst.'"

6 "Ho there! Flee from the land of the north," declares Yahweh, "for I have dispersed you as the four winds of the heavens," declares Yahweh. 7 "Woe, Zion! Escape, you who are living with the daughter of Babylon." 8 For thus says Yahweh of hosts, "After glory He has sent Me against the nations which have taken you as spoil, for he who touches you, touches the apple of His eye. 9 For behold, I will wave My hand over them so that they will be spoil for their slaves. Then you will know that Yahweh of hosts has sent Me. 10 Sing for joy and be glad, O daughter of Zion; for behold, I am coming and I will dwell in your midst," declares Yahweh. 11 "And many nations will join themselves to Yahweh in that day and will become My people. Then I will dwell in your midst, and you will know that Yahweh of hosts has sent Me to you. 12 Then Yahweh will inherit Judah as His portion in the holy land and will again choose Jerusalem.

13 "Be silent, all flesh, before Yahweh; for He is aroused from His holy habitation."

3 Then he showed me Joshua the high priest standing before the angel of Yahweh, and Satan standing at his right hand to accuse him. 2 And Yahweh said to Satan, "Yahweh rebuke you, Satan! Indeed, Yahweh who has chosen Jerusalem rebuke you! Is this not a brand delivered from the fire?" 3 Now Joshua was clothed with filthy garments and standing before the angel.
4 And he answered and spoke to those who were standing before him, saying, "Remove the filthy garments from him." Again he said to him, "See, I have made your iniquity pass away from you and will clothe you with festal robes." 5 Then I said, "Let them put a clean turban on his head." So they put a clean turban on his head and clothed him with garments, while the angel of Yahweh was standing by.

6 And the angel of Yahweh testified to Joshua, saying, 7 "Thus says Yahweh of hosts, 'If you will walk in My ways and if you will keep the responsibility *given by* Me, then you will also render justice in My house and also keep My courts, and I will grant you access to walk among these who are standing *here*. 8 Now listen, Joshua the high priest, you and your friends who are sitting in front of you—indeed they are men who are a wondrous sign, for behold, I am going to bring in My servant the Branch.
9 For behold, the stone that I have put before Joshua; on one stone are seven eyes. Behold, I will engrave an inscription on it,' declares Yahweh of hosts, 'and I will remove the iniquity of that land in one day. 10 In that day,' declares Yahweh of hosts, 'every one

of you will call for his neighbor to *sit* under
his vine and under *his* fig tree.'"

Psalm 147:12–20

12 Laud Yahweh, O Jerusalem!
Praise your God, O Zion!
13 For He strengthened the
bars of your gates;
He blessed your sons within you.
14 *He is* the One who sets peace
in your borders,
He satisfies you with the
finest of the wheat,
15 The One who sends forth His
command to the earth;
His word runs very swiftly,
16 The One who gives snow like wool;
He scatters the frost like ashes,
17 Who casts forth His ice as fragments;
Who can stand before His cold?
18 He sends forth His word
and melts them;
He causes His wind to blow
and so the waters flow,
19 Who declares His words to Jacob,
His statutes and His
judgments to Israel.
20 He has not done so with any nation;
So as for His judgments, they
have not known them.
Praise Yah!

Proverbs 30:21–23

21 Under three things the earth quakes,
And under four, it cannot bear up:
22 Under a slave when he becomes king,
And a wicked fool when he
is satisfied with food,
23 Under an unloved woman
when she gets a husband,
And a servant-girl when she
supplants her mistress.

Revelation 16:1–21

16 Then I heard a loud voice from the
sanctuary, saying to the seven angels,
"Go and pour out on the earth the seven
bowls of the wrath of God."
2 So the first *angel* went and poured
out his bowl on the earth; and it became a
loathsome and malignant sore on the people
who have the mark of the beast and who
worship his image.
3 And the second *angel* poured out his
bowl into the sea, and it became blood like
that of a dead man, and every living thing
in the sea died.
4 Then the third *angel* poured out his bowl
into the rivers and the springs of waters, and
they became blood.
5 And I heard the angel
of the waters saying, "Righteous are You,
who is and who was, O Holy One, because
You judged these things;
6 for they poured
out the blood of saints and prophets, and
You have given them blood to drink. They
deserve it."
7 And I heard the altar saying,
"Yes, O Lord God, the Almighty, true and
righteous are Your judgments."
8 And the fourth *angel* poured out his
bowl upon the sun, and it was given to
it to scorch men with fire.
9 And men
were scorched with fierce heat, and they
blasphemed the name of God who has the
authority over these plagues, and they did
not repent so as to give Him glory.
10 Then the fifth *angel* poured out his
bowl on the throne of the beast, and his
kingdom became darkened; and they
gnawed their tongues because of pain,
11 and they blasphemed the God of heaven
because of their pains and their sores, and
they did not repent of their deeds.
12 And the sixth *angel* poured out his
bowl on the great river, the Euphrates, and
its water was dried up, so that the way would
be prepared for the kings from the east.
13 Then I saw *coming* out of the mouth of
the dragon and out of the mouth of the beast
and out of the mouth of the false prophet,
three unclean spirits like frogs;
14 for they
are spirits of demons, doing signs, which
go out to the kings of the whole world, to
gather them together for the war of the great
day of God, the Almighty.
15 ("Behold, I am
coming like a thief. Blessed is the one who
stays awake and keeps his garments, so that
he will not walk about naked and men will
not see his shame.")
16 And they gathered
them together to the place which in Hebrew
is called Har-Magedon.
17 Then the seventh *angel* poured out
his bowl upon the air, and a loud voice
came out of the sanctuary from the
throne, saying, "It is done."
18 And there
were flashes of lightning and sounds and
peals of thunder; and there was a great
earthquake, such as there had not been
since man came to be upon the earth, so
great an earthquake *was it, and* so mighty.
19 And the great city was split into three

parts, and the cities of the nations fell.
Babylon the great was remembered before
God, to give her the cup of the wine of the
wrath of His rage. 20 And every island fled
away, and the mountains were not found.
21 And huge hailstones, about one talent
each, *came down from heaven upon men;
and men blasphemed God because of the
plague of the hail, because its plague *was
extremely severe.

DECEMBER 27

Zechariah 4:1–6:15

4 Then the angel who was speaking with
me returned and roused me, as a man
who is roused from his sleep. 2 And he said
to me, "What do you see?" And I said, "I see,
and behold, a lampstand all of gold with its
bowl on the top of it, and its seven lamps on
it with seven spouts belonging to each of the
lamps which are on the top of it, 3 also two
olive trees by it, one on the right side of the
bowl and the other on its left side." 4 Then
I answered and said to the angel who was
speaking with me saying, "What are these,
my lord?" 5 So the angel who was speaking
with me answered and said to me, "Do you
not know what these are?" And I said, "No,
my lord." 6 Then he answered and spoke to
me, saying, "This is the word of Yahweh to
Zerubbabel, saying, 'Not by might nor by
power, but by My Spirit,' says Yahweh of
hosts. 7 'What are you, O great mountain?
Before Zerubbabel *you will become* a plain;
and he will bring forth the top stone with
shouts of "Grace, grace to it!"'"

8 Also the word of Yahweh came to me,
saying, 9 "The hands of Zerubbabel have
laid the foundation of this house, and his
hands will finish *it*. Then you will know that
Yahweh of hosts has sent me to you. 10 For
who has despised the day of small things?
But these seven will be glad when they see
the plumb line in the hand of Zerubbabel—
these are the eyes of Yahweh which roam to
and fro throughout the earth."

11 Then I answered and said to him,
"What are these two olive trees on the right
of the lampstand and on its left?" 12 And I
answered the second time and said to him,
"What are the two olive branches which are
beside the two golden pipes, which empty
the golden *oil* from themselves?" 13 So he
spoke to me, saying, "Do you not know
what these are?" And I said, "No, my lord."
14 Then he said, "These are the two anointed
ones who are standing by the Lord of all the
earth."

5 Then I lifted up my eyes again and saw,
and behold, a flying scroll. 2 And he said
to me, "What do you see?" And I said, "I see
a flying scroll; its length is twenty cubits and
its width ten cubits." 3 Then he said to me,
"This is the curse that is going forth over
the face of the whole land; surely everyone
who steals will be purged away according to
the writing on one side, and everyone who
swears will be purged away according to the
writing on the other side. 4 I will make it go
forth," declares Yahweh of hosts, "and it will
enter the house of the thief and the house
of the one who swears falsely by My name;
and it will spend the night within that house
and consume it with its timber and stones."

5 Then the angel who was speaking with
me went out and said to me, "Lift up now
your eyes and see what this is going forth."
6 So I said, "What is it?" And he said, "This is
the ephah going forth." Again he said, "This
is their appearance in all the land 7 (and
behold, a lead cover was lifted up); and
this is a woman sitting inside the ephah."
8 Then he said, "This is Wickedness!" And
he threw her down into the middle of the
ephah and threw the lead weight on its
opening. 9 Then I lifted up my eyes and
saw, and behold, two women were coming
out with the wind in their wings; and they
had wings like the wings of a stork, and
they lifted up the ephah between the earth
and the heavens. 10 And I said to the angel
who was speaking with me, "Where are
they taking the ephah?" 11 Then he said to
me, "To build a house for her in the land of
Shinar; and when it is prepared, she will be
set there on her own pedestal."

6 Then I lifted up my eyes again and saw,
and behold, four chariots were coming
forth from between the two mountains;
and the mountains *were* bronze mountains.
2 With the first chariot *were* red horses, with
the second chariot black horses, 3 with the
third chariot white horses, and with the

fourth chariot dappled horses—*all of them*
mighty. 4 Then I answered and said to the
angel who was speaking with me, "What are
these, my lord?" 5 And the angel answered
and said to me, "These are the four spirits
of heaven, going forth after standing before
the Lord of all the earth, 6 with one of which
the black horses are going forth to the north
country; and the white ones go forth after
them, and the dappled ones go forth to the
south country. 7 Now the mighty ones went
out, and they sought to go to patrol the earth."
And He said, "Go, patrol the earth." So they
patrolled the earth. 8 Then He cried out to me
and spoke to me saying, "See, those who are
going to the land of the north have caused My
Spirit to have rest in the land of the north."

9 And the word of Yahweh came to me,
saying, 10 "Take *an offering* from the exiles,
from Heldai, Tobijah, and Jedaiah; and you
come the same day and come into the house
of Josiah the son of Zephaniah, where they
have come from Babylon. 11 And take silver
and gold, make an *ornate* crown, and set *it*
on the head of Joshua the son of Jehozadak,
the high priest. 12 Then you will say to him,
'Thus says Yahweh of hosts, "Behold, a man
whose name is Branch, and He will branch
out from where He is; and He will build the
temple of Yahweh. 13 Indeed, it is He who
will build the temple of Yahweh, and He
who will bear the splendor and sit and rule
on His throne. Thus, He will be a priest on
His throne, and the counsel of peace will
be between the two offices."' 14 Now the
crown will become a memorial in the temple
of Yahweh to Helem, Tobijah, Jedaiah, and
Hen the son of Zephaniah. 15 And those who
are far off will come and build the temple of
Yahweh." Then you will know that Yahweh
of hosts has sent me to you. And it will
happen if you utterly listen to the voice of
Yahweh your God.

Psalm 148:1–6

1 Praise Yah!
Praise Yahweh from the heavens;
Praise Him in the heights!
2 Praise Him, all His angels;
Praise Him, all His hosts!
3 Praise Him, sun and moon;
Praise Him, all stars of light!
4 Praise Him, heavens of heavens,
And the waters that are
above the heavens!
5 Let them praise the name of Yahweh,
For He commanded and
they were created.
6 He caused them to stand
forever and ever;
He gave a statute and it will
never pass away.

Proverbs 30:24–28

24 Four things are small on the earth,
But they are exceedingly wise:
25 The ants are not a strong people,
But they prepare their food
in the summer;
26 The shephanim are not
a mighty people,
Yet they make their houses in the cliff;
27 The locusts have no king,
Yet all of them go out in rank;
28 The lizard you may grasp
with the hands,
Yet it is in kings' palaces.

Revelation 17:1–18

17 Then one of the seven angels who
have the seven bowls came and spoke
with me, saying, "Come here, I will show you
the judgment of the great harlot who sits
on many waters, 2 with whom the kings of
the earth committed sexual immorality, and
those who dwell on the earth were made
drunk with the wine of her sexual immoral-
ity." 3 And he carried me away in the Spirit
into a wilderness; then I saw a woman sit-
ting on a scarlet beast, full of blasphemous
names, having seven heads and ten horns.
4 And the woman was clothed in purple and
scarlet, and adorned with gold and precious
stones and pearls, having in her hand a gold
cup full of abominations and of the unclean
things of her sexual immorality, 5 and on her
forehead a name *was* written, a mystery,
"BABYLON THE GREAT, THE MOTHER OF
HARLOTS AND OF THE ABOMINATIONS
OF THE EARTH." 6 Then I saw the woman
drunk with the blood of the saints, and with
the blood of the witnesses of Jesus. When I
saw her, I wondered greatly. 7 And the angel
said to me, "Why do you wonder? I will tell
you the mystery of the woman and of the
beast that carries her, which has the seven
heads and the ten horns.

8 "The beast that you saw was, and is not,
and is about to come up out of the abyss and
go to destruction. And those who dwell on

the earth, whose name has not been written in the book of life from the foundation of the world, will wonder when they see the beast, that he was and is not and will come. 9 Here is the mind which has wisdom. The seven heads are seven mountains on which the woman sits, 10 and they are seven kings; five have fallen, one is, the other has not yet come; and when he comes, he must remain a little while. 11 And the beast which was and is not, is himself also an eighth and is *one* of the seven, and he goes to destruction. 12 And the ten horns which you saw are ten kings who have not yet received a kingdom, but they receive authority as kings with the beast for one hour. 13 These have one purpose, and they give their power and authority to the beast. 14 These will wage war against the Lamb, and the Lamb will overcome them, because He is Lord of lords and King of kings, and those who are with Him *are the* called and elect and faithful."

15 And he *said to me, "The waters which you saw where the harlot sits, are peoples and crowds and nations and tongues. 16 And the ten horns which you saw, and the beast, these will hate the harlot and will lay waste to her and make *her* naked, and will eat her flesh and will burn her up with fire. 17 For God gave *it* in their hearts to do His purpose both by doing *their own* common purpose and by giving their kingdom to the beast, until the words of God will be finished. 18 And the woman whom you saw is the great city, which has a kingdom over the kings of the earth."

DECEMBER 28

Zechariah 7:1–9:17

7 Now it happened that in the fourth year of King Darius, the word of Yahweh came to Zechariah on the fourth *day* of the ninth month, *which is* Chislev. 2 And *the town of* Bethel sent Sharezer and Regemmelech and their men to entreat the favor of Yahweh, 3 speaking to the priests, who belong to the house of Yahweh of hosts, and to the prophets, saying, "Shall I weep in the fifth month and abstain, as I have done these many years?" 4 Then the word of Yahweh of hosts came to me, saying, 5 "Speak to all the people of the land and to the priests, saying, 'When you fasted and mourned in the fifth and seventh months these seventy years, was it actually for Me that you fasted? 6 And when you eat and when you drink, are you not eating for yourselves and are you not drinking for yourselves? 7 Are not *these* the words which Yahweh called out by the hand of the former prophets, when Jerusalem was inhabited and at ease along with its cities around it, and the Negev and the Shephelah were inhabited?'"

8 Then the word of Yahweh came to Zechariah saying, 9 "Thus has Yahweh of hosts said, 'Judge with true justice and show lovingkindness and compassion each to his brother; 10 and do not oppress the widow or the orphan, the sojourner or the afflicted; and do not devise evil in your hearts against one another.' 11 But they refused to give heed and turned a stubborn shoulder and dulled their ears from hearing. 12 And they made their hearts diamond-hard so that they could not hear the law and the words which Yahweh of hosts had sent by His Spirit by the hand of the former prophets; therefore great wrath came from Yahweh of hosts. 13 And it happened that just as He called and they would not listen, so they called and I would not listen," says Yahweh of hosts; 14 "but I scattered them with a storm wind among all the nations whom they have not known. Thus the land is desolated behind them so that no one was passing through and returning, for they made the pleasant land desolate."

8 Then the word of Yahweh of hosts came, saying, 2 "Thus says Yahweh of hosts, 'I am jealous with great jealousy for Zion, and with great wrath I am jealous for her.' 3 Thus says Yahweh, 'I will return to Zion and will dwell in the midst of Jerusalem. Then Jerusalem will be called the City of Truth, and the mountain of Yahweh of hosts *will be called* the Holy Mountain.' 4 Thus says Yahweh of hosts, 'Old men and old women will again sit in the streets of Jerusalem, each man with his staff in his hand because of age. 5 And the streets of the city will be filled with boys and girls playing in its streets.' 6 Thus says Yahweh of hosts, 'If it is too difficult in the sight of the remnant of this people in

those days, will it also be too difficult in My
sight?' declares Yahweh of hosts. 7 Thus says
Yahweh of hosts, 'Behold, I am going to save
My people from the land where the *sun* rises
and from the land where the sun sets; 8 and
I will bring them *back*, and they will dwell
in the midst of Jerusalem; and they shall be
My people, and I will be their God in truth
and righteousness.'

9 "Thus says Yahweh of hosts, 'Let your
hands be strong, you who are listening in
these days to these words from the mouth
of the prophets, *those* who *spoke* in the day
that the foundation of the house of Yahweh
of hosts was laid, to the end that the temple
might be built. 10 For before those days there
was no wage for man or any wage for animal;
and for him who went out or came in there
was no peace because of the adversary, and
I set all men one against another. 11 But now
I will not treat the remnant of this people
as in the former days,' declares Yahweh of
hosts. 12 'For *there will be* peace for the seed:
the vine will yield its fruit, the land will yield
its produce, and the heavens will give their
dew; and I will cause the remnant of this
people to inherit all these *things*. 13 And it
will be that just as you were a curse among
the nations, O house of Judah and house
of Israel, so I will save you that you may
become a blessing. Do not fear; let your
hands be strong.'

14 "For thus says Yahweh of hosts, 'Just as
I purposed to bring about evil to you when
your fathers provoked Me to wrath,' says
Yahweh of hosts, 'and I have not relented,
15 so I have again purposed in these days to
do good to Jerusalem and to the house of
Judah. Do not fear! 16 These are the things
which you should do: speak the truth to one
another; judge with truth and judgment for
peace in your gates. 17 Also let none of you
devise evil in your heart against another,
and do not love false oaths; for all these are
what I hate,' declares Yahweh."

18 Then the word of Yahweh of hosts came
to me, saying, 19 "Thus says Yahweh of hosts,
'The fast of the fourth, the fast of the fifth,
the fast of the seventh, and the fast of the
tenth *months* will become joy, gladness,
and merry appointed feasts for the house
of Judah; so love truth and peace.'

20 "Thus says Yahweh of hosts, '*It will* yet
be that peoples will come, even the inhab-
itants of many cities. 21 The inhabitants of
one will go to another, saying, "Let us go at
once to entreat the favor of Yahweh and to
seek Yahweh of hosts; I will also go." 22 So
many peoples and mighty nations will come
to seek Yahweh of hosts in Jerusalem and to
entreat the favor of Yahweh.' 23 Thus says
Yahweh of hosts, 'In those days ten men
from every tongue of the nations will take
hold of the garment of a Jew, saying, "Let
us go with you, for we have heard that God
is with you."'"

9 The oracle of the word of Yahweh
is against the land of Hadrach, with
Damascus as its resting place (for the eyes
of men, especially of all the tribes of Israel,
are toward Yahweh),

2 And Hamath also, which borders on it;
And Tyre and Sidon, because
they are very wise.
3 So Tyre built herself a
tight fortification
And tied up silver like dust
And fine gold like the mire
of the streets.
4 Behold, the Lord will dispossess her
And strike her wealth
down into the sea;
And she will be consumed with fire.
5 Ashkelon will see *it* and be afraid.
Gaza too will writhe in great pain;
Also Ekron, for her hope has
been put to shame.
Moreover, the king will
perish from Gaza,
And Ashkelon will not be inhabited.
6 And those of illegitimate birth
will inhabit Ashdod,
And I will cut off the pride
of the Philistines.
7 And I will remove their blood
from their mouth
And their detestable things
from between their teeth.
Then they also will be a
remnant for our God,
And be like a clan in Judah,
And Ekron like a Jebusite.
8 But I will camp around My
house because of an army,
Because of him who passes
by and returns;
And no taskmaster will pass
over them anymore,
For now I have seen with My eyes.

9 Rejoice greatly, O daughter of Zion!
Make a loud shout, O daughter
of Jerusalem!
Behold, your king is coming to you;
He is righteous and endowed
with salvation,
Lowly and mounted on a donkey,
Even on a colt, the foal of
a pack animal.
10 I will cut off the chariot from Ephraim
And the horse from Jerusalem;
And the bow of war will be cut off.
And He will speak peace to the nations;
And His reign will be from sea to sea
And from the River to the
ends of the earth.

11 As for you also, because of the
blood of your covenant,
I have set your prisoners free
from the waterless pit.
12 Return to the stronghold,
O prisoners who have the hope;
This very day I am declaring that
I will return double to you.
13 For I will bend Judah as My bow;
I will fill the bow with Ephraim.
And I will rouse up your sons, O Zion,
against your sons, O Greece;
And I will make you like a
mighty man's sword.
14 Then Yahweh will appear over them,
And His arrow will go forth
like lightning;
And Lord Yahweh will
blow the trumpet
And will go in the storm
winds of the south.
15 Yahweh of hosts will defend them.
And they will consume and trample
on the stones of a sling;
And they will drink *and*
roar as with wine;
And they will be filled like
a *sacrificial* bowl,
Drenched like the corners of the altar.
16 And Yahweh their God will
save them in that day
As the flock of His people;
For *they are as* the stones of a crown,
Sparkling in His land.
17 For what goodness and what
beauty *will be* theirs!
Grain will make the choice men
flourish, and new wine the virgins.

Psalm 148:7–14

7 Praise Yahweh from the earth,
Sea monsters and all deeps;
8 Fire and hail, snow and clouds;
Stormy wind, doing His word;
9 Mountains and all hills;
Fruit trees and all cedars;
10 Beasts and all cattle;
Creeping things and winged bird;
11 Kings of the earth and all peoples;
Princes and all judges of the earth;
12 Both choice men as well as virgins;
The old with the young.

13 Let them praise the name of Yahweh,
For His name alone is set on high;
His splendor is above
earth and heaven.
14 And He has raised up a
horn for His people,
Praise for all His holy ones;
For the sons of Israel, a
people near to Him.
Praise Yah!

Proverbs 30:29–31

29 There are three things which
are stately in *their* march,
Even four which are stately
when they walk:
30 The lion *which* is mighty
among the animals
And does not turn back before any,
31 The strutting rooster, the
male goat also,
And a king *when his* army is with him.

Revelation 18:1–24

18 After these things I saw another
angel coming down from heaven,
having great authority, and the earth was
illumined with his glory. 2 And he cried out
with a mighty voice, saying, "FALLEN, FALLEN
IS BABYLON THE GREAT! And she has become
a dwelling place of demons and a prison of
every unclean spirit, and a prison of every
unclean bird and a prison of every unclean
and hateful beast. 3 For all the nations have
drunk of the wine of the wrath of her sexual
immorality, and the kings of the earth have
committed sexual immorality with her, and
the merchants of the earth have become
rich by the power of her sensuality."
4 And I heard another voice from heaven,
saying, "Come out of her, my people, so

that you will not participate in her sins and receive of her plagues; 5 for her sins have piled up as high as heaven, and God has remembered her iniquities. 6 Pay her back even as she paid, and give *her* back double according to her deeds; in the cup which she has mixed, mix double for her. 7 To the degree that she glorified herself and lived sensuously, to the same degree give her torment and mourning, for she says in her heart, 'I SIT *as* A QUEEN AND I AM NOT A WIDOW, and will never see mourning.' 8 For this reason in one day her plagues will come, pestilence and mourning and famine, and she will be burned up with fire; for the Lord God who judges her is strong.

9 "And the kings of the earth, who committed sexual immorality and lived sensuously with her, will cry and lament over her when they see the smoke of her burning, 10 standing at a distance because of the fear of her torment, saying, 'Woe, woe, the great city, Babylon, the strong city! For in one hour your judgment has come.'

11 "And the merchants of the earth cry and mourn over her, because no one buys their cargo anymore— 12 cargo of gold and silver and precious stones and pearls and fine linen and purple and silk and scarlet, and every *kind of* citron wood and every article of ivory and every article *made* from precious wood and bronze and iron and marble, 13 and cinnamon and amomum and incense and perfume and frankincense and wine and olive oil and fine flour and wheat and cattle and sheep, and *cargo* of horses and carriages and human beings and human lives. 14 And the fruit you long for has gone from you, and all things that were splendid and shining have passed away from you and *men* will no longer find them. 15 The merchants of these things, who became rich from her, will stand at a distance because of the fear of her torment, crying and mourning, 16 saying, 'Woe, woe, the great city, she who was clothed in fine linen and purple and scarlet, and adorned with gold and precious stones and pearls; 17 for in one hour such great wealth has been laid waste!' And every shipmaster and every passenger and sailor, and as many as make their living by the sea, stood at a distance, 18 and were crying out as they saw the smoke of her burning, saying, 'What is like the great city?' 19 And they threw dust on their heads and were crying out, crying and mourning, saying, 'Woe, woe, the great city, in which all who have ships at sea became rich by her wealth, for in one hour she has been laid waste!' 20 Rejoice over her, O heaven, and you saints and apostles and prophets, because God has pronounced judgment for you against her."

21 Then a strong angel picked up a stone like a great millstone and threw it into the sea, saying, "So will Babylon, the great city, be thrown down with violence, and will not be found any longer. 22 And the sound of harpists and musicians and flute-players and trumpeters will not be heard in you any longer; and no craftsman of any craft will be found in you any longer; and the sound of a mill will not be heard in you any longer; 23 and the light of a lamp will not shine in you any longer; and the voice of the bridegroom and bride will not be heard in you any longer; for your merchants were the great men of the earth, because all the nations were deceived by your sorcery. 24 And in her was found the blood of prophets and of saints and of all who have been slain on the earth."

DECEMBER 29

Zechariah 10:1–12:14

10 Ask rain from Yahweh at the time of the late rain—
Yahweh who makes the storm clouds;
And He will give them showers of rain,
the plant in the field to *each* man.
2 For the teraphim speak wickedness,
And the diviners behold false visions
And speak worthless dreams;
They comfort in vain.
Therefore *the people* journey like sheep;
They are afflicted because there is no shepherd.
3 "My anger burns against the shepherds,
And I will visit *punishment* upon the male goats;
For Yahweh of hosts has visited His flock, the house of Judah,

And will make them like His
splendid horse in battle.
4 "From them will come the cornerstone,
From them the tent peg,
From them the bow of battle,
From them every *good* taskmaster,
all of them together.
5 "And they will be as mighty men,
Treading down *the enemy* in the
mire of the streets in battle;
And they will battle, for Yahweh
will be with them;
And the riders on horses
will be put to shame.
6 "I will make the house of Judah mighty,
And I will save the house of Joseph,
And I will cause them to return,
Because I have had
compassion on them;
And they will be as though I
had not rejected them,
For I am Yahweh their God,
and I will answer them.
7 "And Ephraim will be like
a mighty man,
And their heart will be glad
as if *from* wine;
Indeed, their children will
see *it* and be glad;
Their heart will rejoice in Yahweh.
8 "I will whistle for them to
gather them together,
For I have redeemed them;
And they will be as numerous
as they were before.
9 "And I will sow them among
the peoples,
And they will remember
Me in far countries,
And they with their children
will live and turn back.
10 "Then I will cause them to return
from the land of Egypt
And gather them from Assyria;
And I will bring them into the
land of Gilead and Lebanon
Until no *room* can be found for them.
11 "And they will pass through
the sea *of* distress,
And He will strike the waves in the sea,
So that all the depths of
the Nile will dry up;
And the pride of Assyria will
be brought down,
And the scepter of Egypt will depart.
12 "And I will make them
mighty in Yahweh,
And in His name they will
walk," declares Yahweh.

11 Open your doors, O Lebanon,
That a fire may consume your cedars.
2 Wail, O cypress, for the
cedar has fallen,
Because the mighty *trees*
have been destroyed;
Wail, O oaks of Bashan,
For the impenetrable forest
has come down.
3 There is a sound of the
shepherds' wail,
For their might is destroyed;
There is a sound of the
young lions' roar,
For the pride of the Jordan is destroyed.
4 Thus says Yahweh my God, "Shepherd
the flock *doomed* to slaughter. 5 Those who
buy them slaughter them and are not held
guilty, and *each of* those who sell them says,
'Blessed be Yahweh. Indeed, I have become
rich!' And their own shepherds do not
spare them. 6 For I will no longer spare the
inhabitants of the land," declares Yahweh;
"but behold, I will cause the men to fall, each
into another's hand and into the hand of his
king; and they will crush the land, and I will
not deliver *them* from their hand."
7 So I shepherded the flock *doomed* to
slaughter—hence the afflicted of the flock.
And I took for myself two staffs: the one I
called Favor, and the other I called Union; so
I shepherded the flock. 8 Then I annihilated
the three shepherds in one month, for my
soul was impatient with them, and their soul
also was weary of me. 9 Then I said, "I will
not shepherd you. What is to die, let it die,
and what is to be annihilated, let it be anni-
hilated; and let those who remain consume
one another's flesh." 10 And I took my staff
Favor and cut it in pieces, to break my cov-
enant which I had cut with all the peoples.
11 So it was broken on that day, and thus the
afflicted of the flock who were watching me
knew that it was the word of Yahweh. 12 And
I said to them, "If it is good in your sight,
give *me* my wages; but if not, never mind!"
So they weighed out thirty *shekels* of silver
as my wages. 13 Then Yahweh said to me,
"Throw it to the potter, *that* valuable price
at which I was valued by them." So I took the

thirty *shekels* of silver and threw them to the
potter in the house of Yahweh. 14 Then I cut
in pieces my second staff Union, to break
the brotherhood between Judah and Israel.
15 Then Yahweh said to me, "Take again
for yourself the equipment of a foolish
shepherd. 16 For behold, I am going to raise
up a shepherd in the land who will not care
for those who face annihilation, seek the
young, heal the broken, or sustain the one
standing, but will consume the flesh of the
fat *sheep* and tear off their hoofs.

17 "Woe to the worthless shepherd
Who forsakes the flock!
A sword will be on his arm
And on his right eye!
His arm will be totally dried up,
And his right eye will be
utterly dimmed."

12 The oracle of the word of Yahweh
concerning Israel.
Thus declares Yahweh who stretches
out the heavens, lays the foundation of the
earth, and forms the spirit of man within
him, 2 "Behold, I am going to make Jerusalem
a cup that causes reeling to all the peoples
all around. Now *the one* in siege against
Jerusalem will also *be* against Judah. 3 But it
will be in that day, *that* I will make Jerusalem
a heavy stone for all the peoples; all who
heave it up will be severely injured. And all
the nations of the earth will be gathered
against it. 4 In that day," declares Yahweh,
"I will strike every horse with bewilderment
and his rider with madness. But I will open
my eyes *to watch* over the house of Judah,
while I strike every horse of the peoples
with blindness. 5 Then the clans of Judah
will say in their hearts, 'A strong support for
us are the inhabitants of Jerusalem through
Yahweh of hosts, their God.'
6 "In that day I will make the clans of
Judah like a fiery laver among pieces of
wood and a fiery torch among sheaves, so
they will consume on the right hand and
on the left all the surrounding peoples,
while Jerusalem will again be inhabited in
its own place—in Jerusalem. 7 Yahweh also
will save the tents of Judah first so that the
glory of the house of David and the glory
of the inhabitants of Jerusalem will not be
magnified above Judah. 8 In that day Yahweh
will defend the inhabitants of Jerusalem,
and the one who stumbles among them in
that day will be like David, and the house
of David *will be* like God, like the angel of
Yahweh before them. 9 And it will be in that
day, *that* I will seek to destroy all the nations
that come against Jerusalem.
10 "And I will pour out on the house of
David and on the inhabitants of Jerusalem
the Spirit of grace and of supplication, so
that they will look on Me whom they have
pierced; and they will mourn for Him, as one
mourns for an only son, and they will weep
bitterly over Him like the bitter weeping over
a firstborn. 11 In that day there will be great
mourning in Jerusalem, like the mourning
of Hadadrimmon in the plain of Megiddo.
12 And the land will mourn, each family
alone; the family of the house of David
alone and their wives alone; the family of
the house of Nathan alone and their wives
alone; 13 the family of the house of Levi
alone and their wives alone; the family of
the Shimeites alone and their wives alone;
14 all the families that remain, each family
alone and their wives alone.

Psalm 149:1–4

1 Praise Yah!
Sing to Yahweh a new song,
His praise in the assembly
of the holy ones.
2 Let Israel be glad in his Maker;
Let the sons of Zion rejoice
in their King.
3 Let them praise His name with dancing;
With tambourine and lyre let
them sing praises to Him.
4 For Yahweh takes pleasure
in His people;
He will beautify the afflicted
ones with salvation.

Proverbs 30:32–33

32 If you have been wickedly foolish
in lifting yourself up,
Or if you have schemed *evil, put
your* hand on your mouth.
33 For pressing milk brings forth butter,
And pressing the nose
brings forth blood;
And pressing anger brings forth strife.

Revelation 19:1–21

19 After these things I heard something
like a loud voice of a great crowd in
heaven, saying,

"Hallelujah! Salvation and glory and power belong to our God; 2 BECAUSE HIS JUDGMENTS ARE TRUE AND RIGHTEOUS; for He has judged the great harlot who was corrupting the earth with her sexual immorality, and HE HAS AVENGED THE BLOOD OF HIS SLAVES *shed* BY HER HAND." 3 And a second time they said, "Hallelujah! HER SMOKE RISES UP FOREVER AND EVER." 4 And the twenty-four elders and the four living creatures fell down and worshiped God who sits on the throne saying, "Amen. Hallelujah!" 5 And a voice came from the throne, saying,

"Give praise to our God, all you His slaves, you who fear Him, the small and the great." 6 Then I heard *something* like the voice of a great crowd and like the sound of many waters and like the sound of mighty peals of thunder, saying,

"Hallelujah! For the Lord our God, the Almighty, reigns.

7 "Let us rejoice and be glad and give the glory to Him, for the marriage of the Lamb has come and His bride has made herself ready." 8 And it was given to her to clothe herself in fine linen, bright *and* clean; for the fine linen is the righteous acts of the saints.

9 Then he *said to me, "Write, 'Blessed are those who are invited to the marriage supper of the Lamb.'" And he *said to me, "These are true words of God." 10 Then I fell at his feet to worship him. But he *said to me, "Do not do that! I am a fellow slave with you and your brothers who have the witness of Jesus. Worship God! For the witness of Jesus is the spirit of prophecy."

11 Then I saw heaven opened, and behold, a white horse, and He who sits on it *is* called Faithful and True, and in righteousness He judges and wages war. 12 His eyes *are* a flame of fire, and on His head *are* many diadems; having a name written *on Him* which no one knows except Himself, 13 and being clothed with a garment dipped in blood, His name is also called The Word of God. 14 And the armies which are in heaven, clothed in fine linen, white *and* clean, were following Him on white horses. 15 And from His mouth comes a sharp sword, so that with it He may STRIKE DOWN THE NATIONS, and He will RULE THEM WITH A ROD OF IRON; and HE TREADS THE WINE PRESS OF THE WRATH OF THE RAGE OF GOD, the Almighty. 16 And He has on His garment and on His thigh a name written, "KING OF KINGS, AND LORD OF LORDS."

17 Then I saw an angel standing in the sun, and he cried out with a loud voice, saying to all the birds which fly in midheaven, "Come, assemble for the great supper of God, 18 so that you may eat the flesh of kings and the flesh of commanders and the flesh of strong men and the flesh of horses and of those who sit on them and the flesh of all men, both free men and slaves, and small and great."

19 Then I saw the beast and the kings of the earth and their armies assembled to make war with Him who sits on the horse and with His army.

20 And the beast was seized, and with him the false prophet who did the signs in his presence, by which he deceived those who had received the mark of the beast and those who worshiped his image. These two were thrown alive into the lake of fire which burns with brimstone. 21 And the rest were killed with the sword which came from the mouth of Him who sits on the horse, and all the birds were filled with their flesh.

DECEMBER 30

Zechariah 13:1–14:21

13 "In that day a fountain will be opened for the house of David and for the inhabitants of Jerusalem, for sin and for impurity.

2 "And it will be in that day," declares Yahweh of hosts, "*that* I will cut off the names of the idols from the land, and they will no longer be remembered; and I will also cause the prophets and the unclean spirit to pass away from the land. 3 And it will be that if anyone still prophesies, then his father and mother who gave birth to him will say to him, 'You shall not live, for you have spoken falsely in the name of Yahweh'; and his father and mother who gave birth to him will pierce him through when he prophesies. 4 And it will be in that day, *that* the prophets will each be ashamed of his vision when he prophesies, and they will not put on a hairy mantle in order to deceive; 5 but he will say, 'I am not a prophet; I am

a cultivator of the ground, for a man sold me as a slave in my youth.’ 6 And one will say to him, ‘What are these wounds struck *here* between your arms?’ Then he will say, ‘*Those* with which I was struck in the house of my friends.’

7 “Awake, O sword, against My Shepherd
And against the man, My Associate,”
Declares Yahweh of hosts.
“Strike the Shepherd that the
sheep may be scattered;
And I will turn My hand
against the little ones.
8 “And it will be in all the land,”
Declares Yahweh,
“That two parts in it will be cut
off *and* breathe their last;
But the third will be left in it.
9 “And I will bring the third
part through the fire
And refine them as silver is refined
And test them as gold is tested.
They will call on My name,
And I will answer them;
I will say, ‘They are My people,’
And they will say, ‘Yahweh is my God.’”

14 Behold, a day is coming for Yahweh when the spoil *taken* from you will be divided among you. 2 Indeed, I will gather all the nations against Jerusalem to battle, and the city will be captured, the houses plundered, the women ravished, and half of the city will go forth in exile, but those left of the people will not be cut off from the city. 3 Then Yahweh will go forth and fight against those nations, as the day when He fights on a day of battle. 4 And in that day His feet will stand on the Mount of Olives, which is in front of Jerusalem on the east; and the Mount of Olives will be split in its middle from east to west by a very large valley so that half of the mountain will move toward the north and the other half toward the south. 5 And you will flee by the valley of My mountains, for the valley of the mountains will reach to Azel; indeed, you will flee just as you fled before the earthquake in the days of Uzziah king of Judah. Then Yahweh, my God, will come, *and* all the holy ones with Him!

6 And it will be in that day, *that* there will be no light; the luminaries will dwindle. 7 And it will be a unique day which is known to Yahweh, neither day nor night, but it will be that at evening time there will be light.

8 And it will be in that day, *that* living waters will flow out of Jerusalem, half of them toward the eastern sea and the other half toward the western sea; it will be in summer as well as in winter.

9 And Yahweh will be king over all the earth; in that day Yahweh will be *the only* one, and His name one.

10 All the land will be changed into a plain from Geba to Rimmon south of Jerusalem; but Jerusalem will rise and inhabit its site from Benjamin’s Gate as far as the place of the First Gate to the Corner Gate, and from the Tower of Hananel to the king’s wine presses. 11 And people will inhabit it, and there will no longer be *anything* devoted to destruction, for Jerusalem will be inhabited in security.

12 Now this will be the plague with which Yahweh will plague all the peoples who have gone to war against Jerusalem; their flesh will rot while they stand on their feet, and their eyes will rot in their sockets, and their tongue will rot in their mouth. 13 And it will be in that day, *that* abundant confusion from Yahweh will fall on them; and they will take hold of one another’s hand, and the hand of one will go up against the hand of another. 14 And Judah also will fight at Jerusalem; and the wealth of all the surrounding nations will be gathered, gold and silver and garments in great abundance. 15 And in the same way, the plague on the horse, the mule, the camel, the donkey, and all the cattle that will be in those camps will be like this plague.

16 Then it will be that any who are left of all the nations that went against Jerusalem will go up from year to year to worship the King, Yahweh of hosts, and to celebrate the Feast of Booths. 17 And it will be that whichever of the families of the earth does not go up to Jerusalem to worship the King, Yahweh of hosts, there will be no rain on them. 18 And if the family of Egypt does not go up or enter, then no *rain will fall* on them; it will be the plague with which Yahweh plagues the nations who do not go up to celebrate the Feast of Booths. 19 This will be the punishment of Egypt, and the punishment of all the nations who do not go up to celebrate the Feast of Booths.

20 In that day there will *be inscribed* on the bells of the horses, “Holy to Yahweh.” And the pots in the house of Yahweh will

be like the bowls before the altar. 21 And
every pot in Jerusalem and in Judah will
be holy to Yahweh of hosts; and all who
sacrifice will come and take of them and
boil in them. And there will no longer be a
Canaanite in the house of Yahweh of hosts
in that day.

Psalm 149:5–9

5 Let the holy ones exult in glory;
Let them sing for joy on their beds.
6 *Let* the exaltations of God
be in their throats,
And a two-edged sword in their hand,
7 To execute vengeance on the nations
And punishments on the peoples,
8 To bind their kings with chains
And their honored men
with fetters of iron,
9 To execute on them the
judgment written;
This is the majesty of all His holy ones.
Praise Yah!

Proverbs 31:1–9

31 The words of King Lemuel, the oracle
unto which his mother disciplined
him:
2 What, O my son?
And what, O son of my womb?
And what, O son of my vows?
3 Do not give your excellence
to women,
Or your ways to that which
blots out kings.
4 It is not for kings, O Lemuel,
It is not for kings to drink wine,
Or for rulers to desire strong drink,
5 Lest he drink and forget
what is decreed,
And pervert the justice of
all the afflicted.
6 Give strong drink to him
who is perishing,
And wine to those whose
soul is bitter.
7 Let him drink and forget his poverty
And he will not remember
his trouble any longer.
8 Open your mouth for the mute,
For the justice of all those
passing away.
9 Open your mouth, judge righteously,
And render justice to the
afflicted and needy.

Revelation 20:1–15

20 Then I saw an angel coming down
from heaven, having the key of the
abyss and a great chain in his hand. 2 And
he laid hold of the dragon, the serpent of
old, who is the devil and Satan, and bound
him for a thousand years; 3 and he threw
him into the abyss, and shut *it* and sealed
it over him, so that he would not deceive
the nations any longer, until the thousand
years were finished. After these things he
must be released for a short time.
4 Then I saw thrones, and they sat on
them, and judgment was given to them.
And I *saw* the souls of those who had been
beheaded because of their witness of Jesus
and because of the word of God, and who
also had not worshiped the beast or his
image, and had not received the mark on
their forehead and on their hand. And they
came to life and reigned with Christ for a
thousand years. 5 The rest of the dead did
not come to life until the thousand years
were finished. This is the first resurrection.
6 Blessed and holy is the one who has a part
in the first resurrection. Over these the sec-
ond death has no authority, but they will be
priests of God and of Christ and will reign
with Him for a thousand years.
7 And when the thousand years are
finished, Satan will be released from his
prison, 8 and will come out to deceive the
nations which are in the four corners of
the earth, Gog and Magog, to gather them
together for the war; the number of them
is like the sand of the seashore. 9 And they
came up on the broad plain of the earth
and surrounded the camp of the saints and
the beloved city, and fire came down from
heaven and devoured them. 10 And the devil
who deceived them was thrown into the lake
of fire and brimstone, where the beast and
the false prophet are also, and they will be
tormented day and night forever and ever.
11 Then I saw a great white throne and
Him who sits upon it, from whose presence
earth and heaven fled away, and no place
was found for them. 12 Then I saw the dead,
the great and the small, standing before
the throne, and books were opened; and
another book was opened, which is *the book*
of life. And the dead were judged from the
things which were written in the books,
according to their deeds. 13 And the sea gave
up the dead which were in it, and death and

Hades gave up the dead which were in them, and they were judged, every one *of them* according to their deeds. 14 Then death and Hades were thrown into the lake of fire. This is the second death, the lake of fire. 15 And if anyone's name was not found written in the book of life, he was thrown into the lake of fire.

We are commited as believers to reading this Book, believing this Book, understanding this Book, loving this Book and proclaiming this one Book.

— JOHN MACARTHUR

DECEMBER 31

Malachi 1:1–4:6

1 The oracle of the word of Yahweh to Israel by the hand of Malachi.

2 "I have loved you," says Yahweh. But you say, "How have You loved us?" "*Was* not Esau Jacob's brother?" declares Yahweh. "Yet I have loved Jacob; 3 but I have hated Esau, and I have set his mountains *to be* a desolation and his inheritance for the jackals of the wilderness." 4 Though Edom says, "We have been demolished, but we will return and build up the waste places"; thus says Yahweh of hosts, "They may build, but I will pull down; and *men* will call them a territory of wickedness, and the people toward whom Yahweh is indignant forever." 5 And your eyes will see this, and you will say, "Yahweh be magnified beyond the territory of Israel!"

6 "'A son honors *his* father, and a slave his master. Then if I am a father, where is My honor? And if I am a master, where is the fear of Me?' says Yahweh of hosts to you, O priests who despise My name. But you say, 'How have we despised Your name?' 7 *You* are presenting defiled food upon My altar. But you say, 'How have we defiled You?' In that you say, 'The table of Yahweh is to be despised.' 8 But when you present the blind for sacrifice, is it not evil? And when you present the lame and sick, is it not evil? Please, bring it near to your governor! Would he accept you? Or would he lift up your face?" says Yahweh of hosts. 9 "But now, entreat God's favor, that He may be gracious to us! With this thing which is from your hand, will He lift up any of your faces?" says Yahweh of hosts. 10 "Oh that there were one among you who would shut the gates, that you might not light a *fire on* My altar in vain! I have no delight in you," says Yahweh of hosts, "nor will I accept an offering from your hand. 11 For from the rising of the sun even to its setting, My name *will be* great among the nations, and in every place incense is going to be presented to My name, as well as a grain offering *that is* clean; for My name *will be* great among the nations," says Yahweh of hosts. 12 "But you are profaning it, in that you say, 'The table of the Lord is defiled, and as for its fruit, its food is to be despised.' 13 You also say, 'Behold, *how* tiresome it is!' And you disdainfully sniff at it," says Yahweh of hosts, "and you bring what was taken by robbery and *what is* lame or sick; so you bring the offering! Should I accept that from your hand?" says Yahweh. 14 "But cursed be the swindler who has a male in his flock and vows it, but sacrifices a blemished animal to the Lord, for I am a great King," says Yahweh of hosts, "and My name is feared among the nations."

2 "And now this commandment is for you, O priests. 2 If you do not listen, and if you do not set it upon *your* heart to give honor to My name," says Yahweh of hosts, "then I will send the curse upon you, and I will curse your blessings; and indeed, I have cursed them *already* because you are not setting *it* upon *your* heart. 3 Behold, I am going to rebuke your seed, and I will spread refuse on your faces, the refuse of your feasts; and you will be taken away with it. 4 Then you will know that I have sent this commandment to you, that My covenant may continue with Levi," says Yahweh of hosts. 5 "My covenant with him was *one of* life and peace, and I gave them

to him *as something to be* feared; so he feared Me and stood in awe of My name. 6 Instruction of truth was in his mouth, and unrighteousness was not found on his lips; he walked with Me in peace and uprightness, and he turned many back from iniquity. 7 For the lips of a priest should keep knowledge, and men should seek instruction from his mouth; for he is the messenger of Yahweh of hosts. 8 But as for you, you have turned aside from the way; you have caused many to stumble by the instruction; you have corrupted the covenant of Levi," says Yahweh of hosts. 9 "So I also have made you despised and low before all the people, just as you are not keeping My ways but are showing partiality in the instruction.

10 "Do we not all have one father? Has not one God created us? Why do we deal treacherously each against his brother so as to profane the covenant of our fathers? 11 Judah has dealt treacherously, and an abomination has been done in Israel and in Jerusalem; for Judah has profaned the sanctuary of Yahweh which He loves and has married the daughter of a foreign god. 12 *As* for the man who does this, may Yahweh cut off from the tents of Jacob *everyone* who awakes and answers or who presents an offering to Yahweh of hosts.

13 "And this is a second thing you do: you cover the altar of Yahweh with tears, with weeping, and with groaning because He no longer regards the offering or receives *it as* acceptable from your hand. 14 But you say, 'For what reason?' Because Yahweh has been a witness between you and the wife of your youth, against whom you have dealt treacherously, though she is your companion and your wife by covenant. 15 But not one has done *so*, even *one* who has a remnant of the Spirit. And what did *that* one *do* while he was seeking a godly seed? Be careful then to keep your spirit, and let no one deal treacherously against the wife of your youth. 16 For I hate divorce," says Yahweh, the God of Israel, "and him who covers his garment with wrong," says Yahweh of hosts. "Be careful then to keep your spirit, that you do not deal treacherously."

17 You have wearied Yahweh with your words. But you say, "How have we wearied *Him*?" In that you say, "Everyone who does evil is good in the sight of Yahweh, and He delights in them," or, "Where is the God of justice?"

3 "Behold, I am going to send My messenger, and he will prepare the way before Me. And the Lord, whom you seek, will suddenly come to His temple; and the messenger of the covenant, in whom you delight, behold, He is coming," says Yahweh of hosts. 2 "But who can endure the day of His coming? And who can stand when He appears? For He is like a smelter's fire and like fullers' soap. 3 And He will sit as a smelter and purifier of silver, and He will purify the sons of Levi and refine them like gold and silver, so that they may present to Yahweh offerings in righteousness. 4 Then the offering of Judah and Jerusalem will be pleasing to Yahweh as in the ancient days and as in former years.

5 "Then I will draw near to you for judgment; and I will be a swift witness against the sorcerers and against the adulterers and against those who swear falsely and against those who oppress the wage earner in his wages, the widow and the orphan, and those who turn aside the sojourner and do not fear Me," says Yahweh of hosts. 6 "For I, Yahweh, do not change; therefore you, O sons of Jacob, are not consumed.

7 "From the days of your fathers you have turned aside from My statutes and have not kept *them*. Return to Me, and I will return to you," says Yahweh of hosts. "But you say, 'How shall we return?'

8 "Will a man rob God? Yet you are robbing Me! But you say, 'How have we robbed You?' In tithes and contributions. 9 You are cursed with a curse, for you are robbing Me, the whole nation *of you*! 10 Bring the whole tithe into the storehouse, so that there may be food in My house, and test Me now in this," says Yahweh of hosts, "if I will not open for you the windows of heaven and empty out for you a blessing until it is beyond enough. 11 Then I will rebuke the devourer for you so that it will not corrupt the fruits of the ground; nor will your vine in the field fail to bear," says Yahweh of hosts. 12 "So all the nations will call you blessed, for you shall be a delightful land," says Yahweh of hosts.

13 "Your words have been strong against Me," says Yahweh. "But you say, 'What have we spoken against You?' 14 You have said, 'It is worthless to serve God; and what gain is

it that we have kept His charge and that we
have walked in mourning before Yahweh of
hosts? 15 So now we call the arrogant blessed;
not only are the doers of wickedness built
up, but they also test God and escape.'"
16 Then those who feared Yahweh spoke
to one another, and Yahweh gave heed
and heard *it*, and a book of remembrance
was written before Him for those who fear
Yahweh and who think upon His name.
17 "And they will be Mine," says Yahweh of
hosts, "on the day that I prepare *My* own
treasured possession, and I will spare them
as a man spares his own son who serves
him." 18 So you will return and see *the
distinction* between the righteous and the
wicked, between one who serves God and
one who does not serve Him.

4 "For behold, the day is coming, burning
like a furnace; and all the arrogant and
every worker of wickedness will be chaff;
and the day that is coming will set them
aflame," says Yahweh of hosts, "so that it
will leave them neither root nor branch."
2 "But for you who fear My name, the sun
of righteousness will rise with healing in
its wings; and you will go forth and skip
about like calves from the stall. 3 And you
will tread down the wicked, for they will be
ashes under the soles of your feet on the day
which I am preparing," says Yahweh of hosts.
4 "Remember the law of Moses My ser-
vant, *even the* statutes and judgments which
I commanded him in Horeb for all Israel.
5 "Behold, I am going to send you Elijah
the prophet before the coming of the great
and awesome day of Yahweh. 6 And he
will turn the hearts of the fathers to *their*
children and the hearts of the children to
their fathers, lest I come and strike the land,
devoting it to destruction."

Psalm 150:1–6

1 Praise Yah!
Praise God in His sanctuary;
Praise Him in His mighty expanse.
2 Praise Him for His mighty deeds;
Praise Him according to the
abundance of His greatness.

3 Praise Him with trumpet blast;
Praise Him with harp and lyre.
4 Praise Him with tambourine
and dancing;
Praise Him with stringed
instruments and pipe.
5 Praise Him with resounding cymbals;
Praise Him with clashing cymbals.
6 Let everything that has
breath praise Yah.
Praise Yah!

Proverbs 31:10–31

10 An excellent wife, who can find?
For her worth is far above pearls.

11 The heart of her husband
trusts in her,
And he will have no lack of gain.

12 She deals bountifully with him
for good and not evil
All the days of her life.

13 She searches for wool and flax
And works with her hands in delight.

14 She is like merchant ships;
She brings her food from afar.

15 And she rises while it is still night,
And gives food to her household
And a portion to her young women.

16 She makes plans for a field and buys it;
From the fruit of her hands
she plants a vineyard.

17 She girds herself with strength
And makes her arms strong.

18 She senses that her gain is good;
Her lamp does not go out at night.

19 She stretches out her hands
to the distaff,
And her hands hold fast the spindle.

20 She extends her hand to the poor,
And she stretches out her
hands to the needy.

21 She is not afraid of the snow
for her household,
For all her household are
clothed with scarlet.

22 She makes coverings for herself;
Her clothing is fine linen and purple.

23 Her husband is known in the gates,
When he sits with the
elders of the land.

24 She makes linen garments
and sells *them*,
And gives belts to the tradesmen.

25 Strength and majesty are her clothing,
And she smiles at the future.

26 She opens her mouth in wisdom,
And the instruction of lovingkindness
is on her tongue.

27 She watches over the ways
of her household,
And does not eat the bread of idleness.

28 Her children rise up and bless her;
As for her husband, he also
praises her, *saying*:

29 "Many daughters have done excellently,
But you have gone above them all."

30 Charm is deceitful and beauty is vain,
But a woman who fears Yahweh,
she shall be praised.

31 Give to her from the fruit of her hands,
And let her works praise
her in the gates.

Revelation 21:1–22:21

21 Then I saw a new heaven and a new
earth; for the first heaven and the first
earth passed away, and there is no longer
any sea. 2 And I saw the holy city, new
Jerusalem, coming down out of heaven from
God, made ready as a bride adorned for her
husband. 3 And I heard a loud voice from the
throne, saying, "Behold, the tabernacle of
God is among men, and He will dwell among
them, and they shall be His people, and God
Himself will be among them, 4 and He will
WIPE AWAY EVERY TEAR FROM THEIR EYES; and
there will no longer be *any* death; there will
no longer be *any* mourning, or crying, or
pain. The first things passed away."
5 And He who sits on the throne said,
"Behold, I am making all things new." And
He *said, "Write, for these words are faithful
and true." 6 Then He said to me, "They are
done. I am the Alpha and the Omega, the
beginning and the end. I will give to the one
who thirsts from the spring of the water
of life without cost. 7 He who overcomes
will inherit these things, and I WILL BE HIS
GOD AND HE WILL BE MY SON. 8 But for the
cowardly and unbelieving and abominable
and murderers and sexually immoral
persons and sorcerers and idolaters and
all liars, their part *will be* in the lake that
burns with fire and brimstone, which is the
second death."
9 Then one of the seven angels who
have the seven bowls full of the seven last
plagues came and spoke with me, saying,
"Come here, I will show you the bride, the
wife of the Lamb."
10 And he carried me away in the Spirit to
a great and high mountain, and showed me
the holy city, Jerusalem, coming down out
of heaven from God, 11 having the glory of
God. Her brilliance was like precious stone,
as a stone of crystal-clear jasper. 12 It had a
great and high wall. It had twelve gates and
at those gates, twelve angels; and names
have been written on *those gates*, which are
the names of the twelve tribes of the sons of
Israel. 13 *There were* three gates on the east
and three gates on the north and three gates
on the south and three gates on the west.
14 And the wall of the city had twelve foun-
dation stones, and on them *were* the twelve
names of the twelve apostles of the Lamb.
15 And the one who spoke with me had a
gold measuring rod to measure the city and
its gates and its wall. 16 And the city is laid
out as a square, and its length is as great as
the width; and he measured the city with
the rod, 12,000 stadia; its length and width
and height are equal. 17 And he measured
its wall, 144 cubits, *according to* human
measurements, which are *also* angelic
measurements. 18 And the material of the
wall was jasper, and the city was pure gold,
like pure glass. 19 The foundation stones of
the city wall were adorned with every kind
of precious stone. The first foundation stone
was jasper; the second, sapphire; the third,
chalcedony; the fourth, emerald; 20 the fifth,
sardonyx; the sixth, sardius; the seventh,
chrysolite; the eighth, beryl; the ninth,
topaz; the tenth, chrysoprase; the eleventh,
jacinth; the twelfth, amethyst. 21 And the
twelve gates were twelve pearls; each one of
the gates was a single pearl. And the street of
the city was pure gold, like transparent glass.

22 And I saw no sanctuary in it, for the
Lord God the Almighty and the Lamb are
its sanctuary. 23 And the city has no need of
the sun or of the moon to shine on it, for the
glory of God has illumined it, and its lamp
is the Lamb. 24 And the nations will walk
by its light, and the kings of the earth will
bring their glory into it. 25 And its gates will
never be closed by day, for there will be no
night there; 26 and they will bring the glory
and the honor of the nations into it. 27 And
nothing defiled, and no one who practices
abomination and lying, shall ever come into
it, but only those whose names are written
in the Lamb's book of life.

22 Then he showed me a river of the
water of life, bright as crystal, coming
from the throne of God and of the Lamb, 2 in
the middle of its street. On either side of the
river was the tree of life, bearing twelve *kinds*
of fruit, yielding its fruit every month; and
the leaves of the tree were for the healing of
the nations. 3 And there will no longer be any
curse; and the throne of God and of the Lamb
will be in it, and His slaves will serve Him;
4 and they will see His face, and His name
will be on their foreheads. 5 And there will no
longer be *any* night, and they will not have
need of the light of a lamp nor the light of
the sun, because the Lord God will illumine
them, and they will reign forever and ever.
6 And he said to me, "These words are
faithful and true"; and the Lord, the God of
the spirits of the prophets, sent His angel
to show to His slaves the things which must
soon take place.
7 "And behold, I am coming quickly.
Blessed is he who keeps the words of the
prophecy of this book."
8 I, John, am the one who was hearing
and seeing these things. And when I heard
and saw, I fell down to worship at the feet
of the angel who showed me these things.
9 But he *said to me, "Do not do that! I am
a fellow slave with you and your brothers
the prophets and with those who keep the
words of this book. Worship God!"
10 And he *said to me, "Do not seal up the
words of the prophecy of this book, for the
time is near. 11 Let the one who does unrigh-
teousness, still do unrighteousness; and the
one who is filthy, still be filthy; and let the
one who is righteous, still do righteousness;
and the one who is holy, still keep himself
holy."
12 "Behold, I am coming quickly, and My
reward *is* with Me, to render to every man
according to his work. 13 I am the Alpha and
the Omega, THE FIRST AND THE LAST, the
beginning and the end."
14 Blessed are those who wash their robes,
so that they may have the authority to the
tree of life and may enter by the gates into
the city. 15 Outside are the dogs and the
sorcerers and the sexually immoral persons
and the murderers and the idolaters, and
everyone who loves and practices lying.
16 "I, Jesus, sent My angel to bear witness
to you of these things for the churches. I am
the root and the descendant of David, the
bright morning star."
17 And the Spirit and the bride say,
"Come." And let the one who hears say,
"Come." And let the one who is thirsty
come. Let the one who wishes receive the
water of life without cost.
18 I bear witness to everyone who hears
the words of the prophecy of this book: If
anyone adds to them, God will add to him
the plagues which are written in this book.
19 And if anyone takes away from the words
of the book of this prophecy, God will take
away his part from the tree of life and from
the holy city, which are written in this book.
20 He who bears witness to these things
says, "Yes, I am coming quickly." Amen.
Come, Lord Jesus.
21 The grace of the Lord Jesus be with all.
Amen.

INDEX OF QUOTES

MONETARY UNITS

Assarion (*plural assaria*)	A Roman copper coin, approximately 1/16 of a laborer's daily wage
Daric	A Persian gold coin, weighing approximately 0.3 ounces or 8 grams
Denarius (*plural denarii*)	A Roman silver coin, approximately a laborer's daily wage
Drachma (*plural drachmas*)	A Greek silver coin, approximately a laborer's daily wage
Lepton (*plural lepta*)	Smallest Greek copper coin, approximately 1/128 of a laborer's daily wage
Mina (*plural minas*)	A Greek monetary unit worth approximately 100 days of a laborer's wages
Quadrans	A Roman copper coin, approximately 1/64 of a laborer's daily wage
Shekel	A coin weighing approximately 0.4 ounces or 11 grams
Stater	Literally "standard coin," approximately 4 days of a laborer's wages
Talent	Approximately worth more than 15 years of a laborer's wages

This table contains values regarding monetary units, gathered from widely accepted historical and archeological research. These values are based on the most accurate information available.